French Science Fiction,
Fantasy, Horror
and Pulp Fiction

French Science Fiction, Fantasy, Horror and Pulp Fiction

A Guide to Cinema, Television, Radio, Animation, Comic Books and Literature from the Middle Ages to the Present

by JEAN-MARC LOFFICIER
and RANDY LOFFICIER

FOREWORD BY *Stephen R. Bissette*

McFarland & Company, Inc., Publishers
Jefferson, North Carolina, and London

Cover art by Moebius © 2000 Starwatcher Graphics, Inc.

ISBN 0-7864-0596-1 (softcover: 50# alkaline paper)

Library of Congress and British Library
cataloguing data are available

Manufactured in the United States of America

*McFarland & Company, Inc., Publishers
Box 611, Jefferson, North Carolina 28640
www.mcfarlandpub.com*

To Arlette & Jean-Louis Lofficier,
Max Apfelbaum and Irene Gerken,

who shaped our love
for fantasy and science fiction

Acknowledgments

We are indebted to the following individuals who helped with the research for this book: Michel Bera, François Breuillier, Alain Carrazé, Pierre-Paul Durastanti, Joël Houssin, Michel Jeury, Craig Ledbetter, Frédéric Albert Lévy, Jean-Louis Lofficier, Tim Lucas, Jean-Michel Monnier and Elisabeth Vonarburg.

We are especially grateful to writer/editor Daniel Riche, graphic novelist Stephen R. Bissette and writers Alex Garcia, Jean Pettigrew, Jean-Louis Trudel, Roland C. Wagner and Philippe Ward who, in spite of their busy schedules, managed to find the time to provide invaluable assistance, notes and comments.

Thanks go to *Starlog* Magazine for permission to republish portions of our interviews with Luc Besson (published in *Starlog* no. 85, August 1984) and René Laloux (*Starlog* no. 129, April 1988).

A special note of thanks to our invaluable research assistant, **Henri Rossi**, Docteur ès Lettres, Agrégé de l'Université. There is no way to truly express our gratitude for his hours of tireless research at the *Bibliothèque Nationale*.

J.-M. & R.L., Spring 2000

Table of Contents

Throughout this book, the names of filmmakers, writers, artists, and others that appear in **bold** type are the subject of separate biographical entries in Chapter VI of Book I (for film, television, radio and comic books), or Chapter XI of Book 2 (for literary authors). The titles in ***bold italics*** are the subject of separate entries in their respective categories.

Foreword

by
Stephen R. Bissette

There are so many splendid French books dedicated to the cinema, comics (*la bande dessinée*), animation, and *le fantastique*'s many avenues and auteurs. I have in my library the first book published about horror films, and wouldn't you know it, it was published in France (*Le Fantastique au Cinéma* by Michel Laclos, 1958).

And yet, there has been precious little in the English language dedicated to the Franco-Belgian genre tradition.

You hold in your hand the first full overview of the French *fantastique* in all media.

This is a book I've pined for almost as long as I can remember. If you will bear with me, I'll tell you why.

Long before cable TV, pay-per-view, and home video, broadcast television was all there was. My family were considered relatively lucky to pick up all three American networks (and the fetal stages of ETV) with our TV antenna. Like most American families, we all watched TV. Together, we watched *Ed Sullivan*, *Ozzie and Harriet* and *The Wonderful World of Disney*. My dad watched war movies, my mother watched Lawrence Welk, my older brother watched baseball, my younger sister watched cartoons.

But I craved monster and horror movies.

Precious few of the fantasy and horror films pictured in *Famous Monsters of Filmland* (my Bible back then, you understand) ever surfaced on the movie screens and drive-ins within driving distance; if and when they did, I could rarely convince my parents to go. Like most American kids, my only access was the television in the front room, which never seemed to get the channels the *TV Guide* listed all the really cool stuff on. You know, the cool stuff in *Famous Monsters*! Why didn't *our* TV pick up the Boris Karloff *Frankenstein*, *King Kong*, *Island of Lost Souls*, and *Invasion of the Saucer Men*?

And what about ... *Torticola*? Would I *ever* see *Torticola*?

I find it almost impossible to adequately convey to my own children (who've grown up with my extensive home video and laser disc library at their fingertips) how difficult it used to be to see the movies I so longed to see. When my kids get a handle on my descriptions of "how it used to be," I get the distinct feeling *they don't believe me.* They can't quite grasp that once upon a time you could *only* watch what was being broadcast *while* it was being broadcast. You often had one chance—just *one*—to see a movie or TV show, and if you missed it, it would remain forever out of reach. You couldn't tape it and watch it later. All movies were, naturally, interrupted by commercials every ten-to-fifteen minutes, and most were mindlessly truncated to fit a ninety-minute time slot. Though a few of the movies I ached to see were on *The Early Show* at four in the afternoon, most of the good stuff was on *The Late Show*, starting at 11:30 P.M. or even midnight. Nor could you count on really seeing what was being broadcast, as the vagaries of the wind and weather could change crystal-clear reception to Rorschachian static in minutes.

I was fortunate to have relatively indulgent parents who would permit me to watch *The Late Show* as long as all my homework was done and I got up for school the next morning without dragging my ass.

I was also fortunate that one of the odd advantages of growing up in the backwoods of Northern Vermont in the 1960s was Canadian television. When the weather was clear, our lowly TV antenna picked up three stations from Canada, two in English, and one French.

That was where my education in the cinema *fantastique* began.

1

Canadian TV was a lot more than just travelogues, *The Beachcombers,* and weird imports like *Skippy the Bush Kangaroo.* Channel 6 was my favorite Canadian station, if only for Monday night's *Science Fiction Theater.* It was my first midnight movie, if you will, where I discovered *Carnival of Souls,* Mario Bava's *Black Sunday* (which seemed unbelievably graphic at the time), and a complete *Tarzan* movie retrospective, from Elmo Lincoln to Jock Mahoney. Then there was Channel 10, the French-language station…

Which brings me, finally, to Jean-Marc and Randy's marvelous book.

Despite my name and vague French-Canadian heritage, I can't speak or read a lick of French. My mother and her sisters spoke fluent French, and I've always suspected my brother, sister, and I were discouraged from learning the language so my mom and her sisters could preserve the privacy of their often hyperactive conversations. Like most Americans, I had a smattering of French in school, learning how to ask André about his bicycle long enough to earn a passing grade, but a second language eluded me.

As I've grown older, I've come to envy my friends who can speak and read French. Dear Diana Schutz (with her genuine Canadian background) can read French, my Scottish cartooning pal Cam Kennedy can read French, but not I. Alas, I am but a stupid American. Woe is me. Hence, it is with no little amusement that I now reflect on the fact that, without being particularly impressed by the event at the time, I'd actually read a French novel before I was ten years old.

The first novel I ever labored my way through was none other than Jules **Verne**'s *Voyage au Centre de la Terre* (*Journey to the Center of the Earth*)—a translation, of course, sporting a photo of the crystalline caverns from the 20th Century–Fox movie on its cover.

As you can well imagine, Verne was awfully slow going for an eight year old, but I persevered because I knew from the movie and the *Classics Illustrated* comic book adaptation that dinosaurs appeared in the book. To this day, I'll fight my way through anything if there's a dinosaur in it for me.

I somehow made it to the one-hundred and fiftieth page, by which time Verne's intrepid explorers had wandered into the forest of oversized mushrooms. "Soon!" I thought to myself. "They'll see the dinosaurs soon!"

Pages (days, weeks, *eons!*) later, they found the impressions of monstrous teeth on a crowbar, leading to the marvelous battle in the subterranean sea between the prehistoric aquatic reptiles. Invigorated, I made my way to the final pages, rewarded along the way by Verne's fleeting interludes with empty glyptodon shells, "a whole herd of mastodons," and their shepherd, a twelve-foot prehistoric man (prompting Verne to an outburst of Latin, *Immanis pecoris custos, immanis Ipse!*: "The keeper of gigantic cattle, himself a giant!").

In subsequent months, I wrestled with more Verne novels, including *L'Île Mystérieuse* (*Mysterious Island*), which broke the binge. I was heartbroken to find no giant monsters on Verne's isle, which of course figured prominently in Ray Harryhausen's movie version. By that time, Sir Arthur Conan Doyle, H. G. Wells, and more contemporary authors had caught my attention, making Verne's archaic pioneer efforts seem positively creaky.

Ah, but Verne was the first, appropriately enough. I had, at least, started out on the right foot.

Unable to read French, I remain dependent to this day on the few translations available to us. In my high school years, I lucked into English versions of two of J.-H. **Rosny** Aîné's marvelous prehistoric novels, the Random House 1967 release of *La Guerre du Feu* (*Quest for Fire*) and the Ace paperback translation of *Le Félin Géant* (*The Giant Cat*) retitled *Quest of the Dawn Man.* A few years back, my friend Tim Lucas (co-founder and editor of *Video Watchdog* and author of *Throat Sprockets*) gave me two hardcover translated editions of Marcel **Allain** and Pierre **Souvestre**'s *Fantomas* adventures, *Fantomas* and *The Silent Executioner* (both from William Morrow & Co., 1986 and 1987). Tonight, in my own bed, I will begin the first English translation of Jean **Ray**'s 1943 gothic novel *Malpertuis* (Atlas Press, London, 1998), a book I have long wished to read.

The occasional science fiction collection of European stories further whets my appetite, and my conversations with Jean-Marc during his three-year tenure on this very book often leave me aching to read more (and once you read this book, you'll be aching for the same).

What worlds await me, if only…

But how can I? As I've said, I can neither speak nor read French. Ah, stupid, *stupid* American!

What a sad and sorry state of affairs!

The French cinema, however, was in my reach from a tender age.

I dimly remember watching *Rin Tin Tin* on the French-Canadian TV station with my neighbor and best friend Mitch Casey. We found it inexplicably hilarious that morning, but never again. Thereafter the novelty wore off, and the French station was a curio to pause at, briefly, while spinning the channel dial in search of entertainment.

All that changed when I stumbled on Jean **Cocteau**'s ***La Belle et la Bête*** (*The Beauty and the Beast*) one rainy Sunday afternoon.

I was flicking through the channels in complete boredom when suddenly the face of a werewolf filled the screen. I had seen Lon Chaney as *The Wolfman* only months before, but this wasn't Larry Talbot. This creature was—*different.* Its face was genuinely startling, strangely feline, and alluring. Transfixed, I sat back, further startled when he began to speak French. His words were gibberish to me, but his growling voice was as mesmerizing as his eyes. Though I didn't understand a word, I began to recognize the elements of the fairy tale I knew so well, and watched it through to the end. I shall never forget the confusing rush of emotions it aroused in me, nor the daze it left me in for days afterward.

I was forever changed, but there was no one to talk to about the film, no confidant, no compass, no reference point to draw from.

That evening, my mother translated the tiny blurb in the *TV Guide* for me, the first time in my life I heard the name of Jean Cocteau. Months later, I found a photo of Jean Marais as the Beast in that other '60s monster mag bible, *Castle of Frankenstein*, and began to study the French listings in the *TV Guide* closely, hoping to find more treasure.

One of the early issues of *Famous Monsters* I owned had an article on a French Frankenstein called Torticola, who starred in something called **Torticola contre Frankensberg** (go ahead, look it up). I was fascinated by the pictures of its strange, long-haired, porcelain-faced Karloffian monster, Torticola, and an entourage of equally weird characters, including a cat-man with whiskers. I had vivid dreams about seeing *Torticola* on TV, my unconscious craving an internal landscape to flesh out the terrain inhabited by those grainy black-and-white photos from *Famous Monsters*. The name alone became sort of a totem: Torticola... *Torticola...*

Sadly, I never lucked into *Torticola*, but a listing with the magical name "Cocteau" steered me into a late-night French broadcast of his **Orphée.** I understood nothing of the experience, but was unable to shake the imagery, the truly magical eruptions of fantasy as Orpheus was stalked by silent motorcyclists and literally plunged into netherworlds behind mirrors.

There were new worlds to be explored, and our TV was an occasional doorway to those worlds. How I wished for a map to those uncharted realms: an atlas, a guidebook, some way to tap into the marvels I could only occasionally glimpse.

But there was no such book, there were no such guides.

As I grew older, I found a few reference points. Primary among them was Carlos Clarens' seminal book, *The Illustrated History of the Horror Film,* purchased during a school class trip at the age of twelve. With Clarens as my guide, my fascination with horror films deepened, and the French station synchronistically offered new treasures **Franju**'s **Judex,** Cocteau's **Le Testament d'Orphée,** and the German *Baron Munchausen,* among others (still no *Torticola,* though). ETV broadcast subtitled versions of Cocteau's *La Belle et la Bête* and *Orphée.* I was also given an 8mm movie projector one birthday, and purchased every collection of Georges **Méliès** short films offered by the Blackhawk Films catalogue. According to Clarens' book, it all began with Méliès, and I was fascinated by the films themselves, relics of a pioneer imagination peppered with frantic slapstick, mercurial metamorphoses, and bloodless distortions, dismemberments, and decapitations. By discovering the source of the wellspring, I began to enjoy a sense of order—there was now a history to my obsessions, beyond my personal chronology.

In one remarkable summer, I was able to watch Franju's horrific **Les Yeux sans Visage** (*Eyes Without a Face*) twice—first in English, in a badly-cut late-night broadcast of *The Horror Chamber of Dr. Faustus,* and later in the wee hours of morning on Channel 10 in its original form as *Les Yeux sans Visage.* This proved to be another transformative experience, garnished with a fresh flush of emotions as I watched the French version and stumbled upon that most forbidden of fruit: that which the censor hides from our eyes.

Our local TV station had cut the infamous operation sequence, in which a woman's face is surgically removed, from the already truncated (and poorly dubbed) American version of Franju's classic. This broadcast cut away as soon as the scalpel touched the face. I could hardly believe my eyes weeks later as the French version unflinchingly chronicled more of the gruesome facial surgery, as the blade glided along the unconscious patient's visage and the blood was daubed away, fading out only as the skin was carefully lifted away from the flayed features.

It was not the clinical mayhem alone that made my gorge rise into my throat. It was the dawning realization that I had been denied this experience during the English-language version. This was an awakening for me, a jolt accompanied by a powerful Catholic tangle of shame (at seeing what I now had firm evidence was forbidden, feeling I *should not* look though I *could not* look away); anger (at having been denied this sequence, the terrible black heart of the film); and resolution (I must see everything else I have been denied, whatever the cost).

More than ever before, this secret access I had to the original French films became important. I ached for information, for knowledge, for a guide into these realms that were now even more stimulating and alluring for their hidden horrors.

Again, there was no one among my circle to talk to about this. I internalized these revelations, at least knowing I was not as alone as I felt. I now had Clarens' book and my beloved collection of monster magazines to assure me there were others like me in the world, in other countries, even, in Japan and Germany and Sweden—and France

And the French, I now knew, had a real knack for this sort of thing.

As I grew up, my love affair with French fantasy blossomed. French television offered more rarefied treats, and I was informed enough to seize them: Franju's *La Tête contre les Murs,* **Clouzot**'s *Le Corbeau* and *Le Salaire de la Peur* (*The Wages Of Fear*). Thanks to the University of Vermont's theatrical retrospectives, I was able to savor the subtitled Cocteau classics on the big screen (including a double bill of his **Le Sang d'un Poète** (*Blood of a Poet*) coupled with Buñuel and Dali's delirious *Un Chien Andalou,* and enjoy the genuine *frisson* of seeing Clouzot's **Les Diaboliques**, where a beautiful woman next to me whom I did not know dug her fingernails so deeply into my arm during the film's terrifying climax that she drew blood. While managing the film program as a student at Johnson State College, I "reassembled" Robert Enrico's "lost" Ambrose Bierce anthology feature *Au Coeur de la Vie* for a single evening presentation (a piece of film detective work I am still proud of; sadly, Enrico's masterwork is still known only for a single episode lifted from its context, the Academy-Award winning short film *An Occurrence at Owl Creek Bridge*).

Around this same time, I discovered my first French graphic albums during a trip to Montreal. These were completely unlike any comic I'd ever seen, in both content and format. These were honest-to-God *books,* and the art and printing was far superior to any American comic books. I was quite impressed, but unable to comprehend them; there was no gestalt like that I'd experienced during my first glimpse of Cocteau's ravishing *Beast* or Franju's clinical horrors. My first exposure to *la bande dessinée* was diverting, but little else.

All that changed during my own college years, when my friend Jack Venooker showed me the first issue of *Métal Hurlant*. Raised on the American comics of Kirby and Kubert, flirting with adulthood through the pages of *Creepy* and *Vampirella*, and coming of age with the underground comics of R. Crumb, S. Clay Wilson, and (my favorites) Tom Veitch and Greg Irons, I was by my college years infatuated with the medium of comics. I was already filling my sketchbooks with my own comics, most of them terribly derivative of the more lurid undergrounds, though an occasional drawing or sequential narrative had its own distinctive look. The undergrounds had already begun to wane, and I was restless with the meager diet available.

Métal Hurlant was exactly what it aspired to be: a revelation, a primal scream, a rending of the fabric, a doorway to new visions, new potential. **Moebius**' howling creature on the cover of that first issue was, like Marais' *Beast* and Franju's *Les Yeux sans Visage*, a harbinger of irrevocable and marvelous transformation. I can close my eyes and see it still, years later, as vividly as the moment I first laid eyes upon it.

Though once again the language was a barrier of sorts, making these exotic visions even more exotic, *Métal Hurlant*'s imagery was absolutely galvanizing in its crystalline clarity and immediacy. *Métal Hurlant* changed everything about how I experienced comics and comics thereafter, and profoundly shaped my own evolving efforts to create my own comics. I had never before seen the likes of Philippe **Druillet** and Jean "Moebius" Giraud and their brethren, but now I could not live without them.

A couple of years later, *Heavy Metal* surfaced on the American newsstands, showcasing English translations of Druillet, Moebius, and other French and Belgian *bandes dessinées*. It was the equivalent of seeing Cocteau's work with English subtitles: Finally, I could understand the text. In some cases, however, this was a letdown, as the banality of the writing robbed the visual narratives of their previous exoticism and mystery. How could I be sure these translations were accurate?

Once again, I ached for a guide. Was there more of this magical "stuff," and if so, where? How could I see it, read it, get to it, grasp it, understand it?

And once again, I knew I was not alone.

There have been other delicious discoveries and revelations through the years: **Gance**'s *J'accuse*, **Godard**'s *Alphaville* and *Weekend*, Charlier and Moebius' *Blueberry* graphic novels, **Christin** and **Mézières**' *Valérian* series, Henri Xhonneux's **Marquis**, Jeunet and **Caro**'s *Delicatessen*, and my dear friend Tim Lucas (remember him?) tells me he recently saw a print of *Les Yeux sans Visage* which is even more explicit, as the camera lingers even longer over the facial surgery…

I could go on and on, but what's the point?

Because, you see, there finally *is* a guide, or guides, and they have diligently mapped out these marvels and horrors. Jean-Marc and his wife Randy took it upon themselves to be the cartographers, and you hold in your hand an unprecedented and long-overdue overview of French and Belgian fantasy, horror, and science-fiction in literature, cinema, television, animation and comics.

I know you are in good hands because I have had the privilege to know Jean-Marc and Randy for almost a decade now. I feel very lucky to know them. We met almost by accident, and quickly found in each other a kindred spirit. Our meeting was the first of many encounters, including dinners with Jean Giraud (Moebius) and my publishing the first English language translation of Moebius and Alexandro **Jodorowsky**'s *Les Yeux du Chat* in my ambitious but short-lived horror anthology comic *Taboo*. Jean-Marc also opened my eyes to how dreadful some of the *Heavy Metal* translations of their source materials were, and with Randy launched a series of Moebius collections proffering superior translations.

More importantly, it blossomed into the friendship I enjoy with Jean-Marc and Randy to this day.

In the course of that friendship, they have been marvelous guides. (I am a bit disappointed about Jean-Marc's steadfast refusal to show me *Torticola contre Frankensberg* but other than that, he's been fantastic, and you're damned lucky to have him, really.)

They have much to share with you and I've taken up far too many pages already.

Here is a map of terrain that has been haphazardly charted in the English language. Much will be new to you.

As with all explorations of uncharted territory, one must be patient and pay close attention, and abide by the warning:

Here be monsters…

…including, thank God, Torticola.

> —*Stephen R. Bissette*
> April 1997
> Mountains of Madness, Vermont

Stephen R. Bissette has been a professional cartoonist for twenty years. He is best known for his award-winning collaboration with writer Alan Moore and inker John Totleben on DC Comics' Saga of the Swamp Thing *from 1983 to 1987. His artwork has also graced the pages of* Heavy Metal, Epic Illustrated, Bizarre Adventures, Weird Worlds *and many others. Bissette co-founded, edited and co-published the controversial adult horror comics anthology* Taboo *(1988–95). He has also illustrated special-edition novels, novellas and short stories by Douglas E. Winter, Joe Lansdale, Joe Citro, Rick Hautala and others. As a writer, Bissette's articles on horror films have appeared in* Deep Red, The Video Watchdog, Ecco, Euro-Trash Cinema, Fangoria, Gore Zone *and the book* Cut! Horror Writers on Horror Films. *He has also lectured extensively on the history of horror comics and co-authored the book* Comic Book Rebels *(Donald I. Fine, 1988). His original novella* Aliens: Tribes *won a Bram Stoker Award in 1993. Through his own imprint, SpiderBaby Grafix, Bissette is currently publishing an ambitious serialized graphic novel,* Tyrant, *a rigorously researched portrait of the birth, life and death of a Tyrannosaurus rex in late Cretaceous North America.*

BOOK 1

*Science Fiction, Fantasy,
Horror and Pulp Fiction
in Cinema, Television, Radio,
Animation, and Comic Books*

Preamble

It has always been a source of profound frustration to us that, because of the language barrier, the knowledge of many outstanding non–English works of fiction, be they films, television series, or novels, is denied to the American public. Even scholars are frustrated when it comes to including works of foreign origin in their research.

This failing is particularly heart-wrenching when dealing with the French culture, without a doubt, one of the richest in the world. There was a time when French novels and French films were widely imported in the United States. People were reportedly mobbing the New York harbor waiting for the latest installment of an Alexandre **Dumas** novel. French cinema literally gave its *lettres de noblesse* to the entire medium. But in the age of the global village, this cross-cultural flood appears to have shrunk to a mere rivulet, and we are certainly the poorer for it.

(It should be understood that, throughout this book, we use the word French in the sense of French-language, that is to say, including Belgian, Swiss and, sometimes, French-Canadian works or authors. We have, however, strived to identify non–French-national works or authors whenever possible.)

The purpose of this book is to help remedy this sad state of affairs by providing, if not the works themselves, at least a basic, yet fairly comprehensive, database of information in the particular genres in which we have been active for many years: science fiction, fantasy, horror, and pulp fiction. Because these genres are often regarded as minor by serious scholars on both sides of the Atlantic, we felt that a compilation of works of this nature would be more useful than one dealing with classical or mainstream topics, for which there are at least a few academic sources available to the dedicated researcher.

A note about the French word *fantastique* which crops up in this book. It carries with it a much larger semantic field than its approximate English equivalent, fantasy. As a label, the *fantastique* can encompass fantasy, horror, fairy tales, gothic tales, surrealism, and anything in between. Ultimately, we found it preferable to subscribe to French writer Pierre **Gripari**'s straightforward definition: "The *fantastique* is everything that is not rational."

In this section, we have focused on audio-visual media. Literature will be dealt with in a separate section. Because we consider *les bandes dessinées*, or as the medium is known here, comic books or graphic novels, as a valid art form—indeed, it is called the "Ninth Art" by some French scholars—we decided from the onset to include it in our research. It also seemed to us that, because of its visual connections with animation, a chapter devoted to that medium would fit better in this section than in the one devoted to literature.

No project of this type is ever perfect, or complete. We have tried to be as comprehensive as possible, up to and including the year 1997. Nevertheless, in a book of this scope, no matter how careful one is, omissions are bound to creep in, as well as the occasional mistake. We will be grateful to anyone pointing out such errors or omissions to us, for future reference and inclusion in subsequent reprints.

—Jean-Marc and Randy Lofficier

On Making Science Fiction Films in France and America: Excerpts from an Interview with Luc Besson

*Luc **Besson** is the renowned director of* Subway, Le Grand Bleu, La Femme Nikita, *and the recent spectacular French-American science fiction co-production* The Fifth Element. *He is, perhaps, the only French filmmaker to have achieved a degree of international stardom rivaling that of American directors in recent years. These comments are excerpted from an interview granted to Randy Lofficier in 1984, as Besson had just completed his first, ground-breaking feature, the post-nuclear saga* Le Dernier Combat. *The full interview appeared in* Starlog *No. 85 and is quoted here by permission.*

American cinema is the best in the world, and it would give me great pleasure to know that, at least at the critical and professional level, my film [*Le Dernier Combat*] is appreciated. At the level of the public ... well, I don't know if it corresponds to their taste or what they want to see. Perhaps they will be more likely to accept the originality of it because it comes from another country.

I know that American audiences traditionally don't like pessimistic films, but *Le Dernier Combat* is not a pessimistic film. I didn't want to dramatize the situation, rather find the humor in it. There is not very much we can do about the situation, except take our individual responsibilities, that's all. The system is much too big for us to do anything, we might as well smile.

I think that American films are very well made, and are technically remarkable. The direction, the actors, everything is very good in general. The thing that bothers me a little bit is the stories. There is a tendency for them to talk down to people. Everything is always too simple. I can see the way that ten or eleven year old children react, at least those in France. They are already more advanced than those kinds of stories, they ask more from a film. It's beginning to be difficult to see something that's always the same. For example, the first *Star Wars* surprised a lot of people. It was really excellent. By the second film we started to recognize some of the tricks. By the third one, even if the technique was better and better, and there were more special effects that were better filmed, at the story level there wasn't as much suspense as there was with the first picture.

If I've been influenced by any American director, it's completely unconscious. Of course, there are directors that I respect and adore—for example, Sidney Lumet, Roman Polanski, Milos Forman, also in a different style, Steven Spielberg, who is in my opinion the only person who succeeds in making very good films with good stories that can be seen on several levels. They probably are an influence, in an indirect fashion.

It is very difficult to make a science fiction film in France. All of the producers and distributors that we contacted refused to do *Le Dernier Combat*. Not one said yes. We were forced to set up our own production company, and produce the film ourselves. We formed an investors pool of a dozen private individuals that really love the cinema. Each put in some money and got a profit participation in the film.

10

In the end, we got the money to do almost everything we wanted. When we needed a plane engine to whip up the sandstorm, we got it. Where we saved money was on the salaries. It is people who made the difference, not things. The film was shot in fourteen weeks, but the editing was very painstaking. Because of the absence of dialogue, the sense of the film could only be achieved through images and sounds. There were, therefore, over twenty weeks of editing. The total cost of the production was approximately three million francs ($375,000). From a technical standpoint, all went very well. The practical day-to-day shooting, however, was very difficult, because we were in the ruins all the time. It was extremely dangerous, and there was always the possibility of accidents. In fact, there were several injuries, including a skull fracture. It was extremely tiring to have to work in those tons of rocks all the time. We were dirty from morning to night and we never had a day in a studio to rest. We were always outside in the wind or on the concrete, and

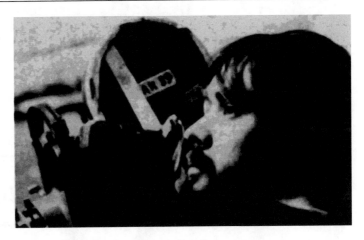

Luc Besson on Le Dernier Combat *(1986).*

it wasn't a pleasant experience. But, everybody was totally committed to the film and very strongly motivated.

CHAPTER I

Cinema

1. Historical Overview

France is, with the United States, the country that has contributed the most to the artistic development of the cinema.

If the credit for the invention of cinema can be fairly divided between Edison's Kinescope (1891) and the Lumière Brothers' Cinématographe (1895), there can be no doubt that fantasy and science fiction cinema was born in France. Its pioneer was Georges **Méliès**. Méliès virtually created the genre with *Le Voyage dans la Lune* (*A Trip to the Moon*, 1902), no less than a loose adaptation, also based on a popular fairground attraction of the times, of Jules **Verne**'s classic novel.

Le Voyage dans la Lune *(A Trip to the Moon, 1902)*

Méliès' success helped launch the careers of a number of "rivals" who exploited the same fantasy vein as he. Among these were Gaston **Velle**, Ferdinand **Zecca,** and Spanish director Segundo de **Chomon**, who produced his own *Voyage à la Lune* (*Journey to the Moon*, 1909), followed by another Verne pastiche, *Voyage au Centre de la Terre* (*Journey to the Center of the Earth,* 1909).

Pioneers of French fantasy and science fiction cinema also included Jean **Durand**, the creator of the comic character of *Onésime*; Alice **Guy-Blaché**, the first woman director; and Victorin **Jasset**, "father" of the serials and author of an adaptation of a Gaston **Leroux** genre story about a "missing link" creature accused of murder, *Balaoo* (*Balaoo*, 1913).

In the 1920s, various artistic influences, such as dadaism; surrealism, as exemplified by writers André **Breton** and Antonin **Artaud**, and painters such as Fernand Léger and Marcel Duchamp, helped foster a surrealist form of cinema which became known as the "avant-garde." Among its most representative filmmakers were Marcel L'Herbier, with *L'Inhumaine* (*The Inhuman*, 1923), Henri Chomette with *Reflets de Lumière et de Vitesse* (*Reflections of Light and Speed*, 1925), Jean Epstein with *La Chute de la Maison Usher* (*The Fall of the House of Usher*, 1928), Germaine **Dulac** with *La Coquille et le Clergyman* (*The Seashell and the Clergyman*, 1928), written by Artaud.

Other French filmmakers who experimented with the "avant-garde" included Abel **Gance** with *La Folie du Dr. Tube* (*The Madness of Dr. Tube*, 1915), René **Clair** with *Entr'acte* (*Intermission*, 1924) and *Le Voyage Imaginaire* (*The Imaginary Journey,* 1926), and Jean Renoir with *La Petite Marchande d'Allumettes* (*The Little Match Girl*, 1928).

Finally, French cinema also welcomed expatriate "avant-garde" artists such as Russian Dimitri Kirsanov, whose *Ménilmontant* (1924) featured the most visual murder scene prior to Hitchcock's *Psycho*; American artist Man Ray, who made a series of surreal shorts: *Le Retour à la Raison* (*The*

Return to Reason, 1925), *Emak Bakia* (1926), *L'Étoile de Mer* (*The Starfish*, 1928) and *Les Mystères du Château de Dé* (*The Mysteries of the Castle of Dice*, 1929), and Spanish director Luis **Buñuel**, who had apprenticed with Epstein on **La Chute de la Maison Usher** (*The Fall of the House of Usher*). Buñuel made both *Un Chien Andalou* (1928), in collaboration with fellow Spanish surrealist painter Salvador Dali, and *L'Age d'Or* (*The Golden Age*, 1930) in Paris.

Buñuel's *L'Age d'Or* and Jean **Cocteau**'s **Le Sang d'un Poète** (*The Blood of a Poet*, 1930) marked the culmination and the end of the "avant-garde." Political reasons, such as the rise of Fascism, as well as economic ones, such as the closure of many French movie studios, caused the movement to fragment and, ultimately, vanish. But it had forced a re-evaluation of the medium of film, and freed it from the artistic shackles of conventional stage melodrama.

Unfortunately, after this auspicious beginning, fantasy and science fiction became marginalized in French cinema until the late 1970s, when the imports of big budget American productions such as *Star Wars* and *Close Encounters of the Third Kind* made them "respectable" in the eyes of producers. Also, the dominance of realism in French cinema, as in French literature, if not totally excluding the *fantastique*, as long as it remained within tasteful boundaries and juvenile forms, practically ruled out any serious science fiction films.

In this review of French genre cinema, we will, therefore, find no series of films comparable to the Universal monster movies of the 1930s, the giant monster movies of the 1950s, or the Hammer horror films of the 1960s. No recurring commercial "conventions," no classic monsters, no school of B movies. It is worth noting that a large number of these types of foreign-made films were either not distributed in France, or distributed in cheap, exploitation houses, and could not, therefore, lift the genre from its commercial ghetto.

French filmmakers who did make incursions, no matter how timid, into the *fantastique* were consequently motivated more by literary pretensions than by the mere desire to terrify their audiences. Overwhelmingly, the themes of early French genre films revolved around the three "D's": Death, Dream, and the Devil (Religion), or traditional folk legends. Abel Gance's *J'accuse* (*I Accuse*, transl. as *They May Live*, 1918, remade 1937), Julien **Duvivier**'s **La Charrette Fantôme** (*The Ghost Cart*, 1939), Maurice **Tourneur**'s **La Main du Diable** (*The Devil's Hand*, transl. as *Carnival of Sinners*, 1942), René Clair's **La Beauté du Diable** (*The Beauty and the Devil*, 1949), or the films of Serge de **Poligny** are good illustrations of this high-brow approach.

The continued influence of the surrealist movement was nevertheless still felt in genre films by Jean Cocteau, such as **La Belle et la Bête** (*The Beauty and the Beast*, 1945) or *Orphée* (1949), and later, in films by Claude **Chabrol**, Alain **Robbe-Grillet,** and Juan Luis Buñuel, the son of the great Spanish director.

Jean Marais in La Belle et la Bête *(*The Beauty and the Beast*, 1945)*

Filmmakers who chose a more popular approach, starting with the great Louis **Feuillade**, who virtually pioneered the art of the serial, and others like him, relied on material drawn from pulp literature: Marcel **Allain** and Pierre **Souvestre**'s master criminal, *Fantômas*, the novels of Gaston **Leroux**, Maurice **Leblanc**, Arthur **Bernède**, and others.

George Franju's horror masterpiece **Les Yeux Sans Visage** (*Eyes Without a Face*, transl. as *The Horror Chamber of Dr. Faustus*, 1959) or, in a strikingly different vein, Roger **Vadim**'s **...Et Mourir de Plaisir** (*...And to Die from Pleasure*, transl. as *Blood and Roses*, 1960) and **Barbarella** (1967), an adaptation of Jean-Claude **Forest**'s popular graphic novel, were all representative of that approach.

In the 1960s, the great directors of the so-called

French "New Wave" made sparse use of the genre, and always as a form of allegory to address social or philosophical concerns: Jean-Luc **Godard**'s *Alphaville* (1965), François **Truffaut**'s *Fahrenheit 451* (1966), and Alain **Resnais**' *Je T'aime, Je T'aime* (*I Love You, I Love You*, 1968) were all serious films using the trappings of science fiction to make a point about life and society.

Virtually the only French filmmaker who could be said to have worked consistently in the genre was Jean **Rollin** who, starting in the late 1960s, began producing a series of mildly erotic vampire films. Rollin's love for the *fantastique* is not in question; however, his relatively undistinguished skills as a filmmaker and his subject matter relegated him and his films to the exploitation (not to say X-rated) distribution circuits, thus furthering the ghettoization problem.

In spite of Méliès' glorious beginnings, science fiction, in the more classic form of space travel and/or alien encounters, remained virtually absent from French movie screens. It is striking to note that, the year before the ground-breaking *2001: A Space Odyssey* impacted the fans' consciousness, French cinema was offering Henri Delanoe's trite comedy *Ne Jouez Pas avec les Martiens* (*Don't Play with the Martians*, 1967).

As always, there were a few exceptions. André Zwobada's *Croisières Sidérales* (*Star Cruises*, 1941) was remarkable only because it dealt with space/time travel at all. More worthy of notice were Abel Gance's grandiose treatment of *La Fin du Monde* (*The End of the World*, 1930) or documentarian Chris **Marker**'s remarkable short feature about time travel, *La Jetée* (*The Pier*, 1964), which inspired *Twelve Monkeys* (1996).

In the 1980s, the genre received a boost from the commercial success of imported American films. Some French filmmakers made occasional tries to follow in the footsteps of their American colleagues. But such attempts remained sporadic, and were often hampered by the lack of budget and special effects know-how. In that vein, one might mention Francis Leroi's *Le Démon dans l'Île* (*The Demon in the Island*, 1982) and Jean-Louis Bertucelli's *Stress* (1984), two effective sci-fi/horror thrillers; Yves **Boisset**'s *Le Prix du Danger* (*The Prize of Peril*, 1982), based on a Robert Sheckley story similar to, but which predated, *The Running Man* (1987) and finally, Arnaud Sélignac's *Gawin* (1990), a feel-good movie that made clever use of modern science fiction icons.

In spite of their good intentions, most of these films seemed to lack a certain conviction, and the French public did not embrace them in the way their producers had hoped. The box office francs instead continued to support the "real thing"—American films.

Modern French filmmakers have produced far more interesting genre films when they have pursued their own path, with stories often strikingly different from Anglo-Saxon models. Over the years, a number of French (and French-language) films have thus struck an original note, although—sad to say—commercial success has more often than not eluded them. Among these, one would single out Pierre **Kast**'s *Les Soleils de l'Île de Pâques* (*The Suns of Easter Island*, 1971); Belgian filmmaker Harry **Kumel**'s *Malpertuis* (1972); Jean Pourtalé's *Demain les Mômes* (*Tomorrow, the Kids*, 1975); Luc **Besson**'s *Le Dernier Combat* (*The Final Combat*, 1982); Alain **Jessua**'s *Paradis pour Tous* (*Paradise for All*, 1982); Claude **Lelouch**'s *Viva la Vie* (*Hurray for Life*, 1984); Luc Besson and Didier Grousset's *Kamikaze* (1986); Enki **Bilal**'s *Bunker Palace Hotel* (1989); Jean-Pierre **Jeunet** and Marc **Caro**'s *Delicatessen* (1992); and René **Manzor**'s *Un Amour de Sorcière* (*A Witch's Love*, 1997).

French co-productions with other countries have also made it possible for French directors to profit from more lavish budgets and better production values. *Fahrenheit 451* (1966), *Barbarella* (1967), *Le Joueur de Flûte* (*The Pied Piper of Hamelin*, 1971), and Pierre-William Glenn's *Terminus* (also transl. as *End of the Line*, 1986), a *Mad Max*–inspired production, were all co-productions. To these, one must add two remarkable films, Bertrand Tavernier's sole incursion into the genre, the uncompromising *La Mort en Direct* (*Death on Live TV*, transl. as *Deathwatch*, 1980) and Jean-Jacques Annaud's recreation of J.-H. **Rosny** Aîné's prehistoric saga, *La Guerre du Feu* (*The War for Fire*, transl. as *Quest For Fire*, 1981). Interestingly, Hollywood has taken notice. Luc Besson recently completed a major French-American science fiction co-production, *Le Cinquième Élément* (*The Fifth Element*, 1997), and Jean-Pierre Jeunet was recruited by 20th Century-Fox to direct *Alien Resurrection* (1997).

Finally, two authentic French fantasy films have recently broken box office records in France and in Europe: Jean-Marie Poiré's comedy *Les Visiteurs* (*The Visitors*, 1994) and Jean-Pierre Jeunet and Marc Caro's *La Cité des Enfants Perdus* (*The City of Lost Children*, 1995). Perhaps they herald a new, vital, promising era for the French fantasy and science fiction cinema.

2. Feature Films

We have attempted to list here every French genre feature film. Our criteria for inclusion in this list have been as follows:

(1) *French*: in today's age of international co-productions, it is sometimes hard to determine a film's nationality. In most cases, we have been guided by the director's nationality, which, but for a few exceptions, ruled out many French/Italian, French/Spanish and, more recently, French/ Eastern European co-productions, such as Peter Fleischmann's *Un Dieu Rebelle* (*Hard to Be a God*, 1990), but did allow us to include **Barbarella** (1967), **Fahrenheit 451** (1966) and **Le Joueur de Flûte** (*The Pied Piper of Hamelin*, 1971). We have also included French-language Belgian, Swiss, and the occasional French-Canadian, films.

There are, however, two exceptions to the above rule:

(a) Luis Buñuel was a controversial Spanish filmmaker who made films in France, written by French writer Jean-Claude **Carrière**, acted by a French cast, and produced with French money. We have therefore included his French-produced genre films in this compilation. His son, Juan Luis **Buñuel**, is treated as a French filmmaker.

(b) Jesus (Jess) Franco is a prolific Spanish B-movie director. Like Buñuel (but for different reasons), he, too, has made a number of French-produced films, as well as French/ Spanish co-productions, usually gore and/or X-rated pictures. We have listed Franco's French productions, but not his foreign co-productions. Readers interested in a more detailed study of Franco's idiosyncratic career are invited to check the following books: *Immoral Tales* by Cathal Tohill and Pete Tombs (St. Martin's, 1995) and the remarkable *Obsession: The Films of Jess Franco* by Lucas Balbo and Peter Blumenstock (in English, Hauffen & Trebbin, Munich, Germany, 1993).

(2) *Genre*: to be included in our list, a film generally had to contain a clear element of *fantastique*: supernatural, fantasy, horror, or science fiction. We have not always deemed it necessary to include minor films with only a very tenuous genre connection, usually in the form of an allegory, e.g.: *Haine* (*Hatred*, 1980) or films dealing purely with religious matters and miracles, e.g.: *Bernadette* (1987), because most people do not consider them *fantastique*. However, we made an exception for Jean-Luc **Godard**'s **Je Vous Salue Marie** (*Hail Mary*, 1984).

On the other hand, we have included films about serial killers and gory murders, such as Bernard **Blier**'s **Buffet Froid** (*Cold Cuts*, 1979), Claude **Chabrol**'s **Le Boucher** (*The Butcher*, 1969), Clouzot's **Les Diaboliques** (*Diabolique*, 1954), **C'est Arrivé Près de Chez Vous** (*It Happened Near Where You Live*, transl. as *Man Bites Dog*, 1992), and Paul Vecchiali's **L'Étrangleur** (*The Strangler*, 1970), because they have a good claim to be at least marginally part of the *fantastique*. We also have included a number of well-known, popular "pulp" heroes such as **Allain** and **Souvestre**'s **Fantômas**, **Leblanc**'s **Arsène Lupin**, **Leroux**'s **Rouletabille** and spy masters **Coplan FX-18** and **OSS 117**, for the same reasons as *Sherlock Holmes*, *The Shadow*, and *James Bond* are often listed in similar works in the English language.

Running times vary slightly according to the sources. When in doubt, we have relied on Jean Tulard's authoritative *Guide des Films*. The year given here is that of the first French release.

L'Abîme des Morts-Vivants [The Abyss of the Living Dead, transl. as **Oasis of the Zombies, Tomb of the Blind Dead]** (Col., 95 min., 1981)
DIR: A. M. Franck (pseudonym of Daniel Lesoeur); WRI: Daniel Lesoeur.
CAST: Manuel Gelin, France Jordan, Jeff Montgomery, Henri Lambert.
STORY: Nazi cannibal zombies protect a treasure hidden in a Moroccan oasis.
NOTE: A Spanish version of the same film exists, directed by Jess Franco, with a different cast.

Ada dans la Jungle [Ada in the Jungle] (Col., 90 min., 1988)
DIR/WRI: Gérard Zingg, based on the eponymous Italian comic book series by Francesco Altan.
CAST: Marie Louisa (Ada), Richard Bohringer, (Pilic), Bernard Blier (Collins), Philippe Léotard, Isaach de Bankolé, Victoria Abril, Charley Boorman, Robert Stephens, Katerine Boorman.
STORY: A British Lord dispatches young Ada to Africa to search for a child he once abandoned in the jungle.
NOTE: This film is an adaptation of a popular Italian comic book series spoofing African adventures *à la Tim Tyler's Luck*.

Adrénaline—Le Film (80 min., 1990)
Compilation of 13 short features (listed here in order of appearance):

1. *Les Aveugles [The Blind]* (Col., 8 min, 1990)
DIR/WRI/CAST: Anita Assal, John Hudson.
STORY: Blind people go to the movies.

2. *Métrovision* (Col., 4 min., 1986)
DIR/WRI/CAST: Yann Piquer.
STORY: The Paris subway suddenly goes insane.

3. *Revestriction [Dream Restriction]* (B&W., 6 min., 1989)
DIR/WRI: Barthélémy Bompard.
CAST: Bernadette Coqueret.
STORY: The walls and ceiling of a room start closing in on its occupant.

4. Graffiti (Col., 3 min., 1990)
DIR/WRI: Barthélémy Bompard.
CAST: Marie-Christine Munchery.
STORY: An old woman draws graffiti with a dead cat.

5. Cimetière des Éléphants [Graveyard of Elephants] (Col., 6 min., 1989)
DIR/WRI: Philippe Dorisson.
CAST: Alain Aithnard.
STORY: Cars go by themselves to a junkyard to die, taking their drivers with them.

6. Embouteillage [Traffic Jam] (B&W., 5 min., 1986)
DIR/WRI: Barthélémy Bompard.
CAST: Franck Baruk.
STORY: A new solution to get rid of traffic jams.

7. Corridor (Col., 7 min., 1989)
DIR: Alain Robak; WRI: Alain Robak, Jean-Marc Toussaint.
CAST: Jean-François Gallotte.
STORY: To be allowed to buy a house, people must first take a cruel exam.

8. Interrogatoire [Interrogation] (Col., 7 min., 1989)
DIR/WRI: Yann Piquer, Jean-Marie Madeddu.
CAST: Jean-Marie Madeddu, Arnaud Chevrier, Carla Teillot.
STORY: Love makes a man agree to submit to a horrible torture.

9. Urgence [Emergency] (Col., 3 min., 1987)
DIR/WRI: Yann Piquer, Jean-Marie Madeddu.
CAST: Jean-Marie Madeddu, Gilbert Duprez.
STORY: A man asking for directions in the countryside unwittingly causes a catatrophe.

10. La Dernière Mouche [The Last Fly] (B&W., 4 min., 1987)
DIR/WRI: Yann Piquer, Jean-Marie Madeddu.
CAST: Jean-Marie Madeddu, Anne-Marie Pisani.
STORY: A lunatic covers the walls of his room with dead insects.

11. TV Buster (Col., 14 min., 1987)
DIR/WRI: Anita Assal, John Hudson.
CAST: Clémentine Célarié, Ged Marlon, Jean-Marie Madeddu, Barthélémy Bompard.
STORY: A television set is possessed by the devil.

12. Cyclope [Cyclops] (Col., 5 min., 1989)
DIR: Anita Assal, John Hudson; WRI: Jean-Marie Madeddu.
CAST: Jean-Marie Madeddu.
STORY: The revolt of a surveillance camera.

13. Sculpture Physique [Physical Sculpture] (Col., 4 min., 1987)
DIR/WRI: Yann Piquer, Jean-Marie Madeddu.
CAST: Jean-Marie Madeddu.
STORY: Beating up someone creates a work of art.

L'Affaire des Divisions Morituri [The Case of the Morituri Department] (B&W., 75 min., 1985)
DIR/WRI: F. Jacques Ossang.
CAST: Gina Lola Benzina, Philippe Sfez, Lionel Tua, Frankie Tavezzano.
STORY: An underground network of modern gladiators.

Ali Baba et les Quarante Voleurs [Ali Baba and the Forty Thieves] (Col., 92 min., 1954)
DIR: Jacques Becker; WRI: Césare Zavattini, Jacques Becker, Marc Maurette, Maurice Griffe.
CAST: Fernandel (Ali Baba), Samia Gamal (Morgiane), Dieter Borsche (Abdul), Henri Vilbert (Cassim), Édouard Delmont, Edmond Ardisson, Manuel Gary, Julien Maffre, Gaston Orbal.
STORY: The legendary tale of Ali Baba retold with famous French comic actor Fernandel in the leading role.

Alice chez les Satyres [Alice Among the Satyrs] (Col., 85 min., 1971)
DIR/WRI: Francis Dubois.
CAST: Diane Dubois, Thierry de Brem, Dominique Cale.
STORY: X-rated version of *Alice in Wonderland*.

Alice, ou La Dernière Fugue [Alice, or The Last Escapade] (Col., 93 min., 1976)
DIR/WRI: Claude **Chabrol**.
CAST: Sylvia Kristel (Alice), Charles Vanel (Vergennes), André Dussolier, Fernand Ledoux, Jean Carmet.
STORY: After a car accident at night on a lonely road, Alice (played by *Emmanuelle* title actress Sylvia Kristel) finds herself in a mysterious mansion where she experiences a series of surreal encounters. In reality, she died in the accident.

L'Alliance [The Alliance] (Col., 90 min., 1970)
DIR: Christian de **Chalonge**; WRI: Christian de **Chalonge**, Jean-Claude **Carrière**, based on his novel.
CAST: Jean-Claude **Carrière** (Hughes), Anna Karina (Jeanne), Isabelle Sadoyan, Jean-Pierre Darras, Tsilla Chelton, Rufus.
STORY: Hughes, a reclusive veterinarian, who conducts ESP experiments, and Jeanne, a mysterious young woman, eventually fall in love after a long courtship, but a final cataclysm upsets their world.

Alphaville—Une Étrange Aventure de Lemmy Caution [Alphaville—A Strange Adventure of Lemmy Caution] (B&W., 100 min., 1965)
DIR/WRI: Jean-Luc **Godard**.
CAST: Eddie Constantine (Lemmy Caution), Anna Karina (Natacha), Akim Tamiroff, Howard Vernon (Von Braun), Laszlo Szabo.

STORY: Tough private eye Lemmy Caution is sent to Alphaville to convince Prof. Von Braun to return. After destroying Alpha-60, the computer which rules the city, he leaves with Von Braun's daughter, Natacha, who has fallen in love with him.

NOTE: The character of Lemmy Caution was created by British thriller writer Peter Cheyney, and was the subject of several French films, all starring expatriate American actor Eddie Constantine.

Les Amazones du Temple d'Or [The Golden Temple Amazons] (Col., 85 min., 1984)

DIR: James Gartner (pseudonym of Jess Franco), Alain Payet; WRI: A. L. Mariaux, George Freeland, based on the story *Akagu, Forbidden Temple* by Jeff Manner.

CAST: Stanley Kapoul, William Berger, Robert Foster, Joan Virly, Françoise Blanchard, Claire Marchal.

STORY: B-movie about a Jungle Queen's revenge on the tribe of amazons who killed her parents.

NOTE: This is a French/Spanish co-production.

L'Amour à Mort [Love Unto Death] (Col., 92 min., 1984)

DIR: Alain **Resnais**; WRI: Jean Gruault.

CAST: Sabine Azema (Elisabeth), Pierre Arditi (Simon), Fanny Ardant (Judith), André Dussolier (Jérôme), Jean Daste.

STORY: Elisabeth and Simon are in love. Simon dies but comes back to life a changed man. When he decides to die again, Elisabeth chooses to join him.

Un Amour de Poche [A Pocket Love, transl. as Girl in His Pocket; Nude in His Pocket] (B&W., 88 min., 1957)

DIR: Pierre **Kast**; WRI: Pierre **Kast**, France Roche, based on the story "*The Diminishing Draft*" (1918) by Waldemar Kaempfert.

CAST: Jean Marais (Prof. Nordmann), Geneviève Page, (Édith), Agnès Laurent (Simone), Amédée, France Roche.

STORY: Prof. Nordmann discovers a way to shrink human beings and uses it to thwart his fiancée's jealousy.

Un Amour de Sorcière [A Witch's Love] (Col., 100 min., 1997)

DIR/WRI: René **Manzor**.

CAST: Jeanne Moreau (Eglantine), Vanessa Paradis (Morgane), Jean Reno (Molok).

STORY: Morgane is a good fairy and the mother of an 11-month-old baby. Her grandmother Eglantine helps her defeat the villainous Molok.

L'Ampélopède (Col., 83 min., 1974)

DIR/WRI: Rachel Winberg.

CAST: Patrizia Pierangeli, Isabelle Huppert, Jean-Marie Marguet, Philippe Lehembre, Louise Dhour.

STORY: A young woman, tired of seeing her beloved countryside ravaged by pollution and home builders, invents a story about a fantastic creature which lives in the woods.

L'An 01 [The Year 01] (B&W., 90 min., 1972)

DIR: Jacques Doillon; WRI: **Gébé** (Georges Blondeaux), based on his novel.

CAST: Romain Bouteille, Cabu, Cavanna, Henri Guybet, Jacques Higelin.

STORY: One day, men stop working and take time to enjoy life, thus beginning a new era.

NOTE: This post-1968, utopian sketch film was made by a number of famous French cartoonists (**Gébé**, Cabu, etc.) and comedians. Alain **Resnais** allegedly directed the Wall Street scene. For **Gébé**, also see Chapter V and ***Rhésus B*** (Chapter II).

L'Âne Qui A Bu la Lune [The Ass Which Drank the Moon] (Col., 95 min., 1986)

DIR/WRI: Marie-Claude Treilhou.

CAST: José Pech (Storyteller), Charles Serres, Marie-Thérèse Rocalve, Francis Serres, Magali Arnaud.

STORY: An Old Man tells five stories adapted from folk tales:

1. Les Trois Jeunes Gens [The Three Young Men]

STORY: Three young peasants go to Paris and are framed for murder.

2. Le Cochon Élu Maire [The Pig Who Was Elected Mayor]

STORY: In a feud-torn village, a pig is elected mayor.

3. Le Moine Changé en Âne [The Monk Who Was Turned Into an Ass]

STORY: A cursed monk turns into an ass.

4. L'Âne Qui A Bu la Lune [The Ass Which Drank the Moon]

STORY: A credulous young farmer believes his donkey has magical powers.

5. Le Carnaval [Carnival]

STORY: A young man meets the ghost of a woman he once loved.

L'Ange [The Angel] (Col., 70 min., 1982)

WRI/DIR: Patrick Bokanowski.

CAST: Maurice Baquet, Jean-Marie Bon, Martine Couture, Jacques Faure.

STORY: A series of symbolic scenes linked together by the thematic image of a man climbing a staircase.

NOTE: This plotless film, which took five years to make, is mostly a technical achievement in weird special effects and image manipulation.

L'Ange et la Femme [The Angel and the Woman] (Col., 90 min., 1977)

DIR/WRI: Gilles Carle.

CAST: Carole Laure, Lewis Furey, Jean Comtois.

STORY: An angel saves a woman from death and falls in love with her.

NOTE: This is a French-Canadian production, shot in French.

Les Anges Gardiens [The Guardian Angels] (Col., 110 min., 1995)

DIR: Jean-Marie Poiré; WRI: J.-M. Poiré, Christian Clavier.

CAST: Gérard Depardieu, Christian Clavier, Eva Grimaldi, Yves Rénier, Alexandre Eskimo, Jennifer Herrera, Zouzou, Fabienne Chaudat, Françoise Bertin, François Morel.

STORY: A French gangster (Depardieu) and a priest (Clavier) face the task of rapatriating a Hong Kong orphan (Eskimo). Their guardian angels (Depardieu, Clavier), acting as their moral opposites, complicate matters.

L'Année Dernière à Marienbad [Last Year in Marienbad] (B&W., 93 min., 1961)

DIR: Alain **Resnais**; WRI: Alain **Robbe-Grillet**.

CAST: Delphine Seyrig, Giorgio Albertazzi, Sacha Pitoeff.

STORY: In a strange hotel seemingly located outside of time, a man (Albertazzi) and a woman (Seyrig) meet, perhaps not for the first time…

NOTE: **Robbe-Grillet**'s story was reportedly inspired by genre novel *La Invencion de Morel* (transl. in 1940 as *The Invention of Morel*) by Argentinian writer Adolfo Bioy

Delphine Seyrig and Giorgio Albertazzi in L'Année Dernière à Marienbad *(Last Year in Marienbad) 1961.*

Casares. The novel deals with the protagonist's search for immortality through the recreation of time-looped holograms. It was filmed as a telefilm in 1967 (see *L'Invention de Morel* in Chapter II) and again in 1974, in Italy, by Emilio Greco as *L'Invenzione di Morel*.

Les Années Lumière [Light Years Away] (Col., 90 min., 1981)

DIR/WRI: Alain Tanner, based on the novel *La Voie Sauvage* [*The Savage Way*] by Daniel **Odier**.

CAST: Trevor Howard, Mick Ford, Bernice Stegers.

STORY: In Ireland, in the year 2000, a bartender learns the secret of flying from an old eccentric.

NOTE: Franco-Swiss co-production.

À Pied, à Cheval et en Spoutnik [On Foot, On Horseback and In a Sputnik, transl. as A Dog, a Mouse and a Sputnik; Hold Tight for the Satellite] (B&W., 100 min., 1958)

DIR: Jean Dréville; WRI: Jean-Jacques Vital, Jacques Grello, Robert Rocca, Noël-Noël.

CAST: Noël-Noël (Léon Martin), Denise Grey (Marguerite), Noël Roquevert, Darry Cowl, Pauline Carton, Misha Auer, Francis Blanche, Nathalie Nerval, Serge Nadaud, Sophie Daumier.

STORY: Léon, a peace-loving Frenchman, finds in his garden a lost Russian satellite and the dog it contains.

L'Araignée d'Eau [The Water Spider] (B&W., 95 min., 1968)

DIR: Jean-Daniel Verhaeghe; WRI: Marcel **Béalu**, based on his novel.

CAST: Marie-Ange Dutheil, Elisabeth Wiener, Marc Eyrault.

STORY: A water spider turns into a beautiful girl to better doom the man who captured her.

NOTE: Marcel **Béalu** is a famous writer of the *fantastique* (see Book 2). Jean-Daniel Verhaeghe directed numerous telefilms such as *L'Étrange Château du Dr. Lerne*, *La Métamorphose* and *La Nuit des Fantômes* (see Chapter II), and an animated short, *Les Marchands d'Armes* (see Chapter IV).

L'Arbre Sous la Mer [The Underwater Tree] (Col., 95 min., 1984)

DIR/WRI: Philippe Muyl, based on the novel *A Naked Young Girl* by Nikos Athanassiadis.

CAST: Christophe Malavoy (Mathieu), Eleni Dragoumi, Julien Guiomar.

STORY: In the Greek islands, Mathieu, a young geologist, falls in love with a beautiful "sea girl" (Dragoumi) but eventually discovers that their love cannot be.

Les Ardentes [The Fiery Ones] (Col., 85 min., 1973)

DIR/WRI: Henri Sala.

CAST: Anne Libert, Sherry Parker, Monique Vila, Yann Keredec.

STORY: X-rated story about a colony of women who live isolated in a strange medieval society.

Armaguedon (Col., 96 min., 1977)

DIR: Alain **Jessua**; WRI: Alain **Jessua**, based on a novel by P. Lippincott.

CAST: Alain Delon (Dr. Ambrose), Jean Yanne, Renato Salvatori.

STORY: Dr. Ambrose is charged by the Government to locate a mysterious terrorist code-named "Armaguedon" (Yanne).

Arsène Lupin

Based on the famous gentleman burglar created by popular writer Maurice **Leblanc** (see Book 2). Genre elements are few and far between, but *Lupin* being the French equivalent of *Sherlock Holmes*, its inclusion in this filmography seems warranted. Also see Chapter II for television adaptations.

1. Arsène Lupin (B&W., 1914)
DIR/WRI: Émile **Chautard**.
CAST: Georges Tréville (Lupin).
STORY: No information available.

2. Arsène Lupin, Détective (B&W., 98 min., 1937)
DIR/WRI: Henri Diamant-Berger.
CAST: Jules Berry (Lupin), Gabriel Signoter (Béchoux), Suzy Prim, Rosine Deréan, Mady Berry, Thomy Bourdelle.
STORY: Lupin impersonates private eye Jim Barnett and matches wits with with inspector Béchoux.

NOTE: Based on *L'Agence Barnett & Cie.*, published in 1928.

3. Les Aventures d'Arsène Lupin [The Adventures of Arsène Lupin] (B&W., 104 min., 1956)
DIR: Jacques Becker; WRI: Albert Simonin, Jacques Becker.
CAST: Robert Lamoureux (Lupin), O. E. Hasse, Liselotte Pulver, Georges Chamarat.
STORY: Original story about an elaborate series of robberies.

4. Signé Arsène Lupin [Signed: Arsène Lupin] (B&W., 100 min., 1959)
DIR: Yves Robert; WRI: Jean-Paul Rappeneau, Yves Robert, François Chavanne, Robert Lamoureux.
CAST: Robert Lamoureux (Lupin), Alida Valli, Jacques Dufilho, Roger Dumas, Yves Robert, Robert Dalban.
STORY: Original story in which Lupin seeks the legendary Golden Fleece.

5. Arsène Lupin contre Arsène Lupin [Arsène Lupin vs. Arsène Lupin] (B&W., 106 min., 1962)
DIR: Édouard Molinaro; WRI: Georges Neveux.
CAST: Jean-Pierre Cassel (Lupin), Jean-Claude Brialy (Lupin) Françoise Dorléac, Geneviève Grad, Michel Vitold, Jean Le Poulain, Henri Virlojeux.
STORY: Original story in which Lupin's sons compete against each other.

NOTE: The character of *Arsène Lupin* also has been the subject of a number of English-language films. A brief filmography follows: *The Gentleman Burglar* (USA, 1908, DIR/WRI: Edwin Stratton Porter, with William Ranows as Lupin); *Arsène Lupin* (UK, 1915, DIR: George L. Tucker, WRI: Bannister Merwin and Kenelm Foss, with Gerald Ames as Lupin); *The Gentleman Burglar* (USA, 1915, DIR: E. A. Martin, WRI: E. Lynn Summers, with William Stowell as Lupin); *Arsène Lupin* (USA, 1917, DIR: John S. Robertson and Paul Scardon, WRI: Garfield Thompson, with Earle Williams as Lupin); *The Teeth of the Tiger* (USA, 1919, DIR: Chester Withey, WRI: Roy Sommerville, with David Powell as Lupin); *813—Arsène Lupin* (USA, 1920, DIR: Scott F. Sidney, WRI: W. Scott Darling, with Wedgewood Nowell as Lupin); *Arsène Lupin* (USA, 1932, DIR: Jack Conway, WRI: Carey Wilson, Lenore Coffee, Bayard Veiller, with John Barrymore as Lupin); *Arsène Lupin Returns* (USA, 1938, DIR: George Fitzmaurice, WRI: James Kevin McGuiness, Howard Emmett Rogers, George Harmon Coxe, with Melvyn Douglas as Lupin); and *Enter Arsène Lupin* (USA, 1944, DIR: Ford L. Beebe, WRI: Bertram Millhauser, with Charles Korvin as Lupin).

L'Atlantide [Atlantis]

Based on the classic novel by Pierre **Benoît** (see Book 2), published in 1919.

Version No.1: (B&W., 90 min., 1921)
Dir/Wri: Jacques Feyder.
Cast: Stacia Napierkowska (Antinéa), Jean Angelo (Morange), Georges Melchior (Saint-Avit), Marie-Louise Iribe.

Version No. 2: (Col., 110 min., 1991)
Dir/Wri: Bob Swaim.
Cast: Victoria Mahoney (Antinéa), Tcheky Karyo (Morhange), Christopher Thompson (Saint-Avit).
Story: Two French officers lost in the Sahara come across the last city of Atlantis, ruled by the cruel Queen Antinéa.
Note: Pierre **Benoît**'s novel was also adapted in Germany in 1932 as *Die Herrin von Atlantis* (Dir: G. W. Pabst, with Brigitte Helm); in the U.S. in 1949 as *Siren of Atlantis* (Dir: Gregg G. Tallas, with Maria Montez); and finally, in Italy in 1961 as *L'Atlantide* (Dir: Edgar G. Ulmer, with Jean-Louis Trintignant and Haya Harareet). Also see Chapter II for a telefilm adaptation.

Au Coeur de la Vie *[In the Midst of Life]* (B&W., 90 min., 1962)
Dir/Wri: Robert Enrico, based on three stories by Ambrose Bierce.

1. Chickamauga
Story: A little deaf boy plays with the ghosts of the soldiers who died during the famous Civil War battle.

2. Mockingbird
Story: A soldier shoots his own twin brother by mistake.

3. La Rivière du Hibou [Owl River, transl. as *An Occurrence at Owl Creek Bridge)* (27 min.)
Cast: Roger Jacquet (Peyton Farquhar), Anne Cornaly (Mrs. Farquhar), Anker Larsen, Stéphane Fey, Jean-François Zeller, Pierre Danny, Louis Adelin (Union Soldiers).
Story: During the Civil War, a Confederate spy who is about to be hung miraculously escapes and manages to return home. But the whole thing was only a dream, and he dies on the gallows.
Note: In order to save money, *The Twilight Zone* producer William Froug purchased the rights to the third short-feature, which had won a prize at the 1962 Cannes Film Festival. A new introduction was recorded by Rod Serling and it was incorporated as episode No. 142 of *The Twilight Zone* and originally broadcast on 28 February 1964. The reedited version went on to win an Oscar.

Au Rendez-Vous de la Mort Joyeuse *[Rendezvous with Joyous Death]* (Col., 90 min., 1972)
Dir: Juan Luis **Buñuel**; Wri: Pierre-Jean **Maintigneux**, Juan Luis **Buñuel**.
Cast: Yasmine Dahm (Sophie), Jean-Marie Bory, Françoise Fabian, Jean-Pierre Darras, Michel Créton, Claude Dauphin, Gérard Depardieu.
Story: A family moves into a haunted house which suc-

ceeds in making all of them, except their daughter, Sophie, leave.

Au Service du Diable *[in the Devil's Service]* (Col., 90 min., 1971) see *La Plus Longue Nuit du Diable*

Les Aventures d'Eddie Turley *[The Adventures of Eddie Turley]* (B&W., 85 min., 1987)
Dir/Wri: Gérard Courant.
Cast: Philip Dubuquoy (Eddie Turley), Françoise Michaud (Lola), Joël Barbouth, Mariola San Martin, Lucia Fioravanti, Joseph Morder, Gérard Tallet.
Story: *La Jetée* meets *Alphaville*. In this feature made of 2400 stills, galactic agent Eddie Turley arrives in Modern City, which he eventually discovers is ruled by a giant computer. He leaves with his new-found love, Lola.

Baby Blood *[transl. as The Evil Within]* (Col., 89 min., 1989)
Dir: Alain Robak; Wri: Alain Robak, Serge Cukier.
Cast: Emmanuelle Escourrou (Yanka), Jean-François Gallotte, Roselyn Geslot, Christian Sinniger, Alain Chabat, Anne Singer, Jean-Claude Romer.
Story: Yanka is a circus woman whose womb is taken over by a creature and later protects the life of the blood-sucking monster to which she eventually gives birth.

Note: French critic Jean-Claude Romer has a small role in this unusual French gore film. Actor Gary Oldman reportedly provided the voice of the creature in the U.S. version.

Ballade de la Féconductrice *[Ballad of the Feconductrix]* (Col., 85 min., 1979)
Dir/Wri: Laurent Boutonnat.
Cast: Orit Mizrahi, Gilles Mathé.
Story: The tale of an evil fairy.

Barbarella (Col., 98 min., 1967)
Dir: Roger **Vadim**; Wri: Terry Southern, Jean-Claude **Forest**, Roger **Vadim**, Vittorio Bonicelli, Brian Degas, Claude Brule, Tudor Gates, Clement Biddle Wood; based on the graphic novel by Jean-Claude **Forest**.
Cast: Jane Fonda (Barbarella), John Philip Law (Pygar), Anita Pallenberg (Black Queen), Milo O'Shea, Marcel Marceau, Ugo Tognazzi, David Hemmings, Claude Dauphin

Jane Fonda is Barbarella *(1967).*

STORY: Barbarella is sent by Earth to planet Sogo to bring back a missing scientist. There, she encounters Pygar, a blind angel, and a lesbian queen.

NOTE: This is a French/Italian co-production. For further information on **Barbarella** and Jean-Claude **Forest**, see Chapter V.

Le Baron Fantôme [The Ghostly Baron] (B&W., 99 Min, 1942)

DIR: Serge de **Poligny**; WRI: Serge de **Poligny**, Louis Chavance, Jean **Cocteau**.

CAST: Odette Joyeux (Elfy), Jany Holt (Anne), Alain Cuny (Hervé), Gabrielle Dorziat (Countess), Claude Sainval, André Lefaur, Aimé Clariond, Jean **Cocteau**.

STORY: The Countess of Saint-Hélié and her two daughters, Elfy and Anne, move into a castle reputedly haunted by their late uncle, baron Carol (**Cocteau**, in a small role). They eventually find the Baron's body in a secret chamber, and the daughters find their true loves.

Baxter (Col., 82 min., 1988)

DIR: Jérôme Boivin; WRI: Jacques Audiard, Jérôme Boivin, based on the novel by Ken Greenhall.

CAST: Maxime Leroux (voice of Baxter), Lise Delamare, Jean Mercure, Jacques Spiesser, Catherine Ferran, Jean-Paul Roussillon, Sabrina Leurquin, Daniel Rialet, Evelyne Didi.

STORY: A thinking, talking dog, Baxter, narrates the grim story of his life.

La Beauté du Diable [The Beauty and the Devil] (B&W., 92 min., 1949)

DIR: René **Clair**; WRI: Armand Salacrou, René **Clair**.

CAST: Michel Simon (Mephistopheles), Gérard Philipe (Henri), Simone Valère, Nicole Besnard, Gaston Modot, Paolo Stoppa.

STORY: A remake of the classic *Faust* story, recast in modern times.

NOTE: This was an Italian-French co-production.

Belle (Col., 93 Min, 1972)

DIR/WRI: André **Delvaux**.

CAST: Jean-Luc Bideau (Mathieu), Adriana Bogdan (Belle), Danièle Delorme (Jeanne), Roger Coggio.

STORY: Mathieu, a writer, falls in love with a mysterious woman (Bogdan) who lives in the woods and never speaks. She drives him to commit murder, but it may all have been a dream.

NOTE: This is a French-language Belgian production.

La Belle Captive [The Beautiful Prisoner] (Col., 88 min., 1983)

DIR/WRI: Alain **Robbe-Grillet**.

CAST: Daniel Mesguich (Walter), Gabrielle Lazure (Marie-Ange), Cyrille Claire (Sara), Daniel Emilfork, Roland Dubillard, François Chaumette.

STORY: Sara entrusts her boyfriend Walter with a mysterious mission. He then encounters the beautiful, vampire-like Marie-Ange, who takes him on a series of surreal adventures.

La Belle et la Bête [The Beauty and the Beast] (B&W., 100 min., 1945)

DIR/WRI: Jean **Cocteau**, based on the classic fairy tale by Mme **Leprince de Beaumont**.

CAST: Josette Day (Belle), Jean Marais (Beast/Prince), Marcel André, Michel Auclair, Mila Parély.

STORY: To save her father's life, a beautiful young woman agrees to spend her life in the castle of a magical beast. Her love will turn the Beast back into a Prince Charming.

La Belle Histoire [A Beautiful Story] (Col., 210 min., 1991)

DIR: Claude **Lelouch**; WRI: Claude **Lelouch**, Marilyne Dupoux.

CAST: Gérard Lanvin, Béatrice Dalle, Patrick Chesnais, Constantin Alexandrov, Vincent Lindon, Paul Préboist, Anémone, Charles Gérard.

STORY: A gypsy (Lanvin) and a young female thief (Dalle) are the reincarnations of a couple who lived at the time of Jesus, and are fated to fall in love.

La Belle Image [The Beautiful Image] (B&W., 90 min., 1950)

DIR: Claude **Heymann**; WRI: Jean Ferry, Claude Heymann, based on the story by Marcel **Aymé**.

CAST: Frank Villard (Raoul), Françoise Christophe (Renée), Pierre Larquey, Junie Astor, Suzanne Flon.

STORY: Raoul, a man with a plain face, magically finds himself transformed into a very handsome man.

NOTE: For other Marcel **Aymé** adaptations, see *Garou-Garou, le Passe-Muraille* below, and Chapter II under ***Aymé, Marcel***.

Les Belles de Nuit [Beauties of the Night] (Col., 89 min., 1952)

DIR: René **Clair**; WRI: René **Clair**, Pierre Barillet, Jean-Pierre Grédy.

CAST: Martine Carol, Gina Lollobrigida, Gérard Philipe.

STORY: A frustrated pianist (Philipe) has vivid dreams in which he is pursued by beautiful women in different historical eras.

NOTE: This was an Italian-French co-production.

Belphegor (B&W., Serial in Four Eps., 1926)

DIR: Henri Desfontaines; WRI: Arthur **Bernède**.

CAST: René Navarre (Chantecoq), Lucien Dalsace (Bellegarde), Elmire Vautier (Simone Desroches), Georges Paulais (Commissioner Ménardier), Jeanne Brindeau (Elsa).

STORY: A ghostly presence is haunting the Louvre. The villains are unmasked by journalist Bellegarde and detective Chantecoq. Belphegor is revealed to be Bellegarde's mistress, Simone.

NOTE: Arthur **Bernède** also created the character of *Judex* (see below). *Belphegor* was later remade as a television series (see Chapter II).

La Bête [The Beast] (Col., 104 min., 1975)

DIR/WRI: Walerian **Borowczyk**.

CAST: Sirpa Lane, Lisbeth Hummel, Pierre Benedetti, Guy Tréjean, Marcel Dalio, Roland Armontel, Jean Martinelli, Pascale Rivault.

STORY: A strange, erotic variation on *La Belle et la Bête*, in which the Beast turns out to be an over-endowed wild boy.

Black Moon (Col., 100 Min, 1975)

DIR/WRI: Louis **Malle**.

CAST: Cathryn Harrison (Lily), Thérèse Giehse, Alexandra Stewart, Joe Dallesandro

STORY: During a war between the sexes, Lily finds refuge in a forest cabin inhabited by an old woman who talks to rats (Giehse), a strange brother-sister couple (Dallesandro, Stewart), a discursive unicorn and a piano-playing cat.

Le Boucher [The Butcher] (Col., 95 min., 1969)

DIR/WRI: Claude **Chabrol**.

CAST: Jean Yanne (Popaul), Stéphane Audran.

STORY: Popaul, the butcher of a small regional village, is suspected of being a serial killer by the new schoolteacher.

Boulevard de l'Étrange [Boulevard of the Weird] (117 min., 1986)

Compilation of 8 short features (listed in order of appearance):

1. Le Mauvais Oeil [The Evil Eye] (Col., 15 min, 1985)

DIR/WRI: Jean-Louis Cros.

CAST: Georges Claisse, Catherine Wilkening, François Capelier.

STORY: A 19th century photographer discovers he has magical powers.

2. Je Reviens De Suite [I'll Be Right Back] (Col., 15 min, 1982)

DIR/WRI: Henri Gruvman.

CAST: Henri Gruvman, Florence Aguttes, Ulrika White.

STORY: A stage magician enables people to enter the world of celluloid film.

3. L'Abygène (B&W., 9 min, 1985)

DIR/WRI: Anne Bocrie.

CAST: Anne Caudry, Samuel Malaval.

STORY: An ordinary woman's breakfast turns into a nightmare.

4. Le Ciel Saisi [The Captured Sky] (Col., 23 min, 1983)

DIR/WRI: Henri Herré.

CAST: Marie Vayssière, Philippe Marbot.

STORY: Omnipresent surveillance cameras spy on an ordinary couple.

5. Le Réacteur Vernet [The Vernet Reactor] (Col., 11 min, 1985)

DIR: Laurent Dussaux; WRI: Laurent Dussaux, Laurent Zerah, based on a story by Lion Miller.

CAST: Claude **Klotz**, Gérard Grobman, Philippe Mareuil.

STORY: A retarded man invents a wonderful machine.

6. La Fonte de Barlaeus [The Melting of Barlaeus] (Col., 15 min, 1983)

DIR/WRI: Pierre-Henri Salfati.

CAST: Roland Dubillard, Sylvie Flepp, Rachel Salik, Michel Caccia.

STORY: A man believes he is made of butter.

7. Game Over (Col., 8 min, 1984)

DIR/WRI: Bernard Villiot.

CAST: Roger Mirmont, Marc Mazza, Roxanne Nouban.

STORY: A killer, his victim, and a witness are trapped in a deadly game.

8. La Consultation (B&W., 21 min, 1985)

DIR/WRI: Radovan Tadic.

CAST: Isabelle Weingarten, Dominique Marcas, Sébastien Floche.

STORY: A troubled mother visits a psychiatrist who turns out to be a monkey.

Buffet Froid [Cold Cuts] (Col., 95 min., 1979)

DIR/WRI: Bertrand **Blier**.

CAST: Gérard Depardieu (Alphonse Tram), Bernard Blier (Inspector), Jean Carmet (Killer), Michel Serrault, Carole Bouquet.

STORY: Alphonse Tram, a police inspector, and a serial killer embark on a murder spree.

Bunker Palace Hotel (Col., 95 min., 1989)

DIR: Enki **Bilal**; WRI: Enki **Bilal**, Pierre **Christin**.

CAST: Jean-Louis Trintignant (Holm), Carole Bouquet (Klara), Maria Schneider (Muriel), Roger Dumas, Yann Collette, Jean-Pierre Léaud, Hans Meyer.

STORY: In an Eastern European country torn by civil war, the former political elite has found refuge in a vast underground bunker. A young rebel, Klara, manages to infiltrate the bunker, but things begin to fall apart.

NOTE: For further information on Enki **Bilal** and Pierre **Christin**, see Chapter V.

La Cage [The Cage] (Col., 83 min., 1963)
DIR: Robert Darene; WRI: Christine Garnier, Alain Bouvette, Pierre Tristan, Marc Boureau, Georges de la Grandière, Robert Darene.

CAST: Marina Vlady, Jean Servais, Philippe Maury, Myriel David, Colette Duval, Alain Bouvette.

STORY: An African spell causes a man to see apparitions of his dead wife.

Calmos [Quiet Please!] (Col., 107 min., 1976)
DIR: Bertrand **Blier**; WRI: Bertrand **Blier**, Philippe Dumarcay.

CAST: Jean-Pierre Marielle (Paul), Jean Rochefort (Albert), Bernard Blier (Priest), Pierre Bertin, Brigitte Fossey.

STORY: A group of men who are tired of women decide to retire to the countryside and live in peace.

La Cavalcade des Heures [The Cavalcade of Hours] (B&W., 99 min., 1943)
DIR/WRI: Yvan Noé.

CAST: Pierrette Caillol (Hora), Fernandel (Antonin), Charles Trenet, Tramel, Gaby Morlay, Jeanne Fusier-Gir, Jean Chevrier, Jules Ladoumègue.

STORY: In this sketch film, the Incarnation of Time (Caillol) helps a series of characters to take control of their destiny.

Cartes sur Table [Cards on the Table, transl. as Attack of the Robots] (B&W., 93 min., 1966)
DIR: Jess Franco; WRI: Jean-Claude **Carrière**.

CAST: Eddie Constantine, Sophie Hardy, Fernando Rey, Alfredo Mayo.

STORY: Men are turned into killer robots.

NOTE: This French-Spanish co-production, directed by renowned Spanish genre filmmaker Jess (Jesus) Franco, is listed here because of its script by Jean-Claude **Carrière**.

C'est Arrivé Près de Chez Vous [It Happened Near You, transl. as Man Bites Dog] (B&W., 95 min., 1992)
DIR: Rémy Belvaux, André Bonzel, Benoît Poelvoorde; WRI: Rémy Belvaux, André Bonzel, Benoît Poelvoorde, Vincent Tavier.

CAST: Benoît Poelvoorde (Ben), André Bonzel, Rémy Belvaux, Jacqueline Poelvoorde Pappaert, Nelly Pappaert, Hector Pappaert, Valérie Parent, Jenny Drye, Malou Madou.

STORY: A television crew follows and interviews Ben, a serial killer, and eventually becomes involved in his insane life.

NOTE: This is a French-language Belgian production, with no specific genre elements, but an incredibly surreal and violent climate.

La Chambre Ardente [The Burning Court] (B&W., 111 min., 1963)
DIR: Julien **Duvivier**; WRI: Julien **Duvivier**, Charles Spaak, based on the novel by John Dickson Carr.

CAST: Jean-Claude Brialy, Nadja Tiller, Balpêtré, Walter Giller, Helena Manson.

STORY: A woman who seems possessed by her ancestor, a famous poisoner, commits a murder.

NOTE: In spite of a rational explanation at the end, the entire film operates on the basis that possession by a spirit is real.

La Chambre Verte [The Green Room] (Col., 94 min., 1978)
DIR: François **Truffaut**; WRI: François **Truffaut**, Jean Gruault, based on the novel by Henry James.

CAST: François **Truffaut** (Davenne), Nathalie Baye (Cécilia), Jean Dasté, Jean-Pierre Moulin, Antoine Vitez, Jane Lobre, Jean-Pierre Ducos.

STORY: Davenne, a man who literally worships the dead, falls in love with Cécilia, a woman who shares his obsession.

NOTE: For other Henry James adaptations, see *Le Tour d'Écrou* below, and Chapter II under "*James, Henry.*"

Les Charlots Contre Dracula [The Charlots vs. Dracula] (Col., 85 min., 1980)
DIR: Jean-Pierre Desagnat; WRI: Les Charlots, Jean-Pierre Desagnat, Olivier Mergault, Fernand Pluot, based on an idea by Vera Belmont and Jacques Dorfmann.

CAST: Les Charlots, Amélie Prevost, Andréas Voutsinas (Dracula), Gérard Jugnot.

STORY: A famous French comedy team (*à la* The Three Stooges) fights the notorious undead Count (who is looking for a magic bottle) in this slapstick farce.

Le Charme Discret de la Bourgeoisie [The Discreet Charm of the Bourgeoisie] (Col., 105 min., 1972)
DIR: Luis Buñuel; WRI: Luis Buñuel, Jean-Claude **Carrière**.

CAST: Fernando Rey (Ambassador), Paul Frankeur (Thévenot), Delphine Seyrig (Mrs Thévenot), Bulle Ogier (Florence), Jean-Pierre Cassel, Stéphane Audran, Michel Piccoli, Claude Piéplu, Julien Bertheau, François Maistre.

STORY: A series of surreal, satirical sketches (often dealing with death and dreams) assembled around the theme of a dinner party held by the same cast of bourgeois characters. Perhaps they are all dead and this is their afterlife?

La Charrette Fantôme [The Ghost Cart] (B&W., 93 min., 1939)

DIR/WRI: Julien **Duvivier**, based on the book by Selma Lagerlöf.

CAST: Pierre Fresnay (David), Louis Jouvet (Georges), Micheline Francey (Edith), Valentine Tessier, Mila Parely, Palau.

STORY: Edith, a Salvation Army worker, tries to save the soul of David, whose nights are haunted by the shade of his late friend Georges, condemned to drive the Ghost Cart because of his evil deeds.

Le Château des Messes Noires [The Castle of Black Masses, transl. as ***The Devil's Plaything]*** (Col., 100 min., 1972)

DIR/WRI: Joseph Sarno.

CAST: Nadia Henkowa, Anke Syring.

STORY: A couple finds refuge in a castle inhabited by vampires.

NOTE: This is a French-language Swiss production.

Le Château du Vice [Castle of Vice] see ***La Plus Longue Nuit du Diable***

Les Chemins de la Violence [The Paths of Violence] see ***Perversions Sexuelles***

Cherchez l'Erreur [Find the Mistake] (Col., 92 min., 1980)

DIR: Serge Korber; WRI: Roland Magdane.

CAST: Roland Magdane (Paul), Roland Dubillard, Henri Virlojeux, Caroline Grimaldi, Micheline Luccioni, Tania Lopert, Marthe Villalonga, Béatrice Lord.

STORY: Paul, an eccentric scientist, discovers a miracle formula that might save the world, or destroy it. After the formula kills his dog, he destroys it.

Le Chevalier de la Nuit [The Knight of the Night] (B&W., 90 min., 1953)

DIR: Robert Darène; WRI: Jean Anouilh, Robert Darène.

CAST: Jean-Claude Pascal, Renée Saint-Cyr, Grégoire Aslan, Max Dalban, Louis de Funès.

STORY: In this *Dr. Jekyll & Mr. Hyde* variation, a man is haunted by two personalities, one good, the other evil.

Les Chevaliers de la Table Ronde [The Knights of the Round Table] (Col., 230 min., 1989)

DIR: Denis Llorca; WRI: Denis Llorca, Philippe Vialèles, based on the classic stories by **Chrétien de Troyes**.

CAST: Alain Cuny (Merlin), Alain Macé (Arthur), Maria Casarès (Viviane), Michel Vitold (Fisher King), Mireille Delcroix (Amythe), Nadine Darmon (Morgaine), Gilles Geisweiller (Perceval), Denis Llorca (Lancelot), Valérie Durin (Guinevere), François Berreur (Galaad), Benoist Brione (Gauvain).

STORY: Faithful if somewhat static translation of the saga of King Arthur and the Quest for the Holy Grail.

NOTE: This was based on an 11-hour-long stage play. Also see ***Perceval le Gallois*** below, and ***Lancelot du lac*** in Chapter II.

Les Chiens [The Dogs] (Col., 99 min., 1979)

DIR: Alain **Jessua**; WRI: Alain **Jessua**, André **Ruellan**.

CAST: Gérard Depardieu (Morel), Victor Lanoux (Dr. Féret), Nicole Calfan (Elisabeth), Pierre Vernier, Gérard Séty, Fanny Ardant.

STORY: Morel, a trainer of aggressive guard dogs, uses fear of crime to gain control of the minds of the inhabitants of a suburban town, until the pent-up violence he has fostered eventually turns against him.

NOTE: André **Ruellan** is the noted science fiction writer Kurt **Steiner**. He also wrote the film's novelization.

Les Chinois à Paris [The Chinese in Paris] (Col., 95 min., 1974)

DIR: Jean **Yanne**; WRI: Jean **Yanne**, Gérard Sire, Robert **Beauvais**, based on a story by Robert **Beauvais**.

CAST: Jean **Yanne** (Régis), Michel Serrault (Grégoire), Nicole Calfan (Stéphanie), Bernard Blier, Paul Préboist, Jacques François, Georges Wilson, Daniel Prévost, Macha Méril, Fernand Ledoux.

STORY: Thinly-veiled political satire about a Chinese invasion of France.

NOTE: Actor-director Jean **Yanne** also wrote the radio serial ***L'Apocalypse est pour Demain*** (see Book 1, Chapter III).

La Chute de la Maison Usher [The Fall of the House of Usher] (B&W., 55 min., 1928)

DIR/WRI: Jean Epstein, based on the story by Edgar Allan Poe.

CAST: Marguerite Gance (Lady Usher), Jean Debucourt (Roderick Usher), Charles Lamy.

STORY: Much praised silent adaptation of Poe's classic story about an evil House inhabited by a cursed family.

NOTE: Luis Buñuel assisted Jean Epstein on this film. The same year, another experimental, expressionistic version of this classic story was made in Rochester, New York, by Dr. James Sibley Watson and Melville Webber. Also see Chapter II under *Histoires Extraordinaires* for a television adaptation.

Le Ciel sur la Tête [The Sky Over My Head] (Col., 107 min., 1964)

DIR: Yves Ciampi; WRI: Yves Ciampi, Alain Satou, Jean Chapot.

CAST: André Smagghe, Jacques Monod, Marcel Bozzuffi, Yves Brainville, Guy Tréjean, Henri Piegay, Bernard Fresson, Béatrice Cenci.

STORY: The crew of a French aircraft carrier must solve the mystery of an unidentified satellite. Is it American, Russian, or extraterrestrial?

Le Cinquième Élément [The Fifth Element] (Col., 127 min., 1997)

DIR: Luc **Besson**; WRI: Robert Mark Kanen, Luc **Besson**.

CAST: Bruce Willis (Korben), Gary Oldman (Zorg), Ian Holm (Cornelius), Milla Jovovich (Leeloo), Chris Tucker.

STORY: In a futuristic world, cab driver Korben Dallas and alien clone Leeloo team up to search for the elusive "Fifth Element" and defeat the forces of darkness.

NOTE: American-French co-production. Visual designs were provided by renowed comic book artists **Moebius** and Jean-Claude **Mézières**.

La Cité de la Peur [The City of Fear] (Col., 90 min., 1994)

DIR: Alain Berberlian; WRI: Les Nuls.

CAST: Chantal Lauby, Alain Chabat, Dominique Farrugia, Gérard Darmon, Valérie Lemercier.

STORY: During the Cannes Film Festival, a serial killer duplicates the murders of a low-budget horror film (*Red is Dead*) being promoted there.

NOTE: Played for laughs. Les Nuls are a famous French troupe of television comics.

La Cité de l'Indicible Peur [The City of Unspeakable Fear] (B&W., 90 min., 1964) (aka *La Grande Frousse [The Great Fear]*)

DIR: Jean-Pierre **Mocky**; WRI: Jean-Pierre **Mocky**, Gérard Klein, based on the novel by Jean **Ray**.

CAST: Bourvil (Inspector Triquet), Jean-Louis Barrault (Douve), Francis Blanche (Franqui), Jean Poiret, Victor Francen, Raymond Rouleau, Jacques Dufilho, René-Louis Lafforgue, Véronique Nordey.

STORY: Triquet, a charming but hapless police inspector, unmasks several murderers in a small provincial town whose residents harbor dark secrets.

NOTE: The Gérard Klein who co-wrote the script is not the homonymous French science fiction writer/editor. For other Jean **Ray** adaptations, see *Malpertuis* below.

La Cité des Enfants Perdus [The City of Lost Children] (Col., 111 min., 1995)

DIR: Jean-Pierre **Jeunet** & Marc Caro; WRI: J.-P. **Jeunet**, M. **Caro**, Gilles Adrien, Guillaume Laurent.

CAST: Ron Perlman, Daniel Emilfork (Krank), Judith Vittet, Dominique Pinon, Jean-Claude Dreyfus, Geneviève Brunet, Odile Mallet, Mireille Mosse, François Hadji-Lazaro, Joseph Lucien.

STORY: Crazed inventor Krank is aging because he can't dream. To counter this, his cyclopean henchmen kidnap children from the local port. A circus strongman (Perlman) teams up with a band of ragamuffins to stop him.

La Cité Foudroyée [The City Struck by Lightning] (B&W., 60 min., 1924)

DIR: Luitz-Morat; WRI: Jean-Louis **Bouquet**.

CAST: Daniel Mendaille, Jeanne Maguenat, Armand Morins.

STORY: A mad scientist (Mendaille) who has found the way to control lightning threatens to destroy Paris, but it all turns out to be events in a novel.

NOTE: Also see the telefilm *Alouqa* in Chapter II.

Clash (Col., 100 min., 1983)

DIR/WRI: Raphaël Delpard.

CAST: Catherine Alric (Martine), Pierre Clémenti (Stranger), Bernard Fresson (Bé), Jean-Claude Benhamou, Igor Galo.

STORY: Martine helps Bé commit a robbery; later, they meet a mysterious Stranger, who turns into a monster. It was all a dream. She is killed by the gangsters, but the Stranger returns to take her away.

NOTE: A French-Yugoslavian co-production.

Clérambard (Col., 100 min., 1969)

DIR: Yves **Robert**; WRI: Yves **Robert**, Jean-Loup Dabadie, based on a novel by Marcel **Aymé**.

CAST: Philippe Noiret (Clérambard), Dany Carrel, Lise Delamare, Roger Carel, Claude Piéplu.

STORY: Clérambard is an odious country squire who becomes a saintly prophet after seeing a vision of St. Francis of Assisi.

Club Extinction see Docteur M

Coma (Col., 85 min., 1994)
DIR: Denys Granier-Defferre; WRI: Jacqueline Carot, based on a novel by Frédéric **Dard**.

CAST: Richard Anconina, Anna Kanakis, Isabelle Candelier.

STORY: A crippled man is the prisoner of two beautiful women in a Portuguese mansion. But it may all be an illusion.

NOTE: Frédéric **Dard** is a famous thriller writer, known for his popular satirical detective character, Police Commissioner *San Antonio* (see below).

La Concentration (Col., 94 min., 1968)
DIR/WRI: Philippe Garrel.

CAST: Jean-Pierre Léaud, Zouzou.

STORY: In a surreal prison, a man and a woman live and fight, until he eventually kills her.

Coplan FX-18
The *Francis Coplan, Agent FX-18* series is the French equivalent of James Bond. The novels are published by Editions Fleuve Noir, and written by Paul Kenny, a pseudonym of writers Jean Libert & Gaston Vandenpanhuyse. These two authors also wrote a number of noted science fiction novels under the pseudonym of Jean-Gaston **Vandel** (See Book 2). Also see Chapter II for an eponymous television series and Chapter V (under *Fleuve Noir*) for comic book adaptations of **Vandel**'s science fiction novels.

1. Coplan, Agent Secret FX-18 [Copan, Secret Agent Fx-18, transl. as Coplan Tries His Luck] (Col., 97 min., 1964)
DIR: Maurice Cloche; WRI: C. Plume, J. Bollo, Maurice Cloche, based on the novel *Coplan Tente sa Chance [Coplan Tries his Luck]* by Paul Kenny.

CAST: Ken Clark (Coplan), Jany Clair, Guy Delorme, Jacques Dacqmine.

STORY: A spy satellite must be destroyed.

2. Coplan FX-18 Casse Tout [Coplan Fx-18 Destroys Everything; transl. as the Exterminators] (Col., 95 min., 1965)
DIR: Ricardo Freda; WRI: Claude Marcel Richard, based on the novel by Paul Kenny.

CAST: Richard Wyler (Coplan), Robert Manuel, Gil Delamare, Jany Clair, Valeria Ciangottini.

STORY: Coplan helps Israeli agents thwart the plans of a neo-nazi tycoon (Manuel) who plots to destroy New York

with a nuclear rocket assembled in a secret underground base.

3. Coplan Ouvre le Feu à Mexico [Coplan Opens Fire in Mexico, transl. as Coplan Between the Nets] (Col., 93 min., 1966)
DIR: Ricardo Freda; WRI: José Antonio de la Loma, based on the novel by Paul Kenny.

CAST: Lang Jeffries (Coplan), Sabine Sun, Silvia Solar, Frank Oliveras, Ida Galli, Anotonio Orengo.

STORY: A Mexican estate owner is building atom bombs to take over the world.

4. Coplan Sauve Sa Peau [Coplan Saves His Skin] (Col., 90 min., 1967)
DIR: Yves **Boisset**; WRI: Claude Veillot, Yves **Boisset**, based on the novel by Paul Kenny.

CAST: Claudio Brook (Coplan), Margaret Lee, Jean Servais, Bernard Blier, Jean Topart, Klaus Kinski.

STORY: In Istanbul, Coplan thwarts the plans of a Count Zaroff-like mad scientist (Servais).

Coup de Jeune [Getting Young] (Col., 88 min., 1992)
DIR: Xavier Gélin; WRI: Philippe Setbon, Xavier Gélin.

CAST: Martin Lamotte, Ludmila Mikaël, Jean Carmet, Daniel Gélin (Gaudéamus), Antonin Lebas Joly, Jean-Pierre Castaldi, Anémone, Patrick Chesnais, Manuel Gélin.

STORY: The 70-year old Prof. Gaudéamus finds a serum which turns him into a 6-year old, while retaining all his memories and personality. His son (Carmet) helps him reach a more satisfying middle age, before eventually reverting to his natural age, having learned that age is a thing of the mind.

NOTE: This film is obviously inspired by Howard Hawks' *Monkey Business*, as well as René **Goscinny** & Coq's comic strip series, **Docteur Gaudéamus** (see Chapter V).

Les Créatures [The Creatures] (B&W., 90 min., 1966)
DIR/WRI: Agnès Varda.

CAST: Michel Piccoli, Catherine Deneuve, Éva Dahlbeck, Britta Petterson, Jacques Charrier, Ursula Kubler, Marie-France Mignal.

STORY: A novelist (Piccoli) on holiday with with his pregnant wife (Deneuve), who lost her voice in a car accident, plots his next book by using real people and twisting their lives through the prism of his imagination.

Le Cri du Hibou [The Cry of the Owl] (Col., 112 min., 1987)
DIR: Claude **Chabrol**; WRI: Claude **Chabrol**, Odile Barski, based on a novel by Patricia Highsmith.

CAST: Christophe Malavoy (Robert), Mathilda May (Juliette), Jacques Penot, Jean-Pierre Kalfon.

STORY: Gory thriller in which two jilted lovers plot a bloody revenge.

Croisières Sidérales [Star Cruises] (B&W., 95 min., 1941)

DIR: André Zwobada; WRI: Pierre Guerlais.

CAST: Madeleine Sologne (Françoise), Julien Carette (Lucien), Suzanne Dehelly, Robert Arnoux, Jean Marchat.

STORY: Two astronauts, Lucien and Françoise, explore outer space in a hot-air balloon (!) and return to Earth to discover that they've aged only two weeks while twenty-five years have elapsed. This leads to holiday cruises in space.

Dans les Griffes du Maniaque [In the Grip of the Maniac* aka *The Diabolical Dr. Z; Miss Death and Dr. Z; Miss Death] (B&W., 86 min., 1965)

DIR: Jess Franco; WRI: Jean-Claude **Carrière**, based on the novel by David Kuhne.

CAST: Mabel Karr, Fernando Montes, Estella Blain.

STORY: Men are turned into killer robots.

NOTE: This French-Spanish co-production, directed by renowned Spanish genre filmmaker Jess (Jesus) Franco, is listed here because of its script by Jean-Claude **Carrière**. This is the third in the Dr. Orloff series (see ***L'Horrible Dr. Orloff*** below).

Le Déclic [Click] (Col., 90 min., 1984)

DIR/WRI: Jean-Louis Richard, based on the Italian graphic novel by Milo Manara.

CAST: Jean-Pierre Kalfon (Fez), Florence Guérin (Claudia), Bernard Kuby, Jasmine Maimone, Lisa Marks.

STORY: Fez, a lovesick scientist, uses an electronic gadget to trigger Claudia's erotic behavior; but her husband becomes jealous.

Delicatessen (Col., 95 min., 1992)

DIR: Jean-Pierre **Jeunet** & Marc **Caro**; WRI: J.-P. **Jeunet**, M. **Caro**, Adrien Gilles.

CAST: Marie-Laure Dougnac, Dominique Pinon, Karin

Marie-Loure Dougnac and Dominique Pinon in Delicatessen *(1992).*

Viard, Jean-Claude Dreyfus, Ticky Holgado, Anne-Marie Pisani, Edith Ker, Patrick Paroux, Jean-Luc Caron.

STORY: In a surreal near-future, a butcher murders to provide the building's other tenants with fresh meat.

Demain les Mômes [Tomorrow, the Kids] (Col., 100 min., 1975)

DIR: Jean Pourtalé; WRI: Jean Pourtalé, Franck Vialle, Raymond Lepoutre.

CAST: Niels Arestrup (Philippe), Brigitte Rouan, Emmanuelle Béart.

STORY: After a mysterious cataclysm, a lone survivor, Philippe, encounters a tribe of children who obstinately refuse all contact with him.

Le Démon dans l'Île [The Demon in the Island] (Col., 102 min., 1982)

DIR: Francis Leroi; WRI: Francis Leroi, Owen T. Rozmann.

CAST: Jean-Claude Brialy (Dr. Marshall), Annie Duperey (Gabrielle) Pierre Santini, Cerise, Gabriel Cattand.

STORY: Gabrielle, a young doctor newly arrived on an island, eventually discovers that a series of deadly accidents have been caused by a psychokinetic child controlled by the evil Dr. Marshall.

Les Démoniaques [Demoniacs] (Col., 84 min., 1973) (aka ***Les Diablesses [The She-Devils]; Deux Vierges pour Satan [Two Virgins for Satan]***)

DIR/WRI: Jean **Rollin**.

CAST: Joëlle Coeur, Live Lone, John Rico.

STORY: Three men and a woman draw passing ships to their doom on a lonely coast.

Le Dernier Combat [The Final Combat] (B&W., 90 min., 1982)

DIR: Luc **Besson**; WRI: Luc **Besson**, Pierre Jolivet.

CAST: Pierre Jolivet, Jean Bouise, Jean Reno, Fritz Wepper, Christiane Kruger.

STORY: In a post-apocalyptic world where men have lost their voices, a survivor (Jolivet) is taken in by a doctor (Bouise) who has managed to save the last woman, and fights a savage warrior (Reno) to the death.

NOTE: Pierre Joliver also directed ***Simple Mortel*** (see below).

Le Dernier Homme [The Last Man] (Col., 82 min., 1969)

DIR/WRI: Charles Bitsch.

CAST: Jean-Claude Bouillon, Corinne Brill, Sophia Torkelli.

STORY: Three spelunkers—one man and two women—are the only survivors after an atomic war.

Deux Vierges pour Satan [Two Virgins for Satan] see *Les Démoniaques*

Le Diable et les Dix Commandements [The Devil and the Ten Commandements] (B&W., 80 min., 1962)

DIR: Julien **Duvivier**; WRI: Julien **Duvivier**, Maurice Bessy, René **Barjavel**, Henri Jeanson, Michel Audiard. ("Thou Shalt Not Kill" based on a story by David Alexander; "Thou Shalt Not Steal" based on a story by William Link & Richard Levinson.)

CAST: Fernandel, Gaston Modot, Jean-Claude Brialy, Charles Aznavour, Danielle Darrieux, Alain Delon, Claude Dauphin, Germaine Kerjean, Françoise Arnoul, Mel Ferrer, Louis de Funès, Lino Ventura, Georges Wilson.

STORY: This often amusing, sometimes sad, star-studded sketch film narrated by the Devil (as a snake) illustrates God's Ten Commandements, and how to twist them.

NOTE: René **Barjavel** is a famous science fiction writer (see Book 2). His science fiction novels *Le Grand Secret* and *Le Voyageur Imprudent* were adapted for television (see Chapter II). Henri Jeanson is a famous historian. William Link & Richard Levinson are the creators of *Columbo*.

Les Diablesses [The She-Devils] see *Les Démoniaques*

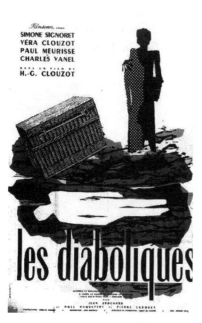

Les Diaboliques [Diabolique] (B&W., 110 min., 1954)

DIR: Henri-Georges Clouzot; WRI: H.-G. Clouzot, Jérôme Geromini, René Masson, Frédéric Grendel, based on the novel by **Boileau-Narcejac**.

CAST: Simone Signoret (Nicole), Véra Clouzot (Christina), Paul Meurisse (Michel), Charles Vanel (Fichet), Jean Brochard, Michel Serrault, Pierre Larquey, Noël Roquevert.

STORY: Christina (his wife) and Simone (his mistress) join forces to murder Michel, the director of a private school. But in reality, it is a diabolical plot conceived by Michel and Simone to get rid of weak-hearted Christina.

NOTE: Pierre **Boileau** and Thomas **Narcejac** are a famous team of mystery writers (see Book 2). They also wrote the screenplay adaptation of the classic and much imitated *Les Yeux Sans Visage* (see below). Their story *Au Bois Dormant* was adapted for television (see Chapter II). *Les Diaboliques* was clearly identified by Hitchcock as a major influence on his making of *Psycho*. **Boileau-Narcejac** later provided the story for Hitchcock's *Vertigo*. The police inspector played by Vanel was reportedly the basis for the popular *Columbo* character. The film was remade in the U.S. in 1996 as *Diabolique*, starring Sharon Stone in the role played by Simone Signoret and Isabelle Adjani in the role played by Véra Clouzot.

Dites-le avec des Fleurs [Say It with Flowers] (Col., 100 min., 1974)

DIR: Pierre Grimblat, WRI: Lucile Laks, Tonino Guerra, Pierre Grimblat, based on the novel by Christian Charrière.

CAST: Delphine Seyrig, John Moulder Brown, Francis Blanche, Fernando Rey, Frédéric Mitterand, Julien Guiomar.

STORY: A German maid (Seyrig) joins a stange family who are hiding a secret linked to World War II.

Docteur Jekyll et les Femmes [Doctor Jekyll and Women, transl. as *Doctor Jekyll and Miss Osborne]* (Col., 95 min., 1981)

DIR/WRI: Walerian **Borowczyk**.

CAST: Udo Kier (Jekyll), Marina Pierro, Howard Vernon, Patrick Magee.

STORY: In this low-budget, mildly pornographic version of Stevenson's novel, Dr. Jekyll chooses to remain Hyde.

Docteur M (Col., 116 min., 1990)(aka *Club Extinction*)

DIR: Claude **Chabrol**; WRI: Solace Mitchell, Claude **Chabrol**, based on the novel by Norbert Jacques.

CAST: Alan Bates (Dr. M), Jan Niklas (Hartmann), Jennifer Beals, Hanns Zischler, Benoît Régent, Alexander Radszun, Peter Fitz, Daniela Poggi, William Berger, Michael Degen, Andrew McCarthy.

STORY: In this French-

German co-production, loosely inspired by Fritz Lang's *Docteur Mabuse* series, a mad scientist uses modern brainwashing techniques to create death and destruction.

Docteur Petiot (Col., 102 min., 1989)

DIR: Christian de **Chalonge**; WRI: Christian de **Chalonge**, Dominique Garnier.

CAST: Michel Serrault (Petiot), Pierre Romans, Bérangère Bonvoisin, Nita Klein.

STORY: The story of a notorious French serial killer of the 1940s.

Dora, ou la Lanterne Magique [Dora, or the Magic Lantern] (Col., 89 min., 1976)

DIR: Pascal Kane; WRI: Pascal Kane, Raoul Ruiz.

CAST: Valérie Mairesse, Nathalie Manet, Rita Maiden, Gérard Boucaron.

STORY: The fairy tale-like adventures of an innocent young woman in a surreal Paris.

Dracula Père et Fils [Dracula, Father and Son, transl. as *Dracula & Son]* (Col., 100 min., 1976)

DIR: Édouard Molinaro; WRI: Alain Godard, Jean-Marie Poiré, based on the novel *Paris Vampire* by Claude **Klotz**.

CAST: Christopher Lee (Dracula), Bernard Menez (His Son), Marie-Hélène Breillat, Raymond Bussières, Gérard Jugnot.

STORY: Dracula is forced to leave Romania and become a horror film star. His son, who is a failure as a vampire, becomes a minimum wage worker. He eventually defies his father to save his fiancée (Breillat).

NOTE: The U.S. version of this film was mutilated by an English adaptation, which totally denatured the light-hearted and often moving nature of the original. This is the last film in which Christopher Lee played Dracula. He was re-dubbed in the aforementioned U.S. version.

Duelle (Col., 118 min., 1976)

DIR: Jacques Rivette; WRI: Eduardo de Gregorio, Marilu Parolini, Jacques Rivette.

CAST: Bulle Ogier (Viva), Juliet Berto (Leni), Jean Babilée, Hermine Karagheuz, Nicole Garcia, Claire Nadeau.

STORY: Two sorceresses, blonde Leni and brunette Viva, battle to recover a magic jewel.

Eclipse sur un Ancien Chemin vers Compostelle [Eclipse on an Old Road Towards Compostelle] (Col., 90 min., 1977)

DIR/WRI: Bernard Férié.

CAST: Jean Martin, Martine Chevalier, Bruno Pradal.

STORY: During a traditional village celebration honoring two local saints, a young witch unearths the memories of old crimes.

Écoute Voir [Hear See] (Col., 105 min., 1978)

DIR: Hugo Santiago; WRI: Claude **Ollier**.

CAST: Catherine Deneuve (Claude), Sami Frey, Florence Delay, Anne Parillaud, Jean-François Stevenin.

STORY: Claude, a woman detective, investigates a mysterious religious sect which controls a paralyzing ray.

NOTE: **Ollier** also wrote some novels (see Book 2) as well as radio dramas such as *L'Attentat en Direct* [*Terrorism On Live TV*] (see Chapter III).

L'Écume des Jours [Froth on the Daydream] (Col., 115 min., 1968)

DIR: Charles Belmont; WRI: Pierre Pelegri, Philippe Dumarçay, Charles Belmont, based on the novel by Boris **Vian**.

CAST: Annie Buron (Chloé), Jacques Perrin (Colin), Marie-France Pisier, Alexandra Stewart, Sacha Pitoeff, Bernard Fresson, Claude Piéplu.

STORY: Colin falls in love with Chloé, but a water lily growing inside her eventually kills her. He steals her coffin and runs away.

NOTE: Boris **Vian** is a famous writer (see Book 2). Also see Chapter II for a television adaptation of another of his novels, *L'Herbe Rouge* [*The Red Grass*].

L'Éden et Après [Eden and Afterwards] (Col., 100 min., 1971)

DIR/WRI: Alain **Robbe-Grillet**.

CAST: Catherine Jourdan, Pierre Zimmer, Lorraine Rainer, Sylvain Corthay, Richard Leduc.

STORY: A Tunisian initiates a young woman (Jourdan) in surreal games of love and death.

Elle Voit des Nains Partout [She Sees Dwarves Everywhere] (Col., 85 min., 1981)

DIR: Jean-Claude Sussfeld; WRI: Jean-Claude Sussfeld, Philippe Bruneau, based on his play.

CAST: Philippe Bruneau (Albert), Marilyn Canto, Christian Clavier, Agnès Daems, Roland Giraud, Martin Lamotte, Gaëlle Legrand, Thierry Lhermitte, Zabou, Jacques Monnet, Renaud, Louis Navarre, Valentine Monnier, Coluche, Josiane Lévêque.

STORY: Parody of Walt Disney's fairy tales, *The Three Musketeers*, *Les Misérables*, *Robin Hood*, *Tarzan*, etc., centered around Snow White's quest for her Prince Charming.

Les Enfants [The Children] (Col., 94 min., 1984)

DIR: Marguerite Duras; WRI: Marguerite Duras, Jean Mascolo, Jean-Marc Turine.

CAST: Alexander Bougosslavsky (Ernesto), Daniel Gélin, Tatiana Moukhine, Martine Chevalier, Pierre Arditi, André Dussolier.

STORY: In this allegoric fable, Ernesto, a seven-year-old child who looks like a thirty-year-old man, is a mental prodigy, but chooses a simple life over the sum of all knowledge.

Un Escargot dans la Tête [A Snail in the Head]
(Col., 90 min., 1980)

DIR/WRI: Jean-Étienne Siry.

CAST: Florence Giorgetti, Renaud Verley, Jean-Claude Bouillon.

STORY: A novelist (Giorgetti) in a hospital for a nervous breakdown meets a strange artist. She then experiences a series of surreal nightmares featuring snails.

…Et Mourir de Plaisir […And to Die from Pleasure, transl. as Blood and Roses] (Col., 80 min., 1960)

DIR: Roger **Vadim**; WRI: Roger **Vadim**, Roger Vailland,

Annette Vadim and Elsa Martinelli in Et Mourir de Plaisir *(1960).*

Claude Brulé, Claude Martin, based on the story by Sheridan Le Fanu.

CAST: Annette Vadim (Carmilla), Elsa Martinelli, Mel Ferrer, Jacques-René Chauffard, Serge Marquand, Marc Allégret.

STORY: Modern version of Le Fanu's classic vampire tale, *Carmilla*. Vampire Carmilla interferes with her cousin's wedding with a nobleman (Ferrer).

NOTE: **Carmilla** was also adapted for television by Paul **Planchon** (see Chapter II).

L'Étrangleur [The Strangler] (Col., 93 min., 1970)

DIR/WRI: Paul Vecchiali.

CAST: Jacques Perrin (Émile), Julien Guiomar, Eve Simonet, Paul Barge, Nicole Courcel, Jacqueline Danno, Hélène Surgère.

STORY: Émile strangles women because he can't stand to see them unhappy. A scavenger nicknamed the "Jackal" (Barge) robs his victims' bodies. A policeman (Guiomar) undertakes a surreal investigation.

L'Évènement Le Plus Important Depuis Que l'Homme A Marché sur la Lune [The Most Important Event Since Man Walked on the Moon, transl. as A Slightly Pregnant Man] (Col., 94 min., 1973)

DIR/WRI: Jacques **Demy**.

CAST: Catherine Deneuve (Irène), Marcello Mastroianni (Mario), Micheline Presle, Marisa Pavan, Mireille Matthieu, Claude Melki, André Falcon, Maurice Biraud, Alice Sapritch, Raymond Gérôme.

STORY: Mario lives with Irène. When he learns that *he* is pregnant, he marries her, but eventually discovers it was only a nervous pregnancy. Irène has a baby.

NOTE: The theme of this film was recycled in *Junior* (1994), starring Arnold Schwarzenegger.

Exorcisme [Exorcism] see Sexorcismes

Les Expériences Érotiques de Frankenstein [Frankenstein's Erotic Experiments] (Col., 90 min., 1972)

DIR/WRI: Jess Franco.

CAST: Britt Nichols, Howard Vernon.

STORY: Cagliostro uses the Frankenstein Monster to kidnap girls whose body parts he needs to build the perfect woman.

NOTE: This is a French-Spanish co-production.

Expériences Sexuelles au Château des Jouisseuses [Sexual Experiences in the Castle of Pleasure] see Sexorcismes

Extraneus (98 min., 1981)

Compilation of eight short features (listed in order of appearance):

1. La Voix du Large [A Voice from the Sea] (Col., 9 min., 1972)
DIR/WRI: François Porcile, Philippe de Poix.
CAST: Anne Dimitriadis.
STORY: A young woman is threatened by a flooding river.

2. Nuit de Noce [Wedding Night] (Col., 15 min., 1974)
DIR/WRI: Bernard Férié.
CAST: Jean Barney, Mireille Férié.
STORY: A newlywed groom is struck by lightning while playing piano.

3. L'Inconnu [The Unknown Man] (Col., 15 min., 1978)
DIR/WRI: Claude Monrond.
CAST: Béatrice Lord, Daniel Peigné.
STORY: A mysterious stranger follows an old woman.

4. La Tache [The Blot] (Col., 19 min., 1976)
DIR/WRI: Nicolas Brachlianoff.
CAST: Muse Dalbray, Bernard Malaterre, Monique Fabre.
STORY: The ghost of a former tenant haunts an apartment.

5. Casse-Tête [Mind-Bender] (Col., 7 min., 1978)
DIR/WRI: Daniel Chevalier.
CAST: Jacques Ebner.
STORY: A man asks a filmmaker to film his suicide.

6. L'Empreinte
(See Chapter IV, Selected Short Features.)

7. Le Motard de l'Apocalypse [The Apocalypse Biker] (Col., 10 min., 1978)
DIR/WRI: Richard Olivier.
CAST: Roland Mahauden, Serge Degroot, Yannick Degroot, Alain Delforge, Michel Lederman, Roland Vanberg.
STORY: In a post-apocalyptic landscape, a German zombie biker fights Hell's Angels mutants.

8. Fracture
(See Chapter IV, Selected Short Features.)

Fahrenheit 451 (Col., 113 min., 1966)
DIR: François **Truffaut**; WRI: François **Truffaut**, Jean-Louis Richard, based on the novel by Ray Bradbury.
CAST: Julie Christie, Oskar Werner, Cyril Cusak, Anton Diffing.
STORY: Truffaut's masterful adaptation of Bradbury's surreal future where

books are routinely burned, and rebels learn to memorize them to preserve culture.
NOTE: This is a British production.

Fantômas

A series of films based on the popular novels by Marcel **Allain** & Pierre **Souvestre** published between 1911 and 1913. Also see Chapter II for a television adaptation.

1. Fantômas (B&W., 1146 M, 1913)

2. Juve Contre Fantômas [Juve vs. Fantômas] (B&W., 1913)

3. Le Mort Qui Tue [The Dead Man Who Kills] (B&W., 1913)

4. Fantômas Contre Fantômas [Fantômas vs. Fantômas] (B&W., 1914)

5. Le Faux Magistrat [The Phony Magistrate] (B&W., 1914)
DIR/WRI: Louis **Feuillade**.
CAST: René Navarre (Fantômas), Bréon (Juve), Georges Melchior (Fandor), Renée Carl (Lady Beltham).
STORY: Master criminal Fantômas outwits police commissioner Juve and journalist Jerôme Fandor.
NOTE: The original silent serial series is faithful to the early novels and displays considerable poetic charm.

6. Fantômas (B&W., 91 min., 1932)
DIR/WRI: Paul Féjos.
CAST: Jean Galland (Fantômas), Thomy Bourdelle (Juve), Tania Fedor (Lady Beltham), Marie-Laure, Gaston Modot, Georges Rigaud.
STORY: Fantômas murders a rich lady, but is unmasked by Juve.

7. Mr. Fantômas (B&W., 20 min., 1937)
DIR/WRI: Ernst Moerman.
CAST: Jean Michel, Trudi Ventonderen, Françoise Bert, Jacqueline Arpé, Susan Samuel, Léa Dumont.
NOTE: This is a Belgian short feature.

8. Fantômas (B&W., 95 min., 1946)
DIR: Jean Sacha; WRI: Jean-Louis **Bouquet**.
CAST: Marcel Herrand (Fantômas), Alexandre Rignault (Juve), André Le Gall (Fandor), Lucienne Le Marchand (Lady Beltham), Simone Signoret (Hélène), Yves Deniaud, Georges Gosset.
STORY: Fantômas tries to prevent Fandor from marrying the arch-villain's daughter, Hélène, but Juve saves the day.
NOTE: Jean-Louis **Bouquet** also wrote *La Cité Foudroyée*.

9. Fantômas Contre Fantômas [Fantomas vs. Fantomas] (B&W., 95 min., 1948)
DIR: Robert Vernay; WRI: Solange Térac.
CAST: Maurice Teynac (Fantômas), Alexandre Rignault (Juve), Yves Furet (Fandor), Aimé Clariond, Balpêtré, Marcelle Chantal.

STORY: Fantômas teams up with a mad surgeon (Clariond) who turns people into assassins.

10. Fantômas (Col., 95 min., 1964)

11. Fantômas Se Déchaîne [Fantômas Strikes Back] (Col., 94 min., 1965)

12. Fantômas contre Scotland Yard [Fantômas vs. Scotland Yard] (Col., 92 min., 1966)
DIR: André Hunebelle; WRI: Jean Halain, Pierre Foucaud.
CAST: Jean Marais (Fantômas/Fandor), Louis de Funès (Juve), Mylène Demongeot.
STORY: Fantômas borrows gadgets from James Bond's panoply (a pocket submarine in the first installment, a flying car in the second). De Funès plays the role for laughs. Jean Marais plays the double role of Fantômas (wearing a very effective green mask) and his nemesis, journalist Fandor.

Le Fantôme de la Liberté [The Phantom of Liberty]
(Col., 103 min., 1974)
DIR: Luis Buñuel; WRI: Luis Buñuel, Jean-Claude **Carrière**.
CAST: Julien Bertheau, Adriana Asti, Michel Lonsdale, Michel Piccoli, Claude Piéplu, Jean-Claude Brialy, Monica Vitti, Paul Frankeur, Adolfo Celi.
STORY: A series of surreal sketches, often satirical in nature, some dealing with dreams and death.

Le Fantôme du Moulin-Rouge [The Ghost of the Moulin-Rouge] (B&W., 90 min., 1924)
DIR/WRI: René **Clair**.
CAST: Georges Vaultier (Julien), Sandra Milowanoff (Yvonne), Madeleine Rodrigue, Albert Préjean, Paul Ollivier.
STORY: In order to marry Yvonne, Julien's astral body helps her father to get rid of a blackmailer.

Fascination (Col., 82 min., 1979)
DIR/WRI: Jean **Rollin**.
CAST: Franka Maï, Brigitte Lahaie, Jean-Marie Lemaire, Fanny Magier.
STORY: A young burglar (Lemaire) finds refuge in a castle inhabited by two vampires.
NOTE: Generally considered the best among **Rollin**'s films.

La Femme aux Bottes Rouges [The Woman with Red Boots] (Col., 95 min., 1974)

DIR: Juan Luis **Buñuel**; WRI: Juan Luis **Buñuel**, Jean-Claude **Carrière**.
CAST: Catherine Deneuve (Françoise), Fernando Rey (Pérou), Adalberto Marias Merli, Jacques Weber.
STORY: Pérou, a rich but aging art collector, meets Françoise, a beautiful enchantress.

La Femme Objet [The Woman Thing] (Col., 90 min., 1981)
DIR/WRI: Frédéric Lansac.
CAST: Richard Allan, Helen Shirley, Laura Clair, Marilyn Jess.
STORY: X-rated (and satirical) adventures of a science-fiction writer who is the victim of satyriasis. Having run out of willing women, he ends up building female androids.

La Fiancée des Ténèbres [The Fiancée of Darkness] (B&W., 100 min., 1944)
DIR: Serge de **Poligny**; WRI: Serge de **Poligny**, Gaston Bonheur.
CAST: Jany Holt (Sylvie), Pierre Richard-Willm (Roland), Simone Valère, Edouard Delmont, Fernand Charpin, Line Noro.
STORY: Two lovers discover a secret, underground cathedral leading to a fairyland where they'll live a wonderful day of love.

Filles Traquées [Hunted Girls] *see* La Nuit des Traqués

La Fin du Monde [The End of the World, transl. as Paris After Dark] (B&W., 103 min., 1930)
DIR: Abel **Gance**; WRI: Camille **Flammarion**.
CAST: Colette Darfeuil, Abel Gance, Victor Francen, Samson Fainsilber, Jean d'Yd, Sylvie Grenade.
STORY: A scientist announces that a comet will soon destroy the Earth. But it eventually spares the planet and helps bring about world unity.
NOTE: Camille **Flammarion** is a famous science fiction

writer (see Book 2). The film was novelized by J. **Renez** (see Book 2).

Le Fou du Labo 4 [The Madman of Lab 4] (Col., 90 min., 1967)

DIR: Jacques Besnard; WRI: Jean Halain, Jacques Besnard, based on a story by Jacques **Chambon**.

CAST: Jean Lefèbvre (Eugène), Bernard Blier (Beauchard), Pierre Brasseur, Michel Serrault, Maria Latour.

STORY: Eugène, a genial scientist, discovers a new, powerful, euphoric gas, which then becomes the target of a spy ring.

France, Société Anonyme [France, Inc.] (Col., 100 min., 1973)

DIR: Alain Corneau; WRI: Alain Corneau, Jean-Claude **Carrière**.

CAST: Michel Bouquet, Roland Dubillard, Allyn Ann Mac Lerie, Ann Zacharias, Michel Vitold, Yves Alfonso, Gérard Desarthe, Daniel Ceccaldi.

STORY: In the year 2222, a former drug lord (Bouquet) comes out of hibernation and tells how corporate power and the legalisation of drugs destroyed his empire.

François 1er [Francis the 1st] (B&W., 100 min., 1936)

DIR: Christian-Jaque; WRI: Paul Fékété.

CAST: Fernandel (Honorin), Mona Goya, Alice Tissot, Henri Bosc.

STORY: In this French *Connecticut Yankee…* comedic variation, Fernandel is hypnotized back to the days of King Francis 1st where, with the help of a pocket encyclopedia, he revolutionizes history.

Frankenstein 90 (Col., 92 min., 1984)

DIR: Alain **Jessua**; WRI: Alain **Jessua**, Paul Gégauff.

CAST: Jean Rochefort (Victor Frankenstein), Eddy Mitchell (Creature), Fiona Gélin.

STORY: Frankenstein's creature falls in love with his creator's fiancée, and vice-versa. The Creature ends up a millionaire.

Les Frères Pétard [The Petard Brothers] (Col., 90 min., 1986)

DIR: Hervé Palud; WRI: Hervé Palud, Igor Aptekman.

CAST: Gérard Lanvin, Jacques Villeret, Josiane Balasko, Valérie Mairesse, Michel Galabru, Dominique Lavanant.

STORY: A French Cheech & Chong–like comedy, which takes place in a near future in which the sale of soft drugs has become legal.

Le Frisson des Vampires [The Vampires' Shiver transl. as Sex and the Vampire; Terror of the Vampire] (Col., 89 min., 1970)

DIR/WRI: Jean **Rollin**.

CAST: Sandra Jullien, Nicole Nancel.

STORY: The semi-parodic adventures of the owners of a castle which houses a female vampire cult.

Le Futur aux Trousses [The Future in Pursuit] (Col., 100 min., 1974)

DIR/WRI: Dolorès Grassian.

CAST: Bernard Fresson, Michel Aumont, Andréa Ferréol.

STORY: In a future when people work only three days a week, a corporation offers everyone the possibility of acquiring another identity to satisfy their fantasies.

Galaxie [Galaxy] (Col., 82 min., 1971)

DIR: Mathias Mérigny; WRI: Mathias Mérigny, Roger Michel, Pierre Latzko.

CAST: Marika Green, Henri Serre, Reinghard Kolidehoff, Jean Gras.

STORY: Five scientists investigate the concept of an "anti-universe." During an experiment, three die and one vanishes. A police inspector investigates.

Garou-Garou, Le Passe-Muraille [Garou-Garou, the Walker Through the Walls] (B&W., 85 min., 1950)

DIR: Jean Boyer; WRI: Marcel Audiard, based on the story by Marcel **Aymé**.

CAST: Bourvil (Dutilleul), Joan Greenwood, Marcelle Arnold, Raymond Souplex, Gérard Oury, Frédéric O'Brady.

STORY: Dutilleul, a modest civil servant, discovers that he has the power to walk through walls and uses it to become a master burglar.

NOTE: Marcel **Aymé** is a popular novelist and dramatist (see Book 2). Other feature film adaptations of his works include *La Belle Image* (above) and *La Vouivre* (below). Also see Chapter II for television adaptations of other stories under **Aymé, Marcel**.

Les Gaspards (Col., 94 min., 1973)
DIR: Pierre Tchernia; WRI: Pierre Tchernia, René **Goscinny**.
CAST: Michel Serrault (Rondin), Philippe Noiret (Gaspard), Chantal Goya, Charles Denner, Michel Galabru.
STORY: Rondin, a meek bookseller, discovers a secret Parisian underground society led by the colorful Gaspard de Montfermeil.
NOTE: René **Goscinny** is better known as the writer of the comic-book series *Astérix* and *Iznogoud* (see Chapter V).

Gawin (Col., 95 min., 1990)
DIR: Arnaud Sélignac; WRI: Arnaud Sélignac, Alexandre Jardin.
CAST: Jean-Hugues Anglade (Nicolas), Wojtek Pszoniak (Pierre), Bruno (Félix), Catherine Samie.
STORY: Nicolas' son, Félix, is dying from leukemia. Knowing that his son's fondest dream is to meet an extra-terrestrial, Nicolas impersonates the alien Gawin, and takes the boy to a glacier which passes as Saturn. Eventually, they meet an old man, who may be a real alien, and who cures Félix.

Le Gendarme et les Extra-Terrestres [The Gendarme and the ETs] (Col., 95 min., 1978)
DIR: Jean Girault; WRI: Jacques Vilfrid.
CAST: Louis de Funès (Cruchot), Michel Galabru (Gerber), Maria Mauban, Maurice Risch, Jean-Pierre Rambal, Guy Grosso, Michel Modo, France Rumilly, Jean-Roger Caussimon, Mario David, Jacques François.
STORY: The fifth in a series of slapstick comedies starring Louis de Funès as a policeman from the French Riviera town of Saint-Tropez. Here, De Funès is outwitted by extra-terrestrials taking human shapes to study mankind.

Giorgino (Col., 177 min., 1994)
DIR: Laurent Boutonnat; WRI: Gilles Laurent, Laurent Boutonnat.
CAST: Mylène Farmer, Jeff Dahlgren, Louise Fletcher, Frances Barber, Jean-Pierre Aumont.
STORY: After World War I, a young Doctor (Dahlgren) finds love in a village haunted by the ghosts of the men who died during the war.

Glissements Progressifs du Plaisir [Progressive Slidings into Pleasure] (Col., 104 min., 1974)
DIR/WRI: Alain **Robbe-Grillet**.
CAST: Anicée Alvina (Alice), Olga Georges-Picot (Nora), Jean-Louis Trintignant, Michel Lonsdale.
STORY: The surreal interrogation of Alice, accused of having murdered Nora.

Le Golem [transl. as The Legend of Prague] (B&W., 100 min., 1935)
DIR: Julien **Duvivier**; WRI: Julien **Duvivier**, André-Paul Antoine, based on the novel by Gustav Meyrinck.
CAST: Harry Baur (The Emperor), Roger Karl, Germaine Aussey, Jany Holt.
STORY: The Jews of Prague create a clay monster to destroy the Emperor.
NOTE: Also see Chapter II for a television adaptation.

Golem, L'Esprit de l'Exil [Golem, the Spirit of Exile] (Col., 105 min., 1991)
DIR/WRI: Amos Gitaï.
CAST: Ophrah Shemesh, Hanna Schygulla (Golem), Samuel Fuller, Mireille Perrier, Vittorio Mezzogiorno, Fabienne Babe, Antonio Carallo, Bernard Levy, Sotigui Kouyaté.
STORY: Modern transposition of the classic tale where the Golem helps those who are exiled from their native land.

Goto, L'Île d'Amour [Goto, Island of Love] (B&W/Col., 93 min., 1968)
DIR/WRI: Walerian **Borowczyk**.
CAST: Pierre Brasseur (Goto), Ligia Branice (Glossia), Ginette Leclerc, René Dary.
STORY: Surreal political fable about the imaginary island of Goto ruled by the dictator Goto and his wife Glossia.

La Goulve [transl. as Erotic Witchcraft] (Col., 87 min., 1971)
DIR: Mario **Mercier**, Bepi Fontana; WRI: Mario **Mercier**.
CAST: Malka Simon (Goulve), Hervé Hendricks, César Torres, Anne Varèse, Marie-Ange Saint-Clair, Manuel Navo.
STORY: The Goulve, an elemental snake goddess, possesses humans and drives them to suicide.
NOTE: Mario **Mercier** was one of the editors of the magazine *Horizons du Fantastique* and the author of several genre novels (see Book 2). He also directed *La Papesse* (1974) (see below).

Les Gourmandes du Sexe [Sex Gluttons] (Col., 85 min., 1978)
DIR/WRI: John Love.
CAST: Cathy Stewart, Dominique Aveline.
STORY: X-rated tale of a revenge from beyond the grave.

Le Gout du Sang [The Taste of Blood] see *Perversions Sexuelles*

La Grande Frousse [The Great Fear] see *La Cité de l'Indicible Peur*

La Grande Trouille [The Great Scare] (Col., 100 min., 1974) *(aka Tendre Dracula [Tender Dracula])*

DIR: Pierre Grunstein; WRI: Justin Lenoir.

CAST: Peter Cushing (Mac Gregor), Alida Valli (Héloise), Miou-Miou (Marie), Nathalie Courval, Bernard Menez, Stéphane Shandor, Julien Guiomar.

STORY: Film producers want to shoot a gothic movie in Dracula's castle.

Jean-Jacques Annaud.

La Guerre du Feu [The War for Fire, transl. as ***Quest for Fire]*** (Col., 96 min., 1981)

DIR: Jean-Jacques Annaud; WRI: Gérard Brach, based on the novel by J.-H. **Rosny** Aîné.

CAST: Everett McGill, Rae Dawn Chong, Ron Perlman, Gari Schwartz, Brian Gill.

STORY: Three cavemen go looking for fire. One of them finds love and eventually learns the secret of making fire.

NOTE: J.-H. **Rosny** Aîné is, with Jules **Verne**, one of the major science fiction writers of the 19th century (see Book 2). Gérard Brach wrote several films for Roman Polanski, and numerous telefilms such as ***L'Étrange Château du Dr. Lerne*** and ***La Nuit des Fantômes*** for director Jean-Daniel Verhaeghe (see Chapter II).

Les Gueux au Paradis [Two Funny Guys in Paradise] (B&W., 85 min., 1945)

DIR: René Le Hénaff; WRI: André Obey, based on a story by G. M. Martens.

CAST: Fernandel, Raimu, Gaby Andreu, Alerme, Armand Bernard.

STORY: After being run over, two funny guys visit Hell and Heaven before being sent back to Earth.

Gwendoline (Col., 105 min., 1983)

DIR/WRI: Just Jaeckin, based on the British bondage comic book series by John Willie.

CAST: Tawny Kitaen (Gwendoline), Brent Huff (Willard), Zabou, Jean Rougerie, Bernadette Lafont.

STORY: The exotic adventures of Gwendoline and Willard in an Oriental fantasy world which includes the savage Kiops and an underground kingdom of Amazons, ruled by a cruel queen.

Hélas Pour Moi [Woe Is Me!] (Col., 84 min., 1992)

DIR/WRI: Jean-Luc **Godard**.

CAST: Gérard Depardieu, Laurence Masliah, Bernard Verley, Jean-Louis Loca.

STORY: A god borrows the body of a garage owner to seduce the man's wife.

Hibernatus (Col., 80 min., 1969)

DIR: Édouard Molinaro; WRI: Jean Halain, Jacques Vilfrid, based on the play by Jean-Bernard Luc.

CAST: Louis de Funès (Hubert), Bernard Alane (Paul), Claude Gensac, Olivier de Funès, Paul Préboist, Claude Piéplu, Michel Lonsdale, Pascal Mazzotti, Jacques Legras.

STORY: Hubert, a 19th-century man trapped in the ice in Greenland, is brought back to life; his descendents must pretend to live in the past in order to not traumatize him.

Histoires Abominables [Abominable Tales] (80 min., 1979)

Compilation of six short features (listed here in order of appearance):

1. Le Blanc des Yeux [The White of the Eyes] (B&W, 11 min, 1977)

DIR/WRI: Henry Colomer.

CAST: Marcel Dalio, Sylvia Badesco, Robert Théophile, Régis Outin, Alain Petit.

STORY: A mad scientist invents a machine that can paint portraits but sucks up the model's life.

2. La Passion d'une Femme Sans Coeur [The Passion of a Heartless Woman] (B&W, 15 min, 1975)

DIR/WRI: Moïse Maatouk, based on a story by Paul Deschelles.

CAST: Niels Arestrup, Catherine Gandois, Piéral.

STORY: A showman exhibits a woman's living head, connected to an artificial life-support machine. The head falls in love with him and ends up killing him.

3. Celui qui Venait d'Ailleurs [He Came from Beyond] (Col., 19 min, 1978)

DIR/WRI: Atahualpa Lichy, Jean-Paul Torok, based on a story by Claude **Seignolle**.

CAST: n/a.

STORY: The inhabitants of a lonely village believe that a stranger is a ghost.

4. Pauvre Sonia [Poor Sonia] (Col., 13 min, 1975)

DIR/WRI: Dominique Maillet, based on a story by Claude **Seignolle**.

CAST: Anicée Alvina, Frank David, Eva Damien, Gérard Boucaron.

STORY: A man follows a young prostitute and discovers that she belongs to the living dead.

NOTE: For further information on Claude **Seignolle**, see ***Le Faucheur*** in Short Features below.

5. La Mémoire [The Memory] (Col., 10 min, 1975)

DIR/WRI: **Gébé**.

CAST: Philippe Léotard, Diane Kurys, Albert Augier, Philippe Mireau.

STORY: A man forgets where he parked his car and panics.

NOTE: For further information on **Gébé**, see ***L'An 01*** above.

6. Le Déjeuner du Matin [The Morning Breakfast] (Col., 12 min, 1978)

DIR/WRI: Patrick Bokanowski.

CAST: n/a.

STORY: Animated short about scenes of daily life.

Histoires Extraordinaires [Extraordinary Tales]

(B&W., 90 min., 1949)

DIR: Jean Faurez; WRI: Jean Faurez, Guy Decomble, based on short stories by Edgar Allan Poe & Thomas de Quincey.

CAST: Fernand Ledoux, Suzy Carrier, Jules Berry, Paul Frankel, Olivier Hussenot, Marina de Berg, Roger Rafal, Roger Blin.

STORY: Three gendarmes swap horror stories, including "The Tell-Tale Heart," "The Cask of Amontillado," and "Thou Art the Man."

Histoires Extraordinaires [Extraordinary Tales,

transl. as **Spirits of the Dead]** (Col., 120 min., 1968)

Film compised of three sketches based on short stories by Edgar Allan Poe, narrated by Vincent Price.

1. Metzengerstein

DIR: Roger **Vadim**; WRI: Roger **Vadim**, Pascal Cousin.

CAST: Peter Fonda, Jane Fonda, Carla Marlier, Philippe Lemaire, James Robertson Justice, Andreas Voutsinas.

STORY: A spurned woman who murdered her lover becomes attracted to a horse who may be his reincarnation.

2. William Wilson

DIR: Louis **Malle**; WRI: Daniel Boulanger.

CAST: Alain Delon, Brigitte Bardot, Katia Cristina, Umberto d'Orsini, Daniele Vargas.

STORY: A man is stalked by his doppleganger.

NOTE: The third sketch, *Toby Dammit*, is directed by Federico Fellini and was filmed in English. Also see Chapter II for a television adaptation of Poe's stories.

L'Homme à l'Oreille Cassée [The Man with the

Broken Ear] (B&W., 75 min., 1934)

DIR/WRI: Robert Boudrioz, based on the novel by Edmond **About**.

CAST: Thomy Bourdelle (Fougas), Jim Gerald, Jacqueline Daix, Alice Tissot.

STORY: Fougas, a Napoleonic Army colonel, is placed in hibernation, then brought back to life. He dislikes the modern world, and marries his granddaughter.

L'Homme au Cerveau Greffé [The Man with the

Transplanted Brain] (Col., 90 min., 1971)

DIR/WRI: Jacques Doniol-Valcroze, based on a story by Victor **Vicas** & Alain Franck.

CAST: Jean-Pierre Aumont (Marcilly), Mathieu Carrière (Franz), Michel Duchaussoy (Degagnac), Nicoletta Machiavelli, Marianne Eggerickx, Martine Sarcey.

STORY: Marcilly, a neurologist afflicted with with a deadly disease, asks one of his colleagues (Duchaussoy) to transplant his brain into the body of a young victim of a traffic accident (Carrière). His own daughter then falls in love with his new self.

NOTE: For other works by Victor **Vicas**, see Chapter II.

L'Homme Qui Vendit Son Âme [Au Diable] [The

Man Who Sold His Soul (To the Devil)]

based on the novel by Pierre **Veber**.

Version No. 1: (B&W., 1920)

DIR/WRI: Pierre Caron.

CAST: Charles Dullin.

NOTE: This is a lost silent film.

Version No. 2: (B&W., 90 min., 1943)

DIR: Jean-Paul Paulin; WRI: Charles Méré.

CAST: Robert Le Vigan (Devil), Michèle Alfa, Mona Goya, André Luguet, Pierre Larquey, Huguette Saint-Arnaud, Renée Thorel.

STORY: A banker sells his soul to the Devil in exchange for worldly riches, but he must then use the money to do evil.

NOTE: Pierre **Veber** (see Book 2) also wrote **Rouletabille Aviateur** (see below).

Les Hommes Veulent Vivre! [Men Want to Live!]

(B&W., 110 min., 1961)

DIR: Leonide Moguy; WRI: Leonide Moguy, Henri Torres.

CAST: Claudio Gora, John Justin, Jacqueline Huet, Yves Massard.

STORY: An anti-atomic research story, featuring a deadly death ray.

L'Horrible Dr. Orloff [The Awful Dr. Orloff aka

Cries in the Night; The Demon Doctor] (B&W., 86 min., 1961)

DIR/WRI: Jess Franco, based on the novel by David Kuhne.

CAST: Howard Vernon, Conrado San Martin, Perla Cristal, Maria Silva.

STORY: Unauthorized variation of **Franju**'s *Les Yeux Sans Visage*, in which mad Dr. Orloff performs monstrous surgery on disfigured people.

NOTE: This is a French/Spanish co-production directed by renowned Spanish B-movie director Jess (Jesus) Franco. It is the first in a series which includes *Les Maîtresses du Dr. Jekyll* (*Dr. Orloff's Monster*, 1964), **Dans les Griffes du Maniaque** (*In the Grip of the Maniac; The Diabolical Dr. Z; Miss Death; and Dr. Z; Miss Death*, 1965), *Les Orgies du Dr. Orloff* (1966), *Orloff et l'Homme Invisible* (1970), etc., and the remake **Les Prédateurs de la Nuit** (see below).

Hu-Man (Col., 90 min., 1974)
DIR: Jerôme Lapperousaz; WRI: André **Ruellan**.
CAST: Terence Stamp, Jeanne Moreau.
STORY: An actor who lost is wife is enlisted by scientists who use him in a time travel experiment.

L'Ibis Rouge [The Red Ibis] (Col., 90 min., 1975)
DIR: Jean-Pierre **Mocky**; WRI: Jean-Pierre **Mocky**, André **Ruellan**, based on a novel by Fredric Brown.
CAST: Michel Serrault (Jérémie), Michel Galabru (Raymond), Michel Simon, Jean Le Poulain.
STORY: Jérémie is a serial killer who strangles women with a scarf embroidered with a red ibis. Raymond who witnessed one of his crimes tries to use him to kill his wife.
NOTE: Fredric Brown is a renowned American science fiction writer (*Martians Go Home*). André **Ruellan**, aka Kurt **Steiner**, is a noted horror writer (see Book 2).

I.F.1 Ne Répond Plus [I.F.1 Does Not Answer] (B&W., 100 min., 1932)
DIR: Karl Hartl; WRI: André Beucler, Walter Reisch, based on the novel by Kurt (Curt) Siodmak.
CAST: Charles Boyer, Jean Murst, Pierre Brasseur, Danièle Parola.
STORY: Air transport companies fight against the existence of a huge sea platform in the Atlantic.
NOTE: This is the French version of a multinational co-production. Two other versions were shot simultaneously with different casts: a German version, *F.P.1 Antwortet Nicht*, with Hans Albers, Sybille Schmitz, Paul Hartmann, and Peter Lorre; and an English version, *F.P.1*, with Leslie Fenton, Conrad Veidt, Jill Esmond, and George Merritt. Kurt (Curt) Siodmak is the writer of *The Wolf Man* (1941) and the classic thriller novel, *Donovan's Brain*.

L'Île d'Épouvante [The Island of Terror] (B&W., 3000 ft., 1913)
DIR/WRI/CAST: No information available (reportedly based on H.G. Wells' *The Island of Dr. Moreau*).
STORY: Mad Dr. Wagner flees to an island to continue his skin grafts transplant research. The shipwrecked hero flees with the doctor's daughter when he discovers that he is to be his next subject.

L'Île Mystérieuse [The Mysterious Island] (Col., 105 min., 1972)
DIR: Henri Colpi, Juan Antonio Bardem; WRI: Jacques Champreux, based on the novel by Jules **Verne**.
NOTE: Feature-length film version edited down from a television series. See Chapter II under **Verne, Jules**.

Ils [They] (Col., 100 min., 1970)
DIR: Jean-Daniel Simon; WRI: Jean-Daniel Simon, J.-P. Petrolacci, based on the novel *Le Seuil du Jardin [The Treshold of the Garden]* by André **Hardellet** (see Book 2).

CAST: Michel Duchaussoy, Charles Vanel, Alexandra Stewart, Vernon Potchess, Pierre Massimi.
STORY: An old man has a machine which enables an artist to realize his unconscious dreams.

Ils Sont Fous, Ces Sorciers [The Wizards Are Crazy] (Col., 95 min., 1978)
DIR: Georges Lautner; WRI: Norbert Carbonneaux, Albert Kantof, Georges Lautner, Claude Mulot.
CAST: Jean Lefèbvre, Daniel Ceccaldi, Henri Guybet, Julien Guiomar, Renée Saint-Cyr, Caterine Lachens.
STORY: Having angered the native gods, two hapless French tourists (Lefèbvre, Ceccaldi) come back from a trip to the islands with a curse on their heads.

Ils Sont Grands, Ces Petits [The Kids Have Grown Up] (Col., 95 min., 1979)
DIR: Joël Santoni; WRI: Daniel Boulanger, Joël Santoni, Jean-Claude **Carrière**.
CAST: Claude Brasseur (Léo), Catherine Deneuve (Louise), Claude Piéplu, Eva Darlan, Jean-François Balmer, Roland Blanche, Yves Robert, Clément Harari.
STORY: When Louise is expropriated by a real estate tycoon (Piéplu), her friend Léo, a gifted inventor, uses his knowledge of robotics to get revenge.

L'Imprécateur [The Imprecator] (Col., 100 min., 1977)
DIR: Jean-Louis Bertucelli; WRI: Jean-Louis Bertucelli, Stéphen Becker, René-Victor **Pilhes**, based on his novel.
CAST: Jean Yanne, Michel Piccoli, Jean-Pierre Marielle, Jean-Claude Brialy, Marlène Jobert, Michel Lonsdale.
STORY: Surreal adventure in which an unknown employee causes chaos and eventually destroys a large multinational corporation from within. Was it all a dream?

L'Inconnu de Shandigor [The Unknown Man from Shandigor] (Col., 90 min., 1967)
DIR: Jean-Louis Roy; WRI: Jean-Louis Roy, Gabriel Arout.
CAST: Marie-France Boyer, Ben Carruthers, Daniel Emilfork, Howard Vernon, Jacques Dufilho.
STORY: A villain discovers a way to make atomic weapons unworkable. He is devoured by his own sea monster at the climax.
NOTE: This is a French-language Swiss production.

J'accuse [I Accuse]
Version No. 1: (B&W., 110 min., 1918)
DIR: Abel **Gance**; WRI: Blaise Cendrars, Abel **Gance**.
CAST: Séverin-Mars (François Laurin), Maryse Dauvray (Édith Laurin), Romuald Joubé (Jean Diaz).
STORY: During World War I, the wife of a French soldier

is raped by a German while her husband and a poet friend fight in the trenches.

NOTE: The film includes a striking ending where the war dead rise to get their revenge on those who stayed safely behind. Blaise Cendrars (Frédéric Sauser, 1887-1961) is a famous poet and essayist.

Version No. 2: (Col., 125 min., 1937 [transl. as *That They May Live*])

DIR: Abel **Gance**; WRI: Steve Passeur, Abel **Gance**.

CAST: Marcel Delaître (François Laurin), Line Noro (Édith Laurin), Victor Francen (Jean Diaz), Jean Max, Renée Devilliers.

STORY: In this version, Diaz is a scientist who survived World War I. Desperately seeking to prevent another war, he invents an indestructible glass. When he learns that a new war is imminent, he raises the dead from the trenches and, this time, is heard. Peace prevails.

J'ai Rencontré le Père Noël [I Have Met Santa Claus, transl. as *Here Comes Santa Claus]* (Col., 85 min., 1984)

DIR: Christian Gion; WRI: Christian Gion, Didier Kaminka.

CAST: Armand Meffre (Santa Claus), Karen Cheryl, Alexia Haudot, Éric Chapuis, Dominique Hulin, Hélène Zidi, Jean-Louis Foulquier.

STORY: A little boy (Chapuis) is reunited with missing parents thanks to Santa Claus.

James Bande 00 Sexe (Col., 65 min., 1981)
DIR/WRI: Michel Baudricourt.

CAST: Guy Royer, Cathy Stewart, Helen Shirley, Dominique Trissou.

STORY: X-rated James Bond parody.

Le Jardinier [The Gardener] (Col., 94 min., 1980)
DIR/WRI: Jean-Pierre Sentier

CAST: Maurice Benichou (Gardener), Jean Bolo, Pierre Bolo, Michèle Marquais, Claude Faraldo.

STORY: In a surreal future where water has become a precious commodity, a gardener revolts against two tyrannical brothers who run the factory where he works.

Je T'aime, Je T'aime [I Love You, I Love You] (Col., 91 min., 1968)
DIR: Alain **Resnais**; WRI: Jacques **Sternberg**.

CAST: Claude Rich, Olga Georges-Picot, Anouk Ferjac.

STORY: A man (Rich) who tried to commit suicide is projected back into the past where he can again live with his late wife (Georges-Picot). But the experiment goes wrong.

NOTE: Jacques **Sternberg** is a famous science fiction writer (see Book 2) who also wrote the animated short *La Planète Verte* (see Chapter IV).

Je Vous Salue Marie [Hail Mary] (Col., 65 min., 1984)
DIR: Jean-Luc **Godard**; WRI: Jean-Luc **Godard**, Anne-Marie Miéville.

CAST: Myriem Roussel (Mary), Thierry Rode, Philippe Lacoste, Juliette Binoche.

STORY: The story of Gabriel, Mary, and Joseph recast in modern-day Switzerland.

Les Jeux de la Comtesse Dolingen de Gratz [The Games of the Countess Dolingen de Gratz] (Col., 114 min., 1980)
DIR/WRI: Catherine Binet, based on story elements from Unica Zürn and Bram Stoker.

CAST: Michel Lonsdale (Bertrand), Carol Kane, Katia Watschenko, Marina Vlady, Roberto Plate.

STORY: Bertrand, a wealthy art collector, brags about the horrible revenge he exacted on a thief who stole from him.

Les Jeux Sont Faits [All Bets Are Off] (B&W., 90 min., 1947)
DIR: Jean Delannoy; WRI: Jean-Paul Sartre, Jean Delannoy, Jacques-Laurent Bost.

CAST: Micheline Presle (Ève), Marcel Pagliero (Pierre), Colette Ripert, Marguerite Moreno, Fernand Fabre, Charles Dullin, Paul Ollivier, Marcel Mouloudji, Danièle Delorme.

STORY: Pierre and Ève have died at the same, exact second; she was poisoned by her husband, he was murdered by a fellow worker. Because they were fated to meet, they are returned to life for a day, but the difference in their origins proves too much, and they fail to fall in love.

NOTE: Novelist, playwright, and existentialist writer Jean-Paul Sartre (1905-1980) needs little introduction.

Le Joueur d'Échecs [The Chess Player]
Version No. 1: (B&W., 82v min., 1927)

DIR: Raymond Bernard; WRI: Henry Dupuy-Mazuel.

CAST: Edith Jehanne, Pierre Blanchar, Charles Dullin.

STORY: A villain is killed by an android chess player.

Version No. 2: (B&W., 90 min., 1938)

DIR: Jean Dréville; WRI: Albert Guyot.

CAST: Conrad Veidt (Kempelen), Françoise Rosay (Catherine II), Bernard Lancret, Micheline Francey, Paul Cambo, Jacques Grétillat, Gaston Modot.

STORY: A romantic tale of young Polish patriots in love (Cambo, Francey) grafted onto the original Kempelen story.

NOTE: Both films are based on the famous story of Kempelen's android chess player. Also see Chapter II for television adaptations.

Le Joueur de Flûte [The Pied Piper of Hamelin]

(Col., 90 min., 1971)

DIR: Jacques **Demy**; WRI: Jacques **Demy**, Andrew Birkin, Mark Peploe.

CAST: Donovan (the Piper), Jack Wild, Donald Pleasance, Cathryn Harrison, Peter Vaughan.

STORY: Faithful adaptation of the classic fairy tale.

NOTE: This is a British production.

Judex

Series of films based on the novels by Arthur **Bernède** (see Book 2), a popular pulp writer who also created the character of ***Belphegor*** (see Chapter II).

1. Judex (B&W., 12 Eps., 1916)

2. La Nouvelle Mission de Judex [Judex's New Mission] (B&W., 12 Eps., 1917)

DIR: Louis **Feuillade**; WRI: Arthur **Bernède**.

CAST: René Cresté (Judex), Louis Leubas (Favraux), Édouard Mathé, Yvonne Dario, Marcel Lévesque, Musidora, André Brunelle.

STORY: The original silent serial series introduces the character of avenging mystery man Judex, who is determined to bring corrupt banker Favraux to justice. Judex eventually falls in love with Favraux's daughter.

3. Judex (B&W., 95 min., 1934)

DIR/WRI: Maurice Champreux.

CAST: René Ferté, Marcel Vallée, Mihalesco, Jean Lefèbvre, René Navarre, Constantini.

STORY: Faithful remake of Louis **Feuillade**'s serial.

4. Judex (B&W., 100 min., 1963)

DIR: Georges **Franju**; WRI: Jacques Champreux, Francis Lacassin.

CAST: Channing Pollock (Judex), Michel Vitold (Favraux), Édith Scob (Jacqueline), Francine Bergé, Jacques Jouanneau, Théo Sarapo, Sylvia Koscina, René Genin.

STORY: Clever remake of Louis **Feuillade**'s serial; a moving and poetic homage to the original.

NOTE: Jacques Champreux is Maurice Champreux's son (see ***Nuits Rouges*** below and ***L'Homme Sans Visage*** and

L'Île Mystérieuse in Chapter II). Francis Lacassin is a renowned comic book scholar.

Juliette, ou la Clé des Songes [Juliette, or the Key to Dreams] (B&W., 100 min., 1951)

DIR: Marcel **Carné**; WRI: Marcel **Carné**, Jacques Viot, Georges Neveux.

CAST: Gérard Philipe (Michel), Suzanne Cloutier (Juliette), Jean-Roger Caussimon, René Guénin, Yves Robert, Édouard Delmont, Roland Lesaffre, Gabrielle Fontan, Max Dejean, Arthur Devere, Marcelle Arnold, Fernand René, Martial Rebe, Marion Delbo.

STORY: Michel is in prison because he stole from his employer at Juliette's behest. His experiences in a strange Land of Dream change his life.

Kamikaze (Col., 90 min., 1986)

DIR: Didier Grousset; WRI: Didier Grousset, Luc **Besson**, Michèle Halberstadt.

CAST: Michel Galabru (Albert), Richard Bohringer (Pascot), Dominique Lavanant, Riton Liebman, Jean-Paul Muel.

STORY: Albert, an embittered, old scientist, builds a weapon which enables him to kill people who appear live on television. After a prodigious manhunt, police commissioner Pascot finds him, but for reasons of national security, the military kills the scientist.

Le Lac des Morts-Vivants [The Lake of the Living Dead, transl. as Zombie's Lake] (Col., 90 min., 1980)

DIR: J. R. Lazer, Jean **Rollin** (uncredited); WRI: Julian Estelim (pseudonym of Daniel Lesoeur).

CAST: Howard Vernon, Pierre Escourrou, Anthony Mayans, Nadine Pascale, Anouchka.

STORY: Avenging Nazi zombies emerge from a lake and eat their victims.

Landru [Bluebeard] (Col., 155 min., 1962)

DIR: Claude **Chabrol**; WRI: Françoise Sagan.

CAST: Charles Denner (Landru), Michèle Morgan, Danielle Darrieux, Stéphane Audran, Juliette Mayniel, Catherine Rouvel.

STORY: The story of a notorious French serial killer of the 1940s.

Léonor (Col., 100 min., 1975)

Dir: Juan Luis **Buñuel**; Wri: Juan Luis **Buñuel**, Jean-Claude **Carrière**, Michel Nuridzani, Pierre Maintigneux, based on a story by Ludwig Tieck.

Cast: Michel Piccoli (Richard), Liv Ullman (Léonor), Ornella Muti (Catherine).

Story: During the Middle Ages, after his wife Léonor's death, Richard marries Catherine. But ten years later, Léonor returns, and may be a vampire.

Lèvres de Sang [Bloody Lips] (Col., 92 min., 1975)

Dir: Jean **Rollin**; Wri: Jean **Rollin**, Jean-Lou Philippe.

Cast: Jean-Lou Philippe, Annie Briand, Nathalie Perrey, Willy Braque, Paul Bisciglia.

Story: A child meets a beautiful woman. Twenty years later, he meets the same woman who has not changed. In fact, she is a vampire.

Les Lèvres Rouges [Red Lips, transl. as ***Daughters of Darkness]*** (Col., 98 min., 1971)

Dir: Harry **Kumel**; Wri: Harry **Kumel**, Jean Ferry.

Cast: Delphine Seyrig (Countess Bathory), Danielle Ouimet, John Karlen, Andréa Rau.

Story: In Ostend, a newlywed couple (Karlen, Ouimet) runs afoul of the vampire Countess Bathory.

Libra (Col., 90 min., 1974)

Dir: Roland Moreau, Georges Perdriaud, Jean Talansier; Wri: Groupe Pattern.

Cast: Pierre Sherley, Kris Frémont, Fabien Dutaillis, Jean-Pierre Pasquier.

Story: Upon their return to Earth, cosmonauts land on a mountain where a group of young people have dreamed a bucolic utopia.

Les Liens de Sang [Blood Relatives] (Col., 100 min., 1977)

Dir: Claude **Chabrol**; Wri: Claude **Chabrol**, Sidney Banks, based on a novel by Ed McBain (Evan Hunter).

Cast: Donald Sutherland (Carella), Stéphane Audran, Aude Landry, Lise Langlois, David Hemmings, Donald Pleasance.

Story: "86th Precinct" story about a gory murder about incest.

Note: French-Canadian co-production.

Le Lit de la Vierge [The Virgin's Bed] (Col., 100 min., 1969)

Dir/Wri: Philippe Garel.

Cast: Pierre Clémenti, Zazou, Jean-Pierre Kalfon.

Story: The surreal adventures of Mary and Jesus.

Litan (Col., 88 min., 1981)

Dir: Jean-Pierre **Mocky**; Wri: Jean-Claude Romer, Jean-Pierre **Mocky**, Patrick Granier, Scott & Suzy Baker.

Cast: Jean-Pierre **Mocky**, Marie-José Nat, Nino Ferrer, Roger Lumont.

Story: In the atmospheric village of Litan, two lovers (Mocky and Nat) become involved in a plot by a mysterious doctor (Ferrer) to control the lifeforce of the dead.

Note: Scott Baker is an American science fiction writer living in Paris. Jean-Claude Romer is one of the foremost French Cinema scholars.

Le Locataire [The Tenant] (Col., 125 min., 1976)

Dir: Roman Polanski; Wri: Gérard Brach, Roman Polanski, based on the novel by Roland **Topor**.

Cast: Roman Polanski (Trelkovsky), Isabelle Adjani (Stella), Melvyn Douglas, Shelley Winters, Héléna Manson, Bernard Fresson, Claude Piéplu, Rufus, Romain Bouteille, Jacques Monod.

Story: Trelkovsky, a meek bureaucrat, rents an apartment previously occupied by a woman who threw herself out of the window. He starts impersonating her, and eventually shares the same fate.

Note: Roland **Topor** is a renowned French writer/cartoonist (see Book 2), who designed René **Laloux**'s *La Planète Sauvage* [*Fantastic Planet*] (see Chapter IV) and *Marquis* (below). He also acted in Werner Herzog's *Nosferatu*.

Lorna l'Exorciste [Lorna the Exorcist] *see* ***Les Possédés du Diable***

Le Loup des Malveneur [The Wolf of Malveneur] (B&W., 99 min., 1943)

Dir: Guillaume Radot; Wri: Francis Vincent-Bréchignac.

Cast: Pierre Renoir (Réginald), Madeleine Sologne (Monique), Michel Marsay, Gabrielle Dorziat, Yves Furet, Louis Salou.

STORY: Réginald, the last descendant of the Malveneur family, is afraid of being struck by his ancestor's werewolf curse. Monique, a governess, solves the mystery.

Le Loup-Garou [The Werewolf] (B&W., 90 min., 1923)

DIR/WRI: Jacques Roullet, Pierre Bressol, based on the novel by Alfred Machard.

CAST: Léon Bernard, Simone Jacquemin, Jeanne Delvair, Pierre Juvenet, Madeleine Guitty.

Story/NOTE: This film is listed here only because many reference works include it as the story of a priest's murderer, who is cursed to turn into a werewolf. In reality, it is about an escaped convict who tries to escape from the police with his young son, and tells the child that they're being pursued by a werewolf. It is *not* a fantasy film.

La Lune dans le Caniveau [The Moon in the Gutter] (Col., 137 min., 1983)

DIR: Jean-Jacques Beinex; WRI: J.-J. Beinex, Olivier Mergault, based on the novel by David Goodis.

CAST: Gérard Depardieu (Gérard), Nastassja Kinski (Loretta), Victoria Abril (Bella), Vittorio Mezzogiorno, Dominique Pinon, Béatrice Reading.

STORY: In a surreal, imaginary city, Gérard, a docker, searches for the man who raped his sister, driving her to kill herself. He then falls passionately in love with Loretta, a woman from the "high city," where rich people live.

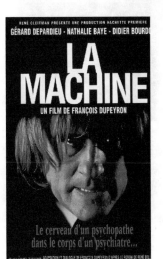

La Machine (Col., 94 min., 1994)

DIR/WRI: François Dupeyron, based on the novel by René **Belletto**.

CAST: Gérard Depardieu, Nathalie Baye, Didier Bourdon, Natalia Woerner, Erwan Baynaud.

STORY: A neuro-psychiatrist (Depardieu) invents a machine which switches his mind with that of a psychotic killer (Bourdon).

La Machine à Découdre [The Killing Machine] (Col., 88 min., 1986)

DIR/WRI: Jean-Pierre **Mocky**.

CAST: Jean-Pierre **Mocky** (Dr. Enger), Patricia Barzyk, Peter Semler.

STORY: A mad doctor embarks on a killing spree.

Ma Femme Est une Panthère [My Wife Is a Panther] (Col., 85 min., 1961]

DIR: Raymond Bailly; WRI: Gérard Carlier.

CAST: Jean Richard, Jean Poiret, Michel Serrault, Silvana Blasi, Marcel Lupovici.

STORY: A woman's soul has transmigrated into a panther's body and can become human at will.

Le Magnifique [The Magnificent One, transl. as How to Destroy the Reputation of the Greatest Secret Agent] (Col., 90 min., 1973)

DIR: Philippe de Broca; WRI: Francis Véber.

CAST: Jean-Paul Belmondo (François/Bob), Jacqueline Bisset (Christine/Tatiana), Vittorio Caprioli, Monique Tarbès, Jean Lefèbvre, Mario David, André Weber, Hubert Deschamps.

STORY: François, a writer of spy thrillers, keeps alternating between his reality and the fictional world of his hero, Bob.

La Main [The Hand] (Col., 90 min., 1969)

DIR: Henri Glaeser; WRI: Henri Glaeser, Paul Parisot.

CAST: Nathalie Delon, Michel Duchaussoy, Henri Serre, Pierre Dux, Roger Hanin.

STORY: A pair of murderers are forced to cut off their victim's hand when they dispose of his body. But the hand returns to haunt them.

La Main du Diable [The Devil's Hand, transl. as Carnival of Sinners] (B&W., 82 min., 1942)

DIR: Maurice **Tourneur**; WRI: Jean-Paul Le Chanois, based on a short story by Gérard de **Nerval**.

CAST: Pierre Fresnay (Roland), Josseline Gaël (Irène), Marcelle Rexlane, Gabrielle Fontan, Pierre Palau, Noël Roquevert, Guillaume de Sax, Pierre Larquey.

STORY: Roland, a failed painter, buys a mysterious mummified hand which makes him rich and famous, and enables him to marry Irène, the woman he loves, but by so doing he has unwittingly sold his soul to the devil.

NOTE: Gérard de **Nerval** is a famous poet and writer of the *fantastique* (see Book 2). Another of his story was adapted for television in *Les Classiques de l'Étrange* (see Chapter II).

Les Mains d'Orlac [The Hands of Orlac] (B&W., 105 min., 1960)

DIR: Edmond T. Gréville; WRI: Edmond T. Gréville, John Baines, based on the novel by Maurice **Renard**.

CAST: Mel Ferrer (Orlac), Dany Carrel, Christopher Lee, Lucile Saint-Simon, Balpétré.

STORY: A surgeon (Balpétré) grafts a killer's hands onto a famous pianist (Ferrer). Before he kills his wife (Carrel), he learns that the killer was in fact innocent.

NOTE: Maurice **Renard** is a famous science fiction writer (see Book 2). This is the third film adaptation based on his story, after *Orlacs Hände* in Germany in 1924 (DIR: Robert

Wiene, starring Conrad Veidt), and *Mad Love* in the U.S. in 1935 (DIR: Karl Freund, starring Peter Lorre). **Les Mains d'Orlac** was also adapted for television in the anthology series **Des Voix dans la Nuit** [*Voices in the Night*]. Two more of Renard's genre novels, **Le Péril Bleu** and **Le Docteur Lerne**, were also adapted for television, the former in the anthology series **Les Classiques de l'Étrange** [*Classics of the Strange*] and the latter as a telefilm, **L'Étrange Château du Dr. Lerne** (see Chapter II). Also see Chapter III for radio adaptations.

Le Maître du Temps [The Time Master] (B&W., 90 min., 1970)

DIR: Jean-Daniel Pollet; WRI: J.-D. Pollet, Pierre **Kast**.

CAST: Jean-Pierre Kalfon, Ruy Guerra.

STORY: A man (Kalfon), who may be an alien, owns a ring that allows him to travel through time; he uses it to visit various eras in Brazilian history.

Les Maîtres du Soleil [The Sun Masters] (Col., 85 min., 1983)

DIR/WRI: Jean-Jacques Aublanc.

CAST: Marcel Amont, Georges Claisse, Maurice Garrel, François Chaumette, Catherine Jarrett, Bernard Marcellin, Jean Davy, Gérard Chaillou.

STORY: A retired scientist (Claisse) investigates the disappearance of a colleague (Davy) who had made break-through discoveries in light energy. The missing scientist now wants to cleanse the world, but is destroyed by ancient, occult powers.

La Malédiction de Belphegor [The Curse of Belphegor] (Col., 98 min., 1966)

DIR: Georges Combret; WRI: Georges Combret, Michel Dubox.

CAST: Paul Guers, Dominique Boschero, Raymond Souplex, Raymond Bussières, Noëlle Noblecourt, Maurice Chevit, Achille Zavatta, Marcel Charvey, Annette Poivre.

STORY: A madman possessed by the pagan god Belphegor, and armed with sophisticated technology, attempts to prevent the staging of what he believes to be a blasphemous play. No relation to the **Belphegor** television series.

Malevil (Col., 119 min., 1980)

DIR: Christian de **Chalonge**; WRI: Christian de **Chalonge**, Pierre Dumayet, based on the novel by Robert **Merle**.

CAST: Michel Serrault (Emmanuel), Jean-Louis Trintignant (Fulbert), Jacques Dutronc, Jacques Villeret, Robert Dhéry.

STORY: After a nuclear war, some survivors learn to live in peace under Emmanuel's guidance, but they come in conflict with another group led by the fascistic Fulbert.

NOTE: Robert **Merle** is a famous writer, author of *The Day of the Dolphin* (1967) (see Book 2).

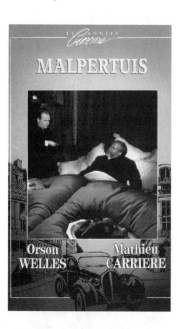

Malpertuis (Col., 110 min., 1972)

DIR: Harry **Kumel**; WRI: Jean Ferry, based on the novel by Jean **Ray**.

CAST: Orson Welles (Cassave), Mathieu Carrière (Yann), Susan Hampshire, Michel Bouquet, Jean-Pierre Cassel.

STORY: After Uncle Cassave's death, Yann, a young sailor, inherits his ancient house, Malpertuis, and its weird occupants, who turn out to be the shades of the Olympian Gods once captured by his uncle.

NOTE: This is a French-language Belgian production. Jean **Ray** is Belgian and a major writer of the *fantastique* (see Book 2). Other adaptations include the feature film **La Cité de l'Indicible Peur** (above) and **L'Homme Qui Osa** in Selected Short Features.

Mama Dracula (Col., 90 min., 1980)

DIR: Boris Szulzinger; WRI: Boris Szulzinger, Pierre Sterckx, Marc-Henry Wajnberg.

CAST: Louise Fletcher (Mama), Maria Schneider, Marc-Henry & Alexandre Wajnberg.

STORY: Another variation of the Countess Bathory/female Dracula tale, used here mostly as a vehicle for two stand-up comedians, the Wajnbergs, two cousins posing as Mama Dracula's twin sons.

NOTE: This is a French-language Belgian production.

Le Mangeur de Lune [The Moon Eater] (Col., 103 min., 1994)

DIR: Dai Sijie; WRI: Dai Sijie, Nadine Perront.

CAST: Chick Ortega, Rufus, Mohamed Camara, Catherine Hiegel, Geneviève Fontanel, Yann Collette.

STORY: Adaptation of a Russian legend in which, in order to be freed from a curse, a flying man must be bathed in human blood.

Manika, Une Vie Plus Tard [Manika, One Life Later] (Col., 100 min., 1988)

DIR: François Villiers; WRI: François Villiers, Jean-Pierre Gibrat, Brian Phelan.

CAST: Julian Sands, Ayesha Dharker, Stéphane Audran.

STORY: A young Indian girl discovers that she is the reincarnation of another woman.

Marguerite de la Nuit [Marguerite of the Night] (Col., 125 min., 1955)

DIR: Claude **Autant-Lara**; WRI: Ghislaine Autant-Lara, Gabriel Arout, based on the novel by Pierre **Mac Orlan**.

CAST: Michèle Morgan (Marguerite), Yves Montand (Léon/Mephistophes), Jean-François Calvé (Faust), Pierre Palau, Massimo Girotti.

STORY: Another variation on the classic *Faust* story, in which Marguerite is willing to sacrifice her soul to save Faust, but because Mephistopheles is in love with her, he releases them both.

Marianne de Ma Jeunesse [Marianne of My Youth] (B&W., 105 min., 1954)

DIR/WRI: Julien **Duvivier**, bssed on the novel by Peter von Mendelssohn.

CAST: Marianne Hold, Pierre Vaneck, Isabelle Pia, Gil Vidal, Jean Yonnel.

STORY: In the midst of the Bavarian forest, a young man (Vaneck) meets a beautiful, mysterious woman (Hold) who transforms his life.

Marie-Chantal Contre Dr. Kha [Marie-Chantal vs. Dr. Kha] (Col., 114 min., 1965)

DIR: Claude **Chabrol**; WRI: Claude **Chabrol**, Christian Yve, based on an idea by Jacques Chazot.

CAST: Marie Laforêt (Marie-Chantal), Akim Tamiroff (Dr. Kha), Francisco Rabal, Serge Reggiani, Charles Denner, Roger Hanin, Stéphane Audran.

STORY: Marie-Chantal accidentally comes into the possession of the secret of a super-weapon, and becomes the target of a variety of spies and the evil Dr. Kha in this lighthearted satire of James Bond movies.

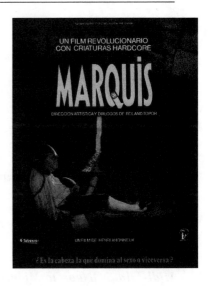

Marquis (Col., 83 min., 1988)

DIR: Henri Xhonneux; WRI: Roland **Topor**, Henri Xhonneux.

Creature Design: Roland **Topor**.

VOICES: François Marthouret (Marquis), Valerie Kling (Colin), Michel Robin (Ambert), Isabelle Canet-Wolfe (Justine), Nathalie Juvet (Juliette), Vicky Messica, René Lebrun, Bob Morel, Roger Crouzet, Willem Holtrop, Éric de Saria, Henri Rubinstein.

HANDLERS: Philippe Bizot (Marquis), Gabrielle Van Damme (Ambert), Bien de Moor (Justine/Juliette), Olivier Dechaveau, Bernard Cognaux, Pierre Decuypère.

STORY: In the 18th century, a liberal writer, Marquis, is jailed in the Bastille. There, he has conversations with his penis (endowed with a separate personality, named Colin), meets other colorful prisoners, and, eventually, escapes.

NOTE: This *Muppet Movie*-like French-Belgian co-production features a remarkable cast of animal caricatures: Marquis is a dog, Ambert his jailer a rat, Governor Preaubois a rooster, etc.

Un Martien à Paris [A Martian in Paris] (B&W., 90 min., 1960)

DIR: Jean-Daniel Daninos; WRI: Jean-Daniel Daninos, Jacques Vilfrid.

CAST: Darry Cowl, Nicole Mirel, Henri Vilbert, Gisèle Grandré, Rolande Ségur, Michèle Verez.

STORY: A Martian lands in Paris to study the emotion called love.

Le Martien de Noël [The Christmas Martian] (Col., 66 min., 1977)

DIR: Bernard Gosselin; WRI: Roch **Carrier**, Louise Forestier.

CAST: Paul Berval, Yvan Canuel, Roland Chenail, François Gosselin, Ernest Guimond.

STORY: Children find a friendly Martian in a forest at Christmas time.

NOTE: French-Canadian production.

La Mémoire Courte [Short Memory] (Col., 90 min., 1979)

DIR: Eduardo de Gregorio; WRI: Edgardo Cozarinsky, Eduardo de Gregorio.

CAST: Philippe Léotard, Nathalie Baye, Bulle Ogier.

STORY: A fantastical investigation in a Jose Luis Borges-like setting.

NOTE: Franco-Belgian co-production.

La Merveilleuse Visite [The Marvellous Visitation]
(Col., 100 min., 1974)

DIR: Marcel **Carné**; WRI: Marcel **Carné**, Didier Decoin, based on the story by H.-G. Wells.

CAST: Gilles Kohler (Angel), Roland Lesaffre, Deborah Berger, Lucien Barjon, Mary Marquet, Jean-Pierre Castaldi, Yves Barsacq, Jacques Debary.

STORY: The inhabitants of a small village in Britanny discover a man who claims to be an angel who fell from the sky.

Midi-Minuit [Noon to Midnight] (Col., 105 min., 1970)

DIR/WRI: Pierre Philippe.

CAST: Sylvie Fennec, Béatrice Arnac, Daniel Emilfork, Jacques Portet, Laurent Vergez, Patrick Jouanne.

STORY: A mysterious killer with vampiric tendencies rips his victims apart with iron-clawed gloves.

Les Mille et Une Nuits [The Thousand and One Nights] (Col., 98 min., 1990)

DIR: Philippe de Broca; WRI: Philippe de Broca, Jérôme Tonnerre.

CAST: Thierry Lhermitte (Sultan), Gérard Jugnot (Genie), Vittorio Gassman, Catherine Zeta-Jones (Sheherazade).

STORY: Comedic transposition of the classic tale, in which a genie from the 20th century uses modern equipment to save Sheherazade from the Sultan.

Le Miracle des Loups [The Miracle of the Wolves]
Version No.1: B&W., 3000 M., 1924

DIR: Raymond Bernard; WRI: Jean-José Frappa, Dupuy-Mazuel.

CAST: Charles Dullin (Louis XI), Vanni Marcoux (Charles le Téméraire), Romuald Joubet (Robert), Yvonne Sergyl (Jeanne), Gaston Modot, Philippe Hériat.

Version No.2: Col., 130 min., 1961

DIR: André Hunebelle; WRI: André Hunebelle, Jean Halain.

CAST: Jean-Louis Barrault (Louis XI), Roger Hanin (Charles le Téméraire), Jean Marais (Robert de Neuville), Rosanna Schiaffino (Jeanne de Beauvais).

STORY: Medieval tale where two lovers are miraculously saved by wolves.

Le Miraculé [The Miracle Victim] (Col., 87 min., 1986)

DIR: Jean-Pierre **Mocky**; WRI: Jean-Pierre **Mocky**, Jean-Claude Romer, Patrick Granier.

CAST: Michel Serrault (Fox-Terrier), Jean Poiret (Papu), Jeanne Moreau.

STORY: Papu pretends to be paralyzed to defraud his insurance company. After a trip to Lourdes, he really becomes paralyzed.

NOTE: Jean-Claude Romer is a well-known film historian.

Mister Freedom (Col., 110 min., 1968)

DIR/WRI: William Klein.

CAST: John Abbey (Mr. Freedom), Donald Pleasance (Dr. Freedom), Jean-Claude Drouot, Philippe Noiret, Delphine Seyrig, Serge Gainsbourg, Yves Montand, Rufus, Sami Frey.

STORY: Mr. Freedom fights Moujik Man over the fate of France; a satire on the clash between super-powers, done in a comic-book style.

Mister Frost (Col., 105 min., 1989)

DIR: Philippe Setbon; WRI: Philippe Setbon, Brad Lynch, Louise Vincent, Deny Hall.

CAST: Jeff Goldblum, Alan Bates, Kathy Baker, Roland Giraud, Jean-Pierre Cassel, François Négret, Daniel Gélin, Maxime Leroux, Vincent Schiavelli.

STORY: A murderer (Goldblum) incarcerated in a lunatic asylum tries to convince his doctor (Baker) that he is the Devil.

Le Moine [The Monk] (Col., 90 min., 1972)

DIR: Ado Kyrou; WRI: Luis Buñuel, Jean-Claude **Carrière**, based on the novel by Matthew Lewis.

CAST: Franco Nero (Ambrosio), Nathalie Delon (Jean), Nicol Williamson, Nadja Tiller.

STORY: Adaptation of Lewis' gothic tale about Ambrosio, a monk who is being tempted by the Devil (Delon).

NOTE: This film was originally written by **Carrière** for Luis Buñuel to direct.

Le Moine et la Sorcière [The Monk and the Witch]
(Col., 98 min., 1986)

DIR: Suzane Schiffman; WRI: Pamela Berger, Suzane Schiffman.

CAST: Tcheky Karyo (Étienne), Christine Boisson (Elda), Jean Carmet, Féodor Atkine.

STORY: In the middle-ages, Étienne, an inquisitor, accuses Elda, a local woman who is knowledgeable about herbs and plants of being a witch; she is eventually rescued by the local priest (Carmet).

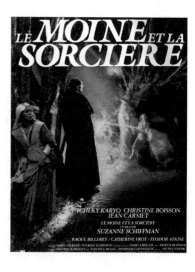

Le Monde Tremblera [The World Will Quake]
(B&W., 108 Min, 1939)

Dir: Richard Pottier; Wri: J. Villard, Henri-Georges Clouzot, based on the novel *La Machine à Prédire la Mort* [*The Death-Predicting Machine*] by Charles **Robert-Dumas** & Roger-Francis **Didelot**.

Cast: Claude Dauphin (Jean), Roger Duchesne, Madeleine Sologne, Erich von Stroheim.

Story: Jean, a young inventor, creates a machine that can accurately predict the time of someone's death—including his.

Monsieur Leguignon, Guérisseur [Mr. Leguignon, Healer] (B&W., 90 Min, 1953)

Dir: Maurice Labro; Wri: Solange Térac, Maurice Labro, based on the radio series by Robert Picq & Pierre Ferrari.

Cast: Yves Deniaud, Jeanne Marken, Nicole Besnard, André Brunot, Michel Roux.

Story: A man discovers that he has the power of healing.

Morgane et ses Nymphes [Morgana and Her Nymphs] (Col., 90 min., 1970)

Dir/Wri: Bruno Gantillon.

Cast: Dominique Delpierre, Alfred Baillou, Mireille Saunin, Régine Motte, Ursule Pauly, Michèle Perello, Nathalie Chaîne.

Story: X-rated tale of the wild adventures of two girls in the Faerie realm.

La Mort de l'Utopie [The Death of Utopia] (Col., 70 min., 1975)

Dir/Wri: Jorge Amat.

Cast: José-Louis Aguire, Charlotte Trench, Emmanuelle Riva, Juliette Noessi.

Story: After his capture by the police, a mad gunman finds refuge in his imagination.

La Mort en Direct [Death on Live TV, transl. as ***Deathwatch]*** (Col., 120 min., 1980)

Dir: Bertrand Tavernier; Wri: David Rayfiel, Bertrand Tavernier, based on the novel *The Continuous Katherine Mortenhoe*, aka *The Unsleeping Eye*, by D. G. Compton.

Cast: Romy Schneider (Katherine), Harvey Keitel (Roddy), Harry Dean Stanton (Vincent), Max von Sydow (Gerard), Thérèse Liotard (dubbed by Julie Christie).

Story: Roddy, a television reporter, has a camera implanted in his eye in order to follow and broadcast the journey of Katherine, a woman dying from an incurable disease, as she looks for Gerard, her estranged husband. Eventually, disgusted by his treachery and voyeurism, he allows himself to go blind. We discover that the woman can be cured—it was all part of a plan by Vincent, the head of the TV network, to guarantee a happy ending and big ratings. But Katherine chooses to die to make a point.

Note: The U.S. release version of this film was badly re-edited by the distributor; in particular, the reasons for Schneider's suicide were completely obfuscated.

Une Mort sans Importance [A Meaningless Death]
(B&W., 80 min., 1948)

Dir/Wri: Yvan Noé.

Cast: Jean Tissier (Duvernay), Suzy Carrier, Jean-Pierre Kerrien, Marcelle Géniat, Jeanne Fusier-Gir.

Story: Death forces a man (Kerrien) to choose another member of his family to take his place.

La Mort Trouble [An Unclear Death] (Col., 84 min., 1968)

Dir: Claude d'Anna, Ferid Boughdir; Wri: Ferid Boughdir.

Cast: Aly Ben Ayed, Ursule Pauly, Sophie Vaillant, S. Céline.

Story: On a deserted island, a strange butler plays games with three young women.

La Morte-Vivante [The Living Dead Girl] (Col., 90 min., 1982)

Dir/Wri: Jean **Rollin**.

Cast: Françoise Blanchard, Marina Pierro, Carina Barone, Mike Marshall, Fanny Magier.

Story: A young girl comes back to life.

Ne Jouez Pas avec les Martiens [Don't Play with Martians] (Col., 90 min., 1967)

Dir: Henri Delanoe; Wri: Henri Delanoe, Joanne Harwood, based on the novel *Les Sextuplés de Loqmaria* [*The Sextuplets of Loqmaria*] by Michel **Labry**.

Cast: Jean Rochefort, Macha Meril, André Vallardy, Frédéric de Pasquale, Haydée Politoff, Pierre **Dac**.

Story: A reporter fakes a Martian landing when sextuplets are born in a Britanny village. Real aliens (not Martians) then arrive to claim the children.

Némo (Col., 97 min., 1984)

Dir: Arnaud Sélignac; Wri: Arnaud Sélignac, Jean-Pierre Esquenazzi, Telsche Boorman, based on the comic strip by Winsor McCay.

Cast: Seth Kibel (Nemo), Mathilda May (Alice), Katrine Boorman, Michel Blanc, Harvey Keitel, Carole Bouquet, Jason Connery, Charley Boorman, Dominique Pinon.

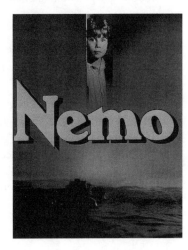

STORY: Little Nemo meets Captain Nemo and Zorro, and saves Alice in Wonderland.

Névrose [Neurosis, transl. as *the Revenge of the House of Usher]* (Col., 90 min., 1983)
DIR: A.M. Franck (pseudonym of Daniel Lesoeur); WRI: Daniel Lesoeur.
CAST: Howard Vernon (Éric Usher), Jean Tolzac, Joan Virly, François Blanchard, Olivier Mathot.
STORY: Sequel to Edgar Allan Poe's classic story.
NOTE: There is a Spanish version with a different cast entitled *El Hundimiento de la Casa Usher.*

Les Noces Rouges [Wedding in Blood] (Col., 90 min., 1973)
DIR/WRI: Claude **Chabrol**.
CAST: Michel Piccoli (Pierre), Stéphane Audran (Lucienne), Claude Piéplu (Paul), Clotilde Joano.
STORY: Pierre, an elected official, murders his wife to be with his lover, Lucienne. But her husband Paul blackmails him.

Notre Histoire [Our Story] (Col., 110 min., 1984)
DIR/WRI: Bertrand **Blier**.
CAST: Alain Delon (Robert), Nathalie Baye (Donatienne), Michel Galabru, Sabine Haudepin, Jean-François Stevenin, Gérard Darmon, Ginette Garcin.
STORY: Robert meets Donatienne, a strange woman with whom he experiences a series of surreal adventures; but he discovers that it was all a dream.

La Nuit de la Mort [The Night of Death] (Col., 90 min., 1980)
DIR: Raphaël Delpard; WRI: Raphaël Delpard, Richard Joffo.
CAST: Isabelle Goguey (Martine), Charlotte de Turckheim (Nicole), Betty Beckers, Michel Flavius, Ernest Menzer.
STORY: Young nurses unwittingly provide fresh flesh and blood to the pensioners of an old folks' home who refuse to age.

La Nuit des Pétrifiés [The Night of the Petrified] see *La Plus Longue Nuit du Diable*

La Nuit des Traquées [The Night of the Hunted] (Col., 90 min., 1980) (aka *Filles Traquées [Hunted Girls]*)
DIR/WRI: Jean Rollin.
CAST: Brigitte Lahaie, Vincent Gardner, Dominique Journet.
STORY: A relentless psychotic killer pursues a young couple.
NOTE: Not to be confused with the eponymous 1959 thriller by Bernard Roland.

La Nuit du Cimetière [The Night at the Cemetery] see *La Rose de Fer*

La Nuit Fantastique [The Fantastic Night] (B&W., 103 min., 1941)
DIR: Marcel L'Herbier; WRI: Louis Chavance.
CAST: Fernand Gravey (Denis), Saturnin Fabre (Thalès), Micheline Presle (Irène), Jean Parédès, Charles Granval, Bernard Blier, Marcel Levesque.
STORY: Denis, a student, helps Irène, a magician's daughter, escape from an unwanted marriage.

La Nuit Tous les Chats Sont Gris [At Night All Cats Are Grey] (Col., 90 min., 1977)
DIR: Gérard Zingg; WRI: Gérard Zingg, Philippe Dumarçay.
CAST: Gérard Depardieu, Laura Betti, Robert Stephens, Charlotte Crow.
STORY: A British writer invents the character of a French bandit to entertain his young niece. The fictional character comes to life and eventually the author must kill him.

Nuits Rouges [Red Nights, transl. as *Shadowman]* (Col., 105 min., 1973)
DIR: Georges **Franju**; WRI: Jacques Champreux.
NOTE: Feature-length film version shot simultaneously with, and edited down from, a television series. See *L'Homme Sans Visage* in Chapter II.

L'Oeil du Malin [The Evil Eye, transl. as *The Third Lover]* (B&W., 80 min., 1961)
DIR/WRI: Claude **Chabrol**.
CAST: Jacques Charrier (Albin), Stéphane Audran (Hélène), Walter Reyer.
STORY: Chilling tale of obsessional evil, in which a journalist, Albin, tries to destroy a couple.

L'Oeil Qui Ment [The Lying Eye, transl. as *Dark at Noon]* (Col., 100 min., 1992)
DIR: Raoul Ruiz; WRI: Raoul Ruiz, Paul Fontaine-Salas.
CAST: John Hurt, Didier Bourdon, Lorraine Evanoff, David Warner, Daniel Prévost.
STORY: After World War I, a surgeon travels to a Portuguese village which is filled with miracles and supernatural occurrences; he eventually learns to accept these events.
NOTE: Chilean director Raoul Ruiz also directed *Les Trois Couronnes du Matelot* (1982) and *Régime Sans Pain* (1985) (see below), and a Menahem Golan-produced version of *Treasure Island* (1986). This is a French-Portuguese co-production.

Ophelia (B&W., 102 min., 1962)
DIR: Claude **Chabrol**; WRI: Paul Gégauff.

CAST: Alida Valli (Claudia), Claude Serval (Adrien), Juliette Mayniel.

STORY: Surreal, Kafkaesque tale which treats Shakespeare's *Hamlet* as a contemporary murder mystery.

Oppressions (Col., 85 min., 1987)
DIR: Jean Cauchy; WRI: Jean Cauchy, Agnès Bromberg.
CAST: Louise Bertaux (Constance), Philippe Lemaire, Hugues Proffy, Didier Cauchy, Philippe Hérisson, Vincent de Bouard.
STORY: In a future where the melting polar ice has created a water world, Constance escapes from her father (Lemaire), and goes looking for her two childhood loves.

L'Or [Gold] (B&W., 120 min., 1934)
DIR: Serge de **Poligny**, Karl Hartl; WRI: Rolf E. Vanloo.
CAST: Brigitte Helm (Florence), Pierre Blanchar (François), Jacques Dumesnil, Rosine Deréan, Line Noro.
STORY: François, a scientist, discovers how to turn lead into gold, but eventually chooses to destroy his research.
NOTE: This is the French version of a French-German co-production with UFA. The German version stars Brigitte Helm, Hans Albers, and Friedrich Kayssler. Some of its special effects were later reused in *Magnetic Monster* (1953).

L'Ordinateur des Pompes Funèbres [The Mortuary Computer] (Col., 85 min., 1975)
DIR: Gérard Pirès; WRI: Jean-Patrick Manchette, Gérard Pirès, based on the novel by Walter Kemply.
CAST: Jean-Louis Trintignant (Fred), Mireille Darc (Charlotte), Bernadette Laffont, Bernard Fresson, Lea Massari, Claude Piéplu.
STORY: Fred, a computer scientist, uses his programming skills to get rid of his wife and all his enemies.
NOTE: Jean-Patrick Manchette is a popular thriller writer.

L'Or et le Plomb [Gold and Lead] (Col., 85 min., 1966)
DIR/WRI: Alain Cuniot, based on *Le Monde Comme Il Va* [*The World as it Goes*] by **Voltaire**.
CAST: Alain Cuniot, Emmanuelle Riva, Max-Paul Fouchet, Michel Legrand, Jean Massin.
STORY: A man from another planet interviews people to decide if Earth is worth saving.

Les Orgies du Comte Porno [The Orgies of Count Porno] (Col., 60 min., 1984)
DIR/WRI: Joanna Morgan.
CAST: Alain L'Yle.
STORY: An evil, leather-masked Master (the Devil?) orders his disciples to torture helpless women.
NOTE: A fairly sick and weird combination of X-rated and gore film.

Orphée [Orpheus]
(B&W., 112 min., 1949)

Le Testament d'Orphée [The Testament Of Orpheus] (B&W., 77 min., 1959)
DIR/WRI: Jean **Cocteau**.
CAST: Jean Marais (Orphée), Marie Déa (Eurydice), Maria Casarès, Jacques Varennes, François Périer, Pierre Bertin, Édouard Dhermitte.
STORY: Modern transposition of the classic Orpheus legend.

OSS 117

This is another series of films based on a popular *James Bond*-like French book series written in the 1950s by Jean **Bruce** (and later continued in the 1960s by his wife, Josette Bruce), starring spymaster extraordinaire Hubert Bonnisseur de la Bath, aka OSS 117.

1. OSS 117 n'est pas mort [OSS 117 is Not Dead] (B&W., 80 min., 1956)
DIR: Jean Sacha; WRI: Jacques Berland, Jean Levitte, based on the novel by Jean **Bruce**.
CAST: Ivan Desny (OSS 117), Magali Noël, Danik Patisson, Georges Lannes, Marie Déa.
STORY: OSS 117 investigates the leak of strategic documents.

2. OSS 117 Se Déchaîne [OSS 117 Strikes Back] (B&W., 110 min., 1963)
DIR/WRI: André Hunebelle, based on the novel by Jean **Bruce**.
CAST: Kerwin Matthews (OSS 117), Irina Demick, Daniel Emilfork, Yvan Chiffre.
STORY: OSS 117 thwarts an enemy spy ring in Corsica.

3. Banco à Bangkok pour OSS 117 [Banco in Bangkok for OSS 117, transl. as *Shadow of Evil or Panic in Bangkok for Agent OSS 117]* (Col., 92 min., 1964)
DIR: André Hunebelle; WRI: Pierre Foucaud, Raymond Borel, André Hunebelle, Michel Lebrun, Richard Caron, Patrice Rondard, based on the novel *Lila de Calcutta* by Jean **Bruce**.
CAST: Kerwin Matthews (OSS 117), Robert Hossein, Anna-Maria PierAngeli, Dominique Wilms, Henri Virlogeux.
STORY: A secret Indian sect plans to use infected rats to create a worldwide epidemic.
NOTE: Robert Hossein directed plays for the **Grand-Guignol**.

4. Furia à Bahia pour OSS 117 [Fury in Bahia for OSS 117, transl. as *Mission for A Killer]* (Col., 84 min., 1965)

DIR: André Hunebelle; WRI: Jean Halain, Pierre Foucaud, André Hunebelle, based on the novel *Dernier Quart d'Heure* [*Last Quarter of an Hour*] by Jean **Bruce**.

CAST: Frederick Stafford (OSS 117), Mylène Demongeot, Raymond Pellegrin, Perrette Pradier, Annie Andersson, François Maistre, Jacques Riberolles.

STORY: OSS 117 goes up against a gang which uses a drug that removes all will power, and turns its victims into zombies.

5. *Atout Coeur à Tokyo pour OSS 117* [*Trump of Hearts in Tokyo for OSS 117,* transl. as *Terror in Tokyo*] (Col., 90 min., 1966)

DIR: Michel Boisrond; WRI: Pierre Foucaud, Marcel Mithois, based on the novel by Jean **Bruce**.

CAST: Frederick Stafford (OSS 117), Marina Vlady, Henri Serre, Colin Drake, Tetsuko Yoshimura.

STORY: OSS 117 thwarts Japanese atomic blackmailers who have built a super-weapon.

6. *Pas de Roses pour OSS 117* [*No Roses for OSS 117,* transl. as *Murder for Sale* or *Double Agent*] (Col., 105 min., 1968)

DIR/WRI: André Hunebelle, based on the novel by Jean **Bruce**.

CAST: John Gavin (OSS 117), Robert Hossein, Margaret Lee, Curd (Curt) Jurgens, Luciana Paluzzi, George Eastman.

STORY: OSS 117 goes after a ring of hitmen who murder politicians.

7. *OSS 117 Prend des Vacances* [*OSS 117 Takes a Vacation*] (Col., 92 min., 1969)

DIR: Pierre Kalfon; WRI: Pierre Kalfon, Josette Bruce, Pierre Philippe, based on the novel by Josette Bruce.

CAST: Luc Merenda (OSS 117), Elsa Martinelli, Edwige Feuillère, Geneviève Grad, Norma Bengell.

STORY: More Brazilian adventures as OSS 117 goes up against secret super-weapons.

Out Un: Spectre (Col., 260 min., 1971-74)

DIR/WRI: Jacques Rivette, based on a story by Honoré de **Balzac**.

CAST: Michel Lonsdale, Bulle Ogier, Jean-Pierre Léaud, Bernadette Laffont, Françoise Fabian.

STORY: In contemporary Paris, a young man tries to locate thirteen people implicated in a mysterious conspiracy.

NOTE: This film was originally conceived as a 12 hour 40 min. production, but was released in a 4 hour 20 min. version. Honoré de **Balzac** is a classic novelist who also wrote some supernatural stories, such as **Melmoth Réconcilié** and **La Peau de Chagrin**, adapted for television (see Book 2 and Chapter II).

Panique [*Panic*] (Col., 90 min., 1977)

DIR: Jean-Claude Lord; WRI: J.-C. Lord, Jean Salvy.

CAST: Paule Bailargeon, Jan Coutu, Lise Thouin.

STORY: A journalist investigates an industrial threat to Canadian ecology.

NOTE: French-Canadian production.

La Papesse (Col., 95 min., 1974)

DIR: Mario **Mercier**; WRI: Robert Paillardon.

CAST: Lisa Lavanne, Érika Maaz, Jean-François Delatour.

STORY: A young couple joins a sect of devil worshippers. During their abominable initiation rituals, he is killed and she goes mad.

NOTE: Mario **Mercier** also directed **La Goulve** (see above).

Papy Fait de la Résistance [*Papy Joins the Resistance*] (Col., 100 min., 1983)

DIR: Jean-Marie Poiré; WRI: Christian Clavier, Martin Lamotte, Jean-Marie Poiré.

CAST: Christian Clavier, Michel Galabru (Papy), Gérard Jugnot, Martin Lamotte (Bourdelle, aka Super-Résistant), Dominique Lavanant, Jacques Villeret, Josiane Balasko, Jean-Claude Brialy, Michel Blanc, Jean Carmet.

STORY: Comedy about the French Resistance.

NOTE: The only genre element is the inclusion of a French super-hero, "Super-Résistant" with the traditional, meek secret identity.

Paradis pour Tous [*Paradise for All*] (Col., 110 min., 1982)

DIR: Alain **Jessua**; WRI: Alain **Jessua**, André **Ruellan**.

CAST: Patrick Dewaere (Alain), Jacques Dutronc (Dr. Valois), Fanny Cottençon (Jeanne), Stéphane Audran (Edith), Philippe Léotard, Jeanne Goupil, Patrice Kerbrat.

STORY: Alain, a chronically depressed man, becomes the first subject of Dr. Valois, a scientist who has discovered a brain operation which turns people into happy, yet soulless, beings. The experiment is a success—a frightening success.

Paradisio (B&W., 90 min., 1961)

DIR: Jacques Henrici; WRI: Laurence Zeitlin, Henri Halle.

CAST: Arthur Howard.

STORY: A man owns a pair of X-ray glasses which make clothes invisible.

NOTE: This is a French/German/British "nudie" film featuring 3-D sequences.

Parano (Col., 82 min., 1994)

Anthology film comprised of six stories, linked together.

DIR: Yann Piquer; WRI: Yann Piquer, Alain Robak, Manuel Flèche, Anita Assal, John Hudson.

CAST: Jean-Marie Madeddu, Gustave Parking, Smaïn, Alain Chabat, Patrick Bouchitey, Jean-François Gallotte.

1. *Parano (linking story)*

STORY: A beautiful paranoid girl tells stories to a shy young man who ends up strangling her to shut her up.

2. Nuit d'Essence [Gasoline Night]
STORY: A pyromaniac is traumatized by the death of his family.

3. Panic FM
STORY: A pizza delivery man hears a horrible news story on the radio.

4. Déroute [Retreat]
STORY: After a car crash, a couple is doomed to relive their recent fight.

5. Sado et Maso Vont en Bateau [Sado & Maso Go Boating]
STORY: A man falls in love with a masochistic woman.

6. Joyeux Anniversaire [Happy Birthday]
STORY: A woman plots her husband's death by getting him into a diving suit and then arranging for him to be carried away in a water-dropping plane.

Paris N'Existe Pas [Paris Does Not Exist] (B&W., 95 min., 1968)
DIR/WRI: Robert Benayoun.
CAST: Danièle Gaubert, Richard Leduc, Serge Gainsbourg, Monique Lejeune.
STORY: A young artist discovers that he can mentally travel back through time.
NOTE: Robert Benayoun is a renowned film critic.

Paris Qui Dort [Paris Sleeps, transl. as *The Crazy Ray]* (B&W., 61 min./1480 M., 1923)
DIR/WRI: René **Clair**.
CAST: Henri Rollan, Albert Préjean, Marcel Vallée, Madeleine Rodrigue.
STORY: A scientist's ray plunges Paris into a cataleptic state, except for the Eiffel Tower watchman and the passengers of an airplane.

Parking (Col., 95 min., 1985)
DIR/WRI: Jacques **Demy**.
CAST: Francis Huster (Orphée), Keito Ito (Eurydice), Jean Marais (Hadès), Marie-France Pisier, Laurent Malet, Gérard Klein, Hugues Quester.
STORY: Another modern transposition of the Orpheus myth; this time, Orpheus is a modern pop star.

Le Passage [The Passage] (Col., 84 min., 1986)
DIR/WRI: René **Manzor**.
CAST: Alain Delon (Jean), Christine Boisson (Catherine), Alain Musy (David), Jean-Luc Moreau, Alberto Lomeo.
STORY: Death itself tries to prevent Jean, an animation director, from making a film about world peace. With the help of his young son, the director outwits Death.

Le Passe-Muraille [The Walker Through the Walls] see *Garou-Garou, Le Passe-Muraille*

Le Pays sans Étoiles [The Starless Country] (B&W., 100 min., 1945)
DIR/WRI: Georges Lacombe, based on the novel by Pierre **Véry**.
CAST: Gérard Philipe (Simon/Frédéric), Pierre Brasseur, Jany Holt.
STORY: A young lawyer experiences visions of a murder he may (or may not) have committed. Are they visions of the past, or of the future?
NOTE: Pierre **Véry** is a noted mystery and fantasy writer (see Book 2). His works include two well-known thrillers, *L'Assassinat du Père Noël* [*The Murder of Santa Claus*] and *Les Disparus de Saint-Agil* [*Disappearances at Saint-Agil*], both made into films. His novel, *Le Gentleman des Antipodes*, was adapted for television (see Chapter II).

Peau d'Âne [Donkey Skin] (Col., 89 min., 1970)
DIR/WRI: Jacques **Demy**, based on the fairy tale by Charles **Perrault**.
CAST: Catherine Deneuve (Donkey Skin), Jean Marais (Blue King), Jacques Perrin (Prince Charming), Delphine Seyrig, Micheline Presle, Fernand Ledoux, Sacha Pitoëff, Henri Crémieux.
STORY: Gorgeous adaptation of the classic fairy tale in which a Princess (Deneuve) who wants to avoid an unwanted marriage flees into the forest and lives disguised by a donkey skin.
NOTE: Charles **Perrault** is the author of a number of classic fairy tales such as *Sleeping Beauty*, *Cinderella*, etc. (see Book 2). For other **Perrault** adaptations, see *Le Petit Poucet* (below) and *La Belle au Bois Dormant* and *Cendrillon* in Chapter II.

Perceval le Gallois (Col., 138 min., 1978)
DIR/WRI: Éric Rohmer, based on the stories by **Chrétien de Troyes**.
CAST: Fabrice Luchini (Perceval), André Dussolier (Gauvain)m, Marc Eyraud (King Arthur), Marie-Christine Barrault (Guinevere), Gérard Falconetti, Arielle Dombasle, Michel Etcheverry.
STORY: The legendary tale of pure-hearted Perceval, who leaves his mother's castle to join King Arthur and his Knights of the Round Table, and eventually searches for the Holy Grail.
NOTE: For other **Chrétien de Troyes** adaptations, see *Les Chevaliers de la Table Ronde* (above) and *Lancelot du Lac* in Chapter II.

Perversions Sexuelles [Sexual Perversions] (Col., 90 min., 1972) (aka *Le Gout du Sang [The Taste of Blood]*, *Le Sang des Autres [The Blood of Others]*, *Les Chemins de la Violence [The Paths of Violence]*, *La Volupté de l'Horreur [Voluptuous Hor-*

ror], Le Secret de la Momie [The Mummy's Secret]).

DIR: Ken Ruder (pseudonym of Pierre Chevalier); WRI: Alexandro Marti Gelabert.

CAST: Catherine Frank, Michael Flynn, Sandra Reeves, Patricia Lee, Julie Prescott, Georges Rigaud.

STORY: A resurrected mummy drains the blood from young women to survive.

NOTE: Not to be confused with Claude Chabrol's 1983 adaptation of Simone de Beauvoir's novel, *Le Sang des Autres*. The final title is explained by the fact that this film was eventually released on the X-rated circuit. There is a Spanish version (*El Secreto de la Momia Egipcia*) directed by Alejandro Martí, starring Teresa Gimpera, Frank Brana, and Martin Trévières.

Le Petit Poucet [Tom Thumb] (Col., 80 min., 1972)

DIR: Michel Boisrond; WRI: Michel Boisrond, Marcel Julian, based on the fairy tale by Charles **Perrault**.

CAST: Titoyo (Tom Thumb), Jean-Pierre Marielle (Ogre), Marie Laforêt, Jean-Luc Bideau, Michel Robin, Marianne Ridoret.

STORY: Adaptation on the classic fairy tale about a boy abandoned in the forest who encounters an Ogre with Seven-League Boots.

NOTE: For other **Perrault** adaptations, see *Peau d'Âne* (above) and *Cendrillon* in Chapter II.

La Petite Bande [The Little Gang] (Col., 91 min., 1982)

DIR: Michel Deville; WRI: Gilles Perrault.

CAST: François Marthouret (Stranger), Roland Amstutz, Nathalie Bécue, Françoise Lugagne.

STORY: Six runaway English boys experience a series of adventures in France, until they are captured by a secret sect which steals little boys' youth; but they are rescued by a mysterious guardian angel-like hero (Marthouret).

NOTE: Gilles Perrault is a famous espionage thriller writer.

Les Petites Jouisseuses [Small Pleasures] (Col., 85 min., 1979)

DIR/WRI: Homère Bongo.

CAST: Lise Badia, Brigitte Blanche.

NOTE: X-rated film about a female vampire.

Plein Soleil [Full Sun] (Col., 120 min., 1959)

DIR: René Clément; WRI: Paul Gégauff, based on a novel by Patricia Highsmith.

CAST: Alain Delon (Ripley), Marie Laforêt, Maurice Ronet, Elvire Popesco, Romy Schneider.

STORY: Tom Ripley kills a young American and takes over his life.

NOTE: Brilliant adaptation of Highsmith's first novel about the charming sociopath Ripley. Music by Nino Rota.

La Plus Longue Nuit du Diable [The Devil's Longest Night, transl. as *the Devil's Nightmare]* (Col., 95 min., 1971) (aka *Au Service du Diable [In the Devil's Service], Le Château du Vice [The Castle of Vice], La Nuit des Pétrifiés [The Night of the Petrified]*)

DIR: Jean Brismée; WRI: Patrice **Rhomm**, Charles Lecocq, André Hunebelle, Jean Brismée.

CAST: Erika Blanc, Jean Servais, Daniel Emilfork (Satan), Jacques Monseu, Ivana Novak, Shirley Corrigan.

STORY: A long night of terror grips the passengers of a coach when it becomes lost in the Black Forest. They find refuge in a castle and become involved in a battle between good and evil. The eldest daughter of a family becomes the agent of the Devil because of an ancient curse.

Le Plus Vieux Métier du Monde [The Oldest Profession in the World] (Col., 120 min., 1967)

Six sketches about prostitution. Only the sixth belongs to the genre.

Anticipation—L'An 2000 [Science Fiction—The Year 2000]

DIR/WRI: Jean-Luc **Godard**.

CAST: Jacques Charrier, Anna Karina, Marilu Tolo, Jean-Pierre Léaud.

STORY: In the year 2000, a prostitute working for the state and a spaceman rediscover the notion of kissing.

Les Portes de la Nuit [The Gates of Night] (B&W., 120 Min, 1946)

DIR: Marcel **Carné**; WRI: Jacques **Prévert**, Joseph Kosma.

CAST: Jean Vilar (Destiny), Yves Montand, Nathalie Nattier, Pierre Brasseur, Serge Reggiani, Saturnin Fabre, Julien Carette, Mady Berry, Dany Robin, Raymond Bussières, Sylvia Bataille, Christian Simon.

STORY: In post-war Paris, Destiny is incarnated as a vagrant whose predictions fail to help a young couple.

Le Portrait de Dorian Gray [The Picture of Dorian Gray] (Col., 90 min., 1977)

DIR/WRI: Pierre Bouteron, based on the story by Oscar Wilde.

CAST: Raymond Gérôme (Lord Henry), Marie-Hélène Breillat, Patrice Alexandre, Denis Manuel.

STORY: Adaptation of a play written by Bouteron based on Wilde's famous story about an ageless man.

Les Possédés du Diable [Possessed by the Devil]
(Col., 85 min., 1974) (aka *Lorna l'Exorciste [Lorna the Exorcist]*)

DIR: Clifford Brown (pseudonym of Jess Franco); WRI: Jesus Franco Manera, Robert de Nesle (also producer).

CAST: Pamela Stanford, Lina Romay, Guy Delorme, Jacqueline Parent.

STORY: A rich industrialist once made a pact to deliver his 18-year old daughter to the mysterious Lorna.

NOTE: This is a French production directed by Spanish director Jess (Jesus) Franco.

Possession (Col., 127 min., 1981)
DIR/WRI: Andrzej Zulawski.

CAST: Isabelle Adjani (Anna), Sam Neill (Marc), Heinz Bennent, Margit Carstensen.

STORY: Anna cheats on her husband, Marc, with a creature of unknown origins, which takes on her husband's form the more she has sex with it. After their deaths, their doppelgangers fall in love.

NOTE: Franco-German co-production.

La Poupée [The Doll] (Col., 90 min., 1961)
DIR: Jacques Baratier; WRI: Jacques **Audiberti**.

CAST: Sonne Teal (Android), Zbigniew Cybulski, Claudio Gora, Daniel Emilfork, Catherine Milinaire, Jacques Dufilho, Sacha Pitoeff.

STORY: In a South American country, a rebel scientist invents a duplicating machine and uses it to create an android double of the dictator's mistress.

La Poupée Rouge [The Red Doll] (Col., 80 min., 1969)
DIR/WRI: Francis Leroi.

CAST: Aude Olivier, Gaétane Lorre, André Oumansky, François Guilloteau.

STORY: Political fiction about a revolution in an imaginary country.

Les Prédateurs de la Nuit [The Night Predators, transl. as Faceless]
(Col., 93 min., 1988)

DIR: Jess Franco, René Château (uncredited); WRI: Fred Castle (pseudonym of René Château).

CAST: Helmut Berger (Dr. Flamand), Chris Mitchum (Sam), Telly Savalas (Terry), Howard Vernon (Orloff), Caroline Munro, Brigitte Lahaie, Stéphane Audran.

Brigitte Lahaie in Les Prédateurs de la Nuit *(1988).*

STORY: In this transposition of **Franju**'s *Les Yeux Sans Visage*, Dr. Flamand (Berger) kidnaps a young model (Munro) to graft her face onto his disfigured sister's (Lahaie). Howard Vernon guest-stars as Dr. Orloff.

NOTE: Also see *L'Horrible Dr. Orloff* (above).

Le Prix du Danger [The Prize of Peril] (Col., 99 min., 1982)
DIR: Yves **Boisset**; WRI: Jean Curtelin, Yves **Boisset**, based on a short story by Robert Sheckley.

CAST: Gérard Lanvin (François), Michel Piccoli (Frédéric Mallaire), Marie-France Pisier, Bruno Cremer, Andréa Ferreol, Gabrielle Lazure, Catherine Lachens.

STORY: *The Prize of Peril* is a TV game show where contestants must escape killers in order to collect their prizes. François, a contestant who has discovered that the games are fixed, is committed.

NOTE: Robert Sheckley is a famous American science fiction writer. He wrote the short story which became the basis for the film *The Tenth Victim* (1965).

Gérard Lanvin and Michel Piccoli in Le Prix du Danger *(1982).*

Le Professeur Raspoutine (Col., 85 min., 1981)
DIR: Gregory; WRI: André White.

CAST: Gabriel Pontello, Laetitia Cruising.

STORY: The Jekyll-Hyde title character hypnotizes his female patients.

NOTE: X-rated film with genre elements.

Providence (Col., 100 min., 1976)
DIR: Alain **Resnais**; WRI: David Mercer.

CAST: John Gielgud (Clive), Dirk Bogarde (Claud), Ellen Burstyn (Sonia), David Warner, Elaine Stritch, Peter Arne, Anna Wing, Tanya Lopert, Dennis Lanson.

STORY: A dying writer's nightmares take on fearsome shapes in the city of Providence.

Queen Lear (Col., 90 min., 1980)
   DIR/WRI: Mokhtar Chorfi.
   CAST: Joe Dallesandro, Laura Garcia Lorca, Fabrice Josso.
   STORY: Ghostly variation on *King Lear*.
   NOTE: Franco-Swiss co-production.

Les Raisins de la Mort [The Grapes of Death,** transl. as **Pesticide] (Col., 89 min., 1978)
   DIR/WRI: Jean **Rollin**.
   CAST: Marie-Georges Pascal, Serge Marquand, Félix Marten, Brigitte Lahaie.
   STORY: Polluted grapes turn grape growers into a blood-thirsty mob.

Régime sans Pain [Regime Without Bread] (Col., 75 min., 1985)
   DIR/WRI: Raoul Ruiz.
   CAST: Anne Alvaro, Olivier Angèle, Gérard Maimone, Gilles Arbona.
   STORY: Surrealistic story about Jason III, king of the rock music-based principality of Vercors, in his search for a new personality.
   NOTE: See *L'Oeil Qui Ment* above.

Rei-Dom, ou la Légende des Kreuls [Rei-Dom, or The Legend of the Kreuls] (Col., 100 min., 1989)
   DIR/WRI: Jean-Claude Gallotta.
   CAST: Pascal Gravat, Christophe Delachaux, Éric Alfieri, Muriel Boulay, Mathilde Altaraz, Robert Seyfried, Deborah Salmirs, Viviane Serry.
   STORY: The survivor of a car crash imagines himself in a heroic-fantasy universe where he is a warrior, the last defender of the peaceful people of Kreul.

La Reine des Vampires [The Queen of Vampires]
   see ***Le Viol du Vampire***

Rendez-Moi Ma Peau [Give Me Back My Skin] (Col., 90 min., 1980)
   DIR/WRI:Patrick Schulmann.
   CAST: Erik Colin, Bee Michelin.
   STORY: In this satirical comedy, a clumsy witch causes two young people to switch bodies (but each retains his own voice).

Rendez-Vous à Bray [Rendezvous at Bray] (Col., 90 min., 1971)
   DIR/WRI: André **Delvaux**, based on a story by Julien **Gracq**.
   CAST: Anna Karina, Bulle Ogier, Mathieu Carrière.
   STORY: In 1917, a young man (Carrière) spends a strange weekend in a mysterious castle.

Requiem pour un Vampire [Requiem for a Vampire]
   see ***Vierges et Vampires***

Réseau Particulier [Singular Network] (Col., 85 min., 1982)
   DIR: Joe de Palmer; WRI: Joe de Lara.
   CAST: Jean-Pierre Armand, Carmelo Petix, Isabelle Tara.
   STORY: Secret Agent James Love 069 (!) battles the inventor of a secret virus in this soft-core erotic parody.

La Revanche des Mortes Vivantes [The Revenge of the Living Dead Girls] (Col., 85 min., 1985)
   DIR/WRI: Peter B. Harsone (pseudonym of Pierre Reinhard).
   CAST: Kathryn Charly, Veronik Cantazaro.
   STORY: Poisoned milk creates a plague of female zombies. This film is x-rated because of sex scenes, including one where a young woman is vaginally impaled.

Rocambole
   Based on the famous character created by popular writer Victor-Alexis **Ponson du Terrail** (see Book 2). Rocambole is a daring adventurer who fights for good but often on the wrong side of the law; he is the first modern literary superhero. Also see Chapter II for television adaptations.

1. Rocambole (B&W., 1914)
   DIR/WRI: Georges Denola.
   CAST: Gaston Silvestre (Rocambole).
   STORY: Serial comprised of three episodes entitled "La Jeunesse de Rocambole" ["Rocambole's Youth"], "Les Exploits de Rocambole" ["Rocambole's Adventures"], and "Rocambole et l'Héritage du Marquis de Morfontaine" [*Rocambole and the Marquess of Morfontaine's Inheritance*"].

2. Rocambole (B&W., 1924)
   DIR/WRI: Charles Maudru.
   CAST: Maurice Thorèze (Rocambole), Claude Mérelle.
   STORY: Serial comprised of two episodes entitled "Les Premières Armes de Rocambole" ["Rocambole's First Adventures"] and "Les Amours de Rocambole" ["Rocambole's Loves"].

3. Rocambole (B&W., 1932)
   DIR/WRI: Gabriel Rosca.
   CAST: Rolla Norman (Rocambole).

4. Rocambole (B&W., 105 min., 1947)

DIR: Jacques de Baroncelli; WRI: Léon Ruth, André-Paul Antoine.

CAST: Pierre Brasseur (Rocambole), Sophie Desmarets (Baccarat), Lucien Nat (Andréa), Robert Arnoux.

STORY: Film in two parts entitled "Rocambole" and "La Revanche de Baccarat" ["Baccarat's Revenge"]. The story is loosely based on the first serial, in which Rocambole and Baccarat start as adversaries and end up joining forces to defeat the evil Sir Williams/Andréa.

5. Rocambole (Col., 100 min., 1962)

DIR: Bernard Borderie; WRI: Ugo Liberatore.

CAST: Channing Pollock (Rocambole), Nadia Gray (Baccarat), Guy Delorme.

STORY: In 1903 London, Rocambole unmasks German spies.

NOTE: Pollock played Judex in **Franju**'s eponymous film.

La Rose de Fer *[The Iron Rose* transl. as *The Crystal Rose]* (Col., 81 min., 1973) (aka *La Nuit du Cimetière [Night at the Cemetery]*)

DIR/WRI: Jean **Rollin**.

CAST: Françoise Pascal, Pierre Dupont, Mireille Dargent.

STORY: Two lovers spend the night in a cemetery.

La Rose Écorchée *[The Flayed Rose,* transl. as *Blood Rose]* (Col., 92 min., 1970)

DIR: Claude Mulot; WRI: Claude Mulot, E. Oppenheimer, Jean Larriaga.

CAST: Philippe Lemaire, Annie Duperey, Howard Vernon, Elisabeth Tessier, Michèle Perello, Olivia Robin.

STORY: A mad doctor tries to restore his wife's disfigured face.

NOTE: Another uncredited remake of *Les Yeux Sans Visage* (see below).

Rouletabille

Based on the famous character of the journalist-detective created by popular writer Gaston **Leroux**, author of the classic *Phantom of the Opera* (see Book 2). Genre elements are few and far between, but Leroux being the French equivalent of Sir Arthur Conan Doyle, the inclusion of *Rouletabille* in this filmography seems warranted. Also see Chapter II for television adaptations.

1. Le Mystère de la Chambre Jaune [The Mystery of the Yellow Room] (B&W., 905 meters, 1913)

DIR/WRI: Maurice **Tourneur**.

CAST: Marcel Simon (Rouletabille), Paul Escoffier (Larsan), Laurence Duluc (Mathilde).

STORY: Rouletabille solves a murder in a locked room.

2. Le Parfum de la Dame en Noir [The Scent of the Woman in Black] (B&W., 1220 meters, 1914)

DIR/WRI: Émile **Chautard**.

CAST: Maurice Le Féraudy (Rouletabille), Jean Garat, Devalence, Mme. Van Doren.

STORY: Rouletabille solves another uncanny murder.

NOTE: A 1919 American version of this serial was also produced, directed by **Chautard**, starring Lorin Baker, Ethel Grey Terry, and George Cowl.

3. Rouletabille chez les Bohémiens [Rouletabille and the Gypsies] (Serial, B&W., 10 eps., 8000 meters, 1922)
1. "Le Livre des Ancêtres" ["The Book of the Ancestors"]; 2. "L'Arrestation" ["The Arrest"]; 3. "L'Instruction" ["The Investigation"]; 4. "La Poursuite" ["The Pursuit"]; 5. "La Page Déchirée" ["The Torn-Up Page"]; 6. "L'Enlèvement" ["The Kidnapping"]; 7. "A Severe Turn"; 8. "Le Signe" ["The Sign"]; 9. "Les Noces" ["The Wedding"]; 10. "Le Châtiment" ["The Punishment"].

DIR: Henri Fescourt; WRI: Gaston **Leroux**.

CAST: Gabriel de Gravone (Rouletabille), Joe Hamman, Romuald Joublé, Edith Jehanne, Jean Dehelly, Suzanne Talba.

STORY: Rouletabille recovers a sacred book stolen from the gypsies.

NOTE: Simultaneously novelized by **Leroux**.

4. Le Mystère de la Chambre Jaune [The Mystery of the Yellow Room] (B&W., 108 min., 1913)

DIR/WRI: Marcel L'Herbier.

CAST: Roland Toutain (Rouletabille), Marcel Vilbert (Larsan), Huguette Ex-Duflos (Mathilde), Edmond Van Daële (Darzac).

5. Le Parfum de la Dame en Noir [The Scent of the Woman in Black] (B&W., 109 min., 1931)

DIR/WRI: Marcel L'Herbier.

CAST: Roland Toutain (Rouletabille), Marcel Vilbert (Larsan), Huguette Ex-Duflos (Mathilde), Edmond Van Daële (Darzac).

6. Rouletabille Aviateur [Rouletabille Aviator] (B&W., 100 min., 1932)

DIR: Étienne Szekely; WRI: Pierre **Veber**.

CAST: Roland Toutain (Rouletabille), Léon Bélières, Lisette Lanvin.

STORY: Rouletabille solves a murder at an airfield.

NOTE: Original story written with the permission of the **Leroux** estate. Pierre **Veber** also wrote *L'Homme Qui Vendit Son Âme Au Diable* (see above).

7. Rouletabille Joue et Gagne [Rouletabille Plays and Wins] (B&W., 95 min., 1947)

DIR: Christian Chamborant; WRI: Pierre Lestringuez.

CAST: Jean Piat (Rouletabille), Marie Déa, Lucas-Gridoux.

Story/NOTE: Original story written with the permission of the **Leroux** estate.

8. Rouletabille Contre la Dame de Pique [Rouletabille vs. the Queen of Spades] (B&W., 88 min., 1948)

DIR: Christian Chamborant; WRI: Pierre Lestringuez.

CAST: Jean Piat (Rouletabille), Marie Déa, Lucas-Gridoux.

STORY/NOTE: Original story written with the permission of the **Leroux** estate.

9. *Le Mystère de la Chambre Jaune [The Mystery of the Yellow Room]* (B&W., 90 min., 1949)

DIR: Henri Aisner; WRI: Wladimir Pozner.

CAST: Serge Reggiani (Rouletabille), Marcel Herrand (Larsan), Hélène Perdrière (Mathilde), Lucien Nat (Darzac).

10. *Le Parfum de la Dame en Noir [The Scent of the Woman in Black]* (B&W., 100 min., 1949)

DIR: Louis Daquin; WRI: Wladimir Pozner.

CAST: Serge Reggiani (Rouletabille), Marcel Herrand (Larsan), Hélène Perdrière (Mathilde), Lucien Nat (Darzac).

Le Sadique aux Dents Rouges [The Sadist with Red Teeth] (Col., 100 min., 1970)

DIR/WRI: Jean-Louis Van Belle.

CAST: Jane Clayton, Albert Simono, Daniel Moosmann.

STORY: A young artist is obsessed by the thought of becoming a vampire.

Les Saisons du Plaisir [The Seasons of Pleasure] (Col., 88 min., 1988)

DIR/WRI: Jean-Pierre **Mocky**.

CAST: Charles Vanel (Van Bert), Denise Grey, Jacqueline Maillan, Bernadette Laffont, Jean Poiret, Eva Darlan, Stéphane Audran, Richard Bohringer, Darry Cowl, Fanny Cottençon.

STORY: Van Bert, a wealthy centenarian, gathers his family and friends to decide who will inherit his fortune. Meanwhile the world is approaching nuclear war.

Salammbô (B&W., 3500 meters, 1924)

DIR/WRI: Pierre Marodon, based on the novel by Gustave **Flaubert**.

CAST: Jeanne de Balzac (Salammbô), Rolla Norman (Matho), Victor Vina (Hamilcar).

STORY: The doomed love story of Salammbô, the daughter of Carthagenian general Hamilcar, with Matho, leader of the rebel mercenaries.

NOTE: Gustave **Flaubert** is a famous novelist. *Salammbô* was remade in Italy in 1959, DIR: Sergio Grieco, starring J. Valerie. It was also adapted as three graphic novels by Philippe **Druillet** (see Chapter V).

San Antonio Ne Pense Qu'à Ça [San Antonio Only Thinks About That] (Col., 90 min., 1981)

DIR/WRI: Joël Seria, based on the character created by Frédéric **Dard**.

CAST: Philippe Gasté, Pierre Doris, Hubert Deschamps.

STORY: Police Commissioner San Antonio (Gasté) fights Miss Tenebra and KGB spies to reclaim a pair of X-ray glasses.

NOTE: Loosely based on a very popular series of humoristic detective novels.

Le Sang des Autres [The Blood of Others] see **Perversions Sexuelles**

Scheherazade (B&W., 90 min., 1962)

DIR: Pierre Gaspard-Huit; WRI: Marc-Gilbert Sauvajon, Pierre Gaspard-Huit.

CAST: Anna Karina (Scheherazade), Gérard Barray, Antonio Vilar, Giulano Gemma, Marilu Tolo, Fernando Rey, Fausto Tozzi, Gil Vidal.

STORY: Another adaptation of *A Thousand and One Nights*.

Le Secret de la Momie [The Mummy's Secret] see **Perversions Sexuelles**

Le Secret de Sarah Tombelaine [The Secret of Sarah Tombelaine] (Col., 90 min., 1990)

DIR: Daniel Lacambre; WRI: Claude Gilbert, Daniel Lacambre.

CAST: Irène Jacob (Sarah) Marc de Jonge, Harry Cleven, François Caron, Rémy Roubakha, Jean-Paul Roussillon, Jenny Alpha, Gabriel Cattand, Jean Markale, Hélène Simonnet.

STORY: Sarah, a young woman, is about to be sacrificed to a dragon living under the Mont Saint-Michel; she is rescued by an engineer (Cleven).

Les Secrets Professionnels du Docteur Apfelgluck [The Professional Secrets of Dr. Apfelgluck] (Col., 86 min., 1990)

DIR: Hervé Palud, Allessandro Capone, Mathias Ledoux, Stéphane Clavier, Thierry Lhermitte; WRI: Philippe Bruneau, Thierry Lhermitte.

CAST: Thierry Lhermitte, Gérard Jugnot, Jacques Villeret, Michel Blanc, Zabou, Christian Clavier, Josiane Balasko.

STORY: Several sketches in this comedy revolve around fantasy elements: an unbeatable game show contestant, true x-ray glasses, a journey through the afterlife, murderous innkeepers.

La Septième Dimension [The 7th Dimension] (Col., 90 min., 1987)

Anthology film comprised of six stories, linked together.

WRI: Laurent Dussaux, Elvire Murail, Nicolas Cuche.

CAST: Francis Frappat (Henri), Marie-Armelle Deguy (Hélène), Jean-Michel Dupuis (Louis).

Le Savant Fou [The Mad Scientist]
DIR: Stéphan Holmes.

Le Mariage [The Wedding]
DIR: Peter Winfield.

Le Chasseur de Rêves [The Dream Hunter]
DIR: Olivier Bourbeillon.

Le Duel
DIR: Laurent Dussaux.

La Fille qui Boit [The Drinking Girl]
DIR: Manuel Boursinhac.

Henri en Egypte [Henri In Egypt]
DIR: Benoît Ferreux.
STORY: Henri searches for his love, Hélène, through time, while fighting his rival, Louis. The stories take the characters: 1. to Doctor Jekyll's lab; 2. to the Middle Ages; 3: to the time of King Arthur; 4: to a sorcerous duel; 5: to a medieval castle during the Inquisition; and finally 6: to Ancient Egypt.

Sérail [Seraglio] (Col., 90 min., 1976)
DIR/WRI: Eduardo de Gregorio.
CAST: Leslie Caron, Bulle Ogier, Marie-France Pisier, Colin Redgrave.
STORY: A novelist (Redgrave) meets three strange women in a house he wants to purchase. He is eventually imprisoned in the house.

Le Seuil du Vide [The Threshold of the Void]
(B&W., 90 min., 1971)

DIR: Jean-François Davy; WRI: J.-F. Davy, André **Ruellan**, based on his novel (written under the pseudonym of Kurt **Steiner**).
CAST: Dominique Erlanger, Pierre Vaneck, Jean Servais, Odette Duc, Catherine Rich, Michel Lemoine.
STORY: A young girl (Erlanger) becomes the prey of a cult of immortals who steal her youth.
NOTE: André **Ruellan** is a noted science fiction and horror writer (see Book 2). See Chapter V under ***Fleuve Noir*** for comic book adaptations of his other novels.

Le Sexe Qui Parle [The Talking Penis, transl. as ***Pussy Talk]*** (Col. 90 min., 1975)

DIR/WRI: Frédéric Lansac (pseudonym of Claude Mulot).
CAST: Pénélope Lamour, Béatrice Harnois, Nils Hotz, Ellen Earl-Coupey, Sylvia Bourdon, Vicky Messica.
STORY: Award-winning X-rated film in which a man discovers his penis can talk. A sequel, *Triples Introductions (Le Sexe Qui Parle II)*, also written and directed by Lansac, starring France Lomay, Richard Lemieuvre, and Gwenda Farnel was released in 1978.

Sexorcismes [Sexorcism] (Col., 93 min., 1975) **(aka *Exorcisme [Exorcism], Expériences Sexuelles au Château des Jouisseuses [Sexual Experiences in the Castle of Pleasure])***
DIR: James P. Johnson (pseudonym of Jess Franco); WRI: David Khune (Jess Franco), James C. Gardner, Henri Bral de Boitselieu.
CAST: Lina Romay, Jess Franck (Jess Franco), Monica Swinn, Lynn Monteil, Catherine Leferrière, Caroline Rivière.
STORY: A religious fanatic tortures people whom he thinks are possessed by the devil.
NOTE: This is a French-Belgian co-production.

Signé Furax [Signed: Furax] (Col., 90 min., 1980)
DIR/WRI: Marc Simenon, based on the radio series by Pierre **Dac** & Francis **Blanche**.
CAST: Bernard Haller (Furax), Mylène Demongeot (Malvina), Jean Le Poulain, Michel Galabru, Jean-Pierre Darras, Pasquali.
STORY: The evil Babus steal Paris' monuments by dehydrating them (!), then pins the blame on retired master criminal Edmond Furax.
NOTE: This is based on the first book adaptation of the popular radio serial. For further information, see Chapter III.

Si J'Avais Mille Ans [If I Was a Thousand Years Old] (Col., 86 min., 1983)
DIR/WRI: Monique Enckell.
CAST: Daniel Olbrychsky, Jean Bouise, Marie Dubois, Dominique Pinon.
STORY: Every year at Halloween, the ghosts of medieval knights invade a small island in Britanny. A thousand years earlier, the villagers refused to turn over to them a girl they had condemned to die.

Simple Mortel [Mere Mortal] (Col., 85 min., 1991)
DIR/WRI: Pierre Jolivet.
CAST: Philippe Volter, Christophe Bourseiller, Nathalie Roussel, Roland Giraud, Marcel Maréchal, Arlette Thomas.
STORY: A linguist (Volter) receives messages in ancient Gaelic from a mysterious, seemingly all-powerful entity who orders him to accomplish a series of actions (including murdering one of his friends) in order to save the world.
NOTE: Pierre Jolivet co-wrote ***Le Dernier Combat*** (above).

Un Soir, par Hasard [One Night, by Chance]

(B&W., 90 min., 1964)

DIR: Ivan Govar; WRI: Ivan Govar, André Allard, Pierre Sabatier, based on the novel by René Collard.

CAST: Pierre Brasseur, Anita Stroyberg, Jean Servais.

STORY: A couple is offered a method of immortality.

Un Soir, un Train [One Night, a Train] (Col., 91 min., 1968)

DIR/WRI: André **Delvaux**, based on a story by Johan Daisne.

CAST: Yves Montand (Mathias), Anouk Aimée (Anne), Adriana Bogdan, François Beukelaers.

STORY: Mathias loses his girlfriend Anne on a train. When the train stops, he finds himself in a strange town. He eventually awakens and discovers that the train had an accident and Anne is dead.

Les Soleils de l'Île de Pâques [The Suns of Easter Island] (Col., 94 min., 1971)

DIR/WRI: Pierre **Kast**.

CAST: Norma Bengell, Françoise Brion, Alexandra Stewart, Jacques Charrier, Maurice Garrel, Marcello Romo, Zozimo Bulbul.

STORY: Extraterrestrials summon six men and women to Easter Island to evaluate mankind's progress. Disgusted by the violence they discover, the aliens leave.

La Sorcière [The Witch] (B&W., 97 min., 1955)

DIR: André Michel; WRI: Jacques Companez.

CAST: Marina Vlady (Aino), Maurice Ronet (Laurent), Nicole Courcel, Michel Etcheverry.

STORY: In a Swedish village, a newly arrived man falls in love with a girl who may be a witch.

La Soupe aux Choux [The Cabbage Soup] (Col., 98 min., 1981)

DIR: Jean Girault; WRI: Louis de Funès, Jean Halain, based on the novel by René **Fallet**.

CAST: Louis de Funès (Claude), Jean Carmet (Le Bombé), Jacques Villeret (La Denrée), Christine Dejoux, Claude Gensac, Henri Genès.

STORY: An extraterrestrial who loves cabbage soup resurrects an old farmer's wife. Eventually, made aware that the world has passed him by, the farmer and his friend leave Earth.

NOTE: René **Fallet** also wrote *La Mort Amoureuse* [*Death in Love*] for television (see Chapter II).

Sous le Soleil de Satan [Under the Sun of Satan]

(Col., 113 min., 1987)

DIR: Maurice Pialat; WRI: Sylvie Danton, based on the novel by Georges **Bernanos**.

CAST: Gérard Depardieu (Abbé Donissan), Sandrine Bonnaire, Maurice Pialat.

STORY: In 1926, the abbot Donissan experiences a crisis of faith and performs a miracle.

Spermula (Col., 110 min., 1976)

DIR/WRI: Charles Matton.

CAST: Dayle Haddon (Spermula), Udo Kier, Ginette Leclerc, Georges Geret, François Dunoyer, Jocelyne Boisseau.

STORY: A sect of telepathic women led by the beautiful Spermula tries to take over the world, but fails. Spermula sacrifices her immortality for a night of true passion.

Stress (Col., 90 min., 1984)

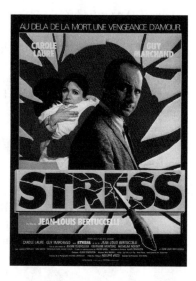

DIR: Jean-Louis Bertucelli; WRI: André Grall.

CAST: Guy Marchand (Alex), Carole Laure (Nathalie), Patrice Kerbrat (Gérard), André Dussolier, Germaine Monero.

STORY: Gérard's heart has been transplanted in Alex and seeks revenge against Nathalie, his former girl-friend who drove him to commit suicide.

Suivez Mon Regard [Follow My Glance] (Col., 85 min., 1986)

DIR/WRI: Jean Curtelin.

CAST: Pierre Arditi, Stéphane Audran, Jean-Claude Brialy, Claude **Chabrol**, Gérard Darmon, Andréa Ferréol, Brigitte Lahaie, Léo Malet, Macha Méril, Zabou.

STORY: Surreal series of very short sketches, often parodic or nonsensical. Genre elements include the return of Christ, what happens after death, mysterious disappearances of people and their dogs, etc.

Sur la Terre Comme au Ciel [On Earth as in Heaven] (Col., 80 min., 1991)

DIR: Marion Hänsel; WRI: Marion Hänsel, Paul Le, Jaco Van Dormael, L. van Keerberger.

CAST: Carmen Maura (Maria), Didier Bezace, Samuel Mussen, Jean-Pierre Cassel, Johan Leysen, Serge-Henri Valcke, Pascale Tison.

STORY: A fetus mysteriously tells his mother that he and the other fetuses have decided not to be born until the world becomes a better place. She eventually convinces him otherwise.

NOTE: This is a Belgian-French-Spanish co-production. Director André **Delvaux** has a small role.

Sylvie et le Fantôme [Sylvie and the Ghost] (B&W., 102 min., 1945)

DIR: Claude **Autant-Lara**; WRI: Jean Aurenche, based on a play by Alfred Adam.

CAST: Odette Joyeux (Sylvie), Pierre Larquey (Baron Édouard), Jacques Tati (The Ghost), François Périer, Jean Desailly, Gabrielle Fontant, Julien Carette, Louis Salou, Claude Marcy.

STORY: Sylvie is in love with a gallant ghost. During a party for her sixteenth birthday, she discovers what real love is.

NOTE: Also see Chapter II for a television adaptation.

Le Syndrome de l'Espion [The Spy Syndrome] (Col., 70 min., 1989)

DIR: Daniel Petitcuenot; WRI: Daniel Petitcueno, Kristine Joray.

CAST: Christian Pageault, Philippe Schmid, Bob Watson Barr, Robert Ground, Liliane David.

STORY: While filming a movie, a filmmaker becomes involved in a three-way battle between American, Russian, and Jupiterian spies, all vying for the same, mysterious mineral.

Le Temps de Mourir [A Time to Die] (Col., 90 min., 1969)

DIR: André Farwagi; WRI: Alain Morineau, André Farwagi.

CAST: Bruno Cremer (Max), Anna Karina, Jean Rochefort, Catherine Rich, Daniel Moosmann, Billy Kearns.

STORY: A mysterious girl (Karina) shows Max a film portraying his own murder. By trying to prevent it, Max actually causes the murder to take place.

Tendre Dracula [Tender Dracula] see La Grande Trouille

La Tendre Ennemie [The Tender Enemy] (B&W., 69 min., 1936)

DIR: Max Ophuls; WRI: Curt Alexander, Max Ophuls, based on a play by André-Paul Antoine.

CAST: Jacqueline Daix (Line), Simone Berriau (Annette), Georges Vitray, Marc Valbel, Catherine Fonteney.

STORY: The ghost of Line's father and her mother's lover join forces to save her from an unwanted marriage.

La Tentation de Barbizon [The Temptation of Barbizon] (B&W., 100 min., 1945)

DIR: Jean Stelli; WRI: André-Paul Antoine.

CAST: François Perier (The Devil), Simone Renant (The Angel), André Bervil, Juliette Faber, Pierre Larquey, Daniel Gélin.

STORY: The Devil (as a film producer) tries to break up a young couple, while an Angel (as a film star) attempts to bring them back together.

Terminus [transl. as End of the Line] (Col., 110 min., 1986)

DIR: Pierre-William Glenn; WRI: P.-W. Glenn, Patrice **Duvic**, based on a story by Alain Gillot.

CAST: Johnny Hallyday, Karen Allen, Jürgen Prochnow, Julie Glenn, Gabriel Damon, Dominique Valera, Dieter Shidor.

STORY: In a post-apocalyptic future, the driver of a giant battletruck (Hallyday) and a girl (Allen) try to escape from a totalitarian regime.

NOTE: This is a French-German co-production. Patrice **Duvic** is a science fiction writer and essayist (see Book 2).

Terreur [Terrror, transl. as The Perils of Paris] (B&W., 90 min., 1924)

DIR/WRI: Édouard José.

CAST: Pearl White, Robert Lee, Henry Bandin, Arlette Marchal.

STORY: Criminals are after the Power Ray invented by the heroine's father.

NOTE: This is second serial in the *Perils of Pauline* series which started in 1914, and later became a Universal serial (starring Evalyn Knapp) in 1933.

Le Testament d'Orphée [The Testament of Orpheus] see Orphée

Le Testament du Dr. Cordelier [The Testament of Dr. Cordelier, transl. as The Doctor's Horrible Experiment; Experiment in Evil] (B&W., 100 min., 16 November 1961)

DIR/WRI: Jean Renoir, based on the novel by Robert-Louis Stevenson.

NOTE: See Chapter II.

Tête à Tête [Head to Head] (Col., 75 min., 1994)

DIR: Jean-Hugues Lime, Yves Benoît; WRI: J.-H. Lime.

CAST: Régie Laspalès (Prosper), J.-H. Lime (Paul), Christian Pernot (Henri), Laurence Semonin, Didier Benureau, Philippe Chevallier.

STORY: Paul and Henri are friends until the latter dies in a plane crash. A goofy undertaker, Prosper, gives Paul Henri's head, which he collected and which has mysteriously remained alive. But Paul finds living with a talking head unbearable.

Thank You, Satan (Col., 85 min., 1988)

DIR: André Farwagi; WRI: André Farwagi, Christian Carini, Nelly Allard, Jean Cosmos.

CAST: Carole Laure, Patrick Chesnais, Marie Fugain, Muriel Brenner, Sandrine Caron, Annie Legrand (Satan), Bernard Le Coq, Éric Blanc.

STORY: A fourteen-year-old girl (Fugain) signs a pact with Satan to solve her family's romantic problems.

NOTE: This sitcom-like comedy is a French-Canadian production whose only genre element is the presence of a female Satan.

Themroc (Col., 105 min., 1972)

DIR/WRI: Claude Faraldo.

CAST: Michel Piccoli (Themroc), Béatrice Romand, Marilu Tolo, Francesca Coluzzi, Jeanne Herviale, Patrick Dewaere, Miou-Miou, Romain Bouteille, Coluche.

STORY: Themroc is a lonely man who leads a savage revolt against society.

Tintin

Based on the popular series of graphic novels created by **Hergé** (see Chapters IV and V).

1. Tintin et le Mystère de la Toison d'Or [Tintin and the Mystery of the Golden Fleece] (Col., 94 min., 1961)

DIR: Jean-Jacques Vierne; WRI: André Barret, Rémo Forlani.

CAST: Jean-Pierre Talbot (Tintin), Georges Wilson (Haddock), Georges Loriot (Calculus), Charles Vanel (Father Alexander), Dario Moreno (Midas Papas), Marcel Bozzuffi (Angorapoulos), Dimitrios Starenios (Scoubidovitch).

STORY: Haddock inherits an old steamer which contains the key to a hidden treasure. Borderline SF only. Prof. Calculus discovers a pill which, when dropped in the fuel tank, makes the boat go incredible speeds.

2. Tintin et les Oranges Bleues [Tintin and the Blue Oranges] (Col., 110 min., 1964)

DIR: Philippe Coudroyer; WRI: André Barret.

CAST: Jean-Pierre Talbot (Tintin), Jean Bouise (Haddock), Félix Fernandez (Prof. Calculus), Francky François, André Marie (Thomson & Thompson), Jenny Orléans, Max Eloy.

STORY: Tintin outwits an Arab Sheik who has kidnaped a scientist who has created a new type of orange that can grow in the desert.

Tom et Lola (Col., 97 min., 1989)

DIR: Bertrand Arthuys; WRI: Bertrand Arthuys, Christian de **Chalonge**, Muriel Teodori, Luc Goldenberg.

CAST: Neil Stubbs (Tom), Mélodie Collin (Lola), Cécile Magnet, Marc Berman, Catherine Frot, Célian Varini, Janine Souchon, Sophie Arthuys, Olivier Belmont, Nadia Chapuis.

STORY: The surreal adventures of two children with immune deficiencies who escape their hospital "bubble."

Le Toubib [The Doc] (Col., 95 min., 1979)

DIR: Pierre Granier-Deferre; WRI: P. Granier-Deferre, P. Jardin, based on the novel by J. Freustié.

CAST: Alain Delon (Desprès), Véronique Jannot (Harmonie), Bernard Giraudeau (François), Francine Bergé, Michel Auclair, Catherine Lachens, Bernard Le Coq.

STORY: During a third world war, Desprès, a cynical, *M.A.S.H.*–type doctor, falls in love with Harmonie, a beautiful, idealistic nurse, but she is eventually killed by a mine.

NOTE: The original novel took place in the present, not the future.

Alain Delon in Le Toubib *(1979).*

Le Tour d'Écrou [The Turn of the Screw] (Col., 92 min., 1992)

DIR/WRI: Rusty Lemorande, based on the novel by Henry James.

CAST: Patsy Kensit (Jenny), Stéphane Audran (Mrs Grose), Julian Sands, Marianne Faithfull.

STORY: Faithful adaptation of the classic story about two children haunted by the ghosts of the previous caretakers.

NOTE: This is a French-British co-production obviously inspired in its approach and style by Jack Clayton's 1961 classic, *The Innocents*. *Le Tour d'Écrou* was also adapted for television. Also see the anthology series *James, Henry* in Chapter II.

Toute Une Vie [A Whole Life, transl. as *And Now My Love]* (Col., 150 min., 1974)

DIR: Claude **Lelouch**; WRI: Claude **Lelouch**, Pierre Uytterhoeven.

CAST: Marthe Keller, André Dussolier, Charles Denner, Carla Gravina, Charles Gérard.

STORY: This multi-generational family saga begins in 1918 and ends in the year 2000, when an expectant couple (Keller, Dussolier) must hide in order to escape compulsory abortion.

Traitement de Choc [Shock Treatment, transl. as *Doctor in the Nude]* (Col., 91 min., 1972)

DIR/WRI: Alain **Jessua**.

CAST: Alain Delon (Dr. Devillers), Annie Girardot (Hélène), Michel Duchaussoy, Robert Hirsch, Jean-François Calve.

STORY: Dr. Devillers secretly uses organs harvested from his Portuguese workers to keep his rich clientele young. A patient, Hélène, discovers the truth and kills him.

NOTE: Alain **Jessua** also wrote the novelization of the film.

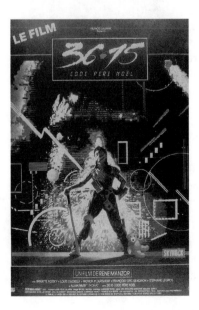

36-15 Code Père Noël [Santaclaus.com] (Col., 90 min., 1989)

DIR/WRI: René **Manzor**.

CAST: Brigitte Fossey, Louis Ducreux, Alain Musy, Patrick Floersheim (Santa Claus), François-Éric Gendron.

STORY: In a deserted house, a nine-year-old child fights a serial killer disguised as Santa Claus. The boy's grandfather eventually comes to his rescue.

Le Trio Infernal [The Infernal Threesome] (Col., 110 min., 1974)

DIR: Francis Girod; WRI: Francis Girod, Jacques Rouffio, based on a novel by Solange Fasquelle.

CAST: Michel Piccoli (Georges), Romy Schneider (Philomène), Mascha Gomska (Catherine), Andréa Ferréol.

STORY: In 1919, Georges, a lawyer, his mistress, Philomène, and her sister Catherine commit numerous murders to collect life insurance premiums.

Triples Introductions see *Le Sexe Qui Parle*

Les Trois Couronnes du Matelot [The Sailor's Three Crowns] (B&W/Col., 117 min., 1982)

DIR: Raoul Ruiz; WRI: Raoul Ruiz, Emilio de Solar, François Ede.

CAST: Jean-Bernard Guillard, Philippe Deplanche, Jean Badin, Claude Derepp, Lisa Lyon, Frank Oger, Paule Brunet.

STORY: For the price of three crowns, a sailor agrees to tell a student three horror tales.

NOTE: Also see *Régime Sans Pain* above.

Le Troisième Cri [The Third Scream] (Col., 90 min., 1973)

DIR/WRI: Igaal Niddam.

CAST: Jacques Denis, Myriam Mézières, Christine Fersen, Leyla Aubert.

STORY: A dozen persons become trapped inside an anti-nuclear bunker.

NOTE: This is a French-language Swiss production.

Trompe l'Oeil (Col., 105 min., 1974)

DIR: Claude d'Anna; WRI: Claude d'Anna, M. F. Bonin.

CAST: Max von Sydow, Laure Deschanel, Micheline Presle.

STORY: A pregnant woman returns after having disappeared and without any memories of what happened to her. She and her husband are then stalked by a mysterious stranger. At the end, the woman flies away with a bird-man.

Le Tronc [The Torso] (Col., 80 min., 1992)

DIR: Karl Zéro, Bernard Faroux; WRI: Karl Zéro.

CAST: Rose Thierry, Jean-Pol Dubois, Alexis Nitzer, Yvon Back, Stéphane Bignon.

STORY: Allegorical comedy in which a man who has been made limbless by his lover (Thierry) undergoes a series of adventures before returning to his love.

NOTE: Karl Zéro is a television comedian.

Trop, C'est Trop [Too Much Is Too Much] (Col., 90 min., 1974)

DIR/WRI: Didier Kaminka.

CAST: Didier Kaminka, Philippe Ogouz, Georges Beller, Claudia Wells, José-Luis de Villalonga.

STORY: Three men born on the same day fall in love with

a girl also born that day. After her death, they commit suicide and find themselves in Hell. There, Lucifer arranges for the girl to bear three boys and one girl identical to the protagonists.

Le Tunnel [The Tunnel] (B&W., 80 min., 1933)

DIR: Kurt Bernhardt; WRI: Kurt Bernhardt, R. Steinbicker, Alexandre **Arnoux**, based on the novel by B. Kellermann.

CAST: Jean Gabin (MacAllan), Madeleine Renaud (Mary), Edmond Van Daele, Robert Le Vigan.

STORY: The engineer in charge of the construction of a transatlantic tunnel succeeds in his task, despite his wife's death at the hands of saboteurs.

NOTE: This is the French version of a multinational co-production. Two other versions were shot simultaneously with different casts: a German version, *Der Tunnel*, DIR: Kurt Bernhardt, with Paul Hartmann, Olly von Flint, and Gustav Gründgens; and an English version, *Transatlantic Tunnel*, DIR: Maurice Elvey, with Richard Dix, Leslie Banks, and Madge Evans (1935). Alexandre **Arnoux** (1884-1973) is a science fiction writer.

Tykho Moon (Col., 107 min., 1997)

DIR: Enki **Bilal**; WRI: Enki Bilal, Dan Franck.

CAST: Julie Delpy, Michel Piccoli, Marie Laforêt, Richard Bohringer, Jean-Louis Trintignant, Johan Leysen.

STORY: The leaders of a lunar colony which looks like Paris are the victims of a spreading cancer which turns their skins blue. The president (Piccoli) searches for the only man with the cure.

NOTE: Graphic novelist Enki **Bilal** also directed **Bunker Palace Hotel** (above). Also see Chapter V.

Ubac (Col., 80 min., 1986)

DIR: Jean-Pierre Grasset; WRI: Pierre Chaussat, Michel Cyprien, Richard Bohringer, Jean-Pierre Grasset.

CAST: Richard Bohringer, Suzanna Borges, Pierre Malet, Larry Lamb, Rufus.

STORY: At fifty year intervals, a hunter (Lamb) and a pulp writer (Bohringer) are drawn to a mysterious lost valley inside the Amazon.

L'Unique [The Only One] (Col., 90 min., 1985)

DIR: Jérôme Diamant-Berger; WRI: Jérôme Diamant-Berger, Olivier Assayas, Jean-Claude **Carrière**.

CAST: Julia Migenes-Johnson, Tcheky Karyo, Sami Frey, Charles Denner, Jezabel Carpi, Fabienne Babe, Thierry Rode.

STORY: A music superstar (Migenes-Johnson) is replaced by a hologram designed by a mad scientist (Frey).

Uranus (Col., 99 min., 1990)

DIR: Claude Berri; WRI: Claude Berri, Arlette Langmann, based on a novel by Marcel **Aymé**.

CAST: Gérard Depardieu, Philippe Noiret, Michel Blanc, Jean-Pierre Marielle, Michel Galabru.

STORY: The turmoils of a small French provincial town immediately after World War II.

NOTE: The film downplays the genre elements (the evil influence of the planet Uranus) contained in the original novel.

La Vampire Nue [The Nude Vampire] (Col., 90 min., 1969)

DIR/WRI: Jean **Rollin**.

CAST: Olivier Martin, Caroline Cartier, Ly Letrong, Michel Delahaye, Maurice Lemaître, Bernard Musson, Jean Aron.

STORY: A scientist (Martin) tries to discover the secret of the vampires' existence and eventually learns that they are mutants.

NOTE: The poster for this film was designed by Philippe **Druillet** (see Chapter V).

Le Vampire de Dusseldorf [The Dusseldorf Vampire] (B&W., 86 min., 1964)

DIR: Robert Hossein; WRI: Robert Hossein, Charles Dessailly.

CAST: Robert Hossein (Kurten), Marie-France Pisier.

STORY: The story of a notorious German serial killer of the 1930s.

Les Vampires [The Vampires] (Serial, B&W., 10 Eps., 1915)

1: "La Tête Coupée" ["The Cut-Off Head"]; 2: "La Bague qui Tue" ["The Killing Ring"]; 3: "Le Cryptogramme Rouge" ["The Red Cryptogram"]; 4: "Le Spectre"; 5: "L'Évasion du Mort" ["The Deadman's Escape"]; 6: "Les Yeux qui Fascinent" ["The Mesmerizing Eyes"]; 7: "Satanas"; 8: "Le Maître de la Foudre" ["The Lightning Master"]; 9: "L'Homme des Poisons" ["A Man of Poisons"]; 10: "Les Noces Sanglantes" ["The Bloody Wedding"].

DIR/WRI: Louis **Feuillade**.

CAST: Édouard Mathé (Philippe), Marcel Levesque (Oscar), Jean Aymé, Musidora.

STORY: A heroic journalist (Mathé) fights the sinister machinations of the "Vampires" gang, led by a series of evil, power-mad villains: the Great Vampire, Satanas, Venenos, etc.

NOTE: Novelized by **Feuillade** and George **Meirs** (see Book 2).

Un Vampire au Paradis [A Vampire in Paradise] (Col., 100 min., 1990)

DIR/WRI: Abdelkrim Bahloul.

CAST: Farid Chopel (Nosfer), Bruno Crémer, Brigitte Fossey, Laure Marsac, Hélène Surgère, Abdel Kechiche, Jean-Claude Dreyfus, Saïd Amadis, Michel Peyrelon, Benoît Giros, Mathieu Poirier, Françoise Rigal.

STORY: A young girl from a bourgeois family (Marsac) is bitten by Nosfer, a Muslim vampire, and begins to speak Arabic. After having located the vampire, who is accidentally shot, she and her family travel to North Africa where she meets a young Arab who suffers from the reverse curse.

La Vérité sur l'Imaginaire Passion d'un Inconnu [The Truth About the Imaginary Passion of An Unknown Man] (Col., 85 min., 1973)

DIR/WRI: Marcel Hanoun.

CAST: Michel Morat, Anne Wiazemsky, Isabelle Weingarten, Michel Lonsdale.

STORY: In the near future, a retarded girl finds an unknown man crucified like Christ. No one can discover the man's identity.

La Vie Amoureuse de l'Homme Invisible [The Invisible Man's Love Life, transl. as **Dr. Orloff and the Invisible Man]** (Col., 86 min., 1971)

DIR/WRI: Pierre Chevalier.

CAST: Howard Vernon.

STORY: X-rated film in which Prof. Orloff creates an amorous invisible monster. (It turns out to be an ape.)

Ma Vie Est un Enfer [My Life Is Hell] (Col., 106 min., 1991)

DIR: Josiane Balasko; WRI: Joël **Houssin**, Josiane Balasko.

CAST: Josiane Balasko (Leah), Daniel Auteuil (Abargadon), Richard Berry, Michael Lonsdale (Gabriel), Catherine Samie, Jean Benguigui, Luis Rego, Catherine Hiegel, Jessica Forde, Max Vialle, Ticky Holgado, Bertrand **Blier**, Joël **Houssin**, Daniel Riche.

STORY: Leah sells her soul to the demon Abargadon, but the archangel Gabriel turns Abargadon back into a mortal, who now needs Leah's help to escape eternal damnation.

NOTE: Joël **Houssin** is a prolific science fiction and television writer (see Book 2, and **Les Hordes** in Chapter II). Daniel Riche is a science fiction editor and essayist (see Book 2).

La Vie Est un Roman [Life Is a Novel, transl. as **Life Is a Bed of Roses]** (Col., 111 min., 1983)

DIR: Alain **Resnais**; WRI: Jean Gruault.

CAST: Vittorio Gassman (Walter), Ruggero Raimondi (Forbek), Géraldine Chaplin, Fanny Ardant, Pierre Arditi, Sabine Azéma, André Dussollier, Robert Manuel, Martine Kelly.

STORY: In the same castle, three stories interconnect: in 1919,

Poster by Bilal for La Vie Est un Roman *(1983).*

Utopian Count Forbek attempts a psychic experiment; in 1982, a conference on imagination proves to be a failure; finally, children project themselves in a fairy tale land of adventure.

NOTE: This film features sets designed by Enki **Bilal** (see Chapter V).

Vierges et Vampires [Virgins and Vampires transl. as **Caged Virgins; Crazed Virgins; Dungeon of Horror]** (Col., 81 min., 1971) (aka **Requiem pour un Vampire [Requiem for a Vampire]**)

DIR/WRI: Jean **Rollin**.

CAST: Marie-Pierre Castel, Mireille d'Argent, Philippe Gaste, Louise Dhour.

STORY: A mildly erotic variation on the theme of vampire women.

Le Viol du Vampire [The Vampire's Rape], Followed by La Reine des Vampires [The Queen of Vampires] (B&W., 90 min., 1968)

DIR/WRI: Jean **Rollin**.

CAST: Solange Pradel, Ursule Pauly, Nicole Romain, Bernard Letrou, Catherine Deville, Marquis Polho, Jacqueline Sieger (Vampire Queen), Ariane Sapriel.

STORY: A young man frees four women vampires and pays the price. After defeating a vampire cult, the young man and his wife, now turned into vampires, sacrifice their lives.

NOTE: First vampire movie directed by Jean **Rollin**, in black-and-white with amateur actors.

Les Visiteurs [The Visitors] (Col., 102 min., 1994)

DIR: Jean-Marie Poiré; WRI: Jean-Marie Poiré, Christian Clavier.

CAST: Jean Reno (Godefroy), Christian Clavier, Valérie Lemercier, Marie-Anne Chazel, Isabelle Nanty, Christian Bujeau, Gérard Séty, Michel Peyrelon, Didier Pain.

STORY: Godefroy, a medieval knight, and his squire (Clavier) are magically transported to the 20th century, where they meet Godefroy's descendant (Lemercier). Eventually, he returns to his own time, but the squire chooses to remain in the present.

NOTE: This comedic fantasy film was an enormous success at the French box office. A version was dubbed in English by Mel Brooks for release in the American market. A sequel was released in 1998.

Les Visiteurs du Soir [The Visitors of the Evening, transl. as *The Devil's Envoys]* (B&W., 123 min., 1942)

DIR: Marcel **Carné**; WRI: Jacques **Prévert**, Pierre Laroche.

CAST: Jules Berry (The Devil), Arletty (Dominique), Alain Cuny (Gilles), Marie Déa, Marcel Herrand, Fernand Ledoux, Simone Signoret.

STORY: The Devil sends Gilles and Dominique, two minstrels, to spread despair among mankind. However, Gilles falls in love with a local baron's daughter (Déa). Nothing the Devil does can break that love.

Viva la Vie [Hurray for Life] (Col., 110 min., 1984)

DIR/WRI: Claude **Lelouch**.

CAST: Michel Piccoli (Perrin), Charlotte Rampling

Jules Berry plays chess in Les Visiteurs du Soir *(1942).*

(Catherine), Jean-Louis Trintignant, Évelyne Bouix, Raymond Pellegrin, Charles Gérard, Laurent Malet.

STORY: Two UFO abductees (Piccoli, Bouix) return with a message of peace for mankind. In reality, it seems to have been an elaborate hoax, or possibly a dream.

La Voie Lactée [The Milky Way] (Col., 92 Min, 1969)

DIR: Luis Buñuel;
WRI: Luis Buñuel, Jean-Claude **Carrière**.

CAST: Paul Frankeur, Laurent Terzieff, Alain Cuny, Édith Scob (Marie), Bernard Verley (Jesus), Michel Piccoli (Marquis de Sade), Julien Bertheau, Georges Marchal, Jean Piat, Delphine Seyrig.

STORY: On their way to Compostelle, two modern-day pilgrims have visions and meet historical figures (Jesus, the Marquis de Sade, etc.).

La Volupté de l'Horreur [Voluptuous Horror] see *Perversions Sexuelles*

La Vouivre (Col., 102 min., 1988)

DIR/WRI: George Wilson, based on the story by Marcel **Aymé**.

CAST: Lambert Wilson (Arsène), Laurence Treil (the

Vouivre), Jean Carmet, Suzanne Flon (Louise), Jacques Dufilho, Macha Méril, Kathie Kriegel, Jean-Jacques Moreau, Paola Lanzi.

STORY: A young soldier back from World War I falls under the deadly spell of a mysterious spirit woman who lives in the swamps of his homeland.

NOTE: Based on a story published in 1949. For other Marcel **Aymé** adaptations, see *Garou-Garou, Le Passe Muraille* (above).

Week-End (Col., 95 min., 1967)
DIR/WRI: Jean-Luc **Godard**.
CAST: Jean **Yanne**, Mireille Darc, Jean-Pierre Kalfon, Jean-Pierre Léaud, Yves Beneyton, Paul Gégauff, Yves Alfonso.
STORY: A Parisian couple go to the country for the weekend; they pass dozens of dead bodies in car wrecks; they meet Emily Brontë and Cagliostro. Later, they are captured by anarchists, whom the wife joins. They kill and eat her husband.

Jean Yanne and Mireille Darc in Week-End *(1967).*

What a Flash (Col., 95 min., 1971)
DIR/WRI: Jean-Michel Barjol.
CAST: Maria Vincent, Bernadette Laffont, Vanina Michel, Catherine Lachens, Jean-Pierre Lombard, Jean-Claude Dauphin, Serge Marquand, Pierre Vassiliu.
STORY: A dozen people are trapped aboard a spaceship.

Les Yeux sans Visage [Eyes Without a Face, transl. as **The Horror Chamber of Dr. Faustus]** (B&W., 88 min., 1959)
DIR: Georges **Franju**; WRI: **Boileau-Narcejac**, Jean **Redon**, Claude Sauter, based on the novel by Jean **Redon**.

CAST: Pierre Brasseur (Dr. Genessier), Edith Scob (Christiane), Alida Valli (Louise), Juliette Mayniel, Béatrice Altariba, Claude Brasseur, François Guérin, Alexandre Rignault.

STORY: Dr. Genessier, a corrupt surgeon, responsible for the accident which disfigured his daughter Christiane, attempts to graft other girls' faces onto hers, but fails. She revolts, goes insane and kills her father.

NOTE: Jean **Redon** is a thriller writer. His novel was published in 1959 by Fleuve Noir's *Angoisse* imprint (see Book 2).

Pierre Brasseur in Les Yeux sans Visage *(1959).*

See Chapter V under *Fleuve Noir* for a comic book adaptation. For **Boileau-Narcejac**, see *Les Diaboliques* above. The same story was the uncredited basis for Jess Franco's *L'Horrible Dr. Orloff*, *Les Prédateurs de la Nuit*, and *La Rose Écorchée* (see above).

Zoo Zéro (Col., 95 min., 1978)
DIR/WRI: Alain Fleischer.
CAST: Catherine Jourdan (Eva), Klaus Kinski (Yavé), Alida Valli (Yvonne), Pierre Clémenti, Rufus, Christine Chappey, Lisette Malidor.
STORY: In a devastated city, Eva, a singer, reaches a zoo owned by her father Yavé, and frees the animals which take over from Man.

3. Selected Short Features

To list each and every French genre short feature—even limiting ourselves to those actually screened or broadcast—would be literally an impossible task.

First, all films made during the early days of cinema by Georges **Méliès** and those who followed in his footsteps were short features, and many of these were genre films or contained genre elements. Listing all these separately here would be confusing. We have, however, made the following exceptions:

La Conquête du Pôle (*The Conquest of the Pole*, 1913), *Le Voyage à Travers l'Impossible* (*Journey Through the Impossible*, 1904) and *Le Voyage dans la Lune* (*A Trip to the Moon*, 1902) by Georges **Méliès**.

Balaoo (1913) by Victorin **Jasset**.

La Folie du Dr. Tube (*The Madness of Dr. Tube*, 1916) by Abel **Gance**.

Entr'acte (*Intermission*, 1924) and *Le Voyage Imaginaire* (*The Imaginary Journey*, 1925) by René **Clair**.

La Petite Marchande d'Allumettes (*The Little Match Girl*, 1928) by Jean Renoir.

Le Sang d'un Poète (*The Blood of a Poet*, 1930) by Jean **Cocteau**.

Otherwise, we have chosen to regroup the early French genre short features under their respective authors' names in Chapter VI. Please refer to the entries for: Germaine **Dulac**, Julien **Duvivier**, Louis **Feuillade**, Abel **Gance**, Georges **Méliès**, **Méliès' rivals** (Early French Filmmakers Before World War I) and Maurice **Tourneur** for additional titles.

Then—and this became particularly true from the mid-1970s on—film festivals, state subsidies, and a very real demand from television channels such as M6 or Canal-Plus encouraged young filmmakers to make an increasingly larger number of short features. There is, sadly, very little material available on these, and what exists is often very cursory, rendering any research extremely difficult. Some of these short features are listed here; others, if they made it to the small screen, are listed in Chapter II under Telefilms.

Our compilation naturally includes all contemporary short features which have attracted a certain degree of fame. Among these, we feel we must single out:

Chris **Marker**'s classic *La Jetée* (*The Pier*, 1964), later the basis for Terry Gilliam's *Twelve Monkeys* (1995) (check Chapter VI for other Chris **Marker** shorts).

Robert Enrico's *La Rivière du Hibou* (*Owl River*, transl. as *An Occurrence at Owl Creek Bridge*), a segment of his anthology film *Au Coeur de la Vie* (*In the Midst of Life*, 1962) (see above), which was incorporated in the television series *The Twilight Zone*.

And, finally, Jean-Pierre **Jeunet** and Marc **Caro**'s *Le Bunker de la Dernière Rafale* (*The Bunker of the Last Gale*, 1981), which is a clear precursor to their later feature films, *Delicatessen* (1992) and *La Cité des Enfants Perdus* (*The City of Lost Children*, 1995).

Finally, we have also sought to track down and list those short features which adapt genre literary works, and have included the ones reviewed in genre magazines or screened at genre festivals.

L'Abygène see *Boulevard de l'Étrange* in Feature Films above.

Adrénaline see Feature Films above.

L'Après-Mémoire [The After-Memory] (B&W., 376 meters, 1969)

Dir/Wri: Luc Hannaux, based on a story by Charles Hatcher.

Cast: No information available.

Story: The end of our civilization, filmed in a style similar to that of *La Jetée*.

Les Arcanes du Jeu [The Arcanas of the Game]

(Col., 26 min., 1982)

Dir/Wri: Chantal Picault.

Cast: Anne Morello, Zazie, Max Vialle, Jacques Rispal, Yves Carlevaris, Bernard Szajner.

Story: A young girl travels back in time to prevent her friend's death.

L'Armoire [The Wardrobe] (Col., 352 meters, 1969)

Dir/Wri: Jean-Pierre Moulin, based on a story by Ambrose Bierce.

Cast: No information available.

Story: A young man kills his parents and hides their bodies in a wardrobe.

Atmosphère (B&W., 3 min., 1985)

Dir/Wri: Yann Piquer, Philippe Dorisson.

Cast: André Obadia, Christine Chiorino.

Story: In a polluted future, wearing oxygen masks has become compulsory.

Attention à la Peinture [Wet Paint] (Col., 10 min., 1989)

Dir/Wri/Cast: Cris Campion.

Story: Everything a painter paints dies.

Les Aveugles [The Blind] see *Adrénaline* in Feature Films above.

Balaoo, ou Des Pas Au Plafond [Balaoo, or Footprints on the Ceiling] (B&W., 652 meters, 1913)

Dir: Victorin **Jasset**, based on the novel by Gaston **Leroux**.

Cast: Lucien Bataille (Balaoo), Camille Bardou, Henri Gouget.

Story: The story of a murderous man-ape.

Note: For further information on Gaston **Leroux**, see *Rouletabille* above, and a separate section devoted to television adaptations in Chapter II. An American film version was produced under the title *The Wizard* in 1927, Dir: Richard Rosson; Wri: Harry Hoyt and Andrew Bennison, with Gustav von Seyfferlitz, Edmund Lowe, and Leila Hyams, and again in 1942 as *Dr. Renault's Secret*, Dir: Harry Lachman; Wri: William Bruckner and Robert F. Metzler, with J. Carrol Naish, George Zucco, and Lynne Roberts.

Le Blédia [The Vilde] (Col., 15 min., 1992)

Dir/Wri: Olivier Legan.

Story: Three modern teenagers accidentally meet the Devil (or "Vilde" in contemporary French slang).

La Bonne Dame [The Good Lady] (B&W., 680 meters, 1966)
DIR/WRI: Pierre Philippe.
CAST: Valeska Gert.
STORY: A vampire lodger preys on her young tenants.

Boulevard de l'Étrange see Feature Films above.

Le Bunker de la Dernière Rafale [The Bunker of the Last Gale] (B&W., 27 min., 1981)
DIR: Jean-Pierre **Jeunet** and Marc **Caro**; WRI: J.-P. **Jeunet**, M. **Caro**, Gilles Adrien.
CAST: Marc **Caro**, Jean-Pierre **Jeunet**, Jean-Marie de Busscher, Bruno Richard.
STORY: In a bunker where the survivors of a future war hide, a countdown begins and destroys the precarious social fabric.

Le Bunker de la Dernière Rafale (The Bunker of the Last Gale) *1981*

Casse-Tête [Mind-Bender] (Col., 7 min., 1978) See ***Extraneus*** in Feature Films above.

Cauchemar Blanc [White Nightmare] (B&W., 8 min., 1991)
DIR/WRI: Mathieu Kassovitz, based on a comic-book story by **Moebius**.
CAST: Yvan Attal, François Toumarkine, Roger Souza, Jean-Pierre Darroussin, Abder El Kebir, Émile Abossolo M'Bo, Laurent Goldstein.
STORY: A gang of racists who sets out to beat up an innocent Arab worker experiences a nightmarish adventure.
NOTE: This short-feature by the director of *La Haine* won a prize at the Cannes Film Festival. For further information on **Moebius**, see Chapter V. The original story was translated into English and included in *H. P.'s Rock City* (Dark Horse Comics, 1996).

Celui Qui Venait d'Ailleurs [He Came from Beyond] (Col., 19 min, 1978) see ***Histoires Abominables*** in Feature Films above.

Le Château du Passé [The Castle of the Past] (B&W., 20 min., 1959)
DIR/WRI: Marc de Gastyne.
CAST: Gaston Modot, Hermine, Jacky.
STORY: Ghosts make two shepherdesses' wishes come true.

Le Chemin d'Azatoth [Azatoth's Path] (Col., 13 min., 1987)
DIR/WRI: Clément Delage.
CAST: Jean Bouise, Jean-Marie Marion, Valérie Steffen, Robert Enrico.
STORY: A gangster on the lam in the countryside meets a strange sect.

Le Ciel Saisi [The Captured Sky] see ***Boulevard de l'Étrange*** in Feature Films above.

Cimetière des Éléphants [Graveyard of Elephants] see ***Adrénaline*** in Feature Films above.

La Comète [The Comet] (Col., 22 min., 1981)
DIR/WRI: Catherine Cohen.
CAST: Christine Fersen, Romain Trembleau.
STORY: A mother and a child fight while a comet threatens to destroy Earth.

La Conquête du Pôle [The Conquest of the Pole] (B&W., 300 meters, 1913)
DIR/WRI: Georges **Méliès**.
CAST: Georges **Méliès**.
STORY: Explorers at the North Pole battle a Snow Giant.
NOTE: A classic **Méliès** and one of his last productions. The special effect Snow Giant was particularly remarkable.

The Snow Giant from La Conquête du Pôle *(1913).*

La Consultation see ***Boulevard de l'Étrange*** in Feature Films above.

Corridor see ***Adrénaline*** in Feature Films above.

Coup D'Fil [Phone Call] (Col., 6 min., 1980)
DIR/WRI/CAST: Marc Jolivet.
STORY: Public telephones take revenge on a vandal.

Du Crime Considéré comme un des Beaux Arts [Of Crime Considered as One of the Fine Arts] (Col., 15 min., 1980)

DIR: Frédéric Compain; WRI: Frédéric Compain, Gilles Taurand.

CAST: Michel Piccoli, Dominique Farro, Rebecca Pauly, Pat Andréa.

STORY: In the future, a detective (Piccoli) investigates a crime.

Pauly, Farro and Piccoli in Du Crime considéré comme un des Beaux Arts *(1980).*

Cyclope [Cyclops] see ***Adrénaline*** in Feature Films above.

La Dernière Mouche [The Last Fly] see ***Adrénaline*** in Feature Films above.

Destin [Destiny] (Col., 13 min., 1977)

DIR: Reynald Chapuis; WRI: Françoise Bourdin.
CAST: Gisèle Chapuis, Françoise Bourdin.
STORY: A woman meets her Death, face to face.

Documents Interdits [Forbidden Files] (B&W/Col., 92 min., 1991)

DIR/WRI: Jean-Teddy Abdi-Filippe.
CAST: N/A.
STORY: Pseudo-documentaries made to look like amateur footage of unexplained, paranormal phenomenon. Includes *Le Soldat* (*The Soldier*), *La Sorcière* (*The Witch*), *Fantômes* (*Ghosts*), etc.

Éden (Col., 13 min., 1982)

DIR/WRI: Robert Réa.
CAST: Jean-Pierre Darroussin, Didier Crespo, Zabou, Philippe Leroy-Beaulieu.
STORY: A man goes to Heaven and meets his father, age ten, and his mother, a young girl.

Embouteillage [Traffic Jam] see ***Adrénaline*** in Feature Films above.

Entr'acte [Intermission] (B&W., 22 min., 1924)

DIR: René **Clair**; WRI: Francis Picabia.
CAST: Jean Borlin (Magician), Man Ray, Marcel Duchamp, Inge Fries, Erik Satie, Marcel Achard, Georges Auric.
STORY: A series of surreal scenes ending with a funeral. A magician comes out of the coffin and causes everyone to disappear.

Équinoxe (Col., 12 min., 1976)

DIR/WRI: Jacques Robiolles.
CAST: No information available.
STORY: A mermaid is discovered on a beach.

Extraneus see Feature Films above.

Les Fanatiques [The Fanatics] (Col., 10 min., 1985)

DIR/WRI: Jean-Philippe Bêche-Dallier.
CAST: Jean-Pierre Rochette, Michèle Pierson, Roger Perrinoz, Philippe Dallier.
STORY: On the eve of World War III, Paris has been evacuated.

Le Faucheur [The Reaper] (B&W., 20 min., 1968)

DIR/WRI: Alain Gassener, based on a story by Claude **Seignolle**.
CAST: André Faure, Adrien Nicati, Stanley White (The Reaper), Lali Holm, Alain Véron.
STORY: A careless driver (Faure) picks up Death as a hitch-hiker.
NOTE: Claude **Seignolle** is a famous writer of the fantastique (see Book 2). Also see *Celui qui Venait d'Ailleurs*, *Le Miroir* and *Pauvre Sonia* below, *Marie la Louve* in Chapter II and *Delphine* in Chapter III.

La Folie du Dr. Tube [The Madness of Dr. Tube] (B&W., 2 reels, 1916)

DIR/WRI: Abel **Gance**.
CAST: Albert Dieudonné.
STORY: Experimental film about a scientist who breaks light down into its basic components.

La Fonte de Barlaeus [The Melting of Barlaeus] see ***Boulevard de l'Étrange*** in Feature Films above.

La Forêt Désenchantée [The Disenchanted Forest] (Col., 28 Min., 1981)

DIR/WRI: Jacques Robiolles.
CAST: Fabrice Luchini, Bojena Horackova, Colin Jorre, Jean-Luc Passereau, Pierre Atterand, Jean-Christophe Rosé.
STORY: A love story among the fantastic inhabitants of a fairy wood threatened by the construction of a highway.

Fourmi Chérie [Darling Ant] (Col., 11 min., 1986)
DIR/WRI: Thierry Barthes, Pierre Jamin.
CAST: Olivier Achard, Alain Flick, Josy Rosier, Karim Chérier.
STORY: An ant's point of view during the demolition of a building.

Frankenstein: La Véritable Histoire [Frankenstein: The True Story] (Col., 26 min., 1981)
DIR: Roland Portiche; WRI: Igor & Grichka **Bogdanoff**.
CAST: Gilles Guillot (Baron Frankenstein), Olivier Hémon (Monster), Gilbert Bahon.
STORY: Satirical take on the Frankenstein story (Frankenstein becomes Einstein).
NOTE: The **Bogdanoff** brothers produced and hosted the television series, *Temps X* (see Chapter II).

Game Over see *Boulevard de l'Étrange* in Feature Films above.

Gas, ou la Peur des Plus Forts [Gas, or Fear of the Strongest] (B&W., 4 min., 1984)
DIR/WRI: Henri Barges.
CAST: Catherine Ussel, Michel Foucaud, Jean-Denis Brulois.
STORY: Two mutants chase a young woman through a ravaged city.

Graffiti see *Adrénaline* in Feature Films above.

Gyro (Col., 13 min., 1976)
DIR/WRI: Patrick Ghnassia.
CAST: Delphine Desyeux, Jean-Marc Torres.
STORY: Filmed ballet about a vampire who transforms into a bird of light.

Haute Pression [High Pressure] (Col., 7 min., 1986)
DIR/WRI: Olivier Ringer.
CAST: Anna Achdian, Jacques Villa.
STORY: A woman accidentally enters a "pneumatic" universe.

Hémophilia (Col., 15 min., 1985)
DIR/WRI: Norbert **Moutier**.
CAST: Eva Sinclair, Guy Penet, Jean-Marie Vauclin.
STORY: In the future, private subways are heavily guarded; yet, mysterious murders occur.
NOTE: **Moutier**, aka Norbert George **Mount**, is a fanzine editor and also contributes to *L'Écran Fantastique*. In 1997, he became the publisher of *Fantastyka* magazine (see Book 2).

Homicide by Night (Col., 17 min., 1984)
DIR/WRI: Gérard Krawczyk, based on a story by Pierre Siniac.

CAST: Mado Maurin, Paul Crauchet, Claude **Chabrol**.
STORY: Old people join forces to catch a serial killer.

L'Homme Qui Osa [The Man Who Dared] (B&W., 860 m, 1966)
DIR/WRI: Jean Delire, based on a story by Jean **Ray**.
CAST: No information available.
STORY: A man meets a mermaid.
NOTE: For other Jean **Ray** adaptations, see *La Cité de l'Indicible Peur* and *Malpertuis* in Feature Films above.

L'Inconnu [The Unknown Man] see *Extraneus* in Feature Films above.

L'Inconnue [The Unknown Woman] (Col., 17 min., 1966)
DIR/WRI: Claude Weisz.
CAST: Gérard Blain, Paloma Matta.
STORY: A beautiful short film about a ghost.

Interrogatoire [Interrogation] see *Adrénaline* in Feature Films above.

Je Ne Sais Pas [I Don't Know] (B&W., 315 m, 1966)
DIR/WRI: Gérard Pires.
CAST: Bernadette Laffont, Jean-Pierre Kalfon.
STORY: A man who broke up with his girlfriend tries to commit suicide, but ends up stepping sideways in time.

Je Reviens De Suite [Back at Once] see *Boulevard de l'Étrange* in Feature Films above.

La Jetée [The Pier] (B&W., 29 min., 1964)
DIR/WRI: Chris **Marker**.
CAST: Davos Hanich, Hélène Chatelain, Jacques Ledoux, Jean Negroni.
STORY: A time traveller (Hanich) tries to escape from a bleak, totalitarian future.
NOTE: This renowned short feature is the basis for Terry Gilliam's 1995 *Twelve Monkeys*.

Le Mauvais Oeil [The Evil Eye] see *Boulevard de l'Étrange* in Feature Films above.

Métrovision see *Adrénaline* in Feature Films above.

Le Miroir [The Mirror] (Col., 13 min., 1976)
DIR/WRI: Dominique Maillet, based on a story by Claude **Seignolle**.
CAST: Anne Jolivet, Albert Pierjac.
STORY: A mysterious woman hides a secret behind the bandages which cover her head.

NOTE: For further information on Claude **Seignolle**, see *Le Faucheur* above.

Mr. Fantômas see *Fantômas* in Feature Films above.

Le Motard de l'Apocalypse [The Biker from Apocalypse] see *Extraneus* in Feature Films above.

Le Mur Blanc [The White Wall] (B&W., 15 min., 1982)
DIR/WRI: Antoine Lacomblez.
CAST: Jean-Hugues Anglade.
STORY: In a strange hotel, a traveller falls under the hypnotic spell of a white wall.

Natural Killer (Col., 6 min., 1985)
DIR/WRI: Bernard Bebargue.
CAST: Laurence Caubet, Eric Espinasse.
STORY: In a post-apocalyptic world, "Natural Killer" exterminates mutants.

Nuit de Noce [Wedding Night] see *Extraneus* in Feature Films above.

Nuit Féline [Feline Night] (Col., 12 min., 1978)
DIR/WRI: Gérard Marx.
CAST: No information available.
STORY: A variation on *Cat People*.

L'Oniromane (Col., 381 meters, 1969)
DIR/WRI: Jean-Philippe Ginet.
CAST: No information available.
STORY: A character drawn on a poster comes to life.

Pas De Linceul pour Billy Brakko [No Shroud for Billy Brakko] (Col., 5 min., 1983)
DIR: Jean-Pierre **Jeunet**, based on a story by Marc **Caro**.
CAST: Marc **Caro**, Zorin, Phil Casoar, Jean Bouise (Narrator).
STORY: A futuristic private eye investigates a murder.

Pauvre Sonia [Poor Sonia] (Col., 12 min., 1975) see *Histoires Abominables* in Feature Films above.

La Pension [The Retirement Home] (Col., 35 min., 1987)
DIR: Marc Cadieux; WRI: Marc Cadieux, Lionel Kopp.
CAST: Christian Charmetant, Isabelle Petit-Jacques, François Nègre, Jimmy-Léonar Aeton, Hervé Briaux, Emmanuelle Devos, Jérôme Keen.
STORY: A mysterious "home" inhabited by eccentrics is revealed to be the antechamber of death.

Le Péril Rampant [The Crawling Menace] (Col., 25 min., 1981)
DIR/WRI: Alberto Yaccelini.
CAST: Pierre Julien, Bernard Born, Maurice Vallier, Jeanne Biras, Gérard Heffmann, Jean-Claude Dreyfus, Michèle Loubet, Jean-Pierre Elga, Gilbert K. Jakubzcyk.
STORY: An homage to serials, presented as the sixth chapter of a fictional serial, *Les Aventures du Serpent* (*Adventures of the Snake*).

La Petite Gare [The Little Train Station] (Col., 9 min., 1976)
DIR/WRI: Emmanuel Ciepka.
CAST: Catherine Rich, Bernard Giraudeau.
STORY: A man and a woman meet in a deserted railway station.

La Petite Marchande d'Allumettes [The Little Match Girl] (B&W., 29 min., 1928)
DIR/WRI: Jean Renoir, based on a story by Hans Christian Andersen.
CAST: Catherine Hessling, Jean Storm, Manuel Raabi.
STORY: Short feature adaptation of the classic story about the poor little match girl who freezes to death. She dreams of toys and a handsome officer who comes flying through the air to rescue her.

Le Phénomène [The Phenomenon] (Col., 7 min., 1977)
DIR/WRI/CAST: Paul Dopff.
STORY: Homage to the special effects masters of the early days of movie-making.

Pourquoi les Martiens Sont-Ils Verts? [Why Are Martians Green?] (Col., 8 min., 1987)
DIR: Caroline Vié; WRI: Claude Scasso, Caroline Vié.
CAST: Caroline Laury, Mitsou, Patrick Laviosa, Yorgos Bontouvis.
STORY: Musical satire about Earth's efforts to repel a Martian invasion.

Le Rat Noir d'Amérique [The American Black Rat] (Col., 21 min., 1982)
DIR/WRI: Jérôme Enrico.
CAST: André Julien, Philippe du Janerand, Philippe Goyard, Louis Julien, Pierre Arditi, Pia Courcelles.
STORY: A writer meets the characters he has just created.

Le Réacteur Vernet [The Vernet Reactor] see *Boulevard de l'Étrange* in Feature Films above.

Rendez-Vous Hier [Rendezvous Yesterday] (Col., 26 min., 1981)
DIR: Gérard Marx; WRI: Gérard Marx, Dominique Lancelot.

CAST: Richard Bohringer, Michel Derville, Peter Berlig, Catherine Jarrett.
STORY: A man travels back in time through his ancestral memory.

Le Rendez-Vous du Petit Matin [Rendezvous at Sunrise] (Col., 5 min., 1978)
DIR: Patrick Rieul; WRI: Éric Goupil.
CAST: Rémy Carpentier.
STORY: A man meets Death.

Revestriction [Dream Restriction] see Adrénaline in Feature Films above.

La Rivière du Hibou [Owl River, transl. as An Occurrence at Owl Creek Bridge] see Au Coeur de la Vie in Feature Films above.

La Saisie [The Repossession] (Col., 7 min., 1975)
DIR/WRI: Robert Cappa.
CAST: Denis Manuel, Émile Coz, Yves Le Garrec, Patrick Ménager.
STORY: A man whose furniture is being repossessed insists on keeping a dresser.

Le Salut Est dans la Fuite [Salvation Lies in Running Away] (Col., 9 min., 1975)
DIR/WRI: Francis Guibert.
CAST: Kathleen Delzant, Alain Pistre, Liliane Vaquero, Claude Coiffier.
STORY: A young woman returns to her ancestral home.

Le Sang d'un Poète [The Blood of a Poet] (B&W., 49 min., 1930)
DIR/WRI: Jean **Cocteau**.
CAST: Enrique Rivero (The Poet), Lee Miller, Feral Benga, Pauline Carton.
STORY: A series of surreal scenes orchestratred by the poetic genius of Jean **Cocteau**.

Sculpture Physique [Physical Sculpture] see Adrénaline in Feature Films above.

Une Seconde Jeunesse [A Second Youth] (Col., 13 min., 1976)
DIR/WRI: Robert Cappa.
CAST: Samson Fainsilber, Anna Gayane, Annie Dana.
STORY: Two old people live alone in a house, locked in silent hate of each other.

Silver Slime (Col., 15 min., 1981)
DIR/WRI: Christophe Gans.

CAST: Isabelle Wendling, Aïssa Djabri.
STORY: Homage to Mario Bava.
NOTE: Christophe Gans is the director of *Crying Freeman* and a former editor of the magazine *Starfix*.

Six Minutes de Demain [Six Minutes from Tomorrow] (Col., 6 min., 1982)
DIR/WRI: Thierry Foulquier.
CAST: Carole Simon, Luc Baptiste.
STORY: An escape from a totalitarian future.

Sous un Soleil d'Été [Under a Summer Sun] (Col., 14 min., 1979)
DIR: Raffy Schart; WRI: Raffy Schart, Maïté Melronian.
CAST: Marjorie Kleeberg, Thomas Nevsa, Florence Pichard du Page, Dominique Kleeberg, Raffy Schart.
STORY: The strange and fantastic universe created by the mind of a little girl.

Star Suburb: La Banlieue des Étoiles (Col., 26 min., 1982)
DIR/WRI: Stéphane Drouot.
CAST: Caroline Appere, Marcelle Turlure.
STORY: In her futuristic apartment, a girl who can't sleep listens to a galactic radio station presenting a new game show.

Subtil Concept (B&W., 21 min., 1980)
DIR/WRI: Gérard Krawczyk, based on the short story "*Mr. Big*" by Woody Allen.
CAST: Allan Wenger, Rebecca Pauly, Nicholas Bang, Daniel Croheim, Ed Marcus.
STORY: A hardboiled private eye is hired to find out who killed God.

Le Suicide de Frankenstein [Frankenstein's Suicide] (Col., 45 min., 1984)
DIR/WRI: René **Manzor**.
CAST: No information available.
STORY: Another variation on the Frankenstein theme.

Sybille (Col., 15 min., 1979)
DIR/WRI: Robert Cappa.
CAST: Manuel Bonnet, Jean Montagne, Brigitte Roudier, Gilles Kohler.
STORY: A man buys a film reel showing a mysterious woman. Everytime he projects the film, new scenes appear until the woman reaches into his reality, killing him.

Synthétique Opérette (Col., 10 min., 1986)
DIR: Olivier Esmein; WRI: Olivier Esmein, F. Favre.
CAST: P. Braoudé, B. Berre, R. Cantarella, C. Carrée.
STORY: Two convention-goers at a beach resort are accidentally connected to a strange cathodic tube.

La Tache [The Blot] see *Extraneus* in Feature Films above.

T'as le Bonjour d'Alfred [Alfred Says Hi!] (Col., 5 min., 1985)
DIR/WRI: Clément Delage.
CAST: Michel Duperret, Valérie Steffen.
STORY: A psychotic killer strikes.

Ténèbres [Darkness] (Col., 323 meters, 1969)
DIR/WRI: Claude Loubarie.
CAST: No information available.
STORY: No one who has ever entered a strangely abandoned neighborhood in a ruined city has ever returned.

Tic Tac [Tick Tock] (Col., 4 min., 1982)
DIR/WRI/CAST: Marc Jolivet.
STORY: Time speeds up.

Le Tigre du Jardin des Plantes [The Tiger of the Botanical Gardens] (Col., 14 min., 1982)
DIR/WRI: Jean-Denis Robert.
CAST: Valérie Chassigneux, Hyppolyte Girardot.
STORY: A man switches minds with a zoo tiger.

Torticola Contre Frankensberg [Torticola vs. Frankensberg] (B&W., 34 min., 1952)
DIR: Paul Paviot; WRI: Albert Vidalie, Louis Sapin.
CAST: Vera Norman (Lorelei), François Patrice (Éric), Roger Blin (Frankensberg), Michel Piccoli (Torticola), Hélèna Manson, Marc Boussac.
STORY: In this surreal parody of gothic horror films, Dr. Frankensberg's monster, Torticola, revolts and frees the beautiful captive Lorelei and Eric the wolf-man.

Le Triangle de Mimizan [The Mimizan Triangle] (B&W., 16 min., 1981)
DIR/WRI: Florence Barnett, Jean-Louis Philippon.
CAST: The inhabitants of the town of Mimizan.
STORY: Based on the real-life shipwreck of a tanker off the western coast of France, the filmmakers build a pseudo-documentary, where local inhabitants convincingly spin a yarn about an ancient curse.

TV Buster see *Adrénaline* in Feature Films above.

Urgence [Emergency] see *Adrénaline* in Feature Films above.

Vibroboy (Col., 28 Min., 1993)
DIR: Jan Kounen; WRI: Jan Kounen, Carlo de Boutiny.
CAST: Dominique Bettenfeld, Valérie Druguet, Michel Vuillermoz, Fabien Béhar.
STORY: Semi pornographic parody of super-hero films. A man is possessed by an Aztec warrior's spirit.
NOTE: Jan Kounen is the director of *Dobermann* (1997), written by Joël **Houssin** (see Book 2).

Le Village de Lilith [Lilith's Village] (B&W., 15 min., 1969)
DIR/WRI: Philippe Durand.
CAST: No information available.
STORY: Fear reigns in a small town.

Voix d'Eau [Water Voices] (Col., 16 min., 1982)
DIR: Alain Robak; WRI: Alain Robak, Michel Tassilly.
CAST: Christian Ugolini.
STORY: A man immerged under water in his bathtub hears a conversation between two lovers, mysteriously carried through the network of pipes.

La Voix du Large [A Voice from the Sea] see *Extraneus* in Feature Films above.

Le Voyage à travers l'Impossible [Journey Through the Impossible, transl. as *The Impossible Journey]* (B&W., 24 min., 1904)
DIR/WRI: Georges **Méliès**.
CAST: Georges **Méliès**, Manuel Delpierre, Fernande Albany, Victor André.
STORY: The members of the Incoherent Geographic Society travel toward the Sun aboard an interplanetary train.

Le Voyage dans la Lune [A Trip to the Moon] (B&W., 14 min., 1902)
DIR/WRI: Georges **Méliès**, inspired by the novel by Jules **Verne**.
CAST: Georges **Méliès**, Bleuette Bernon, Victor André, Henri Delannoy.
STORY: The Astronauts' Club sends a rocket to the Moon, where its passengers are imprisoned by the Selenites before escaping and returning to Earth.
NOTE: Also see "*Verne, Jules*" in Chapter II.

Le Voyage de M. Guitton [Mr. Guitton's Journey] (B&W., 139 m., 1969)
DIR/WRI: Pascal Aubier.
CAST: No information available.
STORY: A man wakes up and discovers that his bedroom is on rails.

Le Voyage Imaginaire [The Imaginary Journey] (B&W., 20 min., 1925)
DIR/WRI: René **Clair**.
CAST: Jean Borlin, Albert Préjean, Jim Gérald, Paul Ollivier, Dolly Davis.

STORY: A bank employee falls asleep and has adventures in the land of dreams.

Zito contre Mesrine, Jr. [Zito vs. Mesrine Jr.] (Col., 4 min., 1985)
DIR/WRI: Gabor Rassov.

CAST: Anita Vanzetto, Lucio Mad, Giorgio Rodriguez, Aaron Yuberg, Catherine Frot.

STORY: Zito fights a psycho-killer in this homage to Italian zombie films.

CHAPTER II

Television

1. Historical Overview

First, a brief historical note on French television itself: French television was first called RTF—for Radio Télévision Française. It changed its name to ORTF in 1964, when it was split into two, then later, three channels. In 1975, these channels were eventually dubbed TF1, A2, and FR3, the last functioning as a regional channel.

French television was partially privatized in 1987, with TF1 becoming private, and A2 (later renamed FR2) and FR3 remaining public. Other private channels, such as Channel 5, M6, Arte, etc., and pay cable channel, *Canal Plus*, were also added to the broadcasting spectrum in the 1980s.

French television has traditionally created less original fiction programming than American or British television because it has relied on a greater diversity of programs, including movies, foreign imports, variety, music, sports, round-table discussions, documentaries, ballet, opera, etc. and whatever series it has produced have generally been either historical or police series, two genres at which French television fairly excels.

Science fiction and the *fantastique* have, therefore, mostly been relegated to literary adaptations of Jules **Verne**, Maurice **Renard**, and Marcel **Aymé**, as well as the stable of ever-popular pulp writers such as Gaston **Leroux**, Maurice **Leblanc**, Arthur **Bernède**, Gustave **Le Rouge**, Marcel **Allain** & Pierre **Souvestre**, etc.

The most memorable of these literary adaptations were made in the 1960s and 1970s, and included:

Claude **Barma**'s *Belphegor* (1965), an overnight ratings sensation and cult series.

Claude Santelli's series of Jules Verne adaptations in the mid–1960s.

A remarkable version of Gustav Meyrinck's *Golem* (1967).

Jacques Champreux teaming with Pierre **Prévert** on *Les Compagnons de Baal* (*The Brotherhood of Baal*, 1968) and

with Georges **Franju** on *L'Homme sans Visage* (*The Faceless Man*, transl. as *Shadowman*, 1975).

Marcel Cravenne's versions of Gaston Leroux's *La Poupée Sanglante* (*The Bloody Puppet*, 1976) and Maurice Leblanc's *L'Île aux Trente Cercueils* (*The Island of the Thirty Coffins*, 1979).

And, finally, Maurice **Frydland**'s wonderfully over-the-top adaptation of Gustave Le Rouge's *Le Mystérieux Docteur Cornelius* (*The Mysterious Dr. Cornelius*, 1984).

Original, made-for-television genre fare of note includes:

Claude Guillemot's fondly remembered and too short-lived *La Brigade des Maléfices* (*The Brigade of Spells*, 1970), a humorous predecessor of *The X-Files*.

Jean Dréville and **Noël-Noël**'s time travel mini-series, *Le Voyageur des Siècles* (*The Traveler of the Centuries*, 1971).

The interesting but often rather tame *Aux Frontières du Possible* (*To the Frontiers of the Possible*, 1971, 1974).

And, finally, writer Alain **Page**'s thrilling, groundbreaking mini-series *Les Compagnons d'Eleusis* (*The Brotherhood of Eleusis*, 1975) and *Le Mutant* (1978).

Also notable was producer Michel **Subiela**'s *Le Tribunal de l'Impossible* (*The Tribunal of the Impossible*) which, from 1967 to 1974, presented a series of made-for-television features dealing with all the various facets of the *fantastique*, the paranormal and the unexplained.

Sadly, as French television became increasingly privatized and commercial in the early 1980s, it almost entirely stopped producing new genre programs, instead relying increasingly on inexpensive American, British, and German imports. A few low-budget genre productions were produced for regional channels, but these were not especially well made, nor did they have any significant impact on the ratings.

However, this changed again in the 1990s, during which a large number of homegrown cop shows were made: *Maigret*, *Navarro*, *Nestor Burma*, *Commissaire Leclerc*, *Julie Lescault*, to name but a few of the more famous. In spite of this abundance of new French productions, and the local success of American genre series such as *The X-Files*, French television producers have not, to date, made any new genre series.

2. Series

Our definition of "series" includes the following types of programs:

Regular Series: hero-driven, open-ended, on-going, self-contained stories, with recurring characters.

Mini-Series: A single story, with beginning, middle and end, split into various episodes for programming purposes.

Anthologies: series of unrelated, self-contained stories with no recurring characters.

Major Authors: For reference's sake, we have chosen to regroup the numerous adaptations of Marcel Aymé, Maurice Leblanc, Gaston Leroux, and Jules Verne under their own names. Separate entries have, however, been retained for cross-reference purposes.

Aéroport 2000 [Airport 2000] (A2, Col., three 60 min. eps., 1980)

Only episode 2 of this airport-themed anthology series belonged to the science fiction genre.

2. Charter 2020 (19 April 1980)

DIR: Pierre Lary; WRI: Fernand Pluot, Pierre Lary.

CAST: Georges Marchal, Tsilla Chelton, Alexandre Rignault, Daniel Mesguich.

STORY: A Concorde lands in 2020 in a future where women reproduce by parthenogenesis.

L'Agence Nostradamus [The Nostradamus Agency] (RTF, B&W., ten 15 min. eps., 9–30 October 1950)

DIR: Claude **Barma**; WRI: Jean-Luc & Pierre Dumayet.

CAST: Denise Provence (Dominique), Jacques Henri Duval (Robert), Henri Demay, P.-J. Montcorbier, Gisèle Chilton, J.-P. Moulinot, Geneviève Morel, Jean-Claude Deret, Jean-Jacques Daubin, Roger Saltel, Pierre Goutas, Bernard Hubrenne.

CONCEPT: A police series mixing crime detection with astrology.

EPISODE GUIDE: No information available.

NOTE: This was the first French television series ever created.

Alice, Où Es-Tu? [Alice, Where Are You?] (ORTF 1, Col., twenty 13 min. eps., August–October 1969)

DIR: Paul Siegrist; WRI: Jean Canolle, Gérard Lucas, Pierre Zimmer.

CAST: Alain Chevallier (Antoine), Hariette Ariel (Alice).

STORY: A young employee leaves his job to pursue a mysterious young woman.

NOTE: Franco-Swiss co-production.

L'Alphomega (ORTF 1, Col., six 60 min. eps., 26 February-2 April 1973)

DIR/WRI: Lazare Iglésis.

CAST: Henri Verlojeux (Tonton), André Weber (Biceps), Mike Marshall.

STORY: Science fiction comedy in which two friends, Tonton and Biceps, run a shop called "The Key to the Galaxies."

Henri Virlojeux in L'Alphomega.

Arsène Lupin see *Leblanc, Maurice*

Astrolab 22 (TF1, Col., thirteen 26-min. eps., 15 June–7 July 1985)

DIR: Pierre Sisser; WRI: Pierre Sisser, Roland Portiche, based on a story by Essam El Maghraby.

CAST: Pierre Londiche, Jean-Yves Gautier, Vincent Siegrist, Véronique Prune, Bruno Guillain.

STORY: French-Saudi co-production about a group of space cadets living aboard a space station and exploring the planets of the solar system.

NOTE: Roland Portiche also worked as a director on **Temps X** (see Non-Fiction below).

Les Atomistes [The Atom-Smashers] (ORTF 1, B&W., twenty-six 13 min. eps., 12 February–18 March 1968)

DIR: Léonard Keigel; WRI: Bernard **Thomas**, Agnès **Van Parys**.

CAST: Marc Michel, Jacques Debary, Simone Bach, Alain Nobis, Philippe Rouleau.

STORY: Scientists create a crystal that boosts human powers.

NOTE: Novelized in 1968 by Bernard **Thomas** and Georges **Van Parys**.

Aux Frontières du Possible [To the Frontiers of the Possible] (ORTF 2, Col., thirteen 60 min. eps., 1971, 1974)

REGULAR CAST: Pierre Vaneck (Yann Thomas), Elga Andersen (Barbara Andersen), Jean-François Rémi (Courtenay-Gabor), Yvette Montier (secretary), Eva Christian (Christa, eps. 9-11 only), Robert Rudel (Chalier, eps. 1-6 only).

CONCEPT: Two young scientists (Vaneck and Andersen) from the International Bureau of Scientific Protection (in French: BIPS) investigate unexplained phenomena *à la The X-Files*. the answers are always based on new, cutting edge scientific discoveries.

1st Season:

1. Le Dossier des Mutations V [The Mutation V File] (4 October 1971)
DIR: Victor **Vicas**; WRI: Jacques **Bergier**, Henri **Viard**.
GUEST CAST: François Chaumette, François Jaubert, Robert Lombard.
STORY: Can a plum tree be genetically modified to grow diamonds?

2. Attention Névroses Mentales [Beware Mental Neuroses] (11 October 1971)
DIR: Victor Vicas; WRI: Jacques Bergier, Henri Viard.
GUEST CAST: Unknown.
STORY: Astronauts exhibit mysterious signs of depression.

3. Terreur au Ralenti [Terror in Slow Motion] (18 October 1971)
DIR: Claude Boissol; WRI: Jacques Bergier, Henri Viard.
GUEST CAST: Michel Garnier, Jean Lelamer, Jean-Pierre Lorrain.
STORY: A man has the power to make people live in slow motion.

4. Menaces sur le 6ème Continent [Threats Over the 6th Continent] (25 October 1971)
DIR: Claude Boissol; WRI: Jacques Bergier, Henri Viard.
GUEST CAST: André Oumansky, Jean Lemaître, Max Amyl.
STORY: Is there intelligent life under water?

5. L'Homme Radar [The Radar Man] (11 October 1971)
DIR: Victor Vicas; WRI: Jacques Bergier, Henri Viard.
GUEST CAST: Jean Aron, Françoise Giret, Hubert Deschamps.
STORY: Scientists are killed in mysterious plane crashes.

6. Protection Spéciale Ultra-Sons U [Special Protection Ultrasound U] (11 November 1971)
DIR: Claude Boissol; WRI: Jacques Bergier, Henri Viard.
GUEST CAST: Jacques Harden, Marcel Gassouk, Roger Bontemps.
STORY: A criminal ring designs the ultimate spying device.

2nd Season:

7. Le Dernier Rempart [The Last Rampart] (23 February 1974)
DIR: Claude Boissol; WRI: Henri Viard.
GUEST CAST: Georges Atlas, Maurice Gautier.
STORY: A Parisian suburb lives under a mysterious spell.

8. Le Cabinet Noir [The Black Cabinet] (2 March 1974)
DIR: Victor Vicas; WRI: Henri Viard.
GUEST CAST: Herta Kravina, Joachim Rake.
STORY: Seemingly random murders are committed in the cinemas.

9. Les Hommes Volants [The Flying Men] (9 March 1974)
DIR: Claude Boissol; WRI: Henri Viard.
GUEST CAST: Unknown.
STORY: The B.I.P.S. investigates UFO sightings in Finland.

10. Meurtres à Distance [Murders at a Distance] (16 March 1974)
DIR: Claude Boissol; WRI: Henri Viard.
GUEST CAST: Michel Auger, Nicole Dessailly, Pierre Hatet.
STORY: Something is interfering with a telepathic communication experiment aboard a nuclear submarine.

11. Alerte au Minotaure [Minotaur Alert] (23 March 1974)
DIR: Victor Vicas; WRI: Henri Viard.
GUEST CAST: Toni Arasse, Jacques Berthier, Philippe Brigaud.
STORY: A new method of doping.

12. Les Créateurs de Visible [The Creators of the Visible] (30 March 1974)
DIR: Victor Vicas; WRI: Henri Viard.
GUEST CAST: Louis Aubert, Guy Lecuyer, Fernande Giroux.
STORY: Someone creates lifelike optical illusions of dead political leaders.

13. L'Effaceur de Mémoire [The Memory Eraser] (6 April 1974)
DIR: Victor Vicas; WRI: Henri Viard.
GUEST CAST: Don Arres, Roland Chenail, Gratien Gelinas.
STORY: A series of mysterious attacks of amnesia.
NOTE: Henri Viard is a journalist and science fiction writer (see Book 2). Jacques Bergier was a renowned specialist in science fiction, fantasy, the occult, and secret intelligence (see Book 2). He was the author of several non-fiction books on borderline genre subjects, including *Le Matin des Magiciens*, co-written with Louis **Pauwels** (see **Le Golem** below).

Aymé, Marcel

The fantastic stories and fairy tales of popular writer Marcel **Aymé** (see Book 2) have been such a staple of French television that we have regrouped them in a single section below. Also see la **Belle Image**, **Garou-Garou**, **Le Passe-Muraille**, and la **Vouivre** in Chapter I for feature film adaptations of other Marcel **Aymé** stories.

Marcel Aymé (A2, Col., five 60 min. eps. 1977-91)

Five delightful adaptations starring the incomparable Michel Serrault and produced by Pierre Tchernia.

1. Le Passe-Muraille [The Walker Through the Walls] (24 December 1977)
DIR/WRI: Pierre Tchernia.

Michel Serrault in Le Passe-Muraille.

CAST: Michel Serrault, Andréa Ferreol, Marco Perrin, Jean Obe, Pierre Tornade, Raoul Curet, Michel Muller, Georges Atlas, Roger Carel, Michel Tugot, Robert Rollis.

STORY: A meek civil servant who discovers that he has the ability to walk through walls becomes a master burglar.

2. La Grâce (21 April 1979)
DIR/WRI: Pierre Tchernia.
CAST: Michel Serrault, Rosy Varte, Roger Carel, Ginette Garcin, Serge Bento, Annie Le Youdec.

STORY: A saintly man is given a halo and must learn to sin to be rid of it.

3. Lucienne et le Boucher [Lucienne and the Butcher] (1983)
DIR/WRI: Pierre Tchernia.
Not a genre story.

4. L'Huissier [The Bailiff] (3 January 1991)
DIR: Pierre Tchernia; WRI: Jean-Claude Grinberg.
CAST: Michel Serrault, Judith Magre, Maurice Chevit, Daniel Prévost, Jean-Paul Roussillon, Pierre Tornade, Georges Wilson.

STORY: A mean-spirited bailiff dies, but is sent back to Earth for a second chance.

5. Héloïse (23 January 1991)
DIR/WRI: Pierre Tchernia.
CAST: Michel Serrault, Françoise Arnoul, Roger Carel, Pierre Doris, Jean Rougerie, Jacqueline Danno, Bernard Woringer.

STORY: A meek photographer turns into a woman at night.

La Bonne Peinture [The Good Paintings] (ORTF 2, Col., 60 min., 24 November 1967)
DIR: Philippe Agostini; WRI: Odette Joyeux.
CAST: Claude Brasseur, Pierre-Jean Vaillard, René Lefèvre, Jacqueline Coué, Raymond Pelletier, France Rumilly.

STORY: A painter's paintings are so realistic that they have the power to appease hunger.

Les Bottes de Sept Lieues [The Seven League Boots]

Version No. 1: (ORTF 2, Col., 90 min., 28 December 1971)
DIR: François Martin; WRI: François Martin, François Chevalier.
CAST: Pascal Sellier, France Darry, Jean Bouise, Fernand Berset, Dominique Vincent, Pascal Gillot, Bernard Dumaine, Gilberte Moutier, Eric Baugin, Louise Roblin.

Version No. 2: (A2, Col., 75 min., 20 December 1990)
DIR: Hervé Baslé; WRI: Jean-Claude Grinberg.
CAST: Christine Boisson, Jérémie Semonin, Jacques Dufilho, Pierre-Alexis Hollenbeck, Maxime Boidron, Benoît Robert, Pierre Baslé, Baptiste Vitez, Jean-Claude Bouillaud.

STORY: A crotchety old shop-keeper owns the legendary seven-league boots.

Les Contes du Chat Perché [The Tales of the Crouching Cat, aka The Wonderful Farm] (ORTF 2, Col., thirteen 20-min. eps. 1968)

1. Les Boîtes de Peinture [The Paint Boxes] (21 December 1968)

2. L'Âne et le Cheval [The Ass and the Horse] (22 December 1968)

3. Les Vaches [The Cows] (23 December 1968)

4. La Patte du Chat [The Cat's Paw] (24 December 1968)

5. Le Problème [The Problem] (25 December 1968)

6. Le Petit Coq Noir [The Little Black Rooster] (26 December 1968)

7. Le Chien Aveugle [The Blind Dog] (27 December 1968)

8. Le Cerf et le Chien [The Deer and the Dog] (28 December 1968)

9. Le Paon [The Peacock] (29 December 1968)

10. Les Boeufs [The Ox] (30 December 1968)

11. Le Canard et la Panthère [The Duck and the Panther] (31 December 1968)

12. Le Mouton [The Sheep] (1st January 1969)

13. Le Loup [The Wolf] (2nd January 1969)
DIR: Arlen Papazian; WRI: Albert Husson.
REGULAR CAST: Christine Chicoine (Delphine), Marie-Claude Breton (Mariette), André Julien (Father), Odette Picquet (Mother).

GUEST CAST: Armand Maistre, Pierre Gualdi, Françoise Bertin, Bernard Tirli, Yveline Moatti, and the voices of Yves Mathieu, Alexandre Rignault, Jean Valton, Roger Carel, Marguerite Cassan, Françoise Arnaud.

STORY: On a farm, two little girls communicate with the animals, and have a series of adventures.

La Fabrique [The Factory] (A2, Col., 90 min., 24 December 1979)

DIR/WRI: Pascal Thomas.

CAST: Emilie Gruel, Brigitte Gruel, Renaud Vincent, Armand Gruel, Hervé Bonjean, Frédéric Duru, Sophie Lamoureux, Alexandre Brunner, Emmanuelle Bot, Bernard Menez.

STORY: A spoiled little rich girl shares Christmas with a poor little boy from the previous century.

La Grâce (RTF, B&W., 23 April 1953)

DIR: Jacques-Gérard Cornu; WRI: J.-L. Descaves.

CAST: André de Chauveron, Jean-Pierre Moulinot, Paul Colline, Annie Duguay.

STORY: A saintly man is given a halo and must learn to sin to be rid of it.

Le Loup [The Wolf] (RTF, B&W., 25 min., 24 December 1958)

DIR/WRI: Jean-Christophe Averty.

CAST: Jacques Fabbri, Jacqueline Bressy, Sylviane Margollé, Paulette Dubost, Jean-Marie Serreau.

STORY: A wolf and two little girls play together.

Le Modèle [The Model] (ORTF 2, Col., 90 min., 5 July 1969)

DIR/WRI: Jacques Pierre.

CAST: Robert Manuel, Maike Jansen, Gabriel Jabbour, Jacques Duby, Jacqueline Danno.

STORY: A young woman helps a writer with writer's block.

Le Nain [The Dwarf] (RTF, B&W., 19 March 1961)

DIR: Pierre Badel; WRI: Jean Cathelin.

CAST: Roland Lacoste, Jean Hoube, Paul Frankeur, Jacques Gripel, Evelyne Lacroix, Fernande Albany, Dominique Davray, Arthur Allan.

STORY: After thirty-five years, a circus dwarf begins to grow taller.

La Belle et son Fantôme [The Beauty and Her Ghost] (RTF, B&W., thirteen 30 min. eps., 1962)

1. *Le Prince de Comagène [The Prince of Comagène]* (7 April 1962)

2. *Le Château de Lestrange [The Castle of Lestrange]* (14 April 1962)

3. *La Nuit Fantôme [The Ghostly Night]* (21 April 1962)

4. *La Fiancée du Premier Clerc [The First Clerk's Fiancée]* (28 April 1962)

5. *Barbara, Morte ou Vivante [Barbara, Living or Dead]* (5 May 1962)

6. *La Nuit de Gustave [Gustave's Night]* (12 May 1962)

7. *Rencontre avec l'Homme Aquarium [Meeting with the Aquarium Man]* (19 May 1962)

8. *Troisième Nuit au Château [Third Night at the Castle]* (26 May 1962)

9. *Charles-Auguste Perd la Partie [Charles-Augustes Loses a Hand]* (2 June 1962)

10. *Minna de Lestrange* (9 June 1962)

11. *La Villa Rose [The Pink Villa]* (16 June 1962)

12. *Week-End pour Charles-Auguste* (23 June 1962)

13. *Le Puit de la Cave [The Cellar's Pit]* (30 June 1962)

DIR/WRI: Bernard Hecht.

CAST: Philippe Ogouz (Charles-Auguste), Anne Tonietti (Barbara), Jacques Monod (Deodat), Josette Vardier (Minna), Jean-Paul Moulinot (Walter), Jean-Marc Tennberg (Poinsot), Bernard Woringer (Oreste), Harry Max, Charles Lavialle, Raymond Jourdan, Madeleine Damiens, Henri Lambert, Annick Allières.

STORY: Amateur detective Charles-Auguste Beauvallet and the beautiful Barbara investigate the gothic mysteries surrounding a haunted castle.

NOTE: The character of Charles-Auguste was first created by Bernard Hecht in 1959 for a television series entitled *Bastoche & Charles-Auguste*.

Belphegor, ou Le Fantôme du Louvre [Belphegor, or the Ghost of the Louvre] (ORTF 1, B&W., thirteen 30 min. eps., Rep. as Four 80 min. eps., 1965)

1. *Le Louvre* (6 March 1965)

2. *Le Secret du Louvre [The Secret of the Louvre]* (13 March 1965)

Yves Renier and Christine Delaroche in Belphegor.

3. Les Rose-Croix [The Rosicrucians] (20 March 1965)

4. Le Rendez-Vous du Fantôme [Rendezvous with the Ghost] (27 March 1965)

DIR: Claude **Barma**; WRI: Claude Barma, Jacques Armand, based on the screenplay by Arthur **Bernède**.

CAST: Juliette Gréco (Laurence Borel), René Dary (Commissioner Ménardier), Yves Renier (André Bellegarde), Christine Delaroche (Colette Ménardier), François Chaumette (Boris Williams), Héléna Bossis (Irène Nando), Paul Cambo, François Chodat, Sylvie, Paul Crauchet, René Alone, Sylvain Levignac, Marguerite Muni, Christian Lude, Jacky Calayatud, Raymond Devime, Jacques Dynam, Maurice Gautier, Germaine Ledoyen, Robert Lombard, Jean Mauvais, Jean Michaud, Pascal Mazzotti, Alain Mottet, Natalie Nerval, Hubert Noel, Pierre Palau, Marcelle Ranson, Nicolas Vogel, Jean-Pierre Zola.

STORY: A ghostly presence is haunting the Louvre. In reality, it is a medium (Gréco) who is manipulated by a secret society led by Boris Williams. They are looking for an ancient alchemical treasure hidden inside the statue of the god Belphegor in the museum. the villains are unmasked by André Bellegarde, an enterprising student, and his girlfriend Colette.

NOTE: Arthur Bernède also created the character of *Judex*. *Belphegor* was adapted from the eponymous 1926 film (see Chapter I).

Bing (FR3, Col., three 60 min. eps., 1991)

1. Bing (3 May 1991)

2. Touche Pas à Mon Antenne [Don't Touch My Antenna] (10 May 1991)

3. Où sont les Confitures? [Where's the Jam?] (17 May 1991)

DIR: Nino Monti; WRI: Nino Monti, Henri Slotine, based on the novel *All Right, Everybody Off the Planet* by Bob Ottum.

CAST: Jean-François Garreaud (Bing/Dieudonné), Jean-Paul Farre (Fiddle), Claire Nadeau (Gabrielle), Marcel Philippot (Narbonne), Valentin Traversi (Destournelles), Sophie Carle (Marie-Lou), Marina Pastor (Ginny), Christian Jolibois (Prof. Brisebois), Marie-Claude Vermorel (Paola).

STORY: Alien visitors send one of their own, Bing, disguised as a journalist, to help Earth decrypt their message, which reads "We come in Peace." In spite of his ignorance of human relationships, Bing stages a successful first contact.

Bing II (FR3, Col., two 90 min. eps., 29 & 30 December 1992)

DIR: Nino Monti; WRI: Henri Slotine, based on the characters created by Bob Ottum in his novel *All Right, Everybody Off the Planet.*

CAST: Jean-François Garreaud (Bing/Dieudonné), Jean-Paul Farre (Fiddle), Claire Nadeau (Gabrielle), Marcel

Philippot (Narbonne), Valentin Traversi (Destournelles), Sophie Carle (Marie-Lou), Marina Pastor (Ginny), Christian Jolibois (Prof. Brisebois), Marie-Claude Vermorel (Paola), Paul Guers (Gen. Bassompierre), Catherine Erhardy (Felicity).

STORY: The aliens leave Earth and erase all memories of their visit, but have mistakenly left behind an "egg" containing their knowledge. Bing returns to Earth to retrieve it. Eventually, he and his human friends use it to build a new Noah's Ark-like spaceship and leave Earth for a more peaceful planet.

Bob Morane (ORTF 2, B&W., twenty-six 30 min. eps., beginning 28 March 1965)

DIR: Robert Vernay; WRI: J. M. Arlaud, Henri **Vernes**, based on his novels.

REGULAR CAST: Claude Titre (Bob Morane), Billy Kearns (Bill Ballantine).

CONCEPT: Based on a long-running series of popular, juvenile adventure novels by Henri Vernes featuring the intrepid French major Robert Morane and his sidekick, a hulking Scotsman named Bill Ballantine (see Book 2).

1. La Cité des Sables [The City in the Sands]
GUEST CAST: Unknown.
STORY: Morane embarks on a Middle-Eastern adventure.
NOTE: Based on Book No.16, 1956.

2. La Galère Engloutie [The Sunken Galley]
GUEST CAST: Unknown.
STORY: Morane goes after an underwater treasure.
NOTE: Based on Book No.2, 1954.

3. L'Héritage du Flibustier [The Pirate's Inheritance]
GUEST CAST: Unknown.
STORY: Another treasure hunt.
NOTE: Based on Book No.5, 1954.

4. Échec à la Main Noire [The Black Hand in Check]
GUEST CAST: Unknown.
STORY: Morane vs. the Mafia.
NOTE: Based on Book No.20, 1957.

5. La Vallée des Brontosaures [The Valley of the Brontosauri]
GUEST CAST: Unknown.
STORY: A hidden graveyard of dinosaurs.
NOTE: Based on Book No.9, 1955.

6. La Fleur du Sommeil [The Flower of Sleep]
GUEST CAST: Unknown.

STORY: Morane fights an opium ring.
NOTE: Based on Book No. 22, 1957.

7. *Le Démon Solitaire [The Lone Demon]*
GUEST CAST: Unknown.
STORY: Morane goes after a wild horse.
NOTE: Based on Book No. 42, 1960.

8. *Le Temple des Crocodiles [The Temple of the Crocodiles]*
GUEST CAST: Unknown.
STORY: Morane discovers a lost Egyptian temple.
NOTE: Based on Book No. 44, 1961.

9. *Le Tigre des Lagunes [The Lagoon Tiger]*
GUEST CAST: Unknown.
STORY: Morane defeats a famous pirate.
NOTE: Based on Book No. 45, 1961.

10. *Le Dragon des Fenstone [The Fenstone Dragon]*
GUEST CAST: Unknown.
STORY: A fake dragon is used to commit a crime.
NOTE: Based on Book No. 46, 1961.

11. *Rafale en Méditerranée [Storm Over the Mediterranean]*
GUEST CAST: Unknown.
STORY: Morane fights a ring of smugglers.
NOTE: Adapted from Book No. 47, *Trafic aux Caraïbes [Traffic in the Caribbean]*, 1961.

12. *Les Semeurs de Foudre [The Sowers of Lightning]*
GUEST CAST: Unknown.
STORY: A gang of villains use controlled lightning as their weapon.
NOTE: Based on Book No. 52, 1962.

13. *Le Club des Longs Couteaux [The Club of the Long Knives]*
GUEST CAST: Unknown.
STORY: Morane defeats a Chinese Tong.
NOTE: Based on Book No. 53, 1962.

14. *La Voix du Mainate [The Mynah's Voice]*
GUEST CAST: Unknown.
STORY: A Mynah bird has been taught secret information.
NOTE: Based on Book No. 54, 1962.

15. *Le Lagon aux Requins [The Shark Lagoon]*
GUEST CAST: Unknown.
STORY: Morane fights a gang of pirates.
NOTE: Based on Book No. 50, 1962.

16. *La Rivière de Perles [The River of Pearls]*
GUEST CAST: Unknown.
STORY: in Hong Kong, Morane searches for a valuable necklace.
NOTE: Based on Book No. 59, 1963.

17. *Mission à Orly [Mission at Orly]*
GUEST CAST: Unknown.

STORY: Morane prevents a kidnapping.
NOTE: Based on Book No. 62, 1964.

18. *Les Joyaux du Maradjah [The Jewels of the Maharadjah]*
GUEST CAST: Unknown.
STORY: Morane prevents a revolution.
NOTE: Based on Book No. 64, 1964.

19. *Le Camion Infernal [The Truck from Hell]*
GUEST CAST: Unknown.
STORY: Morane accepts a suicide mission.
NOTE: Based on Book No. 68, 1964.

20. *Mission à Montellano [Mission in Montellano]*
GUEST CAST: Unknown.
STORY: Morane transports an invaluable rocket part.
NOTE: Based on Book No. 62, 1964.

21. *Le Témoin [The Witness]*
GUEST CAST: Unknown.
STORY: Morane protects a schoolteacher who witnessed a crime (new story).

22. *Le Gardian Noir [The Black Guardian]*
GUEST CAST: Unknown.
STORY: Morane thwarts a plot among the Gypsies (new story).

23. *Le Prince [The Prince]*
GUEST CAST: Unknown.
STORY: Morane impersonates an escape artist (new story).

24. *Complot à Trianon [Plot at the Trianon]*
GUEST CAST: Unknown.
STORY: Morane prevents a political assassination (new story).

25. *Le Cheik Masqué [The Masked Sheik]*
GUEST CAST: Unknown.
STORY: Morane exposes a criminal (new story).

26. *Les Forbans de l'Or Noir [The Black Gold Villains]*
GUEST CAST: Unknown.
STORY: Morane thwarts a sabotage ring (new story).
NOTE: Whereas most of the novels contain science fiction or fantasy elements (such as a deadly Fu Manchu-like enemy called Monsieur Ming and the recurring appearances of friendly Time Patrol operatives from the future), only a few of the television episodes do. However, because of the important place held by *Bob Morane* in French juvenile science fiction, not unlike, say, *Doc Savage* in the United States, we have thought it worthwhile to list the entire series. Also see Chapter V for graphic novel adaptations.

La Brigade des Maléfices [The Brigade of Spells]
(ORTF 2, Col., six 60 min. eps., 1971)
DIR: Claude Guillemot; WRI: Claude Guillemot, Claude Nahon, Monique Lefèbvre.

Claude and Pierre Brasseur in ep. 4 of La Brigade des Maléfices.

REGULAR CAST: Léo Campion (Inspector Gaston Martin Paumier), Marc Lamole (Albert), Jacques François (Police Commissioner), Jean-Claude Balard (Inspector Muselier).

CONCEPT: Inspector Paumier and his faithful assistant Albert investigate supernatural mysteries. Their rival is unbelieving inspector Muselier who always tries (and fails) to find a rational explanation for each mystery.

1. Les Disparus de Rambouillet [Disappearings in Rambouillet] (2 August 1971)

GUEST CAST: Jean-Pierre Andreani (Lancelot), Sylvie Fennec (Fairy), Virginie Vignon (Musidora).

STORY: Fairies are responsible for men disappearing in a forest near Paris.

2. La Septième Chaîne [The Seventh Channel] (9 August 1971)

GUEST CAST: Pierre Brasseur (The Devil), Olivier Lebeaut, Sybille Maas.

STORY: The Devil uses television to drive people to commit murder.

3. Voir Vénus et Mourir [To See Venus and Die] (16 August 1971)

GUEST CAST: Philippe Clay (Adonis), Annie Duperey (Venusine).

STORY: A beautiful Venusian goes after a con artist selling interplanetary vacations.

4. La Créature [The Creature] (23 August 1971)

GUEST CAST: Pierre Brasseur (The Devil), Claude Brasseur, Catherine Jacobsen.

STORY: The Devil uses a beautiful, soulless woman to drive people to suicide.

5. Les Dents d'Alexis [Alexis' Teeth] (30 May 1971)

GUEST CAST: Pierre Vernier (Alexis de Sambleux), Karyn Balme.

STORY: An unhappy vampire falls in love with his dentist, thus lifting his curse.

6. Le Fantôme des HLM [The Ghost of the Housing Project] (6 September 1971)

GUEST CAST: Gérard Sety (Anatole), Paul Ville (Marquis de Palaiseau).

STORY: The ghost of a 17th century nobleman haunts a housing project.

Les Classiques de l'Étrange [Classics of the Strange]
PROD: Michel **Subiela**.

1. La Main Enchantée [The Enchanted Hand] (ORTF 1, Col., 90 min., 5 October 1974)

DIR: Michel **Subiela**; WRI: Michel Subiela, Francis Lacassin, based on a story by Gérard de **Nerval**.

CAST: Pierre Maxence, Nathalie Juvet, Alain Mottet, Thierry Dufour, Roland Monod, Serge Lhorca.

STORY: A magician gives a man a spell which makes his right hand invincible, but it no longer obeys his will.

NOTE: Another Gérard de Nerval story was adapted as a feature film entitled ***La Main du Diable*** (see Chapter I). Francis Lacassin is a well-known comic book scholar.

2. Le Péril Bleu [The Blue Peril] (A2, Col., 90 min., 31 March 1975)

DIR: Jean-Christophe Averty; WRI: Claude **Veillot**, based on the novel by Maurice **Renard**.

CAST: Jean-Roger Caussimon, Bernard Valdeneige, Michel Modo, Eric Colin, France Dougnac, Yvonne Clech, Nicole Norden.

STORY: in 1914, aliens abduct people to study mankind.

NOTE: Claude Veillot is a journalist and science fiction writer (see Book 2). He also adapted René **Barjavel**'s ***Le Grand Secret*** (see below) for television. for further information on Maurice Renard, see Book 2, ***Les Mains d'Orlac*** [*The Hands of Orlac*] in Chapter I. Also see Chapter III for radio adaptations.

3. Le Collectionneur de Cerveaux [The Brain Collector] (A2, Col., 90 min., 23 October 1976)

DIR/WRI: Michel **Subiela**, based on the story "Robots Pensants" ["Thinking Robots"] by George **Langelaan**.

CAST: Claude Jade, François Dunoyer, André Reybaz, Roger Crouzet, Thierry Murzeau.

STORY: Count Saint-Germain grafts human organs inside robot bodies to build perfect androids.

NOTE: This anthology series was intended to take over from ***Le Tribunal de l'Impossible*** [*The Tribunal of the Impossible*] (see below), with a program of four films per year, all adapted from the best literary material. Unfortunately, it was cancelled soon after the first episode and subsequent productions were aired independently at random dates. for more information on George Langelaan, see Book 2 and ***La Dame d'Outre-Nulle Part*** below.

Les Compagnons de Baal [The Brotherhood of Baal] (ORTF 1, B&W., seven 60 min. eps., 1968)

1. Le Secret de Diogène [Diogenes' Secret] (12 July 1968)

2. Les Mystères de l'Île Saint-Louis [The Mysteries of Saint-Louis Island] (29 July 1968)

3. Le Spectre Rouge [The Red Spectre] (5 August 1968)

4. L'Inquiétant Professeur [The Disturbing Professor] (19 August 1968)

5. La Nuit du Huit de Trèfle [The Night of the Eight of Clubs] (26 August 1968)

6. L'Héritage de Nostradamus [The Inheritance of Nostradamus] (2 September 1968)

7. L'Éveil de Liliane [Liliane's Awakening] (9 September 1968)

DIR: Pierre Prévert; WRI: Jacques Champreux.

CAST: Jean Martin (Hubert de Mauvouloir), Jacques Champreux (Claude), Martine Redon (Liliane), René Dary (Commissioner), Raymond Bussières (Diogenes), Jacques Monod, Catherine Alcover, Pierre André Krol, René Lefèvre, Jean Herbert, Roger Desmare, Patrick Lancelot, François Dyrek, André Rousselet, Gérard Larcebeau, Claire Nadeau.

STORY: Claude, a journalist, unmasks a centuries-old criminal conspiracy, the Brotherhood of Baal, led by the mysterious Hubert de Mauvouloir, a man who may be the Count of Saint-Germain.

NOTE: Jacques Champreux is the son of Maurice Champreux, a collaborator of Louis **Feuillade**, and the director of the 1932 version of **Judex**. Jacques Champreux wrote **Franju**'s version of **Judex** (see Feature Films in Chapter I), as well as **L'Homme Sans Visage** (see below). Pierre Prévert is Jacques **Prévert**'s younger brother.

Les Compagnons d'Eleusis [The Brotherhood of Eleusis] (TF1, Col., thirty 15 min. eps., 26 September–16 November 1975)

DIR: Claude Grinberg; WRI: Alain **Page**.

CAST: Marcel Dalio (Mafel), Bernard Alane (Vincent), Thérèse Liotard (Sophie), Catherine Sellers (Emmanuelle), Hubert Gignoux (Verdier), Pierre Tabard (Beaumont), Yves Bureau, Gabriel Cinque, Jacques Goasguen, Maurice Travail, Pierre Hentz, Jean-Jacques Lagarde, Jean Turlier, Jean Berger, Raoul Delfosse.

STORY: A secret society of modern alchemists decides to use vast quantities of gold to destroy the modern world's emphasis on material values.

NOTE: Alain Page also wrote **Le Mutant** (below) and **Le Bal des Affamés** (see Chapter III). a novelisation of **Les Compagnons** written by **Page** was published in 1975.

Les Contes du Chat Perché see **Aymé, Marcel**

Coplan FX-18 (A2, 1989)

Based on the spy thrillers by Paul **Kenny** (see Chapter I).

1. Coups Durs [Hard Blows] (16 April 1989)
DIR: Gilles Behat; WRI: G. Behat, Philippe Madral.

2. L'Aigle et le Serpent [The Eagle and the Serpent] (17 September 1989)
DIR: Peter Kassovitz; WRI: Dominique Robel, Pierre Geller.
CAST: Philippe Caroit (Coplan), Pierre Dux (Le Vieux).
STORY: Spy adventures. See Jean-Gaston **Vandel** in Book 2.

De Bien Étranges Affaires [Some Very Strange Affairs] (FR3, Col., six 60 min. eps., 1982)

1. La Soucoupe de Solitude [A Saucer of Loneliness] (8 September 1982)
DIR: Philippe Monnier; WRI: Philippe Monnier, Michel Picard, based on a story by Theodore Sturgeon.
CAST: Catherine Leprince, André Valardy.
STORY: A small flying saucer confides its cosmic loneliness to an equally lonely girl.
NOTE: Sturgeon's story originally appeared in the magazine *Galaxy* in 1953. It was adapted again as part of the new *Twilight Zone* on CBS on 27 September 1986, directed by John Hancock, written by David Gerrold, starring Shelley Duvall.

2. L'Ami Étranger [The Alien Friend] (15 September 1982)
DIR: Patrick Jamain; WRI: Philippe Setbon.
CAST: Ottavia Piccolo, Marcel Bozzuffi, Roland Bertin.
STORY: A man meets a girl who is the exact double of a girl he loved twenty years ago. In reality, she is an alien who has been sent to study mankind.

3. Lourde Gueuse [Heavy Iron] (22 September 1982)
DIR/WRI: Jean-Luc Miesch, based on a story by Jean-Pierre **Andrevon**.
CAST: Franco Interlenghi, Eddie Constantine, Michel Robin, Isabelle Lacamp, Elisabeth Bourgine, Christian Bouillette.
STORY: The crew of a spaceship revolts against their captain.
NOTE: For further information on Jean-Pierre Andrevon, see Book 2 and the telefilm **Le Travail du Furet** below.

4. L'Amour qui Tue [The Killing Love] (29 September 1982)
DIR/WRI: Laurent Heynemann, based on the story "The Price of Synergy" by Theodore Sturgeon.
CAST: Patrick Chesnais, Stefania Casini, Philippe Lemaire, Jean-Paul Muel, Daniel Laloux.
STORY: A drug kills its victims during love-making.

5. Un Homme Ordinaire [An Ordinary Man] (6 October 1982)
DIR: Juan Luis **Buñuel**; WRI: Hélène Peycharand, based on the short story "Programmation" ["Programming"] by Raoul Gamond.

CAST: Eric Prat, David Pontremoli, Hélène Peychayrand, Michèle Auclair, Danièle Godet.

STORY: in a chaotic post-nuclear future, androids learn to become human.

6. Le Triangle à Quatre Côtés [The Four-Sided Triangle] (13 October 1982)

DIR: Jean-Claude Lubtchansky; WRI: J.-C. Lubtchansky, Paul Gégauff, based on the novel by William Temple.

CAST: Maria Rosaria Ommaggio, Alain Maratrat, François Marthouret, Gabriel Jabbour.

STORY: A girl who is loved by two men is duplicated by the one she has refused.

NOTE: William Temple's novel (originally published as a short story in the magazine *Amazing* in 1939 and expanded in 1949) was also adapted as a 1952 Hammer Film directed by Terence Fisher, starring Barbara Payton.

Destination Xero (1971)

DIR/WRI: Unknown.

CAST: Unknown.

STORY: Children's serial.

Dorothée, Danseuse de Corde see *Leblanc, Maurice*

La Double Vie de Théophraste Longuet see *Leroux, Gaston*

La Duchesse d'Avila [The Duchess of Avila] (ORTF 2, Col., four eps. of 70, 130, 55, and 100 min., 4–25 July 1973)

DIR: Philippe Ducrest; WRI: Philippe Ducrest, Véronique Castelnau (Evelyne Eyfel), Roger Caillois, based on Jean **Potocki**'s *Le Manuscrit trouvé à Saragosse* [*The Ms. Found in Zaragoza*].

CAST: Jean Blaise (Alphonse), José-Luis de Villalonga, Evelyne Eyfel, Sylvie Bréal, Jacqueline Laurent, Michel de Ré, Piéral, François Maistre, Serge Marquand, Jacques Morel, Jean Martin, Jean Franval.

STORY: Alphonse, a young Spanish nobleman, embarks on a fantastic journey.

Fantômas (A2, Col., four 90-min. eps., 1980)

Jean Blaise in La Duchesse d'Avila.

Based on the novels by Marcel **Allain** & Pierre **Souvestre**. See Book 2 and Feature Films in Chapter I.

Regular CAST: Helmut Berger (Fantômas), Jacques Dufilho (Juve), Pierre Malet (Fandor), Gayle Hunnicut (Lady Beltham).

CONCEPT: Arch-criminal Fantômas outwits Police Commisionner Juve and journalist Jerôme Fandor.

1. L'Échafaud Magique [The Magic Scaffold] (4 October 1980)

DIR: Claude **Chabrol**; WRI: Bernard Revon.

GUEST CAST: Kristina Van Eyck (Princess Danidoff), Pierre Douglas (Judge Fuselier), Mario David (Nibet), Hélène Duc.

STORY: Fantômas sends an innocent man to the guillotine.

NOTE: Based on Book 1, 1911.

2. L'Étreinte du Diable [The Devil's Hug] (11 October 1980)

DIR: Juan Luis **Buñuel**; WRI: Bernard Revon.

GUEST CAST: Pierre Douglas (Judge Fuselier), Jean-Paul Zehnacker, Hélène Peycharand.

STORY: Fantômas infiltrates the Paris underground.

NOTE: Based on Book 2, 1911.

3. Le Mort Qui Tue [The Deadman Who Kills] (18 October 1980)

DIR: Juan Luis Buñuel; WRI: Bernard Revon.

GUEST CAST: Kristina Van Eyck (Princess Danidoff), Pierre Douglas (Judge Fuselier), Mario David (Nibet), Maxence Mailfort, Véronique Delbourg, Philippe Laudenbach, Victor Garrivier, Danielle Godet.

STORY: Fantômas impersonates a banker and uses a glove made with human skin to leave false fingerprints behind.

NOTE: Based on Book 3, 1911.

4. Le Tramway Fantôme [The Phantom Trolley] (25 October 1980)

DIR: Claude Chabrol; WRI: Bernard Revon.

GUEST CAST: Peter Wolfsberger, Claudia Messner, Marieli Frohlich.

STORY: Fantômas kidnaps a king.

NOTE: Based on Book 5, 1911.

Fantômette (FR3, Col., twenty-six 30 min. eps., 1993)

DIR: Christiane Leherissey, Christiane Spiero, etc.; WRI: Stéphane Barbier, Jean-Guy Gingembre, Patrick Hutin, Pascal Bancou, Christian Bouveron, etc.; based on the novels by Georges **Chaulet**.

Regular CAST: Katia Sourzac (Fantômette/Françoise), Justine Fraioli (Boulotte), Sabine Franquet (Ficelle), Bertrand Lacy (Oeil-de-Lynx), Arsène Jiroyan (Navarin), Christine Reverho (Cynica), Bruno Raffaelli ("Silver Mask").

STORY: A teenage girl, Françoise, takes on the identity of costumed crime fighter Fantômette to thwart the evil schemes of mad scientists such as Cynica, or super-villains such as "Silver Mask." Stories often rely on science fiction gadgets: cloning in *Fantômette et le Clone*, time travel in *Fantômette et le Passé Recomposé* [*Fantomette and the Made-Up Past*], mind control in *Prise de Tête pour Fantômette* [*Headache for Fantomette*], etc.

NOTE: In addition to his **Fantômette** series, Georges Chaulet is also the writer of a popular series of graphic novels featuring **Les Quatre as** [*The Four Aces*] (see Chapter V).

Le Grand Secret [The Great Secret] (A2, Col., six 60 min. eps., 6 January–10 February 1989)

DIR: Jacques Trébouta; WRI: André Cayatte, Claude **Veillot**, Mark Princi, based on the novel by René **Barjavel**.

CAST: Claude Rich, Louise Marleau, Peter Sattmann, Fernando Rey, Richard Munch, Paul Guers, Martine Sarcey.

STORY: An Indian scientist discovers a virus which confers immortality, but because it is contagious, it threatens the security of the world. the immortals are secretly exiled to a forbidden island in the Pacific.

NOTE: Claude Veillot also adapted Maurice **Renard**'s *Le Péril Bleu* (see above). René Barjavel is a famous science fiction writer (see Book 2) who also worked on **Le Diable et les Dix Commandements** [*The Devil and the Ten Commandments*] (1962) (see Chapter I). Another of his novels, *Le Voyageur Imprudent*, was adapted as a telefilm (see below).

La Guerre des Insectes [The War of the Insects] (A2, Col., four 60 min. eps., 20–28 March 1981)

DIR: Peter Kassovitz; WRI: Giulio Questi, based on the novel by Jean **Courtois-Brieux**.

CAST: Mathieu Carrière, Patrick Chesnais, Victoria Tennant, Miguel Fernandez, André Oumansky, Anémone, Bernard-Pierre Donnadieu, Marie-Pierre Casey.

STORY: A mutated breed of insects threatens to create worldwide starvation by destroying all food supplies on Earth.

Les Habits Noirs [The Men in Black] (ORTF 1, B&W., thirty-one 15 min. eps., 16 October–24 November 1967)

DIR: René Lucot; WRI: Jacques Siclier, based on the novels by Paul **Féval**.

CAST: Jean-François Calvé (Lecoq), Jean-Pierre Bernard (André Maynotte), Julia Dancourt (Julie Maynotte), Jean Lanier (Colonel Bozzo), François Dalou (J.-B. Schwartz), Bernard Jousset, Renée Barell, Gilette Barbier, Raymond Jourdan, Raoul Curet, Roger Jaquet, Maïa Simon, Annie Siniglia, Jean-Pierre Brunot, Jean-Pierre Leroux, Gilles Guillot.

STORY: André Maynotte is framed for a burglary he did not commit. He discovers that the real villains are a Mafia-like secret society, the "Men in Black," whose mysterious leader, Colonel Bozzo, may be hundreds of years old. His adversary is the ruthless Lecoq, inspired by the real-life Vidocq.

NOTE: Paul Féval is one of the major serial writers in French literary history (see Book 2). Also see **Le Loup Blanc**.

Histoires Étranges [Strange Tales] (FR 3, Col., four 90 min. eps., 1980)

PROD: Pierre Badel, Chantal Rémy.

STORY: Pierre Badel plays himself as a filmmaker investigating the supernatural.

1. Un Rêve [A Dream] (9 February 1980)

DIR/WRI: Pierre Badel, based on a story by Ivan Turgenev.

CAST: Philippe Duclos, Geneviève Mnich, William Coryn, Dominique Paturel.

STORY: A child dreams of his father who vanished during World War I.

2. La Loupe du Diable [The Devil's Magnifying Glass] (23 February 1980)

DIR/WRI: Pierre Badel, based on the story "The Portrait" by Nikolai Gogol.

CAST: Rosy Varte, Pierre Michael, Gabriel Jabbour, Pierre Destailles.

STORY: An actress's life is plagued by a cursed painting.

3. La Morte Amoureuse [The Loving Dead] (9 March 1980)

DIR: Peter Kassovitz, based on a story by Théophile **Gautier**.

CAST: François Marthouret, Jean Martion, Gérard Desarthe, Laura Condamines.

STORY: A man's retina preserves the image of the dead woman he once loved.

4. Le Marchand de Sable [The Sandman] (22 March 1980)

DIR: Pierre Badel, based on a story by E.T.A. Hoffmann.

CAST: Paul Le Person, Nathalie Nell, André Landais, Alain Berteau, Elisabeth Bourguine, Victor Garrivier, Thérèse Liotard, Daniel Russo.

STORY: A student recognizes his father's murderer in a painting.

Histoires Extraordinaires [Extraordinary Tales] (FR 3, Col., Six 60 min. eps., 1981)

Based on stories by Edgar Allan Poe.

1. Le Joueur d'Echecs de Maetzel [Maetzel's Chess Player] (7 February 1981)

DIR: Juan Luis **Buñuel**; WRI: Hélène Peychardand, Juan Luis **Buñuel**.

CAST: Jean-Claude Dronot, Diana Bracho, Martin Lasalle.

STORY: Maetzel creates a chess-playing android.

2. Le Scarabée d'Or [The Gold Beetle] (21 February 1981)

DIR: Maurice Ronet; WRI: Napoléon Murat, Maurice Ronet.

CAST: Vittorio Caprioli, Dominique Zardi.
STORY: A macabre treasure hunt.

3. *Ligeia* (7 March 1981)
DIR: Maurice Ronet; WRI: Napoléon Murat, Maurice Ronet.
CAST: Georges Claisse, Joséphine Chaplin, Arielle Dombasle.
STORY: A man's dead wife returns to haunt him.

4. *Le Système du Docteur Goudron et du Professeur Plume [The System of Dr. Tarr and Professor Feather]* (21 March 1981)
DIR: Claude **Chabrol**; WRI: Paul Gégauff.
CAST: Jean-François Garreaud, Coco Ducados, Pierre Le Rumeur, Vincent Gauthier, Ginette Leclerc, Noëlle Noblecourt, Jacques Galland.
STORY: The inmates take over the asylum.

5. *La Lettre Volée [The Purloined Letter]* (4 April 1981)
DIR/WRI: Ruy Guerra.
CAST: Vittorio Caprioli, Pierre Vaneck.
STORY: Detective Dupin finds a stolen letter.

6. *La Chute de la Maison Usher [The Fall of the House of Usher]* (12 April 1981)
DIR: Alexandre Astruc; WRI: Pierre Pelegri.
CAST: Fanny Ardant, Pierre Clementi, Mathieu Carrière, Jacques Daqmine.
STORY: A family curse and a premature burial haunt an ancient house.

Histoires Insolites [Weird Tales] (ORTF 1, Col., six 55 min. eps., 1974)

1. *Monsieur Bébé [Mister Baby]* (19 October 1974)
DIR: Claude **Chabrol**; WRI: Roger Grenier, based on the story "Good and Loyal Services" by Julio Cortazar.
CAST: Daniel Ollier, Denise Gence, François Perrot, Philippine Pascal, Max Doelnitz, Jean-Marie Bernicat.
STORY: An old cleaning woman is hired to take care of the mysterious "Mister Baby."

2. *Les Gens de l'Été [The Summer People]* (26 October 1974)
DIR: Claude Chabrol; WRI: Roger Grenier, based on a story by Shirley Jackson.
CAST: Madeleine Ozeray, François Vibert, Jean-Paul Frankeur, Charles Charras.
STORY: A retired couple falls in love with a holiday town.

3. *Une Invitation à la Chasse [An Invitation to a Hunt]* (2 November 1974)
DIR: Claude Chabrol; WRI: Paul Gegauff, based on a story by George Hitchcock.
CAST: Jean-Louis Maury, Margarethe Trotta, Jean Martin, Dominique Zardi, Henri Attal, Michèle Alexandre.
STORY: An accountant is invited to a hunting party organized by the local nobleman.

4. *Nul n'Est Parfait [Nobody's Perfect]* (9 November 1974)
DIR: Claude Chabrol; WRI: Roger Grenier, based on a story by Georges Mandel.
CAST: Michel Duchaussoy, Caroline Cellier.
STORY: Every morning, a man tries, unsuccessfully, to murder his wife.

5. *Un Jour comme les Autres avec des Cacahuètes [A Day Like Any Other, with Peanuts]* (23 November 1974)
DIR: Édouard Molinaro; WRI: Roger Grenier, based on a story by Shirley Jackson.
CAST: Jean-Pierre Darras, Marie-Hélène Breillat, Christine Kaufmann, Bernard Lecoq.
STORY: A strange man who does good deeds always gives peanuts away afterwards.

6. *Parcelle Brillante [Shining Particle]* (30 November 1974)
DIR: Christian de **Chalonge**; WRI: Roger Grenier, based on a story by Theodore Sturgeon.
CAST: Gert Froebe, Juliet Berto.
STORY: A brilliant but lonely man repairs a female android.

L'Homme de la Nuit see **Leroux, Gaston**

L'Homme sans Visage [The Faceless Man] (TF1, Col., eight 50 min. eps., 1975)

1. *La Nuit du Voleur de Cerveaux [The Night of the Brain Stealer]* (17 July 1975)

2. *Le Masque de Plomb [The Mask of Lead]* (24 July 1975)

3. *Les Tueurs sans Âmes [The Killers Without Souls]* (31 July 1975)

4. *La Mort qui Rampait sur les Toits [Death Stalks the Rooftops]* (7 August 1975)

5. *La Marche des Spectres [The Walk of the Spectres]* (14 August 1975)

6. *Le Sang Accusateur [The Accusing Blood]* (21 August 1975)

7. *Le Rapt [The Kidnapping]* (28 August 1975)

8. *Le Secret des Templiers [The Secret of the Templars]* (4 September 1975)
DIR: Georges **Franju**; WRI: Jacques Champreux.
CAST: Jacques Champreux (The Faceless Man), Gayle Hunnicut (His girlfriend), Clément Harari (Dr. Dutreuil), Roberto Bruni (Maxime de Borrego), Gert Froebe (Commissioner Sorbier), Josephine Chaplin (Martine Leduc), Patrick Préjean (Séraphin Beauminou), Pierre Collet (Grandmaster), Enzo Fisichella (Inspector Peclet), Henry Soskin (Prof. Petrie).
STORY: Maxime and his girlfriend Martine fight a Fantômas-like villain, the Faceless Man, his girlfriend, and a mad

scientist who can turn people into zombies. Eventually, they find themselves competing to discover the Templars' treasure.

NOTE: An edited version of this series was distributed as a feature film under the title **Nuits Rouges** [*Red Nights*, transl. as *Shadowman*] (col., 105 min., 1973). Jacques Champreux also wrote **Judex** and **Les Compagnons de Baal** (see above).

Les Hordes [The Hordes] (Channel 5, Col., four 90 min. eps., 1991)

1. *La Guerre des Gueux* [*The War of the Peasants*] (13 March 1991)

2. *Les Hordes Noires* [*The Black Hordes*] (14 March 1991)

3. *Les Hordes Blanches* [*The White Hordes*] (21 March 1991)

4. *Les Hordes d'Acier* [*The Steel Hordes*] (27 March 1991)
DIR: Jean-Claude Missiaen; WRI: Jacques Zelde, Joël **Houssin**, Daniel Riche, Jean-Luc Fromental, J.-C. Missiaen, based on the novel by Jacques **Zelde**.
CAST: François Dunoyer, Corinne Touzet, Souad Amidou, Simon Eine, Jean-Pierre Kalfon, Philippe Lemaire, Féodor Atkine, Michel Peyrelon, Philippe Laudenbach, Jean-Claude Bouillaud, Bernard Freyd, Jean-Pierre Malo, Dominique Valera, Françoise Brion, Anouk Ferjac, Nils Tavernier, Jacques Ferrière, Pierre Londiche, Gérard Sergue, Louis Navarre.
STORY: in a post-apocalyptic future, hordes of beggars spread chaos and violence. a policeman (Dunoyer) infiltrates the hordes to find their mysterious leader (Lemaire). A conflict erupts between the head of the military (Kalfon) and a demagogue (Eine) trying to use the hordes for political power. Eventually, the hordes win, but the new regime is merely a screen for the establishment of a new totalitarian system.
NOTE: Joël Houssin is a prolific science fiction and television writer (see Book 2), who wrote the feature film **Ma Vie Est Un Enfer** (see Chapter I) and the telefilm **Haute Sécurité** (see below). Daniel Riche is a science fiction editor and essayist (see Book 2).

L'Île aux Trente Cercueils see **Leblanc, Maurice**

L'Île Mystérieuse see **Verne, Jules**

L'Italien, ou Le Confessionnal des Pénitents Noirs [The Italian, or the Confessional of the Black Penitents] (A2, Col., six 60 min. eps., 1977)

1. *L'Italien* (1 July 1977)

2. *L'Enlèvement* [*The Kidnapping*] (8 July 1977)

3. *L'Évasion* [*The Escape*] (15 July 1977)

4. *La Maison du Pêcheur* [*The Fisherman's House*] (22 July 1977)

5. *Le Saint-Office* [*The Holy See*] (29 July 1977)

6. *Révélations* (5 August 1977)
DIR: Alain Boudet; WRI: Marcel Moussy, based on the novel by Ann Radcliffe.
CAST: Pierre-François Pistorio, Aniouta Florent, Maurice Garrel, Odile Versois, Francis Claude, Marcel Imhof, Germaine Delbat.
STORY: The adventures of two star-crossed lovers in 18th century Italy.
NOTE: Adaptation of the classic gothic novel by Ann Radcliffe, published in 1797.

James, Henry (TF 1, Col., two 55 min. eps., 1976)

1. *De Grey* (20 March 1976)
DIR: Claude **Chabrol**; WRI: Roger Grenier.
CAST: Hélène Perdrière, Daniel Lecourtois, Catherine Jourdan, Yves Lefèvre.
STORY: An ancient family curse plagues two young lovers.

2. *Owen Wingrave* (17 April 1976)
DIR/WRI: Paul Seban.
CAST: Mathieu Carrière, Bernard Giraudeau, Patrick Legal, Jean Boissery, Pierre Le Rumeur, Danièle Girard, Louise Conte.
STORY: A young man dies of fright.
NOTE: For other Henry James adaptations, see la **Chambre Verte** and **Le Tour d'Écrou** in Chapter I, and television adaptations of la **Redevance du Fantôme** and **Le Tour d'Écrou** under Telefilms below.

Joseph Balsamo (ORTF 1, Col., seven 52-min. eps., 8 January–19 February 1973)
DIR: André Hunebelle; WRI: Pierre Nivollet, based on the novel by Alexandre **Dumas**.
CAST: Jean Marais (Balsamo), Udo Kier (Gilbert), Henri Guisol (Taverney), Doris Kunstmann (Andrée), Bernard Alane (Philippe), Louise Marleau (Du Barry), Olympia Carlisi (Lorenza), Léonce Corne (Althotas), Guy Tréjean (Louis XV).
STORY: Alchemist and fortune-teller Joseph Balsamo plots the downfall of the French monarchy in the days of Louis XV, using the mediumistic powers of his wife, Lorenza, and manipulating the greedy mistress of the king.
NOTE: Alexandre Dumas is the popular writer who created the *Three Musketeers* and the *Count of Monte-Cristo* (see Book 2).

Leblanc, Maurice
Popular writer Maurice **Leblanc** is the creator of gentleman-burglar Arsène Lupin, the French equivalent of Sherlock Holmes. (In fact, Holmes himself appears several times

in the Lupin novels in the transparent guise of "Herlock Sholmes.") While Arsène Lupin does not, properly speaking, feature any supernatural or *fantastique* elements, its preeminence in pulp fiction warrants its inclusion in this filmography. See Book 2. Also see Chapter I for feature film adaptations.

Arsène Lupin (ORTF 2, Col., twenty-six 60 min. eps., 1971, 1973-74)

REGULAR CAST: George Descrières (Lupin), Yvon Bouchard (Grognard) and Marthe Keller (Natacha), Roger Carel (Guerchard) (French eps. only).

First Season:

1. *Le Bouchon de Cristal [The Cristal Topper]* (18 March 1971)
   DIR: Jean-Pierre Decourt; WRI: Jacques Nahum, René Wheeler.
   GUEST CAST: Daniel Gelin, Nadine Alari.
   STORY: A member of parliament blackmails the government with secret information.
   NOTE: Based on Book 6, 1912.

2. *Victor de la Brigade Mondaine [Victor from the Vice Squad]* (25 March 1971)
   DIR: Jean-Pierre Decourt; WRI: Claude Brûlé.
   GUEST CAST: Bernard Lavalette, Pierre Massimi.
   STORY: Lupin impersonates a police detective.
   NOTE: Based on Book 19, 1934.

3. *Arsène Lupin contre Herlock Sholmes: Le Diamant Bleu [Arsène Lupin vs. Herlock Sholmes: The Blue Diamond]* (1st April 1971)
   DIR: Jean-Pierre Decourt; WRI: Claude Brûlé.
   GUEST CAST: Henri Virlojeux (Sholmes), Charles Millot.
   STORY: Lupin and Sholmes match wits.
   NOTE: Based on Book 2, 1908.

4. *L'Arrestation d'Arsène Lupin [The Capture of Arsène Lupin]* (8 April 1971)
   DIR: Jean-Pierre Decourt; WRI: Claude Brûlé.
   GUEST CAST: William Sabatier, Robert André.
   STORY: Lupin is arrested aboard a transalantic ship.
   NOTE: Based on a short story included in Book 1, 1907.

5. *L'Agence Barnett [The Barnett Agency]* (15 April 1971)
   DIR: Jean-Pierre Decourt; WRI: Jacques Nahum, René Wheeler.
   GUEST CAST: Jacques Balutin, Teddy Bilis.
   STORY: Lupin impersonates a private eye.
   NOTE: Based on Book 15, 1928.

6. *La Fille aux Yeux Verts [The Girl with Green Eyes]* (22 April 1971)
   DIR: Dieter Lemmel; WRI: Albert Simonin, Rolf & Alexandra Becker.
   GUEST CAST: Kathrin Ackermann, Josef Fröhlich.

   STORY: Lupin pursues the secret of the fountain of youth.
   NOTE: German episode. Based on Book 14, 1927.

7. *La Chaîne Brisée [The Broken Chain]* (29 April 1971)
   DIR: Paul Cammermans; WRI: Jean Marcillac, Jacques Armand.
   GUEST CAST: Sjoukje Hooymaayer, Fons Rademakers.
   NOTE: Dutch episode. Original story.

8. *La Femme aux Deux Sourires [The Woman with Two Smiles]* (6 May 1971)
   DIR: Marcello Baldi; WRI: Albert Simonin, Duccio Tessari, Adriano Barraco.
   GUEST CAST: Raffaela Cara, Mario Bernardi.
   STORY: Lupin pursues a mysterious woman.
   NOTE: Italian episode. Based on Book 18, 1933.

9. *La Chimère du Calife [The Caliph's Chimera]* (13 May 1971)
   DIR: Dieter Lemmel; WRI: Albert Simonin, Rolf & Alexandra Becker.
   GUEST CAST: Gunnar Moller, Bernd Schäfer.
   NOTE: German episode. Original story.

10. *Une Femme Contre Arsène Lupin [A Woman vs. Arsène Lupin]* (20 May 1971)
    DIR: Tony Flaadt; WRI: Jacques Armand.
    GUEST CAST: Louis Arbessier, Juliette Mills, François Simon.
    NOTE: Dutch episode. Original story.

11. *Les Anneaux de Cagliostrio [The Rings of Cagliostro]* (27 May 1971)
    DIR: Wolf Dietrich; WRI: Georges Grammont, Wolf & Alexandra Becker.
    GUEST CAST: Christine Buchegger, Hans Holt, Kitty Speiser.
    NOTE: German episode. Original story.

12. *Les Tableaux de Tornbüll [The Paintings of Tornbüll]* (3 June 1971)
    DIR: Dieter Lemmel; WRI: Georges Grammont, Rolf & Alexandra Becker.
    GUEST CAST: Kathrin Ackermann, Hubert Mittendorf, Conny Collins.
    NOTE: German story. Original story.

13. *Le Sept de Coeur [The Seven of Hearts]* (19 June 1971)
    DIR: Jean-Louis Colant; WRI: Nathan Grigorieff.
    GUEST CAST: Janine Patrick, Roger Dutoit, Raoul de Manez (Maurice Leblanc).
    STORY: Lupin tells Maurice Leblanc how he recovered the plans of a secret weapon.
    NOTE: This is based on a short story included in Book 1, 1907.

Second Season:

14. *Herlock Sholmes Lance un Défi [Herlock Sholmes Throws a Challenge]* (18 December 1973)

DIR: Jean-Pierre Desagnat; WRI: Claude Brûlé.
GUEST CAST: Henri Virlojeux (Sholmes), Sophie Agacinski, Bernard Dhéran.
STORY: Lupin and Sholmes match wits again.
NOTE: This is based on another story included in Book 2, 1908.

15. *Arsène Lupin Prend des Vacances* [*Arsène Lupin Takes a Vacation*] (20 December 1973)
DIR: Jean-Pierre Desagnat; WRI: Nathan Gregorieff, Albert Simonin.
GUEST CAST: Claude Degliame, Daniel Sarky.
STORY: Lupin seeks the secret of "813."
NOTE: This is based on Book 5, 1910.

16. *Le Mystère de Gesvres* [*The Mystery of Gesvres*] (22 December 1973)
DIR: Jean-Pierre Desagnat; WRI: Albert Simonin.
GUEST CAST: Bernard Giraudeau (Beautrelet), Thérèse Liotard.
STORY: Lupin hides behind the secret of the "Hollow Needle."
NOTE: Based on Book 4, published in 1909.

17. *Le Secret de l'Aiguille* [*The Secret of the Needle*] (25 December 1973)
DIR: Jean-Pierre Desagnat; WRI: Albert Simonin.
GUEST CAST: Bernard Gireaudeau (Beautrelet), Henri Virlojeux (Sholmes), Catherine Rouvel.
STORY: Sholmes and Beautrelet compete to solve the mystery of the "Hollow Needle."
NOTE: Same as Ep. 16.

18. *L'Homme au Chapeau Noir* [*The Man with the Black Hat*] (27 December 1973)
DIR: Jean-Pierre Desagnat; WRI: Claude Brûlé.
STORY: Lupin and Sholmes match wits again.
NOTE: This is based another story included in Book 2, 1908.

19. *L'Écharpe Rouge* [*The Red Scarf*] (29 December 1973)
DIR: Jean-Pierre Desagnat; WRI: Claude Brûlé.
GUEST CAST: Sacha Pitoeff, Prudence Harrington.
STORY: Lupin seeks a precious sapphire.
NOTE: This is based on a short story included in Book 7, 1913.

20. *La Demeure Mystérieuse* [*The Mysterious Residence*] (5 January 1974)
DIR: Jean-Pierre Desagnat; WRI: Georges Berlot.
GUEST CAST: Evelyne Dress, Marika Green.
STORY: Lupin solves the mystery of an ancient house.
NOTE: Based on Book 16, 1929.

21. *Les Huit Coups de l'Horloge* [*The Eight Strikes of the Clock*] (12 January 1974)
DIR: Jean-Pierre Desagnat; WRI: Robert Scipion, Claude Brûlé.

GUEST CAST: Corinne Le Poulain.
STORY: Lupin unmasks a serial killer.
NOTE: Based on Book 12, 1923.

22. *La Dame au Chapeau à Plumes* [*The Lady with the Feathered Hat*] (19 January 1974)
DIR: Wolf Dietrich; WRI: Rolf & Alexandra Becker.
GUEST CAST: Fritz Muliar, Christine Böhm.
NOTE: German episode. Original story.

23. *La Danseuse de Rottenburg* [*The Dancing Girl from Rottenburg*] (26 January 1974)
DIR: Fritz Umgelter; WRI: Rolf & Alexandra Becker.
GUEST CAST: Dagmar Heller, Charlote Kerr.
NOTE: German episode. Original story.

24. *Le Film Révélateur* [*The Revealing Film*] (2 February 1974)
DIR: Fritz Umgelter; WRI: Rolf & Alexandra Becker.
GUEST CAST: Maria Korber, Marie Versini.
NOTE: German episode. Original story.

25. *Double Jeu* [*Double Game*] (9 February 1974)
DIR: Fritz Umgelter; WRI: Rolf & Alexandra Becker.
GUEST CAST: Andréa Dahmen, Gunther Sporrle.
NOTE: German episode. Original story.

26. *Le Coffre-Fort de Madame Imbert* [*The Safe of Mrs. Imbert*] (16 February 1974)
DIR: Jean-Pierre Desagnat; WRI: Albert Simonin.
GUEST CAST: Pascale Roberts, Jean-Pierre Rambal.
STORY: Lupin commits a daring burglary.
NOTE: This is based on a short story included in Book 1, published in 1907.

Arsène Lupin Joue et Perd [*Arsène Lupin Plays and Loses*] (A2, Col., six 52 min. eps., 12–27 December 1980)

DIR: Alexandre Astruc; WRI: Alexandre Astruc, Roland Laudenbach.
CAST: Jean-Claude Brialy (Lupin), Christiane Kruger (Dolores), Maurice Biraud (Weber), François Maistre (Valenglay), Marco Perrin (Gourel), François Perrot (Altenheim), Jacques Dacqmine, Philippe Mareuil, Elyette Damian, Sacha Briquet, Jeanne Goupil, Hubert Deschamps, Serge Berry, Gérard Buhr, René Bovloc, Valérie Pascal.
STORY: Lupin seeks to solve mystery of "813," which might change the map of Europe.
NOTE: Based on Book 5, 1910.

Les Nouveaux Exploits d'Arsène Lupin (France 3, Col., 90 min. eps., 1996–97)

NOTE: This series is currently in production. Our episode guide is therefore incomplete.
REGULAR CAST: François Dunoyer (Lupin), Paul Le Person, Franck Capillery.

1. Herlock Sholmes s'en mêle [Herlock Sholmes Meddles]
    DIR: Alain Nahum; WRI: Jacques Avanac, Albert Kantof, Philippe Delannoy.
    CAST: Vania Tzvetkova, Joseph Sartchadjiev.

2. Arsène Lupin Rencontre Freud [Arsène Lupin Meets Freud]
    DIR: Vittorio Barino; WRI: Albert Kantof, Jacques Nahum.
    CAST: Eva Grimaldi, Ugo Pagliai, Rugger de Daninos, Silvano Tranquilli, Tamara Dona, Rosetta Salata, Pier Senarica

François Dunoyer as Lupin.

3. Le Masque de Jade [The Mask of Jade]
    DIR: Philippe Condroyer; WRI: Philippe & Mariette Condroyer.
    CAST: Charlotte Kady, Corinne Touzet, Bruno Raffaelli, Yann Babilee, Aurelien Wiik, Christine Lemler.

4. La Robe de Diamants [The Diamond-Studded Dress]
    DIR: Nicolas Ribowski; WRI: Jacques Nahum, Philippe Delannoy.
    CAST: Michèle Laroque, Patrice Kerbrat, Thiam, Roland Lesaffre, Antoine Dulery.

5. Requins à la Havane [Sharks in Havana]
    DIR: Alain Nahum; WRI: Jacques Avanac, Albert Kantof.
    CAST: Jacqueline Arenal, Carlos Cruz, Broselandia Hernandez Boudet.

6. Les Souterrains Étrusques [The Etruscean Tunnels]
    DIR: Vittorio de Sisti; WRI: Jacques Nahum, Christian Watton, based on an idea by Richard Caron.
    CAST: Vittoria Belvedere, Pier Paolo Capponi, Augusto Zucchi, Stafania Orsola Garrello, Paolo Maria Scalondro, Marina Giulia Cavalli, Vincenzo Crocitti.

7. La Tabatière de l'Empereur [The Emperor's Snuff Box]
    DIR: Alain Nahum; WRI: Jacques Avanac, Albert Kantof.
    CAST: Edward Zentara, Henryk Bista, Katarzyna Walter, Agnieszka Wagner, Gabriela Kownacka.

Dorothée, Danseuse de Corde [Dorothy the Rope Dancer] (A2, Col., three 60 min. eps., 1983)

1. L'Assassin du Prince d'Argonne [The Murderer of the Prince of Argonne] (21 December 1983)

2. In Robore Fortuna (22 December 1983)

3. Le Testament du Marquis de Beaugreval (28 December 1982)
    DIR: Jacques Fansten; WRI: Michel Favart, Jacques Fansten.
    CAST: Fanny Bastien (Dorothée), Macha Meril, Féodor Atkine, Patrick Fierry, Jean-Denis Filliozat, Bruno Bouillon, Arnaud Giordano.
    STORY: A young circus acrobat solves the mystery of the treasure of the Kings of France.
    NOTE: This is a sequel to Book 13 in the *Arsène Lupin* series, which does not feature Arsène Lupin.

L'Île aux Trente Cercueils [The Island of the Thirty Coffins] (A2, Col., six 60 min. eps., 21 September–6 October 1979)

DIR: Marcel Cravenne; WRI: Robert Scipion.
    CAST: Claude Jade (Véronique), Yves Beneyton (Philippe), Georges Marchal (d'Hergemont), Jean-Paul Zehnacker (Vorski), Julie Philippe (Elfide), Edith Perret (Gertrude), Pierrette Thévenon (Clémence), Peter Semler (Otto), Armand Babel (Corréjou), Jean Le Mouel (LeGoff), Jen-René Gossart (Conrad).
    STORY: Veronique is stranded on a desolate island off the coast of Britanny, when an ancient curse appears to be coming to life. In reality, the villainous Vorski seeks the secret of a miraculous stone.
    NOTE: Based on Book 10 in the *Arsène Lupin* series, the character of Lupin was removed from this television version for legal reasons.

Leroux, Gaston

Gaston **Leroux** is a major writer of the *fantastique*. His most famous novel is, without a doubt, the notorious *Le Fantôme de l'Opéra [Phantom of the Opera]*. Many of his works have been adapted for film or television, starting with Victorin **Jasset**'s 1913 short feature, ***Balaoo, ou des Pas au Plafond*** (see Chapter I). We have not included here the adaptations of Leroux's more conventional mysteries (such as ***L'Homme Qui Revient de Loin*** [*The Man Who Returned from Far Away*]), or the adventures of his other fictional hero, the former convict *Chéri-Bibi*. Also see Book 2 and Chapter I for feature film adaptations.

Le Coeur Cambriolé [The Stolen Heart] (A2, Col., 90 min., 20 June 1986)

DIR/WRI: Michel **Subiela**.
    CAST: Yann Babilée, Catherine Erhardy, Georges Marchal, Arthur Denberg, Roger Carel, Marc François, Olivia Brunaux, Marcello Leone.
    STORY: A painter uses his psychic powers to steal a young man's bride.
    NOTE: ***Le Coeur Cambriolé*** was also adapted on the anthology series ***Les Soirées du Bungalow*** [*The Evenings at the Bungalow*] (see below).

La Double Vie de Théophraste Longuet [The Double Life of Théophraste Longuet] (TF1, Col., three 90 min. eps., 1981)

1. Le Mystère [The Mystery] (27 October 1981)

2. Le Combat [The Fight] (29 October 1981)

3. Le Trésor [The Treasure] (30 October 1981)
DIR: Yannick Andrei; WRI: Jean-Claude **Carrière**.
CAST: Jean Carmet (Théophraste), Geneviève Fontanel (Marcelline), Gabriel Cattand, Nicolas Silberg (Cartouche), Michel Duchaussoy, Gabriel Jabbour, Jean-Claude Carrière (Eliphas), Marie Bunel, Nicole Carrière.
STORY: Théophraste, a retired merchant, finds himself possessed by the spirit of notorious 18th-century highwayman Cartouche.

Le Fantôme de l'Opéra [The Phantom of the Opera] (A2, Col., 100 min., 28 December 1980)
DIR: Dirk Sanders; CHOREOGRAPHY: Roland Petit; MUSIC: Marcel Landowski; ART DIRECTION: Patrick Flynn.
NOTE: Ballet in 2 acts and 12 scenes.

Le Fauteuil Hanté [The Haunted Chair] (ORTF 1, Col., 115 min., 27 June 1970)
DIR/WRI: Pierre Bureau.
CAST: Jacques Grello (Lalouette), Lucien Nat (Loustalot), Jean Mermet (Dédé), Sacha Pitoeff (Eliphas), Renaud Mary (Patard), Noël Roquevert, Olivier Hussenot.
STORY: A mad academician uses strange weapons to kill those who have discovered his secret: His son is the real inventor of his designs.

La Femme au Collier de Velours [The Woman with the Velvet Necklace] (FR 3, Col., 4 September 1986)
DIR: Jean Sagols; WRI: Jacques Tephany.
CAST: Pierre Vaneck, Rebecca Pauly, Corinne Dacla, Didier Sauvegrain.
STORY: Gothic tale.

L'Homme de la Nuit [The Night Man] (A2, Col., four 60 min. eps., 9–30 September 1983)
DIR: Juan Luis **Buñuel**; WRI: Jacques Armand.
CAST: George Wilson (Maxime Broom), Bulle Ogier (Marthe), Claude Giraud (Franck), Véronique Delbourg (Maria), Mathieu Barbey, Corinne Le Poulain.
STORY: in 1917 Russia, two lovers (Giraud, Delbourg) get rid of the husband (Wilson). Twenty years later, he returns to revenge himself as a mysterious masked man.

La Poupée Sanglante [The Bloody Puppet] (A2, Col., six 60 min. eps., 17 September–22 October 1976)
DIR: Marcel Cravenne; WRI: Robert Scipion.

CAST: Jean-Paul Zehnacker (Benedict Masson), Yolande Folliot (Christine), Ludwig Gaum (Gabriel), Georges Wod (Marquis), Édith Scob (Marquise), Dominique Leverd (Jacques), Julien Verdier (Gaillard), Sacha Pitoeff (Sahib Khan), Cathy Rosier, Georges Lycan, Gabriel Gobin, Germaine Delbat, Florence Brière, Jacqueline Rouillard, Armontel, Jean Rupert.
STORY: The brain of Benedict Masson, a man unjustly guillotined, is transplanted into an android body. He later helps expose and defeat a vampiric cult led by a depraved nobleman (Wod).

Le Roi Mystère [King Mystery] (FR 3, Col., four 90 min. eps., 1991)

1. La Guillotine (23 April 1991)

2. Le Perroquet [The Parakeet] (30 April 1991)

3. La Dent Creuse [The Hollow Tooth] (7 May 1991)

4. Le Châtiment [The Punishment] (14 May 1991)
DIR: Paul **Planchon**; WRI: Marcel Jullian.
CAST: Christopher Bowen (King Mystery/Robert Pascal), Philippe Bouclet (Sinnimari), Piéral (Mac Callan), Aurèle Doazan (Gabrielle), Éva Mazauric (Liliane), Patrick Polvey, Dominique Pinon, Patrick Burgel, Carina Barone, Yan Epstein, Fred Ulysse, Amadeus August, Gaby Fuchs.
STORY: The mysterious King of the Parisian underworld challenges the evil schemes of the corrupt Imperial Prosecutor.

Rouletabille
STORY: Young journalist Rouletabille investigates murders committed in mysterious, often uncanny, circumstances.

1. Le Mystère de la Chambre Jaune [The Mystery of the Yellow Room] (ORTF 1, B&W., 90 min., 27 November 1965)
DIR: Jean Kerchbron; WRI: Jean Gruault, Jean Kerchbron.
CAST: Claude Brasseur (Rouletabille), François Maistre (Larsan), Marika Green (Mathilde), Lucien Nat, Géo Wallery, Jean Champion.

2. Le Parfum de la Dame En Noir [The Scent of the Lady in Black] (ORTF 1, B&W., ten 15 min. eps., 3–14 March 1966)
DIR: Yves **Boisset**; WRI: Bernard Dabry, Guy Jorré.
CAST: Philippe Ogouz (Rouletabille), Raymond Loyer (Darzac), Nicole Maurey (Mathilde), Aimé Demarch, Lucien Raimbourg, Tania Lopert, René Lefèvre.

3. Rouletabille chez le Tsar [Rouletabille and the Czar] (ORTF 1, B&W., ten 15 min. eps., 17–30 March 1966)
DIR: Jean-Charles Lagneau; WRI: Bernard Dabry, Guy Jorré.
CAST: Philippe Ogouz (Rouletabille), Maria Meriko

(Matrena), Julien Guiomar (Trebassof), Paloma Matta, Georges Claisse, Pierre Tornade.

4. *Rouletabille chez les Bohémiens [Rouletabille and the Gypsies]* (ORTF 1, B&W., ten 15 min. eps., 31 March–13 April 1966)

DIR: Robert Mazoyer; WRI: Bernard Dabry, Guy Jorré.

CAST: Philippe Ogouz (Rouletabille), Tania Balachova (Zina), Judith Magre (Calista), Caroline Cellier, Annie Savarin, Henri Piégay, Henri Virlojeux, Jacques Robiolles.

NOTE: Also see Chapters I and V for other adaptations.

Jacques Rosny as The White Wolf.

Le Loup Blanc [The White Wolf] (FR 3, Col., three 55 min. eps., 1977–78)

1. *L'Albinos [The Albino]* (30 December 1977)

2. *La Forêt de Rennes [The Forest of Rennes]* (31 December 1977)

3. *Jean Blanc* (1st January 1978)

DIR: Jean-Pierre Decourt; WRI: J.-P. Decourt, Henri de Turenne, based on the novel by Paul **Féval**.

CAST: Jacques Rosny (Jean Blanc/Loup Blanc), Henri Lambert, Michel Vitold, Claude Giraud, Maryvonne Schiltz, Jean Leuvrais, Sébastien Foure.

STORY: In 18th century Britanny, the peasants revolt against the Regency, led by a mysterious Robin Hood-like figure hiding behind the mask of a white wolf.

NOTE: For further information on Paul Féval, see *Les Habits Noirs* above. *Le Loup Blanc* does not feature any specific fantasy elements, except for the *Zorro*-like theme of revenge and secret identities.

Le Monde Enchanté d'Isabelle [Isabelle's Enchanted World] (ORTF 1, Col., thirteen 30 min., Eps., Avril–June 1973)

DIR/WRI: Jean-Claude Youri.

CAST: Isabelle Youri (Isabelle), Jean Topart, Laurence Badie, Léo Campion, Fabrice Bruno.

STORY: A little girl explores a fantasy world.

Le Mutant (TF1, Col., six 60 min. eps., 15 June–20 July 1978)

DIR: Bernard Toublanc-Michel; WRI: Alain **Page**.

CAST: Fanny Ardant (Jeanne Laurent), Bernard Woringer (Walter), Jacques Dacqmine (Prof. Masson), Nicolas Pignon (Saül Masson), Idwig Stephane (Henri Muller), Anton Diffring (Martin O'Brien), Haydée Politoff (Marie Morand), Stéphane Bouy, Philippe Forquet, Gilles Kohler, Barbara Sommers, Laure Moutoussamy, Rudolph Gessler, Matt Carney, Billy Kearns.

STORY: The mysterious head of an equally mysterious organisation hires Walter to research the life of a mutant boy, Saül Masson, who grew up to become a genius. Eventually, the "head" is revealed to be Saül, who is plotting to take over mankind with mind-controlling implants.

NOTE: Alain Page also wrote *Les Compagnons d'Eleusis* (above) and *Le Bal des Affamés* (see Chapter III). a novelisation of *Le Mutant* written by **Page** was published in 1978.

Le Mystérieux Docteur Cornelius [The Mysterious Dr. Cornelius] (A2, Col., six 60 min. eps., 16 September–21 October 1984)

DIR: Maurice **Frydland**; WRI: Jean-Pierre Petrolacci, Jean-Daniel Simon, Pierre Nivollet, based on the novel by Gustave **Le Rouge**.

CAST: Gérard Desarthe (Cornelius Kramm), Jean Bouise (Fritz Kramm), François Eric Gendron (Harry Dorgan), Hugues Quester (Barruch Jorgel), Renzo Palmer (William Dorgan), Robert Rimbaud (Bondonnat), Caroline Sihol (Isadora Jorgel), Georges Geret (Fred Jorgel), Maurice Vaudaux (Joe Dorgan), Maria Blanco (Frédéricque Bondonnat), Anne Fontaine (Andrée de Maubreuil), Enzo Robutti (M. de Maubreuil), Jacques François (Lord Burydan).

STORY: Two millionaires, their families, and friends fight the evil schemes of the mad scientist Dr. Cornelius Kramm, his brother Fritz, and their secret organisation, the Red Hand, in a series of globe-spanning encounters.

NOTE: See Book 2. Also see Chapter III for a radio adaptation.

Mycènes, Celui Qui Vient du Futur [Mycenes, He Who Comes from the Future] (ORTF 1, Col., two 90 min., Eps., 1972)

1. *La Planète Fermée [The Closed Planet]* (29 January)

2. *La Piste Sans Étoiles [The Starless Arena]* (19 February)

DIR: François Chatel; WRI: André Michel, Louis Rognoni, Stéfan **Wul** (ep. 2 only).

CAST: Armand Ablanalp (Mycènes), Dominique Leverd, Catherine Ciriez, Jean Coste, Frédéric Lambre.

STORY: Mycènes, a robot android from the future, comes to learn about our era.

NOTE: Originally slated for thirteen episodes, this series was cancelled after only two because of its low ratings and viewers' negative reactions. Stéfan Wul is a major science fiction writer (see Book 2). Two of his novels were turned into animated features by René **Laloux** (see Chapter IV).

Noires Sont Les Galaxies [Dark Are the Galaxies]

(A2, four 60 min. eps., April 1981)

DIR: Daniel Moosmann; WRI: Jacques Armand.

CAST: Richard Fontana, Catherine Leprince, François Perrot, Catriona McCall, Stéphane Bouy, Maryvonne Schiltz, Raoul Guillet, Roger Riffard.

STORY: A young doctor discovers that alien exiles have been stealing human corpses to inhabit them. But the exiles are themselves hunted by hostile aliens from their homeworld.

L'Oeil de la Nuit [The Eye of Night] (A2, Col., eight

30 min. eps., 1979, 1981)

DIR/WRI: Jean-Pierre Richard.

Regular CAST: Gérard Séty, Fred Personne, Maurice Bourbon, Jean Bollery.

STORY: Four men meet at the Inn of Legends to tell stories.

1. Le Ballet Inachevé [The Unfinished Ballet] (8 October 1979)

GUEST CAST: Unknown.

STORY: A poor musician hears a man whistling the music he has just composed.

2. Le Chien de la Colonelle [The Colonel's Wife's Dog] (13 October 1979)

GUEST CAST: Unknown.

STORY: A colonel is addicted to gambling, much to his wife's dismay.

3. Le Vin des Carpates [The Wine from the Carpathians] (20 October 1979)

GUEST CAST: Unknown.

STORY: A man visits a haunted castle.

4. La Locataire des Bois [The Tenant in the Woods] (27 October 1979) (previously aired on 23 July 1978 as *La Rose Impossible* [*The Impossible Rose*])

GUEST CAST: Benoist Brione, Jenny Arasse, Maurice Jaquemont.

STORY: A young biker picks up a mysterious female hitchhiker.

5. On L'Appellait l'Américain [They Called Him the American] (17 December 1981)

GUEST CAST: Raymond Bussières, Jérôme Zucca.

STORY: A strange friendship develops between a young sailor and an old tramp.

6. Le Fantôme Est Amoureux [The Ghost Is in Love] (18 December 1981)

GUEST CAST: Jean Bouin, Thérèse Liotard.

STORY: A down on his luck comedian, hired to play a ghost, meets a real ghost.

7. La Fin d'un Cauchemar [The End of a Nightmare] (21 December 1981)

GUEST CAST: Jacques Duby, Pascale Roberts.

STORY: A travel agent is plagued by a recurring nightmare.

8. Le Syndrome de Cendrillon [The Cinderella Syndrome] (22 December 1981)

GUEST CAST: Guy Marchand.

STORY: A traveling salesman accepts the hospitality of two strange sisters.

La Poupée Sanglante see Leroux, Gaston

Rocambole (ORTF 2, B&W., Three Seasons of twenty-

six 15-min. eps., 1964–65)

1st Season: L'Héritage Mystérieux [The Mysterious Inheritance] (18 April–7 May 1964).

2nd Season: Les Étrangleurs [The Stranglers] (8 May–9 June 1964).

3rd Season: La Belle Jardinière [The Beautiful Gardener] (15 April–10 May 1965).

DIR: Jean-Pierre Decourt; WRI: J.-P. Decourt, Anne-Marie Salerne, Louis Falavigna, based on the novels by **Ponson du Terrail**.

REGULAR CAST: Pierre Vernier (Rocambole), Jean Topart (Sir Williams), Marianne Girard (Baccarat), René Clermont (Beaupréau), Alain Dekock (Marmouset), Jean Heynau (Mourax), Paul Bisciglia (Bistoquet), Michel Puterflam (Mort-des-Braves), Jeanne Herviale (La Fipart).

GUEST CAST: Michel Beaune (de Kergaz), Jacques Dynam (Bastien), Cécile Vassort (Cerise), Raoul Curet (Colar), Henri Piegay (Fernand), Jacqueline Corot (Jeanne), Marie-France Boyer (Hermine) (1st Season); Jean-Paul Moulinot (Lord Charring), Hubert Deschamps (Murph), Jean Negroni (Guhri), Mario Pilar (Nively), Raoul Curet (Le Patissier), Élisabeth Wiener (Gipsy), Nadine Alari (Milady) (2nd Season); Francine Bergé (Belle Jardinière), Michel Ruhl (Volovodine), Julien Guiomar (Capendoc), Jacques Seiler (Artoff), Bernard Ceyleron (Serguei), Jean Degrave (Illyne) (3rd Season).

STORY: Taking place in the mid–19th century, this serial-like series narrates the adventures of gentleman-burglar Rocambole against his former master and enemy, the arch-villain Sir Williams and his adversary-turned-lover, Baccarat. In the first season, Rocambole rescues a young heiress. In the second season, he thwarts a gang of Thugees. In the third season, he becomes involved in a war between two Russian secret societies.

NOTE: Victor-Alexis Ponson du Terrail is, with Paul **Féval**, one of the most famous serial writers in French literary history (see Book 2). His other genre work, la *Baronne Trépassée* [*The Dead Baroness*], was adapted for television as **Le Veneur Noir** (see below).

Rouletabille see Leroux, Gaston

Le Sérum de Bonté [The Happiness Serum] (RTF 1, B&W., thirteen 30-min. eps., October-December 1960)
DIR: Jean-Daniel Norman; WRI: Pierre Armand.
CAST: Jean Richard (Dupont), Paulette Dubost, Evelyne Ker, Nicolas Ray, Hélène Vallier.
STORY: In this sitcom, the French government tests on an average family a new drug that is intended to improve people.

Les Soirées du Bungalow [The Evenings at the Bungalow] (ORTF 1, Col., four 60-min. eps., 1969)
REGULAR CAST: Tom Duggan, Gianni Esposito, François Maistre, Jean-Roger Caussimon, Olivier Hussenot, Muse d'Albray.
STORY: Guests at a bungalow tell each other fantasy stories.

1. *La Merveilleuse Histoire du Major Brown [The Marvellous Story of Major Brown]* (26 April 1969)
DIR: Roger Iglésis; WRI: Roger Iglésis, Louis **Pauwels,** based on a story by G. K. Chesterton.
GUEST CAST: Vytte Pedersen, Robert Le Beal, Sacha Pitoeff, Dominique Bernard.
STORY: A doctor meets a ghost.

2. *Histoire d'une Famille de Tyrone [The Story of a Family from Tyrone]* (26 April 1969)
DIR: Roger Iglésis; WRI: Roger Iglésis, Louis Pauwels, based on a story by Sheridan Le Fanu.
GUEST CAST: Marika Green, François Perrot, Katharina Reen.
STORY: An Irish castle is haunted.

3. *Le Coeur Cambriolé [The Stolen Heart]* (7 September 1969)
DIR: Roger Iglésis; WRI: Roger Iglésis, Louis Pauwels, based on the novel by Gaston **Leroux.**
GUEST CAST: Giani Esposito, Juliette Villard, Jean-Pierre Jorris, Raymond Meunier.
STORY: A painter uses his psychic powers to steal a young man's bride.
NOTE: Also see **Leroux, Gaston.**

4. *L'Homme Hanté [The Haunted Man]* (22 December 1969)
DIR: Roger Iglésis; WRI: Roger Iglésis, Louis Pauwels, Paule de Beaumont, based on a story by Charles Dickens.
GUEST CAST: Jean-Roger Caussimon, Edith Scob, Etienne Bierry, Colette Ripert, Henri Poirier, Yves-Marie Maurin.
STORY: A chemist haunted by his memories, discovers that forgetting the past comes with a price.
NOTE: For further information on Louis Pauwels, see *Le Golem* under Telefilms below.

La Sorcellerie [Witchcraft] (FR 3, Col., three 90 min. eps., October-November 1985)

1. *Un Jour entre Chien et Loups [One Day, Between Dogs and Wolves]*

DIR: Patrick Saglio; WRI: Michel Picard, Alain Doutey.
CAST: Valérie Popesco, Xavier Gélin, Vanessa Vaylord.
STORY: After a car accident in the country, a man's wife disappears.

2. *L'Enfant et les Magiciens [The Child and the Wizards]*
DIR: Philippe Arnal; WRI: Paul Wagner, Philippe Arnal.
CAST: Magali Noël, Etienne Berry, Alexandre Sterling, Alain Libolt.
STORY: A warlock and a witch try to teach their trade to their nephew.

3. *L'Oeil du Sorcier [The Wizard's Eye]* (previously aired on 26 September 1979)
DIR: Alain Dhénault; WRI: Patrick Pesnot, Philippe Alfonsi.
CAST: Christian Barbier, Elina Labourdette, Lucienne Lemarchand, Catherine Lafond, Marie Delarue, Edmond Beauchamps, Roger Riffard.
STORY: A medical doctor who has returned to the country to live, is threatened by local witchcraft.

S.O.S. Terre [SOS Earth] (Television Romande, eight eps., 1966)
DIR/WRI: Germaine Epierre.
CAST: Unknown.
STORY: Children's serial.

Sueurs Froides [Cold Sweat] (Canal Plus, Col., eighteen 30-min. eps, 1988)
NOTE: This anthology series of crime thrillers, hosted by Claude **Chabrol,** included three genre episodes:

2. *La Sublime Aventure [The Sublime Adventure]* (6 February 1988)
DIR/WRI: René **Manzor,** based on a story by Louis C. Thomas.
CAST: Guy Marchand, Frédéric Mitterand, A. Zamberlan.
STORY: People turn into gasses and vanish into thin air.

4. *Toi si Je Voulais [You If I Wanted]* (5 March 1988)
DIR/WRI: Patrice Leconte, based on a story by Louis C. Thomas.
CAST: Gérard Jugnot, Julie Jezequel, Christine Amat, Patrick Baroude, Etienne Fernagut.
STORY: A man discovers that he can wish people dead.

8. *Mise à l'Index [Put On the Black List]* (2 April 1988)
DIR: Bernard Nauer; WRI: Philippe de Chauveron, Bernard Nauer, based on a story by Bruno Léandri.
CAST: Jean Carmet, Eva Darlan, Jean Rougerie, Marc Berman, Ticky Holgado.
STORY: A journalist accidentally uncovers the trafficking of human flesh.
NOTE: Bruno Léandri is a famous French humorist.

Tang (ORTF 2, Col., thirteen 26 min. eps., June 1971)
DIR: André Michel; WRI: Jacques Faurie.
CAST: Valery Inkijinoff (Tang), Abbie Kerani (Kyoo), Xavier Gelin (André), Catherine Samie (Léna), Patrick Préjean (Marcel), Jacques Galipeau (Carteau).
STORY: A secret organization led by the evil Tang schemes to control an all-powerful weapon dubbed "327" and take over the world.

La Tante de Frankenstein [Frankenstein's Aunt]
(FR3, Col., thirteen 30 min. eps., February–April 1990)
DIR: Jurad Jakubisko; WRI: Jurad Jakubisko, Jurad Dietl, Allan Rune Petterson.
CAST: Viveca Kindfors (Aunt Frankenstein), Ferdy Mayne (Dracula), Eddie Constantine, Flavio Bucci, Jacques Herlin, Gail Gatterburg.
STORY: The descendents of Frankenstein attempt to carry on his dream in this satirical series of fantastic adventures.
NOTE: This is an international co-production betwen Austria, the then-Czechoslovakia, the then-West Germany, and France.

Traquenards [Traps] (FR3, Col., thirteen 30 min. eps., December 1987–March 1988)
DIR: Bruno Carrière, Raoul Held, Christian Alba, François Labonté, Jean-Claude Charnay; WRI: Daniel Bertolino, Catherine Viau, Bruno Carrière.
Murée Vive [*Buried Alive*]; CAST: Alexis Martin.
Mort à Minuit [*Dead at Midnight*]; CAST: Thomas Hellman.
L'Héritage Maudit [*The Accursed Inheritance*]; CAST: Michel Vitold.
La Caverne des Disparus [*The Cavern of the Vanished*]; CAST: Jacques Godin.
Trésor de Feu [*Treasure of Fire*]; CAST: Hélène Godin.
Quasimodo; CAST: Marcha Grenon.
Le Chevalier de Passignac; CAST: Sophie Léger.
STORY: Thirteen adolescents manage to extricate themselves from seemingly inescapable traps. Many situations contain genre elements (either fantastic or horrific).
NOTE: French-Canadian co-production.

Le Tribunal de l'Impossible [The Tribunal of the Impossible] (ORTF 1, Col., fourteen 90 min. eps., 1967-74)
PROD: Michel **Subiela**.
NOTE: This anthology of telefilms focused on the uncanny, the paranormal, and the unexplained. It was followed by a round-table discussion between a panel of experts, some "believers," others skeptics.

1. *La Bête du Gévaudan [The Beast of Gevaudan]* (3 October 1967)
   DIR: Yves-André Hubert; WRI: Michel Subiela.

Le Tribunal de l'Impossible: La Bête du Gévaudan.

CAST: André Valmy, Georges Chamarat, Pierre Hatet, Guy Tréjan, Maria Meriko, Yvon Sarray, Jean Violette, Bernadette Lange, André Falcon, Marcel Champel, Claude Richard, Patrick Préjean.
STORY: A legendary wolf-like creature plagues the Gevaudan countryside in 18th-century France.

2. *Le Fabuleux Grimoire de Nicolas Flamel [The Fabulous Grimoir of Nicolas Flamel]* (25 November 1967)
   DIR: Guy Lessertisseur; WRI: Alain Decaux.
   CAST: Paul Crauchet (Flamel), Ariette Gilbert, Roger Crouzet, Lucien Nat, Maurice Bourbon, Georges Riquier, Jacques Lalande, Françoise Dorner, Maurice Garrel, Frank Estange, François Dyrek.
   STORY: Cardinal de Richelieu orders the arrest of the grand-nephew of notorious 14th century alchemist Nicolas Flamel, who may have inherited his ancestor's secrets.
   NOTE: Alain Decaux is a renowned historian.

3. *Les Rencontres du Trianon, ou la Dernière Rose [The Trianon Encounters, or the Last Rose]* (10 February 1968)
   DIR: Roger Kahane; WRI: Francis Lacassin.
   CAST: Louise Conte, Jacqueline Jefford, Jacques Alric, Jean Calve, Denise Benoit, Sylvie Vaneck.
   STORY: Two English tourists appear to have mysteriously been transported back through time for an hour at Versailles Castle.
   NOTE: Francis Lacassin is a well-known comics scholar.

4. *Nostradamus, ou Le Prophète en Son Pays [Nostradamus, or a Prophet in His Own Land]* (11 May 1968)
   DIR: Pierre Badel; WRI: Michel Subiela.
   CAST: Jean Topart (Nostradamus), Rosy Varte, Jean Leuvrais, François Maistre, Catherine Le Couey, Robert Murzeau, Lucien Nat.
   STORY: Was the famous seer a charlatan?

5. *Qui Hantait le Presbytère de Borley? [Who Haunted the Borley Presbytery?]* (30 November 1968)

DIR: Alain Boudet; WRI: Michel **Subiela**.

CAST: Guy Tréjean, Catherine Rich, Jean Obé, Bernadette Lange, Jean Martin, Juliette Mills, Guy Pierauld, Hélène Dieudonné, Madeleine Damiens, Catherine Lafond, Sylvain Joubert.

STORY: A haunted-house case from the late 1920s.

6. *Le Sabbat du Mont d'Etenclin [The Sabbath of Mount Etenclin]* (1st March 1969)

DIR: Michel Subiela; WRI: André Desvallées.

CAST: Edith Garnier, Charles Moulin, Serge Duchez, Roger Guillo, Jean-Pierre Herce, Renée Gardes, Marc de Georgi, Frédérique Ruchaud, André Valmy, Jean Vinci.

STORY: The last witch trial held in France in 1668.

7. *La Passion d'Anne-Catherine Emmerich [The Passion of Anne-Catherine Emmerich]* (29 November 1969)

DIR: Michel Subiela; WRI: Marcelle Maurette.

CAST: Anouk Ferjac, Claude Titre, Bernard Verley, Jacques Monod, Sylvie Bourgoin, Gérard Denizot, Maike Jansen, Erwan Kerne.

STORY: An 18th-century German girl experiences visions of Christ, and bears stigmata of his crucifixion.

8. *Un Esprit Nommé Katie King [A Spirit Called Katie King]* (24 January 1970)

DIR: Pierre Badel; WRI: Hélène Misserly.

CAST: Bulle Ogier, Michel Vitold, Loleh Bellon, Robert Party, Maurice Teynac, Hélène Duc, Raymond Pélissier, Clément Bairam.

STORY: In 1874 London, young medium Florence Cook summons the spirit of Katie King, a girl who died under Cromwell.

9. *Un Mystère Contemporain [A Contemporary Mystery]* (14 March 1970)

DIR: Alain Boudet; WRI: Albert Husson.

CAST: Claude Vernier, Dominique Leverd, Marika Green, Christine Audhuy, Arch Taylor, Jacques Riberolles, Jacques Debary, Martine Ferrière.

STORY: A contemporary Belgian medium helps solve a case of kidnapping and a case of murder.

10. *La Cité d'Is [The City of Ys]* (30 May 1970)

DIR/WRI: Michel Subiela.

CAST: André Valmy, Isa Mercure, Jean-Pierre Herce, Roland Monod, Yvon Sarray, Raoul Guillet, Pierre Rich, Mirès Vincent, Eva Simmonet.

STORY: The legendary city of Ys in Britanny is cursed to be swallowed by the ocean because of the sins of its evil queen, Dahuse.

11. *Le Voleur de Cerveau [The Mind Stealer]* (6 February 1971)

DIR: Alain Boudet; WRI: Francis Lacassin.

CAST: Marcel Cuvelier, Gérard Berner, Geneviève Bray, Nita Klein, Jean Barney, Elisabeth Hary.

STORY: Did a murderer act under someone else's hypnotic control?

12. *La Double Vie de Mlle. de la Faille [The Two Lives of Miss de la Faille]* (9 February 1974)

DIR: Michel Subiela; WRI: André Desvallées.

CAST: Muriel Baptiste, Pierre Le Rumeur, Joël Bion, Mirès Vincent, Pascale Berger, Marcel Champel, Serge Merlin, Régis Outin.

STORY: The young bride of an 18th century nobleman looks uncannily like his former lover, who died several years earlier. Is she merely a look-alike or the reincarnation of the dead girl?

13. *Agathe, ou l'Avenir Rêvé [Agatha, or Dreams of the Future]* (24 August 1974)

DIR: Yves-André Hubert; WRI: Hélène Misserly.

CAST: Douchka, Maud Rayer, Janine Souchon, Van Doude, Guy Gerbaud, Christian de Tilière, Marc Cassot, Patrick Guillaumin, Jean-Pierre Moreux, Simone Landry.

STORY: in 19th century Nîmes, a young girl experiences dreams that uncannily come true.

14. *Le Baquet de Frédéric-Antoine Messmer [Messmer's Bucket]* (7 September 1974)

DIR: Michel Subiela; WRI: Daniel Heran, Michel Berthier.

CAST: Bernard Verley, Nicole Hiss, Roger Crouzet, Olivier Nolin, Philippe Kellerson, Teddy Bilis, Jean Lescot, Gérald Denizot, André Valtier, Gilbert Damien, Georges Aubert.

STORY: The biography of the man who pioneered hypnotism.

NOTE: A fifteenth episode, *Enquête Posthume sur un Vaisseau Fantôme [Posthumous Investigation of a Ghost Ship]*, devoted to the mystery of the *Mary-Celeste*, was shot but not broadcast, due to a management change in French television. It starred Diane Kurys, who went on to become a famous director.

Le Veneur Noir [The Dark Hunter] (FR 3, Col., two

85 mins. eps., 29–30 December 1982)

DIR: Paul **Planchon**; WRI: David-André Lang, Paul Planchon, based on the novel *La Baronne Trépassée [The Dead Baroness]* by **Ponson du Terrail**.

CAST: Georges Marchal (Le Veneur), François-Eric Gendron (Philippe), Anne Canovas (Lilly), Pierre Banderet (Simiane), Jean Alibert, Antoine Baud, Julien Couty, Maurice Deschamps, Jean-Claude Hirsch, André Lacombe, Serge Pauthe, André Pomarat, Max Ruire, Yves Prunier, Marcel Specht, Lionel Astier, Isabelle Charraix, René Prost, Robert Chazot, Martine Laisne, Gérard Darrieu, Eddy Roos, Christian Auger.

STORY: A young nobleman who is responsible for his wife's death fights a mysterious masked man, the Dark Hunter, allegedly the 900-year-old son of the Devil. He also meets a woman who is an exact double of his dead wife, and who appears to be possessed by her spirit.

NOTE: For further information on **Ponson du Terrrail**, see *Rocambole* above.

Verne, Jules

As with Marcel **Aymé**, the fantastic stories of popular science fiction writer Jules **Verne** (see Book 2) have also been a staple of French television. We have therefore regrouped them in alphabetical order in a single section below.

La Chasse au Météore [The Meteor Hunt] (ORTF 1, B&W., 90 min., 29 December 1966)

DIR: Roger Iglésis; WRI: Jean-Claude Youri.

CAST: Philippe Avron (Zephyrin), Joseph Paster, Bernard Lajarrige, François Maistre, Jacques de Barry, René Clermont, France Delahalle.

STORY: Scientists track down a meteor.

Le Château des Carpathes [The Castle in the Carpathians] (A2, Col., 120 min., 19 December 1976)

DIR: Jean-Christophe Averty; WRI: Armand Lanoux.

CAST: Jean-Roger Caussimon (Frik), Jean Martin (Orfanik), Mady Mesplé (Stella), Jacqueline Danno (Fausta), Benoît Allemane (Franz), Guy Grosso, Bernard Valdeneige, Nicole Norden, Yves Arcanel, Jacques Legras, Bernard Cara, Annette Poivre, Sacha Pitoëff, Raymond Meunier.

STORY: A lonely nobleman who lost his lover lives in retirement in his castle. a strange inventor uses his devices to preserve the image of the girl and keep strangers away.

Deux Ans de Vacances [A Two Years' Vacation, Transl. as Adrift in the Pacific] (ORTF 1, Col., six 60 min. eps., 1 June–15 July 1974)

DIR: Gilles Grangier; WRI: Claude Desailly.

CAST: Franz Seidenschwan, Didier Gaudron, Marc di Napoli, Dominique Planchot, Frédéric Duru, Rainer Basedow, Werner Pocchard.

STORY: A *Treasure Island*-like story about two shipwrecked teenagers struggling to escape pirates in the South Pacific.

L'Île Mystérieuse [The Mysterious Island]

Version No. 1: (RTF, B&W., two 60 Min eps., 28 April, 5 May 1963)

DIR: Pierre Badel; WRI: Claude Santelli.

CAST: René Arrieu

L'Île Mystérieuse (1st version).

(Nemo), Michel Etcheverry, Jacques Grello, Armand Meffre, Ibrahim Seck, Philippe Coussoneau.

Version No. 2: (ORTF 1, Col., 40 min., 7 December 1969)

DIR/WRI: Claude Santelli.

CAST: Pierre Dux (Nemo), Michel Etcheverry.

Version No. 3: (ORTF 1, Col., six 55 min. eps., 1973)

1. L'Évasion [The Escape] (17 December 1973)

2. Les Naufragés de l'Air [The Castaways of the Air] (19 December 1973)

3. Territoire Interdit [Forbidden Territory] (21 December 1973)

4. L'Abandonné [The Forsaken] (24 December 1973)

5. Le Drapeau Noir [The Black Flag] (26 December 1973)

6. Le Secret de l'Île [The Island's Secret] (28 December 1973)

DIR: Henri Colpi, Juan Antonio Bardem; WRI: Jacques Champreux.

CAST: Omar Sharif (Nemo), Gérard Tichy, Philippe Nicaud, Ambroise Bia, Jess Hahn, Rafaël Bardem, Gabriele Tinti, Vidal Molina, Rik Battaglia.

STORY: Castaways on a desert island are secretly aided by Captain Nemo.

NOTE: This is a sequel to the classic *20,000 Leagues Under the Sea*. An edited version of Version No. 3 was first released as a feature film (see Chapter I). For further information on Jacques Champreux, see *L'Homme Sans Visage* above.

Les Indes Noires [The Black Indies] (ORTF 1, B&W., 95 min., 25 December 1964)

DIR: Marcel Bluwal; WRI: Marcel Moussy.

CAST: Alain Mottet (James), Georges Poujoly (Harry), André Valmy (Simon), Jean-Pierre Moulin (Jack), Paloma Matta (Nell), Geneviève Fontanel, Yvette Étiévant, Christian Barbier, Jean Galland.

STORY: A faithful rendition of **Verne**'s classic novel about an underground industrial civilization.

Maître Zacharius

Version No. 1: (ORTF 3, Col., 55 min. 26 June 1973)

DIR: Pierre Bureau; WRI: Marcel Brion, Pierre Bureau.

CAST: Pierre Vial (Zacharius), Jean-Pierre Sentier, Madeleine Barbulée, Jacques Roussillon, François-Louis Tilly, Jany Gastaldi.

Version No. 2: (TF1, Col., 85 min., 24 March 1984)

DIR: Claude Grinberg; WRI: Serge Ganzl, Claude Grinberg.

CAST: Charles Denner (Zacharius), Emmanuelle Béart, Pierre-Louis Rajot.

STORY: An old clockmaker dreams of controlling time and invents a robot android.

Nemo (ORTF 1, Col., 95 min., 21 March 1970)

DIR: Jean Bacque, based on a play by Alexandre Rivemale.

CAST: Michel Le Royer (Nemo), Lucien Barjon (Arronax), Agnès Desroches, Bernard Cara, Jean Franval, Gilbberte Rivet, Pierre Mirat, Fernand Guiot.

STORY: Captain Nemo decides to retire and leaves the Nautilus.

NOTE: This is not, strictly speaking, a Jules **Verne** story, but an unauthorized sequel.

L'Orgue Fantastique [The Fantastic Organ] (ORTF 1, Col., 73 min., 24 December 1968)

DIR: Jacques Trébouta; WRI: Frédéric Ardant, Claude Santelli.

CAST: Xavier Depraz (Takelbarth), Fernand Ledoux (Hartman), Sabine Haudepin (Christel), Philippe Normand, François Valorbe, Marcel Cuvelier, Jacques Rispal, Francis Lax, François Vibert.

STORY: After an old organist's death, the devil (Depraz) comes to a village and uses its children to create a fantastic new organ.

NOTE: This is based on the short story "M. Ré Dièse et Mlle. Mi Bémol" included in the collection *Hier et Demain* [*Yesterday & Tomorrow*].

Le Secret de Wilhelm Storitz [The Secret of Wilhelm Storitz] (ORTF 1, Col., 110 min., 28 October 1967)

DIR: Eric Le Hung; WRI: Claude Santelli.

CAST: Jean-Claude Drouot (Storitz), Bernard Verley, Pascale Audret, Monique Mélinand, Robert Vattier, Pierre Leproux, Michel Vitold.

STORY/NOTE: This story, about a scientist who has discovered the secret of invisibility, also incorporates elements from another **Verne** novel, *Le Château des Carpathes* [*The Castle in the Carpathians*].

Le Tour du Monde en 80 Jours [Around the World in 80 Days]

Version No. 1: (A2, Col., two 90 min. eps., 29–30 December 1975)

DIR: Pierre Nivollet; WRI: Jean Marsan, Jean Le Poulain. MUSIC: Gérard Calvi; CHOREOGRAPHY: Jean Guélis.

CAST: Jean Le Poulain (Fogg), Pierre Trabaud (Passepartout), Roger Carel.

NOTE: Musical comedy.

Version No. 2: (A2, Col., 25 December 1979)

DIR: André Frédérick; WRI: Pavel Kohout.

CAST: Daniel Ceccaldi (Fogg), Roger Pierre (Passepartout), Jean-Pierre Darras.

Version No. 3: (FR3, Col., twelve 5 min. eps., 22 December 1980–3 January 1981)

DIR/WRI: Serge Danot.

CAST: Jean Pellotier (Fogg), Charles Caunant (Passepartout), Christian Duc, Paul Bisciglia, Michel Bruzat.

STORY: Englishman Phileas Fogg bets that he can travel around the world in 80 days.

NOTE: Serge Danot is the creator of *Le Manège Enchanté* (see Chapter IV).

Les Visiteurs [The Visitors] (TF1, Col., six 60 min. eps., 1980)

1. Zarko (3 April 1980)

2. Alambda (10 April 1980)

3. Pirvii (17 April 1980)

4. Kyrin (24 April 1980)

5. Memno (1st May 1980)

6. Reka (8 May 1980)

DIR: Michel Wyn; WRI: Claude Desailly.

CAST: José-Marie Flotats (Jean-Louis Brosec), Barbara Kramer (Renate Mattiesen), Jacques Balutin (Bob), Piéral, Michèle Bardollet (Colette), François Chaumette (Reka), André Oumansky (Kyrin), Jean-Claude Bouillaud, Jean-René Gossart (Zarko), Pierre Gualdi, Renzo Martini, Feodor Atkine, Amparo Grisales, Patrice Valota, Ronald France.

STORY: Two aliens from a perfect but loveless galactic empire, Arkim and Tolrach, are reincarnated into the bodies of two comatose Earthlings: Jean-Louis and Renate. Their mission is to find out why six previous "visitors" sent to Earth have vanished without a trace. After a globe-spanning quest, they discover that the visitors like their new lives on Earth better and have decided to remain. Now in love, Arkim and Tolrach (who is pregnant) decide to stay, as well.

Des Voix dans la Nuit [Voices in the Night] (TF1, Col., six 60 min. eps., 1991)

1. Succubus (21 July 1991)

DIR: Patrick Dromgoole; WRI: Bob Baker & Dave Martin.

CAST: Barry Foster, Lindsey Baxter, Jeremy Gilley, Aurore Clément.

STORY: A young man believes he is being haunted by female ghosts.

NOTE: Bob Baker and Dave Martin are two British writers who have written many episodes of *Doctor Who*.

2. La Chambre Secrète [The Secret Room] (9 July 1991)

DIR/WRI: Didier Haudepin, based on a story by Robert Aickman.

CAST: Carol Kane, Jean-François Stévenin, Sabine Haudepin, Eléonor Hirt.

STORY: Two children discover a secret room inside a doll house.

3. Une Main dans l'Ombre [A Hand in the Shadow] (16 July 1991)

DIR/WRI: Peter Duffel.

CAST: Sylvie Granottier, Nicola Pagett, Clive Francis, Helen Cherry.

STORY: Two girls have a picnic in a cemetery.

4. L'Hospice [The Home] (23 July 1991)

DIR/WRI: Dominique Othenin-Girard, based on a story by Robert Aickman.

CAST: Marthe Keller, Jack Shepherd, Alan Dobie, Gordon Warnecke, Jonathan Cecil.

STORY: A driver whose car broke down stays at a strange hotel.

5. Les Mains d'Orlac [The Hands of Orlac] (30 July 1991)

DIR: Peter Kassovitz; WRI: Peter Kassovitz, Patrick Pesnot, based on the novel by Maurice **Renard**.

CAST: Jacques Bonnafé, Laszlo Szabo, Henri Serre, Rebecca Potok, Anne Roussel.

STORY: A surgeon grafts a murderer's hands on a pianist.

NOTE: Also see Chapter I for a feature film adaptation of the same story.

6. Les Trains (6 August 1991)

DIR: György Gat; WRI: Unknown.

CAST: Sophie Carle, Nicola Cowper, Robert Koltaï.

STORY: Two young woman become lost in the countryside.

Robert Vattier in Le Voyageur des Siècles.

Le Voyageur des Siècles [The Traveler of the Centuries] (ORTF 1, Col., four 60 min. eps., 1971)

1. L'Homme au Tricorne [The Man with the Three-Cornered Hat] (7 August 1971)

2. L'Album de Famille [The Family Album] (14 August 1971)

3. Le Grain de Sable [The Grain of Sand] (21 August 1971)

4. Le Bonnetier de la Rue Tripette [The Hosier of Tripette Street] (28 August 1971)

DIR: Jean Dréville; WRI: **Noël-Noël**.

CAST: Robert Vattier, Hervé Jolly, Raymond Baillet, Angelo Bardi, Paul Bisciglia, Anne-Marie Carrière, Roger Carel, Georges de Caunes, Gérard Darrieu, François Darbon, Michel Le Royer, Jean-Marie Proslier, Georgette Anys, Lucien Raimbourg, Léonce Corne, France Delahalle.

STORY: An inventor travels back through time to 1884 to meet his great-uncle. Then, together, they travel back to the days of the French Revolution. to save the girl he loves, who is doomed to die on the guillotine. The hero succeeds in preventing the Revolution from taking place, thereby changing the course of history. But the girl nevertheless dies in a balloon accident.

NOTE: Noël-Noël novelized his teleplay (see Book 2).

3. Telefilms

Our definition of telefilms include about twenty short features made for or first broadcast on French television, and which attracted a degree of fame by being reviewed in genre magazines. There are, without a doubt, other short features which are not listed here, primarily because information about them is not readily available. We do not believe, however, that anything of major importance has been omitted. Information about running times was not available for all films.

À l'Heure Où Le Coq Chantera [When the Rooster Crows] (ORTF 2, Col., 18 September 1971)

DIR: Jacques Audoir; WRI: Jacques Audoir, Jean-Charles Lagneau.

CAST: Geneviève Fontanel, Jean-Pierre Moulin, Françoise Petit, Vernon Dobtcheff.

STORY: A ghost story.

Adrian et Jusemina (RTF, B&W., 20 May 1958)

DIR: René Lucot; WRI: Louis Foucher, based on a story by Michel de **Ghelderode**.

CAST: Robert Fontanet, Huguette Hue, Pierre Giraud, Jenny Clève.

STORY: A story about witchcraft.

NOTE: Michel de Ghelderode is a famous Belgian writer of the *fantastique* (see Book 2) This story and *Magie Rouge* (see below) are taken from his collection *Sortilèges [Spells]*.

Alice au Pays des Merveilles [Alice in Wonderland] (ORTF 2, Col., 115 min., 22 December 1970)

DIR: Jean-Christophe Averty; WRI: Henri Parisot, based on a story by Lewis Carroll.

CAST: Marie-Véronique Maurin (Alice), Aimée Fontaine, Guy Grosso, Alice Sapritch, Francis Blanche, Hubert Deschamps, Michel Robin, Michel Muller, Pierre Louki, Annette Poivre, Bernard Cara, Michel Modo, Jacques Balutin, Bernard Valdeneige, Daniel Laloux.

STORY: Remarkable adaptation of Lewis Carroll's classic tale.

Alouqa, ou la Comédie des Morts [Alouqa, or the Comedy of the Dead] (TF1, Col., 80 min., 13 August 1975)

DIR: Pierre Cavassilas; WRI: Francis Lacassin, based on a story by Jean-Louis **Bouquet**.

CAST: Jean Martin, Max Vialle, Catherine Hubeau, Francis Lax, Roger Pelletier, Pascale Rivault, Karen Blanguenon, Georges Sellier.

STORY: A medium hires a troupe of actors to restage a drama that led to an old family curse.

NOTE: Francis Lacassin is a well-known French comics scholar. for further information on Jean-Louis Bouquet, see Book 2 and the feature film *La Cité Foudroyée* in Chapter I.

L'Archange [The Archangel] (1967)

DIR: Olivier Ricard; WRI: Roger **Blondel**, based on his novel.

CAST: Unknown.

STORY: An astronaut is selected to go on a dangerous mission.

NOTE: Roger Blondel also wrote numerous science fiction novels under the pseudonym of B.-R. **Bruss** (see Book 2). His story *Sous un Ciel Couleur d'Aubergine* was adapted for radio (see Chapter III).

L'Atlantide (ORTF 2, Col., 120 min., 24 February 1972)

DIR: Jean Kerchbron; WRI: Jean Kerchbron, Armand Lanoux, based on the novel by Pierre **Benoît**.

CAST: Ludmilla Tcherina (Antinea), Jacques Berthier (Morhange), Denis Manuel (Saint-Avit), Gilles Segal, Marie-Christine Darah, Yves Elliot.

STORY: Two French officers, Morhange and Saint-Avit, lost in the Sahara, come across the lost city of Atlantis, ruled by the cruel Queen Antinea.

NOTE: Also see Book 2 and the feature film adaptations in Chapter I.

Au Bois Dormant [The Sleeping Woods] (TF1, Col., 90 min., 12 February 1975)

DIR/WRI: Pierre Badel, based on the story by **Boileau-Narcejac**.

CAST: Maureen Kervin, Bernard Alane, René Alone, Jenny Astruc.

STORY: a girl succeeds in solving a seemingly supernatural mystery that plagued her boyfriend's ancestor.

NOTE: For further information on Boileau-Narcejac, see Book 2 and *Les Diaboliques* in Chapter I. *Au Bois Dormant* was published in 1956.

Azouk (RTF, B&W., 8 June 1957)

DIR/WRI: Jean Prat, based on a play by Alexandre Rivemale.

CAST: Roger Carel, Lucien Barjon, Jean-Paul Vignon, Henri Virlojeux.

STORY: The revenge of African spirits.

Barbara de Lichtenberg (FR 3, Col., 11 May 1979)

DIR: Paul **Planchon**; WRI: Paul Sonnendrucker, Paul Planchon.

CAST: Danièle Gueble, Yvette Stahl.

STORY: Gothic tale.

La Belle au Bois Dormant [The Sleeping Beauty] (ORTF 1, Col., 120 min., 22 December 1973)

DIR: Robert Maurice; WRI: Romain Weingarten, based on a story by Charles **Perrault**.

CAST: Isabelle Weingarten (Nuit), Michel de Ré, Marie Dubois, Didier Vallée, Gaby Sylvia, Lucienne Bogaert, Tania Balachova, Marc Eyraud.

STORY: In this free adaptation of the classic fairy tale, the Princess (called "Night") must undergo further trials before finding her Prince Charming.

NOTE: For other Charles **Perrault** adaptations, see *Peau d'Âne [Donkey Skin]* and *Le Petit Poucet [Tom Thumb]* in Chapter I, and *Cendrillon* below.

La Belle au Bois Dormant.

Billénium (ORTF 3, Col., 85 min., 10 September 1974)

DIR: Jean de Nesle; WRI: Jacques Goimard, based on a story by J. G. Ballard.

CAST: Claude Debord, Alberto Simono, Rosita Fernandez, Jeanine Souchon, Cyril Robichez, Bernard Claudet, Philippe Peltier, Jacques Mussier, Ronny Coutture.

STORY: In an overpopulated world, someone discovers a whole new empty space.

NOTE: Jacques Goimard is a renowned science fiction critic and editor (see Book 2). This production was intended to be the pilot for an unsold series of science fiction adaptations, entitled *Demain ou Jamais* [*Tomorrow or Never*]. J. G. Ballard is a British science fiction writer who wrote *Empire of the Sun* and *Crash*.

La Bonne Peinture see ***Aymé, Marcel***

Les Bottes de Sept Lieues see ***Aymé, Marcel***

Le Briquet [The Lighter] (RTF, B&W., 1954)

DIR: Marcel Bluwal; WRI: Marcel Bluwal, René Fallet, based on a story by Hans-Christian Andersen.

CAST: Christiane Minazzoli, Paul Guers, Jean Berger, André Valmy.

STORY: A classic fairy tale.

Carmilla, Le Coeur Pétrifié [Carmilla, the Petrified Heart] (FR 3, Col., 60 min., 10 March 1988)

DIR: Paul **Planchon**; WRI: Paul Planchon, Antonin Robert, based on the story by Sheridan Le Fanu.

CAST: Emmanuelle Meyssignac (Carmilla), Aurelle Doazan, Yvette Stahl, Paulette Schlegel, Roland Kieffer, André Pomarat, Dinah Faust.

STORY: Adaptation of Le Fanu's notorious female vampire story.

NOTE: Roger **Vadim** adapted the same story as a feature film under the title *...Et Mourir de Plaisir* (see Chapter I).

Ce Soir à Samarcande [Tonight in Samarkand] (RTF, B&W., 31 October 1953)

DIR/WRI: Maurice Cazeneuve, based on a play by Jacques Deval.

CAST: Gaby Sylvia, Paul Bernard, Abel Jaquin, Francette Vernillat.

STORY: A woman tries to escape from her preordained doom, but in vain.

Cendrillon [Cinderella] (RTF, B&W., 24 December 1953)

DIR: Claude **Barma**; WRI: Pierre Dumayet, based on a story by Charles **Perrault**.

CAST: Christine Carrère, Jean Vinci.

STORY: Musical adaptation of the classic fairy tale.

NOTE: For further information on Charles Perrault, see Book 2 and la **Belle au Bois Dormant** above.

La Chasse au Météore see ***Verne, Jules***

Le Château aux Portiques [The Castle with Porticos] (ORTF 3, Col., 9 October 1973)

DIR: Odette Collet; WRI: Charlotte Mercier.

CAST: Maria Meriko, Olivier Deschamps, Natacha Inutine.

STORY: A vampire story.

Le Château des Carpathes see ***Verne, Jules***

La Chose Qui Ricane [The Cackling Thing] (FR 3, Col., 11 September 1985)

DIR: Joseph Drimal; WRI: Maurice Sarfati, based on a story by Robert-Louis Stevenson.

CAST: Maurice Sarfati, Bernard Tiphaine, Jean Bousquet, Marie Bunel.

STORY: Horror story.

NOTE: The same team also adapted **Le Démon Écarlate** and **La Montre du Doyen** (see below).

Christmas Carol (TF1, Col., 90 min., 25 December 1984)

DIR/WRI: Pierre Boutron, based on a story by Charles Dickens.

CAST: Michel Bouquet (Scrooge), Pierre Clémenti, Georges Wilson, Lisette Maslidor, Pierre Olaf, Jean Martin, Manuel Bonnet.

STORY: Lavish and well interpreted adaptation of Dickens' classic tale.

Chroniques Martiennes [The Martian Chronicles] (ORTF 3, Col., 110 min., 13 December 1974)

DIR: Renée Kammerscheit; WRI: Louis **Pauwels**, based on the stories by Ray Bradbury.

CAST: Guy Shelley, Jean-José Fleury, Jean-Claude Amyl, Olivier Sydney, Philippe Murgier, Virginie Billetdoux, Alain Foures.

STORY: Television version of a play based on Ray Bradbury's classic collection of short stories. Tim Wilder tells the story of the conquest of Mars as lived by his father.

NOTE: For further information on Louis Pauwels, see **Le Golem** below.

Le Coeur Cambriolé see ***Leroux, Gaston***

Le Colchique et l'Étoile [The Colchicum and the Star] (TF1, Col., 26 July 1974)

DIR/WRI: Michel **Subiela**, based on the novel by Nicole Ciravegna.

CAST: Olivier Norin, Catherine Hubeau, Jean-Pierre Jorris, Gérald Denizot.

STORY: Science fiction.

Le Coq Noir [The Black Rooster] (FR 3, Col., 50 min., 3 September 1982)

DIR: Jean-Charles Cabanis; WRI: Paul **Planchon**, Maurice

Sarfati, based on the story "L'Esquisse Mysterieuse" ["The Mysterious Sketch"] by **Erckmann-Chatrian**.

CAST: Bernard Freyd, Jean-Pierre Bagot, Germain Muller, Maurice Sarfati, Dinah Faust, Marcel Spegt, Jean-Marie Holterbach, Paul Bru.

STORY: A painter accidentally paints a murder scene.

NOTE: For further information on Erckmann-Chatrian, see *Hugues Le Loup* below.

La Couleur de l'Abîme [The Color from the Abyss]

(TF1, Col., 55 min., 5 July 1983)

DIR: Pascal Kané; WRI: Gilberto Azevedo.

CAST: Jean-François Stévenin, Evelyne Dress, Rebecca Pauly, Garrick Maul.

STORY: American spelunkers unknowingly awaken a "Color out of Space"–like entity, which then attacks a local family.

NOTE: This story is loosely inspired by H. P. Lovecraft's famous 1927 short story.

Le Cyborg, ou Le Voyage Vertical [The Cyborg, or the Vertical Journey]

(ORTF 2, Col., 85 min., 15 September 1970)

DIR: Jacques Pierre; WRI: Yves Jamiaque.

CAST: Anne Vernon, Clotilde Joano, Laurence Jyl, Roger Pigault, Marc Michel, Armand Mestral, Gérard Depardieu, Max Vialle.

STORY: Seven people from different backgrounds are taken to an underground bunker and told that one of them is a cyborg.

La Dame d'Outre-Nulle Part [The Lady from Beyond Nowhere]

(Television Romande, 1966)

DIR: Jean-Jacques Lagrange; WRI: Jean-Louis Roncoroni, based on a story by Georges **Langelaan**.

CAST: Unknown.

STORY: The tale of a female alien.

NOTE: George Langelaan is a famous writer and journalist who also wrote the classic story *The Fly* (see Book 2). Also see *Temps Mort* below.

Le Démon Écarlate [The Scarlet Demon]

(FR 3, Col., 60 min., 17 March 1988)

DIR: Joseph Drimal; WRI: Maurice Sarfati, based on a story by Sheridan Le Fanu.

CAST: Pierre Vaneck, Pierre Rousseau, Annick Jarry, Tobias Kempf, André Pomarat, Valérie Wolf.

STORY: A judge orders the hanging of his mistress' husband, but the dead man returns to exact revenge.

NOTE: The same team also adapted *La Chose Qui Ricane* and *La Montre du Doyen* as telefilms. for another Le Fanu adaptation, see *Carmilla* above.

La Dépêche de Nuit [The Night Wire]

(A2, Col., 30 min., 2 April 1984)

DIR: Joseph Lewartowski; WRI: Alain Pozzoli, based on a story by H. F. Arnold.

CAST: Olivier Granier, Ariel Semenoff.

STORY: A journalist broadcasts the story of the invasion of a deadly, living fog.

NOTE: H. F. Arnold's original short story was published in the magazine *Weird Tales* in 1926.

Le Devine-Vent [The Guess-Wind]

(FR 3, Col., 26 Decembre 1980)

DIR/WRI: Régis Forrissier, based on a story by Charles Galtier.

CAST: Paul Crauchet, Anne-Marie Besse, Pierre Boutron.

STORY: Provencal folk tale.

Dissimulation: Une Simulation de Philip K. Dick

(La Sept, 15 min., 1993)

DIR/WRI: Hervé Nisic.

CAST: Tomacz Bialkowski (Dick).

STORY: Surreal and made-up video report about Dick's visit to the Metz SF convention.

Le Docteur Lerne see L'Étrange Château du Docteur Lerne

L'Ensorcelée [The Spellbound Girl]

(A2, Col., 11 April 1981)

DIR: Jean Prat; WRI: Jean Prat, Paule de Beaumont, based on the novel by **Barbey d'Aurevilly**.

CAST: Julie Philippe, Jean-Luc Boutté, Elizabeth Kaza, Fernand Berset.

STORY: A woman is seemingly possessed by evil.

NOTE: Jules-Amédée Barbey d'Aurevilly is a famous poet and writer of the *fantastique* (see Book 2).

Entre-Temps [Between Times]

(A2, Col., 29 August 1984)

DIR: José-Maria Berzosa; WRI: Carlos Semprun, José-Maria Berzosa.

CAST: Philippe du Janerand, Jean Bouzid, Servane Ducorps, Aïna Walle.

STORY: Time travel story.

L'Envolée Belle [The Beautiful Flight]

(ORTF 2, B&W., 24 December 1969)

DIR: Jean Prat; WRI: Alexandre Rivemale.

CAST: Ardisson, Dominique Rollin, Jean Pignol, Laurence Imbert.

STORY: Christmas story.

Et Meurent les Géants [And the Giants Died] (FR 3, Col., 19 June 1981)
DIR/WRI: Fernand Vincent, based on a story by Louis-François Caude.
CAST: Patrick Raynal, Dominique Dimey, Cyril Robichez, Dominique Sarrazin.
STORY: Folk tale.

Esprits de Famille [Family Ghosts] (FR 3, Col., 19 April 1975)
DIR/WRI: Marc Pavaux, based on a play by Claude Caron.
CAST: Annette Poivre, Raymond Bussières, Brigitte Fossey.
STORY: Ghost story.

Les Étonnements d'un Couple Moderne [The Astonishments of a Modern Couple] (A2, Col., 90 min., 24 December 1986)
DIR: Pierre Boutron; WRI: Jean-Claude **Carrière**.
CAST: Jean Carmet, Delphine Seyrig, Judith Magre, François Perrot, Henri Garcin, Alain Doutey, Anaïs Jeanneret.
STORY: A couple discovers that their friends are aliens who have been studying Earth for a quarter of a century, and who are about to return home, deeming the planet doomed.

L'Étrange Château du Docteur Lerne [The Strange Castle of Dr. Lerne] (A2, Col., 105 min., 28 December 1983)
DIR: Jean-Daniel Verhaerghe; WRI: Gérard Brach, based on the novel by Maurice **Renard**.
CAST: Jacques Dufilho (Lerne), Pierre Clémenti, Dora Doll, Jean-Pierre Roussillon, Pierre Etaix, Valérie Jeanneret, Henri Guybet, Claude Villers.
STORY: A mad scientist experiments with human grafts.
NOTE: For further information on Maurice Renard, see Book 2 and *Les Mains d'Orlac* [*The Hands of Orlac*] in Chapter I. Jean-Daniel Verhaerghe also directed the feature film *L'Araignée d'Eau* [*The Water Spider*] (see Chapter I), and the telefilms *La Métamorphose* and *La Nuit des Fantômes*. Gérard Brach wrote several films for Roman Polanski, and the screenplay for *La Guerre du Feu* (see Chapter I).

La Fabrique see *Aymé, Marcel*

Le Fantôme des Canterville [The Canterville Ghost] (RTF, B&W., 25 November 1962)
DIR: Marcel Cravenne; WRI: Albert Husson, based on a story by Oscar Wilde.
CAST: Jacques Fabbri, Maria Pacôme, Jacques Berlioz, Claude Rich, Raymone, Pierre Pernet, Claude Nicot.
STORY: Claude Rich is a wonderful ghost in this video adaptation of Wilde's famous story about a crude American family's acquisition of a haunted castle.

Le Fauteuil Hanté see *Leroux, Gaston*

La Femme au Collier de Velours see *Leroux, Gaston*

La Fenêtre [The Window] (ORTF 2, Col., 45 min., 2 August 1970)
DIR/WRI: Jacques Pierre, based on the story "The Spider" by Hanns Heinz Ewers.
CAST: Michel Lonsdale, Jacqueline Danno, Hélène Dieudonné, Alexandre Rignault.
STORY: A spider creature capable of taking the shape of a beautiful young woman lures young men to their deaths.

La Fleur et le Fantôme [The Flower and the Ghost] (RTF, B&W., 1953)
DIR: François Chatel; WRI: Jacques Floran.
CAST: Isa Miranda, André Valmy, Deryeth Mendel, Christian Fourcade.
STORY: A period ghost story.

Frankenstein (ORTF 3, Col., 95 min., 7 May 1974)
DIR: Bob Thénault; WRI: François Chevallier, based on the novel by Mary Shelley.
CAST: Gérard Berner (Victor), Gérard Boucaron (Frobelius/Monster), Karin Petersen (Elisabeth), Bernard Mesguich (Clerval), Nicolas Silberg, Jean Lepage, Françoise Lugagne, Marc Fayolle.
STORY: In this adaptation of Shelley's classic tale, Victor, after having been expelled from the university and repudiated by his family, conducts his experiments on Frobelius, a retarded man. After the latter dies in a mountain accident, Victor brings him back to life.

Le Gentleman des Antipodes [The Gentleman from the Other Side of the World] (A2, Col., 4 November 1976)
DIR: Boramy Tioulong; WRI: Christine Lamorlette, based on the novel by Pierre **Véry**.
CAST: Gilles Segal (Prosper Lepicq), Armand Mestral, Raymond Gérome, Rosy Varte, Jean Martin, Ginette Garcin, Francis Lax, Jean-Paul Zehnacker, Marc Fayolle, Paul Le Person.
STORY: In order to unmask serial killer, Lepicq infiltrates a club made up of people whose faces resemble animals.
NOTE: For other Pierre Véry adaptations, see *Le Pays Sans Étoiles* in Chapter I.

Le Golem (ORTF 2, B&W., 115 Min, 18 February 1967)
DIR: Jean Kerchbron; WRI: Louis **Pauwels**, Jean Kerchbron, based on the novel by Gustav Meyrinck.

CAST: André Reybaz (Pernath), Pierre Tabard, Michel Etcheverry, Marika Green, François Vibert, Robert Etcheverry, Magali Noël, Douking, Françoise Winskill, Alfred Baillou, Serge Merlin.

STORY: Faithful adaptation of Meyrinck's classic novel.

NOTE: Louis Pauwels is a famous writer and journalist, often associated with Jacques **Bergier** (see *Aux Frontières du Possible* above). for television, he wrote number of script adaptations, including the anthology series *Les Soirées du Bungalow* and the telefilms *Chroniques Martiennes* (based on Ray Bradbury's science fiction classic), *Président Faust*, and *Les Roses de Manara* (see below).

La Grâce see *Aymé, Marcel*

Le Grand Poucet [Big Thumb] (A2, Col., 25 December 1980)

DIR/WRI: Claude-Henri Lambert, based on a play by Claude-André Puget.

CAST: Christian Marquand, Bruno Devoldère, Carole Coulombe.

STORY: Fairy tale.

Gueule d'Atmosphère [Funny Face] (FR 3, Col., 52 min., 6 June 1980)

DIR: Maurice Château; WRI: Jean-Pierre **Hubert**.

CAST: Bernard Freyd, Hervé Pierre, Claude Bouchery.

STORY: Survivors try to flee a pollution-caused plague.

NOTE: Jean-Pierre Hubert is a noted science fiction writer (see Book 2).

Haute Sécurité [High Security] (FR 3, Col., 60 min., 17 August 1988)

DIR: Jean-Pierre Bastid; WRI: Joël **Houssin**, Daniel Riche.

CAST: Juliet Berto, Kader Boukhanef, Serge Marquand.

STORY: Out of control robocops wreak havoc on a city.

NOTE: For further information on Joël **Houssin** and Daniel Riche, see *Les Hordes* above. This telefilm was was one of three (the others being *Les Lutteurs Immobiles* and *Le Matin des Jokers*) written by contemporary science fiction authors for Michel Le Bris, the then-programming director of FR3.

L'Herbe Rouge [The Red Grass] (A2, Col., 90 min., 11 September 1985)

DIR: Pierre **Kast**, Maurice Dugowson; WRI: Pierre Kast, based the novel by Boris **Vian**.

CAST: Jean Sorel, Jean-Pierre Léaud, Mijou Kovacs, Yves Robert, Jacques Perrin, Jean-Claude Brialy, Alexandra Stewart, Philippe Clay, Françoise Arnoul.

STORY: In a fantastic universe (where grass is red), an engineer builds a machine that will materialise his fears.

NOTE: Pierre Kast died before finishing this film, which was completed by Maurice Dugowson. for further information on Boris Vian, see *L'Écume des Jours* in Chapter I.

Hilda Muramer (ORTF 2, Col., 65 min., 12 September 1973)

DIR: Jacques Trebouta; WRI: Loys Masson, based on the story *Metzengerstein* by Edgar Allan Poe.

CAST: Loumi Iacobesco (Hilda), Jacques Weber, Paul Crauchet, Dominique Toussaint, Hervé Jolly.

STORY: In this free adaptation of Poe's story, the Muramers and the Malirings are two enemy clans. After Hilda Muramer refuses to save the Malirings from a fatal fire, a horse becomes the instrument of the Malirings' revenge.

L'Histoire Terrible et Douce de la Demoiselle à la Violette [The Terrible and Kind Story of the Damsel with a Violet] (FR 3, Col., 16 April 1983)

DIR: Jean-Luc Mage; WRI: Pierre Dubois.

CAST: Sylvaine Charlet, Hervé Barel, Alain Crampon.

STORY: Fairy tale.

L'Homme d'Orlu [The Man from Orlu] (ORTF 2, Col., 18 May 1971)

DIR/WRI: Jacques Krier.

CAST: Pierre Santini, Jean Lescot, Gérard Darrieu.

STORY: Science fiction.

L'Homme en Rouge [The Man in Red] (FR 3, Col., 16 January 1981)

DIR: Paul **Planchon**; WRI: David-André Lang, Paul Planchon.

CAST: Christian Baltauss, Yvette Stahl, Henri Muller.

STORY: Ghost story.

L'Homme Qui a Perdu Son Ombre [The Man Who Lost His Shadow]

Based on the story *The Wonderful Story of Peter Schlemihl* (1814) by Adalbert von Chamisso.

Version No. 1: (RTF, B&W., 60 min., 12 November 1951)

DIR/WRI: Philippe Agostini, Albert Riera.

CAST: Odette Joyeux, Gérard Oury, Jacques François, Gaston Séverin, Jean Topart, Lucien Blondeau.

Version No. 2: (ORTF 1, Col., 85 min., 16 July 1966)

DIR: Marcel Cravenne; WRI: Albert Husson.

CAST: Claude Nicot, Danièle Lebrun, Julien Guiomar, Henri Guisol, Anne Bertin, Catherine Hiegel, Clément Harari.

STORY: A man sells his shadow to the devil but comes to regret it.

Le Horla (ORTF 1, Col., 80 min., 1966)

DIR/WRI: Jean-Daniel Pollet, based on the story by Guy de **Maupassant**.

CAST: Laurent Terzieff.

STORY: An invisible entity persecutes a man.

NOTE: Guy de Maupassant is a famous writer and poet (see Book 2). *Le Horla* was also filmed in 1963 as *Diary of a Madman*, starring Vincent Price.

Le Hors-Le-Champ [Out of Focus] (ORTF 3, Col., 50 min., 20 February 1973)

DIR: Gérard Guillaume; WRI: Michel Suffran.

CAST: Claude Mann, Christiane Laurent, Jean Pignol, Jean Lepage.

STORY: A young photographer buys an antique camera which takes him into the past.

La Hotte [The Basket] (ORTF 3, Col., 23 December 1973)

DIR/WRI: Daniel Georgeot, based on a story by Hervé **Bazin**.

CAST: Georges Géret, Jean-Jacques Delbo, Anne-Marie Durin.

STORY: Christmas story.

Hugues Le Loup [Hugh the Wolf]

Based on the novel by **Erckmann-Chatrian**. Émile **Erckmann** and Alexandre **Chatrian** are a famous writing team who penned numerous fantastic stories revolving around folk tales (often of their native Alsace) (see Book 2).

Version No. 1: (TF1, Col., 90 min., 29 January 1975)

DIR/WRI: Michel **Subiela**.

CAST: Patricia Callas, Claude Titre, Jean-Claude Dauphin, Bernard Charnacé, André Valmy.

Version No. 2: (FR3, Col., 60 min., 19 January 1979)

DIR: Paul **Planchon**; WRI: Paul Planchon, Maurice Sarfati.

CAST: André Pomarat, Margot Lefèvre, Paul Sonnendrucker, Eric de Dadelsen, Marcel Spegt, Christiane Durry, Robert Fuger.

STORY: Count Nideck and his daughter Odile live in a lonely castle in a countryside plagued by a werewolf.

NOTE: Other television adaptations of Erckmann-Chatrian include **Le Coq Noir**, above, and **La Montre du Doyen** below.

Il n'y a Plus de Héros au Numéro que Vous Avez Demandé [There's No Hero at the Number You Have Dialed] (TF1, Col., 70 min., 9 December 1980)

DIR/WRI: Pierre Chabartier.

CAST: Serge Reggiani, Hélène Vallier, Léo Campion, Claire Maurier.

STORY: A man finds an old telephone which mysteriously connects him with a soldier in the trenches of World War I.

L'Île Bleue [The Blue Island] (A2, Col., 90 min., 21 May 1983)

DIR: Jean-Claude Giudicelli; WRI: J.-C. Giudicelli, Michel **Jeury**.

CAST: Jean-Pierre Kalfon, Aïna Walle, Paul Crauchet, Philippe du Janerand, Féodor Atkine.

STORY: In the far future, man has learned to control time and dreams. Everything is white and blue. However, grey rebels have reclaimed the right to dream and die.

NOTE: Michel Jeury is a major science fiction writer (see Book 2). His television credits also include **Jour "J" Comme Jouet** below.

Image Interdite [Forbidden Image] (A2, Col., 90 min., 24 November 1984)

DIR: Jean-Daniel Simon; WRI: Claude May, J.-D. Simon.

CAST: Sylvie Fennec, Anne Teyssedre, Jacques Serres, Daniel Langlet, Karol Zubert.

STORY: In a future world where images and their transmissions have been forbidden, a young filmmaker discovers a beautiful actress.

NOTE: Jean-Daniel Simon also directed **Ils** (see Chapter I).

Les Indes Noires see Verne, Jules

L'Invention de Morel [Morel's Invention] (ORTF 2, Col., 110 min., 8 December 1967)

L'Invention de Morel.

DIR: Claude-Jean Bonnardot; WRI: C.-J. Bonnardot, Michel Andrieu, based on the novel *La Invencion de Morel* by Adolfo Bioy Casares.

CAST: Alain Saury, Juliette Mills, Didier Conti, Anne Talbot, Anne-Marie Blot, Ursula Kubler, Dominique Vincent, Paula Dehelly, Guy d'Arcangues, Jean Martin.

STORY: Luis (Saury), a prison escapee, arrives on an island where a sophisticated 3-D projection system endlessly replays scenes featuring the now-deceased guests of the inventor, Morel. Luis falls in love with one of the projections and chooses to die to incorporate himself into the projection.

NOTE: Also see **L'Année Dernière à Marienbad** in Chapter I.

Le Jardinier [The Gardener] (ORTF 3, Col., 90 min., 25 December 1973)

DIR: Antoine Léonard; WRI: François Possot.

CAST: Pierre Fresnay, Paul Crauchet, Gérard Lorin, Claude Richard, Philippe Laudenbach.

STORY: Philosophical tale with fantasy elements.

Le Jardinier Récalcitrant [The Rebellious Gardener] (TF1, Col., 95 min., 24 February 1983)

DIR: Maurice Failevic; WRI: Maurice Failevic, Jean-Claude **Carrière**.

CAST: Philippe de Cherisey (Martin Blanchet), Jean-Paul Schneider, Maurice Vaudaux, Pierre Londiche, Gabrielle Lazure.

STORY: In an antiseptic future where all food is industrially produced *in vitro*, a rebellious gardener uses ancient seeds to again grow vegetables.

Je Tue Il [I Kill He] (A2, Col., 90 min., 1982)

DIR: Pierre Boutron; WRI: Jean-Claude **Carrière**.

CAST: Unknown.

STORY: Science fiction.

Jour "J" Comme Jouet [Day "T" for Toy] (FR 3, Col., 13 min., 25 December 1983)

DIR: Jacques Manlay; WRI: Michel **Jeury**.

CAST: Unknown.

STORY: Santa Claus overthrows a 1984-like dictatorship.

NOTE: For further information about Michel Jeury, see ***L'Île Bleue*** above.

Kira (Television Suisse Romande, 1967)

DIR: Unknown; WRI: Serge Leroy & Claude Ligure.

CAST: Unknown.

STORY: An alien woman falls in love.

Lancelot du Lac (ORTF 2, Col., 135 min., 25 December 1970)

DIR/WRI: Claude Santelli, based on **Chrétien de Troyes**.

CAST: Gérard Falconetti (Lancelot), Marie-Christine Barrault (Guenevere), Tony Taffln (Arthur), Arlette Tephany, Jean Chevrier, Jean Bouvier, Paul Rieger, Anne Saint-Mor, Jacques Weber, Mariannik Revillon, Jean-Pierre Bernard, Patrick Verde.

STORY: The story of the famous Knight of the Round Table, shot on location in Britanny, based on the original stories by Chrétien De Troyes. Also see ***Les Chevaliers de la Table Ronde*** and ***Perceval le Gallois*** in Chapter I.

La Légende de la Ville d'Ys [The Legend of the City of Ys] (FR 3, Col., 26 October 1983)

DIR: Renaud Saint-Pierre; WRI: Michel Le Bris.

CAST: Pierre Rousseau, Jenny Arasse, Robert Dadles, Jacques Anton.

STORY: The legendary city of Ys in Britanny is cursed to be swallowed by the ocean, because of the sins of its evil queen Dahuse.

NOTE: Also see ***Le Tribunal de l'Impossible***, Ep. 10 above.

Le Loup see ***Aymé, Marcel***

Les Lutteurs Immobiles [The Motionless Fighters] (FR 3, Col., 60 min., 2 August 1988)

DIR: André Farwagi; WRI: Serge **Brussolo**, based on his novel.

CAST: Bernard-Pierre Donnadieu, Marie Rivière, Fernand Guiot, Jacques Grandjouan, Fernand Kindt, Jean Mourat.

STORY: To eliminate waste and protect everyday objects, a future repressive society creates biological links between criminals and a chosen object.

NOTE: André Farwagi directed ***Le Temps de Mourir*** (see Chapter I). Serge Brussolo is a major science fiction and horror writer (see Book 2). This telefilm was one of three (the others being ***Haute Sécurité*** and ***Le Matin des Jokers***) written by contemporary science fiction authors for Michel Le Bris, the then-programming director of FR3.

Mademoiselle B. (A2, Col., 90 min., 27 August 1986)

DIR: Bernard Queysanne; WRI: Bernard Queysanne, Maurice **Pons**, based on his novel.

CAST: Claude Avril (B), Jean-Baptiste Thiérée, André Weber, Marc Fayolle, Dominique Erlanger, Didier Chevalier.

STORY: A retired writer in the countryside becomes acquainted with a mysterious girl who is dressed in white and shunned by the local villagers.

Magie Rouge [Red Magic] (Ortf 1, Col., 23 February 1973)

DIR/WRI: Daniel Georgeot, based on a play by Michel de **Ghelderode**.

CAST: Jean Le Poulain, Anne Alvaro, Paul Barge, Jean-Roger Caussimon.

STORY: Gothic horror tale.

NOTE: For further information on Michel de Ghelderode, see ***Adrian et Jusemina*** above.

Maître Zacharius see ***Verne, Jules***

Aurélie Gibert in Marie la Louve.

Marie la Louve [Marie the Wolf] (FR 3, Col., 95 min., 10 December 1991)

DIR: Daniel Wronecki; WRI: Daniel Wronecki, Rodolphe-Marie Arlaud, based on a story by Claude **Seignolle**.

CAST: Aurélie Gibert, Frédéric Pellegeay, Pierre Debauche, Dora Doll, Etienne Bierry, Sylvie Herbert, Jean-Paul Roussillon, Marie Pillet.

STORY: A young girl tries, unsuccessfully, to reject the powers she inherited, which enable her to cure wolf bites and lead wolves.

NOTE: Claude Seignolle is a famous writer of the *fantastique*. Also see Book 2, **Le Millième Cierge** and **Roc** below, and the short feature **Le Faucheur** in Chapter I and **Delphine** in Chapter III.

Mars: Mission Accomplie [Mars: Mission Accomplished] (1967)

DIR: Unknown; WRI: Henri **Viard**.

CAST: Unknown.

STORY: A rivalry develops between American and Soviet spacemen en route to Mars.

NOTE: Henri Viard also wrote for **Aux Frontières du Possible** (see above).

Le Matin des Jokers [The Morning of the Jokers]

(FR 3, Col., 60 min., 18 November 1988)

DIR: Robert Mugnerot; WRI: Pierre **Pelot**.

CAST: Greg Germain, Blanche Ravalec, Patrick Messe, Claire de Beaumont.

STORY: A doctor has created cloned twins of his wife (murdered by her clone) and politicians.

NOTE: Pierre Pelot is a major science fiction writer (see Book 2). This telefilm was one of three (the others being **Haute Sécurité** and **Les Lutteurs Immobiles**) written by contemporary science fiction authors for Michel Le Bris, the then-programming director of FR3. Also see la **Mission** below.

Melmoth Réconcilié [Melmoth Reconciled] (RTF, B&W., 15 May 1964)

DIR: Georges Lacombe; WRI: Pierre Latour, based on the novel by Honoré de **Balzac**.

CAST: Robert Porte, François Maistre, Régine Blaess, Anne-Marie Cofflnet.

STORY: The eternal wanderer finally finds peace.

NOTE: Honoré de Balzac is a classic novelist who also wrote some supernatural stories, such as **La Peau de Cha-**

grin and *Le Réquisitionnaire* below; also see *Out Un: Spectre* in Chapter I.

La Métamorphose [The Metamorphosis] (FR 3, B&W., 50 min., 5 June 1983)

DIR: Jean-Daniel Verhaeghe; WRI: J.-D. Verhaeghe, Roger Vrigny, based on the novel by Franz Kafka.

CAST: Madeleine Robinson, Julien Guiomar, Anne Caudry, Pierre Etaix.

STORY: Faithful adaptation of Kafka's classic allegorical novel in which a man wakes up to find himself transformed into a giant insect.

NOTE: For further information on Jean-Daniel Verhaeghe, see **L'Étrange Château du Dr. Lerne** above.

Le Millième Cierge [The Thousandth Candle] (Television Suisse Romande, Col., 80 min., 27 November 1969)

DIR/WRI: Raymond Barrat, based on a story by Claude **Seignolle**.

CAST: Raoul Guillet, Pierre Ruegg, Jacques Richard (The Devil), Serge Nicoloff, Caroline Cartier:

STORY: Folk legend.

NOTE: For other Claude Seignolle adaptations, see **Marie la Louve** above.

Le Miroir Opaque [The Opaque Mirror] (TF1, Col., 90 min., 25 July 1985)

DIR: Alain Boudet; WRI: Christian Watton, Alain Boudet.

CAST: Aïna Walle, Yves Beneyton, Georges Marchal, Roland Monod.

STORY: A young woman's dreams lead her to solve a murder.

La Mission, ou L'Aube du Rat [The Mission, or the Dawn of the Rat] (FR 3, Col., 1986)

DIR: Michel Guillet; WRI: Pierre **Pelot**.

CAST: Unknown.

STORY: A post-apocalyptic saga.

NOTE: For further information on Pierre Pelot, see **Le Matin des Jokers** above.

Le Modèle see Aymé, Marcel

Mon Faust [My Faust] (ORTF 2, Col., 1st December 1970)

DIR/WRI: Daniel Georgeot, Pierre Franck, based on a play by Paul Valéry.

CAST: Pierre Fresnay, Pierre Dux, Danièle Delorme.

STORY: Variation of the *Faust* story.

La Montre du Doyen [The Dean's Watch] (FR 3, Col., 3 January 1988)

DIR: Joseph Drimal; WRI: Maurice Sarfati, based on a story by **Erckmann-Chatrian**.

CAST: André Pomarat, Yves Aubert, Claude Lergenmuller, Marcel Grandidier.

STORY: A tale of rural witchcraft.

NOTE: The same team adapted *La Chose Qui Ricane* and *Le Démon Écarlate* as telefilms (see above). For further information on Erckmann-Chatrian, see *Hugues Le Loup* above.

La Mort Amoureuse [Death in Love] (TF1, Col., 85 min., 16 November 1977)

DIR: Jacques Ertaud; WRI: René **Fallet**.

CAST: Marcel Dalio (God), Françoise Lugagne (Death), Guy Marchand, Myriam Boyer, Michel Creton, Pierre Saintons, Françoise Dupré.

STORY: Death's human lover cheats on her, causing her to become jealous.

NOTE: René Fallet also wrote *La Soupe aux Choux* [*The Cabbage Soup*], adapted into an eponymous 1981 film (see Chapter I).

Le Nain see Aymé, Marcel

Le Navire Étoile [The Starship] (RTF, B&W., 11 December 1962)

DIR: Alain Boudet; WRI: Michel **Subiela**, based on the novel *The Space Born* (1956) by E. C. Tubb.

CAST: Dirk Sanders, Geneviève Casile, Pierre Massimi, François Maistre, René Arrieu, Roger Blin, André Charpak, Yves Brainville.

STORY: A revolution takes place in a generation starship ruled by a computer. It is eventually revealed that the ship is nearing its destination, and the revolt was all part of a plan to restore a sense of initiative in the crew.

Némo see Verne, Jules

La Nonne Sanglante, ou Roberta la Flétrie [The Bloody Nun, or Roberta the Branded] (FR 3, Col., 10 May 1981)

DIR: Bernard Maigrot; WRI: Maurice Sarfati, based on a novel by Albert **Bourgeois**.

CAST: Maria Laborit, Edith Perret, Nathalie Roussel.

STORY: Gothic melodrama.

La Nuit des Fantômes [Night of the Ghosts] (FR 3, Col., 75 min., 18 December 1990)

DIR: Jean-Daniel Verhaeghe; WRI: Gérard Brach.

CAST: Frédéric Deban, Marie Bunel, Jean-Pierre Bisson, Clément Harari, Laurent Paris, Baptiste Roussillon, Pauline Delfau.

STORY: A modern-day teenager (Deban) falls in love with the ghost of a noblewoman from the Crusades (Bunel).

NOTE: For further information on Jean-Daniel Verhaeghe and Gérard Brach, see *L'Étrange Château du Dr. Lerne* above.

La Nuit Se Lève [Night Is Rising] (ORTF 2, Col., 20 October 1970)

DIR: Roland Bernard; WRI: Jean-Claude Brisville.

CAST: Pascale Audret (Karen), Régine Blaess, Paul Bergé, André Julien.

STORY: A contemporary vampire story set in the mountain region of the Gévaudan.

Objets Trop Identifiés [Too Identified Flying Objects] (TF1, Col., 6 August 1984)

DIR: Alain Dhouailly; WRI: Victor Haïm.

CAST: Dominique Arden, Hubert Deschamps, Maurice Chevit.

STORY: UFO story.

On a Feulé Chez M. Sloop [Something Growled at Mr. Sloop's] (A2, Col., 22 November 1981)

DIR/WRI: Claude Ventura, based on a play by Bernard Mazéas.

CAST: Rosine Favey, Bernard Mazéas.

STORY: Gothic story.

L'Oreille Absolue [The Absolute Ear] (ORTF 2, Col., 24 August 1972)

DIR: Philippe Condroyer; WRI: François-Régis Bastide.

CAST: Michel Subor, Hannah Peschar, Jacques Seiler, Guy Tréjean.

STORY: Satirical science fiction.

L'Orgue Fantastique see Verne, Jules

Owen, Thomas

A number of Thomas **Owen**'s short stories (see Book 2) were produced for Belgian television by Pierre Levie.

1. Le Testament de Monsieur Breggins [The Testament of Mr. Breggins] (1965)
DIR: Jean De Lire.

2. Pitié pour les Ombres [Mercy for the Shadows] (1966)
DIR: Lucien Deroisy.

3. Le Voyageur [The Traveler] (1967)
DIR: Françoise Levie

4. Non-Lieu [Innocent] (1968)
DIR: Michel Stameschkine.

5. La Princesse Vous Demande [The Princess Is Asking for You] (1969)
DIR: Jean De Lire.

Les Palmiers du Métropolitain [The Palm Trees of the Metro] (A2, Col., 3 August 1978)
DIR/WRI: Jean-Claude Youri.
CAST: Linda Thorson, Maurice Biraud, Pierre Tornade, Françoise Taillandier.
STORY: Comedy with light fantasy overtones.

La Peau de Chagrin [The Sorrow's Skin] (A2, Col., 150 min., 29 December 1980)
DIR: Michel Favart; WRI: Armand Lanoux, based on the novel by Honoré de **Balzac**.
CAST: Marc Delsaert, Catriona McCall, Anne Faudry, Richard Fontana, Alain Cuny, Alexandre Rignault, Jean-Marie Galey, Raymond Jourdan, Robert Favart.
STORY: A young man receives the gift of a strange talisman which grants his wishes but shortens his life in exchange.
NOTE: For further information about Balzac, see *Melmoth Réconcilié* above.

Le Péril Bleu see *Les Classiques de l'Étrange*

Petit Claus et Grand Claus [Little Claus and Big Claus] (ORTF 2, B&W., 70 min., 25 December 1964)
DIR: Pierre Prévert; WRI: Pierre Prévert, Jacques **Prévert**, based on the story by Hans Christian Andersen.
CAST: Elisabeth Wiener, Maurice Baquet, Roger Blin, Jean-Jacques Steen, Madeleine Damiens, Laure Paillette, Hubert Deschamps, Roger Pigaut (Narrator).
STORY: Big Claus has four horses, while Little Claus has only one. After Big Claus kills his rival's horse, Little Claus plots revenge.

Le Petit Manège [The Little Merry-Go-Round] (FR 3, Col., 30 November 1984)
DIR/WRI: Daniel Tragarz, based on a story by Gilbert Rozes and Michel Rouzière.
CAST: Jean Franval, Vanessa Zaoui, Yolande Gilot, Mimie Mathy.
STORY: Children's fantasy.

Photo-Souvenir [Souvenir Shots] (ORTF 3, Col., 35 min., 10 May 1978)
DIR: Edmond Séchan; WRI: Edmond Séchan, Jean-Claude **Carrière**.
CAST: Jean-Claude Carrière, Vania Vilers, Bernard Lecoq, Danièle Aymé, Ginette Mathieu, Jean-Paul Venel.
STORY: A mysterious camera shows a surgeon pictures of the future.

Pleine Lune [Full Moon] (FR 3, Col., 45 min., 1982)
DIR/WRI: Jean-Pierre Richard.
CAST: Laurent Mallet, Thérèse Liotard.
STORY: A tale of love among vampires.

Président Faust (ORTF 1, Col., 105 min., 12 January 1974)
DIR: Jean Kerchbron; WRI: Jean Kerchbron, Louis **Pauwels**.
CAST: François Chaumette (Faust), François Simon, France Dougnac, Elina Labourdette, Maurice Chevit, André Oumansky, Jacques Mauclair, Jean-Luc Boutté, Laurence Ragon.
STORY: In this modern variation of the classic tale, Faust is a powerful captain of industry who eventually falls in love with the daughter of a trade union leader.
NOTE: Kerchbron and Pauwels also produced *Le Golem* (see above).

Le Prince Porcher [The Pig-Keeping Prince] (RTF, B&W., 20 April 1962)
DIR: Monique Chapelle; WRI: Michèle Angot, based on *The Pig-Keeper and the Princess* by Hans-Christian Andersen.
CAST: Marie Dubois, Jacques Grello, Madeleine Barbulée, Anne Zamire.
STORY: A classic fairy tale.

Le Puits et le Pendule [The Pit and the Pendulum] (ORTF 1, B&W., 45 min., 9 January 1964)
DIR/WRI: Alexandre Astruc, based on the story by Edgar Allan Poe.
CAST: Maurice Ronet.
STORY: Brilliant adaptation of Poe's story. the prisoner escapes by getting rats to chew his bonds.

Que Voyez-Vous, Miss Ellis? [What Do You See, Miss Ellis?] (FR 3, Col., 35 min., 24 August 1975)
DIR: Claude Mourthé; WRI: Anny Mourthé, based on a story by Roderick Wilkinson.
CAST: Edith Scob, Roger Blin, Jean-Paul Cisife, Edgar Duvivier.
STORY: A young girl and her companion are pulled inside a painting.

Le Recyclage de Georges B. [The Recycling of Georges B.] (TV Suisse Romande, 1967)
DIR: Unknown; WRI: Pierre-Henri Zoller.
CAST: Unknown.
STORY: The hero tries to escape from a world where everything is literally kept under wraps.

La Redevance du Fantôme [The Ghost's Rent] (ORTF 1, B&W., 100 min., 17 April 1965)
DIR: Robert Enrico; WRI: Jean Gruault, based on a story by Henry James.
CAST: Stéphane Fey, François Vibert, Marie Laforêt, Reine Courtois, Michel Lonsdale, Philippe Sautrec.
STORY: A classic ghost story.

Le Réquisitionnaire [The Commanding Officer]
(ORTF 1, B&W., 14 May 1968)

DIR: Georges Lacombe; WRI: Didier Goulard, Maurice Fabre, based on a story by Honoré de **Balzac**.

CAST: Alice Sapritch, Jacques Dacqmine, Sylvie Vaneck, Paul Barge.

STORY: Ghost story.

NOTE: For other Balzac adaptations, see *Melmoth Réconcilié* above.

Rhésus B (1967)

DIR: Unknown; WRI: **Gébé** (Georges Blondeau).

CAST: Unknown.

STORY: in 2067, any type of work is prohibited.

NOTE: Also see *L'An 01* (Chapter 1) and Chapter V.

Roc, ou la Malédiction [Roc, or the Curse] (FR 3, Col., 90 min., 6 February 1973)

DIR: Daniel Wronecki; WRI: Daniel Wronecki, Claude **Seignolle**, based on his short story "Le Diable en Sabots" [*The Devil in Clogs*].

CAST: Claude Titre (Roc), Laurence Imbert, François Darbon, Françoise Le Bail, Raymond Meunier, Aline Bertrand, Paul Bisciglia, Thérèse Clay, André Dumas, Arlette Ménard, Jean Nehr.

STORY: Roc, a newcomer, seemingly gifted with mysterious powers, takes over the trade of a smith who hanged himself.

NOTE: For further information on Claude Seignolle, see *Marie la Louve* above.

Les Roses de Manara [The Roses of Manara] (TF1, Col., 24 March 1976)

DIR: Jean Kerchbron; WRI: Louis **Pauwels**, Jean Kerchbron.

CAST: Jean-Claude Drouot, Jean-Roger Caussimon, Jean Rupert, Denise Roland.

STORY: Science fiction.

NOTE: Kerchbron and Pauwels also produced *Le Golem* (see above).

Rubis [Ruby] (A2, Col., 95 min., August 1984)

DIR: Daniel Moosmann; WRI: Jean Bany, based on the short story "To See the Invisible Man" by Robert Silverberg.

CAST: Pierre Vaneck, Claude Mathieu, Georges Chatelain, Stéphane Bouy.

STORY: In the 22nd century, Avignon is ruled by an authoritarian pope. a music teacher who publicly claimed not to like Wagner is condemned to a year of "social invisibility," evidenced by a ruby-like gem implanted on his forehead.

NOTE: This is a loose adaptation of Robert Silverberg's story which originally appeared in the magazine "Worlds of Tomorrow" in 1963. It was adapted again as part of the new *Twilight Zone* on CBS on 31 January 1986, directed by Noel Black, written by Steven Barnes, starring Cotter Smith.

Une Seconde d'Éternité [A Second of Eternity]
(TF1, Col., 70 min., 13 July 1977)

DIR: Gérard Chouchan; WRI: Jean Ferry, based on a story by Daphne du Maurier.

CAST: Loleh Bellon, Catherine Lafond, Pascale Berger, Renée Duchâteau, Anne Denieul.

STORY: A woman is suddenly thrown into a nightmarish reality.

Le Secret de Monsieur L. [The Secret of Mister L.]
(A2, Col., 22 August 1983)

DIR/WRI: Pierre Zucca.

CAST: Pierre Arditi, Michel Bouquet, Irina Brook.

STORY: Satirical tale with fantasy elements.

Le Secret de Rembourg [The Secret of Rembourg]
(ORTF 2, Col., 21 December 1974)

DIR: Jeannette Hubert; WRI: Georges Sonnier, based on a tale by E.T.A. Hoffmann.

CAST: Christian Rist, François Perrot, René Bernan, Jenny Arasse.

STORY: Ghost story.

Le Secret de Wilhelm Storitz see **Verne, Jules**

Sherlock Holmes en Amérique [Sherlock Holmes in America] (RTF, B&W., 24 December 1957)

DIR: Françoise Dumayet; WRI: Unknown.

CAST: Ronald Howard (Holmes), Jean Paqui, Joël Flateau, Georges Janney, Maurice Sarfati.

STORY: Sherlock Holmes pastiche.

Si J'Étais Vous [If I Were You] (ORTF 2, Col., 22 October 1971)

DIR: Ange Casta; WRI: Ange Casta, Robert de Saint-Jean, based on the novel by Julien Green.

CAST: Dominique Maurin, Grégoire Aslan, Jacques Debary, Gérard Darrieu, Henri Virlojeux, Patrick Dewaere, Jean-Paul Moulin.

STORY: An old man (Aslan) gives a young, disillusioned man (Maurin) the power to mentally switch bodies and live other people's lives.

Le Spectre de Tappington [Tappington's Ghost]
(ORTF 2, B&W., 9 April 1965)

DIR: Paul Renty; WRI: Christiane Dupont, based on a story by Richard Harris Barham.

CAST: Pierre Tornade, Cécile Arnold, Jean-Louis Le Goff, Odette Piquet.

STORY: A period ghost story.

Strangers dans la Nuit [Strangers in the Night] (FR 3, Col., 8 October 1991)

DIR: Sylvain Madigan; WRI: Gérard Krawczyk, Marcel Gotlib.

CAST: Karine Viard, Philippe Ulchan, Patrick Braoudé.

STORY: Satirical tale.

NOTE: Marcel Gotlib is a renowned French cartoonist.

La Surprenante Invention du Prof. Delalune [The Surprising Invention of Prof. Delalune] (1964)

DIR/WRI: Albert Husson.

CAST: Unknown.

STORY/NOTE: Science fiction comedy for children included in the program *Théâtre de la Jeunesse [Youth's Theater]*.

Sylvie et le Fantôme [Sylvie and the Ghost] (RTF, B&W., 24 July 1954)

DIR/WRI: Stellio Lorenzi, based on a play by Alfred **Adam**.

CAST: Marianne Lecène (Sylvie), Alfred Adam, Suzanne Dentès, Charles Deschamps, Jean Ozenne, Madeleine Barbulée, Solange Certain, Albert Rémy.

STORY: Sylvie falls in love with a gallant ghost. During a party for her sixteenth birthday, she discovers real love.

NOTE: Also see Chapter I for a feature film adaptation of the same play.

Temps Mort [Dead Time] (Television Suisse Romande, 1969)

DIR: Jean-Jacques Lagrange; WRI: Jean-Louis Roncoroni, based on a story by Georges **Langelaan**.

CAST: Unknown.

STORY: Science fiction.

NOTE: For more information on George Langelaan, see la ***Dame d'Outre-Nulle Part*** above.

Le Testament du Dr. Cordelier [The Testament of Dr. Cordelier, trans. as ***The Doctor's Horrible Experiment, aka Experiment in Evil]*** (RTF, B&W., 100 min., 16 November 1961)

DIR/WRI: Jean Renoir, based on the novel by Robert-Louis Stevenson.

CAST: Jean-Louis Barrault (Dr. Cordelier/Opale), Teddy Bills, Michel Vitold, Jean Topart, Micheline Gary, Gaston Modot.

STORY: French transposition of Stevenson's *Dr. Jekyll and Mr. Hyde.*

NOTE: This film was originally made in 1959 and screened that year at the Venice Film Festival. However, its release was delayed because of a conflict between film and television distributors.

Tête d'Horloge [Clock Head] (ORTF 2, Col., 100 min., 11 April 1970)

DIR: Jean-Paul Sassy; WRI: Jean **Pradeau**, based on his novel.

CAST: Pierre Fresnay (Clock Head), Claude Cerval, Sophie Grimaldi, Bruno Balp, Denise Benoit.

STORY: One day, all of the world's clocks mysteriously stop, except for the watch of an old professor nicknamed "Clock Head" because of his punctuality.

Thanatos Palace Hôtel

Based on the short story by André **Maurois**, a famous writer and essayist (see Book 2).

Version No. 1: (FR3, Col., 60 min., 8 May 1973)

DIR: Pierre Cavassilas; WRI: Maurice **Toesca**

CAST: Max Vialle, Barbara Lass, Jacques Monod, Roger Pelletier.

Version No. 2: (FR3, Col., 14 November 1979)

DIR: James Thor; WRI: Maurice **Toesca**, James Thor.

CAST: Jean-Pierre Bacri, Aïna Walle, Igor Tyczka, Gérard Hérold.

STORY: People wishing to die but afraid to commit suicide come to an hotel where they will be killed painlessly.

NOTE: Maurice Toesca also wrote ***Les Voyageurs de l'Espace*** (see below).

Le Tour d'Écrou [The Turn of the Screw] (ORTF 2, Col., 100 min., 25 December 1974)

DIR: Raymond Rouleau; WRI: Paule de Beaumont, Jean Kerchbron, based on the novel by Henry James.

CAST: Suzanne Flon, Andrée Tainsy, Laure Jeanson, Stéphane Guiraud, Robert Hossein, Marie-Christine Barrault, Robert Rimbaud,.

STORY: Psychoanalytical version of Henry James' classic story in which two children are haunted by the ghosts of an evil gardener and his lover.

NOTE: See Chapter I for a feature film adaptation of the same story. Actor Robert Hossein also directed plays for the **Grand-Guignol**. Also see the anthology series ***James, Henry*** above.

Le Tour du Monde en 80 Jours see ***Verne, Jules***

Tout Spliques étaient les Borogoves [Mimsy Were the Borogoves] (ORTF 2, Col., 85 min., 6 September 1970)

DIR: Daniel Lecompte; WRI: François-Régis Bastide, Daniel Lecompte, Marcel **Schneider**, based on the eponymous short story (published in 1943) by Lewis Padgett, aka Henry Kuttner & Catherine L. Moore.

CAST: Eric Damain, Laurence Debia, Malka Ribowska, William Sabatier, Madeleine Ozeray, Jean-Roger Caussimon, Pierre Didier, Muse Dalbray, Max Desrau.

STORY: Two children find educational toys from another dimension which eventually teach them to travel there.

Le Travail du Furet [The Weasel's Work]

(FR 2, Col., 100 min., 31 January 1994)

DIR: Bruno Gantillon; WRI: Gérard Carré, Alain Minier, based on the novel by Jean-Pierre **Andrevon**.

CAST: Fabrice Eberhard, Marine Delterme, Richard Sammut, Charlie Nelson, Mircea Abulescu, Dan Condurache, Roman Saint-Ourens, Carmen Ionescu, Valentin Uritescu, Luana Stoica.

STORY: In an overpopulated near-future, people are randomly selected to die, and are then killed by a cadre of executioners dubbed "Weasels." One of the Weasels (Eberhard) falls in love with his intended victim (Delterme) and refuses to kill her, then goes on discover that the system is rigged.

NOTE: Jean-Pierre Andrevon is a famous science fiction writer (see Book 2). Another of his books provided the basis for René **Laloux**'s animated feature, *Gandahar* (see Chapter IV). Also see the episode "Lourde Gueuse" in the anthology series *De Biens Étranges Affaires* above.

Vacances au Purgatoire [Holidays in Purgatory]

(FR 3, Col., 90 min., 26 December 1992)

DIR: Marc Simenon; WRI: Valentine Albin.

CAST: Marie-Anne Chazel, Michel Pilorge, Louba Guertchikof, Mylène Demongeot, Thierry de Peretti, Michel Peyrelon.

STORY: After her death, a call-girl is sent back to Earth in the body of a harried housewife.

La Vénus d'Ille [The Venus of Ille]

Based on a story by Prosper **Mérimée**, a famous writer of the *fantastique* (see Book 2).

Version No. 1: (RTF, B&W., 13 December 1957)

DIR: Pierre Badel; WRI: Jean-Claude Youri

CAST: Jacques Castelot, François Vibert, F. Albani, J. Oumanski, Alain Bouvette, Michèle Nadal, Pierre Leproux.

Version No. 2: (FR3, Col., 4 July 1980)

DIR/WRI: Jean-Jacques Bernard, Robert Réa.

CAST: François Marthouret, Jean-Pierre Bacri, Yves Favier, Raymonde Aubray.

STORY: A bridegroom mistakenly places his wedding ring on the finger of the statue of a pagan goddess, and thus seals his doom.

Vie et Mort d'Untel [Life and Death of Anyone]

(FR 3, Col., 55 min., 11 April 1980)

DIR: Fernand Vincent; WRI: Pierre Dupriez, Serge **Martel**.

CAST: Jean-Paul Zehnacker, Alain Doutey, Maud Rayer.

STORY: A man finds a book which tells the story of his life.

NOTE: This script was originally written for a radio play broadcast on *Le Théâtre de l'Étrange* [*Theater of the Weird*] (see Chapter III) on 10 September 1973.

La Voix Venue d'Ailleurs [The Voice from Beyond]

(ORTF 3, Col., 50 min., 20 March 1973)

DIR: Odette Collet; WRI: Pierre Dupriez, Serge **Martel**.

CAST: Elia Clermont, Paul Guers, Michel Fortin.

STORY: A mysterious female voice on the telephone causes the disappearance of a writer.

NOTE: Dupriez and Martel wrote numerous radio scripts for *Le Théâtre de l'Étrange* [*Theater of the Weird*] (see Chapter III). Also see Book 2.

Le Vol d'Icare [The Flight of Icarus] (A2, Col., 100 min., 22 November 1980)

DIR/WRI: Daniel Ceccaldi, based on a novel by Raymond **Quéneau**.

CAST: Michel Galabru, Caroline Cellier, Henri Garcin, Evelyne Buyle, Roger Carel, Pierre Malet.

STORY: A writer hires a detective to locate the hero of his latest novel who has, literally, left the author's manuscript.

NOTE: Raymond Quéneau (see Book 2) was a famous humorist.

Le Voyageur Imprudent [The Careless Traveler]

(A2, Col., 90 min., 2 January 1982)

DIR/WRI: Pierre Tchernia; based on the novel by René **Barjavel**.

CAST: Thierry Lhermitte, Anne Caudry, Jean-Marc Thibault, Lily Fayol, Jean Bouise.

STORY: A time traveler returns to the past and mistakenly kills his grandfather, thus creating a time paradox.

NOTE: For further information on René Barjavel *see Le Grand Secret* above.

Le Voyageur Imprudent.

Les Voyageurs de l'Espace [The Space Travelers]

(ORTF 1, B&W., 22 July 1966)

DIR: Edmond Tybo; WRI: Maurice **Toesca**, based on his play.

CAST: Jacques Duby, Didier Cherreau, Sady Rebot, Bérangère Vattier.

STORY: On another planet, Greek spacemen discover the ancient Greek Gods exiled from Earth 2000 years ago.

NOTE: Maurice Toesca also wrote **Thanatos Palace Hotel** (see above) and **Tête à Tête** for Radio (see Chapter III). He is also the author of a science fiction novel, *Le Singe Bleu* [*The Blue Monkey*] (See Book 2).

Zacharius see **Verne, Jules**

4. Non-Fiction

Fantasy / Fantasy Vision (A2, 30 min., 1986-89)
PROD: Alain Guiot, Alain Carrazé; DIR: Fabrice Maze.
HOSTS: Jean-Luc Delarue, Olivier Dorangeau.
NOTE: Successor of **Temps X** (below), this half-hour show covered science fiction, fantasy, and horror, primarily in the fields of movies and television, using a mix of clips, interviews, etc. the two hosts introduced the topics with trendy banter. The show was programmed as a late-night monthly addition to the music variety anthology *Les Enfants du Rock* [*Children of Rock*].

Temps X (TF1, 60 min., 1979-85)
PROD: Igor & Grichka Bogdanoff, Alain Carrazé, François Jouniaux; DIR: Roland Portiche, Pierre-Alain Beauchard.
HOSTS: Igor & Grichka Bogdanoff.
NOTE: The first television program to cover fantasy and science fiction, as well as science-fact, in depth. the twin hosts posed as cosmonauts on a space station, and introduced a genre series, such as the *Prisoner*, the *Twilight Zone* or *Space: 1999*. More interestingly, they also hosted a wide variety of made-for-order documentaries, covering topics such as superhero comics, genre film festivals, special effects, genre films and television series, science fiction toys and collectibles. We list here a complete episode guide of the show for its first three years.

1. Kurt Steiner (aka André Ruellan), Space travel (21 April 1979).

2. Metz convention, E.T.s, Gérard Klein (28 April 1979).

3. Fashion, E.T.s, Comic books (5 May 1979).

4. Norman Spinrad, *Star Trek*, *Famous Monsters*, Jacques Goimard (12 May 1979).

5. Michel **Jeury**, *Incredible Hulk*, Mutants (19 May 1979).

6. Jacques **Sadoul**, Devo, Robots (26 May 1979).

7. Philippe **Druillet**, Time travel (2 June 1979).

8. Fanzines, Parallel universes (9 June 1979).

9. Jean-Claude **Mézières**, Games, Galactic empires (16 June 1979).

10. Gérard **Klein**, J.R.R. Tolkien, Ends of the world (23 June 1979).

11. Didier Marouani, Futurology (30 June 1979).

12. Philippe **Curval**, René **Barjavel**, Joelle **Wintrebert** (7 July 1979).

13. H.R. Giger, *Alien* (8 September 1979).

14–15. *Star Wars* (22 September/6 October 1979).

16. World Convention (Brighton) (20 October 1979).

17. Jacques Attali, Mad scientists (3 November 1979).

18. *Dracula*, TV series (24 November 1979).

19. J.-M. Jarre, *Time After Time* (1st December 1979)

20. *Lord of the Rings* (15 December 1979).

21. *Meteor*, the Impact of science fiction (29 December 1979).

22. Paris Film Festival (12 January 1980).

23. Avoriaz Film Festival (19 January 1980).

24. Philippe **Druillet** (2 February 1980).

25. *Amityville II* (16 February 1980).

26. Short feature: *L'Horloge Parlante* [*Speaking Clock*] (1st March 1980).

27. *Star Trek: The Motion Picture* (15 March 1980).

28. Short feature: *L'Équation du Plaisir* [*Pleasure Equations*] (29 March 1980).

29. **Pellos**, Arthur C. Clarke (12 April 1980).

30. Paul **Gillon**, Cergy-Pontoise Convention (26 April 1980).

31. Chris Foss, M.H.D. (10 May 1980).

32. Nicollet (24 May 1980).

33. *The Empire Strikes Back*, *The Black Hole* (7 June 1980).

34. Jean-Claude **Mézières**, the *Empire Strikes Back* (21 June 1980).

35–42. *Space: 1999* (broadcast of television episodes).

43. Short feature: *Le Voyageur du Carbonifère* [*Traveller from the Carbonifere*] (13 September 1980).

44–45. Rockets (20/27 September 1980).

46. Black holes (4 October 1980).

47. Short feature: *L'Ultime Creation* [*The Ultimate Creation*] (11 October 1980).

48. Jack Williamson (18 October 1980).

49. Philippe **Druillet**, H.R. Giger (25 October 1980).

50. French comic books, Robots (1st November 1980).

51. *The Shining* (8 November 1980).

52. John Varley (15 November 1980).

53. Paris Film Festival (22 November 1980).

54. *Superman II* (29 November 1980)

55. Robots (II) (6 December 1980).

56. Alexandro **Jodorowsky**, Future foods (13 December 1980).

57. Enki **Bilal**, Cinema: The Year in Review (20 December 1980).

58. W. Siudmak, Short feature: *La Planète Rouge* [*Red Planet*], DIR: Roland Portiche. STORY: The First Expedition to Mars (27 December 1980).

59. Gérard **Klein**, The year 2000 (3 January 1981).

60. A.C. Decouflé, Monsters, Short feature: *La Réponse* [*The Answer*] (10 January 1981).

61. Avoriaz Film Festival (17 January 1981).

62. F*lash Gordon* (24 January 1981).

63. Robert Sheckley, Monsters (II) (31 January 1981).

64. Short feature: *Le Dormeur* [*The Sleeper*], DIR: Roland Portiche. STORY: A man comes out of hibernation every hundred years (7 February 1981).

65. Boris Vallejo, Daniel Garric, Atlantis (14 February 1981).

66. M. Salomon, Theodore Sturgeon (21 February 1981).

67. Jean-Pierre **Andrevon**, *Close Encounters—the Special Edition* (28 February 1981).

68. Jesco con Puttkamer, NASA, Frankenstein (14 March 1981).

69. Short feature: *Frontière Noire* [*Dark Frontier*], DIR: Roland Portiche. STORY: First contact between men and aliens (21 March 1981).

70. Roger Corman, *Battle Beyond the Stars* (28 March 1981).

71. Animation, More robots (4 April 1981).

72. Guéranger, *Scanners* (11 April 1981).

73. Tim White, NASA (II) (18 April 1981).

74. Computer-generated animation, *Somewhere in Time* (25 April 1981).

75. Short feature: *L'Ange Gardien* [*Guardian Angel*], DIR: Roland Portiche. STORY: A computer-controlled house goes wrong (2 May 1981).

76. Alexander Mosley, Utopias (9 May 1981).

77. Colonna, Nostradamus (16 May 1981).

78. Superheroes, Alien worlds (23 May 1981).

79. *Excalibur, A Spaceman in King Arthur's Court* (30 May 1981).

80. Harlan Ellison, *2001* (6 June 1981).

81. Arthur C. Clarke, Bernard **Blanc**, Space travel (20 June 1981).

82. *Clash of the Titans* (27 June 1981).

83–92. *Battlestar Galactica* (broadcast of television episodes).

93. *Outland*, Comic books (12 September 1981).

94. *Raiders of the Lost Ark* (19 September 1981).

95. *After the Apocalypse* (26 September 1981).

96. *Altered States* (3 October 1981).

97. Gorge Ifrah, *Insects* (10 October 1981).

98. John Glenn, *Fantastic Monsters* (17 October 1981).

99. Pierre **Versins**, Lille convention (24 October 1981).

100. *Catastrophes* (31 October 1981).

101. *Heavy Metal* (7 November 1981).

102. Paris Film Festival (14 November 1981).

103. Ray Harryhausen, Jacques Gastineau (21 November 1981).

104. Fantastic animation (28 November 1981).

105. Leonardo da Vinci (5 December 1981).

106–107, 109. UFOs and E.T.s (12/19 December 1981, 2 January 1982).

108. Short feature: *Frankenstein, la Véritable Histoire* [*Frankenstein: The True Story*], DIR: Roland Portiche. STORY: Frankenstein is a ready-to-assemble alien robot (26 December 1981).

CHAPTER III

Radio

1. Historical Overview

The golden age of French radio took place in the 1950s and the early 1960s, when up to fifteen million listeners remained glued to their seats for a variety of programs including music, comedy, game shows, and serials.

If most serials were soaps like the hugely popular *La Famille Duraton* (Radio-Luxembourg, 1937-66!), a few relied on the traditional forms of pulp literature for their inspiration: Fearless heroes fighting mysterious villains bent on world domination. Some played it straight (***L'Homme à la Voiture Rouge*** (*The Man with the Red Car*, 1962–64); others with a hearty dose of humor, like the classic ***Signé Furax*** (*Signed: Furax*, 1951–52; 1956–60); One, ***Ça Va Bouillir*** (*It's Gonna Boil*, 1952–66), managed to have it both ways, featuring a real radio personality playing himself as the hero of incredible adventures.

From 1968 on, television took over the place that had been occupied by radio in the family bosom. Radio was relegated to sports, news, and music until the 1980s, when so-called "free" radio and FM radio exploded on the air waves.

2. Series

L'Apocalypse Est pour Demain [The Apocalypse Is for Tomorrow] (France-Inter, 1977)

WRI/VOICES: Jean **Yanne**.

STORY: A "salubrious and ecological" comedy serial in which movie star/comedian Jean Yanne tells the adventures of Robin Cruso in a world invaded by pollution and cars.

NOTE: Yanne (a noted actor-director who directed ***Les Chinois à Paris*** (see Book 1, Chapter I)) wrote a novelisation of his serial (see Book 2).

Astérix (France-Inter, 1966-68)

VOICES: Roger Carel (Astérix), Jacques Morel (Obélix), Bernard Lavalette.

STORY: Based on the famous graphic novels by **Goscinny** and **Uderzo** (see Chapter V), the radio adaptations expanded the original stories and added new characters (such as the two idiotic Roman spies Romulus and Remus, proud to belong to "very old Roman families") and new layers of plot.

Les Aventures de Peter Gay see *Peter Gay*

Les Aventures de Tchitchklov see *Tchitchklov*

Blake & Mortimer (ORTF/France II, 1960–63)

DIR: Jacques Langeais, Nicole Strauss.

VOICES: Jacques Morel (Mortimer), Roger Carel, Jean Rochefort, Jean-Pierre Marielle.

STORY: Adaptations of two of the popular graphic novels: *SOS Météores* [*SOS Meteors*] and *Le Piège Diabolique* [*The Time Trap*] by Edgar-Pierre **Jacobs** (see Chapter V).

Bons Baisers de Partout [From Everywhere with Love] (France-Inter, 1966–68)

WRI/VOICES: Pierre **Dac**, Louis Rognoni.

STORY: This madcap *James Bond* satire tells the adventures of Nicolas Leroidec, anvil salesman and French intelligence ace. All the characters sport punnish names: Hubert de Guerlasse, l'Adjudant Tifrisse, etc. Some of the stories involve SF elements, as when two agents are sent a year back in time.

Ça Va Bouillir see *Zappy Max*

C'est Parti Mon Zappy see *Zappy Max*

Doyle, Sir Arthur Conan (France-Culture, 1981)

1. *La Main Brune [The Brown Hand]* (19 September 1981)
DIR: Anne Lemaître; WRI: E. Loria.

2. *La Hachette d'Argent* [*The Silver Axe*] (28 September 1981)
DIR: C. Roland-Manuel; WRI: M. Loran, E. Loria.

3. *La Grande Experience de Keinplatz [The Great Keinplatz Experiment]* (5 October 1981)
DIR: G. Delaunay; WRI: M. Loran.

4. *Le Lot No. 249* (12 October 1981)
DIR: Arlette Dave; WRI: M. Loran, E. Loria.

5. *L'Anneau de Toth [The Ring of Toth]* (26 October 1981)
DIR: G. Peyrou; WRI: E. Loria.
STORY/NOTE: A series of adaptations of Conan Doyle's stories dealing with reincarnation, the occult, parapsychology, and ancient curses.

Dracula (France-Culture, 17 Eps., 1982-83)
DIR/WRI: Jacques Bransolle, Jean-Pierre Colas, based on the novel by Bram Stoker.

L'Homme à la Voiture Rouge [The Man with the Red Car] (Radio-Luxembourg, 1962-64)
DIR: Jean Maurel; WRI: Yves Jamiaque.
STORY: Reporter Stéphane Berrier and his red car, Ruby (which seems gifted with some kind of intelligence, as it appears to warn or rescue him from tight spots) fights a worldwide conspiracy led by the "*Grand Patron*" [*Big Boss*], from a secret base under a volcano in Sicily to one protected by a deadly force field in the Amazon Delta.

Littérature Populaire & Fantastique aux 18ème & 19ème Siècle [Fantastic & Popular Literature of the 18th & 19th Century] (France-Culture, 1980)
DIR/HOST: Maurice Sarfati.

1. *Caftan Rouge le Sorcier [Red Caftan the Wizard]* (18 August 1980)
DIR: Bronislav Horowicz; WRI: Nikolai Gogol.

2. *Les Chiennes Blanches [The White Dogs]* (19 August 1980)
DIR: Eveline Fremy; WRI: James Hogg.

3. *Poing de Fer [Iron Fist]* (20 August 1980)
DIR: Anne Lemaître; WRI: Walter Scott.

4. *Le Château d'Otranto [The Castle Of Otranto]* (21 August 1980)
DIR: Bronislav Horowicz; WRI: Horace Walpole.

5. *Wolfstein et Mégalena* (23 August 1980)
DIR: Georges Peyrou; WRI: Percy B. Shelley.
NOTE: A series of adaptations of popular gothic fantasy stories.

Malheur aux Barbus see *Signé Furax*

Le Mystérieux Dr. Cornelius [The Mysterious Dr. Cornelius] (France-Culture, thirty-five 30 min. eps., 1978)
DIR: Alain Barroux; WRI: Édith Loria, based on the novels by Gustave **Le Rouge**.
CAST: Jean Topart (Fritz), Michel Bouquet (Cornelius), Denis Manuel (Harry Dorgan), Guy Tréjean (G. de Maubreuil), Jean Wiener (Bondonnat), Pierre Vaneck (Burydan), Catherine Hubeau (Isidora), Naïa Simon (Andrée), Catherine Laborde (Frédérique).
NOTE: Radio adaptation of the famous pulp serial novel about a mad plastic surgeon and the heroes who band together to defeat him. See Book 2. Also see Chapter II for a television adaptation.

Panix (France Inter, 1973-76)
WRI/VOICES: Claude Villers, Patrice Blanc-Francard.
STORY: The comedic adventures of French super-hero Panix, who protects his girl-friend Mireille Pamieux from the evil schemes of villainous Elvis Sansfin.

Passeport pour l'Inconnu [Passport for the Unknown] (Radio-Genève, 1957)
DIR: Roland Sassi; WRI: Pierre **Versins**.
STORY: Adaptations of classic novels and short stories by Asimov, Van Vogt, Heinlein, etc. Original radio plays include:
Procyon Simple Course [Procyon Simple Run] by Robert Pibouleau (18 February 1959)
Le Robot Mal-Aimé [The Ill-Loved Robot] by Laurent Lourson (18 March 1959)
A-t-il Fait Sauter la Maison? [Has He Blown Up the House?] by Roland Sassi (7 May 1965)
Hier le Jour, Hier la Nuit [Yesterday the Day, Yesterday the Night] by Martine Thomé (16 June 1966)
NOTE: Pierre **Versins** is a renowned science fiction scholar, author of several novels as well as the *Encyclopédie de l'Utopie et de la Science-Fiction* (See Book 2).

Les Aventures de Peter Gay [The Adventures of Peter Gay] (Europe 1, 1963-64)

WRI: Jacques Antoine.

VOICES: Pierre Gay.

STORY: Peter Gay was an aerospace engineer who became involved in adventures blending cutting edge scientific discoveries and spy thrillers. He took part in telepathic experiments between the Pentagon and a nuclear submarine cruising under the Pole; he thwarted a terrorist assassination attempt against UN Secretary Dag Hammarskjöld, etc.

Plate-Forme 70 (RTF, 1946)

DIR: Bernard Gandrey-Réty; WRI: Jean **Nocher**.

VOICES: Jean Nocher.

STORY: Prof. Hélium (Nocher) warns the listeners that Earth is in imminent danger of being destroyed by a freak atomic explosion.

NOTE: This Orson Welles' *War of the Worlds*–like broadcast was taken seriously by many listeners and generated 28,000 letters. It was novelized by Nocher in 1946 (see Book 2).

Le Prisonnier de la Planète Mars [The Prisoner of Planet Mars] (France-Culture, 1978)

DIR/WRI: Marguerite **Cassan**, based on the novels by Gustave **Le Rouge**.

NOTE: Radio adaptation of the famous pulp serial novel about the war against Martian vampires. Marguerite Cassan is a noted writer of the *fantastique* (see Book 2).

Renard, Maurice (France-Culture, 1981)

DIR: E. Frémy; WRI: Marguerite **Cassan**.

1. *La Berlue de Mme d'Estrailles [Mrs. d'Estrailles' Vision]* (9 November)

2. *L'Homme qui Voulait Être Invisible [The Man Who Wanted to Be Invisible]* (16 November)

3. *L'Homme Truqué [The Rigged Man]* (20 November)

4. *L'Homme au Corps Subtil [The Man with a Subtle Body]* (23 November)

5. *Le Brouillard du 26 Octobre [The Mist of October 26th.]* (30 November)

6. *L'Affaire du Miroir [The Mirror Affair]* (7 December)

NOTE: A series of adaptations of science fiction short-stories; for further adaptations of Maurice Renard, see Chapter I (in particular **Les Mains d'Orlac**) and Chapter II.

7. *L'Image au Fond des Yeux [The Image at the Bottom of the Eyes]* (14 December)

Rocambole (RTF, 1941)

Based on the famous character created by popular writer Victor-Alexis **Ponson du Terrail** (see Book 2).

La Science-Fiction (France-Culture, 1980-81)

DIR: Henri Soubeyran; WRI: Catherine Bourd et.

1. *The Dreaming Jewels* (Theodore Sturgeon) *(*26 July 1980)

2. *The Man in the High Castle* (Philip K. Dick) (2 August 1980)

3. *Les Vampires de l'Alfama* (Pierre **Kast**) (19 August 1980)

4. *Le Correcteur* (Isaac Asimov) (21 August 1980)

5. *The Lovers* (Philip Jose Farmer) (25 July 1981)

6. *A Door Into Summer* (Robert A. Heinlein) (1st August 1981)

NOTE: A series of adaptations of classic science fiction novels by major American writers.

Signé Furax

1. *Malheurs aux Barbus [Woe to the Bearded Ones]* (RTF, 1951–1952)

2. *Signé Furax [Signed: Furax]* (Europe 1, 1956–1960)

WRI: Pierre **Dac**, Francis **Blanche**; DIR: Pierre-Arnaud de Chassy-Poulay.

VOICES: Pierre Dac (Black), Francis Blanche (White), Jean-Marie Amato (Furax, Asti), Jeanne Dorival (Malvina), Maurice Biraud (Socrate), Edith Fontaine, Roger Pierre, Jean-Marc Thibault, Raymond Devos, Pauline Carton, Jean Poiret, Laurence Riesner, François Chevrais.

STORY: Retired arch-criminal Edmond Furax and his girlfriend, the beautiful Malvina, help the forces of good, in the persons of Police Commissioner Socrate, private investigators Black and White, former hitman Asti Spumante, genial scientist Hardy-Petit, his daughter Carole, and son-in-law Théo Courant, thwart the nefarious schemes of the evil secret sect of the Babus (originally the "*Barbus*" [*Bearded Ones*]), led by the evil Klakmuf. Plots include the dehydration of Paris' monuments to better steal them, traveling back in time to the Crimean War to change history, a strange light which saps people's wills, a space-travelling atoll which takes our heroes to the planet Asterix, and an invasion of giant spiders. The last episode of the saga, *Le Gruyère Qui Tue (The Swiss Cheese That Kills)* saw Earth being threatened by body-snatching aliens, the Gsbrr, who literally inhabit Swiss cheese. With the help of their friends from planet Asterix, and of some Parmesan cheese, Furax and the gang will defeat the Gsbrr.

NOTE: This legendary series was serialized in the form of daily ten-minutes episodes (weekdays only) and totaled over 1200 episodes. The saga began modestly on RTF as a short-lived series entitled *Malheurs aux Barbus* narrating the fight of private investigators Black and White against the megalomaniacal gangster, Edmond Furax. Four years later, it was reincarnated on Europe No.1 as *Signé Furax* and quickly became a national media event. Also see Chapter I for a feature film adaptation, Chapter V for a comic strip adaptation and Book 2 for a series of novelizations.

Les Aventures de Tchitchklov (17 eps., France-Culture, 1979)

DIR: Sylvie Marville, based on the novel *Dead Souls* by Nikolai Gogol.

Le Théâtre de l'Étrange [Theater of the Weird]

(France-Inter, 1963-74)

DIR/HOST: Frédéric Christian.

NOTE: In addition to covering the genre with interviews, reviews, etc., this anthology show presented monthly radio adaptations of classic novels and short stories by Anderson, Heinlein, Claude **Seignolle** (see *Delphine* below), etc. Original radio plays include:

Akatan Bloc NC 22 by René Brandt (1964).

Le Mal des Mots [*The Evil of Words*] by Stella Matard (1966).

L'Ambassadeur de Xonoi [*The Ambassador from Xonoi*] by Frédéric Christian (1968), in which a computer-generated voice played an alien.

Les Orgues du Vent [*The Organs of the Wind*] by Louis **Thirion** (1968).

Le Petit Homme de San Francisco [*The Little Man of San Francisco*] by Louis Thirion (1968).

Appartement 6000 ou Le Gardien [*Apartment 6000, or The Watchman*] by Louis Thirion (1969).

Eudes, l'Enfant venu d'Ailleurs [*Eudes, the Child from Beyond*] by Louis Thirion (1970).

Tintin (Europe 1, 1964)

VOICES: Jacques Hilling (Haddock), Jacques Dufilho (Tournesol).

STORY: Adaptations of the graphic novels by **Hergé** (see Chapter V).

Les Tréteaux de la Nuit [Night Stage] (France-Inter, 1979-80)

HOSTS: Patrice Galbeau, Jean-Jacques Vierne.

DIRS: Bronislav Horowicz, Claude Roland-Manuel, Bernard Saxe, Georges Godebert, Anne Lemaître, Olivier d'Horrer, Jeanne Rollin-Weisz, Jacques Taroni, Henri Soubeyran, Arlette Dave, Jean-Wilfrid Garrett, etc.

NOTE: A series of weekly 50-minute original plays featuring fantasy, horror or science fiction elements. Stories for the 1979 and 1980 seasons are listed below:

13 January 1979: *La Tête* [*The Head*] by Jacques Mauclair.
20 January 1979: *Le Dernier des Rabasteins* [*The Last of the Rabasteins*] by Philippe Derrez.

27 January 1979: *Le Reportage* [*The Report*] by Marie-Blanche Dumet.
3 February 1979: *Oh! Quelle Famille* [*What a Family!*] by Jean Brach.
10 February 1979: *Djamilia* by Marie O.
17 February 1979: *La Très Humide Histoire de Fusain Canson et de sa Goelette* [*The Very Humid Story of Fusain Canson and of His Schooner*] by Colette Piat.
24 February 1989: *La Caverne de la Nuit* [*The Cavern Night*] by Philippe Brunet-Schneider.
3 March 1979: *Le Vent Kuona* [*The Wind Kuona*] by Jacques Floran.
10 March 1979: *Un Poisson dans la Ville* [*A Fish in the City*] by Jean-François Menard.
17 March 1979: *La Marque* [*The Mark*] by Maurice Dantan.
24 March 1979: *Une Funeste Expérience* [*A Sinister Experiment*] by Dominique Cir.
31 March 1979: *Une Nuit de Solstice* [*Solstice Night*] by Katherine Robineau.
7 April 1979: *Les Cerceaux Domestiques* [*The Domestic Hoops*] by Odile Marcel.
14 April 1979: *M comme Mithra* [*M as in Mithra*] by Catherine d'Etchea.
21 April 1979: *L'Homme en Noir* [*The Man in Black*] by Frédéric Christian.
28 April 1979: *Une Singuliere Journée* [*A Singular Day*] by Louis Rognoni.
5 May 1979: *L'Étrange Partie d'Échecs de Douglas McLloy* [*The Strange Chess Game of Douglas McLloy*] by Catherine Tolstoï.
12 May 1979: *Alex et Odilon* by Jean Emmanuel.
19 May 1979: *La Bombe Glacée* [*The Ice Cream Surprise*] by Michèle Tourneur.
26 May 1979: *Du Cyanure dans la Rivière* [*Cyanide in the River*] by Henri Mitton.
9 June 1979: *C'est Mon Papa Qui a Gagné la Bataille* [*My Daddy Won the Battle*] by J.J. Steen.
16 June 1979: *La Leçon de Chine* [*China Lesson*] by Francis Roure.
23 June 1979: *L'Homme aux Yeux Gris* [*The Man with Grey Eyes*] by Jean-Jacques Varoujean.
30 June 1979: *Un Testament Provençal* [*A Provencal Testament*] by Pierre Magnan.
7 July 1979: *Opération Osiris* by Jacques Idier.
14 July 1979: *La Marée Était en Noir* [*The Tide Wore Black*] by Jean-Claude Danaud.
28 July 1979: *L'Hôtel du Progrès* by Jean Brach.
4 August 1979: *Saint Petersbourg* by Patrick Besson.
11 August 1979: *Mademoiselle Else* by Arthur Schitzer.
18 August 1989: *La Grande Entourloupe* [*The Great Trick*] by Roald Dahl.
25 August 1979: *Bouche Cousue* [*Closed Mouth*] by Charles Goupil.
1st September: *Le Fantôme Inconnu* [*The Unknown Ghost*] by Daniel Zerki.

15 September 1979: *Un Château de Sable* [*A Sand Castle*] by Jacques Bens.

22 September 1979: *Paradise* Barby Gilbert Simourre.

29 September 1979: *Clamuche, ou La Vertu Récompensée* [*Clamuche, or Rewarded Virtue*].

6 October 1979: *Comme à la Fin d'une Danse* [*As at the End of a Dance*] by Marie-Bénédicte Charon.

13 October 1979: *La Mort Caméléon* [*Chameleon Death*] by Martin Lewis.

20 October 1979: *Requiem pour un Inconnu* [*Requiem for an Unknown Man*] by Gerard Houlet.

27 October 1979: *Place Clichy* by Jean-Jacques Varoujean.

3 November 1979: *Un Poète M'a Dit* [*A Poet Told Me*] by Marc Audouard.

17 November 1979: *La Fille de Lady Edwina* [*Lady Edwina's Daughter*] by Gabriel Douchkine.

1st December 1979: *Le Trou* [*The Hole*] by Daniel Goldenberg.

8 December 1979: *Rendez-vous à Sainte Adresse* by Patrick Liegebel.

15 December 1979: *Numéro Huit, au Bout de l'Impasse* [*No.8 at the End of the Dead End*] by Michèle Tourneur.

22 December 1979: *La Visitation* by Henri Weitzmann.

29 December 1979: *Mort d'un Vampire Trop Honnête* [*Death of a Too Honest Vampire*] by Bernard Da Costa.

12 January 1980: *Bonjour Philippine* by Fred Kassak.

26 January 1980: *Dossier CX* by Louis Rognogni.

9 February 1980: *L'Entrée de Service* [*The Service Entrance*] by Guy Haurey.

16 February 1980: *Hasard ou Vengeance* [*Chance or Revenge*] by Ida Savignac.

23 February 1980: *Du Muguet en Hiver* [*Lily in Winter*] by Claude Dufresne.

8 March 1980: *Trains Espace Tour* by Bernard Mazeas.

29 March 1980: *Quai 17* [*Platform 17*] by Pascal Hamel.

12 April 1980: *L'Adjudant* by Patrick Besson.

26 April 1980: *Allo! C'est toi? C'est moi* [*Hello? Is it you? It's Me*] by Philippe Clay.

17 May 1980: *Le Mal d'Aurore* [*Dawn's Disease*] by Catherine Tolstoï.

14 June 1980: *Le Jeune Garçon au Bord de la Rivière* [*The Young Man by the River*] by Guy Haurey.

21 June 1980: *Les Voyageurs de Nulle Part* [*The Travelers from Nowhere*] by Luc Sylvair.

5 July 1980: *Les Gens du Dessus* [*The People from Above*] by Gilles Laurent et Marie Borrel.

2 August 1980: *Angelina et son Armoire* [*Angelina and Her Dresser*] by Daniel Goldenberg.

9 August 1980: *Le Juke-box Jouait du Wagner* [*The Juke-Box Played Wagner*] by Jean-Claude Danaud.

27 September 1980: *Le Tueur de Temps* [*The Time Killer*] by Alain Spiraux.

8 November 1980: *Le Fantôme de la Maoulinière* [*The Ghost of Maouliniere*] by Henri Weitzmann.

6 December 1980: *Attention: Une Sorciere Peut en Cacher Une Autre* [*Watch Out: One Witch Can Hide Another*] by Katherine Robineau.

20 December 1980: *La Planète du Temps* [*Time's Planet*] by Louis Rognoni.

Trois Hommes à la Recherche d'une Comète [*Three Men in Search of a Comet*] (France-Culture, 20 eps., 4–29 August 1980)

WRI: Lazare Kobrynski.

STORY: To avoid nuclear war, the super-powers are duped into sending missiles toward a threatening comet. But the missiles destroy the Moon instead.

Les Tyrans Sont Parmi Nous [*The Tyrants Are Among Us*] (RTF, 1953)

WRI: Jacques Antoine.

STORY: A mysterious, international organisation, Point Zero, has found the secret of making gold ("artificial" gold is, however, slightly radioactive) and prepares to use it to conquer the world.

Vas-y Zappy see *Zappy Max*

Voyages au Bout de la Science [*Voyage to the Ends of Science*] (Radio-Lausanne, 1952)

WRI: Stephen Spriel.

STORY: This thirteen-episode magazine series also broadcast a number of original radio plays written by Stephen Spriel (the co-founder of the science fiction imprint *Le Rayon Fantastique*) and G.-M. Bovay (except where otherwise mentioned):

1. *Ils Sont Parmi Nous* [*They Walk Among Us*].

2. *Les Sur-Animaux* [*The Over-Animals*].

3. *Un Maître du Monde* [*A Master of the World*].

4. *Les Passagers de l'Avenir* [*The Passengers from the Future*].

5. *Fort-de-France Appelle Mont-Pelé* (by René Maurice-Picard).

6. *Menace sur la Terre* [*Menace on Earth*].

7. *La Reine de la Jungle* [*The Queen of the Jungle*].

8. *Le Jour où la Terre s'arrêta* [*The Day the Earth Stood Still*] (adaptation of the film).

9. *Le Congrès de 39* [*The Congress of 39*] (by René Maurice-Picard).

10. *Quand le Soleil Reviendra* [*When the Sun Returns*].

11–12. *Le Nouveau Déluge* [*The New Flood*] (based on a novel by Noelle Roger).

13. *Les Révoltés de l'An 3000* [*Revolt in the Year 3000*].

XT-1 (Radio-Luxembourg, 1957)

DIR/HOST: Georges H. Gallet, Jacques Tourneur.

NOTE: Short-lived magazine series created by the co-founder of the science fiction imprint *Le Rayon Fantastique*. Jacques Tourneur was the son of Maurice **Tourneur**.

Zappy Max

1. *Vas-y Zappy [Go for It, Zappy]* (Radio-Luxembourg, 1952-57)

2. *Ça Va Bouillir [It's Gonna Boil!]* (Radio-Luxembourg, 1957-63)

3. *C'est Parti Mon Zappy [Zappy Max Is Go!]* (Radio-Luxembourg, 1963-66)

WRI: Saint-Julien (Hugo de Hahn).

VOICES: Zappy Max (Himself), Roger Carel, Jacques Balutin, Jean Daurant, André Le Gall.

STORY: Radio personality Zappy Max plays himself as an investigative reporter who thwarts the evil, world-conquering schemes of the obese mad scientist Kurt von Strafenberg (Le Gall), aka the *Tonneau [Barrel]*, and the secret criminal society known as the *Treize [Thirteen]*.

NOTE: This is one of the longest serials on French radio, totaling over 3300 episodes. The name change was due to a change of sponsors in 1963, from Unilever to Procter & Gamble. Also see Chapter V for a comic book adaptation.

3. Plays

Over the years, France-Inter and France-Culture, a cultural channel, have broadcast numerous radio plays featuring fantastic elements; some were original stories, others adaptations of literary classics. A comprehensive listing of such plays is virtually impossible to assemble, as records of these are incomplete and no study has been published. We have listed here a selection of some of the more interesting plays.

L'Arc-en-Ciel, ou Naissance d'un Mutant [The Rainbow, or Birth of a Mutant] (France-Culture, 1966)

DIR/WRI: R.-J. Chauffard.

STORY: Post-cataclysmic tale.

L'Attentat en Direct [Terrorism on Live TV] (France-Culture, 1969)

DIR/WRI: Claude **Ollier**.

STORY: Political fiction.

NOTE: Ollier also wrote novels (see Book 2) and the film *Écoute Voir [Hear See]* (see Chapter I).

L'Autre Monde [The Other World] (France-Culture, 1980)

DIR/WRI: Bronislav Horowicz, based on the story by **Cyrano de Bergerac**.

STORY: Radio dramatization of the famous utopia.

Les Aventures Génétiques [The Genetic Adventures] (France-Inter, 1981)

DIR: O. d'Horrer; WRI: Jean Loisy.

STORY: Two geneticists produce a superbaby.

Le Bal des Affamés [The Ball of the Starving] (France-Inter, 1981)

DIR: J. Taroni; WRI: Alain **Page**.

STORY: A writer's fictional characters assume lives of their own.

NOTE: Alain Page wrote *Le Mutant* (see Chapter II).

La Brume Ne Se Lèvera Plus [The Devil in Clogs] (Radio-Montpellier, 1966)

DIR/WRI: Maurice Bardoulat, based on a story by Claude **Seignolle**.

VOICES: Madeleine Attal.

NOTE: For other Seignolle adaptations, see *Delphine* below.

Ce Que Me Raconta Jacob [What Jacob Told Me] (France-Inter (*Théâtre de l'Étrange*), 1966)

DIR/WRI: René Jentet, based on a story by Claude **Seignolle**.

VOICES: Gérard Darrieu, Léon Spiegelman.

NOTE: For other Seignolle adaptations, see *Delphine* below.

Le Chupador (France-Inter (*Theâtre de l'Étrange*), 1968)

DIR/WRI: Jeanne Rollin-Weisz, based on a story by Claude **Seignolle**.

VOICES: Michel Vitold, François Maistre, France Descaux.

STORY: Ghost story; for other Claude Seignolle adaptations, see *Delphine* below.

Coeur de Chien [Heart of a Dog] (France-Culture, 1981)

DIR: C. Roland-Manuel; WRI: G. Bray, based on the novel by Mikhail Bulgakov.

NOTE: A satire of Soviet society based on a popular Russian genre novel.

Les Cris du Coeur [The Screams of the Heart] (France-Inter, 1981)

DIR: P. Billard; WRI: Robert Nahmias.

STORY: Is personality transferred after a heart transplant?

Le Diable Amoureux [The Devil in Love] (France-Culture, 1980)

DIR: Jeanne Rollin-Weisz; WRI: Henri Weitzmann, based on the novel by Jacques **Cazotte**.

STORY: A nobleman summons a demon.

Le Diable en Sabots [The Devil in Clogs] (Radio-Montpellier, 1964)

DIR/WRI: Maurice Bardoulat, based on a story by Claude **Seignolle**.

VOICES: Madeleine Attal.

NOTE: For other Seignolle adaptations, see **Delphine** below.

Delphine (France-Inter (Théâtre de l'Étrange), 1967; Rep. France-Culture, 1981)

DIR: Alain Baloux; WRI: Hubert Juin, based on a story by Claude **Seignolle**.

VOICES: Michel Bouquet, Fernand Ledoux.

STORY: Ghost story; for other Claude Seignolle adaptations, see **La Brume Ne Se Lèvera Plus, Ce Que Me Raconta Jacob, Le Chupador, Le Diable en Sabots, La Galoup, Marie la Louve,** and **Le Millième Cierge**; also see **Le Faucheur** under Short Features in Chapter I and **Marie la Louve** in Chapter II.

Electrodome 2006 (France-Culture, 1979)

DIR: B. Saxe; WRI: Verell Pennington Ferguson.

STORY: *Rollerball* inside a giant electronic billiard.

Etat Civil [Civil State] (France-Culture, 1968)

DIR: Unknown; WRI: Pierre **Gripari**.

STORY: Social satire.

Le Fantastique Inceste [The Fantastic Incest] (France-Culture, 1967)

DIR: Unknown; WRI: Pierre Le Quellec.

STORY: Time travel story.

Les Fleurs de Systèle [The Flowers of Systele] (France-Culture, 1981)

DIR: E. Cramer; WRI: Myrielle Marc.

STORY: Women of the future revolt by refusing to bear female babies.

Le Galoup (France-Inter (Théâtre de l'Étrange), 1968)

DIR/WRI: Jeanne Rollin-Weisz, based on a story by Claude **Seignolle**.

STORY: Ghost story; for other Claude Seignolle adaptations, see **Delphine**.

Grand-Guignol

Great-Guignol (1923)

Marémoto (1924)

DIR: Georges Godebert; WRI: Gabriel Germinet (*Marémoto* written in collaboration with Pierre Cusy).

NOTE: Radio plays written for the **Grand-Guignol** Theater (see Book 2) and broadcast by the BBC.

Inutile de S'Inquiéter [No Need to Worry] (France-Inter, 1981)

DIR: Anne Lemaître; WRI: Serge Ganzl.

STORY: Two aliens study mankind through the eyes of dogs.

Le Jeune Garçon au Bord de la Rivière [The Young Boy by the River] (France-Inter, 1981)

DIR: J. Taroni; WRI: Guy Haurey.

STORY: Ghost story.

La Lune Comme un Point sur un I [The Moon as a Dot on the I] (France-Inter, 1981)

DIR: H. Soubeyran; WRI: Michelle Tourneur.

STORY: Ghost story.

Marie la Louve [Mary the Wolf]

Version No. 1: Radio-Toulouse, 1965

Version No. 2: Radio-Limoges, 1968

DIR/WRI: Maurice Bardoulat, based on a story by Claude **Seignolle** (both versions).

NOTE: For other Seignolle adaptations, see **Delphine** below.

Le Martien [The Martian] (Radio-Luxembourg, 1954)

DIR: Unknown; WRI: Georges **Chaulet**.

STORY: Phony Martian.

NOTE: Georges Chaulet is the creator of **Fantômette** and **Les Quatre As** (see Chapter V).

Le Matagot (France-Inter [Théâtre de l'Étrange], 1970)

DIR/WRI: Jeanne Rollin-Weisz, based on a story by Claude **Seignolle**.

STORY: Ghost story; for other Claude Seignolle adaptations, see **Delphine**,

Le Millième Cierge [The Thousandth Candle] (France-Inter [Théâtre de l'Étrange], 1968)

DIR/WRI: René Jentet, based on a story by Claude **Seignolle**.

VOICES: Gérard Darrieu, Jean-Roger Caussimon, Catherine Seller.

STORY: Ghost story; for other Claude Seignolle adaptations, see *Delphine*,

La Mort Caméléon [The Chameleon Death] (France-Inter, 1981)
DIR: Anne Lemaître; WRI: Martin Lewis.
STORY: A man acquires chameleon-like powers.

Le Mystère de la Mary-Céleste [The Mystery of the Mary-Celeste] (France-Culture, 1981)
DIR: J.-W. Garrett; WRI: Philippe Clay.
STORY: A shipwreck survivor tells the truth.

Noë, ou L'Épopée d'un Survivant [Noah, or A Survivor's Odyssey] (France-Culture, 1979)
DIR: R. Jentet; WRI: Lazare Kobrynski.
STORY: A post-cataclysmic tale.

Nouvelles Scènes de la Vie Future [New Scenes of a Future Life] (France-Culture, 1981)
DIR: G. Godebert; WRI: Dominique Kergall.
STORY: People are programmed to die at age 75.

On a Sonné! [Someone Rang!] (France-Culture, 1981)
DIR: J.-J. Vierne; WRI: Serge **Martel**.
STORY: Several dreamers dream the same dream.

Où Est Donc la Nuit? [Where Is the Night?] (France-Culture, 1980)
DIR: Anne Lemaître; WRI: Marian Georges Valentini.
STORY: A post-cataclysmic tale.

Le Péril Vert [The Green Peril] (France-Culture, 1980)
DIR: Jeanne Rollin-Weisz; WRI: Serge **Martel**, Pierre Dupriez.
STORY: Deprived of oxygen, plants find a way to steal it from humans.

La Peste Blanche [The White Plague] (France-Culture, 1980)
DIR/WRI: Jean-Wilfrid Garrett.
STORY: The world ends in bacteriological war.

Le Premier Matin [The First Morning] (France-Culture, 1981)
DIR: J. Couturier; WRI: Yann Potocki.
STORY: A post-cataclysmic tale.

Quelques Instants de la Vie de Mon Concierge [Some Instants in the Life of My Concierge] (France-Inter, 1981)
DIR: G. Godebert; WRI: Michèle Angot.
STORY: Dracula as a Parisian concierge.

Rendez-Vous avec le Démon [Rendezvous with the Devil] (RTF, 9 December 1958)
WRI: Jean-Louis **Bouquet**.
NOTE: Bouquet is the writer of *La Cité Foudroyée* (see Chapter I), *Alouqa* (see Chapter II) and several short story collections (see Book 2).

Une Soirée Comme les Autres [An Evening Like Any Other] (France-Culture, 1972)
DIR: Unknown; WRI: Jacques **Sternberg**.
STORY: Social satire.

Sous un Ciel Couleur d'Aubergine [Under an Aubergine-Colored Sky] (France-Culture, 1967)
DIR: Unknown; WRI: Roger **Blondel**.
STORY: Alien encounter.
NOTE: Roger Blondel wrote numerous science fiction novels under the pseudonym B.-R. **Bruss** (see Book 2). His novel *L'Archange* was also adapted for television (see Chapter II).

Le Tabernacle [The Tabernacle] (France-Culture, 1968)
DIR: Unknown; WRI: André Quéderosse.
STORY: Post-cataclysmic story.

Tête à Tête [Head to Head] (France-Culture, 1981)
DIR: J.-J. Vierne; WRI: Maurice **Toesca**.
STORY: After having his limbs amputated, a British Naval officer survives as an immortal head.
NOTE: Maurice Toesca also wrote *Thanatos Palace Hotel* and *Les Voyageurs de l'Espace* (see Book 1, Chapter II) for television. He is also the author of a science fiction novel, *Le Singe Bleu [The Blue Monkey]* (See Book 2).

Le Trio, ou Le Triomphe de la Mécanique [Triangle, or The Triumph of Machines] (France-Inter, 1981)
DIR: G. Gravier; WRI: Daniel Goldenberg.
STORY: Robots in love.

Les Trois Cases Blanches [The Three White Squares] (France-Culture, 1980)
DIR: J.-P. Colas; WRI: Alain Didier.
STORY: Three people are mysteriously omitted from a telephone directory.

3, Rue Bréa [3, Brea Street] (France-Culture, 1981)
DIR: J.-J. Vierne; WRI: Bernard Mazeas.
STORY: In a strange city, everyone is named Berthier, lives at the same address, and works at the same job.

Les Yaquils (France-Culture, 1967)
DIR: Unknown; WRI: Emmanuel Robles.
STORY: Social satire.

4. Non-Fiction

A non-exhaustive list of some major radio shows dealing with science fiction, fantasy and other related topics (e.g., rock music and comics) includes:

À Contre-Courant du Fantastique Français [Against the Flow of French Fantasy] (France-Culture, 25-30 August 1980)
Prods: Pierre Dupriez, Serge **Martel**.
NOTE: Six-part discussion on French *fantastique*; guests included J.-B. **Baronian**, Claude **Cheinisse**, Jacques Goimard, Yves & Ada **Rémy**, Roland Stragliati, Hubert Juin, Jacques **Van Herp**.

L'Anticipation Française [French Science Fiction] (France-Culture, 3-24 August 1979)
Prods: Pierre Dupriez, Serge **Martel**.
NOTE: Four-part discussion on French science fiction; guests included Pierre **Barbet**, J.-B. **Baronian**, Jacques Goimard, Francis Lacassin, Jacques **Van Herp**, Roland Stragliati.

Les Cités, les Villes et Pays Imaginaires [Cities, Towns and Imaginary Countries] (France-Culture, 1966)
HOST: Robert Valette.

La Culture Cyberpunk (France-Culture, 1991)
Prod: Daniel Riche; DIR: Patrice Cresta.
NOTE: Two-hour special devoted to an analysis of the "cyberpunk" literary genre, including telephone interviews with Bruce Sterling, Michael Swanwick, etc.

Futura (France-Inter, 1980)
DIR/HOST: Jacques Pradel.
NOTE: Science fiction and science fact.

Intersidéral (France-Inter, 1982-83)
HOST: Philippe Manoeuvre.
NOTE: Daniel Riche reviewed SF books & films, as well as conducted interviews, etc.

De Jules Verne à L'Odyssée de l'Espace [From Jules Verne to A Space Odyssey] (Europe 1, 1969)

HOSTS: Alain **Dorémieux**, Michel **Demuth**, Jacques Goimard.

Littérature et Paralittérature (France-Culture, 1967)
HOSTS: Pierre **Versins**, Daniel **Drode**, François Le Lionnais.

Panorama de la Science-Fiction (France-Culture, June 1972)
HOST: Frédéric Christian.

Les Récits de Science-Fiction [Science Fiction Tales] (France-Culture, 1969)
HOSTS: Alain **Dorémieux**, Hubert Juin, Stanislas Fumet.

Scènes de Votre Vie Future [Scenes of Your Future Life] (Radio Monte-Carlo, 1961)
HOST: Jimmy **Guieu**.

Science & Science Fiction (France-Culture, 1987)
Prod: Stéphane Deligeorge.
NOTE: One-hour segment of the *La Science et les Hommes [Science & Men]* series devoted to SF, and which included interviews with Michel **Demuth**, Daniel Riche, etc.

L'Utopie et la Littérature [Utopia and Literature] (France-Culture, 1967)
HOST: Robert Valette.
Radio shows dealing with telepathy, parapsychology, ghosts, UFOs, witchcraft, etc. include:

L'Heure du Mystère [The Mystery Hour] (Radio-Luxembourg, 1951–52)
HOST: Jean Thévenot.

Ici l'Ombre [Here Are Shadows] (France-Inter, 1978)
HOSTS: Henri Gougaud, Jacques Pradel.

Radio-Mystère [Radio Mystery] (Radio-Luxembourg, 1956)
HOSTS: Myr & Myroska.

Vous Avez Dit Étrange? [Did You Say Strange?] (France-Inter, 1982)
HOST: Jacques Pradel.

Le Boulevard de l'Étrange [Boulevard of the Weird] (France-Inter, 1985)
HOSTS: Jean-Yves Casgha, Martine Gibert.

CHAPTER IV

Animation

1. Historical Overview

Animation, as well as the technique of stop-motion puppetry, were pioneered in France by Emile **Cohl**, who began producing short cartoons in 1908, often starring his creation, the puppet *Fantoche*. However, World War I crippled French animation, as it did likewise to genre literature and graphic novels.

After World War I, while animation in America resolutely embarked on commercial roads, animation in France remained stuck in experimental, art driven formats. That tradition still survives, to some extent, today. A number of remarkable experimental French animated shorts continue to be produced, with the help of television financing and state subsidies.

In the feature film arena, after Disney established its undisputed artistic and commercial domination, French animators found it virtually impossible to break through. Brave attempts were made, by Jean Image, Paul **Grimault** and, later, by René **Laloux** and Jean-Paul Picha, but they proved, at best, only moderately successful. It is only in the last few years that the *Astérix* series has proved itself a reasonably strong contender in the field.

In television, American animated series and, from the 1980s on, Japanese imports as well, have traditionally dominated French screens. The too-rare exceptions were Jean Image's classic *Joe* series, a 1960 barely animated version of *Tintin*, and the remarkably adult, prime time *Les Shadoks*, which has virtually no counterpart anywhere in the world. A special case was the stop-motion puppet show *Le Manège Enchanté*, which went on to become a cult classic in England under the title of *The Magic Roundabout*.

More recently, French television animation has taken the route of multinational coproductions, with actual animation virtually always produced in Asia. (A good example of this approach was *Ulysse 31*.) Some French-produced and French-designed shows nevertheless have emerged, such as new *Tintin*, *Spirou*, and *Blake & Mortimer* series, based on the popular graphic novels, or the forthcoming *Bob Morane* series.

One area where French producers and animators have recently displayed their brilliance is in the field of computer generated images, with shows like the International Emmy Award–winning *Insektors*, and the brilliantly inventive *Quarxs*.

2. Feature Films

Aladin et la Lampe Merveilleuse [Aladdin and the Magic Lamp] (Col., 70 min., 1970)

DIR: Jean Image; WRI: Jean & France Image.

VOICES: Gaston Guez, Henri Virlojeux, Claire Guibert, Lucie Dolène, Fred Pasquali.

STORY: Fanciful version of the classic *Thousand and One Nights* tale, starring the little thief who finds a Djinn and goes on to defeat the evil vizier and marry the Princess.

Astérix (Col., each about 80 min.)

1. ***Astérix le Gaulois [Asterix the Gaul]*** (1967)

DIR: Studio Belvision; WRI: René **Goscinny**.

STORY: We meet Asterix, Obelix, and the inhabitants of an isolated Gaul village who are successfully resisting Caesar's conquest with the help of a magic potion which confers super strength.

NOTE: Based on Book 1, 1961.

2. ***Astérix et Cléopâtre [Asterix and Cleopatra]*** (1968)

DIR: Studio Belvision; WRI: René **Goscinny**, Pierre Tchernia.

STORY: Asterix helps Queen Cleopatra wins a bet with Caesar.

NOTE: Based on Book 6, 1965.

3. *Les Douze Travaux d'Astérix [The Twelve Tasks of Asterix]* (1976)

DIR: Studio Dargaud; WRI: René **Goscinny**, Pierre Tchernia.

STORY: Caesar challenges Asterix and Obelix to accomplish twelve Herculean tasks (new story).

4. *Astérix et la Surprise de César [Asterix and Caesar's Surprise]* (1985)

DIR: Paul & Gaëtano Brizzi; WRI: Pierre Tchernia.

STORY: Asterix becomes a Roman gladiator to free a fellow Gaul.

NOTE: Based on Book 4, 1964, and Book 10, 1967.

5. *Astérix chez les Bretons [Asterix in Britain]* (1986)

DIR: Pino Van Lamsveerde; WRI: Pierre Tchernia.

STORY: Asterix travels to England to help the British fight off the Romans.

NOTE: Based on Book 8, 1966.

6. *Astérix et le Coup du Menhir [Asterix and the Menhir Blow]* (1989)

DIR: Philippe Grimond; WRI: Yannik Voight, Adolph Kabatek.

STORY: An accidental blow on the head makes the Druid insane.

NOTE: Based on Book 7, 1966.

VOICES: Roger Carel (Asterix), Jacques Morel (Obelix, 1–3), Pierre Tornade (Obelix, 4–6).

NOTE: Based on the graphic novels by René **Goscinny** & Albert **Uderzo** (see Chapter V). A seventh film, *Astérix chez les Indiens* [*Asterix and the Indians*, transl. as *Asterix Conquers America*], taking the intrepid Gaul warrior to America, and based on an original story (loosely inspired from Book 22, 1975), was made in 1994 by a German animation studio.

La Bergère et le Ramoneur [The Shepherdess and the Chimney Sweep] see *Le Roi et l'Oiseau*

Le Big Bang (Col., 80 min., 1986)

DIR: Jean-Paul Picha; WRI: Jean-Paul Picha, Tony Hendra.

VOICES: Luis Rego, Georges Aminel, Perette Pradier, Régine Tessot, Roger Carel.

STORY: After World War III, the world is divided between an American/Russian empire and a women dominated-country. An unemployed superhero falls in love with his female counterpart, but a final war destroys the world.

Le Chaînon Manquant [The Missing Link, transl. as *B.C. Rock]* (Col., 95 min., 1980)

DIR: Jean-Paul Picha; WRI: Jean Paul Picha, Jean Collette, Pierre Berthier, Tony Hendra (U.S. version).

VOICES: Jacques Dacqmine, Richard Darbois, Georges Aminel, Roger Carel, Philippe Nicaud.

STORY: An animated satire of life in the Stone Age.

Chronopolis (Col., 70 min., 1982)

DIR: Piotr Kamler; WRI: Piotr Kamler, Gabrielle Althen.

VOICE: Michael Lonsdale.

STORY: Avant-garde animated film about a city which manufactures time, and a love story between a moment of time and an alien being.

L'Enfant Invisible [The Invisible Child] (Col., 63 min., 1983)

DIR/WRI: André Lindon.

STORY: A little boy on a seaside vacation acquires an invisible playmate: A little girl who comes from the sea. The greyness of city life eventually drives him to join her.

Les Fabuleuses Aventures du Baron de Munchausen [The Fabulous Adventures of Baron Munchausen] (Col., 78 min., 1979)

DIR: Jean Image; WRI: Jean & France Image, Serge Nadaud.

VOICES: Dominique Paturel (Baron), Michel Elias, Francis Laine, Christian Duvaleix.

STORY: The Baron travels on a flying horse to deliver a present to the Sultan from the King of Prussia. During his journey, he meets various super-powered companions. He escapes from the Sultan by riding a cannonball. Later, he travels to the bottom of the sea, meets a mermaid, is swallowed by a giant whale, etc.

La Flûte à Six Schtroumpfs [The Smurfs and the Magic Flute] (Col., 80 min., 1975)

DIR/WRI: **Peyo**, Yvan **Delporte**, based on their graphic novel.

VOICES: William Coryn, Michel Modo, Georges Pradez, Jacques Balutin, Ginette Garcin, Albert Médina, Henri Crémieux, Jacques Dynam.

STORY: Two medieval squires, Johan and Pirlouit (in English: *PeeWee*) try to prevent a magic flute from falling into evil hands; they eventually enlist the help of the flute makers, a tribe a small, blue creatures called Schtroumpfs (in English: *Smurfs*).

NOTE: Based on Book 9 in the *Johan* series, 1960 (see Chapter V). A series of nine 13 min. animated shorts (seven B&W., two in color) starring the **Smurfs** were produced in the 1960s by Eddy Ryssack & Maurice **Rosy**, before the notorious Hanna Barbera series of the 1980s (which is not included here). These included *Le Schtroumpf et le Dragon* [*The Smurfs and the Dragon*] (1963), *Le Schtroumpf Volant* [*The Flying Smurf*] (1964), *Le Schtroumpf à tout faire* [*Handy Smurf*] (1966), etc., based on stories published in *Spirou* magazine in 1963 and later collected in Books 1 and 4 of the **Schtroumpfs** series.

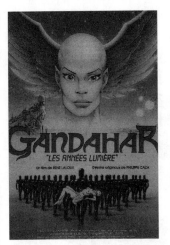

Gandahar [Transl. as Light-years] (Col., 83 min., 1987)

DIR: René **Laloux**; WRI: René Laloux, based on the novel by Jean-Pierre **Andrevon** and the art of Philippe **Caza** (U.S. adaptation: Isaac Asimov).

VOICES: Pierre Marie Escourrou, Catherine Chevallier, Georges Wilson, Anny Duperey.

STORY: Sylvain and Arielle fight to save their peaceful kingdom of Gandahar from the attacks of mysterious metal men from the future.

NOTE: Jean-Pierre Andrevon is a famous science fiction writer. Another of his books, *Le Travail du Furet* [*The Weasel's Work*] was adapted for television. See Chapter II. For further information on Philippe **Caza**, see Chapter V.

Gwen, le Livre du Sable [Gwen, the Book of Sand] (Col., 67 min., 1984)

DIR: Jean-François Laguionie; WRI: Jean-François Laguionie, Jean-Paul Gapari.

VOICES: Michel Robin, Lorella Di Cicco.

STORY: After a nuclear war, the survivors eke out a miserable existence in the desert, terrified of their evil god, Malouk. A fearless little girl, Gwen, helps them challenge their beliefs.

Les Maîtres du Temps [The Time Masters] (Col., 78 min., 1981)

DIR: René **Laloux**; WRI: René Laloux, **Moebius**, Jean-Patrick Manchette, based on the novel *L'Orphelin de Perdide* by Stefan **Wul**.

VOICES: Christian Zanessi, Pierre Tardy, Françoise Bourgoin.

STORY: A spaceman rushes to rescue a child abandoned on a hostile planet with a microphone as their only link. Eventually, he discovers that the old man who has been his companion is the child, who grew up in a different time.

NOTE: For further information on Moebius, see Chapter V. For other Stefan Wul adaptations, see *La Planète Sauvage* (below) and *Mycènes* in Chapter II.

Marquis see Chapter I

Les Minipouss [The Littles] (Col., 75 min., 1985)

DIR: Bernard Deyriès; WRI: Jean Chalopin, based on the novel by John Peterson.

VOICES: Odile Schmitt, Amélie Morin, Jacques Marin, Chris Benard.

STORY: The Littles help rescue an orphan from his evil uncle.

NOTE: Based on the American-produced syndicated cartoon series.

Pinocchio dans l'Espace [Pinocchio in Outer Space] (Col., 90 min., 1962)

DIR/WRI: Ray Goosens, based on the fairy tale by Collodi.

VOICES (U.S. version): Arnold Stang, Jess Cain.

STORY: Young robot Pinocchio and his parrot-like alien friend defeat Astro, the space whale.

La Planète Sauvage [The Savage Planet, transl. as Fantastic Planet] (Col., 72 min., 1973)

DIR: René **Laloux**; WRI: Roland **Topor**, René Laloux, based on the novel *Oms en Série* by Stefan **Wul**.

STORY: On an alien world, men are treated like pets or vermin by giant humanoids, until one of them escapes and eventually succeeds in bringing the two races together.

NOTE: This film won an award at the Cannes Film Festi-

La Planète Sauvage

val. Stéfan Wul is a major science fiction writer. For other adaptations, see *Les Maîtres du Temps* (above) and *Mycènes* in Chapter II. Roland Topor is a renowned French writer/cartoonist, who wrote Roman Polanski's *Le Locataire* and *Marquis* (see Chapter I). He also acted in Werner Herzog's *Nosferatu*.

Pluk, Naufragé de l'Espace [Pluk, Stranded in Space] (Col., 75 min., 1978)

DIR: Jean Image; WRI: Jean & France Image.

STORY: Two young Earth kids and their dog help Pluk, an alien robot, fight various threats and return home.

Pollux et le Chat Bleu [Dougal and the Blue Cat] (Col., 90 Min, 1970)

DIR: Serge Danot; WRI: Serge Danot, Jacques Josselin (English version: Eric Thompson)

STORY: Dougal enters into a conflict with a blue cat who wants everything to be blue.

NOTE: See *Le Manège Enchanté*, under Television below.

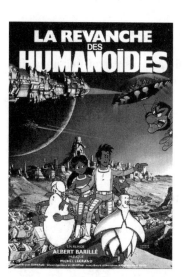

La Revanche des Humanoïdes [The Humanoids' Revenge] (Col., 100 min., 1982)

DIR/WRI: Alain Barillé.

VOICES: Roger Carel, Yves-Marie Maurin, Sady Rebbot, Annie Balestra, Vincent Ropion.

STORY: Pierrot, Psi, and Metro the robot are intergalactic patrolmen working for planet Omega. They thwart the evil designs of a supercomputer called Yama.

Le Roi et l'Oiseau [The King and the Bird, transl. as The Incredible Adventures of Mr. Wonderbird] (Col., 87 min., 1979)

DIR: Paul **Grimault**; WRI: Jacques **Prévert**, based on a tale by Hans Christian Andersen.

VOICES: Jean Martin (The Bird), Pascal Mazzoti (The King), Renaud Marx (The Chimney Sweep), Agnès Viala (The Shepherdess), Raymond Bussières, Roger Blin, Claude Piéplu.

STORY: A tyrannical king falls in love with a shepherdess, who loves a chimney sweep. Thanks to a wily bird, the lovers escape from the king.

NOTE: A shorter version of this film was released in 1953 as *La Bergère et le Ramoneur.*

Le Roman de Renard [The Novel of Renard] (B&W, 70 min., 1926–1930 (Silent); 1939–1940 (Talking))

DIR: Ladislas Starevitch; WRI: Irène Starévitch, based on the medieval folk tales and the version *Reineke Fuchs* by Goethe.

VOICES: Romain Bouquet (Renard), Sylvain Itkine (Ysengrin), Sylvia Bataille (Coard), Claude Dauphin (Monkey).

STORY: Renard the fox is the consummate trickster. Tired of his crimes, the other animals have him tried by King Noble, the Lion.

NOTE: This is the first feature length animated production using puppetry. It is a technical feat (up to a dozen characters in motion in a single frame) as well as an artistic one. Considered lost after World War II, this film was rediscovered in 1990.

Le Secret des Sélénites [The Secret of the Moon People, transl. as Moon Madness; Moon Berserk] (Col., 76 min., 1983)

DIR: Jean Image; WRI: Jean & France Image.

VOICES: Dominique Paturel (Baron), Pierre Destailles, Jacques Marin, Serge Nadaud.

STORY: An 18th-century scientist, Sirius, sends his cousin, Baron Munchausen, to the Moon to fetch the Talisman of Eternal Life. The Baron and his companions travel to the Moon in a flying galleon and fight evil little green men.

Tarzoon, la Honte de la Jungle [Shame of the Jungle; Jungle Burger] (Col., 80 min., 1975)

DIR: Jean-Paul Picha; WRI: Boris Sulzinger, Jean-Paul Picha, Pierre Bartier, Christian Dora.

STORY: A parodic version of *Tarzan* in which an impotent, incompetent jungle lord thwarts the plans of the dreaded Queen Bazonga and her phallic zombies.

Tintin (Col., each about 80 min.)

1. *Tintin et le Temple du Soleil [Tintin and the Temple of the Sun]* (1969)
   DIR: Studio Belvision; WRI: Michel **Greg**.
   STORY: Tintin saves Prof. Calculus from an Inca curse and discovers a hidden Inca civilization in the Andes.
   NOTE: Based on Book No.13: 1948 and Book No.14: 1949.

2. ***Tintin et le Lac aux Requins [Tintin and the Lake of Sharks]*** (1972)
   DIR: Studio Belvision; WRI: Michel **Greg**.
   STORY: Villainous Rastapopoulos plans to use a 3-D projector built by Prof. Calculus to further his evil schemes (new story).
   VOICES: Jacques Careuil (Tintin), Henri Virlojeux (Haddock), Jacques Balutin (Prof. Calculus).
   NOTE: Based on the graphic novels by **Hergé** (see Chapter V). Also see television adaptations below, and two live-action feature films in Chapter I.

3. Television

Blake & Mortimer (Canal +, Col., one season of thirteen 26 min. eps., 1997)
   DIR: Stéphane Bernasconi, Yannick Barbaud.

1. *Le Mystère de la Grande Pyramide [The Mystery of the Great Pyramid]* (WRI: Éric Rondeaux).

2. *La Marque Jaune [The Yellow Mark]* (WRI: Éric Rondeaux).

3. *Le Secret de l'Espadon [The Secret of the Swordfish]* (WRI: Éric Rondeaux).

4. *L'Énigme de l'Atlantide [The Atlantis Mystery]* (WRI: Béatrice Marthouret & Yves Coulon).

5. *SOS Météores [SOS Meteors]* (WRI: Marc Perrier).

6. *Le Piège Diabolique [The Diabolical Trap]* (WRI: Marc Perrier).

7. *L'Affaire du Collier [The Necklace Affair]* (WRI: Véronique Herbaut).

8. *Les Trois Formules du Prof. Sato [The Three Formulas of Prof. Sato]* (WRI: Jean Christophe Derrien).

9. *L'Affaire Francis Blake [The Francis Blake Case]* (WRI: Marc Perrier).

10. *L'Héritage du Viking [The Viking's Inheritance]* (WRI: Russell Craig Richardson).

11. *Le Testament de l'Alchimiste* (WRI: Éric Rondeaux).

12. *Le Secret de l'Île de Pâques [The Secret of Easter Island]* (WRI: Véronique Herbaut).

13. *La Porte du Druide [The Druid's Gate]* (WRI: Jean Christophe Derrien).
   STORY: Adaptation of the famous comic book series by E. P. **Jacobs** (see Chapter V). Eps. 1 9 are based on the original graphic novels; eps. 11–13 are new stories.

Les Contes de la Rue Broca
(FR3/Canal J, Col., thirteen 13 min. eps., 1996)
   DIR: Christian Lapointe, based on the stories by Pierre **Gripari**.

1. *Le Géant aux Chaussettes Rouges [The Giant with Red Socks]*.

2. *Le Gentil Petit Diable [The Nice Little Devil]*.

3. *La Sorcière de la Rue Mouffetard [The Witch of Mouffetard Street]*.

4. *Je ne Sais Qui Je ne Sais Quoi [I Don't Know Who I Don't Know What]*.

5. *La Fée du Robinet [The Tap Fairy]*.

6. *Scoubidou, la Poupée Qui Sait Tout [Scoobidoo, the Doll Who Knew All]*.

7. *Le Prince Blub et la Sorcière [Prince Blub and the Witch]*.

8. *Histoire de Lustucru [Lustucru's Story]*.

9. *La Sorcière du Placard à Balais [The Broom Closet Witch]*.

10. *Le Petit Cochon Futé [The Clever Little Pig]*.

11. *La Paire de Chaussures [The Pair of Shoes]*.

12. *La Maison de l'Oncle Pierre [Uncle Peter's House]*.

13. *Le Roman d'Amour d'une Patate [A Potato's Love Story]*.
   NOTE: Modern fairy tales in the Marcel **Aymé** vein, based on a popular collection of stories published in 1967. This series won the 1996 Best Children's Series Award.

Insektors (Canal +, Col., two seasons of twenty-six 13 min. eps., 1994 95)
   DIR: Georges Lacroix, Renato.
   STORY: On a planet inhabited by intelligent insects, the nature loving Joyces try to contain the industrial, polluting Beurks.

Joe (ORTF 1, Col., three seasons of thirteen 5 min. eps., 1960 63)

1. *Joe chez les Abeilles [Joe Among the Bees]* (released in video as *Joe Petit Boum Boum*).

2. *Joe chez les Fourmis [Joe Among the Ants]*.

3. *Joe aux Merveilleux Royaumes des Mouches [Joe in the Wonderful Kingdoms of the Flies]* (released in video as *Joe et la Sorcière [Joe and the Witch]*).

Dir: Jean Image; Wri: Jean & France Image, Michel Emer.

Voices: Roger Carel (Joe), Laurence Badie, Christian Legrand, Linette Lemercier.

Story: Joe is shrunk to insect size by a friendly bee named Bzz and shares adventures among the insects, first thwarting the evil wasps, then helping the ants against the red ants, and finally capturing the Witch Tsetsebosse whose spell has put the Hive to sleep.

Le Manège Enchanté [The Magic Roundabout] (ORTF 1, B&W/Col., 5 min. eps., 1963 71)

Dir/Wri: Serge Danot.

Story: *The Magic Roundabout* (to adopt its British title) deserves to be listed here because it is clearly fantasy. Djinn-like character Zebulon (Zebedee) takes naive little girl Margot (Florence) to a magic land inhabited by the colorful dog Pollux (Dougal), his friend the snail Ambroise (Brian), and many other quirky characters. Unlike the original French shows, which were mind-numbingly simple, the BBC version was dubbed by comedian Eric Thompson (actress Emma Thompson's father), who added many contemporary double entendres and allusions. The British *Magic Roundabout* justifiably went on to become a cult classic. A feature film was released in 1970, **Pollux et le Chat Bleu** (see Films above).

Les Quarxs (Col., twelve 3 min. eps., 1995)

Dir: Maurice Benayoun, Stéphane Singler.

Story: Microscopic invisible creatures hide among everyday objects, causing ordinary disasters.

Saturnin (1965 70)

Dir: Jean Tourane; Wri: Jean Tourane, R. Lavigne, L. de Vilmorin.

Voices: Ricet Barrier (Saturnin), Robert Lamoureux (Narrator).

Story: Entirely shot with live ducklings and other animals, this French children's show functioned like the British *Tales of the Riverbank*, anthropomorphizing animals and often blending in fantasy elements. A 60 min. special, *Saturnin et la Fée Pas Comme les Autres [Saturnin and a Fairy Unlike Any Other]*, was released in 1969. It dealt with Saturnin's efforts to thwart the evil schemes of a monkey black magician to keep a good fairy imprisoned.

Les Schtroumpfs [The Smurfs] see **La Flûte à Six Schtroumpfs** (see Films above)

Les Shadoks (ORTF 1, Col., 416 two min. eps., 1968 75)

Created by: Jacques Rouxel; Dir: René Borg (1st season), Robert Richez (2nd. season), Jacques Rouxel (3rd season).

Narrator: Claude Piéplu.

Story: This cult series of surreal shorts tells the story of two races of alien creatures, the sweet, smart, hamster like, bowler hat-wearing Gibis, and their nemeses, the mean, stupid, bird-like Shadoks. Both races want to leave their broken-down planet and relocate on Earth.

Spirou (Col., 22 min. eps., 1992)

Dir: Michel Gauthier; Wri: Philippe Tome, based on the graphic novels.

Voices: Vincent Ropion (Spirou), Patrick Guillemin (Fantasio).

Story: Belgian publisher Dupuis teamed up with Ciné-Groupe and French animation studio Pixibox to adapt the adventures of the popular comics character. Several episodes contain science fiction elements.

Note: Based on the **Spirou** graphic novels by Tome & Janry (see Chapter V).

Tintin

Version No. 1: (Belvision, B&W., twelve 5 min. eps., 1957)

1. *Le Sceptre d'Ottokar [King Ottokar's Sceptre]* (Book No.8: 1939).

2. *L'Oreille Cassée [The Broken Ear]* (Book No.6: 1937).
   Dir: Studios Belvision.
   Voices: Jean Nohain (Narrator).
   Note: Daily 5 minute serial forms, devoting about 30 minutes to each album.

Version No. 2: (Belvision, Col., ninety one 5 min. eps, 1957)

1. *Objectif Lune [Destination Moon]* (Book No.16: 1953 & Book No.17: 1954).

2. *Le Crabe aux Pinces d'Or* [*The Crab with the Golden Claws*] (Book No.9: 1941).

3. *Le Secret de la Licorne* [*The Secret of the Unicorn*] (Book No.11: 1943).

4. *Le Trésor de Rackham le Rouge* [*Red Rackham's Treasure*] (Book No.12: 1944).

5. *L'Étoile Mystérieuse* [*The Shooting Star*] (Book No.10: 1942).

6. *L'Île Noire* [*The Black Island*] (Book No. 7: 1938).

7. *L'Affaire Tournesol* [*The Calculus Affair*] (Book No.18: 1956).
DIR: Studios Belvision; WRI: Michel **Greg**.
VOICES: No information available.
NOTE: Daily 5 minute serial forms, devoting about 35 minutes to each album. The animation was very limited.

Version No. 3: (Ellipse/Nelvana, Col., twenty-one 42 min. eps., 1991)

1. *Tintin en Amérique* [*Tintin in America*] (Book No. 3: 1932).

2. *Les Cigares du Pharaon* [*The Cigars of the Pharaoh*] (Book No.4: 1934).

3. *Le Lotus Bleu* [*The Blue Lotus*] (Book No.5: 1936).

4. *L'Oreille Cassée* [*The Broken Ear*] (Book No.6: 1937).

5. *L'Île Noire* [*The Black Island*] (Book No. 7: 1938/1966).

6. *Le Sceptre d'Ottokar* [*King Ottokar's Sceptre*] (Book No.8: 1939).

7. *Le Crabe aux Pinces d'Or* [*The Crab with the Golden Claws*] (Book No.9: 1941).

8. *L'Étoile Mystérieuse* [*The Shooting Star*] (Book No.10: 1942).

9. *Le Secret de la Licorne* [*The Secret of the Unicorn*] (Book No.11: 1943).

10. *Le Trésor de Rackham le Rouge* [*Red Rackham's Treasure*] (Book No.12: 1944).

11. *Les Sept Boules de Cristal* [*The Seven Crystal Balls*] (Book No.13: 1948).

12. *Le Temple du Soleil* [*The Temple of the Sun*] (Book No.14: 1949).

13. *Tintin au Pays de l'Or Noir* [*The Land of Black Gold*] (Book No.15: 1950).

14. *Objectif Lune* [*Destination Moon*] (Book No.16: 1953).

15. *On a Marché Sur la Lune* [*They Walked on the Moon*, transl. as *Explorers on the Moon*] (Book No.17: 1954).

16. *L'Affaire Tournesol* [*The Calculus Affair*] (Book No.18: 1956).

17. *Coke en Stock* [*Coke in Stock*, transl. as *The Red Sea Sharks*] (Book No. 19: 1958).

18. *Tintin au Tibet* [*Tintin in Tibet*] (Book No.20: 1960).

19. *Les Bijoux de la Castafiore* [*The Castafiore Emeralds*] (Book No.21: 1963).

20. *Vol 714 Pour Sidney* [*Flight 714 for Sydney*] (Book No.22: 1968).

21. *Tintin et les Picaros* [*Tintin and the Picaros*] (Book No.23: 1976).
DIR: Stéphane Bernasconi.
VOICES: Thierry Wermuth (Tintin), Christian Pelissier (Haddock), Henri Labussière (Tournesol).
STORY: French studio Ellipse teamed up with Canadian animation company Nelvana to adapt all of Tintin's graphic novels in a form extremely faithful to **Hergé** (see Chapter V).

Ulysse 31 (Col., twenty-six 24 min. eps., 1978)
DIR: Jean Chalopin; WRI: Various.
VOICES: No information available.
STORY: The story of Ulysses and his Odyssey, transposed into the 31st century.

4. Selected Short Features

Also see entries under Émile **Cohl** and René **Laloux** in Chapter VI.

***Les Astronautes* [*The Astronauts*]** (B&W., 15 min., 1960)
DIR/WRI: Walerian **Borowczyk**, Chris **Marker**.
VOICES: Michel Boschet.
STORY: A satirical look at inventors and space travel.

***Ballade Atomique* [*Atomic Ballad*]** (1947)
DIR/WRI: Jean Image.
STORY: Space travel fantasy.

***La Brûlure de Mille Soleils* [*The Burn of a Thousand Suns*]** (Col., 23 min., 1964)
DIR/WRI: Pierre **Kast**, based on the art of Eduardo Luis.
VOICES: Pierre Vaneck, Barbara Laage.
STORY: Short animated feature about a spaceman who lands on an alien planet and discovers a truly alien society and form of love (where six people are needed to make a couple).
NOTE: Chris **Marker** worked on editing this film.

***Le Dernier Fantôme* [*The Last Ghost*]** (Col., 30 min., 1973)
DIR/WRI: Jacques Ansan.
STORY: The last ghost wanders on a post nuclear Earth.

L'Empreinte [The Print] (Col., 8 min., 1975)
DIR/WRI: Jacques Cardon.
STORY: A baby grows up with a prosthetic device shaped like a footprint already provided for the convenience of his future oppression.
NOTE: Anthologized in *Extraneus* (see Chapter I).

Les Escargots [The Snails] (Col., 11 min., 1965)
DIR: René **Laloux**; WRI: René Laloux, Roland **Topor**.
STORY: A poor farmer wishes for bigger heads of lettuce, which in turn create giant snails.

L'Évasion [The Escape] (Col., 8 min., 1977)
DIR/WRI: Jean-Pierre **Jeunet**; PUPPETS: Marc **Caro**.
STORY: A prisoner tries to escape from his cell.
NOTE: Also see the feature films *Delicatessen* and *La Cité des Enfants Perdus* in Chapter I.

La Formule [The Formula] (Col., 6 min., 1976)
DIR/WRI: Jean-Claude Amiot.
STORY: A scientist discovers a doomsday formula.

Fracture [Break] (Col., 18 min., 1977)
DIR/WRI: Paul & Gaëtan Brizzi.
STORY: Mankind's last survivor fights in a plant world.
NOTE: Anthologized in *Extraneus* (see Chapter I).

Le Manège [The Merry Go Round] (10 min., 1979)
DIR/WRI: Jean-Pierre **Jeunet**; PUPPETS: Marc **Caro**.
STORY: Children who win a prize on a merry-go-round are forced below it to power it like galley slaves.
NOTE: See *L'Évasion* (above).

Le Mangeur de Temps [The Time Eater] (Col., 8 min., 1976)
DIR/WRI: Jacques Barsac.
STORY: Surreal allegory about time.

Les Marchands d'Armes [The Weapon Merchants] (Col., 3 min., 1976)
DIR: Jean-Daniel Verhaeghe, based on the art of Desclozeaux and Puig Rossado.
STORY: Political satire mixed with fantasy.
NOTE: J.-D. Verhaeghe directed *L'Araignée d'Eau* (see Chapter I) and *La Métamorphose* and *La Nuit des Fantômes* (see Chapter II).

Monsieur Victor, ou La Machine à Retrouver le Temps [Mr. Victor, or the Machine to Find Lost Time] (1955)
DIR/WRI: Jean Image.
STORY: Time-travel fantasy.

Oiseau de Nuit [Night Bird] (Col., 9 min., 1976)
DIR/WRI: Bernard Palacios.
STORY: The sight of a beautiful woman disturbs a bureaucrat.

Les Passagers de la Grande Ourse [The Passengers of Ursa Major] (1944)
DIR/WRI: Paul **Grimault**.
STORY: Space travel fantasy including a crazy robotic butler.

La Planète Verte [The Green Planet] (Col, 10 Min, 1966)
DIR: Piotr Kamler; WRI/NAR: Jacques **Sternberg**.
STORY: An ecological fable about Planet Actur, 3,000 light years from Earth.
NOTE: Jacques Sternberg also wrote *Je T'Aime, Je T'Aime* (see Chapter I).

Le Poirier de Misère [The Pear Tree of Misery] (Col., 12 Min, 1963)
DIR/WRI: Jean Coignon.
STORY: This beautiful Belgian animated short is based on Brueghel's paintings and tells the legend of an old woman who keeps Death imprisoned in a pear tree.

Rencontre des Nuages et du Dragon [Meeting of the Clouds and the Dragon] (B&W, 33 min., 1980)
DIR: Lam Lê; WRI: Lam Lê, Henri Colomer.
STORY: A magical paint brush prevents a train catastrophe and cures a sick woman.

Rhapsodie de Saturne [Saturnian Rhapsody] (1946)
DIR/WRI: Jean Image.
STORY: Space travel fantasy.

Servais, Raoul
Belgian animator who studied animation at the Academy of Fine Arts in Gent, Belgum. He has made a number of remarkable animated genre short features (all about 3 min.), including: *Chromophobia* (1966), *Sirène [Mermaid]* (1968), *Gold Frame* (1969), *To Speak or Not to Speak* (1970), *Opération X70* (1971), *Pegasus* (1973), *Le Chant de Halewyn [Halewyn's Song]* (1974), *Harpya* (1977), etc.

La Tendresse du Maudit [The Tenderness of the Damned] (Col., 10 min., 1980)
DIR: Jean-Manuel Costa; WRI: J.-M. Costa, Frédéric Grosjean.
STORY: A good vs. evil fight among the gargoyles of a cathedral.
NOTE: Award-winning stop-motion animation film.

Tour d'Ivoire [Ivory Tower] (Col., 6 min., 1975)
DIR/WRI: Bernard Palacios.
STORY: A painter ignores creatures crawling behind his back.

Un [One] (Col., 5 min., 1976)
DIR/WRI: Paul & Gaëtan Brizzi.
STORY: A character is pursued by a nightmarish monster.

Le Voyage d'Orphée [Orpheus' Journey] (Col., 15 min., 1983)
DIR: Jean-Manuel Costa; WRI: J.-M. Costa, Silvia Fabrizio.
STORY: Retelling of the Orpheus myth.

5. Interview with René Laloux

*René **Laloux** is the renowned director of **La Planète Sauvage** [Fantastic Planet, 1973], **Les Maîtres du Temps** [The Time Masters, 1981], and **Gandahar** [Lightyears, 1987]. He is, perhaps, the only French animation director to have achieved a degree of international recognition. These comments are excerpted from an interview granted to Jean-Marc & Randy Lofficier in 1987, as Laloux had just completed his animated science fiction saga **Gandahar**. The full interview appeared in Starlog No. 129 and is reproduced here by permission.*

Violence erupts as a giant blue humanoid is brought low by a group of small, rebellious men. A young orphan boy runs for his life, chased by a buzzing swarm of giant insects. The peaceful realm of Gandahar is attacked by a mindless horde of robots. These scenes are only a few of the animated marvels created by Rene Laloux, the 58-year-old French animation director, winner of the 1973 Cannes Film Festival's Special Jury Prize for his full length animated feature, *La Planète Sauvage [Fantastic Planet]*.

Laloux is in the United States to help promote the release of his third, and most recent, animated feature, *Gandahar [Lightyears]*, which follows his relatively unsuccessful 1982 release, *Les Maîtres du Temps [The Time Masters]*. Laloux speaks no English, therefore this interview was conducted in a lively French, interrupted by puffs of the almost obligatory cigarette that most French directors consider to be the only thing standing between themselves and a nervous breakdown.

Indeed, Laloux, really an artist at heart, has had a difficult life, filled with a bevy of occupations before he settled into that of movie maker. "If I have done many different things in my life," he explains, "it is because I used to be poor. I kept on painting, but I had a great deal of difficulty making a living from it. So, I chose jobs that would enable me to survive. I don't know if I learned much as a bank employee, for example, but my four years of work in a psychiatric hos-

pital was an experience that I consider to be very important. I learned a lot about humanity."

Strangely, it was there, too, that Laloux had the opportunity to first try his hand at animation, with the help of a group of patients. A few years later, between exhibitions of his paintings, Laloux met avant garde artist Roland **Topor**. (Horror-movie buffs may remember Topor as the man who played the part of Renfield in Werner Herzog's *Nosferatu*.) This encounter led to a variety of collaborative projects, culminating in 1973 with the production of *Fantastic Planet*, a Franco-Czechoslovakian production.

Fantastic Planet's imaginative storyline and its bizarre decor brought it considerable fame, as well as the Prize at Cannes. Although a large share of the credit for this success should be given to Laloux's direction and Topor's brilliant designs, the rest belongs to French science fiction author Stefan **Wul**, who wrote *Oms en Série [OMS In Series]*, the original novel upon which the movie was based.

The positive reception of *Fantastic Planet* convinced Laloux, already a science fiction fan, that he had found his perfect source of inspiration. When he returned to France from Czechoslovakia, he began work on the adaptation of yet another science fiction novel, *Les Hommes-Machines contre Gandahar [The Machine Men vs. Gandahar]*, by French writer Jean-Pierre **Andrevon**.

Gandahar, retitled *Lightyears* for its American release, contained much to inspire Laloux. Yet, he needed an artist of a stature equal to Topor to adequately render Andrevon's vision. He found such an artist in the person of Philippe **Caza**, known to the American public for his short, fantastic stories published in *Heavy Metal*, and his recent collection, *Escape from Suburbia*, recently released by NBM. Caza is also famous in France for his science fiction illustrations, including a series of covers designed for the French translations of Jack Vance's novels.

Laloux explains why he looked to the field of comics for his visual inspiration. "For sixty years, *Silly Symphony*–style creatures have dominated cartoons throughout the world. For me, there was no question of adding to that army of cats and mice, drawn in a style that has deteriorated considerably because of television. For my part, I try to approach the design of an animated picture in a completely different manner. There are in Europe, and especially in France, some graphic artists of great poetic talent. Whether they have come up by way of comics or illustration, they often share a taste for realistic fantasy. I would like to lead these artists to cross the frontier between their solitary work on static images, and our teamwork on animated pictures.

"When I returned from Czechoslovakia, I needed to have a project going. I was already familiar with Caza's work as an illustrator of science fiction novels, rather than as a comics artist. In fact, his work as an illustrator seemed to me, at the time, more mature and experimental than his work in comics. This was confirmed when, later, he began drawing his comics in the style that he had developed through his work in illustration. Anyway, I wrote to tell him that I wanted to do this film with him. He agreed, and we began to work on a first adaptation of the novel. That was thirteen years ago."

But in spite of Laloux's best efforts, he could find no backer for **Gandahar**. Then, in 1977, the director conceived yet another ambitious project: a series of six one-hour television films, all based on science fiction novels. In addition, each picture would be designed by a different artist, all culled from the ranks of *Métal Hurlant*, the original French version of *Heavy Metal* magazine, which was phenomenally successful at the time.

For his first picture, Laloux chose *L'Orphelin de Perdide* [*The Orphan of Perdide*], one of his favorite novels, also written by Stefan Wul. For his visual inspiration, Laloux chose Jean "**Moebius**" Giraud, the co founder of *Métal Hurlant* and a man generally acknowledged to be one of the world's leading fantasy artists. Moebius' work has since been translated in *Heavy Metal* and was republished in its entirety in the United States by Marvel and Dark Horse in a series of award-winning graphic novels.

After three years of production at the Oscar-winning Pannonia Film Studios of Budapest, Hungary, the film was eventually released in 1982 under the revised title of **Les Maîtres du Temps** [*The Time Masters*]. However, it performed poorly at the box office.

"Even though **The Time Masters** was in no way as successful as **Fantastic Planet**," Laloux remarks, "it was nevertheless a positive experience for me, in the sense that, afterwards, I never again lacked work. There are many things I still love in that film, such as the two little gnomes, and the core story. But there are also many problems with it. The animation is not always what it should be, and the main female character is graphically atrocious. It all has to do with production compromises because of money. I wish I could put together a new version someday, and take out some of these things."

Then, the **Gandahar** project once again came to life, following a strange series of events. It all began with a trip to North Korea by a group of French Trade Union leaders. During the visit, the Frenchmen were apprised of the existence of a large, and mostly unemployed, North Korean studio, where work could presumably be done at extremely competitive rates. One thing lead to another, producers and financiers became involved, and soon afterwards, Laloux's phone rang with an offer to do **Gandahar** in North Korea.

"At first, I was a bit concerned," the director explained. "North Korea is very far, and life there is not too comfortable, at least by our standards. But it was an offer I couldn't pass up. I was lucky because I was the first western director to use their studio, and they made a big effort, from an artistic and technical standpoint. I had 160 persons to work on the film, and we got an animation that is almost of Disney quality, with superb backgrounds. It was the first time in my life that I had been given the means to make a full length animated feature the way it should be made.

"I had three assistants with me, one for the animation, one for the backgrounds, and a third one for all the technical problems. One of the problems we faced was how to communicate with the Koreans, and make sure we understood their feedback. But we were given two young students as interpreters, who really did wonders.

"We spent almost two years there, which is a rather short schedule for a movie of this kind. In terms of budget, we spent only about 50 percent of what we would have spent if I had had to do the film in France, and we got a quality of animation that I would consider equal or superior, especially considering that our characters are realistic characters, which are always more difficult to animate convincingly.

"We had no problem with the Korean authorities, who were always most cooperative. They were aware we were making quite an effort by going there, and they tried very hard to make our life easy. We did experience some technical difficulties in the beginning, the kind that you always experience when you go to a Third World country: camera problems, electrical problems, etc. For example, I didn't want to shoot anything in color until we got the right kind of camera. So we worked for several months doing line tests only, which was psychologically difficult for the local animators.

"In the end, we had to bring a lot of equipment with us, and supervise its installation. But, when we did get it right, and we began to do color work, they became very happy and enthusiastic. In a way, it was as much of a teaching job as it was a production job. We helped them to organize themselves. But it was an interesting task, and the animation team's enthusiasm was very rewarding.

"The Koreans did all the animation. We lived very dangerously because we didn't have the kind of pre-production time that we should normally have had. One always underestimates how much pre production time one needs in animation. In this instance the production was scheduled to start almost right away, so we left and did everything in Korea.

"When you work with a foreign team, in my opinion, the most crucial step is the lay-out, that is the picture of the background as it will be shot, with the characters shown at the beginning and the end of their animation. We spent a lot of time with the Koreans on this. At first, it wasn't always easy, but by working closely with us, they began to learn to do things the way we wanted them. And even when things weren't right, because we were there, we could always ask for corrections at every step of the way."

Although he didn't go to Korea, Caza remained involved in the new version of the film. "He played an absolutely essential part in the visual conception of the picture," Laloux explains. "And we did a new adaptation together. We ignored the one that we had done thirteen years ago, and started fresh, with only our memories of what seemed good. I think our new adaptation is better, more daring and free.

We made the story more logical. In appearance, it's farther away from the original novel, but in essence, I think it serves it better.

"To me, this is a simple story. It is about an old creature, an entity who is becoming senile and is very, very afraid of dying. So, because it doesn't want to die, it returns to the past to steal the regenerating energy that it needs from a happy planet inhabited by men called Gandahar. There is a time paradox at the end, to the effect that we are, ourselves, creating the monsters that will one day destroy us. I like stories with time paradoxes, but I'm not fixated on them!

"I believe Andrevon, the author of the novel, saw the film recently, and liked it. When a film is good, the author is generally happy, because he realizes that it has not betrayed the spirit of his book. It is a little like translating a poem from one language into another. If you do a literal translation, you are doomed to fail. You need another poet to interpret, and possibly rewrite or change the original, while keeping to its tone and mood. It's the same thing when you go from a book to a movie."

In the case of **Gandahar**, there was a further adaptation: that into the English language. Harvey Weinstein, chairman of Miramax Films, the American distributor of the film, asked science fiction author Isaac Asimov to write an American adaptation of Laloux's original screenplay. At the time of the interview, Laloux had not yet seen the results of Asimov's work, and in any event, felt that, because of his poor command of the English language, he would not be able to comment properly on it. However, his enthusiasm at the idea of working with the great science fiction writer was immediately obvious and convincing.

"I am absolutely delighted that Harvey picked Asimov to do the job. I have an immense admiration for him. He is a wonderful writer. I love his *Robot* stories, and I think *The Gods Themselves* is a superb novel. In fact, I had written several articles about science fiction in which I had mentioned his name, and I had sent him copies. Perhaps he remembered me. We prepared a very literal English translation for him, and he had the complete freedom to take it from there, in accordance with what was happening on the screen. I am impatient to discover the result."

Laloux was equally impatient to hear the American soundtrack of the film. Miramax signed Glenn Close, Christopher Plummer, Jennifer Grey, and even magicians Penn and Teller to provide voices for the American version. "I very much like their choices," Laloux comments, "because I am a firm believer in the importance of voices in animation. In fact, I prefer American voices. I think English sounds more sensual. To me, it has a greater presence on screen. When we did the English version of **The Time Masters**, I preferred it to the French version."

As to the change in title from **Gandahar** to **Lightyears**, Laloux feels that, although it does not quite fit the story as well, it sounds appealing, and adequately conveys the science fiction nature of the picture.

"It is definitely my best film to date, at least from a technical standpoint," Laloux says. "For instance, I was able to do something I did in **Fantastic Planet**, but was unable to do in **The Time Masters**, which was a better outline of the characters with darker lines to better integrate them in the backgrounds. I don't know if the film will have the same amount of success, however, because that depends on whether it answers a need in thepublic, and this is something that always remains unpredictable."

Laloux is determined to stick to science fiction in the future. In addition to Asimov, some of his favorite American authors include Philip K. Dick, Thomas Disch, and Cordwainer Smith, whose planet Shayol is part of **Lightyears** as a character named Shayol. However, it is with French authors that Laloux intends to continue to collaborate.

"I have three projects right now. Two are straight adaptations of two science fiction novels by French author Serge **Brussolo**, whom I find absolutely remarkable. The first is entitled *Le Carnaval de Fer* [*The Iron Carnival*], and I'd like to do that one with artist François **Schuiten**. (American readers may be familiar with Schuiten's work from *The Walls of Samaris*, a graphic novel recently published by NBM.) The next is yet another Brussolo novel entitled *L'Image du Dragon* [*The Image of the Dragon*], for which I don't have any artist in mind yet. The third is an original story entitled *Le Parapluie Qui Parlait Du Nez* [*The Umbrella Which Talked Through Its Nose*], developed by **Brussolo** based on characters and visual concepts created by artist Jacques Colombard, in the Granville style.

"There is also a book by American thriller writer Jerome Charyn that I would like to do someday, but that is still something for the future."

CHAPTER V

Comic Books and Graphic Novels

1. Historical Overview

What are commonly referred to as "comic books," "comic strips," or simply "comics" in English are, in French, called "*bandes dessinées*"—illustrated strips—or BD for short.

Comics are sometimes considered as an indigenous American art form. Yet, they first took root in Europe, and have flourished there beyond the commercial and artistic limitations imposed upon them in the United States. Nowhere else in Europe have comics thrived and been so recognized as in France and Belgium, where they truly deserve the label of "graphic novels."

Some scholars like to trace the ancestry of comics to medieval tapestries or the engravings used during the French Revolution to tell simple stories. However, most experts agree that the first, deliberate attempt at creating comics in a modern form should be credited to Swiss writer-cartoonist Rodolphe **Topffer**, whose first graphic story, *Histoire de M. Vieuxboix* (*The Story of Mr. Vieuxbois*), was published in Geneva in 1827.

One of the first French comics creators signed his work as **Christophe**, and started publishing illustrated stories aimed at children as early as 1887. His *Savant Cosinus* (*Prof. Cosine*, 1900) and ***Malices de Plick et Plock*** (*The Tricks of Plick & Plock*, 1904) were probably the first two forays of comics into the genres of science fiction and fantasy, by way of humor and children's literature.

Other luminaries of the period included Caran d'Ache (Emmanuel Poiré, 1858–1909), the great animal artist, Benjamin Rabier (1864–1939), and science fiction writer-illustrator Albert **Robida**.

Soon, comics took off as a separate branch of French children's literature, and were published in a variety of illustrated magazines, such as:

La Jeunesse Illustrée (*Youth Illustrated Stories*, 1903–1935).

Le Petit Journal Illustré (*The Little Illustrated Journal*, 1904–1914).

La Semaine de Suzette [*Suzette's Weekly*, 1905–1940), for which Joseph P. Pinchon (1871–1953) created the character of a naive, young housemaid from Brittany, the famous *Bécassine*.

L'Épatant (*The Wonderful*, 1908–1937), in which Louis Forton (1879–1934) created an equally famous trio of rogues and con artists, *Les Pieds Nickelés* (*The Nickel-Footed Gang*), the first French comics to use word balloons and also the first to be adapted for animation, by Émile **Cohl** in 1917.

Fillette (*Little Girl*, 1909–1942), which published A. Vallet's classic *Espiègle Lili* (*Naughty Lili*).

As was the case with science fiction magazines, World War I had a severe impact on the budding French comics industry, both artistically and commercially. Nevertheless, the first "albums"—collections of comics stories previously serialized in magazines, and sold in bookstores—began to appear on the children's bookshelves just after World War I. This publishing practice enabled the medium to achieve a degree of economic legitimacy in France which was denied to them in the United States.

In terms of content, the comics stories of the time for the most part remained devoid of genre elements. One of the rare exceptions was *Dans la Planète Mars* (*On the Planet Mars*), published in 1915 in the magazine *Belles Images* (*Beautiful Pictures*, 1904–1936), and signed G. Ri., a pseudonym of artist Victor Mousselet.

The next revolution in comics took place in 1925, when cartoonist Alain **Saint-Ogan**, following the footsteps of Louis Forton, created the characters of ***Zig et Puce*** for *Le Dimanche Illustré* (*Illustrated Sunday*, 1924–1940). *Zig et Puce* was the first modern French comics series, reflecting the influences of not only *Les Pieds Nickelés*, but also of American cartoonists George McManus' *Bringing Up Father* and Martin Branner's *Winnie Winkle*, both published with success in France at the time. *Zig et Puce* used word balloons exclusively, a clear, semi-caricatural drawing line and established modern story-telling comics conventions.

Soon after *Zig et Puce*, Belgian cartoonist **Hergé** created the immortal character of *Tintin* in 1929 for *Le Petit Vingtième* (1928–1940), the illustrated weekly supplement to the local catholic newspaper *Le Vingtième Siècle* (*The 20th Century*); the art form was truly launched.

In 1938, French cartoonist Robert Velter, signing **Rob-Vel**, who had at one time been one of Martin Branner's assistants on *Winnie Winkle*, created the character of *Spirou* as a direct competitor to *Tintin*.

The pre–World War II period was also marked by the growing importation into France of classic American comic strips, such as *Flash Gordon, Brick Bradford, Prince Valiant, Tarzan, Mickey Mouse, Popeye*, etc., published in magazines such as *Le Journal de Mickey, Robinson*, and *Hop-Là!* These had a strong and lasting influence on French and Belgian artists.

Yet, native genre stories created during the period remained the exception. In 1929, Félix Jobbé-Duval (1879–1961) sent his heroes *À la Conquête de la Planète Mars* (*To the Conquest of Planet Mars*) in *Cri-Cri* (1911–1937). Saint-Ogan transported *Zig et Puce* to the future in *Zig et Puce au XXIème Siècle* (*Zig and Puce in the 21st Century*) in 1935. Rob-Vel had *Spirou* fight mad scientist Sosthène Silly in 1939. But these were the exceptions. The only genre comics creation rivaling the American productions was that of writer Martial Cendres and artist **Pellos**, *Futuropolis*, published in 1937-38 in the magazine *Junior* (1936–1942).

When the Nazis banned the importation of American strips during World War II, the French/Belgian comics industry was forced to replace them with local products, thus fostering local talent. Writer-artist Edgar P. **Jacobs** first finished the interrupted publication of *Flash Gordon* (1942), then drew his own *Flash Gordon*–inspired series, *Le Rayon U* (*The U Ray*, 1944), before going on to create his own classic series, *Blake et Mortimer* in 1946. In *Le Téméraire* (*The Fearless*), a pro–Nazi magazine, Auguste **Liquois** wrote and drew another *Flash Gordon* imitation, *Vers les Mondes Inconnus* (*Towards the Unknown Worlds*).

After the war, artists such as **Jijé** (Joseph Gillain), with *Jean Valhardi*; Raymond **Poïvet**, with *Les Pionniers de l'Espérance* (*Hope's Pioneers*); **Sirius**, with *L'Épervier Bleu* (*The Blue Hawk*); and Jacques **Martin**, with *Lefranc* appeared on the scene and created a variety of adventure series in the tradition of American strip artists Milton Caniff, Alex Raymond, Hal Foster, etc. (Poïvet had previously contributed to *Le Téméraire*.)

On the humor front, artists André **Franquin** (who took over *Spirou*), **Will** (who took over *Tif et Tondu*), **Peyo** (with *Johan* and, later, *Les Schtroumpfs* [*The Smurfs*]), did the same, crafting a number of Disney-inspired strips and eventually establishing a unique Belgian graphic style, which still exerts its influence today.

Curiously, the political forces of the Catholic Church and of the Socialist Left combined to keep out American comics, deemed too violent for children by the former, and too imperialistic by the latter. They created a vigilant censorship of comics, which were still perceived as a medium for children. This took the form of a law passed in France in 1949, which effectively prevented the further exploitation of American adventure series.

The French/Belgian comics industry then became dominated by a number of weekly magazines which published humor or adventure series, at first often inspired by, or derivative of, American series, firmly aimed at children and teenagers. These magazines, kept artistically in line by state censorship, were:

Spirou (1938–).
Tintin (1946–1989).
Vaillant, retitled *Pif* in 1969 (1945–1993).
Pilote (1959–1989).

Parallel to these socially respectable publications, a line of cheaper comic books came into existence after World War II, in order to satisfy the continued demand for harder-edged, American-style material. Known as the *petits formats* (*small formats*), these digest-sized comic books published a mix of American, Italian, and Spanish westerns, crime stories, pastiches of *Tarzan*, super-heroes and science fiction sagas, as well as some French material.

The "small format" publishers included Artima (1946–62), later renamed Aredit (1962–), headquartered in Roubaix in the North of France, which published a variety of science fiction titles such as *Cosmos*, *Meteor*, and *Spoutnik*, and Éditions Lug (1950–) and Éditions du Siècle (1946–51), later renamed Imperia (1952–87), both established in Lyons. All fought numerous battles with the state censors, who forced them to go from their original full-color, comic book-size to a black-and-white, digest-size format—hence their name.

Three "small format" genre series made a lasting impression on their readers: **Chott**'s *Fantax* (1946–1949), a French superhero which was soon put out of business by French censorship; **Lortac** and R. & R. **Giordan**'s *Les Conquérants de l'Espace* (*The Space Conquerors*), from the fondly-remembered *Meteor* (1953–1962); and Bob **Dan**'s popular *Tarou*, a Tarzan-like hero that ran uninterrupted from 1949 to 1973!

After the political roots of May 1968, the comics industry began to change. Comics readership was growing older. The artists and writers were becoming tired of the limitations imposed on them by a juvenile market. The age of adult comics was about to begin.

Interestingly, the first adult comic book was the daring science fiction epic **Barbarella**, by illustrator Jean-Claude **Forest**, who had until then been famous among genre fans for his covers for the science fiction magazine *Fiction* (the French edition of the American *F & SF*) and the book imprint *Le Rayon Fantastique*. Published by Losfeld in 1964, *Barbarella* was soon followed by Philippe **Druillet**'s equally daring **Lone Sloane** (1966), which migrated to the pages of *Pilote* in 1970, Nicolas Devil's **Saga de Xam** (1967), Guy Pellaert's **Jodelle** (1966) and **Pravda** (1968), etc.

Other noted genre series of the times included Pierre **Christin** and Jean-Claude **Mézières**' *Valerian*, created in 1967 in *Pilote*, Greg and Eddy **Paape**'s *Luc Orient*, created in 1966 in *Tintin*, Roger **Leloup**'s *Yoko Tsuno*, created in 1970 in *Spirou*, and Forest and Paul **Gillon**'s *Les Naufragés du Temps* (*Castaways in Time*) in the short-lived magazine *Chouchou* (1964–1965).

The "silver age" of French comics eventually came to an end in 1972 when cartoonists Marcel Gotlib, Nikita Mandryka, and Claire Brétécher left *Pilote* to create and

self-publish an adult, underground humor magazine, *L'É-cho des Savanes*. In 1974, **Moebius**, Philippe Druillet, and writer Jean-Pierre **Dionnet** did the same, creating *Métal Hurlant*, the first comics magazine entirely devoted to science fiction and fantasy. (Their publishing company was called Les Humanoïdes Associés, or "Humanos" for short.) In a strange turn of events, *Métal Hurlant* acquired a U.S. edition, *Heavy Metal*, in 1977.

The period ranging from the mid–1970s to the mid–1980s saw the decline of the traditional juvenile humor/adventure comics, with the exception of *Spirou*, which retained its grip on this market, and a rapid increase in the number of series aimed at an older audience. New magazines were created, often featuring genre material. The most notable of these were:

L'Écho des Savanes (1972–).
Métal Hurlant (1975–1987).
Fluide Glacial (1975–).
Circus (1975–1989).
(À Suivre) (1978–98).

The "small format" publishers who had introduced

Marvel Comics superhero characters in 1969 followed suit with their own French-grown versions. Among the most fondly remembered are the short-lived **Wampus** (1969) and **Photonik** (1980-81).

This maturing of French comics proved good for science fiction and fantasy. The major star in the genre was Moebius, who contributed such groundbreaking series as *Arzach* (1975) and **Le Garage Hermétique** (*The Airtight Garage*, 1977) to *Métal Hurlant*. His series **John Difool**, aka **L'Incal** (*The Incal*, 1980–1988), written by cult filmmaker Alexandro **Jodorowsky**, became the major genre event of the 1980s.

Other noted genre creations of the 1980s included Jacques **Tardi**'s nostalgic **Adèle Blanc-Sec** and Didier **Comès**' series of dark fantasies, both published in Casterman's *(À Suivre)* starting in 1978; **Hermann**'s violent, post-nuclear saga **Jeremiah**, created in 1979; Serge **Le Tendre** and Régis **Loisel**'s beautiful heroic fantasy quest **La Quête de l'Oiseau du Temps** (*The Quest for the Time Bird*) in *Charlie*, 1982, virtually the first of its kind in French comics; Benoît **Peeters** and François **Schuiten**'s ambitious **Les Cités Obscures** (*The Dark Cities*) in *À Suivre*, 1983; and finally, Patrick **Cothias** and Serge **Adamov**'s decadent **Les Eaux de Mortelune** (*The Waters of Deadmoon*) in *Circus*, 1985.

The most significant genre artist of the late 1980s was, without a doubt, Yugoslav-born Enki **Bilal**. His graphic novel **La Femme Piège** (*The Woman Trap*), the second volume of the *Nikopol* series (published by Dargaud, 1986), with its nightmarish visions of white-faced, blue-haired women mingling with gods in a post-apocalyptic future, best captured the "no future" sensibilities of the Punk era. Bilal also wrote and directed two live-action feature film: **Bunker Palace Hotel** (1989) and **Tykho Moon** (1997) (see Chapter I).

The glut of the 1980s was followed by an inevitable decline, which forced the publishers to discontinue most of the magazines. *Tintin, Pilote, Charlie, Métal Hurlant*, and others were cancelled. The number of graphic novels, which had increased sharply during the decade, fell. Individual sales went down as well. The "small format" publishers which survived now relied on French translations of American comics or Japanese comics: Manga.

However, a new generation of French publishers had made its appearance among the rubble of the industry. They often published material by young writers and artists, with a strong inclination toward science fiction and, especially, heroic fantasy. The most notable of these publishers were Guy Delcourt (which published Vatine and Cailleteau's *Aquablue*), Soleil (with Arleston and Tarquin's *Lanfeust de Troy*), and Vent d'Ouest and Zenda (which was later taken over by Glénat).

The following abbreviations are used in this chapter to represent the major publishers:

AM: Albin Michel, publisher of the magazine *L'Écho des Savanes*.

Aud: Audie, publisher of the magazine *Fluide Glacial*.

Cast.: Casterman, publisher of the magazine *(À Suivre)*.

Dar.: Dargaud, publisher of the magazines *Pilote* and *Charlie*.

Delc.: Guy Delcourt (no magazine).

Dup.: Dupuis, publisher of the magazine *Spirou*.

Glé.: Glénat, publisher of the magazines *Circus*, *Gomme* and *Vécu*.

Hum.: Les Humanoïdes Associés, publisher of the magazine *Métal Hurlant*.

Lom.: Lombard, publisher of the magazine *Tintin*.

Sol.: Soleil (no magazine).

Vail.: Vaillant, publisher of the magazine *Vaillant*, later retitled *Pif*.

VdO.: Vent d'Ouest (no magazine).

Zen.: Zenda (no magazine).

2. Graphic Novels

A word about series. Series are a number of graphic novels built around a hero, sometime a world or universe, rather than a self-contained story built around a central theme. In this listing, series' titles are indicated as follows: *Jeremiah*, while stand-alone graphic novels are not: *Abominable*.

In those frequent cases where only some episodes, but not all, of a series contain fantasy or science fiction elements (e.g.: *Dan Cooper*, *Jean Valhardi*, *Vincent Larcher*, etc.), we have listed only the genre episodes, but retained their proper numbering in the series' internal chronological order, when applicable.

The exceptions to the above rule are *Astérix*, *Bob Morane*, *Spirou*, *Tarou*, and *Tintin*, because of the special place and importance these five series have in the history of French-language comics. For these works, we have listed the entire series, whether or not individual episodes contain science fiction or fantasy elements.

Series have been alphabetized as individual titles, and not following the rules applying to persons' names. For example, *Jean Valhardi* is listed under the letter "J" and not "V" for *Valhardi, Jean*. We have provided alternative title entries for those series with confusing titles such as "The World of…"

In most cases, we have chosen to list the individual titles in a series and their years of publication according to the order of the graphic novels, and not the original magazine serialization. However, some series—especially those originally serialized in *Vaillant*—were not collected, or were only partially collected, in the graphic novel format, as was traditionally the case. For these, we have listed the original stories as they were serialized.

Finally, there are a few authors whose bodies of work deserve to be considered as a unit, even though they are comprised of mostly unrelated books. We have singled out and given separate, single entries to the following creators: **Bilal**, **Boucq**, **Caza**, **Comès**, **Druillet**, **Foerster**, **Fred**, **Mallet**, **Masse**, and **Moebius**.

Abominable (Glé., 1988)
WRI/ART: **Hermann**.
STORY: Horror stories *à la* H. P. Lovecraft.

Absurdus Delirium
WRI: Bigart; ART: Tha.

1. *Vol. 1* (Aud., 1989)

2. *Vol. 2* (Aud., 1992)
STORY: Nonsensical fantasies *à la* Fredric Brown.
NOTE: Originally serialized in *Fluide Glacial*.

Adam Sarlech
WRI/ART: Frédéric **Bézian**.

1. *Adam Sarlech* (Hum., 1989)

2. *La Chambre Nuptiale* [*The Wedding Suite*] (Hum., 1991)

3. *Testament sous la Neige* [*The Testament Beneath the Snow*] (Hum., 1993)
STORY: Gothic trilogy in which the hero faces Death and other supernatural forces.

Adèle Blanc-Sec (Les Aventures Extraordinaires d') [The Extraordinary Adventures of Adèle Blanc-Sec]
WRI/ART: Jacques **Tardi**.

1. *Adèle et la Bête* [*Adele and the Beast*] (Cast., 1976, transl. Dark Horse/NBM)

2. *Le Démon de la Tour Eiffel* [*The Demon of the Eiffel Tower*] (Cast., 1976, transl. Dark Horse/NBM)

3. *Le Savant Fou* [*The Mad Scientist*] (Cast., 1977, transl. Dark Horse/NBM)

4. *Momies en Folie* [*Mummies on Parade*] (Cast., 1978, transl. Dark Horse/NBM)

5. *Le Secret de la Salamandre* [*The Secret of the Salamander*] (Cast., 1981, transl. Dark Horse/NBM)

6. Le Noyé à Deux Têtes [The Drowned Man with Two Heads] (Cast., 1985)

7. Tous des Monstres [Everyone a Monster] (Cast., 1994)
    STORY: In 1920s Paris, writer Adèle Blanc-Sec faces mad scientists, secret sects of demon worshippers, resurrected Egyptian mummies, etc.
    NOTE: Originally serialized in *Sud-Ouest* in 1976. The more recent stories were serialized in *(À Suivre)*.

Related Works:
    Le Démon des Glaces [The Demon of the Ice] (Dar., 1974, rep. Cast., 1995)
    Adieu Brindavoine (Dar., 1974, rep. Cast., 1979, transl. Dark Horse, 1992)
    STORY: *Le Démon des Glaces* is a Jules **Verne**–inspired story taking place in the 1880s and incorporated into the **Adèle Blanc-Sec** saga. *Brindavoine* is about a World War I veteran who helped Adèle in ep. 5, and is now a regular in the series.
    NOTE: Originally serialized in *Pilote* in 1972.

Adieu, Brindavoine see **Adèle Blanc-Sec**

Adler
    WRI/ART: Sterne.

1. L'Avion du Nanga [The Plane from Nanga] (Lom., 1987)

2. Le Repaire du Katana [The Lair of Katana] (Lom., 1988)

3. Muerte Transit (Lom., 1989)

4. Dernière Mission [Last Mission] (Lom., 1992)

5. Black Bounty (Lom., 1994)

6. L'Île Perdue [The Lost Island] (Lom., 1996)
    STORY: Political fictions and exotic adventures.
    NOTE: Originally serialized in *Tintin* in 1985.

Adolphus Claar (Hum., 1983)
    WRI/ART: Yves **Chaland**.
    STORY: Parodic science fiction in the clear-line style, serialized in *Métal Hurlant* in 1981.

Adrénaline (Hum., 1982)
    WRI/ART: Voss.
    STORY: Hard-rock science fiction from *Métal Hurlant*.

Agar see *Targa*

Agar
    WRI: Claude **Moliterni**; ART: Robert **Gigi**.

1. Les Jouets Maléfiques [The Evil Toys] (Dar., 1974)

2. Les Phantasmes de la Nuit [The Phantasms of the Night] (Dar., 1975)

3. Le Magicien de la Planète Morte [The Wizard of the Dead Planet] (Dar., 1976)
    STORY: A young man fights fantastic menaces in a dreamlike, futuristic universe.
    NOTE: Originally published in Italy in 1972 before being serialised in France in *Lucky Luke* in 1974.

L'Âge de Fer [The Iron Age] (Hors-Série, 1991)
    WRI/ART: **Gébé**.
    STORY: Social satire.

L'Âge d'Ombre [The Age of Darkness]
    WRI/ART: **Caza**.

1. Les Habitants du Crépuscule [The Inhabitants of Twilight] (Dar., 1982)

2. Les Remparts de la Nuit [The Ramparts of Night] (Dar., 1984)
    STORY: Surrealistic, Lovecraftian-inspired stories.

Agence Hermès [The Hermes Agency]
    WRI/ART: Wozniak.

1. La Manière Noire [The Black Manner] (Magic-Strip, 1986)

2. L'Oeil de Dieu [The Eye of God] (Magic-Strip, 1986)
    STORY: Supernatural investigations.

Alain Cardan
    WRI: Yvan **Delporte**; ART: Gérald **Forton**.

1. Alain Cardan (1956)

2. Alain Cardan, Citoyen de l'Espace [Citizen of Space] (1957)

3. Allo, Ici Vénus [Venus Calling] (1958)

4. L'Exode de la Croix Ansée [The Exodus of the Crux Ansata] (1960)
    STORY: Earth colonizes the solar system and launches expeditions to other stars.
    NOTE: Originally serialized in *Risque-Tout* and *Spirou* from 1956 to 1960. Not collected in the graphic novel format.

Alain Landier (Les Extraordinaires Aventures d') [The Extraordinary Adventures of Alain Landier]
    WRI/ART: Albert **Weinberg**.

1. Les Inconnus [The Unknowns] (1962)

2. L'Algue Mystérieuse [The Mysterious Algae] (1962)

3. Exploration Fantastique [Fantastic Exploration] (1962)

4. Les Naufragés des Ténèbres [The Castaways in Darkness] (1962)

5. Le Messager d'un Autre Monde [The Messenger from Another World] (1962)

6. Les Naufragés de l'Espace [The Castaways in Space] (1962)

7. La Planète Insolite [The Strange Planet] (1962)

8. Les Émigrants du Cosmos [The Immigrants of the Cosmos] (1962)

9. Les Cobayes [The Guinea Pigs] (1963)

10. Danger en Amazonie [Danger in Amazonia] (1963)

11. Le Dinosaure [The Dinosaur] (1963)

12. Les Champignons [The Mushrooms] (1963)

13. Le Calendrier de Pierre [The Stone Calendar] (1963)

14. Le Voyageur de l'Espace [The Space Traveller] (1963)

15. Les Pierres de Lune [The Moon Stones] (1963)

16. Cauchemar [Nightmare] (1964)

17. Le Primate (1964)

18. L'Homme Volant [The Flying Man] (1964)

19. Les Lumières de Vénus [The Lights from Venus] (1968)

20. Le Monstre [The Monster] (1970)

STORY: Series of short stories (8 to 12 pages long) starring an archeologist whose explorations into pre–Columbian civilizations lead him to discover extraterrestrial connections. The first ten episodes form a complete story in which Landier discovers alien survivors living inside the Earth; they then take him on a cosmic journey, including a visit to a hollow world.

NOTE: Originally serialized in *Tintin* from 1962 to 1970. Not collected in the graphic novel format.

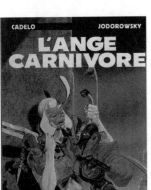

Alandor (La Saga d') [The Saga of Alendor)

WRI: Alexandro **Jodorowsky**; ART: Silvio Cadelo.

1. Le Dieux Jaloux [The Jealous God] (Hum., 1984)

2. L'Ange Carnivore [The Carnivorous Angel] (Hum., 1986)

STORY: A war takes place on a planet fragmented into four continents, adrift in space.

NOTE: Silvio Cadelo is an Italian artist.

Albator

WRI: Claude **Moliterni**; ART: Five Stars Studio (Pierre **Le Guen**, Christian Gaty, Philippe **Luguy**, René **Deynis**, Max Lenvers).

1. Le Corsaire de l'Espace [The Space Corsair] (Dar., 1980)

2. La Revanche d'Albator [Albator's Revenge] (Dar., 1980)

3. Le Triomphe d'Albator [Albator's Triumph] (Dar., 1980)

4. Le Choc des Planètes [The Crash of the Planets] (Dar., 1980)

5. La Bataille de l'Espace [The Space Battle] (Dar., 1980)

6. Albator, Prisonnier du Silence [Prisoner of Silence] (Dar., 1980)

7. La Planète Creuse [The Hollow Planet] (Dar., 1980)

8. Les Silvydres Attaquent [The Silvydres Attack] (Dar., 1981)

9. Le Vaisseau Fantôme [The Ghost Ship] (Dar., 1981)

STORY: French-produced stories featuring the Japanese animation character known in the U.S. as *Captain Harlock*.

Alcester Crowley

WRI/ART: Antonio Cossu.

1. Alcester Crowley (Dup., 1985)

2. Les Gorilles de l'Apocalypse [The Gorillas of the Apocalypse] (Hum., 1990)

STORY: An antique shop owner solves supernatural mysteries.

NOTE: Originally serialized in *Spirou* in 1980. Antonio Cossu is an Italian artist working primarily in the French comics industry.

Alef-Thau (Les Aventures d') [The Adventures of Alef-Thau]

WRI: Alexandro **Jodorowsky**; ART: **Arno**.

1. L'Enfant-Tronc [The Trunk Child] (Hum., 1983)

2. Le Prince-Manchot [The One-Armed Prince] (Hum., 1984)

3. Le Roi Borgne [The One-Eyed King] (Hum., 1986)

4. Le Seigneur des Illusions [The Lord of Illusions] (Hum., 1988)

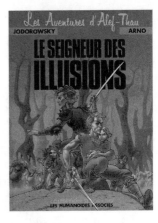

5. *L'Empereur Boîteux* [*The Lame Emperor*] (Hum., 1989)

6. *L'Homme Sans Réalité* [*The Man Without Reality*] (Hum., 1991)

7. *La Porte de la Vérité* [*The Gate of Truth*] (Hum., 1994)
STORY: Heroic fantasy adventures in which a limbless hero eventually succeeds in replacing his missing arms and legs.
NOTE: Originally serialized in *Métal Hurlant* in 1982.

Alerte à La Terre [Alert on Earth] (Samedi-Jeunesse, 1958)
WRI/ART: Christian Mathelot.
STORY: Pulp science-fiction story.
NOTE: Originally serialized in *Coq Hardi* in 1955.

Alertogas
WRI/ART: Hubuc.
Le Labyrinthe [*The Labyrinth*] (Dup., 1964)
STORY: Humorous stories about Ancient Greece.
NOTE: Originally serialized in *Spirou*. Never collected in the graphic novel format.

Alise et les Argonautes [Alise and the Argonauts]
WRI: Patrick **Cothias**; ART: Alfonso Font.

1. *La Nuit du Président* [*The Night of the President*] (Glé., 1987)

2. *La Souris Verte* [*The Green Mouse*] (Glé., 1988)
STORY: Transposition of the Greek legend to a post-apocalyptic future after a bacteriological war.
NOTE: Originally serialized in *Circus* in 1986. Alfonso Font is a Spanish artist.

Allande
WRI/ART: Patrice Garcia.

1. *Le Royaume Perdu* [*The Lost Kingdom*] (Zen., 1990)

2. *Le Secret d'Alcante* [*Alcante's Secret*] (Zen., 1991)

3. *Gaenn* (Zen., 1992)
STORY: Heroic fantasy.

Allo, DMA   see *Guy Lebleu*

Altor
WRI: **Moebius**; ART: Marc **Bati**.

1. *Le Cristal Majeur* [*The Magic Crystal*] (Dar., 1986, transl. Catalan)

2. *Sur l'Île de la Licorne* [*The Island of the Unicorn*] (Dar., 1988, transl. Catalan)

3. *Le Secret d'Aurelys* [*Aurelys' Secret*] (Dar., 1990, transl. Catalan)

4. *Les Immortels de Shinkara* [*The Immortals of Shinkara*] (Dar., 1992)
WRI/ART: Marc **Bati**.

5. *Les Seigneurs Force* [*The Power Lords*] (Dar., 1994)
STORY: An elf-like hero works to help backward planets join a peaceful galactic federation.

Amazones [Amazons] (Hum., 1984)
WRI/ART: Jeronaton (Jean Torton).
STORY: Heroic fantasy.

Amiante
WRI: **Caza**; ART: Patrick Lemordan.

1. *La Cité Perdue de Kroshmargh* [*The Lost City of Kroshmargh*] (Sol., 1993)

2. *L'île du Géant Triste* [*The Island of the Sad Giant*] (Sol., 1994)

3. *Le Labyrinthe de la Lune Pâle* [*The Maze of the Pale Moon*] (Sol., 1995)

4. *La Clef de la Pierre-Étoile* [*The Key to the Star Stone*] (Sol., 1997)
STORY: Red-haired, one-eyed Amiante, Fafnir the Thief, and the wizard Mordecai fight demons and evil wizards.

L'Amour Hologramme [A Holographic Love Story] (Cast., 1993)
WRI: Christian **Lamquet**.
STORY: A cosmonaut and a woman on Earth share a holographic love affair.

L'An 01 [The Year 01] (Square, 1972)
WRI/ART: **Gébé**.
STORY: Men stop working and take time to enjoy life.
NOTE: Also see Chapter I for a feature film adaptation.

Anahire
WRI: Loic Malnati; ART: Anne Ploy.

1. *Le Monstre* [*The Monster*] (Delc., 1996)
STORY: Horror story set in the fantastic city of Anahire.

L'Ange [The Angel]
WRI/ART: Michel Faure.

1. *Les Rois Mages* [*The Three Wise Kings*] (Hum., 1990)
WRI: Nicole Nord; ART: Michel Faure.

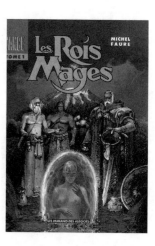

2. Le Ventre de l'Ogresse [The Belly of the She-Ogre] (Hum., 1991)

STORY: To defeat the evil Lilith, three Wizard Kings decide to find a virgin who will bear a cosmic savior.

Anibal Cinq

WRI: Alexandro **Jodorowsky**; ART: Georges Bess.

1. Dix Femmes avant de Mourir [Ten Women Before Dying] (Hum., 1990, transl. *Heavy Metal*)

2. Chair d'Orchidée pour le Cyborg [Orchid Flesh for a Cyborg] (Hum., 1992, transl. *Heavy Metal*)

STORY: Cyborg Annibal Cinq is the enforcing arm of the Council of Five (hence his name; *Cinq* = Five) against tyrants and techno-criminals.

NOTE: Georges Bess is an expatriate American artist working primarily in the French comics industry.

Anita Bomba

WRI: Rufner (Eric Gratien); ART: Cromwell.

1. Aussi Loin Que Je Me Rappelle... [As Far as I Can Recall...] (Cast., 1994)

2. Ce n'Est Pas parce que Je Suis Pauvre... [It's Not Because I'm Poor...] (Cast., 1995)

3. Un Jour J'ai Arrêté de Bosser... [One Day, I Stopped Working...] (Cast., 1996)

STORY: A young, hot-tempered safecracker teams up with a schizoid robot in a series of madcap adventures.

L'Anneau du Nibelung [The Ring of the Nibelung]

WRI: Numa Sadoul, based on Richard Wagner; ART: France Renoncé.

1. L'Or du Rhin [The Rhinegold] (Dar., 1982)

2. La Walkyrie (Dar., 1982)

3. Siegfried (Dar., 1983)

4. Le Crépuscule des Dieux [The Twilight of the Gods] (Dar., 1984)

STORY: Lush and faithful adaptation of Wagner's tetralogy.

Anticipation see *Fleuve Noir*

L'Appel des Étoiles see *Bilal*

L'Appel du Fossoyeur see **Foerster**

Les Apprentis Sorciers [The Sorcerer's Apprentices]

WRI/ART: Yannick.

STORY: Time-traveling teenagers.

NOTE: Originally serialized in *Pif* in 1975-76. This short-lived series was comprised of eight, six-page short stories.

Après l'Apocalypse: Une Nuit, un Lâche [Post-Apocalypse: One Night, a Coward] (Deligne, 1979)

WRI/ART: Anghel.

STORY: Post-apocalyptic drama.

Aquablue

WRI: Thierry Cailleteau; ART: Olivier Vatine.

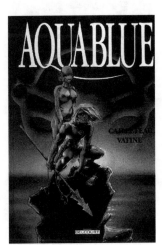

1. Nao (Delc., 1988, transl. Dark Horse)

2. Planète Bleue [Blue-Planet] (Delc., 1989, transl. Dark Horse)

3. Le Mégophias (Delc., 1990)

4. Corail Noir [Black Coral] (Delc., 1993)

WRI: Thierry Cailleteau; ART: Cyrus Tota.

1. Étoile Blanche 1 [White Star] (Delc., 1994)

2. Étoile Blanche 2 [White Star 2] (Delc., 1996)

STORY: The survivor of a spaceship crash grows up on an Eden-like aquatic planet and helps rescue it from the clutches of a greedy interstellar corporation. The *Étoile Blanche* series is a spin-off.

NOTE: Artist Olivier Vatine drew the comics adaptation of Timothy Zahn's *Star Wars: Heir to the Empire* for Dark Horse.

Arabelle, La Petite Sirène [Arabelle, the Little Mermaid]

WRI/ART: Jean **Ache**.

1. Paris by Night (Denoël, 1964)

2. Arabelle en Espagne [Arabelle in Spain] (Poche, 1967)

3. Arabelle et le Bel Canto (Poche, 1967)

4. Opération Cristobal (Poche, 1967)

5. Rendez-vous avec l'Atome [Rendezvous with the Atom] (Poche, 1968)

6. La Dernière Sirène [The Last Mermaid] (Glé., 1978)

STORY: The light comedy, romantic adventures of the last living mermaid, her boyfriend Fleur-Bleue, and pet monkey Kouki.

NOTE: Originally serialized as a daily strip in *France-Soir* (1950–62); later collected in digest-size magazines in the late 1960s. *Arabelle* made a brief return appearance in *Tintin* in 1977.

L'Arbre-Coeur see **Comès**

L'Archer Blanc [The White Archer]

WRI: François **Corteggiani**; ART: Jean-Yves **Mitton**.

1. *Le Retour de l'Archer* [*The Return of the Archer*] (*Mickey* 1840, 1988)

2. *La Cage* [*The Cage*] (*Mickey* 1849, 1988)

3. *Le Cirque* [*The Circus*] (*Mickey* 1853, 1988)

4. *Le Traître* [*The Traitor*] (*Mickey* 1859, 1988)

5. *L'Arc Magique* [*The Magical Bow*] (*Mickey* 1873, 1988)

6. *L'Oeil Qui Voit Tout* [*The All-Seeing Eye*] (*Mickey* 1876, 1988)

7. *La Garde d'Acier* [*The Steel Guard*] (*Mickey* 1880, 1988)

8. *La Proie et l'Ombre* [*The Preyandits Shadow*] (*Mickey* 1889, 1988)

9. *L'Épreuve* [*The Trial*] (*Mickey* 1893, 1988)

10. *Les Otages* [*The Hostages*] (*Mickey* 1902, 1988)

STORY: Heroic fantasy version of Robin Hood with superheroic elements. In a medieval-like future, the masked White Archer and his Merry Men (Professor Arko, young Tork, etc.) fight the tyrannical Klovos and his henchman Yargo.

NOTE: Serialized in *Le Journal de Mickey*; not collected in the graphic novel format.

L'Archimage Robert (Zen., 1991)
WRI: François Froideval; ART: Manini.
STORY: Heroic fantasy.

Ardeur

WRI: Daniel Varenne; ART: Alex Varenne.

1. *Ardeur* (Square, 1980)

2. *Warschau* (AM., 1981)

3. *La Grande Fugue* [*The Great Escape*] (AM., 1982)

4. *Berlin Strass* (AM., 1983)

5. *Ida Mauz* (AM., 1983)

6. *Jack le Vengeur* [*Jack the Avenger*] (AM., 1987)
STORY: After a limited nuclear war, a lone hero tries to survive between a new totalitarian order and organized looters.
NOTE: Originally serialized in *Charlie* in 1979.

Argyll de Marcarande

WRI/ART: Dominique Latil.

1. *L'Héritier du Trône* [*The Heir to the Throne*] (Sol., 1996)
STORY: Heroic fantasy.

Aria

WRI/ART: Michel Weyland.

1. *La Fugue d'Aria* [*Aria's Escape*] (Lom., 1982)

2. *La Montagne aux Sorciers* [*The Mountain of Wizards*] (Lom., 1982)

3. *La Septième Porte* [*The Seventh Gate*] (Lom., 1983)

4. *Les Chevaliers d'Aquarius* [*The Knights of Aquarius*] (Lom., 1984)

5. *Les Larmes de la Déesse* [*The Tears of the Goddess*] (Lom., 1985)

6. *L'Anneau des Elflings* [*The Ring of the Elflings*] (Lom., 1985)

7. *Le Tribunal des Corbeaux* [*The Tribunal of the Crows*] (Lom., 1986)

8. *Le Méridien de Posidonia* [*The Meridian of Posidonia*] (Lom., 1987)

9. *Le Combat des Dames* [*The Battle of the Ladies*] (Lom., 1987)

10. *Oeil d'Ange* [*Angel's Eye*] (Lom., 1988)

11. *Les Indomptables* [*The Untamables*] (Lom., 1988)

12. *Jenessandre* (Lom., 1989)

13. *Le Cri du Prophète* [*The Cry of the Prophet*] (Lom., 1990)

14. *Le Voleur de Lumière* [*The Thief of Light*] (Lom., 1991)

15. *Vendéric* (Lom., 1992)

16. *Ove* (Lom., 1994)

17. *La Vestale de Satan* [*The Vestal of Satan*] (Lom., 1995)

18. *Vénus en Colère* [*The Wrath of Venus*] (Lom., 1996)

19. *Sacristar* [*Holy Star*] (Dup., 1996)
STORY: A wandering swordswoman fights evil wizards and spurned noblemen.
NOTE: Originally serialized in *Tintin* in 1980.

Arkadi (Le Monde d') [The World of Arkadi]

WRI/ART: Caza.

1. *Les Yeux d'Or-Fé* [*The Eyes of Or-Fe*] (Hum., 1989)

2. *Le Grand Extérieur* [*The Great Outside*] (Hum., 1990)

3. *Arkadi* (Hum., 1991)

4. *La Corne Rouge [The Red Horn]* (Hum., 1992)

5. *Les Voyageurs de la Mer Morte [The Travellers of the Dead Sea]* (Hum., 1995)

6. *Noone* (Hum., 1996)
STORY: The son of a barbarian and a sorceress holds the key to survival in a future when Earth no longer spins on its axis, and light and darkness are locked in endless struggle.

Arkel
WRI: Stephen **Desberg**; ART: Marc Hardy.

1. *Les Sept Diables Supérieurs [The Seven Major Devils]* (Dup., 1985)

2. *Arkel* (Palombia, 1992)

3. *Gordh* (Palombia, 1993)

4. *Lilith* (Palombia, 1993)
STORY: A fantasy series set in the Heavens and in Hell.

Arkhé see *Caza*

Arlette Coudrier see *Le Mécano des Étoiles*

Armalite 16
WRI/ART: Michel **Crespin**.

1. *Marseil* (Hum., 1979)

2. *Armalite 16* (Hum., 1980)

3. *Lune Blanche [White Moon]* (Hum., 1981)

4. *Dorianne* (Hum., 1985)

5. *Les Infernés* (Hum., 1987)

6. *La Saison du Cerf [The Season of the Buck]* (Hum., 1988)
STORY: In a post-cataclysmic future, two young men and a young woman try to escape from a new totalitarian state.
NOTE: Originally serialized in *Métal Hurlant* in 1978.

Les Armées du Conquérant see *Arn*

Arn
WRI: Jean-Pierre **Dionnet**; ART: Jean-Claude **Gal**.

1. *La Vengeance d'Arn [Arn's Revenge]* (Hum., 1981)

2. *Le Triomphe d'Arn [Arn's Triumph]* (Hum., 1988) (Co-WRI: Picaret)
STORY: A young prince grows up in captivity, escapes to reclaim his kingdom, and eventually destroy his enemies.
NOTE: Originally serialized in *Métal Hurlant* in 1980.

Related works:
Les Armées du Conquérant [The Conqueror's Armies] (Hum., 1977, transl. *Heavy Metal*, 1978)
STORY: Huge conquering armies embark on an endless series of conquests.
NOTE: Originally serialized in *Métal Hurlant* in 1974.

Arsène Lupin
WRI: André-Paul **Duchateau**, based on the novels by Maurice **Leblanc**; ART: Géron.

1. *Le Bouchon de Cristal [The Crystal Topper]* (Lefrancq, 1989)

2. *813—La Double Vie d'Arsène Lupin [813—The Double Life of Arsène Lupin]* (Lefrancq, 1990)

3. *813—Les Trois Crimes d'Arsène Lupin [813—The Three Crimes of Arsène Lupin]* (Lefrancq, 1991)

4. *La Demoiselle aux Yeux Verts [The Girl with Green Eyes]* (Lefrancq, 1992)

5. *L'Aiguille Creuse [The Hollow Needle]* (Lefrancq, 1994)

WRI/ART: Bourdin.
1–2. *813* (Prifo, 1977)
STORY: The adventures of the famous gentleman burglar.
NOTE: Also see Chapters I and II for film and television adaptations.

Arthur le Fantôme Justicier [Arthur the Avenging Ghost]
WRI/ART: Jean **Cézard**.

1. *Les Hommo-Sapiens* (46 p.) (1962)

2. *Arthur contre César [Arthur vs. Caesar]* (25 p.) (1962)

3. *Aux Arènes de Verderum [The Arenas of Verderum]* (34 p.) (1963)

4. *À la Recherche du Chercheur [Seeking the Seeker]* (64 p.) (1963)

5. *Le Seigneur de Malpartout [The Lord of Illover]* (64 p.) (1964)

6. *L'Insaisissable Prince Noir [The Uncatchable Black Prince]* (1964)

7. *Arthur au Texas [Arthur in Texas]* (51 p.) (1965)

8. *Pour un Bijou de Rien du Tout [For a Worthless Jewel]* (16 p.) (1965)

9. *Maxime a Disparu [Maxime Has Disappeared]* (16 p.) (1965)

10. *Les Trois T [The Three Ts]* (20 p.) (1965)

11. *WWWBZ* (24 p.) 1965)

12. *Le Testament du Corsaire Centenaire [The Testament of a Hundred-Year-Old Pirate]* (20 p.) (1965)

13. *Oncle Hippolyte [Uncle Hyppolite]* (20 p.) 1965)

14. *Les Corsaires du Ciel [The Corsairs of the Sky]* (20 p.) (1965)

15. *Grand Cactus, le Petit Indien [Great Cactus, the Little Indian]* (23 p.) (1966)

16. *Des Bosses sur la Plata [Bumps Over the Plata]* (64 p.) (1966)

17. *Cheveux dans le Vent [Hair in the Wind]* (23 p.) (1966)

18. *Le Fantôme du Cap Vandebou [The Ghost of Cape Vandebou]* (22 p.) (1966)

19. *Arthur, Photographe de Presse [Arthur, Press Photographer]* (28 p.) (1966)

20. *Arthur Passe à l'Attaque [Arthur Attacks]* (28 p.) (1967)

21. *Arthur Pousse à la Consommation [Arthur Encourages Consumption]* (32 p.) (1967)

22. *Arthur Apprend son Métier [Arthur Learns a Trade]* (24 p.) (1967)

23. *Arthur Prolonge ses Vacances [Arthur Extends His Holidays]* (27 p.) (1967)

24. *Arthur Présent dans le Passé [Arthur Present in the Past]* (23 p.) (1967)

25. *La Vallée Heureuse [The Happy Valley]* (20 p.) (1967)

26. *Arthur a Bonne Mine [Arthur Looks Well]* (16 p.) (1967)

27. *Arthur Incorruptible [Untouchable Arthur]* (39 p.) (1968)

28. *Le Mystère de la Villa du Duc d'Os [The Mystery of the Villa of Duke d'Os]* (32 p.) (1968)

29. *Arthur sur la Santa-Billa [Arthur On the Santa Billa]* (20 p.) (1968)

30. *Arthur Touche le Tiercé [Arthur Wins at the Track]* (16 p.) (1968)

31. *La Mystérieuse Météorite [The Mysterious Meteor]* (24 p.) (1968)

32. *Pique-Nique Mouvementé [A Hectic Picnic]* (16 p.) (1968)

33. *Arthur contre les Fantômes de la Ville Fantôme [Arthur Against the Ghosts of the Ghost Town]* (20 p.) 1968)

34. *La Chasse au Trésor [The Treasure Hunt]* (48 p.) (1969)

35. *Mission Exceptionelle [Exceptional Mission]* (20 p.) (1969)

Graphic Novels:

1. *Pistoles en Stock [Coins in Stock]* (Vail., 1963)

2. *Sur la Mer Calmée [On a Calm Sea]* (Vail., 1964)

3. *Le Départ des Revenants [The Ghosts Are Leaving]* (Vail., 1964)

4. *Les Rois de la Flibuste [The Pirate Kings]* (Vail., 1974)

5. *Les Incorruptibles [The Untouchables]* (Vail., 1975)

STORY: Humorous adventures of a time-traveling ghost and his partner, the magician Passe-Passe.

NOTE: Originally serialized in untitled episodes in *Vaillant* from 1953 to 1977. Only five adventures were collected in the graphic novel format. From 1953 to 1960, individual episode titles are impossible to list, as the series went on continuously without any breaks. After 1960, Cézard crafted individual stories (ranging from 20 to 64 pages) until 1969. After episode 35, Cézard began doing seven- and six-page stories. Since their number totals about 110, we have not listed them separately. The **Rigolus** (see below) made their first appearance in a 1969 story. After Cézard's death in 1977, the character was eventually taken over, in 1982, by Marc Arapu.

Related Works:

Père Passe-Passe

STORY/NOTE: Series of short gags featuring Arthur's partner, serialized in *Vaillant* from 1966 to 1971.

Les Rigolus et les Tristus

STORY/NOTE: 45 seven-page stories featuring pinkish good aliens and greenish bad ones introduced in **Arthur**. Serialized in *Pif* from 1969 to 1973.

Aryanne

WRI: Jean-Claude Smit & Terence (Thierri Martens); ART: Michel Guillou.

1. *Les Amants Foudroyés [The Thunderstruck Lovers]* (Magic-Strip, 1986)

2. *Les Voyageurs de la Mort Longue [The Travelers of the Long Death]* (Magic-Strip, 1986)

3. *Les Bannis du Désert [The Exiles in the Desert]* (Magic-Strip, 1987)

4. *Le Nil Noir [The Black Nile]* (Magic-Strip, 1989)

5. *La Dernière Colonne [The Last Column]* (Magic-Strip, 1989)

6. *Le Tueur de la Pluie [The Killer of Rain]* (Magic-Strip, 1990)

7. *Les Entrailles du Paradis [The Bowels of Paradise]* (Magic-Strip, 1990)

8. *A l'Aube des Glaces [At the Dawn of the Ice]* (Magic-Strip, 1991)

9. *La Cité des Sciences [The City of Sciences]* (Magic-Strip, 1991)

STORY: A princess of Atlantis seeks to restore her kingdom. Thierri Martens (a former editor of *Spirou*) writes genre novels under the pseudonym of Yves **Varende** (see Book 2).

Arzach

WRI/ART: **Moebius**.

1. *Arzach* (Hum., 1976, transl. Marvel, 1985)

2. *Arzach Made in USA* (Hum., 1994, transl. as *Visions of Arzach*, Kitchen Sink) (*Ed.*: Jean-Marc & Randy Lofficier)

STORY: The silent adventures of a pterodactyl-riding warrior.

NOTE: Originally serialized in *Métal Hurlant* in 1975.

Les As [The Aces' Gang]

(genre stories only)
WRI/ART: **Greg**.

3. *L'Homme à Deux Têtes [The Man with Two Heads]* (1965; rep. Dar., 1982)

7. *L'Affreux Electronique [The Electronic Ugly]* (1966; rep. Dar., 1978)

10. *L'Alchimiste [The Alchemist]* (1967; rep. Dar., 1981)

12. *Le Désert Humide [The Wet Desert]* (1967; rep. Dar., 1984)

14. *Les Musiciens de Nulle Part [The Musicians from Nowhere]* (1968; rep. Dar., 1983)

15. *L'Homme Qui Vendait du Froid [The Man Who Sold Cold]* (1968; rep. Dar., 1982)

STORY: The adventures of a gang of street-wise kids. Some episodes deal with mad scientists, rogue robots, etc.

NOTE: Originally serialized in *Vaillant* from 1964 to 1973.

Ashe Barrett

WRI/ART: Vincent Hardy.

1. *Berdouille et Techno* (VdO., 1986)

2. *Douze Travaux à fond la Caisse [Twelve Tasks at High Speed]* (VdO., 1987)

STORY: The surreal adventures of a test pilot for the devices and vehicles imagined by mad scientists.

Astérix le Gaulois [Asterix the Gaul]

WRI: René **Goscinny**; ART: Albert **Uderzo**.

1. *Astérix le Gaulois [Astérix the Gaul]* (Dar., 1961, transl. Hodder)

2. *La Serpe d'Or [The Golden Sickle]* (Dar., 1962, transl. Hodder)

3. *Astérix et les Goths [Asterix and the Goths]* (Dar., 1963, transl. Hodder)

4. *Astérix Gladiateur [Asterix the Gladiator]* (Dar., 1964, transl. Hodder)

5. *Le Tour de Gaule [The Tour of Gaul]* (Dar., 1965, transl. as *Asterix and the Banquet*, Hodder)

6. *Astérix et Cléopâtre [Asterix and Cleopatra]* (Dar., 1965, transl. Hodder)

7. *Le Combat des Chefs [The Chieftains' Fight]* (Dar., 1966, transl. as *The Big Fight*, Hodder)

8. *Astérix chez les Bretons [Asterix in Britain]* (Dar., 1966, transl. Hodder)

9. *Astérix et les Normands [Asterix and the Normans]* (Dar., 1966, transl. Hodder)

10. *Astérix Légionnaire [Asterix the Legionary]* (Dar., 1967, transl. Hodder)

11. *Le Bouclier Arverne [The Arverne Shield]* (Dar., 1968, transl. as *The Chieftain's Shield*, Hodder)

12. *Astérix aux Jeux Olympiques [Asterix at the Olympic Games]* (Dar., 1968, transl. Hodder)

13. *Astérix et le Chaudron [Asterix and the Cauldron]* (Dar., 1969, transl. Hodder)

14. *Astérix en Hispanie [Asterix in Spain]* (Dar., 1969, transl. Hodder)

15. *La Zizanie [The Discord]* (Dar., 1970, transl. as *Asterix and the Roman Agent*, Hodder)

16. *Astérix chez les Helvètes [Asterix in Switzerland]* (Dar., 1970, transl. Hodder)

17. *Le Domaine des Dieux [The Mansion of the Gods]* (Dar., 1971, transl. Hodder)

18. *Les Lauriers de César [The Laurels of Caesar]* (Dar., 1972, transl. as *Asterix and the Laurel's Wreath*, Hodder)

19. *Le Devin [The Soothsayer]* (Dar., 1972, transl. Hodder)

20. *Astérix en Corse [Asterix in Corsica]* (Dar., 1973, transl. Hodder)

21. *Le Cadeau de César [Caesar's Gift]* (Dar., 1974, transl. Hodder)

22. *La Grande Traversée [The Great Crossing]* (Dar., 1975, transl. Hodder)

23. *Obélix et Compagnie [Obelix and Co.]* (Dar., 1976, transl. Hodder)

24. *Astérix chez les Belges [Asterix in Belgium]* (Dar., 1979, transl. Hodder)

WRI/ART: Albert **Uderzo**.

25. *Le Grand Fossé [The Great Divide]* (Albert-René, 1980, transl. Hodder)

26. *L'Odyssée d'Astérix [Asterix's Odyssey]* (Albert-René, 1981, transl. Hodder)

27. *Le Fils d'Astérix [Asterix's Son]* (Albert-René, 1983, transl. Hodder)

28. *Astérix chez Rahâzade [Asterix at Rahazade's]* (Albert-René, 1987, transl. Hodder)

29. *La Rose et le Glaive [The Rose and the Sword]* (Albert-René, 1991, transl. as *The Secret Weapon*, Hodder)

30. *La Galère d'Astérix [Asterix's Galley]* (Albert-René, 1996)

STORY: The world-famous adventures of a small but clever Gaul warrior who fights Caesar's invading armies with the help of a potion which confers super-strength.

NOTE: There are, strictly speaking, few fantasy elements in **Astérix**, other than a variety of Druidic magic potions. In the latest installment (No. 30), however, Astérix discovers Atlantis. The **Astérix** stories were originally serialized in *Pilote*. Since René **Goscinny**'s death in 1977, **Uderzo** has continued the series alone.

Related Works:

Les Douze Travaux d'Astérix [The Twelve Tasks of Asterix] (Dar., 1976)

Astérix et la Surprise de César [Asterix and Caesar's Surprise] (Albert-René, 1985)

Le Coup du Menhir [The Menhir Blow, transl. as Operation Getafix] (Albert-René, 1989)

NOTE: These are comic book adaptations of the animated films, and not part of the regular continuity (see Chapter IV).

Atomas
WRI/ART: **Pellos**.
STORY: Science fiction.
NOTE: Originally serialized in *Mon Journal* in 1948.

Atome 21
WRI/ART: **Érik**.
STORY: Juvenile science fiction adventures.
NOTE: Serialized in *Paris-Jeunes* in 1946.

Atomos see *Fleuve Noir*

Attila
WRI: Maurice **Rosy**; ART: **Derib**.

1. *Un Métier de Chien [A Dog's Job]* (Dup., 1969)

2. *Attila au Château [Attila at the Castle]* (Dup., 1969)

3. *Le Mystère Z14 [The Z14 Mystery]* (Dup., 1971)

4. *La Merveilleuse Surprise d'Odée [Odee's Marvellous Surprise]* (Dup., 1974)

STORY: The adventures of an intelligent, talking dog who works for Swiss intelligence.

NOTE: Originally serialized in *Spirou* in 1967. The character was taken over by artist Didgé in 1987.

Aurore et Ulysse see *Les Petits Hommes*

L'Autre see *Wampus*

L'Autre Monde [The Other World]
WRI: **Rodolphe**; ART: Florence Magnin.

1. *Le Pays Roux [The Red Country]* (Vaisseau d'Argent, 1991)

2. *De l'Autre Côté du Ciel [On the Other Side of the Sky]* (Dar., 1992)

STORY: An airplane pilot lands in a fantasy world where the sky is literally falling.

Avant l'Incal see *L'Incal*

Avatars et Coquecigrues [Avatars & Gobbledigooks] (Aud., 1975)
WRI/ART: **Alexis**.
STORY: Fantasy stories originally published in *Pilote* and *Fluide Glacial*.

La Ballade au Bout du Monde [The Ballad of the Edge of the World]
WRI: Pierre **Makyo**; ART: Laurent Vicomte.

1. *La Prison [The Prison]* (Gle., 1982)

2. *Le Grand Pays [The High Country]* (Gle., 1984)

3. *Le Bâtard [The Bastard]* (Gle., 1985)

4. *La Pierre de Folie [The Stone of Madness]* (Gle., 1988)

WRI: Pierre **Makyo**; ART: Eric Herenguel.

5. *Ariane* (Glé., 1992)

6. *A-Ka-Tha* (Glé., 1993)

7. *La Voix des Maîtres [The Voice of the Masters]* (Glé., 1994)

8. *Maharani* (Glé., 1995)

STORY: A young photographer finds himself transported to a medieval land.

NOTE: Originally serialized in *Gomme*, then *Circus* in 1981.

Le Bandard Fou see **Le Garage Hermétique**

Le Banni [The Exile]
WRI/ART: Marcel Coucho.

1. *Le Banni [The Exile]* (Coucho, 1983)

2. *Signé le Banni [Signed: the Exile]* (Goupil, 1985)
STORY: A parody of *Conan*, originally serialized in *Fluide Glacial* in 1982.

Barbarella
WRI/ART: Jean-Claude **Forest**.
1. *Barbarella* (Losfeld, 1964, transl. Grove)

2. *Les Colères du Mange-Minutes [The Wrath of the Minute Eater]* (Kesselring, 1974)

3. *Le Semble-Lune [The False Moon]* (Horay, 1977, transl. as *Barbarella & the Moon Child*, *Heavy Metal*)

WRI: Jean-Claude **Forest**; ART: Daniel Billon.
4. *Le Miroir aux Tempêtes [The Storm Mirror]* (AM., 1982)
STORY: Space wanderer Barbarella has various adventures on the planet Lython. In the second volume, she explores a slow-time planet. In the subsequent volumes, she marries and has a child.
NOTE: Originally serialized in *V-Magazine* in 1962 and, later, in *L'Écho des Savanes*. The first graphic novel was adapted into a feature film by Roger **Vadim** (see Chapter I).
Related Works:
Mystérieuse, Matin, Midi et Soir [Mysterious, Morning, Noon and Evening] (Serg, 1972)
WRI/ART: Jean-Claude **Forest**.
STORY: Barbarella rescues Prof. Alizarine and his friends, stranded on a mysterious planet.
NOTE: Originally serialized in *Pif* in 1971.
Hypocrite
WRI/ART: Jean-Claude Forest.

1. *Hypocrite et le Monstre du Loch Ness [Hypocrite and the Loch Ness Monster]* (Serg, 1971)

2. *Comment Décoder l'Étircopyh [How to Decode Etircopyh]* (Dar., 1973)

3. *N'Importe Quoi de Cheval [Anything But Horses]* (Dar., 1974)
STORY: Prof. Alizarine hires spunky teenager Hypocrite to come work for Yolanda, the zoo-planet.
NOTE: The first story was originally serialized in *France-Soir* in 1971; the other two in *Pilote* in 1973.

Bébé Cyanure
Bébé Cyanure [Baby Cyanide] (Glé., 1975)
NOTE: Earlier prototype of **Hypocrite** serialized in *Chouchou* in 1964.

Batmax (Futuropolis, 1986)
WRI/ART: **Lob**.
Sory: Batman satire.

Beatifica Blues
WRI: Jean **Dufaux**; ART: **Griffo**.

1. *Vol. 1* (Dar., 1986)

2. *Vol. 2* (Dar., 1988)

3. *Vol. 3* (Dar., 1989)
STORY: *Mad Max*-like science fiction.

Le Beau Pays d'Onironie [The Beautiful Land of Onirony] (Helyode, 1992)
WRI/ART: L. Meys.
STORY: Fantasy.

Les Beaux Contes de Fée [Beautiful Fairy Tales]

1. *Les Merveilleuses Aventures de Mark et d'Ermelyne [Mark and Ermelyne's Marvellous Adventures]* (ART: Jobbé-Duval) (SPE, 1926)

2. *Brillantine et Diamantine* (SPE, 1926)

3. *La Forêt Enchantée [The Enchanted Forest]* (ART: André Galland) (SPE, 1926)

4. *Les Aventures de Guénola et de Guiduc [Guenola and Guiduc's Adventures]* (SPE, 1926)

5-6. *Les Extaordinaires Aventures de la Princesse La-Zu-Ti [Princess La-Zu-Ti's Extraordinary Adventures]* (2 vols.) (SPE, 1927)

7. *L'Écuyer du Roi Othon [King Othon's Squire]* (ART: Rolno) (SPE, 1927)

8-9. *Le Nain Bleu [The Blue Dwarf]* (2 vols.) (ART: Jobbé-Duval) (SPE, 1927)

10. *Les Voiles Magiques [The Magic Sails]* (ART: Jobbé-Duval) (SPE, 1927)
STORY: Classic fairy tales.

Bébé Cyanure see **Barbarella**

La Belette see **Comès**

La Belle au Bois Dormant [Sleeping Beauty] (GP, 1947)
WRI/ART: Edmond-François Calvo.
STORY: Classic fairy tale.

Belphégor (1964)

WRI: Unknown; ART: Julio Ribera.

STORY/NOTE: Illustrated adaptation of the renowned television series (see Chapter II) serialized in the daily newspaper, *France-Soir*. Julio Ribera is a Spanish artist working primarily in French comics.

Benoît Brisefer

WRI/ART: **Peyo**.

1. *Les Taxis Rouges [The Red Taxicabs]* (ART ASST.: **Will**) (Dup., 1961)

2. *Madame Adolphine* (ART ASST.: **Will**) (Dup., 1963)

3. *Les 12 Travaux de Benoît Brisefer [The Twelve Tasks of Benoît Brisefer]* (Co-WRI: Yvan **Delporte**; ART ASST.: Walthéry) (Dup., 1967)

4. *Tonton Placide [Uncle Placide]* (Co-WRI: **Gos**; ART ASST.: Walthéry) (Dup., 1968)

5. *Le Cirque Bodoni [The Bodoni Circus]* (ART ASST.: Walthéry, **Gos**) (Dup., 1970)

6. *Lady d'Olphine* (Co-WRI: Yvan **Delporte**; ART ASST.: Walthéry) (Dup., 1972)

WRI: **Peyo**; ART: Albert Blesteau.

7. *Le Fétiche [The Idol]* (Co-WRI: Blesteau) (Dup., 1978)

WRI: Thierry Culliford, Dugomier; ART: Albert Blesteau, Pascal Garray.

8. *Hold-Up sur Pellicule [Hold-Up on Film]* (Lom., 1994)

9. *L'île de la Désunion [The Island of Disharmony]* (Lom., 1995)

10. *La Route du Sud [The Road to the South]* (Lom., 1996)

STORY: A little boy is endowed with super-strength, except when he catches a cold. His opponents include an evil android grandmother.

NOTE: Originally serialized in *Spirou* in 1960.

Le Bibendum Céleste [The Celestial Airship] (Hum., 1995)

WRI/ART: Nicolas de Crécy.

STORY: Fantasy.

Bibi Fricotin

(genre stories only)

WRI: R. **Lortac**; ART: Pierre Lacroix.

42. *Bibi Fricotin et les Lunettes à Lire la Pensée [The Mind-Reading Glasses]* (SPE, 1954)

45. *Bibi Fricotin et les Soucoupes Volantes [The Flying Saucers]* (SPE, 1955)

46. *Bibi Fricotin et les Martiens [The Martians]* (SPE, 1955)

53. *Bibi Fricotin et le Secret de la Momie [The Mummy's Secret]* (SPE, 1962)

54. *Bibi Fricotin et le Nautilus* (SPE, 1962)

60. *Bibi Fricotin et la Fantastique Machine KBX Z2 [The Fantastic Machine KBX Z2]* (SPE, 1963)

62. *Bibi Fricotin en l'An 3000 [In The Year 3000]* (SPE, 1963)

63. *Bibi Fricotin Découvre l'Atlantide [Bibi Fricotin Discovers Atlantis]* (SPE, 1963)

STORY: The adventures of a clever young lad and his companion, an African youth named Razibus. With the help of kindly scientist Prof. Radar, their travels occasionally take them to Mars, through time, or on searches for lost civilizations.

NOTE: Originally created in 1924 by Louis Forton, this *Tintin*-like series was taken over by Gallaud in 1936 and by Pierre Lacroix in 1946.

Bigoudi à Travers les Âges [Bigoudi Through the Ages]

WRI/ART: J. Robin.

1. *L'Âge de Pierre [The Stone Age]* (Bias, 1942)

2. *Les Gaulois [The Gauls]* (Bias, 1942)

3. *Les Romains [The Romans]* (Bias, 1945)

4. *Le Moyen Âge [The Middle Ages]* (Bias, 1945)

STORY: Educational time travel stories.

Bilal, Enki

L'Appel des Étoiles [The Call of the Stars] (Minoutschine, 1975; rep. as *Le Bol Maudit [The Accursed Bowl]* (Futuropolis, 1982); transl. NBM)

Mémoires d'Outre-Espace [Memories from Beyond Space] (Dar., 1978)

Crux Universalis (Hum., 1982)

Images pour un Film [Images for a Film] (Dar., 1983) (WRI: Jean-Marc Thévenet)

Los Angeles (Autrement, 1984) (WRI: Pierre **Christin**)

L'État des Stocks [The State of Stocks] (Futuropolis, 1986)

Hors-Jeu [Out of Play] (Autrement, 1987) (WRI: Patrick Cauvin)

Coeurs Sanglants [Bloody Hearts] (Hum., 1988)

Tykho Moon: *Livre du Film [TM: Book of the Film]* (Christian Desbois, 1996)

STORY/NOTE: The earlier volumes collect science fiction short stories originally serialized in *Pilote*. *Images pour un Film* contain designs drawn for Alain **Resnais**' film, **La Vie Est un Roman** (See Chapter I).

Billy the Cat

WRI: **Desberg**; ART: Colman.

1. *Dans la Peau d'un Chat [In a Cat's Skin]* (Dup., 1990)

2. *Le Destin de Pirmin [Pirmin's Fate]* (Dup., 1991)

3. *L'Été Secret [The Secret Summer]* (Dup., 1994)

4. *Saucisse le Terrible [Sausage the Terrible]* (Dup., 1996)
STORY: A little boy is reincarnated as a cat.

Bizu

WRI/ART: Jean-Claude **Fournier**.

1. *Bonjour Bizu [Hello Bizu!]* (Dup., 1982)

2. *Le Signe d'Ys [The Sign of Ys]* (Fleurus, 1986)

3. *Le Fils de Fa Dièse [The Son of D Sharp]* (Fleurus, 1986)

4. *Le Chevalier Potage [The Soup Knight]* (Dup., 1990)

5. *Le Trio Jabadao [The Jabadao Trio]* (Dup., 1991)

6. *La Croisière Fantôme [The Ghost Cruise]* (Dup., 1992)

7. *La Houle aux Loups [The Howl of the Wolves]* (Dup., 1994)
STORY: A man lives in a magical forest in Britanny, inhabited by all kinds of fairy creatures, including the music-loving Schnokbul.
NOTE: Originally serialized in *Spirou* in 1967.

Black Mary

WRI: Chauvel; ART: Fages.

1. *Quartier des Ombres [The Shadow Quarter]* (Glé., 1993)

2. *Le Jour des Oiseaux [The Day of the Birds]* (Glé., 1995)

3. *Guignol* (Glé., 1997)
STORY: Gothic adventures.

Black-Out (Hum., 1983)
WRI: Gainsbourg; ART: Armand.
STORY: Near-future science fiction.

Blake et Mortimer

WRI/ART: Edgar-Pierre **Jacobs**.
1. *Le Secret de l'Espadon, Vol. 1: La Poursuite Fantastique [The Secret of the Swordfish, Vol. 1: The Fantastic Pursuit]* (Lom., 1950)

2. *Le Secret de l'Espadon, Vol. 2: SX1 Contre-Attaque [The Secret of the Swordfish, Vol. 2: SX1 Strikes Back]* (Lom., 1953)

3. *Le Mystère de la Grande Pyramide, Vol. 1: Le Papyrus de Manethon [The Mystery of the Great Pyramid, Vol. 1: The Papyrus of Manethon]* (Lom., 1954)

4. *Le Mystère de la Grande Pyramide, Vol. 2: La Chambre d'Horus [The Mystery of the Great Pyramid, Vol. 2: The Chamber of Horus]* (Lom., 1955)

5. *La Marque Jaune [The Yellow Mark]* (Lom., 1956)

6. *L'Enigme de l'Atlantide [The Atlantis Mystery]* (Lom., 1957, transl. Catalan)

7. *S.O.S. Météores—Mortimer à Paris [SOS Meteors—Mortimer in Paris]* (Lom., 1959)

8. *Le Piège Diabolique [The Diabolical Trap]* (Lom., 1962, transl. as *The Time Trap*, Catalan)

9. *L'Affaire du Collier [The Necklace Affair]* (Lom., 1967)

10. *Les Trois Formules du Professeur Sato, Vol. 1: Mortimer à Tokyo [The Three Formulas of Prof. Sato, Vol 1: Mortimer in Tokyo]* (Lom., 1972)

11. *Les Trois Formules du Professeur Sato, Vol. 2: Mortimer contre Mortimer [The Three Formulas of Prof. Sato, Vol 2: Mortimer vs. Mortimer]* (ART: Bob **De Moor**) (Lefrancq, 1989)

WRI: Jean **Van Hamme**; ART: Ted Benoît.
12. *L'Affaire Francis Blake [The Francis Blake Case]* (Dar., 1996)
STORY: Col. Francis Blake works for British Intelligence. Prof. Philip Mortimer is a scientist. Together, they take part in a series of fantastic adventures: defeating an Asian take-over the world after World War III (eps. 1 & 2), uncovering the mystery of a hidden treadure chamber beneath the Great Pyramid (eps. 3 & 4), thwarting an evil mastermind who controls a super-powered criminal (ep. 5), discovering the advanced civilization of Atlantis (ep. 6), preventing an invasion of Europe based on weather control (ep. 7), traveling through time (ep. 8) and, finally, fighting life-like androids (eps. 10 & 11). Ep. 9 and 12 do not contain any genre elements.
NOTE: Serialized in *Tintin* since 1946. Ep. 11 was posthumously completed by Bob **De Moor** over **Jacobs**' pencils. ***Blake et Mortimer*** are currently scheduled to be adapted as both a live-action and an animated television series (see Chapter IV). They were also adapted for radio (see Chapter III).

Blanche-Épiphanie

WRI: Jacques **Lob**; ART: Georges **Pichard**.

1. *Blanche-Épiphanie* (Serg, 1972)

2. *Blanche-Épiphanie* (Vol. 2) (Fromage, 1976)

3. *La Croisière Infernale [The Cruise from Hell]* (Hum., 1977)

4. *Blanche à New York [Blanche in New York]* (Hum., 1980)

5. *Le Cavalier Noir [The Dark Rider]* (Leroy, 1987)
STORY: A satire of pulp melodramas; masked hero Defendar rescues innocent Blanche-Épiphanie from a variety of fates worse than death.

NOTE: Originally serialized in *V-Magazine*, *Métal Hurlant* and the daily newspaper *France-Soir*.

Blue
WRI: Joël **Houssin**; ART: Philippe **Gauckler**.

1. Blue (Hum., 1985)

2. Phantom (Hum., 1987)
STORY: In a nightmarish future, gangs are kept prisoners in a sealed city, behind a seemingly impregnable wall.
NOTE: Joël **Houssin** is a well-known science fiction writer, who has also written films and television (see Book 2 and Chapters I and II).

Bob Fish
WRI/ART: Yves **Chaland**.

1. Bob Fish (Hum., 1981)

2. Les Cybers ne sont pas des Hommes [The Cybers Aren't Real Men] (Hum., 1988) (WRI: F. Landon)
STORY: Parody of the 1950s Belgian aventure comics.
NOTE: Originally serialized in *Métal Hurlant* in 1980.

Bob Marone
WRI: **Yann**; ART: Didier **Conrad**.

1. Le Dinosaure Blanc [The White Dinosaur] (Gle., 1984)

2. L'Affrontement [The Clash] (Glé., 1985)
STORY: Parody of **Bob Morane**, in particular the novel *La Chasse aux Dinosaures [The Dinosaur Hunters]*.
NOTE: Originally serialized in *Circus* in 1983.

Bob Morane
WRI: Henri **Vernes**; ART: Dino Attanasio.
1. L'Oiseau de Feu [The Firebird] (Marabout, 1960)

2. Le Secret de l'Antarctique [The Secret of the Antarctic] (Marabout, 1962)

3. Les Tours de Cristal [The Towers of Crystal] (Marabout, 1962)

4. Le Collier de Civa [The Necklace of Shiva] (Marabout, 1963)

5. Bob Morane et la Terreur Verte [The Green Terror] (Marabout, 1963)

WRI: Henri **Vernes**; ART: Gérald **Forton**.
6. Le Mystère de la Zone Z [The Mystery of Zone Z] (Marabout, 1964)

7. La Vallée des Crotales [The Valley of the Rattlesnakes] (Marabout, 1964)

8. L'Epée du Paladin [The Sword of the Paladin] (Dar., 1967)

9. Le Secret des Sept Temples [The Secret of the 7 Temples] (Dar., 1968)

WRI: Henri **Vernes**; ART: William Vance (William Van Cutsem).

10. Opération Chevalier Noir [Operation Black Knight] (Dar., 1969)

11. Les Poupées de l'Ombre Jaune [The Puppets of the Yellow Shadow] (Dar., 1970)

12. Les Fils du Dragon [The Sons of the Dragon] (Dar., 1971)

13. Les Yeux du Brouillard [The Eyes in the Fog] (Dar., 1971)

14. La Prisonnière de l'Ombre Jaune [The Prisoner of the Yellow Shadow] (Dar., 1972)

15. L'Archipel de la Terreur [The Archipelago of Terror] (Dar., 1972)

16. La Ville de Nulle Part [Nowhere City] (Dar., 1973)

17. L'Oeil du Samurai [The Eye of the Samurai] (Dar., 1973)

18. Les Contrebandiers de l'Atome [The Atom Smugglers] (Dar., 1974)

19. Guérilla à Tumbaga [Guerilla in Tumbaga] (Dar., 1974)

20. Les Géants de Mu [The Giants of Mu] (Lom., 1975)

21. Panne Sèche à Serrado [Out of Gas in Serrado] (Lom., 1975)

22. Les Sept Croix de Plomb [The Seven Lead Crosses] (Lom., 1975)

23. Les Sortilèges de l'Ombre Jaune [The Spells of the Yellow Shadow] (Lom., 1976)

24. Le Temple des Dinosaures [The Temple of the Dinosaurs] (Lom., 1977)

25. Les Bulles de l'Ombre Jaune [The Bubbles of the Yellow Shadow] (Lom., 1978)

26. L'Empreinte du Crapaud [The Mark of the Toad] (Lom., 1979)

27. L'Empereur de Macao [The Emperor of Macau] (Lom., 1980)

WRI: Henri **Vernes**; ART: Francisco Coria.
28. Opération Wolf (Lom., 1980)

29. Commando Epouvante [Terror Commando] (Lom., 1981)

30. Les Guerriers de L'Ombre Jaune [The Warriors of the Yellow Shadow] (Lom., 1982)

31. Service Secret Soucoupes [Secret Service Saucers] (Lom., 1982)

32. Le Président Ne Mourra Pas [The President Will Not Die] (Lom., 1983)

33. Les Chasseurs de Dinosaures [The Dinosaur Hunters] (Lom., 1984)

34. Une Rose pour L'Ombre Jaune [A Rose for the Yellow Shadow] (Lom., 1984)

35. La Guerre des Baleines [The War of the Whales] (Lom., 1985)

36. Le Réveil du Mamantu [The Mamantu Awakens] (Lom., 1986)

37. Les Fourmis de l'Ombre Jaune [The Ants of the Yellow Shadow] (Lom., 1987)

38. Le Dragon des Fenstone [The Dragon of Fenstone] (Lom., 1988)

39. Les Otages de l'Ombre Jaune [The Hostages of the Yellow Shadow] (Lom., 1988)

40. Snake (Lom., 1989)

41. Le Tigre des Lagunes [The Lagoon Tiger] (Lom., 1989)

42. Le Temple des Crocodiles [The Temple of the Crocodiles] (Lom., 1990)

43. Le Masque de Jade [The Jade Mask] (Lom., 1990)

44. Trois Petits Singes [Three Little Monkeys] (Lom., 1991)

45. Le Jade de Séoul [The Jade from Seoul] (Lom., 1992)

46. La Cité des Rêves [The City of Dreams] (Lom., 1993)

47. L'Arbre de l'Éden [The Tree from Eden] (Lom., 1994)

48. Un Parfum d'Ylang-Ylang [A Scent of Ylang-Ylang] (Lom., 1995)

49. Alias MDO (Lom., 1996)

50. L'Anneau de Salomon [Solomon's Ring] (Lom., 1996)

51. La Vallée des Brontosaures [The Valley of the Brontosaurus] (Lom., 1997)

Bob Morane Classics
WRI: Henri **Vernes**; ART: Gérald **Forton**.

1. Les Loups sont sur la Piste [The Wolves Are on the Trail] (1967) / *La Malédiction de Nosferat [The Curse of Nosferat]* (1967) (Deligne, 1979)

2. La Piste de l'Ivoire [The Ivory Trail] (1962; Deligne, 1979)

3. L'Île du Passé [The Island of the Past] (1966; Deligne, 1979)

4. L'Ennemi sous la Mer [The Undersea Enemy] (1966; Deligne, 1979)

5. Les Masques de Soie [The Silk Masks] (1967; Deligne, 1970)

6. La Rivière de Perles [The River of Pearls] (1965) / *La Couronne de Golconde [The Crown of Golconde]* (1965) (Deligne, 1980)

7. Échec à la Main Noire [The Black Hand in Check] (1963; Lefrancq, 1992)

8. La Vallée Infernale [The Infernal Valley] (Lefrancq, 1993)

9. La Chasse aux Dinosaures [The Dinosaur Hunters] (1965; Lefrancq, 1994)

10. Le Club des Longs Couteaux [The Club of the Long Knives] (Lefrancq, 1996)

STORY: Bob Morane and his friend Bill Ballantine fight evil throughout the world, in space, and through time. A recurring villain is the diabolical Monsieur Ming, aka The Yellow Shadow, a fiendish Oriental mastermind bent on universal domination. Other recurring villains include SMOG, an international spy ring led by the beautiful but deadly Miss Ylang-Ylang, the mad Dr. Xhatan, and a society of humanoid toad-men living secretly among men.

NOTE: Comics adaptations of the famous juvenile adventure series (also see Chapter II for a television adaptation). Originally serialized in *Femmes d'Aujourd'Hui* (1959) and *Pilote* (1966). Dino Attanasio is an Italian artist; Francisco Coria is a Spanish artist.

Le Bol Maudit see **Bilal**

Bornéo Jo
WRI: Danie Dubos; ART: Georges **Pichard**.

1. Bornéo Jo (Dar., 1983)

2. La Pierre de Passe [The Past Stone] (Dar., 1984)

STORY: Mildly erotic adventures in fantasy jungle settings.

NOTE: Originally serialized in *Charlie* in 1982.

Boskovich
WRI: Raoul **Cauvin**; ART: Antonio Cossu.

1. La Porte du Grand Mhoi [The Gate of the Great Mhoi] (Dup., 1988)

2. La Vengeance du Tambour [The Drummer's Revenge] (Dup., 1988)

STORY: Dark vision of a dehumanized future.

NOTE: Originally serialized in *Spirou* in 1983. Antonio Cossu is an Italian artist working primarily in the French comics industry.

Bouche du Diable see **Boucq**

Boucq, François
Cornet d'Humour [Humor Cone] (WRI: Delan) (Dar., 1980)

Les Leçons du Prof. Bourremou [The Teachings of Prof. Bourremou] (WRI: Pierre **Christin**) (Aud., 1981)

Pas de Deo Gratias pour Rock Mastard [No Deo Gratias for Rock Mastard] (WRI: Delan) (Futuropolis, 1983)

Les Pionniers de l'Aventure Humaine [The Pioneers of the Human Adventure] (Cast., 1984; transl. Catalan)

Point de Fuite pour les Braves [No Escape for the Brave] (Cast., 1986)

La Dérisoire Effervescence des Comprimés [The Desultory Effervescence of Tablets] (Cast., 1991)

La Pédagogie du Trottoir [The Sidewalk's Pedagogy] (Cast., 1987)

La Femme du Magicien [The Magician's Wife] (WRI: Jerôme Charyn) (Cast., 1986; transl. Catalan)

Bouche du Diable [Devil's Mouth] (WRI: Jerome Charyn) (Cast., 1990; transl. as *Billy Budd, KGB*, Catalan)

Les Dents du Recoin [The Corner Teeth] (Cast., 1994)

La Rage de Vivre [The Rage To Live] (Cast., 1996)

STORY: Surreal humor and fantasy, except for the two books written by Charyn, which are dark thrillers often verging on the horrific.

NOTE: The first three volumes were originally serialized in *Fluide Glacial*, later books in *(À Suivre)*.

Bout d'Homme [Little Man]

WRI/ART: Jean-Charles Kraehn.

1. *L'Enfant et le Rat [The Child and the Rat]* (Glé., 1990)

2. *La Parade des Monstres [The Monsters' Parade]* (Glé., 1991)

3. *Vengeance [Revenge]* (Glé., 1993)

4. *Karriguel en Ankou* (Glé., 1994)
   STORY: A teenager faces paranormal threats.

Bran—Légende Née des Tourbillons des Vents du Nord [Bran—Legend Born from the Gales of the North Wind] (Lom., 1993)
   WRI: Jean-Luc **Vernal**; ART: Philippe Delaby.
   STORY: High fantasy.

Bran Ruz (Cast., 1981)
   WRI: Alain Deschamps; ART: Claude **Auclair**.
   STORY: Heroic fantasy.

Le Bras du Démon [The Demon's Arm]

WRI: Christian **Godard**; ART: Florenci Clavé.

1. *À l'Étranger Qui M'habite [To the Stranger Who Lives Within Me]* (Sol., 1996)
   STORY: After an accident in which he lost his right arm, a man is grafted a new, murderous limb.

Brigade Temporelle [Time Brigade]

WRI: Claude-Jacques Legrand; ART: Edmundo Ripoli.

STORY: The adventures of a Time Patrol.

NOTE: Eighteen eps. originally serialized in *Futura* Nos. 1-10 and 19-26 (Ed. Lug, 1972-75); not collected in the graphic novel format. Edmundo Ripoli is a Spanish artist.

Brougue

WRI/ART: **Franz**.

1. *Goff* (Blanco, 1989)

2. *La Renarde [The Fox Woman]* (Blanco, 1991)

3. *Grimpeur [Climber]* (Sol., 1995)
   STORY: Heroic fantasy.

Broussaille [Brush]

WRI: **Bom**; ART: Frank (Frank Pé).

1. *Les Baleines Publiques [The Public Whales]* (Dup., 1987)

2. *Les Sculpteurs de Lumière [The Sculptors of Light]* (Dup., 1987)

3. *La Nuit du Chat [The Night of the Cat]* (Dup., 1989)
   STORY: Fantasy, humor, and poetry for adolescents.
   NOTE: Originally serialized in *Spirou* in 1978.

Bug Hunters

WRI: Scotch Arleston (Christophe Pelinq), Claude **Ecken**; ART: Labrosse.

1. *Le Prisonnier du Virtuel [The Prisoner of Virtuality]* (Sol., 1996)
   STORY: The ghosbusters of cyberspace.

Le Caillou Rouge see **Caza**

Cairn

WRI: Pierre **Dubois**; ART: Jerôme Lereculey.

1. *L'Élu des Armes (Miroir des Eaux) [The Chosen by the Weapons (Mirror of the Waters)]* (Zen., 1995)

2. *La Voie du Guerrier [The Way of the Warrior]* (Glé., 1996)
   STORY: Heroic fantasy.

Canal Choc

WRI: Pierre **Christin**; ART: Various, under the editorship of Jean-Claude **Mézières**.

1. *L'Image Disparue [The Vanished Image]* (Hum., 1990)

2. *Les Capitaines Aveugles [The Blind Captains]* (Hum., 1990)

3. *Les Corps Masqués [The Masked Bodies]* (Hum., 1991)

4. *Les Chasseurs d'Invisible [The Hunters of the Invisible]* (Hum., 1992)
   STORY: A CNN-like team of journalists investigates the presence of invisible aliens on Earth.

NOTE: Each volume includes an illustration by a "guest artist": **Moebius** in ep. 1, **Bilal** in ep. 2, **Druillet** in ep. 3, and Annie Goetzinger in ep. 4.

Canardo (Les Enquêtes de l'Inspecteur) [The Investigations of Inspector Canardo]
WRI/ART: Benoît Sokal.

1. *Premières Enquêtes [First Investigations]* (Pepperland, 1979)

2. *Le Chien Debout [The Upright Dog]* (Cast., 1981, transl. as *Shaggy Dog Story*, Fantagraphics)

3. *La Marque de Raspoutine [The Mark of Rasputin]* (Cast., 1982)

4. *La Mort Douce [The Soft Death]* (Cast., 1983)

5. *Noces de Brume [Misty Wedding]* (Cast., 1985)

6. *L'Amerzone* (Cast., 1986)

7. *La Cadillac Blanche [The White Cadillac]* (Cast., 1990)

8. *L'île Noyée [The Drowned Island]* (Cast., 1992)

9. *Le Canal de l'Angoisse [The Canal of Terror]* (Cast., 1994)

10. *Le Caniveau sans Lune [The Moonless Gutter]* (Cast., 1995)
STORY: A grim duck detective investigates in a gritty, anthropomorphic animal world.
NOTE: Originally serialized in *(À Suivre)* in 1978.

De Cape et De Crocs [Of Cloaks and Fangs]
WRI: Alain Ayroles; ART: Jean-Luc Masbou.

1. *Le Secret du Janissaire [The Secret of the Janissary]* (Delc., 1995)

2. *Pavillons Noirs [Black Flags]* (Delc., 1996)
STORY: Medieval heroic fantasy starring intelligent wolves.

Capricorne see Rork

Captain Fulgur
WRI: Claude **Moliterni**; ART: Five Stars Studio (Pierre **Le Guen**, Christian Gaty, Philippe **Luguy**, René **Deynis**, Max Lenvers).

1. *Captain Fulgur* (Dar., 1981)

2. *L'Étoile Noire [The Dark Star]* (Dar., 1981)
NOTE: Comics adaptation of a Japanese animated series.

Captain Futur (Hum., 1979)
WRI: Philippe Manoeuvre; ART: Serge **Clerc**.
STORY: Parody of American space operas.

Cargal
WRI: Daniel **Pecqueur**; ART: Gilles Formosa.

1. *La Tombe du Borgne [The Tomb of the One-Eyed Man]* (Dar., 1982)

2. *Manhawar* (Dar., 1984)

3. *Le Troisième Monde [The Third World]* (Dar., 1987)

4. *Le Maître de Brumazar [The Master of Brumazar]* (Dar., 1989)
STORY: The prince of the Kingdom of the Two Worlds fights the evil knight Manhawar.
NOTE: Originally serialized in *Pilote* in 1981.

Carland Cross
WRI: M. Oleffe; ART: O. Grenson.

1. *Le Golem* (Lefrancq, 1991)

2. *Le Dossier Carnavon [The Carnavon File]* (Lefrancq, 1992)

3. *Tunnel* (Lefrancq, 1993)

4. *Le Mystère du Loch Ness [The Loch Ness Mystery]* (Lefrancq, 1994)

5. *Le Mystère du Loch Ness 2 [The Loch Ness Mystery 2]* (Lefrancq, 1995)

6. *La Ghoule de Shadwell [The Ghoul of Shadwell]* (Lefrancq, 1996)
STORY: A detective investigates supernatural mysteries.

Carmen Mc Callum
WRI: Olivier Vatine, Fred Duval; ART: Gess, Fred Blanchard.

1. *Jukurpa* (Delc., 1995)

2. *Mare Tranquilitatis* (Delc., 1996)
STORY: In 2053, Carmen McCallum is hired by the Yakuzas and ends up in an orbital prison.

Carnivores
WRI: J. Wacquet; ART: Eric Herenguel.

1. *Terry* (Zen., 1991)

2. *Xiao* (Zen., 1992)
STORY: Science fiction.

Carol Détective
WRI: André-Paul **Duchateau**; ART: Eddy **Paape**.

1. *Les Hallucinés [The Hallucinated]* (Lom., 1991)

2. *Mission Atlantide [Mission Atlantis]* (Lom., 1992)
STORY: The adventures of a futuristic female detective and her intelligent cat.

La Caste des Méta-Barons see **L'Incal**

Caste Magnétique [Magnetic Caste] (Hum., 1989)
WRI: Éric Cartier, P. Naegelen; ART: P. Cartier.
STORY: Science fiction.

Cauchemar Blanc see **Moebius**

Cauchemarrant [Funny Nightmares] (Bédérama, 1979)
WRI/ART: André **Franquin**.
STORY: Funny little monsters.

Ça va, Ça vient see **Fred**

La Caverne du Souvenir [Cave of Memory] (Lom., 1985)
WRI/ART: **Andréas**.
STORY: Gothic fantasy.

Caza, Philippe
Kris Kool (Losfeld, 1970)
Fume, C'est du Caza [Smoke, It's by Caza] (Kesselring, 1975)
Caza 30X30 (Hum., 1980)
Arkhé (Hum., 1982)
Le Caillou Rouge et Autres Contes [The Red Pebble and Other Tales] (Dar., 1985)
Mémoire des Écumes (WRI: Lejalé) *[Memory of the Froth]* (Dar., 1985)
Lailah (Hum., 1988)
Chimères [Chimeras] (Hum., 1988)
STORY/NOTE: Kris Kool is a futuristic James Bond. The other volumes are collections of fantasy and science fiction short stories, originally serialized in *Pilote*.

Cédric
WRI/ART: **Ferry**.
STORY: Medieval saga about alchemists and wizardry.
NOTE: Originally serialized in *Tintin* in 1975; not collected in the graphic novel format.

Celui-Là [That One]
WRI: Alain Riondet; ART: Claude **Auclair**.

1. Celui-là [That One] (Cast., 1989)

2. Celui qui Achève [He Who Finishes] (Cast., 1991)
STORY: Heroic fantasy.
NOTE: Ep. 2 was completed by **Tardi** and **Mézières** after **Auclair**'s death in 1990.

Celui Qui Est Né Deux Fois [He Who Was Twice Born]
WRI/ART: **Derib**.

1. Pluie d'Orage [Rain Storm] (Lom., 1983)

2. La Danse du Soleil [The Dance of the Sun] (Lom., 1984)

3. L'Arbre de Vie [The Tree of Life] (Lom., 1985)
STORY: Tales of Indian magic.

150 Loups-Garous [150 Werewolves]
WRI: P. Mezinski; ART: Jean-Pierre **Danard**, François **Pierre**

1. Sur une Place de Constantinople [On a Constantinople Square] (Dar., 1992)

2. Les Mocassins de Messar Gbo [Messar Gbo's Mocassins] (Dar., 1996)
STORY: The Grand Master of an esoteric sect hires a young man to steal an alchemical painting.

Le Centaure Mécanique [Mechanical Centaur] (Hum., 1982)
WRI: **Rodolphe**; ART: Eberoni.
STORY: Science fiction.

Les Centaures see **Les Petits Hommes**

Certains l'aiment noir see **Foerster**

Ceux-Là [These People] (2 vols., Square, 1980)
WRI: Jean-Pierre **Andrevon**; ART: Georges **Pichard**.
STORY: Adaptation of science fiction short stories by this renowned writer.

Ceux Venus de l'Espace [They Came from Space]
WRI/ART: Polch.

1. Base dans les Andes [Base in the Andes] (Kesselring, 1979)

2. Atlantis (Kesselring, 1979)
STORY: UFO stories *à la* Erich Von Daniken.

Challenger
WRI: André-Paul **Duchateau**, based on the novel by Sir Arthur Conan Doyle; ART: Patrice **Sanahujas**.

1. Vol. 1 (Lefrancq, 1990)

2. Vol. 2 (Lefrancq, 1992)
STORY: Comics adaptation of *The Lost World*.

Le Chaman (Ice Crim's, 1984)
WRI: Frank Giroud; ART: Ab'Aigre.
STORY: Indian magic.

Champakou
WRI/ART: Jeronaton (Jean Torton).

1. Champakou (Hum., 1979, transl. *Heavy Metal*, 1981)

2. L'Oeuf du Monde [The World Egg] (Hum., 1981)

3. Le Grand Passage [The Great Passage] (Magic-Strip, 1982)

4. L'Éternel Voyage 1 [The Eternal Voyage 1] (Bédéscope, 1985)

4. L'Éternel Voyage 2 [The Eternal Voyage 2] (Création, 1986)
   STORY: Pre-Columbian civilizations and extraterrestrial visitations.
   NOTE: Originally serialized in *Métal Hurlant* in 1978.

Chancellor
   WRI: André-Paul **Duchateau**; ART: Patrice **Sanahujas**.

1. L'Aiguille de Feu [The Needle of Fire] (Dar., 1986)

2. La Croisière des Morts-Vivants [The Cruise of the Living Dead] (Dar., 1989)
   STORY: A futuristic detective investigates.

La Chanson de Sigale [Sigale's Song]
   WRI/ART: C. Goux.

1. Aiguesieste (Dar., 1993)

2. Paris la Douce (Dar., 1994)
   NOTE: Provencal science fiction.

Le Chant des Étoiles [The Song of the Stars]
   WRI/ART: Patrice Garcia.

1. L'Arche de Tanathé [The Ark of Tanathe] (Zen., 1995)
   STORY: Science fiction.

Le Chant des Lames [The Song of the Blades]
   WRI: Nordine; ART: Yazghi.

1. Le Chant des Lames [The Song of the Blades] (Sol., 1996)
   STORY: Heroic fantasy.

Chaos see **Moebius**

Charley Delco see **Le Mécano des Étoiles**

Charlot
   (genre stories only)
   WRI: Montaubert; ART: Jean-Claude **Forest** (except where otherwise indicated)

16. Charlot et le Balai Atomique [The Atomic Broom] (ART: Pierre Lacroix) (SPE, 1952)

19. Charlot et les Mammouths [The Mastodons] (SPE, 1954)

20. Charlot contre Mandrago Satanas [Charlot vs. Mandrago Satanas] (SPE, 1954)

24. Charlot Chevalier de la Table Ronde [Knight of the Round Table] (SPE, 1956)

31. Charlot Pionnier Interplanétaire [Interplanetary Pioneer] (SPE, 1960)

33. Charlot et les Robots (SPE, 1961)

37. Charlot sur la Lune [On the Moon] (ART: Serna) (SPE, 1963)
   STORY/NOTE: The adventures of Charlie Chaplin's Little Tramp were originally serialized in *Cri-Cri* and *L'Épatant* in the 1920s, drawn by Thomen. After World War II, Thomen continued the series for fifteen issues, then the art duties were split between Mat (Marcel Trublin) and Jean-Claude **Forest**, who drew a series of parodic science fiction stories.

Charly
   WRI: Denis Lapière; ART: Magda Seron.

1. Jouet d'Enfer [Hell Toy] (Dup., 1991)

2. L'île Perdue [The Lost Island] (Dup., 1992)

3. Le Réveil [The Awakening] (Dup., 1993)

4. Le Piège [The Trap] (Dup., 1994)

5. Cauchemars [Nightmares] (Dup., 1995)

6. Le Tueur [The Killer] (Dup., 1996)
   STORY: A young boy receives an armed spaceship as a gift.
   NOTE: Originally serialized in *Spirou* in 1990.

Le Chat [The Cat]
   WRI/ART: Michel Denys (aka **Greg**).
   STORY: A "cat-man" super-hero fights crime in England.
   NOTE: 26 episodes originally serialized in *Heroic Albums* (Esseo, 1953–56).

Chats [Cats]
   WRI/ART: Didier **Convard**.

1. Not'Dam [Our Lady] (Glé., 1992)

2. Adam et Rêve [Adam and Dream] (Glé., 1992)

3. La Ruche [The Hive] (Glé., 1994)

4. Le Village Immortel [The Immortal Village] (Dar., 1997)
   STORY: Cats have acquired intelligence in a post-nuclear world.

Le Chêne du Rêveur [The Dreamer's Oak] (Bayard, 1984)
   WRI: Benoist, Maurouard; ART: Arno.
   STORY: A group of schoolchildren finds an alien stranded on Earth.

Cherchez le Martien see ***Mallet***

Le Chevalier Printemps [The Knight of Spring]
(Glé., 1977)
WRI/ART: Jean Trubert.
STORY: With the help of his magic sword, a knight and his squire fight evil wizards, dragons, etc.

Les Chevaliers de la Cloche [The Knights of the Bell]
WRI: Didier **Convard**; ART: Juvin.

1. *Les Chevaliers de la Cloche [The Knights of the Bell]*
(Glé., 1990)

2. *Le Clown à la Hache [The Clown with an Axe]* (Glé., 1991)
NOTE: 19th century pulp fiction.

Chimères see ***Caza***

Chroniques de Fin de Siècle [Chronicles of the End of the Century]
WRI: Jan **Bucquoy**; ART: Jacques Santi.

Gérard Craan

1. *Camp de Réforme B [Reform Camp B]* (Deligne, 1982)

2. *Au Dolle Mol* (Deligne, 1983)

Chroniques de Fin de Siècle [Chronicles of the End of the Century]

1. *Autonomes [Autonomous]* (Ansaldi, 1985)

2. *Mourir à Creys-Malville [To Die in Creys-Malville]*
(Ansaldi, 1986)

3. *Chooz* (Alpen, 1988)
STORY: Anarchist Gérard Craan fights the totalitarian forces of a new European power.

Chroniques de l'Impossible [Chronicles of the Impossible]
WRI: Christian Piscaglia; ART: Claude **Laverdure**.

1. *La Maison de Bruges [The House in Bruges]* (Dar., 1987)

2. *Les Tempêtes de Saint-Malo [The Storms of Saint-Malo]*
(Dar., 1988)

3. *La Longue Nuit de Strasbourg [The Long Night of Strasbourg]* (Dar., 1990)
STORY: Two sisters, Lucie and Cécile, investigate supernatural mysteries in ancient European cities.

Chroniques de la Lune Noire [Chronicles of the Black Moon]

WRI: François Froideval; ART: Olivier Ledroit.

1. *Le Signe des Ténèbres [The Sign of Darkness]* (Zen., 1989)

2. *Le Vent des Dragons [The Dragons' Wind]* (Zen., 1990)

3. *La Marque des Démons [The Mark of the Demons]* (Zen., 1991)

4. *Quand Sifflent les Serpents [When Serpents Hiss]* (Zen., 1993)

5. *La Danse Écarlate [The Scarlet Dance]* (Dar., 1994)

WRI: François Froideval; ART: Pontet.
6. *La Couronne des Ombres [The Crown of Shadows]* (Dar., 1995)

7. *De Vents de Jade et de Jais [Of Winds of Jade and Jet]*
(Dar., 1997)
STORY: Rogue knight Wishermill fights the evil wizard Haazel Thorn.

Chroniques de Panchrysia
WRI/ART: **Ferry**.

1. *L'Envol [The Flight]* (Lom., 1995)

2. *Les Rêves [The Dreams]* (Lom., 1996)

3. *Les Statues [The Statues]* (Lom., 1997)
STORY: A young orphan uncovers the secret of an ancient alchemist.

Chroniques de Saint-Cyprien
WRI/ART: Bouchard.

1. *La Chapelle du Démon [The Demon's Chapel]* (Glé., 1981)

2. *Une Valise pour Jupiter [A Suitcase for Jupiter]* (Glé., 1982)
STORY: Science fiction.

Chroniques des Pays de Markal [Chronicles of Markal Country]
WRI: François **Corteggiani**; ART: Jean-Pierre **Danard**, François **Pierre**.

1. *La Couleur de la Vie [The Color of Life]* (Milan, 1986)

2. *Le Lézard aux Yeux Rouges [The Red-Eyed Lizard]*
(Milan, 1987)
STORY: Princess Zara of Go fights against the evil wizard Magor and his lizard men.

Chroniques du Griffon Noir [Chronicles of the Black Gryphon]
WRI/ART: Henri Desclez.

1. *Le Cygne Rouge [The Red Swan]* (1975)

2. *Les Larmes de Squonk [The Squonk's Tears]* (1975)

3. Jkwala (1975)

4. La Maison Espagnole [The Spanish House] (1975)

5. Le Fils de Baal Sjemm [The Son of Baal Sjemm] (1976)

6. Le Berger du Diable [The Devil's Shepherd] (1976)

7. Noeuds de Bruges [Brugian Knots] (1976)

8. Une Nature Bien Morte [A Very Still Life] (1976)

9. Le Diable Cornu [The Horned Devil] (1976)

10. La Soeur de Herr Knopf [The Sister of Herr Knopf] (1976)

11. La Nuit du Cerf [The Night of the Buck] (1976)

12. Les Matous [The Pussycats] (1976)

13. La Barque Bleue [The Blue Skiff] (1977)

14. Les Ancêtres [The Ancestors] (1977)

15. Les Gants Rouges [The Red Gloves] (1978)
STORY: In 1850 Belgium, a miniature-maker, his daughter, and a good wizard fight the forces of darkness.
NOTE: Series of short stories originally serialized in *Tintin* from 1975 to 1978; never collected in the graphic novel format.

Chroniques du Temps de la Vallée des Ghlomes [Chronicles of the Times of the Valley of the Ghlomes]

WRI: Christian **Godard**; ART: Julio Ribera.
1. Chroniques du Temps de la Vallée des Ghlomes [Chronicles of the Times of the Valley of the Ghlomes] (Dar., 1985)

2. La Guerre des Pilons [The War of the Maces] (Dar., 1986)

WRI: Christian **Godard**; ART: Florenci Clave.
3. L'Hydre Mélomane [The Music-Loving Hydra] (Vaisseau d'Argent, 1990)

4. Besache Peau [Besache Skin] (Sol., 1996)
STORY: Mildly erotic heroic fantasy.
NOTE: Julio Ribera and Florenci Clave are Spanish artists.

Chroniques Métalliques see **Moebius**

Chroniques originelles [Chronicles of the Origins]
WRI/ART: Marc **Bati**.

1. Volume 1 (Sol., 1996)
STORY: Science fiction.

La Citadelle Aveugle see **Moebius**

La Citadelle Pourpre [The Purple Citadel] (Delc., 1988)
WRI: Salvetti, Headline; ART: Jacques Terpant.
STORY: Heroic fantasy.

La Cité-Feu see **Moebius**

Les Cités Obscures [The Dark Cities]
WRI: Benoît **Peeters**; ART: François **Schuiten**.

1. Les Murailles de Samaris [The Walls of Samaris] (Cast., 1983, transl. NBM)

2. La Fièvre d'Urbicande [The Fever in Urbikand] (Cast., 1985, transl. Dark Horse/NBM)

3. La Tour [The Tower] (Cast., 1987, transl. Dark Horse/NBM)

4. La Route d'Armilia [The Road to Armilia] (Cast., 1988)

5. Brüsel (Cast., 1992)

6. L'Enfant Penchée [The Leaning Child] (Cast., 1996)

Related Works:

1. Le Mystère d'Urbicande [The Urbikand Mystery] (Cast., 1985)

2. L'Archiviste [The Archivist] (Cast., 1987)

3. Encyclopédie des Transports Présents et à Venir [Encyclopedia of Present & Future Transportation] (Cast., 1988)

4. Le Musée A. Desombres (Cast., 1990)

5. L'Écho des Cités [City News] (Cast., 1993)

6. Le Guide des Cités [City Guide] (Cast., 1996)
STORY: Stories of a world of surreal cities where architecture dominates men's lives.
NOTE: Originally serialized in *(À Suivre)* in 1982.

Clameurs see **Fleuve Noir**

Clotho
WRI: Gérard **Dewamme**; ART: Jacques Bonodot.

1. Le Gambit des Innocents [The Gambit of the Innocents] (Glé., 1989)

2. La Larme de Sang [The Tear of Blood] (Glé., 1990)
STORY: A young Fury spreads love and death.

Le Coeur Couronné [The Crowned Heart]
WRI: Alexandro **Jodorowsky**; ART: **Moebius**.

1. La Folle du Sacré-Coeur [The Madwoman of the Sacred-Heart] (Hum., 1992, transl. Dark Horse)

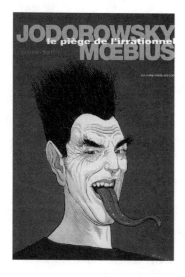

2. Le Piège de l'Irrationnel [The Irrational Trap] (Hum., 1993, transl. as *The Madwoman of the Sacred-Heart*, Dark Horse)

STORY: Religious fanatics and a reluctant university professor become involved in the heralding of a new savior.

Le Coeur de Sang [The Bloody Heart]

WRI: Isabelle Mercier, Roger Seiter; ART: Vincent Bailly.

1. Les Chevaliers Guides [The Guiding Knights] (Delc., 1995)

STORY: Peaceful dwarves are attacked by the evil Baldur's armies of trolls.

Coeurs Sanglants see **Bilal**

Comès, Didier

Silence (Cast., 1980)

La Belette [The Weasel] (Cast., 1983)

L'Ombre du Corbeau [The Shadow of the Crow] (Lom., 1984)

Éva (Cast., 1985)

Iris (Cast., 1991)

L'Arbre-Coeur [The Heart-Tree] (Cast., 1988; transl. Dark Horse)

La Maison Où Rêvent les Arbres [The House Where Trees Dream] (Cast., 1995)

STORY: Series of b&w graphic novels dealing with the myths and legends of the French countryside.

NOTE: Originally serialised in *(À Suivre)*.

Comme un Poulet Sans Tête [Like a Headless Chicken] (Delc., 1995)

WRI/ART: Alex Barbier.

STORY: Science fiction.

Commissaire Finemouche et l'Agent Fiasco [Commissioner Finemouche and Policeman Fiasco]

WRI: Lange; ART: Mahaux.

1. Smog à Gogo [Lotsa Smog] (Dup., 1965)

STORY: Criminals use anti-gravity devices and fake smog to steal monuments.

NOTE: Originally serialized in *Spirou* in 1965; never collected in the graphic novel format.

Les Compagnons du Crépuscule [The Companions of the Dusk]

WRI/ART: François **Bourgeon**.

1. Le Sortilège du Bois des Brumes [The Spell of the Misty Forest] (Cast., 1984; transl. NBM)

2. Les Yeux d'Etain de la Ville Glauque [The Tin Eyes of the Gloomy Town] (Cast., 1986)

3. Le Dernier Chant des Malaterre [The Last Song of Malaterre] (Cast., 1990)

STORY: During the One Hundred Years War, a mysterious Knight and his companions fight the forces of darkness.

NOTE: Originally serialized in *(À Suivre)* starting in 1983.

Les Compagnons du Rêve [The Companions of the Dream]

WRI: Nataël; ART: Béja.

1. L'Ombre du Mangou [The Shadow of the Mangu] (Glé., 1990)

2. La Fenêtre Oubliée [The Forgotten Window] (Glé., 1991)

STORY: Paranormal investigations.

La Complainte de l'Homme Programmé see **Moebius**

Complaintes des Landes Perdues [Laments of the Lost Lands]

WRI: Jean **Dufaux**; ART: Gregor Rosinski.

1. Sioban (Dar., 1993)

2. Blackmore (Dar., 1994)

3. Dame Gerfaut (Dar., 1997)

STORY: Princess Sioban fights to free the Celtic land of Eruin Dulea from the domination of the evil wizard Bedlam.

NOTE: Gregor Rosinski is a Polish artist working primarily in French comics.

Le Concombre Masqué [The Masked Cucumber]

WRI/ART: Nikita Mandryka.

1. Les Aventures Potagères du Concombre Masqué [The Vegetable Adventures of the Masked Cucumber] (Futuropolis, 1971)

2. Les Aventures Potagères du Concombre Masqué (vol. 2) [The Vegetable Adventures of the Masked Cucumber 2] (Dar., 1973)

3. Le Retour du Concombre Masqué [The Return of the Masked Cucumber] (Dar., 1975)

4. Comment Devenir Maître du Monde [How to Become Master of the World] (Dar., 1980)

5. La Vie Quotidienne du Concombre Masqué [The Daily Life of the Masked Cucumber] (Dar., 1981)

6. À la Poursuite du Broutchlaga Mordoré [The Hunt for the Golden Brutchlaga] (Dar., 1982)

7. Le Concombre Masqué contre le Grand Patatoseur [The Masked Cucumber vs. the Great Potatozer] (Dar., 1983)

8. La Dimension Poznave [The Poznave Dimension] (Dup., 1990)

9. La Dimension Poznave (vol. 2) [The Poznave Dimension 2] (Dup., 1991)

10. Le Concombre Dépasse les Bornes [The Cucumber Goes Overboard] (Dup., 1991)

11. Le Concombre Dépasse les Bornes (vol. 2) [The Cucumber Goes Overboard 2] (Dup., 1992)

12. Le Concombre Masqué Fait Avancer les Choses [The Masked Cucumber Helps Move Things Forward] (Dup., 1992)

STORY: The surreal adventures of vegetable characters in a dream-like, *Krazy Kat*-type of land.

NOTE: Originally serialized in *Vaillant* in 1965, in *Pilote* during the 1970s and in *L'Écho des Savanes* in the 1980s.

Les Conquérants de l'Espace [The Conquerors of Space]

WRI: R. **Lortac**; ART: Raoul & Robert **Giordan**.

1. Les Conquérants de l'Espace [The Conquerors of Space] (1953; rep. Meteor 1, Lefrancq, 1990)

2. Vers la Lune [Towards the Moon] (1953; rep. Meteor 1, Lefrancq, 1990)

3. La Planète du Silence [The Silent Planet] (1953; rep. Meteor 1, Lefrancq, 1990)

4. Aventure dans la Lune [Adventure On the Moon] (1953; rep. Meteor 1, Lefrancq, 1990)

5. "Terra"—Monde Nouveau [Terra—a New World] (1953; rep. Meteor 1, Lefrancq, 1990)

6. Invasion Martienne [Martian Invasion] (1953; rep. Meteor 1, Lefrancq, 1990)

7. Au Secours de Mars [To Help Mars] (1953; rep. Meteor 1, Lefrancq, 1990)

8. Croisière Sidérale [Star Cruise] (1954; rep. Meteor 1, Lefrancq, 1990)

9. Titania (1954; rep. Meteor 2, Lefrancq, 1990)

10. Guerre en Utopie [War in Utopia] (1954; rep. Meteor 2, Lefrancq, 1990)

11. Menace sur Arbor [Threat to Arbor] (1954; rep. Meteor 2, Lefrancq, 1990)

12. "Aqua"—Cité Sous-Marine [Aqua—The Underwater City] (1954; rep. Meteor 2, Lefrancq, 1990)

13. Guerre aux Parasites [War Against the Parasites] (1954; rep. Meteor 2, Lefrancq, 1990)

14. Aventure en Kroscopie [Adventure in Kroscopia] (1954; rep. Meteor 3, Lefrancq, 1995)

15. "Mytho"—Planète Fabuleuse [Mytho—The Fabulous Panet] (1954; rep. Meteor 3, Lefrancq, 1995)

16. Invasion de Robots [Robot Invasion] (1954; rep. Meteor 3, Lefrancq, 1995)

17. Alerte sur Pluton [Alert on Pluto] (1954; rep. Meteor 3, Lefrancq, 1995)

18. Le Monde Parallèle [The Parallel World] (1954; rep. Meteor 3, Lefrancq, 1995)

19. La Planète des Mirages [The Planet of Mirages] (1954; rep. Meteor 4, Lefrancq, 1996)

20. Avatars sur la Planète "Sylva" [Trouble on Planet Sylva] (1955; rep. Meteor 4, Lefrancq, 1996)

21. La Guerre des Robots [The War of the Robots] (1955; rep. Meteor 4, Lefrancq, 1996)

22. Voleurs de Radium [Radium Thiefs] (1955; rep. Meteor 4, Lefrancq, 1996)

23. Grandes Chasses sur Orpito [Big Hunts on Orpito] (1955; rep. Meteor 4, Lefrancq, 1996)

24. Le Robinson de l'Espace [The Robinson of Space] (1955)

25. Cataclysme chez les Surhommes [Cataclysm Among the Supermen] (1955)

26. Méfaits et Bienfaits du Bolide "Alpha" [Good and Bad Things About Rocket Alpha] (1955)

27. "Nutricia"—Planète Convoitée [Nutricia—The Coveted Planet] (1955)

28. Voyage dans le Passé [Journey into the Past] (1955)

29. La Planète du Sommeil [The Planet of Sleep] (1955)

30. *La Planète des Amphibies [The Planet of the Amphibians]* (1955)

31. *Menace pour la Terre [Menace to Earth]* (1955)

32. *Conspiration dans les Étoiles [Conspiracy Among the Stars]* (1956)

33. *Les Pirates des Étoiles [The Star Pirates]* (1956)

34. *Les Ravisseurs de l'Espace [The Space Kidnappers]* (1956)

35. *Chercheurs d'Uranium [Uranium Seekers]* (1956)

36. *La Révolte des Animaux [The Revolt of the Animals]* (1956)

37. *Les Vampires de Pomena [The Vampires of Pomena]* (1956)

38. *Révolte sur Héraclos [Revolt on Heraklos]* (1956)

39. *En Route pour Mars [Destination Mars]* (1956)

40. *Les Naufragés de l'Espace [Shipwrecked in Space]* (1956)

41. *Le Rayon Lambda [The Lambda Ray]* (1956)

42. *"Ugol" le Conquérant [Ugol the Conqueror]* (1956)

43. *Aventure au Pays des Merveilles [Adventures in Wonderland]* (1956)

44. *Paradis sous Globe [A Domed Paradise]* (1956)

45. *Le Domino Volant [The Flying Domino]* (1957)

46. *À la Recherche du Domino Volant [Search for the Flying Domino]* (1957)

47. *L'Opération "Déluge" [Operation Flood]* (1957)

48. *La Planète Bagne 117 [Penitentiary Planet 117]* (1957)

49. *La Planète Vagabonde [The Wandering Planet]* (1957)

50. *Deux Enfants dans l'Espace [Two Children in Space]* (1957)
    Special—*Le Satellite en Détresse [The Satellite in Distress] / Les Pirates du Chaos [The Pirates of Chaos]* (1957)

51. *Les Naufragés de l'Infini [Shipwrecked in Infinity]* (1957)

52. *Au Pouvoir des Hommes Verts [In the Green Men's Power]* (1957)

53. *Les Évadés de Disciplina [Escape from Disciplina]* (1957)

54. *Terre Symétrique [Symmetrical Earth] / La Planète Lilliput [The Liliputian Planet]* (1957)

55. *"Ophénia"—La Planète qui Meurt [Ophenia—The Dying Planet]* (1957)

56. *Planète Prohibée [Forbidden Planet]* (1957)

57. *La Comète Écarlate [The Scarlet Comet]* (1958)

58. *Science sans Conscience [Soulless Science]* (1958)

59. *Au Pouvoir des Sorcières [In the Witches' Power]* (1958)

60. *Le Satellte V13 Ne Répond Plus [Satellite V13 Does Not Answer]* (1958)

61. *La Flore de l'Astre Eden [The Flora of the Eden Star]* (1958)

62. *La Planète des Fusées Perdues [The Planet of the Lost Rockets]* (1958)

63. *L'Ère du Prophète Électronique [The Era of the Electronic Prophet]* (1958)

64. *Les Curieux Hommes de Thorp [The Curious Men of Thorp]* (1958)

65. *Le Maître de Malva [The Master of Malva]* (1958)

66. *Les Surhommes de Kander [The Supermen of Kander]* (1958)

67. *La Ronde des Heures [The Dance of the Hours]* (1958)

68. *Les Raccourcis de l'Espace [The Shortcuts of Space]* (1958)

69. *Le Monstre des Sables [The Sand Monster]* (1959)

70. *Aventure Souterraine [Underground Adventure]* (1959)

71. *Les Derniers des Aroukans [The Last of the Arukans]* (1959)

72. *Les Pillards de la Cité Morte [The Looters of the Dead City]* (1959)

73. *Explorateurs des Temps Futurs [Explorers of the Future]* (1959)

74. *L'Étrange Robot [The Strange Robot]* (1959)

75. *"Daphnis"—Astre Convoité [Daphnis—The Coveted Star]* (1959)

76. *Mission Diplomatique [Diplomatic Mission]* (1959)

77. *Planètes Rivales [Rival Planets]* (1959)

78. *Guerre Climatique [Weather War]* (1959)

79. *Croisière de Luxe [Luxury Cruise]* (1959)

80. *Vers la Terre Promise [Towards the Promised Land]* (1959)

81. *Une Planète S'est Évadée [A Planet Has Escaped]* (1960)

82. *Les Cercueils d'Or [The Gold Coffins]* (1960)

83. *Les Naufragés de Zamora [Shipwrecked on Zamora]* (1960)

84. *Étranges Empreintes [Strange Trails]* (1960)

85. *La Chasse aux Satellites [The Satellite Hunt]* (1960)

86. *Bonheur à Perpétuité [Happiness for Life] / Le Mal des Espaces [The Space Sickness]* (1960)

87. *Les Profs des Étoiles [The Star Teachers]* (1960)

88. *La Reine du Cosmos [The Cosmic Queen]* (1960)

89. *La Fin des Invisibles [The End of the Invisibles] / L'Astre des Immortels [The Star of the Immortals]* (1960)

90. *La Terre est Folle [Earth Goes Mad] / Plus Vite que la Lumière [Faster Than Light]* (1960)

91. *Cités Volantes [Flying Cities] / Les Derniers Géants [The Last Giants]* (1960)

92. *La Révolte des Nyctalopes [The Revolt of the Nyctalopes] / Le Paradou* (1960)

93. *Au Pouvoir des Chmoks [In the Chmoks' Power] / Chez les Hommes-Méduses [Among the Medusa Men]* (1961)

94. *Les Hommes-Gymnotes du "Fulgura" [The Gymnote-Men from the Fulgura] / La Boue Vivante d'Eldorado [The Living Mud of Eldorado]* (1961)

95. *Les Diamants de l'Astre Thesaurus [The Diamonds from the Star Thesaurus] / Les Esclavagistes de l'Espace [The Space Slavers]* (1961)

96. *L'Astre des Bien Portants [The Star of the Healthy] / Séjour chez les Métamorphes [Staying Among the Metamorphs]* (1961)

97. *Le Congrès Ne S'amuse Pas [The Congress Is Not Amused] / Les Hommes de Pierre de Gwaldin [The Stone Men of Gwaldin]* (1961)

98. *La Planète des Cyclones [The Hurricane Planet] / Le Robot qui Voulut Être Roi [The Robot Who Wanted To Be King]* (1961)

99. *La Chose [The Thing] / L'Arme Absolue [The Absolute Weapon]* (1961)

100. *"Océania"—Planète sans Terre [Oceania—The Landless Planet] / Traître à la Paix [Traitor to Peace]* (1961)

101. *Planète sans Nom [Nameless Planet]* (1961)

102. *L'Astre des Naufrageurs [The Star of the Ship Wreckers]* (1961)

103. *Survivants sous les Ruines [Survivors in the Ruins]* (1961)

104. *Le Grain de Sable [The Grain of Sand]* (1961)

105. *La Déesse Aveugle [The Blind Goddess]* (1962)

106. *On a Volé le RZ.000 [They Stole the RZ.000]* (1962)

107. *La Croix du Mal [The Evil Cross]* (1962)

108. *La Planète Blessée [The Wounded Planet]* (1962)

109. *Chute dans l'Infini [Fall into Infinity]* (1962)

110. *Planète sans Équilibre [Planet Without Balance]* (1962)

111. *Robots Humains [Human Robots]* (1962)

112. *Le Voleur d'Étoiles [The Star Thief]* (1962)

113. *Trahison à Mulcina [Betrayal in Mulcina]* (1962)

114. *Erreur de Tir [Stray Shooting]* (1962)

115. *Les Hommes Sont Toujours des Hommes [Men Are Still Men]* (1962)

116. *Les Diamants de Ramira [The Diamonds of Ramira]* (1963)

117. *"Experimenta"—Planète Curieuse [Experimenta—The Curious Planet]* (1963)

118. *Le Bagne de l'Espace [The Space Penitentiary]* (1963)

119. *Rendez-vous dans l'Espace [Rendezvous in Space]* (1963)

120. *Révole sur Ténigra [Revolt on Tenigra]* (1963)

121. *Planète Intoxiquée [Intoxicated Planet]* (1963)

122. *Le Voleur d'Orage [The Storm Thief]* (1963)

123. (no story—see **Les Francis**)

124. *Un Homme Perdu... Lequel? [A Man Is Lost, Which One?]* (1963)

125. *Le Virus Timeo [The Timeo Virus]* (1963)

126. *Devant le Nuclerama [Before the Nuclerama]* (1963)

127. *Panique sur le Monde [World Panic]* (1963)

128. *Le Mystère des Ondes Perdues [The Mystery of the Lost Waves]* (1964)

129. *Les Valises Infernales [The Suitcases from Hell]* (1964)

130. *Le Monde a Faim [The World Is Hungry] / Alerte sur la Terre! [Alert On Earth]* (1964)

131. *Voyage sans Retour [Journey of No-Return]* (1964)

132. *Le Maître du Silence [The Master of Silence]* (1964)

133. *Voleur de Satellite [The Satellite Thief]* (1964)

134. *La Planète du Silence [The Silent Planet]* (1964) (not the same story as No. 3)

135. *Le Secret des Montagnes Ennemies [The Secret of the Enemy Mountains]* (1964)

136. *Satellite Pirate [Pirate Satellite]* (1964)

137. *La Planète Sans Nom [The Nameless Planet]* (not the same story as No. 101)

STORY: Dr. Spencer, space pilot Spade, and their me-

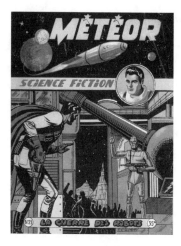

chanic Texas, explore space aboard their rocket, the *Space Girl*, meeting strange new civilizations and strange new worlds *à la Star Trek*.

NOTE: Originally serialized in the small-format magazine *Meteor* and later reprinted in *Cosmos*. Episodes 1 to 13 have been reprinted as two graphic novels by Lefrancq in 1990.

La Conquête des Elohim [Conquest of the Elohim] (Leroy, 1983)

WRI/ART: Gérard Leclaire.
STORY: Bible stories with ETs.

Constant Souci see Le Mystère de l'Homme aux Trèfles

Convoi see Karen Springwell

Cornet d'Humour see ***Boucq***

Cosmo

WRI: J. K. **Melwyn-Nash**; ART: Jean-Yves **Mitton**.
STORY: French super hero.
NOTE: Eight eps. originally serialized in *Mustang* (Series II), Nos. 62-69 (Ed. Lug, 1981); not collected in the graphic novel format.

Cosmopolis

WRI/ART: R. Negrete.

1. *Un Jour de Gloire [A Day of Glory]* (Magic-Strip, 1986)

2. *L'Arbre de Vie [The Tree of Life]* (Magic-Strip, 1987)
STORY: Science fiction.

Cosmos see Fleuve Noir

Coutoo (Delc., 1989; transl. Dark Horse)
WRI/ART: **Andréas**.
STORY: A NY policeman investigates a serial killer infected with a strange virus.

Cranach de Morganloup

WRI: Jean-Luc **Vernal**; ART: Didier **Convard**.

1. *Le Voyageur des Portes [The Gates Traveler]* (Lom., 1987)

2. *La Pierre Bleue de Naja [The Blue Stone of Naja]* (Lom., 1988)
STORY: Young Cranach and his magic sword Gaelle fight villains in a medieval Celtic future.
NOTE: Originally serialized in *Tintin* in 1982.

Cristal

WRI: **Maric**; ART: Carlo Marcello.

1. *Venu d'Ailleurs [He Came from Beyond]* (Dup., 1986)

2. *Les Tueurs d'un Autre Monde [The Killers from Another World]* (Dup., 1986)

3. *Passeport pour l'Angoisse [Passport for Terror]* (Dup., 1987)

4. *Sortilège à Bahia [Spells in Bahia]* (Dup., 1987)

5. *Le Cobaye [The Guinea Pig]* (Dup., 1988)
STORY: An alien stranded on Earth must flee from the military scientists who want to capture him.
NOTE: Originally serialized in *Spirou* in 1983. Carlo Marcello is an Italian artist working primarily in French comics.

Le Cristal Majeur see Altor

Les Crocs d'Ébène [The Ebony Teeth]: L'Ère du Dragon [The Era of the Dragon] (Glé., 1988)

WRI: G. Elton **Ranne** & Juszezak; ART: Juszezak.
STORY: Heroic-fantasy.
NOTE: G. Elton **Ranne** is a science fiction author (see Book 2).

La Croisière Fantastique [The Fantastic Cruise]

WRI: Jean-Claude **Smit Le Bénédicte**; ART: Grégor Rosinski.

1. *L'île des Marées [The Island of Tides]* (Lom., 1987)

2. *Les Déesses d'Eau [The Goddesses of Water]* (Lom., 1988)
STORY: Heroic fantasy on a water world.
NOTE: Gregor Rosinski is a Polish artist working primarily in French comics.

Cromwell Stone

WRI/ART: **Andréas**.

1. *Cromwell Stone* (Deligne, 1984, transl. Dark Horse)

2. *Le Retour de Cromwell Stone [The Return of Cromwell Stone]* (Delc., 1994)
STORY: Cromwell Stone is the pawn of Lovecraftian creatures trapped on Earth.

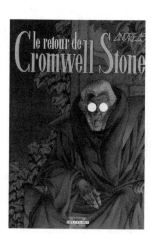

Les Croqueurs de Sable [The Sand Eaters]
WRI/ART: Joly Guth.

1. *La Lèpre Rouge [The Red Leprosy]* (VdO., 1989)

2. *La Luciole d'Or [The Gold Firefly]* (VdO., 1990)

3. *La Blanche Neige [The White Snow]* (VdO., 1992)

4. *L'Âme Braise [The Fiery Soul]* (VdO., 1994)
STORY: In a future desertic France, survivors discover new ways of life.

Crux Universalis see **Bilal**

Cryozone
WRI: Thierry Cailleteau; ART: Denis Bajram.

1. *Sueurs Froides [Cold Sweat]* (Delc., 1996)
STORY: Science fiction.

La Crypte du Souffle Bleu [The Crypt of the Blue Wind]
WRI: René **Durand**; ART: Castaza.

1. *Le Pays Rouillé [The Rusted Land]* (Sol., 1990)

2. *La Barrière des Instants Perdus [The Barrier of the Lost Moments]* (Sol., 1992)

3. *Les Neuf Armées de Rouille [The Nine Armies of Rust]* (Sol., 1993)
STORY: Heroic fantasy in a humoristic vein.

Cupidon [Cupid]
WRI: Raoul **Cauvin**; ART: Malik (William Taï).

1. *Premières Flèches [First Arrows]* (Dup., 1990)

2. *Philtre d'Amour [Love Potion]* (Dup., 1991)

3. *Baiser de Feu [Kiss of Fire]* (Dup., 1991)

4. *Souffle au Coeur [Heart Murmur]* (Dup., 1992)

5. *Arc en Ciel [Rainbow]* (Dup., 1993)

6. *L'Ange et l'Eau [The Angel and the Water]* (Dup., 1994)

7. *Un Amour de Gorille [A Gorilla in Love]* (Dup., 1994)

8. *Je l'Aime un Peu [I Love You a Little]* (Dup., 1995)

9. *Vive la Mariée [Hurray for the Bride]* (Dup., 1996)
STORY: Gags about the little Greek God of Love.
NOTE: Originally serialized in *Spirou* in 1988.

Le Cycle de Cyann
WRI: Claude **Lacroix**; ART: François **Bourgeon**.

1. *La Source et la Sonde [The Source and the Probe]* (Cast., 1994)

2. *Six Saisons sur Ilo [Six Seasons on Ilo]* (Cast., 1996)
STORY: Cyann must save her world from a mysterious disease.
NOTE: Originally serialized in *(À Suivre)* in 1993.

Cyber (Les Aventures de) [Cyber's Adventures] (Losfeld, 1969)
WRI: G. Néry; ART: J. Poirier.
STORY: Parody of adult science fiction.

Le Cycle des Deux Horizons see **Deux Horizons (Le Cycle des)**

Le Cycle d'Oyasu Sang-Dragon see **Oyasu Sang-Dragon**

Cyrrus
WRI/ART: **Andréas**.

1. *Cyrrus* (Hum., 1984)

2. *Mil* (Hum., 1987)
STORY: Archeologist Cyrrus Foxe finds a mysterious temple from before the dawn of man; an occult experiment later sends a child, Mil, traveling back through time to 1924 and beyond.
NOTE: The entire saga was reprinted in one volume with additional material by Delcourt in 1995.

Cythère, l'Apprentie Sorcière see **Fred**

Dan Cooper
(genre stories only)
WRI/ART: Albert **Weinberg**.

1. *Le Triangle Bleu [The Blue Triangle]* (Lom., 1957)

2. *Le Maître du Soleil [The Master of the Sun]* (Lom., 1958)

3. *Le Mur du Silence [The Wall of Silence]* (Lom., 1959)

4. *Cap sur Mars [Destination Mars]* (Lom., 1960)

13. *Le Mystère des Soucoupes Volantes [The Mystery of the Flying Saucers]* (Lom., 1969)

14. Panique à Cap Kennedy [Panic at Cape Kennedy] (Lom., 1970)

16. SOS dans l'Espace [SOS in Space] (Lom., 1971)

23. Opération Jupiter (originally serialized in 1958) (Lom., 1979)

STORY: In the early stories, Canadian Air Force pilot Dan Cooper was involved in futuristic attempts at space exploration. Later stories became more present-day, but occasional episodes would pit Dan against mysterious blue-skinned aliens.

NOTE: Originally serialized in *Tintin* in 1954.

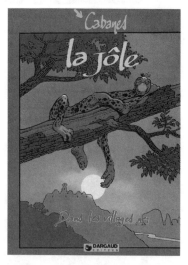

Dans les Villages [In the Villages]

WRI/ART: Max **Cabanes**.

1. Dans les Villages [In the Villages] (Aud., 1978, rep. as *La Jôle*, Dar., 1983)

2. L'Anti-Jôle (Dar., 1982)

3. La Crognote Rieuse [The Laughing Crognote] (Dar., 1984)

4. Le Rêveur de Réalité [The Reality Dreamer] (Dar., 1986)

STORY: In a bleak, surreal world, the hapless Merdouzils are terrified by the annoyingly stupid Joles. Jean-Marie, a young Merdouzil, goes on a quest to free his people and discover the true nature of his dream-like universe.

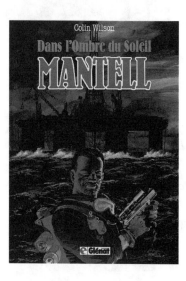

Dans l'Ombre du Soleil [In the Shadow of the Sun]

WRI/ART: Colin Wilson.

1. Rael (Glé., 1984, transl. Eclipse, 1987)

2. Mantell (Glé., 1986)

3. Alia (WRI: Thierry Smolderen) (Glé., 1989)

STORY: In a post-apocalyptic future, Rael is taken prisoner by Dr. Steiner, who rules a huge space station and raids the planet below for slave workers.

NOTE: Originally serialized in *Circus* in 1983.

Das Reich

WRI/ART: **Rodolphe**.

1. La Citadelle [The Citadel] (Sol., 1995)

2. La Route des Svastikas [The Road of the Swastikas] (Sol., 1996)

STORY: Adventures in a universe where the Nazis won World War II.

Dayak

WRI/ART: Philippe **Adamov**.

1. Ghetto 9 (Glé.,1993; transl. *Heavy Metal*)

2. La Chambre Verte [The Green Room] (Glé., 1994)

3. Zaks (Glé., 1995)

STORY: In the far future, mankind lives in a giant, decadent metropolis, ruled by merciless masters.

Déboires d'Outre-Tombe [Mishaps from Beyond the Grave]

WRI: Serge De Beketch; ART: Jean-Marc Loro.

1. Vol. 1 (Publicness, 1971)

2. Vol. 2 (Cygne, 1982)

STORY: Gags on the themes of supernatural monsters.

NOTE: Originally published in *Pilote* in 1969.

Déconan le Barbaresque (Dar., 1979)

WRI: Marcel Coucho; ART: Pailler.

STORY: Parody of *Conan the Barbarian*.

NOTE: Originally published in *Pilote* in 1977.

Dédal

WRI: Éric Corbeyran; ART: Nicolas Guénet.

1. Le Dieu Kolerr [The God Wrath] (Sol., 1993)

2. Les Terres Païennes [The Pagan Lands] (Sol., 1994)

STORY: Barbarian-king Ragnall seeks a magic sword.

Le Démon des Glaces see *Adèle Blanc-Sec*

Demain les Monstres [Tomorrow, the Monsters] (Sol., 1994)

WRI/ART: Jean-Yves **Mitton**.

STORY: Horror stories.

Les Dents du Recoin see *Boucq*

La Dérisoire Effervescence des Comprimés see *Boucq*

Dérives [Adrift] (Delc., 1991)

WRI: Scholz, Gérard Goffaux,

Philippe **Foerster**, Antonio Cossu, **Yann**, Frédéric **Bézian**; ART: **Andréas**.

STORY: Six fantasy stories.

Le Dernier Loup d'Oz [The Last Wolf of Oz]
WRI/ART: Lidwine.

1. *La Rumeur des Eaux [The Murmur of the Waters]* (Delc., 1995)
STORY: The war-like Wolves of Oz steal a mystic talisman.

La Dernière Lune [The Last Moon] (Lom., 1993)
WRI: **Rodolphe**, Serge **Le Tendre**; ART: Antonio Parras.
STORY: In 1947, on a mysterious island, a mad scientist plots to take over the world.
NOTE: Antonio Parras is a Spanish artist.

Le Désintégré Réintégré see **Moebius**

Les Dessous de la Ville see **Masse**

Les Deux du Balcon see **Masse**

Deux Horizons (Le Cycle des) [The Cycle of the Two Horizons]
WRI: Pierre **Makyo**; ART: Christian Rossi.

1. *Jordan* (Delc., 1990; transl. Dark Horse, 1991)

2. *Selma* (Delc., 1991)

3. *Le Coeur du Voyage [The Heart of the Journey]* (Delc., 1993)
STORY: A young Polish student is plagued by supernatural encounters linked to a mysterious black pearl.

La Déviation see **Moebius**

Dick Hérisson
WRI/ART: Didier **Savard**.

1. *L'Ombre du Torero [The Shadow of the Matador]* (Dar., 1984)

2. *Les Voleurs d'Oreilles [The Ear Stealers]* (Dar., 1985)

3. *L'Opéra Maudit [The Cursed Opera]* (Dar., 1987)

4. *Le Vampire de la Côte [The Vampire of the Coast]* (Dar., 1990)

5. *La Conspiration des Poissonniers [The Fishermen's Conspiracy]* (Dar., 1993)

6. *Frères de Cendres [Ash Brothers]* (Dar., 1995)

7. *Le Tombeau d'Absalom [The Tomb of Absalom]* (Dar., 1996)

STORY: A detective investigates mysteries with supernatural overtones.
NOTE: Originally serialized in *Charlie* in 1983.

Digitaline (Lom., 1989)
WRI: Robert De Groot; ART: J. Landrain.
STORY: Science fiction story drawn entirely on computer.

Les Dirigeables de L'Amazone [The Dirigibles of the Amazon]
WRI: René **Durand**; ART: Patrice **Sanahujas**.

1. *Les Dirigeables de l'Amazone [The Dirigibles of the Amazon]* (Glé., 1980)

2. *La Course Aérostiere [The Aerostat Race]* (Glé., 1981)

3. *La Cour des Miracles [The Court of Miracles]* (Glé., 1982)
STORY: A futuristic dirigible race over the Amazon.
NOTE: Originally serialized in *Circus* in 1979.

Les Disques de Feu [The Discs of Fire] (Lom., 1950)
WRI/ART: Rémy Boules.
STORY: Flying saucers attack.
NOTE: Originally serialized in *Tintin* Nos. 89-120; never collected in the graphic novel format.

Le Djinn Toutouffu
WRI/ART: Jean-Marie Brouyère.
STORY: Comical adventures of a young Djinn and his pet dragonfly.
NOTE: Eight short stories serialized in *Tintin* in 1969; never collected in the graphic novel format.

Djumbo Warrior see **Teddy Bear**

Dock 21
WRI: **Rodolphe**; ART: Alain Mounier.

1. *L'Abîme du Temps [The Abyss of Time]* (Dar., 1992)

2. *Je Suis un Autre [I Am Another]* (Dar., 1993)
STORY: Thrillers with science fiction elements.

Docteur Fu Manchu
WRI: Juliette Benzoni; ART: Robert **Bressy**.

1. *Le Maître du Monde [The Master of the World]* (Hachette, 1975)
STORY/NOTE: Over 3,000 daily strips featuring Sax Rohmer's famous Chinese mastermind were serialized in the daily newspaper, *Le Parisien Libéré* (1961-1972). Only one collection was published.

Docteur Fulminate see Prof. Vorax

Docteur Poche

WRI/ART: Marc **Wasterlain**.

1. *Il Est Minuit, Docteur Poche [The Time Is Midnight, Dr. Poche]* (Dup., 1978)

2. *L'Île des Hommes-Papillons [The Island of the Butterfly Men]* (Dup., 1979)

3. *Karabouilla* (Dup., 1980)

4. *La Planète des Chats [The Planet of the Cats]* (Dup., 1981)

5. *Le Géant Qui Posait des Questions [The Giant Who Asked Questions]* (Dup., 1982)

6. *Le Renard Bleu [The Blue Fox]* (Dup., 1984)

7. *Le Petit Singe Qui Faisait des Manières [The Little Monkey with Good Manners]* (Dup., 1985)

8. *Gags en Poche [Pocket Gags]* (Dup., 1986)

9. *La Forêt Magique [The Magic Forest]* (Dup., 1990)

10. *Le Père Noël [Santa Claus]* (Cast., 1995)

STORY: Droll, light fantasy adventures starring an amiable doctor who has the power of flight, and of his girlfriend, Zoe.
NOTE: Originally serialized in *Spirou* in 1975.

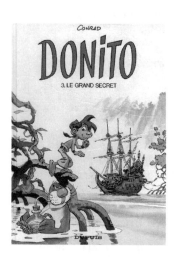

Donito

WRI/ART: Didier **Conrad**.

1. *La Sirène des Caraïbes [The Mermaid of the Caribbean]* (Dup., 1991)

2. *La Pyramide des Tempêtes [The Pyramid of Storms]* (Dup., 1992)

3. *Le Grand Secret [The Great Secret]* (Dup., 1993)

4. *L'Île aux Pirates [The Pirates' Island]* (Dup., 1995)

5. *L'Or Caché du Cachalot [The Whale's Hidden Gold]* (Dup., 1996)

STORY: In the 17th-century Caribbean, a young boy acquires the power to breathe under water and fights an evil mermaid.

Les Dossiers du B.I.D.E. [The B.I.D.E. Files]

WRI: Jean Yanne; ART: Tito Topin.

1. *La Langouste ne Passera Pas [Stop the Lobsters]* (Cast., 1969)

2. *Voyage au Centre de la C...ulture [Voyage to the Center of C...ulture]* (Cast., 1969)
STORY: *Mission: Impossible* pop art parody with science fiction elements.

Dossiers Soucoupes Volantes [The UFO Files]

WRI: Jacques **Lob**; ART: Robert **Gigi**.

1. *Dossiers Soucoupes Volantes [The UFO File]* (Dar., 1972)

2. *Ceux Venus d'Ailleurs [Those from Beyond]* (Dar., 1973)

3. *OVNI: Dimensions Autre [UFO: Another Dimension]* (Dar., 1975)
STORY: Well-researched depictions of authentic UFO encounters.
NOTE: These stories were originally serialized in *Pilote*.

Double Évasion see **Moebius**

Dracurella

WRI: Christian **Godard**; ART: Julio Ribera.

1. *Dracurella* (Dar., 1976)

2. *Le Fils de Dracurella [Dracurella's Son]* (Dar., 1979)

3. *L'Oncle de Dracurella [Dracurella's Uncle]* (MC Prods., 1987)
STORY: Parodic adventures of a young female vampire.
NOTE: Julio Ribera is a Spanish artist.

Dragan

WRI: Éric Corbeyran; ART: C. Bec.

1. *Les Géôles d'Ayade [The Jails of Ayade]* (Sol., 1993)
STORY: A savage rebel in a middle-eastern-like heroic-fantasy universe.

Les Dragons

WRI: Frédéric Contremarche; ART: Joël Mouclier.

1. *Les Jouets Olympiques [The Olympic Toys]* (Delc., 1994)

2. *La Lune pour Témoin [The Moon as a Witness]* (Delc., 1995)
STORY: Three ancient dragons return to a future Earth dominated by cybernetics.

Druillet, Philippe

Vuzz (Dar., 1974; rep. as *Là-Bas [Out There]*, Hum., 1978)
La Nuit [The Night] (Hum., 1976)
Mirages (Hum., 1976)
Druillet (Hum., 1981)
Le Mage Acrylic [The Acrylic Wizard] (ART: Bihannic) (Hum., 1982)

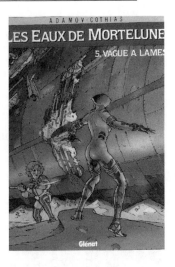

Nosferatu (Dar., 1989 ; transl. Dark Horse)

Manuel, L'Enfant Rêve [Manuel, the Dreamchild] (WRI: Jacques **Attali**) (Stock, 1994)

STORY: Gothic fantasies, originally serialized in *Pilote* and *Métal Hurlant*. *Vuzz* is an anti-hero in a heroic-fantasy universe. *La Nuit* is a dark, post-apocalyptic urban saga about death and decay. *Nosferatu* is a futuristic, vampire story. For further information on Jacques **Attali**, see Book 2.

Duel (Hum., 1984)
WRI: Charles Imbert; ART: Philippe **Gauckler**.
STORY: Punk science fiction.

Durga Rani
WRI: J. Sylvère (René **Thévenin**); ART: **Pellos**.

1-2. La Reine des Jungles (2 vols.) [The Queen of the Jungle] (SPE, 1948)

3. L'Appel du Maître [The Call of the Master] (SPE, 1949)
STORY: Female *Tarzan*.
NOTE: René **Thévenin** is a famous science fiction writer. Originally serialized in *Fillette* in 1946.

Dydo
(genre stories only)
WRI/ART: Durane.

1. Dydo Roi Atomique [Atomic King] (René Touret, 1949)

2. Dydo Pilote Interplanétaire [Interplanetary Pilot] (René Touret, 1949)

3. Dydo Général Saturnien [General on Saturn] (René Touret, 1949)

4. Dydo Chasse la Grand Ourse [Hunts Ursa Major] (René Touret, 1949)

5. Dydo et les Constellations [The Constellations] (René Touret, 1950)

6. Dydo Champion du Ciel [Champion of the Skies] (René Touret, 1950)
STORY: A resourceful young boy in a series of cosmic adventures.

Les Eaux de Mortelune [The Waters of Deadmoon]
WRI: Patrick **Cothias**; ART: Philippe **Adamov**.

1. L'Échiquier du Rat [The Rat's Chessboard] (Glé., 1986, transl. *Heavy Metal*)

2. Le Café du Port [The Harbor Café] (Glé., 1987)

3. Le Prince et la Poupée [The Prince and the Doll] (Glé., 1989)

4. Les Yeux de Nicolas [Nicholas' Eyes] (Glé., 1990)

5. Vagues à Lames [Waves of the Soul] (Glé., 1992)

6. Le Chiffre de la Bête [The Number of the Beast] (Glé., 1994)

7. La Guerre des Dieux [War of the Gods] (Glé., 1995)
STORY: In a decadent future where water and gasoline are scarce, Violhaine and her mutant brother Nicolas become involved in a feud between the Prince of Deadmoon and his rival, Duke Malik. The characters return in a new saga, starting with ep. 6.
NOTE: Originally serialized in *Circus* in 1985.

Eclipso see **Fleuve Noir**

Les Écluses du Ciel [Skylocks]
WRI: **Rodolphe**; ART: Michel **Rouge**.

1. La Marque de Morgane [The Mark of Morgaine] (Glé., 1983)

2. Les Chevaux de la Nuit [The Night Horses] (Glé., 1984)

3. Gwen d'Armor (Glé., 1985)

WRI: **Rodolphe**; ART: François **Allot**.
4. Avalon (Glé., 1988)

5. Le Pays Blanc [The White Land] (Glé., 1990)

6. Tombelaine (Glé., 1991)

7. Tiffen (Glé., 1994)
STORY: Tales of magic and fairy folk in ancient Britanny.
NOTE: Originally serialized in *Circus* in 1981.

L'École Abracadabra [The Abracadabra School]
WRI: François **Corteggiani**; ART: Pierre Tranchand.

1. L'École Abracadabra [The Abracadabra School] (Dar., 1991)

2. Plongeons et Dragons [Dunces and Dragons] (Dar., 1991)

3. Des Balais Roses [Broom Hildies] (Dar., 1992)

4. C'Est pas Sorcier [If This Isn't Witching] (Dar., 1993)

5. *Sabbat Comme vous Voulez [Sabbath Mania]* (Dar., 1995)

6. *Le Philtre a Gaffé [Philterminator]* (Dar., 1996)

7. *Déconfiture au Chaudron [Jam in the Cauldron]* (Dar., 1997)

STORY: Humorous stories about a school for young wizards.

NOTE: Originally serialized in *Le Journal de Mickey* in 1987.

Éden (Zen., 1992)
WRI/ART: Vince.
STORY: Space opera.

Édéna (Le Monde d') [The World of Aedena]
WRI/ART: **Moebius**.

1. *Sur l'Étoile [Upon a Star]* (Hum., 1983, transl. Marvel)

2. *Les Jardins d'Édéna [The Gardens of Aedena]* (Cast., 1988, transl. Marvel)

3. *La Déesse [The Goddess]* (Cast., 1990, transl. Marvel)

4. *Stel* (Cast. 1994., transl. Marvel)

STORY: Stel and Atan (later Atana) are space repairmen who are taken to the planet Aedena, where they confront an underground civilization of faceless drones.

NOTE: The first story was done as a special advertising premium for car manufacturer Citroën. Later stories were originally serialized in *(À Suivre)*.

Editnalta
WRI/ART: Didier **Convard**.

1. *Le Coeur Charbon [The Coal Heart]* (Dar., 1995)

2. *Le Thalamus* (Dar., 1997)

STORY: On the planet Editnalta, the Lords of the Citadel try to preserve their power in spite of the advances of an ever-encroaching desert.

Edmund Bell (Les Enquêtes d') [The Investigations of Edmund Bell]
WRI: Jacques **Stoquart**, based on Jean **Ray**; ART: René **Follet**.

1. *Le Diable au Cou [The Devil on His Heels]* (Lefrancq, 1987)

2. *La Nuit de l'Araignée [The Night of the Spider]* (Lefrancq, 1988)

WRI: Lodewijk, based on Jean **Ray**; ART: René **Follet**.
3. *L'Ombre Rouge [The Scarlet Shadow]* (Lefrancq, 1989)

4. *L'Ombre Noire [The Black Shadow]* (Lefrancq, 1990)

WRI: Duquesnoy, based on Jean **Ray**; ART: René **Follet**.
5. *Le Train Fantôme [The Ghost Train]* (Lefrancq, 1993)

STORY: A teenager finds himself involved in supernatural mysteries.

NOTE: Jean Ray is a major Belgian writer of the *fantastique*. Originally serialized in *Spirou* in 1986.

Electropolis see ***Futuropolis***

Les Elfes de Pomaridus [The Elves of Pomaridus] (Schlirf, 1984)
WRI/ART: Claude **Renard**.
STORY: High fantasy.

L'Empreinte des Chimères [Mark of the Chimeras]
WRI: Gallie; ART: Coronas.

1. *Colin* (Vd'O., 1991)
STORY: Heroic fantasy.

En Vert et Contre tous see ***Mallet***

L'Enclave (Dar., 1993)
WRI/ART: Nicolas Dumontheuil.
STORY: The surreal adventures of a a man who runs alongside an endless wall.

L'Encyclopédie de Masse see ***Masse***

L'Encyclopédie en Bandes Dessinées [The Comics Encyclopedia]
WRI: Imbar; ART: Hubert.

1. *Le Maître de Xurs [The Master of Xurs]* (Ph. Auzou, 1980)

2. *Les Tigres Galactiques [The Galactic Tigers]* (Ph. Auzou, 1980)

3. *Les Sables d'Uracan [The Sands of Uracan]* (Ph. Auzou, 1980)

4. *Birabanor* (Ph. Auzou, 1980)

5. *Objectif Collision [Target: Collision]* (Ph. Auzou, 1980)

6. *Apocalypse* (Ph. Auzou, 1980)

7. *Commando Pollution* (Ph. Auzou, 1980)

8. *Double Menace* (Ph. Auzou, 1980)

9. *Un Aller pour l'Enfer [A One-Way Ticket for Hell]* (Ph. Auzou, 1980)

10. *Le Défi du Barbare [The Barbarian's Challenge]* (Ph. Auzou, 1980)

WRI: Imbar; ART: Pierre **Dupuis**.

11. *Le Virus des Virus* (Ph. Auzou, 1981)

12. *Le Jardin Maudit [The Cursed Garden]* (Ph. Auzou, 1981)

13. *La Bombe Mégastar [The Megastar Bomb]* (Ph. Auzou, 1981)

14. *L'Impératrice Noire [The Dark Empress]* (Ph. Auzou, 1981)

15. *Guerre à Bactéria [War in Bacteria]* (Ph. Auzou, 1981)

WRI: Imbar; ART: André **Chéret**.

16. *Super-Greuhu* (Ph. Auzou, 1982)

17. *État d'Urgence [State of Emergency]* (Ph. Auzou, 1982)

18. *Opération Disco* (Ph. Auzou, 1982)

19. *Extermination* (Ph. Auzou, 1982)

20. *Folie et Cie. [Madness, Inc.]* (Ph. Auzou, 1980)

21. *Le Fils des Lunes [The Son of the Moons]* (Ph. Auzou, 1982)

22. *Le Grand Chemin [The Great Path]* (Ph. Auzou, 1982)

23. *Foresta* (Ph. Auzou, 1982)

24. *Péril Form X* (Ph. Auzou, 1982)

25. *Les Naufrageurs [The Wreckers]* (Ph. Auzou, 1982)
STORY: Educational science fiction for children.

Les Enfants de la Salamandre [The Children of the Salamander]
WRI: Jean **Dufaux**; ART: **Renaud**.

1. *Angie* (Dar., 1988)

2. *Arkadin* (Dar., 1989)

3. *Alicia* (Novedi, 1990)
STORY: Thriller about people with ESP powers.

Les Enfants Terribles [The Terrible Children]
WRI/ART: Jean-Luc Cornette.

1. *Maxime Maximum* (Cast., 1995)
STORY: A little boy has the power to turn into a balloon.

En Pleine Guerre Froide [In the Midst of the Cold War] (Hum., 1987)

WRI: Jean-Luc Fromental; ART: Jean-Louis Floc'h.
STORY: Collection of short science fiction stories.

Les Enragés de la Peste Blanche [The Fury of the White Plague] (Deligne, 1977)
WRI/ART: Jean **Pleyers**.
STORY: Apocalyptic science fiction.

Envahisseurs sur Janus [The Invaders of Janus] (Deligne, 1981)
WRI: Stephen **Desberg**; ART: Musquera.
STORY: Space opera.

L'Envoyé [The Envoy]
WRI: G. Pernin; ART: E. Lepage.

1. *Les Maudits à Maletor [The Accursed of Maletor]* (Lom., 1990)

2. *La Statue d'Or Vivant [The Statue of Living Gold]* (Lom., 1991)
STORY: Gothic fantasy.

L'Épée de Cristal [The Crystal Sword]
WRI: Jacques Goupil; ART: **Crisse**.

1. *Le Parfum des Grinches [The Scent of the Grinches]* (VdO., 1989)

2. *Le Regard de Wenlok [The Gaze of Wenlok]* (VdO., 1991)

3. *La Main de la Mangrove [The Hand of the Mangrove]* (VdO., 1991)

4. *Le Cri du Grouse [The Shriek of the Grouse]* (VdO., 1992)

5. *Le Goût de Sulfur [A Taste of Sulfur]* (VdO., 1995)

6. *Les Arcanes* (Vd'O., 1995)
STORY: Heroic fantasy themed on the five senses and the seven cardinal sins.

L'Épervier Bleu [The Blue Hawk]
(genre stories only)
WRI/ART: **Sirius**.

1. *L'Épervier Bleu [The Blue Hawk]* (Dup., 1948)

2. *Le Pharaon des Cavernes [The Pharaoh of the Caverns]* (Dup., 1950)

4. *Les Pirates de la Stratosphère [The Pirates of the Stratosphere]* (Dup., 1951)

5. *L'Ennemi sous la Mer [The Undersea Enemy]* (Dup., 1952)

6. *La Vallée Interdite [The Forbidden Valley]* (Dup., 1954)

7. *Point Zéro* (Dup., 1954)

8. *La Planète Silencieuse [The Silent Planet]* (Dup., 1954)
WRI: Jean-Marie Brouyère; ART: **Sirius**, J.-M. Brouyère.

9. *Le Puzzle de l'Au-Delà [The Puzzle from Beyond]* (Dup., 1973)

10. *Le Cimetière de l'Infini [The Graveyard of Infinity]* (Dup., 1975)
STORY: Eric, nicknamed the Blue Hawk, his burly friend Larsen, and an Hindu boy named Sheba, discover lost civilizations, undersea cities, and secret moonbases.
NOTE: Originally serialized in *Spirou* in 1942. Eps. 9 and 10 were not collected in graphic novel format. After 1975, Sirius (alone) did three more adventures, but these did not contain any genre elements.

Epoxy (Losfeld, 1968)
WRI: Jacques **Van Hamme**; ART: Paul **Cuvelier**.
STORY: Adult variation on Greek mythology.

Epsilon *(Moi, Epsilon, 15 Ans, Fils du Néant) [I, Epsilon, 15-Year-Old, Son of No One]*
WRI/ART: Jean-Yves **Mitton**.
In Titans:

88-90. *Enfer en Éden [Hell in Eden]* (1986)

91-93. *Évasion, ou Le Secret d'Éden [Escape, or Eden's Secret]* (1986)

94-95. *Hors d'Éden, Point de Salut [Outside of Eden, No Salvation]* (1986)

96-99. *Underground* (1987)

100. *Jeux Barbares [Barbarian Games]* (1987)

101-102. *Cité Haute [High City]* (1987)

103. *Zyklon* (1987)

104. *Déportation* (1987)

105. *Rebellion* (1987)

106-108. *Retour vers Éden [Return to Eden]* (1987)
STORY: In the year 2086, the teenage son of "Psi," the despotic ruler of "Eden," a futuristic European city-state, becomes a rebel gifted with superhuman powers. Epsilon teams up with Foxie and the robot Mentor to fight Psi and search for his mother. It eventually turns out that Epsilon is really the son of Mikros and Saltarella (see **Mikros** below).
NOTE: Originally serialized in *Titans* (Ed. Lug); not collected in the graphic novel format.

Ergun l'Errant [Ergun the Wanderer]
WRI/ART: Didier **Comès**.

1. *Le Dieu Vivant [The Living God]* (Dar., 1974)

2. *Le Maître des Ténèbres [The Master of Darkness]* (Cast., 1981)
WRI: Benoit **Peeters**; ART: Patrick Deubelbeiss.

3. *Mort ou Vif [Dead or Alive]* (Cast., 1987)

4. *Les Jeux Sont Faits [Game Over]* (Cast., 1988)
STORY: A space wanderer exiled from Earth visits various planets and helps their inhabitants.
NOTE: Originally serialized in *Pilote* in 1972.

Escale sur Pharonescia see **Moebius**

L'Esclavage, C'Est la Liberté [Slavery Means Freedom] (Hum., 1984)
WRI/ART: Chantal **Montellier**.
STORY: Bleak, dystopian future.

L'État des Stocks see **Bilal**

L'État Morbide [The Morbid State]
WRI/ART: Daniel **Hulet**.

1. *La Maison Dieu [The House of God]* (Glé., 1987)

2. *Le Passage Avid [The Hungry Passage]* (Glé., 1990)

3. *Waterloo Exit* (Glé., 1992)
STORY: An evil house casts a powerful spell on a new tenant.

L'Éternel Voyage see **Champakou**

Étoile Blanche see **Aquablue**

L'Étoile Ming [The Ming Star]
WRI/ART: J.-L. André.

1. *Passage de l'Étoile Ming dans une Nuit de Jade [Passage of the Ming Star in a Jade Night]* (Dar., 1985)

2. *Les Mutants du Kwantung [The Mutants of Kwantung]* (Dar., 1985)
STORY: Oriental fantasy.

L'Étoile Polaire [The Polar Star]
WRI: Luc Dellisse; ART: Philippe Delaby.

1. *Le Milieu du Ciel [The Middle of Heaven]* (Lom., 1994)

2. *La Nuit Comme un Cheval Arabe [The Night as an Arabian Horse]* (Lom., 1995)

3. *Les Faux Jumeaux [The False Twins]* (Lom., 1996)
STORY: Geoffroy and the witch Polaire try to escape from the Devil's clutches.

L'Étonnante Croisière du Prof. Gromulus see **Professeur Gromulus**

Étrange Apocalypse [Strange Apocalypse] (Futuropolis, 1983)

WRI/ART: Meriaux.
STORY: Apocalyptic science fiction.

L'Étrange Nuit de M. Korb [The Strange Night of Mr. Korb] (Magic-Strip, 1982)
WRI/ART: Frédéric **Bézian**.
STORY: Dark, gothic fantasy.

Étranges Aventures see *Fleuve Noir*

Les Êtres de Lumière [The People of Light]
WRI/ART: Jean **Pleyers**.

1. *L'Exode [The Exodus]* (Hum., 1982)

2. *Le Péril Extrazorien* (Hum., 1984)
STORY: The alien Zors, who have embarked on a millennia-long galactic exodus, come across Earth.

Éva see *Comès*

L'Expédition du Prof. Gromulus see *Professeur Gromulus*

Exterminateur 17 (Hum., 1981; transl. Heavy Metal)
WRI: Jean-Pierre **Dionnet**; ART: Enki **Bilal**.
STORY: An android soldier seeks revenge.

Face de Lune [Moon Face]
WRI: Alexandro **Jodorowsky**; ART: François **Boucq**.

1. *La Cathédrale Invisible [The Invisible Cathedral]* (Cast.,1992)

2. *La Pierre de Faîte [The Capstone]* (Cast., 1996)
STORY: A mysterious moon-faced boy who has the power to tame the waves overthrows a totalitarian regime.
NOTE: Originally serialized in *(À Suivre)*.

Fann le Lion
WRI/ART: Renée Rahir.

1. *Adieu Kilimandjaro* (Cast., 1991)

2. *Hook Stock Farm* (Cast., 1992)

3. *Triple Traque [Triple Hunt]* (Cast., 1993)
STORY: In a future Africa inhabited by lion-men, young Fann, whose father was a human, is torn between the two civilizations.

Fantagas (Delc. 1995)
WRI/ART: Carlos Nine.
STORY: A policeman pursues a mysterious serial killer.

Fantax
WRI: J. K. **Melwyn-Nash**; ART: **Chott**.

1. *Le Gentleman Fantôme [The Gentleman Ghost]* (1946)

2. *Fantax Contre le Mikado [Fantax vs. the Mikado]* (1946)

3. *Fantax chez les Gangsters [Fantax vs. the Gangsters]* (1946)

4. *Fantax Contre l'Homme Qui Terrorisait New York [Fantax vs. the Man Who Terrified New York]* (1946)

5. *Fantax Contre le "Werewolf"* (1946)

6. *Les Pirates de l'Edelweiss [The Pirates of the Edelweiss]* (1946)

7. *La Torture du Corbeau [The Torture of the Raven]* (1946)

8. *Le Vautour de la Jungle [The Vulture of the Jungle]* (1947)

9. *Le Gang de la Mort [The Gang of Death]* (1947)

10. *Fusillade à Brooklyn [Gunfight in Brooklyn]* (1947)

11. *La Mort Noire [The Black Death]* (1947)

12. *Les Six Gardiennes de l'Enfer [The Six She-Guardians of Hell]* (1947)

13. *Fantax Contre le Ku-Klux-Klan [Fantax vs. KKK]* (1947)

14. *La Maison des 7 Géants [The House of the 7 Giants]* (1947)

15. *Le Monde du Silence [The Silent World]* (1947)

16. *La Prêtresse du Soleil [The Priestess of the Sun]* (1947)

17. *Les Écumeurs de Londres [The Reavers of London]* (1947)

18. *Le Château de l'Épouvante [The Castle of Terror]* (1947)

19. *Le Désert de la Peur [The Desert of Fear]* (1947)

20. *Terre de Feu [Land of Fire]* (1947)

21. *Les Buveurs de Sang [The Blood Drinkers]* (1947)

22. *La Jungle en Délire [The Mad Jungle]* (1947)

23. *Les Tigres Noirs [The Black Tigers]* (1947)

24. *La Rose du Levant [The Rose of Sunrise]* (1947)

25. *Coupeurs de Têtes [The Head Shrinkers]* (1947)

26. *La Tour de la Faim [The Tower of Hunger]* (1948)

27. *Dans le Grand Silence Blanc [In the Great White Silence]* (1948)

28. *La Proie du Monstre [The Monster's Prey]* (1948)

29. *Sous le Signe du Cobra [The Mark of the Cobra]* (1948)

Wri/Art: **Chott**.

30. *Évadés de l'Enfer [Escape from Hell]* (1948)

31. *Le Spectre de la Mine [The Spectre of the Mine]* (1948)

32. *Le Monstre de l'Abîme [The Monster from the Abyss]* (1948)

33. *L'Atoll Mystérieux [The Mysterious Atoll]* (1948)

34. *Le Jockey Sans Nom [The Nameless Jockey]* (1948)

35. *Le Bolide Noir [The Black Racer]* (1948)

36. *La Piste Tragique [The Tragic Trail]* (1949)

37. *Échec à Banserman [Banserman in Check]* (1949)

38. *Le Retour d'Al Capy [The Return of Al Capy]* (1949)

39. *Fantax Joue...et Perd! [Fantax Plays...and Loses!]* (1949)

Wri: J.-F. Ronald -Wills.
La Perle de Manille [The Pearl of Manila] (serialized novel in *Fantax Magazine*, Nos. 1-6, 1949)

Wri: **Chott**; Art: Remy.
0. *Les Nouvelles Aventures de Lord Horace Neighbour [The New Adventures of Lord Horace Neighbour]* (serialized in *Reportages Sensationnels*, Nos. 1-5, 1950-51)

1. *L'Homme Noir Prend la Main [The Dark Man Returns]* (1959)

2-3. *L'Ange Noir [The Dark Angel]* (1959)

3-4, 6. *L'Enfer Blanc [The White Hell]* (1959)

5. (reprints)

7-8. *Fantax Contre les Tigres Noirs [Fantax vs. the Black Tigers]* (new version of No. 23) (1959)

Story: Lord Horace Neighbour works as British attaché at the British Embassy in Washington during the day, and fights crime at night as the caped crusader, Fantax.

Note: Because of its violent contents (S&M, bondage, torture, etc.) **Fantax** was virtually single-handedly responsible for the French Law of 1949 which censored adventure comics. Only one collection was reprinted in the graphic novel format, *Fantax Est de Retour [Fantax Returns]* (Bédésup, 1986).

Fantômas

Wri: L. Dellisse, based on the novels by Marcel **Allain** & Pierre **Souvestre**; Art: Claude **Laverdure**.

1. *L'Affaire Beltham [The Beltham Case]* (Lefrancq, 1990)

2. *Juve contre Fantômas [Juve vs. Fantômas]* (Lefrancq, 1991)

3. *Le Mort Qui Tue [The Deadman Who Kills]* (Lefrancq, 1995)

Story: Master criminal Fantomas outwits police commissioner Juve and journalist Jerôme Fandor.

Note: Faithful adaptations of the first three novels by Allain & Souvestre (see Chapters I and II for feature film and television adaptations). A weekly color page written by Allain and drawn by P. Santini was published in *Gavroche* in 1941. A daily b&w strip drawn by Pierre Tabary was syndicated by Opera Mundi from November 1957 to March 1958 (192 strips). A new weekly, color page, written by Agnès Guilloteau and drawn by Jacques Taillefer, was syndicated by Opera Mundi in 1969. Seventeen fumetti magazines adapting Nos 1, 2, 3, and 5 of the book series were published by Del Duca in 1962 and 1963.

Fantômette

Wri: Georges **Chaulet**; Art: François **Craenhals**.

1. *Fantômette Se Déchaîne! [Fantômette Strikes Back!]* (Hachette, 1982)

2. *Fantômette Livre Bataille [Fantômette Goes to War]* (Hachette, 1982)

3. *Fantômette Risque Tout [Fantômette Risks All]* (Hachette, 1983)

Wri: Georges **Chaulet**; Art: Endry.

4. *Fantômette Fends les Flots [Fantômette at Sea]* (Hachette, 1984)

Story: Teenage girl Françoise takes on the identity of costumed crime fighter Fantomette to thwart evil schemes.

Note: Faithful adaptations of the juvenile series (see Chapter II for a television adaptation).

Fariboles Sidérales [Cosmic Jokes] (Hum., 1979)
Wri/Art: Claude **Lacroix**.
Story: Humorous science fiction.

Fatum

Wri: François **Froideval**; Art: Francard

1. *L'Héritier [The Heir]* (Dar., 1996)

2. *Premières Armes [First Weapons]* (Dar., 1997)

Story: A teenager inherits a multiplanetary business empire.

La Fée Aveline

Wri: René **Goscinny**; Art: Coq.

STORY: The humorous adventures of a young and very attractive fairy among men.

NOTE: Originally serialized in the women's weekly, *Jours de France* (1968-69). Coq is a Spanish artist.

Les Fées [The Fairies]

WRI: François Froideval; ART: Patrick Larme.

1. Fées pas Braire [Don't Make Me Laugh] (Dar., 1996)
STORY: The humorous adventures of a gang of naughty fairies.

Fées et Tendres Automates [Fairies and Tender Automata] (VdO., 1996)

WRI/ART: Jam.

STORY: In a baroque futuristic metropolis, a robot and a fairy fall in love.

Félina

WRI: Victor Mora; ART: Annie Goetzinger.

1. Félina (Glé., 1979)

2. Les Mystères de Barcelone [The Mysteries of Barcelona] (Dar., 1982)

3. L'Ogre du Djébel [The Djebel Ogre] (Dar., 1986)
STORY: A black-cloaked heroine who uses circus skills seeks to avenge her husband's death; Felina is ably assisted by a Tibetan wizard.

NOTE: Originally serialized in *Circus* in 1978, then in *Pilote* in 1982.

La Femme du Magicien see *Boucq*

La Ferme des Animaux [The Animal Farm] (Novedi, 1985)

WRI: **Moebius**, based on the novel by Georges Orwell; ART: Marc **Bati**.

STORY: Cartoony but otherwise faithful adaptation of Orwell's classic.

Feu d'Ange [Angel Fire]

WRI: Vanek; ART: Burton.

1. La Nuit de la Chandeleur [The Night of Chandeleur] (Glé., 1995)

2. Le Maître des Oiseaux [The Master of Birds] (Glé., 1996)
STORY: A little Gypsy boy exhibits paranormal powers.

Les Feux d'Askel [The Fires of Askel]

WRI: Scotch Arleston (Christophe Pelinq); ART: Jean-Louis Mourier.

1. L'Onguent Magnifique [The Magnificent Unguent] (Sol., 1993)

2. Retour à Vocable [Return to Vocable] (Sol., 1994)

3. Corail Sanglant [Bloody Coral] (Sol., 1995)
STORY: Heroic fantasy on a waterworld infested with pirates.

Les Fils de la Nuit [The Sons of Night]

WRI/ART: Patrice Garcia.

1. Au-Delà des Portes [Beyond the Gates] (Sol., 1992)

2. Le Maître d'Éternité [The Master of Eternity] (Sol., 1993)

3. Rêves de Mortalité [Dreams of Mortality] (Sol., 1993)
STORY: Heroic fantasy.

Fin de Siècle [End of the Century] (Magic-Strip, 1983)

WRI/ART: Frédéric **Bézian**.
STORY: Gothic fantasy.

La Fin du Monde Est pour Demain [The World Ends Tomorrow] (Samedi-Jeunesse, 1958)

WRI/ART: Christian Mathelot
STORY: Pulp science fiction.
NOTE: Originally serialized in *Coq Hardi* in 1958; not collected in graphic novel format.

Finkel

WRI: Didier **Convard**; ART: Christian **Gine**.

1. L'Enfant de la Mer [The Sea Child] (Delc., 1994)

2. Océane (Delc., 1995)

3. Génos (Delc., 1996)
STORY: On a waterworld, children mutate to become aquatic creatures.

Le Flagada

WRI/ART: Charles Degotte.

1. Le Flagada (Pepperland, 1981)

2. Émilius le Terrible [The Dreaded Emilius] (MC Prods., 1989)

3. Les Classiques du Rire: Le Flagada [Classics of Humor: The Flagada] (Dar., 1995)

STORY: A fantastic animal, round and yellow, lazy, gluttonous, gifted with the power of flight and speech, shares an island with a *Gilligan*-like castaway.

NOTE: Originally appeared in numerous short stories serialized in *Spirou* (1961-current); only a few were collected in graphic novel format.

Fleuve Noir

WRI: Faithful adaptations of novels published in the *Anticipation* (FNA) and *Angoisse* (FNAG) imprints of Éditions Fleuve Noir, a major French publisher of popular literature. A number of spy heroes from the *Espionnage* imprint (such as G.-J. **Arnaud**'s *Commander*) were also adapted.

ART: Mostly anonymous, except where otherwise mentioned.

PUBL: In various magazines published by by Artima/Aredit, except for *Super Boy* which was published by Imperia (see *Magazines* below).

TITLES:

Anticipation:

2-3. *La Foudre Anti-D [The Anti-D Lightning]* (FNA No.73, 1956, by Jean-Gaston **Vandel**) (1977)

5. *Départ pour l'Avenir [Departure for the Future]* (FNA No.56, 1955, by Jean-Gaston **Vandel**) (1978)

9-10. *Bureau de l'Invisible [Bureau of the Invisible]* (FNA No.61, 1956, by Jean-Gaston **Vandel**) (1979)

11. *Le Règne des Mutants [The Reign of the Mutants]* (FNA No.91, 1957, by Jimmy **Guieu**) (1979)

NOTE: The "missing" numbers are adaptations of non-French authors, e.g.: Vargo Statten, Volsted Gridban, etc. Jean-Gaston **Vandel** is the pseudonym of two writers who also created the character of *Coplan FX-18* (see Chapters I and II). Jimmy **Guieu** is a popular Fleuve Noir science fiction author and occult writer with his own imprint.

Atomos:

1. *La Sinistre Mme. Atomos [The Sinister Mrs. Atomos]* (FNAG No.109, 1964, by André **Caroff**) (1968)

2. *Mme. Atomos Sème la Terreur [Mrs. Atomos Spreads Terror]* (FNAG No.115, 1965, by André **Caroff**) (1969)

3. *Mme. Atomos Frappe à la Tête [Mrs. Atomos Strikes at the Head]* (FNAG No.120, 1965, by André **Caroff**) (1969)

4. *Un Linceul pour Mme Atomos [A Shroud for Mrs. Atomos]* (by André **Caroff**) (1969)

5. *Miss Atomos* (FNAG No.124, 1965, by André **Caroff**) (1969)

6. *La Défaite de Mme. Atomos [The Defeat of Mrs. Atomos]* (by André **Caroff**) (1970)

7. *Miss Atomos vs. KKK* (FNAG No.130, 1966, by André **Caroff**) (1970)

8. *Le Retour de Mme. Atomos [The Return of Mrs. Atomos]* (FNAG No.134, 1966, by André **Caroff**) (1970)

9. *Traquenard pour Mme. Atomos [Ambush for Mrs. Atomos]* (by André **Caroff**) (1970)

10. *L'Erreur de Mme. Atomos [The Mistake of Mrs. Atomos]* (FNAG No.136, 1966, by André **Caroff**) (1971)

11. *Mme. Atomos Prolonge la Vie [Mrs. Atomos Prolongs Life]* (FNAG No.140, 1967, by André **Caroff**) (1971)

12. *Les Monstres de Mme. Atomos [The Monsters of Mrs. Atomos]* (FNAG No.143, 1967, by André **Caroff**) (1971)

13. *Mme. Atomos Crache des Flammes [Mrs. Atomos Spits Fire]* (FNAG No.146, 1967, by André **Caroff**) (1971)

14. *Mme. Atomos Croque le Marmot [Mrs. Atomos Eats a Child]* (FNAG No.147, 1967, by André **Caroff**) (1972)

15. *La Ténébreuse Mme. Atomos [The Dark Mrs. Atomos]* (FNAG No.152, 1968, by André **Caroff**) (1972)

16-17. *Mme. Atomos Change de Peau [Mrs. Atomos Sheds Her Skin]* (FNAG No.156, 1968, by André **Caroff**) (1972)

18. *Mme. Atomos Fait du Charme [Mrs. Atomos Charms Her Way]* (FNAG No.160, 1969, by André **Caroff**) (1972)

19-20. *L'Empreinte de Mme. Atomos [The Mark of Mrs. Atomos]* (FNAG No.169, 1969, by André **Caroff**) (1973)

21-22. *Mme. Atomos Jette un Froid [Mrs. Atomos Catches a Cold]* (FNAG No.173, 1969, by André **Caroff**) (1973)

23-24. *Mme. Atomos Cherche la Petite Bête [Mrs. Atomos Seeks Small Creatures]* (FNAG No.177, 1970, by André **Caroff**) (1974)

25-26. *Le Rideau de Brume [The Curtain of Mist]* (FNA No.457, 1971, by André **Caroff**) (1974)

27-28. *La Guerre des Nosiars [The War with the Nosiars]* (FNA No.489, 1972, by André **Caroff**) (1975)

29-30. *Les Êtres du Néant [The People from Nowhere]* (FNA No.513, 1972, by André **Caroff**) (1975)

31. *L'Exilé d'Akros [The Exile from Akros]* (FNA No.567, 1973, by André **Caroff**) (1976)

32-33. *La Planète Infernale [The Planet from Hell]* (FNA No.529, 1972, by André **Caroff**) (1976)

34-35. *Ceux des Ténèbres [Those Who Live in Darkness]* (FNA No.553, 1973, by André **Caroff**) (1977)

36-37. *Le Bagne de Rostos [The Rostos Penitentiary]* (FNA No.613, 1974, by André **Caroff**) (1977)

NOTE: André **Caroff** is the pseudonym of writer André Carpouzis. Mrs. Atomos is a Japanese female mad scientist who unleashes various plagues and monsters on the United States to avenge the bombings of Hiroshima and Nagasaki. After Aredit ran out of *Mrs. Atomos* novels, they adapted various, unrelated science fiction novels by André Caroff.

Clameurs:

1-2. *Nous Avons Tous Peur [We Are All Afraid]* (FNAG No.24, 1956, by B.-R. **Bruss**) (1976)

3. *Un Drame de l'Au-Delà [A Drama from Beyond]* (FNAG No.No. 65, 1960, by E.-J. **Certon**) (1976)

4-5. *Ce Mur Qui Regardait [That Staring Wall]* (FNAG No.55, 1959, by Jean **Murelli**) (1976)

6-7. *Une Morte à Tuer [To Kill a Dead Woman]* (FNAG No.66, 1960, by Jean **Murelli**) (1977)

8. *Phantasmes [Phantasms]* (FNAG No.91, 1962, by Marc **Agapit**) (1977)

9. *Le Visage du Spectre [The Face of the Spectre]* (FNAG No.63, 1960, by Marc **Agapit**) (1977)

10. *La Halte du Destin [The Halt of Fate]* (FNAG No.72, 1961, by D.-H. **Keller**) (1978)

11-12. *L'Ombre qui Tue [The Killing Shadow]* (FNAG No.74, 1961, by D.-H. **Keller**) (1978)

13. *Complexes* (FNAG No.82, 1962, by Marc **Agapit**) (1978)

14. *Griffe de Mort [Death Claw]* (FNAG No.94, 1963, by André **Caroff**) (1979)

15. *Requiem pour les Huits [Requiem for Eight]* (FNAG No.89, 1962, by Jean **Murelli**) (1979)

16. *Le Médium [The Medium]* (FNAG No.96, 1963, by André **Caroff**) (1979)

17. *Lucifera* (FNAG No.107, 1964, by Maurice **Limat**) (1979)

NOTE: B.-R. **Bruss** is the pseudonym of writer Roger **Blondel**. Marc **Agapit** is the pseudonym of writer Adrien **Sobra**. D.-H. **Keller** is the pseudonym of prolific writers François **Richard** and Henri **Bessière** who also wrote numerous science fiction novels under the pseudonym of "**Richard-Bessière**."

Cosmos:

7. *Objectif Soleil [Target: The Sun]* (FNA No.No. 69, 1956, by **Richard-Bessière**) (1968)

8. *Altitude Moins X [Altitude Minus X]* (FNA No.No. 75, 1956, by **Richard-Bessière**) (1968)

Eclipso:

22. *Les Yeux Braqués [The Fixed Eyes]* (FNAG No.122, 1965, by Marc **Agapit**) (1973)

24. *Maléfices [Spells]* (FNAG No.18, 1956, by B.-R. **Bruss**) (1973)

27. *Le Médium* (FNAG No.96, 1963, by André **Caroff**) (1974)

28. *Fenêtres sur l'Obscur [Windows Into Darkness]* (FNAG No.20, 1956, Kurt **Steiner**) (1974)

29. *L'Oiseau de Malheur [The Bird of Ill Omen]* (FNAG No.104, 1963, by André **Caroff**) (1975)

30. *Le Banquet des Ténèbres [The Feast of Darkness]* (FNAG No.22, 1956, by Peter **Randa**) (1975)

32. *Le Fantôme Aveugle [The Blind Ghost]* (FNAG No.8, 1955, by Patrick **Svenn**) (1975)

33. *Une Chose dans la Nuit [A Thing in the Night]* (FNAG No.14, 1955, by Jean **David**) (1976)

37. *Vengeance de l'Inconnu [Revenge of the Unknown]* (FNAG No.21, 1956, by Patrick **Svenn**) (1977)

39-40. *L'Envers du Masque [The Other Side of the Mask]* (FNAG No.33, 1957, by Kurt **Steiner**) (1977)

41 *Sueurs [Sweat]* (FNAG No.37, 1957, by Kurt **Steiner**) (1978)

NOTE: Kurt **Steiner** is the pseudonym of noted writer André **Ruellan**, who has also written scripts for films and television (see Chapters I and II). Peter **Randa** is the pseudonym of writer André Duquesne.

Étranges Aventures:

11. *Croisière dans le Temps [Time Cruise]* (FNA No.6, 1952, by **Richard-Bessière**) (1967)

28. *Le Sang du Cactus [The Blood of the Cactus]* (FNAG No.88, 1962, by André **Caroff**) (1973)

Hallucinations:
1st Series:

1. *Hallucinations* (FNAG No.73, 1960, by André **Caroff**) (1969)

2. *Névrose [Neurosis]* (FNAG No.77, 1961, by André **Caroff**) (1969)

3. *Cruauté Mentale [Mental Cruelty]* (FNAG No.106, 1963, by André **Caroff**) (1969)

4. *La Bête Immonde [The Awful Beast]* (FNAG No.53, 1959, by Marc **Agapit**) (1970)

5. *Clameurs [Clamors]* (FNAG No.83, 1961 by André **Caroff**) (1970)

6. *Agence Tous Crimes [All-Crime Agency]* (FNAG No.40, 1958, by Marc **Agapit**) (1970)

7. *Crucifie le Hibou [Crucify the Owl]* (FNAG No.81, 1961, by Maurice **Limat**) (1970)

9. *Greffe Mortelle [Mortal Transplant]* (FNAG No.43, 1958, by Marc **Agapit**) (1971)

10. *Batelier de la Nuit [Night Boatman]* (FNAG No.85, 1961, by Maurice **Limat**) (1971)

11. *Le Doigt de l'Ombre [The Finger of Shadow]* (FNAG No.51, 1959, by Marc **Agapit**) (1971)

12. *Le Marchand de Cauchemars [The Nightmare Peddler]* (FNAG No.90, 1962, by Maurice **Limat**) (1971)

13. *Parade des Morts-Vivants [Parade of the Living Dead]* (FNAG No.151, 1967, by Marc **Agapit**) (1971)

14. *Créature des Ténèbres [Creature of Darkness]* (FNAG No.93, 1962, by Maurice **Limat**) (1972)

15-16. *La Tour de Frankenstein [The Tower of Frankenstein]* (FNAG No.30, 1957, by Benoît **Becker**) (1972)

17. *Le Pas de Frankenstein [The Step of Frankenstein]* (FNAG No.32, 1957, by Benoît **Becker**) (1972)

18. *La Nuit de Frankenstein [The Night of Frankenstein]* (FNAG No.34, 1957, by Benoît **Becker**) (1972)

19. *Le Sceau de Frankenstein [The Seal of Frankenstein]* (FNAG No.36, 1957, by Benoît **Becker**) (1972)

20. *Frankenstein Rôde [Frankenstein Prowls]* (FNAG No.41, 1958, by Benoît **Becker**) (1972)

21. *La Cave de Frankenstein [The Cellar of Frankenstein]* (FNAG No.50, 1959, by Benoît **Becker**) (1972)

22. *Les Yeux Braqués [The Staring Eyes]* (FNAG 122, 1965, by Marc **Agapit**) (1972)

23. *L'Heure Funèbre [The Funeral Hour]* (FNAG No.2, 1955, by Patrick **Svenn**) (1973)

24. *Expédition Épouvante [Terror Expedition]* (FNAG No.4, 1955, by Benoît **Becker**) (1973)

25. *Laisse Toute Espérance [Abandon All Hope]* (FNAG No.10, 1955, by Benoît **Becker**) (1973)

26. *Le Chien des Ténèbres [The Dog of Darkness]* (FNAG No.6, 1955, by Benoît **Becker**) (1973)

27. *L'Oeil Était dans la Tombe [The Eye Was Inside the Tomb]* (FNAG No.7, 1955, by B.-R. **Bruss**) (1973)

28. *L'Aile de l'Abîme [The Wing of the Abyss]* (FNAG No.9, 1955, by D.-H. **Keller**) (1973)

30. *L'Escalier de l'Ombre [The Staircase of Shadows]* (FNAG No.11, 1955, by Peter **Randa**) (1973)

31. *Le Seuil du Vide [The Treshold of the Void]* (FNAG No.25, 1955, by Kurt **Steiner**) (1974) (also adapted as a feature film — see Chapter I)

32. *Terreur [Terror]* (FNAG No.15, 1956, by Benoît **Becker**) (1974)

33-34. *Le Bruit du Silence [The Sound of Silence]* (FNAG No.13, 1955, by Kurt **Steiner**) (1974)

35. *De Flamme et d'Ombre [Of Flame and Shadows]* (FNAG No.23, 1956, by Kurt **Steiner**) (1974)

36. *Château du Trépas [Castle of the Trespassed]* (FNAG No.19, 1956, by Benoît **Becker**) (1974)

37. *Les Dents Froides [The Cold Teeth]* (FNAG No.31, 1957, by Kurt **Steiner**) (1974)

38. *Les Pourvoyeurs [The Purveyors]* (FNAG No.35, 1957, by Kurt **Steiner**) (1974)

39. *Pour Que Vive le Diable [For the Devil to Live]* (FNAG No.17, 1956, by Kurt **Steiner**) (1974)

40-41. *Veillée des Morts [Wake of the Dead]* (FNAG No.26, 1957, by Peter **Randa**) (1975)

42. *Les Rivages de la Nuit [The Shores of Night]* (FNAG No.27, 1957, by Kurt **Steiner**) (1975)

43. *Les Griffes de l'Oubli [The Claws of Oblivion]* (FNAG No.28, 1957, by Jean **David**) (1975)

44-45. *Je Suis un Autre [I Am Another]* (FNAG No.29, 1957, by Kurt **Steiner**) (1975)

46. *Lumière de Sang [Bood Light]* (FNAG No.44, 1958, by Kurt **Steiner**) (1975)

47-48. *L'Herbe aux Pendus [The Herb of the Hanged Men]* (FNAG No.39, 1958, by Kurt **Steiner**) (1975)

49. *Syncope Blanche [White Fainting]* (FNAG No.45, 1957, by Kurt **Steiner**) (1975)

50. *Terreur en Plein Soleil [Terror Under a Full Sun]* (FNAG No.38, 1958, by B.-R. **Bruss**) (1975)

51. *Le Village de la Foudre [The Village of Lightning]* (FNAG No.47, 1958, by Kurt **Steiner**) (1976)

52. *La Marque du Démon [The Mark of the Demon]* (FNAG No.42, 1958, by Kurt **Steiner**) (1976)

53. *L'Orgue de l'Épouvante [The Organ of Terror]* (FNAG No.49, 1958, by Jean **Murelli**) (1976)

54. *Les Yeux sans Visage [The Eyes Without a Face]* (FNAG No.56, 1959, by Jean **Redon**) (1976) (also adapted as a feature film—see Chapter I)

55. *Le Ventriloque de l'Au-Delà [The Ventriloquist from Beyond]* (FNAG No.54, 1959, by G. **Gauthier**) (1976)

56. *Dans un Manteau de Brume [In a Cloak of Mist]* (FNAG No.57, 1959, by Kurt **Steiner**) (1976)

57. *Parodie à la Mort [Parody to Death]* (FNAG No.62, 1960, by Peter **Randa**) (1976)

58-59. *Puzzle Macabre [Macabre Puzzle]* (FNAG No.58, 1959, by Marc **Agapit**) (1976)

60-61. *Piège Infernal [Infernal Trap]* (FNAG No.60, 1959, by Marc **Agapit**) (1977)

2nd Series:

1-13: Les Noirs Paradis [The Black Paradises] (FNAG no.110, 1964, by Jean **Murelli**); *La Figurine de Plomb [The Lead Statuette]* (FNAG No.119, 1965, by B.-R. **Bruss**); La Mygale *[The Spider]* (FNAG No.123, 1966, by Maurice **Limat**); (#8) Phantasmes (FNAG 91, 1962, by Marc **Agapit**); (#9-10) *Le Visage du Spectre [The Face of the Spectre]* (FNAG 63, 1960 by Marc **Agapit**); (#13) *Complexes* (FNAG 82, 1962, 1960 by Marc **Agapit**); *Les Jardins de la Nuit [The Gardens Of The Night]* (FNAG No.129, 1966, by Maurice **Limat**); and *Comme un Sepulcre Blanchi [As a White Sepulcher]* (FNAG No.132, 1966, by Dominique **Arly**) (1977-78).

NOTE: The "missing" numbers are adaptations of non–French authors. The Frankenstein adaptations (Nos. 16-21 above) by "Benoît **Becker**" (a house pseudonym) were written by noted film writer Jean-Claude **Carrière** (see Chapter I). The other Benoît **Becker** adaptations (Nos. 24-26 and Nos. 32 and 36) were written by José-André **Lacour**.

Névrose:

Névrose [Neuroses] (FNAG No.77, 1961, by André **Caroff**); *Les Nuits de Rochemaure [The Nights of Rochemaure]* (FNAG No.100 by Michel **Talbert**) and *Les Revenantes [The Ghosts]* (FNAG No.126, 1965, by Dominique **Arly**) (1981-83)

NOTE: The other issues did not adapt any Fleuve Noir stories. Michel **Talbert** Is the pseudonym of writer Michel **Bernanos**. Dominique **Arly** is the pseudonym of Constant Pettex.

Sidéral:

1. *Les Conquérants de l'Univers [The Conquerors of the Universe]* (FNA No.1, 1951, by **Richard-Bessière**; ART: Raoul & Robert **Giordan**) (1969)

2. *À l'Assaut du Ciel [To Assault the Sky]* (FNA No.2, 1951, by **Richard-Bessière**; ART: Raoul & Robert **Giordan**) (1969)

3. *Retour du Météore [Return of the Meteor]* (FNA No.3, 1951, by **Richard-Bessière**; ART: Raoul & Robert **Giordan**) (1969)

4. *La Planète Vagabonde [The Wandering Planet]* (FNA No.4, 1952, by **Richard-Bessière**; ART: Raoul & Robert **Giordan**. (1969)

5. *Sauvetage Sidéral [Interstellar Rescue]* (FNA No.37, 1954, by **Richard-Bessière**; ART: Raoul & Robert **Giordan**) (1970)

6. *S.O.S. Terre [SOS Earth]* (FNA No.55, 1955, by **Richard-Bessière**; ART: Raoul & Robert **Giordan**) (1970)

7. *Vingt Pas dans l'Inconnu [Twenty Steps into the Unknown]* (FNA No.60, 1955, by **Richard-Bessière**; ART: Raoul & Robert **Giordan**) (1970)

8. *Feu dans le Ciel [Fire in the Sky]* (FNA No.64, 1956, by **Richard-Bessière**) (1970)

9. *Route du Néant [Road into the Void]* (FNA No.81, 1956, by **Richard-Bessière**) (1970)

10. *Le Pionnier de l'Atome [The Pioneer of the Atom]* (FNA No.5, 1952, by Jimmy **Guieu**; ART: Raoul & Robert **Giordan**) (1970)

11. *La Dimension* (FNA No.27, 1953, by Jimmy **Guieu**; ART: Raoul & Robert **Giordan**) (1971)

12. *Au-Delà de l'Infini [Beyond Infinity]* (FNA No.8, 1952, by Jimmy **Guieu**; ART: Raoul & Robert **Giordan**) (1971)

13. *L'Invasion de la Terre [The Invasion of Earth]* (FNA No.13, 1952, by Jimmy **Guieu**; ART: Raoul & Robert **Giordan**) (1971)

14. *Hantise sur le Monde [Fear Over the World]* (FNA No.18, 1953, by Jimmy **Guieu**; ART: Raoul & Robert **Giordan**) (1971)

15. *L'Univers Vivant [The Living Universe]* (FNA No.22, 1953, by Jimmy **Guieu**; ART: Raoul & Robert **Giordan**) (1971)

17. *Nous, les Martiens [We, the Martians]* (FNA No.31, 1954, by Jimmy **Guieu**; ART: Raoul & Robert **Giordan**) (1972)

19. *Les Astres Morts [The Dead Stars]* (FNA No.11, 1952, by Jean-Gaston **Vandel**) (1972)

20. *La Spirale du Temps [The Spiral of Time]* (FNA No.36, 1954, by Jimmy **Guieu**) (1972)

21. *Alerte aux Robots [Robot Alert]* (FNA No.15, 1952, by Jean-Gaston **Vandel**) (1972)

23. *Frontières du Vide [Frontiers of the Void]* (FNA No.17, 1953, by Jean-Gaston **Vandel**; ART: Raoul & Robert **Giordan**) (1972)

25. *Le Monde Oublié [The Forgotten World]* (FNA No.41, 1955, by Jimmy **Guieu**) (1973)

26. *Les Chevaliers de l'Espace [The Space Knights]* (FNA No.7, 1952, by Jean-Gaston **Vandel**) (1973)

27. *Le Satellite Artificiel [The Artificial Satellite]* (FNA No.10, 1952, by Jean-Gaston **Vandel**) (1973)

28. *Le Soleil sous la Mer [The Sun Under the Sea]* (FNA No.19, 1953, by Jean-Gaston **Vandel**; ART: Raoul & Robert **Giordan**) (1973)

30. *Attentant Cosmique [Cosmic Strike]* (FNA No.21, 1953, by Jean-Gaston **Vandel**; ART: Raoul & Robert **Giordan**) (1973)

32. *Incroyable Futur [Incredible Future]* (FNA No.24, 1953, by Jean-Gaston **Vandel**) (1973)

34. *Agonie des Civilisés [Agony of the Civilisation]* (FNA No.26, 1953, by Jean-Gaston **Vandel**; ART: Raoul & Robert **Giordan**) (1974)

37. *S.O.S. Soucoupes [SOS Saucers]* (FNA No.33, 1954, by B.-R. **Bruss**) (1974)

39. *Fuite dans l'Inconnu [Flight Into the Unknown]* (FNA No.34, 1954, by Jean-Gaston **Vandel**) (1974)

40. *Pirate de la Science [Pirate of Science]* (FNA No.29, 1954, by Jean-Gaston **Vandel**) (1974)

43. *La Guerre des Soucoupes [The War of the Saucers]* (FNA No.40, 1955, by B.-R. **Bruss**) (1974)

44. *Territoire Robot [Robot Territory]* (FNA No.43, 1955, by Jean-Gaston **Vandel**) (1974)

45. *L'Homme de l'Espace [The Man from Outer Space]* (FNA No.45, 1955, by Jimmy **Guieu**) (1975)

48. *Naufragés des Galaxies [Castaways from the Galaxies]* (FNA No.39, 1954, by Jean-Gaston **Vandel**) (1975)

49. *Opération Aphrodite* (FNA No.47, 1955, by Jimmy **Guieu**) (1975)

50-51. *Les Titans de l'Énergie [The Titans of Energy]* (FNA No.48, 1955, by Jean-Gaston **Vandel**) (1975)

53. *Commandos de l'Espace [Space Commandos]* (FNA No.51, 1955, by Jimmy **Guieu**; ART: Raoul & Robert **Giordan**) (1975)

55. *Raid sur Delta [Raid on Delta]* (FNA No.52, 1955, by Jean-Gaston **Vandel**) (1976)

58. *L'Agonie du Verre [The Agony of Glass]* (FNA No.54, 1955, by Jimmy **Guieu**; ART: Raoul & Robert **Giordan**) (1976)

59. *Univers Parallèles [Parallel Universes]* (FNA No.58, 1955, by Jimmy **Guieu**; ART: Raoul & Robert **Giordan**) (1976)

60. *Nos Ancêtres de l'Avenir [Our Ancestors from the Future]* (FNA No.62, 1956, by Jimmy **Guieu**; ART: Raoul & Robert **Giordan**) (1976)

61. *Rideau Magnétique [Magnetic Curtain]* (FNA No.65, 1956, by B.-R. **Bruss**) (1977)

NOTE: The "missing" numbers are adaptations of non-French authors, e.g.: Vargo Statten, Volsted Gridban, etc. No. 46 is an adaptation of Isaac Asimov's (writing as Paul French) *David Starr—Space Ranger*, translated and published in French by Fleuve Noir. Nos. 62-63 are an adaptation of John Wyndham's *The Day of the Triffids*.

Super Boy:

97. *Les Chevaliers de l'Espace [The Space Knights]* (FNA No.7, 1952, by Jean-Gaston **Vandel**; ART: Félix Molinari) (1957)

98. *La Satellite Artificiel [The Artificial Satellite]* (FNA No.10, 1952, under the title *La Cité Morte [The Dead City]*, by Jean-Gaston **Vandel**; ART: Félix Molinari) (1957)

99. *Les Astres Morts [The Dead Stars]* (FNA No.11, 1952, under the title *La Conquête des Astres [Conquest of the Stars]*, by Jean-Gaston **Vandel**; ART: Félix Molinari) (1957)

Floribert

WRI: Mauguli; ART: François Castan.

STORY: A young man uses a magic stone, which turns all it touches to stone, to fight pollution.

NOTE: Numerous stories were serialized in *Fripounet* (Ed. Fleurus, 1978-87), but not collected in the graphic novel format.

Foc

WRI: René **Durand**; ART: Yves **Bordes**.

1. *Les Mangeurs d'Espoir [The Hope Eaters]* (Dar., 1984)

2. *La Confrérie de la Flétrissure [The Brotherhood of the Wilt]* (Dar., 1987)

3. *L'Arc Azur [The Azure Arc]* (Dar., 1989)
WRI: René **Durand**; ART: Amblevert.

4. *Les Cimiers du Sépulcre [Crest of the Sepulchre]* (Sol., 1993)

STORY: Werewoman Foc, resurrected knight Dominique, and gnome Jubal, seek revenge in a 13th century Earth where vegetal aliens have taken human shapes.

NOTE: Originally serialized in *Charlie* in 1983.

Foerster, Philippe

Certains l'aiment noir [Some Like It Dark] (Aud., 1982)
La Soupe aux Cadavres [Cadaver Soup] (Aud., 1983)
Pinocchio (Magic Strip, 1983)

L'Appel du Fossoyeur [The Call of the Gravedigger] (Aud., 1984)

Porte-à-Porte Malheur [Door-to-Door Bad Luck] (Aud., 1984)

Nuits Blanches [White Nights] (Aud., 1987)

Instants Damnés [Accursed Moments] (Aud., 1988)

Les Rendez-Vous de Minuit [The Midnight Rendezvous] (Aud., 1989)

Hantons sous la Pluie [Haunting in the Rain] (Aud., 1990)

La Raison du Plus Mort [Deadman's Reason] (Aud., 1994)

Tous les Haricots Ont une Fin [All the Beans Must Have an Ending] (Aud., 1996)

NOTE: Collections of b&w horror stories in a darkly humorous vein; originally serialized in *Fluide Glacial*. Two stories were translated in *Taboo* (Spiderbaby Grafix).

Foligatto (Hum., 1991)
  WRI: Alexios Troyas; ART: Nicolas de Crécy
  STORY: Heroic fantasy.

La Folle du Sacré-Coeur see **Le Coeur Couronné**

Le Fond de l'Air Est Frais see **Fred**

Foudre
  WRI: Luc Dellisse; ART: C. Durieux.

1. *L'Étincelle [The Spark]* (Lom., 1996)

2. *Clandestin [Clandestine]* (Lom., 1996)

3. *Hong Kong Machine* (Lom., 1997)

4. *Le Dernier Nobel [The Last Nobel]* (Lom., 1997)
  STORY: In 2051, Mankind has become sterile. Emmanuel Carrot investigates.

Foufi
  WRI/ART: Kiko.

1. *Foufi et le Tapis Merveilleux [Foufi and the Magic Carpet]*, aka *L'Héritage Enchanté [The Enchanted Inheritance]* (1965; rep. Dup., 1968)

2. *Les Voleurs Volants [The Flying Thieves]* (1965)

3. *Le Coffret Magique [The Magic Chest]* (1966; rep. Dup., 1968)

4. *Le Nabab* (1967)

5. *Les Attractions d'Orient [The Oriental Attractions]* (1968)

6. *L'Élixir de Charme [The Elixir of Charm]* (1968)

7. *Le Secret de la Montagne [The Secret of the Mountain]* (1969)

8. *La Tournée des Grands Dupes [The Dupes' Walk]* (1973)
  STORY: A young Arab boy and his magic carpet in the world of the Thousand and One Nights.
  NOTE: Originally serialized in *Spirou* in 1964. Only eps. 1 and 3 have been collected in the graphic novel format. Kiko is an Egyptian-born author. He also drew over 30 shorter stories starring *Foufi* between 1964 and 1980.

Les Fourmis [The Ants]
  WRI: Bernard **Werber**; ART: Patrick Serres.

1. *Les Fourmis [The Ants]* (AM., 1994)
  STORY: Comics adaptation of a best-selling science fiction novel depicting the lives of the ants.

Fox
  WRI: Jean **Dufaux**; ART: Jean-François Charles.

1. *Le Livre Maudit [The Accursed Book]* (Glé., 1991)

2. *Le Miroir de la Vérité [The Mirror of Truth]* (Glé., 1992)

3. *Rais el Djemat* (Glé., 1993)

4. *Le Dieu Rouge [The Red God]* (Glé., 1994)

5. *Le Club des Momies [The Club of Mummies]* (Glé., 1995)

6. *Jour Corbeau [Crow Day]* (Glé., 1996)
  STORY: An *Indiana Jones*-like archeologist becomes involved in esoteric mysteries.

Les Francis
  WRI: R. **Lortac**; ART: Raoul & Robert **Giordan**.
  STORY: The adventures of a family of space travelers not unlike the Robinsons of *Lost in Space*.
  NOTE: Untitled short stories originally serialized as a back-up feature in Meteor Nos. 103-110 (Artima, 1962), and No. 123 *(Le Leviathan Ne Répond Plus [Leviathan Does Not Answer]* (Artima, 1963).
  NOTE: These stories have never been collected in the graphic novel format.

Fred
  Le Petit Cirque [The Little Circus] (Dar., 1973)

Le Fond de l'Air Est Fred [The Air Is Fred] (Dar., 1973)
Hum! (Dar., 1974)
Ça Va, Ça Vient [Coming and Going] (Dar., 1977)
Y'a plus de Saisons [No More Seasons] (Dar., 1978)
Le Manu-Manu (Dar., 1979)
Cythère, L'Apprentie-Sorcière [Cythere, the Sorceress's Apprentice] (GP Or, 1980)
Magic Palace-Hôtel (Fred, 1980)
Parade (Fred, 1982)
L'Histoire du Corbac aux Baskets [The Tale of the Crow Who Wore Sneakers] (Dar., 1993)
L'Histoire du Conteur Électrique [The Tale of the Electronic Story-Teller] (Dar., 1995)

STORY/NOTE: Surreal tales originally serialized in *Hara-Kiri* and *Pilote*. A family pulls a little circus car. A man wakes up transformed into a giant crow. Giant hand-shaped creatures roam the countryside. A traveler is lost in a Babel-like hotel. A storyteller talks to the Moon, etc.

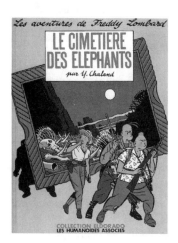

Freddy Lombard
WRI/ART: Yves **Chaland**.

1. *Le Testament de Godefroid de Bouillon [The Testament of Godefroid de Bouillon]* (Magic-Strip, 1981, transl. *Heavy Metal*)

2. *Le Cimetière des Éléphants [The Graveyard of the Elephants]* (Hum, 1984)

    WRI: **Yann**; ART: Yves **Chaland**.

3. *La Comète de Carthage [The Comet of Carthage]* (Hum., 1986)

4. *Vacances à Budapest [Holidays in Budapest]* (Hum., 1988)

5. *F-52* (Hum., 1989)

STORY: Freddy Lombard, his friend Sweep, and the beautiful Dina, have adventures in a "nostalgia" 1950 universe which includes giant stratospheric planes, rockets and other *Tintin*-like devices.

Fulguros
WRI/ART: R. **Brantonne**.

1. *Les Robots Géants [The Giant Robots]*.

2. *L'Élixir de Jeunesse [The Elixir of Youth]*.

3. *Le Fils du Radjah [The Rajah's Son]*.

4. *La Maison Mystérieuse [The House of Mystery]*.

5. *L'Ultimatum*.

6. *La Fin d'un Rêve [The End of a Dream]*.

7. *Fulguros et sa Kronexa*.

8. *L'Ennemi Public No. 1 [The Public Enemy No. 1]*.

9. *Fulguros Contre le Dragon Vert [Fulguros vs. the Green Dragon]*.

10. *Le Gaz Alpha et la Poudre Omega [The Alpha Gas and the Omega Powder]*.

11. *Aventures Extraordinaires [Extraordinary Adventures]*.

12. *La Fuite de Murdock [Murdock's Flight]*.

STORY/NOTE: Short-lived science fiction series about a self-dubbed "Master of Thunder" by the renowned cover artist of Editions Fleuve Noir. Originally serialized in *Audax* in 1946, then *Sylvie* in 1954–55, then in *Meteor* in 1967. Never collected in the graphic novel format.

Fu Manchu see Docteur Fu Manchu

Fume, C'est du Caza see **Caza**

Fusion see **Moebius**

Futuropolis (Glé., 1977)
WRI: René **Thévenin**. ART: **Pellos**.
STORY: A futuristic metropolis is controlled by robots.
NOTE: Reprinting of the classic story originally published in *Junior* in 1937-1938. A pseudo-sequel, **Electropolis**, was published in 1940 but has not been reprinted.

Fuzz et Fizzbi
WRI: Thierry Cailleteau; ART: Cyrus Tota.

1. *Le Mangerunes [The Rune Eater]* (Glé., 1990)

2. *Salmigonde* (Glé., 1991)

3. *Les Caverneux [The Cave Dwellers]* (Glé., 1993)
STORY: Humorous heroic fantasy.

Gadel le Fou [Gadel the Mad]
WRI/ART: Marc N'Guessan.

1. *La Laisse [The Leash]* (VdO., 1993)

2. *L'Esprit du Prince [The Prince's Spirit]* (Vent d'Ouest, 1994)
STORY: Heroic fantasy.

Galax
WRI: Roger **Lecureux**; ART: Roland Garel.
STORY: In the 21st century, space commandos Galax and Janet Dolce, with the help of their friend, crotchety scientist Prof. Jems, protect mankind against evil villains.

NOTE: Numerous stories serialized in *Marco Polo* (Ed. Aventures et Voyages) between 1962-1973. Never collected in graphic novel format.

Le Garage Hermétique (Le Monde du) [The World of the Airtight Garage]
WRI/ART: **Moebius**.

1. *Le Bandard Fou [The Horny Goof]* (Fromage,1974; rep. Hum., 1976; transl. Dark Horse)

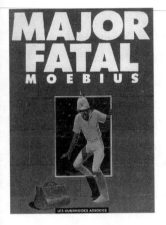

2. *Major Fatal (Hum., 1977), rep. as Le Garage Hermétique [The Airtight Garage]* (Hum., 1988; transl. Marvel)

3. *L'Homme du Ciguri [The Man from the Ciguri]* (Hum., 1995; transl. Dark Horse)
STORY: The "Airtight Garage" is the nickname of a three-leveled private universe created by the godlike Major Grubert inside a small asteroid. The evil Bakalite and the mysterious Jerry Cornelius (Lewis Carnelian in the English version) try to wrest it away.
NOTE: Originally serialized in *Métal Hurlant* in 1974.

Related Works:
WRI: **Moebius**, Jean-Marc & Randy Lofficier; ART: Eric Shanower.

1. *Le Prince Impensable [The Elsewhere Prince]* (Hum, 1990)

2. *Les Quatre Royaumes [The Four Kingdoms]* (Hum., 1990)

3. *Le Retour du Jouk [Return of the Jouk]* (Hum., 1991)
STORY: An artist becomes involved in the Major's attempts at saving the Garage from the monstrous Bouch' Tar'Hai.
NOTE: This story takes place chronologically before *The Airtight Garage*. All three volumes originally appeared in English as *The Elsewhere Prince*, a six-issue comic-book mini-series (Marvel, 1990).

WRI: **Moebius**, Jean-Marc & Randy Lofficier; ART: Jerry Bingham.
4. *Les Terres Aléatoires [The Randomearths]* (Hum., 1992)

5. *Le Seigneur d'Onyx [The Onyx Overlord]* (Hum., 1992)
STORY: The Major and Finnegar, a female detective, save the Garage from an alien slave master.
NOTE: This story takes place chronologically before *The Airtight Garage*. These two volumes originally appeared in English as *Onyx Overlord*, a four-issue comic-book mini-series (Marvel, 1992).

Garulfo
WRI: Bruno Maiorana; ART: Alain Ayroles.

1. *De Mares en Châteaux [From Ponds to Castles]* (Delc., 1995)

2. *De Mal en Pis [From Worse to Worst]* (Delc., 1996)

3. *Le Prince aux Deux Visages [The Prince with Two Faces]* (Delc., 1996)
STORY: A Frog is turned into a Prince.

Gaspard de la Nuit [Gaspar of the Night]
WRI: Stephen **Desberg**; ART: Johan **De Moor**.

1. *De l'Autre Côté du Masque [The Other Side of the Mask]* (Cast., 1987)

2. *Les Chasseurs dans la Nuit [The Night Hunters]* (Cast., 1989)

3. *Le Prince des Larmes Sèches [The Prince of Dried Tears]* (Cast., 1990)

4. *Les Ailes de Naxmaal [The Wings of Naxmaal]* (Cast., 1991)
STORY: When young Gervais puts on a mysterious mask, he finds himself transformed into Gaspar of the Night and transported to a fantasyland inhabited by unicorns, mermaids, and dragons.

Gaudéamus
WRI: René **Goscinny**; ART: Coq.
STORY: The handsome Dr. Gaudéamus has found a potion which enables him to revert to a baby, while retaining his adult memories and wits. With his beautiful wife, Pepita, he uses this "power" to help the police.
NOTE: Originally serialized in the women's weekly, *Jours de France* (1957-67, 1969-71). Coq is a Spanish artist.

Génial Olivier [Olivier the Genius]
WRI/ART: Jacques **Devos**.

1. *L'École en Folie [What a Crazy School]* (Dup., 1974)

2. *Le Génie et sa Génération [The Genius and His Generation]* (Dup., 1975)

3. *Génie, Vidi, Vici* (Dup., 1976)

4. *Un Généreux Génie Gêné [An Embarrassed and Generous Genius]* (Dup., 1977)

5. *Le Génie se Surpasse [The Genius Overdoes It]* (Dup., 1977)

6. *Un Ingénieux Ingénieur Génial [An Ingenius Genial Engineer]* (Dup., 1978)

7. *La Passé Recomposé [The Imperfect Past]* (Dup., 1979)

8. *Électrons, Molécules et Pensums [Electrons, Molecules and Punishment]* (Dup., 1980)

9. *L'Électron et le Blason [The Electron and the Coat of Arms]* (Dup., 1981)

10. *Un Génie Ingénu [An Ingenuous Genius]* (Dup., 1982)

11. *Génie, Péripéties et Facéties [Genius, Adventures and Farces]* (Dup., 1983)

12. *Un Génie Est chez Nous [A Genius at Home]* (Dup., 1984)

13. *Un Génie Gai Nickelé [A Lucky Nickel Genius]* (Dup., 1985)

14. *Un Génie Un Peu Nigaud [A Simple Genius]* (Dup., 1986)

15. *Hi-Fi Génie [Hi-Fi Genius]* (Dup., 1987)

16. *Génie sans Bouillir [Boiling Genius]* (Dup., 1988)

17. *Le Génie se Multiplie [Multiplying Genius]* (Dup., 1989)
STORY: The satirical adventures of a boy genius and his nemesis, Principal Rectitude.
NOTE: Originally serialized in *Spirou*, starting in 1964.

Les Géoles d'Ayade [The Jails of Ayade) (Sol., 1993)
WRI: Bec; ART: Éric Corbeyran.
STORY: Heroic fantasy.

Gérard Craan see Chroniques de Fin de Siècle

Gil et Georges
WRI/ART: Marc **Wasterlain**.

1. *La Machine Perplexe [The Puzzled Machine]* (Bayard, 1986)

2. *Le Maître des Robots [The Robot Master]* (Bayard, 1988)

3. *Les Hommes Transparents [The See-Through Men]* (Bayard, 1989)
STORY: Comical adventures of two friends and their robot in a fantastic world.

Gilles de Chin et du Dragon de Mons (La Geste de)
WRI/ART: P'tiluc.

1. *La Mémoire et la Boue [The Memory and the Mud]* (Vd'O., 1989)

2. *Le Doute et l'Oubli [The Doubt and the Oblivion]* (Vd'O., 1990)
STORY: Extravagant medieval heroic fantasy.

Ginger
WRI/ART: **Jidehem**.

1. *Les Aventures de Ginger [The Adventures of Ginger]* (Bédéscope, 1979)

2. *Les Yeux de Feu [The Eyes of Fire]* (Dup., 1983)

3. *L'Affaire Azinski [The Azinski Case]* (Dup., 1984)

4. *Ginger et le Collectionneur [Ginger and the Collector]* (Bédéscope, 1984)

5. *Le Baron Est Fou [The Baron Is Mad]* (Bédéscope, 1984)

6. *Les Mouches de Satan [The Flies of Satan]* (Dup., 1985)
STORY: A young female private eye takes part in fantastic adventures.
NOTE: The first album collects material originally serialized in *Heroic Albums* in 1954. The series was later continued in *Spirou* starting in 1979.

Gipsy
WRI: Thierry Smolderen; ART: Enrico Marini.

1. *L'Étoile du Gitan [The Star of the Gypsy Star]* (Hum., 1993; transl. as *The Wandering Star*, *Heavy Metal*)

2. *Les Feux de Sibérie [The Fires of Siberia]* (Hum., 1994)

3. *Le Jour du Tsar [The Day of the Czar]* (Hum., 1995)

4. *Les Yeux Noirs [The Black Eyes]* (Dar., 1997)
STORY: A futuristic truck driver travels along a vast highway crossing Europe and Asia.

Gnomes et Lutins [Gnomes and Goblins]
WRI/ART: Jean-Jacques Chabin.

1. *Volume 1* (Sol., 1995)
STORY: Heroic fantasy.

Goldorette
WRI/ART: Lucques (Luc Nisset).

1. *Goldorette* (Fromage, 1980)

2. *Goldorette Contre Supercalin [Goldorette vs. Supersmooch]* (AM., 1982)
STORY: Adult humor featuring a female super-heroine.

Gorn
WRI/ART: Tiburce Oger.

1. *Même la Mort [Even Death Itself]* (VdO., 1992)

2. *Le Pacte [The Pact]* (VdO., 1993)

3. *La Danse des Damnés [The Dance of the Damned]* (VdO., 1994)

4. *Le Sang du Ciel [The Blood of the Sky]* (VdO., 1995)

5. *Ceux Qui Nous Hantent [Those Who Are Haunting Us]* (VdO, 1996)
STORY: Heroic fantasy.

Le Gowap
WRI: **Mythic (Smit Le Benedicte)**; ART: Curd Ridel.

1. *Un Amour de Gowap [A Lovely Gowap]* (Lom., 1996)

2. *Tempête Domestique [Domestic Storm]* (Lom., 1997)

3. *Y a du Gowap dans l'Air [Gowap in the Air]* (Lom., 1997)
STORY: The humorous adventure of a fantastic cartoony animal.

Le Grand Chien [The Big Dog]
WRI: Vulliez; ART: Hugues.

1. *Le Grand Chien [The Big Dog]* (Glé., 1981)

2. *Mort au Mètre [Death by the Meter]* (Glé., 1982)
WRI/ART: Hugues.

3. *Le Sixième Sceau [The Sixth Seal]* (Glé., 1984)
STORY: Serious science fiction saga featuring a mutant rebel in a post-apocalyptic United States.

Le Grand Manque [The Great Shortage]
WRI: Christian **Godard**; ART: Julio Ribera.

1. *Le Grand Manque [The Great Shortage]* (Vaisseau d'Argent, 1989)

2. *Pour Trois Gouttes de Rosée [Three Drops of Dew]* (Sol., 1993)
STORY: Science fantasy.
NOTE: Julio Ribera is a Spanish artist working primarily in French comics.

Le Grand Passage see *Champakou*

Le Grand Pouvoir du Chninkel [The Great Power of the Chninkel] (Cast., 1988; transl. Dark Horse)
WRI: Jean Van Hamme; ART: Gregor Rosinski.
STORY: On a world before time, a brave little elf is on a mission from God.

NOTE: Gregor Rosinski is a Polish artist working primarily in French comics.

Les Griffes du Marais [The Swamp Claws]
WRI: Éric Corbeyran; ART: Amblevert.

1. *Le Raborne* (VdO., 1989)

2. *Annaëlle* (VdO., 1991)

3. *Bras-Faucon [Hawk-Arm]* (VdO., 1994)
STORY: Heroic fantasy.

Grimion Gant de Cuir [Grimion Leather Glove]
WRI/ART: Pierre **Makyo**.

1. *Sirène [Siren]* (Glé., 1984)

2. *Le Corbeau Blanc [The White Raven]* (Glé., 1985)

3. *La Petite Mort [The Little Death]* (Glé., 1987)

4. *Le Pays de l'Arbre [The Country of the Tree]* (Glé., 1992)
STORY: In the 1930s, a young boy whose right hand is like a cat's (and kept hidden under a leather glove, hence his nickname) seeks the secret of his origins.
NOTE: These stories were originally serialized in *Circus* in 1983.

Guerre à la Terre [War Against Earth]
WRI: **Marijac**; ART: Auguste **Liquois** (vol. 1); Pierre Duteurtre (Vol. 2).
STORY: Captain Veyrac and his crew fight the invading hordes of little yellow Martians and their monstrous, invading armies.
NOTE: Originally serialized in *Coq Hardi* in 1946 and 1947; republished in two volumes by Glénat in 1975.

La Guerre des Fées [The War of the Fairies] (Delagrave, 1909)
WRI: Le Cordier; ART: Pinchon.
STORY: Illustrated fairy tale.

La Guerre des Mondes [The War of the Worlds] (Dar., 1986)
WRI: H.G. Wells; ART: Edgar-Pierre **Jacobs**.
STORY: Illustrated adaptation of the classic science fiction novel.

La Guerre du Feu [The War for Fire]
Version No. 1: WRI: J. H. **Rosny** Aîné; ART: **Pellos** (Glé., 1976).
Version No. 2: WRI: J. H. **Rosny** Aîné; ART: Carlo Marcello (GP, 1982).
STORY: Illustrated adaptations of the classic prehistoric saga. Also see Chapter I for a film adaptation (*Quest for Fire*).

Les Guerriers [The Warriors]
WRI: Lalit; ART: Pellet.

1. *La Forteresse de Cormandel [The Fortress of Cormandel]* (Sol., 1996)
STORY: A hero seeks the last woman in a savage prehistoric-type future.

Guilio et le Drôle de Monde [Guilio and the Funny World]
WRI/ART: Laurent Parcelier.

1. *L'Auberge du Bossu [The Hunchback's Inn]* (Cast., 1994)

2. *L'Auberge de la Tarsaque [The Tarask's Inn]* (Cast., 1995)
STORY: Young Guilio and the mysterious Mr. Lasky explore a strange medieval fantasyland.

Guy Lebleu
WRI: Jean-Michel **Charlier**; ART: Raymond **Poïvet**.

1. *Allo, DMA* (134 p.) (1962; rep. 2 vols., Glé., 1976)

2. *Les Pirates de la Nuit [The Pirates of the Night]* (56 p.) (1964)

3. *L'Organisation XXX* (28 p.) (1965)

4. *Mort en Tous Genres [Any Kinds of Death]* (29 p.) (1965)

5. *La Cité Secrète de la Mort [The Secret City of Death]* (34 p.) (1966; rep. Glé., 1976)

6. *15 Milliards de Diamants [Fr15 Billion in Diamonds]* (74 p.) (1967)
STORY: A fearless radio journalist goes against an organization of mad scientists bent on achieving world domination.
NOTE: Originally serialized in *Pilote* in 1961.

Guy Pingaut
WRI/ART: Unknown.

1. *Les Martiens [The Martians]* (1957)

2. *Le Monstre [The Monster]* (1957)

3. *L'Inventeur [The Inventor]* (1957)

4. *Les Kan-Dor* (1968)
STORY: Science fiction adventures.
NOTE: Short-lived series published in *Spirou*. Never collected in the graphic novel format.

La Hache du Pouvoir [The Axe of Power]
WRI: Roger Seiter; ART: Frédéric Pillot.

1. *Le Prince Guerrier [The Warrior Prince]* (Delc., 1996)
STORY: Heroic fantasy.

Halona (Dup., 1993)
WRI/ART: Philippe Berthet.

STORY: An artist who is a suspect in a murder investigation blames his twin brother.

Hallucinations see *Fleuve Noir*

Hans
WRI: André-Paul **Duchateau**; ART: Gregor Rosinski.

1. *La Dernière Île [The Last Island]* (Lom., 1983)

2. *La Prisonnière de l'Éternité [The Prisoner of Eternity]* (Lom., 1985)

3. *Les Mutants de Xanaïa [The Mutants of Xanaia]* (Lom., 1986)

4. *Les Gladiateurs [The Gladiators]* (Lom., 1988)

5. *La Loi d'Ardélia [The Law of Ardelia]* (Lom., 1990)

WRI: André-Paul **Duchateau**; ART: Kas.
6. *La Planète aux Sortilèges [The Planet of Spells]* (Lom., 1992)

7. *Les Enfants de l'Infini [The Children of Infinity]* (Lom., 1994)

8. *Le Visage du Monstre [The Face of the Monster]* (Lom., 1996)

9. *La Princesse d'Ultis [The Princess of Ultis]* (Lom., 1997)
STORY: On a post-nuclear Earth, the mysterious Hans and his companion, the beautiful Orchid, fight against the evil overlord Valsary, with the help of the alien Xanaians.
NOTE: Originally serialized in *Tintin* in 1980. Gregor Rosinski is a Polish artist working primarily in French comics.

Hantons sous la Pluie see *Foerster*

Harry Dickson
Version No.1: WRI: Christian Vanderhaeghe, based on Jean **Ray**; ART: Pascal J. Zanon.

1. *La Bande de l'Araignée [The Gang of the Spider]* (ART BD, 1986)

2. *Les Spectres Bourreaux [The Ghost Executioners]* (ART BD, 1988)

3. *Les Trois Cercles de l'Épouvante [The Three Circles of Terror]* (ART BD, 1990)

4. *Le Royaume Introuvable [The Hidden Kingdom]* (Dar., 1994)

5. *L'Étrange Lueur Verte [The Strange Green Glow]* (Dar., 1997)

Version No.2: WRI: Richard **Nolane**; ART: Olivier Roman.

1. *L'île des Possédés [The Island of the Possessed]* (Sol., 1992)

2. *Le Démon de Whitechapel [The Demon of Whitechapel]* (Sol., 1994)

3. *Les Amis de l'Enfer [The Friends from Hell]* (Sol., 1995)

4. *Les Ombres de Blackfield [The Shadows of Blackfield]* (Sol., 1996)
STORY: Version No.1 adapts Jean **Ray**'s stories about a famous occult detective. Version No.2 uses the same character in all-new stories written by a genre author. Also see the film ***Malpertuis*** in Chapter I.

Hassan et Kadour
WRI: J. Alexander (Van Melkebeke); ART: Jacques Laudy.

1. *Les Mameluks de Bonaparte [Bonaparte's Mameluks]* (RTP, 1975)

2. *La Mission du Major Redstone [The Mission of Major Redstone]* (Bédéscope, 1978)

3. *Les Émeraudes du Conquistador [The Conquistador's Emeralds]* (Bédéscope, 1978)

4. *Le Voleur de Bagdad [The Thief of Bagdad]* (Bédéscope, 1979)

5. *Le Voeu Magique [The Magic Wish]* (Bédéscope, 1980)

6. *Le Miroir Enchanté [The Enchanted Mirror]* (Bédéscope, 1983)
STORY: Two Thousand-and-One Nights street urchins embark on a series of time-traveling adventures.
NOTE: Originally serialized in *Tintin* in 1948.

Hazel et Ogan
Wri: **Bosse**; Art: Norma.

1. *L'Épée de Foudre [The Sword of Lightning]* (Blanco, 1989)

2. *Le Pays des Trolls [The Land of the Trolls]* (Blanco, 1991)

3. *Moon Wolf* (Sol., 1994)
STORY: Heroic-fantasy.

Heilman (Hum., 1978; transl. Heavy Metal, 1979)
WRI/ART: Voss.
STORY: Futuristic punk rock fantasy.

Helgvor du Fleuve Bleu [Helgvor of Blue River] (Opera Mundi, 1980)
WRI/ART: Robert Rigot, based on the novel by J.-H. **Rosny** Aîné.
STORY: Prehistoric adventures.

He Pao see *Le Moine Fou*

Les Héritiers [The Inheritors]
WRI: G. Elton **Ranne**; ART: Juszezak.

1. *Par delà les Montagnes [Beyond the Mountains]* (VdO., 1990)

2. *Dans les Brûmes du Lac [On the Lake of Mists]* (VdO., 1991)
STORY: Life in a savage, future USA.
NOTE: G. Elton **Ranne** is a science-fiction author (see Book 2).

Les Héritiers d'Orphée [The Heirs of Orpheus]
WRI: P. Aubert; ART: Félix **Molinari**.

1. *Le Vol du Condor [The Flight of the Condor]* (Sol., 1992)

2. *La Cité des Orages [The City of Storms]* (Sol., 1993)

3. *La Troisième Lumière [The Third Light]* (Sol., 1994)
STORY: Heroic fantasy.

Les Héritiers du Soleil [The Heirs of the Sun]
WRI/ART: Didier **Convard**.

1. *Le Masque de Mort [The Mask of Death]* (Glé., 1986)

2. *Le Prophète de Sable [The Prophet of Sand]* (Glé., 1987)

3. *La Veuve Mère [The Mother Widow]* (Glé., 1989)

4. *Noir l'Amour [Dark Love]* (Glé., 1990)

5. *Néphérouré* (Glé., 1991)

WRI: Didier **Convard**; ART: F. Bihel.

6. *La Princesse Endormie [The Sleeping Princess]* (Glé., 1994)

7. *L'Architecte Immobile [The Motionless Architect]* (Glé., 1995)

8. *Illusion* (Glé., 1996)

9. *La Nuit de la Lumière [The Night of the Light]* (Glé., 1996)
STORY: Heroic fantasy adventures during the Hebrew exodus from Egypt.
NOTE: Originally serialized in *Vécu* in 1986.

Hispañola
WRI/ART: Fabrice Meddour.

1. *Le Sérum* (VdO., 1995)

2. *Le Grand Silencieux [The Great Silent One]* (VdO., 1996)

3. *Vicky* (VdO., 1996)
STORY: Science fiction adaptation of *Treasure Island* in a *Mad Max*–like universe.

L'Histoire du Conteur Électrique see ***Fred***

L'Histoire du Corbac aux Baskets see ***Fred***

Histoires Alarmantes [Alarming Stories] (Dup., 1987)

WRI: Jasmin; ART: Antonio Cossu.

STORY: Collection of gothic/horror stories.

NOTE: Antonio Cossu is an Italian artist working primarily in French comics.

Homicron

WRI: Claude-Jacques Legrand; ART: Lina Buffolente (eps. 1-2); Paolo Morisi (eps. 3-8).

STORY: An alien super-hero on Earth.

NOTE: Eight episodes originally serialized in *Futura* (Ed. Lug) in 1972-73; not collected in the graphic novel format. Buffolente and Morisi are Italian artists.

L'Homme au Bigos [The Man with the Big Hat]

WRI: **Rodolphe**; ART: Jacques Ferrandez.

1. *L'Homme au Bigos [The Man with the Big Hat]* (Hum., 1980)

2. *Le Maître de la Nuit [The Night Master]* (Hum., 1982)

3. *Villa Ténèbre [House of Darkness]* (Hum., 1984)

4. *Martin Squelette [Martin Skeleton]* (Hum., 1988)

WRI: **Rodolphe**; ART: Mauclère.

5. *Étrangère au Paradis [Stranger in Paradise]* (Hélyode, 1994)

6. *Pierrot la Lune [Pierrot Moon]* (Hélyode, 1997)

STORY: Mystery thrillers with gothic/supernatural overtones.

L'Homme de Java [The Man from Java]

WRI/ART: Gabrion.

1. *Rebelle [Rebel]* (VdO., 1990)

2. *L'Australien [The Australian]* (VdO., 1991)

3. *Pirates* (VdO., 1993)

4. *Mama King* (VdO., 1994)

STORY: Black magic and exotic tales.

L'Homme est-il bon? see **Moebius**

Horde [Zen., 1994)

WRI: Jab Jab Whamo; ART: J.D. Morvan.

STORY: Horde is a virtual-reality game taking place in a heroic-fantasy universe. A hacker uses it to create an archdemon.

Horologiom

WRI/ART: Fabrice Lebeault.

1. *L'Homme sans Clef [The Man Without a Key]* (Delc., 1994)

2. *L'Instant du Damokle [The Time of Damokle]* (Delc., 1995)

3. *Nahedig* (Delc., 1996)

STORY: A mime arrives in a surreal, emotionless, mechanical city.

Hors-Jeu see **Bilal**

L'Horus de Nekhen [The Horus of Nekhen]

WRI: François **Corteggiani**; ART: Georges **Ramaioli**.

1. *L'Horus de Nékhen [The Horus of Nekhen]* (Milan, 1989)

2. *Le Chant du Harpiste [The Song of the Harpist]* (Milan, 1990)

STORY: Tales of Ancient Egypt.

Hugo

WRI/ART: Bédu (Bernard Dumont).

1. *Le Sortilège du Haricot [The Bean Spell]* (Lom., 1986)

2. *Le Nain de Corneloup [The Dwarf of Corneloup]* (Lom., 1987)

3. *Le Pommier de Dieu [God's Appletree]* (Lom., 1988)

4. *Le Château des Mouettes [The Castle of the Seagulls]* (Lom., 1989)

5. *La Perle Bleue [The Blue Pearl]* (Lom., 1990)

STORY: Cartoony fantasy adventures of a medieval troubadour, his pet bear, and a friendly elf.

NOTE: Originally serialized in *Tintin* in 1981.

Les Huit Jours du Diable [Eight Days for the Devil] (Lom., 1983)

Le Neuvième Jour du Diable [The Devil's Ninth Day] (Lom., 1986)

WRI/ART: Didier Convard.

STORY: Short stories showing the spread of evil throughout history.

Hum see **Fred**

Les Hybrides [The Hybrids]

WRI: T. Umbreil, Benoît **Peeters**; ART: Séraphine.

1. *Animal, On est mal [Animal, We're Sick]* (Temps Futurs, 1984)

WRI: Thierry Smolderen; ART: Séraphine.

2. *Le Bouclier d'Orion [The Shield of Orion]* (Glé., 1987)

3. D'un Soleil à l'Autre [From One Sun to Another] (Glé., 1989)

4. Au Loin, une Île [Far Away, an Island] (Glé., 1991)
STORY: On a post-cataclysmic Earth, a young hybrid, Orion, refuses to abandon his human mother.

La Hyène [The Hyena]
WRI: Éric Corbeyran; ART: Stéphane Thanneur.

1. L'Année de Sang [The Year of Blood] (Sol., 1992)
WRI: Éric Corbeyran; ART: Laurent Séroussi.

2. Zodiack (Sol., 1995)
STORY: Heroic fantasy.

Hypérion (Lom., 1981)
WRI: André-Paul **Duchateau**; ART: **Franz**.
STORY: Amazon adventures in a post-cataclysmic England.

Hypocrite see *Barbarella*

Ian Kalédine
WRI: Jean-Luc **Vernal**; ART: **Ferry**.

1. La Nuit Blanche [The White Night] (Lom., 1983)

2. Le Secret de la Taïga [The Secret of the Taiga] (Lom., 1983)

3. La Mémoire du Fond de l'Oeil [The Memory at the Back of the Eye] (Lom., 1984)

4. Shan Pacha (Lom., 1985)

5. La Fée Peri [Peri the Fairy] (Lom., 1986)

6. Le Couteau de Braise [The Ember Knife] (Lom., 1987)

8. Le Grand Complot [The Great Conspiracy] (Lom., 1988)

9. Le Secret de Château Flambard [The Secret of Flambard Castle] (Lom., 1990)

10. Dottore Serpenti [Doctor Serpent] (Lom., 1992)
STORY: A Russian prince, a female journalist, and an Irish giant encounter alien phenomena in early 20th-century Europe.
NOTE: Originally serialized in *Tintin* in 1977.

Ici Même [Same Here] (Cast., 1979)
WRI: Jean-Claude Forest; ART: Jacques Tardi.

STORY: The surreal story of a man who is allowed to live only on the very top of the walls on a country estate.

Idées Noires [Dark Designs] (2 vols.) (Aud., 1981, 1984)
WRI/ART: André **Franquin**.
STORY: Collection of dark, surreal vignettes.

Ikar
WRI: Pierre **Makyo**; ART: René **Follet**.

1. Le Petit Prince Barbare [The Little Barbarian Prince] (Glé., 1995)
STORY: Light fantasy.

L'Île des Morts [The Isle of the Dead]
WRI: Thomas Mosdi; ART: Guillaume Sorel.

1. In Cauda Venenum (VdO., 1991)

2. Mors Ultima Ratio (VdO., 1992)

3. Abyssus Abyssum Invocat (VdO., 1993)

4. Perinde ac Cadaver (VdO., 1994)

5. Acta est Fabula (VdO., 1995)
STORY: Supernatural thrillers.

Images pour un Film see **Bilal**

L'Incal (aka **Les Aventures de John Difool**) *[The Adventures Of John Difool]*
WRI: Alexandro **Jodorowsky**; ART: **Moebius**.

1. L'Incal Noir [The Dark Incal] (Hum.,1981; transl. Marvel)

2. L'Incal Lumière [The Bright Incal] (Hum., 1982; transl. Marvel)

3. Ce Qui Est En Bas [That Which Is Below] (Hum., 1983; transl. Marvel)

4. Ce Qui Est En Haut [That Which Is Above] (Hum., 1985; transl. Marvel)

5. La Cinquième Essence 1: Galaxie qui Songe [The Fifth Essence 1: The Dreaming Galaxy] (Hum., 1988; transl. Marvel)

6. La Cinquième Essence 2: La Planète Difool [The Fifth Essence 2: Difool's Planet] (Hum., 1988; transl. Marvel)

Related Works:

Avant l'Incal *(aka* La Jeunesse de Difool) [John Difool Before the Incal]

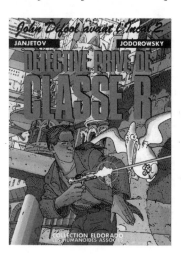

WRI: Alexandro **Jodorowsky**; ART: Zoran Janjetov.

1. *Avant l'Incal,* aka *Les Deux Orphelins [Before the Incal,* aka *The Two Orphans]* (Hum., 1988)

2. *Détective Privé de Classe R [Private Detective Class R]* (Hum., 1988)

3. *Croot* (Hum., 1991)

4. *Anarco Psychotiques [Anarco Psychotics]* (Hum., 1992)

5. *Ouisky, SVP & Homéoputes [Whisky, SVP & Homeowhores]* (Hum., 1993)

6. *Suicide Allée [Suicide Alley]* (Hum., 1995)

La Caste des Méta-Barons [The Saga of the Meta-Barons]

WRI: Alexandro **Jodorowsky**; ART: Juan Gimenez:

1. *Othon le Trisaïeul [Othon the Great]* (Hum., 1992; transl. *Heavy Metal*)

2. *Honorata la Trisaïeule* (Hum., 1993)

3. *Aghnar le Bisaïeul* (Hum., 1995)

4. *Oda la Bisaïeule* (Hum., 1996)

Misc.:

Les Mystères de l'Incal [Mysteries of the Incal] (accompanying text by Jean Annestay) (Hum., 1989, transl. Graphitti)

STORY: The Incal is a mysterious artifact of power coveted by various factions in the galaxy. Hapless private eye John Difool becomes a pawn in a cosmic game. The ***Before the Incal*** series is a prequel to John Difool's adventures, leading to his encounter with the Incal. The ***Meta-Baron*** is a supporting character in the saga. A separate series reveals the history of his ancestors.

NOTE: The early ***Incal*** stories were originally serialized in *Métal Hurlant.* Zoran Janjetov is a Serb artist. Juan Gimenez is a renowned Spanish artist.

L'Indien Français [The French Indian]

WRI: René **Durand**; ART: Georges **Ramaioli**.

1. *L'Indien Français [The French Indian]* (Glé., 1978)

2. *La Lune Enterrée [The Buried Moon]* (Glé., 1980)

3. *Le Scalp et la Peau [The Scalp and the Skin]* (Glé, 1982)

4. *Traqués [Hunted]* (Glé., 1983)

5. *Le Chasseur des Solitudes [The Lonely Hunter]* (Glé., 1985)

6. *Bois Brûlé [Burned Wood]* (Glé., 1987)

7. *Grondements [Growls]* (Glé., 1988)

8. *Hurlements [Howls]* (Sol., 1992)

STORY: In the late 1800s, a French biologist travels to the American West where he accelerates the evolution of a she-wolf who becomes his wife.

NOTE: Originally serialized in *Circus* starting in 1977.

Instants Damnés see ***Foerster***

Iris see ***Comès***

Isabelle

WRI: Raymond Macherot, André **Franquin**, Yvan **Delporte**; ART: **Will**.

1. *Le Tableau Enchanté [The Enchanted Painting]* (Dup., 1972)

2. *Les Maléfices de l'Oncle Hermès [The Spells of Uncle Hermes]* (Dup., 1978)

3. *L'Astragale de Cassiopée [The Astragal of Cassiopea]* (Dup., 1979)

4. *Un Empire de Dix Arpents [A Ten-Acre Empire]* (Dup., 1980)

5. *L'Étang des Sorciers [The Wizards' Pond]* (Dup., 1981)

6. *Isabelle et le Capitaine [Isabelle and the Captain]* (Dup., 1983)

7. *L'Envoûtement de Népenthès [The Spell of Nepenthes]* (Dup., 1986)

WRI: Yvan **Delporte**; ART: **Will**.

8. *La Lune Gibbeuse [The Gibbous Moon]* (Dup., 1991)

9. *La Traboule de la Géhenne [The Wind of Gehenna]* (Dup., 1992)

10. *Le Sortilège des Gâtines [The Spell of the Gatines]* (Dup., 1993)

11. *Le Grand Bonbon [The Great Goody]* (Dup., 1994)

12. *Les Abraxas Pernicieux [The Pernicious Abraxas]* (Dup., 1995)

STORY: The fantastic adventures of a little girl whose uncle is a magician.

NOTE: Originally serialized in *Spirou* in 1971.

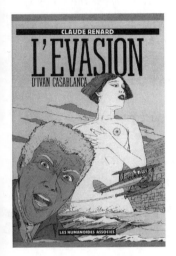

Ivan Casablanca
WRI/ART: Claude **Renard**.

1. *L'Évasion d'Ivan Casablanca [Ivan Casablanca's Escape]* (Hum., 1984)
WRI: Jean-Luc Fromental; ART: Claude **Renard**.

2. *Le Rendez-Vous d'Angkor [Rendezvous in Angkor]* (Hum., 1986)
STORY: A nightmarish parallel universe.

Ivan Zourine
WRI: Jacques **Stoquart**; ART: René **Follet**.

1. *Le Testament de Sibérie [The Siberian Testament]* (Magic-Strip, 1979)

2. *Les Ors du Caucase [The Gold of the Caucasus]* (Magic-Strip, 1979)
STORY: Fantastic adventures.

Iznogoud
WRI: René **Goscinny**; ART: Jean Tabary.

1. *Le Grand Vizir Iznogoud [The Great Vizier Iznogoud]* (Dar., 1966)

2. *Les Complots du Grand Vizir Iznogoud [The Conspiracies of the Great Vizier Iznogoud]* (Dar., 1967)

3. *Les Vacances du Calife [The Caliph's Holidays]* (Dar., 1968)

4. *Iznogoud l'Infâme [Iznogoud the Infamous]* (Dar., 1969)

5. *Des Astres pour Iznogoud [Iznogoud Sees Stars]* (Dar., 1969)

6. *Iznogoud et l'Ordinateur Magique [Iznogoud and the Magic Computer]* (Dar., 1970)

7. *Une Carotte pour Iznogoud [A Carrot for Iznogoud]* (Dar., 1971)

8. *Le Jour des Fous [Madmen's Day]* (Dar., 1972)

9. *Le Tapis Magique [The Magic Carpet]* (Dar., 1973)

10. *Iznogoud l'Archarné [Iznogoud the Determined]* (Dar., 1974)

11. *La Tête de Turc d'Iznogoud [Iznogoud and the Turks]* (Dar., 1975)

12. *Le Conte de Fées d'Iznogoud [Iznogoud's Fairy Tales]* (Dar., 1976)

13. *Je Veux Être Calife à la Place du Calife [I Want to Be Caliph in the Caliph's Stead]* (BD Star, 1978)

14. *Les Cauchemars d'Iznogoud 1 [Iznogoud's Nightmares]* (Séguinière, 1979)

WRI/ART: Jean Tabary.
15. *L'Enfance d'Iznogoud [Iznogoud's Childhood]* (Glé., 1981)

16. *Izonogoud et les Femmes [Iznogoud and Women]* (Séguinière, 1983)

17. *Les Cauchemars d'Iznogoud 2 [Iznogoud's Nightmares 2]* (WRI: Alain Buhler) (Séguinière, 1983)

18. *Le Complice d'Iznogoud [Iznogoud's Accomplice]* (Séguinière, 1984)

19. *Les Cauchemars d'Iznogoud 3 [Iznogoud's Nightmares 3]* (Séguinière, 1985)

20. *L'Anniversaire d'Iznogoud [Iznogoud's Birthday]* (Séguinière, 1987)

21. *Iznogoud Enfin Calife! [Iznogoud Caliph at Last!]* (Tabary, 1989)

22. *Les Cauchemars d'Iznogoud 4 [Iznogoud's Nightmares 4]* (Tabary, 1990)

23. *Le Piège de la Sirène [The Siren's Trap]* (Tabary, 1992)

24. *Les Retours d'Iznogoud [Iznogoud Returns]* (Tabary, 1994)
STORY: An evil vizier uses all kinds of magical devices to try to get rid of a kind but dim-witted caliph; however, they always backfire with hilarious effects.

NOTE: Originally serialized in *Record* in 1962, then in *Pilote* in 1969. **Iznogoud** has also appeared as a weekly strip in *Le Journal du Dimanche* (1974-80) and has recently been adapted as an animated series.

Jabert
WRI: P. Le Gall; ART: A. Geerts.

1. *Jabert Contre l'Adversité [Jabert vs. Adversity]* (Delc., 1990)

2. *La Malédiction des Wladech [The Curse of Wladech]* (Delc., 1992)
STORY: Humorous adventures with fantasy elements.

Jacques Flash

WRI: Jean **Ollivier**; ART: Pierre **Le Guen**.

1. *Jacques Flash contre l'Homme Invisible [Jacques Flash vs. the Invisible Man]* (67 p.) (1957; rep. Vail., 1960)

2-3. *Jeux de Mains, Jeux de Vilains [Hand Games, Evil Games] / Le Retour de l'Homme Invisible [The Return of the Invisible Man]* (56 p.) (1959; rep. Vail., 1961)

WRI: Jean **Ollivier**; ART: Gérald **Forton**.

4. *Contre Cyrano de Bergerac* (26 p.) (1960)

5. *Bagarres en Birmanie [Battle in Burma]* (22 p.) (1960)

6. *Matricule 9929 FK 75 [License Plate 9929 FK 75]* (43 p.) (1961)

WRI: Pierre Castex; ART: René **Deynis**.

7. *Le Trésor de l'Homme Invisible [The Invisible Man's Treasure]* (11 p.) (1961)

8. *Contre les Hommes Invisibles [Against the Invisible Men]* (26 p.) (1962)

9. *Invisiblement Votre [Invisibly Yours]* (30 p.) (1963)

10. *La Fiancée de l'Homme Invisible [The Bride of the Invisible Man]* (32 p.) (1963)

11. *Faites Chauffer la Colle [Heat Up the Glue]* (34 p.) (1964)

12. *L'Homme Invisible Joue et Gagne [The Invisible Man Plays To Win]* (10 p.) (1964)

13. *L'Homme Invisible fait des Siennes [The Invisible Man Plays Tricks]* (63 p.) (1965)

14. *Le Fantôme de l'Homme Invisible [The Ghost of the Invisible Man]* (1965)

15. *Contre 3,1416* (1965)

16. *Cache-Cache Catcheur [Hide and Seek with a Wrestler]* (1965)

17. *Le Grand Chantage [The Great Blackmail]* (1965)

18. *Enlevez, c'est pesé [Take It Away, It's Been Weighed]* (1965)

19. *Les Pirates de l'Air [The Air Pirates]* (1965)

20. *Teuf-Teuf Polka [Jalopy Polka]* (1966)

21. *Les Hercules d'Acier [The Steel Hercules]* (1966)

22. *Ballet Ballon [Balloon Ballet]* (1966)

23. *Le Gang des Tracteurs [The Tractor Gang]* (1966)

24. *Scandale chez les As [Scandal Among the Aces]* (1966)

25. *Branle-bas chez les Radios Pirates [Alert Among the Radio Pirates]* (1966)

26. *Les Pères Noël de l'Épouvante [The Terrifying Santa Clauses]* (8 p.) (1966)

27. *Avez-vous Vu Mirza? [Have You Seen Mirza?]* (1967)

28. *Les Voyageurs du Futur [The Travellers from the Future]* (1967)

29. *Méfiez-vous des Fantômes [Don't Trust the Ghosts]* (1967)

30. *Le Grand Maître de Bornéo [The Master of Borneo]* (1967)

31. *Le Commando Libellule [The Dragonfly Commando]* (1967)

32. *Les Abominables Petits Hommes Verts [The Awful Little Green Men]* (1967)

33. *La Marée Nore [The Black Tide]* (1968)

34. *Le Jour des Dauphins [The Day of the Dolphins]* (1968)

35. *L'Étrange Safari [The Strange Safari]* (1968)

36. *Rapt en Plein Ciel [Skyjacking]* (1968)

37. *Alerte au X43* (1968)

39. *Les Chevaliers de l'Hélibulle [The Knights of the Helibubble]* (1969)

40. *Les Esclaves de la Forêt [The Slaves of the Forest]* (1969)

50. *24 Heures dans l'Autre Monde [24 Hours in the World Beyond]* (1970)

WRI: Pierre Castex; ART: Max Lenvers.

38. *Le Fantôme du Zoo [A Ghost at the Zoo]* (1968)

41. *La Nuit des Vampires [The Night of the Vampires]* (1969)

42. *La Folie des Diamants [The Diamond Madness]* (1969)

43. *Terreur sur la Manche [Terror Over the Channel]* (1969)

44. *Aller sans Retour [One-Way Ticket]* (1969)

45. *Miracle à Colombes* (1969)

46. *Furie sur l'Or Noir [Black Gold Fury]* (1969)

47. *La Cadena de Uro* (1970)

48. *Les Disparus d'Alcatraz [Disappearances in Alcatraz]* (1970)

49. *Le Mur des 9000 Soleils [The Wall of 9000 Suns]* (1970)

51. *Le Mammouth du Ciel [The Sky Mastodon]* (1970)

52. *Bien Joué, Fillette! [Well Played, Little Girl!]*

53. *Safari à l'Héritage [Inheritance Safari]* (1971)
WRI: Pierre Castex; ART: Legoff.

54. *Nuages sur Nouakcholt [Clouds Over Nouakcholt]* (1973)
STORY: A journalist uses Prof. Folven's invisibility serum to fight crime.
NOTE: Originally serialized in *Vaillant* from 1956 to 1973. In spite of its popularity, only the first three episodes were collected in the graphic novel format. Except where otherwise mentioned, the stories were usually 12-pages long (switching to 20 pages from No. 40), and self-contained.

Jaleb le Télépathe

WRI: Claude-Jacques Legrand; ART: Annibale Casabianca (1-16); Yves Chantereau (17-18).
STORY: An alien baby accidentally abandoned on Earth grows up to be a telepathic humanoid and eventually finds his people.
NOTE: Eighteen eps. originally serialized in *Futura*, Nos. 1-18 (Ed. Lug, 1972-73); not collected in the graphic novel format. Annibale Casabianca is an Italian artist.

Les Jardins de la Peur [The Gardens of Fear]

WRI: Jean **Dufaux**; ART: Eddy **Paape**, Sohier.

1. *Le Caveau Harwood [The Harwood Tomb]* (Dar., 1988)

2. *Le Retour de Lady Mongo [The Return of Lady Mongo]* (Dar., 1989)

3. *Les Cauchemars de Nils Fallon [The Nightmares of Nils Fallon]* (Hum., 1991)
STORY: Gothic fantasy and black magic.

Jason Muller see Simon du Fleuve

Jean Cyriaque (Hum., 1982)
WRI: Jean-Pierre **Dionnet**; ART: Jean Solé.
STORY: A man discovers that he originally came from another dimension.
NOTE: Originally serialized in *Pilote*.

Jean Valhardi

(genre stories only)
WRI: Jean-Michel **Charlier**; ART: Eddy **Paape**.

4. *Le Rayon Super-Gamma [The Super-Gamma Ray]* (Dup.,1953)

5. *La Machine à Conquérir le Monde [The World-Conquering Machine]* (Dup., 1954)

WRI/ART: **Jijé**.

6. *Valhardi Contre Soleil Noir [Valhardi vs. Black Sun]* (Dup., 1958)
STORY: Fearless insurance investigator Jean Valhardi fights a variety of crooks and villains, including some mad scientists who want to take over the world.
NOTE: Originally created in 1941 in *Spirou* by writer Jean Doisy and artist **Jijé**. **Charlier** and **Paape** took over the series in 1952 and gave it a more fantastic bent, which remained when Jijé returned in 1957. Jijé dropped *Valhardi* again in 1965. The character reappeared in 1981 for a couple of stories by **Duchateau** and **Stoquart**, and art by **Follet**.

Jeepster

WRI: Patrick Giordano; ART: Francard (Frank Picard).

1. *Rêves de Fantôme [Ghost Dreams]* (Dar., 1992)

2. *Le Secret des Tubulaires [The Secret of the Tubulars]* (Dar., 1993)

3. *Capri, C'est Fini [Capri, It's Over]* (Dar., 1996)
STORY: Space opera, super-heroes, and manga-style (Japanese comic-book-style) adventures.

Jeff Sullivan

WRI: Claude-Jacques Legrand; ART: Luciano Bernasconi.
STORY: A superhero travels to a parallel universe where the Japanese have won World War II.
NOTE: Seven eps. originally serialized in *Futura*, Nos. 27-33 (Ed. Lug, 1974-75); not collected in the graphic novel format. Luciano Bernasconi is an Italian artist.

Jeremiah

WRI/ART: **Hermann**.

1. *La Nuit des Rapaces [The Night of the Predators]* (Fleurus, 1979, transl. as *The Survivors*, Fantagraphics)

2. *Du Sable Plein les Dents [Sand in the Teeth]* (Fleurus, 1979)

3. *Les Héritiers Sauvages [The Savage Inheritors]* (Fleurus, 1980)

4. *Les Yeux de Fer Rouge [The Eyes of Red Iron]* (Fleurus, 1980; transl. Fantagraphics)

5. *Un Cobaye pour l'Eternité [A Guinea Pig for Eternity]* (Hachette, 1981)

6. *La Secte [The Sect]* (Hachette, 1982)

7. *Afroamerica* (Hachette, 1982)

8. *Les Eaux de la Colère [The Angry Waters]* (Hachette, 1983)

9. *Un Hiver de Clown [A Clown Winter]* (Hachette, 1983)

10. *Boomerang* (Hachette, 1984)

11. *Delta* (Hachette, 1985)

12. *Julius et Romea* (Hachette, 1986)

13. *Strike* (Dup., 1988)

14. *Simon Est de Retour [Simon Is Back]* (Dup., 1989)

15. *Alex* (Dup., 1990)

16. *La Ligne Rouge [The Red Line]* (Dup., 1992)

17. *Trois Motos...Ou Quatre [Three Bikes...or Four]* (Dup., 1994)

18. *Caesar* (Dup., 1995)

19. *Zone Frontière [Border Zone]* (Dup., 1996)

STORY: Jeremiah and his companion, the rash and violent Kurdy, try to survive in a post-apocalyptic world where civilization has fallen apart.

Le Jeu de Pourpre [The Purple Game]

WRI: Pierre **Makyo**; ART: Rocco.

1. *Le Rêve Partagé [The Shared Dream]* (Glé., 1994)

2. *Le Corps Dispersé [The Scattered Body]* (Glé., 1995)

3. *La Mort Donnée [The Given Death]* (Glé., 1996)

STORY: In ancient India, a warrior and the son of a farmer become involved in fantastic adventures.

La Jeune Fille et le Vent [The Young Girl and the Wind]

WRI: Martin Ryeland; ART: Jung.

1. *La Jeune Fille et le Vent [The Young Girl and the Wind]* (Delc., 1995)

2. *Soon Li* (Delc., 1996)

STORY: Heroic fantasy.

Les Jeux du Crocodile [The Games of the Crocodile]

WRI: Bogue; ART: Modem.

1. *Niveau 1 [Level 1]* (Dar., 1996)

2. *Niveau 2 [Level 2]* (Dar., 1997)

STORY: A futuristic world is in thrall to electronic games.

Jhen/Xan

WRI: Jacques **Martin**; ART: Jean **Pleyers**.

Xan

1. *L'Or de la Mort [The Gold of Death]* (Lom., 1984)

2. *Jehanne de France* (Lom., 1985)

Jhen

1. *Les Écorcheurs [The Skinners]* (Cast., 1984)

2. *Barbe-Bleue [Bluebeard]* (Cast., 1984)

3. *La Cathédrale [The Cathedral]* (Cast., 1985)

4. *Le Lys et l'Ogre [The Lys and the Ogre]* (Cast., 1986)

5. *L'Alchimiste [The Alchemist]* (Cast., 1989)

6. *Le Secret des Templiers [The Templars' Secret]* (Cast., 1990)

STORY: The fantastic adventures of a young stone cutter in the days of Joan of Arc and Gilles de Rais, aka Bluebeard.

NOTE: Originally serialized in *Tintin* in 1978 as *Xan*; the series changed its name to *Jhen* when it was taken over by Casterman.

Jim Boum

WRI/ART: **Marijac**.

STORY/NOTE: Originally a western hero created by **Marijac** in *Coeurs Vaillants* in 1931. The character's "grandson" was featured in World War II adventures in *Coq Hardi* from 1945 to 1950. During this period, the "new" Jim Boum was also involved in a series of science fiction adventures, traveling to Mars as well as back through time to prehistory. Only the western stories were collected in the graphic novel format.

Jo, Zette et Jocko

(genre stories only)
WRI/ART: **Hergé**.

1. *Le Testament de M. Pump [The Testament of Mr. Pump]* (Lom., 1951)

2. *Destination New York* (Lom., 1951)

3. *Le "Manitoba" ne Répond Plus [The "Manitoba" No Longer Answers]* (Lom., 1952)

4. *L'Éruption du Kamarako [The Karamako Eruption]* (Lom., 1952)

STORY: The two children of engineer Jacques Legrand and their pet chimpanzee become involved in fantastic globe-spanning adventures.

NOTE: Originally serialized in *Coeurs Vaillants* in 1936. After World War II, the series appeared in *Tintin*.

Jodelle/Pravda

WRI: Pierre Bartier; ART: Guy Pellaert.

1. *Jodelle* (Losfeld, 1966)
   WRI: Pascal Thomas; ART: Guy Pellaert.

2. *Pravda la Survireuse* (Losfeld, 1968)
   STORY: Jodelle and Pravda are **Barbarella**-like super female agents fighting tyrants in a pop-art future where Roman Empire-like fashions cohabit with advanced technology.

Johan/Johan et Pirlouit/Les Schtroumpfs
Johan/Johan & Pirlouit

(genre stories only)
WRI/ART: **Peyo**.

2. *Le Maître de Roucy-beuf [The Master of Roucy-boeuf]* (Dup., 1954)

3. *Le Lutin du Bois aux Roches [The Goblin of Rocky Glade]* (Dup., 1955)

4. *La Pierre de Lune [The Moonstone]* (Dup., 1956)

6. *La Source des Dieux [The Spring of the Gods]* (Dup., 1957)

9. *La Flute à Six Schtroumpfs [The Flute with Six Smurfs]* (Dup., 1960)

10. *La Guerre des Sept Fontaines [The War of the Seven Fountains]* (Dup., 1961)

12. *Le Pays Maudit [The Accursed Land]* (Dup., 1964)

13. *Le Sortilège de Maltrochu [The Spell of Maltrochu]* (Dup., 1970)
    WRI: Thierry Culliford, Yvan **Delporte**; ART: Alain Maury

14. *La Horde du Corbeau [The Crow's Horde]* (Lom., 1994)

15. *Les Troubadours de Roc-à-Pic [The Troubadours of Edge-Rock]* (Lom., 1997)
    STORY: Johan and Pirlouit (in English: PeeWee) are two medieval squires who become involved in a variety of mostly fantastic adventures, involving wizards, dragons, etc.
    NOTE: **Johan** was originally serialized in *La Dernière Heure* in 1946, *Le Soir* in 1950, then in *Spirou* in 1954. **Pirlouit** first appeared in ep. 3. The **Smurfs** first appeared in ep. 9 (originally serialized in 1958), which was then turned into an animated feature film (see Chapter IV). They later guest-starred in eps. 10, 12, and 13. After **Peyo**'s death in 1992, the series was revived by his son, Thierry Culliford.

Les Schtroumpfs [The Smurfs]

WRI: Yvan **Delporte**; ART: **Peyo**.

1. *Les Schtroumpfs Noirs [The Black Smurfs]* (Dup., 1963; transl.)

2. *Le Schtroumpfissime [The Smurfissimo]* (Dup., 1965; transl. as *King Smurf*)

3. *La Schtroumpfette [The Smurfette]* (Dup., 1967)

4. *L'Oeuf et les Schtroumpfs [The Egg and the Smurfs]* (Dup., 1968)

5. *Les Schtroumpfs et le Cracoucass [The Smurfs and the Cracoucass]* (Dup., 1969)

6. *Le Cosmoschtroumpf [The Astrosmurf]* (Dup., 1970)

7. *L'Apprenti Schtroumpf [The Apprentice Smurf]* (Dup., 1971)

8. *Histoires de Schtroumpfs [Smurf Tales]* (Dup., 1972)

9. *Schtroumpf Vert et Vert Schtroumpf [Smurf Green and Green Smurf]* (Dup., 1973)

10. *La Soupe aux Schtroumpfs [Smurf Soup]* (Dup., 1976)

11. *Les Schtroumpfs Olympiques [The Olympic Smurfs]* (Dup., 1983)

12. *Le Bébé Schtroumpf [Baby Smurfs]* (Dup., 1984)

13. *Les P'tits Schtroumpfs [The L'il Smurfs]* (Dup., 1988)

14. *L'Aéroschtroumpf* (Cartoon, 1990)

15. *L'Étrange Réveil du Schtroumpf Paresseux [The Strange Awakening of Lazy Smurf]* (Cartoon, 1991)

16. *Le Schtroumpf Financier [Finance Smurf]* (Lom., 1992)

WRI: Thierry Culliford, L. Parthoens; ART: Alain Maury.

17. *Le Schtroumpfeur de Bijoux [Jewel Smurf]* (Lom., 1995)

18. *Docteur Schtroumpf [Doctor Smurf]* (Lom., 1996)
    STORY: The entire world is now familiar with the little blue elves who live in mushroom houses and are constantly plagued by the evil wizard Gargamel and his cat Azrael.
    NOTE: After being introduced in **Johan et Pirlouit**, the **Smurfs** first starred in booklet-sized stories in *Spirou* (1959-1962), before eventually being given full-size treatment. Eps. 1 and 4 consist of small-sized stories redrawn for the larger format. They were the subject of two cartoon series, a short-lived Belgian one in the 1960s and the world-famous Hanna-Barbera series in the 1980s (see Chapter IV).

John Difool see ***L'Incal***

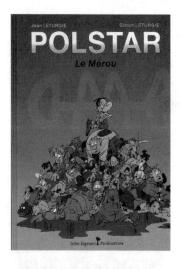

John Eigrutel

WRI: Jean Léturgie; ART: Simon Léturgie.

1. *Le Contrat Polstar [The Polstar Contract]* (Eigrutel, 1996)

2. *Le Contrat Bob Steel [The Bob Steel Contract]* (Eigrutel, 1996)

STORY: Science fiction adventures in a futuristic world.

John Watercolor see ***Moebius***

La Jonque Fantôme Vue de l'Orchestre [The Phantom Junk as Seen from the Orchestra] (Cast., 1981)

WRI/ART: Jean-Claude **Forest.**

STORY: A boy encounters a magician who opens doorways to other dimensions.

Jordan see ***Deux Horizons (Le Cycle des)***

Jordan

WRI: Patrice **Cadot**; ART: P. Richelle.

1. *Les Statues Englouties [The Sunken Statues]* (Lom., 1990)

2. *Les Mannequins de Cire [The Wax Mannequins]* (Lom., 1990)

STORY: Gothic fantasy.

Julius Corentin Acquefacques

WRI/ART: Marc-Antoine Mathieu.

1. *L'Origine [The Origins]* (Delc., 1990)

2. *La Qu...* (Delc., 1991)

3. *Le Processus [The Process]* (Delc., 1993)

4. *L'Épaisseur du Miroir [The Thickness of the Mirror]* (Delc., 1995)

STORY: A Kafkaesque universe discovers that it is part of a comic-book story.

Les Jumeaux Magiques [The Magical Twins] (Hachette, 1987)

WRI: Alexandro **Jodorowsky**; ART: Georges Bess.

STORY: Heroic fantasy.

NOTE: Georges Bess is an expatriate American artist, working primarily in French comics.

Kabur

WRI: Claude-Jacques Legrand; ART: Luciano Bernasconi.

1. *La Saga de Kabur [The Saga of Kabur]* (1975)

2. *L'Exil [The Exile]* (1976)

3. *La Cité des Araignées [The City of Spiders]* (1976)

4. *Les Jeux de Lorgash [The Games of Lorgash]* (1976)

5. *Moloch* (1976)

STORY: Conan-like hero.

NOTE: Five eps. originally serialized in *Kabur* (Ed. Lug.); not collected in the graphic novel format. Luciano Bernasconi is an Italian artist.

Karen Springwell

WRI: Thierry Smolderen; ART: Philippe **Gauckler.**

1. *Convoi [Convoy]* (Hum., 1990)

2. *Les Prisonniers de Convoi [The Prisoners of Convoy]* (Hum., 1991)

3. *Les Joueurs de Convoi [The Players of Convoy]* (Hum., 1993)

4. *Le Ciel de Convoi [The Skies of Convoy]* (Hum., 1995)

STORY: In 2069, against the background of the VR universe *Convoy*, heroine Karen Springwell and space colonies agent Cho Jen expose a planet-wide conspiracy led by the Earth President.

Karga, le 7ème Univers [Karga, 7th Universe]
 Bédéscope, 1979)
   WRI: Henri **Vernes**; ART: André Beautemps.
   STORY: Heroic fantasy.
   NOTE: Henri **Vernes** is the author of the juvenile science fiction series **Bob Morane**.

Kaza le Martien [Kaza the Martian]
   WRI/ART: **Kline**.
   STORY: Kaza, Prince of Mars, is overthrown by the tyrant Agold. He and three Earthmen fight for justice and freedom on the Red Planet.
   NOTE: Originally serialized in *OK Magazine* in 1946-1948.

Kéos
   WRI: Jacques **Martin**; ART: Jean **Pleyers**.

1. *Osiris* (Bagheera, 1992)

2. *Le Cobra* (Helyode, 1993)
   STORY: Tales of magic in ancient Egypt.

Khéna et Le Scrameustache see *Le Scrameustache*

Kim Devil
   WRI: Jean-Michel **Charlier**; ART: Gérald **Forton**.

1. *La Cité Perdue [The Lost City]* (Dup., 1955)

2. *Le Peuple en Dehors du Temps [The People from Outside of Time]* (Dup., 1955)

3. *Le Monde Disparu [The Vanished World]* (Dup., 1957)

4. *Le Mystère du Dieu Blanc [The Mystery of the White God]* (Dup., 1957)
   STORY: An intrepid explorer discovers lost civilizations in the Amazonian jungle.
   NOTE: Originally serialized in *Spirou* in 1953.

Kookaburra
   WRI/ART: **Crisse**.

1. *Planète Dakoi* (Sol., 1996)
   STORY: Science fiction.

Korrigan
   WRI: **Vicq**; ART: **Franz**

1. *Korrigan* (Chlorophylle, 1980)
   STORY: Humorous fantasy.
   NOTE: Originally serialized in *Tintin* from 1970 to 1975.

Krane le Guerrier [Krane the Warrior]
   WRI: Jean-Pierre Gourmelen; ART: Lionel Bret.

1. *Krane le Guerrier [Krane the Warrior]* (Dar., 1982)

   WRI: Jean-Pierre Gourmelen; ART: Marco Patrito.

2. *Le Complot Androïde [The Android Conpiracy]* (Dar., 1986)

3. *La Septième Galaxie [The 7th Galaxy]* (Sol., 1993)
   STORY: In the year 5025, a retired space soldier is forced to reenlist to fight an evil space pirate.
   NOTE: Originally serialized in *Charlie* in 1980.

Kris Kool see *Caza*

Kronos
   WRI: Henri Filippini; ART: Pierre **Dupuis**.

1. *Kronos* (Dar., 1980)

2. *Objectif Kronos* (Dar., 1981)
   STORY: Space opera.

Kronos
   WRI/ART: Jean-Yves **Mitton**.
   In Titans:

115-117. *Noces Mortelles [Deadly Nuptials]* (1988)

118-120. *La Malédiction d'Olphir [The Curse of Olphir]* (1988)
   STORY: Kronos is, in reality, an alien named Zaar who has been hiding on Earth for thousands of years to escape from his people.
   NOTE: Originally serialized in *Titans* (Ed. Lug); never collected in the graphic novel format.

Les Krostons
   WRI: Paul **Deliège**; ART: Arthur Piroton, Paul **Deliège**.

1. *La Menace des Krostons [The Threat of the Krostons]* (Dup., 1972)

   WRI/ART: Paul **Deliège**.

2. *Ballade pour un Kroston [Ballad for a Kroston]* (Dup., 1975)

3. *La Maison des Mutants [The House of Mutants]* (Dup., 1979)

4. *La Vie de Château [Life at the Castle]* (Dup., 1982)

5. *L'Héritier [The Heir]* (Dup., 1984)
   STORY: The Krostons are three little, evil, yet incompetent, green-skinned gnomes who have the power to travel between the second dimension (existing as drawings) and the third. They seek to take over the world but their plans always backfire.
   NOTE: Originally serialized in *Spirou* in 1968. In the first story, the Krostons appeared under the pen of a comic-artist (drawn realistically by Piroton).

Labyrinthes [Labyrinths]
   WRI: Serge **Le Tendre**; ART: Pendanx.

1. *Le Dieu Qui Souffre [The Suffering God]* (Glé., 1993)

2. *La Mort Qui Marche [The Walking Death]* (Glé., 1995)

3. *Agwe Wedo* (Glé., 1996)

STORY: The adventures of a team of spiritualists in the early days of the 20th century.

Lailah see ***Caza***

Laïyna

WRI: Pierre **Dubois**; ART: René **Hausman**.

1. *La Forteresse de Pierre [The Stone Fortress]* (Dup., 1986)

2. *Le Crépuscule des Elfes [The Twilight of the Elves]* (Dup., 1988)

STORY: A human child is raised by elves in a Tolkien-like universe.

Le Lama Blanc [The White Lama]

WRI: Alexandro **Jodorowsky**; ART: George Bess.

1. *Le Lama Blanc [The White Lama]* (Hum., 1988)

2. *La Seconde Vue [The Second Sight]* (Hum., 1988)

3. *Les Trois Oreilles [The Three Ears]* (Hum., 1989)

4. *La Quatrième Voix [The Fourth Voice]* (Hum., 1991)

5. *Main Fermée, Main Ouverte [Open Hand, Closed Hand]* (Hum., 1992)

6. *Triangle d'Eau, Triange de Feu [Water Triangle, Fire Triangle]* (Hum., 1995)

STORY: A white woman's child is raised in Tibet and is chosen of become the vessel of the reincarnation of the Great Lama.

NOTE: George Bess is an expatriate American artist, working primarily in French comics.

Lanfeust de Troy

WRI: Scotch Arleston (Christophe Pelinq); ART: Didier Tarquin.

1. *L'Ivoire du Magohamoth [The Ivory of the Magohamoth]* (Sol., 1994)

2. *Thanos l'Incongru [Thanos the Incongruous]* (Sol., 1995)

3. *Castel Or Azur [Castle Gold Azure]* (Sol., 1995)

4. *Le Paladin d'Eckmul [The Paladin of Eckmul]* (Sol., 1996)

Related Works:
Histoires Trolles [Troll Story]

1. *Troll de Troy* (Sol., 1996)

STORY: In the fantasy world of Troy, everyone is gifted with a magical power. Young Lanfeust, old wizard Nicolède, and his two beautiful daughters leave their village to seek the secret of Lanfeust's powers.

Larry Cannon

WRI: Claude-Jacques Legrand; ART: Annibale Casabianca (19-21, 24-25, 28-30); Yves Chantereau (22-23, 26-27).

STORY: An insurance investigator fights alien parasites who have the power to control minds.

NOTE: Eleven eps. originally serialized in *Futura*, Nos. 19-30 (Ed. Lug, 1973-75); not collected in the graphic novel format. Annibale Casabianca is an Italian artist.

Les Leçons du Prof. Bourremou see ***Boucq***

Lefranc

WRI/ART: Jacques **Martin**.

1. *La Grande Menace [The Great Threat]* (Lom., 1954)

2. *L'Ouragan de Feu [The Fire Storm]* (Lom., 1961)

3. *Le Mystère Borg [The Borg Mystery]* (Cast., 1965)

WRI: Jacques **Martin**; ART: Bob **De Moor**.
4. *Le Repaire du Loup [The Wolf's Lair]* (Cast., 1974)

WRI: Jacques **Martin**; ART: Gilles Chaillet.
5. *Les Portes de l'Enfer [The Gates of Hell]* (Cast., 1978)

6. *Opération Thor* (Cast., 1979)

7. *L'Oasis* (Cast., 1981)

8. *L'Arme Absolue [The Absolute Weapon]* (Cast., 1982)

9. *La Crypte [The Crypt]* (Cast., 1984)

10. *L'Apocalypse* (Cast., 1987)

11. *La Cible [The Target]* (Cast., 1989)

STORY: Free-lance reporter Lefranc and teenager Jean-Jean thwart the megalomaniacal schemes of would-be world conqueror Axel Borg.

NOTE: Originally serialized in *Tintin* in 1952.

La Légende de Kynan [The Legend of Kynan] (Lom., 1993)

WRI: Jean-Luc Sala; ART: Henri-Joseph Reculé.

STORY: The confrontation between the last Celtic King and Arthur, the first Christian one.

Légendes d'Aujourd'hui [Modern Legends]

WRI: Pierre **Christin**; ART: Jacques **Tardi**.

1. *Rumeurs sur le Rouergue [Rumors Over the Rouergue]* (Futuropolis, 1976)

WRI: Pierre **Christin**; ART: Enki **Bilal**.
2. *La Croisière des Oubliés [The Cruise of the Forgotten Ones]* (Dar., 1975; transl. as *The Voyage of Those Forgotten, Heavy Metal*)

3. *Le Vaisseau de Pierre [The Stone Vessel]* (Dar., 1976; transl. as *Progress, Heavy Metal*)

4. *La Ville Qui N'existait pas [The Town That Didn't Exist]* (Dar., 1977; transl. Catalan)

5. *Les Phalanges de l'Ordre Noir [The Phalanxes of the Black Order]* (Dar., 1979; transl. as *The Ranks of the Black Order*, Catalan)

6. *Partie de Chasse [The Hunting Party]* (Dar., 1983; rep. Hum., with additional material, 1990; transl. Catalan)

STORY: This is not, strictly speaking, a series but a very loosely connected number of graphic novels devoted to the political and ecological changes of our society. A mysterious white-haired, dark-eyed, nameless character appears to be the only link between these books.

NOTE: The early stories were originally serialized in *Pilote*, starting in 1972.

Légendes de l'Éclatée aka La Planète Oubliée [Legends of the Scattered aka The Forgotten Planet]

(Kesselring, 1979; Rep. Cygne, 1983)
WRI: **Rodolphe**; ART: Michel **Rouge**.
STORY: Space opera.

Légendes des Contrées Oubliées [Legends of the forgotten Lands]

WRI: Bruno Chevalier; ART: Thierry Ségur.

1. *La Saison des Cendres [The Season of Ashes]* (Delc., 1987)

2. *Le Pays des Songes [The Dream Country]* (Delc., 1989)

3. *Le Sang des Rois [The Blood of Kings]* (Delc., 1992)
STORY: Heroic fantasy.

Leonid Beaudragon

WRI: Jean-Claude **Forest**; ART: Didier **Savard**.

1. *Le Fantôme du Mandchou Fou [The Ghost of the Mad Manchu]* (Bayard, 1986)

2. *La Nuit des Totems [The Night of the Totems]* (Hum., 1990)

3. *Le Scaphandrier du Lundi [The Monday Deep-Sea Diver]* (Hum., 1992)
STORY: Leonid Beaudragon and his faithful assistant Sonia-Solange solve a series of comical supernatural mysteries.

Lettre aux Survivants [Letter to the Survivors] (AM, 1982)
WRI/ART: **Gébé**.
STORY: Social satire.

Le Lièvre de Mars [The Mars Hare]

WRI: Patrick **Cothias**; ART: Antonio Parras.

1. *Vol. 1* (Glé., 1993)

2. *Vol. 2* (Glé., 1994)

3. *Vol. 3* (Glé., 1995)

4. *Vol. 4* (Glé., 1996)
STORY: A man who claims to have been on a secret mission to Mars (and indeed was) has become the target of mysterious assassins.

NOTE: Antonio Parras is a Spanish artist.

Little Nemo

WRI: **Moebius**; ART: Bruno Marchand, based on the character created by Winsor McCay.

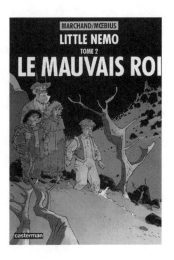

1. *Le Bon Roi [The Good King]* (Cast., 1994)

2. *Le Mauvais Roi [The Bad King]* (Cast., 1995)
STORY: A retelling of the classic adventures of Little Nemo; this time, Nemo protects the Good King of Slumberland and his pretty daughter from the evil Nightmare King.

Lone Sloane

WRI/ART: Philippe **Druillet**.

1. *Le Mystère des Abîmes [The Mystery of the Abyss]* (Losfeld, 1966; rep. Hum., 1977)

2. *Les Six Voyages de Lone Sloane [The Six Voyages of Lone Sloane]* (Dar., 1972; transl. Dark Horse/NBM)

3. *Delirius* (WRI: Jacques **Lob**) (Dar., 1973; transl. Dark Horse/NBM)

4. *Gail* (Hum., 1978)

5. *Salammbo* (Dar., 1981)

6. *Carthago* (Dar., 1982)

7. *Matho* (Dar., 1986)

STORY: Grandiose space opera on a Lovecraftian scale featuring the adventures of a space pirate who deals with dark gods and other-dimensional forces.

NOTE: Eps. 2 and 3 were originally serialized in *Pilote*, starting in 1970. Ep. 4 was serialized in *Métal Hurlant*. Eps. 5-7 adapt of Gustave **Flaubert**'s fantasy epic, *Salammbo* (see Chapter I for a film adaptation), with Lone Sloane retroactively implanted in the story.

The Long Tomorrow see *Moebius*

Los Angeles see *Bilal*

Louison Cresson

WRI/ART: L. **Becker**.

1. *La Nuit des Fantômes [The Night of the Ghosts]* (Dup., 1991)

2. *La Ferme du Fou [The Madman's Farm]* (Dup., 1991)

3. *Le Machin Venu de l'Espace [The Thingy from Outer Space]* (Dup., 1992)

4. *Le Train Fantôme [The Ghost Train]* (Dup., 1993)

5. *Le Rock de la Pastèque [The Watermelon Rock]* (Dup., 1995)

STORY: Comical adventures featuring mad computers, ghostly monks, ETs, etc.

Les Loups [The Wolves] (Cygne, 1982)
WRI/ART: Michel Riu.
STORY: Fantastic tales about wolves.

Lova

WRI/ART: Jean-Claude Servais.

1. *Vol. 1* (Dup., 1992)

2. *Vol. 2* (Dup., 1993)

STORY: Fantasy. The story of a female wolf-child.

Luc Orient

WRI: **Greg**; ART: Eddy **Paape**.

1. *Le Dragon de Feu [The Dragon of Fire]* (Lom., 1969)

2. *Les Soleils de Glace [The Suns of Ice]* (Lom., 1970)

3. *Le Maitre de Terango [The Master of Terango]* (Lom., 1971)

4. *La Planète de l'Angoisse [The Planet of Terror]* (Lom., 1972)

5. *La Forêt d'Acier [The Forest of Steel]* (Lom., 1973)

6. *Le Secret des 7 Lumières [The Secret of the 7 Lights]* (Lom., 1974)

7. *Le Cratère aux Sortilèges [The Crater of Spells]* (Lom., 1974)

8. *La Légion des Anges Maudits [The Legion of the Fallen Angels]* (Lom., 1975)

9. *24 Heures pour la Planète Terre [24 Hours for Planet Earth]* (Lom., 1975)

10. *Le 6ème Continent [The Sixth Continent]* (Lom., 1976)

11. *La Vallée des Eaux Troubles [The Valley of Murky Waters]* (Lom., 1976)

12. *La Porte de Cristal [The Crystal Gate]* (Lom., 1977)

13. *L'Enclume de la Foudre [The Anvil of Thunder]* (Lom., 1978)

14. *Le Rivage de la Fureur [The Shores of Wrath]* (Lom., 1981)

15. *Roubak, Ultime Espoir [Rubak: Ultimate Hope]* (Lom., 1984)

16. *Caragal* (Lom., 1985)

17. *Les Spores de Nulle Part [The Spores from Nowhere]* (Lom., 1990)

18. *Rendez-Vous à 20 Heures en Enfer [Rendezvous at 20:00 in Hell]* (Lom., 1994)

STORY: Luc Orient, his mentor Prof. Hugo Kala, and his girlfriend Lora rescue aliens from the planet Terango, stranded on Earth. They then travel to Terango to thwart the evil tyrant Sectan (eps. 1-5). Subsequent adventures involve a series of scientific mysteries. The characters eventually return to Terango in ep. 14.

NOTE: Originally serialized in *Tintin* in 1966.

Luce

WRI: Toff; ART: Behe.

1. *Luce* (VdO., 1992)

2. *Double Je [Double I]* (VdO., 1993)
STORY: In 2012, religious fundamentalists rule Europe.

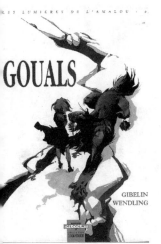

Les Lumières de l'Amalou [The Lights of the Amalou]

WRI: Christophe Gibelin; ART: Claire Wendling.

1. *Théo* (Delc., 1990)

2. *Le Pantin [The Puppet]* (Delc., 1991)

3. *Le Village Tordu [The Twisted Village]* (Delc., 1992)

4. *Gouals* (Delc., 1994)

5. *Cendres [Ashes]* (Delc., 1996)
STORY: Two races of little creatures, the weasel-like Furets and the "Transparent Ones" co-habit in uneasy peace, until they are forced to flee their land to seek the mystic Great Oak.

Les Lutins [The Goblins]

WRI: Pierre **Dubois**; ART: S. Duval.

1. *Bonnie Tom 1* (Delc., 1993)

2. *Bonnie Tom 2* (Delc., 1994)

3. *Puckwood Génies 1* (Delc., 1995)

4. *Puckwood Génies 2* (Delc., 1996)
STORY: In 19th-century England, highwayman Bonnie Tom is going to be hanged unless he is rescued by the elves.

Mac Gallan

WRI/ART: Pierre **Dupuis**.

1. *Les Pirates de l'Infini [The Pirates of Infinity]* (1950; rep. Glé., 1977)
STORY/NOTE: Space opera, originally published in digest-size in *Zorro*.

Les Machinistes (Hum., 1984)

WRI: Claude **Renard**; ART: François **Schuiten**, based on the film *Gwendolin*.

STORY: Techno-fantasy with bondage elements based on the movie starring Gwendolin, John Willie's famous soft-core bondage British comic strip character.

Made in L.A. see **Moebius**

Le Mage Acrylic see **Druillet**

Magellan see **Mr. Magellan**

Magic Palace Hotel see **Fred**

Les Magiciens d'Osinor [The Wizards of Osinor]

WRI/ART: Guérin.

1. *Le Voleur de Grimoires [The Grimoir Thief]* (Sol., 1991)
STORY: Heroic fantasy.

La Main Verte [The Green Hand] (Hum., 1978)

WRI: Zhâ; ART: Nicole **Claveloux**.
STORY: Science fiction.

La Maison où Rêvent les Arbres see **Comès**

Le Maître des Brumes [The Mist Master]

WRI: Jean **Dufaux**; ART: **Éric**.

1. *La Route vers Glimrock [The Road to Glimrock]* (Glé., 1987)

2. *La Prière des Charognards [The Prayer of the Carrion-Eaters]* (Glé., 1988)

3. *La Peste d'Oar [The Plague of Oar]* (Glé., 1989)
STORY: Heroic fantasy.

Les Maîtres Cartographes [The Master Mapmakers]

WRI: Scotch Arleston (Christophe Pelinq); ART: Paul Glaudel.

1. *Le Monde de la Cité [The World of the City]* (Sol., 1992)

2. *Le Glyphe du Bouffon [The Jester's Glyph]* (Sol., 1992)

3. *Les Tours du Floovant [The Towers of Floovant]* (Sol., 1994)

4. *Le Second Fragment [The Second Fragment]* (Sol., 1996)
STORY: Heroic fantasy.

Les Maîtres du Temps see **Moebius**

Major Fatal see *Le Garage Hermétique*

La Malédiction des 7 Boules Vertes [The Curse of the 7 Green Balls]

WRI/ART: Laurent Parcelier

1. *Le Voyageur Imprudent [The Careless Traveler]* (Cast., 1988)

2. *Le Magicien [The Wizard]* (Cast., 1988)

3. *La Poursuite [The Pursuit]* (Cast., 1989)

4. *La Chasse au Dragon [The Dragon's Hunt]* (Cast., 1990)

5. *Le Rire de la Sorcière [The Witch's Laugh]* (Cast., 1991)

6. *Le Lutin Farceur [The Joking Goblin]* (Cast., 1993)
STORY: Juvenile fantasy.
NOTE: Ep. 6 features the same characters but is not part of the series' regular continuity.

Malheig
WRI/ART: Stalner.

1. *Que Rien ne Meure [Let Nothing Die]* (Dar., 1995)

2. *Le Souffle du Dragon [The Dragon's Breath]* (Dar., 1996)

3. *L'Oeil de Wedal [The Eye of Wedal]* (Dar., 1997)
STORY: Heroic fantasy in medieval Scotland.

Les Malices de Plick et Plock [The Tricks of Plick and Plock] (Petit Français, 1904)
WRI/ART: **Christophe**.
STORY: The comical adventures of two small gnomes.

Mallet, Patrick
Xing et Xot
Six mini-books stories, *Spirou* (Dup., 1960–63)

Pegg le Robot

1. *Pegg en Amazonie [Pegg in the Amazon]* (Dup., 1960)

2. *La Tiare de Chouboul-Toukroum [The Tiara of Chouboul-Toukroum]* (Dup., 1962)

3. *Les Malheurs de Pegg [Pegg's Misfortunes]* (Dup., 1965)
NOTE: Some *Pegg* stories written by **Vicq**.

Zoum le Martien
Nineteen 6-page stories, *Pilote* (Dar., 1965-70)

Related Works:
Cherchez le Martien [Seek the Martian] (Dar., 1973)
Le Petit Monde de Pat Mallet [Pat Mallet's Little World] (Dar., 1975)
Les Petits Hommes Verts [The Little Green Men] (Denoël, 1976)
En Vert et Contre Tous [Green and All] (Eurédif, 1984)
Les Petits Hommes Verts Envahissent la Terre [The Little Green Men Invade Earth] (Glé., 1983)
STORY: Xing, Xot, and Zoum and other unnamed Little

Green Men are inept but funny martians who have various misadventures on Earth. Pegg is an intelligent but unlucky little robot, who shares the same universe as Xing and Xot.

La Malvenue [The Illcome]
WRI: Claude **Seignolle**; ART: B. Loisel.

1. *La Malvenue [The Illcome]* (Création, 1986)

2. *Malédiction [Curses]* (Magic-Strip, 1988)
STORY: Adaptation of Claude **Seignolle**'s gothic horror novel about an evil house (see Chapters I and II for film and television adaptations).

Les Mange-Bitume [The Tar Eaters] (Dar., 1974)
WRI: Jacques **Lob**; ART: Jose Bielsa.
STORY: Tales of a future society where everyone lives in cars.
NOTE: Jose Bielsa is a Spanish artist.

Mangecoeur [Heart-Eater]
WRI: Mathieu Gallié; ART: Jean-Baptiste Andreae.

1. *La Chrysalide Diaprée [The Diapered Chrysalis]* (VdO., 1993)

2. *Dans le Jeu des Miroirs [In the Game of Mirrors]* (VdO., 1995)

3. *Le Rêve d'Argemme [The Dream of Argemme]* (VdO., 1996)
STORY: Fantasy.

Manuel, l'Enfant-Rêve see **Druillet**

Le Manu-Manu see **Fred**

Marc Mathieu
WRI/ART: Dominique **Hé**.

1-2. *Le Faucon de Mû [The Hawk of Mu]* (Hum., 1981)

3. *L'Empreinte du Minotaure [The Mark of the Minotaur]* (Hum., 1983)

4. *Le Testament du Dieu Chac [The Testament of the God Chac]* (Hum., 1984)

5. *Le Signe de Shiva [The Sign of Shiva]* (Hum., 1985)

6. *Le Retour de Tangata Manu [The Return of Tangata Manu]* (Hum., 1987)

STORY: An archeologist unearths lost civilizations and forgotten monsters.

NOTE: Originally serialized in *Métal Hurlant* in 1980.

Le Marchand de Temps [The Time Merchant]
WRI: Éric Corbeyran; ART: Chaye.

1. *Procès [Trial]* (Sol., 1992)

2. *Chimères [Chimera]* (Sol., 1993)

3. *Enfers [Hells]* (Sol., 1994)
STORY: Heroic fantasy about a gun merchant in the 13th century.

Le Marchand d'Idées [The Merchant of Ideas]
WRI/ART: Philippe **Berthet** & Antonio Cossu.

1. *Le Marchand d'Idées [The Merchant of Ideas]* (Glé., 1982)

2. *Caron des Glaces [Caron of the Ice]* (Glé., 1984)

3. *Les Naufragés de Lorelei [The Lorelei Castaways]* (Glé., 1985)

4. *Le Semeur d'Étoiles [The Star Sower]* (Glé, 1988)
STORY: A man from the future tries to save mankind.

NOTE: Originally serialized in *Circus* in 1982. Antonio Cossu is an Italian artist working primarily in French comics.

La Mare aux Pirates see *Masse*

Marie la Noire [Black Mary]
WRI: **Rodolphe**; ART: Florence Magnin.

1. *Les Trépassés [The Trespassed]* (Dar., 1995)

2. *Les Autres Mondes [The Other Worlds]* (Dar., 1996)

3. *La Passe de l'Au-Delà [The Passage Beyond]* (Dar., 1997)
STORY: In an alternate 18th-century England, the dead come back to life.

Le Marsupilami see *Spirou*

Martin Milan
WRI/ART: Christian **Godard**.

A1/B9. Destination Guet-Apens [Destination Ambush] (Dar., 1971)

A2/B11. Églantine de Ma Jeunesse [Eglantine of My Youth] (Dar., 1972)

A3/B2. Les Clochards de la Jungle [The Tramps of the Jungle] (Dar., 1973)

A4/B4. L'Émir aux Sept Bédouins [The Emir with Seven Beduins] (Dar., 1974)

A5/B8. Les Hommes de la Boue [The Mud Men] (Dar., 1975)

B1. Mille Ans pour une Agonie [A Thousand Years for an Agony] (Dar., 1978)

B3. Adeline au Bout de la Nuit [Adeline at the End of Night] (Dar., 1979)

B5. L'Enfant a la Horde [The Horde Child] (Dar., 1981)

B6. Il S'appellait Jérôme [His Name Was Jerome] (Dar., 1982)

B7. Une Ombre Est Passée [A Shadow Passed] (Dar., 1982)

B10. L'Ange et le Surdoué [The Angel and the Gifted Kid] (Dar., 1985)

B12. Le Cocon du Désert [The Desert Cocoon] (Dar., 1996)

B13. La Goule et le Biologiste [The Ghoul and the Biologist] (Dar., 1997)
STORY: The bittersweet adventures of a pilot of a taxi plane. Numerous genre elements: ghosts, aliens, mad scientists, etc.

NOTE: Originally serialized in *Tintin* in 1967. Two series of graphic novels were published (A and B), with different numberings.

Masse, Francis
Masse (Fromage, 1976)
Mémoires d'Outre-Terre [Memories from Beyond Earth] (Aud., 1977)
Encyclopédie (2 vols.) (Hum., 1982)
On M'Appelle l'Avalanche [They Call Me Avalanche] (Hum., 1983)
Les Dessoux de la Ville [The Undercity] (Hoebecke, 1985)
Les Deux du Balcon [Two on the Balcony] (Cast., 1985)
La Mare aux Pirates [The Pirates' Pond] (Cast., 1987)
STORY/NOTE: Black-humored, surreal stories (some were translated in *Heavy Metal*).

Master Volume
WRI/ART: Siro.

1. *Master Volume* (Zen., 1992)

2. *Show Time* (Zen., 1994)
STORY: Punk rock super-hero fantasy.

Le Matin des Suaires Brûlés [The Morning of the Burnt Shrouds]
WRI: Gary Lukinburg (Yann Cherrier); ART: Patrick Tandiang.

1. Celui Qui Cherche [He Who Seeks] (Sol., 1995)

2. Souffle des Légendes [Breath of Legends] (Sol., 1996)
STORY: Gothic horror.

Matricule 4500
WRI: Jean-Pierre **Andrevon**; ART: Veronik.

1. Matricule 4500 (Glé., 1982)

2. Neurones Trafic (Glé., 1985)
STORY: Bleak dystopia in a cyberpunk future.
NOTE: Jean-Pierre **Andrevon** is a noted science fiction writer; one of his novels was the basis of the animated feature *Gandahar* (see Chapter IV).

Maya le Sioux
WRI: Unknown; ART: Guy Mouminoux.

1. La Hache de Guerre [The War Hatchet] (1949)

2. La Torture (1949)

3. Les Dieux Parlent [The Gods Speak] (1949)

4. Chasse à l'Homme [Man Hunt] (1949)

5. La Cité Mystérieuse [The Mysterious City] (1949)

6. Combat Décisif [Deciding Battle] (1949)

7. Les Magyors (1949)

8. Le Désert des Ténèbres [The Desert of Darkness] (1949)

9. Course contre la Mort [Death Race] (1949)

10. Vengeance (1949)

11. Héroïque sauvetage [Heroic Rescue] (1949)

12. Le Nain Igsong [Igsong the Dwarf] (1949)

13. Quin-Chin-Ya (1950)

14. Le Pic du Soleil [The Sun Peak] (1950)

15. Les Contrebandiers [The Smugglers] (1950)

16. Guet-Apens [Ambush] (1950)

17. Le Plan d'Attaque [The Attack Plan] (1950)

18. Carcasse (1950)

19. L'Éxécution (1950)

20. Le Vaisseau Fantôme [The Ghost Ship] (1950)

21. L'Épouvante [The Horror] (1950)

22. Chef des Sioux [Chief of the Sioux] (1950)
STORY: A young Indian brave lives through a series of heroic fantasy adventures involving lost civilizations equipped with ray guns and prehistoric monsters.
NOTE: Published in the magazine format by Éd. Elan; never collected in the graphic novel format.

Le Mécano des Étoiles [The Cosmic Mechanic]
(Bayard, 1987)
WRI: Jacques **Lob**; ART: Jean-Pierre **Danard**, François **Pierre**.
STORY: In a future when Earth has colonized the solar system, Charley Delco and Arlette Coudrier fight villains who want to steal the secret of a teleportation device.

Mégalithe
WRI/ART: **Érik**.
STORY: Juvenile adventures of a secret agent in a pseudo-science fiction prehistoric world.
NOTE: Originally serialized in *Record* from 1966 to 1973; never collected in the graphic novel format.

Mégalus—la Planète des Ombres [Megalus—The Planet of Shadows] (Leroy, 1986)
WRI/ART: J. Brunier.
STORY: Space opera.

Melmoth
WRI: **Rodolphe**; ART: Marc Rénier.

1. Sur la Route de Londres [On London Road] (Dar., 1990)

2. Mary Shilling (Dar., 1993)
STORY: Gothic fantasy in 19th century England.

Mélusine
WRI: Gilson; ART: Clarke.

1. Sortilèges [Spells] (Dup., 1995)

2. Le Bal des Vampires [The Vampires' Ball] (Dup., 1995)

3. Inferno (Dup., 1996)
STORY: The humorous adventures of a young witch's apprentice.

La Mémoire Albinos—Le Syndrome des Sorciers [The Albino Memory: The Wizards' Syndrome] (Bédéscope, 1986)
WRI: Alain Streng; ART: Claude **Laverdure**.
STORY: Cyberpunk science fiction.

Mémoire de Sable [Memory of Sand]
WRI/ART: Isabelle Dethan.

1. La Tour du Savoir [The Tower of Knowledge] (Delc., 1993)

2. La Cité-Morgane (Delc., 1994)

3. Lune Noire [Black Moon] (Delc., 1995)
STORY: In a fantasyland, the beautiful Naomi discovers a tower which contains billions of books.

La Mémoire des Celtes [Celtic Memory]
WRI: Jean **Ollivier**; ART: Coelho (Eduardo Texeira).

1. *Les Navigations de Mael Duin [The Journeys of Mael Duin]* (Hachette, 1985)

2. *La Chambre de Cristal [The Crystal Chamber]* (Hachette, 1986)
   STORY: Celtic heroic fantasy.
   NOTE: Coelho is a renowned Portguese artist.

Mémoire des Écumes see **Caza**

La Mémoire du Futur see **Moebius**

Mémoire Vierge [Virgin Memory]
   WRI: Yves Corriger; ART: Nicolas Finet.

1. *Le Chant des Autres [Others' Song]* (Delc., 1992)
   STORY: Six space fugitives, armed with a deadly weapon and protoplasmic matter which can give form to anyone's fantasies, travel from world to world.

Mémoires d'Outre Espace see **Bilal**

Mémoires d'Outre Terre see **Masse**

Memory
   WRI: Patrick **Cothias**; ART: Philippe **Sternis**.

1. *Le Bal des Mandibules [The Ball of the Claws]* (Glé., 1986)

2. *Le Cargo sous la Mer [The Cargo Under the Sea]* (Glé., 1987)

3. *Le Necromobile [The Necromobile]* (Glé., 1988)
   STORY: A Tibetan Lama gathers a team of troubleshooters to thwart the evil Kartel which threatens planet Earth.
   NOTE: Originally serialized in *Circus* in 1985.

Menace Diabolique [Diabolical Menace] (Hum., 1979)
   WRI/ART: Denis Sire.
   STORY: Science fiction satire.

Le Meneur de Chiens [The Pack Leader] (Dar., 1984)
   WRI/ART: Dimitri (Guy Mouminoux).
   STORY: Medieval gothic fantasy.

Messara
   WRI: Philippe Bonifay; ART: Jacques Terpant.

1. *L'Égyptienne [The Egyptian]* (Dar., 1994)

2. *Minos* (Dar., 1995)
   STORY: The heroic fantasy adventures of an Egyptian priestess in Ancient Crete.

Métamorphoses
   WRI/ART: Claude **Renard**, François **Schuiten**.

1. *Aux Médianes de Cymbiolas [The Medians of Cymbiola]* (Hum., 1980)

2. *Le Rail* (Hum., 1982)
   STORY: A series of loosely connected stories which take place in metamorphosing universes, ranging from the desert of Cymbiola to an orbital space station.

Mic Mac Adam
   WRI: Stephen **Desberg**; ART: **Benn**.

1. *Le Tyran de Midnight Cross [The Tyrant of Midnight Cross]* (Dup., 1982)

2. *Morts au Sommet [Death at the Summit]* (Dup., 1985)

3. *Les Mains d'Ivoire [The Hands of Ivory]* (Fleurus, 1987)

4. *Le Bois des Lépreux [The Wood of the Lepers]* (Fleurus, 1987)

5. *Les Cinq Miroirs [The Five Mirrors]* (Fleurus, 1989)
   STORY: Fantasy, humor, and parapsychology.
   NOTE: Originally serialized in *Spirou* in 1981.

Mickey à Travers les Siècles [Mickey Mouse Across the Centuries]
   WRI: Pierre Fallot; ART: Pierre Nicolas.

1. *Mickey chez les Hommes des Cavernes [Mickey Among the Cavemen]* (Hachette, 1970)

2. *Mickey à Babylone [Mickey in Babylon]* (Hachette, 1970)

3. *Mickey et les Travaux d'Hercule [Mickey and the Labors of Hercule]* (Hachette, 1970)

4. *Mickey et Guillaume Tell [Mickey and William Tell]* (Hachette, 1970)

5. *Mickey et Merlin l'Enchanteur [Mickey and Merlin the Wizard]* (Hachette, 1971)

6. *Mickey et le Collier de la Reine [Mickey and the Queen's Necklace]* (Hachette, 1971)

7. *Mickey et le Vrai Comte de Monte-Cristo [Mickey and the Real Count of Monte-Cristo]* (Hachette, 1971)

8. *Mickey Rencontre Henri IV [Mickey Meets Henri IV]* (Hachette, 1971)

9. *Mickey Chez les Peaux-Rouges [Mickey Among the Redskins]* (Hachette, 1972)

10. *Mickey, Écuyer d'Ivanhoe [Mickey, Ivanhoe's Squire]* (Hachette, 1972)

11. *Mickey Corsaire [Mickey Corsair]* (Hachette, 1972)

12. *Mickey, Ami de d'Artagnan [Mickey, d'Artagnan's Friend]* (Hachette, 1978)

13. *Mickey Explore le Temps [Mickey Explores Time]* (Edi-Monde, 1980)

14. *Mickey au Temps des Mousquetaires [Mickey in the Times of the Musketeers]* (Dar., 1991)

15. *Mickey au Temps de Napoléon [Mickey in Napoleon's Times]* (Dar., 1991)

16. *Mickey Découvre l'Amérique [Mickey Discovers America]* (Dar., 1993)

STORY: Thanks to a secret formula created by Prof. Durandus, Walt Disney's Mickey Mouse acquires the power to randomly travel through time when hit upon the head. His subsequent adventures enable him to explore important moments of French history, with rare forays into science fiction.

NOTE: This popular series, made in France for the French readers, was originally serialized one-page a week in *Le Journal de Mickey* (Edi-Monde) from 1952 to 1978.

Mikros, Titan Microscosmique
In Titans:
WRI/ART: Jean-Yves **Mitton**.

35-40. *Voir Venise et Mourir [To See Venice And Die]* (1981-82)

41-43. *Microbios* (1982)

44-46. *Descente aux Enfers [Descent Into Hell]* (1982)

47-49. *Peste Noire [Black Plague]* (1983)

50-52. *Adieux du Troisième Type [Good-Byes of the Third Kind]* (1983)

53. *Pour que Règne le Mal [Let Evil Reign]* (1983)

54-58. *Psi* (1983)

59-61. *Le Beau, La Belle...et les Bites [Handsome, Beauty... And Bytes]* (1984)

62-64. *Destination Néant [Destination Vacuum]* (1984)

65-68. *Psiland* (1984)

69-71. *Piège pour un Insect [Insect Trap]* (1984)

72-74. *Punch* (1985)

75-78. *Outre-Monde [The World Beyond]* (1985)

79-81. *Le Mur de la Lumière [The Light Barrier]* (1985)

82-87. *Passeport pour l'Infini [Passport for Infinity]* (1986)
STORY: Three Harvard entomologists, Mikros, Saltarella,

and Crabb, are mutated into humanoid insects by the alien Svizz, who want to use them to conquer Earth. The characters and one of their arch-enemies, "Psi," return in *Epsilon*.

NOTE: Sixteen eps. originally serialized in *Mustang* (Series II), Nos. 54-70 (Ed. Lug, 1980-81), then the series continued in *Titans*; not collected in the graphic novel format.

Mil see *Cyrrus*

1996
WRI/ART: Chantal **Montellier**.

1. *1996* (Hum., 1978; transl. *Heavy Metal*)

2. *Wonder City* (Hum., 1983)
STORY: The harrowing description of a Fascist future world halfway between *Brave New World* and *THX 1138*.
NOTE: Originally serialized in *Métal Hurlant*.

Mirages see *Druillet*

Le Miroir des Eaux [The Mirror of the Waters] see *Cairn*

Mister X
WRI: André Roger; ART: André Bohan.
First Series:

1. *Les Voleurs d'Or [The Gold Thieves]* (1949)

2. *Le Lac Souterrain [The Underground Lake]* (1949)

3. *Prisonnier! [Prisoner!]* (1949)

4. *Les Robots* (1949)

5. *Le Rayon Fatal [The Deadly Ray]* (1949)

6. *La Cage de Verre [The Glass Cage]* (1950)

7. *Marcalbus le Magicien [Marcalbus the Magician]* (1950)

8. *Le Maître du Mystère [The Master of Mystery]* (1950)

9. *Buddy à la Rescousse [Buddy to the Rescue]* (1950)

10. *La Route des Carvanes [The Caravan Road]* (1950)

11. *Helianas* (1950)

12. *Le Secret de Georginus [The Secret of Georginus]* (1950)

13. *Le Retour de Grisou [The Return of Grisou]* (1950)

14. *Les Guerriers Voilés [The Veiled Warriors]* (1950)

15. *Face aux Monstres [Face-to-Face with the Monsters]* (1950)

16. *Le Docteur Zamos* (1950)

17. *Aventure en Mer [Adventure at Sea]* (1950)

18. *Y23 à l'Oeuvre [Y23 at Work]* (1951)

19. *Noyade Manquée [Unsuccessful Drowning]* (1951)

20. *Étrange Mission [Strange Mission]* (1951)

21. *Les Ennuis de Bill O'Connell [The Troubles of Bill O'Connell]* (1951)

22. *La Planète Inconnue [The Unknown Planet]* (1951)

Second Series:

1. *Le Peuple des Korgs [The People of Korg]* (1951)

2. *L'Île de l'Épouvante [The Island of Terror]* (1951)

3. *Le Maître des Monstres [The Monster Master]* (1951)

4. *Alerte à la Terre [Alert on Earth]* (1951)

5. *La Fin d'une Planète [The End of a Planet]* (1951)

6. *La Cité du Pôle [The Polar City]* (1951)

7. *Dans la Mer de Glace [In the Sea of Ice]* (1951)

8. *Face à la Mort [Face-to-Face with Death]* (1951)

9. *Au Coeur de la Forêt [In the Heart of the Forest]* (1951)

10. *Pablo le Métis* (1951)

STORY: French super-hero.

NOTE: Published in the magazine format by Éd. Elan; never collected in the graphic novel format.

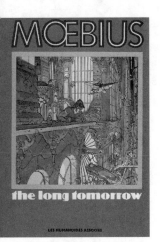

Moebius

John Watercolor (Hum., 1976; rep. as *Les Vacances du Major [The Major's Holidays]*, Hum., 1990; transl. as *The Early Moebius*, Graffiti).

Cauchemar Blanc [White Nightmare] (Hum., 1977; rep. as *La Citadelle Aveugle [The Blind Citadel]*, Hum., 1989; transl. in *Arzach*, Marvel)

L'Homme est-il bon? [Is Man Good?] (Hum., 1977; rep. as *The Long Tomorrow*, Hum., 1989; transl. Marvel)

Les Yeux du Chat [Eyes of the Cat] (WRI: Alexandro **Jodorowsky**) (Hum, 1978; transl. Taboo)

Tueur de Monde [The World Killer] (Hum., 1979; rep. Cast., 1988)

La Déviation [The Detour] (Hum, 1980; rep. as *Escale sur Pharagonescia*, Hum., 1989; transl. as *Pharagonesia*, Marvel)

Moebius 30x30 (Hum., 1980)

Les Maîtres du Temps [The Time Masters] (With René **Laloux**) (Hum., 1982) (comics adaptation of eponymous animated feature film; see Chapter IV)

La Complainte de l'Homme Programmé [The Ballad of the Programmed Man] (Hum., 1982)

La Mémoire du Futur [Memory of the Future] (Gentiane, 1983)

Le Désintégré Réintégré [The Reintegrated Desintegrated Man] (Hum., 1984)

Venise Céleste [Celestial Venice] (Aedena, 1984)

Starwatcher (Aedena, 1986)

Made in L.A. (Cast., 1988)

Chaos (Hum., 1991; transl. Marvel)

Silence On Rêve [Silence, Dreaming] (Cast., 1991)

Chroniques Métalliques (Hum., 1992; transl. as *Metallic Memories*, Marvel)

Fusion (Cast., 1995; trans. Marvel)

STORY: Collections of short stories, for the most part originally published in *Métal Hurlant*.

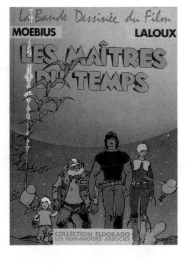

Moi, Epsilon... see Epsilon

Le Moine Fou [The Mad Monk]

WRI/ART: Vink (Vinh Khoa).

1. *Le Moine Fou [The Mad Monk]* (Dar., 1984)

2. *La Mémoire de Pierre [The Memory of Stone]* (Dar., 1985)

3. *Le Brouillard Pourpre [The Purple Mist]* (Dar., 1987)

4. *Le Col du Vent [The Pass of the Winds]* (Dar., 1990)

5. *Le Monastère du Miroir Précieux [The Monastery of the Precious Mirror]* (Dar., 1992)

6. *Les Matins du Serpent [The Mornings of the Serpent]* (Dar., 1993)

7. *Le Tourbillon des Fleurs Blanches [The Whirlpool of the White Flowers]* (Dar., 1994)

8. *Le Voyage de Petit Li [The Journey of Little Li]* (Dar., 1995)

9. *Le Tournoi des Licornes [The Tournament of the Unicorns]* (Dar., 1997)

STORY: In ancient China, a young orphan girl pursues a mad monk gifted with magical powers.

NOTE: Originally serialized in *Charlie* in 1983.

Le Monde d'Arkadi see Arkadi

Le Monde d'Édéna see Édéna

Le Monde du Garage Hermétique see *Le Garage Hermétique*

Les Mondes Engloutis [The Sunken Worlds]
WRI: Wodmark; ART: David Duprez.

1. *Il Faut Sauver Arkadia [We Must Save Arkadia]* (Cast., 1985)

2. *La Cour des Miracles [The Court of Miracles]* (Cast., 1986)

3. *Thot* (Cast., 1986)
STORY: Fantasy.

Monsieur Noir [Mister Dark]
WRI: Duvaux; ART: **Griffo**.

1. *Vol. 1* (Dup., 1994)

2. *Vol. 2* (Dup., 1995)
STORY: Fanny is a guest in the mysterious castle of Blacktales where two strange communities, the Tohus and the Bohus, vie to renew their lease from the castle's mysterious owner, Mister Dark.

Mort à Outrance [Overwhelming Deaths] (VdO., 1995)
WRI: Thomas Mosdi; ART: Guillaume Sorel.
STORY: A collection of fantastic stories.

Mortepierre
WRI: Brice Tarvel; ART: Aoumari.

1. *La Chair et le Souffre [The Flesh and the Sulphur]* (Sol., 1995)
STORY: Heroic fantasy.
NOTE: Brice Tarvel is a pseudonym of science fiction writer François **Sarkel** (see Book 2).

Morte Saison [Dead Season] (Hum., 1979)
WRI: Zhâ; ART: Nicole **Claveloux**.
STORY: Dark science fiction.

Mr. Magellan
WRI: Jean **Van Hamme**; ART: **Geri**.

1. *Mr. Magellan, I.T.O.* (Lom., 1970)

2. *Hold-Up au Vatican [Hold-Up at the Vatican]* (Lom., 1971)
WRI: André-Paul **Ducha-teau**; ART: **Geri**.

3. *Opération Crystal* (Lom., 1972)

4. *L'Ile des Colosses [The Island of the Colossus]* (Lom., 1973)

5. *S.O.S. Tanynka* (Lom., 1975)

6. *La 2ème Mort du Pharaon [The Second Death of the Pharaoh]* (Lom., 1981)

7. *Danger Cosmos* (Lom., 1981)

8. *La Mer à Boire [To Drink the Sea]* (Lom., 1982)
STORY: Mr. Magellan, and his super-strong assistant Capella, work for the International Testing Organisation and fight well-meaning ETs and mad scientists.
NOTE: Originally serialized in *Tintin* in 1969.

Le Mur de Pan [The Wall of Pan]
WRI/ART: Philippe Mouchel.

1. *Mavel Coeur d'Élue [Mavel Chosen Heart]* (Delc., 1995)

2. *La Guerre de l'Aura [The War of the Aura]* (Delc., 1996)
STORY: The Wall of Pan was built eons ago to separate the peaceful lands of Pan from the war-like Doms.

Mustang
WRI: Jack Nolez (Jacques Lennoz); ART: Franco Oneta.
STORY: Native American super-hero.
NOTE: Sixteen eps. originally serialized in *Mustang* (Series II), Nos. 54-61 (Ed. Lug, 1980-81); not collected in the graphic novel format. Franco Oneta is an Italian artist.

Myrtil Fauvette
WRI/ART: Riff Reb.

1. *Parole de Diable... [The Devil's Word]* (Hum., 1990)

2. *Tu Descendras du Ciel [Coming Down from the Sky]* (Hum., 1992)

3. *Mister Clean* (Hum., 1995)
STORY: Myrtil Fauvette fights against the politically correct forces of a world where ecology and cleanliness have become totalitarian values.

Le Mystère de l'Homme aux Trèfles [The Mystery of the Clover Man] (Glé., 1974)

WRI/ART: **Greg**.

STORY: Constant Souci defeats a villain who owes his luck to milk made with four-leaf clover.

NOTE: Originally serialized in *Tintin* in 1966.

Les Mystères de l'Ouest [Wild, Wild West]

WRI: Jean Sanitas; ART: Gérald **Forton**.

1. *Quand l'Enfer se Déchaîne [When Hell Breaks loose]*

2. *La Légion de Fer [The Iron Legion]*

3. *L'Homme Qui ne Respirait pas [The Man Who Did Not Breathe]*

4. *L'Impossible Voleur [The Uncanny Thief]*

5. *Les Hommes sans Visage [The Faceless Men]*

6. *La Lueur Jaune [The Yellow Light]*

7. *L'Étape de l'Épouvante [The Stop of Terror]*

9. *Le Monstre Venu du Passé [The Monster from the Past]*

10. *Le Déluge [The Flood]*

11. *Les Hommes en Conserve [The Men in Cans]*

12. *Le Bruit Silencieux [The Silent Noise]*

13. *Combat avec l'Invisible [Battle with the Invisible Man]*

14. *Le Rocher Attaque [The Rock Attacks]*

15. *Les Monstres du Dr. Burton [Dr. Burton's Monsters]*

16. *Les Mystères de l'Ouest [Wild, Wild West]*

17. *Les Armures Fantômes [The Ghost Armors]*

STORY/NOTE: These were new 12-page stories (not adaptations of television episodes) based on the popular American fantasy western television series. It was originally serialized in *Pif* in 1976-76, then published in *Télé-Junior* in 1978. The series was not collected in the graphic novel format.

Mystérieuse, Matin, Midi et Soir see *Barbarella*

Mythôlogias

WRI: Serge Pradier; ART: Claude Plumial.

1. *L'Ouvrage des Démons [The Work of the Demons]* (Zen., 1995)
STORY: Heroic fantasy.

Nabuchodinosaure

WRI: Herlé; ART: Roger Widenlocher.

1. *Prélude à L'Apeupréhistoire [Prelude to the Semiprehistory]* (Dar., 1991)

2. *Chroniques de l'Apeupréhistoire [Chronicles of the Semiprehistory]* (Dar., 1992)

3. *Du Rififi chez les Sauriens [When Saurians Clash]* (Dar., 1993)

4. *Humo Sapiens* (Dar., 1994)

5. *Commando Reptile Saurien* (Dar., 1995)

6. *Paleolithic Sinfonia* (Dar., 1996)

7. *Panique à Diplodocus-Land* (Dar., 1997)
STORY: Comical adventures of intelligent dinosaurs.

Nahomi

WRI: **Bom**; ART: **Crisse**.

1. *Les Noisettes Magiques [The Magic Hazelnuts]* (Lom., 1985)

2. *La Poudre d'Oubli [The Oblivion Powder]* (Lom., 1986)

3. *La Chanson de Galadrielle [The Song of Galadrielle]* (Lom., 1987)
STORY: Fantastic adventures of a young girl in ancient Japan.

NOTE: Originally serialized in *Tintin* in 1983.

Les Naufragés de l'An 3000 [The Castaways of the Year 3000]

WRI/ART: Fédor.

1. *Les Naufragés de l'An 3000 [The Castaways of the Year 3000]* (1962)

2. *Bienvenue à Cosmonia [Welcome to Cosmonia]* (1962)

3. *Les Chasseurs de Météorites [The Meteor Hunters]* (1962)

4. *La Révolte des Robots [The Revolt of the Robots]* (1962)

5. *Les 4 Coins de l'Impossible [The 4 Corners of the Uncanny]* (1963)

6. *Station BX21* (1963)

7. *Les Habitants de l'Atome [The Dwellers of the Atom]* (1963)
STORY: Space opera in the year 3000.

NOTE: Originally serialized in *Tintin* in 1962-63; never collected in the graphic novel format.

Les Naufragés de l'Espace [The Castaways of Space]

WRI: Raoul **Cauvin**; ART: Guy Counhaye.

STORY: Humor stories about a group of space wanderers.

NOTE: Originally serialized in *Spirou* in 1973; never collected in the graphic novel format.

Les Naufragés du Temps [The Castaways in Time, transl. as *Lost in Time*]

WRI: Jean-Claude **Forest**; ART: Paul **Gillon**.

1. L'Etoile Endormie [The Sleeping Star] (Hachette, 1974)

2. La Mort Sinueuse [The Creeping Death] (Hachette, 1975)

3. Labyrinthes [Labyrinths] (Hachette, 1976; transl. NBM)

4. L'Univers Cannibale [The Cannibal Universe] (Hachette, 1976)

Wri/Art: Paul **Gillon**.

5. Tendre Chimere [Tender Chimera] (Hum., 1977)

6. Les Maitres Reveurs [The Master Dreamers] (Hum., 1978)

7. Le Sceau de Beselek [The Seal of Beselek] (Hum., 1979)

8. Ortho-Mentas (Hum., 1981)

9. Terra (Hum., 1984)

10. Le Cryptomère (Hum., 1989)

STORY: Christopher and Valérie, the last survivors of the 20th century, awake in 2981, a time when Earth is threatened by alien, intelligent rats. They then fight the Tapir, a villain from another universe. Later, they explore new worlds.

NOTE: Originally serialized in *Chouchou* in 1964. Later episodes were serialized in *Métal Hurlant* in 1977.

La Nef des Fous [The Ship of Madmen]
Wri/Art: Turf.

1. Eauxfolles [Crazy Water] (Delc., 1993)

2. Pluvior 627 (Delc., 1994)

3. Turbulences [Troubles] (Delc., 1996)

STORY: In an underwater medieval kingdom ruled by an artificial intelligence, panic reigns when the dome begins to crack.

Neige [Snow]
Wri: Didier **Convard**; Art: Christian **Gine**.

1. Les Brumes Aveugles [The Blind Mist] (Lom., 1987)

2. La Mort-Corbeau [The Raven Death] (Lom., 1988)

3. L'Aube Rouge [The Red Dawn] (Lom., 1989)

4. Intermezzo (Glé., 1991)

5. Il Diavolo (Glé., 1992)

6. Le Pisse-Dieu [The Piss-God] (Glé., 1993)

7. Les Trois Crimes de Judas [The Three Crimes of Judas] (Glé., 1994)

8. La Brèche [The Breach] (Glé., 1995)

9. La Chanson du Muet [The Song of the Dumb Man] (Glé., 1996)

STORY: In the near future, the whole of Europe lives in a state of perpetual winter, trapped behind a force field. Young "Neige" is raised by Northman, one of the twelve "immortals" who created this world and holds the keys to the gates that lead to the world outside.

NOTE: Originally serialized in *Tintin* in 1986.

Nemo see **Little Nemo**

Le Neuvième Jour du Diable see **Les Huit Jours du Diable**

Névrose see **Fleuve Noir**

Nic
Wri/Art: **Hermann**.

1. Hé Nic? Tu rêves? [Hey Nic, Are You Dreaming?] (Dup., 1981)

2. Bonnes Nuits, Nic [Good Night, Nic] (Dup., 1982)

3. Ça C'est Filarmo... Nic [That's Filarmo... Nic] (Dup., 1983)

STORY: Homage to *Little Nemo in Slumberland*.

NOTE: Originally serialized in *Spirou* in 1986.

Nic et Mino
Wri: Claude Dupré; Art: Jean **Ache**.

1. SOS de l'Oncle Octave—Un Appel de l'Antarctique (1958–59)

2. Le Mystère de la Cité Perdue [The Mystery of the Forgotten City] (Edi-Monde, 1962)

3. La Chasse au Vénusien [The Venusian Hunt] (Edi-Monde, 1962)

4. Le Secret de l'île Interdite [The Secret of the Forbidden Island] (Edi-Monde, 1963)

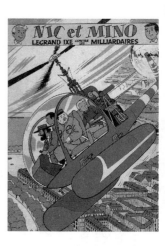

5. *Legrand-Ixe contre les Milliardaires [Legrand-Ixe vs. the Billionaires]* (Edi-Monde, 1964)

6. *Gare aux Sauterelles [Beware the Locusts]*

7. *Les Ratapous à l'Heure Atomique [The Ratapous in the Atomic Age]*

8. *Terrible Tante Amélie [Terrible Aunt Amelia]*

9. *Flash sur l'Amazonie [Flash Over Amazonia]*

10. *Des Artichauts dans le Désert [Artichokes in the Desert]*

11. *Le Fantôme du Fier-à-Bras [The Ghost of the Fier-à-Bras]*

STORY: Nic and Mino Dabarin are two twins (Nic is blond, Mino dark-haired). With their companions, Tao, a Confucius-quoting Chinese; Bob, an annoying American journalist; Sweet Grannie, an American billionaire; and the eccentric Prof. Zaparelli, they became involved in a series of fantastic adventures dealing with a lost civilization of Conquistadors (from which they'll bring back the tempestuous Pistoletas), secret islands, artichoke-headed Venusians, mad scientists, and an international spy ring led by their arch-foe Legrand-Ixe.

NOTE: Originally serialized two-pages a week in *Le Journal de Mickey* (Edi-Monde) from 1958 to 1966. Only stories Nos. 2-5 were collected in the graphic novel format.

Nikopol
WRI/ART: Enki **Bilal**.

1. *La Foire aux Immortels [The Immortals' Fair]* (Dar., 1980; transl. as *Gods in Chaos*, Catalan)

2. *La Femme Piège [The Woman Trap]* (Dar., 1986; transl. Catalan)

3. *Froid Equateur [Cold Equator]* (Hum., 1992)
STORY: A 20th century cosmonaut, a blue-haired journalist, and aliens who look like Egyptian gods are players and pawns in a series of complex games played on a decadent future Earth.

Nobodyland
ART: C. Carré; ART: B. Bittler.

1. *Milena* (Glé., 1991)

2. *Needham* (Glé., 1992)
STORY: Futuristic thriller.

Noël
WRI/ART: André **Franquin**.

1. *Noël et l'Élaoin* (Dup., 1959)
WRI: Serdu; ART: Stibane.

2. *Retrouvailles [Meeting Again]* (Marsu, 1990)
STORY: A multi-purpose robot and his boy.

Nomad
WRI/ART: Morvan, Buchet & Savoia.

1. *Nomad* (Glé., 1994)

2. *Gai-Jin* (Glé., 1995)

3. *Mémoires Mortes [Dead Memories]* (Glé., 1995)
STORY: Manga-like science fiction.

Nombre
WRI: Thierry Smolderen; ART: Egger (**Ab'Aigre**).

1. *La Chanson de l'Ogre [The Ogre's Song]* (Hum., 1991)

2. *La Maison de l'Ogre [The Ogre's House]* (Hum., 1992)
STORY: Dark, gothic fantasy.

Norbert et Kari
(genre stories only)
WRI/ART: Christian **Godard**.

10–11. *Le Maître des Abysses [The Master of the Abyss]* / *Le Peuple des Dito [The Dito People]* (Hachette No. 4, 1975)

13–14. *L'île aux Monstres [Monster Island]* / *Opération Terre Brûlée [Operation Scorched Earth]* (Hachette No. 3, 1975)

15–16. *La Pierre de Nulle Part [The Stone from Nowhere]* / *Le Souffle de l'Enfer [Hell's Breath]* (Glé. No. 6, 1981)

17. *Au Royaume d'Astap [In Astap's Kingdom]* (Hachette No. 1, 1974)
STORY: Cartoony adventures of a Frenchman living on a Polynesian island with his native friend. Genre elements include a secret, underwater civilization, etc.

NOTE: Originally serialised in *Pilote* from 1963 to 1969.

Nosferatu see **Druillet**

La Nuit see **Druillet**

La Nuit de l'Étoile [The Night of the Star] (Aedena, 1986)
WRI/ART: **Moebius**, Marc **Bati**.
STORY: Science fiction and fantasy in Tahiti.

Nuits Blanches see **Foerster**

Les Observateurs de la Terre [Earth Watch]
WRI: J. Goyallon & A. Pros; ART: J. Pruvot.

1. *L'Arche du Cosmos [The Cosmic Ark]* (Total, 1986)
   WRI: J. Goyallon & A. Pros; ART: J.-P. Vomorin.

2. *La Planète Protégée [The Protected Planet]* (Total, 1987)

3. *La Première Colonie [The First Colony]* (Total, 1988)

4. *L'Empire des Dinosaures [The Dinosaur Empire]* (Total, 1990)

5. *Les Mutants du Cénozoïque [The Cenozoic Mutants]* (Total, 1990)

6. *La Planète Menacée [The Threatened Planet]* (Total, 1991)
   STORY: Ecological space opera.

Odyss
WRI/ART: Olivier **Taffin**.

1. *L'Écheveau de l'Amer [The Bitter Spin]* (VdO., 1993)
   STORY: Fantasy.

L'Oeuf du Monde see Champakou

Ogar
WRI/ART: Yves Mondet.

1. *Le Trésor de Montezuma [The Treasure of Montezuma]* (1948)

2. *Les Ravageurs des Amazones [The Reavers of the Amazon]* (1948)

3. *Le Temple du Soleil Rouge [The Temple of the Red Sun]* (1948)

4. *L'Inconnue de Maracaïbo [The Unknown Girl from Maracaibo]* (1949)

5. *Les Mangeurs de Terre [The Earth Eaters]* (1949)

6. *Les Écumeurs de Sumatra [The Raiders of Sumatra]* (1949)

7. *Le Fétiche de Corail [The Coral Idol]* (1949)

8. *L'Homme du Désert [The Desert Man]* (1949)
   STORY: Tarzan-like hero.
   NOTE: Originally serialized in an eponymous magazine by *Le Journal des Jeunes*. Never collected in the graphic novel format.

Olivier Rameau
WRI: **Greg**; ART: **Dany**.

1. *La Merveilleuse Odyssée d'Olivier Rameau et de*

Colombe Tiredaile [The Marvellous Odyssey of Olivier Rameau and Colombe Tiredaile] (Lom., 1970)

2. *La Bulle de Si-C'était-Vrai [The Bubble of If-'Twere-True]* (Lom., 1971)

3. *Le Château des 4 Lunes [The Castle of the 4 Moons]* (Lom., 1972)

4. *La Caravelle de N'Importe-Où [The Caravel of Anywhere]* (Lom., 1973)

5. *Le Grand Voyage en Absurdie [The Great Journey to Absurdia]* (Lom., 1974)

6. *L'Oiseau de Par-Ci, Par-Là [The Bird of Here-and-There]* (Lom., 1975)

7. *Le Miroir à Trois Faces [The Three-Sided Mirror]* (Lom., 1976)

8. *La Trompette du Silence [The Silent Trumpet]* (Lom., 1978)

9. *Le Canon de la Bonne Humeur [The Canon of Good Humor]* (Lom., 1983)

10. *Le Rêve aux Sept Portes [The Seven Gates of Dream]* (Lom., 1985)

11. *L'Océan sans Surface [The Ocean Without Surface]* (Lom., 1987)
    STORY: Young legal clerk Olivier Rameau, kindly solicitor Mr. Pertinent, and the stunningly beautiful Colombe Tiredaile save the amiable fantasyland of Rêverose (Pink Dreams) from various threats.
    NOTE: Originally serialized in *Tintin* in 1968.

L'Ombre du Corbeau see Comès

L'Ombre du Soleil see Dans l'Ombre du Soleil

On M'appelle l'Avalanche see **Masse**

Onkr, l'Abominable Homme des Glaces
WRI: Jean Malac/**Yuan Delporte**; ART: Tenas (Louis Saintels).

1. *Onkr, l'Abominable Homme des Glaces [Onkr, the Abominable Ice Man]*

2. *Les Onkriens Sont Là [The Onkrians Are Here]*

3. *La Chasse à l'Onkrakrikru [The Hunt for the Onkrakrikru]*

STORY: Profs. Schmoll and Dugommier find Onkr, a super-strong caveman, frozen in Siberian ice. After thawing out, Onkr goes on a Hulk-like rampage throughout France, pursued by two other villainous scientists, Profs. Zinzin and Moleskine. Eventually, Onkr mellows out (as do the villains) and returns to Siberia. There, the scientists find a whole tribe of "Onkrians" (including Onkr's father, Papa Onkr), whom they befriend. They later go hunting for the Onkrakrikru, a mischievous, blue-skinned flying sea-horse-like creature.

NOTE: Originally serialized two pages a week in *Le Journal de Mickey* (Edi-Monde) between 1961 and 1972. Fourteen stories in total never reprinted in the graphic novel format.

L'Or et l'Esprit [The Gold and the Mind]

WRI: Legrand; ART: Jean-Marc Rochette.

1. *Le Tribut [The Tribute]* (Cast., 1994)

2. *L'Aigle de Lafcadio [The Eagle of Lafcadio]* (Cast., 1996)
STORY: On the world of Two-Moons, space trooper Gavurio falls in love with ecologist Gilda. Gavurio is disgusted by the massacre of the native population. The spirit of one of the natives, Yul, eventually comes to share the young man's body.

L'Or du Temps [The Gold of Time]

WRI: D. Haziot; ART: F. Baranger.

1. *Fille de l'Ombre [The Daugher of Shadows]* (Dar., 1989)

2. *L'Autre Rive [The Other Bank]* (Dar., 1989)

3. *La Chair des Dieux [The Flesh of the Gods]* (Dar., 1989)
STORY: Retelling of the myth of Orpheus.

Orion, Le Laveur de Planètes [Orion, the Planet Cleaner] (Dar., 1974)

WRI: Claude **Moliterni**; ART: Robert **Gigi**.
STORY: A planet cleaner fights androids.
NOTE: Originally serialized in *Phénix* in 1968.

Orn

WRI: Patrick **Cothias**; ART: Olivier **Taffin**.

1. *Orn, Coeur de Chien [Orn, Heart of a Dog]* (Dar., 1982)

2. *La Fille et la Tortue [The Girl and the Turtle]* (Dar., 1983)

3. *La Croisée du Malin [The Devil's Path]* (Dar., 1984)

4. *Le Maître Loup [The Master Wolf]* (Dar., 1985)

5. *Chien de Coeur [Dog of Heart]* (Dar., 1987)

6. *Orkaëlle* (Dar., 1989)
STORY: At the dawn of time, Earth is ruled by four Elemental Lords. Gé, the Earth Lord, transforms his son, Orn, into a dog in order to hide him from his enemy, Pyros, the Lord of Fire. Orn grows up to reclaim his birthright.

Oscar Hamel

(genre stories only)
WRI/ART: Frédéric-Antonin **Breysse**.

6. *La Cité Oubliée [The Forgotten City]* (Fleurus, 1954)

7. *Les Conquérants de l'Infini [The Conquerors of Infinity]* (1955,. rep. Fleurus, 1982)
STORY: *Tintin*-like adventures; in ep. 7, the heroes travel to the Moon.
NOTE: Originally serialized in *Coeurs Vaillants* from 1945 to 1955.

Osinor see Les Magiciens d'Osinor

L'Ouragan des Âmes Perdues [The Storm of the Lost Souls]

WRI: Chatillon; ART: Lukinburg.

1. *La Justice de l'Aigle [The Justice of the Eagle]* (Sol., 1995)
STORY: Heroic fantasy.

OVNI see Dossiers Soucoupes Volantes

Oyasu Sang-Dragon

WRI/ART: Werner.

1. *L'Éveil de l'Ombre [The Shadow Wakes]* (Cast., 1991)

2. *Jodo Jodo* (Cast., 1992)
STORY: Heroic fantasy in ancient Japan.

Pan et la Syrinx

WRI/ART: Mic Delinx (Michel Houdelinckx).
STORY: The little faun Pan and his girl-friend, the Syrinx, experience various comical adventures in the world of Greek mythology.
NOTE: Originally serialized in a dozen short stories published in *Pilote* from 1967 to 1970; never collected in the graphic novel format.

Pacush Blues

WRI/ART: Ptiluc.

1. *Premières Mesures [First Measures]* (VdO., 1983)

2. *Jefferson, ou le Mal de Vivre [Jefferson, or Sick of Living]* (VdO., 1983)

3. *L'Importance Majeure des Accords Mineurs [The Major Importance of Minor Accords]* (VdO., 1984)

4. *Destin Farceur: Crescendo [Mocking Fate: Crescendo]* (VdO., 1985)

5. *Destin Farceur: Descendo [Mocking Fate: Descendo]* (VdO., 1986)

6. *Le Mal de Mer [Sea Sickness]* (VdO., 1988)

7. *Variations* (VdO., 1991)

8. *La Logique du Pire [The Logic of the Worst]* (VdO., 1993)

9. *Relecture du Mythe de Frankenstein [Rereading of the Myth of Frankenstein]* (VdO., 1996)
STORY: The comical adventures of intelligent rats.

Pandora (Glé., 1983)
WRI/ART: Y. Timouk.
STORY: Fantasy.

Panick
WRI/ART: A. Desneuve.

1. *La Crypte aux Cristaux [The Crystal Crypt]* (Dar., 1984)
STORY: Science fiction.

Papilio
WRI: Hervé Croze, Michel Pierret; ART: Michel Pierret.
STORY: A young blond humanoid and his alien companion, Gekko, seek an hospitable home throughout space and time.
NOTE: Originally serialized in *Tintin* in 1978; never collected in the graphic novel format.

Papyrus
WRI/ART: Lucien **De Gieter**.

1. *La Momie Engloutie [The Sunken Mummy]* (Dup., 1978)

2. *Le Maître des Trois Portes [The Master of the Three Gates]* (Dup., 1979)

3. *Le Colosse Sans Visage [The Faceless Colossus]* (Dup., 1980)

4. *Le Tombeau du Pharaon [The Tomb of the Pharaoh]* (Dup., 1981)

5. *L'Égyptien Blanc [The White Egyptian]* (Dup., 1982)

6. *Les Quatre Doigts du Dieu Lune [The Four Fingers of the Moon God]* (Dup., 1983)

7. *La Vengeance de Ramsès [The Revenge of Ramses]* (Dup., 1984)

8. *Les Métamorphoses d'Imhotep [The Metamorphoses of Imhotep]* (Dup., 1985)

9. *Les Larmes du Gánt [The Giant's Tears]* (Dup., 1986)

10. *La Pyramide Noire [The Dark Pyramid]* (Dup., 1987)

11. *Le Pharaon Maudit [The Accursed Pharaoh]* (Dup., 1988)

12. *L'Obélisque* (Dup., 1989)

13. *Le Labyrinthe* (Dup., 1990)

14. *L'Île Cyclope [The Cyclopean Island]* (Dup., 1991)

15. *L'Enfant Hiéroglyphe [The Hieroglyph Child]* (Dup., 1992)

16. *Le Seigneur des Crocodiles [The Lord of the Crocodiles]* (Dup., 1993)

17. *Toutankhamon* (Dup., 1994)

18. *L'Oeil de Ré [The Eye of Re]* (Dup., 1995)

19. *Les Momies Maléfiques [The Evil Mummies]* (Dup., 1996)
STORY: In ancient Egypt, young page Papyrus and Theti-Chéri, the daughter of the Pharaoh, face a series of supernatural threats.
NOTE: Originally serialized in *Spirou* in 1974

Parade see **Fred**

Parasite (Zen., 1992)
WRI/ART: Stan.
STORY: Science fiction.

Pas de Deo Gratias pour Rock Mastard see **Boucq**

Le Passage de la Saison Morte [The Passing of the Dead Season]
WRI: Philippe Bonifay; ART: Jacques Terpant.

1. *L'Île du Temps [The Isle of Time]* (Glé., 1989)

2. *La Sorcière [The Witch]* (Glé., 1991)
STORY: Heroic-fantasy.

La Passion de Diosamante [Diosamante's Passion] (Hum., 1992)

WRI: Alexandro **Jodorowsky**; ART: Jean-Claude **Gal**.
STORY: A cruel queen decides to redeem herself to be worthy of the love of her king.

Patrick Maudick
WRI/ART: Patrick Dumas.

1. *Les Oiseaux du Diables [The Devil's Birds]* (Glé., 1981)

2. *Les Méandres du Temps [The Meanderings of Time]* (Glé., 1983)
STORY: Science fiction homage to **Blake et Mortimer** (see above).
NOTE: Originally serialized in *Circus* in 1980.

Le Pays Miroir [The Mirror Land]
WRI: Claude Carré; ART: Jean-Marie Michaud.

1. *L'Incendiaire [The Arsonist]* (Dar., 1992)

2. *Représailles [Reprisal]* (Dar., 1993)

3. *La Course du Balancier [The Race of the Balance]* (Dar., 1993)
STORY: Fantastic thriller.

Les Paysages de la Nuit [The Landscapes of Night]
(Delc., 1994)
WRI/ART: Barbier.
STORY: A futuristic murder mystery in a world where androids rule and humans are kept in captivity.

La Pédagogie du Trottoir see **Boucq**

Pegg Le Robot see **Mallet**

Pemberton
WRI/ART: **Sirius**.

1. *Les Voyages Insolites de Pemberton [Pemberton's Strange Journeys]* (Dar., 1976)

2. *Pemberton, C'est Rien qu'un Menteur [Pemberton Is Nothing But a Liar]* (Dar., 1977)

3. *La Vie Ardente et Douloureuse de Pemberton [Pemberton's Intense and Painful Life]* (Dar., 1978)

4. *T'Aurais pas du, Pemberton [You Shouldn't Have, Pemberton]* (Dar., 1981)
STORY: The tall tales of an old sea wolf.
NOTE: Originally serialized in *Pilote* in 1973.

La Pension du Dr. Eon [The Pension of Dr. Eon]
(Lom., 1997)
WRI: Patrick **Cothias**; ART: **Griffo**.
STORY: A young female journalist investigates a mysterious Scottish asylum.

Percevan
WRI: Xavier Fauche, Jean Léturgie; ART: Philippe **Luguy**.

1. *Les Trois Étoiles d'Ingaar [The Three Stars of Ingaar]* (Glé., 1982)

2. *Le Tombeau des Glaces [The Ice Tomb]* (Glé., 1983)

3. *L'Épée de Ganaël [The Sword of Ganael]* (Glé., 1984)

4. *Le Pays d'Aslor [The Country of Aslor]* (Dar., 1985)

5. *Le Sablier d'El Jerada [The Hourglass of El Jerada]* (Dar., 1986)

6. *Les Clefs du Feu [The Keys of Fire]* (Dar., 1988)

7. *Les Seigneurs de l'Enfer [The Lords of Hell]* (Dar., 1992)

8. *La Table d'Émeraude [The Emerald Tablet]* (Dar., 1995)

9. *L'Arcantane Noire [The Black Archantana]* (Dar., 1996)
STORY: A medieval adventurer fights evil wizards and other supernatural threats.
NOTE: Originally serialized in *Gomme* in 1981.

Père Passe-Passe see **Arthur Le Fantôme Justicier**

Perlin et Pinpin
WRI/ART: Marcel **Cuvillier**.

1. *Les Joyeux Nains [The Happy Gnomes]* (Croisade, 1943)

2. *Chez le Prof. Duradar* (Fleurus, 1954)

3. *Chez les Abeilles [With the Bees]* (Fleurus, 1954)

4. *Au Pays des Jouets [In the Land of Toys]* (Fleurus, 1954)

5. *Chez les Poissons [With the Fishes]* (Fleurus, 1956)

6. *Vedettes de Cirque [Circus Stars]* (Fleurus, 1956)

7. *Château de la Peur [Castle of Fear]* (Fleurus, 1957)

8. *Au Pôle Nord [At the North Pole]* (Fleurus, 1957)

9. *Chez les Oiseaux [With the Birds]* (Fleurus, 1957)

10. *Au Pays des Chansons [In the Land of Songs]* (Fleurus, 1957)

11-12. *Chez les Fées (2 vols.) [In Fairyland]* (Fleurus, 1957)

WRI: Escudié; ART: Didier **Savard**.

1. *La Grenouille Noire [The Black Frog]* (Hélyode, 1993)

2. *La Poudre à Remonter le Temps [The Time-Traveling Powder]* (Hélyode, 1993)
STORY: The adventures of two malicious little gnomes.
NOTE: Very famous children's series, originally serialized in *Âmes Vaillantes* in 1940. The expression "Take Perlin Pinpin's powder" is commonly used in French language to define a quasi-magical escape.

Perpette
WRI/ART: Arkas.

1. *Mauvaises Fréquentations [Bad Frequentations]* (Glé., 1991)

2. *Un Rat dans ma Soupe [A Rat in My Soup]* (Glé., 1992)
STORY: Jail stories with a philosophizing rat named Monte-Cristo.

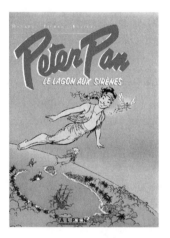

Peter Pan
Version No.1: WRI/ART: Régis **Loisel**.

1. *Londres [London]* (VdO., 1990)

2. *Opikanoba* (VdO., 1992)

3. *Tempête [Storm]* (VdO., 1994)

4. *Mains Rouges [Red Hands]* (VdO., 1996)

Version No.2: WRI: François **Rivière**; ART: Jean-Pierre **Danard**, François **Pierre**.

1. *Le Lagon aux Sirènes [The Mermaid Lagoon]* (Hum., 1990)
STORY: Two very different adaptations of James Barrie's work. The Régis **Loisel** version is considerably grimmer and more adult, and features Jack the Ripper.

Le Petit Cirque see **Fred**

Petite Chronique Vénusienne [Little Venusian Chronicle]
WRI: Geerts; ART: Jean-Marie Brouyère.
STORY: Humorous science fiction.
NOTE: Short stories originally published in *Spirou* in 1977-78.

Les Petits Hommes [The Little Men]
First Series:
WRI: Albert Desprechins; ART: Pierre Séron.

1. *Alerte à Eslapion sous Ravejols [Alert in Eslapion]* (1967; rep. No. 19, 1986)

2. *Les Évadés [The Escapees]* (1968; rep. Sol., 1991)

3. *Le Petit Homme Qui Rit [The Little Man Who Laughs]* (1968; rep. Jordan, 1991)

4. *Le Coq en Pâte [Chicken and Dough]* (1969; rep. Jordan, 1992)

5. *Des Souris et des Petits Hommes [Of Mice and Little Men]* (1970; rep. Sol., 1989)

Second Series:
WRI: Albert Desprechins; ART: Pierre Séron.

1. *L'Exode [Exodus]* (Dup., 1970; rep. 1974)
WRI: Mittei (Jean Mariette); ART: Pierre Seron.
8. *Du Rêve en Poudre [Dream Powder]* (Dup., 1971; rep. 1978)

2. *Des Petits Hommes au Brontoxique [The Little Men in Brontoxic]* (Dup., 1974)

3. *Les Guerriers du Passé [The Warriors of the Past]* (Dup., 1975)

4. *Le Lac de l'Auto [The Car in the Lake]* (Dup., 1975)

5. *L'Oeil du Cyclope [The Eye of the Cyclop]* (Dup., 1976)

6. *Le Vaisseau Fantôme [The Ghost Ship]* (Dup., 1977)

7. *Les Ronces du Samourai [The Thorns of the Samurai]* (Dup., 1978)

9. *Le Triangle du Diable [The Devil's Triangle]* (Dup., 1979)

10. *Le Peuple des Abysses [The People of the Abyss]* (Dup., 1980)

11. *Dans les Griffes du Seigneur [In the Clutches of The Lord]* (Dup., 1981)

12. *Le Guêpier [The Wasps' Nest]* (WRI: Seron) (Dup., 1981)

13. *Les Prisonniers du Temps [The Prisoners of Time]* (WRI: Seron) (Dup., 1982)

14. *Les Hommes-Singes [The Ape Men]* (WRI: Seron) (Dup., 1983)

15. *Mosquito 417* (Dup., 1984)

16. *La Planète Ranxerox* (WRI: Seron) (Dup., 1985)

17. *Le Trou Blanc [The White Hole]* (WRI: Seron) (Dup., 1985)

18. *Le Pickpocket* (WRI: Seron) (Dup., 1986)

20. *Rapt en Sous-Sol [Kidnapping in the Basement]* (Dup., 1986)

WRI/ART: Pierre Seron.

21. *Les 6 Clones* (Dup., 1987)

22. *L'Ermite de Rochafleur [The Hermit of Flower Rock]* (Dup., 1987)

23. *Le Dernier des Petits Hommes [Last of the Little Men]* (Dup., 1988)

24. *Le Volcan d'Or [The Golden Volcano]* (Dup., 1988)

25. *Petits Hommes et Minigags [Little Men and Minigags]* (Dup., 1989)

26. *Voyage entre Deux Mondes [Travel Between Two Worlds]* (Dup., 1990)

27. *C+C = Boum* (Dup., 1991)

28. *Les Catherinettes* (Dup., 1992)

29. *Choucroute et Melba [Sauerkraut Melba]* (Dup., 1993)

30. *Bébé Tango* (Dup., 1994)

31. *Tchakakhan* (Dup., 1995)

32. *Melting Pot* (Dup., 1995)

33. *Vingt Mille Lieues sous les Terres [20,000 Leagues Beneath the Earth]* (Dup., 1996)
STORY: In a French scientific community, everyone who has come in contact with a meteorite suddenly shrinks to doll-size. The resulting "Little Men" build a secret civilization and become involved in a series of fantastic adventures.

Related Work:
Les Centaures (Aurore et Ulysse)
WRI: Stephen **Desberg**; ART: Pierre Seron.

1. *La Porte du Néant [The Gate of the Void]* (Dup., 1982)

2. *Le Loup à 2 Têtes [The Two-Headed Wolf]* (Dup., 1983)

3. *L'Odyssée [The Odyssey]* (Dup., 1984)

4. *Les Amazones [The Amazons]* (Dup., 1985)

5. *Les Châtiments d'Hermès [The Punishment of Hermes]* (MC Prods., 1988)

6. *Kelvinhator III* (Sol., 1989)
STORY: Light fantasy stories starring two young centaurs.
NOTE: **Les Petits Hommes** was originally serialized in *Spirou* in 1967 and **Les Centaures** in 1980. The two series cross over in ep. 24. The **Scrameustache** (see below) appears in ep. 18.

Les Petits Hommes Verts see **Mallet**

Pharaon
WRI: André-Paul **Duchateau**; ART: Daniel **Hulet**.

1. *Philtre pour l'Enfer [Potion for Hell]* (Hachette, 1981)

2. *Le Cerveau de Glace [The Brain of Ice]* (Hachette, 1982)

3. *L'Incarnation de Seth [The Incarnation of Seth]* (Hachette, 1983)

4. *Promenade des Solitudes [Lonely Walk]* (Hachette, 1984)

5. *Dossiers Anti [Anti Files]* (Hachette, 1984)

6. *Des Ombres sur le Sable [Shadows on the Sand]* (Hachette, 1985)

7. *Les Feux de la Mer [The Fires of the Sea]* (Glé., 1996)
STORY: Special agent Pharaoh fights would-be world conquerors, mad scientists, and Egyptian cults.
NOTE: Originally serialized in *Super As* in 1980.

Le Phénix et le Dragon
WRI/ART: P. Son.

1. *Le Prince Sage [The Wise Prince]* (Glé., 1991)

2. *Le Serment de Lung-Nhai [The Serment of Lung-Nhai]* (Glé., 1993)
STORY: Oriental heroic-fantasy.

Phil Korridor
WRI: Alph; ART: A. Koch.

1. *La Nuit des Fulgurs [The Night of the Fulgurs]* (Zen., 1992)

2. *L'Écrivain Repenti [Writer's Repent]* (Zen., 1994)

3. *La Proie des Ombres [The Prey of Shadows]* (Zen., 1994)
STORY: Fantastic thriller.

Philémon
WRI/ART: **Fred**.

1. *Avant la Lettre [Before the Letter]* (Dar., 1966, rep. 1978)

2. *Le Naufragé du A [Stranded on the A]* (Dar., 1972)

3. *Le Piano Sauvage [The Savage Piano]* (Dar., 1973)

4. *Le Château Suspendu [The Hanging Castle]* (Dar., 1973)

5. *Le Voyage de l'Incrédule [The Unbeliever's Journey]* (Dar., 1974)

6. *Sinbabbad de Batbad* (Dar., 1974)

7. *L'Île des Brigadiers [The Island of the Brigadiers]* (Dar., 1975)

8. *A l'Heure du Second T [The Hour of the Second T]* (Dar., 1975)

9. *L'Arche du A [The Ark of the A]* (Dar., 1976)

10. *L'Âne en Atoll [The Ass in an Atoll]* (Dar., 1977)

11. *La Mémémoire [The Grannymemory]* (Dar., 1977)

12. *Le Chat à Neuf Queues [The Cat o' Nine Tails]* (Dar., 1978)

13. *Le Secret de Félicien [The Secret of Felicien]* (Dar., 1981)

14. *L'Enfer des Épouvantails [The Scarecrow Hell]* (Dar., 1983)

15. *Le Diable du Peintre [The Painter's Devil]* (Dar., 1987)

STORY: A farm boy, his wizard uncle Phélicien, and Barthélémy the well-digger, explore the fantastic universe of the letters of that spell the words "Atlantic Ocean" on the maps.

NOTE: Originally serialized in *Pilote* in 1965.

Photonik

WRI/ART: Cyrus Tota.

STORY: Taddeus Tenterhook, a hunchback teenager, turns into the super-hero Phontonik, and with the help of Dr. Ziegler and "Tom Thumb," fights super-powered criminals.

NOTE: Sixteen eps. originally serialized in *Mustang* (Series II), Nos. 54-70 (Ed. Lug, 1980-81), then in *Spidey* starting with No. 22. In 1987, a number of episodes were written and drawn by Jean-Yves **Mitton**; one graphic novel released by Delcourt in 1998.

Pierrot et la Lampe [Pierrot and the Lamp] (Cartoon, 1991)

WRI/ART: **Peyo**.

STORY: A boy and his magic lamp.

NOTE: Originally serialized in *Spirou* in 1966.

Pif Le Chien [Pif the Dog]

Pif is a funny animal, the hero of a Disney-like series centering around this friendly, anthropomorphic dog, his son Pifou, his nemesis, the cat Hercules, etc. Pif was the mascot of the magazine *Vaillant*, which was retitled *Pif* in 1969. It was created by Cabrero Arnal, and later taken over by Roger Mas, Louis Cance, and many others. In the late 1970s, a number of stories written by Corteggiani and drawn by Motti featured science fiction elements, such as robots and extra-terrestrials.

Pinocchio see **Foerster**

Les Pionniers de l'Aventure Humaine see **Boucq**

Les Pionniers de l'Espérance [Hope's Pioneers]

WRI: Roger **Lecureux**; ART: Raymond **Poïvet**.

1. *Les Pionniers de l'Espérance [Hope's Pioneers]* (52 p.) (1947) (rep. as *Vers l'Ourang Mystérieux [Towards Mysterious Ourang,]*, aka *Radia, La Planète aux 1000 Secrets [Radia, the Planet of 1000 Secrets]*, Vail., 1947, 1962; rep. Futuropolis 1, 1984)

2. *La Cité de Bangra [The City of Bangra]* (42 p.) (1948) (rep. Satellite Images, 1960; rep. Futuropolis 1, 1984)

3. *Le Désert Blanc [The White Desert]* (12 p.) (1948) (rep. Futuropolis 2, 1984)

4. *Kataraz la Maudite [Kataraz the Accursed]* (55 p.) (1949) (rep. Vail., 1960; rep. Futuropolis 2, 1984)

5. *Les Pionniers de l'Espérance, aka 500,000 Ans Avant [500,000 Years Before]*, aka *C'était il y a 50.000 Ans [50.000 Years Ago]* (25 p.) (1949) (rep. Vail., 1961; rep. Futuropolis 2, 1984)

6. *Aquatide, la Cité des Ondes [Aquatide—The City of Waves]* (47 p.) (1951) (rep. Vail., 1961; rep. Futuropolis 3 1984)

7. *Le Secret de Jacques Ferrand [The Secret of Jacques Ferrand]*, aka *On a volé les Plans du Satellite Artificiel [They Stole the Artificial Satellite's Blueprints]* (25 p.) (1951) (rep. Vail., 1962; rep. Futuropolis 3, 1984)

8. *Le Prof. Marvel a Disparu [Prof. Marvel Has Vanished]* (27 p.) (1952) (rep. Vail., 1962; rep. Futuropolis 3, 1984)

9. *L'Étang des Solitudes [The Pond of Loneliness]*, aka *Le Jardin Fantastique [Fantastic Garden]* (50 p.) (1953) (rep. Vail., 1961; rep. Futuropolis 4, 1988)

10. *Les Hommes aux Yeux d'Or [The Men with Golden Eyes]*, aka *Caluda* (63 p.) (1958) (rep. Futuropolis 4, 1988)

11. *Échec aux Zions [The Zions in Check]* (80 p.) (1959) (rep. Futuropolis 5, 1989)

12. *Inaccessible 7 [Unreachable 7]* (36 p.) (1960) (rep. Futuropolis 5, 1989)

13. *Nibor* (49 p.) (1961)

14. *Les Forbans de l'Espace [The Space Pirates]* (1963)

15. *Il n'Est Jamais Trop Tard [It's Never Too Late]* (1965)

16. *L'Otage des Profondeurs [The Hostage of the Deep]* (1965)

17. *La Première Fugue [The First Flight]* (1965)

18. *La Terre Sautera Ce Soir [Earth Will Explode Tonight]* (1965)

19. *Les Buveurs de Mer [The Sea Drinkers]* (1965)

20. *Prisonniers du Temps [Prisoners of Time]* (1966)

21. *Le Paradis du Prof. Danvers [The Paradise of Prof. Danvers]* (1966)

22. *Les Naufragés de l'Espace [The Castaways of Space]* (1966)

23. *Le Cas du Dr. Kih [The Case of Dr. Kih]* (1966)

24. *4−2 = 1* (1966)

25. *Les Mirages d'Or [The Golden Mirages]* (1966)

26. *Destination Infini [Destination Infinity]* (1966)

27. *L'Étrange Fin du Capitaine Jork [The Strange End of Captain Jork]* (1966)

28. *Une Chaude Affaire [A Hot Affair]* (1966)

29. *Une Conquête Silencieuse [A Silent Conquest]* (1966)

30. *L'Invulnerable X* (1967)

31. *L'Affaire des Héros [An Affair of Heroes]* (1967)

32. *La Tête d'Épingle [The Head of a Pin]* (1967)

33. *L'Homme de Chaire [The Man of Fleshe]* (1967)

34. *Les Esclaves du Cosmos [The Cosmic Slaves]* (1967)

35. *Un Soleil a Disparu [A Sun Has Disappeared]* (1967)

36. *Les Hommes Papillons [The Butterfly Men]* (1967)

37. *La Mort de Thanga [The Death of Thanga]* (1967)

38. *La Planète Diamant [The Diamond Planet]* (1967)

39. *Les Grands Monstres [The Great Monsters]* (1967)

40. *L'Armada Fantôme [The Phantom Armada]* (1967)

41. *Les Oiseaux Poignards [The Dagger Birds]* (1968)

42. *Le Fléau d'Or [The Golden Plague]* (1968)

43. *Les Robinsons de la Planète X [The Robinsons of Planet X]* (1968)

44. *Le Jour Où la Terre se rendit [The Day Earth Surrendered]* (1968)

45. *Les Garrots Vivants [The Living Tourniquets]* (1968)

46. *L'Homme Poussière [The Man of Dust]* (1968)

47. *Le Hérisson de Métal [The Metal Hedgehog]* (1968)

48. *Un Simple Cauchemar [A Simple Nightmare]* (1968)

49. *La Pierre de Joie [The Stone of Joy]* (1968)

50. *La Créature du 2/10/2069* (1968)

51. *Les Gladiateurs de Tarengo [The Gladiators of Tarengo]* (1969)

52. *Ceux Qui Prévoyaient Tout [Those Who Predicted Everything]* (1969)

53. *Les Hommes d'En Bas [The Men from Below]* (1969)

54. *La Nuit des Horreurs [The Night of Horrors]* (1969)

55. *Le Cerveau de Secours [The Spare Brain]* (1969)

56. *Commando sur l'EMC* (1969)

57. *Les Hommes Squales [The Shark Men]* (1969)

58. *Le Tremblement de Fleurs [Flower Quake]* (1970)

59. *17 Minutes à Vivre [17 Minutes to Live]* (1970)

60. *Le Sanctuaire de Glace [The Ice Sanctuary]* (1970)

61. *La Mousse Verte [The Green Froth]* (1970)

62. *L'Arche de Noé [Noah's Ark]* (1970)

63. *Les Voleurs de Pensée [The Mind Stealers]* (1970)

64. *Une Surprise de Taille [A Big Surprise]* (1970)

65. *Le Monstre Invisible [The Invisible Monster]* (1970)

66. *L'Éponge de l'Espace [The Space Sponge]* (1971)

67. *Station 67* (1971)

68. *Les Mandraghommes [The Mandramen]* (1971)

69. *Les Creatures de Chahawa [The Creatures from Chahawa]* (1971)

70. *Le Sarcophage Zorien [The Zorian Sarcophagus]* (1971)

71. *Les Sept Derniers Jours [The Seven Last Days]* (1971)

72. *Angoisse à l'EMC [Terror at EMC]* (1972)

73. *Le Paradis du Diable [The Devil's Paradise]* (1972)

74. *La Désertion de Thanga [Thanga's Desertion]* (1972)

75. *Le Robot Invulnérable [The Invulnerable Robot]* (1972)

76. *Commando T* (1972)

77. *Les Bracelets G [The G Armbands]* (1972)

78. *Les Explorateurs du Temps [The Explorers of Time]* (1973)

79. *Un Trou dans les Archives [A Hole in the Archives]* (1973)

80. *La Chute d'un Tyran [The Fall of a Tyrant]* (1973)

81. *La Grande Sépulture [A Great Burial Site]* (1973)

Story: In the origin story, the Pioneers are a team of astronauts sent aboard the rocketship *Espérance [Hope]* toward the mysterious planet Radias, which threatens Earth. Eventually, the cast narrows down to four main characters: Maud, Tsin-Lu, Rodion, and Thanga, who become fearless space explorers.

NOTE: Originally serialized in *Vaillant* from 1945 to 1973. Only the first six episodes were collected in the graphic novel format by *Vaillant*. Later, the first twelve adventures were collected in a five-volume set by Futuropolis. The page count of eps. 1-14 is variable; eps. 15-50 are 12 pages long; eps. 51-81 are 20 pages long.

Les Pirates de l'Infini see *Mac Gallan*

Pixies
WRI: Pierre **Dubois**; ART: R. Rivard.

1. *Le Cercle des Caraquins [The Circle of the Caraquins]* (Glé., 1991)

2. *Le Roi des Ombres [The King of Shadows]* (Glé., 1993)
STORY: Medieval heroic fantasy.

La Planète des Clowns [The Clown Planet] (Crocodile, 1980)
WRI/ART: Marc **Wasterlain**.
STORY: Light fantasy.

Plick et Plock see **Les Malices de Plick et Plock**

Plip, la Planète Rectangle [Plip, the Rectangular Planet] (Delc., 1995)
STORY/ART: Michel Pirus.
STORY: Children's tale about the adventures of President Elephant, who lives on a flat, rectangular world.

Point de Fuite pour les Braves see *Boucq*

Les Poisons de Mars [The Poisons of Mars] (Lefrancq, 1992)
WRI: Jacques **Stoquart**, based on Isaac Asimov; ART: E. Loutte.
STORY: Adaptation of Asimov's *David Starr, Space Ranger*. Also adapted under **Fleuve Noir**.

Polka
WRI: Didier **Convard**; ART: Siro.

1. *Le Mal d'Orphée [Orpheus' Sickness]* (Dar., 1995)

2. *Démokratie* (Dar., 1996)
STORY: Futuristic thriller.

Polonius (Hum., 1977; Transl. Heavy Metal)
WRI: Picaret; ART: Jacques Tardi.
STORY: A fantastic adventure in a Roman Empire-like setting.
NOTE: Originally serialized in *Métal Hurlant*.

Le Pont dans la Vase [The Bridge in the Mud]
WRI: Chomet; ART: Chevillard.

1. *L'Anguille [The Eel]* (Glé., 1994)

2. *Orlandus* (Glé., 1995)
STORY: Camille Park is a rebel in a universe made up of cities connected by giant bridges.

Porte à Porte Malheur see *Foerster*

Les Potamoks
WRI: Joann Sfar; ART: Jose Luis Munuera.

1. *Terra Incognita* (Delc., 1995)

2. *La Fontaine Rouge [The Red Fountain]* (Delc., 1996)
STORY: In a fantasy world, a crew of human explorers comes across a ship manned by an intelligent, boar-like race.

Potron et Minet
WRI/ART: H. B. De Bissot.
STORY: Cartoony adventures in a fictional medieval kingdom featuring the alchemist Belphegor; his talking crow, Juju; his two nephews, Potron and Minet; and the irascible Baron des Bosses.
NOTE: Originally published in mini-books in *Spirou* from 1961 to 1970.

Poumo-Thorax (Aud., 1981)
WRI/ART: Marcel Coucho.
STORY: Super-hero satire.

Poussière d'Étoiles [Star Dust] (Glé., 1983)
WRI: **Steiner**; ART: Mako.
STORY: Science fiction.

Poussière d'Étoiles [Star Dust] (Zen., 1990)
WRI: Salvetti & Headline; ART: Alamy.
STORY: Science fiction.

Pravda la Survireuse see **Jodelle**

Processus de Survie [Survival Process] (Hum., 1984)
WRI/ART: Paul **Gillon**.
STORY: Collection of science fiction short stories.

Professeur Canif Contre Docteur Krapotus
WRI/ART: **Érik**.
STORY: Juvenile science fiction adventures.
NOTE: Originally serialized in *Coq Hardi* in 1947; never collected in the graphic novel format.

Professeur Cataral
WRI/ART: **Érik**.
STORY: Juvenile science fiction adventures.
NOTE: Originally serialized in *Record* in 1951-56; never collected in the graphic novel format.

Professeur Globule et Docteur Virus
WRI/ART: **Érik**.
STORY: Juvenile science fiction adventures.
NOTE: Originally serialized in *Gavroche* in 1941-42; never collected in the graphic novel format.

Professeur Gromulus

WRI/ART: **Érik**.

STORY: Juvenile science fiction adventure featuring a lost world inhabited by dinosaurs.

NOTE: Serialized in *L'Intrépide* in 1957.

Professeur Jabirus

WRI/ART: F. de Nussy.

1. *Le Prof. Jabirus et les Envoyés de la Planète Delta [Prof. Jabirus and the Envoys from Planet Delta]* (Vigot, 1945)

2. *Le Prof. Jabirus à Deltapolis* (Vigot, 1945)
   STORY: Juvenile science fiction adventures.

Professeur Lapalme

WRI/ART: D. Briel

1. *Le Mystère de la Plante Tako [The Mystery of the Tako Plant]* (Glé., 1982)

2. *La Grenade Oxy* (Glé., 1983)
   STORY: Fantastic thrillers.

Professeur Stanislas see *Time Is Money*

Professeur Stratus

WRI/ART: Guy Counhaye.

1. *Le Tombeau des Neiges [The Tomb of the Snows]* (Lom., 1990)

2. *La Forteresse Amphibie [The Amphibian Fortress]* (Lom., 1993)

3. *Les Démons de Roquebrou [The Demons of Roquebrou]* (Lom., 1996)
   STORY: Jules **Verne**-like science fiction adventures.

Professeur Vorax

WRI/ART: **Érik**.

1. *Dr. Fulminate & Prof. Vorax*

2. *Tribacil contre Prof. Vorax*
   STORY: Juvenile science fiction adventures created during World War II.
   NOTE: Ep. 1 was originally serialized in *Le Téméraire* in 1943-44; ep. 2 was originally serialized in *Coq Hardi* in 1946; neither were collected in the graphic novel format.

Protéo

WRI: Imbar; ART: André **Chéret**.

1. *Les Bannis [The Banished]* (Auzou, 1985)

2. *Le Dragon du Mont Tombe [The Dragon of Tomb Mountain]* (Auzou, 1985)
   STORY: Prehistoric fantasy.

P'tit Gus

WRI: Rémo Forlani; ART: Raymond **Poïvet**.

STORY: A young farmer arrives in a land where the skies turn red and animal-headed people stalk the countryside.

NOTE: Originally serialized in *Chouchou* in 1964; never collected in the graphic novel format.

Quasar

WRI/ART: Christian **Lamquet**.

1. *Les Biomes* (Dup., 1987)

2. *Quasar* (Hélyode, 1994)
   STORY: In the last days of the 21st century, a special agent, his girlfriend, and their pet robot fight a variety of threats against Earth.
   NOTE: Originally serialized in *Spirou* in 1984; vol. 2 was never collected in the graphic novel format.

Les Quatre As [The Four Aces]

WRI: Georges **Chaulet**; ART: François **Craenhals**.

1. *Le Serpent de Mer [The Sea Serpent]* (Cast., 1964)

2. *L'Aéroglisseur [The Hovercraft]* (Cast., 1964)

3. *La Vache Sacrée [The Sacred Cow]* (Cast., 1964)

4. *Le Visiteur de Minuit [The Midnight Visitor]* (Cast., 1965)

5. *Le Couroucou* (Cast., 1966)

6. *La Coupe d'Or [The Gold Cup]* (Cast., 1967)

7. *Le Dragon des Neiges [The Snow Dragon]* (Cast., 1968)

8. *Le Rallye Olympique [The Olympic Rallye]* (Cast., 1969)

9. *L'Île du Robinson [The Robinson's Island]* (Cast., 1970)

10. *Le Tyran [The Tyrant]* (Cast., 1971)

11. *La Ruée Vers l'Or [The Gold Rush]* (Cast., 1973)

12. *Le Picasso Volé [The Stolen Picasso]* (Cast., 1974)

13. *La Bombe F* (Cast., 1975)

14. *La Saucisse Volante [The Flying Sausage]* (Cast., 1976)

15. *Le Gang des Chapeaux Blancs [The Gang of the White Hats]* (Cast., 1977)

16. *Le Vaisseau Fantôme [The Ghost Ship]* (Cast., 1978)

17. *Le Diamant Bleu [The Blue Diamond]* (Cast., 1979)

18. *La Licorne [The Unicorn]* (Cast., 1980)

19. *L'Iceberg* (Cast., 1981)

20. *Le Château Maléfique [The Evil Castle]* (Cast., 1982)

21. *Le Trésor des Tsars [The Czars' Treasure]* (Cast., 1983)

22. *Le Hold-Up de la Big Bank* (Cast., 1984)

23. *Le Magicien [The Wizard]* (Cast., 1985)

24. *Le Secret de la Montagne [The Secret of the Mountain]* (Cast., 1987)

25. *La Déesse des Mers [The Sea Goddess]* (Cast., 1988)

26. *La Navette Spatiale [The Space Shuttle]* (Cast., 1989)

27. *Le Requin Géant [The Giant Shark]* (Cast., 1990)

28. *L'Empire Caché [The Hidden Empire]* (Cast., 1991)

29. *Le Mystère de la Jungle [The Mystery of the Jungle]* (Cast., 1992)

WRI: Georges **Chaulet**; ART: F. **Craenhals**, Jacques Debruyne.

30. *Les Extraterrestres [The Extraterrestrials]* (Cast., 1993)

31. *Le Fantôme du Mont Saint-Michel [The Ghost of Mount St.Michael]* (Cast., 1994)

32. *Le Robot Vandale [The Vandal Robot]* (Cast., 1995)

33. *L'Atlantide [Atlantis]* (Cast., 1996)

34. *Les Trois Sorcières [The Three Witches]* (Cast., 1996)

35. *Les Dinosaures [The Dinosaurs]* (Cast., 1997)

STORY: Three teenage boys, one girl, and their pet dog embark on a series of adventures, most of which contain genre elements. Georges **Chaulet** is also the author of ***Fantômette***.

421

WRI: Stephen **Desberg**; ART: Éric Maltaite.

1. *L'Épave et les Millions [The Wreck and the Millions]* (Dup., 1983)

2. *Guerre Froide [Cold War]* (Dup., 1984)

3. *Bon Baisers du Septième Ciel [From Seventh Heaven with Love]* (Dup., 1985)

4. *Suicides* (Dup., 1986)

5. *Dans l'Empire du Milieu [In the Middle Empire]* (Dup., 1987)

6. *Scotch Malaria* (Dup., 1987)

7. *Les Enfants de la Porte [The Children of the Gate]* (Dup., 1988)

8. *Falco* (Dup., 1989)

9. *Les Années de Brouillard [The Fog Years]* (Dup., 1990)

10. *Morgane Angel* (Dup., 1991)

11. *Le Seuil de Karlov [The Threshold of Karlov]* (Dup., 1992)

STORY: Science fiction thriller, incorporating time-travel elements.

NOTE: Originally serialized in *Spirou* in 1980.

Quentin Gentil see *Les As*

La Quête de l'Oiseau du Temps [Quest for the Time Bird, transl. as *Roxanna*]

WRI: Serge **Le Tendre**; ART: Régis **Loisel**.

1. *La Conque de Ramor [Ramor's Conch]* (Dar., 1983, transl. NBM)

2. *Le Temple de l'Oubli [The Temple of Oblivion]* (Dar., 1984, transl. NBM)

3. *Le Rige* (Dar., 1985, transl. NBM)

4. *L'Oeuf des Ténèbres [The Egg of Darkness]* (Dar., 1987, transl. NBM)

STORY: To prevent the return of the evil god Ramor, the witch queen Mara sends the knight Bragon and a beautiful girl Pelisse (in English: Roxanna) on a quest to find the mysterious Time Bird.

NOTE: Originally serialized in *Charlie* in 1982.

La Race des Seigneurs [The Race of the Lords]

WRI: Denis Lapiere; ART: Didier Courtois.

1. *La Mémoire Brûlée [The Burned-Out Memory]* (Dar., 1995)

2. *La Tanière de l'Ours Noir [The Lair of the Black Bear]* (Dar., 1996)

STORY: Futuristic thriller.

Radada la Méchante Sorcière [Radada the Nasty Witch]

WRI: Sauger; ART: Gaudelette.

1. *Radada la Méchante Sorcière [Radada the Nasty Witch]* (Aud., 1994)

2. *Waugh!* (Aud., 1995)

3. *Volume 3* (Untitled) (Avd., 1996)

STORY: Humorous tales about a nasty witch and her pet monsters.

NOTE: Originally serialized in *Fluide Glacial*.

Radar

WRI: Unknown; ART: Bob Vinell (Robert Meyer).

1. Course à la Lune [Race to the Moon] (1947)

2. Derrière la Lune [Behind the Moon] (1947)

3. Panique dans la Lune [Panic on the Moon] (1947)

4. La Planète de l'Épouvante [The Planet of Terror] (1947)

5. La Guerre des Robots [The War of the Robots] (1947)

6. L'Enfer aux Rayons Verts [The Green Ray Hell] (1947)

7. Les Titans du Ciel [The Titans of the Sky] (1947)

8. Le Cyclone de Minuit [The Midnight Cyclone] (1947)

9. Les Robinsons de Vénus [The Robinsons of Venus] (1947)

10. La Caverne du Silence [The Cavern of Silence] (1947)

11. Le Prisonnier du Néant [The Prisoner of the Void] (1947)

12. La Lutte Fratricide [A Brotherly Fight] (1947)
STORY: Space opera.
NOTE: Published in its eponymous magazine by Éditions du Siècle/Imperia. Never collected in the graphic novel format.

Rael see ***Dans l'Ombre du Soleil***

Raffington Event see ***Rork***

La Rage de Vivre see ***Boucq***

Rahan

WRI: Roger **Lecureux**; ART: André **Chéret**.
Serialized in *Pif* (first 100 episodes—1969-1977):

1. Le Secret du Soleil [The Secret of the Sun] (1969)

2. La Horde Folle [The Crazy Horde] (1969)

3. Le Piège à Poissons [The Fish Trap] (1969)

4. La Pierre Magique [The Magic Stone] (1969)

5. Le Tombeau Liquide [The Watery Grave] (1969)

6. Le Dieu Mammouth [The Mastodon God] (1969) (rep. Vol. 1, Vail., 1972)

7. Le Pays à Peau Blanche [The Country with White Skin] (1969)

8. La Longue Griffe [The Long Claw] (1969)

9. L'Arc du Ciel [The Celestial Arch] (1970) (rep. Vol. 2, Vail., 1972)

10. La Bête Plate [The Flat Beast] (1970) (rep. as Les Temps Sauvages [The Savage Times], Vol. 2, Vail., 1972)

11. Les Hommes aux Jambes Lourdes [The Men with Heavy Legs] (1970) (rep. as Ceux Qui Marchent Debout [Those Who Walk Upright], Vol. 3, Vail., 1972)

12. Le Petit Homme [The Little Man] (1970) (rep. Vol. 3, Vail., 1972)

13. Comme Aurait Fait Crao [As Crao Would Have Done] (1970) (rep. Vol. 4, Vail., 1973)

14. Le Nouveau Piège [The New Trap] (1970)

15. Mort à la Manta [Death to Manta] (1970) (rep. Vol. 4, Vail., 1973)

16. Le Collier de Griffes [The Necklace of Claws] (1970) (rep. Vol. 5, Vail., 1973)

17. L'Arme Qui Vole [The Flying Weapon] (1970)

18. L'Arbre du Demon [The Demon Tree] (1970) (rep. Vol. 5, Vail., 1973)

19. Le Rivage Interdit [The Forbidden Shore] (1970) (rep. Vol. 6, Vail., 1973)

20. Le Chef des Chefs [The Chief of Chiefs] (1970)

21. La Falaise du Sacrifice [The Sacrificial Cliff] (1970) (rep. Vol. 6, Vail., 1973)

22. La Flèche Blanche [The White Arrow] (1970) (rep. Vol. 7, Vail., 1973)

23. Le Peuple des Arbres [The Tree People] (1970)

24. Le Coutelas d'Ivoire [The Ivory Knife] (1971) (rep. Vol. 1 & 7, Vail., 1972)

25. Le Territoire des Ombres [The Land of Shadows] (1971) (rep. Vol. 8, Vail., 1974)

26. Le Tueur de Mammouths [The Mastodon Killer] (1971)

27. Le Clan du Lac Maudit [The Clan of the Accursed Lake] (1971) (rep. Vol. 8, Vail., 1974)

28. La Terre Qui Parle [The Talking Earth] (1971) (rep. Vol. 9, Vail., 1974)

29. Les Longues Crinières [The Long Manes] (1971)

30. Pour Sauver Alona! [To Save Alona!] (1971) (rep. Vol. 9, Vail., 1974)

31. Le Clan Sauvage [The Savage Clan] (1971) (rep. Vol. 10, Vail., 1974)

32. Plus Vite Que le Zébra [Faster Than the Zebra] (1971)

33. Le Monstre d'un Autre Temps [The Monster from Another Time] (1971) (rep. Vol. 11, Vail., 1974)

34. *La Forêt des Haches [The Forest of Axes]* (1971) (rep. Vol. 10, Vail., 1974)

34b. *Rahan Special: Fils des Âges Farouches [Son of a Savage Age]* (1971)

35. *Le Sorcier de la Lune [The Moon Wizard]* (1971)

36. *Les Singes Hommes [The Men Ape]* (1971)

37. *Le Lagon de l'Effroi [The Lagoon of Terror]* (1972)

38. *Le Signe de la Peur [The Sign of Fear]* (1972) (rep. Vol. 11, Vail., 1974)

39. *Les Liens de Vérité [The Chains of Truth]* (1972) (rep. Vol. 12, Vail., 1974)

40. *Le Dernier Homme [The Last Man]* (1972)

41. *La Falaise d'Argile [The Cliff of Clay]* (1972) (rep. Vol. 12, Vail., 1974)

42. *Le Démon des Marais [The Swamp Demon]* (1972)

43. *L'Île du Clan Perdu [The Island of the Lost Clan]* (1972) (rep. Vol. 13, Vail., 1975)

44. *L'Herbe Miracle [The Miracle Herb]* (1972)

45. *Les Chasseurs de Foudre [The Lightning Hunters]* (1972)

46. *Le Retour des Goraks [The Return of the Goraks]* (1972) (rep. Vol. 13, Vail., 1975)

47. *Les Hommes Sans Cheveux [The Hairless Men]* (1972)

48. *Les Larmes Qui Volent [The Flying Tears]* (1973)

49. *Les Coquillages Bleus [The Blue Shells]* (1973) (rep. Vol. 14, Vail., 1975)

50. *Ceux de la Terre Haute [Those from the Highlands]* (1973) (rep. Vol. 14, Vail., 1975)

51. *Celui Qui Avait Tué le Fleuve [He Who Killed the River]* (1973)

52. *L'Arme à Trois Bras [The Three-Armed Weapon]* (1973) (rep. Vol. 15, Vail., 1975)

53. *Le Petit Homme [The Little Man]* (1973) (rep. Vol. 16, Vail., 1975)

54. *La Mère des Mères [The Mother of Mothers]* (1973)

55. *Celui Qui Fait des Nuages [The Cloud Maker]* (1973)

56. *Les Mangeurs d'Hommes [The Man-Eaters]* (1973) (rep. Vol. 15, Vail., 1975)

57. *Le Pont des Singes [The Monkey Bridge]* (ART: Guido Zamperoni) (1973) (rep. Vol. 21, Vail., 1976)

58. *Le Dieu Bonheur [The God of Happiness]* (1974) (rep. Vol. 16, Vail., 1975)

59. *L'Arbre-Roi [The Tree-King]* (1974) (ART: Guido Zamperoni) (rep. Vol. 19, Vail., 1976)

60. *L'Enfance de Rahan [Rahan's Childhood]* (1974)

61. *La Lance Magique [The Magic Spear]* (1974)

62. *La Part des Chefs [The Chieftains' Share]* (1974) (ART: Guido Zamperoni) (rep. Vol. 20, Vail., 1976)

63. *La Bête Qui Parle [The Talking Beast]* (1974) (rep. Vol. 17, Vail., 1976)

64. *L'Oeil Qui Voit Loin [The Farseeing Eye]* (1974) (ART: G. Zamperoni) (rep. Vol. 22, Vail., 1977)

65. *L'Enfant Chef [The Chief Child]* (1974) (rep. Vol. 17, Vail., 1976)

66. *Les Hommes sans Tête [The Headless Men]* (1974) (rep. Vol. 17, Vail., 1976)

67. *L'Oiseau Qui Court [The Running Bird]* (1974) (rep. Vol. 18, Vail., 1976)

68. *Le Captif du Grand Fleuve [The Prisoner of the Great River]* (1974)

69. *L'Arme Terrifiante [The Terrifying Weapon]* (1974) (rep. Vol. 18, Vail., 1976)

70. *Les Esprits de la Nuit [The Night Spirits]* (1975) (rep. Vol. 20, Vail., 1976)

71. *Le Sacrifice de Maoni [Maoni's Sacrifice]* (1975) (rep. Vol. 17, Vail., 1976)

72. *La Boue Qui Dévore [The Devouring Mud]* (1975)

73. *L'Oeil Bleu [The Blue Eye]* (1975) (rep. Vol. 19, Vail., 1976)

74. *Les Adorateurs de la Mort [The Death Worshippers]* (1975)

75. *Les Enfants du Fleuve [The Children of the River]* (1975) (rep. Vol. 20, Vail., 1976)

76. *La Caverne des Tromperies [The Cavern of Tricks]* (1975)

77. *Le Quatre-Jambes [The Four-Legs]* (1975) (rep. Vol. 23, Vail., 1977)

78. *Le Clan des Hommes Doux [The Clan of the Soft Men]* (1975)

79. *La Vallée des Tourments [The Valley of Pain]* (1976) (rep. Vol. 22, Vail., 1977)

80. *Le Démon de Paille [The Straw Demon]* (1976) (rep. Vol. 23, Vail., 1977)

81. *Les Pierres d'Eau [The Water Stones]* (1976) (rep. Vol. 24, Vail., 1977)

82. *Les Poissons Femmes [The Fish Women]* (1976)

83. *Les Têtes à Corne [The Horn Heads]* (1976)

84. *Le Wampas sans Ailes [The Wingless Wampas]* (1976) (ART: Enrique Romero) (rep. Vol. 26, Vail., 1977)

85. *Les Pierres qui Brûlent [The Burning Stones]* (1976) (rep. Vol. 25, Vail., 1977)

86. *Le Venin de Docilité [The Slave Poison]* (1976) (rep. Vol. 25, Vail., 1977)

87. *Le Secret de Wandaka [Wandaka's Secret]* (1976) (rep. Vol. 27, Vail., 1977)

88. *La Chose Qui s'Étire [The Pulling Thing]* (1977) (rep. Vol. 27, Vail., 1977)

89. *Dans les Entrailles du Gorak [In the Gorak's Belly]* (1977)

90. *Le Dernier Massacre [The Last Massacre]* (1977)

91. *Le Secret des Eaux Profondes [The Secret of the Deep Waters]* (1977)

92. *Le Coutelas Perdu [The Lost Knife]* (1977)

93. *Le Rire de Tanaka [Tanaka's Laugh]* (1977)

94. *Le Piège Fantastique [The Fantastic Trap]* (ART: Enrique Romero) (1977)

95. *La Vallée Heureuse [The Happy Valley]* (1977)

96. *La Mort de Rahan [Rahan's Death]* (1977)

97. *Pour Venger Rahan [To Avenge Rahan]* (1977)

98. *Le Dieu Soleil [The Sun God]* (1977)

99. *La Caverne Hantée [The Haunted Cavern]* (ART: Enrique Romero) (1977)

100. *L'Impossible Capture [The Impossible Capture]* (1977)
Graphic Novels (new material only/no reprints listed):

Vol. 21. L'Île des Morts Vivants [The Island of the Living Dead] (ART: Guido Zamperoni) (Vail., 1976)

Vol. 23. Les Longues Jambes [The Long Legs] (ART: Guido Zamperoni) (Vail., 1977)

Vol. 24. Le Souffle du Ciel [The Breath of the Sky] (ART: Guido Zamperoni) (Vail., 1977)

Vol. 25. L'Oeil de Granit [The Granite Eye] / La Folie de l'Ivoire [The Ivory Madness] (ART: Guido Zamperoni) (Vail., 1977)

Vol. 26. Le Secret de l'Enfance de Rahan [The Secret of Rahan's Childood] / Pour un Quartier de Viande [For a Piece of Meat] (ART: Enrique Romero) (Vail., 1977)

Vol. 27. L'Herbe Miracle [The Miracle Herb] (ART: Enrique Romero) (Vail., 1977)

Vol. 2 (new numbering). Le Trésor de Rahan [Rahan's Treasure] (Vail., 1980)

Vol. 3. Le Spectre de Taroa [The Ghost of Taroa] (Vail., 1981)

Messidor 1. Le Maître des Fauves [The Beast Master] (Mess., 1986)

Messidor 2. Le Grand Amour de Rahan [Rahan's Great Love] (Mess., 1986)

Messidor 3. La Troisième Vie de Rahan [Rahan's Third Life] (Mess., 1987)

Novedi 1. Rahan Contre le Temps [Rahan Against Time] (Novedi, 1991)

Novedi 2. La Mangeuse d'Homme [The Man Eater] (Novedi, 1992)

Novedi 3. Rahan le Tueur [Rahan the Killer] (Dup., 1993)
STORY: Rahan, son of Crao, is a lone, blond caveman who travels throughout prehistoric Earth, teaching the first elements of civilization to the folks he encounters.

NOTE: Originally serialized in *Pif*, **Rahan** (like ***Tounga***) is included here primarily because it depicts Cro-Magnons cohabiting with Neanderthals and various dinosaur species. Later **Rahan** reprint editions included some new stories (often about the character's youth), or linking stories, which have not been listed here.

Rails
WRI: David Chauvel; ART: Fred Simon.

1. *Jaguars* (Delc., 1992)

2. *La Garde Blanche [The White Guard]* (Delc., 1993)

3. *La Chute du Lion [The Lion's Fall]* (Delc., 1994)

4. *Face à Face [Face to Face]* (Delc., 1995)
STORY: Dystopian future about a rail-based society.

La Raison du Plus Mort
see **Foerster**

Rasch see Laïyna

Le Rayon U [The U Ray] (1944; rep. Lom., 1974)
WRI/ART: Edgar-Pierre **Jacobs.**
STORY: A Flash Gordon-type story.

Red Ketchup
WRI: Pierre Fournier; ART: Real Godbout.

1. *Kamarade Ultra* (Croc, 1988; rep. Dar., 1991)

2. *Red Ketchup vs. Red Ketchup* (Dar., 1992)

3. *Red Ketchup S'Est Échappé! [Red Ketchup Has Escaped!]* (Dar., 1994)
STORY: The comedic adventures of an ultra-violent FBI agent and his clones.
NOTE: French-Canadian series originally published in Montreal.

Reflets d'Écume [Foam Reflections]
WRI: Ange; ART: Varanda.

1. *Naïade* (VdO., 1994)

2. *Noyade [Drowning]* (VdO., 1995)
STORY: A new, more adult version of the *Little Mermaid* story.

Région Étrangère [Foreign Area] (Hum., 1989)
WRI: Jean-Pierre **Dionnet**; ART: Bob Deum.
STORY: Science fiction.

Les Remparts d'Écume [The Ramparts of Foam]
WRI: Turf; ART: Joël Mouclier.

1. *Les Yeux Clos [The Eyes Closed]* (Delc., 1990)
WRI: Frédéric Contremarche; ART: Joël Mouclier.

2. *La Nuit des Masques [The Night of the Masks]* (Delc., 1992)
STORY: Post-apocalyptic stories.

Les Remparts de Sang [The Ramparts of Blood]
WRI: Éric Corbeyran; ART: Patrice Garcia.

1. *La Gourbeille* (Sol., 1994)
STORY: Heroic fantasy.

Les Rendez-Vous de Minuit see **Foerster**

Le Résistant [The Resistant]
WRI: François **Corteggiani**; ART: Jean-Yves **Mitton**.
STORY: A man fights alone against an extraterrestrial invasion.
NOTE: Serialized in *Pif* in 1989; not collected in the graphic novel format.

Rêves Écarlates [Scarlett Dreams] (Aedena, 1987)
WRI/ART: Robert **Gigi**.
STORY: Collection of science fiction art & stories.

Richard Bantam
WRI: André-Paul **Duchateau**; ART: Decoster.

1. *Les Sept Périls de Sumor [The Seven Perils of Sumor]* (Rossel, 1975)

2. *Le Châtiment des Cinq Morts [The Punishment of the Five Deaths]* (Rossel, 1976)
STORY: Exotic thriller with science fiction elements.

Les Rigolus et les Tristus see **Arthur, Le Fantôme Justicier**

Robert Franc
WRI/ART: Francis Josse.

1. *La Cité Sous la Mer [The City Under the Sea]* (1947)
STORY: An intrepid adventurer defeats would-be world conquerors.
NOTE: Originally serialized in *Le Conquérant*; never collected in the graphic novel format.

Les Robinsons de la Terre [The Robinsons of Earth] (Vail., 1980)
WRI: Roger **Lecureux**; ART: Alfonso Font.
STORY: Science fiction.
NOTE: Originally serialized in *Pif*. Font is a renowned Spanish artist.

Rocambole
Based on the famous character created by popular writer Victor-Alexis **Ponson du Terrail**.
1. Rocambole (14 issues, Éditions Armand Fleury, 1947)
WRI/ART: Gaston Niezab.

1. *La Vengeance de l'Italien [The Italian's Revenge]*

2. *La Falaise Tragique [The Tragic Cliff]*

3. *La Trahison de Fornarina [Fornarina's Betrayal]*

4. *Les Frères Ennemis [The Enemy Brothers]*

5. *Le Millions de Kerma [Kerma's Millions]*

6. *La Fille du Baron [The Baron's Daughter]*

7. *Le Guet-Apens de Belleville [The Belleville Ambush]*

8. *La Lettre de Baccarat [Baccarat's Letter]*

9. *La Folie de Baccarat [Baccarat's Madness]*

10. *Le Double Piège [Double Trap]*

11. *La Méprise de Bastien [Bastien's Mistake]*

12. *Les Oiseaux en Cage [Birds in Cage]*

13. Le Chevalier Errant [The Wandering Knight]

14. L'Évasion de Baccarat [Baccarat's Escape]
    STORY: Faithful adaptation of the first serial.
        2. *Rocambole* (242 strips, Le Parisien Libéré, 1949–50)
    WRI/ART: André Galland.
        3. *Nouvelles Aventures de Rocambole [Rocambole's New Adventures]* (610 strips, Le Parisien Libéré, 1954-56)
    WRI/ART: André Galland.
        4. *Rocambole* (41 issues, Éditions Aventures & Voyages (Mon Journal), 1964–67)
    WRI/ART: ??

1. La Machination [The Scheme]

2. Le Troisième Larron [The Third Partner]

3. L'Enlèvement [The Kidnapping]

4. Sir Williams N'Est Pas Content! [Sir Williams Is Unhappy!]

5. Pris au Piège [Trapped]

6. Sir Williams Démasqué [Sir Williams Unmasked]

7. Rocambole et le Club des Valets de Coeur [Rocambole and the Club of the Jacks of Hearts]

8. La Toile de l'Araignée [The Spider's Web]

9. Le Moulin des Soupirs [The Windmill of Sighs]

10. Le Château de Dagomar [Dagomar's Castle]

11. L'Héritage de Patricia [Patricia's Inheritance]

12. Le Mystérieux Sosie [The Mysterious Lookalike]

13. Un Rival Diabolique [A Diabolical Rival]

14. Jeu Dangereux [Dangerous Game]

15. Rocambole Contre Mister X [Rocambole vs. Mister X]

16. L'Insaisissable [The Uncatchable]

17. Un Piège Diabolique [A Diabolical Trap]

18. Le Visiteur du Soir [The Visitor of the Evening]

19. La Tabatière de l'Empereur [The Emperor's Snuff Box]

20. Rocambole Pris au Piège [Rocamble Trapped]

21. La Rivière de Diamants [The River of Diamonds]

22. Les Fils du Dragon [The Sons of the Dragon]

23. Le Fantôme de Dagomar [Dagomar's Ghost]

24. L'Ombre de la Potence [The Shadow of the Gallows]

25. L'Enlèvement [The Kidnapping]

26. Le Mystère de la Galerie Raphael [The Mystery of the Raphael Gallery]

27. Échec et Mat [Checkmate]

28. Les Faussaires [The Forgers]

29. L'Énigme du Sphinx [The Mystery of the Sphinx]

30. Le Collier Maudit [The Accursed Necklace]

31. Un Fabuleux Héritage [A Fabulous Inheritance]

32. Défi à la Mort [Defying Death]

33. Une Main dans l'Ombre [A Hand in the Shadow]

34. Le Prisonnier de la Casbah [Prisoner of the Casbah]

35. Le Goeland Noir [The Black Seagull]

36. Le Mystère de Cross Island [The Mystery of Cross Island]

37. À la Poursuite du Fantôme [Pursuing the Ghost]

38. L'Étoile du Matin [The Morning Star]

39. Le Cinquième Homme [The Fifth Man]

40. Bahadus le Cruel [Bahadus the Cruel]

41. La Mort Que l'On N'Attendait Pas [The Unexpected Dead Man]
    STORY: After a fairly faithful adaptation of the original serials in the early issues, Rocambole is depicted as a adventurer who lives in semi-retirement in a castle with his faithful manservant and his dog, Kid. He is periodically summoned to London by the Secret Service to undertake a variety of perilous missions.
    NOTE: With No. 21, *Rocambole* merged with its sister magazine **Rouletabille** (see below) and became **Rocambole et Rouletabille**.

Roc Météor
    WRI/ART: Albert **Weinberg**.
    STORY: The adventures of a space pilot.
    NOTE: Published in *Heroic Albums* in 1955-56; never collected in the graphic novel format.

Roger Fringant (Futuropolis, 1981)
    WRI/ART: Jacques Lob.
    STORY: Satirical science fiction stories.

Rogon Le Leu
    WRI: Didier **Convard**; ART: Chabert.

1. Château Sortilège [Spellbound Castle] (Delc., 1995)

2. Les Enfants de Brocéliande [The Children of Broceliande] (Delc., 1996)
    STORY: The adventures of Merlin's son.

Le Roi Cyclope [King Cyclops]

WRI/ART: Isabelle Dethan.

1. *Le Puits aux Morts [The Well of the Dead]* (Delc., 1996)
STORY: Heroic fantasy.

Roq

WRI: Avossa; ART: Tarquin.

1. *La Prospère Magnifique [The Magnificent Prosper]* (Sol., 1992)

2. *Le Prince Courageux [The Courageous Prince]* (Sol., 1993)
STORY: Heroic fantasy.

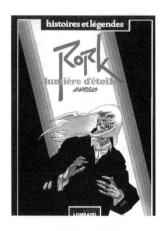

Rork

WRI/ART: **Andréas**.

1. *Fragments* (Lom., 1984; transl. Dark Horse/NBM)

2. *Passages* (Lom., 1984; transl. Dark Horse/NBM)

3. *Le Cimetière des Cathédrales [The Graveyard of Cathedrals]* (Lom., 1988; transl. Dark Horse/NBM)

4. *Lumière d'Etoile [Starlight]* (Lom., 1988; transl. Dark Horse/NBM)

5. *Capricorne [Capricorn]* (Lom., 1990; transl. Dark Horse/NBM)

6. *Descente [Descent]* (Lom., 1992)

7. *Retour [Return]* (Lom., 1993)

Related Works:
Raffington Event, Detective (Lom., 1989)

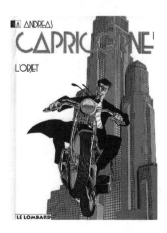

Capricorne:

1. *L'Objet [The Object]* (Lom., 1996)

2. *Électricité [Electricity]* (Lom., 1997)
STORY: Rork is a white-haired "wizard" from another dimension who solves supernatural mysteries, before he uncovers his origins. Supporting characters include Raffington Event, a portly detective of the occult; and astrologer crime-fighter Capricorn, a cross between the *Shadow* and Doc *Savage*.
NOTE: Originally serialized in *Tintin* in 1978.

Rosa Thuringae

WRI: E. Boisset; ART: C. Oudot.

1. *L'Éclipse de Lune [The Lunar Eclipse]* (VdO., 1993)

2. *La Mille et Unième Fleur [The Thousand and One Flowers]* (VdO., 1995)
STORY: Heroic fantasy.

La Rose de Jéricho [The Jericho Rose]

WRI/ART: Uriel.

1. *Premier Jour [First Day]* (VdO., 1995)
STORY: On the eve of World War II, a human scientist attempts to capture the mind of an extra-dimensional entity.

Rouge de Chine [China Red]

WRI/ART: Thierry Robin.

1. *Ville Dragon [Dragon City]* (Delc., 1991)

2. *Masques [Masks]* (Delc., 1992)

3. *Zhan Zheng* (Delc., 1994)
STORY: Heroic fantasy adventures in ancient China.

Rouletabille

Based on the character created by Gaston **Leroux** (also see Chapters I and II for film and television adaptations), starring a journalist detective who investigates fantastic mysteries.

1. Rouletabille (32 issues, Éditions Aventures & Voyages (Mon Journal), 1965-67)
WRI/ART: ??.
STORY: After a fairly faithful adaptation of the original novels in the early issues, *Rouletabille* is suddenly transplanted to the 1960s, and fights enemy spies, etc.
NOTE: With No. 12, *Rouletabille* merged with its sister magazine *Rocambole* (see above) and became *Rocambole et Rouletabille*, No. 12 becoming No. 21 in the new series, which continued until No. 41.

2. Rouletabille
WRI: Éric Cartier (Claude **Moliterni**); ART: Sicomoro.

1. *Le Crâne de Cristal [Crystal Skull]* (Dar., 1985)

2. *La Momie Écarlate [The Scarlet Mummy]* (Dar., 1987)

3. *Le Singe d'Or [The Gold Monkey]* (Dar., 1989)

4. *Sida Connection* (Bagheera, 1993)
NOTE: All-new stories.

3. Rouletabille

WRI: André-Paul **Duchateau**, based on the novels by Gaston **Leroux**; ART: Bernard C. Swysen.

1. *Le Fantôme de l'Opéra [The Phantom of the Opera]* (Lefrancq, 1989)

2. *Le Mystère de la Chambre Jaune [The Mystery of the Yellow Room]* (Lefrancq, 1990)

3. *Le Parfum de la Dame en Noir [The Scent of the Woman in Black]* (Lefrancq, 1991)

4. *La Poupée Sanglante [The Bloody Puppet]* (Lefrancq, 1992)

5. *La Machine à Assassiner [The Killing Machine]* (Lefrancq, 1993)

6. *L'Épouse du Soleil [The Bride of the Sun]* (Lefrancq, 1994)

7. *Le Trésor du Fantôme de l'Opéra [The Treasure of the Phantom of the Opera]* (Lefrancq, 1996)

NOTE: Free adaptations of **Leroux**'s novels, including some which did not originally feature Rouletabille.

La Route des Goëlands [The Seagulls' Road]

WRI: Sylli; ART: **Ab'Aigre**.

1. *La Vengeance du Tiki [The Tiki's Revenge]* (Glé., 1981)

2. *Atoll Tabou* (Glé., 1982)

3. *Le Rêve de l'Alligator [The Alligator's Dreams]* (Glé., 1983)

STORY: The adventures of a young girl and a mysterious Polynesian idol gifted with strange powers.

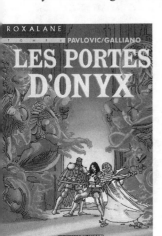

Roxalane

WRI: Patrick Galliano; ART: Boro Pavlovic.

1. *Roxalane* (Hum., 1988)

2. *Les Quatre Chevaliers de Pierre [The Four Stone Knights]* (Hum., 1989)

3. *Alizarine la Rouge [Alizarine the Red]* (Hum., 1990)

4. *Les Portes d'Onyx [The Gates of Onyx]* (Hum., 1991)
STORY: Heroic fantasy.
NOTE: Boro Pavlovic is a Serbian artist.

La Saga d'Alandor see Alandor

Saga de Xam (Losfeld, 1967)
WRI/ART: "Nicolas Devil."

STORY/NOTE: Erotic pop art science fiction. "Nicolas Devil" is a pseudonym used by an artists' studio that included, among others, filmmaker Jean **Rollin** (see Book 2 and Chapter I).

Saisons Voraces see Le Soleil des Loups

Saito

WRI: François **Corteggiani**; ART: Norma.

1. *La Nuit du Oni [The Night of the Oni]* (Sol., 1993)

2. *La Lune Rouge [The Red Moon]* (Sol., 1994)

3. *La Griffe et le Sabre [The Claw and the Sword]* (Sol., 1995)

STORY: Deposed prince Saito and his companion, the dwarf Ooka, seek revenge against the villainous Lord Obata in this medieval japanese heroic-fantasy saga.

Salammbo see Lone Sloane

Salvator (Prifo, 1977)

WRI/ART: Auguste **Liquois**.
STORY: A French superhero, precursor of **Satanax** (see below).
NOTE: Originally serialized in *Tarzan* in 1947.

Samba Bugatti

WRI: Jean **Dufaux**; ART: **Griffo**.

1. *Samba Bugatti* (Glé., 1992)

2. *Monkey Rock* (Glé., 1993)

3. *Le Mystère Bugatti [The Bugatti Mystery]* (Glé., 1995)

4. *L'Oiseau Rouille [The Rusty Bird]* (Glé., 1996)
STORY: Cyberpunk science fiction. Machines can catch a deadly virus transmitted by Man. Samba Bugatti is the hero who must eliminate the virus carriers.

Sang-de-Lune [Blood of the Moon]

WRI: Jean **Dufaux**; ART: Viviane Nicaise

1. *Sang-de-Lune [Blood of the Moon]* (Glé., 1992)

2. *Sang-Marelle [Blood of the Hopscotch]* (Glé., 1994)

3. *Sang-Désir [Blood of Desire]* (Glé., 1994)

4. *Rouge Vent [Red Wind]* (Glé., 1995)

5. *Sang Délire [Blood Delirium]* (Glé., 1996)
STORY: The saga of a family curse.

Santiag

WRI: Jean **Dufaux**; ART: **Renaud**.

1. *Santiag* (Glé., 1991)

2. *Le Gardien de la Nuit [The Night Watchman]* (Glé., 1992)

3. *Rouge comme l'Éternité [Red as Eternity]* (Glé., 1994)

4. *De l'Autre Côté du Rio [From the Other Side of the Rio]* (Glé., 1995)

5. *Le Retour [The Return]* (Glé., 1996)
STORY: Native American legends.

Satanax
WRI: Jean d'Alvignac; ART: Auguste **Liquois**.

1. *Satanax le Superhomme [Satanax the Superman]* (1948)

2. [Untitled] (1948)

3. *Lutte Contre l'Inconnu [Fight Against the Unknown]* (1948)

4. *Satanax Contre les Hommes-Lions [Satanax vs. the Lion Men]* (1948)

5. *Le Défilé des Éléphants [The Canyon of the Elephants]* (1948)

6. *La Colère de Satanax [The Wrath of Satanax]* (1948)

7. *Zacharias Contre Satanas* (1948)

8. *Satanax Joue et Gagne [Satanax Plays and Wins]* (1948)

9. *Bataille de Géants [Battle of Giants]* (1948)

10. *Contre ou Avec Satanax? [For or Against Satanax?]* (1948)

11. *Guerre à la Guerre [War to War]* (1948)

12. *La Chute de l'Archange [The Fall of the Archangel]* (1949)

13. *Menace sur Vallorbe [Threat Over Vallorbe]* (1949)

14. *Le Cauchemar Est Terminé [The Nightmare Is Over]* (1949)

15. *Satanax et les Fantômes [Satanax and the Ghosts]* (1949)

16. *Satanax Contre les Grands Maîtres [Satanax vs. the Grand Masters]* (1949)
STORY: Arsène Satard, a humble court recorder, is given superhuman powers by an old alcheimist. He then decides to fight crime and injustice as Satanax.

NOTE: All sixteen issues of *Satanax* (Ed. Mondiales) were published in 1948-49. They were reprinted in three volumes by Ed. Prifo in 1977.

Scarlett Dream
WRI: Claude **Moliterni**; ART: Robert **Gigi**.

1. *Scarlett Dream* (Losfeld, 1967)

2. *Araigna* (Serg, 1972)

3. *L'Inconnue de Hong Kong [The Unknown Woman from Hong Kong]* (Dar., 1979)

4. *Ombres sur Venise [Shadows Over Venice]* (Dar., 1980)

5. *À Deux Pas de l'Enfer [Two Steps Away from Hell]* (Dar., 1981)

6. *En Double Commande [Double Drive]* (Dar., 1982)
STORY: The beautiful Scarlett Dream works for the International Counter-Intelligence Bureau. Her arch-enemies are Doctor Styx and his beautiful but deadly assistant, Zarda.

NOTE: First serialized in *V Magazine* in 1965, then in the daily newspaper *France-Soir* (1975-76).

Scènes de la Vie de Banlieue [Scenes of Suburban Life]
WRI/ART: **Caza**.

1. *Scènes de la Vie de Banlieue [Scenes of Suburban Life]* (Dar., 1977; transl. NBM, 198?)

2. *Accroche-toi au Balai, J'Enlève le Plafond [Grab the Broom, I'm Taking the Ceiling Away]* (Dar., 1978)

3. *L'Hachèlème Que J'Aime [The Apartment I Love]* (Dar., 1979)
STORY: Fantastic, surreal stories on the theme of suburban life in rent-controlled, low-cost apartment buildings. The hero is a self-portrait of **Caza**.

NOTE: These stories were originally serialized in *Pilote* in 1972.

Les Schtroumpfs see *Johan*

Le Scrameustache
WRI/ART: **Gos**.

1. *L'Héritier de l'Inca [The Inca's Heir]* (Dup., 1973)

2. *Le Magicien de la Grande Ourse [The Magician of Ursa Major]* (Dup., 1974)

3. *Le Continent des Deux Lunes [The Continent of the Two Moons]* (Dup., 1976)

4. *Le Totem de l'Espace [The Space Totem]* (Dup., 1977)

5. *Le Fantôme du Cosmos [The Cosmic Ghost]* (Dup., 1977)

6. *La Fugue du Scrameustache [The Scrameustache Runs Away]* (Dup., 1978)

7. *Les Galaxiens [The Galaxians]* (Dup., 1979)

8. *La Menace des Kromoks [The Threat of the Kromoks]* (Dup., 1980)

9. *Le Dilemne de Khéna [Khena's Dilemma]* (Dup., 1980)

10. *Le Prince des Galaxiens [The Prince of the Galaxians]* (Dup., 1981)

11. *Le Renegat [The Renegade]* (Dup., 1982)

12. *La Saga de Thorgull [The Saga of Thorgull]* (Dup., 1983)

13. *Le Secret des Trolls [The Secret of the Trolls]* (Dup., 1984)

14. *Les Kromoks en Folie [The Kromoks Are Mad]* (Dup., 1985)

15. *Le Stagiaire [The Trainee]* (Dup., 1986)

16. *Le Grand Retour [The Great Return]* (Dup., 1987)

17. *Les Galaxiens s'en Vont en Gags [The Galaxians Leave Laughing]* (Dup., 1988)

18. *D'où Viens-Tu, Scrameustache? [Where Do You Come from, Scrameustache?]* (Dup., 1989)

19. *Les Figueuleuses [The Face-Screamers]* (Dup., 1989)

20. *Le Sosie [The Look-Alike]* (Dup., 1990)

21. *L'Oeuf Astral [The Astral Egg]* (Dup., 1991)

22. *Chroniques Galaxiennes [Galaxian Chronicles]* (Dup., 1992)

23. *La Caverne Tibétaine [The Tibetan Cave]* (Dup., 1992)

24. *Le Cristal des Atlantes [The Atlanteans' Crystal]* (Dup., 1993)

25. *Le Bêtisier Galaxien [The Galaxians' Book of Silly Stories]* (Dup., 1994)

26. *Les Enfants de l'Arc-en-ciel [The Children of the Rainbow]* (Dup., 1994)

27. *Les Naufragés du Chastang [The Castaways of Chastang]* (Dup., 1995)
STORY: Young Khéna; his friend, the mischievous alien Scrameustache; and the Smurf-like Galaxians, fight a variety of cosmic villains, including the ape-like Kromoks.
NOTE: Originally serialized in *Spirou* in 1972.

Le Secret des Hommes-Chiens [The Secret of the Man-Dogs] (Dup., 1995)
WRI: Yves Huppen; ART: **Hermann**.
STORY: A circus of freaks arrives in a mysterious town ruled by a strange countess. Hydrocephalic gnomes walk the streets at night carrying butcher knives.

Semio
WRI: Fred Contramarche; ART: Joël Mouclier.

1. *Les Fleurets [The Swords]* (Delc., 1995)

2. *Ithicène* (Delc., 1996)
STORY: Heroic fantasy.

Séraphin Contre Angelure see *Tracassin*

Sergei Wladi
WRI: Ralph; ART: Riff Reb & Cromwell.

1. *Le Bal de la Sueur [The Ballroom of Sweat]* (EDS, 1985)

2. *Aaargl!* (Glé., 1987)
STORY: Exotic adventures wth genre overtones.

Le Serment de l'Ambre [The Serment in Amber] (Delc., 1995)
WRI: Frédéric Contremarche; ART: Mathieu Lauffray.

1. *L'Amojar* (Delc., 1995)
STORY: Two twin sisters have stolen the fabled Eternity Stone from its eight guardian brothers.

Service des Cas Fous [Service of the Mad Cases] (Dar., 1985)
WRI/ART: **Gébé**.
STORY: Social satire.

Les Shadoks
WRI: Rouxel; ART: Rouxel, Borredou.

1. *Les Shadoks* (Julliard, 1968)

2. *Les Shadoks Pompent à Rebours [The Shadoks Pump Backwards]* (Grasset, 1975)
STORY/NOTE: Based on the television cartoon series (see Chapter IV).

Shekawati
WRI: Gabrion; ART: Antigny.

1. *L'Enfant des Dieux [The Child of the Gods]* (VdO., 1996)
STORY: On an alien planet, a teenager must rescue his tribe, which has been captured by slavers.

Shelter (Hum., 1979)
WRI/ART: Chantal **Montellier**.
STORY: A nuclear alert in a supermarket.

Sherlock Holmes
WRI: André-Paul **Duchateau**, based on the character created by Arthur Conan Doyle; ART: G. Clair & Stibane.

1. La Sangsue Rouge [The Red Leech] (Lefrancq, 1990)

2. Le Chien des Baskerville [The Hound of the Baskerville] (Lefrancq, 1991)

3. La Béquille d'Aluminium [The Aluminium Crutch] (Lefrancq, 1993)

4. Jack l'Éventreur [Jack the Ripper] (Lefrancq, 1994)

5. La Bande Mouchetée [The Speckled Band] (Lefrancq, 1995)

6. Le Rat Géant de Sumatra [The Giant Rat of Sumatra] (Lefrancq, 1996)
STORY: New adventures of the famous detective.

Sibylline
(genre stories only)
WRI/ART: Raymond Macherot.

7. Elixir le Maléfique [Elixir the Maleficent] (Dup., 1979)

8. Bukokratz le Vampire (Dup., 1982)

9. Le Chapeau Magique [The Magic Hat] (Dup., 1983)

10. Le Violon de Zagabor [Zagabor's Violin] (Dup., 1984)

11. Le Kugulde (Dup., 1985)
STORY: The Disney-like adventures of a little field mouse and her friends. Some stories feature fantasy elements.
NOTE: Originally serialized in *Spirou* in 1965.

Sidéral see *Fleuve Noir*

Signé Furax [Signed: Furax] (Pressibus, 1991)
WRI: Pierre **Dac** & Francis **Blanche**; ART: Henry **Blanc**.
STORY: Comic strip adaptation of the famous radio serial (see Chapter III).
NOTE: Originally serialized as 571 daily strips in the newspaper *France-Soir* in 1957-58.

Silence see *Comès*

Silence, On Rêve see *Moebius*

Silver Screen
WRI: Headline & Salvetti; ART: Alamy.

1. Poussière d'Étoiles [Stardust] (Zen., 1990)
WRI: L. Harlé; ART: Brénat.

2. Les Yeux de Cendre [The Eyes of Ashes] (Zen., 1991)
STORY: Cyberpunk science fiction.

Simon du Fleuve [Simon of the River]
WRI/ART: Claude **Auclair**.

0. La Ballade de Cheveux Rouges [The Ballad of Red-Hair] (Lom., 1973; rep. Hommage, 1981)

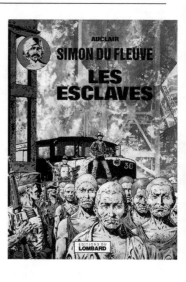

1. Le Clan des Centaures [The Clan of the Centaurs] (Lom., 1976)

2. Les Esclaves [The Slaves] (Lom., 1977)

3. Mailis (Lom., 1978)

4. Les Pélerins [The Pilgrims] (Lom., 1978)

5. Cité NW No.3 (Lom., 1979)
WRI: Alain Riondet;
ART: Claude **Auclair**.

6. L'Éveilleur [The Awaker] (Lom., 1988)

7. Les Chemins de l'Ogam [The Paths of the Ogam] (Lom., 1988)

8-9. Naufrage [Shipwreck] (Lom., 1989)
STORY: The adventures of an idealistic wanderer who travels in a near-future, post-cataclysmic Earth.
NOTE: Originally serialized in *Tintin* in 1973. For legal reasons, ep. 0 was not collected in the graphic novel format until 1981 when it was published in a pirate edition. Auclair left the series in 1979, then returned in 1988, introducing an older and married Simon.

Related Work:
Jason Muller (Hum., 1975)
WRI: Claude **Auclair**, **Moebius**, Pierre **Christin**; ART: Claude **Auclair**.
STORY: Jason Muller is another post-nuclear-war survivor.
NOTE: Originally serialized in *Pilote* in 1970; Jason Muller guest-stars and dies in **Simon** ep. 5.

Simon le Danseur [Simon the Dancer]
WRI; Daniel; ART: **Sirius**.

1. La Rade des Vaisseaux Perdus [The Port of the Lost Ships] (Bédéscope, 1978)

2. Les Étangs de Xyballa [The Ponds of Xyballa] (Bédéscope, 1978)
STORY: Heroic fantasy.
NOTE: Originally serialized in *Spirou* in 1971-72.

666—Succubus
WRI: François Froideval; ART: Tacito.

1. Ante Demonium (Zen., 1993)

2. Allegro Demonio (Zen., 1994)

3. Demonio Fortissimo (Zen., 1995)

4. Lilith Imperatrix Mundi (Zen., 1996)
STORY: Gothic horror.

Le Skblllz
WRI/ART: **Geri**.

1. Skblllz (Pepperland, 1981)
STORY: A fantastic, blue, hairy, intelligent animal expresses himself through consonants, and lays eggs containing virtually anything.
NOTE: Originally serialized as a series of one-page gags in *Tintin* from 1966 to 1970.

Skud
WRI: P. & S. Perna; ART: Stéfane.

1. Les Passeurs d'Egyd [The Traders of Egyd] (VdO., 1992)

2. La Cité Labyrinthe [The Labyrinth City] (VdO., 1994)
STORY: Heroic fantasy.

Snark Saga
WRI: Patrick **Cothias**; ART: Philippe **Sternis**.

1. L'Oiseau Bleu [The Blue Bird] (Bayard, 1982)

2. Le Lapin Blanc [The White Rabbit] (Bayard, 1983)
STORY: Juvenile science fiction series about a race of aquatic creatures.
NOTE: Originally serialized in *Okapi* in 1980.

Les Snorky
WRI: Raoul **Cauvin**; ART: F. Oneta.

1. Le Requin Jaune [The Yellow Shark] (Dup., 1986)

2. Un Snorky à la Dérive [A Snorky Adrift] (Dup., 1986)

3. Mousse en Péril [Cabin Boy in Danger] (Dup., 1987)
STORY: Aquatic version of the Smurfs (see **Schtroumpfs** above), tied in with a cartoon series.

Le Soleil des Loups [The Sun of the Wolves]
WRI: Gilles Gonnort & Ralph; ART: Arthur Qwak.

1. Le Soleil des Loups [The Sun of the Wolves] (VdO., 1987)
WRI: Gilles Gonnort; ART: Arthur Qwak.

2. Le Creuset de la Douleur [The Crucible of Pain] (VdO., 1989)
WRI: Éric Gratien; ART: Arthur Qwak.

3. Saisons Voraces [Voracious Seasons] (VdO., 1995)
STORY: Heroic fantasy.

Les Soleils Rouges de l'Éden [The Red Suns of Eden]
WRI: H. Poudat; ART: S. Fino.

1. Les Amputés [The Amputated] (Sol., 1995)

2. L'Eror (Sol., 1996)
STORY: Heroic fantasy on a world ruled by a theocratic elite.

Songe
WRI: Didier **Convard**; ART: Sonk (Pham Minh Son).

1. Les Forges de la Guerre [The Crucible of War] (Magnard, 1985)
STORY: Heroic fantasy.
NOTE: Sonk is a Vietnamese artist.

Sophie/Starter et Pipette
WRI: Yvan **Delporte**; ART: **Jidehem**.

Starter et Pipette

1. La Révolte des Autos [The Revolt of the Cars] (Dup., 1959)

2. Starter Contre les Casseurs [Starter vs. the Junkmen] (Dup. 1961; rep. Bédéscope, 1983)

Sophie
WRI/ART: **Jidehem**.

1. L'Oeuf de Karamazout [The Egg of Karamazout] (Dup., 1968)
WRI: **Vicq**; ART: **Jidehem**.

2. La Bulle du Silence [The Bubble of Silence] (Dup., 1968)

3. Les Bonheurs de Sophie [Sophie's Fortunes] (Dup., 1969)

4. Qui Fait Peut à Zoé [Who Is Scaring Zoe?] (Dup., 1970)

5. Le Rayon Ka [The Ka Ray] (Dup., 1971)

6. La Maison d'en Face [The House Across the Street] (WRI: Yvan **Delporte**) (Dup., 1963; rep. 1972)

7. Le Cube Qui Parle [The Talking Cube] (Dup., 1972)

8. Les Bonheurs de Sophie 2 [Sophie's Fortunes 2] (Dup., 1973)

9. La Tiare de Matlotl Halatomatl [The Tiara of Matlotl Halatomatl] (Dup., 1973)

10. Le Douanier Rousseau [Custom Officer Rousseau] (Dup., 1974)

11. Le Souffle du Dragon [The Dragon's Breath] (Dup., 1976)

12. Cette Sacrée Sophie [Holy Sophie!] (Dup., 1977)

13. Les Quatre Saisons [The Four Seasons] (Dup., 1978)

14. L'Inspecteur Céleste [Inspector Celeste] (Dup., 1979)

15. Donald Mac Donald (Dup., 1980)

16. *Rétro Sophie* (Dup., 1981)

17. *Sophie et Compagnie [Sophie and Co.]* (Dup., 1984)

18. *Don Giovanni* (Dup., 1990)

19. *L'Odyssée du U522 [The Odyssey of U522]* (Dup., 1991)

20. *Le Tombeau des Glyphes [The Tomb of the Glyphs]* (Dup., 1995)
    STORY: Starter is a car mechanic. Pipette, his friend, is a motorcycle mechanic. In their second adventure (rep. as *Sophie*, ep. 6), they meet Prof. Karamazout and his spunky, resourceful daughter, Sophie. Prof. Karamazout's inventions include the "Egg," an egg-shaped vehicle which can travel over land and water and is propelled by magnetism, and Zoë, an old jalopy equipped with a sentient computer.
    NOTE: Originally serialized in *Spirou* in 1956 (**Starter**) and 1964 (**Sophie**).

Les Sorcières de Thessalie (2 vols.) *[The Witches of Thessalia]* (Glé., 1985-86)
    WRI: Apulée; ART: Georges **Pichard**.
    STORY: Greek mythology.

SOS Bonheur (3 vols.) *[SOS Happiness]* (Dup., 1988-89)
    WRI: Jacques **Van Hamme**; ART: **Griffo**.
    STORY: Political fiction about a near-future society where justice is administered by computers.

La Soupe aux Cadavres see **Foerster**

La Source d'Éternité [The Source of Eternity]
    WRI: Rafael; ART: Birger.

1. *Les Guerriers Oubliés [The Forgotten Warriors]* (Glé., 1985)

2. *La Lumière d'Itsu [The Light of Itsu]* (Glé., 1987)
    STORY: Asian Incas return to life in the Amazonian jungle.

Space Gordon
    WRI: André-Paul **Duchateau**; ART: Raoul **Giordan**.

1. *Les Sept Périls de Corvus [The Seven Perils of Corvus]* (Lefrancq, 1993)
    STORY: *Flash Gordon*–like adventure.

Spartakus
    WRI: Laurent F. Bollée; ART: Michel Valdman.

1. *Fatal Carnaval [Deadly Carnival]* (Dar., 1994)
    STORY: A Terminator-like android pursues terrorists in a future where cloning and space travel are common place.

Spencer see **Les Conquérants de l'Espace**

La Sphère Cubique [The Cubic Sphere] (Hum., 1983)
    WRI/ART: J.-M. Béa.
    STORY: Science fiction.

La Sphère du Nécromant [The Necromancer's Sphere] (Delc., 1987)
    WRI: Thierry Cailleteau; ART: Larnoy.
    STORY: Heroic fantasy.

Spirou
    WRI/ART: **Rob-Vel**.

1. *La Naissance de Spirou [The Birth of Spirou]* (1938–40; rep. Deligne, 1975)

2. *La Seconde Guerre Mondiale [World War II]* (1940–43; rep. Deligne, 1975)

    WRI/ART: **Jijé**.

1. *Spirou et l'Aventure [Spirou and Adventure]* (1943–46; rep. Dup., 1948)

    WRI/ART: André **Franquin**.

2. *Spirou et Fantasio* (1946-48, Dup. 1948; rep. as Vol 1: *L'Héritage [The Inheritance]*; Vol 2 *Radar le Robot*; Dup., 1989)

Spirou et Fantasio:
    WRI/ART: André **Franquin**.

1. *Quatre Aventures de Spirou et Fantasio [Four Adventures of Spirou and Fantasio]* (Dup., 1950)

2. *Il y a un Sorcier à Champignac [There Is a Wizard in Champignac]* (WRI: J. Darc (Henri Gillain)) (Dup., 1951)

3. *Les Chapeaux Noirs [The Black Hats]* (CO-ART: **Jijé**) (Dup., 1952)

4. *Spirou et les Héritiers [The Inheritors]* (Dup., 1953)

5. *Les Voleurs du Marsupilami [The Men Who Stole the Marsupilami]* (WRI: Jo Almo (Geo Salmon)) (Dup., 1954)

6. *La Corne de Rhinoceros [The Horn of the Rhinoceros]* (WRI: Maurice **Rosy**) (Dup., 1955)

7. *Le Dictateur et le Champignon [The Dictator and the Mushroom]* (WRI: Maurice **Rosy**) (Dup., 1956)

8. *La Mauvaise Tête [The Phony Head]* (Dup., 1956)

9. *Le Repaire de la Murène [The Lair of the Moray]* (CO-ART: Roba, **Jidehem**) (Dup., 1957)

10. *Les Pirates du Silence [The Pirates of Silence]* (WRI: Maurice **Rosy**; CO-ART: **Will**) (Dup., 1958)

11. *Le Gorille a Bonne Mine [The Mine of the Gorillas]* (Dup., 1959)

12. *Le Nid des Marsupilamis [The Nest of the Marsupilamis]* (Dup., 1960)

13. *Le Voyageur du Mésozoïque [The Traveler from the Mesozoic]* (Dup., 1960)

14. *Le Prisonnier du Bouddha [The Prisoner of the Buddha]* (WRI: **Greg**; CO-ART: **Jidehem**) (Dup., 1960)

15. *Z Comme Zorglub [Z as in Zorglub]* (WRI: **Greg**; CO-ART: **Jidehem**) (Dup., 1961)

16. *L'Ombre du Z [The Shadow of the Z]* (WRI: **Greg**; CO-ART: **Jidehem**) (Dup., 1962)

17. *Spirou et les Hommes-Bulles [Spirou and the Bubble-Men]* (CO-ART: **Roba**) (Dup., 1964)

18. *QRN sur Bretzelburg [QRN Over Bretzelburg]* (CO-WRI: **Greg**) (Dup., 1966)

19. *Panade à Champignac [Stinking Mess in Champignac]* (CO-WRI/ART: **Jidehem**, **Peyo**, **Gos**) (Dup., 1969)

20. *Tembo Tabou* (WRI: **Greg**; CO-ART: **Roba**) (Dup., 1971)

WRI/ART: Jean-Claude **Fournier**.

21. *Le Faiseur d'Or [The Gold Maker]* (CO-ART: **Franquin**) (Dup., 1970)

22. *Du Glucose pour Noëmie [Glucose for Noëmie]* (Dup., 1971)

23. *L'Abbaye Truquée [The Abbey of Tricks]* (Dup., 1972)

24. *Tora Torapa* (Dup., 1973)

25. *Le Gri-Gri du Niokolo-Koba [The Talisman from Niokolo-Koba]* (Dup., 1974)

26. *Du Cidre pour les Étoiles [Cider for the Stars]* (Dup., 1975)

27. *L'Ankou* (Dup., 1977)

28. *Kodo le Tyran [Kodo the Tyrant]* (Dup., 1979)

29. *Des Haricots Partout [Beans Everywhere]* (Dup., 1980) WRI: Raoul **Cauvin**; ART: Nic Broca.

30. *La Ceinture du Grand Froid [Belt of the Great Cold]* (Dup., 1983)

31. *La Boîte Noire [The Black Box]* (Dup., 1983)

32. *Les Faiseurs de Silence [The Makers of Silence]* (Dup., 1984)

WRI/ART: Philippe Tome (Philippe Vandevelde), Janry (Jean-Richard Guerts)

33. *Virus* (Dup., 1984)

34. *Aventure en Australie [Adventure in Australia]* (Dup., 1985)

35. *Qui Arrêtera Cyanure? [Who Will Stop Cyanide?]* (Dup., 1985)

36. *L'Horloger de la Comète [The Clockmaker of the Comet]* (Dup., 1986)

37. *Le Réveil du Z [The Z Awakens]* (Dup., 1986)

38. *La Jeunesse de Spirou [Young Spirou]* (Dup., 1987)

39. *Spirou et Fantasio à New York [Spirou and Fantasio in New York]* (Dup., 1987)

40. *La Frousse aux Trousses [Fear After Them]* (Dup., 1988)

41. *La Vallée des Bannis [The Valley of the Exiles]* (Dup., 1989)

42. *Spirou à Moscou [Spirou in Moscow]* (Dup., 1990)

43. *Vito la Déveine [Unlucky Vito]* (Dup., 1991)

44. *Le Rayon Noir [The Black Ray]* (Dup., 1993)

45. *Luna Fatale [Fatal Luna]* (Dup., 1995)

STORY: Spirou, originally a groom at the Moustic Hotel; his pet squirrel Spip; and his journalist friend Fantasio are the heroes of a series of fantastic adventures. Genre elements include mad scientists such as Sosthène Silly (ep. 1), the kindly Count of Champignac (introduced in ep. 2), his rival, the crazy but hilarious Zorglub (eps. 15, 16, 19 and 37), and their various, incredible inventions: The "metomol," a mushroom-based gas capable of liquefying metals, the G.A.G., a portable anti-gravity generator, etc. Other genre adventures include the resurrection of a live dinosaur (ep. 13), secret, underwater cities (ep. 17), time travel (eps. 36, 37), various robots and androids, including Cyanide, a deadly Marilyn Monroe-lookalike (ep. 35), and even Death itself, in the person of its Britannic incarnation, the "Ankou" (ep. 27). The ***Marsupilami***, a fantastic animal found in the Amazonian jungle (introduced in ep. 4), now has its own series.

NOTE: Originally serialized in *Spirou*. The Tome & Janry stories have been turned into an animated television series (see Chapter IV).

Le Marsupilami
WRI: **Greg**; ART: Batem.

1. *La Queue du Marsupilami [The Tail of the Marsupilami]* (Marsu, 1987)

2. *Le Bébé du Bout du Monde [The Baby from the End of the World]* (Marsu, 1988)
   WRI: **Yann**; ART: Batem.

3. *Mars le Noir [Black Marsu]* (Marsu, 1989)

4. *Le Pollen du Monte Urticando [The Pollen of Monte Urticando]* (Marsu, 1989)

5. *Baby Prinz* (Marsu, 1990)

6. *Forlandia* (Marsu, 1991)

7. *L'Or de Boavista [The Gold of Boavista]* (Marsu, 1992)

8. *Le Temple de Boavista [The Temple of Boavista]* (Marsu, 1993)
   STORY: The adventures of native Marsupilamis in their Amazonian Jungle. Some supporting characters created by **Franquin** occasionally guest-star in the series.
   NOTE: *Marsupilami* was licensed to Walt Disney Prods. in the early 1990s and was turned into various cartoons. These were creatively unsuccessful.

Spoty et la Lune Alphane [Spoty and the Alphane Moon] (Hum., 1987)
   WRI/ART: Max (Maxime Perramon).
   STORY: The comedic adventures of a wandering robot. The stories parody the clichés of B science fiction movies.

Stan Pulsar
   WRI: Thierry Cailleteau; ART: Olivier Vatine.

1. *L'As des Astres [The Star Ace]* (Delc., 1987)
   STORY: *Flash Gordon* parody.
   NOTE: The *Stan Pulsar* stories were originally serialized in *Fluide Glacial.*

Stany Beule dans la Lune [Stany Beule in the Moon] (1949)
   WRI/ART: **Kline**.
   STORY: Science fiction adventures.
   NOTE: Originally serialized in *Fillette* Nos. 99-142, from January 1948 to April 1949.

Starbuck
   WRI/ART: Philippe **Foerster**.

1. *Le Galion de Minuit [The Midnight Galleon]* (Dup., 1990)

2. *Le Cimetière des Baleines [The Graveyard of the Whales]* (Dup., 1990)

3. *Le Réveil des Oiseaux Prêtres [The Priest-Birds Awaken]* (Dup., 1991)
   STORY: The fantastic adventures of an old sea wolf.
   NOTE: Originally serialized in *Spirou* in 1987.

Starwatcher see **Moebius**

Submerman
   WRI: Jacques **Lob**; ART: Georges **Pichard**.

1. *Submerman* (Glé., 1976)

2. *Les Peuples de la Mer [The Undersea People]* (Glé., 1978)

3. *Les Mémoires de Submerman,* aka *Au-Delà du Grand Bouchon [Submerman's Memoirs,* aka *Beyond the Great Sinkhole]* (Dar., 1979)

4. *L'Aventure Sans Retour [The Adventure of No Return]* (Dar., 1969)

5. *Le Péril Vert [The Green Peril]* (Dar., 1970)
   STORY: The bittersweet tales of Submerman, prince of Atlantis, and his undersea kingdom, which includes the villainous, scaly, green-skinned Hydrons.
   NOTE: Originally serialized in *Pilote* in 1967. Eps. 4 and 5 have not been collected in the graphic novel format.

Suicide Commando (Hum., 1983)
   WRI: Charles Imbert; ART: Philippe **Gauckler**.
   STORY: Science fiction.

Super Boy
   WRI: Robert **Bagage**; ART: Félix **Molinari**.
   STORY: This character, who owes nothing to DC Comics' adventures of *Superman* as a boy, is the son of a scientist who protects Earth against mad scientists and various extraterrestrial threats. He wears belt rockets which enable him to fly, and a radio helmet with a transparent visor à la Judge Dredd.
   NOTE: Published in the digest-sized magazine *Super Boy* Nos. 112–247 (Imperia, 1958–69). Never collected in the graphic novel format.

Super Dupont
   WRI: Jacques **Lob**, Marcel Gotlib; ART: Marcel Gotlib, **Alexis**, Jean Solé.

1. *Super Dupont* (Aud., 1977)

2. *Amour et Forfaiture [Love and Betrayal]* (Aud., 1980)

3. *Opération Camembert* (Aud., 1982)

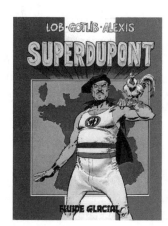

4. Oui Nide You (Aud., 1983)

5. Les Âmes Noires [The Dark Souls] (Aud., 1995)
STORY: The parodic adventures of a wholly French super-hero.

NOTE: Originally created in *Pilote* in 1972, before being serialized in *Fluide Glacial* in 1975. Originally drawn by Gotlib, **Super Dupont** was taken over by **Alexis** in 1974, and, after his death in 1977, by Solé.

Supermatou [Supercat]
WRI/ART: Jean-Claude Poirier.

STORY: A boy turns into Supercat, a masked hero who, with the help of a talking dog, fights crime.

NOTE: This comedy series was comprised of a dozen of six-page stories, serialized in *Pif* starting in 1975. Never collected in the graphic novel format.

Sur l'Étoile see *Édéna (Le Monde d')*

Le Surfer d'Argent: Parabole [The Silver Surfer: Parable] (Cast./Marvel, 1990)
WRI: Stan Lee; ART: **Moebius**.

STORY/NOTE: Galactus returns to Earth and is worshipped as a god. Collaboration between the founder of Marvel Comics and the famous French comics artist on this renowned American super-hero.

Le Surfer d'Argent: La Porte Étroite [The Silver Surfer: the Narrow Gate] (Ed. Lug/Marvel, Nova Nos. 25-26, 1980)
WRI: J. K. **Melwyn Nash**; ART: Jean-Yves **Mitton**.

STORY/NOTE: Mephisto tries to destroy the Earth. Story featuring the famous Marvel Comics super-hero made especially for the French market.

La Survivante [The Survivor]
WRI/ART: Paul **Gillon**.

1. La Survivante [The Survivor] (AM., 1985; transl. NBM, 1993)

2. L'Héritier [The Heir] (AM., 1987; transl. NBM, 1994)

3. La Revanche [The Revenge] (AM., 1988)

4. L'Ultimatum (AM., 1991)
STORY: Aude is the last woman

on Earth in a post-cataclysmic world inhabited by intelligent robots.

Sylfeline
WRI: Marc **Bati**; ART: Bruno Bellamy.

1. Les Cinq Mondes de Sylfeline [The Five Worlds of Sylfeline] (Dar., 1993)

2. Les Pouvoirs de Tchoubou [The Powers of Tchubu] (Dar., 1995)

3. Le Dieu à la Mémoire Perdue [The God with a Lost Memory] (Dar., 1996)
STORY: Lighthearted fantasy.

Sylve
WRI: Brice **Tarvel**; ART: Aouamri.

1. Le Peuple des Racines [The Root People] (Vaisseau d'Argent, 1990)

2. Le Voyage Vertical [The Vertical Journey] (Arboris, 1993)

3. Le Seigneur des Écorces [The Lord of the Bark] (Arboris, 1995)
STORY: In the future, humans live inside a giant tree.

NOTE: Brice **Tarvel** is a pseudonym of science fiction writer François **Sarkel**.

Sylvio
WRI: G. Lions; ART: Philippe **Luguy**.

1. La Menace du Trèfle Rouge [The Menace of the Red Clover] (1974; rep. MC Prods., 1988)

2. Les Libellules Magiciennes [The Magic Dragonflies]
STORY: Sylvio the little cricket; and his girl-friend, Cleo the Bee, thwart the nefarious schemes of cockroach Jack, with the help of their friends, the good fairies.

NOTE: Originally serialized in *Pif* in 1974, and published in six-page installments. Only one graphic novel was published.

Taar le Rebelle [Taar the Rebel]
WRI: Claude **Moliterni**; ART: Jaime Brocal-Remohi.

1. Taar le Rebelle [Taar the Rebel] (Dar., 1976)

2. Le Phare de la Vie [The Lighthouse of Life] (Dar., 1977)

3. Le Géant des Eaux Glauques [The Giant of the Murky Waters] (Dar., 1977)

4. L'Être de Nulle Part [The Being from Nowhere] (Dar., 1978)

5. La Forteresse du Silence [The Fortress of Silence] (Dar., 1979)

6. Le Sablier d'Or [The Golden Hourglass] (Dar., 1981)

7. *La Cité Engloutie [The Sunken City]* (Dar., 1982)

8. *Le Collier de la Mort [The Necklace of Death]* (Dar., 1982)

9. *Le Monde Disparu [The Vanished World]* (Dar., 1984)

10. *L'Empire du Vide [The Empire of the Void]* (Dar., 1985)

11. *Le Cercle de Feu [The Circle of Fire]* (Dar., 1987)

12. *L'Étau [The Vise]* (Dar., 1988)
STORY: *Conan*-like heroic fantasy.
NOTE: Brocal-Remohi is a Spanish artist.

Taï-Dor

WRI: Serge **Le Tendre**, **Rodolphe**; ART: Serrano.

1. *Les Gants de Taï-Dor [The Gloves of Tai-Dor]* (Novédi, 1987)

2. *Le Masque de Taï-Dor [The Mask of Tai-Dor]* (Novédi, 1988)

3. *Gilles de Taï-Dor* (Novédi, 1989)

4. *La Veuve Noire 1 [The Black Widow 1]* (VdO., 1991)

5. *La Veuve Noire 2 [The Black Widow 2]* (VdO., 1992)

6. *Les Enfants Perdus [The Lost Children]* (VdO., 1994)

7. *Le Mage [The Magus]* (VdO., 1996)
STORY: Lighthearted heroic fantasy.

Takuan see *Les Voyages de Takuan*

Tanatha

WRI: Patrick **Cothias**; ART: Dominique **Hé**.

1. *Acte I* (Glé., 1992)

2. *Acte II* (Glé., 1993)

3. *Acte III* (Glé., 1995)

4. *Acte IV* (Glé., 1996)
STORY: Futuristic thriller. Tanatha is a killer who dispatches people whose "life contracts" have expired.

Tandori

WRI: Scotch Arleston (Christophe Pelinq); ART: Curd Ridel.

1. *Le Réveil de l'Éléphant Bleu [The Blue Elephant Awakens]* (Lom., 1993)

2. *La Déesse aux Deux Visages [The Two-Faced Goddess]* (Lom., 1994)

3. *Un Livre dans la Jungle [A Book in the Jungle]* (Lom., 1995)
STORY: A young fakir fights Kali worshippers in ancient India.

Tärhn

WRI/ART: Bernard Dufossé.

1. *Tährn, Prince des Etoiles [The Star Prince]* (Glé., 1979)

2. *Clystar, Planète Océan [Clystar, Ocean Planet]* (Glé., 1980)

3. *Bataille pour Staroth [Battle for Staroth]* (Glé., 1980)

4. *Planète Oubliée [Forgotten Planet]* (Glé., 1981)

5. *Syrul, Menace pour la Terre [Syrul, Menace to Earth]* (Glé., 1981)

6. *La Cité du Ciel [The City in the Sky]* (Glé., 1982)

7. *Les Rêves d'Yscher [The Dreams of Yscher]* (Glé., 1983)

8. *Au-delà des Ténèbres 1: Siann [Beyond the Darkness]* (Glé., 1984)

9. *Au-delà des Ténèbres 2: Athana* (Glé., 1986)
STORY: A young telepath who is also the heir to an alien throne is secretly raised on Earth. After reclaiming his birthright, he embarks on a series of science fiction adventures.
NOTE: Originally serialized in *Djin* in 1978; then in *Triolo* in 1986.

Targa

WRI: Robert **Bagage**; ART: Georges Estève.

1. *Le Totem d'Or [The Gold Totem]* (1947)

2. *Le Maître du Torrent [The Master of the Rapids]* (1947)

3. *L'Anneau d'Ivoire [The Ivory Ring]* (1948)

4. *Le Masque du Diable [The Mask of the Devil]* (1948)

5. *L'Île aux Idoles [The Islands of Idols]* (1948)

6. *Le Requin de Corail [The Coral Shark]* (1948)

7. *L'Empire des Monstres [The Empire of Monsters]* (1948)

8. *La Flèche Vivante [The Living Arrow]* (1948)

9. *Le Trésor des Boucaniers [The Treasure of the Buccaneers]* (1948)

10. *Le Pays Maudit [The Accursed Land]* (1948)

11. *Trapèze aux Tigres [The Tiger Trapeze]* (1948)

12. *L'Oeil du Dragon [The Eye of the Dragon]* (1948)

13. *La Perle Noire [The Black Pearl]* (1948)

14. *Le Palais des Jungles [The Jungle Palace]* (1949)

15. *L'Escalier de Feu [The Stairs of Fire]* (1949)

16. *Les Justiciers d'Ivoire [The Avengers of Ivory]* (1949)

17. *Les Trois Boules Blanches [The Three White Balls]* (1949)

18. *Le Cylindre d'Or [The Gold Cylinder]* (1949)

WRI: Robert **Bagage**; ART: Bob Roc (Robert Rocca).

19. *Les Corsaires de Corail [The Corsairs of Coral]* (1949)

20. *Les Monstres aux Diamants [The Diamond Monsters]* (1949)

21. *Le Monstre du Lac [The Lake Monster]* (1949)

22. *Le Lotus Noir [The Black Lotus]* (1949)

23. *La Fée des Mines [The Fairy of the Mines]* (1949)

24. *La Colonne Maudite [The Accursed Column]* (1949)

25. *La Jungle en Feu [The Jungle On Fire]* (1949)

26. *Le Temple Fantastique [The Fantastic Temple]* (1950)

27. *L'Enfer de la Jungle [Jungle Hell]* (1950)

28. *Le Tombeau du Justicier [The Tomb of the Avenger]* (1950)

29. *L'Homme à la Cagoule [The Man in the Hood]* (1950)

30. *Les Révoltés de la Jungle [Revolt in the Jungle]* (1950)

31. *La Cataracte Maudite [The Accursed Waterfall]* (1950)

WRI: Robert **Bagage**; ART: Carland (André Rey).

32. *La Village de la Peur [The Village of Fear]* (1950)

33. *La Noix de Gor [The Nut of Gor]* (1950)

34. *Le Secret du Silo [The Secret of the Silo]* (1950)
STORY: Tarzan-like character.
NOTE: Originally published by Éditions du Siècle/Imperia in its eponymous magazine. Reprinted later under the name *Agar*.

Tarou

WRI/ART: Bob Dan.

1. *La Jeunesse de Tarou, Maître des Lagons [The Youth of Tarou, Master of Lagoons]* (1949)

2. *L'Héritage de Tarou [Tarou's Inheritance]* (1949)

3. *Le Temple de Bouddha [The Temple of Buddha]* (1949)

4. *La Capture de Tarou [Tarou's Capture]* (1949)

5. *La Vengeance de Tarou [Tarou's Revenge]* (1949)

6. *La Reconnaissance de Tarou [Tarou's Reward]* (1949)

7. *Tarou contre les Pirates [Tarou vs. the Pirates]* (1949)

8. *Prisonnier des Pithécantropes [Prisoner of the Pithecantropes]* (1950)

9. *La Mine d'Émeraude [The Emerald Mine]* (1950)

10. *L'Enlèvement de Tarou [Tarou's Kidnaping]* (1950)

11. *La Grande Peur de Tarou [Tarou's Great Fear]* (1950)

12. *La Cité des Nègres Blancs [The City of the White Negroes]* (1950)

13. *La Reine des Crocodiles [The Queen of the Crocodiles]* (1950)

14. *Pris au Piège [Trapped]* (1950)

15. *La Fin Tragique de Kaarado [Kaarado's Tragic End]* (1950)

16. *Le Lac de l'Anaconda [The Anaconda Lake]* (1950)

17. *Périlleuse Évasion [Dangerous Escape]* (1951)

18. *La Disparition de Tarou [Tarou's Disappearance]* (1951)

19. *L'Évasion de Tarou [Tarou's Escape]* (1951)

20. *Le Retour Agressif de Carver [Carver's Aggressive Return]* (1951)

21. *Les Rubis de Bakouta [The Rubies of Bakuta]* (1951)

22. *Au Secours des Esclaves Blancs [To Rescue the White Slaves]* (1951)

23. *Déluge sur la Jungle [Jungle Flood]* (1951)

24. *Navigation Imprévue [Unforeseen Sea Journey]* (1951)

25. *L'Île Maudite [The Accursed Island]* (1951)

26. *Perdus en Mer [Lost at Sea]* (1951)

27. *Panique au Zoo [Panic at the Zoo]* (1951)

28. *Nouveaux Périls [New Dangers]* (1951)

29. *Le Dieu Salvator [Salvator the God]* (1951)

30. *Le Temple du Soleil [The Temple of the Sun]* (1952)

31. *Le Tatou d'Or [The Gold Tattoo]* (1952)

32. *Prisonniers des Jivaros [Prisoner of the Jivaros]* (1952)

33. *En Péril sur le Tapaua [In Danger on the Tapaua]* (1952)

34. *Face au Jaguar [Face-to-Face with the Jaguar]* (1952)

35. *La Vallée de l'Horreur [The Valley of Horror]* (1952)

36. *Le Pic aux Démons [The Demons' Peak]* (1952)

37. *Le Sacrifice d'Hatapunca [The Sacrifice of Hatapunca]* (1952)

38. *Une Fâcheuse Rencontre [An Unfortunate Encounter]* (1952)

39. *L'Homme de la Mine [The Man from the Mine]* (1952)

In *Tarou*:

1. *Les Démons de la Jungle [The Demons of the Jungle]* (1954)

2. *Justice Immanente [Sudden Justice]* (1954)

3. *Prisonniers des Thugs [Prisoner of the Thuggee]* (1954)

4. *Tragique Évasion [Tragic Escape]* (1954)

5. *Le Grand Maître de Kâli [The Grand Master of Kali]* (1954)

6. *La Fin des Thugs [The End of the Thuggee]* (1954)

7. *La Reine des Fauves [The Queen of the Wild Beasts]* (1954)

8. *Tarou a le Dernier Mot [Tarou Has the Last Word]* (1954)

9. *L'Homme des Cîmes [The Man of the Peaks]* (1954)

10. *Le Tigre Noir [The Black Tiger]* (1954)

11. *Hang-Tchin le Pirate* (1954)

12. *L'île aux Tortues [The Island of Turtles]* (1954)

13. *Face aux Bushmen [Face-to-Face with the Bushmen]* (1955)

14. *Pour Sauver Makiwi [To Save Makiwi]* (1955)

15. *Le Trésor des Hovas [The Hovas' Treasure]* (1955)

16. *L'Or Qui Tue [The Gold That Kills]* (1955)

17. *Au Pays des Nyam-Nyams [In the Nyams-Nyams' Land]* (1955)

18. *Le Sorcier Blanc [The White Wizard]* (1955)

19. *L'Homme aux Éléphants [The Elephant Man]* (1955)

20. *Le Prisonnier de Bengala [The Prisoner of Bengala]* (1955)

21. *La Piste de la Soif [The Trail of Thirst]* (1955)

22. *Le Tombeau de Temasgar [The Tomb of Temasgar]* (1955)

23. *Périls dans la Jungle [Jungle Perils]* (1955)

24. *Aux Prises avec les Tikkis... [Grappling with the Tikkis]* (1955)

25. *Le Tigre de Bali [The Tiger of Bali]* (1956)

26. *Typhon sur l'île [Typhoon on the Island]* (1956)

27. *Mystère à Bord [Mystery on Board]* (1956)

28. *Le Souffleur de Volcan [The Volcano Blaster]* (1956)

29. *La Perle Rouge [The Red Pearl]* (1956)

30. *Le Secret du Samouraï [The Secret of the Samurai]* (1956)

31. *L'Enfant du Mékong [The Child of the Mekong]* (1956)

32. *L'Éléphant Blanc [The White Elephant]* (1956)

33. *La Maison du Klima-n'Djaro [The House of Klima-n'Djaro]* (1956)

34. *L'Homme aux Gorilles [The Gorilla Man]* (1956)

35. *La Cité des Singes [The Ape City]* (1956)

36. *Le Pharaon Noir [The Black Pharaoh]* (1956)

37. *Le Sorcier d'Eau [The Water Wizard]* (1957)

38. *Sous les Chutes du Zambèze [Under the Falls of the Zambeze]* (1957)

39. *Sur la Piste du Roi de l'Or [On the Trail of the Gold King]* (1957)

40. *À la Recherche de Snark [Searching for the Snark]* (1957)

41. *Le Petit Muet de San Felix [The Little Dumb Man of San Felix]* (1957)

42. *Le Temple de Poussière [The Temple of Dust]* (1957)

43. *Dans la Gueule du Serpent à Plumes [In the Jaws of the Feathered Serpent]* (1957)

44. [reprints]

45. *L'Ours de la Cordillère [The Mountain Bear]* (1957)

46. *L'Hacienda des Cactus [The Hacienda of the Cacti]* (1957)

47. *Le Zoo Invraisemblable [The Impossible Zoo]* (1957)

48. *Le Signe du Grand Mahoupa [The Sign of the Great Mahoupa]* (1957)

49. [reprints]

50. *La Grotte du Dragon Noir [The Cave of the Black Dragon]* (1958)

51. *La Vallée de la Solitude [The Valley of Solitude]* (1958)

52. *Le Tigre Vert [The Green Tiger]* (1958)

53. *Sous le Signe de Bouddha [Under the Sign of Buddha]* (1958)

54. *Le Secret de l'Île des Cocotiers [The Secret of Coconut Tree Island]* (1958)

55. [reprints]

56. *Le Château dans les Sables [The Castle in the Sands]* (1958)

57. *Sous l'Oeil de la Caméra [Under the Camera's Eye]* (1958)

58. *La Forêt Interdite [The Forbdden Forest]* (1958)

59. *Le Monstre de Lac Malheur [The Monster of Woe Lake]* (1958)

60. *Le Dernier Couagga [The Last Couagga]* (1958)

61. *Ivoire à Gogo [Ivory in Bulk]* (1959)

62. *La Grande Peur de Bâli [The Great Fear of Bali]* (1959)

67. *L'Homme au Masque de Cire [The Man in the Wax Mask]* (1959)

64. *La Pierre Qui Chante [The Singing Stone]* (1959)

65. *Le Temple Secret d'Azerkh-Amen [The Secret Temple of Azerkh-Amen]* (1959)

66. *La Roche du Ciel [The Rock from the Sky]* (1959)

67. *La Cage aux Requins [The Shark Cage]* (1959)

68. *L'île des Galériens [The Island of the Galley Slaves]* (1959)

69. *Les Démons de la Terre [The Demons of the Earth]* (1959)

70. *Une Bouteille à la Mer [A Bottle Into the Sea]* (1959)

71. *La Piste des Hallucinations [The Trail of Hallucinations]* (1959)

72. *La Tribu des Orchidées [The Orchid Tribe]* (1959)

73. *Passeport pour la Vallée de l'Or [Passport for the Valley of Gold]* (1960)

74. *L'Homme aux Grands Pieds [The Man with Big Feet]* (1960)

75. *Le Secret d'El Dorado [The Secret of El Dorado]* (1960)

76. *La Poupée Indienne [The Indian Doll]* (1960)

77. *L'Hacienda de la Peur [The Hacienda of Fear]* (1960)

76. *L'île Vagabonde [The Wandering Island]* (1960)

79. *Les Écumeurs de I'Amazone [The Reavers of the Amazon]* (1960)

80. *Mutinerie à Bord [Mutiny On Board]* (1960)

81. *La Zone du Silence [The Zone of Silence]* (1960)

82. *La Prison de Bambous [The Bamboo Prison]* (1960)

83. *L'Oiseau Moqueur [The Mocking Bird]* (1960)

84. *Le Sphynx du Lac Victoria [The Sphinx of Lake Victoria]* (1960)

85. *La Pirogue du Grand Caïman [The Canoe of the Great Cayman]* (1961)

86. *La Caravane Fantôme [The Ghost Caravan]* (1961)

87. *Le Palais de Corail [The Coral Palace]* (1961)

88. *Trafic à Pondichéry [Traffic in Pondichery]* (1961)

89. *Seigneur Lion contre Seigneur Tigre [Lord Lion vs. Lord Tiger]* (1961)

90. *Les Rubis du Maharajah [The Rubies of the Maharajah]* (1961)

91. *Le Portrait de Bouddha [The Portrait of Buddha]* (1961)

92. *La Cascade aux Paillettes [The Sparkling Waterfall]* (1961)

93. *La Caverne aux Monstres Marins [The Cave of the Sea Monsters]* (1961)

94. *L'Aigle de Malacca [The Eagle of Malacca]* (1961)

95. *La Pagode aux Cobras [The Pagoda of the Cobras]* (1961)

96. *Le Kriss d'Or [The Gold Kriss] / Les Canons de Pierre [The Stone Cannons]* (1961)

97. *Le Bassin aux Lotus d'Or [The Pond with the Golden Lotus]* (1962)

98. *Les Trois Noix d'Arec [The Three Nuts of Arec]* (1962)

99. *Le Mystérieux Météorite [The Mysterious Meteorite]* (1962)

100. *Les Dauphins du Pacifique [The Dolphins of the Pacific]* (1962)

101. *Le Mystère de Salt River [The Mystery of Salt River]* (1962)

102. *Le Réveil des Aztèques [The Aztecs Awaken]* (1962)

103. *Une Pêche Miraculeuse [A Miraculous Fishing]* (1962)

104. *Voie Interdite [Forbidden Way]* (1962)

105. *L'Aigle du Roc Vert [The Green Rock Eagle]* (1962)

106. *Le Puits d'Enfer [Hell Well]* (1962)

107. *Le Docteur Tatoué [The Tattooed Doctor]* (1962)

108. *Le Gaucho Blanc [The White Gaucho]* (1963)

109. *Le Défilé du Dragon [Dragon's Pass]* (1963)

110. *La Bête du Cap Horn [The Beast of Cape Horn]* (1963)

111. *Le Secret de l'île de Pâques [The Secret of Easter Island]* (1963)

112. *Le Mage des Îles Kermadec [The Magician of Kermadec Island]* (1963)

113. *La Montagne des Hommes Blêmes [The Mountain of the Pale Men]* (1963)

114. *La Forêt Infernale [Hell Forest]* (1963)

115. *Le Roi des Kangourous [The King of the Kangaroos]* (1963)

116. *Le Toboggan de la Montagne Rousse [The Toboggan of Rust Mountain]* (1963)

117. *La Rivière Empoisonnée [The Poisoned River]* (1963)

118. *La Cascade Diabolique [The Devil's Waterfall]* (1963)

119. *La Mine du Glouton [The Glutton's Mine]* (1963)

120. *L'Homme sans Visage [The Faceless Man]* (1964)

121. *Panique sur le Pacific Railway [Panic on Pacific Railway]* (1964)

122. *Le Ranch du Totem [The Totem Ranch]* (1964)

123. *Des Triangles sur le Sable [Triangles on the Sand]* (1964)

124. *Une Fâcheuse Rencontre [An Unfortunate Encounter]* (1964)

125. *Mystère aux Caraïbes [Mystery in the Caribbean]* (1964)

126. *Le Cimetière des Sargasses [The Graveyard of the Sargasso]* (1964)

127. *L'Île du Pot au Noir [The Black Pot Island]* (1964)

128. *Prisonnier des Hommes-Lions [Prisoner of the Lion-Men]* (1964)

129. *Le Casque de Kiriburu [The Helmet of Kiriburu]* (1964)

130. *La Caverne du Léopard [The Leopard's Cave]* (1964)

131. *La Tribu Perdue des Gorilles [The Lost Tribe of the Gorillas]* (1964)

132. *La Vallée des Voix [The Valley of the Voices]* (1965)

133. *On a Volé le Kenia [They Stole Kenya]* (1965)

134. *Le Gouffre aux Varans [The Varans' Pit]* (1965)

135. *Le Lac du Targui [The Lake of Targui]* (1965)

136. *La Prison de Glace [The Ice Prison]* (1965)

137. *Un Tour dans la Préhistoire [A Prehistoric Journey]* (1965)

138. *L'Odyssée de la "Belle Aurore" [The Odyssey of the "Beautiful Dawn"]* (1965)

139. *Les Émeraudes de Li-Fang [The Emeralds of Li-Fang]* (1965)

140. *Echec aux Thugs [The Thuggee in Check]* (1965)

141. *Raha, l'Éléphant Fou [Raha, the Mad Elephant]* (1965)

142. *Le Puits Ardent [The Fiery Pit]* (1965)

143. *Face au Pithécantrope [Face-to-Face with the Pithecantrope]* (1965)

144. *Le Maître des Cobras [The Master of Cobras]* (1966)

145. *La Météorite* (1966)

146. *Le Temple aux Spectres [The Temple of Ghosts]* (1966)

147. *La Rivière aux Favials [The Favial River]* (1966)

148. *L'Île de la Licorne [The Unicorn Island]* (1966)

149. *La Pagode aux Perroquets [The Pagoda of Parrots]* (1966)

150. *Le Gardien du Corail [The Guardian of the Coral]* (1966)

151. *La Perle Noire de Kushimoto [The Black Pearl of Kushimoto]* (1966)

152. *Péril en Alaska [Danger in Alaska]* (1966)

153. *Ursus de la Forêt [Ursus of the Forest]* (1966)

154. *Le Ranch Maudit [The Accursed Ranch]* (1966)

155. *Le Cañon de l'Aigle Rouge [The Red Eagle Canyon]* (1967)

156. *Une Course au Wyoming [A Race in Wyoming]* (1967)

157. *Dans les Cavernes de Wind [In the Caves of the Wind]* (1967)

158. *Le Saloon Hanté [The Haunted Saloon]* (1967)

159. *Les Naufrageurs de Socorro [The Shipwreckers of Socorro]* (1967)

160. *Le Trésor de Moctezuma [The Treasure of Moctezuma]* (1967)

161. *Le Cirque en Folie [The Crazy Circus]* (1967)

162. *Surprise aux Samoa [Surprise in Samoa]* (1967)

163. *Face aux Derniers Cannibales [Face-to-Face with the Last Cannibals]* (1967)

164. *Prisonniers des Baleines [Prisoner of the Whales]* (1967)

165. *Adieu au Cormoran [Farewell to the Cormorant]* (1967)

166. *La Cité du Mystère [The City of Mystery]* (1967)

167. *Le Rendez-Vous des Condors [The Condors' Rendezvous]* (1968)

168. *La Rivière des Malheurs [The River of Woes]* (1968)

169. *Gahanda la Sorcière [Gahanda the Witch]* (1968)

170. *L'Idole qui Tue [The Murderous Idol]* (1968)

171. *La Route dans l'Ombre [The Road Into the Shadows]* (1968)

172. *L'Arme de Cristal [The Crystal Weapon]* (1968)

173. *La Captive du Dragon [The Dragon's Captive]* (1968)

174. *Les Sortilèges de la Forêt [The Spells of the Forest]* (1968)

175. *Le Signe de Granit [The Granite Sign]* (1968)

176. *L'Île Sous-Marine [The Underwater Island]* (1968)

177. *La Tortue d'Or [The Gold Turtle]* (1969)

178. *La Porte du Néant [The Gate into the Void]* (1969)

179. *L'Étrange Message [The Strange Message]* (1969)

180. *La Malédiction du Grand Mokissos [The Curse of Great Mokissos]* (1969)

181. *Le Trou sans Fond [The Bottomless Pit]* (1969)

182. *Le Miroir Magique [The Magic Mirror]* (1969)

183. *Le Serpent à Épines [The Thorny Snake]* (1969)

184. *Un Curieux Pirate [A Curious Pirate]* (!969)

185. *L'Invraisemblable Île Mini [The Impossible Mini Island]* (1969)

186. *Abdou Perle Noire [Abdou Black Pearl]* (1969)

187. *Le Marabout Rouge [The Red Marabout]* (1970)

188. *L'Heure du Soleil Tuera! [The Hour of the Killing Sun]* (1970)

189. *Le Temple du Tigre [The Temple of the Tiger]* (1970)

190. *Le Roi des Yacks [The King of the Yaks]* (1970)

191. *La Rose du Bengale [The Bengal Rose]* (1970)

192. *La Colère de Civa [The Wrath of Shiva]* (1970)

193. *Le Lac des Géants [The Lake of Giants]* (1970)

194. *Le Cratère aux Surprises [The Crater of Surprises]* (1970)

195. *La Piste Oubliée [The Forgotten Trail]* (1970)

196. *L'Inconnu de l'île Siribu [The Unknown Man from Siribu Island]* (1970)

197. *Le Puits du Chinois [The Chinese Well]* (1970)

198. *La Bête de Macassar [The Beast of Macassar]* (1971)

199. *Le Rendez-Vous des Seigneurs [The Rendezvous of the Lords]* (1971)

200. *Un Ami Dangereux [A Dangerous Friend]* (1971)

201. *Tarou, Dieu des Papous [God of the Papous]* (1971)

202. *Le Triangle de Feu [The Triangle of Fire]* (1971)

203. *Un Touriste Bizarre [A Bizarre Tourist]* (1971)

204. *La Jonque Rouge [The Red Junk]* (1971)

205. *Un Homme Cousu d'Or [A Very Wealthy Man]* (1971)

206. *Le Testament du Mongol [The Mongol's Testament]* (1971)

207. *Cavalcade Infernale [Hell Ride]* (1971)

208. *Le Chant des Sables [The Song of the Sands]* (1971)

209. *Un Nid de Dragons [A Dragons' Nest]* (1972)

210. *Un Sport du Tonerre [A Fantastic Sport]* (1972)

211. *La Baie des Phoques [The Bay of the Seals]* (1972)

212. *Le Club des Loups [The Wolves' Club]* (1972)

213. *Le Monde Est en Péril [The World in Peril]* (1972)

214. *Une Bouteille à la Mer [A Bottle into the Sea]* (1972)

215. *Passage Interdit [Forbidden Passage]* (1972)

216. *La Vallée des Mirages [The Valley of Mirages]* (1972)

217. *La Vengeance du Dompteur [The Tamer's Revenge]* (1972)

218. *En Remontant le Colorado [Going Up the Colorado River]* (1972)

219. *Le Réveil des Cherokees [The Cherokee Awaken]* (1972)

220. *L'Homme à la Carabine [The Carbine Man]* (1972)

221. *Le Ranch du Maudit [The Ranch of the Accursed]* (1973)

222. *Jim Black le Trappeur [Jim Black the Trapper]* (1973)
STORY: A remarkable series featuring a Tarzan-like character, who is the son of a French engineer and a Polynesian native woman, and who has been raised by tigers.

NOTE: Originally serialized in *Aventure* (eps. 1–7), *Dynamic* (eps. 8–39), *Ardan* (6 back-up features only, not listed above (1953)), before being granted its own eponymous magazine (1954–73). Never collected in the graphic novel format. Even though many episodes do not contain any genre elements, we have listed the entire series because of its unique importance, mythic quality, and longevity.

La Tchalette et Autres Contes de Magie et de Sorcellerie [The Tchalette & Other Tales of Magic and Witchcraft] (Lom., 1982)
WRI/ART: Jean-Claude Servais.
STORY: Tales of witchcraft and sorcery.

Teddy Bear
WRI/ART: Gess.

1. *Teddy Bear* (Zen., 1992)

2. *Djumbo Warrior* (Zen., 1993)
STORY: Cyberpunk science fiction.

La Teigne
WRI/ART: Tehy.

1. Nuits d'Embrase [Fiery Nights] (VdO., 1990)

2. Haines Flamboyantes [Flaming Hatred] (VdO., 1993)

3. L'Archange [The Archangel] (VdO., 1995)
STORY: Heroic fantasy.

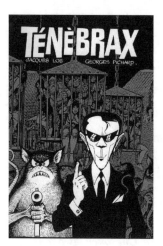

Ténébrax (SERG, 1966)
WRI: Jacques Lob; ART: Georges Pichard.
STORY: Satirical tale of a mad scientist who controls an army of giant, intelligent rats and who plots to take over Paris.
NOTE: Originally serialized in *Chouchou* in 1963.

Terre d'Ailleurs [Earths from Beyond] (Kesselring, 1988)
WRI/ART: M. Riu.
STORY: Collection of fantasy stories.

La Terre de la Bombe [The Earth After the Bomb]
WRI: René **Durand**; ART: Georges **Ramaioli**.

1–2. La Terre de la Bombe (2 vols.) [The Earth After the Bomb] (Glé., 1979, 1981)

3. Les Sortilèges de Perp [The Spells of Perp] (Glé., 1982)

4. Les Cracheuses Oniriques [The Dream Spitters] (Glé., 1984)

5. Pour les Beaux Yeux de la Princesse [For the Princess' Beautiful Eyes] (Glé., 1986)
STORY: Nightmarish description of a savage, post-apocalyptic Earth.

NOTE: Originally serialized in *Circus* from 1977–1986.

Les Terres Creuses [The Hollow Earths]
WRI: Luc Schuiten; ART: François **Schuiten**.

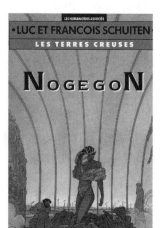

1. Carapaces [Shells] (Hum., 1980)

2. La Tere Creuse, aka *Zara [The Hollow Earth]* (Hum., 1985)

3. Nogegon (Hum., 1990)
STORY: Fantasy adventures about a hollow world whose inhabitants embark on a quest for the truth.
NOTE: Originally serialized in *Métal Hurlant* in 1979.

Terres d'Ombre [Land of Shadows]
WRI: Benoit Springer; ART: Christophe Gibelin.

1. Terres d'Ombre [Land of Shadows] (Delc., 1995)

2. Brèche [Break] (Delc., 1996)
STORY: Heroic fantasy.

Testar le Robot (Fleurus, 1987)
WRI: François **Corteggiani**; ART: Philippe Bercovici.
STORY: The adventures of a friendly robot.

Tetfol
WRI/ART: **Éric**.

1. Le Fils du Loup [The Son of the Wolves] (Lom., 1981)

2. Le Prince du Gévaudan [The Prince of Gevaudan] (Lom., 1981)

3. Les Soleils Perdus [The Lost Suns] (Lom., 1982)

4. Le Grand Livre [The Great Book] (Lom., 1983)

5. La Lumière Noire [The Black Light] (Lom., 1983)

6. Les Héritiers du Crépuscule [The Heirs of Twilight] (Lom., 1984)

7. La Pierre des Certitudes [The Stone of Certainties] (Lom., 1986)
STORY: A young boy who was raised by wolves fights evil wizards and ruthless barons in a pseudo-medieval world.
NOTE: Originally serialized in *Tintin* in 1978.

Thael
WRI: Lanno; ART: Lautussier.

1. La Baie des Diables [The Devils' Bay] (Cygne, 1982)

2. L'Enfer de Nikaïa [The Nikaian Hell] (Cygne, 1983)
STORY: Heroic fantasy.

Thanéros
WRI: C. Carré & D. Parent; ART: E. Larnoy.

1. Le Chant du Majordome [The Majordomo's Song] (Novedi, 1989)

2. Déli d'Enfance [Childhood Crime] (Novedi, 1990)

3. Péliqan (Dup., 1994)
STORY: The eternal battle between Love and Death.

Théophile et Philibert
WRI/ART: Deliège.
Le Phosphopoil (Dup., 1960)
L'Étrange Passe-Temps de B. Kromitch [The Strange Pastime of B. Kromitch] (Dup., 1961)
L'Homme aux Mains d'Or [The Man with the Golden Hands] (Dup., 1962)
STORY: Two heroes outwit an invisible villain; later, they fight a man with the Midas touch.
NOTE: Originally serialized in *Spirou*. Never collected in the graphic novel format.

Thomas Noland
WRI: Daniel **Pecqueur**; ART: **Franz**.

1. *La Glaise des Cimetières [The Clay of the Cemeteries]* (Dar., 1984)

2. *Race de Chagrin [Race of Sorrows]* (Dar., 1984)

3. *L'Orphelin des Étoiles [The Star Orphan]* (Dar., 1987)

4. *Les Naufragés de la Jungle [Stranded in the Jungle]* (Dar., 1989)
STORY: Heroic fantasy.

Thorgal
WRI: Jean **Van Hamme**; ART: Gregor Rosinski.

1. *La Magicienne Trahie [The Betrayed Sorceress]* (Lom., 1980)

2. *L'Île des Mers Gelées [The Island of the Frozen Seas]* (Lom., 1980)

3. *Les Trois Vieillards du Pays d'Aran [The Three Old Men of Aran Country]* (Lom., 1981)

4. *La Galère Noire [The Black Galley]* (Lom., 1982)

5. *Au-Delà des Ombres [Beyond the Shadows]* (Lom., 1983)

6. *La Chute de Brek Zarith [The Fall of Brek Zarith]* (Lom., 1984)

7. *L'Enfant des Étoiles [The Star Child]* (Lom., 1984)

8. *Alinoë* (Lom., 1985)

9. *Les Archers [The Bowmen]* (Lom., 1985)

10. *Le Pays Qâ [The Land of Qa]* (Lom., 1986)

11. *Les Yeux de Tanatoloc [The Eyes of Tanatloc]* (Lom., 1986)

12. *La Cité du Dieu Perdu [The City of the Lost God]* (Lom., 1987)

13. *Entre Terre et Lumière [Between the Earth and the Light]* (Lom., 1988)

14. *Aaricia* (Lom., 1989)

15. *Le Maître des Montagnes [The Mountain Master]* (Lom., 1989)

16. *Louve [She-Wolf]* (Lom., 1990)

17. *La Gardienne des Clés [The Keeper of the Keys]* (Lom., 1991)

18. *L'Épée-Soleil [The Sun Sword]* (Lom., 1992)

19. *La Forteresse Invisible [The Invisible Fortress]* (Lom., 1993)

20. *La Marque des Bannis [The Mark of the Exiles]* (Lom., 1995)

21. *La Couronne d'Ogotaï [The Crown of Ogotai]* (Lom., 1995)

22. *Géants [Giants]* (Lom., 1996)

23. *La Cage [The Cage]* (Lom., 1997)
STORY: Thorgal is a brave Viking warrior who eventually discovers that he is the sole survivor of an alien expedition which was shipwrecked on Earth.
NOTE: Originally serialized in *Tintin* in 1977. Gregor Rosinski is a Polish artist working primarily in French comics.

Thorkael
WRI: Serge de Beketch; ART: Jean-Marc Loro.

1. *L'Oeil du Dieu [The Eye of the God]* (SERG, 1976)

2. *La Porte de Tai-Matsu [The Gate of Taï-Matsu]* (SERG, 1977)
STORY: Thorkael is a clever rogue who fights a variety of gods and thieves in a colorful heroic fantasy world.
NOTE: Originally serialized in *Pilote* in 1971.

Tif et Tondu
(genre stories only)
WRI: Maurice **Rosy**; ART: **Will**.

4. *Tif et Tondu Contre la Main Blanche [Tif and Tondu vs. the White Hand]* (Dup., 1956)

5. *Le Retour de Choc [The Return of Choc]* (Dup., 1957)

6. *Passez Muscade [Hot Potato]* (Dup., 1958)

9. *La Villa du Long-Cri [The Villa of the Long Howl]* (Dup., 1966)

10. *Les Flèches de Nulle Part [The Arrows from Nowhere]* (Dup., 1967)

12. *Le Réveil de Toar [Toar Awakens]* (Dup., 1968)

13. *Le Grand Combat [The Great Clash]* (Dup., 1968)

14. *La Matière Verte [The Green Matter]* (Dup., 1969)

15. *Tif Rebondit [Tif Bounces Back]* (Dup., 1969)

WRI: Maurice Tillieux; ART: **Will**.
16. *L'Ombre sans Corps [The Bodiless Shadow]* (Dup., 1970)

17. *Tif et Tondu Contre le Cobra [Tif and Tondu vs. the Cobra]* (Dup., 1971)

19. *Sorti des Abîmes [Out of the Abyss]* (Dup., 1972)

20. *Les Ressuscités [Resurrections]* (Dup., 1973)

25. *Le Retour de la Bête [The Return of the Beast]* (Dup., 1977)

WRI: Stephen **Desberg**, Maurice Tillieux; ART: **Will**.
26. *Le Gouffre Interdit [The Forbidden Chasm]* (Dup., 1978)

WRI: Stephen **Desberg**; ART: **Will**.
28. *Métamorphoses* (Dup., 1980)

32. *Traitement de Choc [Shock Treatment]* (Dup., 1984)

33. *Choc 235* (Dup., 1985)
STORY: The adventures of two private detectives: Tif, a bald (and bold) adventurer, and his companion, Tondu, a former navy captain who wears a beard. Their arch-enemy is Monsieur Choc, the mysterious leader of the Mafia-like gang of the White Hand. Monsieur Choc wears a tuxedo and hides his face behind a medieval helmet. Many adventures involve fantasy elements: anti-gravity (ep. 6), android duplicates (ep. 8), giant robots (ep. 12), dream travel (ep. 13), invisibility and brain transplant (ep. 16), super-speed (ep. 32), etc.
NOTE: **Tif et Tondu** was originally created by Fernand Dineur for *Spirou* in 1938, then taken over by **Will** in 1948,

who finally retired in 1991. The series is now written by Denis Lapierre and drawn by Sikorski.

Time Is Money (aka *Timoleon and Prof. Stanislas*)
WRI: **Fred**; ART: **Alexis**.

1. *Time Is Money* (Dar., 1974)

2. *Quatre Pas dans l'Avenir [Four Steps into the Future]* (Dar., 1975)

3. *Joseph le Borgne [One-Eyed Joseph]* (Dar., 1975)
STORY: A lonely scientist and a door-to-door salesman try to use a time machine to make money, but their schemes continually backfire.
NOTE: Originally serialized in *Pilote* in 1969.

Timothée Titan
WRI: François **Corteggiani**; ART: Cavazzano.

1. *Rendez-vous sur Proctor 5 [Rendezvous on Proctor 5]* (Hachette, 1987)
STORY: Space opera.

Tintin
WRI/ART: **Hergé**.

1. *Tintin aux Pays des Soviets [Tintin in the Land of Soviets]* (b&w, *Petit Vingtième*, 1930; color, Cast., 1973)

2. *Tintin au Congo [Tintin in Congo]* (b&w, *Petit Vingtième*, 1931; color, Cast., 1946)

3. *Tintin en Amérique [Tintin in America]* (b&w, *Petit Vingtième*, 1932; color, Cast, 1945; transl. Atlantic Little Brown)

4. *Les Cigares du Pharaon [The Cigars of the Pharaoh]* (b&w, Cast., 1934; color, Cast., 1955; transl. Atlantic Little Brown)

5. *Le Lotus Bleu [The Blue Lotus]* (b&w, Cast., 1936; color, Cast., 1946; transl. Atlantic Little Brown)

6. *L'Oreille Cassée [The Broken Ear]* (b&w, Cast., 1937; color, Cast., 1943; transl. Atlantic Little Brown)

7. *L'Île Noire [The Black Island]* (b&w, Cast., 1938; color, Cast., 1943; redrawn edition, Cast., 1966; transl. Atlantic Little Brown)

8. *Le Sceptre d'Ottokar [King Ottokar's Sceptre]* (b&w, Cast., 1939; color, Cast., 1947; transl. Atlantic Little Brown)

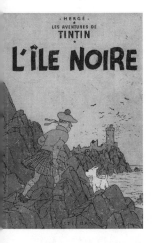

9. *Le Crabe aux Pinces d'Or [The Crab with the Golden Claws]* (b&w, Cast., 1941; color, Cast., 1944; transl. Atlantic Little Brown)

10. *L'Étoile Mystérieuse [The Mysterious Star]* (Cast., 1942 (directly in color, no more b&w editions); transl. as *The Shooting Star*, Atlantic Little Brown)

11. *Le Secret de la Licorne [The Secret of the Unicorn]* (Cast., 1943; transl. Atlantic Little Brown)

12. *Le Trésor de Rackham le Rouge [Red Rackham's Treasure]* (Cast., 1944; transl. Atlantic Little Brown)

13. *Les Sept Boules de Cristal [The Seven Crystal Balls]* (Cast., 1948; transl. Atlantic Little Brown)

14. *Le Temple du Soleil [The Temple of the Sun]* (Cast., 1949; transl. as *Prisoners of the Sun*, Atlantic Little Brown)

15. *Tintin au Pays de l'Or Noir [The Land of Black Gold]* (Cast., 1950; redrawn edition, Cast., 1971; transl. Atlantic Little Brown)

16. *Objectif Lune [Destination Moon]* (Cast., 1953; transl. Atlantic Little Brown)

17. *On a Marché sur la Lune [They Walked on the Moon]* (Cast., 1954; transl. as *Explorers On the Moon*, Atlantic Little Brown)

18. *L'Affaire Tournesol [The Calculus Affair]* (Cast., 1956; transl. Atlantic Little, Brown)

19. *Coke en Stock [Coke in Stock]* (Cast., 1958; transl. as *The Red Sea Sharks*, Atlantic Little Brown)

20. *Tintin au Tibet [Tintin in Tibet]* (Cast., 1960; transl. Atlantic Little Brown)

21. *Les Bijoux de la Castafiore [The Castafiore Emeralds]* (Cast., 1963; transl. Atlantic Little Brown)

22. *Vol 714 Pour Sidney [Flight 714 for Sydney]* (Cast., 1968; transl. Atlantic Little Brown)

23. *Tintin et les Picaros [Tintin and the Picaros]* (Cast., 1976; transl. Atlantic Little Brown)

24. *Tintin et l'Alph Art [Tintin and the Alph'Art]* (Cast., 1986)

STORY: A teenage reporter and his dog Milou (Snowy) travel around the world righting wrongs. Captain Haddock joins Tintin in ep. 9. The brilliant but hearing-impaired Prof. Tournesol (Prof. Calculus) arrives in ep. 11. Other regulars include the inept detectives Dupont & Dupond (Thomson & Thompson), who first appear in ep. 4, the terrifying diva Bianca Castafiore, who first appears in ep. 8, and the villainous Rastapopoulos, who stars in eps. 4, 5, 15, and 22. The character of Mik Ezdanitoff, the human contact between Earth and mysterious aliens (ep. 22), is a caricature of renowned science fiction writer and essayist, Jacques **Bergier** (see Chapter II).

Genre stories include a falling star containing a new chemical element (ep. 10), the curse of an Incan mummy and the subsequent discovery of a hidden Inca civilization (eps. 13 & 14), a journey to the Moon (eps. 16 & 17), a ultra-sound doomsday weapon (ep. 18), the Yeti (ep. 20) and, finally, UFOs (ep. 22).

NOTE: Eps. 1–8 were originally serialized in the daily paper *Le Vingtième Siècle* (1929–38) in Belgium, and eps. 1–15 in the magazine *Coeurs Vaillants* (1930–48) in France. Eps. 9-13 were then serialized in the daily paper *Le Soir* (1940-44) in Belgium. The other stories were serialized in *Tintin* starting in 1946 (in Belgium) and 1950 (in France).

Eps. 1–9 were first drawn and published in b&w editions, and were later redrawn in new color versions after World War II. Because of Hergé's desire to update the stories, ep. 7 was entirely redrawn in 1966, and ep. 15 heavily modified in 1971. The last *Tintin* story (ep. 24) was left uncompleted, drawn in pencils only, before **Hergé**'s death in 1983. It was subsequently published as such.

Tintin was the subject of two live action features, a radio serial, two animated features, and two separate animated television series (see Chapters I, III, and IV respectively).

Tiriel, Héritier d'un Monde [Tiriel, Inheritor of a World] (Nathan, 1975)

WRI: Jean-Pierre **Dionnet**; ART: Raymond **Poïvet**.

STORY: Young Tiriel discovers a gateway to a world of heroic fantasy.

Titan

WRI/ART: Pierre **Dupuis**.

1. *Titan* (1963; rep. Glé., 1977)

2. *Le Retour de Titan [Titan's Return]* (1963; rep. Glé., 1977)

STORY: Space opera.

NOTE: Originally published in an eponymous b&w digest-sized magazine (SNPI).

T.N.T.

WRI: A.-P. **Duchateau**, René **Durand**, M. Borgia (P. Rey); ART: Christian **Denayer**.

1. *Octobre* (Lefrancq, 1989)

2. *Les 7 Cercles de l'Enfer [The 7 Circles of Hell]* (Lefrancq, 1991)
    WRI: A.-P. **Duchateau**, René **Durand**, M. Borgia (P. Rey); ART: F. Brichau.

3. *La Horde d'Or [The Golden Horde]* (Lefrancq, 1992)

4. *La Bête du Goulag [The Gulag Beast]* (Lefrancq, 1995)
    STORY: The adventures of a super-powered mutant.

Tom X

WRI: Robert **Bagage**; ART: Robert **Bagage** (B); Raoul Auger (A).

1. *Panique à Bikini [Panik at Bikini]* (1946) (B)

2. *La Vénus de Tarawa [The Venus of Tarawa]* (1946) (B)

3. *Le Boeuf Musqué [The Musk Ox]* (1946) (B)

4. *Le Tueur Étincelant [The Shining Killer]* (1946) (B)

5. *L'Écran Diabolique [The Devil Screen]* (1946) (B)

6. *Le Piton Infernal [Hell Peak]* (1946) (B)

8. *Le Dragon Bleu [The Blue Dragon]* (1947) (B)

10. *Les 13 Cagoules [The 13 Hoods]* (1947) (B)

11. *L'Oiseau de Feu [The Firebird]* (1947) (A)

12. *La Pagode Sanglante [The Pagoda of Blood]* (1947) (B)

13. *Le Chalet [The Cabin]* (1947) (A)

14. *Les Ravisseurs des Mers Australes [The Kidnappers of the Southern Seas]* (1947) (B)

15. *La Fin du Tyran [The End of a Tyrant]* (1947) (A)

16. *Sang et Ivoire [Blood and Ivory]* (1947) (B)

17. *Le Fantôme des Pyramides [The Ghost of the Pyramids]* (1947) (B)

19. *Le Zéro de la Mort [The Zero of Death]* (1947) (B)

20. *New York Va Sauter [New York Is Going to Be Destroyed]* (1947) (B)

21. *Le Cercle Rouge [The Red Circle]* (1947) (B)

22. *Le Secret de la Sierra [The Secret of the Sierra]* (1947) (B)

23. *L'Héritière du Soleil [The Heiress of the Sun]* (1947) (B)

24. *La Citadelle de l'Abîme [The Citadel of the Abyss]* (1947) (B)

25. *La Terreur des Atlantes [The Terror of the Atlanteans]* (1947) (A)

26. *Les Gladiateurs de l'Océan [The Ocean Gladiators]* (1947) (A)

27. *L'Énigme de Mysore [The Enigma of Mysore]* (1947) (B)

28. *La Marécage des Morts-Vivants [The Swamp of the Living Dead]* (1947) (B)

29. *Document Secret [Secret Document]* (1947) (A)

30. *Le Gang du Castor [The Beaver Gang]* (1947) (A)

31. *La Fusée des Neiges [The Snow Rocket]* (1948) (A)

32. *Le Masque de Soie [The Silk Mask]* (1948) (A)

33. *La Ronde Infernale [Hell Dance]* (1948) (B)

34. *Panique sur la Banquise [Panic on the Ice Flow]* (1948) (B)

35. *Tom X Contre Hitler [Tom X vs. Hitler]* (1948) (B)

36. *Victoire sur les SS [Victory Against the SS]* (1948) (B)

37. *La Griffe du Vautour [The Claw of the Vulture]* (1948) (A)

38. *Le Cheik Rouge [The Red Sheik]* (1948) (A)

39. *Le Crabe des Neiges [The Snow Crab]* (1948) (A)
    STORY: A Doc Savage–like hero fights former Nazis and various mad scientists, discovers lost civilizations, etc.
    NOTE: Originally serialized in its eponymous magazine, published by Éditions du Siècle (later Imperia). Issues Nos. 7, 9 and 18 do not contain any *Tom X* stories. Never collected in the graphic novel format.

Tongue*Lash

WRI: Randy & Jean-Marc Lofficier; ART: Dave Taylor.

1. *La Morsure du Serpent [The Serpent's Tooth]* (Sol., 1996)
    STORY: Two detectives investigate a murder in a pseudo-Mayan fantasy world.
    NOTE: Dave Taylor is a British artist. An American edition of this book was simultaneously published by Dark Horse in the United States.

Tonton Eusèbe

WRI/ART: Jean Lebert.

STORY: Cartoony adventures of a wild and goofy scientist and his nephew.

NOTE: Originally serialized in *Coeurs Vaillants* from 1961 to1967; never collected in the graphic novel format.

Toot et Puit

WRI/ART: Lucien **De Gieter**.

STORY: The adventures of a brave fisherman and his mermaid.

NOTE: Originally published in *Spirou* from 1966 to 1973; never collected in the graphic novel format.

Le Torte

WRI: Pierre **Dubois**; ART: Lucien Rollin.

1. *L'Oeuvre du Fou [The Madman's Work]* (Glé., 1989)

2. *La Geste Sombre [The Dark Saga]* (Glé., 1990)

3. *Éon de l'Étoile [Eon of the Star]* (Glé., 1991)

4. *Tréo Fall* (Glé., 1992)

5. *Le Veneur Noir [The Dark Hunter]* (Glé., 1993)
    STORY: Heroic fantasy.
    NOTE: Pierre **Dubois** is also the author of numerous science fiction and fantasy novels (see Book 2).

Totentanz—La Danse des Morts [The Dance of the Dead] (Magic-Strip, 1986)
WRI/ART: Frédéric **Bézian**.
STORY: Gothic horror.

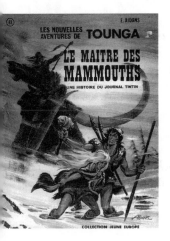

Tounga

WRI/ART: Édouard Aidans.

1. *La Horde Maudite [The Accursed Horde]* (Lom., 1964)

2. *Les Hommes Rouges [The Red Men]* (Lom., 1967)

3. *Le Dieu de Feu [The God of Fire]* (Lom., 1968)

4. *L'Antre de la Mort [The Lair of Death]* (Lom., 1969)

5. *Le Combat des Géants [The Clash of the Giants]* (Lom., 1970)

6. *L'Étalon Noir [The Black Stallion]* (Lom., 1971)

7. *Le Peuple des Arbres [The Tree People]* (Lom., 1972)

8. *Le Maître des Mammouths [The Mastodon Master]* (Lom., 1973)

New Series (reprints not listed):

1. *Noun le Boîteux [Noun the Lame]* (Lom., 1974)

3. *Des Loups et des Hommes [Of Wolves and Men]* (Lom., 1975)

4. *La Grande Peur [The Great Fear]* (Lom., 1976)

5. *Au-Delà des Terres Froides [Beyond the Cold Lands]* (Lom., 1977)

8. *Pour Sauver les Urus [To Save the Urus]* (Lom., 1979)

12. *Le Faiseur de Feu [The Fire Maker]* (Lom., 1982)

13. *La Piste Perdue [The Lost Trail]* (Lom., 1984)

14. *La Dernière Épreuve [The Last Trial]* (Lom., 1985)

15. *La Loi et le Sang [The Law and the Blood]* (Lom., 1986)

16. *La Mort du Géant [The Giant's Death]* (Lom., 1995)
    STORY: A caveman and his pet saber-toothed tiger travel throughout prehistoric Earth.
    NOTE: Originally serialized in *Tintin* since 1961, **Tounga** (like **Rahan**) is included here primarily because it depicts Cro-Magnons cohabiting with Neanderthals and various dinosaur species.

Tous les Haricots ont une Fin see **Foerster**

Les Toyottes

WRI/ART: Louis-Michel **Carpentier**.

1. *La Dalle Maudite [The Accursed Slab]* (Cast., 1980)

2. *Mais Où Est Donc Passé Barnabé? [But Where Has Barnaby Gone?]* (Cast., 1980)

WRI: Raoul **Cauvin**; ART: L.-M. **Carpentier**.
3. *La Dame Blanche [The White Lady]* (Cast., 1980)

4. *La Grande Panique [The Great Panic]* (Cast., 1981)

5. *Les Toyottes Contre Férox [The Toyottes vs. Ferox]* (Cast., 1982)

6. *Histoires de Toyottes [Toyottes Tales]* (Lom., 1989)
    STORY: After a nuclear war, a race of intelligent rats builds a medieval civilization.

Tracassin

WRI/ART: Jean Chakir.

1. *Le Job à Mi-Temps [The Part-Time Job]*

2. *Tracassin au Petit Bonheur [A Little Happiness]*

3. *Quelle Vie de Chien! [What a Dog's Life!]*

4. *La Question Subsidaire [The Final Question]*

5. *Le Satané Gagnant [The Damn Winner]* (Dar., 1974)

6-7. *L'Invasion / La Libération* (rep. as *Le Grand Jumelage [Twin Cities]*, Dar., 1975)
    STORY: Angel Seraphin fights demon Angelure for the conscience of the dim but good-hearted Tracassin.

NOTE: Originally serialized in *Pilote*. Thirty six-to-eight-page stories featuring **Tracassin** were published between 1962 and 1966, but were never collected in the graphic novel format. Only graphic novel-length stories are listed above. Of these, only the last two were eventually collected in the graphic novel format.

Le Transperceneige [The Snowplow Train] (Cast., 1984)

WRI: Jacques Lob; ART: Jean-Marc Rochette.

STORY: In a future Ice Age, the remnants of mankind are confined inside a vast automated train, traveling on a never-ending journey.

NOTE: Originally serialized in *(À Suivre)*.

Le Traque-Mémoire [The Memory Tracker]

WRI: Gibelin; ART: Saint-Servain.

1. *Sanitas* (Delc., 1993)

2. *Alice* (Delc., 1994)

STORY: Working conditions are so harsh on the planet Loon that the miners who extract its precious coral must use an hallucinogenic drug to relax.

Trelawnay

WRI: Dieter; ART: Éric Herenguel.

1. *Trelawnay* (Delc., 1996)
STORY: Heroic fantasy.

Tristan le Ménestrel [Tristan the Minstrel]

WRI: Hélène Cornen; ART: François Plisson.

1. *Le Sortilège d'Ysandrelle [The Spell of Ysandrelle]* (Dar., 1987)

2. *L'Île des Rois Maudits [The Island of the Accursed Kings]* (Dar., 1988)

3. *L'Appel des Druides [The Call of the Druids]* (Dar., 1989)

4. *L'Élixir de l'Oubli [The Elixir of Oblivion]* (Dar., 1990)

5. *Bolbec le Noir [Bolbek the Black]* (Dar., 1991)

6. *Ianna* (Dar., 1994)

7. *Les Conquérants du Soleil [The Conquerors of the Sun]* (Dar., 1995)
STORY: Heroic fantasy.

Les Trois Cheveux Blancs [The Three White Hairs] (Dup., 1993)

WRI: **Yann**; ART: René **Hausman**.

STORY: King Karalius cuts off his people's tongues to keep his secret, but red-haired Vaiva, a witch who lives in the forest, knows what it is.

Troll

WRI: Morevan, Sfar; ART: Boiscommun.

1. *Les Insoumis [The Insurgents]* (Delc., 1996)
STORY: Heroic fantasy.

Tropique des Étoiles [Tropic of the Stars]

WRI/ART: Chris **Lamquet**.

1. *L'Enfant Clone [The Clone Child]* (Hélyode, 1991)

2. *La Phase Végétale [The Vegetal Phase]* (Hélyode, 1992)

3. *Les Boréales [The Boreals]* (Hélyode, 1993)

4. *Le Réveil des Poussières [The Dust Awakens]* (Lefrancq, 1996)
STORY: Ecological science fiction.

Tueur de Monde see **Moebius**

Tueur de Ville [The City Killer]

WRI: Ralph; ART: Kisler.

1. *Vixit* (VdO., 1988)
WRI: Ruffner; ART: Kisler.

2. *Delenda Carthago* (VdO., 1994)
STORY: In the future, the powerful organization which controls Earth sends a commando of thirteen warriors to destroy a rebel city.

Tumak

WRI/ART: B. Linssen.

1. *Les Survivants des Terres Froides [The Survivors of the Cold Earth]* (Deligne, 1979)
STORY: Post-apocalyptic science fiction.

Tumak, Fils de la Jungle [Tumak, Son of the Jungle]

WRI: Unknown; ART: Raymond **Poïvet**.

STORY: Another French *Tarzan*.

NOTE: Originally serialized in Nos. 1–19 of *L'Intrépide* in 1948.

Udolfo
WRI: André-Paul **Duchateau**; ART: Eddy **Paape**.

1. *La Montre aux Sept Rubis [The Watch with 7 Rubies]* (Jonas, 1980)

2. *Le Grimoire de Lucifer [Lucifer's Grimoir]* (Bédéscope, 1986)
   STORY: Gothic fantasy.

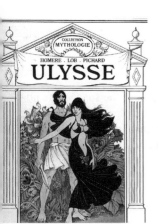

Ulysse (SERG, 1974; transl. Heavy Metal)
WRI: Jacques **Lob**; ART: Georges **Pichard**.
STORY: Science fiction retelling of Homer's *Odyssey*, with space aliens playing the parts of the Greek gods.

Urm Le Fou see *Yragaël*

Les Vacances du Major see *Moebius*

La Vache [The Cow]
WRI: Stephen **Desberg**; ART: Johan **De Moor**.

1. *Pi = 3,1416* (Cast., 1992)

2. *À Mort l'Homme, Vive l'Ozone [Death to Man, Hurray for Ozone]* (Cast., 1994)

3. *Même les Oiseaux Puent [Even Birds Stink]* (Cast., 1995)

4. *Peaux de Vache [Cow Skins]* (Cast., 1995)

5. *Le Silence des Animaux [The Silence of the Beasts]* (Cast., 1996)

STORY: Satirical stories about intelligent farm animals who live among us and monitor man's activities.

NOTE: Originally serialized in *(À Suivre)* in 1991.

Le Vagabond des Limbes [The Vagabond of Limbo]
WRI: Christian **Godard**; ART: Julio Ribera.

1. *Le Vagabond des Limbes [The Vagabond of Limbo]* (Hachette, 1975)

2. *L'Empire des Soleils Noirs [The Empire of the Black Suns]* (Hachette, 1976)

3. *Les Charognards du Cosmos [The Carrion-Eaters of the Cosmos]* (Hachette, 1976)

4. *Les Démons du Temps Immobile [The Demons of Still Time]* (Dar., 1978)

5. *L'Alchimiste Suprême [The Supreme Alchemist]* (Dar., 1979; transl. Dar.)

6. *Quelle Réalité Papa? [What Is Reality, Papa?]* (Dar., 1980; transl. Dar.)

7. *La Guerre des Bonkes [The War of the Bonks]* (Dar., 1981)

8. *Pour Trois Graines d'Éternité [For Three Seeds of Eternity]* (Dar., 1981)

9. *Le Labyrinthe Virginal [The Virginal Maze]* (Dar., 1982)

10. *Le Dernier Prédateur [The Last Predator]* (Dar., 1983)

11. *Le Masque de Kohm [The Mask of Kohm]* (Dar., 1984)

12. *Les Loups de Kohm [The Wolves of Kohm]* (Dar., 1985)

13. *L'Enfant-Roi d'Onirodyne [The Child-King of Onirodyne]* (Dar., 1986)

14. *La Petite Maîtresse [The Little Mistress]* (Dar., 1987)

15. *Le Temps des Oracles [The Time of the Oracles]* (Dar., 1988)

16. *Le Dépotoir des Etoiles [The Cosmic Junkyard]* (Vaisseau d'Argent, 1988)

17. *La Martingale Céleste [The Celestial System]* (Vaisseau d'Argent, 1988)

18. *Les Contrebandiers du Futur [The Smugglers of the Future]* (Vaisseau d'Argent, 1989)

19. *Un Tramway Nommé Délire [A Tramway Called Delirium]* (Vaisseau d'Argent, 1990)

20. *Un Certain Monsieur Ko [A Certain Mister Ko]* (Vaisseau d'Argent, 1990)

21. *La Décharge [The Landfill]* (Vaisseau d'Argent, 1990)

22. *Le Solitaire [The Loner]* (Dar., 1992)

23. *La Rupture [The Rupture]* (Dar., 1993)

24. Muskie Encore et Toujours [Musky Ever and Always] (Dar., 1994)

25. Le Petit Clone [The Little Clone] (Dar., 1995)

26. Le Point de Non-Retour [The Point of No Return] (Dar., 1997)

STORY: Axle Munshine is condemned to wander forever the pathways of space. His only companion is young Muskie, heir to the throne of the powerful Eternals. Axle seeks Chimeer, a beautiful woman whom he saw in a dream, and who is eventually revealed to be Muskie's future self.

NOTE: Julio Ribera is a Spanish artist working primarily in French comics.

Valérian

WRI: Pierre **Christin**; ART: Jean-Claude **Mézières**.

0. Les Mauvais Rêves [The Bad Dreams] (Dar., 1967; rep. 1986)

1. La Cité des Eaux Mouvantes [The City of the Moving Waters] (Dar., 1970)

2. L'Empire des Mille Planètes [The Empire of a Thousand Planets] (Dar. 1971; transl. NBM)

3. Le Pays Sans Étoiles [World Without Stars] (Dar. 1972; transl. Dar.)

4. Bienvenue sur Aflolol [Welcome to Alflolol] (Dar. 1972; transl. Dar.)

5. Les Oiseaux du Maître [The Birds of the Master] (Dar., 1973)

5b. Par les Chemins de l'Espace [Across the Pathways of Space] (Dar. 1968-70, rep. 1979)

6. L'Ambassadeur des Ombres [The Ambassador of the Shadows] (Dar. 1975; transl. Dar.)

7. Sur les Terres Truquées [On the Fixed Earths] (Dar., 1977)

8. Les Héros de l'Equinoxe [The Heroes of the Equinox] (Dar. 1978; transl. Dar.)

9. Métro Châtelet Direction Cassiopée (Dar., 1980)

10. Brooklyn Station Terminus Cosmos (Dar., 1981)

11. Les Spectres d'Inverloch [The Ghosts of Inverloch] (Dar., 1984)

12. Les Foudres d'Hypsis [The Thunder of Hypsis] (Dar., 1985)

13. Sur les Frontières [On the Borders] (Dar., 1988)

14. Les Armes Vivantes [The Living Weapons] (Dar., 1990)

15. Les Cercles du Pouvoir [The Circles of Power] (Dar., 1994)

16. Les Otages de l'Ultralum [The Hostages of the Ultralum] (Dar., 1996)

Related Works:

Mézières, et Christin Avec... [Mézières, and Christin, With...] (Dar., 1983)

Les Habitants du Ciel [The Inhabitants of the Sky] (Dar., 1991)

STORY: The adventures of an agent of the space-time police of Galaxity, a powerful Terran empire from the future. His companion is the red-haired Laureline, originally from medieval France. In ep. 12., Galaxity's future is erased by powerful time-manipulating aliens, stranding Valerian and Laureline in our present.

NOTE: Originally serialized in *Pilote* in 1967.

Valhalla

WRI/ART: P. Madsen.

1. La Rage d'Odin [The Wrath of Odin] (Zen., 1990)

2. Quark le Rebelle [Quark the Rebel] (Zen., 1990)

3. Au Pays des Géants [In the Land of the Giants] (Zen., 1991)

STORY: Heroic fantasy based on Norse mythology.

Valhardi see *Jean Valhardi*

Vanity Benz

WRI: Didier Van Cauwelaert; ART: Franck Bonnet.

1. Cuba Cola (Dar., 1994)

2. L'Enfant Qui Dirigeait la Terre [The Child Who Ruled the World] (Dar., 1995)

3. Le Sommet de Venise [The Venice Summit] (Dar., 1996)

STORY: Political thrillers starring an investigative reporter and incorporating paranormal elements.

Vauriens [Rascals]

WRI: Luc Brunschwig; ART: Laurent Cagniat.

1. Pop Bras d'Argile [Pop Arm-of-Clay] (Delc., 1995)

2. Dame Brèche Dents [Lady Break-Tooth] (Delc., 1996)

STORY: Heroic fantasy.

Vauvert et Séléna

WRI: Thierry Smolderen; ART: Mayall.

1. *Le Détective Extra-Lucide [The ESP Detective]* (Alpen, 1990)
   STORY: Fantastic thriller.

Venise Céleste see **Moebius**

Le Vent des Dieux [The Wind of the Gods]

WRI: Patrick **Cothias**; ART: Philippe **Adamov**.

1. *Le Sang de la Lune [The Blood of the Moon]* (Glé., 1985, transl. *Heavy Metal*)

2. *Le Ventre du Dragon [The Belly of the Dragon]* (Glé., 1986)

3. *L'Homme Oublié [The Forgotten Man]* (Glé., 1987)

4. *Lapin-Tigre [Tiger Rabbit]* (Glé., 1988)

5. *La Ballade de Mizu [The Ballad of Mizu]* (Glé., 1991)

WRI: Patrick **Cothias**; ART: T. Gioux.

6. *L'Ordre du Ciel [The Order of Heaven]* (Glé., 1992)

7. *Barbaries* (Glé., 1993)

8. *Ti Fun* (Glé., 1993)

9. *Cambaluc* (Glé., 1994)

10. *Le Gherkek* (Glé., 1995)

11. *Le Sang de la Lune [The Blood of the Moon]* (Glé., 1996)
    STORY: Heroic fantasy in 13th-century Japan.
    NOTE: Originally serialized in *Vécu* in 1985.

Le Ventre du Minotaure [The Belly of the Minotaur]

(Hum., 1990)
WRI/ART: Beltran.
STORY: Fantasy.

La Vérité Est au Fond des Rêves [The Truth Lies at the Bottom of the Dreams]

(Hum., 1993)
WRI: Alexandro **Jodorowsky**; ART: Jean-Jacques Chaubin.
STORY: Dream-like fantasy.

Vers les Mondes Inconnus [Towards the Unknown Worlds]

(1943)
WRI/ART: Auguste **Liquois**.

STORY: *Flash Gordon* imitation created during World War II.
NOTE: Originally serialized in *Le Téméraire*; never collected in the graphic novel format.

Vic Voyage

WRI/ART: Sergio Macedo.

1. *Le Trésor de Paititi [The Treasure of Paititi]* (Glé., 1983)

2. *À la Recherche d'Agharta [Seeking the Aghartha]* (Glé., 1985)

3. *Pacifique Sud [South Pacific]* (Aedena, 1985)

4. *Le Mystère des Atolls [The Mystery of the Atolls]* (Aedena, 1986)

5. *Brasil* (Vaisseau d'Argent, 1989)
   STORY: Vic Voyage has breen chosen by the Gods to herald the end of the world unless men learn to live in harmony with Earth.
   NOTE: Sergio Macedo is a native Brazilian artist, working primarily in the French comics industry.

Victor Billetdoux

WRI/ART: Wininger.

1. *La Pyramide Oubliée [The Forgotten Pyramid]* (Glé., 1978)

2. *Les Ombres de Nulle Part [The Shadows from Nowhere]* (Glé., 1979)

3. *La Nuit de l'Horus Rouge [The Night of the Red Horus]* (Glé., 1982)
   STORY: Fantastic thrillers involving ancient Egyptian artifacts and myths.

Vihila, Planète des Perversions [Vihila, Planet of Perversions]

WRI: Dominique Verseau (Jimmy **Guieu**); ART: Trébor.

1. *Vol. 1* (Neptune, 1982)

2. *Vol. 2* (Neptune, 1983)
   STORY: Erotic SF by the noted writer (see Book 2).

Les Villages see **Dans Les Villages**

Vincent Larcher

(genre stories only)
WRI/ART: Raymond Reding.

1. *Olympic 2004* (Lom., 1969)

2. *11 Gauchers pour Mexico [11 Left-Handed Players for Mexico]* (Lom., 1970)

3. *Le Zoo du Dr. Ketzal [The Zoo of Dr. Ketzal]* (Lom., 1973)

STORY: A member of the French national soccer team befriends the super-powered son of a mad scientist. They expose a conspiracy to frighten the world into world peace by using faked alien manifestations at global sports events. Finally, they team up to defeat another mad scientist during the 1968 Olympics in Mexico.

NOTE: Originally serialized in *Tintin* in 1963; only the three eps. above (serialized in 1968-69) contained genre elements.

20,000 Lieues Sous les Mers [20,000 Leagues Under the Seas]
Based on the novel by Jules **Verne**.
Version No.1: WRI: Déséchal; ART: Blondeau (Hachette, 1951)
Version No.2: WRI/ART: Gasquet (Nathan, 1975)

Virus (Fromage, 1980)
WRI/ART: Jean Teulé.
STORY: Political science fiction.

Le Voleur de Proxima [The Thief from Proxima]
WRI: Patrick Galliano; ART: Roland Barthélemy.

1. *L'Équilibre Sacré [The Sacred Balance]* (Hum., 1992)

2. *Vulcania* (Hum., 1993)
STORY: Heroic fantasy.

Les Voleurs d'Empire [The Thieves of the Empire]
WRI: Jean **Dufaux**; ART: M. Jamar.

1. *Les Voleurs d'Empire [The Thieves of the Empire]* (Glé., 1993)

2. *Fleurs de Peau [Skin Flowers]* (Glé., 1995)

3. *Un Sale Métier [A Dirty Job]* (Glé., 1996)
STORY: In 1870 during the Franco-Prussian War, a woman makes a pact with Death.

Les Voleurs de Paradis [The Thieves of Paradise]
WRI: Éric Corbeyran; ART: Nicolas Guenet.

1. *Beline* (Sol., 1995)
STORY: Heroic fantasy.

Vorax see Professeur Vorax

Vortex
WRI/ART: Vince.
Tess Wood, Prisonnière du Futur (4 vols.) [Tess Wood, Prisoner of the Future] (Delc., 1994-96)
WRI/ART: Stan.
Cambell, Voyageur du Temps (4 vols.) [Cambell, Time Traveller] (Delc., 1994-96)
STORY: Time travel adventures.
NOTE: Shared universe with the two series released simultaneously.

Voyage au Centre de la Terre [Journey to the Center of the Earth]
Based on the novel by Jules **Verne**.
WRI: Roudolph; ART: R. Polese (Sage, 1978).

Voyage Intemporel [Timeless Voyage] (Glé., 1982)
WRI: Appel-Guery; ART: Sergio Macedo.
STORY: Benevolent aliens help mankind.

Les Voyages de Takuan [The Journeys of Takuan]
WRI: Serge **Le Tendre**; ART: Siméoni.

1. *Les Fous de Dieu [The Madmen of God]* (Dar., 1987)

2. *Le Livre de Sang [The Book of Blood]* (Delc., 1991)
WRI: Serge **Le Tendre**; ART: Taduc.

3. *La Voix de l'Ours [The Bear's Voice]* (Delc., 1994)

4. *La Source Noire [The Black Spring]* (Delc., 1995)

5. *La Mère des Douleurs [The Mother of Pain]* (Delc., 1996)
STORY: Sword and sorcery against witchcraft in the 15th Century.

Voyages en Terres Étrangères [Journeys Through Strange Lands]
WRI/ART: Daniel **Hulet**.

1. *Volume 1* (Sol., 1995)
STORY: Heroic fantasy.

Vuzz see Druillet

Waki
WRI: J. K. **Melwyn-Nash**, Franco Frescura; ART: Luciano Bernasconi.

1. *Le Piège de Glace [The Ice Trap]* (1974)

2. *Un Bruissement d'Ailes [A Flutter of Wings]* (1974)

3. *Histoire d'Amour et de Mort [Tale of Love and Death]* (1974)

4. Le Dieu de Cendres [The God of the Ashes] (1974)

5. Tout le Sable du Monde [All the Sand in the World] (1974)

6. Sortilège [Spell] (1974)

SR 52. Dans la Pierre pour l'Éternité [In Stone for Eternity] / Les Hommes Noirs [The Black Men] (1974)

SR 53. Les Derniers Monstres [The Last Monsters] / La Paroi de Verre [The Glass Wall] (1975)

SR 54. Un Jour Quelqu'un A Dit [One Day Someone Said] (1975)

SR 56. Visions (1975)
STORY: Prehistoric science fiction in a post-cataclysmic world.
NOTE: Originally published by Ed. Lug in six digest-sized magazines. The series was continued in *Special Rodeo* Nos. 52-55. Not collected in the graphic novel format. Franco Frescura and Luciano Bernasconi are Italian artists.

Wampus/L'Autre [The Other]

WRI: J. K. **Melwyn-Nash**, Franco Frescura; ART: Luciano Bernasconi.

1. Wampus (1969)

2. Le Dernier Ricanement [The Last Laugh] (1969)

3. Et Vint le Chaos [And Chaos Came] (1969)

4. La Grande Explosion [The Great Explosion] (1969)

5. Vu du Pont [View from a Bridge] (1969)

6. Toilette du Bourreau [Executioner's Wash] (1969)

7. Le Ciel Est Rouge [The Sky Is Red] (1985)
STORY: An alien monster with shapeshifting powers is sent by an evil cosmic intelligence to destroy Earth. He is discovered and pursued by French secret agent, Jean Sten.
NOTE: Originally published by Ed. Lug in six digest-sized magazines. The series was discontinued in 1969 because of censorship problems. The final episode was finally serialized in *Ombrax* No. 230-233 (1985). The same concept was then continued as **L'Autre** in *Futura* Nos. 11-18 (1972-74). **L'Autre** featured a more humanoid alien (but one using the same unique eye design than **Wampus**) and less nihilistic violence. The character of Jean Sten was replaced by Jean Vlad. Neither series was collected in the graphic novel format. Franco Frescura and Luciano Bernasconi are Italian artists.

Wayne Thunder

WRI: De Kuyssche; ART: Marcello.

1. Le Continent Perdu [The Lost Continent] (Lon., 1987)

2. La Porte de l'Initié [The Initiate's Gate] (Lom., 1988)
STORY: Esoteric SF.

Wen (2 vols., untitled)

(Lom., 1983-84)
WRI: Jacques **Stoquart**; ART: **Éric**.
STORY: A young man gifted with supernatural powers.
NOTE: Originally serialized in *Tintin* in 1977.

William Lapoire

WRI/ART: Ernst.

1. William Lapoire (Lom., 1985)

2. En Son Âme et Inconscience [On His Soul and Inconscience] (Lom., 1986)

3. Dégelées par –40 [Defreeze By –40] (Lom., 1987)

4. Le Big Bagne [The Big Hard Labor Camp] (Lom., 1988)
STORY: Humorous adventures of an agent of the Devil.
NOTE: Originally serialized in *Tintin* in 1978.

Woker

WRI/ART: Achdé & Widenlocher.

1. Le Secret de Tanzania [The Secret of Tanzania] (Dar., 1997)
STORY: Humorous intergalactic safaris.

Wonderman

WRI/ART: J.-A. Dupuich.

1. Wonderman Contre le Cercle Noir [Wonderman vs. the Black Circle] (1949)

2. Le Sauvetage du XB-98 [The Rescue of XB-98] (1949)

3. Échec au Sacrifice [Sacrifice in Check] (1949)

4. Le Secret des Pharaons [The Secret of the Pharaohs] (1949)

5. Les Cinq Gorilles du Diable [The Devil's Five Gorillas] (1949)

6. Énigme au Thibet [Tibetan Enigma] (1949)

7. Wonderman Contre les Espions de l'Atome [Wonderman vs. the Atomic Spies] (1950)

8. Tragédie au Cirque [Tragedy at the Circus] (1950)

9. *Les Trois Perles [The Three Pearls]* (1950)

10. *L'Hercule de Pierre [The Stone Hercules]* (1950)

11. *Le Mystère de la Sierra [The Mystery of the Sierra]* (1950)

12. *Le Précipice de la Mort [The Precipice of Death]* (1950)

13. *Trafic d'Opium [Opium Traffic]* (1951)

14. *Le Gang du Poison [The Poison Gang]* (1951)

15. *Le Trésor du Yucatan [The Treasure of Yucatan]* (1951)
STORY: French superhero.
NOTE: Originally serialized in *Aventure* (eps. 1-7), *Dynamic* (eps. 8-12) and *Audax* (Artima).

Wooly Wan
WRI: Renard; ART: Roels.

1. *Mister K* (Lom., 1996)
STORY: The paranoid adventures of a writer in a futuristic police state.

Xam see Saga de Xam

Xan see Jhen

Xing et Xot see Pegg le Robot

Xoco
WRI: Thomas Mosdi; ART: Olivier Ledroit.
1. *Papillon Obsidienne [Obsidian Butterfly]* (VdO., 1994)
STORY: Heroic fantasy.

Ya Plus de Saisons see Fred

Yan et Mirka
WRI: Harriet; ART: Redondo.

1. *L'Expédition Perdue [The Lost Expedition]* (Litote, 1985)
STORY: Juvenile space opera.

Yann le Migrateur [Yann the Wanderer]
WRI: Robert Génin; ART: Claude **Lacroix**.

1. *La Planète aux Illusions [The Planet of Illusions]* (Glé., 1978)

2. *La Cité des Sept Sages [The City of the Seven Wise Men]* (Glé., 1979)

3. *Le Refus des Étoiles [The Refusal of the Stars]* (Glé., 1980)

4. *L'île des Fous [The Madmen's Isle]* (Glé., 1982)

5. *Les Survivants de Galia [The Survivors of Galia]* (Glé., 1984)

STORY: A space-time traveler and his robot work to preserve cosmic peace.
NOTE: Originally serialized in *Formule 1* in 1975, and in *Gomme* from 1981 to 1984.

Les Yeux du Chat see Moebius

Yoko Tsuno
WRI/ART: Roger **Leloup**.

1. *Le Trio de l'Étrange [A Strange Trio]* (Dup., 1972)

2. *L'Orgue du Diable [The Devil's Organ]* (Dup., 1973)

3. *La Forge de Vulcain [Vulcan's Forge]* (Dup., 1973; transl. Catalan)

4. *Aventures Electroniques [Electronic Adventures]* (Dup., 1974)

5. *Message pour l'Eternité [Message for Eternity]* (Dup., 1975)

6. *Les Trois Soleils de Vinéa [The Three Suns of Vinea]* (Dup., 1976; transl. Catalan)

7. *La Frontière de la Vie [The Frontier of Life]* (Dup., 1977)

8. *Les Titans [The Titans]* (Dup. 1978; transl. Catalan)

9. *La Fille du Vent [The Daughter of the Wind]* (Dup., 1979)

10. *La Lumière d'Ixo [The Light from Ixo]* (Dup. 1980; transl. Catalan)

11. *La Spirale du Temps [The Time Spiral]* (Dup., 1981)

12. *La Proie et l'Ombre [The Prey and the Shadow]* (Dup., 1982)

13. *Les Archanges de Vinéa [The Archangels of Vinea]* (Dup., 1983)

14. *Le Feu de Wotan [The Fire of Wotan]* (Dup., 1984)

15. *Le Canon de Kra [The Cannon of Kra]* (Dup., 1985)

16. *Le Dragon de Hong-Kong [The Dragon from Hong-Kong]* (Dup., 1986)

17. *Le Matin du Monde [The Morning of the World]* (Dup., 1988)

18. *Les Exilés de Kifa [The Exiles of Kifa]* (Dup., 1991)

19. *L'Or du Rhin [The Rhinegold]* (Dup., 1993)

20. *L'Astrologue de Bruges [The Astrologer of Bruges]* (Dup., 1994)

21. *La Porte des Âmes [The Gate of Souls]* (Dup., 1996)
STORY: A female European electronics engineer of Japanese descent takes part in fantastic adventures, some of them involving blue-skinned aliens from the advanced civilization of Vinea.
NOTE: Originally serialized in *Spirou* in 1970.

Yolanda et les Voluptés Cosmiques [Yolanda and the Cosmic Pleasures]
WRI: Dominique Verseau (Jimmy **Guieu**); ART: Trébor.

1. *Vol. 1* (Neptune, 1982)

2. *Vol. 2* (Sedem, 1983)
STORY: Erotic SF by the noted writer (see Book 2).

Yoyo
WRI: **Yann**; ART: Frank Le Gall.

1. *La Lune Noire [The Black Moon]* (Glé., 1986)

2. *Les Sirènes de Wall Street [The Sirens of Wall Street]* (Glé., 1987)
STORY: Cartoony adventures of a little girl in Transylvania.

Yragaël/Urm le Fou [Urm the Mad]
WRI: Michel **Demuth**; ART: Philippe **Druillet**.

1. *Yragaël* (Dar., 1974; transl. *Heavy Metal*)
WRI/ART: Philippe **Druillet**.

2. *Urm le Fou [Urm the Mad]* (Dar., 1975; transl. *Heavy Metal*)
STORY: Inspired by Michael Moorcock's *Elric of Melnibone*, this series tells the story of doomed Prince Yragaël and the fall of the Empire of Cemeroon. Urm is Yragael's hunchback son.
STORY: Originally serialized in *Pilote* in 1972. Michel **Demuth** is a renowned science fiction writer/editor.

Yvain De Kanhéric
WRI: **Maric**; ART: Gérald **Forton**.

1. *Sortilèges [Spells]* (Deligne, 1982)

2. *L'Homme à la Main Coupée [The Man with a Cut-Off Hand]* (Deligne, 1982)
STORY: Medieval sorcery.

Yvain et Yvon
WRI: **Bom**; ART: Patrice **Cadot**.

1. *La Piste du Bahomet [The Trail of the Baphomet]* (Lom., 1987)

2. *Le Roi des Loups [The King of the Wolves]* (Lom., 1988)

3. *Le Cheval des Étoiles [The Star Horse]* (Lom., 1988)

4. *L'Enfant de la Nuit [The Night Child]* (Lom., 1989)
STORY: Humorous werewolf tales.
NOTE: Originally serialized in *Tintin* in 1985.

Yves Le Loup [Yves the Wolf]
WRI: Jean **Ollivier**; ART: René **Bastard**.

1. *Yves le Loup [Yves the Wolf]* (1948)

2. *Au Pays des Géants [In the Land of the Giants]* (1948)

3. *La Conquête du Graal [The Conquest of the Grail]* (1948)

4. *La Grande Croisade [The Great Crusade]* (1949)

5. *La Forêt Chantante [The Singing Forest]* (1949)

6. *La Légende d'Yseult [The Legend of Yseult]* (1949)

7. *Viviane la Blonde [Blonde Vivien]* (1950)

8. *Perceval le Gallois* (1950)

9. *Les Escoliers de Paris [The Students of Paris]* (1950)

10. *[Untitled]* (1951)

11. *L'Enfance d'Yves le Loup [The Childhood of Yves the Wolf]* (1951)

12. *Les Barbares d'Erin [The Barbarians from Erin]* (1952)

13. *Le Château sous le Lac [The Castle Under the Lake]* (1952)

14. *[Untitled]* (1952)

15. *Le Château Maudit [The Accursed Castle]* (1953)

16. *Au Pays Maure [In the Land of the Moors]* (1953)

17. *La Légende de Brocéliande [The Legend of Broceliande]* (1954)

18. *[Untitled]* (1954)

19. *[Untitled]* (1955)

20. *Le Testament de Gauvin [The Testament of Sir Gawin]* (1955)

21. *Le Manoir des Ogres [The Castle of the Ogres]* (1956)

22. *Le Chant de l'Alouette [The Song of the Alouette]* (1956)

23. *[Untitled]* (1957)

24. *La Cité de Feu [The City of Fire]* (1957)

25. *La Tour des Cent Vaillances [The Tower of a Hundred Brave Feats]* (1957)

26. *Debout les Jacques [Raising the Jacks]* (1958)

27. *La Rose Noire de Bagdad [The Black Rose of Bagdad]* (1958)

27b. *Les Pirates de Famagouste [The Pirates of Famagouste]* (5 p.) (1958)

28. *La Mort du Roi Arthur [The Death of King Arthur]* (1959)

29. *La Guerre des Deux Jean [The War of the Two Johns]* (1959)

29b. *Le Défi du Trouvère [The Challenge of the Troubadour]* (3 p.) (1960)

30. *Les Enfances du Preux [A Knight's Childhood]* (ART: E.T. Coelho) (1960)

31. *Le Chevalier de Trèfle [The Knight of Clubs]* (ART: E.T. Coelho) (1961)

32. *Le Complot de Paris [A Parisian Plot]* (ART: E.T. Coelho) (1961)

33. *La Révolte des Flandes [Revolt in Flanders]* (ART: E.T. Coelho) (1961)

34. *L'Unicorne* (1964)

35. *La Coupe d'Or [The Gold Cup]* (1964)

35b. *Le Manoir de Caronaise [The Castle of Caronaise]* (9 p.) (1964)

36. *Les Chevaliers du Roi Arthur [King Arthur's Knights]* (1964)

37. *Le Royaume de Tara [The Kingdom of Tara]* (1965)

38. *Le Siège de Tintagel [The Siege of Tintagel]* (1966)

STORY: Yves the Wolf's mother is King Arthur's sister, Ghislaine. A Knight of the Round Table, Yves meets Merlin and Morgan le Fey, and fights for justice and Camelot.

NOTE: This series, heavily inspired by *Prince Valiant*, was originally serialized in *Vaillant* from 1948 to 1966; only one collection was published in 1954. Eps. ranged in page count from a dozen to well over 40 pages (ep. 36 holds the record with 63 pages).

Zanzie

WRI/ART: **Érik**.

STORY: Juvenile science fiction featuring a lost world inhabited by dinosaurs.

NOTE: Serialized in *L'Intrépide* in 1958.

Zappy Max

WRI: Saint-Julien (Hugo de Haan); ART: Maurice Tillieux.

1. *Vas-y Zappy! [Go Zappy!]* (Champs-Elysées, 1960)
   WRI: Saint-Julien (Hugo de Haan); ART: Jacques Devaux.

2. *Ça Va Bouillir! [It's Gonna Boil]* (1961; rep. Furioso, 1979)
   STORY: Real-life radio DJ Zappy Max thwarts mad scientists.

NOTE: Comics adaptation of the popular radio series (see Chapter III), originally serialized in *Pilote* in 1959-61.

Zig et Puce

(genre stories only)
WRI/ART: Alain **Saint-Ogan**.

9. *Zig et Puce au XXIème Siècle [Zig and Puce in the 21st Century]* (1935)

WRI/ART: **Greg**.

3. *Le Prototype Zéro-Zéro* (Lom., 1967)

4. *La Pierre Qui Vole [The Flying Stone]* (Lom., 1968)
   STORY: Two kids and their pet penguin Alfred find themselves in the future.

NOTE: One of the oldest French adventure strips, created in 1925 by Alain **Saint-Ogan**. After its original publication in *Le Dimanche Illustré*, **Zig et Puce** appeared in a variety of papers until 1952. In 1963, the adventures were taken over by **Greg** and serialized in *Tintin*.

Zor et Mlouf

WRI: Jean Sanitas; ART: Jacques Kamb.

1. *Zor et Mlouf* (1965)

2. *Le Secret de 333* (1966)

3. *Station Pôle 333 [333's Polar Station]* (1966)

4. *Plantasphère 333* (1966)

5. *Roboville 333* (1966)

5b. *Nautlus 333* (5 p.) (1966)

6. *Altitude 333* (1966)

7. *L'Aquariglomo 333* (1966)

7b. *Le Noël de Zor et Mlouf [Zor and Mlouf's Christmas]* (1966)

8. *Aglubulus 333* (1967)

9. *Le Xumucle* (1967)

10. *Au Pays des Translucides [In the Land of the Transparents]* (1967)

10b. 333 Pères Noël [333 Santas] (1967)

11. Captain 333 (1968)

12. Xumuclion (1968)

13. Le Biorayon A.T. Choum (1968)

14. Au Pays des Chimères [In the Land of Chimeers] (1968)

15. Transcosmos ZM 333 (1968)

STORY: A helmeted super-hero (Zor) and his shape-changing pet (Mlouf) thwart the evil schemes of a megalomaniacal robot-maker, 333.

NOTE: Originally serialized in *Vaillant* from 1965 to 1968; never collected in the graphic novel format. Episodes were usually 12 or 26 pages in length (except for ep. 8 which is 46 pages).

Zoum le Martien [Zoum the Martian] see *Pegg le Robot*

Zowie
    WRI: Christian Darasse; ART: **Bosse**.

1. Le Pinceau de Cristal [The Crystal Brush] (Dup., 1983)

2. Le Mystère du An Veskenn [The Mystery of an Veskenn] (Dup., 1985)
    STORY: Juvenile light fantasy.
    NOTE: Originally serialized in *Spirou*; only ep. 1 was collected in the graphic novel format.

3. Selected Magazines

(À Suivre) (Cast., 1978–98)
EDITOR: Jean-Paul Mougin.
Adèle Blanc-Sec, Boucq, Canardo, Les Cités Obscures, Comès, Les Compagnons du Crépuscule, Le Cycle de Cyann, Édéna.

Albator (Dar., 1980–81)
EDITOR: Claude **Moliterni**.
Albator, Captain Fulgur, Kronos.

L'An 2000 [Year 2000] (Ed. du Puits Pelu, 1953–54)
EDITOR: Yves Mondet.

Anticipation (Aredit, 1977–)
EDITOR: Émile Keirsbilk.
Fleuve Noir.

Atomos (Aredit, 1968–77)
EDITOR: Émile Keirsbilk.
Fleuve Noir.

Audax (Artima, 1950–61)
EDITOR: Émile Keirsbilk.
Fulguros, Wonderman.

Aventures Fiction (Artima/Aredit, 1958–60, 1966–78)
EDITOR: Émile Keirsbilk.
Fleuve Noir.

Capitain' Horn (Ed. du Siècle, 1948–1949)
EDITOR: Bagnol.
Capitain' Horn.

Casse-Cou (Ed. de la Foux, 1954)
EDITOR: M. Bourdin.
S.O.S. Terre.

Charlie Mensuel see *Pilote*

Chouchou (Filipacchi, 1964–65)
EDITOR: Jean-Claude **Forest**.
Les Naufragés du Temps, P'tit Gus, Tenebrax.

Circus (Glé., 1975–89)
EDITORS: Jacques Glénat, Henri Filippini.
Alise, La Ballade au Bout du Monde, Les Dirigeables de l'Amazone, Les Eaux de Mortelune, Les Écluses du Ciel, Grimion Gant de Cuir, L'Indien Français, Le Marchand d'Idées, Memory, La Terre de la Bombe.

Clameurs (Aredit, 1977–)
EDITOR: Émile Keirsbilk.
Fleuve Noir.

Coeurs Vaillants (Fleurus, 1929–1963)
EDITORS: Various, esp. **Marijac** (1934–44).
Jim Boum, Jo, Zette et Jocko.

Coq Hardi (Montsouris/Châteaudun, 1944–63)

EDITOR: **Marijac**.
Alerte à la Terre, Guerre à la Terre.

Cosmos (Artima/Aredit, 1956–61, 1967–)
EDITOR: Émile Keirsbilk.
Fleuve Noir.

Dynamic (Artima, 1950–65)
EDITOR: Émile Keirsbilk.
Tarou, Wonderman.

Eclipso (Aredit, 1968–)
EDITOR: Émile Keirsbilk.
Fleuve Noir.

Étranges Aventures (Arédit, 1966–)
EDITOR: Émile Keirsbilk.
Fleuve Noir.

Fantax (Ed. Mouchot, 1946–49, 1950–51)
EDITOR: **Chott**.
Fantax.

Fluide Glacial (Aud., 1975–)
EDITORS: Marcel Gotlib, Jacques Diament.
Absurdus Delirium, Le Banni, Foerster, Radada, Super Dupont.

Futura (Lug, 1972–75)
EDITORS: J. K. **Melwyn-Nash**, Auguste and Claude Vistel.

L'Autre, Brigade Temporelle, Homicron, Jaleb le Télépathe, Larry Cannon.

Gomme (Glé., 1981–84)
EDITORS: Jacques Glénat, Henri Filippini.
La Ballade au Bout du Monde, Percevan.

Hallucinations (Aredit, 1969–77)
EDITOR: Émile Keirsbilk.
Fleuve Noir.

Hello BD see *Tintin.*

Inter-Planètes (Ed. de Lutèce, 1968–69)
EDITOR: Jean Kalistrate.

La Jeunesse Illustrée [Illustrated Youth] (1903–35)
Illustrated text stories including a number of science fiction tales: *Carbodio le Candidat Roi de la Lune* [*The Candidate King of the Moon*] (1912); *Valvérane l'Anticipite* (1922); *L'Aérolithe* (1924); *L'Homme Qui ne Dormait pas* [*The Man Who Could Not Sleep*] (1924); *Le Déguisement de Zéphirine* [*Zephirine's Disguise*] (1926)

Kabur (Lug, 1975–76)
EDITORS: J. K. **Melwyn-Nash**, Auguste and Claude Vistel.
Kabur.

Maya Le Sioux (Elan, 1949–50)
EDITOR: Unknown.
Maya Le Sioux.

Métal Hurlant (Hum., 1975–87)
Métal Aventure (Hum., 1983–85)
EDITORS: Jean-Pierre **Dionnet**, Jean-Luc Fromental.
Alef-Thau, Armalite 16, Arn, Arzach, Bob Fish, Champakou, Freddy Lombard, Le Garage Hermétique, L'Incal, Moebius, 1996, Les Naufragés du Temps, Les Terres Creuses.
Note: Métal Hurlant exerted a powerful influence on American comics through the licensing of a U.S. edition by National Lampoon in 1977, *Heavy Metal.*

Meteor (Artima/Aredit, 1953–77)
EDITOR: Émile Keirsbilk.
Les Conquérants de l'Espace, Les Francis.

Mister X (Elan, 1949–51)
EDITOR: Unknown.
Mister X.

Monstre (Bel-Air, 1965)
EDITOR: Unknown.

Mustang (Series 2) (Lug, 1980–81)
EDITORS: J. K. **Melwyn-Nash**, Auguste and Claude Vistel.
Cosmo, Mikros, Photonik.

Myster (Ed. De La Foux, 1954)
EDITOR: M. Bourdin.
Cagliostro.

Neutron (Promarcy, 1980–81)
EDITOR: Unknown.
Poïvet.

OSS 117 (Aredit, 1966–)
EDITOR: Émile Keirsbilk.
Adaptations of **OSS 117** spy novels (see Chapter I).

Pif-Gadget see **Vaillant**
Pilote (Dar., 1959–74)
Pilote Mensuel (Dar., 1974–86)
Charlie Mensuel (Dar., 1982–86)
Pilote-Charlie (Dar., 1986–89)
EDITORS: Various, Esp. René **Goscinny** (1960–74) and Jean-Michel **Charlier** (1960–72), Guy Vidal (1974–86).
Astérix, Bilal, Bob Morane, Cargal, Caza, Le Concombre Masqué, Dick Hérisson, Dossiers Soucoupes Volantes, Druillet, Foc, Fred, Guy Lebleu, Iznogoud, Krane le Guerrier, Légendes d'Aujourd'hui, Lone Sloane, Le Moine Fou, Orn, Pemberton, Philémon, La Quête de l'Oiseau du Temps, Submerman,

Thorkael, Time Is Money, Le Vagabond des Limbes, Valerian, Yragaël.

Radar (Ed. du Siècle, 1947)
EDITORS: Robert **Bagage**, Jean Guillet.
Radar.

Satanax (Ed. Mondiales, 1948–49)
EDITOR: Auguste **Liquois.**
Satanax.

Satellite Images (Ed. Scientifiques and Littéraires, 1960)
EDITOR: Michel **Benâtre**, Hervé **Calixte.**

Sidéral (Artima/Aredit, 1958–62, 1968–77)
EDITOR: Émile Keirsbilk.
Fleuve Noir.

Spatial (Deligne, 1978–83)
EDITOR: Michel Deligne.

Spirou (Dup., 1938–)
EDITORS: Various, esp. Yvan **Delporte** (1955–68), Thierri Martens.
Alain Cardan, Aleister Crowley, Attila, Benoît Brisefer, Bizu, Boskovich, Broussaille, Cristal, Cupidon, Docteur Poche, Donito, Edmund Bell, L'Épervier Bleu, Foufi, Génial Olivier, Isabelle, Jean Valhardi, Johan/Les Schtroumpfs, Kim Devil, Les Krostons, Mallet, Mic Mac Adam, Papyrus, Les Petits Hommes, 421, Le Scrameustache, Simon le Danseur, Sophie, Spirou/Le Marsupilami, Starbuck, Tif et Tondu, Yoko Tsuno.

Super Boy (Imperia, 1949–87)
EDITORS: Robert **Bagage**, Jean Guillet.
Super Boy.

Targa (Ed. du Siècle/Imperia, 1947–51)

EDITORS: Robert **Bagage**, Jean Guillet.
Targa.

Tarou (Artima/Aredit, 1954–73)
EDITOR: Émile Keirsbilk.
Tarou.

Terreur (Bel-Air, 1965)
EDITOR: Unknown.

Tintin (Belgium: Lom., 1946–88; France: Dar., 1948–72)
Tintin l'Hebdoptimiste (France: Dar., 1973–75)
Nouveau Tintin (France: Edi-Monde/Lom., 1975–78)
Tintin Reporter (Yeti Presse, 1988–89)
Hello BD (1989–93)
  EDITORS: Various, esp. **Greg** (1966–75).

Alain Landier, Aria, Blake et Mortimer, Cranach De Morganloup, Dan Cooper, Hans, Hassan et Kadour, Hugo, Ian Kalédine, Korrigan, Lefranc, Luc Orient, Mr. Magellan, Nahomi, Neige, Olivier Rameau, Rork, Simon du Fleuve, Tetfol, Thorgal, Tintin, Tounga, Vincent Larcher, Yvain et Yvon.

Titans (Ed. Lug, 1976–)
EDITORS: J. K. **Melwyn-Nash**, Auguste and Claude Vistel.
Epsilon, Mikros, Kronos.

Tom X (Ed. du Siècle/Imperia, 1946–48)
EDITORS: Robert **Bagage**, Jean Guillet.
Tom X.

Ulysse 31 (Dynamisme/Gréantori, 1981–83)

EDITOR: Unknown.
Ulysse 31.

Vaillant (Vaillant, 1945–69)
Pif-Gadget (Vaillant, 1969–82)
Nouveau Pif (Vaillant, 1982–93)
EDITORS: Various, esp. Jean **Ollivier** (1945–58), Roger **Lecureux** (1958–63).
Arthur Le Fantôme Justicier, Les As, Jacques Flash, Les Pionners de l'Espérance, Rahan, Yves Le Loup, Zor et Mlouf.

Waki (Lug, 1974)
  EDITORS: J. K. **Melwyn-Nash**, Auguste and Claude Vistel.
  Waki.

Wampus (Lug, 1969)
  EDITORS: J. K. **Melwyn-Nash**, Auguste and Claude Vistel.
  Wampus.

4. Interview with Moebius

Moebius is the co-founder of the magazine Métal Hurlant *(Heavy Metal in the United States) and the author of such classic science fiction and fantasy graphic novel as* **Le Garage Hermétique** *[The Airtight Garage] and* **Arzach**. *He is also a renowned conceptual artist who provided designs for such motion pictures as* **Les Maîtres du Temps** *[The Time Masters], TRON, Willow, The Abyss, and* The Fifth Element. *He is arguably the only French comic book artist to have achieved major international recognition. These comments are excerpted from an interview granted to Jean-Marc Lofficier in 1988.*

Question: In 1973 you, Philippe **Druillet**, and Jean-Pierre **Dionnet** left *Pilote* to create your own magazine, *Métal Hurlant*. Why?

Moebius: We were all in the situation as children vis à vis their parents, the parents being the publisher. At the time, some of the artists, including myself, didn't know if we wanted to express ourselves, or go on exploiting the teenage audience. It was unpleasant for us to see our more personal strips cohabit with strips that were in effect pandering to the teenage market which we were condemning. It was an ambiguous, and ultimately unacceptable, compromise.

Question: How did the idea to self-publish arise?

Moebius: It had never before happened that a small group

of artists sat together and pooled some money together to create their own publishing company. One day, we all went to have a drink and someone said, "What we should do is what the Americans are doing, self-publish." We meant, of course, the undergrounds, which were our model.

We could see that, even though they weren't all actually published by the artists themselves, they were still published by small companies, artisans.

The publishers themselves were like artists, they invented new structures, new formats, new covers, and new ways of reaching the readers. The artists were tapping into cultural references that came from outside the small, traditional comics culture, such as psychedelics, the Vietnam War, etc.

Adult comics started in the United States with the American Underground. They were the first in the world to use comics as a means of communication, to express real emotions. Before, comics were used only to do stories, entertainment. It had some great moments, but it was all very

Moebius

conventional. The American underground showed us in Europe how to express true feelings, how to tell something to the reader through the comics. They blew the mind of the few professionals in Europe who saw them. It showed us the way, helped us create our own stories, express our own emotions. The answer from the public was phenomenal, first in France, then throughout Europe.

People took it more seriously in Europe than they did in the United States because the separation of genres was not so strong there that they could not, not accept the idea that comics could be art, a valid mean of self-expression, with both high and low points, but where the high points can be very good. Like with movies, theatre and any other form of expression.

In the case of *Métal Hurlant*, it was the same thing. From the very start, the magazine looked slicker and more professional, because Jean-Pierre Dionnet was a professional and wanted it to have that very sharp look. We didn't want to simply parody the Undergrounds. We wanted to publish a real professional magazine, but one where the artists would be totally free to do what they wanted—which is a very scary concept!

So we had these two different motivations: one was to create a new tool, a new medium; the other was just searching for freer ways of expression.

Question: What was your first "new" Moebius-style story?

Moebius: *Le Bandard Fou* [*The Horny Goof*]. It was first published in 1974 by the same folks who were putting out the magazine *L'Écho des Savanes*. However, people usually consider my short story "La Déviation" [*The Detour*], which appeared in *Pilote* in 1973, the first Moebius-style story, but it was signed "Gir" and was more like a statement of intention, a manifesto if you wish. *The Horny Goof*, done the following year, is the tangible product of that manifesto, the first real, full-length, adult Moebius story.

All this has to be seen in the context of the spirit of May 1968. In France, the events of May '68 started a cultural explosion, which found its way into the comics. The new state of mind was openness, awareness, and the desire to explore new roads, to tell new stories, to create new patterns, to look for other types of societies. The first comic artists to take the leap were Gotlib, **Mandryka** and Claire Brétecher, who decided to leave *Pilote* at the peak of its success and, in 1973, started their own self-published magazine, *L'Écho des Savanes*. Philippe Druillet and I were champing at the bit

and, a year later, with Jean-Pierre Dionnet, we started our own magazine too, *Métal Hurlant*.

The Horny Goof was drawn during that incubating period, just before the creation of *Métal*. I remember that my inspiration came after an evening spent in the company of other comic artists, most especially Gotlib. I drew that story at night, in small increments, while I was doing *Blueberry* and other jobs during the day. The story came in a state of complete spontaneity—some would say irresponsibility! To that extent, it anticipates *Arzach* and especially *The Airtight Garage*, to which it is an unplanned prequel, in particular in its mixture of science fiction, humor, and the purposefully-kept-mysterious threads of the story.

The Horny Goof was my first "adult" story. To me, "adult" means to be free in spirit, to know no bounds, to accept no moral restrictions, especially those imposed by somebody else. Only the artist himself can impose his own restrictions, and therefore assume full responsibility for his art. That is what it means to be an "adult."

I believe that to become an "adult" is ultimately the only way for a comic artist not to become bored to death. If you have to draw the same characters day after day, with the same faces, the same costumes, if you can't express anything personal, if you have to illustrate the same stories, often given to you by people you don't know or don't respect, you can very well go mad, or start drinking in order to compensate, or maybe even kill yourself. It's a nightmare. The only way to stay alive is to stay fresh and have fun doing what you're doing.

The Horny Goof was one of the first stories I did in that spirit of freedom. It was something incredible. It expresses an emotion, like "I don't know what I've done, but I must continue. I don't know where I'm going, but I must go on." I think the reader feels that. I was not seeking to deliberately put these theories into practice. I was only doing it because I experienced great pleasure doing so. But it just happened that it fit. When you open a door, you don't know what you're going to find behind it.

Question: And then you did *Arzach*, which was received like a kind of explosion.

Moebius: Yes. It really was a small revolution in the world of comics. The public thought it was fantastic. First, the approach that I had taken, which was to tell a story without words, came as a kind of shock. Then, it was not a story that fit within the usual classifications of comic-book stories at the time. I say comic-book stories, because it obviously was a lot more ordinary when compared to the kinds of stories they did in literary works of fantasy. There was also the fact that I had put a lot more work into each panel, in fact the kind of work that was usually more associated with a painting or a full-blown illustration. That, too, impressed people deeply.

Arzach was a kind of statement. With it, I tried to plunge into an alien world, a world literally beyond everything we know. But I didn't want to do just any kind of weird story.

It had to be very personal, carry a lot of my inner feelings…. When one becomes involved in that kind of work, one opens certain doors inside oneself, and then archetypal forms and images begin to appear. For example, the very first image that you see in *Arzach* is that of a huge tower. It is an obvious phallic symbol. And one finds the same symbolism in *Arzach*'s hat, and many more images spread throughout the stories. Of course, it was not done as a deliberate attempt on my part. I didn't sit down at my desk, and tell myself to draw phallic shapes! No, it was far more subtle, a little like a Rorschach inkblot test….

Arzach is full of dream-like images. When an artist puts himself in a state where he wants to draw what exists at the deepest level of his consciousness, just on the edge of the subconscious mind, then strange things begin to happen. The defenses erected by your conscious mind start crumbling, and the intellect's direction yields to messages from the subconscious. A Ouija board works on the same principles, and so does *Arzach*.

Arzach is full of negative images, because, at the time, I had the same frame of mind as most Parisian comic artists, when being negative was considered a criterion of quality. There is a lot of symbolism of death too, which once again, is not deliberate. Arzach's bird, for instance, obviously belongs to an extinct species. It appears to be made of concrete…. At that time, the only way that I had to open myself to the subconscious plane, and free myself from the direction of my intellect, was to go "below," in those darker zones of myself which, at the time, revealed someone who was suffering, someone who was not living a happy existence, someone who was surrounded by a hard and terrible world. When you open those doors inside yourself, the only pictures that you find are images of death and fear.

Question: Tell us about **Le Garage Hermétique** [*The Airtight Garage*].

Moebius: The story of the making of *The Airtight Garage* is a funny one. In those days, I often felt strong bursts of inspiration, and I would go home and draw all night. In the morning, I would look at what I had done and would either shelve it, because I thought it looked absurd or uninteresting, or I would add to it in order to build a four- or six-page story. With *The Airtight Garage*, it all started like that. I drew the first two pages with the feeling of making up a big joke, a complete mystery, something that could not possibly lead anywhere. And yet, at the same time, I was trying to create something that captured a feeling of joy and fantasy that I felt inside me, almost as if I was remembering the incomplete part of a dream.

After I finished these two pages, I put them in a drawer and forgot all about them, until Jean-Pierre Dionnet, then-editor of *Métal Hurlant*, found them and asked me to draw an ending to the story so that he could publish them. I told him that I would do one for the next issue of the magazine. The following month, he called me back and reminded me

about the ending. Of course, I hadn't done anything. So, in a state of panic, I did two more pages to buy myself more time. Since I hadn't even kept a copy of the first two pages, I had no references and, as a result, the second chapter had no continuity with the first one. It is only with the third chapter that I began picking up the loose ends and giving the story a direction. That's when I brought back Major Grubert, for instance. Soon, I decided to experiment with the story-telling itself by challenging myself every month to solve the continuity problems that I had introduced in previous months.

By creating this feeling of permanent insecurity, I was forced to experience the total joy of creating a continuity. Every month, I would try very hard to recreate a coherent story from the existing elements. Then, I would break them apart again in order to create again a feeling of insecurity, so that, the next month, I would again have to pick up the pieces and do it again, and so on until the end of the story. I finally gathered all the threads in the last fifteen pages, which I did in one sitting. You will note, however, that the story ends on yet another open-ended sequence, which introduces a potentially unlimited incoherence factor. The Major finds himself in our reality, which is the epitome of non-coherence.

Question: And then, you worked with screenwriter Dan O'Bannon on **The Long Tomorrow**. How did that happen?

Moebius: *The Long Tomorrow* is part of the period when I was working on the film version of *Dune*, that Alexandro Jodorowsky tried to put together in 1975 and 1976. Alexandro had hired Dan O'Bannon to be in charge of the special effects. Originally, Alexandro and I had gone to Los Angeles to talk to [special effects technician] Douglas Trumbull, but for some reason, things didn't work out, and Dan was hired instead.

Dan had come to stay in Paris, but he did not have much to do, since we were still busy working on the concepts and the designs of the film. So, to keep himself busy, he was drawing stories. In fact, Dan is a very good artist. He could have become a great comic artist with more practice. At the time, he had done many things. He had acted and directed in *Dark Star*, with John Carpenter. He knew special effects. He wrote and he drew. He did many things. So, one day, he showed me a story that he had just finished drawing. It was *The Long Tomorrow*, a kind of classic detective story, but set in the future. I immediately became enthusiastic. I loved the way he had handled it. When we try to do stories like that in Europe, parodies or imitations of the Golden Age American detective story, it always looks fake. If the French are doing it, it looks French. If the Italians do it, it looks Italian. Somehow, the national peculiarities always come back to haunt the final product. But in *The Long Tomorrow*, there was no such thing. It was pure. Suddenly I was reading a pastiche that was not a pastiche, but something even more original than the original source material. In attempting to do a parody, Dan had in fact ended up creating something that was not parodying but reusing and developing the same classic themes. *The Long Tomorrow* may be a short story but, in my opinion, it is as good as [author Raymond] Chandler.

Because it was a very strong story, I felt right away that it would enable me to do some really crazy and wonderful things, The artist has a great deal more freedom, in terms of designing costumes, characters, decors, etcetera, when he deals with a very solid story. Then, one does not have to worry about adding visual elements, whose only purpose is to further the plot. One can concentrate exclusively on the art. That is what I did with *The Long Tomorrow*. I was able to do things that went beyond the traditional conventions of the genre. For example, Pete Club's costume may seem almost ridiculous. Instead of going back to the classical, dark look of the private eye, the Bogart-style of trenchcoat, I chose to give Club a very colorful and fancy costume. I could do that, because the story was strong enough to let me get away with it. And I did basically the same with all the visual elements of the story. I freely injected a very personal sense of aesthetics into the whole thing.

I faithfully followed Dan's story. He had drawn it in its entirety, almost like a storyboard. In fact, someday, I would like to print the two versions of *The Long Tomorrow* side by side. The story carried me so much that I did not feel time go by. It was great. Then, suddenly, I reached the end, and it was over. Everyone loved *The Long Tomorrow*, so I asked Dan to write me a sequel, which he did. But when it came, I did not have a good feel for it. It was not as powerful as the first story. It was just another adventure. So I never drew it. There was, however, another sequel of sorts.

After *Dune* folded, Dan went on to work on *Alien* and he called me to do some designs. So, I met the director, Ridley Scott. Later, Ridley asked me to work on *Blade Runner*, but at the time, I was going to work on another film, ***Les Maîtres du Temps*** [*The Time Masters*], so I could not. Now, I'm a bit sorry that I did not, because I love *Blade Runner*. But I am very happy, touched even, that my collaboration with Dan became one of the visual references of the film.

Question: Where do you see comics going next?

Moebius: I see an even further concentration of publishers, but operating within a different frame of reference. It is likely that we're going to see comics evolving in two directions.

First, there will be products aimed for mass consumption, easily read and easily discarded, probably produced as cheaply as possible. On the other hand, there will also be prestige comics, worthy of being collected, with greater literary and artistic values, reflecting a real investment on the part of their creators. But for these to happen, today's young artists must extract themselves from their present cultural referential system, which is still primarily super-hero oriented, to really express themselves in more open ways. Comics must learn to express personal, internal universes, deal with social or political themes, or truly original visions.

It is important to reach a public that doesn't let itself be trapped in genres or categories. To me, adolescents who are stuck in a single genre, like super-heroes, are already old people. To me, to be young is to be free of prejudice and preconceived ideas.

CHAPTER VI

Selected Biographies

1. Filmmakers

Autant-Lara, Claude (1903–2000)

Paris Qui Dort (*Paris Sleeps*, transl. as *The Crazy Ray*; Asst. Dir., [1923])
Le Voyage Imaginaire (*The Imaginary Journey*; Asst. Dir., [1925])
Sylvie et le Fantôme (*Sylvie and the Ghost*, 1945)
Marguerite de la Nuit (*Marguerite of the Night*, 1955)

Claude **Autant-Lara** began his film career as a set decorator and costume designer for Marcel L'Herbier. In 1923, he served as assistant director on René **Clair**'s *Paris Qui Dort* (*Paris Sleeps*, transl. as *The Crazy Ray*) and in 1925, on the short-feature *Le Voyage Imaginaire* (*The Imaginary Journey*). After a spell in Hollywood, he returned to France, where he embarked on a full-fledged directorial career, often assisted by his wife Ghislaine, also an actress and screenwriter. Autant-Lara gained fame with *Le Diable au Corps* (*Devil in the Flesh*, 1946). Other films of interest include *L'Auberge Rouge* (*The Red Inn*, 1951), an irreverent medieval murder mystery; *La Traversée de Paris* (*Crossing Paris*, 1956), a vitriolic satire of the World War II black market; and *La Jument Verte* (*The Green Mare*, 1959), a bawdy satirical farce based on Marcel **Aymé**'s novel.

Barma, Claude (1918–)

L'Agence Nostradamus (1950, TV)
Cendrillon (*Cinderella*, 1953, TV)
Belphegor (1965, TV)

Director Claude **Barma** joined French television in 1946, and had the honor of having directed the very first French television series, *L'Agence Nostradamus* (*The Nostradamus Agency*, 1950), the first made-for-television feature, *Pas d'Accord pour Mister Blake* (*No Agreement for Mr. Blake*, 1951), a thriller, and the first historical series, *Le Chevalier de Maison-Rouge* (*The Knight of Maison-Rouge*, 1963), based on the novel by Alexandre **Dumas**. In addition to *Belphégor* (1965), Barma also produced and directed the very popular historical mini-series *Les Rois Maudits* (*The Accursed Kings*, 1972/73), television adaptations of **Dumas**' *Les Trois Mousquetaires* (*The Three Musketeers*, 1959), Rostand's *Cyrano de Bergerac* (1960), *Hamlet* (1962) and numerous episodes of police series, including the renowned *Maigret* (with Jean Richard in the role).

Besson, Luc (1959–)

Le Dernier Combat (*The Final Combat*, 1982)
Kamikaze (Wri., 1986)
Le Cinquième Élément (*The Fifth Element*, 1997)

Luc **Besson**'s first feature was the mostly-silent, black-and-white, post-apocalyptic fable, **Le Dernier Combat** (*The Final Combat*, 1982), written with Pierre Jolivet, which immediately established him as a leading genre filmmaker. Both his subsequent surrealistic thriller, *Subway* (1985), starring Christopher Lambert, and his enormously successful *Le Grand Bleu* (*The Big Blue*, 1988), contain borderline fantasy overtones. Besson also co-wrote the script of the science fiction thriller **Kamikaze** (1986), directed by his former assistant, Didier Grousset. The American success of *Nikita* (*La Femme Nikita*, 1991) and *Léon* (*The Professional*, 1994) enabled him to secure American financing for his big budget science fiction epic, **Le Cinquième Élément** (*The Fifth Element*), a prestigious a French-American co-production shot in English, starring Bruce Willis and Gary Oldman (1997).

Blier, Bertrand (1939–)

Calmos (*Quiet Please!*, 1976)
Notre Histoire (*Our Story*, 1976)
Buffet Froid (*Cold Cuts*, 1979)

The son of renowned actor Bernard Blier, director Bertrand **Blier** began his career in the 1960s as assistant on films by Georges Lautner, Christian-Jacque, etc. His first feature film, *Les Valseuses* (*Balls*, transl. as *Going Places*, 1974), an anarchistic, erotic road movie, attracted considerable attention. His *Préparez vos Mouchoirs* (*Get Out Your Handkerchiefs*, 1978) received an Oscar for Best Foreign Film. In addition to his genre films listed below, Blier is also the author of **Buffet Froid** (*Cold Cuts*, 1979), a biting satire on the life of a serial killer.

Boisset, Yves (1939–)

Rouletabille: Le Parfum de la Dame en Noir (*The Scent of the Lady in Black*, 1966, TV)
Coplan Sauve Sa Peau (*Coplan Saves His Skin*, 1968)
Le Prix du Danger (*The Prize of Peril*, 1983)

Yves **Boisset** began his career in the 1960s as assistant to directors Robert Hossein and René Clément. His first feature film, one of the French James Bond-like **Coplan** series, confirmed his knack for the genre of action/adventure thrillers, with political overtones. Several of his later films are, in fact, thinly-disguised versions of French political scandals: *L'Attentat* (*The Assassination*, 1972), *R.A.S.* (*Nothing to Report*, 1973), *Le Juge Fayard* (1977), etc. Other notable films include atmospheric thrillers such as *Un Taxi Mauve* (*The Purple Taxi*, 1977), which makes good use of its Irish locations, and *Radio-Corbeau* (1989), a strange murder mystery about a radio-broadcasting vigilante.

Borowczyk, Walerian (1923–)

Goto, L'Île d'Amour (*Goto, Island of Love*, 1968)
La Bête (*The Beast*, 1975)
Dr. Jekyll et les Femmes (*Dr. Jekyll and Women*, transl. as *Dr. Jekyll and Miss Osborne*, 1981)

A Polish émigré, Walerian **Borowczyk** began his French career in 1958 and quickly became a leading animator of fantasy shorts such as *Terra Incognita*, *Le Magicien* and **Les Astronautes** (all 1959), the latter co-directed with Chris **Marker**. He began directing live-action features in 1967, and produced a number of commercial erotic films, often with fantasy overtones, such as the surrealistic **Goto, L'Île d'Amour** (*Goto, Island of Love*, 1968).

Bourgeois, Gérard (?–?) *see* **Méliès' Rivals**

Buñuel, Juan Luis (1934–)

Au Rendez-Vous de la Mort Joyeuse (*Rendezvous with Joyous Death*, 1972)
La Femme aux Bottes Rouges (*The Woman with Red Boots*, 1974)
Léonor (1975)
Fantômas *Ep. 2. L'Étreinte du Diable* (*The Devil's Hug*, 1980, TV)
Fantômas *Ep. 3. Le Mort Qui Tue* (*The Deadman Who Kills*, 1980, TV)
Histoires Extraordinaires (*Extraordinary Tales*) *Ep. 1. Le Joueur d'Echecs de Maelzel* (*Maelzel's Chess Player*, 1980, TV)

De Bien Étranges Affaires (*Very Strange Affairs*) *Ep. 5. Un Homme Ordinaire* (*An Ordinary Man*, 1982, TV)
L'Homme de la Nuit (*The Night Man*, 1983, TV)

The son of famous Spanish film director Luis Buñuel (1900–1983), Juan Luis **Buñuel**'s directorial debut was the critically well-received **Au Rendez-Vous de la Mort Joyeuse** (*Rendezvous with Joyous Death*, 1972). Buñuel has since established his own brand of fantasy, distinctive from his father's, verging on the gothic (as in **Léonor**), but always with a lighter touch. He has also contributed numerous telefilms to French television, including an adaptation of Gaston **Leroux**'s novel, **L'Homme de la Nuit** (*The Night Man*).

Capellani, Albert (1870–1931) *see* **Méliès' Rivals**

Carné, Marcel (1909–)

Les Visiteurs du Soir (*The Visitors of the Evening*, transl. as *The Devil's Envoys*, 1942)
Les Portes de la Nuit (*The Gates of Night*, 1946)
Juliette, ou La Clé des Songes (*Juliet, or The Key to Dreams*, 1951)
La Merveilleuse Visite (*The Marvelous Visitation*, 1974)

One of the great classic French directors, Marcel **Carné** assisted René **Clair** in the early 1930s before making his directorial debut with *Jenny* (1936), followed by the classic *Drôle de Drame* (*Bizarre, Bizarre*, 1937), *Quai des Brumes* (*Port of Shadows*) and *Hôtel du Nord* (both 1938) and *Le Jour Se Lève* (*Daybreak*, 1939). He reached the peak of his fame with *Les Enfants du Paradis* (*The Children of Paradise*, 1945). His **Les Portes de la Nuit** (*Gates of Night*, 1946), written with Jacques **Prévert**, is a borderline fantasy film in which Fate itself is incarnated as an old tramp played by Jean Vilar.

Caro, Marc (?–) *see* **Jeunet, Jean-Pierre**

Carrière, Jean-Claude (1931–)

Cartes sur Table (*Cards on the Table*, transl. as *Attack of the Robots*; Wri., 1962)
Dans les Griffes du Maniaque (*In the Grip of the Maniac*, transl. as *The Diabolical Dr. Z, Miss Death* and *Dr. Z, Miss Death*; Wri., 1965)
La Voie Lactée (*The Milky Way*, 1969)
L'Alliance (*The Alliance*; Wri., 1970)
Le Charme Discret de la Bourgeoisie (*The Discreet Charm of the Bourgeoisie*; Wri., 1972)
Le Moine (*The Monk*; Wri., 1972)
France, Société Anonyme (*France, Inc.*; Wri., 1973)
La Femme aux Bottes Rouges (*The Woman with Red Boots*; Wri., 1974)
Le Fantôme de la Liberté (*Phantom of Liberty*; Wri., 1974)
Léonor (Wri., 1975)
Photo Souvenir (*Souvenir Shots*; Wri., 1978, TV)
Ils Sont Grands Ces Petits (*The Kids Have Grown Up*; Wri., 1979)
La Double Vie De Théophraste Longuet (*The Double Life of Théophraste Longuet*; Wri., 1981, TV)

Je Tue Il (*I Kill He*; Wri., 1982, TV)
Le Jardinier Récalcitrant (*The Rebel Gardener*; Wri., 1983, TV)
L'Unique (*The Only One*; Wri., 1985)
Les Étonnements d'un Couple Moderne (*The Astonishments of a Modern Couple*; Wri., 1986, TV)

Jean-Claude **Carrière** is a prolific French writer and screenwriter, who has collaborated with Luis Buñuel (including on the cult classic *Belle de Jour*), Juan Luis **Buñuel**, Pierre Etaix, Louis **Malle** (*Le Voleur* (*The Thief*, 1965)), Jacques Deray (*La Piscine* (*The Swimming Pool*, 1969)), Jesus "Jess" Franco, Jean-Luc **Godard** and Volker Schlondorff (*The Tin Drum* (1979)). Among his non-genre film credits are *Le Retour de Martin Guerre* (1982), a medieval mystery starring Gérard Depardieu, *The Unbearable Lightness of Being* (1988), *Valmont* (1989), and the hugely successful *Cyrano* (1990), also starring Depardieu. Jean-Claude Carrière also wrote a series of *Frankenstein* novels in the early 1960s under the pseudonym of "Benoît **Becker**." See Book 2 and Book 1, Chapter V (under *Fleuve Noir*) for comic book adaptations of these novels.

Chabrol, Claude (1930–)

L'Oeil du Malin (*The Evil Eye*, transl. as *The Third Lover*, 1961)
Ophelia (1962)
Landru (*Bluebeard*, 1963)
Marie-Chantal Contre Dr. Kha (*Marie-Chantal vs. Dr. Kha*, 1965)
Le Boucher (*The Butcher*, 1970)
Les Noces Rouges (*Wedding in Blood*, 1973)
Histoires Insolites (*Weird Tales*) *Ep. 1. Monsieur Bébé* (*Mister Baby*, 1974, TV)
Histoires Insolites (*Weird Tales*) *Ep. 2. Les Gens de l'Été* (*The Summer People*, 1974, TV)
Histoires Insolites (*Weird Tales*) *Ep. 3. Une Invitation à la Chasse* (*Invitation to a Hunt*, 1974, TV)
Histoires Insolites (*Weird Tales*) *Ep. 4. Nul N'est Parfait* (*Nobody's Perfect*, 1974, TV)
Alice, ou La Dernière Fugue (*Alice, or The Last Escapade*, 1976)
Henry James Ep. 1. De Grey (1976, TV)
Les Liens de Sang (*Blood Relatives*, 1979)
Fantômas Ep. 1. L'Échafaud Magique (*The Magic Scaffold*, 1980, TV)
Fantômas Ep. 4. Le Tramway Fantôme (*The Phantom Trolley*, 1980, TV)
Histoires Extraordinaires (*Extraordinary Tales*) *Ep. 4. Le Système du Docteur Goudron et du Professeur Plume* (*The System of Dr. Tarr and Professor Fether*, 1980, TV)
Le Cri du Hibou (*The Cry of the Owl*, 1987)
Sueurs Froides (*Cold Sweat*; host, 1988)
Docteur M (1990)

Claude **Chabrol** went from being a writer for *Les Cahiers du Cinéma* magazine in the mid-1950s to directing his first film, *Le Beau Serge* in 1958, thus establishing himself as the first of the so-called "New Wave" directors. From this early period, we shall mention *L'Oeil du Malin* (*The Evil Eye*, transl. as *The Third Lover*, 1961), a chilling tale of obsessional evil, and the surreal, Kafkaesque *Ophelia* (1962), which treats Shakespeare's *Hamlet* as a contemporary murder mystery. Chabrol's well-known admiration for Hitch-

cock can be found in a number of hard-edged, often bloody, thrillers, which verge on the horrific: *Landru* (*Bluebeard*, 1963), the tale of a notorious French serial killer; *Le Boucher* (*The Butcher*, 1970), another serial killer story; *Les Noces Rouges* (*Wedding in Blood*, 1973); *Les Liens de Sang* (*Blood Relatives*, 1979), based on an Ed McBain novel; *Les Fantômes du Chapelier* (*The Hatmaker's Ghosts*, 1982), based on a Georges Simenon novel; *Poulet au Vinaigre* (*Cop au Vin*, 1985) and *Inspector Lavardin* (1986), which launched a series of successful thrillers starring Jean Poiret as the incredibly caustic Inspector Lavardin; and *Le Cri du Hibou* (*The Cry of the Owl*, 1987), based on a Patricia Highsmith novel. Claude Chabrol has also acted as a Rod Serling–like host for the popular French television anthology show, *Sueurs Froides* (*Cold Sweat*), devoted to grim murders, again often verging on the horrific.

Chalonge, Christian de (1937–)

L'Alliance (*The Alliance*, 1970)
Histoires Insolites (*Weird Tales*) *Ep. 6. Parcelle Brillante* (*Shining Particle*, 1974, TV)
Malevil (1980)
Tom et Lola (Wri., 1989)
Docteur Petiot (1990)

Christian de **Chalonge**'s directorial career is not a prolific one, but even those films which are not, strictly speaking, fantasy or science fiction, contain elements worthy of note, such as his recent *Docteur Petiot* (1990), starring Michel Serrault as a notorious French serial killer who, at one point, fantasizes himself giving advice to Murnau's *Nosferatu*!

Chomon, Segundo de (1871–1929) *see* Méliès' Rivals

Clair, René (Chomette, René, 1898–1981)

Paris Qui Dort (*Paris Sleeps*, transl. as *The Crazy Ray*, 1923)
Entr'acte (*Intermission*, 1924)
Le Fantôme du Moulin-Rouge (*The Ghost of the Moulin-Rouge*, 1924)
Le Voyage Imaginaire (*The Imaginary Journey*, 1925)
La Beauté du Diable (*Beauty and the Devil*, 1949)

After World War I, René **Clair** went into acting, and then into writing/directing with *Paris Qui Dort* (*Paris Sleeps*, transl. as *The Crazy Ray*), his first film (1923). His subsequent films exhibit the style, charm, wit and often light fantasy touch which quickly became his trademark. His early talkie, *Le Million* (1931), is universally considered a film classic. During his brief stays in England and in the United States, Clair made a number of fantasy films which are not reviewed here because they were shot directly in English, but should be recorded: *The Ghost Goes West* (UK, 1935), *I Married a Witch* (U.S., 1942), *It Happened Tomorrow* (U.S., 1944), as well as a film version of Agatha Christie's *And Then There Were None* (U.S., 1945).

Cocteau, Jean (1889–1963)

Le Sang d'un Poète (*Blood of a Poet*, 1930)
Le Baron Fantôme (*The Ghostly Baron*; Wri., 1942)
La Belle et la Bête (*Beauty and the Beast*, 1945)
Orphée (*Orpheus*, 1949)
Le Testament d'Orphée (*The Testament of Orpheus*, 1960)

Jean **Cocteau** was a famous French poet, novelist, painter, and filmmaker, and one of the leading lights of the surrealist movement. Cocteau's first film, *Le Sang d'un Poete* (*Blood of a Poet*, 1930), established his obsessive exploration of the themes of inner, spiritual life and death, later revisited in *Orphée* (*Orpheus*, 1949) and *Le Testament d'Orphée* (*The Testament of Orpheus*, 1960). Other films of note not included here include his scripts for Jean Delannoy's *L'Éternel Retour* (*The Eternal Return*, 1943), a modern retelling of the story of Tristan and Isolde, and the beautiful *La Princesse de Clèves* (*Dir.*: Jean Delannoy, 1961), also a tale of impossible love.

Cohl, Émile (1857–1938)

As **Méliès** is to live-action films, Émile **Cohl** is to animation. A political cartoonist, Cohl was hired by Louis **Feuillade** in 1905 and started to work for Gaumont. In 1907, he began producing a series of short animated cartoons, drawing every frame of his films, and puppet films, thereby pioneering the technique of stop-motion animation. Cohl left Gaumont in 1910 to work for Pathé, then joined Éclair in 1912. He eventually moved to the United States, where he worked on the *Newlyweds*, *Baby Snookums,* and *Moving World* cartoons until 1914. After World War I, he found it hard to adapt to new animation techniques, and stopped producing films in 1918. He lived in poverty until his death. An Emile Cohl animation prize in now awarded every year in France. Between 1908 and 1918, Cohl made over 100 films, most if not all having a claim to being fantasy. Some of his most famous genre titles include *Le Cauchemar de Fantoche* (*The Puppet's Nightmare*, 1908), *L'Automate* (*The Automaton*, 1908), *La Lune dans son Tablier* (*Moon in His Apron*, 1909), *Les Lunettes Féeriques* (*The Fairy Spectacles*, 1909), *Clair de Lune Espagnol* (*The Spaniard on the Moon*, 1909), *Monsieur Clown chez les Lilliputiens* (*Mr. Clown in Lilliput*, 1909), *Le Tout Petit Faust* (*A Very Small Faust*, 1910), *Les Aventures du Baron de Crac* (*The Adventures of Baron Munchausen*, 1910), *La Boîte Diabolique* (*The Evil Chest*, 1911), and *La Main Mystérieuse* (*The Mysterious Hand*, 1916).

Delvaux, André (1926–)

Un Soir, un Train (*One Night, a Train*, 1968)
Rendez-Vous à Bray (1971)
Belle (1972)

Belgian filmmaker André **Delvaux** started his career working for Belgian television in the 1960s. His first feature, *The Man Who Had His Hair Cut Short* (1966) won a British Academy Award. His third film, the surreal ***Rendez-Vous à Bray*** (1971), based on a Julien **Gracq** story, won a Louis Delluc Award in France.

Demy, Jacques (1931–1990)

Peau d'Âne (*Donkey Skin*, 1970)
Le Joueur de Flûte (*The Pied Piper of Hamelin*, 1971)
L'Évènement le Plus Important Depuis Que l'Homme a Marché sur la Lune (*The Most Important Event Since Man Walked on the Moon*, transl. as *A Slightly Pregnant Man*, 1973)
Parking (1985)

Jacques **Demy** began his career as assistant to French animator Paul **Grimault**, before making a remarkable directorial debut with *Lola* (1961). He is, however, best remembered for his classic musicals, *Les Parapluies de Cherbourg* (*The Umbrellas of Cherbourg*, 1964) and *Les Demoiselles de Rochefort* (*The Young Girls of Rochefort*, 1967). His incursions into fantasy also include a British co-production, ***Le Joueur de Flûte*** (*The Pied Piper of Hamelin*, 1971) and the marginal genre film ***L'Évènement le Plus Important Depuis Que l'Homme a Marché sur la Lune*** (*The Most Important Event Since Man Walked on the Moon*, transl. as *A Slightly Pregnant Man*, 1973) whose theme was retread by the American film *Junior* (1994), starring Arnold Schwarzenegger.

Dulac, Germaine (1882-1942)

Originally a journalist, Germaine **Dulac** fell in love with films and formed a production company with her husband in 1915. Later, they met with D. W. Griffith and she eventually emerged as one of the leading figures of avant-garde French filmmaking, making a number of shorts, some with fantasy or science fiction elements, including *La Mort du Soleil* (*Death of the Sun*, 1922), *Le Diable dans la Ville* (*The Devil in the City*, 1924) (written by Jean-Louis **Bouquet**) and the famous *La Coquille et le Clergyman* (*The Seashell and the Clergyman*, 1928). Sound eventually put an end to her directing career, and she moved on to supervising newsreel productions.

Durand, Jean (1882–1946) *see* **Méliès' Rivals**

Duvivier, Julien (1896–1967)

Le Golem (1935)
La Charrette Fantôme (*The Ghost Cart*, 1939)
Marianne de Ma Jeunesse (*Marianne of My Youth*, 1954)
Le Diable et les Dix Commandements (*The Devil and the Ten Commandments*, 1962)
La Chambre Ardente (*The Burning Court*, 1963)

Julien **Duvivier**'s first experiences in cinema involved assisting Louis **Feuillade** and Marcel L'Herbier. He began directing silent films in 1919—his *La Réincarnation de Serge Renaudier* (*The Reincarnation of Serge Renaudier*, 1920) is fantasy—but only made his mark in the 1930s with a series of realistic dramas like *Poil de Carotte* (1932), *La Tête d'un Homme* (*The Head of a Man*), based on a Simenon "Maigret" novel (1933), *Maria Chapdelaine* (1934), and the world-famous *Pépé le Moko* (1937), remade in the U.S. in 1938 as *Algiers*. He moved to America during WWII. During this period, one can note another borderline fantasy, *Flesh and Fantasy* (in French: *Obsessions*, 1943)—one of the three stories deals with a prediction which comes true. After the war, Duvivier's most notable films include *Anna Karenina* (1948) and *Le Petit Monde de Don Camillo* (*The Little World of Don Camillo*, 1951), based on Giovanni Guareschi's novel, which spawned a successful series. His *Voici le Temps des Assassins* (*Here Comes the Time of the Murderers*, transl. as *Deadlier Than the Male*, 1956) is a remarkably evil-spirited crime thriller. His **Le Diable et les Dix Commandements** (*The Devil and the Ten Commandments*, 1962) is a borderline fantasy.

Feuillade, Louis (1873–1925)

Fantômas (5 eps.) (1913-14)
Les Vampires (*The Vampires*, 10 Eps., 1915-16)
Judex (12 eps., 1915-16)
La Nouvelle Mission de Judex (*The New Mission of Judex*, 12 eps., 1917)

Louis **Feuillade** is to popular French cinema what Abel **Gance** is to serious filmmaking. The son of a wine broker, Feuillade began his film career as a screenwriter in 1906. The following year, he was appointed production chief at Gaumont, but continued to direct his own projects, including such genre fares as *L'Homme Aimanté* (*The Magnetized Man*, 1907), *La Chatte Métamorphosée en Femme* (*The Cat That Was Changed into a Woman*, 1909), *Le Mort Vivant* (*The Living Dead*, 1912), *L'Anneau Fatal* (*The Deadly Ring*, 1912), *Le Revenant* (*The Spectre*, 1913), and *La Gardienne du Feu* (*Guardian of the Fire*, 1913). Feuillade is, today, considered the father of "serials," the forerunner of German expressionism, and a master of suspense. In 20 years, he directed and wrote well over 800 films in various genres. He is, however, best remembered for his pulp fantasy serials featuring colorful master villains, masked avengers, secret societies, and the like. In addition to the serials reviewed above, some of his best works included *Barrabas* (12 eps.) (1919), *L'Homme sans Visage* (*The Faceless Man*, 1919) and *Vindicta* (5 eps., 1923). Feuillade's work was rediscovered in the 1940s and he has, since then, been included among the great pioneers of French cinema.

Franju, Georges (1912–1987)

Les Yeux sans Visage (*Eyes Without a Face*, 1959)
  Judex (1963)
L'Homme sans Visage (*The Faceless Man*, transl. as *Shadowman*, 1974; TV)

Co-founder of the French Cinemathèque with Henri Langlois, Georges **Franju** first drew fame with *Le Sang des Bêtes* (*The Blood of the Beasts*, 1949), a stark, uncompromising documentary about the Paris slaughterhouse. In ad-

dition to his genre films reviewed here, Franju is also known for a documentary about Georges **Méliès**, *Le Grand Méliès*, (1952). He also directed *Marcel Allain* (1966), a documentary about the co-creator of *Fantômas*, for French television, and later directed a *Fantômas*-like television series, **L'Homme sans Visage** (*The Faceless Man*, transl. as *Shadowman*, 1974).

Frydland, Maurice (1934–)

Le Mystérieux Docteur Cornelius (1982; TV)

Maurice **Frydland** worked as assistant director and director of short features before working as a television reporter and documentary filmmaker. His first fiction program was an adaptation of a François Mauriac story, *Le Mystère Fontenac* (*The Fontenac Mystery*) in 1974. After several telefilms devoted to contemporary political issues, and one remarkable historical series, *L'Épingle Noire* (*The Black Pin*, 1981), he directed the cult classic **Le Mystérieux Docteur Cornelius** (1982), based on a Gustave **Le Rouge** pulp serial. His subsequent career includes stints on many of France's most prestigious police series: *Maigret* (starring Jean Richard), *Les Cinq Dernières Minutes* (*The Last Five Minutes*; *Nestor Burma* (first starring Gérard Desarthe, then Guy Marchand), and other made-for-television features.

Gance, Abel (1889–1981)

La Folie du Dr. Tube (*The Madness of Dr. Tube*, 1915)
J'accuse (*I Accuse*, 1918)
La Fin du Monde (*The End of the World*, transl. as *Paris After Dark*, 1930)
J'accuse (*I Accuse*, transl. as *They May Live*, 1937)

First an actor, then a screenwriter, Abel **Gance** began directing short films such as *Le Masque d'Horreur* (*The Horror Mask*, 1912) before World War I. A pioneer of film technique with his use of close-ups and tracking shots, Gance is better known today for his experimental shorts such as **La Folie du Dr. Tube** (*The Madness of Dr. Tube*, 1916) and *Les Gaz Mortels* (*The Deadly Gasses*, 1916), and *Au Secours!* (*Help!*, 1923), as well as his more ambitious film projects such as **J'accuse** (*I Accuse*, 1918, remade in 1937), *La Roue* (*The Wheel*, 1923), his unqualified masterpiece, *Napoléon* (1927), and the classic, **La Fin du Monde** (*The End of the World*, 1930).

Godard, Jean-Luc (1930–)

Alphaville (1965)
Le Plus Vieux Métier du Monde (*The Oldest Profession in the World*) "In the Year 2000" segment; (1967)
Week-End (1967)
Je Vous Salue Marie (*Hail Mary!*, 1985)
Hélas Pour Moi! (*Woe Is Me*, 1992)

A regular contributor to *Les Cahiers du Cinéma* magazine in the 1950s, Jean-Luc **Godard** became one of the leading representatives of the French "New Wave" cinema with his first feature film, *À Bout de Souffle* (*Breathless*, 1960). Even though Godard's only sience fiction film is *Alphaville* (1965), and only on an allegorical level, most of his early works are imbued with surreal qualities, which are particularly evident in the apocalyptic *Week-End* (1967). After 1968, Godard's career took a more political and wildly experimental turn. It was only in the 1980s that he returned to more traditional themes.

Grimault, Paul (1905–1994)

Le Roi et l'Oiseau (*The King and the Bird*, 1979)

Animation director Paul **Grimault** began his career in advertising, before going into animation in the late 1930s. His short *Le Petit Soldat* (*The Little Soldier*, 1947) won first prize at the Venice Festival the following year. Other famous genre shorts include *L'Épouvantail* (*The Scarecrow*, 1943), *La Flûte Magique* (*The Magic Flute*, 1946), *Le Petit Soldat* (*The Little Soldier*, 1947); currently scheduled to be remade by Pixar), *La Demoiselle et le Violoncelliste* (*The Young Lady and the Cellist*, 1964). His masterpiece remains the animated feature ***Le Roi et l'Oiseau*** (*The King and the Bird*, 1979), which he started in the early 1950s.

Guy-Blaché, Alice (1873–1968) *see* **Méliès' Rivals**

Jasset, Victorin (1862–1913) *see* **Méliès' Rivals**

Jessua, Alain (1932–)

Traitement de Choc (*Shock Treatment*, 1972)
Armaguedon (1977)
Les Chiens (*The Dogs*, 1979)
Paradis pour Tous (*Paradise for All*, 1982)
Frankenstein 90 (1984)

Once an assistant to such distinguished directors as Jacques Becker, Marcel Ophuls, Marcel Carné and Marc Allégret, Alain Jessua started in features with *La Vie à l'Envers* (*Life Upside Down*, 1964), a remarkable study of an increasingly alienated man. In Jessua's films, reality is never as simple or safe as it first seems. His *Jeu de Massacre* (*The Killing Game*, 1967) shows a man who identifies with a comic-book character. *Armaguedon* (1977) is a paranoid thriller about a lonely man turning into a terrorist and challenging the government. Jessua also wrote the novelization of *Traitement de Choc*.

Jeunet Jean-Pierre (1955–) & Caro, Marc (?-)

L'Évasion (*The Escape*, 1977)
Le Manège (*The Merry-Go-Round*, 1979)
Le Bunker de la Dernière Rafale (*The Bunker of the Last Gale*, 1981)
Pas de Linceul pour Billy Brakko (*No Shroud for Billy Brakko*, 1983)
Delicatessen (1992)
La Cité des Enfants Perdus (*City of the Lost Children*, 1995)

Jeunet and **Caro** made their filmmaking debuts with a number of visually striking animated and stop-motion short features such as ***Le Manège*** (*The Merry-Go-Round*, 1979). Their first live-action short feature, ***Le Bunker de la Dernière Rafale*** (*The Bunker of the Last Gale*, 1981), was a critical success and drew attention to them. They confirmed their gift for unique visuals and nightmarish settings with their first feature film, ***Delicatessen*** (1992). Their subsequent ***La Cité des Enfants Perdus*** (*The City of Lost Children*, 1995) was much praised at the Cannes Film Festival. Jeunet and Caro have often been compared to British film director Terry Gilliam. Jean-Pierre Jeunet recently directed *Alien Resurrection*, starring Sigourney Weaver (1997).

Kast, Pierre (1920–1984)

Un Amour de Poche (*Pocket Love*, transl. as *Nude in His Pocket*, 1957)
La Brûlure de Mille Soleils (*The Burn of a Thousand Suns*, 1964)
Le Maître du Temps (*The Time Master*; Wri., 1970)
Les Soleils de l'Île de Paques (*The Suns of Easter Island*, 1971)
L'Herbe Rouge (*The Red Grass*, 1984; TV)

Pierre **Kast** began working for the Cinémathèque Française in 1946, before becoming film director Jean Grémillon's assistant in 1948. He then wrote and directed a number of award-winning short features, live-action and animated, many of them borderline fantasy. His first full-length feature was ***Un Amour de Poche*** (*Pocket Love*, 1957). Many of his films made use of Brazilian or Portuguese history and vistas. He also wrote a vampire novel, *Les Vampires de l'Alfama* (*Vampires of the Alfama*), originally intended to be a treatment for a film. Kast died of a heart attack in 1984, while finishing a made-for-television adaptation of Boris Vian's genre novel, ***L'Herbe Rouge*** (*The Red Grass*). Pierre Kast also produced an excellent 30-minute documentary about French writer/artist Albert **Robida**, entitled *Monsieur Robida, Prophète et Explorateur du Temps* (*Mr. Robida, Prophet and Time Explorer*, 1963).

Kumel, Harry (1940–)

Les Lèvres Rouges (*Red Lips*, transl. as *Daughters of Darkness*, 1971)
Malpertuis (1972)

Belgian film writer-director who began making award-winning short films in his early teens before moving into television. His first feature film was *Mr. Hawarden* (1968), the tale of a man who disguises himself as a woman in order to beat a murder rap. After the commercial failure of the nevertheless brilliant ***Malpertuis***, **Kumel** went back to making television features such as *The Coming of Joachim Stiller* (1975). He recently returned to the cinema with *Eline Verre* (1991), the pessimistic tale of a woman's descent into madness.

Laloux, René (1929–)

Les Escargots (*The Snails*, 1965)
La Planète Sauvage (*The Savage Planet*, transl. as *Fantastic Planet*, 1973)
Les Maîtres du Temps (*The Time Masters*, 1981)
Gandahar (transl. as *Lightyears*, 1987)

Animation director René **Laloux** worked as a painter, a puppeteer and even a male nurse before embarking on an animation career. His first projects included *Les Dents du Singe* (*The Monkey's Teeth*, 1960) and *Les Temps Morts* (*The Dead Times*, 1964), a short feature inspired by the art of illustrator Roland **Topor** and written by Jacques **Sternberg**. Then, again with Topor, he made the award-winning short, *Les Escargots* (*The Snails*, 1965). Afterwards, Laloux decided to produce a series of full-length animated features adapting author Stéfan **Wul**'s science fiction novels. Only two were made: *La Planète Sauvage* (*The Savage Planet*, transl. as *Fantastic Planet*, 1973), using the visual designs of Topor; and *Les Maîtres du Temps* (*The Time Masters*, 1981), using the designs of **Moebius**. His recent *Gandahar* (transl. as *Lightyears*, 1987) was based on a science fiction novel by Jean-Pierre **Andrevon** and used the designs of artist Philippe **Caza**. The relative lack of commercial success of Laloux's last two features has made it difficult for him to produce more films.

Lelouch Claude (1937–)

Toute Une Vie (*A Whole Life*, transl. as *And Now My Love*, 1974)
Viva La Vie (*Hurray for Life*, 1984)
La Belle Histoire (*A Beautiful Story*, 1991)

Claude **Lelouch**'s first film, a short directed when he was 13, won a prize at the Cannes Film Festival. He made his first feature in 1960, and established himself with the classic *Un Homme et une Femme* (*A Man and a Woman*; in 1966. A prolific director, Lelouch has mostly handled romantic dramas and thrillers.

Malle, Louis (1932–1995)

Histoires Extraordinaires—"William Wilson" segment (*Extraordinary Tales*, transl. as *Spirits of the Dead*, 1968)
Black Moon (1975)

After co-directing the famous Captain Cousteau documentary *The Silent World* (1956), Louis **Malle** assisted Robert Bresson on *Un Condamné à Mort S'Est Échappé* (*A Man Escaped*, 1956) before directing his first feature, the crime thriller *Ascenseur pour l'Échafaud* (*Elevator for the Gallows*, transl. as *Frantic*, 1958). Malle established himself as a brilliant, versatile director, in both France and the United States, with films such as *Lacombe Lucien* (1973), *Pretty Baby* (1978), *Atlantic City* (1980), *My Dinner with André* (1981), *Au Revoir les Enfants* (*Good-Bye, Children*, 1987), which have garnered some of the industry's most prestigious awards.

Manzor, René (1960–)

Le Suicide de Frankenstein (*Frankenstein's Suicide*, 1984)
Le Passage (*The Passage*, 1986)
Sueurs Froides (*Cold Sweat*) Ep. 2. *La Sublime Aventure* (*The Sublime Adventure*, 1988; (TV)
3615 Code Père Noël (*Santaclaus.com*, 1989)
Un Amour de Sorcière (*A Witch's Love*, 1997)

Young French director René **Manzor** began his film career with an animation short entitled *Synapse*, before producing his own films. He was chosen by Alain Delon to direct *Le Passage* (1986) and, later, directed various French television series. More recently, he directed two episodes of Lucasfilm's *Young Indiana Jones* television series and *Un Amour de Sorcière* (*A Witch's Love*, 1997), a big-budget fantasy starring Jeanne Moreau and Vanessa Paradis.

Marker Chris (Bouche-Villeneuve, Christian-François) (1921–)

Les Astronautes (*The Astronauts*, 1960)
La Brûlure de Mille Soleils (*The Burn of a Thousand Suns*, 1964)
La Jetée (*The Pier*, 1964)

Writer, poet, essayist, Chris **Marker** is primarily a documentary filmmaker of note. All his films reflect his strong political convictions, and some, among the most recent, deal with science fiction concepts: *Junkopia* (1981), *2084* (co-dir., 1984). Chris Marker has often been involved working with other directors: he co-directed **Resnais**' *Les Statues Meurent Aussi* (*The Statues Also Die*, 1953), **Borowczyk**'s *Les Astronautes* (*The Astronauts*, 1960), edited **Kast**'s *La Brulure de Mille Soleils* (*The Burn of a Thousand Suns*, 1964), was assistant cameraman on Costa Gavras's *L'Aveu* (*The Confession*, 1970) and directed *The Making of Kurosawa's Ran* (1985). His only fictional short feature, *La Jetée* (*The Pier*, 1964) (which was the basis for Terry Gilliam's *Twelve Monkeys*), remains to date one of the most strikingly inventive films ever made about time travel.

Méliès, Georges (1861–1938)

Le Voyage dans la Lune (*A Trip to the Moon*; loosely based on Jules **Verne**'s novel) (1902)
Le Voyage à Travers l'Impossible (*The Journey Through the Impossible*, transl. as *The Impossible Journey*, 1904)
La Conquête du Pôle (*The Conquest of the Pole*, 1912)

The son of a shoe manufacturer, **Méliès** became interested in art, sculpture and puppetry while in school. After completing his military service, and against his father's wishes, he attended the École des Beaux-Arts, one of France's most prestigious art schools. In 1884 he traveled to London, where he became acquainted with the tradecraft of stage magicians. In 1888, after receiving his father's inheritance, Méliès purchased the Robert Houdin Theater and embarked on a full-time career as a stage magician, often incorporating "magic lanterns" as part of his elaborate illusions. In 1895, after witnessing the Lumière Brothers' first cinematographic exhibition, he decided to become a filmmaker.

At first, Méliès' short films (about 20 meters in average length), which he began producing in 1896, were nothing more than recorded daily events, occasionally sprinkled with doses of stage magic for spice. But soon—allegedly following an accidental jamming of his camera—Méliès discovered the potential of trick photography. He began experimenting with studio shooting and artificial lighting, and pioneered virtually all modern special effect techniques: multiple exposures, matte paintings, etc. From magic to fantasy and science fiction was but a small step, and it was therefore not surprising that Méliès quickly came to rely on fantasy and science fiction themes for his work.

When it comes to science fiction and fantasy cinema, it is no exaggeration to state that Méliès invented it all. Most of the genre's classic themes were there: ghosts and haunted castles, wizards and witches, space travel, airships and submarines, the conquest of the Pole and the tunnel under the British Channel, transcontinental car races, flying men and mermaids, giants and microscopic men, living dolls, men turning into monsters, and many, many more. Méliès was to be credited for the very first film adaptations of *She*, *Gulliver's Travels*, Jules **Verne**, *Rip van Winkle*, *Faust*, *Baron Munchausen*, *Cinderella* and *The Thousand and One Nights*.

Eventually, Méliès' career waned. Financial difficulties forced him to sell his studio in 1923, and subsequently, he left the business entirely. However, he was rediscovered in the 1930s, and awarded the Legion of Honor medal. Most of Méliès' films contain elements of fantasy and science fiction. A partial list of titles follows:

L'Hallucination de l'Alchimiste (*The Alchemist's Hallucination*, 1897)
Le Château Hanté (*The Haunted Castle*, 1897)
Magie Diabolique (*Diabolical Magic*, 1898)
La Damnation de Faust (*The Damnation of Faust*, 1898)
Le Rêve d'un Astronaute ou La Lune à un Mètre (*An Astronaut's Dream, or The Moon a Meter Away*, 1898—the first space travel film ever!)
La Caverne Maudite (*The Haunted Cavern*, 1898)
Le Spectre (1899)
Le Diable au Couvent (*The Devil in the Convent*, 1899)
La Danse du Feu (*The Fire Dance*, 1899; loosely based on H. Rider Haggard's *She*)
Le Miroir de Cagliostro (*The Mirror of Cagliostro*, 1899)
Évocation Spirite (*Summoning the Spirits*, 1899)
Cendrillon (*Cinderella*, 1899; based on Charles **Perrault**'s classic fairy tale)
La Forêt Enchantée (*The Enchanted Forest*, 1900)
Le Livre Magique (*The Magic Book*, 1900)
Spiritisme Abracadabrant (*Amazing Spirits*, 1900)
Mésaventures d'un Aéronaute (*Misadventures of an Aeronaut*, 1900)
Chez la Sorcière (*The Witch's House*, 1901)
Le Temple de la Magie (*The Temple of Magic*, 1901)
Le Diable Géant (*The Giant Devil*, 1901)
L'Oeuf du Sorcier (*The Sorcerer's Egg*, 1901)
La Danseuse Microsocopique (*The Microscopic Dancer*, 1901)
L'Homme Mouche (*The Man Fly*, 1902)
La Femme Volante (*The Flying Woman*, 1902)
Les Voyages de Gulliver (*Gulliver's Travels*, 1902; based on Swift's novels; first film adaptation ever made)

Les Filles du Diable (*The Devil's Daughters*, 1903)
La Statue Animée (*The Living Statue*, 1903)
La Flamme Merveilleuse (*The Wondrous Flame*, 1903)
Le Sorcier (*The Wizard*, 1903)
Le Monstre (*The Monster*, 1903)
Le Royaume des Fées (*The Faerie Kingdom*, 1903)
Le Revenant (*The Spectre*, 1903)
Faust aux Enfers (*Faust in Hell*, 1903—a sequel to his 1898's *La Damnation de Faust*)
Le Coffre Enchanté (*The Enchanted Chest*, 1904)
La Damnation du Dr. Faust (*Dr. Faust's Damnation*, 1904—a remake of 1898's *La Damnation de Faust*)
La Sirène (*The Mermaid*, 1904)
La Dame Fantôme (*The Lady Ghost*, 1904)
Le Diable Noir (*The Dark Devil*, 1905)
Le Palais des Mille et Une Nuits (*The Palace of the Thousand and One Nights*, 1905—the first Arabian Adventure film)
La Légende de Rip van Winkle (*The Legend of Rip Van Winkle*; based on Washington Irving's classic tale, 1905)
Le Dirigeable Fantastique (*The Fantastic Airship*, 1906)
La Magie à Travers les Âges (*Magic Through the Ages*, 1906)
Le Fantôme d'Alger (*The Ghost of Algiers*, 1906)
Les 400 Farces du Diable (*Satan's Merry Frolics*, 1906)
L'Alchimiste Parafaragaramus (1906)
La Fée Carabosse (1906)
200,000 Lieues sous les Mers, ou Le Cauchemar d'un Pêcheur (*200,000 Leagues Under the Sea, or A Fisherman's Nightmare*, 1907; loosely based on Jules **Verne**'s novel; that book's first film adaptation)
Le Tunnel sous la Manche, ou Le Cauchemar Franco-Anglais (*The Tunnel Under the Channel, or The Franco-British Nightmare*, 1907)
Satan en Prison (*Satan in Jail*, 1907)
Le Rêve d'un Fumeur d'Opium (*The Dream of an Opium Smoker*, 1908)
La Prophétesse de Thèbes (*The Seeress of Thebes*, 1908)
Le Raid Paris–New York (*The Paris–New York Race*, 1908)
Au Pays des Jouets (*Toyland*, 1908)
La Poupée Vivante (*The Living Doll*, 1908)
Le Fakir de Singapour (*The Singapore Fakir*, 1908)
Le Locataire Diabolique (*The Diabolical Tenant*, 1909)
Le Papillon Fantastique (*The Fantastic Butterfly*, 1910)
Les Hallucinations du Baron de Munchausen (*Baron von Munchausen's Hallucinations*, 1911; the first Munchausen film)
Cendrillon (*Cinderella*, 1912; another remake)

"Méliès' Rivals" (Early French Filmmakers Before World War I)

Georges **Méliès'** success helped launch the careers of a number of lesser-known filmmakers, who largely mined the same vein as he did. Among these are:

Bourgeois, Gérard (?–?)

Author of *La Vie au 21ème Siècle* (*Life in the 21st Century*, 1909).

Capellani, Albert (1870–1931)

One of Pathé's best-known directors, his five-hour-long *Les Misérables* (1912) was regarded as a classic. **Capellani** moved to the United States in 1915. His genre films include *Aladin* (1906), *Cendrillon* (*Cin-*

derella, 1907), and *Le Chat Botté* (*Puss in Boots*, 1908).

Émile Chautard (1881–1934)

Originally an actor, Émile **Chautard** directed several short feature adaptations of **Grand-Guignol** plays by André de **Lorde** (see Book 2) with Victorin **Jasset**: *Une Nuit d'Épouvante* (*A Night of Terror*), *Fumeur d'Opium* (*Opium Smoker*); and *Le Cercueil de Verre* (*The Glass Coffin*). Chautard alone directed *Le Sculpteur Aveugle* (*The Blind Sculptor*), *Malédiction* (*The Curse*; both 1913), *Bagnes d'Enfants* (*Children's Penitentiary*), *Le Faiseur de Fous* (*The Maker of Madmen*; both 1914), also based on de **Lorde**'s plays. In 1914, Chautard directed ***Le Parfum de la Dame en Noir (The Scent of the Woman in Black)***; based on Gaston **Leroux**'s famous novel (which he remade in 1919 in the U.S.), and *Arsène Lupin*. He then emigrated to Hollywood, where he both directed and acted in a number of undistinguished productions.

Chomon, Segundo de (1871–1929)

The Spanish **Méliès**, Segundo de **Chomon** worked in France during the 1906-1909 period during which he produced several, semi-plagiarized Jules **Verne** adaptations. His genre films of the period include *Voyage à la Planète Jupiter* (*Travel to Jupiter*, 1907), *Le Chevalier Mystère* (*The Mystery Knight*, 1907), *La Maison Hantée* (*The Haunted House*, 1907), *Cauchemar et Doux Rêve* (*Nightmare and Sweet Dream*, 1908), *Mars* (1908), *Cuisine Magnétique* (*Magnetic Kitchen*, 1908), *Voyage à la Lune* (*Journey to the Moon*, 1909) and *Voyage au Centre de la Terre* (*Journey to the Center of the Earth*, 1909).

Durand, Jean (1882–1946)

An early French filmmaker, Jean **Durand** was important in the development of the slapstick comedy. Between 1907 and 1929, he turned out scores of silent shorts, including the *Calino* (1907–11) and *Onésime* (1912–13) series. Several contained fantasy elements, such as *Onésime Horloger* (*Onesime Clock-Maker*, 1912), *Onésime aux Enfers* (*Onesime in Hell*, 1912) and *Onésime et la Maison Hantée* (*The Haunted House*, 1913).

Guy-Blaché, Alice (1873–1968)

The first woman director, Alice **Guy-Blaché** made numerous one-reelers for Gaumont between 1896 and 1907, including numerous fantasy films such as *La Fée aux Choux* (*The Cabbage Fairy*, 1896), *Faust et Mephistopheles* (1902), *La Fiancée Ensorcelée* (*The Bewitched Fiancée*, 1903), *La Fève Enchantée* (*The Magic Bean*, 1904) (based on *Jack and the Beanstalk*),

and *La Fée Printemps* (*The Spring Fairy*, 1906). In 1907, Guy-Blaché moved to the United States, where she formed her own production company. In 1922, she returned to France but was not able to continue her career. Most of her other genre output was produced during her years in the United States, e.g. *In the Year 2000* (1912), *The Pit and the Pendulum* (1913), *The Vampire* (1915), etc.

Jasset, Victorin (1862–1913)

A predecessor of Louis **Feuillade**, Victorin **Jasset** was a director of early serials starring *Nick Carter* (1906, 1909, 1911) and *Rifle Bill, King of the Prairie* (1908). He also directed ***Balaoo ou Des Pas au Plafond*** (*Balaoo, or Footprints on the Ceiling*, 1913), an adaptation of Gaston **Leroux**'s genre story about a "missing link" creature accused of murder. In 1911 and 1912, Jasset and Émile **Chautard** directed several short feature adaptations of **Grand-Guignol** plays by André de **Lorde**: *La Justice du Mort* (*Dead Man's Justice*), *Le Cabinet d'Affaires* (*The Business Cabinet*), *Une Nuit d'Épouvante* (*A Night of Terror*), *Fumeur d'Opium* (*Opium Smoker*) and *Le Cercueil de Verre* (*The Glass Coffin*).

Velle, Gaston (?–?)

Author of a number of genre shorts including *Le Chapeau Magique* (*The Magic Hat*, 1903), *Les Invisibles* (1905), *À La Conquête de l'Air* (*The Conquest of the Air*, 1906) and *Le Voyage dans une Étoile* (*The Journey Inside a Star*, 1906).

Zecca, Ferdinand (1864–1947)

Mostly an imitator of **Méliès**, Ferdinand **Zecca** strove not to innovate but to make more commercial films. He eventually became a director of the Pathé organization in 1910. Some of his most famous genre films included *À La Conquête de l'Air* (*The Conquest of the Air*, 1901), *Ce Que Je Vois dans Mon Télescope* (*What I See in My Telescope*, 1902), *Ali-Baba et les Quarante Voleurs* (*Ali-Baba and the Forty Thieves*, 1902), *Le Chat Botté* (*Puss in Boots*, 1903), *Rêve à la Lune* (*Moon Dream*, 1905), *L'Album Magique* (*The Magic Album*, 1908) and *Le Roi de l'Air* (*The King of the Air*, 1913).

Mocky, Jean-Pierre (1929–)

La Cité de l'Indicible Peur (*The City of Unspeakable Fear*) aka *La Grande Frousse* (*The Great Fear*, 1964)
L'Ibis Rouge (*The Red Ibis*, 1975)
Litan (1981)
La Machine à Découdre (*The Killing Machine*, 1986)
Le Miraculé (*The Miracle Victim*, 1987)
Les Saisons du Plaisir (*The Seasons of Pleasure*, 1988)

Jean-Pierre **Mocky** began his film career in the mid-

1940s as an actor (he appeared in **Cocteau**'s *Orpheus*) and began to write and direct films in the late 1950s. His quick, incisive style has enabled him to carve himself a successful niche as a director of social satires and often very dark humored thrillers. A number of his films include borderline genre elements: In *Les Compagnons de la Marguerite* (*The Brotherhood of the Daisy*, 1967), a clever forger revolutionizes the legal state of marriage. In *La Grande Lessive* (*The Great Washing*, 1968), a couple of teachers go to war against television, climbing rooftops at night to remove aerials. In **L'Ibis Rouge** (*The Red Ibis*, 1975), a pitiful serial killer eventually discovers true love and happiness. In *À Mort l'Arbitre* (*Death to the Umpire*, 1984), soccer hooligans quickly turn into a terrifying, bloodthirsty mob. **Le Miraculé** (*The Miracle Victim*, 1987) deals with Lourdes miracles. **La Machine à Découdre** (*The Killing Machine*, 1986) follows the descent into madness of a murderous doctor. **Les Saisons du Plaisir** (*The Seasons of Pleasure*, 1988) ends with a nuclear catastrophe.

Planchon, Paul (1949–)

Barbara de Lichtenberg (1979) (TV)
Hugues Le Loup (*Hugh the Wolf*, 1979) (TV)
L'Homme En Rouge (*The Man in Red*, 1981; TV)
Le Coq Noir (*The Black Rooster*, 1982; TV)
Le Veneur Noir (*The Dark Hunter*, 1982; TV)
Carmilla, Le Coeur Pétrifié (*Carmilla, the Petrified Heart*, 1988; TV)
Le Roi Mystère (*King Mystery*, 1991; TV)

Paul **Planchon** worked in live theater in Lyon before assisting film director André Hunebelle. He began to direct television programs in 1971. His output has since then comprised virtually every genre and type of programming, including the famous French soap *Châteauvallon* and the renowned police series *Commissaire Moulin*.

Poligny, Serge de (1903–1983)

L'Or (*Gold*, 1934)
Le Baron Fantôme (*The Ghostly Baron*, 1942)
La Fiancée des Ténèbres (*Fiancée of Darkness*, 1944)

Serge de **Poligny** began his career as a set decorator for the French Paramount studios, but eventually began to direct films in the early 1930s. He produced a series of commercial films, showing little influence from American cinema and relying on French themes—medieval legends and folklore—as source material for genre films.

Prévert, Jacques (1900–1977)

Les Visiteurs du Soir (*The Visitors of the Evening*, transl. as *The Devil's Envoys*; Wri., 1942)
Les Portes de la Nuit (*The Gates of Night*; Wri., 1946)
Petit Claus et Grand Claus (*Little Claus and Big Claus*; Wri., 1964; TV)
Le Roi et l'Oiseau (*The King and the Bird*; Wri., 1979)

Screenwriter and a member of the surrealist movement,

Jacques **Prévert** began writing poetry and screenplays in the 1930s. He penned numerous classics in collaboration with Jean Renoir and Marcel **Carné**, including *Drôle de Drame* (*Bizarre, Bizarre*, 1937), *Quai des Brumes* (*Port of Shadows*, 1938), *Le Jour Se Lève* (*Daybreak*, 1939), *Les Enfants du Paradis* (*Children of Paradise*, 1945) (for which he won an Oscar nomination), and *Sortilèges* (*Spells*; Wri., 1944) with Christian-Jaque. Prévert also collaborated with Paul **Grimault** on several animation projects including *Le Petit Soldat* (*The Little Soldier*, 1947). His brother, Pierre Prévert (1906-1988) was a director.

Resnais, Alain (1922–)

L'Année Dernière à Marienbad (*Last Year in Marienbad*, 1961)
Je T'aime, Je T'aime (*I Love You, I Love You*, 1968)
L'An 01 (*The Year 01*) "Wall Street" segment, 1972)
Providence (1976)
La Vie Est un Roman (*Life Is a Novel*, transl. as *Life Is a Bed of Roses*, 1983)
L'Amour à Mort (*Love Unto Death*, 1984)

Even though Alain **Resnais** had directed short 16mm films before, his professional film career could be said to have begun with a series of striking documentaries made in the early 1950s: *Van Gogh* (1948), *Guernica* (1950), *Les Statues Meurent Aussi* (*The Statues Also Die*; co-dir. with Chris **Marker**, 1953), *Nuit et Brouillard* (*Night and Fog*, 1956). Resnais' first feature film, Hiroshima Mon Amour (1959), immediately established him as a leader of the French New Wave. Many of Resnais' subsequent films contain fantasy elements, as they all share the filmmaker's obsession with the themes of memory and reality.

Robbe-Grillet, Alain (1922–)

L'Année Dernière à Marienbad (*Last Year in Marienbad*; Wri., 1961)
L'Éden et Après (*Eden and Afterwards*, 1971)
Glissements Progressifs du Plaisir (*Progressive Slidings Into Pleasure*, 1974)
La Belle Captive (*The Beautiful Prisoner*, 1983)

Novelist, director, and screenwriter, Alain **Robbe-Grillet** is a proponent of a deconstructionist approach to narrative techniques, inspired by Proust and Bergson. His first work in films was the script for **Resnais'** *L'Année Dernière à Marienbad* (*Last Year in Marienbad*, 1961). In Robbe-Grillet's subsequent films, the same approach prevails: the narration is never linear, reality is subjective, memories are never to be trusted. His films also contain a rich catalog of dream-like erotic images. In *L'Immortelle* (*The Immortal*, 1962), a man finds a woman, loses her, and searches for her in Istanbul. In **Glissements Progressifs du Plaisir** (*Progressive Slidings into Pleasure*, 1974), a woman, alone, naked in a white cell, is relentlessly interrogated about a murder she may, or may not, have committed. (Also see Book 2.)

Rollin, Jean (1939–)

Le Viol du Vampire (*The Vampire's Rape* aka *La Reine des Vampires* [*The Vampires' Queen*] 1968)
La Vampire Nue (*The Nude Vampire*, 1969)
Le Frisson des Vampires (*The Vampires' Shiver*, transl. as *Sex and the Vampire, Terror of the Vampires*, 1970)
Vierges et Vampires (*Virgins and Vampires*, transl. as *Caged Virgins*; *Crazed Virgins* aka *Requiem pour un Vampire* [*Requiem for a Vampire*], 1971)
La Rose de Fer (*The Iron Rose*, transl. as *The Crystal Rose* aka *La Nuit du Cimetière* [*Night at the Cemetery*], 1973)
Les Démoniaques (*Demoniacs*, 1973)
Lèvres de Sang (*Bloody Lips*, 1975)
Les Raisins de la Mort (*Grapes of Death*, transl. as *Pesticide*, 1978)
Fascination (1979)
Le Lac des Morts-Vivants (*Lake of the Living Dead*, transl. as *Zombie Lake*; using the pseudonym of J. R. Lazer, 1980)
La Nuit des Traqués (*Night of the Hunted* aka *Filles Traquées* [*Hunted Girls*], 1980)
La Morte-Vivante (*The Living Dead Girl*, 1982)

A fan of fantasy and gothic literature, Jean **Rollin** began his filmmaking career as a general assistant on Jean Delannoy's *Notre-Dame de Paris* (1956) and George Lampin's French version of *Crime and Punishment* (1956). Rollin's first feature was the amateur production of *La Vampire Nue* (*The Nude Vampire*, 1968), which showed literary influences of Gaston **Leroux** and Louis **Feuillade**. During this period, Rollin also associated with fellow science fiction and fantasy fans, including comics artists Philippe **Druillet** and **Caza**. Druillet drew the posters for *Le Viol du Vampire*, *La Vampire Nue* and *Le Frisson des Vampires*, and played small parts in *Le Viol du Vampire* and *Vierges et Vampires*. Caza contributed art for *Lèvres de Sang*. Rollin was also part of the collective "Nicholas Devil" art team that created the *Saga de Xam* graphic novel for publisher Losfeld. Because of the soft-core erotic nature of his films, Rollin was ghettoized in the X-rated exploitation circuits. Under the pseudonym of Michel Gentil, he is also the author of many X-rated films, and he wrote the script for *Emmanuelle 6*. Rollin's undeniable visual qualities are generally hampered by rock bottom low budgets and often incoherent narratives. More recently, Rollin has turned to writing horror novels: *Anissa*, *Les Voyageuses*, *Les Pillardes*, *Les Incendiaires*, *Bestialité*, etc. (see Book 2).

Ruellan, André (1922–)

Le Seuil du Vide (*The Threshold of the Void*; Wri., based on his novel, 1971)
Hu-Man (Wri., 1974)
L'Ibis Rouge (Wri.; *The Red Ibis*, 1975)
Les Chiens (*The Dogs*; Wri., 1979)
Paradis Pour Tous (*Paradise for All*; Wri., 1982)

André **Ruellan**, aka Kurt **Steiner**, is a major science fiction and horror writer, with over thirty-five novels to his credit. See Chapter V (under *Fleuve Noir*) for comic book adaptations of some of his novels and Book 2 for his literary career.

Subiela, Michel (1935–)

Le Navire Étoile (*The Starship*, 1962; TV)
Le Tribunal de l'Impossible (*The Tribunal of the Impossible*) Ep. 1. La Bête du Gévaudan (*The Beast of Gevaudan*; Wri., 1967; TV)
Le Tribunal de l'Impossible (*The Tribunal of the Impossible*) Ep. 4. Nostradamus, ou Le Prophète en Son Pays (*Nostradamus, or A Prophet in His Own Land*; Wri., 1968; TV)
Le Tribunal de l'Impossible (*The Tribunal of the Impossible*) Ep. 5. Qui Hantait le Presbytère de Borley? (*Who Haunted the Borley Presbytery?*; Wri., 1968; TV)
Le Tribunal de l'Impossible (*The Tribunal of the Impossible*) Ep. 6. Le Sabbat du Mont d'Étenclin (*The Sabbath of Mount Etenclin*, 1969; TV)
Le Tribunal de l'Impossible (*The Tribunal of the Impossible*) Ep. 7. La Passion d'Anne-Catherine Emmerich (*The Passion of Anne-Catherine Emmerich*, 1969; TV)
Le Tribunal de l'Impossible (*The Tribunal of the Impossible*) Ep. 10. La Cité d'Is (*The City of Ys*, 1970; TV)
Le Tribunal de l'Impossible (*The Tribunal of the Impossible*) Ep. 12. La Double Vie de Mlle. De La Faille (*The Two Lives of Miss de la Faille*, 1974; TV)
Le Tribunal de l'Impossible (*The Tribunal of the Impossible*) Ep. 14. Le Baquet de Frédéric-Antoine Messmer (*Messmer's Bucket*, 1974; TV)
Les Classiques de l'Étrange (*Classics of the Strange*) Ep. 1. La Main Enchantée (*The Enchanted Hand*, 1974; TV)
Les Classiques de l'Étrange (*Classics of the Strange*) Ep. 3. Les Voleurs de Cerveaux (*The Brain Stealers*, 1976; TV)
Le Colchique et l'Étoile (*The Colchicum and the Star*, 1974; TV)
Hugues Le Loup (*Hugh the Wolf*, 1975; TV)
Le Coeur Cambriolé (*The Burglared Heart*, 1986; TV)

Michel **Subiela** studied filmmaking at the French cinema school IDHEC in 1952, before going to work for French television. He was one of the first writer/directors to adapt contemporary literary classics for the small screen. He is, in particular, responsible for the first French Science Fiction television production ever made, *Le Navire Étoile* (*The Space Born*, 1962), based on the novel by E. C. Tubb. From 1967 to 1974, Subiela produced, and often wrote and directed, the classic anthology series *Le Tribunal de l'Impossible* (*The Tribunal of the Impossible*), devoted to the unexplained. Subiela then went on to write and/or direct a number of non-genre telefilms and series, including the renowned *Maigret* (starring Jean Richard).

Tourneur, Maurice (Thomas, Maurice) (1876–1961)

Rouletabille: Le Mystère de la Chambre Jaune (*The Mystery of the Yellow Room*, 1913)
La Main du Diable (*The Devil's Hand*, transl. as *Carnival of Sinners*, 1942)

Maurice **Tourneur** was first a book illustrator and an assistant to renowned sculptor Auguste Rodin in the early 1900s. After a brief time on the stage, he became a film director for the Éclair Studios in 1912, producing a number of shorts, some with fantasy elements, such as an adaptation of Poe's *Le Système du Docteur Goudron et du Professeur*

Plume (*The System of Dr. Tarr and Professor Fether*), *Figures de Cire* (*Waxworks*; both 1912), and a serial of Gaston **Leroux**'s popular detective **Rouletabille** (1913). Tourneur left France in 1914 to go to Hollywood, where he made a number of classics such as *Treasure Island* (1920) and *Lorna Doone* (1922). In 1926, after a dispute with MGM over the film adaptation of Jules **Verne**'s *Mysterious Island* (which was eventually completed by Lucien Hubbard and released in 1929), he returned to France. In 1934, he shot a short feature, *Obsession ou L'Homme Mystérieux* (*Obssession, or The Mysterious Man*), based on a **Grand-Guignol** play by André de **Lorde** and Alfred **Binet**. After a car accident in 1949, he retired from filmmaking.

His son, Jacques Tourneur (1904-1977), became a successful Hollywood director, making a number of genre movies: *Cat People* (142), *I Walked with a Zombie* (1943), *Curse of the Demon* (1957), *The Comedy of Terrors* (1963), *War Gods of the Deep* (1965) as well as *Night Call* (1964), the 139th episode of *The Twilight Zone*.

Truffaut, François (1932–1984)

Fahrenheit 451 (1966)
La Chambre Verte (*The Green Room*, 1978)

François **Truffaut** was a film critic for *Cahiers du Cinéma* magazine before emerging as an "auteur" (a theory he had helped create) with his first feature film, *Les Quatre Cents Coups* (*The 400 Blows*) in 1959. Truffaut's films were mostly autobiographical, following the life of fictional character Antoine Doinel (played by Jean-Pierre Léaud) from age 12 to middle-age. An admirer of Jean Renoir and American cinema (in particular Alfred Hitchcock), Truffaut won an Oscar for *La Nuit Américaine* (*Day for Night*) in 1973. His excursions into the fantasy genre remain marginal. In addition to the films listed below, he helped produce Jean **Cocteau**'s *Le Testament d'Orphée* (*The Testament of Orpheus*, 1960), but his most visible role (as an actor) may well be that of a French UFO scientist in Steven Spielberg's *Close Encounters of the Third Kind* (1977).

Vadim, Roger (1928–2000)

...Et Mourir De Plaisir (*...And to Die from Pleasure*, transl. as *Blood and Roses*, 1960)
Barbarella (1967)
Histoires Extraordinaires—"Metzengerstein" segment (*Extraordinary Tales*, transl. as *Spirits of the Dead*, 1968)

Roger **Vadim** was an actor, a journalist, and the assis-

tant to director Marc Allégret before making a sensational film debut with *Et Dieu Créa la Femme* (*And God Created Woman*, 1956), which starred his then-wife, Brigitte Bardot. Vadim went on to direct a series of visually remarkable, mildly erotic films, often containing borderline fantasy elements. However, his popularity waned as he became somewhat typecast and the victim of changing fashions in the 1970s. Vadim had small parts in Jean **Cocteau**'s *Le Testament d'Orphée* (*The Testament of Orpheus*, 1960) and John Landis' *Into the Night* (1985). Vadim also edited a collection of short-stories about vampires (1961, Robert Laffont).

Velle, Gaston (?–?) *see* Méliès' Rivals

Vicas, Victor (1918-1985)

Aux Frontières du Possible (*To the Frontiers of the Possible*) *Ep. 1. Le Dossier des Mutations V* (*The Mutation V File*, 1971; TV)
Aux Frontières du Possible (*To the Frontiers of the Possible*) *Ep. 2. Attention Névroses Mentales* (*Beware Mental Nevroses*, 1971; TV)
Aux Frontières du Possible (*To the Frontiers of the Possible*) *Ep. 5. L'Homme Radar* (*The Radar Man*, 1971; TV)
Aux Frontières du Possible (*To the Frontiers of the Possible*) *Ep. 8. Le Cabinet Noir* (*The Black Cabinet*, 1971; TV)
Aux Frontières du Possible (*To the Frontiers of the Possible*) *Ep. 11. Alerte Au Minotaure* (*Minotaur Alert*, 1974; TV)
Aux Frontières du Possible (*To the Frontiers of the Possible*) *Ep. 12. Les Créateurs de Visible* (*The Creators of the Visible*, 1974; TV)
Aux Frontières du Possible (*To the Frontiers of the Possible*) *Ep. 13. L'Effaceur de Mémoire* (*The Memory Eraser*, 1974; TV)
L'Homme au Cerveau Greffé (*The Man with a Brain Transplant*; Wri., 1974)

Born in Berlin, Victor **Vicas** studied film in Paris and became an assistant cameraman in the 1930s. In 1940, he moved to the United States where he worked as an assistant director. After the war, he returned to Europe, where he directed half a dozen feature films in Germany, England, Switzerland, and France. He eventually settled in France and began working steadily as a television director. His output includes *Aux Frontières du Possible*, *L'Étrange Monsieur Duvallier* (*The Strange Mr. Duvallier*, 1979), a series about a Saint-like character based on the novel by Claude **Klotz**, and the cult favorite *Les Brigades du Tigre* (*The Tiger's Brigades*, 1974–78, 1982–83), about Prime Minister Clémenceau's "Untouchables" before World War I.

Zecca, Ferdinand (1864–1947) *see* Méliès' Rivals

2. Comic Book Writers and Artists

Ab'aigre (Habegger, Pascal) (1949–) *(Artist)*

A native of Switzerland, **Ab'aigre**

began his comics career in *Circus* with *La Route des Goëlands* (*Seagulls' Road*) in 1980. He also drew *Le Chaman* for *Ice Crim's* in 1984.

Ache, Jean (Huet, Jean) (1923– 1985) *(Artist/Writer)*

His pseudonym was an homage to

273

the famous illustrator Caran d'Ache. After working on numerous children's magazines during World War II, Jean **Ache** created the mermaid *Arabelle* for the daily newspaper *France-Soir* in 1950 and the long-running juvenile adventure series *Nic et Mino* for *Le Journal de Mickey* in 1958. He was also the author of a number of popular children's series, such as *Archibald, Achille,* and *Pat'apouf.*

Adamov, Philippe (?–) *(Artist/Writer)*

After working as a book illustrator, Adamov published his first comics work in the magazine *Okapi* in 1983. His genre work includes: *Dayak* (also Wri.), *Les Eaux de Mortelune* (*The Waters of Deadmoon*), and *Le Vent des Dieux* (*Wind of the Gods*).

Alexis (Vallet, Dominique) (1946–1977) *(Artist/Writer)*

Talented humorist who collaborated on a series of parodies published in *Pilote* in the early 1970s, including *Cinemastock* and the famous *Super Dupont* with Gotlib, *Al Crane* with Lauzier, and *Time Is Money* with **Fred**. He also wrote and drew short, fantastic vignettes collected in *Avatars et Coquecigrues* (*Avatars and Gobbledygooks*).

Alexis

Alf *see* Pierre, François

Allot, François (1958–) *(Artist)*

After designing the SF cartoon series *Ulysse 31* (see Book IV), **Allot** col-

laborated with writer **Rodolphe** on the series *Les Écluses du Ciel* (*Skylocks*), originally created by Michel **Rouge**.

Andréas (Martens, Andreas) (1951–) *(Artist/Writer)*

A native of Germany, **Andréas** studied at the St. Luc comics school in Belgium, assisting Eddy **Paape** on *Udolfo*, before relocating to France. His genre series include *Cromwell Stone*, *Cyrrus*, *Rork* and a number of single works such as *La Caverne du Souvenir* (*Cave of Memory*), *Coutoo*, *Dérives* (*Adrift*), *Aztèques, Révélations Posthumes* (*Posthumous Revelations*), etc.

Arno (Dombre, Arnaud) (1961–1995) *(Artist)*

Arno began working in comics with *Le Chêne du Rêveur* (*The Dreamer's Oak*) published in *Okapi* in 1983. He then embarked on the *Alef-Thau* series, written by Alexandro **Jodorowsky**.

Auclair, Claude (1943–1990) *(Artist/Writer)*

Auclair's early comics works were influenced by Jean **Giraud**. After contributing illustrations to SF magazines, he drew his first genre series, the post-apocalyptic *Jason Muller*, for *Pilote* in 1969, and then its spin-off, *Simon du Fleuve* (*Simon of the River*), for *Tintin* in 1973. Auclair's work matured in the 1980s with the graphic novel *Bran Ruz* (1981) and a flamboyant heroic-fantasy saga, *Celui-Là* (*That One*). Auclair died of cancer in 1990.

Auclair

Bagage, Robert (?–?) *(Artist/Writer)*

After starting as a sports illustrator, **Bagage** became editor of the Éditions du Siècle, later renamed Imperia, which published a line of digest-sized comics magazine. Genre series he created include *Z.302*, *Tom X*, *Super Boy* (drawn by Félix **Molinari**) and *Targa*. He retired after Imperia ceased its operations in 1987.

Bastard, René (1900–1975) *(Artist/Writer)*

After working on various children's series during World War II, **Bastard** joined the editorial team of *Vaillant* in 1946, for which he drew the Arabian adventures of *Nasdine Hodja*, written by Roger **Lecureux**, and the Arthurian *Yves Le Loup* (*Yves the Wolf*), written by Jean **Ollivier**.

Bati, Marc (1958–) *(Artist/Writer)*

Bati began his professional comics career in the footsteps of **Moebius**, collaborating on a number of graphic novels such as *La Ferme aux Animaux* (*Animal Farm*) and *La Nuit de l'Étoile* (*Night of the Star*) (1985). In 1986, he embarked on the light fantasy saga, *Altor*, written by Moebius. More recently, he wrote the *Sylfeline* series for Bruno Bellamy.

Benn (Beniest, André) (1950–) *(Artist/Writer)*

After starting as **Peyo**'s assistant on *Les Schtroumpfs* (*The Smurfs*), **Benn** drew a number of children's adventure series in *Spirou* and *Tintin* in the early 1970s. He created *Mic Mac Adam* with **Desberg** in 1978.

Berthet, Philippe (1956–) *(Artist/Writer)*

After studying comics at the St. Luc school in Belgium, **Berthet** joined the editorial team of *Spirou* where he met fellow artist, Italian Antonio Cossu, with whom he collaborated on the SF saga *Le Marchand d'Idées* (*Merchant* *of Ideas*). Berthet has also collaborated with **Andréas**, **Foerster**, etc. More recently, he produced the solo work, *Halona*.

Bézian, Frédéric (1960–) (Artist/Writer)

After studying comics at the St. Luc school in Belgium, **Bézian** embarked on a series of dark but not humorless stories, often tapping a gothic vein, like *L'Étrange Nuit de M. Korb* (*Mr. Korb's Strange Night*) and *Fin de Siècle* (*End of the Century*). He has also written and drawn the *Adam Sarlech* series.

Bilal, Enki (1951–) (Artist/Writer)

A native of the former Yugoslavia, **Bilal** started publishing a series of Lovecraftian-inspired short stories in *Pilote* in 1972, later collected in various books. In 1974, he teamed up with writer Pierre **Christin** on the series *Légendes d'Aujourd'hui* (*Modern Legends*). In 1980, he started his own series, *Nikopol*, which has garnered considerable commercial and critical success. Other notable works include the solo graphic novel *Exterminateur 17* (1981), written by Jean-Pierre **Dionnet**. More recently, he has embarked on a film-directing career. His first feature, *Bunker Palace Hotel*, was released in 1989, and his second, *Tykho Moon*, in 1997. Bilal is one of the major comics influences of the late 1980s.

Bilal

Blanc, Henry (1921–) (Artist)

Primarily a cartoonist and humor artist, **Blanc** became one of *France-Soir*'s major daily strip providers, with the adaptation of the popular radio serial *Signé Furax* (1957), *Les Nouveaux Mystères de Paris* (*The New Mysteries of Paris*) and *Commissaire San-Antonio*.

Bom (de Bom, Michel) (1950–) (Writer)

Prolific Belgian writer who contributed numerous children's adventure series to both *Spirou* and *Tintin* throughout the 1980s. His genre work includes *Broussaille* (*Brush*), *Nahomi* and *Yvain et Yvon*.

Bordes, Yves (1953–) (Artist)

Bordes' first comics works were historical adventures produced for children's magazines in the late 1970s. He is the artist of *Foc*.

Bosse (Bosmans, Serge) (1954–) (Artist)

Bosse joined the editorial team of *Spirou* in 1978 with the light fantasy *Zowie*. He has contributed various series to both *Spirou* and *Tintin*, including *Kogaratsu* and the genre series *Hazel et Ogan*.

Boucq, François (1955–) (Artist/Writer)

Boucq began his professional career signing political cartoons in daily papers and magazines. With **Christin**, he then produced a number of humor series, always with some light fantasy overtones, for *Fluide Glacial* (*Les Leçons du Prof. Bourremou* (*The Teachings of Prof. Bourremou*). In 1981, he embarked on a series of brilliant, surreal stories for *(A Suivre)*, later collected in a number of graphic novels, starting with *Les Pionniers de l'Aventure Humaine* (*Pioneers of the Human Adventure*). Boucq has also drawn a number of more serious, yet still fantastic, collaborations with American

writer Jerôme Charyn, such as (*La Femme du Magicien* (*The Magician's Wife*) and Alexandro **Jodorowsky**, with whom he worked on *Face de Lune* (*Moon Face*).

Bourgeon, François (1945–) (Artist/Writer)

After working in glass-making and stained glass, **Bourgeon** drew various children's series before creating his first commercial success, the historical saga of *Les Passengers du Vent* (*Passengers of the Wind*) (1978–1984). He then wrote and drew the medieval fantasy *Les Compagnons du Crépuscule* (*Companions of the Twilight*, 1982–1986), and has recently embarked on a science fiction series, written by Lacroix, *Le Cycle de Cyann*.

Brantonne, René (1903–1979) (Artist)

One of the foremost French SF illustrators, **Brantonne** began his career as a commercial artist in the late 1920s, drawing French film posters for Paramount and creating logos for Standard Oil (later Exxon). He lived in the United

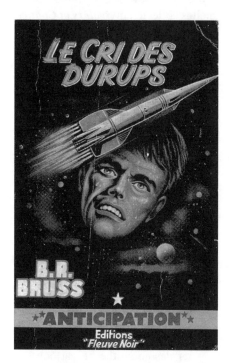

Cover art by Brantonne.

States during World War II, where he drew film posters for all the major studios. After the war, he returned to France and began working as a comics artist on a vast number of disposable adventure series for a variety of digest-sized magazines: *Fulguros* and *Johnny Speed* for *Artima* (later *Aredit*), *Praline*, *Buffalo Bill* for *Remparts*, etc. (He even drew a short-lived French version of *Brick Bradford*.) During that time, he also became the cover artist *par excellence* of the *Anticipation* imprint of Éditions **Fleuve Noir**, drawing the covers of Nos. 1–273 (1954–1965) and Nos. 562–795 (1973–1977), influencing virtually every French SF reader of the 1950s and 1960s.

Bressy, Robert (1924–) *(Artist)*

After having worked as an animator for director Paul **Grimault**, **Bressy** began working as a daily strip artist for Opera Mundi in 1952. His works include adaptations of classic novels (Balzac, Hugo, etc.), television series, Disney characters, etc. His major genre work is the strip *Docteur Fu Manchu*, based on Sax Rohmer's character.

Breysse, Frédéric-Antonin (1907–) *(Artist/Writer)*

Initially a lithographer, **Breysse** started working as an artist with *Coeurs Vaillants* just before the war, and eventually became one of its editors. During this period, he created the character of *Oscar Hamel*. He retired from comics in 1955, to become a commercial artist in the fields of automobiles and aeronautics.

Bucquoy, Jan (1945–) *(Writer)*

Belgian writer who began his comics career with the celebrated thriller *Jaunes* in *Circus*. His genre credits include the political **Gérard Craan** and **Chroniques de Fin de Siècle** (*Chronicles of the End of the Century*).

Cabanes, Max (1947–) *(Artist/Writer)*

Cabanes is better known for his re-membrances of French provincial life in the 1950s and 1960s à la *American Graffiti*, such as the award-winning *Colin-Maillard*. He is also the author of the mystical and surreal series **Dans Les Villages** (*In the Villages*) which he began in *Fluide Glacial* in black and white in 1978, and later continued in *Pilote*.

Cadot, Patrice (1959–) *(Artist/Writer)*

Cadot began his career in comics at *Spirou* in the late 1970s, and later contributed to *Tintin*. He is the artist of **Yvain et Yvon** (written by **Bom**) and the writer of **Jordan**.

Calvo, Edmond-François (1892–1958) *(Artist/Writer)*

One of the most famous children's illustrators of the 1930s, **Calvo** also was a superb animal artist. His masterpiece is *La Bête Est Morte* (*The Beast is Dead*), a transposition of WW II with animals, written by Victor Dancette. Calvo illustrated numerous children's fairy tales, including a masterful version of **La Belle au Bois Dormant** (*Sleeping Beauty*) and adventure stories (*Robin des Bois* (*Robin Hood*), *Moustache and Trotinette*, etc. after the war.

Carpentier, Louis-Michel (1944–) *(Artist)*

After working as an animator on the *Lucky Luke*, *Astérix* and *Tintin* features (see Chapter IV), **Carpentier** began illustrating a series of children's books in 1975. He eventually co-created the strange and surreal series, *Les Toyottes* with **Cauvin** in 1980.

Cauvin, Raoul (1938–) *(Writer)*

One of the leading writers of humor series for *Spirou*, **Cauvin** began his career in the late 1960s with *Les Naufragés* (*Shipwrecked*) for Brétécher and *Les Mousquetaires* (*Musketeers*) for Mazel. His most famous series are *Sammy* (for Berck) and *Les Tuniques Bleues* (*The Blue Coats*) for Salvérius. His genre series include **Boskovich**, **Cupidon**, *Les Naufragés de l'Espace* (*Castaways in Space*), **Les Snorky**, a brief stint on **Spirou** (with Nic Broca) and **Les Toyottes** with **Carpentier**.

Caza (Cazaumayou, Philippe) (1941–) *(Artist/Writer)*

After starting as an advertising artist, **Caza** published his first graphic novel, **Kris Kool**, a pop art-inspired story of a futuristic James Bond, in 1970. He then contributed numerous short genre stories to *Pilote*, including a fierce satire of suburban life as seen though a SF spectrum, gathered in the **Scènes de la Vie de Banlieue** (*Scenes of Suburban Life*, 1975–79) and the more serious **L'Âge d'Ombre** (*Age of Darkness*, 1982–84) series. Caza created several heroic fantasy stories for *Métal Hurlant* in the 1980s, including his **Arkadi** series. More recently, he has begun writing such series, such as **Amiante**, for other artists as well. Caza is one of France's leading SF illustrators, having contributed most of the covers to the SF imprint of Éditions J'ai Lu. His SF art was gathered in the book **Chimères** (*Chimera*). He also provided the designs for René **Laloux**'s animated feature **Gandahar**, based on a novel by Jean-Pierre **Andrevon**. Caza's wife, Scarlett Smulkowski, is one of France's leading colorists.

Cézard, Jean (César, Jean) (1925–1977) *(Artist/Writer)*

One of the leading members of the editorial team at *Vaillant* after World War II, for which he created the famous character of **Arthur le Fantôme Justicier** (*Arthur the Avenging Ghost*) in 1953. **Cézard** also worked on a number of humor series, including *Kiwi* (which he created) and *Pim, Pam, Poum*, the French version of *The Katzenjammer Kids*.

Chaland, Yves (1957–1990) *(Artist/Writer)*

One of the leading representatives of the "clear line" style, **Chaland** began publishing satirical strips paying homage to the Belgian adventure comics of the 1950s in *Métal Hurlant* in the late 1970s. His own series, ***Adolphus Claar***, ***Bob Fish***, and ***Freddy Lombard*** (written by **Yann**), also done for *Métal Hurlant*, tapped into the same nostalgic feel of yesterday's SF. Chaland died in a car accident in 1990. His wife, Isabelle, is a renowned French colorist.

Charlier, Jean-Michel (1924–1989) *(Writer)*

A former law student and airplane pilot, **Charlier** became the single, major writer of adventure series for *Spirou* in the 1950s and *Pilote* (which he co-edited) in the 1960s. His most famous non-genre creations included the *Terry and the Pirates*-inspired *Buck Danny* (for Hubinon), the boy scout adventures of *La Patrouille des Castors* (*Beavers' Patrol*; for Mitacq), the French air force hero *Michel Tanguy* (for **Uderzo** and later **Jijé**), the pirate adventures of *Barbe-Rouge* (*Red-Beard*; also for Hubinon), the western series *Lt. Blueberry* (for **Giraud**), journalist *Marc Dacier* (for **Paape**), etc. He never created any major genre series but used genre elements in some of his adventure series: ***Guy Lebleu***, ***Jean Valhardi***, and ***Kim Devil***. These represented only a minor fraction of his prodigious output.

Charlier

Chéret, André (1937–) *(Artist)*

After drawing numerous historical adventures in *Coeurs Vaillants* in the early 1960s, **Chéret** joined the editorial team of *Vaillant*, for which he co-created (with Roger **Lecureux**) the popular ***Rahan***. Chéret has also contributed to ***L'Encyclopédie en Bandes Dessinées*** (*The Comics Encyclopedia*), and co-created the character of ***Protéo***.

Chott (Mouchotte, Pierre) (1911-1966) *(Artist)*

After drawing children's adventure strips during World War II, **Chott** founded his own publishing company in 1945, and created one of the first French costumed heroes, ***Fantax***. Unfortunately, he experienced many problems with French censorship, which ultimately drove him out of business.

Christin, Pierre (1938–) *(Writer)*

Also a distinguished SF writer (see Book 2), **Christin** co-created and wrote the space-opera series ***Valerian*** with his childhood friend **Mézières**. He first used the pen-name "Linus." Another, more recent, collaboration with Mézières, is the futuristic thriller ***Canal-Choc***. His other famous genre series is the grim and political ***Légendes d'Aujourd'hui*** (*Modern Legends*) with **Bilal**. Christin has also worked with **Auclair** (on ***Jason Muller***), **Boucq** (***Les Leçons du Prof. Bourremou***; *The Teachings of Prof. Bourremou*), and **Tardi**.

Christin

Christophe (Colomb, Marie-Louis-Georges) (1856-1945) *(Artist/Writer)*

Professor of Natural Sciences and Assistant Director of the Botanical Laboratory at the Sorbonne, **Christophe** discovered that he could use his real talent as an illustrator to teach and entertain. He published his first illustrated story in *Mon Journal* in 1887. In 1889, he created the first "graphic novel" after **Topffer**, *La Famille Fenouillard*, which was collected in book form in 1893, thereby setting the precedent of serializing a comics story before publishing it as a book. In 1896, Christophe created the *Sapeur Camember*; in 1900, the *Savant Cosinus* (*Savant Cosine*) and, finally, in 1904 his classic ***Les Malices de Plick et Plock*** (*The Tricks of Plick & Plock*). During that time, he also produced numerous shorter strips, including his famous *L'Arroseur Arrosé*, which became the basis for one of Lumière's first films in 1895. Artistically, after Topffer, Christophe was the first to develop comics' modern graphic language.

Claveloux, Nicole (1940–) *(Artist/Writer)*

Initially a children's illustrator and the author of the comedic, poetic series *Grabote*, **Claveloux** also drew several SF graphic novels for *Métal Hurlant*, including ***La Main Verte*** (*Green Hand*) and ***Morte Saison*** (*Dead Season*).

Clerc, Serge (1957–) *(Artist/Writer)*

Like **Chaland**, **Clerc** was one of the representatives of the "clear line" style at *Métal Hurlant* in the 1980s. He, too, created a number of nostalgic, homage series, including ***Captain Futur***, *Phil Perfect*, *Sam Bronx*, etc.

Comès, Didier (Dieter Herman) (1942–) *(Artist/Writer)*

Belgian artist Didier **Comès** began his comics career with more traditional stories: the adventures of space wanderer ***Ergün*** in *Pilote* in 1973, and the graphic novel ***L'Ombre du Corbeau*** (*Shadow of the Crow*) in *Tintin* in 1975. However, starting in 1979, with

Silence, he embarked on a series of critically acclaimed, black-and-white graphic novels for *(A Suivre)*, which were revolutionary both in visual terms as well as literary content. Deeply in love with the countryside, and well versed in ancient occult lore, Comès has become one of the major genre artists working in the field of gothic comics today.

Conrad, Didier (1959–) (Artist/ Writer)

With **Yann**, **Conrad** is one of the young cartoonists who revolutionized *Spirou* magazine in the 1980s, with series such as *Les Innommables (The Unmentionables)*. Together, they also produced an hilarious parody of *Bob Morane* entitled *Bob Marone*. Alone, Conrad has also written and illustrated such work as *Donito* and the much-acclaimed *Le Piège Malais (The Malaysian Trap)*.

Convard, Didier (1950–) (Artist/ Writer)

Convard is a prolific writer/artist who began writing and/or drawing short adventure strips in the 1970s. He joined the editorial team at *Tintin* in the early 1980s, and contributed a series of fantastic stories later collected in *Les 8 Jours du Diable (8 Days for the Devil)* and *Le 9ème Jour du Diable (The Devil's Ninth Day)*. Also for *Tintin*, he drew the fantasy series, *Cranach De Morganloup* (1983) written by **Vernal**, and wrote the critically acclaimed *Neige (Snow, 1985)* for artist **Gine**. For *Vécu*, he wrote and drew the historical fantasy, *Les Héritiers du Soleil (Heirs of the Sun, 1986)*. Since then, Convard has written a number of genre series for a variety of other artists: *Les Chevaliers de la Cloche (The Knights of the Bell)*, *Finkel*, *Polka* and *Songe*. More recently, he has embarked on two new solo series, *Chats (Cats)* and *Editnalta*.

Corteggiani, François (1953–) (Writer)

Prolific writer who began writing various children's and adventure series, often with historical themes, for *Pif*, *Mickey*, *Gomme*, etc. in the mid-1970s. In the fantasy genre, **Corteggiani** created a number of pseudo-historical sagas, such as *Chroniques des Pays de Markal (Chronicles of Markal Country)*, *L'Archer Blanc*, *L'Horus de Nekhen*, and the Japanese sword & sorcery series, *Saito*. He has also written light fantasy in a humor vein with *L'École Abracadabra (The Alakazam School)*, *Timothée Titan*, and *Testar le Robot*.

Cothias, Patrick (1948–) (Writer)

Writer **Cothias** began his comics career by writing historical adventure series in *Pif* in the mid-1970s, including the hugely popular *Masquerouge (Redmask)*; later *Les Sept Vies de l'Épervier (Sparrowhawk's Seven Lives)* with André Juillard. His genre collaborations include two best-selling series with artist **Adamov**: *Le Vent des Dieux (Wind of the Gods)* and *Les Eaux de Mortelune (Waters of Deadmoon)*. He has also written *Alise et les Argonautes* for Font, *Le Lièvre de Mars (Mars Hare)* for Parras, *Orn* for **Taffin**, *Memory* and *Snark Saga* for **Sternis**, and *Tanatha* for **Hé**, making him one of the most popular and prolific genre writers in French comics.

Craenhals, François (1926–) (Artist/Writer)

Craenhals joined the editorial team of *Tintin* in 1950; there, he wrote and drew the adventure series *Pom & Teddy* as well as a celebrated medieval saga, *Chevalier Ardent*. He is also the artist of *Fantômette* and *Les Quatre As (Four Aces)*, based on the novels by Georges **Chaulet**.

Crespin, Michel (1955–) (Artist/ Writer)

A student of the Beaux-Arts School in Nice, **Crespin** is the author of the remarkable post-apocalyptic saga *Armalite 16* published in *Métal Hurlant*.

Crisse (Chrispeels, Didier) (1960–) (Artist)

Belgian artist **Crisse** created *Nahomi* in 1980 for *Tintin* and recently embarked on the well-received sword & sorcery saga, *L'Épée de Crystal (Crystal Sword)*.

Cuvelier, Paul (1923–1978) (Artist/Writer)

One of the first artists to have worked for *Tintin*, **Cuvelier** created the cult favorite *Corentin*. His only incursion in the genre is the erotic *Epoxy*, written by **Van Hamme**.

Cuvillier, Marcel (1897–1957) (Artist/Writer)

Prolific cartoonist and children's illustrator, he created two of the most famous and long-running children's series, *Perlin et Pinpin* (1940–58) and *Sylvain & Sylvette* (1941–58).

Dan, Bob (Dansler, Robert) (1900–1973) (Artist/Writer)

Prolific writer/artist and author of numerous adventure stories, starting in 1935: *Jim Mystère*, *Zorro*, *Les Fils du Vents (Sons of the Wind)*, *Bill Tornade*, *Jack Sport*, etc. One of his best creations is the Tarzan-like *Tarou*.

Danard, Jean-Pierre (aka Dan) (1956–) & Pierre, François (aka Alf) (?–) (Artists)

Two young artists who began collaborating on a number of juvenile series in the mid-1980s, including *Chroniques du Pays de Markal (Chronicles of Markal Country)*, *Peter Pan*, and *Le Mécano des Étoiles (Cosmic Mechanic)*. More recently, they drew the intricate and exotic *150 Loup-Garous (150 Werewolves)*.

Dany (Henrotin, Daniel) (1943–) (Artist/Writer)

A former student of Mitteï and Greg, **Dany** published his first hit series, the dream-like and romantic *Olivier Rameau* (written by Greg) in

Dany

Tintin in 1968. Dany has also drawn adventure series such as *Bernard Prince*, *Arlequin*, and *Equateur*. He is also the artist of a popular series of X-rated humor books.

De Gieter, Lucien (1932–) (Artist/Writer)

A former student of **Peyo**, **De Gieter** published his first series in *Spirou*, including **Toot et Puit** in 1966. However, his first hit was the fantastic and well-researched adventures of young Egyptian page **Papyrus**, which have remained a constant best-seller.

Deliège, Paul (1931–) (Artist/ Writer)

One of the staff cartoonists with *Spirou* during the 1960s, he wrote and/or drew numerous funny characters such as *Bobo*, *Cabanon*, *Superdingue*, *Sam*, etc. He is also the creator of the hilarious **Krostons**, three evil, incompetent cartoony characters who constantly try to take over the world.

Delporte, Yvan (1928–) (Writer/ Editor)

Delporte joined the editorial team of *Spirou* in 1945 and became one of its major humor writers, eventually being promoted to editor-in-chief (from 1955 to 1968). He is responsible for the development (if not the actual creation) of the world-famous **Schtroumpfs** (*Smurfs*) and **Benoît Brisefer** for **Peyo**; *Isabelle* for **Will** and *Sophie* for **Jidéhem**. In a more se-

rious vein, he wrote the ahead-of-its-times space opera series **Alain Cardan** for **Forton**.

De Moor, Johan (?–) (Artist)

The son of Bob **De Moor**, Johan **De Moor** created his own series, **Gaspard de la Nuit** (*Gaspar of the Night*) with **Desberg**, in 1987 after having worked at the *Tintin* studio on *Quick & Flupke*. He is also the artist on the dark, satirical strip **La Vache** (*The Cow*), also created with Desberg.

De Moor, Robert "Bob" (1925–) (Artist)

A prolific Belgian artist, Bob **De Moor** joined the *Tintin* studio in 1950 and ably assisted **Hergé** on *Tintin* until his death. He then took over the **Blake et Mortimer** and **Lefranc** series. His other series include insurance investigator *Mr. Barelli*, *Cori le Moussaillon*, and the cartoony *Balthazar*.

Denayer, Christian (1945–) (Artist)

After assisting artist Tibet (Gilbert Gascard) on *Ric Hochet* and Jean Graton on *Michel Vaillant*, **Denayer** co-created the adventure series *Yalek* with A.-P. **Duchateau** in 1969. He also launched another hero, *Alain Chevalier*, for *Tintin* in 1971. His genre series is *T.N.T.*, also with Duchateau.

Derib (De Ribeaupierre, Charles) (1944–) (Artist/Writer)

Swiss artist who began his comics career in *Spirou* in 1966 with *Arnaud de Casteloup* and the popular talking dog, **Attila**. He is also the creator of the popular western series *Buddy Longway* and the artist on the juvenile western *Yakari*. His knowledge of the west enabled him to create the mystic **Celui Qui Est Né Deux Fois** (*He Who Was Born Twice*) in 1981.

Desberg, Stephen (1954–) (Writer)

Prolific writer who started his career

at *Spirou* in 1978, taking over the writing chores on the classic thriller, **Tif et Tondu**. He then went on to create and script a number of popular genre series, also for *Spirou*: **Arkel**, **Mic Mac Adam**, **Les Centaures** (*The Centaurs*) and **421**. **Desberg**'s collaboration with Johan **De Moor** have produced **Gaspard de la Nuit** (*Gaspar of the Night*) and the satirical **La Vache** (*The Cow*). He is also the writer of the graphic novel, **Envahisseurs sur Janus** (*Invaders of Janus*).

Devos, Jacques (1924–) (Artist/ Writer)

Cartoonist who began working for *Spirou* in the early 1960s, **Devos** has created a number of humor series, including the borderline genre **Génial Olivier** and *Victor Sébastopol*.

Dewamme, Gérard (1953–) (Writer)

Dewamme's first published comics story was the instant classic romantic thriller *Tendre Violette* with Servais for (*A Suivre*). The author of numerous thrillers, his genre contribution is **Clotho** with Jacques Bonodot.

Deynis, René (1930–) (Artist)

Deynis joined the editorial team of *Vaillant* in 1959 and worked on *Jean et Jeanette* and **Jacques Flash**. After working for various children's magazine in the 1970s, he helped fund the Five Stars Studio, where he worked on comics adaptation of Japanese animation series such as **Albator** and **Captain Fulgur**. Deynis is now retired.

Dionnet, Jean-Pierre (1947–) (Writer)

Initially a fan writer, **Dionnet** began contributing several short genre stories to *Pilote* in the early 1970s, and one longer story, the beautiful **Jean Cyriaque** (with Solé). In 1973, Dionnet, with artists **Moebius** and Philippe **Druillet**, founded the genre magazine *Métal Hurlant*. For *Métal*, Dionnet wrote **Exterminateur 17** for **Bilal**, *Arn* for **Gal** and *Région Étrangère* (*Foreign Area*) for Deum. He is also the author of a remarkable fantasy graphic novel, *Tiriel*, with **Poïvet**. After *Métal*'s initial bankruptcy (the magazine was taken over by other publishers), Dionnet became a radio and television personality and a comics editor for publisher Albin Michel.

Druillet, Philippe (1944–) (Artist/Writer)

Druillet burst onto the French comics scene with his *Lone Sloane* graphic novel, published in 1966 by the same adult publisher who had previously released *Barbarella*. In 1969, he made waves again when he began serializing new *Lone Sloane* stories in *Pilote*. And in 1973, with **Moebius** and **Dionnet**, he was one of the four founding fathers of *Métal Hurlant*. Druillet continued to be one of comics' most radical ground-breakers throughout the 1970s with stories such as *La Nuit* (*The Night*, 1975), the Elric-inspired *Yragaël* (1974), *Nosferatu* (1978–89), and finally his epic trilogy based on Gustave **Flaubert**'s *Salammbo* (1980–88). Druillet's career has now taken a turn toward fine arts.

Duchateau, André-Paul (1925–) (Writer)

Also a writer of detective fiction, **Duchateau** joined the editorial team of *Tintin* in 1955 when he created the popular investigative journalist *Ric Hochet*, with Tibet (Gilbert Gascard). He contributed numerous police and adventure series to *Tintin* throughout the 1960s and 1970s. Even his science fiction and fantasy series usually contain an element of detection. His genre works include *Udolfo* and *Carol Detective* with **Paape**, *Chancellor* with **Sanahujas**, *Hans* with Rosinski, *Hyperion* with **Franz**, *Mr. Magellan* with **Geri**, *Pharaon* with **Hulet**, *Richard Bantam* and *T.N.T.* Because of his affinity for mysteries, he was also chosen by publisher Claude Lefrancq to adapt in comics form the adventures of classic detectives such as Arthur

Duchateau

Conan Doyle's *Challenger* and *Sherlock Holmes* as well as Maurice **Leblanc**'s *Arsène Lupin* and Gaston **Leroux**'s *Rouletabille*.

Dufaux, Jean (1949–) (Writer)

After having studied at a Belgian film school and worked as a journalist, **Dufaux** began writing comics for *Tintin* in 1983. A prolific writer, Dufaux likes to cross genre boundaries, mixing history with fantasy or SF with thrillers. His genre series include *Beatifica Blues* and *Samba Bugatti* with **Griffo**, *La Complainte des Landes Perdues* (*Lament of the Lost Lands*) with Rosinski, *Les Enfants de la Salamandre* (*Children of the Salamander*) and *Santiag* with **Renaud**, *Les Jardins de la Peur* (*Gardens of Fear*) with **Paape**, *Le Maître des Brumes* (*Mist Master*) with **Éric**, *Sang de Lune* (*Moon Blood*) with **Nicaise**, *Fox* and *Les Voleurs d'Empire* (*Thieves of Empire*). He also is well known for the *film noir*-like thriller *Jessica Blandy*, also with **Renaud**.

Dupuis, Pierre (1931–) (Artist/Writer)

Prolific artist who studied with **Gillon**, then went on to work for *Vaillant* in 1949, and then *Spirou*. **Dupuis** produced numerous historical and adventure series for a variety of magazines. His genre efforts include *Mac Gallan* and *Titan*. He also drew *Kronos* for *Fulgur* in 1980. But he is bet-

ter known for his biographies and a detailed history of World War II in comics form.

Durand, René (1948–) (Writer)

A professor of literature, **Durand**'s first comics series was *La Terre de la Bombe* (*Earth After the Bomb*), with **Ramaioli**, published in *Circus* in 1976. His other genre series include the popular *L'Indien Français* (*French Indian*), also with Ramaioli, *Foc* with **Bordes**, *Les Dirigeables de l'Amazone* (*Dirigibles of the Amazon*) with **Sanahujas** and, more recently, *T.N.T.* and *La Crypte du Souffle Bleu* (*Crypt of the Blue Wind*). Durand is also known for his remarkable South African saga, *Zoulouland*, also with Ramaioli.

Éric (Delzant, Frédéric) (1947–) (Artist/Writer)

After working as an interior architect, **Éric** began working in comics with **Wen**, a series written by **Stoquart** for *Tintin* in 1973. His other genre works include the juvenile heroic fantasy *Tetfol*, which he created in 1977, and the more recent *Le Maître des Brumes* (*Mist Master*), with **Dufaux**, in 1986.

Erik (Jolly, René) (1911–1974) (Artist/Writer)

Prolific cartoonist who produced numerous children's adventure series starting in the 1930s. His genre works include *Atome 21*, *Prof. Vorax*, *L'Expédition du Prof. Gromulus* (*Prof. Gromulus' Expedition*), *Prof. Canif*, *Prof. Cataral*, and the popular *Mégalithe*. **Erik** died of cancer in 1974.

Ferry (Vosselen, Van) (1944–) (Artist/Writer)

After learning his craft at the Saint-Luc comics school in Belgium, **Ferry** began working in comics in 1970 with *Savary*. In 1975, he created *Cédric* and in 1978, he and **Vernal** created the popular *Ian Kalédine*, both for *Tintin*. More recently, Ferry has embarked on

Ferry

a new fantasy series, *Chroniques de Panchrysia*.

Foerster, Philippe (1954–) (Artist/Writer)

Belgian artist and alumnus of the Saint-Luc comics school, **Foerster** began contributing to *Tintin* in 1979, before contributing a series of dark, gothic short-stories to *Fluide Glacial*, starting in 1980, collected in a series of nine remarkable albums. He is also the author of a macabre retelling of *Pinocchio* (1983), and the writer/artist of the series *Starbuck*, published in *Spirou* since 1987.

Foerster

Follet, René (1931–) (Artist)

Originally an illustrator, **Follet** began contributing comic-book stories to *Spirou* in 1949, and to *Tintin* in 1954. He has illustrated two adventure series written by **Stoquart**, often containing genre elements: *Jean Valhardi* and *Ivan Zourine*. His best-known work is *Edmund Bell*, a supernatural investigator, based on the works of Jean **Ray**. He has recently embarked

on a fantasy series, *Ikar*, written by **Makyo**.

Forest, Jean-Claude (1930–1998) (Artist/Writer)

After illustrating numerous children's stories in the 1950s, including the popular *Charlot* series, loosely based on Charlie Chaplin's famous *Little Tramp* character, **Forest** burst onto the comics scene with the creation of *Barbarella* in 1964. Prior to that, he had already distinguished himself as a science fiction illustrator by contributing numerous covers to the magazine *Fiction* (French edition of *F & SF*) and the paperback imprint Le Rayon Fantastique. *Barbarella* was followed by a number of spin-offs such as *Bébé Cyanure* (1964), *Mystérieuse, Matin, Midi et Soir* (*Mysterious, Morning, Noon and Evening*, 1971), and *Hypocrite* (1971), originally serialized in the daily *France-Soir*. Forest was editor of the short-lived *Chouchou* magazine in 1964, for which he co-created and wrote the popular SF series *Les Naufragés du Temps* (*Castaways in Time*) for artist **Gillon**. As a writer, Forest has also co-created *Leonid Beaudragon* with **Savard** and a remarkable graphic novel with **Tardi**, *Ici Même* (*Same Here*). His last solo genre work is the beautiful album *La Jonque Fantôme Vue de l'Orchestre* (*The Phantom Junk as Seen from the Orchestra*) published in 1981. Forest later stopped drawing to concentrate on writing. He wrote a juvenile fantasy novel, *Lilia Entre l'Air et l'Eau* (*Lilia Between Air And Water*, 1983) (See Book 2).

Forton, Gérald (?–) (Artist)

The grandson of Louis Forton, creator of *Les Pieds Nickelés*, Gérald **Forton** started working in comics in the early 1950s, collaborating to *Spirou* (*Alain Cardan*, *Kim Devil*) and *Vaillant* (*Teddy Ted*, *Jacques Flash*). In the 1960s, he took over the popular *Bob Morane* series that appeared in *Pilote*. In 1976, he co-created the fantasy series *Yvain De Kanheric*, while draw-

ing a number of comic adaptations of television series, such as *Les Mystères de l'Ouest* (*Wild Wild West*), *Spider-Man*, etc. Forton emigrated to the United States in the early 1980s, where he has worked on a number of comic-book series (*Jonah Hex*, *Arak*, with Randy & Jean-Marc Lofficier, etc.) as well as animated television series (*Masters of the Universe*, *BraveStarr*).

Fournier, Jean-Claude (1943–) (Artist/Writer)

French artist with strong British roots, **Fournier** took over the *Spirou* series from **Franquin** in 1968. He also wrote and drew the poetic series *Bizu*, also for *Spirou* magazine.

Franquin, André (1924–1997) (Artist/Writer)

With **Hergé**, one of the most influential Belgian artists. **Franquin** took over *Spirou* in 1946 and continued the series until 1968. For it, he created a gallery of colorful characters such as the fantastic *Marsupilami*; *Gaston*, the perennial office goof; Zorglub, the funny mad scientist; *Noël*; the Count of Champignac, etc. For *Spirou*, Franquin assisted on the writing of *Isabelle*. In the 1970s and early 1980s, Franquin produced a series of dark, surreal vignettes gathered in *Idées Noires* (*Dark Designs*) and *Cauchemarrants* (*Funny Nightmares*).

Franz (Drappier, Franz) (1948–) (Artist/Writer)

Belgian artist who began his career in 1968 by drawing short stories published in *Spirou* and *Tintin*. His best-known series are the humorous fantasy *Korrigan* and the pseudo-historical *Jugurtha*. Other genre works include *Hyperion* with A.-P. **Duchateau** and *Thomas Noland* with **Pecqueur**. Recently, he has embarked on a solo heroic-fantasy series, *Brougue*.

Fred (Aristidès, Othon-Frédéric) (1931–) (Artist/Writer)

After working as a cartoonist for

various daily papers, **Fred** was one of the founders of the humor magazine *Hara-Kiri*, for which he created the **Manu-Manu** and *Le Petit Cirque* (*The Little Circus*). He joined the editorial team of *Pilote* in 1965, and created the character of **Philémon**. He also continued to write and draw dream-inspired fables, collected in various graphic novels. For artist **Alexis**, Fred wrote the humorous adventures of two incompetent time-travelers, *Time Is Money*. In 1979, he created the character of *Cythère* for *Pif*. More recently, Fred embarked on a series of surreal moralistic fables.

Gal, Jean-Claude (1944–) (Artist)

An art teacher, **Gal** contributed some short stories to *Pilote* before producing the lavish heroic sagas of **Arn** and **La Passion de Diosamante** (*Diosamante's Passion*) for *Métal Hurlant*.

Gauckler, Philippe (1960–) (Artist)

Young artist who began illustrating science fiction stories for *Métal Hurlant* in 1982—later collected in **Duel** and **Suicide Commando**. He illustrated Joel **Houssin**'s science fiction saga, **Blue**, and Thierry Smolderen's "Convoy" series, aka **Karen Springwell**.

Geri (Ghion, Henri) (1934–) (Artist/Writer)

Geri began contributing various cartoons to *Tintin* magazine in 1954,

Geri

for which he eventually created the fabulous **Skblllz**. He also illustrated the adventures of **Mr. Magellan** for **Van Hamme** and **Duchateau**.

Gigi, Robert (1926–) (Artist)

After illustrating numerous children's adventure series in the 1940s and 1950s, **Gigi** teamed up with writer **Moliterni** in 1965 to create **Scarlett Dream**. They also produced **Orion** in *Phénix* in 1968 and **Agar** in the mid–1970s. For *Pilote*, Gigi illustrated the **Dossiers Soucoupes Volantes** (*UFO Files*), written by **Lob**.

Gillon, Paul (1926–) (Artist/Writer)

Gillon joined the editorial team of *Vaillant* in 1947, illustrating numerous adventure stories. In 1959, he started drawing the famous *13, Rue de l'Espoir* (*13 Hope St.*) daily romance strip for *France-Soir*. His science fiction series include **Les Naufragés du Temps** (*Castaways in Time*), co-created with Jean-Claude **Forest** for *Chouchou* in the mid-1960s; and **La Survivante** (*The Survivor*) for *L'Écho des Savanes* in the mid-1980s.

Gine (Martinez, Christian) (1947–) (Artist)

Initially a cartoonist, **Gine** began drawing adventure comics for *Tintin* in 1979. In 1986, he embarked on the science fiction series, **Neige** (*Snow*), his major work so far. He has also illustrated the fantasy series, **Finkel**.

Giordan (Raoul) (1926–) & (Robert) (1922–1980s) (Artists)

The **Giordan** brothers began drawing comics for a variety of children's magazines in the late 1940s, but their major works were published by Artima (later Aredit) in the 1950s: **Les Conquérants de l'Espace** (*Space Conquerors*) and **Les Francis** in the classic *Meteor*, and **Tom Tempest** in *Audax*. In the 1970s, they were assigned to illustrate the comics adaptations of the

science fiction novels of Éditions *Fleuve Noir* for *Sidéral* and *Anticipation*. Robert passed away in the 1980s. Raoul briefly returned to comics with **Space Gordon** in 1993.

Giraud, Jean see Moebius

Godard, Christian (1932–) (Artist/Writer)

Godard (no relation to the filmmaker) began writing and drawing comics in 1954. He eventually joined the editorial team of *Pilote*, for which he created the cartoony semi-genre series **Norbert et Kari**. In 1966, he created his second popular series, air-taxi pilot **Martin Milan** for *Tintin*. As a writer, Godard has often worked with Spanish artist Julio Ribera, producing a number of genre series: **Dracurella**, **Chroniques du Temps de la Vallée des Ghlomes** (*Chronicles of the Times of the Ghlomes' Valley*), **Le Grand Manque** (*The Great Shortage*), and the popular **Vagabond des Limbes** (*Vagabond of Limbo*). Godard is also much in demand as a humor writer.

Gos (Goossens, Roland) (1937–) (Artist/Writer)

Not to be confused with humor cartoonist Daniel Goossens (no relation), **Gos** joined **Peyo**'s studio, working on **Les Schtroumpfs** (*Smurfs*) and **Benoît Brisefer**, until creating his own, very successful series, **Le Scrameustache**, for *Spirou* in 1972.

Goscinny, René (1926–1977) (Writer)

One of the most important and influential writers in French comics history, **Goscinny** is the co-creator (with artist **Uderzo**) of the world-famous **Astérix**. Goscinny launched **Astérix** in the first issue of *Pilote*, a magazine which he co-created (with Uderzo and writer **Charlier**) in 1959, and which he edited until his death. Goscinny worked in the United States from 1945 to 1951 with Harvey Kurtzman, Will Elder, and John Severin. Back in Europe, before creating *Pi-*

lote, he wrote scripts for many popular humor series, such as the western *Lucky Luke* with Morris (Maurice de Bévère), *Spaghetti*, *Strapontin*, *Modeste & Pompon*, etc. During that period, he also created *Iznogoud* with Tabary, *Gaudéamus* with Coq (and later *La Fée Aveline* as well), and *Le Petit Nicolas* with Sempé.

Greg (Regnier, Michel) (1931–1999) *(Artist/Writer)*

One of the most prolific creators in comics, **Greg** started his career as a writer/artist in 1947 and, in the early 1950s, produced a superhero series, *Le Chat*, under the name of Michel Denys. In 1958, he joined the editorial team of *Tintin*, which he edited from 1965 to 1975. There, he wrote and drew a number of humorous adventure series including *Rock Derby*, *Zig et Puce*, and the classic *Le Mystère de l'Homme aux Trèfles* (*The Mystery of the Clover Man*). As a writer, he co-created a number of cutting-edge, modern adventure heroes, such as *Bernard Prince* and *Comanche* for **Hermann**, *Bruno Brazil* for William Vance, and *Luc Orient* for Eddy **Paape**. He also wrote the poetic *Olivier Rameau* for **Dany**. During the 1960s, Greg also wrote and drew the hugely successful humor series *Achille Talon* for *Pilote* and the juvenile *Les As* for *Vaillant*. Greg also wrote some of the best stories for *Spirou* and *Le Marsupilami*, and several successful detective novels.

Griffo (Goelen, Werner) (1949–) *(Artist)*

Belgian artist who, after an aborted start in the early 1970s, returned to comics with *SOS Bonheur* (*SOS Happiness*) for *Spirou* in 1981, written by **Van Hamme**. Since then, he has illustrated two remarkable science fiction series, *Beatifica Blues* and *Samba Bugatti*, and more recently, *Monsieur Noir*.

Hausman, René (1936–) *(Artist)*

After working in animation, **Haus-**man joined the editorial team of *Spirou* in 1957. He subsequently illustrated numerous fairy tales and children's books. He returned to comics in the mid-1980s with the superb heroic-fantasies, *Laïyna* and *Les Trois Cheveux Blancs* (*The Three White Hairs*), written by **Yann**.

Hé, Dominique (1949–) *(Artist)*

A student of **Moebius**, **Hé** began contributing stories to *Pilote* in 1973. In 1980, he created *Marc Mathieu* for *Métal Hurlant*. After several historical series, he recently embarked on *Tanatha*, a heroic fantasy adventure.

Hergé (Rémi, Georges) (1907–1983) *(Artist/Writer)*

Belgian cartoonist **Hergé**'s first regular comics series was about a boy-scout hero, *Totor*, created in 1926. In 1929, he created the world-famous character of *Tintin*, which turned him into a superstar—the only European artist to rival Disney—and one of the founding fathers of French-language comics. The eponymous magazine *Tintin* was started in 1946. His characters—Tintin, Captain Haddock, Prof. Calculus, etc.—have become modern archetypes. Other characters created by Hergé include the short-lived *Jo, Zette et Jocko* and a series of gags about two Belgian tots, *Quick & Flupke*.

Hermann (Huppen, Hermann) (1938-) *(Artist/Writer)*

Belgian artist **Hermann** made a strong debut in *Tintin* in 1965 as co-creator of the action adventure series *Bernard Prince*, and again in 1969 with the western *Comanche*—both written by **Greg**. During this period, Hermann also co-created the historical saga *Jugurtha*, and illustrated the western novels starring *Dylan Stark* by Pierre **Pelot**. In 1979, Hermann created his own science fiction saga, the post-apocalyptic *Jeremiah*. In 1984, he also launched a medieval epic, *Les Tours de Bois-Maury*. His horror stories have

been collected in *Abominable* (1988). In 1995, he illustrated the more whimsical *Le Secret des Hommes-Chiens* (*Secret of the Man-Dogs*) written by his son, Yves.

Hulet, Daniel (1947–) *(Artist/Writer)*

Belgian artist **Hulet** began publishing in *Tintin* in 1975. In 1981, he teamed up with **Duchateau** to create superspy *Pharaon*. In 1987, he began writing and drawing his own, gothic series, *L'État Morbide* (*Morbid State*), and recently, has embarked on a heroic fantasy saga, *Voyages en Terres Étrangères* (*Journeys through Strange Lands*).

Jacobs, Edgar-Pierre (1904–1987) *(Artist/Writer)*

Commercial illustrator, fashion designer, and even opera baritone, **Jacobs** entered the comics field during World War II, when, in 1942, he was asked to complete the adventures of *Flash Gordon*, which had been banned by the Nazis. In 1944, his publisher asked him to create a similar series, which he did: *Le Rayon U*. In 1943, he joined the **Hergé** studio and collaborated on some of the *Tintin* stories. When *Tintin* magazine was launched in 1946, he created the powerful science fiction saga *Blake et Mortimer*, which has become one of the true milestones of French-language comics. Jacobs, almost as much as Hergé, is responsible for the "clear line" style of Belgian comics.

Jidehem (De Mesmaeker, Jean) (1935–) *(Artist)*

Belgian artist **Jidehem** started his comics career with *Ginger* in the early 1950s, then joined the editorial team of *Spirou*, for which he created the popular characters of *Sophie* and *Starter*. He also assisted **Franquin** on *Spirou* and *Gaston Lagaffe*, lending his real name to a character of that series.

Jijé (Gillain, Joseph) (1914–1980) *(Artist/Writer)*

One of the founding fathers of French comics, **Jijé** worked in comics beginning in the 1930s. He was one of the first artists to work for *Spirou* magazine, taking over the title character from **Rob-Vel** from 1940 to 1946, and creating *Jean Valhardi*, *Blondin & Cirage*, and the popular western series *Jerry Spring*. In the early 1960s, he took over the art chores on *Michel Tanguy* for *Pilote*. Jijé worked in the tradition of Hal Foster, Alex Raymond, and Milton Caniff, and taught numerous French artists, including Jean **Giraud**.

Jodorowsky, Alexandro (1929–) *(Writer)*

Born in Chile, cult filmmaker **Jodorowsky** (*El Topo*, *The Holy Mountain*) met **Moebius** in the late 1970s while working in Paris on an aborted film adaptation of Frank Herbert's *Dune*. He then turned to a prolific writing career, producing numerous genre series with superior artists: the classic *Incal* with Moebius, *Alandor* with Italian artist Silvio Cadelo, *Alef-Thau* with **Arno**, *Le Lama Blanc* (*The White Lama*) with expatriate American Bess, *Face-De-Lune* (*Moon Face*) with **Boucq**, *La Passion de Diosamante* (*Diosamante's Passion*) with **Gal**, etc. Even though he is not a native French-speaker, Jodorowsky is included here because of the profound impact his works have had on the French-language comics industry.

Kline (Chevallier, Roger) (1922–) *(Artist/Writer)*

Prolific author of numerous juvenile adventure series published in *Coq Hardi* (*Robin Hood*, *Colonel X*), "*Vaillant*" (*Davy Crockett*, *Loup Noir*) and *Fillette* (**Stany Beule dans la Lune**; *Stany Beule in the Moon*). His first series was the genre classic *Kaza le Martien* (*Kaza the Martian*), published in 1946.

Lacroix, Claude (1944–) *(Artist/Writer)*

Prolific French cartoonist and illustrator who also contributed covers and illustrations to the French editions of *F & SF* and *Galaxy*. His first genre comics series was **Yann le Migrateur** with writer Genin in 1979. He also wrote and drew various humoristic SF stories for *Métal Hurlant*, collected in **Fariboles Sidérales** (*Cosmic Jokes*). He has recently embarked on a new series, **Le Cycle de Cyann**, drawn by **Bourgeon**. Claude Lacroix is not related to Pierre Lacroix (1912–), the artist of *Les Pieds Nickelés*, **Charlot**, and **Bibi Fricotin**.

Lamquet, Christian (1954–) *(Artist/Writer)*

Young Belgian artist who assisted Édouard Aidans on **Tounga** in the 1970s, before creating **Quasar** for *Spirou* in 1984, whose themes he later revisited in his **Tropique des Étoiles** (*Tropic of the Stars*) series. In 1993, **Lamquet** produced a remarkable graphic novel, **L'Amour Hologramme** (*Holographic Love*).

Laverdure, Claude (1947–) *(Artist)*

After working in advertising and assisting Édouard Aidans throughout the 1970s, **Laverdure** illustrated the graphic novel **La Mémoire Albinos** (*Albino Memory*) in 1986. Since then, he has worked on **Fantômas** and **Chroniques de l'Impossible** (*Chronicles of the Impossible*).

Lecureux, Roger (1925–1999) *(Writer)*

Prolific writer who joined the editorial team of *Vaillant* in 1945 and later became its editor-in-chief from 1958 to 1963. There, he created many adventure series, such as **Les Pionniers de l'Espérance** (*Hope's Pioneers*) with **Poïvet**, *Nasdine Hodja* with **Bastard**, *Teddy Ted* with Gérald **Forton**, *Lynx* with Bob Sim, *Fils de Chine* with **Gillon**, *Le Grêlé 7/13* with Christian

Gaty, *Rahan* with **Chéret**, *Les Robinsons de la Terre* (*Robinsons from Earth*) with Alfonso Font, and many others. During that time, he also contributed numerous stories to a variety of various digest-sized comics magazines, including the space opera, *Galax*.

Le Guen, Pierre (1929–) *(Artist)*

After drawing *Tangor* in *O.K.* magazine from 1947 to 1949, **Le Guen** joined the editorial team of *Vaillant* in 1950, where he co-created **Jacques Flash** with Jean **Ollivier**. After working for various children's magazine in the 1970s, he helped fund the Five Stars Studio, where he worked on comics adaptation of Japanese animation series such as **Albator** and **Captain Fulgur**.

Leloup, Roger (1933–) *(Artist/Writer)*

Leloup joined the **Hergé** studio in 1955 and worked on the new version on **Tintin**'s *Black Island*. He also worked with Jacques **Martin** on *Alix*. In 1970, he created the popular character of **Yoko Tsuno** for *Spirou*.

Le Tendre, Serge (1946–) *(Writer)*

Le Tendre started his comics writing career in 1975 with numerous short stories for a variety of magazines. In 1982, he co-created with **Loisel** the hugely popular heroic fantasy, **La Quête de l'Oiseau du Temps** (*Quest for the Time Bird*, transl. as *Roxanna*) for *Charlie*. His other genre series include *Les Voyages de Takuan* (*Takuan's Journeys*), **Taï-Dor** (co-written with **Rodolphe**), and the more recent **Labyrinthe**.

Liquois, Auguste (1902–1969) *(Artist)*

This classic comic artist and illustrator from the 1930s and 1940s is fondly remembered for two genre series, **Guerre à la Terre** (*War against Earth*) and two early French super-heroes, *Satanax* and *Salvator*. He also took over *Tarzan* after the Nazis banned the import of American strips, and drew a *Flash Gordon* imitation: *Vers les Mondes Inconnus* (*Towards the Unknown Worlds*). Liquois retired in 1959.

Lob (Loeb, Jacques) (1932–1990) *(Writer)*

Originally a science fiction cartoonist, **Lob** contributed to *Planète*, *Fiction* (the French edition of *F & SF*), *Hara-Kiri*, and various other magazines in the 1950s. In the 1960s, he teamed up with Georges **Pichard** to create **Submerman** for *Pilote*, **Ténébrax** for *Chouchou*, **Ulysse** for *Linus* and **Blanche-Épiphanie** for *V Magazine*. In the 1970s, he wrote a number of stories for *Pilote*: *Delirius*, a chapter in the **Lone Sloane** saga with **Druillet**, *Les Mange-Bitume* with Bielsa, *Dossiers Soucoupes Volantes* (*UFO Files*) with **Gigi**. In 1972, Lob and cartoonist Marcel Gotlib created the hugely popular super-hero parody, **Super Dupont**. In the 1980s, Lob signed *Le Mécano des Étoiles* (*Cosmic Mecano*) and the remarkable **Le Transperceneige** (1982) with Rochette, published in *(A Suivre)*. His own cartoony parodies of science fiction themes were collected in **Roger Fringant**, *Batmax*, and *L'Homme au Landau* (*The Man in the Baby Cart*).

Loisel, Régis (1951–) *(Artist/Writer)*

After a few stories published in the early 1970s, **Loisel** illustrated the hugely popular heroic-fantasy, **La Quête de l'Oiseau du Temps** (*Quest for the Time Bird*, transl. as *Roxanna*) written by **Le Tendre** for *Charlie*, from 1982 to 1987. More recently, he embarked on an adult retelling of Barrie's **Peter Pan**.

Lortac, R. (Colliard, Robert) (1884–1973) *(Writer)*

Prolific writer who contributed numerous stories (prose and comics) to

various magazines from the turn of the century to the early 1960s. His genre contributions include *Démonax* for *Gavroche* in 1941, **Bibi Fricotin** (with Pierre Lacroix) and, especially, **Les Conquérants de l'Espace** (*Space Conquerors*) and **Les Francis** with R. & R. **Giordan** for *Meteor* in the 1950s.

Luguy, Philippe (Liéron, Guy) (1948–) *(Artist)*

After working for a number of digest-sized adventure magazines in the 1960s and 1970s, **Luguy** co-created **Sylvio** in 1974 for *Pif*. In 1982, he co-created the popular heroic-fantasy series, **Percevan**. Luguy also helped fund the Five Stars Studio, where he worked on comics adaptation of Japanese animation series such as **Albator** and **Captain Fulgur**.

Makyo, Pierre (Fournier, Pierre) (1952–) *(Artist/Writer)*

Fournier began working in comics as an artist under his real name in 1977. After illustrating a number of children's series, he joined the editorial team of *Spirou* as Pierre **Makyo** in 1982. There, he began contributing scripts on a regular basis, including on *Jerôme K. Jerôme Bloche*. As a writer, his first big success was **La Ballade au Bout du Monde** (*Ballad to the Edge of the World*) for artist **Vicomte**, published in *Circus*. Since then, he has written other genre series, such as **Le Cycle des Deux Horizons** (*Cycle of the 2 Horizons*) for Christian Rossi, **Ikar** for **Follet**, and **Le Jeu de Pourpre** (*The Purple Game*) for Rocco. From 1983 to 1987, Makyo also wrote and drew the surreal **Grimion Gant de Cuir** (*Grimion Leather-Glove*), also for *Circus*.

Maric (Chiavarino, Raymond) (1927–) *(Writer)*

Maric wrote numerous children's adventure stories during the 1940s and 1950s, including **Bibi Fricotin**, *Charlot*, and *Les Pieds Nickelés*. He also co-created **Cristal** for *Spirou* in 1983

and **Yvain De Kanhéric** with Gérald **Forton**.

Marijac (Dumas, Jacques) (1904–) *(Artist/Writer)*

A popular and prolific artist/writer of the 1930s, **Marijac** was involved in the French Resistance during World War II, and launched the popular *Coq Hardi* after the war, thus becoming one of the leading publishers of French comics in the 1950s. His creations include *Capitaine Fantôme*, *Colonel X* and, in the genre, the multi-faceted **Jim Boum** and **Guerre à la Terre** (*War Against Earth*), with **Liquois**.

Martin, Jacques (1921–) *(Artist/Writer)*

Martin was one of the first artists to join the editorial team of *Tintin* in 1948, for which he created the hugely popular *Alix* and, in 1952, *Lefranc*. In 1970, he let other artists take over the drawing of *Lefranc*, and began writing pseudo-historical genre series such as **Jhen** (aka **Xan**) and **Kéos**, both with **Pleyers**.

Masse, Francis (1948–) *(Artist/Writer)*

Renowned French cartoonist who started publishing idiosyncratic, black-and-white stories in *Le Canard Sauvage* in 1973. He has since contributed to virtually every comics magazine, including *Fluide Glacial*, *Métal Hurlant*, *(A Suivre)*, etc. His stories have been collected in a number of books.

Melwyn-Nash, J. K. (Navarro, Marcel) (1919–) *(Writer)*

Lyon-based journalist and writer, **Navarro** started his career in comics by contributing stories to **Chott**'s *Fantax* in 1946. He then co-founded the Aventures & Voyages publishing house, which published a number of children's adventure stories. In 1950, with Auguste Vistel, Navarro founded Éditions Lug, which became one of the leading publisher of French and Italian digest-sized comics and later (starting in 1969), licensed editions of Marvel Comics characters. It is in this capacity that Navarro (always using the pseudonym of **Melwyn-Nash**) co-created a number of popular characters such as the western avenger, *Ombrax*; the Tarzan-like *Zembla*; and a number of super-heroes such as **Homicron**, **Mikros**, **Photonik**, and **Wampus**. Melwyn-Nash also wrote a special episode of Marvel's *Silver Surfer*, especially drawn by **Mitton** for the French market.

Mézières, Jean-Claude (1938–) (Artist)

French artist **Mézières** attended the same art school as **Moebius** and **Mallet** in the 1950s. He joined the editorial team of *Pilote* in the early 1960s, and co-created *Valerian*, the most popular SF series in French comics, with **Christin** in 1967. He also supervised *Canal-Choc* in 1990.

Mitton, Jean-Yves (1945–) (Artist)

French artist who joined Éditions Lug as a staff artist in 1964 after working on a number of digest-sized magazines. He wrote and drew *Epsilon*, **Mikros**, **Cosmo**, **Kronos**, **L'Archer Blanc**, **Photonik**, etc. He also drew a special episode of Marvel's *Silver Surfer* for the French market.

Moebius (Giraud, Jean) (1938–) (Artist/Writer)

Jean **Giraud**, aka **Moebius**, is an artist whose work as an illustrator has garnered him many of the world's most prestigious awards. Giraud has been widely acknowledged as being one of the major, modern-day influences in the visual arts field. While still in art school (with **Mézières** and **Mallet**), he wrote and drew various western strips published in *Coeurs Vaillants* in the late 1950s. In 1960, Giraud worked as **Jijé**'s assistant on *Jerry Spring*. It is at that time that he created the punnish signature of Moebius, which he used to sign

dark-humored strips in the satirical magazine, *Hara-Kiri*. In 1963, Giraud met writer Jean-Michel **Charlier** and, together, they created the popular western series, *Lieutenant Blueberry* for *Pilote*. In the late 1960s, Moebius began illustrating and doing covers for French science fiction books and magazines. In 1975, Moebius co-founded the magazine *Métal Hurlant*, for which he created a number of seminal, breakthrough science fiction and fantasy stories, such as *Arzach* and *Le Garage Hermétique* (*The Airtight Garage*) and *L'Incal*, the latter written by cult filmmaker Alexandro **Jodorowsky**. In the 1980s, Moebius embarked on the more personal *Édéna* saga, *Le Coeur Couronné* (*The Crowned Heart*, written by Jodorowsky, and drew a special *Silver Surfer* graphic novel, written by Marvel Comics legend Stan Lee. As a writer, Moebius has worked with **Auclair** on *Jason Muller*, Marc **Bati** on *Altor*, and *La Nuit de l'Étoile* (*Night Of The Star*) and Bruno Marchand on *Little Nemo*. Finally, Moebius has also worked as a visual conceptualist for the motion picture industry on Jodorowsky's aborted production of *Dune*, Ridley Scott's *Alien*, René **Laloux**'s *Les Maîtres du Temps* (*The Time Masters*), Walt Disney's *TRON*, *Masters of the Universe*, Ron Howard's *Willow* (1987), Jim Cameron's *The Abyss* (1988), and Luc **Besson**'s *The Fifth Element* (1997).

Molinari, Félix (1931–) (Artist/Writer)

Molinari began his career as a comics artist with *L'Aigle des Mers* (*Sea Eagle*) in the late 1940s, before creating the popular World War II adventure series, *Garry* in 1948, and the equally popular SF super-hero *Super Boy* (no relation with DC Comics' character) in 1958. Molinari recently came out of retirement to work on *Les Héritiers d'Orphée* (*Orpheus' Heirs*).

Moliterni, Claude (1932–) (Writer)

Renowned comics expert and histo-

rian, **Moliterni** created the magazine *Phénix* in the 1960s before joining the editorial team of *Pilote* in the early 1970s. As a writer, he has co-created *Scarlett Dream*, *Orion*, and *Agar* with **Gigi**, and *Taar le Rebelle* with Remohi. He also wrote a comics version of the Bible as well as adaptations of popular Japanese cartoon series, *Albator* and *Captain Fulgur*. Under the pseudonym of Éric Cartier, Moliterni is also the writer of a series of adaptations of Gaston **Leroux**'s *Rouletabille*.

Montellier, Chantal (1947–) (Artist/Writer)

Montellier first appeared in comics with grim, realistic strips published in *Charlie* in 1973. A strong advocate of left-wing politics, she produced a series of dystopias about Fascistic near-futures for *Métal Hurlant* in the late 1970s and early 1980s: *1996*, *Shelter*, and *L'Esclavage, C'est la Liberté* (*Slavery Means Freedom*). She also created the character of *Andy Gang*, a grim detective.

Navarro, Marcel *see* Melwyn-Nash, J.K.

Ollivier, Jean (1921–) (Writer)

One of the major writers of *Vaillant* and its editor-in-chief until 1958, **Ollivier** co-created *Yves le Loup* (*Yves the Wolf*) for **Bastard**, *Jacques Flash* for **Le Guen**, *Ragnar the Viking* for Coelho, *Davy Crockett* for **Kline**, *Docteur Justice* for Marcello, and many other historical and adventure heroes. More recently, he wrote *La Mémoire des Celtes* (*Celtic Memory*), illustrated by Coelho. Ollivier also is a prolific author of juvenile novels.

Paape, Eddy (1920–) (Artist)

Prolific Belgian artist who joined the editorial team of *Spirou* in 1946, taking over *Jean Valhardi* from **Jijé**. In 1958, he and **Charlier** created their own globe-trotting adventure hero, *Marc Dacier*. In 1965, he moved to *Tintin*, where he and **Greg** created the *Flash Gordon*-inspired popular science fiction series, *Luc Orient*. More recent genre series include *Udolfo* and *Carol Détective* with **Duchateau**, and *Les Jardins de la Peur* (*Gardens of Fear*) with **Dufaux**.

Pecqueur, Daniel (1948–) (Writer)

After a career in race car driving, **Pecqueur** starting writing *Cargal* for *Pilote* in 1981 and, later, *Thomas Noland* with **Franz** in *Charlie*.

Peeters, Benoît (1958–) (Writer)

After several novels and scholarly books about **Hergé**, **Peeters** co-created the series *Les Cités Obscures* with **Schuiten**. He also took over the writing of *Ergün* from **Comes**, and co-created *Les Hybrides*.

Pellos (Pellarin, René) (1900–1998) (Artist/Writer)

After a prolific career as a sport cartoonist in the 1930s, **Pellos** began drawing children's comics. In 1937-38, he and **René Thevenin** created *Futuropolis* in *Junior*, one of the milestones of French-language SF comics. He remained extremely prolific in the field of children's comics, during and after World War II, taking over *Les Pieds Nickelés* in 1948. His other genre series include *Electropolis* (1940); *Atomas* (1948); a female *Tarzan*-like series, *Durga Rani* (1946-1953); and a remarkable adaptation of J. H. **Rosny** Aîné's *La Guerre du Feu* (*Quest for Fire*) (1951).

Peyo (Culliford, Pierre) (1928–1992) (Artist/Writer)

After a brief stint as an animator, **Peyo** created the character of medieval page *Johan* in *La Dernière Heure* in 1946. He brought *Johan* to *Spirou* in 1952, adding the comical Pirlouit and, in 1958, the hugely successful *Les Schtroumpfs* (*The Smurfs*). He is also the creator of *Benoît Brisefer*. His son, Thierry Culliford, has taken over the writing of some of his father's creations.

Pichard, Georges (1920–) (Artist)

After a successful career as a commercial artist, cartoonist, and illustrator, **Pichard** entered the field of comics in a big way in the 1960s, teaming up with writer **Lob** on a number of genre series such as *Submerman* (in *Pilote*), *Ténébrax* (in *Chouchou*), *Ulysse* (in *Phénix*), and *Blanche-Épiphanie* (in *V Magazine*). In addition to a number of remarkable erotic works, Pichard is also the artist of *Bornéo Jo*, done with Danie Dubos, and *Ceux-Là* (*These People*) with Jean-Pierre **Andrevon**, done in the 1980s. A more recent work is a loose adaptation from a classic Greek tragedy, *Les Sorcières de Thessalie* (*Witches of Thessalia*).

Pierre, François see Danard, Jean-Pierre

Pleyers, Jean (1943–) (Artist/Writer)

After working as an assistant on various adventure series in the 1960s, **Pleyers** made a first incursion into science fiction comics with *Les Enragés de la Peste Blanche* (*Fury of the White Plague*) in 1977. He then became Jacques **Martin**'s assistant on *Alix*, and eventually co-created with him *Jhen* and *Kéos*. Pleyers continued to work solo on a new science fiction series, *Les Êtres de Lumière* (*Beings of Light*) in the 1980s.

Poïvet, Raymond (1910–1999) (Artist)

Poïvet worked as a fashion artist in the 1940s and had contributed to *Le Téméraire*, before joining the editorial team of *Vaillant* in 1945, where he and **Lecureux** created the first modern French science fiction series, *Les Pionniers de l'Espérance* (*Hope's Pioneers*). During that period, he also co-created *Colonel X* with **Marijac** in 1947 and a *Tarzan*-like series, *Tumak* in 1948. In 1961, he and **Charlier** co-created *Guy Lebleu* for *Pilote*. In 1964, he collaborated to the short-lived *Chou-*

chou magazine with *P'tit Gus*. With **Dionnet**, Poïvet created the remarkable fantasy *Tiriel*, started in 1974 and completed in *Métal Hurlant* in 1982.

Ramaioli, Georges (1945–) (Artist)

A student of Jean **Giraud**, **Ramaioli**'s first comics series was the post-cataclysmic classic *La Terre de la Bombe* (*Earth After the Bomb*) published in *Circus* in 1977. With René **Durand**, Ramaioli created the popular western with SF elements *L'Indien Français* (*The French Indian*), and *Zoulouland*. More recently, he created *L'Horus de Nekhen*, a series about ancient Egypt, with **Corteggiani**.

Renard, Claude (1946–) (Artist/Writer)

After working for *Spirou* in the early 1960s, **Renard** started an art studio which included **Schuiten**, Sokal, etc. among its students. With Schuiten, Renard co-created *Les Machinistes* and *Métamorphoses*. His own solo works include *Ivan Casablanca* and *Les Elfes de Pomaridus*.

Renaud (Denauw, Renaud) (?–) (Artist)

An alumnus of the St. Luc comics school in Belgium, **Renaud** worked in advertising and contributed to the comics adaptations of the *Fleuve Noir* novels for Arédit. In 1975, he started drawing juvenile adventure series for *Spirou*. In 1980, he switched to *Tintin*. Finally, in 1987 he teamed up with writer **Dufaux** to co-create *Jessica Blandy*, and two remarkable genre series, *Les Enfants de la Salamandre* (*Children of the Salamander*) and *Santiag*.

Rob-Vel (Velter, Robert) (1909–1991) (Artist/Writer)

French artist Robert **Velter** assisted Martin Branner on *Winnie Winkle* before returning to Europe in 1935 and creating the daily strip, *Monsieur*

Subito (using the pseudonym "Bozz"). In 1938, he created the character of *Spirou* for the eponymous magazine, which he relinquished to *Jijé* in 1943. He continued to be a popular cartoonist and comic-strip artist until his retirement in the 1970s.

Rodolphe (Jacquette, Rodolphe) (1948–) (Writer)

Prolific French writer who began working with Floc'h and Goetzinger for *Pilote* in 1975. His numerous genre contributions include *Légendes de l'Éclatée* (*Legends of the Scattered*) and *Les Écluses du Ciel* (*Skylocks*) with Michel **Rouge**; *L'Autre Monde* (*The Other World*) and *Marie-La-Noire* (*Black Mary*) with Florence Magnin; *Dock 21* with Mounier; *Le Centaure Mécanique* (*Mechanical Centaur*) with Eberoni; *L'Homme au Bigos* (*The Man with the Hat*) with Ferrandez; *Melmoth* with Marc Rénier; *La Dernière Lune* (*The Last Moon*); and *Taï-Dor*, on which he partnered with Serge **Le Tendre**.

Rosy, Maurice (1927–) (Artist/Writer)

Rosy joined the editorial team of *Spirou* in the early 1950s. He contributed stories to *Tif et Tondu* (creating the unforgettable character of Monsieur Choc) and *Spirou*. In 1967, he co-created *Attila* with **Derib**. His other popular creation is the cartoony convict, *Bobo*. Rosy retired from comics in the late 1960s to go into advertising.

Rouge, Michel (1950–) (Artist)

A student of Jean **Giraud**, **Rouge** began his comics career by assisting **chéret** on *Rahan*. With **Rodolphe**, he has produced two genre series, *Légendes de L'Éclatée* (*Legends of the Scattered*) and *Les Écluses du Ciel* (*Skylocks*). He has since taken over *Comanche* from **Hermann**.

Saint-Ogan, Alain (1895–1974) (Artist/Writer)

With **Hergé**, **Saint-Ogan** is the founding father of French-language comics. He started as a cartoonist in 1913, publishing in a variety of newspapers and magazines. In 1925, he created *Zig et Puce* and was the first French artist to use word balloons. He continued producing *Zig et Puce*, as well as other less memorable children's series, until the late 1940s. He eventually entrusted the series to **Greg**. *Zig et Puce*'s pet penguin, Alfred, was for a long time used to designate a major French comics award. Alain Saint-Ogan also co-wrote a 1945 fantasy novel, *Le Voyageur Immobile* (*The Motionless Traveller*) with Camille **Ducray**.

Sanahujas, Patrice (1952–) (Artist)

After working for a number of digest-size magazine publishers, **Sanahujas** began *Les Dirigeables de l'Amazone* (*Dirigibles of the Amazon*) in 1980 with **Durand**. With **Duchateau**, he later co-created *Chancellor* and an adaptation of Arthur Conan Doyle's *Challenger*. He has also provided the covers for a series of *Bob Morane* reprints.

Savard, Didier (1950–) (Artist/Writer)

French artist **Savard** created *Dick Hérisson* in 1981 for *Charlie* magazine. He also worked with **Forest** on *Léonid Beaudragon* and, more recently, illustrated a new version of *Perlin et Pinpin*.

Schuiten, François (1956–) (Artist)

An alumnus of the St. Luc comics school in Belgium, **Schuiten** began publishing in 1977 in *Métal Hurlant*, for which he co-created *Les Machinistes* and *Métamorphoses* with **Renard**, and *Les Terres Creuses* (*The Hollow Earths*) with his brother, Luc. But his major work is the remarkable series *Les Cités Obscures* (*The Dark Cities*), written by **Peeters** and published in *(A Suivre)* since 1978.

Sirius (Mayeu, Max) (1911–1997) (Artist/Writer)

One of the first artists to join the editorial team of *Spirou* in 1942, **Sirius** created the science fiction adventure series, *L'Épervier Bleu* (*The Blue Hawk*). After some censorship problems, he created in 1953 the popular historical saga, *Timour*, which is still continuing today. Other genre creations include the short-lived fantasy *Simon le Danseur* (*Simon the Dancer*) and the dark-humored and more cartoony *Pemberton*, created for *Pilote* in 1972.

Sternis, Philippe (1952–) (Artist)

Sternis published a number of children's stories in *Record* in the early 1970s, before working as a cartoonist in Spain. Back in France, he co-created *Snark Saga* and *Memory* with **Cothias**, the former for *Okapi* in 1980 and the latter for *Circus* in 1985.

Stoquart, Jacques (1931–) (Writer)

Stoquart's first comics story was *Wen* written for **Éric** and serialized in *Tintin* in 1970. He then worked steadily with **Follet**, co-creating *Edmund Bell* and *Ivan Zorine*, and working on *Jean Valhardi*. He is also the writer of the superb historical series *Ramiro*, drawn by William Vance. In 1992, Stoquart wrote a comics adaptation of Isaac Asimov's first *Lucky Starr* novel, *Les Poisons de Mars* (*Poisons of Mars*).

Taffin, Olivier (1946–) (Artist/Writer)

French artist who was first published in *Pilote* in 1973. After working as a children's book illustrator, he returned to comics in 1982 with *Orn*, written by **Cothias**. He then embarked on solo series such as *Allaive* (1986) and *Odyss*.

Tardi, Jacques (1946–) (Artist/Writer)

Tardi's first comic-book story

(written by **Moebius**) was published in *Pilote* in 1970. He then illustrated the first story in **Christin**'s *Légendes d'Aujourd'hui* (*Modern Legends*) saga, later taken over by **Bilal**. In 1977, he and Picaret created the pseudo-historical fantasy *Polonius* for *Métal Hurlant*. In 1978, he illustrated **Forest**'s graphic novel, *Ici Même* (*Same Here*), and created his masterwork, *Adèle Blanc-Sec*, for (*A Suivre*). The *Adèle* saga tied in with two previous graphic novels, published in the 1970s in *Pilote*: *Adieu Brindavoine* and *Le Démon des Glaces* (*Demon of the Ice*). Tardi has also produced a number of graphic novels featuring French writer Léo Malet's popular hard-boiled detective, *Nestor Burma*.

Topffer, Rodolphe (1799–1846) *(Artist/Writer)*

Swiss artist **Topffer** can justifiably claim to be the man who invented comics. In 1827, Topffer wrote and drew his *Histoire de M. Vieutboix*, the first modern comic strip, using panels and cinematic storytelling techniques. Because of its revolutionary nature, it was not published until 1837. Meanwhile, Topffer wrote the novel *Docteur Festus* (which features a proto-"Lost World"), and then drew his own graphic adaptation which he published separately. Its success encouraged him to draw *M. Cryptogame* (1830), *M. Jabot* (1831), *M. Pencil* (1831), and, later, *M. Crépin* (1837) and *Histoire de Jacques* (1844). Topffer not only created comics but studied and defined them in articles and reviews. Of his work, he said: "The art without the text would be obscure; the text without the art would be meaningless."

Uderzo, Albert (1927–) *(Artist/Writer)*

Uderzo's career as a comic artist really took off after World War II with a number of humorous historical series such as *Flamberge*, *Arys Buck*, and *Belloy*. In 1952, he met writer René **Goscinny** and, together, they created *Jehan Pistolet* and *Luc Junior*. But their first success was the proto-*Astérix* tale of an American Indian, *Oumpah-Pah*, created for *Tintin* in 1958. In 1959, Uderzo, Goscinny, and **Charlier** founded the magazine *Pilote*, for which Uderzo co-created *Astérix* (with Goscinny) and *Michel Tanguy* (with Charlier). *Astérix* quickly became the most successful French-language comics series since *Tintin*. Since Goscinny's death in 1977, Uderzo has continued *Astérix* alone.

Van Hamme, Jean (1939–) *(Writer)*

Belgian writer and novelist whose comics career began in the late 1960s when he co-created a number of adventure series (mostly for *Tintin*) such as *Arlequin*, *Domino*, *Tony Stark*, and the genre series *Epoxy* (with **Cuvelier**) and *Mr. Magellan* (with **Geri**). His best-known genre creation, however, was the popular *Thorgal* series, with Rosinski. With Rosinski, he produced the remarkable graphic novel, *Le Grand Pouvoir du Chninkel* (*The Chninkel's Great Power*), and with **Griffo**, a two-volume political fiction, *SOS Bonheur* (*SOS Happiness*). In the 1980s, Van Hamme co-created two hugely successful series, both thrillers dealing in political and international intrigues: *XIII* (with William Vance) and *Largo Winch* (with Francq). Van Hamme has also written for the cinema, including *Diva* (1980) for Jean-Jacques Beinex and *Meurtres à Domicile* (*Murders At Home*, 1982) based on a novel by Thomas **Owen**.

Vernal, Jean-Luc (1944–) *(Writer)*

A former journalist, **Vernal** joined the editorial team of *Tintin* in 1976, where he wrote *Jugurtha* for **Hermann** and, later, **Franz**. He eventually became *Tintin*'s last editor-in-chief, from 1979 to 1988. His genre series include *Cranach De Morganloup* with **Convard**, and *Ian Kalédine* with **Ferry**. He is also the writer of *Bran— Légende Née Des Tourbillons Des Vents Du Nord* (*Bran—Legend Born Out of the Gales of the North Wind*).

Vernes, Henri (Dewisme, Charles-Henri) (1918–) *(Writer)*

Writer of *Bob Morane* and *Karga*.

Vicq (Raymond, Antoine) (1936-1987) *(Writer)*

Prolific Belgian writer who wrote numerous humor series for *Spirou* and *Tintin* in the 1960s and 1970s, including *Korrigan* for **Franz**, *Sophie* for **Jidehem**, *Pegg* for **Mallet**, *La Ribambelle* for Roba, *Taka Takata* for Azara, etc.

Wasterlain, Marc (1946–) *(Artist/Writer)*

An alumnus of **Peyo**'s studio, **Wasterlain** worked on *Les Schtroumpfs* (*The Smurfs*) and *Benoît Brisefer* before creating his own, whimsical series, *Docteur Poche*, in 1976 for *Spirou*. Other creations include *Gil et Georges* for *Okapi*, *Jeanette Pointu* for *Spirou*, and the graphic novel *La Planète des Clowns* (*Clown Planet*).

Weinberg, Albert (1922–) *(Artist/Writer)*

After assisting Victor Hubinon and **Jijé**, **Weinberg** joined the editorial team of *Tintin* in 1950, for which he created two science fiction series, the remarkable *Alain Landier* and *Dan Cooper*. After a few episodes, the latter took a mundane turn and became a regular adventure series. From 1949 to 1956, he wrote and drew *Luc Condor* and *Roc Météor* for *Heroic-Albums*. Weinberg still works on *Dan Cooper* today.

Will (Maltaite, Willy) (1927–2000) *(Artist)*

Will was a colleague of **Jijé** and one of the first artists to join the editorial team of *Spirou* in 1948. He took over *Tif et Tondu* from Dineur, and worked on it regularly until 1991. He also assisted **Peyo** on *Benoît Brisefer* and **Franquin** on *Spirou*. His other genre series is the whimsical fantasy, *Isabelle*, co-created with **Franquin**, **Delporte**, and Macherot. His son, Éric Maltaite, is also an artist.

Yann (Le Pennetier, Yann) (1954–) *(Writer)*

With **Conrad**, **Yann** is one of the young cartoonists who revolutionized *Spirou* in the 1980s, with series such as *Les Innommables* (*The Unmentionables*). Together, they also produced an hilarious parody of *Bob Morane* entitled *Bob Marone*. Yann has also written *Freddy Lombard* for **Chaland**, *Yoyo* for Le Gall, and *Les Trois Cheveux Blancs* (*The Three White Hairs*, 1993) for **Hausman**. He recently took over the writing of the new adventures of *Le Marsupilami*. Under the pseudonym of "Balac," he wrote the remarkable historical saga *Sambre* with Hislaire.

BOOK 2

*Science Fiction,
Fantasy, Horror and
Pulp Fiction in Literature*

Preamble

When embarking on any study about fantasy and science fiction in literature, it is often customary to start with an attempt to define these genres.

In French, the word *"fantastique"* carries with it a much larger definition, or "semantic field," than its approximate English equivalent, which would be "fantasy." Because it is easy to lose oneself in complex arguments about definitions, and about what belongs to the genre and what does not, we subscribe to Pierre **Gripari**'s simple definition: "The *fantastique* is everything that is not rational."

Within this definition, science fiction can be viewed, as Belgian writer Jacques **Sternberg** once did, as nothing more than a *succursale* (*branch*) of the *fantastique*. However, while recognizing that Sternberg has a point, we shall nevertheless treat science fiction as a wholly separate genre from the *fantastique*, and not as a mere subset. We do this because we believe that, from their very inceptions, the two genres, *fantastique* and science fiction, reflected two sharply different literary objectives on the part of their writers, as well as filled two sharply different literary needs from the standpoint of their readers.

For the purpose of this book, we shall construe as *fantastique* all of that which appeals to the heart, to the emotions, to the soul. The *fantastique* relies on irrational beliefs, a sense of the marvelous (*merveilleux*). It stems from faith: faith in established religions as well as in folkloric legends, faith in ancient or modern myths, such as what is commonly known as the occult or, more accurately, what the French dub *ésotérisme* (*esoterica*), meaning that which is hidden, occult, obscure, or secret. Faith traditionally opposes science and material progress, which science fiction naturally embraces and advocates.

Like religion, the *fantastique*, whether expressed through the forms of drama, poetry, or fables, first helped medieval people begin to illuminate the fearsome darkness in which they lived, before the age of humanism and "enlightenment."

Its lighter, more baroque side, mutated into the *merveilleux*: fairy tales which evolved into 19th-century classic fantasy and high fantasy, its romantic, symbolic and surrealistic variants, and later, modern-day heroic-fantasy and sword and sorcery, often following the Anglo-Saxon templates borrowed from J. R. R. Tolkien and Robert E. Howard.

The darker side of the *fantastique* evolved into gothic literature, the *romans noirs* and *romans frénétiques*, as well as occult literature and other forms of "classic" *fantastique*, before ultimately branching out into modern horror (*Horreur* and *Angoisse*) and supernatural fiction. A literary tradition which began following in the footsteps of E.T.A. Hoffman and Edgar Allan Poe eventually produced a rich catalog of authors ranging from the popular, such as Gaston **Leroux** and Marcel **Aymé** in France and Jean **Ray** in Belgium, to the highly literate, such as Michel de **Ghelderode** and Alain **Robbe-Grillet**.

Science fiction, on the other hand, and unlike the *fantastique*, appeals to the head, the intellect, and the mind. Its true roots lie with humanism, the Renaissance, and the 18th-century *Esprit des Lumières* (*Enlightenment*). It is, ultimately, based on logic, on science, and on testing hypotheses. Science fiction, even when used as a social allegory, which it often is, always relies on a shared pretense of verisimilitude between the writer and his reader.

Science fiction started with the Utopias of the 16th century, which eventually turned into the *Voyages Extraordinaires* (*Extraordinary Voyages*), a subset of literature eventually popularized by the great master himself, Jules **Verne**. Verne single-handedly launched modern science fiction by combining the Extraordinary Voyages with scientific anticipation, and was soon widely imitated. The formula devised by Verne, rather than the more sophisticated one used by H. G. Wells, was the template borrowed by Hugo Gernsback (1884–1967), the Luxembourg-born father of American science fiction.

But Verne's impact on science fiction was not entirely positive. Scholars have observed that because he was published and characterized as a writer of juvenile novels, the genre itself became tarred with that brush in the eye of the critics and the literary establishment. Because of the dominance of realism imposed by 19th-century values, and the French literary establishment's rejection of science and progress, the growth of French science fiction, unlike that of its American counterpart, became somewhat stunted, often relegated to the province of juvenile entertainment.

Yet, in spite of this, the genre flourished in the 1920s and 1930s, which are, in the eyes of many, the true golden age of French science fiction. In the United States, *Amazing Stories* was created in 1928 and *Astounding Science Fiction* in 1930. Yet, in France, between the wars, magazines like *Sciences & Voyages*, *Je Sais Tout*, *Lectures pour Tous*, and others like them published authors such as J.-H. **Rosny** Aîné, Maurice **Renard**, etc., who easily surpassed their English-speaking colleagues in imagination, maturity, and sophistication.

The year 1950 represented an important dividing line in the history of science fiction and, to a lesser extent, the *fantastique*, in French literature. In that year, American science fiction began to be translated and published in France on a regular basis. Publishing imprints such as *Le Rayon Fantastique* (est. in 1951) and *Présence du Futur* (est. in 1954), and magazines like *Fiction* (the French edition of *F & SF*, est. in 1953), changed the nature of the genre, dramatically and virtually overnight,

Until then, French science fiction had been slowly developing a specific and unique voice. However, the publication in the early 1950s, in one fell swoop, of American masterpieces by writers such as Isaac Asimov, A. E. Van Vogt, Ray Bradbury, and others delivered French science fiction a blow from which it took almost twenty years to recover.

Today, however, one can firmly state that science fiction, fantasy and horror are healthier in France than in any other western country outside of the United States.

It is often too common to hear American and even British pundits deplore the state of science fiction outside the English-speaking world. It must be said that such statements arise out of ignorance, fostered in the most part by the inability to process information written in another language, and perhaps by a lack of curiosity from the part of Americans and a lack of proselytism on the part of the French.

If quantity alone is a yardstick of health, French science fiction can be said to be very healthy, with no less than several imprints putting out half-a-dozen novels by native French writers *every month,* and several magazines as well. (And this does not include juvenile novels and genre works published in more mainstream imprints.) This represents an output of well over a hundred new works each year, certainly unmatched in Italy, Spain, Germany (excluding *Perry Rhodan*), Scandinavia, and other European nations.

Quality is, of course, a more subjective argument. Yet, contemporary French science fiction, fantasy and horror, whether from the 1960s, 1970s, 1980s, or 1990s, boasts many talented voices, fully equal to those of their American counterparts.

These, then, are our terms of reference, the literary canvas against which we propose to paint the history of French *fantastique* and science fiction.

It should be understood that, throughout this book, we use the word French in the sense of French-language, that is to say, including Belgian, Swiss, and French-Canadian works and/or authors. We have, however, strived to identify non French-national works and/or authors whenever possible.

No project of this type is ever perfect, or complete. We have tried to be as comprehensive as possible, up to and including the year 1997. Nevertheless, in a book of this scope, no matter how careful one is, omissions are bound to creep in, as well as the occasional mistake. We will be grateful to anyone pointing out such errors or omissions to us, for future reference and inclusion in subsequent reprints.

Finally, an editorial note: Throughout this book, the authors whose names are printed in **bold** type are the subject of separate bibliographical entries in our Authors' Bibliographies in Chapter XI.

On Writing and Publishing Science Fiction in France and the United States: Excerpts from an Interview with Pierre Barbat

Pierre Barbet is one of the few contemporary French science fiction authors to have been regularly translated in the United States. His historical fantasies such as Baphomet's Meteor, The Enchanted Planet, *and* Games Psyborgs Play, *were published by DAW books in the late 1970s. Barbet (his real name was Claude Avice but he also used the pseudonyms of David Maine and Olivier Sprigel) was born in 1925 in Le Mans. By profession he was a Doctor of Pharmacy. His silver-haired grace and gentility was a welcome presence at science fiction conventions around the world. He was also a positive force behind the scenes in the promotion of French science fiction to the English-language market. Pierre Barbet passed away in 1995. These comments are excerpted from an interview granted to Jean-Marc Lofficier in 1977, a transitional period when French science fiction was still heavily politicized and was looking for new avenues to explore. The full interview appeared in the Canadian fanzine* Asterisks *No. 10.*

I am wont to compare science fiction to a tree with many branches. There is not only heroic fantasy and historical fiction, but also classical space opera. Some writers have specialized in science fantasy, or heroic-fantasy, without totally abandoning science fiction. A good example of this in France is Kurt **Steiner**, who writes both good science fiction and good science fantasy. Now must be added speculative and political fiction. All these branches co-exist and have their own readers. New branches will no doubt burgeon because science fiction is an extremely vital literary form.

French science fiction has a flavor all of its own in the field of polemics: There is a whole range of French science fiction which deals with the themes of destruction and anarchy. As far as I can gather, particularly from the American publishers, the New Wave did not have as weighty an impact in the USA as we were led to believe here in France. However, in France, it had a far greater success, and certain imprints have published many works in that political vein. But I don't think that any of these are particularly apt for the international market. I don't think that these French novels would have any great impact abroad. Besides, there are

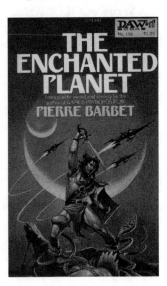

very few French novels abroad. I believe one must either confine oneself to those areas derived exclusively from French literature by taking up in the heroic-fantasy mold traditional themes of French fantasy or, alternatively, launching into political fiction concerned with present-day problems in the speculative fiction manner, but seen from the French angle.

It is easy to write such "futurology" and make it happen on a distant planet. After all, that's all **Voltaire** did in his novella, *Micromegas*; he looked for escapism. But just because a story is taking place on another planet does not mean that one cannot deal with a futuristic problem absolutely the same as the problems that face us today. It is, perhaps, a little more interesting, for some, to read stories set amongst the stars but, generally, when one writes a book of political or speculative fiction, it is set on Earth in the not too distant future.

French "classics" like J.-H. **Rosny** Aîné might have a chance of reaching the American audience. But, to my way of thinking, other French authors have nothing really new to bring to the American market. The American market is a businessman's market: When they buy a novel, it's because they expect a return on their money through sufficient sales. If one gave them a French novel or space opera of the anarchic type, they would get scarcely any return, it would not work. But heroic fantasy about French literary problems or historical fiction specifically about French problems would interest the American reader because he could recognize it as being something "French." I think there is always a certain level of success assured to French themes, but one could not go as far as to say that they advance literature, my own works included. My historical fiction is amusing, but little more than that. The same goes for heroic fantasy; if I write of *Mélusine*, or *Huon of Bordeaux*, it may be interesting and pleasant to read, but to say that it advances literature one jot is quite another matter. When I was young, I read Jules **Verne** and H.G. Wells, and after having been cut off from all science fiction during the war, René **Barjavel**'s *Ravage* and *Le Voyageur Imprudent* (*The Careless Traveller*), which opened up a whole new vista, the discovery of what a writer

could achieve with science fiction. I had to wait a long time for translations of the anglophone "greats" and also before we had caught up with them due to the complete cessation of production of French science fiction during the war. It was this that spurred me on to write science fiction myself. When I read the first of the American translations in the *Rayon Fantastique* imprint in 1951, I said to myself, "I could write like that" and offered my first manuscript to their publisher, Gallimard, who accepted it. My favorite authors remain Americans: I like Alfred Bester very much, and Isaac Asimov and A. E. Van Vogt. In France, Gérard **Klein** particularly interests me. In Poland, Stanislaw Lem and in Romania, Vladimir Colin.

Through science fiction conventions, it is of the greatest importance to have close contacts with authors from all countries to ensure that one's own production might be readable on a world scale. Contact with French fandom is easily established through conventions, where one can meet many young science fiction fans. There is a small science fiction circle in Grenoble, a similar one in the region around Marseilles, but, of course, in Paris, we are luckier since both publishers and writers can meet on Mondays and discuss our problems.

As far as Europe is concerned, the European Convention is an excellent opportunity to establish contacts in all the European countries, including Eastern Europe, from which we get little information, to have open discussions with other authors and to find out what interests them and the publishers. Worldcons are also very stimulating. I went to the Toronto World Convention and the European convention held in Poznan, Poland [in 1976]. The difference was obvious: American fandom is far richer than its French counterpart. Their material means are not as slender as ours, they are better organized and there are more of them, proportionately, to raise funds for the conventions. What we lack are funds. As regards the Eastern countries, at Poznan, none of the fans could come; we saw only technicians there, i.e. publishers, critics, writers, but hardly any fans—only those who lived nearby.

CHAPTER I

The Middle Ages (1100–1500)

French language, and therefore French literature, first took form in the Middle Ages.

After the Roman Conquest, the Gaul dialects gave way to Latin, which evolved into a number of Romance languages, and eventually into something called "Old French."

It is worth noting that this development was not uniform. The language remained divided into the *langue d'oil*, employed in Northern France, and the *langue d'oc*, employed in Southern France. (These terms derived from their respective expressions for "yes.") As Northern France became politically dominant, so did the *langue d'oil*, even though the *langue d'oc* did not entirely disappear, and still survives today as *Provençal* (or Occitan).

The first texts written in Old French appeared during the reign of Emperor Charlemagne (742-814). It was under Charlemagne's rule that the feudal ideals of knightly behavior—courtesy, generosity, modesty, loyalty to one's liege, consideration for the weak—first took root. Charlemagne was a great warrior-king, fighting for Christendom against the Saracens. His reign was a time of unique political stability and economic prosperity. Finally, Charlemagne encouraged scholars and writers. All these factors combined to foster a legend-making process which gave birth to French literature.

As for the *fantastique*, it was virtually defined in the Middle Ages. This was a time when the supernatural was perceived as something perhaps to be preferably avoided, but still not outrageous or unbelievable. It was during the Middle Ages that the old Celtic, Frankish, and Germanic myths were translated from the cultural sphere more commonly associated with religion (implying serious belief and worship) into that of popular folklore (implying belief but not worship).

The Catholic Church, as the dominant religion of the times, made sure that the old myths, since they could not be totally eradicated, would remain just that: folklore, the latter being obviously less important than religion. In some

cases, such as the Arthurian Romances, the Church even ensured that the myths were redressed in Christian trappings.

Finally, the Middle Ages were the period during which all the various tales dealings with supernatural concepts such as angels, demons, fairies, witches and warlocks, etc. were consolidated, unified, and given modern form. Concepts and characters such as Mélusine, Harlequin, Oberon, Morgan Le Fey, etc. which are, today, considered an integral part of fantasy, were first given their definitive shapes at the time.

For purposes of convenience, we have divided medieval French literature into four sub-genres:

1. The *Chansons de Geste (Songs of Deeds)*

The *Chansons de Geste* were poetic sagas that began as "oral literature," that is to say, they were sung by wandering minstrels and troubadours, and were an integral part of a vast oral tradition. Starting around the 12th century, they were eventually committed to paper by pious monks working in monastic libraries. About a hundred *Chansons de Geste* are known to have existed. Most dealt with knightly epics, courtly love, and the miracle-filled lives of the saints (see **Religious Drama** below).

One of the earliest and most deservedly famous *Chanson de Geste* was *La Chanson de Roland* (*The Song of Roland*, c. 1100), which told of the desperate fight of Knight Roland, Charlemagne's own son, against the Saracens, and his eventual doom in the Pyrenean mountain pass of Roncevaux, after having been betrayed by the evil Ganelon. In reality, historical evidence would suggest that Roland was ambushed by Basque brigands, but no minstrel ever let truth stand in the way of a great song!

La Chanson de Roland, like most *Chansons de Geste*,

contained its usual array of supernatural phenomena: celestial visitations, etc. However, it was memorable in that it featured the first, invulnerable magical blade, Roland's sword, Durandal, as well as Roland's magical horn, Oliphant. Heroic fantasy fans may recall that British author Michael Moorcock sent his famous hero, Elric of Melniboné, to Roncevaux to collect Durandal. *La Chanson de Roland* was first "translated" into modern French in 1837 by Francisque **Michel**. Numerous editions and revisions followed, by Francis Génin (1850), Léon Gautier (1872), Petit de Julleville (1878), Léon Clédat (1886), Gaston Paris (1887), etc. One of the best modern-language editions of was Joseph **Bédier**'s (1922, revised 1937).

By the 12th century, as Old French came into being, formally educated poets started expanding their repertoire by using dramas drawn either from "classic" (i.e.: Roman or Greek) sources, but also, more interestingly, from Celtic or Germanic legends, imported into France by other scholars. (The fact that Latin was still the *lingua franca* of the literary elite greatly facilitated international communication.) In these new songs, Christian miracles were replaced with pagan ones.

One such epic was the popular *Le Roman de Tristan et Iseult* (*The Novel of Tristan Isolde*), which made its first appearance circa 1170 and became an overnight success. (Joseph Bédier also provided a modern-language edition of *Le Roman de Tristan et Iseult*.) Another natural candidate for the epic treatment was the life-story of King Arthur of Britain, adapted from Geoffrey of Monmouth's 1136 historical tome, *History of the Kings of Britain*.

The most important French poet of the times was **Chrétien de Troyes**, who became the virtual founder of Arthurian romance. Chrétien de Troyes had already produced a number of more conventional works, such as *Erec et Enide*, *Cligès* (which used the *Tristan and Isolde* motif), etc. His first Arthurian saga was *Lancelot, ou Le Chevalier à la Charette* (*Lancelot, or the Knight with a Cart*; c. 1177), which related how brave knight Lancelot rescued beautiful Queen Guinevere. Lancelot's success eventually led Chrétien de Troyes to write his masterpiece, *Perceval, ou le Conte du Graal* (*Perceval, or the Tale of the Grail*, c. 1182).

In *Perceval*, the eponymous character was a brave but innocent knight, who discovered the accursed land of the *Roi Pêcheur* (*Fisher King*), who was the guardian of the Grail, and suffered from a mysterious wound that would not heal. Perceval could have healed the King and become the Grail's guardian, but missed his opportunity.

Few people today realize that, in its original version, *Perceval* was not a Christian work. The Grail was not yet "holy," and bore no relation to the latter version of the cup used by Joseph of Arimathea to gather Christ's blood. Instead, *Perceval* drew on a variety of pagan myths and symbols. Some were clearly Celtic in nature and echoed druidic ceremonies; others were more obscure. Some scholars have theorized that *Perceval* contained Greek Mythology (i.e.,

the Mysteries of Eleusis) and even Middle-Eastern (i.e., the cult of Mithra) esoteric influences.

In 1215, the Roman Catholic Church held its Council of Lateran, which formally established the dogma of the Eucharist—Christ's flesh and blood being mystically present in the wafer host and wine taken during the Holy Communion. It certainly was no coincidence that, at the same time, Robert de **Boron**, elaborating on Chrétien de Troyes' work, tied together the Arthurian legends of Lancelot and Perceval, and placed them firmly within a Christian context. It was de Boron, and not Chrétien de Troyes, who established the now well-known origins of the "Holy" Grail, with Joseph of Arimathea and the blood of Christ. He also added the characters of Lancelot, King Arthur, Merlin, Morgan Le Fey, etc. and, more generally, gave the entire saga the form that we know today.

Between 1215 and 1235, de Boron published five books: *Histoire du Saint-Graal* (*The Story of the Holy Grail*), *Histoire de Merlin* (*The Story of Merlin*), *Le Livre de Lancelot du Lac* (*The Book of Lancelot of the Lake*), *La Quête du Saint-Graal* (*The Quest for the Holy Grail*), and *La Mort du Roi Arthu* (*The Death of King Arthur*). These books formed the basis for all subsequent Arthurian legends, including the later retelling by Sir Thomas Malory (?-1471).

Among other *Chansons de Geste* told and/or written during the 13th century, there were three which include strong genre elements and deserve to be mentioned here because of the archetypes they established for later works of fantasy:

The first was *Huon de Bordeaux*, an anonymous epic in which Huon, one of Charlemagne's proud knights, met the fairy king Aubéron, whom Shakespeare would later turn into Oberon for *A Midsummer Night's Dream*, and who was described there as the son of Julius Cesar and Morgan Le Fey. Cesar was, clearly, a great, almost magical emperor from a long-buried past. As to Morgan, she was originally a fairy queen named Morgue, whose origins predated that of the Arthurian legends. Aubéron gave Huon a magic ring, and a magic horn which enabled him to summon the legions of fairyland. Huon fought an evil Saracen sorcerer-king, and eventually freed and married the beautiful Esclarmonde.

Amadas et Ydoine, another anonymous epic, was a tale of thwarted love between Ydoine, betrothed to the Count of Nevers, and her brave lover, Amadas. It featured witches and sorcery aplenty, and the mysterious character of the Maufé, who was either the Devil himself, or one of his agents. The Maufé (a deformation of the French "*mauvais*" meaning bad, evil) was not like the crude and grotesque devils depicted until then in **Religious Dramas**. He was, on the contrary, a seductive, clever, charismatic character, imbued with evil supernatural powers, but bound by certain rules. The Maufé was the model for all subsequent "Prince of Darkness" types, from Faust's Mephistopheles to the devil character played by Jules Berry in the classic film *Les Visiteurs du Soir* (see Book 1, Chapter I).

Le Paradis de la Reine Sybille (*Queen Sybil's Paradise*; c. 1200), credited to Antoine de la **Salle**, told the story of a knight who discovered a hidden fairyland, ruled by the beautiful Queen Sybil. The Queen and her maidens were succubae of some kind—they periodically turned into snakes. As was often the case in such legends, the Knight could leave the kingdom only on certain days. Eventually, he did leave, but the memories of the sexual delights he experienced proved too great a temptation, and he chose to return to Queen Sybil's paradise, thereby losing his eternal soul. *Le Paradis de la Reine Sybille* was the model for numerous, similar tales, including Richard Wagner's *Tannhauser*. It also most clearly and emphatically condemned the pleasures of the flesh—more evidence of the "Christianization" of the old legends.

The *Chansons de Geste* survived throughout the centuries and, in various modernized versions, are still on French bookshelves today. Chrétien de Troyes and Robert de Boron's Arthurian stories are available in modern retellings by Jacques **Boulenger** (*Les Romans de la Table Ronde* [*Novels of the Round Table*]), Jean **Markalé** (*Merlin l'Enchanteur* [*Wizard Merlin*] and *Le Graal* [*The Grail*]) and even in a five-volume juvenile version by François **Johan**.

The Huon de Bordeaux story, as well as numerous others, were collected in a remarkable series of books, the **Contes et Légendes** (*Tales and Legends*) imprint, written by various authors and still in print today. They have also been retold in modern form by François **Suard**.

Finally, other Arthurian novels, such as *Méliador* by famous historian Jean **Froissart**, *Méraugis de Portlesguez* by Raoul de **Houdenc**, *La Demoiselle à la Mule* (*The Lady with a Mule*) by Païën de Maisières, *Perlesvaus, Le Livre de Caradoc* (*The Book of Caradoc*), *Le Chevalier à l'Épée* (*The Knight with a Sword*), *Hunbaut, L'Atre Périlleux* (*The Perilous Hearth*), *Gliglois, Le Roman de Jaufré* (*The Novel of Jaufre*), *Blandin de Cornouaille* (*Blandin of Cornwall*), *Les Merveilles de Rigomer* (*The Wonders of Rigomer*), and *Le Chevalier au Papegau* (*The Knight with the Papegau*), and others have been collected in *La Légende Arthurienne*, a remarkable anthology prepared by Danielle **Régnier-Bohler**.

Film adaptations included **Les Chevaliers de la Table Ronde** (*The Knights of the Round Table*) (see Book 1, Chapter I), as well as a television version, **Lancelot Du Lac** (see Book 1, Chapter II).

2. The *Fabliaux (Fables)*

Another aspect of French medieval literature were the *Fabliaux*, satirical fables which relied on the tradition well-established by Aesop of using anthropomorphic animals in order to poke fun at, or criticize, the world's various ills.

The most famous of these *Fabliaux* was, without a doubt, the *Roman de Renart* (*The Novel of Reynart*). It chronicled the feud between sly Renart (or Renard in modern French, i.e.: the fox) and his rival, the loutish wolf, Ysengrin. The animals were portrayed as inhabiting Man's world—Renart stole chickens from human farmers—but also as having a medieval society of their own, ruled by the benevolent King Noble the lion. In *Renart*, the animals all were noblemen, usually barons, and it went without saying that they all were Roman Catholics.

Renart himself was a consummate con artist, totally devoid of scruples yet not without roguish charm. He periodically landed himself in trouble, was caught, tried, condemned, escaped, fled to his castle (Maupertuis), was besieged by his enemies, but, every time, he managed to outwit his foes and came out on top. Through ruse and betrayal, he even usurped Noble's throne when the king was away, fighting a Saracen army composed of camels, elephants, and other exotic animals.

Le Roman de Renart was attributed to poet Pierre de **Saint-Cloud**, who chronicled the first Renart-Ysengrin battles circa 1175. But other writers soon jumped into the act and Renart's saga grew to epic proportions. By the 14th century, *Le Roman de Renart* included over 30 "branches."

Le Roman de Renart was first assembled and put into coherent form by D. M. **Méon**, using manuscripts from the 13th, 14th, and 15th centuries, preserved in the Royal Library and published in a four-volume edition in 1826. There also was a three-volume edition published by Ernest Martin in 1881-1887. a more modern, and fairly definitive, edition is Léopold **Chauveau**'s 315-page volume.

Le Roman de Renart has the honor of being the basis for one of the very first animated features ever made (see Book 1, Chapter IV).

3. Poetry

French medieval poetry was lyrical, elegant, and full

of allegorical meanings. As such, it often employed the supernatural as a mean of literary artifice. The famous *Le Roman de la Rose* (*The Romance of the Rose*; c. 1230), by Guillaume de **Lorris**, which celebrated courtly love, depicted a young couple venturing into a dream-country where the plucking of a rose symbolized an amorous victory. (It was later completed by Jean de **Meung** in the 14th century.)

Lesser-known works, such as the Celtic ballads of Marie de **France** (c. 1170), were filled with fantasy: *Lanval* featured a fairy queen; *Yonec*, a lover who turned into a bird (an earlier version of what would likely become the inspiration for *L'Oiseau Bleu* [*The Blue Bird*]); *Milon*, an enchanted ring; *Eliduc*, a magic potion. Marie de France—who may be a composite of several poets—was likely the first artist to have sung the magical doom of Ys, a mythical city off the coast of Brittany which was reputed to have sunk in the 5th century. (See Book 1, Chapter II for two television adaptations of this legend.)

Le Jeu de la Feuillée (*The Game of the Leaves*; c. 1275) by Adam de la **Halle** was an epic poem which also featured fairy creatures and introduced the character of King Hellequin, patterned after a Germanic storm god. Hellequin was the Lord of the Wild Hunt, the Master of Spells. In the 14th century, Dante (1265-1321) took the character and renamed him Harlequin. In the original poem, Hellequin was madly in love with Morgue the fairy—again, the Morgan Le Fey or Fata Morgana of later incarnations.

In the anonymous *Le Livre de la Fontaine Périlleuse* (*The Book of the Perilous Fountain*, c. 1425), a young man sought the Fountain of Life. When he peered into its waters, an arm made of fire came out and stabbed him. In order to be cured, he had to undergo a series of mystic tests. The poem was demonstrably written as an allegory of the alchemical *Grand Oeuvre* (*Great Work*), and the young protagonist eventually found enlightenment when he discovered and worshipped the "hermetic sun." This was one of the first recorded literary works in which the frontier between the occult and fantasy was easily crossed.

The famous fairy queen *Mélusine* (also known as *Ondine*) took modern form in Jehan d'**Arras**' 1475 poem. One day of every week, the lovely bride Mélusine sought isolation in order to revert to her natural form. She begged her husband, Raimondin de Lusignan, to not try to find out her secret. Unfortunately, he did and discovered that his wife was half-human, half-reptile. This cost poor Mélusine her soul. She was forced to turn back into a winged serpent and fly away.

4. Religious Dramas

Classic Roman and Greek theater had all but vanished after the fall of Rome. Serious drama was reborn during the Middle Ages, somewhat surprisingly, within the folds of the Catholic Church, which sponsored religious dramatizations of the life of Jesus or of the Saints, called *Mystères* (*Mysteries*) or *Miracles*, performed at Easter and Christmas times.

The Mysteries and Miracles were first performed in Latin, then in Old French. They often took several days to perform, and included spectacular stage effects. Among the most noted plays performed during the 12th, 13th, and 14th centuries were: *Le Jeu d'Adam* (*Play of Adam*); *La Résurrection du Sauveur* (*Our Savior's Resurrection*); *Le Jeu de Saint Nicolas* (*Play of Saint Nicolas*) by Jean Bodel d'Arras; the monumental *Le Mystère de la Passion* (*Mystery of the Passion*, or *Passion Play*), which took four days to perform, by Arnoul Gréban, organist and choirmaster at Notre-Dame; *Les Miracles de Théophile* (*Theophile's Miracles*), which contained an early variation of the Faust theme; *Les Miracles de Notre-Dame* (*Miracles of Notre-Dame*) by Gautier de Coincy; and others.

Religious drama was eventually codified into a series of prose stories purported to be the "true stories" of the lives of the Saints, which became known as *La Légende Dorée* (*The Golden Legends*). Like *Le Roman de Renart*, the texts which comprised *La Légende Dorée* were eventually gathered and collected c.1264 by the Dominican monk Jacques de **Voragine**, aka Jacques de Varazze, who later became Archbishop of Genoa. They were translated into French in 1900 by the Abbot Roze in a modern edition which is still in print today.

Jacques de Voragine
La Légende Dorée
*
GF-Flammarion

CHAPTER II

The Renaissance (1500–1650)

The 16th century was marked by the emergence of new ideas and literary trends, often as a reaction against what was perceived as the "obscurantism" of the Middle Ages.

Among the factors which contributed to the Renaissance were: (i) the discoveries of new continents by Christopher Columbus (1451-1506), Vasco da Gama (1460-1524), Magellan (1480-1521), Verrazano (1485-1528) and Jacques Cartier (1491-1557), which offered new imaginary vistas in which to locate stories; (ii) the scientific and technical discoveries of scientists such as Copernicus (1473-1543) and Ambroise **Paré** (1517-1590); and, finally, (iii) Gutenberg's (1390-1468) discovery of the printing press c. 1450, which made the greater circulation of literary works possible.

After the fall of Constantinople in 1453, Greek intellectuals moved to Italy, which quickly became the cultural center of the Renaissance, drawing talent from all over Europe. From the Latin word *humanitas* (*culture*) then came the humanists, who taught humanism, a school of thought based on the ancient Greco-Roman ideals of wisdom, tolerance, and rational thought. One of foremost humanists of the times was philosopher Erasmus (1467-1536) who, although born in Holland, spent a considerable amount of time in France.

The Renaissance bloomed in France during the reign of King François 1st (1494-1547). As Charlemagne had done before, François 1st created a favorable environment for the development of letters, arts, and sciences. He founded several scientific colleges, attracted foreign artists, such as Leonardo da Vinci (1452-1519), to the French Court and, more generally, gave a seal of official tolerance towards the publication of the new philosophy.

It was during the French Renaissance that proto-science fiction first split away from the *fantastique*. The thirst for learning combined with a natural sense of optimism in science and progress to produce the Utopias.

It was also during the Renaissance that the traditional *fantastique* derived from myths, legends, and folklore also split into two forms: one which continued the poetic tradition of the Middle Ages and eventually led to the *Merveilleux* (*Marvelous*) and the *Contes de Fées* (*Fairy Tales*), and the other, the darker side of the same literary coin, dealing with witchcraft, devil worship, sorcery and, generally speaking, all matters pertaining to the occult.

1. The Utopias

The invention of the first Utopia has been credited to British writer Sir Thomas More (1478-1535) who, inspired by Erasmus, wrote *The Utopia* in 1516 in Latin. In it, a Portuguese sailor returned from his journeys and described the perfect, humanistic society he discovered on the Island of Utopia. Even though More's *Utopia* was translated into French in 1550 (and in English only in 1551!), it clearly inspired French writer François **Rabelais,** who, in a unique literary cross-over, chose to locate several of his stories in the same island.

Rabelais was a scholar, a humanist, a physician, and a writer. His works constituted an extraordinary blend of political and sociological satire, extraordinary voyages, pre-Utopia utopias, and heroic-fantasy quests. His literally larger-than-life, colorful characters with "gargantuan" appetites were also literary archetypes that spawned many imitations. Rabelais, a former monk who had studied medicine, strongly believed that Man's body and spirit should be freed from medieval restrictions. He trusted nature and progress, and saw unlimited horizons ahead for mankind. This, combined with his vivid imagination and prodigious sense of satire, led him to create an array of imaginary lands and societies which remains, today, among the most complex ever devised in imaginary literature.

Furthermore, Rabelais' fantastic worlds were not places serving only satirical or comparative purposes, i.e., designed to be contrasted by the reader with the real society of the time. They also contained clearly drawn speculative statements about the future, making him the first proto-science fiction author in French literature.

For example, Rabelais' masterpieces, *Pantagruel* (1532) and *Gargantua* (1534), about the adventures of two giant kings—Gargantua was King of the Dipsodes and Pantagruel's father—mentioned a trip to the Moon, advanced surgical techniques (such as organ grafts), advanced military tactics (such as fortifications, deep sea diving), as well as more fantastic concepts, such as that of miniaturization *à la Fantastic Voyage*. On another level, the gigantism of Gargantua and Pantagruel was not only literal, but allegorical. For Rabelais, mankind itself was the giant ready to awaken. In this, he anticipated Jonathan Swift (1667-1745), Olaf Stapledon (1886-1950), and, closer to modern times, Frank Herbert.

With the Reformation and its ensuing series of civil wars, including the infamous massacre of St. Bartholomew's day in 1572, the political climate changed during the second half of the 16th century; religious and political intolerance gained new ground, and Rabelais' works were forbidden. Even though his *Third* (1546), *Fourth* (1548-52) and *Fifth* (published posthumously in 1564 and of dubious authenticity) *Books* were much "safer" politically, they nevertheless caused their author many problems, even forcing him into internal exile for a while. From a science fiction standpoint, however, these later works remained interesting because, in them, Rabelais developed the literary device of the *Voyage Imaginaire* (*Imaginary Journey*) to a heretofore unprecedented extent.

Borrowing from a tradition going back to Homer's *Odyssey*, and inspired by the real-life journey of explorer Jacques Cartier, Rabelais described how French travelers to India (who used the legendary North-West passage) came across and explored twenty-one islands, each one with a strange society of its own: an island where people fed on wind, one where sound could be frozen and unfrozen at will, one where the local king used magnetic force to stop cannonballs. In these books, Rabelais gave form to a genre which was later exploited by such luminaries as **Cyrano de Bergerac**, Jonathan Swift, Jules **Verne** and, in modern times, Jack Vance.

The other great writer of the French Renaissance was Michel Eyquem, aka Michel de **Montaigne**, a formidable essayist and philosopher, whose life-work, the introspective three-volume *Essais* (*Essays*, 1580-1588), still carries a deep influence on French philosophy today.

Even though less inclined towards the Imaginary than Rabelais, Montaigne's profound hatred for dogmatism of any kind led him to take an occasional journey to Utopia himself. In Chapter XXXI of Book 1 of the *Essays*, entitled *Des Cannibales* (*Of Cannibales*), Montaigne described a mythical land peopled by "good savages." We shall note in passing that Montaigne was aware of the existence of Plato's fabled Atlantis, since he took pains to rule it out as the location of his own imaginary island.

Rabelais was not alone in breaking new literary grounds. Other, lesser known writers worthy of being mentioned here included:

Bonaventure des Périers, with his *Cymbalum Mundi* (1537), a book comprised of four dialogues, allegedly told by the author/translator to a man named Pierre Tryocam, in which the god Hermes made fun of philosophers and then discovered that someone stole the Book of Destinies that Zeus had entrusted to him.

Raoul **Spifame**, with his *Dicacarchia Henrici, Regis Christianissimi, Progymnasmata* (1556).

Béroalde de Verville, with *L'Idée de la République* (*The Idea of the Republic*, 1584) and *Discours de Jacophile à Limne* (1605).

Finally, one should also note a remarkable work by the noted physician and medical pioneer Ambroise **Paré**, *Les Monstres, Tant Terrestres Que Marins, avec Leurs Portraits* (*Monsters, Terrestrials as Well as Sea-Faring, with Their Portraits*, 1579), in which the "scientific" evidence of the existence of dragons, hermaphrodites, and unicorns was taken for granted.

2. The *Merveilleux (Marvelous)*

From 1550 until 1650, a strange, almost schizophrenic, form of literary cohabitation existed between humanist philosophy (devoted to the material universe), and the *fantastique* (dealing with the supernatural); and between pagan influences (harking back to the Greeks), and Christian faith. For example, the great 16th-century French poet **Ronsard** (1524-1585), founder of the literary group *La Pleïade* (called thus as an homage to a group of seven 3rd-century BC Alexandrian poets who had placed themselves under the protection of this constellation), published a number of works belonging to the *fantastique*. In his earlier *Odes* (1550), Ronsard often drew heavily on the superstitions of his native Vendômois country, writing about witches and witchcraft. Then, at the peak of his literary fame, he devoted several of his more famous *Hymnes* (1552) to supernatural subjects such as "Daimons" and astrology. Baïf (1532-1589), another member of *La Pléïade*, celebrated the pagan goddess Hecate.

Ronsard

In a remarkable poem entitled *Les Sepmaines* (1578), which may well be the first heroic-fantasy-type work in French literature, Guillaume **Du Bartas** described the creation of the world by God, including scenes of battles with monsters, the Garden of Eden, etc

The ensuing Baroque period continued to rely heavily

on warlocks and witches, often drawn from antiquity (such as Medea, Circe, and the Witches of Thessalia) for dramatic purposes, in an imitation of the increasingly successful pastoral literature from Italy and Spain, in which Greek-Roman myths still played a strong role.

The classic novel *L'Astrée* (*Astrea*, 1607-27) by Honoré d'**Urfé** was obviously inspired by the prose romance of chivalry *Amadis of Gaul*, a neo-*Chanson de Geste* which had been circulating in various forms since the late 13th century, but reached its pinnacle when reassembled by Spanish writer Garcia Rodriguez Montalvo. *Amadis of Gaul* was originally based on myths derived from the Celtic Arthurian legends, but in its 16th-century form, came to embody all the ideals of the now-vanished Age of Chivalry: a virtually invincible, handsome Christian knight who was totally loyal to his God-anointed King, and who was courtly and chaste to his princess love. What once was fiery, mystic, raw legend had become literary convention, if not clichés. The true belief was gone; only the sense of wonder remained—the sense of the *Merveilleux*.

In the same fashion, *L'Astrée*, with its druid Climante, his magic mirror, and his Fountain of Truth, functioned not as a first-degree romance but as a stylized, artificially contrived romance. From *L'Astrée* to famous playwright Pierre **Corneille**'s lesser-known but classic tragedies, *Médée* (1635) and *Circé* (1675), the warlocks and the witches became the popular *deus ex machina* of French literature.

Raymond Lebègue, in his article *Le Merveilleux Magique en France dans le Théâtre Baroque* (*Magical Marvelous in France in Baroque Theater*; in *Revue d'Histoire du Théâtre,* Jan-Mar., 1963) listed no less than seventy-five plays where warlocks played a major part, often appearing in several plays written by different authors. Ismen the Magician, created by Le Tasse, appeared in Chrétien des Croix's *Les Amantes* (*The Lovers*, 1613). In *La Bague d'Oubli* (*The Ring of Oblivion*, 1628), Jean de **Rotrou** introduced Alcandre the Sorcerer, who went on to star in Bazire's *Arlette* (1638). Rotrou was a playwright who wrote a number of baroque plays and (with the more famous Corneille) heralded the advent of Classic Theater. His *Crisante* took place in a room draped in black and featured a decapitated head, one murder, and three suicides, all performed on stage.

With Corneille and Molière (1622-1673), Jean **Racine** was one of the best playwrights of the 17th century. A number of his plays, such as *Andromaque* (1667), *Iphigénie* (1674), and the famous *Phèdre* (1676), borrowed elements from Greek mythology.

Similar themes, borrowed from classic Greco-Roman authors such as Ovid, Apuleius, Ariosto, etc. were also the source of inspiration of numerous opéras performed at the court of the Sun King, and written by Philippe **Quinault** (for composer Jean-Baptiste Lully), d'**Albaret** (for composer Jean-Marie Leclair Aîné), Pierre-Joseph **Bernard**, Louis de **Cahusac**, Louis **Fuzelier**, Adrien-Joseph **Le Valois d'Orville**, Jean-François **Marmontel** and the Abbott **Pelle**-grin (for composer Jean-Philippe Rameau), Antoine **Houdar de la Motte** (for composer Marin Marais), Antoine **Danchet** (for composer André Campra), etc. (For a more complete listing, see "**Opéra**" in Chapter XI.)

Operas were prodigious re-users of mythology, folk tales, and legends. Early operatic works were classic dramas featuring larger-than-life deeds and high passions. They were the successors of medieval mystery plays and sagas, and the precursor of modern heroic fantasy or space opera films.

Finally, one should mention here Jean de **La Fontaine**, the popular fabulist who adapted Aesop's tales into French verse (1668; revised in 1678; revised again in 1693).

3. The *Romans Ésotériques (Esoteric Novels)*

During the Middle Ages, there was generally no difference between a magician and a sorcerer. Merlin, Vivian, and Morgan were each considered on their own merits, and their connections, if any, with Christian dogma were loose and informal. Religious persecution began in the 13th century, when the Roman Catholic Church formally defined a sorcerer as a heretic who obtained his powers from a pact with Satan, while a magician was someone who practiced the ancient divining arts. The former was deemed to be anathema, and was usually condemned to be burned at the stake, while the latter, though held in dubious regard, was not automatically assumed to have diabolical connections.

In the early part of the 14th century, French King Philip IV (the Fair, 1268-1314) used trumped up accusations of witchcraft and sorcery to justify the elimination of the powerful Order of the Knights Templar, burning their Grand-Master Jacques de Molay at the stake in 1314. Then, the Black Death struck (1347-1351), which both strengthened and weakened the Church. The calamity strengthened the Church because it seemingly justified its persecution of witches and heretics, and gave it more temporal power; however, spiritually, the plague weakened the Church because it revealed the institution's sheer powerlessness before the plague, costing it many of the minds and souls of the common folk. A number of grief-stricken people began to turn away from the Church, and secretly started to worship revamped avatars of old gods, such as the Horned One (which was not Satan, the Fallen Angel, but was treated by the Church as such), or at least looked to them for succor.

No one will ever know the actual number of real "witches," but undeniably, the pressure was growing and the Church had to react to prevent what it saw as an unacceptable return to pagan worship, or worse. Big scale witch hunts therefore started in the 15th century. Joan of Arc (b. 1412), deemed guilty of sorcery, was burned at the stake in 1431. Gilles de Rais (b. 1404), who later provided inspiration for Charles **Perrault**'s infamous "Blue Beard," was also tried for sorcerous practices, and was executed in 1440.

Finally, in 1484, the newly-appointed Pope Innocent VIII (1432-1492) published his famous bull, *Summis Desiderantes Affectibus* (*Desiring with the Most Profound Anxiety*). In it, the Pope complained that the work of two fanatical, sadistic Dominican inquisitors, Heinrich Kramer (?-?) and Jakob Sprenger (?-?) lacked support because—a surprisingly candid admission!—neither the clergy nor the laity were convinced of the extent and seriousness of the "crime" of witchcraft! The Pope went on to warn everyone to support the madmen's investigations, or else "upon him shall fall the wrath of God Almighty." *Summis Desiderantes Affectibus* had the nefarious result of fastening on European powers the duty of fighting the Devil and eradicating witchcraft, justifying the most merciless persecutions for at least the next two centuries.

(As a *fantastique* footnote, contemporary chroniclers noted that, toward the end of his life, Innocent VIII was kept alive by blood transfusions from young boys, and was thus responsible for the deaths of three lads.)

So while Humanism and its enlightened creed was spreading throughout Europe in the 16th century, another, darker storm was brewing. In 1486, the aforementioned Jakob Sprenger wrote and published the infamous *Malleus Maleficarum*, the *Hammer of Witches*, undoubtedly the most important and sinister work on demonology ever written. While this book was not considered a work of fiction by his author or his readers, it nevertheless belongs squarely in this study to the extent that it catalogued and codified all magical practices known at the time.

For a purely literary standpoint, like any contemporary best-seller, the *Malleus Maleficarum* spawned a large number of imitations. Among French works directly or indirectly deriving from it were Jean Bodin's (?-?) *La Démonomanie des Sorciers* (*Demonology of Sorcerers*, 1580), *De la Démonomanie* (*Of Demonology*, 1587), and *Le Fléau des Démons et ses Sorciers* (*Plague of Demons and Sorcerers*, 1616); Henri Boguet's (?-?) *Discours Exécrables des Sorciers* (*Awful Discourses of Sorcerers*, 1603), Pierre de Lancre's (?-?) *Tableau de l'Inconstance des Mauvais Anges* (*Table of the Inconstancies of Fallen Angels*, 1613) and *L'Incrédulité et Mescréance du Sortilège* (*Incredulity and Unbelief of Spells*, 1622). As unpalatable as the fact may be, these books, far more real and awful than H. P. Lovecraft's (1890-1937) fictional *Necronomicon* or August Derleth's (1909-1971) *Culte des Ghoules*, were among the true ancestors of today's modern horror fiction.

Occult literature was not all demons and witches. The tradition of esoteric writings, originated by the medieval alchemists, remained strong. There was a tenuous line between the non-fictional writings of these proto-scientists, and the transparent, symbolical allegories that they often used to hide their knowledge, in plain sight as it were, and to avoid persecution. We have already mentioned *Le Livre de la Fontaine Périlleuse* (*The Book of the Perilous Fountain*; c. 1425) as an example of this approach.

Alchemy likely originated with Greek, Egyptian, and Middle Eastern scientific traditions brought into Europe through Italy or through the Moorish Conquest of Spain during the 8th century. Indeed, words like elixir, alcohol, and alembic all have Arabic roots.

The University of Montpellier, in the South of France, was established in 1181, and became the cradle of alchemy. Among its students and/or teachers were such notorious alchemists as Albert le Grand, aka Albertus Magnus (1193-1280), who wrote five books about alchemy, including the treatise *De Alchemia*; Raymond Lulle (1235-1315), who wrote *Ars Magna*; Arnauld de Villeneuve (1240-1313), who wrote *Le Grand Rosaire* (*Great Rosary*); Roger Bacon (1214-1294). The University of Montpellier also counted at one time or another Erasmus, **Rabelais**, and even the notorious Nostradamus (1503-1566) among its staff.

Another notorious alchemist of the times was the legendary "gold-maker," Nicolas Flamel (1330-1418), who wrote *Explication des Figures Hiéroglyphiques* and whose mysterious life has since then provided much grist for the fictional mill. Eventually, with such proto-scientists as Paracelsius (1493-1541) and Agrippa de Nettesheim (1486-1535), a branch of alchemy turned into regular science, like medicine and chemistry, while the other remained hidden in the domain of the occult.

A note about alchemy: The popular misconception was that alchemists sought the secret of the philosopher's stone, which was said to have the power to transmute base metal—usually lead—into gold. The reality was somewhat more complex. The alchemist was dedicated to the *Grand Oeuvre* (*great work*), a life-long, time-consuming, spiritual and chemical process whose end-result was the production of an elixir of long life. The so-called philosopher's stone was, by all accounts, a reddish powder dubbed "projection powder." A small portion of it, wrapped in paper, was thrown into molten lead and, according to various witnesses, did turn it into gold.

The fact that lead has an atomic weight of 82 in the periodic table of elements, while mercury (a vital element in the alchemical process) is 80 and gold is 79 gives cause to wonder. How could the alchemists, in an age where earth, water, air, and fire were considered "elements," link these three metals together? How could they imagine methods of transmutation not requiring massive energy bombardments of the sort that we now know as cold nuclear fusion? In any event, the "philosopher's stone" was but the final test, a chemical proof in the process leading to the true goal: the elixir of long life.

Whether alchemy is fact or fantasy may never be fully known; however, it is interesting to remark that, in an age where the average life span was 38 years, all the above-mentioned alchemists lived to reach their eighties.

CHAPTER III

The Enlightenment (1650–1800)

The 18th century is known to historians as the *Siècle des Lumières* (*Century of Lights*), or Enlightenment. Starting with the ascension to the throne in 1643 of Sun King Louis XIV (1638-1715), France entered a period of political, artistic, and scientific *grandeur*, before settling into the decadent reigns of Louis XV (1710-1774) and Louis XVI (1754-1793).

Religious persecution and witch hunts finally stopped in 1670, after the personal intervention of Louis XIV, who overruled the local Parliament of the city of Rouen, in an affair where five hundred persons were under suspicion of witchcraft.

Enlightenment could be arguably said to have started with René Descartes (1596-1650) in 1637 with his *Le Discours de la Méthode*, or in 1687 when Isaac Newton (1643-1727) published his *Mathematical Principles of Natural Philosophy*, the basis for a comprehensive, mathematical description of the universe, which demonstrated the power of science over the material world.

The prevailing modes of Enlightenment thinking were rational thought and skepticism. Throughout the use of reason, Man would master nature and himself. Nothing exemplified this better than Denis **Diderot**'s massive, seventeen-volume *Encyclopedia* (1751-72), a sum of knowledge whose advocated purpose was to disseminate information, reduce superstition, and improve the human condition.

In literature, the baroque was replaced by classicism during the reign of the Sun King, with its roster of great playwrights: **Corneille**, **Racine,** and Molière. The so-called "Quarrel of the Ancients and the Moderns" (c. 1690) freed French writers from the need to imitate the literature of antiquity. Finally, the passion for new philosophical ideas, incarnated by the great **Voltaire**, and the spread of cosmopolitan influences, such as those of Spinoza (1632-1677), Newton and Goethe (1749-1832), fostered a climate of debate that would eventually produce the blueprints for a new, modern society.

That "new society" would be the project—and ultimate

failure—of the French Revolution, which could therefore be said to be the brainchild of the proto-science fiction writers of the 17th and 18th centuries.

1. The *Voyages Imaginaires (Imaginary Journeys)*

It was during the late 17th century that a growing distinction began to appear between the pure utopias, the purpose of which remained social satire and philosophical discourse, and the first *Voyages Imaginaires*, which aimed to entertain. It was also during the 18th century that many of the now-classic themes, such as journeys through the cosmos, to the center of the Earth or even to the future, were first defined in literary terms.

a. Cosmic Journeys

Following in the footsteps of **Rabelais**, and a contemporary of Roger Bacon (whose *New Atlantis* was published in 1629), Tommaso Campanella (1568-1639; whose *City of the Sun* was published in 1637), and Francis Godwin (1562-1633; whose the *Man in the Moone* was published in 1638), was Charles **Sorel**, the author of the three-volume *Le Berger Extravagant* (*The Extravagant Shepherd*, 1627), and *La Maison des Jeux* (*The House of Games*), which included the *Récit du Voyage de Brisevent* (*Tale of Brisevent's Journey*, 1642), which both contained fantastic utopias inhabited by equally fantastic beings.

In it, Sorel wrote, "Some men have affirmed that there are many worlds, which some have placed in the planets, and others in the fixed stars; for my part, I believe there is a world on the moon." In describing a trip there, Sorel imagined a "Prince as ambitious as Alexander, who shall come to conquer this world," doing so using "great engines, to descend or ascend."

A writer undoubtedly influenced by Sorel was French nobleman Hector Savinien **Cyrano de Bergerac**, whose *Histoire Comique des Etats et Empires de la Lune* (*Comical History of the States and Empires of the Moon*) was published posthumously in 1657, soon followed by *Histoire Comique des Etats et Empires du Soleil* (*Comical History of the States and Empires of the Sun*) in 1662, eventually collected as *L'Autre Monde* (*Other Worlds*).

Cyrano de Bergerac is famous as the hero of a superb 1898 play by Edmond Rostand (1868-1918), which made his swordsmanship and the size of his nose illustrious. But he was also a poet, soldier of fortune, and a distinguished man of letters, whose writings were published after his death in order to avoid persecution for heresy. He wrote two remarkable utopias-cum-social satires which were also noteworthy because of their author's attempts to devise various methods of space travel, some of them clearly fanciful (even at the time), others more scientific (rockets, parachutes, use of magnetism). Cyrano de Bergerac certainly influenced the later works of Voltaire and Jonathan Swift.

Well versed in esoteric matters—the Rosicrucians were mentioned in passing in his *L'Autre Monde*—Cyrano de Bergerac described magical rituals and alchemical processes in various of his letters, collected in *Pour et Contre les Sorciers* (*For and Against Sorcerers*; published in 1663), even making use of the real-life alchemist Agrippa de Nettesheim as a fictional character. In the same fashion, he had the ghosts of Campanella and Descartes "guest-star" in *L'Autre Monde*.

But what made *L'Autre Monde* remarkable as a work of proto-science fiction, perhaps the first of its kind, and different from all the utopias which preceded it, was that Cyrano de Bergerac added to the usual satirical and philosophical discourse elements based on his knowledge of physics and astronomy. The book featured the concepts of rocket power, hot-air ballooning, and the phonograph. Another remarkable innovation was the creation of "real" alien societies, such as that of the Bird-Men who live on the "dark side" of the Sun and hate men. In Cyrano de Bergerac's colorful universe, Man was not only no longer the sole sentient species in the universe, but he was not even the most important one.

In 1686, Corneille's nephew, Bernard Le Bovier de **Fontenelle** took the theme of cosmic exploration one step further and published his *Entretiens sur la Pluralité des Mondes* (*Conversations on the Plurality of Worlds*), a pseudo-documentary work about the possibilities of life on other planets. This was one of the earliest works popularizing the concepts of astronomy and possible life on other planets. It proved an enormous influence on all subsequent proto-science fiction works. The book was written as a series of exchanges between the author and the fictional Marquise de G***, and did much to popularize scientific astronomical concepts. In his foreword, Fontenelle stated that he "did not want to imagine anything about the inhabitants of

these other worlds that could be either entirely impossible or chimerical; (he) tried to describe everything that could reasonably be formulated, and even the visions (he) added had to have some foundations in reality." This was, clearly, an approach characteristic of a work of science fiction, not fantasy.

The success of Cyrano de Bergerac's works popularized the concept of journeys into outer space and to other planets, and spawned many imitators, such as **Nolant de Fatouville**'s *Arlequin Empereur de la Lune* (*Harlequin, Emperor of the Moon*, 1684).

The next thematic leap was accomplished by the distinguished satirist François-Marie Arouet, aka Voltaire, in his novella *Micromegas*, published in 1752. The title character was a giant alien from Sirius who, accompanied by an equally gigantic Saturnian, had come to visit Earth. Even though Voltaire's primary purpose was satire, he nevertheless relied on well-researched scientific foundations, as shown in this excerpt: "Our space traveler was well acquainted with the laws of gravity, and all of its attractive and repulsive nature." Voltaire went on to state how comets and solar rays can be used to travel between planets.

Once exposed, the theme of cosmic voyages grew and developed, usually as the pretext for some thinly-disguised utopias, but more often than not including some startling proto-science fiction contents. For example, in 1750, the Chevalier de **Béthune** published a *Relation du Monde de Mercure* (*Tale of the World Mercury*), a colorful utopia about the immortal, winged beings inhabiting the planet Mercury.

In 1753, in *Amilec, ou la Graine d'Hommes qui Sert à Peupler les Planètes* (*Amilec, or the Seed of Man Who Is Used to Seed the Planets*), Charles-François **Tiphaigne de la Roche** conceived the concept of journeys through both the macro-cosmos and the micro-cosmos.

In 1757, Swiss writer Emmerich **Vattel** penned probably the first novel ever written about a journey to the world of insects. In *Les Fourmis* (*The Ants*), a man transferred his mind into that of an ant and discovered the new perspectives of a microscopic world.

In 1761, Daniel de Villeneuve, aka **Listonai**, wrote *Le Voyageur Philosophe dans un Pays Inconnu aux Habitants de la Terre* (*The Philosophical Traveler in a Country Unknown from the Inhabitants of Earth*), an elaborate utopia featuring a flying space galley, complete with pilot, astronavigator, and crew.

In 1765, Marie-Anne de **Roumier-Robert** wrote *Voyage de Milord Céton dans les Sept Planètes ou le Nouveau Mentor* (*Voyage of Lord Ceton in the Seven Planets or the New Mentor*) in which the hero and his sister travel to seven different planets on the wings of the angel Zachiel. In this space travel story, the inhabitants of each planet were chosen to represent a human character trait—Martians were bellicose, Venusians lovers, etc.

In 1775, Louis-Guillaume de **La Follie**, a scientist and industrial chemist, penned *Le Philosophe sans Prétention*

(*The Philosopher Without Pretention*), an utopia which featured an electric-powered starship remarkably ahead of its time. Through dreams, the protagonist learned of a wondrous spaceship invented on the planet Mercury by the scientist Scintilla. The ship itself was patterned after a static electricity machine.

Finally, in the 1790s, the noted utopist, playwright, and journalist Louis-Abel Beffroy de Reigny, better known as "**Cousin Jacques**," wrote a number of satirical plays taking place on other planets: *Nicodème dans la Lune, ou la Révolution Pacifique* (*Nicodeme on the Moon, or the Peaceful Revolution*, 1791), *Les Deux Nicodèmes, ou les Français dans la Planète Jupiter* (*The Two Nicodemes, or the French on the Planet Jupiter*, 1791), and a novella, *La Constitution de la Lune* (*The Moon's Constitution*, 1793). Cousin Jacques also self-published *Les Lunes du Cousin Jacques, ou le Courrier des Planètes* (*The Moons of Cousin Jacques, or the Planetary Mail*, 1785-1791), the first proto fanzine in the history of science fiction.

After the French Revolution, the theme of cosmic journeys eventually became trivialized. In 1875, one of composer Jacques Offenbach's operettas (libretto written by A. **Vanloo**, E. **Leterrier**, and A. **Mortier**) was even entitled *Le Voyage dans la Lune* (*The Journey to the Moon*; see **Opéra**). It would take the prodigious talent of Jules **Verne** to restore luster and scientific credibility to the concept of space travel.

b. Other Lands

To differentiate himself from those writers sending their characters on cosmic journeys, Gabriel de **Foigny** (aka Jacques Sadeur) wrote *La Terre Australe Connue* (*The Known Austral Land*, 1676), later reissued as *Les Aventures de Jacques Sadeur dans la Découverte et le Voyage de la Terre Australe* (*The Adventures of Jacques Sadeur in the Discovery and the Jouney of the Austral Land*, 1693), an elaborate utopia about an enlightened Antipodean race.

Denis **Veiras** penned a four-volume *Histoire des Sévarambes* (*The History of the Serarites or Sevarambi*, 1677-79), another utopian description of the mores of the fictional people inhabiting the "Austral Land" (Terrae Australes Icognitae). Interestingly, Veiras' work was first published anonymously in English in 1675.

In 1683, the Abbot **Maillot** published *Relation du Voyage Mystérieux de l'Île de la Vertu* (*Tale of the Mysterious*

Voyage to the Island of Virtue). And in 1690, Gabriel **Daniel** penned *Voyage du Monde de Descartes* (*A Voyage to the World of Descartes*, 1690), a utopia centered around the ideas of philosopher René Descartes.

Simon **Tyssot de Patot** dispatched his heroes to an imaginary land located near South Africa in *Voyages et Aventures de Jacques Massé* (*Voyages and Adventures of Jacques Massé*), published in 1710. Again, the book's contents did not range much beyond the traditional confines of the utopias; they did, however, include "living fossils," giant birds, and strange flora that survived from prehistoric times, arguably making it the first modern Lost World novel.

More conventional utopias continued to rely on fictional lands. Even a renowned literary figure such as famous writer and essayist **Montesquieu** devoted Letters XI to XIV of his *Lettres Persanes* (*Persan Letters*, 1721) to the fictional *Histoire des Troglodytes* (*History of the Troglodytes*). This essay used a fictional lost race to depict a utopian society.

In 1759, in *Candide*, Voltaire described the mythical country of Eldorado, the ancient land of the Incas.

In 1760, **Tiphaigne de la Roche** sent his heroes to the secret land of *Giphantie* in Africa, where a race of secret supermen lived in royal isolation. (The novel also featured a concept remarkably similar to that of television.) The following year, in *L'Empire des Zaziris sur les Humains ou la Zazirocratie* (*The Empire of the Zaziris Over Mankind, or The Zazirocracy*) Tiphaigne de la Roche anticipated many future tales of secret alien invasions by postulating that mysterious beings, the eponymous "Zaziris," descendents of the mythical sylphs and djinns, lived hidden among us and secretly controlled the destinies of mankind.

Of greater interest is Nicolas-Edmé **Restif de la Bretonne**, a prolific author of semi-autobiographic and somewhat pornographic novels. The proto-science fictional works of Restif de la Bretonne were virtually "discovered" by noted researcher Pierre **Versins**, who devoted a full eight pages to them in his prodigious 1972 *Encyclopédie de l'Utopie, des Voyages Extraordinaires et de la Science Fiction*, and called Restif de la Bretonne a "master of conjecture, utopia, and science fiction."

In *La Découverte Australe par un Homme Volant* (*The Southern Discovery by a Flying Man*), published in 1781, a young scientist invented a flying machine with wings and parachute which enabled him to reach speeds of over 100 miles per hour. The Flying Man then went on to create his own city-state, accessible only by air, and to conquer the girl he loved. He even considered using air power to become master of the world. Eventually, he embarked on the exploration of the Southern Hemisphere. Like Rabelais before him, Restif de la Bretonne described various islands inhabited by colorful societies of animal-men.

Cyrano de Bergerac's *L'Autre Monde*, Tiphaigne de la Roche's *Giphantie*, Restif de la Bretonne's *La Découverte Australe*, as well as French translations of More, Campanella

LES LUNES
D U
COUSIN JACQUES.

SECONDE ANNÉE.
21.ᴹᴱ NUMÉRO.

NOUVELLE LUNE DE SEPTEMBRE
1786.

Ridendo dicere verum.

*Abonnement pour Paris, 18 liv. par an;
pour la province 21 livres franc de port.*

A PARIS;

ᴄʜᴇᴢ LESCLAPART, Libraire de MONSIEUR,
Frere du ROI, rue du Roule, N°. 11, près du
Pont-Neuf.

1786.

and Swift, were reprinted in *Voyages aux Pays de Nulle Part* (*Voyages to the Nowhere Lands*) by publisher Robert Laffont in 1993.

The concept of a journey to the center of the Earth was first introduced by Simon **Tyssot de Patot** in his 1720 novel, *La Vie, les Aventures et le Voyage de Groenland du Révérend Père Cordelier Pierre de Mésange* (*The Life, Adventures and Trip to Greenland of the Rev. Father Pierre de Mesange*). This was the first time that the notion of a journey to the center of the Earth was introduced in a realistic, pseudo-scientific fashion, as opposed to the various mythological journeys to Hell, such as Dante's the *Divine Comedy* of the early 14th century. (The other seminal work on this theme is Danish writer Ludvig Holberg's [1684-1754] *Voyage of Nikolas Klimius*, but is dated from 1741.)

One hundred forty-four years before Jules Verne's classic, Tyssot de Patot described how his protagonists discover a hidden, underground kingdom located near the North Pole. That kingdom was inhabited by the descendants of African colonists who had left their homeland four thousand years earlier. This proto–*Pellucidar* was lit by a mysterious fireball and was also inhabited by small man-bat creatures. (The novel also featured the character of the Wandering Jew.)

In 1721, an anonymous author published the self-evident *Relation d'un Voyage du Pôle Arctique au Pôle Antarctique par le Centre du Monde avec la Description de ce Périlleux Passage et les Choses Merveilleuses et Étonnantes qu'on a découvertes sous le Pôle Antarctique* (*Tale of a Journey from the North Pole to the South Pole Through the Center of the Earth, with the Description of This Dangerous Passage and the Wondrous and Amazing Things We Discovered Under the South Pole*).

Finally, in 1737-38, Charles de Fieux, Chevalier de **Mouhy** wrote the two volumes of *Lamékis, ou les Voyages Extraordinaires d'un Égyptien dans la Terre Intérieure avec la Découverte de l'Île des Sylphides* (*Lamekis, or the Extraordinary Voyages of an Egyptian in the Inner Earth with the Discovery of Sylphides' Island*), in which his hero, an Egyptian boy, rescued a blue-skinned man who came from an underground land called Trifolday, located at the center of the Earth. The fugitive told the boy how he fought there against races of snake-men, toad-men, and worm-men. Fans of Edgar Rice Burroughs (1875-1950) would feel quite comfortable in the Chevalier de Mouhy's colorful descriptions of the fantastic kingdoms existing at the center of the Earth.

c. The Future

For those who preferred not to travel to outer or inner space, there was always the future. In 1659, an obscure contemporary of Cyrano de Bergerac, Jacques **Guttin** wrote *Epigone, Histoire du Siècle Futur* (*History of the Future Century*). In it, the author did not resort to the well-known literary trick of dreams or imaginary journeys, but merely told a story that took place in the future, not unlike

Robert Heinlein's *Future History* novels. Guttin described the future history of France, ruled by the "Clodovist" kings, and the peregrinations of the young heir to the French throne.

In *Telliamed*, a visionary book published in 1748 and dedicated to Cyrano de Bergerac, sub-titled "Conversations of an Indian Philosopher with a French Missionary on the Decrease of the Seas, the Origins of Earth and of Man," Benoît de **Maillet** anticipated Olaf Stapledon by telling the story of the evolution of man, from his origins in the sea—a startling breakthrough concept if there ever was one—to his future among the stars.

Louis-Sébastien **Mercier**'s *L'An 2440, Rêve s'il en Fut Jamais* (*The Year 2440, a Dream If There Ever Was*), published in 1771, depicted a future France governed according to the principles of Enlightenment. It was one of the first literary works to make the transition from utopia to scientific anticipation, as it featured intercontinental dirigible flights. Its importance had less to do with its literary value—in it, the author just wakes up seven hundred years later—than its historical consequences. *L'An 2440* not only helped shape the philosophies that led to the French Revolution, but it was also the first utopia of its kind to be translated in America, in 1772.

Mercier was not the only thinker whose works of fiction paved the way for the French Revolution. Others included the pseudonymous **Morelly** with his *Naufrage des Isles Flottantes, ou Basiliade du Célèbre Pilpai* (*Wreck of the Floating Islands*, 1753), Listonai, Voltaire, and La Follie.

Mercier's *Voyages Imaginaires, Songes, Visions et Romans Cabalistiques* (*Imaginary Journeys, Dreams, Visions and Cabalistic Novels*, 1788) also featured a scientific device anticipating communications between the Earth and the Moon, achieved through the equivalent of a modern-day laser.

Restif de la Bretonne's *L'An 2000* (*The Year 2000*, 1789), in spite of its prophetic title—perhaps the first time that a now such common title was used in the history of science fiction—was only a comedy of manners.

In 1791, with *Ma République* (*My Republic*), **Delisle de Sales** penned one of the first parallel history or "what if" novellas in the history of science fiction by describing what the French Revolution might have been had King Louis XVI been a better politician.

Finally, there is one, prodigious novel which combined in a dazzling display of imagination all of these proto-science fiction themes, and more. It was *Les Posthumes* (*Posthumous Writings*), a four-volume work, again by Restif de la Bretonne, published only in 1802. Its hero, the Duke of Multipliandre, mastered the ability to free his mind from his body, using a process which the author took pains to qualify as "physical and not supernatural." Multipliandre first used this power (as well as that of invisibility) to take over the bodies of various kings and thus create world peace. Then, like the hero of Olaf Stapledon's *Star Maker*, he embarked on a vast journey through space, occupying the bodies of various alien races and eventually traveling farther in space to the very center of the universe. Later, Multipliandre used his mental powers to travel into the future, where he encountered races of supermen and mutants. Finally, the immortal Multipliandre watched Earth as it plummeted toward the Sun some three million years in the future. Pierre Versins dubbed *Les Posthumes* a brilliant, visionary, but scattered work.

This chapter on Imaginary Journeys would not be complete without a mention of editor-publisher Charles-Georges-Thomas **Garnier**, who in 1787 launched a 36-volume specialized collection—perhaps the first science fiction imprint ever—entitled *Voyages Imaginaires, Songes, Visions et Romans Cabalistiques* (*Imaginary Journeys, Dreams, Visions and Occult Novels*). During the two years of its existence, *Voyages Imaginaires* reprinted and popularized works by French authors such as Cyrano de Bergerac, Montesquieu, Mouhy, Foigny, Veiras, Voltaire, Mercier, Cazotte, and others (See complete table of contents under "**Voyages Imaginaires**" in Chapter XI.)

2. The *Contes de Fées & Féeries* (Fairy Tales)

Baroque (whether in the form of the novel, the theater, or even opera) was the link between the *Merveilleux* of the Renaissance and the more formalized *Contes de Fées*, or *Féeries*, of the Enlightenment period. The undeniable popularity of the genre was, in great part, attributable to the fact that *Féeries* were safe; they did not imperil the soul—a serious concern for a nation which had just come out of an era of great religious persecution—and they appropriately reflected the *grandeur* of the Sun King's reign.

The precursor to the genre was the Baroness d'**Aulnoy** (aka Madame d'Aulnoy) who, in 1690, introduced in her rambling novel *Histoire d'Hyppolite, Comte de Douglas* (*Story of Hippolyte, Count of Douglas*) a fairy tale entitled *L'Île de la Félicité* (*The Island of Happiness*). (It was later reprinted by Garnier in his *Voyages Imaginaires*.) In 1695, another novelist, Madame Lhéritier, included four fairy tales in her *Oeuvres Mêlées* (*Mixed Works*).

But it was in 1697 that the true genius of the *Féerie* appeared on the scene. Charles **Perrault**, until then a renowned literary figure, a man who was a champion of sciences, the author of a decisive article in the so-called "Quarrel of the Ancients and Moderns"—on the side of the latter—released under the name of his son, Pierre Perrault Darmancourt (1678-1700), also a folklorist, *Histoires ou Contes du Temps Passé* (*Histories or Tales of Past Times*) aka *Contes de ma Mère l'Oie* (*Tales of Mother Goose*). In it, Perrault had carefully collected a number of popular folk tales and legends, such as *Cendrillon* (*Cinderella*), *La Belle au Bois Dormant* (*Sleeping Beauty*), *Peau d'Âne* (*Donkey Skin*), *Le Petit*

Chaperon Rouge (*Little Red Riding Hood*), *Barbe-Bleue* (*BlueBeard*), *Le Chat Botté* (*Puss in Boots*), and others.

These ancient stories were retold in a style free of affectation, and were always accompanied by a moral, taking a leaf from the popular *Fables* of **La Fontaine**. The book proved incredibly successful and immediately spawned many imitators. However, it is worth noting that, unlike some of these, Perrault had not softened or prettified his fairy tales. His yarns preserved the cruelty, some would say savagery and goriness, of the original medieval tales. In his stories, sorcery was still very real. A number of his literary successors, on the other hand, chose to emphasize nicer sentiments and gentle magic.

After Perrault, the Baroness d'Aulnoy followed suit with a remarkable, three-volume collection entitled simply *Contes de Fées* (*Fairy Tales*), and then her *Contes Nouveaux ou les Fées à la Mode* (*New Tales or Fairies in Fashion*). Unlike Perrault, Madame d'Aulnoy used her tales for satirical purposes, deliberately aiming them at an adult readership. As a result, her tales were a little more complex and sophisticated, and, perhaps unfairly, did not survive the test of time as well. Her best-remembered stories are *L'Oiseau Bleu* (*The Blue Bird*), *La Chatte Blanche* (*The White She-Cat*) and *Le Nain Jaune* (*The Yellow Dwarf*), which spawned a popular board-and-card game. *L'Oiseau Bleu* (*The Blue Bird*) introduced one of the very first "Prince Charmings" in the world of fairy tales.

The *Féeries* was a genre in which many women writers excelled. Between 1697 and 1702, some of the best of these authors included:

Madame de **La Force**, with *Les Fées: Contes des Contes* (*The Fairies: Tales of Tales*).

The Countess de **Murat**, with *Les Contes de Fées* (*The Fairy Tales*) and *Les Nouveaux Contes des Fées* (*The New Fairy Tales*).

The Chevalier de **Mailly**, with *Les Illustres Fées* (*The Illustrious Fairies*).

The Marquise d'**Aulneuil**, with *La Tyrannie des Fées Détruites* (*The Tyranny of Destroyed Fairies*).

Jean de **Préchac**, with *Contes moins Contes que les Autres, Sans Paragon et la Reine des Fées* (*Tales Less Tales Than Others, Without Paragon, and the Fairy Queen*).

Perrault and Madame d'Aulnoy virtually defined the first boundaries of modern fantasy. After them, magicians, ogres, dragons, dwarves and fairies were definitively integrated in the realms of fantasy.

Not coincidentally, the classic *Thousand and One Nights* were simultaneously first "translated" into French—and quite possibly made up from very thin or non-existent sources, as no earlier Arabic manuscripts of *Aladdin* and *Ali-Baba* are known to exist—by Antoine **Galland** from 1704 to 1717, contributing to increase the popular appeal of the *Féeries*, and their sense of disconnection from reality.

As with the *Féeries*, the Oriental fantasy tradition created by Galland was continued with much success by a number of imitators, who all claimed to have "translated" a number of "Oriental" collections, such as:

François **Petis de la Croix**, with *Les Mille et Un Jours* (*The Thousand and One Days*).

Thomas-Simon **Gueulette**, with *Les Mille et Un Quarts d'Heures* (*The Thousand and One Quarters of An Hour*), *Les Mille et Une Heures* (*The Thousand and One Hours*) and *Les Mille et Une Soirées* (*The Thousand and One Evenings*).

The Abbott Jean-Paul **Bignon**, with *Les Aventures d'Abdalla, Fils d'Hanif* (*The Adventures of Abdallah, Son of Hanif*).

The Chevalier de **Mailly**, with *Voyage et les Aventures de Trois Princes de Serendib* (*Voyage and Adventures of Three Princes from Serendib*).

In the same vein were the "Arlequinades," plays featuring the famous character from the Comedia Dell'Arte, many of which incorporated the popular fantasy concepts of the times. In addition to **Nolant de Fatouville**'s *Arlequin Empereur de la Lune* (*Harlequin, Emperor of the Moon*, 1684) we could also include a number of titles by popular playwright and novelist Alain René **Lesage** such as *Arlequin Roi de Serendib* (*Harlequin King of Serendib*, 1713), *Arlequin Mahomet* (1714), *L'Île des Amazones* (*Amazon Island*, 1718), and others. (Lesage also wrote a celebrated three-volume, historical swashbuckling novel, *Gil Blas de Santillane* [1715, 1724, 1735].)

After a twenty-or-so years' pause, a "second wave" of fairy tales hit the market in the mid-1700s, this time written by authors such as Dame **Lévesque**, Mademoiselle de **Lubert**, Madame de **Lintot**, the Abbott Joseph de **La Porte** (with his *Bibliothèque des Fées et des Génies* [*Library of Fairies and Djinns*], 1765), the Comte de **Caylus**, Encyclopedist Denis Diderot, and, most especially, the talented Jeanne-Marie **Leprince de Beaumont**, whose classic *La Belle et la Bête* (*Beauty and the Beast*, 1757) has transcended the ages.

Leprince de Beaumont authored forty collections of tales (dubbed "Magasins" or Stores), published in London between 1750 and 1780. *La Belle et la Bête* was, itself, based on an earlier fairy tale by Gabrielle-Suzanne **Barbot de Gallon de Villeneuve**, included in her collection *Les Contes Marins ou La Jeune Américaine* (*Sea Stories or the Young American Girl*, 1740).

This abundance of material eventually led an enterprising publisher, the Chevalier Charles-Joseph de **Mayer**, to gather the best fairy tales of the times in a prodigious, forty-one volume anthology, entitled *Le Cabinet des Fées*

(*The Fairies' Cabinet*), published in Amsterdam and Geneva between 1785 and 1789. *Le Cabinet* thus has the honor of being the first specialized fantasy imprint ever published. (See specific entry under **Cabinet des Fées** in Chapter XI.)

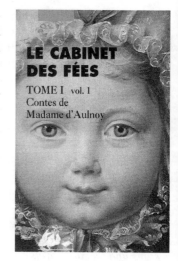

To each action a reaction: in *Zadig* (1747), Voltaire mocked his contemporaries' predilection for the *Féeries*— while making use of the same literary devices.

Jacques **Cazotte**, who had started as a writer of *Féeries*, such as *La Patte du Chat* (*Cat's Paw*, 1741) and *Les Mille et Une Fadaises* (*A Thousand and One Silly Stories*, 1742), soon tired of the increasingly precious and effete *Féeries* of latter years, and eventually ended up writing much darker tales such as *Le Diable Amoureux* (*The Devil in Love*, 1772), in which a young nobleman conjured up a demon who assumed the shape of a beautiful woman. In his "*Ollivier*," a poem written in 1773, the inhabitants of an island who lost the power of speech used music to express themselves.

In this fashion, the literary evolution of the *Féeries* paralleled that of French royalty, with the decadence and corruption of Louis XV replacing the aristocratic grandeur of Louis XIV. Cazotte well embodied the transition between the *Contes de Fées* and a darker and grimmer *fantastique*.

Eventually, the French Revolution came and, in an act tantamount to a literary execution, guillotined the heads of, if not the fairies and the little people, then those of many of the people who had become so much associated with this *Ancien Régime* genre.

(For film adaptations of **Perrault**'s tales, see *Peau d'Âne* and the section on Georges **Méliès** in Book 1, Chapter I, and *Le Petit Poucet*, *La Belle Au Bois Dormant* and *Cendrillon* in Book 1, Chapter II. *La Belle et la Bête* was also the subject of a classic French film by Jean **Cocteau**.)

3. The *Romans Philosophiques (Philosophical Novels)*

Even in the Age of Enlightenment, there were those who strenuously opposed the scientific and "positive" spirits of the times.

As the spiritual influence of the Catholic Church waned, thinkers dreamt of new universal faiths. Many of these based their thinking on occult knowledge handed (or allegedly handed) down through the ages, from the far-flung Orient to the Knights Templars and, finally, to the Freemasons and the Rosicrucians who flourished during the Enlightenment.

The line between proto-scientists like Franz Mesmer (1734-1815), real philosophers like Emanuel Swedenborg (1688-1772), "illuminists" like Louis-Claude de **Saint-Martin**, the author of *L'Homme de Désir* (*The Man of Desire*, 1790), in which a man reached total unity with the universe, and more mysterious figures such as the notorious alchemist/seer Count de Saint-Germain (1710-1784?) and his Masonic disciple, Giuseppe Balsamo, aka Cagliostro (1743-1795), was indeed a fragile and argumentative one.

The impact of these philosophers on the *fantastique* was, nevertheless, unquestionable, as their ideas acted as the starter which inflamed the imagination of many writers. Eventually, as had been the case during the Middle Ages when religious concepts slowly evolved into fantasy, a number of esoteric theories and writings were bowdlerized and trivialized to become merely adjuncts of the *fantastique*. This transition was perfectly illustrated by the fact that writer Alexandre **Dumas** used both Saint-Germain and Cagliostro as fictional characters in his novels, *Joseph Balsamo* and *Le Collier de la Reine* (*The Queen's Necklace*).

We already have mentioned Cyrano de Bergerac's letters, *Pour et Contre les Sorciers* (*For and Against Sorcerers*, 1663), which made fictional use of real-life alchemists. In 1670, the Abbott Nicolas-Pierre-Henri de Montfaucon de **Villars** published the thinly disguised occult fiction, *Le Comte de Gabalis* (*The Count of Gabalis*) sub-titled *Entretiens sur les Sciences Secrètes* (*Conversations on Secret Sciences*). Interestingly, the latter was reprinted in 1788 by Garnier in his *Voyages Imaginaires* imprint, proving once again how thin the delineation between the genres was. Having disclosed secret knowledge supposedly led to the Abbott's murder by Rosicrucians in 1675.

In 1707, Alain René **Lesage** penned a famous play about the demon Asmodeus, *Le Diable Boîteux* (*The Lame Devil*), inspired by a Spanish novel by Luis Velez de Guevara.

In 1731, the Abbott Jean **Terrasson** wrote *Séthos, Histoire ou Vie Tirée des Monuments, Anecdotes de l'Ancienne Égypte* (*Story or Life Drawn from Monuments and Anecdotes from Ancient Egypt*), whose pseudo-Egyptian and occult themes were later plagiarized by Mozart (1756-1791) for his opera the *Magic Flute* (1791), which also incorporated the composer's Masonic beliefs and various Masonic imagery.

One of the most interesting philosophical novels of the times was *Le Diable Amoureux* (*The Devil in Love*, 1772) by Jacques Cazotte, sub-titled "*un roman fantastique*"—a novel of the *fantastique*—perhaps the first time in literary history that a work was so clearly labeled. This alone marked it as one of the most important precursors in the genre. As briefly mentioned above, the hero, Alvaro, a young Spanish nobleman, conjured up the Devil, who assumed the shape of Biondetta, a seemingly innocent, very beautiful young woman. Biondetta eventually succeeded in drawing Alvaro into her bed, at which point she reverted to her true form: that of a hideous devil from Hell. However, thanks to his strong faith

and subsequent confession, Alvaro saved his soul from eternal damnation.

Le Diable Amoureux was truly the first modern French horror novel. In it, the supernatural was not treated as a fantamasgory, or for satirical or philosophical purposes. It was intended to be real and to induce fear in the reader. Even though Cazotte was not a member of any occult societies at the time, *Le Diable Amoureux* nevertheless drew much attention from occult circles because of its mystic and esoteric contents. Indeed, an 1845 reprinting was prefaced at great length by noted occultist/writer Gérard de **Nerval**.

Another work in the same vein was *Vathek*, a novel written directly into French in 1787 by English-born writer William **Beckford**. A Byronian figure steeped in occult knowledge and sexual perversions, Beckford allegedly wrote his novel non-stop in three days and two nights in a state of trance prefiguring the surrealists' automatic writing. *Vathek* told the story of the damnation of a Caliph who succumbed to the charms of the Giaour, a sorcerer ogre, and ended up worshipping the Oriental demon, Eblis. Vathek was eventually fated to suffer eternal damnation, his heart forever ablaze in his chest.

Other, lesser known examples of the proto-*fantastique* and worth mentioning were:

La Poupée (*The Doll*, 1747), by Jean **Galli de Bibbiéna**, in which a porcelain doll turned into a young woman.

Valérie (1792), by Jean-Pierre **Claris de Florian**, a continuator of La Fontaine, in which the eponymous heroine was, herself, a ghost.

Finally, in 1813, the very strange *Le Manuscrit Trouvé à Saragosse* (*Ms. Found in Saragosa*) was published in Paris. It did not properly belong to the *Roman Noir* so popular at the time, being more like a work of proto-*fantastique* (hence its inclusion in this chapter). Like *Vathek*, it was written directly into French by a non-French writer, the Polish count and scientist Jan **Potocki**. In it, a young captain stopped at a Spanish inn and heard tales-within-tales of horrific nature. *Le Manuscrit* featured a pair of sisters who were either vampires or succubae, as well as an assortment of ghosts and demons and the character of the Wandering Jew, which had now been made popular by Matthew Lewis' the *Monk* (1796). It also virtually created the archetypes of bandits living in secret underground caverns, Gypsies being the practitioners of contemporary versions of the medieval witches' Sabbaths, which would later become perennially popular staples of works of pulp fiction by 19th-century authors such as **Ponson du Terrail**, Paul **Féval**, Eugène **Sue**, and Gaston **Leroux**.

Paradoxically, *Le Manuscrit* featured another modern characteristic: Its macabre imagery was contrasted by Potocki's deliberate attempt (through his hero) to find rational explanations for his horrible adventures—for example, drug-induced nightmares—before diving again mercilessly into the murky waters of the *fantastique*.

(*Le Manuscrit* was partially filmed by Polish director Wojcieck Has in 1965.)

CHAPTER IV

19th Century Fantastique *(1800–1914)*

The 19th century was a period of great turmoil in French history. After the French Revolution, France successively experienced Napoléon's First Empire, a Monarchic Restauration, a Second Republic, a Second Empire, and a Third Republic. During the First and Second Empires, periods of proud, military glory alternated with crushing, humiliating defeats.

It was in this ever-boiling cauldron of historical upheaval that French literature exploded into a bouquet of heretofore unknown and abundant colors—and so did the *fantastique.*

French literature of the 19th century was dominated by three currents: the *romantisme* (*romanticism*), the *réalisme* (*realism*, or *naturalism*), and the *symbolisme* or *décadent* (*symbolism*, or *decadence*) which, while distinctive in terms of works, nevertheless intermingled in the lives of their respective writers. For example, Honoré de **Balzac**, a founder of realism, also had his romantic period; Victor **Hugo** and Gérard de **Nerval**, to name but two, moved easily between romanticism and symbolism. We were therefore forced to resort to some degree of arbitrariness when choosing where to classify an author's works.

In addition to the literary currents mentioned above, the French *fantastique* of the 19th century was influenced by a number of powerful, visionary authors:

The English Gothic writers, especially Ann Radcliffe (1764-1823), Matthew Lewis (1775-1818), and Charles-Robert Maturin (1782-1824).

The German writer, E. T. A. Hoffmann (1776-1822).

The American writer, Edgar Allan Poe (1809-1849).

The British poets, Lord Byron (1788-1824) and Oscar Wilde (1854-1900), the latter lived in Paris in 1883 and 1892 and professed his admiration for both **Gautier** and **Baudelaire**.

The German composer, Richard Wagner (1813-1883).

And, finally, the two occult writers Eliphas **Lévi** and Allan **Kardec**.

From a literary—if not historical—standpoint, it could be argued that the 19th century came to a crashing halt not in 1901, as per the calendar, but with the advent of World War I in 1914, hence our decision to include in this chapter works published in the first decade of the 20th century as well. The period between 1900-1914 is known as the *belle époque* (*beautiful era*).

Finally, it is worth noting that it was during this incredibly rich century that we started to see the formation of a clear split between the more lurid and exploitative forms of the *fantastique* which catered to the masses and are dubbed here *fantastique populaire*, and the more literary and refined works of both major and minor mainstream writers, dubbed *fantastique littéraire*.

Our overview of the century begins with the gothic novels.

1. The *Romans Noirs* and *Romans Frénétiques* (Gothic Novels)

As the 19th century was about to begin, the English gothic novels hit the French literary scene with a bang. Their extravagant and macabre nature tapped into the emotions released during the French Revolution, and eventually helped the genre to seamlessly evolve into the more modern forms of the *fantastique.*

Horace Walpole's (1717-1797) the *Castle of Otranto* had already been published in 1765, but it was Ann Radcliffe, with her the *Mysteries of Udolfo* (1794), and Matthew Lewis, with the *Monk* (1796), which both proved enormously successful in their French translations. A subsequent, but no less influential, author was Charles-Robert Maturin, whose *Melmoth the Wanderer* (1820) was praised by distinguished writers such as **Baudelaire** and Balzac—the latter even writing a sequel to it.

Imitation being the sincerest form of flattery, the English gothic writers helped launch a wave of what the French called *romans noirs* (*black novels*), or *romans frénétiques* (*frantic novels*), which became the first sub-genre of popular literature.

One of the first French writers to borrow from the English gothics was the infamous Donatien Alphonse François, Marquis de **Sade**, an indomitable rebel and notorious *débauché* whose erotic novels *Justine* (1791) and *Juliette* (1798), although they contained no true fantastic elements, were clearly gothic in inspiration, and obviously anticipated the trend toward the gothic in French literature. Also, by becoming the first of the *écrivains maudits* (*accursed writers*), **Sade** started another modern trend, that of pushing the envelope, challenging the mores of the times, thumbing his nose at society, daring his literary successors to further explore and test the boundaries of what is acceptable in the genre.

In 1798, Jacques-Antoine **Reveroni Saint-Cyr** imitated Sade with *Pauliska, ou la Perversité Moderne* (*Pauliska, or Modern Perversity*). But the first real French *roman noir* is usually considered to be *Coelina, ou l'Enfant du Mystère* (*Coelina, or the Child of Mystery*), written in 1799 by François-Guillaume **Ducray-Duminil**, and quickly turned into an equally successful stage play by Guilbert de **Pixérécourt**—himself the author of a number of over a hundred plays in the gothic, *roman noir*, and melodramatic veins, such as *Le Château des Appenins* (*The Castle in the Appenins*, 1799) and *Le Solitaire de la Roche Noire* (*The Hermit of Black Rock*, 1806).

From 1800 onward, French enthusiasm for the *roman noir* grew by leaps and bounds. For example, *Les Barons de Flesheim* (*The Barons of Flesheim*, 1798) by Charles **Pigault-Lebrun**; *Le Monstre* (*The Monster*, 1824), and *Le Damné* (*The Damned*, 1824) by Eugène de **Lamerlière**; and the anonymous *Fantômes Nocturnes ou la Terreur des Coupables, le Théâtre des Forfaits, Offrant par Nouvelles Historiques des Visions Infernales de Monstres Fantastiques, d'Images Funestes, de Lutins Homicides, de Spectres et d'Échafauds Sanglants, Supplices Précurseurs des Scélérats* (*Nocturnal Ghosts or the Terror of the Guilty, Theater of Evil Deeds, Offering Through Historical Stories Infernal Visions of Fantastic Monsters, Nefarious Images, Murderous Goblins, Specters and Bloody Scaffolds, Tortures Worthy of the Worst Villains*, 1821)—the title pretty much spells it out!—were all major commercial successes.

In 1819, a translation of John-William Polidori's (1795-1821) notorious vampire tale, the *Vampyre*, falsely attributed to Lord Byron, was published in France. It proved enormously successful and was immediately copied by Cyprien **Bérard**, who authored *Lord Rutwen ou les Vampires* in 1820, which was then promptly adapted into a stage play by Charles **Nodier** the same year. The character of the vampire, which had previously been satirized by **Voltaire** in his *Dictionnaire Philosophique* (1764), suddenly became a Byronesque romantic icon which took the literary establishment by storm. Judging by the popularity of Anne Rice's present-day *Lestat*, one may hazard that this literary icon, while over one hundred seventy-five years old, is still powerful today.

Vampires were suddenly fashionable. In 1823, the Théâtre de la Gaité in Paris featured a play entitled *Polichinelle Vampire*. In 1825, in the three-volume *La Vampire*, Étienne-Léon de **Lamothe-Langon** told the story of a young Napoleonic army officer who brought his Hungarian fiancée home to later discover that she was, in reality, a vampire. It is worth noting that this story predated Bram Stoker's *Dracula* (published in 1897) by seventy-two years!

In 1820, the great Honoré de **Balzac**, still an aspiring writer, paid his dues to the *roman noir*. Balzac became a renowned, prolific writer of mainstream literature, justly famous for a series of novels called *La Comédie Humaine* (*The Human Comedy*), which helped establish the orthodox classical novel. But his early works were very much influenced by the popular gothic novels of the times. *Falthurne* (1820), for example, was a novel about a virgin prophetess who knew occult secrets that dated all the way back to ancient Mesopotamia.

In his youth, Balzac was a prolific gothic novelist. In 1822, he wrote *L'Héritière de Birague* (*The Heir of Birague*), *Jean-Louis, ou la Fille Trouvée* (*Jean-Louis, or the Found Girl*), and *Clotilde de Lusignan* (aka *L'Israélite*), all signed "Lord R'Hoone," an anagram of Honoré, and *Le Vicaire des Ardennes* (*The Vicar of the Ardennes*), heavily inspired by Lewis' *The Monk*, signed "Horace de Saint-Aubin." In 1823, as "Saint-Aubin," he penned *La Dernière Fée* (*The Last Fairy*), and in 1824, *Annette et le Criminel* (*Annette and the Criminal*; aka *Argow le Pirate*), and in 1825, *Wann-Chlore* (aka *Jane la Pâle*)—all *romans noir* which **Balzac** later disavowed.

More pertinent to this study is *Le Centenaire, ou les Deux Beringheld* (*The Hundred-Centenarian, or the Two Beringheld*), clearly inspired by *Melmoth* and published in 1822. Unlike Maturin, however, Balzac did not use the convenient cliché of a pact with the Devil, but instead drew on his own occult knowledge—specifically, Rosicrucian beliefs—to create the character of a four-hundred-year-old vampire who, in order to prolong his existence, did not drain blood but the very essence of life itself.

Maturin's influence on Balzac's approach to the *fantastique* was even more pronounced with *L'Élixir de Longue*

Vie (*The Elixir of Long Life*, 1830) and *La Peau de Chagrin* (*The Skin of Sorrow*, 1831). In the former, the protagonist, Don Juan Belvidero, was not only obsessed with the secret of immortality, but he was also a monster of pride who felt only contempt for mankind and for God. In the latter, Balzac focused on the theme of the destruction of the precious life essence. The power and consequences of the unchecked passions which imbued these two novels became his trademark theme, which he later put to good use in the more realistic settings of his *Comédie Humaine* novels.

Finally, in *Melmoth Réconcilié* (*Melmoth Reconciled*, 1835), Balzac took the last, logical step. Reusing Maturin's own character, and drawing from the "illuminist" philosophies of Louis-Claude de **Saint-Martin**, he concocted a yarn that showed Melmoth a path to salvation.

Even after Balzac had become a respected and successful mainstream writer, and even though he is credited today as the creator of realism and naturalism in the novel, he still chose to incorporate mystical and philosophical speculations in some of his works. His knowledge of, and interest in, the occult, and especially his search for "higher" planes of existence, manifested itself in some of his latter novels, which belong to the *fantastique symboliste* school (see below). Among these were *Louis Lambert* (1832), which featured a man seeking higher dimensions; the aptly-named *La Recherche de l'Absolu* (*The Search for the Absolute*, 1834), whose hero was an alchemist; and *Seraphita* (1835), a novel clearly inspired by Swedenborg's philosophy about a perfect, angelic hermaphrodite—a recurring theme in the *symboliste* movement.

Having begun with *Falthurne* and ended with *Seraphita*, and through the very salvation of Melmoth's soul, Balzac could be said to have completed his personal initiation. He left behind the negative energies of the *roman noir* and instead focused on the positive aspects of his personal spiritual quest. a remarkable literary journey by any standards.

With Charles **Rabou** and Philarète **Chasles**, Balzac compiled a notable anthology, *Contes Bruns* (*Brown Tales*, 1832), which included stories such as "Tobias Guarnerius" and "Le Ministère Public" ("The Public Ministry"). Other tales included: "*Le Mannequin*" ("*The Mannikin*", 1831), "La Danse des Morts" ("The Dance of the Dead", 1832) and "L'Homme aux Échéances" ("The Man with the Bill Book, 1833). Rabou was also the author of gothic novels such as *L'Allée des Veuves* (*Widows' Alley*, 1845) and *La Fille Sanglante* (*The Bloody Girl*, 1857).

(*La Peau de Chagrin* and *Melmoth Réconcilié* were adapted by French Television (see Book 1, Chapter II); one of **Balzac**'s short stories became the basis for the 1971-74 film *Out Un: Spectre* (see Chapter I).)

In 1821, the talented Charles **Nodier** wrote *Smarra ou les Démons de la Nuit* (*Smarra, or the Demons of the Night*), a series of terrifying dream-based tales. An inventive and talented writer, Nodier also began his literary career by penning popular gothic novels such as *Les Proscrits* (*The Pro-*scribed*, 1802), *Le Peintre de Salzbourg* (*The Painter of Salzbourg*, 1803), and *Les Méditations du Cloître* (*The Meditations of the Cloister*, 1803). But his true career in the genre began after the Restoration in 1820, when he wrote the play *Lord Rurthwen* based on the famous Polidori story. *Smarra*, too, was a fantasy saga, in which a Byronesque hero encountered fairies and vampires, perhaps the first mixture of traditional and modern fantastic elements under a single cover.

Then, in 1825, Nodier published *Infernaliana*, an anthology of stories about the Devil and possession. In 1837, he wrote *Ines de la Sierra* and, finally, in 1839, *Lydie*, two gothic novels. But Nodier's heart was not with the *roman noir*. As early as 1822, with his *Trilby ou le Lutin d'Argail* (*Trilby, or the Goblin of Argail*), a novel based on an old Scot legend in which a woman was psychically enslaved by a supernatural creature, he demonstrated that his literary gifts belonged to other areas of the *fantastique*: that of the fairy tale. In 1830, with the publication of *L'Histoire du Roi de Bohême et de ses Sept Châteaux* (*The Story of the King of Bohemia and of His Seven Castles*), Nodier, having taken to heart the lessons of Hoffmann's *Tales*, embarked on a more romantic type of *fantastique*, and helped steer the genre in other directions. (That aspect of Nodier's career is reviewed below.)

Meanwhile, also in 1821, the Vicomte Charles-Victor d'**Arlincourt** combined Walter Scott's (1771-1832) sense of historical epic with Ann Radcliffe's gothic passions, and penned the genre's first historical gothic novel, *Le Solitaire* (*The Hermit*). *Le Solitaire* was a *roman frénétique* with genre elements. It postulated that, from a Swiss hideaway, the hidden hand of Charles le Téméraire, who in reality died in 1477, continued to secretly control all the major events of history until the early 1500s. In many ways, it was also the first modern conspiracy novel!

The public loved it, and *Le Solitaire*, too, spawned several imitations, such as:

The medieval gothic novels *La Danse Infernale* (*The Hellish Dance*, 1829) and *Les Deux Fous* (*The Two Madmen*, 1830) by Paul **Lacroix**.

Le Manteau d'un Sous-Lieutenant (*The Sub-Lieutenant's Coat*, 1832) by Auguste **Jeancourt**.

L'Écuyer Dauberon (*The Squire Dauberon*, 1832) by Mélanie **Waldor**.

Another celebrated writer, Victor **Hugo**, the author of *Les Misérables* (1862), was also influenced by Walter Scott when he wrote his renowned novel, *Notre-Dame de Paris* (aka the *Hunchback of Notre-Dame*, 1831), which contained numerous horrific elements as well as one of the first "classic" monsters after Frankenstein (1818) and Lord Ruthwen the Vampire (1819). But, prior to this, Hugo, too, had paid his dues to the *roman frénétique* by penning *Han d'Islande* (*Han of Iceland*, 1823), a bloody tale featuring two monstrous heroes, one a Viking warrior who drank blood from his victims' skulls, and the other a semi-mythical bear. In

1826, in *Bug-Jargal*, Hugo told the story of a native revolt on the island of Saint-Domingue, and included the description of a terrifying witch doctor. One of Hugo's short-stories, "*Claude Gueux*," was even adapted into a **Grand-Guignol** play by **Chancerel**.

Hugo's penultimate novel, the morbid and romantic *L'Homme qui Rit* (*The Man Who Laughs*, 1869) was about a horribly disfigured man who lived in 17th-century England. Its 1928 film version, starring Conrad Veidt, was credited as the model for Batman's notorious adversary, the Joker. *L'Homme qui Rit* showed a marked return to Walter Scott and the gothic influences. In it, Hugo created a sublime, horrific figure, one matching that of his earlier Quasimodo and the Frankenstein Monster. The hero, Gwynplaine, is the son of a 17th-century English nobleman who rebelled against the King. As a result, the King ordered the boy's mouth to be sliced open to his ears, and the boy himself sold to the Gypsies. When he grew up, Gwynplaine's hideous grin turned him into a tragic circus freak, known as the "Man Who Laughs," one who hated the society which inflicted such a monstrous and unfair punishment upon him.

(French film versions of Hugo's works included a 1956 Franco-Italian co-production of *Notre-Dame de Paris*, directed by Jean Delannoy, and no less than seven filmed versions of *Les Misérables*.)

In 1829, *L'Âne Mort et la Femme Guillotinée* (*The Dead Donkey and the Guillotined Woman*) by Jules **Janin** was hailed by some as a new masterpiece of the macabre—often verging on the pastiche—but was criticized by others for being just too bloody and horrible. Gore, pure horror fiction had arrived. Excessive amounts of gore had already been featured in the works of Philarète **Chasles**, such as *Le Père et la Fille* (*The Father and the Daughter*, 1824) and *La Fiancée de Bénares* (*The Fiancée from Benares*), but it was Janin who made it popular and enabled it to reach new audiences, anticipating the Grand-Guignol by sixty-eight years.

Bloodthirstiness also was a trademark of Pétrus **Borel**, a noted romantic author praised by Théophile **Gautier**, who wrote *Champavert, Contes Immoraux* (*Immoral Tales*, 1833), an anthology featuring macabre, morbid, and gory tales rather than immoral ones. Some of these tales contained the first modern exploration of the theme of the werewolf, adding one more "classic" monster to the gallery listed above. A romantic who was nicknamed the "lycanthrope" by his friends, **Borel** became one of the most outrageous purveyors of *romans frénétiques*. His *Madame Putiphar* (written in 1833 but published only in 1839) is often listed as one of the true masterpieces of the French gothics. It, too, anticipated what eventually emerged as the Grand-Guignol. At the same time, it proved to be one of the last *romans frénétiques* of the period, the genre having run out of blood (as it were) and being progressively replaced by more classic forms of the *fantastique*.

Meanwhile, 1830 saw the publication of *Césaire* by Alexandre **Guiraud**, a member of the French Academy.

In 1832, Jacques **Boucher de Perthes**, a famous archeologist who, in a five-volume treatise entitled *De la Création* (*Of Creation*, 1838-41), first postulated the then-controversial theories about the real age of mankind, published *Nouvelles*, a collection of short stories including "*Paola*," the tale of a 300-year-old vampire countess.

Also in 1832, *Le Diable* (*The Devil*) by Étienne-Léon de **Lamothe-Langon** introduced the incredibly charming yet wholly corrupt character of the Chevalier Draxel, virtually evil incarnate, one more modern literary archetype shaped from the cauldron of gothic literature. Lamothe-Langon, a writer known for his memoirs, also penned an impressive number of gothic novels with lurid titles such as: *Le Monastère des Frères Noirs, ou l'Étendard de la Mort* (*The Monastery of the Black Friars, or the Standard of Death*, 1825), *L'Hermite de la Tombe Mystérieuse, ou les Fantômes du Vieux Château* (*The Hermit of the Mysterious Grave, or the Ghosts of the Old Castle*, 1829), *La Cloche du Trépassé, ou les Mystères du Château de Beauvoir* (*The Bell of the Deceased, or the Mysteries of the Castle of Beauvoir*, 1839), etc.

The almost sadistic description of the slow, pernicious influence of evil was particularly well handled by writer Frédéric **Soulié** who, in 1832, published his first *roman noir*, *Les Deux Cadavres* (*The Two Corpses*), which was followed by *Le Vicomte de Béziers* (*The Viscount of Beziers*) in 1834 and, in 1838, by his masterwork, the classic *Les Mémoires du Diable* (*The Devil's Memoirs*). In it, Soulié combined the techniques of the *roman frénétique* with the passions of Sade—the reading of *Justine* is actually used as a means of torture in the novel!—to orchestrate a series of crimes, murders, adulterous and incestuous liaisons, which all took place under the malevolent eye of a dandified Satan. The prolific Soulié wrote over one hundred other novels, many of which dealt with Napoleon's First Empire.

After so much blood, so much gore and so much evil, the *roman frénétique* began to justifiably display signs of exhaustion. Other successful works of the genre and the times included:

Le Mutilé (*The Mutilated Man*, 1832), by Xavier-Boniface de **Saintine**, a gothic novel about a poet whose tongue and hands are cut off to prevent him from expressing himself.

Les Contes de Sainte-Pélagie (*Tales from Saint-Pelagie*, 1833), by Alphonse **Choquart**, a collection of gothic and supernatural tales told by prisoners of the famous jail.

Les Roueries de Trialph (*Trialph's Lies*, 1833), by Charles **Lassailly**.

Le Cimetière d'Ivry (*The Ivry Cemetery*, 1834), by **Arthaud** and **Poujol**.

The grim *Album d'un Pessimiste* (*Album of a Pessimist*, 1835), by Alphonse **Rabbe**, greatly admired by **Baudelaire**.

Ugolino (1835), by Aloysius **Block**, inspired by Hoffmann.

Le Magicien (*The Magician*, 1838), by Alphonse **Esquiros**, a friend of Pétrus Borel who later turned to politics and became a senator.

Une Promenade de Bélial (*Belial's Walk*, 1848), by Alfred de **Poittevin**.

Les Nuits du Père Lachaise (*The Nights of the Père Lachaise*, 1845), about the famous Parisian cemetery, *Les Veuves du Diable* (*The Devil's Widows*, 1858) and *Le Vampire du Val-de-Grâce* (*The Vampire of the Val-de-Grâce Hospital*, 1861), by Léon **Gozlan**.

Prolific author Albert **Bourgeois**, who penned well over two hundred melodramas, contributed *La Nonne Sanglante* (*The Bloody Nun*, 1835), in which a ghostly nun sought revenge on the former lover who sealed her fate. (It was adapted for television—see Book 1, Chapter II). He also wrote *Les Pilules du Diable* (*The Devil's Pills*, 1867), in which a witch turned a man into a turkey!

Eventually, the *roman noir* gave way to more modern forms of the *fantastique*. On the one hand, it continued along the paths of the popular novel, published in inexpensive formats and catering to large audiences. This tradition of the *fantastique populaire*, which had begun with the pre-Revolutionary imprints of *Le Cabinet des Fées* (*The Fairies' Cabinet*) and the *Voyages Imaginaires* (*Imaginary Journeys*), continued and gained momentum with the publication of the more lurid and exploitative samples of the *romans frénétiques*. The more brutal, gorier, brand of horror, as exemplified by the notorious performances of the Grand-Guignol theater in Paris (which began in 1897), was published in small, inexpensive pamphlets, labeled "*horreur*" (*horror*), or "*épouvante*" (*fright*). In the true tradition of popular fiction, they were considered cheap thrills, good only for the barely educated masses.

At the other end of the literary spectrum, the *roman noir* was alchemically transformed by the influences of Hofmann and Poe, and evolved into a more poetic and literary form of the *fantastique*, which attracted major writers, such as Gustave **Flaubert**, Honoré de Balzac, Victor Hugo, Théophile **Gautier**, Prosper **Mérimée**, George **Sand**, and Guy de **Maupassant**, to name but a few of the more famous. Thus did the *fantastique* gain entrance—even if sometimes through the back door—in "classic" French literature, forming a sub-set referred to here as the *fantastique littéraire*.

2. The *Fantastique Populaire*

a. Before 1900

The pioneer, and one of the most successful representatives ever, of the *fantastique populaire* was Eugène **Sue**, whose *Les Mystères de Paris* (*The Mysteries of Paris*) was serialized in 1843 in the daily newspaper *Le Journal des Débats* and directly inspired Hugo's *Les Misérables*. *Les Mys* *tères de Paris* was the *Dallas* or *Dynasty* of its times. It was a hugely popular social-gothic serial pitting the mysterious Prince Rodolphe and the beautiful Fleur-de-Marie against the villainous Maître d'École (*Schoolmaster*), Chourineur (*Stabber*), and La Chouette (*Owl*) in the dark mazes and haunts of the Paris underworld. Its initial serialization in a daily newspaper—hence the label *roman feuilleton* (*feuille* [*leaf*] being a term for a newspaper's page) employed for this type of novels—rather than publication in the more traditional and higher-brow book form, was a clear evidence of the distinction between popular entertainment and works with more respectable literary and cultural aspirations.

Sue wrote in a style which was a captivating combination of gothic melodrama and social realism. He was one of the first French writers to denounce some of the social ills that accompanied the Industrial Revolution. His earlier works, such as *Kernock le Pirate* (1830), *Atar-Gull* (1831), *La Salamandre* (1832), *Paula Monti, ou L'Hotel Lambert* (1842) and *La Morne au Diable* (*The Devil's Morn*, 1842) were all traditional *romans noir*, borrowing themes from Radcliffe or Fenimore Cooper—tales of grisly murders, bloodthirsty pirates, and high adventure. His *Latréaumont* (1837) was an historical gothic novel which inspired Isidore **Ducasse** to choose the pseudonym of **Lautréamont**.

With *Le Juif Errant* (*The Wandering Jew*), serialized in 1844-45, Sue wrote his first, full-blown *fantastique* novel. In it, the Wandering Jew and his sister Herodiade met every hundred years across the Straits of Bering. Throughout the centuries, they have waged a secret war against the powerful Jesuits, using men and even real-life historic events— such as the cholera epidemic which struck Paris in 1832— as chess pieces in their time-spanning game.

The seminal novel on the subject of the Wandering Jew was *Ahasvérus*, a lengthy and sophisticated poetic narrative published eleven years before in 1833 by Edgar **Quinet**, also the author of a remarkable book about Merlin, *Merlin l'Enchanteur* (*Merlin the Enchanter*, 1895). The character of the Wandering Jew, which had previously appeared in **Tyssot de Patot**'s *La Vie, les Aventures et le Voyage de Groenland du Révérend Père Cordelier Pierre de Mésange* (*The Life, Adventures and Trip to Greenland of the Rev. Father Pierre de Mesange*) and **Potocki**'s *Le Manuscrit Trouvé à Saragosse* (*Ms. Found in Saragosa*), returned in Alexandre **Dumas**' *Isaac Laquedem* (1853).

Some of these novels were turned into stage plays, directed by Sue himself: *Les Mystères de Paris* in 1843, *Le Juif Errant* in 1849. *Les Mystères de Paris* were filmed in 1943 by Jacques de Baroncelli (starring Marcel Herrand as Rodolphe and Caecilia Paroldi as Fleur de Marie), and in 1962 by André Hunebelle (starring Jean Marais—the Beast from *La Belle et la Bête*—as Rodolphe and Dany Robin as Fleur de Marie.)

The undisputed master of French popular literature was, without a doubt, the prodigious Alexandre **Dumas**, known throughout the world for his classic adventure nov els, *Les Trois Mousquetaires* (*The Three Musketeers*, 1844) and *Le Comte de Monte-Cristo* (*The Count of Monte Cristo*, 1845), both based on real-life characters and events. a number of Dumas' lesser known works, such as *Le Château d'Eppstein* (*The Castle of Eppstein*, 1844) and *Le Trou d'Enfer* (*The Hell Hole*, 1851), were *romans noir*.

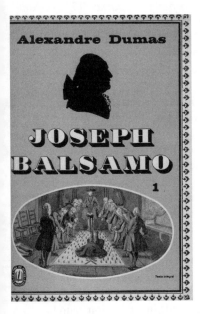

But like Balzac, Dumas had a strong interest in, and knowledge of, the occult. One of his earliest works was a collaboration with Gérard de **Nerval** entitled *L'Alchimiste* (*The Alchemist*, 1839). Later, his *Joseph Balsamo* (1846) starred the eponymous freemason who was shown using the mediumnistic powers of a young virgin to pave the way for the destruction of the French Monarchy and the advent of the Revolution. In its sequel, *Le Collier de la Reine* (*The Queen's Necklace*, 1849), Balsamo was succeeded by Cagliostro, who was now pulling the strings. *Isaac Laquedem* (1853) was Dumas' own version of **Sue**'s *Wandering Jew*, happily mixing occult conspiracies and historical events. (*Joseph Balsamo* was adapted by French television—see Book 1, Chapter II.)

Dumas was gifted with a prodigious imagination and was a born storyteller. He was also finely attuned to the trends and fashions that were popular in the marketplace. The success of Hoffmann's *Tales* and of the *Thousand and One Nights* undoubtedly influenced him to write *Les Mille et Un Fantômes* (*A Thousand and One Ghosts*, 1849), an anthology of macabre tales, linked by the now-classic device of guests sharing ghostly tales at a dinner party. Among its contents was a story about a vampire who preyed on a girl and was eventually destroyed by being nailed in his coffin with a consecrated sword. Vampires sold books and Dumas returned to the theme with the elaborate *Le Vampire* (1851), recasting his protagonist in a more romantic mode. Finally, in 1857, Dumas penned one of the first modern werewolf stories—and still one of the best—with *Le Meneur de Loups* (*The Leader of Wolves*), the tale of a man who became a werewolf after a pact with the devil.

Another famous author of serial novels was Paul **Féval**, whose popularity easily equaled that of Dumas, **Ponson du Terrail**, and Sue. Féval, like Dumas, was the author of numerous popular swashbuckling novels, such as *Le Loup Blanc* (*The White Wolf*, 1843), a provincial *Monte-Cristo* tale, and *Le Bossu* (*The Hunchback*, 1857), in which the hero, Lagardère, a prodigious swordsman, disguised himself as a hunchback to take revenge against his enemies.

Féval's *Les Mystères de Londres* (*The Mysteries of London*, 1844) was an obvious attempt at cashing in on **Sue**'s success; however, Féval made it more lurid by including a mad scientist performing human experiments. But when it came to occult conspiracies and mysterious secret societies working behind the scenes pursuing nefarious goals, Féval outdid both Sue and Dumas. *Le Fils du Diable* (*The Devil's Son*, 1847), *La Fée des Grèves* (*The Fairy of the Shores*, 1851), *La Soeur des Fantômes* (*The Sister of Ghosts*) aka *Les Revenants* (*The Phantoms*, 1853), *Les Compagnons du Silence* (*The Brotherhood of Silence*, 1857), *Jean Diable* (*John the Devil*, 1862) and *La Fille du Juif Errant* (*The Daughter of the Wandering Jew*, 1864)—yes, him again!— all dealt with the desperate plights of innocents caught in the sinister webs spun by the forces of evil. Unlike the works of Dumas, Ponson du Terrail, and Sue, all of Féval's novels contained some fantastic elements, e.g. *La Fille du Juif Errant* featured a transfer of souls between two characters, embedded in a deeply surreal atmosphere. Thus, Féval helped the gothic novel merge with the *fantastique*.

Féval's masterpiece was unarguably *Les Habits Noirs* (*The Black Coats* or the *Men in Black*, 1863-75), a huge, sprawling saga comprised of eight separate novels. *Les Habits Noirs* told the story of an innocent man framed by a brotherhood of criminals led by a mysterious immortal, the Colonel Bozzo-Corona. The Colonel was the Moriarty-like godfather of a criminal empire which dated back centuries and anticipated the Mafia. The Colonel's right-hand man was the mysterious Monsieur Lecoq, clearly inspired by the real-life master criminal turned Prefect of Police, Vidocq. (No relation to **Gaboriau**'s detective mentioned below.) Féval made the mistake of killing off the Colonel at the end of the first volume, but like Conan Doyle, yielding to his readers' pressure, he brought him back, again and again. The brotherhood's password was "*Fera-t-il jour demain?*" (*Will there be daylight tomorrow?*), meaning, will a crime be committed? and the sinister reply was, "*It will be daylight from midnight to noon if it's the will of the father.*" By its methods, themes and characters, *Les Habits Noirs*, while only marginally a genre work, was another precursor of today's conspiracy thrillers.

Finally, even more so than Sue and Dumas, Féval was the only author of *romans feuilletons* (or *feuilletoniste*) of the times who never shrank from using classic fantastic concepts because of fear of rejection by the public. His *Le Chevalier Ténèbre* (*The Knight of Darkness*, 1862) related the criminal exploits of two vampire brothers. It was followed by the macabre *Les Drames de la Mort* (*The Dramas of Death*, 1867), and by an outrageous vampire novel, *La Ville Vampire* (*The Vampire City*, 1874). In it, Féval parodied Ann Radcliffe, even making her his fictional hero! *La Ville Vampire* opened with the news of a vampire plaguing the English countryside where Ms. Radcliffe lived. To save one of her cousins, the indomitable novelist—or rather, her fictional counterpart—gathered a group of fearless vampire hunters. This was, perhaps, the first such group in literary history, this novel predating Stoker's *Dracula* by twenty-three years. Then, Radcliffe and her band traveled to the vampire city of Selené, located in Serbia, not far from Transylvania. Selené turned out to be a giant necropolis carved from black marble. There, Radcliffe and her companions succeeded in tearing out the heart of the vampire lord Goetzi and burning it, thus putting an end to the undead menace. They then made their escape from the accursed city.

La Ville Vampire was, like *Les Habits Noirs*, remarkable because of its themes and its characters. It was arguably the first true, popular *fantastique* epic, unabashedly commercial, without any literary pretensions. "You want vampires, I'll give you vampires," Féval seemed to tell his readers. The book's tremendous success only proved the justness of his commercial instincts.

(**Le Loup Blanc** and **Les Habits Noirs** were adapted by French television—see Book 1, Chapter II. *Le Bossu* was filmed four times.)

One could hardly cover the field of 19th-century *roman feuilleton* without mentioning Victor-Alexis **Ponson du Terrail**, the author of the saga of *Rocambole* or *Les Drames de Paris* (*The Dramas of Paris*), comprising twenty-five volumes published between 1857 and 1867.

Rocambole was an adventurer who did good but was often on the wrong side of the law, like Arsène Lupin and the Saint. As did Sherlock Holmes and the Shadow, Rocambole gathered around him a group of assistants, selected from various slices of society, ready to drop everything to help their "Master." Like Doc Savage, Rocambole mastered the physical skills of the Orient and inherited some of the secrets of ancient Tibetan (or equally exotic) civilizations. Rocambole was more than a mere man, he was the first modern, literary super-hero.

Rocambole's sometimes lover, sometimes rival, was the beautiful Baccara, a former courtesan who was a fearless shooter, rider, and swordswoman. In one of the novels of the saga, it was revealed that she eventually emigrated to the New World and became Calamity Jane! Rocambole's archenemy was the satanic Sir Williams, whose extraordinarily devious schemes were always thwarted at the last minute. In fact, the term "*rocambolesque*" became common in French to label any kind of fantastic adventure. While incurably evil, Sir Williams nevertheless had a sense of panache and doomed grandeur about him. Rocambole, whose origins remained shrouded in mystery, started as a minor, supporting character helping Sir Williams in one of his nefarious plot to steal an inheritance. Then the pupil overtook and surpassed his master. Rocambole always referred to Sir Williams as "my good Master" and it was clear that the two adversaries liked and respected each other. *Rocambole* was often sprinkled with fantastic elements, such as a sect of Kali-worshipping thugs, and a Russian exiled

prince who was also a mad scientist plotting to conquer the world, but like *Les Habits Noirs*, it was primarily a crime thriller/adventure series. Unlike Féval's work, however, *Rocambole* created and virtually defined all the archetypes of modern heroic and super-heroic fiction.

Ponson du Terrail's only other excursion in the genre was his early novel *La Baronne Trépassée* (*The Dead Baroness*, 1852), in which the reader never knew if the title character was truly dead or not, and if she was dead, did she return to life as a vampire? The ending, which offered no rational explanation, made *La Baronne Trépassée* a genre novel.

Rocambole and *La Baronne Trépassée* (under the title **Le Veneur Noir**) were adapted by French television—see Book 1, Chapter II.

Finally, no overview of this period would be complete without a mention of Émile **Gaboriau**, the founding father of the modern detective story with his character of Monsieur Lecoq. Lecoq (no first-name was ever given by Gaboriau) was an agent of the dreaded Sureté. He was a methodical, scientifically minded detective who, like Sherlock Holmes, carefully gathered minute clues from the scene of the crime and, from them, drew conclusions which, at first, amazed his colleagues but proved eminently logical when explained.

Sir Arthur Conan Doyle paid homage to Gaboriau when he first introduced Holmes and, indeed, Monsieur Lecoq was a worthy precursor of the Great Detective, who owed him more than a passing debt. Like Holmes, Lecoq was more than a mere crime-solver: he was a Vidocq-like character, a master of disguise with a secret identity in the Paris underworld; in the amateur detective Father Tabaret, he even had an older mentor who, like Mycroft Holmes, helped him solve particularly challenging puzzles from the comfort of his bed. Monsieur Lecoq first appeared as a supporting character, a student of the methods of Tabaret in *L'Affaire Lerouge* (*The Lerouge Affair*, 1866) but quickly graduated to full-blown "hero" status in *Le Crime d'Orcival* (*The Orcival Crime*, 1867). The newspaper serializing Lecoq's adventures saw its sales skyrocket, which encouraged Gaboriau to write the classic *Le Dossier No.113* (*File 113*, 1867), *Les Esclaves de Paris* (*The Slaves of Paris*, 1868) and, finally, *Monsieur Lecoq* (1869), which told the story of Lecoq's first case. An unauthorized sixth volume, *La Vieillesse de Monsieur Lecoq* (*Mr. Lecoq's Old Age*) was written by Fortuné de Boisgobey in 1875, anticipating the modern publishing phenomenon of Sherlock Holmes pastiches.

b. La Belle Époque (1900-1914)

With the end of the 19th century, and the advent of the *Belle Époque*, the *fantastique populaire* became increasingly modern. The haunted castles and period sagas of Dumas and Féval made room for more contemporary dramas. with the influence of Edgar Allan Poe and Jules **Verne**, gothic and/or supernatural elements were digested and incorporated in adventures in which science and logic could no longer be ignored.

In fact, many of the authors of the times happily straddled the line between *fantastique* and science fiction. Depending on the works, Gaston **Leroux**, Maurice **Leblanc**, Marcel **Allain** and Pierre **Souvestre**, Jean de la **Hire**, Gustave **Le Rouge**, and Maurice **Renard**, to name but a few, were equally prominent in both genres, but at heart belonged in the *fantastique populaire* because their style and themes made them the literary successors of Sue, Dumas, and Féval rather than of **Verne** and **Rosny**.

The leading *feuilletoniste* of the *Belle Époque* was Gaston **Leroux**, a writer best known for his classic *Le Fantôme de l'Opéra* (*The Phantom of the Opera*, 1910), about which little need be said. What few people know, however, is that the original novel, never faithfully adapted to the screen, contained memorable horrific moments, such as the exploration of the civilization beneath the Opera, with the mysterious creatures who lived there, and the heroes' grueling fight in the Phantom's mirrored chamber of horrors. Trained as a lawyer, Leroux was a renowned investigative journalist who even traveled to, and reported from, Russia just before the Bolshevik Revolution. His journalistic skills helped the *fantastique* emerge from the gothic and romantic literary morass of the end of the 19th century, and, by making it more contemporary and real, gave it a new lease on life.

In *Le Fantôme de l'Opéra*, Leroux skillfully mixed fantastic events with real-life facts, such as the existence of an underground lake under the Opera. The same held true of *Le Fauteuil Hanté* (*The Haunted Chair*, 1909), a fantastic mystery novel in which a mad scientist used ingenious, murderous devices to rid himself of applicants at the French Academy who have uncovered his dark secret. These novels read like sensational newspaper accounts of the surreal.

Leroux's eclectic curiosity conferred upon his *oeuvre* a wildly diverse nature. His first novel, *La Double Vie de Theophraste Longuet* (*The Double Life of Theophraste Longuet*, 1903), belonged squarely to the *fantastique*. In it, a retired merchant found himself possessed by the spirit of notorious 18th-century French highwayman, Cartouche. He went on to discover a secret, underground society which had been living in vast caverns under Paris since the 14th century. Later, Leroux shied away from purely supernatural themes, a couple of exceptions being short stories such as

the Hoffmannesque "L'Homme qui a Vu le Diable" ("The Man Who Saw the Devil," 1908), and "Le Coeur Cambriolé" ("The Burglared Heart," 1920).

When **Leroux** dealt with fantastic themes, it was in ways that were resolutely modern, and often derivative of the works of other popular writers. His classic *Balaoo* (1911) was about a murderous ape-man *à la* Poe's *Murder in the Rue Morgue*. *L'Épouse du Soleil* (*The Bride of the Sun*, 1912) was a Lost World story with pure H. Rider Haggard elements. Finally, *La Poupée Sanglante* (*The Bloody Puppet*, 1923) and *La Machine à Assassiner* (*The Killing Machine*, 1924) were strange combinations of classic *fantastique* and science fiction. In the first volume, the brain of a man framed for murder and later guillotined was transplanted into the body of an android. In its sequel, the characters exposed a vampire cult—one without some of the more supernatural characteristics usually associated with vampirism—led by a depraved nobleman.

Leroux's literary idols being Dumas and Féval, it was no surprise that he was equally comfortable chronicling extravagant tales of murders, revenge, masked men, swooning women, mysterious dwarves, and secret societies meeting in underground caverns, with or without fantastic elements. Like their American pulp counterparts of the 1930s, these sagas were *fantastique* more in terms of their atmosphere than because of any specific supernatural concepts. In this vein, the ever-prolific Leroux penned *Le Roi Mystère* (*King Mystery*, 1908), an Alexandre Dumas-like *Monte-Cristo* story (a format he reused in several other novels), *La Reine du Sabbat* (*The Queen of the Sabbath*, 1910), *L'Homme de la Nuit* (*The Night Man*, 1911), *L'Homme Qui Revient de Loin* (*The Man Who Returned from Afar*, 1916), *Le Sept de Trèfle* (*The Seven of Clubs*, 1921) and *Les Mohicans de Babel* (*The Mohicans of Babel*, 1926).

Finally, Leroux was also the author of a series of mystery novels, starring the character of dashing young journalist, Joseph Rouletabille, clearly an idealized projection of the author. Like Dupin, Lecoq, Holmes and Poirot, Rouletabille solved his cases by pure deductive reasoning. The *Rouletabille* series included few genre elements, but its gothic atmosphere justified its inclusion here. The series was comprised of seven novels, starting with the classic *Le Mystère de la Chambre Jaune* (*The Mystery of the Yellow Room*, 1907), plus two novels written by Noré Brunel adapted from film scripts.
La Double Vie de Théophraste Longuet, Balaoo, Le Fauteuil Hanté, Le Roi Mystère, Rouletabille, and

most of Leroux's novels have been adapted into films and television movies and series. See Book 1, Chapters I and II. a series of **Rouletabille** graphic novels also exist—see Book 1, Chapter V.

Easily the equal of Leroux in fame, and arguably his superior in style, was writer Maurice **Leblanc**, the creator of the character of gentleman-burglar Arsène Lupin who, in France, has enjoyed a popularity as long-lasting and considerable as Sherlock Holmes in the English-speaking world. There were twenty-two volumes in the *Lupin* series written by Leblanc, and five sequels written by the notorious mystery writing team of **Boileau-Narcejac**. While the *Arsène Lupin* saga rarely featured any purely fantastic elements, its preeminence in modern pulp fiction also warranted its inclusion here.

Lupin was introduced in a series of short stories serialized in the magazine *Je Sais Tout* (*I Know Everything*), starting in 1905. a literary descendent of Ponson du Terrail's *Rocambole*, Lupin was, like Holmes, an archetype. Although he was on the other side of the law, he was clearly a force for good, and those he defeated, always with characteristic gallic style and panache, were worse villains than he. In other words, Lupin was the Simon Templar (aka The Saint) of the 19th century. Another thing Lupin shared with Holmes was that Leblanc spared no effort in making him "real," including playing the part of John D. Watson and appearing as Lupin's own biographer in several of the books. Also, like Doyle's hero, some of Lupin's best adventures dealt with burning political issues of the times—torn from the headlines, as it were. and finally, like Doyle, Leblanc often alluded to other stories that had not yet been told.

Indeed, the two characters were bound to meet and, in an unprecedented act of literary pastiche and cross-over, Sherlock Holmes himself appeared several times in the *Lupin* novels in the transparent guise of "Herlock Sholmes" —after some legal objections from Conan Doyle. In "Her-

lock Sholmes arrive trop tard" ("Herlock Sholmes Arrives Too Late"; a short story included in the first collection, *Arsène Lupin, Gentleman Cambrioleur* (*Arsene Lupin, Gentleman Burglar*), (1907)), Sholmes met a young Lupin for a brief time, unaware that he was, in fact, Lupin. Called in to solve an ancient riddle, Sholmes succeeded, but only to find out that Lupin slipped in the night before and got away with the treasure. However, having anticipated that the riddle would be easily solved by the great English detective, Lupin, as a mark of respect and admiration, left his car waiting for Sholmes at the exit of the secret tunnel.

This meeting marked the beginning of a stormy relationship between the two characters. As Lupin confided to Leblanc, when he met Sholmes, he felt scrutinized to the core of his being and realized at once that, should he meet the Detective again, Sholmes would recognize him, whatever the disguise. (Lupin, like Rocambole, Lecoq and Holmes, is a master of disguise.)

And meet again they did in two more stories collected in *Arsène Lupin contre Herlock Sholmes* (*Arsene Lupin vs. Herlock Sholmes*, 1908). In the first story, Sholmes was called to Paris to help solve some mysterious robberies. The truth was that Lupin had been using secret passages built in houses designed by himself in the guise of an architect. Sholmes and his biographer (Dr. Wilson) had a chance meeting with Lupin and Leblanc in a restaurant. The two foes took each other's measure and the reader was led to the conclusion that, although the law made these two enemies, they could very well be friends under different circumstances. The story ended with many twists: first, Lupin managed to outwit Sholmes by having him captured and shipped back to England; but as he was himself ready to escape the following day, whom did he find barring the way but Sholmes, who tricked the captain of the ferry by moving the clock's hand, then managed to take the train back to Paris in time to stop Lupin! The great detective delivered the gentleman burglar into the hands of the police and left; whereupon Lupin made a daring escape and then was there at the station to say good-bye to Sholmes.

In the second story, the same pattern was reenacted. This time, the final chapter had Lupin and Sholmes refusing to leave a sinking boat, each wanting the other to be the first to display a sign of weakness. Eventually, Sholmes was rescued by the police while Lupin was believed to have drowned. He popped up again on the ferry crossing the English Channel and, this time, Sholmes let him go rather than drag an innocent girl into the clutches of the law.

Sholmes appeared twice more in the *Arsène Lupin* saga. In the prodigious battle for the secret of *L'Aiguille Creuse* (*The Hollow Needle*, 1909), Sholmes made a brief appearance at the end. Summoned by the baffled police, he had, naturally, solved the mystery. The "Needle" was a huge natural rock formation off the Normandy coast; in his novel, **Leblanc** postulated that it was hollow and housed the secret treasure of the Kings of France. This was only fiction, yet to this day, a large number of tourists, influenced by Lupin's adventure, have been shown to believe that the Needle is indeed hollow!

At the end of the novel, Sholmes and his men have cornered Lupin who, unbeknownst to them, had decided to "go straight" and live a peaceful life with his new wife, Raymonde. Unfortunately, in the encounter, Sholmes captured Raymonde who has been, until then, unaware of her husband's real identity. Moved by the irresistible compulsion to stop Lupin, Sholmes blurted out the truth. A shocked Raymonde attempted to escape. Lupin shot first. Chaos ensued. In the resulting gun battle, Raymonde was killed when she threw herself in front of Lupin to save him from a bullet fired by Sholmes. Sholmes was stunned by this unexpected and unwanted tragic development; Lupin was wracked with grief. The two giants grappled briefly, but Lupin got away and returned to a life of crime.

The last time Sholmes is mentioned in the Lupin saga was in what may be the gentleman burglar's greatest epic: *813* (1910). In it, the formidable enigma of "813," which may lead to the redrawing of the political map of Europe, had the Kaiser of Germany baffled. Lupin, from his cell in a Paris jail—he had been captured after successfully impersonating the head of the French Sureté—learned that Sholmes had been called, but had failed to solve the riddle. Freed by the Kaiser's intervention, Lupin found the solution, but fairness forces one to acknowledge that he did so in circumstances that may have given him an edge over Sholmes. In this book, Lupin's real adversary appeared to be a more-than-human, black-clad, merciless killer, whom Lupin referred to as the "monster" or the "vampire."

Finally, several *Arsène Lupin* novels contain some remarkable genre elements: a radioactive "god-stone" that cured people and caused mutations was the object of a surreal battle in *L'Île aux Trente Cercueils* (*The Island of the Thirty Coffins*, 1920); the secret of the Fountain of Youth, a mineral water source hidden under a lake in the Auvergne,

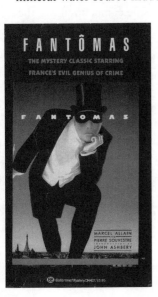

was the goal sought by the protagonists in *La Demoiselle aux Yeux Verts* (*The Damsel with Green Eyes*, 1927); finally, in *La Comtesse de Cagliostro* (*The Countess of Cagliostro*, 1924), Lupin's adversary was none other than Josephine Balsamo, the granddaughter of Cagliostro himself.

(The *Arsène Lupin* novels have been adapted into films and television movies and series. See Book 1, Chapters I and II.)

Lupin was a villain, but one who generally fought for good. Not so Fantômas, another superior literary creation of the period, the brainchild of Marcel **Allain** and Pierre **Souvestre**. Fantômas was created in 1911 and appeared in a total of thirty-two volumes written by the two collaborators, then a subsequent eleven volumes written by Allain alone after Souvestre's death in 1914. Allain went on to become the prolific author of well over 500 adventure, romance, detective novels, and serials. His best-known achievement, however, remained the Fantômas series.

Arch-criminal Fantômas was one of the most popular characters in the history of French pulp literature. His adversaries were determined policeman Juve (who may be Fantômas' brother?) and young journalist Jérôme Fandor, who eventually fell in love with Fantômas' daughter. Another recurring character was the tragic figure of Fantômas' lover, Lady Beltham, who was constantly torn between her passion for the villain and her horror at his criminal schemes.

The character and the monstrously complicated plots designed by Allain and Souvestre were greatly admired by the surrealists. The *Fantômas* novels were rich in gruesome scenes, such as Fantômas sending an innocent man made-up to look like him to the guillotine, in *Fantômas*, 1911; or Fantômas using gloves made of human skin to leave a deceased man's fingerprints on his victims in *Le Mort qui Tue* (*The Dead Man Who Kills*, 1911); or Fantômas holding a king prisoner in a secret chamber under the Place de la Concorde, in *Un Roi Prisonnier de Fantômas* (*A King Prisoner of Fantomas*, 1911); or Fantômas hi-

jacking an entire subway train; or Fantômas commandeering a hansom cab driven by a dead man to spread the plague through the streets of Paris, in *Le Fiacre de Nuit* (*The Night Hansom Cab*, 1911); and even, on a more mundane level, Fantômas placing razor blades in all the shoes sold in a department store, and filling their perfume sprays with acid! As was often the case, however, the truly evil nature of Fantômas was somewhat diluted in the latter novels.

The first *Fantômas* book cover, showing a contemplative masked man dressed in a dinner jacket and holding a dagger, boldly stepping over Paris, was so well known that it has almost become a cliché today. Just as Sherlock Holmes was the archetypal modern detective, Fantômas was the archetypal modern arch-villain. Among his better-known (and even more horrific) literary descendents were the Italian super-villains Diabolik, Satanik and Kriminal.

(The *Fantômas* series was adapted into films, television series and comic books—see Book 1, Chapters I, II and V.)

A lesser pulp hero, and one that has not gained the recognition of, nor survived the test of time as well as, Rouletabille, Lupin, or Fantômas, was the Nyctalope by Jean de **La Hire**, a prolific writer of numerous popular adventure series, many of which included fantastic or science fiction elements.

The Nyctalope was Léo Sainte-Claire, or Jean de Sainclair (depending on the novel, continuity not being La Hire's strong point), a super-powered avenger who could see in the dark and who sported an artificial heart. He made his first appearance in *L'Homme Qui Peut Vivre dans l'Eau* (*The Man Who Could Live Underwater*), serialized in the daily newspaper *Le Matin* in 1908. His adventures comprised seventeen, luridly entitled volumes, the most famous being *Le Mystère des XV* (*The Mystery of the XV*, 1911), *Lucifer* (1920), *L'Antéchrist* (*The Antichrist*, 1927), *Titania* (1929), *Belzébuth* (1930), and *Gorillard* (1932). (Also see Chapter V.)

The Nyctalope, even more than Rocambole, Lupin, or Fantômas, was the first, full-fledged super-hero in the history of pulp literature. What made him so were not only his super-powers, secret origins, and devoted band of fearless assistants, but his colorful rogues gallery that even Doc Savage or Superman would envy. These included the megalomaniacal Baron Glo von Warteck, aptly nicknamed "Lucifer," the mad monk Fulbert, the devilish Oxus, the "Red Princess" Diana Ivanovna Krosnorow, Queen of the Hashishins, the mad Engineer Korridès, and finally, Leonid Zattan, truly evil incarnate. The Nyctalope's allies included his fiancée (later, wife and mother of his son, Pierre) Sylvie Mac Dhul, the Japanese Gno Mitang, the mysterious Jewish wizard, Mathias Lumen, and finally, the international C.I.D. (Committee of Information and Defense (against Evil)) which he, himself, created. The Nyctalope's adventures took place on Earth, under water, in Tibet, on Rhea (an unknown satellite of Earth), on Mars; and even in the future.

It was just at the turn of the century that another modern literary archetype made its first appearance in popular literature: the mad doctor. The character of Dr. Caresco, introduced in *Le Mal Nécessaire* (*The Necessary Evil*, 1899), written by André **Couvreur**, himself a medical doctor, was undoubtedly one of the first mad surgeons in popular literature. Caresco returned in *Caresco Surhomme ou le Voyage en Eucrasie* (*Caresco the Superman, or the Voyage to Eucrasia*, 1904), a novel describing a sado-masochistic utopia (Eucrasia) built by surgery and ruled by Caresco. In 1909, with *Une Invasion de Macrobes* (*An Invasion of Macrobes*), Couvreur then embarked on a series of adventures featuring another mad scientist, Professor Tornada. These will be covered in greater detail in our next chapter. By comparison, Sax Rohmer's (1883-1959) Fu Manchu was first published in 1913.

A worthy and more famous literary successor of Dr. Caresco was Dr. Cornelius Kramm, the star of *Le Mystérieux Dr. Cornélius* (*The Mysterious Dr. Cornelius*), a sprawling saga serialized in eighteen volumes during 1912 and 1913 and written by another prolific writer of adventure stories, Gustave **Le Rouge**. Cornélius Kramm and his brother, Fritz, ruled an international crime empire called the "Red Hand." Cornélius was a mad surgeon nicknamed the "Sculptor of Human Flesh"—he could alter people's likenesses, and did so to further his evil ends, and even "cloned" them. He was eventually defeated by a vast alliance of heroes after a world-spanning battle. (*Le Mystérieux Dr. Cornelius* was adapted for television and radio; see Book 1, Chapter II and III.)

Less prolific than Le Rouge, but more important from a literary standpoint, especially in the field of science fiction, was Maurice **Renard**. Renard was the author of two archetypal "mad doctor" novels: *Le Docteur Lerne—Sous-Dieu* (*Dr. Lerne—Undergod*, 1908), a novel which he dedicated to H. G. Wells. In it, a Dr. Moreau-like mad scientist transplanted not only organs between men and animals, but also between plants, and even machines. In 1920, Renard wrote the classic *Les Mains d'Orlac* (*The Hands of Orlac*), in which a virtuoso pianist received the transplanted hands of a murderer and turned into a killer himself. (*Le Docteur Lerne* and *Les Mains d'Orlac* have been adapted as films and television movies—see Book 1, Chapters I and II.)

Deserving of a footnote in this sub-genre is Guillaume **Livet**, whose creation was *Miramar, L'Homme aux Yeux de Chat* (*Miramar, the Man with Cat Eyes*, 1913), another arch-villainous mad scientist out to conquer the world. Miramar did not gain the recognition of the more famous Fantômas, yet like the Nyctalope, he saw in the dark, and like Dr. Cornélius, he performed strange organ grafts and mad surgery on his victims. A potentially deadly combination!

Another product of the more bloodthirsty aspirations of the *Belle Époque* was the notorious **Grand-Guignol** theater. The Grand-Guignol was a theater specializing in gory horror plays and dark comedies. It was located on Impasse Chaptal in Paris (in the 9th *arrondissement*) and operated from April, 1897 to June, 1962. Its sole competition was the Theatre des Deux Masques, which opened in February 1921, but three years later, chose to concentrate instead on more conventional murder mysteries. The Grand-Guignol derived its name from "Guignol," a character from a French Punch & Judy-like show, created in Lyons by Laurent Mourguet (1769-1844). Before it became a theater, the Grand-Guignol premises were first a chapel, then became the atelier of the painter Rochegrosse (1859-1938), who was appropriately infamous for his gory, realistic depictions of massacres and scenes of torture of the saints.

The first director of the Grand-Guignol was its founder, playwright Oscar **Méténier**. Prior to establishing the theater, Méténier worked for the Paris police; his duties included assisting condemned men on their way to the guillotine. He started the theater as a place to produce his own plays. Méténier's plays started as a combination of crime stories and naturalistic, social studies. One of his first plays, *Made-*

moiselle Fifi (after a story by Guy de **Maupassant**, 1896), showed material that had never before been displayed on stage: a prostitute plunging a knife into the throat of an officer who insulted her. The play's considerable success indicated that gory crimes could sell seats, and Grand-Guignol was born. Subsequently, Méténier had occasional problems with censorship which, on several occasions, closed him down, but that did not stop the theater from creating the first, modern representation of horror.

The next director of the Grand-Guignol was Max **Maurey** who, from 1899 to 1914, increasingly shifted the emphasis of the plays from naturalistic dramas to gore. It was Maurey (who also wrote numerous comedies for the theater) who had the idea of hiring a doctor to assist fainting spectators, and who discovered playwright André de **Lorde**.

The Grand-Guignol produced short plays of one or two acts with no mood-breaking intermission between the acts. It offered four to six plays a night, alternating vaudeville, boulevard comedies, and horrific, gory dramas. Literary influences included Edgar Allan Poe (whose "The System of Doctor Tarr and Professor Fether" was the subject of a hugely popular and gory adaptation, featuring a madman scooping an eyeball out of his victim's socket) and Guy de Maupassant. The stories contained few ghosts, vampires, devils, and monsters. Instead, they relied on "real" monsters: the ones that exist within normal-looking human beings. The Grand-Guignol plays dramatized the then-new to the stage "penny dreadful" concepts of serial killers, mad surgeons, insane alienists, murderers with uncontrollable urges, twisted psychoses, weird erotic obsessions, and dubious heredity.

The writing displayed a surgical-like sense of brevity and effectiveness. Overcome by fear or horror, many people fainted. Some spectators, outraged by what they beheld, loudly summoned the police. Finally, women were said to attend the Monday matinées with their lovers often as a prelude to their illicit affairs.

The Grand-Guignol has been the subject of a comprehensive study in Agnès Pierron's remarkable anthology, *Le Grand-Guignol: Théâtre des Peurs de la Belle Époque* (*The Grand-Guignol: Theater of the Fears of the Belle Époque*; Laffont, 1995). (For a list of authors and plays, see separate entry under "**Grand-Guignol**" in Chapter XI.)

Another branch of the *fantastique populaire* of the *Belle Époque* which straddled the line between science fiction and *fantastique* was the Extraordinary Voyage/Lost World exotic adventure, featuring hidden lands, secret civilizations, dastardly villains, and other melodramatic elements inherited from gothic literature. These novels borrowed just as much from Jules **Verne** as they did from H. Rider Haggard (1856-1925), whose *King Solomon's Mines* had been published in 1885 and *She* in 1886. Examples included Gaston Leroux with *L'Épouse du Soleil* (*The Bride of the Sun*, 1912), mentioned above, and Maurice **Maindron**

with *La Gardienne de l'Idole Noire* (*The Guardian of the Black Idol*, 1910), an Indiana Jones-like novel taking place in India in the 1500s, featuring the efforts of a brave Spanish Captain to rescue a young princess from the unspeakable clutches of the evil worshippers of Kali.

The pulp magazines of the times, such as *Le Journal des Voyages* (*The Journal of Voyages*, 1877-1947), *Lectures Pour Tous* (*Readings for All*, 1898-1940), *Je Sais Tout* (*I Know Everything*, 1905-1921), and *L'Intrépide* (*The Fearless*, 1910-1937), as well as a bevy of pulp paperback imprints by publishers such as Ollendorff, Méricant, Férenczi, Lafitte, and Baudinière happily mixed the formats of traditional adventures à la, say, Jack London, with crime fiction (with or without fantastic elements), science fiction, and *fantastique* (see Chapters V and VII). In addition to Leroux, Leblanc, Renard, La Hire, Allain, and Le Rouge, all reviewed above, the true heirs of Soulié, Dumas, Féval, and Sue were writers such as:

Louis **Boussenard**, with *Les Étrangleurs du Bengale* (*The Stranglers of Bengal*) (1899).

René **Thévenin**, with *La Cité des Tortures* (*The City of Tortures*, 1906).

Georges **Le Faure**, with *Le Secret du Glacier* (*The Secret of the Ice Flow*, 1907) and *Un Descendant de Robinson* (*A Descendent of Robinson*, 1910).

Charles **Derennes**, with *Le Peuple du Pôle* (*The People of the Pole*, 1907).

Maurice **Champagne** with *Les Reclus de la Mer* (*The Recluse of the Sea*, 1907) and *Les Sondeurs d'Abîmes* (*The Probers of the Abyss*, 1911).

Pierre **Giffard**, with *Le Tombeau de Glace* (*The Tomb of Ice*, 1908).

Octave **Béliard**, with *Les Merveilles de l'Île Mystérieuse* (*The Wonders of Mysterious Island*, 1911).

René-Marcel de **Nizerolles**, with his 1800-page serial *Les Voyages Aériens d'un Petit Parisien à travers le Monde* (*The Aerial Voyages of a Little Parisian Across the World*, 1910-12).

These authors, and others, continued to enrich the field after World War I. But because of the increasing blending of genres, these types of works, if lacking clear supernatural elements, will now be reviewed in our science fiction chapters.

3. The *Fantastique Littéraire*

On the more respectable side of the literary fence, the 19th century *fantastique* literature after 1830 was dominated, as mentioned above, first by the influence of E.T.A. Hoffmann, and then by that of Edgar Allan Poe.

Hoffmann's famous *Tales* were translated in a twenty volume-collection published between 1829 and 1833 by publisher Renduel, who also published Honoré de Balzac and Théophile **Gautier**. They featured supernatural characters moving in and out of men's lives, thereby revealing the tragic or monstrous sides of human nature, and had an immediate and huge effect on French writers. They were so successful that it is not an exaggeration to say that the mid-1800s belonged to the *fantastique romantique*. (Having discussed the works of Balzac and Hugo under the *roman noir* section, they shall not be mentioned again in this chapter.)

a. Fantastique Romantique

The first of Hoffmann's literary followers was Charles **Nodier** who, in an article entitled "*Du Fantastique en Literature*" (*Of the Fantastic in Literature*, 1830), published in the famous magazine *Revue de Paris*, condemned the *roman frénétique* and hailed the *fantastique* as the "only essential literature."

Nodier's manifesto was enthusiastically endorsed by poets Gérard de **Nerval** and Alfred de Musset (1810-1857) in articles published in 1831. Faithful to his principles, Nodier took an interest in classic fantasy and penned a number of more traditional fairy tales, such as *L'Histoire du Roi de Bohême et de Ses Sept Châteaux* (*The Story of the King of Bohemia and of His Seven Castles*, 1830), *Trésor des Fèves et Fleur de Pois* (*Treasure of the Beans and Flower of Peas*, 1837), the Oriental tale *Le Songe d'Or* (*The Golden Dream*), as well as religious dramas, such as *La Combe de l'Homme Mort* (*The Valley of the Dead Man*, 1833), *Soeur Beatrix* (*Sister Beatrix*, 1837) and *La Neuvaine de la Chandeleur* (*The Rosary of the Chandeleur*, 1839), all drawing their inspiration from medieval sources.

But a writer of Nodier's immense talent could not be satisfied by just following in the classic footsteps of **Perrault** and Madame d'**Aulnoy**. In *Smarra* (1821), his Byronesque hero travelled through enchanted forests and into Arabian Nights territory before eventually confronting an evil vampire. Nodier's fairy tale masterpiece was *La Fée aux Miettes* (*The Crumb Fairy*, 1832). In it, Michel, a young carpenter, was devoted to the eponymous Crumb Fairy, an old beggar woman who may be Belkiss, the legendary Queen of Saba. In order to restore her to her true form, he searched for the magical Singing Mandragore. In *La Fée aux Miettes*, Nodier, like Hoffmann, succeeded in breaking down the walls between fantasy and reality. The reader was ultimately left to wonder whether Michel was mad or in touch with a higher plane of reality. Nodier could rightfully lay claim to being one of the world's first "high fantasy" writers, sixty years before William Morris' (1834-1896) *The Wood Beyond the World* (1890).

Before joining the ranks of France's leading romantic poets, Gérard de **Nerval**, one of the first symbolist and surrealist writers in French literature, translated Goethe's *Faust* (1827). He then embarked on the writing of a series of fantastic tales, all exhibiting a strong Hoffmann influence: "Soirée d'Automne" ("Autumn Evening"), "Le Portrait du Diable" (The Devil's Portrait), "La Reine des Poissons" (The Queen

of the Fish), "Le Monstre Vert" (The Green Monster), "La Main Enchantée" (The Enchanted Hand), etc., all collected in *La Main de Gloire* (*The Glory Hand*, 1832). In 1839, Nerval collaborated with Dumas on *L'Alchimiste* (*The Alchemist*).

Mentally unhinged after a lover's death, Nerval developed an interest in mystical beliefs. After a journey through Egypt and the Middle East in 1843, he became fascinated by ancient religions, such as the cults of Isis, Cybele, and Mithra, as well as various esoteric secrets such as the Illuminati and the theories of reincarnation, dreams, and the means of communication with supernatural realms. In *Voyage en Orient* (*Voyage to the Orient*, 1851), he wrote an account of his journeys, in which he included some adapted Arabic legends such as "The Tale of Caliph Hakem and the Queen of the Morning." In *Les Illuminés* (*The Illuminati*, 1852), he penned a series of biographies of **Cazotte**, **Restif de la Bretonne**, Cagliostro, and other famous adepts.

Committed to an asylum several times, Nerval nevertheless managed, in his intervals of sanity, to become one of France's most renowned poets. After being institutionalized, his work began taking on an increasing visionary quality, with *Aurélia* (1853-54), *Les Filles du Feu* (*Daughters of Fire*, 1854), which included the story "*Sylvie*," and *Pandora* (1854). All were obsessive visions, dreams, or nightmares, deeply steeped in Oriental mythologies and dealing with the themes of damnation and salvation of the soul. They reflected with admirable lucidity a man's descent into madness, and his morbid, yet beautiful, exploration of the land of the dead. *Aurelia* also featured one of the first, modern variations on the theme of the doppleganger. Nerval's fantastic poetry was collected in *Les Chimères* (*Chimeras*, 1854). A year later, his body was found mysteriously hanging from a lampost near the Chatelet in Paris. Perhaps he had at last met his doppleganger?

Gustave **Flaubert**, the author of the classic *Madame Bovary* (1857), combined romanticism and realism. Some of his early works nevertheless featured alchemists, pacts with the devil, and all the traditional elements of gothic and supernatural fiction. Between 1835 and 1838, he wrote a series of fantastic short stories, such as "Bibliomanie," "Voyage en Enfer" ("Voyage to Hell", 1835), "Rêve d'Enfer" ("A Dream of Hell", 1837), "La Danse des Morts" ("The Dance of the Dead", 1838), etc. Of greater interest was *Smarh* (1839), a *Faust*-like novel clearly labeled as *fantastique*, the title of which was probably borrowed from Nodier's *Smarra*. Flaubert returned to the Faustian theme with *La Première Tentation de St. Antoine* (1849), revised in 1874 as *La Tentation de St. Antoine* (*The Temptation of St. Anthony*). This was an extravagant Christian fantasy in which he tried to reconcile science and religion.

Finally, in 1858, Flaubert produced what may very well be the first work of modern heroic fantasy in the French languange, *Salammbô*. It was a brash, colorful, and exotic novel about ancient Carthage, the North-African city-state which challenged Roman domination during the Punic Wars

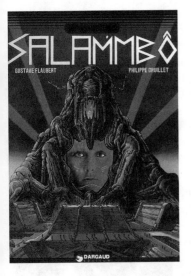

in the 2nd century B.C., and was loosely based on an incident reported by Roman historian Polybius. In it, Flaubert created the fictional character of Salammbô, the daughter of Carthagenian general Hamilcar, and told of her doomed love story with Matho, the leader of the rebel mercenaries who were besieging Carthage. While the supernatural was, at best, understated, *Salammbô* was a worthy precursor of the opulent, colorful, savage fantasies of Robert E. Howard (1906-1936), and Matho was a true proto-Conan.

Salammbô was adapted into a series of graphic novels by artist Philippe **Druillet** as part of his **Lone Sloane** series (see Book 1, Chapter V) and twice adapted for the cinema (see Book 1, Chapter I).

Théophile **Gautier**, a leading writer of the Romantic movement, is today best remembered for his swashbuckling novel *Capitaine Fracasse* (1863). Gautier first embraced the *fantastique* with classic gothic stories or tales heavily influenced by Hoffmann. *Albertus* (1832) was a novel in verse about an artist who damned himself for the love of a witch. The concept of impossible love, often love between the living and the dead, became a recurrent theme throughout Gautier's career. In *La Morte Amoureuse* (*The Loving Dead*, 1836), he told the story of a young priest who fell in love with a beautiful female vampire, but was eventually forced by his superior to kill her. *La Morte Amoureuse* was a remarkably modern precursor to the romantic vampire novels of Chelsea Quinn Yarbro and Anne Rice, in that its vampire was not a soulless creature of the night, but a loving, sensitive, and incredibly erotic woman.

Like his friend Nerval, Gautier exhibited a strong interest in the occult, metaphysics, and Oriental philosophies. His numerous journeys inspired *Arria Marcella* (1852), a time-travel love story which took us back to the days of ancient Pompei; *Jettatura* (1856), the story of a man victim of a curse. Both *Avatar* (1857) and *Spirite* (1866) are *roman spirites* which dealt with the theme of life after death. The former featured an exchange of souls and bodies, made possible by using Doctor Miracle's forbidden Oriental knowledge. The latter told of the romantic liaison between a young man and his ghostly lover. Gautier also translated Eric Raspe's *Baron Munchausen's Narrative of His Marvellous Travels and Campaigns in Russia* (1875) into French. The French edition was illustrated by renowned artist Gustave Doré (1833-1883).

Prosper **Mérimée**, a writer and journalist well known for his *Colomba* (1840) and *Carmen* (1845), took some of the exotic concepts already developed by Nerval and Gautier and added his own dose of realism, and even of skepticism. His first excursion into the genre was *La Guzla* (1827), a literary hoax comprised of ballads about murder, revenge and vampires, allegedly translated from the Illyrian by "Hiacynthe Maglanowich." The book even included a pseudo-academic study of vampirism! In 1829, Mérimée's *Vision de Charles X*, a tale about a Swedish king cursed with second sight, looked so authentic to the critics—even though it was mostly made up—that it confirmed Mérimée's talent of journalist of the *fantastique*. In 1830, Mérimée traveled to Spain and wrote about witchcraft. His *Les Âmes du Purgatoire* (*The Souls of Purgatory*, 1834) retold the famous Don Juan legend.

Mérimée's eye for realistic details, even when describing fantastic events, was particularly notable in his *La Vénus d'Ille* (1837), which became an immediate classic. In it, a young man fell in love with a pagan statue and made the mistake of giving her a wedding ring. The statue eventually came to life and crushed her groom. Mérimée used no spells and no fancy mysticism to explain the incredible event, just pure fantasy. *Lokis* (1869) reversed the roles: this time, it was the bride who was devoured by her husband, a monstrous "werebear." Two of his latter works, *La Chambre Bleue* (*The Blue Room*, 1872) and the posthumous *Djoumâne* (written in 1870; published in 1873), based on a North African legend, also showed Mérimée's fascination with the supernatural. It is worth noting that Mérimée translated Pushkin's *Queen of Spades* (1834), and wrote a study about Russian fantasy writer, Nikolai Gogol.

La Vénus d'Ille was twice adapted for French television (see Book 1, Chapter II); *Lokis* was made into a film in 1970 by Polish filmmaker Janusz Majewski.

Like Nodier and Nerval, George **Sand** also wrote an essay, entitled "Essai sur le Drame Fantastique" ("Essay on Fantastic Tragedies"), in which she perceptively stated that "the world of the *fantastique* is neither outside nor above nor below, but inside us." After toying with the form of the *Roman Noir* with *Consuelo* (1842) and *La Contesse de Rudolstadt* (1844), Sand found her own voice in a series of rustic novels which drew their inspiration from the folkloric legends of her native Berry countryside: *La Mare au Diable* (*The Devil's Pond*, 1845), *La Petite Fadette* (*The Little Fadette*, 1849) and *François le Champi* (1849). However, her *Légendes Rustiques* (*Rustic Legends*, 1858) and her *Contes d'une Grand-Mère* (*Grandmother's Tales*, 1872) represented an attempt at recreating the fairy tale genre in rustic trappings.

Rustic legends also were the main sources of inspiration of Émile **Erckmann** and Alexandre **Chatrian**, an Alsatian writing team who signed their works **Erckmann-Chatrian**. They are known today mostly for their richly drawn novels about life in the French countryside. Their first novella, however, *Science et Génie* (*Science and Genius*,

1850), told the story of an alchemist who invented a potion that could turn people into stone. Erckmann-Chatrian then embarked on a series of rustic horror stories, often incorporating the theme of men transforming into beasts. Their stories were collected in four volumes: *Les Contes Fantastiques* (*Fantastic Tales*, 1847), which included the classic short story "L'Araignée Crabe" (*The Crab-Spider*), about a blood-sucking lake monster with the body of a spider and the head of a man; *Contes de la Montagne* (*Mountain Tales*, 1860); *Contes du Bord du Rhin* (*Rhine Tales*, 1862); and finally, *Contes Populaires* (*Popular Tales*, 1866). Erckmann-Chatrian also wrote the novel *Hughes-le-Loup* (*Hugh-the-Wolf*, 1863), about a noble family, victims of a werewolf curse, combining the then-popular theme of lycanthropy with story elements taken from the *roman noir*.

(**Hughes-le-Loup** and several of Erckmann-Chatrian's tales were adapted by French television—see Book 1, Chapter II.)

Anatole **France** won the 1921 Nobel Prize for literature. Some of his earlier works, like *L'Abeille* (*The Honey Bee*, 1883) and *Balthazar et la Reine Balkis* (*Balthazar and Queen Balkis*, 1889), were classic fairy tales. France also wrote a number of Christian-themed fantasies, in the vein of Flaubert's *Tentation de St. Antoine*, such as *L'Étui de Nacre* (*The Mother-of-Pearl Casket*, 1892) and *Le Puits de Sainte Claire* (*The Well of Saint Clara*, 1895). His *Sur La Pierre Blanche* (*The White Stone*, 1905) and *L'Île des Pingouins* (*Penguin Island*, 1908) were sometimes classified as science fiction, but they were better described as allegorical philosophical tales which used the elements of fantasy purely for satirical purposes (see Chapter V). France did pen a major work of fantasy, however, one which was truly revolutionary and represented a thematic bridge between Milton's (1608-1674) *Paradise Lost* (1667) and more modern renditions of the Prince of Darkness. In *La Révolte des Anges* (*The Revolt of the Angels*, 1914), France wrote a startling tale in which the fallen angel Arcade schemed to organize a new revolt among the fallen angels who were living on Earth, generally posing as artists; but Lucifer, who lived as a peaceful gardener, stopped him by convincing him that the next battle needed to be won not on the celestial battlefield but in the hearts and minds of men.

Other notable authors of the period included:

Samuel-Henry **Berthoud**, who penned *Contes Misanthropiques* (*Misanthropic Tales*, 1831), *Le Cheveu du Diable* (*The Devil's Hair*, 1833), *L'Anneau de Salomon Légende Hollandaise* (*Solomon's Ring, A Dutch Legend*, 1850), *Le Dragon Rouge, ou l'Art de Commander au Démon et aux Esprits Infernaux* (*The Red Dragon, or the Art of Commanding the Devil and the Infernal Spirits*, 1861) and *Le Baiser du Diable* (*The Devil's Kiss*, 1861), among others.

Jules de la **Madelène**, the author of *Les Années en Peine* (*The Years of Pain*, 1857), a collection of fantastic tales including "Rosita" and "La Dernière Heure d'un Stradivarius" ("A Stradivarius' Last Hour").

Armand **Silvestre**, with *Contes à la Brune* (*Tales of Mist*, 1889), *Histoires Abracadabrantes* (*Alakazam Tales*, 1893), *La Planète Enchantée* (*The Enchanted Planet*, 1896) and *Contes Irrévérencieux* (*Irreverent Tales*, 1896).

Of all the writers who, like Sand, Erckmann-Chatrian, and Berthoud, used regional folklore as a source of inspiration, none was more famous or influential than Anatole **Le Braz**, whose many works were entirely devoted to the preservation of the "soul" of ancient Britanny. Le Braz's books were praised and recognized by the French Academy. They included a novel, *Le Gardien du Feu* (*The Guardian of the Fire*, 1900), several fantastic stories collections such as *Pâques d'Islande* (*Icelandic Easter*, 1897) and *Le Sang de la Sirène* (*The Blood of the Mermaid*, 1901), and numerous books collecting and preserving the rich heritage of Britannic folk tales, such as the classic *La Légende de la Mort chez les Bretons Armoricains et en Basse Bretagne* (*The Legend of Death Among Armorican Britons and in Lower Britanny*, 1893), *Vieilles Histoires du Pays Breton* (*Old Tales From Britanny*, 1897), *La Terre du Passé* (*Land of the Past*, 1902), *Le Théâtre Celtique* (*Celtic Theatre*, 1905) and *Contes du Soleil et de la Brume* (*Tales of Sun and Mist*, 1913).

Nobel prize winner Frédéric **Mistral**'s classic *Mireille* (*Mireio*, 1859) was an epic poem written in the Provencal language of Southern France; it featured a good witch and various spirits. It was adapted into an opera by Michel **Carré**.

Finally, one could not complete this overview of the *fantastique romantique* of the 1800s without mentioning the field of the **Opera**, where Hoffmann's tales and other fantastic stories were much in demand. Among the most notable works were:

La Damnation de Faust (*Faust's Damnation*, 1846) by Hector **Berlioz**.

La Poupée de Nuremberg (*The Nuremberg Doll*, 1852; music by Adolphe Adam) by Adolphe de **Leuven** and A. de **Beauplan**.

Faust (1859; music by Charles Gounod) and *Les Contes d'Hoffmann* (1881; music by Jacques Offenbach) by Michel **Carré** and Jules **Barbier**.

Le Sabbat (*The Sabbath*, 1877; music by Emmanuel Chabrier) by Armand **Silvestre**.

Le Roi d'Ys (1888) about the legendary sunken city off the coast of Britanny (music by Édouard Lalo) and *Esclar-*

monde (*with Louis de Gramont*, 1889; music by Jules Massenet) by Alfred **Blau**. (For a more detailed list of authors and composers, see separate entry under **Opéra** in Chapter XI.)

Of all opera writers, none was as prolific in the genre as Eugène **Scribe**, whose works included *La Dame Blanche* (*The White Lady*, 1825) based on Walter Scott's stories (music by François-Adrien Boieldieu); *Robert le Diable* (*Robert the Devil*, 1831; music by Giacomo Meyerbeer); *Le Cheval de Bronze* (*The Brass Horse*, 1835; music by Daniel Auber); *Le Lac des Fées* (*The Fairy Lake*, 1839; music by Daniel Auber), and *La Part du Diable* (*The Devil's Share*, 1843), the latter taking place on planet Venus (music by Daniel Auber); *Le Juif Errant* (*The Wandering Jew*, 1852; music by Fromental Halévy, written in collaboration with Jules-Henri **Vernoy de Saint-Georges**, 1852) and *La Chatte Métamorphosée en Femme* (*The Cat Who Turned Into a Woman*; music by Jacques Offenbach, written in collaboration with **Mélesville**, 1858).

Even the ballet reflected the fantastic mood of the times, as demonstrated by the prodigious success of Eugène Lami's fantasy ballet, *La Sylphide* (1832), starring Marie Taglioni (1804-1884), which drew enormous crowds, or that of Théophile Gautier's *Giselle* (1842).

b. Fantastique Réaliste

And then came Edgar Allan Poe.

Poe's stories were translated and collected in *Histoires Extraordinaires* (*Extraordinary Stories*) in 1856 by the notorious *poète maudit* (*accursed poet*) Charles Baudelaire. While Hoffmann appealed to the imagination, Poe used a merciless, inescapable form of logic. Where Hoffmann relied on metaphysics, Poe used mathematics. Unlike the romantics and their unbridled fears, Poe contributed a logical, almost rational approach to the supernatural. He also cast a darker light than Hoffmann, in the sense that his stories rarely offered any hope or salvation. Finally, he also made the genre more respectable, to the extent that its stories proved popular and influential even among writers of so-called "mainstream" literature; those authors began to write material in the same vein.

Guy de **Maupassant**, one of the most famous writers of the naturalist school, is often held to be one of the greatest French short-story writers ever. A literary disciple of Gustave Flaubert, Maupassant wrote, throughout his life, about thirty genre stories or novellas, from the macabre "La Main Coupée" ("*The Severed Hand*," 1875) to "Qui Sait?" ("Who Knows," 1890). Maupassant followed in the footsteps of Poe, and clearly anticipated H. P. Lovecraft (1890-1937). Like the writer from Providence, he was obsessed with the notion of insanity and the slow descent into madness. He, himself, suffered from congenital syphilis. His brother was retarded and, before being eventually committed in 1888, had allegedly told Maupassant, "It is you who

are mad; you are the crazy one in the family." Indeed, by his mid-thirties, Maupassant began to suffer from chronic neuralgia, compounded by his use of drugs and his latent psychoses. He started to hallucinate the presence of mysterious, hostile, invisible beings, and became haunted by the idea of death. Maupassant was finally committed in 1892 and died shortly afterwards.

During his last years, Maupassant wrote a number of short stories reflecting those fears: In "Sur l'Eau" ("On the Water," 1881), a simple boat ride took its protagonists into another, invisible alien universe. "Apparition" (1883) dealt with a man who did not believe in ghosts and whose sanity was severely shaken when he was confronted with a true, supernatural phenomenon. "Lui?" ("*Him?*," 1883) and "L'Auberge" ("The Inn," 1886) dealt with hallucinations. "Un Fou?" ("*A Madman?*," 1884) with schizophrenia before its nature became known or understood.

Maupassant's masterpiece was "Le Horla" (1887), which was the basis for the 1963 film *Diary of a Madman*, starring Vincent Price. In it, it was revealed that Man shared the Earth with invisible beings of great powers to whom we were only cattle, and who were destined to be our successors. with its pseudo-scientific and psychoanalytic explanations, "Le Horla" was in the same vein as Bulwer-Lytton's (1803-1873) the *Coming Race* (1871), and anticipated Charles Fort's (1874-1932) *The Book of the Damned* (1919) and Eric Frank Russell's (1905-1978) *Sinister Barrier* (1943). The origin of the word "Horla" was never fully explained, but could derive from "*hors-là*" ("*out there*") or from the local *patois* word "*horzain*" ("*stranger*").

Unlike most of his predecessors, Maupassant dealt with the *fantastique* in a natural and yet immensely disturbing fashion. He did not rely on devils, witches, or other supernatural forces, but on the objective, fundamental alienness of the universe, blissfully ignorant of its deadly nature. For Maupassant, as for Lovecraft, to get a glimpse of the true reality was to risk madness, death—or worse.

The eclectic **Villiers de l'Isle-Adam** was another naturalist writer whose *Contes Cruels* (*Cruel Tales*, 1883) and *Nouveaux Contes Cruels* (*New Cruel Tales*, 1888) seemed directly inspired by Poe and shared the same sensibilities and taste for the macabre. Like Poe, Villiers was also tempted by science fiction. His *Tribulat Bonhomet* (1887) used ornate literary twists oin a horror tale involving possession and hideous paroxysms of female guilt.

In the same vein, Octave **Mirbeau** penned a series of truly sadistic and mean-spirited tales of murders, cannibalism, and ghostly revenge in *Le Jardin des Supplices* (*Torture Garden*, 1899) and *Les Vingt et un Jours d'un Neurasthénique* (*The 21 Days of a Neurasthenic*, 1901).

Poe's influence was also noticeable in many of the works of the lesser known genre writers of the period:

Minuits, Récits de la Veillée (*Midnight, Tales of the Watch*, 1856) by Claude **Vignon**, the wife of occultist Eliphas **Lévi**.

La Double Vie (*The Double Life*, 1858), a collection of supernatural stories that included the classic "Le Mensonge" ("The Lie") by Charles **Asselineau**, a writer better known for his literary studies and his friendship with Baudelaire.

Contes Extraordinaires (*Extraordinary Tales*, 1879) by Ernest **Hello**.

Contes Abracadabrants (*Alakazam Tales*, 1880) by **Lemercier de Neuville**.

Histoires Incroyables (*Incredible Stories*, 1885), *Nouvelles Histoires Incroyables* (*New Incredible Tales*, 1888) and *L'Élixir de Vie* (*The Elixir of Life*, 1890), a novel about a man who must steal others' life-forces in order to remain alive, by Jules **Lermina**.

Sueurs de Sang (*Blood Sweat*, 1893) and *Histoires Désobligeantes* (*Uncomfortable Stories*, 1894), two collections of short stories that incorporate the horrific elements of the *roman frénétique* with modern supernatural concepts, by Léon **Bloy**.

A special mention should be made of humorist Eugène **Mouton**, whose *Nouvelles et Fantaisies Humoristiques* (*Humoristic Short Stories*, 1872) and *Fantaisies* (*Fantasies*, 1883) were Swiftian, macabre, dark-humored stories mixing the fantastique with the burlesque, such as "Histoire de l'Invalide à la Tête de Bois" (*Tale of the Invalid with a Wooden Head*), the story of a soldier with a transplanted wooden head.

As we shall see in the next chapter, Poe's influence was felt not only on the *fantastique* but also on science fiction, through Jules **Verne**, who greatly admired him, to the point of writing his own sequel to Poe's the *Narrative of Arthur Gordon Pym*, *Le Sphinx des Glaces* (*The Sphinx of the Ices*, 1897), but also on a number of distinguished authors such as J.-H. **Rosny** Aîné and Maurice **Renard** who, unlike Verne, crossed the line between the *fantastique* and science fiction, and yet owed to Poe their rational, lucid, logical approach to the supernatural. Examples of this type of *fantastique réaliste* could be found in Rosny's *La Sorcière* (*The Witch*) and *L'Immolation* (both 1887), and Renard's *Fantômes et Fantôches* (*Ghosts and Puppets*, 1905).

As mentioned above, Poe also enticed a number of so-called "mainstream" writers to cross the literary boundaries between realism, social satire, science fiction, and the *fantastique*.

Claude **Farrère**, the first recipient of the French Goncourt Award—the equivalent of the British Booker Prize or the American Pulitzer Prize—wrote *La Maison des Hommes Vivants* (*The House of Living Men*, 1911). In it, Farrère described a sect of secret immortals, founded by the Count of Saint-Germain, who must steal others' life-forces through electro-chemical means in order to preserve their own immortality. (*La Maison des Hommes Vivants* was adapted into a Grand-Guignol play by Pierre-Louis **Rehm**.)

Among other notable "mainstream" authors who followed in the footsteps of Poe were:

Jean **Richepin**, with *Les Morts Bizarres* (*The Bizarre*

Deaths, 1876), *Théâtre Chimérique* (*Chimerical Theater*, 1896), and *Le Monstre* (*The Monster*, 1896).

Gaston **Danville**, with *Contes de l'Au-Dela* (*Tales from Beyond*, 1893).

Laurent **Montesiste**, with *Histoires Vertigineuses* (*Dazzling Tales*, 1896).

Victor-Émile **Michelet**, with *Contes Surhumains* (*Superhuman Tales*, 1900).

Edmond **Vibert**, with *Pour Lire en Automobile, Nouvelles Fantastiques* (*To Read in a Car, Fantastical Short Stories*, 1901).

Gabriel **Legué**, with *La Messe Noire* (*The Black Mass*, 1903).

Edmond **Haraucourt**, with *La Peur* (*The Fear*, 1907).

c. Fantastique Symboliste

Toward the later part of the 19th century, the morbid fascination for the supernatural that was obvious in the works of Poe combined with the decadent and erotic influences of the works of Lord Byron and Oscar Wilde, and the esoteric operas of German composer Richard Wagner, to fuel the growth of the *fantastique symboliste*, also dubbed *fantastique décadent*.

As symbolist manifesto was published by Jean Moréas in the daily newspaper *Le Figaro* on September 18, 1886. But the true precursor of the *fantastique symboliste* was without a doubt Charles **Baudelaire**. a renowned poet and the French translator of Poe, Baudelaire was prosecuted for obscenity and blasphemy for his morbid poetry, which included verses about lost civilizations, ghouls, vampires, etc. His oeuvre, steeped in the macabre and the *fantastique*, was collected in *Les Fleurs du Mal* (*The Flowers of Evil*, 1857). Rejecting the posings of the romantics, Baudelaire anticipated the symbolists' and, later, the surrealists' spiritual quests. He virtually revolutionized poetry and influenced the creation of the symbolist movement. Indeed, the leaders of that movement attended his funeral and adopted him as their guide and inspiration.

Another *avant-garde poète maudit* of the decadent movement was Isidore Ducasse, who used the pseudonym of **Lautréamont**—a name borrowed from a fictional character created by Sue. His poems, collected in *Les Chants de Maldoror* (*The Songs of Maldoror*, 1869), owed their inspiration to both Sade and Byron, as well as the gothic excesses of the *roman frénétique*.

Baudelaire and Lautréamont were among the first to fully focus on the exploration of evil and the dark recesses of the human soul. Jules-Amédée **Barbey d'Aurevilly**, a devout catholic, novelist, and renowned literary critic, was critical of the naturalist school (e.g., Émile **Zola**), but a great admirer of Baudelaire. His novels were tales of terror in which morbid passions were acted out in bizarre crimes, often told against the bloody background of the French Revolution. In *Les Diaboliques* (*The Diabolical Women*; written in 1858, published in 1874, and not to be confused with the famous **Boileau-Narcejac** thriller), Barbey broke new ground, describing with a minutiae of psychological details the diabolical nature of perversity, sadism, and eroticism. Throughout his other works, such as *L'Ensorcelée* (*The Spellbound*, 1854), *Le Chevalier des Toches* (*The Knight of Toches*, 1864), and *Une Histoire sans Nom* (*A Nameless Story*, 1881), Barbey exhibited a profound belief in the existence of pure evil, and its ability to take possession of the human soul. His works later inspired such classic writers as George **Bernanos** and André Mauriac. Interestingly, his nearest English-language counterpart, Robert Louis Stevenson (1850-1894) did not publish his *Strange Case of Dr. Jekyll and Mr. Hyde* until 1888.

Joris-Karl **Huysmans** continued Barbey's obsession with the description of evil by creating new dramatic templates for old concepts, such as the Devil, the witches' black mass, etc. What Ira Levin did with *Rosemary's Baby*, Huysmans achieved in *À Rebours* (*Backwards*, 1884) and *Là-Bas* (*Over There*, 1891), which became the "manifestos" of the symbolists and the decadents. The character of the Duke des Esseintes, who felt only contempt for the century in which he lived, and instead chose to go to a magical land, perfectly embodied the secret desire of the decadents to turn back the clock to another, mythical time.

Another major writer of the *fantastique décadent* was Rémy de **Gourmont**, also a renowned literary critic, whose face was hideously marred by lupus. His *Lilith* (1892) was a Satanic play. His darkly horrific tales were collected in *Proses Moroses* (*Morose Prose*, 1894), *D'un Pays Lointain* (*From a Far-Away Land*, 1898), and *Histoires Magiques* (*Magical Stories*, 1902). His *Le Pèlerin du Silence* (*The Pilgrim of Silence*, 1896) took place in Persia and related an initiatic journey. In the short story "Péhor" (included in *Histoires Magiques*), the eponymous incubus crawled his way up through the belly and the throat of his female victim and, as she expired, drank her soul directly from the inside of her mouth.

The works of Jean **Lorrain**, also a writer of plays and operas, reflected a similar, lifelong obsession with the nature of evil, corruption, and decadence in all its varied forms. In his novels, the supernatural was only one of the means through which the human soul could be degraded. Lorrain's books included *Buveurs d'Âmes* (*Soul Drinkers*, 1893), *Un Démoniaque* (*Demoniacal*, 1895), *Sensations et Souvenirs* (*Feelings and Remembrances*, 1895), *Une Femme par Jour* (*A Woman a Day*, 1896), the kabbalistic novel *La Mandragore* (1899) and *Histoires de Masques* (*Stories of Masks*, 1900). But his masterpiece was *Monsieur de Phocas* (1901), a novel featuring the character of Claudius Ethal, who, like Huysman's Duke des Esseintes, cultivated and fed on evil, except that, unlike the Duke, Ethal was not handsome but a grotesque Mr. Hyde, a Toulouse-Lautrec-like misfit, a manifestation of Lorrain's tortured soul.

Marcel **Schwob** was another master of the *fantastique*

symboliste of the late 19th century. His collection *Coeur Double* (*Twin Hearts*, 1891) was dedicated to Stevenson, and explored the nature of true terror. Like Lorrain, Schwob also focused on the horrid reality hidden behind the masks of the ordinary. His other collection, the justifiably famous *Le Roi au Masque d'Or* (*The King In the Golden Mask*, 1892) was dedicated to J.-H. Rosny Aîné and contained some short stories that could be equally considered science fiction or horror. The title piece was about an Oriental king who wore a gold mask and lived surrounded by priests, concubines, jesters, and eunuchs, all wearing gold masks. One day, the king took off his mask and discovered that he was a leper; he then blinded himself and abandoned his throne to travel to a City of Lepers, with a still-loyal woman by his side, unaware that she, too, is a leper.

Maurice **Level** was Marcel Schwob's cousin, and he too contributed several notable genre works including *On?* (*They?*, 1908), *Lady Harrington* (1908), *L'Épouvante* (*The Horror*, 1908), *Les Portes de l'Enfer* (*The Gates of Hell*, 1910), and the collection *Contes de l'Heure Présente* (*Tales of the Present Times*, 1914), written with Charles **Robert-Dumas** (also see Chapter VI).

Symbolist poetry, already influenced by Baudelaire, Villiers, and Huysmans, took an increasingly elliptical and esoteric style with Arthur Rimbaud (1854-1891), Paul Verlaine (1844-1896) and Stéphane **Mallarmé**. Mallarmé's poems *Hérodiade* (1864) and *L'Après-Midi d'un Faune* (*The Afternoon of a Faun*, 1876), in turn, influenced composer Debussy and Belgian poet Maurice **Maeterlinck**, whose play *Pelléas et Mélisande* (1892), with its dream-like atmosphere, was perfectly representative of this current of symbolist thought.

Another famous symbolist writer was Paul **Adam**, who wrote *Volontés Merveilleuses* (*Marvellous Wills*, 1888-90), a trilogy comprised of *Être* (*To Be*), *En Décor* (*In the Background*), and *Essence de Soleil* (*Essence of the Sun*), in which a sorceress used dark forces to escape from her father.

Henri de **Régnier**'s fantastic tales, collected in *La Canne de Jaspe* (*The Stick of Jaspe*, 1897) and *Histoires Incertaines* (*Uncertain Tales*, 1919), could also be linked to the symbolist current, to the extent that they read like updated fairy tales of ghosts and monsters set against the cold palaces and forests of past centuries.

Pierre **Louÿs**' stories, collected in *Sanguines* (*Bloody Tales*, 1903), used the familiar themes of the decadent school, but gave them a refreshingly ironical twist: in one tale, an ancient Egyptian princess was spooked by the sight of a modern cigarette; in another, a madman climbed a mountain to hear a goddess sing; in yet another, a woman portrayed very differently from what she really was in a Balzac novel failed to convince the great writer than she was herself, and not a fictional character!

Other notable symbolist writers included:

Élémir **Bourges**, who penned a number of elaborate,

dark and esoteric novels, including the classic *Le Crépuscule des Dieux* (*The Twilight of the Gods*, 1884) and *La Nef* (*The Ship*), a metaphysical epic which took him almost twenty years to write (1904-1922).

Édouard **Dujardin**, with *Les Hantises* (*The Hauntings*, 1886).

Bernard **Lazare**, with *Le Miroir des Légendes* (*The Mirror of Legends*, 1892).

Alfred **Le Bourguignon**, with *La Chouette* (*The Owl*, 1893).

Joseph de **Gobineau,** with *Nouvelles Asiatiques* (*Asian Short Stories*, 1896).

Gustave **Kahn**, with *Le Conte de l'Or et du Silence* (*The Tale of Gold and Silence*, 1898), dedicated to Mallarmé.

The symbolist movement eventually reached its peak in the early 1900s before declining and, eventually, giving way to surrealism after World War I. A special note should be made of five other writers who, while not symbolists nor decadents, appeared to anticipate the currents of thoughts that eventually led to surrealism after World War I:

Aloysius **Bertrand**'s strange *Gaspard de la Nuit* (*Gaspar of the Night*, 1842) collected forty-eight short stories subtitled "dark fantasies *à la* Rembrandt and Callot," and harked back to a medieval occult tradition.

Xavier **Forneret**'s *Un Oeil Entre Deux Yeux* (*One Eye Between Two Eyes*, 1838) and short fiction "Le Diamant de l'Herbe" ("The Diamond in the Grass," 1840) anticipated the formal word games of the surrealists.

Paul **Claudel**'s *La Ville* (*The City*, 1892) was a social and religious allegory taking place in a fantastical, godless city.

Satirical writer Alfred **Jarry**, creator of the grotesque and wildly amusing *Ubu Roi* (1896), was a forerunner of the Theatre of the Absurd; his *Gestes et Opinions du Docteur Faustroll* (*Deeds and Opinions of Dr. Faustroll*, 1911) contained a so-called treatise of "pataphysics," and was later embraced by the dadaists and the surrealists.

Finally, Raymond **Roussel** was a true precursor of surrealism with his elaborate word games in *Impressions d'Afrique* (*Impressions of Africa*, 1910) and the bizarre *Locus Solus* (1914), a book comprised of surreal scenes in which corpses replayed their lives in a store window, a woman assembled a mosaic made of human teeth, a girl was seen swimming inside a diamond, etc.

As the 20th century began, old-fashioned horror became less popular among the classical and mainstream writers, being increasingly relegated to the popular side of literature and the Grand-Guignol. Romanticism fell out of fashion. The naturalists were more interested in the sociological and psychological horrors inflicted by society rather than the vampires and werewolves of gothic literature. a case, for example, could be made that Émile **Zola**'s descriptions of the sordid underbelly of French society belonged to the horror genre.

The symbolists and the decadents fought against the growing popularity of the naturalist works of Zola, Flaubert, and Goncourt. They sought to tame the shadows, explore the darkness, map the horrors of hell and the human soul, unveil the faces of evil and make them a subject of seduction. As the year 1900 approached, the notion of *fantastique décadent* became associated with that of *fantastique fin de siècle* (*end of the century*). And, as a reaction to the naturalist school, it took more and more refuge in subject matters whose roots lay deep in the occult.

d. Fantastique Ésotérique *and* Fantastique Fin de Siècle

More than ever before, the occult and esoteric philosophies continued to fire the imaginations of those opposing the currents of thoughts of Cartesian naturalist literature, especially during the latter part of the 19th century. Two dominant figures of the times became the guiding lights of this type of *fantastique*:

The first was Eliphas **Lévi**, who wrote *Histoire de la Magie* (*The History of Magic*, 1860), *La Clef des Grands Mystères* (*The Key to the Great Mysteries*, 1860), *Dogme et Rituel de la Haute Magie* (*Dogma and Rituals of High Magic*, 1861), *Fables et Symboles* (*Fables and Symbols*, 1862), *La Science des Esprits* (*The Science of Spirits*, 1865), and the posthumously-published *Le Livre des Splendeurs* (*The Book of Splendors*, 1894) and *Le Grand Arcane, ou l'Occultisme Dévoilé* (*The Great Arcana, or Occultism Unveiled*, 1898).

Lévi was the first modern occultist to combine various occult and previously secret branches of research, such as alchemy, kabbala, and witchcraft, into a coherent and modern system of thought. His influence on the genre was enormous; it is no exaggeration to say that the entire field of occult literature and occult books would not exist without him. Unlike the "old masters" of previous centuries, Lévi simplified, vulgarized, democratized and, in effect, made the occult accessible to one and all. He reassured the Christians by expelling the old concepts of the Devil, and emphasized the word "science." Lévi was the first to propose a unified theory of the occult, in which the paranormal and the supernatural are nothing but an as-yet-undiscovered part of science.

Lévi became, directly or indirectly, the unavoidable reference in the field, the source which all subsequent writers using occult themes—whether they were believers or unbelievers—felt bound to use. He, himself, became a fictional character, appearing as the White Magician Unken in **Péladan**'s *La Victoire du Mari* (*The Husband's Victory*, 1889) and as Gaston Leroux's mysterious magus, Eliphas de Saint-Elme de Taillebourg de la Nox, in *Le Fauteuil Hanté* (*The Haunted Chair*, 1910). Ironically, Lévi denounced all his works on his death bed!

The other major figure of the *fantastique ésotérique* was Allan **Kardec**, whose *Le Livre des Esprits* (*Book of*

Spirits, 1857), and its numerous "sequels," notably *Le Livre des Mediums* (*The Book of Mediums*), launched the *spiritisme*, and virtually created the sub-set of the *roman spirite*, devoted to the theme of communication between the living and the dead.

Kardec's work influenced such renowned writers as Hugo, Baudelaire, Balzac (with *Séraphita*), Gautier (with *Spirite*), Villiers de l'Isle-Adam (with *Tribulat Bonhomet*), **Flammarion**, Oscar Wilde, and others.

In addition to these, other notable authors of *roman spirites* included:

Clément de **La Chave**, with *La Magicienne des Alpes* (*The Magician of the Alps*, 1861).

Henri **Rivière**, with *La Main Coupée* (*The Severed Hand*, 1862), *La Possédée, ou la Seconde Vie du Dr. Roger* (*The Possessed Woman, or the Second Life of Dr. Roger*, 1863), *Les Méprises du Coeur* (*The Mistakes of the Heart*, 1865), and *L'Envoûtement* (*The Spell*, 1870). *Les Méprises du Coeur* collected a number of notable genre tales including "Les Voix Secrètes de Jacques Lambert" ("Jacques Lambert's Secret Voices"), "Le Rajeunissement" ("Growing Younger") and "Les Visions du Lieutenant Féraud" ("Lt. Feraud's Visions").

Jules **Claretie**, with *Jean Mornas* (1885).

Charles **Richet** (writing as "Charles Epheyre"), with *Possession* (1887).

Léon **Hennique**, with *Un Caractère* (*A Character*, 1889).

Of all the many occult-inspired writers of the late 19th century, such as Stanislas de Guaïta (1861-1898), Édouard Schuré (1841-1919), Papus (1865-1916), Saint-Pol Roux, and Puvis de Chavannes, the most prominent was undoubtedly Josephin **Péladan**, also known for his numerous aliases such as the Sâr Merodack, Princess Dinska, Miss Sarah, and the Marquis de Valognes!

Péladan's first novel, *Le Vice Suprême* (*The Supreme Vice*, 1884), was prefaced and praised by Barbey d'Aurevilly. In 1890, with writer Élémir **Bourges**, Péladan spearheaded a split from the Kabbalistic Order of the Rosicrucians (established in 1988 by Stanislas de Guaïta) and founded his own neo-Catholic Rosicrucian Order, thus starting a famous feud between the two orders dubbed the "war of the two roses." Borrowing from Lévi, Kardec, and various Eastern (or pseudo-Eastern) mystic sources, Peladan embarked on the writing of a fourteen-volume saga entitled *La Décadence Latine* (*The Latin Decadence*), of which *Le Vice Suprême* is the first, and which was meant to be an occult version of Balzac's renowned *Human Comedy* series.

In these novels, Péladan was more concerned with the development of his occult philosophies—such as the notion of androgyny explored in *L'Androgyne* (1891)—than he was with the construction of a classic dramatic structure. In *La Victoire du Mari* (*The Husband's Victory*, 1889), the evil sorcerer Sexthenthal cast a spell on Izel, a newlywed French girl during the Wagner Festival at Bayreuth. Her husband,

Adar, enlisted the help of white magician Unken to defeat Sexthenthal. His *La Torche Renversée* (*The Spilled Torch*, 1925) was a sequel to the Round Table Mythos. Péladan's alter ego, the magus-like Sar Merodack, starred in some of the books.

Following in the wake of Péladan was his fellow occultist Jules **Bois**, a noted expert and author of numerous books on satanism and magic, whose *L'Ève Nouvelle* (*The New Eve*, 1896) and *Le Mystère et la Volupté* (*The Mystery and the Voluptuousness*, 1901) were novels about magical love.

Writers representative of this *fantastique fin de siècle* included Paul Adam, Jean Lorrain, Joris-Karl Huysmans, all mentioned previously, but also the following:

Catulle **Mendès**, with *Zo'Har* (1886).

Rachilde, with *Monsieur Vénus* (1889), *L'Animale* (*The She-Beast*, 1893), *Le Démon de l'Absurde* (*The Demon of the Absurd*, 1894) and *La Princesse des Ténèbres* (*The Princess of Darkness*, 1896).

Camille **Mauclair**, with *Le Soleil des Morts* (*The Sun of the Dead*, 1898) and *L'Ennemie des Rêves* (*The Dream Foe*, 1900).

Finally, before closing this chapter, there were three very unique and virtually unclassifiable writers who must be added as a footnote to an otherwise incredibly prolific century:

Émile **Deschamps** was a writer semingly gifted with authentic Edgar Cayce-like paranormal powers. Known as a literary critic and dabbler—he wrote some librettos for Berlioz and Meyerbeer—Deschamps penned a fantastic autobiography entitled *Les Réalités Fantastiques* (*Fantastic Realities*, 1854). In it, he casually detailed his heretofore unrevealed encounters with the supernatural, since his childhood: instances of divination, successful readings, encounters with ghost-like spirits, and the story of his dealings with a young Jewish woman who was his spiritual soul-mate.

While Deschamps was, in every respect, a normal person, Alexis-Vincent-Charles **Berbiguier de Terre-Neuve du Thym** was a man afflicted with an acute and most unique form of mental sickness. Virtually all of his adult life, Berbiguier genuinely believed himself to be persecuted by the *Farfadets* (*Little People*, or *Goblins*), and saw their agents in his everyday encounters with doctors, lawyers, neighbors, and the rest of society. Berbiguier wrote an amazing, three-volume autobiography, *Les Farfadets, ou Tous les Démons ne sont pas de l'Autre Monde* (*The Goblins, or Not All Demons Come from Another World*, 1821), which was also a wildly imaginative treatise on the *Farfadets*, their powers and methods of operation, and which contained *Ghostbusters*-like strategies on how to fight them effectively.

Finally, Gabriel Antoine Jogand-Pagès, using the pseudonym of "Léo **Taxil**," wrote *Le Diable au XIXème Siècle ou les Mystères du Spiritisme* (*The Devil In the 19th Century*, 1892-95), a pseudo-documentary book about the

Freemasonry, which included some truly grotesque and utterly unbelievable descriptions of secret underground rituals, the summoning and worship of monstrous devils, and other horrors. Jogand-Pagès also was known under his other pseudonym of "Henry Bataille," not to be confused with the playwright Henry **Bataille**.

CHAPTER V

19th Century Science Fiction (1800–1914)

The distinction between the *fantastique*, reviewed in our previous chapter, and science fiction became clearly apparent during the 19th century. In spite of all its excesses, the French Revolution succeeded in imposing the values of scientific progress and so-called Cartesian thinking on French society, thus setting the stage for the Industrial Revolution, which itself gave rise to the socialist ideas of Pierre Proudhon (1809-1865) in France, and Karl Marx (1818-1883) in England. The 19th century was also a period of colonial expansion, with fierce competition between France and the other European powers for most of Africa, a good part of Asia, and many Pacific Islands.

Literature being the mirror of society, some of these notions were bound to be reflected in the novels of the times, and indeed they were among the powerful social forces that shaped modern science fiction. During the early part of the 19th century, the subset of the *fantastique* which had previously been devoted to proto-science fiction, such as utopias and imaginary journeys, evolved into the *voyages extraordinaires* and, from 1864 onward, thanks to the incomparable Jules **Verne**, the first, true works of modern science fiction.

From the onset, what distinguished science fiction from the *fantastique* was that it was a literature of ideas rather than style, of concepts rather than characters. This dichotomy was a direct result of the conflict present in French society between the past and the future, conservative and radical ideas, literature and science, classicism and progress. The concerns of science fiction—"what if" scenarios, considerations of the impact of technology and scientific anticipation of the future—were, by their very nature, deemed by the guardians of French culture to be inferior to the nobler concerns of true literature.

This perception, which to some extent still exists today, was reinforced by the fact that the works of Jules Verne were arbitrarily, and somewhat unjustly, catalogued as being aimed at young adults. Even worse, science fiction proved to be a fertile field for all kinds of pulp-like, popular adventure serials, where thrills were more important than a well-turned sentence. As a result, science fiction was firmly categorized as second-rate literature, at best juvenile, at worst obscene, no matter how talented some of its authors, or enlighened some of its novels.

Whereas we were able, in our previous chapter, to contrast literary and popular forms of the *fantastique*, there was, sadly, very little science fiction that was published as "real" literature, and when it happened, it certainly was never labelled as such. A good novel, by a startling example of circular logic, could never be a science fiction novel. In America and England, Poe and Wells are universally regarded today as major literary figures. Sadly, in France, Verne and **Rosny Aîné** are still treated as marginal and/or juvenile authors.

1. From Imaginary Journeys to *Voyages Extraordinaires*

Prior to Jules Verne's grand entrance onto the science fiction stage in 1864, the earlier part of the century showed no clean break with the literary tradition inherited from before the French Revolution. In fact, the Napoleonic regime which followed the Revolution even encouraged a return to a certain literary classicism. In spite of this, however, a deliberate and growing scientific spirit was applied to even the most old-fashioned utopias of the pre-Revolutionary period. Some works emerged from this period as true, conceptual breakthroughs which established and defined new boundaries for the growing new genre.

As we did in Chapter III, we have somewhat arbitrarily grouped the pre-Verne science fiction according to three themes: Outer Space, Other Lands, and the Future.

a. Cosmic Journeys

Cosmic journeys were a tradition firmly established by **Cyrano de Bergerac**. They continued to thrive during the first half of the 19th century, remaining more often than not a pretext for thinly veiled social satire. However, as we mentioned above, these stories increasingly incorporated scientific elements and began to aim for believability, an essential ingredient of modern science fiction.

In 1832, in his collection of short stories simply entitled *Nouvelles* (*Short Stories*), Jacques **Boucher de Crèvecoeur de Perthes** included "*Mazular*," the tale of a journey to the Moon.

In chapters 14 and 16 to 18 of *Les Aventures Amphibies de Robert-Robert et de son fidèle compagnon Toussaint Lavenette* (*The Amphibian Adventures of Robert-Robert and His Faithful Companion Toussaint Lavenette*, 1853), a sprawling juvenile saga serialized in the *Journal des Enfants* (*Children's Journal*), Louis **Desnoyers** described the travels of Cousin Laroutine on the Moon. In a typical pre-Revolutionary style, however, our satellite was reached via hot air balloon, and the tone was one of social satire.

The same means of travel was employed in *Les Aventures d'un Aéronaute Parisien dans les Mondes Inconnus* (*The Adventures of a Parisian Aeronaut in the Unknown Worlds*, 1856) by Alfred **Driou**.

The most remarkable novel of the period, and perhaps the first modern "space opera" ever, certainly the first interstellar epic in genre history, was without a doubt *Star, ou Psi de Cassiopée* (1854) by Charles-Ischir **Defontenay**. This astonishing novel described in amazing details the long history of an alien civilization based on a far-off planet with three stars and five satellites. Not much was known about Defontenay, a French doctor who, a full forty years before H. G. Wells, wrote this remarkable science fiction novel, distinguished not only by its content but by its mature, poetic, literary style, a far cry from the latter works of Verne and his followers.

Star opened with a poem, anticipating the "free" verse of the surrealists, describing the discovery in the Himalayas of a hollow meteor, which was revealed to be a cosmic cache of alien books and manuscripts. Once translated, these documents turned out to be a correspondence between two wise men from the far-off world of Star. Through them, we learned of the existence of a planetary system with four suns (including a red dwarf), one planet, and five satellites. Defontenay's amazing powers of imagination provided us with wonderfully realistic descriptions of the alien seasons, flora, and fauna of Star, including its "bramiles" and "psarginos," and described the slow progress of its inhabitants on the road to planetary civi-

lization. Star is peopled by various races: the "Savelces," the "Treliors," the "Ponarbates," and others. We witnessed their histories, their wars, their natural disasters and were offered a glimpse into their alien cultures. The "Nemsedes," for example, were asexual beings who lived for a thousand years, and used their wisdom for the benefit of the other races. The "Eras," on the other hand, were evil and used "devolution" to enslave others. Finally, Defontenay told us of the end of the Starrian civilization, brought about by a plague. But the novel did not end there. Some Starrians escaped the plague and, using a starship powered by anti-gravity, fled to Tassul, the planet's inner satellite. (This device was very similar to Wells' "cavorite" from his 1901 *First Men in the Moon*.) Eventually, overpopulation drove more Starrians to emigrate to Lessur, the second satellite, which turned out to be a living planetary organism. Two centuries later, more Starrians moved to Rudar, the third satellite. Finally, the Starrians travelled to their fourth moon, Elier, which was transparent and, therefore, uninhabitable. They eventually returned to their homeworld, reconquered it, and founded a new interplanetary civilization, one that gathered all the races and cultures they met during their cosmic travels.

The history of the Starrian race, as presented by Defontenay, was comprised of a collection of poems, plays, and sagas culled from its various centuries. Their quality was such that they could be real poems from a real culture. In *Star*, Defontenay single handedly anticipated many of the now-classic themes of space opera in this novel. His "Farewell to the Reader" showed that he was conscious of the originality, if not sheer uniqueness, of his novel. The expression "ahead of its times" barely began to describe *Star*. Unlike most of the novels of the period, it is still readable today, and was warmly greeted by the public when it was reprinted in 1972. One is tempted to speculate about the future of science fiction had *Star* been emulated instead of ignored—*Star Maker* in 1860, *Foundation* in 1900, *Dune* in 1920?

Famous astronomer, author, and publisher Camille **Flammarion** popularized astronomy and cosmology, and was fascinated by the possibility of alien life. In *La Pluralité des Mondes Habités* (*The Plurality of Inhabited Worlds*, 1862), *Les Habitants de l'Autre Monde* (*The Inhabitants of Another World*, 1862), and *Les Mondes Imaginaires et les Mondes Réels* (1864), Flammarion speculated on the physiological properties of extraterrestrial life. He was also one of the first writers to seriously study science fiction as a separate genre.

At the time when Jules Verne was about to write his notorious *De la Terre à la Lune* (*From the Earth to the Moon*), two other writers also penned similar cosmic journeys:

Alexandre **Dumas**, the renowned author of *Les Trois Mousquetaires* (*The Three Musketeers*) and *Le Comte de Monte-Cristo* (*The Count of Monte Cristo*) wrote the novella, "*Voyage à la Lune*" ("*Trip to the Moon*"), in which our satellite was reached by a spacecraft powered by a substance "repelled by the Earth."

The second writer was Achille **Eyraud**, with *Voyage à Vénus* (*Voyage to Venus*, 1865), in which space travel was achieved through the use of a "reaction engine" which some genre scholars construed as rockets. In fact, **Eyraud** used the recoil effect to propel his spacecraft; however, since the water expelled was recovered in a container towed behind the craft, it would not have been scientifically workable. On the planet Venus, **Eyraud**'s hero discovered a utopian society, in which the sexes were equal and solar-powered robots toiled in the fields.

Finally, two other "cosmic" works of note were also published in 1865:

François-Henri **Peudefer de Parville** published *Un Habitant de la Planète Mars* (*An Inhabitant of Planet Mars*), in which the calcified body of a Martian, taken away from the red planet by a comet a long time ago, was dug up and recovered in America.

The Baron Alfred d'**Espiard de Colonge** wrote *La Chute du Ciel ou les Antiques Météores Planétaires* (*The Fall from the Sky or the Ancient Planetary Meteors*, 1865), a pseudo-scientific treatise in which he hypothesized that life on Earth had originated on another world and had come to our planet as a result of a collision with that other world.

b. Other Lands

Atlantis was the subject of Belgian author Charles-Joseph de **Grave**'s three-volume *République des Champs-Elysées ou Monde Ancien* (*Republic of the Elysean Fields, or the Ancient World*, 1806), a pseudo-erudite treatise on the existence of an antediluvian world that preceded recorded history.

In the same vein, a little later, Népomucène-Louis **Lemercier** wrote *L'Atlantiade, ou la Théogonie Newtonienne*, an epic poem about ancient Atlantis published in 1812. and Godefroy de **Roisel** penned *Les Atlantes* (*The Atlanteans*, 1874).

Swiss writer-artist Rodolphe **Toepffer** was not only the pioneer of modern comic books (see Book 1, Chapters V and VI), but was also one of the first modern writers to have introduced the concept of the "Lost World" in his prose novel *Voyages et Aventures du Docteur Festus* (*Voyages and Adventures of Dr. Festus*, 1833; not to be confused with the eponymous graphic novel). In it, Toepffer's hero flew above Antarctica, where he spotted a myterious Lost World inhabited by prehistoric creatures.

Other notable works in this vein included:

Étienne **Cabet**'s *Voyage et Aventures de Lord W. Carisdall en Icarie* (*Voyage and Adventures of Lord W. Carisdall in Icaria*, 1840), a Communist utopia.

Isidore **Grandville**'s *Un Autre Monde* (*Another World*, 1844), was illustrated by "Taxile Delord"—in reality another of Grandville's pseudonyms. The novel revealed the existence of intelligent marine races such as the Tritons and the Nereids, but was mostly remarkable for its illustrations. It probably was the first, fully illustrated science fiction novel.

In 1864, Henry de **Kock**'s *Les Hommes Volants* (*The Flying Men*) was, to a large extent, a retread of **Restif de la Betonne**'s *La Découverte Australe* (see Chapter III).

Finally, in 1865, the renowned female author George **Sand** wrote *Laura, ou le Voyage dans le Cristal* (*Laura or the Voyage Inside the Crystal*), in which Alexis, a young geologist, first mind-travelled to a crystalline universe located inside a gem. Then, the hero embarked on a physical journey to reach the center of the Earth—Jules Verne's notorious novel had been published the preceding year and certainly inspired Sand. At the North Pole, Alexis discovered a warm-climate sea and a Lost World island inhabited by "living fossils"—long-extinct creatures still alive. At the center of the island was a tall mountain where Alexis eventually found the passage to the Earth's Core.

c. The Future

The earliest and most notable work in this sub-genre was *Le Dernier Homme* (*The Last Man*, 1805) by Jean-Baptiste Cousin de **Grainville**, which was possibly the first novel ever written on this now-popular theme. In it, the narrator met an Incarnation of Time who told him the saga of Omegare, the last man on Earth. A bleak vision of the future emerged, of a time when a dying Earth became totally sterile. Omegare travelled to Brazil where the last men found refuge. Ormus, the "God of Earth," tried to manipulate Omegare to make him father a new race of monstrous cannibals, doomed to live in eternal darkness, but the vision of this awful future terrified Omegare, who instead chose death.

A number of startlingly accurate predictions about the future were made in Pierre-Marc-Gaston de **Levis**' two-volume *Les Voyages de Kang-Hi, ou Nouvelles Lettres Chinoises* (*Kang-Hi's Journeys, or New Chinese Letters*, 1810), a proto-scientific anticipation which mentioned the concepts of the Suez canal, air conditioning, air pollution, railways and other futuristic technologies and problems.

Strangely enough, the saga of Omegare, the last man on Earth, was not over, and gave rise to one of the first unauthorized spin-offs in literary history. In 1831, Auguste-François **Creuzé de Lesser** published an expanded version of Grainville's work, including a description of aerial cities and a failed attempt at leaving Earth to colonize another planet.

The character of Omegar (this time, without an "e") returned again in *L'Unitéide, ou la Femme Messie* (*The Uniteide or the Messiah Woman*, 1858), a vast philosophical-poetic saga, self-published by Paulin **Gagne**. *L'Unitéide* took place in the year 2000, when, according to the author, there were only twelve countries. In it, God sent the eponymous female messiah to save the world.

Finally, the following year, Gagne's wife, Élise **Gagne**, wrote *Omégar ou Le Dernier Homme* (*Omegar, or the Last Man*, 1859), yet another poetic epic about the final days of the Earth.

The future doom forecasted by Antoine-François-Marius **Rey-Dussueil** in *La Fin du Monde* (*The End of the World*, 1830) and *Le Monde Nouveau* (*The New World*, 1831) was far more immediate. In the first volume, the 1832 comet pushed Earth off its axis, causing the ice caps to melt and the world to be flooded. A man and three women survived at the top of the Mont-Blanc. The building of massive Noah's Arks was a pretext for the author to criticize the politics of the times. The second novel was mostly political satire. While **Rey-Dussueil** failed to fully exploit the theme of a cosmic catastrophe bringing about the end of the world as we know it, he nevertheless earned the right to be considered the first serious "cataclysmic" author of the 19th century.

The future of Man was also a concern of Charles **Nodier** (see Chapter IV) who, in 1833, penned *Hurlubleu*, in which the hero, Berniquet, who lived a hundred years in Nodier's future (i.e.: in 1933), was placed in suspended animation and was awakened 10,000 years in the future. What Nodier achieved was to tell the tale of two different worlds: that of the year 1933, and that of the future kingdom of Hurlubière, located on a top-shaped Earth, made bigger by the inclusion of the Moon. In the far future, Berniquet embarked on a picaresque, ten-year search for the perfect android, manufactured four thousand years before by the great scientist Zeretochthro-Schah.

Closer to us was Félix **Bodin**'s *Le Roman de l'Avenir* (*The Novel of the Future*, 1834). a historian himself, Bodin wrote an amazing novel, for which he coined the term "futuristic literature." In it, he tried to predict the events of the late 20th century, allegedly revealed to him by an Italian magus. Some of his predictions included the devaluation of the currency, the growth in power of North Africa, the creation of the Panama Canal, the reform of Islam, flying fortresses and parachutes, the breakup of the Russian Empire, the creation of a new Babylonian Empire, the establishment of a new Jewish State in Palestine, and other wonders.

The same year, Louis **Desnoyers**, in the last chapters of his four-volume *Paris Révolutionnaire* (*The Paris Revolution*, 1833-34), also attempted to predict what the future of the French capital would be, up to the end of the 19th century.

In 1841, Alexandre-Jean-Joseph de **La Ville de Mirmont** staged a futuristic play merely entitled *L'An 1928* (*The Year 1928*).

In 1846, Émile **Souvestre** published the ambitious *Le Monde Tel Qu'il Sera* (*The World as It Will Be*), a full-blown dystopia and scientific anticipation which featured some remarkable predictions. In it, Maurice and Marthe were taken to the year 3000 by a man named "John Progress" on a flying, steam-powered, time-travelling locomotive. There, they found steam-powered metros, submarines, synthetic materials imitating real wood, marble, etc., telephone, air conditioning, and giant fruits and vegetables obtained through what we would call today genetic engineering. The world was one, single society, the center of which was Tahiti. As in Huxley's *Brave New World*, eugenics and genetic manipulation were used to manufacture races of men tailored to various tasks.

Other visions of the future in the tradition of Nodier and Souvestre included:

Joseph **Déjacque**'s *L'Humanisphère* (1859), an anarchist utopia.

Hippolyte **Mettais**' *L'An 5865 ou Paris dans 4000 Ans* (*The Year 5865 or Paris in 4000 Years*, 1865), in which Paris in the future reverted to being a village.

Samuel-Henry **Berthoud**'s *L'Homme depuis Cinq Mille Ans* (*Man for Five Thousand Years*, 1865), a scientific novel about the history of Man, which began with a prehistoric prologue and ended with a grand finale taking place in the year 2865.

Fernand **Giraudeau**'s prophetic *La Cité Nouvelle* (*The New City*, 1868), a visionary dystopia describing the ultra-capitalistic world of 1998, and a society enslaved by the use of small steam- or wind-powered motorcars.

Ernest **Jonchère**'s *Clovis Bourbon: Excursion dans le 20ème Siècle* (*Clovis Bourbon: Travel to the 20th Century*, 1868).

Tony **Moilin**'s *Paris en l'An 2000* (*Paris in the Year 2000*, 1869).

Alfred-Louis **Franklin**'s *Les Ruines de Paris* (*The Ruins of Paris*, 1875), in which archeologists from a New Caledonian civilization from the year 4875 unearthed the ruins of Paris.

Even the renowned writer Victor **Hugo**, in his poetic epic *La Légende des Siècles* (*The Legend of the Centuries*, 1859), felt obliged to write a section anticipating the 20th century.

It was a short leap from visions of the future to visions of alternate Earths, parallel histories, and worlds that might have been. The first tale of a totally fictional, and yet "real" alternate universe, one in which Napoleon subdued Russia in 1812, invaded England in 1814, and went on to become the enlightened ruler of the world, was written by Louis **Geoffroy** in 1836. Entitled *Napoléon et la Conquête du Monde* (*Napoleon and the Conquest of the World*, 1812-32; revised in 1841 as *Napoléon Apocryphe*), it detailed with great and methodical precision the conquests of the Emperor, and the technical and scientific achievements made by a united planet under Napoleon's wise leadership: electric-powered zeppelins, weather control, flying cars, typewriters (dubbed "writing pianos"), miracle cures, technology to make sea water drinkable, the discovery of a new planet, Vulcan (!), and more.

In 1848, noted writer Théophile **Gautier** penned the novella *Les Deux Étoiles* (*The Two Stars*) about a plan to rescue Napoleon from St. Helens by sub-marine.

More elaborate was *Hurrah!!! ou La Révolution par les Cosaques* (*Hurrah!!! or the Revolution of the Cossacks*), published in French in London in 1854 by Ernest **Coeurderoy**. In it, the decadence of Western Europe was followed by an invasion of barbarians from the North, the death of civilization as we know it and, finally, the glorious rebirth of a new socialist era led by the Cossacks and, behind them, the Asians. *Hurrah!!!* may well have the dubious honor of being the first "yellow peril" novel in genre history, followed closely by Belgian writer Iwan **Gilkin**'s *Jonas* (1900).

2. Jules Verne

And then came Jules **Verne** and everything changed forever.

Verne made his genre beginnings with two novellas entitled *Un Voyage en Ballon* (*A Voyage in a Balloon*), an adventure tale published in 1851, and "*Maître Zacharius*," a story belonging to the *fantastique* featuring a clockmaker and the Devil, published in 1854. Verne's literary influences were Edgar Allan Poe, from whom he drew his sense of wonder and the ability to project the cold light of scientific logic upon the wildest of notions, Victor **Hugo** for his romantic spirit, and Alexandre **Dumas**, for his sense of drama and adventure. In 1850, Verne had a play, *Les Pailles Rompues* (*The Broken Straws*), produced at Dumas' *Theâtre Historique* in Paris. and in 1897, he penned his own sequel to Poe's the *Narrative of Arthur Gordon Pym* entitled *Le Sphinx des Glaces* (*The Sphinx of the Ice*). It is also worth noting that Verne, who was born in the Atlantic port city of Nantes, had tried to embark on a ship when he was young.

Verne burst onto the literary scene with the serialized version of *Cinq Semaines en Ballon* (*Five Weeks in a Balloon*), the tale of a trans-African balloon journey, published in 1863 in a magazine founded by visionary publisher Pierre-Jules Hetzel, who immediately realized **Verne**'s enormous potential.

Strangely, Verne and Hetzel's relationship began with a rejection. The second novel—or more appropriately novella—submitted by Verne to Hetzel in 1863 was entitled *Paris au 20ème Siècle* (*Paris in the 20th Century*). It was a grim, Orwellian story about a young poet, Michel, who desperately tried to fit into a soulless, technological society dominated by huge corporations, and who, having failed in his efforts, eventually died from the cold, homeless.

(The handwritten manuscript of *Paris in the 20th Century* was found by accident in 1994 by Verne's great grandson, Jean, in a forgotten safe that had belonged to Verne's son, Michel. The safe's key had been lost, but this was unimportant, as the strongbox was believed to be empty. The manuscript was thoroughly checked by Verne experts, who unanimously pronounced it authentic. a further proof of its veracity comes from the fact that its margins bore numerous, handwritten annotations by Hetzel, who rejected it,

telling the 35-year old author to return to writing adventure stories.)

One can understand Hetzel's rejection because, even though *Paris in the 20th Century* was a stunning display of forecasting, probably unique and towering in the annals of science-fiction, it nevertheless was a meandering, mawkish, sentimental novel, even by the standards of the times. Yet, in it, Verne foresaw a world suffering from overpopulation and illiteracy, pollution and deforestation, a world where wars were no longer waged by vast armies but by powerful machines, a world

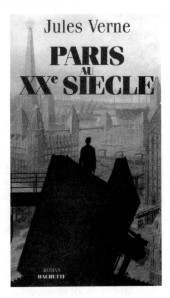

of political apathy, unemployment, and homeless people dying from the cold. Uncannily, Verne's predictions even included accurate descriptions of music made with synthesizers, staged sitcoms produced by teams of writers, male fashion (long hair), and single-parent families. Verne depicted a fully-electrified Paris where streets were jammed with automobiles (proudly and accurately detailing their principles and operation!) and where commuters piled themselves into elevated trains. Some of today's metro stations are exactly as foreseen by Verne. The offices contained elevators, computers (giant calculating machines), photocopiers, faxes, and even automated alarm systems, which could trap would-be burglars—and the electric chair was the preferred means of capital punishment. Verne even mentioned a 500-foot tall lighthouse dominating Paris' skyline and built on the very same spot where the Eiffel Tower was erected 26 years later!

In order to fully appreciate Verne's staggering predictions, one must recall that, at the time the book was written, America was in the throes of the Civil War. Gasoline-powered engines were developed in 1864 (even though the principles were known since 1859), typewriters were introduced in 1867, telephones in 1876, phonographs in 1877, filament lightbulbs in 1879, the electric chair in 1888 and the Paris Metro in 1898.

Paris in the 20th Century went against the traditional view of Verne, which often contrasted him with Wells, as the provider of thrilling but somewhat superficial adventure stories heralding the wonder of future science. Instead, as early as 1863, Verne saw the 20th century as a foreboding time, where technology and money all but eradicated literature and poetry. (In a satirical scene, a librarian cannot fulfill the hero's request for a novel by Victor Hugo, having never heard of him.) As mentioned above, this was not the type of novel Hetzel expected from Verne. As he put it in his rejection letter: "You undertook an impossible task, and you did not pull it off. Nobody will ever believe your prophecies." Meekly, the author followed his publisher's advice, buried the manuscript in a drawer, and never returned to it, only cannibalizing an occasional idea or quote for his later works.

Verne's first, full-blown genre novel was therefore the enormously successful *Voyage au Centre de la Terre* (*Journey to the Center of the Earth*, 1864), which introduced all the elements which became characteristic of his style, and indeed of much of later science fiction: an initial fantastic concept, a thrilling adventure, a sense of wonder, some wonderful vistas, a few momentary views into even more fantastic elements, but always careful to not go too far in order to never become unbelievable. For example, in this novel the heroes crossed a vast, inner sea and glimpsed the occasional living, prehistoric monster, but nothing more. In a startling break with the past, and in a fashion that has since become a hallmark of science fiction writers, Verne was always careful to strive for believability before all. Another of Verne's archetypal contributions to the genre was the character of the daring, often eccentric, even renegade, scientist-hero, whose genius is doubted by his peers, and whose will and boundless curiosity drives the plot forward. Professor Liddenbrock from *Journey to the Center of the Earth* was but the first in a very long line of similar characters who are still with us today.

De la Terre à la Lune (*From the Earth to the Moon*, 1865) and its sequel, *Autour de la Lune* (*Around the Moon*, 1870), were the seminal works on spaceflight of the 19th century, having inspired real-life rocketeers Tsiolkovsky, Goddard, Oberth, Braun, and Gagarin. In it, a group of American industrialists concocted a scheme to fire a cannon shell to the Moon from the fictional "Stony Hill," near Tampa, less than a hundred miles from Cape Canaveral. The shell eventually carried three passengers, including the French adventurer, Michel Ardan. The spacecraft orbited the Moon, upon which the remains of an ancient civilization could be glimpsed, then returned to Earth.

In *From the Earth to the Moon*, Verne did his scientific homework. No less an authority than Professor Wernher von Braun stated that Verne's calculations were "nearly as accurate as the knowledge of the time permitted." While it was true that the passengers would have been crushed by the acceleration, Verne was well aware of this and even voiced these objections himself in the novel. But he was striving for believability, in effect deliberately sacrificing scientific accuracy for the sake of fictional verisimilitude. Again, his was a process that became characteristic of science fiction writers. For example, had Verne chosen to use rockets, by the standards of the times, he would have had to make his craft either a huge powder keg, or combine tens of thousands of small rockets, either of which would have been deemed ludicrous by readers. In any event, Verne's accurate foretelling of space travel far outweighed any purposeful liberties he took.

The success of *From the Earth to the Moon* was enormous and proved that Verne's approach was right. The story was further popularised in an 1875 **Offenbach** opera whose libretto was written by Albert **Vanloo**, E. **Leterrier** and A. **Mortier**; and of course the 1902 **Méliès** film, ***Le Voyage dans la Lune*** (*A Trip to the Moon*; see Book 1, Chapter I). In 1867, Hetzel granted Verne his own imprint dubbed *Voyages Extraordinaires* (*Extraordinary Voyages*), a first in publishing history. For almost forty years thereafter, Verne produced a regular, steady flow of novels.

His next seminal work was *Vingt Mille Lieues Sous les Mers* (*Twenty Thousand Leagues Under the Sea*, 1870), which, with its sequel, *L'Île Mystérieuse* (*Mysterious Island*, 1875), introduced the character of Captain Nemo. Nemo has since joined the ranks of Sherlock Holmes, Tarzan, and Superman as one of the most famous modern fictional characters. He is a Byronesque figure: a brilliant scientist, an adventurer, a loner who exists beyond the reaches of man's society, a law unto himself, like Dumas' Count of Monte-Cristo, a man so wronged that he committed unspeakable deeds in the name of revenge. Nemo was an avenger who stood for freedom and justice. He was almost an anarchist, a modern anti-hero. The prodigious odyssey of Professor Arronax and harpooner Ned Land aboard Nemo's nuclear-powered submarine, the *Nautilus*— a name as well known today as *Star Trek*'s *Enterprise*, and which was given in homage to Verne by the U.S. Navy to the world's first nuclear submarine in 1954—is too well known to need retelling. In addition to the various technological wonders described by Verne, from deep-sea diving suits to navigation under the North Pole, we should mention the glimpses of sunken Atlantis presented to the heroes.

Other significant Verne novels included *Les Indes Noires* (*The Child of the Cavern*, 1877), a story about an underground civilization; and *Hector Servadac* (1877), in which an inhabited piece of Earth (located near Algeria) was carried away after a collision with a small asteroid, christened "Gallia" by its unwilling passengers. During its eccentric orbit, which took them as far as Saturn, one of the cosmic travelers, an astronomer, calculated the precise moment when Gallia was to swing by Earth again. Then, using a makeshift hot air balloon, they returned to our world. *Hector Servadac* accurately described the physical conditions of life on a planetoid, the problems of survival in deep space and the beautiful, cosmic vistas of Jupiter and Saturn. *Sans Dessus Dessous* (*Topsy Turvy*, 1889) saw the return of the cannon-loving protagonists of *From the Earth to the Moon*, and featured a crazy scheme to move the Earth off its axis.

Robur le Conquerant (*Robur the Conqueror*, 1886), and its sequel, *Maître du Monde* (*Master of the World*, 1904), were variations on a theme already explored in *Twenty Thousand Leagues Under the Sea*, except that, in this case, it was a flying machine, the *Albatros*, not a submarine, that terrorized the world. Its creator was very unlike the romantic Nemo: indeed, the steely, grim, megalo-maniacal engineer Robur, who became a dangerous mad-man in the second volume, represented the dangers of un-fettered science. Robur was one of the first mad scientists in science fiction history, and his plan to make himself "Master of the World" was to become one of the most no-torious of all genre clichés.

In *Face au Drapeau* (*Facing the Flag*, 1896), Verne's fictional inventor Thomas Roch designed a rocket-powered missile intended to be launched from a submarine—the first time ever this military device was postulated. Amusingly, the real-life French chemist Eugene Turpin, a pioneer of rocket engineering, enraged by what he saw as unpleasant simi-larities between him and Roch, sued the writer for libel—and lost.

The pessimism that had originally been present in *Paris in the 20th Century* and suppressed during most of Verne's prolific career, resurfaced in tales like the short story "L'Éternel Adam" ("The Eternal Adam"), written in 1905 but published in the collection *Hier et Demain* (*Yesterday & To-morrow*, 1910), in which a far-future historian discovered that our civilization was destroyed by a cataclysm, and that Adam and Eve were cyclical reoccurrences; and *L'Éton-nante Aventure de la Mission Barsac* (*The Amazing Adven-ture of the Barsac Mission*), written in 1903, published in 1914, in which a scientist was shown to be unwittingly work-ing on nefarious projects in a secret scientific city.

On the other hand, *La Chasse au Météore* (*The Chase of the Golden Meteor*), written in 1902, published in 1908, was a lighthearted romp in which the delightful scientist Zephyrin Xirdal found a way to cause a meteor made of gold to fall to Earth; and *Le Secret de Wilhelm Storitz* (*The Secret of Wilhelm Storitz*), written in 1902, published in 1910, was a beautiful, romantic novel on the theme of invisibility, in which the invisible heroine was finally able to become vis-ible again when she gave birth to her child.

It is impossible to overestimate the impact of Jules Verne on modern science fiction. As we have seen, many of the classic themes had already appeared sporadically in genre literature before Verne started writing; he did not so much create as reshape. Defontenay and others may have been more brilliant, more visionary, and better writers, but it was Verne who reached the masses, who popularized the concepts of science fiction and gave them their modern form.

Like Robert Heinlein much later, Verne made scientific anticipation popular with both younger and older readers. He came to exert such a powerful influence on the genre that it can safely be claimed that, without him, there would be no science fiction. The Luxembourg-born father of modern American science fiction, Hugo Gernsback, was a fan of Verne and published translations of his stories in his maga-zine *Modern Electrics* starting in 1908. This led to the cre-ation of *Amazing Stories* in 1926.

In France, Verne cast an enormous shadow on the en-tire genre, until World War II. Jules Verne's huge commer-cial success virtually created an industry overnight. It can be claimed that by tying science fiction to the juvenile mar-ket, Verne contributed to the fostering of the French cultural prejudice that the genre could not be a mature form of lit-erature. Yet, before Verne, science fiction novels were few and far between, usually the result of some writer's indi-vidual attempt at breaking new ground. After Verne, we are confronted by a literary phenomenon, where one can no longer group a few isolated titles along thematic lines, but is forced to look at an entire industry, the output of which is numbered in the hundreds. with Jules Verne, the Golden Age of French science fiction had begun.

3. The Golden Age

The Hetzel imprint devoted to Jules Verne, *Voyages Ex-traordinaires* (*Extraordinary Voyages*, 1867-1910) was the first of a series of imprints that contributed to create the Golden Age of French science fiction.

Other pre-World War I imprints of note which followed included:

Romans d'Aventures (*Adventure Novels*, 1884-1905), also published by Hetzel, devoted mostly to Verne's occa-sional collaborator, André **Laurie**.

Voyages Scientifiques Extraordinaires (*Extraordinary Scientific Voyages*, 1892-94), published by Fayard and fea-turing works by Georges **Le Faure**.

Les Grandes Aventures (*The Great Adventures*, 1888-1900), published by **Flammarion** and featuring works by Louis **Boussenard**.

Le Roman d'Aventures (*The Adventure Novels*, 1908-11), retitled *Les Récits Mystérieux* (*Mysterious Tales*, 1912-14), published by Albert Méricant and featuring works by Gustave **Le Rouge** and Paul d'**Ivoi**.

In a more popular vein, publisher Jules Tallandier's *Livre National* (*National Book*) published two imprints, *Ro-mans d'Aventures et d'Explorations* (*Novels of Adventure and Exploration*, 1900-1920) and *Romans Populaires* (*Pop-ular Novels*, 1900-1935), which both featured numerous genre works by Louis Boussenard and Jean de **La Hire**.

Finally, the Golden Age of French science fiction was also the result of the publication of numerous illustrated pulp magazines such as the monumental weekly *Le Jour-nal des Voyages* (*The Journal of Voyages*) which started in 1875 as *Sur Terre and Mer* (*On Land and on Sea*), then took its definitive title in 1877. Its publishing history spanned over seventy years: 1st series (1877-1896), 1012 issues pub-lished; 2nd series (1896-1915): 941 issues published; 3rd se-ries (1924-25): 29 issues published; 4th series (1925-29): 159 issues published; and finally, 5th series (1946-1949): 149 issues published. Chauvinistic, somewhat xenophobic, yet visionary, *Journal des Voyages* serialized novels by Louis Boussenard, Paul d'**Ivoi**, René **Thévenin**, Maurice

Champagne, G. **Le Wailly**, Capitaine **Danrit**, and many others.

Other pre-World War I magazines of note included:

La Science Illustrée (*Illustrated Science*, 1887-1905), edited by Adolphe Bitard and Louis Figuier, featuring works by Boussenard, **Flammarion**, **Robida**, and H. G. Wells.

The monthly *Lectures Pour Tous* (*Readings for All*, 1898-1940), 581 issues in all, published by Hachette and featuring works by J.-H. **Rosny** Aîné, Octave **Béliard**, Raoul **Bigot**, and Albert **Bailly**.

Its direct competitor, the monthly *Je Sais Tout* (*I Know Everything*, 1905-39), published by Pierre Lafitte and featuring works by J.-H. Rosny Aîné, Gaston **Leroux**, Henri **Lambs**, and Maurice **Renard**.

And, finally, *L'Épatant* (*The Wonderful*, 1908-37) and *L'Intrépide* (*The Fearless*, 1910-37), subtitled "Aventures, Voyages, Explorations," both published by Offenstadt, aimed at young adults and publishing a mix of comics and adventure novels, including works by José **Moselli**, Pierre **Adam**, André **Falcoz** (writing as "Élie Montfort"), and Guy d'**Armen**. (Offenstadt eventually became the Société Parisienne d'Édition and *L'Épatant* returned as a full-blown comic-book magazine from 1951-69; *L'Intrépide* was sold to Del Duca and also returned as a comic-book magazine from 1948-62.)

a. Major Authors

Of all the authors who followed in the footsteps of Jules Verne, perhaps the most important was Albert **Robida**, a writer/artist who also deserves a place in genre history as (with the exception of Isidore Grandville, mentioned above) the founding father of science fiction illustration. Robida not only illustrated genre stories by **Rabelais**, **Cyrano de Bergerac**, and **Flammarion**, but he also wrote and illustrated his own scientific anticipations, starting with a deliberate homage to Verne entitled *Voyages Très Extraordinaires de Saturnin Farandoul dans les 5 ou 6 Parties du Monde et dans tous les Pays Connus et même Inconnus de M. Jules Verne* (*The Very Extraordinary Voyages of Saturnin Farandoul in the 5 or 6 Continents of the World and in All the Lands Known or Even Unknown to Mr. Jules Verne*), a *Voyage Extraordinaire*-like novel serialized over a hundred issues in 1879 and later collected in a single volume in 1883.

Robida's masterpiece of scientific anticipation was *Le Vingtième Siècle* (*The 20th Century*), a *Dinotopia*-type of book, serialized in 50-plus issues in 1882-83, and entirely devoted to the visual description of scenes of daily life of the mid-to-late 1950s. Robida proved constantly inventive in the imagining of futuristic devices, such as videophones, flying taxis, etc. The book also included the idea of the Moon being drawn closer to the Earth by a battery of giant magnets, which may have influenced Laurie's *Les Exilés de la Terre* (*Exiled from Earth*)—see below. So popular was *Le Vingtième Siècle* that Robida continued in this vein with *La*

Guerre au Vingtième Siècle (*War in the 20th Century*, 1883), set in 1975, and *La Vie Électrique* (*The Electric Life*, 1890), set in 1955, which offered more of his satirical, pessimistic view of the future, and often contained frighteningly accurate predictions, such as the possibility of germ warfare.

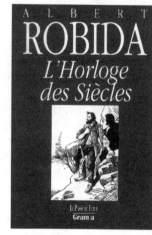

But Robida was not only a gifted artist and the author of remarkable scientific anticipations. In a startlingly different vein, he also wrote a clasic novel, *L'Horloge des Siècles* (*The Clock of the Centuries*, 1902), in which time started running backwards, the dead came back to life, and human society was thrown into utter chaos. The novel concludes when time had regressed to the battle of Waterloo. The book remains one of the most striking novels ever written on this classic theme, later explored in Philip K. Dick's *Counterclock World* (1967), among others. Another notable Robida work was *L'Ingénieur von Satanas* (*Engineer Von Satanas*, 1919).

Like Verne, André **Laurie** was another discovery of publisher Hetzel, and indeed had collaborated with Verne on *Les Cinq Cent Millions de la Begum* (*The 500 Millions of the Begum*, 1879), *L'Étoile du Sud* (*The Southern Star*, 1884), and *L'Épave du "Cynthia"* (*Salvage from the "Cynthia"*, 1885). Prior to this, Laurie's political activities on behalf of the Commune had caused him to temporarily exile himself to England. One of his most interesting genre novels was *Les Exilés de la Terre, Séléné Company Ltd.* (*Exiled from Earth*, 1887), probably one of the most fanciful cosmic tales of all times. In it, a consortium which intended to exploit the Moon's mineral resources decided that, since our satellite was too far to be reached, it must be brought closer to the Earth. A Sudanese mountain composed of pure iron ore became the headquarters of a newly established Selene Company. Solar reflectors were used to provide the energy required to convert the mountain into a huge electro magnet, with miles of cables wrapped around it. A spaceship-cum-observatory was built on top of the mountain. When the experiment began, the mountain was ripped away from the Earth and catapulted to the Moon. There, the protagonists had various adventures and eventually returned to Earth by re-energizing the mountain.

Other notable works by Laurie included *De New York à Brest en Sept Heures* (*New York to Brest in Seven Hours*, 1888), which predicted a transatlantic tunnel; *Le Secret du Mage* (*The Secret of the Magician*, 1890), in which evidence of an advanced antediluvian civilization was discovered; *Le Rubis du Grand Lama* (*The Ruby of the Great Lama*, 1894), which featured a steam-powered flying island; *Atlantis*

(1895), which described how the mythical kingdom survived under a glass dome at the bottom of the sea near the Azores; *Le Maître de l'Abîme* (*The Master of the Abyss*, 1905), featuring a revolutionary submarine; and finally *Spiridon le Muet* (*Spiridon the Mute*, 1907), a remarkable novel about a human-sized, intelligent ant.

In it, a young surgeon, Dr. Cordat, discovered an island off the coast of Corsica inhabited by sentient ants. Their king, Spiridon, was remarkably brilliant and conversed with Cordat through telepathy. Curious about human society, Spiridon travelled with Cordat to Paris. There, using his advanced knowledge, he became a famous doctor effecting seemingly miraculous cures. However, jealous competitors unmasked him. Forced to protect himself, Spiridon revealed his alien nature and became a killer. Eventually wounded, Spiridon lost his intelligence on the operating table. The character of Spiridon, depicted as a non-human alien, gifted with great knowledge, an insatiable scientific curiosity but no human feelings or emotions, the victim of mankind's petty jealousies and racial fears, was a striking departure from the Vernian influence that permeated the rest of Laurie's works.

Another thriving successor of Verne was Louis **Boussenard**, whose popular adventure novels were serialized in the *Journal des Voyages*. His most memorable novels were *Les Secrets de Monsieur Synthèse* (*The Secrets of Mr. Synthesis*, 1888) and its sequel, *Dix Mille Ans dans un Bloc de Glace* (*Ten Thousand Years in an Ice Block*, 1889). In the former, we were introduced to the hero, "Mr. Synthesis," a mad scientist who sought to control the evolution of Man and then modify the orbit of the Earth. In the latter, the same Mr. Synthesis woke up from ten thousand years of hibernation in a future where Earth is now inhabited by the "cerebrals," little men with huge mental powers, who were descended from the Chinese and the Africans. Other notable Boussenard novels included *Les Français au Pole Nord* (*The Frenchmen at the North Pole*, 1893); *L'Île en Feu* (*Island on Fire*, 1898), which featured a liquid hydrogen-propelled dirigible, and *Les Gratteurs de Ciel* (*The Sky Scrapers*, 1908), an aerial saga featuring young Dicky, the self-proclaimed "king of the reporters," in which super-powered dirigibles fought with weapons that looked suspiciously like tactical nuclear devices ("nuclear grenades").

The four-volume *Les Aventures Extraordinaires d'un Savant Russe* (*The Amazing Adventures of a Russian Scientist*) by Georges **Le Faure** and Henry de **Graffigny** (1888-96) was a much more ambitious cosmic saga. Introduced by Camille Flammarion, it told the story of the exploration of the solar system and beyond. Both authors were familiar with rocket science; in 1904, de Graffigny actually flew a rocket-powered model airplane and, in 1915, proposed catapulting a capsule into orbit using centrifugal force. Their scientific speculations were therefore more advanced than Verne's. In the first volume, a spaceship was launched from a cannon built inside a volcano, the explosive being the sud-

denly released lava. The heroes protected themselves against the acceleration with mattresses. The ship was made of a nickel-magnesium alloy. Oxygen was stored in tablet form and carbon dioxide was removed with potassium hydroxide. Electricity provided light and heat. Once on the Moon, the travellers encountered a jet-propelled craft. Their subsequent flight from the Moon to Venus, and later to Mercury, was achieved by using the pressure of the light from the sun on a hollow sphere. The heroes then pursued their journey on a fragment of Mercury torn away by a comet; as it passed near Phobos, which was atmospherically connected to Mars, they travelled in a balloon down to the red planet, wearing pressure suits. The travellers then flew from Mars to Jupiter in a barrel-shaped, reaction-powered starship, which sucked interplanetary debris at one end and expelled it at the other. Another remarkable prediction was a means of communication between planets through beams of light picked up and modulated by selenium photocells.

Alone, Georges Le Faure was also responsible for a number of Jules Verne-inspired adventure novels such as *Quinze Mille Lieues dans l'Espace* (*Fifteen Thousand Leagues in Space*, 1893) and *Les Robinsons Lunaires* (1893), in which a propellor-driven airship crashed on the Moon. Le Faure also wrote two of militaristic anticipations that will be reviewed below.

Henry de Graffigny was an engineer drawn to the subject of cosmic journeys, which he explored in *De La Terre aux Etoiles* (*From the Earth to the Stars*, 1887), in which Earthmen travel to the Moon, then to Venus, and then aboard a comet throughout the Solar System; and *La Ville Aérienne* (*The Aerial City*, 1910), about a flying city.

By far the most commercially prosperous and influential successor of Verne was Paul d'**Ivoi**, whose 21-volume series, *Les Voyages Excentriques* (*Eccentric Voyages*), was published by Furne (and sometimes serialized in *Le Journal des Voyages*) between 1894 and 1914. D'Ivoi's best-known book was an *Around the World in 80 Days* variant entitled *Les Cinq Sous de Lavarède* (*The Five Pennies of Lavarede*, 1894), the first in the *Eccentric Voyages* series, in which a young, daring hero embarked on a Phileas Fogg-like journey around the world with only five pennies in his pocket. Lavarède returned in more genre-oriented stories such as *Cousin de Lavarède* (*Lavarede's Cousin*, 1897), which featured a super-powered flying speedster. D'Ivoi's novels were more adventure-oriented, in a pulp/serial sense, and faster-paced than **Verne**'s. They included a variety of futuristic planes, submarines, rocketships, super-powered weapons, and other wonders. Their heroes circumnavigated the globe, in the air or under the oceans, fought a variety of mad scientists, international conspiracies, and megalomaniacal tyrants, discovered evidence of advanced, ancient civilizations. Among the most notable volumes of the series were *Corsaire Triplex* (*Corsair Triplex*, 1898), a variation on *Twenty Thousand Leagues Under the Sea* featuring a Captain Nemo-like hero; *Docteur Mystère* (*Doctor Mystery*, 1900), with a plethora of

gadgets; *Miss Mousqueterr* (1907), in which light was used as an all-purpose weapon by Violet Mousqueterr and her companions to defeat a secret Hindu cult; *L'Aéroplane Fantôme* (*The Phantom Airplane*, 1910); and *Le Chevalier Illusion* (*The Illusion Knight*, 1913), featuring a mind-control device. D'Ivoi also collaborated with Colonel **Royet** on several other serials—see below.

Not all genre writers of the times felt compelled to imitate Jules Verne. The prolific Jules **Lermina**, who was mentioned in Chapter IV in connection with a number of Poe-inspired collections of fantastic tales, was one of these. In his *Histoire Incroyable à Bruler* (*Incredible Tale to Be Burned*, 1988), Lermina introduced a secret society of Hindu sorcerers who have inherited the scientific secrets of ancient Atlantis, a theme later developed in Talbot Mundy's *The Nine Unknown* (1924). *Le Secret des Zippelius* (*The Secret of the Zippelius*, 1889) featured the controlled disintegration of water. The two-volume *La Bataille de Strasbourg* (*The Battle of Strasburg*, 1892) was one of the first novels on the infamous theme of the "yellow peril." In it, a scientist used telluric energy to fight the invading Asian hordes. In *L'Effrayante Aventure* (*The Frightful Adventure*, 1910), Lermina used Bulwer-Lytton's "vril"-force (borrowed from the *Coming Race* (1871)) to create the "vriliogyre," a vril-powered flying machine. The novel also featured the resurrection of prehistoric monsters frozen in ice in caverns under Paris. Lermina's most interesting novel was *Mystère-Ville* (*Mystery City*, 1905), written under the pseudonym of William Cobb, and illustrated by Robida. In it, he postulated that Protestants who had fled from French persecution created a secret, futuristic city in a hidden Chinese valley. The so-called "Mystery-City" used advanced technology based on the properties of sound and light.

In the more traditional field of popular adventure serials, Jean de **La Hire** and Gustave **Le Rouge** dominated the period, and were both already mentioned in Chapter IV. La Hire's prodigious superhero, the Nyctalope, made his first appearance in *L'Homme Qui Peut Vivre dans l'Eau* (*The Man Who Could Live Underwater*, 1908) and continued to delight audiences until the mid-1950s. The Nyctalope's adventures were pure, unbridled science fiction: in *L'Homme Qui Peut Vivre dans l'Eau*, mad scientist Oxus grafted a shark's gills onto a man; in *Le Mystère des XV* (*The Mystery of the XV*, 1911), Oxus tried to conquer Mars; in *Lucifer* (1920), Glo von Warteck tried to impose his will on Earth using "Omega Rays" and the "teledyname"; in *Le Roi de la Nuit* (*The King of the Night*, 1923), the Nyctalope flew to Rhea, an unknown satellite of Earth, using a spacecraft

patented by Dr. Cavor (La Hire's tip of the hat to Wells) and settled a war between its winged day-siders and night-siders; in *Belzébuth* (1930), the villainous Mezarek sent the Nyctalope's wife and son to the future year 2100. La Hire was also the author of *La Roue Fulgurante* (*The Fiery Wheel*) (1908), a classic space opera in which five Earthmen were abducted in the eponymous "fiery wheel" (a flying saucer?) and taken to Mercury by aliens who looked like columns of light; and *Le Corsaire Sous-Marin* (*The Undersea Corsair*, 1912-13), a 79-issue Verne-inspired serial.

Le Rouge's archetypal mad scientist story, *Le Mystérieux Dr. Cornélius* (*The Mysterious Dr. Cornelius*), was an 18-volume saga serialized in 1912-13. Prior to this, Le Rouge, with Gustave **Guitton**, had written *La Conspiration des Milliardaires* (*The Billionaires' Conspiracy*, 1899-1900), in which billionnaire William Boltyn used American technology and the power of mediums to try to become master of the world. *Les Conquérants de la Mer* (*The Conquerors of the Sea*), *La Princesse des Airs* and *Le Sous-Marin "Jules Verne"* (*The Submarine "Jules Verne"*), all written with Guitton and published in 1902, were Jules Verne-inspired adventure serials featuring a variety of futuristic vehicles and colorful, larger-than-life villains. *L'Espionne du Grand Lama* (*The Spy of the Great Lama*, 1906) introduced a Lost World inhabited by prehistoric creatures. *La Reine des Éléphants* (*The Queen of Elephants*, 1906) featured a society of intelligent elephants.

Le Rouge's masterpiece was *Le Prisonnier de la Planète Mars* (*The Prisoner of Planet Mars*, 1908) and its sequel, *La Guerre des Vampires* (*The War of the Vampires*, 1909), in which Robert Darvel, a young American engineer, built a psychic-powered spaceship and, with Hindu help, travelled to Mars. (Curiously, La Hire's *La Roue Fulgurante*, mentioned above, as well as Henri **Gayar**'s *Les Aventures Merveilleuses de Serge Myrandhal sur la Planète Mars* (*The Wondrous Adventures of Serge Myrandhal on the Planet Mars*)—see below—all published in 1908, use psychic-powered spaceships.) Le Rouge's Mars was elaborately described, with its fauna, flora, and various races of inhabitants, à la C. S. Lewis's *Out of the Silent Planet* (1938). Darvel ran afoul of Mars' hostile, bat-winged, blood-sucking natives, a once-powerful civilization now ruled by the Great Brain, a giant brain-like entity, perhaps the first time that this now clichéd idea was used in modern science fiction. The Great Brain got rid of Darvel by sending him back to Earth, unfortunately with some of the vampires. The second volume dealt with the war on Earth against the vampires, who wanted Darvel to return to Mars to destroy the Great Brain.

On the eve of the Paris Universal Exposition of 1900 and, ultimately, of World War I, the single author who best embodied the evolution of a subset of modern science fiction away from the juvenile, one-dimensional scientific anticipations of Verne, or the pulp serials of d'Ivoi, La Hire and Le Rouge, to a more mature, literary form was Belgian author J.-H. **Rosny** Aîné—the "Elder," to distinguish him from his younger brother, also a writer.

Rosny Aîné was very much like H.G. Wells or Olaf Stapledon in his concepts and his way of dealing with them in his novels. He was, without a doubt, the second most important figure after Verne in the history of modern French science fiction. Rosny, who was a member of the distinguished Goncourt literary academy, was also the first writer to straddle the line between mainstream and science fiction literature, even though his genre fiction was unjustly, but not unsurprisingly, neglected by literary scholars.

Rosny's first science fiction tale was the short story "Les Xipehuz" (1887), in which primitive humans (the story took place a thousand years before Babylonian times) encountered inorganic aliens, with whom all forms of communication proved impossible. Men eventually drove away the invaders, but the hero mourned the loss of another life, another thought. This was the first time that science fiction had abandoned its usual anthropomorphic approach in the description of alien life. The story "Un Autre Monde" ("Another World", 1895) established that humans shared the Earth with the land-bound Moedingen and the air-borne Vuren, two infinitely flat and invisible species who cohabited with us. Only a mutant whose vision was superior to that of ordinary men could see them. In "Le Cataclysme" ("The Cataclysm", 1896), an entire region of France saw the physical laws of nature change, as a result of the arrival of a mysterious electro-magnetic entity from outer space.

Rosny's short novel, *La Mort de la Terre* (*The Death of the Earth*, 1910), took place in the far future, when Earth had all but dried out. In it, the last descendents of mankind became aware of the emergence of a new species, the metal-based "Ferromagnetals," fated to replace us. *La Mort de la Terre* was one of the most moving tales ever written about the extinction of Man. One of the striking concepts of this poetic, evocative epic was that our disappearance was not the result of some kind of war or cataclysm, but merely that of natural evolution, the same evolution that was once responsible for the passing away of the dinosaurs. The "Ferromagnetals" were another of Rosny's mysterious alien races, not evil, merely beyond communication—not unlike Abraham Merritt's the *Metal Monster* (1920).

Another novel, *La Force Mystérieuse* (*The Mysterious Force*, 1913), told of the destruction of a portion of the light spectrum by a "mysterious force"—possibly aliens from outer space who, for a brief while, shared our physical ex-

istence. This caused panic, then a progressive and potentially deadly cooling of the world. Social upheaval followed, before order was restored. *La Force Mystérieuse* was, coincidentally, similar to Doyle's *The Poisoned Sky*, published at the same time.

L'Énigme de Givreuse (*The Enigma of Givreuse*, 1917) was another remarkable novel about the bipartition—cloning—of a human being into two totally similar individuals, each naturally believing himself to be the original. The novella "La Jeune Vampire" ("The Young Vampire", 1920) was perhaps the first time that vampirism was described as a genetic mutation, transmissible by birth—not unlike Richard Matheson's *I Am Legend*. *L'Étonnant Voyage d'Hareton Ironcastle* (*The Amazing Journey of Hareton Ironcastle*, 1922) was a more traditional adventure novel, where explorers eventually discovered a fragment of an alien world, with its fauna and flora, attached to Earth.

Rosny's masterpiece was *Les Navigateurs de l'Infini* (*The Navigators of Infinity*, 1925) and its sequel *Les Astronautes* (*The Astronauts*; written at the same time, but published only in 1960) in which the word "astronautique" was coined for the first time. In it, Rosny's heroes travelled to Mars in the "Stellarium," a spaceship powered by artificial gravity and made of "argine," an indestructible, transparent material, not unlike Larry Niven's spaceships in his *Known Space* series. on Mars, the human explorers came in contact with the gentle, peaceful, six-eyed, three-legged "Tripèdes," a dying race slowly being replaced by the "Zoomorphs," alien entities who bore some resemblance to the "Ferromagnetals" of *La Mort de la Terre*. In the sequel, a young Martian female, capable of bearing children parthenogetically by merely wishing it, gave birth after falling in love with one of the human explorers, undoubtedly the first romance ever written between a man and an alien female. This heralded the rebirth of the Martian race and, with Man's help, the eventual reconquest of their planet.

Les Navigateurs de l'Infini was a colorful, poetic ode to the powers of love and science, a plea for understanding between races, and the view that all living creatures—men as well as aliens—are somehow connected in the greater scheme of things. This was a sharp departure from the xenophobic approach shaped by Wells with *War of the Worlds* in 1898, which eventually dominated Anglo-Saxon science fiction until Stanley Weinbaum's *A Martian Odyssey* (1934).

Like Verne, Rosny exerted a powerful influence on French science fiction. Among the authors indebted to him were Maurice **Renard**, H.-J. **Proumen**, B.-R. **Bruss**, Stefan **Wul**, and Francis **Carsac**. Finally, Rosny was also, if not the creator, the author who virtually defined the sub-genre of the prehistoric novel and the Lost World story in French literature. These will be reviewed under **Other Lands** below.

André **Couvreur**, a medical doctor turned writer, was mentioned in Chapter IV for his character of Dr. Caresco, one of the first mad surgeons in genre literature introduced in *Le Mal Nécessaire* (*The Necessary Evil*, 1899). (Wells' Dr. Moreau had been created in 1896.) In 1909, with *Une Invasion de Macrobes* (*An Invasion of Macrobes*), Couvreur embarked on a series of adventures featuring another mad scientist, Professor Tornada. In it, Tornada unleashed a plague of giant microbes on Paris. In its sequel, *L'Androgyne—Les Fantaisies du Professeur Tornada* (*The Androgyne—the Fantasies of Prof. Tornada*, 1922), Tornada turned a man into a woman. In *Le Valseur Phosphorescent* (*The Phosphorescent Waltzer*, 1923), he created a phosphorescent android. In *Les Mémoires d'un Immortel* (*Memoirs of An Immortal*, 1924), he tackled the concept of immortality. Finally, in *Le Biocole* (1927), Tornada did achieve a form of immortality through organ replacements, but it led to social chaos. The last Tornada story was *Le Cas de la Baronne Sasoitsu* (*The Case of Baroness Sasoitsu*, 1939), in which the now-reformed mad genius tried to help mankind with his "psychovisor." Before his death in 1944, Couvreur had started a new Tornada novel, *La Mort du Soleil* (*The Death of the Sun*), which remained uncompleted. Another of Couvreur's novels, *Le Lynx* (1911), written with Michel **Corday**, was about artificial telepathy induced by a serum.

Couvreur's Dr. Caresco and Wells' Dr. Moreau undoubtedly influenced Maurice **Renard** in his own "mad doctor" novel, *Le Docteur Lerne—Sous-Dieu* (*Dr. Lerne—Undergod*, 1908), which was dedicated to Wells. In it, a mad scientist transplanted not only organs between men and animals, but also between plants, and even machines. Renard's impact was more considerable in the 1920s and 1930s (see Chapter VII). However, he had already published several major collections of stories blending science fiction and *fantastique* before World War I: *Fantômes et Fantôches* (*Ghosts and Puppets*), written under the pseudonym of "Vincent Saint-Vincent" (1905), *Le Voyage Immobile* (*The Motionless Journey*, 1909) and *M. D'Outremort* (*Mr. Beyonddeath*, 1913), which treated themes as varied as the resurrection of prehistoric monsters, a pseudo-scientific journey to the world behind the looking-glass, and the invention of the "Aerofix," a device impervious to Earth's rotation.

Renard's 1912 novel, *Le Péril Bleu* (*The Blue Peril*), which many considered to be his masterpiece, postulated the existence of unimaginable, invisible creatures who lived in the upper strata of the atmosphere and fished for men the

Renard

way men captured fish. These aliens, dubbed "Sarvants" by the human scientists who discovered them, felt threatened by our incursions into space the way men would be threatened by an invasion of crabs, and retaliated by capturing men, keeping them in a space zoo, and studying them. Eventually, when the Sarvants came to the realization than men were intelli-

gent, they released their captives. In the end, the blood-thirstiness and savagery was on the side of men, not the Sarvants.

Le Péril Bleu predated Charles Fort's *Book of the Damned* (1919) and subsequent works in that vein, and retained a humanistic and tolerant philosophy rather than fearful and xenophobic one. The conceptual leap taken in less than fifty years between Verne's first timid steps into space in 1865 and Rosny's and Renard's close-encounter stories was staggering. By comparison with the United States, as mentioned above, Hugo Gernsback had just published *Ralph 124C41+* in *Modern Electrics* (1911) and *Amazing Stories* magazine was still fifteen years in the future.

b. Other Notable Writers

In this section, we will review other notable genre works written by genre writers prior to World War I, regrouping them along thematic lines.

COSMIC JOURNEYS

In 1883, Alexandre Bessot de **Lamothe** published *Quinze Mois dans la Lune* (*Fifteen Months on the Moon*), a Vernian fantasy aimed at young adults.

In 1889, Charles **Guyon** published *Voyage dans la Planète Vénus* (*Voyage to the Planet Venus*), a utopian tale in which the heroes travelled to Venus in a hot air balloon. However, the Venusians had to build an enormous cannon to launch them back to Earth in an obvious tip of the hat to Verne.

In 1890, A. de **Ville d'Avray** wrote *Voyage dans la Lune avant 1900* (*Journey to the Moon Before 1900*), a book with fifty color plates which detailed a journey to the Moon, again made in a hot air balloon—the *Intrépide*—and the adventures that its passengers had on our satellite.

In 1894, Théodore **Cahu** penned *Perdus dans l'Espace* (*Lost in Space*).

In 1896, Pierre de **Sélènes** wrote *Un Monde Inconnu, Deux Ans sur la Lune* (*An Unknown World, Two Years on the Moon*), an unauthorized sequel to Verne's *From the Earth to the Moon*, in which the very same cannon was used to send a crew of explorers to the Moon. There, they met an advanced race of Selenites who were able to absorb in gaseous form the elements they needed to feed themselves.

The popular writer of adventure serials Arnould **Galopin** showed more imagination in his *Le Docteur Oméga—Aventures Fantastiques de Trois Français dans la Planète Mars* (*Dr. Omega—Fantastic Adventures of Three Frenchmen on Planet Mars*, 1905), in which the eponymous hero invented a spacecraft dubbed *Cosmos* to travel to the Red Planet. *Cosmos* was a projectile-shaped vehicle built using an antigravitational substance called "repulsite." It could also function on land and under water. (In a revised version published in 1908-09, Galopin changed the name of the ship to *Excelsior* and the substance to "stellite.") The planet turned out to be inhabited by extremely ugly aliens, and the story had mild xenophobic overtones.

Mars remained in fashion in *Les Aventures Mer-*

veilleuses de Serge Myrandhal sur la Planète Mars (*The Wondrous Adventures of Serge Myrandhal on the Planet Mars*, 1908) by Henri **Gayar**. In it, the Red Planet is reached via psychic powers, just as in La Hire's *La Roue Fulgurante* and Le Rouge's *Le Prisonnier de la Planète Mars*—see above. Gayar's Mars was inhabited by the Houas, small, red-furred anthropoids who live underground, and by the Zoas, beautiful winged humanoids, also referred to as "Elohim." The psychic-powered ship was named "Velox." In a later version, published in 1925 as *Les Robinsons de la Planète Mars* (*The Robinsons of Planet Mars*) under the pseudonym of "Cyrius," Gayar got rid of the psychic energies and instead used the planetary force of attraction; he also added German villains to the plot and prophetically rechristened the rocketships *V1* and *V2*.

Sylvain **Déglantine**'s *Les Terriens sur Vénus* (*Earthmen on Venus*, 1907), on the other hand, was a rather naive story about a journey to and the exploration of Venus.

In Abbott Théophile **Moreux**'s *Le Miroir Sombre* (*The Dark Mirror*, 1911), reprinted as *Mars va nous Parler* (*Mars Will Talk to Us*) in the *Journal des Voyages* (which the Abbott briefly edited) in 1924, scientists communicated with Mars through a radio-telescope-like device, the eponymous "dark mirror"; curiously, the novel established a link between sun spots and eathquakes.

Finally, popular adventure serial writer and engineer André **Mas**' novel, *Les Allemands sur Vénus* (*The Germans on Venus*, 1914), was a chauvinistic novel in which the Germans used centrifugal force to launch a space expedition to take over the planet Venus. In 1913, the author had, in fact, proposed launching a projectile from the rim of a spinning wheel. In his novel, Mas later divided the solar system between the various Earth powers: Russia got the Moon, the United States, Saturn, Japan, Jupiter, France, Mars, etc.

In addition to space travel, there was one notable time-travel novel published in 1909, Octave **Béliard**'s *Les Aventures d'un Voyageur qui Explora le Temps* (*The Adventures of a Voyager Who Explored Time*), which told the story of a scientist who invented a time-travel machine which was then unwittingly hijacked by his two young sons. He eventually discovered that they went on to become the founders of ancient Rome.

OTHER LANDS AND MAD SCIENCE

As indicated above, the sub-genre known as the prehistoric novel was not the creation of J.-H. Rosny Aîné. Technically, that credit belonged to Samuel-Henry **Berthoud**'s *L'Homme depuis Cinq Mille Ans* (*Man for Five Thousand Years*, 1865; see above) and Élie **Berthet** with his four-part serial, *Le Monde Inconnu* (*The Unknown World*, 1876), revised as *Paris Avant l'Histoire* (*Paris Before History*, 1885), which described in great detail the life of Parisians during the Stone Age, the building of the first Lake City and, finally, the foundation of Paris.

Ernest d'**Hervilly**'s *Aventures d'un Petit Garçon*

Préhistorique en France (*Adventures of a Prehistoric Boy in France*, 1887) was the first adventure-oriented prehistoric novel, although satirical in intent and aimed at a juvenile market.

Rosny gave nobility to the genre with five powerful classic novels: *Vamireh* (1892), *Eyrimah* (1893), the world-renowned classic *La Guerre du Feu* (*Quest for Fire*, 1909), *Le Félin Géant* (*The Giant Cat*, 1918; sometimes known as *Quest of the Dawn Man*) and *Helgvor du Fleuve Bleu* (*Helgvor of the Blue River*, 1930). In it, Rosny combined the notions of modern drama with the ability to depict Man's early days in a colorful, yet totally believable fashion. The dialogue between the prehistoric man and the mastodon of *La Guerre du Feu* was not very different from the attempts at communicating with the Xipehuz. Rosny's prehistoric novels became so popular and widely respected that *La Guerre du Feu* was even included in schools' curriculum.

Following **Rosny**'s prehistoric trail were:

Raymond **Auzias-Turenne**, with *Le Dernier Mammouth* (*The Last Mastodon*, 1901-02).

Ray **Nyst**, with *La Caverne* (*The Cave*, 1909).

Paul **Max**, with *Volcar le Terrible* (*Volcar the Terrible*, 1913).

Edmond **Haraucourt** with *Daâh, Le Premier Homme* (*Daah, the Fist Man*, 1914).

In this vein one should also mention André **Lichtenberger**'s *Les Centaures* (*The Centaurs*, 1904), which told how prehistoric man exterminated the enlightened Centaur race.

Rosny was also a precursor of the Lost World genre—Haggard's *She* dating from 1887 and Doyle's eponymous classic dating from 1912. *Nymphée* (1893) featured a Lost World located near the river Amour in Siberia in which amphibious humans lived. *Les Profondeurs de Kyamo* (*The Depths of Kyamo*) and *La Contrée Prodigieuse des Cavernes* (*The Prodigious Land of the Caverns*; both 1896) were more exotic versions of Verne's *Journey to the Center of the Earth*, and featured giant, intelligent bats who lived in underground caverns. Finally, *Les Femmes de Setné* (*The Women of Setné*, 1903), written under the pseudonym of "Enacryos," dealt with a Lost World situation in the days of ancient Egypt. *Les Hommes-Sangliers* (*The Boar Men*, 1929), later expanded as *La Sauvage Aventure* (*The Savage Adventure*, 1932), took place on a mysterious Antipodean island inhabited by savage Boar-Men, with locales called the Blue Forest, the Red Forest, the Infernal Rocks, and the Vlugt Pass.

The *Journal des Voyages* was otherwise, as its title

indicated, the natural home for tales dealing with exotic lands and uncanny adventures in which daring heroes and their virginal girl-friends fought would-be masters of the world and mad scientists, often of Germanic or Asian origins. Among the authors of note published within its pages, and that of other similar magazines, were:

Louis **Jacolliot**, who wrote adventure tales featuring exotic locations and futuristic vehicles such as *La Cité des Sables* (*The City of the Sands*, 1877), *L'Afrique Mystérieuse* (*Mysterious Africa*, 1877) and *Les Mangeurs de Feu* (*The Fire Eaters*, 1885-87), which featured an aerial battle between submersible planes.

François **Teissier**, who followed Verne's model with *Voyage Aérien de New York à Yokohama* (*Aerial Journey from New York to Yokohama*, 1878) and *Les Merveilles et Mystères de l'Océan, ou Voyage Sous-Marin de Southampton au Cap Horn* (*Wonders and Mysteries of the Ocean, or Underwater Journey from Southampton to the Cape Horn*, 1900).

Jules **Gros**, with novels such as *Un Volcan dans les Glaces* (*A Volcano in the Ice*, 1879), the adventures of a scientific expedition at the North Pole; and *L'Homme Fossile* (*The Fossil Man*, 1898), the adventures of a scientific expedition at sea.

Alphonse **Brown**, with novels such as *Les Mohicans du Sahara* (*The Mohicans of the Sahara*, 1885), *Les Conquérants de l'Air* (*The Conquerors of the Air*, 1880), and *Une Ville de Verre* (*A City of Glass*, 1890).

The Commandant Gaston de **Wailly**, who wrote *Le Monde de l'Abîme* (*The World of the Abyss*), serialized in *À Travers le Monde* (*Throughout the World*) in 1904, in which Earth was revealed to be hollow and the protagonists discovered a race of peaceful, scientifically advanced bat-like humanoids living under our feet. They spent their time hunting living dinosaurs which threatened their existence. In *Le Roi de l'Inconnu* (*The King of the Unknown*), also serialized in *À Travers le Monde* in 1905, another secret underground kingdom was discovered, this time ruled by an enlightened scientist. Finally, in *Le Meurtrier du Globe* (*The Murderer of the Globe*, 1910), a madman who lost his family in an earthquake believed that Earth itself was a living organism, which he tried to kill.

René **Thévenin** was the author of pulpish yarns such as *La Cité des Tortures* (*The City of Tortures*, 1906), about an underground Australian city where the Chinese secretly prepared to take over the world; and *Le Collier de l'Idole de Fer* (*The Necklace of the Iron Idol*, 1912), about an idol of living metal created by Inca survivors to guard their Lost City.

Maurice Champagne contributed novels such as *Les Reclus de la Mer* (*The Recluse of the Sea*, 1907), a *Twenty Thousand Leagues Under the Sea* variation; *Les Sondeurs d'Abîmes* (*The Probers of the Abyss*, 1911), in which brave explorers discover an evil Tibetan underground empire; *L'Âme du Dr. Kips* (*The Soul of Dr. Kips*, 1912), and *La Vallée Mystérieuse* (*The Mysterious Valley*, 1914).

Pierre **Luguet**'s *Une Descente au Monde Sous-Terrien* (*A Descent Into a Sub-Terranean World*, 1906) was another tale of underground exploration.

Charles **Derennes** contributed another notable addition to the genre with *Le Peuple du Pôle* (*The People of the Pole*, 1907), in which aviators discovered a race of peaceful, reptilian humanoids living in a secret valley at the North Pole; and *Les Conquérants d'Idoles* (*The Conquerors of Idols*, 1908), about a hidden race of Incas who turned out to be descendents of Atlantis.

Finally, René-Marcel de **Nizerolles**'s serial, *Les Voyages Aériens d'un Petit Parisien à travers le Monde* (*The Aerial Voyages of a Little Parisian Throughout the World*, 1910-12), serialized in 382 chapters, or 1776 pages in total, featured the fantastic globe-trotting adventures of a young hero named "Tintin" (no relation to **Hergé**'s character).

Couvreur's Caresco and Tornada, Le Rouge's Cornelius, La Hire's Oxus, Renard's Lerne, Livet's Miramar, etc. were not the only examples of unfettered science. The works of Jules **Claretie** were scientific anticipations based on the physiological and physchological research of the times. After *La Mer Libre* (*The Open Sea*, 1878), a banal Extraordinary Voyage, Claretie penned *Jean Mornas* (1882), a novel about the criminal use of hypnosis; *L'Oeil du Mort* (*Deadman's Eye*, 1887), based on the theory that the image of the murderer remained fixed on the victim's eye; and *L'Obsession* (*The Obsession*, 1905), which featured the materialization of a twin personality.

In the short story "Le Coeur de Tony Wandel" ("The Heart of Tony Wandel") in the collection *Kermesses* (*Fiestas*, 1884), Belgian writer Georges **Eekhoud** was one of the first to postulate a personality transfer following a heart transplant.

In 1853, Alexandre **Dumas** Fils (*Son*) had written a short story entitled "La Boîte d'Argent" ("The Silver Box") on the same theme.

Notable adventure writers and novels in this vein included:

André **Bleunard** with *La Babylone Électrique* (*The Electric Babylon*, 1888), about an electric-powered city in Mesopotamia; *La Vengeance d'un Savant* (*A Scientist's Revenge*, 1890), about radio transmission; and *Toujours Plus Petits* (*Always Smaller*, 1893), in which men were shrunk down to microbe-size—probably one of the first modern novels on the theme of the "Shrinking Man."

Henri **Austruy**'s *L'Eupantophone* (1901) was a novel about a telepathic device.

Danielle d'**Arthez**' *Le Trust du Soleil* (*The Sun Company*, 1906) was a prophetic novel about weather control.

Pierre **Giffard**'s Professor Lionel-Prospero Macduff, in *Le Tombeau de Glace* (*The Tomb of Ice*, 1908), succeeded in performing a heart transplant operation during a perilous mission to the Pole.

More interestingly, that same year, in *Le Mystérieux Dajann-Phinn* (*The Mysterious Dajann-Phinn*), polytechnician Michel **Corday** penned a variation on the Frankenstein theme, featuring a scientist who created a perfect humanoid.

Finally, in Jean de **Quirielle**'s remarkably prescient *L'Oeuf de Verre* (*The Glass Egg*, 1912), androids were artificially grown in a glass container. This may well be the first use of the word "android," predating Karel Capek's *R.U.R.* by nine years. De Quirielle's *La Joconde Retrouvée* (*The Mona Lisa Recovered*, 1913) was based on an original concept: Leonardo da Vinci used "living paint" to paint the Mona Lisa, who was therefore "trapped" within the painting. The Mona Lisa was briefly stolen from the Louvre—an historical fact—to enable the thief to recreate the young woman.

THE FUTURE

Many scholars long considered *Prodigieuse Découverte et ses Incalculables Conséquences sur les Destinées du Monde Entier* (*Prodigious Discovery and Its Incalculable Consequences on the Fate of the Entire World*) credited to one "X. **Nagrien**" and published by Hetzel in 1867 as an unsigned Jules Verne novel. The book was even released under Verne's name in Spain and Italy. However, it was a novel by A. Audois, in which in the near future an inventor discovered two elements, dubbed "pos" and "neg" which, when brought together, nullified gravity. The inventor then built a craft dubbed the *Negopos*, which led to a revolution in transports—for example, the introduction of regular air shuttles between Paris and Strasbourg. The consequences of the introduction of the *Negopos* proved to be staggering: the new craft challenged the notion of national borders, and led to the redrawing of the political map of the world.

Following in the tradition of Souvestre and Robida, Didier de **Chousy** with *Ignis* (1883) penned a remarkable scientific anticipation which forecasted robot-driven cars, moving sidewalks, recorded music, as well as the use of geothermal energy as a power source and the manufacturing of robots, which were described as mechanical, metal beings whose various shapes were designed for specific tasks. These "Atmophytes" (steam-powered men) eventually petitioned for human rights, almost forty years before Capek's *R.U.R.* (1921).

Other notable scientific anticipations included:

Georges **Pellerin**'s *Le Monde dans 2000 Ans* (*The World in 2000 Years*, 1878).

Émile **Calvet**'s *Dans Mille Ans* (*In a Thousand Years*, 1883), a utopia in which three men used a drug to induce hibernation and travel to the future, where they discovered that compounded interest had made them rich.

A Swiss author signing "**Verniculus**" wrote *Histoire de la Fin du Monde, ou La Comète de 1904* (*Story of the End of the World, or the Comet of 1904*, 1882), in which the eponymous comet threatened to turn Earth's atmosphere into a flammable gas. Jules Verne himself was a fictional character in the novel.

Léo **Claretie**, the cousin of Jules Claretie (see below), wrote *Paris depuis ses Origines jusqu'en l'An 3000* (*Paris from Its Origins Until the Year 3000*, 1886), in which the three final chapters detailed the future of Paris: "1987," the self-explanatory "Ruins of Paris," and, finally, the more optimistic "Year 3000."

Poet Jean **Rameau**'s 1887 collection, *Fantasmagories* (*Phantasmagorias*), in which he described the mores and technology of the year 1987 in a satirical mode.

Alfred de **Ferry**'s *Un Roman en 1915* (*A Novel of 1915*, 1889), a political anticipation about a socialist politician who started a civil war.

Alain **Le Drimeur**'s *La Cité Future* (*The Future City*, 1890).

A. **Vilgensofer**'s *La Terre dans Cent Mille Ans* (*Earth in 100,000 Years*, 1893), which postulated that all Earthmen eventually spoke French, the only living language left on the planet at that time—was this conceited vision any more fanciful than the notion of aliens speaking English?

Maurice **Spronck**'s *L'An 330 de la République* (*The Year 330 of the Republic*, 1894), subtitled "In the 22nd Century of the Christian Era," which may have been the first utopia to use a non-Gregorian calendar and featured a Europe invaded by Africans.

Jean Gabriel de **Tarde**'s *Fragment d'Histoire Future* (*Fragment of Future History*, 1894) was translated into English with a foreword by Wells; it depicted a utopian-like society which was forced to move underground as the Sun's energy became depleted.

Camille **Debans**' *Le Vainqueur de la Mort* (*The Man Who Vanquished Death*, 1895).

Han **Ryner**'s *Un Roman Historique* (*An Historical Novel*, 1896; published under his real name of Henri Ner), dated from "Old Paris in the Year 2347 of the Abominable Social Era."

In 1900, Guy de **Téramond**, one of the future editors of the *Journal des Voyages* (see Chapter VII) wrote *L'Homme qui peut tout* (*The Man Who Could Do Anything*), in which brain surgery transformed a former criminal into a prodigious scientist who planned to turn Earth into a new utopia.

Fernand **Kolney**'s *L'Amour dans 5000 Ans* (*Love in 5000 Years*, 1905, reprinted in 1928).

Jean **Grave**, who published a number of anarchist utopias "masquerading" as children's books, such as *Les Aventures de Nono* (*The Adventures of Nono*, 1901) and *Terre Libre* (*Free Earth*, 1908).

Gustave **Guitton**, who collaborated with Gustave Le Rouge (see above), also wrote a number of novels speculating about the future: *Terre Abandonnée* (*Abandoned Land*, 1901), *Les Têtards (Futures Femmes)* (*The Tadpoles [Future Women]*, 1904) and *Ce Que Seront les Hommes de l'An 3000* (*What Men from the Year 3000 Will Be Like*, 1907), dedicated to H. G. Wells. The latter was a deliberately op-timistic utopia, meant to contrast with Wells' pessimistic visions. In it, a young man awakened from a "belzevorine"-induced sleep in the year 3000 and discovered a technolog-ically perfect utopia with fiberglass, typewriters, computers, electronic showers, synthetic foods, etc. Earth had been turned into a vast garden with only two industrial zones at the poles, with planetary weather control and energy pro-vided by the harnessing of the planet's rotation.

Less optimistic was Jules **Sageret**'s short story "La Race qui Vaincra" ("The Race Which Will Win," 1908), an anticipation taking place in "the 21lst Year of the Second Cycle" and one of the very first genre novels dealing with the theme of the mutants fated to replace the human race. Here, these mutants were called "Whistlers."

On a somewhat similar theme, Marcel **Roland** penned a series of novels dubbed "novels of future times" which in-cluded *Le Presqu'Homme* (*The Almost-Man*, 1907), *Le Déluge Futur* (*The Future Flood*, 1910), and *La Conquête d'Anthar* (*The Conquest of Anthar*, 1913).

Émile **Solari**'s *La Cité Rebâtie* (*The Rebuilt City*, 1907) also featured a universal flood.

Louis de **Meurville**'s *La Cité Future* (*The Future City*, 1910).

The prolific Dr. Octave **Béliard**, whose further works will be reviewed in Chapter VII, penned the aptly named *La Journée d'un Parisien au XXIème Siècle* (*A Day in the Life of a Parisian in the 21st Century*, 1910) and *Une Exploration Polaire aux Ruines de Paris* (*A Polar Exploration in the Ruins of Paris*, 1911). The former was particularly interest-ing. It showed a colossal, futuristic Paris where monuments like the Eiffel Tower were dwarfed by *Blade Runner*-like towers. Business was run by multinational corporations. The Moon had been terraformed since the 1950s, and fitted with an artificial atmosphere. The latter described a Europe buried under the ice and Paris being excavated by archeol-ogists from Madagascar.

In 1911, the writing team of Victor Cyril and Dr. Eugène Berger, signing **Cyril-Berger**, penned *La Merveilleuse Aventure de Jim Stappleton* (*The Wondrous Adventure of Jim Stappleton*, 1911), the description of a future America and the story of a future boxer whose sparring partner is a robot. It was later adapted into a play by **Yorril Hansewick** for the **Grand Guignol**.

Belgian writer, François **Léonard**, wrote *Le Triomphe de l'Homme* (*The Triumph of Man*, 1911), an odd Stapledon-like story set ten thousand years in the future, when Earth, under the leadership of a brilliant scientist, Prof. Neick, was turned into a giant spaceship travelling toward Vega. After detailing the huge social upheavals entailed by the start of its journey, the novel chronicled the survival of mankind. After centuries, the new men faced the Green Enemy—in-telligent plants who have appeared on Earth—and the Red Enemy, the star Vega itself, which ended up consuming the planet.

In 1912, René **Lorraine** penned the juvenile *Un Petit Monde d'Aviateurs en l'An 2000* (*A Small World of Aviators in the Year 2000*, 1912) which described the future as a flying utopia.

Another juvenile futuristic tale was *Le Déluge de Feu* (*The Fire Flood*), by Swiss author Eugène **Pénard**, serial-ized in *Pages Illustrées* in 1911-12.

Finally, Belgian writer Alex **Pasquier** penned *Le Secret de ne Jamais Mourir* (*The Secret of Never Dying*, 1913), a tale of automatons.

Charles **Renouvier** coined the term "Uchronia" to label alternate futures of the type already described by Louis **Geoffroy** in his *Napoléon Apocryphe* (see above). In his *Uchronie (L'Utopie dans l'Histoire): Esquisse Historique Apocryphe du Développement de la Civilisation Européenne tel qu'il n'a pas été, tel qu'il aurait pu être* (*Uchronia (Utopia in History): Apocryphal Sketch of the Development of European Civilization, as It Was Not, as It Could Have Been*, 1876), Renouvier chronicled a parallel history of Eu-rope, starting in the year 175 A.D., then the untimely death of Emperor Constantine, topsy-turvy Crusades where the Easterners attempted to take Rome back from the Western Church, and finishing in the 8th century, dubbed the 16th century because in that world, years were counted from the date of the first Olympics.

In R. F. **Géris**' *Quo Vadimus?* (1903), sub-titled "Story of Future Times," the Duke of Orleans restored French monarchy and saved the country France from evil Freema-sons.

In Louis **Millanvoy**'s *Seconde Vie de Napoléon* (*Napoleon's Second Life*, 1913), Napoleon escaped his fate on Saint-Helens but ended up a king in Africa after a ship-wreck.

During the 19th century, France also had the dubious honor of having an entire sub-genre of scientific anticipa-tion devoted to chauvinistic, militaristic tales of future or near-future wars pitting the French against pretty much the rest of the universe and featuring super-weapons, improved killing machines, and invasions of all kinds.

The major representative of that "school" was the prolific Émile-Auguste-Cyprien Driant who, under the pseu-donym of "Capitaine **Danrit**," penned a plethora of bellicose anticipations, such as the eight-volume *La Guerre de De-main* (*Tomorrow's War*, 1889-96), in which the French fought the Germans; the four-volume *L'Invasion Noire* (*The Black Invasion*, 1895-96), in which the French fought the Muslims and the Africans; the three-volume *La Guerre Fa-tale* (*The Fatal War*, 1901-02), in which the French fought the British; the three-volume *L'Invasion Jaune* (*The Yellow Invasion*, 1905–06), in which the French fought the Asians; *L'Aviateur du Pacifique* (*The Aviator of the Pacific*, 1909-10), in which the French helped the Americans fight the Japan-ese (which prophetically included an attempt by the Japan-ese to invade Midway); *L'Alerte* (*The Alert*, 1910), in which the French once again fought the Germans; plus some ideological wars against radical teachers, anarchists, and Bolsheviks, conducted with various degrees of carnage under water, as in *Robinsons Sous-Marins* (*Robinsons Under the Sea*, 1907-08), in the air (*Robinsons de l'Air* (*Robinsons of the Air*, 1908-09); underground as in (*Robinsons Souterrains* (*Underground Robinsons*, 1912-13); or in the future, as depicted in (*La Révolution de Demain* (*Tomorrow's Revolution*), written with Arnould **Galopin** (1909-10)). Honored during his life—he was awarded the Great Medal of Honor of the Society for the Promotion of Good in 1905, and a commemorative stamp was issued in 1956, forty years after his death—Danrit was justifiably forgotten, remaining no more than a curious footnote in the history of modern French science fiction.

Other aggressive works in this vein included:

La Guerre sous l'Eau (*The Underwater War*, 1890) and the candidly entitled *Mort aux Anglais* (*Death to the British*, 1892), by Georges Le Faure (see above).

Les Malheurs de John Bull (*John Bull's Problems*, 1884), by Camille **Debans**, in which a man bought an island, founded a new state, then declared war on England.

Pierre **Ferreol**'s *La Prise de Londres au XXème Siècle* (*The Taking of London in the 20th Century*, 1891).

Eugène **Demolder**'s *L'Agonie d'Albion* (*The Agony of Albion*, 1901) depicted an England conquered by the Boers.

Colonel **Royet** and Paul d'Ivoi's *La Patrie en Danger* (*France Threatened*, 1905) was the tale of yet another futuristic war; and their *Un, La Mystérieuse* (*One, the Mysterious*, 1905), featured the brilliant French inventor Darger, who used a plethora of gadgets (including the *Proteus*, a super-vehicle which could travel both in the air and underground) to fight the Bolsheviks.

Both Rodolphe **Martini**'s *La Guerre Aérienne Berlin-Bagdad* (*The Aerial War Berlin-Baghdad*, 1907) and Marc **Gouvieux**' *Haut les Ailes!* (*Up the Wings!*, 1914) prophetically predicted that air power would win the next war.

Finally, Roger **Duguet** and G. **Thierry**'s *Le Capitaine Rex* (1910) featured a Catholic France which allied itself with Spain and Italy to fight Protestant Anglo-Saxon imperialism.

Three particularly notable authors were:

Han **Ryner**, with *Le Sphinx Rouge* (*The Red Sphinx*, 1905) and *Les Pacifiques* (*The Pacifics*, 1914), perhaps the only genre author to have stood for peace in these troubled times. In the former, both Paris and Berlin were surrounded by the forces of their respective armies. Political assassins murdered the military leaders in an attempt to force peace, but they were captured, tried, convicted, and executed, so that war could go on. In the latter, humans shipwrecked in the Sargasso Sea encountered peaceful Atlanteans who have domesticated the universal "pandyname" energy.

Pierre **Giffard**, with the thirty-issue serial *La Guerre Infernale* (*The Infernal War*, 1908), illustrated by Robida, which depicted with a prodigious wealth of details an apocalyptic world war pitting westerners against the Chinese; in

it, the war was fought in the air, on and under water, and under ground, with a multitude of weapons capable of freezing the oceans or setting them afire, of spreading vast clouds of toxic gases over huge distances, etc.

Belgian writer François **Léonard**, with *La Conquête de Londres* (*The Conquest of London*), written in 1912 but not published until 1917, which depicted an Anglo-German war that featured radium-powered rockets, magnetic-powered flying dreadnaughts, and the discovery of the virus of death itself.

c. Mainstream Writers

Some authors produced literary works that would, by any normal standards, be regarded as science fiction, or at least containing science fiction elements, were nevertheless published outside the field, and therefore not labelled as such.

Among the more notable of these was astronomer-writer Camille **Flammarion** (see above). Throughout the 19th century, Flammarion continued his exploration of the cosmos in a number of brilliant, groundbreaking stories collected in *Récits de l'Infini* (*Stories of Infinity*, 1872), revised as *Lumen* (1887), and *Rêves Etoilés* (*Starry Dreams*, 1888). In the title story "*Lumen*," a man learned about the universe by conversing with an entity made of pure mind. Other stories dealt with the notion of an Earth where time ran backwards, extra-sensory perception enabling a man to see into other dimensions, and a description of the migration of souls among the Sirian alien race.

Flammarion's masterpiece was a novel entitled *La Fin du Monde* (*The End of the World*, 1893), loosely adapted into an eponymous 1930 film by Abel **Gance** (see Book 1, Chapter I). In an essay-like style, the book revealed in great detail the future history of Man in the 25th century, and then the eventual disappearance of Earth's atmosphere in ten million years. Perhaps not surprisingly for someone so well versed in the history of the genre, Flammarion's last man, like Granville's (see above), was named "Omegar." Another notable work was the novel *Stella* (1897), in which a dying man and a woman found themselves reincarnated on Mars.

Flammarion's interest in reincarnation and hauntings eventually overtook his more scientific avocations and, like Doyle, whom he knew well, he eventually became a major defender of spiritualism, writing several pseudo-documentary works on the subject, such as *Les Maisons Hantées* (*The Haunted Mansions*) and *La Mort et son Mystère* (*Death and Its Mystery*). However, Flammarion's contribution to modern science fiction cannot be underestimated, including the fact that, like Verne, he was widely translated into English and,

Flammarion

therefore, contributed to shaping the evolution of the genre, from Wells to America.

Humorist Eugène **Mouton**'s short story collection, *Nouvelles* (*Short Stories*, 1872) also included a tale entitled "La Fin du Monde" ("The End of the World"), in this case a grim dystopia that featured "monstrous" cattle and sheep "modified" (genetically engineered) to better serve man's needs. His 1883 collection *Fantaisies* (*Fantasies*) included a tale entitled "L'Origine de la Vie," in which life on Earth was attributed to a collision with another world; and "L'Historioscope," in which a scientist invented a device that could look into the past.

In 1860, French journalist and satirist Edmond **About** wrote *Le Cas de M. Guérin* (*The Case of Mr. Guerin*), in which a man became pregnant. His classic *L'Homme à l'Oreille Cassée* (*The Man with the Broken Ear*, 1862), adapted into an eponymous 1962 film (see Book 1, Chapter I), featured the reanimation in 1859 of a Napoleonic Army colonel who had been preserved in suspended animation since 1813. Finally, *Le Nez d'un Notaire* (*The Notary's Nose*, 1862) dealt with organ transplants, in this case in a humorous fashion since the transplanted organ is a nose.

Writer, poet, and inventor Charles **Cros** was a friend of Rimbaud, Verlaine, Allais, Huysmans, and Manet, and was a well-known literary figure of the 19th century. His works later inspired the surrealists. *Un Drame Interastral* (*An Interplanetary Drama*, 1872) was about an unlawful love between an Earthman and a Venusian woman. Cros also discovered an earlier version of the phonograph (called "paléophone").

In 1872, Auguste **Blanqui**, a notorious arnarchist who spent over thirty years of his life in jail, penned *L'Éternité par les Astres* (*Eternity Through the Stars*, 1872), an elaborate cosmogony based on the universal repetition of some kind of primordial pattern.

In 1873, Alphonse **Daudet**, a mainstream author famous for his series of Provencal tales collected in *Lettres de mon Moulin* (*Letters from My Windmill*, 1866), wrote the remarkable short story "Wood's Town," which is a tale of the revolt of plants against men.

In 1888, the famous communard Louise **Michel** penned *Le Monde Nouveau* (*The New World*), an anarchist utopia.

Jean-Marie-Matthias-Philippe Auguste, Comte de **Villiers de l'Isle-Adam**, an important writer of the *fantastique* better known for his *Contes Cruels* (*Cruel Tales*; see Chapter IV), more than dabbled in science fiction. His short story "La Machine à Gloire" ("The Glory Machine") (1874), included in *Contes Cruels*, featured robot-like "andreids" manufactured by Edison. Villiers reused the idea in a more elaborate form in *L'Ève Future* (*The Eve of the Future*, 1886), a bitterly ironic novel in which a boorish young lord sought to love a female robot. His *Axel* (1890) was a prose poem in which the eponymous hero was a wealthy Rosicrucian scientist whose supernaturally impregnable fortress defied the armies of a dying world. *Axel*'s world anticipated the effete, decadent universes of writers Jack Vance and

Moorcock. The hero's final words, "Live? Our servitors will do that for us!" summed up rather well Villiers' rejection of a future world with no room for aristocrats.

A few of Guy de **Maupassant**'s stories could just as easily be classified as science fiction: "Le Horla" (1887; see Chapter IV) and "L'Homme de Mars" ("The Man from Mars", 1888), in which a man saw a Martian spaceship, described as a luminous, transparent globe, fall into the Atlantic Ocean near Etretat.

In 1893, mainstream writer André **Gide** penned *Le Voyage d'Urien* (*The Voyage of Urien*), an Extraordinary Voyage novel in which the hero discovered a Utopia while exploring the Sargasso Sea and the North Pole.

The same year, novelist Paul **Adam** wrote *Le Conte Futur* (*A Tale of the Future*), the utopian tale of a future war that eventually led mankind to universal peace. Some of the more interesting notions featured in the book included sophisticated machines taking over farming labors.

Even the renowned Émile **Zola**, the founder of the naturalist movement in literature, wrote three novels before his untimely accidental death in 1902 that would be classifiable as science fiction: *Fécondité* (*Fecundity*, 1899), *Travail* (*Labor*, 1901) and *Vérité* (*Truth*; published posthumously in 1903). a fourth novel, *Justice*, was meant to complete the tetralogy, entitled *Les Quatre Evangiles* (*The Four Gospels*), but was not written. The books followed the lives of four brothers in seemingly divergent futures, the events taking place from 1925 to 1980: in *Travail*, for example, the workers' revolt has succeeded, but the world is then ravaged by a cataclysmic war. There are other instances of scientific and social anticipations in the other two novels.

The advent of the 20th century brought a number of notable works of "mainstream" science fiction. *La Force Ennemie* (*The Enemy Force*, 1903) by John-Antoine **Nau** actually won the first Goncourt literary prize ever. The novel dealt with a mind transfer over cosmic distances. The hero was locked in a lunatic's asylum because he was possessed by an alien mind named Kmohoûn, originating from Tkoukrah, a hellish world orbiting the star Aldebaran, starkingly described by Nau.

Daniel **Halévy**'s *Histoire de Quatre Ans, 1997-2001* (*Four Years' History*, 1903) was an attempt at creating a future history, including an Arabic invasion.

Nobel prize winner Anatole **France** contributed *Sur La Pierre Blanche* (*The White Stone*, 1905), in which a group of intellectuals theorized about the rise of socialism; and *L'Île des Pingouins* (*Penguin Island*, 1908), a *Planet of the Apes*-like novel in which mankind's evolution was paralled in a satirical fashion through a race of penguins who, after they have been baptized, became human (also see Chapter IV for France's fantasies).

In 1909, Belgian writer Henry **Kistemaekers**, known mostly for his romance novels, penned *Aéropolis* (1909), sub-titled "A Comic Novel of Aerial Life," a satirical tale of a "yellow peril" invasion of Europe.

In 1910, Jacques **Constant** portrayed a fate almost as dreadful in *Le Triomphe des Suffragettes* (*The Triumph of the Suffragettes*), a novel taking place in 1995 and forecasting a grim future when women take over.

The same concept had previously been treated in Henri **Desmarest**'s *La Femme Future* (*Future Woman*, 1890), which showed the dangers of a world ruled by females.

Jean **Richepin**, a member of the French Academy, and the author of notable collections of fantastic stories (see Chapter IV), wrote *L'Aile, Roman des Temps Nouveaux* (*The Wing, Novel of Modern Times*, 1911), in which Earth's lei lines were harnessed to power a fleet of flying machines, and the ruins of precataclysmic civilisations were discovered.

Finally, Gaston de **Pawlowski**, in his *Contes Singuliers* (*Singular Tales*, 1912) and *Voyage au Pays de la 4ème Dimension* (*Voyage in the Fourth Dimension*, 1912), wrote a number of classic, satirical stories mocking progress and technology.

CHAPTER VI

The Fantastique *Entre-Deux Guerres (Between the Wars) (1918–1945)*

The confidence displayed by French society in the early 1900s was sapped by the slaughter of World War I in which, out of 8 million Frenchmen drafted, 1.3 million were killed and 1 million severely crippled. Large sections of France were devastated and industrial production fell by 60 percent. Even deeper and longer-lasting, however, were the psychological wounds left by the war, and the awareness that such a fate could never be endured again.

It was, therefore, not surprising that French culture between the wars gave rise to an abundance of new ideas intending to break with the past: Cubism, the music of Erik Satie (1866-1925), and the search for a sense of spiritual exaltation as demonstrated in the films of Jean **Cocteau**, Marcel L'Herbier, Luis Buñuel and René **Clair**.

In French literature, the Dadaist and Surrealist movements exemplified that desire to break violently with the past, but the more conventional forms of the novel remained otherwise less innovative. The period was dominated by family-saga novels, or *roman-fleuve (river novels)*; working-class novels in the tradition of **Zola**; and regional novels advocating a return to the old-fashioned values of peasant life. This began to change only in the mid-1930s with the popularity of writers like André Malraux (1901-1976), Albert Camus (1913-1960), and Louis-Ferdinand Céline (1894-1961), and the influences of American writers such as William Faulkner (1897-1962), John Dos Passos (1896-1970), and even the Irishman James Joyce (1882-1924).

In the *fantastique*, the split between *fantastique littéraire* and *fantastique populaire* was definitively formed. The former was written by literary-minded writers, and followed a tradition that had begun with Hoffmann, Poe, the romantics, and the symbolists. The latter was written by popular writers, walking in the footsteps of the *roman noir*, **Dumas**, **Sue**, and **Féval**.

1. *Fantastique Littéraire*

The *fantastique littéraire* between the wars reflected the dichotomy mentioned above, torn between the extremes of Surrealism and Dadaism on the one hand; and more traditional modes of expression, relying on old-fashioned supernatural devices in the vein of Hoffmann and Poe on the other. The only new foreign influence was that of Henry James (1843-1916). A non-literary influence, especially on the surrealists, was that of Sigmund Freud (1856-1939), whose theories were used by numerous writers as keys to unlock closed doors in their explorations of the attics of the human soul.

a. Fantastique Surréaliste

The desire of both the dadaists and their literary successors, the surrealists, was to destroy existing social structures and the notion of ordered text. Dadaism began as a nihilistic artistic movement that paralleled the political anarchist movements of the times. in France, it was heralded in literary form by writers Alfred **Jarry** and Guillaume **Apollinaire**

Jarry was the inventor of "pataphysics," a logic of the absurd. He displayed a biting sense of satire when dealing with human evil and irrationality. Apollinaire was an avant-garde poet who penned a series of vivid, sometimes whimsical, often wildly fantastic, stories, always exhibiting a daring sense of the outrageous. in order to shock his readers, Apollinaire liked to experiment with the form of the text; he also liked to defeat expectations, challenge dogmas, and question matters of faith, always with a sense of the bizarre. *L'Enchanteur Pourrissant* (*The Rotting Enchanter*, 1909) was a poetic dialog between Merlin and Viviane. *L'Hérésiarque et Cie.* (1910) was a collection of short stories written between 1899 and 1910, which dealt with a variety of fantasy themes such as magic and invisibility. The story "Le Passant de Prague" ("The Pedestrian from Prague") featured the Wandering Jew telling his own story, making references to those who previously wrote about him, such as Goethe, Sue, **Quinet,** and **Richepin**. The twist was that, far from being a cursed, unhappy figure, Ahasverus was a contented, even festive man.

Because of his somewhat anarchistic outlook, and his love for typographical experimentation, Apollinaire was the first, true herald of surrealism. By the time of his death in 1918, he had made it possible for the never-ending search for the bizarre in literature to be viewed not just as an amusing but pointless game, but as a true method, a metaphysical quest, reflecting more profound concerns and higher literary ambitions.

It was no coincidence that, in 1918, poet Tristan Tzara published the first dadaist manifesto, displaying the desire to submit the content and the form of poetry to an uncontrolled eruption of social violence: "I want to destroy the compartments of the brain as well as those of social order; I want to throw the hand of heaven into hell and the eyes of hell into heaven."

After 1922, the dadaist movement began to lose its force as its participants turned toward surrealism. By emphasizing the subconscious and using devices such as automatic writing, the surrealists also sought to destroy the "rationalistic" culture that had led France into the horror of World War I. But unlike the dadaists, whose emphasis was on negation, the surrealists embraced a mutated form of the earlier romanticism: they praised **Baudelaire**, **Nerval**, **Sade**, **Lautréamont**, **Rimbaud,** and **Mallarmé**. They glorified pulp heroes such as **Allain** and **Souvestre**'s *Fantômas* and **Le Rouge**'s *Docteur Cornélius*.

Surrealism was a means of reuniting the conscious and the unconscious, reality and fantasy, and let dreams loose on the day-time world. Its major spokesman was André **Breton**, a former medical student who had worked as a neuro-psychiatrist, and was well acquainted with the writings of Freud, whom he met in 1921. In 1919, Breton joined forces with writer Louis **Aragon** (1897-1982; also a medical doctor) and Philippe Soupault to launch the magazine *Littérature*, which published the first surrealist texts.

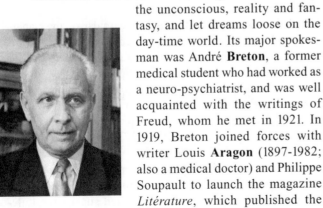

Louis Aragon

André Breton

In 1924, Breton published his first surrealist manifesto, which defined surrealism as "pure psychic automatism through which one can express verbally, through writing or any other medium, the real process of thought, transcribing it without any control exercised by reason, and free of any aesthetic and moral concern." In 1930, Breton published a second manifesto, but by then, various internecine quarrels, splinters, and political problems arising from the cohabitation with communism, had brought the disintegration of the movement.

As mentioned above, surrealism embraced fantasy. "The *merveilleux* (*marvelous*) is always beautiful," wrote Breton. "Anything marvelous is beautiful; indeed only the marvelous is beautiful." Breton himself showed the way with *Nadja* (1928), a novel which mixed everyday occurrences with surreal and psychological aberrations.

Blaise **Cendrars**, writer, poet, and journalist, openly declared his admiration for Le Rouge's *Dr. Cornelius*. His *La Fin du Monde Filmée par l'Ange* (*The End of the World Filmed by an Angel*, 1919), and *Moravagine* (1926) were surrealist novels. The latter was named after, and told the story of, an evil madman who escaped from a lunatic asylum and caused a spree of terror and destruction on the world that rivaled those of *Dr. Cornelius* and *Fantômas*. But unlike its popular predecessors, *Moravagine* transformed its popular fiction characters and situations through the use of vivid poetry and surreal imagery. It was an ode to sheer violence, evil and chaos unleashed, a foreboding herald of the events that would come during World War II.

Other major writers stood out among the current of *fantastique surréaliste* that arose in the 1920s and 1930s:

Playwright Jean **Giraudoux** created an impressionistic form of drama by emphasizing dialogue and style rather than realism, combining tragedy, humor, and fantasy in a heretofore unknown and brilliant manner. in *Intermezzo* (1937), a timid ghost revolutionized a small provincial town. *Ondine* (1939) was about a water sprite who fell in love with a mortal.

Julien **Gracq**'s first novel, *Au Château d'Argol* (*At the Castle of Argol*, 1938), was immediately hailed by the surrealists because it combined the literary effects of the *roman noir* with the poetry of Rimbaud. The book took place in a *Gormenghast*-like castle where the young owner, his friend, and the beautiful Heide spent their time playing morbid and decadent games. in 1951, Gracq published the equally brilliant *Le Rivage des Syrtes* (*The Shores of the Syrtes*), which was awarded the Goncourt literary award. It took place in the imaginary land of Farghestan, which had been at war with its neighbor for three hundred years.

The *fantastique surréaliste* contributed, in an almost

logical fashion, to the development of some unique and remarkable fantastic poetry. In *Les Nouvelles Révélations de l'Être* (*The New Revelations of Being*, 1938), poet Antonin **Artaud** crafted a tapestry of surreal prophecies inspired by the Tarot imagery. His *Les Tarahumaras* (1945) was a collection of magical texts written under the influence of peyote.

Jean **Cocteau** produced such acclaimed works as the poems of *L'Ange Heurtebise* (*The Angel Heurtebise*, 1925), the plays *Orphée* (*Orpheus*, 1926) and *Les Chevaliers de la Table Ronde* (*The Knights of the Round Table*, 1937), and the hauntingly beautiful and surreal 1945 film version of *La Belle et la Bête* (*Beauty and the Beast*; See Book 1, Chapter I).

Finally, Jules **Supervielle**, a writer of Basque descent, incorporated hispanic vistas and themes in *L'Homme de la Pampa* (*The Man from the Pampa*, 1923), *Le Survivant* (*The Survivor*, 1928), his novel *L'Enfant de la Haute Mer* (*The Child from the High Sea*, 1931), and plays *La Belle au Bois* (*The Beauty in the Wood*, 1932) and *Robinson* (1949).

Many other surrealist writers used fantastic elements such as dreams, alternate realities, exotic or initiatic journeys to surreal lands and places, in their works. Among the most notable were:

Non-conformist Benjamin **Péret**, who wrote a number of fantastical tales in the 1920s and 1930s, collected in *Main Forte* (*Strong Hand*, 1946) and *Dernier Malheur, Dernière Chance* (*Last Woe, Last Chance*, 1946).

Ethnologist Michel **Leiris**, whose *Aurora* (1928) owed its title to a pun on the word "horrora" and harked back to the influences of the *roman noir*.

Georges **Limbour**, an admirer of **Mallarmé** and Rimbaud, whose fantastical stories were collected in *L'Illustre Cheval Blanc* (*The Illustrious White Horse*, 1930).

René **Crevel** (who committed suicide at 35), with the wildly surreal *Mon Corps et Moi* (*My Body and I*, 1925), *La Mort Difficile* (*The Difficult Death*, 1926), *Babylone* (1927) and *Êtes-Vous Fou?* (*Are You Mad?*, 1929).

And, finally, Robert **Desnos** with *La Liberté ou l'Amour!* (*Liberty or Love!*, 1927).

More mainstream writers who also dabbled in the genre included Paul Éluard (1895-1952), Max Jacob (1876-1944), and Pierre Reverdy (1889-1960).

b. Traditional Fantastique

Outside of the more extravagant arena of surrealism, the presence of the *fantastique* continued to grace the pages of mainstream literature, often through a discreet intrusion of the supernatural into the novel, especially among the more "highbrow" authors. It was not intended to shock or surprise the reader, as it did in surrealist works, but simply to cohabit in parallel with our more mundane reality. This approach to the *fantastique* was a precursor of today's magical realism.

For example, **Alain-Fournier**'s *Le Grand Meaulnes* (1913, translated as *The Lost Domain*) was a classic romantic novel in which a runaway boy encountered a strange,

other-worldly girl. It was adapted in an eponymous 1967 film directed by Jean-Gabriel Albicocco, which ignored the underlying fantasy elements of the novel.

The same theme was carried over in the Faustian variation, *Marguerite de la Nuit* (*Marguerite of the Night*, 1922), by Pierre **Mac Orlan**, which also was made into a film (see Book 1, Chapter I). Mac Orlan's other novels showed a wide variety of influences, ranging from **Nerval** and **Schwob** to Stevenson. In *Le Rire Jaune* (*The Yellow Laugh*, 1914), mankind eventually perished from irrepressible laughter. *La Bête Conquérante* (*The Conquering Beast*, 1920) was an *Animal Farm*-like parable. *Le Nègre Léonard et Maître Jean Mullin* (1920) depicted the catastrophic consequences of the disappearance of evil from Earth. In *La Cavalière Elsa* (*Elsa the Rider*, 1921), Russia invaded Europe. Finally, *Malice* (1923) was the morbid yet erotic tale of the Devil's progressive corruption of a man through lascivious sex and money.

The Devil was also very much the focus of Georges **Bernanos**'s *Sous le Soleil de Satan* (*Under the Sun of Satan*, 1926), a much celebrated religious novel in which the Devil materialized to tempt a country priest. (This novel was filmed in 1987 by Maurice Pialat – see Book 1, Chapter I.)

The *fantastique* of Pierre **Benoît** was equally unobtrusive: it discreetly seeped through his many colorful novels, rightly famous for their exotic locales, eccentric characters, and steamy plots. The classic *L'Atlantide* (1919) was a superb literary reread of H. Rider Haggard's *She*, in which two French officers

Georges Bernanos

found the last city of Atlantis in the midst of the Sahara Desert. There, Queen Antinea turned them into her lovers before casting them into metal statues. *L'Atlantide* was the subject of numerous film and television adaptations (see Book 1, Chapters I and II). Other Benoît novels worthy of mention included *La Chaussée des Géants* (*The Giants' Path*, 1922), *Le Puit de Jacob* (*Jacob's Well*, 1925), *Le Roi Lépreux* (*The Leper King*; AM, 1927) and *Le Soleil de Minuit* (*The Midnight Sun*, 1930).

In the second tiers of literary (or mainstream) writers, the *fantastique*, when present, was more deliberate, often relying more fully on the true and tested supernatural elements crafted in past centuries. By far, the most remarkable author in this category was Claude **Farrère**, who had become famous first through his exotic novels of Indochina and then his character studies. In parallel with his mainstream production, Farrère penned a number of truly outstanding genre works such as *La Maison des Hommes Vivants* (*The House of Living Men*, 1911), mentioned in chapter IV. He continued his production between the wars with collections of fantastic tales such as *Contes d'Outre et d'Autres Mondes* (*Tales from Beyond and Other Worlds*, 1921), *Histoire de Très Loin ou d'Assez Près* (*Tales of Very Far or Near Enough*, 1923), which included his classic "Où?" ("Where?"), *L'Autre Côté* (*The Other Side*, 1928), *La Marche Funèbre* (*The Funeral March*, 1929) and *La Porte Dérobée* (*The Hidden Door*, 1930).

Farrère's *fantastique* clearly owed its inspiration from **Maupassant**, and easily crossed into the domain of science fiction. (One of Farrère's novels, a dystopia, is in fact reviewed in chapter VII.) "Où?" was a remarkable exploration of the "out there," a fourth dimension which followed different laws of time and space. Surprisingly, *L'Autre Côté* won the very first prestigious Goncourt literary award in 1928, showing that the *fantastique* still carried its letters of nobility.

Like Farrère, Pierre **Frondaie** was an author who was better known for his realistic novels. Nevertheless, his *Contes Réels et Fantaisistes* (*Real and Fantastic Tales*, 1930), *Quand le Diable s'en mêle* (*When the Devil Meddles*, 1935), and *Les Fatidiques* (*Fated Tales*, 1946) were all fantastic tales, many of which featured the character of Jean Pharg, a mysterious narrator in the tradition of William Hope Hodgson's Carnacki the Ghost-Finder, perhaps the first of its kind in French literature.

Frédéric **Boutet**, who wrote a famous *Dictionnaire des Sciences Occultes* (*Dictionary of Occult Sciences*, 1937), also penned a number of Poe-like novels such as *Le Reflet de Claude Mercoeur* (*Claude Mercoeur's Reflection*, 1921), *Le Spectre de M. Imberger* (*The Ghost of Mr. Imberger*, 1922), and *Les Aventuriers du Mystère: Tableau de l'Au-Delà* (*The Adventurers of Mystery: Scene from Beyond*, 1927).

In the midst of an abundant production of mainstream novels devoted to French farmers, Ernest **Pérochon** produced a true *roman spirite*, *Les Ombres* (*The Shadows*, 1923), as well as a number of collections of fantasy tales such as *Huit Gouttes d'Opium* (*Eight Drops of Opium*, 1925), and *Contes des Cent Un Matins* (*Tales of 101 Mornings*, 1930).

Léon **Daudet**'s *Un Jour d'Orage* (*A Stormy Day*, 1925) was also a provincial fantasy, taking place in Provence and featuring the famous seer Nostradamus. Another novel in the same vein was *Le Sang de la Nuit* (*The Blood of the Night*, 1926).

Other notable authors of the period included:

Maurice **Magre**, the author of *Lucifer* (1929) and *Interventions Surnaturelles* (*Supernatural Interventions*, 1939).

Jean **Cassou**, who penned *La Clef des Songes* (*The Key to Dreams*, 1929), *De l'Étoile au Jardin des Plantes* (*From the Étoile to the Botanical Gardens*, 1935) and *Les Enfants sans Âge* (*The Ageless Children*, 1946).

Laurence **Albaret**, whose collection *Le Grand Ventre* (*The Great Belly*, 1944) contained some very bizarre stories.

Maurice **Level** (see Chapter IV), a contributor to the **Grand-Guignol**, who wrote *Les Morts Étranges* (*Strange Deaths*, 1921), *La Cité des Voleurs* (*City of Thieves*, 1924), and *L'Énigme de Bellavista* (*The Mystery of Bellavista*, 1929), the last title co-written with Jean **Prudhomme**.

Joseph-Charles-Victor **Mardrus**, who continued the tradition of Arabian tales *La Reine de Saba* (*The Queen of Sheba*, 1919) and a rewritten, updated version of the Thousand and One Nights, *Le Livre des Mille et Une Nuits* (*The Book of Thousand and One Nights*, 1920-24).

A special place in the history of the *fantastique* ought to be reserved for to Marcel **Aymé**, novelist, playwright, and master of social satire and modern fairy tales. **Aymé**'s fantastic universe mixed broad country wit such as *La Jument Verte* (*The Green Mare*, 1933) with local folk legends such as *La Vouivre* (1943), a book about a snake woman who lived in a swamp. Aymé's later collections of short stories combined a lighter but nevertheless piercing wit with fantasy elements, treated as disarmingly common place occurrences. *Le Passe-Muraille* (*The Walker Through the Walls*, 1943) was a classic yarn about an obscure civil servant who turned into a daring super-criminal after acquiring the power to walk through solid objects. *Le Nain* (*The Dwarf*, 1934) was about a dwarf who finally began to grow at age 30. Finally, Aymé's short animal fables, *Les Contes du Chat Perché* (*The Tales of the Crouching Cat*, 1931) and *Autres Contes du Chat Perché* (*Other Tales of the Crouching Cat*, 1954), easily made him an equal of **La Fontaine** or **Perrault**.

Marcel Aymé
Les contes du chat perché

Marcel Aymé's tales have been a godsend for film and television adaptations: *La Belle Image*, *Clérambard*, *Le Passe-Muraille*, *Les Contes du Chat Perché*, *Uranus*, and *La Vouivre*, as well as many others, were all adapted (see Book 1, Chapters I and II).

Another fantasy tale which defied classification is Antoine de **Saint-Exupéry**'s world-famous *Le Petit Prince* (*The Little Prince*, 1943).

2. *Fantastique Populaire*

Between the wars, the *fantastique populaire* continued to cater to the masses by providing cheap entertainment in the form of the *romans feuilletons*, pulp-like magazines such as *Le Journal des Voyages* (*The Journal of Voyages*, 1877-1947), *Lectures pour Tous* (*Readings for All*, 1898-1940) and *L'Intrépide* (*The Fearless*, 1910-1937), and paperback imprints from publishers such as Ollendorff, Méricant, Férenczi, and Tallandier.

To the names of **Leroux**, **Renard**, **Rosny Aîné**, **La Hire**, **Le Rouge**, **Béliard**, and **Couvreur** should be added those of **Magog**, **Thévenin**, **Armandy**, **Varlet**, **Valleret**, **Toudouze**, **Limat**, **Dazergues**, and many more, who all continued to write a unique blend of science fiction, fantasy, and adventure. (These authors are reviewed in chapters V and VII.)

The writing team of Charles and Henri **Omessa** was notable for *Anaïtis, Fille de Carthage* (*Daughter of Carthago*, 1922), a proto-heroic fantasy in the vein of Gustave **Flaubert**'s *Salammbô* (see Chapter IV). They also penned *Le Troisième Oeil de Civa* (*The Third Eye of Shiva*, 1932) and *Histoire de l'Autre Monde* (*Tale from Another World*, 1934).

Another notable author was the prolific Arthur **Bernède**, who wrote popular adventure novels in the tradition of Sue and Féval. Bernède was the creator of the dark-clad crime avenger, *Judex* (1917), adapted into serial form by Louis **Feuillade** and later remade as a film by Georges **Franju** (see Book 1, Chapter I). Judex returned in *La Nouvelle Mission de Judex* (*Judex's New Mission*, 1919). Others writing

Belphégor

in this vein were Edward Brooker, Gilles Mersay and Norbert Sévestre. Another famous Bernède creation was the ghostly figure of *Belphégor* (1928), the puppet of a sect of Rosicrucians seeking a dark secret hidden within the walls of the Louvre Museum. *Belphegor*, too, was made into a serial and remade in 1965 as a popular television series (see Book 1, Chapter II). Other notable Bernède novels included *La Devineresse* (*The Seeress*, 1930), *Le Sorcier de la Reine* (*The Queen's Wizard*, 1930), *Mephisto* (1931), *La Fille du Diable* (*The Devil's Daughter*, 1932) and *Vampiria* (1932).

Jean **Joseph-Renaud** wrote popular *fantastique* for magazines, but in a more supernatural vein. He was one of the first French writers to credit Ambrose Bierce as an influence in his collection of Bierce-inspired tales and Bierce translations *Le Clavecin Hanté* (*The Haunted Harpsichord*, 1920). His novel *La Vivante Épingle* (*The Living Needle*, 1922) used the then-popular myths of ancient Egypt in the tradition of **Gautier**. Again like Bernède, Joseph-Renaud was a prolific writer, happily mixing genres between adventure, detective and supernatural fiction. Among his best genre novels or story collections were *Les Doigts qui*

Parlent (*The Talking Fingers*, 1917), *Lumières dans la Nuit* (*Lights in the Night*, 1923), *La Vasque d'Or* (*The Golden Basin*, 1925), *Le Seigneur Mystère* (*Lord Mystery*, 1929), *Au-Delà* (*Beyond*, 1932), and *Les Deux Idoles* (*The Two Idols*, 1932). Joseph-Renaud also contributed a play entitled *La Visionnaire* (*The Visionary*, 1936) to the Grand-Guignol.

The **Grand-Guignol** theater reached its pinnacle between the wars and continued to reign supreme in the subgenre of pure horror fiction. Camille Choisy managed the Grand-Guignol from 1914 to 1930. Unlike his predecessors, **Méténier** and **Maurey**, Choisy was not a writer but a former stage decorator. He was responsible for the development of the many, spectacular, gory special effects which became associated with the theater. Choisy discovered lead actress Paula Maxa and even bought a fully equipped and functional surgical theatre to serve as a prop/set for the plays. After Choisy came Jack **Jouvin**, who managed the Grand-Guignol from 1930 to 1938. Under his stewardship, psychology was added to gore and the characters became more fleshed out. However, Jouvin lacked in other managerial areas and, with changing times and fashions, decline began to set in.

The greatest writing discovery of the Grand-Guignol was André de **Lorde**, nicknamed the "Prince of Terror," who became the French Stephen King of his day. A small and polished man, Lorde was a prolific playwright who also wrote fashionable comedies as well as social novels. He penned over one hundred and fifty plays, often in collaboration with other writers, such as Pierre **Chaine**, Henri **Bauche**, Alfred **Binet**, Georges **Montignac**, Charles **Foleÿ**, and others. His celebrity during the period easily rivaled that of Alexandre **Dumas** or Edmond de Goncourt. Lorde became the Grand Guignol writer *par excellence* and probably the first bestselling gore writer in the genre's history. Lorde's own brand of horror relied on medicine and psychiatry rather than the supernatural. For him, a man who saw ghosts or conversed with spirits was a dangerous lunatic, possibly a potential murderer, not someone who communicated with the occult. Lorde's works were collected in various volumes, including *Théâtre d'Épouvante* (*Theater of Horror*, 1909), *Cauchemars* (*Nightmares*, 1912), *Théâtre Rouge* (*Red Theater*, 1922), *Les Drames Célèbres du Grand-Guignol* (*Famous Tragedies of the Grand-Guignol*, 1924), *Théâtre de la Peur* (*Theater of Fear*, 1924), *Théâtre de la Mort* (*Theater of Death*, 1928), and *La Galerie des Monstres* (*The Gallery of Monsters*, 1928).

One of the most distinctive genre writers of the 1930s, and one who also blended genres with deceptive facility, was famous mystery writer Pierre **Véry**, whose novels almost always incorporated surreal, virtually supernatural elements, explained away at the end, but not necessarily in a fully rational fashion. Some of Véry's works squarely belonged in the fantasy genre, such as *Le Pays sans Étoiles* (*The Starless Country*, 1945), adapted into an eponymous

McFarland & Company, Inc. Publishers

Box 611, Jefferson, North Carolina 28640
Tel. 336-246-4460   FAX 336-246-5018

Enclosed please find

Lofficier. French Science Fiction, Fantasy, Horror and Pulp Fiction

Pub. date: **September 2000**

Price: $95

Postpaid Price: $99

This book is sent to you

__XX__ for review. Please send us **two copies** of your *published review for our files. We ask that you include our address (and our 800 order line) in any review.*

_____ with the compliments of the author/publisher.

_____ for examination.

_____ as your desk copy, with our compliments.

_____ in accordance with our agreement.

_____ for subsidiary rights consideration.

Promotion Department
McFarland & Company, Inc.

1945 feature film (see Book 1, Chapter I), and *Tout Doit Disparaître le 5 Mai* (*Everything Must Go on May 5th*, 1961), his last book, a collection of fantastic tales. His first novel, the brilliant *Pont Égaré* (*Lost Bridge*, 1929), was clearly inspired by the surrealists. And so were *Les Métamorphoses de Jean Sucre* (*The Metamorphoses of Jean Sucre*, 1931) and *Le Meneur de Jeu* (*The Game Master*, 1934), which already displayed his talent for crafting quirky, odd little enigmas.

It was for his mystery novels that Véry won his literary fame. After winning a genre award for his *Le Testament de Basil Crookes* (*The Testament of Basil Crookes*, 1930),

published under the pseudonym of "Toussaint-Juge," Véry created the character of Prosper Lepic, a lawyer and poet whose face resembled that of an owl. Lepic solved mysteries that almost, but never quite, fell into the supernatural or the bizarre: *Le Gentleman des Antipodes*, (*The Gentleman from the Other Side of the World*, 1936) featured a club of animal-faced individuals. (It was adapted for television—see Book 1, Chapter II.) *Le Thé des Vieilles Dames* (*The Tea of the Old Ladies*, 1937) was another Lepic thriller which took place in an odd little village with a dream-like quality. **Véry**'s best known mystery novels were the surreal *L'Assassinat du Père Noël* (*The Murder of Santa Claus*, 1934), in which the inhabitants of a mountain village closed in by the snow discovered the corpse of a mysterious man dressed as Santa Claus, and *Les Disparus de Saint-Agil* (*The Saint-Agil Disappearances*, 1935) about strange events at a boys' school. Both were made into popular films.

Like Véry, Claude **Aveline** straddled the line between the *fantastique* and detective fiction. He was the author of several collections of strange and fantastic stories, such as *Trois Histoires de la Nuit* (*Three Stories of Night*, 1931), *C'est Vrai mais il ne faut pas le croire* (*It's True But You Can't Believe It*, 1939) and *Temps Mort* (*Dead Time*, 1945). Aveline became justly famous for creating the character of detective Frédéric Belot. The Belot series included titles such as *Voiture 7, Place 15* (*Train Car 7, Seat 15*, 1962), *La Double Mort de Frédéric Belot* (*The Two Deaths of Frederic Belot*, 1962), *Le Jet d'Eau* (*The Water Fountain*, 1962), *L'Abonné de la Ligne U* (*The Subscriber to the U Line*, 1964), and *L'Oeil de Chat* (*Cat's Eye*, 1970). *L'Abonné de la*

Ligne U was adapted in 1964 into a television series of forty 15-minute episodes directed by Yannick Andrei and starring Jacques Dacqmine as Belot.

The prolific Alexandre **Arnoux** was another author who liked to blend genres, easily crossing the lines between science fiction, fantasy, and mainstream literature. A number of his novels and plays were modern retelling of classic legends, such as *Légende du Roi Arthur et des Chevaliers de la Table Ronde* (*Legend of King Arthur and the Knights of the Round Table*, 1920), *Huon de Bordeaux* (1922), and *Merlin l'Enchanteur* (*Merlin the Enchanter*, 1931); others were pure fantastical tales such as *Abisag, ou l'Église Transportée par la Foi* (*The Church Transported By Faith*, 1918), *Indice 33* (*Indicia 33*, 1920), and the collections *Suite Variée* (*Varied Suite*, 1925) and *Sortilèges* (*Spells*, 1949).

Charles **Guyon** also relied on classic fairy tales and folk legends, with *Les Bons Petits Lutins* (*The Good Little Goblins*, 1923), *Les Contes de rand'Maman* (*Granny's Tales*, 1926), *Les Petits Lutins de Carnac* (*The Little Goblins of Carnac*, 1926), *Récits Légendaires des Bords du Rhin* (*Legendary Tales of the River Rhine*, 1926), *La Caverne de la Fée Cocasse* (*The Cavern of the Funny Fairy*, 1927), and *Légendes du Roi de Thulé* (*Legends of the King of Thule*, 1931).

In the 1930s, Édouard **Letailleur** penned a dozen notable gothic horror thrillers, including *Le Cimetière des Lépreux* (*The Graveyard of Lepers*), *La Demeure de Satan* (*The House of Satan*) and *Perkane, le Démon de la Nuit* (*The Night Demon*) (all 1934).

Finally, Léo **Gestelys** contributed a number of popular adventure novels with gothic or exotic genre elements. Among these were *Le Trésor des Derviches* (*The Treasure of the Derviches*, 1937), and *La Maison de la Mort* (*The House of Death*, 1938). After the war, **Gestelys** alternated between horror novels such as Nuit d'Épouvante (*Night of Terror*, 1946), *Le Fluide d'Or* (*The Golden Fluid*, 1949) and *L'Île des Malédictions* (*The Island of Curses*, 1955), and fantasy-oriented romance novels like *La Tour des Korrigans* (*The Tower of the Korrigans*, 1952) and *Le Fantôme de la Fiancée* (*The Fiancée's Ghost*, 1958).

3. Belgian *Fantastique*

Unlike in France, where the *fantastique* was either a marginal phenomenon existing on the edges of mainstream literature, or something relegated to the entertainment of the lower classes, in Belgium the *fantastique* became a major literary current. One can legitimately speak of a Belgian "school" of the *fantastique*, both in terms of quantity and quality—quantity because Belgium produced a disproportionately high number of first-rate authors; quality because, in spite of each writer's individuality, there was a certain commonality among Belgian-born writers in terms of themes and approach to the *fantastique*.

Some scholars have explained this richness and propensity for the *fantastique* in Belgian literature by pointing out the Flemish taste for the baroque and the bizarre, a long fascination for ghost stories and other supernatural phenomenon, and a natural inclination towards the *fantastique* as a refuge, if not a rebellion, against a bleak life, history, and surroundings.

a. Traditional Fantastique

As French-language Belgian literature began to mature in the late 1800s, it incorporated the traditional Flemish and French-language (i.e., Wallon) folklore. Romanticized versions of folkloric tales were the subject of the works of:

Marcellin **La Garde**, with *Le Val de l'Amblève* (*The Valley of Ambleve*, 1879) and *Légendes Ardennaises* (*Legends from the Ardennes*, 1886).

Henri de **Nimal**, with *Légendes de la Meuse* (*Legends of the Meuse*, 1898).

Eugène **Demolder**, with *Contes d'Yperdamme* (*Tales from Yperdamme*, 1891) and *La Légende d'Yperdamme* (*The Legend of Yperdamme*, 1897).

The Germanic influences of authors such as Hoffman and H. H. Ewers combined with the folkloric material to give rise to a tradition of writers producing collections of fantastic tales which eventually became known as the "Belgian School of the Strange." What characterized these stories were their initial firm rooting in everyday reality, a reality of Brueghellian proportions, followed by an abrupt transition into, or eruption from, the supernatural, the latter presented not in vaporous terms but as another, equally tangible, always terrifying, form of reality. Among the early proponents of this Belgian "school" were:

Georges **Eekhoud**, with his *Kermesses* (*Fiestas*, 1884), *Cycle Patibulaire* (*Evil-Looking Cycle*, 1892), *L'Autre Vue* (*The Other View*, 1904) and *La Danse Macabre du Pont de Lucerne* (*The Danse Macabre of Lucerne Bridge*, 1920).

Hubert **Stiernet**, with his *Contes au Perron* (*Tales of the Balcony*, 1893) and *Histoires Hantées* (*Haunted Stories*, 1907).

Pol **Demade**, with *Contes Inquiets* (*Worried Tales*, 1898), *Les Âmes qui Saignent* (*The Bleeding Souls*, 1910), and *Le Cortège des Ombres* (*The Procession of the Shadows*, 1925).

This tradition continued through the 1920s and 1930s with popular authors such as:

Horace **Van Offel**, who penned a number of commercial works such as *Le Tatouage Bleu* (*The Blue Tattoo*, 1917), *La Terreur Fauve* (*The Fawn Terror*, 1922), *Le Jongleur d'Épées* (*The Juggler of Swords*, 1930), *La Flûte Corsaire* (*The Corsair Flute*, 1933) and *Le Capitaine du Vaisseau-Fantôme* (*The Captain of the Ghost-Ship*, 1943).

Jean de **Bosschère**, the author of numerous fantastic tales collected posthumously in *Contes de la Neige et de la Nuit* (*Tales of Snow and Night*, 1954); his novel *Satan l'Obscur* (*Satan the Obscure*, 1933) dealt with the Devil in terms similar to Bernanos or Mac Orlan.

The Devil was very much at the center of the works of one of the greatest literary figures in Belgian history—the eccentric playwright Michel de **Ghelderode**. He was a true visionary whose folkish morality plays and stories resonated with violence, demonism, holy madness, and typically Belgian, Hyeronimus Bosch-like humor and fantasy. His plays, such as *Fastes d'Enfer* (*Feasts of Hell*, 1929), *Magie Rouge* (*Red Magic*, 1934), and *La Ballade du Grand Macabre* (*The Ballad of the Great Macabre*, 1935), brought to life the macabre tradition of Flemish culture. The plays were eventually embraced by the avant-garde theater and exerted a powerful influence on the art. Ghelderode's collection *Sortilèges* (*Spells*, 1941) contained twelve dark, anguished stories, all told in the first person narrative, which contributed to a claustrophobic sense of inescapable doom. Together, these stories formed a uniquely beautiful panorama of horrors. (*Magie Rouge* and "**Adrian et Jusemina**" [from *Sortilèges*] were adapted for television—see Book 1, Chapter II.)

b. Fantastique Symboliste

Parallel to this current, Belgian fantastic literature was also powerfully influenced by the symbolists, the best example being poet Maurice **Maeterlinck**. Already known in the 1890s, Maeterlinck consolidated his literary reputation in the years following World War I, winning the Nobel Prize for Literature in 1911. The author of the classic *Pelléas et Mélisande* (1892), he also wrote the perennial classic *L'Oiseau Bleu* (*The Blue Bird*, 1908), an allegorical fantasy conceived as a play for children.

Other Belgian writers influenced by the symbolists included:

Roland de **Marès**, with *En Barbarie* (*Among the Barbarians*, 1895).

Albert **Mockel**, the author of *Clartés* (*Lights*, 1901) and *Contes pour Enfants d'Hier* (*Tales for Yesterday's Children*, 1908).

Charles **Van Lerberghe**, with *Selection Surnaturelle* (*Supernatural Selection*, 1905).

Jehan **Maillart**, with *Contes Chimériques* (*Chimerical Tales*, 1905).

One should also mention Robert **Poulet**, whose entire fiction challenged the very notion of "being," such as in *Handji* (1930), where two soldiers created a human avatar to rescue them from oblivion, *Le Trottoir* (*The Pavement*, 1931), *Ténèbres* (*Darkness*, 1934) and *Prélude à l'Apocalypse* (*Prelude to the Apocalypse*, 1944).

The one author who contributed the most to the creation and embellishment of the notion of "fantastic reality" was Franz **Hellens**.

A precursor of the surrealists, Hellens displayed from his earliest collections of tales a lyrical, romantic approach to fantasy. *Les Hors-le-Vent* (*The Out-Wind*, 1909), *Les Clartés Latentes* (*The Latent Clarities*, 1912) and *Nocturnal* (1919) were his first explorations into the land of dreams, which he later dubbed the "second life." His novel *Mélusine* (1920) was generally considered a pre-surrealist novel. A friend of Maeterlinck, Supervielle, Éluard, etc., Hellens published the magazine *Le Disque Vert* (*The Green Disk*) in 1922, which he edited with Henri **Michaux**. A prolific writer, Hellens always returned to the *fantastique*, contributing several milestones in the genre, such as *Réalités Fantastiques* (*Fantastic Realities*, 1923), *Nouvelles Réalités Fantastiques* (*New Fantastic Realities*, 1941) and *Fantômes Vivants* (*Living Ghosts*, 1944).

Last but not least, Hellens' fellow editor, Henri **Michaux**, with *Un Barbare en Asie* (*A Barbarian in Asia*, 1932), *Voyage en Grande Garabagne* (*Voyage in Great Garabagne*, 1936), *Au Pays de la Magie* (*In the Land of Magic*, 1941), and *Ici, Poddema* (*Here, Poddema*, 1946), created a series of novels which read like *voyages extraordinaires* of the surreal. Like a French Jack Vance, Michaux loved creating imaginary lands peopled with colorful inhabitants who followed strange customs. One of his imaginary societies lived in perpetual anxiety, another refused to acknowledge the past and the future; in the land of magic, physical laws were subject to psychic rules.

c. Jean Ray

The most famous author of Belgian fantastique was, without a doubt, Jean **Ray** who, like Jules **Verne** in science fiction, deserves his own section. Ray, whose real name was Jean Raymond de Kremer, was generally regarded by genre scholars as the French-language equivalent of Poe and Lovecraft. He began his career as a pulp writer, writing anything and everything, using a variety of aliases, the most famous being that of "John Flanders." He even had several stories published under that name in the magazine *Weird Tales* magazine. Ray lived the adventurous life of some of his characters, sailing across the seven seas, engaging in colorful, improbable exploits, and during that time, caring little for his literary reputation.

Ray's gigantic output can be divided into three parts. Under his own name, he wrote many short stories, which were collected in a number of volumes and have since become horror classics. His stories were steeped in the rich, mist-shrouded atmosphere of his native Flanders. In them, unspeakable creatures stalked the wintry darkness, pathetic neighbors hid unmentionable secrets and committed gruesome murders. Ray's major collections were *Les Contes du Whisky* (*The Tales of Whiskey*,

1925), *La Croisière des Ombres* (*The Cruise of Shadows*, 1932), *Les Cercles de l'Epouvante* (*The Circles of Terror*, 1943), *Les Derniers Contes de Canterbury* (*The Last Tales of Canterbury*, 1944), *Le Livre des Fantômes* (*The Book of Ghosts*, 1947), *Le Carrousel des Maléfices* (*The Spellbound Merry-Go-Round*, 1964) and *Les Contes Noirs du Golf* (*Dark Tales of Golf*, 1964).

In 1943, Ray wrote two novels, *Malpertuis* (1943) and *La Cité de l'Indicible Peur* (*The City of the Unspeakable Fear*, 1943). *Malpertuis* was about an ancient, terror-filled mansion where a dying warlock had trapped the aging gods of Olympus inside the "skins" of ordinary Flemish citizens. It was immediately hailed as a classic of the genre, and in 1972 was made into an eponymous film by Belgian film-maker Harry **Kumel** (see Book 1, Chapter I). *La Cité de l'Indicible Peur* was

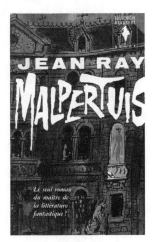

more of a horror thriller. In it, a series of ghastly deeds and creatures plagued the small, isolated British village of Ingersham. Eventually, there was a rational explanation—except for a single ghost, who turned out to be harmless. It, too, was made into a 1964 film, unfortunately in a comedic vein (see Book 1, Chapter I).

Under the name of "John Flanders," or any of his other pseudonyms, Ray wrote (often in Flemish) a number of juvenile adventure novels, many incorporating science fiction or fantasy elements, as well as an estimated 300 stories in various French, Belgian, and Flemish magazines, including the famous *Vlaamse Filmkens* (1930-45).

The third part of Ray's literary output was even more interesting. Europe, too, had its age of pulps. Some were translations of American series such as *Nick Carter*, but many others were written by native authors. Among these, the best and the most famous of all was an unauthorized Sherlock Holmes pastiche, *Harry Dickson*, sub-titled "the American Sherlock Holmes."

The original series began in Germany in 1907, and was comprised of 230 issues in total. The name Sherlock Holmes was actually used for the first ten issues, and replaced by that of *Harry Dickson*, or *Harry Taxon* (depending on the editions), afterwards, after some concern about the legitimate wrath of Sir Arthur Conan Doyle's lawyers.

Sixteen issues of the original German series were

adapted into French in 1907-08 by Fernand Laven for the magazine *La Nouvelle Populaire* under the title *Les Dossiers Secrets du Roi des Détectives* (*The Secret Files of the King of Detectives*). A Dutch/Flemish edition was later launched in 1929. In1931, publisher Hip Janssens asked Jean Ray to translate the Dutch edition into French.

Quickly, Ray became tired of translating the mediocre original stories.Using the titles and the covers (by noted German artist Alfred Roloff, a member of the Berlin Academy) as starting points, he began to write his own stories. Out of 178 published *Harry Dickson* tales, experts agree that Ray totally recreated 109, and adapted perhaps another dozen. It is no exaggeration to say that Roloff's covers greatly contributed to the series' success since, when they stopped, it had to be discontinued. Because the covers generally depicted events taking place before World War I, although the stories themselves were supposed to take place in the 1930s, Ray had to draw on his fertile imagination to create an atmosphere of musty death and decadence, of small villages where time and fashions had stood still.

The adventures of Harry Dickson and his young-assistant, Tom Wills, have delighted several generations of readers. Because they were written by a master of the *fantastique*, they quickly became more fantasy-oriented than the Holmesian canon. The best and most fondly remembered *Harry Dickson* stories were not those where the great detective fought a spy or a blackmailer in true Holmesian fashion, but those that pit him against some monstrous fallen angel. What the intellect lost in logic and deduction, the readers gained in pure entertainment and fantasy.

Although a rational explanation—often itself leaning heavily toward science fantasy—was always provided at the end of each story, under Ray's pen, Dickson battled a series of villains that even Holmes would never have dreamed of:

Euryale Ellis, a beautiful woman who had the power to turn her victims into stone and who may have been a reincarnation of the legendary Gorgon, Medusa (No. 163); Gurrhu, a living Aztec god who hid in an underground temple located beneath the very heart of London, filled with scientifically advanced devices (No. 93); the last, living Babylonian mummies who found refuge under a Scottish lake (No. 147); a nefarious blood-drinking serial killer dubbed the "Vampire with red eyes" (No. 81); the enigmatic, tuxedo-suited avenger known as "Cric-Croc, the Walking Dead" (No. 146); a death-dealing android with a silver face (No. 151); the-murderous spy code-named the Blue Stork (No. 119); the super-villain Mysteras, who relied on elaborate and deadly illusions (Nos. 103-104); the bloodthirsty Hindu god-Hanuman (No. 68), the killing sect of the Moon Knights; and many more. *Harry Dickson*'s fame in France rivals that of *Sherlock Holmes* and *Arsène Lupin*. Filmmaker Alain **Resnais** tried, unsuccessfully, to get a live-action *Harry Dickson* feature off the ground in the 1960s. *Harry Dickson* thrives today as two competing comic-book series (see Book 1, Chapter IV).

Loved by a growing number of fans, Jean Ray was sadly only "discovered" by the critics and the mainstream public just before his death, in the early 1960s. Ray's fiction provided a transition between the purely supernatural horrors of past centuries and modern concepts such as parallel dimensions and alien entities *à la* Lovecraft. His protagonists, however, were resolute and more likely to face the forces of darkness than go mad or cringe away from them in terror. There is no way to overestimate Ray's importance in French-language horror fiction. Ray left a powerful mark not only upon French, but also Flemish, genre literature. Like Lovecraft, he was the forefather of a modern school of horror writers.

CHAPTER VII

Science Fiction
Entre-Deux Guerres
(Between the Wars) (1918–1950)

World War I, with its 2.3 million dead and crippled, definitely buried the 19th century and sapped the confidence of French society. Deep wounds were created in the collective psyche: On the one hand, France had won the war, and chauvinistic pride and xenophobic arrogance were at an all-time high. On the other hand, things could never be the same again. This almost schizoid conflict between the illusion of superiority that boosted the desire to preserve traditional values, and the emergence of new—and therefore threatening—ideas intending to break with the past was played out, with dramatic results, in the field of science fiction.

Science fiction between the wars became the theater of another battle, between the forces of conservatism and the forces of progress. Unfortunately, the contribution of science and technology to the slaughter of World War I was only too obvious: Aviation, tanks, the machine gun, rockets, and deadly gas. had not carried people to the moon or across the globe, but instead had killed millions of young Frenchmen. The emphasis being on "young," for one of the unintended consequences of World War I was that it polarized the conflict between "old" values and "young" ones, and the young ones lost.

Since Jules **Verne**, French science fiction had made prodigious conceptual leaps forward, not unlike what happened in the United States in the 1930s and 1940s. If the comforting, optimistic scientific anticipations of Verne had not entirely disappeared, they had nevertheless been submerged in a more ambitious, constantly expanding genre. By the time World War I erupted, the prodigious **Rosny** Aîné had evoked the end of our civilization; **Le Faure** & De **Graffigny** had explored the solar system; **La Hire** and **Le Rouge** had investigated the use of mind powers; **Renard** and **Couvreur** had worried about medical experiments; De

Quirielle and **Corday** had created artificial life; **Béliard** and **Robida** had travelled through time. This was an unparalleled thematic record, unmatched by what was happening at the time in England and America.

After the war, however, because the new science fiction embodied the future and represented values that were perceived by the older French cultural elite as threatening the stability and conservatism of society, it was increasingly relegated to the shelves of juvenile publishing; and ultimately, even there, it was fought and driven out on philosophical and ideological grounds. The same reactionary forces that, in 1941, stood behind Marshal Petain and literally split France in half, the same conservative forces that equated science with "heretic" Darwinism, thought that the heavens should be inhabited by angels, not aliens, and generally believed that their mission was to protect France and the *Occident Chrétien* (*Christian Occident*) from the depraved forces of progress and the outside world, pilloried the new science fiction.

Belgian scholar Jacques **Van Herp** found that, between 1923 and 1925, the publishers of the magazines *L'Intrépide* and *Sciences et Voyages* lost no less than five libel suits against various Catholic organizations that had slandered them, their authors, and their publications. Other magazines, such as *Science et Vie* and authors like Maurice **Renard** were also targeted by the same reactionary forces. The words of one of the judgments rendered against *Sciences et Voyages* in 1925 leave no room for doubt: The court found that the magazine exerted a "pernicious influence on the imagination and intelligence of children"!

Ideas, like men, can be killed in battle. This was exactly what happened to French science fiction. The conservatives' message was heard loudly and clearly throughout the French publishing establishment. The next few years saw a gradual end to the publication of ground-breaking novels about interplanetary exploration, biological experiments, and mind powers. Instead, we saw a return to the tamer, non-threatening, Earth-based adventures of the late 19thcentury. Publisher Hachette sought refuge behind the politically correct name of Jules Verne and created a "Jules Verne Award" in 1926; with one exception, however, it was awarded to mediocre novels and was abandoned in 1933.

By the end of the 1920s, just as Hugo Gernsback's *Amazing Stories* (1926) was preparing to bloom on the other side of the Atlantic Ocean, the Golden Age of French science fiction had effectively ended, shot down on the ideological battlefield by the more powerful, conservative elements of a society which refused progress. It can be said with some degree of validity that French science fiction never recovered.

1. The End of the Golden Age

World War I had, directly or indirectly, been responsible for the cancellation of virtually all the major genre imprints. After the war, science fiction was mostly relegated to popular adventure imprints that carried little or no literary respectability.

Publisher Jules Tallandier was one of the most active in the field with:

The long-lived *Bibliothèque des Grandes Aventures* (*Library of Great Adventures*, 1923-30), renamed *Grandes Aventures-Voyages Excentriques* (*Great Adventures-Eccentric Voyages*, 1930-42), then simply *Grandes Aventures* (*Great Adventures*, 1949-53).

Les Romans Mystérieux (*Mysterious Novels*, 1927-50).

Voyages Lointains-Aventures Étranges (*Far Voyages-Strange Adventures*, 1927-32).

À Travers l'Univers (*Throughout the Universe*, 1932-33 and 1952-53).

Les Chevaliers de l'Aventure (*The Knights of Adventure*, 1930-34).

Les Meilleurs Romans d'Aventures (*The Best Adventure Novels*, 1937-38).

Le Livre d'Aventures (*The Book of Adventures*, 1937-38 and 1952-53).

Le Lynx (*The Lynx*, 1940-41).

And, finally, *Univers-Aventures* (*Adventure Universe*, 1949-53).

Among the writers published by these various imprints were **Boussenard**, d'**Ivoi**, **Falcoz**, **Bonneau**, **Thébault**, **Groc**, **Petithuguenin**, de **Wailly**, **Armandy**, **Couvreur**, and **Magog**.

Tallandier's main competitor was a Hungarian expatriate, J. Ferenczi, who published:

Les Romans d'Aventures (*Adventure Novels*, 1921-29).

Le Livre de l'Aventure (*The Book of Adventure*, 1929-31).

Voyages et Aventures (*Voyages and Adventures*, 1933-41).

Le Petit Roman d'Aventures (*The Little Adventure Novels*, 1936-39)

Mon Roman d'Aventures (*My Adventure Novels*, 1942-1956).

Among the writers published by these various imprints were **La Hire**, **Thévenin**, **Dazergues** (writing as "Mad"), de **Graffigny**, and **Limat**.

To this impressive list should be added:

Collection d'Aventures (*Adventure Collection*, 1918-27), by publisher Offenstadt, featuring novels by Pierre **Adam** and **Moselli**.

Contes et Romans Pour Tous (*Tales and Novels for All*, 1927-36), by publisher Larousse, featuring works by **Allorge**, **Bernay**, and **Le Rouge**.

Aventures et Voyages (*Adventures and Voyages*, 1929-48), by publisher Fernand Nathan.

L'Aventure (*Adventure*, 1929-30), by publisher Fayard, featuring works by d'**Agraives** and **Thébault**.

Romans pour la Jeunesse (*Novels for the Young*, 1932-35), by publisher Rouff.

The magazines continued to fulfill their important function. In addition to the weeklies, *Le Journal des Voyages* (*The Journal of Voyages*) and *L'Intrépide* (*The Fearless*), and the monthlies *Lectures Pour Tous* (*Reading for All*) and *Je Sais Tout* (*I Know Everything*), new magazines started between the wars included:

The important *Sciences et Voyages* (*Science and Voyages*, 1919-1935), published by Offenstadt (which already published *L'Intrépide*), featuring works by **Groc**, **Moselli** and **Thévenin**.

The short-lived *À l'Aventure* (*To Adventure*, 1920-21), which serialized some genre novels under the editorship of Louis-Frédéric **Rouquette**.

Oeuvres Libres (*Free Works*, 1921-40), published by Fayard, featuring works by **Couvreur**, **Farrère**, and **Vallerey**.

a. Major Authors

Two major science fiction authors of the period were J.-H. **Rosny** Aîné, with the ground-breaking *Les Navigateurs de l'Infini* (*The Navigators of Infinity*, 1925), already reviewed in Chapter V, and Maurice **Renard**.

Renard had already made his mark on the genre with the two classics, *Le Docteur Lerne* (*Dr. Lerne*, 1908) and *Le Péril Bleu* (*The Blue Peril*, 1912). In a 1913 short story, *Le Brouillard du 26 Octobre* (The Mist of Oc-

tober 26th), he told how two scientists were transported back in time to the Miocene Era and encountered winged beings. In 1920, Renard wrote *Les Mains d'Orlac* (*The Hands of Orlac*), in which the hands of a killer were transplanted onto a pianist. *L'Homme Truqué* (*The Phony Man*, 1921) featured the graft of "electroscopic" eyes onto a man blinded during the war. The result was the strange description of a world perceived through artificial senses. *L'Homme Qui Voulait Être Invisible* (*The Man Who Wanted to Be Invisible*, 1923) dealt excellently with the issue of invisibility; in it, **Renard** exposed the scientific fallacy inherent in Wells' famous novel. Since, in order to function, the human eye must perform as an opaque darkroom, any truly invisible man would also be blind! In the controversial *Le Singe* (*The Monkey*, 1924), written with Albert **Jean**, Renard imagined the creation of artificial lifeforms through the process of "radiogenesis," a sort of human electrocopying process. The novel was ferociously attacked by the Catholic press, which saw it as sacrilegious, and blacklisted by public libraries.

Un Homme chez les Microbes: Scherzo (*A Man Amongst the Microbes: Scherzo*, 1928) was one of the first scientific novels on the theme of miniaturization, not forgetting **Bleunard**'s *Toujours Plus Petits* (*Always Smaller*, 1893), certainly one of the first to introduce the concept of a micro-world where atoms were microscopic solar systems with planets. Renard's hero submitted himself willingly to a shrinking process that eventually ran out of control. As in Richard Matheson's 1956 classic, *The Shrinking Man,* the hero was then attacked by insects and other menaces before eventually arriving on an electron-size planet, where scientifically advanced people were able to reverse the process and send him home. Finally, *Le Maître de la Lumière* (*The Light Master*, 1933) anticipated Bob Shaw's notorious "slow glass" by introducing the concept of a glass that condensed time. Because of his understanding and knowledge of the genre—he even wrote an article on the "*merveilleux scientifique*" (scientific marvellous) in 1914 for a major newspaper—Renard could have been a major literary breakthrough figure, comparable to a Clarke or an Asimov in England and the United States. Instead, because of the conservative pressures mentioned above, and the French context of the period, he remained a minor writer, known only to specialists.

The treatment accorded to José **Moselli** was ever more unjust, since all of his works were published only in magazine form, and none were collected in book form until the 1970s, even though all scholars agree that he was one of the most interesting genre authors of the 1920s and 1930s. Moselli was one of the most prolific and popular "house authors" of Offenstadt and most of his literary output was published in *L'Intrépide* and *Sciences et Voyages*. Like Renard, Moselli could have become another H. G. Wells had the publishing opportunities existed. He embodied many of the qualities of modern science fiction writers: A seemingly endless variety of daring ideas, introduced seriously and not

for satirical purposes, exploited logically and not serving merely as a pretext for a wild adventure; featuring fully developed, believable characters rather than cardboard hero figures.

A brief panorama of some of Moselli's early genre output remains, even today, an impressive catalog of ideas: *Le Téléluz* (1918) was about a helmet that enabled his wearer to see and hear scenes that took place miles away. *La Prison de Glace* (*The Ice Prison*, 1920) dealt with a form of controlled hibernation. *Le Rayon Phi* (*The Phi Ray*, 1921) was a powerful death ray. *La Corde d'Acier* (*The Rope of Steel*, 1921) featured a gang of criminals whose scheme involved dropping transparent corpses from the air. In *Les Conquérants de l'Abîme* (*The Conquerors of the Abyss*, 1922), a scientist devised a mean to modify the course of the Gulf Stream. In *Le Maître de la Foudre* (*The Lightning Master*, 1922), a Japanese mad scientist used a death ray-like device to destroy ships at a distance. *Le Voyage Éternel* (*The Eternal Voyage*, 1923) was the tale of the first failed Moon exploration venture in which a space prospector discovered he could not return to Earth. *La Cité du Gouffre* (*The City of the Pit*, 1925) featured an underwater city. *L'Archipel de l'Épouvante* (*The Archipelago of Terror*, 1926) was a Lost World story.

Two works of this period particularly stood out. *Le Messager de la Planète* (*The Messenger of the Planet*, 1924) was not unlike John W. Campbell's classic "Who Goes There?" aka "The Thing" in that it featured the discovery of an alien whose ship crashed near the South Pole. But here, the alien turned out to be an advanced and peaceful being from the planet Mercury. Unfortunately, the sled dogs killed the alien before he could share his knowledge with the Earthmen who rescued him.

The visionary *La Fin d'Illa* (*The End of Illa*, 1925) began with the emergence of a new Pacific island on which were found a cache of ancient documents and a small fragment of "zero-stone." A San Francisco scientist then managed to decypher the documents, which told the tale of the final, apocalyptic clash between the now-lost Gondwanan cities of Illa and Nour. Later, his maid unwittingly threw the "zero-stone" fragment into the fireplace, thus causing the famous 1905 earthquake. *La Fin d'Illa* not only featured an array of impressive technological predictions, such as atom bombs, solar-powered cities, force fields, and flying saucers, but also a grim catalog of social predictions. The Illians were described as a technologically advanced race who lost their will to fight and their feelings of humanity. They were served by undermen, genetically manufactured from apes for use as slave labor. Their leader was Rair, a proto-Hitler with a Fascist police force who violently suppressed any opponents to the regime. Rair's dreams of conquest eventually led Illa to total destruction after the dictator obtained the secret of nuclear disintegration (the "zero-stone") and used it on the neighboring city-state of Nour. In *La Fin d'Illa*, Moselli not only anticipated the sociological and technological horrors of World War II and Naziism, but was also the first to equate nuclear conflict—even one clearly won by one of the two combatants—with mutual destruction. *La Fin d'Illa* may well be one of the stories responsible for the harsh, unjust 1925 verdict rendered by the court against *Sciences et Voyages*, where it was published.

Moselli was a perfect example of self-censorship at work as a result of the pressures described above. His later works evidenced a return to safer, tamer ideas. Three novels could nevertheless be mentioned: In *La Guerre des Océans* (*The War of the Oceans*, 1929), Fédor Ivanovitch Sarraskine, like a vengeful Captain Nemo, used his science to attack the British and American fleets; he also surgically turned his victims into unwilling fish-men, thereby ensuring their obedience. In *L'Empereur du Pacifique* (*The Emperor of the Pacific*, 1932-35), mad scientist Ambrose Vollmer turned a Pacific atoll into a nightmarish Doctor Moreau-like kingdom of radio-controlled zombies and human experiments. Finally, *L'Île des Hommes Bleus* (*The Island of the Blue Men*, 1939) was yet another variation in the same theme. In it, millionaire Wasili Tchorok used the knowledge of scientist Antoine Chantour to build a giant floating city in a geostationary orbit; the eponymous "blue men" were surgically modified to breathe in the upper atmosphere.

Renard and Moselli were, without a doubt, the two major genre authors of the 1920s. However, H.-J. **Magog**, while not as significant as they, deserves special recognition. Magog was the author of many popular adventure novels, many of which displayed a wild and unique imaginative streak. But from a literary standpoint, they were often marred by their pulpish nature. In *Extraordinaire Aventures de Deux Fiancés à travers le Monde* (*Extraordinary Adventures of Two Fiancés Across the World*, 1922), which took place in 2050, a Japanese mad scientist used the heat from the Earth's core to cause the oceans to dry up, but the ensuing volcanic eruptions ended up destroying Japan. In *L'Île Tombée du Ciel* (*The Island Which Fell From the Sky*, 1923), a piece of a wandering planet fell near Australia; its human explorers discovered that it was inhabited by invisible aliens who turned out to be benevolent. *Trois Ombres sur Paris* (*Three Shadows Over Paris*, 1928) also took place in the 21st century and featured the artificial creation of a race of supermen, and their conflict with the political powers of the times. Its conclusion was remarkably similar to the 1935 Olaf Stapledon novel, *Odd John*, in which the supermen were exiled to an island where they eventually destroyed themselves.

H.-J. Magog also collaborated with the son of prolific serial writer Paul **Féval** (see Chapter IV), Paul **Féval** Fils, on a sprawling, rambling serial entitled *Les Mystères de Demain* (*The Mysteries of Tomorrow*, 1922-23), an obvious homage to **Sue**'s *Les Mystères de Paris*. In it, the good scientist Oronius fought the evil schemes of the evil German scientist, Hantzen, and his Hindu female mystic, Yogha. *Les Mystères de Demain* took a kitchen sink approach to the genre, including all the possible clichés: secret base on top of the Everest, "carnoplastic" surgery, soul transfers, mud-eating mountain dwarfs, salamander beings living at the Earth's core, germ warfare, and the rebirth of prehistoric Atlantis.

Maurice **Leblanc**, the father of the popular gentleman-burglar Arsène Lupin (see Chapter IV), would undoubtedly have made an excellent science fiction writer, one to rival Renard and Moselli, had he continued in that vein, but time allowed him to write only two genre novels. *Les Trois Yeux* (*The Three Eyes*, 1919) was a remarkable novel about communication between alien races. In it, a scientist discovered how to receive images from Venus, whose inhabitants turned out to be three-eyed aliens. At first, the Venusians transmitted images from Earth's past, then pictures of their own, almost incomprehensibly alien society, seemingly based on triangular logic. **Leblanc** also wrote *Le Formidable Evènement* (*The Formidable Event*, 1920), in which an earthquake caused a new land mass to emerge between France and England.

Finally, René **Thévenin**, already mentioned in Chapter V, was another good example of a writer of popular but undistinguished adventure serials, such as *Le Maître des Vampires* (*The Master of Vampires*, 1923), *La Jungle Insurgée* (*The Insurgent Jungle*, 1926), *Sous les Griffes du Monstre* (*Under the Claws of the Monster*, 1926), and *La Forêt Sanglante* (*The Bloody Forest*, 1927), who suddenly, like Moselli, rose above the pulpish nature of the medium and penned two genuine classics. *Les Chasseurs d'Hommes* (*The Manhunters*, 1930) took place in Darkest Africa and told the story of two superpowered mutants who hunt men to feed on their lifeforce. The mutants used their parapsychic powered to recreate an Eden-like garden behind a force field, in which they studied two humans. The male mutant was eventually killed by a free man ("wolf"); his mate, who may have been pregnant, disappeared after being saved by a slave ("dog"). Thévenin also wrote a good prehistoric novel, *L'Ancêtre des Hommes* (*The Ancestor of Men*, 1932), and is also credited by science fiction scholars with *Sur l'Autre Face du Monde* (*On the Other Side of the World*, 1935), a novel written under the pseudonymn of "André **Valérie**." Anticipating Arthur C. Clarke's classic *Against the Fall of Night*, the novel told the story of the confrontation between the civilized men who survived an ice age in a fortified city and the savage hunters who managed to survive on the surface of the planet. The lone explorer sent by the city to explore the outside world was eventually torn between two societies that were not yet ready to cohabit peacefully. (See *Futuropolis* in Book 1, Chapter V.)

b. Other Notable Writers

In this section, we will review other notable genre works published in the 1920s and 1930s, grouping them along thematic lines.

COSMIC JOURNEYS

This section covers journeys through time and space, as well as encounters with alien lifeforms.

Mars was still very much the preferred destination when it came to space travel. The oddly-entitled *D'Amra sur Azulba* (*Of Amra on Azulba*, 1917) by Prince Louis de **Bourbon**, was sub-titled "Diary of a Marsian (sic) on Earth" and was the satirical tale of a Martian who came to Earth (called "Azulba" in his language) on a radium-powered ship, during World War I.

In Marcel **Laurian**'s *L'Étrange Voyage* (*The Strange Journey*, 1912), a Persian Magus transported an entire Earth mountain and its inhabitants to Mars. Laurian's Red Planet was inhabited by prehistoric monsters, electro-magnetic beings, black-skinned and red-skinned anthropoids, winged sphinxes, mermaids, and cyclops. The heroes even met the famous seer Nostradamus!

In **Miral-Viger**'s *L'Anneau de Feu* (*The Ring of Fire*, 1922; aka *L'Anneau de Lumière* (*The Ring of Light*)), a rocket used the controlled disintegration of "virium"—a fictional material 60,000 more powerful than radium—to propel itself through space.

The writing team of Théo **Varlet** and Octave **Jonquel** wrote a two-volume epic, *Les Titans du Ciel* (*The Titans of the Sky*, 1921) and *L'Agonie de la Terre* (*The Agony of Earth*, 1922), which was clearly influenced by Wells' classic *War of the Worlds*. In it, the Jovians intervened after another Martian attack on Earth. The Jovians then destroyed Mars, using focused solar energy. But the Martians migrated to Earth en masse, our planet being revealed as the place where Martian souls reincarnate. Souls are alleged to travel inward from Mars, to the Earth, to Venus, to Mercury, to end up one with the Sun. This explained the original invasion. Curiously, Varlet and Jonquel's Martians were described as creatures not at all like Wells' but more like **Le Rouge**'s Martians. In the second volume, the Earthmen fought the body-snatching Martians, this time with the help of the Venusians.

Varlet alone also wrote *La Grande Panne* (*The Great Breakdown*, 1930), which featured Aurore Lescure, a character who may well be the first fictional woman astronaut, and the theme of a deadly virus—in this case, one devouring electricity—brought back to Earth by a spaceship. Its sequel, *Aurore Lescure, Pilote d'Astronef*, written soon after, was not published (and then only posthumously) until 1943.

The writing team of Victor Cyril and Dr. Eugène Berger, signing **Cyril-Berger**, penned *L'Adversaire Inconnu* (*The Unknown Adversary*, 1922), in which the egg of a small, chameleon-like, vampiric alien arrived on Earth on a meteorite. After hatching, the creature became stranded on Earth.

Two other notable works of interplanetary fiction were Belgian author Pierre **Nothomb**'s *La Rédemption de Mars* (*The Redemption of Mars*, 1922); and Michel **Epuy**'s *Anthéa, ou l'Étrange Planète* (*Anthea, or the Strange Planet*, 1923).

Henri **Allorge**, in *Ciel contre Terre* (*Heaven vs. Earth*, 1924), described an attack on our planet by vampire-like Martians who owed much to Le Rouge's 1908 *Le Prisonnier de la Planète Mars* (*The Prisoner of Planet Mars*). These Martians, however, were defeated by alcohol.

Henri de **Graffigny** (see Chapter V) returned to the more ambitious theme of the exploration of the solar system with *Voyage de Cinq Américains dans les Planètes* (*Voyage of Five Americans on the Planets*, 1925), and penned *Les Diamants de la Lune* (*The Diamonds of the Moon*, 1930), which featured a rocket-plane and the mineral exploitation of our satellite. Another notable novel by de Graffigny was *Electropolis* (1933), a lost world novel.

René **Trotet de Bargis** followed in the same vein with *La Mission de Quatre Savants* (*The Mission of Four Scientists*, 1925).

The prolific Jean de **La Hire** penned the thirty-volume serial, *Les Grandes Aventures d'un Boy Scout* (*The Great Adventures of a Scout*, 1926), which included many interplanetary adventures with lurid titles such as *Les Hommes de Mars* (*The Men From Mars*), *Chasses Martiennes* (*Martian Hunts*), *Le Rayon-Ardent* (*The Fiery Ray*), *La Vengeance des Kolops* (*The Revenge of the Kolops*), *Vers le Tour du Monde Saturnien* (*Across the World of Saturn*), and *Le Drame des Hommes-Taureaux* (*The Tragedy of the Men-Bull*).

Jean **Petithuguenin**, in *Une Mission Internationale sur la Lune* (*An International Mission on the Moon*, 1926) included a modern description of a rocket trip to the Moon, taking into account acceleration, weightlessness, the use of lateral rockets to turn the ship prior to landing, airlocks, and spacesuits.

In 1928, writer/illustrator Henri **Lanos**, whose art had graced the covers for *Je Sais Tout* since 1905 and *Lectures Pour Tous* since 1910, wrote and illustrated *Le Grand Raid Paris-La Lune* (*The Great Paris-Moon Race*), serialized in *Pierrot*, another juvenile magazine.

Also in 1928, an unknown writer who used the pseudonym "**Cabarel**" published the two-volume imaginative yet naive *Dans l'Étrange Inconnu* (*Into the Strange Unknown*), in which the author, using hypnosis and astral projection, visited two unseen satellites of Earth, Ersa and Nemea, as well as other planets of the solar system and other star systems, including Sirius. The second volume included a trip to Ancient Lemuria, or Mu, 60,000 years in the past, and the resurrection of the ancient priestess, Oris.

In a somewhat more serious vein, Albert **Bailly**'s *L'Éther-Alpha* (1929), the best novel to be awarded the Jules Verne Award, imagined a spaceship made of coagulated aether, the eponymous "ether-apha," a substance both hard and transparent. In the novel, the ship travelled to the Moon, where the explorers encountered the "Radios," energy-based Selenites. After testing the humans, the Radios eventually decided they did not want to live next to them and took our satellite far away from Earth.

Another Martian novel was Paul **Darcy**'s *La Conquête de la Planète Mars* (*The Conquest of Planet Mars*), serialized in *Le Petit Illustré* in 1929.

In René **Pujol**'s *Le Soleil Noir* (*The Black Sun*, 1929), a cataclysm threatened to destroy Earth. In his *La Planète Invisible* (*The Invisible Planet*, 1931), a new planet was discovered in the solar system. Finally, in *Au Temps des Brumes* (*In the Times of the Mist*, 1932), Earth was enveloped by a mysterious cosmic black cloud that stopped all sunlight.

In Pierre **Lavaur**'s *La Conquête de la Terre* (*The Conquest of Earth*, 1931), it was the telekinetic Jovians who attacked our planet, and were defeated through "atomic power."

Raoul **Brémond**'s dry and academic *Par-Delà l'Univers* (*Beyond the Universe*, 1931) was undoubtedly one of the first novels ever written to deal with the theme of a journey through the fourth dimension on a purely scientific basis.

On the other hand, Étienne de **Riche**'s *Le Raid Fantastique* (*The Fantastic Raid*, 1931) dismissed the notion of rocket-powered space travel because of the lack of atmosphere to push against!

"Les Anekphantes," one of the two stories contained in Roger **Farney**'s collection *Deux Histoires Fabuleuses* (*Two Fabulous Stories*, 1931), featured microscopic, cell-like alien intelligences living among us on Earth, who became aware of man's existence following the discovery of radio.

Marcel **Jeanjean**'s *La Merveilleuse Invention de l'Oncle Pamphile* (*Uncle Pamphile's Marvellous Invention*, 1930) was published as a juvenile novel, illustrated by the author (who was the official painter of the Air Ministry), but was both a space travel and a time travel story, including themes such as the colonization of other worlds, the dangers of excess reliance on robots, and the modification of Earth's rotation.

But the definitive time travel novel of the period was Jacques **Rigaut**'s *Un Brillant Sujet* (*A Brilliant Subject*, 1921), in which a scientist built a time machine and travelled seven years back into the past. There, he met an old flame and his younger self. Travelling on, he met his mother and, unlike in the movie *Back to the Future*, discovered that he may well be his own father. The daring hero pursued his journey into the past, not afraid of killing Jesus, cutting off Cleopatra's nose and teaching the Incas about steam power and electricity. He finally died of old age before reaching the Genesis.

OTHER LANDS AND MAD SCIENCE

The tradition of the adventure serial that had been perfectly embodied before the war by writers such as Paul d'**Ivoi** (see Chapter V) continued with a vengeance between the wars. by then, the ingredients were familiar: Fast-paced, globe-trotting adventures, centering around a single genre concept such as super-powered vehicle, a futuristic weapon, the discovery of a Lost World, a Hidden Empire or a Secret City; featuring brave heroes, demure girlfriends and dastardly villains, megalomaniacal would-be world conquerors, and mad scientists, often of Germanic or Asian origins.

Old hands at this craft included Gustave **Le Rouge** who, in 1923, penned *Les Aventures de Todd Marvel, Détective Milliardaire* (*The Adventures of Todd Marvel, Billionaire Detective*), and Jean de **La Hire**, who continued his prolific serial writing career with adventure novels such as *La Prisonnière du Dragon Rouge* (*The Prisoner of the Red Dragon*, 1923), *Les Dompteurs de Forces* (*The Tamers of Forces*, 1925), *La Captive du Soleil d'Or* (*The Captive of the Golden Sun*, 1926), the six-volume *Les Aventures de Paul Ardent* (*The Adventures of Paul Ardent*, 1928), *Les Amazones* (*The Amazons*, 1930) and numerous others.

Even Gaston **Leroux**, the "father" of *Rouletabille* and the *Phantom of the Opera* (see Chapter IV), contributed *Les Aventures Effroyables de Herbert de Renich* (*The Frightful Adventures of Herbert De Renich*, 1917-20), an epic undersea saga which was his answer to Verne's *Twenty-Thousand Leagues Under the Sea*.

Other notable practitioners in this vein included:

Georges G.-**Toudouze** who, in *Le Petit Roi d'Ys* (*The Little King of Ys*, 1913), featured a submarine tank looking for the legendary city. His *Les Sous-Marins Fantômes* (*The Phantom Submarines*, 1921) also dealt with the exploitation of the ocean. *Les Compagnons de l'Iceberg en Feu* (*The Companions of the Burning Iceberg*, 1922) featured a frozen sailor of the Spanish Armada brought back to life. Other ocean-themed adventure novels by Toudouze included *Le Corsaire du Pacifique* (*The Corsair of the Pacific*, 1929) and *Le Secret de l'Île d'Acier* (*The Secret of the Island of Steel*, 1934). His best-known work was a loosely-connected series of novels entitled *Les Aventuriers de la Science* (*The Adventurers of Science*), whose first volume, *L'Homme qui Volait le Gulf-Stream* (*The Man Who Stole the Gulf-Stream*, 1925), featured the descendent of an Aztec king who compelled a misguided scientist to create a new form of coral to divert the Gulf Stream; and *L'Éveilleur de Volcans* (*The Awakwener of Volcanos*, 1926), about the taming of erupting peaks.

Pierre **Adam**, like Moselli, was a regular contributor to *L'Intrépide* throughout the 1920s and 1930s. According to some scholars, "Pierre Adam" may have been a pseudonym for writer Antonin **Seuhl** (see below). Adam's most notorious serials included *La Sirène aux Yeux Fauves* (*The Mermaid with Fawn Eyes*, 1916), *Les Yeux d'Acier* (*The Eyes of Steel*, 1916), *L'Usine Infernale* (*The Infernal Factory*, 1919-20), and *Les Buveurs d'Espace* (*The Drinkers of Space*, 1922), in which the heroes use a super-plane/submarine to explore a heretofore unknown land. In the Lost World tradition, Adam penned *Le Maître des Abîmes* (*The Master of the Abyss*, 1927), *Le Royaume du Silence* (*The Kingdom of*

Silence, 1929) and *La Reine des Mayas* (*The Queen of the Mayas*, 1933). Adam also wrote *Le Grand Choc* (*The Great Clash*, 1922), in which a mad scientist tried to reverse Earth's magnetic poles, and *Le Gouffre aux Surprises* (*The Pit of Surprises*, 1932), in which another mad scientist brainwashed his victims in order to transfer other people's personalities into their minds.

Journal des Voyages editor Guy de **Téramond** contributed the sprawling 25-issue serial, *Vingt Mille Lieues à travers le Monde* (*20,000 Leagues Across the World*, 1923-24), which included a grab-bag of classic themes such as a Lost World located at the Pole, a Journey to the center of the Earth, the flying island of Laputa, telepathy, Hindu yoghi, vampires, evil Germans, and even a full-blown prehistoric novel insert, *À la Recherche du Plésiosaure* (*In Search of the Plesiosaurus*). Other notable works by de Téramond included *Ravengar* (1922), a novel on the theme of invisibility; *L'Homme qui Voit à travers les Murailles* (*The Man Who Could See Through Walls*, 1913), about a radium-powered superman; and *Le Faiseur de Monstres* (*The Monster Maker*, 1930), featuring a mad surgeon.

With *Rapa Nui* (1923) André **Armandy** explored the mysteries of Easter Island. His *Le Démon Bleu* (*The Blue Demon*, 1926) introduced a race of powerful mole men. Other notable Armandy titles included *L'Île de Corail* (*The Coral Island*, 1927) and *Terre de Suspicion* (*Land of Suspicion*, 1926).

Jean d'**Agraives** wrote novels such as *La Cité des Sables* (*The City of the Sands*, 1924), which featured a giant flying ship armed with paralysing rays; *Le Rayon Svastika* (*The Swastika Ray*, 1926); *Le Virus 34* (*The Virus 34*, 1929); *Le Sorcier de la Mer* (*The Wizard of the Sea*, 1927), about a mad scientist who used radiation to control the creatures who live underwater and threaten the world with mass starvation; the novel also included some interesting notions like making oil from fish and an Inca Lost World in Tierra del Fuego; and *L'Empire des Algues* (*Empire of Seaweed*, 1935), in which a chemist who discovered "algol," a new super-fuel made from algae, was kidnapped by the Germans and the Japanese and forced to work for them in their secret Sargasso Sea base. D'Agraives also penned the more noteworthy *L'Aviateur de Bonaparte* (*Bonaparte's Aviator*, 1926), which theorized that Napoleon owed his victories to secret aerial reconnaissance.

Albert **Bonneau**'s best novels included *La Cité sans Soleil* (*The City Without Sun*, 1927), which told the story of the battle between two secret Egyptian kingdoms; and the six-volume *Les Samourais du Soleil Pourpre* (*The Samurais of the Purple Sun*, 1928-31), a sprawling "Yellow Peril" epic all too typical of the times.

Maurice **Champagne** (already mentioned in Chapter V) wrote exotic adventures such as *La Cité des Premiers Hommes* (*The City of the First Men*, 1928), featuring the descendents of Hebrews who did not take refuge on Noah's Ark; *L'Île Engloutie* (*The Sunken Island*, 1929); *La Terre Perdue* (*The Lost Land*, 1930), and *L'Île Terrestre* (*The Terrestrial Island*, 1936).

André **Falcoz**, in *Le Soleil du Monde* (*The Sun of the World*, 1927), told the tale of a lost Inca city with advanced technology. Falcoz wrote novels under the pseudonyms of "Élie Montfort" and "L. Morvers." In *Les Rescapés de l'Île Verte* (*The Survivors of Green Island*, 1929), a mad scientist manufactured mutants. In *Le Semeur de Feu* (*The Sower of Fire*, 1925), another mad scientist, hidden in an underground Himalayan lair, defied the world with a death ray that could detonate explosives at a distance. Finally, in *La Poudre de Mort* (*The Powder of Death*, 1929), the evil Konserson mutated children into gnomes with hypertrophied brains to master a death ray that would enable him to conquer an Asian throne.

Guy d'**Armen** in his classic *La Cité de l'Or et de la Lèpre* (*The City of Gold and Leprosy*, 1928) featured a secret underground Tibetan city ruled by an evil, while-haired immortal called Natas (Satan spelled backwards). Anyone who escaped immediately died of leprosy. Natas was eventually defeated by the brave Francis Ardant. Armen explored variations of the same theme in *Les Troglodytes du Mont Everest* (*The Troglodytes of Mount Everest*, 1929), in which the villainous Mendax ransomed ocean liners with his superplane-cum-submarine; and *Les Géants du Lac Noir* (*The Giants of the Dark Lake*, 1931), in which the villainous Khyzil Kaya ruled a secret city protected by giant spiders, giant microbes, and giant mutants. Later, Armen included more scientific anticipations in his works. *Le Semeur de Cyclones* (*The Seeder of Cyclones*, 1931), published under the pseudonym of "Francis Annemary," introduced a mad scientist who controlled a captive volcano. His *Les Rayons Ultra-Z* (*The Ultra-Z Rays*, 1932) was a device to detect mineral deposits. *Le Secret de Frigidopolis* (*The Secret of Frigidopolis*, 1933) was about a secret, artificial city located near the Cape Horn. Finally, *La Fin d'Iramonda* (*The End of Iramonda*, 1935), published under the pseudonym of "Jacques Diamant," featured one more lost city of scientifically advanced, green-skinned men who can regenerate themselves and control various death rays.

Luc **Alberny**'s *Le Glaive sur le Monde* (*The Sword Over the World*, 1928) may well be one of the first modern conspiracy novels, and revealed that the Cathars were secretly fomenting wars, and were, in particular, responsible for World War I. In his *L'Étrange Aventure du Prof. Pamphlegme* (*The Strange Adventure of Prof. Pamphlegme*, 1933), music enabled a man to travel into the fourth dimension. Finally, in *Le Mammouth Bleu* (*The Blue Mastodon*, 1935), Alberny revealed that the Basque language originated with a race of intelligent mastodons who still lived in vast, underground caverns.

Jean **Petithuguenin**, in a more popular vein, penned *Le Roi de l'Abîme* (*The King of the Abyss*, 1928-29) and *Le Secret des Incas* (*The Secret of the Incas*, 1931).

Dr. Augustin **Galopin** wrote *Excursions du Petit Poucet*

à travers le Corps Humain (*Journeys of Tom Thumb Through the Human Body*, 1886), another novel on the theme of the "Shrinking Man," this time anticipating the film *Fantastic Voyage*. Dr. **Galopin** was the father of Arnould **Galopin** (see Chapter V and below) and the physician of Vincent Van Gogh, who painted a celebrated portrait of him.

Finally, Max-André **Dazergues** wrote *Du Sang sur les Nuages* (*Blood on the Clouds*, 1930) under the pseudonym of "André Mad." It was about a gang of sky pirates led by a genial gnome and an android woman. The hero and the female android ended up married and became the rulers of a race of Selenites on the Moon. *L'Île de Satan* (*Satan's Island*, 1931) featured an artificial island built by a mad scientist and camouflaged to look like a real island. *L'Île Aérienne* (*The Aerial Island*, 1931), written under the pseudonym of "André Star," was about another flying city. Finally, *La Fusée des Glaces* (*The Ice Rocket*, 1938) featured a super-powered submarine able to navigate under the polar ice shelf.

Some notable novels featuring Extraordinary Voyages by authors not named above included:

Pierre de **La Batut**'s *La Jeune Fille en Proie au Monstre* (*The Young Girl Who Became the Prey of a Monster*, 1920) was about an archaeologist who, exploring the ruins of an ancient Assyrian city, discovered proof of the existence of an advanced antediluvian civilisation, that of the Kirubim, a race of winged bulls with human faces. The archeologist's assistant's fiancee was kidnapped by the Kirubim, who turned out to still live in a vast underground city where they kept men as their slaves and plotted to conquer Earth. La Batut theorized in the novel that Earth's rotation around the Sun actually eroded the planet, ultimately condemning what lived on its surface to extinction, and releasing other species who lived underground.

Engineer Léon **Creux**'s *Le Voyage de l'Isabella au Centre de la Terre* (*The Journey of the Isabella at the Center of the Earth*, 1922) was another interesting underground saga. In it, explorers used a giant mole machine, the *Isabella*, to journey to the center of the Earth. There, they found mountains of pure gold, copper, nickel, and other useful minerals. At 6000 meters deep, they discovered a giant radioactive cavern filled with aether. Finally, at the Earth's core itself, they found another cavity housing a veritable miniature solar system, composed of a sun-like liquid platinum sphere, surrounded by miniature satellites including a 40-km diameter "Anti-Earth."

Two more novels on this theme included Jean **Duval**'s *Au Centre de la Terre* (*At the Earth's Core*, 1925), in which

giant ants inhabited the Earth's core; and Camille **Audigier**'s *La Révolte des Volcans* (*The Revolt of the Volcanos*, 1935), the tale of yet another journey to the Center of the Earth, except that this time, it was inhabited by ancient Romans who had found refuge there after the fall of their empire.

Paul **Vimereu**'s *César dans l'Île de Pan* (*Caesar on the Island of Pan*, 1923) featured Napoleon, who managed to avoid imprisonment on Saint-Helens through the substitution of a lookalike and who, after being shipwrecked in the Pacific, ended up on a Lost World-type island inhabited by intelligent primates and prehistoric animals. Coincidentally, in Pierre **Veber**'s *La Seconde Vie de Napoléon 1er* (*Napoleon's Second Life*), also published in 1923, Napoleon escaped from Saint-Helens to live a secret life in France until his natural death at age 80.

In the tradition of Rosny's *Quest for Fire*, prehistorian Max **Begouën** penned two well-documented novels about life in prehistoric times, *Les Bisons d'Argile* (1925) and *Quand le Mammouth Ressuscita* (*When the Mastodon Revived*, 1928), which won the Jules Verne Award. In it, a mastodon and seven cavemen trapped in ice were brought back from frozen slumber.

Other notable prehistoric and last world novels of the times included:

André **Legrand**'s *L'Île sans Amour* (*The Loveless Island*, 1921).

André **Lichtenberger**'s *Raramené* (1921), a missing-link story, and *Houck et Sla* (1930).

Claude **Anet**'s *La Fin d'un Monde* (1922), about the end of an advanced prehistoric civilization.

Victor **Forbin**'s *Les Fiancés du Soleil* (*The Fiancés of the Sun*, 1923).

René **Trotet de Bargis**' *Kh'ia, la Fille des Gorilles* (*Kh'ia, Daughter of Gorillas*, 1923) about a young girl raised by apes.

Fernand **Mysor**'s *Les Semeurs d'Épouvante, Roman des Temps Jurassiques* (*The Sowers of Terror, Novel of Jurassic Times*, 1923), in which two people travelled back in time to the Jurassic era, where they were eaten by a prehistoric monster, and *Va'Hour l'Illuminé* (*Va'Hour the Mad*, 1924).

Pierre **Goemaere**'s *Le Pèlerin du Soleil* (*The Pilgrims of the Sun*, 1927).

Léon **Lambry**'s *Rama, Fille des Cavernes* (*Rama, Daughter of the Caverns*, 1928) and *La Mission de Run le Tordu* (*The Mission of Twisted Run*, 1929).

Jean de **Kerlecq**'s *Urfa, l'Homme des Profondeurs* (*Urfa, Man of the Depths*, 1931).

René **Thévenin**'s *L'Ancêtre des Hommes* (*The Ancestor of Men*, 1932; see above).

H.-J. **Proumen**'s *Ève, Proie des Hommes* (*Eve, Prey of Men*, 1934; see below).

Charles de **L'Andelyn**'s *Nara le Conquérant* (*Nara the Conqueror*, 1936).

Guy de **Larigaudie**'s *Yug* (1945) and *Yug en Terres Inconnues* (*Yug in Unknown Lands*, 1946).

Raymond de **Rienzi**'s startlingly original novel, *Les Formiciens* (*The Ant-Men*, 1932), sub-titled "A Novel of the Secondary Era," told the detailed story of the life of an antman named Hind in a semi-barbaric civilization of insectmen during Earth's Secondary Era.

Atlantis had already been the subject of Jean **Carrère**'s *La Fin d'Atlantis ou Le Grand Soir* (*The End of Atlantis, or the Great Night*, 1903-4) and Pierre **Benoît**'s classic *L'Atlantide* (1919; see Chapter VIII). It was also the theme of numerous novels written during the 1920s and 1930s, such as:

Paul **Féval** Fils and H.-J. **Magog**'s *Le Réveil d'Atlantide* (*Atlantis Awakens*), the third volume of their serial *Les Mystères de Demain* (*The Mysteries of Tomorrow*, 1922-23; see above).

Georges **Grandjean**'s *Antinéa, La Nouvelle Atlantide* (*Antinea, the New Atlantis*, 1922).

Georges **Spitzmuller** and J.-A. **Barbier-Daumont**'s *Héliodora en Atlantide* (*Heliodora in Atlantis*, 1923).

Jean d'**Esme**'s *Les Dieux Rouges* (*The Red Gods*, 1923), in which the survivors of the lost continent of Gondwana found refuge in Vietnam.

Léon **Groc**'s *2000 Ans Sous la Mer* (*2000 Years Under the Sea*, 1924; see below).

Noelle **Roger**'s *Le Soleil Enseveli* (*The Buried Sun*, 1928; see below).

P. **Couteaud**'s *Chez les Atlantes* (*With the Atlanteans*, 1928).

Roger **Devigne**'s *Mon Voyage en Atlantide* (*My Journey to Atlantis*, 1929).

Charles **Magué**'s trilogy, comprised of *Les Survivants de l'Atlantide* (*The Survivors of Atlantis*, 1929), *La Cuve aux Monstres* (*The Vat of Monsters*, 1930) and *L'Archipel des Demi-Dieux* (*The Archipelago of Demigods*, 1931).

Pierre **Legendre**'s *Le Dernier des Atlantes* (*The Last of the Atlanteans*, 1930).

Eugène **Thébault**'s *Nira, Australe Mystérieuse* (*Nira, Mysterious Australian*, 1930) described a secret Atlantean civilization located in the Antarctic which used magnetic power and anti-gravity discs.

P.-A. de **Cassagnac**'s *Le Couloir de Lumière* (*The Corridor of Light*), a more generic Lost World tale serialized in *L'Intrépide* in 1932.

Claude **Saint-Yves**' *Le Marabout des Atlantes* (*The Priest of Atlantis*, 1932).

Annette **Godin**'s *La Dernière Atlante, ou Le Second Péché d'Ève* (*The Last Atlantean, or Eve's Second Sin*), published in Algiers in 1933.

J. **Fardet**'s *Dans l'Éclatante Atlantis* (*In the Shimmering Atlantis*, 1935).

Finally, Alin **Monjardin**'s colorful *L'Extraordinaire Voyage* (*The Extraordinary Journey*, 1934), in which the Atlantean survivors lived in an underwater domed city also inhabited by octopus-men and dinosaurs.

H. de **Volta**'s twenty-part serial, *L'Île Merveilleuse* (*The Marvellous Island*), published in 1921, featured virtually every theme in fashion at the times, with chapters entitled "Cinq Cent Lieues sous la Terre" ("500 Leagues Underground"), "Ressuscités après 100.000 Ans" ("Brought Back to Life After 100,000 Years"), "Vers les Mondes Inconnus" ("Towards the Unknown Worlds"), "La Découverte de l'Atlantide" ("The Discovery of Atlantis") and "Scientific City."

Jules d'**Ottange** wrote a four-volume serial, *La Chasse aux Milliards* (*The Hunt for the Billions*, 1926-31), in which a billionaire created cities at the bottom of the sea.

Jean **Bonnéry** was another popular adventure writer who liked to craft pseudo-scientific thrillers such as *1 = 2 = 3* (1927), *Le Visage de Lumière* (*The Face of Light*, 1927), and *La Ville Invisible* (*The Invisible City*, 1933).

Gaston **Pastre** followed more blandly in Verne's footsteps with titles such as *La Ville Aérienne* (*The City in the Air*, 1928); *Le Secret des Sables* (*The Secret of the Sands*, 1928), which won the Jules Verne Award; *Le Palace à la Dérive* (*A Palace Adrift*, 1929) and *L'Île d'Épouvante* (*The Island of Terror*, 1932).

Before he became a famous mainstream writer, and the creator of the immortal Commissaire Maigret, the prolific Georges Simenon penned a number of pulp adventure novels under the pseudonym of "Georges **Sim**," such as *Le Roi des Glaces* (*The King of the Ice*, 1927), *Le Secret des Lamas* (*The Secret of the Lamas*, 1928) and *Le Gorille-Roi Ching* (*of the Gorillas*, 1929).

Pierre **Demousson** contributed pulp-like adventure novels with genre elements such as *Les Compagnons du Dragon Noir* (*The Companions of the Black Dragon*, 1929), *Les Briseurs de Continents* (*The Continent Breakers*, 1930-31) and *Le Secret de l'Antarctide* (*The Secret of Antarctica*, 1930).

Louis-Frédéric **Rouquette**, the editor of *À l'Aventure*, wrote *L'Homme qui Vint...* (*The Man Who Came...*, 1921), *Le Grand Silence Blanc* (*The Great White Silence*, 1921), *L'Épopée Blanche* (*The White Epic*, 1926) and *Le Secret du Pôle* (*The Secret of the Pole*, 1926).

Finally, Paul Yves **Sébillot**, penned the four-volume *L'Île Volante* (*The Flying Island*, 1923) and *Le Roi de l'Épouvante* (*The King of Terror*, 1930).

Other notable novels of the period about mad scientists, mutants, and various perversions of science included:

Henri **Falk**'s *Le Maître des Trois États* (*The Master of Three States*, 1917), written with Paul **Plançon**, in which a scientist invented a density-altering machine.

Jules **Chancel**'s *Sous le Masque Allemand* (*Under the German Mask*, 1917), featured advanced cosmetic surgery; his *L'Étreinte de la Main de Fer* (*The Grip of the Iron Hand*, 1925), a device that sees through walls, and *Le Tour du Monde Involontaire* (*The Involuntary Around-The-World Journey*, 1929), a laser-like death ray.

The brother-sister team of Marie and Frédéric Petitjean de la Rosière, who later became famous as the renowned authors of Harlequin-like romance novels under the pseudonym of "**Delly**," wrote *Les Maîtres du Silence* (*The Masters of Silence*, 1918-19), a two-volume serial about a Chinese secret society who fought tyranny with paranormal powers. Another renowned romance novelist, Max du **Veuzit**, wrote *L'Automate* (*The Automaton*) in 1935.

Raoul **Bigot**'s *Nounlegos* (1919), sub-titled "The Man Who Read Brains," was a remarkable novel about telepathy. In collaboration with E.M. **Laumann**, Bigot also penned *L'Étrange Matière* (*The Strange Matter*, 1921), about the discovery of the "crystallopyr," a substance that could generate exteme heat and cold; and *Le Visage dans la Glace* (*The Face in the Ice*, 1922). Laumann and Henri **Lanos** (see above) wrote *L'Aéro-Bagne 32* (*Air Penitentiary 32*, 1920) about a futuristic aerial prison.

Léon **Baranger**'s *Le Maître de la Force* (*The Master of the Force*, 1919) featured stories dealing with a hate-concentrating ray and a mental collector.

Jean de **La Hire**'s *Joe Rollon, l'Autre Homme Invisible* (*Rollon, Another Invisible Man*, 1919), written under the pseudonym of "Edmond Cazal," was another variation on Wells' *Invisible Man*.

The self-explanatory *Les Voleurs de Cerveaux* (*The Brain Stealers*, 1916) by Jean de **Quirielle** featured a mad scientist coupled human brains together to make a giant power battery.

Henry **Du Roure**'s *Le Secret de l'Or* (*The Secret of Gold*, 1920) featured a scientist who, having discovered the secret of gold-making, used it to ruin France.

J. **Bruno-Ruby** (a pseudonym of female author Madame Jean Vignaud) with *Celui Qui Supprima la Mort* (*He Who Got Rid of Death*, 1921) crafted a Christian allegory in which Satan was depicted as a 30th-century scientist who sought the secret of immortality but was defeated by the power of the cross.

Pierre **Desclaux**'s *Les Morts de Bronze* (*The Dead Men in Bronze*, 1921) featured criminals who used a special ray to turn their victims into metal. His *Le Maître du Monde* (*The Master of the World*, 1921) was about an invisible mastermind named Robur (like the Jules Verne character). And *Le Secret d'Hermano* (*The Secret of Hermano*, 1926), written under the pseudonym of "Jean Frick," was about an evil secret society which uses brain surgery to turn people into mindless zombies.

In Gabriel **Bernard**'s *La Volonté de John Harry Will* (*The Will of John Henry Will*, 1921), a tycoon's mental energy was used as an energy source. His *Satanas* (1922) featured men with telepathic powers. In *Les Compagnons de la Haine* (*The Companions of Hate*, 1928), a scientist devised a machine that could accurately predict people's actions.

In **Cyril-Berger**'s *L'Expérience du Dr. Lorde* (*The Experiment of Dr. Lorde*, 1922), the eponymous protagonist discovered the scientific reality of the soul, which he called the "odic fluid," and for revenge, transferred that of a murderer into another man.

In 1923, Clément **Vautel** imagined *La Machine à Fabriquer des Rêves* (*The Dream-Making Machine*).

In 1924, Noelle **Roger** wrote *Le Nouvel Adam* (*The New Adam*, 1924; see below), about an artificial man.

In Raoul **Gain**'s *Le Donneur de Jeunesse* (*The Youth Giver*, 1927), a mad scientist used organ grafts to prolong life.

Paul **Féval** Fils, the author of *Les Mystères de Demain* (*The Mysteries of Tomorrow*) with H.-J. Magog (see above), penned *Miriakris, Amie d'Enfance de Jésus* (*Miriakris, Jesus' Childhood Friend*, 1927), with Henri **Allorge**, which featured an Egyptian priest awakened from suspended animation; *Félifax* (1929), a serial about the offspring of a woman inseminated with tiger's sperm; and *La Lumière Bleue* (*The Blue Light*, 1930), with Henri **Boo-Silhen**, in which a machine could print thoughts like photographs.

Henri **Bernay** and René **Pujol**'s *La Pastille Mystérieuse* (*The Mysterious Pill*, 1925) featured controlled nuclear explosions. In *on a Volé Un Transatlantique* (*They Stole a Transatlantic Ship*, 1927), "lambda rays" could be used to control people's wills. *Le Secret de la Sunbeam Valley* (*The Secret of Sunbeam Valley*, 1928), written with René Pujol (see above) used solar energy to grow food in the Australian desert.

Roger **Fribourg**'s *Des Éclairs dans la Nuit* (*Lightning Bolts in the Night*, 1927) concerned a man who had been struck by lightning subsequently develop the ability to see magnetic waves.

In Arnould **Galopin**'s *Le Bacille* (*The Bacillus*, 1928), a mad scientist plotted to poison drinking water. Galopin was the author of the 1905 Martian epic, *Docteur Omega* (see Chaper V) and a number of pedestrian Verne-like adventure serials, such as *Le Tour du Monde en Sous-Marin* (*Around the World in a Sub-Marine*, 1925-26), *Aventures d'un Apprenti Parisien, ou Le Tour du Monde en Hydroplane* (*Adventures of a Parisian Apprentice, or Around the World in a Hydroplane*, 1928), and *Le Tour du Monde en Aéroplane* (*Around the World in an Airplane*, 1929), co-written with Henri de la **Vaulx**.

In Henri **Darblin**'s *La Horde des Monstres* (*The Horde of Monsters*, 1928), a lost valley in the Rocky Mountains was inhabited by giant insects created by a mad scientist—one of the first novels on this theme, with Jean **Duval**'s *Au Centre de la Terre* (*At the Earth's Core*, 1925; see above).

Curiously, that same year, Norbert **Sévestre** published *La Révolte des Monstres* (*The Revolt of the Monsters*, 1928), in which mankind also fought giant insects, on a larger scale. Sévestre had previously written Verne-like novels such as *Le Tour du Monde en 14 Jours* (*Around the World in 14 Days*, 1921) and *Trois Jeunes Aéronautes au Pôle Sud* (*Three Young Airmen at the South Pole*, 1927).

In Étienne **Gril**'s *La Machine à Guérir de la Vie* (*The Machine to Cure Life*, 1929), written under the pseudonym of "Stéphane Corbière" with J. **Fouquet**, a scientist invented a ray that could just as easily kill cancer cells as kill people.

Octave **Béliard**'s *Les Petits Hommes de la Pinède* (*The Little Men in the Pine Forest*, 1928) was the tale of the impossible love between a man and an ant-sized woman genetically created by a mad scientist. The "Little Men" developed at a faster pace than man and would eventually have threatened our species had a fire not destroyed the pine forest where they lived. (Béliard won the first Jules Verne award with the unremarkable *La Petite Fille de Michel Strogoff* (*Michel Strogoff's Grand-Daughter*, 1927)).

Eugène **Thébault**'s *Radio-Terreur* (*Radio-Terror*, 1928) had the rare privilege of having been translated in the American magazine *Wonder Stories* in 1933. The story took place in 1952 and told of the attempt by a mad scientist to blackmail the world. Finally, in *Le Soleil Ensorcelé* (*The Spellbound Sun*, 1930), another mad scientist, Colquorès, used a red diamond star which emitted the mysterious "Rays 55" to alter the very shape of Earth and turn Paris into a jungle.

In Maurice **Landay**'s *L'Antenne Mystérieuse* (*The Mysterious Antenna*, 1931), the hero was transformed into a living radio, and was able to defeat the evil schemes of a German super-villain who was plotting to kick the French out of Vietnam!

L'Ombre Inaccessible (*The Unreachable Shadow*), published in *L'Intrépide* in 1931-32 under the pseudonyms of "**Mettra**" and "**Nubé**," was a colorful Fu-Manchu pastiche in which the villain was named Karma and was the Lord of the Tulpakhangs, the so-called city of the ice ghosts.

Finally, Hervé de **Peslouan**'s *L'Étrange Menace du Prof. Iouchkoff* (*The Strange Threat of Prof. Iouchkoff*, 1931), which won the Jules **Verne** Award, brought together a school monitor and the eponymous Russian mad scientist, a Robur-like engineer who created a formidable flying machine called the "Menace."

THE FUTURE

Novels in the tradition of Souvestre and Robida and De Chousy, which tried to predict what life would be in the year 2000 or 3000 continued to be fashion. Among the notable titles published during the period were:

Joseph-Louis **Lecornu**'s *Cinquante Ans Après: Une Exposition à Verdun en 1967* (*Fifty Years Later: An Exhibit in Verdun in 1967*, 1918).

Gérard d'**Houville**'s *En l'An 2000* (*In the Year 2000*, 1921).

André **Lebey**'s *Tenue du... 16 Septembre 5924* (*Review of... Sept. 7th, 5924*, 1922).

Pierre **Mille**'s *Dans Trois Cents Ans* (*In 300 Years*, 1922), which postulated a future that had reverted to barbarism after global war.

Georges **Spitzmuller**'s *Une Expédition aux Ruines de Paris* (*An Expedition to the Ruins of Paris*, 1923).

Edmond **Caraguel**'s *Napoléon V, Dictateur* (1926).

Charles **Rivet** and Michel **Goriellof**'s self-explanatory *Le Triomphe de Lénine (Anno Diaboli 310) 2227—Roman Soviétique* (*The Triumph of Lenin [Anno Diaboli 310] Yr. 2227—Soviet Novel*, 1927).

Bernard **Audry**'s *La Dictatrice* (1928), about a woman taking power in France.

Banville d'Hostel's *Z, Anticipation Dramatique sur le Dernier Jour de la Terre* (*Z, Dramatic Anticipation on the Last Day of the Earth*, 1929).

Henri **Bernay**'s *L'Homme qui Dormit Cent Ans* (*The Man Who Slept for a Hundred Years*, 1928), about a modern Rip Van Winkle who awoke in the 21st century.

Catholic writer Louis **Artus** deserves a special mention for a series of stories collected in *La Maison du Fou* (*The House of the Madman*, 1918), *La Maison du Sage* (*The House of the Wise Man*, 1920) and *Les Chiens de Dieu* (*God's Dogs*, 1928) which portrayed with chilling details a future dystopian Europe where communism and technology had triumphed and Christians were persecuted.

These were supplemented by a variety of novels dealing with castrophes and social upsets befalling our planet. As early as 1913, Henri **Allorge** had predicted the dire consequences of the disappearance of iron in *La Famine de Fer* (*The Iron Famine*). His more elaborate *Le Grand Cataclysme* (*The Great Cataclysm*, 1927) took place in the 100th century and featured a world where electricity suddenly vanished. (Interestingly, in that future, love had long been found to be caused by a virus!).

The disappearance of iron was also explored in Raoul **Bigot**'s *Le Fer qui Meurt* (*The Death of Iron*, 1918) and Serge **Held**'s *La Mort du Fer* (*The Death of Iron*, 1931), in which alien spores carried to Earth by a meteorite destroyed all iron. (This story was later translated into English by Fletcher Pratt.)

In Colonel **Royet**'s *La Tempête Universelle de l'An 2000* (*The Universal Tempest of the Year 2000*, 1921), a solar eruption killed all life on Earth, except for an American man and a French woman; the new Adam and Eve then fought giant worms for possession of the planet. Royet also penned the eloquent *À Deux Doigts de la Fin du Monde* (*Two Inches Away From the End of the World*, 1929).

In Henri **Falk**'s *L'Âge de Plomb* (*The Age of Lead*, 1918), increased solar radiation forced men to live behind lead-lined walls.

Noelle **Roger**'s *Le Nouveau Déluge* (*The New Flood*, 1922; see below) posited a watery catastrophe.

Aslan's *Adieu, Britannia!* (1923) showed the British Isles submerged under a giant tide.

Pierre **Dominique**'s *Le Feu du Ciel* (*Fire From the Sky*, 1926) was a vision of a new apocalypse.

André **Armandy**'s *Le Grand Crépuscule* (*The Great Twilight*, 1928) prophetically dealt with the exhaustion of petroleum resources.

Charles de **L'Andelyn**'s *Les Derniers Jours du Monde* (*The Last Days of the World*, 1931) featured a new Ice Age, which threatened mankind's survival.

Social upheavals occurred in Antonin **Seuhl**'s *La Grève*

des Machines (*The Machines on Strike*, 1924) and Étienne **Gril**'s *Les Chevaliers de l'Incertain* (*The Knights of Uncertainty*, 1929), about a world transformed by rampant anarchy.

In *Jean Arlog, Le Premier Surhomme* (*Jean Arlog, the First Superman*, 1921), Georges **Lebas** wrote about a self-made superman who tried to stop the rotation of the Earth through sheer telekinetic power, but died in the process. Lebas then described how Earth was captured by a wandering star in *L'Heure Perdue* (*The Lost Hour*, 1930).

Further in the future, Han **Ryner** in *Les Surhommes, Roman Prophétique* (*The Supermen, Prophetic Novel*, 1929) told the story of the emergence of a new sun and a new race of thinking mastodons.

In *Tréponème* (1931) by Dr. Marc **La Marche**, it was a virus that turned men into supermen.

And then, there was the ever-constant flow of stories about future wars:

As early as 1915, Louis-Jules **Gastine**'s eighteen-issue serial, *La Guerre de l'Espace* (*The Space War*), with titles such as *L'Invasion Chinoise* (*The Chinese Invasion*) and *La Revanche Barbare* (*Barbarous Revenge*), foresaw a worldwide aerial war with Asia. Gastine returned to the theme with *La Ruée des Jaunes* (*The Yellow Rush*, 1933). Pierre-Barthélemy **Gheusi**'s *Le Mascaret Rouge* (*The Red Tide*, 1931) also fanned the same fear of a universal "Yellow Peril."

Arthur **Bernède**'s *Chantecoq* (1916) retold the war between France and Germany, this time using super-weapons.

Roger **Chanut**'s *Les Ombres de Demain* (*Tomorrow's Shadows*, 1920) also predicted a futuristic war conducted with deadly weapons.

Doctor Rochard, using the pseudonyms of "Professor **Motus**" and "Professor X," penned the grimly prophetic *L'Offensive des Microbes, Roman d'une Guerre Future* (*The Microbes' Attack, Novel of a Future War*, 1923); aka *La Guerre Microbienne, La Fin du* Monde (*The Microbian War, the End of the World*), in which a German scientist attacked France with a bacteriological weapon.

Ch. **Duhemme**'s *Français, Garde à Vous!* (*Frenchmen, to Arms!*, 1930), co-written with **Hubert-Jacques**, was subtitled "The Aero-Chemical War That Germany Is Preparing."

Colonel **Royet**'s twenty-issue serial, *1932: La Guerre est Déclarée* (*1932: War Is Declared*, 1931) anticipated the real thing by less than ten years. More novels in this vein followed until World War II actually broke out.

Two works stood out amongst the others:

Anarchist Victor **Méric**'s *La Der des Der* (*The Next Last War*, 1929) described the next conflict in bitter and cynical tones.

Jean **Petithuguenin**'s *Le Grand Courant* (*The Great Current*, 1931) was about a future war between a technologically advanced Europe and an ecologically conscious Asia.

Finally, the period saw the publication of two interest-

ing uchronias by René **Jeanne**: *Napoléon-Bis* (1932), in which it was revealed that the real Napoleon had been kidnapped and replaced by a look-alike during the Russian Campaign, hence its failure; and the earlier *Si le 9 Thermidor...* (*If on 9 Thermidor*, 1929), co-written with E. M. **Laumann**, a "What if Robespierre had not died" novel.

c. Mainstream Writers

As in previous years, a number of writers generally catalogued among mainstream authors penned works that, for all intents and purposes, belonged to the science fiction genre.

One of the best was Claude **Farrère**, the first recipient of the literary Goncourt Award, and the author of the 1911 fantastic novel, *La Maison des Hommes Vivants* (*The House of Living Men*; see chapters IV and VI). Farrère's works encompassed both the *fantastique* and science fiction. *Les Condamnés à Mort* (*Those Condemned to Die*, 1920) showed machines leading men into a Communist dystopia, but the revolutionaries were eventually defeated by a scientist and his disintegrating ray. His collection *Histoire de Très Loin ou d'Assez Près* (*Tales of Very Far or Near Enough*, 1923) included his classic short story "Où?" ("Where?"), a remarkable exploration of the "out there," a fourth dimension which followed different laws of time and space. The 1927 story "Fin de Planète" ("End of a Planet") featured a disgruntled chemist who, unable to marry the aristocratic girl he loved, instead caused the disintegration of his world, which was revealed to be the missing fifth planet of our solar system.

Henri **Barbusse**, a novelist famous for his award-winning *Le Feu* (*Under Fire*, 1916), a novel about a soldier's life during World War I, penned *Les Enchaînements* (1925), which featured a hero whose visionary experiences enabled him to travel through time.

The first professional woman writer of science fiction was Swiss author Noëlle **Roger**. In reality Hélène Pittard ("Roger" was a pseudonym), she was the daughter of a literary scholar, specialist in Jean-Jacques Rousseau, and the wife of a famous anthropologist. She began writing proto-feminist tales at age 22 and served as a nurse during World War I. She travelled with her husband in the Middle East and Asia, and wrote a number of genre works, nevertheless published by mainstream publishers such as Calmann-Lévy and Albin Michel, and recognized by the French Academy. Her *Le Nouveau Déluge* (*The New Flood*, 1922) depicted the sinking of the entire European continent, thereby letting the waters of the Atlantic Ocean flood France. The ensuing exodus and fight for survival were narrated with uncharacteristic sobriety and subtlety, anticipating the British novels of John Wyndham and Edmund Cooper. *Le Nouvel Adam* (*The New Adam*, 1924) was about the deliberate attempt to scientifically create a new, superior race of men. *L'Hôte Invisible* (*The Invisible Host*, 1926), about a monster who appeared every century or so, and *Celui Qui Voit* (*He Who Sees*, 1926) were variations on the theme of invisibility. *Le Livre qui fait Mourir* (*The Book That Kills*, 1927) revolved around a cursed book. *Le Soleil Enseveli* (*The Buried Sun*, 1928) told of the emergence of a new island which revealed the existence of Atlantis. *Le Chercheur d'Ondes* (*The Wave Seeker*, 1931) dealt with parapsychology, and *Le Nouveau Lazare* (*The New Lazarus*, 1935) with resurrection. Roger's later works included *La Vallée Perdue* (*The Lost Valley*, 1940), an interesting prehistoric novel where the eponymous Lost World is located in a hidden Swiss Valley, and *Au Seuil de l'Invisible* (*On the Treshold of the Unseen*, 1949), a collection of stories originally published in the 1930s.

Another woman author of the period was Renée **Dunan**, whose first book, *Baal ou La Magicienne Passionée, Livre des Ensorcellements* (*Baal or the Impassioned Magician, Book of Spells*, 1924) was a science fiction treatment of psi powers, magic, and alchemy. In it, the modern sorceress Palmyre taught her female assistant the secret of her magic, including the ability to travel from one dimension to another. They met the Lovecraftian entity Baal, whose octopus-like form was described as a three-dimensional projection from a multi-dimensional creature. *La Dernière Jouissance* (*The Last Pleasure*, 1925) told the future history of the human race after it was decimated by a deadly underground gas called "necron." A scientific dictatorship ensued, and was eventually overthrown by a Messianic revolution. The rebel leader used an atom bomb-like explosive, the "klazzite," whose explosion could only be triggered by the detonation of the less powerful "klazzite 2." Other later novels included *La Montagne de Diamants* (*The Mountain of Diamonds*, 1934) and *L'Épouvantable Secret* (*The Awful Secret*, 1934).

Other mainstream authors of the 1920s who dabbled in the genre included:

Félicien **Champsaur**, with the novella "Le Dernier Homme" ("The Last Man"), 1907), in which a comet increased the oxygen in the Earth's atmosphere and caused the forests to take over Paris and man to revert to an ape-like condition. Champsaur's *Les Ailes de l'Homme* (*The Wings of Man*, 1917) was a remarkably accurate description of a rocket-powered plane. He also penned three satirical novels about beast-men: *Ouha, Roi des Singes* (*Ouha, King of the Apes*, 1923), *Homo Deus, le Satyre Invisible* (*Homo Deus, the Invisible Satyr*, 1924) and *Nora, La Guenon Devenue Femme* (*Nora, the She-Monkey Made Woman*, 1929).

Omer **Chevalier** checked in with *L'Avatar d'Yvan Orel* (*Yvan Orel's Avatar*, 1919), in which an Earthman was reincarnated on a utopian Venus.

Gabriel de **Lautrec**, whose collection *La Vengeance du Portrait Ovale* (*The Revenge of the Oval Portrait*, 1922) included such science fiction tales as "Dans Le Monde Voisin" ("In the Next World"), featuring creatures from the Fourth

Dimension, and "Fragment de Conte Futur" ("Fragment of Future Tale"), about the slow disappearance of oxygen.

Jacques **Chenevière**, whose *Jouvence ou la Chimère* (*Youth, or the Chimera*, 1922) was about a scientist who died, leaving an immortality formula behind.

Playwright and fantasy author Alexandre **Arnoux** (see Chapter VI) wrote *Le Règne du Bonheur* (*The Reign of Happiness*, 1924), a modern utopia in which space travellers who journeyed faster than light returned to a future Earth which has reverted to primitive innocence; and *Petite Lumière et l'Ourse* (*Little Light and the She-Bear*, 1923), about a superhuman robot.

Ernest **Pérochon**, another Goncourt Award winner and normally the author of novels extolling the glory of French farmers, wrote a remarkable scientific anticipation, *Les Hommes Frénétiques* (*The Frenetic Men*, 1925). The novel took place in the 30th century, then renamed the 5th century of the Universal Era, after a global war with the Asians, won thanks to a young female physicist, Noelle Roger (an homage?) and a bacteriological war. The secrets of radium and aether had been discovered by the great French scientist, Averine. (In the future, French is, of course, the universal language.) Energy was provided by the controlled disintegration of potassium salts, and cities stretched like conducting wires along the meridians that formed a planet-wide grid. In the novel, another war between rival meridians started. New, horrible weapons were used which mutated men: In Australia, their skeletons became soft; in South America, they became blind; in Central America, cannibals; in the Middle East, werewolf-like beings; some grew new organs; others, new senses. The novel ended with a new Adam and a new Eve. Pérochon's novel was an apocalyptic warning against unchecked technology. Another of his notable genre works was *Le Crime Étrange de Lise Balzan* (*Lise Balzan's Strange Crime*, 1929). Pérochon also penned some fantasy works reviewed in Chapter VI.

Odette **Dulac**'s *(L'Amour)...Tel qu'il est* [(*Love*)...*As It Were*, 1926] was a colorful esoteric novel postulating the existence of an ancient, technologically and psychically advanced civilization, a Gaia-like sentient Earth, secret initiates living hidden among us for thousands of years, etc.

The son of Alphonse **Daudet**, Léon **Daudet**, a noted political writer and polemist (also see Chapter VI) wrote *Le Napus, Fléau de l'An 2227* (*The Nomore, Plague of the Year 2227*, 1927), in which people started disappearing without explanation and war ensued. His *Les Bacchantes* (1931) featured the discovery of "time waves" which enabled scientists to bring images back from the past. *Ciel de Feu* (*Sky of Fire*, 1934) was about a futuristic Franco-German war.

André **Arnyvelde**'s *L'Arche* (*The Ark*, 1920) was a novel about the coming of a race of superhuman mutants, the "Arcandres," born from ordinary men and women and gifted with extrasensory perception.

Finally, the renowned essayist, biographer and novelist André **Maurois**, the author of the satirical, best-selling

André Maurois

World War I novel, *The Silences of Colonel Bramble* (1918), penned several science fiction satires such as the Swiftian *Voyage au Pays des Articoles* (*A Voyage to the Island of the Articoles*, 1927); *Deux Fragments d'Une Histoire Universelle 1992* (*Two Fragments of a Universal History—1992*, 1928), in which the inhabitants of Uranus failed to understand Earthmen; *Relativisme* (*Relativity*, 1930), a collection of fantastic tales; and the classic *Le Peseur d'Âmes* (*The Weigher of Souls*, 1931), in which a doctor discovered that the soul was a gas that escaped the body upon death, and who attempted to posthumously blend his soul with that of his lover. Maurois' *La Machine à Lire les Pensées* (*The Thought-Reading Machine*, 1937; see below), like Paul Féval Fils & Henri Boo-Silhen's *La Lumière Bleue* (*The Blue Light*; see above), dealt with a machine capable of recording thoughts like photographs

2. A Period of Transition

During the late 1930s and 1940s, while science fiction in the United States blossomed, the genre was allowed to flounder in France, the victim of censorship and spiralling economic pressures, attributable to a loss of readership, an increase in the cost of paper and, from 1935 on, the competition of magazines publishing translations of American stories and comic strips.

By the start of World War II, the field was severely depressed. *Sciences et Voyages* (*Science and Voyages*) magazine had stopped publication in 1935, *L'Intrépide* (*The Fearless*) in 1937, *Je Sais Tout* (*I Know Everything*) in 1939, *Lectures Pour Tous* (*Reading for All*) and *Oeuvres Libres* (*Free Works*) in 1940. Only the *Journal des Voyages* (*The Journal of Voyages*) carried on until 1949.

Five years of war and Nazi occupation completed the devastation of what had been the Golden Age of French science fiction. Quantitatively, the field was severely hit. Qualitatively, however, there were a few glimmers of hope. However, these came not from the authors of the previous decades, like **Renard** and **Moselli**, whose

spirits had been effectively crushed, but from new voices, often originating from mainstream culture. The flame was kept alive, if only barely, by André **Maurois'** *La Machine à Lire les Pensées* (*The Thought-Reading Machine*, 1937; see above), René **Barjavel's** *Ravage* (1943) and Jacques **Spitz**, who followed the lead of the surrealists.

In the popular field, a few new names emerged, such as Maurice **Limat**, Yves **Dermèze** and the talented B.-R. **Bruss**, who followed in the footsteps of **Rosny** Aîné.

Finally, it was during that wartime period that the first elements of a true French science fiction fandom began to emerge, with names like Georges Gallet, Jacques **Bergier**, Jacques **Van Herp**, Pierre **Versins**, and others, who eventually not only preserved the rich heritage of the Golden Age, but were instrumental in orchestrating a revival of science fiction in the 1950s, when the genre finally reemerged from its long slumber.

a. Major Authors

Writer Léon **Groc** embodied the evolution of French science fiction between the wars, with a career that began in 1913 with *Ville Hantée* (*The Haunted City*, 1913) and *L'Autobus Évanoui* (*The Vanished Bus*, 1914), two stories in a Maurice Renard vein that dealt with paranormal powers in a pseudo-scientific fashion. In *L'Autobus Évanoui*, for example, an artificial form of telepathy was created through the use of radioactivity and the appropriate thought-harnessing equipment. *2000 Ans Sous la Mer* (*2000 Years Under the Sea*, 1924) was typical of its times, featuring the descendents of ancient Phenicians who lived underwater in vast, domed cities. The same was true of *Le Chasseur de Chimères* (*The Hunter of Chimeras*, 1925), which anticipated the concept of nuclear desintegration.

Groc's works began to evolve with the more original *La Révolte des Pierres* (*The Revolt of the Stones*, 1929), in which the inhabitants of the Moon were portrayed as mineral, radioactive beings who lived in gestalt-like triads. A Norwegian scientist succeeded in transporting a Selenite to Earth. Eventually, a madman kidnapped one of the Selenites and used his power to control stones to cause much havoc, such as the throwing of the Obelisk, the demolition of Notre-Dame, and the destruction of the Alps, before being stopped. Another notable Groc work of the period was *L'Impossible Ransom* (*The Impossible Ransom*, 1937).

As the war neared its end, Groc was once again at the forefront of popular anticipation with *La Planète de Cristal* (*The Crystal Planet*, 1944), which featured two-dimensional beings living on a quasi-invisible crystal moon above Earth. They perished when Men touched them, but in a *Flatland*-like twist, so did men when coming into contact with four-dimensional aliens! Finally, *L'Univers Vagabond* (*The Wandering Universe*, 1950), written with Groc's wife Jacqueline **Zorn**, featured a generational starship en route to Alpha Centauri. There, the human colonists were defeated by radioactive mineral aliens and were forced to return to Earth. Other notable works of this period included *Le Tour du Sorcier* (*The Wizard's Tower*, 1944), *Le Maître du Soleil* (*The Master of the Sun*, 1946) and *L'Émetteur Inconnu* (*The Unknown Transmitter*, 1949), also written with Zorn.

During this period, notorious Belgian writer Jean **Ray** (see Chapter VI) penned many stories which often straddled the line between *fantastique* and science fiction, such as the novella *La Ruelle Ténébreuse* (*The Dark Street*, 1932), about a street that led into another, frightening dimension, and many *Harry Dickson* tales, such as "L'Homme au Masque d'Argent" ("The Man in the Silver Mask"; No.151, 1936), about a death-dealing silver android.

Belgian writer Henri-Jacques **Proumen** was more chararacteristic of the evolution of the genre during the 1930s and 1940s. Proumen, who knew both Rosny and Renard, wrote *Sur le Chemin des Dieux* (*On the Path of the Gods*, 1928), in which a scientist discovered the secrets of mind control; at first, he used them for peace, but then he succumbed to his megalomaniacal impulses. *La Boîte aux Marionnettes* (*The Puppet Box*, 1930) was a superb collection of genre stories, including "Surhommes" ("Supermen", 1926), a satirical look at men with hypertrophied brains. His *Le Sceptre Volé aux Hommes* (*The Scepter Stolen From Men*, 1930) was a novel in which the next race of supermen, the "hyperanthropes," enslaved mankind and lived on an island, as in Olaf Stapledon's *Odd John* and H.-J. Magog's *Trois Ombres sur Paris* (*Three Shadows Over Paris*, 1928). While some men served the mutants of their own free will, others revolted and, eventually, caused the destruction of the island. *Ève, Proie des Hommes* (*Eve, Prey of Men*, 1934) was a prehistoric novel featuring a cavewoman. *La Brèche d'Enfer* (*The Hellish Breach*, 1946) was a warning written initially about a new, fictional weapon of mass destruction called "fulgurium," but the bombing of Hiroshima overtook the author and Proumen had to rewrite his novel to make it about the atom bomb. Finally, Proumen's other genre tales were collected in *L'Homme qui a été mangé* (*The Man Who Was Eaten*, 1950).

After Maurice Renard, the French writer who most characterized the pre-World War II period, and one of the few original voices of that time, was Jacques **Spitz**. Spitz's novels were generally dark and pessimistic; they also contained some fierce satirical observations and were always extremely well documented, contrasting the realistic attention brought to the description of the details of everyday life with the outlandishness of their events. In term of literary influences, Spitz had come out of surrealism, as evidenced by his first novels, *La Croisière Indécise* (*The Indecisive Cruise*, 1926) and *Le Vent du Monde* (*The Wind of the World*, 1928). His genre career began with *L'Agonie du Globe* (*The Agony of the Globe*, 1935), in which Earth was bissected into two hemispheres, one of which eventually crashed into the Moon. The novel established the use of realistic details that became characteristic of Spitz's style. The more pedes-

trian *Les Évadés de l'An 4000* (*The Escapees From Year 4000*, 1936) told of a new Ice Age which drove men underground, the ensuing scientific dictatorship and finally, an escape to Venus. *La Guerre des Mouches* (*The War of the Flies*, 1938) featured the conquest of Earth by mutated flies animated by a gestalt intelligence. The flies kept only a few men (among them the narrator) in a reserve. In *L'Homme Élastique* (*The Elastic Man*, 1938), one of Spitz's best novels, a means to compress and decompress atoms was found, enabling the creation of tiny super-soldiers and flaccid giants. *L'Expérience du Dr. Mops* (*The Experiment of Dr. Mops*, 1939) and *L'Oeil du Purgatoire* (*The Eye of Purgatory*, 1945) both explored the theme of seeing into the future; in the former, the hero found he could not see beyond his own death; in the latter, Dr. Dagerloff's unhappy guinea pig saw not the real future but an increasingly aging present, where death and decay became overpowering sights.

Later Spitz works included *La Parcelle "Z"* (*Particle Z*, 1942) and *Les Signaux du Soleil* (*The Signals of the Sun*, 1943), in which the Martians and Venusians mined Earth's atmosphere for its components, but stopped once they came to realize our planet was inhabited by intelligent life—this was accomplished by encrypting "pi" into the ionization of the atmosphere. *Ceci Est Un Drame* (*This Is a Tragedy*, 1947) was a play set in the far future. Finally, and most regrettably, two of Spitz's genre novels, *Alpha du Centaure* (*Alpha Centauri*) and *La Troisième Guerre Mondiale* (*World War III*), did not find any publisher, a perfect illustration of the difficulties encountered by science fiction in the 1940s.

Another notable author of the late 1930s was Régis **Messac**. Less prolific than Renard, Spitz, and others, Messac was nevertheless a groundbreaking writer, as well as an editor who launched a short-lived science fiction imprint, *Les Hypermondes* (*The Hyperworlds*) in 1935. He would undoubtedly have contributed even more significant works to the field had he not died in the German concentration camps in 1943. As it was, Messac wrote only three novels, one of which was not published until 1973! a veteran of World War I, Messac had foreseen the evils of World War II in his classic *Quinzinzinzili* (1935), which featured a society of children who reverted to savagery after a chemical world war. Written twenty years before William Golding's *Lord of the Flies*, *Quinzinzinzili* postulated that a party of school children, isolated from the outside world, saw civilization as we know it collapse amongst them. Messac's narrator was a lone, embittered adult. Since the children quickly evolved a new simplified language, he progressively found himself incapable of understanding his former charges. For him, there was no happy ending, only an inescapable tragedy. For Messac, not only was the veneer of civilization brittle, but Man was, by nature, amoral. The book's title came from the name of the children's totemistic god, derived from a mangled, badly remembered prayer, "Pater Noster *Qui es in coelis*"—Quinzinzinzili. The relationship of religion to myth and ritual was carefully described by Messac as the children reverted to a primitive stage of development.

Messac's other novel, *La Cité des Asphyxiés* (*The City of the Asphyxiated*, 1937), featured a "chronoscope" enabling its protagonists to peer into the future. One of them was accidentally transported to the eponymous underground futuristic city, where air had become a commercial commodity. The book then became a biting social satire.

René **Barjavel** was the last "grandmaster" of the period and the first to emerge during World War II. His works formed a bridge between the popular science fiction of the 1930s and the mainstream literature of the 1940s. Barjavel's vision of the world was pessimistic and firmly positioned against progress and science, which was precisely the type of ideology that made him respectable with the cultural elite. In Barjavel's world, Man is born good, Machine is what made him evil. His novels showed how science fiction theme could be assimilated by mainstream literature, to the extent that, through a peculiar form of circular logic, they became not-science fiction. (A contemporaneous critic wrote, "Science fiction is by nature badly written and pro-technology; Barjavel is a good writer and against technology; therefore his works are not science fiction.")

Barjavel's first novel, *Ravage* (1943), took place in 2052 and portrayed a post-holocaust France turning away from the evils of technology and returning to an agricultural, utopian setting after the mysterious disappearance of electricity, a theme already explored in Henri Allorge's 1927 *Le Grand Cataclysme* (*The Great Cataclysm*; see above). *Le Voyageur Imprudent* (*The Careless Traveller*, 1944) was a time-travel story that took Barjavel's Wellsian protagonist through various, monstrous, dystopic futures, before ending on what was then a still new idea: A time paradox where the hero erases himself by accidentally killing one of his ancestors. (*Le Voyageur Imprudent* was adapted as a television movie—see Book 1, Chapter II.) *L'Homme Fort* (*The Strong Man*, 1946) featured an artificial superman who, like Philip Wylie's *Gladiator*, tried to impose peace on the world but failed. *Le Diable l'Emporte* (*The Devil Takes It*, 1948) introduced the character of Mr. Gé, a powerful billionnaire who built a gigantic Noah's Ark beneath Paris to preserve the human race. Destruction eventually came in the form of "thick water," a substance which raised the freezing point of water above even a human body's temperature and, like Kurt Vonnegut's Ice-9 from *Cat's Cradle*, killed off all life on Earth. However, a desperate couple of survivors managed to flee in a rocket. The novel's dedication summed up Barjavel's belief in future self-destruction: It was dedicated to both our ancestors and descendents, the cavemen.

Barjavel, even more so than Rosny, was the first genre writer to break out of the science fiction ghetto. Like Kurt Vonnegut in the United States, he became one of the most distinguished purveyors of both science fiction and fantasy tales under the guise of mainstream literature. His later works will be discussed in chapters VIII and IX.

Like Barjavel, the author known as "B.-R. **Bruss**" (a pseudonym of writer René Bonnefay) came to represent a transition—that between the popular science fiction of the 1930s and the popular science fiction of the 1950s and 1960s. Bruss' first genre novel was *Et la Planète Sauta...* (*And the Planet Exploded...*, 1946), which told of the self-annihilation of a world that turned out to be the fifth planet. The novel began with the discovery of a cache of documents found in a meteor. Once deciphered, these were revealed to be the diary of an alien nuclear scientist who ultimately chose to disintegrate his own world rather than allow its population to be totally enslaved by a tyrant with mind-controlling powers. *Apparition des Surhommes* (*Appearance of the Supermen*, 1953) was another novel on the theme of the coming race of supermen fated to replace men. Like Thévenin's *Les Chasseurs d'Hommes* (*The Manhunters*, 1930) and Proumen's *Le Sceptre Volé aux Hommes* (*The Scepter Stolen From Men*, 1930), Bruss' mutants are beautiful, angelic beings whose existence split mankind into two camps: "dogs" who serve them faithfully, and "wolves" who dream of destroying them. Bruss became one of the best of the science fiction and horror writers of Fleuve Noir throughout the 1950s, 1960s, and 1970s; his later works are reviewed in chapters VIII and IX.

Finally, two notable single works also stood out during the period:

Belgian writer Marcel **Thiry**'s *Échec au Temps* (*Time in Check*) was written in 1939 but not published until 1945. (Thiry had written collections of surreal poetry in the 1920s. His fantasy works are mentioned in Chapter VIII.) *Échec au Temps* was a famous alternate-history novel in which Napoleon won the battle of Waterloo. Coincidentally, the same theme was explored by mainstream author Robert **Aron** in *Victoire à Waterloo* (*Victory at Waterloo*, 1937).

Journalist Marc **Wersinger**'s *La Chute dans le Néant* (*The Fall Into Nothingness*, 1947) was an odd novel featuring a man who discovered he had the power to materialize and control a mysterious, ectoplasmic substance. At first, he used his powers to become a stage magician, but the ectoplasm eventually escaped his control and began to cause havoc and destruction. The hero's desperate attempts to regain control of his powers caused him to begin to start shrinking. The ending of the novel was much like Richard Matheson's 1956 classic the *Shrinking Man*.

b. Other Notable Writers

COSMIC JOURNEYS

One of the most nefarious consequences of the self-censorship imposed on science fiction in the 1930s was the suppression of space opera as a sub-genre. While the unbridled imagination of authors was given free rein in America, in France, writers wisely preferred to remain Earthbound. Works like Gustave Le Rouge's 1908 *Le Prisonnier de la Planète Mars* (*The Prisoner of Planet Mars*) and Jean de La Hire's *Les Grandes Aventures d'un Boy Scout* (*The Great Adventures of a Scout*, 1926), which were the French equivalent of Edgar Rice Burroughs' 1912 *A Princess of Mars*, could have inspired others to follow and helped the genre to blossom. But it was not to be.

Nothing illustrated this better than Alin **Monjardin**'s 1934 novel, *L'Extraordinaire Voyage* (*The Extraordinary Journey*; see above), which was rewritten by the author to change its setting from interplanetary space to Atlantis.

By the end of the 1930s, American science fiction welcomed the talents of Isaac Asimov, Robert Heinlein, and A. E. Van Vogt, to name but a few, while in France, Renard, Moselli, and Thévenin had virtually deserted the genre, and Spitz was a lonely voice.

One of the last, grand space operas was René-Marcel de **Nizerolles**' 108-issue serial, *Les Aventuriers du Ciel: Voyages Extraordinaires d'un Petit Parisien dans la Stratosphère, la Lune et les Planètes* (*The Adventurers of the Sky: Extraordinary Voyages of a Little Parisian in the Stratosphere, the Moon and the Planets*, 1935-37), a sequel to his 1912 *Les Voyages Aériens d'un Petit Parisien à travers le Monde* (*The Aerial Voyages of a Little Parisian Across the World*), featuring the adventures of the indomitable Tintin (no relation to **Hergé**'s character). In it, Tintin used the hydrogen-powered spaceship "Bolide" to explore the solar system. On Venus, he found descendents of the Greek Gods ruling a race of giant cyclops. On Mars, he came across a race of little men served by giant robots. The saga also included time-travel; anticipating Pierre **Boulle**'s classic *Planet of the Apes*, Tintin discovered that apes had superseded men five thousand years in the future.

The year 1935 also saw the publication of *Un Français dans la Lune* (*A Frenchman on the Moon*) by Jean **Loisy**; and *La Visite des Martiens* (*The Visit of the Martians*) by Jacques **Loria**.

The following year, *Les Fiancés de la Planète Mars* (*The Fiancés of Mars*, 1936), was among the first of many adventure novels by Maurice **Limat**. Limat, like Bruss, later became one of the regular contributors of the *Anticipation* and *Angoisse* imprints of Fleuve Noir in the 1950s, 1960s, and 1970s (see chapters VIII and IX). Limat followed in the footsteps of Gustave Le Rouge with novels such as *L'Avion Mystérieux* (*The Mystery Plane*, 1937) and *Les Naufragés de la Voie Lactée* (*The Castaways of the Milky Way*, 1939), but this was still science fiction that followed the templates of 1914.

Henri **Duvernois**' *L'Homme qui s'est Retrouvé* (*The Man Who Found Himself*, 1936) was a cosmic journey with a unique twist. In it, a man travelled to Proxima Centauri and arrived on a planet that was just like Earth, but thirty-five years earlier.

Louis **Grivel**'s *À la Conquête de Venus* (*The Conquest of Venus*) was published in Tunisia in 1942 and depicted Venus as a prehistoric planet.

Finally, a few notable juvenile or young-adult genre novels were published just before World War II. These included:

Le Mystère de la Nuit Sans Lune (*The Mystery of the Moonless Night*, 1942), a novel about the explosion of the Moon, by Christiane **Fournier**.

Panique sur le Monde (*Panic Over the World*, 1942), *S.O.S.! Ici Paris* (*SOS! Paris Calling*, 1942) and *On a Volé No. 2 de la Rue* (*They Stole No. 2 of the Street*, 1947), by Henri **Suquet**.

OTHER LANDS AND MAD SCIENCE

One of the last and most remarkable authors to come out of the adventure magazines and imprints of the 1920s and 1930s was Tancrède **Vallerey**. In his *Celui qui Viendra* (*He Who Shall Come*, 1929), a young scientist and his mentor, Dr. Fauster, were visited by a mysterious being who turned out to be an alien from Aldebaran. The alien told them that his world was willing to share its scientific wonders with Earth, but could take only one man back with him. Fauster went, but because of the time factor, he would not return for several centuries. The novel ended with the young hero's tragic plight, speculating about the wonders he will never know and telling his successors to wait for Fauster's return. *L'Île au Sable Vert* (*The Island with Green Sand*, 1930) won the Jules Verne Award but was an ordinary adventure novel featuring underground tunnels linking various parts of the globe. *L'Avion Fantastique* (*The Fantastic Plane*, 1936) was about a remote-controlled, pilotless plane. Far more interesting was *Un Mois sous les Mers* (*A Month Undersea*, 1937), in which it was revealed that a piece of Mercury had fallen to the bottom of the Pacific Ocean and created an underwater alien eco-system, complete with intelligent, giant ants and a crystalline vegetation. The ant-like aliens were at war with each other ("just like men") and used weapons that harnessed radioactivity.

Giant insects were also featured in Charles de **Richter**'s *La Menace Invisible* (*The Invisible Threat*, 1934), in which a mad scientist led an invasion of termites to destroy Paris and almost conquer the world. (The novel was translated by Fletcher Pratt in *Wonder Stories* magazine as *The Fall of the Eiffel Tower*.) Other notable works by de Richter included *Les Vierges du Soleil* (*The Virgins of the Sun*, 1944) and *L'Homme qui Voulut le Déluge* (*The Man Who Wanted the Flood*, 1945), about a mad scientist who tried to create a new flood.

Also in 1934, Jean **Cotard**'s *Le Flot d'Épouvante* (*The Flood of Terror*) featured an invasion of the French coastline by giant crabs. Another particularly vile supervillain was Robert **Collard**'s *Demonax* (1938). And in Jean-Pierre **Besson**'s *Le Monstre de St. Basile* (*The Monster of St. Basile*, 1941), a giant, mutated fly attacked Paris.

In 1936, the prolific Maurice **Limat** began his career with *La Montagne aux Vampires* (*The Mountain of Vampires*, 1936), about a man who could control vampires. It was followed by *L'Araignée d'Argent* (*The Silver Spider*, 1936), featuring a robot spider created by an ancient civilisation, *Les Hommes d'Acier* (*The Men of Steel*, 1936), *L'Empereur des Scaphandriers* (*The Emperor of Deep-Sea Divers*, 1937), *Le Septième Cerveau* (*The Seventh Brain*, 1939), *Le Zodiaque de l'Himalaya* (*The Zodiac of the Himalaya*, 1942), *Les Rescapés de la Préhistoire* (*Escape From Prehistory*, 1947) and *La Comète Écarlate* (*The Scarlet Comet*, 1948), to name but a few.

Also in 1936, Paul **Alpérine** wrote *L'Île des Vierges Rouges* (*The Island of the Red Virgins*), about a Lost World of Amazons hidden in the Brazilian jungle. Other notable Alpérine novels included *Ombres sur le Thibet* (*Shadows Over Tibet*, 1945), about a Tibetan mountain made of radium; *La Citadelle des Glaces* (*The Citadel of the Ice*, 1946); *Les Secrets de la Mer Morte* (*The Secrets of the Dead Sea*, 1949), and *Demain dans le Soleil* (*Tomorrow Inside the Sun*, 1950).

Finally, Paul Bérato also known as "Paul **Béra**" and "Yves **Dermèze**," began a prolific career as a writer of juvenile adventure novels with *La Cité dans les Glaces* (*The City in the Ice*, 1942), *Les Buveurs d'Océan* (*The Drinkers of Oceans*, 1943), *Le Pays sans Soleil* (*The Land Without Sun*, 1948), and *Les Pirates du Ciel* (*The Sky Pirates*, 1949). Like Bruss and Limat, Béra eventually joined the team of the *Anticipation* and *Angoisse* imprints of Fleuve Noir (see chapters VIII and IX).

Three notable novels of the period were:

L'Île sous Cloche (*The Domed Island*) by Xavier de **Langlais**, first published in Breton as *Enez ar Rod* (*The Island of the Wheel*) in 1944 and translated into French by the author in 1946.

Fabrique d'Hommes (*Man Factory*, 1946) by Jean **Bucline**, about a secret Master of the World living on an artificial island, who used agents to sow discord and foment wars.

Les Rayons M.V. (*The MV Rays*, 1947) by Émile **Couture**.

Other notable authors and works of the 1930s and 1940s in the popular adventure vein included:

J.-H. **Rosny** Jeune, Rosny's younger brother, with

L'Énigme du Redoutable (*The Enigma of the Redoutable*, 1930), in which a lost underwater colony of Britons was discovered; and *Le Destin de Martin Lafaille* (*The Fate of Martin Lafaille*, 1945), featuring a brilliant mathematician who solved the mysteries of the universe.

Raoul **Le Jeune** contributed *Prisonniers au Fond des Mers* (*Prisoners at the Bottom of the Sea*, 1931), *Le Pays de la Mort* (*The Land of Death*, 1931), *Le Maître des Sargasses* (*The Master of the Sargasso Sea*, 1932), and *Prisonnier des Invisibles* (*Prisoner of the Invisibles*, 1933).

V. **Géraud**, with *Sous les Sables du Sahara* (*Under the Sands of the Sahara*), serialized in the *Petit Illustré* in 1932, told of the exploration of the underground sea and the vast oil fields that lay hidden under the Sahara, which was rather prophetic considering that no one suspected the existence of oil there at the time.

Maurice **Boué** and Édouard **Aujay**, with *Le Tour du Monde en... Un Jour* (*Around the World in One Day*, 1933), which featured a method of travel which involved remaining motionless while letting the Earth rotate underneath.

Georges **Delhoste**, with *Le Maître du Jour et du Bruit* (*The Master of Day and Noise*, 1933), which featured the television-like transmission of sounds and images; and *La Science Folle* (*Science Gone Mad*, 1934), in which a dwarf mad scientist transformed the Sahara into a futuristic empire.

Gustave **Gailhard**, with *La Cité Fantôme* (*The Phantom City*, 1934) and *Le Lac des Mirages* (*The Lake of Mirages*, 1938).

Félix **Celval**, with *Les Robinsons de l'Espace* (*The Space Robinsons*, 1934), *Le Rayon Infernal* (*The Hellish Ray*, 1935), *Le Monstre de l'Île sans Nom* (*The Monster of the Nameless Island*, 1936) and *Les Flibustiers de l'Espace* (*The Corsairs of Space*, 1938).

Félix **Léonnec**, with *Le Secret de l'Immortalité* (*The Secret of Immortality*, 1934), *L'Île d'Épouvante* (*Island of Terror*, 1936) and *Le Dragon Volant* (*The Flying Dragon*, 1937).

René **Duchesne**, with *Le Maître de la Mort* (*The Master of Death*, 1936), *Les Forbans de l'Océan* (*The Ocean Bandits*, 1936), *L'Extraordinaire Voyage du Loriot* (*The Extraordinary Journey of the Loriot*, 1937) and *Les Hommes sans Visage* (*The Faceless Men*, 1938).

Michel **Darry**, with *La Course au Radium* (*The Race for Radium*, 1936), *La Chambre de la Mort Lente* (*The Chamber of Slow Death*, 1937), *La Vallée de la Mort Rouge* (*The Valley of the Red Death*, 1937) and *L'Île des Singes Rois* (*The Island of the Monkey Kings*, 1939).

Robert **Jean-Boulan**, with *L'Île des Centaures* (*Centaur Island*, 1936), *La Ville des Tritons* (*The City of Tritons*, 1937), *Au Paradis des Étoiles* (*In the Paradise of Stars*, 1938) and *Les Aventuriers de la Planète Mars* (*The Adventurers of Planet Mars*, 1941).

André **Michel**, with *Le Mystère de la Pyramide* (*The Mystery of the Pyramid*, 1936), *L'Oiseau du Pôle* (*The Bird* *of the Pole*, 1937), *Au Coeur du Cyclone* (*In the Heart of the Hurricane*, 1938) and *Le Secret des Huit* (*The Secret of the Eight*, 1939).

Maurice **Pérot**, with *L'Expérience du Dr. Hortner* (*The Experiment of Dr. Hortner*, 1937), *Le Royaume de l'Épouvante* (*The Kingdom of Terror*, 1937), *Les Explorateurs de l'Espace* (*The Explorers of Space*, 1938) and *La Cité des Réprouvés* (*The City of the Shunned*, 1939).

Mona **Gloria**, with *Au Pays des Géants Rouges* (*In the Land of the Red Giants*, 1937), *Les Mystérieuses Catacombes* (*The Mysterious Catacombs*, 1938) and *Au Pays des Demi-Hommes* (*In the Land of the Half-Men*, 1941).

Jean **Normand**, with *Les Vengeurs du Soleil* (*The Avengers of the Sun*, 1928), *Le Poignard de Verre* (*The Glass Dagger*, 1936) and *La Cité du Mystère* (*The City of Mystery*, 1937).

George **Fronval**, with *L'Énigmatique Fen-Chu* (*The Mysterious Fen-Chu*, 1944) revised as *Le Maître des Robots* (*The Robot Master*, 1946).

Pierre **Olasso**, with *Le Sorcier de la Jungle* (*The Wizard of the Jungle*, 1938) and *Le Monstre Préhistorique* (*The Prehistoric Monster*, 1952).

Léopold **Frachet**, with *Mille Lieues sous les Terres* (*A Thousand Leagues Under the Earth*, 1939), *La Guerre des Robots* (*War of the Robots*, 1939) and *La Reine de l'Amazone* (*The Amazon Queen*, 1939), a colorful Lost World story.

Jean **Kery**, with *Les Conjurés de l'Île Secrète* (*The Plotters of the Secret Island*, 1939), *La Secte Infernale* (*The Infernal Sect*, 1949), *La Reine du Pôle* (*The Queen of the Pole*, 1950) and *Les Mystères d'Atomeville* (*The Mysteries of Atom-City*, 1951).

Roger-Henri **Jacquart**, with *Cet Étrange Docteur Lang* (*That Strange Dr. Lang*, 1940), *La Prison sous l'Océan* (*The Prison Under the Ocean*, 1944) and *Le Dernier Couple* (*The Last Couple*, 1945).

And, finally, Swiss writer Jacques **Chable**, with *Le Maître du Soleil* (*The Master of the Sun*, 1942) and the juvenile *Flammes dans le Ciel* (*Fire in the Sky*, 1943).

THE FUTURE

The perspective of a new conflict with Germany continued to fill the pages of the science fiction imprints and magazines throughout the 1930s and 1940s, with novels such as Jean **Bardanne**'s *L'Allemagne Attaquera Le...* (*Germany Will Attack On...*, 1932), followed by the grimly prophetic *La Guerre et les Microbes* (*War and Microbes*, 1937).

In Colonel **Brat**'s "Paris Sera-t-il Détruit en 1936?" ("Will Paris Be Destroyed in 1936?," 1933), the French thwarted a sneak German attack. This story was written as an explicit response to a German novel *How Paris Will Be Destroyed in 1936* (1932) by German author Major von Helders, in which France was attacked by the British.

Albert de **Pouvourville**'s *Pacifique 39* (1934) and the

thirty-issue serial *La Guerre Prochaine/ L'Héroïque Aventure* (*The Next War/The Heroic Adventure*, 1934-35) were military anticipations of World War II, just as Capitaine **Danrit**'s novels (see Chapter V) were military anticipations, of World War I. What was especially ironic in this case was that reality overtook fiction and the real war forced the author to stop writing in the middle of his story.

Gaston **Pastre** was another provider of adventure novels and military anticipations such as *L'Île Z* (*Z Island*, 1936), *Le Grand Complot de 1950* (*The Great Plot of 1950*, 1938), *Les Avions de la Mort* (*The Planes of Death*, 1939), and *Les Sous-Marins Fantômes* (*The Ghost Submarines*, 1939). What made Pastre's military fiction rather lame was that he "cheated" by boosting the performances of French machines and unrealistically lowering that of German equipment, and did not hesitate to employ hoary "deus ex machina" devices to guarantee a French victory.

More serious was the five-issue serial *La Guerre! La Guerre!* (*War! War!*, 1939) written by Jean de **La Hire** under the pseudonym of "Commandant Cazal." Appearing on the eve of the war, it prophesied the enormously important role played by oil in the future conflict.

The same year, a writer using the pseudonym "Commandant **Verdun**" released two volumes of *Face à l'Ennemi* (*Facing the Enemy*), which included an underground war and a "tornado squad."

Other novels about the future included:

E.-G. **Perrier**'s *En l'An 2000* (*In the Year 2000*, 1931).

Georges **Duhamel**'s *Les Jumeaux de Vallangoujard* (*The Twins From Vallangoujard*, 1931), a young adult novel about the discovery of the secret of happiness, which ended up standardizing mankind.

Pierre de **Nolhac**'s *Saison en Auvergne* (*Season in Auvergne*, 1932), in which an earthquake created an inland sea in the center of France.

Jean **Quatremarre**'s *Alors la Terre s'arrêta...* (*Then the Earth Stood Still*, 1934), in which an asteroid crashed into the Moon, which fell to Earth killing everyone except a couple of humans.

Belgian writer Ege **Tilms**' *Hodomur, l'Homme de l'Infini* (*Hodomur, Man of Infinity*, 1934).

Charles de **L'Andelyn**'s *La Prodigieuse Découverte de Georges Lefranc* (*The Prodigious Discovery of Georges Lefranc*, 1935), about an immortality serum and a future where perfumes were personalized and food came in tablets.

Elga **Dimt**'s *Et La Vie Continue* (*And Life Goes On*, 1941), sub-titled "An Idyll in Lausanne in the Year 2234."

Étienne **Gril**'s *L'Ovipare* (1942), which described an odd near-future in which a woman started laying eggs.

Pierre **Devaux**'s *Uranium*, written in 1944 but not published until 1946, which was a prophetic warning against the atom bomb.

Belgian author Stéphane **Hautem**'s *Le Retour au Silence* (*The Return to Silence*, 1945), a dystopia subtitled

"Diary of the Homo Citroensis No.K228b" after the famous French car make.

Aimé **Blanc**'s *Le Drame de l'An 3000* (*The Drama of Year 3000*, 1946).

And, finally, Christophe **Paulin**'s *S'Il n'en reste qu'un* (*If Only One Is Left*, 1946), in which a young French physicist and an American girl were the only survivors on an Earth "purified" of all living matter by a mad scientist; together, they had to recreate civilization.

Finally, a special place should be reserved for Swiss writer Léon **Bopp**, whose unique and unclassifiable *Jacques Arnaut et la Somme Romanesque* (*Jacques Arnaut and the Sum of His Novels*, 1933) was a literary hoax-like book about a fictional writer. Bopp's four-volume *Liaisons du Monde* (*World Relations*, 1938-44) was a detailed epic describing a parallel France under Soviet domination from 1935 to 1944. Bopp's genre stories were collected in *Drôle de Monde* (*Funny World*) in 1940.

c. Mainstream Writers

André **Maurois** remained the most notable mainstream writer dabbling with science fiction themes during the period. His classic *La Machine à Lire les Pensées* (1937; *The Thought-Reading Machine*, 1937), already mentioned above, featured a camera-like device capable of capturing thoughts on film. Another story on the same theme was A. **Clouet**'s "La Machine à Capter la Pensée" ("The Machine to Capture Thoughts," 1941].)

Raymond **Desorties**'s *Le Tétrabie* (1933) was about a fantastic machine that could travel in the air, on land, and under the sea. The tale symbolized how the Vernian spirit of invention had infiltrated mainstream litterature.

Another notable futuristic allegory was Jean **Talabot**'s *R'Adam et R'Eve ou Le Vestige* (*R'Adam and R'Eve or the Remains*, 1934).

Belgian thriller writer Stanislas-André **Steeman**, the author of the character of Monsieur Wens, penned a sequel to Gaston **Leroux**'s 1911 missing link novel *Balaoo* (see Chapter IV) with *Les Fils de Balaoo* (*The Sons of Balaoo*, 1934), and one novel dealing with robots, *Ennemi sans Visage* (*Faceless Enemy*, 1938), reissued as *Monsieur Wens et l'Automate* (*Mr. Wens and the Automaton*, 1943).

In *Voyage au Pays des Bohohoms* (*Voyage to the Lands of the Bohohoms*, 1938), Luc **Durtain** told the story of a man who discovered that the clouds were inhabited by nearly insubstantial beings. Durtain also penned *La Guerre n'existe pas* (*War Dies Not Exist*, 1939) and a collection of genre tales, *Histoires Fantastiques* (*Fantastic Stories*, 1942).

In 1946, André H. **Balnec** described the colonization of the Moon in *Sélèné*. In it, the first man to land on the Moon was a Frenchman, Émile Durand. The Moon, now dubbed the Satellite and its inhabitants the Satellians, was partitioned into various colonies, each affiliated to a different nation. The novel went on to examine in great detail the social, economic, religious, and political problems created by the existence of a Moon colony.

Finally, the names of Romain **Gary**, Henri d'**Amfreville**, Yves **Gandon**, and Raymond **Abellio** should be added here, as they began to contribute genre novels in the late 1940s. Their works will be more appropriately reviewed in Chapter IX.

CHAPTER VIII

Modern Fantastique
After World War II

World War II exacted both a huge physical and a devastating psychological toll on French culture. France's defeat in 1940, followed by four years of occupation and, in some cases, of collaboration or resistance, confronted writers with choices they had never before had to face. The ensuing development of the atom bomb, and the polarization of the political conflict between East and West, introduced sharp new fears into the cauldron of the collective unconscious.

After World War II, mainstream French culture increasingly frowned upon works of unbridled imagination and preferred instead to embrace the more naturalistic and political concerns of the existentialists, embodied by writers such as Jean-Paul Sartre (1905-1980), Albert Camus (1913-1960), Simone de **Beauvoir**, and Boris **Vian**. The existentialists depicted Man as being alone in a bleak, godless universe. In the 1950s, the *Nouveau Roman* (*New Novel*), pioneered by Françoise Sagan (1935-), continued the literary experiments of the surrealists by rejecting the traditional framework of fiction. Some of its most notorious contributors included Marguerite Duras (1914-), Alain **Robbe-Grillet**, Jean **Cayrol**, Michel **Butor**, and Nathalie Sarraute.

Yet, paradoxically, in spite of being deliberately marginalized by literary critics and the literary establishment, the *fantastique* thrived as it never had before. Both in terms of quality and quantity, the modern period is the richest, and some of its authors among the best, in the history of the genre.

For this chapter, we have divided the previous fifty years into three chronological subdivisions: the first, dubbed the "1950s and 1960s," starts in the immediate postwar period of the late 1940s, continues through the 1950s and the early 1960s, when France shed its colonial past and experienced a postwar economic boom and a period of unprece-

dented stability, and ends approximately in 1970, when the political and sociological upheavals caused by the notorious "events" of May 1968 created a virtual cultural revolution and a sharp shift to the left in France's cultural scene.

The second subdivision, dubbed the "1970s," reflects this period of transformation and ends in the mid-1980s, after the full impact of the left's election to power in 1981, a factor which paradoxically broke its stranglehold on culture.

The third and last subdivision, dubbed the "1980s and 1990s," runs from the mid-1980s to the late 1990s.

We have also retained our previous division between the *fantastique littéraire* on the one hand, comprised of works with literary ambition and generally published by mainstream houses, and the *fantastique populaire*, on the other hand, written for entertainment and/or shock value, and generally published in specialized paperback imprints. This division, however, and more so than at any other time in history, becomes increasingly arbitrary and difficult to determine as we approach the 1980s. In the 1960s, authors such as Roger **Blondel**/B.-R. **Bruss** and Michel **Bernanos**/Michel **Talbert** used different pseudonyms depending on which sides of the literary fence they wrote. In the 1980s, popular authors such as Claude **Klotz**, Georges-Olivier **Châteaureynaud**, and René **Réouven** were published by mainstream literary houses.

Finally, within our chronological outline, we have attempted to regroup authors by sub-genres, but that is also a difficult and often debatable notion. The proliferation of styles and the explosion of approaches to the *fantastique* during the past fifty years is nothing short of remarkable. Modern French *fantastique* does not speak with one voice, or even a few, but with many. The sources of inspiration range from the traditional *fantastique* based on classic supernatural concepts, to new surrealism, regional *fantastique* rooted in country folk legends, symbolism, and esoterism.

Major foreign influences on modern French *fantastique* include Franz Kafka (1883-1924), who was translated into French in 1933 (*The Trial*) and 1938 (*The Castle, Metamorphosis*); Jorge Luis Borges (1899-1986); H. P. Lovecraft (1890-1937), whose works were greatly admired by Jean **Cocteau**, by then a member of the French Academy; Dino Buzzati (1906-1972); Julio Cortazar (1914-1984); Vladimir Nabokov (1899-1977); Gabriel Garcia-Marquez (1928-) and Richard Matheson (1926-). These writers virtually redefined modern *fantastique* by showing that it could embrace much more than mere ghost stories.

Other, more recent, influences included the American and Italian "gore" movies, Stephen King, Robert E. Howard (whose *Conan* did not become a household name in France until the early 1980s), role-playing games such as *Dungeons & Dragons*, R. L. Stine's *Goosebumps* series, and more. The growth of gore fiction and sword & sorcery during the last decade is a dubious tribute to the Americanization of world culture.

Still, when considered in its entirety, French modern *fantastique* looks like a gigantic melting pot, or a huge orchestra in which all the instruments have successfully blended their music together in order to achieve a wholly new vision of the world, a vision that could only be created through the unique medium of the *fantastique*.

1. The 1950s and 1960s

a. Fantastique Littéraire

Traditional Fantastique

Marcel **Béalu** was easily one of the leading writers of the *fantastique littéraire* of the immediate postwar period. His tales were halfway between prose and poetry, and his fantasy followed the classic path of Hoffman, Poe, and Gérard de **Nerval**. In Béalu's fiction, hapless souls became slowly trapped in dream-like realities where inhuman forces held sway. *L'Expérience de la Nuit* (*The Experience of Night*, 1945) dealt with the power to see into other dimensions. His classic *L'Araignée d'Eau* (*The Water Spider*, 1948) was about an impossible love between a man and a watery creature who slowly turned into a girl. Rejected by her human lover, she drowned him. (The novel was adapted into an eponymous 1968 feature film—See Book 1, Chapter I.) Béalu's shorter stories, collected in *Mémoires de l'Ombre* (*Memoirs of Shadow*, 1941; rev. 1959) and *L'Aventure Impersonelle* (*The Unpersonal Adventure*, 1954; rev. 1964), were a series of sometimes poetic, often morbid, vignettes in terror, all built around the theme of trafficking with the darkness. Another, more recent novel, *La Poudre des Songes* (*The Dust of Dreams*, 1977), followed the same pattern.

Marcel **Brion** was, with Béalu, the other major writer of the *fantastique* of the immediate postwar period Unlike Béalu, however, Brion's approach of the supernatural almost always referred to the romantic tradition and the search for a mystical absolute. Brion was, at heart, a dreamer. *De l'Autre Côté de la Forêt* (*On the Other Side of the Forest*, 1966), *Les Miroirs et les Gouffres* (*Mirrors and Abysses*, 1968) and *Nous Avons Traversé la Montagne* (*We Have Crossed the Mountain*, 1972) were all about esoteric journeys where love enabled the protagonists to go beneath the surface of things and find the true reality. *L'Ombre de l'Arbre Mort* (*The Shadow of the Dead Tree*, 1970) and *Le Journal du Visiteur* (*The Diary of a Traveller*, 1980) were about love defying death; in the latter, a man fell in love with a woman who had been dead for three hundred years, and succeeded in bringing her back to life for a brief moment. Brion's most famous collections of stories were *Les Escales de la Haute Nuit* (*The Shore Leaves of the Deepest Night*, 1942) and *La Chanson de l'Oiseau Étranger* (*The Song of a Strange Bird*, 1958).

André **Pieyre de Mandiargues** loved fairy tales, and everything that was baroque and fabulous. This elegant author wrote numerous short stories, collected in *Le Musée Noir* (*The Black Museum*, 1946; rev. 1974), *Soleil des Loups* (*The Sun of the Wolves*, 1951) and *Feu de Braise* (*Ember Fire*, 1959). His tales owed their inspiration to sources as varied as **Sade**, the *roman noir*, **Nodier**, **Mérimée** and Bierce. Pieyre de Mandiargues' gift was to make the invisible visible with an implacable sense of logic and an almost maniacal precision. His stories did not try to terrify as much as they attempted to convey a sense of "wrongness." Erotic love and death were easily intertwined in his nightmarish visions, such as in his latter novel *La Motocyclette* (*The Motorbike*, 1963).

André **Dhôtel** was an explorer of the *fantastique*, a cartographer who wandered through strange lands where the rules of logic rarely seemed to apply. Influenced by the folk legends of his native Ardennes—a forest-covered mountain range located between France and Belgium—Dhôtel used adolescents as his protagonists to make us experience weird and wondrous events, which were inevitably presented in a disturbingly matter-of-fact way. His *La Chronique Fabuleuse* (*The Fabulous Chronicle*, 1955) and *Le Pays où l'on n'arrive Jamais* (*The Unreachable Country*, 1955) belonged to that vein. His classic *Les Voyages Fantastiques de Julien Grainebis* (*The Fantastic Voyages of Julian Grainebis*, 1958) featured a young man who first experienced life as a tree, then visited a robotic utopia and eventually brought his mother back from a village which suffered from the curse of invisibility.

Noël **Devaulx** was the last major French *fantastique* author of the immediate postwar period. Devaulx' own brand of *fantastique* relied of the intrusion of strange, subtle, mysterious, unexplained, and ultimately unexplainable, elements into everyday reality. His short stories were dubbed by critics "allegories without explanations, parables without keys."

His best collections were *L'Auberge Parpillon* (*The Parpillon Inn*, 1945), *Le Pressoir Mystique* (*The Mystic Press*, 1948), *Bal chez Alféoni* (*Ball at the Alféoni's*, 1956) and *Le Lézard d'Immortalité* (*The Lizard of Immortality*, 1977). Devaulx also wrote a novel, *Sainte Barbegrise* (*Saint Greybeard*, 1952).

Other genre writers of note who emerged during this period included:

André de **Richaud** who, like a French Richard Matheson, was one of the first authors to introduce the concepts of modern psychology into the *fantastique*. In *La Nuit Aveuglante* (*The Blinding Night*, 1945), for example, the protagonist could not remove a devil's face-shaped mask because it reflected the evil contained within his soul. *Je ne suis pas mort* (*I Am Not Dead*, 1965) was another notable work by Richaud in this vein.

Marcel **Schneider** was the author of a remarkable *Histoire de la Littérature Fantastique en France* (*History of Fantastic Literature in France*, 1964), and also a talented writer who followed the traditions laid out by Nodier and Nerval. His novels mixed classic themes, such as impossible loves and ancient gods and goddesses, with images pulled from the subconscious mind. *La Première Île* (*The First Island*, 1951) was about the theme of the androgyne; *Le Guerrier de Pierre* (*The Stone Warrior*, 1969) featured a man turned into stone. Schneider's best short story collections, where the fantastic intrudes upon modern settings with disturbing consequences, included *Aux Couleurs de la Nuit* (*In the Colors of Night*, 1953) and *Opéra Massacre* (*Opera Slaughter*, 1965).

Like Schneider, Roger **Caillois** was an historian of the genre, the writer of *Approches de l'Imaginaire* (*Approach of the Imaginary*, 1970) and the editor of a deservedly famous *Anthologie du Fantastique* (*Anthology of Fantasy*, 1977). But Caillois was also the author of numerous genre works, such as *Méduse* (1960), *Trois Leçons des Ténèbres* (*Three Lessons of Darkness*, 1978), and *La Lumière des Songes* (*The Light of Dreams*, 1984), all traditional in inspiration.

Michel **Bernanos** was the fourth son of renowned writer Georges **Bernanos**, the author of *Sous le Soleil de Satan* (see Chapter VI). Young Bernanos lived an adventurous life, including two stays in Brazil in 1938 and 1948, which inspired him to write the classic novel *La Montagne Morte de la Vie* (*The Dead Mountain of Life*, 1967), which was published only after his untimely death in 1964. *La Montagne Morte de la Vie* was about the terrifying experiences encountered by two men who are shipwrecked on a mysterious desert island, and eventually discovered that the mountain which dominated the island was home to a mysterious, Lovecraftian entity. Bernanos also wrote the poetic *Le Murmure des Dieux* (*The Whisper of the Gods*, 1964) under the pseudonym of "Michel Drowin," and several popular horror novels under the pseudonym of "Michel Talbert" (see **Fantastique Populaire** below).

Another notable writer was André **Beucler**, whose

strange short fictions were collected in *Trois Oiseaux* (*Three Birds*, 1957) and *Ténèbrus* (*Darkness*, 1968). Even the renowned existentialist writer Simone de **Beauvoir** was to be credited for her *Tous les Hommes sont Mortels* (*All Men Are Mortals*, 1946), in which a 13th century man who became immortal regretted his past.

Finally, playwright Maurice **Toesca** wrote a number of allegorical genre novels such as *Le Singe Bleu* (*The Blue Monkey*, 1948), *Le Bruit Lointain du Temps* (*Time's Far-Away Sound*, 1961), and *Les Loups-Garous* (*The Werewolves*, 1966). Toesca also adapted genre material for radio and television (see Book 1, chapters II and III).

One could not write a panorama of the French *fantastique* of the 1950s and 1960s without mentioning the monthly magazine *Fiction*, created in 1953, which started as a French edition of the American magazine *F & SF*, but also published a number of French fantastic authors until about 1968, after which it devoted itself entirely to science fiction. During this period, *Fiction* published stories by such distinguished foreign authors as Borges, Matheson, Calvino, and Buzzati, and also works by French writers such as **Albaret**, **Cassou**, and **Véry**. Several noted French genre authors made their first appearance in the pages of *Fiction*.

Among these were Alain **Dorémieux**, who eventually became *Fiction*'s editor in 1957, and also wrote polemical reviews under the pseudonym of "Serge-André Bertrand." Dorémieux's short stories, later collected in *Mondes Interdits* (*Forbidden Worlds*, 1967), *Promenades au bord du Gouffre* (*Walks on the Edge of the Pit*, 1978), and *Couloirs sans Issue* (*No Exit Corridors*, 1981) showed the influence of Richard Matheson, and were charmingly morbid in tone. A recurring Dorémieux theme is the presence of strange, almost always deadly, female creatures. Finally, Dorémieux became one of France's foremost anthologist of horror fiction, compiling several anthologies of various authors (including one devoted to Richard Matheson) and editing the ten-volume series, *Territoires de l'Inquiétude* (*Territories of Worry*, 1991-96; see below).

Another *Fiction* alumni of note was Fereydoun **Hoveyda**, an Iranian-born writer who also contributed articles and reviews to the magazine under the pseudonym of "F. Hoda." Hoveyda's short stories were classic little gems, collected in *Dans une Terre Étrange* (*On a Strange Earth*, 1968) and *Le Losange* (*The Losange*, 1968).

Also notable were Pierre **Ferran**, whose *Sans Tambour Ni Trompette* (*With Neither Drum Nor Trumpet*, 1979) struck an original note in the production of the times; Jacques **Sternberg**; **Topor** (both reviewed under **Modern Surreal-**

ists below); Gabriel **Deblander** (reviewed under **Belgian Fantastique** below); Julia **Verlanger**, and Christine **Renard** (both reviewed under **Female Writers** below). All in all, a very impressive record for *Fiction*.

Modern Surrealists

Even though the surrealists lost some of their appeal because of the war and were no longer at the forefront of the literary scene after it, a number of writers such as Julien **Gracq**, whose *Le Rivage des Syrtes* (*The Shores of the Syrtes*) was published in 1951, continued to produce genre works.

Lise **Deharme** was a such a writer. Deharme had previously collaborated with both **Breton** and Gracq. She was the "lady with a glove" in Breton's *Nadja*. Her fantasy novel *La Porte à Côté* (*The Next Door*, 1949) featured a female succubus who cast her spell on the modern-day descendent of an 18th-century nobleman she once cursed. The ending, in which the succubus turned into a movie star, was, however, resolutely modern and ironic. Deharme's collections of short stories, such as *Cette Année-là* (*That Year*, 1945) and *Le Pot de Mousse* (*The Pot of Mousse*, 1946), or later novels such as *Le Château de l'Horloge* (*The Castle of the Clock*, 1955), also mixed fantastic and surreal elements with a sense of finely tuned irony.

More reflective of the period was Boris **Vian**, a literary descendent of Alfred **Jarry**—he was a "transcendental satrap" in Jarry's "College of Pataphysics"—and a fine dramatist of the absurd. Many of Vian's plays and novels contained elements borrowed from surrealism, traditional *fantastique,* and even science fiction: *L'Écume des Jours* (*Froth on the Daydream*, 1947), adapted into an eponymous 1968 feature film (see Book 1, Chapter I), was a surreal narrative; *L'Arrache-Coeur* (*Heartsnatcher*, 1953) was a fable about metamorphosis. The stories gathered in *Les Fourmis* (*The Ants*, 1949) blended surrealism and fantasy. Vian will also be discussed as a science fiction author in Chapter IX.

Filmmaker and dramatist Alain **Robbe-Grillet** is justifiably famous for the minute precision with which he describes situations that are totally strange and surreal. In *Le Labyrinthe* (*In the Labyrinth*, 1959), Robbe-Grillet showed us a soldier carrying a package under his arm lost in a mysterious, maze-like city, buried under everlasting snow. We never learned who the soldier was, what the package contained, or to whom he was to deliver it. *Instantanés* (*Snap Shots*, 1962) was a collection of tales loaded with surreal imagery: a living mannikin, an escalator going nowhere, a secret chamber that cannot be accessed, the paintings of Chirico. Other significant Robbe-Grillet works included *La Maison de Rendez-Vous* (*The House of Rendezvous*, 1965), *Topologie pour une Cité Fantôme* (*Topology for a Phantom City*, 1976) and *Djinn* (1981).

Robbe-Grillet's special brand of Kafkaesque, metaphysical *fantastique* was also very much in evidence in the films that he wrote and/or directed such as *L'Année Dernière*

à Marienbad (*Last Year in Marienbad*, 1961), directed by Alain **Resnais**; *L'Éden et Après* (*Eden and Afterwards*, 1971), *Glissements Progressifs du Plaisir* (*Progressive Slidings Into Pleasure*, 1974) and *La Belle Captive* (*The Beautiful Prisoner*, 1983; see Book 1, Chapter I).

Jacques **Sternberg** is a Belgian writer, but he deserves to be profiled in this section, as well as discussed as a science fiction author in Chapter IX. Like Robbe-Grillet, Sternberg also wrote for film director Alain Resnais, penning the script of his 1968 surreal time-travel feature, *Je t'aime, Je t'aime* (see Book 1, Chapter I). Like Vian, Sternberg also wrote just as much science fiction as *fantastique*. In fact, he once wrote that he considered science fiction to be only a "*succursale*" (branch) of the *fantastique*. Sternberg's approach to the *fantastique* is complex and resolutely modern. In his works, the causes of terror are not ghosts or vampires but the present-day city, often depicted as a giant, evil entity, ready to crush the hapless humans who dare live within its body. This theme reappears in novels such as *L'Employé* (*The Employee*, 1958), *L'Architecte* (*The Architect*, 1960) and *La Banlieue* (*The Suburb*, 1976). Sternberg's short fiction, collected in *La Géométrie dans l'Impossible* (*The Impossible Geometry*, 1953), *La Géométrie dans la Terreur* (*The Terror Geometry*, 1958), *Contes Glacés* (*Icy Tales*, 1974) and *Contes Griffus* (*Clawed Tales*, 1993), to name but a few, successfully mix several diverse elements: a very dark sense of humor, an almost British knack for pure nonsense, a Kafkaesque notion of the absurd, a taste for the macabre, and finally, a somber, pessimistic vision of the world and the future. In Sternberg's fiction, love is never a source of redemption, but something impossible, almost alien, as in *Sophie, la Mer, la Nuit* (*Sophie, the Sea, the Night*, 1976) or *Le Navigateur* (*The Navigator*, 1977).

Roland **Topor** began his career in the *fantastique* as a renowned artist and cartoonist—he designed René **Laloux**'s animated feature, *La Planète Sauvage* (see Book 1, Chapter IV)—but was soon recognized as a talented writer. Topor became associated with filmmakers Fernando Arrabal and Alexandro **Jodorowsky** in the 1960 neo-surrealist movement dubbed "Panique," about which he later wrote *Café Panique* (*Panic Café*, 1982). Topor published some of his first short stories in the pages of *Fiction*, crafting brilliantly sarcastic, horribly mocking, sadistic little vignettes, collected in titles such as *Quatre Roses pour Lucienne* (*Four Roses for Lucienne*, 1967). He quickly became known as a writer of unbounded imagination, blessed with a uniquely dark sense of humor. His *La Cuisine Cannibale* (*Cannibal Cooking*, 1970) remains a masterpiece in that vein. His novel *Le Locataire Chimérique* (*The Imaginary Tenant*, 1964) was adapted into the 1976 film *Le Locataire* (*The Tenant*) by Roman Polanski (see Book 1, Chapter I).

Other notable, modern surrealist writers of the 1950s and 1960s included:

Pierre **Bettencourt** was the author of several, self-published collections of very short, surreal, absurd little tales, such as *La Folie Gagne* (*Madness Is Winning*, 1950), *Fragments d'Os pour un Squelette* (*Bone Fragments for a Skeleton*, 1950), *Histoires à Pendre ou à Laisser* (*Stories to Take or Leave*, 1951) and *Histoires comme il faut* (*Stories as They Are*, 1955). Bettencourt's fiction is remarkable for its humor, which is comparable to that of American writer Fredric Brown.

Maurice **Blanchot** wrote Kafkaesque utopias such as *Le Très-Haut* (*The Most High*, 1948), *Le Ressassement Éternel* (*The Eternal Repetition*, 1951) and *Le Dernier Homme* (*The Last Man*, 1957).

Jean Marie Amédée **Paroutaud** in *La Ville Incertaine* (*The Uncertain City*, 1950) told the story of a man who was condemned to death for murder and managed to flee to another country. But that country was subject to total chaos and anarchy. Eventually, the murderer preferred to return to his homeland, finding the certain death that awaits him preferable to pure, insane irrationality. Another notable work by Paroutaud is *La Descente Infinie* (*The Infinite Descent*, 1977).

François **Valorbe** was another author whose works, such as *Soleil Intime* (*Intimate Sun*, 1949), *La Vierge aux Chimères* (*The Virgin with Chimeras*, 1957) and *L'Apparition Tangible* (*The Tangible Apparition*, 1969), featured surrealistic elements. His later novel, *Voulez-Vous Vivre en Eps?* (*Do You Want to Live in Eps?*, 1969), was notable for its wonderful blend of fantasy and surrealism.

René Bonnefoy, like Michel Bernanos, wrote numerous popular horror (and science fiction) novels under a pseudonym – that of "B.-R. **Bruss**." (Bruss is reviewed under **Fantastique Populaire**, below, and discussed as a science fiction author in Chapter IX.) as "Roger **Blondel**," Bonnefoy wrote a number of beautifully crafted, surreal novels in the vein of Vian and Borges, such as *Le Mouton Enragé* (*The Rabid Sheep*, 1956), *L'Archange* (*The Archangel*, 1963), the literary tale of a man about to embark on a cosmic journey; and *Le Boeuf* (*The Ox*, 1965), a bitterly acid and surreal tale about teaching. Blondel's best work is *Bradfer et l'Éternel* (*Bradfer and the Eternal*, 1964), a picaresque, satirical novel about a simple man who travels through imaginary lands with a stubborn desire to "get to the bottom of things" as his only weapon.

One writer who truly defied any attempt at classification was Pierre **Gripari**, who broke onto the literary scene with a number of truculent, colorful genre novels, such as *Pierrot la Lune* (*Pierrot-of-the-Moon*, 1963) and *La Vie, la Mort et la Resurrection de Socrate-Marie Gripotard* (*Life, Death and Resurrection of Socrate-Marie Gripotard*, 1968), a novel about a Candide-like superman. *L'Incroyable Equipée de Phosphore Noloc* (*The Incredible Voyage of Phosphore Noloc*, 1964) was an homage to Jules **Verne**'s Extraordinary Voyages and Utopias in which the hero, Phosphore Noloc ("Colon" spelled backwards), discovered that our cosmos was really inside a woman's womb during an incomprehensible act of cosmic copulation. Earth was a fe-

male egg moving inside the placenta of a giant uterus (the stars were small dots lining the uterus' inner walls) and every day, each "new" sun was but a dying sperm, but one day, one of these sperm would hit Earth and fertilize it. Gripari's novels could all just as easily be classified as science fiction, fantasy, satire, or surrealism. His works reflect a dazzling variety of influences, ranging from the occult to Dickens, **Rabelais**, Voltaire, and Russian literature. Gripari also published two collections of genre stories, *Diable, Dieu et autres Contes* (*Of the Devil, God and Other Tales*, 1965) and *Contes de la Rue Broca* (*Tales of Broca Street*, 1967), a collection of modern fairy tales, which became very popular in the late 1970s and were eventually adapted for animation (see Book 1, Chaper IV).

FEMALE WRITERS

While one would be hard-pressed to find any special stylistic differences between the works of the female writers reviewed in this section and those of, say, Béalu or Brion, it nevertheless remains that the emergence of women as major writers of the *fantastique* is one of the most interesting aspects of the immediate postwar period.

As mentioned above, many of these women were first published in the pages of *Fiction* in the late 1950s and early 1960s. Some wrote both science fiction and *fantastique*, and are therefore reviewed at greater length in Chapter IX. The works of authors that belonged squarely in the domain of the *fantastique* included:

Démons et Merveilles (*Demons and Wonders*, 1951) by Françoise d'**Eaubonne**.

Lumière d'Épouvante (*Light of Terror*, 1956) by Marianne **Andrau**.

The stories of Julia **Verlanger**, later collected in *Les Portes Sans Retour* (*The Gates of No Return*, 1976) and *La Flûte de Verre Froid* (*The Flute of Cold Glass*, 1976).

The stories of Christine **Renard**, later collected in *La Mante au Fil des Jours* (*The Mantis on the Flow of the Days*, 1977).

The stories of Nathalie **Henneberg**, later collected in *L'Opale Entydre* (*The Entydre Opal*, 1971).

The fact that most of these collections were often published ten or fifteen years after the original publication of the stories themselves is evidence that the publishing market of the 1950s and 1960s had not yet reached a maturity capable of dealing with the concept of women as authors of straightforward *fantastique*.

Other female writers of the postwar period were drawn to a more traditional, more literary type of *fantastique*, and were published by mainstream houses. While they arguably never gained the fame of their male counterparts, they nevertheless represent an outstanding body of work that is simply impossible to ignore.

André **Frédérique** wrote numerous short stories collected in *Histoires Blanches* (*White Tales*, 1945) and *Aigremort* (*Bitterdeath*, 1947). She displayed a flair for the macabre and the ability to evoke fear with soft, paranoid touches.

Yvonne **Escoula**'s *fantastique* is romantic, full of poetic notions about lost youth, desires and dreams, reminiscences of past lives, and evocations of parallel realities. Her most notable books included *Poursuite du Vent* (*Pursuit of the Wind*, 1947), *Promenade des Promesses* (*Boulevard of Promises*, 1948), *Contes de la Ventourlière* (*Tales of the Ventourliere*, 1965) and *La Peau de la Mer* (*The Skin of the Sea*, 1972).

Geneviève **Gennari** also liked to cross the border between reality and dream, causing the reader to lose his hold on physical existence. *La Fontaine Scellée* (*The Sealed Fountain*, 1950), *Le Rideau de Sable* (*The Curtain of Sand*, 1957), *Nouvelles du Temps et de l'Espace* (*Stories of Time and Space*, 1964) and the more recent *Dieu et son Ombre* (*God and His Shadow*, 1981) and *Le Manuscrit* (*The Manuscript*, 1989) are among her best works.

Mainstream writer and film director Nelly Kaplan used the pseudonym of "**Bélen**" to pen a number of erotic short stories based on either fantastic or science fiction themes. These were collected in *Et Délivrez-nous du Mâle* (*And Free Us from the Males*, 1960), *La Géométrie dans les Spasmes* (*Geometry in Spasms*, 1961) and *La Reine des Sabbats* (*The Queen of the Sabbath*, 1962).

Other noted female writers of the *fantastique* who could be found on the edges of the literary mainstream of the 1960s included:

The surreallistically inclined Simone **Balazard**, with *Le Château des Tortues* (*The Castle of Turtles*, 1962) and *Le Rocher Rouge* (*The Red Rock*, 1972).

The wonderful Marguerite **Cassan**, whose mischievous sense of Lewis Carrollesque humor shone in tales gathered in *Histoires à Coté* (*Sideway Stories*, 1963), *Fil à Fil* (*Thread to Thread*, 1965), and *À Développer dans l'Obscurité* (*To Develop in the Dark*, 1967).

The gothic writer Martine **Chevrier**, with *La Fontaine de Sang* (*The Fountain of Blood*, 1966) and *La Fête des Morts* (*The Festival of the Dead*, 1974) also contributed significantly.

Marie-Thérèse de **Brosses** wrote *Assunrath* (1967), a Richard Matheson-like tale of a woman shrunk down to insect-size.

FANTASTIQUE RÉGIONAL

The traditional connections between the *fantastique littéraire* and the folk tales and legends of the French countryside were reactualized in the earlier part of the 20th century by the efforts of scholars such as Pierre Saintyves (Émile Nourry, 1870-1975), who published *Les Contes de Perrault et les Récits Parallèles* (*Perrault's Tales and Parallel Stories*, 1923) and *En Marge de la Légende Dorée* (*On the Margins of the Golden Legend*, 1930); Arnold Van Gennep, with his *Manuel de Folklore Français Contemporain*

(*Manual of Contemporary French Folklore*, 1943); and Henri Pourrat, with his thirteen-volume collection, *Trésor des Contes* (*Treasure of Folk Tales*, 1948-62). In the late 1930s, publisher Fernand Nathan even started a popular imprint of folk tales retold in a modern style accessible to children and young adults, called *Contes et Légendes*.

In the literary field, the tradition of **Berthoud**, **Sand**, and **Le Braz** was upheld by the prodigious and prolific Claude **Seignolle**, who wrote numerous books collecting and preserving authentic country legends, as well as many short stories and novels making use of the local folklore, including gruesome peasant witchcraft rituals, devil worship, werewolves, etc.

In the first category, we could include *En Sologne* (1945), the two-volume *Contes Populaires de Guyenne* (*Popular Tales of Guyenne*, 1946), *Le Diable dans la Tradition Populaire* (*The Devil in Popular Traditions*, 1959), *Le Folklore du Languedoc* (1960), *Le Folklore de la Provence* (1963), *Les Évangiles du Diable* (*The Devil's Gospel*, 1964) – the devil is a recurrent theme in Seignolle's work and this 900-page book collected and annotated all of the popular beliefs on the subject—*Le Berry Traditionnel* (1969), *Contes Fantastiques de Bretagne* (1969), and others.

Seignolle's own brand of fictional *fantastique* was influenced by his "sorcerous childhood"—the title of a 1994 collection—spent in the misty plains of his native Sologne, and a terrifying encounter with the Devil incarnated in a local warlock, which he claimed to have experienced at age 15 in 1932. This conferred a real sense of authenticity to Seignolle's books, which were almost devoid of any literary artifices. His major works included *La Malvenue* (*The Ill-come*, 1952; rev. 1965), *Le Bahut Noir* (*The Black Dresser*, 1958), *Le Diable en Sabots* (*The Devil in Clogs*, 1959), *La Brume ne se lèvera plus* (*The Mist Will No Longer Rise*, 1959; rev. 1963), *Histoires Maléfiques* (*Maleficent Tales*, 1965), *Contes Macabres* (*Macabre Stories*, 1966), *Les Chevaux de la Nuit* (*The Night Horses*, 1967), *La Nuit des Halles* (*The Night of the Halles*, 1965), *Invitation au Château de l'Étrange* (*Invitation to the Castle of the Weird*, 1969), *Histoires Vénéneuses* (*Poisonous Tales*, 1970) and *Contes Sorciers* (*Sorcerous Stories*, 1974). A number of Seignolle's stories have been adapted as short features or television movies—see Book 1, ***Le Faucheur*** under Short Features in Chapter I, ***Marie la Louve*** in Chapter II, and ***Delphine*** in Chapter III.

Other writers who used the rich French country folklore as a source of inspiration included:

Jean **Blanzat**, the author of numerous stories featuring the Devil, such as *L'Orage du Matin* (*The Morning Storm*, 1942), *La Gartempe* (1957), *L'Iguane* (*The Iguana*, 1966), and *Reflets dans un Ciel d'Or* (*Reflections in a Golden Sky*, 1973).

Eugène **Bressy**, the author of *Légendes de Provence* (*Legends of Provence*, 1963).

Jean-Loup **Trassard**, whose tales embellished the western French province called Mayenne, with *L'Érosion Intérieure* (*The Inner Erosion*, 1965), *L'Ancolie* (*The Ancoly*, 1975), and *Histoires Fraîches* (*Fresh Tales*, 1981).

Interestingly, two African authors from the state of Benin chose to write their native legendary tales in French: Olympe **Bhély-Quénum**, the author of *Le Chant du Lac* (*The Song of the Lake*, 1965), in which a lake spirit interferes with the local villagers' lives, and other African mythological tales such as *Un Piège sans Fin* (*An Endless Trap*, 1978), *L'Initié* (*The Initiate*, 1979), and *Les Appels du Vodou* (*Call of the Voodoo*, 1994); and Jean **Pliya**, the author of *L'Arbre Fétiche* (*The Fetish Tree*, 1963) and *Kondo le Requin* (*Kondo the Shark*, 1965)

Benjamin **Matip**, an African author from the state of Cameroon, wrote a collection of native fairy tales, *À la Belle Étoile* (*Under the Night Sky*, 1962).

Algerian writer Mohammed **Dib** wrote *Baba Férane* (1959), a collection of Algerian folk tales, as well as *Qui se Souvient de la Mer?* (*Who Remembers the Sea?*, 1962), a dream-like novel about a man trapped in a strange, living city. Other notable works included *Cours sur la Rive Sauvage* (*Run on the Wild Shore*, 1964), which dealt with the intersection between dimensions; and *Le Talisman* (1966).

b. *Fantastique Populaire*

HORROR

After a brief economic and artistic lull caused by the war, the *fantastique populaire* thrived again in the postwar period, following in the footsteps of the now-classic tradition established by the **Grand-Guignol** theater.

Among the celebrities who were seen attending the Grand-Guignol during World War II were Hermann Göring, Ho Chi Minh and General George Patton. Eventually, piling horror upon horror led to auto-parody and a general lack of believability. World War II, with its parade of true-life horrors, could be said to have contributed to the decline and fall of the Grand-Guignol. Reality appeared to have, temporarily at least, overtaken fiction. The theater's last manager, Charles Nonon, declared in an interview granted to *Time* magazine (30 Nov. 1962): "We could not compete with Buchenwald."

For the record, the last directors of the Grand-Guignol theater were: Éva Berkson (1939-1952), Marcel Maurey (1952-1953), Raymonde Machard (1954-1958), Christiane Wiegant (1959-1960) and Charles Nonon (1961-1962). After 1946, outside directors were hired to stage the plays. These included Paul Ratineau (1946-47), Éva Berkson (1947-50), Alexandre Dundas (1947-50), Jacques Polieri (1951), Jean Gobert (1952), Jean Dout (1952), Georges Vitaly (1952-53), Michel de Ré (1953-55), Robert Hossein (1954-55)—who went on to direct the film **Le Vampire de Dusseldorf** (*The Dusseldorf Vampire*, 1964), numerous mainstream plays, and who acted in the *Angelique* and **OSS 117** film series; see Book 1, Chapter I—René Rocher (1955-56), Antoine Marin

(1956), Fred Pasquali (1956-59), Eddy **Ghilain** (1960-61), Bernard Charlan (1962), and M. Renay (1962).

In the literary field, the popular *fantastique* was more than ever synonymous with horror, and was primarily meant to thrill, entertain and shock the readers, not offer them a subtle, sophisticated, literary experience. Its niche existed between the thriller genre, especially when it involved gory or surreal crimes, and the popular adventure/science fiction literature developed in the 1920s and 1930s. As we will see, many of the authors easily crossed from one genre into another, but a few, more specialized writers nevertheless emerged.

By far the most distinguished was Jean-Louis **Bouquet**, whose early works included *romans-cinémas* (film novelizations) and film scripts, such as Luitz-Morat's **La Cité Foudroyée** (1924) and Germaine **Dulac**'s *Le Diable dans la Ville* (*The Devil in the City*, 1924)—see Book 1, Chapter I. Under the pseudonym of "Nevers-Severin," Bouquet later wrote a number of surreal, popular murder mysteries such as *Doum* (1943), *Les Mystères de Montmartre* (*The Mysteries of Montmartre*, 1944) and *L'Homme des Antipodes* (*The Man from the Other Side of the World*, 1944). His best genre fiction, however, was published under his own name and collected in *Le Visage de Feu* (*The Face of Fire*, 1951) and *Les Filles de la Nuit* (*The Daughters of Night*, 1951), which was retitled *Aux Portes des Ténèbres* (*At the Gates of Darkness*) by the publisher. In his works, Bouquet gave a new lease on life to such classic themes as witches' curses, reincarnation and spells enabling men to enter occult realms. His classic story "**Alouqa**" was adapted into a 1975 telefilm (see Book 1, Chapter II), and another story, "**Rendez-Vous avec le Démon**," was turned into a radio play (see Book 1, Chapter III).

The notorious writing team of **Boileau-Narcejac** acquired justified worldwide fame for their famous thriller *Celle qui n'était plus* (*She Who Was No More*, 1952), which was later filmed by H.-G. Clouzot as **Les Diaboliques** (see Book 1, Chapter I). The pair wrote the screenplay adaptation of the classic and much-imitated **Les Yeux Sans Visage** (see Book 1, Chapter I), based on Jean **Redon**'s novel (see below). Finally, their novel *D'Entre les Morts* (*From the Dead*, 1956) provided the story for Hitchcock's *Vertigo*. While Boileau-Narcejac's thrillers were always resolved with rational explanations, they succeeded in creating an unforgettable atmosphere of fear, relying on seemingly surreal events. *Le Mauvais Oeil* (*The Evil Eye*, 1956) and **Au Bois Dormant** (*The Sleeping Woods*, 1956; the latter adapted for television— see Book 1, Chapter II) made use of classic folk legends and fairy tales. *Les Magiciennes* (*The Magicians*, 1957) and *Maléfices* (*Spells*, 1961) explored the darkest recesses of the human soul. *...Et Mon Tout Est un Homme* (*...And What Is Left Is a Man*, 1965) was a variation on the Frankenstein myth. Lastly, Boileau-Narcejac were chosen to continue Maurice **Leblanc**'s popular *Arsène Lupin* series, for which they produced five successful novels.

Like Boileau-Narcejac, Frédéric **Dard** is better known as a prolific mystery writer, and the author of a popular series of detective novels noted for their creative use of French slang, written under the byline and featuring the character of Police Commissioner San-Antonio. Using the pseudonym of "Frédéric Charles," Dard also wrote two grand-guignolesque horror novels, *La Maison de l'Horreur* (*The House of Horror*, 1952) and *La Main Morte* (*The Dead Hand*, 1954). Under his own name, he wrote a number of brilliant hard-boiled thrillers, some of which included genre elements, such as *Coma* (1959) and *Puisque les Oiseaux Meurent* (*Since the Birds Die*, 1960). Dard also penned a number of fantastic stories, which were later collected as *Histoires Déconcertantes* (*Unsettling Tales*, 1977).

Unlike the works of Boileau-Narcejac and Dard, the novels of Raoul de **Warren** belonged to the traditional *fantastique*, making use of such time-tested concepts as spectres, ghouls, and demons. *L'Énigme du Mort Vivant* (*The Mystery of the Living Dead*, 1950) and *La Bête de l'Apocalypse* (*The Beast of the Apocalypse*, 1956) were among this popular author's best genre works. A number of his works, written in the late 1940s and early 1950s, were reprinted by the publisher L'Herne in the 1980s, including *L'Insolite Aventure de Marina Sloty* (*Marina Sloty's Strange Adventure*, 1981), *Rue du Mort-qui-Trompe* (*Street of the Dead Who Cheats*, 1984), *Et le Glas Tinta Trois Fois* (*And the Bell Tolled Three Times*, 1989) and *Les Portes de l'Enfer* (*The Gates of Hell*, 1991).

The 1950s saw the emergence of popular paperback imprints entirely devoted to horror novels, following a pattern previously established with adventure and science fiction novels by publishers such as Tallandier and Ferenczi. Most of these imprints, however, were short-lived. Among these were:

Épouvante (*Terror*), with seven volumes published in 1954 and 1955 by publisher La Corne d'Or.

Another *Épouvante* imprint, with a single volume published in 1954 by publisher Édica.

Frayeurs (*Fears*), with five volumes published in 1954 and 1955 by publisher L'Arabesque.

L'Étrange (*Strange*), with four volumes published in 1956 by publisher Robert Laffont.

Some notable authors published by these imprints included Robert **Georges-Méra** with *Que le Diable l'Emporte!* (*Let the Devil Take Her!*, 1952), *L'Inhumaine Création du Professeur Lynk* (*Prof. Lynk's Inhuman Creation*, 1954), *La Mort aux Vifs* (*Death to the Living*, 1954) and *Le Monstrueux Professeur Lynk* (*The Monstrous Prof. Lynk*, 1960).

The major genre imprint that dominated the 1950s and 1960s, however, was publisher Fleuve Noir's *Angoisse* (*Anguish*), which was started in 1954 in the wake of the company's successful science fiction imprint, *Anticipation*, and continued monthly until 1974, publishing a total of 261 volumes, a feat probably unique in the annals of horror litera-

ture. *Angoisse* relied heavily on its sister imprint *Anticipation* for its stable of authors, and therefore published only French writers, with five exceptions: American writers David Keller, Evangeline Walton, and Donald Wandrei, British author Virginia Lord, and German author Roger Sattler.

Among the best authors published by *Angoisse*, first and foremost was André **Ruellan**, a medical doctor who used the pseudonym of "Kurt **Steiner**" for his popular works. Whether writing as Ruellan or Steiner, he was also one of France's best science fiction authors of the period; his other works are reviewed in Chapter IX. For *Angoisse*, Steiner penned twenty-two horror novels, mastering all the classic themes and creating some new ones as well. Zombies appeared in *Le Bruit du Silence* (*The Sound of Silence*, 1955); other dimensions in *Fenêtres sur l'Obscur* (*Windows Into Darkness*, 1956) and *Les Pourvoyeurs* (*The Purveyors*, 1957); modern vampires in *Le Seuil du Vide* (*The Threshold of the Void*, 1956; which was made into a small-budget horror film – see Book

1, Chapter I) and *Syncope Blanche* (*White Faint*, 1958); witchcraft in *La Marque du Démon* (*The Mark of the Demon*, 1958); haunted castles in *Lumière de Sang* (*Blood Light*, 1958); pacts with the Devil in *Pour Que Vive Le Diable* (*For the Devil to Live*, 1956). Other notable titles included: *De Flamme et d'Ombre* (*Of Flame and Shadow*, 1956), *Je Suis Un Autre* (*I Am Other*, 1957), *Les Dents Froides* (*The Cold Teeth*, 1957), *L'Envers du Masque* (*The Other Side of the Mask*, 1957), *Dans un Manteau de Brume* (*In a Cloak of Mist*, 1959) and *Glace Sanglante* (*Bloody Ice*, 1960).

Perhaps because of Steiner's medical background, the strength of his novels lay in their detailed, almost clinical, atmosphere of heavy, oppressive, bludgeoning horror, which anticipated the stronger, gorier books of the next decades. In 1979, Ruellan signed the script and novelization of a remarkable modern horror movie, **Les Chiens** (*The Dogs*; see Book 1, Chapter I), in which an attack-dog trainer, played by Gérard Depardieu, used people's fears to slowly take over a town.

Like André Ruellan, René Bonnefoy (aka "René Blondel"—see above) wrote most of his popular books under a pseudonym, "B.R. **Bruss**." Like Steiner, Bruss was also one of France's best popular science fiction authors of the period, whose works are reviewed in Chapter IX. For *Angoisse*, Bruss wrote nine novels, including *L'Oeil était dans la*

Tombe (*The Eye Was in the Tomb*, 1955); *Maléfices* (*Spells*, 1956), about a local bridge cursed by two Egyptian talismans incorporated into its metal; *Nous Avons Tous Peur* (*We Are All Afraid*, 1956), about a nightmarish creature who stalks an isolated village; *Terreur en Plein Soleil* (*Terror Under a Full Sun*, 1958), about a telepath who sadistically drives people to commit suicide; *Le Tambour d'Angoisse* (*The Drum of Terror*, 1962), about the members of an Australian ethnological expedition who are driven insane by the drumbeats of invisible natives; *Le Bourg Envoûté* (*The Spellbound Burg*, 1964), about evil forces which return to plague a village every two centuries; *La Figurine de Plomb* (*The Lead Statuette*, 1965), about a mystical object which enables its owner to change the course of his fate; and finally, *Le Mort qu'il faut Tuer* (*The Dead Man Who Must Be Killed*, 1971), a variation on the theme of the Curt Siodmak novel, *Donovan's Brain*. Like Belgian author Jean **Ray**, Bruss liked to depict strange and pathetic characters, moving in a mundane, yet suffocating, environment. The horrific elements were introduced slowly, but implacably, in a clear and colorful style. In his novels, men were usually the predestined victims of unspeakable Lovecraftian-like forces. The Bruss horror novels have few equals in their spellbinding atmosphere of oppressive horror.

Unlike André Ruellan and René Bonnefy, Adrien Sobra, a former English teacher, was already a mainstream, if little-known, novelist who had published a few novels and thrillers (using the anagrammatic pseudonym of "Ange Arbos") before he turned to writing popular horror fiction under the pseudonym of "Marc **Agapit**." Agapit wrote forty-three novels for *Angoisse* and was one of the imprint's best and most respected authors. Unlike Steiner and Bruss, Agapit

used the supernatural sparsely, his catalog of horrors being somewhat more akin to a Ruth Rendell rewritten by the Grand-Guignol. Agapit delighted in throwing a light on the perversity of the human soul, showing sordid, lonely, ordinary people ravaged by time, sinking slowly into madness. His heroes often came from cursed families. They exhibited an unhealthy sexuality and may even have had physical handicaps, as in *La Bête Immonde* (*The Awful Beast*, 1959), whose hero is blind, and *École des Monstres* (*Monster School*, 1963). Agapit's protagonists were often young boys who became natural preys for decrepit, evil females, or innocently trafficked with the most monstrous, unnatural creatures, as in the classic *Greffe Mortelle* (*Mortal Transplant*, 1958), which was praised by no less than Jean **Cocteau**, and *Le Miroir Truqué* (*The Trick Mirror*, 1973).

Agapit's supernatural elements, when he chose to use any, were more likely to be Hell and the Christian Devil, as in *Agence Tous Crimes* (*All-Crime Agency*, 1958) and *L'Héritage du Diable* (*The Devil's Inheritance*, 1971), or borrowed from classical mythology, such as the Minotaur in *La Nuit du Minotaure* (*The Night of the Minotaur*, 1965), the Furies in *Les Ciseaux d'Atropos* (*The Scissors of Atropos*, 1973), Oedipus in *Piège Infernal* (*Infernal Trap*, 1960), Shakespeare's *The Tempest* in *L'Île Magique* (*The Magical Island*, 1967), and the Wandering Jew in *Monsieur Personne* (*Mister Nobody*, 1967). Other notable titles included: *Puzzle Macabre* (*Macabre Puzzle*, 1959), *Opéra de la Mort* (*Death Opera*, 1960), *Phantasmes* (1962), *Le Voyage en Rond* (*The Circular Journey*, 1964), *Les Yeux Braqués* (*The Staring Eyes*, 1965), *La Guivre* (1966), *La Goule* (*The Ghoul*, 1968), *La Dame à l'Os* (*The Lady with the Bone*, 1969), *Une Sorcière m'a dit* (*A Witch Told Me*, 1970), and *Le Poids du Monde* (*The Weight of the World*, 1970).

Another writer of note who contributed to *Angoisse* was renowned film writer Jean-Claude **Carrière** (see Book 1, chapters I, II and VI), who wrote six *Frankenstein* pastiches (with plotting assistance from Guy Bechtel for the first), continuing the adventures of Mary Shelley's immortal creature: *La Tour de Frankenstein* (*The Tower of Frankenstein*, 1957), *Le Pas de Frankenstein* (*The Step of Frankenstein*, 1957), *La Nuit de Frankenstein* (*The Night of Frankenstein*, 1957), *Le Sceau de Frankenstein* (*The Seal of Frankenstein*, 1957), *Frankenstein Rôde* (*Frankenstein Prowls*, 1958), and *La Cave de Frankenstein* (*The Cellar of Frankenstein*, 1959). Carrière's approach to Mary Shelley's character was startlingly different from both the Universal and Hammer film versions. In his novels, Carrière followed the footsteps of the Monster, christened "Gouroull," as he made his way back from Iceland, to Scotland, and then Germany and

Switzerland, from the late 1800s to the 1920s. Unlike its predecessors, Carrière's Monster was a ruthless, demoniacal thing, the very incarnation of evil. His yellow, unblinking eyes hid a cunning, inhuman intelligence. The Monster barely spoke, but used his razor-sharp teeth to slit his victims' throats. Carrière insisted on the physical inhumanity of the creature: the Monster did not breathe, his skin was white as chalk, but strangely impervious to flames, his strength and speed were prodigious, what ran in his veins was not blood, and he had no normal heartbeat; even his thought process was shown to be alien. The plots have the Monster pursuing his own, evil agenda, generally unafraid of the weaker humanity, and woe to anyone standing in his way. Even people who tried to help or reason with him were just as likely to be killed by the inhuman fiend.

Carrière's *Frankenstein* novels were released under the pseudonym of "Benoît **Becker**," a house name created by the publisher and also used by writer/journalist José-André **Lacour**, who wrote six other *Angoisse* novels, without the character of *Frankenstein*.

André **Caroff** wrote seventeen *Angoisse* novels, starting in 1964 with *La Sinistre Mme Atomos* (*The Sinister Mrs. Atomos*), which starred the character of the deadly *Madame Atomos*, a brilliant but twisted female Japanese scientist out to revenge herself against the United States for the bombings of Hiroshima and Nagasaki. A sample *Madame Atomos* plot had the evil title character unleash a deadly new threat, such as radioactive zombies, only to be stopped in the nick of time by the heroes. Prior to creating *Madame Atomos*, Caroff had penned the adventures of Dr. François Petit, a sociopath *à la* Hannibal Lecter, visibly inspired by the real-life French serial killer, Dr. Petiot. (Dr. Petit appeared in Nos. 73, 77, and 83 of the imprint.) in the 1970s, after the cancellation of *Angoisse*, Caroff continued his prolific writing career in the *Anticipation* imprint.

Leading *Anticipation* writer **Richard-Bessière** contributed five novels to *Angoisse* under the name "Dominique H. Keller," a pseudonym created especially by editor François Richard, who was reluctant to lose the benefit of the name recognition that came from having published a translation of American writer David Henry Keller's the *Solitary Hunters* (*Weird Tales*, 1934; coll. 1948).

Other *Anticipation* writers who contributed to *Angoisse* during the 1950s and 1960s included:

Jimmy **Guieu**, with one novel;

Peter **Randa**, with five novels, including *Parodie à la Mort* (*Death Parody*, 1960), which was adapted into a Grand-Guignol play by M. **Renay**; and

Maurice **Limat**, with thirty-three novels, most of which were devoted to two interconnected series, the first following the adventures of Teddy Verano, a ghostbuster and detective of the supernatural mysteries, introduced in *Mandragore* (1963), and the second dedicated to Mephista, a spin-off of the *Verano* series about an evil female demon, introduced in *Mephista* (1969). The Mephista character proved

popular with the readers and went on to appear in twelve more titles.

Writers who wrote exclusively for *Angoisse* included:

Michel **Bernanos**, the son of Georges Bernanos (see above), who contributed three novels under the pseudonym of "Michel Talbert" and whose *Les Nuits de Rochemaure* (*The Nights of Rochemaure*, 1963) has since become a cult classic.

Dominique **Arly**, who penned nineteen supernatural thrillers (1965-74) with mildly erotic elements, a number of which starred the attractive Rosamond Lew, introduced in *Les Pistes Maudites* (*The Accursed Trails*, 1970).

José **Michel** (in reality, a collaboration between Caroff and his mother), with six novels (1966-70), including *La Dernière Fuite* (*The Last Flight*, 1966).

Jean **Murelli**, with twelve titles (1958-69), including *Ce Mur Qui Regardait* (*That Staring Wall*, 1959), and *Ma Peau de Fantôme* (*My Ghostly Skin*, 1969).

Patrick **Svenn**, with three novels (1955-56); Jean **David**, with two novels (1956-57); G. **Gauthier** (1959); E.-J. **Certon** (1960); Franc **Puig** (1960), and Marcel G. **Prêtre** (1968).

Last but not least, thriller writer Jean **Redon** published only one *Angoisse*—but it was the classic *Les Yeux Sans Visage* (*The Eyes Without a Face*, 1959). This novel about a brilliant but crazed surgeon who killed women to transplant their faces onto his disfigured daughter was adapted into a Grand-Guignol play by M. Renay, and into a classic eponymous 1959 horror film by director Georges **Franju**, written by Boileau-Narcejac (see above). It also helped inspire a series of other horror films.

ESOTERISM

The *fantastique ésoterique* is a category that can itself be split into two separate sub-sections. The first consists of novels which derive their inspiration from the occult, following in the footsteps of the symbolists and the *roman spirite*, such as:

Noël de **La Houssaye**'s *L'Apparition d'Arsinoë* (*The Apparition of Arsinoe*, 1947), in which the author-narrator is a white magician who uses Cornelius Agrippa's secrets to invoke the ghost of Arsinoe, the first Queen of Egypt.

Marguerite **Yourcenar**'s *L'Oeuvre au Noir* (*The Dark Work*, 1968; translated as the *Abyss*), in which a Renaissance Italian warlock attempts to use alchemy to understand and, ultimately, control the universe.

Patrick **Ravignant**'s *La Peau de l'Ombre* (*The Skin of the Shadow*, 1963), a novel about immortality and metaphysical initiation.

The tradition of the *roman initiatique*, that is to say of

a novel describing an initiation, an esoteric journey at the end of which the protagonist grasps the true nature of reality, was upheld by André **Hardellet**. In his classic *Le Seuil du Jardin* (*The Treshold of the Garden*, 1958), Hardellet's hero, painter Steve Masson, meets an inventor who has created a "magic lantern" that can give life to memories, but the device is eventually destroyed by a mysterious organization. *Le Parc des Archers* (*The Park of the Bowmen*, 1962) focused a writer's rebellion against a totalitarian tyranny located in an alternate universe Paris. Steve Masson appeared in the book in a cameo. *Lourdes, Lentes* (*Heavy, Slow*, 1969), a novel originally credited to "Steve Masson" and later republished under Hardellet's own name, also starred Masson, this time in a dreamlike quest for a lost love. In *Lady Long Solo* (1971), Hardellet himself explored a dead Paris where he met ghosts and fictional characters. *Les Chasseurs* (*The Huntsmen*, 1966) was a collection of fantastic tales. (*Le Seuil du Jardin* was adapted into a 1970 feature film entitled ***Ils*** (*They*) by Jean-Daniel Simon—see Book 1, Chapter I.) in Hardellet's works, the hero may be crushed by reality on our plane, but ultimately triumphs on another. The recurring character of Steve Masson is the magus who unlocks the eternal mysteries of life and the universe.

The second category is that of the "vulgarization" books intending to popularize occult concepts. While technically beyond the scope of our research, and even though we have not included most of the authors listed below in our dictionary, we feel that some of these works deserve to be mentioned here, for several reasons. First, their theories are often reflected in the fantastic fiction of the times, as was the case with the works of Éliphas **Lévi**, Allan **Kardec**, Madame Blavatsky and occultists of the Golden Dawn. However, unlike the occultists and esoteric writers of previous eras, who were addressing a selected audience, the modern authors have reached a vast, uninformed, undiscriminating readership. Second, in the same fashion as Richard S. Shaver, Erich Von Daniken, or Charles Berlitz, they have often incorporated outlandish concepts in their historical (or pseudo-historical) research, blurring the line between fact and fiction, science and fantasy. In Gérard de Sède's *La Race Fabuleuse* (*The Fabulous Race*), for example, the Merovingian Kings were said to carry alien genes!

The popularity of esoteric vulgarization books can be said to have started with the best-selling book *Le Matin des Magiciens* (*The Morning of the Magicians*) by Jacques **Bergier** and Louis **Pauwels**, published in 1960. In it, information about the Nazis' presumed connections with the occult, the role of secret societies in behind-the-scenes political manipulation, the nature of alchemy, and the practice of sorcery, were evoked in a modern, investigative documentary style *à la The X-Files*. The considerable knowledge of Bergier in both the fantastic and esoteric fields combined with Pauwels' literary skills to create a best-selling book. *Le Matin des Magiciens'* commercial success, as well as that of the magazine *Planète* (*Planet*), also edited by Pauwels

along the same lines, contributed to the creation of a full-blown industry of esoteric vulgarization books.

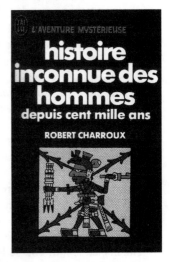

Among the authors who followed in the footsteps of Bergier and Pauwels in the 1960s, the foremost was Robert Charroux, a French variant of Erich Von Daniken or Richard S. Shaver who specialized in ancient, technologically advanced societies and ancient extraterrestrial visitations. Charroux's first best-seller, *Histoire Inconnue des Hommes depuis 100.000 Ans* (*Unknown History of Man for the Last 100,000 Years*) was published in 1963 and was followed by *Le Livre des Maîtres du Monde* (*The Book of the Masters of the World*), *Le Livre du Mystérieux Inconnu* (*The Book of the Mysterious Unknown*), *Le Livre du Passé Mystérieux* (*The Book of the Mysterious Past*), and half-a-dozen other similar titles.

Gérard de Sède wrote a dozen or so best-selling works about the Templars, the Cathars, the Holy Grail, and the Merovingian Kings, which among other things, inspired the recent best-seller *Holy Grail, Holy Blood*. De Sède's career began with *Les Templiers sont parmi nous* (*The Templars Are Among Us*) in 1962 and continued with *Le Trésor Maudit de Rennes-le-Château* (*The Accursed Treasure of Rennes-Le-Château*), *La Race Fabuleuse* (*The Fabulous Race*), *Le Secret des Cathares* (*The Secret of the Cathars*), *Le Sang des Cathares* (*The Blood of the Cathars*), and others. Another specialist of the Templars was Louis Charpentier, whose *Les Mystères Templiers* (*The Templar Mysteries*), published in 1967, followed the same vein.

Other notable authors included:

Jacques **Sadoul**, with *Le Trésor des Alchimistes* (*The Alchemists' Treasure*).

Guy Tarade, with *Les Dossiers de l'Étrange* (*The Strange Files*).

Denis **Saurat**, with *L'Atlantide et le Règne des Géants* (*Atlantis and the Reign of the Giants*).

ESP expert Jean Prieur, with *Les Témoins de l'Invisible* (*The Witnesses of the Invisible*), and *Les Visiteurs de l'Autre Monde* (*The Visitors from Another World*).

Science fiction writer Jimmy **Guieu**, with two tomes about UFOs, *Les Soucoupes Volantes viennent d'un Autre Monde* (*The Flying Saucers Come from Another World*) and *Black-Out sur les Soucoupes Volantes* (*Black-Out on the Flying Saucers*). As if to prove the circularity of this literary phenomenon, the latter was prefaced by Jean **Cocteau**, himself a member of an alleged Templar-derived secret society dubbed the Prieuré de Sion.

JUVENILES

The postwar period saw a boom in specialized imprints aimed at children and young adults. Some of the most famous were Hachette's *Bibliothèque Rose* (*Pink Library*) for children, which published Enid Blyton's *Fearless Five* novels; Hachette's *Bibliothèque Verte* (*Green Library*) for young adults, which reprinted condensed versions of **Dumas**, **Verne**, etc.; G.P.'s *Bibliothèque Rouge & Or* (*Red and Gold Library*); Delagrave's *Aventure & Jeunesse* (*Adventure and Youth*); Gasnier's *Jeunesse de France* (*French Youth*); Rageot's *Bibliothèque de l'Amitié* (*Library of Friendship*); Alsatia's *Signe de Piste* (*Trail Sign*), all for young adults, and many more.

To the extent that French educators still believed that the *fantastique* (and even more so, science fiction) were harmful to the young minds in their charge, children's books and young adult books were kept carefully free of genre elements, except of course for sanitized, recycled fairy tales and folk legends, such as Fernand Nathan's imprint **Contes et Légendes**, mentioned above, or material of a similar nature aimed at children, and a few adventure or swashbuckling classics for young adults.

Nevertheless, a few authors made original contributions to the field of "juvenile" *fantastique*. Alice **Coleno** wrote a series of modern fairy tales, remarkable both for their style and imagination: *La Forêt de Cristal* (*The Crystal Forest*, 1946), *Contes de Diamant* (*Diamond Tales*, 1957), *Les Jardins de la Licorne* (*The Gardens of the Unicorn*, 1957), and *La Montagne des Démons* (*The Mountains of Demons*, 1963) are all fantasy classics for children, worthy of **Perrault** or the Baroness d'**Aulnoy**.

Renée **Aurembou**'s novels were young adult adventures which drew their inspiration from some of the most mysterious aspects of French history: *La Maison des Fonds Noirs* (*The House of Dark Recesses*, 1954), *Le Mystère de l'Abbaye Brûlée* (*The Mystery of the Burned Abbey*, 1966), and *Le Trésor de Montségur* (*The Treasure of Montsegur*, 1966) are among her most notable works.

Other writers of juvenile novels who occasionally invoked mild fantasy elements included Henriette **Robitaillie**, with *Le Château des Malices* (*The Castle of Tricks*, 1945), *Contes des Bois et de la Lande* (*Tales of Woods and Moors*, 1949), *Le Secret de l'Oeil Jaune* (*The Secret of the Yellow Eye*, 1949), and *Le Monstre des Abîmes* (*The Monster from the Abyss*, 1951). Robitaillie was also the author of the juvenile novel *Norr le Mystérieux* (*Norr the Mysterious*, 1957).

Mainstream romance novelist Guy des **Cars** penned the delightful *Mon Ami Touche-à-Tout* (*My Friend Touches-Everything*, 1946), a children's fantasy in which a boy invokes a pantheon of modern muses and fairies (for electricity, science, etc).

Also worthy of note was Belgian writer Jean-Claude **Alain**'s five-volume light fantasy series devoted to the exploits of *Mikhaïl, Prince d'Hallmark* (*Mikhail, Prince of Hallmark*, 1953-55). Other works of similar nature included:

Jean-François **Pays**' three-volume series, *Sous le Signe de Rome* (*Under the Mark of Rome*, 1961-63), in which a young Gaul boy named Loic and a young Roman boy named Marcus (the future emperor Marcus-Aurelius) chase after a sacred bull called Toukaram.

Pierre **Debresse**'s *Samorix et le Rameau d'Or* (*Samorix and the Golden Branch*, 1965) and *Le Trésor de Carthage* (*The Treasure of Carthage*, 1967).

X. B. **Leprince**'s two volume fantasy, *La Quête Fantastique* (*The Fantastic Quest*, 1969). Leprince was also the author of numerous juvenile adventure novels, many with mild fantasy elements, such as *Le Tesbi de Nacre* (*The Mother of Pearl Tesbi*, 1958) and *Le Crapaud d'Ambre Jaune* (*The Yellow Amber Toad*, 1965).

Michel **Peyramaure**, with novels such as *La Vallée des Mammouths* (*The Valley of the Mastodons*, 1966), *Les Colosses de Carthage* (*The Colossus of Carthage*, 1967), *La Citadelle Ardente* (*The Fiery Citadel*, 1978), *La Tête du Dragon* (*The Dragon's Head*, 1978), *Quand Surgira l'Étoile Absinthe* (*When the Absinthe Star Rises*, 1980), *La Porte Noire* (*The Black Gate*, 1985), and *La Chair et le Bronze* (*The Flesh and the Bronze*, 1985).

Serge **Dalens** was one of the editors and most popular writers of the *Signe de Piste* imprint, for which he contributed collections of fantastic tales such as *Les Contes du Bourreau* (*Tales of the Executioner*, 1955) and *2 + 2 font... 5* (*2+2 = 5*, 1969), as well as two popular series, the adventures of Prince Éric, starting in 1957 with *Le Bracelet de Vermeil* (*The Vermillion Bracelet*, 1937) and *Les Enquêtes du Chat-Tigre* (*The Tiger-Cat Investigates*), a series of juvenile investigations, written with Jean-Louis **Foncine** under the pseudonym of "Mik Fondal."

Finally, with *Les Exploits de Fantômette* (*The Exploits of Fantomette*), published in 1961 by the *Bibliothèque Rose*, writer Georges **Chaulet** created one of the most popular and endearing characters in modern juvenile fiction. Fantômette is a masked teenage girl whose real name is Françoise Dupont. With the help of her two goofy but well-intentioned friends, Boulotte and Ficelle, Fantômette thwarts criminals and evil-doers everywhere. Her adventures are liberally sprinkled with fantasy and science fiction elements. The Fantômette series continued for over fifty volumes, the last one being published in the 1990s. It also spun off a popular television and a comic-book series (see Book 1, chapters II and V).

c. Belgian Fantastique

During the 1950s and 1960s, Belgian *fantastique* was dominated by the existence of the *Marabout* imprint of Belgian publisher Gérard. *Marabout* began in the late 1940s as a general literature and non-fiction paperback imprint, and began publishing a line of juvenile adventure novels in 1953, including the famous Bob Morane series by Henri **Vernes**, reviewed under science fiction in Chapter IX. By 1960, *Marabout* had published a series of new editions of classic novels by Alexandre **Dumas**, when it decided to add Edgar Allan Poe and, a year later, Jean **Ray** to its catalog, the latter with its famous collection, *25 Histoires Noires et Fantastiques* (*25 Dark and Fantastic Tales*, 1961). Its considerable success led to more reprints of classic genre works by Eugène **Sue**, Paul **Féval**, **Ponson du Terrail**, Frédéric **Soulié**, Gérard de **Nerval**, Théophile **Gautier**, and **Erckmann-Chatrian**, as well as translations of Bram Stoker (*Dracula*), Mary Shelley (*Frankenstein*), Hanns Heiz Ewers, M. G. Lewis, and Charles Maturin, establishing *Marabout* as Belgium's first popular paperback *fantastique* imprint.

More Jean Ray titles followed, reprints as well as new collections such as *Le Carrousel des Maléfices* (*The Spellbound Merry-Go-Round*, 1964) and *Les Contes Noirs du Golf* (*Dark Tales of Golf*, 1964). Between 1961 and 1966, *Marabout* published eight Jean Ray volumes and then embarked on a reprinting of the *Harry Dickson* series that lasted for sixteen volumes. They also published collections by Michel de **Ghelderode**, Franz **Hellens**, Marcel **Béalu**, André **Pieyre de Mandiargues**, and several volumes of Claude **Seignolle** stories. Another author reprinted by *Marabout* was poet Marcel **Thiry** who, like Henri **Michaud**, had published some genre poetry in the 1920s. Thiry's collection of fantastic tales, *Nouvelles du Grand Possible* (*Tales of the Great Possible*), was published by *Marabout* in 1949 and reprinted in 1967.

Another author reprinted by *Marabout* was "Thomas **Owen**," the pseudonym of writer Gérald Bertot. The name "Thomas Owen" first appeared as that of a policeman in *Ce Soir, Huit Heures* (*Tonight at 8*, 1941), a mystery thriller with mild genre undertones, written by Bertot under the pseudonym of "Stéphane Rey." Bertot, now writing as Owen, introduced his amateur detective character, Madame Aurelia, in *Destination Inconnue* (*Destination Unknown*, 1941). Madame Aurelia appeared in *Un Crime Swing* (*A Swing Crime*, 1942), *L'Or Indigo* (*Indigo Gold*; written in 1942 but published only in 1995), and *Hôtel Meublé* (*Furnished Hotel*, 1943). The latter was made into a 1982 film entitled **Meurtres à Domicile** (*Murders at Home*) by director Marc Lobet, scripted by noted comic-book writer Jean **Van Hamme**, with Anny Duperey as Madame Aurelia.

Owen's first true genre books were *Initiation à la Peur* (*Initiation to Fear*, 1942) and *Les Chemins Étranges* (*The Strange Paths*, 1943), the latter a collection of fantastic tales

prefaced by Jean Ray. All of Owen's subsequent books—except one mainstream novel, *Les Grandes Personnes* (*The Adults*, 1954)—were fantastic collections: *La Cave aux Crapauds* (*The Toad Cave*, 1945), *Pitié pour les Ombres* (*Mercy for the Shadows*, 1961), *Cérémonial Nocturne* (*Night Ceremonies*, 1966), *La Truie* (*The Sow*, 1972), *Le Rat Kavar* (*Kavar the Rat*, 1975), and others. Owen is also the author of two genre novels: *Le Livre Interdit* (*The Forbidden Book*, 1944) and *Le Jeu Secret* (*The Secret Game*, 1950).

In Owen's stories, the focus is on fear itself. It is the ultimate expression of despair that the characters face when they finally succumb to supernatural events beyond mortal comprehension. Throughout his works, Owen used the same style and methods that he used when he was writing Agatha Christie-like detective novels: an objective, methodical approach, starting with ordinary, mundane events, such as marital discord or business disputes, and then bringing in not a murder but a vampire, or a ghoul, or a ghost seeking revenge from beyond the grave. Some of his most interesting tales, such as *The Sow* and *Kavar the Rat*, used animals to create fear.

Meanwhile, during this period, Franz **Hellens** continued to be one of Belgium's most prolific genre contributors with *Contes Choisis* (*Selected Tales*, 1956), *Les Yeux du Rêve* (*The Eyes of the Dream*, 1964), *Herbes Méchantes* (*Bad Herbs*, 1964) and *Le Dernier Jour du Monde* (*The Last Day of the World*, 1967).

Another prolific author whose career had begun before the war was Robert **Poulet**, with *L'Enfer-Ciel* (*The Heaven-Hell*, 1952), *La Lanterne Magique* (*The Magic Lantern*, 1956) and *Les Sources de la Vie* (*The Sources of Life*, 1967).

New Belgian genre authors who appeared during the 1950s and 1960s included Monique **Watteau**, who made a remarkable beginning with *La Colère Végétale* (*The Vegetable Wrath*, 1954), a novel about the revolt of the vegetable kingdom. Watteau's subsequent novels, such as *La Nuit aux Yeux de Bête* (*The Night with Eyes of Beasts*, 1956), *L'Ange à Fourrure* (*The Angel with Fur*, 1958), and *Luciferian—Je Suis le Ténébreux* (*I Am the Dark One*, 1962), expanded on the theme of metamorphosis and devolution, creating strange intrreractions between man and animal, and animal and vegetable. In Watteau's works, devolution is not a fall from grace from the presumably superior status of humanity, a mere degeneration, but on the contrary, a wonderful transformation from one state into another, that can be interpreted as a liberation, a transition toward a new form of happiness.

Like Monique Watteau, Anne **Richter** (not to be confused with French-Canadian writer Anne **Richter**) liked to blur the boundaries between men and animals. Her first collection, *La Fourmi a fait le Coup* (*The Ant Did It*, 1955), established the interdependence of all living things. Here again, passage from one form to another was depicted as a liberation. In another collection, *Les Locataires* (*The Tenants*, 1967), Richter showed that the *fantastique* is only a natural extension of reality, and there can be no happiness unless one submits willingly to the supernatural.

Another writer obssessed with the triumph of the *fantastique* over the mundane was Jean **Muno**, whose classic novel, *L'Hipparion* (1962), set the stage for a confrontation between the imaginary and the real, not to the latter's advantage. Muno's subsequent works, such as *L'Homme qui s'efface* (*The Man Who Disappeared*, 1963), and his recent collections of short stories, *Histoires Singulières* (*Singular Tales*, 1979) and *Histoires Griffues* (*Clawed Tales*, 1985), continued to explore this theme.

This notion of imagining other forms of reality is a recurrent theme in the Belgian *fantastique*. Two more examples are *Octobre, Long Dimanche* (*October, Long Sunday*, 1957), in which writer Guy **Vaes** imagined the plight of a man whose rhythm of life is so different that it is no longer possible for him to speak or even see his surroundings; and *La Longueur du Temps* (*The Length of Time*, 1968), in which author Albert **Dasnoy**, with great stylistic precision, studied the notion of schizoid realities.

Other notable Belgian authors of the period included:

Raymond **Mottart**, with *Bételgeuse* (1956).

José **Hervyns**, with *Cette Race Indécrottable* (*That Incorrigible Race*, 1956).

Paul **Bay**, with *Descendit aux Enfers* (*Descending to Hell*, 1958), in which Jesus visited a futuristic hell which was portrayed as a science fiction metropolis.

Bernard **Manier**, with *Histoires d'Ailleurs et de Nulle Part* (*Tales of Elsewhere and Nowhere*, 1961).

Pierre **Nothomb**, with *Le Prince du Dernier Jour* (*The Prince of the Last Day*, 1960) and *Les Miracles* (*The Miracles*, 1962).

2. The 1970s

a. Fantastique Littéraire

TRADITIONAL FANTASTIQUE

The student revolt of 1968 was reflected in French literature, with the publishing of left-wing ideological novels, feminist books, and post-*nouveau roman* works. Traditional fantastic subjects (such as vampires, ghosts, etc.) were in-

creasingly relegated to the field of popular literature, or used for satirical purposes.

Writers who sought to modernize classic genre themes included:

Yves **Olivier-Martin**, with *Isolina* (1968).

Michel **Treignier**, with *Spectrales* (1974) and *Le Chemin des Abîmes* (*The Path to the Abyss*, 1976), published by *Marabout*.

Writer/filmmaker Pierre **Kast**, whose classic vampire novel *Les Vam-*

pires de l'Alfama (*The Vampires of the Alfama*, 1975) was originally a film project and is perhaps the first modern vampire novel to present vampires as romantic heroes.

Pierre-Jean **Rémy**, whose *Une Figure dans la Pierre* (*A Figure in the Stone*, 1976), *Cordélia, ou l'Angleterre* (*Cordelia, or England*, 1979), and *Pandora* (1980) were modern gothic fantasies.

Jacques **Sadoul**'s trilogy of the *Domain of R.*, comprised of *La Passion Selon Satan* (*The Passion According to Satan*, 1960), *Le Jardin de la Licorne* (*The Garden of the Unicorn*, 1977) and *Les Hautes Terres du Rêve* (*The High Country of Dreams*, 1979), drew its inspiration from a variety of classic sources, ranging from H. P. Lovecraft, Robert Bloch, and the author's notorious knowledge of alchemy and witchcraft.

Henri **Gougaud**, with *Départements et Territoires d'Outre-Mort* (*Departments and Territories Beyond Death*, 1977).

In a satirical vein, Claude **Klotz**, also a mainstream writer of note under the pseudonym of "Patrick Cauvin," wrote a satirical prehistoric novel, *Les Innommables* (*The Unmentionables*, 1971), and a remarkably funny novel about Dracula forced to move to Paris and become a horror film star, *Paris-Vampire* (1974). The latter was made into a 1976 feature film entitled **Dracula Père et Fils**, starring Christopher Lee (see Book 1, Chapter I). Another notable **Klotz** genre novel was *Les Aventures Fabuleuses d'Anselme Levasseur* (*The Fabulous Adventures of Anselme Levasseur*, 1976).

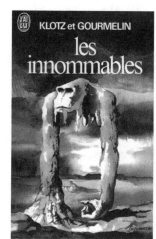

Writers who chose a symbolist approach to genre themes included:

Patrick **Ravignant**, with *Idiot Cherche Village (Le Livre du Chaos); (Idiot Seeks Village [The Book of Chaos]*, 1976), an apocalyptic novel filled with philosophical questions, depicting an esoteric quest which becomes a battle for the ultimate truth. Other notable **Ravignant** novels included *La Comtesse des Ténèbres* (*The Countess of Darkness*, 1979) and *Les Empires Secrets de Napoléon* (*Napoleon's Secret Empires*, 1979).

Mario **Mercier**, one of the editors of the magazine *Horizons du Fantastique* and the director of two genre films, **La Goulve** (1971) and **La Papesse** (1974) (see Book 1, Chapter I), wrote three novels mixing classic genre themes such as vampires and necrophilia with erotic and esoteric elements: *La Cuvée de Singes* (*A Bucketful of Monkeys*, 1970), *Le Nécrophile* (1970) and *L'Odyssée Fantastique d'Arthur Dément* (*Arthur Dement's Fantastic Odyssey*, 1976).

In Paul **Wagner**'s poetic *L'Enfant et les Magiciens* (*The*

Child and the Wizards, 1977), a pair of sorcerers attempted to transplant the soul of their deceased child into the body of an orphan.

Blending the surrealist approach with the classic themes of the *fantastique* was the approach of Maurice **Pons**. His novel *Rosa* (1967) starred a prostitute who magically dispatches all her unhappy clients into her womb. *Mademoiselle B.* (1973) was an original, surreal vampire story. In *La Maison des Brasseurs* (*The House of the Brewers*, 1978), each chapter ends with the description of a painting in which the action takes place.

Jacques **Hamelink**, with *Horror Vacui* (1970), a collection of fantastical horror tales.

Corsican writer Jean-Claude **Rogliano**, whose *Le Berger des Morts* (*The Shepherd of the Dead*) was a classic Corsican gothic novel written directly in Corsican in 1975 (under the title *Mal'Concilio*) and translated and published in French in 1980.

MODERN SURREALISTS

A number of authors, generally considered to be mainstream writers, followed in the footsteps of the surrealists, and wrote what would otherwise be considered genre novels, published by mainstream houses.

One of the best authors in this neo-surrealist category was Michel **Tournier** who, in *Vendredi, ou Les Limbes du Pacifique* (*Friday, or Limbo of the Pacific*, 1967), rewrote the classic Daniel Defoe novel. Here, Friday is the incarnated double of Robinson, the fruit of his union with the Land. Robinson becomes like Prospero, and Friday serves as his Ariel—or Caliban. Tournier continued to display his amazing blend of myth and parable in *Le Roi des Aulnes* (*The King of the Elms*, 1970), *Pierrot ou les Secrets de la Nuit* (*Pierrot, or the Secrets of the Night*, 1979), and *Le Vol du Vampire* (*The Vampire's Flight*, 1981), using classic images to propose a new place for Man in the universe. In Tournier's works, we exist between myth and reality, and legends can only help us find our place in the cosmic order.

The fantastic works of Hubert **Haddad** also relied on mythology, but in a more explicit and romantic fashion: *Un Rêve de Glace* (*A Dream of Ice*, 1974), *La Cène* (*The Last Supper*, 1975), *Les Grands Pays Muets* (*The Great Silent Countries*, 1978), *La Rose de Damoclès* (*The Rose of Damocles*, 1982), and *Les Effrois* (*The Fears*, 1983) are among his most notable works.

Another author whose works re-examined the fundaments of mythology was Jean **Cayrol**, with his series *Histoire d'une Prairie* (*Tale of a Field*, 1969), *Histoire d'un Désert* (*Tale of a Desert*, 1972), *Histoire de la Mer* (*Tale of the Sea*, 1973), *Histoire de la Forêt* (*Tale of a Forest*, 1975), *Histoire d'une Maison* (*Tale of a House*, 1976), and *Histoire du Ciel* (*Tale of the Sky*, 1979).

The tradition of the absurdist novel inherited from the surrealists could be found in the works of Jean-Marie **Le Clézio**, the author of surreal novels such as *Haï* (1971), *Les*

Géants (*The Giants*, 1973), which is set in a nightmarish shopping center; *Voyages de l'Autre Côté* (*Journeys to the Other Side*, 1975), in which the hero undergoes various metamorphoses before being transported into another universe; and *L'Inconnu sur la Terre* (*The Unknown Man on Earth*, 1978). Le Clézio's works displayed an amazing ability to translate madness and aberrations in mundane terms, and open windows into other realities.

The same absurdist tradition was also present in the novels of:

Jean-Charles **Rémy**, such as *La Randonnée* (*The Journey*, 1970) and *L'Arborescence* (1977), in which a bureaucrat is slowly metamorphosed into a sequoia.

Claude **Louis-Combet**, who displayed influences ranging from both Borges to Matheson, such as *Infernaux Paluds* (*Infernal Paluds*, 1970) and *Voyage au Centre de la Ville* (*Voyage to the Center of Town*, 1974).

The works of Georges-Olivier **Châteaureynaud** also displayed the combined influences of both Borges and Kafka, and were remarkable because of their macabre beauty and romantic nature. In *Les Messagers* (*The Messengers*, 1974), two men—a master and his disciple—carry a mysterious message to a no less mysterious recipient and undergo several severe trials in their strange journey. Eventually, the Master dies and the Disciple is expected to carry on without ever learning the purpose of his mission. Explanations are not necessary for they would destroy the fine allegory crafted by Châteaureynaud. *La Belle Charbonnière* (*The Beautiful Coal Lady*, 1976) was a collection of pseudo-medieval legends, one about eternal youth, the other challenging the very concept of gravity. *Le Verger* (*The Orchard*, 1978) took place in a mysterious concentration camp; there, a child finds a path to a secret orchard that only he can reach, but he eventually chooses to die with the other inmates rather than suffer the curse of being alone in his private paradise. Another notable Châteaureynaud work of the period was *Mathieu Chain* (1978).

Among other writers published by mainstream houses who incorporated into their works elements belonging to the surreal or the *fantastique* were:

Hubert **Monteilhet**, with *Les Pavés du Diable* (*The Devil's Cobblestones*, 1970), *Non-Sens* (*Nonsense*, 1971), *Les Bourreaux de Cupidon* (*Cupid's Executioners*, 1972), *Esprit, es-tu là?* (*Spirit, Are You Here?*, 1977), *Un Métier de Fantôme* (*A Ghostly Business*, 1979), and *Les Queues de Kallinaos* (*The Tails of the Kallinaos*, 1981), to name but a few.

Syrian-born Kamal **Ibrahim**, with *Celui-ci, Celui-moi* (*This One, This Me*, 1971), *Corps en Friche* (*Fallow Bodies*, 1974) and *Le Voyage de Cent Mètres* (*The 100-Meter Journey*, 1979).

Gilbert **Lascault**, with *Un Monde Mimé* (*A Mimed World*, 1975), *Voyage d'Automne et d'Hiver* (*Travel of Autumn and Winter*, 1979), *Destinée de Jean-Simon Castor* (*The Destiny of Jean-Simon Castor*, 1981), *420 Minutes dans* *la Cité des Ombres* (*420 Minutes in the City of Shadows*, 1988) and *Enfers Bouffons ou la Nuit de Satan Dément* (*Jesting Hells, or the Night of the Mad Satan*, 1996).

Finally, Pierre **Gripari** continued to produce a series of remarkably surreal books, such as a wonderful collection of genre stories, *L'Arrière-Monde* (*The Backworld*, 1972), and the novel *Gueule d'Aminche* (1973), a translation of the Gilgamesh story as a gangster saga in a fictional Mediterranean republic. Other notable Gripari books of the period included *Rêveries d'un Martien en Exil* (*Dreams of a Martian in Exile*, 1976) and *Pedigree du Vampire* (*Pedigree of the Vampire*, 1977).

FEMALE WRITERS

Female writers continued to excel in the more traditional realms of the *fantastique*. The works of Pierrette **Fleutiaux**, such as *Histoire du Gouffre et de la Lunette* (*Story of the Pit and the Glasses*, 1967), *Histoire de la Chauve-Souris* (*Tale of the Bat*, 1975), *Histoire du Tableau* (*Story of a Painting*, 1977), and *Métamorphoses de la Reine* (*Metamorphosis of the Queen*, 1984), were praised by Cortazar, who wrote an introduction to one of her collections. In Fleutiaux's stories, reality is ultimately less fulfilling than the darkness, which must be embraced. Her revisited fairy tales were dark and erotic, full of strange things waiting for the opportunity to grab us. Fleutiaux has been compared to both Kafka and Poe.

Gabrielle **Wittkop** also displayed a fine taste for the morbid and clinical horror in books such as *Le Nécrophile* (1972) and *La Mort de C. Christian* (*The Death of C. Christian*, 1975). Her more recent works include *Les Rajahs Blancs* (*The White Rajahs*, 1986), *Hemlock, ou Les Poisons* (1988), and the collection, *Les Départs Exemplaires* (*Exemplary Departures*, 1996).

Jehanne **Jean-Charles** wrote a numbr of Poe-like short stories collected in *Les Plumes du Corbeau* (*The Raven's Feathers*, 1973), *La Mort, Madame* (*Death, Madam*, 1974), and *Vous avez dit Horrible?* (*Did You Say Awful?*, 1980).

Jeanne **Champion** chronicled the supernatural events of a small French village in *Vautour-en-Privilège* (*Vulture-In-Privilege*, 1973), hallucinatory remembrances of things past in *Dans les Jardins d'Esther* (*In Esther's Garden*, 1975) and penned a remarkable gothic murder mystery set in a monastery in *Les Gisants* (*The Tombs*, 1977).

Yvonne **Caroutch** wrote literary genre novels suffused with esoteric themes, such as *Le Gouvernement des Eaux* (*The Government of Waters*, 1970) and *La Voie au Coeur de Verre* (*The Way of the Heart of Glass*, 1972).

In the same vein, Sarane **Alexandrian**'s *L'Oeuf du Monde* (*The Egg of the World*, 1975) contemplated the ability of the human mind to control space and time. Also notable was her *Les Terres Fortunées du Songe* (*Dream's Happy Lands*, 1979).

Odile **Marcel** made her mark with the poetic *L'Eau qui Dort* (*Sleeping Water*, 1977) and *L'Amazonie* (1981).

Finally, Suzy **Morel** blended legends and romanticism with such intimate novels as *L'Enfant Cavalier* (*The Child Rider*, 1977), *Les Pas d'Orphée* (*Orpheus' Steps*, 1982), *Le Chemin des Loups* (*The Wolves' Path*, 1985) and *L'Office des Ténèbres* (*The Office of Darkness*, 1989).

Other notable female writers of the period included: Christia **Sylf**, with her collection *La Patte de Chat* (*The Cat's Paw*, 1974), Nicole **Avril** and Claire **Bonnafé**, who will all be reviewed under **Heroic Fantasy** below.

b. Fantastique Populaire

HORROR

The *Angoisse* imprint of Éditions Fleuve Noir continued publishing horror novels until 1974, and was then followed by their *Horizons de l'Au-Delà* (*Horizons from Beyond*) imprint, which mostly reprinted earlier titles, until 1985. Among the authors introduced in *Angoisse* during its last few years were a number of distinguished science fiction writers from the *Anticipation* imprint who dabbled with horror, such as:

G.-J. **Arnaud**, who penned such classics as *Le Dossier Atrée* (*The Atreus File*, 1972) and *La Dalle aux Maudits* (*The Slab of the Accursed*, 1974). Arnaud became one of the regular contributors to the *Anticipation* imprint in the 1980s with his *Ice Company* series (see Chapter IX). He had previously written a dozen mysteries for Hachette (1952-54), Ferenczi (1959-60), and L'Arabesque (1972-79), using the pseudonyms of "Saint-Gilles" and "Georges Murey," and over seventy-five novels for the Fleuve Noir *Special-Police* imprint (1960-88). These mysteries were almost gothic, featuring pseudo-fantasy elements, and a deep sense of paranoia and unreality. Their protagonists were often women trapped in unrelentingly evil schemes. The books were influenced by the writings of **Simenon** and the films of Hitchcock. Some of Arnaud's thrillers could arguably be labelled *fantastique*. One of the most notorious, *Enfantasme*, was made into a 1978 feature film entitled *L'Enfant de la Nuit* (*The Night Child*) by Sergio Gobbi.

Paul **Béra**, also a well-known science fiction writer under the pseudonym of "Yves **Dermèze**," chronicled the adventures of Léonox, starting with *Léonox, Monstre des Ténèbres* (*Leonox, Monster of Darkness*) in 1971. Léonox subsequently appeared in Nos. 211, 225, 242, and 249 of the *Angoisse* imprint, and made his last appearance in *L'Être Mystérieux* (*The Mysterious Being*), a 1977 novel written

under the pseudonym of "John Luck" for the short-lived fantasy series of the *Le Masque* imprint of the Librairie des Champs-Élysées. The *Léonox* series focused on the adventures of humans who became the agents of supernatural forces beyond human ken, as well as the incarnation of even more dreaded powers, such as Death, which appeared in the form of a meek civil servant called "Mr. Mower."

Other *Anticipation* writers who wrote for *Angoisse* included:

Pierre **Pelot**, writing as "Pierre Suragne," with *La Peau de l'Orage* (*The Skin of the Storm*, 1973), *Duz* (1973), and *Je Suis la Brume* (*I Am the Mist*, 1974).

Jean-Pierre **Andrevon**, writing as "Alphonse **Brutsche**," with *Un Froid Mortel* (*A Deadly Cold*, 1971) and *Le Reflux de la Nuit* (*The Reflux of Night*, 1972).

Max-André **Rayjean**, with six novels (1969-74), featuring the occult detective Henri Gil. Gabriel **Jan**, with two novels (1973-74).

Other writers published by *Angoisse* before its cancellation included:

Dominique **Rocher**, with ten novels (1968-75) including *Les Voyances du Docteur Basile* (*The Visions of Dr. Basile*, 1970).

Agnès **Laurent**, with six novels (1970-73) including *Le Sang des Étoiles* (*Blood of the Stars*, 1973).

Michel **Saint-Romain**, with four novels (1971-72); Anthony **Feek** with two novels (1973-74); "Éric **Verteuil**" (the pseudonym of the writing team of Alain Bernier and Roger Maridat); and Chris **Burger** with two novels, *Incubation* (1974) and *Le Sorcier* (*The Wizard*, 1975), for the *Horizons de l'Au-Delà* imprint.

Conversely, the first writer to have introduced horror themes to the classic science fiction *Anticipation* imprint of Fleuve Noir was Robert **Clauzel**, whose brand of horror relied on a mixture of Lovecraftian forces from beyond the known universe and Dean Koontz-like scientific projects. In *L'Horreur Tombée du Ciel* (*The Horror That Fell from the Sky*, 1971), an alien germ threatened to engulf Earth; in *La Terrible Expérience de Peter Home* (*The Dreadful Experi-*

ment of Peter Home, 1973), the experiments of a terrible new Prometheus could destroy the world; in *Le Nuage qui Vient de la Mer* (*The Cloud Which Came from the Sea*, 1974), mysterious aliens manipulated a corner of England to test our ability to deal with incomprehensible cosmic forces released accidentally in our universe.

Other horror imprints of the 1970s included:

La Bibliothèque de l'Étrange (*The Library of the Strange*), published by Galliéra.

Terrific, published by Monnet, which released works by Agnès **Laurent**, a series of horror thrillers by "Maïk **Vegor**," as well as a series of novels by Maurice **Périsset**, a writer whose genre career spanned several decades, from his classic *Les Eaux Noires* (*The Black Waters*, 1946) to *Le Jeu de Satan* (*The Game of Satan*, 1972) and *Le Visage Derrière la Nuit* (*The Face Behind the Night*, 1973).

Mémoires d'Outre Ciel (*Memoirs from Beyond the Sky*), published by Garry from 1979 to 1982. Its catalog included genre novels such as Jacques **Hurtaud**'s *La Révolte des Arbres* (*The Revolt of the Trees*, 1979) and *Ombre* (*Shadow*, 1979), Bastien **Dorion**'s *Le Fantôme de Sang* (*The Phantom of Blood*, 1980), and *Les Orgues de l'Infini* (*The Organs of Infinity*, 1982); Jean **Scapin**'s *La Maison du Frisson* (*House of Shivers*, 1982); Jean **Mauhourat**'s *Le Singe Jaune* (*The Yellow Monkey*, 1982); as well as novels by Belgian writer Jean **Sadyn** (see below), Robert **Clauzel** (writing as "Roy Morrisson"), Gabriel **Jan** (writing as "Yann Delmon"), and others.

Finally, one should mention a series of thrillers with horrific elements, such as *La Baie des Trépassés* (*The Bay of the Trespassed*, 1973) and *Robinson Cruauté* (*Robinson Cruelty*, 1974) written by Catherine **Arley** and published by Eurédif in the mid-1970s.

HEROIC FANTASY

French heroic fantasy could be said to have started with Gustave **Flaubert**'s *Salammbô* published in 1862 (see Chapter IV).

André Ruellan, writing as "Kurt **Steiner**," was arguably the first writer to introduce modern heroic fantasy in the *Anticipation* imprint of Fleuve Noir with his *Aux Armes d'Ortog* (*Under Ortog's Arms*, 1960), and its sequel *Ortog et les Ténèbres* (*Ortog and the Darkness*, 1969). The world of Dal Ortog Dal of Galankar is a futuristic Earth where sophisticated science cohabits with a pseudo-medieval society. In the first novel, Ortog was sent by the ruling Sopharc, Karella, to find a cure for the slow death that is killing Earth and its inhabitants after a devastating interplanetary war. Ortog eventually returned with such a cure, but too late to save his love, Karella's daughter, Kalla. In the sequel, Ortog and his friend Zoltan, embarked on an Orpheus-like quest through the dimensions of Death to find Kalla's soul and bring her back to Earth. Ortog is armed with the devastating "Blue Weapon" in the form of a sword whose blade disintegrates everything it touches. He eventually found Kalla,

ORTOG ET LES TÉNÈBRES

lost her again, and returned to Earth, cursed with immortality.

Another precursor of modern French heroic-fantasy was Nathalie **Henneberg**, the Russian-born wife of German-born science fiction writer, Charles **Henneberg** who, in the 1950s, penned a series of flamboyantly gothic space operas, featuring superhuman protagonists, often soldiers or mercenaries, victims of violent, romantic passions. After Charles' death in 1959, Nathalie (who, at first, signed Nathalie-Charles Henneberg) pursued her late husband's writing career, but relied increasingly on fantasy rather than science fiction elements.

LA PLAIE

le rayon fantastique

Les Dieux Verts (1961) told the romance of Argo and Atlena during the future Emerald Age of Earth, when Man's empire is on the decline and the world is ruled by the eponymous "Green Gods," powerful entities from the vegetable kingdom. *Le Sang des Astres* (*The Blood of the Stars*, 1963) was a colorful gothic fantasy in which an astronaut from the year 2700 journeys to a medieval Earth-like world ruled by kabbala, where legends live, and where he falls in love with a female salamander.

Nathalie Henneberg's masterpiece was *La Plaie* (*The Plague*, 1964), a sprawling 600-page novel that told of the desperate battle by a handful of humans and angel-like mutants against a wave of pure, malevolent evil sweeping the galaxy, and which incarnates itself in the bodies of the "Nocturnes" (*Nocturnals*). Henneberg's works stood alone in the literary landscape of the 1960s, even in the world of science fiction and the *fantastique*. Her use of the French language, betraying Germanic and Russian influences, was unusually well-suited to creating larger-than-life heroic characters and epic romances. Like the British and American masters of the genre, Henneberg knew how to build full-blown, intricately detailed baroque and colorful universes. Her fantasy short-stories were later collected in *Démons et Chimères* (*Demons and Chimeras*, 1977) and *D'Or et de Nuit* (*Of Gold and Night*, 1977).

Henneberg's heroic fantasy relied on basic themes bor-rowed from space opera. Christia **Sylf**'s novels, on the other hand, were pure heroic fantasy. *Kobor Tigan't* (1969) and its sequel, *Le Règne de Ta* (*The Reign of Ta*, 1971), took place thirty throusand years ago, during the reign of the Giants, a mythical pre-Atlantean race which preceded ours. The novel told of the conflict between the sorcerous Queen-Mother, Abim, and her daughters Opak, who rules Kobor Tigan't, the five-levelled City of the Giants, and her sister, Ta. The world of Kobor Tigan't was inhabited by a race of reptilian bisexual humanoids, theT'los, who were used as sex slaves by the Giants. The novels also featured the crystal-like Elohim, messengers of occult alien powers from beyond, dragons, and a host of other fantastic creatures. The *Kobor Tigan't* novels were clearly heroic fantasy, yet would be hard to compare to anything published in England or America. They contained numerous erotic scenes as well as esoteric elements that one rarely finds in the more literary worlds of Tolkien or the juvenile savagery of Howard's *Conan* series. They were written in a rich, colorful prose, and even included a glossary of the language of the Giants.

Sylf continued her saga with *Markosamo le Sage* (*Markosamo the Wise*, 1973), this time with a story featuring the reincarnations of all her principal characters, but set twenty thousand years ago, during the Age of Atlantis. A fourth volume, *La Reine au Coeur Puissant* (*The Strong-Hearted Queen*, 1979), carried on with a tale taking place in ancient China two thousand years ago. **Sylf** had announced the publication of five more volumes in her series: *La Geste d'Amoïnen* (*The Saga of Amoinen*), set in Nordic Finland; *Amiona la Courtisane* (*Amiona the Courtesan*), set in Renaissance Venice; *Ertulie de Fons l'Abîme* (*Ertulia of Fons-The-Abyss*), set during the reign of the French Sun King; and the two-volume *L'Apocalypse de Kébélé* (*Kebele's Apocalypse*), featuring her immortal narrator and set in the far future. Unfortunately, these works were never published.

Charles **Duits** belonged to the same rich and colorful tradition of fantasy world-building as Flaubert and Sylf. With *Ptah Hotep* (1971) and *Nefer* (1978), Duits wrote a prodigious heroic fantasy saga that took place on a parallel Earth with two moons—Athenade and Thana—during the time of Ancient Egypt and the Roman Empire. *Ptah Hotep* was the story of the ascension of a young prince to the throne of Caesar. *Nefer*, which took place several centuries later, told of the adventures of a young Egyptian priest who fell in love with a sacred prostitute. The supernatural was intelligently used as an integral part of Duits' intensely spiritual "otherworld" rather than as an artificial literary device

to be exploited for cheap thrills. Even the erotic passages were, as with Sylf, an integral part of the magic. Duits was a friend of André Breton and the surrealists. A gifted poet and a man who had experimented with peyote, he was also influenced by the *Thousand and One Nights* and the Indian *Ramayana*. *Ptah Hotep* and *Nefer* were prodigious descriptions of alternate realities, comparable to no other fantasy works in the Anglo-Saxon tradition.

Jean **Tur** created a Polynesian-like world of island empires, lost on a vast Pacific-like ocean, in a world that never was. In his series the *Memoirs of the Arkonn Tecla*, that began with *L'Archipel des Guerrières* (*The Archipelago of the Warrior-Women*, 1973) and continued with *La Harpe des Forces* (*The Harp of Power*, 1974) and *Sterne Dorée* (*Golden Sterne*, 1976), Tur narrated, in painstaking detail, the story of a peace expedition led by the Arkonn Tecla, a warrior prince of the Mavae Empire, who has been sent to the neighboring Aginn Archipelago to cement an alliance. The Aginn turned out to be fierce Amazon-like women, and by the end of the third volume, Tecla had only begun entreaties with them. (Two more volumes have reportedly been self-published by Tur since then.) The seafaring world of Tur—perhaps the lost Empire of Mû?—owed little to the modern world as we know it. The first-person narrative device used by Tur was both poetic and epic, with many erotic scenes devoted to Tecla's tumultuous love life. As with Duits, the role of magic was sparse, the supernatural powers manifesting themselves during a religious ceremony in the form of a celestial harp.

The *fantastique* of Yves and Ada **Rémy** was baroque and colorful. In their collection, *Les Soldats de la Mer* (*The Soldiers from the Sea*, 1968), and their novel, *Le Grand Midi* (*The Great South*, 1971), they chronicled the tales of a mysterious neverland dubbed the "Federation," through its myths, legends and, ultimately, military history.

Another author who dabbled with heroic fantasy was Christian **Charrière**, who wrote novels that would fit between the high fantasy of a William Morris and symbolist literature. Charrière's *L'Enclave* (*The Enclave*, 1971), *Mayapura* (1973), and *Le Sîmorgh* (1977) were all anachronistic quests taking place in imaginary lands. Mayapura is an imaginary city that could just as well be located on Jack Vance's *Dying Earth*. The Simorgh is a colorful bird gifted

with the curse of prophecy—whoever follows him, or so the legends say, can, after a perilous journey, find a land of paradise. Both novels created their own supernatural mythology, filled with religious icons, talking skeletons, animated stones giving birth to monsters, monuments carved with secret symbols, and other wonders.

Other literary works of high fantasy written during the decade included:

Nicole **Avril**'s *Les Gens de Misar* (*The People of Misar*, 1972), about a fantasy city located in an imaginary world.

Mainstream science fiction writer René **Barjavel**'s collaboration with Olenka de **Veer**, *Les Dames à la Licorne* (*The Ladies of the Unicorn*, 1974), and its sequel, *Les Jours du Monde* (*The Days of the World*, 1977).

Claire **Bonnafé**'s poetic *Le Bruit de la Mer* (*The Sound of the Sea*, 1978).

Sous l'Araignée du Sud (*Under the Southern Spider*) by Dominique **Roche** and Charles **Nightingale** (1978), a fantasy odyssey mixing Tolkienesque and Lovecraftian themes.

Finally, in 1980, the writing team of Marcelle Perriod and Jean-Louis Fraysse, using the nom-de-plume of "Michel **Grimaud**," and also known for their juvenile novels (see below) and science fiction works (see Chapter IX), penned one notable high fantasy novel for *Présence du Futur*: *Malakansâr*, sub-titled *L'Éternité des Pierres* (*The Eternity of Stones*). It was a literary work of classic fantasy, telling the story of the dramatic quest by three characters for the eponymous mythical city through the Lands of the Morning and the Lands of the Evening.

The 1970s were also years when British and American fantasy began to appear in France. Tolkien's *The Hobbit* had been translated in 1967, but had remained generally unnoticed. *The Lord of the Rings* was first published in 1972, but did not energize the field to the extent that it did in England and America. Robert E. Howard's *Conan* also had two volumes published in 1972 (sporting attractive covers by Philippe **Druillet**), but made no major impact. It was only in 1980 that the *Conan* saga, helped by the release of the 1982 film, became a best-selling phenomenon. More influential were the works of Jack Vance, in particular *The Eyes of the Overworld* which had been serialised in *Fiction* in the early 1960s, Michael Moorcock's *Elric*, translated in 1969, and Fritz Leiber's *Fafhrd and Gray Mouser* stories, published in 1970.

Under editor Alain Dorémieux, *Fiction* began publishing some heroic fantasy short stories by writers Daniel **Walther** and Jean-Pierre **Fontana** in the early 1970s.

Fontana, using the pseudonym "Guy Scovel," embarked on *La Geste du Halaguen* (*The Saga of the Halaguen*), a Jack Vance-inspired heroic fantasy saga, that was eventually collected in 1975 by *Marabout*. *La Geste* described the battle between the brave warrior Silgan and the barbarian chief known only as the "Sequençaire" to protect the Kingdom of Occitanie. The universe it described was more science-fantasy rather than pure sword & sorcery. Sil-

FLEUVE NOIR

FLEUVE NOIR

gan's world was eventually revealed to be a huge, star-travelling worldship out of control, and Silgan himself the reincarnation of his pilot. *La Geste du Halaguen* was recently expanded by Fontana with the recent 1997 publication by L'Atalante of *Naalia de Sanar*, a prequel to the 1975 novel, telling the origins of Silgan.

Another regular contributor to *Fiction,* Jean-Pierre **Andrevon**, wrote *Les Hommes-Machines contre Gandahar* (*The Machine Men vs. Gandahar*, 1969), another science fantasy also owing much to Jack Vance and taking place on the colorful, peaceful world of Gandahar. Gandahar is a lost Earth colony inhabited by a gentle medieval society which uses ecologically friendly technology. In the novel, Gandahar was invaded by robotic Machine Men who turned out to have been sent from its future. The heroic Sylvin Lanvere, Queen Ambisextra's knight, saved the day. The novel became the basis for the eponymous 1987 animated feature by René **Laloux**, released in the United States as **Lightyears** (see Book 1, Chapter IV). Andrevon recently returned to the colorful world of Gandahar with *Gandahar et l'Oiseau-Monde* (*Gandahar and the World-Bird*, 1997), published in a juvenile imprint, in which the planet is revealed to be a giant bird's egg.

At Fleuve Noir's *Anticipation* imprint, Pierre **Barbet** followed suit with *À Quoi Songent les Psyborgs?* (*What Do Psyborgs Dream About?*, 1971), in which his Galactic Temporal Investigator Setni explored a planet where a trio of powerful, disembodied

brains have recreated the fantasy legends of Amadis of Gaul for their own entertainment. Barbet continued to mine this vein with *La Planète Enchantée* (1973) and *Vénusine* (1977), the latter written under the pseudonym "Olivier Sprigel." He also penned a historical fantasy, *L'Empire du Baphomet* (*The Empire of Baphomet*, 1972), in which an alien attempted to manipulate the Templar Knights to take over the world during the Crusades.

Also at *Anticipation*, the writing team of Jean-Louis & Doris **Le May** flirted with heroic-fantasy with *Les Créateurs d'Ulnar* (*The Creators of Ulnar*, 1972), in which space explorers acquired god-like powers on the planet Ulnar, recreated a fantasy world, and ended up waging an apocalyptic war.

In 1976, publisher Librairie des Champs-Élysées was the first to offer a short-lived imprint of fantasy novels, with translations of Robert E. Howard, Gardner Fox, and Fritz Leiber, as well as reprints of Nathalie Henneberg, and two collection of heroic-fantasy stories by Julia Verlanger, *Les Portes Sans Retour* (*The Gates of No Return*, 1976) and *La Flûte de Verre Froid* (*The Flute of Cold Glass*, 1976).

Using the pseudonym of "Gilles Thomas," **Verlanger** then contributed the remarkable *Magie Sombre* (*Dark Magic*, 1977) to Fleuve Noir. In it, a young man found an old book of spells and, after having adapted the spells to replace medieval ingredients with modern ones (blood of salamander, for instance, is replaced with engine oil), acquired the power to control demons. But he quickly dis-

covered the evil that he unwittingly unleashed, and must join forces with the benevolent "Lords of the Fern" to banish the demons.

ESOTERISM

Esoteric fiction and pseudo-documentary books continued to be a staple of publishing throughout the 1970s.

Jean **Markalé** proved to be a worthy successor of Anatole **Le Braz** with works like *La Tradition Celtique en Bretagne Armoricaine* (*Celtic Tradition in Armorican Britanny*, 1975), *Histoire Secrète de la Bretagne* (*Secret History of Britanny*, 1977), *Merlin l'Enchanteur* (*Wizard Merlin*, 1981), and *Le Graal* (*The Grail*, 1982). Since then, Markalé has continued to bring to light not only Celtic myths and legends, but also other myths connected with the Templars, the Cathars, and other medieval elements.

Yann **Brékilien** also continued Le Braz' work on Britannic legends with *Récits Vivants de Bretagne* (*Living Tales from Britanny*, 1979), *La Reine Sauvage* (1980), *Les Cavaliers du Bout du Monde* (*The Riders of World's End*, 1990), and *Le Druide* (*The Druid*, 1994).

Jean-Paul **Bourre** made his mark on the field with works dealing with witchcraft and magic, such as *Les Sectes Lucifériennes Aujourd'hui* (*Luciferian Sects Today*, 1978), before contributing more recent works about vampires such as *Dracula et les Vampires* (*Dracula and the Vampires*, 1981), a fictionalized essay painting vampires as initiates looking for immortality.

JUVENILES

Throughout the 1970s, Georges **Chaulet** continued to produce *Fantômette* novels, as well as several other popular children's adventure series, such as *Béatrice*, *Candy*, *Étincelle*, *Le Petit Lion* (*The Little Lion*), *Le Prince Charmant* (*Prince Charming*), *Les Quatre As* (*The Four Aces*), and others, most of which contained genre elements. He also wrote novelisations of Walt Disney's *Mickey Mouse* and DIC's *Inspector Gadget*.

René **Guillot** was another writer who alternated between children's fantasy series, such as the *Kiriki* novels (1970) and *L'Extraordinaire Aventure de Messire Renart* (*The Extraordinary Adventure of Sir Renart*, 1972), and juvenile exotic adventures, such as *Le Chef au Masque d'Or* (*The Chief with a Golden Mask*, 1973) and *Le Chevalier Sans Visage* (*The Knight Without a Face*, 1973).

Michèle **Angot** updated the art of fairy tales with *Les Contes de la Lune Bleue* (*Tales of the Blue Moon*, 1970), *Les Contes de la Lune Rousse* (*Tales of the Rust Moon*, 1970), and *La Grotte aux Fées* (*The Fairies' Cave*, 1971).

Henri **Gougaud** also managed to combine the fairy tales and folk legends of the past with more modern sensibilities in collections such as *Contes de la Huchette* (*Tales of the Small Basket*, 1973), *L'Arbre à Soleil* (*The Sun Tree*, 1979), *L'Arbre aux Trésors* (*The Treasure Tree*, 1987), and

L'Arbre d'Amour et de Sagesse (*The Tree of Love and Wisdom*, 1992).

Another writer in this vein was Philippe **Dumas**, who penned several delightful collections of modern fairy tales, such as *Le Professeur Ecrouton-Creton* (1977), *Contes à l'Envers* (*Inside-Out Tales*, 1977), *La Petite Géante* (*The Little Giantess*, 1979), and *Ondine au fond de l'Eau* (*Ondine Beneath the Water*, 1979).

Finally, the success of Pierre **Gripari**'s *Contes de la Rue Broca* (*Tales of Broca Street*, 1967) led him to embark on a series of modern fairy tales such as *Histoire du Prince Pipo, de Pipo le Cheval et de la Princesse Popi* (*Tale of PrInce Pipo, Pipo the Horse and Princess Popi*, 1976), *Nanasse et Gigantel* (1977), *La Sorcière de la Rue Mouffetard* (*The Witch of Mouffetard St.*, 1980), *Le Gentil Petit Diable* (*The Kind Little Devil*, 1980), *Patrouille du Conte* (*Fairy Tale Patrol*, 1983), and others, which made him the contemporary equivalent of Marcel **Aymé**.

In the young-adult field, "Michel **Grimaud**" (see above) turned out a number of juvenile fantasies (as well as science fiction novels) such as *Amaury, Chevalier Cathare* (*Amaury, Cathar Knight*, 1971), *La Ville sans Soleil* (*The City Without Sun*, 1973), *La Terre des Autres* (*Others' Land*, 1973), *Le Peuple de la Mer* (*The People of the Sea*, 1974), and the prehistoric saga of *Rhôor l'Invincible* (*Rhoor the Invincible*), published by Alsatia in 1971.

Other authors of young adult fantasies included:

Michel **Cosem**, with *Haute Erre* (*High Wandering*, 1972), *La Chasse Artus* (*The Artus Hunt*, 1974), and *Alpha de la Licorne* (*Alpha of the Unicorn*, 1979).

Xavier **Armange**, with *L'Arbre de l'An Bientôt* (*The Tree of Soon Year*, 1979).

c. Belgian Fantastique

In 1969, writer Jean-Baptiste **Baronian**, himself a genre author, took over the editorship of *Marabout* and expanded the *fantastique* imprint by introducing a number of new authors who continued the traditions and styles of Jean Ray and Thomas Owen. Baronian was the author of *Scènes de la Vie Obscure* (*Scenes of the Dark Life*, 1977) and *Le Diable Vauvert* (*The Devil Vauvert*, 1979), as well as a number of remarkable genre anthologies and an authoritative *Panorama de la Littérature Fantastique de Langue Française* (*Panorama of Fantastic Literature in the French Language*, 1978).

Among the most notable authors published by *Marabout* was Gérard **Prévot**, with *Le Démon de Février* (*The February Demon*, 1970), *Celui Qui Venait De Partout* (*That Which Came from Everywhere*, 1973), *La Nuit du Nord* (*The Night of the North*, 1974), and *Le Spectre Large* (*The Large Spectre*, 1975). A realist writer in the tradition of Sternberg, Prévot depicted a world where everyday life is *fantastique*. In his universe, somber men moved like grim specters through the cold, wind-swept cities of Flanders.

The world order was always susceptible to replacement by evil and chaos.

Jean **Sadyn**, with *La Nuit des Mutants* (*The Night of the Mutants*, 1970), straddled science fiction and horror. Sadyn went on to to write *Haute Magie* (*High Magic*, 1980) and *Cosmos* (1982) for the *Mémoires d'Outre-Ciel* imprint (see above), before eventually turning to spinning yarns derived from Flemish folklore, such as *Fables et Contes Flamands* (*Fables and Flemish Tales*, 1993) and *Flandres Fantastiques* (*Fantastic Flanders*, 1994).

Gaston **Compère**, with *La Femme de Putiphar* (*Putiphar's Wife*, 1975) sublimated the reassuring certainties of reality, then proceeded to destroy them with his sarcastic, laser-sharp wit. His vision of what dwells within the human spirit was that of a surgeon of the soul. Compère was also the author of *Sept Machines à Rêver* (*Seven Machines for Dreaming*, 1974), a collection of tales where the burlesque competed with derision, in a manner that was equally joyful and scary, scandalous and serious. Later, notable Compère works included *La Constellation du Serpent* (*The Constellation of the Snake*, 1983) and *Les Eaux de l'Achéron* (*The Waters of the Acheron*, 1985).

Other notable *Marabout* writers included:

Jean-Paul **Raemdonck**, with *Han* (1972), a chaotic novel full of arresting images.

Daniel **Mallinus**, with *Myrtis and Autres Histoires de Nuit and de Peur* (*Myrtis and Other Tales of Night and Fear*, 1973), a collection of fear stories cleverly reworking classic themes.

Jean-Pierre **Bours**, with *Celui Qui Pourrissait* (*He Who Rots*, 1977), a collection of genre stories often centered around the theme of searching for one's true identity.

Marabout ceased publication in 1981. Other Belgian *fantastique* writers of the 1970s included:

Gabriel **Deblander**, the author of numerous short stories published in *Fiction* in the 1960s and collected in *Le Retour des Chasseurs* (*The Return of the Hunters*, 1970). Deblander later penned *L'Oiseau sous la Chemise* (*The Bird Under the Shirt*, 1976), a novel dealing with ancient folk legends, making him a Belgian Claude Seignolle.

Georges **Thinès** was another notable Belgian author with *L'Oeil de Fer* (*The Eye of Iron*, 1977) and *Les Objets vous trouveront* (*Objects Will Find You*, 1979). In his stories, every seemingly ordinary day became a prodigious field of dreams filled with unexpected surprises, impossible probabilities, and strangely behaving objects. More recent works by Thinès included *Le Désert d'Alun* (*The Alun Desert*, 1986) and *La Face Cachée* (*The Hidden Face*, 1994).

3. The 1980s and 1990s

a. Fantastique Littéraire

The *fantastique*, in all its diversity of expression, has continued to be well represented during the last two decades among the works published by mainstream publishers and generally deemed to be part of so-called mainstream literature. By necessity, considering the lack of historical perspective, we shall refrain from classifying authors too specifically, following instead a chronological perspective and providing a potpourri-like selection of some of the most interesting works.

Fréderic **Tristan** is a renowned and prolific author whose genre career could easily said to have began as early as 1959 with his novel *Le Dieu des Mouches* (*The God of the Flies*). Yet, it is only with *Les Tribulations Héroïques de Balthasar Kober* (*The Heroic Tribulations of Balthasar Kober*, 1980), a *roman picaresque*, that he embarked on a series of strikingly original esoteric novels, each depicting an initiatic, spiritual journey. In *Les Tribulations*, a divinely inspired madman seeks the light by exploring the secrets of kabbala and alchemy. *L'Histoire Sérieuse et Drolatique de l'Homme sans Nom* (*The Serious and Funny Tale of the Nameless Man*, 1980) features a nameless adventurer who has lived for centuries. Other notable Tristan works in this vein include *L'Oeil d'Hermès* (*The Eye of Hermes*, 1982), *Naissance d'un Spectre* (*Birth of a Spectre*, 1983), *Le Fils de Babel* (*The Son of Babel*, 1985), *Le Singe Égal du Ciel* (*The Ape Equal to Heaven*, 1986), *L'Ange dans la Machine* (*The Angel in the Machine*, 1989), and *Le Dernier des Hommes* (*The Last Man*, 1993).

Hubert **Haddad** and Georges-Olivier **Châteaureynaud**, already mentioned in our previous sections, continued to pen a number of finely crafted, literary fantasies. The former with novels such as *La Ville sans Miroir* (*The City Without Mirrors*, 1984), *Oholiba des Songes* (*Oholiba of the Dreams*, 1989), *L'Âme de Buridan* (*Buridan's Soul*, 1992), and *La Falaise de Sable* (*The Sand Cliff*, 1997). The latter with works like *La Faculté des Songes* (*The Faculty of Dreams*, 1982), *Le Congrès de Fantômologie* (*The Congress of Phantomology*, 1985), *Le Jardin dans l'Île* (*The Garden in the Island*, 1989), *Le Château de Verre* (*The Glass Castle*, 1994), and *Les Messagers* (*The Messengers*, 1996).

Michel **Tournier** also continued to produce a number of notable young adult and juvenile works, as well as remarkable genre novels such as *Le Crépuscule des Masques* (*The Twilight of the Masks*, 1992) and *Le Miroir à Deux Faces* (*The Mirror with Two Faces*, 1994).

Claude **Louis-Combet** offered such fine works as *Le Roman de Mélusine* (*The Novel of Melusine*, 1986), *Figures de Nuit* (*Night Figures*, 1988), and *Augias et Autres Infâmes* (*Augias and Other Infamous Actions*, 1993).

Jean-Marie **Le Clézio** contributed *La Genèse* (*Genesis*, 1987) and *L'Étoile Errante* (*The Wandering Star*, 1992).

Mainstream novelist Jean d'**Ormesson** penned the notable *Histoire du Juif Errant* (*Story of the Wandering Jew*, 1991).

René **Réouven**, an author of thrillers and Sherlock

Holmes pastiches (see below), also wrote several science fiction novels under the name of René **Sussan**. As Sussan, he published *Les Insolites* (*Strange Tales*, 1984), a collection of fantastical and science fiction tales which won the 1985 French Science Fiction Grand Prize. As Réouven, he wrote *Les Grandes Profondeurs* (*The Lower Depths*, 1991) and *Les Survenants* (*The Overghosts*, 1996), a prodigious novel about a man stalked by another version of himself from a "what if" reality. With Donna Sussan, he co-authored *Les Nourritures Extra-Terrestres* (*Extra-Terrestrial Food*, 1994), which won the 1995 Grand Prize of Imagination.

Some of the best new authors included:

Roger **Vrigny** made a remarkable appearance with *Un Ange Passe* (*An Angel Passes*, 1979), the striking tale of an exterminating angel, followed by *Accident de Parcours* (*Accident in Transit*, 1985), a collection of three fantastic stories. Other, more recent notable works by Vrigny include *Le Garçon d'Orage* (*The Storm Boy*, 1994) and *Instants Dérobés* (*Purloined Moments*, 1996).

Pierre-Jean **Rémy**, wrote some wonderful modern, gothic fantasies, such as *Cordélia, ou l'Angleterre* (*Cordelia, or England*, 1979) and *Pandora* (1980).

Georges de **Lorzac** penned *La Loque à Terre* (*The Wreck of a Tenant*, 1980), the surreal tale of a man trapped in a high-rise staircase.

François **Sonkin** published *Le Petit Violon* (*The Small Violin*, 1981), a remarkable collection of fantastic tales.

Gérard **Macé** penned a number of short stories that read like prose poems, collected in *Bois Dormant* (*Sleeping Woods*, 1983), *Les Trois Coffrets* (*The Three Boxes*, 1985), *Vies Antérieures* (*Previous Lives*, 1991), and *L'Autre Hémisphère du Temps* (*The Other Half of Time*, 1995).

Sony Labou **Tansi** is a Congolese French-speaking writer whose first novel, *Conscience de Tracteur* (*Tractor Consciousness*, 1979) dealt with a sentient tractor in his native Africa. Other notable works by him include *Les Sept Solitudes de Lorsa Lopez* (*The Seven Solitudes of Lorsa Lopez*, 1985) and *Les Yeux du Volcan* (*The Eyes of the Volcano*, 1988).

Belgian writer Alain **Berenboom** is another notable author, with works such as *La Position du Missionnaire Roux* (*The Red Missionary Position*, 1989), *La Table de Riz* (*The Rice Table*, 1992), and *La Jerusalem Captive* (*Captive Jerusalem*, 1997).

Finally, Jeremy **Bérenger** is a poet of the supernatural. His *Allison la Sybilline* (1994) and *La Rousseur des Bananes à l'Été finissant* (*The Redness of Bananas at the End of Summer*, 1997) are written in a flamboyant style that perfectly transcribes his rich imagination. In *Allison*, as in most of his writings, Bérenger was inspired by a story of his own life. The result is an endearing and gripping tale of a man who has fallen in love with a woman whom he cannot have but who will, eventually, become his writing muse.

Notable female writers of the last decade included:

Danièle **Sallenave** with *La Vie Fantôme* (*The Ghost Life*, 1986) and *Les Trois Minutes du Diable* (*The Devil's Three Minutes*, 1994), in which the world stops every day for three minutes.

Colette **Fayard**, with *Les Chasseurs au Bord de la Nuit* (*The Hunters at the Edge of Night*, 1989), *Par Tous les Temps* (*By All Time*, 1990), and *Le Jeu de l'Éventail* (*The Game of the Fan*, 1992).

Katherine **Quénot**, with *Rien que des Sorcières* (*Nothing But Witches*, 1993), the tale of three women with strange powers, and *Blanc comme la Nuit* (*White as Night*, 1993).

Jeanne **Faivre d'Arcier**, one of the very few French authors published by Presses-Pocket, mined the vein exploited by Anne Rice with *Rouge Flamenco* (*Flamenco Red*, 1993) and *La Déesse Écarlate* (*The Scarlet Goddess*, 1997), two very colorful gothic novels about vampires.

Laurence **Cossé** with *Le Coin du Voile* (*The Corner of the Veil*, 1996), in which a priest discovers an unarguable proof of the existence of God, but the world cannot live with it.

Marie **Darrieussecq**, one of 1996's literary successes, with *Truisme*, in which a woman is gradually changing into a sow.

b. *Fantastique Populaire*

HORROR

With the advent of the 1980s, films such as George Romero's *Dawn of the Dead* (1978), John Carpenter's *Halloween* (1978), David Cronenberg's *Scanners* (1981), and many others, as well as cheap Italian "rip-offs" of such works, became a definite influence in shaping the forms of modern French horror fiction. The translation and success of Anglo-Saxon authors such as Stephen King, Dean R. Koontz, and Clive Barker also had a marked impact on the French literary marketplace.

A number of dedicated popular horror imprints were launched during the last two decades:

Fantastique/Science Fiction (1979-88) by Nouvelles Éditions Oswald, which reprinted classic works by Hodgson, Merritt, Buchan, Stapledon, and others.

Les Fenêtres de la Nuit (*The Windows of Night*, 1980-83) by publisher Seghers, edited by Gérard **Klein** and Bernard Oudin, which translated works by Le Guin, Herbert, and Moorcock.

Paniques (*Panics*, 1981-86) by publisher Presses de la Cité, which translated works by Frank de Felitta, F. Paul Wilson and John Saul.

Épouvante (*Horror*), retitled *Ténèbres* (*Darkness*, 1986-ongoing), by publisher J'ai Lu, edited by Jacques **Sadoul**, which translated works by Stephen King, Dean R. Koontz, Peter Blatty, and Peter Straub.

Terreur (*Terror*, 1989-ongoing) by publisher Presses-Pocket, edited by Patrice **Duvic**, which translated works by Thomas Harris, James Herbert, Ramsay Campbell, Dean R. Koontz, Anne Rice, and Graham Masterton, with a few, select works by French authors such as Pierre Pelot and Jeanne Faivre d'Arcier.

Spécial Fantastique (*Special Fantastic*, 1987-88) by publisher Albin Michel, which translated works by Clive Barker and James Herbert.

Présence du Fantastique (*Presence of the Fantastic*, 1990-98) by publisher Denoël, edied by Jacques Chambon, which transated works by Robert Holdstock, Lisa Tuttle, Richard Matheson and K.,W. Jeter, and also published French works by Serge **Brussolo**, Jean-Marc **Ligny**, Anne **Duguël** and a series of anthologies by Alain Dorémieux, entitled *Territoires de l'Inquiétude* (*Territories of Worry*).

Outside of the exceptions mentioned above, French horror novels were mostly published by Éditions Fleuve Noir, first sporadically in the early 1980s in their classic science fiction *Anticipation* imprint (novels by Serge Brussolo and Joël Houssin), then in a dedicated imprint called *Gore* started in 1985 by editor Daniel Riche, which also published translations of Herschell Gordon Lewis, Shaun Hutson, and Joe Russo. *Gore* was taken over in 1989 by Juliette Raabe, who then edited the short-lived *Angoisses* (*Anguishes*) imprint in 1993-94, which was almost immediately replaced by the *Frayeurs* (*Scares*) imprint, edited by writer/filmmaker Jean **Rollin** from 1994 to 1996.

Another short-lived French horror imprint of the late 1980s was *Media 1000* which introduced the adventures of Michael **Honaker**'s ghost-busting Commander Ebnezer Grimes, whose adventures were later continued at Fleuve Noir's *Anticipation*.

Also, Serge Brussolo was granted his own horror imprint by publisher Gérard de Villiers from 1990 to 1992.

If France has its Clive Barker, it undoubtedly is Serge **Brussolo**, an amazingly prolific writer who has (so far) written well over ninety novels in various popular genres ranging from science fiction to horror, fantasy, crime, and others. Like filmmaker David Cronenberg, Brussolo appeared fascinated by the endless mutations of the flesh, and like Barker, he displayed a dark and radical vision, unafraid of delving into the extremes of pain and organic horror. At Fleuve Noir's *Anticipation*, his horror novels included *Le Puzzle de Chair* (*The Jigsaw Puzzle of Flesh*, 1983) which was about radical organ transplants; *Les Semeurs d'Abimes* (*The Abyss Sow-*

ers*, 1983), which took place in the same universe and revolved around living, symbiotic tattoos; *La Colère des Ténèbres* (*Ira Mélanox; the Wrath of Darkness*, 1986) which featured a disease that made human bones as fragile as glass, a werewolf, and diamond-hard locusts; *Catacombes* (*Catacombs*, 1986) the grim story of a mad sculptor and his female model in a haunted house; *Docteur Squelette* (*Doctor Skeleton*, 1987) another tale of the mutation of human bones; *La Nuit du Venin* (*The Night of the Poison*, 1987) which featured a carnivorous micro-organism; *Les Animaux Funèbres* (*The Funeral Beasts*, 1987) and *L'Ombre des Gnomes* (*The Shadow of the Gnomes*, 1987), both of which took place in a sun-baked, Central American village overrun by necrophagous monkeys.

In his own imprint, Brussolo published a number of powerful, morbid horror novels, such as *Cauchemar à Louer* (*Nightmare for Rent*, 1990), a variation on the "Hell House" theme; *La Meute* (*The Pack*, 1990), about the crazy son of a mad hunter who sacrificed girls to his father's hunting trophies; *Les Bêtes* (*The Beasts*, 1990), a gory novel about men turning into animals; *Les Démoniaques* (*The Demoniacals*, 1991), a superb gothic novel about an ancient, hellish book; *Krucifix* (1990); *Les Emmurés* (*Walled Up*, 1991); *Les Rêveurs d'Ombre* (*The Dreamers of Shadows*, 1991); *Le Vent Noir* (*The Black Wind*, 1991); and *Les Inhumains* (*The Inhumans*, 1992).

Other **Brussolo** works were *La Nuit du Bombardier* (*The Night of the Bomber*, 1989), which took place in a city haunted by the memory of a a plane which crashed there, killing thousands; the wreck of the plane was, itself, inhabited by a vampiric lifeform; *Boulevard des Banquises* (*Ice Shelf*

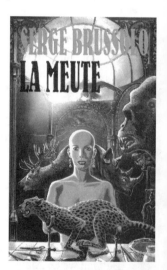

Boulevard, 1990), took place in a strange city located near the Arctic Circle, whose sadomasochistic residents once wrecked ships, and told of the grisly revenge of their long-dead victims, both published by Denoël. More recent works published in Fleuve Noir's *Anticipation* imprint included *Abîmes* (*Abyss*, 1993); *De l'Autre Côté du Mur des Ténèbres* (*On the Other Side of the Wall of Darkness*, 1993), about nightmares breaking through into the real world; and a trilogy entitled *Les Brigades du Chaos* (*The Brigades of Chaos*; Nos. 1962, 1970, 5, 1995-97), which took place in a future Los Angeles where the dead returned to life, objects were inhabited by weird life, and chaos reigned.

Joel **Houssin** was another prolific French writer who began his literary career in the late 1970s with a number of excellent science-fiction novels. He became a best-selling author with a series of detective thrillers featuring a tough cop nicknamed the *Dobermann* (recently made into a feature film directed by Jan Kounen). Houssin's first science fiction horror novel published in Fleuve Noir's *Anticipation* was *Angel Felina* (1981), which featured a virus that caused a bloody revolt of animals. *Le Pronostiqueur* (*The Handicapper*, 1981) began with a man receiving letters advising him of the winner of tomorrow's races, and ended up with the revelation of horrible human experiments. *Lilith* (1982) was about the spirit of a panther-like entity who possessed people and forced them to kill. *Le Chasseur* (*The Hunter*, 1983) was a monstrous gestalt created by handicapped children whose home had been destroyed. *Voyeur* (1983) was a David Cronenberg-like story in which a new synthetic biological organism infected people, making them commit acts of sexual perversion and cannibalism. Finally, *Les Vautours* (*The Vultures*, 1984) was a horror thriller about organ transplants.

In 1985, Houssin had two more horror novels published in the *Gore* imprint of Fleuve Noir: *L'Autoroute du Mas-sacre* (*Massacre Highway*), about a cannibal family which waylaid travelers, *à la* Wes Craven's film, *The Hills Have Eyes*; and *L'Écho des Supplicés* (*The Echo of the Tortured*), about the terrible, ritual revenge exacted by the dead innocents slaughtered throughout history on the descendents of their torturers.

Both Brussolo and Houssin won critical recognition and commercial success. Their stylish books won media attention and compared favorably with those of their American and British counterparts. However, the power of Brussolo's and Houssin's gut-twisting imagery was also what separates them from the literary establishment.

Michel **Honaker**'s first three novels, *Le Démon du Bronx* (*The Demon of the Bronx*), *D'Argile et de Sang* (*Of Clay and Blood*), and *La Maison des Cauchemars* (*The House of Nightmares*), all published in 1988 by *Media 1000*, featured the character of the Commander, a grim devil hunter named Ebenezer Graymes. The series was continued with Fleuve Noir's *Anticipation* (Nos. 1759, 1771, 1783, 1795, 1810, 1822, 1990-91). Honaker was also the author of an excellent vampire novel, *Terminus Sanglant* (*Bloody Terminus*), published in *Gore* in 1988.

Thanks to the editorship of Daniel Riche, many other renowned science fiction authors contributed to *Gore*. Pascal Marignac, a renowned thriller writer under the pseudonym "**Kâa**," used the pseudonym of "Corsélien" to pen *L'État des Plaies* (*The State of the Wounds*, 1987), about a cannibal monster, and *Bruit Crissant du Rasoir sur les Os* (*The Grating Sound of Razor Over Bones*, 1988).

Jean **Mazarin**, another renowned science fiction and thriller writer, used the pseudonym of "Charles Nécrorian" to pen *Blood Sex* (1985), about a horror writer who needed to kidnap and torture victims in order to fuel his imagination; *Impacts* (1986), a *First Blood* variation; and *Skin Killer* (1987), about a serial killer who skinned his victims.

G.-J. **Arnaud**, with *Le Festin Séculaire* (*The Secular Feast*, 1985), about a living house feeding on human flesh, and *Grouillements* (*The Swarming*, 1986), about humans living symbiotically with worms.

Pierre **Pelot**, with *Aux Chiens Écrasés* (*The Run-Over Dogs*, 1987).

André Ruellan writing as "Kurt **Steiner**," with *Grand Guignol 36-88* (1988).

Christian **Vilà**, writing alone with *Clip de Sang* (*Bloody Video Clip*, 1985), about a devil-worshipping rock star, and *L'Océan Cannibale* (*The Cannibal Ocean*, 1987), about an underwater monster; and writing with Jean-Pierre **Hubert** as "Jean Viluber," with *Coupes Sombres* (*Dark Cuts*, 1987) and *Greffes Profondes* (*Deep Grafts*, 1990).

Daniel **Walther**, with *La Marée Purulente* (*The Foul Tide*, 1986), about an evil spirit using leprosy to attack the world.

Jean-Pierre **Andrevon**, with *Cauchemars de Sang* (*Bloody Nightmares*, 1986), the tale of a bloody revenge.

Claude **Ecken**, with *La Peste Verte* (*The Green Plague*, 1987), about a mad doctor spreading contagious diseases.

Emmanuel **Jouanne** and Jacques **Barbéri**, with *Rêve de Chair* (*Dream of Flesh*, 1988).

Bruno **Lecigne**, with the *Immolations* series (1987-88), written with Sylviane **Corgiat** and Thierry **Bataille**.

The writing team of Alain Bernier and Roger Maridat, who began their career under the pseudonym of "Éric **Verteuil**" in 1974 in the classic *Angoisse* imprint of Fleuve Noir, returned to *Gore* with *Horreur à Maldoror* (*Horror in Maldoror*, 1987), about a madwoman who created a living horror museum. They went on to publish over half a dozen novels, including *Monstres sur Commande* (*Monsters to Order*, 1988), *Les Horreurs de Sophie* (*The Horrors of Sophie*, 1989), and *Le Tour du Monde en Quatre-Ving Cadavres* (*Around the World with Eighty Corpses*, 1990).

New *Gore* writers included:

Gilles **Bergal**, with *Cauchemar à Staten Island* (*Nightmares in Staten Island*, 1987), about sewer monsters, and *Camping Sauvage* (*Savage Camping*, 1989).

Yves **Ramonet**, who used the pseudonym "Axelman," with *La Massacreuse* (*The Massacrer*, 1988), *Aux Morsures Millénaires* (*At the Millennial Bites*, 1989), and *Dunes Sanglantes* (*Bloody Dunes*, 1990).

Magazine editor Norbert Moutier, signing "Norbert **Mount**," with *Neige d'Enfer* (*Hellish Snow*, 1988) and *L'Équarisseur de Soho* (*The Soho Equerry*, 1990).

Fétidus, with *La Mort Putride* (*Putrescent Death*, 1989).

François **Sarkel**, with *La Chair sous les Ongles* (*The Flesh Under the Nails*, 1990).

Mort **Humann**, a pseudonym of André Jammet, with *Fantôme de Feu* (*Ghost of Fire*, 1989) and *Horrific Party* (1990).

Boris and François **Darnaudet** with *Collioures Trap* (written in collaboration with C. Rabier, 1989) and *Andernos Trap* (1990).

Gilles **Santini**, who penned *Morte Chair* (*Dead Flesh*, 1989), *Éventrations* (*Disembowelings*, 1990), and others.

Following *Gore*, in 1992, Fleuve Noir published the short-lived John Sinclair series, a series of horror-themed thrillers credited to "Jason **Dark**."

In 1993, the short-lived *Angoisses* imprint published nine novels, by Jean-Pierre Andrevon, Kââ (Pascal Marignac), Jean Mazarin, François Sarkel, and Jean Rollin, as well as:

Incarnations (1994) by Yves Ramonet, again writing as "Axelman," about a multiple-personality-disorder patient who managed to incarnate her personalities.

Magna Mater (1993) by Laurent Fétis, about a young girl from Brazil who used her evil powers to destroy the Earth.

In 1994, Rollin launched the *Frayeurs* imprint, subtitled a "blood-red series for your white nights," in the wake of *Angoisses*. For *Frayeurs,* Rollin himself contributed his pulp-like series, *Les Deux Orphelines Vampires* (*The Two Orphan Vampire Girls*), which started with the eponymous novel in *Angoisses* in 1993 and continued in *Frayeurs* with *Anissa* (1994); *Les Voyageuses* (*The Travellers*, 1995); *Les Pillardes* (*The Female Looters*, 1995), and *Les Incendiaires* (*The Female Arsonists*, 1995).

Anne **Duguël**, otherwise a prolific children's books writer under the pseudonym of "Gudule" (see below), penned *Asylum* (1994), a novel about a child gifted with psychic powers who avenged his parents' murder; *Gargouille* (*Gargoyle*, 1995), about a Catholic girls' school; *Lavinia* (1995), a mixture of political fiction and horror; and *La Baby-Sitter* (1995). Duguël continued her production at *Présence du Fantastique* with *Le Chien qui Rit* (*The Dog That Laughs*, 1995) and *La Petite Fille aux Araignées* (*The Little Girl with Spiders*, 1995).

Kââ (Pascal Marignac) wrote *Criant de Vérité* (*Screaming with Truth*, 1995), about a sect of mad sculptors who use human limbs for their works.

Renowned science fiction writer Serge **Lehman** (see Chapter IX) contributed *Le Haut-Lieu* (*The High Place*, 1995), by about a cursed apartment—a concept not dissimilar to that of Kurt Steiner's *Le Seuil du Vide* published in the classic *Angoisse* imprint.

Frayeurs also introduced a number of new writers, such as:

Alain **Venisse**, with *Le Clown de Minuit* (*The Midnight Clown*, 1994), about a murderous phantom that appeared in the guise of a clown; *Symphonie pour l'Enfer* (*Symphony for Hell*, 1994), a Lovecraftian homage; and *Dans les Pro-*

fondeurs du Miroir (*In the Depths of the Mirror*, 1994), a novel about an evil doppleganger.

Lori **Anh**, with *Dégénérescence* (1994), about a girl pursued by a mutant that is half-plant, half-human.

Félix **Brenner**, with *L'Araignée de Yoshiwara* (*Yoshiwara's Spider*, 1994), a vampiric tale recast as a Japanese legend.

Anissa **Berkani-Rohmer**, with *Catacombes* (*Catacombs*, 1995), about a monster prowling the Paris catacombs.

Pascal **Françaix**, with *Le Cercueil de Chair* (*The Coffin of Flesh*, 1995) and *Kamarde* (1995), an interesting supernatural variation on the Frankenstein theme.

Bernard **Florentz**, with *La Femme Morte* (*The Dead Woman*, 1994), a doomed love story, and *La Correction* (1994), a *Tales from the Crypt*-like tale of revenge.

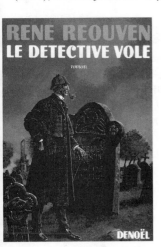

At Denoël, on a different note, the Sherlock Holmes pastiches of René **Réouven** proved equally successful. Réouven became the French equivalent of Philip Jose Farmer, bringing together popular fiction characters from sources as diverse as Doyle, Poe, Dumas, Verne as well as real-life characters such as Vidocq, Poe, etc. The novels included *Élémentaire, mon cher Holmes* (*Elementary, My Dear Holmes*, 1982), *Le Bestiaire de Sherlock Holmes* (*Sherlock Holmes' Bestiary*, 1987), *Le Détective Volé* (*The Stolen Detective*, 1988), in which Holmes investigated Poe's Purloined Letter case and met Vidocq; *Les Passe-Temps de Sherlock Holmes* (*Sherlock Holmes' Passtimes*, 1989), *Histoires Secrètes de Sherlock Holmes* (*Secret Histories of Sherlock Holmes*, 1993) and *Voyage au Centre du Mystère* (*Journey to the Center of Mystery*, 1995), which made use of Jules Verne's classic tale.

Another author of Holmesian pastiches was Belgian writer Yves **Varende**, the author of *Sherlock Holmes Revient* (*Sherlock Holmes Returns*, 1996), *Le Requin de la Tamise* (*The Shark of the Thames*, 1996), and *Le Tueur dans le Fog* (*The Killer in the Fog*, 1997).

François **Rivière**, a renowned essayist and writer of graphic novels, also paid homage to the classics in novels such as *Le Manuscrit d'Orvileda* (*The Orvileda Manuscript*,

1980), *Profanations* (1982), *Tabou* (*Taboo*, 1985), *Julius Exhumé* (*Julius Exhumed*, 1990) and *Kafka* (1992), which incorporated a variety of influences, ranging from Agatha Christie to H. P. Lovecraft, German cinema to Hollywood. *Profanations*, for example, featured Lovecraft himself in a novel-within-a-novel tale of the desecration of a sacred Indian site.

More notable recent genre works included the following:

In 1979, Jean-Pierre **Andrevon** published *Les Revenants de l'Ombre* (*The Shadow Ghosts*), a novel in which Nazis fought zombies; Andrevon then revised the novel in 1989 for publisher NéO, and again in 1997 for *Présence du Fantastique*.

In 1983, Pierre **Pelot** wrote *La Nuit sur Terre* (*Night on Earth*) for Denoël, a superb novel of suspense and terror in which a young woman was lured to a deserted mountain house by a religious sect. It was reprinted by Presses-Pocket in 1997.

Michel **Pagel**'s *Sylvana* (1989), published by Fleuve Noir's *Anticipation*, was an excellent novel about vampires; Pagel's latest novel, *Nuées Ardentes* (*Fiery Clouds*, 1997), was another major work of the *fantastique*.

With *Yoro Si* (1991), renowned science fiction author Jean-Marc **Ligny** wrote the beautiful story of a young European musician confronted with African magic in the state of Burkina Faso ("yoro si" means "nowhere" in the local language). In *La Mort Peut Danser* (*Death Can Dance*, 1994), Ligny mixed modern rock 'n' roll with Celtic fantasy, in what is now considered a cult book. Both novels were published by Denoël's *Présence du Fantastique*.

In 1993, Alain **Dorémieux** wrote a hauntingly beautiful ghost novel, *Black Velvet*, also published by Denoël.

Brigitte **Aubert** staked out the niche claimed in the United States by Thomas Harris (*The Silence of the Lambs*) with a series of harrowing thrillers featuring mysterious serial killers, such as *Les Quatre Fils du Dr. March* (*The Four Sons of Dr. March*, 1992), in which the killer was one of four brothers; *La Mort des Bois* (*Death in the Woods*, 1996), in

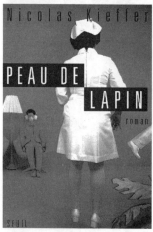

which the protagonist was a blind, speechless quadraplegic; and the colorful *Requiem Caraïbe* (1997). Her *Ténèbres sur Jacksonville* (*Darkness Over Jacksonville*, 1994) was an *Evil Dead*-like story about evil zombies terrorizing a New Mexico town.

The theme of the elusive serial killer was also featured in *Monsieur Malaussène*, a 1995 novel by mainstream thriller writer Daniel **Pennac**. Pennac's latest novel, *Messieurs les Enfants* (*Mister Children*, 1997), was about children and adults trading places, and featured a very modern ghost.

Nicolas **Kieffer**, in *Peau de Lapin* (*Rabbit Skin*, 1994), wrote a thriller with fantasy elements taking place in a mysterious Colorado lunatic asylum, where the patients may not be insane but simply in contact with other realities.

Yvon **Hecht**, in *Helena Von Nachtheim* (1996), penned a gothic vampire story not unlike Chelsea Quinn Yarbro's *Saint-Germain* saga. (Another notable gothic vampire series was Jeanne **Faivre d'Arcier**'s *Rouge Flamenco*; see above).

Jean-Jacques **Nguyen** was one of the rising stars of French fandom and the author of numerous genre short-stories collected in *Rêves d'Arkham* (*Arkham Dreams*, 1996; for the Lovecraft-inspired) and *Rêves d'Ailleurs* (*Elsewhere Dreams*, 1997; for the rest).

Philippe **Ward**'s *Artahe* (1997), released by new publisher CyLibris, was a novel about the modern worshippers of an ancient bear-god spirit and took place in the author's native Pyrennées.

In 1997, Francis **Valéry**, also a renowned critic, journalist, editorialist, and science fiction scholar, created the shared-world series of the *Agence Arkham*, a group of investigators of the supernatural. The series was short-lived but included Valéry's *Les Messagers de Saumwatu* (*The*

Messengers of Saumwatu, 1997), Roland C. **Wagner**'s *Le Nombril du Monde* (*The Navel of the World*, 1997), and Boris and François Darnaudet's *Daguerra* (1997).

In the same vein, publisher Khom-Heidon released a number of shared-world horror series such as the three-volume *Scales* (1996-97) by G. Elton **Ranne** (a writing team comprised of Gérard & Anne Guéro); and the three-volume *Nightprowler* (1996-97) by Christian **Jacq.**

HEROIC FANTASY

Heroic fantasy thrived in the 1980s and 1990s as never before, with most examples following the well-established templates of Tolkien, Robert E. Howard's *Conan*, Michael Moorcock's *Elric,* and the TSR role-playing game-derived series of *Dragonlance* and *Dungeons & Dragons*.

Also, in 1995, both David Eddings and Robert Jordan were translated in dedicated fantasy imprints like *Fantasy* and *Dark Fantasy* at Presses-Pocket, edited by Jacques Goimard, and *Fantasy* at J'ai Lu, edited by Jacques **Sadoul**.

One of the first dedicated heroic fantasy imprints of the 1980s was the short-lived *Plasma*, edited by Bruno **Lecigne**, which published a series of novels taking place in the shared world of the *Cycle des Chimères* (*The Saga of the Chimeras*). Among these were:

Le Titan de Galova (*The Titan of Galova*, 1983) and *Océane* (1983), by Lecigne and Sylviane **Corgiat**.

Jean-Marc **Ligny**'s *Succubes* (*Succubi*, 1983), which was revised in 1990 for a Fleuve Noir *Anticipation* reprint, along with its sequel, *Sorciers* (*Wizards*).

Jean-Pierre **Hubert**'s *Séméla* (1983).

Alain **Paris**' *Chasseur d'Ombres* (*Shadows Hunter*, 1983).

And Jean-Pierre **Vernay**'s *Le Sang des Mondes* (*The Blood of the Worlds*, 1983).

Another short-lived heroic fantasy imprint was *Temps Futurs* (*Future Times*), which published translations of Michael Moorcock's *Eternal Champion* stories and Stephen R. Donaldson's *Thomas Covenant* saga. The French "star" of *Temps Futurs* was Francis **Berthelot**, with the novel *Khanaor* (1983), comprised of two separate books, *Solstice de Fer* (*Iron Solstice*) and *Équinoxe de Cendre* (*Ash Equinox*), which were revised for a 1986 Fleuve Noir *Anticipation* reprint.

In the mainstream, renowned writer René **Barjavel** penned a brilliant retelling of the saga of Merlin with *L'Enchanteur* (*The Enchanter*, 1984), which became a best-seller. This trend also included Florence **Trystram**'s *Lancelot* (1987) and Isabelle **Hausser**'s *Célubée* (1986).

Another mainstream success was Bernard **Simonay**, published by the Éditions du Rocher. His novels *Phénix* (1986), and its sequel *Graal* (1988), were science fantasies not unlike Fred Saberhagen's *Swords* or Michael Moorcock's *Runestaff* series, taking place in a pseudo-medieval future Europe where post-nuclear technology has become like magic. In *Phénix*, the brother and sister team of Dorian and Solyane must find the secret of their origins as well as save their peaceful kingdom of Syrdahar. *Graal* took place twenty years later, when Solyane must defeat an evil Prophet. **Simonay** continued his prolific production with *La Malédiction de la Licorne* (*The Curse of the Unicorn*, 1990), *La Porte de Bronze* (*The Gate of Brass*, 1994), and the thee-volume series *Les Enfants de l'Atlantide* (*The Children of Atlantis*, 1994-96).

In the mid-1980s, the *Anticipation* imprint of Fleuve Noir began to regularly publish works of heroic fantasy, and in 1992, eventually created its own dedicated sub-imprint, *Legend*. Hugues **Douriaux** quickly became one of *Legend*'s most prolific and popular writers. He was the author of numerous sprawling, multi-volume sagas, as well as many stand-alone novels. Douriaux began his career with a huge post-nuclear science fantasy saga entitled *Un Homme Est Venu...* (*A Man Came...*), originally published in the *Grands Romans* (*Great Novels*) imprint

of Fleuve Noir in 1981, and reprinted in *Anticipation* as six volumes in 1987 and 1988. It was followed by *Le Chemin des Mondes* (*The Path of Worlds*, 1982). Douriaux's major heroic-fantasy series included: *La Biche de la Forêt d'Arcande* (*The Doe from the Forest of Arcande*; Nos. 1642, 1646, 1653, 1988); *Les Chroniques de Vonia* (*The Chronicles of Vonia*; Nos. 1718, 1730, 1742, 1753, 1766, 1777, 1790, 1989-90); *Les Fleurs et le Vent* (*The Flowers and the Wind*; Nos. 1807, 1808, 1809, 1991); *L'Anneau-Feu de Gundhera* (*The Fire-Ring of Gundhera*; Nos. 1866, 1870, 1874, 1878, 1907, 1992-93); and *La Porte de Flamme* (*The Gate of Fire*; Nos. 1945, 1957, 1967, 1994-95). His last novel for the *Legend* imprint, *Les Pierres de Lumière* (*The Stones of Light*, 1996), was also a fantasy.

Under the pseudonym of "Gilles **Thomas**," and until her death in 1985, Julia Verlanger continued to produce heroic fantasy works such as *La Croix des Décastés* (*The Cross of the Outcasts*, 1977), *D'un Lieu Lointain Nommé Soltrois* (*From a Far Place Called Solthree*, 1979), *La Porte des Serpents* (*The Gate of the Serpents*, 1980), and *Les Cages de Beltem* (*The Cages of Beltem*), a novel

first published in condensed form in 1982, and reissued as two volumes, *Acherra* and *Offren*, in 1995.

Daniel **Walther** contributed the science fantasy trilogy of *Swa*, comprised of *Le Livre de Swa* (1982), *Le Destin de Swa* (1982) and *La Légende de Swa* (*Shai's Legend*, 1983), to *Anticipation*, as well as *Nocturne sur Fond d'Epées* (*Nocturne on a Field of Swords*, 1984) to publisher NéO.

André **Caroff** penned the heroic fantasy saga of the *Reds* (Nos. 1117, 1147, 1175, 1203, 1983), in which Hem-The-Red freed an occupied Europe from the tyrannic Masters.

Gabriel **Jan** wrote a heroic-fantasy series taking place in the post-cataclysmic world of the *Blue Deluge* (Nos. 1334, 1350, 1984).

Alain **Paris** and Jean-Pierre **Fontana** created the *Chroniques de la Lune Rouge* (*Chronicles of the Red Moon*; Nos 1341, 1398, 1419, 1515, 1984-87), detailing the adventures of the warrior Zarko in a post-cataclysmic Central/South America that had reverted to savagery.

Paris alone wrote the *Chroniques d'Antarcie* (*Chronicles of Antarcia*; Nos. 1408, 1502, 1549, 1985-87), the story of the ancient civilization that thrived in Antarctica ten thousand years ago; followed by the *Pangea* trilogy (Nos. 1705, 1711, 1717, 1989); and finally by his masterpiece, *Le Monde de la Terre Creuse* (*The World of the Hollow Earth*; Nos 1629, 1635, 1640, 1645, 1749, 1754, 1760, 1824, 1830, 1834, 1988-91), a prodigious ten-volume saga taking place in an alternate reality where the Nazis have won World War II,

and where the world may really be hollow. The series also became a popular role-playing game. Single heroic fantasy novels included *Ashermayam* (1986), in which a warrior-wizard fought a female demon; and *Le Dieu de la Guerre* (*The God of War*, 1989).

After writing esoteric pseudo-documentary books such as *Quand l'Atlantide resurgira* (*When Atlantis Will Rise Again*, 1979), *Châteaux Forts Magiques de France* (*Magi-*

cal Castles of France, 1982) and *Vercingétorix et les Mystères Gaulois* (*Vercingetorix and the Gallic Mysteries*, 1983), Roger **Facon** wrote a number of heroic fantasy novels for *Anticipation*, such as *Par Le Sabre des Zinjas* (*By the Sword of the Zinjas*, 1986) and *Les Compagnons de la Lune Blême* (*The Fellowship of the Pale Moon*, 1992).

Bruno Lecigne and Sylviane Corgiat penned *Le Jeu de la Trame* (*The Game of the Weave*; Nos 1486, 1527, 1555, 1610, 1986-88), the tale of the quest of the warrior Keido for the thirty-nine major arcana of the magic Game of the Weave, which he needed in order to return his dead sister to life.

Pierre **Bameul**, who had written *Par Le Royaume d'Osiris* (*By the Kingdom of Osiris*, 1981) for OPTA, wrote a saga entitled *Pour Nourrir le Soleil* (*To Feed the Sun*; Nos. 1458, 1489, 1986) for *Anticipation*. It told the story of a parallel universe in which the Viking warrior Arne Marsson became Quetzalcoatl, and conquered the Aztec Empire.

Popular horror writer Serge **Brussolo** contributed two heroic fantasy novels with strong horror elements: *Le Tombeau du Roi Squelette* (*The Tomb of the Skeleton King*, 1988) and *Le Dragon du Roi Squelette* (*The Dragon of the Skeleton King*, 1989), in which legless Shagan, Junia the giantess, who carried him on her back, and their master, the mastersmith-sorcerer Massalian, teamed up to face the demonic hordes of the Skeleton King. Since then, Brussolo also wrote the more literary medieval saga of *Hurlemort— Le Dernier Royaume* (*DeathScream—the Last Kingdom*, 1993). Finally, Brussolo, using the pseudonym of "Kitty Doom," was also the author of two dark fantasies, *L'Empire des Abîmes* (*The Empire of the Abyss*, 1997) and *Les Invisibles* (*The Invisible Ones*, 1997), published by *Présence du Futur*.

Michel **Pagel** wrote *L'Ange du Désert* (*The Desert Angel*; Nos. 1403, 1457, 1985-86), which took place in a barbaric world where a biker nicknamed "Angel" searched for the mythical city of Lankor; and *Les Flammes de la Nuit* (*The Flames of Night*; Nos. 1433, 1493, 1513, 1563, 1986-87), where the Sorceress Rowena, who was once banished from the Kingdom of Fuinor, a hollow-Earth-type world, eventually returned to conquer it. *L'Antre du Serpent* (*The Lair*

of the Serpent; No. 1794, 1990) and *Le Refuge de l'Agneau* (*The Refuge of the Lamb*; No. 1801, 1991) formed a novel entitled *Les Antipodes* (*The Antipodean*). Writing as "Félix Chapel," Pagel also penned the series *L'Oiseau de Foudre* (*The Bird of Lightning*; Nos. 1739, 1757, 1768, 1786, 1819, 1990-91).

Jean-Claude **Dunyach** penned *Le Jeu des Sabliers* (*The Game of the Hourglasses*; Nos.1592, 1609, 1987-88), which featured four characters who were incarnations of a tarot-like set of cards searching for three hourglasses supposed to confer immortality. Dunyach also wrote *La Guerre des Cercles* (*The War of the Circles*, 1995).

Alain **le Bussy** created the adventures of *Yorg*, another barbarian in a post-cataclysmic Earth (Nos. 1956, 1958, 1960, 1979, 1981, 1982, 1995). Le Bussy has reportedly written six more volumes in this series, which to date, have not yet been published. He was also the author of *Chatinika* (1995) and *Le Dieu Avide* (*The Hungry God*, 1996), the latter the first volume of a new heroic-fantasy series.

Claude **Castan** penned the tetralogy of *Galaë* (Nos. 1978, 1983, 1984, 1987, 1996). In it, young Celian was raised by a friend of his dead mother, eventually learned that his father was the King of the Elves, and that only he could save the kingdom from a cataclysmic war.

Phil **Laramie** wrote the *Akantor* series (Nos. 1507, 1525, 1986-87).

Jean-Christophe **Chaumette** penned *Le Neuvième Cercle* (*The Ninth Circle*; Nos. 1780, 1785, 1792, 1797, 1804, 1812, 1990-91) and, more recently, *Le Niwaâd* (1997).

Manuel **Essard** wrote *La Forteresse Pourpre* (*The Purple Fortress*, 1993).

G. Elton **Ranne** wrote *La Mâchoire du Dragon* (*The Jaws of the Dragon*, 1996).

Christophe **Loubet** wrote *La Saga des Bannis* (*The Saga of the Banished*; Nos 17, 18, 1997).

Finally, Valérie **Simon** penned *Arkem, La Pierre des Ténèbres* (*Arkem, the Stone of Darkness*; Nos. 22, 23, 1997).

The same publishing group which backed Fleuve Noir also financed Éditions Vaugirard, which published translations of the *Blade* series, E.C. Tubb's *Dumarest,* and the multi-author *Destroyer* novels. Vaugirard dedicated an entire paperback imprint to the adventures of *Rohel Le Conquérant* (*Rohel the Conqueror*), a sprawling science-fantasy saga created by science fiction writer Pierre **Bordage** (see Chapter IX). In this series, the hero, Rohel the Vioter, was forced to travel from world to world, seeking the sword Lucifal to avenge his people, the Genesians of Antiter, who were murdered by the evil Garloups (*Werwolves*). The Garloups originally came from within a black hole, and took Rohel's true love, the beautiful Saphyr, prisoner. Rohel stole the ultimate equation, the Mentral, which controlled the passage between the worlds, from the Jahad, the fanatical worshippers of the One True Oak. The *Rohel* saga was comprised of three "Cycles" of five volumes each: *Dame Asmine of Alba* (1992-94), *Lucifal* (1995-96), and *Saphyr of Antiter* (1996-97).

New publisher L'Atalante, which released Bordage's notable space opera trilogy, *Les Guerriers du Silence* (*The Warriors of Silence*, 1993-95), also published Gilles **Servat**'s heroic fantasy trilogy, *Les Chroniques d'Arcturus* (*The Chronicles of Arcturus*, 1996-97). Mostly known as a singer and lyricist of classic Breton themes, Servat came to write novels in order to tell the longer stories that he could not tell in songs. His *Arcturus* novels, based on the ancient legends of Britanny, were filled with epic and sensual scenes, larger-than-life characters. The first novel told of how Skinn Mac Dana came to the world of Bré, and of his fight for survival.

Other L'Atalante heroic fantasy works included Jean-Pierre **Fontana**'s revised *Halaguen* saga (1997; see above).

Other recent notable genre works include:

Two heroic fantasy novels written in Occitan by Joan-Frédéric **Brun**, *Lo Retrach dau Dieu Negre* (1987) and *Septembralas* (1994).

Michel **Novy**'s *Le Châtiment des Rois Frères* (*The Punishment of the Brother Kings*, 1994), the beautiful, poetic tale of two brothers, one good and one evil, who fought for a kingdom. The story was epic and reminiscent of the classic fairy tales.

Hervé **Carn**'s *Issek* (1997).

Harry **Morgan**'s baroque *La Reine du Ciel* (*The Queen of the Sky*, 1997), published by Rivages in their new *Fantasy* imprint. "Harry **Morgan**" is the nom-de-plume of a French writer living in Alsace.

Also in 1997, renowned science fiction writer **Ayerdhal** (see Chapter IX) published *Parleur, ou La Chronique d'un Rêve Enclavé* (*Speaker, or the Chronicle of an Embedded Dream*) at J'ai Lu. It was a unique political fantasy, with no supernatural or magical elements, in which a group of revolutionaries attempted to resist the encroachments of the medieval authorities.

Finally, another very recent development was the creation by yet another new publisher, Mnemos, established in 1995, of an entire line of heroic fantasy novels written by young French authors. Among these were:

Mathieu **Gaborit**, with *Les Chroniques du Crépusculaire* (*Chronicles of Twilight*; Nos. 1, 3, 6, 1995-96), which starred a young female magician called Agone; and the saga of the city of *Abyme* (*Abyss*), a mix of fantasy and *film noir* (Nos. 12, 15, 1996).

David & Isabelle **Collet**, with the *Nephilim* series (Nos. 9, 13, 19, 1995-96), which was based on a French role-playing game. The Nephilim were body-snatching entities which have plagued Mankind since the dawn of time. They were

fought by an occult alliance of Templar Knights, alchemists, etc. Sébastien **Pennes**'s trilogy *Le Cycle des Phénix* (*The Cycle of the Phenix*; Nos. 2, 4, 7, 1995-96) also took place in the *Nephilim* universe.

Pierre **Grimbert**, with the award-winning *Le Secret de Ji* (*The Secret of Ji*; Nos. 11, 14, 20, 22, 1996-97), a series of novels in which the heroes were heirs to a mysterious magical secret.

Editor Stéphane **Marsan**'s *Les Carnets de la Constellation* (*The Notebooks of the Constellation*; Nos. 5, 8, 10, 1996) took place in the universe of the Guild, a series of island kingdoms located on a vast ocean; the novels dealt with the changes created by the emergence of a new continent.

Other Mnemos heroic fantasy authors included Laurent **Kloetzer** and Erik **Wietzel**.

In 1997, Mnemos created a new imprint, *Daemonicon*, featuring three more heroic fantasy sagas, *L'Éclipse des Dragons* (*The Eclipse of Dragons*) by "Duncan Eriksson," *L'Âme des Rois Nains* (*The Soul of the Dwarf Kings*) by "William Hawk," and *Le Sanctuaire des Elfes* (*The Sanctuary of the Elves*) by "Edwyn Kestrel," in reality three French writers using English-sounding pseudonyms.

The same editorial policy was followed by publisher Khom-Heidon for a series by Christian **Jacq** entitled *Chroniques des Sept Cités* (*Chronicles of the Seven Cities*, 1997); and another by Bernard **Rastouin** entitled *Shaan—Le Cercle des Réalités* (*The Circle of Realities*, 1996-97).

JUVENILES

The field of children's books and young-adult literature virtually exploded in the 1980s and 1990s, and genre works became superabundant, especially after the successful translations of American series like R. L. Stine's *Goosebumps*.

We are providing here a selection of the major writers with selected works, starting with previously mentioned authors:

The writing team signing "Michel **Grimaud**" created children's books such as *Les Contes de la Ficelle* (*Tales from the String*, 1982), juvenile fantasies such as *L'Enfant de la Mer* (*The Child from the Sea*, 1986) and *Le Coffre Magique* (*The Magical Chest*, 1990), as well as more modern horror-slanted thrillers such as *L'Assassin crève l'Écran* (*The Murderer Steps Through the Screen*, 1991), and *L'Inconnu dans le Frigo* (*The Stranger Inside the Refrigerator*, 1997).

The distinguished Michel **Tournier** penned *La Fugue du Petit Poucet* (*Tom Thumb's Escape*, 1988), as well as the delightful *Les Contes du Medianoche* (*Tales from the Me-*

dianoche, 1989) and *Le Medianoche Amoureux* (*The Medianoche in Love*, 1989).

Another mainstream writer, Robert **Escarpit**, the author of the classic *Contes de la Saint Glinglin* (*Tales of Any Saint*, 1973), returned to the field with a vengeance with *L'Enfant qui Venait de l'Espace* (*The Child Who Came from Outer Space*, 1984), *Tom, Quentin et le Géant Bila* (*Tom, Quentin and Bila the Giant*, 1994), *Hugo, Charlie et la Reine Isis* (*Hugo, Charlie and Queen Isis*, 1995), and *La Poudre du Père Limpinpin* (*The Powder of Father Limpinpin*, 1996).

Science fiction writer Jean-Pierre **Andrevon** authored *Le Jour du Grand Saut* (*The Day of the Great Jump*, 1997) and *La Bête sur le Parking* (*The Beast on the Parking Lot*, 1997), as well as *Gandahar et l'Oiseau-Monde* (*Gandahar and the World-Bird*, 1997; see above).

Jean-Marc **Ligny** published *Les Ailes Noires de la Nuit* (*The Black Wings of Death*, 1995).

Michel **Cosem** wrote *Le Chapeau Enchanté* (*The Enchanted Hat*, 1984) and *Le Chemin du Bout du Monde* (*The Path at the End of the World*, 1993).

Xavier **Armange** contributed *Dragon d'Ordinaire* (*Dragon of the Ordinary*, 1985) and a series of novel entitled *Cache-Cache* (*Hide-&-Seek*, 1986).

To follow on the footsteps of Georges **Chaulet**, particularly in the wake of the American *Goosebumps* series, proved a winning strategy more than ever. Some of the most recent successful juvenile series include:

Basile (1995-96) by Véronique **Le Normand**.

Lapoigne (1995-97), a juvenile fantasy/thriller saga by Thierry **Jonquet**.

Abdallah (1995-97) by Paul **Thiès**.

A special mention goes to the wonderful *Jonathan Cap* series (1986-90) by François **Rivière**, which wonderfully blended young adult adventure and old-fashioned pulp traditions: *Le Labyrinthe du Jaguar* (*The Jaguar's Labyrinth*, 1986), *La Samba du Fantôme* (*The Ghost's Samba*, 1986), *La Clinique du Docteur K.* (*Dr.K's Clinic*, 1986), *Jonathan Cap contre les Chevaliers de Satan* (*Jonathan Cap vs. Satan's Knights*, 1986), *Les Formules de Zoltan* (*Zoltan's Formulas*, 1986), and *Le Spectre du Mandarin* (*The Mandarin's Ghost*, 1988) were among the best volumes in the series.

Among the newest writers, François **Sautereau** easily jumped from science fiction, as in *La Cinquième Dimension* (*The Fifth Dimension*, 1979), to modern magical realism, as in *Léonie et la Pierre de Lumière* (*Leonie and the Stone of Light*, 1980) and *Nicolas et la Montre Magique* (*Nicolas and the Magic Watch*, 1981). Sautereau's young-adult novels were elaborate fantasies, remarkable for their sense of detail and exotism. Notable titles included *L'Héritier de la Nuit* (*The Night Heir*, 1985), *La Cité des Brumes* (*The City of Mists*, 1986), and *La Forteresse de la Nuit* (*The Fortress of Night*, 1989).

Evelyne **Brisou-Pellen** wrote juvenile fantasies in a style not unlike that of Ursula K. Le Guin's *Earthsea* novels. Notable titles included *La Porte de Nulle Part* (*The Gate*

of Nowhere, 1980), *La Cour aux Étoiles* (*Courtyard of the Stars*, 1982), *La Grotte des Korrigans* (*The Korrigans' Cave*, 1985), *Le Maître de la Septième Porte* (*The Master of the Seventh Gate*, 1986), and *Le Défi des Druides* (*The Challenge of the Druids*, 1988).

Odile **Weulersse** penned action-oriented, young-adult adventures with solid plots and exotic locales. Notable titles included *Le Messager d'Athènes* (*The Messenger from Athens*, 1985), *Le Secret des Catacombes* (*The Secret of the Catacombs*, 1986), *Le Cavalier de Bagdad* (*The Rider of Baghdad*, 1988), and *L'Aigle de Mexico* (*The Eagle from Mexico*, 1992).

Béatrice **Tanaka** used classic fairy tales to create new, colorful tales, aimed at younger audiences. Notable titles included *Ytch et les Choumoudoux* (*Ytch and the Choomoodoos*, 1982), *La Princesse aux Deux Visages* (*The Princess with Two Faces*, 1987), *Trois Sorcières* (*Three Witches*, 1988), and *La Quête du Prince de Koripan* (*The Quest of the Prince of Koripan*, 1992).

Évelyne **Reberg** similarly relied on classic fairy tales and folk legends for her inspiration. Notable titles included *Le Dragon Chanteur* (*The Singing Dragon*, 1980), *La Princesse Muette* (*The Silent Princess*, 1980), and *La Machine à Contes* (*The Storytelling Machine*, 1981).

Michèle **Kahn**'s modern fairy tales were more somber and reflective, yet shone with a special poetic light. Notable titles included *De l'Autre Côté du Brouillard* (*On the Other Side of the Fog*, 1980), *Contes du Jardin d'Eden* (*Tales of the Garden of Eden*, 1982), and *De I'Autre Côté du Miroir* (*On the Other Side of the Mirror*, 1985).

Christian **Poslaniec**'s books were filled with a strange sense of humor and a weird notion of reality. Notable titles included *Histoires Horribles et Pas si Méchantes* (*Awful and Not So Nasty Tales*, 1986), *L'Escargot de Cristal* (*The Crystal Snail*, 1986), *Le Marchand de Mémoire* (*The Memory Merchant*, 1988), *Le Treizième Chat Noir* (*The Thirteenth Black Cat*, 1992), and *Le Jour des Monstres* (*The Day of the Monsters*, 1994).

Jean **Alessandrini**'s brand of juvenile *fantastique* relied on a slightly surrealist conception of the adventure novel. Notable titles included *Le Prince d'Aéropolis* (*The Prince of Aeropolis*, 1986), *Le Détective de Minuit* (*The Midnight Detective*, 1987), and *La Malédiction de Chéops* (*The Curse of Cheops*, 1989).

The prolific Anne Dugüel, signing "**Gudule**," also knew how to take classic concepts such as monsters, witches, and devils, and give them a weird, modern twist. Notable titles included *Prince Charmant Poil aux Dents* (*Prince Charming My Foot*, 1987), *Agence Torgnole, Frappez Fort!* (*Slap Agency, Hit Harder!*, 1990), *L'École qui n'existait pas* (*The School That Did Not Exist*, 1994), *Le Dentiste est un Vampire* (*The Dentist Is a Vampire*, 1996), *La Sorcière est dans l'École* (*The Witch Is in the School*, 1996), *Le Manège de l'Oubli* (*The Merry-Go-Round of Oblivion*, 1997), *Bonjour, Monsieur Frankenstein* (*Hello, Mr. Franken-*

stein, 1997), to name but a few books among Dugüel's generally outstanding production.

Jean-Louis **Craipeau** followed in the same vein with *L'Oeil de Belzébuth* (*Beelzebub's Eye*, 1986), *L'Ogre-Doux* (*The Sweet Ogre*, 1989), *Le Dragon Déglingué* (*The Broken Dragon*, 1989), *La Sorcière des Cantines* (*The Witch of the Cantina*, 1997), and *Dracula fait son Cinéma* (*Dracula Makes a Movie*, 1997).

So did Alain **Surget** with *Gare à la Bête!* (*Beware the Beast!*, 1989), *Le Fils des Loups* (*The Son of the Wolves*, 1989), *L'Abominable Gosse des Neiges* (*The Abominable Snow Kid*, 1990), *Le Bal des Sorcières* (*Witches' Ball*, 1994), and *Le Gouffre aux Fantômes* (*The Ghost Pit*, 1994).

Marie **Farré** was another proponent of the updating of classic monsters, with *Papa est un Ogre* (*Dad Is an Ogre*, 1983), *Mon Maître d'École Est le Yéti* (*My Principal Is the Yeti*, 1984), and *Mon Oncle est un Loup-Garou* (*My Uncle Is a Werewolf*, 1985).

Others in this genre included:

Olivier **Cohen**, with *Je m'appelle Dracula* (*My Name Is Dracula*, 1987) and *La Fiancée de Dracula* (*The Bride of Dracula*, 1988).

Martine **Bourre**, with *Ne Dérangez pas les Dragons!* (*Don't Disturb the Dragons!*, 1988).

Philippe **Barbeau**, with *L'Ami de l'Ogre* (*The Ogre's Friend*, 1990).

Stories leaning more toward horror and the more traditional types of *fantastique* included:

Yak **Rivais**'s *Les Sorcières sont N.R.V.* (*The Witches Are Annoyed*, 1988), *Les Contes du Miroir* (*Tales of the Mirror*, 1988), and *Contes du Cimetière après la Pluie* (*Tales from the Cemetery After the Rain*, 1997).

Hervé **Fontanières**, with *Rendez-vous en Enfer* (*Rendezvous in Hell*, 1997), which took place at a lonely lighthouse.

Éric **Sanvoisin**, with *Bizarre le Bizarre* (1996) and *Les Chasseurs d'Ombre* (*The Shadow Hunters*, 1997).

Jacques **Barnouin** delighted younger readers with the

nocturnal tales of *Le Fantôme Sparadrap et Autres Histoires Sans Sucre* (*The Band-Aid Ghost and Other Sugarless Stories*, 1984) and *Bonjour, la Nuit!* (*Hello, Night!*, 1985).

Young readers also loved Yves-Marie **Clément**'s *Le Petit Dragon Qui Toussait* (*The Little Dragon Who Coughed*, 1996).

Lorris **Murail** was a noted science fiction writer and scholar who contributed *Le Marchand de Cauchemars* (*The Nightmare Peddler*, 1990), and *La Poubelle d'Ali-Baba* (*Ali-Baba's Dustbin*, 1991); while Marie-Aude **Murail** wrote *Graine de Monstre* (*Monster Seed*, 1986), *Le Visiteur de Minuit* (*The Midnight Visitor*, 1988), and *Le Docteur Magicus* (1988).

Finally, heroic fantasy began to make an appearance among juvenile novels with Éric **Bisset**'s *Le Grimoire d'Arkandias* (*The Grimoir of Arkandias*, 1997) and numerous, young-adult genre novels written by Michel **Honaker**, including the trilogy *Le Chevalier de Terre Noire* (*The Knight of Blackland*, 1996); *Le Chant de la Reine Froide* (*The Song of the Cold Queen*, 1996), *La Cantate des Anges* (*Angels' Cantata*, 1996), *La Symphonie du Destin* (*The Symphony of Fate*, 1996), *Nocturne pour une Passion* (*Nocturne for a Passion*, 1996), *Les Héritiers du Secret* (*The Heirs of the Secret*, 1996), *La Flûte Enchantée* (*The Enchanted Flute*, 1997), and others.

Honaker also contributed some young adult horror novels, such as *Magie Noire dans le Bronx* (*Black Magic in the Bronx*, 1996), a reworking of his first *Commander* novel, *Le Démon du Bronx* (*The Demon of the Bronx*, 1988; see above), *La Créature du Néant* (*The Creature from the Void*, 1997), and *Rendez-Vous à Apocalypse* (*Rendezvous at Apocalypse*, 1997).

Modern Science Fiction
(After 1950)

Until the early 1950s, French science fiction was limping along, not having recovered from the double blows of the censorship of the late 1920s and World War II.

Renard and **Moselli** were lost to the genre. **Spitz** had not cultivated any followers. And **Barjavel** was on his way to becoming a full-fledged mainstream author.

All magazines, except for the now outmoded *Journal des Voyages* (*Journal of Voyages*) were dead, and it too stopped publication in 1949. A short-lived *Anticipations* was started in Brussels in 1945 but lasted only fifteen issues.

The situation was just as bleak with popular paperback imprints. Nathan's *Aventures & Voyages* (*Adventures & Voyages*) had been cancelled in 1948; Tallandier's *Grandes Aventures* (*Great Adventures*, 1949-53) and *Le Livre d'Aventures* (*The Book of Adventure*, 1951-54), as well as Ferenczi's *Mon Roman d'Aventures* (*My Adventure Novels*, 1942-56), limped along, but published a type of science fiction that had not basically changed since 1914, and could even be said to have regressed compared to the heights of the late 1920s. A small adult imprint, *Horizons Fantastiques* (*Fantastic Horizons*) by publisher Le Sillage released only four titles between 1949 and 1953.

All this began to change in 1951.

As in the previous chapter, we have divided the last fifty years into chronological subdivisions, but in this instance four instead of three.

The first, dubbed the "1950s and 1960s," started in 1950 and ended approximately in 1970, just after the cultural revolution of May 1968. It was the "silver age" of French science fiction. The second subdivision, dubbed the "1970s," was marked by a politicization of French science fiction as well as "new wave" stylistic experiments, the emergence of

major new authors, and a commercial boom that lasted until the middle of the next decade. The third subdivision, dubbed the "1980s," saw the end of the boom and a retrenchment of science fiction. Finally, the fourth and last subdivision, dubbed the "1990s," runs from the late-1980s to the present. It is characterized by a new, more modest upswing in authors and publishing, as well as a return to more traditional storytelling techniques.

1. The 1950s and 1960s (The Silver Age)

The 1950s and 1960s could be dubbed the "silver age" of French science fiction. It was a period of rebirth, growth, and consolidation. It was during that period that a new slate of major, modern authors began to emerge.

It was also, unfortunately, a period during which French science fiction, which had been in a literary coma since the 1920s, discovered in one massive, collective blow the best of American science fiction of the 1940s and 1950s. As a result, and for the next thirty years or so, French science fiction lived under the shadow of American science fiction, always comparing itself to it and playing catch up. More subtly, the very themes and modes of expression of the genre were now defined according to American criteria. Even at its best, French science fiction was forced to play by the literary rules established in American science fiction, and if it did not always lose in quality, it often did in originality.

a. The Publishers

The notion that an allegedly new literary genre dubbed

science fiction was about to emerge was first broached in a series of articles published in the press: in 1950, in the major daily newspaper, *Le Figaro*; in 1951, in literary magazines such as *Critique*, *Les Temps Modernes*, *Cahiers du Sud* and *Esprit*; and, finally, in 1952, as a full-page blast in the major popular daily newspaper, *France-Dimanche*. Science fiction had arrived. It was naturally linked to the great pioneers, Jules **Verne** and H.G. Wells, but in a surprising act of collective amnesia, all the prodigious works of the first half of the century, which had not been labeled science fiction since that label had not existed then, were completely forgotten and left unmentioned.

The idea of a dedicated, adult science fiction book imprint had been pitched to various publishers by notable fans such as Jacques **Bergier**, Georges Gallet, and Michel Pilotin since after the war. In January 1951, publishers Hachette and Gallimard, rather than competing, joined forces to create the first, modern French science fiction imprint, *Le Rayon Fantastique* (*The Fantastic Bookshelf*), jointly edited by Gallet and Pilotin. The *Rayon Fantastique* published both golden age American classics (selected by Gallet) and more contemporary works (selected by Pilotin), such as novels by Asimov, Clarke, Van Vogt, Sturgeon, Hamilton, Heinlein, Leiber, Williamson, and Moore. It also introduced French authors such as Francis **Carsac**, Nathalie C. **Henneberg**, Albert **Higon** aka Michel **Jeury**, Gérard **Klein**, and Philippe **Curval**. The *Rayon Fantastique* sported attractive covers by noted French artist Jean-Claude **Forest**, the creator of ***Barbarella*** (see Book 1, Chapter IV). The imprint eventually fell victim to lukewarm sales, as well as a tug of war between its two rival co-owners, and stopped publication in 1964 after having released 124 titles. (During its existence, it resurrected the Jules Verne Award.)

Eight months later, in September 1951, publisher Marc de Caro whose company, Fleuve Noir, was specializing in popular "pulp" paperback imprints such as police thrillers (*Special Police*), espionage novels (*Espionnage*), adventure stories (*L'Aventurier*) and, later, war stories (*Feu*), decided to launch a science fiction imprint called *Anticipation*. (A horror imprint entitled *Angoisse* followed in 1954; see Chapter VIII.) The new imprint was entrusted to editor François Richard—half of the writing team of **Richard-Bessière**. The particularity of *Anticipation* was that it cultivated in-house authors: Richard-Bessière, Jean-Gaston **Vandel** (another writing team better known as "Paul **Kenny**," creator of French James Bond-like hero, Coplan), Jimmy **Guieu**, Stéfan **Wul**, and B.-R. **Bruss**, to which were later added Maurice **Limat**, Max-André **Rayjean**, Kurt **Steiner**, Peter **Randa**, Gérard **Klein** (writing as "Gilles d'Argyre"), Pierre **Barbet**, and Jean-Louis & Doris **Le May**. Another particularity was that the authors' style owed relatively little, at least at first, to their American counterparts. The early volumes of the imprint followed the literary traditions established by **Rosny** and Renard. *Anticipation* also published a few selected novels by American or British authors, such as

Anderson, Asimov (the first *Lucky Star* novel), Brackett, Clarke, Fearn (writing as "Vargo Statten"), Hubbard, Leinster, Tubb (writing as "Volsted Gridban"), Van Vogt, and Wyndham, as well as translations of the successful German *Perry Rhodan* series.

In 1953, an exhibit entitled *Présence du Futur* (*Presence of the Future*) was held at the bookstore La Balance, owned by Valerie Schmidt, which had become a meeting place for well-known fans and professionals of the period: Established figures such as Bergier, Pilotin, Sternberg, and Vian met newcomers such as Curval, Carsac, Versins, Ruellan, Sadoul, and Klein. (La Balance, later renamed L'Atome, closed in 1962.)

The following year, in March 1954, publisher Denoël borrowed the name to launch its *Présence du Futur* imprint, edited by Robert Kanters. With a first slate of titles initially selected by Pilotin, *Présence du Futur* introduced Bradbury, Lovecraft, Bester, Matheson, Blish, Brown, Aldiss, Vonnegut, Simak, Ballard, Galouye, and others. To the French public. It also published early works by Gérard **Klein**. In terms of French authors, during this period, *Présence du Futur* concentrated on works by mainstream-oriented writers, such as Jérôme **Sériel**, Jacques **Sternberg**, René **Barjavel**, Marianne **Andrau**, Jean-Louis **Curtis**, Jean **Hougron**, and René Réouven aka René **Sussan**.

Meanwhile, in October 1953, publisher Maurice Renault, whose company OPTA had been putting out *Mystère-Magazine*, a French edition of *Ellery Queen's Magazine*, since 1948, decided to launch *Fiction*, a French edition of the American *Magazine of Fantasy & Science Fiction*. *Fiction* was edited initially by Renault, with the help of his partner Daniel Domange and Jacques Bergier. Then, writer Alain **Dorémieux** took over in 1957. *Fiction* published many science fiction and fantastic stories by French genre authors from the start (also see Chapter VIII). OPTA was an acronym for "Office de Publicité Technique & Artistique" (*Office of Artistic and Technical Advertising*) reflecting the fact that the company had started as an advertising agency, and remained so until Domange's death in 1971.

In 1959, under Dorémieux' direction, OPTA began publishing a series of yearly, book-length *Specials*, several of which were devoted entirely to French authors. In 1964, Renault picked up *Galaxie* (a French edition of *Galaxy*), which had previously been published from 1953 to 1959. In 1965, it launched the hardcover imprint *Club du Livre d'Anticipation* (at first co-edited with Jacques **Sadoul**) and the paperback imprint *Galaxie-Bis*. Both published mostly American classics until the 1970s.

Other short-lived imprints of the mid-1950s included:
Visions Futures (*Future Visions*, 1952-53), by publisher La Flamme d'Or, which published ten volumes including works by **Keller** & **Brainin** and Kurt Steiner writing as "Kurt Wargar."

Grands Romans-Sciences-Anticipations (*Great Novels of Science & Anticipation*, 1953-54), by publisher Le Trotteur, which published eight volumes including works by Keller & Brainin.

Série 2000 (1954-56), by publisher Métal, which published twenty-five volumes including works by Charles Henneberg, Maurice Limat, Pierre **Versins** and Paul **Béra** writing as "Yves **Dermèze**."

Cosmos (1955-57), by publisher Grand Damier, which issued twelve volumes, including works by Keller & Brainin and Maurice Limat.

In January 1958, a new magazine entitled *Satellite* was launched by Michel **Benâtre** and Hervé **Calixte** (also assisted by Jacques Bergier) to compete with *Fiction*. It lasted only forty-seven issues, until January 1963, but during that time, it published stories by Francis Carsac, Charles Henneberg, Gérard Klein, Philippe **Curval**, Michel **Demuth**, and Pierre Versins. *Satellite* also published a short-lived paperback imprint, *Les Cahiers de la Science-Fiction* (*The Science Fiction Notebooks*, 1958-60), which published ten volumes.

Versins also published the remarkable fanzine *Ailleurs* (*Elsewhere*) from 1956 to 1963. Other notable fanzines of the 1960s included Jacqueline Osterrath's *Lunatique* and Jean-Pierre **Fontana**'s *Mercury*.

Three more short-lived genre imprints made their appearance in the 1960s:

Science-S-Fiction by Ditis, which released only eight titles in 1960.

Espions de Demain (*Tomorrow's Spies*) by Arabesque, which published ten novels in 1960.

Science-Fiction Suspense (1960-61) by Daniber, which published seventeen volumes, including works by Del Rey and Wollheim.

Finally, Belgian publisher Marabout (see Chapter VIII) began issuing science fiction novels regularly as part of its fantastic imprint, starting in 1964 with an anthology by Hubert Juin, followed by novels by Anderson, **Langelaan**, Van Vogt, and others, then gave the genre its own dedicated imprint, *Science-Fiction*, under the editorship of Jean-Baptiste **Baronian** in 1969.

b. Major Authors

Gérard **Klein** was the first among a new wave of science fiction fans turned writers, inspired by American science fiction. He began to publish a series of Bradbury-influenced short stories in *Satellite* in 1955 when he was 18, which were later collected in *Les Perles du Temps* (*The Pearls of Time*), for *Présence du Futur*. In 1958, he published two minor space operas, *Agent Galactique* (*Galactic Agent*) under the pseudonym of "Mark Starr" in *Satellite*, and *Embûches dans l'Espace* (*Ambushes in Space*), written with Richard **Chomet** and Patrice **Rondard**, for the *Rayon Fantastique*. Klein also wrote a major novel, the Van Vogt-influenced *Le Gambit des Étoiles* (*Starmasters' Gambit*, 1958) for the *Rayon Fantastique*. In it, the secret immortal

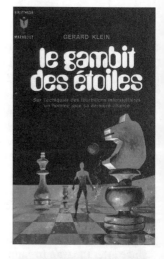

masters of the Federation played galactic chess with the human agent of mysterious cosmic powers, who turned out to be sentient stars. *Le Gambit des Étoiles* established Klein as any major new talent, and from that point on, he has remained one of the best French science fiction writers.

Klein followed up with the popular *Argyre* saga, describing the future history of Man's conquest of the Solar System. Written for *Anticipation*, and originally published under the pseudonym of "Gilles d'Argyre," These were comprised of *Chirurgiens d'une Planète* (*The Planet Surgeons*, 1960; it was revised in 1987 as *Le Rêve des Forêts* (*A Dream of Forests*)), which described the terraforming of Mars by the enterprising Georges Beyle; *Les Voiliers du Soleil* (*The Solar Sailors*, 1961), in which Beyle, now linked to a giant computer, defeated an alien invader; and *Le Long Voyage* (*The Long Journey*, 1964), in which Beyle returned to launch a plan to turn a terraformed Pluto into a starship. Other notable works of the period included another Van Vogtian time-thriller, *Le Temps n'a pas d'Odeur* (*Time Has No Scent*, 1963) for *Présence du Futur*, and *Les Tueurs de Temps* (*The Time Killers*, 1965) for *Anticipation*, which reprised the theme of a chess game spanning time and space. Klein also published a collection of literary stories, *Un Chant de Pierre* (*A Song of Stone*, 1966), and *Le Sceptre du Hasard* (*The Scepter*

of Chance, 1968), the latter a political space opera of the far future, in which Beyle had a passing mention.

In 1969, Klein, who by then had become a renowned critic and essayist, launched the prestigious *Ailleurs & Demain* (*Elsewhere & Tomorrow*) science fiction imprint at Robert Laffont (see below). There, he published one major new novel, *Les Seigneurs de la Guerre* (*The Overlords of War*, 1971), and another excellent short story collection, *La*

Loi du Talion (*The Law of Retaliation*, 1973). *Les Seigneurs de la Guerre* was a sophisticated space-time opera, still reminiscent of Van Vogt, but incorporating more challenging philosophical implications. Its hero, Colson, was a lone warrior caught in a future war who found himself thrown back and forth between two segments of time separated by 6,000 years. The prime movers were the mysterious Gods of Aergistal, omnipotent chess players who lived a complex "hyper-life" (infinitely replaying their own existence) at the end of time, and built a simulated battlefield where all the various wars of time were waged anew. Their goals were both simple and complex: War was to be abolished, war was to be understood, war was to be preserved (in case the universe needed it someday). War was depicted as a negative, yet indispensable factor in human evolution, almost a biological imperative. It is interesting to note that Klein declared in an interview that a large part of *Overlords* had been written during his military service during the Algerian war of independence, which officially ended in 1962. Since the early 1970s, Klein has devoted all his energies to his work as editor and anthologist.

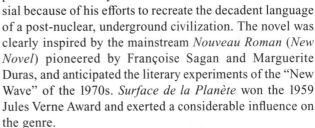

"Francis **Carsac**," the pseudonym of university professor and prehistorian François Bordes, bridged the gap between French science fiction of the 1930s and 1940s, and the American-influenced space operas of the 1950s. All of his works, except for the last, were published by the *Rayon Fantastique*, and were characterized by a profoundly humanistic, tolerant philosophy, often absent from the American works of the period. *Ceux de Nulle Part* (*Those from Nowhere*, 1954) featured an average Earthman volunteering to help an interstellar civilization fight a war against the Misliks, alien metallic intelligences not unlike Rosny's "ferromagnetics" who turned off suns. *Les Robinsons du Cosmos* (*The Robinsons of the Cosmos*, 1955) was a *When Worlds Collide*-like tale of men colonizing another world. *Terre en Fuite* (*Fleeing Earth*, 1960) described how a future scientist turned Earth into a giant ship to escape the death of our sun.

Ce Monde est Notre (*This World Is Ours*, 1962) took place in the same universe as *Ceux de Nulle Part*, but several centuries later. It dealt intelligently and with great sensitivity with the problem of three different cultures sharing the same planet: One was a colony of Basque humans, the other survivors from a lost Terran ship who built a pseudo-medieval society, the third a peaceful, primitive cold-blooded reptilian race. Because galactic law stated that there can be only one race per planet, a team of investigators was sent to decide who would stay and who would be removed.

Pour Patrie, l'Espace (*For Homeland, Space*, 1962) was a Poul Anderson-like space opera about space-faring gypsies and the galactic empire from which they sprang and which they defied. Finally, **Carsac**'s last novel, *La Vermine du Lion* (*The Vermin of the Lion*, 1967), published by *Anticipation*, featured Terai Laprade, an anthropologist who fought to protect an unspoiled world and its natives from a ruthless mining company. The novel was ahead of its times in terms of its political and ecological concerns.

Other notable authors published by the *Rayon Fantastique* included:

"Albert **Higon**," a pseudonym of writer Michel **Jeury** (see below), who contributed two space operas, *Aux Étoiles du Destin* (*Destiny's Stars*, 1960), featuring a cosmic battle between the alien T'Loons and the incomprehensible Glutons, whose only communication is the wonderfully nonsensical sentence, "Sacred whirlpool matures green water," and *La Machine du Pouvoir* (*The Machine of Power*, 1960), which won the 1960 Jules Verne Award.

"Philippe **Curval**," a pseudonym of journalist Philippe Tronche, with *Les Fleurs de Vénus* (*The Flowers of Venus*, 1960) and *Le Ressac de l'Espace* (*The Breakers of Space*, 1962), which won the 1963 Jules Verne Award, featured the alien Txalqs who must live in symbiosis with humans to realize their ideal of beauty. These were early works, however; the considerable impact of both Jeury and Curval was not felt until the 1970s (see below).

Daniel **Drode**, whose only novel, *Surface de la Planète* (*Surface of the Planet*, 1959) proved immediately controversial because of his efforts to recreate the decadent language of a post-nuclear, underground civilization. The novel was clearly inspired by the mainstream *Nouveau Roman* (*New Novel*) pioneered by Françoise Sagan and Marguerite Duras, and anticipated the literary experiments of the "New Wave" of the 1970s. *Surface de la Planète* won the 1959 Jules Verne Award and exerted a considerable influence on the genre.

Serge **Martel**, who won the 1958 Jules Verne Award for *L'Adieu aux Astres* (*Farewell to the Stars*, 1958), a nostalgia-filled space opera, which was followed by *L'Aventure Alphéenne* (*The Alphean Adventure*, 1960). (With Pierre Dupriez, Serge Martel wrote radio scripts for **Le Théâtre de l'Étrange** [*Theater of the Weird*]; see Book 1, Chapter III.)

"Jérôme **Sériel**" was the pseudonym of renowned scientist Jacques Vallée, better known for a number of serious books studying the so-called UFO phenomenon. Sériel's first novel, *Le Sub-Espace* (*The Sub-Space*, 1961), won the 1961 Jules Verne Award and featured an astonishing cosmic battle using what was at the time cutting-edge physics. Sériel continued to explore the theme of alien intelligences existing in a multi-dimensional universe in his next novel, *Le Satellite Sombre* (*The Dark Satellite*, 1963), published by *Présence du Futur*. (A 1986 genre novel about artificial intelligence, *Alintel*, was released under Vallée's own name.)

Vladimir **Volkoff**, the son of exiled Russians, penned the satirical, surrealist novel, *Métro pour l'Enfer* (*Metro for Hell*, 1963), which won the 1963 Jules Verne Award. Volkoff then wrote the *Langelot* juvenile series under the pseudonym of "Lieutenant X" (see below). Volkoff eventually returned to science fiction in the 1980s with two novels, *Le Tire-Bouchon du Bon Dieu* (*The Corkscrew of God*, 1982), in which Earth was surrendered by the humans to an alien fungus; and *La Guerre des Pieuvres* (*The War of the Octopuses*, 1983). Meanwhile, he had established himself as a major writer of critically acclaimed John Le Carré-like thrillers such as *Le Retournement* (*The Turning*, 1979) and *Le Montage* (*The Machination*, 1982).

Finally, the *Rayon Fantastique* published two remarkable female writers:

Françoise d'**Eaubonne** had already written a number of fantastic stories collected in *Démons et Merveilles* (*Demons and Wonders*, 1951; see Chapter VIII), when she penned the ambitious future-history novel, *Les Sept Fils de l'Étoile* (*The Seven Sons of the Star*, 1962), for the *Rayon Fantastique*. It was followed by *L'Échiquier du Temps* (*Time's Chessboard*, 1962) and *Rêve de Feu* (*Dream of Fire*, 1964).

Similarly, Christine **Renard** was another female writer who had contributed short stories to *Fiction* and wrote *À Contre-Temps* (*Against Time*, 1963), a love story with a time paradox, for the *Rayon Fantastique*.

Another notable female author was Marianne **Andrau**, whose *Les Mains du Manchot* (*The Hands of the One-Armed*

Man, 1953), a novel about the Kafkaesque city of Parsepol, which existed in another dimension, was originally published in a mainstream imprint by Denoël. Andrau followed it with *Le Prophète* (*The Prophet*, 1955), *Lumière d'Épouvante* (*Light of Terror*, 1956), a collection of fantastic tales (see Chapter VIII), *D.C. (Doom City)* (1957), and finally, *Les Faits d'Eiffel* (*The Feats of Eiffel*, 1960), another short story collection, this time published in *Présence du Futur*. Another Andrau genre novel was *L'Architecte Fou* (*The Mad Architect*, 1964), a dystopia telling the story of three immortals from the 20th century who discovered the world of the 22nd century.

Of all the authors published by *Anticipation* during the period, none was more remarkable than "Stefan **Wul**," the pseudonym of dental surgeon Pierre Pairault. Wul's eleven novels, published between 1956 and 1959, were all classics, enlivened by their colorful, poetic imagery and their operatic stories, which took pulp clichés and turned them into powerful dramas. *Niourk* (1957) told the story of a mutant child who came to rediscover civilization in the ruins of a post-cataclysmic New York (Niourk). Another interesting aspect of this novel was that its protagonist was black, an unusual choice for the times. *OMS en Serie* (*OMS in Series*, 1957) and *L'Orphelin de Perdide* (*The Orphan of Perdide*, 1958) were the basis for two of René **Laloux**'s animated features, **La Planète Sauvage** (*Fantastic Planet*) and **Les Maîtres du Temps** (*Time Masters*; see Book 1, Chapter IV). In the former, men have become the pets of an advanced race of alien giants. In the latter, a boy abandoned on a hostile world was linked to his rescuers through a space radio. The novel ended with a clever time paradox in which one of the rescuers turned out to be the same boy, but much older.

Other notable Wul works included: *Le Temple du Passé* (*The Temple of the Past*, 1958), in which spacemen who crashed on an alien world were swallowed by a giant whale-like creature and, in order to save themselves, caused it to evolve, eventually creating a new race of intelligent lizards. the lone survivor was ultimately revealed to be an Atlantean; *La Mort Vivante* (*The Living Death*, 1958), about a scientist who, in order to recreate a billionaire's dead daughter, created a protoplasmic entity which ended up swallowing the world; the futuristic spy thrillers, *Piège sur Zarkass* (*Trap on Zarkass*, 1958) and *Odyssée Sous Contrôle* (*Odyssey Under Control*, 1959), which anticipated today's virtual-reality sagas.

Writer André **Ruellan** contributed many remarkable horror novels to Fleuve Noir's *Angoisse* imprint under his pseudonym of "Kurt **Steiner**" (see Chapter VIII). As Steiner, he also penned two heroic fantasy novels starring the futuristic knight, Dal Ortog Dal of Galankar (also see Chapter VIII). For *Anticipation*, Steiner wrote a few no less remarkable science fiction novels. *Salamandra* (1959) described a love affair between an Earthman and a Mercurian woman. The remarkable *Le 32 Juillet* (*July 32nd*, 1959) described how a man found himself in another dimension

and explored the vast insides of a giant, living entity. *Les Improbables* (1965) told of a time war between two future cities, Babelia and Kaltarborog, and the attempts by their descendents to manipulate events to increase their probability of existence. *Les Océans du Ciel* (*The Oceans of the Sky*, 1967) was a colorful space opera featuring a method of birth involving cosmic exchanges between two worlds. *Les Enfants de l'Histoire* (*The Children of History*, 1969) was a thinly disguised allegory of the political events of May 1968 recast in future guise.

In the 1970s, Steiner continued to pen a series of well-crafted novels for *Anticipation*. *Le Disque Rayé* (*The Scratched Record*, 1970) was an interesting saga involving a complex time loop. *Brebis Galeuses* (*Black Sheep*, 1974) was a medical dystopia. *Un Passe Temps* (*A Pastime*, 1979) another clever time paradox tale. More importantly, in 1974, Steiner wrote the remarkable novel, *Tunnel*, under his own name (**Ruellan**) for *Ailleurs & Demain*. It depicted the flight of a man through a garbage jungle surrounding a bleak, futuristic Paris. The man is dragging behind him the body of his dead lover, searching for a way to resurrect her. In 1979, Ruellan also novelized his script for Alain **Jessua**'s remarkable movie, *Les Chiens* (*The Dogs*; see Book 1, Chapter I). Finally, in 1984, Ruellan wrote *Mémo* for *Présence du Futur*, a novel in which a scientist's experiments with a new drug intended to stimulate memory ended in a nightmarish disaster.

After Wul and Steiner, one of the most interesting authors of *Anticipation* was the prolific "B.-R. **Bruss**" (René Bonnefoy) who, like Steiner, also contributed to the *Angoisse* imprint (see Chapter VIII). Bruss had begun to write science fiction in the 1940s (see Chapter VII), and under the other pseudonym of "Roger **Blondel**," also wrote a number of beautifully crafted, surreal novels in the vein of Vian and Borges in the 1950s and 1960s (see Chapter VIII). Bruss wrote

over forty novels for *Anticipation* between 1954 and 1975. His first three novels formed a trilogy about an Earth vs. Flying Saucers war (Nos. 33, 40, 65, 1954-56). Bruss' novels were lessons about the need for mutual respect and tolerance between different lifeforms. One of his most notable earlier works was the *Cerel* (*Cerveaux Électroniques* [*Electronic Brains*]) trilogy (Nos. 136, 143, 225, 1959-63), in which mankind learned to live in peace alongside the giant computers which had once enslaved them.

Men falling in love and eventually marrying alien females, often belonging to races with superior powers, were the subject of novels such as *L'Otarie Bleue* (*The Blue Otter*, 1963), *L'Étrange Planète Orga* (*The Strange Planet Orga*, 1967), *L'Espionne Galactique* (*The Galactic Spy*, 1968), in which the love interest was revealed to be a cyborg, and the beautiful *Les Enfants d'Alga* (*The Children of Alga*, 1968), in which the sterile Algans come to Earth to father children.

Men coming in contact with alien entities of vast, extraordinary powers, who at first barely took notice of our existence, included *Une Mouche Nommée Drésa* (*A Fly Named Dresa*, 1964), *L'Énigme des Phtas* (*The Enigma of the Phtas*, 1965), *La Créature Éparse* (*The Fragmented Creature*, 1966), and *Le Mystère des Sups* (*The Mystery of the Sups*, 1967).

Men being experimented upon by aliens and the two species ultimately gaining a form of mutual understanding included *Les Translucides* (*The Transparents*, 1964), in which human guinea pigs were turned into transparent giants; and *La Planète Glacée* (*The Ice Planet*, 1965), which featured a man whose brain was transplanted into an alien robot.

Some of Bruss' best novels were *Le Grand Feu* (*The Great Fire*, 1964), in which the children of men and young alien sentient robots made contact on a post-cataclysmic Earth in spite of their elders' reluctance; later, the robots helped rescue men from giant ants; *Planètes Oubliées* (*Forgotten Planets*, 1965), where each planet was seeded with a specific profession (surgeons, artists, psychologists, etc.), generating colorful, split cultures; *L'Astéroïde Noir* (*The Black Asteroid*, 1964), a harrowing exploration of the dimension of dreams; the self-explanatory *Le Trappeur Galactique* (*The Galactic Trapper*, 1967), for its colorful alien fauna; *La Planète Introuvable* (*The UnfIndable Planet*, 1968), in which an alien planet seemed to exist simultaneously in different time zones; and *Parle, Robot!* (*Speak, Robot!*, 1969), a moving first-person history of a sentient robot. Later Bruss works, however, took a more pessimistic slant, as evidenced

LA PLANETE INTROUVABLE

FLEUVE NOIR

in *La Planète aux Oasis* (*The Oasis Planet*, 1970), where mankind was casually exterminated by superior cosmic entities, and *Une Si Belle Planète* (*Such a Beautiful Planet*, 1970), where a human colony had to abandon a world previously seeded by another race.

"**Richard-Bessière**" was another of the major writers of Fleuve Noir's *Anticipation* imprint, writing almost one hundred novels between 1951 and 1985. Henri-Richard Bessière's father was a friend and writing partner of François Richard, who became the first editor of the imprint. Together, the two men had used the signature of "F. Richard-Bessière" On previous collaborations. When *Anticipation* started in 1951, the contracts for the novels written by young Henri-Richard Bessière, and edited by his father and François Richard, were signed by his father. The novels were therefore released under the "F. Richard-Bessière name. After his father's death, Henri-Richard Bessière asked that the books be released under his own name, but the publishers did not want to risk losing the benefits of what they considered a "valuable house name." A compromise was reached and, starting with *Les Maîtres du Silence* (*The Masters of Silence*, 1965), the books were signed "Richard-Bessière"—sometimes with, sometimes without, a hyphen.

Bessière's first science fiction series (Nos. 1-4, 37, 1951-54) featured the so-called *Conquérants de l'Universe* (*Conquerors of the Universe*), a band of Earthmen led by Professor Bénac, the inventor of a spaceship called *Meteor*, and comprised of a young French engineer, an American journalist and a young British woman. The Conquerors explored the Solar System, helping friendly aliens and thwarting evil tyrants. The novels, originally written in the mid-1940s, owed more to Verne, and **Le Faure** & de **Graffigny**, than to post-World War II science fiction. The somewhat naïve adventures of these brave men were close in style to *Flash Gordon* and the *Lensmen* series, and embodied the transition between the French science fiction of the 1920s and 1930s, and that of the 1950s and 1960s, influenced by American authors. Bessière updated the saga in a two-volume remake entitled *Les Pionniers du Cosmos* (*The Pioneers of the Cosmos*; Nos. 264, 268, 1965).

Bessière's most popular series featured the adventures of American journalist Sydney Gordon, his ditzy wife Margaret, his catastrophe-prone son, Bud, and his scientist friends, Archie and Gloria Brent. The series began in *Création Cosmique* (*Cosmic Creation*; No. 89, 1957) and continued through numerous novels (Nos. 97, 121, 129, 198, 210, 232, 255, 289, 342, 372, 438, 482, 646, 809, 903, 1032,

1957-80). The Sydney Gordon adventures were initially fairly serious tales of alien or extra-dimensional invaders, but eventually took a tongue-in-cheek turn with *Les Mages de Dereb* (*The Wizards of Dereb*; No. 289, 1966), in which Sydney and his friends discovered the Land of Fiction, where they faced the demented products of the imagination of a science fiction writer; and *Ne Touchez Pas Aux Borloks* (*Don't Touch the Borloks*; No. 342, 1968), in which alien toys created chaos on Earth. A recurring opponent of Gordon and his friends became the Machine, a giant, intelligent, extra-dimensional computer with god-like powers introduced in *La Machine Venue d'Ailleurs* (*The Machine from Beyond*; No. 372, 1969), which created pocket universes in which it ran fanciful simulations. Bessière's other popular series involved the hard-boiled adventures of Dan Seymour, a futuristic James Bond, introduced in *Agent Spatial No. 1* (*Space Agent No. 1*; No. 293, 1966). Seymour went on to appear in another eight novels (Nos. 329, 359, 380, 422, 473, 516, 531, 615, 1967-74).

Bessière made his mark through a number of non-connected novels that featured an original blend of horror and science fiction. He had previously contributed to Fleuve Noir's *Angoisse* imprint under the pseudonym of "Dominique Keller" (see Chapter VIII). These were among his best novels. Monstrous aliens threatening to take over mankind were featured in *Escale chez les Vivants* (*Stop-Over Among the Living*, 1960); evil entities from beyond human ken whose only weakness was sound invaded Earth in *Les Maîtres du Silence* (*The Masters of Silence*, 1965); *Cette Lueur Qui Venait Des Ténèbres* (*That Light Which Came from the Dark*, 1967) featured ghastly alien body-snatching parasites; *Le Vaisseau de l'Ailleurs* (*The Ship from Beyond*, 1972) was based on Wagnerian mythos; *Les Seigneurs de la Nuit* (*The Lords of Night*, 1973) described the triumph of a Nazi-like dark power. The ultimately doomed reconquest of a hellish, post-cataclysmic Earth, ruled by mutants and strange, deadly lifeforms, was the subject of *Légion Alpha* (1961), *Les Sept Anneaux de Rhéa* (*The Seven Rings of Rhéa*, 1962), in which Earth was described as seven concentric spheres with Hell at its core; *Les Jardins de l'Apocalypse* (*The Gardens of the Apocalypse*, 1963) and *Des Hommes, Des Hommes Et Encore Des Hommes* (*Men, Men and Always Men*, 1968). *Les Marteaux de Vulcain* (*The Hammers of Vulcan*, 1969) described a nightmarish planet where survival was all but impossible. The *Coburn* saga (Nos. 1293 and 1346) featured a spaceman constantly returned to life on yet another

RICHARD-BESSIÈRE

LES MARTEAUX DE VULCAIN

FLEUVE NOIR

hellish planet, Xambo. *Je m'appelle... Tous* (*I'm Called... All*, 1965) featured a lone spaceman who crashed on an alien planet and cloned himself in huge numbers before eventually succumbing to madness.

Finally, Bessière also wrote almost a hundred spy thrillers for the *Espionnage* imprint of Fleuve Noir under the pseudonym of "F.-H. Ribes." Many of these starred a hero called Gérard Lecomte; some featured genre elements, such as *Lecomte—Objectif OVNI* (*Lecomte—Target UFO*, 1976).

Another notable writer published by *Anticipation* was "Jean-Gaston **Vandel**," the pseudonym of the writing team of Jean Libert and Gaston Vandenpanhuyse, who also used the alias of "Paul **Kenny**" To create a popular James Bond-like hero, Coplan FX-18, whose adventures were published by Fleuve Noir in its *Espionnage* imprint. The success of the *Coplan* series caused the writers to abandon Vandel's career after only twenty novels published between 1952 and 1956. Vandel's production, like Bruss', emphasized the importance of tolerance and communication between different species: alien lifeforms in *Les Astres Morts* (*The Dead Stars*, 1952), where a machine called "transferator" was used; *Attentat Cosmique* (*Cosmic Strike*, 1953) and *Incroyable Futur* (*Incredible Future*, 1953), where the aliens forced a third age of enlightenment upon mankind; sentient robots in *Alerte aux Robots* (*Alert: Robots*, 1952), where robots revolted until men agreed to treat them more humanely, and *Territoire Robot* (*Robot Territory*, 1955), in which Martian robots enslaved men; and finally, mutants, such as the "Vitelians" introduced in *Fuite dans l'Inconnu* (*Flight Into the Unknown*, 1954) and *Raid sur Delta* (*Raid Over Delta*, 1955), who were mutants who were artificially created when mankind seemed to be doomed by incurable disease; and *Le Troisième Bocal* (*The Third Jar*, 1956), where it was aliens who helped create mutants to save Mankind.

The survival of the species was a recurrent theme in Vandel's rather pessimistic fiction: The dangers of overpopulation, pollution and the evils of science unchecked were featured in *Agonie des Civilisés* (*Agony of the Civilized*, 1953), *Les Titans de l'Energie* (*The Energy Titans*, 1955), where the alien Ktongs tried to save Mankind in spite of itself, *Départ pour l'Avenir* (*Departure for the Future*, 1955), in which thirty children were voluntarily sent into space, away from a polluted Earth, and *La Foudre Anti-D* (*The Anti-D Lightning*, 1956), a terrifying picture of the world running toward its doom.

Some other notable novels by Vandel included *Les Chevaliers de l'Espace* (*The Space Knights*, 1952) and its sequel, *Le Satellite Artificiel* (*The Artificial Satellite*, 1952), in which an order of space knights used a space station as a base to protect Earth; *Frontières du Vide* (*Frontiers of the Void*, 1953), which revealed that the dead lived on a distant planet; and *Bureau de l'Invisible* (*Office of the Invisible*, 1956), which was about an organization of crime-solving psychics led by the mysterious Kerrick, who used an alien artifact to control his agents' powers. Before a villain could

use the artifact for evil ends, an alien ship came to Earth and destroyed it.

Michel **Demuth**, who later became one of the most influential editors of OPTA during the 1970s, and is a renowned translator (Frank Herbert's *Dune* is among his credits), began publishing a series of interconnected short stories in *Fiction* in the 1960s. That series formed a 2000-year future history *à la* Heinlein or Asimov, and was eventually collected in two volumes as *Les Galaxiales* (*The Galaxials*) in the 1970s. Demuth also penned numerous other short stories and novellas for *Satellite*, collected in

La Clé des Étoiles (*The Key to the Stars*, 1960), and for *Fiction* (sometimes using the pseudonym "Jean-Michel Ferrer"), collected in *Les Années Metalliques* (*The Metal Years*, 1977).

Finally, German-born Charles **Henneberg** penned a a series of flamboyant, gothic space operas featuring superhuman protagonists, often soldiers or mercenaries, victims of violent, romantic passions. *La Naissance des Dieux* (*The Birth of the Gods*, 1954), published by *Séries 2000*, mixed Greek and Norse mythologies in a science fiction context. In it, a scientist, an astronaut and a poet found they could psychically recreate life, and eventually vied for supremacy on another planet which turned out to be Earth in the far future. In accordance with Henneberg's philosophy, the astronaut was the hero, and the poet the misguided villain. The novel won the Rosny Award. *Le Chant des Astronautes* (*The Astronauts' Song*, 1958), serialized in *Satellite*, dealt with the battle against energy creatures from Algol. An *Premier, Ere Spatiale* (*Year 1 of*

the Space Era, 1959), serialized in *Fiction*, was about the first faster-than-light ship. Finally, *La Rosée du Soleil* (*The Dew of the Sun*, 1959), published by the *Rayon Fantastique*, told the adventures of the four crewmen of a spaceship stranded on the fantastic alien world of Bellatrix.

After Charles Henneberg's death in 1959, his works were continued by his wife, Russian-born Nathalie **Henneberg**, who had anonymously collaborated with her husband on the above novels. Nathalie Henneberg's works, starting with *Les Dieux Verts* (*The Green Gods*, 1961), became increasngly gothic and fantastic, and are reviewed under heroic fantasy in Chapter VIII.

c. Other Notable Writers

Of all the authors published by Fleuve Noir's *Anticipation* imprint, Jimmy **Guieu** is, without a doubt, the one who has achieved the most surprising commercial success. His first novel, *Le Pionnier de l'Atome* (*The Pioneer of the Atom*, 1952), dealt with the classic theme of a journey into the microcosmos and used the by then old-fashioned concept of a Hindu's psychic powers. With his second novel, *Au-delà de l'Infini* (*Beyond Infinity*; No. 8, 1952), Guieu introduced the character of American biologist Jerry Barclay and reversed the theme. This time, it was our universe that was a microcosmos contained within the knee of a beautiful woman from a macrocosmos. Guieu continued the Barclay series for three more books (Nos. 13, 18, 22, 1952-53), usually teaming Jerry with good aliens in order to defeat evil aliens, and returning him to the macrocosmos for further adventures.

With *La Dimension X* (*Dimension X*; No. 27, 1953) and, especially, *Nous les Martiens* (*We the Martians*; No. 31, 1954), Guieu introduced a new hero: archeologist Jean Kariven. In the *Kariven* series, Guieu began to explore his favorite themes such as UFOs, secret alien encounters, von Daniken-like theories of ancient astronauts, esoteric secrets, and occult societies, sprinkling his novels with footnotes claiming that the various facts upon which he was basing his tales were indeed "authentic." In *Nous les Martiens* (*We the Martians*), Kariven discovered that, in the far distant past, men had emigrated to Earth from Mars. Eight more Kariven novels followed (Nos. 36, 41, 45, 47, 51, 54, 58, 62, 1954-56), dealing with time travel, lost civilizations, plus a tetralogy featuring a space war between the good Polarians and the evil Denebians, with Earth secretly caught in the middle: *L'Homme de l'Espace* (*The Man from Space*), *Opération Aphrodite*, *Commandos de l'Espace* (*Space Commandos*), and *Nos Ancêtres de l'Avenir* (*Our Ancestors from the Future*). One of the Kariven novels, *Univers Parallèles* (*Parallel Universes*; No. 58, 1955), even featured a cross-over with Jerry Barclay, who was said to live in a parallel universe.

Guieu continued to exploit the UFO and occult vein with increasing success. After the Kariven adventures, he penned a number of non-connected novels, except for two that featured a team of American investigative reporters, Ericksson and Wendell: *Les Monstres du Néant* (*The Monsters from the Void*, 1956) and *Les Êtres de Feu* (*The Beings of Fire*, 1956). He also wrote two successful non-fiction books about UFOs, *Les Soucoupes Volantes viennent d'un Autre Monde* (*The Flying Saucers Come from Another World*) and *Black-Out sur les Soucoupes Volantes* (*Black-Out on the Flying Saucers*; the latter prefaced by Jean **Cocteau**). By the 1970s, Guieu had become a major French figure in UFO circles.

Simultaneously, Guieu began to chronicle the exploits of two daring space traders of the future, Blade and Baker.

The series began with *Les Forbans de l'Espace* (*The Space Pirates*; No. 224, 1963) and continued in *Les Destructeurs* (*The Destroyers*; No. 237, 1963), *Joklun-N'Ghar la Maudite* (*Joklun-N'Ghar the Accursed*; No. 352, 1968), and nine more (Nos. 395, 447, 470, 504, 521, 618, 662, 707, 730, 1969-76).

In 1967, with *Le Retour des Dieux* (*The Return of the Gods*; No. 337), Guieu revamped the Kariven character into that of journalist of the occult Gilles Novak who, with the help of his girl-friend Régine Véran, and various friends and allies (often real-life friends of Guieu or thinly disguised real-life figures), fought against would-be tyrants, Communists, terrorists, the drug cartel, and various alien menaces. Novak was helped in his battles by Michael Merkavim, the head of a new, powerful Templar Order, equipped with futuristic weapons and based in a parallel dimension. Merkavim was introduced in *Les Sept Sceaux du Cosmos* (*The Seven Seals of the Cosmos*; No. 343, 1968) and *L'Ordre Vert* (*The Green Order*; No. 384, 1969). The *Gilles Novak* series was comprised of Nos. 360, 425, 439, 459, 480, 496, 547, 568, 578, 602, 647, 688, 851, and 1273, *Les Fils du Serpent* (*The Sons of the Serpent*, 1984), the last of the eighty-two novels Guieu wrote directly for *Anticipation*.

Due to the phenomenal growth in popularity of his novels, Guieu was granted his own imprint in 1979. At first, it reprinted rewritten, updated versions of his original novels, then it began publishing a series of share-cropping spin-off novels, featuring Gilles Novak, Blade & Baker, the planet Joklun N'Ghar, etc., written by other writers, mostly Roland C. **Wagner** (using the pseudonym "Richard Wolfram"), but also Philippe **Randa**, Nicolas **Gauthier**, Laurent **Genefort** (using the pseudonym "S. Grey"), and others. A separate, short-lived spin-off series, the *Chevaliers de Lumière* (*The Knights of Light*), devoted to the New Templars, was published from 1987 to 1989. Today, Jimmy Guieu has become a trademarked phenomenon, unique in the annals of science fiction, and certainly without equivalent in England or America. His success is attributable to his clever mix of occult facts, mild eroticism, ultra-conservative and somewhat bigoted politics, and a forceful if simple storytelling style successfully imitated by his successors. Most regular Guieu readers are drawn from the general public rather than the science fiction audience—as is the case with *The X-Files*—and are not science fiction fans but only Jimmy Guieu fans.

Pierre **Barbet**'s first two science fiction novels, *Vers un Avenir Perdu* (*Towards a Lost Future*, 1962) and *Babel 3805* (1962) were published by the *Rayon Fantastique*. After the cancellation of that imprint in 1964, Barbet (a pseudonym of Dr. Clauve Avice) moved to Fleuve Noir's *Anticipation* in 1966, and became a steady provider of classic space operas, such as *Vikings de l'Espace* (*Space Vikings*, 1969), the tale of the conquest of the galaxy by a Viking-like warlord whose planet's sun is dying. Barbet was among the first writers to introduce heroic fantasy to *Anticipation* as part of his *Temporal Investigator Setni* series, which started with *L'Exilé du Temps* (*The Exile of Time*; No. 392, 1969) and continued with Nos. 479, 544, 609, 1254, 1298, 1483, and 1560 (see Chapter VIII). Setni was a special agent for a Galactic Federation ruled by preserved brains. Barbet's other notable novels included the *Napoleons of Eridani* trilogy (Nos. 426, 1169, 1284, 1970-84), in which a squadron of Napoleonic soldiers kid-napped by aliens ended up conquering a space em-pire, a theme reminiscent of Poul Anderson's *High Crusade*. Barbet's other series included the adven-tures of the dashing Alex Courville (Nos. 835, 932, 1099, 1199, 1347, 1401, 1505, 1547, 1620, 1978-88), a hero not unlike An-derson's Dominic Flan-dry, and the saga of the *Cities in Space* (Nos. 951, 1071, 1131, 1284, 1371, 1979-85), reminiscent of James Blish's renowned series. Barbet produced sixty-two novels for Fleuve Noir between *Les Limiers de l'Infini* (*The Trackers of Infinity*, 1966) and *L'Ere du Spatiopithèque* (*The Era of the Spatiopithecus*, 1991). He also produced a few more se-rious, politically oriented works, and some novels for other publishers under the pseudonyms of "David Maine" And "Olivier Sprigel."

The husband and wife writing team of Jean-Louis and Doris **Le May** penned numerous colorful, literary, even po-etic, space operas for *Anticipation*, most of which took place in the same future Galactic Federation introduced in their first novel, *La Chasse à l'Impondérable* (*The Hunt for the Weightless Element*; No. 304, 1966). This novel, and several others, were eventually regrouped in a loose series entitled *Enquêtes Galactiques* (*Galactic Investigations*), because they featured the Federation's multi-species police force, Interco. *La Chasse à l'Impondérable* and its sequel, *L'Oenips d'Orlon* (*The Oenips of Orlon*; No. 312, 1967), starred the same investigative team, agents Rockenret and Gerdavid, and their female partners, involved in the pursuit of drug traffickers. The trilogy ended with a huge space battle in *Les Drogfans de Gersande* (*The Drogfans of Gersande*; No. 327, 1967). Rockenret and Gerdavid returned in *Irimanthe*

(No. 436, 1970). As the series progressed, other novels began to depict different facets of the Federation's life, such as *La Quête du Frohle d'Esylée* (*The Quest of the Frohle of Esyleum*, 1969), *La Plongée des Corsaires d'Hermos* (*The Dive of the Cor-sairs of Hermos*, 1970), where the point of view shifted to that of corsairs fighting Interco, and *La Mission d'Eno Granger* (*The Mission of Eno Granger*, 1970; also see Chapter VIII for a heroic fantasy novel). Other, non-Feder-ation stories—possibly myths of the Federation?—were regrouped in another series, entitled *Contes et Légendes du Futur* (*Tales and Legends of the Future*). Among the best of these were *Arel d'Adamante* (*Arel of Adamante*, 1968), the tale of a water world

AREL D'ADAMANTE

F L E U V E   N O I R

where men live in harmony with cetaceans; *Les Fruits du Métaxylia* (*The Fruits of the Metaxylia*, 1972), the trilogy of the *Érémides*, powerful beings who could freely roam un-seen through space (Nos. 550, 564, 624, 1973), and the saga of a bittersweet love story between two proud contestants in a cosmic regatta across the solar system (Nos. 759, 777, 785, 824, 1976-77). The Le May's forty-third novel, *L'É-paisse Fourrure des Quadricornes* (*The Thick Fur of the Quadricorns*, 1978), an Interco thriller about illegal poach-ing, was the last one they wrote together.

Alone, Jean-Louis **Le May** continued the *Contes et Lé-gendes du Futur* series, but not the *Enquêtes Galactiques*, and added two other series, *Chroniques des Temps à Venir* (*Chronicles of Times to Come*), starting with *L'Ombre dans la Vallée* (*The Shadow in the Valley*, 1979), about the slow rebuilding of civilization in Southern France after an unspecified disaster, and the trilogy of the *Hortans* (*Out-side Time*; Nos. 1176, 1272, 1357, 1982-85), somewhat reminiscent of the earlier *Érémides* series. He penned twenty-three further nov-els, until *L'Hérésie Magicienne* (*The Magical Heresy*, 1987).

By the time he began writ-ing for *Anticipation* in 1959, Maurice **Limat** was already a veteran author, having penned numerous popular adventure novels since the late 1930s (see Chapter VII). During the 1950s, he contributed a series of science fiction novels to Ferenczi's *Mon Roman d'Aventures*

imprints, such as *Les Faiseurs de Planètes* (*The Planet Makers*, 1951), *Comète 73* (1953), *Courrier Interplanétaire* (*Interplanetary Courrier*, 1953), *Le Mal des Étoiles* (*Star Sickness*, 1954), *Attaque Cosmique* (*Cosmic Attack*, 1954), *Les Forçats de l'Espace* (*The Convicts of Space*, 1954), and others, even hiding his abundant production under the pseudonyms of "Maurice Lionel," "Maurice d'Escrignelles," and "Lionel Rex." In 1955, he contributed *SOS Galaxie* (*SOS Galaxy*) to *Série 2000* and then began to write for *Cosmos*. His *Monsieur Cosmos* (1956) dealt with the theme of the macrocosmic man, creator of universes. Other titles included *Planète sans Soleil* (*Planet Without Sun*, 1956) and *Pas de Planète pour les Terriens* (*No Planets for the Earthmen*, 1957). These began to reflect the influence of American space operas.

Les Enfants du Chaos (*The Children of Chaos*, 1959), in which men used psychic power to create a world, but then asked themselves whether they had earned the right to play God, was Limat's first novel for *Anticipation*, and somewhat characteristic of his subsequent production. Limat continued to be a prolific writer, penning numerous, lyrical, sometimes even religious, space operas for *Anticipation*— one hundred and seven in total, until *Atoxa-des-Abysses* (*Atoxa-Of-The-Abyss*, 1987)—as well as some horror novels for the *Angoisse* imprint (see Chapter VIII). His best titles included: *Moi, Un Robot* (*I, Robot*, 1960), which pondered if robots had souls; *Message des Vibrants* (*Message from the Vibrating Ones*, 1961), about souls separated from their bodies (a recurring Limat theme); *Lumière Qui Tremble* (*Shivering Light*, 1962), in which a little boy created a fantasy world; and *Le Sang Vert* (*The Green Blood*, 1963), which detailed the transformation of a stranded spaceman into a giant, sentient tree that eventually gave birth to new lifeforms.

Limat introduced the character of futuristic police commissioner Robin Muscat in *Les Foudroyants* (*The Lightning Men*; No. 164, 1960), in which a hapless young man was turned into an electromagnetic force. But his most popular, long-running hero was the green-eyed, telepathic Chevalier Coqdor, and his pet, the bat-winged pstor, Rax, introduced in *L'Étoile de Satan* (*The Star of Satan*; No. 241, 1964). Muscat and Coqdor soon teamed up and they appeared, separately or together, in a vast number of subsequent volumes, including Nos. 252, 257, 262, 266, 274, 296, 302, 308, 341, 379, 398, 411, 441, 453, 464, 497, 526, 556, 676, 689, 749, 821, 971, 1143, 1184, 1231, 1279, and 1465. The *Coqdor* adventures usually

MAURICE LIMAT

LES PORTES DE L'AURORE

FLEUVE NOIR

celebrated the power of love and tolerance, and a genuine belief in God, the Great Architect of the Universe, something unusual in science fiction. A recurring theme was that secrets that lay beyond mortal ken should not, indeed could not, be fathomed. In *Ici Finit Le Monde* (*Here Ends the Universe*, 1964), Coqdor reached the literal end of the universe, but could go no farther and the mystery of the white flashes that occurred beyond the final border were not solved. In *Les Portes de l'Aurore* (*The Gates of Dawn*, 1967), Coqdor travelled into the dimension of Death but was stopped before he could reach beyond the eponymous Gates of Light. Other unfathomable cosmic secrets were the topics of *Le Treizième Signe du Zodiaque* (*The Thirteenth Sign of the Zodiac*, 1969) and *Flammes sur Titan* (*Flames Over Titan*, 1969), which featured a Prometheus-like, star-travelling scientist trying to solve the mystery of the first emergence of life on another world. Two other short-lived Limat series featured Luc Delta, a spaceship test pilot (Nos. 351, 362, 1968), and Luxman, a man condemned to death who acquired super-powers (Nos. 1291, 1345, 1984).

"Peter **Randa**" was the pseudonym of a former French soldier who already had written several thrillers for *Angoisse* (see Chapter VIII) when he penned *Survie* (*Survival*, 1960) for *Anticipation*, the first of seventy-nine militaristic space operas, usually starring loners, soldiers, or mercenaries, trapped on alien battlefields, in hopeless wars and/or missions, or stranded on alien worlds. His last novel was *Escale à Hango* (*Stop-Over in Hango*, 1980). Randa's heroes ultimately succeeded against all odds in elevating themselves to positions of supreme power.

Some of his best novels included *Commando de Transplantation* (*Transplanted Commando*, 1961), *Humains de Nulle Part* (*Humans from Nowhere*, 1963), *Zone de Rupture* (*Breaking Zone*, 1964), *La Grande Dérive* (*The Great Drift*, 1967), *Les Ides de Mars* (*The Ides of Mars*, 1967), *L'Héritier des Sars* (*The Heir of the Sars*, 1968), *L'Homme Éparpillé* (*The Scattered Man*, 1969) and *L'Univers des Torgaux* (*The Universe of the Torgaux*, 1970). Randa's major series was that of *Les Ancêtres* (*The Ancestors*; Nos. 220, 258, 346, 522, 1963-72), about the unique society formed by the crews of light-speed starships which were the sole links between the human planets of a star-spanning civilization; their name was due to the fact that, to planet-bound humans, they appeared to age more slowly. They also controlled a greater variety of technology. Another series was the saga of the conquering hero, Elteor (Nos. 757, 787, 799, 1976-77).

PETER RANDA

LES IDES DE MARS

FLEUVE NOIR

In a phenomenon unique in the annals of science fiction, Peter Randa's career was continued, in the same style and inspiration, by his son, who signed "Philippe **Randa**," and who began with *Les Fusils d'Ekaistos* (*The Guns of Ekaistos*, 1981). Philippe Randa wrote a total of twenty-two space operas, ending with *Le Mal d'Ibrator* (*The Disease of Ibrator*, 1988). His best series included *L'Empire Terrien* (*The Terran Empire*; Nos. 1052, 1124, 1155, 1173, 1264, 1981-83); *Les Voyageurs de Vestera* (*The Travellers of Vestera*; Nos. 1238, 1354, 1514, 1983-87), and *Les Pirates de l'Espace* (*The Space Pirates*; Nos. 1372, 1436, 1550, 1985-87).

The last of Fleuve Noir's *Anticipation* regular contributors of the 1950s and 1960s was the equally prolific "Max-André **Rayjean**" (another pseudonym), whose novels often dealt with alien contacts and strange biological mutations. Rayjean's first novel was *Attaque Sub-Terrestre* (*Subterranean Attack*, 1956), about a microscosmic invasion. His seventy-seventh and last was *Le Dernier Soleil* (*The Last Sun*, 1987). *Le Péril des Hommes* (*The Peril of Men*, 1960) was about human sterility; *Le Quatrième Futur* (*The Fourth Future*, 1967) and *L'An Un des Kreols* (*Year One of the Kreols*, 1969) featured in the former the artificial creation, in the latter the natural emergence of new races of men. Unlike most other *Anticipation* novels, some of Rayjean's books had bleak endings, often dealing with the disappearance of the human race. Among these were *Ere Cinquième* (*Fifth Era*, 1959), *Les Magiciens d'Andromède* (*The Wizards of Andromeda*, 1961), and *Terrom, Âge "Un"* (*Terrom Age One*, 1963). Some depicted humans being experimented upon by exceedingly strange alien lifeforms, such as *Round Végétal* (*Vegetable Battle*, 1964), *Le Zoo des Astors* (*The Zoo of the Astors*, 1966), and *Relais Kéra* (*The Kera Relay*, 1969). A notable work was *Les Forçats de l'Energie* (*The Energy Convicts*, 1965), which depicted microbes as intelligent aliens and told the story of their desperate travel from body to body from the viewpoints of both the microbes and their infected human host. Rayjean's regular series included the adventures of TV investigative reporter Joe Maubry, introduced in *La Folie Verte* (*The Green Madness*; No. 114, 1958), and continued in Nos. 167, 217, 229, 291, 344, 437, and 778 (1960-77); and space security agent Jé Mox, introduced in *L'Arbre de Cristal* (*The Crystal Tree*; No. 512, 1972), and continued in Nos. 712, 753, 796, 815, and 896 (1975-79).

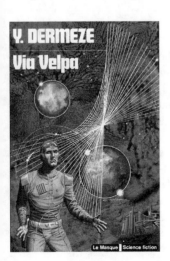

Like Maurice Limat, "Yves **Dermèze**" (a pseudonym of Paul Bérato aka Paul **Béra**) was an experienced writer who had been producing popular adventure and ju-venile genre novels since the early 1940s (see Chapter VII), using a myriad of pseudonyms ("Jean Vier," "Michel Avril," "Jean Mars," "Paul Mystère," etc.), making his bibliography hard to research. In the 1950s, Dermèze produced *La Folie Rouge* (*The Red Madness*, 1954) for Arabesque. Then for *Série 2000*, he wrote *Le Titan de l'Espace* (*The Titan of Space*, 1954), about the conflict between two energy beings on Earth, a novel which was, at the time, deemed to have been influenced by Van Vogt's *Black Destroyer*, even though Dermèze had written his book prior to the latter's translation. He also penned *Via Velpa* (1955), a prodigious space opera ahead of its times, in which an Altairian rebel used time travel and passages between universes to defeat the terrifying threat of the alien, sand-like Mobiks. Other Dermèze works of the period included *La Pierre Vivante* (*The Living Stone*, 1958) and *Les Envoyés du Paradis* (*The Envoys of Paradise*, 1963). In 1970, the author, now signing "Paul Béra," began writing for the *Anticipation* and *Angoisse* imprints of Fleuve Noir (see Chapter VIII). His later works will be discussed in the next section.

Série 2000 also published several space operas by renowned genre historian "Pierre Versins" (a pseudonym of Jacques Chamson), who published and edited the fanzine *Ailleurs* (*Elsewhere*). A Swiss resident, Versins produced the radio series ***Passeport pour l'Inconnu*** (see Book 1, Chapter III). His novels included *Les Étoiles ne s'en foutent pas* (*The Stars Do Care*) (1954), *En Avant Mars!* (*Towards Mars*, 1955), and *Feu d'Artifice* (*Fireworks*, 1956) and offered a radical—in the political sense of the word—brand of space opera, something unusual at the time.

Among the other notable French genre authors published by the *Rayon Fantastique* were:

"**Arcadius**" (a pseudonym), who also wrote a number of well-received, literary science fiction stories for *Fiction* in the 1960s. In *La Terre Endormie* (*The Sleeping Earth*, 1961), mankind was placed in a coma by the "green bomb" and the world was taken over by plants. He wrote only one more novel, *Planète d'Exil* (*Planet of Exile*, 1963).

Alain Yawache, signing "Lieutenant **Kijé**," penned a number of militaristic space operas, such as *La Guerre des Machines* (*The War of the Machines*, 1959), *Celten Taurogh* (1961), *L'Épée de l'Archange* (*The Sword of the Archangel*, 1963) and, later, *Les Cendres de la Terre* (*The Ashes of Earth*) (1976). As "Alain Yaouanc," Yawache was famous for his espionage thrillers.

In John **Amila**'s *Le Neuf de Pique* (*The Nine of Hearts*, 1956), space travellers discovered that we lived in a microcosmos contained inside a card player's eye in a macrocosmos.

Finally, in Yvon **Hecht**'s striking *La Fin du Quaternaire* (*The End of the Quaternary*, 1962), humans gave birth to the insect-like race that was fated to replace them.

The writing team of Henri **Keller** and Grégoire **Brainin** provided a number of easy-to-read if somewhat unoriginal space operas to *Visions Futures* (*Future Visions*), *Grands*

Romans-Sciences-Anticipations (*Great Novels of Science & Anticipation*), *Cosmos,* and *Série 2000.* These included *Planète Atlante* (*Atlantean Planet,* 1953), *L'Attaque des Vénusiens* (*The Attack of the Venusians,* 1953), *La Machine à Explorer le Rêve* (*The Dream Machine,* 1955), *Le Tour du Soleil en 80 Jours* (*Around the Sun in 80 Days,* 1955), *Au Centre de l'Univers* (*At the Center of the Universe,* 1956), and *Et le Temps s'arrêtera* (*And Time Shall Stop,* 1956).

With Maurice Limat, Léopold **Massiéra** was one of the regular contributors to Ferenczi's *Mon Roman d'Aventures* imprint, for which he penned a variety of genre titles such as *L'Énigme des Soucoupes Volantes* (*The Mystery of the Flying Saucers,* 1953), *Le Monde des Abîmes* (*The World of the Abyss,* 1954), *Les Troupeaux de la Lune* (*The Cattle of the Moon,* 1955), and *Le Guide de l'Avenir* (*The Guide from the Future,* 1956). Another regular contributor was Gil **Roc**, with *L'Univers des Gouffres* (*The Universe of the Pits,* 1955) and *L'Horrible Planète* (*The Awful Planet,* 1956).

Other notable genre writers of the period included:

Belgian author R. **Kulavik**, with *Terre contre Mars, La Bataille des Hommes de Fer* (*Earth vs. Mars, the Battle of the Iron Men,* 1948).

Robert **Teldy-Naïm**, with *Paradis Atomiques* (*Atomic Paradises,* 1949) and *Cela Arrivera Hier* (*It Will Happen Yesterday,* 1954).

Lucien **Bornert**, with *Le Péril Vient du Ciel* (*The Danger Comes from the Sky,* 1953) and *Robots Sous-Marins* (*Underwater Robots,* 1953).

Denis Gabriel **Guignard**, with *Pyramidopolis* (1953).

Jean **Lec**, with *L'Être Multiple* (*The Multiple Being,* 1954) and *La Machine à Franchir la Mort* (*The Machine to Cross Death,* 1955).

Claude **Yelnick**, with *L'Homme Cette Maladie* (*Man, This Disease,* 1954), in which a man found access to another world through a lighthouse.

Y.F.J. **Long**, with *Les Atlantes du Ciel* (*The Atlanteans from the Sky,* 1955).

Belgian authors Albert and Jean **Crémieux**, with *Chute Libre* (*Freefall,* 1955) and its sequel, *La Parole Perdue* (*The Lost Word,* 1956), about the exploration of Earth by an alien from planet "54."

Jacques-Henri **Juillet**, with *Atomes à Vendre* (*Atoms for Sale,* 1955) and *Les Visiteurs de l'An 2000* (*The Visitors from Year 2000,* 1956).

Adrien Sobra aka "Marc **Agapit**" (see Chapter VIII), with *Portes sur l'Inconnu* (*Doors Into the Unknown,* 1956).

Satellite founder Michel Bénâtre writing as "Jean **Cap**," With *Nurma* (1956) and *La Brigade du Temps* (*The Time Brigade,* 1960).

Serge **Alkine**, with the space operas, *La Révolte de la Terre* (*The Revolt of Earth,* 1956) and *L'Or de la Lune* (*Gold on the Moon,* 1957).

François **Lourbet**, with *Les Bagnes de l'Espace* (*The Space Penitentiaries,* 1960) and *Sortilège Temporel* (*Time Spell,* 1960).

René **Cambon**, with *L'Homme Double* (*The Double Man,* 1960).

D.A.C. **Danio**, with *Les Cuirs Bouillis* (*The Boiled Leathers,* 1961).

P.-A. **Hourey**, with *Vuzz* (1955).

M. and T. **Tavera**, with *L'Ogive du Monde* (*The World Cone,* 1959).

Jean **Bommart**, the author of a popular series of mysteries starring the elusive *Poisson Chinois* (*Chinese Fish*) used the pseudonym of "Kemmel," penned *Je Reviens De...* (*I Come Back From...,* 1957) and *Au Bout du Ciel* (*At the End of the Sky,* 1962).

Finally, from 1945 to 1948, the Éditions & Revues Françaises published a pulp series of *Fu-Manchu*–like adventure novels featuring the dreaded Pao Tchéou, so-called *Master of the Invisible.* Episodes 1 to 20 were attributed to "Edward **Brooker**" and episodes 21 to 36 to "Sam P. **Norwood**"—obviously pseudonyms. Bound volumes collecting installments of the series were issued in the 1950s under different titles.

d. Mainstream Writers

Because science fiction was perceived as a new genre, and one coming from far-off, exotic America, it immediately attracted mainstream literary personalities such as Boris **Vian**, Jean **Cocteau**, André **Maurois**, Michel **Butor**, Raymond **Quéneau**, and others.

The editorial policies of Robert Kanters at publisher Denoël's *Présence du Futur* were to attract to science fiction mainstream writers who normally would not have contributed to the genre. The results were excellent, with works of high literary quality and, often, genuinely new ideas, including:

Jean-Louis **Curtis**' *Un Saint au Néon* (*A Neon Saint,* 1956) was a collection of five satirical short stories about the future.

Jean **Paulhac**'s *Un Bruit de Guêpes* (*The Sound of Wasps,* 1957) was another collection of biting, satirical stories.

Jean **Hougron**'s *Le Signe du Chien* (*The Sign of the Dog,* 1960) was a remarkable novel on the difficulties of communication between alien species. In 1980, Hougron returned to the genre and penned another epic novel on a similar theme, *Le Naguen.*

René **Sussan**, aka René **Réouven** (see Chapter VIII), contributed *Les Confluents* (*The Confluence,* 1960), a novel about a future human race that produced children through artificial means and, upon discovery that these

children eventually became sexless, tried to modify key moments in history to alter the future. Sussan also contributed *L'Anneau de Fumée* (*The Smoke Ring*) to *Présence du Futur* in 1974.

Finally, Edward de **Capoulet-Junac** penned *Pallas ou la Tribulation* (*Pallas, or Tribulations*, 1967), in which human beings were abducted by bizarre aliens.

Kanters also reprinted Jean **Ray**'s *Malpertuis* (see Chapter VI) and René **Barjavel**'s *Le Voyageur Imprudent* (*The Careless Traveller*) and *Le Diable l'Emporte* (*The Devil Takes It*; see Chapter VII). Barjavel's *Colomb de la Lune* (*Colombus of the Moon*, 1962), also published by Denoël, took place in the same universe, but earlier, and featured Mr. Gé and the first, doomed Moon expedition.

Neo-surrealist Belgian author Jacques **Sternberg** straddled the line between the *fantastique* and science fiction, which he stated was was only a subset of the former in a notorious essay, *Une Succursale du Fantastique nommée Science-Fiction* (*A Branch of the Fantastic Called Science Fiction*), published in 1958 by Losfeld—one of the first non-fiction genre works published in France. Sternberg's career as a dark humorist of the *fantastique* is reviewed in Chapter VIII. His science fiction tales followed the same biting, absurdist tradition, and were gathered in various collections, such as *La Géométrie dans l'Impossible* (*The Impossible Geometry*), published in 1953 by Losfeld; *Entre Deux Mondes Incertains* (*Between Two Uncertain Worlds*), published in 1957 by *Présence du Futur*; *Univers Zéro* (*Universe Zero*), published in 1970 by Marabout; and *Futurs sans Avenir* (*Future Without Future*), published in 1971 by Gérard Klein in his prestigious *Ailleurs & Demain* (*Elsewhere & Tomorrow*) imprint. Themes included aliens misguidedly posing as African-Americans to invade America, the 533rd crucifixion of Jesus, and the casual destruction of Earth by aliens who cannot understand humans. Sternberg's stories anticipated the more experimental texts of the New Wave, or the humor of Douglas Adams. His novels had the same dark, nihilistic, misanthropic characteristics, minus the humor. In *La Sortie est au Fond de l'Espace* (*The Exit Lies at the End of Space*, 1956), aliens who despised mankind caused microbes to grow and, ultimately, utilized euthanasia to kill the few human survivors who had found refuge on their world. *Attention, Planète Habitée* (*Beware, Inhabited Planet*, 1969) followed the same, merciless logic.

Existentialist author Boris **Vian** (see Chapter VIII) also blended elements borrowed from surrealism and traditional *fantastique* with science fiction. One of the main literary personalities of the 1950s, Vian translated American authors such as A. E. Van Vogt and Ray Bradbury. Vian was himself a writer of "new wave"-like speculative fiction ahead of his times. His *L'Herbe Rouge* (*The Red Grass*, 1950), adapted for television in 1985 by Pierre **Kast** (see Book 1, Chapter II), blended time travel with nostalgia. *L'Automne à Pékin* (*Autumn in Peking*, 1947) was a desert utopia set in an alternate universe. Vian skillfully used the imagery of science

fiction to create hostile environments which assaulted his protagonists' sense of individuality, in an almost Philip K. Dick-like fashion.

Of all the mainstream authors who penned works that could easily be labelled science fiction, none was as important as Pierre **Boulle**, whose 1963 classic *La Planète des Singes* (*Planet of the Apes*) became one of the world's best-known science fiction stories and spawned a series of successful movies and television series. Boulle—also the author of the non-genre the *Bridge on the River Kwai*—used science fiction to tell moral fables sprinkled with heavy doses of satire. His short stories were collected in *Les Contes de l'Absurde* (*Absurd Tales*, 1953) and $E = MC^2$ (1957). In the latter's eponymous story, Einstein's formula reversed itself, energy became matter again, and the citizens of Hiroshima found themselves buried under uranium flowers. The short story "Une Nuit Interminable" ("An Endless Night", 1957) told the story of the protracted time wars between Badarian from the far past and Pergolians from the far future, in which each side paradoxically ended up becoming its own opponent. Other notable Boulle works included *Le Jardin de Kanashima* (*Kanashima's Garden*, 1964), which dealt with the conquest of the Moon; *Quia Absurdum* (1970); and the dystopia, *Les Jeux de l'Esprit* (*Mind Games*, 1971).

Just as interesting as Boulle was the renowned Romain **Gary**, a former diplomat turned writer and winner of the Goncourt Award. Like Boulle, Gary used genre elements to morally dissect situations that were rarely (if ever) brought up in ordinary science fiction. In *Tulipe* (*Tulip*, 1946), the blacks inherited the Earth. *Gloire à nos Illustres Pionniers* (*Glory to Our Illustrious Pioneers*, 1962) was a collection which included some genre tales. In *La Danse de Gengis Cohn* (1967), the ghost of a Jewish comedian possessed the body of his Nazi assassin. Finally, in *Charge d'Âme* (*Soul Power*, 1978), men's souls were used for fuel and energy, including the conduct of war.

Of almost equal importance was Jacques **Audiberti**, a prolific mainstream writer and playwright who often used genre themes in his works. *La Nâ* (1944)—the "snow" In savoyard patois—and *Les Tombeaux Ferment Mal* (*The Tombs Don't Close Properly*, 1963) revealed that survivors of Atlantis lived in underground cities and controlled the Earth's crust. (*Les Tombeaux* also dealt with time travel.) *L'Opéra du Monde* (*The Opera of the World*, 1947) postulated the existence of an ancient, pre-cataclysmic Lemurian civilization. *Marie Dubois* (1952) and *Infanticide Préconisé* (*Recommended Infanticide*, 1958) were, respectively, stories about a superman, and mutant children who lived among us. *Les Naturels du Bordelais* (*The Naturals of Bordeaux*, 1953) was a play in which intelligent crickets eventually replaced man. Finally, **La Poupée** (*The Doll*, 1956) was made into an eponymous film (see Book 1, Chapter I).

In Yves **Gandon**'s *Le Dernier Blanc* (*The Last White Man*, 1945), a virus killed all white men. His *La Ville Invis-*

ible (*The Invisible City*, 1953) was a daring novel in which men used advanced mental manipulation techniques to reinvent a new past for themselves. *Après les Hommes* (*After Men*, 1963) featured an intelligent, ethical race of ferromagnetic creatures, not unlike those depicted by Rosny in his 1910 *La Mort de la Terre* (*The Death of the Earth*). Gandon's genre stories were collected in *En Pays Singulier* (*In a Singular Country*, 1949) and *Pour un Bourbon Collins* (*For a Bourbon Collins*, 1967).

Other notable mainstream writers who penned genre works during the period included:

Henri d'**Amfreville** was a surrealist writer who wrote *La Terre Est Chaude* (*Earth Is Hot*, 1946), a novel in which animals threatened to replace man, and *L'Homme Nu* (*The Naked Man*, 1951), about the man of the future who had acquired god-like powers.

Raymond **Asso** in *Les Hors-La-Vie* (*The Out-Life*, 1946) theorized that it was possible to travel between dimensions by assembling sophisticated puzzles.

Romain **Rolland**, better known for his masterpiece *Jean-Christophe*, wrote *La Révolte des Machines ou La Pensée Déchaînée* (*The Revolt of Machines, or Thought Unbound*, 1947).

Swiss writer Dominique **André**'s *Conquête de l'Éternel* (*Conquest of the Eternal*, 1947) was yet one more sequel to Poe's *The Narrative of A. Gordon Pym in Nantucket*. In it, he described a secret Antarctic civilization of perfect, immortal beings. Eventually, its protagonist, a female mad scientist, destroyed Earth after having plunged its inhabitants into comas.

Gustave **Thibon** wrote the apocalyptic *Face à la Peur—La Fin du Monde est pour Demain* (*Facing the Fear—the End of the World Is for Tomorrow*, 1947). In his *Vous Serez Comme des Dieux* (*You Will Be Like Gods*, 1954), public and private transportation were relegated to the rooftops of Paris.

Raymond **Abellio**'s *Les Yeux d'Ézéchiel Sont Ouverts* (*The Eyes of Ezekiel Are Open*, 1949) was an esoteric novel in which we discovered that supermen were hidden among us and had secretly been controlling the events of World War II. Abellio's *La Fosse de Babel* (*The Pit of Babel*, 1962) showed the future decadence of the western society.

Raymond **Caen**'s *Les Stas, ou Le Journal d'un Dieu* (*The Stabs, or the Diary of a God*, 1950) was about a race of indestructible men whose lives had been "stabilized."

Claude **Saint-Yves**, who had already penned an Atlantis novel in 1932 (see Chapter VII), returned to the theme with two romantic fantasies, *Les Aventures du Dernier Atlante* (*The Adventures of the Last Atlantean*, 1950) and *La Fiancée du Dernier Atlante* (*The Fiancée of the Last Atlantean*, 1953). Later, in *Le Serpent* (*The Serpent*, 1957) and *Tes Yeux m'ont vu* (*Your Eyes Saw Me*, 1957), Maryse **Choisy-Clouzet** wrote about cyberneticists who were descendents of Atlantis and created Golem-like creatures.

Jules **Romains** penned the pessimistic anticipations,

Violation de Frontières (*Border Violation*, 1951) and *Passagers de cette Planète, Où allons-nous?* (*Passengers of This Planet, Where Are We Going?*, 1955).

Roger **Ikor**'s *Les Grands Moyens* (*Powerful Means*, 1951) depicted a bleak post-nuclear, communist Europe, where everything of importance was buried beneath tons of rubble. New, powerful and, ironically, even more destructive means were used to move the Earth's crust. **Ikor**'s six-volume saga, *Si Le Temps...* (*If Time...*, 1960-69), was a series of novels attempting to map out man's future progress, beginning with a mystic who wished to rid the world of money, the root of all evil.

Writer/artist "**Vercors**" (a pseudonym of Jean Bruller) wrote several allegorical genre stories, including *Les Animaux Dénaturés* (*The Unnatural Animals*, 1952), in which a new race of primates, discovered in New Guinea, challenged the differences that exist between man and ape. His *Colères* (*Wrath*, 1956) dealt with the quest for immortality, and in *Sylva* (1961), a female fox was turned into a woman, before reverting to type.

Louis **Velle**'s *Ma Petite Femme* (*My Little Woman*, 1953) was a novel about the miniaturisation of a woman.

Michel **Carrouges**' *Les Portes Dauphines* (*The Dauphine Gates*, 1954) featured a slot-machine which turned out to be a gate leading onto another world. His *Les Grands-Pères Prodiges* (*The Prodigal Grandfathers*, 1957) illustrated the social problems that could be caused by the introduction of techniques of rejuvenation. Carrouges is also the author of one of the first serious UFO research works published in French, the luridly mistitled *Apparitions de Martiens* (*Martian Apparitions*, 1954).

René **Albérès** was another mainstream writer who produced two collections of short stories centered around science fiction themes: *L'Autre Planète* (*The Other Planet*, 1958) and *Manuscrit Enterré dans le Jardin d'Éden* (*Ms. Buried in the Garden of Eden*, 1967).

In Georges **Blond**'s *Les Naufragés de Paris* (*Castaways of Paris*, 1959), the disintegration of paper provoked a social collapse. Coincidentally, in the earlier *2 Morts... 20 Milliards* (*2 Dead... 20 Billion*, 1949), Robert **Collard** had imagined a paper-destroying ray.

Jean de **Patmos** penned *Anthropothéose* (*Anthropotheosis*, 1958), a novel about supermen.

La Fusée (*The Rocket*) was a 1958 stage play written by Roger **Gadeyne** and Adelin **Tilman** about a dozen couples who left Earth to colonize another planet. Another genre play was *Chroniques d'une Planète Provisoire* (*Chronicles of a Temporary Planet*, 1962), by Armand **Gatti**, in which Earth astronauts observed the evolution of an alien planet not unlike ours, but were unable to intervene to change the course of events.

In Henri **Gillet**'s *Le Voleur d'Instants* (*The Thief of Moments*, 1959), a scientist found a way to record and preserve the best moments of a man's life.

In *Les Grenouilles* (*The Frogs*, 1962), Belgian writer

Raymond **Duesberg** penned the description of a weird post-nuclear society.

In *Le Sud* (*The South*, 1962), Yves **Berger** depicted an alternate Virginia before the Civil War.

In 1967, Robert **Escarpit** (also see Chapter VIII) penned *Honorius, Pape* (*Pope Honorius*), a satirical novel in which Earth was reduced to a handful of islands inhabited by the descendants of a scientific congress.

Finally, the same year, Jean **Rignac** penned *Le Réveil des Titans* (*The Titans Awake*), an occult novel that mixed esoteric elements with science fiction concepts.

A genre which became increasingly popular in the late 1950s and throughout the 1960s was that of thrillers and espionage novels, many of which more than dabbled with science fiction themes.

In 1957, journalist and espionage author Georges **Langelaan** wrote his famous short story "La Mouche"("The Fly"), later reprinted in his remarkable collection, *Nouvelles de l'Anti-Monde* (*Stories of the Anti-World*, 1962). This well-known horror story was filmed twice, by Kurt Neumann in 1958, with Vincent Price; and by David Cronenberg in 1986. *Le Dauphin Parle Trop* (*The Dolphin Spoke Too Much*, 1964) and *Le Zombie Express* (*Zombi Express*, 1964) were espionage thrillers with science fiction elements. Another notable Langelaan work was *Le Vol de l'Anti-G* (*The Flight of the Anti-G*, 1967).

Another thriller writer, Henri Viard, used the pseudonym of "Henry **Ward**" to pen *Les Soleils Verts* (*The Green Suns*, 1956), in which a parallel universe intersected with ours, neutralizing all atom bombs and making the West and the East believe the other has found a new weapon. Ward's other genre novel was *L'Enfer est dans le Ciel* (*Hell Is in the Sky*, 1958).

Also in 1956, George-Marie **Bernanose** wrote *La Porte Interdite* (*The Forbidden Door*), a detective novel taking place in the future 1975, pitting a policeman against a mad scientist.

The Cold War and the ever-present threat of World War III were the themes of *La Troisième Guerre Mondiale Durera Six Heures* (*WWIII Will Last Six Hours*, 1950) by Hector **Ghilini**, and *La Guerre est pour Demain* (*War Is for Tomorrow*, 1956), in which Henry **Clérisse** detailed a hypothetical invasion of Europe by the Soviets. Marcel **Guichard** in *Feu Paris* (*Exit Paris*, 1958) also showed the destruction of the French capital.

Science fiction made further inroads in the espionage genre through specialized imprints such as *Espions de Demain* (*Tomorrow's Spies*) by Arabesque, which published ten genre novels in 1960, such as:

Michel **Rosel**'s *Trafic de Cerveaux* (*Brain Traffic*, 1960).

Franck **Erboy**'s *Mat aux Automates* (*The Automatons' Checkmate*, 1960).

Éric **Cartier**'s *Les Inhumains* (*The Inhumans*, 1960).

"Ex-Agent **SR 27**"'s *Ici, Base Spatiale 15* (*Here, Space Base 15*, 1960).

Mark **Banon** was the pseudonym used by the author(s?) of seventeen science-fiction espionage thrillers published in the early 1960s by the Presses Internationales (*Inter-Espions* and *Espionnage-Choc* imprints) and by A. Martel (*Le Crabe Espionnage* and *Start* imprints). The Banon novels included *Fusées sous le Pacifique* (*Rockets Under the Pacific*, 1962), *Trahison dans l'Espace* (*Betrayal in Space*, 1963) and *Les Surhommes* (*The Supermen*, 1964).

Another author of science fiction espionage was Luc **Barsac**, who wrote six genre thrillers for Arabesque's *Espionnage* imprint (1954), such as *Duel chez les Jaunes* (*Duel Among the Yellows*, 1958) and *Évadé de l'Espace* (*Escape in Space*, 1963).

Even popular spy heroes in the tradition of James Bond often engaged in science fictionesque adventures. Among the most notable were:

The most famous of all fiction super-spies was OSS 117, the hero of over a hundred thrillers written by Jean **Bruce**, and the subject of a series of films (see Book 1, Chapter I). After Bruce's death, his wife, Josette (née Przybyl), continued the series. A number of *OSS 117* novels featured genre elements, such as *Arizona Zone A* (1959), in which OSS 117 unmasked alien invaders, and *Magie Blanche pour OSS 117* (*White Magic for OSS 117*, 1969).

Coplan FX-18 by "Paul **Kenny**" (see above)—some of the Coplan stories, such as *Bataillon Fantôme* (*Ghostly Battalion*, 1959), featured genre elements. Coplan, too, was the subject of several films and television adaptations—see Book 1, chapters I and II.

Other notable super-spies included:

H by Bruno **Bax** (a dozen novels between 1956 and 1960).

Lecomte by "F.-H. Ribes" (**Richard-Bessière**).

Luc Ferran and Le Commander by G.-J. **Arnaud** (see below).

Mr. Suzuki by Jean-Pierre **Conty** including genre novels such as *Horizons Fantastiques pour Mr. Suzuki* (*Fantastic Horizons for Mr. Suzuki*, 1975), *Project Cyclope* (*Project Cyclops*, 1976) and *Dr. Suzuki et Mr. Hyde* (1978).

Bonder by André **Caroff** (see below).

Face d'Ange by Adam **Saint-Moore** (see below).

Marc Avril by Christopher **Stork** (see below).

Finally, in a completely different vein, the 1950s saw the novelization of the riotously funny radio serial *Signé Furax* by Pierre **Dac** and Francis **Blanche** (see Book 1, Chapter III), in which a colorful cast of characters fought an international crime cartel of bearded villains. Furax's

FRANCIS BLANCHE & PIERRE DAC

LE GRUYERE QUI TUE

roman

incredible adventures included travelling back in time to change history, and journeying through space on a flying atoll to the far-off planet Asterix. In 1968, Furax returned to the airwaves and the bookshelves one last time to defeat a horde of parasitic, alien invaders in *Le Gruyère qui Tue* (*The Gruyere That Kills*).

In the same vein, Robert **Beauvais'** *Quand Les Chinois...* (*When the Chinese...*, 1966), about a hypothetical Chinese invasion of France, was adapted into a comedy, ***Les Chinois à Paris***, a 1974 film by Jean Yanne (see Book 1, Chapter I).

e. Juveniles

Just after World War II, Pierre **Devaux** founded the young adult imprint *Sciences & Aventures* with publisher Magnard, which released twelve, Heinlein-like juvenile science fiction novels between 1946 and 1962, including detailed afterwords to provide the readers with scientific explanations of what was possible, and what was not. Another publisher, Mame, followed suit with *Succes Anticipation*, which published five volumes (among them were translations of some Heinlein juveniles) between 1955 and 1958.

Among the novels written and/or published by Devaux's in his imprint were *XP 15 en Feu!* (*XP15 on Fire!*, 1946) and its sequel, *L'Exilé de l'Espace* (*Exiled in Space*, 1947), both about the conquest of space. Devaux' writing partner, Henri-Georges **Viot**, penned *La Cité Fantastique* (*The Fantastic City*, 1947) and *Chronastro* (1953), a time travel story. Together, Devaux and Viot wrote *L'Écolier Invisible* (*The Invisible Schoolboy*, 1950), *La Minute Dérobée* (*The Purloined Minute*, 1952), a sequel to *Chronastro*, *La Conquête d'Almériade* (*The Conquest of Almeriade*, 1954), and *Explorations dans le Micro-monde* (*Explorations in the Microworld*, 1957).

In 1952, Belgian publisher Marabout launched a new young-adult imprint, entitled *Marabout Junior*, which released a steady flow of adventure novels, including some space operas, such as:

Jacques **Pierroux'** *Pilotes pour Demain* (*Pilots for Tomorrow*, 1956) and *Police Spatiale* (*Space Police*, 1961).

J.-J. **Mézière**'s *Satellite Lune* (*Moon Satellite*, 1955).

Paul **Vallène**'s *Aller-Simple pour l'Anadyr* (*One-Way Ticket for Anadyr*, 1964).

And several novels by Jimmy **Guieu**, writing under the pseudonym of "Claude Vauzière," such as *Traffic Interstellaire* (*Interstellar Trafic*, 1960) and *Échec aux Végans* (*The Vegans in Check*, 1962).

By far the most popular series of *Marabout Junior* adventures featured *Nick Jordan*, an espionage hero created by André **Fernez**, and whose adventures, such as *Virus H-84* (1960), occasionally contained genre elements; and *Bob Morane*, by Henri **Vernes**, which began in 1963 and has continued to this day, totalling a staggering 177 volumes!

In 1967, *Marabout Junior* changed its name to *Marabout Pocket*, and added several new adventure series: *Kim Carnot*, another spy hero by Jacques **Legray;** one of the Carnot novels, *Destination Espace* (*Destination Space*, 1967), featured plans to settle another planet; *Gil Terrail*, a daring investigator; *Jo Gaillard*, a sea captain; as well as translations of *Doc Savage* and a western series, *Dylan Stark*, by Pierre **Pelot** (see below). But throughout, the focus remained on *Bob Morane*, the undisputed star of the imprint.

One of the longest and most popular juvenile adventure series in the world, *Bob Morane* was also the subject of one television series (see Book 1, Chapter II) and an ongoing series of graphic novels (see Book 1, Chapter V). An animated series was released in 1999. The basic concept was pure adventure: Bob Morane, a retired Air Force major, and his friend, a tough, burly scotsman, Bill Ballantine, fought evil throughout the world, sometimes in space and even through time itself.

Bob Morane's colorful rogues' gallery included: (a) the diabolical Monsieur Ming, aka the "Yellow Shadow," A fiendish Oriental mastermind bent on universal domination, who appeared in Nos. 33, 35, 37, 38, 43, 50, 57, 63, 72, 75, 76, 87, 122, 135, 137, 144, 147, 148, and 157, plus the *Cycle du Temps* episodes listed below; (b) SMOG, an international spy cartel led by the beautiful but deadly Miss Ylang-Ylang and Roman Orgonetz, her ruthless henchman, a professional assassin with teeth of gold (Nos. 41, 45, 53, 71, 78, 83, 88, 96, 100, 107, 123, 155); (c) the mad Dr. Xhatan, master of light, who is served by an artificially created breed of green-skinned men (Nos. 79, 80, 106); (d) the humanoid Toadmen, descendents of an alien race stranded on our world long ago, secret masters of robotics (Nos. 86, 89, 129); and (e) the Tiger, an ordinary tramp whose intelligence was boosted with the memories of several brilliant scientists— and that of a deadly man-eating tiger (Nos. 124, 125, 145, 148, 149).

One sub-set of Bob Morane's adventures was *Le Cycle du Temps* (*The Time Saga*), which pitted Bob Morane and the Time Patrol (previously encountered in Nos. 20 and 69 of the series) against the Yellow Shadow, who was always trying to change the course of history to conquer the world (Nos. 90, 91, 92, 93, 99, 105, 115, 126, 139, 143, 149). Another notable sub-set series was *Le Cycle d'Ananké* (*The Ananke Saga*), in which Morane and Ballantine tried to escape from a nightmarish, other-dimensional world (Nos. 127, 130, 134, 141, 146).

Another popular young-adult series of the 1960s and 1970s was *Langelot*, published by publisher Hachette's long-standing, popular young-adult imprint, *Bibliothèque Verte* (*Green Library*). Written under the pseudonym of "Lieutenant X," But long attributed to renowned thriller author Vladimir **Volkoff** (see above), *Langelot* began in 1965 and, to date, number forty volumes, the last published in 1986. The series starred the eponymous young French secret agent, member of SNIF, a super-secret French intelligence department. Several of the novels pitted Langelot against megalomaniacal villains, such as Mister T, an obese and crippled mad scientist whose lair was a satellite orbiting the Earth (Nos. 6-8); the international spy cartel SPHINX (Nos. 12, 14, 15, 16, 19, 20, 31, 34); the BIDI, another spy ring led by an indomitable, evil granny (No. 3); the mysterious "Country 4584"; and the arch-traitor Cordovan. A spin-off series included two volumes about Corinne, a young SNIF agent and Langelot's occasional girlfriend.

Another popular genre series for young adults featured a group of fearless time travellers and was called *IST* (*Investigations Spatio-Temporelles*; *Spatio-Temporal Investigations*). It was written by Swiss author Jean-Claude **Froelich** for publisher Magnard, and was comprised of *Voyage au Pays de la Pierre Ancienne* (*Voyage to the Land of Old Stones*, 1962), *Naufrage dans le Temps* (*Castaways in Time*, 1965), *La Horde de Gor* (*The Horde of Gor*, 1969), *Le Masque du Taureau* (*The Mask of the Bull*, 1969), and *La Gaule Appelle IST* (*Gaul Is Calling IST*, 1971).

Other notable authors of juvenile science fiction published after World War II and during the 1950s and 1960s included:

Guy **Séverac**, with *Les Conquérants de l'Infini* (*The Conquerors of Infinity*, 1945).

Roger **Trubert**, with *L'Astre Rouge* (*The Red Star*, 1945).

Lucien **Prioly**, with *Nous Étions Sept Astronautes* (*We Were Seven Astronauts*, 1946), *L'Île des Hommes de Fer* (*The Island of the Iron Men*, 1948), and *Alerte aux Martiens* (*Martian Alert*, 1954).

André **Baruc**, with *Gobe-Lune* (*Moon Swallower*, 1948), *Contes de la Zérozième* (*Tales from the Zeroth Grade*, 1949), and *Les Pantins de Cristal* (*The Crystal Puppets*, 1957).

Fanny **Clar**, with *Dix-Sept et Un* (*17 and 1*, 1950), in which Earth, under pressure from underground gas, might explode.

Belgian writer Jean-Claude **Alain**, with *Demain il fera jour* (*Tomorrow the Sun Will Rise*, 1952), an H. G. Wells-inspired novel in which one race toiled underground while another one lived in the Golden City above.

Speleologist Norbert **Casteret**, with two novels about underground explorations conducted with a giant mole machine, *La Montagne Creuse* (*The Hollow Mountain*, 1962) and *Mission Centre Terre* (*Mission Center Earth*, 1964). Casteret also penned *Muta, Fille des Cavernes* (*Muta, Daughter of the Caverns*, 1965), a prehistoric novel.

In the same vein, Jean **Darrau** had previously written

À la Conquête du Mammouth (*The Conquest of the Mastodon*, 1947) about the discovery of the bones of a mastodon in a cave.

Georges **Duhamel**, with *Les Voyageurs de l'Espérance* (*The Voyagers of the Hope*, 1953), about the flight of men trying to escape Earth's destruction from "Z bombs."

Paul **Berna**, with a series of books about the conquest of the Moon, such as *Nous Irons à Lunaterra* (*We Shall Go to Lunaterra*, 1954), *La Porte des Étoiles* (*The Gate of Stars*, 1954), *Le Continent du Ciel* (*The Continent of the Sky*, 1955), and *Le Jardinier de la Lune* (*The Gardener of the Moon*, 1955).

Emil **Anton**, with *Les Robots du Mont Maudit* (*The Robots of the Accursed Mountain*, 1954) and *On se Bat sur la Lune* (*Battle on the Moon*, 1956).

Renowned science fiction scholar Jacques **Van Herp** used a variety of pseudonyms, such as "Michel Jansen," "André Jouly," And "Michel Goissert" To pen a number of young-adult novels, such as *Les Raiders de l'Espace* (*Space Raiders*, 1955; with Jean **Erland**) about a gang of space pirates, *La Porte sous les Eaux* (*The Gate Under the Sea*, 1960), based on a story by Jean Ray, and *Rona sur l'Amazone* (*Rona of the Amazon*, 1963), a novel about antigravity.

Pierre de **Sarcus**, with *La Ville Souterraine* (*The Underground City*, 1957).

Jacques **Chabar**, with *L'Étoile au Fond des Mers* (*The Star at the Bottom of the Sea*, 1958), in which a rocket travels undersea before going into space. Chabar also penned a fantasy-oriented novel, *La Cité du Serpent à Plumes* (*The City of the Feathered Serpent*, 1954).

Françoise d'**Eaubonne** (see above) teamed up with Jacques Bergier and L. **Jean-Charles** to pen a juvenile space opera describing the exploration of the asteroid Icarus, *Le Sous-Marin de l'Espace* (*The Space Submarine*, 1959).

Henriette **Robitaillie** (see Chapter VIII) penned two poetic science fiction novels, *Algue* (*Algae*, 1959) and *Les Sept Portes d'Ebène* (*The Seven Ebony Doors*, 1959).

André **Massepain** wrote several novels in which young heroes thwarted villainous plots involving marginal science fiction elements, such as *La Fusée Mystérieuse* (*The Mysterious Rocket*, 1959), *Une Affaire Atomique* (*An Atomic Affair*, 1961), and *Les Flibustiers de l'Uranium* (*The Uranium Pirates*, 1974). He also wrote two novels with prehistoric elements, *La Grotte aux Ours* (*The Bear Cave*, 1966) and *L'Île aux Fossiles Vivants* (*The Island of the Living Fossils*, 1967).

Christian **Pineau**, with

La Grotte aux Ours

La Planète aux Enfants Perdus (*The Planet of Lost Children*, 1960), which featured cosmonauts landing on Venus and finding an Eden-like world ruled by a good fairy and peopled with lost children and pets.

Christian **Fontugne** and Mary **Carey**, with the self-explanatory *Disparus dans l'Espace* (*Vanished in Space*, 1961). Another "Lost in Space" novel was *Le Chant des Abîmes* (*Songs of the Abyss*, 1962) by X. B. **Leprince** (see Chapter VIII), who also wrote *Dans le Sillage de l'Altaïr* (*In the Wake of the Altair*) (1970).

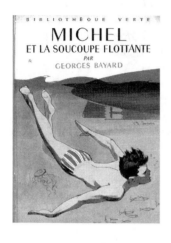

Georges **Bayard** with *Les Pionniers du Déluge* (*The Pioneers of the Flood*, 1961), in which a mad scientist threatened to drown the Earth in a new flood. Bayard was also the author of the series *Michel*, about the adventures of a clever and spunky teenager (over 20 volumes published by *Bibliothèque Verte* from 1958 to 1980). Two Michel adventures contained marginal genre elements: *Michel et la Soucoupe Flottante* (*Michel and the Floating Saucer*, 1963) and *Michel et les Maléfices* (*Michel and the Evil Spells*, 1979).

In the same vein, Paul-Jacques **Bonzon** wrote a dozen, popular juvenile novels in the 1960s and 1970s, featuring *Les Six Compagnons* (*The Six Companions*), a group of teenagers from Lyon who solved crimes and fought a variety of evil-doers. *Les Six Compagnons et L'Homme des Neiges* (*The Six Companions and the Yeti*) and *Les Six Compagnons et la Pile Atomique* (*The Six Companions and the Nuclear Pile*) contained marginal genre elements.

Marie-Louise **Vert** took her readers across a cosmic tour of various planets in *Le Bal des Étoiles* (*Ballroom of the Stars*, 1962), and entertained younger children with *Un Grillon dans la Lune* (*A Cricket on the Moon*, 1973).

Suzanne **Pulicani**'s *Monsieur Touminou Cosmonaute* (*Mr. Pussycat Cosmonaut*, 1964) was also a charming space adventure for young children.

Claude **Cénac**, with several, excellent genre novels, such as *La Planète Bonheur* (*Planet Happiness*, 1963), *La Citadelle de l'Espoir* (*The Citadel of Hope*, 1964), *Le Robot Sauvage* (*The Savage Robot*, 1966) and *Des Milliards de Soleils* (*Billions of Suns*, 1971).

Jean-Luc **Beno**, with *1990, ou Les Moins de 15 Ans à l'Assaut du Cosmos* (*1990, or the Under-15s at the Assault of the Cosmos*, 1963), illustrated by Jean-Claude **Forest** (see Book 1, Chapter IV).

A minor classic was René **Guillot**'s *La Planète Ignorée* (*The Unknown Planet*, 1963), in which a student came in contact with humanoid aliens who lived hidden among us, and came from a dying counter-Earth-type planet located on the other side of the Sun. A genre children's book by Guillot (see Chapter VIII) was *Un Petit Chien va dans la Lune* (*A Little Dog Goes to the Moon*, 1970).

Another remarkable young-adult novel was Henry **Thilliez**'s *La Planète sans Rivage* (*Planet Without Shores*, 1964), in which explorers of Venus discovered an underground civilization.

Marcelle **Manceau**, with a prehistoric novel, *Le Talisman du Soleil* (*The Talisman of the Sun*, 1966).

Maurice **Vauthier** with *La Planète Kalgar* (*The Planet Kalgar*, 1966), in which two races fought on an alien planet in the 24th century. Vauthier had also written *La Terrible Bombe X* (*The Dreaded X Bomb*, 1964).

2. The 1970s

The 1970s was a decade of expansion for French science fiction.

The famous events of May 1968 shook French political and cultural life, and their consequences were naturally felt in the field of science fiction. French science fiction became increasingly political, leaning toward the radical left, bringing together a variety of causes such as opposition to the Vietnam war, nuclear power, industrial polution, capitalism, and imperialism into a style that became known as "New Science Fiction." The translations of "new wave" American and British authors including Harlan Ellison, Norman Spinrad, etc., 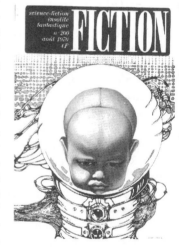 as well as the emergence of younger, radical French authors of "new science fiction" In the pages of *Fiction*, such as Jean-Pierre **Andrevon**, provoked irate letters from older readers.

As a new generation came of age, science fiction exploded commercially, and a plethora of new imprints were started all throughout the 1970s, reaching a peak in 1977, when virtually every French publisher had at least one genre imprint, if not more, creating a boom that lasted until the early 1980s. And as fans turned pro, these imprints were edited by new talent as well.

a. The Publishers

The major publishing event of the decade was the creation in 1969 of the *Ailleurs & Demain* (*Elsewhere & Tomorrow*) imprint by Gérard **Klein** at publisher Robert

Laffont. This silver-foiled, trade paperback line published some of the best American works of the period (including Frank Herbert's *Dune*), as well as providing a forum for French authors such as Michel Jeury, Philippe Curval, and André Ruellan. Klein also edited the short-lived juvenile imprint, *L'Âge des Étoiles* (*The Age of the Stars*, 1977-79), *Ailleurs & Demain Classiques* (*Elsewhere & Tomorrow Classics*, 1970-), a reprint imprint, and a short-lived series of essays.

Denoël's *Présence du Futur* (*Presence of the Future*) also began to publish newer French writers, including Jean-Pierre Andrevon, Philip **Goy**, and Philippe Curval. In 1976, editor Robert Kanters was replaced by Elisabeth Gille, who continued and expanded her roster with names like Daniel Walther, Pierre Pelot, Patrice **Duvic**, Serge **Brussolo**, and Emmanuel **Jouanne** (see next section).

Fleuve Noir's monolithic *Anticipation* started attracting some new blood in 1968 with Louis **Thirion**, then in 1970 came Robert **Clauzel**, in 1971 Andrevon (under a pseudonym) and G.-J. **Arnaud**, in 1972 Pierre **Pelot** (also under a pseudonym), and in 1976 Julia Verlanger (also under a pseudonym). The previously independent Fleuve Noir was taken over by the giant publishing group, Presses de la Cité, in 1966 and increased its number of releases from two to six titles a month! In 1974, control of the editorship passed into the hands of Patrick Siry, who also supervised a reprint program of older titles.

Two imprints started during the decade, concentrated on publishing French authors:

Nebula, launched in 1975 by OPTA and edited by Alain Dorémieux, alternated between American/British and French "new science fiction" authors and published the first novels of Dominique **Douay**, Joël **Houssin**, and Jean-Pierre **Hubert**. It was cancelled in 1977.

Alerte! n°2

Ici & Maintenant (*Here & Now*), launched in 1977 by Swiss publisher Kesselring and edited by Bernard **Blanc**, published radical political "new science fiction" titles by Yves **Frémion** and Maxime **Benoit-Jeannin**. It also published the magazine *Alerte,* edited by Blanc.

Other genre imprints (for obvious reasons, many simply called "Science-Fiction"—note the hyphen in French) created during this prolific decade included:

Science-Fiction, launched in 1970 by J'ai Lu, and edited by Jacques Sadoul, became one of the most important paperback lines of the decade, making science fiction classics accessible to a large public. During the 1970s, J'ai Lu published a few selected French authors—

Michel Jeury, Dominique Douay, and Pierre Pelot—and concentrated mostly on classic American science fiction. It also put out a quarterly magazine, *Univers*, started in 1975, and edited by Yves **Frémion**.

Science-Fiction, launched in 1969 by Marabout, and edited by Jean-Baptiste **Baronian**, published mostly reprints, but also put out some new titles by Jean-Pierre Fontana (as "Guy Scovel"), Daniel **Walther**, Bernard **Villaret**, and Landry **Merillac**, and two noted French anthologies edited by Henry-Luc **Planchat**.

Science-Fiction, launched tentatively in 1968 by Albin Michel, and relaunched in 1972, was a line of silver-foiled paperbacks edited by George Gallet and Jacques Bergier. A separate line of trade paperbacks was added in 1977 under the name *Super+Fiction*. It published mostly classic American authors, with a few French reprints and some new works by Nathalie Henneberg and Pierre Barbet (under a pseudonym).

Anti-Mondes (*Anti-Worlds*), launched in 1972 by OPTA and edited by Michel Demuth, published mostly contemporary American science fiction. It was cancelled in 1977.

Dimensions, launched in 1973 by Calmann-Levy, and edited by Robert Louit, published mostly contemporary American and British authors, plus a few French writers such as Dominique Douay and Philippe Curval.

Le Masque Science-Fiction, launched in 1974 by Librairie des Champs-Élysées, and edited successively by Jacques Van Herp and Michel Demuth, published mostly works by classic American and French authors, such as Nathalie Henneberg and Yves Dermèze.

Science-Fiction, launched in 1974 by Livre de Poche/Hachette, and edited by Michel Demuth and Gérard Klein, published mostly reprints of classic genre novels, with no French authors.

Science-Fiction, launched in 1977 by Presses Pocket, and edited by Jacques Goimard, also published mostly reprints of classic genre novels, but added some new French works by Michel Jeury, Pierre Pelot, Vladimir Volkoff, and Philippe Curval.

Other significant imprints included:

Autres Temps, Autres Mondes (*Other Times, Other Worlds*, 1966-1983), by Casterman, a series of hardcover anthologies edited by Alain Dorémieux.

Science-Fiction (1972-77) followed by *Titres SF* (*Titles SF*, 1979-83), by J.-C. Lattès, the latter edited by Marianne **Leconte**.

Champ Libre (*Open Field*, 1974-78), by Chute Libre.

Futurama (1974-82), by Presses de la Cité, edited by J.-P. Manchette & J.-P.Bouyxou.

Constellation (1975-77), by Seghers, edited by Gérard Klein.

Marginalia (1975-79), by comic-book publisher Jacques Glénat, followed by *Train d'Enfer—SF* (*Hell Train SF*, 1980).

Autrepart (*Otherwhere*, 1977), by Presses de la Renaissance.

Bibliothèque des Utopies (*Utopia Library*, 1977-78), by Adel-Balland, edited by Pierre Versins.

Bibliothèque Aérienne (*Aerial Library*, 1977-78) and *Horizons Illimités* (*Unlimited Horizons*, 1977), by comic-book publisher Les Humanoïdes Associés.

Changez de Fiction (*Change Fiction*, 1977-78), by Le Dernier Terrain Vague, edited by Lionel Hoebke.

Travelling sur le Futur (*Traveling on the Future*, 1977-81), by Duculot.

Écrits Possibles (*Possible Writings*, 1978-80) and *Espaces Mondes* (*Space Worlds*, 1979-80), by Ponte Mirone.

L'Utopie Tout de Suite (*Utopia Right Now*, 1979-80), by Encre, edited by Bernard Blanc.

Mémoires d'Outre-Ciel (*Memoirs from Beyond the Sky*, 1979-82), by Garry.

Fantastique/Science Fiction (1979-88) by Nouvelles Éditions Oswald.

S.F. (1980-81) by Fernand Nathan.

On the magazine front, in addition to *Fiction* and *Galaxie* (which was cancelled in 1977), OPTA launched *Marginal* (1973-77). Editors included Alain Dorémieux until 1974, Michel Demuth, then Daniel Riche from 1977 to 1980.

Horizons du Fantastique (*Horizons of the Fantastic*) was published between 1967-76, co-created by Alain Schlockoff, edited by Dominique Besse & Louis Guillon, and covered science fiction, fantasy, and esoterism in books, films, and comics. Its contribution included Joëlle **Wintrebert**.

Other notable but short-lived magazines included *Imagine* (1975), *Mouvance* (1977), *SF Magazine* (1976-77), a translation of the British *SF Monthly*, and two versions of *Futurs* (1978).

b. Major Authors

The first of the French "new wave" writers was Jean-Pierre **Andrevon**, whose career began in the pages of *Fiction*, coincidentally in the May 1968 issue, and heralded the French "new wave" of the 1970s. Andrevon was then at the forefront of an informal movement of left-wing political science fiction authors whose themes included socialist ideology, ecology, anti-nuclear power, and anti-militaristic concepts. His first novels were published by *Présence du Futur*. These included the delightful science fantasy *Les Hommes-Machines contre Gandahar* (*The Machine Men vs. Ganda-*

har, 1969; see Chapter VIII), then four collections of political short stories, *Aujourd'hui, Demain et Après* (*Today, Tomorrow and After*, 1970), *Cela Se Produira Bientôt* (*It Will Happen Soon*, 1971), *Repères dans l'Infini* (*Markings in Infinity*, 1975), and *Dans les Décors Truqués* (*Inside the Phony Backgrounds*, 1979), and novels like *Le Temps des Grandes Chasses* (*The Time of the Great Hunts*, 1973) and the remarkable *Le Désert du Monde* (*The Desert of the World*, 1977), an evocative tale of the last days of man on Earth. Also at *Présence du Futur*, Andrevon launched and edited a three-volume series of ecological science fiction anthologies, *Retour à la Terre* (*Back to the Earth*, 1974, 1975, 1977).

Simultaneously, from 1971 to 1975, Andrevon took the pseudonym "Alphonse **Brutsche**" to pen three non-political space operas for Fleuve Noir's *Anticipation* imprint and four horror novels for *Angoisse* (see Chapter VIII). Paradoxically, some of these were among his best works of the period. *La Guerre des Gruulls* (*The War Against the Gruulls*, 1971) featured a space war between Earth and the alien Gruulls which was the result of a misunderstanding. In *Le Dieu de Lumière* (*The God of Light*, 1973), a star probe discovered an Earth-like world in the Orion system. In 1984, Andrevon returned to Fleuve Noir, having abandoned the

"Brutsche" pseudonym, and contributed four more science fiction novels, plus three horror novels (see Chapter VIII). *Soupçons sur Hydra* (*Suspicions Over Hydra*, 1984) and *Le Premier Hybride* (*The First Hybrid*, 1985) dealt with a colonial conflict between Earthmen and the native inhabitants of Hydra. Previous "Brutsche" Works were revised by Andrevon and reissued under his own name.

During the 1980s, Andrevon continued to produce novels and short story collections that were still imbued with his political slant, but with less dogmatism than before and featuring greater emotional nuances and richer characters. Among these were *Neutron* (1981), *Il Faudra Bien Se Résoudre à Mourir Seul* (*We Must Accept to Die Alone*, 1983), *C'est Arrivé mais on n'en a rien su* (*It Happened But We Never Found Out*, 1984), and *Sukran* (1989) for *Présence du Futur*. The last described a Europe where the sea level was rising and an anti-Islamic crusade was raging. At J'ai Lu, Andrevon published *Cauchemar... Cauchemars!* (*Nightmare... Nightmares!*, 1982), the tale of an identity search, and *Le Travail du Furet à l'Intérieur du Poulailler* (*The Weasel's Work Inside the Chicken Coop*, 1983) for J'ai Lu. The latter described a *Logan's Run*-like world where the government used hired killers nicknamed "weasels" to "retire" people whose economic usefulness was at an end. This moving love story between such a "weasel" and his intended victim was adapted into an eponymous 1994 television movie—see Book 1, Chapter II. *La Trace des Rêves* (*The Trace of Dreams*, 1988), also written for J'ai Lu, described a pseudo-fantasy world in which the human survivors of a nuclear conflict had been reduced to five inches in height in order to survive and eventually reclaim Earth.

Through the 1980s and 1990s, Andrevon diversified his career further, producing crime thrillers, adventure novels,

and juvenile novels, as well as horror, fantasy, and science fiction. Among his best juveniles were the earlier fantasy, *La Fée et le Géomètre* (*The Fairy and the Surveyor*, 1981), contrasting the fairy people and the modern, materialistic world; *Le Grand Combat Nucléaire de Tarzan* (*Tarzan's Great Nuclear Fight*, 1986), *Le Chevalier, l'Autobus et la Licorne* (*The Knight, the Bus and the Unicorn*, 1987), *La Bête sur le Parking* (*The Beast on the Parking Lot*, 1997) and *Gandahar et l'Oiseau-Monde* (*Gandahar and the World-Bird*, 1997), for Denis **Guiot**'s new *Vertige* imprint (see below).

Michel **Jeury** burst upon the French science fiction scene with the Philip K. Dick-inspired *Le Temps Incertain* (*The Uncertain Time*, 1973), published in *Ailleurs & Demain*. Jeury had previously written two space operas for the *Rayon Fantastique* under the pseudonym of "Albert **Higon**" (see above). It was his *Ailleurs & Demain* novels, such as *Le Temps Incertain* and *Les Singes du Temps* (*The Time Monkeys*, 1974), which both took place in the same universe, that made him one of the most important writers of the 1970s. Both novels dealt with time and its manipulation through the use of "chronolytic" drugs. Their protagonists were "psychronauts," helpless explorers of a confusing, multidimensional universe, facing threats from alternate realities, such as Harry Krupp Hitler 1st, Emperor of the Undetermined, or the mysterious "Phords" from the future world of Garichankar. The psychronauts always searched for, and often found, secret paradises, such as the tropical realm of the Divers of Ruaba, hidden within the folds of space and

time. In *Soleil Chaud, Poisson des Profondeurs* (*Warm Sun, Fish from the Deep*, 1976), Jeury returned to the same jumble of alternate realities. This time, the novel took place in 2039, when the world was torn between two warring megacorporations and their rival computer systems, which permeated every facet of reality. Meanwhile, psychiatric patients escaped through fugues that seemed to carry them either to a peaceful tropical island, or to the serenity of an underwater world.

Throughout the 1970s and 1980s, Jeury continued to produce a number of remarkably original novels for *Ailleurs & Demain*, always of the highest literary quality. While he was certainly representative of a certain style of French science fiction popular in the 1970s and 1980s, he was nevertheless not a part of the political "new science fiction" movement. *Le Territoire Humain* (*The Human Territory*, 1979) featured yet another oasis of humanity existing on the borders of a dehumanized megastate. *Les Yeux Géants* (*The Giant Eyes*, 1980) theorized that modern-day UFOs were projections of mankind's collective unconscious in the late 20th century, and imagined what the next century's manifestations would be like. The remarkable *L'Orbe et la Roue* (*The Orb and the Wheel*, 1982) featured a twenty thousand-year-old rebel brought back to life in a far future, when the entire solar system had become a giant Dyson's Sphere, controlled by the rival powers of the Orb (its Lords) and the Wheel (its cosmic engineers). Finally, *Le Jeu du Monde* (*The World Game*, 1985) returned to the universe of the first three volumes, featuring an Earth which had become a giant gaming arena, and a conflict between two organizations, one representing chance, the other the eponymous World-Game. Its hero eventually found refuge on space islands orbiting the planet.

Throughout the 1970s, the prolific Jeury also managed to write genre novels for virtually every other publisher. He resurrected the pseudonym of "Albert Higon" for J'ai Lu, for which he wrote *Les Animaux de Justice* (*The Justice Animals*, 1976), about aliens who used humans to tell right from wrong, and *Le Jour des Voies* (*The Day of the Ways*,

1977), about a false prophet whose predictions of a new and better universe surprisingly come true. He returned to J'ai Lu in 1986 to pen *La Croix et la Lionne* (*The Cross and the She-Lion*, 1986), about the adventures of an Earthwoman on an alien world inhabited by a race of Lion-people. During this period, Jeury also contributed two juvenile genre novels, *Le Sablier Vert* (*The Green Hourglass*, 1977) and *Le Monde du Lignus* (*The World of the Lignus*, 1978), to Gérard Klein's short-lived juve-

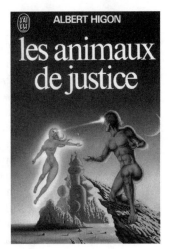

nile imprint, *L'Âge des Étoiles*; one political genre novel, *Poney-Dragon* (1978) for *Ici & Maintenant*; and two more elaborate Dickian novels, *L'Univers-Ombre* (*The Shadow Universe*, 1979) and *Les Enfants de Mord* (*The Children of Mord*, 1979), the latter for Presses-Pocket.

In 1979, Michel Jeury became a regular contributor to Fleuve Noir's *Anticipation* imprint, for which he wrote a total of nineteen novels between 1980 and 1992. The first, *Les Îles de la Lune* (*The Islands of the Moon*, 1979), started an interconnected series of books (Nos. 945, 992, 1003, 1034, 1062, 1091, 1979-81) that developed elements that had already been hinted at in the *Ailleurs & Demain* works, progressively building the notion of a "Jeury Universe" that included "chronolysis," space islands and history being manipulated by the "geoprogrammers." Other series included the future history of the Hebrew-like Goer race, a saga that began with *La Planète du Jugement* (*The Planet of Judgment*; No. 1133, 1982) and continued in Nos. 1181, 1260, 1394 (1982-85); and *Le Dernier Paradis* (*The Last Paradise*; Nos. 1365, 1376, 1985), about the survivors of Paradise 5, the last city of men on Earth after the planet was abandoned. Other notable *Anticipation* titles included *Les Tours Divines* (*The Divine Towers*, 1983), *L'Anaphase du Diable* (*The Devil's Anaphase*, 1984), and *Aux Yeux la Lune* (*The Eyes of the Moon*, 1988; originally intended for *Ailleurs & Demain*).

In parallel with his production for *Anticipation*, Jeury developed the saga of the *Colmateurs* (*The Pluggers*) for Presses-Pocket, starting in 1981 with *Cette Terre* (*That Earth*) and continuing with *Le Vol du Serpent* (*The Flight of the Serpent*, 1982) and *Les Démons de Jerusalem* (*The Demons of Jerusalem*, 1985). This ambitious trilogy told the story of a pandimensional corps of monitors set up by the mysterious "geoprogrammers" to "plug" holes between alternate Earths. Their enemies were the equally mysterious "Brownians" who attempted to open such holes and facilitate interworld travel. The *Colmateurs* series was ar-

guably Jeury's masterpiece, combining strong, dramatic characters, tightly-paced narration, cutting-edge science, and epic conflicts on a truly mind-boggling scope. Unfortunately, the series was left unfinished when, in the late 1980s, Jeury turned to writing a stream of mainstream best-selling novels about life in his native southwestern France at the turn of the century. In order to keep his two literary careers separate, Jeury then reused the "Albert Higon" pseudonym when Fleuve Noir published his last two genre novels, *La Chimère Infernale* (*The Infernal Chimera*) and *Le Vaisseau-Démon* (*The Demon-Ship*), in 1992. Jeury recently returned to writing science fiction, penning a 1998 juvenile novel with his daughter, Dany, for Denis Guiot's *Vertige* imprint (see below).

Like Michel Jeury, Philippe **Curval** first published two space operas for the *Rayon Fantastique* in the 1960s (see above). He then contributed another, *Les Sables de Falun* (*The Sands of Falun*), to *Fiction* in 1970. Simultaneously, he published two literary works, *La Forteresse de Coton* (*The Fortress of Cotton*, 1967) and a collection of short stories, *Attention, Les Yeux* (*Watch Out for the Eyes*, 1973). His first new style novel was *L'Homme à Rebours* (*The Backwards Man*, 1974), published by *Ailleurs & Demain*, a complex work on the theme of parallel universes, and the ability to choose one's reality. *Cette Chère Humanité* (*That Dear Mankind*, 1976), also published by *Ailleurs & Demain*, became an instant classic. It took place in a near-future Europe dubbed "Marcom" (Common Market), closed off from the rest of the planet. An oniromancer from the Marcom sent a mysterious SOS toward the "Payvoides" (Developing Countries), who then sent an agent to investigate. What he found was a strange dystopia where space and time have been dilated by the experiments of a mad genius. Another Marcom novel, which dealt with time travel, was *En Souvenir du Futur* (*In Remembrance of the Future*, 1983), also published by *Ailleurs & Demain*.

Curval's novels were poignant, often bitterly dark, character-driven social satires. *Le Dormeur s'éveillera-t-il?* (*Will the Sleeper Awaken*, 1979), published by *Présence du Futur*, was another major work presenting a mutating world that had fallen apart, where new myths were possibly tools implanted by the old masters to prepare their reconquest. In many of Curval's novels, space and time seemed to obey biological rather than physical laws. In the old-fashioned, satirical space opera, *Rut aux Étoiles* (*Rutting Stars*, 1979), hyperspace was portrayed like an artery crossing the body of the galaxy. Alternate universes

interpenetrated like living amoebas in *Un Soupçon de Néant* (*A Touch of Nothingness*, 1977), which took place in the "Solar Social System" and featured a protagonist who had acquired the power to materialize beings created by his own subconscious; and *Y-a-quelqu'un?* (*Anyone There?*, 1979), where a man searched for his girlfriend, the victim of the merging of parallel Earths. Aliens lived on separate mental planes in *La Face Cachée du Désir* (*The Hidden Face of Desire*, 1980), where ethnological communication between Earthmen and the blue-furred Chulies who inhabited the strategically important hyperspatial world of Standard is all but impossible. The same feeling of true alienness pervaded *L'Odeur de la Bête* (*The Scent of the Beast*, 1981), in which a Russian investigator attempted to discover the connection between two decadent races of natives on a Russian space colony.

Curval also edited two remarkable anthologies of new French authors for *Présence du Futur*, *Futurs au Présent* (*Present-Day Futures*, 1978) and *Superfuturs* (*Superfutures*, 1986), in which he "discovered" most of the major names of the 1980s and 1990s, including **Brussolo**, and **Ligny**. *Présence du Futur* also gathered Curval's short stories in a number of collections, such as *Regarde, Fiston, s'il n'y a pas un Extra-Terrestre Derrière la Bouteille de Vin* (*Sonny, Look and See If There Isn't an E.T. Behind the Wine Bottle*, 1980), *Debout les Morts, le Train Fantôme Entre en Gare* (*Get Up, Dead Men, the Ghost Train Is Entering the Station!*, 1984), *Comment Jouer à l'Homme Invisible en Trois Leçons* (*How to Play Invisible Man in Three Lessons*, 1986), and *Habite-t-on Réellement Quelque Part?* (*Do We Really Live Anywhere?*, 1989). Like Jeury, Curval shifted toward mainstream literature in the 1990s.

Pierre **Pelot** was already a prolific author of young-adult novels, including the popular *Dylan Stark* western series for *Marabout Pocket* and two genre novels, *Les Étoiles Ensevelies* (*The Buried Stars*, 1972) and *Une Autre Terre* (*Another Earth*, 1972), when he began publishing a series of remarkably mature space operas for Fleuve Noir's *Anticipation* (and modern horror thrillers for *Angoisse* as well—see Chapter VIII) under the pseudonym of "Pierre **Suragne**." Between 1972 and 1980, Pelot contributed fourteen science fiction novels and seven horror novels to Fleuve Noir. His *Anticipation* novels were notable for their bleak endings, which was unusual at the time, as well as for their new concepts, often incorporating post-1968 political ideas. They were written in a hard-hitting style borrowed from

thrillers rather than from space opera, and included occasional sexual scenes. *La Septième Saison* (*The Seventh Season*, 1972) saw man fail to master another world after having hopelessly polluted Earth. *Mal Iergo le Dernier* (*Mal Iergo the Last*; as *Pierre Suragne*, 1972) was the story of a doomed quest. The poetic *L'Enfant Qui Marchait sur le Ciel* (*The Child Who Walked on the Sky*, 1972) featured a child trying to escape from a closed world. *Et puis les Loups Viendront* (*And Then the Wolves Will Come*; as *Pierre Suragne*, 1973) was a violent *Mad Max*-like tale. *Ballade pour Presqu'un Homme* (*Ballad for Almost a Man*, 1974) was another tale of Man having reverted to savagery. The best "Suragne" novel was *Mais si les Papillons Trichent?* (*But What If the Butterflies Cheat?*, 1974), in which mental illnesses in a dystopic future were revealed to be the manifestation of the psychosis of the creator of that universe. Later novels, such as *Virgules Téléguidées* (*Remote-Controlled Commas*, 1980) and *Dérapages* (*Out of Control*, 1980) were increasingly political in tone.

Starting in 1977, and throughout the 1980s, Pelot produced a huge number of novels for virtually every genre publisher. Most, if not all, carried the same message, vilifying the evils of the modern, capitalistic, military-industrial world. They all described dystopic police states cohabiting with either savage no man's lands or peaceful utopias, and featured doomed rebels who tried to see beyond the veil of their protected lives.

For *Ailleurs & Demain*, Pelot penned *Transit* (1977), one of his most accomplished novels, which returned to the concepts of *Mais si les Papillons Trichent?* In it, an experimental hypnotic journey led a researcher to a peaceful utopia. For *Ici & Maintenant*, Pelot wrote *Le Sommeil du Chien* (*The Sleep of the Dog*, 1978), an ecological novel. For *Dimensions*, he wrote *Les Pieds dans la Tête* (*The Feet in the Head*, 1982), where the technology of "Bifurcated Paradoxal Sleep" enabled the government to beam dreams directly into the brain.

For J'ai Lu, Pelot wrote six novels between 1977 and 1983, including *Les Barreaux de l'Éden* (*The Bars of Eden*, 1977), about a religious dystopia; and *Delirium Circus* (1977), about a future actor who rebelled against his simulacrum existence. Other notable dystopias were depicted in *Parabellum Tango* (1980), *Kid Jesus* (1981), and *La Foudre au Ralenti* (*The Slow-Motion Lightning*, 1983).

For *Présence du Futur*, Pelot wrote four novels between 1977 and 1982, including *Foetus-Party* (1977), de-

picting a euthanasia-based world ruled by the "Holy Management"; *Canyon Street* (1978), about a planet-wide city; *La Guerre Olympique* (*The Olympic War*, 1980) where future sports were used as an alternative to war; and *Mourir au Hasard* (*To Die Randomly*, 1982), depicting a world where everyone's death is programmed from birth.

Pelot's major stream of dystopic novels during the 1980s were produced for *Presses-Pocket*, for which he wrote twelve novels between 1977 and 1990, starting with *Le Sourire des Crabes* (*The Smile of the Crabs*, 1977). Most of these fit in a series entitled *Les Hommes sans Futurs* (*Men Without a Future*), which began with *Les Mangeurs d'Argile* (*The Clay Eaters*; No. 5126, 1981). Other episodes were Nos. 5135, 5157, 5173, 5190, 5209. These portrayed the desperate and often all too futile wanderings of the last men and women on an Earth now inhabited by unfathomable new mutants. Other notable Pelot novels included *La Rage dans le Troupeau* (*The Rage in the Flock*, 1979), *Le Ciel Bleu d'Irockee* (*The Blue Sky of Irockee*, 1980) and *Les Îles du Vacarme* (*The Islands of Clamor*, 1981).

In 1985, Pelot returned to Fleuve Noir's *Anticipation*, for which he created another eighteen science fiction novels (and several horror ones—see Chapter VIII) until 1991. Some of these were regrouped in series, such as *Chromagnon Z* (Nos. 1355, 1369, 1426, 1469, 1985-86), about a future ruled by merciless multinational corporations; *Tony Burden* (Nos. 1482, 1495, 1553, 1565, 1580, 1986-87), about a future war veteran who carried a psychic virus; *Les Raconteurs de Nulle Part* (*The Story Tellers from Nowhere*; FNAs 1732, 1737, 1743, 1750, 1990); and finally, a *Conan* parody, *Konnar* (Nos. 1788, 1796, 1802, 1811, 1831, 1990-91). In the 1990s, Pelot, like Andrevon, diversified his career further, producing crime thrillers, adventure novels, and a few more science fiction works, such as the recent *Messager des Tempêtes Lointaines* (*Messenger of the Far Storms*, 1996) for *Présence du Futur*.

The first author to herald a change at Fleuve Noir's *Anticipation* was not Pelot, however, but Louis **Thirion**, who had previously written the surreal *La Résidence de Psycartown* (*The Psycartown Residence*) for Losfeld in 1968. For *Anticipation*, Thirion wrote a total of twenty-one literary space operas, starting with *Les Stols* (No. 354, 1968) and concluding with *Requiem pour une Idole de Cristal* (*Requiem for a Crystal Idol*, 1991). Several of these starred a semi-existentialist spaceman, Commodore Jord Maogan

(Nos 354, 377, 393, 427, 456, 543, 1968-73). Maogan's role in these colorful, poetic novels was often that of a mediator between mankind and alien lifeforms, like the Stols, the ancient empire of Antephaes (No. 377), or the powerful Ysee-A (No. 427), herself pursued by the even more indescribably powerful Glorvd. Another series featured the temporal adventures of *Gern Enez Sanders* (FNAs 1348, 1442, 1455, 1509, 1644, 1673, 1985-89). One of these novels, *Que l'Eternité Soit avec Vous!* (*May Eternity Be with You!*; No.1442, 1986) was a Sherlock Holmes pastiche.

Thirion also wrote a number of radio scripts for **Le Théâtre de l'Étrange** (*Theater of the Weird*; see Book 1, Chapter III).

Other authors signalled a change at Fleuve Noir's *Anticipation* during the early 1970s included:

Georges-Jean **Arnaud** made his first appearance in *Anticipation* in 1971 with *Les Croisés de Mara* (*The Crusaders of Mara*), the first volume of a trilogy comprised of Nos. 469, 509, and 538 (1971-72), and entitled *Chroniques de la Longue Séparation* (*Chronicles of the Long Separation*), in which a group of characters from the lost human colony of Mara, which had reverted to feudalism, rediscovered its origins and embarked on a quest through space to find Earth. Arnaud was a prolific writer, the au-

thor of well over three hundred novels in different genres, including espionage thrillers, detective fiction, science fiction, horror, erotic fiction and mainstream literature. His espionage fiction incuded two series: *Luc Ferran*, with sixteen novels written under the pseudonym of "Gil Darcy" for publisher L'Arabesque from 1963 to 1969; and *Le Commander* for Fleuve Noir's *Espionnage*, with about thirty novels written between 1967 and 1980. Arnaud also wrote non-series espionage novels under the pseudonyms of "Saint-Gilles" And "Georges Murey" for Ferenczi (1958-60) and L'Arabesque (1957-65), and another fifty-odd novels under his own name for Fleuve Noir's *Espionnage* imprint (1961-86). Some of these thrillers featured James Bond-like science fiction elements. Eight *Commander* novels were adapted into digest-sized graphic novels (see Book 1, Chapter V under *Fleuve Noir*). **Arnaud** also wrote horror novels and thrillers (see Chapter VIII). He made his lasting mark in science fiction in the 1980s with his series *La Compagnie des Glaces* (*The Ice Company*), which is reviewed in our next section.

Yann Menez wrote six novels for *Anticipation* between 1974 and 1980, all remarkable for their well-constructed plots that eventually culminated in clever climaxes, such as *Un Monde de Héros* (*A World of Heroes*, 1975), in which androids were implanted with the personalities of great artists of the past; *Appelez-moi Dieu* (*Call Me God*, 1976), a complex futuristic battle between good and evil involving scientific astrology, religion, messianic power, reincarnation, and time travel; and *Demandez le Programme* (*Ask for the Program*, 1980), in which gifted children hacked into computers.

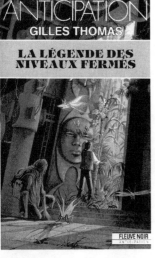

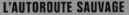

Julia **Verlanger**, also known for her works in the *fantastique* (see Chapter VIII), used the pseudonym of "Gilles Thomas" to pen over a dozen of science fiction and heroic-fantasy novels for Fleuve Noir's *Anticipation* between 1976 and 1980. Notable science fiction titles included *L'Autoroute Sauvage* (*The Savage Highway*), a trilogy that followed the adventures of a young survivor in a post-cataclysmic France (Nos. 742, 772, 910, 1976-79); *Les Voies d'Almagiel* (*The Ways of Almagiel*, 1978), the fascinating study of an alien society divided between masters and slaves; *La Légende des Niveaux Fermés* (*The Legend of the Closed Levels*, 1978); *L'Ange aux Ailes de Lumière* (*The Angel with Wings of Light*, 1978), about the colorful planet Malvie; and *Horlemonde* (*Worldbeyond*, 1980), the description of a deadly space penitentiary.

At OPTA, under the editorship of Alain Dorémieux, "new science fiction" authors were given room to express themselves in the pages of *Fiction* and through the *Nebula* imprint. Two anthologies were published that tried to emulate Michael Moorcock's *New Worlds* or Harlan Ellison's *Dangerous Visions*: *Les Soleils Noirs d'Arcadie* (*The Black Suns of Arcadia*, 1975), edited by Daniel **Walther**, and *Banlieues Rouges* (*Red Suburbs*, 1976), edited by Joël **Houssin** and Christian **Vilà**.

Daniel **Walther** had been publishing science fiction and heroic fantasy stories in *Fiction* since the 1960s. In 1972, he self-published his first novel, a surreal, new-wavish space opera, *Mais l'Espace, Mais le Temps...* (*But Space, But Time...*). After *Les Soleils Noirs d'Arcadie*, he published a collection of short stories, *Requiem pour Demain* (*Requiem for Tomorrow*) at Marabout in 1976; *Krysnak, ou le Complot* (*Krysnak, or the Conspiracy*), a new-wave apocalyptic novel at *Présence du Futur* in 1978; and finally, what may be his best work, *L'Épouvante* (*The Terror*) at J'ai Lu in 1979. *L'Épouvante* was influenced by McKenna's *The Sand Pebbles*, Buzzati's *The Desert of the Tartars,* and Conrad's *Heart of Darkness*, and described the harrowing odyssey of a lieutenant of the Earth forces as his gunboat travelled upstream on a nightmarish planet.

In 1982, Walther began contributing to Fleuve Noir's *Anticipation*, for which he wrote the heroic fantasy trilogy of *Swa* (see Chapter VIII), as well as half-a-dozen novels such as *Embuscade sur Ornella* (*Ambush on Ornella*, 1983), in which powerful aliens ended a long-standing space war; *Apollo XXV* (1983), an interesting speculation on the role of God in space; *La Pugnace Revolution de Phagor* (*The Pugnacious Revolution of Phagor*, 1984), the tale of an alien revolution; *Le Veilleur à la Lisière du Monde* (*The Watcher on the Edge of the World*, 1985), and *La Planète Jaja* (*The Jaja Planet*, 1989). During the period, he also

wrote *Happy End* (1982), a picaresque variation on the classic utopia *City of the Sun*, and several collections of short stories, such as *L'Hôpital* (*The Hospital*, 1982), *Coeur Moite* (*Moist Heart*, 1984) and *Sept Femmes de mes Autres Vies* (*Seven Women of My Other Lives*, 1985) for NéO.

Joël **Houssin**'s first new wave novel, *Locomotive Rictus*, was published by *Nebula* in 1975. Houssin then contributed a series of science fiction thrillers and horror novels to Fleuve Noir's *Anticipation* and *Gore* imprints (see Chapter VIII). His science fiction works included *Le Champion des Mondes* (*The Champion of the Worlds*, 1982), the description of a frightening world revolving entirely around games; *Blue* (1982), which took place in a claustrophobic city full of mutant gangs who were kept prisoner there by unseen forces; (*Phantom*, an original comic-book sequel, was written by Houssin and drawn by **Gauckler** in 1987—see Book 1, Chapter V). *City* (1983) was the story of a duel between a policeman and a mad motorcyclist in a crumbling

futuristic city; *Game Over* (1983) was a *Damnation Alley*-like odyssey in a *Mad Max* world. The success of the *Dobermann* series and of Houssin's television writing career eventually took him in a different literary direction, but he returned to science fiction in 1989 to pen two remarkable, award-winning novels: *Argentine* (1989) took place in a surreal, desert prison universe where naked men fought under the shadows of huge, black zeppelins; and the cyberpunk, rock-themed *Le Temps du Twist* (*The Time of Twist*, 1990), both for *Présence du Futur*.

Two other major authors to have come out of *Nebula* were Dominique **Douay** and Jean-Pierre **Hubert**. Dominique Douay's first novel was *Éclipse*, the story of the fall of a futuristic military dictator-ship, published by *Nebula* in 1975. It was followed by a number of Philip K. Dick–influenced novels, such as *L'Échiquier de la Creation* (*The Chessboard of Creation*, 1976), published by J'ai Lu, in which two entities, the white king Galaad and the black king Aumaire, played a game of planetary chess; *Strates* (*Strata*, 1978), published by *Présence du Futur*, in which a mental illness dubbed "lostime" enabled people to escape a politically harsh world by escaping into the past; *La Vie Comme une Course de Chars a Voile* (*Life as a Sailcar Race*, 1978), published by *Dimensions*, a novel following the narrative pattern of a race, in which a man discovered that his universe was not real; and *Le Principe de l'Oeuf* (*The Principle of the Egg*, 1980), also published by *Dimensions*, in which the eponymous fetus-like entity recreated a uchronic history. A collection of short stories of the period was *Cinq Solutions pour en Finir* (*Five Solutions to End It All*, 1978).

With *L'Impasse-Temps* (*Impasse Time*), published by *Présence du Futur* in 1980, Douay struck a more personal note. The novel concerned a man who found a mysterious object which enabled him to freeze time; at first, he used it to commit petty crimes, but then realized to his horror that the device was slowly turning him into a grey-skinned, carnivorous, reptilian monster, let loose upon a defenseless world. *Rhino* (1985), published by Fleuve Noir's *Anticipation*, took place in a galactic future where the mysterious

alien Qalaqs were the only ones who could guide space-ships through hyperspace. Order was maintained by three super-beasts, a rhinoceros, a unicorn, and a mastodon, psychically connected a human handler. Rhino, the rhinoceros handler, eventually realized that they, too, could do what the Qalaqs did, and fought Licorice, the unicorn handler, for the future of mankind. Other notable works included the collection *Le Monde est un Théâtre* (*The World Is a Stage*, 1982) and *La Fin des Temps et Après* (*The End of Time and After*, 1991), a novel featuring the unexpected appearance of time bubbles from the past; both were published by *Présence du Futur*.

Jean-Pierre **Hubert**'s first novel was *Planète à Trois Temps* (*Three Time Planet*), the story of three artists from decadent Earth on a galactic tour, published by *Nebula* in 1975. It was followed by two political science-fiction novels published by *Ici & Maintenant*, *Mort à l'Etouffée* (*Death by Suffocation*, 1977) and *Couple de Scorpions* (*Couple of Scorpions*, 1980). Throughout the 1980s, Hubert wrote a series of grim, colorful and powerful novels, published by *Presence du Futur*: in *Le Champ du Rêveur* (*The Dreamer's Field*, 1983), an alien civilization became contaminated by the dreams of an Earth child; *Les Faiseurs d'Orage* (*The Storm Makers*, 1984) featured an Earth subject to the capricious whims of five powerful, god-like figures which had once been created by mankind to explore the cosmos; *Ombromanies* (*Shadowmania*, 1986) won the Rosny award; finally, *Roulette Mousse* (*Soft Roulette*, 1987) was a collection of short stories. Hubert also wrote some horror novels with Christian Vilà under the pseudonym of "Jean Viluber" (see Chapter VIII). He recently returned to science fiction with a juvenile novel, *Le Bleu des Mondes* (*The Blue of the Worlds*, 1997).

Other notable authors published by *Présence du Futur* included:

Philip **Goy**, with *Le Père Eternel* (*The Eternal Father*, 1974), a satirical novel in which a megalomaniacal biologist, Jerome Stereod, tried to perpetuate himself through a dynasty; the new wave *Le Livre-Machine* (*The Machine-Book*,

1975), a caricatural utopia; a collection of short stories, *Vers la Révolution* (*Towards the Revolution*, 1977), and finally, *Faire le Mur* (*To Jump the Wall*, 1980). Goy's works were either too political in content or too avant-garde in style to be widely apreciated, but they became representative of a period of literary experimentation.

Jean-Pierre **Fontana** had already edited the fanzine *Mercury* and contributed numerous science fiction and

heroic fantasy stories to *Fiction* (see Chapter VIII) when *Présence du Futur* published *Shéol* (1976), about a "bubble-city" and its cortege of nomads searching for energy on a devastated Earth. Fontana went on to pen *La Femme Truquée* (*The Phony Woman*, 1980) for publisher NéO, about a parallel universe where Paris was divided, like Berlin, into two blocs. Then, in 1984, he embarked on a long series of collaborations with Alain **Paris** (see below) for Fleuve Noir's *Anticipation*, including numerous works of heroic fantasy (see Chapter VIII). His stand-alone science fiction novels for *Anticipation* were *La Jaune* (*The Yellow*, 1986), a contemporary novel about a military experiment that went dramatically wrong, and *La Colonne d'Émeraude* (*The Emerald Column*, 1992).

During the 1970s, J'ai Lu published two remarkable novels by journalist and thriller writer Claude **Veillot**. In *Misandra* (1974), Veillot depicted in strikingly memorable terms a savage world ruled by amazon-like women who hunted men, a work not unlike Suzy McKee Charnas' novels. *La Machine de Balmer* (*Balmer's Machine*, 1978) was an original time-travel romance in which a man oscillated between 1925 and the present, searching for the beautiful Cassandra.

In 1978, *Ailleurs & Demain* published *La Maison du Cygne* (*House of the Swan*) by two renowned authors of the *fantastique*, Yves and Ada **Rémy** (see Chapter VIII); it told the story of two warring cosmic entities, the Swan and the Eagle, who fought on Earth through human agents.

"New science fiction" blossomed toward the end of the 1970s with the appearance of Kesselring's *Ici & Maintenant* (*Here & Now*) imprint, labelled thus as a manifesto-like

challenge to Klein's classic *Ailleurs & Demain* (*Elsewhere & Tomorrow*) imprint, and *L'Utopie Tout de Suite* (*Utopia Right Now*), put out by small publisher Encre. Both were edited by Bernard **Blanc**, the author of a much-publicized essay entitled "Why I Killed Jules Verne," which read as a virulent manifesto in favor of "new science fiction."

At Kesselring, Blanc co-edited *Alerte* and several political anthologies with eloquent titles such as *Ciel Lourd, Béton Froid* (*Heavy Sky, Cold Concrete*), *Planète Socialiste* (*Socialist Planet*), *Quatre Milliards de Soldats* (*Four Billion Soldiers*; all 1977), and others. He also published a variety of titles by established writers such as Jeury, Pelot, Hubert, as well as new authors such as Yves Frémion, Maxime **Benoit-Jeannin**, Philippe **Cousin**, and Pierre **Marlson**. Blanch also published Joëlle **Wintrebert**'s first novel, *Les Olympiades Truquées* (*The Trick Olympics*, 1980), which she revised in 1987 and for which she won the 1988 Rosny Award (see below).

ciel lourd béton froid / collectif n°1

Journalist Yves **Frémion**, also the editor of *Universe* for J'ai Lu, was the first author published by *Ici & Maintenant* with a collection of stories entitled *Octobre, Octobres* (*October, Octobers*, 1977). Frémion then edited two notable anthologies, *La Planète Larzac* (*Planet Larzac*, 1980) and *Territoires du Tendre* (*Territories of Tenderness*, 1982), and published *Rêves de Sable, Châteaux de Sang* (*Dreams of Sand, Castles of Blood*, 1986) at J'ai Lu. His juvenile novel, *Tongre* (1986), told the sentimental story of the life of a centaur-like creature of the alien world of Soline; it received a mainstream juvenile literature award. Frémion then wrote *Ronge* (*Gnaw*, 1988) for

Yves Frémion
Tongre
folio junior
PIRANHA

Fleuve Noir's *Anticipation* and the Rosny award-winning *L'Hétéradelphe de Gane* (*The Heteradelph of Gane*, 1989), before being elected on a "green party" platform to the European Parliament.

Maxime **Benoit-Jeannin** penned two novels for *Ici & Maintenant*: *La Terre était ici* (*Earth Was Here*, 1978) and *L'Adieu des Industriels* (*Farewell to the Industrials*, 1980); he also wrote a more traditional space opera for OPTA's *Galaxie-Bis* imprint, *L'Ami des Ambrosiens* (*The Ambrosians' Friend*, 1981).

Philippe **Cousin**'s first short story collection for *Ici &*

Maintenant was *Le Retour du Boomerang* (*The Return of the Boomerang*, 1980), also the last title published by the imprint. Cousin went on to collaborate with Jean-Pierre Andrevon (see above) on several notable anthologies with ecological/urban themes for *Présence du Futur*, such as *L'Immeuble d'En Face* (*The Building Across the Street*, 1982), *Hôpital Nord* (*North Hospital*, 1984), and *Gare Centrale* (*Central Station*, 1985). Cousin also published the collection *Mange ma Mort* (*Eat My Death*, 1983) and *La Solution du Fou* (*The Madman's Solution*, 1989) at *Présence du Futur*.

"Pierre **Marlson**," a pseudonym of Martial-Pierre Colson, had collaborated with Michel Jeury on *L'Empire du Peuple* (*The People's Empire*, 1977) for Albin Michel and written "new science fiction"-type works for small publisher Ponte Mirone, *Hyménophage* (1978) and the anhology *Des Métiers d'Avenir* (*Future Jobs*, 1979). For *Ici & Maintenant*, Marlson wrote *Désert* (1979). He then penned *Les Compagnons de la Marciliague* (*The Companions of Marciliague*, 1979) for Encre.

At Encre, Blanc published Michel Jeury's *L'Univers-Ombre* (*The Shadow Universe*, 1979) and Jacques **Boireau**'s *Les Années de Sable* (*The Years of Sand*, 1979).

"New science fiction" ultimately proved to be an experiment that remained commercially unsuccessful but was nevertheless important and influential. Some of that influence was positive in that these works opened new vistas and made the field more relevant; but it also had a negative side, alienating casual readers who did not find it sufficiently entertaining.

c. Other Notable Writers

Yves **Dermèze** (see above) made his appearance in Fleuve Noir's *Anticipation*, using the pseudonym of Paul **Béra**, with *Planète Maudite* (*Accursed Planet*; No. 423) in 1970. It was the first episode of the adventures of a self-aware robot with three brains called *Robi*, which continued in Nos. 443, 458 and 498 (1970-72). Béra also contributed the *Léonox* horror series to the *Angoisse* imprint (see Chapter VIII). In total, he penned twenty-one novels for *Anticipation* between 1970 and 1983. Another series was that of the parallel world of *Oeus* (Nos. 517, 856, 1972-78). Other notable novels included *Le Vieux et son Implant* (*The Old Man and His Implant*, 1975), in which a disease killed young people, forcing them to become attached to old people; *Jar-Qui-Tue* (*Jar-Who-Kills*, 1978), in which three men from different eras became aware of each other's existence; *Ceux d'Ailleurs* (*Those from Beyond*, 1979), a colorful journey beyond death; *La Horde Infâme* (*The Awful Horde*, 1980), a prehistoric novel; *Changez de Bocal* (*Change of Jars*, 1981), featuring a society where people can change their ages at will; and *L'Ombre du Tueur* (*The Shadow of the Killer*, 1983), a *Tenth Victim*-like story. During that period, Béra

also used the "Dermèze" pseudonym for two well-crafted science fiction novels published by Librairie des Champs Élysées in their *Le Masque Science-Fiction* imprint, *L'Image de l'Autre* (*The Image of the Other*, 1974) and *Les Lumières* (*The Lights*, 1976), about an Earth inhabited by savage mutants with deadly powers; as well as one juvenile novel, *Le Sharoun de Gallicad* (*The Sharoun of Gallicad*, 1974), published by Marabout.

Robert **Clauzel** began the series of the mind-bogglingly cosmic adventures of Claude Éridan with *La Tâche Noire* (*The Black Spot*; No. 418) in 1970. Eridan was a galactic trouble-shooter from the advanced planet of Gremchka who, with the help of his Earth friends, Gus and Arièle Béranger, uncovered Lovecraftian secrets about the "true" nature of the universe, and the indescribable forces which inhabit it. The series included Nos. 418, 434, 455, 468, 481, 499, 518, 527, 559, 583, 684, 763, 800, 854, and 946 (1970-79). Clauzel's other works tended to be straightforward horror novels using science fiction themes and concepts to create a sense of utter powerlessness at the hands of incomprehensibly powerful alien entities (see Chapter VIII). In total, Clauzel wrote thirty-one novels for *Anticipation*, until *Les Survivants de la Mer Morte* (*The Survivors of the Dead Sea*, 1984)

Jan de **Fast** made his entrance at Fleuve Noir's *Anticipation* in 1972 with *L'Envoyé d'Alpha* (*The Emissary from Alpha*; No. 495), the first episode of the adventures of Dr. Alan. Alan traveled across the galaxy on his ship the *Blastula*, acting as a trouble-shooter for a peace-loving human civilization based on planet Alpha, led by the seductive Artificial Intelligence, Nora. De Fast being a medical doctor, many of his plots were based on, or made use of, biology. The Alan novels included Nos. 514, 539, 560, 579, 593, 600, 614, 634, 637, 652, 661, 678, 694, 709, 725, 738, 764, 782, 791, 869, 874, 893, 927 and 967 (1972-80). De Fast wrote forty-three novels between 1972 and 1981, his last one being *Il Fera Si Bon Mourir...* (*It Will Be So Good to Die...*, 1981), about a galactic rebellion.

Jean-Pierre Garen was another prolific author of space operas for Fleuve Noir's *Anticipation* imprint. He made his debut with *Le Bagne d'Edenia* (*The Edenia Penitentiary*, 1974). But his major contribution was the adventures of the *Surveillance Service of Primitive Planets*, often starring an agent called Marc Stone, the galactic troubleshooting arm of the Terrestrial Union. It was introduced in *Le Dernier des Zwors* (*The Last of the Zwors*; No. 1167, 1982) and totalled thirty-eight novels to date. Its

considerable commercial success (not unlike that of Germany's *Perry Rhodan* series) recently granted it its own imprint.

Jacques **Hoven**'s first novel, *Adieu, Cered* (*Farewell to Cered*, 1972), was a moving tale about a space convict fraternizing with powerful aliens. Hoven wrote nine novels for *Anticipation*, but each of them imbued with humanistic ideals and, often, strange time paradoxes. In *Sombre est l'Espace* (*Dark Is Space*, 1973), men went searching in space for their cosmic roots; *Les Intemporels* (*The Intemporals*, 1974) featured three characters from three different futures; *La Porte des Enfers* (*The Gates of Hell*, 1978) described an endless journey through terrifying parallel universes. Also notable were *Robinson du Cosmos* (*Cosmic Robinson*, 1980) and Hoven's last novel, *Les Non-Humains* (*The Non-Humans*, 1981).

When Fleuve Noir cancelled its *Angoisse* horror imprint, André **Caroff**, the creator of *Madame Atomos*, moved to *Anticipation* with *Le Rideau de Brume* (*The Curtain of Mist*, 1971). Caroff produced thirty-four novels between 1971 and 1989. His series included the adventures of a futuristic space trooper named Rod (Nos. 962, 974, 1026, 1035, 1980); and the series *Abel 6666* (Nos. 1245, 1327, 1342, 1361, 1378, 1396, 1404, 1418, 1983-85), which took place in a computerized future. Caroff also penned the heroic fantasy saga of the Reds (see Chapter VIII) and a series of spy thrillers featuring the character of Bonder for the *Espionnage* imprint. Several *Bonder* novels contain minor genre elements: *Bonder Super-Tueur* (*Bonder Super-Killer*, 1974), *Bonderscopie* (1975), *Bonder contre Dr. Astro* (*Bonder vs. Dr.Astro*, 1976), *Bonder Opération Magie* (*Bonder Operation Magic*, 1976), *Bonder Mach 3* (1977), *Bonder Connexion 12* (1978), *Bonder Stade Zombi 4* (1979), and others.

Gabriel **Jan** had previously contributed two horror novels to Fleuve Noir's *Angoisse* (see Chapter VIII), when he published *La Planète aux Deux Soleils* (*The Planet with Two Suns*, 1974) at *Anticipation*. Jan wrote thirty-five science fiction novels for Fleuve Noir between 1974 and 1987, his last novel being *Les Elus de Tôh* (*The Elects of Toh*, 1987). The most notable included a series about a future polluted Earth where humans lived in domed cities (Nos. 830, 868, 1978), the *Surmonde des Gofans* (*Overworld of the Gofans*) trilogy (Nos. 1102, 1123, 1141, 1981-82), in which bisexual entities could be split into two separate individuals; and a heroic fantasy series (see Chapter VIII).

Paul-Jean **Hérault**'s first novel for Fleuve Noir's *Anticipation*, *Le Rescapé de la Terre* (*The Survivor from Terra*; No. 691, 1975) featured Cal of Ter, a spaceman from Earth's future, who found himself stranded on a prehistoric world. Using suspended animation and advanced technology, Cal returned periodically to check on his adopted world's progress, helping its evolution across the centuries. The series was comprised of Nos. 714, 776, 895, 933, 1005, and 1281 (1975-84). Two other notable series were *Durée des Équipages: 61 Missions* (*The Crews Will Last 61 Missions*),

featuring the adventures of space pilot Gurvan in a warlike, overpopulated future (Nos. 1562, 1584, 1612, 1987-88); and *La Treizième Génération* (*The Thirteenth Generation*; Nos. 1772, 1778, 1990). Hérault wrote twenty-two novels, concluding with *Ceux qui ne voulaient pas Mourir* (*Those Who Refused to Die*, 1996).

Jean **Mazarin** was already known for his police thrillers (also written under the pseudonym "Emmanuel Errer") when he contributed *Pas Même un Dieu* (*Not Even a God*, 1976), a sad novel about a young savage who believed himself to be the son of a god, to Fleuve Noir's *Anticipation*. Mazarin contributed twenty novels to the imprint until 1986, before writing horror fiction under the pseudonym of "Charles Nécrorian" (see Chapter VIII). His best works included a trilogy about a star-spanning Terran Empire (Nos. 769, 790, 817, 1977) and a remarkable unchronia, *L'Histoire Détournée* (*The Hijacked History*, 1984), which took place in a universe where, ten days after Hitler's suicide in 1945, "V-6" atomic weapons destroyed London, Washington and Moscow. The story was about a coup attempt in Burgundy that threatened to start a new war between the Great Reich and Japan. Mazarin also penned two novels about Face, a murderous female android, *Poupée Tueuse* (*Killer Doll*, 1985) and *Poupée Cassée* (*Broken Doll*, 1986), his last novel.

Other Fleuve Noir's *Anticipation* authors of the period included:

Gérard **Marcy**, with space opera thrillers such as *La Neige Bleue* (*The Blue Snow*, 1969), *La Force Secrète* (*The Secret Force*, 1970), and *Le Missile Hyperspatial* (*The Hyperspatial Missile*, 1972).

Georges **Murcie**, who wrote thirty-one novels, starting with *Garadania* (1970), including *La Folie du Capitaine Sangor* (*The Madness of Captain Sangor*, 1975), *La Courte Eternité d'Hervé Girard* (*The Short Eternity of Hervé Girard*, 1977), and *Tetras* (1980), his last novel.

Pierre **Courcel**, with three novels, *Equipages en Péril* (*Crews in Danger*, 1970), *Bases d'Invasion* (*Invasion Bases*, 1971) and *Escales Forcées* (*Forced StopOver*, 1972).

"Dan **Dastier**" was a house pseudonym created by Fleuve Noir and shared by at least two writers, Marc **Bréhal** and Yves **Chantepie**. Chantepie was also the author of another genre novel published by Albin Michel under their house pseudonym of "Jean-Yves **Chanbert**," *Les Sirènes de Lusinia* (*The Sirens of Lusinia*, 1974). Dastier's first novel for *Anticipation* was *Les Déracinés d'Humania* (*Uprooted* *from Humania*, 1972). Chantepie reportedly took over from Bréhal around 1975. In total, Dastier penned thirty-four novels, the last being *Le Sixième Symbiote* (*The Sixth Symbiote*, 1987). The best featured the daring space explorer, Julian de Cerny, who first appeared in *La Planète aux Diamants* (*The Diamond Planet*; No. 584, 1973) and returned in Nos. 607, 620 and 985 (1974-80).

Daniel **Piret** also started his *Anticipation* career in 1972 with *Année 500.000* (*Year 500,000*, 1972). Piret wrote thirty-four novels for Fleuve Noir, the last being *La Parole* (*The Spoken Word*, 1984). He also contributed five more genre novels to the short-lived *Mémoires d'Outre-Ciel* (*Memoirs from Beyond the Sky*), from publisher Garry under the pseudonym of "Red Ilan." *Prométhée* (*Prometheus*, 1982) and *Le Fils de Prométhée* (*The Son of Prometheus*, 1983) formed a somewhat ambitious time-travel novel subtitled *Les Ellipses Temporelles* (*Temporal Ellipses*).

Christian **Mantey** began to write for *Anticipation* in 1976 with *Transit pour l'Infini* (*Transit for Infinity*, 1976). He wrote six novels between 1976 and 1984, including the Mel Titcht series (Nos. 1093, 1193, 1219, 1280, 1981-84), about a detective of the Bureau of Parallel Cases who investigated extra-dimensional entities. With Jean-Philippe **Berger**, Mantey used the pseudonym of "Jean-Christian Bergman" to pen three more novels in 1979-80. Finally, with Pierre **Dubois**, Mantey used the pseudonym of "Budy Matieson" to pen two more novels, the post-apocalyptic *Chroniques du Retour Sauvage* (*Chronicles of the Savage Return*; Nos. 993, 1019, 1980).

Frank **Dartal**'s first novel for *Anticipation* was *Les Brumes du Sagittaire* (*The Mists of Sagittarius*, 1977). Dartal wrote fifteen novels, until *L'Épopée du Draco* (*The Draco's Odyssey*, 1988). Notable titles were *Le Règne du Serpent* (*The Reign of the Serpent*, 1979), *Civilisations Galactiques—Providence* (*Galactic Civilisations—Providence*, 1980), *Et Un Temps Pour Mourir* (*And a Time to Die*, 1982) and *Eridan VII* (1986).

Chris **Burger** had already contributed two *Angoisse* novels (see Chapter VIII) prior to penning *Quand Elles Viendront* (*When They Will Come*, 1977) and *Le Temps des Autres* (*The Time of Others*, 1977) for *Anticipation*.

Finally, Vincent **Gallaix** wrote only two novels for *Anticipation*, *Orbite d'Attente* (*Waiting Orbit*, 1977) and *Zoomby* (1977), about an all-too perfect android, rejected by the human race.

Other notable authors of the period were published by other imprints:

Bernard **Villaret** made his debut at Marabout with a grim space opera, *Mort au Champ d'Étoiles* (*Death on a Field of Stars*, 1970). He then moved to *Présence du Futur* where he published two novels, *Deux Soleils pour Artuby* (*Two Suns for Artuby*, 1971) and *Le Chant de la Coquille Kalasai* (*The Song of the Kalasai Shell*, 1976), which illustrated the dangers of introducing Earth culture to a Polynesian-like planet. Having spent time in French Polynesia, Villaret knew how to give his novel a strong ring of authenticity and feeling. Villaret also published one collection of stories, *Visa pour l'Outre-Temps* (*Visa for Beyond Time*, 1976), two juvenile genre novels, *Pas d'Avenir pour les Sapiens* (*No Future for Homo Sapiens*, 1980) and *L'Infini Plus Un Mètre* (*Infinity Plus One Meter*, 1981), and one more novel, *Quand Reviendra l'Oiseau-Nuage* (*When the Cloud Bird Returns*, 1983), for Albin Michel.

Other genre authors published by Marabout included:

Landry **Merillac**, with an ambitious space opera, *Les Sept Soleils de l'Archipel Humain* (*The Seven Suns of the Human Archipelago*, 1973).

Belgian writer Vincent **Goffart**, with a romantic time-travel story, *Jonathan à Perte de Temps* (*Jonathan Losing Time*, 1975).

Another Belgian author, Paul **Hanost**, with a modern space opera, *Le Livre des Étoiles* (*The Book of Stars*, 1977).

Publisher Albin Michel published novels by "David Maine" (Pierre Barbet—see above) and "Jean-Yves Chanbert" (Dan Dastier—see above), but also by a renowned writer of the *fantastique*, Patrick **Ravignant** (see Chapter VIII), who penned *Les Mutants de la Voie* (*The Mutants of the Way*, 1972).

Another author published by Albin Michel was Belgian writer Yves **Varende** (also see Chapter VIII), who wrote *Le Gadget de l'Apocalypse* (*The Apocalypse Gadget*, 1978). Varende went on to pen a trilogy of novels in 1980 for comic-book publisher Jacques Glénat, *Tamaru*, *Les Tueurs de l'Ordre* (*The Killers of Order*) and *Tuez-les Tous!* (*Kill Them All!*).

Gerard Klein's *Ailleurs & Demain* published a number of outstanding collections of genre stories by various authors:

Tellur (1975) by Pierre-Jean **Brouillaud**.

Les Prédateurs Enjolivés (*The Beautified Predators*, 1976) by Pierre **Christin**, better known for being the writer of the popular comic-book space opera *Valérian* (see Book 1, Chapter V). Christin went on to pen *Le Futur est en Marche Arrière* (*The Future Is in Reverse*) for Encre in 1979.

L'Hippocampe (*The Sea-Horse*, 1981) by Lorris **Murail**, who had already written two surreal novels for publisher Jean-Claude Lattès, *Omnyle* (1975), and *La Secte* (*The Sect*, 1977).

And, finally, *Tous ces Pas vers le Jaune* (*All These Steps Towards Yellow*, 1979), the first novel by Christian-Yves **Lhostis**, the surreal tale of people living their lives in a completely green-colored environment.

Other notable works published elsewhere included:

Georges **Soria**'s *La Grande Quincaillerie* (*Great Hardware*, 1975), published by *Présence du Futur*.

Jean **Le Clerc de la Herverie**'s *Ergad le Composite* (1976), published by *Nebula*.

Pierre **Giuliani**'s *Séquences pour le Chaos* (*Sequences for Chaos*, 1977), published by Lattès and *Les Frontières d'Oulan-Bator* (*The Borders of Ulan-Bator*, 1979), published by *Dimensions*.

Pierre **Bameul**'s *Je Paye Donc Je Suis* (*I Pay Therefore I Am*, 1977) and *Écrit dans le Passé* (*Written in the Past*, 1978), published by OPTA.

And Cyrille **Kaszuk**'s *L'Épreuve de Judith* (*Judith's Test*, 1978), published by J'ai Lu.

Finally, one should note Louis **Bayle**'s two-volume collection *Aièr e Deman* (1970), meaning "Elsewhere and Tomorrow" In the Provencal regional language; it was a collection of fourteen fantastic tales retelling the history of mankind from 200,000 BC to the far future, written directly in that language.

d. Mainstream Writers

The most interesting mainstream writer to have contributed to science fiction in the 1970s was Robert **Merle**, a Goncourt Award winner, who in 1968 penned the famous *Un Animal Doué de Raison* (*An Animal Gifted with Reason*), a fascinating examination of the political and scientific consequences of communication with dolphins, translated and better known as the *Day of the Dolphin*, and made into an eponymous 1973 film. Merle's 1972 novel, *Malevil*, was a starkly realistic description of the rebuilding of civilization after a nuclear conflict. It, too, became a best-seller and was also adapted into a feature film in 1980. *Les Hommes Protégés* (*The Protected Men*, 1974) was an elaborate social satire that featured the destruction by an epidemic of the male population of the United States, with the resulting consequence of women taking over. Other notable works by Merle included *Madrapour* (1976), *Homme Invisible, Pour Qui Chantes-tu?* (*Invisible Man, for Whom Do You Sing?*, 1984) and *L'Enfant-Roi* (*The Child-King*, 1993).

The other best-selling mainstream genre writer of the decade was René **Barjavel**, who made a startling return to science fiction with *La Nuit des Temps* (*The Dawn of Time*, 1968), which became an immediate commercial success, tapping into the spirit of youthful revolt of the times. In it, a man and a woman, the survivors of a pre-cataclysmic civilization that destroyed itself, were found frozen in a giant sphere at the South Pole. Their revival, and the tale of their doomed love, ignited social upheavals *à la* May 1968. Barjavel followed it with *Le Grand Secret* (*The Great Secret*, 1973), a novel that began as a political thriller with the discovery of the secret of a contagious form of immortality which could destroy the world, by an Indian scientist in the 1950s, and ended up describing a doomed island utopia *à la* Olaf Stapledon's *Odd John*. (**Le Grand Secret** was adapted as a television movie—see Book 1, Chapter II.) *Une Rose au Paradis* (*A Rose in Paradise*, 1981) was a touching love story taking place in the same universe as *Le Diable l'Emporte* (*The Devil Takes It*, 1948) and *Colomb de la Lune* (*Colombus of the Moon*, 1962), featuring the character of Mr. Gé, the builder of the Last Ark. Finally, *La Tempête* (*The Tempest*, 1982) was a panorama of various ills perpetrated by mankind upon itself in the near-future.

Other notable mainstream authors who penned genre works during the period included:

Emmanuelle **Arsan**, with *Nouvelles de l'Érosphere* (*Stories from the Erosphere*, 1969), a collection of short, erotic fiction, many containing genre elements, by the author of the renowned erotica classic, *Emmanuelle*.

Michel **Butor**, with *La Rose des Vents* (*The Rose of Winds*, 1970), another collection of short, poetic stories about the future of mankind.

Jean-Marie **Fonteneau**, with *Les Champignons* (*The Mushrooms*, 1970), an allegorical novel n which the world is taken over by mushrooms.

Gilbert **Beau de Loménie**, with *Le Monde Sans Grand-Mères* (*The World Without Grand-Mothers*, 1970), in which the nuclear fallout turned women into men when they reached the age of forty.

Swiss author Jérôme **Deshusses**, with a striking anarchist utopia, *Le Grand Soir* (*The Big Night*, 1971); other notable works in this vein by Deshusses included *Sodome-Ouest* (1966) and *Délivrez Prométhée* (*Free Prometheus*, 1979).

Jean **Marabini**, with *Les Enfants Fous—an 2021* (*The Mad Children—Year 2021*, 1971), and *Les Hommes du Futur* (*Future Men*, 1965).

Claude **Ollier**, with *La Vie sur Epsilon* (*Life on Epsilon*, 1972), a surreal novel in which four astronauts, stranded on the eponymous planet, experienced psychogical attacks, not unlike what happened in Lem's *Solaris*. Its style was somewhat similar to that of satirist arry Malzberg. Ollier also wrote the 1978 film **Écoute Voir** (*Hear See*; see Book 1, Chapter I) and radio dramas such as **L'Attentat en Direct** (*Terrorism on Live TV*; see Book 1, Chapter III).

Jean **Raspail**, with *Le Camp des Saints* (*The Camp of the Saints*, 1973), about an overpopulated world in which Europe succumbed to a Third World invasion; other notable works by Raspail included *Le Jeu du Roi* (*The King's Game*, 1976) and *Septentrion* (1979).

Jean-Michel **Barrault** with the self-explanatory *...Et Les Bisons Brouteront à Manhattan* (*...And the Buffalo Will Graze in Mahattan*, 1973).

Pierre **Daninos**, with *La Première Planète à Droite en sortant par la Voie Lactée* (*The First Planet on the Right When You Exit at the Milky Way*, 1975), a satirical science-fantasy by a renowned humorist, better known for his satire, *Les Carnets du Major Thompson* (*Major Thompson's Notebooks*).

Frantz-André **Burguet**, with *Vanessa* (1977), a fictional future biography of the author's daughter, written as if it were the year 2004, when she has grown up to become a famous concert pianist.

Laurence **Korb**, with *Paris-Lézarde* (*Paris-Lizard*, 1977), about the destruction of Paris.

Philippe d'**André**, with *Les Ruses de l'Assaillant* (*The Ruses of the Attacker*, 1978), a collection of genre stories.

Marius-Pierre **Guibert**, with *Étranges Retours* (*Strange*

Returns, 1978), a novel in which a spaceman returned to a post-nuclear Earth.

Willy de **Spens**, with *La Nuit des Long Museaux* (*The Night of the Long Snouts*, 1978), featuring a revolt of domesticated animals.

Jacques **Massacrier**, with *Outre-Temps* (*Beyond Time*, 1978), where the survivors of a global ice melt created a utopian society.

Michel **Polac**, with *Le Q.I. Ou le Roman d'un Surdoué* (*The I.Q. Or a Novel of the Gifted*, 1978), a shocking novel where mankind, after discovering that intelligence could be increased by eating brains, fell prey to a cannibal holocaust and a genetic apocalypse.

Hugo **Verlomme**, with *Mermère* (1978), the tale of a conflict between mankind and an underwater civilisation.

Florence **Vidal**, with *L'Aolès Férox* (*Aloes Ferox*, 1978), an African political satire with science fiction elements.

Finally, in the futuristic espionage category, in 1971, Fleuve Noir launched a dedicated imprint called *Espiomatic Infra-Rouge* (*Espiomatic Infrared*), featuring the adventures of super-agent Vic Saint-Val and written under the pseudonym of "Vic Saint-Val" by one of the *Espionnage* imprint's regular conbributors, Gilles **Morris**. The *Vic Saint-Val* adventures totalled sixty novels, published until 1979. Most included science fiction elements in the form of advanced technology. Morris continued Vic Saint-Val's adventures under his own name in the *Kamikaze* trilogy published in the *Anticipation* imprint (Nos. 1269, 1287, 1301, 1984), in which Saint-Val defeated an evil organization that was trying to forcibly bring peace to the world through the use of deadly, miniature flying saucers.

e. Juveniles

The 1970s saw the blossoming of true science fiction in the field of young-adult and children's books, with a slate of new authors, who also occasionally contributed to regular adult imprints. In spite of the failure of Gérard Klein's short-lived imprint, *L'Âge des Étoiles* (*The Age of the Stars*), which published eleven volumes between 1977 and 1979), attracting works by Michel Jeury, Christian Léourier, and sporting covers by renowned French artists such as Jean-Claude **Mézières** and **Moebius**, young-adult science fiction was healthily represented in the catalogs of publishers such as Magnard, Hatier, Hachette (in its *Bibliothèque Verte* (*Green Library*) imprint), and others.

Christian **Léourier** was probably the best and most famous author to have continually crossed the fence between young-adult and regular science fiction. Léourier's first novel was *Les Montagnes du Soleil* (*The Mountains of the Sun*), a novel featuring the adventures of a savage warrior rediscovering the secrets of Old Earth after a cataclysmic flood. It was published by **Klein** in his prestigious *Ailleurs & Demain* imprint in 1972. Léourier later contributed one

more novel to *Ailleurs & Demain*, *La Planète Inquiète* (*The Worried Planet*, 1979), about an Earth colony mysteriously falling prey to chaos; and one novel to *L'Âge des Étoiles*, *L'Arbre-Miroir* (*The Mirror-Tree*, 1977), a coming-of-age tale on a planet torn between the human colonists and the natives. Meanwhile, in 1974, with *Le Messager de la Grande Île* (*The Messenger from the Great Island*, 1974) Léourier embarked on his most famous series, the cosmic adventures of a group of colorful characters from the waterworld of Thalassa who, led by Jarvis de Helan, search the galaxy for the legendary mother Earth. Eight *Jarvis* novels were published between 1974 and 1980.

In the 1980s, Léourier continued to alternate between regular genre novels and young-adult books. The former were published at J'ai Lu, and included *Ti-Harnog* (1984), in which a human observer challenged the rigid caste system of an alien society; *L'Homme Qui tua l'Hiver* (*The Man Who Killed Winter*, 1986), in which a female archeologist and a native searched for a mythical lost city; *Mille Fois Mille Fleuves* (*A Thousand Times a Thousand Rivers*, 1987), a love story between an alien woman and an Earthman on a waterworld; *Les Racines de l'Oubli* (*The Roots of Oblivion*, 1988), *La Loi du Monde* (*The Law of the World*, 1990), *Les Masques du Réel* (*The Masks of Reality*, 1991), and *La Terre de Promesse* (*The Earth of the Promise*, 1994), all novels which featured intricate alien cultures. The latter included *Petit Dragon* (*Little Dragon*, 1986), *Eli le Rêveur* (*Eli the Dreamer*, 1988), and *E.V.A. Ou l'Été de la Lune* (*EVA or the Summer of the Moon*, 1991).

Christian **Grenier** was by far the most prolific provider of young-adult science fiction throughout the 1970s and 1980s. In 1972, Grenier penned a remarkable non-fiction book, *Jeunesse et Science-Fiction* (*Youth and Science Fiction*), one of the first essays on this topic. His first novel was *Sabotage sur la Planète Rouge* (*Sabotage on the Red Planet*, 1972), which was followed by *Aïo, Terre Invisible* (*Aio, Invisible Land*, 1973), *Messier 51, ou l'Impossible Retour* (*Messier 51, or the Impossible Return*, 1975), and *Le Secret des Mangeurs d'Étoiles* (*The Secret of the Star Eaters*, 1978), all well-crafted space operas for publisher Hatier. More notable were the intricate *La Machination* (*The Machination*, 1973), which won a mainstream juvenile literary prize awarded by French television, the first volume in a series of young adult novels written for publisher GP and featuring remarkable characterizations, sophisticated concepts worthy of any "adult" science fiction novel, and strong narratives worthy of Robert Heinlein. These included a two-volume saga co-written with William **Camus** (see below), devoted to a planet colonized by Native Americans, *Cheyenne 6112* (1974) and *Une Squaw dans les Étoiles* (*A Squaw Among the Stars*, 1975), as well as stand-alone novels like *Le Satellite Venu d'Ailleurs* (*The Satelite from Beyond*, 1975), *Les Fleurs de l'Espace* (*The Space Flowers*, 1976), and *Le Soleil va Mourir* (*The Sun Will Die*, 1977). Grenier also contributed *Le Montreur d'Étincelles* (*The Spark Per-*

former), about an alien world resisting colonization, to Klein's *L'Âge des Étoiles* in 1978. His *Les Cascadeurs du Temps* (*The Time Stuntmen*, 1977) won another major juvenile literature award.

In the 1980s and 1990s, Grenier continued his career with novels like *L'Habitant des Étoiles* (*The Star Dweller*, 1985) and the award-winning *Le Coeur en Abîme* (*The Heart in the Abyss*, 1985). In 1995, he launched the juvenile series of *Aina, Fille des Étoiles* (*Daughter of the Stars*) for publisher Nathan (three volumes so far), and yet another award-winning series for young adults, the saga of the Multimonde (Multiworld), a mysterious gateway leading into other universes that seemed to be patterned after the novels written by the uncle of one of the young heroes. It was comprised of *La Musicienne de l'Aube* (*The Musician of Dawn*, 1996); *Les Lagunes du Temps* (*The Lagoon of Time*, 1997), which took place in an alternate future Venice; *Cyberpark* (1997), featuring a devastated future Earth crawling with killer robots; and *Mission en Mémoire Morte* (*Mission in Dead Memory*, 1997), the last three published by Denis **Guiot** in his new imprint, *Vertige* (see below).

Like Christian Léourier, the writing team using the pseudonym of "Michel **Grimaud**" alternated between young-adult and regular science fiction and fantasy novels. They began their genre career with two volumes featuring the adventures of the young savage Rhôor l'Invincible (Rhoor the Invincible) published by Alsatia in 1971 (see Chapter VIII). It was followed by a series of literary juvenile science fiction and fantasy novels, such as *La Ville sans Soleil* (*The City Without Sun*, 1973), *Soleil à Crédit* (*Sun on Credit*, 1975), and the remarkable *L'Île sur l'Ocean Nuit* (*The Island on the Night Ocean*), published in *L'Âge des Étoiles* in 1978. Grimaud also contributed two of the bext young adult novels published by Duculot's short-lived *Travelling sur le Futur* imprint, *Les Esclaves de la Joie* (*Slaves of Joy*, 1977) and *Le Temps des Gueux* (*The Time of the Poor*, 1980).

In the 1980s, Michel Grimaud penned three notable adult genre novels for *Présence du Futur*: a high fantasy, *Malakansâr* (1980; see Chapter VIII), and two science fiction works, *La Dame de Cuir* (*Leather Lady*, 1981), a love story between a man and an alien woman, the latter treated as an animal in order to render the colonization of her world legally possible; and *L'Arbre d'Or* (*The Gold Tree*, 1983), a humorous romp through a colorful, anachronistic universe. In the young-adult field, Grimaud continued to produce such notable novels as *Le Passe-Monde* (*The Passworld*, 1982) and *Le Tyran d'Axilane* (*The Tyrant of Axilane*, 1982), as well as juvenile fantasies and, more recently, horror-slanted thrillers (see Chapter VIII).

Another major contributor of young-adult genre novels was the prolific Philippe **Ébly** who, throughout the 1970s and 1980s, penned several major series. The best known was *Les Conquérants de l'Impossible* (*The Conquerors of the Impossible*), published by Hachette's *Bibliothèque Verte*,

which began in 1971 with *Destination Uruapan* and is still continuing to date after twenty-five volumes. The series featured the adventures of Serge, Thibaut, the beautiful Souhi, and their teenage companions, in the present, involving aliens (*...Et les Martiens Invitèrent les Hommes* (*...And the Martians Invited Men*, 1974)), robots (*La Montagne aux Robots* (*Robot Mountain*, 1987), in the past (*L'Évadé de l'An II* (*Escape from Year II*, 1973), *Le Matin des Dinosaures* (*Morning of the Dinosaurs*, 1982)), in the future, with a trilogy comprised of *La Grande Peur de l'An 2117* (*The Great Fear of the Year 2117*, 1983), *2159 La Fin des Temps Troublés* (*2159 the End of the Troubled Times*, 1985), and *Les Parias de l'An 2187* (*The Pariahs of the Year 2187*, 1986), featuring a time where oceans have expanded and civilization collapsed. Other series by Ébly included *Les Évadés du Temps* (*Escape in Time*), comprised of seven novels published by *Bibliothèque Verte* between 1977 and 1985; and the short-lived *Les Patrouilleurs de l'An 4003* (*The Patrollers of the Year 4003*), comprised of four novels published in 1984 and 1985.

Huguette **Carrière** created the spunky character of Tony in 1971 with *Tony et l'Homme Invisible* (*Tony and the Invisible Man*, 1971). The *Tony* series was published by Hachette's *Bibliothèque Rose* (*Pink Library*), a children's imprint. The imprint comprised of twenty novels, many featuring genre elements, such as *Le Garçon de l'Autre Planète* (*The Boy from Another Planet*, 1972) and *Tony au Carnaval des Robots* (*Tony at the Robots' Carnival*, 1980). Carrière also penned a remarkable young-adult series, *L'Envoyé* (*The Envoy*), comprised of *Maletor* and *L'Étoile Perdue* (*The Lost Star*) for Alsatia in 1977 and 1978.

Robert **Alexandre**'s series, *Mykir*, was also published by Alsatia and began with *Le Survivant* (*The Survivor*, 1973). It continued through four more volumes, until *Les Orphelins d'Almeray* (*The Orphans of Amray*, 1981). For Alsatia, Alexandre also penned *Sandrihar* (1975), *Tiguir* (1977) and *Les Héritiers des Sept Mondes* (*The Inheritors of the Seven Worlds*, 1982); he also wrote one adult novel for Fleuve Noir's *Anticipation*, *Yriel* (1989).

Other notable authors of juvenile science fiction published during the period included:

William **Camus**, with *Opération Clik-Clak* (1975), *Un Bonheur Électronique* (*An Electronic Happiness*, 1977), and *Une Drôle de Planète* (*A Funny Planet*; GP, 1978). Camus also collaborated with Christian Grenier (see above) and Pierre Pelot and J. **Coué** for *Le Canard à Trois Pattes* (*The Three-Legged Duck*, 1978), and with Jacky **Soulier** for *Le Péril Vient de la Terre* (*The Danger Comes from Earth*, 1981).

Claude & Jacqueline **Held**, with *Le Chat de Simulombula* (*The Cat from Simulombula*, 1971), *Expédition Imprévue sur la Planète Éras* (*Unforeseen Expedition to Planet Eras*, 1978), *L'Antre de Starros* (*The Lair of Starros*, 1979), *Trois Enfants dans les Étoiles* (*Three Children Among the Stars*, 1980) and, more recently, *La Poudre des Sept Planètes* (*The Powder of Seven Planets*, 1990).

François **Celier**, with the adventures of Éric Matras, published by the *Bibliothèque Verte*, including *Les Chevaliers de l'Océan* (*The Knight of the Ocean*, 1969) and *La Vallée Fantastique* (*Fantastic Valley*, 1970), which featured giant anthropoids.

Adrien **Martel**, with the adventures of Gil, *Gil dans le Cosmos* (*Gil in the Cosmos*, 1971) and *Gil Revient sur Terre* (*Gil Returns to Earth*, 1971).

Jean **Cernaut**, with *Zone Interdite* (*Forbidden Zone*, 1972).

Yvonne **Meynier**, with *Delphine, Reine de la Lumière* (*Delphine, Queen of Light*, 1972).

Geoffrey X. **Passover**, with *Joar de l'Espace* (*Joar of Space*, 1972) and *Les Survivants de l'An 2000* (*The Survivors of the Year 2000*, 1977).

Philippe V. **Rivages**, with *La Planète de l'Eau Bleue* (*The Planet of Blue Water*, 1973).

Jacqueline **Monsigny**, with *Freddy Ravage*, a series about the adventures of a super-agent, that comprised seven volumes published between 1975 and 1977. Of particular interest were *Freddy Ravage et les Diplodocus* (*Freddy Ravage and the Diplodocus*, 1975) and *Freddy Ravage Prisonnier des Pharaons* (*Freddy Ravage Prisoner of the Pharaohs*, 1976).

Daniel **Valiant**, with *La Légende du Goéland Blanc* (*The Legend of the White Seagull*), comprised of *Ciel des Sables* (*Sky of the Sands*, 1976) and *La Caverne du Temps* (*The Cavern of Time*, 1977).

Finally, Pierre **Probst**, who in 1965 had taken his fearless heroine, Caroline, to the Moon in *Caroline sur la Lune* (*Caroline on the Moon*, 1965), continued her fantastic adventures through the 1970s and 1980s with *Caroline et la Petite Sirène* (*Caroline and the Little Mermaid*, 1977), *Caroline chez les Lilliputiens* (*Caroline in Lilliput*, 1984), *Caroline à travers les Âges* (*Caroline Throughout the Ages*, 1985), and *Caroline et le Robot* (*Caroline & the Robot*, 1986).

3. The 1980s

The 1980s was a decade of transition for French science fiction.

The political experimentations of the "new science fiction" of the 1970s eventually ended, for the most part because of its lack of commercial success. The election of Socialist president François Mitterand in 1981 demonstrated that left-wing ideology was not the panacea for France's ills, and put to rest the influence of May 1968. Also, the books were ultimately rejected by all readers except for a small circle of fans. As the commercial boom of the 1970s ended, publishers were forced to refocus on what actually sold in the marketplace.

Yet another generation of new writers emerged; these were more likely to follow their own voices, and less encumbered by the baggage of previous generations, who had had to stick together to face a hostile literary world. The success of *Star Wars* and other big-budget motion pictures, cartoons, and comics, meant that science fiction had now become part of the French cultural mainstream. It was easier than ever for a number of writers to leave the confining economic restrictions of the dedicated imprints, and turn to more general and financially rewarding pursuits.

Indeed, one of the most notable experiments of the decade was the Limites (Limits) group, comprised of authors such as Emmanuel **Jouanne** and Antoine **Volodine**. Limites Attempted to merge science fiction with highly stylized general literature, as a reaction against both traditional space opera and the political "new science fiction" of the 1970s. By cutting itself off from the genre's popular roots, however, Limites ultimately failed to enlist enough readers to become a commercially viable movement.

a. The Publishers

The 1980s saw the progresssive disappearance of most of the imprints that had been launched, often too quickly, in the 1970s:

Kesselring's *Ici & Maintenant* (*Here & Now*) was cancelled in 1980.

Marabout's *Science-Fiction* and Librairie des Champs-Élysées's *Le Masque Science-Fiction* were cancelled in 1981.

Garry's *Mémoires d'Outre-Ciel* (*Memoirs from Beyond the Sky*) and Presses de la Cité's *Futurama* were cancelled in 1982.

Jean-Claude Lattes' *Titres SF* (*Titles SF*) and Casterman's *Autres Temps, Autres Mondes* (*Other Times, Other Worlds*) were cancelled in 1983.

Calmann-Levy's *Dimensions* and Albin Michel's *Science-Fiction* were cancelled in 1984.

OPTA's *Galaxie-Bis* was cancelled in 1988.

Finally, even *Fiction*, the magazine that had been the most dominant voice of the French science fiction community since 1953, was cancelled in February 1990.

The most active imprint remained Fleuve Noir's *Anticipation* which, under the inspired editorship of Patrick Siry, managed to attract authors like Michel Jeury in 1980, Joël Houssin and Daniel Walther in 1981, Serge Brussolo in 1982, Jacques **Mondoloni** and Jean-Pierre Andrevon in 1984 and Jean-Marc Ligny in 1988. It also fostered new talent such as Michel Pagel, Alain Paris, Roland C. Wagner, and Michel Honaker.

Under Elisabeth Gille's equally inspired editorship, *Présence du Futur* continued to publish some of the best French science fiction of the decade: Jean-Pierre Andrevon, Pierre Pelot, Jean-Pierre Hubert and also new authors such as Serge **Brussolo** and Jean-Marc **Ligny**. *Présence du Futur* championed the efforts of Limites, publishing the works of Emmanuel **Jouanne**, Antoine **Volodine**, Francis **Berthelot**, and the group's anthology, *Malgré le Monde* (*In Spite of the*

World, 1987). Gille left the editorship of *Présence du Futur* in 1986 and was replaced by Jacques Chambon.

The other three major imprints, Klein's *Ailleurs & Demain*, Sadoul's *Science Fiction* at J'ai Lu, and Goimard's *Science Fiction* at Presses-Pocket, published a few French authors (**Jouanne**, **Jeury**, **Pelot**, **Volkoff**, etc.), but on a more occasional basis than before.

b. Major Authors

One of the most important genre writers to come out of the 1980s was the prolific Serge **Brussolo**. Like Stefan Wul, he relied on powerful visual imagery rather than on conventionally structured plots, on disturbing images rather than characters, on strikingly original and bizarre ideas rather than standard concepts. His strength lay in the accumulation of dark, obscene, often disgusting details. Brussolo constantly straddled the line between horror and science fiction, thrillers, and even heroic fantasy. Indeed, a number of his works are reviewed in Chapter VIII.

Brussolo received the French Science Fiction Grand Prize for his short story "Funnyway" (1978), published in Philippe Curval's anthology, *Futurs au Présent* (*Present-Day Futures*), about a surreal prison-maze, and for his first collection of short stories, *Vue en Coupe d'une Ville Malade* (*Cut-Out View of a Sick City*, 1980), published by *Présence du Futur*. At *Présence du Futur*, he followed it with *Aussi Lourd que le Vent* (*Heavy as the Wind*, 1981), *Sommeil de Sang* (*Sleep of Blood*, 1982), featuring a decadent society of carnivores who ate the flesh of fabulous animals frozen inside mountains; *Portrait du Diable en Chapeau Melon* (*Portrait of the Devil Wearing a Bowler*, 1982), another striking novel exploring the world of Funnyway; and *Le Carnaval de Fer* (*The Iron Carnival*, 1983), the tale of a grim pilgrimage in a dark fantasy world.

During the same period, Brussolo penned a juvenile genre novel, *Les Sentinelles d'Almoha* (*The Sentinels of Almoha*, 1981) for Nathan (revised in 1994 for publication in Fleuve Noir's *Anticipation* imprint) and *Traque-La-Mort* (*Death Tracker*, 1982) for *Titres SF*, the latter also taking place in the Almohan universe and featuring men functioning as living bombs. Brussolo also embarked on a career as an author of very dark thrillers with *Le Nuisible* (*The Harmful*, 1982), for the aptly-named *Cold Sweat* imprint of Denoël.

In 1982, with *Les Mangeurs de Murailles* (*The Eaters of Walls*), a novel about a bunker-like cubic city threatened by giant termites, Brussolo began producing a steady flow of novels for Fleuve Noir's *Anticipation*, twenty-seven in total until 1989. Eight of these were straightforward horror stories, and two heroic fantasy novels (see Chapter VIII). Some of the most notable titles were: *Territoire de Fièvre* (*Fever Land*, 1983), taking place in the Almohan universe, featured a planet-sized beast floating in space. *Les Lutteurs Immobiles* (*The Motionless Fighters*, 1983) was based on

the concept of the protection of objects taken to its limits: If someone broke an object, one of his bones was broken as a punishment. Monstrous worlds where men were victims of ghastly plagues, mutations, and inexplicably hostile environments were pictured in *Les Bêtes Enracinées* (*The Rooted Beasts*, 1984), *Ce Qui Mordait Le Ciel...* (*What Bit the Sky...*, 1984) and its sequel, *Crache-Béton* (*Spit-Concrete*, 1984), where a disease caused people to spit gravel; and the *Cycle des Ouragans* (*Saga of Storms*) series (Nos. 1399, 1414, 1424, 1985-86), taking place in the Almohan universe, on the planet Santal, plagued by hellishly destructive winds. There, a teenage girl, Nathalie, and her Dobermann, Cedric, encountered slaughterhouse concerts and fled from mad priests. Novels about mercilessly hostile futures included the award-winning series *Les Soldats de Goudron* (*The Tar Soldiers*; Nos. 1330, 1366, 1382, 1537, 1984-87), with its underwater subway, cannibal ambulances and inextinguishable fires, *Enfer Vertical en Approche Rapide* (*Vertical Hell Rapidly Approaching*, 1986), with its tower-like prison of Shaka-Kandarec where convicts can be set free if they win twenty ghastly trials, one for each floor of the tower, and *Danger Parking Miné!* (*Danger: Mined Parking!*, 1986), where concrete was poured inside buildings to defeat the homeless.

In the late 1980s, Brussolo was given his own horror imprint by publisher Gérard de Villiers (see Chapter VIII), and returned to *Présence du Futur* with a new series of brilliant novels, just as horrific, and always exploring biological themes, such as *Procédure d'Évacuation Immédiate des Musées Fantômes* (*Procedure for the Immediate Evacuation of the Phantom Museums*, 1987), in which the souls of the departed were used as a source of energy; *Le Château d'Encre* (*The Castle of Ink*, 1988), featuring shadows serving as medical symbiotes; *L'Homme aux Yeux de Napalm* (*The Man with the Napalm Eyes*, 1989), a grim, hallucinatory Christmas tale; *Le Syndrome du Scaphandrier* (*The Diver's Syndrome*, 1992), and *Mange-Monde* (*World-Eater*, 1993), a collection of short stories.

In the 1990s, Brussolo diversified his production even further: more thrillers, including the *Conan Lord* series at Librairie des Champs-Élysées; more horror novels, under his own name at Fleuve Noir's *Anticipation*, and dark fantasies under the pseudonym of "Kitty Doom" at *Présence du Futur*; as well as some mainstream and historical fiction. Brussolo returned to *Anticipation* in 1992 with a few genre novels, such as *Rinocérox*, about berserker-like robot tanks; and *Capitaine Suicide* (*Captain Suicide*, 1992), about a living planet.

One of the major genre achievements of the 1980s was G.-J. **Arnaud**'s prodigious, award-winnng series, *La Compagnie des Glaces* (*The Ice Company*) published at Fleuve Noir's *Anticipation*, starting with *La Compagnie des Glaces* (*The Ice Company*; No. 997, 1980). The *Ice Company* was the sprawling saga of a future Earth that lived under a new Ice Age. The population lived in domed cities, connected by extended rail networks, which carried power as well as trains and goods. The world of the *Ice Company* was ruled by a variety of powerful organizations, such as the rail companies, the sect-like Dispatchers' Guild, and the Church of the Neo-Catholics. On the ice shelf lived tribes of mysterious, red-furred humanoids who could stand the freezing cold, and whose origins were a baffling mystery. A scientist, Lien Rag, embarked on an odyssey to discover the secret origins of his world. As the series progressed, other major characters were established: the Gnome, a dwarf who founded the powerful Ice Shelf Company on top of the frozen Pacific; Lady Diana, the head of the Transamerican Company and one of the few persons to know the secrets origins of the companies; Yeuse, the beautiful, former cabaret singer who eventually climbed to a position of power; Kurts the pirate, a mutant with a powerful computerized rogue locomotive. Lien's quest eventually took him into space, where all the secrets of his world were at last revealed. Reclaiming Earth from its frozen state then became the focus of his adventures.

For its sheer scope and ambition, and unrivalled craftmansip, the *Ice Company* ranks with such established masterpieces as Isaac Asimov's *Foundation* and Frank Herbert's *Dune*. It quickly became a best-seller, won the 1982 French science fiction Grand Prize, spawned a popular role-playing game, and was awarded its own dedicated imprint in 1988. Arnaud reached a conclusion of sorts with Volume 62, *Il Était Une Fois La Compagnie Des Glaces* (*Once Upon a Time, the Ice Company*) (1992), but has now started to write new stories taking place several centuries earlier in the saga in a new series entitled *Chroniques Glaciaires* (*Ice Chronicles*).

During the 1980s, Denoël's *Présence du Futur* introduced most of the major new authors of the decade. After Brussolo, the most notable new writer presented by *Présence du Futur* was Jean-Marc **Ligny**, who had also been included in Curval's anthology, *Futurs au Présent* (*Present-Day Futures*). Ligny's first novel, *Temps Blancs* (*White Times*), was published in 1979. It featured a city governed by powerful computers which also regulated time itself. Outside was a white, icy wilderness inhabited by mutants and telepathic wolves. Ligny continued to pen a series of dark, pessimistic novels for *Présence du Futur* throughout the 1980s. *Biofeedback* (1979) was a Philip K. Dick–like novel about a near-future world caught in the madness of a giant computer. *Furia!* (1982) was the first in a series of novels influenced by rock music. *Yurlunggur* (1987) showed the Australian Aborigines' eponymous dream-snake invade the grim reality of the modern Paris suburbs. Finally, *D.A.R.K.* (1988) was a nihilistic vision of World War III.

In 1988, Ligny began to write more traditional novels for Fleuve Noir's *Anticipation*, starting with two collaborations with Dominique Goult, *Kriegspiel* and *Dreamworld* (1988), followed by his series *Les Voleurs de Rêves* (*The Stealers of Dreams*; FNA 1670, 1681, 1694, 1706, 1719, 1731,

1989-90); a two-volume heroic-fantasy saga *Succubes* (*Succubi*; see Chapter VIII); the trilogy of *Op Tao* (Nos. 1779, 1784, 1791, 1990), which was itself included and continued in the series, *Chroniques des Nouveaux Mondes* (*Chronicles of the New Worlds*; Nos. 1817, 1829, 1846, 1852, 1991), taking place in a galactic civilisation where humans cohabited with two other alien species. Other notable novels included *Aqua* (1993) and *Cyberkiller* (1993) for Fleuve Noir, and the award-winning *Inner City* (1996), a cyberpunk novel for J'ai Lu. Ligny also wrote *Slum City* (1996), a juvenile cyberpunk role-playing game novel for Denis Guiot's *Vertige* juvenile imprint (see below), which took place in the same universe as *Inner City*.

Emmanuel **Jouanne** was one of the founder of most notable member of the Limites group. He tried to bring science fiction and mainstream literature closer together by writing a number of highly literary, poetic works that emphasized style over content. His fist novel, *Damiers Imaginaires* (*Imaginary Squares*, 1982), published by *Présence du Futur*, featured a futuristic mankind living in vast, floating palaces which behaved like chess pieces on an invisible board in an unimaginable game. His next novel, *Nuage* (*Cloud*, 1983), published by *Ailleurs & Demain*, was a variation on the *Solaris* concept of a world materializing people's unconscious desires; in this case, only Prune, a little girl, was able to adapt and survive. Jouanne then returned to *Présence du Futur* for a series of stylistically striking novels and short story collections, such as *Ici Bas* (*Here Below*, 1984), *Dites-le avec des Mots* (*Say It with Words*, 1985), co-written with Jean-Pierre **Vernay** (see above), *Cruautés* (*Cruelties*, 1987), *Terre* (*Earth*, 1988), *Le Rêveur de Chats* (*The Dreamer of Cats*, 1988), and *La Trajectoire de la Taupe* (*The Mole's Trajectory*, 1989). (Jouanne also penned one *Gore* novel for Fleuve Noir with Jacques **Barbéri**—see Chapter VIII.)

Finally, the single, major new female writer of the decade was Joëlle **Wintrebert**, whose first novel, *Les Olympiades Truquées* (*The Trick Olympics*), had originally been published in 1980 in *Ici & Maintenant* (see above), but which won the Rosny award in its revised version, published in 1987 by Fleuve Noir's *Anticipation*. Wintrebert followed it with *Les Maîtres-Feu* (*The Fire Masters*, 1982), published by J'ai Lu, which featured the adventures of Jordane, a young human linguist, and Beni, a young sentient native dinosaur, on the volcanic planet of Dante. Her next novel, *Chromoville* (1983), also published by J'ai Lu, told how various exotic characters were reluctantly forced to foment a revolution in a futuristic city. *Le Créateur Chimérique* (*The Chimerical Creator*, 1988), still at J'ai Lu, won the French Science-Fiction Award. It took place on the water world of Farkis, among the native Ouqdars, who worshipped the goddess Khimer. But nothing was as it seemed, and Farkis was ultimately revealed to be an artificial eco-system manipulated by men. Other notable works included *Bébé-Miroir* (*Mirror Baby*, 1988) for Fleuve Noir's *Anticipation*, a collection of short stories, *Hurlegriffe* (*Screamclaw*, 1996) and numerous excellent young-adult novels (see below).

Other notable authors of the 1980s published by *Présence du Futur* included:

Francis **Berthelot**'s first novel was *La Lune Noire d'O-rion* (*The Black Moon of Orion*, 1980), a gay-themed space opera for *Dimensions*. He then went on to write a major heroic-fantasy work, *Khanaor* (see Chapter VIII). Berthelot then followed in the footsteps of Jouanne and the "Limites" group with the allegorical *La Ville au Fond de l'Oeil* (*The City at the Bottom of the Eye*, 1986) for *Présence du Futur*, which won the prestigious Rosny Award. It was followed by the award-winning *Rivage des Intouchables* (*Beach of the Untouchables*, 1990), also for *Présence du Futur*. It took place on the planet Erda-Rann, where the sea was a living entity acting as the natives' collective unsconscious.

Another Limites author was Jacques **Barbéri**, who wrote five novels for *Présence du Futur*, starting with *Kosmokrim* (1985), and continuing with *Une Soirée à la Plage* (*An Evening on the Beach*, 1988), *Narcose* (1989), *Guerre de Rien* (*War of Nothing*, 1990), and *La Mémoire du Crime* (*The Memory of the Crime*, 1992). **Barbéri** also collaborated with Yves **Ramonet** under the pseudonym of "Oscar Valetti" to pen three space operas for Fleuve Noir's *Anticipation* (Nos. 1880, 1896, 1913, 1992-93).

Belgian author Alain **Dartevelle** made a notable debut in 1984 with *Borg, ou l'Anatomie d'un Monstre* (*Borg, or the Anatomy of a Monster*), which was followed by *Script* (1989), published at *Présence du Futur*, an experimental, Kafkaesque novel taking place in the city of Newgorod. *Imago* (1994), published by J'ai Lu, was yet another surreal journey through an imaginary city, organized according to the laws of Freudian theories. More recently, Dartevelle penned a two-volume juvenile fantasy, *Le Cycle de Vertor* (*The Saga of Vertor*, 1997).

Antoine **Volodine** also made a notable debut in 1985 with *Biographie Comparée de Jorian Murgrave* (*Comparative Biography of Jorian Murgrave*), published by *Présence du Futur*. The book was assembled as a mosaic of fragments of texts composing the biography of the eponymous character, who came to Earth after his native world had been destroyed by war, but did not find peace. Other Volodine novels published at *Présence du Futur* included *Un Navire de Nulle Part* (*A Ship from Nowhere*, 1986), which painted a striking image of Russia submerged under a luxuriant jungle; the award-winning *Rituel du Mépris, Variante Moldscher* (*Ritual of Contempt, the Moldscher Variation*, 1987), and *Des Enfers Fabuleux* (*Some Fabulous Hells*, 1987), all of which belonging to the Limites current. In the 1990s, Volodine turned his back on science fiction and committed himself entirely to mainstream literature, producing a string of critically acclaimed novels for publisher Minuit. However, a number of these, such as *Le Nom des Singes* (*The Name of the Apes*, 1994), *Le Port Intérieur* (*The Inner Harbor*, 1996), and *Nuit Banche en*

Balkhyrie (*White Night in Balkiria*, 1997), contained marginal genre elements.

Several other notable new authors published by Fleuve Noir's *Anticipation* during the 1980s, were:

Michel **Pagel**'s first *Anticipation* novel was *Demain Matin au Chant du Tueur!* (*Tomorrow Morning When the Killer Sings*, 1984), a post-cataclysmic tale of survival in a France destroyed by earthquakes. Pagel wrote twenty-two novels for *Anticipation*, concluding with *Orages en Terre de France* (*Storms Over the Land of France*, 1991). Some of these titles included several heroic fantasy series, written under both his own name and the pseudonymn of "Félix Chapel," and a vampire novel (see Chapter VIII). Among the more notable science fiction works were *La Taverne de l'E-spoir* (*The Inn of Hope*, 1984), the moving portrayal of a dystopian world; *Le Viêt-Nam au Futur Simple* (*Future Tense Vietnam*; FNA 1320, 1984), a tale of World War III; *Pour Une Poignée d'Helix Pomatias* (*For a Fistful of Helix Pomatias*, 1988), a parody of the hard-boiled detective novel; and *Le Cimetière des Astronefs* (*The Graveyard of the Spaceships*, 1991).

Alain **Paris** wrote thirty-three novels for *Anticipation*, including nine in collaboration with Jean-Pierre Fontana, starting with *Les Bannières de Persh* (*The Banners of Persh*, 1984) in which an Earth astronaut stranded on an alien world becomes a pawn in a game played by intelligent insects. Paris' other collaborations with Fontana included the trilogy of *Les Ravisseurs d'Éternité* (*The Kidnappers of Eternity*; No. 1323, 1359, 1484, 1984-86), a tale about a post-cata-clysmic world where men lived in closed cities such as New Jericho; the four-volume heroic-fantasy series of *Chroniques de la Lune Rouge* (*Chronicles of the Red Moon*; see Chapter VIII) and *Le Désert des Cendres* (*The Desert of Ashes*, 1992).

Alone, Paris penned several other heroic fantasy series, such as the trilogy *Chroniques d'Antarcie* (*Chronicles of Antarctia*); the trilogy of *Pangea* and the prodigious ten-volume saga of *Le Monde de la Terre Creuse* (*The World of the Hollow Earth*; see Chapter VIII). His more notable science fiction works included the *Soldat-Chien* (*Dog Soldier*) series (Nos 1434, 1600, 1986-87) about a mercenary operating in a *Bladerunner*-like future; "Reich" (1986), based on the idea that the Nazis had discovered time travel in 1945; and *AWACS* (1993). In 1988, Paris also penned *Achéron* for publisher Aurore, and *Daïren* for J'ai Lu.

Jacques **Mondoloni**'s first novel was *Je Suis Une Herbe* (*I Am an Herb*, 1982) for J'ai Lu, and featured a mutant vegetable. It was followed by *Papa 1er* (*Daddy 1st.*, 1983) for *Présence du Futur* and then the *Goulags Mous* (*Soft Gulags*) series (Nos. 1289, 1343, 1529, 1576, 1984-87) for Fleuve Noir's *Anticipation*, in which the world was a semi-Communist state monitored by telepaths.

Finally, Pierre **Stolze** enjoyed a cult following for *Le Serpent d'Éternité* (*The Serpent of Eternity*) (1979) and *Kamtchatka* (1980), both published by OPTA in their

Galaxie-Bis imprint. Later **Stolze** penned the humorous *Marilyn Monroe et les Samourais du Père Noël* (*Marilyn Monroe and Santa Claus' Samurais*, 1986) for J'ai Lu and *Intrusions* (1990), a collection of strong, imaginative short stories. Other notable works include *Theophano 960* (1995) for Fleuve Noir's *Anticipation* and *La Maison Usher ne Chutera pas* (*The House of Usher Shall Not Fall*, 1996) for *Destination Crépuscule*.

c. Other Notable Writers

At the very end of the 1970s, as science fiction became more popular, a number of Fleuve Noir authors who had previously been writing espionage and detective thrillers segued to the *Anticipation* imprint to write genre novels.

The first of these was Piet **Legay**, whose first genre novel was *Demonia, Planète Maudite* (*Demonia, Cursed Planet*, 1977). In total, Legay penned fifty-five novels until *Shaan!* (1994). Some of the most notable included *Vega IV* (1978), the story of a forbidden romance between an Earthwoman and an alien, a theme reversed in *Le Défi Génétique* (*The Genetic Challenge*, 1980); *L'Ultime Test* (*The Ultimate Test*, 1980) was a clever murder mystery set on a planetoid; *Un Monde Si Noir* (*Such a Dark World*, 1982) and *Elle s'appelait Loan* (*Her Name Was Loan*, 1982) featured a beautiful alien woman whose job was to find human bodies for her people; *Dimension Quatre* (*Dimension Four*, 1983), subtitled "Time's Law," was about the secret Illuminati living among us who could access another dimension; *Viol Génétique* (*Genetic Rape*, 1985) saw mankind attempt to force an alien race into slavery. Later novels were loosely connected through the series *Dossiers Maudits* (*Accursed Files*), which started with *Mortel Contact* (*Deadly Contact*; No. 1520, 1987), in which the entire personnel of a space outpost had inexplicably vanished; another notable entry in the series included *Les Portes de l'Enfer* (*The Gates of Hell*, 1987), in which a man was found to be both alive and dead. The series continued with Nos. 1558, 1579, 1648, 1679, 1744, 1756, and 1774 (1987-90). Another important series was *Chronos* (Nos. 1799, 1814, 1826, 1991).

Gilles **Morris** had been writing the *Vic Saint-Val* series for Fleuve Noir since 1973; when it was discontinued in 1979, he naturally segued to *Anticipation* with *Facteur Vie* (*Life Factor*, 1979). Morris penned a total of fifty-seven genre novels, concluding with *Psychosphère* (1992). A large number of his novels were grouped in trilogies, often published several years apart. The most notable included the post-nuclear world of the *Villes-Corolles* (*Corolla Cities*; Nos. 959, 1087, 1151, 1979-82); *La Nappe Verte* (*The Green Slick*), in which a living organism attacked planets (Nos. 979, 1021, 1095, 1980-81); *Les Cervoboules* (*The Ball-Brains*), in which the crew of a spaceship fought brain creatures (Nos. 1070, 1129, 1137, 1981-82); *Les Calins* (*The Kitties*), cute alien felines which used their mental powers to take over the world (Nos. 1165, 1188, 1221, 1982-83); *Hellium*,

about the colonization of an alien planet (Nos. 1322, 1337, 1344, 1984); *Apocalypse* (Nos. 1313, 1363, 1381, 1984-85); *Le Talion*, about an ultra-violent future society (Nos. 1409, 1416, 1423, 1985-86); *La Medicarchie*, about a future world where doctors ruled (Nos. 1452, 1461, 1478, 1986); *Les Oumladrs*, where Earth was threatened by extra-dimensional beings (Nos. 1481, 1488, 1498, 1986); *Les Mitochondres*, about an alien intelligence which tested and gave supranormal powers to men (Nos. 1528, 1530, 1546, 1987).

Christopher **Stork** also made his debut at *Anticipation* in 1979 with *L'Ordre Établi* (*The Established Order*). In total, Stork wrote forty-seven novels for *Anticipation* concluding with *Alter Ego* (1988). Some of his more notable works included *Achetez Dieu!* (*Buy God!*, 1980), the description of a world-wide theocracy; *L'Usage de l'Ascenseur est Interdit aux Enfants de Moins de Quatorze Ans Non Accompagnés* (*The Use of the Elevator Is Forbidden to Unaccompanied Children Under 14*, 1980), which featured a race of alien children who considered adulthood as a disease; *Les Derniers Anges* (*The Last Angels*, 1981), which showed how Earth's religions were manipulated by alien entities; *L'An II de la Mafia* (*Year II of the Mafia*, 1982), which described a post-cataclysmic USA ruled by the Mafia; *Pièces Détachées* (*Spare Parts*, 1984), a frightening look at organ smuggling, not unlike Niven's *A.R.M.* stories; *Les Lunatiques* (*The Lunatics*, 1985), a thriller taking place inside a Lunar hospital; and *Billevesées et Calembredaines* (*Nonsense and Gobbledygook*, 1985), where Stork himself was the hero, pitted against two intelligent insects who have shrunk him to their size. From 1973 to 1988, Stork also used the pseudonym "Marc Avril" to pen a series of espionage novels written in the first person, starring Marc Avril, the leader of a team of four gifted freelance intelligence agents. The series was comprised of over thirty titles, several of which included genre elements: super-weapons, space stations, Nazi conspiracies, devil worshippers, parapsychologists and mediums working for the CIA and KGB, a love potion, and others.

Finally, the last prolific author of Fleuve Noir who shifted to writing for *Anticipation* in 1979 was Adam **Saint-Moore**, who penned eight novels belonging to a series entitled *Chroniques de l'Ère du Verseau* (*Chronicles of the Age of Aquarius*) between 1979 and 1985. These depicted the history of a post-nuclear future where Earth was under the domination of a matriarchal society. Saint-Moore also wrote numerous espionage novels featuring the character *Face d'Ange* (*Angel Face*). Some of these included marginal genre elements such as *Face d'Ange, la Dame et l'Ogre* (*Angel Face, the Lady and the Ogre*, 1976), *Face d'Ange dans le Cercle Magique* (*Angel Face in the Magic Circle*, 1977), and *Face d'Ange et le Dinosaure* (*Angel; Face and the Dinosaur*, 1979).

Other *Anticipation* writers of the decade included:

Michel **Honaker**, whose first *Anticipation* novel was *Planeta Non Grata* (1983), featuring alien vampire birds holding a world in thrall. **Honaker** wrote nineteen novels blending horror and science fiction, until *L'Oreille Absolue* (*Absolute Ear*, 1992). Notable titles included *Le Semeur d'Ombres* (*The Sower of Shadows*, 1985), in which a space outpost was invaded by an alien plant; *Lumière d'Abîme* (*Light of the Abyss*, 1985), in which regulators hunted missing clones; *Building* (1987), about a planet-wide city; and the *Vorkul* trilogy (Nos. 1441, 1496, 1575, 1986-87), about mysterious aliens with strange powers. In 1989, with *Bronx Ceremonial* (No. 1723), Honaker brought the character of the Commander, a grim devil hunter named Ebenezer Graymes created for *Media 1000*, to *Anticipation* and continued the series there (see Chapter VIII). He also penned some horror novels for the *Gore* imprint, and more recently, a series of juvenile heroic fantasy works (also see Chapter VIII).

Hugues **Douriaux** was one of Fleuve Noir's steady providers of heroic fantasy novels (see Chapter VIII). Douriaux's first novel for *Anticipation*, however, was *Les Démoniaques de Kallioh* (*The Demons of Kallioh*; Nos. 1307, 1391, 1984-85), in which an alien princess and her Terran lover fight demon-like beings. Douriaux's other science fiction titles included the aptly entitled *Galax-Western* (1985); *P.L.U.M. 66-50* (Nos. 1428, 1468, 1986), about a female android from Vega-II on the run on Earth; *Tragédie Musicale* (*Musical Tragedy*, 1986), a sci-fi rock tale of murder and revenge; *Vermine* (*Vermin*, 1987), *Syndrome Apocalypse* (1989), *Roche-Lalheue* (1991), *Malterre* (1992), *Symphonie Pastorale* (*Pastoral Symphony*, 1993), *Warrior* (1994), and *Interférences* (1996). All genres included, Douriaux produced thirty-eight novels for Fleuve Noir.

Th. **Cryde** wrote five novels between 1984 and 1993, including the *Insects* trilogy (Nos. 1336, 1356, 1415, 1984-85) about mutated insects which ended up creating a third race that was half-insect, half human.

Thierry **Lassalle** wrote *Nord* (*North*, 1984) and *La Piste du Sud* (*Trail of the South*, 1986), a single novel in which the son of the Southern King escaped from the frigid North.

Gilbert **Picard** contributed four novels in 1985 and 1986, including *Le Miroir du Passé* (*The Mirror of the Past*, 1985), featuring a mirror that showed images from the past; and *Le Volcan des Sirènes* (*The Mermaids' Volcano*, 1985) and *Les Combattants des Abysses* (*The Fighters of the Abyss*, 1986) which took place in the post-cataclysmic world of the 26th century, where survivors tried to build a new, marine-based society

Claude **Ecken** wrote six novels for *Anticipation*, from *La Mémoire Totale* (*The Total Memory*, 1986), about an amnesia plague; the *Chroniques Télématiques* (*Telematic Chronicles*), about a hyper-computerized future (No. 1521, 1987); *L'Ère du Pyroson* (*The Pyroson Era*; Nos. 1683, 1690, 1989); and *Le Cri du Corps* (*The Body Scream*, 1990).

Gérard **Delteil**, who had already written numerous detective novels for Fleuve Noir, penned four futuristic thrillers, including *Transfert* (*Transfer*, 1986), about body transfer; *Hors-Jeu* (*Out of the Game*, 1987), and *Tchernobagne* (*Chernocamp*, 1989).

Guy **Charmasson**, whose previous genre credits included *Le Crépuscule des Surhommes* (*The Twilight of the Supermen*) published by Marabout in 1978, began writing for *Anticipation* in 1986 with *L'Heure Perdue* (*The Lost Hour*). He wrote four novels, including the two-volume *Les Tueurs d'Elmendorf* (*The Killers of Elmendorf*; Nos. 1634, 1639, 1988).

Also notable were *Adonai* (Nos. 1328, 1392, 1984-85) by "Michaël Clifden" (a pseudonym of H.-M. **Jaouen**); *Quand Souvenirs Revenir, Nous Souffrir et Mourir* (*When Memories Return, We Suffer and Die*, 1986) by **Dagory**; and *Roulette Russe* (*Russian Roulette*, 1985) by **Daridjana**.

Other notable authors of the period published by other imprints included:

Patrice **Duvic**, whose first novel was the Van Vogt-inspired *Poisson-Pilote* (*Pilot Fish*), published by *Présence du Futur* in 1979. Duvic also wrote *Naissez, Nous Ferons le Reste* (*Be Born, We'll Take Care of the Rest*) for Presses-Pocket in 1979 and novelized his script for the motion picture *Terminus* (see Book 1, Chapter I) for J'ai Lu in 1982.

The eclectic Jean-Pierre **Vernay** published *L'Enfer en ce Monde* (*Hell in This World*, 1980) at Ponte Mirone; then *Dites-le avec des Mots* (*Say It with Words*, 1985) in collaboration with Emmanuel Jouanne (see below) and *Fragments du Rêve* (*Dream Fragments*, 1989) for *Présence du Futur*.

Présence du Futur also published Maurice **Mourier**'s *Parcs de Mémoire* (*Memory Park*, 1985).

The twin hosts of the popular television show, *Temps X* (see Book 1, Chapter II), Igor and Grichka **Bogdanoff**, wrote *La Machine Fantôme* (*The Ghost Machine*, 1985) for J'ai Lu; a juvenile novel, *La Mémoire Double* (*The Double Memory*, 1989), and a remarkable study on the perception and definition of science fiction by mainstream figures, *L'Effet Science-Fiction* (*The Science Fiction Effect*, 1979).

Marianne **Leconte**'s *Titres SF* imprint published two striking genre novels by guitarist and film director Marc **Bourgeois**, *Altiplano* (1980), about a baroque future Earth, and *Vautours* (*Vultures*, 1982), which took on a space colony threatened by native flying creatures.

Titres also published Michel **Calonne**'s *Hurleville* (*Screamcity*, 1981), about a future Europe threatened by a new Ice Age. Calonne had previously published a collection, *Le Plus Jeune Fils de l'Écureuil* (*The Squirrel's Youngest Son*, 1958), which included several genre stories, and a novel, *Une Folie au Bord de la Mer* (*A Folly at the Sea Shore*, 1960), in which a new construction material was used to build a futuristic, sixteen-story residence.

Garry's short-lived *Mémoires d'Ourte-Ciel* (*Memoirs from Beyond the Sky*) imprint published a mix of *fantastique* (see Chapter VIII) and science fiction, including works by "Yves Dermèze" (Paul Béra), "Red Ilan" (Daniel Piret), "Lionel Rex" (Maurice Limat), "Roy Morrisson"

(Robert Clauzel). Among the genre writers published by Garry were:

Maurice **Merault**, with *Meurtres Transtemporels* (*Transtemporal Murders*, 1980) and *L'Être de la Grande Spirale* (*The Being from the Great Spiral*, 1982).

Janine **Renaud**, with *La Base Interdite* (*The Forbidden Base*, 1979) and *Les Suppliciés d'Iryknos* (*The Tortured Men of Iryknos*, 1982).

And **Guadalcazar**, with *Le Dernier Combat* (*The Last Battle*, 1979) and *Xirlo* (1980).

A publishing phenomenon of the mid-1980s was that of the franchised book: paperback series such as the *Executioner*, the *Destroyer*, and their French counterparts, super-agent Malko Linge aka *S.A.S.*, sold in huge numbers through newstands and paperback bookstores. This was extended to science fiction with dedicated imprints devoted to *Perry Rhodan*, Jeffrey Lord's *Blade*, E.C. Tubb's *Dumarest*, and Jimmy Guieu (see above). Three notable imprints in this vein were:

Jag le Félin (*Jag the Feline*), published under the house name of "Zeb **Chillicothe**," was started in 1985 by Christian Mantey, and included thirty-four volumes by 1994. Mantey wrote and/or plotted the majority of the series; some novels were written in collaboration with Serge Brussolo, Pierre Dubois, Joël Houssin, and Jacques Barbéri. Jag was a fierce warrior in a futuristic, post-cataclysmic Earth, devastated by the realisation that the universe is no longer expanding but contracting.

The *Russ Norton* character, published under the house name of "Terence **Corman**" and "Don A. **Seabury**," was started in 1987 by Richard D. **Nolane**. Only six volumes were published. It was a post-nuclear saga taking place in world plagued by mutants and monsters.

La Compagnie des Glaces (*The Ice Company*) was started by Fleuve Noir in 1988 (see above).

Finally, *Rohel Le Conquérant* (*Rohel the Conqueror*) was started in 1992 by Pierre **Bordage** and is reviewed under heroic fantasy in Chapter VIII.

d. Mainstream Writers

Perhaps the most surprising mainstream author to write genre fiction during the 1980s was famous writer, economist, and politician Jacques **Attali**, a special advisor to French president François Mitterand. Attali wrote a series of themed novels including *La Figure de Fraser* (*Fraser's Figure*, 1984) and, especially, *La Vie Éternelle* (*Eternal Life*, 1989), a novel in space travellers stranded on an alien world replayed mankind's history.

Professor Rémy **Chauvin**, a renowned popular psychologist, penned a number of genre novels on the cutting-edge of science and philosophy, such as *Voyage Outre-Terre* (*Journey Beyond Earth*, 1983), *Les Veilleurs du Temps* (*The Time Watchers*, 1984), and *Le Nouveau Golem* (*The New Golem*, 1993).

Other notable genre works published in mainstream imprints included:

André **Audureau**'s *Feminapolis* (1979), a novel in which women ruled the world.

Le Dernier de l'Empire—K'harmattour (*The Last of the Empire*, 1981) by an African author from Senegal, Smbeme **Ousmane**, who wrote this fascinating two-volume African political novel.

Michel **Braudeau**'s *Fantôme d'une Puce* (*Ghost of a Chip*, 1982), a proto-cyberpunk tale.

Michel **Arrivé**'s *L'Horloge sans Balancier* (*The Clock Without Pendulum*, 1983), the diary of a mutant.

René **Dzagoyan**'s *Le Système Aristote* (1984).

And, finally, Alain **Nadaud** with *L'Envers du Temps* (*The Other Side of Time*, 1985), a wonderful novel in which a Roman legionary discovered that time was running backards.

e. Juveniles

The popularity of *Star Wars* and other media products ensured that genre concepts showed up with increasing regularity in juvenile novels produced throughout the decade.

One of the best authors of the period was Thérèse **Roche**, who won the 1984 juvenile category of the French science fiction award for her series of humorous, creative novels about children and alien lifeforms, done for publisher Magnard. Among her best novels were *Garlone et les Snils* (*Garlone and the Snils*, 1982), *Le Naviluk* (1983), *Les Extra-Chats* (*The Extra-Cats*, 1984), *Lily Moon et la Lucarne* (*Lily Moon and the Small Window*, 1988), and *Appoline et la Porte du Temps* (*Appoline and the Gate of Time*, 1989).

Joëlle Wintrebert (see above) made a notable entry in the genre with *Nunatak* (1983), published by Casterman. She then continued to produce a series of colorful young-adult novels characterized by their skillful handling of difficult or sophisticated themes. Her best works in this category included *La Fille de Terre Deux* (*The Girl from Earth-Two*, 1987), *L'Océanide* (1992), the award-winning *Les Diables Blancs* (*The White Devils*, 1993) and, more recently, *Les Ouraniens de Brume* (*The Ouranians of Mist*, 1996) and *Les Gladiateurs de Thule* (*The Gladiators of Thule*, 1997).

Science fiction-themed series remained as popular as ever. Some of the best entries were:

Maurice **Bitter**'s time-travelling *Les Robinsons du Temps* (*The Robinsons of Time*), published by La Farandole, starting in 1982.

Emmanuel **Baudry** and Alain **Royer**'s *Les Invisibles* (*The Invisibles*), also starting in 1982.

Jean **Chalopin** and Nina **Wolmark**'s *Ulysse 31* (1982), based on a popular animated series (see Book 1, Chapter IV) transplanting the tale of Ulysses into the 31st century.

Other notable genre works included:

Lucien-Guy **Touati** and Claude **Rose**'s *Guillou dans les Étoiles* (*Guillou Among the Stars*, 1979).

René **Escudié**'s *L'Enfant Qui Avait accroché la Lune* (*The Child Who Had Hooked the Moon*, 1980) and *La Charrette à Traverser le Temps* (*The Cart Which Travelled Through Time*, 1982).

Dominique **Peko**'s *La Planète des Norchats* (*Planet of the Norcats*, 1981).

René **Durand**'s *Ludine de Terrève* (1981).

Georges **Goetz**'s *L'Efface-Temps* (*The Time Eraser*, 1983).

Valérie **Groussard**'s *Caravane Interstellaire* (*Interstellar Caravan*, 1984) and *Le Tour de Xrom* (*The Tower of Xrom*, 1986).

And, finally, Michel **Lamart**'s *Le Rire du Robot dans les Champs Magnétiques* (*The Laughter of the Robot in the Magnetic Fields*, 1984).

4. The 1990s

The 1990s was a decade of recovery for French science fiction.

Commercially, science fiction regained some of the ground it had lost during the 1980s. By the late 1990s, with slightly over one hundred new novels per year, and numerous new authors and magazines, French science fiction was both quantitatively and qualitatively again florishing.

Creatively, a new generation of writers generally returned to more conventional themes and narratives, ensuring greater readability. The influences of American science fiction and of French science fiction of the 1950s and 1960s were more pronounced, and yet more fully assimilated, leading to novels that could arguably compete with the best of American production.

a. The Publishers

In 1992, Fleuve Noir split its classic *Anticipation* imprint into five sub-imprints: *Legend*, devoted to heroic fantasy (see Chapter VIII); *Space*, for space operas; *Métal* for cyberpunk novels; *Delirius*, for satirical novels; and *Panik*, for horror-oriented science fiction. In 1997, *Anticipation* finally discontinued its numbering and started again with a new imprint simply called *SF*, comprised of five new sub-imprints: *Zone Rouge* (*Red Zone*), *Métal*, *Space*, *Polar*, and *Mystère*, the latter two for mystery-themed science fiction, and a new numbering system, starting from No.1. Throughout this period, editors such as Daniel Riche, Nicole Hibert, and Philippe Hupp managed to foster a slate of new talents, such as **Ayerdhal**, Richard **Canal**, Serge **Lehman**, Roland C. **Wagner**, Jean-Claude **Dunyach**, and Alain **le Bussy**.

At Denoël, Jacques Chambon continued to edit *Présence du Futur*, publishing new works by Houssin, Brussolo, Douay, and Ruellan. Chambon also added two new imprints, *Présence du Fantastique* (see Chapter VIII) and the more literary-oriented *Présences*.

Jacques Sadoul's J'ai Lu published Ayerdhal and Canal. Klein's *Ailleurs & Demain* and Goimard's Presses-Pocket did not play significant roles in terms of French authors.

The torch was picked up by new publishers, including:

L'Atalante, a small company based in Nantes in Western France, which introduced Pierre **Bordage** and Paul **Borrelli**, and also published translations of Terry Pratchett and Michael Moorcock (see Chapter VIII); *Destination Crépuscule* (*Destination Twilight*), created by Gilles **Dumay** (see below); Mnemos, which published mostly heroic fantasy novels (see Chapter VIII); SENO, under the direction of editor Stéphane **Marsan**; Lefrancq (which mostly reprinted classic works by Wul, Carsac, etc.); Khom-Heidon; CyberLibris and others.

A number of new magazines also made their first apparances in the late 1990s: *Bifrost*, *CyberDreams* (edited by Francis **Valéry**), *Étoiles Vives* (*Living Stars*), *Galaxies* (co-edited by J.-C. Dunyach), and *Ozone*, recently retitled *Science-Fiction Magazine*.

b. Major Authors

One of the best new science fiction writers revealed by Fleuve Noir's *Anticipation* imprint during the 1990s was **Ayerdhal**. His books formed complex, richly textured, multi-chaptered sagas, taking place in elaborate space empires *à la* Frank Herbert, who was an acknowledged influence, worthy of a Dan Simmons or Iain Banks. Ayerdhal's first saga was *La Bohême et l'Ivraie* (Nos. 1763, 1769, 1775, 1781, 1990), in which a group of artists eventually challenged the power of the galactic Homeocracy. It was followed by the intricate galactic epic, *Mytale* (Nos. 1803, 1813, 1832, 1991), *Demain, une Oasis* (*Tomorrow, an Oasis*, 1991), the two-volume *Le Chant du Drille* (*The Drille's Song*; Nos. 1871, 1875, 1992), *Cybione* (1992) and, finally, *Polytan* (1993).

In 1993, Ayerdhal moved to J'ai Lu, for which he created the *Dune*-like *Daym* Universe in two brilliant novels, *L'Histrion* (*The Histrionic*, 1993) and *Sexomorphoses* (*Sexomorphosis*, 1994). The Daym universe was a galaxy in turmoil, filled with conflicting powers such as the Empire, the Confed, the Nauts, the Scients, the Church, and the mystic Taj Ramanes. At the center of the plots and counterplots was Genesis, the planet-wide living computer, who sought to bring peace to it all. Genesis' tool was Aimlin(e), a two-brained sexomorph whose role was to act as a galactic jester, but whose origins remained shrouded in mystery. For J'ai Lu, Ayerdhal also wrote *Ballade Choréiale* (*Choreial Ballad*, 1994), a C. J. Cherryh-like tale exploring the moral and political consequences of exposing a medieval planet to the advanced technology of the Human Federation, *Parleur* (*Speaker*, 1997), a political fantasy work (see Chapter VIII); and edited *Génèses* (*Genesis*, 1996), a remarkable original anthology of modern French science fiction à la *Dangerous Visions*.

Pierre **Bordage** was, without a doubt, the other major new French science fiction author of the 1990s. In his trilogy of *Les Guerriers du Silence* (*The Warriors of Silence*), comprised of three 500-page volumes—*Les Guerriers du Silence* (*The Warriors of Silence*, 1993), *Terra Mater* (1994), and *La Citadelle Hypénéros* (1995), published by L'Atalante—Bordage recaptured most of the strengths of Dan Simmons' *Hyperion*. *Les Guerriers du Silence* was a rich and strongly structured space opera, with numerous characters and subplots, telling the story of a Galactic Empire in chaos, threatened by the mysterious alien Scaythes of Hypeoneros, tools of a power which wished to uncreate the universe. Against them stood the "Warriors of Silence," a band of reluctant heroes with unique abilities, selected by the forces of Life to save the cosmos. Bordage also wrote the science fantasy series, *Rohel Le Conquérant* (*Rohel the Conqueror*; see Chapter VIII). In 1996-97, Bordage wrote *Wang*, a two-volume series taking place in the year 2211 on a planet divided into two worlds separated by a mysterious "curtain." Wealth and technological comfort existed on its Western side, savagery and poverty reigned on its Eastern side. The hero, Wang, broke the law of Assol the Mongol, an Eastern clan leader, and was condemned to exile in the West. He crossed the Curtain at Most, a town located in Bohemia, unaware of what existed on the other side, for no one had ever before returned from the West. *Wang* won the 1997 Best Novel Eiffel Tower Grand Prize award.

Other major writers of the decade included:

Currently living in Senegal, Richard **Canal** wrote exotic, poetic, and intriguing novels influenced by African tribes and traditions. Canal's earlier works included *La Malédiction de l'Éphémère* (*The Curse of the Ephemereal*, 1986), in which aliens interested in mankind's arts kept it prisoner within the solar system; the *Animamea* trilogy published by Fleuve Noir's *Anticipation* (Nos. 1536, 1554, 1582, 1986-87), which also published *La Guerre en ce Jardin* (*The War in This Garden*, 1991); and *Villes-Vertiges* (*Vertigo-Cities*, 1988), for Aurore. In 1990, Canal began producing a series of major novels for J'ai Lu, starting with *Swap-Swap* (1990), *Ombres Blanches* (*White Shadows*, 1993), *Aube Noire* (*Black Dawn*, 1994), each won the coveted Rosny Award. These novels formed an "African" trilogy in which racial and economic conflicts tore up a near-future grain-producing Africa and industrially exhausted America. More recent works included *Le Cimetière des Papillons* (*The Graveyard of the Butterflies*, 1995) and *Les Paradis Piégés* (*The Trapped Paradises*, 1997), also published by J'ai Lu.

Serge **Lehman**'s first novel was *La Loi Majeure* (*The Major Law*; No. 1738, 1990), written under the pseudonym of "Don Herial" for Fleuve Noir's *Anticipation*. It became the first volume in a trilogy entitled *La Guerre des Sept Minutes* (*The Seven-Minute War*) (Nos. 1738, 1762, 1990) that remained uncompleted for contractual reasons. Lehman's next

novel, *Espion de l'Étrange* (*Spy of the Weird*, 1992), was signed "Karel Dekk," which also was the name of the book's main character. During the four years that followed, Lehman wrote mostly short stories. In 1995, he published his fourth novel, *Le Haut-Lieu* (*The High Place*; see Chapter VIII), followed by a collection, *La Sidération* (*Sideral*, 1996). (Most of his stories took place in roughly the same fictional universe.) in 1996, Fleuve Noir launched Lehman's latest series, *F.A.U.S.T.* (three volumes 1996-97), in its own dedicated imprint. This best-selling series was set at the beginning of the next century, when two huge megacorps joined forces to take over the world. The self-styled "Defenders" were a group of men and women dedicated to fight them. More recent works, also published by Fleuve Noir, included a *F.A.U.S.T.* spin-off, *Wonderland* (1997), the colorful tale of a near-future garbage dump, and *L'Ange des Profondeurs* (*The Angel of the Depth*, 1997), the first of a new series featuring Martin Dirac, a man haunted by the disappearance of his father, whose quest brought him face to face with the secrets behind modern myths such as lycanthropy and Hollow Earth. In 1998, Lehman also edited *Escales sur l'Horizon* (*Stopovers Over the Horizon*) for Fleuve Noir, an original anthology comprised, like Ayerdhal's *Géneses* (*Genesis*), of contemporary stories.

Roland C. **Wagner** had discovered science fiction through Fleuve Noir's *Anticipation* imprint in the 1960s, and grew up to become one of its most prolific and popular writers in the 1990s. Wagner's novels blended humor, action, and rock music weirdness, in a fast-paced, easy to read narrative. His first novel for *Anticipation* was *Le Serpent d'Angoisse* (*The Terror Snake*; FNA 1585, 1987), later incorporated into the series *Histoire du Futur Proche* (*Tales of the Near Future*). He has since then written nineteen novels for Fleuve Noir, including the following series: *Le Faisceau Chromatique* (*The Chromatic Cluster*; Nos. 1614, 1770, 1787, 1820, 1988-91). *Poupée aux Yeux Morts* (*Dead-Eyed Doll*; FNA 1649, 1654, 1659, 1988) was a long novel split into three separate novels because of its length. It told the story of Kerl, an astronaut who returned to Earth after a fifty-year cosmic journey, to be confronted by several mysteries, such as why he aged fifty years, while his girlfriend, who stayed on Earth, did not. Guided by a Fouinain, a cartoon-like alien, Kerl embarked on a complex journey of discovery that ended with a battle between two Gestalt entities, one embodying the forces of neo-puritanism, tyranny, and repression, the other the future of mankind among the stars. The third volume of *Poupée aux Yeux Morts*, entitled *Les Futurs Mystères de Paris* (*The Future Mysteries of Paris*), gave its name to, and anticpated the themes of, Wagner's most-popular series (Nos. 1988, 1998, 2001, 15, 1996-97). *Les Futurs Mystères de Paris* featured the adventures of private detective Tem (short for "Temple Sacré de l'Aube Radieuse" (*Sacred Temple of the Radiant Dawn*)), a mutant who had the power of going unnoticed. Tem was not invisible, just "transparent" to other people. The series took place in 2063, fifty years after the mysterious "Great Terror" which shook up civilization.

Wagner's other series included *Histoire du Futur Proche* (*Tales of the Near Future*; FNA 1585, 1678, 1695, 1702, 1987-89), *La Sinsé Gravite au 21* (*The Sinsey Gravitates at 21*; FNA 1806, 1825, 1991), another long novel split into two parts, written under the pseudonym of "Red Deff." (*Les Psychopompes de Klash* (*The Psychopumps of Klash*, 1990), a space opera, was also written as "Red Deff," but recently reprinted by Mnémos under Wagner's name. Wagner also wrote, under the name of "Richard Wolfram," a parodic series of short stories making fun of French fandom, collected in *Quelqu'un Hurle Mon Nom* (*Someone Howls My Name*, 1993). He also used the "Wolfram" pseudonym to pen numerous novels published under Jimmy Guieu's name in the Jimmy Guieu imprint. Finally, he contributed a horror novel to Francis Valéry's *Agence Arkham* series (see Chapter VIII).

Jean-Claude **Dunyach** is a scientist, as well as one of the editors of *Galaxies*. His first book, *Autoportrait* (*Self-Portrait*), published by *Présence du Futur* in 1986, was a collection of poetic, sensitive stories. He made his mark at Fleuve Noir's *Anticipation* with a series of novels including fantasies like *Le Jeu des Sabliers* (*The Game of the Hourglasses*; see Chapter VIII) and the award-winning series *Étoiles Mortes* (*Dead Stars*; Nos. 1837, 1838, 1858, 1991-92). In the latter, giant alien creatures the size of a city enabled mankind to reach the stars, but only wealthy people could use their services. More recent works by Dunyach include *Roll Over, Amundsen* (1993).

Laurent **Genefort** is a prolific young writer whose first novel for *Anticipation* was *Le Bagne des Ténèbres* (*The Penitentiary of Darkness*; No. 1655, 1988), the first volume in the *Era of the Vangke*, a series taking place in the far future, when the eponymous, mysterious alien race has left behind strange artifacts. The series also featured another mysterious race, the godlike Yuweh, who had the power to build worlds. The following novels were part of the *Vangke* universe: Nos. 1655, 1861, 1884, 1932, 1954, 1961, 1966, 1974, 1980, 10, and 25 (1988-97). Nos. 1993 and 1994 (1996) formed a separate subset of the *Vangke* series, entitled *L'Opéra de l'Espace* (*The Space Opera*). In it, an opera singer, after losing his voice, embarked on a quest to find a Yuweh who might help him regain what he had lost. During his travels, he assembled a company of various other artists. Genefort's novels emphasized adventure and action, and displayed his concern for ecology. He was particularly skilled at building colorful yet believable alien worlds and cultures. Another notable series was that of the *Interregnum* era (Nos. 1872, 1922, 1944, 1992-94), which included the award-winning *Arago* (No. 1922, 1993). In total, Genefort has written seventeen novels for Fleuve Noir to date.

Belgian author Alain **le Bussy** was an active member of French fandom for years before finally publishing his first novel, the award-winning *Deltas*, in *Anticipation* in 1992.

Deltas was the first volume of the *Cycle d'Aqualia* (*The Aqualia Cycle*; Nos.1885, 1908, 1931, 1992-93), the story of the one-legged space pilot Carvil. Le Bussy also penned a number of heroic-fantasy works, including the saga of *Yorg* (see Chapter VIII). His other works included *Deraag* (1993), *Garmalia* (1994), *Quête Impériale* (*Imperial Quest*, 1994), *Soleil Fou* (*Crazy Sun*, 1995) and *Équilibre* (*Balance*, 1997), the story of a waterworld, the sole meeting point between mankind and an alien reptilian race.

After studying psychology and playing keyboards for a free-jazz band in the '80s, Paul **Borrelli** decided to become a writer. His first novel, *L'Ombre du Chat* (*The Shadow of the Cat*), published by L'Atalante in 1994, was a detective story set in Marseilles in a *Bladerunner*-like 21st century. The hero was an illegal weapon manufacturer who was suspected of being a serial killer and had to find the real murderer. *Désordres* (*Disorders*, 1997) was yet another serial-killer story, featuring some of the same characters.

Finally, Swiss writer Wildy **Petoud** wrote *La Route des Soleils* (*The Road of the Suns*, 1994) for *Anticipation*. It was a space opera filled with parodic elements of previous novels published by the imprint, while offering a more subtle and complex read on another level. *Tigre au Ralenti* (*Tiger in Slow Motion*), published by *Destination Crépuscule* in 1996, related a very strange and unsettling story, fascinating in the way it was told and structured.

c. *Other Notable Writers*

At *Anticipation*, other notable writers who came out of the last decade included:

Alain **Billy**, with *L'Orchidée Rouge de Madame Shan* (*Mrs. Shan's Red Orchid*, 1988), *Maaga-la-Scythe* (1988), and *Les Fruits Sataniques* (*Satan's Fruits*, 1993).

Gilles **Bergal** (using the pseudonym of "Milan"), with *Le Clone Triste* (*The Sad Clone*, 1988) and *Le Rire du Klone* (*The Klone's Laughter*, 1988).

Samuel **Dharma**, with *Traqueur* (*Tracker*, 1988) and *Nécromancies* (1988).

Bertrand **Passegué**, with the *Bêta IV Hydri* series (Nos 1658, 1677, 1691, 1707 and 1720, 1988-89), the *Troglo Blues* series (Nos. 1805, 1815, 1991), and *Métacentre* (*Metacenter*, 1992).

François **Rahier**, with *Le Crépuscule du Compagnon* (*The Twilight of the Companion*, 1988) and *L'Ouragan des Enfants Dieux* (*The Storm of the God Children*, 1991).

Max **Anthony**, with *L'Androïde Livide de l'Asteroïde Morbide* (*The Livid Android of the Morbid Asteroid*, 1989), *Le Huitième Crystal du Docteur Mygale* (*The Eighth Crystal of Doctor Tarentula*, 1993), and *Boulevard des Miroirs Fantômes* (*Boulevard of the Phantom Mirrors*, 1993).

Yves **Carl**, with *Jhedin Ovoghemma* (1989).

Patrick **Lacheze**, with *Fleur* (*Flower*, 1989).

Jean-Claude **Lamart**, with *Top Niveau* (*Top Level*, 1989).

Gérard **Néry**, with a series entitled *1999* (Nos. 1688, 1713, 1724 and 1736, 1989-90).

Philippe **Guy**, with *Dernière Tempête* (*Last Tempest*, 1989) and *Phalènes* (1996).

Manuel **Essard**, with a series entitled *Au Nom du Roi* (*In the King's Name*; Nos. 1827, 1848, 1991).

Dominique **Brotot**, with *Penta* (1992), one of the first cyberpunk novels published in France, *Neurovision* (1993), and *Le Voleur d'Organes* (*The Organ Thief*, 1994).

Marc **Lemosquet**, with *Plug-In* (1992) and *Cobaye* (*Guinea Pig*, 1993).

Oscar **Valetti**, with *Labyrinth-Jungle* (1992), *L'Ombre et le Fléau* (*The Shadow and the Plague*, 1992), and *Chair Inconnue* (*Unknown Flesh*, 1993).

Daniel **Ichbiah** and Yves **Uzureau**, with *Xyz* (1993), a purposefuly confusing, satirical, nonsensical novel about a man who is the last hope of humanity and who is sent down to a mysterious planet from which no one has ever returned.

Thierry **Pastor**, with *Les Yeux de la Terre Fo*lle (*The Eyes of the Crazy Earth*, 1993).

C. **Kauffman**, with *Nickel le Petit* (*Nickel the Small*, 1994) and *Jalin Ka* (FNA 1949, 1994).

Franck **Morrisset**, with *Alice qui dormait* (*Alice Who Slept*, 1996) and *La Résolution Andromède* (*The Andromeda Resolution*, 1997).

Philippe **Renford**, with *Plus Proche que vous ne Pensez* (*Closer Than You Think*, 1997), the story of an amnesiac mutant in search of his past and of the purple-eyed woman he loves, set in an apocalyptic background where every plant, animal, and insect can be lethal.

Serge **Séguret**, with his *Zone Rouge* (*Red Zone*) trilogy (Nos. 4, 12, 21, 1997), about futuristic bikers in a *Damnation Alley*-like world.

The writing team signing "G. Elton **Ranne**," with *Double Jeu* (*Double Game*, 1997) and *Chute Libre* (*Free Fall*, 1997).

Gore writer Christian **Vilà** returned to science fiction with *Ice Flyer* (1997).

Other notable authors of the period published by other imprints included:

Gilles **Dumay** was, for many years, one of the major writers in French science fiction fandom, where he published a great number of short stories. In the late 1980s, Dumay created *Destination Crépuscule* (*Destination Twilight*), a publishing house that quickly grew, first in association with Encrage, an already well-established company, and later by itself, changing its name to Orion in 1997. Dumay is now at the head of a small press which has, throughout the years, gained in respect and reputation. He is also the editor-in-chief of a semi-annual professional magazine, *Étoiles Vives* (*Living Stars*), and is an occasional illustrator. As he became more involved in editing, he wrote less frequently. He is the author of one novel, *Strange Rock Anathema* (1993). Other notable authors published by *Destination Crépuscule* included: Guillaume **Thiberge** with

L'Appel de l'Espace (*The Call from Space*, 1996); Nicole **Bouchard** with *Terminus Fomalhaut* (1997), and Thierry **Di Rollo** with *Number Nine* (1997).

Another fan turned writer turned publisher was Francis **Valéry**, also a renowned essayist and book-seller. Valéry's best novel was *Les Voyageurs sans Mémoires* (*The Travellers Without Memories*), published by *Destination Crépuscule* in 1997. Other notable works included *L'Arche des Rêveurs* (*The Ark of the Dreamers*, 1991) and *Altneuland* (1995). Valéry established the imprints *Cyberdreams* and *Agence Arkham* (see Chapter VIII) with publisher DLM. One of the best authors published by *Cyberdreams* was Sylvie **Denis** with *Jardins Virtuels* (*Virtual Gardens*, 1995).

Mnemos' leading author was Mathieu **Gaborit** (see Chapter VIII) with the saga of *Ecryme* (1994), co-written with Guillaume **Vincent**; also notable was Fabrice **Colin** for *Neuvième Cercle* (*Ninth Circle*, 1997) and *Les Cantiques de Mercure* (*The Canticles of Mercury*, 1997), about underground life in 1999 New York.

Another active member of French fandom, Raymond **Milési**, co-edited the renowned anthology *Mouvance* in the 1980s. His novels included *Chien Bleu Couronné* (*Crowned Blue Dog*, 1991) at *Anticipation* and *Salut Delcano!* (*Hello Delcano!*, 1996) and *Futur sans Étoiles* (*Starless Future*, 1997), the first two installments in a space opera series published by new publisher SENO.

Another notable SENO author was Éric **Cowez** with *Island One: L'Arche des Outre-Ciel* (*The Ark from Beyond the Sky*, 1995) and *Geminga, La Civilisation Perdue* (*Geminga, the Lost Civilization*, 1996), a Martian space opera taking place in the year 3115.

Convention organizer, fanzine editor, reviewer, radio DJ, and short-story writer Jean **Millemann** wrote *Fumeterre* (*SmokeyEarth*, 1994), a collection of dark science fantasy stories.

Alain **Duret** penned *Kronikes de la Fédérasion* (*Kronikles of the Federation*, 1997) for Belgian publisher Lefrancq.

Finally, François **Tessier**, with *Les Foudres de l'Abîme – La Directive Exeter* (*The Lightning from the Abyss—the Exeter Directive*, 1997), wrote the first in a series of futuristic thrillers entitled *Polaris*, published by Khom-Heidon.

d. Mainstream Writers

The most astounding success of the decade for a genre novel published as mainstream literature was Bernard **Werber**'s *Les Fourmis* (*The Ants*, 1991), recently translated into English. Werber combined his knowledge of ants with a real talent of scientific vulgarization to offer a startling if anthropomorphized inside look at the world seen through the eyes of ants. The lack of conventional dramatic structure helped legitimize the novel as something other than a science fiction novel. Two sequels were published, *Le Jour des Fourmis* (*The Day of the Ants*, 1992) and *La Révolution des*

Fourmis (*The Revolution of the Ants*, 1996). Werber also applied his talents to *Les Thanatonautes* (*The Thanatonauts*, 1994), a novel dealing with the exploration of death.

Another major genre author was Maurice G. Dantec, whose notorious, best-selling thriller *Les Racines du Mal* (*The Roots of Evil*) was published by the famous *Série Noire* crime imprint in 1995, even though it featured cyberpunk themes, such as the recording of the entire contents of a man's mind into a computer and the survival of his electronic personality after his physical death.

Other works in the same vein included René **Belletto**'s *La Machine* (1990), a novel about mind transfer, adapted into an eponymous 1994 film; and some of Serge Brussolo's recent thrillers, such as the *Conan Lord* series (1995).

Other notable genre works published as mainstream literature included:

Amin **Maalouf**'s *Le Premier Siècle Après Béatrice* (*The First Century After Beatrice*, 1992), in which a new drug enabled women to give birth only to boys.

Jean-Pierre **Berbier**'s *Le Soleil et la Mort en Face* (*The Sun and Death in My Face*, 1994), in which the hero received the thoughts of a murderer from the future.

Hervé **Bazin**'s *Le Neuvième Jour* (*The Ninth Day*, 1994).

Vladimir **Makanine**'s *La Route est Longue* (*The Road Is Long*, 1994), which described a future world where animals were no longer butchered for food.

Loup **Durand**'s *Le Grand Silence* (*The Great Silence*, 1994), a novel about telepathy.

And, finally, Tunisian author Alia **Marbrouk**'s *Le Futur est déjà là* (*The Future Is Already Here*, 1997).

e. Juveniles

As outlined in Chapter VIII, the publishing of genre books for children and young adults exploded in the 1990s. New imprints were created, such as *Livre de Poche Jeunesse*, *Pleine Lune* (*Full Moon*), and *Vertige Science-Fiction*, edited by Denis Guiot.

Classic novels by Stefan Wul (such as *Niourk*) were reprinted for a new public; famous authors like Jean-Pierre Andrevon, Michel Honaker, Jean-Marc Ligny, Michel Jeury (with his daugher Dany), and François Sautereau, contributed new works (see Chapter VIII).

The most successful genre writers for young adults to have come out of the decade were the writing team of Alain **Grousset** and Danielle **Martinigol** (who also used the pseudonym "Kim Aldany") with novels like *Les Oubliés de Vulcain* (*Forgotten on Vulcan*, 1995), *L'Enfant-Mémoire* (*The Memory Child*, 1996), *Les Mondes Décalés* (*The Out-of-Line Worlds*, 1997), plus the popular series of Kerri & Megane.

François **Appas** created the series of *Les Quatre Voyageurs* (The Four Travellers), four time-travelling children, for younger readers in 1992 with *Les Quatre Voyageurs à la Poursuite d'Aspirinus* (*The Four Travellers Pursue Aspirinus*).

Other notable authors included:

Pascal **Garnier** with *À rebrousse temps* (*Time Backwards*, 1993); and Robert **Belfiore** with *La Pieuvre de Xeltar* (*The Octopus of Xeltar*, 1995; written with Philippe Henri **Turin**) and *Le Maître de Juventa* (*The Master of Juventa*, 1996).

LAST WORD

Hundreds of writers. Thousands of novels.

This is a considerable achievement for France, a country with a population one-fifth that of the United States, and a mainstream literary, scientific, and economic environment generally dismissive, if not hostile, to the *fantastique* and science fiction.

Like any form of literature, French science fiction and *fantastique* have known both glorious and difficult times; but always, the flame has stayed alive.

In spite of the material obstacles thrown in their path, such as having to compete economically and creatively with major American authors, and the extreme difficulty of making a living from writing purely genre fiction, French authors of unassailable talent, the equals of their English-speaking colleagues, have managed to make a powerful mark on the history of the genre.

As the new millennium approaches, French science fiction and *fantastique* face new challenges resulting from the same economic pressures exerted upon publishers, especially niche publishers, everywhere; they also can look forward to greater opportunities as new writers increasingly grow up in a friendlier and more receptive environment.

Across the centuries, the children of Rabelais, Cyrano de Bergerac, and Jules Verne are still embarking on imaginary journeys and extraordinary voyages, adding new lands to the same ancient maps, continuing the exploration of the mindscapes of imagination.

CHAPTER X

French-Canadian Science Fiction & Fantastique

by Jean-Louis Trudel

Any discussion of French-language speculative fiction in Canada should start with definitions. For science fiction, Jean-Marc **Gouanvic** has pointed out in his article "*La SFQ dans son Histoire: Quelques RemarquesRétrospectives et Prospectives*" (*Imagine* No. 49) the dubious usefulness of listing works as falling into this category before the concept was even fully developed. Science fiction nowadays encompasses a wide range of themes, stories, and treatments, not all of which existed in the past. The same is true of speculative fiction, a sometimes denigrated label which remains an extremely convenient way to designate works variously identified as science fiction, fantasy, *fantastique*, or horror. This is especially important since, in French, fantasy is a semantically empty word. Instead, several categories inhabit the same semantic space: *insolite*, *merveilleux*, and the many ramifications of the *fantastique* or fantastical.

The term most widely used in Québec's *milieu* of writers and critics is SFQ: *Science-Fiction Québécoise*. It will not be used here. Many writers of French-language science fiction in Canada were not natives of the province of Québec or did not reside there when they wrote. Even today, its descriptive value remains doubtful, though it has a powerful prescriptive one. An additional initial is often tacked on in order to speak of "*la science-fiction et le fantastique québécois*," but the dominant position of science fiction within the community may be due to the fact it is the one genre the community can most easily lay a claim to.

In French-speaking Canada, the *fantastique*, which subsumes to an extent both fantasy and supernatural horror, has much older roots than science fiction, clearly predating the formation of a united community, and its practitioners are, for the most part, found outside the self-identified community of SFFQ writers. When speaking generally, this survey will refer to speculative fiction (abbreviated as SF) to discuss all the genres or sub-genres mentioned above. Otherwise, the appropriate labels will be used. Even though it is anachronistic for at least half the period considered here, the term science fiction will be understood to describe stories which present situations and plot devices incorporated within the modern genre so designated, such as future societies, fantastic voyages, or superhuman characters. Science fiction will involve an unavoidable rational component, often but not always appealing to the authority of science. As a result, its bounds will be time-dependent: a story which might have qualified as science fiction in the 19th century may be termed outright fantasy if penned in the 20th (unless it is a conscious throwback).

This essay surveys most of the history of French-language SF in French-speaking Canada.To a certain extent, it overemphasizes early works of science fiction whileskimming over the contemporary production of fantastical stories. Still, for all genres, it can only qualify as a summary presentation of an evolving scene after 1945.

THE PRECURSORS: FANTASY

The French-language fantasy literature in Canada is rooted in the old oral tradition of the settlers, in the literary tradition of France itself (the settlement of New France is contemporaneous with the first literary reworking of fairy tales by Charles **Perrault**), and also in similar currents of world literature. As part and parcel of the oral tradition, many cautionary tales incorporated, in a Canadian context, the supernatural figures of the Catholic religion—the devil especially, but also damned souls metamorphosing into werewolves or coming back as ghosts—as well as references to the mysterious powers of Native American medicine men.

Such motifs are used in the first novel of French-Canadian letters, *L'Influence d'un Livre* (1837; transl. as the *Influence of a Book*, 1993). The earliest known Canadian SF tales in French appear there for the first time in the printed form. While the novel's romantic treasure quest is certainly the work of its avowed author, Philippe **Aubert de Gaspé**, Jr., it is usually assumed that the fantastical episodes were contributed by the author's father, Philippe Aubert de Gaspé, Sr. (1786-1871), whose skeptical outlook shaped by the Enlightenment tended to treat supernatural elements with caution.

Other 19th-century writers such as Guillaume **Lévesque**, Paul Stevens or Honoré **Beaugrand** mined the same oral tradition, at first uncritically and even pietistically. Often, their stories exploited the horrific potential of the original tales. For instance, Beaugrand's story the *Werwolves* (1898),only published in English in the author's lifetime, is set in 1706 and tells of a band of Iroquois at the mouth of the Richelieu River, who feed on human flesh when they turn into werewolves. In 1913, it was made into a movie by theCanadian director Henry McCrae, which arguably stands as the world's first werewolf film. (Don Hutchison and Peter Halasz in their article "*Blood on the Snow: A Survey of Canadian Horror Fiction*" (*The Scream Factory* No. 18) attribute the story to *Henry* Beaugrand (1855-1929), but the reference is clearly to *Honoré* Beaugrand.)

A growing skepticism becomes evident in the later stories of authors like Pamphile **Lemay** and, especially, Louis **Fréchette**, whose ostensibly fantastical tales often subvert in fact the traditional beliefs by remaking them into stories of misperception. Themes imported from abroad, such as the *poltergeist*, start appearing instead of the old standbys like witchcraft. An excellent sampling of all these stories is found in Aurélien **Boivin**'s modern anthology *Le Conte Fantastique Québécois au XIXème Siècle* (*Fantastical Tales from Quebec in the 19th Century*, 1987).

In the first half of the 20th century, another element of the oral tradition, folk tales reflecting the legacy of European fairy tales, was systematically unearthed by ethnographers such as Marius Barbeau, who published the two resulting collections as children's books, beginning in 1942. One recurring hero in this popular pantheon is an avatar of the archetypal Jack, who often carries the day through a mixture of guile, luck, and virtue rewarded by higher powers. Called Ti-Jean, or "Little John," his name connects him to St. John the Baptist, patron saint of French-Canadians, often represented in Québec iconography as a young boy carrying (away?) a sheep. The entire corpus of legendary stories and motifs has undergone periodic revivals, in various forms ranging from folk music to beer labels, without ever enjoying any massive popularity or intellectual respect. Nevertheless, they remain as an enduring and pervasive substratum of fantastical literature in the culture of French-speaking Canada.

THE PRECURSORS: SCIENCE FICTION

The earliest piece of French-language Canadian science fiction is usually traced back to 1839. A Swiss immigrant, Aimé-Nicolas **Aubin**, published it under the name of Napoléon Aubin as an unfinished serial, *Mon Voyage à la Lune* (*My Journey to the Moon*). The first six episodes appeared irregularly in the newspaper *Le Fantasque,* edited and published by Aubin himself in Québec City, coming out on July 9 and 21, August 3, September 2 and 17, and October 1 of 1839.

Aimé-Nicolas Aubin himself is a fascinating figure. Born in 1812, in Chêne-Bougeries, Switzerland, he emigrated to the United States at the age ofseventeen. After a stay of six years, he moved to Montréal and then to Québec City, where he founded *Le Fantasque* In August 1837. The irreverent tone of his articles once netted him two months in jail. After *Le Fantasque* died, Aubin became a chemistry teacher, published the first two volumes of the *Histoire du Canada* by François-Xavier Garneau, and invented a gas-lighting device.

The science fiction component of the serial is most evident in the first episode. The hero's means of travel to the Moon is more whimsical than ingenious, reminiscent of **Cyrano de Bergerac**'s solutions. Though humbler in scope than **Voltaire**'s *Micromégas*, the serial does offer a broad critique of earthly prejudices. After the first episode, *Mon Voyage à la Lune* veers from social criticism to a Swiftian satire of the mores and customs of Québec's society in particular. Despite the closeness in dates and subject, as well as Aubin's links with the United States, there seems to be no connection between Edgar Allan Poe's *The Unparalleled Adventure of One Hans Pfall* (1835)—which in fact offers much more interesting science fictional speculations—and Aubin's serial. However,the green-skinned Lunatics are an early occurrence of the green alien motif in SF.

Other characteristics of the work and of its author should be noted. First of all, Napoléon Aubin was still a newcomer when he wrote it: French-language Canadian science fiction has continued to be shaped by immigrants from abroad (arguably, this is also true of English-language Canadian science fiction). This is far less true of fantasy or *fantastique* works in French, whose authors are more often home-grown.

Second, *Mon Voyage à la Lune* was an artifact of a small press manned by Aubin himself: Again, small presses have been a natural haven for native SF of every stripe in Québec throughout its history. However, whereas the fantastical works of authors such as Louis **Fréchette**, Jacques **Ferron**, or Anne **Hébert** have frequently found a mainstream audience, science fiction, with very few exceptions, has been almost entirely relegated to the small presses.

Finally, the story's content itself is typical of another enduring trend. After Aubin, science fiction in francophone Canada was used again and again as a literary device that allowed a present society to be criticized, either by pointing out its shortcomings through future improvements, or by proposing a different and better society.

Two 19th-century short stories unequivocally belong to the genre of science fiction: *Le Carnaval à Québec en 1996 (Écrit à distance d'un Siècle, en Février 1896)* (*Carnival in Quebec in 1996* [*Written a Century Before*]) (1896), by Nazaire Levasseur, and *La Tête de Saint Jean-Baptiste, ou Légende pour nos Arrières-petits-neveux en 1980* (*The Head of St. John the Baptist, or Legend for Our Great-Grand-Nephews in 1980*, 1880), by Wenceslas-Eugène Dick. Both stories belong to the robust traditionof "decimal futurism": the tendency to look ahead by an exact decade, century, or millennium.

The stories' themes are not vastly different. In both cases, the 20th century fulfills the hopes of Québec. Its new-found prosperity is symbolized by new railways and bridges, an increased population, the cultivation of new lands, an unshaken Catholic faith. Independence is at most alluded to, however. In *La Tête de Saint Jean-Baptiste*, Lake St. Jean has been drained, and the Province of Saguenay has a population of three million out of seven million French Canadians. Québec owes its new wealth to a gift from Saint John the Baptist, who came down to Earth in order to reward the province's piety. In *Le Carnaval à Québec en 1996*, a railway circles the Île d'Orléans and a new bridge crosses the Saint-Lawrence upstream from Québec City.

In these texts, it is of course not so much the stories that are interesting as the speculation about the future, which reflects a society torn between its religious past and the allure of a technological future. This is even more evident in the last known science fiction work of the 19th century.

Canada's first French-language science fiction novel, *Pour la Patrie* (1895; transl. As for *My Country*, 1975) by Jules-Paul **Tardivel**, builds on the same patriotic and religious themes, and also starts its narrative in the 20th century. It advocates the founding of a reborn New France, to extend in North America a French and Catholic civilization. Ironically, this landmark novel in French-Canadian letters was written by a Franco-American, for Tardivel was born in Covington, Kentucky. (The hundreds of thousands of Quebecers who emigrated to theUnited States are known as Franco-Americans. The most notable of them may be another Franco-American writer, Jack Kerouac.) This goes a long way towards explaining the radicalism of his vision, considering the role of the church in the survival—and later the assimilation—of the Franco-American diaspora. The novel bears the imprint of Tardivel's ardent Catholic faith and ultramontane beliefs, and might be classified as fantasy, despite the political speculation, if the author did not believe as firmly in the reality of his religion as any modern hard science fiction writer believes in the truth of science. Still, it makes for a bizarrecounterpart to H. G. Wells' novels.

Another work partially intended as propaganda is *Sim-*

ilia Similibus, ou La Guerre au Canada (*The War in Canada*, 1916), by Ulric **Barthe**. In it, Québec City is conquered by the Prussian army. This may be the first alternate-history novel of Québec, though it is finally revealed as a mere dream. The author defends the pro-British cause and Canada's participation in the war that is going on in Europe.

Much lighter in tone, *Les Aventures Extraordinaires de Deux Canayens* (*The Extraordinary Adventures of Two Canucks*, 1918), by Jules **Jéhin**, has no polemical intent. Two French Canadians use a superior flying machine to set up a short-lived Empire of Space (not of Outer Space, but actually of the Airs). Two elements lighter than hydrogen are introduced to justify the flying machine, which harks back to Jules **Verne**'s *Robur le Conquérant*, but it's all a simple excuse for a humorous jaunt. The son of a famous Belgian violinist who worked with Calixa Lavallée, Doctor Jules Jéhin de Prume seems to have spent much of his life in New York.

On the other hand, *La Cité dans les Fers* (*The City in Chains*, 1926), by Ubald **Paquin**, is a grim anticipation of a bid for Québec independence, perhaps inspired by the 1916 Easter uprising in Ireland. It features a full-scale revolt bankrolled by a Franco-American millionaire, defeated by British might and treason from within. Strictly speaking, it is a hybrid, melding the *Zukunftskrieg* (future war) genre and the political thriller, but lacking in science fictional elements.

Also intended as popular entertainment, *L'Impératrice de l'Ungava* (*The Empress of Ungava*, 1927), by Alexandre **Huot**, tells of an undiscovered city in the Ungava. The SF tincture is extremely dilute and it is much more in the line of the traditional adventure stories of the time. It does offer the amusing twist that in this tale, Québec nationalism is answered by Amerindian pride and self-determination.

La Fin de la Terre (*The End of the Earth*, 1931), by Emmanuel **Desrosiers**, is more modern in its conception. Earth's agony, caused by overpopulation, famine, lack of fertile soil, natural catastrophes, and exhaustion of non-renewable resources, is described, but the ending is optimistic about the technological (and ethical) progress of mankind: With the consent of the Martians, the survivors remove themselves to the Red Planet. The grandeur of the ideas is noteworthy and the like was not seen again for several years. The author also managed to write a full-length novel without a single female character.

Siraf, Étranges Révélations, Ce Qu'On Pense de Nous par-delà la Lune (*Siraf, Strange Revelations, What They Think of Us Beyond the Moon*, 1934) was written by a Frenchman who had emigrated to Alberta, Georges **Bugnet**. Here, science fiction is a literary framing device that allows an astral entity to converse with a human about various philosophical problems of interest to the author. Unlike a rare but hardy strain of modern Québec pseudo-SF novels, the author was not half-postulating that this entity really-existed, but merely using it as his mouthpiece.

Armand **Grenier**'s novels, on the other hand, tried to

uphold Québec's "race," religion, and language. *Erres Boréales* (*Northern Impetus*, 1944) was published by the Éditions Laurin under Grenier's pseudonym of "Florent Laurin." It takes place in 1968. A new invention has warmed the sea off the coasts of Labrador and the Eastern Arctic, so that the French-Canadian "race" has colonized and exploited northern territories that are chock-full of precious ore deposits. Nationalist feeling is exalted; the courage and spirit of the pioneers is glorified. A map of the new lands with their French names is glued inside the book's cover and drawings are included. *Défricheur de Hammada* (*Hammada Pioneer*, 1953) was published under Grenier's pseudonym of "Guy René de Plour." In it, the ideal Québec society is transplanted in the middle of the Sahara, under domes where Christian and family values are fully adhered to. Grenier announced that he was preparing to write, presumably in English, a work called the *Future Laid Out in the Unknown*, but it seems never to have materialized.

In the same tradition of proof by science fiction, *Eutopia* (1944), written under the pseudonym Jean **Berthos**, and improbably attributed to Thomas-Alfred Bernier (1844-1908) instead of plain old Thomas Bernier, combines technological inventions and a strange socialism that protects order, justice, and Christian virtue. Some have seen Fascism in this strange mix.

Other books are sometimes added to exhaustive lists for this period: *L'Île du Savoir* (*The Island of Knowledge*, 1947), a possible juvenile by Victor Boisson and Jean Conterno (not "Canteno" as sometimes mentioned). The book was printed in Canada soon after the end of the war but written in Lyons, France, between 1941 and 1942. It is not mentioned in the *Dictionnaire des Oeuvres Littéraires du Québec*, nor was it ever acquired by the National Library in Ottawa. Furthermore, it is among the first of several books published by Victor A. Boisson, whose later works were released in France, some of them in the Lyons area. Conterno's only claim to literary fame rests on the part-authorship of this book, while all evidence points to Victor A. Boisson being French and probably from Southern France. It has been suggested, rather plausibly, that the book was printed in Canada because the Second World War cast its authors (very) temporarily on the country's shores. All in all, it seems that it cannot be included as a genuine part of the corpus.

Lipha: Ses Étapes (*Lipha: His Stops*, 1931), by J.-O. Léger, has often been mistaken for science fiction because of its unusual title. In fact, it is a reprint collection of articles on political and agricultural matters, written under the pseudonym of "Lipha," the persona of an imaginary journalist. It has nothing to do with SF.

Marcel Faure (1922), by Jean-Charles **Harvey**, is a mix of the utopian novel and of the future-tense political thriller, with a dash of star-crossed love. It is less dramatic in its extrapolation than Paquin's work but can still be considered borderline SF, like Huot's Amerindian utopia. The agrarian utopias of Antoine Gérin-Lajoie, *Jean Rivard, Défricheur*

(*Jean Rivard, Pioneer*, 1862) and *Jean Rivard, Économiste* (*Jean Rivard, Economist*, 1864), are sometimes brought up also, but it is hard to speak of science fiction in connection with works where the author, towards the end of the second book, reminds readers who might find implausible the progress of the imaginary village of Rivardville that the real-life village of L'Industrie (now Joliette), in Montcalm county, has undergone exactly the same improvements.

Thus, at the end of this first period, French-language Canadian science fiction can be divided between the broadly utopian (from Tardivel to Grenier), the philosophical (Aubin, Bugnet, Desrosiers), the propagandistic (Barthe and most others to some degree), and the adventure tale (Jéhin, Huot, Paquin). In several cases, a considerable reluctance to get to the speculative part of the story is noticeable. Tardivel's novel does start right away forty years into the future, but Jéhin, Huot, Harvey, and Paquin incorporate long build-ups that stay on the safe side of the unknown. In Huot's case especially, the payoff is in the very last few chapters alone.

Yesterday

An era ended with *Défricheur de Hammada* in more than one way. While Catholic cultural and liturgical motifs still surface today in French-language Canadian SF, the Catholic discourse proper has quite simply vanished. Indeed, not only was Grenier's book the last real gasp of a Catholic literary tradition stretching back to Tardivel and Guillaume **Lévesque**, but it also marked the end of dilettante SF in French-speaking Canada. In the years which followed World War II, exhaustiveness becomes chimerical in all fields as more and more authors choose SF as their main writing avocation.

In marked contrast to the philosophical and propagandistic works of the older writers, the new popular serials put out as cheap pamphlets In post-war Québec used science fiction tropes to entertain. In the forthrightly science fictional *Les Aventures Futuristes de Deux Savants Canadiens-Français* (*The Futuristic Adventures of Two French-Canadian Scientists*, 1949), by Louis **Champagne**, the pseudonym of a series of forgotten hacks, the adventures of the heroes are reminiscent of early pulp science fiction in the United States. Indeed, that same year, Yves **Thériault** published at least one story in English, "*The Barren Field*," a tale of black magic, in the November issue of *Weird Tales*, one of the U.S. pulps. The most enduring of these serials, *Les Aventures Étranges de l'Agent Ixe-13, l'As des Espions Canadiens* (*The Strange Adventures of Agent X-13, the Ace of Canadian Spies*), put out by Pierre Daignault under the pen name of Pierre **Saurel**, included fifteen or so space-opera episodes published in 1960.

Stirrings of change were already evident during the war years. When Rodolphe **Dubé** published his speculative essay "Lepic et l'Histoire Hypothétique" ("Lepic and the Hypothetical History", 1940) in the book *Mondes Chimériques-*

(*Chimerical Worlds*) under the pseudonym of François Hertel, it was an early example of an alternate history in Québec SF. In fact, it is one of the rare instances of a francophone scenario based on a victory of the French over the English in the Seven Years' War.

However, in SF as a whole, the post war years were remarkably fallow and it was not until 1960 or so that a sea change occurred. The beginnings of the Space Age may suffice to explain the growing interest for science fiction. On the other hand, the recognition won by magical realism in world literature presumably played a role in the resurgence of French-language fantastical literature in Canada after 1960, just as the tremendous popularity in English-speaking countries of generic fantasy and horror clearly sparked the writing of works in the same vein after 1980. Furthermore, during the last couple of decades, various New Age cults and ideologies have generated literary echoes, usually on the margins of fantasy proper, though several of Esther **Rochon**'s books evince a Buddhist approach to both the myth-making and moral aspects of fantasy.

In French-speaking Canada, the transition from traditional to modern fantasy may be dated to Yves Thériault's *Contes pour un Homme Seul* (*Tales for a Man Alone*, 1944). His rural tales are crafted sparingly, proceeding directly to a character's inexplicable doom. More recently, his daughter, Marie José **Thériault**, has been writing, on the other hand, consciously archaic stories, as in the collection *La Cérémonie* (1978),which was translated as *The Ceremony* in 1980, or in her novel *Les Demoiselles de Numidie* (*The Maidens of Numidia*, 1984), both distinguished by a lush prose style.

The tradition of dark fantasy in short fiction was continued by several writers, though in new guises. Maurice **Émond**'s recent gathering of such stories in *Anthologie de la Nouvelle et du Conte Fantastiques Québécois au XXème Siècle* (*Anthology of Short Stories and Fantastical Tales from Quebec in the 20th Century*, 1987) serves up an excellent array of modern fantastical fiction in French by Canadian authors.

On the novel side, Marie-Claire **Blais** transposed the changes wrenching Québec's society in *La Belle Bête* (*The Beautiful Beast*, 1959), translated in 1960 as *Mad Shadows*, where evil is a tangible force occupying a phantasmagoricallandscape. Like authors Anne **Hébert** and Daniel **Sernine**, she was extending the lineage of Québec Gothic by adapting it to the changing times.

Up to 1974, the best literary works clearly belong to the fantastical strain within SF. During this period, the *fantastique* surfaces in intelligent short story collections like Claude **Mathieu**'s *La Mort Exquise* (*Delightful Death*, 1965) or Jacques **Brossard**'s *Le Métamorfaux* (*The Metamorfalse*, 1974), which are both wonderfully Borgesian in spots; or in such poignant collections as Roch **Carrier**'s *Jolis Deuils* (*Pretty Mournings*, 1964) and Claudette **Charbonneau-Tissot**'s *Contes pour Hydrocéphales Adultes* (*Tales for Adult Hydrocephalics*, 1974).

The *Fantastique* also was skillfully handled in the novels of Jacques **Ferron**, such as *La Charrette*(1968), which was translated as the *Cart* in 1980, or *L'Amélanchier*(1972), which was translated as the *Juneberry Tree* in 1975, both coming, at times, within hailing distance of South American magical realism. Antonine **Maillet**'s *Don l'Orignal* (1972), translated as the *Tale of Don l'Orignal* in 1978, is a more Rabelaisian kind of fantasy.

Closer to traditional fantasy, we find Michel **Tremblay**'s novel *La Cité dans l'Oeuf* (*The City in the Egg*, 1969), with a pleasantly original mix of folklore, Greek myths, and original ideas, while his short-fiction collection *Contes pour Buveurs Attardés* (1966), translated as *Stories for Late Night Drinkers* in 1977, is more traditional fare along *fantastique* lines.

Another noteworthy author is Claire de **Lamirande**, whose first novels appeared during this period. *Jeu de Clefs* (*A Game of Keys*, 1974) is an effective ghost story. In fact, SF motifs also appear in several of her later books, such as *L'Opération Fabuleuse* (*The Fabulous Operation*, 1978), though they tend to be overwhelmedby the mainstream sensibility she brings to her writing.

Finally, the traditional fairy tales for children collected and published early in this period by adapters following in the footsteps of Barbeau gradually made way for more original fantasies, as in Claude **Aubry**'s *Les Îles du Roi Maha Maha II: Conte Fantaisiste Canadien* (1960), translated as *The King of the Thousand Islands: a Canadian Fairy Tale* in 1963; Henriette **Major**'s*Le Club des Curieux* (*The Club for Inquisitive Folks*, 1967); or Danièle **Simpson**'s *Le Voleur d'Étoiles* (*The Star Thief*, 1971). In fact, Claude **Aubry**, who was a translator and chief librarian of the Ottawa Public Library from 1953 to 1979, spans the transition, since he also published early on a collection of folk tales.

As far as science fiction is concerned, the first blooms of a renewal in the sixties were probably not unrelated to the *révolution tranquille* that had begun to modify the old rules in Québec. Science fiction has always been the literature of change. Between 1960 and 1973, several writers were the first to publish more than one or two isolated science fiction stories, as had been the case until then, mostly because they shared in the surge of science fiction in juvenile literature.

In 1960, Guy **Bouchard** was among the first, publishing *Vénus via Atlantide*. Suzanne **Martel** followed, with her young-adult classic, *Surréal 3000 (Quatre Montréalais en l'an 3000, 1*963), translated as the *Underground City* (1964), with its still very readable account of life underground centuries after a nuclear war. From 1965 to 1968, Maurice **Gagnon** published the *Unipax* series of novels describing a worldwide organization devoted to peace and equipped with fabulous machines. Even Yves **Thériault** tried his hand at science fiction, between 1966 and 1967, with the *Volpek* series starring a secret agent in the James Bond mold who uses various nifty gadgets and tangles a few times with extraterrestrials.

While these short novels had aimed for a younger readership, Monique **Corriveau**'s *Compagnon du Soleil* (*Companion of the Sun*, 1976) was a trilogy meant for more mature adolescents. It dealt with repression and revolt, totalitarianism and freedom. For more than ten years, it stood as the only French-language SF trilogy in Canada. Starting in 1971, the *Jeunesse-Pop* Imprint of the Éditions Paulines (Médiaspaul) started to include regular SF offerings for its young readers, most often a blend of science fiction and adventure. Normand Côté, writing under the pseudonym of "Louis **Sutal**," and Jean-Pierre **Charland**, were among the more prominent names. By the end of the decade, Charles **Montpetit** and Daniel **Sernine** published their first books in the line. **Sernine** took over the imprint's editorship around 1985.

On the adult side, Ronald **Després** published in 1962 *Le Scalpel Ininterrompu* (*The Uninterrupted Scalpel*), in which the whole of humanity is vivisected within twenty years. In spirit, it is closer to some surrealists and their predecessors, **Lautréamont** or **Forneret**. Yves Thériault also wrote science fiction for adults: a collection of nuclear-war short stories *Si la Bombe m'était Contée* (*If the Bomb Was Told to Me*, 1962), and a novel *Le Haut Pays* (*The High Country*, 1973), occupying the borderlands of SF—since it refers to parallel worlds—and esoterism—since it mentions secret knowledge, initiates, and Great Ones. Classification can be hard.

Jacques **Benoit** specialized in a more flamboyant style, sometimes funny, sometimes cruel, producing a kind of skewed SF. His first novel, *Jos Carbone* (1967), translated in 1974, has occasionally been classified as SF: it is certainly not science fiction, and it is hard even to justify the label of "speculative fiction." The story does take place in an imaginary wood and the mood is surreal, but the place-names and the general atmosphere are not really distinct from Québec's old storytelling tradition and saint-laden toponymy. The setting is as real and as imaginary as Mariposa, Manawaka, or Yoknapatawpha counties, differing from them only in degree: It is a conceivable extension of Québec geography. Benoit's next novel, *Patience et Firlipon* (1970), was definitely SF: It spices a wonderful love story with futuristic gadgets in a Montréal of tomorrow. Finally, *Les Princes* (1973), translated as the *Princes* in 1977, describes a city that cannot fit on the known globe or in the known past, but where no overt magic is present. Call it "speculative fiction." More somber, it echoes the October Crisis, dealing with repression and discrimination.

Emmanuel **Cocke** was born in France, moved to Québec, and died in India in 1973, but his novels *Va Voir au Ciel si j'y suis* (*Go to Heaven and See If I'm There*, 1971) and *L'Emmanuscrit de la Mère Morte* (*The Emmanuscript of the Dead Mother*, 1972), portray 21st century Montréal. While Québec City dominated the future of Québec in the science fiction of the 19th century and early 20th century, at least till Ubald Paquin's work, in which Montréal and Québec City share equal billing, Montréal has come to be the center of Québec's future in its science fiction. If Ubald Paquin marked a turning point, then Suzanne **Martel** and Emmanuel Cocke probably confirmed Montréal's ascendancy. Cocke's hero presents himself as the savior of humanity, who will prevent Earth's end. References to Québec's self-determination underscore the political nature of the hero's project. The rediscovery of human dignity and the transformation of society lead to a new Québec. Cocke's writing is deliriously pedantic, characterized by acidic puns and an often boring psychedelic self-centeredness. As in the novels of Tardivel, Grenier, and Berthos, science fiction is used to invent tomorrow's Québec. Up to a point, Jean-Pierre **April** may be considered an heir to the baroque style of writers like Cocke, Roger DesRoches, and Patrick **Straram**, who flourished in the seventies.

In 1972, Maurice **Gagnon** returned to SF with a somewhat traditional novel, *Les Tours de Babylone* (*The Towers of Babylone*). The choice the protagonist has to make between two kinds of societies could be read as an allegory of Québec's situation … or perhaps not.

At the end of this second age of French-language Canadian science fiction, what common traits link the stories listed here? In his survey of English-language Canadian speculative fiction, John Robert Colombo found polar lands, catastrophe scenarios, alienation, and more fantasy than hard science fiction.

Up to 1974, similar traits characterize the French-Canadian works. Most of the stories included here as science fictional are stronger on political or social speculation than hard science. Of course, alienation is a central theme, whether it is manifested in the yearning for a different society or in the fear of unearthly entities and powers. Outright catastrophe scenarios are actually rare, aside from the novels of Paquin, Desrosiers, or **Després**. However, Colombo included in his catastrophe scenarios the separation of Québec from the rest of Canada. In French-language science fiction, a disaster occurs only if Québec fails to separate successfully, as in Paquin's novel. Several stories and novels deal with a more powerful, if not fully independent, Québec. They are the obverse of Colombo's catastrophe scenario: the national redemption scenario. As for Colombo's polar lands, Huot's work and *Erres Boréales* would be the main examples of the same affinity in French-language science fiction. Since 1974, a few more works could be cited, such as Jean-Pierre April's *Le Nord Électrique* (*The Electrical North*, 1986) or Pierre **Billon**'s acclaimed novel *L'Enfant du Cinquième Nord* (1982), which was translated as the *Children's Wing* in 1995.

TODAY: INCUBATION

The year 1974 marks the beginning of a new phase that has not yet ended. Occasional SF authors like Jacques Benoit, Yves Thériault, and Maurice **Gagnon** essentially abandoned the field. Jacques **Brossard**'s pre-1974 incursion into modern fantasy was only followed by a science fiction work in 1989. Cocke was dead.

A new generation of writers still active today appeared on the scene. In 1974, Esther **Rochon** published *En Hommage aux Araignées* (*In Homage to Spiders*); its revised version as a juvenile novel, *L'Étranger sous la Ville* (*The Stranger Under the City*), was published in 1986. The sequel, *L'Épuisement du Soleil* (*The Exhaustion of the Sun*, 1985), is a minor classic in the field, and Rochon is still publishing books set in the same universe.

Also in 1974, *Requiem*, a small science fiction and *fantastique* magazine, was launched in Longueuil. Apart from one lonely attempt to produce a high-school fanzine in the late sixties, *Requiem*, under Frenchman Norbert **Spehner**, was the first periodical to focus on science fiction, fantasy and *fantastique* in francophone Canada. The reason for the choice of name remains obscure. It may or may not be a reference to Heinlein's famous short story. Legend has it that the name was the suggestion of the original staff's only woman. In 1975, *Requiem* published Daniel **Sernine**'s first short story, as well as Jean-Pierre April's in 1977, and those of René **Beaulieu**, Denis **Côté**, and French-born Élisabeth **Vonarburg** in 1978.

After 1974, books with a more audacious outlook and a more mature style started appearing, such as *La Manufacture de Machines* (*The Machine Factory*, 1976), by Louis-Philippe **Hébert**, and *Un Été de Jessica* (*A Summer of Jessica*, 1978), by Alain **Bergeron**. Science fiction was catching up to the literary headstart of the fantastical.

On the fantasy side, however, 1974 is not as well-marked a turning point. Certainly, the appearance of *Requiem* was also important for young authors such as Michel **Bélil** and Daniel **Sernine**, who wished to explore fantastical themes, new and old. However, well-established Québec writers hardly needed to notice its existence.

At times, new fantastical works still recycled 19th-century motifs. Thus, the most famous instance of Québec Gothic is probably Anne **Hébert**'s novel *Les Enfants du Sabbat* (1975), translated as *Children of the Black Sabbath* in 1977. The vampire is another 19th-century creature, though mostly unknown in Québec literature until the 20th century; **Hébert** used them too in *Héloïse* (1980), translated in 1982.

Notable books from the second half of the decade owe little, if anything, to the emerging SF community. This applies to Jacques **Godbout**'s novel, *L'Isle au Dragon* (1976), translated as *Dragon Island* in 1978, featuring a dragon as a defender of the environment; to André **Carpentier**'s novel *L'Aigle Volera à travers le Soleil* (*The Eagle Will Fly Through the Sun*, 1978), as well as to Négovan **Rajic**'s intriguing allegory of political oppression, *Les Hommes-Taupes* (1978), which was translated as the *Mole Men* in 1980. In a more horrific vein, Pierre **Turgeon** published *Un, Deux, Trois* (*One, Two, Three*, 1978), about a strange being who haunts a ghost town, while Jacques **Ferron**'s *Les Roses-*

Sauvages (1971), translated as *Wild Roses* in 1976, is a chilling portrayal of insanity.

The same lack of connection with the *milieu* is true of André **Berthiaume**'s collections *Le Mot pour Vivre* (*A Word InLifewise*, 1978) and *Incidents de Frontière* (*Border-Incidents*, 1984), though the latter snagged the *Grand Prix de la Science-Fiction et du Fantastique Québécois*.

On the other hand, Michel Bélil was closely associated from the first with the new creative scene, though his literary career may have peaked early on with the publication of his collections *Le Mangeur de Livres* (*The Book-Eater*, 1978) and *Déménagement* (*Moving Day*, 1981), and his novel *Greenwich* (1981).

Finally, Daniel Sernine demonstrated a precocious prolificity with his collections *Les Contes de l'Ombre* (*Tales of Shadows*, 1979), *Légendes du Vieux Manoir* (*Legends of the Old Manor*, 1979), *Le Vieil Homme et l'Espace* (*The Old Man and Space*, 1981), and *Quand Vient la Nuit* (*When Night Comes*, 1983), in addition to his numerous young adult books which started appearing in 1979.

TODAY: MATURITY

In 1979, several events combined to launch a most remarkable decade for French-language SF in Canada.

The second lasting SF magazine, *Imagine*, was born in the fall, with Jean-Marc **Gouanvic**, another Frenchman, as fiction editor: it eventually published the first works of Jean **Pettigrew**, Agnès **Guitard**, Jean-Louis **Trudel**, and Natasha Beaulieu, among others. Also in 1979, *Requiem* changed its name to *Solaris*, paying homage to Russian writer Stanislaw Lem. The first Boréal convention of French-language science fiction and *fantastique* took place in Chicoutimi, adding impetus to the nascent SF community in Québec. In following years, the convention launched the literary careers of young writers like Francine **Pelletier**, in 1981, and Yves **Meynard**, in 1986. (Since 1979, four Boréal conventions have been held in Québec City, two more in Chicoutimi, four in Montréal, one in Longueuil, and two in Ottawa.)

In 1980, the publications of *L'Oeil de la Nuit* (*The Eye OfNight*), by Élisabeth Vonarburg, and *La Machine à Explorer la Fiction* (*The Machine for Exploring Fiction*), by Jean-Pierre April, launched the first serious SF line in Québec, known as *Chroniquesdu Futur* (*Chronicles of the Future*), by the Éditions Le Préambule. In 1983 appeared the first three French-language Canadian SF anthologies. *Aurores Boréales 1* (*Northern Lights I*) was edited by Norbert Spehner, also in charge of the *Chroniques du Futur* imprint. *Espaces Imaginaires 1* (*ImaginarySpaces I*) was edited by Jean-Marc Gouanvic and Stéphane **Nicot** from France; it included stories by authors from both Canada and France. Finally, *Les Années-Lumières* (*Light-Years*), was also the work of Gouanvic, who only used Canadian stories in the French language. Since then, several more anthologies have been issued.

The decade of the eighties also saw new signs of recognition of French-language Canadian SF in France, English-speaking Canada, and elsewhere. In 1982, the *Grand Prix de la Science-Fiction Française* was awarded to an Élisabeth-Vonarburg novel, *Le Silence de la Cité* (published in English in 1988 as *The Silent City* in Canada, England, and then the United States). In 1983, the same award was won by a Swiss residing in Ottawa, Pierre **Billon**, for *L'Enfant du Cinquième Nord* (*The Child of the Fifth North*). In 1988, *Les Visiteurs du Pôle Nord* (*The North Pole Visitors*), by a Paris-born Ottawa writer, Jean-François **Somcynsky** (who now writes as **Somain**) won the 1987 PrixLouis-Hémon from the Académie du Languedoc, in France.

Even if they did not always win awards, other works bear mentioning. Jean **O'Neil**'s delightful *Giriki et le Prince de Quécan* (*Girikiand the Prince of Quecan*, 1982) is an offbeat satire and love story, not unlike some of Jacques Benoit's earlier efforts. Louky **Bersianik**'s *L'Euguélionne* (1976), translated as *The Euguelionne* in 1981, is an extraordinary feminist and anti-Freudian manifesto which combines a fragmented SF narrative and numerous digressions; the central story is eerily reminiscent in parts of the *Female Man* (1975) by Joanna Russ, though **Bersianik** composed it between 1972 and 1974. It inspired a National Film Board video. Agnès **Guitard**'s *Les Corps Communicants* (*The Communicating Bodies*, 1981) must stand as one of the best novels in French ever to deal with telepathy and the power a mindlink could grant one person over another; as such, it is far superior to Daniel Sernine's competent but too earnest *Les Méandres du Temps* (*The Meanders of Time*, 1983). Claude-Michel Prévost's dense and involving prose made for hard-hitting stories like "Procrastination City" (1987), just as the author known as "Michel Martin," fusing the talents of Jean Dion and Guy Sirois, deserves to be remembered for a handful of excellent short stories, including "Geisha Blues" (1988).

Finally, Jacques **Brossard**'s first volume of five in the series *L'Oiseau de Feu* (*The Firebird*), *Les Années d'Apprentissage* (*The Years of Apprenticeship*, 1989), garnered unanimous praise and all three French-language SF awards given in Canada. Though this first book was a masterful depiction of life in a strange and oppressive city, the books that followed have by and large been disappointments.

Still, science fiction had come into its own. If the caliber of writing did not always match the raw power of the authors' imaginations, the eighties did demonstrate that French-Canadian science fiction could be as good as works published in France or the United States.

On the other hand, the good news did not last: the *Chroniques du Futur* imprint died in 1988 after publishing an eleventh book, a short-story collection by Francine **Pelletier**, *Le Temps des Migrations* (*The Time of Migrations*). The Éditions Les Imaginoïdes, specializing in SF, stopped publishing SF after putting out a fourth anthology. The challenge of creating a home for SF was picked up by the Logiques publishing house, which chose Gouanvic to edit the *Autres Mers, Autres Mondes* (*Other Seas, Other Worlds*) imprint, which also folded after putting out eleven books, lasting from 1988 to 1991.

Until then, all efforts to sustain the publication of local SF works had been backed by what were essentially small presses. However, things changed in 1991 when **Pettigrew** started working for the Québec/Amérique publishing house, one of the major players in the French-speaking Canadian market. Major novels by Joël Champetier, Daniel Sernine, and Élisabeth Vonarburg were included alongside mainstream works. Next, in 1994, when Pettigrew became Québec/Amérique's principal editor, he created for the first time a mass market imprint called *Sextant* which would be open to various genres, including science fiction, *fantastique*, horror, mysteries, and thrillers of all kinds. However, the *Sextant* line came to a standstill after Pettigrew was forced to leave by which point the imprint had published seven original works of Canadian SF.

Currently, the hopes of French-speaking Canadian SF writers are pinned on Pettigrew's new initiative, the Alire publishing house devoted entirely to putting out books in the same genres covered by *Sextant*. It has put out the long-awaited *Tyranaël* pentalogy by Vonarburg, as well as books by Champetier, Rochon, and other authors.

In practice, many writers continue to write books for young readers, which represent a steady, if not lucrative, outlet. Publishing constraints restrict the length of the resulting works, but Charles **Montpetit**, with *TempsPerdu* (*Lost Time*, 1984), and Vonarburg, with *Les Contes dela Chatte Rouge* (*Tales of the Red Mother-Cat*, 1993), are among those authors who have managed to shine in spite of such limitations. The *Jeunesse-Pop* imprint is now almost entirely devoted to SF, but other publishers are also editing authors like Denis **Côté** and Jacques **Lazure**.

Beginnings are easier to describe than the struggles of adolescence and maturity. French-language Canadian SF has lived through many abortive beginnings. However, since 1974, it may finally have entered an era of sustained, if slow, growth. Writers still at work, including Aude (Claudette **Charbonneau-Tissot**), René Beaulieu, Alain Bergeron, Esther Rochon, Daniel Sernine, and Élisabeth Vonarburg, can trace their careers to the seventies, or to the early issues of *Requiem/Solaris* and *Imagine*. A second generation of authors, such as Joël Champetier, Denis Côté, Michel **Lamontagne**, and Francine Pelletier, is now well-established.

Meanwhile, younger authors like Yves Meynard and Jean-Louis Trudel have given notice they are ready to make their mark. Meynard's collection *La Rose du Désert* (*The Desert Rose*, 1995) demonstrated an unchecked imagination and a gift for sensitive story-telling. Trudel's novel *Pour des Soleils Froids* (*For Some Cold Suns*, 1994) was an ambitious attempt tomeld speculative physics and a far future thriller. (Both Meynard and Trudel also write in English, having published several short stories. In 1998, Meynard's first novel for an adult readership was published in English in the United States.)

Nevertheless, the field is still dominated by a few entrenched figures. Jean-Pierre April may be remembered more for some of his better short stories such as "Le Fantôme du Forum" ("The Forum's Ghost," 1981), "L'Avaleuse d'Oiseaux" ("The Bird Swallower," 1983), and "Impressions de Thaï Deng" ("Thai Deng Impressions," 1985), than for relatively recent and unconvincing novels such as *Berlin-Bangkok* (1989) and *Les Voyages Thanatologiques de Yan Malter* (*The Thanatological Voyages of Yan Malter*, 1995). Still, even in these later works, it remains possible to catch glimpses of his uniquely ironic viewpoint.

Joël Champetier is still defining his career, but *La Taupe et le Dragon* (*The Mole and the Dragon*, 1991) nicely illustrates his talent for gripping science fiction, though he has been turning towards darker and darker fantasy.

Élisabeth Vonarburg towers above the field, since few can match her zest for telling details, her talent for psychological insight, or the scope of her storytelling. Her masterpiece, *Chroniques du Pays des Mères* (1992), translated as *In the Mothers' Land* in 1992, is an engaging account of a woman's coming of age in a post-feminist and post-catastrophe society lacking in men.

That same year, when it could only be overshadowed by Vonarburg's achievement, Daniel Sernine published his best novel to date, *Chronoreg*, linking his future history with an alternate history of our times. However, when he is not writing science fiction, Sernine probably boasts the most sustained project of Québec fantasy. His deliberately nostalgic multi-volume saga known as the *Granverger* cycle conflates Gothic fantasy, archetypal Québec settings, and Canadian history to create a true Québec Gothic. Since most of his books are aimed at young readers, they usually avoid truly horrific elements, with occasional exceptions as in *Le Trésor du Scorpion* (1980) translated as *Scorpion's Treasure* in 1990, and *Le Cercle Violet* (*The Indigo Circle*, 1984). However, his latest adult novel, *Manuscrit Trouvé dans un Secrétaire* (*Manuscript Found in a Secretary*, 1994), is a new variation on an intriguing motif in French-Canadian fantasy—the influence of a book within the book, fictional or not. And the book within is a very Gothic (and relatively gory) tale called "Adeline." Harking back to *L'Influence d'un Livre*, this motif also recurs in the short fiction of 20th century authors like Michel **Bélil**, André **Carpentier**, Claude **Mathieu**, and Marie José **Thériault**.

Another author who has shuttled with success between science fiction and fantasy is Bertrand **Bergeron**, whose collection *Transits* (1990) illuminates his versatility. The *fantastique* proper also numbers skilled practitioners not yet noted, such as Anne **Dandurand**, Claire **Dé**, or Gilles **Pellerin**, whose collection *Ni le Lieu, Ni l'Heure* (*Neither the Time, Nor the Place*, 1987) may best illustrate his thematic range.

Generic fantasy, by comparison, is hard to find. A dozen books may qualify as low-high fantasy, by a medley

of authors including Sernine and Vonarburg. Tellingly, all were published for a juvenile readership. No author has yet found generic fantasy appropriate for handling and developing adult themes or stories. However, in the closely linked genre of supernatural horror in the commercial mold, Champetier has fashioned *La Mémoire du Lac* (*The Memory of the Lake*, 1994), an efficient and suspenseful tale set in Northern Québec. In a similar vein, Stanley **Péan** has written a Haitian remake of Poe in *Le Tumulte de mon Sang* (*The Tumult of My Blood*, 1991). More recently, we find Esther Rochon's *Lame* (*Blade*, 1995), which has some horrific elements, though it belongs to a more metaphysical species of horror, closer to Dante's *Inferno* than to Stephen King or Clive Barker. Older works include Jean-Yves **Soucy**'s *Chevaliers de la Nuit* (1980), translated in 1994 as *Knights of Darkness*, and Normand **Rousseau**'s *Le Déluge Blanc* (*The White Flood*, 1981).

But these past few years, a new generation of young Québec authors weaned on Stephen King and horror movies have started to publish generic horror tales, sometimes derivative, sometimes not. Outgrowing the popular translations of U.S. horror scribes such as R. L. Stine, these new writers have started to explore the possibilities of homegrown horror tales just like their elders once were inspired by foreign examples to write science fiction in French.

Foremost among these young new writers are Natasha **Beaulieu**, Hugues **Morin**, and Claude **Bolduc**, the latter being the author of the young-adult horror novel *Dans la Maison de Müller* (*In Muller's House*, 1995) and the editor of a young-adult horror anthology, *La Maison Douleur et Autres Histoires de Peur* (*The House of Pain and Other Tales of Fear*, 1996). In coming years,we may yet see them produce major works of French-Canadian horror.

Leaving aside the pseudo-fantasy works of disguised esoterica, there remains a number of books inhabiting the uneasy fringes between fantasy and speculative fiction. Esther Rochon, best known for *Coquillage* (1986), translated as *The Shell* in 1990, often dwells in this borderland. While clearly closer to fantasy, Annick **Perrot-Bishop**, the author of *Les Maisons de Cristal* (*The Houses of Crystal*, 1990), may also belong here, as well as Denys **Chabot** for *L'Eldorado dans les Glaces* (*The Eldorado of the Ice*, 1978).

TOMORROW?

In French-speaking Canada, short fiction is the natural home of fantasy and the fantastical, and many magazines, including mainstream ones, publish such stories. Merging easily with the literary mainstream, the fantastical also surfaces in collection after collection. Novels are more rare, though it is the favored format of generic fantasy, mostly in the form of young adult books. Better adapted to short fiction, the fantastical plays on the chill of the unknown, while generic fantasy is a venture into lands already explored. The popularity of the former may or may not need explaining in a country with an uncertain future.

At shorter lengths, science fiction is almost exclusively found in the magazines and collections of the *milieu*, which may be now defined as consisting of faithful readers of *Imagine* and *Solaris*, regular attendees of the Boréal conventions, fanzine publishers, survivors of the *Requiem* era, and selected imprints or publishers. While not exclusively wedded to science fiction by any means, the *milieu* is distinguished not only by a more professional approach to its subject matter, but also by the fact that many of the people involved, and especially the writers, are at least casual acquaintances. It comprises people who actually read SF before trying to write or review it. It is dominated by writers who have made SF their preferred writing genre.

Science fiction novels, while more numerous than ever before, also include a number of works penned by novelists from other fields, trying their hand at SF for a couple of books before moving on. The novels of these "tourists" tend to appear outside the specialized small presses or collections. The science fictional culture of their authors often seems limited to a few SF blockbuster movies or to juvenile adventure novels. Their plots are often derivative, or messianic, featuring Atlantis or wise extraterrestrials. Their frequent reinvention of the wheel unfortunately highlights to what extent theworks produced by the *milieu* go unremarked. If Alire or another publishing house succeeds in creating a presence for the local product, it maybe that such ignorance will become untenable.

The future of French-language SF in Canada remains uncertain. The market is small. The progress that has been made since 1974 is fragile. Nevertheless, Canada's Francophones live in the most technologically, if not scientifically, sophisticated society of the entire Francophonie. Young readers devour SF works, showing a marked preference for horror and fantasy, but not disdaining science fiction. Indeed, it may be plausibly argued that a larger percentage of the SF genre's top French-speaking writers are Canadian than for most other literary forms in French. Furthermore, these writers often enjoy a privileged access to the English-language markets.

For example, the *Tesseracts* (1996) anthology, exclusively devoted to English translations of French-Canadian SF, was probably the first English-language anthology entirely comprised of French-language SF since Damon Knight's. In fact, it was the series of *Tesseracts* anthologies which made possible the inclusion of so many Canadian Francophones in *Northern Stars*(1994), an anthology published by Tor in the U.S.

Overcoming these weakness and turning these strengths to advantage is the challenge faced by the *milieu*.

OTHER MEDIA

SF is harder to identify in other media. in Canada, the history of French-language SF in the cinema and on television screens, or in comic books and graphic novels (*bandes dessinées*) remains to be written.

Genre feature films include *L'Ange et la Femme* (*The Angel and the Woman*, 1977), written and directed by Gilles Carle, starring Carole Laure; and ***Thank You, Satan*** (1988), directed by André Farwagi, written by Farwagi, Christian Carini, Nelly Allard, and Jean Cosmos, and also starring Carole Laure. The National Film Board's endearing science fiction tale *Le Martien de Noël* (*The Christmas Martian*, 1977), by Bernard Gosselin, was produced for a juvenile audience, using a script co-written by Roch **Carrier** and Louise Forestier (see Book 1, Chapter I).

Television SF has most often been aimed at children and teenagers, such as the Christmas movie, *Matusalem* (1993) by Roger Cantin, featuring a pirate's ghost. One recent telefilm that was definitely not intended for children was Yves Simoneau's science fiction thriller *Dans le Ventre du Dragon* (*In the Belly of the Dragon*, 1988). As in most countries outside the U.S., the paucity of SF movies may be due in part to the high cost of special effects.

In the field of comics, the most distinctive series is ***Red Ketchup***, written by Pierre Fournier and drawn by Real Godbout (see Book 1, Chapter V). One must also mention artist Serge Gaboury's strip, *Alyx*, which appeared in 1983-84 in the short-lived magazine *Titanic*, and which tackled science fiction themes. On the fantasy side, in 1979, the comics magazine *Odyssée* offered mythological stories in its two issues. And *Solaris* has long provided a home for short SF strips.

AWARDS

Three major SF awards recognize outstanding or popular works of French-language Canadian SF. The oldest is the Prix Boréal, established at the 1980 Boréal convention in Québec City; the categories have changed over the years, but it remains governed by a popular vote. The Prix Aurora Awards (formerly known as the Casper) are formally known as the Canadian Science Fiction and Fantasy Association Awards. Established in 1980, they did not have any French-language categories before 1986, when Daniel **Sernine**was the first French-speaking winner. They also are decided by a popular vote. Finally, the *Grand Prix de la Science-Fiction et du Fantastique Québécois* was born in 1984; it is the only one to offer a monied prize and to be awarded by a jury. (Also see Chapter XII.)

SOURCES

L'Année de la Science-Fiction et du Fantastique Québécois 1984, 1985, 1986, 1987, 1988, 1989, 1990, 1991, 1992. Éditions Le Passeur, Beauport.

Bélil, Michel. "Le Fantastique Québécois au XIXème Siècle" in *Imagine* No. 6.

_____. "La Science-Fiction Canadienne Française" in *Imagine* No. 19.

Boivin, Aurélien. *Bibliographie Analytique de la Science-Fiction et du Fantastique Québécois: 1960-1985*. Nuit Blanche, Québec, 1992.

Boivin, Aurélien. *Le Conte Fantastique Québécois au XIXème Siècle*. Fides, Montréal, 1987.

Dictionnaire des Oeuvres Littéraires du Québec. Fides, Montréal, 1978.

Émond, Maurice. *Anthologie de la Nouvelle et du Conte Fantastique Québécois au XXème Siècle*. Fides, Montréal, 1987.

Gagnon, Claude-Marie. "Littérature Populaire Québécoise: L'incursion Interplanétaire dans Les Aventures Étranges de l'Agent Ixe-13, l'As des Espions Canadiens" in *Présence Francophone* No. 19, 1979.

Gouanvic, Jean-Marc. "Rational Speculations in French Canada: 1839-1974" in *Science Fiction Studies*, Vol. 15, No 44, 1988.

_____. "La SFQ dans son histoire: Quelques Remarques Rétrospectives et Prospectives" in *Imagine* No. 49.

_____. "La Tête de Saint Jean-Baptiste: Entre la Science-Fiction et le Mythe" in *Imagine* No. 19.

Hutchison, Don, and Peter Halasz. "Blood on the Snow: a Survey of Canadian Horror Fiction" in *The Scream Factory*" No. 18.

Janelle, Claude. "La Science-Fiction au Québec" in *Solaris* No. 50.

Ketterer, David. *Canadian Science Fiction and Fantasy*. Indiana University Press, 1992.

Pomerleau, Luc. "La BD Québécoise" in *Canuck Comics*, John Bell, ed., Matrix Books, 1986.

Sernine, Daniel. "Historique de la SFQ" in *Solaris* No. 79.

Tremblay, Jean-Paul. *Napoléon Aubin*. Fides, Montréal, 1972.

Trudel, Jean-Louis, "Canada: 2. French" in the *Encyclopedia of Fantasy*, John Clute and John Grant, eds. Orbit, 1997.

_____. "Les Pseudonymes dans la SFQ" in *Temps Tôt* No. 8, 1990.

_____. "Science Fiction in Francophone Canada (1839-1989)" In *Out of This World: Canadian Science Fiction and Fantasy Literature*, Andrea Paradis, Hugh Spencer and Allan Weiss, eds. Quarry Press, 1995.

Vonarburg, Élisabeth, and Norbert **Spehner**. "Science-Fiction in Québec: a Survey" in *Science Fiction Studies* No. 21, 1980.

CHAPTER XI

Dictionary of Authors

1. Introduction

While we have tried to be as reasonably exhaustive as possible, it will be obvious to all that a totally satisfactory, comprehensive list of genre authors and genre works in any single language cannot be practically achieved. There are, therefore, a number of reservations that we feel we must state beforehand:

Inclusions and Exclusions: To the best of our experience, no one has ever agreed, nor is likely to ever agree, on what constitutes the intangible boundaries of the *fantastique*. Unlike science fiction, which is much easier to encapsulate, the *fantastique* is often as much a matter of intention or treatment as it is of literary content.

The frontier between mainstream literature and the *fantastique* has always been left purposefully vague by writers. A consequence of this vagueness is that a number of genre, or marginally genre, novels were, and still are, written by non-genre authors and published in non-genre imprints. (For example, many non-genre scholars may be surprised to see entries here for such luminaries of French literature as **Apollinaire**, **Balzac**, **Hugo**, and **Zola**.) To produce a comprehensive list that would include all of these would require having read and/or being able to read the entire French literary output—an impossible task. So, while we have endeavored to keep track of as many of these literary "UFOs" as possible, it is likely that: (a) we have missed quite a few of them, and (b) we have mistakenly included books that we have not read (based on their authors, titles, or secondary information) and which really should not be included here under any standards.

Adventure novels, mysteries, thrillers, and horror novels have also presented us with an acute problem of definition. The line between what should be included here, and what should not, is in many cases highly debatable, even more so than with mainstream novels. For example, while it is obvious that the French equivalents of Agatha Christie's Poirot, Raymond Chandler's Marlowe and John Le Carré's Smiley do not belong in this book, we strongly feel that the French equivalents of Sir Arthur Conan Doyle's Sherlock Holmes, Edgar Rice Burroughs' Tarzan, Walter Gibson's The Shadow, and Ian Fleming's James Bond do. While we realize that all of these heroes technically do not belong to the *fantastique*, they are nevertheless considered by many as "good neighbors." Their fearless, often superhuman protagonists explore hidden lands, discover forbidden cities, and foil mad scientists; they challenge megalomaniacal villains equipped with super-weapons and bent on world domination. Certainly, they deserve to be included in any study of the genre.

In our opinion, a dictionary of the French *fantastique* would be much poorer without such perennially popular heroes as arch-criminal Fantômas (by **Allain** & **Souvestre**), spy extraordinaire OSS 117 (by Jean **Bruce**), gentleman-burglar *Arsène Lupin* (by Maurice **Leblanc**), investigative journalist Rouletabille (by Gaston **Leroux**), master escape artist Rocambole (by **Ponson du Terrail**), ghostbuster *Harry Dickson* (by Jean **Ray**), and fearless adventurer *Bob Morane* (by Henri **Vernes**), to name but a few.

Similarly, in the horror genre, while no one would dispute the inclusion of, say, Stephen King, many would argue about Thomas Harris, whose Hannibal (the Cannibal) Lecter is nevertheless a dominant figure of contemporary horror fiction. In the same fashion, and as a result of these blurred lines, we have had to make many arbitrary choices. Some mysteries and thrillers have been listed here because they contain ghostly and/or gothic elements. Others are here because they feature gore and/or serial killers that could otherwise classify them as horror novels. (We have, for example, included a listing of the **Grand-Guignol** plays, even though most do not include genre elements.) At the same time, we had to draw a line somewhere, and there are undoubtedly some works that we chose not to list here, that would have arguably qualified just as well as others.

The Difficulties of Research: First, as mentioned above, no one can claim to have read the entire French literary output and, therefore, a dictionary like ours is bound to not only contain omissions but also a number of factual errors inherited from secondary or tertiary sources.

This is as good a place as any to pay homage to those researchers whose precious works have formed the architecture of the present volume: Jean-Baptiste **Baronian**, Henri Delmas & Alain Julian, Jean Pettigrew, René **Beaulieu** and the team of *L'Année de la SFF Québécoise*, Jacques Sadoul, Marcel Schneider, Francis Valery, Jacques Van Herp, and the inescapable Pierre Versins, whose *Encyclopédie de l'Utopie, des Voyages Extraordinaires et de la Science-Fiction* remains a never-equalled monument and an indispensable tool to any serious researcher.

In spite of all this, one should note that research into pre-19th century works cannot be as complete as one would wish since literary history has generally been unkind (often not undeservedly so!) towards genre works—utopia, extraordinary voyages, gothic novels, etc.—which have generally been deemed to be too minor to be properly catalogued and studied.

Then, the pulp-like adventure magazines that were immensely popular before World War I and between the wars serialized a staggering number of novels, many of which were never properly collected in book form. To the extent that the stories published by these magazines covered many genres, from the western to scientific anticipation, and that no truly exhaustive compilation of their contents exists, it is a virtually impossible task to list *all* genre novels published during the period.

While our invaluable research assistant, Dr. Henri Rossi, has attempted to check every entry included here against the Bibliothèque Nationale catalog, it is likely that, if only because of human error, a number of inaccuracies may have crept in. As we point out in our introduction, no project of this type is ever perfect, or complete. We will be grateful to anyone pointing out such errors or omissions to us, for future reference and inclusion in subsequent reprints.

2. Publishers and Magazines

The following abbreviations are used in this chapter to represent the major imprints, magazines and publishers:

AA: *À l'Aventure* (*Towards Adventure*); (1920-21). Illustrated magazine which serialized some genre novels under the editorship of Louis-Frédéric **Rouquette**. Seventy-two issues published.

A&D: *Ailleurs & Demain* (*Elsewhere & Tomorrow*; 1969-present), Robert Laffont, publisher. A silver-foil-covered series of trade paperbacks edited by Gérard **Klein** which publishes major names in American and French science fiction: Frank Herbert, Dan Simmons, Philip

K. Dick and Michel **Jeury**, Philippe **Curval**, etc. Over one hundred titles published.

A&D Class.: *Ailleurs & Demain Classiques* (*Elsewhere & Tomorrow Classics*; 1970-present), Robert Laffont, publisher. A gold-foil-covered series of trade paperbacks edited by Gérard **Klein** which reprints classic science fiction novels, including works by Stéfan **Wul**, Jacques **Spitz**, etc. Over twenty titles published. Three non-fiction essays were published in the same imprint under copper-foiled covers.

AdE: *L'Âge des Étoiles* (*The Age of the Stars*; 1977-79), Robert Laffont, publisher. A short-lived series of juvenile science fiction novels edited by Gérard **Klein** featuring new works by Michel **Jeury**, Christian **Léourier**, etc., with covers by renowned French artists such as Jean-Claude **Mézières**, **Moebius**, etc. Eleven titles published.

AdH: L'Âge d'Homme. Swiss publisher who publishes literary works including some genre fiction by Pierre **Gripari**, etc., as well as Pierre **Versins'** massive *Encyclopedia of Science Fiction*.

AdP: *L'Ami de Poche"* (*A Pocket Friend*; 1980-85), Casterman publisher. A paperback imprint of juvenile novels, often featuring fantasy works. Over sixty titles published.

Ailleurs (*Elsewhere*; 1956-67). Pierre **Versins**, editor/publisher. One of France's best-known classic fanzines. Fifty-three issues published.

AL: *Alire* (1997-), Alire, publisher. French-Canadian science fiction imprint edited by Jean Pettigrew, presenting works by Joël **Champetier**, Élisabeth **Vonarburg**, etc.

AM: Albin Michel, publisher. They published two specialized science fiction imprints (see AMSF and AMSF2, below), as well as much mainstream literature.

AMAM: *Autres Mers, Autres Mondes* (*Other Seas, Other Worlds*; 1988-91), Éditions Logiques, publisher. A dedicated French-Canadian science fiction imprint edited by Jean-Marc **Gouanvic**, which published works by Jean-Pierre **April**, Michel **Bélil**, and a remarkable series of anthologies. Eleven titles published.

AMSF and **AMSF2**: *Science-Fiction* and *Super-Fiction* (1972-74; 1975-84), Albin Michel, publisher. Two paperback series of silver-foil-covered science fiction novels edited by George H. Gallet and Jacques **Bergier**, presenting mostly American novels, but with a few French names as well (David **Maine** aka Pierre **Barbet**, Albert **Higon**, aka Michel **Jeury**). Thirty-one volumes published in AMSF and seventy-nine in AMSF 2. The later volumes were trade paperbacks.

Antarès: (1981-present). Magazine. Jean-Pierre Moumon, editor/publisher.

Arabesque: *Espions de Demain* (*Tomorrow's Spies*; 1960) and *Frayeurs* (*Frights*; 1954-55), Arabesque, publisher. Arabesque published nine volumes under a short-lived paperback imprint combining science fiction and spy thriller elements.

Atalante: *Bibliothèque de l'Évasion* (*Library of Escape*; 1994-), Atalante publisher. A series of trade paperbacks devoted to heroic-fantasy authors, including titles by Pierre **Bordage**, Jean-Pierre **Fontana**, Michael Moorcock, Terry Pratchett, etc.

ATAM: *Autres Temps, Autres Mondes* (*Other Times, Other Worlds*; 1966-83), Casterman, publisher. A series of hardcover thematic anthologies and novels edited by Alain **Dorémieux**. Fifty titles published, including thirty-six anthologies.

AV: *Aventures & Voyages* (*Adventures & Travels*; 1929-48), Fernand Nathan, publisher. A series of popular adventure novels.

AVF: *L'Aventure* (*Adventure*; 1929-30), Arthème Fayard, publisher. A series of popular adventure novels, including titles by Jean d'**Agraives**, Eugène **Thébault**, etc. Twenty titles published.

Belfond: *Domaine Fantastique* (*Fantastic Domain*; 1969-75), Belfond, publisher. Trade paperback reprints of classic fantastique novels by Lovecraft, Maurice **Renard** and Claude **Seignolle**. Eight titles published.

BGA: *Bibliothèque des Grandes Aventures* and *Grandes Aventures-Voyages Excentriques* (*Library of Great Adventures/Great Adventures-Eccentric Voyages*; 1923-42, 1949-53), Tallandier, publisher. A series of popular adventure novels, including titles by André **Falcoz**, Charles **Magué**, Eugène **Thébault**, etc. About 660 titles published in the first series, forty-three titles published in the second series.

BR: *Bibliothèque Rose* (*Pink Library*; 1956-present), Hachette, publisher. A series of popular juvenile (under ten) adventure paperbacks with characteristic pink spines) featuring heroes such as Georges **Chaulet**'s *Fantômette*, etc. Over one thousand titles published.

BV: *Bibliothèque Verte* (*Green Library*; 1956-present), Hachette, publisher. A series of popular juvenile/young-adult adventure paperbacks (with a characteristic green spine) featuring heroes such as Lieutenant **X**'s young secret agent *Langelot* and Philippe **Ébly**'s *Les Conquérants de l'Impossible*, etc. Over one thousand titles published.

CA: *Chevalier de l'Aventure* (*Knights of Adventure*; 1930-34), Tallandier, publisher. A series of popular adventure novels, including titles by André **Falcoz**, Jean **Petithuguenin**, etc. About one hundred titles published.

Calmann-Levy: Publisher of mainstream literature. They also published the *Dimensions* (see Dim. below) specialized imprint.

Cast.: Casterman. Renowned Belgian publisher, which publishes numerous graphic novel series including *Tintin*, *Adèle Blanc-Sec*, *Édéna*, etc. (See Book 1, Chapter V). They also published the specialized imprint *Autre Temps, Autres Mondes* (see ATAM above) and the juvenile imprint *L'Ami de Poche* (see AdP above).

CdA/CdF: *Chroniques de l'Au-Delà/du Futur* (*Chronicles of Beyond/The Future*; 1980-88), Éditions du Préambule, publisher. First dedicated French-Canadian *fantastique*/science fiction imprints, edited by Norbert **Spehner** and featuring works by Jean-Pierre **April**, Elisabeth **Vonarburg**, etc. Eleven titles published.

CDAv: *Collection d'Aventures* (*Adventures Collection*; 1918-27). A series of popular adventure novels, including a few titles by José **Moselli**. About six hundred titles published.

CL: *Chute Libre* (*Free Fall*; 1974-78), Champ Libre, publisher. A short-lived series of trade paperbacks edited by Jean-Claude Lattès (see JCL below), which published a mix of adult science fiction by P. J. Farmer, Samuel R. Delany, etc. Twenty titles published.

Cosmos: *Cosmos* (1955-57), Grand Damier, publisher. A paperback series of popular science fiction novels edited by Roger de la Fuye, including titles by Maurice **Limat**, etc. Twelve titles published.

CRNI: Car Rien n'a d'Importance, publisher. See DLM below.

CRT: *Contes et Romans Pour Tous* (*Tales and Novels for All*; 1927-36), Larousse, publisher. A series of popular adventure novels, including titles by Henri **Allorge**, Henri **Bernay**, etc. About forty titles published.

Dan.: *Science-Fiction-Suspense, Anticipation, Mystère* (1960-61), Daniber, publisher. Series of science fiction paperbacks edited by Daniel Bernstein which published mostly American space operas (e.g. Don A. Wollheim). Seventeen titles published.

Den.: Denoël, publisher. They publish the dedicated PdF and PdFant. imprints (see below), as well as thrillers in the *Sueurs Froides* (*Cold Sweat*) imprint and literary genre novels in their *Présences* (*Presences*) imprint.

Dim.: *Dimensions* (1973-84), Calmann-Levy, publisher. A series of trade paperbacks edited by Robert Louit, which published some major names in English-language and French science fiction: Ian Watson, J.G. Ballard and Dominique **Douay**, Philippe **Curval**, etc. Fifty-six titles published.

Ditis: *Science-Fiction* (1960), Ditis, publisher. Short-lived paperback series. No French authors. Eight titles published.

DLM: Publisher of the *Car Rien n'a d'Importance* (*For Nothing is Important*) and *Arkham* (1995-98) paperback imprints. Niche books and specialty editions, edited by Francis **Valéry**. Six titles published in the *Arkham* series.

Encre: *L'Utopie Tout De Suite* (*Utopia Right Now*; 1979-80), Encre, publisher. Series of science fiction trade paperbacks edited by Bernard Blanc. Five titles published.

Fayard: Arthème Fayard, publisher. Publisher of *L'Aventure* (see AVF above), *Voyages Scientifiques Extraordinaires* (see VSE below), and numerous paperback imprints of popular science fiction, crime, and thriller novels.

Ferenczi: Publisher of popular paperback science fiction and adventure imprints such as *Le Livre de l'Aventure* (see LA below), *Mon Roman d'Aventure* (see MRA below), *Le Petit Roman d'Aventure* (see PRA below), *Romans d'Aventures* (see RDA below), and *Voyages & Aventures* (see VA below).

Flamm.: Flammarion, publisher. Mainstream literature publisher. They also published the *Grandes Aventures* (*Great Adventures*; see GA below) imprint and currently publish juvenile genre novels in their *Castor Poche* (*Pocket Beaver*) imprint. They are the publisher of the renowned paperback imprint J'ai Lu (see JL below).

FN: Fleuve Noir/Presses de la Cité, publisher. Fleuve Noir is one of the popular imprints of the Presses de la Cité, a major French publishing group. They publish(ed) a number of dedicated genre imprints (see FN below), as well as police thrillers (*Special Police, Crime, Engrenage, Noire* imprints), espionage novels (*Espionnage, Infra Rouge* imprints), adventure stories (*L'Aventurier* imprint,) and war stories (*Feu* imprint).

FNA: *Anticipation* (1951-97), Fleuve Noir/Presses de la Cité, publisher. A paperback series of popular French science fiction novels launched and edited until the early 1980s by François **Richard**. Writers include B.-R. **Bruss**, Jimmy **Guieu**, J. & D. **Le May**, Maurice **Limat**, Peter **Randa**, M.-A. **Rayjean**, **Richard Bessière**, Louis **Thirion**, Jean-Gaston **Vandel**, and Stefan **Wul**. Subsequent editors included Patrick Siry, Nicole Hibert, and Philippe Hupp. Newer authors included G.-J. **Arnaud**, **Ayerdhal**, Serge **Brussolo**, Hugues **Douriaux**, J.-P. **Garen**, Michel **Honaker**, G. **Morris**, Pierre **Pelot,** Christopher **Stork**, and Roland C. **Wagner**. In 1992, the imprint split into five sub-imprints: *Legend* (heroic-fantasy), *Space, Métal* (various types of science fiction ranging from space opera to cyberpunk), "*Delirius*" (satirical SF), and *Panik* (horror SF). In 1997, it discontinued its numbering and started again with a new imprint simply called *SF* (FNSF) and comprised of five, new sub-imprints: *Zone Rouge, Métal, Space, Polar,* and *Mystère*, and a new numbering starting from No.1. The covers (Nos.1-273, 562-792) were by **Brantonne**. 2002 titles published.

FNAG: *Angoisse* (*Anguish*; 1954-75), Fleuve Noir/Presses de la Cité, publisher. A paperback series of popular French horror novels edited by François **Richard**, including works by Marc **Agapit**, B.-R. **Bruss**, André **Caroff**, and Kurt **Steiner**. The covers were by Gourdon. Two hundred sixty-one titles published.

FNASF: *Aventures sans Frontières* (*Adventures Without Frontiers*; 1995-97), Fleuve Noir/Presses de la Cité publisher. A paperback series of popular adventure/exotic novels launched and edited by Daniel Riche. A dozen titles published.

FNAV: *Aventures & Mystères* (*Adventures & Mysteries*; 1995-97), Fleuve Noir/Presses de la Cité, publisher. A paperback series of popular adventure/gothic novels launched and edited by Daniel Riche. A dozen titles published.

FNBM: *Bob Morane* (1988-91), Fleuve Noir/Presses de la Cité, publisher. A paperback series reprinting the popular juvenile adventure series by Henri **Vernes**, with some new novels thrown in. FNBM was a successor to MBN (see below) and preceded publisher Claude Lefrancq. About forty titles published, including reprints.

FNCG: *Compagnie des Glaces* (*The Ice Company*; 1988-92), Fleuve Noir/Presses de la Cité, publisher. A paperback series reprinting the first thirty-seven volumes of this popular science fiction series by G.-J. **Arnaud** previously published in FNA, and continuing the series until the final, 62nd volume.

FNCL: *Chevaliers de Lumière* (*The Knights of Light*; 1987-90), Fleuve Noir/Presses de la Cité, publisher. A paperback series continuing this popular science fiction series by Jimmy **Guieu** previously published in FNA. A dozen volumes published. It was eventually superseded by the more ambitious Jimmy **Guieu** imprint (see VG below) at Vaugirard.

FNFR: *Frayeur* (*Fright*; 1994-96), Fleuve Noir/Presses de la Cité, publisher. A paperback series of popular French horror novels edited by Jean **Rollin**, and later by Daniel Riche, including works by Jean **Rollin**, Serge **Lehman**, etc. Twenty-eight titles published.

FNG: *Gore* (1985-89), Fleuve Noir (except for Nos. 105-118 published by Vaugirard)/Presses de la Cité, publisher. A paperback series of popular French horror novels edited by Daniel Riche, and later by André **Ruellan** and Juliette Raabe, who also edited the short-lived *Angoisses* (*Anguishes*) imprint, including works by Jean-Pierre **Andrevon**, Joël **Houssin**, etc. Over 120 titles published.

FNSF: (1997-), continuation of FNA (see above).

FNSL: *Super-Luxe* (1974-86), Fleuve Noir/Presses de la Cité, publisher. A paperback series edited by Patrick Siry reprinting some classic FNA novels under the imprint *Lendemains Retrouvés* (*Found Tomorrows*) and FNAG novels under the imprint *Horizons de l'Au-Delà* (*Horizons from Beyond*), with some new novels thrown in. About 170 titles published.

Futurs: (1978; 1981), Futurs Presse, publisher. Nine issues published.

GA: *Grandes Aventures* (*Great Adventures*; 1888-1900). Flammarion, publisher. Imprint launched to publish the works of Louis **Boussenard**.

Gall.: Gallimard publisher. Mainstream literature publisher; they were partnered with Hachette in the specialized RF imprint (see below). They publish the *Folio* paperback imprint and its juvenile *Folio Junior* companion.

GdV: Gérard de Villiers, publisher. Publisher of police novels, supernatural thrillers (by Serge **Brussolo**), and erotic novels under the name and aegis of the author of the famous *S.A.S* spy fiction line.

GRAM: *Grands Romans d'Aventures Modernes* (*Great Novels of Modern Adventures*), Baudinière, publisher.

Hac.: Hachette, publisher. Major French publishing group. It publishes the renowned paperback imprint *Livre de Poche* (see LdP below) and the magazine *Lectures pour Tous* (see LPT below). Hachette was partnered with Gallimard in the specialized *Rayon Fantastique* imprint (see RF below). Hachette also publishes the *Bibliothèque Verte* (see BV above), *Bibliothèque Rose* (see BR above), *Jeunesse Pop Anticipation* (see JPA below), *Poche Rouge* (see PR below), and other juvenile imprints, such as the recent *Vertige* (*Vertigo*) imprint (1996-); itself subdivided into *SF*, *Policier*, *Fantastique*, and *Cauchemar* (*Nightmare*)), edited by Denis **Guiot**; which published novels by Jean-Pierre **Andrevon**, Christian **Grenier**, etc.

HdF: *Horizons du Fantastique* (*Horizons of the Fantastic*; 1967-76), Ekla, publisher. Magazine containing articles, interviews, reviews, and short stories. Thirty-eight issues published.

HF: *Les Horizons Fantastiques* (*Fantastic Horizons*; 1949-54), Le Sillage, publisher. Short-lived series of science fiction paperbacks. Four titles published.

Imagine: (1979-) French-Canadian science fiction magazine founded and edited by Jean-Marc **Gouanvic**.

Intrep.: *L'Intrépide* (*The Fearless*; 1910-37). Illustrated magazine which serialized novels by Pierre **Adam**, Guy d'**Armen**, José **Moselli**, Élie **Montfort**, etc. About 1400 issues published.

JCL: Jean-Claude Lattès, publisher. In parallel with the *Chute Libre* (*Free Fall*; see CL above) and *Titres* (see below) imprints, Jean-Claude Lattès published a series of paperbacks and trade paperbacks featuring Robert E. Howard's *Conan* (three vols), Edgar Rice Burroughs' *Tarzan* (twelve vols), John Carter (five vols) and Pellucidar (two vols), Michael Moorcock's *Hawkmoon* (2 vols), and reprints of Régis **Messac** (three vols), and Pierre **Dac** & Francis **Blanche**'s *Furax* (three vols), plus various other titles (ten vols). The cover art often was by Philippe **Druillet**.

JDH: *Jean de La Hire* (1952-55), Jaeger-d'Hauteville, publishers. Paperback series devoted to the works of Jean de **La Hire** with covers by Brantonne. Twenty-one titles published.

JDV: *Journal des Voyages* (*Journal of Voyages*; 1877-1949). Illustrated magazine which serialized novels by Louis **Boussenard**, Paul d'**Ivoi**, René **Thévenin**, etc. 1st series (1877-1896): 1012 issues; 2nd series (1896-1915): 941 issues; 3rd series (1924-25): 29 issues; 4th series (1925-29): 159 issues; 5th series (1946-1949): 149 issues.

JL: *Science-Fiction* (1970-present), Flammarion, publisher. Paperback series of science fiction novels edited by Jacques **Sadoul**, presenting mostly American novels, but with a few French names as well: **Ayerdhal**,

Richard **Canal**, Christian **Léourier**, Joëlle **Wintrebert**, etc. The cover art is often by renowned artist Philippe **Caza**. About four hundred titles published.

JP: *Jeunesse-Pop* (1971-present), Médiaspaul, publisher. French-Canadian imprint of juvenile science fiction novels edited by Daniel **Sernine**, presenting works by Jean-Louis **Trudel**, Esther **Rochon**, etc. Over one hundred titles published.

JPA: *Jeunesse Pop Anticipation* (1971-74), Hachette, publisher. Series of juvenile science fiction novels. Thirty-four titles published.

JST: *Je Sais Tout* (*I Know Everything*; 1905-1939). Illustrated magazine published by Pierre Laffitte and eventually taken over by LPT (see below) which serialized novels by Maurice **Leblanc**, Gaston **Leroux**, Maurice **Renard**, etc.

Kes.: *Ici & Maintenant* (*Here & Now*; 1977-82), Kesselring, publisher. Swiss-based imprint of science fiction trade paperbacks, including titles by Bernard **Blanc**, Pierre **Pelot**, etc., often with a left-wing political agenda. Twenty-two titles published.

LA: *Le Livre de l'Aventure* (*Book of Adventure*; 1929-31), Férenczi, publisher. Paperback series of popular adventure novels by Jean de **La Hire**, René **Thévenin**, etc. forty-eight titles published.

Lar.: Larousse, publisher. Publisher of novels, non-fiction, and academic books.

LdA: *Le Livre d'Aventures* (*Book of Adventures*; 1937-39; 1951-54), Tallandier, publisher. A series of popular adventure novels. About fifty titles published in the first series.

LdP: *Science-Fiction* (1974-present), Hachette, publisher. Paperback series of science fiction novels edited by Gérard **Klein** and Jacques Goimard, presenting mostly American novels. Over forty anthologies and one hundred titles published.

Lefrancq: Claude Lefrancq, publisher. Belgian publisher of paperbacks and graphic novels, reprinting classics of popular literature such as Henri **Vernes**' Bob Morane, Stefan **Wul**, and Francis **Carsac**.

Libr. Champs-Élysées: Librairie des Champs-Élysées. Publisher of the famous paperback detective/thriller imprint *Le Masque* (*The Mask*), as well as *Le Masque Science Fiction*, *Le Masque Fantastique*, and *Le Masque Bob Morane* imprints (see MSF, MF, and MBN below).

LN: *Le Livre National: Romans d'Aventures et d'Exploration* (*The National Book: Novels of Adventures and Exploration*; 1900-35), Tallandier, publisher. A series of popular adventure novels, including titles by Louis **Boussenard**, Jean de **La Hire**, etc. Over one thousand titles published.

Los.: *Le Terrain Vague* (*The Wasteland*) and *Le Dernier Terrain Vague* (*The Last Wasteland*; 1977-78), Éric Losfeld, publisher.

LPT: *Lectures pour Tous* (*Reading for All*; 1898-1940). Illustrated magazine published by Hachette which serialized novels by Octave **Béliard**, J.-H. **Rosny** Aîné, etc. 581 issues published.

Lynx: *Le Lynx* (1940-41), Tallandier, publisher. Paperback series of mystery, adventure, and science fiction novels, including titles by André **Couvreur**, Léon **Groc**, etc.

Magnard: Publisher of juvenile novels and the *Science & Aventures* (*Science & Adventures*; see S&A below) imprint.

MarF: *Fantastique* (1960-81), Marabout, publisher. Paperback series of *fantastique* novels edited by J.-B. **Baronian**, including reprints of **Balzac**, Théophile **Gautier**, Gérard de **Nerval**, **Ponson du Terrail**, and Jean **Ray**. About one hundred titles published.

MarJ: *Junior* (1953-67), Marabout, publisher. Paperback series of juvenile adventure novels, including Henri **Vernes'** Bob Morane character and André Fernez' spy hero Nick Jordan. Over two hundred titles published.

MarP.: *Pocket* (1967-77), Marabout, publisher. Continuation of MarJ above. In addition to Bob Morane and Nick Jordan, it also published Doc Savage translations and Pierre **Pelot**'s western hero, Dylan Stark. About one hundred titles published.

MarSF: *Science-Fiction* (1960-81), Marabout, publisher. Paperback series of science fiction novels edited by J.-B. **Baronian**, presenting mostly American novels (Van Vogt, Spinrad, Dick, Simak, etc.), but with a few French names as well: Gérard **Klein**, Jacques **Spitz**, Bernard **Villaret**, etc. About sixty titles published.

MBN: *Masque Bob Morane* (1978-80), Librairie des Champs-Élysées, publisher. A paperback series reprinting the popular juvenile adventure series by Henri **Vernes**, with some new novels thrown in. MBN was a successor to MarP. and preceded FNBM (see above). Thirty-four titles published, including reprints.

MdF: Mercure de France, publisher. Publisher of mainstream literature.

Méricant: Publisher of *Le Roman d'Aventures* and *Les Récits Mystérieux* (see RM below), popular paperback imprints.

Métal: *Série 2000* (1954-56), Métal, publisher. Paperback series of silver-foil-covered science fiction novels presenting a mix of American (Raymond F. Jones) and French (Charles **Henneberg**, Maurice **Limat**, Pierre **Versins**) science fiction novels. Twenty-five titles published.

MF: *Masque Fantastique* (1976-81), Librairie des Champs-Élysées, publisher. Paperback series of science fiction novels presenting a mix of American (Robert E. Howard, Gardner Fox, Fritz Leiber) and French (Nathalie **Henneberg**, Kurt **Steiner**, Julia **Verlanger**) *fantastique* novels. Twenty titles published.

Mnémos: Publisher of an imprint of heroic-fantasy paperbacks (1996-). Over thirty titles published as of early 1998.

MOC: *Mémoires d'Outre-Ciel* (*Memories from Beyond the Sky*; 1979-82), Garry, publisher. Series of paperback science fiction and fantastic novels. Twenty-six titles published.

MSF: *Masque Science-Fiction* (1974-81), Librairie des Champs-Élysées, publisher. Paperback series of science fiction novels presenting a mix of American (Isaac Asimov, Philip K. Dick, Eric Frank Russell) and French (Michel **Demuth**, Nathalie **Henneberg**, Olivier **Sprigel** aka Pierre **Barbet**) science fiction novels. 116 titles published.

MRA: *Mon Roman d'Aventure* (*My Adventure Novels*; 1942-56), Férenczi, publisher. Digest-sized series of adventure novels, including works by Maurice **Limat** and Max-André **Dazergues**. About four hundred titles published.

MRAV: *Meilleurs Romans d'Aventures* (*Best Adventure Novels*; 1937-38), Tallandier, publisher. A series of popular adventure novels, including titles by Louis **Boussenard**, etc., reprinting titles initially published in BGA (see above).

Nathan: Fernand Nathan. Publisher of non-fiction and academic books. They also published the *Aventures & Voyages* imprint (see AV above) as well as a number of juvenile paperback imprints such as *SF* (1980-81; eight titles published), *Lune Noire* (*Black Moon*) and *Pleine Lune* (*Full Moon*), which published titles by **Gudule**, François **Sautereau**, etc.

NéO: *Fantastique/Science-Fiction* (1979-1988), Nouvelles Éditions Oswald, publisher. Trade paperback series of reprints of classic Anglo-Saxon and French authors edited by Hélène Oswald. Over 150 titles published.

OAM: "*Anti-Mondes*" (1972-77), Opta, publisher. Trade paperback series of "new wave"-type American and British science fiction edited by Michel **Demuth**. Thirty-four titles published.

OCLA: *Club du Livre d'Anticipation* (1965-89), Opta, publisher. Limited-edition hardcover collection whose editors included Jacques **Sadoul**, Alain **Dorémieux**, and Michel **Demuth**, devoted almost entirely to translations of classics of English and American science fiction (Francis **Carsac** being a French exception). About 130 titles published.

OF: *Fiction* (1953-89), Opta, publisher. Magazine containing articles, reviews, and short stories translated from *F&SF* and other sources. Editors included Alain **Dorémieux**. Over 350 issues published.

OG: *Galaxie* (1953-59, 1964-77), Opta, publisher. Magazine containing mostly short stories translated from *Galaxy* and *If*. Editors included Michel **Demuth**. First series: sixty-five issues published; second series: 223 issues published.

OGB: *Galaxie-Bis* (1965-89), Opta, publisher. Paperback series of mostly classic American science fiction novels. About 120 volumes published.

ON: *Nebula* (1975-77), Opta, publisher. Trade paperback series of "new wave"-type French science fiction edited by Alain **Dorémieux**. Fifteen titles published.

PC: Presses de la Cité, publisher. One of the largest French publishers (with Hachette). They publish the *Presses-Pocket*, now *Pocket* (see PP below), *Fleuve Noir* (see FN- above), and *Vaugirard/Vauvenargues* (see Vaug. & VG below) specialized imprints.

PdE: *Portes de l'Étrange* (*Doors into the Strange*; 1969-76), Robert Laffont publisher. Series of trade paperbacks devoted to occult/esoteric novels, which published Christia **Sylf** and Jean **Tur**. About twelve volumes published.

PdF: *Présence du Futur* (*Presence of the Future*; 1954-present), Denoël, publisher. Paperback series of science fiction novels launched by Robert Kanters and later taken over by Elizabeth Gille. PdF publishes major names in American and French science fiction: Isaac Asimov, Ray Bradbury, James Blish, Roger Zelazny, and Jean-Pierre **Andrevon**, Serge **Brussolo**, Philippe **Curval**, Pierre **Pelot**, etc. Over four hundred titles published, plus fifteen Étoile Double (*Double Star*) twin compilations.

PdFant.: *Présence du Fantastique* (*Presence of the Fantastic*; 1990-present), Denoël, publisher. Paperback series of fantastique novels launched as a companion to PdF. Over fifty titles published.

Plasma: *Fantasy* (1983), Plasma, publisher. Trade paperback series of heroic-fantasy novels. Six titles published.

PP: *Science-Fiction* (1977-present), Presses-Pocket/Pocket/Presses de la Cité, publisher. Paperback series of science fiction and horror (*Terreur* (*Terror*)) novels edited by Jacques Goimard, reprinting American and French (Philippe **Curval**, Michel **Jeury**, Pierre **Pelot**) classics. Noted for covers by renowned artist Siudmak. Over 250 titles published.

PR: *Poche Rouge* (1980-), Hachette, publisher. Juvenile SF imprint.

PRA: *Le Petit Roman d'Aventure* (*The Little Adventure Novels*; 1936-39), Férenczi, publisher. Digest-sized series of adventure novels, including works by Maurice **Limat** and Max-André **Dazergues**. Over two hundred titles published.

Q/A: *Sextant* (1991-96), Québec/Amérique, publisher. French-Canadian science fiction novels by Joël **Champetier**, Élisabeth **Vonarburg**; under the editorship of Jean Pettigrew.

RA: *Romans d'Aventures* (*Adventure Novels*; 1884-1905), Hetzel, publisher. Parallel imprint to VE, devoted mostly to the publication of the works of André **Laurie**. Eleven titles published.

Rageot: Publisher of juvenile fantasy novels in their *Cascade* (*Waterfall*) imprint.

RDA: *Romans d'Aventures* (*Adventure Novels*; 1921-23, 1925-29), Férenczi, publisher. Paperback series of ad-

venture and genre novels, which published Jean de **La Hire**, Léon **Groc**, etc. First series: twenty-one titles published; second series: sixty-one titles published.

Requiem: (1974-) French-Canadian science fiction magazine founded and edited by Norbert **Spehner**. It changed its name to *Solaris* in 1979.

RF: *Le Rayon Fantastique* (*The Fantastic Bookshelf*; 1951-64), Hachette/Gallimard, publishers (Gallimard from No. 7 onward). Paperback series of science fiction novels edited by George H. Gallet (Nos.1-6), then with Michel Pilotin ("Stephen Spriel"), presenting mostly American novels; it also introduced most of the major French authors of the 1960s: Francis **Carsac**, Nathalie C. **Henneberg**, Albert **Higon** aka Michel **Jeury**, Gérard **Klein**, etc. 124 titles published.

RJ: *Romans pour la Jeunesse* (*Novels for the Youth*; 1932-35), Rouff, publisher. Paperback series of adventure and genre novels. About 170 titles published.

RL: Robert Laffont, publisher. Publisher of mainstream literature and non-fiction. It also published the specialized imprints *Ailleurs & Demain* (see A&D above), *Ailleurs & Demain Classiques* (see A&D Class above). It also published a short-lived juvenile SF imprint, *L'Âge des Étoiles* (see AdE above) and an adult fantasy imprint, *Les Portes de l'Étrange* (see PdE above).

RM: *Le Roman d'Aventures* (*Adventure Novels*) and Les Récits Mystérieux (*Mysterious Tales*; 1908-11; 1912-14), Méricant, publisher. Paperback series of adventure and genre novels, by Léon **Groc**, Gustave **Le Rouge**, Paul d'**Ivoi**, etc. About thirty titles published.

RMY: *Romans Mystérieux* (*Mysterious Novels*; 1927-50), Tallandier, publisher. A series of popular adventure novels, including titles by J. **Petithuguenin**, A. **Bernède**, etc.

Sat.: *Satellite* (1958-63), Satellite, publisher. Monthly magazine edited by Hervé **Calixte**, which published a mix of American and French (**Curval**, **Demuth**, **Henneberg**, **Klein**) material. Forty-seven issues and ten novels published.

S&A: *Science & Aventures* (*Science & Adventures*; 1948-62), Magnard, publisher. Trade paperback series of science fiction novels, by Anglo-Saxon authors. Twelve titles published.

S&V: *Sciences & Voyages* (*Science & Journeys*; 1919-1935), Offenstadt, publisher. One of the best of the magazines, which published serialized genre novels (by Léon **Groc**, José **Moselli**, René **Thévenin**, etc.) between the wars. 836 issues published.

SdP: *Signe de Piste* (*Trail Sign*), famous juvenile imprint, Alsatia, publisher. Started in 1936 by Pierre Joubert, subdivided into sub-imprints depending on reader ages, such as "black labels," "red labels," etc. From 1954-1969, *Signe de Piste* was edited by Serge **Dalens** & Jean-Louis **Foncine**, with a new numbering. In total, 201 titles were published, including a sub-imprint for younger children, *Signe de Piste Junior*, launched in 1957 (listed here as **SdP Jr**, thirty-four titles published). From 1971-1975, Alsatia teamed up with Hachette to launch a *Safari-Signe de Piste* imprint, with yet a new numbering (listed here as **SdPSF**). About eighty titles were published. From 1975-1989, Alsatia teamed up with Épi to launch the *Nouveau Signe de Piste* (*New Trail Sign*) imprint, with yet a new numbering (listed here as **SdP 2**). About 150 volumes were published.

SI: *La Science Illustrée* (*Illustrated Science*; 1887-1905). Weekly magazine edited by Adolphe Bitard & Louis Figuier, which published serialized novels by Louis **Boussenard**, etc. Over one thousand issues published.

Solaris *see* **Requiem**.

Tallandier: Publisher of popular paperback science fiction and adventure imprints such as *Bibliothèque des Grandes Aventures* and *Grandes Aventures—Voyages Excentriques* (see BGA above), *Chevalier de l'Aventure* (see CA above), *Le Livre d'Aventures* (see LdA above), *Le Livre National: Romans d'Aventures et d'Exploration* (see LN above), *Le Lynx* (see Lynx above), Meilleurs Romans d'Aventures (see MRAV above), Romans Mystérieux (see RMY above), *Voyages Lointains, Aventures Étranges*, and *À Travers l'Univers* (see VLAE below).

TF: *Travelling sur le Futur* (*Travelling to the Future*; 1977-81), Duculot, publisher. Paperback series of juvenile science fiction novels, including titles by Michel **Grimaud**. Sixteen titles published.

Titres: *Titres SF* (1979-83), Jean-Claude Lattès, publisher. Paperback series of science fiction and fantasy novels edited by Marianne **Leconte**, publishing mostly American authors (including Robert E. Howard's *Conan*) but also a few French names as well (Serge **Brussolo**, Michel **Calonne**). Sixty-eight titles published.

TR: La Table Ronde. Publisher of mainstream literature.

VA: *Voyages & Aventures* (*Voyages & Adventures*; 1933-41), Ferenczi, publisher. Series of paperback science fiction novels publishing a mix of adventure and genre novels, the latter by Jean de **La Hire**, Maurice **Limat**, etc. 380 titles published.

Vaug.: Vaugirard/Vauvenargues, Presses de la Cité, publisher (until 1997), independent thereafter. Imprint launched by the Presses de la Cité to publish series written by house names such as *Jag*, Jimmy **Guieu**, etc.

VE: *Voyages Extraordinaires* (*Extraordinary Voyages*; 1867-1910), Hetzel, publisher. Imprint launched to publish the works of Jules **Verne**. Forty-seven titles published.

VF: *Visions Futures* (*Future Visions*; 1952-53), Flamme d'Or, publisher. Series of science fiction paperbacks. Ten titles published.

VG: *Jimmy Guieu* (1979-present), Plon/Vaugirard/Vauvenargues/Presses de la Cité, publisher. Paperback series reprinting the works of FNA author Jimmy **Guieu**. Over 120 titles published.

VI: *Voyages Imaginaires, Songes, Visions & Romans Cabalistiques* (*Imaginary Voyages, Dreams, Visions & Cabalistic Novels*; 1787-89), Charles-Joseph **Garnier**, editor and publisher. Possibly the first dedicated science fiction imprint ever. Published a mix of foreign (Swift, Berington) and French (**Cyrano de Bergerac**, **Voltaire**) authors. Thirty-six titles published.

VLAE: *Voyages Lointains, Aventures Étranges* and *À Travers l'Univers* (*Far Voyages, Strange Adventures* and *Throughout The Universe*) (1927-33; 1952-53), Tallandier, publisher. Paperback series of adventure novels with some genre titles (Jean de **La Hire**, Louis, **Boussenard**, Albert **Bonneau**). One hundred forty-two titles published in the first series and twelve in the second series.

VSE: *Voyages Scientifiques Extraordinaires* (*Extraordinary Scientific Journeys*; 1892-94), Arthème Fayard, publisher. Published mostly novels by **Le Faure**. 20 titles published.

3. Authors' Bibliographies

Abeille, Jacques (?-); *Le Corps Perdu* (*The Lost Body*; Même & Autre; 1977); *Muraille* (*Walls*; Toril; 1977); *Le Plus Commun des Mortels* (*The Most Common of Mortals*; Cahiers de Brisants; 1980); *Le Cycle des Contrées* (*The Cycle of the Lands*; Zulma; 1982); *Les Jardins Statuaires* (*The Statuary Gardens*; Flamm.; 1982); *Fable* (Deleatur; 1983); *Les Branches dans les Chambres* (*Branches in the Rooms*; Phalène; 1984); *Un Cas de Lucidité* (*A Case Of Clairvoyance*; Deleatur; 1984); *L'Homme Nu* (*The Naked Man*; Deleatur; 1986); *Le Veilleur de Jour* (*The Day Watchman*; Flamm.; 1986); *Les Voyages du Fils* (*The Son's Journey*; Lézard; 1986); *Les Lupercales Forestieres* (*The Forest Festival*; Lézard; 1988); *La Clef des Ombres* (*The Key to Shadows*; Zulma; 1991); *En Mémoire Morte* (*In Dead Memory*; Zulma; 1992); *Les Carnets de l'Explorateur Perdu* (*The Notebooks of the Lost Explorer*; Ombres, 1993); *Le Gésir* (*The Lying*; Tournefeuille; 1993); *La Guerre entre les Arbres* (*The War Between the Trees*; Cadex; 1997); *Divinité du Rêve* (*God of Dreams*; L'Escampette; 1997)

Abellio, Raymond (Soulès, Jean-Jacques; 1907-1986); *Les Yeux d'Ézéchiel Sont Ouverts* (*The Eyes of Ezekiel Are Open*; Gall.; 1949); *La Fosse de Babel* (*The Pit of Babel*; Gall., 1962); *Visages Immobiles* (*Motionless Faces*; Gall., 1984); *La Structure Absolue* (*The Absolute Structure*; Gall., 1988); *Note*: See Chapter IX.

About, Edmond (1828-1885); *Le Cas de M. Guérin* (*The Case of Mr. Guerin*; Lévy, 1860); *L'Homme à l'Oreille Cassée* (Hac., 1862; transl. as *The Man with the Broken Ear*, 1867); *Le Nez d'un Notaire* (Lévy, 1862; transl. as *The Notary's Nose*, 1864); *Tolla* (Hac., 1889); *Note*: See

Chapter V. **L'Oreille Cassée** was adapted into an eponymous 1962 film (see Book 1, Chapter I).

Abric, Léon (1869-?) *see* **Grand-Guignol**

Acar, Jacques *see* **Gallaix, Vincent**

Achard, Eugène (?-); *Le Petit Chaperon Rouge* (*Little Red Riding Hood*; Libr. Gén. Canadienne, n.d.); *Le Petit Prince d'Égypte* (*The Little Prince of Egypt*; Libr. Gén. Canadienne, n.d.); *La Boule d'Or* (*The Golden Ball*; Libr. Gén. Canadienne, n.d.); *La Messe des Petits* (*The Children's Mass*; Libr. Gén. Canadienne, n.d.); *Note*: French-Canadian writer. Children's tales.

Achaume, Auguste (1891-1977) *see* **Grand-Guignol**

Adam, E. (Roy, Yvon; 1947-); *Utopie II* (*Utopia II*; Presses d'Amérique, 1994); *Note*: French-Canadian writer writing under a pseudonym.

Adam, Paul (1862-1920); *Volontés Merveilleuses* (*Marvellous Wills*; A. Savine, 1888-90); *L'Essence du Soleil* (*The Essence of the Sun*; Tresse & Stock, 1890); *Le Conte Futur* (*A Tale of the Future*; L'Art Indep., 1893); *Le Mystère des Foules* (*The Mystery of the Crowds*; Ollendorff, 1895); *La Force du Mal* (*The Power of Evil*; A. Colin, 1896); *Lettres de Malaisie* (*Letters from Malaysia*; Revue Blanche, 1898); *La Force* (*The Strength*; Ollendorff, 1899); *L'Enfant d'Austerlitz* (*The Child of Austerlitz*; SELEA, 1902); *Le Serpent Noir* (*The Black Serpent*; Ollendorf, 1905); *Les Feux du Sabbat* (*The Fires of the Sabbath*; Auteurs Modernes, 1907); *La Ville Inconnue* (*The Unknown City*; Ollendorf, 1911); *Le Culte d'Icare* (*The Cult of Icarus*; Flamm., 1924); *La Bataille d'Uhde* (*The Battle of Uhde*; Flamm., 1925); *Note*: See chapters IV and V.

Adam, Pierre (?-?); *La Sirène aux Yeux Fauves* (*The Mermaid with Fawn Eyes*; L'Intrépide, 1916; rev. CDAv, 1920); *Les Yeux d'Acier* (*The Eyes of Steel*; L'Intrépide, 1916; rev. 4 vols. CDAv, 1921); 1. *Les Yeux d'Acier* (*The Eyes of Steel*); 2. *Dans les Eaux Polaires* (*In the Polar Waters*); 3. *L'Île Mécanique* (*The Mechanic Island*); 4. *La Marche à la Navaja* (*The Navaja Run*); *L'Usine Infernale* (*The Infernal Factory*; L'Intrépide, 1919-20; rev. in 5 vols, CDAv, 1924); 1. *L'Usine Infernale* (*The Infernal Factory*); 2. *L'Escorte Invisible* (*The Invisible Escort*); 3. *L'Évasion de Philibert* (*Philibert's Escape*); 4. *Le Breuvage Magique* (*The Magical Drink*); 5. *L'Implacable Vengeance* (*The Implacable Revenge*); *Les Buveurs d'Or* (*The Gold Drinkers*; CDAv, 1920); *Le Grand Choc* [*The Great Clash*] (*L'Intrépide*, 1921-22; rev. as 6 vols., CDAv, 1925); 1. *Le Grand Choc* (*The Great Clash*); 2. *Les Bandits du Pont de Brooklyn* (*The Bandits of Brooklyn Bridge*); 3. *L'Étrange Invention de Falauvel* (*Falauvel's Strange Invention*); 4. *Vers le Pôle Magnétique* (*Towards the Magnetic Pole*); 5. *L'Éc-*

umeur d'Archipels (*The Archipelago Reaver*); 6. *Le Dompteur de Planètes* (*The Planet Tamer*); *Le Serpent de Cristal* (*The Crystal Snake*; L'Intrépide, 1921); *Les Buveurs d'Espace* (*The Drinkers of Space*; S&V, 1922); *Les Pirates des Grands Fonds* (*The Pirates of the Deep*; L'Intrépide, 1923); *Le Disque de Bronze* (*The Bronze Disc*; 7 vols., CDAv, 1926); 1. *Le Disque de Bronze* (*The Bronze Disc*); 2. *Le Palais des Roches Grises* (*The Palace of the Grey Rocks*); 3. *Au Pouvoir de Kadrassy* (*In Kadrassy's Power*); 4. *La Découverte de Bergal* (*Bergal's Discovery*); 5. *Le Parent du Grand-Esprit* (*The Parent of the Great Spirit*); 6. *Les Émotions de Gastarac* (*Gastarac's Emotions*); 7. *La Tragique Épave* (*The Tragic Wreck*); *Le Maître des Abîmes* (*The Master of the Abyss*; L'Intrépide, 1927); *Le Royaume du Silence* (*The Kingdom of Silence*; L'Intrépide, 1929); *Le Tremplin Magique* (*The Magical Springboard*; as Pierre Mada; L'Intrépide, 1930-31); *Le Gouffre aux Surprises* (*The Pit of Surprises*; L'Intrépide, 1932); *Le Roi du Silence* (*The King of Silence*; L'Intrépide, 1933); *La Reine des Mayas* (*The Queen of the Mayas*; as Pierre Mada; L'Intrépide, 1933); *La Couronne Arc-en-Ciel* (*The Rainbow Crown*; VA, 1934); *Hercule & Co.* (*L'Intrépide*, 1934-35); *La Vallée des Monstres* (*The Valley of Monsters*; L'As, 1937); *Le Petit Monsieur* (*The Little Sir*; n.d.); *Note*: See Chapter VII. According to some scholars, Pierre **Adam** may be a pseudonym of Antonin **Seuhl**.

Adornier, Pierre (?-); *Contres Gris et Roses* (*Grey and Pink Tales*; Tablettes, 1926)

Adriet, Georges (?-?) *see* **Grand-Guignol**

Aeck, Urban G. (1944-); *Le Chasseur* (*The Hunter*; Rocher, 1995)

Agapit, Marc (Sobra, Adrien; 1897-1985); *La Juive d'Oran* (*The Jewess of Oran;* as Ange Arbos; Pensée Latine, 1926); *L'Esprit de la Boîte aux Lettres* (*The Spirit of the Mail Box;* as Ange Arbos; Ferenczi, 1935); *L'Épouvantable Piège* (*The Awful Trap;* as Ange Arbos; Ferenczi, 1935); *Le Robot Fantôme* (*The Ghost Robot;* as Ange Arbos; Ferenczi, 1935); *La Tour du Silence* (*The Tower of Silence*; as Ange Arbos; Ferenczi, 1936); *Le Valet* (*The Butler;* as Adrien Sobra; Bordas, 1949); *La Maison du Robot* (*The House of the Robot;* as Ange Arbos; Ferenczi, 1951); *Le Crime de la Soucoupe Volante* (*The Flying Saucer Crime;* as Ange Arbos; Ferenczi, 1951); *On a tué Dejanire* (*They Killed Dejanire;*

as Ange Arbos; Ferenczi, 1952); *Morts sans Fleurs* (*Dead Without Flowers*; as Adrien Sobra; Métal Pol., 1956); *Portes sur l'Inconnu* (*Doors Into the Unknown*; as Adrien Sobra; Métal 20, 1956); *Les Cuisines de Sirius* (*The Kitchens of Sirius;* as Adrien Sobra; publ. in Italian as *Universo Fantasma* (*Ghostly Universe*, Mondadori, 1957); *Agence Tous Crimes* (*All-Crime Agency*; FNAG 40, 1958); *Greffe Mortelle* (*Mortal Transplant*; FNAG 43, 1958); *Le Doigt de l'Ombre* (*The Shadow Finger*; FNAG 51, 1959); *La Bête Immonde* (*The Awful Beast*; FNAG 53, 1959); *Puzzle Macabre* (*Macabre Puzzle*; FNAG 58, 1959); *Piège Infernal* (*Infernal Trap*; FNAG 60, 1960); *Le Visage du Spectre* (*The Face of the Spectre*; FNAG 63, 1960); *Nuits Rouges* (*Red Nights*; FNAG 67, 1960); *Opéra de la Mort* (*Death Opera*; FNAG 69, 1960); Complexes (FNAG 82, 1962); *Ténèbres* (*Darkness*; FNAG 87, 1962); *Phantasmes* (FNAG 91, 1962); *École des Monstres* (*Monster School*; FNAG 99, 1963); *Guignol Tragique* (*Tragic Puppet Show*; FNAG 105, 1964); *Le Voyage en Rond* (*The Circular Journey*; FNAG 113, 1964); *La Nuit du Minotaure* (*The Night of the Minotaur*; FNAG 118, 1965); *Les Yeux Braqués* (*The Staring Eyes*; FNAG 122, 1965); *Le Fluide Magique* (*The Magical Fluid*; FNAG 125, 1965); *L'Appel de l'Abîme* (*The Call of the Abyss*; FNAG 128, 1966); *La Guivre* (FNAG 131, 1966); *La Ville Hallucinante* (*The City of Hallucinations*; FNAG 133, 1966); *Monsieur Personne* (*Mister Nobody*; FNAG 137, 1967); *L'Île Magique* (*The Magical Island*; FNAG 142, 1967); *Les Santons du Diable* (*The Devil's Nativity Figures*; FNAG 148, 1968); *Parade des Morts-Vivants* (*Parade of the Living Dead*; FNAG 151, 1968); *La Goule* (*The Ghoul*; FNAG 155, 1968); *La Dame à l'Os* (*The Lady with the Bone*; FNAG 159, 1969); *La Poursuite Infernale* (*The Pursuit from Hell*; FNAG 163, 1969); *Opération Lunettes Magiques* (*Operation Magic Glasses*; FNAG 170, 1969); *L'Antichambre de l'Au-Delà* (*The Antechamber of Beyond*; FNAG 176, 1970); *Une Sorcière m'a dit* (*A Witch Told Me*; FNAG 181, 1970); *Le Mur des Aveugles* (*Blind Men's Wall*; FNAG 185, 1970); *Le Poids du Monde* (*The Weight of the World*; FNAG 189, 1970); *Le Pays des Mutants* (*The Land of the Mutants*; FNAG 195, 1971); *L'Héritage du Diable* (*The Devil's Inheritance*; FNAG 205, 1971); *L'Ogresse* (*The Ogress*; FNAG 214, 1972); *La Croix de Judas* (*The Judas Cross*; FNAG 217, 1972); *Le Temps des Miracles* (*The Time of Miracles*; FNAG 223, 1972); *La Bouche d'Ombre* (*The Mouth of Shadows*; FNAG 234, 1973); *Le Miroir Truqué* (*The Trick Mirror*; FNAG 240, 1973); *Les Ciseaux d'Atropos* (*The Scissors of Atropos*; FNAG 244, 1973); *Le Chasseur d'Âmes* (*The Hunter of Souls*; FNAG 254, 1974); *Le Dragon de Lumière* (*The Dragon of Light*; FNAG 260, 1974); *Note:* See Chapter VIII and IX. A number of **Agapit**'s novels were adapted into digest-sized graphic novels (see Book 1, Chapter V under **Fleuve Noir**).

Aghion, Max (?-) *see* **Saint-Granier**

Agraives, Jean d' (Causse, Frédéric; 1892-1951); *La Cité des Sables* (*The City of the Sands*; S&V, 1923); *L'Enjoleuse* (*The Enchantress*; Mon Ciné, 1924); *Le Diamant Roi* (*The King Diamond*; L'Intrépide, 1925); *Le Rayon Svastika* (*The Swastika Ray*; JDV, 1926); *L'Oeil d'Émeraude* (*The Emerald Eye*; L'Intrépide, 1926); *L'Aviateur de Bonaparte* (*Bonaparte's Aviator*; Hac., 1926); *Le Corsaire Borgne* (*The One-Eyed Corsair*; Hac., 1926); *Le Château du Reliquaire* (*The Castle of the Relics*; Gedalge, 1926); *Les Ailes de l'Aigle* (*The Wings of the Eagle*; Hac., 1927); *Le Dernier Faune* (*The Last Faun*; Ren. Du Livre, 1927); *Le Sorcier de la Mer* (*The Wizard of the Sea;* Hac., 1927); *La Princesse aux Dragons Verts* (*The Princess with the Green Dragons*; Hac., 1929); *Les Aventures de Chafustard* (*Chafustard's Adventures*; Boivin, 1929); *Le Virus 34* (*Virus 34*; Cosmopolites, 1929); *Le Serpent de Kali* (*The Serpent of Kali*; Cosmopolites, 1930); *L'Énigme du Pastel* (*The Mystery of the Pastel*; Hac., 1930); *Le Sorcier Jaune* (*The Yellow Wizard*; Berger-Levrault, 1931); *Le Maître-Coq du Kamtchatka* (*The Cook of the Kamtchatka*; Plon, 1932); *Le Tueur de Navires* (*The Ship Killer*; Berger-Levrault, 1932); *Le Petit Roi du Lac* (*The Little King of the Lake*; Nathan, 1932); *L'Ancre sous les Ailes* (*The Anchor Under the Wings*; Berger-Levrault, 1933); *La Gloire sous les Voiles* (*Glory Under the Sails*; Berger-Levrault, 1933); *Le Fléau de Neptune* (*The Bane of Neptune*; Berger-Levrault, 1934); *Les Deux Sirènes* (*The Two Mermaids*; Berger-Levrault, 1934); *L'Empire des Algues* (*The Empire of Seaweed;* serialized as 2 issues, *L'Avion Perdu* (*The Lost Plane*) and *La Mer en Flammes* (*The Sea in Flame*, Cosmopolites, 1935); *Le Trois-Mâts Fantôme* (*The Phantom Schooner*; Hac., 1935); *Un Cargo dans la Nuit* (*A Cargo in the Night*; Hac., 1935); *L'Espionne de Nelson* (*Nelson's Spy*; Hac., 1936); *Le Dernier Pirate* (*The Last Pirate*; Hac., 1937); *Empreintes sur le Vase* (*Prints on the Vase*; Hac., 1937); *Petite Source sous les Palmes* (*Little Spring Under the Palms*; Loisirs, 1938); *Du Sang sur l'Étrave* (*Blood on the Prow*; Fayard, 1939); *La Marque d'Attila* (*The Mark of Attila*; Hac., 1939); *La Maison des Sept Sirènes* (*The House of the Seven Mermaids*; Colbert, 1942); *Le Jardin au Clair de Lune* (*The Garden in the Moonlight*; Colbert, 1942); *Sur la Piste des Dieux* (*On the Trail of the Gods*; Colbert, 1943); *Le Cimetière de Tamerland* (*Tamerlans's Graveyard*; Deux Sirènes, 1947); *Les*

Portes du Monde (*The Gates of the World*; Flore, 1948); *Appel de la Lumière* (*Call of the Light*; Ed. De Paris, 1949); *Note:* See Chapter VII.

Aguilard, André-Albert d' *see* **Armandy, André**

Aguzan, Jean d' (1882-1951) *see* **Grand-Guignol**

Ainsley, Luc (1965-); *Kadel* (Fides, 1986); *Note:* French-Canadian writer. Heroic fantasy.

Ajasson de Grandsagne, J.-B.-F.-E. *see* **Jeancourt, Auguste**

Alain, Jean-Claude (?-); *La Marque de Sang* (*The Mark of Blood*; Petite Ourse, 1946); *La Maison du Bord des Sables* (*The House at the Edge of the Sands*; SdP, 1950); *L'Équipier* (*The Teammate*; SdP, 1951); *La Nuit Merveilleuse de la Cigogne* (*The Marvellous Night of the Stork*; Casterman, 1951); *L'Enfant des Ténèbres* (*The Child of Darkness*; Dumas, 1952); *Demain il fera jour* (*Tomorrow the Sun Will Rise; 1952); La Nuit des Saints Innocents* (*The Night of the Innocent Saints*; Gigord, 1953); *Le Royaume Près de la Mer* (*The Kingdom Near the Sea*; SdP, 1954); *Le Roi Mezel* (*King Mezel*; SdP, 1954); *Pierrot Lunaire* (*Moon Pierrot*; SdP, 1956); *La Piste 116* (*Trail 116*; SdP, 1958); Series *Mikhaïl, Prince d'Hallmark* (*Mikhail, Prince of Hallmark*): *Mikhaïl, Prince d'Hallmark"* (*Mikhail, Prince of Hallmark*; SdP, 1953); *Le Chemin sans Étoiles* (*The Path Without Stars*; SdP, 1953); *Le Fils du Lac* (*The Son of the Lake*; SdP, 1953); *Transfiguration* (SdP, 1954); *La Fin d'Hallmark* (*The End of Hallmark*; SdP, 1955); *Note:* Belgian writer. Juvenile novels. See chapters VIII and IX.

Alain-Fournier (Fournier, Henri Alban; 1886-1914); *Le Grand Meaulnes* (Émile-Paul, 1913; transl. as the *Lost Domain*, 1959); *La Femme Empoisonnée* (*The Poisoned Woman*; Seghers, 1944); *Note:* See Chapter VI.

Albaret, d' (?-?) *see* **Opéra**

Albaret, Laurence (?-); *Le Grand Ventre* (*The Great Belly*; Balzac, 1944); *Note:* See Chapter VI.

Albérès, René-Marill (1921-1982); *L'Autre Planète* (*The Other Planet*; AM, 1958); *Manuscrit Enterré dans le Jardin d'Éden* (*Ms. Buried in the Garden of Eden*; Panorama, 1967); *Note:* See Chapter IX.

Alberny, Luc (1890-?); *Le Glaive sur le Monde* (*The Sword Over the World*; Radot, 1928); *L'Enlèvement de la Cité* (*The Taking of the City*; Jordi, 1930); *L'Étrange Aventure du Prof. Pamphlegme* (*The Strange Adventure of Prof. Pamphlegme*; Figuière, 1933); *Le Mammouth Bleu* (*The Blue Mastodon*; Malfère, 1935); *Note:* See Chapter VII.

Albert-Birot, Pierre (1885-1967); *L'Homme Coupé en Morceaux* (*The Man Cut Into Pieces*; Sic, 1921); *Gra-*

binoulor (Den., 1933); *Théâtre 1: Matoum et Tevibar / Larountala* (Rougerie, 1977); *Théâtre 2: L'Homme Coupé en Morceaux* (*The Man Cut Into Pieces*) / *Le Bon Dieu* (Rougerie, 1978); *Les Femmes Pliantes* (*Pliant Women*; Rougerie, 1978); *Les Mémoires d'Adam et les Pages d'Ève* (*Adam's Memoirs and Eve's Pages*; Allée, 1986)

Aldany, Kim *see* **Grousset, Alain**

Alebert-Weil, Jean-Claude (?-); *Sont les Oiseaux* (*Are the Birds*; Rocher, 1996)

Alessandrini, Jean (1942-); *Henri à l'Amuséum* (*Henri at the Amuseum*; École des Loisirs, 1974); *Le Père Cafetière* (*Father Coffeepot*; Hac., 1981); *Le Zapoyoko* (Centurion, 1984); *Paul et le Takin* (Centurion, 1985); *Le Prince d'Aéropolis* (*The Prince of Aeropolis*; Amitié, 1986); *Le Détective de Minuit* (*The Midnight Detective*; Amitié, 1987); *La Malédiction de Chéops* (*The Curse of Cheops*; Amitié, 1989); *Note:* Juveniles. See Chapter VIII.

Alévy (?-?) *see* **Grand-Guignol**

Alexandre, Robert (?-); *Sandrihar* (SdP 2 6, 1975); *Tiguir* (SdP 2 42, 1977); *La Parenthèse* (*The Parenthesis*; SdP 2 68, 1978); *Les Héritiers des Sept Mondes: Oriane* (*The Inheritors of the Seven Worlds: Oriane*; SdP 2 129, 1982); *Yriel* (FNA 1697, 1989); Series *Mykir: Le Survivant* (*The Survivor*; SdPSF 52, 1973); *Les Révoltés d'Aramanthe* (*The Rebels of Aramanth*; SdPSF 69, 1974); *Les Gardiens de l'Univers* (*The Guardians of the Universe*; SdP 2 12, 1976); *Escale sur Mytilia* (*Shore Leave on Mytilia*; SdP 2 34, 1976); *Les Orphelins d'Almeray* (*The Orphans of Amray*; SdP 2 113, 1981); *Note:* Juvenile SF. See Chapter IX.

Alexandrian, Sarane (?-); *Danger de Vie* (*Danger of Life*; Den., 1969); *L'Oeuf du Monde* (*The Egg of the World*; Filipacchi, 1975); *Les Terres Fortunées du Songe* (*Dream's Happy Lands*; Gallilée, 1979); *Le Déconcerto* (Galilée, 1980); *Le Grand Astrosophe* (Los., 1994); *Note:* See Chapter VIII.

Alkine, Serge (?-); *La Révolte de la Terre* (*The Revolt of Earth*; MRA, 1956); *L'Or de la Lune* (*Gold on the Moon*; MRA, 1957); *En Mains Propres* (*With Clean Hands*; Ferenczi, 1959); *Pour le Grand Voyage* (*For the Great Journey*; Ferenczi, 1959); *Note:* See Chapter IX.

Allain, Marcel (1885-1970); *Le Tour* (With Pierre **Souvestre**; Libr. De l'Auto, 1909); *Paradis d'Amour* (*Love Paradise*; Fayard, 1925); *L'Incroyable Aventure* (*The Incredible Adventure*; SFEPI, 1942); Series *Tigris* (26 vols., Ferenczi, 1928-1930): *1. Tigris; 2. Coeur de Bandit* (*Heart of a Bandit*); *3. Âme d'Amoureuse* (*Soul of a Lover*); *4. L'Audience Rouge* (*The Red Audience*); *5. Rude se venge* (*Rude's Revenge*); *6. L'Impossible Al-*

liance (*The Impossible Alliance*); *7. La Dame en Violet* (*The Lady in Purple*); *8. L'Homme au Masque de Verre* (*The Man in the Glass Mask*); *9. Qui?* (*Who?*); *10. Une Sainte* (*A Saintly Woman*); *11. Crime de Femme* (*Womanly Crime*); *12. Le Mariage de Léon Rude* (*The Wedding of Leon Rude*); *13. Matricule 227* (*Number 227*); *14. Haut et Court* (*High and Short*); *15. Le Fantôme Rouge* (*The Red Ghost*); *16. Le Troisième Squelette* (*The Third Skeleton*); *17. La Roulotte Maudite* (*The Accursed Trailer*); *18. Crucifiée* (*Crucified*); *19. Volonté d'Altesse* (*His Highness' Will*); *20. L'Homme Noir* (*The Dark Man*); *21. Villa des Glycines; 22. L'Instant Tragique* (*Tragic Moment*); *23. Le Fossoyeur de Minuit* (*The Midnight Gravedigger*); *24. Le Garage Rouge* (*The Red Garage*); *25. Tigris Vaincu* (*Tigris Defeated*); *26. Si c'était Tigris?* (*If It Was Tigris?*); Series *Fatala* (22 vols., Ferenczi, 1930-1931): *1. Fatala; 2. La Goule aux Cheveux d'Or* (*The Ghoul with Golden Hair*); *3. Bébert le Courtaud; 4. Meurtrière?* (*Murderess?*); *5. Les Morts Vivants* (*The Living Dead*); *6. Un Ange!* (*An Angel!*); *7. Masquée!* (*Masked!*); *8. L'Autre* (*The Other*); *9. L'Esclave* (*The Slave*); *10. Jésus... Beau Gosse!* (*Jesus... Pretty Kid!*); *11. Partie!* (*Gone!*); *12. Elle!* (*She!*); *13. L'Oeillet Rouge!* (*The Red Carnation!*); *14. Maudite!* (*Accursed!*); *15. Brelan de Haines!* (*Three Hatreds!*); *16. Poupées d'Amour!* (*Love Puppets!*); *17. Secret de Femme!* (*Womanly Secret!*); *18. Peur!* (*Fear!*); *19. Midinette? ; 20. Complice!* (*Accomplice!*); *21. Enfer d'Amour!* (*Hellish Love!*); *22. Notre Maître!* (*Our Master!*); Series *Miss Téria* (12 vols., Ferenczi, 1931): *1. Miss Téria; 2. Du Sang sur une Fleur* (*Blood on a Flower*); *3. Son Homme* (*Her Man*); *4. Coeur de Gosse!* (*Heart of a Kid!*); *5. Une du Trottoir* (*She from the Sidewalk*); *6. Je vous en prie...* (*I Beg You...*); *7. Son Altesse!* (*His Highness!*); *8. Sous l'Ombrelle?* (*Under the Umbrella?*); *9. Le Poison des Lèvres* (*The Poison on the Lips*); *10. Coquette?* (*Coquettish?*); *11. Vendue* (*Sold*); *12. Les Yeux qui Mentent* (*The Lying Eyes*); Series *Dix Heures d'Angoisse* (*Ten Hours of Terror*) (12 vols., Ferenczi, 1932-1933): *1. Crime d'Amour* (*Crime of Love*); *2. Lui ou Elle* (*He Or She*); *3. Deux Blondes* (*Two Blondes*); *4. Ce n'est pas lui* (*It's Not Him*); *5. Vilaine Histoire* (*Dirty Business*); *6. Le Client du Numéro 16* (*The Client of No.16*); *7. Torture; 8. L'Atroce Menace* (*The Awful Threat*); *9. L'Empreinte Sanglante* (*The Bloody Trail*); *10. Le Piège à Hommes* (*The Man Trap*); *11. Un Crime de Minuit* (*The Midnight Crime*); *12. Perfidie!* (*Perfidy!*); *Férocias* (26 vols., Ferenczi, 1933) (individual titles not available);

L'Incroyable Aventure (*The Incredible Adventure*; SFEP, 1940); Series *Fantômas* (with Pierre **Souvestre**): *1. Fantômas* (Fayard, 1911; transl. as *Fantomas*, 1915; retransl. 1986); *2. Juve contre Fantômas* (*Juve vs. Fantomas*; Fayard, 1911; transl. as the *Exploits of Juve*, 1916; retransl. as the *Silent Executioner*, 1987); *3. Le Mort qui Tue* (*The Dead Man Who Kills*) aka *Fantômas Se Venge* (*The Vengeance of Fantomas*; Fayard, 1911; transl. as *Messengers of Evil*, 1917); *4. L'Agent Secret* (*The Secret Agent*) aka *Une Ruse de Fantômas* (*A Ruse of Fantomas*; Fayard, 1911; transl. as *A Nest of Spies*, 1917); *5. Un Roi Prisonnier de Fantômas* (*A King Prisoner of Fantomas*; Fayard, 1911; transl. as *A Royal Prisoner*, 1919); *6. Le Policier Apache* (*The Apache Policeman*) aka *Le Policier Fantômas* (*Fantomas Policeman*; Fayard, 1911; transl. as *The Long Arm of Fantomos*, 1924); *7. Le Pendu de Londres* (*The Hanged Man of London*) aka *Aux Mains de Fantômas* (*In the Hands of Fantomas*; Fayard, 1911 trans. as *Slippery as Sin*, 1920); *8. La Fille de Fantômas* (*The Daughter of Fantomas*; Fayard, 1911); *9. Le Fiacre de Nuit* (*The Night Hansom Cab*) aka *Le Fiacre de Fantômas* (*The Hansom Cab of Fantomas*; Fayard, 1911); *10. La Main Coupée* (*The Severed Hand*) aka *Fantômas à Monaco* (*Fantomas in Monaco*; Fayard, 1911; transl. as the *Limb of Satan*, 1924); *11. L'Arrestation de Fantômas* (*The Capture of Fantomas*; Fayard, 1911); *12. Le Magistrat Cambrioleur* (*The Burglar Judge*) aka *Le Juge Fantômas* (*Judge Fantomas*; Fayard, 1912); *13. La Livrée du Crime* (*The Livery of Crime*) aka *La Livrée de Fantômas* (*The Livery of Fantomas*; Fayard, 1912); *14. La Mort de Juve* (*The Death of Juve*) aka *Fantômas Tue Juve* (*Fantomas Kills Juve*; Fayard, 1912); *15. L'Evadée de Saint-Lazare* (*The Escapee from Saint-Lazare*) aka *Fantômas, Roi du Crime* (*Fantomas, King of Crime*; Fayard, 1912); *16. La Disparition de Fandor* (*The Disappearance of Fandor*) aka *Fandor Contre Fantômas* (*Fandor vs. Fantomas*; Fayard, 1912); *17. Le Mariage de Fantômas* (*The Wedding of Fantomas*; Fayard, 1912); *18. L'Assassin de Lady Beltham* (*The Assassin of Lady Beltham*) aka *Les Amours de Fantômas* (*The Loves of Fantomas*; Fayard, 1912); *19. La Guêpe Rouge* (*The Red Wasp*) aka *Un Défi de Fantômas* (*The Challenge of Fantomas*; Fayard, 1912); *20. Les Souliers du Mort* (*The Dead Man's Shoes*) aka *Fantômas Rôde* (*Fantomas Prowls*; Fayard, 1912); *21. Le Train Perdu* (*The Lost Train*) aka *Le Train de Fantômas* (*The Train of Fantomas*; Fayard, 1912); *22. Les Amours d'un Prince* (*The Love of a Prince*) aka *Fantômas s'amuse* (*Fantomas Has Fun*; Fayard, 1912); *23. Le Bouquet Tragique* (*The Tragic Bouquet*) aka *Le Bouquet de Fantômas* (*The Bouquet of Fantomas*; Fayard, 1912); *24. Le Jockey Masqué* (*The Masked Jockey*) aka *Fantômas, Roi du Turf* (*Fantomas, King of the Turf*; Fayard, 1913); *25. Le Cercueil Vide* (*The Empty Coffin*) aka *Le Cercue il de Fantômas* (*The Coffin of Fantomas*; Fayard, 1913); *26. Le Faiseur de*

Reines (The Queen Maker) aka Fantômas Contre l'Amour (Fantomas vs. Love; Fayard, 1913); *27. Le Cadavre Géant (The Giant Corpse) aka Le Spectre de Fantômas (The Spectre of Fantomas*; Fayard, 1913); *28. Le Voleur d'Or (The Gold Thief) aka Prisonniers de Fantômas! (Prisoners of Fantomas!*; Fayard, 1913); *29. La Série Rouge (The Red Series) aka Fantômas s'évade (Fantomas Escapes*; Fayard, 1913); *30. L'Hôtel du Crime (Crime Hotel) aka Fantômas Accuse! (Fantomas Accuses!)* (Fayard, 1913); *31. La Cravate de Chanvre (The Hemp Necktie) aka Le Domestique de Fantômas (The Servant of Fantomas*; Fayard, 1913); *32. La Fin de Fantômas (The End of Fantomas) aka Fantômas Est-Il Mort? (Is Fantomas Dead?*; Fayard, 1913); Series *Fantômas* (by Marcel **Allain** alone): *33. Fantômas est-il ressuscité? (Is Fantomas Resurrected?*; SPE, 1925/Fayard, 1934; transl. as the *Lord of Terror*, 1925); *34. Fantômas, Roi des Recéleurs (Fantomas, King of the Fences*; SPE, 1926/Fayard, 1934; transl. as *Juve in the Dock*, 1926); *35. Fantômas en Danger (Fantomas in Danger*; SPE, 1926/Fayard, 1935, transl. as *Fantomas Captured*, 1926); *36. Fantômas prend sa Revanche (Fantomas Takes His Revenge*; SPE, 1926/Fayard, 1935; transl. as the *Revenge of Fantomas*, 1927); *37. Fantômas Attaque Fandor (Fantomas Attacks Fandor*; SPE, 1926/Fayard, 1935; transl. as *Bulldog and Rats*, 1928); *38. Si c'était Fantômas? (If It Was Fantomas?*; (*Le Petit Journal*, 1933; Fayard, 1935); *39. Oui, c'est Fantômas! (Yes, It Is Fantomas!*; *Le Petit Journal*, 1934; Fayard, 1937); *40. Fantômas Joue et Gagne (Fantomas Plays and Wins*; *La Dépêche*, 1935; Fayard, 1947); *41. Fantômas Rencontre l'Amour (Fantomas Meets Love*; *France-Soir*, 1946; Fayard, 1947); *42. Fantômas Vole des Blondes (Fantomas Steals from the Blondes*; *Ce Soir*/Fayard, 1948); *43. Fantômas Mène le Bal (Fantomas Leads the Dance*; *Constellation*, 1963); *Note:* See Chapter IV. The **Fantômas** series was adapted into films, television series and comic books (see Book 1, chapters I, II, and V).

Allard-Lacerte, Rolande *see* **Lacerte, Rolande**

Allorge, Henri (1878-1938); *Le Secret de Maître Christophorus (The Secret of Master Christophorus*; Revue Maurice, 1905); *La Famine de Fer (The Iron Famine*; 1913); *Le Mal de la Gloire (The Evils of Glory*; Sansot, 1919); *Le Grand Cataclysme (The Great Cataclysm*; Lar., 1922); *Petits Poèmes Électriques et Scientifiques (Little Electric and Scientific Poems*; Provost-Perrin, 1924); *Ciel contre Terre (Heaven vs. Earth*; Hac., 1924); *Le Roi des Perles (The Pearl King*; SET, 1926); *Miriakris, Amie d'Enfance de Jésus (Miriakris, Jesus' Childhood Friend*; with Paul **Féval**, Fils; Baudinière, 1927); *Les Étoiles Mortes (The Dead Stars*; Bonne Presse, 1928); *Le Bagne sans Sommeil (The Sleepless Penitentiary*; SET, 1929); *L'Espoir Obstiné (Obstinate*

Hope; Perrin, 1930); *L'Énigme de la Crypte (The Mystery of the Crypt*; Gautier-Languereau, 1931); *Les Débuts de Deux Inventions (The Beginnings of Two Inventions*; Lar., 1932); *Les Rayons Ensorcelés (The Spellbound Rays*; Nathan, 1935); *Note:* See Chapter VII.

Almira, Jacques (?-); *Le Marchand d'Oubliés (Merchant of the Forgotten*; Gall., 1979)

Alpérine, Paul (?-); *Nuit d'Écosse (Scottish Night*; Lemerre, 1935); *L'Île des Vierges Rouges (The Island of the Red Virgins*; Lemerre, 1936); *Le Rire de la Sorcière (The Witch's Laughter*; Tallandier, 1941); *Ombres sur le Thibet (Shadows Over Tibet*; Myrte, 1945); *La Citadelle des Glaces (The Citadel of the Ice*; VLAE, 1946); *Les Secrets de la Mer Morte (The Secrets of the Dead Sea*; VLAE, 1949); *Demain dans le Soleil (Tomorrow Inside the Sun*; VLAE, 1950); *Quand Paracelse Ressuscita (When Paracelsius Came Back to Life*; Mari, 1979); *Note:* See Chapter VII.

Alsace, René d' (?-); *L'Enfant Artificiel (The Artificial Child*; Anquetil, 1926); *L'Homme Greffé (The Grafted Man*; Mercure Universel, 1932)

Amboise, Valéry d' (?-); *L'Humanité se Meurt (Mankind Is Dying*; Frontières, Espionnage Fantastique 1, 1972)

Amfreville, Henri d' (1905-1964); *Les Fanatiques (The Fanatics*; Grasset, 1937); *La Terre Est Chaude (Earth Is Hot*; Grasset, 1946); *L'Homme Nu (The Naked Man*; Grasset, 1951); *Note:* See Chapter VII.

Amila, John (Meckert, Jean; 1910-); *La Ville de Plomb (The City of Lead*; as Jean Meckert; Gall., 1949); *Le Neuf de Pique (The Nine of Hearts*; RF 43, 1956); *La Lune d'Omaha (Omaha Moon*; Gall., 1970); *Le Grillon Enragé (The Rabid Cricket*; Gall., 1970); *La Vierge et le Taureau (The Virgin and the Bull*; PC, 1971); *Les Noces de Soufre (Sulphur Wedding*; Gall., 1972); *Terminus Iéna* (Gall., 1973); *Le Boucher des Hurlus (The Butcher of the Hurlus*; Gall., 1982); *Langes Radieux (Brilliant Napkins*; Gall., 1984); *Note:* See Chapter IX.

Andrau, Marianne (1905-); *Les Mains du Manchot (The Hands of the One-Armed Man*; Den., 1953); *Le Prophète (The Prophet*; Den., 1955); *Lumière d'Épouvante (Light of Terror*; Den., 1956); *D.C. (Doom City*; Den., 1957); *Les Faits d'Eiffel (The Feats of Eiffel*; PdF 37, 1960); *L'Architecte Fou (The Mad Architect*; Den., 1964); *Franchir la Mort (To Cross Into Death*; RL, 1985); *Note:* See chapters VIII and IX.

André, Dominique (?-); *Le Baiser Froid (Cold Kiss*; Portiques, 1930); *Cassandre (Cassandra*; Impr. Alençon, 1933); *Mademoiselle Colin* (Portiques, 1934); *Les Auréoles (Haloes*; Divan, 1939); *Suite à Cassandre (Sequel to Cassandre*; Impr. Alençon, 1946); *Conquête de* *l'Éternel* (*Conquest of the Eternal*; Grund, 1947); *Note:* Swiss writer. See Chapter IX.

André, Philippe d' (?-); *Les Clefs* (*The Keys*; RL, 1972); *La Momie* (*The Mummy*; RL, 1974); *Les Ruses de l'Assaillant* (*The Ruses of the Attacker*; RL, 1978); *Le Cabanon* (*The Cabin*; RL, 1980); *Note:* See Chapter IX.

Andrès, Bernard J. (1949-); *La Trouble-Fête* (*The Trouble Maker*; Leméac, 1986); *Note:* French-Canadian writer. Baroque novel about the future occupation of Canada by the U.S.

Andrevon, Jean-Pierre (1937-); *Les Hommes-Machines contre Gandahar* (*The Machine Men vs. Gandahar*; PdF 118, 1969); *Aujourd'hui, Demain et Après* (*Today, Tomorrow and After*; PdF 124, 1970); *Cela Se Produira Bientôt* (*It Will Happen Soon*; PdF 135, 1971); *La Guerre des Gruulls* (*The War Against the Gruulls*; as Alphonse Brutsche; FNA 452, 1971; rev. as Andrevon, FNSL 163, 1985); *Un Froid Mortel* (*A Deadly Cold*; as Alphonse Brutsche; FNAG 201, 1971; rev. as Andrevon, FNSL 159, 1984); *Le Reflux de la Nuit* (*The Reflux of Night*; as Alphonse Brutsche; FNAG 213, 1972; rev. PdFant 26, 1992); *Le Temps des Grandes Chasses* (*The Time of the Great Hunts*; PdF 162, 1973); *Retour à la Terre 1* (*Back to the Earth 1*; anthology; PdF 189, 1974); *Le Dieu de Lumière* (*The God of Light*; as Alphonse Brutsche; FNA 540, 1973; rev. as Andrevon, FNA 1656, 1988); *Le Temps Cyclothymique* (*The Cyclothymic Time*; as Alphonse Brutsche; FNA 631, 1974; rev. As Andrevon, FNA 1680, 1989); *Une Lumière entre les Arbres* (*A Light Between the Trees*; as Alphonse Brutsche; FNAG 253, 1974; rev. as Andrevon, FNSL 168, 1985); *Utopies 75* (*Utopia '75*; anthology/with Philippe **Curval**, Christine **Renard** & Michel **Jeury**; A&D 36, 1975); *Les Enfants de Pisauride* (*The Children of Pisauride*; as Alphonse Brutsche; FNSL 10, 1975; rev. as Andrevon, FNA 1770, 1990); *Repères dans l'Infini* (*Markings in Infinity*; PdF 198, 1975); *Retour à la Terre 2* (*Back to the Earth 2*; anthology; PdF 216, 1975); *Le Désert du Monde* (*The Desert of the World*; PdF 235, 1977); *Retour à la Terre 3* (*Back to the Earth 3*; anthology; PdF 242, 1977); *C'est Tous Les Jours Pareil* (*Every Day Is the Same*; Los., 1977); *La Mémoire Transparente* (*The Transparent Memory*; Atelier du Gué, 1977); *Paysages de Mort* (*Deathscapes*; PdF 253, 1978); *Dans les Décors*

Truqués (*Inside the Phony Backgrounds*; PdF 269, 1979); *Avenirs en Dérive* (*Futures Adrift*; anthology/ with Bernard **Blanc**; Kes., 1979); *Les Revenants de l'Ombre* (*The Shadow Ghosts*; Jean Goujon, 1979; rev. NéO, 1989; rev. PdFant 59, 1997); *Compagnons en Terre Etrangère 1* (*Companions in a Strange Land 1*; anthology; Pdf 284, 1980); *Compagnons en Terre Etrangère 2* (*Companions in a Strange Land 2*; anthology; Pdf 293, 1980); *L'Oreille contre les Murs* (*The Ear Against the Wall*; PdF 310, 1980); *Le Livre d'Or d'Alain Dorémieux* (*The Golden Book of AD*; anthology; PP 5094, 1980); *Cent Monstres du Cinéma Fantastique* (*One Hundred Monsters of the Cinema Fantastique*; with Alain Schlockoff; Non-Fiction; Glénat, 1980); *La Fée et le Géomètre* (*The Fairy and the Surveyor*; AdP 15, 1981); *Neutron* (PdF 320, 1981); *L'Immeuble d'En Face* (*The Building Across the Street*; with Philippe **Cousin**; anthology; PdF 344, 1982); *Des Îles dans la Tête* (*Islands in the Head*; Léon Faure, 1982); *Cauchemar... Cauchemars!* (*Nightmare... Nightmares!*; JL 1281, 1982); *Le Travail du Furet à l'Intérieur du Poulailler* (*The Weasel's Work Inside the Chicken Coop*; JL 1549, 1983); *Il Faudra Bien Se Résoudre à Mourir Seul* (*We Must Accept to Die Alone*; PdF 363, 1983); *La Nuit des Bêtes* (*The Night of the Beasts*; Gall., 1983); *Le Livre d'Or de Jean-Pierre Andrevon* (*The Golden Book of JPA*; PP 5177, 1983); *Hôpital Nord* (*North Hospital*; with Philippe **Cousin**; anthology; PdF 373, 1984); *C'est Arrivé mais on n'en a rien su* (*It Happened But We Never Found Out*; PdF 383, 1984); *Ce Qui Vient de la Nuit* (*That Which Comes Out of the Night*; NéO 112, 1984); *Soupçons sur Hydra* (*Suspicions Over Hydra*; FNA 1304, 1984); *Gare Centrale* (*Central Station*; with Philippe **Cousin**; anthology; PdF 424, 1985); *Le Premier Hybride* (*The First Hybrid*; FNA 1362, 1985); *Cauchemars de Sang* (*Bloody Nightmares*; FNG 26, 1986); *Bandes Interdites* (*Forbidden Strips*; Magnard, 1986); *Le Grand Combat Nucléaire de Tarzan* (*Tarzan's Great Nuclear Fight*; Magnard, 1986); *Ne Coupez Pas!* (*Don't Cut !*; La Découverte, 1986) *Le Train des Galaxies* (*The Train of the Galaxies*; Bordas, 1987); *Le Chevalier, l'Autobus et la Licorne* (*The Knight, the Bus and the Unicorn*; Magnard, 1987); *Ce qu'il y avait derrière l'Horizon* (*What Lay Behind the Horizon*; Siry SF 2, 1988; rev. FNA 1836, 1991); *La Trace des Rêves* (*The Trace of Dreams*; JL 2372, 1988); *Sukran* (PdF 493, 1989); *Comme une Odeur de Mort* (*Like a Smell of*

Death; FNG 85, 1989); *Tout à la Main* (*All by Hand*; Carrère-Kian, 1989); *Sous le Regard des Étoiles* (*Under the Eyes of the Stars*; Aurore, Futurs 7, 1989); *Attention Science-Fiction et Écologie!* (non-fiction; CRNI, 1989); *Sherman* (Flamm., 1989); *Visiteurs d'Apocalypse* (*Apocalyptic Visitors*; FNA 1741, 1990); *Tout Va Mal* (*Everything Is Going Wrong*; CRNI, 1991; rev. DLM, 1997); *Il y a un Bandit Sous Mon lit* (*There Is a Bandit Under My Bed*; Syros, 1992); *Coup de Sang* (*Bloody Blow*; FN Crime 26, 1992); *Leur Tête à Couper* (*Their Head to Cut Off*; FN Crime 37, 1993); *La Mort Blonde* (*The Blonde Death*; FN Crime 45, 1993); *Incendie d'Août* (*August Fire*; Incertain, 1993); *Cauchemars d'Acier* (*Steel Nightmares*; FN Angoisses 2, 1993); *Une Mort Bien Ordinaire* (*A Very Ordinary Death*; PdFant. 32, 1993); *Chères Bêtes* (*Dear Beasts*; Gall., 1994); *La Nécessité Écologique* (*The Ecological Necessity*; non-fiction; CRNI, 1994); *L'Homme aux Dinosaures* (*Dinosaur Man*; with Silvio Cadelo & Stephen Jay Gould; Seuil, 1994); *L'Arche / Le Bal* (*The Ark / the Ball*; Alfil, 1995); *Où sont passés les Éléphants* (*Where Have the Elephants Gone?*; Alfil, 1995); *Le Dernier Dimanche de Monsieur le Chancelier Hitler* (*The Last Sunday of Mister Chancellor Hitler*; Canaille, 1995); *Le Masque au Sourire de Crocodile* (*The Mask with the Crocodile Smile*; FNAV 8, 1995); *Huit Morts dans l'Eau Froide* (*Eight Dead in Cold Water*; FNASF 8, 1995); *Chasse à Mort* (*Death Hunt*; FNAV 16, 1996); *Manuscrit d'un Roman de SF Trouvé dans une Poubelle* (*Ms. Of a SF Novel Found in a Trashcan*; Encrage, 1996); *Six Étages à Monter* (*Six Floors to Climb*; DLM, 1996); *Gorilles en Péril* (*Gorillas in Danger*; Hac., n.d.); *Le Jour du Grand Saut* (*The Day of the Great Jump*; Hac., 1997); *La Bête sur le Parking* (*The Beast on the Parking Lot*; Magnard, 1997); *Gandahar et l'Oiseau-Monde* (*Gandahar and the World-Bird*; Hac., 1997); *Le Parking Mystérieux* (*The Mysterious Parking*; Magnard, 1997); *Fins d'Après-Midi* (*Ends of Afternoons*; La Voute, 1997); *Note:* See Chapters VIII and IX. **Gandahar** was adapted into the eponymous 1987 animated feature by René **Laloux** (see Book 1, Chapter IV). **Le Travail du Furet** was adapted into an eponymous 1994 television movie (see Book 1, Chapter II). **Andrevon** is also a major French anthologist, and the writer of the following graphic novels: *Ceux-Là* (*These People*; 2 vols., Square, 1980); art by George **Pichard**; *Édouard* (Square, 181); art by George **Pichard**; *Matricule 4500* (2 vols., Glénat, 1982, 1985); art by Veronik.

Andriat, Frank (?-) *see* **Smit Le Bénédicte, Jean-Claude**

Anet, Claude (Schopfer, Jean; 1868-1931); *La Fin d'un Monde* (Grasset, 1922; transl. as the *End of a World*, 1927); *Note:* Swiss writer. See Chapter VII.

Angot, Michèle (1925-); *Les Contes de la Lune Bleue* (*Tales of the Blue Moon*; Magnard, 1970); *Les Contes de la Lune Rousse* (*Tales of the Rust Moon*; Magnard, 1970); *La Grotte aux Fées* (*The Fairies' Cave*; Magnard, 1971); *Note:* Juveniles. See Chapter VIII.

Angremy, Jean-Pierre *see* **Rémy, Pierre-Jean**

Anh, Lori (1971-); *Dégénérescence* (FNFR 2, 1994); *Note:* See Chapter VIII.

Anjou, Paul d' (?-); *L'Élément 93* (*Element 93*; Cahiers Libres, 1931)

Ann et Gwen (Legrand, Ilka; ?-); *Note:* Belgian writer. See **Pasquiez, J.-C.**

Annemary, Francis *see* **Armen, Guy d'**

Anonymous; *Les Aventures de Florinde, Habitant de la Basse Région de la Lune* (*The Adventures of Florinde, Inhabitant of the Moon's Lower Regions*; Cabinet du Livre, 1928)

Anonymous; *Le Passage du Pôle Arctique au Pôle Antarctique par le Centre de la Terre* (*The Passage from the Arctic Pole to the Antarctic Pole Through the Center of the Earth*; Noël Pissot, 1721)

Anquetil (?-); *Satan conduit le Bal* (*Satan Leads the Dance*; Anquetil, 1925)

Ansennes, Jean d' *see* **Bouquet, Jean-Louis**

Anthony, Max (?-); *Onze Bonzes de Bronze* (*Eleven Brass Monks*; FNA 1667, 1989); *Fantasmes en Stock* (*Phantasms in Stock*; FNA 1685, 1989); *L'Androïde Livide de l'Asteroïde Morbide* (*The Livid Android of the Morbid Asteroid*; FNA 1714, 1989); *Les Autos Carnivores* (*The Carnivorous Cars*; FNA 1751, 1990); *Panique chez les Poissons Solubles* (*Panic Among the Soluble Fish*; FNA 1798, 1991); *Le Huitième Crystal du Docteur Mygale* (*The Eighth Crystal of Doctor Tarentula*; FNA 1900, 1993); *Boulevard des Miroirs Fantômes* (*Boulevard of the Phantom Mirrors*; FNA 1910, 1993); *Note:* See Chapter IX.

Antin, Guy d'; *Note:* French pseudonym under which four American *Doc Savage* (renamed "Frank Sauvage") adventures were loosely translated/adapted in French in the late 1940s.

Antoine, André-Paul (1892-1982) *see* **Grand-Guignol**

Anton, Emil (Debard, Émile) (?-) & Fage-Antonelli, Jeanne (?-); *L'Île des Hommes Perdus* (*Island of the*

Lost Men; Clocher, 1952); *Le Mort qui Rit* (*The Laughing Dead*; Masque, 1952); *Momies Vivantes* (*Living Mummies*; Clocher, 1953); *Les Robots du Mont Maudit* (*The Robots of the Accursed Mountain*; Mame, 1954); on *se Bat sur la Lune* (*Battle on the Moon*; Mame, 1956); *Le Sortilège Mexicain* (*The Mexican Spell*; Dauphin, 1958); *Le Secret de Tyi* (*The Secret of Tyi*; Remparts, 1960); *La Princesse Embaumée* (*The Embalmed Princess*; Delagrave, 1963); *Note:* Juvenile SF. See Chapter IX.

Anton, Robert (?-); *Avant le Premier Jour* (*Before the First Day*; RF 70, 1960)

Apollinaire, Guillaume (Kostrowitzky, Wilhelm de; 1880-1918); *L'Enchanteur Pourrissant* (*The Rotting Enchanter*; Kahnweiler, 1909); *Le Toucher à Distance* (*Touching from Afar*; MdF, 1910); *La Disparition d'Honoré Subrac* (*The Disappearance of Honore Subrac*; MdF, 1910); *L'Hérésiarque et Cie* (Stock, 1910; transl. as the *Heresiarch & Co.*, 1965); *Le Départ de l'Ombre* (*The Departure of the Shadow*; Le Matin, 1911); *La Fiancée Posthume* (*The Posthumous Bethrothed*; Le Matin, 1911); *Arthur, Roi Passé, Roi Futur* (*Arthur, Past and Future King*; MdF, 1914); *Le Roi-Lune* (*The Moon King*; MdF, 1916); *Les Épingles* (*The Needles*; Cahiers Libres, 1928); *Les Diables Amoureux* (*The Devils in Love*; Gall., 1981); *Note:* See Chapters IV and VI. Also see **Opéra.**

Appas, François (?-); Series *Les Quatre Voyageurs* (*The Four Travellers*): *Les Quatre Voyageurs à la Poursuite d'Aspirinus* (*The Four Travellers Pursue Aspirinus*; BR, 1992; *Les Quatre Voyageurs à Saint-Plume* (*The Four Travellers Pursue Aspirinus*; BR, 1992); *Les Quatre Voyageurs contre l'Ignoble Clam* (*The Four Travellers vs. The Ignoble Clam*; BR, 1992); *Les Quatre Voyageurs et l'Introuvable Huec Huec* (*The Four Travellers and the Unfindable Huec Huec*; BR, 1992); *Les Quatre Voyageurs chez le Marquis Rikiki* (*The Four Travellers and the Marquess Rikiki*; BR, 1994); *Les Quatre Voyageurs contre les Gros Mammouths* (*The Four Travellers vs. The Big Mastodons*; BR, 1995); *Les Quatre Voyageurs et le Secret de Louis XVI* (*The Four Travellers and the Secret of Louis XVI*; BR, 1995); *Les Quatre Voyageurs dans la Ville Fantôme* (*The Four Travellers and the Ghost Town*; BR, 1996); *Les Quatre Voyageurs et l'Immortel Empereur* (*The Four Travellers and the Immortal Emperor*; BR, 1996); *Les Quatre Voyageurs et le Viking Amoureux* (*The Four Travellers and the Viking in Love*; BR, 1996); *Note:* Juvenile SF. See Chapter IX.

Appel, Kira (?-) & M.-R. (?-); *Les Aventures du Génial Ferdinand* (*The Adventures of the Brilliant Ferdinand*; Perret-Gentil, 1964); *Note:* Swiss writers.

Appell, Claude (?-); *Dans l'Espace* (*In Space*; Charpentier, 1960); *Quinze Aventures de l'Espace* (*Fifteen Space Adventures*; Gautier-Languereau, 1972)

April, Jean-Pierre (1948-); *La Machine à Explorer la Fiction* (*The Machine for Exploring Fiction*; CdF 2, 1980); *TéléToTaliTé* (*TeleToTaliTy*; HMH, 1984); *Le Nord Électrique* (*The Electric North*; CdF 10, 1986); *Berlin-Bangkok* (AMAM 5, 1989; rev. JL 3419, 1993); *Chocs Baroques* (*Baroque Shocks*; BQ, 1991); *N'Ajustez Pas Vos Hallucinettes* (*Don't Adjust Your Hallucisets*; Q/A, 1991); *Les Voyages Thanatologiques de Yan Malter* (*The Thanatological Voyages of Yan Malter*; Q/A, 1995); *Note:* French-Canadian writer. See Chapter X. *TéléToTaliTé* is a collection of five stories. *Nord Électrique* sees Northern Quebec turned into an inland sea. In *Berlin-Bangkok*, Bangkok has become a new Babel in the 21st century.

Apruz, Daniel (1937-); *Le Bêlamour* (*Goodlove*; Buchet-Chastel, 1970); *Le Bon Temps* (*Good Times*; Buchet-Chastel, 1972); *Au Bord du Monde* (*At the World's Edge*; Buchet-Chastel, 1976); *Banlieues Lointaines* (*Far Suburbs*; Buchet-Chastel, 1979); *Les Pendules de Malac* (*The Clocks of Malac*; Calmann-Lévy, 1982); *Méfiez-Vous des Arbres* (*Don't Trust the Trees*; Calmann-Lévy, 1983); *Un Hiver en Ville* (*Winter in the City*; Calmann-Lévy, 1984); *10.000 Jours* (*10,000 Days*; Calmann-Lévy, 1986); *L'An 2000* (*The Year 2000*; Méréal, 1996); *Le Coq* (*The Rooster*; Méréal, 1997)

Aquin, Emmanuel (1968-); *Incarnations* (Boréal, 1990); *Désincarnations* (Borál, 1991); *Réincarnations* (Boréal, 1992); *Icare* (*Icarus*; Boréal, 1995); *Le Sandwich au Nilou-Nilou* (*The Nilou-Nilou Sandwich*; Boréal, 1996); *Le Pigeon Doudou* (*The Doodoo Pigeon*; Boréal, 1997); *Note:* French-Canadian writer. *Le Sandwich* and *Le Pigeon* are part of a juvenile fantasy series entitled *Chroniques Glubiennes* (*Glubian Chronicles*).

Aragny, Jean (?-1939) *see* **Grand-Guignol**

Aragon, Louis (1897-1982); *Les Aventures de Télémaque* (*The Adventures of Telemachus*; Gall., 1922)

Arbaud, Joseph d' (1874-1950); *La Bête du Vaccarès* (*The Beast of Vaccares*; Grasset, 1926); *La Sauvagine* (*The Wild One*; Bibl. Faubourg Papier, 1959)

Arbos, Ange *see* **Agapit, Marc**

Arcadius (Hilleret, Marcel-Alain; 1932-); *La Terre Endormie* (*The Sleeping Earth*; RF 81, 1961); *Planète d'Exil* (*Planet of Exile*; RF 111, 1963); *Note:* See Chapter IX.

Arcourt, Luc d' (?-); *L'Avion Fantôme* (*The Ghost Plane*; L'Essor, 1944); *Note:* Belgian writer.

Arcy, Maurice (Baudu, René; ?-); *Les Puissances Se-*

crètes—*La Formule Rouge* (*The Secret Powers—the Red Formula*; Gall., 1934); *Les Puissances Secrètes—Le Maître de la Guerre* (*The Secret Powers—the Master of War*; Gall., 1936); *Le Tueur de Cerveaux* (*The Brain Killers*; Gall., 1937)

Ardisson, Thierry (1949-); *La Bilbe* (Seuil, 1975)

Argyre, Gilles d' *see* **Klein, Gérard**

Ariel, F. (Delagny, Georges; ?-); *Nos Ancêtres du 20ème Siècle* (*Our Ancestors from the 20th Century*; Scorpion, 1963)

Ariste, Jean-Paul (?-); *Néolithis* (Argo, 1931); *Virus* (Saillard, 1936)

Arley, Catherine F. (?-); *La Femme de Paille* (*The Straw Woman*; Eurédif, 1972); *Le Talion* (*An Eye for an Eye*; Eurédif, 1972); *La Baie des Trépassés* (*The Bay of the Trespassed*; Eurédif, 1973); *Robinson Cruauté* (*Robinson Cruelty*; Eurédif, 1974); *Les Valets d'Épée* (*The Jacks of Swords*; Eurédif, 1974); *Les Armures de Sable* (*The Armors of Sand*; Eurédif, 1976); *La Banque des Morts* (*The Bank of the Dead*; Eurédif, 1977); *L'Enfer, Pourquoi Pas?* (*Hell, Why Not?*; Eurédif, 1978); *L'Homme de Craie* (*The Man of Chalk*; Libr. Champs-Elysées, 1980); *L'Ogresse* (*The Ogress*; Libr. Champs-Elysées, 1981); *Le Battant et la Cloche* (*The Clapper and the Bell*; Libr. Champs-Elysées, 1982); *Une Femme Piégée* (*A Woman Trapped*; Libr. Champs-Elysées, 1982); *Note:* See Chapter VIII.

Arlincourt, Charles-Victor Prevot, Vicomte d' (1789-1856); *Charlemagne ou la Croleïde* (Le Normant, 1818); *Le Solitaire* (*The Hermit*; Béchet, 1821); *Le Rénégat* (*The Renegade*; Béchet, 1822); *Ipsiboé* (Béchet, 1823); *L'Étrangère* (*The Stranger*; Béchet, 1825); *Ismalie, ou La Mort et l'Amour* (*Ismalia, or Death and Love*; Ponthieu, 1828); *Les Rebelles sous Charles V* (*The Rebels Under Charles V*; Levavasseur, 1832); *Le Brasseur Roi* (*The Brewer King*; A. Dupont, 1834); *Ida* (Dumont, 1841); *Les Anneaux d'une Chaîne* (*The Links of a Chain*; L. de Porter, 1845); *Les Fiancés de la Mort* (*The Fiancés of Death*; Allouard & Kaeppelin, 1850); *Note:* See Chapter IV.

Arly, Dominique (Pettex, Constant; ?-); *Les Revenantes* (*The Ghosts*; FNAG 126, 1966); *Comme un Sépulcre Blanchi* (*As a White Sepulcher*; FNAG 132, 1966); *Leur Âme au Diable* (*Their Souls to the Devil*; FNAG 145, 1967); *L'Image Fantôme* (*The Phantom Image*; FNAG 153, 1968); *Le Monstre de Green Castle* (*The Monster of Green Castle*; FNAG 157, 1968); *Les Grelots de la Folie* (*The Bells of Madness*; FNAG 164, 1969); *La Dernière Sorcière* (*The Last Witch*; FNAG 172, 1969); *Les Pistes Maudites* (*The Accursed Trails*; FNAG 180, 1970); *Les Ailes de Flamme* (*The Wings of Flame*;

FNAG 187, 1970); *L'Immonde Banshee* (*The Awful Banshee*; FNAG 193, 1971); *Maléfique Hermès* (*Maleficent Hermes*; FNAG 200, 1971); *Les Abominables* (*The Abominations*; FNAG 208, 1971); *Écrit de l'Au-Delà* (*Written from Beyond*; FNAG 215, 1972); *Tout ce qui Tombe* (*All That Falls*; FNAG 220, 1972); *La Chair du Démon* (*The Flesh of the Demon*; FNAG 224, 1972); *La Prison de Chair* (*The Prison of Flesh*; FNAG 236, 1973); *Le Manuscrit Maudit* (*The Accursed Manuscript*; FNAG 245, 1973); *Perfide Asmodée* (*Perfidious Asmodeus*; FNAG 250, 1974); *Au-Delà du Cauchemar* (*Beyond Nightmare*; FNAG 258, 1974); *Nouée d'un Ruban Noir* (*Tied with a Black Ribbon*; FN Special-Police, 1974); *Le Soleil et la Mort* (*The Sun and Death*; FN Special-Police, 1974); *Froide Comme du Marbre* (*Cold as Marble*; FN Special-Police, 1975); *Isabelle et la Bête* (*Isabelle and the Beast*; FN Special-Police, 1976); *Le Forcené* (*The Maniac*; FN Special-Police, 1977); *Les Raisins de la Mort* (*The Grapes of Death*; FN Special-Police, 1978); *Note:* See Chapter VIII.

Armand, Pierre (?-); *Sérum de Bonté* (*Goodness Serum*; Aujourd'hui, 1957)

Armandy, André (Aguilard, André-Albert d'; 1882-1958); *Rapa Nui* (Calmann-Lévy, 1923); *Le Yacht Callirhoé* (*The Yach Callirhoe*; Tallandier, 1924); *Le Nord qui Tue* (*The Murderous North*; Tallandier, 1925); *Terre de Suspicion* (*Land of Suspicion*; Tallandier, 1926); *L'Étrange Traversée (Pour l'Honneur du Navire)* (*The Strange Journey (For a Ship's Honor)*; Calmann-Lévy, 1926); *Le Château de la Fée Morgane* (*The Castle of Morgan Le Fey*; Baudinière, 1926); *Âmes de Joyeux: Les Réprouvés* (*Joyous Souls: The Forgotten*; Baudinière, 1926); *Le Démon Bleu (Miss Démon)* (*The Blue Demon*; serialized as 2 issues, GRAM, 1926; rev. RMY, 1930-31); *1. Le Roi du Chewing-Gum* (*The King of Chewing-Gum*); *2. La Cité Oubliée* (*The Forgotten City*); *L'Île de Corail* (*The Coral Island*; RMY, 1927); *Le Satanic* (serialized as 2 issues, RMY, 1928; rep. as *Les Epaves Dorées* (*The Golden Shipwrecks*, 1954); *1. Les Épaves Dorées* (*The Golden Shipwrecks*); *2. L'Île de la Morte* (*The Dead Woman's Island*); *Le Trésor des Îles Galapagos* (*The Treasure of the Galapagos Islands*; Hac., 1928); *Les Loups Cerviers* (*The Buck Wolves*; serialized as 2 issues, RMY, 1928); *1. Le Maëlstrom; 2. Le Secret de Nicolas Bramberger* (*Nicolas Bramberger's Secret*); *Le Rénégat* (*The Renegade*; Lemerre, 1929); *Le Grand Crépuscule* (*The Great Twilight*; serialized as 2 issues, RMY, 1928); *1. Le Triple Joug du Monde* (*The Triple Hold Over the World*); *2. La Mer des Sables* (*The Sea of Sands*); *La Nuit sans Astres* (*The Starless Night*; serialized as 2 issues, RMY, 1930); *1. Silverhell; 2. Barranco, Ltd.*; *Les Cribleurs d'Océan* (*The Ocean Diggers*; Lemerre, 1930); *La Voie sans Disque* (*The Discless Way*; Lemerre, 1931); *Soho* (Lemerre,

1931); *Dalila* (RMY, 1932); *Le Dictateur des Sables* (*The Dictator of the Sands*; Tallandier, 1932); *Régates* (*Regattas*; Lemerre, 1932); *L'Enchantement* (*The Enchantment*; Tallandier, 1934); *La Quatrième Corde* (*The Fourth Rope*; Lemerre, 1935); *Hommes de Roc, Forteresses d'Argile* (*Men of Rock, Fortresses of Clay*; Lemerre, 1936); *Le Paradis de Satan* (*Satan's Paradise*; Lemerre, 1937); *Le Pardaõ* (*L'Illustration*, 1937); *La Cité Profonde* (*The City of the Deep*; Plon, 1938); *L'Arc-en-ciel de Lune* (*The Moon Rainbow*; Plon, 1939); *Sur la Mer Jolie* (*On a Beautiful Sea*; Tallandier, 1939); *Le Chantier des Rêves* (*The Site of Dreams*; Plon, 1940); La Coframo (Tallandier, 1946); Bocabelle (Tallandier, 1948); *La Toison d'Or* (*The Golden Fleece*; Tallandier, 1949); *La Dernière Plongée* (*The Last Dive*; Tallandier, 1950); *En Rupture de Ban* (*On the Run*; Tallandier, 1952); *Fossiles en Sursis* (*Suspended Fossils*; Tallandier, 1954); *L'Or Noir* (*Black Gold*; Tallandier, 1957); *Le Bar du Bout du Monde* (*The Bar at the End of the World*; Tallandier, 1974); *Note:* See Chapter VII.

Armange, Xavier (1947-); *L'Arbre de l'An Bientôt* (*The Tree of Soon Year*; La Farandole, 1979); *Le Calife que Personne n'aimait* (*The Caliph No One Loved*; J'aime Lire, 1979); *Dragon d'Ordinaire* (*Dragon of the Ordinary*; Flamm., 1985); *Cache-cache à la Ville* (*Hide-&-Seek in the City*; Deux Coqs d'Or, 1985); *Cache-cache à la Campagne* (*Hide-&-Seek in the Country*; Deux Coqs d'Or, 1986); *Cache-cache en Voyage* (*Hide-&-Seek Travels*; Deux Coqs d'Or, 1986); *Une Histoire peu Commune* (*An Uncommon Story*; Armange, 1990); *Le Prisonnier de la Bibliothèque* (*The Prisoner of the Library*; Armange, 1992); *La Malle Sanglante du Puits d'Enfer* (*The Bloody Trunk of Hell's Well*; Orbestier, 1997); *Note:* Juveniles. See Chapter VIII.

Armen, Guy d' (?-?); *Les Ondes Mystérieuses* (*The Mysterious Waves*; L'Intrépide, 1927-28); *La Cité de l'Or et de la Lèpre* (*The City of Gold and Leprosy*; S&V, 1928); *Les Troglodytes du Mont Everest* (*The Troglodytes of Mount Everest*; "L'Intrépide," 1929); *L'Onde Infernale* (*The Infernal Wave*; L'Intrépide, 1930); *Les Géants du Lac Noir* (*The Giants of the Dark Lake*; L'Intrépide, 1931); *Le Semeur de Cyclones* (*The Seeder of Cyclones*; as Francis Annemary; L'Intrépide, 1931); *Les Rayons Ultra-Z* (*The Ultra-Z Rays*; L'Intrépide, 1932); *Le Secret de Frigidopolis* (*The Secret of Frigidopolis*; L'Intrépide, 1933); *Le Secret des Perles Noires* (*The Secret of the Black Pearls*; as Francis Annemary; L'Intrépide, 1934); *La Fin d'Iramonda* (*The End of Iramonda*; as Jacques Diamant; L'Intrépide, 1935); *Terre Infernale* (*Hellish Land*; L'Intrépide, 1936); *Note:* See Chapter VII.

Armont, Paul (?-?) *see* **Grand-Guignol**

Armory (?-); *Le Monsieur aux Chrysanthèmes* (*The Gen-*

tleman with Chrysanthemus; Molière, 1902); *Défense de Mourir* (*Forbidden to Die*; with René **Trintzius**; Jean Renard, 1943)

Arnau, Yves E. (?-); *Le Fils du Soleil* (*The Son of the Sun*; Tisseyre, 1988); *Laurence* (Tisseyre, 1991); *Note:* French-Canadian writer. *Le Fils* is an adventure of detective Edgar Allan, featuring an Egyptian mummy brought back to life.

Arnaud, C.-L. (?-); *Le Second Voyage de Micromégas* (*The Second Journey of Micromégas*; Ed. Nouvelles, 1935); *Note:* Sequel to **Voltaire**'s classic.

Arnaud, Georges-Jean (1928-); *Virus* (FN Special-Police 226, 1960); *Tel un Fantôme* (*As a Ghost*; FN Special-Police 543, 1966); *Les Croisés de Mara* (*The Crusaders of Mara*; FNA 469, 1971); *Les Monarques de Bi* (*The Monarchs of Bi*; FNA 509, 1972); *Lazaret 3* (FNA 538, 1972); *Tendres Termites* (*Tender Termites*; FN Special-Police 966, 1972); *Le Dossier Atrée* (*The Atreus File*; FNAG 216, 1972); *La Mort Noire* (*The Black Death*; FNAG 230, 1973); *Ils Sont Revenus* (*They Came Back*; FNAG 241, 1973); *La Dalle aux Maudits* (*The Slab of the Accursed*; FNAG 248, 1974); *L'Homme Noir* (*The Dark Man*; FN Spécial-Police 1190, 1975); *La Peste aux Mille Milliards de Dents* (*The Plague with a Billion Teeth*; FN Espionnage 1291, 1976); *Enfantasme* (*The Ghost Child*; FN Spécial-Police 1235, 1976); *L'Enfer du Décor* (*The Dark Side of the World*; FN Spécial-Police 1343, 1977); *Les Jeudis de Julie* (*Julie's Thursdays*; FN Spécial-Police 1389, 1978); *Le Vent des Morts* (*The Wind of the Dead*; FN Espionnage 1492, 1979); *Colonel Dog* (FN Espionnage 1518, 1980); *Coquelicot-Party* (FN Espionnage 1551, 1980); *Le Coucou* (*The Cuckoo*; FN Spécial-Police 1574, 1980); *Le Festin Séculaire* (*The Secular Feast*; FNG 8, 1985); *Grouillements* (*The Swarming*; FNG 28, 1986); *Mère Carnage* (*Mother Carnage*; FN Special-Police 2000, 1986); *Cerveaux Empoisonnés* (*Poisoned Brains*; FN Espionnage 1852, 1986); *Une Si Longue Angoisse* (*Such a Long-Lasting Fear*; FN Noire 5, 1988); *Crâne d'Argent* (*Silver Skull*; Julliard, 1992); *Léa de Port-Galère* (*Lea from Port-Galley*; Julliard, 1993); *Les Compagnons d'Éternité* (*The Companions of Eternity*; FNAV 7, 1995); *La Forêt des Hommes Volants* (*The Forest of the Flying Men*; FNAV 15, 1996); *L'Atoll des Bateaux Perdus* (*The Atoll of Lost Ships*; FNSF 14,

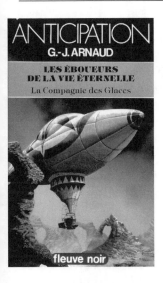

1997); Series *Luc Ferran* (as Gil Darcy): *Luc Ferran du N.I.D.* (*Luc Ferran from the N.I.D.*; Arabesque Espionnage 74, 1958); *Luc Ferran Liquide* (*Luc Ferran Liquidates*; Arabesque Espionnage 78, 1958); *Luc Ferran s'acharne* (*Luc Ferran Persists*; Arabesque Espionnage 82, 1958); *Sérénade pour Luc Ferran* (*Serenade for Luc Ferran*; Arabesque Espionnage 90, 1959); *Luc Ferran Boit du Pulque* (*Luc Ferran Drinks Pulque*; Arabesque Espionnage 94, 1959); *Luc Ferran Feinte en Finlande* (*Luc Ferran Plays in Finland*; Arabesque Espionnage 105, 1959); *Luc Ferran et la Veuve* (*Luc Ferran and the Widow*; Arabesque Espionnage 116, 1959); *Luc Ferran Cravache* (*Luc Ferran Whips*; Arabesque Espionnage 147, 1960); *Luc Ferran dans le Brouillard* (*Luc Ferran in the Fog*; Arabesque Espionnage 171, 1961); *Luc Ferran Quitte le N.I.D.* (*Luc Ferran Leaves the N.I.D.*; Arabesque Espionnage 430, 1966); *Luc Ferran et son Noël Rouge* (*Luc Ferran and His Red Christmas*; Arabesque Espionnage 435, 1966); *Luc Ferran est trahi* (*Luc Ferran Betrayed*; Arabesque Espionnage 440, 1966); *Luc Ferran sauve la Base* (*Luc Ferran Saves the Base*; Arabesque Espionnage 445, 1966); *Luc Ferran Joue les Beatnicks* (*Luc Ferran Plays a Beatnik*; Arabesque Espionnage 455, 1966); *Luc Ferran et le Réseau Radio-Actif* (*Luc Ferran and the Radioactive Network*; Arabesque Espionnage 465, 1966); *Amère Mission pour Luc Ferran* (*Bitter Mission for Luc Ferran*; Arabesque Espionnage 585, 1969); Series: *Commander Le Commander Rit Jaune* (*The Commander Gives a Forced Laugh;* FN Espionnage 614, 1967); *Double pour le Commander* (*Two for the Commander*; FN Espionnage 654, 1968); *Le Commander Souffle la Torche* (*The Commander Blows the Torch*; FN Espionnage 669, 1968); *Le Commander Prend la Piste* (*The Commander Follows the Trail*; FN Espionnage 715, 1969); *Le Commander et l'Évadé* (*The Commander and the Escapee*; FN Espionnage 733, 1969); *Un Amiral pour le Commander* (*An Admiral for the Commander*; FN Espionnage 784, 1970); *Échec au Froid, Commander* (*The Cold in Check, Commander*; FN Espi-

onnage 828, 1970); *Coup de Vent pour le Commander* (*Gust of Wind for the Commander*; FN Espionnage 855, 1971); *Le Commander et la Mamma* (*The Commander and the Mamma*; FN Espionnage 877, 1971); *Le Commander dans un Fauteuil* (*The Commander in an Armchair*; FN Espionnage 911, 1971); *Jouez Serré, Commander* (*Play Close to the Vest, Commander*; FN Espionnage 939, 1972); *Le Commander et le Révérend* (*The Commander and the Reverend*; FN Espionnage 957, 1972); *Le Commander et la Combine* (*The Commander and the Rip-Off*; FN Espionnage 989, 1972); *Le Commander et les Spectres* (*The Commander and the Ghosts*; FN Espionnage 1024, 1973); *Le Commander et la Voyante* (*The Commander and the Fortune-Teller*; FN Espionnage 1064, 1973); *Pour Mémoire, Commander* (*FYI, Commander*; FN Espionnage 1071, 1973); *Le Commander et la Tueuse* (*The Commander and the Female Killer*; FN Espionnage 1094, 1974); *Le Commandeur et le Déserteur* (*The Commander and the Deserter*; FN Espionnage 1104, 1974); *Smog pour le Commander* (*Smog for the Commander*; FN Espionnage 1161, 1975); *Le Commander et le Vigile* (*The Commander and the Watchman*; FN Espionnage 1183, 1975); *Trio Infernal pour le Commander* (*Infernal Trio for the Commander*; FN Espionnage 1196, 1975); *Du Blé pour le Commander* (*Wheat for the Commander*; FN Espionnage 1234, 1976); *Aux Armes, Commander* (*To Arms, Commander*; FN Espionnage 1280, 1976); *Le Commander enterre la Hache* (*The Commander Buries the Hatchet*; FN Espionnage 1330, 1977); *Peur Banche pour le Commander* (*Livid Fear for the Commander*; FN Espionnage 1359, 1977); *Le Mauve sied au Commander* (*Mauve Is Fetching for the Commander*; FN Espionnage 1399, 1978); *Coupe Sanglante pour le Commander* (*Bloody Cut for the Commander*; FN Espionnage 1428, 1978); *Pas de Miracle pour le Commander* (*No Miracles for the Commander*; FN Espionnage 1483, 1979); Series: *La Compagnie des Glaces* (*The Ice Company*) 1. *La Compagnie des Glaces* (*The Ice Company*; FNA 997, 1980); 2. *Le Sanctuaire des Glaces* (*The Ice Sanctuary*; FNA 1038, 1981); 3. *Le Peuple des Glaces* (*The Ice People*; FNA 1056, 1981); 4. *Les Chasseurs des Glaces* (*The Ice Hunters*; FNA 1077, 1981); 5. *L'Enfant des Glaces* (*The Ice Child*; FNA 1104, 1981); 6. *Les Otages des Glaces* (*The Ice Hostages*; FNA 1116, 1982); 7. *Le Gnome Halluciné* (*The Visionary Dwarf*; FNA 1122, 1982); 8. *La Compagnie de la Banquise* (*The Pacific Shelf Company*; FNA 1139, 1982); 9. *Le Réseau de Patagonie* (*The Patagonia Network*; FNA 1157, 1982); 10. *Les Voiliers du Rail* (*The Rail Sailboats*; FNA 1180, 1982); 11. *Les Fous du Soleil* (*The Sun Fanatics*; FNA 1198, 1983); 12. *Network-Cancer* (*Cancer Network*; FNA 1207, 1983); 13. *Station-Fantôme* (*Ghost Station*; FNA 1224, 1983); 14. *Les Hommes-Jonas* (*The Jonah Men*; FNA 1249, 1983); 15. *Terminus Amertume* (*Terminus Despair*; FNA

1267, 1983); *16. Les Brûleurs de Banquise* (*The Ice Melters*; FNA 1271, 1984); *17. Le Gouffre aux Garous* (*The Were-Pit*; FNA 1286, 1984); *18. Le Dirigeable Sacrilège* (*The Sacrilegious Airship*; FNA 1303, 1984); 19. *Liensun* (FNA 1321, 1984); *20. Les Éboueurs de la Vie Éternelle* (*The Dumpsters of Eternity*; FNA 1333, 1984); *21. Les Trains Cimetières* (*The Graveyard Trains*; FNA 1351, 1985); *22. Les Fils de Lien Rag* (*The Sons of Lien Rag*; FNA 1364, 1985); *23. Voyageuse Yeuse* (*Voyager Yeuse*; FNA 1388, 1985); *24. L'Ampoule de Cendres* (*The Glass Urn*; FNA 1405, 1985); 25. *Sun Company* (FNA 1431, 1986); *26. Les Sibériens* (*The Siberians*; FNA 1449, 1986); *27. Le Clochard Ferroviaire* (*The Mysterious Hobo*; FNA 1460, 1986); *28. Les Wagons Mémoires* (*The Memory Trains*; FNA 1477, 1986); *29. Mausolée pour une Locomotive* (*The Fabulous Locomotive*; FNA 1490, 1986); *30. Dans le Ventre d'une Légende* (*In the Belly of a Legend*; FNA 1503, 1986); *31. Les Échafaudages d'Épouvante* (*The Scaffolds of Fear*; FNA 1516, 1987); *32. Les Montagnes Affamées* (*The Hungry Mountains*; FNA 1541, 1987); *33. La Prodigieuse Agonie* (*The Prodigious Agony*; FNA 1552, 1987); *34. On m'appelait Lien Rag* (*They Called Me Lien Rag*; FNA 1571, 1987); *35. Train Spécial Pénitentiaire 34* (*Special Penitentiary TraIn 34;* FNA 1581, 1987); *36. Les Hallucinés de la Voie Oblique* (*The Madmen of the Oblique Way*; FNA 1596, 1987); *37. L'Abominable Postulat* (*The Abominable Verdict*; FNCG 37, 1988); *38. Le Sang des Ragus* (*The Blood of the Ragus*; FNCG 38, 1988); *39. La Caste des Aiguilleurs* (*The Dispatchers*; FNCG 39, 1988); *40. Les Exilés du Ciel Croûteux* (*The Castaways of a Crusty Sky*; FNCG 40, 1988); *41. Exode Barbare* (*Savage Exodus*; FNCG 41, 1988); *42. La Chair des Étoiles* (*The Flesh of the Stars*; FNCG 42, 1988); *43. L'Aube Cruelle d'un Temps Nouveau* (*The Bloody Dawn of the New Times*; FNCG 43, 1988); *44. Les Canyons du Pacifique* (*The Canyons of the Pacific*; FNCG 44, 1989); *45. Les Vagabonds des Brumes* (*The Wanderers in the Mist*; FNCG 45, 1989); *46. La Banquise Déchiquetée* (*The Wrecked Ice Shelf*; FNCG 46, 1989); *47. Soleil Blême* (*Wan Sun*; FNCG 47, 1989); *48. L'Huile des Morts* (*The Oil of the Dead*; FNCG 48, 1989); *49. Les Oubliés de Chimère* (*The Forsakens of Chimera*; FNCG 49, 1989); *50. Les Cargos-Dirigeables du Soleil* (*The Airships of the Sun*; FNCG 50, 1990); *51. La Guilde des Sanguinaires* (*The Bloody Guild*; FNCG 51, 1990); *52. La Croix Pirate* (*The Pirate Cross*; FNCG 52, 1990); *53. Le Pays de Djoug* (*The Land of Djoug*; FNCG 53, 1990); *54. La Banquise de Bois* (*The Pontoons of Lacustra*; FNCG 54, 1990); 55. *Iceberg-Ship* (FNCG 55, 1991); 56. *Lacustra City* (FNCG 56, 1991); *57. L'Héritage du Bulb* (*The Bulb's Inheritance*; FNCG 57, 1991); *58. Les Millénaires Perdus* (*The Lost Millenia*; FNCG 58, 1991); *59. La Guerre du Peuple du Froid* (*The War of the Ice People*; FNCG 59, 1991); *60.

Les Tombeaux de l'Antarctique* (*The Tombs of Antarctica*; FNCG 60, 1992); *61. La Charogne Céleste* (*The Cosmic Remains*; FNCG 61, 1992); *62. Il Était Une Fois La Compagnie Des Glaces* (*Once Upon a Time, the Ice Company;* FNCG 62, 1992); Series *Chroniques Glaciaires* (*Ice Chronicles*): *1. Les Rails d'Incertitude* (*The Rails of Uncertainty*; FNA 1995, 1996); *2. Les Illuminés* (*The Illuminated Ones*; FNSF 26, 1997); *Note:* See Chapters VIII and IX.

Arnothy, Christine (1930-); *Chiche!* (*You Bet!*; Flamm., 1970); *L'Ami de Famille* (*Family Friend*; Grasset, 1984)

Arnoux, Alexandre (1884-1973); *Mort de Pan* (*Pan's Death*; Fasquelle, 1909); *Abisag, ou l'Église Transportée par la Foi* (*The Church Transported by Faith*; AM, 1918); *Légende du Roi Arthur et des Chevaliers de la Table Ronde* (*Legend of King Arthur and the Knights of the Round Table*; Piazza, 1920); *Indice 33* (*Indicia 33*; Fayard, 1920); *Huon de Bordeaux* (AM, 1922); *Petite Lumière et l'Ourse* (*Little Light and the She-Bear*; Le Divan, 1923); *Le Règne du Bonheur* (*The Reign of Happiness*; Fayard, 1924; rev. PdF 40, 1960); *Suite Variée* (*Varied Suite*; Grasset, 1925); *Le Chiffre* (*The Number*; Grasset, 1926); *Merlin l'Enchanteur* (*Merlin the Enchanter*; Plon, 1931); *Le Rossignol Napolitain* (*The Napolitan Nightingale*; Grasset, 1937); *La Thébéenne* (*The Thebeian*; Crès, 1945); *L'Amour des Trois Oranges* (*The Love of the Three Oranges*; Grasset, 1947); *Algorithme* (Grasset, 1948); *Sortilèges* (*Spells*; La Passerelle, 1949); *L'Enchantement de Grenade: Le Cavalier de Fer, La Rose de l'Alhambra* (*The Spell of Granada: The Iron Horseman, the Alhambra Rose*; Gall., 1951); *Crimes Innocents* (*Innocent Crimes*; AM, 1952); *Le Royaume des Ombres* (*The Kingdom of Shadows*; AM, 1954); *Faut-il Brûler Jeanne?* (*Must We Burn Jeanne?*; Gall., 1954); *Le Seigneur de l'Heure* (*The Lord of the Hour*; Gall., 1955); *Zulma l'Infidèle* (*Zulma the Unfaithful*; AM, 1960); *Visite à Mathusalem* (*Visiting Methuselah*; AM, 1961); *Le Siège de Syracuse* (*The Siege of Syracuse*; AM, 1962); *Roi d'un Jour* (*King for a Day*; Cercle du Bibl., 1971); *Note:* See Chapters VI and VII. Also see **Opéra**.

Arnyvelde, André (1881-1942); *Le Roi de Galande* (*The King of Galande*; Monde Ill., 1910); *L'Arche* (*The Ark*; Sté Mutuelle, 1920); *Le Bacchus Mutilé* (*The Mutilated Bacchus*; AM, 1922); on *Demande un Homme, ou L'Étrange Tournoi d'Amour* (*They Need Men, or Love's Strange Tourney*; Flamm., 1924); *Note:* See Chapter VII.

Aron, Robert (?-); *Victoire à Waterloo* (*Victory at Waterloo*; 1937); *Note:* See Chapter VII.

Arosa, Paul (1874-?); *L'Âme Heureuse* (*Happy Soul*; Stock, 1904); *Les Chapeaux de Ste. Catherine* (*St. Catherine's Hats*; Stock, 1905); *Mémoires d'une 50 HP* (*Memoirs of a 50 HP; Stock, 1909); *Les Mystérieuses Études du Professeur Kruhl* (*The Mysterious Studies of Prof. Kruhl*; JST, 1912); *Note:* Also see **Grand-Guignol**.

Arquillière, d' (?-?) *see* **Grand-Guignol**

Arraou, Louis (?-); *Pomponius, le Dernier des Chevaliers* (*Pomponius, the Last Knight*; Plon, 1919); *Un Martien sur Terre* (*A Martian on Earth*; Figuière, 1932)

Arras, Jehan d' (?-?); *Mélusine* (c. 1475); *Note:* See Chapter I.

Arrivé, Michel (?-); *Les Remembrances du Vieillard Idiot* (*Remembrances of a Stupid Old Man*; Flamm., 1977); *La Réduction de Peine* (*On Parole*; Flamm., 1978); *L'Horloge sans Balancier* (*The Clock Without Pendulum*; Flamm., 1983); *L'Éphémère, ou La Mort contre Elle* (*The Ephemereal, or Death Against Her*; Klincksieck, 1989); *Note:* See Chapter IX.

Arrou-Vignod, Jean-Pierre (?-); *L'Homme du Cinquième Jour* (*The Man from Day 5*; Gall., 1997)

Arsan, Emmanuelle (1938-); *Nouvelles de l'Érosphere* (*Stories from the Erosphere*; Losfeld, 1969); *Note:* See Chapter IX.

Artaud, Antonin (1896-1948); *L'Ombilic des Limbes* (*The Umbilicus of Limbo*; Gall., 1925); *Le Pèse-Nerfs* (*The Nerve Weigher*; Cahiers du Sud, 1927); *Héliogabale, ou l'Anarchiste Couronné* (*The Crowned Anarchist*; Den., 1934); *Les Nouvelles Révélations de l'Être* (*The New Revelations of Being*; Den., 1937); *Les Tarahumaras* (Revue Fontaine, 1945); *La Pierre Philosophale* (*The Philosopher's Stone*; La Pléiade, 1949); *Lettres à la Voyante* (*Letters to the Fortune-Teller*; Botteghe Oscure, 1952); *L'Éperon Malicieux* (*The Malicious Spur*; Botteghe Oscure, 1952); *Correspondance de la Momie / Invocation à la Momie / L'Osselet Toxique* (*The Mummy's Correspondence / Invocation of the Mummy / Toxic Bone*; Gall., 1956); *Il n'y a plus de Firmament* (*There's No More Heaven*; Gall., 1961); *Note:* See Chapter VI.

Arthaud, E. (?-?); *Inesilla* (Leroux, 1830); *La Borne* (*The Milestone*; Ménard, 1833); *Le Cimetière d'Ivry* (*The Ivry Cemetery*; with Auguste **Poujol**; Sylvestre Fils, 1834); *Angèle ou La Tombe de Gentilly* (*The Tomb of Gentilly*; Bourdin, 1837); *Note:* See Chapter IV.

Arthez, Danielle d' (?-); *Le Trust du Soleil* (*The Sun Company*; Hac., 1906); *Note:* See Chapter V.

Artus, Louis (1870-1960); *Duchesse Putiphar* (Libr. Theatr., 1903); *La Maison du Fou (Chronique de St. Léonard)* (*The House of the Madman (Chronicles of St. Leonard)*; Grasset, 1918); *La Maison du Sage (Histoire d'un Crime)* (*The House of the Wise Man (Tale of a Crime)*; Émile-Paul, 1920); *Le Vin de Ta Vigne* (*The Wine of Your Grapes*; Grasset, 1922); *Les Chiens de*

Dieu (*God's Dogs*; Grasset, 1928); *Paix sur la Terre* (*Peace on Earth*; Grasset, 1932); *Mon Mal et Moi* (*Evil and I*; Baudinière, 1936); *Terrible Affaire (Folie en Un Acte)* (*Dreadful Business (Folly in One Act)*; Billaudet, 1947); *Doktor Jedermann ou Le Neveu de Faust* (*Dr. Dermann, or Faust's Nephew*; Grasset, 1947); *Trois Prophéties* (*Three Prophecies*; Colombe, 1952); *Note:* See Chapter VII.

Ascain, Claude (?-); *Le Secret du Palais de Bronze* (*The Secret of the Bronze Palace*; Ferenczi, 1936); *La Confrérie du Scarabée* (*The Brotherhood of the Beetle*; Police & Mystère, 1937); *L'Homme qui s'escamote* (*The Vanishing Man*; Ferenczi, 1938); *L'Aventure du Matelot Rampagne* (*The Adventure of Salor Rampagne*; Ferenczi, 1939); *Potion No. 18.099* (ABC, 1941); *Le Monstre Antédiluvien* (*The Antediluvian Monster*; ABC, 1942); *Accident à 9h40* (ABC, 1942)

Aslan (?-); *Adieu, Britannia!* (1923); *Note:* See Chapter VII.

Asselin, Marcel (?-); *Le Spectre des Champs-Élysées* (*The Ghost of the Champs- Élysées*; Janicot, 1944)

Asselineau, Charles (1821-1874); *Double Vie* (*Double Life*; Poulet-Malassis-De Broissie, 1858); *Note:* See Chapter IV.

Asso, Raymond (?-); *Les Hors-la-Vie* (*The Out-Life*; Naville, 1946)

Assollant, Alfred (1827-1886); *Aventures Merveilleuses et Authentiques du Capitaine Corcoran* (*Marvellous and Authentic Adventures of Captain Corcorant*; Hac., 1868); *Histoire Fantastique du Célèbre Pierrot* (*Fantastical Tale of the Famous Pierrot*; Combet, 1901); *Note:* Juvenile fantasy. Fearless Captain Corcoran and his faithful tigress, Luison, and Hindu prince Holkar, fight the evil British Empire.

Astorg, Jean d' (?-?); *Monseigneur* (Livre Moderne, 1926); *Note:* Also see **Grand-Guignol**.

Astous, Claude d' (1953-); *L'Étrange Monument du Désert Libyque* (*The Strange Monument of the Libyan Desert*; CLF, 1986); *La Licorne des Neiges* (*The Snow Unicorn*; Tisseyre, 1993); *Note:* French-Canadian writer. In *L'Étrange*, ancient aliens created life on Earth.

Attal, Jean-Pierre (?-); *Les Chats* (*The Cats*; Julliard, 1961)

Attali, Jacques (1943-); *Les Trois Mondes* (*The Three Worlds*; Fayard, 1981); *Histoire du Temps* (*History of Time*; Fayard, 1982); *La Figure de Fraser* (*Fraser's Figure*; Fayard, 1984); *Un Homme d'Influence* (*A Man of Influence*; Fayard, 1985); *La Vie Éternelle* (*Eternal Life*; Fayard, 1989); *Lignes d'Horizon* (*Horizon Lines*; Fayard, 1990); *Le Premier Jour Après Moi* (*The First Day After Me*; Fayard, 1990); *Il Viendra* (*He'll Come*; Fayard, 1994); *Au-Delà de Nulle Part* (*Beyond Nowhere*; Fayard, 1997); *Note:* See Chapter IX.

Aubert, Brigitte (1956-); *Les Quatre Fils du Dr. March* (*The Four Sons of Dr. March*; Seuil, 1992); *La Rose de Fer* (*The Iron Rose*; Seuil, 1993); *Ténèbres sur Jacksonville* (*Darkness Over Jacksonville*; Seuil, 1994); *La Mort des Bois* (*Death in the Woods*; Seuil, 1996); *Requiem Caraïbe* (Seuil, 1997); *Note:* See Chapter VIII

Aubert, Jacques (?-); *Montmirel* (Egloff, 1943); *La Guerre des Mannequins* (*The War of the Mannequins*; Rhône-Genève, 1945)

Aubert, Mélanie (?-); *Contes Borgnes* (*One-Eyed Tales*; Rupture, 1982)

Aubert, O.-L. (?-); *Legendes Traditionelles de la Bretagne* (*Traditional Legends of Britanny*; L. Aubert, 1965); *Note:* Folk tales.

Aubert de Gaspé, Jr., Philippe Ignace François (1814-1841); *L'Influence d'un Livre* (1837; transl. as the *Influence of a Book*, 1993); *Note:* French-Canadian writer. The earliest known genre tale in French Canada.

Aubignac (Abbé; ?-?); *Relation du Royaume de Coquetterie* (*Tale of the Kingdom of Coquettishness*; 1654; rep. VI, 1788)

Aubin, Napoléon (Aubin, Aimé-Nicolas; 1812-1890); *Mon Voyageà la Lune* (*My Journey to the Moon*; 1839); *Note:* French-Canadian writer (of Swiss origins). One of the earliest known French-Canadian science fiction stories. For further information, see *Napoléon Aubin* by Jean-Paul Tremblay, Éditions Fides, Montréal, 1972.

Aubry, Claude (1914-1984); *Les Îles du Roi Maha Maha II: Conte Fantaisiste Canadien* (Pélican, 1960; transl. as the *King of the Thousand Islands: A Canadian Fairy Tale*, 1963); *Le Violon Magique* (*The Magic Violin*; Deux Rives, 1968); *Légendes du Canada Français* (*Legends of French Canada*; L'Espoir, 1977); *Note:* French-Canadian writer.

Aubry-Morin, Jacqueline *see* **Morin, Jacqueline**

Aude (Charbonneau-Tissot, Claudette; 1947-); *Contes pour Hydrocéphales Adultes* (*Tales for Adult Hydrocephalics*; CLF, 1974); *La Contrainte* (*The Constraint*; Tisseyre, 1976; transl. as *Compulsion*, 1989); *La Chaise au Fond de l'Oeil* (*The Chair in the Eye*; as Aude; Tisseyre, 1979); *L'Assembleur* (*The Assembler*; as Aude; Tisseyre, 1985); *Banc de Brume* (*Fog Bank*; as Aude; Roseau, 1987); *Note:* French-Canadian writer. *L'Assembleur* is the story of a programmed revenge.

Audiberti, Jacques (1899-1965); *Abraxas* (Gall., 1938); *Carnage* (Gall., 1942); *La Nâ* (Gall., 1944); *La Fin du Monde* (*The End of the World*; Temps Perdu, 1944);

L'Opéra du Monde (*The Opera of the World*; Fasquelle, 1947); *Marie Dubois* (Gall., 1952); *Les Naturels du Bordelais* (*The Naturals of Bordeaux*; Gall., 1953); *La Poupée* (*The Doll*; Gall., 1956); *Infanticide Préconisé* (*Recommended Infanticide*; Gall., 1958); *Le Manteau d'Arlequin* (*Harlequin's Cloak*; Gall., 1959); *Les Tombeaux Ferment Mal* (*The Tombs Don't Close Properly*; Gall., 1963); *Note:* See Chapter VII.

Audigier, Camille (?-); *La Révolte des Volcans* (*The Revolt of the Volcanos*; Feuilletons Bleus, 1935); *Note:* See Chapter VII.

Audin, Maurice (?-1957); *Bacchanales* (Grasset, 1946); *Les Maisons du Ciel* (*The Houses of the Sky*; Bordas, 1946); *Dieu-Le Diable, ou Le Démon de la Prophétie* (*God-The-Devil, or the Demon of Prophecy*; Homme Méditant, 1951)

Audois, F. *see* **Nagrien, X**

Audry, Bernard (?-); *La Danse sur la Cime* (*Dancing on the Top*; Lutèce, 1927); *La Dictatrice* (Argo, 1928); *Note:* See Chapter VII.

Audry, Colette (1906-1990); *Derrière la Baignoire* (*Behind the Bathtub*; Gall., 1962); *L'Autre Planète* (*The Other Planet*; Gall., 1972); *La Statue* (Gall., 1983)

Audureau, André (?-); *Feminapolis* (Cercle d'Or, 1979); *Un Merveilleux Dimanche* (*A Wonderful Sunday*; Mazarine, 1980); *Note:* See Chapter IX.

Augay, Ed. (?-); *L'Île Infernale* (*The Hellish Island*; Dupuis, 1950)

Augé de Lassus (?-?) *see* **Opéra**

Aujay, Édouard (?-) *see* **Boué, Maurice**

Aulnettes, M.-H. des (?-); *Le Corsaire sans Pavillon* (*The Corsair Without a Flag*; Stael, 1947)

Aulneuil (Louise de Bossigny, Comtesse d'; ?-?); *La Tyrannie des Fées Détruites* (*The Tyranny of Destroyed Fairies*; J. Fournil, 1703); *Note:* Also see **Cabinet des Fées** and Chapter III.

Aulnoy, Marie-Catherine Le Jumel de Berneville, Baronne d' (1650-1705); *L'Histoire d'Hippolyte, Comte de Douglas* (*The Story of Hippolyte, Count of Douglas*; L. Sevestre, 1690); *Les Contes de Fées* (*The Fairy Tales*; 3 vols.; Vve. Girard, 1697; transl. as *Tales of the Fairies*, 1699; rev. 1721); *Contes Nouveaux ou Les Fées à la Mode* (*New Tales or Fairies in Fashion*; Vve. Girard, 1698); *Les Illustres Fées* (*The Illustrious Fairies*; Brunet, 1699); *Note:* Also see **Cabinet des Fées** and Chapter III.

Aunillon, Pierre-Charles-Fabiot (?-); *Azor, ou Le Prince Enchanté, Histoire Nouvelle pour Servir de Chronique*

à celle de la Terre des Perroquets (*Azor, or the Enchanted Prince, New Story Serving as a Chronicle to the Land of Parrots*; 1750; rev. VI, 1788)

Aurembou, Renée (1908-); *La Maison des Fonds Noirs* (*The House of Dark Recesses*; Rouge et Or, 1954); *Le Mystère de l'Abbaye Brûlée* (*The Mystery of the Burned Abbey*; GP, 1966); *Le Trésor de Montségur* (*The Treasure of Montsegur*; GP, 1966); *Retour à l'Abbaye Brûlée* (*Return to the Burned Abbey*; GP, 1968); *Le Disparu des Villes Mortes* (*Disappeared from the Dead Cities*; GP, 1975); *Note:* Juveniles. See Chapter VIII.

Ausloos, Pierre (?-); *Catalep-6 ou Descente de Psychoflics dans un Cerveau Humain* (*Raid by Psychocops in a Human Brain*; Pensée U., 1977)

Austruy, Henri (1871-?); *L'Eupantophone* (*Nlle. Revue*, 1901); *L'Ère Petitpaon, ou La Paix Universelle* (*The Petitpaon Era, or Universal Peace*; Michaud, 1908); *Note:* See Chapter V.

"Auteurs en Herbe" (Young Authors); *À la Conquête du Futur* (*To the Conquest of the Future*; anthology; BV, 1979)

Autier, J.-J. (?-); *Opération Avion Sous-marin* (*Operation Submarine Plane*; France-Empire, 1980)

Autier, Paul (?-?) *see* **Grand-Guignol**

Autreau, J. (?-?) *see* **Opéra**

Auvray, Jean (1907-1988); *La Légende de Geneviève de Brabant* (Amitié par la Plume, 1952); *Le Banquet des Muses* (*The Muses' Feast*; La Goliardica, 1953); *Petits Contes Illustrés de Tante Agathe* (*Aunt Agatha's Little Illustrated Fairy Tales*; Amitié par la Plume, 1954); *Le Calvaire d'une Citadine* (*The Torture of a City-Dweller*; Amitié par la Plume, 1958); *Les Bas-Fonds de l'Au-delà* (*The Underworld of the Beyond*; Amitié par la Plume, 1964); *Le Briviste dans l'Enfer de Jupiter* (*The Brivist in Jupiter's Hell*; 3 vols.; with Claude Auvray; Amitié par la Plume, 1966; 1967; 1970); *Le Monde des Esprits* (*The World of Spirits*; Amitié par la Plume, 1968); *L'Ange du Mystère, ou Les Métamorphoses du Vampire* (*The Mystery Angel, or Metamorphoses of the Vampire*; Amitié par la Plume, 1969); *Les Destinées Brisées* (*Broken Destinies*; Amitié par la Plume, 1970); *La Voix du Cosmos* (*The Voice of the Cosmos*; Amitié par la Plume, 1974); *Histoires Comme Ça!* (*Tales Like That!*; Club Intell. Fr., 1974); *Les Castors de Ganymède* (*The Ganymede Beavers*; with Claude Auvray; Amitié par la Plume, 1981)

Auzias-Turenne, Raymond (1861-?); *Le Roi du Klondike* (*King of the Klondike*; Calmann-Lévy, 1901); *Le Dernier Mammouth* (*The Last Mastodon*; LPT, 1901-02); *Note:* See Chapter V.

Avard, François (?-); *Le Dernier Continent* (*The Last Continent*; Les Intouchables, 1997); *Note:* French-Canadian writer. SF novel.

Aveline, Claude (1901-1993); *La Merveilleuse Légende de Siddhartha* (*The Wondrous Legend of Siddartha*; Artisan du Livre, 1928); *Trois Histoires de la Nuit* (*Three Stories of Night*; Émile-Paul, 1931); *L'Homme de Phalère* (*The Man from Phalera*; Émile-Paul, 1935); *Baba Diène et Morceau de Sucre* (*Baba Diene and Sugar Cube*; Gall., 1937); *C'est Vrai mais il ne faut pas le croire* (*It's True But You Can't Believe It*; Émile-Paul, 1939); *Les Plus Belles Histoires de Peur* (*The Most Beautiful Tales of Fear*; Émile-Paul, 1942); *Temps Mort* (*Dead Time*; Minuit, 1945); *Pégomancie* (Émile-Paul, 1948); *Voiture 7, Place 15* (*Train Car 7, Seat 15*; MdF, 1962); *La Double Mort de Frédéric Belot* (*The Two Deaths of Frederic Belot*; MdF, 1962); *Le Jet d'Eau* (*The Water Fountain*; MdF, 1962); *Le Poids du Feu* (*The Weight of Fire*; Cercle du Bibl., 1963); *L'Abonné de la Ligne U* (*The Subscriber to the U Line*; MdF, 1964); *L'Oiseau qui n'existe pas* (*The Bird Which Does Not Exist*; Cavallino, 1966); *Le Prisonnier* (*The Prisoner*; Club de la Femme, 1969); *L'Oeil de Chat* (*Cat's Eye*; MdF, 1970); *Hoffman, Canada* (Buchet-Chastel, 1977); *L'Arbre Tic-Tac* (*The Tick-Tock Tree*; Gall., 1982); *Par le Silence et par la Voix* (*By Silence and Voice*; Tuilerie Tropicale, 1987); *Histoires Nocturnes et Fantastiques* (*Nocturnal and Fantastic Tales*; Impr. Nationale, 1989); *D'un Lion, entre un Éléphant et un Pucereau* (*Of a Lion, Between an Elephant and a Flea*; Loisirs, 1991); *Note:* See Chapter VI.

Avice, Claude *see* **Barbet, Pierre**

Avril, Jean d' (Maynial, Édouard; 1879-1966); *La Lande d'Or* (*The Golden Moor*; Mame, 1909); *Griselinde* (Mame, 1909); *Les Aventures de la Princesse Marphise* (*The Adventures of Princess Marphise*; Mame, 1912)

Avril, Marc *see* **Stork, Christopher**

Avril, Nicole (1939-); *Les Gens de Misar* (*The People of Misar*; AM, 1972); *Les Remparts d'Adrien* (*Adrian's Ramparts*; Club du Livre, 1975); *Le Jardin des Absents* (*The Garden of Those Who Aren't Here*; AM, 1977); *La Disgrâce* (Fr. Loisirs, 1980); *Sur la Peau du Diable* (*On the Devil's Skin*; Flamm., 1987); *Note:* See Chapter VIII.

Avril, René d' (?-?) *see* **Opéra**

Axelman *see* **Ramonet, Yves**

Ayerdhal (1959-); *Ylvain, Rêve de Vie* (*Ylvain, Dream of Life*; FNA 1763, 1990); *Made, Concerto pour Salmen et Bohème* (*Made, Concerto for Salmen and Boheme*; FNA 1769, 1990); *La Naïa, Hors Limites* (*The Naia, Beyond Limits*; FNA 1775, 1990); *Ely, l'Esprit Miroir* (*Ely, Mirror Spirit*; FNA 1781, 1990); *Promesse d'Ille* (*Ille's*

Promise; FNA 1803, 1991; rev. as *Mytale*, JL 4641, 1997); *Honneur de Chasse* (*Hunting Honor*; FNA 1813, 1991; rev. as *Mytale*, JL 4641, 1997); *Le Choix du Ksin* (*The Ksin's Choice*; FNA 1832, 1991; rev. as *Mytale*, JL 4641, 1997); *Demain, une Oasis* (*Tomorrow, an Oasis*; FNA 1845, 1991); *Le Syndrome des Baleines* (*The Whale Syndrome*; FNA 1871, 1992); *Le Mystère Lyphine* (*The Lyphine Mystery*; FNA 1875, 1992); *Cybione* (FNA 1886, 1992); *Polytan* (FNA 1935, 1993); *L'Histrion* (*The Histrionic*; JL 3526, 1993); *Balade Choreïale* (*Choreial Ballad*; JL 3731, 1994); *Sexomorphoses* (*Sexomorphosis*; JL 3821, 1994); *Génèses* (*Genesis*; anthology; JL 4279, 1996); *Parleur, ou La Chronique d'un Rêve Enclavé* (*Speaker, or the Chronicle of an Embedded Dream*; JL 4317, 1997); *Note:* See Chapters VIII and IX.

Aymé (Dr.; ?-); *Calès ou L'Humanité Souterraine* (*Calès or the Underground People*; Nef de Paris, 1960)

Aymé, Marcel (1902-1967); *Les Jumeaux du Diable* (*The Devil's Twins*; Gall., 1928); *Les Contes du Chat Perché* (*The Tales of the Crouching Cat*; Gall., 1931; transl. as *The Wonderful Farm*, 1951); Pastorale (Gall., 1931); *Le Puit aux Images* (*The Well of Images*; Gall., 1932); La Jument Verte (Gall., 1933; transl. as *The Green Mare*, 1938; rev. 1955); *Le Nain* (*The Dwarf*; Gall., 1934); *Derrière chez Martin* (*Behind Martin's*; Gall., 1938); *La Belle Image* (*The Beautiful Image*; Gall., 1941; transl. as *The Second Face*, 1951); *Le Passe-Muraille* (*The Walker Through the Walls*; Gall., 1943; transl. as *Across Paris and Other Stories*, 1957, also incl. stories selected from *Le Puit*, *Le Nain*, *Le Vin*, and *En Arrière*); La Vouivre (Gall., 1943; transl. as *The Fable and the Flesh*, 1949); *Le Vin de Paris* (*The Wine of Paris*; Gall., 1947); Uranus (Gall., 1948; transl. as *Fanfare in Blémont*, 1950); *Clérambard* (Grasset,

1950; transl. 1952); *En Arrière* (*Backwards*; Gall., 1950); *Autres Contes du Chat Perché* (*Other Tales of the Crouching Cat*; Gall., 1954; transl. as *Return to the Wonderful Farm*, 1954); *Les Oiseaux de Lune* (*Birds of the Moon*; Gall., 1956); *Le Minotaure* (*The Minotaur*; Gall., 1967); *Note:* See Chapter VI. Numerous Marcel Aymé tales have been adapted for film and television: **La Belle Image, Le Passe-Muraille, Clérambard, Uranus, Les Contes du Chat Perché,** and **La Vouivre**, as well as many others (see Book 1, chapters I and II).

Babinski, Joseph *see* **Olaf**

Bac, Ferdinand (1859-1952); *Le Fantôme de Paris* (*The Ghost of Paris*; Fasquelle, 1908); *Le Mystère Vénitien* (*The Venetian Mystery*; Fasquelle, 1909); *L'Aventure Singulière d'Odysseus* (*Odysseus' Singular Adventure*; Conard, 1923); *L'Extraplanétaire* (*The Extraplanetary*; Conard, 1926)

Bachér, Ingrid (?-); *La Maison des Enfants* (*The Children's House*; OCDL, 1982); *L'Été des Hommes Volants* (*The Summer of the Flying Men*; Bordas, 1983)

Badet, C.-H. (?-); *La Dixième Planète* (*The Tenth Planet*; Métal 1, 1954)

Bailly, Albert (1886-?); *L'Éther-Alpha* (LPT, 1929); *Pardonnons à Dieu (Roman du Futur)* (*Let's Forgive God— a Novel of the Future*; 1960); *Note:* Belgian writer. See Chapter VII.

Balazard, Simone (?-); *Le Château des Tortues* (*The Castle of Turtles*; Flamm., 1962); *Le Rocher Rouge* (*The Red Rock*; Grasset, 1972); *Zita Zoll* (Flamm., 1992); *Note:* See Chapter VIII.

Balbi, André-Jean *see* **Bonelli, André-Jean**

Baldwin-Beneich, Denis *see* **Beneich, Denis**

Ballanche, Pierre-Simon (1776-1847); "Vision d'Hébal, Chef d'un Clan Écossais" (Vision of Hebal, Laird of a Scottish Clan; *Didot, 1831)* is included in *La Ville des Expiations* (*The City of Expiations*; in fragments, Pinard, 1832-1909); *L'Homme sans Nom* (*The Man with No Name*; France-Empire, 1989)

Balleyguier, Noémi (?-?); *Mignonettes: Contes pour les Petis Enfants* (*Tales for Little Children*; Quantin, 1887); *Les Rogimbot* (Quantin, 1887); *Aux Garennes* (Libr. Imprim. Réunis, 1891); *Futurs Chevaliers* (*Future Knights*; Delagrave, 1894); *Seul sur l'Océan* (*Alone on the Ocean*; with Louis **Gastine**; CMM, 1895)

Ballini, Georges (?-); *Brume de Sable* (*Sand Mist*; Ed. Fr. Réunis, 1965); *Cosmos, Pain Quotidien* (*Cosmos, Daily Bread*; Palais Royal, 1970); *Note: Cosmos* is a stage play in 5 acts.

Balloffet, Pierre (?-); *Apocalypse* (as Pierre Irt; Bressane,

1952); *L'Esclave de Brorsk* (*The Slave of Brorsk*; Métal 24, 1956)

Balnec, André H. (?-); *Séléné* (Pavois, 1946); *Pierre Duverger, Veuve Chanasse* (Scorpion, 1964); *Note:* See Chapter VII.

Balzac, Honoré de (1799-1850); *Falthurne* (wri. c. 1820; publ. Corti, 1950); *L'Héritière de Birague* (*The Heir of Birague*; as M.A. de Viellerglé & Lord R'Hoone; Hubert, 1822); *Jean-Louis, ou La Fille Trouvée* (*Jean-Louis, or the Found Girl*; as M.A. de Viellerglé & Lord R'Hoone; Hubert, 1822); *Clotilde de Lusignan* (*aka L'Israélite*; as M.A. de Viellerglé & Lord R'Hoone; Hubert, 1822); *Le Vicaire des Ardennes* (*The Vicar of the Ardennes*; as Horace de Saint-Aubin; Hubert, 1822); *Le Centenaire ou les Deux Berlingheld* (*The Centenarian*; as Horace de Saint-Aubin; Pollet, 1822; transl. 1976); *La Dernière Fée* (*The Last Fairy*; as Horace de Saint-Aubin; Barba, 1823); *Annette et le Criminel* (*Annette and the Criminal*; aka *Argow le Pirate*; as Horace de Saint-Aubin; Buissot, 1824); *Wann-Chlore (aka Jane la Pâle* (*Jane the Pale*; as Horace de Saint-Aubin; Maresq, 1825); *Les Deux Rêves (The Two Dreams; aka Le Petit Souper* (*The Small Dinner*; Revue de la Mode, 1830); *L'Élixir de Longue Vie* (*The Elixir of Long Life*; Revue de Paris/Gosselin, 1830; transl. as *Elixir of Life*, 1901); *La Peau de Chagrin* (*The Skin of Sorrow*; Gosselin, 1831; transl. as *Luck and Leather*, 1842; rev. as *The Wild Ass's Skin*, 1888); *Romans et Contes Philosophiques* (*Novels and Philosophical Tales*; Gosselin, 1831); *Le Chef d'Oeuvre Inconnu* (H. Souverain, 1831; transl. as *The Unknown Masterpiece*, 1843); *Louis Lambert* (Gosselin, 1832; transl. 1889); *La Comédie du Diable* (*The Devil's Comedy*; Gosselin, 1831); *Contes Bruns* (*Brown Tales*; anthology/with **Chasles** & **Rabou**; Guyot, 1832); *La Recherche de l'Absolu* (*The Quest of the Absolute*; H. Souverain, 1834; transl. as *The Philosopher's Stone*, 1844); *Séraphita* (Werdet, 1835; transl. 1889); *Melmoth Réconcilié* (*Melmoth Reconciled*; Allardin, 1835; transl. 1896); Note: See Chapter IV. ***La Peau de Chagrin*** and ***Melmoth Réconcilié*** were adapted by French television (see Book 1, Chapter II); one of Balzac's short stories became the basis for the 1971-74 film ***Out Un: Spectre*** (see Chapter I). Balzac's genre short stories not listed separately above include "Zéro" (1830), "La Danse des Pierres" (The Dance of the Stones; 1830), "La Tour de Birette" (The Tower of Birette; 1830), "L'Église" (The Church; 1831), "Les Proscrits" (The Proscribed; 1831), "Le Réquisitionnaire" (The Requisitioneer; 1831), "L'Auberge Rouge" (The Red Inn; 1831), "Le Dôme des Invalides: Hallucination" (The Dome of the Invalides: An Hallucination; 1832), "Maître Cornélius" (1832) and "Aventures Administratives d'une Idée Heureuse" (Administrative Adventures of a Fortunate Idea; 1834).

Bameul, Pierre (1940-); *Je Paye Donc Je Suis* (*I Pay Therefore I Am*; OG 151-152, 1977); *Écrit dans le Passé* (*Written in the Past*; OF 292-293, 1978); *Par Le Royaume d'Osiris* (*By the Kingdom of Osiris*; GB 75, 1981); *La Saga d'Arne Marsson* (*The Saga of Arne Marsson*; FNA 1458, 1986); *Le Choix des Destins* (*A Choice of Destinies*; FNA 1489, 1986); *Note:* See Chapter IX.

Bammert, Jacques-Joseph (?-) *see Contes et Légendes*

Banon, Mark (?-); *Fusées sous le Pacifique* (*Rockets Under the Pacific*; Inter-Espions 12, 1962); *Trahison dans l'Espace* (*Betrayal in Space*; Inter-Espions 20, 1963); *Les Surhommes* (*The Supermen*; Martel "Start" 16, 1964); *Note:* See Chapter IX.

Banville d'Hostel (?-?); *Z, Anticipation Dramatique sur le Dernier Jour de la Terre* (*Z, Dramatic Anticipation on the Last Day of the Earth; aka Le Drapeau Noir* (*The Black Flag*; Esope, 1929); *L'Homme qui lui Volait sa Pensée* (*The Man Who Stole His Thoughts*; Soutraine, 1942); *Note:* See Chapter IX.

Baranger, Léon (1877-?); *Les Contes Arabes de M. Laroze* (*Arabian Tales*; Grès, 1913); *Le Maître de la Force* (*The Master of the Force*; EFI, 1919); *Note:* See Chapter VII.

Barbe, Hurl (?-); *Alice-Crime, ou Meurtres en Série* (*Alice Crime, or Serial Murders*; Deleatur, 1979); *Les Celtes Mercenaires* (*Mercenary Celts*; Brigandine, 1982); *Pompe le Mousse* (Brigandine, 1982)

Barbeau, Marius (?-); *Le Phénix Doré* (*The Golden Phoenix*; Chatecler, 1950); *Le Fin Voleur de Valenciennes* (*The Slick Thief of Valenciennes*; Chatecler, 1950); *L'Eau qui Rajeunit* (*The Rejuvenating Water*; Chantecler, 1950); *Note:* French-Canadian writer. Children's tales.

Barbeau, Philippe (1952-); *L'Ami de l'Ogre* (*The Ogre's Friend*; Belfond, 1990); *Accroche-toi Faustine!* (*Hold on Tight, Faustine!*; Flamm., 1991); *Note:* Juveniles. See Chapter VIII.

Barbéri, Jacques (1954-); *Kosmokrim* (PdF 407, 1985); *Une Soirée à la Plage* (*An Evening on the Beach*; PdF 477, 1988); *Rêve de Chair* (*Dream of Flesh*; with Emmanuel **Jouanne**; FNG 78, 1988); *Narcose* (PdF 498, 1989); *Guerre de Rien* (*War of Nothing*; PdF 514, 1990); *La Mémoire du Crime* (*The Memory of the Crime*; PdF 534, 1992); *Labyrinth-Jungle* (as Oscar Valetti/with Yves **Ramonet**; FNA 1880, 1992); *L'Ombre et le Fléau* (*The Shadow and the Plague*; as Oscar Valetti/with Yves **Ramonet**; FNA 1896, 1992); *Chair Inconnue* (*Unknown Flesh*; as Oscar Valetti/with Yves **Ramonet**; FNA 1913, 1993); *Carcinoma Tango* (CRNI, 1993); *Note:* See Chapter IX.

Barbet, Pierre (Claude Avice; 1925-1995); *Vers un Avenir Perdu* (*Towards a Lost Future*; RF 98, 1962); *Babel*

3805 (RF 106, 1962); *Les Limiers de l'Infini* (*The Trackers of Infinity*; FNA 285, 1966); *Les Cavernicoles de Wolf* (*The Cavern-Dwellers of Wolf*; FNA 292, 1966); *L'Étoile du Néant* (*The Void Star*; FNA 309, 1967); *Le Secret des Quasars* (*The Secret of the Quasars*; FNA 319, 1967); *Hallali Cosmique* (*Cosmic Hunt*; FNA 330, 1967); *La Planète des Cristophons* (*The Planet of the Christophons*; FNA 345, 1968); *Évolution Magnétique* (*Magnetic Evolution*; FNA 350, 1968); *Vikings de l'Espace* (*Space Vikings*; FNA 371, 1969); *Les Chimères de Seginus* (*The Chimeras of Seginus*; FNA 383, 1969); *L'Exilé du Temps* (*The Exile of Time*; FNA 392, 1969); *Étoiles en Perdition* (*Doomed Stars*; FNA 404, 1970); *Les Maîtres des Pulsars* (*The Masters of the Pulsars*; FNA 413, 1970); *Les Grognards d'Éridan* (FNA 426, 1970; transl. as *The Napoleons of Eridanus*, 1976); *L'Agonie de la Voie Lactée* (*The Agony of the Milky Way*; FNA 435, 1970); *Les Conquistadores d'Andromède* (*The Conquistadores of Andromeda*; FNA 446, 1971); *Le Transmetteur de Ganymède* (*The Ganymede Transmitter*; FNA 463, 1971); *Azraec de Virgo* (*Azraec of Virgo*; FNA 471, 1971); *A Quoi Songent les Psyborgs?* (*What Do Psyborgs Dream About?*; FNA 479, 1971; transl. as *Games Psyborgs Play*, 1973); *L'Empire du Baphomet* (*The Empire of Baphomet*; FNA 494, 1972; transl. as *Baphomet's Meteor*, 1972); *Les Insurgés de Laucor* (*The Insurgents of Laucor*; FNA 508, 1972); *La Planète Empoisonnée* (*The Poisoned Planet*; FNA 523, 1972); *Tremplins d'Étoiles* (*Jumping Point to the Stars*; FNA 532, 1972); *Les Disparus du Club Chronos* (*The Disappeared Members of the Chronos Club*; as David Maine; AMSF 9,

1972); *La Planète Enchantée* (FNA 544, 1973; transl. as *The Enchanted Planet*, 1975); *Liane de Noldaz* (FNA 563, 1973; transl. as *The Joan of Arc Replay*, 1978); *Les Bioniques d'Atria* (*The Bionics of Atria*; FNA 572, 1973); *Le Bâtard d'Orion* (*The Bastard of Orion*; FNA 582, 1973); *L'Univers des Géons* (*The Universe of the Geons*; FNA 598, 1974); *Magiciens Galactiques* (*Galactic Magicians*; FNA 609, 1974); *Les Mercenaires de Rychna* (*The Mercenaries of Rychna*; FNA 622, 1974); *Croisade Stellaire* (FNA 638, 1974; transl. as *Stellar Crusade*, 1980); *La Nymphe de l'Espace* (*The Space Nymph*; FNA 673, 1975); *Patrouilleur du Néant* (*Void Patrol*; FNA 716, 1976); *Ambassade Galactique* (*Galactic Embassy*; FNA 756, 1976); *Guérilléro Galactique* (*Galactic Guerillero*; as David Maine; AMSF2 17, 1976); *Crépuscule du Futur* (*Twilight of the Future*; as Olivier Sprigel; MSF 34, 1976); *Vénusine* (as Olivier Sprigel; MSF 61, 1977); *Commandos sur Commande* (*Commandos to Order*; FNA 835, 1978); *Odyssée Galactique* (*Galactic Odyssey*; FNA 871, 1978); *Lendemains Incertains* (*Uncertain Futures*; as Olivier Sprigel; MSF 78, 1978); *Trafic Stellaire* (*Interstellar Traffic*; FNA 932, 1979); *Oasis de l'Espace* (*Space Oasis*; FNA 951, 1979); *Périple Galactique* (*Galactic Journey*; FNA 994, 1980); *Le Maréchal Rebelle* (*The Rebel Marshal*; FNA 1027, 1980); *Renaissance Planétaire* (*Planetary Rebirth*; as David Maine; AMSF2 47, 1980); *Cité des Astéroïdes* (*City of the Asteroids*; FNA 1071, 1981); *Les Psychos de Logir* (*The Psychos of Logir*; FNA 1099, 1981); *Cités Interstellaires* (*Interstellar Cities*; FNA 1131, 1982); *Survivants de l'Apocalypse* (*Survivors of the Apocalypse*; FNA 1152, 1982); *Invasion Cosmique* (*Cosmic Invasion*; as David Maine; AMSF2 53, 1982); *L'Empereur d'Éridan* (FNA 1169, 1982; transl. as *The Emperor of Eridanus*, 1983); *Les Charognards de Snien* (*The Carrion-Eaters of Snien*; FNA 1199, 1983); *Rome Doit Être Detruite* (*Rome Must Be Destroyed*; FNA 1254, 1983); *Les Colons d'Éridan* (*The Eridani Colonists*; FNA 1284, 1984); *Carthage Sera Détruite* (*Carthago Will Be Destroyed*; FNA 1298, 1984); *Eldorado Stellaire* (*Interstellar Eldorado*; FNA 1347, 1985); *Cités Biotiques* (*Biotic Cities*; FNA 1371, 1985); *Téléclones* (FNA 1384, 1985); *Putsch Galactique* (*Galactic Putsch*; FNA 1401, 1985); *Glaciation Nucléaire* (*Nuclear Ice Age*; FNA 1440, 1986); *La Croisade des Assassins* (*The Assassins' Crusade*; FNA 1483, 1986); *Temps Changeants* (*Chang-

ing Times; FNA 1505, 1986); *Défense Spatiale* (*Space Defense*; FNA 1518, 1987); *Captifs de Corvus* (*Prisoners of Corvus*; FNA 1547, 1987); *Un Reich de 1000 Ans* (*A 1000-Year Reich*; FNA 1560, 1987); *Objectif: Mars 2005* (*Target: Mars 2005*; FNA 1586, 1987); *Option Zéro* (*Zero Option;* FNA 1620, 1988); *Soleil de Mort* (*Death Sun*; FNA 1755, 1990); *L'Ere du Spatiopithèque* (*The Era of the Spatiopithecus*; FNA 1850, 1991); *Note:* See Chapters VIII and IX.

Barbey d'Aurevilly, Jules-Amédée (1808-1889); *L'Ensorcelée* (*The Spellbound*; Lemerre, 1854); *Le Chevalier des Toches* (*The Knight of Toches*; M. Lévy, 1864); *Les Diaboliques* (*The Diabolical Women*; wri. 1858; pub. Dentu, 1874); *Une Histoire sans Nom* (*A Nameless Story*; Lemerre, 1881); *Le Cachet d'Onyx* (*The Onyx Seal*; Petite Bibl., 1921); *Note:* See Chapter IV.

Barbier, Jules (1825-1901) *see* **Opéra**

Barbier-Daumont, J.-A. (?-); *Héliodora en Atlantide* (With Georges **Spitzmuller**; France-Edition, 1923); *Le Capteur d'Âmes* (*The Soul Catcher*; SEDL, 1947)

Barbot, Henri (?-); *Paris en Feu!* (*Paris on Fire!*; BLF, 1914); *Saint-Front* (Stock, 1918)

Barbot de Gallon de Villeneuve, Gabrielle-Suzanne (1695-1755); *Les Contes Marins ou La Jeune Américaine* (*Sea Stories or the Young American Girl*; La Haye, 1740); *Note:* See Chapter III.

Barbusse, Henri (1873-1935); *Les Enchaînements* (Flamm., 1925; transl. as *Chains*, 1925); *Trois Films* (*Three Films*; Flamm., 1926); *Note:* See Chapter VII.

Barcelo, François (1941-); *Agénor, Agénor, Agénor et Agénor* (Quinze, 1980); *La Tribu* (*The Tribe*; Libre Expression, 1981); *Ville-Dieu* (*God City*; Libre Expression, 1982); *Aaa, Aâh, Ha ou les Amours Malaisées* (*The Uneasy Loves*; L'Hexagone, 1986); *Longues Histoires Courtes* (*Long Short Stories*; Libre Expression, 1992); *Note:* French-Canadian writer. Satirical fantasies.

Bardanne, Jean (?-); *L'Allemagne Attaquera Le...* (*Germany Will Attack On...*; Baudinière, 1932); *La Guerre et les Microbes* (*War and Microbes*; Baudinière, 1937); *Note:* See Chapter VII.

Barde, André (?-?); *Au Bord de la Folie* (*On the Edge of Madness*; Simonis Empis, 1901); *Note:* Also see **Grand-Guignol**.

Bardet, Gaston (?-); *Demain, C'est l'An 2000* (*Tomorrow Is the Year 2000*; Plon, 1952)

Baredhyo, Youan de (?-) *see* **Contes et Légendes**

Bargone, Frédéric-Charles *see* **Farrère, Claude**

Barilier, Étienne (?-); *La Créature* (Julliard/AdH, 1984)

Barjavel, René (1911-1985); *Roland, le Chevalier Plus Fier que le Lion* (*Roland, a Knight Prouder Than the Lion*; Den., 1942); *Ravage* (Den., 1943; transl. as *Ashes, Ashes*, 1967); *Le Voyageur Imprudent* (*The Careless Traveller*; Den., 1944; rev.

PdF 23, 1958; transl. as *Future Times Three*, 1970); *Les Enfants de l'Ombre* (*The Shadow Children*; Portulan, 1945;* rev. as *Le Prince Blessé* (*The Wounded Prince*, Flamm., 1974); *La Fée et le Soldat* (*The Fairy and the Soldier*; Ancolie, 1945); *Tarendol* (Den., 1946); *Le Diable l'Emporte* (*The Devil Takes It*; Den., 1948; rev. PdF 33, 1960); *Journal d'un Homme Simple* (*Diary of a Simple Man*; Chambriand, 1951); *Jour de Feu* (*Day of Fire*; Den., 1957); *Colomb de la Lune* (*Colombus of the Moon*; Den., 1962); *La Nuit des Temps* (*The Dawn of Time*; PC, 1968; transl. as *The Ice People*, 1970); *Les Chemins de Katmandou* (*The Road to Katmandu*; PC, 1969); *Les Années de la Lune* (*The Years of the Moon*; PC, 1972); *Le Grand Secret* (*The Great Secret*; PC, 1973; transl. as *The Immortals*, 1974); *Les Dames à la Licorne* (*The Ladies of the Unicorn*; with Olenka de **Veer**; PC, 1974); *Les Années de Liberté* (*The Years of Freedom*; PC, 1975); *Les Années de l'Homme* (*The Year of the Man*; PC, 1976); *Les Jours du Monde* (*The Days of the World*; with Olenka de **Veer**; PC, 1977); *La Charrette Bleue* (*The Blue Cart*; Den., 1980); *Une Rose au Paradis* (*A Rose in Paradise*; PC, 1981); *La Tempête* (*The Tempest*; Den., 1982); *L'Enchanteur* (*The Enchanter*; Den., 1984); *La Peau de César* (*Caesar's Skin*; MdF, 1985); *Demain, le Paradis* (*Tomorrow, the Paradise*; Den., 1986); *Note:* See chapters VII, VIII, and IX. *Le Voyageur Imprudent* and *Le Grand Secret* were adapted as television movies (see Book 1, Chapter II).

Barney, Céline W. *see* **Chéreau, Fred & Ramonet, Yves**

Barnouin, Jacques (1950-); *Le Fantôme Sparadrap et Autres Histoires Sans Sucre* (*The Band-Aid Ghost and Other Sugarless Stories*; Messidor-La Farandole, 1984); *Bonjour, la Nuit!* (*Hello, Night!*; Messidor-La Farandole, 1985); *Alerte Noire* (*Black Alert*; Hac., 1989); *Note:* Juveniles. See Chapter VIII.

Baronian, Jean-Baptiste (1942-); *Récits de Science-Fiction de J.-H. Rosny Aîné* (anthology; MarSF 523, 1975); *La France Fantastique* (anthology; MarF, 1975); *La Belgique Fantastique* (anthology; MarF, 1975); *L'Un l'Autre*

(*The One the Other*; Robert Morel, n.d.); *Le Grand Chalababa* (*The Great Chalababa*; OAM 33, 1977); *Scènes de la Vie Obscure* (*Scenes of the Dark Life*; RL, 1977); *Le Diable Vauvert* (*The Devil Vauvert*; RL, 1979); *Place du Jeu de Balle* (*Place of the Ball Game*; RL, 1980); *Les Quatre Coins du Monde* (*The Four Corners of the World*; RL, 1982); *Sept Simulacres* (*Seven Simulacra*; Valberghe, 1982); *La Vie Continue* (*Life Goes On*; Bourgois, 1989); *La Bibliothèque de Feu* (*The Library of Fire*; Pierre d'Alun, 1990); *Potions Rouges* (*Red Potions*; anthology; Julliard, 1990); *Enfants Rouges* (*Red Children*; anthology; Julliard, 1991); *Livre Rouge* (*Red Book*; anthology; Julliard, 1991); *La Nuit Aller-Retour* (*Return Night*; Bourgois, 1991); *Le Tueur Fou* (*The Mad Killer*; Rivages, 1994); *Le Vent du Nord* (*The North Wind*; Métailie, 1996); **Non-Fiction:** *Panorama de la Littérature Fantastique de Langue Française* (*Panorama of Fantastic Literature in the French Language*; Stock, 1978); *Note:* Belgian writer. See chapters VIII and IX. Jean-Baptiste Baronian was the editor of the *Marabout* science fiction & *fantastique* imprints, and a renowned essayist.

Barrack, Jo (?-); Series *Lord Bionic*: *1. Lord Bionic Entre en Scène* (*Enter Lord Bionic*; Enclos, 1979); *2. Lord Bionic Sort de l'Ombre* (*Lord Bionic Comes Out of the Shadows*; Enclos, 1979); *3. Lord Bionic Aau Service de la Reine* (*Lord Bionic on Her Majesty's Service*; Enclos, 1980); *4. Lord Bionic Va à Dames* (*Lord Bionic Plays Checkers*; Enclos, 1980); *5. Lord Bionic Coupe et Gagne* (*Lord Bionic Plays and Wins*; Enclos, 1980)

Barral, M. (?-) *see **Contes et Légendes***

Barrault, Jean-Michel (?-); *...Et Les Bisons Brouteront à Manhattan* (*...And the Buffalo Will Graze in Mahattan*; Julliard, 1973); *Note:* See Chapter IX.

Barrière, Marcel (1860-1954); *Le Monde Noir* (*The Dark World*; Lemerre, 1909); *La Nouvelle Europe* (*The New Europe*; Lemerre, 1911)

Barsac, Luc (?-); *Duel chez les Jaunes* (*Duel Among the Yellows*; Libr. De La Cité, 1958); *Évadé de l'Espace* (*Escape in Space*; Libr. De la Cité, 1963); *Note:* See Chapter IX.

Barthe, Ulric (1853-1921); *Similia Similibus, ou La Guerre au Canada* (*The War in Canada*; 1916); *Note:* French-Canadian writer. Quebec is conquered bythe Prussian army (though it is all a dream).

Bartillat, Christian de (?-); *Christophe ou La Traversée* (*The Crossing*; Julliard, 1979); *Les Flames de la St. Jean* (*The Fires of St. John's*; AM, 1982); *La Brie qui Rêve: Contes et Légendes de Brie* (*The Dreaming Brie: Tales and Legends of the Brie*; Presses du Village, 1983)

Baruc, André (?-); *Gobe-Lune* (*Moon Swallower*; Mag-

nard, 1948); *Contes de la Zérozième* (*Tales from the Zeroth Grade*; Magnard, 1949); *Les Pantins de Cristal* (*The Crystal Puppets*; Magnard, 1957); *Note:* Juveniles. See Chapter IX.

Barzel, Charles (?-); *Mort et Vivant* (*Dead and Alive*; SELF, 1946)

Basdevant, Denise (?-); *De Monts en Merveilles* (*From Mountains to Wonders*; Flamm., 1963)

Basile, Jean (Bezroudnoff, Jean; 1932-); *Lorenzo* (Jour, 1963); *Les Voyages d'Irkousz* (HMH, 1970); *L'Acide* (*The Acid*; Grasset, 1970); *Le Piano-Trompette* (*The Piano Trumpet*; VLB, 1983); *Note:* French-Canadian writer. In a post-nuclear world, Canada is occupied by the U.S. ("Irkousz" is also spelled "Irkoutsk" in the book.)

Bassan, Élie de (?-?) *see **Grand-Guignol***

Basset, Serge (1865-?) *see **Grand-Guignol***

Bassot, Hubert (?-); *Le 13 Octobre 2017* (France Empire, 1989); *Courage, Perdons!* (*Courage! Let's Lose!*; Carrière, 1993); *Ariane de Tinchebray* (Carrière, 1995)

Bastia, Jean (1878-?); *Tous Avariés* (*All Rotten*; Chavat & Girier, 1903); *Missel Pourpre* (*Purple Prayerbook*; Figuière, 1931); *Note:* Also see **Grand-Guignol**.

Bastia, Pascal (?-); *Quand l'Air Vint à Manquer* (*When Air Ran Out*; Générales, 1946)

Bastid, Jean-Pierre (1937-); *Le Transafricain* (*The Transafrican*; FNASF 12, 1996)

Bataille, Henry Félix (1872-1922); *La Chambre Blanche* (*The White Room*; MdF, 1895); *Ton Sang* (*Your Blood*; MdF, 1898); *La Lépreuse* (*The Woman Leper*; Eschig, 1912)

Bataille, Henry *see **Taxil, Léo***

Bataille, Th. (?-) *see **Lecigne, Bruno***

Battestini, Monique (?-); *Le Grandiose Avenir* (*The Great Future*; anthology/with Gérard **Klein**; Seghers, 1975); *Ce Qui Vient des Profondeurs* (*That Which Came from Below*; anthology/with Gérard **Klein**; Seghers, 1977); *Les Lolos de Vénus* (*Venus' Tits*; anthology/with Bernard **Blanc**; Kes., 1978)

Bauche, Henri (1880-?); *Note:* See Chapter VI, **Grand-Guignol**, and André de **Lorde**.

Bauchy, Jacques-Henry (?-); *Douze Légendes de France* (*Twelve French Legends*; Nathan, 1971); *Fables pour Notre Temps* (*Fables for Our Times*; JH Bauchy, 1979); *Note:* Also see **Contes et Légendes**.

Baudat, Henry (?-); *La Terre en Folie* (*Earth Goes Mad*; Scorpion, 1964)

Baudelaire, Charles (1821-1867); *Les Fleurs du Mal* (*The Flowers of Evil*; Poulet Malassis-De Brise, 1857; transl. 1869); *Note:* See Chapter IV.

Baudry, Emmanuel (1945-); *Histoire de Fous, de Clous, de Sous et Tout* (*Story of Madmen, Nails, Money Et Al.*; with Alain **Royer**; Hac., 1981); *Le Voyage Immobile* (*The Motionless Journey*; Amitié, 1981); *Les Rêves du Président Songecreu* (*The Dreams of President Hollowdream*; Hac., 1984); *Les Rugissements de M. Léo Léopart* (*The Roars of Mister Lepart*; Hac., 1996); *Un Prof à Éclipses* (*A Teacher with Eclipses*; with Alain **Royer**; BR, 1982); *La Kermesse aux Espions* (*The Spy Festival*; with Alain **Royer**; BR, 1982); *Fantômes en Folie* (*Ghosts on Parade*; with Alain **Royer**; BR, 1982); *Le Mystère des Chats Chanteurs* (*The Mystery of the Singing Cats*; with Alain **Royer**; GP, 1983); *Taram et le Chaudron Magique* (*Taram and the Magic Cauldron*; with Alain **Royer**; Hac., 1985); *Note:* Juveniles. See Chapter IX. *Taram* is a French novelisation of Disney's *The Black Cauldron*.

Baudu, René *see* **Arcy, Maurice**

Bauduret, Thomas *see* **Dharma, Samuel**

Bauer, Edmond Édouard (?-); *Le Neveu de Gulliver* (*Gulliver's Nephew*; RDA, 1923)

Baux, Raymond (?-); *Les Fantômes de la Chapelle Pol* (*The Ghosts of the Chapel of Pol*; SdP, 1952); *Note:* Juvenile.

Bavoux, Gérard (?-); *Le Cheval de Dieu* (*God's Horse*; Pygmalion, 1995); *Le Porteur de Lumière* (*The Light Bearer*; Pygmalion, 1996)

Bax, Bruno (?-); Series *"H": H et l'Esionne Ingénue* (*H and the Ingenuous Spy*; Ditis Chouette, 1955); *H et la Bouée Baladeuse* (*H and the Wandering Buoy*; Ditis Chouette 16, 1956); *H et le Sous-Marin Volé* (*H and the Stolen Sub-Marine*; Ditis Chouette, 1956); *H et la Petite Irlandaise* (*H and the Little Irish Girl*; Ditis Chouette 24, 1956); *H et l'Opération Manchot* (*H and Operation One-Armed Man*; Ditis Chouette 32, 1956); *H contre le Réseau Baleine* (*H vs. The Whale Network*; Ditis Chouette 46, 1957); *H et le Hollandais Volant* (*H vs. The Flying Dutchman*; Ditis Chouette 59, 1957); *H et l'Opération Fado* (*H and Operation Fado*; Ditis Chouette 77, 1958); *H et la Dangereuse Africaine* (*H and the Dangerous African*; Ditis Chouette 100, 1958); *H et l'Opération Mer Libre* (*H and the Operation Open Sea*; Ditis Chouette 114, 1958); *H et le Dossier Rouge* (*H and the Red File*; Ditis Chouette 123, 1959); *H et l'Accusée de Varsovie* (*H and the Accused of Warsaw*; Ditis Chouette 148, 1960); *Un Coup de H* (*H Strikes Again*; PC Espionnage, 1960); *Aurore Mortelle* (*Mortal Dawn*; PC Espionnage, 1960); *La Bête Fauve* (*The Wild Beast*; PC Espionnage, 1960); *Office de Mort* (*Deadly Office*; PC Espionnage, 1960); *Note:* See Chapter IX.

Bay, Paul (1887-?); *Mort aux Anges* (*Death to the Angels*; Triolet, 1949); *Descendit aux Enfers* (*Descending to Hell*; La Sève, 1958); *Les Femmes en Pantalon* (*Women in Trousers*; Brabançonne, 1966); *Note:* Belgian writer. See Chapter VIII.

Bayard, Georges (1918-); *Les Pionniers du Déluge* (*The Pioneers of the Flood*; Delagrave, 1961); *L'Urganda, Yacht Fantôme* (*Urganda, Phantom Yacht*; Fleurus-Mame, 1962); *Note:* Juveniles. See Chapter IX.

Bayle, Louis (?-); *Contes de la Mer et des Îles* (*Tales of the Sea and the Islands*; Scorpion, 1959); *Aièr e Deman* (2 vols.; Astrado/Scorpion, 1970); *Note:* See Chapter IX.

Bazin, Hervé (?-); *Le Neuvième Jour* (*The Ninth Day*; Grasset, 1994); *Note:* See Chapter IX.

Bazin, Jean-François (?-); *L'Abbaye des Effrayés* (*The Abbey of the Terrified*; SdP 158, 1960); *Note:* Juvenile.

Béalu, Marcel (1908-1993); *Les Yeux Ouverts* (*Open Eyes*; Figuière, 1936); *Écrit dans la Ville* (*Written in the City*; Sagittaire, 1937); *La Rivière* (*The River*; Goeland, 1938); *Coeur Vivant* (*Living Heart*; Flory, 1941); *Mémoires de l'Ombre* (*Memoirs of Shadow*; Debresse, 1941; rev. Gall., 1944; rev. Los., 1959; rev. MarF 402, 1972; rev. Phébus, 1986); *Miroirs* (*Mirrors*; Bettencourt, 1943; incl. in *Contes du Demi-Sommeil*, Phébus, 1979); *L'Expérience de la Nuit* (*The Experience of Night*; Gall., 1945; rev. Phébus, 1990); *Journal d'un Mort* (*Diary of a Dead Man*; Gall., 1947; rev. Phébus, 1978); *L'Araignée d'Eau* (1948; rev. Belfond, 1969; rev. Phébus, 1994; transl. as *The Water Spider*, 1979); *La Millanderie* (Deux-Rives, 1949); *La Pérégrination Fantasque* (*The Fantastic Journey*; Vrille, 1950; incl. in *Contes du Demi-Sommeil*, Phébus, 1979); *La Bouche Ouverte* (*Open Mouth*; Blanchet, 1952; incl. in *Contes du Demi-Sommeil*, Phébus, 1979); *Ocarina* (poems; Seghers, 1952); *Lampions & Coloquintes* (Rougerie, 1953); *L'Aventure Impersonelle* (*The Unpersonal Adventure*; Arcanes, 1954; rev. Los., 1964; rev. MarF 257, 1966; rev. Phébus, 1985); *L'Herbier de Feu* (*The Herb Book of Fire*; poems; Rougerie, 1955); *Les Messagers Clandestins* (*The Clandestine Messengers*; Los., 1956; rev. Belfond, 1969; incl. in *Contes du Demi-Sommeil*, Phébus, 1979); *Trois Récits* (*Three Stories*; Subervie, 1956); *L'Air de Vie* (*Air of Life*; poems; Seghers, 1958); *Contes du Demi-Sommeil* (*Tales of Half-Sleep*; Fanlac, 1960; rev. Phébus, 1979); *Amour Me Cèle Cell que j'aime* (*Love Hides She Whom I Love*; poems; Seghers, 1962); *La Dormeuse* (*The Sleeping Lady*; Chambelland, 1964); *Le Rêve Rusé* (*The Cunning Dream*; Vodaine, 1964); *Les Lys et le Sang* (*Lys and Blood*; Rougerie,

1964); *Le Bruit du Moulin* (*The Noise of the Mill*; Rougerie, 1966; rev. Corti, 1986); *La Voix sans Nom* (*The Nameless Voice*; poems; Rougerie, 1967); *Le Bien Rêver* (*Good Dreams;* Robert Morel, 1968; rev. as *La Vie en Rêve* (*Life as a Dream*, Phébus, 1992); *Passage de la Bête* (*Passage of the Beast*; Belfond, 1969); *D'Où Part le Regard* (*From Where the Eyes Look*; poems; Rougerie, 1971); *La Grande Marée* (*The Great Tide*; Belfond, 1973); *Hâmes et Konscience* (*Shoul and Konscience*; Daily-Bul, 1974); *Août 73* (*August '73*; Castor Astral, 1975); *Yamira* (poems; Pont Traversé, 1975); *La Poudre des Songes* (*The Dust of Dreams*; Belfond, 1977); *Journal d'un Mort* (*Diary of a Deadman*; Phébus, 1978); *Le Chapeau Magique* (*The Magic Hat*; 3 vols.; Autobiography; Belfond, 1980); *La Mort à Bénidorm* (*Death in Benidorm*; Fanlac, 1985); *Paix du Regard sans Désir* (*Peace of the Eyes Without Desire*; poems; Corti, 1988); *Contes Aigre-Doux (Bittersweet Tales;* L'Anneau du Pain, 1989; rev. as *L'Amateur de Devinettes* (*The Charade Lover*, La Différence, 1992); *Dans la Loi Hors des Lois* (*Within the Law Outside the Law*; poems; Rougerie, 1989); *La Statue de Gladys* (*Gladys' Statue*; Hors du Temps, 1993); *Note:* See Chapter VIII.

Beauchamp, Suzanne (1958-); *Une Chance sur Trois* (*One Chance in Three*; L'Actuelle, 1974); *Note:* French-Canadian writer.

Beauchesne, Yves (1948-1992); *Nuit Battante* (*Beating Night*; Léméac, 1982); *Le Don* (*The Gift*; with David **Schinkel**; Tisseyre, 1987); *Note:* French-Canadian writer.

Beau de Loménie, Gilbert (?-); *Le Monde Sans Grand-Mères* (*The World Without Grand-Mothers*; Rocher, 1970); *Note:* See Chapter IX.

Beaude, Pierre-Marie (?-); *Flora, l'Inconnue de l'Espace* (*Flora, the Unknown Girl from Space*; Flamm., 1994); *Note:* Juvenile SF.

Beaugrand, Honoré (1848-1906); *La Chasse-Galerie: Légendes Canadiennes* (*The Gallery Hunt: Canadian Legends*; 1900; rev. Fidès, 1973; Presses de l'Université de Montréal, 1989; transl. as *La Chasse Galerie and Other Canadian Stories*, 1900); *Note:* French-Canadian writer of fairy tales based on Native American legends.

Beaulieu, René (1957-); *Légendes de Virnie* (*Legends from Virnia*; CdF 3, 1981); *Les Voyageurs de la Nuit* (*The Voyagers of Night*; L'Avenir, 1997); *Un Fantôme d'Amour* (*The Ghost of a Love*; Ashem Fictions, 1997); *Note:* French-Canadian writer. The last two titles are collections of SF stories.

Beaulieu, Victor-Lévy (1945-); *Race de Monde* (*World Race*; Jour, 1969); *Les Grands-Pères* (Jour, 1971; transl.

as *The Grandfathers*, 1975); *La Nuitte de Malcomm Hudd* (*Malcomm Hudd's Night*; Jour, 1973); *Oh, Miami Miami Miami* (Jour, 1973); *Don Quichotte de la Démanche* (*Don Quixote of the Demanche*; L'Aurore, 1974; transl. as *Don Quixote in Nighttown*, 1977); *Un Rêve Québécois* (*A Quebec Dream*; VLB, 1977); *Blanche Forcée* (*Forced White*; Flamm., 1978); *Cérémonial pour l'Assassinat d'un Ministre* (*Ceremonial for the Assassination of a Minister*; VLB, 1978); *La Tête de Monsieur Ferron ou les Chians* (*Mr. Ferron's Head*; VLB, 1979); *Una* (romaman; VLB, 1980); *Steven le Héraut* (*Steven the Herald*; Stanbée, 1985); *Note:* French-Canadian writer. *Una* is the surreal odyssey of a little girl.

Beaumier, Jean-Paul (1954-); *L'Air Libre* (*Open Air*; L'Instant Même, 1988); *Note:* French-Canadian writer. Collection of fantastical tales.

Beaunier, André (1869-1925); *Le Roi Tobol* (*King Tobol*; Fasquelle, 1905); *L'Homme qui a Perdu son Moi* (*The Man Who Lost Himself*; Plon, 1911); *La Révolte* (*The Revolt*; Plon, 1914); *Contes à Psyché* (*Tales of Psyche*; Flamm., 1922); *Picrate et Siméon* (Flamm., 1924); *Le Dernier Jour* (*The Last Day*; Flamm., 1925)

Beauplan, A. de (?-?) *see* **Opéra**

Beauvais, Robert (?-); *Quand Les Chinois...* (*When the Chinese...*; Fayard, 1966); *Note:* Adapted into **Les Chinois à Paris**, a 1974 film by Jean Yanne (see Book 1, Chapter I).

Beauvoir, Simone de (1908-1986); *Tous les Hommes sont Mortels* (Gall., 1946; transl. as *All Men Are Mortal*, 1955); *Note:* See Chapter VIII.

Beccognée, M. (?-); *Les Espions du Ciel* (*The Spies of the Sky*; Satellite 31, 1960)

Beck, Béatrix (1914-); *Contes à l'Enfant Né Coiffé* (*Tales for a Child Born Lucky*; Gall., 1953); *L'Enfant Chat* (*The Cat Child*; Grasset, 1984)

Becker, Benoît; *Expédition Epouvante* (*Expedition Terror*; FNAG 4, 1954); *Le Chien des Ténèbres* (*The Dog of Darkness*; FNAG 6, 1955); *Laisse Toute Espérance* (*Abandon All Hope*; FNAG 10, 1955); *Terreur* (*Terror*; FNAG 15, 1956); *Château du Trépas* (*Castle of Death*; FNAG 19, 1956); *La Chair et la Corde* (*The Flesh and the Rope*; FN Special-Police, 1957); *La Nuit des Traqués* (*Night of the Hunted*; FN Special-Police, 1957); *Le Souffle Coupé* (*Short of Breath*; FNAG 46, 1958); *Guillotine pour Demain* (*Guillotine for Tomorrow*; FN, 1988); Series *Frankenstein*: *La Tour de Frankenstein* (*The Tower of Frankenstein*; FNAG 30, 1957); *Le Pas de Frankenstein* (*The Step of Frankenstein*; FNAG 32, 1957); *La Nuit de Frankenstein* (*The Night of Frankenstein*; FNAG 34, 1957); *Le Sceau de Frankenstein* (*The*

Seal of Frankenstein; FNAG 36, 1957); *Frankenstein Rôde* (*Frankenstein Prowls*; FNAG 41, 1958); *La Cave de Frankenstein* (*The Cellar of Frankenstein*; FNAG 50, 1959); *Note:* See Chapter VIII. "Benoît Becker" was a Fleuve Noir house name which, in the case of the dozen novels published in the *Angoisse* imprint, stood for renowned film writer Jean-Claude **Carrière** (see Book 1, chapters I, II and VI), who wrote all the *Frankenstein* titles (with plot assistance from Guy Bechtel for the first volume), and journalist José-André **Lacour**, who wrote the other six FNAG novels. (Other writers having written under the "Becker" pseudonym include Stéphan Jouravieff and Christiane Rochefort.) The Becker FNAG novels were adapted into digest-sized graphic novels (see Book 1, Chapter V under ***Fleuve Noir***).

Beckford, William (1760-1844); *Histoire du Calife Vathek* (*Tale of Caliph Vathek*; Poinçot, 1787); *Note:* See Chapter III.

Bedel, Maurice (1884-1954); *Jérôme 60° Latitude Nord* (*Jerome 60 Degrees Latitude North*; Gall., 1928); Zulfu (Gall., 1932); *La Nouvelle Arcadie* (*New Arcadia*; Gall., 1934); *L'Alouette aux Nuages* (*The Skylark in the Clouds*; Gall., 1935); *Tropiques Noirs* (*Black Tropics*; Hac., 1950)

Bédier, Joseph (?-); *La Chanson de Roland* (*The Song of Roland*; L'Édition d'Art H. Piazza, 1922, rev. 1937); *Le Roman de Tristan et Iseult* (*The Novel of Tristan and Ysolde*; L'Édition d'Art H. Piazza, 1946); *Note:* See Chapter I.

Beffroy de Reigny, Louis-Abel *see* **Cousin Jacques**

Begouën, Max (1893-1961); *Les Bisons d'Argile* (Fayard, 1925; transl. as *Bison of Clay*, 1926); *Quand le Mammouth Ressuscita* (*When the Mastodon Revived*; LPT, 1928); *Tisik et Katé, Aventure de Deux Enfants à l'Époque du Renne* (*Adventure of Two Children in the Time of the Reindeer*; Diderot, 1946); *Note:* See Chapter VII.

Béhémoth *see* **Marignac, Pascal**

Beigbeder, Marc (?-); *Les Cacagons* (Beigbeder, 1947; pub. Morel, 1966); *La Bouteille à l'Air / Les Enfants sur le Toi* (*Air Bottle / Children on the You*; Beigbeder, 1972); *La Clarté des Abysses* (*Clarity of the Abyss*; Morel, 1977); *L'Apprentissage du Surnaturel* (*Apprenticeship of*

the Supernatural; Bouteille à la Mer, 1979); *Note:* Belgian writer who wrote *Les Cacagons*, a detailed description of an alien civilization. *La Clarté et L'Apprentissage* are studies of ESP and the Supernatural.

Belcayre, Jean de (?-); *Le Secret de la Muette* (*The Secret of the Dumb Woman*; Bonne Presse, 1925); *Le Trésor du Croisé* (*The Crusader's Treasure*; Mame, 1926); *Hors les Griffes* (*All Claws Out*; Bonne Presse, 1928); *Le Petit Chevalier* (*The Little Knight*; Bonne Presse, 1928); *Jardins Secrets* (*Secret Gardens*; Bonne Presse, 1931); *L'Ombre Tragique* (*The Tragic Shadow*; Bonne Presse, 1935); *La Princesse Clair de Lune* (*The Princess Moonlight*; Clocher, 1937); *Le Choix de Reynald* (*Reynald's Choice*; Bonne Presse, 1939); *Audoin le Tors* (*Audoin the Twisted*; Clocher, 1940); *Les Faucons de la Maronne* (*The Hawks of Maronne*; Clocher, 1940); *Les Prisonniers du Pacifique* (*The Prisoners of the Pacific*; Clocher, 1941); *Le Rayon Invisible* (*The Invisible Ray*; Clocher, 1941); *Le Jardin des Chimères* (*The Garden of Chimeras*; Vieux Colombier, 1946); *Le Dragon d'Or* (*The Gold Dragon*; Clocher, 1947); *Le Château du Silence* (*The Castle of Silence*; Vieux Colombier, 1949)

Bélen (Kaplan, Nelly; 1934-); *Et Délivrez-nous du Mâle* (*And Free Us from the Males*; Los., 1960); *La Géométrie dans les Spasmes* (*Geometry in Spasms*; Los., 1961); *La Reine des Sabbats* (*The Queen of the Sabbath*; Los., 1962); *Le Réservoir des Sens* (*Reservoir of the Senses*; Jeune Parque, 1966); *Le Collier de Ptyx* (*Ptyx' Necklace*; as Nelly Kaplan; Pauvert, 1971); *Note:* See Chapter VIII.

Belfiore, Robert (1951-); *Une Fille de Caïn* (*A Daughter of CaIn*; JL 1800, 1985); *La Huitième Vie du Chat* (*The Eighth Life of the Cat*; JL 2278, 1987); *Petite, ou L'Âge d'Or* (*Little One, or the Golden Age*; Flamm., 1990)*La Pieuvre de Xeltar* (*The Octopus of Xeltar;* with Philippe Henri **Turin**; Milan, 1995)*Le Maître de Juventa* (*The Master of Juventa*; Hac., 1996); *Note:* See Chapter IX.

Béliard, Octave (1876-1951); *Les Aventures d'un Voyageur qui Explora le Temps* (*The Adventures of a Voyager Who Explored Time;* LPT, 1909; rev. as *Le Passé Merveilleux* (*The Wondrous Past),* incl. in *Le Décapité Vivant* (*The Living Beheaded Man*), Livre de Paris, 1944); *La Journée d'un Parisien au XXIème Siècle* (*A Day in the Life of a Parisian in the 21st Century*; LPT, 1910); *Une Exploration Polaire aux Ruines de Paris* (*A Polar Exploration in the Ruins of Paris;* LPT, 1911; rev. as *La Découverte de Paris* (*The Discovery of Paris),* incl. in *Le Décapité Vivant* (*The Living Beheaded Man*), Livre de Paris, 1944); *Les Merveilles de l'Île Mystérieuse* (*The Wonders of Mysterious Island*; LPT, 1911); *La Petite Fille de Michel Strogoff* (*The Grand-Daughter of Michel Strogoff*; LPT, 1927); *Le Message Mystérieux* (*The Mysterious Message*; VLAE, 1928); *Les Petits Hommes de la Pinède* (*The Little Men in the Pine Forest*; NSE,

1928); *Le Filon d'Or* (*The Gold Mine*; SEP, 1933); *Le Décapité Vivant* (*The Living Beheaded Man*; Livre de Paris, 1944); *Note:* See Chapters V and VII. **Béliard** also wrote *Sorciers, Rêveurs et Démoniaques* (*Sorcerers, Dreamers and Demon-Worshippers*; Lemerre, 1920), a history of black magic.

Bélil, Michel (1951-); *Le Mangeur de Livres* (*The Book-Eater*; Tisseyre, 1978); *Déménagement* (*Moving Day*; Chasse-Galerie, 1981); *Greenwich* (Leméac, 1981); *La Ville Oasis* (*The Oasis City*; AMAM 7, 1990); *La Grotte de Toubouctom* (*The Cavern of Toubouctom*; Q/A, 1993); *Note:* French-Canadian writer. The first two titles are collections of fantastical tales. *Greenwich* is the surreal odyssey of a man fleeing his past. *La Grotte* is a juvenile fantasy.

Bellay, Jerôme (?-); *Le Seigneur des Dos-Pelés* (*The Lord of the Bare-Backs*; Tchou, 1979); *Le Chercheur d'Opale* (*The Seeker of Opals*; JCL, 1983)

Belletto, René (1945-); *Le Temps Mort* (*Dead Time*; MarF 474, 1974); *Les Traîtres Mots ou Sept Aventures* (*Wrong Words, or Seven Adventures*; Flamm., 1976); *Film Noir* (Hac., 1980); *L'Enfer* (*Hell*; Pol., 1985); *Le Revenant* (*The Ghost*; JL 2841, 1990); *La Machine* (Pol, 1990); *Remarques* (*Observations*; Pol, 1990); *Sur la Terre comme au Ciel* (*On Earth as in Heaven*; JL 2943, 1991); *La Vie Rêvée et Autres Nouvelles* (*Dream Life and Other Stories*; JL, 1994); *Régis Mille, l'Éventreur* (*Regis Mille the Ripper*; POL, 1996); *Note:* See Chapter IX. **La Machine** was adapted into an eponymous 1994 film (see Book 1, Chapter I).

Bellevales, Pierre (?-); *Naissance d'un Quatrième Continent* (*Birth of a Fourth Continent*; Fauconnier, 1926)

Bellion, Roger *see* **Rabiniaux, Roger**

Bellot, Andrée (?-); *Une Pluie Horsaine* (*An Horsaine Rain*; Nlle. Pléiade, 1994)

Belmont, Georges (?-); *Le Grand Pressoir* (*The Big Press*; RL, 1957); *Un Homme au Crépuscule* (*A Man in the Twilight*; Julliard, 1966); *Ex* (Den., 1969)

Belvianes, Marcel (?-); *La Farce du Diable et de la Munière* (*The Farce of the Devil and the Muniere*; Eugène Rey, 1927); *Non! Dieu est Allemand* (*No! God Is German*; Cahiers Libres, 1931); *Le Combat Singulier* (*Single Fight*; Émile-Paul, 1932)

Benâtre, Michel *see* **Cap, Jean**

Beneich, Denis (Baldwin-Beneich, Denis; 1953-); *Softwar* (With Thierry **Breton**; RL, 1984); *Fausse Donne* (*Bad Hand*; Balland, 1990); *L'Imposteur* (*The Impostor*; Balland, 1992)

Ben Kemoun, Hubert (?-); *Le Dernier Jour* (*The Last Day*; Nathan, n.d.)

Beno, Jean-Luc (?-); *1990, ou Les Moins de 15 Ans à l'Assaut du Cosmos* (*1990, or the Under-15s at the Assault of the Cosmos*; Boucherit, 1963); *Note:* Juvenile SF. See Chapter IX.

Benoit, François (?-); *Carcasses* (Boréal Jr., 1992); *Note:* French-Canadian writer. Juvenile SF.

Benoit, Jacques (1941-); *Jos Carbone* (Jour, 1967; transl. 1974); *Patience et Firlipon* (Jour, 1970); *Les Princes* (Jour, 1973; transl. as *The Princes*, 1977); *Gisèle et le Serpent* (*Gisele and the Snake*; Libre Expression, 1981); *Rodolphe Stiboustine* (Boréal, 1993); *Note:* French-Canadian writer. *Patience* tells a wonderful love story with futuristic gadgets in a Montréal of tomorrow. *Les Princes* takes place in an imaginary city.

Benoît, Pierre (1886-1962); *L'Atlantide* (AM, 1919; transl. as *The Queen of Atlantis*, 1920); *La Chaussée des Géants* (*The Giants' Path*; AM, 1922); *L'Oubliée* (*The Forgotten Woman*; AM, 1922); *Le Puit de Jacob* (*Jacob's Well*; AM, 1925); *Le Roi Lépreux* (*The Leper King*; AM, 1927); *Axelle* (AM, 1928); *Le Soleil de Minuit* (*The Midnight Sun*; L'Illustration, 1930); *L'Homme qui était trop grand* (*The Man Who Was Too Tall*; MdF, 1936); *Bethsabée* (AM, 1938); *Lunegarde* (*Moonkeep*; AM, 1942); *L'Oiseau des Runes* (*The Rune Bird*; AM, 1947); *Aïno* (AM, 1948); *Les Agriates* (AM, 1950); *La Sainte Vehme* (*The Holy Vehme*; Mame, 1954); *Ville Perdue* (*Lost City*; AM, 1954); *Montsalvat* (AM, 1957); *Note:* See Chapter VI. **L'Atlantide** was adapted into numerous eponymous film and television movies (see Book 1, chapters I and II).

Benoit-Jeannin, Maxime (1946-); *Plagiaire Planant, Plage Hier Planante* (Panique, 1976); *La Terre était ici* (*Earth Was Here*; Kes. I&M 3, 1978); *L'Adieu des Industriels* (*Farewell to the Industrials*; Kes. I&M 8, 1980); *L'Ami des Ambrosiens* (*The Ambrosians' Friend*; OGB 72, 1981); *La Croisière d'Einstein* (*Einstein's Cruise*; with Philippe **Cousin**; Stock, 1983); *Colonel Laurence* (Le Cri, 1992); *Note:* See Chapter IX.

Ber, André (1920-); *Le Mystère des Trois Roches* (*The Mystery of the Three Rocks*; Fidès, 1953); *Le Repaire des Loups Gris* (*The Lair of the Grey Wolves*; Fidès, 1962); *Segoldiah!* (Déom, 1964); *Note:* French-Canadian writer born in France. *Le Mystère* is about strange happenings on a Guadeloupe plantation. In *Segoldiah*, a man is possessed by an alien intelligence.

Béra, Paul (Bérato, Paul; 1915-); *La Cité dans les Glaces* (*The City in the Ice*; as Yves Dermèze; Mickey, 1942); *L'Étreinte de l'Invisible* (*The Hug of the Invisible*; as Yves Dermèze; NEF, 1942; rev. as *Victime de l'Invisible* (*Victim of the Invisible*, Mérimée, 1952); *Les Buveurs d'Océan* (*The Drinkers of Oceans*; as Yves Dermèze; NEF, 1943); *Les Prisonniers de l'Île sans Nom* (*The

Prisoners of the Nameless Island; as Yves Dermèze; Mickey, 1943); *Les Quatre Châteaux* (*The Four Castles*; as Yves Dermèze; Chantal, 1944); *Le Pays sans Soleil* (*The Land Without Sun*; as Yves Dermèze; Coq Hardi, 1948); *Les Pirates du Ciel* (*The Sky Pirates*; as Yves Dermèze; STAEL Junior 44, 1949); *Jim et Sa Dynamite* (*Jim and His Dynamite*; as Yves Dermèze; STAEL Junior 65, 1950); *La Folie Rouge* (*The Red Madness*; as Yves Dermèze; Arabesque, 1954); *Le Titan de l'Espace* (*The Titan of Space*; as Yves Dermèze; Métal 10, 1954); *Via Velpa* (as Yves Dermèze; Métal 16, 1955); *La Ceinture du Robot* (*The Robot's Belt*; 1955); *La Pierre Vivante* (*The Living Stone*; as Yves Dermèze; Fleurus, 1958); *Les Envoyés du Paradis* (*The Envoys of Paradise*; as Yves Dermèze; Elfes, 1963; rev. MOC 1, 1979); *Planète Maudite* (*Accursed Planet*; FNA 423, 1970); *Les Êtres de Lumière* (*The Beings of Light*; FNA 443, 1971); *Terre d'Arriérés* (*Land of the Backwards*; FNA 458, 1971); *Léonox, Monstre des Ténèbres* (*Leonox, Monster of Darkness*; FNAG 207, 1971); *Espace Interdit* (*Forbidden Space*; FNA 498, 1972); *Race de Conquérants* (*Race of Conquerors*; FNA 517, 1972); *Léonox et la Mort* (*Leonox and Death*; FNAG 211, 1972); *Les Mains Sanglantes de Léonox* (*The Bloody Hands of Leonox*; FNAG 225, 1972); *Bulles d'Univers* (*Universe Bubbles*; FNA 557, 1973); *Léonox et le Mage* (*Leonox and the Magician*; FNAG 242, 1973); *Les Crocs d'Acier de Léonox* (*The Steel Jaws of Leonox*; FNAG 249, 1974); *Planète Polluée* (*Polluted Planet*; FNA 623, 1974); *L'Image de l'Autre* (*The Image of the Other*; as Yves Dermèze; MSF 7, 1974); *Le Sharoun de Gallicad* (*The Sharoun of Gallicad*; as Yves Dermèze; Mar. P2000 14, 1974); *Le Vieux et son Implant* (*The Old Man and His Implant*; FNA 657, 1975); *La Nuit est Morte* (*The Night Is Dead*; FNA 710, 1975); *Les Lumières* (*The Lights*; as Yves Dermèze; MSF 38, 1976); *Comme un Liseron* (as *a Clinging Vine*; FNA 741, 1976); *Nuit d'Émeute* (*Riot Night*; FNA 820, 1977); *L'Être Mystérieux* (*The Mysterious Being*; as John Luck; MF 12, 1977); *Jar-Qui-Tue* (*Jar-Who-Kills*; FNA 842, 1978); *L'Ongle de l'Inconnu* (*The Nail of the Unknown*; FNA 856, 1978); *Dieu Ne Veut Pas Mourir* (*God Does Not Want to Die*) (as Martin Slang; MSF 68, 1978); *Ceux d'Ailleurs* (*Those from Beyond*; FNA 900, 1979); *Marée Noire sur Altéa* (*Black Tide on Altea*; FNA 929, 1979); *Les Manipulateurs* (*The Manipulators*; FNA 965, 1980); *La Horde Infâme* (*The Awful Horde*; FNA 981, 1980); *Nous Irons à Kalponéa* (*We Shall Go to Kalponea*; FNA 1009, 1980); *Q.I.* (*IQ*; FNA 1028, 1980); *Changez de Bocal* (*Change of Jars*; FNA 1059, 1981); *L'Ombre du Tueur* (*The Shadow of the Killer*; FNA 1209, 1983); *Note:* See chapters VII, VIII, and IX.

Bérard, Cyprien (?-?); *Lord Ruthwen ou Les Vampires* (*Lord Ruthwen or the Vampires*; 2 vols.; Ladvocat, 1820; rep. UGE, 1981); *Note:* See Chapter IV and also see Charles **Nodier**. This was an unauthorized sequel to Polidori's classic tale, *The Vampyre* (1819).

Berbier, Jean-Pierre (?-); *Le Soleil et la Mort en Face* (*The Sun and Death in My Face*; Swing, 1994); *Note:* See Chapter IX.

Berbiguier de Terre-Neuve du Thym, Alexis-Vincent-Charles (1776-1861); *Les Farfadets, ou Tous les Démons ne sont pas de l'Autre Monde* (*The Goblins, or Not All Demons Come from Another World*; 3 vols.; Berbiguier, 1821); *Note:* See Chapter IV.

Berck, F. (?-); *Un Monstre Va Naître* (*A Monster Shall Be Born*; Monnet Terrific 5, 1974)

Berenboom, Alain (?-); *La Position du Missionnaire Roux* (*The Red Missionary Position*; Le Cri, 1989); *La Table de Riz* (*The Rice Table*; Ramsay, 1992); *La Jerusalem Captive* (*Captive Jerusalem*; Verticales, 1997); *Note:* Belgian writer. See Chapter VIII.

Bérenger, Jeremy (?-); *Allison la Sybilline* (Sol'Air, 1994); *La Rousseur des Bananes à l'Été finissant* (*The Redness of Bananas at the End of Summer*; Sol'Air, 1997) *Note:* See Chapter VIII.

Bergal, Gilles (Gallerne, Gilbert; 1954-); *L'Appel de la Banshee* (*The Call of the Banshee*; F. Valery, 1981); *Créatures des Ténèbres* (*Creatures of Darkness*; Corps 9, 1985); *Cauchemar à Staten Island* (*Nightmares in Staten Island*; FNG 36, 1987); *Amok* (FNG 63, 1988); *Le Clone Triste* (*The Sad Clone*; as Milan; FNA 1616, 1988); *Le Rire du Klone* (*The Klone's Laughter*; as Milan; FNA 1618, 1988); *Camping Sauvage* (*Savage Camping*; FNG 99, 1989); *L'Oublié Éternel* (*The Eternal Forgotten*; as Gilbert Gallerne; Lueurs Mortes, 1994); *Le Fils du Tyrannosaure* (*The Son of the Tyrannosaurus*; as Gilbert Gallerne; FNAV 14, 1995); *Note:* See Chapters VIII and IX.

Bergen, Christian (?-); *Le Robot de Chair* (*The Robot of Flesh*; VF 5, 1953)

Berger, Eugène *see* **Cyril-Berger**

Berger, Jean-Philippe *see* **Bergman, Jean-Christian**

Berger, Yves (1931-); *Le Sud* (*The South*; Cercle du Bibliophile, 1962; transl. as *The Garden*, 1963); *La Pierre et le Saguaro* (*The Stone and the Saguaro*; Grasset, 1990); *L'Attrapeur d'Ombres* (*The Shadows Catcher*; Grasset, 1992); *Immobile dans le Courant du Fleuve* (*Motionless in the River Flow*; Grasset, 1994); *Note:* See Chapter IX.

Bergeron, Alain (1950-); *Un Été de Jessica* (*A Summer of Jessica*; Quinze, 1978); *Le Chant des Hayats* (*The Song of the Hayats*; JP 83, 1992); *L'Ombre dans le Cristal*

(*The Shadow in the Crystal*; JP, 1995); *Corps-Machines et Rêves d'Anges* (*Machine Bodies and Angel Dreams*; Vents d'Ouest, 1997); *Note:* French-Canadian writer born in France. Also see **Eaglenor.**

Bergeron, Bertrand (1948-); *Parcours Improbables* (*Improbable Itinerary*; L'Instant Même, 1986); *Maisons pour Touristes* (*Houses for Tourists*; L'Instant Même, 1988); *Transits* (L'Instant Même, 1990); *Visa pour le Réel* (*Visa for Reality*; L'Instant Même, 1993); *Note:* French-Canadian writer. Collection of short stories.

Bergeron, Thérèse (1951-); *Sika ou la Porte des Cauchemars* (*The Gate of Nightmares*; Éd. du Gaymont, 1996); *Note:* French-Canadian writer. Fantastical novel.

Bergeron-Hogue, Marthe (1902-1980); *Le Défi des Dieux* (*The Challenge of the Gods*; Éd. de l'An 2000, 1972; rev. Naaman, 1977); *Note:* French-Canadian writer. This novel about a futuristic society of godlike immortals was originally published in Haiti.

Bergier, Jacques (1912-1978); *Visa pour Demain* (*Visa for Tomorrow*; Gall., 1954); *Les Dompteurs de Force* (*The Power Tamers*; Del Duca, 1958); *Le Sous-Marin de l'Espace* (With Françoise d'**Eaubonne** & L. **Jean-Charles**) (*The Space Submarine*; Gautier-Languereau, 1959); *Le Matin des Magiciens* (*Morning of the Magicians*; with Louis **Pauwels**; Gall., 1960); *À l'Écoute des Planètes* (*Listening to the Planets*; Fayard, 1963); *Admirations* (Non-Fiction; Christian Bourgois, 1970); *L'Homme Éternel* (*The Eternal Man*; with Louis **Pauwels**; Gall., 1973); *Note:* See chapters VIII and IX. Jacques Bergier was a renowned specialist in science fiction, fantasy, the occult, and secret intelligence. Bergier also co-edited the magazine *Planète.* He was the inspiration for the character of Mik Ezdanitoff in **Tintin**'s *Flight 714* (see Book 1, Chapter V).

Bergman, Jean-Christian (Berger, Jean-Philippe; ?-) *see* **Mantey, Christian**

Berkani-Rohmer, Anissa (?-); *Catacombes* (*Catacombs*; FNFR 14, 1995); *Note:* See Chapter VIII.

Berleux, Jean (Quentin-Bauchard, Maurice; 1881-1916) *see* **Grand-Guignol**

Berlioz, Hector (1803-1869) *see* **Opéra**

Berma *see* **Verteuil, Éric**

Berna, Paul (Sabran, Jean; 1910-); *Nous Irons à Lunaterra*

(*We Shall Go to Lunaterra*; GP, 1954); *La Porte des Étoiles* (*The Gate of Stars*; GP, 1954); *Le Continent du Ciel* (*The Continent of the Sky*; GP, 1955); *Le Jardinier de la Lune* (*The Gardener of the Moon*; GP, 1955); *Tommy, Chien Parlant* (*Tommy the Talking Dog*; GP, 1956); *Le Carrefour de la Pie* (*The Crossroads of the Magpie*; GP, 1957); *Le Kangourou Volant* (*The Flying Kangaroo*; GP, 1957); *Les Pèlerins de Chiberta* (*The Pilgrims of Chiberta*; GP, 1958); *La Grande Alerte* (*The Great Alert*; GP, 1960); *Le Bout du Monde* (*The End of the World*; GP, 1961); *Le Témoignage du Chat Noir* (*The Testimony of the Black Cat*; GP, 1963); *Opération Oiseau Noir* (*Operation Black Bird*; GP, 1970); *Un Pays sans Légende* (*A Country Without Legends*; GP, 1970); *La Piste du Souvenir* (*The Memory Trail*; GP, 1972); *La Dernière Aube* (*The Last Dawn*; GP, 1974); *Rocas d'Esperanza* (GP, 1977); *Millionnaires en Herbe* (*Young Millionnaires*; Hac., 1977); *Le Cheval sans Tête* (*The Headless Horse*; Poche, 1980); Series *Iris & Co.*: *Les Vagabonds du Pacifique* (*The Wanderers of the Pacific*; SdPSF 50, 1973); *La Grande Nuit de Mirabal* (*Mirabal's Great Night*; SdPSF 56, 1973); *Note:* Juvenile SF. See Chapter IX.

Bernac, Jean (?-?) *see* **Grand-Guignol**

Bernadet, Jeanine (1938-); *L'Enfant au Dahu* (*The Dahu Child*; Hac., 1970)

Bernanos, Georges (1888-1948); *Sous le Soleil de Satan* (*Under the Sun of Satan*; Plon, 1926; transl. as *Star of Satan*, 1927); *Note:* See Chapter VI. Adapted into a 1987 film (see Book 1, Chapter I).

Bernanos, Michel (1923-1964); *Les Nuits de Rochemaure* (*The Nights of Rochemaure*; as Michel Talbert; FNAG 100, 1963); *La Grande Bauche* (*The Great Bauche*; as Michel Talbert; FNAG 102, 1963); *Le Mort Veille* (*Deadman's Watch*; as Michel Talbert; FNAG 108, 1964); *Le Murmure des Dieux* (*The Whisper of the Gods*; as Michel Drowin; TR, 1964); *La Montagne Morte de la Vie* (*The Dead Mountain of Life*; Pauvert, 1967; transl. as *The Other Side of the Mountain*, 1968); *Ils Ont Déchiré Son Image* (*They Tore Up His Image*; Pensée U., 1982); *L'Envers de l'Éperon* (*The Other Side of the Spur*; TR, 1983); *La Neige qui Tue* (*The Killing Snow*; Librairie Bleue, 1985); *La Forêt Complice* (*The Forest His Accomplice*; Castor Astral, 1987); *Note:* See Chapter VIII.

Bernanose, Georges-Marie (1898-1974); *Ténèbres* (*Darkness*; La Bruyère, 1946); *La Porte Interdite* (*The Forbidden Door*; Masque 547, 1956); *Note:* See Chapter IX. Also See **Grand-Guignol.**

Bernard, Chris (?-); *Le Grand Maître Nostradamus* (*The Great Master Nostradamus*; Puyméras, C. Bernard, 1985); *Les Incidents de l'Âge d'Argent* (*The Incidents* *of the Silver Age*; Puyméras, C. Bernard, 1986); *Jupitos invente le monde* (*Jupitos Invents the World*; Vaison-la-Romaine, C. Bernard, 1985); *Nostradamus 432* (Puyméras, C. Bernard, 1985); *Respirs* (La Ravoire, Ed. Gap, 1994); *Sur le Chemin avec Nostradamus* (*On the Road with Nostradamus*; Puyméras, C. Bernard, 1985); *Trois Perles d'Âme* (*Three Soul Pearls*; L'Etrave, 1988); *La Maison de M.* (*M's House*; Phénix, n.d.)

Bernard, Evelyne (1948-); *La Vaironne* (Guérin, 1988); *Le Coeur d'une Femme: Parapsychologie* (*The Heart of a Woman*; Estavel, 1989); *Note:* French-Canadian writer.

Bernard, Gabriel (1885-1934); *La Volonté de John Harry Will* (*The Will of John Henry Will*; S&V, 1921); *Satanas* (serialized in 5 issues, Tallandier, 1922); *1. La Comtesse Éléonore* (*Countess Eleonor*); *2. Les Chevaliers de l'Étoile* (*The Knights of the Star*); *3. L'Énigme du Désert* (*The Mystery of the Desert*); *4. La Cité des Prodiges* (*The City of Miracles*); *5. Le Secret de Patrice Oriel* (*Patrice Oriel's Secret*); *Le Secteur Fatal* (*The Deadly Sector; S&V, 1923*); *Le Champion des Deux Mondes* (*The Champion of Two Worlds*; BGA, 1925); *La Croisière de l'Énergique* (*The Cruise of the Energic*; BGA, 1925); *Les Compagnons de la Haine* (*The Companions of Hate*; RMY, 1928); *La Preuve d'Amour* (*The Proof of Love*; serialized in 2 issues, RMY, 1930); *1. Laquelle des deux?* (*Which of the Two?*); *2. Les Trois Rivaux* (*The Three Rivals*); *L'Agent No.12* (BGA, 1930); *Le Château de X* (*The Castle of X*; BGA, 1930); *Les Fantômes de Versailles* (*The Ghosts of Versailles*; BGA, 1930); *Le Secret du Casque* (*The Secret of the Helmet*; BGA, 1930); *Le Comte de Lucernay* (BGA, 1931); *Les Condamnés de Caracas* (*Condemned in Caracas*; BGA, 1931); *Dossiers Secrets* (*Secret Files*; BGA, 1931); *Le Drame du Pars-Calais* (*The Tragedy of the Paris-Calais*; BGA, 1931); *Les Cinq Détectives* (*The Five Detectives*; RMY, 1931); *Le Député de St. Sauveur* (*The Deputy of St.Sauveur*; BGA, 1932); *Note:* See Chapter VII.

Bernard, Guy (?-?) *see* **Grand-Guignol**

Bernard, Jean (1907-); *Le Jour où le Temps s'est arrêté* (*The Day Time Stopped*; Odile Jacob, 1997)

Bernard, Jean-Jacques (1888-1972); *New Chicago* (Europe 139-140, 1957)

Bernard, Octave (?-?) *see* **Grand-Guignol**

Bernard, Pierre (?-); *L'Aluminium* (AM, 1953); *La Faute* (*The Fault*; n.d.)

Bernard, Pierre-Joseph (?-?) *see* **Opéra**

Bernard, Tristan (1866-1947); *Vous m'en direz tant* (*Tell Me About It*; Flamm., 1894); *Note:* Famous playwright.; Also see **Grand-Guignol**.

Bernard-Walker, J. (?-); *La Chute de l'Amérique* (*The Fall of America; LPT, 1916; rev as La Vengeance du Kaiser* (*New York Bombardé*) (*The Kaiser's Revenge* (*The Bombing of New York*, Hac., 1916)

Bernay, Henri (?-); *La Pastille Mystérieuse* (*The Mysterious Pill*; *CRT, 1925); *La Scolopendre* (*The Scolopendrium*; *CRT, 1927); *La Montagne du Silence* (*The Mountain of Silence*; *CRT, 1927); *On a Volé Un Transatlantique* (*They Stole a Transatlantic Ship*; *CRT, 1927); *Le Secret de la Sunbeam Valley* (*The Secret of Sunbeam Valley*; *CRT, 1928); *L'Homme qui Dormit Cent Ans* (*The Man Who Slept for a Hundred Years*; CRT, 1928; transl. 1948); *La Fortune Errante* (*The Wandering Fortune*; *CRT, 1930); *La Terrible Invention* (*The Awful Invention*; *L'Épatant*, 1932); *Les Chasseurs de Papillons* (*The Hunters of Butterfly*; CRT, 1933); *Le Dragon Volant* (*The Flying Dragon*; *CRT, 1933); *L'Armure du Magyar* (*The Magyar's Armor*; *CRT, 1933); *Le Brick en Dérive* (*Ship Adrift*; *CRT, 1934); *L'Embouteillage de St.Nazaire* (*The St.Nazaire Jam*; RJ, 1945); *Le Maître du Capricorn* (*The Master of the Capricorn*; L'Étrave, 1946); *Batailles Navales au Radar* (*Sea Battles with Radar*; RJ, 1947); *Note:* See Chapter VII. * = with René **Pujol** writing as René Pons.

Bernède, Arthur (1871-1937); *Contes à Nicette* (*Tales of Nicette*; Fishbacher, 1892); *Chantecoq, Grand Roman National* (*Chantecoq, Great National Novel*; Tallandier, 1916; rev. 1920); *Judex* (Tallandier, 1917); *La Nouvelle Mission de Judex* (*Judex's New Mission*; Tallandier, 1919); rev. as *Les Nouveaux Exploits de Judex* (*Judex's New Adventures*; Tallandier, 1925); *La Dernière Incarnation de Judex* (*Judex's Last Incarnation*; Tallandier, 1925); *Belphégor* (RMY, 1928); *Poker d'As* (*Royal Flush*; RMY, 1929); *Les Nouveaux Exploits de Chantecoq* (*Chantecoq' New Feats*; Tallandier, 1929); *La Devineresse* (*The Seeress*; Tallandier, 1930); *Le Sorcier de la Reine* (*The Queen's Wizard*; Tallandier, 1930); *Mephisto* (Tallandier, 1931); *La Fille du Diable* (*The Devil's Daughter*; Tallandier, 1932); *Vampiria* (Blanchon, 1932); *L'Homme aux Sortilèges* (*The Man with Spells*; Technique du Livre, 1939); *L'Homme aux Trois Masques* (*The Man with Three Masks*; Tallandier, 1939); *Un Homme de Proie* (*A Man of Prey*; Tallandier, 1939); *Le Capitaine Anthéor* (*Captain Antheor*; Tallandier, 1939); *Note:* See Chapter VI. Bernède also wrote the script for the 1926 serial **Belphégor** (see Book 1, Chapter I) which was remade into a television series in 1965 (see Book 1, Chapter II).

Bernier, Alain *see* **Verteuil, Éric**

Bernier, Jean (1894-1975) *see* **Grand-Guignol**

Bernier, Thomas *see* **Berthos, Jean**

Béroalde de Verville (?-?); *L'Idée de la République* (*The*

Idea of the Republic; 1584); *Discours de Jacophile à Limne* (1605); *Note:* See Chapter II.

Bersianik, Louky (Durand, Lucille; 1930-); *L'Euguélionne* (La Presse, 1976; transl. 1981); *Note:* French-Canadian writer. Feminist and anti-Freudian manifesto.

Berteaux, Eugène (?-?) *see* **Grand-Guignol**

Berthelot, Francis (1946-); *La Lune Noire d'Orion* (*The Black Moon of Orion*; Dim. 41, 1980); *Solstice de Fer* (*Iron Solstice*; Temps Futurs, 1983; rev. FNA 1420, 1986); *Équinoxe de Cendre* (*Ash Equinox;* Temps Futurs, 1983; rev. FNA 1438, 1986); *La Ville au Fond de l'Oeil* (*The City at the Bottom of the Eye*; PdF 429, 1986); *Rivage des Intouchables* (*Beach of the Untouchables*; PdF 507, 1990); *Note:* See chapters VIII and IX.

Berthet, Élie (1815-1891); *Les Catacombes de Paris* (*The Catacombs of Paris*; Grimaux, 1854); *Le Spectre de Châtillon* (*The Ghost of Chatillon*; Bureaux du Siècle, 1858); *La Dryade de Clairefort* (*The Clairefort Dryad*; Dentu, 1875); *Le Monde Inconnu* (*The Unknown World*; serialized in 4 issues, Dentu, 1876; rev. as *Paris Avant l'Histoire* (*Paris Before History*, Boivin, 1885); *1. Un Rêve* (*A Dream*); *2. Les Parisiens à l'Âge de Pierre* (*Parisians in the Stone Age*); *3. La Cité Lacustre* (*The Lake City*); *4. La Fondation de Paris* (*The Foundation of Paris*); *Les Trois Spectres* (*The Three Ghosts*; Degorce-Cadot, 1877); *Les Drames du Cloître* (*The Dramas of the Cloisters*; Plon, 1880); *Les Crimes du Sorcier* (*The Crimes of the Wizard*; Roy, 1880); *Le Martyre de la Boscotte* (*The Martyrdom of Boscotte*; Dentu, 1880); *La Maison du Malheur* (*The House of Unhappiness*; Dentu, 1886); *Note:* See Chapter V.

Berthet, Marguerite (?-); *La Fée aux Oiseaux* (*The Bird Fairy*; Gastein-Serge, 1912); *L'Ascète du Mont Mérou* (*The Ascetic Man of Mount Merou*; Fauconnier, 1929); *Contes de la Tache d'Huile* (*Tales of a Spot of Oil*; Fauconnier, 1938)

Berthiaume, André (1938-); *Contretemps* (*Countertime*; CLF, 1971); *Le Mot pour Vivre* (*A Word InLifewise*; Parallèles, 1978); *Incidents de Frontière* (*BorderIncidents*; Leméac, 1984); *Presqu'Îles dans la Ville* (*Peninsulas in the City*; XYZ, 1991); *Note:* French-Canadian writer. *Contretemps* is a collection of fantastical tales. *Incidents* was awarded the *Grand Prix de la Science-Fiction et du Fantastique Québécois.*

Berthier, Paul (1948-); *Dérive ou La Terre Prochaine* (*Adrift, or the Promised Land*; JCL, 1978); *La Partie d'Échecs* (*The Game of Chess*; JCL, 1981); *Le Voyage du Maître d'Hôtel* (*The Voyage of the Maitre d'*; Den., 1992)

Berthos, Jean (Bernier, Thomas; ?-); *Eutopia* (Le Quotidien, 1944); *Note:* French-Canadian writer. This utopia combines technological inventions and socialism to achieve order, justice, and Christian virtue.

Berthoud, Samuel-Henry (1804-1891); *Chroniques et Traditions Surnaturelles de la Flandres* (*Chronicles and Supernatural Tradition of Flanders*; 3 vols.; Werdet, 1831-34); *Contes Misanthropiques* (*Misanthropic Tales*; Werdet, 1831); *Le Cheveu du Diable* (*The Devil's Hair*; Mame-Delaunay, 1833); *Le Cocher* (*The Coachman*; Werdet, 1835); *Voyage au Ciel* (*Voyage to Heaven*; La Presse, 1840); *Simar le Maudit* (*Simar the Accursed*; Livre des Feuilletons, 1843); *Le Logis du Diable* (*The Devil's Home*; Livre des Feuilletons, 1843); *La Nuit de la Toussaint* (*All Saints' Night*; Livre des Feuilletons, 1843); *L'Anneau de Salomon (Légende Hollandaise)* (*Solomon's Ring (A Dutch Legend)*; Berck, 1850); *Le Dragon Rouge, ou L'Art de Commander au Démon et aux Esprits Infernaux* (*The Red Dragon, or the Art of Commanding the Devil and the Infernal Spirits*; Renault, 1861); *Le Baiser du Diable* (*The Devil's Kiss*; Renault, 1861); *Contes du Docteur Sam* (*Tales of Dr. Sam*; Garnier, 1862); *Aventure des Os d'un Géant, Histoire Familière du Globe Terrestre avant les Hommes* (*Adventures of the Bones of a Giant, Familiar Tale of the Earth Before Men*; Dupray de la Mahérie, 1862); *Contes à Dodo et à Dedele* (*Tales of Dodo and Dedele*; Dupray de la Mahérie, 1863); *L'Homme depuis Cinq Mille Ans* (*Man for Five Thousand Years*; Garnier, 1865); *Les Féeries de la Science* (*The Magics of Science*; Garnier, 1866); *La Cassette des Sept Amis* (*The Chest of the Seven Friends*; Garnier, 1869); *La Veuve du Diable* (*The Devil's Widow*; Boulé, n.d.); *Note:* See chapters IV and V.

Berton, René (1872-1934); *Le Grand Tailhada ou Les Limousins au Front* (*The Great Tailhada, or Limousins at the Front*; Guillemot Lamothe, 1915); *Le Roi du Cuir* (*The Leather King*; AM, 1929); *Note:* Also see **Grand-Guignol**.

Bertot, Gérald *see* **Owen, Thomas**

Bertrand, Aloysius Louis Jacques Napoléon (1807-1841); *Gaspard de la Nuit* (*Gaspar of the Night*; Labite, 1842); *Note:* See Chapter IV.

Bertrand, René (?-); *Les Bateaux Maudits* (*The Accursed Ships*; Ancre de Marine, 1995); *Note:* Novelized tales of real-life "curses."

Bertrand, P. (?-?) *see* **Grand-Guignol**

Bérys, José de (1883-1957) *see* **Grand-Guignol**

Besnard, Paul (?-); *La Pierre de Jade* (*The Jade Stone*; Bibl. Indép. d'Édition, 1907); Note: Collection of stories, including "L'Épouse Invisible" ("The Invisible Bride"), a variation on Wells' *The Invisible Man.*

Bessand-Massenet, Pierre (?-); *Magie Rose* (*Pink Magic*; Plon, 1955)

Besse, Jules *see* **Clavigny, Georges**

Bessette, Camille (1952-); *Le Complice du Retour Impossible* (*The Accomplice of an Impossible Return*; Fides, 1990); *Note:* French-Canadian writer. Catholic SF.

Bessette, Gérard (1920-); *Les Anthropoïdes* (*The Anthropoids*; La Presse, 1977); *Note:* French-Canadian writer. Prehistoric adventures.

Bessière, Henri-Richard *see* **Richard-Bessière**

Bessières, Albert (1877-1953); *L'Agonie de Cosmopolis* (*The Agony of Cosmopolis*; Spes, 1929)

Besson, André (?-) *see* ***Contes et Légendes***

Besson, Jean-Pierre (?-); *Le Monstre de St. Basile* (*The Monster of St. Basile*; Agence Par. de Distrib., 1941); *100.000 Lieues dans la Stratosphère* (*100,000 Leagues in the Stratosphere*; SFEP, 1940); *Note:* See Chapter VII.

Betant, Liliane (?-); *Actos* (Pensée U., 1975); *Note:* Swiss writer.

Béthune, Chevalier de (?-?); *Relation du Monde de Mercure* (*Tale of the World Mercury*; 1750; rev. VI, 1787); *Note:* See Chapter III.

Bettencourt, Pierre (1917-); *Ni Queue Ni Tête* (*Neiher Head Nor Tail*; Bettencourt, n.d.); *La Folie Gagne* (*Madness Is Winning*; Bettencourt, 1950); *L'Oeil Nu* (*The Naked Eye*; Bettencourt, 1950); *Fragments d'Os pour un Squelette* (*Bone Fragments for a Skeleton*; Bettencourt, 1950); *Histoires à Pendre ou à Laisser* (*Stories to Take Or Leave*; Bettencourt, 1951); *Le Jeune Homme Lunaire* (*The Lunatic Young Man*; Bettencourt, 1951); *Non, Vous ne m'aurez pas Vivant* (*No, You Won't Catch Me Alive*; Bettencourt, 1951); *Trois Petits Tours* (*Three Little Turns*; Bettencourt, 1951); *Terentiatus Maurus* (BN, 1951); *Histoires comme il faut* (*Stories as They Are*; Bettencourt, 1955); *Les Plaisirs du Roi* (*The King's Pleasures*; as Jean Sadinet; Los., 1968); *Note:* See Chapter VIII.

Beucler, André (1898-1985); *Le Mauvais Sort* (*The Evil Eye*; Gall., 1928); *Trois Oiseaux* (*Three Birds*; 1957); *Ténèbrus* (*Darkness*; RL, 1968); *Note:* See Chaper VIII.

Bezian, Huguette *see* **Carrière, Huguette**

Beziau, Claude (?-); *Le Mal des Étoiles* (*Star Sickness*; Cercle d'Or, 1972); *Nationale 137* (Cercle d'Or, 1976); *Les Exorcistes Parlent* (*Exorcists Speak*; Cercle d'Or, 1978); *Bons Baisers du Paradis* (*From Paradise with Love*; France-Empire, 1984)

Bezroudnoff, Jean *see* **Basile, Jean**

Bhély-Quénum, Olympe (1928-); *Le Chant du Lac* (*The Song of the Lake*; Présence Africaine, 1965); *Un Piège sans Fin* (*An Endless Trap*; Présence Africaine, 1978); *L'Initié* (*The Initiate*; Présence Africaine, 1979); *Les Appels du Vodou* (*Call of the Voodoo*; L'Harmattan, 1994); *Note:* Benin writer. See Chapter VIII.

Bianchi, Gérard (?-); *Jours de Cendres* (*Ash Days*; Citron Hallucinogène, 1979)

Bibeau, Paul-André (1944-); *Fréquences Interdites / Le Château d'Ombre* (*Forbidden Frequences / the Castle of Shadows*; L'Actuelle, 1975); *Le Fou de Bassan* (*The Madman of Bassan*; Lune Occidentale, 1980); *La Tour Foudroyée* (*The Tower Struck by Lightning*; Parti Pris, 1984); *Figures du Temps* (*Figures of Time*; Triptyque, 1987); *Note:* French-Canadian writer. Collections of fantastical tales.

Bienvaut, Hervé (?-) *see* ***Contes et Légendes***

Bignon, Jean-Paul (Abbé; 1662-1743); *Les Aventures d'Abdalla, Fils d'Hanif* (*The Adventures of Abdallah, Son of Hanif*; Pierre Witte, 1712); *Note:* See Chapter III.

Bigot, Raoul (?-); *Le Fer qui Meurt* (*The Death of Iron*; LPT, 1918); *Nounlegos* (LPT, 1919); *L'Étrange Matière* (*The Strange Matter*; with E. M. **Laumann**; LPT, 1921); *Le Visage dans la Glace* (*The Face in the Ice*; with E. M. **Laumann**; LPT, 1922); *Note:* See Chapter VII.

Billeter, Jean-Bernard (?-); *Les Règles de Quel Jeu?* (*The Rules of What Game?*; Noir, 1978)

Billon, Pierre (1937-); *L'Ogre de Barbarie* (*The Ogre Grinder*; RL, 1972); *L'Enfant du Cinquième Nord* (*The Child of the Fifth North*; Q/A, 1982; rev. Seuil, 1989; transl. as *The Children's Wing*, 1995); *Le Livre de Seul* (*The Book of Alone*; Archambault, 1983); *L'Ultime Alliance* (*The Ultimate Alliance*; Seuil, 1990); *Note:* French-Canadian writer born in Geneva. Both novels became best-sellers. *L'Ultime* is about man's alliance with the collective consciousness of Earth.

Billot, Renée (?-); *Les 777 Pouvoirs* (*The 777 Powers*; Nathan, 1994)

Billotey, Pierre (?-); *Le Pharmacien Spirite* (*The Pharmacist Conjuring Spirits*; Malfère, 1922); *Le Cuistre Ensorcelé* (*The Spellbound Boor*; AM, 1922); *Le Trèfle à Quatre Feuilles* (*The Four-Leaves Clover*; AM, 1926); *Sao-Kéo ou le Bonheur Immobile* (*The Motionless Happiness*; AM, 1930)

Billy, Alain (?-); *Braises d'une Légende* (*Embers of a Legend*; AM, 1981); *La Sarrasine* (AM, 1984); *Pavel de Fol-en-Fleurs* (Temps Parallèle, 1985); *Au Pays des Femmes* (*In the Land of Women*; AM, 1986); *Le Rideau de Glace* (*The Ice Curtain*; FNA 1542, 1987); *L'Orchidée Rouge de Madame Shan* (*Mrs. Shan's Red Orchid*; FNA 1613,

1988); *Maaga-la-Scythe* (FNA 1636, 1988); *Le Souffle de Lune* (*The Moon Breeze*; FNA 1684, 1989); *Les Fruits Sataniques* (*Satan's Fruits*; FNA 1902, 1993); *Le Peintre des Orages* (*The Storm Painter*; FNA 1943, 1994); Parasol 27 (FNA 1952, 1994); *Note:* See Chapter IX.

Billy, André (Le Roy, Edmond; 1882-1971); *La Malabée in Banlieue Sentimentale* (*Sentimental Suburb*; SLF, 1917)

Bilodeau, François (1930-); *La Naissance d'un Prophète* (*Birth of a Prophet*; Courteau, 1987); *Note:* French-Canadian writer. Esoteric SF.

Bilstein, Jacques-Thomas (?-); *L'Oeil du Diable* (*The Devil's Eye*; Dricot, 1984)

Binet, Alfred (?-1911); *Note:* See Chapter VI, **Grand-Guignol**, and André de **Lorde**.

Binet-Valmer (1875-1940); *Le Sphinx de Plâtre* (*The Plaster Sphinx*; MdF, 1900); *Le Plaisir* (*The Pleasure*; Ollendorff, 1912); *L'Enfant qui Meurt* (*The Dying Child*; Flamm., 1921); *La Créature* (Flamm., 1923); *Le Désordre* (*The Disorder*; Flamm., 1923); *Le Sang* (*The Blood*; Flamm., 1924); *Les Exaltées* (*The Exalted Women*; Flamm., 1925); *Les Fantômes* (*The Ghosts*; Fayard, 1926); *Le Village près du Ciel* (*The Village Near the Sky*; Flamm., 1926); *Maîtres du Monde* (*Masters of the World*; Flamm., 1933); *Le Bois qui Parle* (*The Talking Wood*; n.d.); *Une Morte* (*A Dead Woman*; n.d.); *Note:* Also see **Grand-Guignol**.

Bins, Otwell (?-); *Le Revenant des Neiges* (*The Ghost of the Snows*; VLAE, 1928); *Le Trésor du Lagon* (*The Lagoon Treasure*; VLAE, 1929)

Birdchiren, Olivier (?-) *see* **Conrad, Daniel.**

Bisk, Anatole *see* **Bosquet, Alain**

Bissainthe, Emmanuel (1966-); *Cornélius, le Poète Maudit* (*Cornelius, the Accursed Poet*; Z-25, 1992); *Note:* French-Canadian writer.

Bisset, Éric (1965-); *Le Grimoire d'Arkandias* (*The Grimoir of Arkandias*; Magnard, 1997); *Note:* Juvenile fantasy. See Chapter VIII.

Bitter, Maurice (?-); *La Vie en Transit* (*Life in Transit*; Émile-Paul, 1979); *Les Robinsons du Temps* (*The Robinsons of Time*; La Farandole, 1982); *Les Robinsons du Temps dans la Préhistoire* (*The Robinsons of Time in Prehistory*; La Farandole, 1982); *Les Robinsons à la Guerre de Troie* (*The Robinsons at the Trojan War*; Farandole, 1983); *Les Robinsons dans le Pacifique* (*The Robinsons in the Pacific*; Farandole, 1985); *L'Ombre d'un Oiseau* (*The Shadow of a Bird*; 7 Vents, 1990); *Note:* See Chapter IX.

Bival, Roland (?-); *Le Dernier des Aloukous* (*The Last of the Alukus*; Phébus, 1996)

Biver, Camille (?-); *L'An 2000* (*The Year 2000*; Durendal, 1957)

Blais, Ginette (1955-); *Kazar* (Créations Réalisations YAG, 1992); *Note:* French-Canadian writer. SF novel.

Blais, Marie-Claire (1939-); *La Belle Bête* (*The Beautiful Beast*; Flamm., 1959; transl. as *Mad Shadows*, 1960); *Manuscrits de Pauline Archange* (*Ms. Of Pauline Archangel*; Jour, 1968); *Les Nuits de l'Underground* (*Nights in the Underground*; Stanké, 1978); *Visions d'Anna ou Le Vertige* (*Visions of Anna or Vertigo*; Gall., 1982); *Le Sourd dans la Ville* (*A Deafman in the City*; Gall., 1988); *L'Ange de la Solitude* (*The Angel of Loneliness*; Belfond, 1989); *Soifs* (*Thirst*; Boréal, 1995); *Note:* French-Canadian writer. In *La Belle Bête*, evil is a tangible force occupying a phantasmagorical-landscape, not unlike **Benoit**'s *Jos Carbone*.

Blanc, Aimé (?-); *Le Drame de l'An 3000* (*The Drama of Year 3000*; Debresse, 1946); *La Part du Diable* (*The Devil's Share*; Solidarité par le Livre, 1964); *Le Grand Barrage* (*The Big Dam*; Solidarité par le Livre, 1972); *Barbe-Lune* (*Moon-Beard*; Solidarité par le Livre, 1973); *Les Moissons du Rêve* (*Dream Harvest*; Solidarité par le Livre, 1974); *Le Poids d'un Home* (*The Weight of a Man*; Solidarité par le Livre, 1976); *Le Vin Tiré* (*Drawn Wine*; Solidarité par le Livre, 1978); *Chantegrive* (*Thrushsong*; Solidarité par le Livre, 1979); *Note:* See Chapter VII.

Blanc, Bernard (1951-); *Alerte Nos.1-5* (anthology; Kes., 1977-79); *Ciel Lourd, Béton Froid* (*Heavy Sky, Cold Concrete*; anthology; Kes., 1977); *Planète Socialiste* (*Socialist Planet*; anthology/with Michel **Jeury**; Kes., 1977); *Quatre Milliards de Soldats* (*Four Billion Soldiers*; anthology; Kes., 1977); *Les Lolos de Vénus* (*Venus' Tits*; anthology/with Monique **Battestini**; Kes., 1978); *Avenirs en Dérive* (*Futures Adrift*; anthology/with Jean-Pierre **Andrevon**; Kes., 1979); *C'est la Lune Finale* (*It's the Final Moon*; anthology; Encre 5, 1980); *Que Sont les Fantômes Devenus?* (*What Happened to the Ghosts?*; anthology; NéO 12, 1980); *Note:* See Chapter IX. Bernard Blanc was the editor of the science fiction imprint of Kesselring.

Blanc, H.-F. (?-); *Extreme Fiction* (Actes Sud, 1997)

Blanc, Lou *see* **Lecler, Michel**

Blanche, Caroline (1921-); *Des Nouvelles d'Ailleurs* (*News from Beyond*; Magnard, 1970); *La Bouteille Vagabonde* (*The Wandering Bottle*; Magnard, 1975); *Note:* Juveniles.

Blanche, Francis (1921-1974) *see* **Dac, Pierre**

Blanchot, Maurice (1907-); *Aminadab* (Gall., 1942); *Le Très-Haut* (*The Most High*; Gall., 1948); *Le Ressassement Éternel* (*The Eternal Repetition*; Gall., 1951); *Le*

Dernier Homme (*The Last Man*; Gall., 1957); *Note:* See Chapter VIII.

Blandin, André (?-) *see* **Varlet, Théo**

Blanqui, Auguste (1805-1881); *L'Éternité par les Astres* (*Eternity Through the Stars*; Baillère, 1872); *Note:* See Chapter V.

Blanzat, Jean (1906-1977); *Septembre* (*September*; Grasset, 1936); *L'Orage du Matin* (*The Morning Storm*; Grasset, 1942); *La Gartempe* (Gall., 1957); *Le Faussaire* (*The Forger*; Gall., 1964); *L'Iguane* (*The Iguana*; Gall., 1966); *Reflets dans un Ciel d'Or* (*Reflections in a Golden Sky*; Gall., 1973); *Note:* See Chapter VIII.

Blatière, Raoul (1924-); *SOS Cosmos* (Pensée U., 1972)

Blau, Alfred (?-?) *see* **Opéra**

Blau, Édouard (?-?) *see* **Opéra**

Blenod, Pierre *see* **Demousson, Pierre**

Bleunard, André (?-?); *La Babylone Électrique* (*The Electric Babylon*; Quantin, 1888); *La Vengeance d'un Savant* (*A Scientist's Revenge*; Quantin, 1890); *Toujours Plus Petits* (*Always Smaller*; SI, 1893); *Note:* See Chapter V.

Bloch, Jean-Richard (?-); *Le Dernier Empereur* (*The Last Emperor*; Petite Ill., 1927); *Note:* Theater play.

Bloch, Muriel (1954-); *365 Contes pour tous les Âges* (*365 Tales for All Ages*; Hatier, 1986); *365 Porte-Bonheur* (*365 Lucky Charms*; Hatier, 1987)

Block, Aloysius *see* **Brucker, Raymond**

Blonay, Didier (?-); *Le Roi des Femmes* (*The King of Women*; Gall., 1980); *Séducteur en Détresse avec Photo* (*Seducer in Danger with Photo*; Gall., 1982); *L'Enfance aux Trousses* (*Childhood in Pursuit*; Gall., 1983); *L'Hippopotagne* (*The Hippopotain*; Gall., 1984); *Le Grand Nègre Immortel* (*The Great Immortal Negro*; Flamm., 1993)

Blond, Georges (1906-1989); *Les Naufragés de Paris* (*Castaways of Paris*; Livre Contemporain, 1959); *Note:* See Chapter IX.

Blondeaux, Georges *see* **Gébé**

Blondel, Roger *see* **Bruss, B.-R.**

Blondin, Jacques (?-); *Goldorak l'Invincible* (*The Invincible Goldorak*; BV, 1982); *Goldorak contre les Monstres de l'Espace* (*Goldorak vs. The Space Monsters*; BV, 1983); *Note:* Novelizations of a Japanese anime television series.

Blondy, Bille (?-); *Le Signe Inca* (*The Inca Mark*; La Loupe, 1956)

Bloy, Léon (1846-1917); *La Chevalière de la Mort* (*The Ring*

of Death; Siffer, 1891); *Sueurs de Sang* (*Blood Sweat*; Dentu, 1893); *Histoires Désobligeantes* (*Impolite Stories*; Dentu, 1894; rep. MdF, 1945); *Au Seuil de l'Apocalypse* (*On the Eve of the Apocalypse*; MdF, 1916); *Note:* See Chapter IV.

Blum, Jean-Marc (?-); *La Double-Vie de Peters Petersohn* (*The Double Life of Peters Petersohn*; Oeuvres Libres, 1934)

Boca, Gaston (Poncetton, François; 1877-1950); *Le Visage de l'Au-Delà* (*The Face from Beyond*; L'Oeuvre, 1931); *L'Ombre du Jardin* (*The Shadow in the Garden*; Marianne, 1933)

Bodin, Félix (1795-1837); *Le Roman de l'Avenir* (*The Novel of the Future*; Lecointe & Pougin, 1834); *Athènes en 1840* (*Athens in 1840*; Lecointe & Pougin, 1835); *Note:* See Chapter V.

Bodin, Paul (?-); *Les Aventures Extraordinaires de Didier Lambert* (*The Extraordinary Adventures of Didier Lambert*; Seuil, 1945)

Boell, Jacques (?-); *L'Or de la Muzelle* (*The Gold of the Musel*; S&A 9, 1959)

Boëx, Joseph-Henri *see* **Rosny, J. H. Aîné**

Boëx, Séraphin-Justin *see* **Rosny, J. H. Jeune**

Bogdanoff, Igor (1949-) & Grishka (1949-); *Clés pour la Science-Fiction* (*Keys to Science Fiction*; non-fiction; Seghers, 1976); *L'Effet Science-Fiction* (*The Science Fiction Effect*; non-fiction; RL, 1979); *Chroniques du Temps X* (*Chronicles of Time X*; Guépard, 1981); *La Machine Fantôme* (*The Ghost Machine*; JL 1921, 1985); *La Mémoire Double* (*The Double Memory*; Hac., 1989); *Note:* See Chapter IX. I. & G. Bogdanoff were also the hosts of the television series **Temps X** (see Book 1, Chapter II).

Boigey, Maurice (1877-1933); *Les Confidences d'un Tréponème Pâle* (*The Confidences of a Pale Treponeme*; Payot, 1918)

Boileau-Narcejac (Boileau, Pierre (1906-1989) & Narcejac, Thomas (1908-1998)); *Slim et les Soucoupes Volantes* (*Slim and the Flying Saucers*; as John Silver Lee: pseudonym of Serge Laforest, Léo Malet & Thomas Narcejac; Portulan, 1950); *Celle qui n'était plus (Les Diaboliques)* (*She Who Was No More*; Den., 1952); *D'Entre les Morts* (*From the Dead*; Den., 1956); *Le Mauvais Oeil / Au Bois Dormant* (*The Evil Eye / the Sleeping Woods*; Den., 1956); *Les Magiciennes* (*The Magicians*; Den., 1957); *Maléfices* (*Spells*; Den., 1961); *...Et mon Tout est un Homme* (*...And What Is Left Is a Man*; Den., 1965); *Note:* See Chapter VIII. Boileau-Narcejac wrote **Les Diaboliques** and the screenplay adaptation of the classic and much imitated **Les Yeux**

Sans Visage (see Book 1, Chapter I) and *D'Entre les Morts* provided the story for Hitchcock's *Vertigo*. Their story *Au Bois Dormant* was adapted for television (see Book 1, Chapter II). Also see **Grand-Guignol** and Maurice **Leblanc** (*Arsène Lupin*).

Boily, Carol (1942-); *L'Odyssée sur Terre* (*The Odyssey on Earth*; Phidal, 1988); *Note:* French-Canadian writer.

Boireau, Jacques (?-); *Les Années de Sable* (*The Years of Sand*; Encre 2, 1979); *Chroniques Sarrasines* (*Saracen Chronicles*; Atelier du Tayrac, 1988)

Bois, Jules (1871-1943); *L'Éternelle Poupée* (*The Eternal Doll*; Ollendorf, 1894); *Le Satanisme et la Magie* (*Satanism and Magic*; Chailley, 1895); *L'Ève Nouvelle* (*The New Eve*; Chailley, 1896); *Le Mystère et la Volupté* (*The Mystery and the Voluptuousness*; Ollendorf, 1901); *L'Au-Delà et les Forces Inconnues* (*Beyond and Unknown Forces*; Ollendorf, 1902); *Le Monde Invisible* (*The Invisible World*; Flamm., 1902); *Le Miracle Moderne* (*The Modern Miracle*; Ollendorff, 1907); *Le Vaisseau des Caresses* (*Ship of Caresses*; Fasquelle, 1908); *Le Couple Futur* (*The Future Couple*; Annales Polit. & Litt., 1912); *Note:* Most titles are esoteric essays about metaphysics, magics, etc. See Chapter IV.

Boisjoli, Charlotte (1923-); *13, Rue de Buci* (XYZ, 1989); *Note:* French-Canadian writer. Detective story starring Commissioner Leroy, with fantastical elements.

Boissier, Raymond (?-?) *see* **Grand-Guignol**

Boisson, Marius (1881-); *Le Tour du Monde en Aéroplane* (*Around the World in an Airplane*; Guyot, 1910); *L'Ombre Noire* (*The Black Shadow*; Petits Chefs d'Oeuvre, 1918)

Boissy, Philippe de (?-); *Contes Tristes* (*Sad Tales*; Imprim. Mod. Dreux, 1961); *Balladoèmes... (CRNI, n.d.; Le Temps de Sourire... (A Time to Smile...; CRNI, n.d.; Le Vague à l'Oeil* (*The Eye Out of Focus*; CCL, 1986); *Nivéales* (ULQ Motus, 1988); *Le Lapin Montre les Dents* (*The Rabbit Shows Its Teeth*; Aurore, Futurs, 1988)

Boisvert, Claude (1945-); *Parendoxe* (Asticou, 1978); *Tranches de Néant* (*Slices of Nothingness*; Biocreux, 1980); *Rocamadour/Diogène* (Asticou, 1985); *Le Relais Abitibien* (*The Abitibian Relay*; round-robin novel by C. **Boisvert**, D. **Chabot**, J. Ferguson, R. Godard, M. Lemire & D. St-Germain; Meera, 1987); *Symphonie pour une Main* (*Symphony for One Hand*; Meera, 1987); *Note:* French-Canadian writer. Collections of short stories.

Boisvert, France (1959-); *Les Samourailles* (Hexagone, 1987); *Note:* French-Canadian writer. Nuclear-winter novel.

Boisyvon, Lucien (1886-1967); *Les Repères de l'Île Azurine* (*The Lair of Azurine Island*; with **Dorsenne**; Crès, 1921)

Boisyvon, Y. (?-) & J. (?-); *Au Pays du Fantastique* (*In the Land of the Fantastical*; Janicot, 1946)

Boivin, Aurélien (1945-); *Le Conte Fantastique Québécois au 19ème Siècle* (*Fantastical Tales from Quebec in the 19th Century*; anthology; Fides, 1987; rev. 1997); *Bibliographie Analytique de la Science-Fiction et du-Fantastique Québécois: 1960-1985* (Nuit Blanche, 1992); *Note:* French-Canadian anthology.

Bolduc, Claude (1960-); *Visages de l'Après-Vie* (*Faces of the Afterlife*; L'A Venir, 1992); *Sourires* (*Smiles*; anthology; L'A Venir, 1994); *Dans la Maison de Müller* (*In Muller's House*; JP, 1995); *La Maison Douleur et Autres Histoires de Peur* (*The House of Pain and Other Tales of Fear*; anthology; Vents d'Ouest, 1996); *La Clairière Bouchard* (*The Bouchard Clearing*; Vents d'Ouest, 1996); *Le Maître des Goules* (*The Ghoul Master*; Vents d'Ouest, 1997); *Note:* French-Canadian writer. *Visages* is a collection of fantastical tales.

Bolloré, Gwen-Aël (?-); *Moïra la Naufrageuse* (*Moira the Shipwrecker*; TR, 1958); *Contes Fiction* (*Fictional Tales*; Scorpion, 1961)

Bommart, Jean (1894-1979); *Le Revenant* (*The Ghost*; Lemerre, 1932); *Sourcils Joints* (*Frowning*; Lemerre, 1932); *U-31: Le Sang Neuf* (*The New Blood*; Lemerre, 1933); *Hélène et le Poisson Chinois* (*Helen and the Chinese Fish*; Libr. Champs-Élysées, 1938); *La Dame de Valparaiso* (*The Lady from Valparaiso*; Libr. Champs-Élysées, 1940); *L'Épouvantable Nuit* (*The Dreadful Night*; Libr. Champs-Élysées, 1940); *Aux Mains des Invisibles* (*In the Hands of the Invisibles*; Colbert, 1941); *Je Reviens De...* (*I Come Back From...*; as Kemmel; FNA 84, 1957); *Au Bout du Ciel* (*At the End of the Sky*; as Kemmel; FNA 193, 1962); *Bataille pour Arkhangelsk* (*Battle for Arkhangelsk*; LdP, 1970); *Le Poisson Chinois a tué Hitler* (*The Chinese Fish Killed Hitler*; LdP, 1972); *Le Poisson Chinois à Cuba* (*The Chinese Fish in Cuba*; LdP, 1973); *Le Poisson Chinois à Téhéran* (*The Chinese Fish in Tehran*; LdP, 1974); *Le Poisson Chinois et l'Homme Sans Nom* (*The Chinese Fish and the Man with No Name*; LdP, 1974); *Monsieur Scrupule, Gangster* (*Mr. Scruples, Gangster*; LdP, 1975); *Note:* See Chapter IX.

Bon, Frédéric (?-); *Si Mai Avait Gagné* (*If May Had Won*; with Michel-Antoine **Burnier**; Pauvert, 1968); *Note:* Political satire based on the May 1968 events in France.

Bonaventure, Michel (?-) *see* ***Contes et Légendes***

Bonaventure des Périers (1498-1540); *Cymbalum Mundi* (B. Bonnyn, 1537); *Note:* See Chapter II.

Boncoeur, Jean-Louis (?-); *Le Village aux Sortilèges* (*The Village of Spells*; Fayard, 1980)

Bonelli, André-Jean (Balbi, André-Jean; 1933-); *Loona* (Hélios, 1974; rev. Triangle 20, 1977); *Le Village au Bout du Chemin* (*The Village at the End of the Road*; Humbert, 1976); *Un Pont d'Érable* (*A Maple Bridge*; Pensée U., 1987); *Note:* French-Canadian writer. *Loona* is an anti–pollution novel sub-titled "When the Sky Used to Be Blue."

Bonifacy, Pierre (?-); *Voyage au Pays de la Bonté* (*Journey to the Land of Goodness*; PJ Oswald, 1972); *La Montagne de la Reine Noire* (*The Mountain of the Black Queen*; Bonifacy, 1981); *Pré-Histoire* (*Pre-History*; Bonifacy, 1983); *Les Vingt-Deux Portes du Château de l'Émeraude* (*The 22 Gates of Emerald Castle*; Cahiers Bleus, 1991); *Les Larmes de l'Aurore / Tombeaux pour Neuf Étoiles* (*The Tears of Dawn / a Tomb for Nine Stars*; Libr. Bleue, 1995); *Note:* Also see **Opéra**.

Bonis-Charancle, Marc (?-?) *see* **Grand-Guignol**.

Bonnafé, Claire (?-); *Le Bruit de la Mer* (*The Sound of the Sea*; Balland, 1978); *Le Guetteur Invisible* (*The Invisible Watcher*; Balland, 1990); *Une Lumière dans l'Île* (*A Light on the Island*; Seuil, 1997); *Note:* See Chapter VIII.

Bonnard, Arthur de *see* **Gallus**

Bonneau, Albert (1898-1967); *La Cité sans Soleil* (*The City Without Sun*; BGA, 1927); *Les Samourais du Soleil Pourpre* (*The Samurais of the Purple Sun*; serialized in 6 vols., VLAE, 1928-31); *1. Les Samourais du Soleil Pourpre* (*The Samurais of the Purple Sun*; VLAE, 1928); *2. Les Mystères de Chinatown* (*The Mysteries of Chinatown*; VLAE, 1928); *3. Les Damnés de Sakhaline* (*The Damned of Sakhalin*; VLAE, 1928); *4. La Jonque aux Cercueils* (*The Junk of the Coffins*; VLAE, 1931); *5. Le Trésor du Shogun* (*The Treasure of the Shogun*; VLAE, 1931); *6. La Reine du Hara-Kiri* (*The Queen of Hara-Kiri*; VLAE, 1931); *Le Désert aux Cent Nuages* (*The Desert with a Hundred Clouds*; Ren. du Livre, 1933); *La Maison du Cauchemar* (*The Nightmare House*; Ren. du Livre, 1933); *Le Claim Hanté* (*The Haunted Claim*; as Maurice de Moulins; VLAE, 1937); *Le Complot des Météores* (*The Meteor Plot*; as Maurice de Moulins; VLAE, 1937); *Le Convoi Perdu* (*The Lost Convoy*; VLAE, 1937); *Le Diable de Mallicob* (*The Devil of Mallicob*; as Maurice de Moulins; VLAE, 1937); *La Case aux Têtes Coupées* (*The Hut with Decapitated Heads*; as Jean Voussac; VA, 1937); *Le Lac sans Fond* (*The Bottomless Lake*; as Jean Voussac; VA, 1937); *Les Gangsters des Tropiques* (*The Gangsters from the Tropics*; VLAE, 1938); *Le Centaure de Sierra Blanca* (*The Centaur of Sierra Blanca*; VA, 1938); *La Dette de l'Homme Rouge* (*The Red Man's Debt*; VA, 1938); *Le Volcan du Mortel Oubli* (*The Volcano of Deadly Oblivion*; as Maurice de Moulins; VLAE, 1939); *Le Cargo sans Âmes* (*The Soulless Cargo*; as Maurice de Moulins; VLAE, 1939); *Les Fauves à Face Humaine* (*The Beasts with Human Faces*; as Jean Voussac; VA, 1940); *Nakimbo le Maudit* (*Nakimbo the Accursed*; Tallandier, 1941); *La Nuit des Neuf Errants* (*The Night of the Nine Wanderers*; Tallandier, 1942).

Bonnefoy, René *see* **Bruss, B.-R.**

Bonnefoy, René (?-); *Bacchus Roi* (*King Bacchus*; NSE, 1930); *La Plaque Tournate* (*The Rotating Plate*; NSE, 1931); *La Roche Noire* (*The Black Rock*; NSE, 1931)

Bonnerive, Georges de *see* **Lys, Georges de**

Bonnéry, Jean (?-); *L'Égorgeur de Femmes* (*The Women's Ripper*; Inédits Populaires, 1925); *Les Mains Sanglantes* (*The Bloody Hands*; Inédits Populaires, 1926); *1 = 2 = 3* (Férenczi, 1927); *Le Visage de Lumière* (*The Face of Light*; Férenczi, 1927); *La Ville Invisible* (*The Invisible City*; VA, 1933); *Les Morts qui Tuent* (*The Dead Who Kill*; La Voûte, 1997); *X, le Coupeur de Mains* (*X, the Cutter of Hands*; La Voûte, 1997); *Note:* See Chaper VII.

Bonnet, François (?-); *La Montagne de Beurre* (*The Mountain of Butter*; Zoe, 1980)

Bonvalot (?-?); *Les Enfers en Révolution* (*Revolution in Hell*; MdF, 1831)

Bonvicini, H. (?-); *Suramanath ou La 1000ème Femme* (*The 1000th Woman*; Pensée U., 1976); *Note:* Tale of an underground superior civilization.

Bonzom, Louis (?-); *Les Monstres aux Grandes Oreilles* (*The Monsters with Big Ears*; PRA, 1937); *La Nuit du Diable* (*The Night of the Devil*; Férenczi, 1937)

Bonzon, Paul-Jacques (1908-1978); *Le Viking au Bracelet d'Argent* (*The Viking with a Silver Bracelet*; GP, 1956); *Le Voyageur sans Visage* (*The Faceless Traveller*; Fleurus, 1958); *La Princesse sans Nom* (*The Nameless Princess*; Hac., 1958); *Contes de l'Hiver* (*Winter Tales*; Bias, 1960); *Le Bâteau Fantôme* (*The Ghost Ship*; Hac., 1970); *Note:* Juveniles. See Chapter IX.

Boo-Silhen, Henri *see* **Féval, Paul (Fils)**

Bopp, Léon (1896-1977); *Jacques Arnaut et la Somme Romanesque* (*Jacques Arnaut and the Sum of His Novels*; Gall., 1933); *Drôle de Monde, Contes Drôles et Irritants* (*Funny World, Funny and Irritating Tales*; Gall., 1940); *Liaisons du Monde* (*World Relations*; 4 vols.; Gall., 1938-44); *Note:* Swiss writer. See Chapter VII.

Bor, Karol *see* **Fast, Jan de**

Bordage, Pierre (1955-); *Les Guerriers du Silence* (*The Warriors of Silence*; Atalante, 1993); *Terra Mater* (Atalante, 1994); *La Citadelle Hypénéros* (Atalante, 1995); *Wang 1: Les Portes d'Occident* (*The Western Gates*; Atalante, 1996); *Wang 2: Les Aigles d'Orient* (*The Eastern Eagles*; Atalante, 1997); Series *Rohel Le Conquérant* (*Rohel the Conqueror*): A. Cycle de Dame Asmine d'Alba: *1. Le Chêne Vénérable* (*The Venerable Oak*; Vaug., 1992); *2. Les Maîtres Sonneurs* (*The Ring Masters*; Vaug., 1993); *3. Le Monde des Franges* (*The Edge World*; Vaug., 1993); *4. Lune Noire* (*Black Moon*; Vaug., 1994); *5. Asmine d'Alba* (Vaug., 1994); b. Cycle de Lucifal: *6. Les Anges de Fer* (*The Iron Angels*; Vaug., 1995); *7. Le Grand Fleuve-Temps* (*The Great River of Time*; Vaug., 1995); *8. L'Enfant à la Main d'Homme* (*The Child with a Man's Hand*; Vaug., 1995); *9. Les Portes de Babûlon* (*The Gates of Babulon*; Vaug., 1995); *10. Lucifal* (Vaug., 1996); c. Cycle de Saphyr: *11. Terre Intérieure* (*Inner Earth*; Vaug., 1996); *12. Les Feux de Tarphagène* (*The Fires of Tarphagene*; Vaug., 1996); *13. Le Coeur du Vent* (*The Heart of the Wind*; Vaug., 1997); *14. Saphyr d'Antiter* (Vaug., 1997); *Note:* See chapters VIII and IX.

Bordes, François *see* **Carsac, Francis**

Bordonove, Georges (1920-); *Les Quatre Cavaliers* (*The Four Horsemen*; Julliard, 1962); *Les Atlantes* (*The Atlanteans*; RL, 1965)

Borel, Pétrus (Borel d'Hauterive, Joseph-Pierre; 1809-1859); *Champavert, Contes Immoraux* (*Immoral Tales*; Renduel, 1833); *Madame Putiphar* (wri. 1833; pub. Ollivier, 1839); *Le Fou du Roi de Suède* (*The King of Sweden's Jester*; n.d.); *Note:* See Chapter IV.

Bornert, Lucien (?-); *La Femme Étranglée* (*The Strangled Woman*; Technique du Livre, 1939); *Le Péril Vient du Ciel* (*The Dangers Comes from the Sky*; Trotteur SF 4, 1953); *Robots Sous-Marins* (*Underwater Robots*; Trotteur SF 5, 1953); *Note:* See Chaper IX.

Boron, Robert de (12th-13th Century); *Histoire du Saint-Graal* (*The Story of the Holy Grail*; 1215); *Histoire de Merlin* (*The Story of Merlin*; 1220); *Le Livre de Lancelot du Lac* (*The Book of Lancelot of the Lake*; 1225); *La Quête du Saint-Graal* (*The Quest for the Holy Grail*; 1225-30); *La Mort du Roi Arthur* (*The Death of King Arthur*; 1230-35); *Note:* See Chapter I.

Borrelli, Paul (1959-); *L'Ombre du Chat* (*The Shadow of the Cat*; L'Atalante, 1994); *Désordres* (*Disorders*; Atalante, 1997)

Bosch, Roger-Victor (?-); *La Comète Diabolique* (*The Diabolical Comet*; Promo Édition, 1970)

Bosco, Henri (1888-1976); *Mon Compagnon de Songes* (*My Dream Companion*; Gall., 1968); *Note:* Mainstream writer known for his novels about Provence.

Bosquet, Alain (Bisk, Anatole; 1912-); *À la Mémoire de ma Planète* (*In the Memory of My Planet*; Sagittaire, 1948); *La Grande Éclipse* (*The Great Eclipse*; Sagittaire, 1952); *Ni Singe, ni Dieu* (*Neither Ape Nor God*; Sagittaire, 1953); *Quel Royaume Oublié?* (*What Forgotten Kingdom?*; MdF, 1955); *Le Mécréant* (*The Miscreant*; TR, 1960); *Un Besoin de Malheur* (*A Need for Unhappiness*; Grasset, 1963); *Les Petites Éternités* (*The Small Eternities*; Grasset, 1964); *Les Tigres de Papier* (*The Paper Tigers*; Grasset, 1968); *L'Amour à Deux Têtes* (*Two-Headed Love*; Grasset, 1970)

Bosquet, Luce (?-) *see* **Contes et Légendes**

Bosschère, Jean de (1878-1953); *Ulysse bâtit son Lit* (*Ulysses Makes His Bed*; Fourcade, 1929); *Satan l'Obscur* (*Satan the Obscure*; 1933); *Le Dieu d'Or* (*The Golden God*; Nlles. Ed. Europ., 1936); *Lumière sur l'Obscur* (*Light Onto the Obscure*; Den., 1937); *L'Obscur à Paris* (*The Obscure in Paris*; Den., 1937); *Contes de la Neige et de la Nuit* (*Tales of Snow and Night*; Amitié par le Livre, 1954); *Note:* Belgian poet, novelist, and book illustrator. See Chapter VI.

Bossus, Francis (1931-); *Quand la Mort est au Bout* (*When Death Is at the End*; Tisseyre, 1992); *Note:* French-Canadian writer. Collection of fantastical tales.

Botto, Ernest *see* **Ossau, Jean d'**

Bouchacourt, J.-L. *see* **Perdhubert, Eugène**

Bouchard, Camille (1955-); *Les Griffes de l'Empire* (*The Claws of the Empire*; CLF, 1986); *L'Empire Chagrin* (*The Sorrow Empire*; Héritage, 1991); *Absence* (Héritage, 1996); *Les Démons de Babylone* (*The Demons of Babylon*; Héritage, 1996); *Note:* French-Canadian writer. in the far future of Les Griffes, animals rule over men. L'Empire takes place several centuries later in the same universe.

Bouchard, Claude (1942-); *La Mort Après la Mort* (*Death After Death*; Quinze, 1980); *Note:* French-Canadian writer. Near-death experience.

Bouchard, Guy (1942-); *Vénus via Atlantide* (Fides, 1960); *L'Utopie Aujourd'Hui* (*Utopia Today*; Essay; Presses Université Montréal, 1985); *Les Gélules Utopiques* (*The Utopian Capsules*; AMAM 2, 1988); *Les 42,210 Univers de la Science-Fiction* (Passeur, 1993); *Note:* French-Canadian writer. In *Les Gélules*, a scientist creates a race of telepaths.

Bouchard, Marjolaine (1958-); *Entre l'Arbre et le Roc* (*Between the Rock and the Tree*; JCL, 1997); *Note:* French-Canadian writer.

Bouchard, Nicolas (?-); *Terminus Fomalhaut* (Encrage/Destination Crépuscule, 1997); *Note:* See Chapter IX.

Boucher, Denis (1940-); *Pionniers de la Baie James* (*Pioneers of James Bay*; JP 13, 1973); *Note:* French-Canadian writer. Science fiction.

Boucher, Jean-Pierre (1944-); *La Vie n'est pas une Sinécure* (*Life Is Not a Bed of Roses*; Boréal Jr., 1995); *Note:* French-Canadian writer. Juvenile fantasy.

Boucher de Crèvecoeur de Perthes, Jacques (1788-1868); *Nouvelles* (*Short Stories*; Treuttel & Würz, 1832); *Note:* See chapters IV and V.

Boucher-Mativat, Marie-Andrée (1945-); *Ram, le Robot* (*Ram the Robot*; with Daniel **Mativat**; Héritage, 1984); *La Clé Mystérieuse* (*The Mysterious Key*; Tisseyre, 1989); *Le Fantôme du Rocher* (*The Ghost of the Rock*; with Daniel **Mativat**; La Salle, 1992); *Anatole le Vampire* (*The Vampire Anatole*; HMH, 1996); *Voyageur malgré lui* (*Traveller in Spite of Himself*; Tisseyre, 1996); *Note:* French-Canadian writer. Children's fantasies.

Bouchery, Émile (Froulay (Abbé); ?-?); *Les Petits-Neveux de Gulliver* (*Gulliver's Grand-Nephews*; Libr. Pittoresque de la Jeunesse, 1845)

Bouchet, Paul (?-); *Les Derniers Atlantes* (*The Last Atlanteans*; Colbert, 1943); *Hu Gadarn, le Premier Gaulois* (*Hu Gadarn, the First Gaul*; Fulgur, 1956); *La Princesse de Vix et Hu, Empereur des Gaules* (*The Princess of Vix and Hu, Emperor of Gaul*; Amitié par le Livre, 1968); *Science et Philosophie des Druides* (*Science and Philosophy of the Druids*; Amitié par le Livre, 1968)

Boudet, Robert (?-); *Le Temps Vol'Heures* (*Time Hour Stealer*; Magnard, 1986); *Objectif Terre!* (*Target: Earth!*; Milan, 1990); *Les Mille Vies de Léon Camet* (*The Thousand Lives of Leon Camet*; Milan, 1992); *Le Royaume des Ogres* (*The Kingdom of Ogres*; Nathan, 1993); *Ralentir, Collège Hanté!* (*Slow Down! Haunted School*; Casterman, 1994); *La Ballade d'Aïcha* (*The Ballad of Aicha*; Nathan, 1996); *L'Extraordinaire Aventure de Monsieur Potiron* (*The Extraordinary Adventure of Mr. Pumpkin*; Nathan, 1996); *Le Roman de Renart* (*The Novel of Renart*; École des Loisirs, 1997)

Boudjedra, Rachid (1941-); *L'Escargot Entêté* (*The Stubborn Snail*; Den., 1982)

Boudot, Pierre (?-); *La Louve* (*The She-Wolf*; J-M. Laffont, 1981)

Boué, Maurice (?-); *Le Tour du Monde en... Un Jour* (*Around the World in One Day*; with Édouard **Aujay**; BGA, 1933); *Vendetta* (Dupuis, 1936); *Les Trésors du Pirate* (*The Pirate's Treasure*; Dupuis, 1938); *Le Gouffre d'Or* (*The Golden Abyss*; with Édouard **Aujay**; Dupuis, 1938); *Le Secret du Fétiche* (*The Secret of the Idol*; with Édouard **Aujay**; Dupuis, 1939); *Le Mystère de Kervos* (*The Mystery of Kervos*; Dupuis, 1939); *Le Secret de la Dame Noire* (*The Secret of the Black Lady*; Ed. Nouvelles, 1944); *Note:* See Chapter VII.

Bougeant, Guillaume-Hyacinthe (1690-1743); *Voyage Merveilleux du Prince Fan-Féredin dans la Romancie contenant plusieurs Observations Historiques, Géographiques, Physiques, Critiques et Morales* (*Marvellous Voyage of Prince Fan-Feredin in Romancia Containing Several Historical, Georaphical, Physical, Critical, and Moral Observations*; 1735; rep. VI, 1788)

Bouguennec, Rémy (?-); *Entrez sans Frapper* (*Come in Without Knocking*; anthology; Diz. du Fant., 1980)

Bouhier, F. (?-); *Ruptures* (St. Germain, 1984); *Jeu d'Enfant* (*Child's Play*; CRNI, 1994); *Note:* Juvenile fantasy.

Bouillon, Bernard (?-); *La Planète dans le Bocal / Les Bruits Qui Courent* (*The Planet in a Bowl / Running Noises*; Pensée U., 1977); *Note:* Humorous SF.

Boukay, Maurice (?-?) *see* **Opéra**

Boulenger, Jacques (1879-1944); *Les Romans de la Table Ronde* (*Novels of the Round Table*; Plon, 1924); *Contes de ma Cuisinière* (*My Cook's Tales*; Gall., 1935); *Adam ou Eve* (*Adam Or Eve*; Gall., 1937); *L'Histoire de Merlin l'Enchanteur—Les Enfances de Lancelot* (*The Story of Merlin the Enchanter—the Childhood of Lancelot*; Plon, 1939); *Nostradamus et ses Prophéties* (*Nostradamus and His Prophecies*; Colbert, 1943); *Les Amours de Lancelot du Lac* (*The Loves of Lancelot*; Club Libr. Édit. Ass., 1958); *La Légende du Roi Arthur* (*The Legend of King Arthur*; Terre de Brume, 1993); *Note:* See Chapter I.

Boulle, Pierre (1912-1994); *Les Contes de l'Absurde* (*Absurd Tales*; Julliard, 1953); *E = MC²* (Julliard, 1957; transl. as *Time Out of Mind*, 1966); *La Planète des Singes* (Julliard, 1963; transl. as *Planet of the Apes*, 1963); *Le Jardin de Kanashima* (*Kanashima's Garden*; Julliard, 1964; transl. as *Garden on the Moon*, 1965); *Histoires Charitables* (*Charitable Tales*; Julliard, 1965); *Quia Absurdum* (Julliard, 1970); *Les Jeux de l'Esprit* (*Mind Games*; Julliard, 1971); *Les Oreilles de la Jungle* (*The Ears of the Jungle*; Flamm., 1972); *Les Vertus de l'Enfer* (*The Virtues of Hell*; Flamm., 1974); *Histoires Perfides* (*Perfidious Tales*; Flamm., 1976); *Le Bon Léviathan* (*The Good Leviathan*; Julliard, 1978); *L'Energie du Désespoir* (*The Energy of Despair*; Julliard, 1981); *Miroitements* (*Mirror Images*; Flamm., 1982); *À Nous Deux, Satan* (*Fight with Satan*; Julliard, 1992); *Note:* See Chapter IX. La Planète des Singes was adapted into a classic 1968 film. Boulle is also the author of the non-genre *The Bridge on the River Kwai*.

Boullet, Jean (?-); *D'Icare aux Soucoupes Volantes* (*From Icarus to the Flying Saucers*; Casablanca, 1953); *La*

Belle et la Bête (*Beauty and the Beast*; Los., 1958); *Dix Ans d'Épouvante et de Fantastique* (*Ten Years of Horror and Fantasy*; La Méthode, 1962)

Bouquet, Jean-Louis (1898-1978); *Le Sorcier Mystérieux* (*The Mysterious Wizard*; with André **Dollé**; Ren. du Livre, 1921); *La Main Invisible* (*The Invisible Hand*; with André **Dollé**; Ren. du Livre, 1921); *Le Maître des Ténèbres* (*The Master of Darkness*; with André **Dollé**; Ren. du Livre, 1921); *La Cité Foudroyée* (*The City Struck by Lightning*; Pathé Journal, 1923); *Le Diable dans la Ville* (*The Devil in the City*; Pathé Journal, 1924); *La Porte aux Étoiles* (*The Stargate*; as Jean d'Ansennes; Libr. Champs-Élysées, 1941); Series *Doum* (as Nevers-Severin; Janicot, 1943; rev. as *L'Ombre du Vampire* (*The Shadow of the Vampire*), MarF 1059, and *Irène, Fille Fauve* (*Irene, the Wild Girl*, MarF 1060, 1978): *1. L'Homme aux Fétiches* (*The Man with Idols*); *2. Le Caveau des Angoisses* (*The Cave of Terrors*); *3. La Reine des Ténèbres* (*The Queen of Darkness*); *4. Le Fantôme du Parc Monceau* (*The Ghost of Parc Monceau*); *5. Irène, Fille Fauve* (*Irene, the Wild Girl*); Series *Les Mystères de Montmartre* (*The Mysteries of Montmartre*; as Nevers-Severin; Janicot, 1944): *1. Les Mystères de Montmartre* (*The Mysteries of Montmartre*); *2. Les Aventuriers de la Butte* (*The Adventurers of the Mount*); *3. L'Énigme du Bal Tabarin* (*The Mystery of the Tabarin Ball*); *4. Du Sang Place Pigalle* (*Blood on Place Pigalle*); *5. 20 Hommes aux Abois* (*20 Hunted Men*); Series *L'Homme des Antipodes* (*The Man from the Other Side of the World*; as Nevers-Severin; Janicot, 1944; rev. as *Le Dock des Suicidés* (*The Dock of the Suicides*, MarF 1061, 1979); *1. Drame au Bout du Monde* (*Tragedy at the End of the World*); *2. Le Dock des Suicidés* (*The Dock of the Suicides*); *3. L'Inconnue d'Anvers* (*The Unknown Woman of Antwerp*); *4. Crime au Sérail* (*Crime in the Seraglio*); *5. La Couronne Sanglante* (*The Bloody Crown*); *L'Affaire des Squelettes* (*The Skeleton Case*; as Nevers-Severin; Janicot, 1945); *La Vengeance de l'Araignée* (*The Revenge of the Spider*; as Nevers-Severin; Janicot, 1945); *Le Visage de Feu* (*The Face of Fire*; Robert Marin, 1951; rev. MarF 640, 1978); *Aux Portes des Ténèbres* (*At the Gates of Darkness;* PdF 11, 1956; rev. as *Les Filles de la Nuit* (*The Daughters of Night*, MarF 641, 1978); *Mondes Noirs* (*Dark Worlds*; UGE, 1980); *Note:* See Chapter VIII. Bouquet wrote the 1924 Luitz-Morat film **La Cité Foudroyée** and *Le Diable dans la Ville* (*The Devil in the City*; also 1924) for Germaine **Dulac** (see Book 1, Chapter I). His short story "**Alouqa**" (incl. in *Le Visage de Feu*) was adapted into a 1975 telefilm (see Book 1, Chapter II). Another, "**Rendez-Vous avec le Démon**," was turned into a radio play (see Book 1, Chapter III).

Bouquet, Marcel (?-); *Chant d'Élyssa, Princesse de Tyr* (*The Song of Elyssa, Princess of Tyre*; L. Poyet, 1949);

Et Ce Fut la Guerre Atomique (*And It Was Atomic War*; Métal 2, 1954)

Bourbon, Prince Louis de (?-); *D'Amra sur Azulba* (L. Saussac-Gamon, 1914-17); *Note:* See Chapter V.

Bourgeade, Pierre (?-); *Violoncelle qui résiste* (*Resisting Cello*; Los., 1971); *L'Aurore Boréale* (*Aurora Borealis*; Gall., 1973); *L'Armoire* (*The Dresser*; Gall., 1978); *Une Ville Grise* (*A Grey City*; Gall., 1978); *Le Lac d'Orta* (*The Lake of Orta*; Belfond, 1981); *Les Serpents* (*The Snakes*; Gall., 1983); *La Fin du Monde* (*The End of the World*; Den., 1984); *L'Autorisation* (*The Permit*; Avant-Scène, 1995); *Éros Mécanique* (*Mechanical Eros*; Gall., 1995)

Bourgenay, Henri (?-); *Éphélia, l'Île des Enfants Perdus* (*Ephelia, Island of Lost Children*; SdP 104, 1958); *Note:* Juvenile.

Bourgeois, André (?-) *see **Contes et Légendes***

Bourgeois, Anicet (1806-1871); *La Nonne Sanglante* (*The Bloody Nun*; Boitel, 1835); *Le Spectre et l'Orpheline* (*The Ghost and the Orphan*; Barba, 1836); *La Corde du Pendu* (*The Hanged Man's Rope*; Tresse, 1844); *Le Docteur Noir* (*The Dark Doctor*; Lévy, 1846); *La Sonnette du Diable* (*The Devil's Bell*; Lévy, 1849); *Le Diable d'Argent* (*The Silver Devil*; Libr. Théâtrale, 1857); *Les Pilules du Diable* (*The Devil's Pills*; Marchant, 1867); *Note:* See Chapter IV. *La Nonne* was adapted into an **Opéra** by Eugène **Scribe**.

Bourgeois, Eugène (?-?) *see **Grand-Guignol***

Bourgeois, Marc (1950-); *Altiplano* (Titres 30, 1980); *Vautours* (*Vultures*; Titres 53, 1982); *Note:* See Chapter IX.

Bourgeon, Charles (?-); *A l'Aube d'un Monde Nouveau* (*On the Dawn of a New World*; Pensée Moderne, 1960); *Camerone* (Pensée Moderne, 1963)

Bourges, Élémir (1852-1925); *Le Crépuscule des Dieux* (*The Twilight of the Gods*; Libr. Parisienne, 1884); *Sous la Hache* (*Under the Axe*; Giraud, 1885); *La Nef* (*The Ship*; Stock, 1904-22); *Les Oiseaux s'envolent et les Fleurs tombent* (*Birds Are Flying and Leaves Are Falling*; Plon, 1920); *Note:* See Chapter IV.

Bourillon, Henri *see **Hamp, Pierre***

Bourliaguet, L. (?-); *Contes du Mille-Pattes* (*Tales of the Centipede*; Nlles. Presses Fr., 1946); *Les Mystères du Vervelu* (*The Mysteries of Hairyworm*; Nlles. Presses Fr., 1946)

Bourneuf, Roland (1934-); *Reconnaissances* (*Recognitions*; Parallèles, 1981); *Mémoires du Demi-Jour* (*Memories of Half-Day*; L'Instant Même, 1990); *Chronique des Veilleurs* (*Chronicles of the Watchers*; L'Instant Même, 1993); *Note:* French-Canadian writer born in France. *Chroniques* is a collection of fantastical tales.

Bourre, Jean-Paul (?-); *Les Fils du Feu* (*The Sons of Fire*; JP Bourre, 1971); *Les Enfants Extra-Sensoriels et leurs Pouvoirs* (*ESP Children and Their Powers*; Tchou, 1978); *Magie et Sorcellerie (Essai)* (*Magic and Witchcraft* (essay*)*; Promedit, 1978); *Les Sectes Luci*f*ériennes Aujourd'hui* (*Luciferian Sects Today*; Belfond, 1978); *Le Vampirisme Aujourd'hui: J'ai rencontré des Morts-Vivants* (*Vampirism Today: I Met the Living Dead*; Lefeuvre, 1978); *Le Tarot Tantrique* (*Tantric Tarot*; MNC, 1978); *L'Orgueil des Fous* (*The Pride of Madmen*; Encre, 1979); *Messes Rouges et Romantisme Noir* (*Red Masses and Dark Romanticism*; Lefeuvre, 1980); *Dracula et les Vampires* (*Dracula and the Vampires*; Rocher, 1981); *Les Immortels* (*The Immortals*; Média 1000, 1981); *Les Nonnes Rouges* (*The Red Nuns*; Média 1000, 1981); *La Mecque de Glace* (*The Ice Mecca*; RL, 1981); *Le Sang, la Mort et le Diable* (*Blood, Death and the Devil*; Veyrier, 1985); *Rencontres avec l'Invisible* (*Encounters with the Invisible*; MA, 1986); *Les Vampires* (MA, 1986); *L'Or des Druides* (*The Gold of the Druids*; Veyrier, 1989); *Les Derniers Matins du Monde* (*The Last Mornings of the World*; Nuées Volantes, 1992); *Voyage au Centre de la Vie* (*Journey to the Center of Life*; RL, 1993); *Le Buveur d'Enfance* (*The Drinker of Childhood*; Littéra, 1994); *Le Graal et l'Ordre Noir* (*The Grail and the Black Order*; L'Aencre, 1995); *Mondes et Univers Parallèles: À travers l'Imaginaire et les Sciences* (*Worlds and Parallel Universes: Through Imagination and Sciences*; Filipacchi, 1996); *Note:* See Chapter VIII.

Bourre, Martine (1949-); *Les Piquants de Goz* (*The Thorns of Goz*; Flamm., 1986); *Ne Dérangez pas les Dragons!* (*Don't Disturb the Dragons!*; Flamm., 1988); *Note:* Juveniles. See Chapter VIII.

Bours, Jean-Pierre (1945-); *Celui Qui Pourrissait* (*He Who Rots*; MarF 625, 1977); *Note:* Belgian writer. Collection of supernatural stories.

Boussenard, Louis (1847-1910); *Le Tour du Monde d'un Gamin de Paris* (*The Trip Around the World of a Parisian Kid*; JDV, 1880); *Les Dix Millions de l'Opossum Rouge* (*The Ten Millions of the Red Possum*; GA, 1880); *Les Secrets de Monsieur Synthèse* (*The Secrets of Mr. Synthesis*; SI, 1888); *Dix Mille Ans dans un Bloc de Glace* (GA, 1889; transl. as *Ten Thousand Years in a Block of Ice*, 1898); *Le Mystère de la Guyane* (*The Mystery of Guyana*; Libr. Ill., 1890); *Le Mystère de la Forêt Vierge* (*The Mystery of the Virgin Jungle*; Libr. Ill., 1892); *Le Secret de l'Or* (*The Secret of Gold*; Libr. Ill., 1892); *Le Sultan de Bornéo* (*The Borneo Sultan*; Libr. Ill., 1892); *Les Pirates des Champs d'Or* (*The Pirates of the Gold Fields*; Libr. Ill., 1892); *Aventures d'un*

Gamin de Paris à travers l'Océanie (*Adventures of a Parisian Kid in Oceania*; Libr. Ill., 1892); *Aventures d'un Gamin de Paris au Pays des Bisons* (*Adventures of a Parisian Kid in the Land of the Buffalos*; Libr. Ill., 1892); *Aventures d'un Gamin de Paris au Pays des Lions* (*Adventures of a Parisian Kid in the Land of the Lions*; Libr. Ill., 1892); *Aventures d'un Gamin de Paris au Pays des Tigres* (*Adventures of a Parisian Kid in the Land of the Tigers*; Libr. Ill., 1892); *Aventures d'un Héritier à Travers le Monde* (*Adventures of an Heir Around the World*; Libr. Ill., 1892); *Aventures Périlleuses de Trois Français au Pays des Diamants* (*Perilous Adventures of Three Frenchmen in the Land of Diamonds*; Libr. Ill., 1892); *Le Trésor des Rois Cafres* (*The Treasure of the Caphre Kings*; Libr. Ill., 1892); *Les Français au Pôle Nord* (*The Frenchmen at the North Pole*; JDV, 1892-93); *L'Île en Feu* (*The Island on Fire*; JDV, 1898); *Les Étrangleurs du Bengale* (*The Stranglers of the Bengal;* JDV, 1899); *Les Bandits de la Mer* (*The Bandits of the Sea*; LN 1900); *L'Enfer de Glace* (*The Icy Hell*; LN, 1902); *Monsieur... Rien!* (*Aventures Extraordinaires d'un Homme Invisible*) (*Mister... Nothing!* (*Extraordinary Adventures of an Invisible Man*); JDV, 1907); *Aventures de Roule-ta-Bosse* (*Adventures of Roule-ta-Bosse*; Tallandier, 1907); *Les Gratteurs de Ciel* (*The Sky Scrapers*) aka *Les Aventuriers de l'Air* (*The Adventurers of the Air*; JDV, 1908); *Le Zouave de Malakoff* (*The Zouave of Malakoff*; Tallandier, 1908); *Le Fils du Gamin de Paris* (*The Son of the Parisian Kid*; Tallandier, 1909); *La Terreur en Macédoine* (*Terror in Macedonia*; Tallandier, 1912); *Le Maître du Cuare* (*The Master of Curare*; Tallandier, 1937); *Les Chasseurs de Caoutchouc* (*The Rubber Hunters*; Tallandier, 1938); *Les Robinsons de la Guyane* (*The Robinsons of Guyana*; Tallandier, 1938); *Note:* See Chapter V.

Boutet, Frédéric (1874-1941); *Contes dans la Nuit* (*Tales in the Night*; Chamuel, 1898); *Les Victimes Grimacent* (*The Grimacing Victims*; Chamuel, 1900); *Contes dans la Nuit* (*Tales in the Night*; Carrington, 1903); *Bal Masqué* (*Masked Ball*; Carrington, 1903); *Le Reflet de Claude Mercoeur* (*Claude Mercoeur's Reflection*; Flamm., 1921); *Le Spectre de M. Imberger* (*The Ghost of Mr. Imberger*; Flamm., 1922); *L'Homme Sauvage / Julius Pingouin* (*The Wild Man*; Flamm., 1922); *La Scène Tournante* (*The Rotating Stage*; Gall., 1926); *Les Aventuriers du Mystère: Tableau de l'Au-Delà* (*The Adventurers of Mystery: Scene from Beyond*; Gall., 1927); *Le Dieu Aveugle* (*The Blind God*; Nlle. Revue Critique, 1930); *Note:* See Chapter VI. The author also wrote a *Dictionnaire des Sciences Occultes* (*Dictionary of Occult Sciences*; 1937).

Boutet, Jean-Jacques (?-); *Paranopolis* (Chateau-Renard, 1978)

Bouvard, Roland *see* **Maltravers, Michaël**

Bouyxou, Jean-Pierre *see* **Razat, Claude**

Boverat, Fernand (?-); *La Bataille de l'Océan* (*The Battle of the Ocean*; Ed. M & J de Brunhoff, 1930); *Note:* Franco-German sea battles.

Boyer (Abbé; ?-?) *see* **Opéra**

Boyer d'Argens (?-?); *Lettres Cabalistiques* (*Kabbalistic Letters*; Paupie, 1741)

Boyle, Frank (?-); *L'Agonie de la Cité Bleue* (*The Agony of the Blue City*; Glénat, 1980)

Brac, Virginia (?-); *Coeur-caillou* (*Stone Heart*; FN Crime, 1997); *Note:* Police thriller taking place after a nuclear accident.

Brack, Ludy (?-); *L'Encéphale* (CPE, 1955)

Bracops, Charles *see* **Souvelier, Charles L.**

Bradley, Richard (1948-); *Les Nouveaux Départs* (*The New Departures*; Bradley, 1984); *Note:* French-Canadian writer. Collection of fantasy stories.

Brainin, Grégoire (?-); *Planète Atlante* (*Atlantean Planet*; with Henri **Keller**; VF 10, 1953); *L'Attaque des Vénusiens* (*The Attack of the Venusians*; with Henri **Keller**; Trotteur, 1953); *La Machine à Explorer le Rêve* (*The Dream Machine*; with Henri **Keller**; Cosmos 1, 1955); *La Guerre des Ondes* (*The War of the Waves*; with Henri **Keller**; Cosmos 2, 1955); *Le Tour du Soleil en 80 Jours* (*Around the Sun in 80 Days*; with Henri **Keller**; Cosmos 3, 1955); *Celui Qui Vient De Nulle Part* (*The Man from Nowhere*; with Henri **Keller**; Cosmos 4, 1955); *Au Centre de l'Univers* (*At the Center of the Universe*; with Henri **Keller**; Cosmos 7, 1956); *Et le Temps s'arrêtera* (*And Time Shall Stop;* with Henri **Keller**; Métal 21, 1956; rev. as *Les Derniers Hommes* (*The Last Men*, R.B., 1958); *Au-delà de la Fin du Monde* (*Beyond the End of the World*; with Yves **Jacob**; Cercle d'Or, 1978); *Note:* See Chapter IX.

Brancas-Villeneuve, Abbé François de (?-1748); *Histoire ou Police du Royaume de Gala* (*History or Police of the Kingdom of Gala*; Londres, 1754)

Brat (Colonel; ?-); *Paris Sera-t-il Détruit en 1936?* (*Will Paris Be Destroyed in 1936?*; LPT, 1933); *Note:* See Chapter VII.

Braudeau, Michel (1946-); *Vaulascar* (Seuil, 1977); *Passage de la Main d'Or* (*Passage of a Golden Hand*; Seuil, 1980); *Fantôme d'une Puce* (*Ghost of a Chip*; Seuil, 1982); *Naissance d'une Passion* (*Birth of a Passion*; Seuil, 1985); *L'Objet Perdu de l'Amour* (*The Lost Object of Love*; Seuil, 1988); *L'Amazone* (*The Amazon*; Seuil, 1988); *Le Livre de John* (*The Book of John*; Seuil,

1992); *Mon Ami Pierrot* (*My Friend Pierrot*; Seuil, 1993); *Esprit de Mai* (*Spirit of May*; Gall., 1995)

Brave, Jean-Louis (?-); *Les Goëlands* (*The Seagulls*; Signor, 1978)

Brefford, Alexandre (?-); *Paradis, Fin de Section* (*Paradise, End of Section*; Élan, 1947)

Brehal, Marc *see* **Dastier, Dan**

Breitman, Michel (?-); *Le Montreur et la Princesse* (*The Showman and the Princess*; Impr. Moderne, 1948); *Vetrino, Bonhomme de Verre* (*Vetrino, Little Man of Glass*; Hac., 1956); *Le Mal de Dieu* (*God's Sickness*; Den., 1957)

Brékilien, Yann (?-); *Dieu renverse les Temples* (*God Overthrows Temples*; Scorpion, 1960); *La Révolte des Tracteurs* (*The Tractors' Revolt*; TR, 1968); *Récits Vivants de Bretagne* (*Living Tales from Britanny*; anthology; Hac., 1979); *La Reine Sauvage* (Delarge, 1980); *La Mythologie Celtique* (*Celtic Mythology*; Picollec, 1981); *Une Secte et son Mystère* (*A Sect and its Mystery*; Coop Breizh, 1982); *Les Cavaliers du Bout du Monde* (*The Riders of World's End*; Rocher, 1990); *Le Druide* (*The Druid*; Rocher, 1994); *Contes et Légendes du Pays Breton* (*Tales and Legends of Britanny*; Nature & Bretagne, 1994); *Le Fauve de l'Arrée* (*The Wild Beast of arrée*; Liv'Ed., 1996); *Note:* See Chapter VIII. Also see **Contes et Légendes**.

Brémond, Raoul (?-); *Par-Delà l'Univers* (*Beyond the Universe*; S&V, 1931); *Note:* See Chapter VII.

Brenner, Félix (?-); *L'Araignée de Yoshiwara* (*Yoshiwara's Spider*; FNFR 6, 1994); *Note:* See Chapter VIII.

Brèque, Jean-Daniel (?-); *Malenfances* (*Illchild*; Destination Crépuscule, 1995)

Bressy, Eugène (?-); *Légendes de Provence* (*Legends of Provence*; Flamm., 1963); *Note:* See Chapter VIII.

Breton, André (1896-1966); *Nadja* (Gall., 1928); *Note:* See Chapter VI.

Breton, Gabriel (?-?) *see* **Grand-Guignol**

Breton, Thierry (1955-) *see* **Beneich, Denis**

Bretonneau (Père; ?-?) *see* **Opéra**

Brière, Paule (1959-); *Par Ici La Sortie!* (*This Way to the Exit*; Boréal Jr., 1991); *Esprit, es-tu là?* (*Spirit, Are You There?*; Boréal Jr., 1993); *Note:* French-Canadian writer. Children's fantasies.

Brightmill, Allan (?-); *Opérations Soucoupe* (*Operation Saucer*; VF 2, 1953); *Stop à l'Invasion* (*To Stop the Invasion*; VF 7, 1953)

Bringer, Rodolphe (1871-1943) *see* **La Fouchardière, Georges de**

Brion, Marcel (1895-1984); *La Folie Céladon (The Celadon Madness*; R.A. Corrêa, 1935); *Le Théâtre des Esprits (The Theater of Spirits*; W. Egloff, 1941); *Les Escales de la Haute Nuit (The Shore Leaves of the Deepest Night*; RL, 1942; rep. MarF 374, 1971); *Château d'Ombres (Castle of Shadows*; Libr. Université, 1942); *Le Portrait de Belinda (The Portrait of Belinda*; RL, 1945); *Le Pré du Grand Songe (The Field of the Great Dream; RL, 1946); L'Enchanteur (The Enchanter*; W. Egloff, 1947); *La Révolte des Gladiateurs (Revolt of the Gladiators*; Amiot, 1952); *La Chanson de l'Oiseau Étranger (The Song of a Strange Bird*; AM, 1958); *La Ville de Sable (The City of Sand*; AM, 1959); *La Rose de Cire (The Wax Rose*; AM, 1964); *De l'Autre Côté de la Forêt (On the Other Side of the Forest*; AM, 1966); *Les Miroirs et les Gouffres (Mirrors and Abysses*; AM, 1968); *L'Ombre de l'Arbre Mort (The Shadow of the Dead Tree*; AM, 1970); *Nous Avons Traversé la Montagne (We Have Crossed the Mountain*; AM, 1972); *La Fête de la Tour des Âmes (The Festival of the Tower of Souls*; AM, 1974); *La Résurrection des Villes Mortes (The Resurrection of Dead Cities*; Beauval, 1975); *Les Princes de Francalanza (The Princes of Francalanza*; Den., 1979); *Le Journal du Visiteur (The Diary of a Traveller*; AM, 1980); *Le Château de la Princesse Ilse (The Castle of Princess Ilse*; AM, 1981); *L'Ermite au Masque de Miroir (The Hermit in the Mirror Mask*; AM, 1982); *Villa des Hasards (Villa of Chances*; AM, 1984); *Les Vaines Montagnes (Vain Mountains*; AM, 1985); *Contes Fantastiques (Fantastic Tales*; AM, 1989); *Note:* See Chapter VIII.

Brisay, Henri de (?-); *Le Secret de l'Abbé Fauvel (The Secret of Abbot Fauvel*; Delhomme-Briguet, 1891); *Les Contes de l'Épée (Tales of the Sword*; Mame, 1897); *Trémor aux Mains Rouges (Tremor of the Red Hands*; Mame, 1913); *Plus Fort que la Force (Stronger Than Power*; Mame, 1921)

Brisou-Pellen, Evelyne (1947-); *La Porte de Nulle Part (The Gate of Nowhere*; Bayard, 1980); *Le Mystère de la Nuit des Pierres (The Mystery of the Night of the Stones*; Amitié, 1980); *La Cour aux Étoiles (Courtyard of the Stars*; Amitié, 1982); *Prisonnière des Mongols (Prisoner of the Mongols*; Amitié, 1985); *L'Étrange Chanson de Sveti (Sveti's Strange Song*; Flamm., 1985); *L'Homme Rouge de Hang-Tchéou (The Red Man of Hang-Tcheou*; Hac., 1985); *La Grotte des Korrigans (The Korrigans' Cave*; Centurion, 1985); *Le Maître de la Septième Porte (The Master of the Seventh Gate*; Amitié, 1986); *Le Trésor des Aztèques (The Aztecs' Treasure*; Flamm., 1987); *Le Défi des Druides (The Challenge of the Druids*; Amitié, 1988); *Les Concombres du Roi (The King's Cucumbers*; Centurion, 1988); *Dix Contes de Fée (Ten Fairy Tales*; Albums en Fête, 1988); *L'Héritier du Désert (The Heir of the Desert*; Rageot,

1996); *Un Si Terrible Secret (Such a Terrible Secret*; Rageot, 1997); *Note:* Juveniles. See Chapter VIII.

Brissette, Louise (1951-); *Les Ailes de l'Espoir (The Wings of Hope*; Mots-Agis, 1984); *Note:* French-Canadian writer. Modern fairy tale.

Brochard, Hippolyte-Aimé de (1811-1896); *Le Fleuve sous la Seine, ou Les Aventures Rocambolesques du Baron d'Espignac (The River Under the Seine, or the Extraordinary Adventures of the Baron Espignac*; Conquet, 1890)

Brochet, Jean *see* **Bruce, Jean**

Brochon, Pierre (?-); *Le Canari ne Chante Plus (The Canary No Longer Sings*; Horay, 1959); *Samadhi (E. Thomas, 1978); Des Vents et des Flots (Of Wind and Flows*; Le Croît Vif, 1997)

Brochu, Yvon (1949-); *L'Extra-Terrestre (The E.T.*; Jour, 1975); on *Ne Se Laisse Plus Faire (We Won't Let Them Get Away with It Again*; Q/A, 1989); *Tonton l'Ouragan (Uncle Hurricane*; Héritage Jeunesse, 1995); *La Muse de Monsieur Buse (Mr. Buse's Muse*; Héritage Jeunesse, 1996); on *n'est pas des Monstres (We're Not Monsters*; Q/A, 1992); *Arrête de faire le Clown (Stop Clowning Around*; Q/A, 1993); *Note:* French-Canadian writer. Children's fantasies.

Brodeur, Michel (?-); *Le Jardin du Diable (The Devil's Garden*; Q/A, 1981); *Note:* French-Canadian writer.

Bromberger, Dominique (?-); *L'Itinéraire de Parhan au Château d'Alamut et au-delà (The Itinerary of Parhan in Castle Alamut and Beyond*; Fayard, 1978); *Le Grand Manège: Rencontre avec les Maîtres du Monde (The Great Merry-Go-Round: Meeting with the Masters of the World*; Plon, 1993)

Brooker, Edward (?-) / Norwood, Sam P. (?-); Series *Le Maître de l'Invisible (The Master of the Invisible)*: Menace de l'Invisible *(Threat of the Invisible*; rep. 1953): *1. Le Vol de la Bombe Atomique (The Stealing of an Atom Bomb*; Éditions & Revues Françaises, 1945); *2. Demain New York Sautera (Tomorrow New York Will Be Destroyed*; Éditions & Revues Françaises, 1945); *3. Menace sur l'Angleterre (Threat Over England*; Éditions & Revues Françaises, 1945); *4. Lapertot Engage le Combat (Lapertot Starts to Fight*; Éditions & Revues Françaises, 1945); *Dans les Griffes de l'Invisible (In the Clutches of the Invisible*; rep. 1954): *5. Mo-Hang, l'Île Mysterieuse (Mo-Hang, Mysterious Island*; Éditions & Revues Françaises, 1945); *6. Un Plan Diabolique (A Diabolical Plan*; Éditions & Revues Françaises, 1945); *7. La Lutte des Invisibles (The Clash of the Invisibles*; Éditions & Revues Françaises, 1945); *8. Tsan-Tsan le Mangeur d'Hommes (Tsan-Tsan, Eater of Men*; Édi-

tions & Revues Françaises, 1945) (title unknown; rep. 1954): *9. La Vengeance du Grand Sorcier* (*The Revenge of the Great Wizard*; Éditions & Revues Françaises, 1946); *10. Les Esclaves de Satan* (*The Slaves of Satan*; Éditions & Revues Françaises, 1946); *11. Le Docteur Faustulus* (*Dr. Faustulus*; Éditions & Revues Françaises, 1946); *12. Un Curieux Soupirant* (*A Bizarre Pretender*; Éditions & Revues Françaises, 1946); *À l'Assaut des Planètes* (*To Assault the Planets*; rep. 1955): *13. La Fuite dans l'Espace* (*Flight in Space*; Éditions & Revues Françaises, 1946); *14. Le Royaume de P'to-P'to* (*The Kingdom of P'to-P'to*; Éditions & Revues Françaises, 1946); *15. Au Pays des Hurkas* (*In the Land of the Hurkas*; Éditions & Revues Françaises, 1946); *16. Voyage à travers Mars* (*Journey Through Mars*; Éditions & Revues Françaises, 1946); *Les Sorciers de l'Invisible* (*The Wizards of the Invisible*; rep. 1955): *17. Le Secret de la Jungle* (*The Secret of the Jungle*; Éditions & Revues Françaises, 1946); *18. La Déesse Blanche* (*The White Goddess*; Éditions & Revues Françaises, 1946); *19. La Cité Lacustre* (*The Lake City*; Éditions & Revues Françaises, 1946); *20. Mawamba* (Éditions & Revues Françaises, 1946); *Croisière de l'Épouvante* (*Horror Cruise*; rep. 1955): *21. La Forêt Qui Tue* (*The Killing Forest*; Éditions & Revues Françaises, 1946); *22. Le Radeau de la Mort* (*The Raft of Death*; Éditions & Revues Françaises, 1947); *23. La Guerre des Robots* (*War of the Robots*; Éditions & Revues Françaises, 1947); *24. La Vengeance du Radium* (*The Revenge of Radium*; Éditions & Revues Françaises, 1947); *Angoisse dans la Ville* (*Terror Over the City*; rep. 1955): *25. Les Secrets de l'Atome* (*The Secrets of the Atom*; Éditions & Revues Françaises, 1947); *26. La Ville Sous-Marine* (*The Undersea City*; Éditions & Revues Françaises, 1947); *27. Le Voleur de Pensées* (*The Stealer of Thoughts*; Éditions & Revues Françaises, 1947); *28. La Vengeance de l'Invisible* (*The Revenge of the Invisible*; Éditions & Revues Françaises, 1947); *La Terre Sera-t-elle Préservée?* (*Shall Earth Be Saved?*; rep. 1956): *29. La Guerre des Astres* (*The War of the Stars*; Éditions & Revues Françaises, 1947); *30. Le Maître des Séismes* (*The Master of Earthquakes*; Éditions & Revues Françaises, 1947); *31. Échec à l'Invisible* (*The Invisible in Check*; Éditions & Revues Françaises, 1947); *32. Panique dans la Ville* (*Panic in the City*; Éditions & Revues Françaises, 1947); *Départ pour Mars* (*Departure for Mars*; rep. 1956): *33. Dans les Entrailles de la Terre* (*In the Belly of Earth*; Éditions & Revues Françaises, 1947); *34. L'Île aux Monstres* (*Monster Island*; Éditions & Revues Françaises, 1948); *35. Bagarre à Mo'Ang* (*Clash in Mo'Ang*; Éditions & Revues Françaises, 1948); *36. La Fusée de Faustulus* (*Faustulus' Rocket*; Éditions & Revues Françaises, 1948); *Note:* See Chapter IX.

Brossard, Jacques (1933-); *Le Métamorfaux* (*The Metamorphosis*; HMH, 1974); *Le Sang du Souvenir* (*The Blood of Memories*; La Presse, 1976); *L'Oiseau de Feu 1: Les Années d'Apprentissage* (*The Firebird 1: The Years of Apprenticeship*; Leméac, 1989); *L'Oiseau de Feu 2A: Le Recyclage d'Adakhan* (*The Firebird 2A: Adakhan's Recycling*; Leméac, 1990); *L'Oiseau de Feu 2B: Le Grand Projet* (*The Firebird 2B: The Great Project*; Leméac, 1993); *L'Oiseau de Feu 2C: Le Sauve-Qui-Peut* (*The Firebird 2C: Run for the Hills*; Leméac, 1995); *L'Oiseau de Feu 3: Les Années d'Errance* (*The Firebird 3: The Years of Wandering*; Leméac, 1997); *Note:* French-Canadian writer. *Le Métamorfaux* is a collection of fantastic stories. *L'Oiseau de Feu* is a vast heroic fantasy saga.

Brosses, Marie-Thérèse de (?-); Assunrath (Los., 1967); *De l'Autre Côté de la Vitre* (*On the Other Side of the Glass*; RL, 1985); *Je t'emmènerai à Syracuse* (*I'll Take You to Syracuse*; RL, 1989); *Enquête sur les Enlèvements Extra-Terrestres* (*Investigation on ET Abductions*; Plon, 1995); *Note:* See Chapter VIII.

Brot, Alphonse (?-?); *Salmigondis, Contes de Toutes les Couleurs* (*Salmigondis, Tales of Every Color*; Fournier, 1832); *Note: Includes the classic gothic tale "La Cheminée Gothique"* ("The Gothic Fireplace") originally published in *L'Artiste* in 1832.

Brotot, Dominique (?-); *Chair à Supplices* (*Tortured Flesh*; Siry Maniac 6, 1988); *Penta* (FNA 1889, 1992); *Neurovision* (FNA 1930, 1993); *Le Voleur d'Organes* (*The Organ Thief*; FNA 1940, 1994); *L'Égaré d'Outre-Ciel* (*Lost Beyond the Sky*; ST-Magazine, 1996); *Note:* See Chapter IX.

Brouillaud, Pierre-Jean (?-); *Tellur* (A&D 37, 1975); *Note:* See Chapter IX.

Brouillet, Raymond (?-); *Histoire des Hommes Lunaires* (*History of the Moon Men*; Scorpion, 1961); *Rois Sacrés, Sacrés Rois* (*Sacred Kings, Kings Sacred*; 1975)

Broussan-Gaubert, Jeanne (?-) *see* **Humble, Pierre**

Brown, Alphonse (1841-?); *Voyage à Dos de Baleine* (*Journey on Whaleback*; Librairie Illustrée, 1877); *L'Oasis (Perdus dans les Sables) aka Les Mohicans du Sahara* (*The Oasis (Lost in the Sands) aka The Mohicans of the Sahara*; JDV, 1885); *La Conquête de l'Air aka Les Conquérants de l'Air* (*The Conquest of the Air aka The Conquerors of the Air*; Charavay, 1880); *Une Ville de Verre* (*A City of Glass*; SI, 1890); *La Guerre à Mort* (*War to the Death*; Libr. Ill., 1893); *La Station Aérienne* (*The Aerial Station*; JDV, 1894); *La Tirelire d'Alice* (*Alice's Piggybank*; Charavay, Mantour, Martin, 1896); *La Goëlette Terrestre* (*The Land Schooner*; Libr. Educ. Je-*

unesse, 1900); *Les Faiseurs de Pluie* (*The Rain Makers*; JDV, 1901); *Les Tribulations d'un Pêcheur à la Ligne* (*The Tribulations of a Fisherman*; Sté. d'Ed. & Public., 1910); *Note:* See Chapter V.

Bruce, Jean (Brochet, Jean; 1921-1963); Series *OSS 117: À Tuer: OSS 117* (*To Kill OSS 117*); *Affaire N°1* (*No.1 Case*); *Agonie en Patagonie* (*Agony in Patagonia*); *Alerte: OSS 117* (*Alert OSS 117*); *Alerte à Rangoon pour OSS 117* (*Alert in Rangoon for OSS 117*); *Angoisse pour OSS 117* (*Terror for OSS 117*); *Arizona Zone a* (*Arizona Zone A*); *L'Arsenal Sautera* (*The Arsenal Will Blow Up*); *Atout Coeur à Tokyo* (*Trump Heart in Tokyo*); *Cache-Cache au Cachemire* (*Hide and Seek in Kashmir*); *Cadavre au Détail* (*Corpses on Retail*); *Carte Blanche pour OSS 117* (*Blanck Check for OSS 117*); *Cessez d'Émettre* (*Stop Transmissions*); *Chasse aux Atomes* (*Atom Hunt*); *Chinoiseries pour OSS 117* (*Chinese Tricks for OSS 117*); *Cité Secrète* (*Secret City*); *Contact Impossible* (*Impossible Contact*); *Délire en Iran* (*Madness in Iran*); *Dernier Quart d'Heure* (*The Last 15 Minutes*); *Documents à Vendre* (*Documents for Sale*); *Double Bang à Bangkok* (*Double Bang in Bangkok*); *Du Lest à l'Est* (*Dead Weight in the East*); *L'Espionne s'évade* (*The Female Spy Escapes*); *Les Espions du Pirée* (*The Spies of the Pireus*); *Festival pour OSS 117* (*Festival for OSS 117*); *Fidèlement Vôtre, OSS 117* (*Faithfully Yours, OSS 117*); *Gâchis à Karachi* (*Mess in Karachi*); Hara-Kiri; *Ici OSS 117* (*OSS 117 Is Here*); *Magie Blanche pour OSS 117* (*White Magic for OSS 117*); *Les Marrons du Feu* (*The Chestnuts in the Fire*); *Les Monstres du Holy Loch* (*The Monsters of Holy Loch*); *Ne Jouez Pas avec les Filles* (*Don't Play with Girls*); *Noël pour un Espion* (*Christmas for a Spy*); *OSS 117 à l'École* (*OSS 117 Back to School*); *OSS 117 à Mexico* (*OSS 117 in Mexico*); *OSS 117 Appelle* (*OSS 117 Calls*); *OSS 117 au Liban* (*OSS 117 in Lebanon*); *OSS 117 contre X* (*OSS 117 vs. X*); *OSS 117 et Force Noire* (*OSS 117 and Black Power*); *OSS 117 Franchit le Canal* (*OSS 117 Crosses the Canal*); *OSS 117? Ici Paris!* (*OSS 117? Paris Speaking!*); *OSS 117 Joue le Jeu* (*OSS 117 Plays the Game*); *OSS 117 n'est pas Aveugle* (*OSS 117 Is Not Blind*); *OSS 117 n'est pas Mort* (*OSS 117 Is Not Dead*); *OSS 117 Préfère les Rousses* (*OSS 117 Prefers Redheads*); *OSS 117 Prend le Maquis* (*OSS 117 Goes Into Hiding*); *OSS 117 Rentre dans la Danse* (*OSS 117 Opens the Dance*); *OSS 117 Répond Toujours* (*OSS 117 Always Answers*); *OSS 117 s'en occupe* (*OSS 117 Is Taking Care of It*); *OSS 117 Top Secret*; *OSS 117 Voit Rouge* (*OSS 117 Sees Red*); *Pan, Dans la Lune!* (*Bang! Hit the Moon!*); *Partie de Manille pour OSS 117* (*A Game of Cards for OSS 117*); *Pays Neutre* (*Neutral Country*); *Piège dans la Nuit* (*Trap in the Night*); *Plan de Bataille pour OSS 117* (*Battle Plan for OSS 117*); *Plein Gaz pour OSS 117* (*Full Speed for OSS 117*); *Le Sbire de Birmanie* (*The Birman Henchman*); *Les Secrets font la Valise* (*The Secrets Have Gone AWOL*); *Sous Peine de Mort* (*Under Sentence of Death*); *Strip-Tease pour OSS 117* (*Strip-Tease for OSS 117*); *Tactique Arctique* (*Arctic Tactic*); *Tortures pour OSS 117* (*Tortures for OSS 117*); *Trahison* (*Betrayal*); *Travail sans Filet* (*Working Without a Net*); *Valse Viennoise pour OSS 117* (*Viennese Waltz for OSS 117*); *Visa pour Caracas* (*Visa for Caracas*); *Vous avez trahi* (*You Have Betrayed*); *Note:* See Chapter IX. The *OSS 117* novels were originally published in the 1950s and 1960s by Presses de la Cité/Presses-Pocket, and later reprinted in the 1970s by Edito-Service (often combining two volumes in one), *Fleuve Noir* in the 1980s and M. Lafon in the 1990s. A number of *OSS 117* stories were adapted into films—see Book 1, Chapter I).

Brucker, Raymond (Block, Aloysius; 1800-1875); *Le Spectre* (Revue de Paris, 1831); *Les Deux Notes* (*The Two Notes*; Revue de l'Artiste, 1831); *Ugolino* (Allardin, 1835); *Note:* See Chapter IV.

Bruckner, Pascal (?-); *Monsieur Tac* (Sagittaire, 1976); *Allez Jouer Ailleurs* (*Go Play Elsewhere*; Sagittaire, 1977); *Lune de Fiel* (*Bitter Moon*; Seuil, 1981); *Parias* (*Pariahs*; Seuil, 1985); *Le Palais des Claques* (*The Palace of Slaps*; Seuil, 1986); *Qui de nous deux inventa l'Autre?* (*Who of Us Two Invented the Other?*; Gall., 1988); *Le Divin Enfant* (*The Divine Child*; Seuil, 1992); *La Tentation de l'Innocence* (*The Temptation of Innocence*; Grasset, 1995); *Les Voleurs de Beauté* (*The Beauty Thieves*; Grasset, 1997)

Brûlé, Michel (1964-); *Ail, Aïe!* (*Ouch! Garlic*; Les Intouchables, 1993); *Note:* French-Canadian writer. Fantastical novel.

Bruller, Jean *see* Vercors

Brulotte, Gaétan (1945-); *L'Emprise* (*The Hold*; Ed. de l'Homme, 1978); *Ce Qui Nous Tient* (*That Which Holds Us*; Leméac, 1988); *Le Surveillant* (*The Watcher*; Quinze, 1980); *Note:* French-Canadian writer.

Brun, Joan-Frédéric (1956-); *Lo Retrach dau Dieu Negre* (Inst. Études Occitanes, 1987); *Septembralas* (Inst. Études Occitanes, 1994); *Note:* Occitan writer. See Chapter VIII.

Brunel, Noré (?-); *L'Émigme de Mal-Pas* (*The Mystery of Evil-Step*; Fayard, 1932); *Les Étreintes Maudites* (*Accursed Embraces*; Lugdunum, 1934); *Les Semeurs de Mort* (*The Sowers of Death*; Savoie, 1946)

Brunelle, Alain (1970-); *Enfer* (*Hell*; Alien, 1992); *Vampyres* (Alien, 1993); *Note:* French-Canadian writer. *Enfer* is a collection of fantastical tales. *Vampyres* a fantastical novel.

Bruno-Ruby, J. (Vignaud, Jean (Mrs.); ?-); *Madame Cotte* (Lafitte, 1913); *L'Exemple de l'Abbé Jouve* (*The*

Example of Abbot Jouve; AM, 1919); *Celui Qui Supprima la Mort* (*He Who Got Rid of Death*; Lafitte, 1921); *Sig l'Aventurier* (*Sig the Adventurer*; Portiques, 1930); *Dix sur la Route* (*Ten on the Road*; Fasquelle, 1937); *Note:* See Chapter VII.

Bruss, B.-R. (Bonnefoy, René; 1895-1980); *Et la Planète Sauta...* (*And the Planet Exploded*; Portulan, 1946); *Apparition des Surhommes* (*Appearance of the Supermen*; Froissard, 1953; rev. Rencontre, 1970); *SOS Soucoupes* (*SOS Saucers*; FNA 33, 1954); *La Guerre des Soucoupes* (*The War of the Saucers*; FNA 40, 1955); *L'Oeil était dans la Tombe* (*The Eye Was in the Tomb*; FNAG 7, 1955); *Le Mouton Enragé* (*The Rabid Sheep*; as Roger Blondel; Gall., 1956); *Rideau Magnétique* (*Magnetic Curtain*; FNA 65, 1956); *Substance "Arka"* (FNA 82, 1956); *Maléfices* (*Spells*; FNAG 18, 1956); *Nous Avons Tous Peur* (*We Are All Afraid*; FNAG 24, 1956); *Le Grand Kirn* (*The Great Kirn*; FNA 112, 1958); *Terreur en Plein Soleil* (*Terror Under a Full Sun*; FNAG 38, 1958); *Terre, Siècle 24...* (*Earth, 24th Century...*; FNA 136, 1959); *An... 2391* (*Year... 2391*; FNA 143, 1959); *L'Anneau des Djarfs* (*The Ring of the Djarfs*; FNA 180, 1961); *Bihil* (FNA 186, 1961); *Le Cri des Durups* (*The Scream of the Durups*; FNA 195, 1962); *Le Mur de la Lumière* (*The Light Barrier*; FNA 200, 1962); *Les Horls en Péril* (*The Horls in Peril*; FNA 208, 1962); *Le Tambour d'Angoisse* (*The Drum of Terror*; FNAG 86, 1962); *Complot Vénus-Terre* (*Venus-Earth Conspiracy*; FNA 225, 1963); *L'Otarie Bleue* (*The Blue Otter*; FNA 233, 1963); *L'Archange* (*The Archangel*; as Roger Blondel; RL, 1963); *Une Mouche Nommée Drésa* (*A Fly Named Dresa*; FNA 239, 1964); *Les Translucides* (*The Transparents*; FNA 246, 1964); *L'Astéroïde Noir* (*The Black Asteroid*; FNA 251, 1964); *Le Grand Feu* (*The Great Fire*; FNA 256, 1964); *Le Bourg Envoûté* (*The Spellbound Burg*; FNAG 111, 1964); *La Figurine de Plomb* (*The Lead Statuette*; FNAG 119, 1965); *Le Soleil s'éteint* (*The Sun Is Dying*; FNA 260, 1965); *Planètes Oubliées* (*Forgotten Planets*; FNA 267, 1965); *La Planète Glacée* (*The Ice Planet*; FNA 273, 1965); *L'Énigme des Phtas* (*The Enigma of the Phtas*; FNA 277, 1965); *Bradfer et l'Éternel* (*Bradfer and the Eternal*; as Roger Blondel; RL, 1964); *Le Boeuf* (*The Ox*; as Roger Blondel; RL, 1965); *La Guerre des Robots* (*The War of the Robots*; FNA 287, 1966); *L'Espace Noir* (*The Black Space*; FNA 294, 1966); *La*

Créature Éparse (*The Fragmented Creature*; FNA 301, 1966); *Le Mystère des Sups* (*The Mystery of the Sups*; FNA 318, 1967); *L'Étrange Planète Orga* (*The Strange Planet Orga*; FNA 324, 1967); *Le Trappeur Galactique* (*The Galactic Trapper*; FNA 328, 1967); *Quand l'Uranium Vint à Manquer* (*When Uranium Ran Out*; FNA 338, 1968); *L'Espionne Galactique* (*The Galactic Spy*; FN 348, 1968); *La Planète Introuvable* (*The Unfindable Planet*; FNA 356, 1968); *Les Enfants d'Alga* (*The Children of Alga*; FNA 366, 1968); *Les Centauriens Sont Fous* (*The Centaurians Are Mad*; FNA 386, 1969); *Parle, Robot!* (*Speak, Robot!*; FNA 394, 1969); *La Planète aux Oasis* (*The Oasis Planet*; FNA 419, 1970); *Une Si Belle Planète* (*Such a Beautiful Planet*; FNA 429, 1970); *Les Harnils* (*The Harnils*; FNA 448, 1971); *Le Grand Marginal* (*The Great Outsider*; FNA 472, 1971); *Le Mort qu'il faut Tuer* (*The Dead Man Who Must Be Killed*; FNAG 199, 1971); *Luhora* (FNA 486, 1972); *Les Êtres Vagues* (*The Vague Beings*; FNA 511, 1972); *Guet-Apens sur Zifur* (*Ambush on Zifur*; FNA 551, 1973); *Brang* (FNA 562, 1973); *L'Objet Maléfique* (*The Evil Thing*; FNAG 226, 1973); *La Grande Parlerie* (*The Great Speaking Room*; as Roger Blondel; JCL, 1973); *Un Endroit Nommé La Vie* (*A Place Called Life*; as Roger Blondel; JCL, 1973); *Oh! Oh!* (as Roger Blondel; JCL, 1974); *Penelcoto* (FNA 651, 1975); *Les Graffiti* (as Roger Blondel; JCL, 1975); *Les Fontaines Pétrifiantes* (*The Petrified Fountains*; as Roger Blondel; JCL, 1978); *Les Espaces Enchevêtrés* (*The Intertwined Spaces*; NéO 4, 1979); *Note:* See chapters VII, VIII, and IX. *L'Archange* was adapted for television by the author (See Book 1, Chapter II). A number of Bruss's FNAG novels were adapted into digest-sized graphic novels (see Book 1, Chapter V under ***Fleuve Noir***).

Brussolo, Serge (1951-); *Vue en Coupe d'une Ville Malade* (*Cut-Out View of a Sick City*; PdF 300, 1980); *Aussi Lourd que le Vent* (*Heavy as the Wind*; PdF 315, 1981); *Les Sentinelles d'Almoha* (*The Sentinels of Almoha*; Nathan SF 8, 1981; rev. FNA 1938, 1994); *Sommeil de Sang* (*Sleep of Blood*; PdF 334, 1982); *Portrait du Diable en Chapeau Melon* (*Portrait of the Devil Wearing a Bowler*; PdF 348, 1982); *Traque-La-Mort* (*Death Tracker*; Titres 60, 1982); *Le Nuisible* (*The Harmful*; Den. Sueurs Froides, 1982); *Les Mangeurs de Murailles*

LES ENFANTS D'ALGA

B.R.BRUSS

FLEUVE NOIR

(*The Eaters of Walls*; FNA 1183, 1982); a *l'Image du Dragon* (*In the Dragon's Image*; FNA 1190, 1982); *Le Carnaval de Fer* (*The Iron Carnival*; PdF 359, 1983); *Le Puzzle de Chair* (*The Jigsaw Puzzle of Flesh*; FNA 1225, 1983); *Les Semeurs d'Abîmes* (*The Abyss Sowers*; FNA 1244, 1983); *Territoire de Fièvre* (*Fever Land*; FNA 1251, 1983); *Les Lutteurs Immobiles* (*The Motionless Fighters*; FNA 1257, 1983); *Les Bêtes Enracinées* (*The Rooted Beasts*; FNA 1275, 1984); *Ce Qui Mordait Le Ciel...* (*What Bit the Sky...*; FNA 1290, 1984); *Crache-Béton* (*Spit-Concrete*; FNA 1315, 1984); *Les Foetus d'Acier* (*The Steel Fetuses*; FNA 1330, 1984); *La Maison Vénéneuse* (*The Poisonous House*; FN Special-Police, 1984; rev. as *Bunker*, GDV, 1993); *Ambulance Cannibale Non Identifiée* (*Unidentified Cannibal Ambulance*; FNA 1366, 1985); *Le Rire du Lance-Flammes* (*The Laughter of the Flame-Thrower*; FNA 1382, 1985); *Rempart des Naufrageurs* (*Rempart of the Shipwreckers*; FNA1399, 1985); *Abattoir-Opéra* (*Slaughterhouse Opera*; FNA 1414, 1985; rev. as *La Petite Fille et le Dobermann* (*The Little Girl and the Dobermann*, PdF 557, 1995); *Naufrage sur une Chaise Électrique* (*Sinking in an Electric Chair*; FNA 1424, 1986); *Enfer Vertical en Approche Rapide* (*Vertical Hell Rapidly Approaching*; FNA 1446, 1986); *La Colère des Ténèbres (Ira Mélanox)* (*The Wrath of Darkness*; FNA 1464, 1986); *Danger Parking Miné!* (*Danger: Mined Parking!*; FNA 1475, 1986); *Catacombes* (*Catacombs*; FNA 1491, 1986); *Docteur Squelette* (*Doctor Skeleton*; FNA 1517, 1987); *Operation "Serrures Carnivores"* (*Operation "Carnivorous Locks"*; FNA 1537, 1987); *La Nuit du Venin* (*The Night of the Poison*; FNA 1551, 1987); *Les Animaux Funèbres* (*The Funeral Beasts*; FNA 1572, 1987); *Procédure d'Évacuation Immédiate des Musées Fantômes* (*Procedure for the Immediate Evacuation of the Phantom Museums*; PdF 447, 1987); *L'Ombre des Gnomes*

(*The Shadow of the Gnomes*; FNA 1594, 1987); *Le Château d'Encre* (*The Castle of Ink*; PdF 453, 1988); *Le Voleur d'Icebergs* (*The Iceberg Thief*; FNA 1615, 1988); *Le Tombeau du Roi Squelette* (*The Tomb of the Skeleton King*; FNA 1627, 1988); *Les Écorcheurs* (*The Skinners; Siry SF 1, 1988; rev. as *L'Épave* (*The Wreck*, GDV 5, 1990); *Le Dragon du Roi Squelette* (*The Dragon of the Skeleton King*; FNA 1664, 1989); *La Nuit du Bombardier* (*The Night of the Bomber*; Den. Sueurs Froides, 1989); *Le Murmure des Loups* (*The Whisper of the Wolves*; Den. Sueurs Froides, 1990); *Boulevard des Banquises* (*Ice Shelf Boulevard*; PdFant. 2, 1990); *L'Homme aux Yeux de Napalm* (*The Man with the Napalm Eyes*; PdF 501, 1989); *Cauchemar à Louer* (*Nightmare for Rent*; GDV 1, 1990); *La Meute* (*The Pack*; GDV 2, 1990); *Krucifix* (GDV 3, 1990); *Les Bêtes* (*The Beasts*; GDV 4, 1990); *Les Emmurés* (*Walled Up*; GDV 6, 1991); *Les Rêveurs d'Ombre* (*The Dreamers of Shadows*; GDV 7, 1991); *Les Démoniaques* (*The Demoniacals*; GDV 8, 1991); *Le Vent Noir* (*The Black Wind*; GDV 9, 1991); *Les Inhumains* (*The Inhumans*; GDV 10, 1992); *Le Syndrome du Scaphandrier* (*The Diver's Syndrome*; PdF 526, 1992); *3, Place de Byzance* (*No.3, Byzantium Square*; Den., 1992); *L'Armure Maudite* (*The Accursed Armor*; GDV 12, 1992); *Rinocérox* (FNA 1882, 1992); *Capitaine Suicide* (*Captain Suicide*;

FNA 1894, 1992); *Sécutité Absolue* (*Total Security*; GDV, 1993); *La Route Obscure* (*The Dark Road*; Den. Sueurs Froides, 1993); *Derelict (GDV, 1993; rev. as Avis de Tempête* (*Storm Warning*, GDV, 1997); *La Route Obscure* (*The Dark Road*; Den., 1993); *Hurlemort—Le Dernier Royaume* (*DeathScream—the Last Kingdom*; Den., 1993); *Abîmes* (*Abyss*; FNA 1906, 1993); *De l'Autre Côté du Mur des Ténèbres* (*On the Other Side of the Wall of Darkness*; FNA 1926, 1993); *Mange-Monde* (*World-Eater*; PdF 543, 1993); *Chants Opératoires* (*Surgery Songs*; CRNI, 1993); *Armés et Dangereux* (*Armed and Dangerous*; Libr. Champs-Élysées Masque 2157, 1993); *Le Sourire Noir* (*The Black Smile*; Libr. Champs-Élysées, 1994); *Le Visiteur sans Visage* (*The Faceless Visitor*; Libr. Champs-Élysées Masque 2174, 1994); *Le Chien de Minuit* (*The Midnight Dog*; Libr. Champs-Élysées Masque 2188, 1994); *La Maison de l'Aigle* (*The House of the Eagle*; Den., 1994); *La Moisson d'Hiver* (*The Winter Harvest*; Den., 1995); *Profession: Cadavre* (*Business: Corpse*; FNA 1962, 1995); *La Main Froide* (*The Cold Hand*; Libr. Champs-Élysées, 1995); *Conan Lord, Carnets Secrets d'un Cambrioleur* (*Conan Lord, Secret Notebooks of a Burglar*; Libr. Champs-Élysées Masque 2219, 1995); *Conan Lord: Le Pique-Nique du Crocodile* (*The Crocodile's Picnic*; Libr. Champs-Élysées Masque, 1996); *Ma Vie chez les Morts* (*My Life Among the Dead*; Den. Présences, 1996); *La Fille de la Nuit* (*The Night Girl*; Libr. Champs-Élysées, 1996); *La Promenade du Bistouri* (*The Walk of the Scalpel*; FNA 1970, 1996); *Les Ombres du Jardin* (*The Shadows in the Garden*; Den., 1996); *Le Poing de Dieu* (*The Fist of God*; LdP, 1996); *L'Empire des Abîmes* (*The Empire of the Abyss*; as Kitty Doom; PdF 580, 1997); *Les Invisibles* (*The Invisible Ones*; as Kitty Doom; PdF 581, 1997); *Le Château des Poisons* (*The Castle of Poisons*; Libr. Champs-Élysées, 1997); *La Cicatrice du Chaos* (*The Scar of Chaos*; FNSF 5, 1997); *Les Enfants du Crépuscule* (*The Children of Twilight*; Libr. Champs-Élysées, 1997); as **Chillicothe, Zeb** (see below): Series *Jag*: Nos. 8, 10, 14 are by Serge Brussolo; *Note:* See Chapters VIII and IX. Animation director René **Laloux** has twice worked on an animated adaptation of *À l'Image du Dragon,* first using the working title of *Le Monde des Dieux-Nains (The World of the Dwarf Gods)* in 1986, then again in 1995 as *À l'Ombre du Dragon* (*In the Shadow of the Dragon*), but so far without success. **Les Lutteurs Immobiles** was adapted into a 1988 telefilm (see Book 1, Chapter II).

Brutsche, Alphonse *see* **Andrevon, Jean-Pierre**

Buchard, Robert (1934-); *30 Secondes sur New York* (*30 Seconds for New York*; AM, 1969); *Ce Sacré Vieil Harry* (*That Dear Old Harry*; AM, 1986); *Parole d'Homme* (*My Word as a Man*; AM, 1989); *Meurtres à Missoula* (*Murders in Missoula*; AM, 1995)

Bucline, Jean (?-); *L'Amour... Pour voir* (*Love... To See*; Revue Mondiale, 1931); *Fabrique d'Hommes* (*Man Factory*; Ariane, 1946); *L'An 3000 et la Suite* (*The Year 3000 and After*; La Bruyère, 1990); *Note:* See Chapter VII.

Bugnet, Georges (1879-1981); *Siraf, Étranges Révélations, Ce qu'on pense de nous par-delà la Lune* (*Siraf, Strange Revelations, What They Think of Us Beyond the Moon*; Totem, 1934); *Note:* Frenchman who emigrated to Alberta, Canada. Anastral entity converses with a human.

Bugnet, Nicolas (?-) *see* **Jaunez-Sponville, Pierre-Ignace**

Buhler, Michel (1945-); *La Machine* (*The Machine*; 1967); *Avril 1990 (Si tout se casse la Gueule; April 1990; If All Things Fall Apart*; Kes., 1973); *Note:* Swiss writer.

Burg, Charles-Gustave (?-); *Le Pentacle de l'Ange Déchu* (*The Pentacle of the Fallen Angel*; MarF 495, 1974; rev. NéO 36, 1982)

Burger, Chris (?-); *Incubation* (FNSL 6, 1974); *Le Sorcier* (*The Wizard*; FNSL 11, 1975); *Quand Elles Viendront* (*When They Will Come*; FNA 788, 1977); *Le Temps des Autres* (*The Time of Others*; FNA 806, 1977); *Note:* See chapters VIII and IX.

Burguet, Frantz-André (?-); *Vanessa* (Grasset, 1977); *Les Mouettes Noires* (*The Black Seagulls*; Belfond, 1982); *Note:* See Chapter IX.

Burko-Falcman, Berthe (?-); *La Dernière Vie de Madame K...* (*The Last Life of Mrs. K*; Hac., 1982)

Burnet, Philine (?-) *see* **Couteaud, P.**

Burnier, Michel-Antoine *see* **Bon, Frédéric**

Burnol, Maurice (?-) *see* ***Contes et Légendes***

Bussac, Michel (?-); *Le Réfractaire* (*The Resistant;* Hac., 1978); *Note:* Juvenile SF.

Bussi-Taillefer, Henri (?-); *Faits et Gestes du Dr. Bonus* (*Actions and Reactions of Dr. Bonus*; Nicolas, 1961); *Voyage à la Capitale des Microbes* (*Journey to the Capital of Microbes*; Nicolas, 1962)

Butor, Michel (Fourier, Charles; 1926-); *La Rose des Vents* (*The Rose of Winds*; Gall., 1970); *Note:* See Chapter IX. Also see **Opéra.**

Cabarel (?-); *Dans l'Étrange Inconnu* (*Into the Strange Unknown*; 2 vols.; Pelletan, 1928); *Note:* See Chapter VII.

Cabet, Étienne (1788-1856); *Voyage et Aventures de Lord W. Carisdall en Icarie* (*Voyage and Adventures of Lord W. Carisdall in Icaria*; Souverain, 1840); *Note:* See Chapter V.

Le Cabinet des Fées (Fairies' Cabinet); First specialized genre imprint devoted only to fairy tales. This 41-volume imprint was edited and published by the Chevalier Charles-Joseph de **Mayer** in Amsterdam and Geneva between 1785 and 1789. A modern, seven-volume reissue, edited by Élisabeth Lemirre, was published by Picquier in 1988-1994. Among the authors published in *Le Cabinet* were the Baronne d'**Aulnoy**, the Comte de **Caylus**, Antoine **Galland**, Thomas-Simon **Gueulette**, Madame de **La Force**, the Abbott Joseph de **La Porte**, Madame **Leprince de Beaumont**, Dame **Lévesque**, Madame de **Lintot**, Mademoiselle de **Lubert**, the Chevalier de **Mailly**, and the Comtesse de **Murat**.

Cabridens, Max-Henri (?-?) *see* **Grand-Guignol**

Cacaud, Michel (?-); *Côte d'Amour* (*Coast of Love*; Livres Nouveaux, 1939); *La Guerre des Ailes* (*War of the Wings*; Clocher, 1942); *Corsaires de l'Éther* (*Corsairs of the Ether*; Clocher, 1942); *Note:* Juvenile SF.

Caccia, Fulvio (1952-); *Golden Eighties* (Balzac, 1994); *Note:* French-Canadian writer.

Cade, Michel *see* **Lecler, Michel**

Caen, Raymond (1905-1957); *Les Stas, ou Le Journal d'un Dieu* (*The Stabs, or the Diary of a God*; Lib. 3 Mousquetaires, 1950); *Le Paradis vous attend* (*Paradise Is Waiting*; with François Caen; Nlles. Ed. Latines, 1952); *Ma Boule* (*My Ball*; Vandevelde, 1954); *Note:* See Chapter IX.

Cahu, Jules Nicolas Théodore (1854-1928); *Perdus dans l'Espace* (*Lost in Space*; Lecène-Oudin, 1894); *Note:* See Chapter V.

Cahusac, Louis de (?-?) *see* **Opéra**

Caillet, Gérard (?-) *see* **Opéra**

Caillois, Roger (1913-1978); *Méduse* (Gall., 1960); *Ponce Pilate* (Gall., 1961); *Approches de l'Imaginaire* (*Approach of the Imaginary*; Stock, 1970); *Fenosa* (Mourlot, 1972); *Anthologie du Fantastique* (*Anthology of Fantasy*; anthology; Gall., 1977); *Le Fleuve Alphée* (*The River Alphea*; Gall., 1978); *Babel* (Gall., 1978); *Trois Leçons des Ténèbres* (*Three Lessons of Darkness*; Fata Morgana, 1978); *Chroniques de Babel* (*Chronicles of Babel*; Den., 1981); *La Lumière des Songes* (*The Light of Dreams*; Fata Morgana, 1984); *Les Démons de Midi* (*The Demons of Noon*; Fata Morgana, 1991); *Le Mythe de la Licorne* (*The Myth of the Unicorn*; Fata Morgana, 1991); *Naissance de Lucifer* (*Birth of Lucifer*; Fata Morgana, 1992); *Note:* See Chaper VIII.

Cain, Henri (?-?) *see* **Opéra**

Calixte, Hervé (Rondard, Patrice; 1931-); *Note:* with Jean **Cap**, the co-founder and editor of *Satellite*. See **Klein, Gérard**.

Callebat, Paul (?-); *Orages sur ma Planète* (*Storms on My Planet*; Regain, 1957); *La Débâcle* (*The Retreat*; Debresse, 1959)

Calmet, Dom (?-?); *Dissertation sur les Apparitions des Anges, des Démons et des Esprits* (*Dissertation on the Appearances of Angels, Demons and Spirits*; Bure l'Aîné, 1746)

Calonne, Michel (1927-); *Le Plus Jeune Fils de l'Écureuil* (*The Squirrel's Youngest Son*; RL, 1958); *Une Folie au Bord de la Mer* (*A Folly at the Seashore*; 1960); *Hurleville* (*Screamcity*; Titres 45, 1981); *Les Enfances ou La Couleur de la Nuit des Temps* (*Childhood, or the Color of the Night of Time*; V. Hamy, 1990); *La Graine de Folie* (*The Seed of Madness*; Cairn, 1992); *Le Sac à Histoires* (*The Story Bag*; 4 vols.; Calonne, 1994); *Note:* See Chapter IX.

Calvet, Émile (?-); *Dans Mille Ans* (*In a Thousand Years*; Delagrave, 1883); *Note:* See Chapter V.

Calvez, Jean-Michel (1961-); *Planète des Vents* (*Wind Planet*; FNSF 16, 1997)

Calvo, David (?-); *Délius (Une Chanson d'Été)* (*A Summer Song*; Mnemos 26, 1997); *Note:* See Chapter IX.

Cambon, René (?-); *L'Homme Double* (*The Double Man*; RF 74, 1960); *Nos Chers Disparus* (*Our Dearly Departed*; Den., 1970); *Le Bon Grain est livré* (*The Wheat Has Been Delivered*; Den., 1972); *Machination pour un Cocu* (*Schemes for a Cheated Husband*; Den., 1972); *La Verrue* (*The Wart*; Den., 1974); *Note:* See Chapter IX.

Cambri, Gérard (?-); *Le Président du Monde* (*The President of the World*; Star, 1976); *La Tourmente des Invisibles* (*The Storm of the Invisibles*; as William Stone; Star, 1976); *Les Destructeurs* (*The Destroyers*; as William Stone; Star, 1976); *La Bataille de Buenos Aires* (*The Battle of Buenos Aires*; FN, 1979); *Cash* (FN, 1979); *Massacre à Manhattan* (*Massacre in Manhattan*; FN, 1979); *Ouragan sur la Maison-Blanche* (*Storm Over the White House*; FN, 1979); *Épouvante à Los Angeles* (*Terror in Los Angeles*; FN, 1979); *Holocauste à Paris* (*Holocaust in Paris*; FN, 1980); *Terreur à Haïti* (*Terror in Haiti*; FN, 1980); *Assaut sur New York* (*Assault on New York*; FN, 1980); *Le Carrousel des Vautours* (*The Merry-Go-Round of Vultures*; FN, 1980); *Complot à Washington* (*Plot in Washington*; FN, 1980); *L'Enfer Californien* (*Californian Hell*; FN, 1981); *Le Paradis des Chacals* (*The Jackals' Paradise*; FN, 1981); *Le Sang du Texas* (*The Blood of Texas*; FN, 1981)

Cami, Henri (1884-1958); *Les Aventures du Baron de Crack* (*The Adventures of Baron Munchausen*; Hac., 1926); *Le Jugement Dernier* (*The Last Judgment*; Baudinière, 1928); *Le Scaphandrier de la Tour Eiffel* (*The Diver of the Eiffel Tower*; Baudinière, 1929); *Les Mémoires de*

Dieu le Père (*The Memoirs of God the Father*; Baudinière, 1930); *Les Amants de l'Entre-Ciel* (*The Lovers of Between-The-Sky*; Baudinière, 1933); *Voyage Inouï de M. Rikiki* (*Amazing Journey of Mr. Rikiki*; Baudinière, 1938); *Krik-Robot, Détective à Moteur* (*Mechanical Detective*; Paul Dupont, 1945); *Les Kidnappés du Panthéon* (*Kidnaped in the Pantheon*; Paul Dupont, 1947); *Le Voyage Inouï de M. Rikiki* (*The Amazing Journey of Mr. Rikiki*; Technique du Livre, 1947); *Note:* Children's SF.

Camiglieri, Laurence (1919-) *see* **Contes et Légendes**

Campos, Elisabeth *see* **Sheldon, S. K.**

Camproux (?-) *see* **Contes et Légendes**

Camus, Renaud (1946-); *Roman Roi* (P.O.L., 1983)

Camus, William (1923-); *Le Faiseur de Pluie* (*The Rainmaker*; GP, 1974); *Vers les Terres de Grand-Mère* (*Towards Granma's Lands*; GP, 1974); *Cheyennes 6112* (With Christian **Grenier**; GP, 1974); *Une Squaw dans les Étoiles* (*A Squaw Among the Stars*; with Christian **Grenier**; GP, 1975); *Opération Clik-Clak* (GP, 1975); *Les Aubes Rouges* (*The Red Dawns*; GP, 1976); *Les Éléphants d'Hannibal* (*Hannibal's Elephants*; GP, 1976); *Les Deux Mondes* (*The Two Worlds*; Duculot, 1976); *Les Ferrailleurs* (*The Junk Dealers*; Duculot, 1976); *Un Bonheur Électronique* (*An Electronic Happiness*; GP, 1977); *Le Poulet* (*The Chicken*; GP, 1977); *Les Bleus et les Gris* (*The Blues and the Grays*; GP, 1977); *Une Drôle de Planète* (*A Funny Planet*; GP, 1978); *Un Os au Bout de l'Autoroute* (*A Bone at the End of the Freeway*; GP, 1978); *Le Canard à Trois Pattes* (*The Three-Legged Duck*; with Pierre **Pelot** & J. **Coué**; Duculot, 1978); *Les Oiseaux de Feu et Autres Contes Peaux-Rouges* (*The Firebirds and Other Redskin Tales*; Gall., 1978); *Une Idée Saugrenue* (*A Strange Idea*; Magnard, 1979); *Légendes de la Vieille Amérique* (*Legends of Old America*; Bordas, 1979); *Légendes Peaux-Rouges* (*Redskin Legends*; Magnard, 1980); *La Grande Peur* (*The Great Fear*; Bordas, 1980); *Le Péril Vient de la Terre* (*The Danger Comes from Earth*; with Jacky **Soulier**; Bordas, 1981); *Face au Péril* (*Face-To-Face with the Danger*; Bordas, 1981); *Robots* (La Farandole, 1981); *Extra-Terrestres* (*Extra-Terrestrials*; Hum., 1983); *1000 Ans de Contes* (*1000 Years of Fairy Tales*; Milan, 1996); *Note:* See Chapter IX.

Canal, Richard (1953-); *La Malédiction de l'Éphémère* (*The Curse of the Ephemereal*; La Découverte, 1986; rev. JL 4156, 1996); *Animamea 1: Les Ambulances du Rêve* (*The Ambulances of Dreams*; FNA 1536, 1986); *Animamea 2: La Légende Etoilée* (*The Starry Legend*; FNA 1554, 1987); *Animamea 3: Les Voix Grises du Monde Gris* (*The Grey Voices of the Grey World*; FNA 1582, 1987); *Villes-Vertiges* (*Vertigo-Cities*; Aurore, Fu-

turs 3, 1988); *Swap-Swap* (JL 2836, 1990); *La Guerre en ce Jardin* (*The War in This Garden*; FNA 1818, 1991); *Ombres Blanches* (*White Shadows*; JL 3455, 1993); *Aube Noire* (*Black Dawn*; JL 3669, 1994); *Le Cimetière des Papillons* (*The Graveyard of the Butterflies*; JL 3908, 1995); *Les Paradis Piégés* (*The Trapped Paradises*; JL 4483, 1997); *Note:* See Chapter IX.

Cantin, Reynald (1946-); *Le Lac Disparu* (*The Vanished Lake*; Q/A, 1992); *La Lecture du Diable* (*The Devil's Reading Materials*; Q/A, 1994); *Mon Amie Constance* (*My Friend Constance*; Héritage, 1996); *Note:* French-Canadian writer. Juvenile fantasies. *Le Lac* was written collectively by a class of 14-16-year-olds under the guidance and editorship of Reynald Cantin.

Cantin, Roger (?-); *Matusalem* (Boréal, 1993); *Note:* French-Canadian writer. Juvenile SF novel.

Cap, Jean (Benâtre, Michel; ?-); *Nurma* (Cosmos 9, 1956); *La Brigade du Temps* (*The Time Brigade*; Satellite 28, 32-33, 1960); *À la Recherche de l'Homme Cosmique* (*Searching for the Cosmic Man*; Satellite CSF 10, 1960); *Note:* with Hervé **Calixte**, the co-founder and editor of *Satellite*.

Caplain-Dol, Robert (?-?) *see* **Grand-Guignol**

Capoulet-Junac, Edward de (1930-); *L'Ordonnateur des Pompes Nuptiales* (*The Ordinator of Weddings*; Gall., 1961); *Pallas ou la Tribulation* (*Pallas, or Tribulations*; PdF 100, 1967); *Note:* See Chapter IX.

Caputo, Natha (1904-1967); *Contes des Quatre Vents* (*Tales of Four Winds*; Nathan, 1954)

Caraguel, Edmond P. (?-); *Napoléon V, Dictateur* (Georges-Anquetil, 1926); *Note:* See Chapter VII.

Carducci, Lisa (1943-); *Affaire Classée* (*Case Closed*; Humanitas, 1992); *À l'Encre de Chine* (*In China Ink*; Humanitas, 1994); *Note:* French-Canadian writer. *Affaire* is a collection of fantastical tales.

Carey, Mary (?-) *see* **Fontugne, Charles**

Carl, Yves (?-); *Jhedin Ovoghemma* (FNA 1672, 1989); *Note:* See Chapter IX.

Carlini, Marcel de (?-); *Les Voyages de l'Explorateur Clandestin* (*The Voyages of the Clandestine Explorer*; Labor & Fides-Genève, 1948)

Carn, Hervé (1949-); *Issek* (Diabase, 1997); *Note:* See Chapter VIII.

Caroff, André (Carpouzis, André; 1924-); *Hallucinations* (FNAG 73, 1961); *Le Barracuda* (FNAG 75, 1961); *Névrose* (*Neuroses*; FNAG 77, 1961); *Le Dernier Taxi* (*The Last Taxi*; FNAG 80, 1961); *Clameurs* (*Clamors*; FNAG 83, 1962); *Le Sang du Cactus* (*The Blood of the*

Cactus; FNAG 88, 1962); *Griffe de Mort* (*Death Claw*; FNAG 94, 1963); *Le Médium* (FNAG 96, 1963); *L'Heure des Morts* (*The Hour of the Dead*; FNAG 103, 1963); *L'Oiseau de Malheur* (*The Bird of Ill Omen*; FNAG 104, 1964); *Cruauté Mentale* (*Mental Cruelty*; FNAG 106, 1964); *La Sinistre Mme Atomos* (*The Sinister Mrs. Atomos*; FNAG 109, 1964); *Mme Atomos Sème la Terreur* (*Mrs. Atomos Spreads Terror*; FNAG 115, 1965); *Mme Atomos Frappe à la Tête* (*Mrs. Atomos Strikes at the Head*; FNAG 120, 1965); *Miss Atomos* (FNAG 124, 1965); *Miss Atomos contre KKK* (*Miss Atomos vs. KKK*; FNAG 130, 1966); *Le Retour de Mme Atomos* (*The Return of Mrs. Atomos*; FNAG 134, 1966); *L'Erreur de Mme Atomos* (*The Mistake of Mrs. Atomos*; FNAG 136, 1966); *Mme Atomos Prolonge la Vie* (*Mrs. Atomos Prolongs Life*; FNAG 140, 1967); *Les Monstres de Mme Atomos* (*The Monsters of Mrs. Atomos*; FNAG 143, 1967); *Mme Atomos Crache des Flammes* (*Mrs. Atomos Spits Fire*; FNAG 146, 1967); *Mme Atomos Croque le Marmot* (*Mrs. Atomos Eats a Child*; FNAG 147, 1967); *La Ténébreuse Mme Atomos* (*Dark Mrs. Atomos*; FNAG 152, 1968); *Mme Atomos Change de Peau* (*Mrs. Atomos Sheds Her Skin*; FNAG 156, 1968); *Mme Atomos Fait Du Charme* (*Mrs. Atomos Charms Her Way*; FNAG 160, 1969); *L'Empreinte de Mme Atomos* (*The Mark of Mrs. Atomos*; FNAG 169, 1969); *Mme Atomos Jette Un Froid* (*Mrs. Atomos Throws a Cold*; FNAG 173, 1969); *Mme Atomos Cherche la Petite Bête* (*Mrs. Atomos Seeks Small Creatures*; FNAG 177, 1970); *La Nuit du Monstre* (*The Night of the Monster*; FNAG 192, 1970); *Le Rideau de Brume* (*The Curtain of Mist*; FNA 457, 1971); *La Guerre des Nosiars* (*The War of the Nosiars*; FNA 489, 1972); *Les Êtres du Néant* (*The Void Beings*; FNA 513, 1972); *La Planète Infernale* (*The Infernal Planet*; FNA 529, 1972); *Ceux des Ténèbres* (*Those from Darkness*; FNA 553, 1973); *L'Exilé d'Akros* (*The Exile from Akros*; FNA 567, 1973); *Le Bagne de Rostos* (*The Penitentiary of Rostos*; FNA 613, 1974); Electronic Man (FNA 833, 1978); Rhesus Y-2 (FNA 850, 1978); *Les Combattants de Serkos* (*The Fighters of Serkos*; FNA 872, 1978); *Les Sphères Attaquent* (*The Spheres Attack*; FNA 950, 1979); *Bactéries 3000* (*Bacteria 3000*; FNA 956, 1979); *Rod, Combattant du Futur* (*Rod, Future Fighter*; FNA 962, 1980); *Rod, Menace sur Oxima* (*Rod, Threat Over Oxima*; FNA 974, 1980); *Rod, Patrouille de l'Espace* (*Rod, Space Patrol*; FNA 1026, 1080); Rod, Vacuum-02 (FNA 1035, 1980); *Un Autre Monde* (*Another World*; FNA 1105, 1981); *Captif du Temps* (*Time's Captive*; FNA 1117, 1982); *Métal en Fusion* (*Molten Metal*; FNA 1147, 1982); *Terreur Psy* (*Psi Terror*; FNA 1161, 1982); *Le Piège des Sables* (*The Sand Trap*; FNA 1175, 1982); *L'Oiseau dans le Ciment* (*The Bird in Cement*; FNA 1203, 1983); *Élimination* (FNA 1237, 1983); *Ordinator-Labyrinthus* (FNA 1245, 1983); *Simulations* (FNA 1250, 1983); *Deux Pas dans le Soleil* (*Two Steps Towards the

Sun*; FNA 1309, 1984); *Ordinator-Macchabées* (FNA 1327, 1984); *Ordinator-Phantastikos* (FNA 1342, 1984); *Ordinator-Erotikos* (FNA 1361, 1985); *Ordinator-Criminalis* (FNA 1378, 1985); *Ordinator-Ocularis* (FNA 1396, 1985); *Ordinator-Craignos* (FNA 1404, 1985); *Ordinator-Rapidos* (FNA 1418, 1985); *Extermination* (FNG 83, 1989); *Note:* See chapters VIII and IX. Most of Caroff's earlier novels were adapted into digest-sized graphic novels (see Book 1, Chapter V under **Fleuve Noir**). André Caroff's mother also wrote novels for FNAG under the pseudonym of José **Michel**.

Caroutch, Yvonne (?-); *Le Gouvernement des Eaux* (*The Government of Waters*; Bourgois, 1970); *Le Grand Transparent et le Grand Écorché* (*The Great Transparent and the Great Unskinned*; St. Pierre Capelle, 1972); *La Voie au Coeur de Verre* (*The Way of the Heart of Glass*; Libr. St. Germain, 1972); *Giordano Bruno, le Voyant de Venise* (*The Seer of Venice*; Culture, Arts, Loisirs, 1975); *La Licorne Alchimique* (*The Alchemical Unicorn*; Ed. Philosophiques, 1981); *Le Livre de la Licorne* (*The Book of the Unicorn*; Pardès, 1989); *Note:* See Chapter VIII.

Carpentier, André (1947-); *L'Aigle Volera à travers le Soleil* (*The Eagle Will Fly Through the Sun*; HMH, 1978); *Rue Saint-Denis* (HMH, 1978); *Du Pain, Des Oiseaux* (*Bread, Birds*; VLB, 1982); *Dix Contes et Nouvelles Fantastiques par Dix Auteurs Québécois* (*Ten Fantastic Tales and Short Stories by Ten Authors from Quebec*; anthology; Quinze, 1983); *Dix Nouvelles de Science-Fiction Québécoise* (*Ten SF Short Stories from Quebec*; anthology; Quinze, 1985); *Carnet sur la Fin Possible d'un Monde* (*Notebook on the Possible End of the World*; XYZ, 1992); *Note:* French-Canadian writer.

Carpouzis, André *see* **Caroff, André**

Carpouzis (Mme.) *see* **Michel, José**

Carré, Gérard (1952-); *La Troisième Guerre Mondiale n'aura pas lieu* (*World War III Will Not Happen*; Gall., 1987); *Une Souris et un Homme* (*Of Mouse and Man*; Syros, 1989)

Carré, Lydie (?-); *La Rose de Noumah* (*The Rose of Noumah*; Rocher, 1994)

Carré, Michel (1819-1872) *see* **Opéra**

Carre, Pierre (?-); *Mare Crisium* (Cahiers Nouvel Humanisme, 1952)

Carrère, Emmanuel (?-); *Le Détroit de Behring* (*The Straits of Behring*; POL, 1986); *Je Suis Vivant et Vous Êtes Tous Morts* (*I'm Alive and You're All Dead*; Seuil, 1993)

Carrère, Jean (1868-1932); *La Dame du Nord* (*The Lady

of the North; Grasset, 1909); *Les Chants Orphiques* (*The Orphic Songs*; Plon, 1923); *La Fin d'Atlantis ou Le Grand Soir* (*The End of Atlantis, or the Great Night*; 1903–04; rev. Plon, 1926); *Note:* See Chapter VII.

Carrier, Roch (1937-); *Jolis Deuils* (*Pretty Mournings*; Jour, 1964); *La Guerre, Yes, Sir!* (*The War, Yes, Sir!*; Jour, 1968); *Floralie, Où es-tu?* (*Floralie, Where Are You?*; Jour, 1969); *Le Deux Millième Étage* (*The 2000th Floor*; Jour, 1973); *Il n'y a pas de Pays sans Grand-Père* (*There Are No Countries Without Grandfathers; Stané, 1977); Les Enfants du Bonhomme dans la Lune* (*The Children of the Man in the Moon*; Stané, 1979); *La Céleste Bicyclette* (*The Celestial Bicycle*; Stané, 1980); *Les Fleurs Vivent-Elles Ailleurs que sur la Terre?* (*Do Flowers Live Elsewhere Than on Earth?*; Stané, 1981); *La Dame qui avait des Chaînes aux Chevilles* (*The Lady Who Wore Chains on Her Ankles*; Stané, 1981); *Le Cirque Noir* (*The Black Circus*; Stané, 1982); *De l'Amour dans la Ferraille* (*Love in the Junkyard*; Stané, 1984); *L'Ours et le Kangouro* (*The Bear and the Kangaroo*; Stané, 1986); *Un Chameau en Jordanie* (*A Camel in Jordan*; Stané, 1988); *Le Martien de Noël* (*The Christmas Martian*; Q/A, 1991); *Note:* French-Canadian writer. *Jolis Deuils* is a collection of fantastic stories. *La Céleste Bicyclette* is a stage play. **Le Martien de Noël** is the novelization of an eponymous 1977 feature film by Bernard Gosselin (see Book 1, Chapter I).

Carrière, Huguette (Bezian, Huguette; 1914-); *L'Envoyé 1: Maletor* (*The Envoy 1: Maletor*; SdP 36, 1977); *L'Envoyé 2: L'Étoile Perdue* (*The Envoy 2: The Lost Star*; SdP 61, 1978); Series *Tony: Tony et l'Homme Invisible* (*Tony and the Invisible Man*; BR, 1971); *Tony et l'Énigme de la Zimbollina* (*Tony and the Zimbollina Mystery*; BR, 1971); *Tony et le Garçon de l'Autre Planète* (*Tony and the Boy from Another Planet*; BR, 1972); *Tony et le Masque aux Yeux Verts* (*Tony and the Green-Eyed Mask*; BR, 1972); *Tony et l'Homme en Habit* (*Tony and the Well-Dressed Man*; BR, 1973); *Tony sur l'Île Interdite* (*Tony on the Forbidden Island*; BR, 1973); *Tony et le Secret du Cormoran* (*Tony and the Cormorant's Secret*; BR, 1973); *Tony et la Maison des Ombres* (*Tony and the House of Shadows*; BR, 1974); *Tony et le Transistor* (BR, 1974); *Tony et les Gens du Voyage* (*Tony and the Travellers*; BR, 1974); *Tony et les Drôles de Pistolets* (*Tony and the Funny Guns*; BR, 1975); *Tony et la Cité en Folie* (*Tony and the Mad City*; BR, 1975); *Tony Lève les Masques* (*Tony Lifts the Masks*; BR, 1975); *Tony et le Secret des Pendules* (*Tony and the Clocks' Secret*; BR, 1976); *Tony et la Perle Noire* (*Tony and the Black Pearl*; BR, 1976); *Tony Tire les Ficelles* (*Tony Pulls the Strings*; BR, 1977); *Tony et la Valise Fantôme* (*Tony and the Phantom Suitcase*; BR, 1978); *Tony et le Secret du Guardian* (*Tony and the*

Guardian's Secret; BR, 1978); *Tony au Carnaval des Robots* (*Tony at the Robots' Carnival*; BR, 1980); *Note:* Juvenile SF. See Chapter IX.

Carrière, Jean-Claude (1931-); *Simon le Mage* (*Simon the Magus*; Plon, 1993); *Note:* Also see **Becker, Benoît**.

Carrière, Paul (?-?) *see* **Grand-Guignol**

Carrouges, Michel (Couturier, Louis; ?-); *Les Portes Dauphines* (*The Dauphine Gates*; Gall., 1954); *Les Grands-Pères Prodiges* (*The Prodigal Grandfathers*; Plon, 1957); *Note:* Carrouges is also the author of one of the first serious UFO research works published in French, the luridly mistitled *Apparitions de Martiens* (1954). Also see Chapter IX.

Cars, Guy des (?-); *Mon Ami Touche-à-Tout* (*My Friend Touches-Everything*; Nlles. Presses Fr., 1946); *La Boule de Cristal* (*The Crystal Ball*; Flamm., 1974); *Le Mage* (*The Magus*; Flamm., 1974); *Note:* Popular author of romance novels. See Chapter VIII.

Carsac, Francis (Bordes, François; 1919-1981); *Ceux de Nulle Part* (*Those from Nowhere*; RF 23, 1954); *Les Robinsons du Cosmos* (*The Robinsons of the Cosmos*; RF 34, 1955); *Terre en Fuite* (*Fleeing Earth*; RF 72, 1960); *Ce Monde est Notre* (*This World Is Ours*; RF 91, 1962); *Pour Patrie, l'Espace* (*For Homeland, Space*; RF 104, 1962); *La Vermine du Lion* (*The Vermin of the Lion*; FNA 310, 1967); *Note:* See Chapter IX.

Cartier, Éric (?-); *Les Inhumains* (*The Inhumans*; Arabesque 144, 1960); *Le Furet ne croit pas au Père Noël* (*The Weasel Doesn't Believe in Santa Claus*; Arabesque 246, 1961); *En Double Commande* (*Double Drive*; Arabesque 301, 1962); *Note:* See Chapter IX.

Cassabois, Jacques (1947-); *L'Homme de Pierre* (*The Stone Man*; Messidor-La Farandole, 1981); *Le Bonhomme de Nuit* (*The Night Man*; Magnard, 1983); *Le Port Englouti* (*The Sunken Harbor*; Gall., 1989)

Cassagnac, P.-A. de (?-); *Le Couloir de Lumière* (*The Corridor of Light*; L'Intrépide, 1932); *Note:* See Chapter VII.

Cassagne, Lucien (?-); *Les Hogs* (Horay, 1973)

Cassan, Marguerite (?-); *Histoires à Coté* (*Sideway Sto-*

ries; RL, 1963); *Fil à Fil* (*Thread to Thread*; RL, 1965); *À Développer dans l'Obscurité* (*To Develop in the Dark*; RL, 1967); *Note:* See Chapter VIII. Marguerite Cassan also adapted Gustave **Le Rouge**'s *Le Prisonnier de la Planète Mars* for radio (see Book 1, Chapter III).

Cassou, Jean (1897-1986); *Éloge de la Folie* (*In Praise of Madness*; Émile-Paul, 1925); *La Maison sous la Neige* (*The House Under the Snow*; Émile-Paul, 1926); *Le Pays qui n'est à Personne* (*The Country Which Belongs to Nobody*; Émile-Paul, 1928); *La Clef des Songes* (*The Key to Dreams*; Émile-Paul, 1929); *Comme une Grande Image* (*Like a Big Image*; Émile-Paul, 1931); *Les Inconnus dans la Cave* (*Unknown Men in the Cellar*; Gall., 1933); *De l'Étoile au Jardin des Plantes* (*From the Étoile to the Botanical Gardens*; Gall., 1935); *Les Massacres de Paris* (*The Massacres of Paris*; Gall., 1935); *Légion* (Gall., 1939); *Le Centre du Monde* (*The Center of the World*; Sagittaire, 1945); *Les Enfants sans Âge* (*The Ageless Children*; Sagittaire, 1946); *La Mémoire Courte* (*The Short Memory*; Minuit, 1953); *Obsèques* (*Funerals*; Rougerie, 1971); *Le Voisinage des Cavernes* (*The Neighborhood of Caverns*; AM, 1971); *Si j'étais un Caïd* (*If I Were a Kingpin*; Garnier, 1977); *Note:* See Chapter VI.

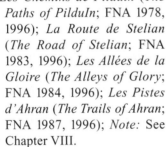

Castan, Claude (1961-); *Les Chemins de Pilduin* (*The Paths of Pilduin*; FNA 1978, 1996); *La Route de Stelian* (*The Road of Stelian*; FNA 1983, 1996); *Les Allées de la Gloire* (*The Alleys of Glory*; FNA 1984, 1996); *Les Pistes d'Ahran* (*The Trails of Ahran*; FNA 1987, 1996); *Note:* See Chapter VIII.

Casteret, Norbert (1897-1987); *La Terre Ardente* (*The Fiery Earth*; Didier, 1950); *La Montagne Creuse* (*The Hollow Mountain*; MarJ 225, 1962); *Mission Centre Terre* (*Mission Center Earth*; Perrin, 1964; transl. as *Mission Underground*, 1968); *Muta, Fille des Cavernes* (*Muta, Daughter of the Caverns*; 1965); *Note:* See Chapter IX.

Castex, Pierre (?-); *Les Hercules d'Acier* (*The Steel Hercules*; PC, 1967)

Castilhon, Jean-Louis (1720-1793); *Zingha, Reine d'Angola* (*Zingha, Queen of Angola*; Bouillon-Lacombe, 1769); *Le Mendiant Boîteux ou les Aventures d'Ambroise Gurnett, Balayeur du Pavé de Spring Garden* (*The Lame Beggar, or the Adventures of Ambrose Gur-*

nett, Street Sweeper at Spring Garden; Bouillon-Lacombe, 1771)

Castle, Fred (Château, René; ?-); *Les Prédateurs de la Nuit* (*The Night Predators*; Média 1000, 1988); *Note:* Novelization of the 1988 Jess Franco horror film written by René Château under his pseudonym of Fred Castle. The story is transposition of **Franju**'s **Les Yeux Sans Visage**.

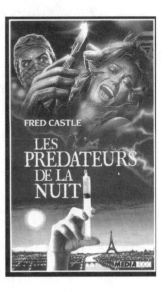

Caters, Christian de *see* **Falcoz, André**

Caudéran, Jean & Denise *see* **Le May, J. & D.**

Cauquelin, Anne (?-); *La Ville la Nuit* (*The City at Night*; PUF, 1977); *Potamor* (Seuil, 1978); *Les Prisons de César* (*Caesar's Jails*; Seuil, 1979); *Tardivo* (Porte du Sud, 1994)

Causse, Charles (?-) *see* **Maël, Pierre**

Causse, Frédéric *see* **Agraives, Jean d'**

Cauvin, Patrick *see* **Klotz, Claude**

Cayatte, André (1909-1989) *see* **Ribon, Robert de**

Caylus, Anne-Claude-Philippe de Tubières de Grimoard de Pestels de Lévi, Marquis d'Esternay, Baron de Bransac, Comte de (1692-1765); *Contes Orientaux tirés des Manuscrits de la Bibliothèque du Roi de France* (*Oriental Tales Drawn from the Library of the King of France*; 1743); *Cinq Contes de Fées* (*Five Fairy Tales*; 1745); *Histoire du Vaillant Chevalier Tyran le Blanc* (*Tales of the Valiant Knight Tyrant the White*; 1775); *Féeries Nouvelles* (*New Fairy Tales*; 1787); *Nouveaux Contes Orientaux* (*New Oriental Tales*; 1787); *Note:* Also see Chapter III, and ***Cabinet des Fées***.

Cayrol, Jean (1911-); *Histoire d'une Prairie* (*Tale of a Field*; Seuil, 1969); *Histoire d'un Désert* (*Tale of a Desert*; Seuil, 1972); *Histoire de la Mer* (*Tale of the Sea*; Seuil, 1973); *Histoire de la Forêt* (*Tale of a Forest*; Seuil, 1975); *Histoire d'une Maison* (*Tale of a House*; Seuil, 1976); *Histoire du Ciel* (*Tale of the Sky*; Seuil, 1979); *L'Homme dans le Rétroviseur* (*The Man in the Mirror*; Seuil, 1981); *Les Enfants Pillards* (*The Looting Children*; Hac., 1981); *Note:* See Chapter VIII.

Cazal, Edmond (Commandant) *see* **La Hire, Jean de**

Cazalbou, Jean (1913-); *Le Pêcheur de Sable* (*The Sand Fisher*; Privat, 1977); *Les Sages de Noukim et les Deux*

Étés (*The Wise Men of Noukim and the Two Summers*; La Farandole-Messidor, 1982); *Fabrice et les Passeurs de I'Ombre* (*Fabrice & the Shadow Travellers*; Flamm 1986); *L'Énigme de la Main Verte* (*The Enigma of the Green Hand*; Milan, 1986)

Cazals, Patrick (?-) *see Contes et Légendes*

Cazes, Bernard (?-); *Histoire des Futurs* (*History of the Futures*; Seghers, 1985)

Cazotte, Jacques (1720-1792); *Ollivier* (Esprit, 1763); *La Patte du Chat* (*The Cat's Paw*; Tilloobalaa, 1741); *Les Mille et Une Fadaises* (*A Thousand and One Silly Stories*; L'Endormy, 1742); *Le Diable Amoureux* (1772; transl. as *The Devil in Love*, 1793); *La Belle par Accident* (*Beauty by Accident*; Esprit, 1776-1788); *Note:* See chapters III and IV.

Celier, François (?-); *Démarcation* (*Boundary*; St. Germain-des-Prés, 1971); Series *Éric Matras:*; *Les Chevaliers de l'Océan* (*The Knight of the Ocean*; BV, 1969); *La Vallée Fantastique* (*Fantastic Valley*; BV, 1970) *Note:* Juvenile SF. See Chapter IX.

Celval, Félix (?-); *Les Robinsons de l'Espace* (*The Space Robinsons*; RJ, 1934); *Le Monstre du Loch Ness* (*The Loch Ness Monster*; VA, 1934); *Les Incendiaires de l'Opéra* (*The Opera Arsonists*; VA, 1934); *Le Château du Paradis* (*The Castle of Paradise*; RJ, 1934); *Le Rayon Infernal* (*The Hellish Ray*; RJ, 1935); *Le Monstre de l'Île sans Nom* (*The Monster of the Nameless Island*; RJ, 1936); *Les Flibustiers de l'Espace* (*The Corsairs of Space*; VA, 1938); *La Marque de la Bête* (*The Mark of the Beast*; VA, 1939); *Note:* See Chapter VII.

Cénac, Claude (Raynaud, Claudine; 1924-); *La Planète Bonheur* (*Planet Happiness*; Magnard, 1963); *La Citadelle de l'Espoir* (*The Citadel of Hope*; Magnard, 1964); *Le Robot Sauvage* (*The Savage Robot*; BR, 1966); *Les Cavernes de la Rivière Rouge* (*The Caverns of Red River*; Magnard, 1967); *Le Coeur sur la Patte* (*Heart in Paw*; Magnard, 1968); *Le Printemps Viendra Deux Foix* (*Spring Will Come Twice*; Hac., 1970); *Des Milliards de Soleils* (*Billions of Suns*; Magnard, 1971); *Demain l'An Mil* (*Tomorrow the Year 1000*; RL, 1976); *Bonhomme Rouge, Bonhomme Vert* (*Red Man, Green Man*; Magnard, 1983); *Les Sorciers de la Rivière Rouge* (*The Wizards of Red River*; Magnard, 1984); *Souviens-toi de la Rivière Rouge* (*Remember the Red River*; Magrwd, 1988); *Les Robestiques* (*The Robestics*; Milan, 1990); *Le Tonnerre de Madrazès* (*The Thunder of Madrazes*; Hac., 1993); *Note:* Juveniles. See Chapter IX.

Cendrars, Blaise (Sauser, Frédéric-Louis; 1887-1961); *La Fin du Monde Filmée par l'Ange* (*The End of the World Filmed by an Angel*; La Sirène, 1919); *L'Eubage* (Au Sans Pareil, 1926); *Moravagine* (Grasset, 1926); *Note:* See Chapter VI.

Cerbelaud-Salagnac, Georges (?-); *Sous le Signe de la Tortue* (*Under the Sign of the Turtle*; SdP, 1937); *Le Mystère du Croiseur 'Toulouse'* (*The Mystery of the Cruiser 'Toulouse'*; SdP, 1948); *Le Sceau du Prince Henri* (*The Seal of Prince Henry*; SdP, 1950); *Note:* Juveniles.

Cernaut, Jean (1919-); *Le Grand Roux* (*The Big Red*; Rouge et Or, 1969); *Zone Interdite* (*Forbidden Zone*; Messidor-La Farandole, 1972); *Le Secret de Miltombe* (*The Secret of Miltombe*; Messidor-La Farandole, 1977); *Comptes à Rendre* (*Accounts to Be Told*; Messidor-La Farandole, 1980); *Terre Franche* (*Free Earth*; Duculot, 1985); *Note:* Juveniles.

Certigny, Henri (1919-); *Les Automates* (*The Automatons*; Gall., 1954); *Le Bal Masqué de Montparnasse* (*The Masked Ball of Montparnasse*; Gall., 1957)

Certon, Erik J. (Certoncini, Frédéric; ?-); *Émeraude* (*Emerald*; Corne d'Or, 1950); *Un Drame de l'Au-Delà* (*A Drama from Beyond*; FNAG 65, 1960)

Certoncini, Frédéric *see* **Certon, Erik J.; Cervières, Paul (?-);** *En Avion Vers la Cité Déserte* (*Flying Towards the Desert City*; Gédalge, 1934); *Le Cousin Météore* (*Cousin Meteor*; Ed. Ouvrières, 1949); *L'Énigme* (*The Enigma*; Dupuis, 1952)

Cervon, Jacqueline (Moussard, Jacqueline; 1924-); *Sélim, le Petit Marchand de Bonheur* (*Selim, the Little Happiness Peddler*; Rouge et Or, 1966); *Benoit, l'Arbre et la Lune* (*Benoit, the Tree and the Moon*; Rouge et Or, 1968); *Djinn la Malice* (Rouge et Or, 1971); *Le Tambour des Sables* (*The Drum of the Sands*; Duculot, 1971); *Django de l'Île Verte* (*Django from the Green Isle*; Rouge et Or 1972); *Coumba du Pays Oublié des Pluies* (*Coumba from the Land Forgotten by the Rains*; Rouge et Or, 1973); *Djilani et l'Oiseau de Nuit* (*Djilani and the Night Bird*; Rouge et Or, 1978); *Le Dernier Mirage* (*The Last Mirage*; Duculot, 1980); *Les Enfants de la Planète* (*The Children of the Planet*; Duculot, 1983); *Note:* Juveniles.

Cesbron, Gilbert (1913-1979); *D'Outremonde* (*From the World Beyond*; Guilde du Livre, 1949); *La Ville Couronnée d'Épines* (*The City Crowned by Thorns*; Livre de Paris, 1976); *Un Vivier sans Eau* (*A Waterless Fishpond*; RL, 1979); *Note:* Mainstream writer.

Cézembre, Jacques (?-); *Le Fantôme de l'Atlantique* (*The Ghost of the Atlantic*; S&V, 1922); *Les Nègres Blonds de l'Île Maudite* (*The Blond Negroes of the Accursed Island*; BGA, 1927); *Le Champion Fantôme* (*The Phantom Champion*; Tallandier, 1932); *La Maisons des Pendus* (*The House of Hanged Men*; Pub. Tech., 1944); *Meurtre sans Victime* (*Victimless Murder*; Pub. Tech., 1944)

Chabar, Jacques (?-); *La Cité du Serpent à Plumes* (*The City of the Feathered Serpent*; Fleurus, 1954); *Le Retour du Serpent à Plumes* (*The Return of the Feathered Serpent*; Fleurus, 1957); *L'Étoile au Fond des Mers* (*The Star at the Bottom of the Sea*; Fleurus, 1958); *Le Marabout du Désert* (*The Desert Witch Doctor*; Fleurus, 1966); *Note:* Juvenile SF. See Chapter IX.

Chabin, Laurent (1957-); *Le Peuple Fantôme* (*The Ghost People*; Boréal, 1996); *Le Rêveur Polaire* (*The Polar Dreamer*; Boréal, 1996); *L'Argol et Autres Histoires Curieuses* (*The Argol and Other Strange Stories*; Boréal, 1997); *Chasseur de Rêves* (*Dream Hunter*; Borál, 1997); *Note:* French-Canadian writer. Juveniles.

Chable, Jacques Édouard (?-); *Le Maître du Soleil* (*The Master of the Sun*; Payot, 1942); *Flammes dans le Ciel* (*Fire in the Sky*; L'Ermitage, 1943); *Du Sang sur le Soleil* (*Blood on the Sun*; Presse, 1958); *Note:* Swiss writer. See Chapter VII.

Chabot, Denys (1945-); *L'Eldorado dans les Glaces* (*The Eldorado of the Ice*; HMH, 1978); *La Province Lunaire* (*The Moon Province*; HMH, 1980); *Le Relais Abitibien* (*The Abitibian Relay*; round-robin novel by C. **Boisvert**, D. **Chabot**, J. Ferguson, R. Godard, M. Lemire, and D. St-Germain; Meera, 1987); *Note:* French-Canadian writer.

Chabot, Vincent (1951-); *Le Maître de Chichen Itza* (*The Master of Chichen Itza*; Q/A, 1990); *Note:* French-Canadian writer. A novel of the Mayans.

Chaboud, Jack (?-); *La Nuit du 8 Décembre* (*The Night of December 8th*; Magnard, 1997); *Note:* Juvenile fantasy.

Chabrey, François *see* **Prêtre, Marcel G.**

Chaieb, Rached (?-); *Les Mortimorts* (*The Deaderdead*; Los., 1970)

Chailley, Beaudoin *see* **Legay, Piet**

Chaine, Pierre (1882-?); *Les Mémoires d'un Rat* (*The Memoirs of a Rat*; À l'Oeuvre, 1917); *Les Scrupules de M. Bonneval* (*Mr. Bonneval's Scruples*; Grasset, 1921); *Contes Fantaisistes* (*Fantasy Tales*; Portiques, 1928); *Note:* See Chapter VI. Also see **Grand-Guignol** and André de **Lorde.**

Chaland, Paul (?-); *L'Aérocrobe* (RL, 1956)

Chalopin, Jean (?-); *La Planète des Croisés d'Argent* (*The Planet of the Silver Crusaders*; Hac., 1987); *Le Mystère de la Pyramide* (*The Mystery of the Pyramid*; AM, 1993); Series *Ulysse 31* (with Nina **Wolmark**): *Les Lestrigons* (BR, 1982); *La Planète Perdue* (*The Lost Planet*; BR, 1982); *La Révolte des Compagnons* (*Revolt of the Companions*; BR, 1982); *La Trahison d'Hératos* (*Heratos' Betrayal*; BR, 1982); Le Sphinx (BR, 1982); *La Cité de Cortex* (*The City of Cortex*; BR, 1983); *Note:* See Chapter IX. *Ulysse 31* is the novelisation of the chil-dren's animated television series (see Book 1, Chapter IV) retelling Ulysses' odyssey in the 31st century.

Chalvin, Antoine (?-); *Les Yeux d'Emma* (*Emma's Eyes*; Alfil, 1994)

Chambe, Émile (?-); *Droit au Pôle Sud* (*Right to the South Pole*; JDV, 1901); *Au Faîte de la Terre* (*At the Top of the Earth*; Tallandier, 1903)

Chambon, Jacques de (?-); *La Fée du Bled* (*The Fairy of the Desert*; SEP, 1934); *Le Puy des Auberges* (*The Village of Inns*; SEP, 1934); *La Capture du Loup Hurlant* (*The Capture of Screaming Wolf*; Ferenczi, 1939); *L'Enterré Vivant* (*Buried Alive*; Ferenczi, 1939); *Le Serpent Lumineux* (*The Serpent of Light*; VA, 1940); *Les Naufragés de l'Iceberg* (*The Castaways of the Iceberg*; Livre Moderne, 1941); *Le Shérif Rouge* (*The Red Sheriff*; Livre Moderne, 1941); *Note:* Chambon is a pseudonym for Albert Bonneau. Not to be confused with editor/anthologist Jacques Chambon.

Chambost, Germain (1935-); *Les Chevaliers de l'Apocalypse* (*The Knights of the Apocalypse*; Picollec, 1980); *Un Bref Instant d'Éternité* (*A Brief Moment of Eternity*; Debresse, 1993)

Chambure, Simone de *see* **Erigny, Simone d'**

Chamelet, Henri *see* **Juillet, Jacques-Henri**

Chamoiseau, Patrick (1953-); *Manman Dio contre la Fée Carabosse* (*Mamy Dio vs. The Evil Fairy*; Ed. Caribéennes, 1988); *Au Temps de l'Antan, Contes du Pays Martinique* (*Tales of Yesterday, from the Martinique*; Hatier, 1988)

Champagne, Carole (?-); *Tobi et le Gardien du Lac* (*Tobi and the Guardian of the Lake*; Héritage, 1985); *Note:* French-Canadian writer. Children's book.

Champagne, Louis; *Series "Les Aventures Futuristes de Deux Savants Canadiens-Français"* (*The Futuristic Adventures of Two French-Canadian Scientists*; Police-Journal, 1949): *1. Les Hommes Sphériques* (*The Spherical Men*); *Note:* French-Canadian series of eight pulp novels starring scientists Marcel Larouche and Robert Morin, and their assistant Adèle Lafrance, who explore the cosmos in a spaceship of their own design. "Louis Champagne" is a house name, possibly used by several different writers.

Champagne, Louise (1953-); *Chroniques du Métro* (*Subway Chronicles*; Triptyque, 1992); *Note:* French-Canadian writer. Collection of fantastical tales.

Champagne, Maurice (1868–1951); *Les Reclus de la Mer* (*The Recluse of the Sea*; as Maurice Champagne; JDV, 1907); *Les Sondeurs d'Abîmes* (*The Probers of the Abyss*; as Maurice Champagne; Delagrave, 1911); *L'Âme du Dr. Kips* (*The Soul of Dr. Kips*; as Maurice Cham-

pagne; JDV, *1912; rev. as Le Secret du Yogi (The Yogi's Secret,* BGA, 1927); *Huit Millions sous les Flots (Eight Millions Under Water*; as Maurice Champagne; Delagrave, 1912); *L'Île du Solitaire (The Island of the Lonely Man*; as Maurice Champagne; Delagrave, 1913); *La Vallée Mystérieuse (The Mysterious Valley*; as Maurice Champagne; Delagrave, 1914); *L'Aventure de Nicolas Corbin (Nicholas Corbin's Adventure*; as Maurice Champagne; Delagrave, 1925); *Les Chercheurs d'Épaves (The Seekers of Shipwrecks*; as Maurice Champagne; Delagrave, 1927); *Le Refuge Mystérieux (The Mysterious Refuge*; as Maurice Champagne; VLAE, 1928); *La Cité des Premiers Hommes (The City of the First Men*; as Maurice Champagne; VLAE, 1928); *L'Île Engloutie (The Sunken Island; as Maurice Champagne;* AVF, 1929; rev. as *L'Auto sous la Mer (The Underwater Car,* Tallandier, 1950); *La Terre Perdue (The Lost Land*; as Maurice Champagne; AVF, 1930); *L'Île Terrestre (The Terrestrial Island*; as Maurice Champagne; BGA, 1936); *La Cage sous la Mer (The Undersea Cage*; as Maurice Champagne; Bonne Presse, 1936); *La Maison du Silence (The House of Silence*; as Maurice Champagne; BGA, 1937); *La Maison qui Descend (The House Which Descends*; as Maurice Champagne; BGA, 1937); *Le Piège sous la Mer (The Undersea Trap*; as Maurice Champagne; BGA, 1938); *Le Signe du Soleil (The Sign of the Sun*; as Maurice Champagne; Tallandier, 1952); *La Maison dans l'Abîme (The House in the Abyss*; as Maurice Champagne; Delagrave, 1965); *Note:* See chapters V and VII.

Champetier, Joël (1957-); *La Mer au Fond du Monde (The Sea at the Bottom of the World*; JP 71, 1990); *La Requête de Barrad (Barrad's Request*; JP 73, 1991); *La Prisonnière de Barrad (Barrad's Prisoner*; JP 76, 1991); *La Taupe et le Dragon (The Mole and the Dragon*; Q/A, 1991; transl., 1999); *Le Jour-de-trop (The Day-Too-Much*; JP 85, 1993); *Le Voyage de la Sylvanelle (The Journey of the Sylvanelle*; JP 88, 1993); *La Mémoire du Lac (The Memory of the Lake*; Q/A, 1994); *Le Secret des Sylvaneaux (The Secret of the Sylvanans*; JP 93, 1994); *Le Prince Japier (Prince Japier*; JP 98, 1995); *Escales sur Solaris (Shore Leave on Solaris*; anthology; with Yves **Meynard**; Vent d'Ouest, 1995); *La Peau Blanche (The White Skin*; AL, 1997); *Coeur de Fer (Iron Heart*; Orion/Étoiles Vives, 1997); *Note:* French-Canadian writer. *The Barrad* series is a heroic-fantasy saga. *La Taupe* takes place on a planet colonized by the Chinese in the 24th century.

Champion, Jeanne (1931-); *Vautour-en-Privilège (Vulture-In-Privilege*; Calmann-Levy, 1973); *Dans les Jardins d'Esther (In Esther's Garden*; Calmann-Levy, 1975); *Les Gisants (The Tombs*; Calmann-Levy, 1977); *Les Frères Montaurian (The Brothers Montaurian*; Grasset, 1979); *La Hurlevent (The Windscream*; Renaissance,

1987); *La Maison Germanicus (The Germanicus House*; Grasset, 1996); *Note:* See Chapter VIII.

Champsaur, Félicien (1838-1934); *Entrée de Clowns (The Clowns' Entrance*; Nlle. Revue Critique, 1886); *Les Deux Singes (The Two Monkeys*; incl. *Le Premier Homme (The First Man)* and *Le Dernier Homme (The Last Man*; AM, 1907); *Les Ailes de l'Homme (The Wings of Man*; Ren. Du Livre, 1917); *Ouha, Roi des Singes (Ouha, King of the Apes*; Charpentier-Fasquelle, 1923); *Homo Deus, le Satyre Invisible (Homo Deus, the Invisible Satyr*; Ferenczi, 1924); *Nora, La Guenon Devenue Femme (Nora, the She-Monkey Made Woman*; Ferenczi, 1929); *Le Crucifié (The Crucified Man*; Ferenczi, 1930); *L'Attirante (The Attactive One*; Ferenczi, 1931) *Note:* See Chapter VII.

Champsoin, M.C. de (?-?) *see* **Grand-Guignol**

Chamson, Jacques *see* **Versins, Pierre**

Chanbert, Daniel-Yves *see* **Dastier, Dan**

Chancel, Jules (1867-1944); *Sous le Masque Allemand (Under the German Mask*; Delagrave, 1917); *L'Étreinte de la Main de Fer (The Grip of the Iron Hand*; Delagrave, 1925); *Le Tour du Monde Involontaire (The Involuntary Around-The-World Journey*; Delagrave, 1929); *Note:* See Chapter VII.

Chancerel, Léon (1886-1965) *see* **Grand-Guignol**

Chantel, Lucien (?-?) *see* **Grand-Guignol**

Chantepie, Robert *see* **Kerlecq, Jean de**

Chantepie, Yves *see* **Dastier, Dan**

Chanut, Roger (?-); *Les Ombres de Demain (Tomorrow's Shadows*; Roman Nouveau, 1920); *Note:* See Chapter VII.

Chapel, Félix *see* **Pagel, Michel**

Chapleau, Bernard (?-); *Les Mirages du Vide (The Mirages of the Void*; Boréal Jr., 1993); *Note:* French-Canadian writer.

Chapouton, Anne-Marie (?-); *L'Année du Mistouflon (The Year of the Mistouflon*; Flamm., 1975); *Millie et la Petite Clé (Millie and the Small Key*; Flamm., 1996); *Note:* Juvenile SF.

Chapuis, Alfred (1880-1958); *L'Homme dans la Lune (The Man in the Moon*; Attinger, 1929); *Le Monde des Automates (The World of Robots*; Slatkine, 1984); *Note:* Swiss writer.

Chapuis, Bernard (1945-); *Terminus Paris* (Formes du Secret, 1978); *Le Moulag: Conversation de Nuit (Night Conversation*; Fayard, 1983)

Charbonneau, Louis (1924-); *Le Grand Ordinateur (The Great Computer*; PC, 1982)

Charbonneau-Tissot, Claudette *see* **Aude**

Chardonnet, Janine (?-); *Les Trolkis de Wawagoya (The Trolkis of Wawagoya*; Magnard, 1982); *Note:* Juvenile SF.

Charland, Jean-Pierre (1954-); *Les Insurgés de Véga 3* (*The Rebels of Vega 3*; JP 11, 1973); *L'Héritage de Bhor* (*Bhor's Inheritance*; JP 17, 1974); *Le Naufrage* (*The Shipwreck*; Jour, 1975); *Note:* French-Canadian writer.

Charles, Éliane (?-?) *see* **Grand-Guignol**

Charles, Frédéric *see* **Dard, Frédéric**

Charmasson, Guy (?-); *Le Crépuscule des Surhommes* (*The Twilight of the Supermen*; MarSF 700, 1978); *L'Heure Perdue* (*The Lost Hour*; FNA 1443, 1986); *L'Incroyable Odyssée* (*The Incredible Odyssey*; FNA 1611, 1988); *Les Tueurs d'Elmendorf—La Vengeance* (*The Killers of Elmendorf: The Revenge*; FNA 1634, 1988); *Les Tueurs d'Elmendorf—La Mission* (*The Killers of Elmendorf: The Mission*; FNA 1639, 1988); *Note:* See Chapter IX.

Charmois, Pierre (?-); *Le Dernier Quartier* (*The Last Quarter*; Pensée U., 1973)

Charon, Gaston *see* **Nocher, Jean.**

Charon, Jean-Émile (?-); *La Femme de la Génèse* (*The Woman of Genesis*; Rocher, 1983)

Charpentier, André (1884-1966); *Le Rapide 115* (Ferenczi, 1927); *Une Énigme entre Ciel et Terre* (*An Enigma Between Heaven and Earth*; Gautier-Languereau, 1928); *Le Stylet d'Argent* (*The Silver Stylus*; Gautier-Languereau, 1928); *Le Train Évanoui* (*The Vanished Train*; Gautier-Languereau, 1928); *Un Pari Peu Banal* (*An Odd Bet*; Tallandier, 1932); *Lui et l'Autre* (*He and the Other*; Tallandier, 1933); *Les Pirates des Abîmes* (*The Pirates of the Abyss*; BGA, 1937); *Le Mystère de l'Île aux Phoques* (*The Mystery of Seal Island*; Tallandier, 1939)

Charpentier, Gustave (1860-1956) *see* **Opéra**

Charrière, Christian (1939-); *L'Enclave* (*The Enclave*; Fayard, 1971); *Mayapura* (Fayard, 1973); *Les Vergers du Ciel* (*The Grapes of Heaven*; Fayard, 1975); *Le Sîmorgh* (Fayard, 1977); *La Forêt d'Iscambe* (*The Forest of Iskamb*; JCL, 1980); *Le Baptême de l'Ombre* (*The Baptism of Shadow*; JCL, 1982); *Le Corbeau Rouge, ou La Deuxième Mort de Leonid Illich* (*The Red Crow, or Leonid Illich's Second Death*; JCL, 1987); *Le Maître d'Âme* (*The Soulmaster*; AM, 1990); *Note:* See Chapter VIII.

Chasles, Philarète (1798-1873); *Le Père et la Fille* (*The Father and the Daughter*; Lecointe & Durey, 1824); *La Fiancée de Bénarès* (*The Fiancée from Benares*; Canel, 1825); *Contes Bruns* (*Brown Tales*; anthology/with **Balzac** & **Rabou**; Guyot, 1832); *Caractères et Paysages* (*Characters and Landscapes*; Mame Delaunay, 1833); *Note:* See Chapter IV. The noted short story "L'Oeil sans Paupière" ("The Lidless Eye") was published in *L'Artiste* in 1831.

Chassaignon, André (?-) *see* **Contes et Légendes**

Chassin, F. *see* **Séverac, Guy**

Château, René *see* **Castle, Fred**

Châteaureynaud, Georges-Olivier (1947-); *Le Fou dans la Chaloupe* (*The Madman in the Lifeboat*; Grasset, 1973); *Les Messagers* (*The Messengers*; Grasset, 1974); *La Belle Charbonnière* (*The Beautiful Coal Lady*; Grasset, 1976); *Le Verger* (*The Orchard*; Balland, 1978); *Mathieu Chain* (Grasset, 1978)*La Faculté des Songes* (*The Faculty of Dreams*; Grasset, 1982); *Le Congrès de Fantômologie* (*The Congress of Phantomology*; Grasset, 1985); *Le Tiroir Secret* (*The Secret Drawer*; with Danièle Thompson; Grasset, 1986); *Le Héros Blessé au Bras* (*The Hero Wounded in the Arm*; Grasset, 1987); *Le Jardin dans l'Île* (*The Garden in the Island*; Renaissance, 1989); *Le Combat d'Odiri* (*Odiri's Fight*; Bayard, 1991); *La Seule Mortelle* (*The Only Mortal*; Nonpareille, 1992); *Le Jardin des Narcisses* (*The Lilies Garden*; La Différence, 1992); *Zinzolins et Nacarats* (*Alfil, 1993*)*Le Kiosque et le Tilleul* (*The Kiosk and the Lime Blossom*; Julliard, 1993); *Le Château de Verre* (*The Glass Castle*; Julliard, 1994); *Le Styx* (Littéra, 1995); *Les Messagers* (*The Messengers*; Babel, 1996); *Les Ormeaux (The Elms; Rocher, 1996)La Fortune* (*The Fortune*; Castor Astral, 1996); *Note:* See Chapter VIII.

Châtillon, Pierre (1939-); *La Mort Rousse* (*The Red Death*; Jour, 1974); *L'Île aux Fantômes* (*Ghost Island*; Jour, 1977); *Philédor Beausoleil* (Leméac/RL, 1978); *La Fille Arc-en-ciel* (*The Rainbow Girl*; Libre Expression, 1983); *Le Violon Vert* (*The Green Violin*; Forges, 1987); *La Vie en Fleurs* (*Life with Flowers*; XYZ, 1988); *L'Atlantidien* (Héritage, 1991); *L'Enfance est une Île* (*Childhood Is an Island*; Triptyque, 1997); *Note:* French-Canadian writer.

Chatrian, Alexandre *see* **Erckmann-Chatrian**

Chaulet, Georges (1931-); *Mémoires du Père Noël* (*Memoirs of Santa Claus*; GP, 1961); *Le Bathyscaphe d'Or* (*The Golden Batyscaph*; BR, 1966); Series: *Fantômette 1. Les Exploits de Fantômette* (*The Exploits of Fantômette*; BR, 1961); *2. Fantômette contre le Hibou* (*Fantômette vs. The Owl*; BR, 1962); *3. Fantômette contre le Géant* (*Fantômette vs. The Giant*; BR, 1963); *4. Fantômette au Carnaval* (*Fantômette at the Carnival*; BR, 1963); *5. Fantômette et l'Île de la Sorcière* (*Fantômette and the Witch's Island*; BR, 1964); *6. Fan-*

tômette contre Fantômette (*Fantômette vs. Fantômette*; BR, 1964); *7. Pas de Vacances pour Fantômette* (*No Holidays for Fantômette*; BR, 1965); *8. Fantômette et la Télévision* (*Fantômette and Television*; BR, 1967); *9. Opération Fantômette* (BR, 1966); *10. Les Sept Fantômette* (*The Seven Fantômette*; BR, 1967); *11. Fantômette et la Dent du Diable* (*Fantômette and the Devil's Tooth*; BR, 1967); *12. Fantômette et son Prince* (*Fantômette and Her Prince*; BR, 1968); *13. Fantômette et le Brigand* (*Fantômette and the Crook*; BR, 1968); *14. Fantômette et la Lampe Merveilleuse* (*Fantômette and the Wondrous Lamp*; BR, 1969); *15. Fantômette chez le Roi* (*Fantômette and the King*; BR, 1969); *16. Fantômette et le Trésor du Pharaon* (*Fantômette and the Treasure of the Pharaoh*; BR, 1970); *17. Fantômette et la Maison Hantée* (*Fantômette and the Haunted House*; BR, 1970); *18. Fantômette contre la Main Jaune* (*Fantômette vs. The Yellow Hand*; BR, 1971); *19. Fantômette à la Mer de Sable* (*Fantômette at the Sea of Sand*; BR, 1971); *20. Fantômette Viendra ce Soir* (*Fantômette Will Come Tonight*; BR, 1972); *21. Fantômette dans le Piège* (*Fantômette in the Trap*; BR, 1972); *22. Fantômette et le Secret du Désert* (*Fantômette and the Secret of the Desert*; BR, 1973); *23. Fantômette et le Masque d'Argent* (*Fantômette and the Silver Mask*; BR, 1973); *24. Fantômette contre Charlemagne* (*Fantômette vs. Charlemagne*; BR, 1974); *25. Fantômette chez les Corsaires* (*Fantômette and the Corsairs*; BR, 1973); *26. Fantômette et la Grosse Bête* (*Fantômette and the Big Beast*; BR, 1974); *27. Fantômette et le Palais sous la Mer* (*Fantômette and the Undersea Palace*; BR, 1974); *28. Fantômette contre Diabola* (*Fantômette vs. Diabola*; BR, 1975); *29. Appelez Fantômette* (*Call Fantômette*; BR, 1975); *30. Olé, Fantômette!* (BR, 1975); *31. Fantômette Brise la Glace* (*Fantômette Breaks the Ice*; BR, 1976); *32. Les Carnets de Fantômette* (*The Notebooks of Fantômette*; BR, 1976); *33. C'est quelqu'un, Fantômette* (*Fantômette Is a Real Somebody*; BR, 1977); *34. Fantômette dans l'Espace* (*Fantômette in Space*; BR, 1977); *35. Fantômette fait tout sauter* (*Fantômette Blows It All Up*; BR, 1977); *36. Fantastique Fantômette* (*Fantastic Fantômette*; BR, 1978); *37. Fantômette et les Quarante Milliards* (*Fantômette and the Forty Billions*; BR, 1978); *38. Fantômette en Plein Mystère* (*Fantômette in Deep Mystery*; BR, 1979); *39. Fantômette et le Mystère de la Tour* (*Fantômette and the Mystery of the Tower*; BR, 1979); *40. Fantômette et le Dragon d'Or* (*Fantômette and the Golden Dragon*; BR, 1980); *41. Fantômette contre Satanix* (*Fantômette vs. Satanix*; BR, 1981); *42. Fantômette est la Couronne* (*Fantômette and the Crown*; BR, 1981); *43. Mission Impossible pour Fantômette* (*Mission Impossible for Fantômette*; BR, 1982); *44. Fantômette Risque Tout* (*Fantômette Risks Everything*; BR, 1982); *45. Fantômette en Danger* (*Fantômette in Danger*; BR, 1983); *46. Fantômette Fend les Flots* (*Fantômette Breaks the Waves*; BR, 1983); *47. Fantômette et le Château Mystérieux* (*Fantômette and the Mysterious Castle*; BR, 1984); *48. Fantômette Ouvre l'Oeil* (*Fantômette Keeps Watch*; BR, 1984); *49. Fantômette se Méfie* (*Fantômette Is Wary*; BR, 1985); *50. Fantômette Passe à l'Attaque* (*Fantômette Attacks*; BR, 1986); *51. C'est toi, Fantômette!* (*It Is You, Fantômette!*; BR, 1987); *52. Fantômette s'envole* (*Fantômette Flies Away*; BR, 1990); *Note:* See Chapter VIII. **Fantômette** has also been adapted for television and comics (see Book 1, Chapters II and V). Series *Étincelle: Mlle. Étincelle et l'Alchimiste* (*The Alchemist*; Cast., 1961); *Mlle. Étincelle et l'Usurpateur* (*The Usurpator*; Cast., 1962); *Mlle. Étincelle et le Transistor* (Cast., 1965); *Note:* A series about a resourceful young girl. Series *Inspector Gadget: Les Astuces de l'Inspecteur Gadget* (*Inspector Gadget's Tricks*; Hac., 1987); *L'Inspecteur Gadget chez les Pirates* (*Inspector Gadget and the Pirates*; Hac., 1987); *L'Inspecteur Gadget et la Princesse* (*Inspector Gadget and the Princess*; Hac., 1987); *L'Inspecteur Gadget est arrivé* (*Inspector Gadget Has Arrived*; Hac., 1988); *L'Inspecteur Gadget ne s'en fait pas* (*Inspector Gadget Does Not Worry*; Hac., 1988); *L'Inspecteur Gadget va se marier* (*Inspector Gadget Is Going to Marry*; Hac., 1988); *L'Inspecteur Gadget dans le Cosmos* (*Inspector Gadget in the Cosmos*; Hac., 1988); *L'Inspecteur Gadget se débrouille* (*Inspector Gadget Finds a Way*; Hac., 1988); *L'Inpecteur Gadget est incroyable* (*Inspector Gadget Is Incredible*; Hac., 1988); *L'Inspecteur Gadget contre le Docteur Gang* (*Inspector Gadget vs. Dr. Gang*; Hac., 1989); *L'Inspecteur Gadget est un as* (*Inspector Gadget Is an Ace*; Hac., 1989); *L'Inspecteur Gadget passe à l'attaque* (*Inspector Gadget Attacks*; Hac., 1989); Series *Le Petit Lion* (*The Little Lion*): *Le Petit Lion se fâche* (*The Little Lion Gets Angry*; Hac., 1969); *Le Petit Lion Astronaute* (*The Little Lion Astronaut*; Hac., 1970); *Le Petit Lion Va Se Marier* (*The Little Lion Is Going to Marry*; Hac., 1970); *Le Petit Lion dans la Tempête* (*The Little Lion in a Storm*; Hac., 1971); *Le Petit Lion tourne un Grand Film* (*The Little Lion Shoots a Big Movie*; Hac., 1972); *Le Petit Lion à l'École* (*The Little Lion at School*; Hac., 1973); *Le Petit Lion Inventeur* (*The Little Lion Inventor*; Hac., 1974); *Le Petit Lion Cow-Boy* (*The Little Lion Cowboy*; Hac., 1975); *Le Petit Lion Grand Chasseur* (*The Little Lion Hunter*; Hac., 1975); *Le Petit Lion au Palais des Merveilles* (*The Little Lion in the Palace of Wonders*; Hac., 1976); *Le Petit Lion Premier Ministre* (*The Little Lion Prime Minister*; Hac., 1977); *Le Petit Lion et la Source Enchantée* (*The Little Lion and the Enchanted Source*; Hac., 1978); *Le Petit Lion et les Sept Pingouins* (*The Little Lion and the Seven Penguins*; Hac., 1979); Series *Le Prince Charmant* (*Prince Charming: Le Trésor du Prince Charmant* (*Prince Charming's Treasure*; Hac., 1978); *Le Prince Charmant* *chez la Fée Pervenche* (*Prince Charming and the Purple Fairy*; Hac., 1979); *Le Prince Charmant et le Magicien* (*Prince Charming and the Magician*; Hac., 1979); *Le Prince Charmant Face au Géant* (*Prince Charming Against the Giant*; Hac., 1980); *Le Prince Charmant contre la Sorcière Verte* (*Prince Charming and the Green Witch*; Hac., 1980); *Le Prince Charmant et les Sept Princesses* (*Prince Charming and the Seven Princesses*; Hac., 1981); *Le Prince Charmant et le Cheval Volant* (*Prince Charming and the Flying Horse*; Hac., 1981); Series *Les Quatre As* (*The Four Aces*): *see* Book 1, Chapter V.

Chaumette, Jean-Christophe (1961-); *Le Jeu* (*The Game*; FN Noire, 1989); *L'Homme-Requin* (*The Man-Shark*; FNA 1780, 1990); *La Cité sous la Terre* (*The Underground City*; FNA 1785, 1990); *Aoni* (FNA 1792, 1990); *La Prophétie* (*The Prophecy*; FNA 1797, 1991); *Les Epées de Cristal* (*The Crystal Swords*; FNA 1804, 1991); *Le Guerrier sans Visage* (*The Faceless Warrior*; FNA 1812, 1991); *Le Niwaâd* (FNSF 8, 1997); *Note:* See Chapter VIII.

Chausson, Ernest (1855-1899) *see* **Opéra**

Chauveau, Léopold (?-?); *Le Roman de Renard* (*The Novel of Reynard*; Payot, 1924); *Note:* See Chapter I.

Chauveau, Philippe (1960-); *Robots et Robots Inc.* (Boréal, 1989); *Note:* French-Canadian writer.

Chauvin, Rémy (?-); *Les Défis de la Guerre Future* (*The Challenges of Future Wars*; France Empire, 1978); *Des Fourmis et des Hommes* (*Of Ants and Men*; France-Empire, 1979); *Voyage Outre-Terre* (*Journey Beyond Earth*; Rocher, 1983); *Les Veilleurs du Temps* (*The Time Watchers*; Rocher, 1984); *Le Nouveau Golem* (*The New Golem*; Rocher, 1993); *Note:* See Chapter IX.

Chauvire, Roger (?-); *La Geste de la Branche Rouge, ou L'Iliade Irlandaise* (*The Geste of the Red Branch, or the Irish Iliad*; Libr. de France, 1926); *L'Incantation* (Firmin-Didot, 1929); *Contes d'un Autre Monde* (*Tales from Another World*; Flamm., 1947); *Le Cycle de Finn, Contes Ossianiques* (*The Finn Cycle, Ossianic Tales*; Terre de Brume, 1995)

Cheinisse, Claude (1931-1982) *see* **Renard, Christine**

Chenevière, Jacques (1886-1976); *L'île Déserte* (*The Desert Island*; Sté. Litt. France, 1918); *Jouvence ou la Chimère* (*Youth, or the Chimera*; Grasset, 1922); *Les Messagers Inutiles* (*The Useless Messengers*; Grasset, 1926); *La Jeune Fille de Neigle* (*The Young Snow Girl*; Calmann-Levy, 1929); *Les Captives* (*The Captives*; AdH, 1992); *Note:* See Chapter VII.

Chénier, Claude (1950-); *Ls Oiseaux Chantent à l'Aurore* (*The Birds Sing at Dawn*; Petite Nation, 1984); *Ulti-*matum (Petite Nation, 1985); *Note:* French-Canadian writer. In *Les Oiseaux*, peaceful aliens arrive on Earth. in Ultimatum, a group of scientists tries to impose peace on Earth.

Chéreau, Fred (?-); *Guillotine!* (as Céline W. Barney/with Yves **Ramonet**; FNG 95, 1989); *Rap Killer* (FN Angoisses 1, 1993)

Chery, Romel (1954-); *L'Adieu aux Étoiles* (*Farewell to the Stars*; Vents d'Ouest, 1997); *Note:* French-Canadian writer. Fantasy.

Chevalier, Omer (1860-1930?); *L'Avatar d'Yvan Orel* (*Yvan Orel's Avatar*; Plon, 1919); *Note:* See Chapter VII.

Chevrette, Christiane (1952-); Series *Camille et Dominique*: *1. Contre l'Artdinateur* (*Vs. The Artputer*; with Danielle **Cossette**; Fides, 1988); *2. En Péril dans l'île* (*In Danger on the Island*; with Danielle **Cossette**; Fides, 1989); *3. Dans Court-Circuit* (*In Short Circuit*; with Danielle **Cossette**; Fides, 1990); *4. Prises au Piège* (*Trapped*; with Danielle **Cossette**; Fides, 1991); *Note:* French-Canadian writer. The adventures of young telepathic twin girls.

Chevrier, Martine (?-); *La Fontaine de Sang* (*The Fountain of Blood*; Corti, 1966); *La Fête des Morts* (*The Festival of the Dead*; Fayard, 1974); *Note:* See Chaper VIII.

Cheynel, Hélène (?-) *see* *Contes et Légendes*

Chillicothe, Zeb; Series *Jag le Félin*: *1. Jag le Félin* (*Jag the Feline*; CM, PD; Plon, 1985); *2. Le Collier de la Honte* (*The Necklace of Shame*; CM, PD; Plon, 1985); *3. La Compagnie des Os* (*The Company of Bones*; CM, PD; Plon, 1985); *4. La Poudre de Vie* (*The Powder of Life*; JH; Plon, 1985); *5. Le Peuple Ailé* (*The Winged People*; JH; Plon, 1986); *6. Le Monde Fracturé* (*The Fractured World*; JH; Plon, 1986); *7. La Ville Piège* (*The Trap City*; JH; Plon, 1986); *8. Les Hommes Tritons* (*The Triton Men*; SB; Plon, 1986); *9. La Cité de Fer* (*The Iron City*; JH; Plon, 1986); *10. Les Tourmenteurs* (*The Tormenters*; SB; Plon, 1987); *11. Le Maître des Orages* (*The Storm Master*; JH; Plon, 1987); *12. Le Doigt du Seigneur* (*The Finger of the Lord*; CM; Plon, 1987); *13. Le Coeur Noir* (*The Black Heart*; JH; Plon, 1987); *14. Les Enfants de Feu* (*The Children of Fire*; SB; Plon, 1987); *15. Les Yeux d'Encre* (*The Eyes of Ink*; JH; PC, 1988); *16. Les Vierges de Pierre* (*The Virgins of Stone*; CM; PC, 1988); *17. L'île de Lune* (*The Moon Island*; CM; PC, 1988); *18. Désert Mécanique* (*Mechanical Desert*; CM; PC, 1988); *19. Les Mangeurs d'Âme* (*The Eaters of Soul*; CM; PC, 1988); *20. Les Ventres Mous* (*The Soft Bellies*; CM, JB; PC, 1989); *21. Station Labyrinthe* (*Labyrinth Station*; CM; PC, 1989); *22. Cloaque Bay* (*Cesspool Bay*; CM; PC, 1989); 23. Destination Apocalypse (CM; PC, 1989); *24. La Mort Métal*

(*The Metal Death*; Vaug., 1990); *25. Métalmorphose* (*Metalmorphosis*; Vaug., 1990); *26. Les Faiseurs d'Acier* (*The Steel Makers*; Vaug., 1990); *27. Les Naufragés de l'Arche* (*The Castaways from the Ark*; Vaug., 1990); *28. L'Univers du Barillet* (*The Barrel Universe*; Vaug., 1991); *29. Les Portes de Lumière* (*The Gates of Light*; Vaug., 1991); *30. Les Loups d'Osborne* (*The Wolves of Osborne*; Vaug., 1991); *31. Noire Prairie* (*Black Prairie*; Vaug., 1992); *32. Ceux du Miroir* (*Those from the Mirror*; Vaug., 1992); *33. L'Oiseau de Cristal* (*The Crystal Bird*; Vaug., 1992); *34. Les Guerriers de Verre* (*The Glass Warriors*; Vaug., 1994); *Note:* See Chapter IX. Jag was created by Christian **Mantey** (CM), with various volumes written in collaboration with Serge **Brussolo** (SB), Pierre **Dubois** (PD), Joël **Houssin** (JH) and Jacques **Barbéri** (JB).

Chimot, Jean-Philippe (?-); *Trois Contre les Invisibles* (*Three Against the Invisibles*; La Farandole, 1980)

Choisy-Clouzet, Maryse (1903-); *Mon Coeur donne une Formule C6 H8 (AzO3)6* (*My Heart Gives a Formula*; Cahiers Suridéalistes, 1927); *Les Atlantides* (4 vols.): *1.* (*title unknown*; 1943); *2. Le Serpent* (*The Serpent*; Caractères, 1957); *3. Tes Yeux m'ont vu* (*Your Eyes Saw Me*; Caractères, 1957); *4.* (*title unknown*; n.d.); *Note:* See Chapter IX.

Chollier, Antoine (1894-1935?); *La Mer des Sargasses* (*The Sargasso Sea*; with H. **Lesbros**; Baudinière, 1923); *Suffétula, Histoire Métempsychique* (*Metempsychic Tale*; Pensée U., 1923); *La Vengeresse, ou La Nouvelle Bethsabée* (*The Avenging Woman, or the New Bethsabea*; Fasquelle, 1925); *Le Fiel du Calice* (*The Bitter Gall of the Chalice*; Vraie France, 1927)

Chomet, Richard (?-) *see* **Klein, Gérard**

Choquart, Alphonse (?-?); *Les Contes de Sainte-Pélagie* (*Tales from Sainte Pelagie*; 1833); *Note:* See Chapter IV.

Choquet, Gaston (?-); *Le Prince Napoudja* (*L'Intrépide*, 1919); *L'Explorateur Fantôme* (*The Ghostly Explorer*; serialized in 3 issues, Coll. d'Aventures, 1920); *1. L'Explorateur Fantôme* (*The Ghostly Explorer*; Coll. d'Aventures, 1920); *2. Le Cratère du Diable* (*The Devil's Crater*; Coll. d'Aventures, 1920); *3. Le Triomphe de l'Aile* (*The Triumph of the Wing*; Coll. d'Aventures, 1920); *Le Signe du Malheur* (*The Sign of Woe*; serialized in 4 issues, Coll. d'Aventures, 1920); *1. Le Signe du Malheur* (*The Sign of Woe*; Coll. d'Aventures, 1920); *2. Le Contrepoison Malais* (*The Malaysian Counterpoison*; Coll. d'Aventures, 1920); *3. Le Maître du Monde* (*The Master of the World*; Coll. d'Aventures, 1920); *4. Le Vaisseau Aérien* (*The Air Ship*; Coll. d'Aventures, 1920)

Choquette, Robert (1905-1991); *Le Sorcier d'Anticosti*

(*The Wizard of Anticosti*; Fides, 1975); *Note:* French-Canadian writer.

Chouinard, Suzanne *see* **Martel, Suzanne**

Chousy, Didier de (?-?); *Ignis* (Berger-Levrault, 1883); *Note:* See Chapter V.

Chrétien de Troyes (1135?-1183?); *Lancelot, ou le Chevalier à la Charette* (*Lancelot, or the Knight with a Cart*; c. 1177); *Perceval, ou le Conte du Graal* (*Perceval, or the Tale of the Grail*; c. 1182); *Note:* See Chapter I.

Christian-Yve, Guy (?-); *Carnaval pour un Décès* (*Carnival for a Death*; Hautefeuille, 1957); *À Tombeaux Ouverts* (*Open Graves*; Julliard, 1958); *Avez-vous vu Glock?* (*Did You See Glock?*; Julliard, 1961)

Christin, Pierre (1938-); *Les Prédateurs Enjolivés* (*The Beautified Predators*; A&D 40, 1976); *Le Futur est en Marche Arrière* (*The Future Is in Reverse*; Encre 4, 1979); *ZAC* (Grasset, 1981); *Note:* See Chapter IX. Pierre Christin is also the writer of the renowned comic-book series **Valerian** (see Book 1, Chapter V).

Chung, Ook (1963-); *Nouvelles Orientales et Désorientées* (*Oriental and Disoriented Tales*; L'Hexagone, 1994); *Note:* French-Canadian writer.

Cincin, Sylvain (?-); *Le Passé Décomposé* (*Decomposed Past*; Den., 1969); *20 Decembre 1998* (Den., 1972)

Cixous, Hélène (?-); *Partie* (*Gone*; Des Femmes, 1979)

Clairville (Nicolaie, Louis-François; ?-?) *see* **Opéra**

Clar, Fanny (?-); *Les Mains Enchantées* (*The Enchanted Hands*; Rose Rouge, 1924); *Les Trois Souhaits de Babette* (*Babette's Three Wishes*; École Émancipée, 1928); *L'Île aux Épouvantails* (*Scarecrow Island*; ESI, 1936); *Le Jardin des Mille Soucis* (*The Garden of 1000 Worries*; SVEL, 1939); *Dix-Sept et Un* (*17 and 1*; Écureuil, 1950); *Note:* Juvenile SF. See Chapter IX.

Claretie, Jules (1840-1913); *La Mer Libre* (*The Open Sea*; JDV, 1878); *Jean Mornas* (1882); *L'Oeil du Mort* (*Deadman's Eye; Flamm.*, 1887; rev. as *L'Accusateur* (*The Accuser*); *L'Obsession* (*The Obsession*; JST, 1905; rev. as *Moi et l'Autre* (*Me and the Other*; Lafitte, 1912); *L'Homme aux Mains de Cire* (*The Man with Wax Hands*; Glénat, 1978); *Note:* See chapters IV and V. Also see **Opéra**.

Claretie, Léo (1862-1924); *Paris depuis ses Origines jusqu'en l'An 3000* (*Paris from Its Origins Until the Year 3000*; Charavay, 1886); *Note:* Cousin of Jules **Claretie**. See Chapter V.

Clarinard, Raymond (1961-); *L'Ombre de Mars* (*The Shadow of Mars*; with Mikaël Ollivier; FNASF 2, 1997)

Claris de Florian, Jean-Pierre (1755-1794); *Fables* (Didot

Aîné, 1792); *Valérie* (Tiger, 1792); *Note:* See Chapter III.

Claudel, Paul (1868-1955); *La Ville* (*The City*; Lib. Art Indep., 1892; rev. MdF, 1948); *Note:* Mainstream writer. See Chapter IV. Also see **Opéra**.

Clauzel, Raymond (1871-1935?); *L'Aube Rouge* (*The Red Dawn*; Leclerc, 1914); *L'île des Femmes* (*The Island of Women*; Monde Nouveau, 1923); *L'Île des Hommes* (*The Island of Men*; Monde Nouveau, 1924)

Clauzel, Robert (?-); *La Tâche Noire* (*The Black Spot*; FNA 418, 1970); *Aux Frontières de l'Impossible* (*To the Frontiers of the Uncanny*; FNA 434, 1970); *L'Horreur Tombée du Ciel* (*The Horror That Fell from the Sky*; FNA 455, 1971); *La Planète qui n'existait pas* (*The Planet Which Did Not Exist*; FNA 468, 1971); *Destination Épouvante* (*Destination Terror*; FNA 481, 1971); *Comme Il Était Au Commencement* (*As It Was in the Beginning*; FNA 499, 1972); *Le Monde de l'Incrée* (*The World of the Uncreated*; FNA 518, 1972); *La Galaxie Engloutie* (*The Sunken Galaxy*; FNA 527, 1972); *À L'Aube du Dernier Jour* (*On the Dawn of the Last Day*; FNA 545, 1973); *Les Cathédrales d'Espace-Temps* (*The Cathedrals of Space-Time*; FNA 559, 1973); *La Terrible Expérience de Peter Home* (*The Dreadful Experiment of Peter Home*; FNA 573, 1973); *Les Étoiles Meurent Aussi* (*The Stars Also Die*; FNA 583, 1973); *La Fantastique Énigme de Pentarosa* (*The Fantastic Enigma of Pentarosa*; FNA 597, 1974); *Le Nuage qui Vient de la Mer* (*The Cloud Which Came from the Sea*; FNA 617, 1974); *Plate-Forme Epsilon* (*Platform Epsilon*; FNA 643, 1974); *Et la Nuit Garda son Secret* (*And the Night Kept Its Secret*; FNA 672, 1975); *Princesse des Étoiles* (*Star Princess*; FNA 684, 1975); *La Terre, Échec et Mat* (*Earth, Checkmate*; FNA 744,

1976); *La Planète Suppliciée* (*The Tortured Planet*; FNA 760, 1976); *Le Cylindre d'Épouvante* (*The Cylinder of Terror*; FNA 763, 1977); *Le Ciel sous la Terre* (*The Sky Under the Earth*; FNA 784, 1977); *L'Oeuf d'Antimatière* (*The Antimatter Egg*; FNA 800, 1977); *Les Naufragés de l'Invisible* (*The Castaways of the Unseen*; FNA 827, 1977); *Le Prince de Métal* (*The Metal Prince*; FNA 854, 1978); *Le Secret des Secrets* (*The Secret of Secrets*; FNA 875, 1978); *Comme un Orgue d'En-*

fer... (*As an Infernal Organ...*; FNA 908, 1979); *La Flamme des Cités Perdues* (*The Flame of the Lost Cities*; FNA 946, 1979); *Si Claire Était la Nuit* (*So Clear Was the Night*; as Roy Morrisson; MOC 10, 1979); *Pour une Pluie d'Étoiles* (*For a Rain of Stars*; as Roy Morrisson; MOC 18, 1980); *L'Horrible Découverte du Dr. Coffin* (*The Horrible Discovery of Dr. Coffin*; FNA 1166, 1982); *L'Anneau de Fer* (*The Ring of Iron*; as Roy Morrisson; MOC 30, 1982); *Les Cendres de la Nuit* (*The Ashes of Night*; FNA 1236, 1983); *La Cité de l'Eternelle Nuit* (*The City of Eternal Night*; FNA 1259, 1983); *Les Survivants de la Mer Morte* (*The Survivors of the Dead Sea*; FNA 1302, 1984); *Les Aventures Extraordinaires de Michel Clarence—Le Secret de la Boîte Rouge* (*The Extraordinary Adventures of Michel Clarence—the Secret of the Red Box*; Le Crâne, 1987); *Note:* See chapters VIII and IX.

Clavel, Bernard (1923-); *L'Arbre qui Chante* (*The Singing Tree*; Farandole, 1978); *Le Mouton Noir et le Loup Blanc* (*The Black Sheep and the White Wolf*; Flamm., 1984); *Le Roi des Poissons* (*The King of Fishes*; AM, 1984); *L'Oie qui avait perdu le Nord* (*The Goose Who Lost the North*; Flamm. 1985); *Au Cochon qui Danse* (*To the Prancing Pig*; Flamm. 1986); *Note:* Also see **Contes et Légendes**.

Clavigny, Georges (Besse, Jules; 1873-1935?); Series *L'Aéronef Pirate* (*The Pirate Airship*; all Geoffroy, c. 1900): 1. *Le Marchand de Secrets* (*The Merchant of Secrets*); 2. *Sur les Toits de Paris* (*On the Rooftops of Paris*); 3. *Le Premier Coup de Fusil* (*The First Rifle Shot*); 4. *Manger et Boire?* (*Eat and Drink?*); 5. *Sur les Toits d'Alexandrie* (*On the Rooftops of Alexandria*); 6. *L'Oasis;* 7. *En Panne dans le Désert* (*Breakdown in the Desert*); 8. *Chez Menelik* ; 9. *L'Aéronef Rencontre le "Patrie"* (*The Airship Meets the "Homeland"*); 10. *Chez les Anthropophages* (*Meet the Cannibals*); 11. *Un Bagne Asiatique* (*An Asian Labor Camp*); 12.*Dans le Palais du Sultan Rouge* (*In the Palace of the Red Sultan*); 13. *Vers les Glaces Polaires* (*Towards the Polar Ice*); 14. *La Grande Course Chicago-Porte Maillot* (*The Great Chicago-Paris Race*); 15. *Terrible Aventure* (*Deadly Adventure*); 16. *La Guerre aux Singes* (*War with the Apes*); 17. *Un Repaire de Bandits* (*A Lair of Bandits*); 18. *Dans le Domaine de Lord Roberts* (*In Lord Roberts' Domain*); 19. *L'Asie Mystérieuse* (*Mysterious Asia*); 20. *Un Prodigieux Coup de Filet* (*A Prodigious Capture*); 21. *En Birmanie* (*In Burma*); 22. *Les Brossard se sont faits Moines* (*The Brossards Get Religion*); 23. *Nouveaux Dangers* (*New Dangers*); 24. *Les Coureurs de Prairie* (*The Prairie Racers*); 25. *En Plein Far-West* (*In the Far West*); 26. *Un Pélerinage à la Mecque* (*A Pilgrimage to Mecca*); 27. *Dernières Aventures Américaines* (*Last American Adventures*); 28. *Les Chercheurs d'Or* (*The Gold Seekers*); 29. *De l'Or et du Sang* (*Of*

Gold and Blood); *30. Un Drame dans les Airs* (*A Drama in the Air*)

Clément, Monique (?-); *Alice de Brocéliande* (Ramsay, 1996)

Clément, Yves-Marie (?-); *Au Pays des Kangourous Roux* (*In the Land of Red Kangaroos*; Rageot, 1994); *Billy Crocodile* (Rageot, 1994); *La Griffe du Jaguar* (*The Jaguar's Claw*; Rageot, 1994); *Tropicales* (FNASF 2, 1995); *Jararaca* (FNASF 17, 1996); *Le Petit Dragon qui Toussait* (*The Little Dragon Who Coughed*; Hatier, 1996); *Prisonniers des Sables* (*Prisoners of the Sands*; Nathan, 1996); *Le Puma aux Yeux d'Émeraude* (*The Puma with Emerald Eyes*; Nathan, 1997); *Note:* Juvenile fantasies. See Chapter VIII.

Clérisse, Henry (?-); *J'avais des Camarades* (*I Had Friends*; Den., 1939); *La Guerre est pour Demain* (*War Is for Tomorrow*; Scorpion, 1956); *Note:* See Chapter IX.

Clermont, Camille (?-?) *see* **Grand-Guignol**

Cléry, Frank (?-); *La Chambre de Souffre* (*The Sulphur Room*; Monnet Terrific 6, 1974)

Clifden, Michaël *see* **Jaouen, Hervé-Marie**

Cloquemin, Paul (?-?) *see* **Grand-Guignol**

Closets, François de (1933-); *Scénarios du Futur* (*Scenarios of the Future*; 2 vols.; Den., 1978-79); *Le Monde de l'An 2000* (*The World of the Year 2000*; Club Fr. du Livre, 1979); *Note:* Collection of scientific anticipations by a renowned science television personality.

Clouatre, Jean (?-) *see* **Rivard, Gilles.**

Clouet, A. (?-); *La Machine à Capter la Pensée* (*The Machine to Capture Thoughts*; VA, 1941); *Note:* See Chaper VII.

Cobb, William *see* **Lermina, Jules**

Cocke, Emmanuel (1945-1973); *Va Voir au Ciel si j'y suis* (*Go To Heaven and See If I'm There*; Jour, 1971); *L'Emmanuscrit de la Mère Morte* (*The Emmanuscript of The Dead Mother*; Jour, 1972); *Sexe-Fiction* (L'Heure, 1973); *Note:* French-Canadian writer born in France. These novels portray 21st-century Montréal.

Cocteau, Jean (1889-1963); *L'Ange Heurtebise* (*The Angel Heurtebise*; 1925); *Les Chevaliers de la Table Ronde* (*The Knights of the Round Table*; 1937); *Note:* See Chapter VI. Jean Cocteau was a renowned filmmaker and dramatist, best-known for **La Belle et la Bête** (see Book 1, Chapters I and VI). Also see **Opéra.**

Coeurderoy, Ernest (1825-1862); *Hurrah!!! Ou La Révolution par les Cosaques* (*Hurrah!!! Or the Revolution of the Cossacks*; Londres, 1854); *Note:* See Chapter V.

Cogan, Paul (1921-1976); *Les Pionniers de l'Espace* (*The Space Pioneers*; Fleurus, 1959); *Note:* Non fiction. See Chapter IX.

Cohen, Olivier (1949-); *Je m'appelle Dracula* (*My Name Is Dracula*; Hac., 1987); *La Fiancée de Dracula* (*The Bride of Dracula*; Hac., 1988); *Note:* Juveniles. See Chapter VIII.

Coleno, Alice (1903-1993); *La Forêt de Cristal* (*The Crystal Forest*; Tisné, 1946); *Contes de Diamant* (*Diamond Tales*; Hatier, 1957); *Les Jardins de la Licorne* (*The Gardens of the Unicorn*; Hatier, 1957); *La Montagne des Démons* (*The Mountains of Demons*; GP, 1963); *Note:* Juveniles. See Chapter VIII.

Colette (Sidonie-Gabrielle; 1873-1954) *see* **Opéra**

Colin, Fabrice (?-); *Neuvième Cercle* (*Ninth Circle*; Mnemos 16, 1997); *Les Cantiques de Mercure* (*The Canticles of Mercury*; Mnemos 28, 1997); *Note:* See Chapter IX.

Collard, Robert (?-); *Démonax* (as Lortac, Raoul; BGA, 1938); *L'Aventure Commencera Ce Soir* (*The Adventure Will Start Tonight*; Colbert, 1943); *La Reine au Masque Vert* (*The Queen with the Green Mask*; Colbert, 1946); *Ida Yakowna, Petit Prodige* (*Little Prodigy*; Montsouris, 1947); *2 Morts... 20 Milliards* (*2 Dead... 20 Billion*; SEPE Bandeau Noir, 1949); *Les Bagnards du Ciel* (*The Convicts of Space*; Métal 4, 1954); *Note:* See Chapter IX.

Colle, Jean Robert (?-) *see* ***Contes et Légendes***

Collet, Henri (1885-1951); *L'Île de Barataria* (*The Island of Barataria*; AM, 1929)

Collet, Isabelle (?-) & David (?-); *Le Chant de la Terre* (*The Song of Earth*; Mnemos 9, 1996); *Diapason d'Orichalque* (*Orichalque Tuning Fork*; Mnemos 13, 1996); *La Part du Diable* (*The Devil's Share*; Mnemos 19, 1997); *Note:* See Chapter VIII. Also see Sébastien **Pennes.**

Colonna, Philippe (?-); *Holon* (With Jean-Christophe **Colonna**; Seuil, 1985)

Colson, Martial-Pierre *see* **Marlson, Pierre**

Combard, Serge (?-); *Le Ministère du Gel* (*The Ministry of Frost*; RL, 1967)

Combes, Francis (?-) *see* ***Contes et Légendes***

Combet, Fernand (?-); *Schrumm Schrumm ou l'Excursion Dominicale aux Sables Mouvants* (*Schrumm Schrumm or the Sunday Excursion to the Quiksands*; Pauvert, 1966); *Mort et Passion de Délix C. Scribator* (*Death and Passion of Felix C. Scribator*; Pauvert, 1971)

Compère, Daniel (?-); *Historilune* (*Storymoon*; Magnard, 1983); *Note:* Juvenile SF.

Compère, Gaston (1924-); *Sept Machines à Rêver* (*Seven Machines for Dreaming*; Belfond, 1974); *La Femme de Putiphar* (*Putiphar's Wife*; MarF 519, 1975); *Écrits de la Caverne* (*Written from the Cave*; J. Antoine, 1976); *L'Office des Ténèbres* (*The Office of Darkness*; Belfond, 1979); *Derrière l'Oeil* (*Behind the Eye*; J. Antoine, 1980); *La Constellation du Serpent* (*The Constellation of the Snake*; Belfond, 1983); *Les Eaux de l'Achéron* (*The Waters of the Acheron*; AdG, 1985); *Songes de l'Oeil Bleu* (*Dreams of a Blue Eye*; Dur-An-Ki, 1985); *Licornes* (*Unicorns*; Duculot, 1989); *Cimmerie, Divagations à Travers un Paysage* (*Cimmeria, Divigations Through a Landscape*; La Manufacture, 1992); *Note:* Belgian writer. See Chapter VIII.

Comte, Jean-François (1933-); *Sylvie et les Vivisecteurs* (*Sylvie and the Vivisectionists*; Marcel Jullian, 1978); *Les Géants Couverts d'Algues* (*The Giants Covered in Seaweed*; Aurore, Futurs 2, 1988); *Le Doge des Miroirs / Alice y-es-tu?* (*The Doge of Mirrors / Alice Are You There?*; Aurore, Futurs 6, 1988)

Conia, Jacques *see* **Hoven, Jacques**

Condroyer, Mariette (?-); *Contes d'Amour et de Mort* (*Tales of Love and Death*; Gall., 1980)

Conil, Jean-Emmanuel *see* **Page, Alain**

Conrad, Daniel (?-); *Le Syndrome Frankenstein* (*The Frankenstein Syndrome*; with Olivier **Birdchiren**; Lueurs Mortes, 1995)

Considerant, Victor (1808-1893); *Publication Complète des Nouvelles Découvertes de Sir John Herschel dans le Ciel Austral et dans la Lune* (*Complete Publication of the New Discoveries of Sir John Herschel in the Souhern Sky and on the Moon*; 1836); *Description du Phalanstère* (Dain & D'Ilsaguier, 1848)

Constant, Alphonse-Louis *see* **Lévi, Éliphas**

Constant, Jacques (?-); *Le Triomphe des Suffragettes* (*The Triumph of the Suffragettes*; Lib U., 1910); *Note:* See Chapter V.

Constantin, Yves de (1897-?); *Liquidation du Monde* (*Liquidating the World;* Émile-Paul, 1935; rev. as *Discours de Réception du Diable à l'Académie Française* (*Inauguration Speech by the Devil at the French Academy*, Péladan, 1982); *Le Paradis Empoisonné* (*The Poisoned Paradise*; Émile-Paul, 1980)

Contes et Légendes (Tales & Legends); The *Contes et Légendes* series (published by Fernand Nathan) was started in the 1930s. It is not limited to France, but includes volumes dealing with all parts of the world. However, only these volumes dealing with France, French history, and French regions have been listed below: **Bammert, Jacques-Joseph** *La Montagne Vos-* *gienne;* **Baredhyo, Youan de** *La Vallée de Barèges;* **Barral, M.** *Le Languedoc* (With **Camproux**); **Bauchy, Jacques-Henry** (q.v.) *L'Orléanais;* **Besson, André** *Le Pays Comtois;* **Bienvaut, Hervé** *Le Val de Loire;* **Bonaventure, Michel** *L'Étang de Thau;* **Bosquet, Luce** *Le Dauphiné;* **Bourgeois, André** *La Puisaye;* **Brékilien, Yann** (q.v.) *Le Pays Breton;* **Burnol, Maurice** *La Montagne Bourbonnaise;* **Camiglieri, Laurence** *La Bresse et le Bugey;* *Les Chevaliers de la Table-Ronde;* *Le Lyonnais;* *Le Poitou et les Charentes;* **Camproux** *see* **Barral, M.;* **Cazals, Patrick** *L'Occitanie;* **Chassaignon, André** *La Picardie;* **Cheynel, Hélène** *Le Vivarais;* **Clavel, Bernard** (q.v.) *Le Bordelais;* **Colle, Jean Robert** *Le Poitou;* **Combes, Francis** *Le Franc-Moisin;* **Deceneux, Marc** *Le Mont Saint-Michel;* **Defrasne, Jean** *Le Berry;* *La Franche-Comté;* *La Renaissance;* **Delample, F.** *see* **Mir, M.;* **Dorsay, Jules** *La Bretagne;* **Durand, Honoré** *Les Causses;* **Fauliot, Pascal** *La Beauce;* **Fischmann, Patrick** *La Sologne;* **Fronval, Georges** (q.v.) *La Flibuste;* **Gardès, Jean-Marc** *Le Plateau Ardéchois;* **Grenier, Christian** (q.v.) *La Conquête du Ciel et de l'Espace;* **Guy, Lucien** *Le Faucigny;* **Hinzelin, Émile** *L'Alsace;* **Huisman, Marcelle & Georges** *Le Moyen Âge;* *La Révolution Française;* **Jacq, Christian** (q.v.) *Le Temps des Pyramides;* **Jean-Mariat, Madeleine** *Les Charentes;* **Lallemand, Y.** *Le Vieux Pays Haut-Marnais;* **Lannion, Philippe** *La Champagne;* *La Normandie;* **Laurent de la Barre, Ernest du** *see* **Souvestre, Émile;* **Lauwereyns de Rosendaele, Antonia de** *Les Flandres;* **Le Breton, P.** *Le Pays de Guipry;* **Le Guen, Annick** *Le Pays de Lorient;* **Levron, Jacques** *L'Anjou;* *L'Auvergne;* **Luzel, François-Marie** *see* **Souvestre, Émile;* **Mège-Privet, Odile** *Le Pays d'Arnay-le-Duc en Terroir Bourguignon;* **Mir, M.** *Le Pays Toulousain* (With F. **Delample**); **Mirande, Jacqueline** (q.v.); *Les Chevaliers de la Table Ronde* (*The Knights of the Round Table*); *Le Moyen-Âge* (*Middle Ages*); *Le Pays d'Oc;* **Montgon, Adhémar de** (q.v.) *see* **Quinel, Charles;* **Lenotre, Thérèse;** **Perron-Louis** *La Bourgogne;* **Peyresblanques, Jean** *Les Landes;* **Pézard, André** *La Provence;* **Pézard, Fanette** (q.v.) *La Gascogne;* **Pinguilly, Yves** (q.v.) *Bretagne;* **Pitz, L.** *La Lorraine;* **Portail, Jean** (q.v.) *La Camargue et les Gitans;* *La Marche et le Limousin;* *Le Pays Niçois;* *La Savoie;* **Poulain, Albert** *La Haute-Bretagne;* *Le Pays de Redon;* **Quinel, Charles** *La Corse* (With Adhémar de **Montgon**); *Le Grand Siècle* (With Adhémar de **Montgon**); *Paris et Montmartre* (With Adhémar de **Montgon**); **Remize, Félix** *Le Gévaudan;* **Sandkühler, Conrad** *Le Catharisme;* **Sautereau, François** (q.v.) *La Naissance de Rome;* **Sorokine, Dimitri** *Le Premier Empire;* *Les Opéras Célèbres;* *Les Ballets et les Opéras Comiques;* **Souvestre, Émile** (q.v.) *La Basse Bretagne* (With Ernest du **Laurent de la Barre** & François-Marie **Luzel**); **Thieblement, Françoise** *Le Pays de Carnac;*

Thomasset, René (q.v.) *Le Pays Basque*; **Toudouze, Georges G. (q.v.)** *L'Île-de-France*; **Toussaint-Samat, Maguelonne (q.v.)** *Les Châteaux de la Loire*; *Les Croisades*; *La Gaule et les Gaulois*; *Le Périgord et le Quercy*; *Les Pyrénées*; **Vidal, Adolphe** *Saint-Jean de Fos*; **Vivier, Robert** *La Touraine*; **Voisin, Michel** *Le Pays de Thône*

Conty, Jean-Pierre (1917-); *M. Suzuki et la Lueur Bleue* (*Mr. Suzuki and the Blue Light*; FN Espionnage 545, 1966); *Horizons Fantastiques pour Mr. Suzuki* (*Fantastic Horizons for Mr. Suzuki*; FN Espionnage, 1975); *Project Cyclope* (*Project Cyclops*; FN Espionnage, 1976); *Dr. Suzuki et Mr. Hyde* (FN Espionnage, 1978); *Le Congres des Sorcières* (*The Congress of Witches*; FN Espionnage, 1979); *Note:* See Chapter IX.

Coppens, Yves (?-) *see* **Pelot, Pierre**

Coquiot, Gustave (1865-1926); *Le Charriot Errant* (*The Wandering Cart*; Monde Ill., 1910); *La Terre Frottée d'Ail* (*Earth Rubbed with Garlic*; Delpech, 1925); *Note:* Also see **Grand-Guignol**.

Corbedanne, Ralph (?-); *Le Hasard est Maître* (*Hazard Is Master*; Livres Nouveaux, 1941); *Le Dernier Templier* (*The Last Templar*; Ed. Ludogr., 1943); *Le Gardien de l'Image* (*The Guardian of the Image*; Ed. Ludogr., 1943); *Au Sud, Rien à Signaler* (*Nothing to Report in the South*; Ed. Ludogr., 1945); *Énigme dans le Temps Perdu* (*Enigma in Lost Time*; Ed. Ludogr., 1958)

Corbeil, Pierre (1947-); *La Concession* (*Imagine* Nos. 55 to 58, 1991); *Note:* French-Canadian writer. Alternate-history where North America speaks French.

Corbière, Stéphane *see* **Gril, Étienne**

Corday, Michel (1870-1937); *Le Mystérieux Dajann-Phinn* (*The Mysterious Dajann-Phinn*; JST, 1908); *Le Fiancé aux Deux Visages* (*The Two-Faced Fiancé*; Libr. Mondiale, 1908); *Le Lynx* (With André **Couvreur**; Lafitte, 1911); *En Tricogne: Un an chez les Tricognes* (*In Tricony: A Year Among the Tricons*; Flamm., 1926); *La Flamme Éternelle* (*The Eternal Flame*; Flamm., 1931); *Ciel Rose* (*Pink Sky*; Flamm., 1933); *Note:* See Chapter V.

Cordier, Jules (?-?) *see* **Opéra**

Corentin, Michel *see* **Lacq, Gilles**

Corgiat, Sylviane (1955-); *Les Trafiquants de Mémoire* (*The Memory Traffickers*; L'Amitié, 1988); *Note:* See chapters VIII and IX. Also see **Lecigne, Bruno**.

Corman, Terence (?-); Series *Russ Norton*: *1. Les Parasites de l'Horreur* (*The Parasites of Terror*; with Don A. **Seabury**; Media 1000 Apocalypse, 1987); *2. Les Murailles de l'Angoisse* (*The Walls of Anguish*; with Don A. **Seabury**; Media 1000 Apocalypse, 1987); *3. Les En-*

fants du Diable (*The Children of the Devil*; with Don A. **Seabury**; Media 1000 Apocalypse, 1987); *4. Carnage aux Caraïbes* (*Massacre in the Caribbean*; with Don A. **Seabury**; Media 1000 Apocalypse, 1987); *5. Les Hommes d'Acier* (*The Men of Steel*; Media 1000 Apocalypse, 1987); *6. Le Rituel des Damnés* (*The Ritual of the Accursed*; Media 1000 Apocalypse, 1987); *Note:* See Chapter IX. Novels written by various French writers using these house names, including Richard D. **Nolane** (No. 1) and Michel **Pagel** (No. 4, heavily rewritten and unacknowledged).

Cormier, Jean-Marc (1948-); *La Symphonie Déconcertante* (*The Unsettling Symphony*; Rimouski, 1984); *Note:* French-Canadian writer. Collection of short stories.

Corneille, Pierre (1606-1684); *Médée* (1635); *Andromède* (1650); *Circé* (1675); *Note:* See Chapter II.

Corneille, Thomas (1625-1709); *Note:* Brother of Pierre **Corneille**. See **Opéra** and **Quinault, Philippe**.

Cornut, Tania (?-); *Le Manteau Rouge Grenat* (*The Dark Red Coat*; Chatelaine, 1961); *Note:* French-Canadian writer. The tale of an enchanted coat.

Coronel (?-) *see* **Vercors**

Corriveau, Hugues (1948-); *Courants Dangereux* (*Dangerous Currents*; L'Instant Même, 1994); *Attention, tu dors debout* (*Watch Out! You're Asleep as You Stand*; L'Instant Même, 1996); *Note:* French-Canadian writer.

Corriveau, Monique(1927-1976); *Le Témoin* (*The Witness*; Cercle du Livre de France, 1969); *Patrick et Sophie en Fusée* (*Patrick and Sophie on a Rocket*; Héritage, 1975); *Compagnon du Soleil* (*Companion of the Sun*; Fides, 1976); *1. L'Oiseau de Feu* (*The Firebird*); *2. La Lune Noire* (*The Black Moon*); *3. Le Temps des Chats* (*The Time of the Cats*); *Note:* French-Canadian writer. Trilogy dealing with repression and revolt, totalitarianism and freedom.

Corsélien *see* **Marignac, Pascal**

Cortambert, Richard (1836-1884); *Un Drame au Fond de la Mer* (*A Drama at the Bottom of the Sea*; JDV, 1877)

Cortanze, Gérard de (?-); *Le Livre de la Morte* (*The Book of the Dead Woman*; Aubier-Montaigne, 1981)

Corthouts, C. (?-); *Virtual World* (Lefrancq, 1997)

Cosem, Michel (1939-); *Haute Erre* (*High Wandering*; RL, 1972); *Fruits et Oiseaux des Magies* (*Fruits and Birds of Magic*; Encres Vives, 1972); *La Chasse Artus* (*The Artus Hunt*; RL, 1974); *Découvrir la S-F* (*Discover SF*; anthology; Seghers, 1975); *Vols de Vanneaux sur la Région des Lacs* (*Flights of Thre Vans Over the Lake Country*; Ostraka, 1977); *Territoire du Multiple* (*Terri-*

tory of Multiple; Ed. Fr. Réunis, 1978); *Alpha de la Licorne* (*Alpha of the Unicorn*; La Farandole, 1979); *Découvrir les Contes Étranges et Merveilleux* (*Discover Strange and Wondrous Tales*; anthology; Seghers, 1980); *Découvir les Animaux Fabuleux* (*Discover Fabulous Animals*; anthology; Seghers, 1980); *Les Doubles Territoires* (*The Double Territories*; RL, 1981); *Les Neiges Rebelles de l'Artigou* (*The Rebel Snows of the Artigou*; Messidor-La Farandole, 1982); *Le Chapeau Enchanté* (*The Enchanted Hat*; Farandole, 1984); *Arbre-Loup* (*Wolf-Tree*; L'École, 1985); *Aux Yeux de la Légende* (*In the Eyes of Legends*; Bedou, 1986); *La Chevauchée de la Délivrance* (*The Freedom Ride*; Milan, 1986); *L'Enlèvement de Brunissen* (*The Taking of Brunissen*; Milan, 1988); *La Colombe et l'Épervier* (*The Dove and the Hawk*; Loubatières, 1989); *Le Chemin du Bout du Monde* (*The Path at the End of the World*; Milan, 1993); *Note:* Juveniles. See Chapter VIII.

Cossé, Laurence (?-); *Le Coin du Voile* (*The Corner of the Veil*; Gall., 1996); *Note:* See Chapter VIII.

Cossette, Danielle (?-) *see* **Chevrette, Christiane**

Costa, André (?-); *L'Appel du 17 Juin* (*The Call of June 17th*; JCL, 1981)

Costins, R.-A. (?-); *Le Fils de Schess* (*The Son of Schess*; Grassin, 1957); *Contes du Bois Joli* (*Tales of Pretty Wood*; SFIL, 1966); *Contes des Alentours* (*Tales of the Neighborhood*; SFIL, 1968); *Moktar Cissé* (CEDA, 1990)

Cotard, Jean (?-); *Chère Petite Thi Haï* (*Dear Little Thi Haï*; L. Fournier, 1929); *Le Ventre du Grand Bouddha: Contes Extraordinaires et Coloniaux* (*The Belly of the Big Buddha: Extraordinary Colonial Tales*; L. Fournier, 1931); *Le Flot d'Épouvante* (*The Flood of Terror*; Figuière, 1934); *L'Opale de Shezady* (*Shezady's Opal*; Baudinière, 1945); *La Porte du Diable* (*The Devil's Gate*; Technique du Livre, 1946); *Solange dans le Silence Blond* (*Solange in Blond Silence*; Baudinière, 1946); *La Belle Nephertys* (*The Beautiful Nephertys*; Baudinière, 1947)

Côté, Denis (1954-); *Les Hockeyeurs Cybernétiques* (*The Cybernetic Hockey-Players*; 1983; transl. as *Shooting for the Stars*, 1990); *Les Parallèles Célestes* (*The Celestial Parallels*; HMH, 1983); *Les Géants de Blizzard* (*The Blizzard Giants*; Courte Échelle, 1985); *La Pénombre Jaune* (*The Yellow Penumbra*; JP, 1986); *Nocturnes pour Jessie* (*Nocturnals for Jessie*; Q/A, 1987); *Les Prisonniers du Zoo* (*The Prisoners of the Zoo*; Courte Échelle, 1988); *L'Idole des Inactifs* (*The Idol of the Idles*; Courte Échelle, 1989); *Le Voyage dans le Temps* (*The Travel in Time*; Courte Échelle, 1989); *La Nuit du Vampire* (*Night of the Vampire*; Courte Échelle, 1990); *La Révolte des Inactifs* (*The Revolt of the Idles*; Courte

Échelle, 1990); *Le Retour des Inactifs* (*The Return of the Idles*; Courte Échelle, 1990); *Terminus Cauchemar* (*Terminus Nightmare*; Courte Échelle, 1991); *Les Yeux d'Émeraude* (*The Emerald Eyes*; Courte Échelle, 1991); *L'Arrivée des Inactifs* (*The Coming of the Idles*; Courte Échelle, 1993); *Je Viens du Futur* (*I Come from the Future*; Tisseyre, 1993); *Aux Portes de l'Horreur* (*The Gates of Horror*; Courte Échelle, 1994); *Le Parc aux Sortilèges* (*The Spellbound Park*; Courte Échelle, 1994); *La Trahison du Vampire* (*The Vampire's Betrayal*; Courte Échelle, 1995); *L'Île du Savant Fou* (*The Island of the Mad Scientist*; Courte Échelle, 1996); *Les Prédateurs de l'Ombre* (*The Predators in the Shadow*; Courte Échelle, 1997); *Note:* French-Canadian writer. *Les Parallèles* is a *Close Encounters*-like story. *Les Géants* follows the adventures of galactic troubleshooters Braal and Chrysalide. *La Pénombre* is a satire of Henri **Vernes'** **Bob Morane**. The saga of the *Inactifs* is a sequel to *Hockeyeurs* and follows the adventures of hockey player Michel Lenoir and journalist Virginia Lynx in the futuristic dystopian state of Lost Ark. *Les Prisonniers, Le Voyage, La Nuit,* and *Les Yeux* feature the fantasy adventures of two contemporary children, Maxime and Jo.

Côté, Jean (1929-); *Échec au Président* (*The President in Check*; Point de Mire, 1974); *Le Parfum de la Terreur* (*The Scent of Terror*; Quebecor, 1995); *Note:* French-Canadian writer. In *Échec*, aliens help a man save our planet.

Côté, Laurier (1955-); *Je Crée Donc Je Suis* (*I Create Therefore I Am*; Tisseyre, 1986); *L'Abominable Homme des Mots* (*The Abominable Man of Words*; Tisseyre, 1994); *Note:* French-Canadian writer.

Côté, Normand *see* **Sutal, Louis**

Coué, J. (1929-); *Kopoh, le Renne-Guide* (*Kopoh, the Reindeer Guide*; RL, 1967); *Les Veillées d'Alouma* (*The Evenings of Alouma*; Messidor-La Farandole, 1967); *La Colère de Maipu* (*The Wrath of Maipu*; RL, 1972); *L'Homme de la Rivière Kwai* (*The Man of River Kwai*; RL, 1973); *Le Lys de Messidor* (*The Lys of Messidor*; PC, 1973); *Pierre est Vivant* (*Pierre Lives*; Amitié, 1977); *Le Canard à Trois Pattes* (*The Three-Legged Duck*; with William **Camus** & J. **Coué**; Duculot, 1978); *Un Soleil Glacé* (*An Icy Sun*; Amitié, 1978); *Les Sept Feux de l'Enfer* (*The Seven Fires of Hell*; Amitié, 1981); *L'Infini des Sables* (*The Infinity of Sand*; Hac., 1987)

Coupry, François (1947-); *Mille Pattes Sans Tête* (*Headless Centipede*; Hallier, 1975); *La Vie Ordinaire des Anges* (*The Ordinary Life of Angels*; RL, 1983); *Le Rire du Pharaon* (*The Laugh of the Pharaoh*; RL, 1984); *Le Fils du Concierge de l'Opera* (*The Son of the Concierge of the Opera*; Gall., 1991)

Courant, Paul (?-); *Les Bruits de l'Enfer* (*The Sounds of Hell*; Mari, 1980)

Courcel, Pierre (?-); *Equipages en Péril* (*Crews in Danger*; FNA 415, 1970); *Bases d'Invasion* (*Invasion Bases*; FNA 454, 1971); *Escales Forcées* (*Forced Stopover*; FNA 487, 1972); *Note:* See Chapter IX.

Courret, G. (?-); *La Révolte Libératrice* (*The Freeing Revolt*; Gémeaux, 1925)

Courtiaud, Laurent (?-); *Les Enfants de Sang* (*The Children of Blood*; FNFR 18, 1995); *Les Voleurs de Vie* (*The Stealers of Life*; FNFR 26, 1995)

Courtois, Jean-Marie (?-); *Trois Contes* (*Three Tales*; Arcel, 1964); *Note:* French-Canadian writer. Children's tales.

Courtois-Brieux, Jean (?-); *La Guerre des Insectes* (*The War of the Insects*; PC, 1977); *Note:* Adapted into an eponymous 1981 television series (see Book 1, Chapter II).

Cousin, Philippe (1947-); *Le Retour du Boomerang* (*The Return of the Boomerang*; Kes. I&M 12, 1980); *L'Immeuble d'En Face* (*The Building Across the Street*; with Jean-Pierre **Andrevon**; anthology; PdF 344, 1982); *La Croisière d'Einstein* (*Einstein's Cruise*; with Maxime **Benoit-Jeannin**; Stock, 1983); *Mange ma Mort* (*Eat My Death*; PdF 362, 1983); *L'Oeuf du Diable* (*The Devil's Egg*; Stock, 1984); *Hôpital Nord* (*North Hospital*; with Jean-Pierre **Andrevon**; anthology; PdF 373, 1984); *Gare Centrale* (*Central Station*; with Jean-Pierre **Andrevon**; anthology; PdF 424, 1985); *La Solution du Fou* (*The Madman's Solution*; PdF 494, 1989); *Les Destins Minuscules* (*The Tiny Fates*; CRNI, 1989); *Le Pacte Pretorius* (*The Praetorius Pact*; AM, 1988); *Brutales* (*Brutal*; Julliard, 1993); *Note:* See Chapter IX.

Cousin Jacques (Beffroy de Reigny, Louis-Abel; 1757-1811); *Turlututu, ou La Science du Bonheur* (*Turlututu, or the Science of Happiness*; Froullé, 1783); *Nicodème dans la Lune, ou La Révolution Pacifique* (*Nicodeme on the Moon, or the Peaceful Revolution*; Froullé, 1791); *Les Deux Nicodèmes, ou les Français dans la Planète Jupiter* (*The Two Nicodemes, or the French on the Planet Jupiter*; Froullé, 1791); *La Constitution de la Lune* (*The Moon's Constitution*; Froullé, 1793); *Turlututu, Empereur de l'Île Verte* (*Turlututu, Emperor of the Green Island*; Froullé, 1797); Note: See Chapter III. Cousin Jacques also self-published *Les Lunes du Cousin Jacques, ou le Courrier des Planètes* (*The Moons of Cousin Jacques, or the Planetary Mail*; 1785-1791), the first proto-fanzine.

Couteaud, P. (?-); *Chez les Atlantes* (*With the Atlanteans*; Ste. d'Ed. Geo., 1928); *À la Conquête du Grand Serpent de Mer* (*The Conquest of the Great Sea Serpent*; with Philine **Burnet**; Mame, 1928); *L'Île de Tulipatan* (*The Island of Tulipatan*; AV, 1929); *Note:* See Chapter VII.

Coutet, Alex (1880-1952); *Le Miroir de l'Invisible* (*The Mirror of the Invisible*; Ren. du Livre, 1921); *Stop (U contre U)* (*U vs.U*; Libr. Champs-Élysées, 1930); *Le Dragon Vert était pour Tchoung-King* (*The Green Dragon Was for Tchoung-King*; Didier, 1945); *La Bête Fantôme* (*The Phantom Beast*; Impr. Toulouse 3AAA, 1946); *Le Magicien des Mers* (*The Wizard of the Seas*; STAEL, 1947)

Couture, Émile (?-); *De Paris à Montevideo, l'Extraordinaire Aventure de Deux Enfants* (*From Paris to Montevideo, the Extraordinary Adventure of Two Children*; SUEL, 1944); *Les Rayons M.V.* (*The MV Rays*; NPF, 1947); *Le Trésor du Soleil* (*The Treasure of the Sun*; Delagrave, 1957); *Note:* See Chapter VII.

Couture, Guillaume (1966-); *Les Forêts de Flume* (*The Forests of Flume*; JP, 1995); *La Sphère Incertaine* (*The Uncertain Sphere*; JP, 1995); *Note:* French-Canadian writer.

Couture, Yvon-H. (1946-); *Le Voyage de Zomlok* (*Zomlok's Journey*; Asticou, 1988); *Note:* French-Canadian writer. Philosophical SF.

Couturier, Louis see **Carrouges, Michel**

Couty, Jean-Pierre (?-?) see **Grand-Guignol**

Couvreur, André (Achille Émile Henri; 1863-1944); *Le Mal Nécessaire* (*The Necessary Evil*; Plon, 1899); *Caresco Surhomme ou Le Voyage en Eucrasie* (*Caresco the Superman, or the Voyage to Eucrasia*; Plon, 1904); *Une Invasion de Macrobes* (*An Invasion of Macrobes*; L'Illustration, 1909/Lafitte, 1910); *Le Lynx* (With Michel **Corday**; Lafitte, 1911); *L'Androgyne—Les Fantaisies du Professeur Tornada* (*The Androgyne—the Fantasies of Prof. Tornada*; Oeuvres Libres, 1922; rev. AM, 1923); *Le Valseur Phosphorescent* (*The Phosphorescent Waltzer*; Oeuvres Libres, 1923); *Les Mémoires d'un Immortel* (*Memoirs of an Immortal*; Oeuvres Libres, 1924); *Le Biocole* (Oeuvres Libres, 1927); *En Au-Delà* (*In the Beyond*; Oeuvres Libres, 1936); *Le Cas de la Baronne Sasoitsu* (*The Case of Baroness Sasoitsu*; Oeuvres Libres, 1939); *Note:* See chapters IV and V.

Cowez, Éric (?-); *Island One: L'Arche des Outre-Ciel* (*The Ark from Beyond the Sky*; SENO 1, 1995); *Geminga, La Civilisation Perdue* (*Geminga, the Lost Civilization*; SENO 2, 1996); *Les Andros de Miranda* (*The Andros of Miranda*; SENO 3, 1996); *Les Naufragés d'Hélix* (*The Castaways of Helix*; SENO 8, 1997); *Note:* See Chapter IX.

Cox, Paul (1959-); *L'Étrange Croisière du Pepeurcouque* (*The Strange Cruise of the Paperhull*; Dargaud, 1987);

Le Mystère de l'Eucalyptus (*The Mystery of the Eucalyptus*; Parution, 1987); *L'Énigme de l'Île Flottante* (*The Enigma of the Floating Island*; Parution, 1988); *Note:* Juveniles.

Craipeau, Jean-Louis (1948-); *L'Oeil de Belzébuth* (*Beelzebub's Eye*; Syros, 1986); *L'Ogre-Doux* (*The Sweet Ogre*; Nathan, 1989); *Le Dragon Déglingué* (*The Broken Dragon*; Nathan 1989); *Alice et le Konce* (Belfond, 1989); *Toto le Balai* (*Toto the Broom*; Mango, 1992); *Polochon, le Cochon qui portait un Caleçon* (*Polochon, the Pig Who Wore Boxers*; Mango, 1994); *Gazoline & Grenadine* (Nathan, 1995); *Mamie Coton* (*Cotton Granny*; Bayard, 1996); *Pépé Grognon* (*Grumpy Pappy*; Syros, 1996); *Drôle de Nom pour un Chien* (*Funny Name for a Dog*; Castor Poche, 1996); *Un Noël à Poil Doux* (*Christmas with Soft Fur*; Nathan, 1996); *À l'Abordage, Mamadou Courage* (*Board the Ship, Mamadou Courage*; Nathan, 1996); *Trois Aventures de l'Ogre-Doux* (*Three Adventures of the Sweet Ogre*; Nathan, 1997); *Gare au Carnage, Amédée Petitpotage* (*Watch Out for the Killing, Amedee Petitpotage*; Nathan, 1997); *Le Petit Chaperon Rouge* (*The Little Red Riding Hood*; Hac., 1997); *La Sorcière des Cantines* (*The Witch of the Cantina*; Père Castor, 1997); *Tiny MacTimid, Fantôme d'Écosse* (*Tiny MacTimid, Scottish Ghost*; Père Castor, 1997); *Dracula fait son Cinéma* (*Dracula Makes a Movie*; Castor Poche, 1997); *Le Kangourou d'Ooz* (*The Kangaroo from Ooz*; Nathan, 1997); *Panique et Chocolat* (*Panic and Chocolate*; Nathan, 1997); *Ma Victoire sur le Cauchemar* (*My Victory Over Nightmare*; Nathan, 1997); *Note:* Juvenile fantasies. See Chapter VIII.

Crayencour, Marguerite de *see* **Yourcenar, Marguerite**

Crémieux, Albert (1865-?) & Jean (?-?); *Le Grand Soir* (*The Big Night*; NSE, 1929); *L'Homme Qui Parlait Aux Bêtes* (*The Man Who Spoke to Animals*; Goelette, 1946); *Chute Libre* (*Freefall*; Métal 12, 1955); *La Parole Perdue* (*The Lost Word*; Métal 22, 1956); *Note:* Belgian writers. See Chapter IX.

Crémieux, Hector (?-?) *see* **Opéra**

Creux, Léon (?-); *Le Voyage de l'Isabella au Centre de la Terre* (*The Journey of the Isabella at the Center of the Earth*; Ducrocq, 1922); *Le Secret de la Dourada* (*The Secret of the Dourada*; Ducrocq, 1925); *Note:* See Chapter VII.

Creuzé de Lesser, Auguste-François (1771-1839); *Le Dernier Homme, poème imité de Grainville* (*The Last Man, Poem Inspired by Grainville*; 1832); *Note:* See Chapter V.

Crevel, René (1900-1935); *Mon Corps et Moi* (*My Body and I*; Kra, 1925); *La Mort Difficile* (*The Difficult Death*; Kra, 1926); *Babylone* (Kra, 1927); *Êtes-Vous Fou?* (*Are You Mad?*; Kra, 1929); *Les Pieds dans le Plat* (*The Feet in the Dish*; Costypo., 1933); *Note:* Surrealist writer. See Chapter VI.

Crisenoy, Maurice de (?-); *Le Secret du Rayon Vert* (*The Secret of the Green Ray*; Printemps 30-31, 1926); *Au Pays des Sortilèges* (*In the Land of Spells*; Bloud & Gay, 1935)

Crocq, Jean (?-); *Les Blasons* (*The Armories*; Debresse, 1957)

Cros, Charles Hortensius Émile (1842-1888); *Un Drame Interastral* (*An Interplanetary Drama*; 1872); *La Science de l'Amour* (*The Science of Love*; 1874); *Note:* See Chapter V.

Cryde, Th. (Debardieux, Cédric; ?-); *La Nuit des Insectes* (*Night of the Insects*; FNA 1336, 1984); *Osmose* (*Osmosis*; FNA 1356, 1985); *La Semaine Carnivore* (*The Carnivorous Week*; FNA 1415, 1985); *L'Endroit Bleu* (*The Blue Place*; FNA 1500, 1986); *La Falaise* (*The Cliff*; FNA 1904, 1993); *Note:* See Chapter IX.

Curel, François de (1854-1928); *Le Solitaire de la Lune* (Stock, 1922)

Curtis, Jean-Louis (Lafitte, Louis; 1917-1995); *Siegfried* (Julliard, 1946); *Gibier de Potence* (*Bad Seed*; Julliard, 1949); *Chers Corbeaux* (*Dear Crows*; Julliard, 1951); *Un Saint au Néon* (*A Neon Saint*; PdF 13, 1956; transl. as *The Neon Halo*, 1958); *À la Recherche du Temps Posthume* (*Searching for Posthumous Times*; Fasquelle, 1957); *Le Cygne Sauvage* (*The Wild Swan*; Julliard, 1962); *Les Forêts de la Nuit* (*The Forests of Night*; UGE, 1963); *La Quarantaine* (*The Quarantine*; Julliard, 1966); *Un Miroir le Long du Chemin* (*A Mirror Along the Path*; Julliard, 1969); *Note:* See Chapter IX.

Curval, Philippe (Tronche, Philippe; 1929-); *Les Fleurs de Vénus* (*The Flowers of Venus*; RF 75, 1960); *Le Ressac de l'Espace* (*The Breakers of Space*; RF 100, 1962); *La Forteresse de Coton* (*The Fortress of Cotton*; Gall., 1967); *Les Sables de Falun* (*The Sands of Falun*; OF 202-204, 1970); *Attention, Les Yeux* (*Watch Out for the Eyes*; Den., 1973); *L'Homme à Rebours* (*The Backwards Man*; A&D 28, 1974); *Utopies 75* (*Utopia '75*; anthology/with Jean-Pierre* **Andrevon**,

présence du futur

philippe curval
la forteresse de coton

denoël

Christine **Renard** & Michel **Jeury**; A&D 36, 1975); *Cette Chère Humanité* (*That Dear Mankind*; A&D 41, 1976; transl. as *Brave Old World*, 1981); *Un Soupçon de Néant* (*A Touch of Nothingness*; PP 5006, 1977); *Futurs au Présent* (*Present-Day Futures*; anthology; PdF 256, 1978); *Ah! Que c'est Beau, New York* (*Ah! New York Is So Beautiful*; Den., 1979); *Rut aux Étoiles* (*Rutting Stars*; PP 5054, 1979); *Y-a-quelqu'un?* (*Anyone There?*; Dim. 39, 1979); *Le Dormeur s'éveillera-t-il?* (*Will the Sleeper Awaken?*; PdF 282, 1979); *Regarde, Fiston, s'il n'y a pas un Extra-Terrestre Derrière la Bouteille de Vin* (*Sonny, Look and See If There Isn't an E.T. Behind the Wine Bottle*; PdF 305, 1980); *Le Livre d'Or de Philippe Curval* (*The Golden Book of Philippe Curval*; PP 5079, 1980); *La Face Cachée du Désir* (*The Hidden Face of Desire*; Dim. 43, 1980); *Tous vers l'Extase* (*All Towards Ecstasy*; Titres 42, 1981); *L'Odeur de la Bête* (*The Scent of the Beast*; PdF 329, 1981); *En Souvenir du Futur* (*In Remembrance of the Future*; A&D 80, 1983); *Debout les Morts, le Train Fantôme Entre en Gare* (*Get Up, Dead Men, the Ghost Train Is Entering the Station!*; PdF 391, 1984); Yann Kersalé (JL, 1985); *Comment Jouer à l'Homme Invisible en Trois Leçons* (*How to Play Invisible Man in Three Lessons; PdF 420, 1986); Superfuturs* (*Superfutures*; anthology; PdF 427, 1986); *Akiloë* (Flamm., 1988); *Habite-t-on Réellement Quelque Part?* (*Do We Really Live Anywhere?*; PdF 484, 1989); *Gillet* (L'Amateur, 1994); *L'Éternité n'est pas la Vie* (*Eternity Is Not Life*; Julliard, 1995); *Les Évadés du Mirage* (*The Escapees from the Mirage*; Den., 1995); *L'Arc Tendu du Désir* (*The Strung Bow of Desire*; L'Astronaute Mort, 1995); *Note:* See Chapter IX.

Cusy, Pierre (?-?) *see* **Grand-Guignol**

Cyr, Céline (1954-); *Les Prisonniers de M. Alphonse* (*The Prisoners of Mr. Alphonse*; Q/A, 1986); *Note:* French-Canadian writer. Children's book.

Cyrano de Bergerac, Hector Savinien (1619-1655); *Histoire Comique des Etats et Empires de la Lune* (*Comical History of the States and Empires of the Moon*; Le Bret, 1657); *Histoire Comique des Etats et Empires du Soleil* (*Comical History of the States and Empires of the Sun*; Charles de Sercy, 1662; Both transl. as *Other Worlds* (1965)); *Pour et Contre les Sorciers* (*For and Against Sorcerers*; 1663); *Note:* See Chapter III.

Cyril-Berger (Cyril, Victor (?-?) & Berger, Eugène (1875-1925)); *La Merveilleuse Aventure de Jim Stappleton* (*The Wondrous Adventure of Jim Stappleton*; Ollendorff, 1911; rev. Crès, 1919); Cri-Cri (Ollendorff, 1913); *Pendant qu'il se bat* (*While He Fights*; Flamm., 1918); *L'Expérience du Dr. Lorde* (*The Experiment of Dr. Lorde*; Crès, 1922); *L'Adversaire Inconnu* (*The Unknown Adversary*; Ferenczi, 1922); *Note:* See Chapters V and VII.

Cyrius *see* **Gayar, Henri**

Czmara, Jean-Claude (1949-); *Homo Spiritus* (Pensée U., 1975); *Solstice* (Ponte Mirone, 1978)

D., Élisabeth (1959-); *L'Ogre-Capitaine* (*Captain Ogre*; Gall., 1987)

Dac, Pierre (1893-1975); *Du Côté d'Ailleurs* (*From Elsewhere*; Julliard, 1966); *Du Côté d'Ailleurs et Réciproquement* (*From Elsewere and Back*; Julliard, 1966); *Le Jour le plus c...* (*The Stupidest Day*; Julliard, 1967); Series *Signé Furax* (With Francis **Blanche**): First Series: *1. Malheur aux Barbus* (*Woe to the Bearded Ones*; Martel, 1952); *2. Confession de Furax* (*Furax's Confession*; Martel, 1952); *3. Mangez de la Salade* (*Eat Salad*; Martel, 1952); *4. Les Barbus de l'Espace* (*The Bearded Ones in Space*;

Martel, 1953); Second Series: *1. Le Boudin Sacré* (*The Sacred Sausage*; JCL, 1970); *2. Malheur aux Babus* (*Woe to the Babus*; JCL, 1970); *3. Crimée... Châtiment* (*Crimea... Punishment*; JCL, 1971); *4. La Lumière qui Éteint* (*The Light That Dims*; JCL, 1971); *Signé Furax* (incl. eps. 1-3, JCL, 1971); *Furax et les Autres* (incl. ep. 4 plus ep. 5. *L'Atoll Anatole* (The Atoll Anatole) and Ep. 6. *Les Babus dans l'Espace* (*The Babus in Space*, JCL, 1973); *7. Le Gruyère qui Tue* (*The Gruyere That Kills*; JCL, 1976); *Note:* See Chapter IX. Novelizations of the eponymous radio serial (see Book 1, Chapter III).

Dagory (Jean-Michel; 1946-); *À la Recherche du Sang Perdu* (*Looking for the Lost Blood*; AM, 1982); *Les Aventures du Captain Élysée* (*The Adventures of Captain Elysee*; FN, 1984); *Quand Souvenirs Revenir, Nous Souffrir et Mourir* (*When Memories Return, We Suffer and Die*; FNA 1425, 1986); *Six Assassins Assassinés* (*Six Murdered Murderers*; Syros, 1987); *Maison qui Pleure* (*Weeping House*; Actes Sud, 1997)

Dahin, Michel (?-); *La Sérénade au Fantôme* (*Ghost Serenade*; SAELT, 1949); *Prisonniers des Diplodocus* (*Prisoners of the Diplodocus*; MRA, 1955)

Dahl, André (1886-1932); *Le Soleil ne se leva pas* (*The Sun Did Not Rise*; Baudinière, 1928); *Le Sleeping en Folie* (*The Mad Train Car*; Nlle. Revue Crit., 1928); *Jeanne d'Arc revint* (*Joan of Arc Came Back*; Nlle. Revue Crit., 1929); *Le Fauteuil à Roulettes, Voyage Imaginaire en France* (*The Wheel Chair, Imaginary Journey in France*; Nlle. Revue Crit., 1930); *Quand te tues-tu?* (*When Shall You Kill Yourself?*; Baudinière, 1930); *Trou-les-Bains* (Baudinière, 1930); *Contes pour la Comtesse* (*Tales for the Countess*; Baudinière, 1933); *Les Trois Aviateurs* (*The Three Airmen*; Baudinière, 1933); *Le Conteur est ouvert* (*The Storyteller Is Here*; Baudinière, 1934)

Daignault, Pierrre *see* **Saurel, Pierre**

Daigneault, Claude (1942-); *Les Frincekanoks* (Logiques, 1995); *Noël, Autos et Cantiques* (*Christmas, Cars and Canticles*; Logiques, 1995); *Note:* French-Canadian writer.

Dalens, Serge (Verdilhac, Yves de; 1910-1998); *Le Jeu sans Frontière* (*The Game Without Frontier*; with Jean-Louis **Foncine**; SdP, 1948); *Les Contes du Bourreau* (*Tales of the Executioner*; SdP, 1955); *La Plume Verte & Autres Contes* (*The Green Feather and Other Tales*; SdP Jr 6, 1957); *2 + 2 font... 5* (*2+2 = 5*; SdP, 1969); Series *Le Prince Éric* (*Prince Eric*): *Le Bracelet de Vermeil* (*The Vermillion Bracelet*; SdP, 1937); *Le Prince Éric* (*Prince Eric;* SdP, 1940); *La Tache de Vin* (*The Wine Spot*; SdP, 1942); *La Mort d'Éric* (*The Death of Eric*; SdP, 1944); *Éric le Magnifique* (*Eric the Magnificent*; SdP 2, 1985); *Ainsi Régna le Prince Éric* (*Thus Ruled Prince Eric*; SdP 2, 1989); Series *L'Étoile de Pourpre* (*The Purple Star*): *Les Prisonniers* (*The Prisoners*; SdPSF 61, 1974); *Les Lépreux* (*The Lepers*; SdPSF 68, 1974); Series *Les Enquêtes du Chat-Tigre* (*The Tiger-Cat Investigates*; as Mik Fondal/with Jean-Louis **Foncine**): *L'Auberge des Trois Guépards* (*The Inn of the Three Leopards*; SdP 88, 1956); *Les Galapiats de la Rue Haute* (*The Kids of High Street*; SdP 96, 1957); *L'Assassinat du Duc de Guise* (*The Assassination of the Duke of Guise*; SdP 101, 1957); *Pas de Chewing-Gum pour Pataugas* (*No Chewing-Gum for Pataugas*; SdP 111, 1958); *Le Piano des Prince Damakine* (*The Piano of the Damakine Princes*; SdP

116, 1958); *La Bible de Chambertin* (*The Bible of Chambertin*; SdP 128, 1959); *La DS de Creil* (*The Citroen from Creil*; SdP 140, 1960); *Telemik, ou le Crime de Mitou* (*Telemik, or Mitou's Crime*; SdP 160, 1962); *La Guêpe et les Frelons* (*The Wasp and the Yellowjackets*; SdP, 1964); *Panique sur la Butte* (*Panic on the Butte*; SdP, 1968); *Versailles-Vougeot ou l'Affaire de Larches* (*Versailles-Vougeot or the Larches Case*; SdP, 1970); *Mik et la Pierre du Soleil* (*Mik and the Sun Stone*; SdP, 1970); *Note:* Juveniles. See Chapter VIII.

Dallix, Géo (?-?) *see* **Grand-Guignol**

Danchet, Antoine (?-?) *see* **Opéra**

Dancray, Paul (?-); *Au Pays des Fakirs* (*In the Land of the Fakirs*; France Ed., 1924); *La Pagode au Miroir d'Argent* (*The Pagoda with the Silver Mirror*; BGA, 1925); *Les Maîtres de l'Himalaya* (*The Masters of Himalaya*; BGA, 1927); *Le Secret de l'Île Noire* (*The Secret of Black Island*; VLAE, 1928); *Le Démon Fauve de Java* (*The Scarlet Demon of Java*; VLAE, 1929); *Le Signe de Khâli* (*The Mark of Kali*; VLAE, 1930); *Le Sorcier du Feu* (*The Fire Wizard*; BGA, 1930); *Le Pirate du Pacifique* (*The Pirate of the Pacifique*; BGA, 1931); *Les Rôdeurs de Brousse* (*The Reavers of the Bush*; BGA, 1931); *Les Révoltés de Wandpoor* (*Revolt in Wandpoor*; VLAE, 1931); *Watahah la Mystérieuse* (*The Mysterious Watahah*; CDA, 1932); *Les Millions du Squatter* (*The Squatter's Millions*; CDA, 1933); *Ls Millions de Tchantoung* (*Tchantoung's Millions*; CDA, 1934); *Le Roi des Hommes Rouges* (*The King of the Red Men*; BGA, 1941)

Dandurand, Anne (1953-); *La Louve-Garou* (*The She-Werewolf*; with Claire **Dé**; Pleine Lune, 1982); *Voila C'est Moi, C'est rien, J'angoisse* (*Here I Am, It's Nothing, I'm Anxious*; Triptyque, 1987); *Note:* French-Canadian writer, twin sister of Claire **Dé**. Collection of short stories.

Dandurand, Claire *see* **Dé, Claire**

Daney, Louis (?-); *Les Hésitations de l'Ingénieur Marel* (*The Hesitations of Engineer Marel*; Crès, 1919); *L'Âne Bleu* (*The Blue Ass*; Hac., 1954)

Dangéry, Jean (?-); *Le Secret de la Mer Saharienne* (*The Secret of the Saharian Sea*; VA, 1936); *L'Afrique se refroidit* (*Africa Is Cooling*; VA, 1940)

Danheux, Paul (Danheux, Pol; 1934-); *In Extremis* (anthology; AECQ, 1989); *Note:* French-Canadian anthology.

Daniel, Gabriel (1649-1728); *Voyage du Monde de Descartes* (1690; transl. as *A Voyage to the World of Cartesius*, 1692); *Note:* See Chapter III.

Daninos, Pierre (1913-); *Eurique et Amérope* (Jeune Parque, 1946); *Les Carnets du Bon Dieu* (*God's Notebooks*; Plon, 1947); *La Première Planète à Droite en sortant par la Voie Lactée* (*The First Planet on the Right When You Exit at the Milky Way*; Fayard, 1975); *Note:* See Chapter IX.

Danio, D.A.C. (?-); *Les "Cuirs Bouillis"* (*The "Boiled Leathers"*; RF 76, 1961); *Note:* See Chapter IX.

Dann, Maurice *see* **Grand-Guignol**

Danrit (Capitaine; Driant, Émile-Auguste-Cyprien; 1855-1916); *La Guerre de Demain* (*Tomorrow's War*; 8 vols.; Flamm., 1889-96); *1-2. La Guerre de Forteresse* (*The Fortress War*); *3-4. La Guerre en Rase Campagne* (*War on Open Land*); *5-6. La Guerre en Ballon* (*War in Balloons*); *7-8. Le Journal de Guerre du Lt. Von Piefke* (*Lt. Von Piefke's War Diary*); *L'Invasion Noire* (*The Black Invasion*; 4 vols.; Flamm., 1895-96); *1. La Mobilitation Africaine* (*The African Mobilization*); *2. Concentration et Pélerinage à La Mecque* (*Concentration and Pilgrimage in Mecca*); *3. À Travers l'Europe* (*Throughout Europe*); *4. Autour de Paris* (*Around Paris*; 3 & 4 later rev. as *Fin de L'Islam Devant Paris* (*The End of Islam Before Paris*); *Ordre du Tzar* (*Orders from the Czar*; Flamm., 1900); *La Guerre Fatale—France-Angleterre* (*The Fatal War—France vs. England*; 3 vols.; Flamm., 1901-02); *1. À Bizerte* (*To Bizerte*); *2. En Sous-Marin* (*On a Submarine*); *3. En Angleterre* (*In England*); *Évasion d'Empereur* (*The Emperor Escapes*; JDV, 1903-04; rev. Flamm., 1911); *Si nous Avions eu la Guerre* (*If We Had War*; JST, 1905); *L'Invasion Jaune* (*The Yellow Invasion*; 3 vols.; Flamm., 1905-06); *1. La Mobilisation Sino-Japonaise* (*The Sino-Japanese Mobilization*); *2. Haine de Jaunes* (*Yellow Hatred*); *3. À Travers l'Europe* (*Throughout Europe*); *Robinsons Sous-Marins* (*Robinsons Under the Sea*; Flamm., 1907-08); *Robinsons de l'Air* (*Robinsons of the Air*; Flamm., 1908-09; rev. as *Un Dirigeable au Pôle Nord* (*A Dirigible at the North Pole*), Flamm., 1910); *L'Aviateur du Pacifique* (*The Aviator of the Pacific*; Flamm., 1909-10); *La Révolution de Demain* (*Tomorrow's Revolution*; with Arnould **Galopin**; Tallandier, 1909-10); *L'Alerte* (*The Alert*; Flamm., 1910); *Au-Dessus du Continent Noir* (*Above the Black Continent*; Flamm., 1911); *Robinsons Souterrains* (*Underground Robinsons*; Flamm., 1912-13; rev. as *La Guerre Souterraine* (*The Underground War*, Flamm., 1915); *Note:* See Chapter V.

Dansler, Robert (?-); *À 300 Mètres sous le Pôle* (*300 Meters Under the Pole*; Oeil de Faucon, 1939); *Les Géants du Titoradium* (*The Giants of Titoradium*; Oeil de Faucon, 1940); *Le Cabanon de la Mort* (*The Cabin of Death*; SFEP, 1941); *La Mare de Sang* (*The Pool of Blood*; SFEP, 1941); *La Princesse de la Jungle* (*The Jungle Princess*; SFEP, 1941); *Le Bal des Serpents* (*The Dance of the Snakes*; SFEP, 1942); *Dans les Griffes du*

Serpent Vert (*In the Claws of the Green Snake*; SFEP, 1942); *Quatre Clous dans un Carré* (*Four Nails in a Square*; SFEP, 1942)

Dantec, Maurice G. (?-); *La Sirène Rouge* (*The Red Siren*; Gall., 1993); *Les Racines du Mal* (*The Roots of Evil*; Gall. Série Noire 2379, 1995); *Note:* See Chapter IX.

Danville, Gaston (1870-?); *Les Infinis de la Chair* (*The Infinity of Flesh*; Lemerre, 1892); *Contes d'Au-Delà* (*Tales from Beyond*; MdF, 1893); *Vers la Mort* (*Towards Death*; Lemerre, 1897); *L'Amour Magician* (*Magician Love*; MdF, 1902); *Le Parfum de Volupté* (*The Scent of Voluptuousness*; MdF, 1905); *Magnétisme et Spiritisme* (MdF, 1908); *Le Mystère Psychique* (*The Psychic Mystery*; Félix Alcan, 1914); *Note:* See Chapter IV.

Darblin, Henri (?-); *La Horde des Monstres* (*The Horde of Monsters*; S&V, 1928); *Quatre Scouts dans les Balkans* (*Four Scouts in the Balkans*; De Brouwer, 1940); *Bellinha de Macao* (Chantal, 1942); *Note:* See Chapter VII.

Darcy, Gil *see* **Arnaud, G.-J.**

Darcy, Paul (?-); *La Conquête de la Planète Mars* (*The Conquest of Planet Mars*; Petit Illustré, 1929); *Le Vampire de Warnaga* (*The Vampire of Warnaga*; Fayard, 1930); *La Prison Aérienne* (*The Airborne Prison*; RJ, 1934); *L'Ange de la Mort* (*The Angel of Death*; Tallandier, 1935); *Le Prisonnier des Sachedds* (*The Prisoner of the Sachedds*; Tallandier, 1938); *L'Idole aux Yeux de Jade* (*The Idol with Jade Eyes*; Tallandier, 1939); *L'Infernale Planète* (*Infernal Planet*; SFP, 1941); *Note:* See Chapter VII.

Dard, Frédéric (1921-) as Frédéric Charles: *La Maison de l'Horreur* (*The House of Horror*; Loupe Épouvante, 1952); *L'Horrible M. Smith* (*The Horrible Mr. Smith*; Loupe Épouvante, 1952; *La Main Morte* (*The Dead Hand*; Loupe Épouvante, 1952; *N'ouvrez pas ce Cercueil* (*Don't Open This Coffin*; Loupe Épouvante, 1954; rev. FNSL 3, 1974); *J'ai peur des Mouches* (*I'm Afraid of Flies*; as San-Antonio; FN Special-Police 141, 1957); *Coma* (FN, 1959); *Puisque les Oiseaux Meurent* (*Since the Birds Die*; PP, 1960); *Le Gala des Emplumés* (*The Ball of the Feathered*; as San-Antonio; FN Special-Police, 1963); *Histoires Déconcertantes* (*Unsettling Tales*; FN, 1977); *Note:* See Chapter VIII. Also see **Grand-Guignol**.

Dard, Michel (?-); *Histoires Confidentielles* (*Confidential Tales*; Grasset, 1970); *Les Sentiers de l'Enfance* (*The Paths of Childhood*; Seuil, 1977); *Mélusine* (LdP, 1979); *Le Rayon Vert* (*The Green Ray*; Seuil, 1979)

Daridjana (?-); *Roulette Russe* (*Russian Roulette*; FNA 1406, 1985); *Note:* See Chapter IX.

Darien, G. (?-?) *see* **Grand-Guignol**

Darios, Louise (Pacheco de Céspedes, Daria-Luisa; 1913-

1986); *Contes Étranges du Canada* (*Strange Tales of Canada*; Beauchemin, 1962); *L'Arbre Étranger* (*The Alien Tree*; Naaman, 1977); *Le Retable des Merveilles* (*The Table of Wonders*; Naaman, 1979); *Le Soleil des Morts* (*The Sun of the Dead*; Naaman, 1982); *Note:* French-Canadian writer. *Le Soleil* is a collection of fantastic tales.

Dark, Jason (?-); Series *John Sinclair, Chasseur de Spectres* (*Ghost Hunter*): *1. Peur sur Londres* (*Fear Over London*; FN, 1992); *2. La Bombe Magique* (*The Magic Bomb*; FN, 1992); *3. L'Horoscope de l'Horreur* (*The Horror Horoscope*; FN, 1992); *4. Une Vie parmi les Morts* (*A Life Among the Dead*; FN, 1992); *Note:* See Chapter VIII.

Darnaudet, Boris (?-) & François (?-); *Collioures Trap* (With C. **Rabier**; FNG 103, 1989); *Andernos Trap* (FNG 115, 1990); *Le Taxidermiste* (*The Taxidermist*; with **Daurel**; Corps 9, 1995); *Daguerra* (DLM, Arkham 5, 1997); *Note:* See Chapter VIII.

Darrau, Jean (?-); *À la Conquête du Mammouth* (*The Conquest of the Mastodon*; STAEL, 1947); *Note:* See Chapter IX.

Darrieussecq, Marie (?-); *Truisme* (P.O.L., 1996); *Note:* See Chapter VIII.

Darry, Michel (?-); *La Course au Radium* (*The Race for Radium*; PRA, 1936); *La Chambre de la Mort Lente* (*The Chamber of Slow Death*; VA, 1937); *La Vallée de la Mort Rouge* (*The Valley of the Red Death*; VA, 1937); *L'Infernale Croisière* (*The Cruise from Hell*; Ferenczi, 1937); *La Malédiction des Andes* (*The Curse of the Andes*; Ferenczi, 1937); *Démon Rouge* (*Red Demon*; Ferenczi, 1938); *Le Trésor des Bolos* (*The Bolos' Treasure*; Ferenczi, 1938); *L'Île des Singes Rois* (*The Island of the Monkey Kings*; PRA, 1939); *La Dernière Inca* (*The Last Inca*; VA, 1939); *Le Pirate des Sables* (*The Pirate of the Sands*; Ferenczi, 1939); *Dans la Gueule du Dragon* (*In the Mouth of the Dragon*; VA, 1940); *Note:* See Chapter VII.

Dartal, Frank (1920-); *Les Brumes du Sagittaire* (*The Mists of Sagittarius*; FNA 775, 1977); *Les Neuf Dieux de l'Espace* (*The Nine Gods of Space*; FNA 807, 1977); *Les Seigneurs de Kalaâr* (*The Lords of Kalaar*; FNA 831, 1978); *Le Livre d'Éon* (*The Book of Eon*; FNA 853, 1978); *Les Roches aux Cent Visages* (*The Rocks of Hundred Faces*; FNA 897, 1979); *Le Règne du Serpent* (*The Reign of the Serpent*; FNA 918, 1979); *Au Quatre Vents de l'Univers* (*The Four Winds of the Universe*; FNA 939, 1979); *La Terre est une Légende* (*Earth Is a Legend*; FNA 977, 1980); *Civilisations Galactiques—Providence* (*Galactic Civilisations—Providence*; FNA 1006, 1980); *Message de Bâl 188* (*Message from Bal 188*; FNA 1120, 1982); *Les Glaces du Temps* (*The Ice of Time*; FNA

1163, 1982); *Et un Temps pour Mourir* (*And a Time to Die*; FNA 1197, 1982); *Eridan VII* (FNA 1472, 1986); *Un Temps pour la Guerre* (*A Time for War*; FNA 1557, 1987); *L'Épopée du Draco* (*The Draco's Odyssey*; FNA 1622, 1988); *Note:* See Chapter IX.

Dartevelle, Alain (1951-); *Borg, ou l'Anatomie d'un Monstre* (*Borg, or the Anatomy of a Monster*; Solidaritude, 1984); *Les Mauvais Rêves de Marthe* (*Martha's Bad Dreams*; Aurore, Futurs 9, 1989); *Script* (PdF 482, 1989); *Imago* (JL 3601, 1994); *Le Cycle de Vertor 1: L'Astre aux Idiots* (*The Star of Idiots*; Cast., 1997); *Le Cycle de Vertor 2: Le Grand Transmutateur* (*The Great Transmutator*; Cast., 1997); *Note:* See Chapter IX.

Dartois, Yves (Ruelle, Yves; 1901-1974); *Le Démon des Bateaux sans Vie* (*The Demon of the Lifeless Boats*; Ren. du Livre, 1927); *La Maison de la Licorne* (*The House of the Unicorn*; Tallandier, 1937); *L'Horoscope du Mort* (*The Dead Man's Horoscope*; Libr. Champs-Élysées, 1937); *Les Réfugiés de la Maison Verte* (*The Refugees of the Green House*; Tallandier, 1940); *La Muraille aux Atlantes* (*The Wall of the Atlanteans*; Den., 1965); *Le Grand-Prêtre des Guanches* (*The High Priest of the Guanches*; Den., 1970); *Mélusine* (Den., 1971); *Le Berceau Fantôme* (*The Phantom Cradle*; Den., 1972); *La Montagne des Druses* (*The Mountain of the Druses*; Den., 1973); *Le Voile de la Madonne* (*The Madonna's Veil*; Grasset, 1973)

Da Silva, Viviane *see* **Julien, Viviane**

Dasit, Jacques (?-); *On a Volé la Bombe Atomique* (*They Stole the Atom Bomb*; Dumas, 1946)

Dasnoy, Albert (1901-); *La Longueur du Temps* (*The Length of Time*; Laconti, 1968); *Note:* Belgian writer. See Chapter VIII.

Dastier, Dan (Brehal, Marc (1940-) / Chantepie, Yves (?-)); *Les Déracinés d'Humania* (*Uprooted from Humania*; FNA 493, 1972); *Les Secrets d'Hypnoz* (*The Secrets of Hypnoz*; FNA 533, 1972); *Messies pour l'Avenir* (*Messiahs for the Future*; FNA 558, 1973); *Les Replis du Temps* (*The Folds of Time*; FNA 570, 1973); *La Planète aux Diamants* (*The Diamond Planet*; FNA 584, 1973); *Les Immortels de Cephalia* (*The Immortals of Cephalia*; FNA 607, 1974); *Les Mutants de Pshuria* (*The Mutants of Pshuria*; FNA 620, 1974); *La Porte du Monde Alpha* (*The Door Into the Alpha World*; FNA 658, 1975); *Zarnia, Dimension Folie* (*Zarnia, Dimen-*

sion of Madness; FNA 697, 1975); *Les Sirènes de Lusinia* (*The Sirens of Lusinia*; as Jean-Yves Chanbert; AMSF 28, 1974); *Les Autos de l'Apocalypse* (*The Cars of Apocalypse*; as Jean-Yves Chanbert; AM, 1976); *Le Feu de Klo-Ora* (*The Fire of Klo-Ora*; FNA 735, 1976); *Au-Delà des Trouées Noires* (*Beyond the Black Holes*; FNA 805, 1977); *Les Maîtres de Gorka* (*The Masters of Gorka*; FNA 826, 1977); *Les Vengeurs de Zyléa* (*The Avengers of Zylea*; FNA 839, 1978); *La Louve de Thar-Gha* (*The She-Wolf of Thar-Gha*; FNA 863, 1978); *Obsession Terzium 13* (FNA 879, 1978); *Les Sequestrés de Kappa* (*Sequestered on Kappa*; FNA 884, 1978); *Le Soleil des Arians* (*The Sun of the Arians*; FNA 891, 1978); *Les Androïdes Meurent Aussi* (*Androids Also Die*; FNA 909, 1979); *Le Talef d'Alkoria* (*The Talef of Alkoria*; FNA 919, 1979); *Naia de Zomkaa* (FNA 943, 1979); *Et Les Hommes Voulurent Mourir* (*And Men Wanted to Die*; FNA 955, 1979); *Une Autre Eternité* (*Another Eternity*; FNA 963, 1980); *Les Sphères de Penta* (*The Spheres of Penta*; FNA 985, 1980); *Les Intemporels* (*The Intemporals*; FNA 996, 1980); *Stade Zéro* (*Stage Zero*; FNA 1017, 1980); *La Métamorphose des Schaftes* (*The Metamorphosis of the Schaftes*; FNA 1046, 1981); *Les Dieux Maudits d'Alphéa* (*The Cursed Gods of Alphea*; FNA 1073, 1981); *L'Enfant de Xéna* (*Xena's Child*; FNA 1096, 1981); *Le Règne d'Astakla* (*The Reign of Astakla*; FNA 1110, 1981); *Le Secret d'Irgoun* (*The Secret of Irgoun*; FNA 1134, 1982); *L'Ère des Bionites* (*The Era of the Bionites*; FNA 1145, 1982); *Les Héritiers d'Antinéa* (*The Heirs of Antinea*; FNA 1189, 1982); Shan-Aya (FNA 1240, 1983); *Le Sixième Symbiote* (*The Sixth Symbiote*; FNA 1559, 1987); *Note:* See Chapter IX. "Dan Dastier" is a house pseudonym created by Fleuve Noir and shared by at least two writers, Marc **Bréhal** and Yves **Chantepie** (also see Jean-Yves **Chanbert**).

Daudet, Alphonse (1840-1897); *Un Réveillon dans les Marais* (*Christmas' Eve in the Swamps*; n.d.); *Les Fées de France* (*Fairies of France*; n.d.); *L'Homme à la Cervelle d'Or* (*The Man with the Golden Brain*; 1869); *Wood's Town* (in *Études et Paysages*, (*Studies and Landscapes*, Lemerre, 1873); *Note:* See chapters IV and V. His story "*Le Siège de Berlin*" was adapted into a **Grand-Guignol** play by Charles **Hellem** & Pol d'**Estoc**.

Daudet, Léon (1867-1942); *Les Morticoles* (Fayard, 1894); *L'Astre Noir* (*The Black Star*; Charpentier, 1894); *Un Jour d'Orage* (*A Stormy Day*; Flamm., 1925); *Le Sang de la Nuit* (*The Blood of the Night*; Flamm., 1926); *Le Napus, Fléau de l'An 2227* (*The Nomore, Plague of the Year 2227*; Flamm., 1927); *Les Bacchantes* (Flamm., 1931); *Ciel de Feu* (*Sky of Fire*; Flamm., 1934); *Note:* Son of Alphonse **Daudet**. See chapters VI and VII.

Daumal, René (1908-1944); *La Grande Beuverie* (*The*

Great Drinking Party; Gall., 1938); *Le Mont Analogue, Récit Véridique* (*The Analogous Mountain, a True Story*; Gall., 1952)

Daurel (?-) *see* **Darnaudet**

Dautan, Fanny (?-); *Le Satellite du Sex-Temps* (*The Satellite of Sex-Time*; Enclos, 1980); *Note:* Erotic SF.

Dave, Max (?-); *Terreur au Château* (*Terror at the Castle*; Bel-Air 1, 1966)

David, Jean (1923-); *Les Passes du Silence* (*The Passage of Silence*; Seuil, 1954); *Une Chose dans la Nuit* (*A Thing in the Night*; FNAG 14, 1956); *Les Griffes de l'Oubli* (*The Claws of Oblivion*; FNAG 28, 1957); *Le Crépuscule du Matin* (*The Twilight of the Morning*; Seuil, 1957); *Les Survivants* (*The Survivors*; Seuil, 1958); *Le Diable est puissant* (*The Devil Is Powerful*; CPE-PIC, 1959); *Assassin* (*Murderer*; Seuil, 1965)

Davidson, Jean (?-); *Histoires Accélérées* (*Accelerated Tales*; Del Duca, 1958); *Les Laboratoires de la Mort Euphorique* (*The Laboratories of Joyous Death*; Den., 1960)

Davor, Yann (?-); *L'Île des Démons* (*The Island of Demons*; Stael, 1947); *Note:* Juvenile SF.

Day, Georges (?-); *L'Anneau de Gygès* (*The Ring of Gyges*; Figuière, 1932)

Day, Pierre (?-?) *see* **Grand-Guignol**

Dazergues, Max-André (?-); *Les Mystères de l'Atlantique* (*The Mysteries of the Atlantic*; LA, 1929); *Du Sang sur les Nuages* (*Blood on the Clouds*; as André Mad; LA, 1930); *L'Île de Satan* (*Satan's Island*; as André Mad; LA, 1931); *L'Oeuf De Nacre* (*The Pearly Egg*; as André Star; VLAE, 1931); *L'Île Aérienne* (*The Aerial Island*; as André Star; BGA, 1931); *Le Vampire de la Montagne d'Or* (*The Vampire of Gold Mountain*; as André Star; BGA, 1931); *Le Traîneau Fantôme* (*The Phantom Sled*; Printemps, 1933); *L'Empereur des Crabes* (*The Emperor of Crabs*; as André Star; BGA, 1933); *La Charmeuse de Monstres* (*The Monster Charmer*; as André Mad; VA, 1934); *Le Fantôme de la Baie des Tigres* (*The Phantom of Tiger Bay*; as André Star; BGA, 1934); *L'Homme Qui Incendia le Pôle* (*The Man Who Set the Pole on Fire*; VA, 1935); *Le Maître du Vertige* (*The Vertigo Master*; VA, 1935); *Les Dés d'Ébène* (*The Ebony Dice*; as André Star; LdA, 1935); *La Déesse des Nuages* (*The Cloud Goddess*; PRA, 1936); *Le Tunnel de l'Épouvante* (*The Tunnel of Horror*; VA, 1936); *Le Requin Volant* (*The Flying Shark*; VA, 1937); *La Sixième Parte du Monde* (*The Sixth Part of the World*; VA, 1937); *Le Traîneau du Diable* (*The Devil's Sled*; PRA, 1937); *La Déesse de Jade* (*The Jade Goddess*; SEPIA, 1937); *La Fusée des Glaces* (*The Ice Rocket;* VA, 1938); *Vengeance de Sor-*

cier (*Sorcerer's Revenge*; Ferenczi, 1938); *Les Yeux de l'Idole* (*The Idol's Eyes*; Ferenczi, 1938); *Le Château des Vampires* (*The Castle of Vampires*; Ferenczi, 1938); *Les Noces d'Angoisse* (*Wedding of Fear*; Mon Livre Préféré, 1938); *La Baleinière de l'Épouvante (The Whaler Ship of Terror*; PRA, 1939; rev. as *La Sirène de la Banquise* (*The Siren of the Ice Shelf*, MRA, 1955); *L'Âme Habite le Crâne* (*The Soul Resides in the Skull*; Ferenczi, 1939); *La Sorcière Blanche* (*The White Witch*; Ferenczi, 1940); *L'Araignée d'Or* (*The Gold Spider*; LA, 1941); *Aéros, Empereur des Nuages* (*Emperor of the Clouds*; Puits Pelu, 1943); *Le Trésor des Achantis* (*The Achantis' Treasure*; SAETL, 1945); *Le Marteau d'Ivoire* (*The Ivory Hammer*; Savoie, 1945); *Minuit chez le Sphinx* (*Midnight at the Sphinx*; R. Bonnefon, 1946); *La Gondole aux Sorciers* (*The Wizards' Gondola*; Duclos, 1946); *Le Sphinx de Cire* (*The Sphinx of Wax*; Puits Pelu, 1946); *Les Briseurs de Montagnes* (*The Mountain Breakers*; JDV, 1947); *Photonox, L'Homme de la Nuit* (*Photonox, the Night Man*; serial. in *Plutos*, 1950-52); *Le Carnaval des Épouvantes* (*The Carnival of Horrors*; Arabesque Frayeurs, 1954); *La Spirale du Diable* (*The Devil's Spiral*; MRA, 1954); *En Avion Au Centre de la Terre* (*By Plane at the Earth's Core*; MRA, 1955); *La Sphère Engloutie* (*The Sunken Sphere*; MRA, 1955); *La Soucoupe de Cire* (*The Wax Saucer*; MRA, 1955); *De la Terre à l'Éther* (*From Earth to the Ether*; MRA, 1956); *Note:* See Chapter VII.

Dé, Claire (1953-); *La Louve-Garou* (*The She-Werewolf*; with Anne **Dandurand**; Pleine Lune, 1982); *Le Désir comme Catastrophe Naturelle* (*Desire as a Natural Catastrophe*; Étincelle, 1989); *Note:* French-Canadian writer, twin sister of Anne **Dandurand**. Collection of short stories.

Debans, Camille (1834-?); *La Peau du Mort* (*Deadman's Skin*; Dentu, 1880); *Histoires de tous les Diables* (*Tales of All the Devils*; Dentu, 1882); *Les Malheurs de John Bull* (*John Bull's Problems*; Flamm., 1884); *Le Vainqueur de la Mort* (*The Man Who Vanquished Death*; SI, 1895); *Note:* See Chapter V.

Debard, Émile *see* **Anton, Emil**

Debardieux, Cédric *see* **Cryde, Th.**

Debellerive, P. (?-); *Voyage dans les Airs* (*Journey Through the Airs*; Gaillard, 1895)

Deberly, Henri (?-); *Prosper et Broudifagne* (Gall., 1924); *Tombes sans Lauriers* (*Graves Without Laurels*; Gall., 1929); *L'Agonisant* (*The Dying Man*; Gall., 1931); *Le Supplice de Phèdre* (*Phaedra's Torture*; Gall., 1934)

Deblander, Gabriel (1934-); *Le Retour des Chasseurs* (*The Return of the Hunters;* RL, 1970); *L'Oiseau sous la Chemise* (*The Bird Under the Shirt*; RL, 1976); *La Chute d'Icare* (*The Fall of Icarus*; Duculot, 1978); *Note:* Belgian writer. See Chapter VIII.

Debresse, Pierre (?-); *Samorix et le Rameau d'Or* (*Samorix and the Golden Branch*; Magnard, 1965); *Le Trésor de Carthage* (*The Treasure of Carthage*; Magnard, 1967); *Les Enfants Immortels Aux Temps Barbares* (*The Immortal Children in Barbarian Times*; GP, 1977); *Un Pont sur le Temps* (*A Bridge Over Time*; Magnard, 1986); *Les Larmes d'Isis* (*The Tears of Isis*; Magnard, 1992); *Note:* Juvenile fantasies. See Chapter VIII.

Debure, H. (?-); *L'Évanouissement du Pôle* (*The Vanishing of the Pole*; BGA, 1933); *Le Secret du Loch Ness* (*The Secret of Loch Ness*; VA, 1934); *Le Phare Sanglant* (*The Bloody Lighthouse*; VA, 1935); *Le Cercle de Serpents* (*The Circle of Serpents*; PRA, 1936)

Debussy, Claude (1862-1918) *see* **Opéra**

Debuys, Pierre (?-); *Les Gardiennes d'Espérance* (*The Guardians of Hope*; FNA 1893, 1992)

Décary, Marie (1953-); *L'Incroyable Destinée* (*The Incredible Destiny*; La Courte Échelle, 1993); *Note:* French-Canadian writer.

Deceneux, Marc (?-) *see* ***Contes et Légendes***

Declausse, Philippe (?-); Series *Les 7* (*The Seven*): *Les Fanfares du Potomac* (*The Orchestra of the Potomac*; JCL, 1973); *Le Président Carabine* (*President Carbine*; JCL, 1973)

Decoin, Didier (1945-); *Le Rendez-Vous du Monstre* (*The Monster's Rendezvous*; Hac., 1988); *Note:* Juvenile.

Décotte, Alex (1944-); *Et Malville Explosa* (*And Malville Exploded*; with Jacques **Neirynck**; Faure, 1988); *Note:* Novel about a French Three-Mile Island incident.

Deff, Red *see* **Wagner, Roland C.**

Deflez, Gilbert (?-); *Je suis vivant mais j'ai peur* (*I'm Alive But I'm Afraid*; Galliera, 1974)

Defontenay, Charlemagne-Ischir (1819-1856); *Star, ou Psi de Cassiopée* (Le Doyen, 1854; rep. PdF 145, 1972; transl. as *Star,* 1985); *Note:* See Chapter V.

Defrasne, Jean (?-) *see* ***Contes et Légendes***

Déglantine, Sylvain (?-); *Les Terriens sur Vénus* (*Earthmen on Venus*; Flamm., 1907); *Le Calvaire d'une Hypnotisé* (*The Torture of an Hypnotised Woman*; La Vie Myst., 1910); *La Nouvelle Babel* (*The New Babel*; LdA, 1954); *Note:* See Chapter V.

Degrelle, Léon *see* **Doutreligne, Jean**

Deharme, Lise (?-1980); *Cette Année-là* (*That Year*; Gal., 1945); *Le Pot de Mousse* (*The Pot of Mousse*; Fontaine, 1946); *La Porte à Côté* (*The Next Door*; Gall., 1949); *Le*

Château de l'Horloge (*The Castle of the Clock*; Julliard, 1955); *Les Quatre Cents Coups du Diable* (*The Devil's 400 Blows*; Deux-Rives, 1956); *Pierre de la Mermorte* (Julliard, 1962); *L'Enchanteur* (*The Enchanter*; Grasset, 1964); *Le Téléphone est Mort* (*The Telephone Is Dead*; Los., 1973); *La Marquise d'Enfer* (*The Marquess of Hell*; Grasset, 1976); *La Caverne* (*The Cave*; Libr. Bleue, 1984); *Note:* See Chapter VIII.

Deincourt, Jean (Hannezo, Gustave-Joanny; 1890-); *Le Sosie de l'Aigle* (*The Eagle's Lookalike*; Chat-Huant, 1932); *L'Inconscient* (*The Unconscious*; Chat-Huant, 1935); *Napoléon avait raison* (*Napoleon Was Right*; Vernaut, 1937)

Déjacque, Joseph (1822-1867); *L'Humanisphère* (serial. 1858-59; rev. Bibl. Temps Nouveaux, 1899); *Note:* See Chapter V.

Dekk, Karel *see* **Lehman, Serge**

Dekobra, Maurice (Tessier, Maurice; 1885-1973); *Hamydal le Philosophe* (*Hamydal the Philosopher*; Baudinière, 1927); *Pourquoi Mourir?* (*Why Die?*; Baudinière, 1931); *Les Lèvres qui Mentent: Le Sphinx a parlé* (*The Lying Lips: The Sphinx Spoke*; Parizeau, 1944); *Le Carnaval des Spectres* (*The Carnival of Spectres*; Sfelt, 1947); *L'Armée Rouge est à New York* (*The Red Army Is in New York*; Scorpion, 1954); *L'Homme qui Mourut Deux Fois (Les Vestales du Veau d'Or)* (*The Man Who Died Twice (The Vestals of the Golden Calf*; Karolus, 1960); *Note: Le Carnaval* is a play in four acts. Also see **Grand-Guignol**.

Delafosse, Bernard (?-); *Terres et Ciels: Réflexions sur l'Univers Humain et sur les Autres* (*Heavens and Earths: Thoughts on the Human Universe and Others*; Omnium Litt., 1957); *À Dieu Vat...* (*God Willing...*; Copelat, 1960); *Des Vies de Lumière* (*Lives of Light*; Trédamiel, 1990); *Chimères Bleues* (*Blue Chimeras*; Trédamiel, 1993)

Delagny, Georges *see* **Ariel, F.**

Delamare, George (1886-1975); *Les Voleurs d'Âmes* (*The Stealer of Souls*; Vraie France, 1925; rev. Cosmopolites, 1929); *Le Roi de Minuit* (*The King of Midnight*; AM, 1926); *Théoclée* (AM, 1929); *Note:* Famous journalist and TV personality.

Delample, F. (?-) *see* ***Contes et Légendes***

Delavigne, Casimir (?-?) *see* **Opéra**

Delbe, Alain (?-); *Les Îles Jumelles* (*The Twin Islands*; Phébus, 1997)

Delcamp, André (?-); *L'Homme au Masque de Chair* (*The Man in the Mask of Flesh*; Fayard, 1935)

Delcour, Bertrand (?-); *Mezcal Terminal* (Climats, 1988);

En Pure Perte (*Total Loss*; Clo, 1994); *Pourquoi nous sommes Morts* (*Why We Are Dead*; Climats, 1995); *Blocus Solus* (Gall., 1996)

Delcourt, Christian (?-); *Discordances* (Cercle d'Or, 1973)

Delerm, Philippe (1950-); *Sortilège au Museum* (*Spell in the Museum*; Magnard, 1997); *Note:* Juvenile fantasy.

Deleutre, Paul *see* **Ivoi, Paul d'**

Delhoste, Georges (?-); *Le Maître du Jour et du Bruit* (*The Master of Day and Noise*; S&V 1933); *La Science Folle* (*Science Gone Mad*; S&V, 1934); *Note:* See Chapter VII.

Delisle de Sales (?-?); *Ma République* (*My Republic*; 1791); *Note:* See Chapter III.

Dellfos *see* **Losfeld, Éric**

Delly (Petitjean de la Rosière, Marie [1875-1947] & Frédéric [1876-1949]); *Les Maîtres du Silence (2 vols.)* (*The Masters of Silence*; Plon, 1918-19); *1. Sous le Masque* (*Under the Mask*); *2. Le Secret de Kou-Kou-Noor* (*The Secret of Koo-Koo-Noor*); *Note:* See Chapter VII.

Delmas, Jean (?-); *Stupefax* (Hac., 1980); *Note:* Juvenile SF.

Delmon, Yann *see* **Jan, Gabriel**

Delmotte, Henri (1798-1836); *Voyage Pittoresque et Industriel dans le Paraguay-Roux et dans la Palingénésie Australe par Tridace-Nafe Theobrome de Kaout't'-Chouk, Gentilhomme Breton* (*Pittoresque & Industrial Journey in the Red Paraguay and in Southern Palingenesia by Tridace-Nafe Theobrome of Kaout't'Chouk, Britannic Genleman*; Hoyois-Derely, 1835)

Delord, Taxile *see* **Grandville, Isidore**

Delteil, Gérard (1939-); *Coup de Cafard* (*Roach Attack*; FN Special-Police 1942, 1985); *Transfert* (*Transfer*; FNA 1453, 1986); *La Septième Griffe de Togor* (*The Seventh Claw of Togor*; FNA 1583, 1987); *Hors-Jeu* (*Out of the Game*; FNA 1597, 1987); *K3* (Carrère, 1987); *Le Miroir de l'Inca* (*The Inca's Mirror*; L. Lévi, 1988); *Tchernobagne* (*Chernocamp*; FNA 1709, 1989); *Le Fils Capet Se Fait La Malle* (*Capet's Son Got Away*; Syros, 1989); *Les 8 Dragons de Jade* (*The 8 Jade Dragons*; Picquier, 1989); *La Nuit de l'Apagón* (*Night of the Apagón*; FNASF 3, 1995); *Au Nord du Rio Balsa* (*To the North of the Rio Balsa*; FNASF 15, 1996); *Piège sur Internet* (*Trap on the Internet*; Hac., 1996); *Note:* See Chapter IX.

Delval, Jacques (1939-); *Le Mystère de l'Océanor* (*The Mystery of the Oceanor*; Centurion, 1985); *Mystère et Boule de Neige* (*Mystery and Snowball*; Centurion, 1988)

Delvart, Roger *see* **Gestelys, Léo**

Del Vidre, Pierre (?-?) *see* **Grand-Guignol**

Demade, Pol (1863-1936); *Contes Inquiets* (*Worried Tales*; 1898); *Les Âmes qui Saignent* (*The Bleeding Souls*; Dewit, 1910); *Le Cortège des Ombres* (*The Procession of the Shadows*; 1925); *Les Âmes Nues* (*The Naked Souls*; Casterman, 1938); *Note:* Belgian writer. See Chapter VI.

Demarcy, Richard (?-); *Albatros* (Bourgois, 1984)

Demolder, Eugène (1862-1919); *Le Massacre des Innocents* (*The Innocents' Massacre*; Monnom, 1891); *Contes d'Yperdamme* (*Tales from Yperdamme*; Lacomblez, 1891); *La Légende d'Yperdamme* (*The Legend of Yperdamme*; MdF, 1897); *La Route d'Émeraude* (*The Emerald Road*; MdF, 1899); *L'Agonie d'Albion* (*The Agony of Albion*; MdF, 1901); *Le Coeur des Pauvres* (*Paupers' Heart*; MdF, 1901); *L'Arche de Monsieur Cheunus* (*The Ark of Mr. Cheunus*; MdF, 1904); *Note:* Belgian writer. See chapters V and VI.

Demont, Jean *see* **Jan, Gabriel**

Demousson, Pierre (?-); *Le Roi des Lacs* (*The King of the Lakes*; Tallandier, 1922); *La Croisière du Floréal* (*The Cruise of the Floreal*; Tallandier, 1928); *L'Amazone du Nicaragua* (*The Nicaraguan Amazon*; Tallandier, 1928); *Le Gnome de la Cathédrale* (*The Gnome of the Cathedral*; Mode Nationale, 1928); *Le Destructeur du Monde* (*The Destroyer of the World*; VLAE, 1929); *Les Compagnons du Dragon Noir* (*The Companions of the Black Dragon*; BGA, 1929); *L'Émeraude du Lama* (*The Lama's Emerald*; Mode Nationale, 1929); *Le Secret du Cabinet des Laques* (*The Secret of the Lacquered Cabinet*; Livre National, 1930); *Le Targui au Litham Vert* (*The Targui with the Green Litham*; Impr. Fr. de l'Éd., 1930); *Le Billet de Galipode* (*Galipode's Ticket*; BGA, 1930); *Le Secret de l'Antarctide* (*The Secret of Antarctica*; BGA, 1930); *La Vengeance du Fétiche* (*The Idol's Revenge*; BGA, 1930); *Terre de Mystère* (*Land of Mystery*; BGA, 1931); *Un Drame dans la Mer Rouge* (*A Tragedy on the Red Sea*; BGA, 1932); *Les Mystères du Bardo* (*The Mysteries of the Bardo*; BGA, 1932); *La Pierre Noire* (*The Black Stone*; BGA, 1932); *Les Pionniers de Fachoda* (*The Pioneers of Fachoda*; CA, 1932); *Les Captifs de la Vierge Rouge* (*The Captives of the Red Virgin*; CA, 1932); *Le Commandant de l'Aquilon* (*The Commander of the Aquilon*; CA, 1932); *Le Frère Novi* (*The Brother Novi*; BGA, 1933); *Les Prisonniers du Sultan Bleu* (*The Prisoners of the Blue Sultan*; BGA, 1933); *La Steppe de la Faim* (*The Steppe of Hunger*; CA, 1933); *La Fille du Prophète* (*The Prophet's Daughter*; BGA, 1936); *L'Idole au Trésor* (*The Treasure Idol*; SEPIA, 1937); *Le Secret du Lac des Hemiones* (*The Secret of the Lake of Hemiones*; Tallandier, 1954);

Note: See Chapter VII. Also used the pseudonym of "Pierre Blenod" for non-genre adventure stories.

Demouzon, Alain (?-); *Dernière Station avant Jérusalem* (*Last Station Before Jerusalem*; Gall. Série Noire, 1994)

Demuth, Michel (1939-); *La Clé des Étoiles* (*The Key to the Stars*; Sat. 26, 1960); *Les Années Metalliques* (*The Metal Years*; A&D 46, 1977); *Les Galaxiales* (*The Galaxials*; 2 vols; JL 693, 1976; JL 996, 1979); *Toxicofuturis* (anthology; OF Special 28, 1977); *Note:* See Chapter IX.

Denis, Guy (?-); *Une Phrase pour Orphée* (*A Sentence for Orpheus*; L'Ardoisière, 1984)

Denis, Pierre (?-); *Les Apprentis Sorciers* (*The Sorcerer's Apprentices*; Nlle. France, 1947)

Denis, Sylvie (1963-); *Jardins Virtuels* (*Virtual Gardens*; DLM, CyberDreams, 1995); *Century XXI* (La Nouvelle Fiction; Encrage, 1995); *L'Invité de Verre* (*The Glass Guest*; DLM, Arkham 4, 1997); *Note:* See Chapter IX.

Denouviac, Edmond (?-?) *see* **Grand-Guignol**

Denz, Jean-Henri (?-); *L'Épée de Zaddok* (*The Sword of Zaddok*; SdP 179, 1968); *Note:* Juvenile.

Derems, Pierre-François (?-); *Tous Aux Abris* (*All in the Shelter*; Los., 1982)

Derennes, Charles (1882-1930); *Le Peuple du Pôle* (*The People of the Pole*; MdF, 1907); *Les Conquérants d'Idoles* (*The Conquerors of Idols*; 1908; MdF, 1919); *Note:* See Chapter V.

Dereves, Jean (?-); *La Seconde Naissance du Monde* (*The Second Birth of the World*; Georges Fr., 1944)

Dermèze, Yves *see* **Béra, Paul**

Derobien, Thibaut (?-); *Le Testament de Princeton* (*The Testament of Princeton*; Simoën, 1977)

Dervin, Sylvie (?-); *La Jument de la Nuit* (*The Nightmare*; AM, 1980)

Desachy, Paul (?-?) *see* **Grand-Guignol**

Desbruères, Michel (?-); *La France Fantastique 1900* (anthology; Phébus, 1978)

Descaves, Lucien (1861-1949); *Les Emmurés* (*The Walled-Ins*; Tresse & Stock, 1894); *La Maison Anxieuse* (*The*

Anxious House; Crès, 1916); *L'Enfant Enragé* (*The Rabid Child*; Coquette, 1922); *Le Faustin* (Fasquelle, 1923); *Note:* Also see **Grand-Guignol**.

Deschamps, Émile (1791-1871); *Réalités Fantastiques* (*Fantastic Realities*; Henneton, 1854); *Note:* See Chapter IV.

Deschamps, Jacques-Marie (?-?) *see* **Opéra**

Deschenes, Jean-Claude (1943-); *La Pipe dans le Mur* (*The Pipe in the Wall*; Griffon d'Argile, 1986); *Note:* French-Canadian writer.

Desclaux, Pierre (1885-); *Les Morts de Bronze* (*The Dead Men in Bronze*; S&V, 1921); *Le Maître du Monde* (*The Master of the World;* S&V, 1921; rev. as *Robur, Maître de l'Or* (*Robur the Gold Master*, Hublot, 1945); *Le Secret d'Hermano* (*The Secret of Hermano*; as Jean Frick, *L'Épatant*, 1926; rev. as Desclaux, as *Le Secret du Bagnard* (*The Convict's Secret*, *Le Moustique*, 1937); *Laboratoire d'Épouvante* (*Laboratory of Terror*; Hublot, 1945); *Note:* See Chapter V.

Desfontaines (Abbé Pierre-François Guyot; 1685-1745); *Le Nouveau Gulliver* (*The New Gulliver*; Vve. Clouzier, 1730); *Note:* Unauthorized sequel to Swift's classic novel penned by his French translator. It narrates the adventures of Gulliver's son.

Desforges, André (?-); *Une Vie de Chien* (*A Dog's Life*; Pensée U., 1975); *Le Chien des Étoiles* (*The Star Dog*; Dossiers d'Aquitaine, 1987)

Desforges, Régine (?-); *La Révolte des Nonnes* (*The Revolt of the Nuns*; TR, 1981)

Desfosses, Jacques (?-); *Pourri comme la Gloire* (*Rotten Like Glory*; Tisseyre, 1997); *Note:* French-Canadian writer.

Des Gachons, Jacques (1868-1945); *Le Mauvais Pas* (*The Wrong Step*; Gautier, 1906); *Le Ballon Fantôme* (*The Phantom Balloon*; Mame, 1911); *Le Chemin de Sable* (the *Sand Path*; Lafitte, 1920); *Les Patins de Gargantua* (*Gargantua's Shoes*; Baudinière, 1924); *Sur Pieds: Contes pour les Petits des Hommes* (*On Their Feet: Tales for the Children of Men*; Monde Moderne, 1925); *La Maison du Passé* (*The House of the Past*; Litt. & Art Fr., 1926)

Deshusses, Jérôme (?-); *Sodome-Ouest* (Flamm., 1966); *Le Grand Soir* (*The Big Night*; Flamm., 1971); *Délivrez Prométhée* (*Free Prometheus*; Flamm., 1979); *Note:* Swiss writer. See Chapter IX.

Deslinières, Lucien (?-); *La Résurrection du Dr. Valbel* (*The Resurrection of Dr. Valbel*; with Jean **Marc-Py**; France-Ed., 1921)

Desmarest, Henri (?-?); *La Femme Future* (*Future Woman*;

Victor Havard, 1890); *Hors le Monde* (*Out of This World*; Victor Havard, 1891); *Le Diamant Vert* (*The Green Diamond*; E. Guérin, 1897); *Note:* See Chapter V.

Desmazures, Florence (1944-); *Les Poches à Petits Secrets* (Cast., 1986); *Le Roi Extraordinaire, la Traversée de la Manche* (*The Extraordinary King and the Channel Crossing*; Grasset, 1988); *Pardon! Je suis un Ornithorynque, tout simplement!* (*Sorry, I'm Just an Ornithorynk*; Grasset, 1988); *Note:* Juveniles.

Desnos, Robert (1900-1945); *La Liberté ou l'Amour!* (*Liberty or Love!*; Kra, 1927; rep. Gall., 1978); *Note:* See Chapter VI.

Desnoyers, Louis (1805-1868); *Paris Révolutionnaire* (*The Paris Revolution*; 4 vols.; 1833-34); *Les Aventures Amphibies de Robert-Robert et de son fidèle compagnon Toussaint Lavenette* (*The Amphibian Adventures of Robert-Robert and His Faithful Companion Toussaint Lavenette*; Passard, 1853); *Note:* See Chapter V.

Desorties, Raymond (?-); *Le Tétrabie* (Gall., 1933); *Note:* See Chapter VII.

Després, Ronald (1935-); *Le Scalpel Ininterrompu* (*The Uninterrupted Scalpel*; À la Page, 1962); *Note:* French-Canadian writer. Surrealist novel in which the whole of humanity is vivisected within twenty years.

Desriaux, Jean (?-); *Les Pantoufles de l'Homme en Noir* (*The Slippers of the Man in Black*; Jeune Parqu (sic), 1972); *La Solution* (Belfond, 1974)

Desrochers, Pierre (1950-); *Le Canissimius* (Q/A, 1990); *Note:* French-Canadian writer. A novel about a dog-chimpanzee hybrid.

Desrosiers, Danièle (?-); *Mougalouk de Nulle Part* (*Mougaluk from Nowhere*; Héritage, 1989); *Au Secours de Mougalouk* (*To Rescue Mougaluk*; Héritage, 1991); *Note:* French-Canadian writer. Children's science fiction tales.

Desrosiers, Emmanuel (1897-1945); *La Fin de la Terre* (*The End of the Earth*; Libr. Action Canadienne Fr., 1931); *Note:* French-Canadian writer. Earth's agony is caused by overpopulation, famine, lack of fertile soil, natural catastrophes, and exhaustion of non-renewable resources.

Desrosiers, Sylvie (1954-); *Les Princes ne sont pas tous Charmants* (*Not All Princes Are Charming*; Courte Échelle, 1995); *Note:* French-Canadian writer.

Destez, R. (?-) *see* **Hue, Edmond**

Désy, Jean (1954-); *Un Dernier Cadeau pour Cornélia* (*One Last Gift for Cornelia*; XYZ, 1989); *L'Horreur Est Humaine* (*Horror Is Human*; anthology; Palindrome, 1989); *La Saga de Freydis Karlsevni* (Hexagone, 1990); *La Rêverie du Froid* (*A Dream of Cold*; Palindrome, 1991); *Note:* French-Canadian writer. *Saga* is a heroic fantasy viking adventure.

Devaulx, Noël (1905-); *L'Auberge Parpillon* (*The Parpillon Inn*; Gall., 1945); *Le Pressoir Mystique* (*The Mystic Press*; Gall., 1948); *Sainte Barbegrise* (*Saint Greybeard*; Gall., 1952); *Bal chez Alféoni* (*Ball at the Alfeoni's*; Gall., 1956); *La Dame de Murcie* (*The Lady of Murcy*; Gall., 1961); *Frontières* (*Borders*; Gall., 1966); *Avec Vue sur la Zone* (*With View Over the Zone*; Corti, 1974); *Le Lézard d'Immortalité* (*The Lizard of Immortality*; Gall., 1977); *La Plume et la Racine* (*The Pen and the Root*; Gall., 1979); *Le Manuscrit Inachevé* (*The Uncompleted Manuscript*; Gall., 1981); *Le Vase de Gurgan* (*Gurgan's Vase*; Gall., 1983); *Le Visiteur Insolite* (*The Strange Visitor*; Gall., 1985); *Instruction Civique* (*Civic Education*; Gall., 1986); *Capricieuse Diane* (*Capricious Diana*; Gall., 1989); *Mémoires du Perroquet Papageno* (*Memoirs of the Parrot Papageno*; Dumerchez, 1993) *Visite au Palais Pompeien* (*Visit to a Pompeian Palace*; Gall., 1994); *Note:* See Chapter VIII.

Devaux, Pierre (1897-1969); *Gaïlen* (Plon, 1937); *Automates et Automatismes* (*Automatons and Automatisms*; PUF, 1941); *L'Avenir Fantastique* (*Fantastic Future*; Den., 1942); *Les Aventuriers de la Science* (*The Adventurers of Science*; Gall., 1943); *Les Dieux Verts* (*The Green Gods*; Nlle. Revue Critique, 1943); *Uranium* (Médicis, 1946); *XP 15 en Feu!* (*XP15 on Fire!*; S&A 1, 1946); *Les Derniers Miracls de la Science* (*The Latest Miracles of Science*; Grandes Techniques Modernes, 1947); *L'Exilé de l'Espace* (*Exiled in Space;* S&A 3, 1947); *L'Écolier Invisible* (*The Invisible Schoolboy*; with H.-G. **Viot**; S&A 4, 1950); *L'Univers Optimiste* (*Optimist Universe*; Amiot-Dumont, 1951); *La Minute Dérobée* (*The Purloined Minute*; with H.-G. **Viot**; S&A 5, 1952; transl. in *Science Fiction* + magazine, ed. Hugo Gernsback, 1953); *La Conquête d'Almériade* (*The Conquest of Almeriade*; with H.-G. **Viot**; S&A 7, 1954); *Explorations dans le Micro-monde* (*Explorations in the Microworld*; with H.-G. **Viot**; S&A 8, 1957); *Cosmonautes Contre Diplodocus* (Hatier, 1971); *Note:* See chapters VII and IX.

Devigne, Roger (1885-1960); *Janot, Le Jeune Homme aux Ailes d'Or* (*Janot, the Young Man with Wings of Gold*; Le Livre, 1925); *Mon Voyage en Atlantide* (*My Journey to Atlantis*; L'Encrier, 1929); *Les Vies Merveilleuses de Rip* (*Rip's Wonderful Lives*; Joie de nos Enfants, 1929); *Les Douze Plus Belles Fables du Monde* (*The Twelve Most Beautiful Fables in the World*; Berger-Levrault, 1931); *L'Atlantide: Sixième Partie du Monde* (*Atlantis: 6th Part of the World*; 1924; rep. Oeuvres Représentatives, 1931); *Note:* See Chapter VII.

Devil, Luc (?-); *Orbite Secrète* (*Secret Orbit*; SEG Espionnage 76, 1967); *Mission Cosmos* (SEG Espionnage 110, 1967); *Note:* SF spy thrillers.

Dewisme, Charles-Henri *see* **Vernes, Henri**

Dex, Léo (1864-?); *Le Record du Tour de la Terre en 29 Jours, 1 Heure, 10 Minutes* (*The Record of Around the World in 29 Days, 1 Hour, 10 Minutes*; Furne, c. 1900); *Note:* Also wrote under the name of "Deburaux."

Dharma, Samuel (Bauduret, Thomas; ?-); *Traqueur* (*Tracker*; FNA 1602, 1988); Nécromancies (FNA 1637, 1988); *Le Chemin d'Ombres* (*The Path of Shadows*; FNA 1666, 1989); *Comme une Odeur de Tombeau* (*Like the Smell of the Grave*; FNA 1773, 1990); *Born Killer* (as Patrick Éris; SENO 5, 1997); *Note:* See Chapter IX.

Dhôtel, André (1900-1991); *Nulle Part* (*Nowhere*; Gall., 1943); *Les Chemins du Long Voyage* (*The Paths of the Long Journey*; Gall., 1949); *La Chronique Fabuleuse* (*The Fabulous Chronicle*; Minuit, 1955); *Le Pays où l'on n'arrive Jamais* (*The Unreachable Country*; Horay, 1955); *Mémoires de Sébastien* (*Memoirs of Sebastian*; Grasset, 1955); *L'Île aux Oiseaux de Fer* (*The Island of the Iron Birds*; Fasquelle, 1956); *Les Voyages Fantastiques de Julien Grainebis* (*The Fantastic Voyages of Julian Grainebis*; Horay, 1958); *Le Neveu de Parencloud* (*Parencloud's Nephew*; Grasset, 1960); *La Plus Belle Main du Monde* (*The Most Beautiful Hand in the World*; Cast., 1962); *La Tribu Bécaille* (*The Becaille Tribe*; Gall., 1963); *La Maison du Bout du Monde* (*The House at World's End*; Horay, 1970); *Un Soir* (*One Evening*; Gall., 1977); *L'Île de la Croix d'Or* (*The Island of the Gold Cross*; Gall., 1978); *La Route Inconnue* (*The Unknown Road*; Phébus, 1980); *La Princesse et la Lune Rouge* (*The Princess and the Red Moon*; Cast., 1982); *Rhétorique Fabuleuse* (*Fabulous Rhetoric*; Garnier, 1983); *Le Bois Enchanté et Autres Contes* (*The Enchanted Wood and Other Tales*; Cast., 1983); *La Nouvelle Chronique Fabuleuse* (*The New Fabulous Chronicle*; Horay, 1984); *Vaux Étranges* (*Strange Places*; Gall., 1986); *Le Chemin du Rêve* (*The Path of Dreams*; Amateur d'Estampes, 1985); *Retour* (*Return*; Le Temps qu'il Fait, 1990); *Contes d'Hiver* (*Winter Tale*; n.d.); *Note:* See Chapter VIII.

Diamant, Jacques *see* **Armen, Guy d'**

Diamant-Berger, Marcel (?-); *Les Étoiles nous sont contées* (*The Stars as They Are Told*; Gédalge, 1947)

Dib, Mohammed (1920-); *Baba Férane—Contes d'Algérie* (*Algerian Tales*; Farandole, 1959); *Qui se Souvient de la Mer?* (*Who Remembers the Sea?*; Seuil, 1962); *Cours sur la Rive Sauvage* (*Run on the Wild Shore*; Seuil, 1964); *Le Talisman* (Seuil, 1966); *Note:* Algerian writer. See Chapter VIII.

Dick, Wenceslas-Eugène (1848-1919); *"La Tête de Saint Jean-Baptiste, ou Légende pour nos Arrières-petits-neveux en 1980"* (*"The Head of St. John the Baptist, or Legend for our Great-Grand-Nephews in 1980"*) (1880); *Note:* French-Canadian writer. This is a short story in which Québec's future prosperity is due to a miracle by St. John the Baptist.

Dickie, Francis (?-); *Le Solitaire de la Vallée* (*The Lonely Man in the Valley*; BGA, 1929)

Didelot, Roger-Francis (1902-); *La Machine à Prédire la Mort* (*The Death-Predicting Machine*; with Charles **Robert-Dumas**; Fayard, 1938); *La Nuit des Fétiches* (*Night of the Idols*; Colbert, 1941); *Marée Jaune* (*Yellow Tide*; Métal, 1954); *Feu sur le Mage* (*Fire on the Magus*; Fayard, 1956); *Note: La Machine à Prédire la Mort* was adated into a 1939 film, ***Le Monde Tremblera*** (*The World Will Quake*; see Book 1, Chapter I).

Dideral, Jean (?-); *Le Charmeur de Voitures* (*The Charmer of Cars*; Ed. Français Réunis, 1976)

Diderot, Denis (1713-1784); *Les Bijoux Indiscrets* (*The Indiscrete Jewels*; Au Monomotapa, 1748); *L'Oiseau Blanc, Conte Bleu* (*The White Bird, Blue Tale*; 1748; publ. Diderot, 1798); *Note:* See Chapter III.

Diesbach, Ghislain de (1931-); *Le Grand Mourzouk* (*The Great Mourzouk*; Julliard, 1968); *Iphigénie en Thuringe* (*Iphigenia in Thuringia*; Julliard, 1988)

Dieudonné, Albert (?-); *Le Tsar Napoléon* (*Czar Napoleon*; Baudinière, 1928); *Note:* Also see **Grand-Guignol.**

Dimonat (?-); *Vengeance Atomique* (*Atomic Revenge*; Gall., 1979)

Dimt, Elga (?-); *Et La Vie Continue* (*And Life Goes On*; Aelf, 1941); *Note:* See Chapter VII.

Dirand, Georges (?-); *Les Présidentielles n'auront pas lieu* (*The Presidential Elections Will Not Take Place*; ATP, 1978)

Di Rollo, Thierry (?-); *Number Nine* (Encrage, 1997); *Note:* See Chapter IX.

Dixmer, Jacques (?-); *L'Aurore des Dieux* (*Dawn of the Gods*; Aléas, 1993); *La Septième Arrhe* (*The Seventh Deposit*; Aléas, 1995)

Djian, Philippe (?-); *50 contre 1* (*50 vs. 1*; BFB, 1981)

Doazit, Nicolas (?-); *La Légende des Mutants* (*The Legend of the Mutants*; Elfes, 1963); *Les Constructions de Nestor Loupion* (*The Constructions of Nestor Loupion*; Atlantic, 1963)

Dobzynski, Charles (1929-); *Dans les Jardins de Mitchourine* (*In Mitchourine's Gardens*; Seghers, 1951); *L'Opéra de l'Espace* (*Space Opera*; Gall., 1963); *Daniel sur la Lune* (*Daniel on the Moon*; Farandole, 1977); *Taromancie* (Ed. Français Réunis, 1977); *Contes à Raconter* (*Tales to Tell*; La Noria, 1980); *Le Commerce des Mondes* (*The Trade of Worlds*; Messidor, 1985); *Cyrille et le Chameau Méthode* (*Cyril and the Camel Method*; Messidor, 1987); *L'Escalier des Questions* (*The Staircase of Questions*; Bedou, 1988)

Docquois, Georges (?-?) *see* **Grand-Guignol**

Dodeman, Charles (1873-?); *Le Secret du Livre d'Heures* (*The Secret of the Prayer Book*; Mame, 1912); *La Bombe Silencieuse* (*The Silent Bomb*; Mame, 1914); *L'Arbre aux Pièces d'Or* (*The Tree with Gold Coins*; Bonne Presse, 1934)

Dolingher, Benjamin (1929-); *Le Bistrot de Fantômes* (*The Bar of Ghosts*; AdH, 1981); *Note:* Romanian-born Swiss writer.

Dollé, André (?-) *see* **Bouquet, Jean-Louis**

Dominique, André (?-); *Conquête de l'Éternel* (*Conquest of the Eternal*; Grund, 1947)

Dominique, Pierre (Lucchini (Dr.); 1889-?); *Le Feu du Ciel* (*Fire from the Sky*; Oeuvres Libres, 1926); *Selon St. Jean* (*According to St. John*; Grasset, 1927); *Colère sur Paris* (*Wrath Over Paris*; Flamm., 1938); *Sous le Joug du Veau d'Or* (*Under the Yoke of the Golden Calf*; Bonne Presse, 1943); *Note:* See Chapter VII.

Dompierre, Violaine (1969-); *Les Gardiens des Ténèbres* (*The Guardians of Darkness*; Guy Saint-Jean, 1995); *Note:* French-Canadian writer.

Don *see* **Vernes, Henri**

Donat, Marc (?-); *Le Mort Vivant* (*The Living Dead*; AM, 1950)

Donner, Chris (?-); *Trois Minutes de Soleil en plus* (*Three More Minutes of Sun*; Gall., 1987); *Le Chagrin d'un Tigre* (*A Tiger's Sorrow*; Gall., 1988)

Doom, Kitty *see* **Brussolo, Serge**

Dorac, Henri *see* **Kubnick, Henri**

Dorémieux, Alain (1933-); *Fiction Specials* (anthologies of French Authors Only): *No.1* (1959), *No.2* (1960), *No.4* (1962), *No.5* (1963), *No.12* (1970), *No.17* (1975); *Mondes Interdits* (*Forbid-*

den Worlds; Los., 1967); *Voyages dans l'Ailleurs* (*Journeys Into the Beyond*; anthology; ATAM, 1971); *Promenades au bord du Gouffre* (*Walks on the Edge of the Pit*; PdF 264, 1978); *Couloirs sans Issue* (*No Exit Corridors*; PdF 323, 1981); *Le Livre d'Or d'Alain Dorémieux* (*The Golden Book of AD*; PP 5094, 1980); *Black Velvet* (Den., 1993; rev. as *Anna et ses Fantômes* (*Anna and Her Ghosts*, France-Loisirs, 1994); *Territoires de l'Inquiétude* (*Territories of Worry*; Anthologies) Vols. 1-9 (PdFant., 1991-96); *Note:* See chapters VIII and IX.

Doret, Louis (?-); *Contes Préhistoriques* (*Prehistoric Tales*; Larousse, 1924)

Dorgelès, Roland (1885-1973); *La Machine à Finir la Guerre* (*The Machine to End Wars*; AM, 1917); *Si c'était vrai?* (*If It Was True?*; AM, 1934)

Dorion, Bastien (?-); *Le Fantôme de Sang* (*The Phantom of Blood*; MOC 16, 1980); *Les Orgues de l'Infini* (*The Organs of Infinity*; MOC 22, 1982)

Dormandi, Ladislas (?-); *Pas si fou* (*Not So Crazy*; Gall., 1952); *La Vie des Autres* (*Others' Lives*; Gall., 1950)

Dornac, Charles (?-?) *see* **Grand-Guignol**

Dorra, Max (?-); *Nuit Blanche avec Reflet Fauve* (*White Night with Fawn Reflections*; Flamm., 1992); *La Qualité du Silence* (*The Quality of Silence*; Den., 1997); **Non-Fiction:** *Le Masque et le Rêve* (*The Mask and the Dream*; Flamm., 1994)

Dor-Rivaux, Étienne (?-); *Thésée ou la Force de l'Ordre* (*Theseus, or the Power of Order*; Pensée U., 1974); *Le Testament de la Baleine* (*The Whale's Testament*; AM, 1976); *Le Tombeau de Minos* (*The Tomb of Minos*; AM, 1978); *Pharaon Blues* (Hatier, 1995)

Dorsay, Jules (?-) *see* **Contes et Légendes**

Dorsenne *see* **Boisyvon, Lucien**

Douay, Dominique (1944-); *Éclipse* (ON 4, 1975); *L'Échiquier de la Creation* (*The Chessboard of Creation*; JL 708, 1976); *Strates* (*Strata*; PdF 249, 1978); *Cinq Solutions pour en Finir* (*Five Solutions to End It All*; PdF 261, 1978); *La Vie Comme une Course de Chars a Voile* (*Life as a Sailcar Race*; Dim. 35, 1978); *Temps Mort, Les Vallées de son Corps* (*Dead Time, the Valleys of Her Body*; Brémont, 1979); *Le Principe de l'Oeuf* (*The Principle of the Egg*; Dim. 44, 1980); *L'Impasse-Temps* (*Impasse Time*; PdF

302, 1980); *Le Monde est un Théâtre* (*The World Is a Stage*; PdF 331, 1982); *Rhino* (FNA 1360, 1985); *Passé Recomposé* (*Past Recomposed*; Aurore, Futurs 4, 1988)*Les Voyages Ordinaires d'un Amateur de Tableaux* (*The Ordinary Voyages of a Painting Lover*); with Michel **Maly**; Valpress, 1988); *La Fin des Temps et Après* (*The End of Time and After*; PdF 511, 1991); *Note:* See Chapter IX.

Doucet, Martin (1976-); *La Trappe* (*The Trapdoor*; Vaixe, 1995); *Note:* French-Canadian writer.

Douriaux, Hugues (1948-); *Un Homme Est Venu... (A Man Came...*; FN Grands Romans, 1981; rev. as *Le Monde d'Après* (*The World After*; FNA *1510, 1986), Les Errants* (*The Wanderers*; FNA 1531, 1987), *Les Guerriers* (*The Warriors*; FNA 1548, 1987), *Les Gladiateurs de Nephers* (*The Gladiators of Nephers*; FNA 1574, 1987), *La Chasse* (*The Hunt*; FNA 1607, 1988), *Le Loup* (*The Wolf*; FNA 1619, 1988)); *Le Chemin des Mondes* (*The Path of Worlds*; FN Grands Romans, 1982); *Les Démoniaques de Kallioh* (*The Demons of Kallioh*; FNA 1307, 1984); *Galax-Western* (FNA 1352, 1985); *Le Château des Vents Infernaux* (*The Castle of the Infernal Winds*; FNA 1391, 1985); *P.L.U.M. 66-50* (FNA 1428, 1985); *Les Androïdes du Désert (P.L.U.M. 2)* (*The Androids of the Desert*; FNA 1468, 1985); *Tragédie Musicale* (*Musical Tragedy*; FNA 1479, 1986); *Vermine* (*Vermin*; FNA 1593, 1987); *Le Monde au-delà des Brumes* (*The World Beyond the Mists*; FNA 1642, 1988); *Thorn le Guerrier* (*Thorn the Warrior*; FNA

1646, 1988); *Les Mortels et les Dieux* (*The Mortals and the Gods*; FNA 1653, 1988); *Syndrome Apocalypse* (FNA 1676, 1989); *Le Lévrier de Varik* (*The Greyhound of Varik*; FNA 1718, 1989); *La Soie Rouge de Xanta* (*The Red Silk of Xanta*; FNA 1730, 1990); *La Dame d'Alkoviak* (*The Lady of Alkoviak*; FNA 1742, 1990); *La Révolte des Barons* (*The Revolt of the Barons*; FNA 1753, 1990); *Arasoth* (FNA 1766, 1990); *Les Enfants de Vonia* (*The Children of Volnia*; FNA 1777, 1990); *Les*

Ballades du Temps Futur (*The Ballads of the Future Time*; FNA 1790, 1990); *Orbret* (FNA 1807, 1991); *Zelmane* (FNA 1808, 1991); *Les Amants Pourchassés* (*The Hunted Lovers*; FNA 1809, 1991); *Roche-Lalheue* (FNA 1844, 1991); Malterre (FNA 1859, 1992); *La Cité des Mille Plaisirs* (*The City of a Thousand Pleasures*; FNA 1866, 1992); *La Déesse de Cimbariah* (*The Goddess of Cimbarriah*; FNA 1870, 1992); *Le Monstre de Palathor* (*The Monster of Palathor*; FNA 1874, 1992); *Le Gouffre du Volcan Céleste* (*The Pit of the Celestial Volcano*; FNA 1878, 1992); *Symphonie Pastorale* (*Pastoral Symphony*; FNA 1899, 1993); *Les Guerriers de Glace* (*The Ice Warriors*; FNA 1907, 1993); *Les Sortilèges de Maïn* (*The Spells of Main*; FNA 1923, 1993); *Warrior* (FNA 1937, 1994); *La Porte de Flamme* (*The Gate of Fire*; FNA 1945, 1994); *Le Dernier des Aramandars* (*The Last of the Aramandars*; FNA 1957, 1995); *Le Prisonnier de l'Entre-Deux-Mondes* (*The Prisoner of Between-Two-Worlds*; FNA 1967, 1995); *Interférences* (FNA 1975, 1996); *Les Pierres de Lumière* (*The Stones of Light*; FNA 1989, 1996); *Note:* See Chapters VIII and IX.

Dournan, Jacques (?-); *An 3000* (*Year 3000*; SEOSC, 1946)

Doutreligne, Jean (Degrelle, Léon; 1906-); *La Grande Bagarre* (*The Great Fight*; Flamm., 1951); *Note:* Belgian writer.

Doyon, Paule (1934-); *Windigo* (Naaman, 1984); *Rue de l'Acacia* (*Acacia Street*; Naaman, 1985); *Note:* French-Canadian writer. *Windigo* is about a Native Canadian folk legend. *Rue* is a collection of fantastical tales.

Dreyfus, Roland (?-?) *see* **Grand-Guignol**

Driant, Émile-Auguste-Cyprien *see* **Danrit (Capitaine)**

Drieu, Patrick (?-); *Le Voleur d'Étoiles* (*The Star Thief*; Debresse, 1978)

Driou, Alfred (1810-?); *Les Aventures d'un Aéronaute Parisien dans les Mondes Inconnus* (*The Adventures of a Parisian Aeronaut in the Unknown Worlds*; Barbou, 1856); *Note:* See Chapter V. Also wrote under the pseudonyms of Charles de Falleville and A. de Villeneuve.

Drode, Daniel (1932-1984); *Surface de la Planète* (*Surface of the Planet*; RF 63, 1959; rev. A&D Class. 11, 1976); *Note:* See Chapter IX.

Drolet, Stéphane (1968-); *Sprotch et le Tuyau Manquant* (*Sprotch and the Missing Pipe*; Q/A, 1987); *Note:* French-Canadian writer. Juvenile SF.

Drouin, Henri (?-); *L'Île des Vertus* (*The Island of Virtues*; Armand Fleury, 1945)

Drowin, Michel *see* **Bernanos, Michel**

Druon, Maurice (1918-); *Tistou les Pouces Verts* (*Tistou Green Thumb*; Del Duca, 1957)

Du Bartas, Guillaume-Salluste (1544-1590); *Les Sepmaines* (1578); *Note:* See Chapter II.

Dubé, Jasmine (1957-); *La Tête de Line Hotte* (*The Head of Line Hotte*; Q/A, 1989); *Note:* French-Canadian writer. Children's fantasy.

Dubé, Rodolphe (?-?); *Les Mondes Chimériques* (*Chimerical Worlds*; 1940); *Note:* French-Canadian writer.

Dubeux, Alfred (?-?) *see* **Lorde, André de**

Dubois, Pierre (1945-); *Bidochet, le Petit Ogre* (*Bidochet, the Little Ogre*; Hac., 1979); *La Botte Secrète de Bidochet* (*Bidochet's Secret Weapon*; Hac., 1980); *Survivance* (*Survival*; as Budy Matieson/with Christian **Mantey**; FNA 1019, 1980); *Till Eulenspiegel* (Hac., 1981); *Capitaine Trèfle* (*Captain Clover*; Cast., 1981); *La Chute de Robin des Bois* (*The Fall of Robin Hood*; Cast., 1982); Shea (as Budy Matieson/with Christian **Mantey**; FNA 1135, 1982); *L'Almanach Sorcier* (*The Wizard's Almanach*; Cast., 1982); *Bidochet et les 55 Plumes de l'Indien* (*Bidochet and the Indian's 55 Feathers*; Hac., 1989); *La Grande Encyclopédie des Lutins, Nains, Gobelins, Gnomes et Farfadets* (*The Great Encyclopedia of Spirits, Dwarves, Goblins, Gnomes and Imps*; with Roland **Sabatier**; Hoëbeke, 1992); *La Forteresse Oubliée, Contes Jurassiens* (*The Forgotten Fortress, Tales of the Jura*; Centre Jurassien du Patrimoine, 1993); *Petits Contes Licencieux des Bretons* (*Small Licentious Tales from Britanny*; Terre de Brume, 1996); *La Grande Encyclopédie des Fées* (*The Great Encyclopedia of Fairies*; Hoëbeke, 1996); *L'Elficologue* (Delcourt, 1996); *Note:* Also see **Chillicothe, Zeb.** Pierre **Dubois** is also the writer of the following comic-book series: **Cairn, Laïyna, Les Lutins, Pixies** and **Le Torte** (see Book 1, Chapter V).

Dubois La Charte, André (?-); *Journal Intime d'Hercule* (*Private Diary of Hercules*; 1957); *Note:* Flat-Earth utopia.

Dubouis-Bonnefond, Marcel (?-); *Extraordinaire Voyage dans la Nuit des Temps* (*Extraordinary Journey at the Dawn of Time*; André Martel, 1959)

Dubreuil, Linda (?-); *Sexe en Fleur* (*Flowering Sex*; Siècle, 1973); *Note:* French-Canadian writer. Erotic fantasy.

Ducasse, Isidore Lucien *see* **Lautréamont (Comte de)**

Duchateau, Jean (?-); *Zinga 8* (Gall., 1967); *Meurtre à l'Élysée* (*Murder at the Elysee-Palace*; Calmann-Lévy, 1987); *Meurtre à TF1: 5 Jours qui ébranlèrent la République* (*Murder at TF1: 5 Days That Shook the Republic*; Calmann-Lévy, 1988)

Duchêne, Ferdinand (1868-?); *Thamil'a* (AM, 1923); *Au Pied des Monts Éternels* (*At the Feet of the Eternal*

Mountains; AM, 1925); *Les Fantaisies du Dr. Mysti* (*The Fantasies of Dr. Mysti*; Soubiron, Algiers, 1934)

Duchesne, Christiane (1949-); *La Bergère de Chevaux* (*The Horse Shepherdess*; Q/A, 1995); *Note:* French-Canadian writer. Juvenile fantasy.

Duchesne, René (?-); *À la Dérive* (*Adrift*; Tallandier, 1933); *L'Ombre du Passé* (*The Shadow of the Past*; Tallandier, 1933); *Le Dirigeable Disparu* (*The Vanished Dirigible*; RJ, 1933); *Le Maître de la Mort* (*The Master of Death*; VA, 1936); *Les Forbans de l'Océan* (*The Ocean Bandits*; VA, 1936); *Blazac, Cambrioleur Amateur* (*Blazac, Amateur Burglar*; RJ, 1937); *Le Roc des Hommes Volants* (*The Rock of the Flying Men*; VA, 1937); *L'Île de la Lente Agonie* (*The Island of Slow Death*; VA, 1937); *L'Extraordinaire Voyage du Loriot* (*The Extraordinary Journey of the Loriot*; VA, 1937); *L'Idole aux Yeux d'Émeraude* (*The Idol with Emerald Eyes*; VA, 1937); *Le Drame du Studio S* (*The Tragedy of Studio S*; RJ, 1938); *La Chasse à l'Homme* (*Man Hunt*; VA, 1938); *L'Effroyable Aventure* (*The Frightful Adventure*; VA, 1938); *Les Hommes sans Visage* (*The Faceless Men*; VA, 1938); *Le Voilier Perdu* (*The Lost Sailboat*; VA, 1939); *Le Royaume des Épaves* (*The Kingdom of the Shipwrecks*; VA, 1939); *Zourka l'Invincible* (*Zurka the Invincible*; VA, 1939); *L'Île des Aveugles* (*The Island of Blind Men*; Livre Moderne, 1941); *L'Île Morte* (*The Dead Island*; Livre Moderne, 1942); *Note:* See Chapter VII.

Duchesne, Suzanne (1953-); *L'Esprit Tourmenté* (*The Tormented Spirit*; Héritage, 1995); *Note:* French-Canadian writer.

Ducray, Camille (?-); *Le Voyageur Immobile* (*The Motionless Traveller*; with Alain **Saint-Ogan**; Ed. Sociales Fr., 1945); *Le Gouffre de la Nuit* (+*The Pit of Night*; Ed. Sociales Fr., 1946); *Note:* Alain **Saint-Ogan** (who also illustrated *Le Gouffre*) is the creator of the famous comic heroes **Zig et Puce** (see Book 1, Chapter V).

Ducray-Duminil, François-Guillaume (1761-1819); *Alexis ou la Maisonette dans les Bois* (*Alexis or the Little House in the Woods*; Maradan, 1789); *Coelina ou l'Enfant du Mystère* (*Coelina or the Child of Mystery*; Le Prieur, 1799); *Contes de Fées* (*Fairy Tales*; Ménard & Desenne, 1819); *Nouveaux Contes de Fées* (*New Fairy Tales*; Le Bailly, 1844); *Les Petits Orphelins du Hameau* (*The Little Orphans of the Village*; Bernardin-Béchet, 1877); *L'Enfant de la Forêt* (*The Forest Child*; Libr. Ill., 1893); *Note:* See Chapter IV. Also see Frédéric **Soulié**.

Duesberg, Raymond (?-); *Les Grenouilles* (*The Frogs*; Plon, 1962); *Note:* Belgian writer. See Chapter IX.

Duffau, S. (?-?); *Le Principe Vital* (*The Vital Principle*; MdF, 1831)

Dufour, Michel (1958-); *Passé la Frontière* (*Past the Border*; L'Instant Même, 1991); *N'arrêtez pas la Musique!* (*Don't Stop the Music!*; L'Instant Même, 1995); *Note:* French-Canadian writer. Collections of fantastic tales.

Dufreigne, Jean-Pierre (?-); *La Prochaine Polaire* (*The Next Polar*; Flamm., 1978); *Je danse pour les Cannibales* (*I Dance for Cannibals*; Flamm., 1980); *Supplique au Roi de Norvège* (*Plea to the King of Norway*; Flamm., 1983); *La Vie est un Jeu d'Enfant* (*Life Is a Child's Play*; Grasset, 1984); *Mémoires d'un Homme Amoureux* (*Memoirs of a Man in Love*; Grasset, 1990); *Le Dernier Amoureux d'Aramis* (*Aramis' Last Lover*; Grasset, 1993); *Boire* (*To Drink*; Grasset, 1996)

Dufresne, Michel (1947-); *Histoires, Contes et Légendes* (*Stories, Tales and Legends*; Cosmos, 1971); *Note:* French-Canadian folk stories anthology.

Dugall, H. L. *see* **Durand, Loup**

Duguël, Anne (Karali, Anna; 1945-); *Prince Charmant Poil aux Dents* (*Prince Charming My Foot*; as Gudule; Syros, 1987); *Rosaloche-la-Moche* (*Ugly Rosaloche*; as Gudule; Syros, 1987); *Bye-bye Maman* (*Goodbye, Mommy*; as Gudule; Syros, 1988); *Agence Torgnole, Frappez Fort!* (*Slap Agency, Hit Harder!*; as Gudule; Syros, 1990); *Une Jeune Fille au Sourire si Fragile* (*A Young Girl with Such a Fragile Smile*; Den., 1991); *Amazonie sur Seine* (Den., 1991); *Le Corridor* (PdFant. 21,

1991); *Mémé est Amoureuse* (*Granny Is in Love*; as Gudule; *Syros*, 1992); *La Vie à Reculons* (*Life Backwards*; as Gudule; Hac., 1994); *Asylum* (FNFR 3, 1994); *L'École qui n'existait pas* (*The School That Did Not Exist*; as Gudule; Nathan, 1994); *Après Vous, M. de la Fontaine* (*After You, Mr. De la Fontaine*; as Gudule; Hac., 1995); *La Bibliothécaire* (*The Librarian*; as Gudule; Hac., 1995); *Gargouille* (*Gargoyle*; FNFR 13, 1995); *Lavinia* (FNFR 21, 1995); *La Baby-Sitter* (FNFR 25, 1995); *Le Chien qui Rit* (*The Dog That Laughs*; PdFant. 39, 1995); *La Petite Fille aux Araignées* (*The Little Girl with Spiders*; FNFR 31, 1995; rev. PdFant. 58, 1996); *Petite Chanson dans la Pénombre* (*Little Song in the Dark*; F. Massot, 1996); *Les Poilantes Aventures de René le Virus* (*The Hilarious Adventures of Rene the Virus*; as Gudule; Bayard, 1996); *L'Envers du Décor* (*The Other Side of the Stage*; as Gudule; Hac., 1996); *Le Château des Chiens Perdus* (*The Castle of Lost Dogs*; as Gudule;

Hac., 1996); *Le Dentiste est un Vampire* (*The Dentist Is a Vampire*; as Gudule; BR, 1996); *La Sorcière est dans l'École* (*The Witch Is in the School*; as Gudule; BR, 1996); *La Révélation* (*The Revelation*; as Gudule/with Julia **Verlanger**; Hac., 1996); *Les Ogres du Centre Commercial* (*The Ogres of the Shopping Center*; as Gudule; BR, 1997); *Le Fantôme du Panier à Linge* (*The Ghost of the Laundry Basket*; as Gudule; BR, 1997); *Un Requin dans la Piscine* (*A Shark in the Swimming Pool*; as Gudule; BR, 1997); *Ne Vous Disputez jamais avec un Spectre* (*Never Argue with a Spectre*; as Gudule; Hac., 1997); *Au Secours Je Suis Invisible* (*Help! I'm Invisible*; as Gudule; Nathan, 1997); *Le Manège de l'Oubli* (*The Merry-Go-Round of Oblivion*; as Gudule; Nathan, 1997); *En Colo avec les Demons* (*To Camp with Demons*; as Gudule; BR, 1997); *Bonjour, Monsieur Frankenstein* (*Hello, Mr. Frankenstein*; as Gudule; Hac., 1997); *La Forêt des Hurlements* (*The Forest of Howls*; as Gudule; Hac., 1997); *Mon Papi s'appelle Barbe-Bleue* (*My Daddy's Name Is Blue-Beard*; as Gudule; Hac., 1997); *Note:* See Chapter VIII.

Duguet, Roger (?-?); *L'Amazone Blanche* (*The White Amazon*; Bonne Pesse, 1909); *Le Capitaine* Rex (With G. **Thierry**; Bonne Presse, 1910); *Note:* See Chapter V.

Duhamel, Georges (1884-1966); *Scènes de la Vie Future* (*Scenes of Future Life*; MdF, 1930); *Les Jumeaux de Vallangoujard* (*The Twins from Vallangoujard*; Hartman, 1931); *Les Voyageurs de l'Espérance* (*The Voyagers of the Hope*; Gédalge, 1953); *Note:* Juvenile SF. See Chapters VII and IX.

Duhamel, Marcel (?-?) *see* **Grand-Guignol**

Duhemme, Ch. (?-?); *Français, Garde à Vous!* (*Frenchmen, to Arms!*; with **Hubert-Jacques**; Bossard, 1930); *Note:* See Chapter VII.

Duits, Charles (1925-1991); *Le Pays de l'Éclairement* (*The Land of Illumination*; Den., 1967); *Ptah Hotep* (Den., 1971); *Les Miférables* (*The Miferables*; Los., 1971); *La Conscience Démonique* (*Demonic Consciousness*; Den., 1974); *Nefer* (Henri Veyrier, 1978); *Fruit sortant de l'Abîme* (*Fruit from the Abyss*; Bois d'Orion, 1993); *Note:* See Chapter VIII.

Dujardin, Édouard (1861-1849); *Les Hantises* (*The Hauntings*; 1886); *Note:* See Chapter IV.

Dulac, Françoise (?-); *Étrange Mésaventure* (*Strange Misadventure*; Grange Frères, 1955); *Note:* French-Canadian writer. Children's tales.

Dulac, Odette (?-1939); *La Houille Rouge* (*Red Coal*; Figuière, 1916); *Faut-il?...* (*Must We?...*; Calmann-Lévy, 1919); *(L'Amour) ...Tel qu'il est* (*(Love)...As It Were*; J. Snell, 1926); *Note:* See Chapter VII.

Dumaine, Ferdinand (?-); *Berlingot et Ouistiti: Les Exploits Fantastiques d'un Mousse et d'un Arpète* (France Éd., 1922); *1. L'Île Décapitée* (*The Beheaded Island*); *2. La Caverne aux Squelettes* (*The Skeleton Cave*); *3. La Sorcière Blanche* (*The White Witch*); *4. La Proie des Pieuvres* (*The Prey of the Octopus*); *Nouveaux Exploits Fantastiques de Berlingot et Ouistiti* (France Éd., 1923-24)

Dumarchey, Pierre *see* **Mac Orlan, Pierre**

Dumas, Alexandre (1802-1870); *L'Alchimiste* (*The Alchemist*; with Gérard de **Nerval**; Dumont, 1839); *Le Château d'Eppstein* (L. de Potter, 1844; transl. as *The Castle of Eppstein*, 1903); *Joseph Balsamo* (Fellens et Dufour/Cadot, 1846); *Le Collier de la Reine* (*The Queen's Necklace*; Cadot, 1849); *Les Mille et Un Fantômes* (*A Thousand and One Ghosts*; Cadot, 1848-51; transl. as *Tales of the Supernatural*, 1907); *Le Vampire* (Michel Lévy, 1851); *Le Trou de l'Enfer* (*The Hell Hole*; Cadot, 1851); *Isaac Laquedem* (Libr. Théâtrale, 1853; transl. as *Isaak Lakadam*, 1853); *Le Meneur de Loups* (Cadot, 1857; transl. as *The Wolf Leader*, 1904); *L'Île de Feu* (*The Island of Fire; aka Le Medecin de Java* (*The Doctor of Java*); with Gaspard-Georges **Pescow**; Michel Lévy, 1870); *Note:* See chapters IV and V. **Joseph Balsamo** was adapted by French television—see Book 1, Chapter II.

Dumas, Alexandre (Fils) (Son; 1824-1895); *Tristan le Roux* (*Tristan the Red*; Cadot, 1856); *Note:* Son of Alexandre **Dumas** and author of *Camille*. See Chapter V.

Dumas, Henri (?-); *Nouvelles de la Pleine Lune* (*Tales of the Full Moon*; Dumillon, 1985)

Dumas, Philippe (1940-); *Le Professeur Ecrouton-Creton* (Ecole des Loisirs, 1977); *Contes à l'Envers* (*Inside-Out Tales*; Ecole des Loisirs, 1977); *La Petite Géante* (*The Little Giantess*; Ecole des Loisirs, 1979); *Ondine au fond de l'Eau* (*Ondine Beneath the Water*; Ecole des Loisirs, 1979); *Le Convive comme it faut* (*A Proper Guest*; Ecole des Loisirs, 1988); *Victor Hugo s'est égaré* (*Victor Hugo Is Lost*; Ecole des Loisirs, 1996); *Note:* Juveniles. See Chapter VIII.

Dumay, Gilles (1971-); *Strange Rock Anathema* (QLVD-CVG, 1993; rev. *Destination Crépuscule*, 1994)

Dumesnil, Robert (?-) *see* **Opéra**

Dumont, Claude (?-); *Zaira* (Legrain-Bourtembourg, 1992); *Les Courbes de Bernstein* (*Bernstein's Curves*; Octa, 1996)

Dumoulin, Gilles-Maurice *see* **Morris, Gilles**

Dunan, Renée (1892-1936); *Baal ou La Magicienne Passionée, Livre des Ensorcellements* (*Baal or the Impassioned Magician, Book of Spells*; Malfère, 1924); *La*

Dernière Jouissance (*The Last Pleasure*; France-Édition, 1925); *Les Amantes du Diable* (*The Devil's Lovers*; L. Querelle, 1929); *Le Chat-Tigre du Service Secret* (*The Tiger-Cat of the Secret Service*; Livre de l'Avenir, 1933); *Le Mystère du Soleil des Tombes* (*The Mystery of the Sun of the Tombs*; Livre de l'Avenir, 1934); *La Montagne de Diamants* (*The Mountain of Diamonds*; Livre de l'Avenir, 1934); *L'Épouvantable Secret* (*The Awful Secret*; Livre de l'Avenir, 1934); *Note:* See Chapter VII.

Dunant, Mathias (?-); *Les Chevaux de Soulimane / La Onzième Lune* (*Suleyman's Horses / The Eleventh Moon*; AM, 1988)

Dunyach, Jean-Claude (1957-); *Autoportrait* (*Self-Portrait*; PdF 415, 1986); *Le Temple de Chair (Le Jeu des Sabliers 1)* (*The Temple of Flesh—the Game of the Hourglasses 1*; FNA 1592, 1987); *Le Temple d'Os (Le Jeu des Sabliers 2)* (*The Temple of Bones—the Game of the Hourglasses 2*; FNA 1609, 1988); *Étoiles Mortes 1: Nivôse* (*Dead Stars 1: Nivose*; FNA 1837, 1991); *Étoiles Mortes 2: Aigue-Marine* (*Dead Stars 2: Aigue-Marine*; FNA 1838, 1991); *Étoiles Mortes 3: Voleurs de Silence* (*Dead Stars 3: Thieves of Silence*; FNA 1858, 1992); *Roll Over, Amundsen* (FNA 1912, 1993); *La Guerre des Cercles* (*The War of the Circles*; FNA 1963, 1995); *Note:* See Chapter IX.

Dupé, Gilbert (?-); *Les Sourciers de l'Or Noir* (*The Dowsers of Black Gold*; Nlles. Presses Fr., 1946); *Pique la Baleine* (*Pick the Whale*; Nlles. Presses Fr., 1946)

Dupin, Aurore *see* **Sand, George**

Dupont, Étienne (?-); *Les Légendes du Mont Saint-Michel* (*Legends of Mount St. Michael*; OCEP, 1981); *Note:* Folk tales.

Dupont, Louis (?-); *La Légende de Thogoruk* (*The Legend of Thogoruk*; Presses d'Amérique, 1993); *Note:* French-Canadian writer.

Dupriez, Pierre (?-) *see* **Martel, Serge**

Dupuis-Déri, Francis (1966-); *L'Erreur Humaine* (*Human Error*; Leméac, 1991); *Love & Rage* (Leméac, 1995); *Note:* French-Canadian writer. *L'Erreur* is a political satire in a world where animals are sentient.

Duquesne, André *see* **Randa, Peter**

Duquesne, Philippe *see* **Randa, Philippe**

Durand, Claude (1938-); *L'Autre Vie* (*The Other Life*; Seuil, 1963); *La Nuit Zoologique* (*Zoological Night*; Grasset, 1979)

Durand, François *see* **Miomandre, Francis de**

Durand, Honoré (?-) *see* ***Contes et Légendes***

Durand, Loup (?-); *La Porte d'Or* (*The Golden Gate*; with Henri **Galissian**/as H. L. Dugall; Fayard, 1967); *Un Temps pour Tuer* (*A Time to Kill*; with Henri **Galissian**/as H. L. Dugall; Fayard, 1969); *Un Amour d'Araignée* (*A Spider's Love*; Libr. Champs-Élysées, 1976); *Le Caïd* (*The Kingpin*; Den., 1976); *Jaraï* (Den., 1980); *Le Seigneur des Tempêtes* (*The Storm Lord*; Den., 1983); *Daddy* (France-Loisirs, 1987); *Le Jaguar* (Orban, 1989); *Les Cavaliers aux Yeux Verts (La Porte de Kerkabanac)* (*The Green-Eyed Riders (The Gate of Kerkqabanac)*; Libr. Gen. Fr., 1989); *Le Grand Silence* (*The Great Silence*; Plon, 1994); *Note:* See Chapter IX.

Durand, Lucille *see* **Bersianik, Louky**

Durand, René (?-); *Ludine de Terrève* (Magnard, 1981) *Note:* Juvenile SF. See Chapter IX.

Duret, Alain (?-); *Le Ciel est par dessus le Toit* (*The Sky Is Above the Roof*; Aurore, Futurs 10, 1990); *Kronikes de la Fédérasion* (*Kronikles of the Federasion*; Lefrancq, 1997); *Note:* See Chapter IX.

Durieux, Raymond (?-?) *see* **Grand-Guignol**

Du Roure, Henry (?-); *La Princesse Alice* (Bloud, 1911); *Le Secret de l'Or* (*The Secret of Gold*; Lafitte, 1916); *Note:* See Chapter VII.

Duroy, Lionel (?-); *Priez Pour Nous* (*Pray for Us*; JL, 1990); *Je Voudrais Descendre* (*I'd Like to Get Off*; Seuil, 1993); *Il ne m'est rien arrivé* (*Nothing Happened to Me*; MdF, 1994); *Comme des Héros* (*Like Heroes*; Fayard, 1996); *Mon Premier Jour de Bonheur* (*My First Day of Happiness*; Julliard, 1996)

Durtain, Luc (Nepveu, A.; 1881-1959); *Manuscrit Trouvé dans un Île* (*Manuscript Found on an Island*; Crès, 1913); *Vers la Ville Kilomètre 3* (*Towards the City Km. 3*; Flamm., 1933); *Frank et Marjorie* (Flamm., 1934); *Yagouta aux Cavaliers* (*Yagouta and the Riders*; Flamm., 1935); *Le Globe sous le Bras* (*The Globe Under My Arm*; Flamm., 1936); *La Femme en Sandales* (*The Woman in Sandals*; Flamm., 1937); *Voyage au Pays des Bohohoms* (*Voyage to the Lands of the Bohohoms*; Flamm., 1938); *La Guerre n'existe pas* (*War Does Not Exist*; Flamm., 1939); *Histoires Fantastiques* (*Fantastic Stories*; Flamm., 1942); *Note:* See Chapter VII.

Duthuit, Florent (?-?); *L'Avion Sous-Marin* (*The Underwater Plane*; same text; two editions: 1) as Émile Lutz/ with Dr. Antoine **Rodiet**; 2) as Florent Duthuit/with

Antoine **Teidor**; Tallandier, 1928); *Note:* Also see **Grand-Guignol**.

Dutourd, Jean (1920-); *2024* (Gall., 1975); *Le Feld-Maréchal Von Bonaparte* (Flamm., 1996)

Dutrisac, Billy Bob (Dutrisac, Robert; 1961-); *Une Photo Vaut Mille Morts* (*A Photo Is Worth a Thousand Dead*; VLB, 1987); *Note:* French-Canadian writer. Horror novel.

Duval, Jean (?-); *Au Centre de la Terre* (*At the Earth's Core*; La Nef, 1925); *Note:* See Chapter VII.

Duval, Paul *see* **Lorrain, Jean**

Duverne, René (1893-1967); *Le Reflet dans la Mare* (*The Reflection in the Pond*; Bonne Presse, 1926); *Michelle et le Demi-Dieu* (*Michelle and the Demi-God*; Fayard, 1932); *Charmanteville* (*Prettytown*; Bonne Presse, 1932); *Le Veau d'Or* (*The Golden Calf*; Stella, 1933); *La Tête Déformée* (*The Malformed Head*; P. Téqui, 1934); *Le Jardin Enchanté* (*The Enchanted Garden*; Garnier, 1936); *La Croisière Immobile* (*The Motionless Cruise*; Bloud & Gay, 1936); *Le Mystère du Château Maudit* (*The Mystery of the Accursed Castle*; Hac., 1945); *Alerte sur le Monde* (*Alert Over the World*; Bonne Presse, 1946); *Le Lac Mystérieux* (*The Mysterious Lake*; Bonne Presse, 1947); *Cinq Enfants dans une Île* (*Five Children on an Island*; Hac., 1949); *Le Lac sans Fond* (*The Bottomless Lake*; Fleurus, 1950); *L'Étrange Menace* (*The Strange Threat*; Bias, 1960); *Note: Le Jardin* is a *Féerie* stage play in 3 acts.

Duvernois, Henri (Schwabacher, Henri-Simon; 1875-1937); *La Marchande d'Oubli* (*The Merchant of Oblivion*; AM, 1909); *Le Chien qui Parle* (*The Talking Dog*; Fayard, 1920); *Les Voyages de M. Pimperneau* (*Mr. Pimperneau's Travels*; Flamm., 1927); *Les Contes d'Henri Duvernois* (*Tales*; 2 vols.; Flamm., 1930); *L'Homme qui s'est Retrouvé* (*The Man Who Found Himself*; Grasset, 1936); *Note:* See Chapter VII. Also see **Grand-Guignol**.

Duveyrier, Anne-Honoré-Joseph *see* **Mélesville**

Duvic, Patrice (1946-); *Monstres et Monstruosités* (*Monsters and Monstrosities*; AM, 1973); *Poisson-Pilote* (*Pilot Fish*; PdF 286, 1979); *Naissez, Nous Ferons le Reste* (*Be Born, We'll Take Care of the Rest*; PP 5064, 1979); *Terminus* (JL 2122, 1982); *Demain les Puces* (*Tomorrow, the Chips*; anthology; PdF 421, 1986); *Autant en Emporte le Divan* (*Gone with the Sofa*; FNA 1997, 1996); *Note:* See Chapter IX. *Terminus* is a novelization of the eponymous 1986 film, written by Duvic (see Book 1, Chapter I).

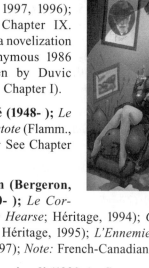

Dzagoyan, René (1948-); *Le Système Aristote* (Flamm., 1984); *Note:* See Chapter IX.

Eaglenor, Brian (Bergeron, Alain; 1950-); *Le Corbillard* (*The Hearse*; Héritage, 1994); *Grignotements* (*Gnawings*; Héritage, 1995); *L'Ennemie* (*The Enemy*; Héritage, 1997); *Note:* French-Canadian writer.

Eaubonne, Françoise d' (1920-); *Comme un Vol de Gerfauts* (*Like a Flight of Falcons*; Julliard, 1947); *Démons et Merveilles* (*Demons and Wonders*; Seghers, 1951); *Le Sous-Marin de l'Espace* (*The Space Submarine*; with Jacques **Bergier** & L. **Jean-Charles**; Gautier-Languereau, 1959); *Planète sans Adieu* (*Planet Without Farewell*; Oeuvres Libres, 1960); *Les Sept Fils de l'Étoile* (*The Seven Sons of the Star*; RF 88, 1962); *L'Échiquier du Temps* (*Time's Chessboard*; RF 99, 1962); *Rêve de Feu* (*Dream of Fire*; RF 124, 1964); *Le Satellite de l'Amande* (*The Satellite of the Almond*; Ed. Des Femmes. 1975); *Les Bergères de l'Apocalypse* (*The Shepherdesses of the Apocalypse*; Simoën, 1978); *Je Ne Suis Pas Née Pour Mourir* (*I Was Not Born Only to Die;* Den., 1982); *À la Limite des Ténèbres* (*At the Boundaries of Darkness*; Encre, 1983); *Les Enfants de l'Horreur* (*Children of Horror*; Encre, 1984); *Toutes les Sirènes sont Mortes* (*All the Sirens Are Dead*; De Magrie, 1992); *Floralies du Désert* (*Flower Shows in the Desert*; Samizdat, 1995); *Note:* See chapters VIII and IX.

Ébly, Philippe (1920-); Series *Les Conquérants de l'Impossible* (*The Conquerors of the Impossible*): *1. Destination Uruapan* (BV, 1971); *2. Celui Qui Revenait De Loin* (*He Who Came Back from Faraway*; BV, 1972); *3. L'Éclair Qui Effaçait Tout* (*The Erasing Lightning Bolt*; BV, 1972); *4. L'Évadé de l'An II* (*Escape from Year II*; BV, 1973); *5. Pour Sauver le Diamant Noir* (*To Save the Black Diamond*; BV, 1973); *6. ...Et les Martiens Invitèrent les Hommes* (*...And the Martians Invited Men*; BV, 1974); *7. Le Navire qui Remontait le Temps* (*The Ship Which Travelled Back Through Time*; BV, 1974); *8. La Ville qui n'existait Pas* (*The City Which Did Not Exist*; BV, 1975); *9. La Voûte Invisible* (*The Invisible*

Ceiling; BV, 1976); *10. L'Île Surgie de la Mer* (*The Island That Came Out of the Sea*; BV, 1977); *11. Le Robot qui Vivait sa Vie* (*The Robot Which Lived Its Life*; BV, 1978); *12. SOS Léonard de Vinci* (BV, 1979); *13. Le Naufragé des Étoiles* (*Shipwrecked in the Stars*; BV, 1980); *14. Le Matin des Dinosaures* (*Morning of the Dinosaurs*; BV, 1982); *15. La Grande Peur de l'An 2117* (*The Great Fear of the Year 2117*; BV, 1983); *16. 2159 La Fin des Temps Troublés* (*2159 The End of the Troubled Times*; BV, 1985); *17. Les Parias de l'An 2187* (*The Pariahs of the Year 2187*; BV, 1986); *Les Marais de la Mort* (*The Swamps of Death*; BV, 1986); *Objectif Nulle Part* (*Target Nowhere*; BV, 1986); *L'Ordinateur qui Semait le Désordre* (*The Computer Which Sowed Disorder*; BV, 1986); *L'Île aux Pieuvres* (*Octopus Island*; BV, 1987); *La Montagne aux Robots* (*Robot Mountain*; BV, 1987); *Les Dix Jours Impossibles* (*Ten Impossible Days*; BV, 1988); *Mission sans Retour* (*Mission of No Return*; BV, 1996); Series *Les Évadés du Temps* (*Escape in Time*): *1. Les Trois Portes* (*The Three Doors*; BV, 1977); *2. Le Voyageur de l'Au-Delà* (*The Traveller from Beyond*; BV, 1978); *3. Volontaires pour l'Inconnu* (*Candidate for the Unknown*; BV, 1980); *4. Un Frère au Fond des Siècles* (*A Brother at the End of the Centuries*; BV, 1981); *5. Chasse au Tigre en Corrèze* (*Tiger Hunt in Correze*; BV, 1982); *6. Le Monstre aux Deux Têtes* (*The Two-Headed Monster*; BV, 1984); *7. Descente au Pays sans Nom* (*Descent Into the Nameless County*; BV, 1985); Series *Les Patrouilleurs de l'An 4003* (*The Patrollers of the Year 4003*): *1. La Forêt des Castors* (*The Forest of Beavers*; Masque jeunesse, 1984); *2. Au Pouvoir des Corsaires* (*In the Power of the Corsairs*; Masque jeunesse, 1984); *3. La Vallée des Cyclopes* (*The Valley of Cyclops*; Masque jeunesse, 1984); *4. L'Enlèvement du Dieu Blanc* (*The Taking of the White God*; Masque jeunesse, 1985); *Note:* Popular juvenile SF series. See Chapter IX.

Ebrard, Hippolyte (?-); *La Grande Espérance* (*The Great Hope*; Debresse, 1956)

Ecken, Claude (1954-); *La Mémoire Totale* (*The Total Memory*; FNA 1422, 1986); *La Peste Verte* (*The Green Plague*; FNG 38, 1987); *L'Univers en Pièce (Chroniques Télématiques)* (*The Universe in Pieces (Telematic Chronicles)*; FNA 1521, 1987); *De Silence et de Feu* (*Of Silence and Fire*; FNA 1683, 1989); *Les Enfants du Silence* (*The Children of Silence*; FNA 1690, 1989); *L'Autre Cécile* (*The Other Cecilia*; FNA 1727, 1989); *Le Cri du Corps* (*The Body Scream*; FNA 1793, 1990); *Le Monde, Tous Droits Réservés* (*The World, All Rights Reserved*; La Geste, 1994); *Note:* See Chapters VIII and IX.

Eekhoud, Georges (1854-1927); *Kermesses* (*Fiestas*; Libr. Nouvelle, 1884); *La Nouvelle Carthage* (*The New Carthago*; Kistermaekers, 1888); *Cycle Patibulaire* (*Evil-Looking Cycle*; MdF, 1892); *Burch Mitsu* (Govaerts, 1896); Escale-Vigor (MdF, 1899); *La Faneuse d'Amour* (*Love Tedder*; MdF, 1900); *L'Autre Vue* (*The Other View*; MdF, 1904); *La Danse Macabre du Pont de Lucerne* (*The Danse Macabre of Lucerne Bridge*; Dechenne, 1920); *Magrice en Flandre, ou Le Buisson des Mendiants* (*The Beggars' Bush*; Les Cinquante, 1927); *Le Quadrille du Lancier & Autres Nouvelles* (*The Lancer's Quadrille & Other Stories*; Gai-Kitsch-Camp., 1992); *Un Illustre Uraniste* (*An Illustrious Uranist*; Gai-Kitsch-Camp., 1996); *Note:* Belgian writer. See chapters V and VI.

Egasel, Roger (Lesage, Roger; 1928-); *Le Cycle Épouvantable* (*The Awful Cycle*; Corne d'Or, 1954); *Go!* (as Roger Lesage; France-Empire, 1954); *Crèvecoeur* (*Heartbreaker*; as Roger Lesage; France-Empire, 1955); *Chauffeur de Morts* (*Driver of the Dead*; Corne d'Or, 1955); *Les Troupeaux de la Lune* (*The Herd of the Moon*; as Roger Lesage; Del Duca, 1956); *Tout vient du Ciel* (*All Comes from Heaven*; as Roger Lesage; Pensée Moderne, 1958)

Egleton, Dominique (1915-); *Étude, Commentaire et Texte Original des Prophéties Perpétuelles* (*Study, Commentary and Original Text of the Eternal Prophecies*; Gauthier Fr., 1946)

Elia, Lucien (?-); *Les Types* (*The Guys*; Flamm., 1967); *Les Ratés de la Diaspora* (*The Losers of the Diaspora*; Flamm., 1969); *Fer-Blanc* (*Tin Plate*; Flamm., 1973); *Pub* (Flamm., 1979)

Élie, Jérôme (1945-); *La Morte du Pont de Varole* (*The Dead Woman of Varole Bridge*; La Pleine Lune, 1996); *Note:* French-Canadian writer.

Emery, Andréa (1950-); *Enfer d'enfer* (*Hell's Hell*; Garnier, 1982); *Le Sang est Salé comme l'Océan* (*Blood Is Salty Like the Ocean*; Magnard, 1984)

Émile-Pignot *see* **Pignot, Émile**

Émond, Louis (1957-); *La Guéguenille* (*The R-Rags*; Tisseyre, 1994); *Trois Séjours en Sombres Territoires* (*Three Stays in Dark Territories*; Tisseyre, 1996); *Note:* French-Canadian writer.

Émond, Maurice (1941-); *Anthologie de la Nouvelle et du Conte Fantastiques Québécois au XXème Siècle* (*Anthology of Short Stories and Fantastical Tales from Quebec in the 20th Century*; anthology; Fides, 1987); *Note:* French-Canadian anthology.

Enacryos *see* **Rosny, J. H. Aîné**

Ennery, d' (?-?) *see* **Verne, Jules**

Entrevaux, V. d' (?-) *see* **Rosmer, Jean**

Epheyre, Charles *see* **Richet, Charles**

Epistolier, Théophraste *see* **Frémion, Yves**

Epstein, Doubi (1947-); *Les Extra-Terrestres Arrivent Samedi* (*The ETs Arrive Saturday*; Kes., 1979)

Epuy, Michel (Vaury, Louis; 1876-?); *Le Champ de Diamants* (*The Field of Diamonds*; Dimanche Illustré, 1908-1909); *Anthéa, ou l'Étrange Planète* (*Anthea, or the Strange Planet*; Fayard, 1923); *La Maison du Chat qui Revient* (*The House of the Cat Which Came Back*; Spès, 1926); *Contes des Garrigues* (*Tales of the Moors*; Aubanel Frères, 1927); *Note:* See Chapter VII.

Erboy, Franck (?-); *Mat aux Automates* (*The Automatons Checkmate*; Arabesque 131, 1960); *Fumée d'Or* (*Golden Smoke*; Arabesque 138, 1960); *Tornades sur Commande* (*Tornado to Order*; Arabesque 156, 1961); *Note:* See Chapter IX.

Erckmann-Chatrian (Erckmann, Emile [1822-1899] & Chatrian, Alexandre [1826-1890]); *Science et Génie, Conte Fantastique* (*Science and Genius, a Fantastical Tale*; Impr. Silbermann, 1850); *L'Illustre Docteur Matheus* (Bourdillat, 1859); *Contes Fantastiques* (Hac., 1860); *L'Araignée-Crabe* (*The Crab-Spider*; Hetzel, 1860); *Contes de la Montagne* (*Mountain Tales*; Michel Lévy, 1860); *Contes du Bord du Rhin* (*Rhine Tales*; Hetzel, 1862); *L'Invasion ou Le Fou Yégoff* (*The Invasion, or Yegof the Mad*; Dentu, 1862); *L'Ami Fritz* (*My Friend Fritz*; Hac., 1863); *Hughes-le-Loup* (*Hugh-The-Wolf*; Hetzel, 1863); *Madame Thérèse* (Hetzel, 1863); *Histoire d'un Conscrit de 1813* (*Story of a Conscripted Man in 1813*; Hetzel, 1864); *Histoire d'un Homme du Peuple* (*Story of a Man of the People*; Hetzel, 1865); *Confidences d'un Joueur de Clarinette* (*Confidences of a Pipe Player*; Hetzel & Lacroix, 1865); *La Maison Forestière* (*The Forest House*; Hetzel & Lacroix, 1866); *Contes Populaires* (*Popular Tales*; Hetzel, 1866); *Histoire d'un Paysan* (*Story of a Peasant*; Hetzel, 1869); *Histoire d'un Sous-Maître* (*Story of an Under-Master*; Hetzel, 1871); *Le Juif Polonais* (Hetzel, 1871; transl. as the *Polish Jew*); *Les Deux Frères* (*The Two Brothers*; Hetzel, 1873); *Le Brigadier Frédéric* (Hetzel, 1874); *Les Années de Collège de Maître Mablot* (*Master Mablot's College Years*; Impr. Du Rappel, 1874); Maître Gaspar Fix (Imprimerie du Rappel, 1875); *Contes Vosgiens* (*Vosgian Tales*; Hetzel, 1877-78); *Les Vieux de la Vieille* (*The Old Man of the Ages*; Hetzel, 1880); *Le Grand-Père Lebigre* (*Grandpa Lebigre*; Hetzel, 1881); *Fables Alsaciennes et Vosgiennes* (*Alsatian and Vosgian Fables*; Hetzel, 1895); *L'Oreille de la Chouette* (*The Owl's Ear;* n.d.); *Note:* See Chapter IV. Hughes-le-Loup and several of Erckmann-Chatrian's tales were adapted for television (see Book 1, Chapter II). English translations do not always follow the French editions and include: *The Forest House* (1871), *Popular Tales and Romances* (1872), *Confessions of a Clarinet Player* (1874), *Stories of the Rhine* (1875), *The Man-Wolf* (1876), *The Wild Huntsman* (1877) and *Strange Stories* (1880).

Erigny, Simone d' (Chambure, Simone de; ?-); *L'Étrange Volonté du Prof. Lorrain* (*The Strange Will of Prof. Lorrain*; Libr. Champs-Élysées Masque 132, 1933)

Eriksson, Duncan (?-); *L'Éclipse des Dragons 1: La Prophétie des Flammes* (*The Eclipse of Dragons 1: The Prophecy of the Flames*; Mnémos Daemonicon, 1997); *Note:* "Duncan Eriksson" is a pseudonym for one of Mnémos' house authors (**Gaborit, Grimbert**, etc). See Chapter VIII.

Éris, Patrick *see* **Dharma, Samuel**

Erland, Jean (?-) *see* **Van Herp, Jacques**

Errer, Emmanuel *see* **Mazarin, Jean**

Escarpit, Robert (1918-); *Contes du Pays Gris* (*Tales of the Grey Country*; Presses Coop., 1936); *Le Littératron* (Flamm., 1954); *Honorius, Pape* (*Pope Honorius*; Flamm., 1967); *Les Somnambidules* (*The Somnanthings*; Flamm., 1971); *Contes de la St. Glinglin* (*Tales of Any Saint*; Magnard, 1973); *Le Jeune Homme et la Nuit* (*The Young Man and the Night*; Flamm., 1979); *Les Voyages d'Hazembat* (*Hazembat's Journeys*; Flamm, 1984); *L'Enfant qui Venait de l'Espace* (*The Child Who Came from Outer Space*; Je Bouquine, 1984); *Le Petit Dieu Okrabe* (*Okrabe the Little God*; La Faranole, 1987); *Papa 1000* (*Daddy 1000*; Magnard, 1988); *Egon le Gascon* (Vivisques, 1989); *Le Secret du Pilfastron* (*The Secret of the Pilfastron*; Bayard, 1991); *Contes de l'Aigle et du Serpent* (*Tales of the Eagle and the Snake*; Magnard, 1992); *Tom, Quentin et le Géant Bila* (*Tom, Quentin and Bila the Giant*; Hac., 1994); *Hugo, Charlie et la Reine Isis* (*Hugo, Charlie and Queen Isis*; Hac., 1995); *La Poudre du Père Limpinpin* (*The Powder of Father Limpinpin*; Chardon Bleu, 1996); *Note:* See Chapters VIII and IX.

Escomel, Gloria (1941-); *Ferveurs* (*Fervors*; St. Germain-des-Prés, 1971); *Exorcisme du Rêve* (*Exorcism of Dreams*; St. Germain-des-Prés, 1973); *Fruit de la Passion* (*Passion Fruit*; Trois, 1988); *Les Eaux de la Mémoire* (*The Waters of Memory*; Boréal, 1994); *Note:* French-Canadian writer.

Escoula, Yvonne (1913-1987); *Poursuite du Vent* (*Pursuit of the Wind*; Gall., 1947); *Promenade des Promesses* (*Boulevard of Promises*; Gall., 1948); *L'Apatride* (Gall., 1951); *Sur la Piste du Mûrier* (*On the Trail of the Mulberry Tree*; Gall., 1953); *Tulipan* (Gall., 1958); *Mémoires d'un Chien* (*Memoirs of a Dog*; Gall., 1960); *Contes de la Ventourlière* (*Tales of the Ventourliere*;

Gall., 1965); *Le Temps Infini* (*Infinite Time*; Gall., 1968); *La Peau de la Mer* (*The Skin of the Sea*; Gall., 1972); *Six Chevaux Bleus* (*Six Blue Horses*; Gall., 1980); *Note:* See Chapter VIII.

Escrignelles, Maurice d' *see* **Limat, Maurice**

Escudié, René (1941-); *Sanarin* (Nathan 1979); *L'Enfant qui avait accroché la Lune* (*The Child Who Had Hooked the Moon*; Pomme d'Api, 1980); *Sanarin et la Bête à Manger les Vilains* (*Sanarin and the Beast Who Ate Villains*; Magnard, 1980); *Une Petite Fille Si Petite* (*Such a Small Little Girl*; Pomme d'Api, 1981); *Les Peurs de Petit Jean* (*Little John's Fears*; Centurion, 1982); *La Charrette à Traverser le Temps* (*The Cart Which Travelled Through Time*; Nathan, 1982); *Mais où est-donc passé le Pulpul?* (*But Where Has the Pulpul Gone?*; Magnard, 1985); *L'Inventeur* (*The Inventor*; Nathan, 1988); *Histoires au Long Cou* (*Tales with a Long Neck*; ZEP 5 Marseilles, 1995); *Note:* Juveniles. See Chapter IX.

Esme, Jean d' (1893-1966); *Les Dieux Rouges* (*The Red Gods*; Ren. Du Livre, 1923); *Les Barbares* (*The Barbarians*; AM, 1925); *L'Île de la Solitude* (*The Island of Loneliness*; Nlle. Revue Critique, 1928); *La Marche vers le Soleil* (*Marching Towards the Sun*; Colbert, 1947); *Épaves Autrales* (*Southern Wrecks*; Nlle. Revue Critique, 1948); *Note:* See Chaper VII.

Espiard de Colonge, Alfred, Baron d' (?-?); *La Chute du Ciel ou Les Antiques Météores Planétaires* (*The Fall from the Sky or the Ancient Planetary Meteors*; Plon, 1865); *Note:* See Chapter V.

Espie de la Hire, Adolphe d' (1878-1956) *see* **La Hire, Jean de**

Esquier, Charles (1874-1931) *see* **Grand-Guignol**

Esquiros, Alphonse (1814-1876); *Le Magicien* (*The Magician;* Desessart, 1838); *Les Vierges Folles* (*The Mad Virgins*; Le Gallois, 1840); *Les Vierges Sages* (*The Wise Virgins*; Delavigne, 1842); *Charlotte Corday* (Desessart, 1845); *Les Vierges Martyres* (*The Martyred Virgins*; Delavigne, 1846); *Le Château Enchanté* (*The Enchanted Castle*; Dentu, 1877); *Note:* See Chapter IV.

Essard, Manuel (?-); *De Bitume et de Sang* (*Of Tar and Blood*; FNA 1827, 1991); *Une Si Jolie Prison* (*Such a Beautiful Prison*; FNA 1848, 1991); *Saigneur de Guerre* (*War Bleeder*; FNA 1891, 1992); *La Forteresse Pourpre* (*The Purple Fortress*; FNA 1917, 1993); *Note:* See Chapters VIII and IX.

Estoc, Pol d' (1854-1948) *see* **Grand-Guignol**

Esvé, Claude (?-); *Le Saut dans l'Inconnu* (*The Leap Into the Unknown*; SdP, 1962); *Face au Maître du Monde* (*Face-To-Face with the Master of the World*; SdP, 1963); *Note:* Juvenile SF.

Étienne, Charles-Guillaume (?-?) *see* **Opéra**

Étienne, Gérard (1936-); *Un Ambassadeur Macoute à Montreal* (*A Macoute Ambassador in Montreal*; Nouvelle Optique, 1979); *Note:* French-Canadian writer.

Étienne, Jean-Claude (?-); *Barbeboule* (Phenix, n.d.)

Étienne, Just-Jean (?-?) *see* **Opéra**

Even, Daniel (?-); *Amours Astrales* (*Astral Loves*; Scorpion, 1959); *Regards sur les Mystères de l'Infini* (*A Look Upon the Mysteries of the Infinite*; with Blanche Even; Pensée U., 1983)

Evrard, A. (?-); *La Femme Artificielle* (*The Artificial Woman*; Scorpion, 1964)

Ex-Agent SR 27 *see* **SR 27**

Eymery, Marguerite *see* **Rachilde**

Eyquem, Michel *see* **Montaigne, Michel de**

Eyraud, Achille (?-); *Voyage à Vénus* (*Voyage to Venus*; Lévy, 1865); *Note:* See Chapter V. **Eyraud** also wrote under the pseudonym of "Achille Lafont."

Faber, Jean (?-); *Le Flacon Noir* (*The Black Bottle*; with P. **Garbani**; RMY, n.d.); *La Ronde des Fantômes* (*The Dance of the Ghosts*; Nlle. Revue Critique, 1930); *Le Bal du Vingt Janvier* (*The Ball of January 20th*; Lutèce, 1951)

Fabien, Jacques (?-); *Paris en Songe* (*Paris in Dreams*; Dentu, 1863); *Note:* Utopia.

Fabre, A. (?-) *see* **Jacquin, J.**

Fabre-Luce, Alfred (1899-1983); *Haute-Cour* (*High Court*; JFG Lausanne, 1963); *Note:* Political fiction about the "trial" of De Gaulle.

Fabrice, Paul (?-); *La Cargaison du Léviathan* (*The Cargo of the Leviathan*; Fleurus, 1955); *L'Indien au Collier d'Or* (*The Indian with the Gold Necklace*; STAEL, 1959); *La Route de Sumatra* (*The Road to Sumatra*; Fleurus, 1962); *Note:* Juvenile fantasies.

Facon, Roger (1950-); *Quand l'Atlantide resurgira* (*When Atlantis Will Rise Again*; RL, 1979); *Mort au Gourou* (*Death to the Guru*; Eurédif, 1980); *Les Meurtres de l'Occulte* (*Murder of the Occult*; Lefèvre, 1981); *La Flandre Insolite & Le Plat Pays des Magiciens* (*Weird Flanders & the Flat Land of the Magicians*; with Jean-Marie **Parent**; RL, 1981); *Châteaux Forts Magiques de France* (*Magical Castles of France*; RL, 1982); *Vercingétorix et les Mystères Gaulois* (*Vercingetorix and the Gallic Mysteries*; RL, 1983); *Par Le Sabre des Zinjas* (*By the Sword of the Zinjas*; FNA 1512, 1986); *La Planète des Femmes* (*The Planet of Women*; FNA 1589, 1987); *Divine Entreprise* (FNA 1621, 1988); *Les Servi-*

teurs de la Force (*Servants of the Force*; with Jean-Marie **Parent**; FNA 1643, 1988); *Les Compagnons de la Lune Blême* (*The Fellowship of the Pale Moon*; FNA 1881, 1992); *Note:* See Chapter VIII.

Fage-Antonelli, Jeanne *see* **Anton, Emil**

Faindt, R. (?-); *Le Souffle du Passé* (*The Breath of the Past*; Marie-Noëlle, 1997)

Faivre d'Arcier, Jeanne (?-); *Rouge Flamenco* (*Flamenco Red*; PP 9127, 1993); *La Déesse Écarlate* (*The Scarlet Goddess*; PP 9183, 1997); *Note:* See Chapter VIII.

Fajeau, Raymond (?-); *Les Enfants de l'Atome* (*Children of the Atom*; Romans & Idées, c. 1960)

Falcoz, André (Caters, Christian de; ?-); *Du Fond de la Mer* (*From the Bottom of the Sea*; L'Intrépide, 1922); *Le Semeur de Feu* (*The Sower of Fire*; as Élie Montfort, L'Intrépide, 1925; rev. as Falcoz, BGA, 1930); *Le Soleil du Monde* (*The Sun of the World*; as Élie Montfort, L'Intrépide, 1926-27; rev. as Falcoz, BGA, 1930); *Le Fou des Mers du Sud* (*The Madman of the Southern Seas*; as Élie Montfort, L'Intrépide, 1926-27; rev. as Falcoz, BGA, 1930); *La Poudre de Mort* (*The Powder of Death*; as L. Morvers, L'Intrépide, 1928-29; rev. as Falcoz, BGA, 1934); *Le Rio de la Bête Silencieuse* (*The Rio of the Silent Beast*; BGA, 1928); *Les Rescapés de l'Île Verte* (*The Survivors of Green Island*; BGA, 1929); *Le Camping aux Têtes Fumées* (*The Camping of Smoked Heads*; BGA, 1932); *Le Pays des Hommes Fous* (*The Country of Madmen*; BGA, 1937); *Zimbabwé la Secrète* (*Zimbabwe the Secretive*; BGA, 1940); *Le Péril Vert* (*The Green Peril*; ABC, 1941); *La Sauterelle Améthyste* (*The Amethyst Locust*; BGA 1952); *Les Naufragés de l'Air* (*Castaways in the Air*; BGA, n.d.); *Note:* See Chapter VII.

Falk, Henri (1881-1937); *La Main d'Or* (*The Golden Hand*; Libr. Universelle, 1913); *Le Maître des Trois États* (*The Master of Three States;* MdF, 1917; rev. as *La Fantastique Invention de César Pitoulet* (*The Fantastic Invention of Cesar Pitoulet*; with Paul **Plançon**), Ferenczi, 1939); *L'Âge de Plomb* (*The Age of Lead*; À l'Oeuvre, 1918); *Note:* See Chapter VII.

Fallet, René (1927-1983); *La Soupe aux Choux* (*The Cabbage Soup*; Den., 1980); *Note:* Adapted into an eponymous 1981 film by Jean Girault starring Louis de Funès (see Book 1, Chapter I). Fallet also wrote **La Mort Amoureuse** (*Death in Love*) for television (see Book 1, Chapter II).

Fanchon, Claude (?-); *Le Whisky Électrique* (*Electric Whisky*; Guy, 1941)

Faraggi, Claude (?-); *Le Passage de l'Ombre* (*The Passage of the Shadow*; Flamm., 1981)

Fardet, J. (?-); *Dans l'Éclatante Atlantis* (*In the Shimmering Atlantis*; VA, 1935); *Note:* See Chapter VII.

Fardoulis-Lagrange, Michel (?-); *Les Hauts Faits* (*The High Feats*; Debresse, 1957); *Memorabilia* (Belfond, 1968); *Sébastien, l'Enfant et l'Orange* (*The Child and the Orange*; Castor Astral, 1986); *Le Grand Objet Extérieur* (*The Big Outside Object*; Castor Astral, 1988); *L'Inachèvement* (*The Uncompletion*; Corti, 1992); *Les Enfants d'Edom et Autres Nouvelles* (*The Children of Edom and Other Stories*; Corti, 1996).

Fargue, Léon-Paul (1876-1947); *Tancrède* (A. Raymond, 1911); *Espaces / Vulturne / Épaisseurs* (*Spaces / Vulturne / Thicknesses*; Gall., 1929); *Les Ludions* (*The Ludions*; Fourcade, 1930); *Haute Solitude* (*High Loneliness*; Émile-Paul, 1941); *Fantôme de Rilke* (*Rilke's Ghost*; Émile-Paul, 1942); *Contes Fantastiques* (*Fantastic Tales*; Galerie Charpentier, 1944); *La Lanterne Magique* (*The Magic Lantern*; RL, 1944); *Une Saison en Astrologie* (*An Astrological Season*; astrolabe, 1945); *Poisons* (*Poisons*; Daragnès, 1946); *Illuminations Nouvelles* (*New Illuminations*; Textes Prétextes, 1953).

Farigoule, Louis *see* **Romains, Jules**

Farney, Roger (?-); *Deux Histoires Fabuleuses* (*Two Fabulous Stories*; Attinger, 1931); *Consciences Fugitives* (*Fugitive Consciences*; Attinger, 1956); *Note:* See Chapter VII.

Farragut, Jean (?-?) *see* **Grand-Guignol**

Farré, Marie (1944-) & Farré, Raymond (1941-); *La Petite Fille qui s'appelait Mali* (*A Little Girl Called Mali*; Hac., 1977); *Les Murs ont des Oreilles* (*Walls Have Ears*; Bordas, 1978); *La Folle Histoire de Grand-Mère Pirate* (*The Crazy Story of Granny Pirate*; Hac., 1978); *Malice et les Gourmands de Minuit* (*Malice and the Midnight Gluttons*; Hac., 1978); *L'Incroyable Secret de Bobbie Boulon* (*The Incredible Secret of Bobby Nutbolt*; Hac., 1979); *Ah! Si j'étais un Monstre* (*Ah! If I Was a Monster*; Hac., 1979); *Malice au Pays des Bisbilles* (*Malice in Quarrelland*; Hac., 1979); *Les Aventures Extraordinaires de Géraldine* (*Geraldine's Extraordinary Adventures*; Hac., 1979); *Le Jour où Clémentine Retrécit* (*The Day Clementine Shrunk*; Hac., 1980); *La Longue Route des Savants Fous* (*The Long Road of the Mad Scientists*; Hac., 1980); *Mais qui sont les mis d'Ariane?* (*But Who Are Ariane's Friends?*; Hac., 1980); *Les 1001 Barbes* (*The 1001 Beards*; Gall., 1981); *Ah! Si j'étais un Monstre* (*Ah! If I Was a Monster*; Hac., 1983); *Les Aventures de Papagayo* (*Papagayo's Adventures*; Gall., 1983); **Farré, Marie (alone);** *Papa est un Ogre* (*Dad Is an Ogre*; Gall., 1983); *Mon Maître d'École est le Yéti* (*My Principal Is the Yeti*; Gall., 1984); *Mon Oncle est un Loup-Garou* (*My Uncle Is a Werewolf*; Gall., 1985); *Ventripôtame et Colégram* (Gall. 1985); **Farré,**

Raymond (alone) *Le Roi qui ne croyait pas aux contes de Fées* (*The King Who Did Not Believe in Fairy Tales*; Gall., 1984); *Note:* Juveniles. See Chapter VIII.

Farrère, Claude (Bargone, Frédéric-Charles; 1876-1957); *Les Civilisés* (*The Civilized*; Ollendorf, 1905); *L'Homme qui Assassina* (*The Man Who Killed*; Ollendorf, 1907); *La Maison des Hommes Vivants* (*The House of Living Men*; Libr. Des Annales, 1911; transl. as *The House of the Secret*, 1923); *Les Corsaires* (*The Corsairs*; Ollendorf, 1914); *Les Condamnés à Mort* (*Those Condemned to Die*; Édouard Joseph, 1920; transl. as *Useless Hands*, 1926); *La Dernière Déesse* (*The Last Goddess*; Flamm., 1920); *Contes d'Outre et d'Autres Mondes* (*Tales from Beyond and Other Worlds*; Dorlon Aîné, 1921); *Histoire de Très Loin ou d'Assez Près* (*Tales of Very Far Or Near Enough;* incl. *Où?* (*Where?*; Flamm., 1923); *Danger de Mort: Récits Péruviens* (*Danger of Death: Peruvian Tales*; Excelsior, 1926); *Le Dernier Dieu* (*The Last God*; Flamm., 1926); *Cent Millions d'Or* (*One Hundred Millions in Gold*; Flamm., 1927); *L'Autre Côté* (*The Other Side*; Flamm., 1928); *La Marche Funèbre* (*The Funeral March*; Flamm., 1929); *La Porte Dérobée* (*The Hidden Door*; Flamm., 1930); *Le Chef* (*The Boss*; Flamm., 1930); *L'Homme qui était trop grand* (*The Man Who Was Too Tall*; Ed. De France, 1936); *Les Imaginaires* (*The Imaginaries*; Flamm., 1938); *La Fin de Psyché* (*Psyche's End*; n.d.); *Note:* See chapters IV, VI, and VII. *La Maison* was adapted into a **Grand-Guignol** play by **Pierre-Louis Rehm.**

Fast, Jan de (?-); *Atlantide 1980* (as Karol Bor; Arabesque, 1961); *L'Envoyé d'Alpha* (*The Emissary from Alpha*; FNA 495, 1972); *La Planète Assassinée* (*The Murdered Planet*; FNA 514, 1972); *Infection Focale* (*Focal Infection*; FNA 539, 1973); *L'Impossible Retour* (*The Impossible Return*; FNA 560, 1973); *Quatrième Mutation* (*Fourth Mutation*; FNA 579, 1973); *Cancer dans le Cosmos* (*Cancer in the Cosmos*; FNA 593, 1974); *Les Tueurs d'Âme* (*The Soul Killers*; FNA 600, 1974); *La Mort Surgit du Néant* (*Death Comes from the Void*; FNA 614, 1974); *La Drogue des Étoiles* (*Star Drugs*; FNA 634, 1974); *Quand les Deux Soleils Se Coucheront* (*When the Two Suns Set*; FNA 637, 1974); *Sécession à Procyon* (*Secession on Procyon*; FNA 652, 1974); *Les Hordes de Céphée* (*The Hordes of Cepheus*; FNA 661, 1975); *La Saga des Étoiles* (*The Saga of the Stars*; FNA 667, 1975); *Dans la Gueule du Vortex* (*In the Mouth of the Vortex*; FNA 678, 1975); *Le Salut de l'Empire Shékara* (*The Salute of the Shekaran Empire*; FNA 683, 1975); *Tourbillon Temporel* (*Time Whirlpool*; FNA 694, 1975); *Nurnah aux Temples d'Or* (*The Golden Temples of Nurnah*; FNA 705, 1975); *Les Walkyries des Pléiades* (*The Valkyries of the Pleiades*; FNA 709, 1975); *Une Porte sur Ailleurs* (*A Door to Elsewhere*; FNA 713, 1975); *La Loi Galactique* (*The Galactic Law*; FNA 725,

1976); *Par le Temps qui Court...* (*As Time Goes By...*; FNA 731, 1976); *Les Tziganes du Triangle Austral* (*The Gypsies of the Southern Triangle*; FNA 738, 1976); *SOS Andromède* (*SOS Andromeda*; FNA 748, 1976); *La Planète des Normes* (*The Planet of the Norms*; FNA 764, 1977); *Un Pas De Trop Vers Les Étoiles* (*One Step Too Many Towards the Stars*; FNA 770, 1977); *Involution Interdite* (*Forbidden Involution*; FNA 782, 1977); *Mondes en Dérive* (*Worlds Adrift*; FNA 791, 1977); *Les Esclaves de Thô* (*The Slaves of Tho*; FNA 808, 1977); *Seules les Étoiles Meurent* (*Only Stars Die*; FNA 823, 1977); *Hier Est Né Demain* (*Yesterday Was Born Tomorrow*; FNA 836, 1978); *Pas de Berceau pour les Ushas* (*No Cradles for the Ushas*; FNA 860, 1978); *Le Plan de Clivage* (*The Cutting Plane*; FNA 869, 1978); *Les Jeux de Nora et du Hasard* (*The Games of Nora and Luck*; FNA 874, 1978); *Le Piège de l'Oubli* (*The Oblivion Trap*; FNA 893, 1978); *Le Fils de l'Etoile* (*The Son of the Star*; FNA 899, 1979); *Aux Confins de l'Empire Viédi* (*On the Borders of the Vedian Empire*; FNA 901, 1979); *Plus Belle Sera l'Aurore* (*Prettier Will Be the Dawn*; FNA 922, 1979); *La Cité où le Soleil n'entrait jamais* (*The City Where the Sun Never Shone*; FNA 927, 1979); *L'Ultimatum des Treize Jours* (*The Ultimatum of Thirteen Days*; FNA 967, 1980); *La Dernière Bataille de l'Espace* (*The Last Space Battle*; FNA 1018, 1980); *Le Secret des Pierres Radieuses* (*The Secret of the Radiant Stones*; FNA 1051, 1981); *Pas de Passeport pour Anésia* (*No Passport for Anesia*; FNA 1082, 1981); *Il Fera Si Bon Mourir...* (*It Will Be So Good to Die...*; FNA 1111, 1981); *Note:* See Chapter IX.

Fauchois, René (1882-1962) *see* **Grand-Guignol** and **Opéra**

Fauconnier, Bernard (?-); *Kairos* (Grasset, 1997)

Fauconnier, Geneviève (1886-1969); *Trois Petits Enfants Bleus* (*Three Little Blue Children*; Stock, 1927)

Faudrin, René (?-); *Les OVNIS* (*UFOs*; Géos, 1975); *Et la Planète se Désintégra* (*And the Planet Disintegrated*; Pensée U., 1975); *Sequians* (Pensée U., 1977); *Note:* The last two titles are collections of short stories.

Fauliot, Pascal (?-) *see* ***Contes et Légendes***

Faure, Michel (?-); *Le Rêve d'Icare* (*Icarus' Dream;* SEPE, 1947)

Faust, Camille Laurent Séverin *see* **Mauclair, Camille**

Fauvel, Jacky (?-); *Les Peuples Vivaient sous la Terre* (*The Underground People*; Ferenczi, 1956)

Fayard, Colette (?-); *Effacement* (*Erasure*; Théâtre Ouvert, 1987); *Les Chasseurs au Bord de la Nuit* (*The Hunters at the Edge of Night*; PdF 487, 1989); *Le Jeu de l'Éventail* (*The Game of the Fan*; PdF 532, 1990); *Par*

Tous les Temps (*By All Times*; PdF 564, 1990); *Note:* See Chapter VIII.

Faye, E. (?-); *Parij* (Serpent à Plumes, 1997)

Feaudière, Maurice *see* **Serge**

Feek, Anthony (Franco, A.; ?-); *La Mantille Espagnole* (*The Spanish Mantilla*; FNAG 233, 1973); *Cimetière pour Femme Seule* (*Cemetery for Single Women*; FNAG 259, 1974)

Fénelon, François de Salignac de la Mothe (1651-1715) *Voyage à l'Île des Plaisirs / Voyage Supposé* (*Voyage to the Isle of Pleasures / Imaginary Voyage*; 1700); *Les Aventures de Télémaque* (1717; transl. as *The Adventures of Telemachus*, 1768); *Note:* French cleric who penned this story of the adventures of Odysseus' son looking for his father. An incomplete 1699 edition was published without the author's consent.

Féraud, Marie (1945-); *Le Magicien de Hambourg* (*The Wizard of Hamburg*; Hac., 1975); *Contes d'Afrique* (*African Tales*; Hac., 1977); *Les Plumes de l'Ange* (*Angel's Feathers*; Duculot, 1978); *Contes de Sicile* (*Sicilian Tales*; Hac., 1979); *La Sorcière de Kerguélen* (*The Witch of Kerguelen*; Hac., 1983); *Télépirate à votre service* (*Telepirate at Your Service*; Hac., 1983); *Note:* Juveniles.

Feraudy, Jacques de (?-); *La Grande Aventurière* (*The Great Adventuress*; Tallandier, 1930); *Le Sous-Marin de Cristal* (*The Crystal Sub-Marine*; Tallandier, 1939)

Feray, Louise-Evelyne (?-); *Épopée des Bords du Chemin* (*Saga of the Sides of the Road*; Julliard, 1980)

Ferguson, Jean (1939-); *Contes Ardents du Pays Mauve* (*Fiery Tales of the Mauve Country*; Leméac, 1974); *Les Humanoïdes* (*The Humanoids*; 1977); *Frère Immondice* (*Brother Garbage*; 1980); *Le Relais Abitibien* (*The Abitibian Relay*; round-robin novel by C. **Boisvert**, D. **Chabot**, J. **Ferguson**, R. Godard, M. Lemire, and D. St-Germain; Meera, 1987); *Valdabie* (Asticou, 1988); *Note:* French-Canadian writer.

Ferjault, Jacky (?-); *Humeurs* (*Moods*; Ferjault, n.d.); *Note:* SF poetry.

Fermont, René (?-); *Mon Voisin, le Prophète* (*My Neighbor, the Prophet*; Sté. d'Ed. Litt. & Techniques, 1932)

Fernez, André (?-); *Virus H-84* (MarJ 164, 1960); *Note:* See Chapter IX.

Féron, José (1940-); *Le Prince Bleu* (*The Blue Prince*; Garnier, 1979; rep. as *Rama, le Prince Bleu*, Hatier, 1989); *Le Téryel et le Cheval Rouge* (*Teryel and the Red Horse*; Hatier, 1985)

Ferragus (Ulbach, Louis; 1822-1889); *Les Secrets du Diable* (*The Devil's Secrets*; M. Lévy, 1858); *La Voix du Sang* (*The Voice of Blood*; Libr. Nouvelle, 1858); *L'Île des Rêves, Aventures d'un Anglais qui s'ennuie* (*The Island of Dreams, Adventures of a Bored Englishman*; Libr. Internationale, 1860); *La Chauve-Souris* (*The Bat*; Libr. Internationale, 1867); *Le Comte Orphée* (*Count Orpheus*; Calmann-Lévy, 1878); *Le Château des Épines* (*The Castle of Thorns*; Calmann-Lévy, 1880); *Le Crime de Martial* (*Martial's Crime*; Calmann-Lévy, 1880); *Note:* Also wrote under the pseudonym of "Madeleine."

Ferran, Pierre (?-); *Sans Tambour Ni Trompette* (*With Neither Drum Nor Trumpet*; St.Germain-des-Prés, 1979); *La Terre est Bleue comme un Orange* (*Earth Is Blue Like an Orange*; anthology; Ed. Ouvrières, 1986); *La Grande Naine et le Petit Géant* (*The Tall Dwarf and the Little Giant*; Magnard, 1987); *Note:* See Chapter VIII.

Ferrané, Jean-François (1949-); *Nabiscounaberne* (Amitié, 1979); *Le Miroir de Pierre* (*The Stone Mirror*; Flamm., 1980); *La Jardin Zoopaslogique* (*The Zooillogical Garden*; Amitié, 1981); *Les Métamorphoses de Corenton* (*Corenton's Metamorphoses*; Amitié, 1981)

Ferreol, Pierre (?-); *Au Fond du Cratère* (*At the Bottom of the Crater*; Boulanger, 1890); *La Prise de Londres au XXème Siècle* (*The Taking of London in the 20th Century*; Boulanger, 1891); *La Bande* (*The Gang*; Boulanger, 1895); *Decavé* (Boulanger, 1895); *Note:* See Chapter V.

Ferrer, Jean-Michel *see* **Demuth, Michel**

Ferron, Jacques (1921-1985); *Contes du Pays Incertain* (*Tales from the Uncertain Country*; Orphée, 1962; transl. 1972); *Contes Anglais* (*English Tales*; Orphée, 1964; incl. in *Contes*, HMH, 1968); *Papa Boss* (Parti Pris, 1966; incl. in *Contes*, HMH, 1968); *Contes* (*Tales*; HMH, 1968); *La Charrette* (1968; transl. as *The Cart*, 1980); *Historiettes* (*Small Tales*; Jour, 1969); *L'Amélanchier* (Jour, 1970; transl. as *The Juneberry Tree*, 1975); *Cotnoir* (*Blackcot*; Jour, 1970); *Les Roses-Sauvages* (1971, transl. as *Wild Roses*, 1976); *Les Confitures de Coings et Autres Textes* (*Quince Jam and Other Tales*; Parti Pris, 1972; rev. 1977; transl. as *Quince Jam*, 1977); *Le Saint-Élias* (Jour, 1972); *La Chaise du Maréchal-Ferrant* (*The Smith's Chair*; Jour, 1972); *Du Fond de mon Arrière-Cuisine* (*From the Back of My Kitchen*; Jour, 1973); *La Nuit* (*The Night*; France-Québec-Nathan, 1979); *La Tête de Monsieur Ferron ou Les Chians, Épopée Drôlatique* (*Mr. Ferron's Head, or the Pains, Funny Saga*; VLB, 1979); *Rosaire* (*Rosary*; VLB, 1981); *La Barbe de François Hertel* (*François Hertel's Beard*; VLB, 1981); *La Conférence Inachevée, Le Pas de Gamelin et Autres Récits* (*The Unfinished Conference, Gamelin's Step and Other Stories*; VLB, 1987); *Note:* French-Canadian writer. *La Charrette* and *L'Amelanchier* are novels of fantastic realism. *Les Roses* is a chilling portrayal of insanity. Most other titles are short-story collections.

Ferron, Madeleine (1922-); *La Fin des Loups-Garous* (*The End of Werewolves*; HMH, 1966); *Coeur de Sucre* (*Sugar Heart*; HMH, 1966); *Le Baron Écarlate* (*The Crimson Baron*; 1971); *Le Chemin des Dames* (*The Ladies' Path*; La Presse, 1977); *Sur le Chemin Craig* (*On the Craig Road*; Stanké, 1983); *Un Singulier Amour* (*A Singular Love*; Boréal, 1987); *Note:* French-Canadian writer.

Ferry, Alfred de (?-); *Un Roman en 1915* (*A Novel of 1915*; Calmann-Lévy, 1889); *Note:* See Chapter V.

Fétidus (?-); *La Mort Putride* (*Putrescent Death*; FNG 96, 1989); *Occupation des Corps* (*Occupation of the Bodies*; FNG 108, 1990); *Note:* See Chapter VIII.

Fétis, Laurent (?-); *Le Mal du Double-Bang* (*The Double-Bang Sickness*; Gall., 1992); *Magna Mater* (FN Angoisses 8, 1993); *Chien Froid* (*Cold Dog*; Gall., 1993); *Innocent X* (Gall., 1995); *Noces de Bois* (*Wood Wedding*; Treize Étrange, 1996); *Puzzle* (Gall., 1997); *Note:* See Chapter VIII.

Feutry, Aimé-Ambroise Joseph (1720-1789); *Le Temple de la Mort* (*The Temple of Death*; Durand, 1753); *Note:* The story of a hellish dream.

Féval, Paul Henri Corentin (Père; 1816-1887); *Les Mystères de Londres* (*The Mysteries of London*; Comptoir des Imprimeurs Réunis, 1844); *Le Fils du Diable* (*The Devil's Son*; Meline, Cans & Cie., 1847); *Le Loup Blanc* (*The White Wolf*; Boisgard, 1851); *La Fée des Grèves* (*The Fairy of the Shores*; Cadot, 1851); *La Soeur des Fantômes (The Sister of Ghosts), aka Les Revenants* (*The Phantoms*; Cadot, 1853); *Les Drames de la Mort* (*The Dramas of Death*; Charlier & Huillery, 1856); *Les Compagnons du Silence* (*The Brotherhood of Silence*; 1857); *Le Chevalier Ténèbre* (*The Knight of Darkness*; Dentu, 1862); *Jean Diable* (*John the Devil*; Dentu, 1862); *La Ville Vampire* (*The Vampire City*; Dentu, 1874); *Les Habits Noirs* (*The Black Coats / the Men in Black*; Hac., 1863-75): *1. Les Habits Noirs* (*The Black Coats*); *2. Coeur d'Acier* (*Heart of Steel*); *3. La Rue de Jérusalem* (*Jerusalem Street*); *4. L'Arme Invisible* (*The Invisible Weapon*); *5. Maman Léo; 6. L'Avaleur de Sabres* (*The Sword Swallower*); *7. Les Compagnons du Trésor* (*The Brotherhood of the Treasure*);*8. La Bande Cadet* (*The Cadet Gang*); *La Fille du Juif Errant* (*The Daughter of the Wandering Jew*; V. Palmé, 1878); *Nuits de Terreur* (*Nights of Terror*; Glénat, 1978); *Note:* See Chapter IV. **Le Loup Blanc** and **Les Habits Noirs** were adapted by French television—see Book 1, Chapter II.

Féval, Paul (Fils; 1860-1933); *Les Mystères de Demain* (*The Mysteries of Tomorrow*; with H.-J. **Magog**; serialized in 5 issues, Ferenczi, 1922-23): *1. Les Fiancés de l'An 2000* (*The Fiancés of the Year 2000*); *2. Le Monde des Damnés* (*The World of the Damned*); *3. Le Réveil d'Atlantide* (*Atlantis Awakens*); *4. L'Humanité Enchaînée* (*Mankind in Chains*); *5. Le Faiseur de Folles* (*The Maker of Madwomen*); *Miriakris, Amie d'Enfance de Jésus* (*Miriakris, Jesus' Childhood Friend*; with Henri **Allorge**; Baudinière, 1927); *Félifax* (serialized in 2 issues, Baudinière, 1929-30): *1. L'Homme-Tigre* (*The Tiger-Man*); *2. Londres en Folie* (*London Goes Mad*); *La Lumière Bleue* (*The Blue Light*; with Henri **Boo-Silhen**; Querelle, 1930); *Note:* Son of Paul **Féval** (above). See Chapter VII.

Fieux de Mouhy *see* **Mouhy, Charles de Fieux, Chevalier de**

Filion, Michel (1955-); *"C" comme dans... Cauchemar* (*N as In... Nightmare*; Presses d'Amérique, 1995); *Note:* French-Canadian writer.

Fillol, Luce (1918-); *L'Allumeur de Rêves* (*The Dream Lighter*; Amitié, 1980); *Le Cheval de Mer* (*The Sea Horse*; Duculot, 1984); *L'Enfer Noir* (*Black Hell*; Flamm., 1987)

Finné, Jacques (?-); *Trois Saigneurs de la Nuit (2 vol.)* (*Three Blood-Lords of the Night*; NéO 157, 184, 1987)

Finot, Louis-Jean (?-) *see* **Grand-Guignol**

Fischmann, Patrick (?-) *see* **Contes et Légendes**

Fitoussi, Michelle (?-) *see* **Petitcastelli, Claude.**

Flach, Marcelle (?-); *Allons-nous encore une fois faire sauter la Terre?* (*Are We Going to Blow Up the Earth Again?*; Pau, 1946)

Flambart des Bords (?-?); *Dix Pas dans l'Inconnu* (*Ten Steps Into the Unknown*; UIE, 1910)

Flammarion, Camille (1842-1925); *La Pluralité des Mondes Habités* (*The Plurality of Inhabited Worlds*; 1862); *Les Habitants de l'Autre Monde* (*The Inhabitants of Another World*; 1862); *Les Mondes Imaginaires et les Mondes Réels* (Flamm., 1864; transl. as *Real and Imaginary Worlds*, 1865); *Récits de l'Infini* (Didier, 1872, rev. as *Lumen*, Flamm., 1887; transl. as *Stories of Infinity*, 1874, *Lumen*, 1897); *Rêves Etoilés* (Flamm., 1888); *Uranie* (Flamm., 1889; trans. 1890); *La Fin du Monde* (SI, 1893; transl. as *Omega: The Last Days of the World*, 1897); *Chroniques et Contes* (*Chronicles and Tales*; Flamm., 1895); *Stella* (Flamm., 1897); *Clairs de Lune* (*By Moonlight*; Flamm., 1903); *Les Maisons Hantées* (*The Haunted Mansions*; JL, 1970); *La Mort et son Mystère* (*Death and Its Mystery*; JL, 1974); *La Mort, le Rêve et l'Univers* (*Death, Dream and the Universe*; Kirmé, 1992); *Note:* See Chapter V. **La Fin du Monde** was loosely adapted into an eponymous 1930 film by Abel **Gance** (see Book 1, Chapter I).

Flanders, John *see* **Ray, Jean**

Flaubert, Gustave (1821-1880); *Voyage en Enfer* (*Voyage to Hell*; 1835); *Rêve d'Enfer* (*A Dream of Hell*; 1837); *La Danse des Morts* (*The Dance of the Dead*; 1838); *Smarh* (1839); *Les Mémoires d'un Fou* (*The Memoirs of a Madman*; 1842); *La Première Tentation de St. Antoine* (1849; transl. as *The First Temptation of St. Anthony*, 1910; rev. 1874 as *La Tentation de St. Antoine*; transl. as *The Temptation of St. Anthony*, 1895); *Salammbô* (M. Lévy, 1862; transl. 1886); *Trois Contes* (*Three Tales*; Charpentier, 1877; transl. 1903); *Note:* See Chapter IV.

Fleg, Edmond (?-) *see* **Opéra**

Fleischmann, Hector (1882-1914); *L'Explosion du Globe* (*The Explosion of the Globe*; AM, 1908); *L'Incendie du Pôle* (*The Conflagration at the Pole*; AM, 1908); *Note:* Belgian writer.

Fleurent, Jacques (?-); *La Chiourme* (PJ Oswald, 1975); *Celteries* (Liv'Editions, 1994); *Note:* Novelized legends from Britanny.

Fleuret, Fernand (1884-1945); *Jim Click ou La Merveilleuse Invention* (*Jim Click or the Wonderful Invention*; Gall., 1930)

Fleutiaux, Pierrette (?-); *Histoire du Gouffre et de la Lunette* (*Story of the Pit and the Glasses;* Julliard, 1967); *Histoire de la Chauve-Souris* (*Tale of the Bat;* Julliard, 1975); *Histoire du Tableau* (*Story of a Painting*; Julliard, 1977); *La Forteresse* (*The Fortress*; Julliard, 1979); *Métamorphoses de la Reine* (*Metamorphosis of the Queen*; Gall., 1984); *La Femme de l'Ogre* (*The Ogre's Wife*; Gall., 1984); *Nous Sommes Éternels* (*We Are Eternal*; Gall., 1990); *Sauvée!* (*Saved!*; Gall., 1993); *Allons-Nous Être Heureux?* (*Shall We Be Happy?*; Gall., 1994); *Mon Frère au Degré X* (*My Brother to the Xth Degree*; École des Loisirs, 1994); *Note:* See Chapter VIII.

Floor, Alan (?-); *Le Voyage de l'Innocent* (*The Journeys of the Innocent*; Edit & Public. Premières, Eroscope 88, 1978); *L'Innocent dans les Jardins* (*The Innocent in the Gardens*; Edit & Public. Premières, Eroscope 95, 1979); *L'Innocent chez les Trolls* (*The Innocent Meets the Trolls*; Edit & Public. Premières, Eroscope 112, 1980); *La Chair de l'Étoile* (*The Flesh of the Star*; Edit & Public. Premières, Eroscope 121, 1980); *L'Île Mauve* (*The Mauve Island*; Edit & Public. Premières, Eroscope 134, 1980); *Note:* Erotic SF.

Florentz, Bernard (?-); *La Femme Morte* (*The Dead Woman*; FNFR 4, 1994); *La Correction* (FNFR 7, 1994); *Créature* (FNFR 29, 1995); *Noces d'Enfer* (*Wedding from Hell*; Rivages/Effroi, 1996); *Note:* See Chapter VIII.

Fobster, Philip (?-); *Soucoupes Volantes* (*Flying Saucers*; André Martel, 1955)

Foëx, Évelyne (1947-); *Voyages sans Retour... Parfois* (*Journey Without Return... Sometimes*; Ed. d'Acadie, 1994); *Note:* French-Canadian writer.

Foigny, Gabriel de (aka Sadeur, Jacques; 1650-1692); *La Terre Australe Connue* (J. Verneuil, 1676, rev. as *Les Aventures de Jacques Sadeur dans la Découverte et le Voyage de la Terre Australe*; transl. as *A New Discovery of Terra Incognita Australis*, 1693; rep. VI, 1788); *Note:* See Chapter III.

Foleÿ, Charles (?-?); *Les Colonnes Infernales* (*The Columns from Hell*; Juven, 1903); *L'Anneau Fayal* (*The Deadly Ring*; Mame, 1908); *La Source aux Rêves* (*The Source of Dreams*; Tallandier, 1914); *Un Roi de Prusse, Voleur de Géants* (*A King of Prussia, Giant Stealer*; Lafitte, 1919); *Kowa la Mystérieuse* (*Kowa the Mysterious*; Lafitte, 1920); *Le Cygne au Collier d'Or* (*The Swan with a Golden Necklace*; Flamm., 1924); *La Cloche des Pendus* (*The Bell of the Hanged Men*; Flamm., 1928); *Un Visage dans la Nuit* (*A Face in the Night*; Marpon, 1929); *La Grotte au Sphinx* (*The Sphinx's Cavern*; Flamm., 1933); *L'Angoisse des Ténèbres* (*The Terror of Darkness*; Flamm., 1936); *Note:* See Chapter VI and **Grand-Guignol**.

Folon, Jean-Michel (1934-); *Le Message* (*The Message*; Hermann, 1967); *L'Homme Invisible* (*The Invisible Man*; Chêne, 1994); *Note:* Folon is a famous painter; this is an illustrated book.

Foncine, Jean-Louis (?-); *La Caverne aux Épaves* (*The Cavern of Ship Wrecks*; SdP, 1949); *Le Glaive de Cologne* (*The Sword of Koln*; SdP 71, 1956); Series *Le Pays Perdu* (*The Lost Land*): *Le Relais de la Chance au Roy* (*The Stop of the Lucky King*; SdP, 1937); *La Bande des Ayacks* (*The Ayacks Tribe*; SdP, 1938); *La Forêt qui n'en Finit Pas* (*The Never-Ending Forest*; SdP, 1946); *Le Foulard de Sang* (*The Bloody Scarf*; SdP, 1946); *Note:* Juveniles. Also see Serge **Dalens**.

Fonclare, Yvette de (?-); *L'Enfant des Étoiles* (*The Star Child*; Hac., 1979); *Les Fées sont Folles à Farlingdon* (*The Fairies Are Mad at Farlingdon*; Hac., 1990); *Hippolyte le Dragon et Autres Contes* (*The Dragon Hippolyte and Other Tales*; Nathan, 1991); *Note:* Juvenile fantasies.

Fondal, Mik *see* **Dalens, Serge**

Fontaine, Clément (1950-); *Merveilles au Pays d'Alice* (*Wonders in Alice's Land*; Tisseyre, 1992); *Note:* French-Canadian writer. Juvenile fantasy.

Fontaines, Sieur de Saint-Marcel, Louis (?-?); *Relation du Pays de Jansénie* (*Tale of the Land of Jansenia*; Claude Barbin, 1660)

Fontana, Jean-Pierre (1939-); *La Geste du Halaguen (The Saga of the Halaguen;* as Guy Scovel; MarSF 537, 1975; rep. as Fontana, NéO 41, 1982; exp. as *Book 1: Naalia de Sanar,* Atalante, 1997); *Shéol* (PdF 222, 1976); *La Femme Truquée (The Phony Woman;* NéO 15, 1980); *Les Bannières de Persh (The Banners of Persh;* with Alain **Paris**; FNA 1308, 1984); *Dernier Étage avant la Frontière (Last Floor Before the Border;* with Alain **Paris**; FNA 1323, 1984); *Sarkô des Grandes Zunes (Sarko of the Great Zunes;* with Alain **Paris**; FNA 1341, 1984); *Le Syndrome Karelmann (The Karelmann Syndrome;* with Alain **Paris**; FNA 1359, 1985); *Le Temple du Dieu Mazon (The Temple of the Mazon God;* with Alain **Paris**; FNA 1398, 1985); *Le Clan du Brouillard (The Clan of the Mists;* with Alain **Paris**; FNA 1419, 1986); *La Jaune (The Yellow;* FNA 1451, 1986); *Les Hommes Lézards (The Lizard Men;* with Alain **Paris**; FNA 1484, 1986); *La Cité des Hommes de Fer (The City of the Iron Men;* with Alain **Paris**; FNA 1515, 1987); *La Colonne d'Émeraude (The Emerald Column;* FNA 1856, 1992); *Le Désert des Cendres (The Desert of Ashes;* with Alain **Paris**; FNA 1868, 1992); *Note:* See Chapters VIII and IX.

Fontanières, Hervé (1958-); *Rendez-vous en Enfer (Rendezvous in Hell;* Rageot, 1997); *Note:* Juvenile. See Chapter VIII.

Fonteneau, Jean-Marie (1931-); *Les Champignons (The Mushrooms;* Grasset, 1970); *Note:* See Chapter IX.

Fontenelle, Bernard Le Bovier de (1657-1757); *Entretiens sur la Pluralité des Mondes (Conversations on the Plurality of Worlds;* 1686; transl. as *The Plurality of Worlds* (1929)); *Note:* Also see Philippe **Quinault** and Chapter III.

Fontis, Henri (?-); *L'Homme aux Trois Visages (The Man with Three Faces;* with J. Ricard; RMY, 1928); *To... Go... Lo...* (With J. Ricard; RMY, 1928)

Fontugne, Christian (Camille; 1905-); *Disparus dans l'Espace (Vanished in Space;* with Mary **Carey**; Delagrave, 1961); *Note:* Juvenile SF. See Chapter IX.

Forbin, Victor (?-); *Les Fiancés du Soleil (The Fiancés of the Sun;* Lemerre, 1923); *Le Secret de la Vie (The Secret of Life;* Baudinière, 1925); *La Fée des Neiges (The Snow Fairy;* Baudinière, 1926); *La Chanson du Puit (The Song of the Pit;* Baudinière, 1927); *Les Justiciers du Pôle (The Avengers of the Pole;* Baudinière, 1933); *Le Pipe-Line sous les Murs de Ninive (The Pipeline Under the Walls of Nineveh;* Baudinière, 1933); *Le Bourreau des Crocodiles (The Crocodile Executioner;* Technique du Livre, 1939); *La Piste Dangereuse (The Dangerous Trail;* Hac., 1976); *Note:* See Chapter VII.

Forest, Jean-Claude (1930-); *Lilia Entre l'Air et l'Eau*

(*Lilia Between Air and Water*; AdP, 1983); *Note:* Novel by the famous comic artist who created **Barbarella** (see Book 1, Chapter V).

Forgit, Michel (1932-); *Épreuves par Neuf (Proof by Nine;* Nathan SF 2, 1980); *La Tour des Miracles (The Tower of Miracles;* Nathan SF 6, 1981); *L'Homme Reconstruit (The Rebuilt Man;* Hermé, 1991)

Forneret, Xavier (1809-1884); *Un Oeil entre Deux Yeux (One Eye Between Two Eyes;* 1838); *Le Diamant de l'Herbe (The Diamond in the Grass;* Pièce de Pièces, Duverger, 1840); *Note:* See Chapter IV.

Forst, John-Christian & John-Sébastien *see* **Smit Le Bénédicte, Jean-Claude**

Fortin, Réal (1945-); *Contes de ma Rivière (Tales of My River;* Musée Régional Haut-Richelieu, 1984); *Le Secret du 7ème Fils (The Secret of the 7th Son;* Coïncidence, 1989); *Note:* French-Canadian writer. Children's fantasy.

Foucher, Jacques (1949-); *Les Secrets de l'Ultra-Sonde (The Secrets of the Ultra-Probe;* Boréal Jr., 1992); *Le Zoo Hanté (The Haunted Zoo;* Héritage, 1993); *Note:* French-Canadian writer. Juvenile SF.

Foucher, Louis (?-); *Éponine et le Puma* (Seghers, 1961); *Argyne et les Gypaètes* (Seghers, 1967); *Carmagnole des Khongres* (Seghers, 1969)

Fouquet, J. (?-) *see* **Gril, Étienne**

Fourier, Charles *see* **Butor, Michel**

Fournel, Victor (1829-?); *Paris Nouveau et Paris Futur (New Paris and Future Paris;* Lecoffre, 1865; rev.1868)

Fournier, Christiane (?-); *Adam, Ève et le Serpent (Adam, Eve and the Snake;* Monde Nouveau, 1923); *Moun, Vierge Folle (Crazy Virgin;* Radot, 1927); *La Pierre de Longue Vie (The Stone of Long Life;* SFEP, 1942); *Le Mystère de la Nuit Sans Lune (The Mystery of the Moonless Night;* SFEP, 1942); *Les Feux de la Saint-Jean (The Fires of St. John's;* Nlles. Presses Fr., 1946); *On a Volé mon Âme (Someone Stole My Soul;* Iris, 1970); *Note:* See Chapter VII.

Fournier, Henri Alban *see* **Alain-Fournier**

Fournier, Maurice (1946-); *La Maison du Diable* (*The Devil's House*; Beffroi, 1989); *Note:* French-Canadian writer. Collection of fantastic tales.

Fournier, Pierre *see* **Gascar, Pierre**

Fourquez, Sabine (?-) *see* **Thomas, Jean**

Frachet, Léopold (?-); *Au Pays de la Lumière Bleue* (*In the Land of Blue Light*; VA, 1936); *L'Explorateur Sous-Marin* (*The Undersea Explorer*; PRA, 1936); *La Cité Sous-Marine* (*The Undersea City*; VA, 1937); *L'Extra-ordinaire Aventure* (*The Extraordinary Adventure*; PRA, 1938); *Sur la Piste des Géants* (*On the Trail of the Giants*; VA, 1938); *Le Royaume des Épaves* (*The Kingdom of the Shipwrecks*; VA, 1938); *Le Mystère du Pacifique* (*The Pacific Mystery*; VA, 1938); *Mille Lieues sous les Terres* (*A Thousand Leagues Under the Earth*; VA, 1939); *La Guerre des Robots* (*The War of the Robots*; VA, 1939); *Le Courrier du Bengale* (*The Bengal Courrier*; VA, 1939); *La Reine de l'Amazone* (*The Queen of the Amazon*; VA, 1940); *La Fosse aux Squelettes* (*The Skeleton Pit*; VA, 1940); *Le Maître du Gulf-Stream* (*Master of the Gulf Stream*; MRA, 1946); *La Route de l'Atlantique* (*The Atlantic Road*; MRA, 1948); *Note:* See Chapter VII.

Frain le Pohon, Irène (?-); *Contes du Cheval Bleu les Jours de Grand Vent* (*Tales of the Blue Horse on Days of Strong Winds*; Picollec, 1980); *Note:* Britannic folk tales.

Fraïssé, Marie-Hélène (?-); *Julienne et le Vélo Cosmique* (*Julian and the Cosmic Bike*; Amitié, 1979)

Françaix, Jean (1912-1997) *see* **Opéra**

Françaix, Pascal (?-); *Le Cercueil de Chair* (*The Coffin of Flesh*; FNFR 16, 1995); *Kamarde* (FNFR 23, 1995); *Laide Mémoire* (*Ugly Memory*; Massot, 1996); *Note:* See Chapter VIII.

France, Anatole (Thibault, François-Anatole; 1844-1924); *Jocaste et le Chat Maigre* (*Jocasta and the Thin Cat*; Calmann-Lévy, 1879); *L'Abeille* (*The Bee*; Charavay, 1883; transl. as *The Honey Bee*, 1911); *Balthazar et la Reine Balkis* (*Balthazar and Queen Balkis*; Calmann-Lévy, 1889; transl. 1909); *L'Étui de Nacre* (Calmann-Lévy, 1892; transl. as *Tales from a Mother-Of-Pearl Casket*, 1896); *Le Puits de Sainte Claire* (Calmann-Lévy, 1895; transl. as *The Well of Santa Clara*, 1903); *Sur la Pierre Blanche* (Calmann-Lévy, 1905; transl. as *The White Stone*, 1910); *La Descente de Marbode aux Enfers* (*The Descent of Marborde to Hell*; 13, rue St. Georges, 1907); *L'Île des Pingouins* (Calmann-Lévy, 1908; transl. as *Penguin Island*, 1909); *Les Contes de Jacques Tournebroche* (*The Tales of Jacques Tournebroche*; Calmann-Lévy, 1908); *Les Sept Femmes de Barbe-Bleue* (Calmann-Lévy, 1909; transl. as *The*

Seven Wives of Bluebeard, 1920); *La Caution* (*The Guarantee*; F. Ferroud, 1912); *La Révolte des Anges* (Calmann-Lévy, 1914; transl. as *The Revolt of Angels*, 1914); *Note:* See Chapters IV and V.

France, Marie de (12th Century); *Les Lais de Marie de France* (*The Ballads of Marie de France*; c.1170); *Note:* Includes *Lanval, Yonec, L'Oiseau Bleu* (*The Blue Bird*), Milon, Eliduc, etc. See Chapter I.

Francheville, Robert (?-1943); *100.000 Lieues en Aéroplane* (*100.000 Leagues in an Airplane*; Tallandier, 1910); *Fin du Monde* (*World's End*; Tallandier, 1910); *Note:* Also see **Grand-Guignol**.

Francillon, Clarisse (1899-1976); *La Mivoie* (*The Halfway*; Gall., 1935); *Coquillage* (*Sea Shell*; Gall., 1937); *Le Plaisir de Dieu* (*God's Pleasure*; Gall., 1938); *Les Nuits sans Fêtes* (*The Joyless Nights*; L'Abbaye du Livre, 1942); *Les Fantômes* (*The Ghosts*; Egloff, 1945); *Les Meurtrières* (*The Crenelles*; Gall., 1952); *Le Carnet à Lucarnes* (*The Skylight Sketchbook*; Den., 1968); *Vingt-Neuf Contes* (*29 Tales*; PJ Oswald, 1968)

Franco, A. *see* **Feek, Anthony**

François (?-?); *Une Visite du Diable* (*A Devil's Visit*; Blaut, 1847)

François (1937-); *La 6ème Colonne* (*The Sixth Column*; Stock, 1979)

Frank, Alain (?-) *see* **Vicas, Victor**

Frank, Christopher (?-); *Mortelle* (*Deadly*; Seuil, 1983)

Franklin, Alfred-Louis (1830-1917); *Les Ruines de Paris, Documents Officiels et Inédits* (*The Ruins of Paris, Official and Unpublished Documents*; Willem-Daffis, 1875; rev. as *Les Ruines de Paris en 4908*, Flamm., 1908); *Note:* See Chapter V.

Fraudet, René *see* **Frondaie, Pierre**

Fraysse, Jean-Louis *see* **Grimaud, Michel**

Fréchette, Louis Honoré (1839-1908); *Feuilles Volantes* (*Flying Leaves*; Darveau, 1890); *Contes de Jos Violon* (*Jos Violon's Tales*; L'Aurore, 1974); *Contes* (*Tales*; Fidès, 1974-76); *Note:* French-Canadian writer of fairy tales based on Quebec folklore.

Frédérique, André (?-); *Ana* (1944); *Histoires Blanches* (*White Tales*; Gall., 1945); *Aigremort* (*Bitterdeath*; GLM, 1947); *Poésies Sournoises* (*Underhanded Poetry*; 1957); *La Grande Fugue* (*The Great Escape*; Plasma, 1980); *Note:* See Chapter VIII.

Fréjaville, Gustave (1883-?) *see* **Grand-Guignol**

Fréjean, Pascal *see* **Lehman, Serge**

Frémion, Yves (1942-); *Univers Nos. 1-19* (anthologies;

JL, 1975-1979); *Ploum, Ploum, Tralala* (as Theophraste Epistolier; Kes., 1975); *La Revanche de Zarathoustra* (*Zaratustra's Revenge*; as Theophraste Epistolier; Vermont, 1977); *Octobre, Octobres* (*October, Octobers*; Kes. I&M 1, 1977); *Les Mauvais Jours Finiront* (*The Bad Days Will End*; as Theophraste Epistolier; Citron Hallucinogène, 1980); *La Planète Larzac* (*Planet Larzac*; anthology; Ponte Mirone, 1980); *Territoires du Tendre* (*Territories of Tenderness*; anthology; PdF 335, 1982); *Les Amazonardes* (Frémion, 1984); *Rêves de Sable, Châteaux de Sang* (*Dreams of Sand, Castles of Blood*; JL 2054, 1986); *Tongre* (Gall., 1986); *Ronge* (*Gnaw*; FNA 1647, 1988); *L'Hétéradelphe de Gane* (*The Heteradelph of Gane*; Aurore, Futurs 8, 1989); *Note:* See Chapter IX.

Fribourg, Roger (?-); *Des Éclairs dans la Nuit* (*Lightning Bolts in the Night*; Gloria, 1927); *Note:* See Chapter VII.

Frick, Jean *see* **Desclaux, Pierre**

Frigerio, Vittorio (1958-); *Au bout de la Rue* (*At the End of the Street*; Vent d'Ouest, 1995); *Note:* French-Canadian writer.

Froelich, Jean-Claude (1914-1972); *Voyage au Pays de la Pierre Ancienne* (*Voyage to the Land of Old Stones*; Magnard, 1962); *Naufrage dans le Temps* (*Castaways in Time*; Magnard, 1965); *La Horde de Gor* (*The Horde of Gor*; Magnard, 1969); *Le Masque du Taureau* (*The Mask of the Bull*; Magnard, 1969); *La Gaule Appelle IST* (*Gaul Is Calling IST*; Magnard, 1971); *Note:* Swiss writer. See Chapter IX.

Froissart, Jean (1337-1414?); *Le Roman de Jaufré* (*The Novel of Jaufré*; c. 1360); *Méliador* (1370); *Note:* See Chapter I.

Frondaie, Pierre (Fraudet, René; 1884-1948); *Le Voyageur Fantastique* (*The Fantastic Traveller*; 1905); *Les Pierres de la Lune* (*The Monstones*; Ollendorf, 1907); *Les Bijoux de la Morte* (*The Dead Woman's Jewels*; Ollendorf, 1907); *La Côte des Dieux* (*The Gods' Coast*; Émile-Paul, 1929); *Contes Réels et Fantaisistes* (*Real and Fantastic Tales*; Émile-Paul, 1930); *Quand le Diable s'en mêle* (*When the Devil Meddles*; Baudinière, 1935); *Les Fatidiques* (*Fated Tales*; Baudinière, 1946); *Note:* See Chapter VI.

Fronval, George (1904-1975); *L'Épave Vivante* (*The Living Wreck*; Tallandier, 1930); *Le Mystère du Temple en Ruines* (*The Mystery of the Temple in Ruins*; Tallandier, 1938); *L'Énigmatique Fen-Chu* (*The Mysterious Fen-Chu*; SEN, 1944 rev. as *Le Maître des Robots* [*The Robot Master*]; Chardon, 1946); *Les Fantômes de Ghost City* (*The Ghosts of Ghost City*; Ed. Revue Fr., 1944); *Le Sorcier des Cheyennes* (*The Cheyennes' Witch Doctor*;

Duclos, 1946); *Le Totem de la Mort* (*The Totem of Death*; Duclos, 1946); *La Ville aux Fantômes* (*The Ghost Town*; Duclos, 1947); *Le Ranch du Mystère* (*The Ranch of Mystery*; Duclos, 1947); *Note:* See Chapter VII. Also see **Contes et Légendes**.

Froulay (Abbé) *see* **Bouchery, Émile**

Fuga, François (?-); *Holocauste à un Dieu* (*Holocaust for a God*; Pensée U., 1972); *Note:* Revolt in utopia.

Fulgence, Jacques (?-); *Les Yeux de l'Amour* (*The Eyes of Love*; Seuil, 1982)

Fuval, Pierre (?-); *Le Mystère du Lac de Laffrey* (*The Mystery of Laffrey Lake*; SdP, 1938); *Note:* Juveniles.

Fuzelier, Louis (?-?) *see* **Opéra**

Gaboriau, Émile (1832-1873); *L'Affaire Lerouge* (*The Lerouge Affair*; Dentu, 1866); *Le Crime d'Orcival* (*The Orcival Crime*; Dentu, 1867); *Le Dossier No.113* (*File 113*; Dentu, 1867); *Les Esclaves de Paris* (*The Slaves of Paris*; Dentu, 1868); *Monsieur Lecoq* (Dentu, 1869); *Note:* See Chapter IV. An unauthorized sixth volume, *La Vieillesse de Monsieur Lecoq* (*The Old Age of Mr. Lecoq*) written by Fortuné de Boisgobey was published by Dentu in 1875.

Gaborit, Mathieu (1973-); *Ecryme* (with Guillaume **Vincent**; Tritel, 1994); *Les Faucheurs de Brise* (*The Wind Reapers*; with Guillaume **Vincent**; Tritel, 1994); *Souffre-Jour* (*Suffer-day*; Mnemos 1, 1995); *Les Danseurs de Lorgol* (*The Dancers of Lorgol*; Mnemos 3, 1995); *Agone* (Mnemos 6, 1996); *Aux Ombres d'Abyme* (*In the Shadows of Abyme*; Mnemos 12, 1996); *La Romance du Démiurge* (*The Demiurge's Romance*; Mnemos 15, 1997); *Les Rives d'Antipolie* (*The Shores of Antipolie*; Mnemos 21, 1997); *Revolutsya* (Mnemos 27, 1997); *Note:* See chapters VIII and IX.

Gabriel, Paul (?-); *Rosalie* (Homont, 1900); *Contes d'Islam* (*Islamic Tales*; Debresse, 1954); *Messages Martiens* (*Martian Messages*; Debresse, 1957)

Gadeyne, Roger (?-); *La Fusée* (*The Rocket*; with Adelin **Tilman**; Jose Milles-Martin, 1958); *Note:* See Chapter IX.

Gagne, Élise (1813-?); *Omégar ou Le Dernier Homme* (*Omegar, or the Last Man*; Didier, 1859); *Note:* See Chapter V.

Gagne, Paulin (1808-1876); *L'Unitéide, ou la Femme Messie* (*The Uniteide or the Messiah Woman*; Gagne, 1858); *L'Histoire des Miracles* (*The Tale of Miracles*; Gagne, 1860); *Note:* Husband of Élise **Gagne**; see Chapter V.

Gagné, Sylvain (1973-); *Le Mystère des Cinq Sabres* (*The Mystery of the Five Sabers*; Asticou, 1988); *Note:* French-Canadian writer. Children's fantasy.

Gagnier, Hélène (1955-); *Le Secret de François* (*Francois' Secret*; Tisseyre, 1990); *Les Enfants de l'Eau* (*The Water Children*; Tisseyre, 1991); *Le Mystère de la Chambre 7* (*The Mystery of Room 7);* Tisseyre, 1996); *Note:* French-Canadian writer. Children's books. In *Le Secret*, a young alien comes to Earth to learn the meaning of love.

Gagnon, Alain (1943-); *Le Pour et le Contre* (*For and Against*; CLF, 1970); *La Grenouille et le Bulldozer* (*The Frog and the Bulldozer*; CLF, 1973); *Le Gardien Des Glaces* (*The Guardian of the Ice*; Tisseyre, 1984); Gilgamesh (JCL, 1986); *La Langue des Abeilles* (*The Language of Bees*; JCL, 1990); *Note:* French-Canadian writer. Gilgamesh is a retelling of the classic legend. The hero of La Langue must choose between two alien species (nicknamed "Bees" and "Wasps") vying for Earth.

Gagnon, Cécile (1936-); *L'Herbe qui Murmure* (*The Whispering Grass*; Q/A, 1992); *Note:* French-Canadian writer. Juvenile. Collection of fantastic tales.

Gagnon, Daniel (1946-); *La Fille à Marier* (*The Daughter to Marry*; Leméac, 1985); *Le Péril Amoureux* (*The Love Peril*; Castor Astral, 1986); *La Fée Calcinée* (*The Charred Fairy*; Castor Astral, 1987); *Ô ma Source!* (*Oh My Source*; Guérin Litt., 1988); *Note:* French-Canadian writer. *La Fée* is a novel of the fantastique.

Gagnon, Denys (1954-); *Le Village et la Ville, Sorcelleries Lyriques* (*The Village and the City, Lyrical Sorceries*; Fleury, 1981); *Haute et Profonde la Nuit* (*High and Deep the Night*; Fleury, 1982); *Note:* French-Canadian writer. Collections of fantastic tales.

Gagnon, Geneviève (1955-); *22,222 Milles à l'Heure* (*22,222 Miles/Hour*; Actuelle, 1972); *Note:* French-Canadian writer. Juvenile novel.

Gagnon, Gilles (?-); *L'Armée du Sommeil* (*The Army of Sleep*; Q/A, 1986); *Note:* French-Canadian writer. A child makes contact with aliens from Neptune.

Gagnon, Jocelyn (1952-); *Les Petits Cris* (*Small Cries*; Q/A, 1985); *Note:* French-Canadian writer. Collection of short stories.

Gagnon, Jocelyne (1947-); *Karkan* (Émeraude, 1991); *Note:* French-Canadian writer.

Gagnon, Maurice (1912-); *L'Anse aux Brumes* (*The Misty Creek*; CLF, 1958); *Le Chasseur d'Ombres* (*The Shadow Hunters*; CLF, 1959); *Les Tours de Babylone* (*The Towers of Babylon*; L'Actuelle, 1972); The *Unipax* series: *Unipax Intervient* (*Unipax Intervenes*; Lidec 101, 1965); *Les Savants Réfractaires* (*The Rebel Scientists*; Lidec 102, 1965); *Le Trésor de la "Santissima Trinidad"* (*The Treasure of the "Santissima Trinidad";* Lidec 103,

1966); *Une Aventure d'Ajax* (*An Adventure of Ajax*; Lidec 104, 1966); *Opération Tanga* (Lidec 105, 1966); *Alerte dans le Pacifique* (*Alert in the Pacific*; Lidec 106, 1967); *Un Complot à Washington* (*Plot in Washington*; Lidec 107, 1968); *Servax à la Rescousse* (*Servax to the Rescue*; Lidec, 1968); *Note:* French-Canadian writer. The Unipax series is a series of novels about a world-wide U.N.C.L.E.-like organizationdevoted to peace and equipped with fabulous machines.

Gail, Otto Willy (?-); *Un Voyage dans la Lune* (*A Trip to the Moon*; AM, 1930)

Gailhard, Gustave (?-); *Amrou B'ba, Marchand d'Esclaves* (*Slave Merchant*; Ferenczi, 1924); *La Démone* (*The She-Demon*; Fayard, 1925); *Au Temps des Bûchers* (*In the Times of the Stakes*; Baudinière, 1926); *Le Festin des Loups* (*The Wolves' Feast*; Fayard, 1926); *Les Compagnons de la Cité Fantôme* (*The Companions of the Ghost Town*; Fayard, 1930); *Le Pays de la Folie* (*The Land of Madness*; Nlle. Revue Critique, 1931); *La Cité Fantôme* (*The Phantom City*; VA, 1934); *Les Yeux du Fauve* (*The Eyes of the Beast*; Baudinière, 1935); *L'Homme sans Visage* (*The Faceless Man*; Baudnière, 1936); *L'Affaire du Yach Poseidon* (*The Case of the Yach Poseidon*; Baudinière, 1937); *Le Lac des Mirages* (*The Lake of Mirages*; VA, 1938); *Un Cadavre sur une Route* (*A Corpse on the Road*; Ferenczi, 1938); *Le Nid du Diable* (*The Devil's Nest*; Ferenczi, 1938); *Le Secret du Masque de Fer* (*The Secret of the Iron Mask*; Tallandier, 1938); *L'Auberge des Trois Pendus* (*The Inn of the Three Hanged Men*; Tallandier, 1941)

Gaillard, Jean (?-); *Le Rallye Fantastique* (*The Fantastic Car Race*; Gédalge, 1956)

Gaillard, Yann (?-); *Le Sirène du Jardin des Plantes* (*The Siren of the Botanical Gardens*; Belfond, 1981); *L'Amateur d'Épouvante* (*The Fear Lover*; Belfond, 1985)

Gain, Raoul (1877-); *Ilots dans le Fleuve* (*Islets in the River*; Images de Paris, 1922); *Recherches pour l'Enchantement* (*Searches for an Enchantment*; Images de Paris, 1924); *Le Jeu Sexuel* (*The Sexual Game*; Monde Moderne, 1926); *Le Donneur de Jeunesse* (*The Youth Giver*; Montaigne, 1927); *Des Américains chez nous* (*Americans Here*; Montaigne, 1928); *Aux Crochets de Dieu* (*On God's Charity*; Montaigne, 1929); *À chacun sa volupté* (*To Each His Pleasure*; AM, 1931); *Autour des Ravalets* (*Around the Ravalets*; Artistes & Écrivains Normands, 1934); *Note:* See Chapter VII.

Galbert de Campistron, Jean (?-?) *see* **Opéra.**

Galet, Jean-Louis (?-); *Pénombres* (*Semi-Shadows*; Fanlac, 1945); *Contes et Légendes de la Forêt d'Oc* (*Tales and Legends of the Forest of Oc*; Perfrac, 1948); *Les Paladins d'Auberoche* (*The Paladdins of Auberoche*;

S&A 11, 1961); *Meurtre à Hautefaye* (*Murder in Hautefaye*; Fanlac, 1970); *Noël en Périgord* (*Christmas in Perigord*; Libro-Liber, 1993)

Gali, Éric (?-); *Les Seigneurs de la Nuit* (*The Lords of Night*; SdPSF 76, 1975); *Note:* Juvenile.

Galissian, Henri (?-) *see* **Durand, Loup**

Gallaix, Vincent (Acar, Jacques; 1937-1976); *La Clairière Oubliée* (*The Forgotten Clearing*; FN, 1975); *Orbite d'Attente* (*Waiting Orbit*; FNA 708, 1977); *Zoomby* (FNA 719, 1977); *Note:* See Chapter IX.

Galland, Antoine (1646-1715); *Les Mille et Une Nuits* (*The Thousand and One Nights*; 1704-17); *L'Histoire de la Sultane de Perse et des Vizirs* (*The Tale of the Sultan of Persia and the Viziers*; 1707); *Contes et Fables Indiennes de Bidpaï et de Iockman* (*Indian Tales and Fables from Bidpai and Iockman*; 1724); *Note:* Also see **Cabinet des Fées** and Chapter III.

Gallerne, Gilbert *see* **Bergal, Gilles**

Gallet, Adrien (?-); *L'Île aux Chiens* (*The Island of Dogs*; Bonne Presse, 1946); *La Menace de Kali* (*The Threat of Kali*; Bonne Presse, 1951)

Gallet, Louis (?-?) *see* **Opéra**

Galli de Bibbiéna, Jean (1709-1779); *La Poupée* (*The Doll*; P. Paupie, 1747); *Note:* See Chapter III.

Gallo, Max (1932-); *La Grande Peur de 1989* (*The Great Fear of 1989);* as Max Laugham; RL, 1966); *L'Oiseau des Origines* (*The Bird of the Origins*; RL, 1974); *Les Hommes Naissent Tous le Même Jour* (*Men Are All Born on the Same Day*; RL, 1978); *La Bague Magique* (*The Magic Ring*; Cast., 1981); *Les Rois sans Visage* (*The Faceless Kings*; Fayard, 1994); *Le Faiseur d'Or* (*The Gold Maker*; Fayard, 1996); *La Femme Derrière le Miroir* (*The Woman Behind the Mirror*; Fayard, 1997)

Gallon, Dominique Anne (?-); *Basa Jaun* (J&D, 1995); *Note*: A monster stalks the Basque country.

Gallus (Bonnard, Arthur de; 1805-1875); *La Marmite Libératrice, ou Le Commerce Transformé* (*The Freedom Cooking Pot, or Trade Transformed*; Gand & Bruxelles, 1865); *Note:* Utopia.

Galopin, Arnould (1865-1934); *Les Voyants de Tilly-sur-Seulles* (*The Seers of Tilly-sur-Seulles*; Ollendorf, 1896); *Les Enracinés* (*The Rooted Ones*; Fayard, 1903); *Le Docteur Oméga—Aventures Fantastiques de Trois Français dans la Planète Mars* (*Dr.Omega—Fantastic Adventures of Three Frenchmen on Planet Mars*; Lib. Mondiale, c. 1905; rev. as *Les Chercheurs d'Inconnu* (*Seekers of the Unknown*, serialized in 12 issues, Tallandier, 1908 (Nos.1-9, 1909 (Nos. 10-12); *1. L'Homme Sous-Marin* (*The Underwater Man*); *2. Le Gouffre Ram-*

pant (*The Creeping Abyss*); *3. La Vallée Rouge* (*The Red Valley*); *4. La Ville de Feu* (*The City of Fire*); *5. Le Fils de la Mort* (*The Son of Death*); *6. La Guerre dans Mars* (*The War on Mars*); *7. La Fête du Sang* (*The Feast of Blood*); *8. Le Roi des Rayons Verts* (*The King of the Green Rays*); *9. L'Oiseau Géant* (*The Giant Bird*); *10. L'Horrible Vision* (*The Awful Vision*); *11. Les Yeux Sanglants* (*The Bloody Eyes*); *12. Les Vainqueurs de l'Espace* (*The Conquerors of Space*); *Le Tour du Monde de Deux Gosses* (*Two Kids Around the World*; with Henri de la **Vaulx**; serialized in 46 issues, Tallandier, 1908; rev. as 23 issues, Tallandier, 1925); *1. Le Tour du Monde de Deux Gosses* (*Two Kids Around the World*); *2. Sur la Terre Hindoue* (*On Hindu Land*); *3. L'Idole de Rhagalpour* (*The Idol of Rhagalpur*); *4. Les Rescapés du Sous-Marin* (*The Survivors of the Submarine*); *5. La Route Sans Fin* (*The Endless Road*); *6. Terre de Misère* (*Land of Misery*); *7. Les Robinsons de la Banquise* (*The Robinsons of the Ice Shelf*); *8. Les Vainqueurs du Pôle* (*The Conquerors of the Pole*); *9. L'Ennemi Invisible* (*The Invisible Enemy*); *10. Le Vapeur Mystérieux* (*The Mysterious Steamship*); *11. Les Écumeurs du Pacifique* (*The Reavers of the Pacific*); *12. Le Prisonnier du Big* (*The Prisoner of the Big*); *13. Les Chercheurs d'Or* (*The Gold Seekers*); *14. Les Étrangleurs de la Sierra* (*The Stranglers of the Sierra*); *15. Le Roi de la Montagne* (*The King of the Mountain*); *16. La Caverne de la Mort* (*The Cavern of Death*); *17. L'Attaque du Pacific Railway* (*The Attack of the Pacific Railway*); *18. La Randonnée Tragique* (*The Tragic Journey*); *19. Le Chemin des Nuages* (*The Path of the Clouds*); *20. L'Oiseau Blanc* (*The White Bird*); *21. Dans la Pampa* (*On the Pampa*); *22. L'Hacienda Maudite* (*The Accursed Hacienda*); *23. La Capture du Tigre* (*The Capture of the Tiger*); *L'Homme à la Figure Bleue* (*The Man with a Blue Face*; Tallandier, 1909); *La Révolution de Demain* (*Tomorrow's Revolution*; with Capitaine **Danrit**; Tallandier, 1909-10); *La Ténébreuse Affaire de Green-Park* (*The Mysterious Affair of Green Park*; Tallandier, 1910); *L'Homme au Complet Gris* (*The Man with a Grey Suit*; Tallandier, 1910; rev. AM, 1931); *Un Aéroplane autour du Monde* (*An Airplane Around the World*; Tallandier, 1910); *La Sandale Rouge* (*The Red Sandal*; AM, 1914); *La Cité Perdue* (*The Lost City*; Tallandier, 1921); *Aventures de Julot, Tueur de Tigres* (*Adventures of Julot, the Tiger-Killer*; Libr. Romans Choisis, 1924); *Le Tour du Monde en Sous-Marin* (*Around the World in a Submarine*; AM, 1925-26); *Un Aviateur de 15 ans* (*A 15-Year-Old Aviator*; Fontenay-aux-Roses, 1926); *Aventures d'un Apprenti Parisien, ou Le Tour du Monde en Hydroplane* (*Adventures of a Parisian Apprentice, or Around the World in a Hydroplane*; Fontenay-aux-Roses, 1928); *Le Bacille* (*The Bacillus*; AM, 1928); *Une Aventure de M. Paturel* (*An Adventure of Mr. Paturel*; Fontenay-aux-Roses, 1926); *Le Tour du Monde en Aéro-*

plane (*Around the World in an Airplane*; with Henri de la Vaulx; AM, 1929); *Aventures d'un Petit Buffalo* (*Adventures of a Small Buffalo*; Fontenay-aux-Roses, 1930); *Aventures d'un Écolier Parisien* (*Adventures of a Parisian Schoolboy*; AM, 1931-33); *Le Tour du Monde d'un Boy-Scout* (*A Boy Scout Around the World*; AM, 1932); *La Dernière Incarnation d'Edgar Pipe* (*The Last Incarnation of Edgar Pipe*; AM, 1934); *Aventures d'un Petit Explorateur* (*Adventures of a Little Explorer*; n.d.; *Ténébras, le Bandit Fantôme* (*Tenebras, the Ghostly Villain*; Libr. Contemporaine, n.d.; *Note:* See chapters V and VII.

Galopin, Augustin (Dr.; ?-); *Excursions du Petit Poucet à travers le Corps Humain* (*Journeys of Tom Thumb Through the Human Body*; 1886; rep. AM, 1928); *Note:* Father of Arnould **Galopin** (above). See Chapter VII.

Gandon, Yves (1899-1975); *Le Grand Départ* (*The Great Departure*; AM, 1939); *Prières de la Dernière Nuit* (*Prayers of the Last Night*; Protat, 1943); *Le Dernier Blanc* (RL, 1945; transl. as *The Last White Man*, 1948); *En Pays Singulier, Histoires Insolites* (*In a Singular Country, Strange Stories*; Lefebvre, 1949); *Zulmé* (Mar 30, 1950); *La Ville Invisible* (*The Invisible City*; Grasset, 1953); *Après les Hommes* (*After Men*; RL, 1963); *Pour un Bourbon Collins* (*For a Bourbon Collins*; RL, 1967); *Monsieur Miracle* (RL, 1968); *Destination Inconnue* (*Destination Unknown*; RL, 1975); *Captain Lafortune* (Plon, 1978); *Note:* See Chapter IX.

Garbani, P. *see* **Faber, J.**

Gardès, Jean-Marc (?-) *see Contes et Légendes*

Garen, Jean-Pierre (Goiran, Jean-Pierre; 1962-); *Le Bagne d'Edenia* (*The Edenia Penitentiary*; FNA 654, 1974); *Orage Magnétique* (*Magnetic Storm*; FNA 703, 1975); *Les Damnés de l'Espace* (*The Damned of Space*; FNA 723, 1976); *Attaque Parallèle* (*Parallel Attack*; FNA 747, 1976); *Le Secret des Initiés* (*The Secret of the Initiates*; FNA 794, 1977); *Opération Epsilon* (FNA 814, 1977); *Mémoire Génétique* (*Genetic Memory*; FNA 844, 1978); *Mission sur Mira* (*Mission to Mira*; FNA 904, 1979); *Capitaine Pluton* (*Captain Pluto*; FNA 1060, 1981); *Génie Génétique* (*Genetic Genius*; FNA 1211, 1983); *L'Emprise du Cristal* (*The Mark of the Crystal*; FNA 1288, 1984); Series *Service de Surveillance des Planètes Primitives* (*Surveillance Service of Primitive Planets*): *1. Le Dernier des Zwors* (*The Last of the Zwors*; FNA 1167, 1982); *2. L'Ordre des Ordres* (*The Order of Orders*; FNA 1338, 1984); *3. L'Inconnue de Ryg* (*The Unknown Woman of Ryg*; FNA 1393, 1985); *4. La Fleur Pourpre* (*The Purple Flower*; FNA 1439, 1986); *5. Opération Bacchus* (FNA 1470, 1986); *6. Le Gladiateur de Venusia* (*The Gladiator of Venusia*; FNA 1492, 1986); *7. Le Dragon de Wilk* (*The Dragon of Wilk*; FNA

1511, 1986); *8. Les Guerrières de Lesban* (*The Warrior-Women of Lesban*; FNA 1532, 1987); *9. Le Chariot de Thalia* (*The Chariot of Thalia*; FNA 1561, 1987); *10. Les Démons de la Montagne* (*The Demons of the Mountain*; FNA 1590, 1987); *11. Le Maître de Juvénia* (*The Master of Juvenia*; FNA 1608, 1988); *12. La Vengeance de l'Androïde* (*The Revenge of the Android*; FNA 1630, 1988); *13. La Quête du Graal* (*The Quest for the Grail*; FNA 1652, 1988); *14. Piège sur Korz* (*Trap on Korz*; FNA 1669, 1989); *15. Des Enfants Très Doués* (*Some Very Gifted Children*; FNA 1682, 1989); *16. Les Pierres de Sang* (*The Stones of Blood*; FNA 1699, 1989); *17. Le Roi de Fer* (*The Iron King*; FNA 1712, 1989); *18. La Chute des Dieux* (*The Fall of the Gods*; FNA 1729, 1989); *19. Safari Mortel* (*Deadly Safari*; FNA 1747, 1990); *20. Chasse Infernale* (*Infernal Hunt*; FNA 1765, 1990); *21. Le Gardien du Cristal* (*The Guardian of the Crystal*; FNA 1789, 1990); *22. Les Pirates de Sylva* (*The Pirates of Sylva*; FNA 1816, 1991); *23. L'Ombre des Rhuls* (*The Shadow of the Rhuls*; FNA 1828, 1991); *24. Astronef Mercure* (*Spaceship Mercury*; FNA 1839, 1991); *25. La Planète des Lykans* (*The Planet of the Lykans*; FNA 1854, 1991); *26. Le Camp des Inadaptés* (*The Camp of the Unadapted*; FNA 1862, 1992); *27. Les Possédés du Démon* (*Possessed By the Demon*; FNA 1879, 1992); *28. Recyclage* (*Recycling*; FNA 1883, 1992); *29. Mission Secrète* (*Secret Mission*; FNA 1895, 1992); *30. Le Temps et l'Espace* (*Time and Space*; FNA 1905, 1993); *31. Les Moines Noirs* (*The Black Monks*; FNA 1916, 1993); *32. Les Mangeurs de Viande* (*The Meat Eaters*; FNA 1924, 1993); *33. Les Mines de Sarkal* (*The Mines of Sarkal*; FNA 1936, 1994); *34. Les Adorateurs de Kaal* (*The Worshippers of Kaal*; FNA 1947, 1994); *35. L'Araignée de Verre* (*The Glass Spider*; FNA 1951, 1994); *36. Les Hommes du Maître* (*The Master's Men*; FNA 1971, 1995); *37. Justice Galactique* (*Galactic Justice*; FNA 1976, 1995); *38. La Montagne Rouge* (*The Red Mountain*; FNA 1985, 1996); *Note:* See Chapter IX.

Garin, Charles (1903-1972) *see* **Grand-Guignol**

Garnier, Charles-Georges-Thomas (1746-1795); Editor and publisher of the first specialized science fiction imprint in history: *Voyages Imaginaires, Songes, Visions et Romans Cabalistiques* (*Imaginary Journeys, Dreams, Visions and Occult Novels*; 36 vols., 1787-88). See **Voyages Imaginaires** and Chapter III.

Garnier, Pascal (?-); *À rebrousse temps* (*Time Backwards*; Mango, 1993); *Note:* See Chapter IX.

Garnung, Francis (?-); *La Pomme Rouge* (*The Red Apple*; Phébus, 1996)

Garrel, Nadine (1939-); *Au pays du Grand Condor* (*In the Land of the Great Condor*; Gall., 1977); *Les Princes de l'Exil* (*The Exiled Princes*; Gall. 1984)

Gary, Romain (Kacew, Romain; 1914-1980); *Tulipe* (*Tulip*; Calmann-Lévy, 1946); *Les Racines du Ciel* (*The Roots of Heaven*; Gall., 1956); *Gloire à nos Illustres Pionniers* (*Glory to Our Illustrious Pioneers*; Gall., 1962; transl. as *Hissing Tales*, 1964); *La Danse de Gengis Cohn* (Gall., 1967; transl. as *The Dance of Gengis Cohn*, 1968); *La Tête Coupable* (Gall., 1968; transl. as the *Guilty Head*, 1969); *Charge d'Âme* (*Soul Power*; Gall., 1978); *Note:* See Chapter IX.

Gascar, Pierre (Fournier, Pierre; 1916-); *Visages Clos* (*Closed Faces*; Gall., 1951); *Les Bêtes / Le Temps des Morts* (*The Beasts / The Time of the Dead*; Gall., 1955); *Voyage chez les Vivants* (*Voyage Among the Living*; Gall., 1958); *Les Vertiges du Présent* (*The Vertigo of the Present*; Arthaud, 1962); *Les Charmes* (*The Charms*; Gall., 1965); *Chimères* (*Chimeras*; Gall., 1969); *L'Arche* (*The Ark*; Gall., 1971); *Le Présage* (*The Omen*; Gall., 1972); *Charles VI: Le Bal des Ardents* (*The Ball of the Fiery Ones*; Gall., 1977); *Le Boulevard du Crime* (*Boulevard of Crime*; Hac., 1980); *La Fleur de Feu* (*The Flower of Fire*; Cast., 1984); *L'Ange Gardien* (*The Guardian Angel*; Plon, 1987)

Gascogne, André (?-); *Le Démon du Néant* (*The Demon from the Void*; Chardon, 1946)

Gastine, Louis-Jules (1858-1930); *Apôtre* (*Apostle*; Genonceaux, 1892); *Seul sur l'Océan* (*Alone on the Ocean*; with Noémi **Balleyguier**; CMM, 1895); *L'Âme Errante* (*The Wandering Soul*; Boulanger, 1895); *Énigme dans l'Espace* (*Mystery in Space*; France Automobile, 1909); *Les Torpilleurs de l'Air* (*Torpedoes in the Air*; with Louis **Perrin**; Livre Moderne, 1912); *La Guerre de l'Espace* (*The Space War*; serialized in 18 issues, Livre Moderne, 1915); *1. Princesse! ... Ou Bagnarde!* (*Princess ... Or Convict!*); *2. Le Coeur de Ninette* (*Ninette's Heart*); *3. Amoureuse* (*In Love*); *4. Les Trois Rivales* (*The Three Rivals*); *5. Bonheur Volé* (*Stolen Happiness*); *6. La Folie d'Aimer* (*The Madness of Love*); *7. Ce Que Femme Veut...* (*What Woman Wants...*); *8. Flambée d'Amours* (*Fires of Love*); *9. L'Invasion Chinoise* (*The Chinese Invasion*); *10. Sous l'Oeil des Celestes* (*Under the Celestials' Eyes*); *11. La Fille du Ciel* (*The Daughter of the Sky*); *12. La Revanche d'Hélène* (*Helen's Revenge*); *13. L'Angoisse de la Sûreté* (*The Sureté's Anguish*); *14. Prisonnier Récalcitrant* (*Unwilling Prisoner*); *15. L'Amour Vainqueur* (*Love Triumphant*); *16. La Force de l'Or* (*The Force of Gold*); *17. La Revanche Barbare* (*Barbarous Revenge*); *18. Les Sept-Sept* (*The Seven-Seven*); *La Ruée des Jaunes* (*The Yellow Rush*; Baudinière, 1933); *Le Roi de l'Espace* (*The King of Space*; Livre Moderne, n.d.); *Note:* See Chaper VII.

Gattefossé, René Marc (1881-); *Adam, L'Homme Tertaire* (*The Tertiary Man*; P. Argence, 1919); *Paradis, Société Anomyme* (*Paradise, Inc.*; Derain-Raclet, 1942); *La*

République des Anges (*The Republic of Angels*; Berger-Levrault, 1948)

Gatti, Armand (1924-); *Envoyé Spécial dans la Cage aux Fauves* (*Special Enjoy in the Lion's Den*; Seuil, 1955); *Le Crapaud-Buffle* (*The Bullhorn Frog*; L'Arche, 1959); *Chroniques d'une Planète Provisoire* (*Chronicles of a Temporary Planet*; 1962); *La Vie Imaginaire de l'Éboueur Auguste Geai* (*The Imaginary Life of Garbageman Auguste Geai*; Avant-Scène, 1962); *La Naissance* (*The Birth*; Seuil, 1968); *Un Homme Seul* (*A Man Alone*; Seuil, 1969); *Les Analogues du Réel* (*The Analogies of Reality*; Ether Vague, 1988); *Note:* See Chapter IX.

Gaucher, Irène (?-); *Quand les Savants sont Magiciens* (*When Scientists Are Wizards*; SUDEL, 1948); *La Terre Tourne* (*Earth Turns*; Ed. Des Gazettes, 1949)

Gaudar, Louis (?-); *Luraméné* (Nef de Paris, 1959)

Gaudette, Pierre (1952-); *Les Problèmes du Diable* (*The Devil's Problems*; with Alkaly **Kaba**; Naaman, 1978); *Note:* French-Canadian writer.

Gaudreault-Labrecque, Madeleine (1931-); *La Dame de Pique* (*The Queen of Spades*; Hexagone, 1988); Series *Les Aventures de Michel Labre: Vol à Bord du Concordia* (*Flight Aboard the Concordia*; Jeunesse, 1968); *Sur La Piste Du Dragon* (*On the Trail of the Dragon*; 2 vols.; HMH, 1986); *Note:* French-Canadian writer. *La Dame* is a fantastic novel. *Michel Labre* is a Canadian Bob Morane, a fearless hero whose adventures often bring him in contact with science fiction themes and elements.

Gauthier, G. (?-); *Le Ventriloque de l'Au-Delà* (*The Ventriloquist from Beyond*; FNAG 54, 1959)

Gauthier, Nicolas (?-) see **Guieu, Jimmy**

Gauthier, Philippe (1965-); *L'Héritage de Qader* (*The Inheritance of Qader*; JP 68, 1990); *Le Château de Fer* (*The Iron Castle*; JP 75, 1991); *Le Destin de Qader* (*The Fate of Qader*; JP 81, 1992); *Note:* French-Canadian writer. Heroic fantasy saga.

Gautier, Philippe (1934-); *La Toussaint Blanche* (*White All Saints' Day*; Pensée U., 1981); *Une Nuit Blanche à Honfleur* (*White Night in Honfleur*; 5 Léopards, 1989)

Gautier, Théophile (1811-1872); *Giselle ou Les Willis* (Pollet, 1842); *Les Deux Étoiles* (*The Two Stars*; Tarride, 1848); *Jettatura* (Lévy, 1857); *Le Roman de la Momie* (*The Novel of the Mummy*; Lévy, 1858); *Romans et Contes* (*Novels and Tales*; Charpentier, 1863); *Spirite* (Charpentier, 1866); *Contes Fantastiques* (*Fantastic Tales*; Corti, 1962); *Note:* See Chapters IV and V. *Giselle* is a ballet with fantasy elements. Gautier's numerous genre tales (most of which are collected in *Romans et Contes* *and Contes Fantastiques)* include "La Cafetière" *("The Coffee Pot"*; 1831, *"Onuphrius"* (1832), *"Albertus ou L'Homme et le Péché"* ("Albertus or Man and Sin") (1832), "Omphale" (1834), "La Morte Amoureuse" (The Loving Dead) (1836), "Fortunio" (1837), "La Pipe d'Opium" (The Opium Pipe) (1838), "Une Larme du Diable" (A Devil's Tear) (1839), "Le Chevalier Double" (The Twin Knight) (1840), "Le Pied de Momie" (The Mummy's Foot) (1840), "Deux Acteurs pour un Rôle" (Two Actors for a Single Part) (1841), "La Mille et Deuxième Nuit" (The Thousand and Second Night) (1842), "Une Visite Nocturne" (A Nocturnal Visit) (1843), "La Péri" (1843), "Le Club des Haschischins" (The Haschischins' Club) (1846), "L'Enfant aux Souliers de Pain" (The Child with Bread Shoes) (1849), "Arria Marcella" (1852), "Le Nid des Rossignols" (The Nightingales' Nest) (1854) and "Avatar" (1865).

Gautier de Montdorge, Antoine (?-?) *see* **Opéra**

Gautier de Téramond, François *see* **Téramond, Guy de**

Gautron, Micheline (?-) *see* **Opéra**

Gavarni (?-?); *L'Homme Seul* (*The Man Alone*; La Mode, 1831)

Gayar, Henri (?-1937); *Les Aventures Merveilleuses de Serge Myrandhal sur la Planète Mars* (*The Wondrous Adventures of Serge Myrandhal on the Planet Mars*; Laumonier, 1908) / *Les Robinsons de la Planète Mars* (*The Robinsons of Planet Mars*; Laumonier, 1908); both rev. as *Les Robinsons de la Planète Mars* (as Cyrius, BGA, 1925); *La Fille des Incas* (*The Daughter of the Incas*; BGA, 1932); *La Bague au Doigt* (*The Ring on the Finger*; BGA, 1932); *Vouée au Diable* (*Sworn to the Devil*; Fayard, 1937); *Note:* See Chapter V.

Gay-Lussac, Bruno (?-); *Le Voyage Enchanté* (*The Enchanted Journey*; Gall., 1981)

Gébé (Blondeaux, Georges; 1929-); *Sept Cartouches* (*Seven Cartridges*; Hac., 1983); *Les Résistants du Square* (*The Square's Resistants*; PC, 1991); *Note:* Famous cartoonist who worked for *Pilote* and *Hara-Kiri*, and author of the graphic novel (also feature film) *L'An 01* (see Book 1, chapters I and IV).

Gehri, Alfred (?-?) *see* **Grand-Guignol**

Gehu, Edmond P. (?-); *Le Voyage du Prolémée* (*The Voyage of the Ptolemee*; Mame, 1934); *La Station du Bout du Monde* (*The Station at the End of the World*; Mame, 1935); *Tempête dans la Stratosphère* (*Tempest in the Stratosphère*; Mame, 1937); *Le Rocher de Semiramis* (*Semiramis' Rock*; Mame, 1937)

Gélinas, Isabelle (1971-); *Le Mystère du Marloland* (*The Mystery of Marloland*; Fidès, 1992); *Note:* French-Canadian writer. Juvenile SF.

Gélinas, Pierre (1925-); *Saisons: La Neige* (*Seasons: The Snow*; Triptyque, 1996); *Note:* French-Canadian writer.

Gendron, Emma (?-); *La Babylone des Mots ou Le Pays Merveilleux* (*The Babylon of Words or the Wondrous Country*; Marquis, 1944); *Note:* French-Canadian writer. Children's tales.

Genefort, Laurent (1968-); *Le Bagne des Ténèbres* (*The Penitentiary of Darkness*; FNA 1655, 1988); *Le Monde Blanc* (*The White World*; FNA 1861, 1992); *Elaï* (FNA 1872, 1992); *Les Peaux Épaisses* (*The Thick Skins*; FNA 1884, 1992); *Rézo* (FNA 1909, 1993); *Arago* (FNA 1922, 1993); *Haute Enclave* (*High Enclave*; FNA 1932, 1993); *Les Chasseurs de Sève* (*The Sap Hunters*; FNA 1944, 1994); *La Troisième Lune* (*The Third Moon*; FNA 1954, 1994); *Le Labyrinthe de Chair* (*The Labyrinth of Flesh*; FNA 1961, 1995); *De Chair et de Fer* (*Of Flesh and Iron*; FNA 1966, 1995); *L'Homme qui n'existait plus* (*The Man Who Was No More*; FNA 1974, 1996); *Lyane* (FNA 1980, 1996); *La Compagnie des Fous* (*The Company of Madmen*; FNA 1993, 1996); *Les Voies du Ciel* (*The Pathways of the Sky*; FNA 1994, 1996); *Le Sang des Immortels* (*The Blood of the Immortals*; FNSF 10, 1997); *Le Continent Déchiqueté* (*The Torn Apart Continent*; FNSF 25, 1997); *Typhon* (Seno, 1997); *Note:* See Chapter IX. Laurent Genefort (using the pseudonym S. Grey) also wrote a novel published under Jimmy **Giueu**'s name in the Jimmy **Guieu** imprint.

Geners, Marc-Émile (?-); *Le Maître du Monde* (*The Master of the World*; Mar. P2000 19, 1975)

Gennari, Geneviève (1920-); *La Fontaine Scellée* (*The Sealed Fountain*; Horay, 1950); *Le Rideau de Sable* (*The Curtain of Sand*; Horay, 1957); *Les Nostalgiques* (*The Nostalgiacs*; Grasset, 1963); *Nouvelles du Temps et de l'Espace* (*Stories of Time and Space*; Perrin, 1964); *L'Étoile Napoléon* (*The Napoleon Star*; Plon, 1964); *La Robe Rouge* (*The Red Dress*; Tchou, 1978); *La Neuvième Vague* (*The Ninth Wave*; Julliard, 1980); *Dieu et son Ombre* (*God and His Shadow*; Perrin, 1981); *Les Portes du Palais* (*The Palace Doors*; Julliard, 1983); *Le Manuscrit* (*The Manuscript*; Rocher, 1989); *Note:* See Chapter VIII.

Gentil-Bernard, Pierre-Joseph (?-?) *see* **Opéra**

Genvrin, Jean-Émile (?-); *Hitler et son ami Concombre* (*Hitler and His Friend Cucumber*; Stock, 1983)

Geoffroy, Louis (Geoffroy-Château, Louis-Napoléon; 1803-1858); *Napoléon et la Conquête du Monde (1812-1832)* (*Napoleon and the Conquest of the World*; Delloye, 1836; rev. as *Napoléon Apocryphe*, Paulin, 1841); *Note:* See Chapter V.

Georges-Méra, Robert (?-); *Que le Diable l'Emporte!* (*Let the Devil Take Her!*; La Tarente, 1952); *L'Inhumaine Création du Professeur Lynk* (*Prof. Lynk's Inhuman Creation*; Corne d'Or, 1954); *La Mort aux Vifs* (*Death to the Living*; Corne d'Or, 1954); *Le Monstrueux Professeur Lynk* (*The Monstrous Prof. Lynk*; Champ de Mars, 1960); *Note:* See Chapter VIII.

Gérard, Jean-Ignace Isidore *see* **Grandville, Isidore**

Géraud, V. (?-); *Sous les Sables du Sahara* (*Under the Sands of the Sahara*; "Petit Illustré," 1932); *Note:* See Chapter VII.

Gerbeault, Jean-Marie *see* **Jackson, Ben**

Gérin, Pierre (1919-); *Dans les Antichambres de Hadès* (*In the Antechambers of Hades*; Garneau, 1970); *De Boue et de Sang* (*Of Blood and Mud*; Garneau, 1975); *Note:* French-Canadian writer. Collection of fantastic tales.

Géris, R. F. (?-); *Quo Vadimus? Histoire des Temps Prochains* (*Story of Future Times*; Gabriel Beauchesnes, 1903); *Note:* See Chapter V.

Germain, Anne (?-); *L'Oeil Marin* (*Eye of the Sea*; AdH, 1980

Germain, José (1884-1964) *see* **Grand-Guignol**

Germinet, Gabriel (1882-1969) *see* **Grand-Guignol**

Gestelys, Léo (Delvart, Roger; ?-); *Alix et son Mystère* (*Alix and Her Mystery*; Tallandier, 1933); *Le Magicien: Amour* (*The Wizard: Love*; Tallandier, 1934); *Le Maître de la Guerre* (*The War Master*; as Roger Delvart; PRA, 1936); *Le Trésor des Derviches* (*The Treasure of the Derviches*; VA, 1937); *La Maison de la Mort* (*The House of Death*; Ferenczi, 1938); *La Fiancée de Barbe-Bleue* (*Bluebeard's Fiancée*; Ferenczi, 1939); *La Flèche d'Acier* (*The Arrow of Steel*; Livre Moderne, 1941); *Nuit d'Épouvante* (*Night of Terror*; Ferenczi, 1946); *Le Fluide d'Or* (*The Golden Fluid*; MRA, 1949); *Le Don Merveilleux* (*The Marvellous Gift*; Remparts Mirabelle, 1952); *Doho l'Enchanteresse* (*Doho the Enchantress*; Remparts Mirabelle, 1952); *La Tour des Korrigans* (*The Tower of the Korrigans*; Remparts Mirabelle, 1952); *À l'Ombre du Moulin* (*In the Shadow of the Windmill*; Remparts Mirabelle, 1952); *Le Bosquet de Diane* (*Diana's Grove*; Remparts Mirabelle, 1952); *La Vie d'un Autre* (*Another's Life*; Remparts Mirabelle, 1952); *Ce n'étaient que des Rêves* (*They Were Only Dreams*; Remparts Mirabelle, 1952); *Le Faiseur de Miracles* (*The Miracle Workers*; Remparts Mirabelle, 1952); *L'Île des Malédictions* (*The Island of Curses*; MRA, 1955); *Le Fantôme de la Fiancée* (*The Fiancée's Ghost*; Remparts, 1958); *Si le Masque Tombait* (*If the Mask Fell*; Remparts, 1960); *Le Fou d'Amour* (*Insane with Love*; Remparts, 1975); *La Douce Victime* (*The Soft Victim*; Remparts, 1982); *La Fille aux Yeux de Mystère* (*The Girl with Mystery Eyes*; Remparts, 1983); *La Flaque de Sang* (*The Pool of Blood*; La Voûte, 1997); *Note:* See Chapter VI.

Gévry, Gérard (1946-); *L'Esprit en Fureur* (*The Angry Spirit*; XYZ, 1990); *Note:* French-Canadian writer. Collection of fantastic tales.

Ghelderode, Michel de (1898-1962); *La Corne d'Abondane* (*The Horn of Plenty*; Vache Rose, 1925); *Kwiebe-Kwiebuas* (Ren, d'Occident, 1926); *Fastes d'Enfer* (*Feasts of Hell*; 1929); *Magie Rouge* (*Red Magic*; 1934); *La Ballade du Grand Macabre* (*The Ballad of the Great Macabre*; Tréteaux, 1935); *Le Cavalier Bizarre* (*The Bizarre Rider*; Ça ira, 1938); *Sortilèges* (*Spells*; L'Essor, 1941); rep. MarF 234, 1967); *La Farce de la Mort qui faillit Trépasser* (*The Farce of Death Who Almost Died*; Sirène, 1952); *Contes et Dicts Hors du Temps* (*Tales and Stories from Out of Time*; Musin, 1975); *Note:* Belgian writer. See Chapter VI. *Magie Rouge* and *Adrian et Jusemina* (from *Sortilèges*) were adaped for television (see Book 1, Chapter II). Also see **Grand-Guignol**.

Gheorgiu, Georges (1926-); *Homo Galacticus* (Debresses, 1961)

Gheusi, Pierre-Barthélémy (1865-); *Le Serpent de Mer* (*The Sea Serpent*; Flamm., 1899); *Sous le Volcan* (*Under the Volcano*; Flamm., 1903); *Les Atlantes* (*The Atlanteans*; with Ch. **Lomon**; Nlle. Revue, 1905); *Le Puit des Âmes* (*The Pit of Souls*; Fasquelle, 1906); *Le Miracle* (*The Miracle*; Choudens, 1910); *Le Tueur de Rois* (*The Killer of Kings*; Gall., 1926); *Le Mascaret Rouge* (*The Red Tide*; Hac., 1931); *Note:* See Chapter VII. *Le Miracle* is a five-act play.

Ghilain, Eddy (1902-1974) *see* **Grand-Guignol**

Ghilini, Hector (?-); *Le Secret du Docteur Voronoff* (*The Secret of Dr. Voronoff*; Fasquelle, 1926); *Selksar, Fils de la Bête* (*Selksar, Son of the Beast*; Jean Renard, 1943); *Galères en Paradis* (*Galleys in Paradise*; Jean Renard, 1943); *La Troisième Guerre Mondiale Durera Six Heures* (*WW III Will Last Six Hours*; Seban, 1950); *Note:* See Chapter IX.

Giaffreri, Charles de (?-?) *see* **Le Gentil, René**

Gibert, Michel (?-); *Blockhaus* (Cercle d'Or, 1973);

Quatuor (Cercle d'Or, 1981); *La Nuit Défigurée* (*The Disfigured Night*; Dary, 1984)

Gide, André (1869-1951); *Le Voyage d'Urien* (*The Voyage of Urien*; Librairie de l'art Indépendent, 1893); *Note:* See Chapter V. Also see **Opéra**.

Giffard, Pierre (1853-1922); *La Fin du Cheval* (*The End of the Horse*; A. Colin, 1899); *Lunes Rouges et Dragons Noirs* (*Red Moons and Black Dragons*; Juven, 1907); *Le Tombeau de Glace* (*The Tomb of Ice*; RM, 1908); *La Guerre Infernale* (*The Infernal War*; serialized in 30 issues, RM, 1908); *1. La Planète en Feu* (*The Planet on Fire*); *2. Les Armées de l'Air* (*The Armies of the Air*); *3. Les Semeurs d'Épouvante* (*The Sowers of Terror*); *4. Prisonniers dans les Nuages* (*Prisoners of the Clouds*); *5. Paris Bouleversé* (*Paris Upset*); *6. Les Chevaliers de l'Abîme* (*The Knights of the Abyss*); *7. Tragédies sous la Mer* (*Tragedies Under the Sea*); *8. Le Siège de Londres* (*The Siege of London*); *9. Moletown, la Ville des Taupes* (*The City of Moles*); *10. La Bataille Aérienne* (*The Air Battle*); *11. Le Sang des Samourais* (*The Blood of the Samurais*); *12. Perdus dans l'Atlantique* (*Lost in the Atlantic*); *13. La Colline des Fous* (*Madmen's Hill*); *14. La Croisière du "Krakatoa"* (*The Cruise of the "Krakatoa"*); *15. La Mer qui brûle* (*The Burning Sea*); *16. La Mer qui gèle* (*The Frozen Sea*); *17. La Tuerie Scientifique* (*The Scientific Massacre*); *18. Jap contre am* (*Jap vs. Sam*); *19. Le Hibou de l'Océan* (*The Owl of the Ocean*); *20. L'Invincible Armada* (*The Invincible Armada*); *21. La Muraille Blanche* (*The White Wall*); *22. Nitchevo!*; *23. Les Fourmis Jaunes* (*The Yellow Ants*); *24. Le Choc des Deux Races* (*The Clash of Two Races*); *25. À Nous le Choléra!* (*Beware the Cholera!*); *26. Le Train Sanitaire* (*The Sanitary Train*); *27. Désespoirs et Vengeance* (*Despair and Revenge*); *28. Les Chinois à Moscou* (*The Chinese in Moscow*); *29. Dans l'Avenue des Supplices* (*On Torture Avenue*); *30. La Fin d'un Cauchemar* (*The End of a Nightmare*); *Les Drames de l'Air* (*Dramas in the Air*; serialized as 8 issues, RM, 1909); *1. La Torpille Volante* (*The Flying Torpedo*); *2. Les Chevaliers de l'Infini* (*The Knights of Infinity*); *3. À l'Assaut du Ciel* (*To Assault the Sky*); *4. Perdus dans l'Espace* (*Lost in Space*); *5. Les Vampires de l'Océan* (*The Ocean Vampires*); *6. Face à la Tempête* (*Face-To-Face with the Storm*); *7. Le Nuage en Feu* (*The Cloud on Fire*); *8. La Chute aux Abîmes* (*The Fall Into the Abyss*); *L'Enfer de Neige* (*The Snowy Hell*; RM, 1909); *Note:* See Chapter V.

Gignoux, Régis (1878-1931); *La Machine à Finir la Guerre* (*The Machine to End War*; AM, 1917); *Le Tabac du Bouc* (*The Goat's Tobacco*; Crès, 1921); *Note:* Also see **Grand-Guignol**.

Gilbert, Charles (1928-); *Soldats Bleus dans l'Ombre* (*Blue Soldiers in the Shadow*; Cercle dOr, 1977); *Les*

Otages de l'Atome (*The Hostages of the Atom*; Cercle d'Or, 1978); *La Montagne Héroïque* (*The Heroic Mountain*; Cercle d'Or, 1980-81); *Le Monde Souterrain de l'Anjou* (*Anjou's Underground World*; Nlle. République, 1986)

Gilbert, Claude (1652-1720); *Histoire de Calejava* (Claude Gilbert, 1700); *Note:* Utopia about "The Island of Reasonable People."

Gilbert, Edmond (?-?) *see* **Grand-Guignol**

Gilkin, Iwan (1858-1924); *La Nuit* (*The Night*; Barral, 1897); *Prométhé* (*Prometheus*; Fischbacher, 1899); *Jonas* (Lamertin, 1900); *Savonarole* (Lameryin, 1906); *Le Roi Cophetua* (*King Cophetua*; Cahiers Indép., 1919); *Note:* Belgian writer. See Chapter V.

Gille, Philippe (?-?) *see* **Opéra**

Gilles, René (?-); *La Dernière Fille des Pharaons* (*The Last Daughter of the Pharaohs*; SdP, 1946); *La Peau de Joie* (*The Skin of Joy*; MdF, 1946)

Gillet, Henri (?-); *Le Voleur d'Instants* (*The Thief of Moments*; Émile-Paul, 1959); *Note:* See Chapter IX.

Gilson, Paul (1904-1963); *Merveilleux* (*Wonderful*; Calmann-Lévy, 1945); *La Boîte à Surprises* (*The Crackerjack Box*; Ed. Nlle. France, 1946); *Ballade pour Fantômes* (*Ballads for Ghosts*; Seghers, 1950); *L'Homme qui a Perdu son Ombre* (*The Man Who Lost His Shadow*; France Ill., 1954); *Énigmarelle* (Seghers, 1963); *Le Monde Merveilleux* (*The Wondrous World*; 1973); *Note: L'Homme* is a two-act play.

Gingras, Lucie (1957-); *La Terreur Bleue* (*The Blue Terror*; Actuelle, 1972); *Note:* French-Canadian writer.

Girardet, Philippe (?-); *Le Professeur d'Avenir* (*Professor of the Future*; Berger-Levrault, 1928)

Girardin, Jules-Marie-Alfred *see* **Levoisin, J.**

Giraudeau, Fernand (?-?); *La Cité Nouvelle* (*The New City*; Amyot, 1868); *Note:* See Chapter V.

Giraudoux, Jean (1882-1944); *Elpénor* (Émile-Paul, 1926); *Intermezzo* (Grasset, 1937); *Ondine* (Grasset, 1939); *Note:* See Chapter VI.

Girieud, Maxime (?-1961); *Contes du Temps Jamais* (*Tales of Never Time*; Sirène, 1919); *Le Voyage Merveilleux de la Nef Aréthuse* (*The Marvellous Journey of the Ship Arethuse*; Lib. De France, 1922)

Gisors, Philippe (?-); *Les Otages du Président, ou La Raison et la Folie* (*The President's Hostages, or Reason and Folly*; Seuil, 1980); *Note:* Political fiction.

Giuliani, Pierre (1947-); *Séquences pour le Chaos* (*Sequences for Chaos*; JCL, 1977); *Les Frontières d'Oulan-Bator* (*The Borders of Ulan-Bator*; Dim. 37, 1979)

Gloria, Mona (?-); *L'Énigme de la Chambe Close* (*The Enigma of the Closed Room*; Baudinière, 1937); *Au Pays des Géants Rouges* (*In the Land of the Red Giants*; VA, 1937); *La Vénus Jaune* (*The Yellow Venus*; Petit Livre, 1937); *Les Mystérieuses Catacombes* (*The Mysterious Catacombs*; VA, 1938); *Le Laboratoire de la Faim* (*The Laboratory of Hunger*; VA, 1941); *Au Pays des Demi-Hommes* (*In the Land of the Half-Men*; VA, 1941); *La Roche qui Pleure* (*The Weeping Rock*; Ferenczi, 1946); *Note:* See Chapter VII.

Gobineau, Joseph de (?-?); *Nouvelles Asiatiques* (*Asian Short Stories*; 1896); *Note:* See Chapter IV.

Godard, Marc (1959-); *La Porte* (*The Door*; Guy Saint-Jean, 1993); *Note:* French-Canadian writer.

Godard, Pierre-Abel (?-); *Les Croix, La Barrière* (*Crosses, the Barrier*; Taurium, 1991)

Godard d'Aucourt de Saint-Just (?-?) *see* **Opéra**

Godbout, Jacques (1933-); *Carton-Pâte* (*Cardboard Paste*; Seghers, 1956); *L'Aquarium* (Seuil, 1962); *Le Couteau sur la Table* (*The Knife on the Table*; Seuil, 1965); *L'Isle au Dragon* (Seuil, 1976; transl. as *Dragon Island*, 1978); *Le Murmure Marchand* (*The Trading Whisper*; Boréal, 1984); *Note:* French-Canadian writer.

Godin, Annette (1895-); *Au Pays du Myrte* (*In the Land of Myrta*; Lemerre, 1921); *L'Erreur de Nedjma* (*Nedjma's Mistake*; Lemerre, 1923); *Contes pour Eux* (*Tales for Them*; Ren. Provinciale, 1931); *La Dernière Atlante, ou Le Second Péché d'Ève* (*The Last Atlantean, or Eve's Second Sin*; Terre d'Afrique, Algiers, 1933); *Note:* See Chapter VII.

Godin, Marcel (1932-); *La Cruauté des Faibles* (*The Cruelty of the Weak*; Jour, 1961); *Ce Maudit Soleil* (*That Damned Sun*; RL, 1965); *Une Dent contre Dieu* (*A Grudge Against God*; RL, 1969); *Confettis* (Stanké, 1976); *Manuscrit* (*Manuscript*; Stanké, 1978); *Maude et les Fantômes* (*Maud and the Ghosts*; Hexagone, 1985); *Après l'Éden* (*After Eden*; Hexagone, 1986); *Les Anges* (*The Angels*; RL, 1988); *Note:* French-Canadian writer.

Goemaere, Pierre (1894-1976); *Le Pèlerin du Soleil* (*The Pilgrims of the Sun*; AM, 1927); *Le Vignes Blanches* (*The White Vines*; Dupuis, 1939); *Les Chevaliers du Tombeau Vide* (*The Knights of the Empty Grave*; Dessart, 1967); *Note:* Belgian writer. See Chapter VII.

Goetz, Georges (1910-); *L'Efface-Temps* (*The Time Eraser*; École des Loisirs, 1983); *Voyage en Outre-Monde* (*Journey to the World Beyond*; École des Loisirs, 1984); *Note:* Juvenile SF. See Chapter IX.

Goffart, Vincent (1942-); *Jonathan à Perte de Temps* (*Jonathan Losing Time*; MarSF 512, 1975); *Note:* Belgian writer. See Chapter IX.

Goffin, Robert (1898-1984); *Le Chat Sans Tête* (*The Headless Cat*; Maison Française, New York, 1941); *Sabotages dans le Ciel* (*Sabotage in the Sky*; Maison Française, New York, 1942); *Passeports pour l'Au-Delà* (*Passport for Beyond*; Maison Française, New York, 1944); *Le Temps des Noires Épines* (*The Time of the Black Thorns*; Paix, 1947); *Le Nouveau Sphinx* (*The New Sphinx*; Maison Française, New York, 1949)

Goiran, Jean-Pierre *see* **Garen, Jean-Pierre**

Goissert, Michel *see* **Van Herp, Jacques**

Goldring, Maurice (?-); *La République Populaire de France (1949-1981)* (*The People's Republic of France (1949-1981)*; Belfond, 1984); *Note:* Political fiction in which French-speaking Belgium is annexed by France in 1949.

Goldschmidt, Maurice (?-); *Altaïr, l'Homme d'Alpha* (*Altaïr, the Man from Alpha*; Pensée U., 1979)

Gomez-Arcos, Agustin (?-); *L'Agneau Carnivore* (*The Carnivorous Lamb*; Stock, 1975); *Ana Non* (Stock, 1977); *Pré-Papa* (Stock, 1979); *L'Enfant Miraculée* (*The Miraculous Child*; France-Loisirs, 1981); *L'Enfant Pain* (*The Bread Child*; Seuil, 1983); *Un Oiseau brûlé vif* (*A Bird Burned Alive*; Seuil, 1984); *Bestiaire* (*Bestiary*; Pré aux Clercs, 1986); *L'Aveuglon* (*The Blinder*; Stock, 1990); *L'Ange de Chair* (*The Flesh Angel*; Stock, 1995)

Gonnet, Charles-A. (?-); *Sur la Piste Blanche* (*On the White Trail*; Gall., 1928); *Sortilège d'Amazon* (*Amazon Spell*; Tallandier, 1937); *Himalaya* (OPTIC, 1945); *Un Avion s'est perdu* (*A Plane Was Lost*; OPTIC, 1945); *L'Envoyé Spécial a disparu* (*The Special Envoy Has Vanished*; Concorde, 1946); *Terreur sur Londres* (*Terror Over London*; Concorde, 1946); *Aloha, le Chant des Îles* (*Aloha, the Song of the Islands*; Concorde, 1946); *Une Flamme dans le Ciel* (*A Flame in the Sky*; Flamme d'Or, 1952); *On a Volé le Canon Atomique* (*They Stole the Atom Gun*; Flamme d'Or, 1953); *Mister Bob* (VF 9, 1953); *La Tendresse de Satan* (*The Tenderness of Satan*; Le Merle, 1980

Gordon, René (?-); *La Croisière de l'Alligator* (*The Cruise of the Alligator*; VF 3, 1953)

Goriellof, Michel (?-) *see* **Rivet, Charles**

Gorka, Lucas (?-); *Mascarad-City* (FNA 1897, 1993)

Gorsse, Henry de (1868-); *Les Marrainnes du Siècle* (*The Godmothers of the Century*; La Cigale, 1901); *Petit Jeannot, La Fée Totorote* (*Little Jeannot and the Fairy Totorote*; Hac., 1904); *L'Aéroplane Invisible* (*The Invisible Airplane*; Hac., 1921); *Cinq Semaines en Aéroplane* (*Five Weeks in an Aiplane*; Hac., 1923); *Le Yacht Mystérieux* (*The Mysterious Yacht*; Impr. Du Palais, 1929); *Note: Les Marraines* is a fairy tale stage play.

Henry de Gorsse also collaborated with Maurice **Leblanc** on an *Arsène Lupin* play, *Arsène Lupin Contre Herlock Sholmès* (1910).

Gouanvic, Jean-Marc (1944-); *Les Années-Lumières* (*Light-Years*; anthology; VLB, 1983); *Espaces Imaginaires 1* (*ImaginarySpaces 1);* anthology/with Stéphane **Nicot**; Imaginoïdes, 1983); *Espaces Imaginaires 2* (*ImaginarySpaces 2);* anthology/with Stéphane **Nicot**; Imaginoïdes, 1984); *Espaces Imaginaires 3* (*Imaginary-Spaces 3);* anthology/with Stéphane **Nicot**; Imaginoïdes, 1985); *Espaces Imaginaires 4* (*ImaginarySpaces 4);* anthology/with Stéphane **Nicot**; Imaginoïdes, 1986); *Dérives 5* (*Adrift 5);* anthology; AMAM 1, 1988); *SF: Dix Années de Science-Fiction Québécoise* (*Ten Years of Quebec SF*; anthology; AMAM 3, 1988); *C.I.N.Q.* (*F.I.V.E.*; anthology; AMAM 4, 1989); *Demain, l'Avenir* (*Tomorrow, the Future*; anthology; AMAM 9, 1990); *Sol* (anthology; AMAM 11, 1991); *Note:* French-Canadian anthologies. Gouanvic is the main founder/editor of *Imagine*.

Goubely, J. (?-?) *see* **Grand-Guignol**

Goudet, François (1930-); *Marinette contre Mozart* (*Marinette vs.Mozart*; Cast., 1987); *Marinette et la princesse de Thulé* (*Marinette and the Princess of Thule*; Cast., 1987)

Gougaud, Henri (1936-); *Les Animaux Magiques de notre Univers* (*Magical Beasts of Our Universe*; Solar, 1973); *Contes de la Huchette* (*Tales of the Basket*; Cast., 1973); *Démons et Merveilles de la S-F* (*Demons and Wonders of Science Fiction*; Julliard, 1974); *Départements et Territoires d'Outre-Mort* (*Departments and Territories Beyond Death*; Julliard, 1977); *Les Dits de Maître Shongland* (*The Lays of Master Shongland*; Gougaud, 1977); *Souvenirs Invivables* (*Unlivable Memories*; Ipomée, 1977); *Le Grand Partir* (*The Great Departure*; Seuil, 1978); *L'Arbre à Soleil* (*The Sun Tree*; Seuil, 1979); *Le Trouveur de Feu* (*The Fire Finder*; Seuil, 1980); *La Rue du Puits qui Parle* (*The Street of the Speaking Well*; Gall., 1981); *Contes du Vieux Moulin et de la Fruchette* (*Tales of the Old Mill*; Cast., 1983); *Le Fils de l'Ogre* (*The Ogre's Son*; Seuil, 1986); *L'Arbre aux Trésors* (*The Treasure Tree*; Seuil, 1987); *L'Homme à la Vie Inexplicable* (*The Man with the Inexplicable Life*; Seuil, 1989); *L'Arbre d'Amour et de Sagesse* (*The Tree of Love and Wisdom*; Seuil, 1992); *La Bible du Hibou* (*The Owl's Bible*; Seuil, 1993); *Les Sept Plumes de l'Aigle* (*The Seven Feathers of the Eagle*; Seuil, 1995); *Note:* See Chapter VIII.

Goulet, Pierre (1948-); *Contes de Feu* (*Tales of Fire*; Q/A, 1985); *Note:* French-Canadian writer. Collection of fantastic tales.

Goulet, Stella (?-); *Mille Baisers, Grand-Père* (*A Thousand Kisses, Grandad*; Q/A, 1991); *Note:* French-Canadian writer. Children's book with a time-travel element.

Goulet, Yves (1940-); *Le Temps Providentiel* (*Providential Time*; Plein Cadre, 1992); *Note:* French-Canadian writer.

Goult, Dominique (?-) *see* **Ligny, Jean-Marc**

Goupil, Mylène (1972-); *Le Détonateur* (*The Trigger*; Fidès, 1992); *Note:* French-Canadian writer. Surrealist fiction in the vein of Boris **Vian**.

Gourmont, Rémy de (1858-1915); *Sixtine, Roman de la Vie Cérébrale* (*Sixtine, a Novel of Cerebral Life*; MdF, 1889); *Lilith* (Presses des Essais d'Art Libre, 1892; transl. 1946); *Le Fantôme* (*The Ghost*; MdF, 1893); *Proses Moroses* (*Morose Prose*; MdF, 1894); *Le Pèlerin du Silence* (*The Pilgrim of Silence*; MdF, 1896); *Les Chevaux de Diomède* (*Diomede's Horses*; MdF, 1897); *D'un Pays Lointain* (*From a Far-Away Land*; MdF, 1898); *Le Deuxième Livre des Masques* (*The Second Book of Masks*; MdF, 1898); *Histoires Magiques* (*Magical Tales*; MdF, 1902); *Une Nuit au Luxembourg* (MdF, 1906; transl. as *A Night in the Luxembourg*, 1912); *Lettres d'un Satyre* (*Letters from a Satyr*; MdF, 1913; transl. as *Mr. Antiphilos, Satyr*, 1922); *Le Château Singulier* (*The Singular Castle*; Contre-Moule, 1989); *Note:* See Chapter IV.

Goursat, Victor (?-?) *see* **Grand-Guignol**

Goutierre, Guy (1939-); *L'Encadreur de Rêves* (*The Framer of Dreams*; Hac., 1980); *Un Matin de Chien* (*A Dog's Morning*; Hac., 1988)

Gouvieux, Marc (?-); *Haut les Ailes!* (*Up the Wings!*; Lafitte, 1914); *Note:* See Chapter V.

Goy, Philip (1941-); *Le Père Eternel* (*The Eternal Father*; PdF 176, 1974); *Le Livre-Machine* (*The Machine-Book*; PdF 193, 1975); *Vers la Révolution* (*Towards the Revolution*; PdF 247, 1977); *Faire le Mur* (*To Jump the Wall*; PdF 307, 1980); *Note:* See Chapter IX.

Gozlan, Léon (1803-1866); *Une Nuit Blanche* (*A White Night*; Souverain, 1840); *Le Dragon Rouge* (*The Red Dragon*; Comptoir des Imprimeurs Unis, 1843); *Les Nuits du Père Lachaise* (*The Nights of the Père Lachaise*; Lemerre, 1845); *Aventures Merveilleuses et Touchantes du Prince Chenevis et de sa Jeune Soeur* (*Wondrous and Moving Adventures of Prince Chenevis and His Young Sister*; Hetzel, 1846); *Les Méandres* (*The Meanderings*; Lecou, 1851); *De 9 Heures à Minuit* (*From Nine to Midnight*; Lecou, 1852); *La Folle du Logis* (*The Madwoman in the House*; Libr. Nouvelle, 1855); *Le Tapis Vert* (*The Green Carpet*; Michel Lévy, 1855); *Les Émotions de Polydore Marasquin ou Trois Mois dans le Royaume des Singes* (*The Emotions of*

Polydore Marasquin or Three Months in the Kingdom of the Apes; Journal Pour Tous, 1856); *Un Fou Couronné* (*A Crowned Madman*; De Vresse, 1857); *Les Veuves du Diable* (*The Devil's Widows*; 1858); *Le Baril de Poudre d'Or / La Marquise de Belverano* (*The Barrel of Gold Dust /* the *Marquise of Belverano*; M. Lévy, 1860); *Le Vampire du Val-de-Grâce* (*The Vampire of the Val-de-Grâce Hospital*; Dentu, 1862); *L'Oeil Noir et l'Oeil Bleu de Mlle. Diane* (*Miss Diana's Black and Blue Eyes*; Dentu, 1864); *La Dame Verte* (*The Green Lady*; Lemerre, 1872); *Histoire de 130 Femmes* (*The Story of 130 Women*; M. Lévy, 1875); *Le Faubourg Mystérieux* (*The Mysterious Suburb*; Bureaux du Siècle, 1875); *Histoire d'un Diamant* (*Story of a Diamond*; Calmann-Lévy, 1882); *La Clef de Cristal / Le Capitaine Maubert* (*The Crystal Key / Captain Maubert*; Flamm., 1890); *Polydore Marasquin au Royaume des Singes* (*Polydore Marsasquin in the Kingdom of the Apes*; Oeuvres Représenatives, 1933); *La Main Cachée* (*The Hidden Hand*; Alfil, 1993); *Note:* See Chapter IV.

Gracq, Julien (Poirier, Louis; 1910-); *Au Château d'Argol* (*At the Castle Argol*; Corti, 1939); *Le Rivage des Syrtes* (*The Shores of the Syrtes*; Corti, 1951); *Note:* See Chapter VI. His story *"Rendez-Vous à Bray"* was made into a 1971 film by André **Delvaux** (see Book 1, Chapter I).

Graffigny, Henry de (Marquis, Raoul; 1863-1942); *Les Voyages Fantastiques* (*The Fantastic Voyages*; Delagrave, 1887); *De La Terre aux Étoiles* (*From the Earth to the Stars*; Libr. Pub. 5cts., 1888); *Les Aventures Extraordinaires d'un Savant Russe* (*The Amazing Adventures of a Russian Scientist*): *1. La Lune* (*The Moon*; with Georges **Le Faure**; Edinger, 1888; rev. as 2 vols., VSE, 1894); *Les Aventures Extraordinaires d'un Savant Russe* (*The Amazing Adventures of a Russian Scientist*): *2. Le Soleil et les Petites Planètes* (*The Sun and the Small Planets*; with Georges Le Faure; Edinger, 1889; rev. as 2 vols., VSE, 1894); *Récits d'un Aéronaute* (*Tales of an Aeronaut*; Libr.Pub. 5cts., 1889); *Les Aventures Extraordinaires d'un Savant Russe* (*The Amazing Adventures of a Russian Scientist*): *3. Les Planètes Géantes et les Comètes* (*The Giant Planets and the Comets;* with Georges Le Faure; Edinger, 1891; rev. as 2 vols., *Les Grandes Planètes* (*The Great Planets*, VSE, 1894); *Les Aventures Extraordinaires d'un Savant Russe* (*The Amazing Adventures of a Russian Scientist*): *4. Le Désert Sidéral* (*The Sidereal Desert*; with Georges Le Faure; VSE, 1896); *À Travers l'Espace—Aventures d'un Aéronaute* (*Throughout Space—Adventures of an Aeronaut*; Alcide Picard, 1908); *Perdus en Mer* (*Lost at Sea*; Ed. Modernes, c. 1908); *Un Sauvage à Paris* (*A Savage in Paris*; Mame, c. 1909); *La Ville Aérienne* (*The Aerial City; Vermot, 1910; rev. RDA, 1926; rev. as Les Naufragés du Sahara* (*Shipwrecked in the Sahara*, VA,

1933); *Voyage de Cinq Américains dans les Planètes* (*Voyage of Five Americans on the Planets*; Gédalge, 1925); *La Caverne au Radium* (*The Radium Cavern*; RDA, 1927); *L'Île des Proscrits* (*The Island of the Banished*; RDA, 1929); *Les Diamants de la Lune* (*The Diamonds of the Moon*; Hac., 1930); *Le Dock Mystérieux* (*The Mysterious Docking Bay*; RJ, 1932); *Electropolis* (Mame, 1933); *Les Martyrs du Pôle* (*The Martyrs of the Pole*; Gédalge, 1934); *Au Fond des Abîmes* (*At the Bottom of the Abyss*; VA, 1934); *Le Bolide d'Or* (*The Golden Rocket*; RJ, 1948); *Note:* See Chapters V and VII.

Grainville, Jean-Baptiste Cousin de (1746-1805); *Le Dernier Homme* (*The Last Man*; Deterville, 1805); *Note:* See Chapter V.

Grainville, Patrick (?-); *La Toison* (*The Fleece*; Gall., 1972); *L'Abîme* (*The Abyss*; Gall., 1974); *Les Flamboyants* (*The Fiery Ones*; Seuil, 1976); *Les Forteresses Noires* (*The Black Fortresses*; Seuil, 1976); *La Diane Rousse* (*The Red Diana*; Seuil, 1978); *Le Dernier Viking* (*The Last Viking*; Seuil, 1980); *L'Ombre de la Bête* (*The Shadow of the Beast*; Balland, 1981); *La Caverne Céleste* (*The Celestial Cavern*; Seuil, 1984); *Le Paradis des Orages* (*The Paradise of Storms*; Seuil, 1986); *L'Arbre Piège* (*The Trap Tree*; Seuil Jeunesse, 1993); *Le Secret de la Pierre Noire* (*The Secret of the Black Stone*; Nathan, 1995)

Grall, Louis (?-); *Le Voleur d'Étoiles* (*The Star Thief*; Bretagnes, 1987)

Gramont, Louis de (?-?) *see* **Opéra**

Gramont, Monique de (?-); *L'Homme Étoile* (*The Star Man*; Libre Expression, 1996); *Note:* French-Canadian writer.

Grand-Guignol; Authors: This list does not generally include the authors of comedies performed at the Grand-Guignol; it is, however, reasonably comprehensive (but not totally exhaustive) as far as dramatic authors are concerned. The authors whose names are followed with (q.v.) have separate entries in this chapter. Also see chapters IV, VI, and VIII. **Abric, Léon** *see* **Héros, Eugène; Achaume, Auguste** *La Maison Vide* (*The Empty House*; with André **Montenis**; 1921); *Les Moribonds* (*The Dying*; 1923); **Adriet, Georges** *Un Drame à Bord* (*Tragedy on Board*; 1926); *La Prison du Vice* (*The Prison of Vice*; 1927); **Aguzan, Jean d'** *La Revenante* (*The Ghostly Woman*; 1906); *Le Sacrifice* (*The Sacrifice*; based on a story by Henri **Duvernois**; 1912); Also see **Lenormand, Henri-René; Alévy** *L'Angelus* (with Marcel **Nadaud**; 1917); **Antoine, André-Paul** *Le Démon Noir* (*The Black Demon*; 1922); *Les Crucifiés* (*The Crucified*; with Charles **Poidloué**; 1923); *La Nuit Tragique de Raspoutine* (*The Tragic Night of Rasputin; aka:*

La Dernière Nuit de Raspoutine; The Last Night of Rasputin; 1924); *La Tueuse* (*The Woman Killer*; 1955); **Aragny, Jean** *Les Yeux du Spectre* (*The Eyes of the Spectre*; 1923); *Le Spectre Sanglant* (*The Bloody Spectre*; 1926); *Le Poignard Malais* (*The Malaysian Dagger*; based on a story by Tristan **Bernard**; 1928); *Le Baiser de Sang* (*The Kiss of Blood*; with Francis **Neilson**; 1929); *Le Tambour de Kovno* (*The Drum of Kovno*; with Albert **Dieudonné**; 1932); *Bourreau d'Enfants* (*Torturer of Children*; 1939); *La Machine à Tuer la Vie* (*The Machine That Killed Life*; 1939); *Note: Les Yeux* features one of the rare ghosts used in the Grand-Guignol. **Aragny** died on the eve of the premiere of *La Machine*; **Armont, Paul** *La Maison du Passeur* (*The House of the Ferryman*; with Louis **Verneuil**; 1924); **Arosa, Paul (q.v.);** *Ensevelis* (*Buried Alive*; 1921); **Arquillière, d' Névrose** (*Neuroses*; 1923); **Astorg, Jean d' (q.v.);** *Le Viol* (*The Rape*; 1918); *Une Fille* (*A Girl*; 1921); *Le Linceul d'Or* (*The Gold Shroud*; 1922); **Autier, Paul** *Gardiens de Phare* (*Guardians of the Lighthouse*; with Paul **Cloquemin**; 1905); **Barde, André (q.v.);** *Un Vol* (*A Burglary*; 1901); *Maison de Rendez-Vous* (*Brothel*; 1901); **Bassan, Élie de** *Les Opérations du Professeur Verdier* (*Prof. Verdier's Operations*; 1907); **Basset, Serge** *Une Partie de Manille* (*A Game of Manila*; 1916); **Bastia, Jean (q.v.);** *Un Fait Divers* (*A News Item*; with André **Lévy-Oulmann**; 1923); *À l'Ombre de la Guillotine* (*In the Shadow of the Guillotine*; 1928); **Bauche, Henri** *Derrière le Voile* (*Behind the Veil*; 1922); *Le Spectre Blanc* (*The White Spectre*; 1949); Also see **Laumann, E.M.; Lorde, André de; Berleux, Jean** *Carrier, Horloger-Bijoutier* (*Carrier, Clockmaker-Jeweler*; 1901); *Note:* A cuckholded husband hangs himself; first "live death" on stage; **Bernac, Jean** *Sol Hyams, Brocanteur* (*Sol Hyams, Junkman*; based on a story by W. Jacobs; 1907); *Le Poison Noir* (*The Black Poison*; with Albert **Jean**; based on a story by Edgar Allan Poe; 1917); *Les Monstres* (*The Monsters*; with Alin **Monjardin**; 1917); Also see **Lorde, André de; Bernanose, Georges-Marie (q.v.);** *Erotikos* (1948); **Bernard, Guy** *Le 2 Août 1914* (1929); **Bernard, Octave** *La Dangereuse Expérience* (*The Dangerous Experiment*; 1942); *Morte et Vivante* (*Dead and Alive*; with Alin **Monjardin**; 1947); **Bernard, Tristan (q.v.);** *L'Étrangleuse* (*The Strangling Woman*; 1948); **Bernier, Jean** *Charlot, la Grande Vache* (*Charlot, the Big Cow*; based on a story by Albert Touchard; 1936); **Berteaux, Eugène** *see* **Thierry, Augustin; Berton, René (q.v.);** *Après Coups! Ou Tics!* (*After Blows or Ticks*; 1908); *L'Euthanasie ou le Devoir de Suer* (*Euthanasia, or Sweating Duty*; 1923); *La Cible* (*The Target*; 1925); *Oeil pour Oeil* (*An Eye for an Eye*; 1926); *L'Homme qui a tué la Mort* (*The Man Who Killed Death*; 1928); *Gott mit uns* (aka *La Lumière dans le Tombeau; The Light Inside the Tomb*; 1929); *La Drogue* (*Drugs*; 1930); **Bertrand, P.** *see* **Lecalire; Bérys, José**

de *Un Cri dans la Nuit* (*A Shout in the Night*; 1935); *Les Ondes Tragiques* (*Tragic Waves*; 1935); *L'Étrangleur Invisible* (*The Invisible Strangler*; 1937); *L'Égorgement de Mme de Praslin* (*The Murder of Mrs de Praslin*; 1939); **Binet, Alfred** *see* **Lorde, André de; Binet-Valmer (q.v.);** *Le Désir* (*The Desire*; 1904); **Boileau-Narcejac (q.v.);** *Meurtre au Ralenti* (*Murder in Slow-Motion*; 1956); **Boissier, Raymond** *Le Cargo de l'Épouvante* (*Cargo of Terror*; 1939; **Bonis-Charancle, Marc** *Les Loups* (*The Wolves*; 1899); *La Maison Hantée* (*The Haunted House*; 1902); **Bourgeois, Eugène** *Le Pendu* (*The Hanged Man*; 1900); **Breton, Gabriel** *L'Appel du Sang* (*The Call of Blood*; 1947; **Cabridens, Max-Henri** *La Fin du Monde* (*The End of the World*; based on a story by Jacques Natanson; 1958); **Caplain-Dol, Robert** *L'Énigme de Deux Nuits* (*The Mystery of Two Nights*; 1936); **Carrière, Paul** *see* **Laumann, E.M.; Chaine, Pierre (q.v.);** *Les Damnés* (*The Damned*; 1923); Also see **Lorde, André de; Champsoin, M.C. de** *Prisonniers des Hommes Bleus* (*Prisoners of the Blue Men*; 1916); **Chancerel, Léon** *Amis de Prison* (*Jail Friends*; with Léon **Guillot de Saix**; based on the story "Claude Gueux" by Victor **Hugo**; 1935); **Chantel, Lucien** *Qui m'a tué?* (*Who Killed Me?*; 1932); *Hystérie* (*Hysteria*; 1932); **Charles, Éliane** *Pas d'Orchidées pour Miss Blandish* (*No Orchids for Miss Blandish*; with Marcel **Duhamel**; based on a story by James Hadley Chase; 1950); **Clermont, Camille** *see* **Martial, Régine; Cloquemin, Paul** *see* **Autier, Paul; Coquiot, Gustave (q.v.)** *see* **Lorrain, Jean; Couty, Jean-Pierre** *L'Assassin* (*The Assassin*; 1956); **Cusy, Pierre** *see* **Germinet, Gabriel; Dallix, Géo** *La Maison dans la Brume* (*The House in the Mist*; with René **Jeanne**; 1916); **Dann, Maurice** *Casque à Pointe* (*Pointy Helmet*; 1932); **Dard, Frédéric (q.v.);** *Du Plomb pour ces Demoiselles* (*Lead for the Ladies*; 1953); *La Garce et l'Ange* (*The Bitch and the Angel*; 1953); *Les Salauds vont en Enfer* (*Bastards Go to Hell*; 1954); *Dr. Jekyll et Mr. Hyde* (based on a story by R.-L. Stevenson; 1954); *La Chair de l'Orchidée* (*The Orchid's Flesh*; with Marcel **Duhamel**; based on a story by James Hadley Chase; 1955); *Les Assassins de Montchat* (*The Montchat Murderers*; based on a story by Paul Gordeaux; 1955); **Darien, G.** *L'Ami de l'Ordre* (*Friend of Order*; 1898); **Day, Pierre** *see* **Sartène, Jean; Dekobra, Maurice (q.v.);** *Le Bateau des Mille Caresses* (*The Boat of a Thousand Caresses*; 1946); *Le Carnaval des Spectres* (*The Carnival of Spectres*; 1947); **Del Vidre, Pierre** *La Mort qui Rode* (*The Prowling Death*; based on a story by Walsworth Camp; 1923, *L'Inconnu* (*The Unknown*; based on a story by Agatha Christie; 1935); **Denouviac, Edmond** *Le Coup du 8 Mai* (*The Event of 8 May*; based on a story by Albert Touchard; 1934); **Desachy, Paul** *see* **Esquier, Charles; Descaves, Lucien (q.v.)** *Atelier d'Aveugles* (*Workshop of the Blind*; 1911); **Dieudonné,**

Albert (q.v.) *see* **Aragny, Jean**; **Docquois, Georges** *Après l'Opéra* (*After the Opera*; 1906); **Dornac, Charles** *Et de Père Inconnu* (*Of Unknown Father*; 1938); **Dreyfus, Roland** *La Cellule 13* (*Cell 13*)*;* 1926); *Le Rendez-Vous du 4* (*Meeting on the 4th*; 1928); *Pigall's—Chambre No. 3* (*Pigall's—Room No. 3*)*;* 1932); *L'Auberge Rouge* (*The Red Inn*; 1934); **Duhamel, Marcel** *see* **Charles, Éliane**; **Dard, Frédéric**; **Durieux, Raymond** *La Nuit de la Saint-Jean* (*The Night of St. John*; 1934); **Duthuit, Florent (q.v.)** *see* **Laumann, E.M.**; **Duvernois, Henri (q.v.)**; *La Dame de Bronze et le Monsieur de Cristal* (*The Brass Woman and the Crystal Man*; 1921); *La Maison des Confidences* (*The House of Confidences*; 1933); **Esquier, Charles** *Nocturne Basque* (with Paul **Desachy**; 1923); **Estoc, Pol d'** *see* **Hellem, Charles**; **Farragut, Jean** *Un Visage dans la Nuit* (*A Face in the Night*; 1942); **Fauchois, René** *Cauchemar* (*Nightmare*; 1943); **Finot, Louis-Jean** *Du Sang dans les Ténèbres* (*Blood in the Darkness*; 1939); *Les Bourreaux* (*The Executioners*; 1940); *Une Garce* (*A Bitch*; 1944); *La Morte* (*The Dead Woman*; 1947); *Règlement de Comptes* (*Settling Accounts*; 1948); **Foleÿ, Charles (q.v.)**; *Le Vieux de la Rouquine* (*The Old Man of the Rouquine*; 1904); *Les Nuits du Bagne* (*The Nights of the Penitentiary*; 1928); Also see **Lorde, André de**; **Francheville, Robert (q.v.)**; *Le Chemin de Ronde* (*The Night Watch*; 1902); *La Porte Close* (*The Closed Door*; 1910); *Le Beau Régiment* (*Pretty Squad*; 1912); *Le Cyclope* (*The Cyclops*; 1916); **Fréjaville, Gustave** *Une Nuit à Londres* (*A Night in London*; based on a story by Charles Dickens; 1922); **Garin, Charles** *Le Délégué de la 3ème Section* (*The Delegate from Section 3*)*;* 1909); *Hioung-Pe-Ling, ou l'Alouette Sanglante* (*The Bloody Nightingale*; 1911); **Gehri, Alfred** *La Femme au Masque* (*The Masked Woman*; 1935); **Germain, José** *La Mort qui Passe, ou Dans l'Ombre* (*Death Going By, or in the Shadow*; 1923); **Germinet, Gabriel** *Great-Guignol* (1923); *Marémoto* (with Pierre **Cusy**; 1924); *Note:* Radio plays (dir: Georges Godebert) written for broadcast by the BBC; **Ghelderode, Michel de (q.v.)**; *La Farce des Ténèbres* (*The Farce of Darkness*; 1952); **Ghilain, Eddy** *L'Espionne* (*The Spying Woman*; 1957); *La Loterie de la Mort ou Sept Crimes dans un Fauteuil* (*The Lottery of Death, or Seven Crimes in an Armchair*; with Pierre **Larroque**; 1957); *La Violeuse* (*The Female Rapist*; 1957); *La Torpille Humaine* (*The Human Torpedo*; 1958); *Le Saut de la Mort* (*The Leap of Death*; based on the story "Salto Mortale" by Alfred **Machard**; 1958); *La Rage au Ventre* (*Rage in the Belly*; 1959); *La Mort qui Tue* (*The Killing Death*; 1960); *Les Coupeurs de Têtes* (*The Head Cutters*; 1960); *Le Cercueil Flottant* (*The Floating Coffin*; 1960); *Hara-Kiri* (1960); *La Sorcière* (*The Witch*; 1961); *Les Blousons Sanglants* (*The Bloody Jackets*; 1961); **Gignoux, Régis (q.v.)**; *Lou la Louve* (*Lou the She-Wolf*; 1930); **Gilbert, Edmond** *Le*

Presbytère de l'Épouvante (*The Presbytery of Horror*; 1929); *Dans la Zone Rouge* (*In the Red Zone*; 1934); **Goubely, J.** *Lit 31* (*Bed 31*)*;* 1935); **Goursat, Victor** *Nuit Blanche* (*White Night*; 1916); **Gravier, Johannès (q.v.)**; *Le Chirurgien de Service* (*The Surgeon on Duty*; with A. **Lebert**; 1905); *Le Rouge est Mis* (*Red Is On*; 1906); *La Suicidette* (*Little Suicide*; 1907); *La Fée Déçue* (*The Disappointed Fairy*; 1911); **Grendel, Maurice de** *see* **Le Bret, André**; **Guillot de Saix, Léon** *see* **Chancerel**; **Hansewick, Yorril** *L'Expérience du Dr. Lorde* (*Dr. Lorde's Experiment*; with P. de **Wattyne**; based on a story by **Cyril-Berger**; 1916); *Les Yeux de Warmeloo* (*The Eyes of Warmeloo*; with P. de **Wattyne**; 1917); *Pâques Juives* (*Jewish Easter*; 1923); *Magie Noire* (*Black Magic*; 1923); **Hellem, Charles** *Aveugle!* (*Blind!*; with Pol d'**Estoc**; 1907); *Sabotage* (with William **Valcros** & Pol d'**Estoc**; 1910); *Le Siège de Berlin* (*The Siege of Berlin*; with Pol d'**Estoc**; based on a story by Alphonse **Daudet**; 1913); *La Maison des Ténèbres* (*The House of Darkness*; with Pol d'**Estoc**; 1917); *Une Heure d'Amour* (*An Hour of Love*; with Pol d'**Estoc**; 1920); *Vers l'Au-Delà* (*Towards the Beyond*; with Pol d'**Estoc**; based on the story "Le Secret de l'Échafaud" ("The Secret of the Gallows") by **Villiers de l'Isle-Adam**; 1922); *Léa, Fille de Joie* (*Pleasure Girl*; with Pol d'**Estoc**; 1922); *Le Droit de Mort* (*The Right of Death*; with Pol d'**Estoc**; 1923); *L'Horrible Volupté* (*The Awful Joy*; with Pol d'**Estoc**; 1924); *Le Faiseur de Monstres* (*The Monster Maker*; with Pol d'**Estoc** and Max **Maurey**; 1929); *La Caresse qui Tue* (*The Killing Caress*; with Pol d'**Estoc**; 1938); *Nuits Corses* (*Corsican Nights*; with Pol d'**Estoc**; 1951); **Hély, Marc** *La Monstrueuse Étreinte* (*The Monstrous Hug*; 1936); *Les Cadavres Vivants* (*The Living Cadavers*; 1937); *Le Sang de la Bête* (*The Blood of the Beast*; 1937); **Héros, Eugène** *La Veuve* (*The Widow*; with Léon **Abric**; 1906); *Note:* Famous guillotine play; **Hesse, Jean (q.v.)**; *La Goule* (*The Ghoul*; 1933); **Ibels, André (q.v.)**; *Il Neige* (*It Is Snowing*; 1922); **Jean, Albert (q.v)**; *Les Morts Étranges d'Albury* (*The Strange Deaths of Albury*; 1914); *Le Poison Noir* (*The Black Poison*; with Jean **Bernac**; based on a story by Edgar Allan Poe; 1917); **Jeanne, René (q.v.)** *see* **Dallix, Géo**; **Laumann, E.M.**; **Jeanniot, Pierre** *La Fugue de Mme Caramon* (*Mrs. Caramon's Escape*; 1917); **Joseph-Renaud, Jean (q.v.)**; *La Visionnaire* (*The Visionary*; 1936); *Le Vampire* (*The Vampire*; 1952); **Joullot, E.** *L'Expérience du Major Dik* (*Major Dik's Experiment*; with Marguerite **Perney**; 1934); **Jouvin, Jack** *Dans le Bled Marocain* (*In the Moroccan Bled*; 1925); *Le Coup de Gong* (*The Strike of the Gong*; 1931); *La Martin Lévesque* (based on a story by Guy de **Maupassant**; 1932); *Sexualité* (*Sexuality*; based on a story by Max Dorian; 1932); *Incognito* (1932); *Une Passe* (*A Lay*; with André-Charles **Mercier**; 1933); *L'Étrangleur* (*The*

Strangler; based on a story by Pierre Nezelov; 1933); *L'Auto 6 827-S.4* (1934); *L'Accident du Studio 16* (*The Accident of Studio 16); 1934); Incognito Tragique* (*Tragic Incognito*; 1936); **Jubin, George** *see* **Mouëzy-Éon, André; Juvenet, Fernand** *Vers le Pôle* (*Towards the Pole*; 1922); **Karquel, André** *Le Bâtard de Vauru* (*The Bastard of Vauru*; 1937); **Kenis, Paul** *Le Chemin du Songe* (*The Path of Dreams*; based on a story by Jean **Ray**; 1914); **Lailler, Jean** *Le Croissant Noir* (*The Black Crescent*; 1913); **Larroque, Pierre** *Le Crime de La Toussaint* (*The Crime of All Saints' Day*; 1958); Also see **Ghilain, Eddy; Lascaris, Théodore** *see* **Lorde, André de; Laumann, E.M. (q.v.);** *En Plongée* (*Diving*; with Paul **Olivier**; 1907); *Nuit d'Illyrie* (*Illyrian Nights*; with Paul **Olivier**; 1909); *Dans les Soutes* (*Inside the Cargo Hold*; 1910); *La Marque de la Bête* (*The Mark of the Beast*; based on a story by Rudyard Kipling; 1916); Catherine Goulden (1917); *La Chute de la Maison Usher* (*The Fall of the House of Usher*; based on a story by Edgar Allan Poe; 1918); *Le Diagnostic* (with Paul **Carrière**; 1921); *L'Ombre d'une Peur* (*The Shadow of a Fear*; with Florent **Duthuit**; 1922); *L'Île du Dr. Moreau* (*The Island of Dr. Moreau*; with Henri **Bauche**; based on a story by H.G. Wells; 1922); *Le Rire de Rosalba* (*Rosalba's Laughter*; with René **Jeanne**; 1948); **Lebert, A.** *see* **Gravier, Johannès; Le Bret, André** *La Maison du Fossoyeur* (*The Gravedigger's House*; with Maurice de **Grendel**; 1948); **Lecalire** *In Extremis* (with P. **Bertrand**; 1916); **Legrand, Henri (q.v.);** *L'Homme qui a Tué la Douleur* (*The Man Who Killed Pain*; 1918); **Lenormand, Henri-René (q.v.);** *La Folie Blanche* (*White Madness*; 1905); *La Grande Mort* (*The Big Death*; with Jean d'**Aguzan**; 1909); *L'Esprit Souterrain* (*The Underground Spirit*; based on a story by Fedor Dostoievski; 1912); *Terres Chaudes* (*Warm Lands*; 1913); **Leroux, Gaston (q.v.);** *L'Homme qui a Vu le Diable* (*The Man Who Saw the Devil*; 1911); **Lesneveu, Henri** *Le Document 528-V* (1916); **Level, Maurice (q.v.);** *Le Boulet* (*The Ball*; with Jacques **Mounier**; 1906); *Sous la Lumière Rouge* (*Under the Red Light*; with Étienne **Rey**; 1912); *Le Baiser dans la Nuit* (*A Kiss in the Night*; 1912); *S.O.S.* (with Charles **Muller**; 1913); *Taiaut!* (1917); *Le Crime* (1918); *Le Sorcier* (*The Wizard*; 1920); *L 'Assassin* (with Charles **Muller**; 1921); *La Malle Sanglante* (*The Bloody Chest*; 1931); **Lévy-Oulmann, André** *see* **Bastia, Jean; Lignereux, G.** *see* **Scheffer, R.; Limat, Maurice (q.v.);** *Les Yeux de l'Autre* (*The Eyes of the Other*; 1948); **Lindauer, Madeleine** *Dix Ans et Une Seconde* (*Ten Years and One Second*; based on a story by Marcellus Schiffer; 1930); **Lorde, André de (q.v.);** *Le Post-Scriptum* (comedy; 1900); *La Dormeuse* (*The Sleeping Woman*; 1901); *La Vieille* (*The Old Woman*; based on a story by Guy de **Maupassant**; 1902); *Héritiers* (*Heirs*; based on a story by Guy de **Maupassant**; 1902); *Le Système du Docteur Goudron*

et du Professeur Plume (*The System of Dr. Tarr and Prof. Fether*; based on a story by Edgar Allan Poe; 1903); *La Dernière Torture* (*The Last Torture*; with Eugène **Morel**; 1904); *L'Obsession ou Les Deux Forces* (*The Obssession, or the Two Forces*; with Alfred **Binet** & Max **Maurey**; 1905); *Baraterie* (based on a story by Masson-Forestier; 1906); *Au Rat Mort—Cabinet 6* (*The Dead Rat—Cabinet 6); with Pierre **Chaine**; 1907); *La Petite Fille* (*The Little Girl*; with Pierre **Chaine**; 1907); *Une Leçon à la Salpêtrière* (*A Lesson at the Salpetriere*; aka: *Un Drame à la...*; *A Tragedy At...*; 1908); *Un Concert chez les Fous* (*A Concert Among Madmen*; with Charles **Foleÿ**; 1909); *L'Horrible Expérience* (*The Awful Experiment*; with Alfred **Binet**; 1909); *Figures de Cire* (*Waxworks*; with Georges **Montignac**; 1910); *L'Homme Mystérieux* (*The Mysterious Man*; with Alfred **Binet**; 1910); *L'Obsédé* (*The Man Obssessed*; with Théodore **Lascaris**; 1912); *Madame Blanchard* (comedy; 1913); *Le Mystère de la Maison Noire* (*The Mystery of the Black House*; with Henri **Bauche**; 1915); *Le Château de la Mort Lente* (*The Castle of Slow Death*; with Henri **Bauche**; 1916); *La Grande Épouvante* (*The Great Fear*; with Henri **Bauche**; 1916); *Le Laboratoire des Hallucinations* (*The Laboratory of Hallucinations*; 1916); *Celles qu'on regrette* (*The Ones We Regret*; comedy; 1919); *Les Pervertis* (*The Perverted*; with Pierre **Chaine**; 1920); *Au Petit Jour* (*At Dawn*; with Jean **Bernac**; 1921); *L'Homme de la Nuit* (*The Night Man*; with Léo **Marchès**; 1921); *Au Téléphone* (*On the Phone*; with Charles **Foleÿ**; created in 1901, rev. 1922); *Le Jardin des Supplices* (*Torture Garden*; with Pierre **Chaine**; based on a story by Octave **Mirbeau**; 1922); *L'Expert* (comedy; 1922); *Sur la Dalle* (*On the Slab*; with Georges **Montignac**; 1923); *L'Étreinte* (*The Hug*; with Pierre **Chaine**; 1925); *Un Crime dans une Maison de Fous, ou Les Infernales* (*A Crime at a Lunatic Asylum, or the Infernal Ones*; with André **Binet**; 1925); *Une Femme dans le Coeur* (*A Woman in My Heart*; comedy; 1925); *Le Cabinet du Docteur Caligari* (*The Cabinet of Dr. Caligari*; with Henri **Bauche**; based on a story by Carl Mayer et Hans Janowitz; 1925); *L'Étrangleuse* (*The Strangler Woman*; 1926); *Les Nuits Rouges de la Tcheka* (*The Red Nights of the Tcheka*; with Henri **Bauche**; 1926); *La Chambre Ardente* (The Fiery Room; with Henri **Bauche**; 1928); *L'Horrible Passion* (*The Awful Passion*; with Henri **Bauche**; 1934); *Jack L'Éventreur* (*Jack the Ripper*; with Pierre **Chaine**; 1934); *Magie Noire* (*Black Magic*; with Henri **Bauche**; 1935); *Le Crime de la Rue Morgue* (*The Murder of the Rue Morgue*; with Eugène **Morel**; based on a story by Edgar Allan Poe; 1936); *L'Horrible Torture* (*The Awful Torture*; 1937); *Marchand de Cadavres* (*Corpse Peddler*; with Henri **Bauche**; 1940); **Lorrain, Jean (q.v.);** *Deux Heures du Matin Quartier Marboeuf* (*Two A.M. In the Marboeuf Neighborhood*; with Gustave **Coquiot**;

1903); *Hotel de l'Ouest... Chambre 22* (*Western Hotel, Room 22);* with Gustave **Coquiot**; 1904); **Machard, Alfred (q.v.);** *Deux Filles de Brest* (*Two Girls from Brest*; 1947); *L'Orgie dans le Phare* (*The Orgy at the Lighthouse*; 1956); **Manchez, Marcel** *Le Retour* (*The Return*; based on a story by Guy de **Maupassant**; 1902); **Manoussi, Jean** *see* **Nancey, Marcel**; **Marchand, Léopold** *L'Amulette Rouge* (*The Red Amulet*; 1936); Also see **Savoir, Alfred**; **Marchès, Léo** *Les Trois Messieurs du Havre* (*The Three Men from Le Havre*; with Clément **Vautel**; 1906); *L'Attentat* (*The Terrorist Act*; with Gaston-Charles **Richard**; 1909); *La Cellule Blanche* (*The White Cell*; with Gaston-Charles **Richard**; 1914); Also see **Lorde, André de**; **Martial, Régine** *À Saint-Lazare!* (with Camille **Clermont**; 1900; **Maurette, Marcelle (q.v.);** *Celle qui Revient* (*She Who Came Back*; 1934); *La Tour d'Amour* (*The Tower of Love*; based on a story by Mme. Rachilde; 1938); *L'Étreinte Sanglante* (*The Bloody Hug*; 1944); **Maurevert, Georges (q.v.);** *Le Coeur Révélateur* (*The Tell-Tale Heart*; based on a story by Edgar Allan Poe; 1900); **Maurey, Max** *L'Atroce Volupté* (*The Horrible Joy*; with Georges **Neveux**; 1919); *La Fosse aux Filles* (*The Girls' Pit*; based on a story by Alexandre Kouprine; 1926); *Le Navire Aveugle* (*The Blind Ship*; based on a story by Jean Barreyre; 1927); *Le Faiseur de Monstres* (*The Monster Maker*; with Charles **Hellem** and Pol d'**Estoc**; 1929); Also see **Lorde, André de**; **Mauris, Jules** *La Vipère* (*The Viper*; 1921); *Un Soir de Bachot* (*An Evening Before the Baccalaureat Examination*; 1941; **Mauvert, G.** *see* **Milliet, Paul**; **Mercier, André-Charles** *see* **Jouvin, Jack**; **Méré, Charles** *Les Trois Masques* (*The Three Masks*; 1908); *Une Nuit au Bouge* (*A Night at the Brothel*; 1919); *Le Marquis de Sade* (1921); *L'Homme Nu* (*The Naked Man*; 1928); *Les Pantins du Vice* (*The Puppets of Vice*; 1929); *Les Nuits d'un Damné* (*The Nights of the Damned*; 1941); **Métayé, Jean** *Le Crime de Mme. Vallier* (*Mrs. Vallier's Crime*; 1946); **Méténier, Oscar (q.v.);** *Mademoiselle Fifi* (based on a story by Guy de **Maupassant**; 1896); *Lui!* (*Him!*; 1897); *En Famille* (*In the Family*; 1898); *La Revanche de Dupont l'Anguille* (*The Revenge of Dupont-The-Eel*; 1898); *Son Poteau!* (*His Pal!*; comedy; with Raoul **Ralph**; 1901); *Note:* In *Lui!* a prostitute realizes that her client (a butcher!) is a serial killer; **Mille, Pierre (q.v.);** *L'Angoisse* (*The Terror*; with Ceylia de **Vylars**; 1908); **Milliet, Paul** *La Découverte du Docteur Malocry* (*Dr. Malocry's Discovery*; with G. **Mauvert**; 1919); **Mitchell, G.** *L'Affaire Moncel* (*The Moncel Affair*; 1901); **Monjardin, Alin (q.v.)** *see* **Bernac, Jean**; **Bernard, Octave**; **Montenis, André** *see* **Achaume, Auguste**; **Montignac, Georges (q.v.)** *see* **Lorde, André de**; **Montrel, Pierre** *L'Invalidation* (*Invalidity*; 1908); **Morel, Eugène (q.v.);** *Le Baiser Mortel* (*The Deadly Kiss*; 1917); Also see **Lorde, André de**;

Mouëzy-Éon, André *Les Nuits du Hampton-Club* (*The Nights of the Hampton Club*; based on a story by R.L. Stevenson; 1908); *Dichotomie* (*Dichotomy*; with Georges **Jubin**; 1911); **Mounier, Jacques** *see* **Level, Maurice**; **Muller, Charles** *see* **Level, Maurice**; **Nadaud, Marcel (q.v.)** *see* **Alévy**; **Nancey, Marcel** *La Ventouse* (*The Blood-Sucker*; with Jean **Manoussi**; 1916); *Note:* Comedic vampire; **Neilson, Francis** *see* **Aragny, Jean**; **Neveux, Georges** *see* **Maurey, Max**; **Nunes, Robert** *La Main de Singe* (*The Monkey's Paw*; based on a story by J. Parker et W. Jacobs; 1921); **Olaf (Babinski, Joseph)** *see* **Palau, Pierre**; **Olivier, Paul** *see* **Laumann, E.M.**; **Orval, Claude (q.v.)**; *La Nuit du 12 au 13* (*The Night of the 12th to the 13th*; 1928); *La Machine Rouge* (*The Red Machine*; 1931); *La Disparue* (*The Woman Who Disappeared*; 1931); *Outre-Tombe* (*Beyond the Grave*; 1932); *Le Masque de la Mort* (*The Mask of Death*; 1941); *Couleur de Sang* (*Color of Blood*; 1941); *Le Souffle de l'Au-Delà* (*The Blow from Beyond*; 1942); *Les Suppliciés* (*The Tortured*; 1943); *Épouvante* (*Horror*; 1944); **Palau, Pierre (q.v.)** *Les Détraquées* (*The Twisted Ones*; with **Olaf**; 1921); *Solitude* (*Loneliness*; 1922); *La Peur* (*The Fear*; 1922); *Les Avortées* (*The Aborted Ones*; 1922); *L'Icone qui s'éteint* (*The Icon Which Passed Away;* based on the story "La Steppe Rouge" ("The Red Steppe") by Joseph Kessel; 1929); *Ombres Rouges* (*Red Shadows*; 1930); *L'Homme dans l'Ombre* (*The Man in the Shadow*; with Maurice **Leblanc**; 1935); **Perney, Marguerite** *see* **Joullot, E.**; **Pérye, André (q.v.)** *Hixe Légionnaire* (*Hixe the Legionary*; 1930); **Poidloué, Charles** *see* **Antoine, André-Paul**; **Quillarbet** *see* **Thalasso**; **Ralph, Raoul (q.v.)** *see* **Méténier, Oscar**; **Randal, M.** *L'Étreinte du Mort* (*Deadman's Hug*; 1946); **Ransan, André (q.v.)** *Les Jeux du Mystère et de la Mort* (*The Games of Mystery and Death*; 1947); **Rehm, Pierre-Louis (q.v.)** *G.Q.G. d'Amour* (*HQ of Love*; 1919); *L'Égorgée* (*The Disemboweled Woman*; 1921); *La Maison des Morts Vivants* (*The House of the Living Dead*; based on a story by Claude **Farrère**; 1922); **Renard, Maurice (q.v.)** *L'Amant de la Morte* (*The Dead Woman's Lover*; based on his story "Le Rendez-Vous"; 1925); **Renaud, Jean-Joseph** *see* **Joseph-Renaud, Jean**; **Renay, M.** *Parodie à la Mort* (*Death Parody*; based on a story by Peter **Randa**; 1962); *Les Yeux sans Visage* (*The Eyes Without a Face*; based on a story by Jean **Redon**; 1962); **Rey, Étienne** *see* **Level, Maurice**; **Richard, Gaston-Charles (q.v.)** *Dans la Pouchkinskaia* (*In the Pouchkinskaia*; 1913); Also see **Marchès, Léo**; **Rieu, Marcel** *La Tête* (*The Head*; 1922); **Roger (Prof.);** *L'Enquête* (*The Investigation*; 1932); **Roland, Claude** *L'Aiguilleur* (*The Dispatcher*; 1899); **Rousseau, René** *L'Atroce Désir* (*The Awful Desire*; 1937); **Salomon, Fernand** *L'Ermite du Cap Nord* (*The Hermit of Cape North*; 1948); **Sartène, Jean** *Nitchevo* (1905); *L'Autre* (*The Other*;

1917); *Hara-Kiri* (with Pierre **Day**; 1919); *Le Rapide No.13* (*Express Train No.13*); 1921); *La Griffe* (*The Claw*; 1930); **Savoir, Alfred (Posznanski, Alfred)**; *Devant la Mort* (*Before Death*; with Léopold **Marchand**; 1920); *La Nurse* (1935); **Scheffer, R.** *La Petite Maison d'Auteuil* (*The Little House in Auteuil*; with G. **Lignereux**; 1907); **Solar, Fabien** *Sur la Lande* (*On the Moor*; 1925); **Sonniès, Paul (Peyssonié, Paul; q.v.)** *Lulu-Jo* (1904); *Note:* Comedy featuring a carnival freak; **Talmours, André** *see* **Valona, Louis; Thalasso, Adolphe (q.v.)** *Pendant l'Orage* (*During the Storm*; with **Quillarbet**; 1903); **Thierry, Augustin** *Le Puits No.4* (*Pit No.4*); with Eugène **Berteaux**; 1908); **Tiercelin, Louis** *Le Sacrement de Judas* (*The Sacrament of Judas*; 1898); **Trébal** *see* **Viterbo, Max; Valcros, William** *see* **Hellem, Charles; Valona , Louis** *L 'Accident* (*The Accident*; with André **Talmours**; 1902); **Vaucaire, Maurice (q.v.)** *Le Cas de Mme. Luneau* (*The Case of Mrs. Luneau*; based on a story by Guy de **Maupassant**; 1917); **Vautel, Clément (q.v.)** *see* **Marchès, Léo; Verneuil, Louis** *see* **Armont, Paul; Vernières, André** *Le Thanatographe* (1913); **Viterbo, Max** *L'Embraseuse* (*The Fire Woman*; with **Trébla**; 1922); **Vois, Ernest** *Elle!* (*She!*; 1899); **Vylars, Cilia de** *see* **Mille, Pierre; Wattyne, P. de** *see* **Hansewick, Yorril; Wisner, René** *Le Chien qui Hurle* (*The Howling Dog*; 1923); **Wissant, Georges de** *Atavisme* (*Heredity*; 1916); **Zuylen de Nyevelt, Hélène baronne de (née de Rotschild; 1863-1947)** *La Mascarade Interrompue* (*The Interrupted Masquerade*; based on the story "*Masque of the Red Death*" by Edgar Allan Poe; 1905)

Grandjean, Georges (?-); *Antinéa, La Nouvelle Atlantide* (*Antinea, the New Atlantis*; Roman Nouveau, 1922); *Les Loups de la Grand'Montagne* (*The Wolves of Big Mountain*; Ollendorff, 1925); *La Kahéna, par l'Or, par le Fer, par le Sang* (*Kahena, By Gold, By Steel, By Blood*; Monde Moderne, 1926); *Le Secret des Temples sans Portes* (*The Secret of the Temples Without Doors*; Fleurus, 1954); *La Guerre des Éléphants* (*War of the Elephants*; Fleurus, 1956); *Note:* See Chapter VII.

Grandville, Isidore (Gérard, Jean-Ignace Isidore; 1803-1847); *Un Autre Monde* (*Another World*; Fournier, 1844); *Note:* See Chapter V. Illustrated by Taxile Delord, another pseudonym of the author.

Grangier, René (?-); *Les Étranges Inventions du Prof. Atomicus* (*The Strange Inventions of Prof. Atomicus*; Scorpion, 1957); *Note:* Swiss writer.

Granier de Cassagnac, Jean *see* **Saint-Granier**

Graux, Lucien (Dr.; ?-); *Sous le Signe d'Horus* (*Under the Sign of Horus*; J. Rousset, 1905); *Le Mouton Rouge* (*The Red Sheep*; Ed. Fr. Illustrée, 1918); *Reincarné!* (*Reincarnated!*; Crès, 1920); *Hanté!* (*Haunted!*; Crès, 1921);

Initié! (*Initiated!*; Crès, 1922); *Saturnin le Saturnien* (*Saturnin the Saturnian*; Crès, 1924); *Le Docteur Illuminé* (*The Illuminated Doctor*; Fayard, 1927); *El Mansour le Doré, Sultan de Marrakech* (*El Mansour the Golden, Sultan of Marrakesh*; Fayard, 1928); *Étripe-Loup* (*Wolf Disemboweler*; Fayard, 1929); *Et Ce Fut La Nuit Blanche* (*And It Was a White Night*; P. Dupont/Lucien Graux, 1938)

Grave, Charles-Joseph de (?-?); *République des Champs-Elysées ou Monde Ancien* (*Republic of the Elysean Fields, or the Ancient World*; 3 vols.; P. Goesin-Verhaeghe, 1806); *Note:* Belgian writer. See Chapter V.

Grave, Jean (1854-1939); *Les Aventures de Nono* (*The Adventures of Nono*; Stock, 1901); *Malfaiteurs!* (*Evil-Doers!*; Stock, 1903); *Le Coin des Enfants* (*Children's Corner*; Temps Nouveaux, 1905-1907); *Terre Libre* (*Free Earth*; Temps Nouveaux, 1908); *Note:* See Chapter V.

Gravel, François (1951-); *La Note de Passage* (*Note of Passage*; Boréal, 1985); *Corneilles* (*Crows*; Boréal, 1989); *Zamboni* (Boréal, 1990); *Le Cercueil de Klonk* (*Klonk's Coffin*; Q/A, 1995); *Le Cauchemar de Klonk* (*Klonk's Nightmare*; Q/A, 1997); *Note:* French-Canadian writer. The characters of *La Note* use mushrooms to travel to a dimension where they meet dead celebrities (Lenin, etc.). The *Klonk* novels are juvenile fantasies.

Gravier, Johannès (1873-?); *La Marchande de Beauté* (*The Beauty Merchant*; Ollendorff, 1914); *Note:* Also see **Grand-Guignol.**

Grée, Alain (?-); *Les Ratons Laveurs dans la Lune* (*The Raccoons on the Moon*; Deux Coqs d'Or, 1967); *Les Ratons Laveurs font le Tour du Monde* (*The Raccoons Around the World*; Deux Coqs d'Or, 1970); *Flap, le Petit Poisson qui voulait d'ecouvrir l'Océan* (*Flap, the Little Fish Who Wanted to Discover the Ocean*; Cast. CBS France, 1972); *César, le Petit Canard qui voulait faire le Tour du Monde* (*Caesar, the Little Duck Who Wanted to Travel Around the World*; Cast. CBS France, 1972); *Note:* Children's books.

Greeff, Étienne de *see* **Hautem, Stéphane**

Grégoire, Claude (1962-); *Le Fantastique Même* (*The Very Fantasy*; anthology; L'Instant Même, 1997); *Note:* French-Canadian writer.

Grégoire, Ménie (?-); *Tournelune* (Flamm., 1983); *Note:* A 19th century woman relives her life in the 20th century.

Gremont, Henri (?-?) *see* **Opéra**

Grendel, Maurice de (?-?) *see* **Grand-Guignol**

Grenier, Armand (1910-); *Erres Boréales* (*Northern Im-*

petus; as Florent Laurin; 1944); *Défricheur de Hammada* (*Hammada Pioneer*; as Guy René de Plour; Laurin, 1953); *Note:* French-Canadian writer. The pseudonym Guy René (Grenier) de Plour reflects both Grenier's name and that of his mother, who was called Plourde. In *Erres*, a new invention enables French-Canadians to colonize the northern territories. In *Défricheur*, Québecois live in domed cities in the Sahara.

Grenier, Christian (1945-); *Jeunesse et Science-Fiction* (*Youth and Science Fiction*; non-Fiction; Magnard, 1972); *Sabotage sur la Planète Rouge* (*Sabotage on the Red Planet*; Hatier JPA 23, 1972); *La Machination* (*The Machination*; GP, 1973); *Aïo, Terre Invisible* (*Aio, Invisible Land*; Hatier JPA 30, 1973); *Cheyenne 6112* (with William **Camus**; GP, 1974); *Une Squaw dans les Étoiles* (*A Squaw Among the Stars*; with William **Camus**; GP, 1975); *Messier 51, ou l'Impossible Retour* (*Messier 51, or the Impossible Return*; Hatier, 1975); *Face au Grand Jeu* (*Facing the Great Game*; La Farandole, 1975); *Le Satellite Venu d'Ailleurs* (*The Satelite from Beyond*; GP, 1975); *Les Fleurs de l'Espace* (*The Space Flowers*; GP, 1976); *Le Soleil va Mourir* (*The Sun Will Die*; GP, 1977); *Les Cascadeurs du Temps* (*The Time Stuntmen*; Magnard, 1977); *Il y a Deux Soleils chez les Tortupatons* (*There Are Two Suns on Turpaton*; Magnard, 1978); *Le Montreur d'Étincelles* (*The Spark Performer*; AdE 8, 1978); *Le Secret des Mangeurs d'Étoiles* (*The Secret of the Star Eaters*; Hatier, 1978); *Le Coeur des Poireaux* (*The Heart of the Leeks*; Amitié, 1978); *Le Moulin de la Colère* (*The Mill of Wrath*; Amitié, 1979); *Le Complot Ordrien* (*The Ordian Plot*; TF 15, 1981); *Un Homme contre la Ville* (*A Man vs. The City*; Gall., 1981); *La Montagne sans Nom* (*The Nameless Mountain*; Gall., 1981); *Dans la Comète et Autres Récits du Cosmos* (*On the Comet and Other Cosmic Tales*; Gall., 1982); *La Lune était Verte et Autres Récits de Fin du Monde* (*The Moon Was Green and Other Tales of the End of the World*; Gall., 1983); *Faiseurs d'Univers* (*Universe Makers*; Gall., 1984); *Les Autos Sauvages* (*The Wild Cars*; Gall., 1985); *L'Habitant des Étoiles* (*The Star Dweller*; Gall., 1985); *Le Coeur en Abîme* (*The Heart in the Abyss*; Hac., 1985); *Futurs Antérieurs* (*Futures Past*; Milan, 1989); *La Bête et dans l'Escalier* (*The Beast Is on the Stairs*; GP, 1989); *Quand la Terre Grondonne* (*When Earth Rumbles*; Maubeuge, 1993); *Virtuel, Attention, Danger* (*Virtual, Beware, Danger*; Milan, 1994); *Le Pianiste Sans Visage* (*The Piano Player Without a Face*; Rageot, 1995); *Aina, Fille des Étoiles* (*Daughter of the Stars*; Nathan, 1995); *Aina et le Secret des Oglonis* (*The Secret of the Oglonis*; Nathan, 1996); *Le Château des Enfants Gris* (*The Castle of the Grey Children*; Nathan, 1996); *La Fille de Troisième B* (*The Girl from Third Grade*; Rageot, 1996); *La Musicienne*

de l'Aube (*The Musician of Dawn*; Rageot, 1996); *Aina et le Pirate de la Comète* (*The Pirate of the Comet*; Nathan, 1997); *L'Ordinateur* (*The Computer*; Rageot, 1997); *Les Lagunes du Temps* (*The Lagoon of Time*; Hac., 1997); *Cyberpark* (Hac., 1997); *Mission en Mémoire Morte* (*Mission in Dead Memory*; Hac., 1997); *Aina Kaha Supermaki* (Nathan, 1997); *Note:* See Chapter IX. Also see **Contes et Légendes**

Gressier, James (?-); *Le Légat Holigon* (*The Legate Holigon*; Ch. Bourgois, 1968)

Grey, S. *see* **Genefort, Laurent**

Gril, Étienne (?-); *Les Chevaliers de l'Incertain* (*The Knights of Uncertainty*; Gall., 1929); *La Machine à Guérir de la Vie* (*The Machine to Cure Life*; as Stéphane Corbière/with J. **Fouquet**; Gall., 1929); *L'Aventure sans Voyage* (*Adventure Without Travel*; L'Épi, 1929); *Le Contrat de Mort* (*The Death Contract*; L'Épi, 1929); *Le Grand-Père sans Enfant* (*The Childless Grand-Father*; L'Épi, 1930); *Béloar* (Nlle. Sté. d'Edition, 1930); *Simples Contes* (*Simple Tales*; M. Sarcou, 1935); *L'Ovipare* (Ed. Romans & Nouvelles, 1942); *Le Cogneur de la Chapelle* (*The Fighter from the Chapel*; SAGE, 1942); *Ulysse chez les Jivaros* (*Ulysses Among the Jivaros*; V. Michon, 1949); *La Chambre Clouée* (*The Nailed Room*; n.d.; *Note:* See Chapter VII.

Grimaître, Héliane *see* **Verlanger, Julia**

Grimaud, Michel (Perriod, Marcelle (1937-) & Fraysse, Jean-Louis (1946-)); *Amaury, Chevalier Cathare* (*Amaury, Cathar Knight*; RL, 1971); *La Ville sans Soleil* (*The City Without Sun*; RL, 1973); *La Terre des Autres* (*Others' Land*; Amitié, 1973); *Le Peuple de la Mer* (*The People of the Sea*; Hatier, 1974); *Des Hommes Traqués* (*Hunted Men*; RL, 1975); *Soleil à Crédit* (*Sun on Credit*; L'Amitié, 1975); *Une Chasse en Été* (*A Summer Hunt*; Rouge et Or, 1976); *Les Esclaves de la Joie* (*Slaves of Joy*; TF 4, 1977); *L'Île sur l'Ocean Nuit* (*The Island on the Night Ocean*; AdE 7, 1978); *Les Vacances de Madame Nuit* (*The Holidays of Mrs. Night*; Amitié, 1978); *Le Grand Voyage d'Alexandre Tolpe* (*Alexander Tolpe's Great Journey*; Amitié, 1979); *Le Temps des Gueux* (*The Time of the Poor*; TF 14, 1980); *Malakansâr* (PdF 296, 1980); *La Dame de Cuir* (*Leather Lady*; PdF 325, 1981); *Le Par-*

adis des Autres (*Others' Paradise*; Amitié, 1981); *Le Jour du Gombo* (*The Day of the Gombo*; La Farandole, 1982); *Le Passe-Monde* (*The Passworld*; La Farandole, 1982); *Le Tyran d'Axilane* (*The Tyrant of Axilane*; Gall., 1982); *Les Contes de la Ficelle* (*Tales from the String*; Amitié, 1982); *L'Arbre d'Or* (*The Gold Tree*; PdF 370, 1983); *Les Pataplafs* (La Farandole, 1985); *L'Enfant de la Mer* (*The Child from the Sea*; Centurion, 1986); *Le Coffre Magique* (*The Magical Chest*; Centurion, 1990); *L'Assassin crève l'Écran* (*The Murderer Steps Through the Screen*; Rageot, 1991); *Le Fantôme des Cassegrain* (*The Ghost of the CassegraIn*; Hac., 1994); *L'Inconnu dans le Frigo* (*The Stranger Inside the Refrigerator*; Flamm., 1997); Series *Rhôor: Rhôor l'Invincible* (*Rhoor the Invincible*; SdPSF 2, 1971); *Rhôor et les Pillards* (*Rhoor and the Looters*; SdPSF 22, 1971); *Note:* See chapters VIII and IX.

Grimbert, Pierre (1971-); *Six Héritiers* (*Six Heirs*; Mnemos 11, 1996); *Le Serment Orphelin* (*The Orphan Pledge*; Mnemos 14, 1996); *L'Ombre des Anciens* (*The Shadow of the Ancients*; Mnemos 20, 1997); *Le Doyen Éternel* (*The Eternal Elder*; Mnemos 22, 1997); *Note:* See Chapter VIII.

Gripari, Pierre (1925-1990); *Pierrot la Lune* (*Pierrot-Of-The-Moon*; TR, 1963); *L'Incroyable Equipee de Phosphore Noloc* (*The Incredible Voyage of Phosphore Noloc*; TR, 1964); *Diable, Dieu et autres Contes* (*Of the Devil, God and Other Tales*; TR, 1965); *Contes de la Rue Broca* (*Tales of Broca Street*; TR, 1967); *La Vie, la Mort et la Resurrection de Socrate-Marie Gripotard* (*Life, Death and Resurrection of Socrate-Marie Gripotard*; TR, 1968); *L'Arrière-Monde* (*The Backworld*; Robert Morel , 1972); *Gueule d'Aminche* (Robert Morel, 1973); *Rêveries d'un Martien en Exil* (*Dreams of a Martian in Exile*; AdH, 1976); *Histoire du Prince Pipo, de Pipo le Cheval et de la Princesse Popi* (*Tale of Prince Pipo, Pipo the Horse and Princess Popi*; Grasset, 1976); *Pedigree du Vampire* (*Pedigree of the Vampire*; AdH, 1977); *Nanasse et Gigantel* (Grasset, 1977); *Vies Parallèles de Roman Branchu* (*Parallel Lives of Roman Branchu*; AdH, 1978); *Le Conte de Paris* (*The Count of Paris*; AdH, 1980); *La Sorcière de la Rue Mouffetard* (*The Witch of Mouffetard St.*; Gall., 1980); *Le Gentil Petit Diable* (*The Kind Little Devil*; Gall., 1980); *Paraboles et Fariboles* (*Parables and Fables*; AdH, 1981); *Moi, Mitounet Joli* (*I, Pretty Mitounet*; AdH, 1982); *Les Contes de la Folie Méricourt* (*Tales of Folie Méricourt Street*;

PIERRE GRIPARI
CONTES CUISTRES

Grasset, 1983); *Patrouille du Conte* (*Fairy Tale Patrol*; AdH, 1983); *Inspecteur Toutou* (*Inspector Doggy*; Grasset, 1984); *Contes Cuistres* (*Rude Tales*; AdH, 1987); *Marelles* (*Hopscotch*; Grasset, 1988); *Contes d'Ailleurs et d'Autre Part* (*Tales of Elsewhere and Other Parts*; Grasset, 1990); *Les Derniers Jours de l'Éternel* (*The Last Days of the Eternal*; AdH, 1990); *Monoméron* (AdH, 1991); *Note:* See Chapter VIII.

Grivel, Guillaume (1735-1810); *L'Île Inconnue, ou Mémoires qui font suite à Ceux du Chevalier des Gastines* (*The Unknown Island, or Memoirs Following Those of the Chevalier des Gastines*; Moutard, 1783; rev. VI, 1787); *Note:* The survivors of a shipwreck discover a Utopia.

Grivel, Louis (?-); *À la Conquête de Venus* (*The Conquest of Venus*; Bonici, Tunis, 1942); *Note:* French-Tunisian writer. See Chapter VII.

Groc, Léon (1882-1956); *Ville Hantée* (*The Haunted City*; RM, 1913; rev. as *La Place Maudite* (*The Accursed Square*, Tallandier, 1942); *L'Autobus Évanoui* (*The Vanished Bus*; RM, 1914); *L'Étrange Alibi* (*The Strange Alibi*; JST, 1917); *La Guerre en Masques* (*War in Masks*; Rouff, 1918); *Perdus dans le Labyrinthe* (*Lost in the Labyrinth*; Rouff, 1918); *La Caverne du Dragon* (*The Dragon's Cave*; Rouff, 1918); *Le Gaz de Démence* (*The Insanity Gas*; S&V, 1921); *Le Disparu de l'Ascenseur* (*The Man Who Disappeared in an Elevator*; AM, 1922); *On a Volé la Tour Eiffel* (*They Stole the Eiffel Tower*; RDA, 1923); *La Maison des Morts Étranges* (*The House of Strange Deaths*; Ferenczi, 1923; rev. as *La Maison des Morts* (*The House of the Dead*, Cosmopolites, 1930); *2000 Ans Sous la Mer* (*2000 Years Under the Sea;* S&V, 1924; rev. as *La Cité des Ténèbres* (*The City of Darkness*, BGA, 1926); *Le Chasseur de Chimères* (*The Hunter of Chimeras*; France-Ed., 1925); *Le Bourreau Fantôme* (*The Phantom Executioner*; Le Masque, 1927); *La Révolte des Pierres* (*The Revolt of the Stones;* Nlle. Revue Critique, 1929; rev. as *Une Invasion de Sélénites* (*An Invasion of the Selenites*, BGA, 1941); *Le Maître de l'Étoile* (*The Master of the Star*; Baudinière, 1933); *Arcana* (Loisirs, 1937); *L'Impossible Rançon* (*The Impossible Ransom*; Fayard, 1937); *L'Homme Qui Fait Chanter Les Astres* (*The Man Who Made the Stars Sing*; Le Masque, 1941); *La Villa du Cauchemar* (*The Nightmarish Villa*; Tallandier, 1941); *L'Assassinée du Téléphone* (*The Woman Murdered on the Telephone*; Tallandier, 1941); *Le Testament du Professeur "Triple G"* (*The Testament of Prof. Triple G*; Tallandier, 1941); *La Fuite du Radium* (*The Escape of Radium*; Office Fr. du Livre, 1944); *Une Nuit* (*One Night*; SEN, 1944); *La Tour du Sorcier* (*The Wizard's Tower*; Rouff, 1944); *La Planète de Cristal* (*The Crystal Planet*; Janicot, 1944); *Le Maître du Soleil* (*The Master of the Sun*; Chantal,

1946); *La Course à la Bombe Atomique* (*The Race for the Atom Bomb*; Rouff, 1947); *L'Émetteur Inconnu* (*The Unknown Transmitter*; with Jacqueline **Zorn**; BGA, 1949); *L'Univers Vagabond* (*The Wandering Universe*; with Jacqueline **Zorn**; Horizons Fantastiques 2, 1950); *SOS à 3200 Mètres d'Altitude* (*SOS 3200 Meters High*; Rouff, 1950); *Note:* See Chapter VII.

Gros, Jules (1829-1891); *Un Volcan dans les Glaces: Aventures d'une Expédition Scientifique au Pôle Nord* (*A Volcano in the Ice: Adventures of a Scientific Expedition at the North Pole*; Dreyfous, 1879); *L'Homme Fossile: Aventures d'une Expédition Scientifique dans les Mers* (*The Fossil Man: Adventures of a Scientific Expedition on the Seas*; Mantoux-Martin Charavay, 1898); *Note:* See Chapter V.

Grosdemange, Pierre *see* **Pelot, Pierre**

Grosjean, Didier (1955-); *Moi, Néfertiti* (*I, Nefertiti*; with Claudine **Roland**; Cast., 1988); *Moi, Barberousse* (*I, Red-Beard*; with Claudine **Roland**; Cast., 1989); *Bonjour, Monsieur Rousseau* (with Claudine **Roland**; Cast., 1989)

Grosmaire, Jean-Louis (1944-); *Un Clown en Hiver* (*A Clown in the Winter*; Vermilion, 1988); *Note:* French-Canadian writer. Near-future tale.

Groussard, Valérie (1948-); *Grodular* (Centurion, 1981); *Caravane Interstellaire* (*Interstellar Caravan*; Ecole des Loisirs, 1984); *Le Tour de Xrom* (*The Tower of Xrom*; Ecole des Loisirs, 1986); *Drôle de Passagère pour Christophe Colomb* (*A Funny Passenger for Christopher Columbus*; Flamm., 1994); *Note:* Juvenile SF. See Chapter IX.

Grousset, Alain (1956-); *Les Mangeurs de Châtaignes* (*The Chestnut Eaters*; Trihan, 1983); *La Citadelle du Vertige* (*The Citadel of Vertigo*; Hac., 1990); *Les Chasse-Marée* (*The Tide Hunters*; Hac., 1994); *Les Oubliés de Vulcain* (*Forgotten on Vulcan*; with Danielle **Martinigol**; LdP Jeunesse 541, 1995); *Kerri et Mégane et les Mange-Forêts (The Forest Eaters*; as Aldany, Kim/with Danielle **Martinigol**; Nathan, 1994); *Kerri et Mégane et les Transmiroirs* (*The Transmirrors*; as Aldany, Kim/with Danielle **Martinigol**; Nathan, 1996); *L'Enfant-Mémoire* (*The Memory Child*; as Aldany, Kim/with Danielle **Martinigol**; Hac., 1996); *Les Mondes Décalés* (*The Out-Of-Line Worlds*; with Danielle **Martinigol**; Flamm., 1997); *Kerri et Mégane—Brocantic Trafic* (as Aldany, Kim/with Danielle **Martinigol**; Nathan, 1997); *Note:* See Chapter IX.

Grousset, Paschal *see* **Laurie, André**

Gsell, Paul (1870-1947); *Nouvelles Scientifiques* (*Scientific News*; Libr. Imprim. Réunis, 1896); *La Science en Histoires* (*Science Through Stories*; L-Henry May, 1897);

Histoires Instructives (*Instructional Tales*; L-Henry May, 1898); *Le Carnet Subline* (*The Sublime Notebook*; Larousse, 1916); *L'Homme qui Lit dans les Âmes* (*The Man Who Read Souls*; Grasset, 1928); *TSF avec les Étoiles* (*Radio with the Stars*; Nlle. Sté. Éd., 1930); *Les Clefs d'Or: Histoire Merveilleuse pour les Gosses de Six à Cent Ans* (*The Gold Keys: Wondrous Tale for Children from Age 6 to 100);* Revue Mondiale, 1931); *Note:* In spite of its title, *Nouvelles* is actually a novel.

G.-Toudouze, Georges *see* **Toudouze, Georges G.**

Guadalcazar (?-); *Le Dernier Combat* (*The Last Battle*; MOC 8, 1979); *Xirlo* (MOC 21, 1980)

Gudule *see* **Duguël, Anne**

Guégan, Gérard (?-); *Technicolor* (Sagittaire, 1975); *Un Silence de Mort* (*A Deathly Silence*; JCL, 1975); *À Feu Vif* (*Burned Alive*; JCL, 1976); *L'Avenir est en Retard* (*The Future Is Late*; AM, 1978); *Oui Mai* (*Yes May*; Sagittaire, 1978); *On Revient Toujours Chez Soi* (*We Always Come Home*; Eibel, 1979); *Le Sang dans la Tête* (*Blood in the Head*; Renaissance, 1980); *Le Requin Vengeur* (*The Avenging Shark*; Slatkine, 1981); *Pour Toujours* (*For Ever*; Grasset, 1984); *La Vie est un Voyage* (*Life Is a Journey*; Bourgois, 1984); *La Terreur, Roman Cruel* (*The Terror, Cruel Novel*; Grasset, 1987); *Le Dernier des Rêveurs* (*Last of the Dreamers*; Flamm., 1990); *Un Cavalier à la Mer* (*Horseman Overboard*; F. Bourin, 1991); *Eurydice ne répond plus* (*Eurydice Does Not Answer*; L'Olivier, 1995); *Les Vivants sont Ceux qui Luttent* (*The Living Are the Ones Fighting*; Cahiers du Futur, 1996)

Gueulette, Thomas-Simon (1683-1766); *Soirées Bretonnes, Nouveaux Contes de Fées* (*Briton Evenings, New Fairy Tales*; 1712); *Les Mille et Un Quarts d'Heures (Contes Tartares)* (*The Thousand and One Quarters of an Hour [Tartar Tales]*; Mazuel, 1715); *Les Comédiens par Hasard* (*Comedians by Chance*; 1718); *Arlequin-Pluton* (*Pluto Harlequin*; 1719); *Les Aventures Merveilleuses du Mandarin Fum Hoam (Contes Chinois)* (*The Wondrous Adventures of Mandarin Fun Hoam [Chinese Tales]*; 1723); *Les Sultanes de Guzarate, ou Le Songe des Hommes Éveillés (Contes Mongols)* (*The Sultanas of Guzarate, or the Dream of Woken Men [Mongol Tales]*; 1732); *Les Mille et Une Heures (Contes Péruviens)* (*The Thousand and One Hours [Peruvian Tales]*; 1733); *Les Mille et Une Soirées (Contes Mogols)* (*The Thousand and One Evenings [Mogol Tales]*; 1749); *Note:* See Chapter III.

Guénot, Jean-Paul (?-); *La Morte Vie* (*The Dead Life*; Belfond, 1989); *La Peau Soleil* (*The Sun Skin*; Paris, 1994)

Guérin, Michelle (1936-); *Les Oranges d'Israël* (*The Oranges of Israel*; CLF, 1972); *Le Ruban de Moebius* (*The*

Moebius Strip; CLF, 1974); *Note:* French-Canadian writer. *Le Ruban* is a collection of fantastic tales.

Guermonprez, Michel (?-); Homo Potens (Scorpion, 1961)

Guéro, Gérard & Anne *see* **Ranne, G. Elton**

Guesviller, Gustave (1865-?); *Oreilles Fendues (Histoires de Sorcellerie; Broken Ears (Tales of Witchcraft)*; Calmann-Lévy, 1891); *En Musique (In Music*; Calmann-Lévy, 1893); *Le Roman de Génevotte (The Novel of Genevotte*; Calmann-Lévy, 1894); *Pauvre Sourire (Poor Smile*; Calmann-Lévy, 1896); *Le Droit Chemin (The Right Path*; Plon, 1900); *Idole (Idol*; Juven, 1910); *La Fille de M. Mahout (Mr. Mahout's Daughter*; Grasset, 1911); *Le Cou Blanc (The White Neck*; RM, 1912); *La Présidente* (Calmann-Lévy, 1914)

Guibert, Marius-Pierre (1902-); *Étranges Retours (Strange Returns*; JCL, 1978); *Note:* See Chapter IX.

Guichard, Marcel (?-); *Feu Paris (Exit Paris*; Scorpion, 1958); *Note:* See Chapter IX.

Guidicelli, Jean-Claude (?-) *see* **Jeury, Michel**

Guieu, Jimmy (1926-); *Le Pionnier de l'Atome (The Pioneer of the Atom*; FNA 5, 1952; rev. VG 84); *Au-delà de l'Infini (Beyond Infinity*; FNA 8, 1952; rev. VG1); *L'Invasion de la Terre (The Invasion of Earth*; FNA 13, 1952; rev. VG3); *Hantise sur le Monde (Fear Over the World*; FNA 18, 1953; rev. VG5); *L'Univers Vivant (The Living Universe*; FNA 22, 1953; rev. VG7); *La Dimension X (Dimension X*; FNA 27, 1953; rev. VG9); *Nous les Martiens (We the Martians*; FNA 31, 1954; rev. VG12); *La Spirale du Temps (The Spiral of Time*; FNA 36, 1954; rev. VG 11); *Le Monde Oublié (The Forgotten World*; FNA 41, 1955; rev. VG 13); *L'Homme de l'Espace (The Man from Space*; FNA 45, 1955; rev. VG 15); *Opération Aphrodite* (FNA 47, 1955; rev. VG 17); *Commandos de l'Espace (Space Commandos*; FNA 51, 1955; rev. VG 19); *L'Agonie du Verre (The Death of Glass*; FNA 54, 1955; rev. VG 21); *Univers Parallèles (Parallel Universes*; FNA 58, 1955; rev. VG 22); *Nos Ancêtres de l'Avenir (Our Ancestors from the Future*; FNA 62, 1956; rev. VG 24); *Les Monstres du Néant (The Monsters from the Void*; FNA 70, 1956; rev. VG 2); *Prisonniers du Passé (Prisoners of the Past*; FNA 72, 1956; rev. VG 26); *Les Êtres de Feu (The Beings of Fire*; FNA 80, 1956; rev. VG 4); *La Mort de la Vie (The Death of Life*; FNA 87, 1957; rev.

VG 34); *Le Règne des Mutants (The Reign of Mutants*; FNA 91, 1957; rev. VG 36); *Créatures des Neiges (Creatures of the Snows*; FNA 95, 1957; rev. VG 56); *Cité Noë No. 2 (Noah City No. 2;* FNA 100, 1957; rev. VG 38); *Le Rayon du Cube (The Cubic Ray*; FNA 103, 1957; rev. VG 77); *Convulsions Solaires (Solar Convulsions*; FNA 110, 1958; rev. VG 6); *Réseau Dinosaure (Dinosaur Network*; FNA 115, 1958; rev.

VG 8; *La Force sans Visage (The Faceless Force*; FNA 118, 1958; rev. VG 57); *Expédition Cosmique (Cosmic Expedition*; FNA 134, 1959; rev. VG 41); *Les Cristaux de Capella (The Crystals of Capella*; FNA140, 1959; rev. VG 42); *Piège dans l'Espace (Trap in Space*; FNA 145, 1959; rev. VG 27); *Chasseurs d'Hommes (Man Hunters*; FNA 149, 1960; rev. VG 10); *Les Sphères de Rapa-Nui (The Spheres of Rapa-Nui*; FNA 156, 1960; rev. VG 78); *L'Ere des Biocybs (The Era of the Biocybs*; FNA 160, 1960; rev. VG 16); *Expérimental X. 35 (Experiment X. 35);* FNA 163, 1960; rev. VG 18); *Traffic Interstellaire (Interstellar Traffic*; as Claude Vauzière; MarJ 167, 1960; rev. as Jimmy Guieu, VG 81); *Planète en Péril (Planet in Danger*; FNA 174, 1961; rev. VG 20); *La Caverne du Futur (The Cavern of the Future*; FNA 181, 1961; rev. VG 79); *La Grande Épouvante (The Great Terror*; FNA 187, 1961; rev. VG 23); *L'Invisible Alliance (The Invisible Alliance*; FNA 191, 1961; rev. VG 25); *Spoutnik VII a disparu (Sputnik VII Has Disappeared*; as Claude Vauzière; MarJ 197, 1961; rev. as Jimmy Gieu, VG 86); *Le Secret des Tshengz (The Secret of the Tshengz*; FNA 199, 1962; rev. VG 29); *Opération Ozma* (FNA 203, 1962; rev. VG 44); *L'Âge Noir de la Terre (The Dark Age of the Earth*; FNA 212, 1962; rev. VG 47); Oniria (FNAG 92, 1962; rev. VG 72); *Échec aux Végans (The Vegans in Check*; as Claude Vauzière; MarJ 235, 1962; rev. as Jimmy Guieu, VG 85); *Mission "T"* (FNA 219, 1963); ep. VG 14); *Les Forbans de l'Espace (The Space Pirates*; FNA 224, 1963; rev. VG 33); *Projet King (Project King*; FNA 231, 1963; rev. VG 80); *Les Destructeurs (The Destroyers*; FNA 237, 1963; rev. VG 32); *Captifs de la Main Rouge (Prisoners of the Red Hand*; as Claude Vauzière; MarJ, 1963, rev. by RCW, VG 94, 1994); *Les Portes de Thulé (The Gates of Thule*; FNA 242, 1964; rev. VG 28); *Le Retour des Dieux (The Return of the Gods*; FNA 337, 1967; rev. VG 48); *Les Sept Sceaux du Cosmos (The Seven Seals of the Cosmos*; FNA 343, 1968; rev. VG 50); *Joklun-N'Ghar la

Maudite (*Joklun-N'Ghar the Accursed*; FNA 352, 1968; rev. VG 35); *La Terreur Invisible* (*The Invisible Terror*; FNA 360, 1968; rev. VG 52); *Refuge Cosmique* (*Cosmic Refuge*; FNA 367, 1968; rev. VG 30); *L'Ordre Vert* (*The Green Order*; FNA 384, 1969; rev. VG 54); *Traquenard sur Kenndor* (*Ambush on Kenndor*; FNA 395, 1969; rev. VG 37); *Demain l'Apocalypse* (*Tomorrow the Apocalypse*; FNA 402, 1969; rev. VG 31); *L'Arche du Temps* (*The Ark of Time*; FNA 407, 1970; rev. VG 82); *Le Triangle de la Mort* (*The Triangle of Death*; FNA 425, 1970; rev. VG 55); *Plan Catapulte* (*Plan Catapult*; FNA 439, 1970; rev. VG 59); *Les Orgues de Satan* (*The Organ of Satan*; FNA 447, 1971; rev. VG 40); *La Voix Qui Venait d'Ailleurs* (*The Voice from Beyond*; FNA 459, 1971; rev. VG 60); *Le Grand Mythe* (*The Great Myth*; FNA 470, 1971; rev. VG 39); *La Charnière du Temps* (*The Hinges of Time*; FNA 480, 1971; rev. VG 61); *Yolanda et les Voluptés Cosmiques* (*Yolanda and the Cosmic Pleasures;* as Dominique Verseau; Python 1, 1971; rev. as *Éros à l'Infini* (*Eros in Infinity*, Redon, 1972); *Yolanda et la Planète aux Supplices* (*Yolanda and the Torture Planet;* as Dominique Verseau; Python 2, 1971; rev. as *Les Esclaves de l'Espace* (*Slaves of Space*, Redon, 1972); *Enjeu Cosmique* (*Cosmic Stakes*; FNA 496, 1972; rev. VG 63); *Les Maîtres de la Galaxie* (*The Masters of the Galaxy*; FNA 504, 1972; rev. VG 43); *Les Rescapés du Néant* (*The Survivors of the Void*; FNA 521, 1972; rev. VG 45); *Torturez les Bourreaux— Yolanda se venge* (*Torture the Executioners—Yolanda's Revenge*; as Dominique Verseau; Python 4, 1972; rev. Redon, 1972); *L'Univers Érotique* (*Erotic Universe*; as Dominique Verseau; Python 5, 1972; rev. Redon, 1972); *La Mission Effacée* (*The Erased Mission*; FNA 547, 1973; rev. VG 64); *Opération Neptune* (FNA 568, 1973; rev. VG 65); *Les Germes du Chaos* (*The Germs of Chaos*; FNA 578, 1973; rev. VG 66); *Les Veilleurs de Poseidon* (*The Watchers of Poseidon*; FNA 602, 1974; rev. VG 67); *L'Exilé de Xantar* (*The Exile from Xantar*; FNA 618, 1974; rev. VG 46); *Le Maître du Temps* (*The Master of Time*; FNA 630, 1974; rev. VG 68); *Manipulations Psi* (*Psi Manipulations*; FNA 647, 1974; rev. VG 69); *Les Pièges de Koondra* (*The Traps of Koondra*; FNA 662, 1975; rev. VG 49); *Les Fugitifs de Zwolna* (*The Fugitives of Zwolna*; FNA 674, 1975; rev. VG 51); *Les Krolls de Vorlna* (*The Krolls of Vorlna*; FNA 688, 1975; rev. VG 70); *Le Bouclier de Boongoha* (*The Shield of Boongoha*; FNA 707, 1975; rev. VG 53); *La Stase Achronique* (*The Achronic Stasis*; FNA 718, 1975; rev. VG 71); *La Colonie Perdue* (*The Lost Colony*; FNA 730, 1976; rev. VG 58); *La Lumière de Thot* (*The Light of Thot*; FNA 779, 1977; rev. VG 73); *Les Légions de Bartzouk* (*The Legions of Bartzouk*; FNA 802, 1977; rev. VG 62); *Les Yeux de l'Epouvante* (*The Eyes of Terror*; FNA 851, 1978; rev. VG 74); *Hieroush, la Planète Promise* (*Hieroush, Promised Planet*; FNA 941, 1979;

rev. VG 76); *La Clé du Mandala* (*The Key of the Mandala*; FNA 982, 1980; rev. VG 75); *Les Fils du Serpent* (*The Sons of the Serpent*; FNA 1273, 1984; rev. VG 83); Series *Les Chevaliers de Lumière* (*The Knights of Light*): *La Force Noire* (*The Black Force*; FNCL 1, 1987; rev. VG 96); *Le Pacte de Kannlor* (*The Pact of Kannlor*; FNCL 2, 1987); *La Terreur Venue du Néant* (*The Terror That Came from the Void*; FNCL 3, 1988; rev. VG 98); *Narkoum: Finances Rouges* (*Narkum: Red Finances*; FNCL 4, 1988; rev. VG 101); *Plan d'Extermination* (*Extermination Plan*; FNCL 5, 1988; rev. VG 104); *Réseau Alpha* (*Alpha Network*; FNCL 6, 1989; rev. VG 107); *L'Héritage de Noé* (*The Inheritance of Noah*; FNCL 7, 1989; rev. VG 109); *Les Sentiers Invisibles* (*The Invisible Paths*; FNCL 8, 1989; rev. VG 112); *L'Empire des Ténèbres* (*The Empire of Darkness*; FNCL 9, 1989; rev. VG 114); *Le Piège du Val Maudit* (*The Trap of the Accursed Valley*; FNCL 10, 1989; rev. VG 116); Series *Jimmy Guieu: Magie Rouge* (*Red Magic*; PR; VG 87, 1992); *Les Rebelles de N'Harangho* (*The Rebels of N'Harangho*; PR; VG 88, 1992); *Le Serpent-Dieu de Joklun-N'Ghar* (*The Serpent God of Joklun-N'Ghar*; RCW; VG 89, 1992); *Le Poison de Thogar'Min* (*The Poison of Thogar'Min*; LG; VG 90, 1993); *Les Maudits d'Hertzvane* (*The Accursed of Hetzvane*; PR/NG; VG 91, 1993); *Les Albinos de Sulifuss* (*The Albinos of Sulifuss*; RCW; VG 92, 1993); *Les Naufragés du Temps* (*The Castaways in Time*; PR/NG; VG 93, 1993); *Échec au Destin* (*Fate in Check*; RCW; VG 95, 1994); *Les Magiciens des Mondes Oubliés* (*The Magicians of the Forgotten Worlds*; RCW; VG 97, 1994); *L'Ombre du Dragon Rouge* (*The Shadow of the Red Dragon*; RCW; VG 99, 1994); *Le Maître de la Main Rouge* (*The Master of the Red Hand*; RCW; VG 100, 1995); *Les Brumes de Joklun-N'Ghar* (*The Mists of Joklun-N'Ghar*; RCW; VG 102, 1995); *Les Voleurs de Dieux* (*The God Stealers*; RCW; VG 103, 1995); *Flammes sur Batoog* (*Flames Over Batoog*; RCW; VG 105, 1995); *Au Coeur de Kenndor* (*In the Heart of Kenndor*; RCW; VG 106, 1996); *La Fin de Gondwana* (*The End of Gondwana*; RCW; VG 108, 1996); *Embuscade sur Eileena* (*Ambush on Eileena*; RCW; VG 110, 1996); *L'Offensive des Frotegs* (*The Attack of the Frotegs*; RCW; VG 111, 1996); *L'Alliance des Invincibles* (*The Alliance of the Invincibles*; RCW; VG 113, 1997); *La Planète sans Nom* (*The Nameless Planet*; RCW; VG 115, 1997); *Panique sur Wondlak* (*Panic Over Wondlak*; RCW; VG 117, 1997); Misc.: *Psiboy, l'Enfant du Cosmos* (*Psyboy, the Cosmic Child*; FN Hors-Série, 1996); *Note:* See Chapters VIII and IX. Due to the popularity of Guieu's novels, he was granted his own imprint in the late 1970s/early 1980s, first at Plon's, then with Vaugirard. At that time, the Guieu books became share-cropping, formulaic novels, written by other writers, such as Roland C. **Wagner** (RCW; using the pseudonym Richard Wolfram), Philippe

Randa (PR), Nicolas **Gauthier** (NG), and Laurent **Genefort** (LG; using the pseudonym S. Grey). A number of Guieu's novels were adapted into digest-sized graphic novels (see Book 1, Chapter V under **Fleuve Noir, Vihila** and **Yolanda**).

Guignard, Denis Gabriel (?-); *Pyramidopolis* (Trotteur, 1953); *Le Rayon Orange* (*The Orange Ray*; Trotteur, 1954)

Guihard, Henri-Antoine (?-); *L'Extra-Terrestre* (*The Extra-Terrestrial*; Pensée U., 1975)

Guilbert, Jean-Claude (?-); *Chronique de la Horde* (*Chronicle of the Horde*; J-D, 1972); *D'un Ciel à Vivre* (*From a Living Sky*; Nouveau Gong, 1976); *Ils Ont Tué Tous Les Héros* (*They've Killed All the Heroes*; AM, 1978)

Guillard (?-?) *see* **Opéra**

Guillaume, Jean-Louis (?-); *Les Entretiens de Montparnasse* (*The Montparnasse Talks*; 2 vols.; J. Renard, 1943); *L'Homme Nu de Monaco* (*The Naked Man from Monaco*; SEPE, 1944); *Obsession* (SEPE, 1945); *Laquelle des Deux?* (*Which of the Two?*; SEPE, 1946); *Les Morts se Taisent* (*Deadmen Keep Quiet*; SEPE, 1946); *Les Soeurs Enemies* (*Enemy Sisters*; SEPE, 1946)

Guillaumes, Pascal (?-); *La Bête de Moebius* (*The Mobius Beast*; DLM, Arkham 3, 1997)

Guillet, Jean-Pierre (1953-); *Le Paradis Perdu* (*The Lost Paradise*; Héritage, 1991); *Destinées* (*Destinies*; Héritage, 1993); *L'Odyssée du Pénélope* (*The Odyssey of the Penelope*; Héritage, 1997); *Note:* French-Canadian writer. *Le Paradis* is a time-travel story. *Destinées* is a collection of fantastic tales. *L'Odyssée* is about Mars exploration.

Guillois, Patrice (?-); *Futino Venu du Ciel* (*Futino Who Came from the Sky*; GP, 1962); *Note:* Children's book.

Guillot, René (1900-1969); *La Planète Ignorée* (*The Unknown Planet*; BV, 1963); *Kiriki et la Flèche Magique* (*Kiriki and the Magic Arrow*; Delagrave, 1969); *Kiriki et le Nain Vert* (*Kiriki and the Green Dwarf*; Delagrave, 1970); *Un Petit Chien va dans la Lune* (*A Little Dog Goes to the Moon*; Hac., 1970); *L'Extraordinaire Aventure de Messire Renart* (*The Extraordinary Adventure of Sir Renart*; Delagrave, 1972); *Le Chef au Masque d'Or* (*The Chief with a Golden Mask*; Hac., 1973); *Le Chevalier Sans Visage* (*The Knight Without a Face*; Hac., 1973); *Il Était Mille et Une Fois* (*Once Upon a Thousand and One Times*; Magnard, 1974); *Contes de la Brousse Fauve ou les Contes qui s'étaient perdus* (*Tales of the Fawn Savanna, or Lost Tales*; Gall., 1979); *Le 397ème Éléphant Blanc* (*The 397th White Elephant*; Nathan, 1986); *Les Éléphants de Sargabal* (*The Ele-* *phants of Sargabal*; Sang de la Terre, 1989); *Contes des 1001 Bêtes* (*Tales of 1001 Beasts*; Magnard, 1995); *Le Maître des Éléphants* (*The Master of the Elephants*; Magnard, 1995); *Note:* Juvenile SF. See chapters VIII and IX.

Guillot de Saix, Léon (1885-?) *see* **Grand-Guignol**

Guiod, Jacques (?-); *La Vie Secrète de l'Homme Invisible* (*The Secret Life of the Invisible Man*; Edit & Public. Premières, Eroscope, 1977); *Note:* Erotic SF.

Guiot, Denis (?-); *Pardonnez-Nous Vos Enfances* (*Forgive Us Your Childhood*; anthology; PdF 250, 1978); *Note:* Editor of the "Vertige" juvenile imprint, Guiot is also the publisher of the magazine *Ozone*.

Guiraud, Alexandre, Baron (?-?); *Césaire, Révélation* (Levavasseur, 1830); *Note:* See Chapter IV.

Guitard, Agnès (1954-); *Les Corps Communicants*(*The Communicating Bodies*; Q/A, 1981); *Note:* French-Canadian writer. The novel deals with telepathy and the power a mindlink could grantone person over another.

Guitet-Vauquelin, Pierre (1882-); *Mendiandou* (Nlle. Revue, 1906); *Le Triomphe de la Chair* (*The Triumph of the Flesh*; Theuveny, 1906); *Les Immobiles* (*The Motionless*; Ed. Modernes, 1907); *Le Marchand d'Illusions* (*The Merchant of Illusions*; Grasset, 1909); *Le Sang des Vignes* (*The Blood of the Grapes*; Fasquelle, 1910); *L'Aéroplane Invisible* (*The Invisible Airplane*; Hac., 1921); *Les Génèses Passionées: L'Île Exaltée* (*The Impassionate Genesis: The Exalted Island*; Ren. du Livre, 1928); *Les Tigres du Silence* (*The Tigers of Silence*; Livre Moderne, 1943); *Le Météore* (*The Meteor*; Floréal, n.d.)

Guitton, Gustave (1870-1918); *La Conspiration des Milliardaires* (*The Billionaires' Conspiracy;* with Gustave **Le Rouge**; serialized in 8 issues, *Guyot*, 1899-1900); condensed as *L'Empereur des Dollars* (*The Dollar Emperor*, Roger & Chernovitz, 1914); *1-2. La Conspiration des Milliardaires* (*The Billionaires' Plot*); *3-4. À Coups de Milliards* (*Throwing Billions Around*); *5-6. Le Régiment des Hypnotiseurs* (*The Hypnotists' Brigade*); *7-8. La Revanche du Vieux Monde* (*The Old World's Revenge*); *Contes à la Vapeur pour Rire en Wagon* (*Steam-Powered Tales to Laugh in a Train*; Didier-Méricant, 1900); *Terre Abandonnée* (*Abandoned Land*; Lafolye, 1901); *Les Conquérants de la Mer* (*The Conquerors of the Sea;* with Gustave **Le Rouge**; serialized in 4 issues, Méricant, 1902); *1. La Flibuste Sanglante* (*The Bloody Pirates*); *2. Les Preneurs de Ville* (*The City Takers*); *3. Les Mangeurs d'Hommes* (*The Man Eaters*); *4. Le Trésor des Crocodiles* (*The Treasure of the Crocodiles*); *La Princesse des Airs* (*The Princess of the Air;* with Gustave **Le Rouge**; serialized in 4 issues, *Guyot*, 1902);

condensed as *Les Dompteurs de Nuages* (*The Cloud Tamers*, Roger & Chernovitz, 1913); *1. En Ballon Dirigeable* (*In Dirigible Balloon*); *2. Les Robinsons de l'Himalaya* (*Robinsons of the Himalaya*); *3. De Roc en Roc* (*From Rock to Rock*); *4. Au Pays des Bouddhas* (*In the Land of the Buddhas*); *Le Sous-Marin "Jules Verne"* (*The Submarine "Jules Verne";* with Gustave **Le Rouge**; serialized in 2 issues, *RM,* 1902); condensed as *La Captive des Flots* (*The Prisoner of the Sea*, Roger & Chernovitz, 1913); *1. Un Drame de la Haine* (*A Drama of Hate*); *2. La Bataille Sous-Marine* (*The Undersea Battle*); *Les Têtards* (*Futures Femmes; The Tadpoles;Future Women*; Méricant, 1904); *Ce Que Seront les Hommes de l'An 3000* (*What Men from the Year 3000 Will Be Like*; Tallandier, 1907); *Note:* See Chapter V.

Gurik, Robert (1932-); *Hamlet, Prince du Québec* (Ed. de l'Homme, 1968); *API 2967—La Palissade* (*The Fence*; Léméac, 1971); *Le Tabernacle à Trois Étages* (*The Three-Storied Tabernacle*; Léméac, 1972); *Note:* French-Canadian writer. Stage plays.

Gus (1911-1997); *La Machine du Prof. Douille* (*The Machine of Prof. Douille*; Ségur, 1951); *Le Corbillard des Anges* (*The Angels' Hearse*; Den., 1980)

Guttin, Jacques (?-?); *Epigone, Histoire du Siècle Futur* (*History of the Future Century*; P. Lamy, 1659); *Note:* See Chapter III.

Guy, Lucien (?-) *see* **Touati**

Guy, Philippe (?-); *Cocons* (*Coccoons*; FNA 1524, 1987); *Dernière Tempête* (*Last Tempest*; FNA 1696, 1989); *Phalènes* (FNA 1977, 1996)

Guy, Lucien (?-) *see* ***Contes et Légendes***

Guy, Robert (1907-); *Candide au Temps des Soucoupes Volantes* (*Candide in the Time of Flying Saucers*; Debresse, 1955); *Pangloss* (Debresse, 1955); *La Maison du Sorcier* (*The Wizard's House*; Terras, 1980); *Le Diable, La Vierge, Les Ermites* (*The Devil, the Virgin, the Hermits*; Siloé, 1989)

Guyne, Alca (?-); *Le Cas Maillard* (*The Maillard Case*; Regain, Monte-Carlo, 1955)

Guyon, Charles (1848-?); *Voyage dans la Planète Vénus* (*Voyage to the Planet Venus*; Lecène-Oudin, 1888); *La Fée Gentillette / Le Trésor des Nains / Trois Géants de la Meuse* (*The Kindly Fairy* / the *Dwarves' Treasure* / *Three Giants from the Meuse*; Lecène-Oudin, 1890); *Vif-Argent, Contes et Légendes* (*Quicksilver, Tales and Legends*; Lecène-Oudin, 1890); *Pâquerette, Contes et Légendes* (*Paquerette, Tales and Legends*; Lecène-Oudin, 1890); *La Canne Enchantée* (*The Enchanted Cane*; Lecène-Oudin, 1890); *Le Rubis Magique* (*The Magic Ruby*; Lecène-Oudin, 1890); *Vers l'Autre Planète*

(*Towards the Other Planet*; Ste. Fr. d'Imprim. & Libr., 1892); *Légendes d'Alsace* (*Alsatian Legends*; Ste. Fr. d'Imprim. & Libr., 1910); *Contes des Vosges* (*Tales from the Vosges*; Larousse, 1914); *Légendes de la Forêt Noire* (*Legends of the Black Forest*; Larousse, 1914); *La Haine du Fakir* (*The Fakir's Hatred*; Larousse, 1919); *Contes du Maroc* (*Moroccan Tales*; Larousse, 1921); *Nouveaux Contes de Noël* (*New Xmas Tales*; Larousse, 1923); *Les Bons Petits Lutins* (*The Good Little Goblins*; Larousse, 1923); *Les Contes de Grand'Maman* (*Granny's Tales*; Larousse, 1926); *Les Petits Lutins de Carnac* (*The Little Goblins of Carnac*; Larousse, 1926); *Récits Légendaires des Bords du Rhin* (*Legendary Tales of the River Rhine*; Larousse, 1926); *La Caverne de la Fée Cocasse* (*The Cavern of the Funny Fairy*; Larousse, 1927); *Légendes de Noël* (*Xmas Legends*; Larousse, 1928); *Contes et Légendes Arabes* (*Arabian Tales and Legends*; Larousse, 1929); *Contes et Légendes d'Islande* (*Icelandic Tales and Legends*; Larousse, 1931); *Légendes du Roi de Thulé* (*Legends of the King of Thule*; Larousse, 1931); *Note:* See chapters V and VI.

Guyot, Charles (?-); *La Légende la Ville d'Ys* (*The Legend of the City of Ys*; L'Édition d'Art H.Piazza, 1982); *Note:* Folk tales.

Guyotat, Pierre (?-); *Tombeau Pour 500.000 Soldats* (*A Tomb for 500,000 Soldiers*; Gall., 1967); *Éden, Éden, Éden* (Gall., 1969); *Bond et Avant* (*Forward Jump*; Gall., 1973); *Prostitution* (Gall., 1975); *Le Livre* (*The Book*; Gall., 1984); *Vivre* (*To Live*; Gall., 1984)

Haddad, Hubert (1947-); *Le Charnier Déductif* (*The Deductive Charnel*; Debresse, 1969); *Un Rêve de Glace* (*A Dream of Ice*; AM, 1974); *La Cène* (*The Last Supper*; AM, 1975); *Les Grands Pays Muets* (*The Great Silent Countries*; AM, 1978); *Les Derniers Jours d'un Homme Heureux* (*The Last Days of a Happy Man*; AM, 1980); *La Rose de Damoclès* (*The Rose of Damocles*; AM, 1982); *Les Effrois* (*The Fears*; AM, 1983); *Retour d'Icare Ailé d'Abîme* (*Return of Winged Icarus from the Abyss*; Thot, 1983); *La Ville sans Miroir* (*The City Without Mirrors*; AM, 1984); *Perdus dans un Profond Sommeil* (*Lost in a Deep Sleep*; AM, 1986); *Le Visiteur aux Gants de Soie* (*The Visitor with Silk Gloves*; AM, 1987); *Oholiba des Songes* (*Oholiba of the Dreams*; TR, 1989); *Armelle ou l'Éternel Retour* (*The Eternal Return*; Castor Astral, 1989); *Kronos et les Marionettes* (*Kronos and the Puppets*; Dumerchez, 1991); *Saintes Beuveries* (*Holy Drinking Binges*; Corti, 1991); *Le Secret de l'Immortalité* (*The Secret of Immortality*; Critérion, 1991); *L'Âme de Buridan* (*Buridan's Soul*; Zulma, 1992); *Le Chevalier Alouette* (*The Skylark Knight*; L'Aube, 1992); *Meurtre sur l'Île des Marins Fidèles* (*Murder on the Island of the Faithful Sailors*; Zulma, 1994); *Le Pont Renversé* (*The Overthrown Bridge*; Littera, 1995); *Le Bleu* *du Temps* (*The Blue of Time*; Zulma, 1995); *La Falaise de Sable* (*The Sand Cliff*; Rocher, 1997); *La Condition Magique* (*The Magical Condition*; Zulma, 1997); *Note:* See Chapter VIII.

Haigh, Alan (?-); *La Porte des Ténèbres* (*The Gate of Darkness*; MFant 18, 1977)

Halévy, Daniel (1872-1962); *Histoire de Quatre Ans, 1997-2001* (*Four Years' History*; Cahiers de la Quinzine, 1903); *Note:* See Chapter V.

Halévy, Dominique (?-); *Céline ou La Multiplication* (Den., 1960); *L'Enfant et l'Étoile* (*The Child and the Star*; Gall., 1978)

Halévy, Ludovic (1834-1908) *see* **Opéra**

Halle, Adam de la (?-?); *Le Jeu de la Feuillée* (*The Game of the Leaves*; c. 1275); *Note:* See Chapter I.

Hamel, Jean-Claude (1953-); *Quatre Fois Rien* (*Four Times Nothing*; CLF, 1974); *Note:* French-Canadian writer. Collection of fantastic tales.

Hamelin, Jean (1920-1970); *Nouvelles Singulières* (*Singular Tales*; HMH, 1964); *Un Dos pour la Pluie* (*A Back for the Rain*; Déon, 1967); *Note:* French-Canadian writer. Collections of fantastic tales.

Hamelink, Jacques (?-); *Le Règne Végétal* (*The Vegetal Kingdom*; AM, 1966); *Horror Vacui* (AM, 1970); *Note:* See Chapter VIII.

Hamp, Pierre (Bourillon, Henri; 1876-1962); *Dix Contes Écrits dans le Nord* (*Ten Tales Written in the North*; Cahiers de la Quinzaine, 1908); *Vieille Histoire: Contes Écrits dans le Nord* (*Old Story: Tales Written in the North*; Gall., 1912); *Les Chercheurs d'Or* (*The Gold Seekers*; Gall., 1920); *La Mort de l'Or* (*The Death of Gold*; Flamm., 1933)

Hannezo, Gustave-Joanny *see* **Deincourt, Jean**

Hanost, Paul (1949-); *Le Livre des Étoiles* (*The Book of Stars*; MSF 52, 1977); *Note:* Belgian writer. See Chapter IX.

Hanotte, Xavier (?-); *Manière Noire* (*Dark Manner*; Belfond, 1995); *Note:* Belgian writer.

Hansewick, Yorril (?-?) *see* **Grand-Guignol**

Hanstein, O. (?-); *Radipolis* (Delachaux & Niestlé, 1944/Nathan, 1945); *Jusqu'à la Lune en Fusée* (*To the Moon in a Rocket*; Nathan, 1948); *10.000 Lieues dans les Airs* (*10,000 Leagues in the Air*; n.d.); *Note:* Swiss writer.

Haraucourt, Edmond (1857-1941); *Les Naufragés* (*The Castaways*; Fasquelle, 1902); *La Traversée de Paris* (*Crossing Paris*; Crès, 1904); *La Peur* (*The Fear*;

Fasquelle, 1907); *Daâh, Le Premier Homme* (*Daah, the First Man*; Flamm., 1914); *Le Poison* (*The Poison*; Kieffer, 1920); *Le Musée de la Double Soif* (*The Museum of Double Thirst*; Cusenier, 1925); *Note:* See chapters IV and V.

Harbitz, Alf (?-); *L'Homme de l'Autre Monde* (*The Man from Another World*; Dupuis, 1950

Hardellet, André (1911-1974); *La Cité Montgol* (Seghers, 1952); Le Luisant et la Sorgue (Seghers, 1954); *Le Seuil du Jardin* (*The Treshold of the Garden*; Julliard, 1958); *Sommeils* (*Sleeps*; Seghers, 1960); *Le Parc des Archers* (*The Park of the Bowmen*; Julliard, 1962); *Les Chasseurs* (*The Huntsmen*; Pauvert, 1966); *Lourdes, Lentes* (*Heavy, Slow*; as Steve Masson; Pauvert, 1969); Lady Long Solo (Pauvert, 1971); *Les Chasseurs Deux* (*Hunters Two*; Pauvert, 1973); *Donnez-moi le Temps* (*Give Me Time*; Julliard, 1973); *La Promenade Imaginaire* (*The Imaginary Walk*; MdF, 1974); *L'Essuyeur de Tempêtes* (*The Tempest Washer*; Plasma, 1979); *Note:* See Chapter VIII. *Le Seuil* was adapted into a 1970 feature film entitled **Ils** (*They*) by Jean-Daniel Simon (see Book 1, Chapter I).

Hartoy, Maurice d' (?-); *Des Cris dans la Tempête* (*Screams in the Tempest*; Perrin, 1919); *L'Homme Bleu, Aventures Merveilleuses du XXème Siècle* (*The Blue Man: Marvellous Adventures in the 20th Century*; Malfère, 1924); *Avec la Femme au Nez Coupé* (*With the Woman with a Cut-Off Nose*; SFIA, 1927); *Enradis Terrestres* (*Terrestrial Inradise*; SFI, 1928); *Au Jardin du Monastère* (*Vieilles Légendes de Normandie; In the Monastery's Garden* (*Old Legends from Normandy*); d'Hartoy, 1933); *Les Fémorales ou l'Éternelle Rencontre* (*The Femorals, or the Eternal Encounter*; St. Germain des Prés, 1953)

Harvey, Azade (1925-); *Contes et Légendes des Îles de la Madeleine 1: Les Contes d'Azade* (*Tales and Legends of the Madeleine Islands 1: Azade's Tales*; Aurore, 1975); *Contes et Légendes des Îles de la Madeleine 2: Azade, Raconte-moi tes Îles d'Azade* (*Tales and Legends of the Madeleine Islands 2: Azade, Tell Me About Your Islands*; Intrinsèque, 1976); *Contes et Légendes des Îles de la Madeleine 3: Azade nous Ramène dans ses Îles d'Azade* (*Tales and Legends of the Madeleine Islands 3: Azade Brings Us Back to His Islands*; Intrinsèque, 1977); *Contes et Légendes des Îles de la Madeleine* (sic) *4* (*Tales and Legends of the Madeleine Islands* (sic) *4;* Marquise, 1983); *Note:* French-Canadian writer. Collections of folk legends.

Harvey, Jean-Charles (?-?); *Marcel Faure* (1922); *Note:* French-Canadian writer.

Hausard, Marie-Claire (?-); *L'Intemporelle* (*The Intemporal*; Satellite 29, 1960

Hausser, Isabelle (?-); *Célubée* (Julliard, 1986); *Une Nuit* (*One Night*; Julliard, 1987); *Nitchevo* (Fallois, 1993); *Les Magiciens de l'Âme* (*The Wizards of the Soul*; Fallois, 1996); *Note:* See Chapter VIII.

Hautem, Stéphane (De Greeff, Étienne; 1898-1961); *Le Retour au Silence* (*The Return to Silence*; Dessart, 1945); *Note:* Belgian writer. See Chapter VII.

Hawk, William (?-); *L'Âme des Rois Nains 1: Le Roi Déchu* (*The Soul of the Dwarf Kings 1: The Overthrown King*; Mnémos Daemonicon, 1997); *Note:* "William Hawk" is a pseudonym for Mnémos' house authors (**Gaborit, Grimbert**, etc). See Chapter VIII.

Hébert, Anne (1916-); *Le Temps Sauvage* (*Savage Time*; HMH, 1967); *Le Torrent* (*The Torrent*; HMH, 1976); *Les Enfants du Sabbat* (*The Children of the Sabbath*; Seuil, 1975; transl. as *Children of the Black Sabbath*, 1977); *Héloïse* (Seuil, 1980; transl. 1982); *Les Fous de Bassan* (*The Gannets of Bassan*; Seuil, 1982); *Les Chambres de Bois* (*The Chambers of Wood*; Seuil, 1985); *L'Enfant chargé de Songes* (*The Child Burdened with Dreams*; Seuil, 1992); *Note:* French-Canadian writer. *Heloïse* is a novel about Parisian vampires.

Hébert, Louis-Philippe (1946-); *Les Mangeurs de Terre* (*The Eaters of Earth*; Jour, 1970); *Le Roi Jaune* (*The King in Yellow*; Jour, 1971); *Le Petit Catéchisme: La Vie Publique de W et ON* (*The Little Catechism: The Public Life of W and ON*; Hexagone, 1972); *Récits des Temps Ordinaires* (*Tales of Ordinary Times*; Jour, 1972); *La Manufacture de Machines* (*The MachineFactory*; Quinze, 1976); *Manuscrit Trouvé Dans Une Valise* (*Ms. Found in a Suitcase*; Quinze, 1979); *Note:* French-Canadian writer.

Hecht, Yvon (?-); *La Fin du Quaternaire et la Suite* (*The End of the Quaternary and the Rest*; RF 90, 1962); *Faergus, ou La Seconde Mort de l'Assassin de Trotsky* (*Faergus, or the Second Death of Trotsky's Murderer*; Encre, 1979); *Alexis, Contribution à l'Étude des Phénomènes Occultes* (*Alexis, Contribution to the Study of Occult Phenomenon*; Londreys, 1986); *Helena Von Nachtheim* (PdFant 51, 1996); *Note:* See chapters VIII and IX.

Hédoin, Raymond-A. (?-); *L'Agent 33* (Cast., 1930); *L'Oiseau de France: Voyage d'une Famille Française autour du Globe* (*The Firebird: Journey of a French Family Around the World*; Cast., 1937); *Ivan des Valdaï* (Cast., 1938); *Amnorix le Carnute* (Cast., 1947); *Quand le Monde était Rome* (*When the World Belonged to Rome*; Cast., 1947); *L'Odyssée du Professeur Moor* (*The Odyssey of Prof. Moor*; Cast., 1953)

Hée, Louis d' (?-); *Une Fumée dans la Nue* (*A Smoke in the Sky*; RM, 1913); *Frontière* (*Frontier*; RM, 1913); *Amour Sacrilège* (*Sacrilegious Love*; LN, 1925); *Le Droit de Maître* (*The Master's Right*; Tallandier, 1933); *Talepsie* (SPE, 1946)

Heidsieck, Christian (?-); *La Ferme d'Ugo* (*Ugo's Farm*; L'Aire, 1982)

Heim, Gérard (?-); *L'Âme Double* (*The Double Soul*; H. Mauger, 1949); *L'Étrange Destin de Jacques Coeur* (*The Strange Fate of Jacques Coeur*; H. Mauger, 1953); *Le Rayon Phi* (*The Phi Ray*; Aventures, 1956); *Paraphrénia* (Groupe Poésie Combat, 1975)

Heimer, Marc (?-); *Surhommes et Surmodes (Essai; Supermen and Overworlds (Essay)*; Julliard, 1961); *Premières Vacances sur la Lune* (*First Holidays on the Moon*; PC, 1967)

Held, Claude (1936-) & Jacqueline (?-); *Le Chat de Simulombula* (*The Cat from Simulombula*; Hac., 1971); *Expédition Imprévue sur la Planète Éras* (*Unforeseen Expedition to Planet Eras*; Bordas, 1978); *Le Pêcheur de Soleil* (*The Sun Fisher*; Dessain & Tobra, 1978); *Les Voyages Interplanétaires de Grand-Père Coloconte* (*The Interplanetary Journeys of Granpa Colonconte*; École des Loisirs, 1979); *L'Antre de Starros* (*The Lair of Starros*; Claude Held alone; Magnard, 1979); *Trois Enfants dans les Étoiles* (*Three Children Among the Stars*; Seghers, 1980); *Le Dragon Bariton et la Petite Sylvie Trop Sérieuse* (*The Baritone Dragon and Little Sylvie Too Serious*; Claude Held alone; Magnard, 1980); *Le Marchand de Sable* (*The Sandman*; Magnard, 1981); *L'Antre de Starros* (*Starros' Lair*; Magnard, 1981); *La Voiture Sauvage* (*The Wild Car*; Jacqueline Held alone; Bordas, 1981); *L'inconnu des Herbes Rouges* (*The Unknown Man from the Red Grass*; Jacqueline Held alone; Bordas, 1983); *Il Était Une Fois Demain* (*Once Upon a Time Tomorrow*; Farandole, 1983); *Contes de Terre et de Lune* (*Tales of Earth and Moon*; Jacqueline Held alone; Ecole des Loisirs, 1983); *Histoires Bicornues* (*Crooked Tales*; Magnard, 1985); *Le Fantôme du Vicomte* (*The Viscount's Ghost*; Jacqueline Held alone; Bordas, 1985); *Eve, le Brontosaure et le Diplodocus* (Jacqueline Held alone; Magnard, 1986); *Alpha, Bêta, Etcaetera* (Claude Held alone; Folle Avoine, 1985); Series *Crocktou, Drôle de Loup* (*Crockall, Funny Wolf*; Jacqueline Held alone; individual titles not available; Bordas, 1987-89); *La Poudre des Sept Planètes* (*The Powder of Seven Planets*; Hac., 1990); *Note:* Juvenile SF. See Chapter IX.

Held, Serge Simon (?-); *La Mort du Fer* (*The Death of Iron*; Fayard, 1931; transl. (by Fletcher Pratt); *Note:* See Chapter VII.

Héléna, André (?-); *La Planète des Cocus* (*The Cuckholds' Planet*; Fleury, 1952); *Aristo et le Fantôme* (*Aristo and the Ghost*; Flamme d'Or, 1954); *Le Festival des Macchabées* (*The Festival of the Dead*; UGE, 1986); *La Vic-*

time (*The Victim*; Fanval, 1988); *Les Anges de la Mort* (*The Angels of Death*; Fanval, 1988); *Les Compagnons du Destin* (*The Companions of Fate*; Fanval, 1988); *Passeport pour l'Au-Delà* (*Passport for Beyond*; Fanval, 1988); *Rencontre dans la Nuit* (*Encounter at Night*; F. Massot, 1997)

Hellem, Charles (1876-1954) *see* **Grand-Guignol**

Hellens, Franz (Van Ermenghem, Frédéric; 1881-1972); *Les Hors-le-Vent* (*The Out-Wind*; Libr. Moderne, 1909); *Les Clartés Latentes* (*The Latent Clarities*; Ass. Des Écrivains Belges, 1912); *Vingt Contes et Paraboles* (*Twenty Tales and Parables*; Libr. Gén. des Sciences, des Arts & des Lettres, 1912); *Nocturnal* (Cahiers Indépendants, 1919); *Mélusine* (Le Voile Rouge, 1920); *Base Basina Boulou* (F. Rieder, 1922); *Réalités Fantastiques* (*Fantastic Realities*; Gall., 1923); *Au Repos de la Santé* (*Healhy Rest*; Commerce d'Esprit, 1932); *Nouvelles Réalités Fantastiques* (*New Fantastic Realities*; Gall., 1941); *Fantômes Vivants* (*Living Ghosts*; Lumière, 1944); *La Vie Seconde ou Les Songes sans la Clef* (*The Second Life, or Dreams Without a Key*; Sablon, 1945); *Le Diable et le Gendarme* (*The Devil and the Gendarme*; Disque Vert, 1954); *Contes Choisis* (*Selected Tales*; Vanderlinden, 1956); *Les Yeux du Rêve* (*The Eyes of the Dream*; Brepols, 1964); *Herbes méchantes* (*Bad Herbs*; MarFant 194, 1964); *Entre le Sommeil et la Mort* (*Between Sleep and Death*; Dynamo, 1964); *Le Dernier Jour du Monde* (*The Last Day of the World*; Belfond, 1967); *Mes Fantômes* (*My Ghosts*; J. Antoine, 1971); *Le Fantastique Réel* (*Real Fantasy*; Labor, 1991); *Note:* Belgian writer. See chapters VI and VIII.

Hello, Ernest (1828-1885); *Contes Extraordinaires* (*Extraordinary Tales*; Perrin, 1879); *Note:* See Chapter IV.

Hély, Marc (?-?) *see* **Grand-Guignol**

Hendrick, Fernand (?-); *L'Agonie dans les Ténèbres* (*The Agony in Darkness*; Albert, 1934)

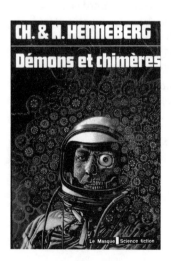

Henneberg (zu Irmelshausen Wasungen, Charles; 1899-1959); *La Naissance des Dieux* (*The Birth of the Gods*; Métal 6, 1954; rev. MSF 51, 1977); *Le Chant des Astronautes* (*The Astronauts' Song*; Sat. 10-11, 1958; rev. MSF 26, 1975); *An Premier, Ere Spatiale* (*Year 1 of the Space Era; OF 71-73,* 1959; rev. by Nathalie-Charles **Henneberg** as *Le Mur de la Lumière* (*The Light Barrier,* AMSF 2, 1972); *La Rosée du Soleil* (*The Dew of the Sun*; RF 65, 1959); *Les Dieux Verts* (with Nathalie-Charles

Henneberg; RF 83, 1961; rev. MSF 30, 1975; transl. as *The Green Gods*, 1974); *La Forteresse Perdue* (*The Lost Fortress*; with Nathalie-Charles **Henneberg**; RF 94, 1962); *Le Sang des Astres* (*The Blood of the Stars*; with Nathalie-Charles **Henneberg**; RF 116, 1963; rev. MFant 4, 1976); *Démons et Chimères* (*Demons and Chimeras*; with Nathalie-Charles **Henneberg**; MSF 66, 1977); *D'Or et de Nuit* (*Of Gold and Night*; with Nathalie-Charles **Henneberg**; MFant 13, 1977); *Note:* See chapters VIII and IX.

Henneberg, Nathalie-Charles (1917-1977); *Les Dieux Verts* (with Charles **Henneberg**; RF 83, 1961; transl. as *The Green Gods*, 1974); *La Forteresse Perdue* (*The Lost Fortress*; with Charles **Henneberg**; RF 94, 1962); *Le Sang des Astres* (*The Blood of the Stars*; with Charles **Henneberg**; RF 116, 1963); *La Plaie* (*The Plague*; RF 122-123, 1964; rev. AMSF 31, 1974); *L'Opale Entydre* (*The Entydre Opal*; Bourgois, 1971); *Le Mur de la Lumière* (*The Light Barrier;* revised version

of *An Premier, Ere Spatiale* (*Year 1 of the Space Era*) by Charles **Henneberg**; AMSF 2, 1972); *Le Dieu Foudroyé* (*The Thunderstruck God*; AMSF2 13, 1976); *Démons et Chimères* (*Demons and Chimeras*; with Charles **Henneberg**; MSF 66, 1977); *D'Or et de Nuit* (*Of Gold and Night*; with Charles **Henneberg**; MFant 13, 1977); *Les Anges de la Colère* (*The Angels of Wrath*; MSF 72, 1978); *Note:* See chapters VIII and IX.

Hennique, Léon (1852-1935); *Un Caractère* (*A Character*; 1889); *Note:* See Chapter IV.

Henriot (Maigrot, Henry; 1857-1933); *Napoléon aux Enfers* (*Napoleon in Hell*; L. Conquet, 1895); *Aventures Prodigieuses de Cyrano de Bergerac* (*Prodigious Adventures of Cyrano de Bergerac*; Imagerie d'Épinal, 1900); *Un Prix de 5 Millions* (*The 5 Million Prize*; Mame, 1903); *Paris en l'An 3000* (*Paris in the Year 3000);* Laurens, 1911); *Note:* Not to be confused with Émile Henriot (1889-1961).

Henry, Frank (?-); *Carnaval des Vampires* (*Vampire Carnival*; FNG 107, 1990

Henry, Michel (1922-); *L'Amour les Yeux Fermés* (*Love with Closed Eyes*; Gall., 1976); *Le Fils du Roi* (*The King's Son*; Gall., 1981); *La Barbarie* (*Barbarism*; Grasset, 1987); *Le Cadavre Indiscret* (*The Indiscreet Corpse*; AM, 1996)

Henry, René (?-); *Face aux Martians* (*Face-To-Face with the Martians*; Zimmerman, 1946)

Hensenne, René (?-); *L'Inconcevable Aventure de Jean Duret* (*The Inconceivable Adventure of Jean Duret*; Maréchal, 1944); *Note:* Belgian writer.

Héran, Danièle (?-); *Une Chaleur d'Enfer* (*A Hellish Heat*; L'Atalante, 1989)

Hérault, Paul-Jean (?-); *Le Rescapé de la Terre* (*The Survivor from Terra*; FNA 691, 1975); *Les Bâtisseurs du Monde* (*The World Builders*; FNA 714, 1975); *La Planète Folle* (*The Mad Planet*; FNA 776, 1977); *Hors Contrôle* (*Out of Control*; FNA 895, 1979); *37 Minutes pour Survivre* (*37 Minutes to Survive*; FNA 933, 1979); *Chak de Palar* (FNA 1005, 1980); *La Fresque* (*The Fresco*; FNA 1040, 1981); *Cal de Ter* (FNA 1281, 1984); *Le Dernier Pilote* (*The Last Pilot*; FNA 1331, 1984); *Le Bricolo* (*The Handyman*; FNA 1437, 1986); *Le Raid Infernal* (*Infernal Raid*; FNA 1499, 1986); *La Famille* (*The Family*; FNA 1540, 1987); *Sergent-Pilote Gurvan* (*Pilot-Sergeant Gurvan*; FNA 1562, 1987); *Gurvan: Les Premières Victoires* (*Gurvan's First Victories*; FNA 1584, 1987); *Officier-Pilote Gurvan* (*Pilot-Officer Gurvan*; FNA 1612, 1988); *Ross et Berkel* (FNA 1772, 1990); *Pédric et Bo* (FNA 1778, 1990); *Danger: Mémoire* (*Danger: Memory*; FNA 1823, 1991); *Le Loupiot* (*The Lamp*; FNA 1849, 1991); *Hors Normes* (*Beyond Norms*; FNA 1890, 1992); *Le Chineur de l'Espace* (*The Space Whiner*; FNA 1973, 1995); *Ceux qui ne voulaient pas Mourir* (*Those Who Refused to Die*; FNA 1986, 1996); *Note:* See Chapter IX.

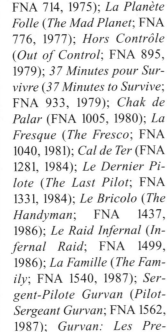

Herbart, Pierre (1904-1974); *Le Rôdeur* (*The Prowler*; Gall., 1931); *Alcyon* (Gall., 1945); *L'Âge d'Or* (*The*

Golden Age; Gall., 1953); *La Licorne* (*The Unicorn*; Gall., 1964)

Herial, Don *see* **Lehman, Serge**

Herly, Jim d' (?-); *Tatiana, L'Île aux Mystères* (*Tatiana, the Island of Mystery*; STAEL, 1947); *Note:* Juvenile fantasy.

Hermary-Vieille, Catherine (?-); *Le Grand Vizir la Nuit* (*The Great Vizier at Night*; Gall., 1981); *L'Épiphanie des Dieux* (*The Gods' Epiphany*; Gall., 1983); *La Marquise des Ombres* (*The Marquess of Shadows*; O. Orban, 1983); *Le Jardin des Henderson* (*The Hendersons' Garden*; Gall., 1988); *La Piste des Turquoises* (*The Trail of the Turquoises*; Flamm., 1992); *L'Initié* (*The Initiate*; Plon, 1996)

Hérold, Ferdinand (?-?); See **Opéra.**

Héron, Jean Olivier (1938-); *La Maison Brule* (*The House Burns*; RL, 1970); *Vita Nova, Chronique de l'Âge de Viande* (*Vita Nova, Chronicles of the Age of Meat*; Cerf, 1978); *Une Pomme de Terre en or Massif* (*A Solid Gold Potato*; Gall., 1983); *Adam 1er, Roi de l'Univers* (*Adam 1st., King of the Universe*; Cerf, 1984); *Les Contes du Septième Jour* (*Tales of the Seventh Day*; Cerf, 1984); *Le Jardinier du Paradis* (*The Gardener of Paradise*; Cerf, 1984); *Victor, le Chat-Botté* (*Victor, the Puss-in-Boots*; AM, 1991); *Le Grand Secret* (*The Great Secret*; AM, 1991); *Le Livre qui avait un Trou* (*The Book with a Hole*; with Domitille Héron; AM, 1992); *L'Ogre qui devint Bon* (*The Ogre Who Became Good*; AM, 1993); *Arrête de Faire des Miracles* (*Stop Performing Miracles*; Cerf, 1996)

Héros, Eugène (?-?) *see* **Grand-Guignol**

Hersay, Gilles (?-); *La Vénus au Nénuphars* (*The Venus of the Water Lillies*; Tallandier, 1934); *Les Amants de Diane* (*Diana's Lovers*; Tallandier, 1934); *Les Ravageurs du Pôle* (*The Ravagers of the Pole*; VA, 1935); *L'Île aux Monstres Bleus* (*The Island of Blue Monsters*; VA, 1936); *La Vengeance des Haschichins* (*The Revenge of the Haschichins*; VA, 1936); *Victime du Mystère* (*Victim of the Mystery*; VA, 1936); *Le Hollandais Volant* (*The Flying Dutchman*; VA, 1937); *L'Ogre de la Brousse* (*The Brush Ogre*; VA, 1937); *La Ville aux Parfums* (*The Perfumed City*; SEPIA, 1937); *L'Homme à la Barbiche Grise* (*The Man with a Grey Beard*; 1937); *Le Chien de M. Gallard* (*Mr. Gallard's Dog*; Ferenczi, 1938); *La Mariée Disparu* (*The Vanished Bride*; Ferenczi, 1938); *Coureurs de Brousse* (*Brush Runners*; Tallandier, 1938); *Les Monstres de Malaïter* (*The Monsters of Malaiter*; Tallandier, 1938); *La Fosse du Pain-Bénit* (*The Pit of Pain-Benit*; Tallandier, 1939); *Les Monstres de Malaita* (*The Monsters of Malaita*; LdA, 1954); *Le Vampire du Couvent Noir* (*The*

Vampire of the Black Convent; Jacquier, 1954); *Les Messagers Mystérieux* (*The Mysterious Messengers*; Didier, 1967)

Hersin, Marguerite (?-); *La Prochaine Dernière* (*The Next Last One*; Kaganski, 1945); Exils (Maroc 45, 1946)

Hérubel, Michel (?-); *L'Amour Cruel* (*Cruel Love*; Plon, 1958); *Le Temple sous la Mer* (*The Undersea Temple*; Fayard, 1975); *Les Caravelles du Soleil* (*The Caravels of the Sun*; Fayard, 1976); *Le Chapelain de Cork* (*The Chaplain from Cork*; Claire Vigne, 1995)

Hervieu, Paul-Louis (?-); *L'Île à la Dérive* (*The Island Adrift*; Plon, 1946)

Hervilly, Ernest d' (1839-1911); *Contes pour les Grandes Personnes* (*Tales for Adults*; Charpentier, 1874); *Timbales d'Histoires à la Parisienne* (*Potpourri of Parisian Tales*; Flamm., 1883); *Aventures d'un Petit Garçon Préhistorique en France* (*Adventures of a Prehistoric Boy in France*; Lib. Mondaine, 1887); *La Statue de Chair* (*The Statue of Flesh*; L. Frinzine, 1887); *L'Île des Parapluies* (*The Island of Umbrellas*; Lemerre, 1890); *Aventures du Prince Frangipane* (*Adventures of Prince Frangipane*; Delagrave, 1890); *La Vision de l'Écolier Puni* (*The Vision of a Punished Schoolboy*; Delagrave, 1891); *L'Île des Parapluies: Aventures du Gâte-Sauce Talmouse* (*The Island of Umbrellas: The Adventures of Cook Helper Talmouse*; Lemerre, 1891); *En Bouteille à travers l'Atlantique* (*Crossing the Atlantic in a Bottle*; Fume, 1894); *À Cocagne* (Lemerre, 1898); *Les Chasseurs d'Édredrons* (*The Pillow Hunters*; Boivin, 1924); *Jack-le-Gel et ses Contes* (*Jack-le-Gel and His Tales*; NLJ, n.d.; *Note:* See Chapter V.

Hervyns, Marie-José (?-); *Cette Race Indécrottable* (*That Incorrigible Race*; Bruylant, 1956); *Note:* Belgian writer. See Chapter VIII.

Herzfeld, Elen (?-) *see* **Klein, Gérard**

Herzog, Émile Salomon *see* **Maurois, André**

Hesse, Jean (?-?); *Un Voyage en Fusée* (*A Journey in a Rocket*; Larousse, 1937); *Les Tribulations d'un Savant* (*A Scientist's Misadventures*; Larousse, 1937); *La Poupée de Caoutchouc* (*The Rubber Doll*; Larousse, 1937); *L'Inventeur des Allumettes* (*The Inventor of Matches*; Larousse, 1939); *Note:* Also see **Grand-Guignol**.

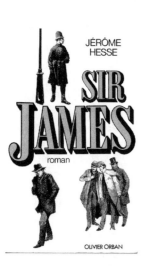

Hesse, Jérôme (1959-); *Sir James* (Orban, 1985); *Note:*

Thriller about Jack the Ripper, featuring the character of Victorian detective Sir James Houseboard.

Hetzel, Pierre-Jules *see* **Stahl, P. J.**

Higon, Albert *see* **Jeury, Michel**

Hilleret, Marcel-Alain *see* **Arcadius**

Hinzelin, Émile (?-) *see* **Contes et Légendes**

Hirshing, Nicolas de (1956-); *Le Navire Ensorcelé* (*The Spellbound Ship*; Bayard, 1981); *Treizes Gouttes de Magie* (*Thirteen Drops of Magic*; Bayard, 1983); *La Sorcière habite au No. 47* (*The Witch Lives at No.47*); Centurion, 1985); *Le Zibou de l'Espace* (*The Zibou from Space*; Bayard, 1986); *Canal Différent* (*Different Channel*; Gall., 1987); *Mon Copain, le Monstre* (*My Pal, the Monster*; Amitié, 1987); *Père Noël Maboul* (*Crazy Santa Claus*; Centurion, 1988); *L'Atroce Monsieur Terroce* (*The Awful Mr. Terroce*; Centurion, 1989); *Perdu dans l'Espace* (*Lost in Space*; Rouge et Or, 1990); *Note:* Juvenile SF.

Hoche, Jules (18.̄9-1926); *Le Faiseur d'Hommes et sa Formule* (*The Maker of Men and His Formula*; Juven, 1906); *Gil Dax, Empereur des Airs* (*Gil Dax, Emperor of the Air*; serialized in 20 issues, Ferenczi, 1914); *Le Secret des Paterson* (*The Paterson's Secret*; RM, 1912); *Le Mort Volant* (*The Flying Deadman*; RM, 1912); *L'Effarante Aventure* (*The Stupefying Adventure*; Ramlot, 1923); *Le Mauvais Rêve* (*The Bad Dream*; France Ed., 1925)

Hoda, F. *see* **Hoveyda, Fereydoun**

Hodeir, André (1921-); *Les Trois Bouteilles de Warwick* (*The Three Bottles of Warwick*; Ecole des Loisirs, 1976); *La Dent du Petit Serpent* (*The Tooth of the Little Snake*; Ecole des Loisirs, 1976); *La Maison du Trompe-l'Oeil* (*The Trompe-l'Oeil House*; Ecole des Loisirs, 1976); *L'Étoile de Léonardo* (*Leonardo's Star*; Ecole des Loisirs, 1977); *Mouna et le Petit Fantôme* (*Mouna and the Little Ghost*; Amitié, 1980

Hoebeke, Lionel (?-); *Bonnes Vacances* (*Happy Holidays*; anthology; Los., 1978)

Hoffmann, François-Bernard (?-?) *see* **Opéra**

Hoffmann, Georges (1894-1962); *Les Faiseurs d'Or* (*The Gold Makers*; Masque, 1932); *Six, Trente-Cinq* (*6-35*); Impr. Fr. de l'Éd., 1935); *Note:* Swiss writer.

Högue, Sylvie (1956-); *Les Mésaventures d'un Magicien* (*The Misadventures of a Magician*; with Gisèle **Internoscia**; Héritage, 1993); *Note:* French-Canadian writer. Juvenile.

Hollande, Eugène (?-); *La Cité Future* (*The Future City*; Fasquelle, 1903)

Honaker, Michel (1958-); *Planeta Non Grata* (FNA 1194, 1983); *Ballade du Voivode* (*Ballad of the Voivode*; FN Espionnage 1768, 1984); *Le Semeur d'Ombres* (*The Sower of Shadows*; FNA 1377, 1985); *Lumière d'Abîme* (*Light of the Abyss*; FNA 1402, 1985); *Le Chant du Vorkul* (*The Song of the Vorkul*; FNA 1441, 1986); *Le Rêve du Vorkul* (*The Dream of the Vorkul*; FNA 1496, 1986); *Canyon Rouge* (*Red Canyon*; FNG 40, 1986); *Building* (FNA 1523, 1987); *La Haine du Vorkul* (*The Hate of the Vorkul*; FNA 1575, 1987); *Le Fouilleur d'Âmes* (*The Searcher of Souls*; Siry SF 3, 1988); rep. FNA 1835, 1991); *Terminus Sanglant* (*Bloody Terminus*; FNG 54, 1988); *Le Démon du Bronx* (*The Demon of the Bronx*; Média 1000, 1988; rev. as *Bronx Ceremonial* (FNA 1723, 1989; rev. as *Magie Noire dans le Bronx* (*Black Magic in the Bronx*, Rageot, 1996); *D'Argile et de Sang* (*Of Clay and Blood*; Media 1000, 1988; rev. as *The Verb of Life* (FNA 1735, 1990); *La Maison des Cauchemars* (*The House of Nightmares*; Média 1000, 1988; rev. as *Return of Emeth* (FNA 1748, 1990); *Enfer et Purgatoire* (*Hell and Purgatory*; FNA 1693, 1989); *King of Ice* (FNA 1759, 1990); *Secret of Bashamay* (FNA 1771, 1990); *Evil Game* (FNA 1783, 1990); *Troll* (FNA 1795, 1991); *Apocalypse Junction* (FNA 1810, 1991); *Dark Spirit* (FNA 1822, 1991); *L'Oreille Absolue* (*Absolute Ear*; FNA 1863, 1992); *Le Coq à la Crête d'Or* (*The Rooster with a Golden Crest*; Rageot, 1994); *Croisière en Meurtre Majeur* (*Cruise in Major Murder*; Rageot, 1994); *Le Prince d'Ébène* (*The Ebony Prince*; Rageot, 1994); *La Sorcière de Midi* (*The Witch of Noon*; Rageot, 1994); *L'Hydre de Tswamba Salu* (*The Hydra of Tswamba Salu*; FNAV 1, 1995); *La Couronne de Sang* (*The Crown of Blood*; FNAV 9, 1995); *Erwan le Maudit* (*Erwan the Accursed*; Rageot, 1995); *Le Chevalier de Terre Noire 1: L'Adieu au Domaine* (*The Knight of Blackland 1 – Farewell to the Domain*; Rageot, 1996); *Le Chevalier de Terre Noire 2: Le Bras de la Vengeance* (*The Arm of Vengeance*; Rageot, 1996); *Le Chevalier de Terre Noire 3: Les Héritiers du Secret* (*The Inheritors of the Secret*; Rageot, 1996); *Le Chant de la Reine Froide* (*The Song of the Cold Queen*; Rageot, 1996); *La Cantate des Anges* (*Angels' Cantata*; Rageot, 1996); *La Symphonie du Destin* (*The Symphony of Fate*; Rageot, 1996); *Nocturne pour une Passion* (*Nocturne for a Passion*; Rageot, 1996); *Les Héritiers du Secret* (*The Heirs of the Secret*; Rageot, 1996); *Le*

Démon de San Marco (*The Demon of San Marco*; Rageot, 1997); *La Citadelle de Cristal* (*The Crystal Citadel*; FNSF 1, 1997); *La Flûte Enchantée* (*The Enchanted Flute*; Rageot, 1997); *Musicien des Princes* (*Musician of Princes*; Rageot, 1997); *Le Chant des Aulnes* (*The Song of the Elms*; Rageot, 1997); *Les Morsures du Passé* (*The Bites of the Past*; Rageot, 1997); *Le Grand Maître des Mémoires* (*The Grand Master of Memories*; Rageot, 1997); *La Créature du Néant* (*The Creature from the Void*; Rageot, 1997); *Rendez-Vous à Apocalypse* (*Rendezvous at Apocalypse*; Rageot, 1997); *Note:* See chapters VIII and IX.

Hoppenot, Henri (?-) *see* **Opéra**

Horvéno, Grégoire (?-); *L'Appel du Fond des Temps* (*The Call from the End of Time*; Flamm., 1994); *Note:* Juvenile fantasy.

Horx, Mathias (?-); *Ah, ça ira* (*Let It Go*; Stock,1983)

Houdar de la Motte, Antoine (1672-1731) *see* **Opéra**

Houdenc, Raoul de (?-?); *Méraugis de Portlesguez* (c. 1200); *Note:* See Chapter I.

Hougron, Jean (1923-); *Rage Blanche* (*White Rage*; Club Fr. du Livre, 1952); *Les Portes de l'Aventure* (*The Gates of Adventure*; Domat, 1954); *La Terre du Barbare* (*The Land of the Barbarian*; Del Duca, 1958); *Le Signe du Chien* (*The Sign of the Dog*; PdF 44, 1960); *Par Qui le Scandale...* (*By Whom Scandal...*; Del Duca, 1960); *Soleil au Ventre* (*Sun in the Belly*; Ed. Mondiales, 1960); *Mort en Fraude* (*Death By Fraud*; Club de la Femme, 1961); *Les Asiates* (*The Asians*; LdP, 1962); *L'Homme de Proie* (*The Man of Prey*; France-Loisirs, 1974); *Le Naguen* (Plon, 1980); *Note:* See Chapter IX.

Houle, Mario (1966-); *Le Voisin Maléfique* (*The Evil Neighbor*; Boréal Jr., 1995); *Note:* French-Canadian writer. Juvenile.

Houlet, Florence (?-); *Calendal, Contes de Noël* (*Calendal, Xmas Tales*; SdP Jr 25, 1964); *Le Char Mysterieux and Autres Contes* (*The Mysterious Cart and Other Tales*; SdP Jr 31, 1965); *Note:* Children's tales.

Hourey, P.-A. (?-); *Maeva* (Francex, 1946); *Vuzz* (RF32, 1955)

Houssin, Joël (1953-); *Locomotive Rictus* (ON 6, 1975);

Banlieues Rouges (*Red Suburbs*; anthology/with Christian **Vilà**; ON 12, 1976); *Angel Felina* (FNA 1088, 1981); *Le Pronostiqueur* (*The Handicapper*; FNA 1106, 1981); *Le Champion des Mondes* (*The Champion of the Worlds*; FNA 1126, 1982); *Blue* (FNA 1144, 1982); *Masques de Clown* (*Clown Masks*; FNA 1160, 1982); *Lilith* (FNA 1185, 1982); *Le Chasseur* (*The Hunter*; FNA 1215, 1983); *City* (FNA 1235, 1983); *Game Over* (FNA 1252, 1983); *Voyeur* (FNA 1265, 1983); *L'Autoroute du Massacre* (*Massacre Highway*; FNG 2, 1985); *L'Écho des Suppliciés* (*The Echo of the Tortured*; FNG 14, 1985); *Les Vautours* (*The Vultures*; FN Grands Succes, 1985); rep. FNA 1466, 1986); *Argentine* (PdF 486, 1989); *Le Temps du Twist* (*The Time of Twist*; PdF 512, 1990); as **Chillicothe, Zeb** (see above): Series *Jag*: Nos. 4, 5, 6, 7, 9, 11, 13, and 15 are by Joël Houssin; *Note:* See Chapters VIII and IX. *Blue* was adapted into a graphic novel (with a never-published-before sequel written by Houssin) by artist Philippe Gauckler (see Book 1, Chapter V). For Fleuve Noir, Houssin created the best-selling crime series featuring the character the Dobermann (recently made into a motion picture). That led him to write for television police series such as *Commissaire Moulin*, *Navarro*, and *Les Boeufs Carotte*. His other genre credits include the television mini-series **Les Hordes** and the telefilm **Haute Sécurité** (see Book 1, Chapter II, and the feature film **Ma Vie Est Un Enfer** (see Book 1, Chapter I).

Houville, Gérard d' (Marie-Louise Antoinette de Hérédia, Madame Henri de Régnier; 1875-1963); *En l'An 2000* (*In the Year 2000*); LPT, 1921); *Note:* See Chapter VII. Also see Henri de **Régnier**.

Hoven, Jacques (Conia, Jacques; ?-); *Mourir pour XA* (*To Die for XA*; FN, 1964); *Adieu, Cered* (*Farewell to Cered*; FNA 488, 1972); *Il Etait Une Fois Dans L'Espace* (*Once Upon a Time in Space*; FNA 548, 1973); *Sombre est l'Espace* (*Dark Is Space*; FNA 585, 1973); *Les Intemporels* (*The Intemporals*; FNA 627, 1974); *La Venus de l'Himmenadrock* (*The Venus of the Himme-*

nadrock; FNA 693, 1975); *La Porte des Enfers* (*The Gates of Hell*; FNA 877, 1978); *Triplix* (FNA 917, 1979); *Robinson du Cosmos* (*Cosmic Robinson*; FNA 968, 1980); *Les Non-Humains* (*The Non-Humains*; FNA 1084, 1981); *Note:* See Chapter IX.

Hoveyda, Fereydoun (1925-); *Les Quarantaines* (*The Quarantines*; Gall., 1962); *L'Aérogare* (*The Airport*; Gall., 1965); *Dans une Terre Étrange* (*On a Strange Earth*; Gall., 1968); *Le Losange* (*The Losange*; Los., 1968); *Le Glaive de l'Islam* (*The Sword of Islam*; Den., 1984); *Les Miroirs du Mollah* (*The Mullah's Mirrors*; Vertiges, 1985); *Note:* See Chapter VIII.

Huant, Ernest (?-); *Voyage en Assuro-Socyalie* (*Voyage to Insuro-Socialy*; Debresse, 1965); *La Nouvelle Face de Méduse* (*The New Face of Medusa*; Pensée U., 1976); *La Base Minos* (*Antinoüs II; The Minos Base*; Debresse, 1986); *Les Étranges Courses du Colonel d'Hourdoff* (*The Strange Races of Colonel Hourdoff*; Moreau. 1986); *Réfléchissons, Porphyre!* (*Think, Porphyre!*); Moureau, 1986); *Le Septaméron* (Debresse, 1989)

Hubert, André (?-); *Hypnose* (Cercle d'Or, 1973)

Hubert, Jean-Pierre (1941-); *Planète à Trois Temps* (*Three Time Planet*; ON 8, 1975); *Mort à l'Etouffée* (*Death By Suffocation*; Kes. I&M 2, 1977); *Noël Noir* (*Black Christmas*; as Jean Viluber/with with Christian **Vilà**; Sanguine, 1979); *Couple de Scorpions* (*Couple of Scorpions*; Kes. I&M 11, 1980); *Scènes de Guerre Civile* (*Scenes of a Civil War*; OGB 82, 1982); *Séméla* (Plasma 3, 1983); *Le Champ du Rêveur* (*The Dreamer's Field*; PdF 355, 1983); *Les Faiseurs d'Orage* (*The Storm Makers*; PdF 376, 1984); *Ombromanies* (*Shadowmania*; PdF 412, 1986); *Roulette Mousse* (*Soft Roulette*; PdF 446, 1987); *Coupes Sombres* (*Dark Cuts*; as Jean Viluber/with Christian **Vilà**; FNG 42, 1987); *Cocktail* (Siry SF 5, 1988;

rev. PdF 531, 1992); *Décharges* (*Discharges*; as Jean Viluber/with Christian **Vilà**; FNG 93, 1989); *Greffes Profondes* (*Deep Grafts*; as Jean Viluber/with Christian **Vilà**; FNG 110, 1990); *Le Bleu des Mondes* (*The Blue of the Worlds*; Hac., 1997); *Note:* See chapters VIII and IX.

Hubert-Jacques *see* **Duhemme, Ch**

Hue, Edmond (?-); *L'Équation du Treizième Degré* (*The Thirteenth Degree Equation*; with R. **Destez**; AM, 1920

Hugo, Abel (?-?); *L'Heure de la Mort* (*The Hour of Death*; Le Conteur, 1833)

Hugo, Victor (1802-1885); *Han d'Islande* (*Han of Iceland*; Persan, 1823); *Bug-Jargal* (U. Canel, 1826); *Notre-Dame de Paris* (*The Hunchback of Notre-Dame*; Gosselin, 1831); *La Légende des Siècles* (*Vingtième Siècle; The Legend of the Centuries—20th Century*; Hetzel, Méline, Crans, 1859); *L'Homme qui Rit* (*The Man Who Laughs*; Libr. Intl., 1869); *Note:* See chapters IV and V. Also see **Opéra**.

Hugues, Monica (?-); *Raz-de-marée sur Aquarius* (*Tsunami on Aquarius*; Hac., 1996)

Huisman, Marcelle (?-) & Georges (?-) *see* **Contes et Légendes**

Humann, Mort (Jammet, André; ?-); *Nécrose* (*Necrosis*; Siry Maniac 8, 1988); *Fantôme de Feu* (*Ghost of Fire*; FNG 97, 1989); *Horrific Party* (FNG 104, 1990); *Piège à Djakarta* (*Trap in Djakarta*; FNG 114, 1990); *Rendez-Vous à Khusdar* (*Appointment on Khusdar; as André Jammet; FNASF 4, 1995)Les Marchands de Bali* (*The Merchants of Bali*; as André Jammet; FNASF 9, 1995); *Note:* See Chapter VIII.

Humble, Pierre (?-); *Caddy-Caddy* (Hac., 1929); *La Malle de Léocadie* (*Leocadie's Trunk*; with Jeanne **Broussan-Gaubert**; Hac., 1929); *Un Colon de 13 Ans* (*A 13-Year-Old Colonist*; with Marguerite **Reynier**; Hac., 1933); *Note:* Juvenile SF. *Caddy* is illustrated by Alain **Saint-Ogan**.

Humières, Robert d' (?-?) *see* **Opéra**

Humour (Lord) *see* **Thiaudière, Edmond**

Huot, Alexandre (1897-1953); *L'Impératrice de l'Ungava* (*The Empress of Ungava*; Édouard Garand, 1927); *Note:* French-Canadian writer. The discovery of an unknown city in the vein of H. Rider Haggard.

Hurault de Vibraye, Ludovic-François *see* **Valorbe, François**

Hurtaud, Jacques (?-); *La Révolte des Arbres* (*The Revolt of the Trees*; MOC 3, 1979); *Ombre* (*Shadow*; MOC 15, 1979); *Note:* See Chapter VIII.

Huys, Roger (?-); *Histoires en Toutes Dimensions* (*Tales of All Dimensions*; Debresse, 1961)

Huysmans, Joris-Karl (1848-1907); *À Rebours* (*Reversed*; Charpentier, 1884; transl. as *Against the Grain*, 1922); *Là-Bas* (*Over There*; Tresse & Stock, 1891; transl. as *Down There*, 1928); *Note:* See Chapter IV.

Ibels, André (1872-?); *Gamliel: Une Orgie au temps de Jésus* (*An Orgy in Jesus' Times*; Offenstadt, 1901); *La Maison de l'Enfer* (*The House from Hell*; Fasquelle, 1926); *Note:* Also see **Grand-Guignol**.

Ibrahim, Kamal (1942-); *Celui-ci, Celui-moi* (*This One, This Me*; P.J. Oswald, 1971); *Corps en Friche* (*Fallow Bodies*; St. Germain-des-Prés, 1974); *Vivre en Cas de Terre* (*To Live in Case of Land*; Benanteur, 1975); *L'Existerie* (*The Existery*; Grames, 1978); *Intacter le Jour* (*To Intact the Day*; Récipiendaire, 1978); *Le Voyage de Cent Mètres* (*The 100-Meter Journey*; P.J. Oswald, 1979); *Mètres Cubes de Chambre* (*Cubic Meters of Room*; NéO, 1981); *Vénitiennes* (*Venetians*; Flamm., 1989); *Villes Entrouvertes* (*Open Cities*; Flamm., 1990); *Note:* Syrian-born writer. See Chapter VIII.

Ichbiah, Daniel (?-); *Xyz* (with Yves **Uzureau**; FNA 1920, 1993); *Note:* See Chapter IX.

Idier, Jacques (?-); *La Vallée de Rosena* (*The Valley of Rosena*; Seuil, 1974); *L'Ambassadeur de Venise* (*The Ambassador of Venice*; Tchou, 1978)

Ikor, Roger (1912-1986); *À Travers nos Déserts* (*Through Our Deserts*; AM, 1950); *Les Grands Moyens* (*Powerful Means*; AM, 1951); *Les Fils d'Avrom* (*The Sons of Avrom*; AM, 1955); *Ciel Ouvert* (*Open Sky*; AM, 1959); *Si Le Temps...* (*If Time...*; 6 vols.): *1. Le Semeur de Vent* (*The Wind Sower*; AM, 1960); *2. Les Murmures de Guerre* (*The Whispers of War*; AM, 1961); *3. La Pluie sur la Mer* (*Rain Over the Sea*; AM, 1962); *4. La Ceinture de Ciel* (*The Sky Belt*; AM, 1964); *5. Les Poulains* (*The Poneys*; AM, 1966); *6. Frères Humains* (*Human Brothers*; AM, 1969); *Gloucq ou La Toison d'Or* (*Gluck or the Golden Fleece*; Flamm., 1965); *Le Tourniquet des Innocents* (*The Turnstile of the Innocents*; AM, 1972); *Note:* See Chapter IX.

Ilan, Red *see* **Piret, Daniel**

Illide (?-); *L'Envol* (*The Departure*; Libr. Intégrale, 1934); *Sur la Lune* (*On the Moon*; with **Lesly**; Libr. Intégrale, 1935)

Imbar, Jean-Gérard (?-); *L'Armoire du Fou* (*The Madman's Closet*; FNASF 18, 1996)

Internoscia, Gisèle (?-) *see* **Högue, Sylvie**

Ionesco, Eugène (1912-1994); *La Photo du Colonel* (*The Colonel's Photo*; Gall., 1962); *Note:* Ionesco first wrote the themes of his famous plays (many incorporating genre elements) in the form of short stories collected in the above-listed book.

Irt, Pierre *see* **Ballofet, Pierre**

Isabelle, David (?-); *Invasion Extraterrestre* (*Extraterrestrial Invasion*; La Plume d'Oie, 1997); *Note:* French-Canadian writer.

Ivoi, Paul d' (Deleutre, Paul-Charles; 1856-1915); Series *Voyages Excentriques* (*Eccentric Voyages*): *1. Les Cinq Sous de Lavarède* (*The Five Pennies of Lavarede;* Furne, 1894; rev. as 2 vols, *Les Cinq Sous de Lavarède* (*The Five Pennies of Lavarede*) and *Les Compagnons du Lotus Blanc* (*The Companions of the White Lotus*, BGA, 1924); *2. Le Sergent Simplet* (*Sergeant Simple;* Furne, 1895; rev. as 2 vols., *Le Sergent Simplet* (*Sergeant Simple*) and *Miss Diana*, BGA, 1929); *3. Cousin de Lavarede* (*Lavarede's Cousin;* Furne, 1897; rev. as 2 vols., *Le Diamant d'Osiris* (*Osiris' Diamond*) and *Le Bolide de Lavarède* (*Lavarede's Speedster*, BGA, 1924); *4. Jean Fanfare* (Furne, 1897; rev. as 2 vols., *Le Diane de l'Archipel* (*The Diana of the Archipelago*) and *La Forteresse Roulante* (*The Fortress on Wheel*, BGA, 1930); *5. Corsaire Triplex* (*Corsair Triplex;* Furne, 1898; rev. as 2 vols., *L'Ennemi Invisible* (*The Invisible Enemy*) and *L'Île d'Or* (*The Golden Island*, BGA, 1925); *6. La Capitaine Nilia* (*Captain Nilia;* Furne, 1898; rev. as 2 vols., *La Capitaine Nilia* (*Captain Nilia*) and *Le Secret de Nilia* (*Nilia's Secret*, BGA, 1925); *7. Docteur Mystère* (*Doctor Mystery;* Furne, 1900; rev. as 2 vols., *L'Ours de Siva* (*Shiva's Bear*) and *Le Brahme d'Ellora* (*The Brahmin from Ellora*, BGA, 1926); *8. Cigale en Chine* (*China Cricket;* Furne, 1901; rev. as 2 vols., *Cigale en Chine* (*China Cricket*) and *La Princesse Roseau-Fleuri* (*Princess Flowery Reed*, BGA, 1927); *9. Massiliague de Marseille* (*Massiliague from Marseilles;* Furne, 1902; rev. as 2 vols., *Massiliague de Marseille* (*Massiliague from Marseilles*) and *Le Voeu des Incas* (*The Incas' Wishes*, BGA, 1926); *10. Les Semeurs de Glace* (*The Seeders of Ice;* JDV/Furne, 1903; rev. as 2 vols., *Les Semeurs de Glace* (*The Seeders of Ice*) and *Le Poison Bleu* (*The Blue Poison*, BGA, 1926); *11. Le Serment de Daalia* (*Daalia's Oath;* JDV, 1903/Furne, 1904; rev. as 2 vols., *Le Serment de Daalia* (*Daalia's Oath*) and *La Chasse au Mystère* (*The Mystery Hunt*, BGA, 1925); *12. Le Prince Virgule* (*Prince Comma;* JDV, 1905; rev. as *Millionnaire Malgré Lui* (*Millionnaire in Spite of Himself,* Furne, 1905; rev. as 2 vols., *Millionnaire Malgré Lui* (*Millionnaire in Spite of Himself*) and *Le Prince Virgule* (*Prince Comma*, BGA, 1928); *13. Le Maître du Drapeau Bleu* (*The Master of the Blue Flag;* Furne, 1907; rev. as 2 vols., *Les Masques d'Ambre* (*The Amber Masks*) and *Le Maître du Drapeau Bleu* (*The Master of the Blue Flag*, BGA, 1927); *14. Miss Mousqueterr* (Furne, 1907; rev. as 2 vols., *Miss Mousqueterr* and *Vers la Lumière* (*Towards the Light*, BGA, 1928); *15. Jud Allan, Roi des Lads* (*Jud Allan, King of the Lads;* Furne, 1907; rev. as 2 vols., *Jud Allan* and *Le Roi des Gamins* (*The King of the Lads*, BGA, 1928); *16. Le Roi du Radium* (*The King of Radium;* JDV, 1909; rev. as *La Course au Radium* (*The Radium Race*, Furne, 1909; rev. as 2 vols., as *La Course au Radium* (*The Radium Race*) and *La Radium qui Tue* (*The Killing Radium*, BGA, 1927); *17. L'Aéroplane Fantôme* (*The Phantom Airplane;* Furne, 1910); rev. as 2 vols., *Le Voleur de Pensées* (*The Stealer of Thoughts*) and *Le Lit de Diamants* (*The Bed of Diamonds*, BGA, 1929); *18. Les Voleurs de Foudre* (*The Stealers of Lightning;* serialized in 2 issues, *L'Automobile de Verre* (*The Glass Automobile*, JDV, 1907-08, and *Les Trois Demoiselles Pickpockets* (*The Three Lady Pickpockets*, JDV, 1909-10; rev. as *Les Voleurs de Foudre* (*The Stealers of Lightning*, Furne, 1910; rev. as 2 vols., *Les Voleurs de Foudre* (*The Stealers of Lightning*) and *Les Bonzes Bleus d'Angkhor* (*The Blue Bonzes of Angkhor*, BGA, 1925); *19. L'Ambassadeur Extraordinaire* (*The Extraordinary Ambassador;* JDV, 1911; rev. as *Message du Mkado* (*Message from the Mikado*, Furne, 1911); rev. as 2 vols., *Le Message du Mikado* (*The Message from the Mikado*) and *Une Fillette contre un Empire* (*A Little Girl vs. An Empire*, BGA, 1925); *20. Le Chevalier Illusion* (*The Illusion Knight;* JDV, 1913; rev. as *Les Dompteurs de l'Or* (*The Gold Tamers*, Furne, 1913; rev. as 2 vols., *Les Dompteurs de l'Or* (*The Gold Tamers*) and *L'Épreuve de l'Irréel* (*The Trial of the Unreal*, BGA, 1926); *21. L'Évadé Malgré Lui* (*Escaped in Spite of Himself;* JDV, 1913-14; rev. as *Match de Milliardaires* (*Billionaires' Fight*, Furne, 1914); *Jaima la Double* (*Jaima the Twin;* Tallandier, 1905); *La Patrie en Danger* (*France Threatened;* with Colonel **Royet**; Juven, 1905); *Un, La Mystérieuse* (*One, the Mysterious;* with Colonel **Royet**; serialized in 88 issues, rev. as 2 vols. Juven, 1905); *1. Les Briseurs d'Épées* (*The Sword Breakers*); *2. Le Capitaine Matraque* (*Captain Bludgeon*); *Espion X323—L'Homme Sans Visage* (*Spy X 323—the Faceless Man;* RM, 1908); *Espion X323—Le Canon du Sommeil* (*Spy X 323—the Sleep Gun;* RM, 1908; rev. as *L'Obus de Cristal* (*The Crystal Shell*, RM, 1912); *Le Puits du Maure* (*The Maur's Pit*; RM, 1912); *Note:* See chapter V.

Ixigrec (?-); *L'Avenir est-il Prévisible?* (*Can We Predict the Future?*; Rivet, 1949); *Panurge au Pays des Machines* (*Panurge in the Land of Machines*; 1950); *Les Essais Fantastiques du Dr. Rob* (*The Fantastic Tests of Dr. Rob*; Ruche Ouvrière, 1966)

Izard, Christophe (?-); *Voilà les Zabars* (*Here Come the Zabars*; GP, 1982); *Les Zabars et Ding-Ding* (GP, 1982); *Note:* Juvenile fantasy series based on a children's television show.

Izieu, Jean d' (?-); *Baldur de la Forêt* (*Baldur of the Forest*; SdPJr 3, 1957); *Note:* Juvenile.

Jackson, Ben (Gerbault, Jean-Marie; ?-?); *L'Âge Alpha, ou La Marche du Temps* (*The Alpha Age, or the March of Time*; Méridien, 1942)

Jacob, Louis (1954-); *Les Temps Qui Courent* (*The Running Times*; Hexagone, 1990); *La Vie qui Penche* (*The Leaning Life*; L'Hexagone, 1993); *Note:* French-Canadian writer. *Les Temps* is a post-cataclysmic novel.

Jacob, Yves (?-); *Au-delà de la Fin du Monde* (*Beyond the End of the World*; with Grégoire **Brainin**; Cercle d'Or, 1978); *Soleils Gris* (*Grey Suns*; Filipacchi, 1991); *Il Était Une Fois un Monstre* (*Once Upon a Time a Monster*; Corlet, 1981); *Les Deux Vies de Marie Salmon* (*The Two Lives of Marie Salmon*; Tallandier, 1994)

Jacolliot, Louis (1837-1890); *Le Spiritisme dans le Monde* (*Essai; Spiritism in the World*; Lacroix, 1875); *La Cité des Sables* (*The City of the Sands*; Decaux, 1877); *L'Afrique Mystérieuse* (*Mysterious Africa*; JDV, 1877); *Les Mangeurs de Feu* (*The Fire Eaters*; JDV, 1885-87); *Le Coureur des Jungles* (*The Jungle Racer*; JDV, 1887-89); *Le Crime du Moulin d'Usor* (*The Crime of the Mill of Usor*; Flamm., 1888); *Vengeance de Forçats* (*Convicts' Revenge*; Flamm., 1888); *Les Chasseurs d'Esclaves* (*The Slave Hunters*; Flamm., 1888); *Les Ravageurs de la Mer* (*The Sea Reavers*; Flamm., 1890); *Le Capitaine de Vaisseau* (*The Ship's Captain*; Dentu, 1890); *Perdus sur l'Océan* (*Lost on the Ocean*; JDV, 1892-94); *Note:* See Chapter V.

Jacq, Christian (?-); *La Confrérie des Sages du Nord* (*The Brotherhood of the Northern Sages*; Rocher, 1980); *L'Empire du Pape Blanc* (*The Empire of the White Pope*; Garancière Av. Fant. 9, 1986); *La Reine Soleil* (*The Sun Queen*; Julliard, 1988); *L'Affaire Toutankhamon* (*The King Tut Affair*; Grasset, 1992); *Le Moine et le Vénérable* (*The Monk and the Venerable Man*; RL, 1992); *La Pyramide Assassinée* (*The Murdered Pyramid*; Plon, 1993); *Barrage sur le Nil* (*Dam Over the Nile*; RL, 1994); *Le Temple des Millions d'Années* (*The Million Years Temple*; RL, 1995); *Les Fils de la Lumière* (*The Sons of Light*; Grand Livre du Mois, 1995); *La Bataille de Kadesh* (*The Battle of Kadesh*; Grand Livre du Mois, 1996); *La Dame d'Abou Simbiel* (*The Lady of Abu Simbiel*; RL, 1996); *La Fiancée du Nil* (*The Fiancée from the Nile*; Magnard, 1996); *Nightprowler 1 – Premiers Sangs* (*First Blood*; Khom-Heidon, 1996); *Nightprowler 2 – La Voie du Sang* (*The Way of Blood*; Khom-Heidon, 1996); *Nightprowler 3 – Le Prix du Sang* (*The Price of Blood*; Khom-Heidon, 1997); *Chroniques des Sept Cités* (*Chronicles of the Seven Cities*; Khom-Heidon, 1997); *Note:* See Chapter VIII. Also see *Contes et Légendes*

Jacquart, Roger-Henri (?-); *Cet Étrange Docteur Lang* (*That Strange Dr. Lang*; La Concorde, 1940); *La Prison sous l'Océan* (*The Prison Under the Ocean*; L'Essor, 1944); *Le Dernier Couple* (*The Last Couple*; La Concorde, 1945); *Luc Mahor Contre l'Inconnu: Demonios* (*Luc Mahor vs. The Unknown: Demonios*; Dupuis, 1954); *Note:* See Chapter VII.

Jacquemard, Serge (?-); *Hécatombe dans l'Ombre* (*Holocaust in the Shadows*; FN Combat de l'Ombre, 1977)

Jacques *see* **Cousin Jacques**

Jacquier, Y. du (?-) *see* **Villois, Florent**

Jacquin, J. (?-); *Le Chien de Serlock (sic) Holmes* (*Serlock Holmes' Dog*; with A. **Fabre**; Hac., 1912); *Le Premier Homme de son Espèce* (*The First Man of His Kind*; LPT, 1912); *Les Petits Naufragés du Titanic* (*The Little Castaways of the Titanic*; Hac., 1913); *Entre Ciel et Terre: Aventures d'un Détective Aviateur* (*Between Heaven and Earth: Adventures of an Air Detective*; with A. **Fabre**; Hac., 1914); *Monsieur Tapinois Aviateur* (*Mr. Tapinois, Aviator*; with A. **Fabre**; Hac., 1927); *Le Sommeil sous les Blés* (*Asleep Under the Wheat Fields;* with A. **Fabre**; *LPT,* 1927; rev. as *Celle Qui Dormait Sous La Terre* (*She Who Slept Under the Earth*, Tallandier, 1930); *Le Chemin des Hirondelles* (*Skylark Path*; Crété-Hac., 1928); *Les Cinq Crimes de Monsieur Tapinois* (*The Five Crimes of Mr. Tapinois*; Crété-Ren. du Livre, 1932); *Un Train Sifflait dans la Nuit* (*A Train Whistled in the Night*; with Hervé de **Peslouan**; Hac., 1935)

Jagot, Henry *see* **Valade, Frédéric**

Jammet, André *see* **Humann, Mort**

Jan, Gabriel (Demont, Jean; 1946-); *Au Seuil de l'Enfer* (*The Treshold of Hell*; FNAG 238, 1973); *La Main du Spectre* (*The Spectre's Hand*; FNAG 255, 1974); *La Planète aux Deux Soleils* (*The Planet with Two Suns*; FNA 648, 1974); *Pandémoniopolis* (FNA 679, 1975); *Les Zwuls de Rehan* (*The Zwuls of Rehan*; FNA 690, 1975); *La Chair des Vohuz* (*The Flesh of the Vohuz*; FNA 720, 1976); *Terreur sur Izaad* (*Terror on Izaad*; FNA 740, 1976); *L'An 22704 des Wans* (*Year 22704 of the Wans*; FNA 751, 1976); *Enfants d'Univers* (*Children of the Universe*; FNA 766, 1977); *Maloa* (FNA 786, 1977); *Les Robots de Xaar* (*The Robots of Xaar*; FNA 801, 1977); *Concentration 44* (FNA 830, 1978); *La Forêt Hurlante* (*The Screaming Forest*; FNA 849, 1978); *Les Maîtres Verts* (*The Green Masters*; FNA 868, 1978); *Reviens, Quémalta* (*Come Back, Quemalta*; FNA 885, 1978); *Impalpable Vénus* (*Untouchable Venus*; FNA 906, 1979); *Ballet des Ombres* (*Ballet of Shadows*; FNSL 74, 1979); *L'Étrange Éliphas* (*The Strange Eliphas*; as Yann Delmon; MOC 4, 1979); *L'Homme Alphoméga* (*The Alphomega Man*; FNA 920, 1979); *Planète des Anges* (*Planet of Angels*; FNA 972, 1980); *Dingue de Planète* (*Crazy Planet*; FNA 984, 1980);

Rêves en Synthèse (*SynThetic Dreams*; FNA 1020, 1980); *Tamkan le Paladin* (*Tamkan the PaladIn*; FNA 1042, 1981); *Étoile sur Mentha* (*Star Over Metha*; FNA 1057, 1981); *Un Drahl Va Naître* (*A Drahl Will Be Born*; FNA 1069, 1981); *Sheena* (FNA 1102, 1981); *Nadar* (FNA 1123, 1982); *Tu Vivras, Céréluna* (*You Will Live, Cereluna*; FNA 1141, 1982); *Le Voyage de Baktur* (*The Voyage of Baktur*; FNA 1153, 1982); *Chasse au Serpent* (*Serpent Hunt*; as Yann Delmon; MOC 31, 1982); *Brigade de Mort* (*Death Brigade*; FNA 1195, 1983); *Les Jardins de Xantha* (*The Gardens of Xantha*; FNA 1205, 1983); *La Grande Prêtresse de Yashtar* (*The High Priestess of Yashtar*; FNA 1216, 1983); *Un Jeu Parmi Tant d'Autres* (*A Game Among Many Others*; FNA 1268, 1983); *On Ne Meurt Pas Sous Le Ciel Rouge* (*No One Dies Under the Red Sky*; FNA 1285, 1984); *La Guerre de la Lumière* (*The War of Light*; FNA 1334, 1984); *La Troisième Puissance* (*The Third Power*; FNA 1350, 1985); *Le Feu du Vahad'Har* (*The Fire of the Vahad'Har*; FNA 1450, 1986); *Cacophonie du Nouveau Monde* (*Cacophony of the New World*; FNA 1494, 1986); *Les Elus de Tôh* (*The Elects of Toh*; FNA 1598, 1987); *Un Fils de Salomon* (*A Son of Solomon*; Foyer de Cachan, 1996); *Note:* See Chapters VIII and IX.

Janier, Gabrielle (?-); *Quand Bébé-Lune sera Grand-Père* (*When Baby Moon Becomes a Grand-Father*; Capricorne, 1958); *L'Oiseau de Brume* (*The Bird of Mist*; St. Germain-des-Prés, 1971); *Le Clair d'Étoiles* (*Clear of Stars*; St. Germain-des-Prés, 1982); *Avant l'Oubli* (*Before Oblivion*; Orbec-F. Rozé, 1986)

Janin, Jules (1804-1874); *L'Âne Mort et la Femme Guillotinée* (*The Dead Ass and the Guillotined Woman*; Baudoin, 1829); *La Double Méprise* (*The Double Misunderstanding*; Levavasseur-Mesnier, 1832); *Contes Fantastiques et Contes Littéraires* (*Fantastical and Literary Tales*; Levavasseur-Mesnier, 1833); *Les Catacombes* (*The Catacombs*; Werdet, 1839); *Note:* See Chapter IV.

Janin, Marc (?-?); *Les Aviateurs des Andes* (*The Andes Aviators*; Boivin, 1912); *Un Grognard de 12 Ans* (*A 12-Year-Old Soldier*; Boivin, 1914); *L'Empire de la Sierra* (*The Empire of the Sierra*; Garnier, 1918)

Jansen, Michel *see* **Van Herp, Jacques**

Jaouen, Hervé-Marie (1946-); *Toilette des Morts* (*Washing the Dead*; FN, 1983); *Le Celte Noir* (*The Dark Celt*; as Michaël Clifden; FNA 1328, 1984); *Les Hommes-Vecteurs* (*The Vector Men*; as Michaël Clifden; FNA 1392, 1985); *La Mariée Rouge* (*The Red Bride*; NéO, 1986); *L'Adieu aux Îles* (*Farewell to the Islands*; Mazarine, 1986); *Histoires d'Ombres* (*Tales of Shadows*; Den., 1986); *Le Monstre du Lac Noir* (*The Monster of Dark Lake*; Syros, 1987); *Les Douze Chambres*

de Monsieur Hannibal (*The 12 Rooms of Mr. Hannibal*; Stock, 1992); *Toutes les Couleurs du Noir* (*All the Colors of Black*; Den., 1995); *Note:* See Chapter IX.

Jarci, Félix (?-); *La Paix par la Terreur—Télépénétration* (*Peace Through Terror—Telepenetration*; with M. **Jarci**; Jarci, 1933)

Jarry, Alfred (1873-1907); *Ubu Roi* (*King Ubu*; MdF, 1896); *Ubu Enchaîné* (*Ubu in Chains*; Revue Blanche, 1900); *Le Surmâle* (*The Supermale*; Fasquelle, 1902); *Gestes et Opinions du Docteur Faustroll* (*Deeds and Opinions of Dr. Faustroll*; Fasquelle, 1911); *Note:* See chapters IV and VI.

Jasmin, Claude (1930-); *Délivrez-Nous du Mal* (*Deliver Us from Evil*; À la page, 1961); *La Corde au Cou* (*The Rope Around the Neck*; RL, 1961); *Blues pour un Homme Averti* (*Blues for an Informed Man*; Parti Pris, 1964); *Éthel et le Terroriste* (*Ethel and the Terrorist*; Déom, 1964); *Et puis tout est Silence* (*And Then All Is Silence*; L'Homme, 1965); *Nicole Sans Micro Ni Caméra* (*Nicole Without Microphone Nor Camera*; Québec-Presse, 1969); *Le Loup de Brunswick City* (*The Wolf of Brunwisck City*; Léméac, 1976); *Le Veau Dort* (*The Calf Sleeps*; Léméac, 1979); *L'Armoire de Pantagruel* (*Pantagruel's Dresser*; Léméac, 1982); *Le Crucifié du Sommet Bleu* (*The Man Crucified on Blue Summit*; Léméac, 1984); *Partir? (To Go?;* Vidéo-Presse, 1991; rev. as *Partir à l'Aventure, Loin, Très Loin* (*To Go Adventuring, Far, Very Far*, Quebecor, 1995); *Note:* French-Canadian writer. *Nicole* is about a sect of Amazons. *Partir* is about alien contact.

Jasper, Ron (?-); *Trust* (Delachaux & Niestlé, 1981); *Crescent Street* (Domino, 1984); *Note:* French-Canadian writer. *Crescent Street* is a political fiction about a secret invasion of Canada by super-powered Russians.

Jaunez-Sponville, Pierre-Ignace (?-?); *La Philosophie de Ruravebohni* (with Nicolas **Bugnet**; Le Normant, 1809); *Note:* Sub-titled "A Country the Discovery of Which Would Seem of Great Interest to Mankind, or Dialogued Narration of the Means Through Which the Ruraveheuxis, Inhabitants of That Same Country, Have Been Led to True and Stable Happiness."

Jayat, Sandra (1939-); *Les Deux Lunes de Savyo* (*The Two Moons of Savyo*; Cast., 1972)

Jean, Albert (1892-); *Le Passant du Monde* (*The World's Pedestrian*; 78 Blvd St. Germain, 1919); *Le Singe* (*The Monkey*; with Maurice **Renard**; Crès, 1925; transl. as *Blind Circle*, 1928); *La Proie de l'Homme* (*Man's Prey*; Gall., 1928); *Le Secret de Barbe-Bleue* (*Bluebeard's Secret*; Sfelt, 1950); *Note:* Also see **Grand-Guignol**.

Jean-Boulan, Robert (?-); *L'Île des Centaures* (*Centaur Island*; VA, 1936); *La Ville des Tritons* (*The City of Tri-*

tons; VA, 1937); *Le Sortilège Malgache* (*The Malgache Spell*; SEPIA, 1937); *La Reine des Chercheurs d'Or* (*The Queen of the Gold Hunters*; SEPIA, 1938); *Au Paradis des Étoiles* (*In the Paradise of Stars*; SEPIA, 1938); *Le Placer de l'Épouvante* (*The Place of Terror*; Tallandier, 1938); *Les Aventuriers de la Planète Mars* (*The Adventurers of Planet Mars*; SEPIA, 1941); *Note:* See Chapter VII.

Jean-Charles, Jehanne (?-); *Les Plumes du Corbeau* (*The Raven's Feathers*; Pauvert, 1973); *La Mort, Madame* (*Death, Madam*; Flamm., 1974); *Vous avez dit Horrible?* (*Did You Say Awful?*; Jean Goujon, 1980); *La Nuit de l'Engoulevent* (*Night of the Nightjar*; Flamm., 1985); *Note:* See Chapter VIII.

Jeancourt, Auguste (Ajasson de Grandsagne, J.-B.-F.-E.; ?-?); *Le Manteau d'un Sous-Lieutenant* (*The Sub-Lieutenant's Coat*; 1832); *Note:* See Chapter IV.

Jeanjean, Marcel (?-); *La Merveilleuse Invention de l'Oncle Pamphile* (*Uncle Pamphile's Marvelous Invention*; 1930); *Note:* See Chapter VII.

Jean-Mariat, Madeleine (?-) *see* **Contes et Légendes**

Jeanne, Henri-Georges *see* **Magog, H.-J.**

Jeanne, René (1887-1946); *L'Image qui Tue* (*The Killing Image*; Coquette, 1922); *Le Château de la Mort Lente* (*The Castle of Slow Death*; Tallandier, 1926); *L'Île Enchantée* (*The Enchanted Island*; Tallandier, 1927); *Les Mystères d'Hollywood* (*The Mysteries of Hollywood*; with E. M. **Laumann**; RMY, 1928); *Si le 9 Thermidor...* (*If on 9 Thermidor*; with E. M. **Laumann**; Tallandier, 1929); *Le Cargo de la Mort* (*The Cargo of Death*; with Pierre **Mariel**; RMY, 1929); *La Griffe du Lion* (*The Lion's Claw*; with Pierre **Mariel**; RMY, 1931); *Napoléon-Bis* (Oeuvres Libres, 1932); *Le Voilier des Hommes sans Âmes* (*The Sailship of the Soulless Men*; Janicot, 1944); *Celui qui Voulait Fabriquer du Bonheur* (*He Who Wanted to Manufacture Happiness*; Vigneau, 1947); *Note:* See Chapter VII. Also see **Grand-Guignol**.

Jeannequin, Michel (?-); *Voyage dans Vénus* (*Voyage to Venus*; Scorpion, 1959)

Jeanniot, Pierre (?-?) *see* **Grand-Guignol**

Jéhin, Jules (1870-1947); *Les Aventures Extraordinaires de Deux Canayens* (*The Extraordinary Adventures of Two Canucks*; 1918); *Note:* French-Canadian writer. Two French-Canadians use a superior flying machine to set up a short-lived Empire of the Air.

Jelinek, Henriette (?-); *La Marche du Fou* (*The Madman's Walk*; Gall., 1974); *Dans la Nuit des Deux Mondes* (*In the Night of Two Worlds*; Gall., 1975); *Ann Lee rachète les Âmes* (*Ann Lee Buys Back Souls*; Julliard, 1978); *Le Porteur de Dieu* (*The God Bearer*; Julliard, 1979);

Madame le Président de la République Française (*Madam President*; Stock, 1981); *Une Goutte de Poison* (*A Drop of Poison*; Ramsay, 1987)

Jessua, Alain (1932-); *Traitement de Choc* (*Shock Treatment*; Seghers, 1973); *Note:* Novelization of the eponymous 1972 film (see Book 1, Chapter I).

Jeury, Michel (1934-); *Aux Étoiles du Destin* (*Destiny's Stars*; as Albert Higon; RF 68, 1960; rev., OGB 108, 1984); *La Machine du Pouvoir* (*The Machine of Power*; as Albert Higon; RF 71, 1960; rev., Néo 16, 1980); *Le Temps Incertain* (*The Uncertain Time*; A&D 22, 1973); *Les Singes du Temps* (*The Time Monkeys*; A&D 31, 1974); *Utopies 75* (*Utopia '75*); anthology/with Jean-Pierre **Andrevon**, Philippe **Curval** & Christine **Renard**; A&D 36, 1975); *Soleil Chaud, Poisson des Profondeurs* (*Warm Sun, Fish from the Deep*; A&D 43, 1976); *Les Animaux de Justice* (*The Justice Animals*; as Albert Higon; JL 640, 1976); *Le Jour des Voies* (*The Day of the Ways*; as Albert Higon; JL 761, 1977); *L'Empire du Peuple* (*The People's Empire*; as Albert Higon/with Pierre **Marlson**; AMSF2 23, 1977); *Planète Socialiste* (*Socialist Planet*; anthology/with Bernard **Blanc**; Kes., 1977); *Le Sablier Vert* (*The Green Hourglass*; AdE 5, 1977; rev. PP 5154, 1983); *Le Monde du Lignus* (*The World of the Lignus*; AdE 9, 1978; rev. PP 5161, 1983); *Poney-Dragon* (Kes. I&M 4, 1978); *Les Enfants de Mord* (*The Children of Mord*; PP 5053, 1979); *L'Univers-Ombre* (*The Shadow Universe*; Encre 1, 1979; rev. FNA 1544, 1987); *Le Territoire Humain* (*The Human Territory*; A&D 54,

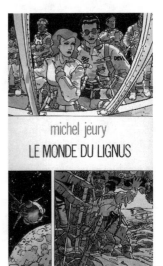

michel jeury
LE MONDE DU LIGNUS

collection "l'âge des étoiles" / robert laffont

ALBERT HIGON

le jour des Voies

SCIENCE-FICTION
Michel Jeury

LES ENFANTS DE MORD

1979); *Les Îles de la Lune* (*The Islands of the Moon*; FNA 945, 1979); *Le Livre d'Or de Gérard Klein* (*The Golden Book of GK*; anthology; PP 5056, 1979); *Les Écumeurs du Silence* (*The Reavers of Silence*; FNA 992, 1980); *Le Sombre Eclat* (*The Dark Shining*; FNA 1003, 1980); *Le Seigneur de l'Histoire* (*The Lord of History*; FNA 1034, 1980); *Les Yeux Géants* (*The Giant Eyes*; A&D 59, 1980); *Nuit et Voyage* (*Night and Travel*; Snake, 1980); *Cette Terre* (*That Earth*; PP 5111, 1981); *La Sainte Espagne Programmée* (*The Holy Programmed Spain*; FNA 1062, 1981); *Les Hommes-Processeurs* (*The Processor Men*; FNA 1091, 1981); *Le Vol du Serpent* (*The Flight of the Serpent*; PP 5145, 1982); *La Planète du Jugement* (*The Planet of Judgment*; FNA 1133, 1982); *Goer-le-Renard* (*Goer-The-Fox*; FNA 1181, 1982); *L'Orbe et la Roue* (*The Orb and the Wheel*; A&D 75, 1982); *Le Livre d'Or de Michel Jeury* (*The Golden Book of Michel Jeury*; PP 5133, 1982); *Les Tours Divines* (*The Divine Towers*; FNA 1206, 1983); *Quand le Temps Soufflera* (*When Time Blows*; FNA 1239, 1983); *Vers l'Âge d'Or* (*Towards the Golden Age*; FNA 1260, 1983); *L'Île Bleue* (*The Blue Island*; with Jean-Claude **Guidicelli**; Plasma, 1983); *L'Anaphase du Diable* (*The Devil's Anaphase*; FNA 1316, 1984); *Les Louves Debout* (*The She-Wolves Standing*; FN Engrenage, 1984); *Les Démons de Jerusalem* (*The Demons of Jerusalem*; PP 5216, 1985); *Le Dernier Paradis* (*The Last Paradise*; FNA 1365, 1985); *Les Survivants du Paradis* (*The Survivors from Paradise*; FNA 1376, 1985); *La Marée d'Or* (*The Golden Tide*; FNA1394, 1985); *Le Jeu du Monde* (*The World Game*; A&D , 1985); *La Croix et la Lionne* (*The Cross and the She-Lion*; JL 2035, 1986); *Aux Yeux la Lune* (*The Eyes of the Moon*; FNA 1623, 1988); *Les Mondes Furieux* (*The Angry Worlds*; Siry SF 8, 1988); rep. as Higon, FNA 1840, 1991); *La Chimère Infernale* (*The Infernal Chimera*; as Albert Higon; FNA 1855, 1992); *Le Vaisseau-Démon* (*The Demon-Ship*; as Albert Higon; FNA 1867, 1992); *Note:* See Chapter IX. Jeury's television credits include the co-written 1983 *L'Île Bleue* and the short-feature *Jour "J" Comme Jouet* (see Book 1, Chapter II).

Jimenes, Guy (1954-); *Noël le Corbeau* (*Noel the Crow*; Centurion, 1982); *L'Arche du Diable* (*The Devil's Ark*; Nathan, 1985); *Le Grand Réparateur* (*The Great Repairman*; Flamm., 1988); *Le Boulanger de Roc-Noir* (*The Baker of Black Rock*; Centurion, 1989); *Note:* Juveniles.

Jobin, François (1946-); *Max ou le Sens de la Vie* (*Max or the Meaning of Life*; Q/A, 1992); *La Deuxième Vie de Louis Thibert* (*Louis Thibert's Second Life*; Q/A, 1996); *Note:* French-Canadian writer.

Jodorowsky, Alexandro (1929-); *Le Paradis des Perroquets* (*The Parrots' Paradise*; Flamm., 1984); *Les Araignées sans Mémoires* (*Spiders Without Memories*; Humanos, 1980); *L'Arbre du Dieu Pendu* (*The Tree of the Hanged God*; Métailié, 1996); *Note:* Chilean-born film director and writer of graphic novels. See Book 1, Chapters V and VI.

Joesbourg (?-); *Histoire d'Avant le Déluge* (*Story from Before the Flood*; Regain, 1952)

Jogand-Pagès, Gabriel-Antoine *see* **Bataille, Henry**

Johan, François (?-); *Les Enchantements de Merlin* (*Merlin's Spells*; AdP 1, 1980); *Lancelot du Lac* (AdP 11, 1980); *Perceval le Gallois* (AdP 17, 1981); *La Quête du Graal* (*Quest for the Grail*; AdP 22, 1981); *La Fin des Temps Chevaleresques* (*The End of the Knightly Times*; AdP 24, 1981); *Le Roman de la Violette* (*The Novel of the Violet*; Cast., 1982); *Till l'Espiègle* (*Till the Sly*; Cast., 1982); *Floire et Blanchefleur* (Cast., 1983); *Ls Quatre Fils Aymon* (*The Four Aymon Sons*; Cast., 1983); *Les Chevaliers de la Table Ronde* (*The Knights of the Round Table*; Cast., 1987); *Note:* See Chapter I.

Jolicoeur, Louis (1957-); *L'Araignée du Silence* (*The Spider of Silence*; L'Instant Même, 1987); *Note:* French-Canadian writer. Collection of fantastic tales.

Jolly, Thérèse (?-); *Aux Couleurs du Diable* (*The Devil's Colors*; Cercle d'Or, 1979); *Note:* Folk tales.

Jolyot De Crébillon, Claude-Prosper (1707-1777); *Le Sopha* (1740, transl. 1742); *Note:* Erotic tale about a vizir turned into a sopha. Also published *"A Gazrah, de l'imprimerie du très-pieux, très clément et très-auguste Sultan des Indes, an de l'Hégire 1120"* (*To Gazrah, from* *the Presses of the Very Pious, Very Merciful and Very August Sultan of India, Year of the Hegira 1120).*

Jonchère, Ernest (?-?); *Clovis Bourbon: Excursion dans le 20ème Siècle* (*Clovis Bourbon: Travel to the 20th Century*; Libr. Internationale, 1868); *Note:* See Chapter V. Also wrote socio-political texts under the pseudonym of "Ernest Brelay."

Joncquel, Octave (?-) *see* **Varlet, Théo**

Jonquelle, Népomucène (1904-1957); *Monsieur Lune et Ses Amis* (*Mr. Moon and His Friends*; Bourrelier, 1950); *Les Avatars de Pilou* (*Pilou's Misadventures*; Delarge, 1977); *Le Pays Hors du Monde* (*The Land Outside the World*; Ecole des Loisirs, 1991); *Note:* Juveniles.

Jonquet, Thierry (?-); *La Bombe Humaine* (*The Human Bomb*; Syros, 1994); *Mygale* (Gall, 1995); *Mémoire en Cage* (*Caged Memory*; Gall., 1995); *Lapoigne et la Chasse aux Fantômes* (*Lapoigne and the Ghost Hunt*; Nathan, 1995); *Lapoigne et la Fiole Mystérieuse* (*Lapoigne and the Mysterious Vial*; Nathan, 1996); *Lapoigne à la Foire du Trône* (*Lapoigne and the Big Fair*; Nathan, 1996); *Lapoigne et l'Ogre du Métro* (*Lapoigne and the Subway Ogre*; Nathan, 1997); *Note:* Juveniles. See Chapter VIII.

Joseph-Renaud, Jean (1874-1946); *Le Chercheur de Merveilleux* (*The Seeker of Wonders*; Calmann-Lévy, 1907); *Un Amateur de Mystères* (*A Lover of Mysteries*; Lafitte, 1910); *Une Nuit Tragique* (*A Tragic Night*; Lafitte, 1913); *Les Doigts qui Parlent* (*The Talking Fingers*; Ren. du Livre, 1917); *Le Clavecin Hanté* (*The Haunted Harpsichord*; Lafitte, 1920); *La Vivante Épingle* (*The Living Needle*; Lafitte, 1922); *Lumières dans la Nuit* (*Lights in the Night*; Ferenczi, 1923); *Le Marquis Tragique* (*The Tragic Marquess*; Ollendorff, 1924); *La Vasque d'Or* (*The Golden Basin*; Fasquelle, 1925); *Un Mystérieux Message* (*A Mysterious Message*; Hac., 1925); *Les Barbonnes* (Fasquelle, 1926); *Le Seigneur Mystère* (*Lord Mystery*; Ren. Du Livre, 1929); *Le Document 127* (*Document 127*); Plon, 1931; *Au-Delà* (*Beyond*; Oeuvres Libres, 1932); *Les Deux Idoles* (*The Two Idols*; Plon, 1932); *L'Épingle Verte* (*The Green Needle*; Baudinière, 1933; rev. as *L'Épingle de Jade* (*The Jade Needle*, La Frégate, 1946; *Seza et Circé* AM, 1935); *Le Violon Fantôme* (*The Ghostly Violin*; R. Simon, 1938); *La Cascade Rouge* (*The Red Waterfall*; Fayard, 1938); *Le Losange Rouge* (*The Red Losange*; Tallandier, 1941); *Note:* See Chapter VI. Also see **Grand-Guignol.**

Jouanne, Emmanuel (1960-); *Damiers Imaginaires* (*Imaginary Squares*; PdF 336, 1982); *Nuage* (*Cloud*; A&D 78, 1983); *Ici Bas* (*Here Below*; PdF 384, 1984); *Dites-le avec des Mots* (*Say It with Words*; with Jean-Pierre **Vernay**; PdF 410, 1985); *Cruautés* (*Cruelties*; PdF 433, 1987); *L'Âge de Fer* (*The Iron Age;* Siry SF 4, 1988*);*

rep. as *L'Hiver Aller-Retour* (*Winter Back and Forth*, PdF 563, 1995); *Terre* (*Earth*; Den., 1988); *Rêve de Chair* (*Dream of Flesh*; with Jacques **Barbéri**; FNG 78, 1988); *Le Rêveur de Chats* (*The Dreamer of Cats*; PdF 479, 1988); *La Trajectoire de la Taupe* (*The Mole's Trajectory*; PdF 503, 1989); *Note:* See chapters VIII and IX.

Joubert, Jean (1928-); *Les Neiges de Juillet* (*The Snows of July*; Julliard, 1963); *La Forêt Blanche* (*The White Forest*; Grasset, 1972); *L'Homme de Sable* (*The Sandman*; Grasset, 1975); *Le Sphinx et Autres Récits* (*The Sphinx and Other Tales*; Cherche-Midi, 1978); *Les Sabots Rouges* (*The Red Clogs*; Grasset, 1979); *Histoire de la Lune et de quelques Étoiles* (*Story of the Moon and a Few Stars*; Amitié, 1981); *Mystère à Papendroch* (*Mystery in Papendroch*; Ecole des Loisirs, 1982); *Histoires de la Forêt Profonde* (*Tales of the Deep Forest*; Ecole des Loisirs, 1984); *Le Lézard Grec* (*The Greek Lizard*; Grasset, 1984); *Les Enfants de Noé* (*The Children of Noah*; École des Loisirs, 1987); *Note:* Juveniles.

Joubert, Noël (?-); *Adelaide, les Montagnes de l'Oubli* (*The Mountains of Oblivion*; Émeraude, 1997); *Note:* French-Canadian writer.

Jouglet, René (1884-1953); *Le Nouveau Corsaire* (*The New Corsair*; Plon, 1926); *Le Bal des Ardents* (*The Fiery Ball*; Plon, 1926); *Voyage à la République des Piles* (*Voyage to the Republic of Piles*; Grasset, 1928); *Les Aventuriers* (*The Adventurers*; Calmann-Lévy, 1930); *La Ville Perdue* (*The Lost City*; Grasset, 1936); *La Nuit Magique* (*The Magical Night*; L'Illustration, 1939); *Le Masque et le Visage* (*The Mask and the Face*; Grasset, 1945)

Joullot, E. (?-?) *see* **Grand-Guignol**

Jouly, André *see* **Van Herp, Jacques**

Jourat, Stéphane *see* **Stork, Christopher**

Jouravieff, Ovide *see* **Stork, Christopher**

Jouve, Pierre-Jean (?-); *La Scène Capitale* (*The Capital Scene*; Gall., n.d.)

Jouvenel, Bertrand de (?-) *see* **Prat, Marcelle**

Jouvet, Pierre (?-); *L'Araignée de la Nuit* (*The Night Spi-*

der; Jouvet, 1942; rev. as *L'Île de l'Araignée* (*The Island of the Spider*; Jouvet, 1978); *L'Étrange Faculté d'Antoine Santaille* (*The Strange Faculty of Antoine Santaille*; Sézanne, 1944); *L'Impossible Enquête* (*The Impossible Investigation;* Jouvet, 1946; rev. as *L'Infernal Périple* (*The Hellish Journey*; Jouvet, 1979); *Le Sphinx Tête de Mort* (*The Death-Head Sphinx*; Lyon, rue Trarieux, 1947); *Le Dilemme ou Dix Mille Hommes pour Refaire le Monde* (*The Dilemma, or 10,000 Men to Remake the World*; Jouvet 1979)

Jouvin, Jack (?-?) *see* **Grand-Guignol**

Jubin, Georges (1868-?) *see* **Grand-Guignol** and **Max Maurey**

Judenne, Roger (1948-); *La Colère du Dieu Serpent* (*The Wrath of the Snake God*; Amitié, 1986); *L'Enfant-Chevreuil* (*The Deer Child*; Amitié, 1987); *Le Propriétaire de la Cathédrale* (*The Owner of the Cathedral*; Flamm., 1988); *Contes de Fées* (*Fairy Tales*; Amitié, 1988); *Les Diables de Séville* (*The Devils of Seville*; Amitié, 1988); *Note:* Juveniles.

Juillet, Jacques-Henri (?-); *L'Enfer est à Tout le Monde* (*Hell Belongs to Everyone*; as Roland Patrick; Pic, 1953); *Le Soleil de la Chair: Histoires d'un Autre Monde* (*The Sun of Flesh: Tales from Another World*; as Roland Patrick; Pic, 1953); *De l'Amour et et du Vent* (*Love and Wind*; as Carol Paterson; Grand Damier, 1954); *Vénus des Neiges* (*Venus of the Snows*; as Yann R. Patrick; L'Arabesque, 1955); *Atomes à Vendre* (*Atoms for Sale*; as Henri Chamelet; Grand Damier, 1955); *Le Diable à Sept Queues* (*The Seven-Tailed Devil*; as Henri Chamelet; Grand Damier, 1955); *Les Paladins du Ciel* (*Paladins of the Sky*; Cosmos 5, 1955); *Les Visiteurs de l'An 2000* (*The Visitors from Year 2000;* Cosmos 6, 1956); *Le Septième Ciel* (*The Seventh Heaven*; Cosmos 8, 1956); *La Montagne aux Ivresses* (*The Mountain of Drunkenness*; as Carol Paterson; Grand Damier, 1956); *Nuits Écossaises* (*Scottish Nights*; as Carol Paterson; Grand Damier, 1956); *Un Certain M. X* (*A Certain Mr. X*; as Henri Chamelet; Grand Damier, 1956); *Le Pêcheur de Lune (ou Les Voluptés Interdites)* (*The Fisher of Moons (or Forbidden Pleasures)*; M. Grillet, 1956); *Massacre au Clair de Lune* (*Massacre in Moonlight*; as Henri Chamelet; Grand Damier, 1957); *Haute Flibuste* (*High Piracy*; Styx, 1957); *Fort 3... Clair 4* (Mykta, 1997); *Note:* See Chapter IX.

Julien, Suzanne (Julien, Susanne) (1954–); *Le Moulin Hanté* (*The Haunted Windmill*; Tisseyre, 1990); *Le Retour du Loup-Garou* (*The Return of the Werewolf*; Tisseyre, 1993); *Une Voix Troublante* (*A Troubling Voice*; Tisseyre, 1996); *Note:* French-Canadian writer. Children's ghost story/thriller.

Julien, Viviane (Da Silva, Viviane; 1936-); *Ce N'est Pas* *Parce Qu'On Est Petit Qu'On Peut Pas Être Grand* (*It's Not Because One Is Small That One Can't Be Tall*; based on a script by David Sigmund; Q/A, 1987); *Le Jeune Magicien* (*The Young Magician*; based on a script by Waldemar Dziki; Q/A, 1987); *Danger Pleine Lune* (*Danger Full Moon*; Q/A, 1993); *Le Retour des Aventuriers du Timbre Perdu* (*The Return of the Raiders of the Lost Stamp*; Q/A, 1994); *Note:* French-Canadian writer. Children's-book fantasies.

Jullien, Jean (1854-1919); *Enquête sur le Monde Futur* (*Investigation on the Future World*; Fasquelle, 1909)

Junod, Roger-Louis (?-); *Alice Rivaz* (Ed. Universitaires Fribourg, 1980); *Les Enfants du Roi Marc* (*The Children of King Marc*; B. Galland, 1980); *Une Ombre Éblouissante* (*A Dazzling Shadow*; AdH, 1989); *Nouvelle Donne en Arkadia* (*New Deal in Arkadia*; AdH, 1993)

Jurdant, Louis Thomas (?-); *Orient-Express* (Rex, 1933); *Le Secret de la Maison Verte* (*The Secret of the Green House*; Ed. de France, 1936); *L'Épouvante sur la Ville* (*Terror Over the City*; 2 vols; Bonne Presse, 1937); *1. Le Porte-Mines d'Argent* (*The Silver Pen*); *2. Le Dragon Noir* (*The Black Dragon*); *Agence Deck and Cie.* (*The Deck and Co. Agency*; Dupuis, 1937); *Cent Mille Dollars au-dessus du Lac Michigan* (*$100,000 Above Lake Michigan*; Bonne Presse, 1938); *La Fiancée de Mob et Parkle* (*Mob and Parkle's Fiancee*; Dupuis, 1938); *Le Cercle d'Or* (*The Golden Circle*; Dupuis, 1938); *La Horde Noire* (*The Black Horde*; Dupuis, 1939); *Service Secret Office B* (Dupuis, 1939); *Le Gardien de la Porte Noire* (*The Guardian of the Black Gate*; Libr. Champs-Élysées, 1940); *La Maison du Soleil Noir* (*The House of the Black Sun*; Arc-en-Ciel, 1940); *Profondeurs* (*The Depths*; Lethielleux, 1942); *Tricheurs* (*Cheaters*; Bonne Presse, 1951); *Dérive* (*Adrift*; Dupuis, 1951); *L'Homme au Manteau Vert Pomme* (*The Man with the Apple Green Coat*; Dupuis, 1951); *Les Gens qui avaient perdu la Tête* (*The People Who Lost Their Heads*; Dupuis, 1954); *Nomades* (Dupuis, 1957); *Le Cercueil de Laque* (*The Lacquered Coffin*; n.d.; Conquistador, n.d.).

Jurgenson, Liuba (?-); *Avoir Sommeil* (*To Feel Sleepy*; Gall., 1981); *Note:* Russian-born writer. Fantastic tales written in French.

Juteau, Marjolaine (?-); *Le Pouvoir d'Olivier* (*Olivier's Power*; Tisseyre, 1990); *Note:* French-Canadian writer. Children's book about a boy who talks with spirits.

Juvenet, Fernand (?-?) *see* **Grand-Guignol**

Ka, Olivier (1967-); *Bioutifoul Weurld* (Zébu, 1995)*Je suis Venu te Dire que je suis Mort* (*I Came to Tell You That I'm Dead*; Florent Massot, 1997)

Kâá *see* **Marignac, Pascal**

Kaba, Alkaly (1936-); *Contes de l'Afrique Noire* (*Tales* *from Dark Africa*; Naaman, 1973); *Walanda, la Leçon* (*Walanda, the Lesson*; St. Germain-des-Prés, 1976); *Les Problèmes du Diable* (*The Devil's Problems*; with Pierre **Gaudette**; Naaman, 1978); *Note:* French-Canadian writer born in Mali.

Kacew, Romain *see* **Gary, Romain**

Kahn, Gustave (1859-1936); *Limbes de Lumières* (*Limbos of Light*; Demqan, 1897); *Le Conte de l'Or et du Silence* (*The Tale of Gold and Silence*; MdF, 1898); *Les Petits Âmes Pressées* (*The Little Pressed Souls*; Ollendorff, 1898); *Le Cirque Solaire* (*The Solar Circus*; Revue Blanche, 1899); *Contes Hollandais* (*Dutch Tales*; Fasquelle, 1903); *Mourle* (Rieder, 1925); *Contes Juifs* (*Jewish Tales*; Fasquelle, 1926); *Note:* See Chapter IV.

Kahn, Michèle (1940-); *Les Promeneurs de la Nuit* (*The Night Wanderers*; Le Cerf/Gamma, 1972); *De l'Autre Côté du Brouillard* (*On the Other Side of the Fog*; Hac., 1980); *Contes du Jardin d'Eden* (*Tales of the Garden of Eden*; Magnard, 1982); *Un Ordinateur pas Ordinaire* (*An Extraordinary Computer*; Bordas, 1983); *De l'Autre Côté du Miroir* (*On the Other Side of the Mirror*; Bordas, 1985); *David et Salomon* (Magnard, 1985); *L'Autre Bout du Monde* (*The Other End of the World*; Bordas, 1987); *La Vague Noire* (*The Dark Wave*; Hac., 1989); *Note:* Juveniles. See Chapter VIII.

Kalogridis, Jeanne (?-); *Pacte avec le Vampire* (*Pact with the Vampire*; Rivages, n.d.)

Kancer, Serge (1928-); *Les Loups dans la Ville* (*The Wolves in the City;* Julliard, 1962; rev. as *Les Enfants de la Colère* (*The Children of Wrath*, Julliard, 1968); *L'Anti-Soleil* (*The Anti-Sun*; Julliard, 1965); *Urabatok, ou Le Navire Ébloui* (*Urabatok, or the Dazzled Ship*; Den., 1969); *La Fille du Dr. Ziegenbock* (*The Daughter of Dr. Ziegenbock*; Or du Temps, 1971)

Kaplan, Nelly *see* **Bélen**

Karali, Anna *see* **Duguël, Anne**

Karch, Pierre-Paul (1941-); *Nuits Blanches* (*White Nights*; Prise de Parole, 1981); *Note:* French-Canadian writer. Collection of fantastic tales.

Kardec, Alan (Rivail, Hippolyte; 1804-1869); *Le Livre des Esprits* (*The Book of Spirits*; 1857); *Note:* See Chapter IV.

Karnauch, Rémi (?-); *Le Fort Intérieur* (*The Inner Fort*; CRNI, n.d.; **Karquel, André (?-?)** *see* **Grand-Guignol**

Karrel, Pierre (?-); *Le Songe de Chronos* (*The Dream of Chronos*; AMSF 2 38, 1979); *Note:* Czech-born French writer.

Kast, Pierre (1920-1984); *Les Vampires de l'Alfama* (*The Vampires of the Alfama*; Orban, 1975); *L'Herbe Rouge:*

Les Lurettes Fourrées (*The Red Grass*; Livre de Paris, 1975); *La Mémoire du Tyran: Treize Miroirs pour l'Empereur Tibère* (*The Tyrant's Memory: 13 Mirrors for Emperor Tiberius*; JCL, 1981); *Note:* See Chapter VIII. Pierre Kast was also a renowned filmmaker (see Book 1, chapters I, II, and VI). *L'Herbe Rouge* is based on his film adaptation of a Boris **Vian** novel.

Kaszuk, Cyrille (?-); *L'Epreuve de Judith* (*The Trail of Judith*; JL 871, 1978); *Les Sorciers de Sundgan* (*The Wizards of Sundgan*; L'Orfraie, 1981); *Note:* See Chapter IX.

Kauffman, Christophe (?-); *Nickel le Petit* (*Nickel the Small*; FNA 1946, 1994); *Jalin Ka* (FNA 1949, 1994); *Note:* See Chapter IX.

Keller, Dominique H. *see* **Richard Bessière**

Keller, Henri (?-); *Planète Atlante* (*Atlantean Planet*; with Grégoire **Brainin**; VF 10, 1953); *L'Attaque des Vénusiens* (*The Attack of the Venusians*; with Grégoire **Brainin**; Trotteur, 1953); *La Machine à Explorer le Rêve* (*The Dream Machine*; with Grégoire **Brainin**; Cosmos 1, 1955); *La Guerre des Ondes* (*The War of the Waves*; with Grégoire **Brainin**; Cosmos 2, 1955); *Le Tour du Soleil en 80 Jours* (*Around the Sun in 80 Days*; with Grégoire **Brainin**; Cosmos 3, 1955); *Celui Qui Vient De Nulle Part* (*The Man from Nowhere*; with Grégoire **Brainin**; Cosmos 4, 1955); *Au Centre de l'Univers* (*At the Center of the Universe*; with Grégoire **Brainin**; Cosmos 7, 1956); *Et le Temps s'arrêtera (And Time Shall Stop;* with Grégoire **Brainin**; Métal 21, 1956; rev. as *Les Derniers Hommes* (*The Last Men*, R.B., 1958); *Note:* See Chapter IX.

Kemmel *see* **Bommart, Jean**

Kemp, Daniel (1957-); *Il n'y a pas de Terre, Il n'y a pas d'Autres Hommes* (*There Is No Earth, There Are No Other Men*; 1980); *La Cité de Cet* (*The City of Cet*; E=MC2, 1990); *Note:* French-Canadian writer. In *La Cité*, benevolent time travellers attempt to save the Earth.

Kenis, Paul (?-?) *see* **Grand-Guignol**

Kenny, Paul *see* **Vandel, Jean-Gaston**

Kergal, Dominique-André (?-); *Nouvelles Scènes de la Vie Future* (*New Scenes of Future Life*; Atelier Jullian,

1979); *L'Avenir se Présente Bien* (*The Future Looks Good*; Ouest-France, 1984)

Kerlecq, Jean de (Chantepie, Robert; 1882-1937); *L'Envoûtement, Carnets de l'Abominable* (*The Spell, Notebooks of Abomination*; Revue Internationale, 1909); *Le Secret de la Forêt* (*The Secret of the Forest*; France-Édition, 1923); *Contes à Faire Frémir* (*Tales to Make You Shiver*; France-Édition, 1924); *Fantinet au Paradis des Animaux* (*Fantinet in Animals' Heaven*; Delagrave, 1925); *La Pantera* (J. Port, 1927); *Urfa, l'Homme des Profondeurs* (*Urfa, Man of the Depths*; CRT, 1931); *Contes des Temps Héroïques* (*Tales of Heroic Times*; CRT, 1931); *Légendes Syriennes* (*Syrian Tales*; CRT, 1931); *Contes Orientaux* (*Oriental Tales*; CRT, 1932); *Le Forgeron de la Douleur* (*The Smith of Pain*; Mame, 1934); *Contes du Vieil Heidelberg* (*Tales of Old Heidelberg*; CRT, 1939); *Les Nuits Égyptiennes* (*Egyptian Nights*; Baudinière, 1945); *Princesse de Légende* (*Princess of Legend*; Belle Hélène, 1957); *Note:* See Chapter VII.

Kerloc'h, Jean-Pierre (1935-); *L'Enfant qui avait la Mer au fond du Coeur* (*The Child with the Sea in His Heart*; Ecole des Loisirs, 1981); *Luciole* (*Firefly*; Ecole des Loisirs, 1982); *Complètement Dragon!* (*Totally Dragon!*; Cluny, 1988); *Note:* Juveniles.

Kern, Alfred (?-); *Le Clown* (*The Clown*; Gallimard, 1957); *L'Amour profane* (*Profane Love*; Gallimard, 1974); *Le Jardin Perdu* (*The Lost Garden*; Rombaldi, 1979); *Gel et Feu* (*Frost and Fire*; Arfuyen, 1989); *Le Point Vif* (*The Live Point*; Arfuyen, 1991)

Kérouan, Jean (?-); *Les Chasseurs de Comètes* (*The Comet Hunters*; Hac., 1927); *La Fortune de Chienfou* (*Maddog's Fortune*; Hac., 1927); *Les Désirs de Riquette* (*What Riquette Wants*; Hac., 1929); *Chienfou dans sa Maison* (*Maddog in His House*; Hac., 1930

Kerruish, J. D. (?-); *Le Monstre Immortel* (*The Immortal Monster*; Ed. de France, 1939)

Kery, Jean (Le Covec de Keryvallon, Jean; 1893-); *Galaor contre Galaor* (*Galaor vs. Galaor*; Tallandier, 1926); *L'Énigme des Mains Coupées* (*The Enigma of the Cut-Off Hands*; Tallandier, 1933); *Le Lotissement Maudit* (*The Accursed Residence*; Baudinière, 1933); *Le Secret du Squelette* (*The Skeleton's Secret*; Tallandier, 1934); *L'Étrange Affaire du Diamant Bleu* (*The Strange Affair of the Blue Diamond*; Baudinière, 1934); *La Blonde Fée de Kerreval* (*The Blonde Fairy of Kerreval*; SEPIA, 1935); *Sylvette et le Fantôme* (*Sylvette and the Ghost*; SEPIA, 1936); *Au Bord de l'Abîme* (*On the Edge of the Abyss*; SEPIA, 1936); *La Baie du Malheur* (*The Bay of Woes*; SEPIA, 1938); *Cendrillon se marie* (*Cinderella Is Getting Married*; SEPIA, 1939); *Les Conjurés de l'Île Secrète* (*The Plotters of the Secret Island*; VA, 1939); *La Secte Infernale* (*The Infernal Sect*; BGA, 1949); *La Reine du Pôle* (*The Queen of the Pole*; BGA, 1950); *Les Mystères d'Atomeville* (*The Mysteries of Atom-City*; BGA, 1951); *Qui est à l'Appareil?* (*Who Is on the Phone?*; Libr. Champs-Élysées, 1952); *Note:* See Chapter VII.

Kesselring, Rolf (?-); *Martiens d'Avril* (*April Martians*; Egraz, 1969); *Note:* Swiss writer and genre publisher.

Kestrel, Edwyn (?-); *Le Sanctuaire des Elfes 1: Le Secret des Faylings* (*The Sanctuary of the Elves 1: The Secret of the Faylings*; Mnémos Daemonicon, 1997); *Note:* "Edwyn Kestrel" is a pseudonym for Mnémos' house authors (**Gaborit**, **Grimbert**, etc). See Chapter VIII.

Ketou, Safia (?-); *La Planète Mauve* (*The Mauve Planet*; Naaman, 1983); *Note:* Algerian writer.

Kevin, Jacques (?-); *La Carte Glissée* (*The Slided Card*; Pauvert, 1978)

Keyser, Édouard de (Romazières, Edmond; 1883-1974); *Le Chercheur de Mystères* (*The Seeker of Mysteries*; Lebègue, 1913); *Le Gouffre* (*The Pit*; Chevalier, 1913); *Baraka* (AM, 1921); *Le Sommeil à Distance* (*Long-Distance Sleep*; S&V, 1922); *La Mer Souterraine* (*The Subterranean Sea*; Fama, 1923); *L'Appel de l'Inconnu* (*The Call of the Unknown*; Nlle. Revue Critique, 1926); *L'Île des Seins Nus* (*The Island of Bare Breasts*; Louis Querelle, 1931); *Le Secret de la Tête Tranchée* (*The Secret of the Decapitated Head*; as Edmond Romazières; Tallandier, 1932); *L'Aviatrice* (*The Aviatrix*; Flamm., 1940); *Rivage du Pacifique* (*Pacific Shores*; as Edmond Romazières; RMY, 1947)

Khaldus (?-); *La Grande Cramignole* (*The Great Cramignole*; PEG, 1947)

Khemir, Nacer (1950-); *L'Ogresse* (La Découverte, 1975); *Le Soleil Emmuré* (*The Walled Sun*; La Découverte, 1978); *Le Conte des Conteurs* (*The Story of Storytellers*; La Découverte, 1982); *Grand-Père est né* (*Grandpa Is Born*; Le Mascaret, 1984); *Shéhérazade* (Le Mascaret, 1988)

Kieffer, Nicolas (1964-); *Peau de Lapin* (*Rabbit Skin*; Seuil, 1994); *Note:* See Chapter VIII.

Kijé (Lieutenant; Yawache, Alain; 1932-); *La Guerre des Machines* (*The War of the Machines*; RF 66, 1959); *Celten Taurogh* (RF 78, 1961); *L'Épée de l'Archange* (*The Sword of the Archangel*; RF 117, 1963); *Les Cendres de la Terre* (*The Ashes of Earth*; AMSF2 10, 1976); *Note:* See Chapter IX.

Kistemaekers, Henry (1872-1938); *Aéropolis* (Fasquelle, 1909); *Note:* Belgian writer. See Chapter V.

Klein, Gérard (1937-); *Agent Galactique* (*Galactic Agent*; as Mark Starr; Sat. 1-5,9, 1958); *Embûches dans l'E-*

space (*Ambushes in Space*; as François Pagery/with Richard **Chomet** & Patrice **Rondard**; RF 53, 1958); *Le Gambit des Étoiles* (RF 62, 1958; transl. as *Starmasters' Gambit*, 1973); *Les Perles du Temps* (*The Pearls of Time*; PdF 26, 1958); *Chirurgiens d'une Planète* (*The Planet Surgeons;* as Gilles d'Argyre; FNA 165, 1960; rev. as *Le Rêve des Forêts* (*A Dream of Forests*, JL 2164, 1987); *Les Voiliers du Soleil* (*The Solar Sailors*; as Gilles d'Argyre; FNA 172, 1961; rev., JL 2247, 1987); *Le Temps n'a pas d'Odeur* (*Time Has No Scent*; PdF 63, 1963; transl. as *The Day Before Tomorrow*, 1972); *Le Long Voyage* (*The Long Journey*; as Gilles d'Argyre; FNA 243, 1964; rev., JL 2324, 1988); *Les Tueurs de Temps* (*The Time Killers*; as Gilles d'Argyre; FNA 263, 1965; rev., PP 5091, 181; transl. as *The Mote in Time's Eye*, 1975); *Un Chant de Pierre* (*A Song of Stone*; Los., 1966); *Le Sceptre du Hasard* (*The Scepter of Chance*; as Gilles d'Argyre; FNA 357, 1968; rev., PP 5077, 1980); Les Seigneurs de la Guerre (A&D 8, 1971; transl. as *The Overlords of War*, 1973); *La Loi du Talion* (*The Law of Retaliation*; A&D 21, 1973); *Histoires Comme Si...* (*Stories as If...*; 10/18 924, 1975); *Le Grandiose Avenir* (*The Great Future*; anthology/with Monique **Battestini**; Seghers, 1975); *En Un Autre Pays* (*In Another Land*; anthology; Seghers, 1976); *Ce Qui Vient des Profondeurs* (*That Which Came from Below*; anthology/with Monique **Battestini**; Seghers, 1977); *Malaise dans la S-F* (*Malaise in Science Fiction*; HL Planchat, 1977); *Le Livre d'Or de Gérard Klein* (*The Golden Book of GK*; PP 5056, 1979); *Le Livre d'Or de Michel Jeury* (*The Golden Book of Michel Jeury*; anthology; PP 5133, 1982); *La Ligne Bleue des Mômes* (*Children's Blue Line*; P-M Favre, 1982); *Les Mondes Francs* (*The Free Worlds*; anthology/with Ellen **Herzfeld** & Dominique **Martel**; LdP 7096, 1988); *L'Hexagone Halluciné* (*The Hallucinations of the Hexagon*; anthology/with Ellen **Herzfeld** & Dominique **Martel**; LdP 7101, 1988); *La Frontière Éclatée* (*The Shattered Frontier*; anthology/with Ellen **Herzfeld** & Dominique **Mar-**

tel; (LdP 7113, 1989); *Les Mosaïques du Temps* (*The Mosaics of Time*; anthology/with Ellen **Herzfeld** & Dominique **Martel**; LdP 7130, 1990); *Note:* See Chapter IX.

Kloetzer, Laurent (?-); *Mémoire Vagabonde* (*Wandering Memory*; Mnemos 24, 1997); *Note:* See Chapter VIII.

Klotz, Claude (1932-); *Les Innommables* (*The Unmentionables*; Bourgois, 1971); *Cosmos-Cross* (Bourgois, 1973); *Putsch-Punch* (Bougois, 1974); *Les Mers Adragantes* (*The Adragantine Seas*; JCL, 1974); *Paris-Vampire* (JCL, 1974; rev. as *Dracula Père et Fils* (*Dracula Father and Son*, LdP 5797, 1983); *Achète-Moi les Amériques* (*Buy Me the Americas*; JCL, 1975); *Les Aventures Fabuleuses d'Anselme Levasseur* (*The Fabulous Adventures of Anselme Levasseur*; JCL, 1976); *Darakan* (JCL, 1978); *Kobar* (AM, 1992); *Killer Kid* (AM, 1989); *Note:* See Chapter VIII.

Kock, Henry de (?-); *Les Mystères du Village* (*The Mysteries of the Village*; Cadot, 1863); *Les Hommes Volants* (*The Flying Men*; Cadot, 1864); *L'Auberge des Treize Pendus* (*The Inn of the 13 Hanged Men*; Walder, 1874); *Mademoiselle Croquemitaine* (Cadot, 1877); *La Fée aux Amourettes* (*The Love Fairy*; Cadot, 1877); *Je Me Tuerai Demain* (*I Shall Kill Myself Tomorrow*; Cadot, 1879); *Note:* See Chapter V.

Kohler, Pierre (?-); *Les Gouffres du Comos* (*The Pits of the Cosmos*; France-Empire, 1978); *Derniers Jours du Monde* (*Last Days of the World*; France-Empire, 1980); *Note: Les Gouffres* is novelized science fact *à la* Fred Hoyle on black holes and quasars.

Kolney, Fernand (1868-1930); *L'Amour dans 5000 Ans* (*Love in 5000 Years*; Kolney, 1905; rev. Quignon, 1928); *La Grève des Ventres* (*The Bellies on Strike*; Génération Consciente, 1908); *Note:* See Chapter V.

Konopnicki, Guy (?-); *1920-2020—Vive le Centennaire du PCF* (*100 Years of French Communist Party History*; Hallier, 1979)

Korb, Laurence (1951-); *Paris-Lézarde* (*Paris-Lizard*; Calmann-Lévy, 1977); *Les Passants du Dimanche* (*The Sunday Pedestrians*; Calmann-Lévy, 1979); *Note:* See Chapter IX.

Korb, Liliane (?-); *Temps sans Frontières* (*Time Without Borders*; Flamm., 1989); *Jasper et les Ombres Électriques* (*Jasper and the Electric Shadows*; with Laurence **Lefèvre**; Hac., 1996); *Mon Père le Poisson Rouge* (*My Father the Gold Fish*; with Laurence **Lefèvre**; Flamm., 1997)

Kostrowitzky, Wilhelm de *see* **Apollinaire, Guillaume**

Kremer, Jean Raymond de *see* **Ray, Jean**

Kruse, Max (?-); *Plodoc et la Planète Inconnue* (*Plodoc and the Unknown Planet*; BR, 1975); *Note:* Juvenile SF.

Kruss, James (1926-); *Le Chasseur d'Étoiles* (*The Hunter of Stars*; Nathan, 1969); *Note:* Juvenile SF.

Kubnick, Henri (?-); *Histoires à Dormir Debout* (*Unbelievable Tales*; Nelson, 1937); *Mésaventures du Fils Noël* (*Misadventures of Kid Noël*; Nelson, 1938); *Aventures d'Autrefois* (*Yesterday's Adventures*; Spès, 1938); *Le Beau Navire* (*The Beautiful Ship*; Gründ, 1938); *Le Cirque* (*The Circus*; Gründ, 1938); *Nuit au Zoo* (*Night at the Zoo*; Gründ, 1938); *Le Roi-Soleil au Clair de Lune* (*The Sun King in the Moonlight*; Palatine, 1960); *La Grande Peur de l'An 2000* (*The Great Fear of the Year 2000);* AM, 1974); *Le Diable dans la Ville* (*The Devil in Town*; JCL, 1978); *Le Clan de Krah* (*Krah's Clan*; JCL, 1982); *La Grande Déesse* (*The Great Goddess*; JCL, 1982); *Dji la Magicienne* (*Dji the Sorceress*; JCL, 1984); *Les Mémoires de la Bastille* (*Memoirs of the Bastille*; JCL, 1989); *Le Narcotique No. 23* (*Sleeping Drug No.23);* as Henri Dorac; Cast., n.d.; *La Capitale Endormie* (*The Sleeping Capital*; as Henri Dorac; Paul Duval, n.d.?

Kulavik, R. (?-); *Terre contre Mars, La Bataille des Hommes de Fer* (*Earth vs. Mars, the Battle of the Iron Men*; Wrill, 1948); *Note:* Belgian writer. See Chapter IX.

Kupferman, Sigfrid (1939-) & Kupferman, Fred (1934-1988); *La Nuit des Dragons* (*The Night of the Dragons*; Hac., 1986); *Le Complot du Télégraphe* (*The Telegraph Plot*; Hac., 1988)

Laani, Abdellatif (1942-); *Saida et les Voleurs de Soleil* (*Saida and the Sun Stealers*; Messidor-La Farandole

La Batut, Pierre de (?-); *L'Homme aux Trois Peaux* (*The Man with Three Skins*; Crès, 1919); *La Jeune Fille en Proie au Monstre* (*The Young Girl Who Became the Prey of a Monster*; JST, 1920); *La Ville Sans Amour* (*The City Without Love*; Oeuvres Libres, 1929); *L'Homme d'Affaires* (*The Business Man*; Gall., 1943); *Le Fétiche de Peau Humaine* (*The Idol of Human Skin*; Janicot, 1944); *La Fille aux Diables* (*The Girl with Devils*; Gall., 1944); *Note:* See Chapter VII.

Labat, Pierre (?-); *Le Manteau Blanc* (*The White Coat*; SdP, 1948); *Le Merveilleux Royaume* (*The Wonderful Kingdom*; SdP, 1950); *Note:* Juveniles.

La Blanchère, Henri Moullin du Coudray de (1821-1880); *Voyage au Fond de la Mer* (*Voyage to the Bottom of the Seas*; Furne & Jouvet, 1868); *Le Club des Toqués* (*The Club of the Crazies;* Lefèvre, 1890, incl. *Le Testament de Faragus* (*Faragus' Testament,* Lefèvre, 1890; rev. as *Sous les Eaux* (*Under Water*, JDV, 1892)

Laboulaye, Édouard (?-); *Contes Bleus* (*Blue Tales*; Char-

pentier, 1877); *Nouveaux Contes Bleus* (*New Blue Tales*; Combet, 1900); *Note:* Folk tales.

Labrèche, Gilles (1956-); *Tom Blake contre le Docteur Strauss* (*Tom Blake vs. Dr. Strauss*; D'Ici et d'Ailleurs, 1995); *Note:* French-Canadian writer.

Labrecque, Brigitte (1961-); *Row, Row, Row Your Boat* (Québec-Trek, 1992); *Note:* French-Canadian writer. *Star Trek* fan fiction.

Labric, Roger (1893-); *Les Champs Bleus* (*The Blue Fields*; Édouard-Joseph, 1923); *On se bat dans l'Air* (*They Fight in the Air*; Baron, 1933); *L'Avion de Minuit* (*The Midnight Plane*; Nlles, Éd. Latines, 1935); *La Grande Escadrille* (*The Great Squadron*; Causse, Graille & Castelnau, 1941); *L'Escadre Invisible* (*The Invisible Squadron*; Chantal, 1943); *Carnet de Vol* (*Flight Log*; Pavois, 1944)

Labro, Jean (?-); *Dénuement* (*Poverty*; Didier, 1944); *Le Geste de Caïn* (*Cain's Gesture*; Didier, 1945); *La Voie Sans Issue* (*The Way Without Exit*; Didier, 1947)

Labrousse, Jacqueline *see* **Mirande, Jacqueline**

Labrunie, Gérard *see* **Nerval, Gérard de**

Labry, Michel (?-); *Les Sextuplés de Loqmaria* (*The Sextuplets of Loqmaria*; Julliard, 1962); *Note:* This novel was adapted into the 1967 feature film ***Ne Jouez Pas Avec Les Martiens*** (*Don't Play with Martians*; see Book 1, Chapter I).

Lacascade, Renée (?-?) *see* **Pérye, André**

Lacasse, Lise (1938-); *La Facilité du Jour* (*The Facility of the Day*; Bellarmin, 1981); *La Corde au Ventre* (*A Rope Around the Belly*; Trois, 1990); *Note:* French-Canadian writer. *La Corde* is a feminist SF novel about a dystopia à la *The Handmaid's Tale*.

Lacassin, Francis (?-); *Vampires de Paris* (*Parisian Vampires*; anthology; UGE, 1981); *Note:* Renowned comics scholar.

Lacerte, Rolande (Allard-Lacerte, Rolande; ?-?); *Les Aventures de Kilucru / L'Étoile Chance* (*The Adventures of Whodbelievit / The Lucky Star*; Beauchemin, 1963); *Le Soleil des Profondeurs* (*The Sun of the Deep*; Jeunesse, 1968); *Note:* French-Canadian writer. Juvenile SF.

Lachance, Laurent (1931-); *Les Rêves ne mentent pas* (*Dreams Do Not Lie*; RL, 1983); *Ailleurs plutôt que Demain / L'Île du Chila-Chila* (*Elsewere Rather Than Tomorrow / The Island of the Chila-Chila*; Héritage, 1991); *Note:* French-Canadian writer. Collection of fantastic tales.

Lachance, Lise *see* **Yance, Claude-Emmanuelle.**

La Chave, Clément de (?-); *Siamora la Druidesse* (*Siamora the She-Druid*; Vanier, 1860); *La Magicienne des Alpes* (*The Magician of the Alps*; Vanier, 1861); *Note:* See Chapter IV.

Lacheze, Patrick (?-); *Fleur* (*Flower*; FNA 1703, 1989)

Laclavetine, Jean-Marie (?-); *Demain la Veille* (*Tomorrow Is Yesterday*; Gall., 1995)

Lacombe, Alain (1947-1992); *Bétonnade pour Sladek* (*Concrete for Slsdek*; Dullis, 1974); *Jeu Blanc pour Sladek* (*White Game for Sladek*; Dullis, 1974); *Les Pions de la Lune* (*The Pawns of the Moon*; Orban, 1975)

Lacotte, Daniel (?-); *La Dame Blanche* (*The White Lady*; Luneau Ascot, 1980); *Note:* Folk tales from Normandy.

Lacour, José-André (?-) *see* **Becker, Benoît**

Lacq, Gil (?-); *L'Or des Romains* (*The Gold of the Romans*; PC, 1968); *Le Roi sans Mémoire* (*The King Without Memory*; GP, 1969); *La Conquête de la Sibérie* (*The Conquest of Siberia*; GP, 1969); *L'Herbe des Sarrasins* (*The Herb of the Saracens*; GP, 1969); *Les Bannis de l'Île aux Huitres* (*Banished on Oyster Island*; GP, 1975); *L'Énergie du Désespoir* (*The Energy of Despair*; with Michel **Corentin**; TF 5, 1978); *Les Enfants de la Guerre* (*The Children of War*; Hac., 1979); *Ni Ongles, Ni Dents* (*Neither Nails Nor Teeth*; TF 13, 1980); *Note:* Juvenile SF.

Lacroix, Francy (?-); *Un Tremblement d'Éther* (*Aether-Quake*; Rex, 1935); *Note:* Belgian writer.

Lacroix, Paul (1806-1884); *La Danse Infernale* (*The Hellish Dance*; 1829); *Les Deux Fous* (*The Two Madmen*; 1830); *La Danse Macabre* (*The Macabre Dance*; Renduel, 1832); *Note:* Aka le Bibliophile Jacob. See Chapter IV.

Lacroix, Pierre D. (1950-); *La Peur au Ventre* (*Fear in the Stomach*; Carfax-bis 2, 1985); *Histoires Simples* (*Simple Stories*; Carfax, 1987); *Note:* French-Canadian writer. Collection of fantastic tales.

La Dixmerie, M. de (?-?); *L'Île Taciturne et l'Île Enjouée, ou Voyage du Génie Alaciel dans ces Deux Îles* (*Taciturn Island and Happy Island, or the Journey of the Djinn Alaciel in These Two Islands*; 1759; rep. VI, 1788)

Ladoix, Jenny (1951-); *Le Château de la Tortue* (*The Castle of the Turtle*; Gall., 1983)

Laet, Danny de (?-); *Histoires de Trains Fantastiques* (*Fantastic Train Stories*; anthology; Libr. Champs-Élysées, 1980); *Note:* Belgian writer/essayist.

Lafargue, Freddie (?-); *Game Over* (Gall., 1993); *Ibrahim Lancelot* (Dagorno, 1994)

Laffite, Louis *see* **Curtis, Jean-Louis**

Lafforest, Roger de (?-); *Les Figurants de la Mort* (*The Stage Extras of Death*; Grasset, 1939); *Si le Ciel tombe...* (*If the Sky Falls...*; Colbert, 1942); *Ces Maisons qui Tuent* (*These Killing Houses*; RL, 1970); *La Réalité Magique* (*Magical Reality*; RL, 1977); *Présence des Invisibles* (*Presence of the Invisibles*; RL, 1983); *La Magie des Énergies* (*The Magic of Energies*; RL, 1985)

Laflamme, Henri (Laflamme, Hermenegilde; 1936-); *Les Farfelus du Cosmos* (*The Cosmic Jokers*; JP 16, 1974); *Note:* French-Canadian writer. Juvenile SF.

Lafleur, Jacques (1946-); *Décors à l'Envers* (*Backgrounds Upside Down*; Naaman, 1981); *Note:* French-Canadian writer. Collection of fantastic tales.

La Follie, Louis-Guillaume de (1739-1780); *Le Philosophe sans Prétention* (*The Philosopher Without Pretention*; Clousier, 1775); *Note:* See Chapter III.

La Fontaine, Jean de (1621-1695); *Fables* (Barbin, 1668; rev. 1678; rev. 1693); *Note:* See Chapter II.

La Force, Charlotte Rose de Caumont de (1646-1724); *Les Fées: Contes des Contes* (*The Fairies: Tales of Tales*; Libr. Revue Indep., 1697); *Note:* Also see **Le Cabinet des Fées** and Chapter III.

Laforgue, Jules (1860-1887); *Moralités Légendaires* (*Legendary Moral Tales*; Libr. Revue Indépendante, 1887); *Note:* Sixth reinterpretations of the tales of Hamlet, Salome, Pan, Lohengrin, etc.

La Fouchardière, Georges de (1874-1946); *Le Diable dans le Bénitier* (*The Devil in the Font*; Montaigne, 1898); *La Machine à Galoper* (*The Galloping Machine*; Tournayre, 1910; rev. as *L'Affaire Peau-de-Balle* (*The Bullet-Skin Case*, AM, 1919); *L'Araignée du Kaiser* (*The Kaiser's Spider*; Payot, 1916); *L'Homme qui Réveille les Morts* (*The Man Who Awoke the Dead*; with Rodolphe **Bringer**; AM, 1918); *Monsieur Mézique* (with Clément **Vautel**; AM, 1914); *La Grande Rafle* (*The Great Dragnet*; with Clément **Vautel**; AM, 1929); *L'Héritier de Don Quichotte* (*Don Quixote's Heir*; Ferenczi, 1930

Laframboise, Michèle (1960-); *Pianissimo* (Zone Convective, 1997); *Note:* French-Canadian writer.

La France, Henri (1914-); *À l'Aube du Verseau* (*The Dawn of Aquarius*; Presses Sélect, 1980); *Les Capsules du Temps* (*Time Capsules*; Bergeron, 1982); *Note:* French-Canadian writer. Atlantis returns.

La France, Micheline (1944-); *Le Fils d'Ariane* (*Ariane's Son*; Pleine Lune, 1987); *Note:* French-Canadian writer. Daughter of Henri **La France**.

Lagabrielle, Michèle (1928-); *Les Deux Vies de Jérémie* (*The Two Lives of Jeremie*; Amitié, 1985)

La Garde, Marcellin (1818-1889); *Le Val de l'Amblève* (*The Valley of Ambleve*; 1879); *L'Enfant du Carrefour Maudit* (*The Child of the Accursed Crossroad*; Blériot & Gauthier, 1883); *Récits de la Vesprée* (*Tales of the Evening*; H. Gautier, 1885); *Les Voies du Châtiment* (*The Ways of Punishment*; H. Gautier, 1886); *Le Val de l'Ourthe: Légendes Ardennaises* (*The Ourthe Valley: Legends from the Ardennes*; Petitpas, 1976); *Note:* Belgian writer. See Chapter VI.

Lagarde, Pierre (1903-); *Ci-gît l'Amout* (*Here Lies Love*; Émile-Paul, 1934); *Poison* (Technique du Livre, 1936); *Crime* (Baudinière, 1938); *Valmaurie* (Technique du Livre, 1944); Clinique B (Baudinière, 1951)

Laguerre, Philippe *see* **Ward, Philippe**

Laguionie, Jean-François (?-); *Les Puces de Sable* (*The Sand Fleas*; Léon Faure, 1980); *Image-Image* (Léon Faure, 1981); *Note:* Juvenile fantasies.

Lahaie, Christiane (1960-); *Insulaires* (*Insulars*; L'Instant Même, 1996); *Note:* French-Canadian writer.

La Hire, Jean de (Espie De La Hire, Adolphe d'; 1878-1956); *Le Trésor dans l'Abîme* (*The Treasure in the Abyss*; *L'Écho*/Boivin, 1907); *La Roue Fulgurante (The Fiery Wheel; Le Matin*/Tallandier, 1908); rep. under the title *Soucoupe Volante* (*Flying Saucer*, Jaeger, 1952 (see below); *Le Corsaire Sous-Marin* (*The Undersea Corsair*; serialized as 79 issues, Ferenczi, 1912-13); *1. Le Vol du Sous-Marin* (*The Stealing of the Sub-Marine*); *2. La Nuit Tragique* (*The Tragic Night*); *3. L'Exploit de Jean l'Anguille* (*The Amazing Feat of John the Eel*); *4. La Grotte d'Épouvante* (*The Cave of Terror*); *5. Le Radeau Fantôme* (*The Ghost Raft*); *6. Le Monstre Vengeur* (*The Avenging Monster*); *7. Dans les Abîmes* (*In the Abyss*); *8. Le Camp des Coupe-Têtes* (*The Camp of the Head-Cutters*); *9. Le Trésor du Corsaire* (*The Corsair's Treasure*); *10. Les Aéroplanes Contre le Cyclope* (*The Airplanes vs. The Cyclops*); *11. La Conquête de l'Île* (*The Conquest of the Island*); *12. Les Traces de Sang* (*Traces of Blood*); *13. La Première Victoire* (*First Victory*); *14. La Revanche du Pavilion Noir* (*The Revenge of the Black Flag*); *15. Le Combat sous les Eaux* (*Underwater Battle*); *16. La Disparition des Forbans* (*The Villains Disappear*); *17. La Découverte de Jean l'Anguille* (*The Discovery of John the Eel*); *18. La Potence Infernale* (*The Hellish Gallows*); *19. L'Exploit de l'Homme-Torpille* (*The Amazing Feat of the Torpedo-Man*); *20. La Terreur du Pacifique* (*The Terror of the Pacific*); *21. Le Corsaire et l'Américain* (*The Corsair and the American*); *22. L'Eau qui Monte* (*Rising Waters*); *23. L'Évasion d'Archibald* (*Archibald's Escape*); *24. La Trombe de Feu* (*The Fire Vortex*); *25. Mort ou Vivant?...* (*Dead or Alive?*); *26. L'Escadre Monstre* (*The Monstrous Ar-*

mada); *27. Le Père de Jean l'Anguille* (*The Father of John the Eel*); *28. L'Idée du Corsaire Noir* (*The Black Corsair's Idea*); *29. Perdus dans l'Air* (*Lost in the Air*); *30. Les Robinsons de l'Air* (*Robinsons of the Air*); *31. L'Étreinte du Serpent* (*The Hug of the Serpent*); *32. La Voix de l'Honneur* (*The Voice of Honor*); *33. La Locomotive Infernale* (*The Infernal Locomotive*); *34. La Poursuite Folle* (*The Mad Pursuit*); *35. La Fusillade Invisible* (*The Invisible Gun Battle*); *36. Et Jean l'Anguille?* (*What About John the Eel?*); *37. La Rencontre Fatale* (*The Fatal Encounter*); *38. La Monstrueuse Bataille* (*The Monstrous Battle*); *39. La Marche à l'Abîme* (*Marching Towards the Abyss*); *40. Le Capitaine Ouragan* (*Captain Hurricane*); *41. La Courte-Paille* (*The Short Straw*); *42. Les Glaces du Pôle* (*The Ice of the Pole*); *43. Les Naufragés du Montroë* (*Shipwreckd on the Montroe*); *44. Des Pas dans la Neige* (*Footsteps on the Snow*); *45. Le Mystère de la Banquise* (*The Mystery of the Ice Shelf*); *46. Le Cercle de la Mort* (*The Circle of Death*); *47. Le Truc de Jim* (*Jim's Trick*); *48. L'Aéro-Fantôme* (*The Air-Ghost*); *49. Le Supplice du Feu* (*The Fire Torture*); *50. L'X Mystérieux* (*The Mysterious X*); *51. Le Précieux Otage* (*The Precious Hostage*); *52. Les Ruses Tragiques* (*Tragic Ruses*); *53. Le Mort Vivant* (*The Living Dead*); *54. Rires de Démons* (*Demons' Laugh*); *55. La Montagne Creuse* (*The Hollow Mountain*); *56. Les Indiens Banivas* (*The Banivas Indians*); *57. Le Feu des Chiquitos* (*The Fire of the Chiquitos*); *58. Oeil-de-Vautour* (*Eye-Of-Vulture*); *59. Le Fils Vengeur* (*The Avenging Son*); *60. Dave Smith and Co.*; *61. L'Effroyable Revanche* (*The Awful Revenge*); *62. La Sorcière du Trou-d'Enfer* (*The Witch of the Hell-Hole*); *63. Le Drame du Fortin* (*The Tragedy of the Fort*); *64. L'Insaisissable* (*The Uncatchable*); *65. Le Calvaire Sanglant* (*The Bloody Calvary*); *66. Fin d'Aventure* (*End of an Adventure*); *67. Mission Dangereuse* (*Dangerous Mission*); *68. Le Serment du Corsaire* (*The Corsair's Oath*); *69. L'Île aux Perles* (*Pearl Island*); *70. Enlevez l'Amiral!* (*Capture the Admiral!*); *71. L'Expiation* (*The Punishment*); *72. Le Corsaire Noir contre Santa-Fe* (*The Black Corsair vs. Sante Fe*); *73. La Contre-Mine* (*The Anti-Mine*); *74. La Mort Prévue* (*The Planned Death*); *75. Le Triomphe du Mal* (*The Triumph of Evil*); *76. Le Mort Parle* (*The Deadman Speaks*); *77. Vers le Drame* (*Towards a Drama*); *78. Le Drame final* (*The Final Drama*); *79. La Fin du Corsaire Noir* (*The End of the Black Corsair*); (serialized again by Ferenczi as 75 issues with variant titles in 1936-37); *Au-Delà des Ténèbres* (*Beyond Darkness*; 1916); rep. Ferenczi, 1921); *Joe Rollon, l'Autre Homme Invisible* (*Joe Rollon, Another Invisible Man;* as Edmond Cazal; ed. Fse. Ill., 1919; rev. as *La Hire, L'Invisible* (*The Invisible*, Jaeger, 1953); *Le Labyrinthe Rouge* (*The Red Labyrinth; À l'Aventure*, 1920); *Raca* (2 vols.; 1922/RDA, 1922); *La Prisonnière du Dragon Rouge*

(The Prisoner of the Red Dragon; 1923/Ollendorf, 1923); rev. as *La Captive du Dragon Noir* (*The Captive of the Black Dragon,* BGA, 1937); *La Captive du Soleil d'Or* (*The Captive of the Golden Sun;* Ferenczi, 1926); *L'Épave Sanglante* (*The Bloody Wreck;* Ferenczi, 1926); *Les Grandes Aventures d'un Boy Scout* (*The Great Adventures of a Boy Scout;* serialized as 30 issues, Ferenczi, 1926); *1. La Volonté de Franc-Hardi* (*The Will of Franc-Hardi*); *2. Le Prodigieux Voyage* (*The Prodigious Journey*); *3. Le Mystère des Souterrains* (*The Mystery of the Tunnels*); *4. La Révolte des Ziouits* (*The Revolt of the Ziouits*); *5. La Lutte Formidable* (*The Formidable Clash*); *6. Les Hommes de Mars* (*The Men from Mars*); *7. Franc-Hardi et les Martiens* (*Franc-Hardy and the Martians*); *8. Les Martiens Capturés* (*The Martians Taken Captives*); *9. Dramatiques Mystères* (*Dramatic Mysteries*); *10. Chasses Martiennes* (*Martian Hunts*); *11. Le Rayon-Ardent* (*The Fiery Ray*); *12. La Pierre Tournante* (*The Turning Stone*); *13. Les Cyclopes à Trompes* (*The Cyclops with a Trunk*); *14. La Vengeance des Kolops* (*The Revenge of the Kolops*); *15. Vers le Tour du Monde Saturnien* (*Across the World of Saturn*); *16. Le Drame des Hommes-Taureaux* (*The Tragedy of the Men-Bull*); *17-30.* (no information available; *Le Zankador* (Ferenczi, 1927); *Les Dompteurs de Forces* (*The Tamers of Forces;* Ferenczi, 1925); *Les Aventures de Paul Ardent* (*The Adventures of Paul Ardent;* serialized in 6 issues, VLAE, 1927-28); *1. Le Sphinx du Labrador* (*The Labrador Sphinx*); *2. La Marque des Deux Tigres* (*The Mark of the Two Tigers*); *3. L'Énigme des Pôles* (*The Mystery of the Poles*); *4. L'Homme aux Hélicoptères* (*The Helicopter Man*); *5. Le Monstre au Coeur d'Acier* (*The Monster with a Heart of Steel*); *6. Les Démons de l'Apatcha* (*Demons of the Apatcha*); *Les Ravageurs du Monde* (*The Ravagers of the World;* VLAE, 1929); *L'Oeil de la Déesse* (*The Eye of the Goddess;* VLAE, 1929); *Le Secret des Cent Îles* (*The Secret of the Hundred Islands;* VLAE, 1929); *Le Roi des Catacombes* (*The King of the Catacombs;* VLAE, 1929); *Les Hommes Sans Yeux* (*The Eyeless Men;* LA, 1930); rep. as *Les Crypte des Maudits* (*Crypt of the Accursed,* VA, 1935); *Le Cercueil de Nacre* (*The Mother-Of-Pearl Coffin;* LA, 1930); *Kaitar* (2 vols., *Kaitar* and *La Nouvelle Judith* (*The New Judith,* LN, 1930); *Les Amazones* (2 vols., *Les Amazones* (*The Amazons*) and *Le Mystère Vaincu* (*The Mystery Solved,* LN, 1930); rep. as 2 vols., *Le Pays Inconnu* (*The Unkonown Land*) and *Les Amazones* (*The Amazons,* Jaeger, 1955); *Le Fils du Soleil* (*The Son of the Sun;* LA, 1931); *Sous l'Oeil de Dieu* (*Under God's Eye;* Fayard, 1932); *Les Chasseurs de Mystères* (*The Hunters of Mysteries;* Tallandier, 1933); *Le Secret des Torelwoch* (*The Secret of Torelwoch;* Ed. de France, 1934); *Le Maître du Monde* (*The Master of the World;* VA, 1934); *Le Regard Qui Tue* (*The Killing Eyes;* VA, 1934); *La Mort de Sardanapale*

(The Death of Sardanapale; 2 vols. as *Les Envoûtés* (*Spellbound,* LN, 1935; rev. as 2 vols., *Les Envoûtés* (*The Spellbound*) and *La Fille au Double Cerveau* (*The Girl with Two Brains,* Jaeger, 1954); *Tu seras folle!* (*You Will Be Mad!;* VA, 1935); *L'Énigme de l'Oeil Sanglant* (*The Mystery of the Bloody Eye;* VA, 1935); *Le Volcan Artificiel* (*The Artificial Volcano;* VA, 1936); *Le Mort-Vivant* (*The Living Dead;* VA, 1936); *L'Antre aux Cent Démons* (*The Lair of a Hundred Demons;* BGA, 1935); *Les Envoûtées* (*The Spellbound;* BGA, 1935); *Le Démon de la Nuit* (*The Night Demon;* BGA, 1937); *Le Million des Scouts* (*The Scouts' Million;* serialized as 22 issues, Ferenczi, 1937-38); *1. Le Million des Scouts* (*The Scouts' Million*); *2. L'Attaque Mystérieuse* (*The Mysterious Attack*); *3. L'Échelle Vertigineuse* (*The Vertiginous Ladder*); *4. Le Navire Tragique* (*The Tragic Ship*); *5. Nos vies à defendre* (*To Defend Our Lives*); *6. Drames de Foret-Vierge* (*Jungle Tragedies*); *7. Surprises du Pacifique* (*Surprises in the Pacific*); *8. Les Derniers Cannibales* (*The Last Cannibals*); *9. Les Jaguars de la Lagune* (*The Lagoon Jaguars*); *10. La Ruse des Gangsters* (*The Gangsters' Ruse*); *11. Un Coup de Marius* (*Something Signed Marius*); *12. Carrington-Junction*; *13. La Reine des Krokis* (*The Queen of the Krokis*); *14. Le Destin d'Olivia* (*Olivia's Fate*); *15. La Grotte aux Outangs* (*The Outang Cave*); *16. Les Bandits de ltor* (*The Bandits of Itor*); *17. Terrible Affaire!* (*Dreadful Business*); *18. L'Avion Bleu* (*The Blue Plane*); *19. Pistes Menacantes* (*Deadly Trails*); *20. Terrible Chassé-croisé* (*Dreadful Crossover*); *21. Fantômes dans le Brouillard* (*Ghosts in the Mist*); *22. Pour la France et la paix* (*For France and Peace*); *La Guerre! La Guerre!* (*War! War!*; as Commandant Cazal; serialized as 5 issues, Tallandier, 1939); *1. La Guerre! La Guerre!* (*War! War!*); *2. Maginot-Siegfried*; *3. Batailles pour la Mer* (*Battles for the Sea*); *4. L'Afrique en Flammes* (*Africa in Flame*); *5. La Fin... par le Pétrole* (*The End... By Oil*); The Nyctalope Series: *1. L'Homme Qui Peut Vivre dans l'Eau* (*The Man Who Could Live Underwater; Le Matin,* 1908/Juven, 1910; rev. as 2 vols., *L'Homme Qui Peut Vivre dans l'Eau* (*The Man Who Could Live Underwater*) and *Les Amours de l'Inconnu* (*The Loves of the Unknown,* RDA, 1921); *2. Le Mystère des XV* (*The Mystery of the XV; Le Matin,* 1911); rep. as 2 vols., *Le Secret des XII* (*The Secret of the XII*) and *Les Conquérants de Mars* (*The Conquerors of Mars,* Jaeger, 1954); *3. Lucifer* (*Le Matin,* 1920; rev. as 2 vols., *Lucifer* and *Nyctalope vs. Lucifer,* RDA, 1922); *4. Le Roi de la Nuit* (*The King of the Night; Le Matin,* 1923; rev. as *Planète Sans Feu* (*Planet Without Fire,* Jaeger, 1953); *5. L'Amazone du Mont Everest* (*The Amazon of Mount Everest; Le Matin/RDA,* 1925); rep. as *La Madone des Cimes* (*The Madonna of the Mountains,* VA, 1933); rep. as *Le Mystère de l'Everest* (*The Mystery of the Everest,* Jaeger, 1953); *6. L'Antéchrist* (*The Antichrist; Le Matin,*

1927); rep. as 2 vols., *La Captive du Démon (Captive of the Demon)* and *La Princesse Rouge (The Red Princess*, Fayard, 1931); *7. Titania (Le Matin*, 1929); rep. as 2 vols., *Titania and Écrase ta Vipère (Squash Your Viper*, LN, 1929); *8. Belzébuth (Le Matin*, 1930); rep. as 2 vols., *Belzébuth and L'Île d'Épouvante (The Island of Terror*, Fayard, 1930); *9. Gorillard (Le Matin*, 1932); rep. as 2 vols., *Gorillard* and *Le Mystère Jaune (The Yellow Mystery*, Fayard, 1932); *10. L'Assassinat du Nyctalope (The Assassination of the Nyctalope*; Ren. du Livre, 1933); *11. Les Mystères de Lyon (The Mysteries of Lyons;* 2 vols., *Les Mystères de Lyon (The Mysteries of Lyons)* and *Les Adorateurs du Sang (The Blood Worshippers*, LN, 1933); *12. Le Sphinx du Maroc (The Moroccan Sphinx*; 1935); *13. La Croisière du Nyctalope (The Nyctalope's Cruise*; Fayard, 1936); rep. as *Wanda*, Jaeger, 1953); *14. La Croix de Sang (Cross of Blood*; Simon, 1941); *15. Rien qu'une Nuit (Only One Night*; 1944); *16. La Sorcière Nue (The Naked Sorceress*; Jaeger, 1954); *17. L'Énigme du Squelette (The Skeleton Enigma*; Jaeger, 1955); *Note:* cee Chapters IV and V. La Hire's novels appeared frequently in new editions. From 1952 to 1955, his son-in-law published 22 volumes containing truncated versions of some of the novels under the imprint of Jaeger-d'Hauteville (with covers by **Brantonne**). We have listed here only the editions with alternate titles.

La Houssaye, Noël de (?-); *L'Apparition d'Arsinoë (The Apparition of Arsinoe*; La Colombe, 1947); *Note:* See Chapter VIII.

Lailler, Jean (?-?) *see* **Grand-Guignol**

Lallemand, Y. (?-) *see Contes et Légendes*

Laloy, Louis (?-?) *see* **Opéra**

Lalonde, Robert (1936-); *Ailleurs est en ce Monde (Elsewhere Is in This World*; Arc, 1966); *Les Contes du Portage (Tales of the Portage*; Léméac, 1973); *La Belle Épouvante (The Beautiful Terror*; Julliard, 1981); *Le Dernier Été des Indiens (The Indians' Last Summer*; Seuil, 1982); *Une Belle Journée d'Avance (A Beautiful Day Ahead*; Seuil, 1986); *Le Fou du Père (The Father's Madman*; Boréal, 1988); *Le Diable en Personne (The Devil in Person*; Seuil, 1989); *L'Ogre des Grands Remous (The Ogre of the Rapids*; Seuil, 1992); *Sept Lacs plus au Nord (Seven Lakes Further North*; Seuil, 1993); *Note:* French-Canadian writer.

La Marche, Marc (Marceron, Dr.; ?-); *Tréponème* (Jeune Cadémie, 1931); *Note:* See Chapter VII.

Lamare, Patrice (?-); *La Galerie des Horreurs (The Gallery of Horrors*; FNG 58, 1987)

Lamarque, B. (?-); *Paris Brûlera (Paris Will Burn*; Sept Couleurs, 1966)

Lamart, Jean-Claude (?-); *Top Niveau (Top Level*; FNA 1708, 1989)

Lamart, Michel (?-); *Au Bord du Gaffre (Near the Edge of the Abyss*; Orcca/MCAM, 1983); *Le Rire du Robot dans les Champs Magnétiques (The Laughter of the Robot in the Magnetic Fields*; Hac., 1984); *Rien N'est Parfait... (Nothing Is Perfect...*; CRNI, n.d.) *Note:* Juvenile SF. See Chapter IX.

Lamartine, Alphonse de (1790-1869); *La Chute d'un Ange (The Fall of an Angel*; Gosselin & Coquebert, 1838)

Lambert, C. (?-); *La Nuit des Mutants (Night of the Mutants*; Hac., 1996)

Lambert, Louis (?-); *Prélude à l'Apocalypse, ou les Derniers Chevaliers du Graal (Prelude to Apocalypse, or the Last Knights of the Grail*; Criterion, 1982)

Lambotte, Emma (1880-?); *L'Aventureux (The Adventurer*; Ed. de Belgique, 1933); *May et le Monstre du Loch Ness (May and the Loch Ness Monster*; CNF, 1937); *Le Roman de Pénélope (Penelope's Novel*; P. Mourousy, 1952)

Lambry, Léon (?-); *Rama, Fille des Cavernes (Rama, Daughter of the Caverns*; Semaine de Suzette, 1928); *La Mission de Run le Tordu (The Mission of Twisted Run*; 1929; rev. Desclée de Brouwer, 1931); *Sur la Terre qui Change (On the Changing Earth*; BGA, 1930); *L'Antre du Sorcier (The Lair of the Wizard*; Tallandier, 1938); *Les Démons d'Annam (The Demons of Annam*; Tallandier, 1938); *Les Hommes des Dunes (The Men from the Dunes*; Tallandier, 1938); *Note:* See Chapter VII.

Lamerlière, Eugène de (?-?); *Le Monstre (The Monster*; U. Canel, 1824); *Le Damné (The Damned*; U. Canel, 1824); *Note:* See Chapter IV.

Lamirande, Claire de (1929-); *Jeu de Clefs (A Game of Keys*; Jour, 1974); *Signé de Biais (Signed Diagonally*; Quinze, 1976); *L'Opération Fabuleuse (The Fabulous Operation*; Quinze, 1978); *Le Grand Élixir (The Great Elixir*; Quinze, 1980); *Papineau, ou L'Épée à Double Tranchant (Papineau, or the Double-Edged Sword*; Quinze, 1980); *L'Occulteur (The Occultor*; Q/A, 1982); *La Rose des Temps (The Rose of Time*; Q/A, 1984); *Note:* French-Canadian writer. *Jeu* is an effective ghost story

Lamontagne, Ann (?-); *La Flèche du Temps (The Arrow of Time*; HMH, 1994); *Note:* French-Canadian writer.

Lamontagne, Michel (1954-); *L'Arbre Noir (The Black Tree*; JP, 1996); *Note:* French-Canadian writer.

Lamothe, Alexandre Bessot de (?-); *La Fée des Sables* (*The Sand Fairy*; Blériot, 1865); *Légendes de tous les Pays* (*Legends from All Countries*; Blériot, 1869); *Les Mystères de Machecoul* (*The Mysteries of Machecoul*; Blérot, 1871); *L'Auberge de la Mort* (*The Inn of Death*; Blériot, 1872); *Le Roi de la Nuit* (*The King of Night*; Blériot, 1873); *La Reine des Brumes et l'Émeraude des Mers* (*The Queen of Mists and the Sea Emerald*; Blériot, 1873); *Le Secret du Pôle* (*The Secret of the Pole*; Blériot, 1878; rev. 1882); *Les Secrets de l'Océan: Le Capitaine Ferragus* (*The Secrets of the Ocean: Captain Ferragus*; Blériot, 1879); *Foedora la Nihiliste* (Blériot, 1880); *Le Fou du Vésuve* (*The Madman of Vesuvius*; Blériot, 1881); *Le Puit Sanglant* (*The Bloody Well*; Blériot, 1881); *Le Secret de l'Équateur* (*The Secret of the Equator*; Blériot & Gautier, 1882); *Flora chez les Nains* (*Flora Among the Dwarves*; Blériot & Gautier, 1883); *Quinze Mois dans la Lune* (*Fifteen Months on the Moon*; Blériot & Gautier, 1883); *Les Faucheurs de la Mort* (*The Reapers of Death*; Ed. Universitaires, 1893); *Les Fils du Martyr* (*The Sons of the Martyr*; H. Gautier, 1903); *Note:* See Chapter V.

Lamothe-Langon, Étienne-Léon de (?-?); *Les Apparitions du Château de Tarabel, ou le Protecteur Invisible* (*The Apparitions at the Castle of Tarabel, or the Invisible Protector*; Dentu, 1822); *La Vampire ou la Vierge de Hongrie* (*The Vampire or the Hungarian Virgin*; 3 vols.; Mme Cardinal, 1825); *Le Monastère des Frères Noirs, ou l'Étendard de la Mort* (*The Monastery of the Black Friars, or the Standard of Death*; Pollet, 1825); *L'Hermite de la Tombe Mystérieuse, ou les Fantômes du Vieux Château* (*The Hermit of the Mysterious Grave, or the Ghosts of the Old Castle*; Mame & Delaunay, 1829); *Le Diable* (*The Devil*; Lachapelle, 1832); *Souvenirs d'un Fantôme* (*A Ghost's Memoirs*; C. Le Clere, 1838); *La Cloche du Trépassé, ou les Mystères du Château de Beauvoir* (*The Bell of the Deceased, or the Mysteries of the Castle of Beauvoir*; Lachapelle, 1839); *L'Homme de la Nuit, ou les Mystères* (*The Night Man, or the Mysteries*; C. Schwarz & A. Cagnot, 1842); *Le Spectre de la Galerie du château d'Estalens, ou le Sauveur Mystérieux* (*The Spectre of the Gallery of the Castle of Estalens, or the Mysterious Savior*; n.d.); *Note:* See Chapter IV.

Lamoureux, Henri (1942-); *Le Fils du Sorcier* (*The Wizard's Son*; JP 45, 1982); *Le Grand Départ* (*The Big Departure*; XYZ, 1993); *Note:* French-Canadian writer. Juvenile SF.

Lance, Pierre (?-); *Le Premier Président* (*The First President*; Filipacchi, 1993); *Note:* Ecological SF.

Lancelot, Michel (?-); *Julien des Fauves* (*Julian of the Beasts*; AM, 1979)

Landay, Maurice (1873-); *Les Robes Noires* (*The Black Dresses*; Ollendorff, 1904); *Les Avariés* (*The Spoiled*; Tallandier, 1904-05); *L'Étrange Amant du Mal* (*Evil's Strange Lover*; with André de **Lorde**; Ren. du Livre, 1923); *L'Assassin Mystère* (*The Mysterious Killer*; Inédits Populaires, 1925); *La Malle à Gouffé* (*Gouffe's Chest*; Inédits Populaires, 1925); *L'Antenne Mystérieuse* (*The Mysterious Antenna*; L'Intrépide, 1930-31); *L'Homme qui a Vaincu la Mort* (*The Man Who Defeated Death*; Tout Savoir, 1930); *Carot Coupe-Tête* (*Carot Head-Cutter*; 25 vols., Fayard, 1933); *Note:* See Chapter VII.

L'Andelyn, Charles de (?-); *Les Derniers Jours du Monde* (*The Last Days of the World*; Jullien, 1931); *La Prodigieuse Découverte de Georges Lefranc* (*The Prodigious Discovery of Georges Lefranc*; Figuière, 1935); *Nara le Conquérant* (*Nara the Conqueror*; Attinger, 1936); *Entre la Vie et le Rêve* (*Between Life and Dream*; Perret-Gentil, 1943); *Le Réveil d'Alexis Deschamps* (*The Awakening of Alexis Deschamps*; Aigle, 1948); *Voyage à la Lune et Au-delà* (*Voyage to the Moon and Beyond*; Connaître, 1960); *Il ne faut pas Badiner avec le Temps* (*Don't Joke with Time*; Perret-Gentil, 1964); *Note:* Swiss writer. See Chapter VII.

Landowski, Marcel (?-) *see* **Opéra**

Landoy, J. A. C. (?-); *Du Fond des Âges: Chronique de la Race Noyée* (*From Ages Long Gone: Chronicle of the Drowned Race*; ProArte, 1948); *Note:* Belgian writer.

Landreau, Max (?-); *La Vengeance du Rhin* (*The Revenge of the Rhine*; SdP, 1946)

Landry, François (?-); *Le Comédon* (Triptyque, 1993); *Note:* French-Canadian writer.

Landry, Louis (1929-); *Fables* (Cercle du Livre de France, 1964); *Glausgab, Créateur de Monde* (*Glausgab, Creator of Worlds*; JP, 1981); *Glausgab, le Protecteur* (*Glausgab, the Protector*; JP, 1981); *Note:* French-Canadian writer.

Lang, André (1893-1941); *Le Responsable* (*The Responsible Party*; AM, 1921); *Fausta* (AM, 1922); *La Paix est pour Demain* (*Peace Is for Tomorrow*; Oeuvres Libres, 1937)

Langelaan, George (1908-1972); *Nouvelles de l'Anti-Monde* (*Stories of the Anti-World*; RL, 1962; transl. as *Out of Time*, 1964); *Le Dauphin Parle Trop* (*The Dolphin Spoke Too Much*; RL, 1964); *Le Zombie Express* (*Zombie Express*; RL, 1964); *Le Vol de l'Anti-G* (*The Flight of the Anti-G*; Planète, 1967); *Les Faits Maudits* (*The Damned Facts*; Planète, 1967); *Treize Fantômes* (*13 Ghosts*; AM, 1971); *Note:* See Chapter IX.

Langlais, Xavier de (Langleiz, Xavier de; ?-1975); *L'Île* *sous Cloche (The Domed Island;* First published in Briton as *Enez ar Rod (The Island of the Wheel,* Skrid ha Skeuidenn, 1944; transl. in French by the author, Portes du Large, 1946; rev. PdF 86, 1965); *Le Roman du Roi Arthur (The Novel of King Arthur;* 1965); *Marzhin* (Al Liamm, 1975); *Tristan et Yseut* (Terre de Brume, 1994); *Note:* French writer from Britanny (hence the alternative Briton spelling of his name). See Chapter VII.

Lannes, Maurice (?-); *Huit Jeunes Filles Ont Disparu (Eight Young Girls Have Vanished;* Le Pelletier, 1945); *Le Bar des Épaves (The Bar of the Wrecks;* L'Arabesque, 1969); *La Belle Révoltée (The Beautiful Rebel;* L'Arabesque, 1969); *Jours Noirs et Nuits Blanches (Dark Days and White Nights;* L'Arabesque, 1969)

Lannion, Philippe (?-) *see Contes et Légendes*

Lanos, Henri (?-); *Un Monde sur le Monde (A World on the World;* with Jules **Perrin**; *Nos Loisirs,* 1910); *L'Aéro-Bagne 32 (Air Penitentiary 32);* with E. M. **Laumann**; LPT, 1920); *Le Grand Raid Paris-La Lune (The Great Paris-Moon Race;* Pierrot, 1928); *Les Hommes de Fer du Dr. Hax (The Iron-Men of Dr. Hax;* Pierrot, 1932); *Note:* See Chapter VII.

Lanzman, Jacques (?-); *Le Têtard (The Tadpole;* RL, 1976); *Uranimus, Fantaisie Romanesque (Uranimus, Romanesque Fantasy;* Lieu Commun, 1982); *L'Arbre Magique (The Magic Tree;* GP, 1982); *La Baleine Blanche (The White Whale;* RL, 1982); *Le Lama Bleu (The Blue Lama;* Gr. Livre du Mois, 1983); *Le Septième Ciel (The Seventh Heaven;* JCL, 1984); *Le Dieu des Papillons (The Gods of the Butterflies;* JCL, 1993); *La Horde d'Or (The Golden Horde;* Gr. Livre du Mois, 994); *Le Fils de l'Himalaya (The Son of the Himalayas;* Ramsay, 1997)

Lapauze, Daniel (?-); *Match Nul (The Game Is a Draw;* L'Arabesque, 1957); *Parallèle 83* (Mar. P2000 6, 1974)

Lapeyrière, Jean de (?-); *L'Homme du Volcan (The Man from the Volcano;* Argo, 1928); *Les Trois Dames et Celle d'Atout (Three Queens and a Trump;* Fasquelle, 1929); *La Caresse Perdue (The Lost Caress;* Lemerre, 1932); *Le Vertige des Impurs (Vertigo of the Impure;* Lemerre, 1932); *La Sirène des Mers du Sud (The Siren of the Southern Seas;* Dupuis, 1937); *Le Tourbillon Bleu (The Blue Maelstrom;* Dupuis, 1938); *Larmes d'un Soir (Tears of an Evening;* Tallandier, 1938); *Au Bout du Fleuve (At the End of the River;* Dupuis, 1938); *L'Aventure Étoilée (The Starry Adventure;* Fayard, 1939)

Lapierre, Dominique (?-); *Le Cinquième Cavalier (The Fifth Horseman;* with Larry Collins; RL, 1980)

Laplace, Louis-Jean (?-); *À 4 Heures, Maître Richard ne sera plus (At 4 O'Clock, Master Richard Will Be No*

More; SPE, 1942); *L'Oeil de Vénus (The Eye of Venus;* Ed. du Marais, 1973); *La Chronique de Cosnie (Chronicles of Cosnia;* Salamandre, 1973); *Des Guignes au Vitriol (Vitriolic Tales;* Laplace, 1976)

Laplante, Michèle de (1944-); *Grand Remous (Big Turbulence;* La Tombée, 1982); *Note:* French-Canadian writer. In the woods, a geologist encounters a living native legend.

La Porte, Abbé Joseph de (1718-1779); *Bibliothèque des Fées et des Génies (Library of Fairies and Djinns;* 1765); *Note:* See *Cabinet des Fées* and Chapter III.

Laramie, Phil (?-); *Le Viol du Dieu Ptah (The Rape of the God Ptah;* FNA 1507, 1986); *La Folle Ruée des Akantor (The Mad Rush of the Akantor;* FNA 1525, 1987); *Les Squales de la Cité Engloutie (The Sharks of the Sunken City;* FNA 1566, 1987); *Le Grand Hurlement (The Great Howling;* FNA 1633, 1988); *Note:* See Chapter VIII.

Larguier, Léo (1878-1950); *L'Abdication de Ris-Orangis (The Ris-Orangis Abdication;* Ed. Fr. Ill., 1918); *François Pain, Gendarme* (Ed. Fr. Ill., 1919); *Le Faiseur d'Or Nicolas Flamel (Nicolas Flamel the Gold Maker;* Nationales, 1935); *L'An Mille (The Year 1000);* AM, 1937); *Le Soldat Inconnu (The Unknown Soldier;* Plon, 1939); *Au Vieux Saint de Bois (The Old Wooden Saint;* Aubanel, 1944); *Le Roi sans Reine (The King Without Queen;* R. Simon, 1947)

Larigaudie, Guy de (1908-1940); *Le Tigre et sa Panthère (The Tiger and His Panther;* SdP, 1938); *L'îlot du Grand Étang (The Island of the Great Pond;* Jean de Gigord, 1939); *Raa la Buse (Raa the Buzzard;* Scouts de France, 1944); *La Frégate Aventurière (The Adventurous Frigate;* Scouts de France, 1945); *Yug* (Jean de Gigord, 1945); *Yug en Terres Inconnues (Yug in Unknown Lands;* Jean de Gigord, 1946); *Harka le Barzoï (SdP Jr 20, 1959); *Étoile au Grand Large (Star in Deep Waters;* Seuil, 1994); *Le Messager de Clotilde (Clotilde's Messenger;* Python, 1996); *Note:* See Chapter VII.

Laroche, Madeleine (1925-); *Le Château du Soleil (The Castle of the Sun;* Blé, 1984); *Note:* French-Canadian writer. Medieval fairy tale inspired by Britannic legends.

La Rochefoucauld, Gabriel de (?-); *Le Professeur Néant (Prof. Void;* Ren. Du Livre, 1922); *L'Homme qui perd la Vue (The Man Who Lost His Sight;* Ed. de France, 1928); *La Dame Verte (The Green Lady;* Ed. de France, 1937); *Le Vol Nuptial (The Wedding Flight;* Ed. de France, 1937)

Larouche, Nadya (1956-); *Les Prisonniers de l'Autre Monde (The Prisoners of Another World;* HRW, 1995); *Note:* French-Canadian writer.

Larroque, Pierre (?-?) *see* **Grand-Guignol**

La Salle, Bruno de (1943-); *Le Coeur du Monstre* (*The Heart of the Monster*; Cast., 1985); *L'Oiseau de Vérité* (*The Bird of Truth*; Cast., 1985); *L'Épine* (*The Thorn*; Cast., 1988)

Lascaris, Théodore (?-?) *see* **Grand-Guignol**

Lascault, Gilbert (1930-); *Un Monde Mimé* (*A Mimed World*; Bourgois, 1975); *Un Îlot Tempéré* (*A Moderate Islet*; Bourgois, 1977); *Voyage d'Automne et d'Hiver* (*Travel of Autumn and Winter*; Bourgois, 1979); *Destinée de Jean-Simon Castor* (*The Destiny of Jean-Simon Castor*; Bourgois, 1981); *Encyclopédie Abrégée de l'Empire Vert* (*Abbreviated Encyclopedia of the Geen Empire*; Papyrus, 1983); *Marmottes à l'Imparfait* (*Imperfect Dormouses*; Ryoân-Ji, 1983); *420 Minutes dans la Cité des Ombres* (*420 Minutes in the City of Shadows*; Ramsey, 1988); *Le Petit Chaperon Rouge, Partout* (*Little Red Riding Hood, Everywhere*; Seghers, 1989); *La Vie des Louvoyantes* (*The Life of the Slipperies*; Gardiens du Schibloleth, 1992); *Enfers Bouffons ou la Nuit de Satan Dément* (*Jesting Hells, or the Night of the Mad Satan*; Fata Morgana, 1996); *Note:* See Chapter VIII.

Laselle, Jean-Pol *see* **Sarkel, François**

La Spina, Greye (?-); *Les Envahisseurs de la Nuit* (*The Invaders of Night*; Galliera 10, 1973)

Lassailly, Charles (?-?); *Les Roueries de Trialph* (*Trialph's Lies*; Silvestre, 1833); *Note:* See Chapter IV.

Lassalle, Thierry (1953-); *Nord* (*North*; FNA 1324, 1984); *La Piste du Sud* (*Trail of the South*; FNA 1427, 1986); *Note:* See Chapter IX.

Lassay, Armand de Madaillan de Lesparre, Marquis de (1652-1738); *Recueil de Différentes Choses (incl. Relation du Royaume de Félicie; Collection of Various Things (incl. Narration of the Kingdom of Felicia);* 4 vols.; Bousquet, 1727); *Note:* Utopia.

Las Vergnas, Anne-Marie-Suzanne *see* **Soulac, Anne-Marie**

Lataillade, Louis (?-); *Les Goélands Aventureux* (*The Adventurous Seagulls*; Didier, 1927); *Le Groupe Sud* (*Group South*; Gall., 1959)

Latil, Pierre de (?-); *Les Voyages des Animaux* (*Animals' Journeys*; Stock, 1948); *Aventures au Jamboree ou Le Noeud de Carrick* (*Adventures at the Jamboree or Carrick's Knot*; L'Arc, 1948); *La Légende des Santons* (*The Legends of the Santons*; Solar, 1950); *Bouya-Bouya* (Plon, 1955); *Le Château des Surprises* (*The Castle of Surprises*; Gautier-Languereau, 1956); *Il Faut Tuer les Robots* (*We Must Kill the Robots*; Grasset, 1957); *Ainsi Vivrons-nous Demain* (*How We Shall Live Tomorrow*;

Centurion, 1958); *Opération Lune* (*Operation Moon*; Hac., 1969); *La Terre* (*Earth*; Hac., 1973); *Micromégas, Le Temps et la Cybernétique* (*Micromegas, Time and Cybernetics*; Fabr. d'Assortiments Réunis, 1975)

Latour, Léon (?-); *Pitremoux chez les Lacustres* (*Pitremoux Among the Lake People*; Suzérenné, 1953); *Note:* Juvenile fantasy.

La Tour, Maxime (?-); *Kaffra Kan* (Tallandier, 1921); *La Tireuse de Cartes* (*The Card Reader*; SET, 1926); *La Vie d'une Morte* (*A Dead Woman's Life*; SET, 1926)

Latour, Sylvain (?-); *Les Mains* (*The Hands*; Milieu du Monde, 1960

Latzarus, Marie-Thérèse (1881-1966); *Une Mystérieuse Petite Fille* (*A Mysterious Little Girl*; Hac., 1938); *Et le Fantôme Entra* (*And the Ghost Walked In*; Bonne Presse, 1949)

L'Aude, Renaud de (?-); *Bergella la Blanche, ou la Volupté qu'elles me doivent* (*Bergella the White, or the Pleasure They Owe Me*; Frontières, 1970); *Note:* Erotic SF about a man abducted by female extraterrestrials.

Laugham, Max *see* **Gallo, Max**

Laumann, E. M. (1863-1928); *Jacques le Résolu* (*Jack the Resolute*; with Pierre **Lostin**; Hac., 1906); *L'Aéro-Bagne 32* (*Air Penitentiary 32);* with Henri **Lanos**; LPT, 1920); *L'Étrange Matière* (*The Strange Matter*; with Raoul **Bigot**; LPT, 1921); *Le Visage dans la Glace* (*The Face in the Ice*; with Raoul **Bigot**; LPT, 1922); *Sous la Banquise* (*Under the Ice Shelf*; BGA, 1928); *Les Mystères d'Hollywood* (*The Mysteries of Hollywood*; with René **Jeanne**; RMY, 1928); *Si le 9 Thermidor...* (*If on 9 Thermidor*; with René **Jeanne**; Tallandier, 1929); *La Closerie des Genêts* (Libr. Contemporaine, 1933); *L'Aventure Amoureuse et Tragique* (*The Tragic and Amorous Aventure*; Tallandier, 1936); *Le Roman d'un Mousse* (*The Novel of a Cabin Boy*; Tallandier, 1937); *L'Alcyon* (L'Hydre, 1986); *Note:* See Chapter VII. Also see **Grand-Guignol**.

Launay, Louis de (1860-1938); *Les Fumées de l'Encens: Vieux Sanctuaires et Rite Anciens* (*The Smoke of Incense: Old Sanctuaries and Ancient Rites*; La Vraie France, 1925); *Les Entretiens d'Ahasvérus* (*Conversations with Ahasverus*; Courrier Politique, 1938)

Laureillard, Rémi (1938-); *Fred le Nain et Maho le Géant* (*Fred the Dwarf and Maho the Giant*; Gall., 1978); *Une Fée sans Baguette* (*A Fairy Without a Wand*; Gall., 1979); *Le Tailleur d'Ulm* (*The Tailor from Ulm*; Gall., 1981); *Moi, Ulysse...* (*I, Ulysses*; Atelier Lyrique de Tourcoing, 1985); *Les Terribles Zerlus* (*The Terrible Zerlus*; Gall., 1986); *Idriss, ou La Fête Interrompue* (*Idriss, or the Interrupted Party*; Gérard Billaudot, 1988)

Laurendeau, Pierre (?-) *Qu'il Est Doux... (How Sweet He Is...*; CRNI, n.d.)

Laurent, Agnès (Simart, Hélène; ?-); *Au Coeur de ma Nuit (In the Heart of My Night;* FNAG 182, 1970); *L'Ultime Rendez-Vous (The Ultimate Rendezvous;* FNAG 188, 1970); *Le Justicier (The Justice-Giver;* FNAG 194, 1971); *L'Ennemi dans l'Ombre (The Enemy in Shadow;* FNAG 205, 1971); *Chimères (Chimeras;* Tallandier, 1971); *Le Magicien Noir (The Dark Magician;* Tallandier, 1971); *Le Sang des Étoiles (Blood of the Stars;* FNAG 228, 1973); *Requiem pour un Fantôme (Requiem for a Ghost;* FNAG 237, 1973); *D Comme Feu (D as in Fire;* Monnet Terrific 9, 1974); *L'Homme qui avait un Secret (The Man Who Had a Secret;* Tallandier, 1976); *La Perle de Sitra (The Pearl of Sitra;* Tallandier, 1977); *Amoureux d'une Ombre (In Love with a Shadow;* Tallandier, 1978); *Le Maître des Aigles (The Master of Eagles;* Tallandier, 1979); *Prisonnier d'une Ombre (Prisoner of a Shadow;* Tallandier, 1980); *Le Sorcier (The Wizard;* Panthéon, 1995); *Note:* See Chapter VIII.

Laurent de la Barre, Ernest du (?-) *see Contes et Légendes*

Laurian, Marcel (?-); *L'Étrange Voyage de Monsieur Barbibon (The Strange Journey of Mr. Barbibon;* Cri-Cri, 1912; rev. as 2 vols. as *Les Hommes-Singes (The Ape-Men)* and *La Guerre des Nains et des Géants (The War of Dwarves and Giants,* CDAv, 1919); *Note:* See Chapter VII.

Laurie, André (Grousset, Paschal; 1844-1909); *Le Rêve d'un Irréconciliable (The Dream of an Irreconcilable Man;* as Paschal Grousset, Madre, 1869); *Les Cinq Cent Millions de la Begum (with Jules* **Verne;** VE, 1879; transl. as *The 500 Millions of the Begum,* 1879); *L'Étoile du Sud (The Southern Star;* with Jules **Verne;** VE, 1884; transl. as *The Vanished Diamond,* 1885); *L'Héritier de Robinson (Robinson Crusoe's Heir;* RA, 1884); *L'Épave du "Cynthia" (with Jules* **Verne;** RA, 1885; transl. as *Salvage from the "Cynthia,"* 1958); *Les Exilés de la Terre, Séléné Company Ltd. (Exiled from Earth;* RA, 1887; transl. as *The Conquest of the Moon,* 1889); *De New York à Brest en Sept Heures (RA,* 1888; transl. as *New York to Brest in Seven Hours,* 1890); *Le Capitaine Trafalgar (RA,* 1888); *Le Nain de Radamèh (The Dwarf of Radameh;* RA, 1888); *Le Secret du Mage (RA,* 1890; transl. as *The Secret of the Magician,* 1892); *Aventure Nautique (Nautical Adventure;* Armand Colin, 1891); *Axel Eberson (RA,* 1891); *Le Rubis du Grand Lama (The Ruby of the Great Lama;* RA, 1894); *Un Roman dans la Planète Mars (A Novel on Planet Mars;* Revue Illustrée, 1895); *Atlantis (RA,* 1895; transl. as *The Crystal City Under the Sea,* 1896); *Le Géant de l'Azur (The Giant of the Azure;* RA, 1903); *Le Filon de Gérard (Gerard's Claim;* RA, 1903); *L'Oncle de Chicago (The Uncle from Chicago;* RA, 1903); *Le Tour du Globe d'un Bachelier (A Graduate Around the World;* RA, 1904); *Le Maître de l'Abîme (The Master of the Abyss;* RA, 1905); *Spiridon le Muet (Spiridon the Mute;* RJ, 1907); *Note:* See Chapter V.

Laurier, Andrée (1956-); *L'Étrange Maison d'Elseva (Elseva's Strange House;* Humanitas, 1995); *Note:* French-Canadian writer.

Laurin, Florent *see* **Grenier, Armand**

Lautréamont (Comte de; Ducasse, Isidore Lucien; 1846-1870); *Les Chants de Maldoror (The Songs of Maldoror;* Chant I: Quesnoy & Cie., 1868); Chants I-VI, Lacroix, Verboeckhoven & Cie., 1869; transl. as *The Lays of Maldoror,* 1924); *Note:* See Chapter IV.

Lautrec, Gabriel de (1867-1938); *Les Histoires de Tom Joë (Tom Joe's Stories;* Ed. Fr. Ill., 1920); *La Vengeance du Portrait Ovale (The Revenge of the Oval Portrait;* Roseau, 1922); *La Semaine des Quatre Jeudis (The Week of Four Thursdays;* Roseau, 1922); *Le Serpent de Mer (The Sea Serpent;* Siècle, 1925); *L'Invalide à la Tête de Bois (The Invalid with a Wooden Head;* Lafitte, 1925); *Note:* See Chapter VII.

Lauwereyns de Rosendaele, Antonia de (?-) *see Contes et Légendes*

Lauzach, J.-J. (?-) *see* **Rachilde**

Lauzon, Vincent (1969-); *Bouh, le Fantôme (Bouh the Ghost;* Héritage, 1992); *Note:* French-Canadian writer. Juvenile fantasy.

Lavacour, André (?-); *Les Français de la Décadence (The Decadent Frenchmen;* Gall., 1960

La Vaulx, Henri de *see* **Galopin, Arnould**

Lavaur, Pierre (?-); *Les Mésaventures d'un Rajeuni (The Misadventures of a New Youth;* LN, 1931); *L'Amour Féroce de l'Étrangleur (The Strangler's Fierce Love;* Tallandier, 1931); *Enterré Vif (Buried Alive;* Tallandier, 1931); *La Conquête de la Terre (The Conquest of Earth;* BGA, 1931); *De la Mort à l'Amour (From Death to Love;* Tallandier, 1932); *La Vengeance du Fiancé (The Fiance's Revenge;* Tallandier, 1932); *Le Fou de la Tour Eiffel (The Madman of the Eiffel Tower;* BGA, 1932); *Le Diable au Magasin (The Devil in the Store;* BGA, 1932); *Un Drame par TSF (A TSF Tragedy;* Libr. Contemporaine, 1932); *L'Oil de Tigre (The Eye of the Tiger;* BGA, 1933); *Elle Croyait Rêver (She Thought She Was Dreaming;* Poche 6, 1937); *Les Captifs du Tawawour (Prisoners of the Tawawour;* BGA, 1939); *L'Énigme de l'Alcyon (The Mystery of the Alcyon;* with Paul **Ternoise;** Dupuis, 1939)

La Ville de Mirmont, Alexandre-Jean-Joseph de (?-?); *L'An 1928 (The Year 1928);* Allouard, 1841); *Note:* Stage play. See Chapter V.

Lay, André (?-); *Vallespi et les Soucoupes Volantes* (*Vallespi and the Flying Saucers*; FN Special-Police 909, 1971)

Lazare, Bernard (1865-1903); *La Fiancée de Corinthe* (*The Bethrothed of Corinth*; Dalou, 1888); *Le Miroir des Légendes* (*The Mirror of Legends*; Lemerre, 1892); *La Porte d'Ivoire* (*The Ivory Gate*; A. Colin, 1897); *Les Porteurs de Torches* (*The Torch Bearers*; A. Colin, 1897); *Le Fumier de Job* (*Job's Compost Heap*; Rieder, 1903)

Lazure, Jacques (1956-); *La Valise Rouge* (*The Red Suitcase*; Q/A, 1987); *Le Domaine des Sans-Yeux* (*The Domain of the Eyeless*; Q/A, 1989); *Pellicule-Cités* (*Film-Cities*; Q/A, 1992); *Monsieur N'importe Qui* (*Mister Anybody*; Q/A, 1993); *Le Rêve Couleur d'Orange* (*The Orange-Colored Dream*; Q/A, 1996); *Note:* French-Canadian writer. *Le Domaine* is heroic fantasy. The other novels are juvenile SF.

Lebas, Georges (1862-1934); *Jean Arlog, Le Premier Surhomme* (*Jean Arlog, the First Superman*; RJ, 1921); *L'Heure Perdue* (*The Lost Hour*; Gautier-Languereau, 1930); *La Mouette* (*The Seagull*; Mode Nationale, 1932); *Note:* See Chapter VII.

Lebert, A. (?-?) *see* **Grand-Guignol**

Lebey, André (1877-1938); *Le Roman de la Mélusine* (*The Novel of Melusine*; MdF, 1895); *Les Pigeons d'Argile* (*The Clay Pigeons*; Juven, 1905); *Tenue du... 16 Septembre 5924* (*Review Of... Sept. 7th, 5924); 1922); *Ameno Kamato* (Crès, 1924); *Les Sept Idées des Sept Dîners des Sept* (*The 7 Ideas of the 7 Dinners of the 7); Ren. du Livre, 1925); *L'Initiation de Vercingétorix* (*The Initiation of Vercingetorix*; AM, 1926); *Le Vénérable et le Curé* (*The Venerable One and the Priest*; AM, 1928); *Le Secret du Temple* (*The Secret of the Temple*; Glottow, 1931); *Main Votive aux Gracques* (*Holy Hand to the Gracques*; AM, 1932); *Note:* See Chapter VII. Also used the pseudonym of "André Yebel."

Leblanc, Benoit (1968-); *Compte à Rebours: TRE 22660*(*Countdown*; HMH, 1994); *Note:* French-Canadian writer.

Leblanc, Léo (?-); *Les Incommunicants* (*The Uncommunicating*; Presses Libres, 1971); *Note:* French-Canadian writer.

Leblanc, Maurice (1864-1941); *Les Trois Yeux* (*The Three Eyes;* 2 vols., *Les Trois Yeux* (*The Three Eyes*) and *Le Rayon B* (*The B Ray*, JST, 1919; rev. Lafitte, 1921); *Le Formidable Evènement* (*The Formidable Event*; JST, 1920; rev. Lafitte, 1921); *L'Homme Truqué* (JST, 1920); *Les Clefs Mystérieuses* (*The Mysterious Keys*; Glénat, 1975); *De Minuit à Sept Heures* (*From Midnight to Seven*; Glénat, 1978); *La Robe d'Écailles Roses* (*The Dress with Pink Shells*; Glénat, 1979); Series *Arsène Lupin:1. Arsène Lupin, Gentleman Cambrioleur* (*Arsene Lupin, Gentleman Burglar*; JST, 1905/07; rev. Lafitte, 1907); *2. Arsène Lupin contre Herlock Sholmes* (*Arsene Lupin vs. Herlock Sholmes*; JST, 1907; rev. Lafitte, 1908); *3. Arsène Lupin, Pièce en 4 Actes* (*Arsene Lupin, Play in Four Acts;* Ill. Théatrale, 1909); *4. L'Aiguille Creuse* (*The Hollow Needle*; JST/Lafitte, 1909); *5. 813 (2* vols., *La Double Vie d'Arsène Lupin* (*The Double Life of Arsene Lupin*) and *Les Trois Crimes d'Arsène Lupin* (*The Three Crimes of Arsene Lupin*, Lafitte, 1910); *6. Le Bouchon de Cristal* (*The Crystal Stopper*; Lafitte, 1912); *7. Les Confidences d'Arsène Lupin* (*The Confidences of Arsene Lupin*; JST, 1911-13; rev. Lafitte, 1913); *8. L'Éclat d'Obus* (*The Shell Shard*; *Le Journal*, 1915; rev.

Lafitte, 1916); *9. Le Triangle d'Or* (*The Golden Triangle; Le Journal*, 1917-18; rev. as 2 vols., *La Pluie d'Étincelles* (*The Rain of Sparks*) and *La Victoire d'Arsène Lupin* (*The Victory of Arsene Lupin*, Lafitte, 1921); *10. L'Île aux Trente Cercueils* (*The Island of Thirty Coffins; Le Journal*, 1919-20; rev. as 2 vols., *Véronique* and *La Pierre Miraculeuse* (*The Miracle Stone*, Lafitte, 1920); *11. Les Dents du Tigre* (*The Teeth of the Tiger; Le Journal*, 1920; rev. Laffite, 1921); *12. Le Retour d'Arsène Lupin* (*The Return of Arsene Lupin*; JST, 1920); *13. Les Huit Coups de l'Horloge* (*The Eight Strokes of the Clock*; Lafitte, 1923); *14. La Comtesse de Cagliostro* (*The Countess of Cagliostro; Le Journal*/Laffite, 1924); *15. La Demoiselle aux Yeux Verts* (*The Damsel with Green Eyes*; *Le Journal*/Laffite, 1927); *16. L'Agence Barnett et Cie.* (*The Barnett and Co. Agency*; Laffite, 1928); *17. La Demeure Mystérieuse* (*The Mysterious Mansion*; *Le Journal*, 1928; rev. Lafitte, 1929); *18. La Barre-y-va* (*Le Journal,* 1930; rev. Lafitte, 1931); *19. La Femme aux Deux Sourires* (*The Woman with Two Smiles*; *Le Journal*, 1932; rev. Laffite, 1933); 20. *Victor de la Brigade Mondaine* (Laffite, 1934); *21. La Cagliostro se venge* (*The Revenge of the Countess of*

Cagliostro; Laffite, 1935)*; 22. Les Milliards d'Arsène Lupin* (*The Billions of Arsene LupIn*; *L'Auto,* 1939; rev. Hac., 1941); By **Boileau-Narcejac**: *1. Le Secret d'Eunerville* (*The Secret of Eunerville*; Libr. Champs-Élysées, 1973); *2. La Poudrière* (*The Powder Keg*; Libr. Champs-Élysées, 1974); *3. Le Second Visage d'Arsène Lupin* (*The Other Face of Arsene Lupin*; Libr. Champs-Élysées, 1975); *4. La Justice d'Arsène Lupin* (*The Justice of Arsene Lupin*; Libr. Champs-Élysées, 1977); *5. Le Serment d'Arsène Lupin* (*The Oath of Arsene Lupin*; Libr. Champs-Élysées, 1979); *Note:* See chapters IV and VII. The **Arsène Lupin** novels have been adapted into films and television movies and series. See Book 1, chapters I and II. Maurice Leblanc also collaborated with Pierre **Palau** on a **Grand-Guignol** play, *L'Homme dans l'Ombre* (1935).

Leblanc du Rollet (?-?) *see* **Opéra**

Leboeuf, Gaétan (?-); *Simon Yourn* (Q/A, 1986); *Boudin d'Air* (*Air Sausage*; Q/A, 1990); *Note:* French-Canadian writer. *Simon* is a humorous time-travel fantasy written for a young-adult market. *Boudin* describes a comical parallel universe.

Le Bourguignon, Alfred (?-?); *La Chouette* (*The Owl*; Chamuel, 1893); *Note:* See Chapter IV.

Le Bovier de Fontenelle, Bernard *see* **Fontenelle, Bernard Le Bovier de**

Lebras, Yves-Marie (?-); *Un Homme Dormit Mille Ans* (*A Man Slept for a Thousand Years*; EDIP, 1930)

Le Braz, Anatole (1859-?); *Pâques d'Islande* (*Icelandic Easter*; Calmann-Lévy, 1897); *Le Gardien du Feu* (*The Guardian of the Fire*; Calmann-Lévy, 1900); *Le Sang de la Sirène* (*The Blood of the Mermaid*; Calmann-Levy, 1901); *Âmes d'Occident* (*Western Souls*; Calmann-Lévy, 1911); *Note:* See Chapter IV. **Folk Tales:** *La Légende de la Mort chez les Bretons Armoricains et en Basse Bretagne* (*The Legend of Death Among Armorican Britons and in Lower Britanny*; Champion, 1893; rev. 1902, 1912, 1922, 1945, 1989); *Les Saints Bretons d'après la Tradition Populaire en Cornouailles* (*Briton Saints According to Popular Cornish Traditions; Annales de Brretagne, 1894); Au Pays des Pardons* (*In the Land of Pardons*; Lemerre, 1894); *Vieilles Histoires du Pays Breton* (*Old Tales from Britanny*; Champion, 1897); *La Terre du Passé* (*Land of the Past*; Calmann-Lévy, 1902); *Le Théâtre Celtique*

ANATOLE LE BRAZ

MAGIES DE LA BRETAGNE

LE GARDIEN DU FEU
LE SANG DE LA SIRÈNE
ÂMES D'OCCIDENT
CHANSONS POPULAIRES
DE LA BASSE-BRETAGNE
LE THÉÂTRE CELTIQUE
COGNOMBRUS
ET SAINTE TRÉFINE
CROQUIS DE BRETAGNE
ET D'AILLEURS
VIEILLES CHAPELLES
DE BRETAGNE
ÎLES BRETONNES
LA TERRE DU PASSÉ

BOUQUINS

(*Celtic Theatre*; Calmann-Lévy, 1905); *Contes du Soleil et de la Brume* (*Tales of Sun and Mist*; Delagrave, 1913); *Note:* See Chapter IV.

Le Bret, André (?-?) *see* **Grand-Guignol**

Le Breton, P. (?-) *see* ***Contes et Légendes***

Lebrun, Michel *see* **Lecler, Michel**

Lebugle, André (1942-); *Les Portes Secrètes du Rêve* (*The Secret Gates of Dream*; Fides, 1989); *Les Visiteurs de Minuit* (*The Visitors of Midnight*; Fides, 1991); *La Chasse aux Vampires* (*The Hunt for Vampires*; Héritage, 1992); *Voyages dans l'Ombre* (*Journeys Into Shadows*; Tisseyre, 1995); *Note:* French-Canadian writer. Collections of fantastical tales and juvenile fantasies.

le Bussy, Alain (1947-); *L'Homme qui a Perdu son Âme* (*The Man Who Lost His Soul*; Xuense, 1991); *Deltas* (FNA 1885, 1992); *Tremblemer* (*Shakesea*; FNA 1908, 1993); *Deraag* (FNA 1919, 1993); *Envercoeur* (*Towardheart*; FNA 1931, 1993); *Garmalia* (FNA 1939, 1994); *Quête Impériale* (*Imperial Quest*; FNA 1948, 1994); *Yorg de l'Île* (*York of the Island*; FNA 1956, 1995); *Rork des Plaines* (*Rork of the Plains*; FNA 1958, 1995); *Hou des Machines* (*Hou of the Machines*; FNA 1960, 1995); *Soleil Fou* (*Crazy Sun*; FNA 1965, 1995); *Chatinika* (FNA 1972, 1995); *L'Angoisse que je lis dans mes Yeux dans le Miroir* (*The Fear I Read in My Eyes in the Mirror*; Lueurs Mortes, 1995); *Jana des Couloirs* (*Jana of the Corridors*; FNA 1979, 1996); *Jorvan de la Mer* (*Jorvan of the Sea*; FNA 1981, 1996); *Djamol de Kiv* (FNA 1982, 1996); *Le Dieu Avide* (*The Hungry God*; FNA 1992, 1996); *Équilibre* (*Balance*; FNSF 11, 1997); *Note:* See chapters VIII and IX.

Lec, Jean (?-); *L'Être Multiple* (*The Multiple Being*; Métal 5, 1954); *La Machine à Franchir la Mort* (*The Machine to Cross Death*; Métal 15, 1955); *Note:* See Chapter IX.

Lecalire (?-?) *see* **Grand-Guignol**

Lecarre, Alain (?-); *Les Oiseaux et le Méchant Bûcheron* (*The Birds and the Nasty Woodsman*; Scorpion, 1961); *Les Animaux du Cosmos* (*The Animals of the Cosmos*; Scorpion, 1964)

Lecaye, Alexis (?-); *Les Pirates du Paradis* (*The Pirates of Paradise*; Den., 1981); *L'Île des Magiciennes* (*The Island of Magicians*; Fayard, 1982)

Lecigne, Bruno (?-); *Le Titan de Galova* (*The Titan of Galova*; with Sylviane **Corgiat**; Plasma 1, 1983); *Océane* (with Sylviane **Corgiat**; Plasma, 1983); *Une Souris Verte* (*A Green Mouse*; with Sylviane **Corgiat**; FN Engrenage 82, 1983); *Dépression Venue de l'Atlantique* (*Depression from the Atlantic*; FN, 1985); *Le Rêve et l'Assassin* (*The Dream and the Assassin*; with Sylviane **Corgiat**; FNA 1486, 1986); *Le Programme*

Troisième Guerre Mondiale (*The WWIII Program*; with Sylviane **Corgiat**; FNA 1506, 1986); *L'Araignée* (*The Spider*; with Sylviane **Corgiat**; FNA 1527, 1987); EMO (FNA 1534, 1987); *Le Souffle de Cristal* (*The Crystal Breath*; with Sylviane **Corgiat**; FNA 1555, 1987); *Immolations* (with Sylviane **Corgiat** & Th. **Bataille**; FNG 44, 1987); *Le Masque d'Écailles* (*The Mask of Scales*; with Sylviane **Corgiat**; FNA 1610, 1988); *Immolations 2* (with Sylviane **Corgiat** & Th. **Bataille**; FNG 70, 1988); *Une Ombre en Cavale* (*A Shadow on the Loose*; with Sylviane **Corgiat**; Amitié, 1988); *Note:* See Chapters VIII and IX.

Lecler, Michel (Cade, Michel; 1930-1996); *Virus B29* (Arabesque, 1955); *Rêves Interdits* (*Forbidden Dreams*; Métal 13, 1955); *Velvet ou l'Éducation, Aventures Picaresques, Angoissantes, Érotiques* (Martineau, 1978); *Erotix* (as Lou Blanc; Edit & Public. Premières, Eroscope, 1980); *L'Envoûteur est dans l'Escalier* (*The Witch Doctor Waits on the Stairs*; FN, 1985); *Les Ogres* (*The Ogres*; Libr. Champs-Élysées, 1990); *Le Géant* (*The Giant*; Rivages, 1996); *Note:* Also wrote under the pseudonym of "Michel Lebrun."

Leclerc, Claude (1949-); *Goldorak: Le Grand Duel Interplanétaire* (*Goldorak: The Great Interplanetary Duel*; Desclez, 1980); *Le Maître des Ténèbres* (*The Master of Darkness*; Desclez, 1981); *Note:* French-Canadian writer. *Le Maître* is a collection of fantastical tales.

Le Clerc de la Bruyère, Charles-Antoine (?-?) *see* **Opéra**

Le Clerc de la Herverie, Jean (?-); *Ergad le Composite* (ON 10, 1976)

Leclercq, P.-R. (?-); *Le Phallus du Petit Jésus* (*The Phallus of Little Jesus;* CRNI, n.d.)*Les Larmes de Jean-Ro* (*The Tears of Jean-Ro*; CRNI, n.d.)

Le Clézio, Jean-Marie (1940-); Haï (Skira, 1971); *Les Géants* (Gall., 1973; transl. as *The Giants*, 1975); *Voyages de l'Autre Côté* (*Journeys to the Other Side*; Gall., 1975); *L'Inconnu sur la Terre* (*The Unknown Man on Earth*; Gall., 1978); *Voyage au Pays des Arbres* (*Journey to the Land of Trees*; Gall., 1978); *Vers les Icebergs* (*Towards the Icebergs*; Fata Morgana, 1978); *Lullaby* (Gall., 1980); *Désert* (Gall., 1980); *Le Chercheur d'Or* (*The Gold Seeker*; Gall., 1985); *Villa Aurore* (Gall., 1985); *La Genèse* (*Genesis*; Gall., 1987); *Le Déluge* (*The Flood*; Gall., 1989); *Onitsha* (Gall., 1991); *Peuple du Ciel* (*Sky People*; Gall., 1991); *Pawana* (Gall., 1992); *L'Étoile Errante* (*The Wandering Star*; Gall., 1992); *Mydriase* (Fata Morgana, 1993); *Poisson d'Or* (*Gold Fish*; Gall., 1997); *La Montagne du Dieu Vivant* (*The Mountain of the Living God*; n.d.); *Orlamonde* (*Worldbeyond*; n.d.); *Note:* See Chapter VIII.

Le Coeur, René (?-); *Le Formidable Secret* (*The Formidable Secret*; Cosmopolites, 1930); *Les Amants de Diane* (*Diana's Lovers*; Prima, 1935); *Le Bateau chargé d'Or* (*The Gold-Filled Boat*; SEPIA, 1938)

Lecompte, Luc (1951-); *Le Dentier d'Énée* (*Aeneas' Teeth*; Hexagone, 1988); *Note:* French-Canadian writer.

Leconte, Marianne (?-); *Les Pièges de l'Espace* (*The Traps of Space*; anthology; MSF 53, 1977); *Les Champs de l'Infini* (*The Fields of Infinity*; anthology; MSF 67, 1977); *L'Araignée de Mer* (*The Sea Spider*; Den., 1993); *Note:* See Chapter IX.

Le Cordier, G. (?-); *Le Pauvre Madapolam* (*Poor Madapolam*; Delagrave, 1901); *Kamara-Badaboum, Roi des Miams-Miams* (*Kamara-Badaboum, King of the Miams-Miams*; Delagrave, 1902); *Terrible Histoire de Sorciers* (*Terrible Tale of Wizards*; Delagrave, 1902); *La Guerre des Fées* (*War of the Fairies*; Delagrave, 1909); *Légende des Bêtes* (*Legends of the Beasts*; Delagrave, 1913)

Lecornu, Joseph-Louis (?-); *Cinquante Ans Après: Une Exposition à Verdun en 1967* (*Fifty Years Later: An Exhibit in Verdun in 1967);* LPT, 1918); *Le Vol de la Golconde* (*The Flight of the Golconde*; LPT, 1918); *De la Terre à la Lune* (*From the Earth to the Moon*; LPT, 1919); *L'Homme Double* (*The Duplicate Man*; LPT, 1924); *Note:* See Chapter VII.

Le Covec de Keryvallon, Jean (1893-) *see* **Kery, Jean**

Lécrivain, Olivier (1957-); *Les Voleurs de Secrets* (*The Thieves of Secrets*; Amitié, 1985)

Le Drimeur, Alain (?-?); *La Cité Future* (*The Future City*; Savine, 1890); *Note:* See Chapter V.

Lee, John Silver *see* **Boileau-Narcejac**

Le Faure, Georges (1856-1953); *La Guerre sous l'Eau* (*The Underwater War*; Dentu, 1890; rev. as 2 vols., VSE, 1893); *Les Aventures Extraordinaires d'un Savant Russe* (*The Amazing Adventures of a Russian Scientist*): 1. *La Lune* (*The Moon*; with Henri de **Graffigny**; Edinger, 1888; rev. as 2 vols., VSE, 1894); *Les Aventures Extraordinaires d'un Savant Russe* (*The Amazing Adventures of a Russian Scientist*): 2. *Le Soleil et les Petites Planètes* (*The Sun and the Small Planets*; with Henri de **Graffigny**; Edinger, 1889; rev. as 2 vols., VSE, 1894); *Les Aventures Extraordinaires d'un Savant Russe* (*The Amazing Adventures of a Russian Scientist*): 3. *Les*

Planètes Géantes et les Comètes (The Giant Planets and the Comets; with Henri de **Graffigny**; Edinger, 1891; rev. as 2 vols., *Les Grandes Planètes (The Great Planets*, VSE, 1894); *Les Robinsons Lunaires (The Moon Robinsons; Soleil du Dimanche,* 1891; rev. Dentu, 1892; rev. as 2 vols., VSE, 1894); *Mort aux Anglais (Death to the British;* VSE, 1892; rev. as *La Croix Blanche (The White Cross;* BGA, 1929); *Les Mésaventures de M. Corpiquet (The Misadventures of Mr. Corpiquet;* VSE, 1892); *Quinze Mille Lieues dans l'Espace (Fifteen Thousand Leagues in Space;* VSE, 1893); *Les Robinsons Lunaires (The Moon Robinsons;* 1893); *Les Orphelins de l'Alaska (The Orphans from Alaska;* VSE, 1893); *L'Île de Glace (The Ice Island;* VSE, 1893); *Les Exploits de Cabreloche (Cabreloche's Amazing Feats;* 2 vols.; VSE, 1893); *Coeur de Soldat (Heart of a Soldier;* with **Gugenheim**; 3 vols.; VSE, 1893); *Les Aventures Extraordinaires d'un Savant Russe (The Amazing Adventures of a Russian Scientist): 4. Le Désert Sidéral (The Sidereal Desert;* with Henri de **Graffigny**; VSE, 1896); *Le Secret du Glacier (The Secret of the Ice Flow;* JDV, 1907; rev. LDA, 1937); *Un Descendant de Robinson (A Descendent of Robinson;* SEP, 1910; rev. BGA, 1924); *Kadidjar le Rouge (Kadidjar the Red;* BGA, 1925); *Le Carré Diabolique (The Diabolical Square;* BGA, 1926); *Le Fils du Bonaparte Noir (Son of the Black Napoleon;* BGA, 1926); *La Main Noire (The Black Hand;* BGA, 1927); *La Mystérieuse Aventure de Fridette (Fridette's Mysterious Adventure;* Firmin Didot, 1927); *La Cité Tentatrice (The Temptress City;* Libr. Contemporaine, 1933); *Dans la Peau d'un Singe (In a Monkey's Skin;* BGA, 1937); *La Voix d'En-Face (The Voice from Across;* SEPIA, 1937); *Le Poste 37* (BGA, 1938); *Petite Étoile (Little Star;* Fayard, 1939); *La Louve de Penandru (The She-Wolf of Penandru;* BGA, 1941); *Le Nid de Singes (Monkeys' Nest;* BGA, 1941); *Un Drame sous la Banquise (A Tragedy Under the Ice Shelf;* BGA, 1949); *Note:* See Chapter V.

Lefebvre, René (?-); *Paris en Amérique (Paris in America;* Charpentier, 1868); *La Roulotte Jaune (The Yellow Wagon;* Libr. Champs-Élysées, 1941); *Le Mystère du Chapelier Ganté (The Mystery of the Gloved Hatter;* Trémois, 1945)

Lefebvre, Reynald (1955-); *Les Voyageurs du Temps (The Time Travellers;* Fidès, 1978); *Note:* French-Canadian writer.

Lefèvre, Laurence (1951-); *Jasper et les Ombres Électriques (Jasper and the Electric Shadows;* with Liliane **Korb**; Hac., 1996); *Mon Père le Poisson Rouge (My Father the Gold Fish;* with Liliane **Korb**; Flamm., 1997); *Week-end Infernal (Hellish Week-End;* Hac., 1997)

Lefèvre, R. (?-); *Les Musiciens du Ciel (Musicians of the*

Sky; Gall., 1938); *Le Rescapé de la "Chimère" (The Survivor from the "Chimera";* Balzac, 1943); *L'Inventeur (The Inventor;* Deux Sirènes, 1947)

Legault, Anne (1958-); *Récits de Médilhault (Tales of Medilhaut;* L'Instant Même, 1994); *Note:* French-Canadian writer.

Legay, Piet (Chailley, Beaudoin; ?-); *Demonia, Planète Maudite (Demonia, Cursed Planet;* FNA 771, 1977); *Le Sursis d'Hypnos (The Reprieve of Hypnos;* FNA 795, 1977); *Les Sphères de l'Oubli (The Spheres of Oblivion;* FNA 829, 1978); *Les Pétrifiés d'Altaïr (The Petrified Men of Altair;* FNA 859, 1978); *Vega IV* (FNA 881, 1978); *Les Passagers du Temps (The Passengers of Time;* FNA 894, 1978); *L'Exilé de l'Infini (The Exile of Infinity;* FNA 911, 1979); *Projet Phoenix (Project Phoenix;* FNA 921, 1979); *Le Maître des Cerveaux (The Brain Master;* FNA 961, 1980); *Transfert Psi! (Psi Transfer!;* FNA 975, 1980); *Le Défi Génétique (The Genetic Challenge;* FNA 1011, 1980); *L'Ultime Test (The Ultimate Test;* FNA 1025, 1980); *L'Étrange Maléfice (The Strange Spell;* FNA 1039, 1981); *Obsession Temporelle (Temporal Obsession;* FNA 1048, 1981); *Le Mystère Varga (The Varga Mystery;* FNA 1061, 1981); *Échec aux Ro'has (The Ro'Has in Check;* FNA 1068, 1981); *Au Nom de l'Espèce (In the Name of the Species;* FNA 1112, 1981); *Hypothèse "Gamma" (Gamma Hypothesis;* FNA 1138, 1982); *Un Monde Si Noir (Such a Dark World;* FNA 1150, 1982); *Elle s'appelait Loan (Her Name Was Loan;* FNA 1168, 1982); *Une Peau si... Bleue! (Such A... Blue Skin!;* FNA 1179, 1982); *Perpetuum* (FNA 1196, 1983); *Anticorps 107 (Antibody 107);* FNA 1212, 1983); *Ce Coeur dans la Glace... (That Heart in the Ice...;* FNA 1223, 1983); *Dimension Quatre (Dimension Four;* FNA 1241, 1983); *Génération Satan* (FNA 1277, 1984); *L'Autre Race (The Other Race;* FNA 1295, 1984); *Psy-Connection* (FNA 1306, 1984); *Les Décervelés (The Debrained;* FNA 1335, 1984); *Viol Génétique (Genetic Rape;* FNA 1373, 1985); *Ultime Solution... (Ultimate Solution...;* FNA 1508, 1986); *Mortel Contact (Deadly Contact;* FNA 1520, 1987); *Les Portes de l'Enfer (The Gates of Hell;* FNA 1539, 1987); *Le Dernier Témoin (The Last Witness;* FNA 1558, 1987); *Cette Vérité Qui Tue (That Truth That Kills;* FNA 1579, 1987); *Aqualud!* (FNA 1606, 1988); *Survival* (FNA 1625, 1988); *L'Enfer des Homosimiens (The Hell of the Homosimians;* FNA 1648, 1988); *Dernière Chance: l'Humanité (Last Chance: Mankind;* FNA 1665, 1989); *Genesis II* (FNA 1679, 1989); *Shândoah!* (FNA 1689, 1989); *Egrégore* (FNA 1700, 1989); *Le Rire du Clone (The Clone's Laughter;* FNA 1715, 1989); *O Gamesh, Prince des Ténèbres (O Gamesh, Prince of Darkness;* FNA 1726, 1989); *Vous Avez Dit "Humain!" (Did You Say, "Human!";* FNA 1744, 1990); *Emergency!* (FNA 1756, 1990); *Le Profanateur (The Desecrator;* FNA 1774,

1990); *Le Temps de l'Effroi* (*The Time of Fear*; FNA 1799, 1991); *Le Temps des Lumières* (*The Time of Light*; FNA 1814, 1991); *Le Temps des Révélations* (*The Time of Revelations*; FNA 1826, 1991); *L'Énigme du Squalus* (*The Squalus Enigma*; FNA 1860, 1992); *Révélations Interdites* (*Forbidden Revelations*; FNA 1876, 1992); *La Mandragore* (*The Mandragore*; FNA 1888, 1992); *Rawâhlpurgis* (FNA 1914, 1993); *Shaan!* (FNA 1950, 1994); *Note:* See Chapter IX.

Legendre, Pierre (?-?); *Crackville* (SEL Furne, 1898); *Au Fond du Maëlstrom* (*At the Bottom of the Maelstrom*; Boivin, 1926); *Le Mystère de Eingall* (*The Mystery of Eingall*; Boivin, 1926); *Londres en Feu* (*London in Flames*; Boivin, 1928); *Les Trois Moustiquaires* (*The Three Mosquiteers*; Boivin, 1929); *Le Dernier des Atlantes* (*The Last of the Atlanteans*; Boivin, 1930); *Note:* See Chapter VII.

Le Gentil, René (1881-?); *La Seconde Vie du Chevalier* (*The Knight's Second Life*; Ren. du Livre, 1922); *Par Desus les Tombeaux* (*Over the Tombs*; Valois, 1931); *Le Secret de Christophe Colomb* (*The Secret of Christopher Columbus*; with Charles de **Giaffreri**; Berger-Levrault, 1937)

Le Gloupier, Georges (?-); *L'Odieux Tout-Puissant* (*The Odious Almighty*; Brigandine, 1981)

Legrand, André (?-); *L'Île sans Amour* (*The Loveless Island*; Crès, 1921); *Note:* See Chapter VII.

Legrand, Benjamin (?-); *La Mécanique des Ombres* (*The Mechanic of Shadows*; Den., 1996)

Legrand, Claude J. (?-); *Projet Nouvelle-Vénus* (*Project New Venus*; FNA 1638, 1988)

Legrand, Henri (1873-1930); *Les Terriens* (*The Earthmen*; as Gabriel **Maurière**; Ambert, 1920); *L'Homme qui meurt pas* (*The Man Who Did Not Die*; as Gabriel **Maurière**; Vraie France, 1926); *Aïno* (as Gabriel **Maurière**; Gédalge, 1929); *Le Semeur Aveugle* (*The Blind Sower*; as Gabriel **Maurière**; Gédalge, 1933); *Note:* Also see **Grand-Guignol**.

Legrand, Ilka (?-) *see* **Ann et Gwen**

Legrand, Marc-Antoine (1673-1728); *Le Roi de Cocagne* (*The King of Cocagne*; Ribou, 1719); *Les Aventures du Voyageur Aérien* (*The Adventures of an Aerial Traveler*; 1724); rep. VI, 1788); *Le Fleuve d'Oubli* (*The River of Oblivion*; Briasson, 1732); *L'Épreuve Réciproque* (*The Reciprocal Test*; Van Ghelen, 1752); *Note: Le Roi* is a three-act play.

Legras, Alain *see* **Marillac, Alain**

Legray, Jacques (?-); *La Vallée Enchantée* (*The Enchanted Valley*; Julliard, 1953); *Les Amazones du Roi* (*The Ama-*

zons of the King; Plon, 1961); *Destination Espace* (*Destination Space*; MarP, 1967); *Note:* See Chapter IX.

Legué, Gabriel (?-1913); *La Messe Noire* (*The Black Mass*; Fasquelle, 1903); *Note:* See Chapter IV.

Le Guen, Annick (?-) *see* **Contes et Légendes**

Le Guillon, Philippe (?-); *Les Portes de l'Apocalypse* (*The Gates of the Apocalypse*; MdF, 1984)

Lehaineux, Victor (?-) *Le Projet* (*The Project*; CRNI, n.d.

Lehman, Serge (Fréjean, Pascal; 1964-); *La Loi Majeure* (*La Guerre des Sept Minutes 1); The Major Law—the Seven-Minute War 1);* as Don Herial; FNA 1738, 1990); *Hydres (La Guerre des Sept Minutes 2); Hydra—the Seven-Minute War 2)* ; as Don Herial; FNA 1762, 1990); *Espion de l'Étrange* (*Spy of the Weird*; as Karel Dekk; FNA 1842, 1991); *Le Haut-Lieu* (*The High Place*; FNFR 15, 1995); *La Sidération* (*Sideral*; Encrage, 1996); *F.A.U.S.T.* (FN Faust 1, 1996); *Les Défenseurs* (*The Defenders*; FN Faust 2, 1996); *Le Mensys* (Destination Crépuscule, 1996); *Wonder-*  *land* (FNA 2000, 1997); *Tonnerre Lointain* (*Distant Thunder*; FN Faust 3, 1997); *L'Ange des Profondeurs* (*The Angel of the Depth*; FNSF 24, 1997); *Note:* See chapters VIII and IX.

Leiris, Michel (1901-); *Le Point Cardinal* (*The Cardinal Point*; Kra, 1927); *Aurora* (Kra, 1928; rep. Gall., 1946); *La Néreide de la Mer Rouge* (*The Nerid of the Red Sea*; Mesures, 1936); *Nuits sans Nuit et Quelques Jours sans Jour* (*Nightless Night and Some Dayless Days*; Gall., 1988); *Haut Mal / Autres Lancers* (*High Evil / Other Throws*; Gall., 1988); *Zébrage* (Gall., 1992); *L'Évasion Souterraine* (*Underground Escape*; Fata Morgana, 1992); *Grande Fuite de Neige* (*Great Fall of Snow*; Fata Morgana, 1992); *Note:* See Chapter VI.

Le Jeune, Raoul (1880-?); *La Secte de la Perle Noire* (*The Sect of the Black Pearl*; France-Édition, 1924); *En l'An 2125* (*In the Year 2125);* Bibl. Mode Nat., 1928); *La Chimère aux Ailes d'Or* (*The Chimera with Golden Wings*; Ed. Modernes, 1929); *Prisonniers au Fond des Mers* (*Prisoners at the Bottom of the Sea*; CA, 1931); *Le Pays de la Mort* (*The Land of Death*; Tallandier, 1931); *Le Trésor des Chibchas* (*The Treasure of the Chibchas*;

Tallandier, 1931); *Le Maître des Sargasses* (*The Master of the Sargasso Sea*; BGA, 1932); *L'Homme Rouge* (*The Red Man*; Tallandier, 1932); *Prisonnier des Invisibles* (*Prisoner of the Invisibles*; RJ, 1933); *La Prêtresse du Mont-Loï* (*The Priestess of Mount Loi*; Tallandier, 1937); *Dans les Airs* (*In the Air*; Tallandier, 1938); *Le Pirate du Pacifique* (*The Pirate of the Pacific*; Tallandier, 1938); *Derrière les Paupières Closes* (*Behind Closed Eyelids*; SEPIA, 1939); *Au Pied du Sphinx* (*At the Sphinx's Feet*; Parisienne, 1941); *Note:* See Chapter VII.

Leloup, Roger (?-); *Le Pic des Ténèbres* (*The Peak of Darkness*; Duculot, 1989)

Lemaire, Ferdinand (?-?) *see* **Opéra**

Lemaire, Gérard (?-) *Le Jour de la Grande Nuit* (*The Day of the Great Night*; Archers, 1977); *Note:* Belgian writer.

Le May, Jean (Cauderan, Jean; ?-) & Le May, Doris (Cauderan, Denise; ?-); *La Chasse à l'Impondérable* (*The Hunt for the Weightless Element*; FNA 304, 1966); *L'Oenips d'Orlon* (*The Oenips of Orlon*; FNA 312, 1967); *Les Drogfans de Gersande* (*The Drogfans of Gersande*; FNA 327, 1967); *L'Odyssée du Delta* (*The Odyssey of the Delta*; FNA 339, 1968); *Message pour l'Avenir* (*Message for the Future*; FNA 347, 1968); *La Planète des Optyrox* (*The Planet of the Optyrox*; FNA 358, 1968); *Arel d'Adamante* (*Arel of Adamante*; FNA 368, 1968); *Solution de Continuité* (*Solution of Continuity*; FNA 382, 1969); *Demain, le Froid* (*Tomorrow, the Cold*; FNA 389, 1969); *La Quête du Frohle d'Esylée* (*The Quest of the Frohle of Esyleum*; FNA 399, 1969); *La Plongée des Corsaires d'Hermos* (*The Dive of the Corsairs of Hermos*; FNA 408, 1970); *La Mission d'Eno Granger* (*The Mission of Eno Granger*; FNA 416, 1970); *Irimanthe* (FNA 436, 1970); *Les Montagnes Mouvantes* (*The Moving Mountains*; FNA 444, 1971); *Les Landes d'Achernar* (*The Moors of Achernar*; FNA 462, 1971); *Les Trophées de la Cité Morte* (*The Trophies of the Dead City*; FNA 475, 1971); *Les Cristaux de Sigel Alpha* (*The Crystals of Sigel Alpha*; FNA 484, 1971); *Vacances Spatiales*

(*Space Holidays*; FNA 500, 1972); *Les Hydnes de Loriscamp* (*The Hydnes from Loriscamp*; FNA 515, 1972); *Les Fruits du Métaxylia* (*The Fruits of the Metaxylia*; FNA 524, 1972); *Les Créateurs d'Ulnar* (*The Creators of Ulnar*; FNA 535, 1972); *L'Empreinte de Shark Ergan* (*The Mark of Shark Ergan*; FNA 550, 1973); *Dame Lueen* (FNA 564, 1973); *Les Trésors de Chrysoréade* (*The Treasures of Chrysoreade*; FNA 581, 1973); *Les Gardiens de l'Almucantar* (*The Guardians of the Almucantar*; FNA 592, 1974); *Yetig de la Nef Monde* (*Yetig of the World Ship*; FNA 611, 1974); *Stellan* (FNA 624, 1974); *Un Pilote a Disparu* (*A Pilot Is Missing*; FNA 650, 1974); *Entre Perlame et Santarène* (*Between Perlame and Santarene*; FNSL 2, 1974); *Échec à la Raison* (*Reason in Check*; FNA 664, 1975); *Claine et les Solandres* (*Claine and the Solandres*; FNA 675, 1975); *Ce Monde Qui n'est Plus Nôtre* (*This World Which is No Longer Ours*; FNA 715, 1975); *Plus Jamais le "France"* (*No More "France"*; FNA 729, 1976); *Énigme aux Confins* (*Mystery on the Rim*; FNA 736, 1976); *L'Ophrys et les Protistes* (*The Ophrys and the Protists*; FNA 745, 1976); *Il était une Voile parmi les Étoiles* (*There Was a Sail Among the Stars*; FNA 759, 1976); *L'Étoile Régatone* (*The Star Regatta*; FNA 777, 1977); *Défi dans l'Uniformité* (*Challenge in the Uniformity*; FNA 785, 1977); *Dal'Nim* (FNA 811, 1977); *Inu Shivan, Dame de Shtar* (*Inu Shivan, Lady of Shtar*; FNA 824, 1977); *Quelques Lingots d'Iridium* (*A Few Bars of Iridium*; FNA 845, 1978); *L'Hypothèse Tétracérat* (*The Tretracerat Hypothesis*; FNA 883, 1978); *L'Épaisse Fourrure des Quadricornes* (*The Thick Fur of the Quadricorns*; FNA 889, 1978); *Note:* See chapters VIII and IX.

Le May, Jean-Louis (Cauderan, Jean); *L'Ombre dans la Vallée* (*The Shadow in the Valley*; FNA 915, 1979); *Le Viaduc Perdu* (*The Lost Viaduct*; FNA 934, 1979); *Safari pour un Virus* (*Safari for a Virus*; FNA 954, 1979); *Le Verbe et la Pensée* (*The Word and the Thought*; FNA

958, 1979); *L'Alizé Pargélide* (*The Pargelide Breeze*; FNA 976, 1980); *Heyoka Wakan* (FNA 989, 1980); *Deux Souris pour un Concorde* (*Two Mice for a Concorde*; FNA 1015, 1980); *Les Volcans de Mars* (*The Volcanos of Mars*; FNA 1067, 1981); *La Révolte des Boudragues* (*The Revolt of the Boudragues*; FNA 1086, 1981); *Lacunes dans l'Espace* (*Gaps in Space*; FNA 1107, 1981); *Sept Soleils dans la Licorne* (*Seven Suns of the Unicorn*; FNA 1125, 1982); *Ald'haï* (FNA 1162, 1982); *Livradoch le Fou* (*Livradoch the Mad*; FNA 1176, 1182); *Dérive sur Kimelunga* (*Adrift on Kimelunga*; FNA 1226, 1983); *Un Peu de Vin d'Antan* (*A Little Elder Wine*; FNA 1243, 1983); *Reflets d'Entre-Temps* (*Reflections from Between Time*; FNA 1272, 1984); *Le Calumet de l'Oncle Chok* (*The Pipe of Uncle Chok*; FNA 1318, 1984); *Illa et son Etoile* (*Illa and Her Star*; FNA 1326, 1984); *Ehecatl, Seigneur le Vent* (*Ehecatl, Lord of the Wind*; FNA 1357, 1985); *Sur Qui Veillent les Achachilas* (*Whom Do the Achachilas Watch*; FNA 1407, 1985); *Sahra* (FNA 1429, 1986); *O Tuha'd et les Chasseurs* (*O Tuha'd and the Hunters*; FNA 1454, 1986); *L'Hérésie Magicienne* (*The Magical Heresy*; FNA 1567, 1987); *Note:* See Chapter IX.

Le May, Pamphile (1837-1918); *Picounoc le Maudit* (*Picounoc the Accursed*; Hurtubise, 1972); *Contes Vrais* (*True Tales*; Soleil de Québec, 1899; rev. Fidès, 1980; rev. Presses de l'Université de Montreal, 1993); *Note:* French-Canadian writer of fairy tales based on Quebec folklore.

Lemercier, Népomucène-Louis (1771-1840); *L'Atlantiade, ou La Théogonie Newtonienne* (Pichard-Didot, 1812); *Note:* See Chapter V.

Le Mercier de la Rivière, Pierre-Paul-François-Joachim-Henri (?-?); *L'Heureuse Nation, ou Relations du Gouvernement des Féliciens* (*The Happy Nation, or Narration of the Government of the Felicians*; Creuze-Béhal, 1792); *Note:* Utopia.

Lemercier de Neuville, Louis (1830-1918); *Contes Abracadabrants* (*Alakazam Tales*; Boulanger, 1880); *Note:* See Chapter IV.

Lemey, Jean-Sébastien (?-); *Le Grand Dépotoir* (*The Great Junkyard*; Silence, 1978)

Lemon, Peter (?-); *L'Épervier II Ne Répond Plus* (*Sparrowhawk II Does Not Answer*; Daniber 11, 1960); *L'Affaire du X-29* (*The X-29 Affair*; Daniber 13, 1960);

Coup de Poing dans le Vide (*Fist Fight in the Void*; L'Alouette 24, 1960

Lemosquet, Marc (?-); *Le Gymnase de l'Ogre* (*The Ogre's Gymnasium*; FNA 1865, 1992); *Plug-In* (FNA 1892, 1992); *Cobaye* (*Guinea Pig*; FNA 1928, 1993)

Le Mouel, Eugène (1859-?); *Jannic le Guetteur* (*Jannic the Watchman*; 1890); *Les Trois Gros Messieurs Mirabelle* (*The Three Big Mirabelle Gentlemen*; Lemerre, 1894); *Les Deux Gars de Roz-Gouët* (*The Two Guys from Roz-Gouët*; A. Colin, 1923); *L'Héritage de Joris Perperdyk* (*Joris Peperdyk's Inheritance*; Nlles. Ed. pour la Jeunesse, 1924); *Un Pension en Aérobus* (*A Pension in Airbus*; Hac., 1925)

Léna, Maurice (?-?) *see* **Opéra**

Lenain, Thierry (1959-); *Un Pacte avec le Diable* (*A Pact with the Devil*; Syros, 1988); *La Fille de Sable* (*The Girl of Sand*; Hac., 1989); *Les Seins d'Aïssata* (*Aissata's Breasts*; Hac., 1989); *Un Marronnier sous les Étoiles* (*A Chestnut Tree Under the Stars*; Syros, 1990); *L'Étrange Madame Mizu* (*The Strange Mrs. Rizu*; Nathan, 1997); *Note:* Juveniles.

Lenglé, Ferdinand (?-?); *L'Âme en Peine* (*The Soul in Pain*; Allardin, 1833)

Lenormand, Henri-René (1852-1951); *Le Jardin sur la Glace* (*The Garden on the Ice*; Stock, 1906); *Le Penseur et le Crétine* (*The Thinker and the Stupid Woman*; Crès, 1920); *Le Mangeur de Rêves* (*The Dream Eater*; Crès, 1922); *À l'Ombre du Mal* (*In the Shadow of Evil*; Hébertot, 1924); *L'Armée Secrète* (*The Secret Army*; Nlle. Revue Fr., 1925); *L'Homme et ses Fantômes* (*The Man and His Ghosts*; Crès, 1925); *Le Simoun* (Rieder, 1930); *La Maison des Remparts* (*The Remparts House*; Nlle. Revue Belgique, 1942); *Note:* Also see **Grand-Guignol**.

Le Normand, Véronique (?-); *Basile et les Dinosaures* (*Basil and the Dinosaurs*; BR, 1995); *Basile et les Extra-Terrestres* (*Basil and the ETs*; BR, 1995); *Basile et les Fantômes* (*Basil and the Ghosts*; BR, 1995); *Basile et la Confiture de Crapauds* (*Basil and the Toad Jam*; BR, 1996); *Basile et la Télé Magique* (*Basil and the Magic TV Set*; BR, 1996); *Note:* Juvenile fantasies. See Chapter VIII.

Lenôtre, Thérèse (1894-1987); *Le Miroir Magique* (*The Magic Mirror*; Larousse, 1931); *Les Deux Visages* (*The Two Faces*; Hac., 1933); *Un Cri dans l'Espace* (*A Scream in Space*; with Adhémar de **Montgon**; Mame, 1935); *Le Serpent Noir* (*The Black Serpent*; Tallandier, 1952); *Contes de la Maison Rose* (*Tales of the Pink House*; Hac., 1953)

Lenteric, Bernard (?-); *La Nuit des Enfants Rois* (*The*

Night of the Children Kings; Orban, 1981); *Voyante* (*Seeress*; Orban, 1982); *La Guerre des Cerveaux* (*The War of the Brains*; Orban, 1985); *Substance B* (*Element B*; Orban, 1986); *Les Enfants de Salonique* (*The Children of Salonica*; Orban, 1988); *La Femme Secrète* (*The Secret Woman*; Orban, 1989); *Vol avec Effraction Douce* (*Stolen with Soft Fracture*; Stock, 1991); *Ennemi* (*Enemy*; JCL, 1992); *La Fortune des Laufer* (*The Laufers' Wealth*; Plon, 1996); *L'Empereur des Rats* (*The Emperor of the Rats*; Plon, 1997)

Léomar, Jac (?-); *Le Tour du Monde en 23 Heures* (*Around the World in 23 Hours*; Desoer, 1943); *Note:* Belgian writer.

Léonard, François (1883-); *Le Triomphe de l'Homme* (*The Triumph of Man*; Lamberty, 1911); *La Conquête de Londres* (*The Conquest of London*; Atar, 1917); *Note:* Belgian writer. See Chapter V.

Léonnec, Félix (?-); *Sous la Griffe du Lion* (*Under the Lion's Claws*; as Éric Stanley; Ferenczi, 1926); *Le Chef Noir* (*The Black Chief*; as Éric Stanley; Ferenczi, 1926); *Aux Mains des Cannibales* (*In the Hands of the Cannibals*; as Éric Stanley; Ferenczi, 1927); *L'Auto Diabolique* (*The Diabolical Car*; Ferenczi, 1927); *Le Feu qui Sauve* (*The Saving Fire*; Radot, 1927); *Le Vampire de Düsseldorf* (*The Vampire of Dusseldorf*; Ferenczi, 1930); *Sous les Pyramides* (*Under the Pyramids*; as Éric Stanley; LA, 1931); *Perdus dans le Désert* (*Lost in the Desert*; as Éric Stanley; Ferenczi, 1931); *La Perfide Thi-Baï* (*Perfidious Thi-Baï*; Tallandier, 1932); *L'Âme d'une Femme* (*The Soul of a Woman*; as Éric Stanley; Ferenczi, 1933); *Le Roi des Pampas* (*The King of the Pampas*; as Éric Stanley; Ferenczi, 1933); *Le Roi du Film* (*The King of Film*; as Éric Stanley; Ferenczi, 1933); *Fin de Cauchemar* (*Nightmare's End*; Libr. Contemporaine, 1933); *Le Secret de l'Immortalité* (*The Secret of Immortality*; VA, 1934); *L'Île d'Épouvante* (*Island of Terror*; VA, 1936); *Le Dragon Volant* (*The Flying Dragon*; RJ, 1937); *Un Cri dans le Brouillard* (*A Scream in the Mist*; RJ, 1937); *Le Mystère du Rapide* (*The Mystery of the Rapid*; RJ, 1937); *Note:* See Chapter VII.

Léourier, Christian (1948-); *Les Montagnes du Soleil* (A&D 14, 1972; transl. as *The Mountains of the Sun*, 1973); *L'Arbre-Miroir* (*The Mirror-Tree*; AdE 3, 1977); *La Planète Inquiète* (*The Worried Planet*; A&D 56, 1979); *Ti-Harnog* (JL 1722, 1984); *Petit Dragon* (*Little Dragon*; Magnard, 1986); *L'Homme qui tua l'Hiver* (*The Man Who Killed Winter*; JL 1946, 1986); *Mille Fois Mille*

Fleuves (*A Thousand Times a Thousand Rivers*; JL 2223, 1987); *Les Ailes de l'Été* (*The Wings of Summer*; Hac., 1988); *Eli le Rêveur* (*Eli the Dreamer*; Hac., 1988); *Les Racines de l'Oubli* (*The Roots of Oblivion*; JL 2405, 1988); *La Loi du Monde* (*The Law of the World*; JL 2736, 1990); *Le Chemin de Rungis* (*The Road of Rungis*; Gall. Folio Jr., 1990); *Le Cavalier Arverne* (*The Arverne Rider*; Hac., 1990); *Les Masques du Réel* (*The Masks of Reality*; JL 2976, 1991); *E.V.A. ou l'Été de la Lune* (*EVA or the Summer of the Moon*; Hac., 1991); *La Terre de Promesse* (*The Earth of the Promise*; JL 3709, 1994); Series *Jarvis: 1. Le Messager de la Grande Île* (*The Messenger from the Great Island*; PR, 1974); *2. Le Paradis des Hommes Perdus* (*The Paradise of Lost Men*; PR, 1975); *3. L'Envoyé du Quatrième Règne* (*The Envoy from the Fourth Reign*; PR, 1976); *4. Les Rebelles de la Soif* (*The Rebels of Thirst*; PR, 1976); *5. La Cité des Hauts Remparts* (*City of the High Remparts*; Hac., 1977); *6. L'Astéroïde Noir* (*The Black Asteroid*; Hac., 1978); *7. Le Gwémen Sacré* (*The Sacred Gwemen*; Hac., 1979); *8. L'Appel des Ondins* (*The Call of the Mermen*; Hac., 1980); *Note:* See Chapter IX.

Leprince, Albert (Dr.; ?-); *Les Cerveaux Cambriolés* (*The Burglared Brains*; Jean Renard, 1943); *Lumières de l'Au-Delà* (*Lights from Beyond*; Jean Renard, 1943); *Le Secret du Bouddha* (*The Secret of the Buddha*; Ariane, 1945); *Envoûtements* (*Spells*; Sté. Litt. Fr., 1947); *Les Immortels de Rock Island* (*The Immortals of Rock Island*; Sté. Litt. Fr., 1947)

Leprince, X. B. (?-); *La Table de Tacfarinas* (*The Tacfarinas Table*; SdP, 1957); *Le Tesbi de Nacre* (*The Mother of Pearl Tesbi*; SdP 95, 1958); *Les Signes de l'Empire* (*The Marks of the Empire*; SdP 115, 1959); *Le Chant des Abîmes* (*Songs of the Abyss*; SdP, 1962); *La Croix d'Agadès* (*The Agades Cross*; SdP, 1962); *Le Crapaud d'Ambre Jaune* (*The Yellow Amber Toad*; SdP, 1965); *Guillery de Saint-Gril* (SdP, 1966); *Dans le Sillage de l'Altaïr* (*In the Wake of the Altair*; GP, 1970); Series *La Quête Fantastique* (*The Fantastic Quest*): *Le Raid des Quatre Châteaux* (*The Four Castles' Raid*; SdP 83, 1969); *La Neuvième Croisade* (*The Ninth Crusade*; SdP 84, 1969); *Note:* Juveniles. See chapters VIII and IX.

Leprince de Beaumont, Jeanne-Marie (1711-1780); *Le Magasin des Enfants (The Children's Store)* incl. *La Belle et la Bête* (*The Beauty and the Beast*; J. B. Reguillat, 1756; transl. as *The Young Misses Magazine*, 1757); *Magasin des Adolescents* (*Teenagers' Store*; J. B. Reguillat, 1760); *Contes Moraux* (*Moral Tales*; Bruysset-Ponthus, 1774); *Nouveaux Contes Moraux* (*New Moral Tales*; Bruysset-Ponthus, 1776); *Note:* Also see **Cabinet des Fées** and Chapter III.

Le Ratz (Louis-Edmond; ?-); *L'Ange, la Bête et l'Homme* (*The Angel, the Beast and Man*; Grasset, 1928); *Le Dialogue Solitaire* (*Solitary Dialogue*; Grasset, 1929); *Re-*

vanche de l'Automne (*Revenge of the Fall*; Grasset, 1931); *George dans la Lune* (*George in the Moon*; Grasset, 1932)

Le Riche de la Pouplinière, Alexandre (?-?) *see* **Opéra**

Lerme-Walter, Marcelle (1906-); *Les Enfants de Pompeï ou Le Jeu du Roi* (*The Children of Pompei, or the King's Game*; Deux Coqs d'Or, 1968); *Les Voyageurs Sans Souci* (*The Worriless Travellers*; Nathan, 1970

Lermina, Jules (1839-1915); *Les Loups de Paris* (*The Wolves of Paris*; 2 vols., Dentu, 1876); *1. Le Club des Morts* (*The Deadmen's Club*); *2. Les Assises Rouges* (*The Red Assises*); *Les Mariages Maudits* (*Accursed Marriages*; Rouff, 1880); *La Comtesse Mercadet* (Boulanger, 1885); *Le Fils de Monte-Cristo* (*Monte-Cristo's Son*; Boulanger, 1881); *Histoires Incroyables* (*Incredible Tales*; Boulanger, 1885); *Nouvelles Histoires Incroyables* (*New Incredible Tales*; Boulanger, 1888); *L'Élixir de Vie* (*The Elixir of Life*; Carré, 1890); *Les Loups de Paris* (*The Wolves of Paris*; 1889-90); *La Magicienne* (*The Sorceress*; Chamuel, 1892); *Le Secret des Zippelius* (*The Secret of the Zippelius*, 1889; Didier-Méricant, 1893); *La Succession Tricoche et Cacobet* (*The Tricoche and Cacobet Inheritance*; Boulanger, 1894); *La Bataille de Strasbourg* (*The Battle of Strasburg*; 2 vols., 1892; Boulanger, 1895); *L'Énigme* (*The Enigma*; Boulanger, 1895); *La Deux Fois Morte* (*The Twice Dead*; Charmuel, 1895); *Dix Mille Lieues sans le vouloir* (*10,000 Leagues Without Willing It*; Tallandier, 1903); *Mystère-Ville* (*Mystery City*; as William Cobb; JDV, 1905); *Magie Pratique: Étude sur les Mystères de la Vie et de la Mort* (*Practical Magic: Study on the Mysteries of Life and Death*; Durville Fils, 1910); *L'Effrayante Aventure* (*The Frightful Adventure*; Tallandier, 1910); *La Criminelle* (*The Criminal*; Tallandier, 1919); *Note:* See chapters IV and V.

Le Rouge, Gustave (1867-1938); *La Conspiration des Milliardaires (The Billionaires' Conspiracy;* with Gustave **Guitton**; serialized in 8 issues, Guyot, 1899-1900); condensed as *L'Empereur des Dollars* (*The Dollar Emperor*, Roger & Chernovitz, 1914); *1-2. La Conspiration des Milliardaires* (*The Billionaires' Plot*); *3-4. À Coups de Milliards* (*Throwing Billions Around*); *5-6. Le Régiment des Hypnotiseurs* (*The Hypnotists' Brigade*); *7-8. La Revanche du Vieux Monde* (*The Old World's Revenge*); *Les Conquérants de la Mer* (*The Conquerors of the Sea*; with Gustave **Guitton**; serialized in 4 issues, Méricant, 1902); *1. La Flibuste Sanglante* (*The Bloody Pirates*); *2. Les Preneurs de Ville* (*The City Takers*); *3. Les Mangeurs d'Hommes* (*The Man Eaters*); *4. Le Trésor des Crocodiles* (*The Treasure of the Crocodiles*); *La Princesse des Airs* (*The Princess of the Air;* with Gustave **Guitton**; serialized in 4 issues, Guyot, 1902); condensed as *Les Dompteurs de Nuages (The Cloud*

Tamers, Roger & Chernovitz, 1913); *1. En Ballon Dirigeable* (*In Dirigible Balloon*); *2. Les Robinsons de l'Himalaya* (*Robinsons of the Himalaya*); *3. De Roc en Roc* (*From Rock to Rock*); *4. Au Pays des Bouddhas* (*In the Land of the Buddhas*); *Le Sous-Marin "Jules Verne"* (*The Submarine "Jules Verne"*; with Gustave **Guitton**; serialized in 2 issues, RM, 1902); condensed as *La Captive des Flots* (*The Prisoner of the Sea*, Roger & Chernovitz, 1913); *1. Un Drame de la Haine* (*A Drama of Hate*); *2. La Bataille Sous-Marine* (*The Undersea Battle*); *Le Voleur de Visage* (*The Face Stealer*; serialized in 4 issues, RM, 1904); *1. Le Voleur de Visage* (*The Face Stealer*); *2. Le Dompteur de Requins* (*The Shark Tamer*); *3. Les Pirates de la Science* (*The Pirates of Science*); *4. L'Îlot Mystérieux* (*The Mysterious Island*); *L'Espionne du Grand Lama* (*The Spy of the Great Lama*; 2 vols.; RM, 1906); *La Reine des Éléphants* (*The Queen of Elephants;* RM, 1906; rev. as *Aventures d'un Vieux Savant* (*Adventures of an Old Scientist*, Bottereau, 1914); *Le Prisonnier de la Planète Mars* (*The Prisoner of Planet Mars;* RM, 1908; rev. as *Le Naufragé de l'Espace* (*The Castaway of Space*, RM, 1912); *La Guerre des Vampires* (*The War of the Vampires;* RM, 1909; rev. as *L'Astre d'Épouvante* (*The Star of Terror*, RM, 1913); *La Mandragore Magique* (*The Magic Mandragora*; Daragon, 1912); *Le Mystérieux Docteur Cornélius* (*The Mysterious Dr. Cornelius*; serialized in 18 issues, Maison du Livre Moderne, 1912-13; rev. as 9 vols, Tallandier, 1918-20); *1. L'Énigme du Creek Sanglant* (*The Mystery of the Bloody Crick*); *2. Le Manoir aux Diamants* (*The Manor of Diamonds*); *3. Le Sculpteur de Chair Humaine* (*The Sculptor of Human Flesh*); *4. Les Lords de la Main Rouge* (*The Lords of the Red Hand*); *5. Le Secret de l'Île des Pendus* (*The Secret of Hanged Man's Island*); *6. Les Chevaliers du Chloroforme* (*The Knights of Chloroform*); *7. Un Drame au Lunatic Asylum* (*Tragedy at the Lunatic Asylum*); *8. L'Automobile Fantôme* (*The Phantom Motorcar*); *9. Le Cottage Hanté* (*The Haunted Cottage*); *10. Le Portrait de Lucrece Borgia* (*The Portrait of Lucrezia Borgia*); *11. Coeur de Gitane* (*Gipsy Heart*); *12. La Croisière du Gorill-Club* (*The Cruise of the Gorill-Club*); *13. La Fleur du Sommeil* (*The Flower of Sleep*); *14. Le Buste aux Yeux d'Émeraude* (*The Bust with Emerald Eyes*); *15. La Dame aux Scabieuses* (*The Scab Lady*); *16. La Tour Fiévreuse* (*The Fevered Tower*); *17. Le Dément de la Maison Bleue* (*The Madman of the Blue House*); *18. Bas les Masques* (*Masks Off*); *Le Masque de Linge* (*The Mask of Cloth*; Nilsson, 1913); *La Rue Hantée* (*The Haunted Street*; Nilsson, 1913); *Le Fantôme de la Danseuse* (*The Ghost of the Ballerina*; Nilsson, 1914); *La Vengeance du Dr. Mohr* (*The Revenge of Dr. Mohr*; Nilsson, 1914); *Les Aventures de Todd Marvel, Détective Milliardaire* (*The Adventures of Todd Marvel, Billionaire Detective*; serialized in 20 issues,

Nilsson, 1923); *La Vallée du Désespoir* (*The Valley of Despair*; JDV, 1927-28); *Note:* See Chapters IV and V. **Le Mystérieux Dr. Cornelius** was adapted for television and radio; see Book 1, chapters II and III.

Leroux, Denis (1966-); *Mauvaise Chair* (*Bad Flesh*; FNFR 9, 1994); *Le Ventre de la Sirène* (*The Belly of the Siren*; FNFR 30, 1995); *Alain au Pays du Vermeil* (*Alan in Vermilion Land*; Treize Étrange, 1995); *La Mésaventure de Jean l'Oli: Le Jeune Chat-Huant* (*The Misadventure of John-the-Oli: The Young Brown Owl*; Treize Étrange, 1996)

Leroux, Gaston (1868-1927); *La Double Vie de Theophraste Longuet* (*Le Matin*, 1903; rev. Flamm., 1904; transl. as *The Double Life*, 1909; rev. as *The Man with the Black Feather*, 1912); *L'Homme qui a vu le Diable* (*The Man Who Saw the Devil*; JST, 1908); *Le Roi Mystère* (*King Mystery*; *Le Matin*, 1909-09; rev. Fayard, 1910); *Le Fauteuil Hanté* (JST, 1909-10; rev. Lafitte, 1911; transl. as *The Haunted Chair*, 1931); *Le Fantôme de l'Opéra* (Lafitte, 1910; transl. as *The Phantom of the Opera*, 1911); *La Reine du Sabbat* (*The Queen of the Sabbath*; *Le Matin*, 1910-11; rev. Fayard, 1913); *L'Homme de la Nuit* (*The Night Man*; Fayard, 1911); *Balaoo* (*Le Matin*, 1911; rev. Tallandier, 1912; transl. 1913); *L'Épouse du Soleil* (JST, 1912; rev. Lafitte, 1913; transl. as *The Bride of the Sun*, 1915); *La Colonne Infernale* (*The Infernal Column*; *Le Matin*, 1916; rev. 2 vols. as *La Colonne Infernale* (*The Infernal Column*) and *La Terrible Aventure* (*The Dreadful Adventure*, Fayard, 1917); *L'Homme Qui Revient de Loin* (*The Man Who Returned from Afar*; JST, 1916-17; rev. Lafitte, 1917; transl. as *The Man Who Came Back from the Dead*, 1916); *Les Aventures Effroyables de Herbert de Renich* (*The Awful Adventures of Herbert De Renich;* as *Le Sous-Marin "Le Vengeur"* (*The Sub-Marine "Avenger,"* *Le Matin*, 1917; rev. 2 vols. as *Le Capitaine Hyx* (*CaptaIn Hyx*) and *La Bataille Invisible* (*The Invisible Battle*, Lafitte, 1920; transl. as *The Amazing Adventures of Carolus Herbert*, 1922 and *The Veiled Prisoner*, 1923); *Le Coeur Cambriolé* (*The Stolen Heart*; JST, 1920; rev. Lafitte, 1922; transl. as *The Burgled Heart*, 1925); *Le Sept de Trèfle* (*The Seven of Clubs;* *Le Matin*, 1921; rev. 2 vols. as *L'Enfer Parisien* (*Parisian Hell*) and *Toujours Plus Au Fond* (*Always Deeper Below*, Lafitte, 1924); *La Poupée Sanglante* (*The Bloody Puppet;* *Le Matin* as *La Sublime Aventure de Benedict Masson* (*Benedict Masson's Sublime Adventure*, 1923; rev. Tallandier, 1924; transl. included in *The Machine to Kill; La Machine à Assassiner* (*The Killing Machine*; *Le Matin* as *Gabriel*, 1923; rev. Tallandier, 1924; transl. as *The Machine to Kill*, 1935); *Les Ténébreuses* (*The Dark Ones;* *Le Matin*, 1924; rev. 2 vols. as *La Fin d'un Monde* (*The End of a World*) and *Du Sang sur la Néva* (*Blood on the Neva*, Tallandier, 1925); *Les Mohicans de Babel* (*The Mohicans of Babel;*

Le Journal, 1926; rev. Baudinière, 1928); *Mister Flow* (*Le Journal*/Baudinière, 1927); *Les Chasseurs de Danse* (*The Dance Hunters*; JDV/Larousse, 1927); *Les Fils de Balaoo* (*The Sons of Balaoo;* with Stanislas-André **Steeman**; *Paris-Soir*, 1934; rev. Libr. Champs-Élysées, 1937); Series *Rouletabille*: *1. Le Mystère de la Chambre Jaune* (*The Mystery of the Yellow Room*; *L'Illustration*, 1907; rev. Lafitte, 1908; transl. 1908); *2. Le Parfum de la Dame en Noir* (*The Scent of the Lady in Black*; *L'Illustration*, 1908; rev. Lafitte, 1909); *3. Rouletabille chez le Tsar* (*Rouletabille and the Czar*; *L'Illustration*/Lafitte, 1913); *4. Rouletabille à la Guerre* (*Rouletabille at War*; *Le Matin*, 1914; rev. 2 vols. as *Le Château Noir* (*The Black Castle*) and *Les Étranges Noces de Rouletabille* (*The Strange Wedding of Rouletabille*, Lafitte, 1916); *5. Rouletabille Chez Krupp* (*Rouletabille at Krupp's*; JST, 1917; rev. Lafitte, 1920); *6. Le Crime de Rouletabille* (*The Crime of Rouletabille*; JST, 1921; rev. Lafitte, 1923); *7. Rouletabille chez les Bohémiens* (*Rouletabille and the Gypsies*; *Le Matin*, 1922; rev. Lafitte, 1923); by Noré Brunel: *8. Rouletabille contre la Dame de Pique* (*Rouletabille vs. The Queen of Spades*; *Soir*, 1947); *9. Rouletabille Joue et Gagne* (*Rouletabille Plays and Wins*; *Soir*, 1947); *Note:* See Chapters IV and VII and **Grand-Guignol**. **La Double Vie, Le Fauteuil Hanté, Le Roi Mystère, Le Coeur Cambriolé,** and most of Leroux's novels have been adapted into films and television movies and series. See Book 1, chapters I and II for details. A series of **Rouletabille** graphic novels also exists (see Book 1, chapter V).

Le Roux, Hugues (1860-1925); *Portraits de Cire* (*Waxworks*; Lecène Oudin, 1891); *Les Hommes de l'Air* (*The Aerial Men*; Juven, 1910); *Le Maître de l'Heure* (*The Hour Master*; Lafitte, 1911)

Le Roy, Edmond *see* **Billy, André**

Leroy de la Brière, A. (?-?); *La Maîtresse du Diable* (*The Devil's Mistress*; in *L'Artiste*, 1833)

Leruitte, Carlos (?-); *Jim l'Hypnotiseur* (*Jim the Hypnotist*; Soledi, 1941); *Note:* Belgian writer.

Lesage, Alain René (1668-1747); *Le Diable Boîteux* (*The Lame Devil*; Vve. Barbin, 1707); *Arlequin Roi de Serendib* (*Harlequin King of Serendib*; E. Ganeau, 1713); Arlequin Mahomet (E. Ganeau, 1714); *L'Île des Amazones* (*Amazon Island*; 1718); *Le Monde Renversé* (*The World Upside Down*; 1718); *Note:* See Chapter III. *Le Diable* was adapted for opera by Jean **Françaix** (see **Opera**).

Lesage, Roger *see* **Egasel, Roger**

Lesbros, H. *see* **Chollier, Antoine**

Lescap, Julien (?-); *L'Homme qui fabriquait de la Chair*

(*The Man Who Manufactured Flesh*; LA, 1929); *L'Effrayante Découverte* (*The Frightful Discovery*; VA, 1934); *L'Or dans le Désert* (*Gold in the Desert*; Ferenczi, 1936)

Lesconvel, Pierre (1650-1722); *L'Île d'un Règne Heureux, ou Relation du Voyage du Prince de Montberand dans l'Île de Naudely* (*The Island of the Happy Kingdom, or the Tale of the Voyage of Prince De Montberand in the Island of Naudely*; Merinde Democrite, 1706)

Lesly *see* **Illide**

Lesneveu, Henri (?-?) *see* **Grand-Guignol**

Lesprit, Éric (1937-); *La Caravane du Bout du Monde* (*The Caravan at the End of the World*; Hac., 1972); *L'Île du Dragon Pourpre* (*The Island of the Purple Dragon*; as Éric Lestier; Hac., 1973); *Le Désert Sacré* (*The Holy Desert*; SdP, 1975); *Note:* Juveniles.

Lessard, Francyne (1955-); *Shawksa et le Conte Secret* (*Shawksa and the Secret Tale*; Camédu, 1991); *Note:* French-Canadian writer. Juvenile.

Lessard, Marc (1959-); *Le Miroir aux Assassins* (*The Mirror of Assassins*; Guy Saint-Jean, 1994); *Rumeurs de Morts* (*Rumors of Death*; Guy Saint-Jean, 1996); *Note:* French-Canadian writer.

Lessard, Paulin (?-); *Les Deux Petits Nains* (*The Two Little Dwarves*; La Baie, 1947); *Note:* French-Canadian writer. Children's tales.

Lessay, Jean (?-); *Le Large* (*The Horizon*; Léon Faure, 1982); *Note:* Collection of juvenile fantasies.

Lestier, Éric *see* **Lesprit, Éric**

Letailleur, Édouard (?-); *Le Cimetière des Lépreux* (*The Graveyard of Lepers*; Gall., 1934); *La Demeure de Satan* (*The House of Satan*; Gall., 1934); *Perkane, le Démon de la Nuit* (*The Night Demon*; Gall., 1934); *Note:* See Chapter VI.

Leterrier, E. (?-?) *see* **Opéra**

Leuven, Adolphe de (?-?) *see* **Opéra**

Le Valois d'Orville, Adrien-Joseph (?-?) *see* **Opéra**

LeVasseur, Nazaire (1848-1927); *Têtes et Figures* (*Heads and Figures*; Cie. de Publ. *Le Soleil*, 1920); *Note:* French-Canadian writer. Collection including the short story "Le Carnaval à Québec en 1996 (Écrit à distance d'un Siècle, en Février 1896)" ("Carnival in Quebec in 1996 (Written from a Century Ago)"; 1896).

Level, Maurice (1875-1926); *Contes Cruels* (*Cruel Tales*; n.d.; *On?* (*They?*; JST, 1908); Lady Harrington (1908; transl. 1909); *L'Épouvante* (*The Horror*; Monde Ill., 1908); *Les Portes de l'Enfer* (*The Gates of Hell*; Monde

Illustré, 1910); *Contes de l'Heure Présente* (*Tales of the Present Times*; with Charles **Robert-Dumas**; Diesterweg, 1914); *Les Oiseaux de Nuit* (*The Night Birds*; Flamm., 1914); *L'Alouette* (*The Sylark*; Flamm., 1918); *Le Crime* (*The Crime*; Ferenczi, 1921); *Les Morts Étranges* (*Strange Deaths*; Ferenczi, 1921); *L'Ombre* (*The Shadow*; Flamm., 1921); *La Cité des Voleurs* (*City of Thieves*; Flamm., 1924); *L'Énigme de Bellavista* (*The Mystery of Bellavista*; with Jean **Prudhomme**; RMY, 1929); *Le Marchand de Secrets* (*The Merchnt of Secrets*; with Jean **Prudhomme**; RMY, 1929); *L'Île sans Nom* (*The Nameless Island*; Cosmopolites, 1929); *L'Emprise de la Forêt* (*The Grip of the Forest*; Cuénot-Bourges, 1932); *La Malle Sanglante* (*The Bloody Trunk*; Glénat, 1977); *Note:* See chapters IV and VI. Also see **Grand-Guignol**.

Lévesque, Guillaume (?-); *Note:* French-Canadian writer of fairy tales based on Native American legends.

Lévesque, Louise Cavelier, Dame (1703-1745); *Le Prince des Aigues-Marines* (*The Prince of Aigues-Marines*; Vatel, 1722); *Le Prince Invisible* (*The Invisible Prince*; Vatel, 1722); *Célénie* (P. Prault, 1733); *Lilia, Histoire de Carthage* (*History of Carthago*; 1736); *Sancho Pansa Gouverneur* (N. Desbordes, 1738); *Note:* Also see **Cabinet des Fées** and Chapter III.

Lévesque, Louise (1955-); *Les Enfants d'Ydris* (*The Children of Ydris*; Q/A, 1990); *Entre Deux Temps* (*Between Two Times*; Q/A, 1992); *Note:* French-Canadian writer. Children's fantasies.

Lévesque, Pierre-Charles (?-?); *Les Rêves d'Aristobule, Philosophe Grec* (*The Dreams of Aristobule, Greek Philosopher*; 1761); rep. VI, 1788)

Lévesque, Richard (1944-); *Les Yeux d'Orages* (*The Storm Eyes*; Castelriand, 1978); *Note:* French-Canadian writer. Collection of fantastical tales.

Lévesque, Robert (1952-); *Énigme à Mururoa* (*Mystery in Mururoa*; Compton, 1990); *Note:* French-Canadian writer. The young-adult adventures of French-Canadian secret agent Richard Lewis. The first story reveals the descendents of the Lost Continent of Mu.

Lévi, Éliphas (Constant, Alphonse-Louis; 1810-1875); *Histoire de la Magie* (*The History of Magic*; Bailly-Baillère, 1860); *Note:* See Chapter IV; also see Claude **Vignon**.

Levis, Pierre-Marc-Gaston, Duc de (1775-1830); *Les Voyages de Kang-Hi, ou Nouvelles Lettres Chinoises* (*Kang-Hi's Journeys, or New Chinese Letters*; 2 vols.; 1810); *Note:* See Chapter V.

Levoisin, J. (Girardin, Jules-Marie-Alfred; ?-?); *Les Aventures du Baron de Münchausen* (*The Adventures of*

Baron of Munchausen; Hac., 1879); *Contes sans Malice* (*Tales Without Malice*; Hac., 1880); *La Chasse au Léviathan par le Capitaine Mayne-Reid, ouvrage imité de l'anglais* (*The Hunt for Leviathan By Captain Mayne-Reid, Work Inspired from the English*; Hac., 1882); *Les Théories du Docteur Wurz* (*Dr. Wurz's Theories*; Hac., 1882); *Le Fiancé de Léonora* (*Leonora's Fiancé*; Hac., 1882); *Les Voyages du Docteur van den Kruis* (*Dr. Van Den Kruis' Journeys*; Hac., 1882); *Contes à Jeannot* (*Tales for Jeannot*; Hac., 1888); *Contes à Pierrot* (*Tales for Pierrot*; Hac., 1888); *La Lanterne Magique* (*The Magic Lantern*; Hac., n.d.)

Levron, Jacques (?-) *see* **Contes et Légendes**

Lévy-Oulmann, André (?-?) *see* **Grand-Guignol**

Leyris, Pierre (1907-); *Le Rêve d'Angus Og* (*Angus Og's Dream*; Hatier, 1986); *La Bataille des Oiseaux* (*The Battle of the Birds*; Hatier, 1988); *Note:* Juveniles.

Lhassa, Jean (?-) *see* **Smit Le Bénédicte, Jean-Claude**

L'Heureux, Christine (1946-); *Le Dernier Recours* (*The Last Recourse*; Libre Expression, 1984); *Note:* French-Canadian writer. A virus kills all women.

Lhostis, Christian-Yves (?-); *Tous ces Pas vers le Jaune* (*All These Steps Towards Yellow*; A&D 59, 1979); *Gare aux Chasseurs de Têtes* (*Beware the Head Hunters*; RL, 1985); *Les Yeux au Chaud* (*The Warm Eyes*; RL, 1986); *Note:* See Chapter IX.

Lhotte, Céline (1888-1963); *Sous le Doux Règne des Jouets* (*Under the Kind Reign of the Toys*; Mariage & Famille, 1933)

Libert, Jean (1913-1995) *see* **Vandel, Jean-Gaston**

Lichtenberger, André (1870-1940); *Contes Héroïques* (*Heroic Tales*; Fischbacher, 1897); *Mon Ptit Trott* (*My Little Trott*; Plon, 1898); *La Petite Soeur de Trott* (*Trott's Little Sister*; Plon, 1898); *Les Centaures* (*The Centaurs*; Calmann-Lévy, 1904); *La Folle Aventure* (*The Crazy Adventure*; Calmann-Lévy, 1908); *Poupette, Fille d'Allah* (*Poupette, Daughter of Allah*; Berger-Levrault, 1918); *Raramené, Histoire d'Ailleurs* (*Tale from Beyond*; Ferenczi, 1921); *Pickles ou Récits à la Mode Anglaise* (*Pickles, or British Tales*; Crès, 1923); *Des Enfants dans un Jardin* (*Children in the Garden*; Plon, 1927); *Des Voix dans la Nuit* (*Voices in the Night*; Ferenczi, 1929); *Houck et Sla* (Nathan, 1930); *L'Enfant aux Yeux de Chat* (*The Child with Cat's Eyes*; Ferenczi, 1932); *Vent du Sud* (*Southern Wind*; Fayard, 1932); *Le Noël de Trott* (*Trott's Christmas*; Plon, 1934); *Trott et l'Escargot* (*Trott and the Snail*; Plon, 1934); *Deux Morts et le Vivant* (*Two Dead and a Live One*; Fayard, 1936); *La Main de Sang* (*The Hand of Blood*; Ferenczi, 1939); *La Dompteuse de Tamanoirs* (*The Ant-Eater Tamer*; Gautier-Languereau,

1939); *Gorri le Forban* (*Gorri the Villain*; Nelson, n.d.; *Note:* See chapters V and VII.

Lienhardt, Jean-Michel (1943-); *La Mémoire des Hommes* (*The Memory of Men*; JP 62, 1988); *Note:* French-Canadian writer. Post-nuclear odyssey.

Lieutenant X *see* **Volkoff, Vladimir**

Ligeron, Jean-Michel (?-); *La Malédiction de la Dame Blanche* (*The Curse of the White Lady*; Ramuel, 1997)

Light, Lucius (Colonel; ?-); *L'Opération Adam et Ève* (*Operation Adam and Eve*; Debresse, 1961)

Lignereux, G. (?-?) *see* **Grand-Guignol**

Ligny, Jean-Marc (1956-); *Temps Blancs* (*White Times*; PdF 273, 1979); *Biofeedback* (PdF 289, 1979); *Furia!* (PdF 346, 1982); *Succubes* (*Succubi*; Plasma 2, 1983); rep. FNA 1761, 1990); *Yurlunggur* (PdF 439, 1987); *Kriegspiel* (with Dominique **Goult**; FNA 1632, 1988); *Dreamworld* (with Dominique **Goult**; FNA 1661, 1988); *D.A.R.K.* (PdF 473, 1988); *Les Semeurs de Mirages* (*The Mirage Sowers*; FNA 1670, 1989); *L'Art du Rêve* (*The Art of Dreams*; FNA 1681, 1989); *A la Recherche de Faërie* (*Searching for Faerie*; FNA 1694, 1989); *Labyrinthe de la Nuit* (*Night Labyrinth*; FNA 1706, 1989); *Hypnos et Psyché* (FNA 1719, 1989); *Traqueur d'Illusions* (*Illusion Tracker*; FNA 1731, 1990); *Succubes II:*  *Sorciers* (*Succubi II: Wizards*; FNA 1767, 1990); *Rasalgethi* (FNA 1779, 1990); *Apex M.57* (FNA 1784, 1990); *Bérénice* (FNA 1791, 1990); *Le Voyageur Solitaire* (*The Lone Traveller*; FNA 1817, 1991); *Un Eté à Zédong* (*A Summer in Zedong*; FNA 1829, 1991); *Albatroys* (FNA 1846, 1991); *Albatroys 2* (FNA 1852, 1991); *Le Voyageur Perdu* (*The Lost Traveller*; Bayard, 1991); *Yoro Si* (PdFant. 15, 1991); *Aqua* (FNA 1898, 1993); *Cyberkiller* (FNA 1933, 1993); *La Mort Peut Danser* (*Death Can Dance*; PdFant. 35, 1994); *Les Ailes Noires de la Nuit* (*The Black Wings of Death*; Rageot, 1995); Inner City (J'ai Lu 4159, 1996); *La Fille de l'Abbaye* (*The Girl from the Abbey*; Liv'Éditions, 1996); *Slum City* (Hac., 1996); *Note:* See chapters VIII and IX.

Limat, Maurice (1913-); *La Montagne aux Vampires* (*The Mountain of Vampires*; PRA, 1936); *L'Aéronef C-3* (*Air-*

ship C3); VA, 1936); *Le Fantôme Volant (The Flying Phantom;* PRA, 1936); *L'Aquarium de Jade (The Jade Aquarium;* as Maurice Lionel; PRA, 1936); *Drame au Fond de la Mer (Tragedy at the Bottom of the Sea;* as Maurice Lionel; PRA, 1936); *L'Araignée d'Argent (The Silver Spider;* PRA, 1936); *Les Fiancés de la Planète Mars (The Fiancés of Planet Mars;* VA, 1936); *Les Hommes d'Acier (The Men of Steel;* as Maurice Lionel; VA, 1936); *Au Royaume de Satan (In the Kingdom of Satan;* VA, 1936); *L'Avion Mystérieux (The Mystery Plane;* as Maurice Lionel; PRA, 1937); *La Prêtresse du Zodiaque (The Priestess of Zodiac;* PRA, 1937); *L'Empereur des Scaphandriers (The Emperor of Deep-Sea Divers;* as Maurice d'Escrignelles; VA, 1937); *L'Île du Grand Serpent (The Island of the Great Snake;* as Maurice Lionel; PRA, 1937); *Le Mystère des Hommes-Volants (The Mystery of the Flying Men;* PRA, 1938); *L'Île Fantôme (The Phantom Island;* VA, 1938); *Le Monarque de l'Abîme (The Monarch of the Abyss;* as Maurice Lionel; VA, 1938); *Les Hommes Blancs de l'Inconnu (The White Men of the Unknown;* VA, 1938); *L'Île de la Mort Rouge (The Island of the Red Death;* PRA, 1938); *Le Navire Volant (The Flying Ship;* as Maurice Lionel; PRA, 1938); *Radio-Infernale (Hell Radio;* PRA, 1938); *Les Hommes-Perroquets (The Parrot-Men;* VA, 1938); *Les Naufragés de la Voie Lactée (The Castaways of the Milky Way;* as Maurice Lionel; VA, 1939); *Le Septième Cerveau (The Seventh Brain;* Techniques de Livre, 1939); *L'Île aux Idoles (Idols Island;* MRA, 1941); *Le Zodiaque de l'Himalaya (The Zodiac of the Himalaya;* MRA, 1942); *L'Île Foudroyante (Lightning Island;* as Maurice Lionel; MRA, 1942); *L'Hallucinante Aventure (The Visionary Adventure;* ABC, 1942); *La Femme aux Pieuvres (The Octopus Woman;* as Maurice Lionel; SEG, 1942); *Alerte aux Bolides (Alert to the Speedsters;* MRA, 1947); *Un Drame en Astronef (Tragedy on a Starship;* as Maurice Lionel; MRA, 1947); *Les Rescapés de la Préhistoire (Escape from Prehistory;* SEG, 1947); *La Comète Écarlate (The Scarlet Comet;* as Maurice Lionel; SEG, 1948); *Le Cercueil de Fer (The Iron Coffin;* as Maurice Lionel; SEG, 1948); *Les Yeux de l'Autre (The Eyes of the Other;* **Grand-Guignol**, 1948); *Le Nuage Rouge (The Red Cloud;* SEG, 1949); *Le Trésor du Roi d'Ys (The Treasure of the King of Ys;* SEG, 1949); *La Forêt qui Tue (The Killing Forest;* Coq Hardi, 1948); *L'Évasion des Agents X (The Escape of the X-Agents;* SEG, 1950); *Les Faiseurs de Planètes (The Planet Makers;* MRA, 1951); *Révolte en Plein Ciel (Revolt on Open Sky;* MRA, 1952); *Corsaires Invisibles (Invisible Corsairs;* MRA, 1952); *Au-delà du Vertige (Beyond Vertigo;* MRA, 1953); *Comète 73 (Comet 73);* MRA, 1953); *Courrier Interplanétaire (Interplanetary Courrier;* MRA, 1953); *A-117 a Disparu (A117 Has Disappared;* MRA, 1953); *La Cité des Étoiles de Mer (The City of the Starfish;* as Lionel Rex;

Spes, 1953); *Le Mal des Étoiles (Star Sickness;* MRA, 1954); *Crocodilopolis* (as Maurice Lionel; MRA, 1954); *Attaque Cosmique (Cosmic Attack;* as Maurice Lionel; MRA, 1954); *Les Forçats de l'Espace (The Convicts of Space;* MRA, 1954); *La Révolte des Spectres (The Revolt of the Spectres;* Arabesque, 1954); *Opération Ténèbres (Operation Darkness;* Arabesque, 1954); *Au Soleil de l'Épouvante (Sun of Terror;* MRA, 1955); *Satellites Inconnus (Unknown Satelites;* MRA, 1955); *L'Oiseau des Ténèbres (The Bird of Darkness;* MRA, 1955); *Chasseur de Comètes (Comet Hunters;* as Maurice Lionel; MRA, 1955); *Les Passagers du Silence (The Passengers of Silence;* MRA, 1955); *SOS Galaxie (SOS Galaxy;* Metal 18, 1955); *Le Vampire Tombé du Ciel (The Vampire Who Fell from the Sky;* MRA, 1956); *Monsieur Cosmos* (Cosmos 10, 1956); *Planète sans Soleil (Planet Without Sun;* Cosmos 11, 1956); *Pas de Planète pour les Terriens (No Planets for the Earthmen;* Cosmos 12, 1957); *Les Enfants du Chaos (The Children of Chaos;* FNA 141, 1959); *Le Sang du Soleil (The Blood of the Sun;* FNA 147, 1959); *J'écoute l'Univers (I Listen to the Universe;* FNA 154, 1960); *Métro Pour l'Inconnu (Metro for the Unknown;* FNA 159, 1960); *Les Foudroyants (The Lightning Men;* FNA 164, 1960); *Moi, Un Robot (I, Robot;* FNA 170, 1960); *Le Carnaval du Cosmos (The Cosmic Carnival;* FNA 173, 1961); *Océan, Mon Esclave (Ocean, My Slave;* FNA 178, 1961); *Message Des Vibrants (Message from the Vibrating Ones;* FNA 184, 1961); *Les Damnés de Cassiopée (The Damned of Cassiopea;* FNA 190, 1961); *Crucifie le Hibou (Crucify the Owl;* FNAG 81, 1961); *Batelier de la Nuit (Night Boatman;* FNAG 85, 1962); *Lumière Qui Tremble (Shivering Light;* FNA 196, 1962); *Les Fils de l'Espace (The Sons of Space;* FNA 204, 1962); *L'Anti-Monde (The Anti-World;* FNA 211, 1962); *Dans Le Vent Du Cosmos (In the Cosmic Winds;* FNA 215, 1962); *Le Marchand de Cauchemars (The Nightmare Peddler;* FNAG 90, 1962); *Créature des Ténèbres (Creature of Darkness;* FNAG 93, 1963); *Chantespectre (Ghostsong;* FNAG 95, 1963); *L'Ombre du Vampire (The Shadow of the Vampire;* FNAG 97, 1963); *Les Créatures d'Hypnôs (The Creatures of Hypnos;* FNA 218, 1963); *Le Crépuscule des Humains (The Twilight of Mankind;* FNA 226, 1963); *Le Sang Vert (The Green Blood;* FNA 230, 1963); *Les Sortilèges d'Altaïr (The Spells of Altair;* FNA 235, 1963); *Mandragore* (FNAG 101, 1963); *Lucifera* (FNAG 107, 1964); *L'Étoile de Satan (The Star of Satan;* FNA 241, 1964); *Échec au Soleil (The Sun in Check;* FNA 248, 1964); *Particule Zéro (Particle Zero;* FNA 252, 1964); *Ici Finit Le Monde (Here Ends the Universe;* FNA 257, 1964); *Le Miroir (The Mirror;* FNAG 112, 1964); *La Prison de Chair (The Prison of Flesh;* FNAG 114, 1964); *Le Manchot (The One-Armed Man;* FNAG 117, 1965); *Le Moulin des Damnés (The Mill of the Damned;* FNAG 121, 1965); *Les Soleils Noirs (The Black*

Suns; FNA 262, 1965); *Fréquence ZZ* (*Frequency ZZ*; FNA 266, 1965); *Le Flambeau du Monde* (*The Torch of the World*; FNA 274, 1965); *Methoodias* (FNA 278, 1965); *La Mygale* (*The Spider*; FNAG 123, 1965); *Moi, Vampire* (*I, Vampire*; FNAG 127, 1966); *Les Jardins de la Nuit* (*The Gardens of Night*; FNAG 129, 1966); *Planétoïde 13* (*Planetoid 13;* FNA 283, 1966); *Rien Qu'une Étoile* (*Only a Star*; FNA 288, 1966); *La Terre n'est pas Ronde* (*Earth Is Not Round*; FNA 296, 1966); *Le Soleil de Glace* (*The Sun of Ice*; FNA 302, 1966); La Maleficio (FNAG 135, 1966); *Ici le Bourreau* (*I, the Executioner*; FNAG 141, 1967); *L'Aquarium de Sang* (*The Bloody Aquarium*; FNA 144, 1967); *Le Dieu Couleur de Nuit* (*The Night-Colored God*; FNA 308, 1967); *Les Oiseaux de Véga* (*The Birds of Vega*; FNA 317, 1967); *Les Portes de l'Aurore* (*The Gates of Dawn*; FNA 325, 1967); *La Nuit des Géants* (*The Night of the Giants*; FNA 334, 1967); *En Lettres de Feu* (*In Fiery Letters*; FNAG 150, 1968); *Amazone de la Mort* (*Death Amazon*; FNAG 154, 1968); *La Planète de Feu* (*The Planet of Fire*; FNA 341, 1968); *Les Sirènes de Faô* (*The Sirens of Fao*; FNA 351, 1968); *Le Septième Nuage* (*The Seventh Cloud*; FNA 362, 1968); *Ici, l'Infini* (*Infinity Here*; FNA 370, 1968); *Mephista* (FNAG 166, 1969); *Métalikus* (FNA 374, 1969); *Le Treizième Signe du Zodiaque* (*The Thirteenth Sign of the Zodiac;* FNA 379, 1969); *Flammes sur Titan* (*Flames Over Titan*; FNA 391, 1969); *Tempête sur Goxxi* (*Tempest Over Goxxi*; FNA 398, 1969); *Mephista contre Mephista* (*Mephista vs. Mephista*; FNAG 171, 1969); *Le Voleur de Rêves* (*The Dream Stealer*; FNA 411, 1970); *Plus Loin Qu'Orion* (*Farther Than Orion*; FNA 417, 1970); *Les Cosmatelots de Lupus* (*The Spacesailors of Lupus*; FNA 430, 1970); *Et la Comète Passa* (*And the Comet Flew By*; FNA 441, 1970); *Mephista et le Clown Ecarlate* (*Mephista and the Scarlet Clown*; FNAG 183, 1970); *Mephista et la Lanterne des Morts* (*Mephista and the Lantern of the Dead*; FNAG 190, 1970); *Un Astronef Nommé "Péril"* (*A Starship Named "Peril";* FNA 453, 1971); *Un de la Galaxie* (*One of the Galaxy*; FNA 464, 1971); *Moissons du Futur* (*Future Harvests*; FNA 474, 1971); *La Planète aux Chimères* (*The Planet of Chimeras*; FNA 485, 1971); *Mephista et la Croix Sanglante* (*Mephista and the Bloody Cross*; FNAG 197, 1971); *Danse Macabre pour Mephista* (*Macabre Dance for Mephista*; FNAG 203, 1971); *Quand le Ciel s'embrase* (*When the Sky Lights Up*; FNA 497, 1972); *Les Pêcheurs d'Étoile* (*The Fishermen of the Stars*; FNA 507, 1972); *L'Empereur de Métal* (*The Metallic Emperor*; FNA 526, 1972); *Mephista et la Mort Caressante* (*Mephista and the Caressing Death*; FNAG 210, 1972); *Mephista et le Chasseur Maudit* (*Mephista and the Accursed Hunter*; FNAG 219, 1972); *Mephista et le Guignol Noir* (*Mephista and the Black Puppet Show*; FNAG 227, 1972); *Robinson du Néant* (*Robinson of the Void*; FNA 537, 1973); *SOS...*

Ici, Nulle Part! (*SOS from Nowhere!*; FNA 556, 1973); *L'Étoile du Silence* (*The Star of Silence*; FNA 574, 1973); *La Jungle de Fer* (*The Iron Jungle*; FNA 588, 1973); *Mephista Belle à Faire Peur* (*Mephista Beautiful Enough to Scare*; FNAG 232, 1973); *Mephista contre l'Homme de Feu* (*Mephista vs. The Man of Fire*; FNAG 239, 1973); *Ton Sang, Mephista* (*Your Blood, Mephista*; FNAG 246, 1973); *Vertige Cosmique* (*Cosmic Vertigo*; FNA 608, 1974); *L'Iceberg Rouge* (*The Red Iceberg*; FNA 635, 1974); *L'Espace d'un Éclair* (*In the Space of a Lightning Flash*; FNA 642, 1974); *Mephista et le Chien Hurlamor* (*Mephista and the Howling Dog*; FNAG 252, 1974); *Les Sub-Terrestres* (*The Sub-Terrestrians*; FNA 665, 1975); *Où Finissent les Étoiles?* (*Where Do the Stars End?*; FNA 676, 1975); *Le Maelstrom de Kjor* (*The Maelstrom of Kjor*; FNA 689, 1975); *Il est Minuit à l'Univers* (*It Is Midnight in the Universe*; FNA 699, 1975); *La Lumière d'Ombre* (*The Shadowlight*; FNA 717, 1975); *Astres Enchaînés* (*Chained Stars*; FNA 732, 1976); *Les Incréés* (*The Uncreated*; FNA 749, 1976); *Miroirs d'Univers* (*Mirrors of Universes*; FNA 758, 1976); *Cap sur la Terre* (*Direction: Earth*; FNA 768, 1977); *Les Diablesses de Quiwâm* (*The Devil-Women of Quiwam*; FNAG 789, 1977); *La Tour des Nuages* (*The Tower of Clouds*; FNA 803, 1977); *Mortels Horizons* (*Deadly Horizons*; FNA 821, 1977); *Principe Omicron* (*Omicron Principle*; FNA 837, 1978); *Les Fontaines du Ciel* (*The Fountains of the Sky*; FNA 857, 1978); *La Cloche de Brume* (*The Foghorn*; FNA 892, 1978); *Dô, Coeur De Soleil* (*Do, Heart of the Sun*; FNA 913, 1979); *Écoutez la Nuit* (*Listen to the Night*; as Lionel Rex; MOC 6, 1979); *Moi, Le Feu* (*I, Fire*; FNA 971, 1980); *Le Zénith... Et Après?* (*Zenith, and Beyond?*; FNA 1000, 1980); *Le Proscrit de Delta* (*Proscribed from Delta*; FNA 1031, 1980); *La Légende Future* (*The Future Legend*; FNA 1047, 1981); *Une Morsure de Feu* (*A Fire Bite*; FNA 1063, 1981); *La Nuit Solaire* (*The Solar Night*; FNA 1083, 1981); *Le Troubadour de Minuit* (*The Midnight Troubadour*; FNA 1097, 1981); *Les Rénégats d'Ixa* (*The Renegades of Ixa*; FNA 1118, 1982); *Coup-Dur sur Déneb* (*Hard Blow on Deneb*; FNA 1143, 1982); *Les Esclaves de Xicor* (*The Slaves of Xicor*; FNA 1164, 1982); *Le Mécaniquosmos* (*The Mecanicosmos*; FNA 1184, 1982); *Les Presque Dieux* (*The Almost Gods*; FNA 1210, 1983); *Comme un Vol de Chimères* (as *a Flight of Chimeras*; FNA 1231, 1983); *Le Grand Oiseau des Galaxies* (*The Great Bird of the Galaxies*; FNA 1247, 1983); *L'Oeil Écarlate* (*The Scarlet Eye*; FNA 1266, 1983); *Les Vikings de Sirius* (*The Vikings of Sirius*; FNA 1279, 1984); *L'Homme de Lumière* (*The Man of Light*; FNA 1291, 1984); *L'Élixir Pourpre* (*The Purple Elixir*; FNA 1314, 1984); *Les Idoles du Lynx* (*The Idols of Lynx*; FNA 1345, 1984); *L'Hydre Acéphale* (*The Acephalic Hydra*; FNA 1349, 1985); *Rouge est la Chute du Soleil* (*Red Is the Sunfall*; FNA

1374, 1985); *La Cité du Vent Damné* (*The City of the Accursed Winds*; FNA 1387, 1985); *Ceux de la Montagne de Fer* (*Those of the Iron Mountain*; FNA 1397, 1985); *Wân, l'Iconoclaste* (*Wan the Iconoclast*; FNA 1421, 1986); *Khéoba-la-Maudite* (*Kheoba-The-Accursed*; FNA 1465, 1986); *Le Sphinx des Nuages* (*The Sphinx of the Clouds*; FNA 1474, 1986); *Et la Pluie Tomba sur Mars* (*And Rain Fell on Mars*; FNA 1497, 1986); *Le Serpent de Rubis* (*The Ruby Snake*; FNA 1526, 1987); *Lointaine Étoile* (*Far Star*; FNA 1545, 1987); *La Croix de Flamme* (*The Firecross*; FNA 1568, 1987); *Atoxa-des-Abysses* (*Atoxa-Of-The-Abyss*; FNA 1599, 1987); *Note:* See chapters VII, VIII, and IX. A number of Maurice Limat's novels were adapted into digest-sized graphic novels (see Book 1, Chapter V under **Fleuve Noir**). Also see **Grand-Guignol**.

Limbour, Georges (1900-1970); *Le Cheval de Venise* (*The Horse from Venice*; 1924); *L'Illustre Cheval Blanc* (*The Illustrious White Horse*; Gall., 1930); *L'Enfant Polaire* (*The Polar Child*; Fontaine, 1945); *La Chasse au Mérou* (*The Grouper Hunt*; Leiris, 1959); *Contes and Récits* (*Tales and Stories*; Gall., 1973); *La Pie Voleuse* (*The Thieving Magpie*; Gall., 1995); *Note:* See Chapter VI.

Limite; *Malgré le Monde* (*In Spite of the World*; anthology; PdF 452, 1987); *Note:* Limite is a writers' collective.

Lindauer, Madeleine (?-?) *see* **Grand-Guignol**

Lintot, Catherine Caillot, Madame de (?-?); *Trois Nouveaux Contes de Fées* (*Three New Fairy Tales*; Didot, 1735); *Note:* Also see **Cabinet des Fées** and Chapter III.

Linville, André (?-); *L'Oiseau sans Ailes* (*The Wingless Bird*; LPT, 1921); *La Dernière Traversée* (*The Last Crossing*; Chantel, 1935)

Lionel, Maurice *see* **Limat, Maurice**

Liotard-Schneider, Maxime (?-); *L'Homme d'Armes au Pays Vert* (*The Man of Arms in the Green Country*; Soleil des Lièvres, 1978)

Listonai (Villeneuve, Daniel de; ?-); *Le Voyageur Philosophe dans un Pays Inconnu aux Habitants de la Terre* (*The Philosophical Traveller in a Country Unknown from the Inhabitants of Earth*; 1761); rep. VI, 1788); *Note:* See Chapter III.

Livache, Christian (1947-); *Les Effacés du Nôveau World* (*The Erased from the New World*; Lettres Libres, 1984)

Livet, Guillaume (?-); *Pietro Durena, Le Semeur de Morts* (*Pietro Durena, the Sower of Deaths*; Tallandier, 1913); *Miramar, L'Homme aux Yeux de Chat* (*Miramar, the Man with Cat Eyes*; Tallandier, 1913); *Note:* See Chapter IV.

Livrozet, S. (?-); *Jeva de Nazareth* (Livrozet, 1980

Locle, Camille de (?-?) *see* **Opéra**

Lo Duca, Joseph-Marie (?-); *La Sphère de Platine* (*The Platinum Sphere*; Fasquelle, 1945); *Journal Secret de Napoléon Bonaparte (1769-1869); The Secret Diary of Napoleon* (1769-1869); Amis du Livre, 1961); *Le Huitième Sceau* (*The Eighth Seal*; Pauvert, 1968); *Et Le Ciel Se Retira...* (*And the Sky Pulled Back; trilogy including Le Huitième Sceau* (*The Eighth Seal, Le Neuvième Sceau* (*The Ninth Seal), and Le Dixième Sceau* (*The Tenth Seal*, Opta, 1980); *Note:* Italian-born French writer; *La Sphère* was originally written in Italian in 1927 but rewritten in French by Lo Duca for the 1945 ediion.

Loiseau, Yvette-Marie (1930-); *Le Mur du Froid* (*The Wall of Cold*; Hac., 1971); *Le Secret des Nomades d'Iran* (*The Secret of the Iranian Nomads*; Hac., 1975); *Opération Pra-Loup* (GP, 1979); *L'Odyssée de Sandrine* (*Sandrine's Odyssey*; Duculot, 1982); *Note:* Juvenile SF.

Loiseleur de Longchamps, Guillaume (?-?) *see* **Opéra**

Loisy, Jean (?-); *Un Français dans la Lune* (*A Frenchman on the Moon*; Oeuvres Françaises, 1935); *Les Enfants des Vainqueurs* (*The Winners' Children*; RL, 1943); *De la Mort à l'Espérance* (*From Death to Hope*; Points & Contrepoints, 1955); *Aux Frontières de ce Monde* (*To the Frontiers of This World*; Beauchesne, 1966); *Note:* See Chapter VII.

Lombard, Jacques (1893-?); *Les Amants Damnés* (*The Accursed Lovers*; Lemerre, 1922); *Les Serpents Rôdent* (*Snakes on the Prowl*; Lemerre, 1924); *La Route Obscure* (*The Dark Road*; Lemerre, 1927); *Cocktails Après Minuit* (*Cocktails After Midnight*; Lemerre, 1929); *Bagheera* (Lemerre, 1930); *Cadavres de Cristal* (*Crystal Cadavers*; Del Duca, 1951)

Lombard, Jean *see* **Rayjean, Max-André**

Lomon, Ch. (?-) *see* **Gheusi, P.-B.**

Lompech, H. (?-) *see* **Maudru, P.**

Long, Y.F.J. (1921-); *Les Atlantes du Ciel* (*The Atlanteans from the Sky*; Métal 8, 1955); *Note:* See Chapter IX.

Lopez, José (?-); *Mi-figue, Misanthrope* (*Neither Fowl, NorMal*; CRNI, n.d.)

Loranger, Francine (1946-); *Chansons pour un Ordinateur* (*Songs for a Computer*; Fidès, 1980); *Note:* French-Canadian writer. Juvenile SF.

Lord, Michel (1949-); *Anthologie de la Science-Fiction Québécoise Contemporaine* (*anthology of Contemporary Quebec SF*; anthology; BQ, 1988); *Note:* French-Canadian writer.

Lorde, André de Latour, Comte de (1871-1942); *Théâtre d'Épouvante* (*Theater of Horror*; incl. *Une Leçon à la Salpêtrière, L'Obsession, La Dormeuse, Au Rat Mort—Cabinet 6, Le Système du Docteur Goudron et du Professeur Plume, La Dernière Torture, Sur la Dalle*; Fasquelle, 1909); *L'Horrible Expérience* (*The Awful Experiment*; with Alfred **Binet**; Ondet & Viterbo, 1910); *Cauchemars* (*Nightmares*; Ollendorff, 1912); *Les Invisibles* (*The Invisible Ones*; with Alfred **Binet**; Monde Illustré, 1912); *Théâtre Rouge* (*Red Theater*; incl. *Des Yeux dans l'Ombre, Figures de Cire, L'Enfant Mort, Attaque Nocturne*; Figuière, 1922); *L'Étrange Amant du Mal* (*Evil's Strange Lover*; with Maurice **Landay**; Ren. du Livre, 1923); *Les Drames Célèbres du Grand-Guignol* (*Famous Tragedies of the Grand-Guignol*; incl. *Le Château de la Mort Lente, La Grande Épouvante, Le Laboratoire des Hallucinations*; Stock, 1924); *Théâtre de la Peur* (*Theater of Fear*; incl. *L'Horrible Expérience*, Baraterie, *L'Acquittée, Les Infernales*; Libr. Théâtrale, 1924); *Le Cercueil de Chair* (*The Coffin of Flesh*; with Henri **Bauche**; Libr. Théâtrale, 1924); *Un Crime dans une Maison de Fous* (*A Crime in a Lunatic Asylum*; Libr. Théâtrale, 1925); *Le Cabinet du Dr. Caligari* (*The Cabinet of Dr. Caligari*; Nlle. Revue, 1927); *Les Maîtres de la Peur* (*The Masters of Fear*; with Albert Dubeux; Delgrave, 1927); *Théâtre de la Mort* (*Theater of Death*; incl. *Les Charcuteurs, Le Vaisseau de la Mort, L'Homme Mystérieux*; Ollendorff, 1928); *La Galerie des Monstres* (*The Gallery of Monsters*; Figuière, 1928); *Le Jardin des Supplices* (*The Garden of Tortures*; with Pierre **Chaine**; Libr. Théâtrale, 1929); *Grand-Guignol* (incl. *Jack l'Éventreur, L'Horrible Passion, Magie Noire*; anthology/with Henri **Bauche** & Pierre **Chaine**; Figuière, 1936); *Contes du Grand-Guignol* (*Tales of the Grand-Guignol*; FN, 1993); *Note:* See chapters IV and VI and **Grand-Guignol**.

Loria, Jacques (?-); *La Visite des Martiens* (*The Visit of the Martians*; Figuière, 1935); *Note:* See Chapter VII.

Lorrain, Jean (Duval, Paul-Alexandre-Martin; 1855-1906); *La Forêt Bleue* (*The Blue Forest*; Lemerre, 1882); *Sonyeuse* (Charpentier, 1891); *Buveurs d'Âmes* (*Drinkers of Souls*; Charpentier, 1893); *Un Démoniaque* (*Demoniacal*; Dentu, 1895); *Sensations et Souvenirs* (*Feelings and Remembrances*; Charpentier & Fasquelle, 1895); *Une Femme par Jour* (*A Woman a Day*; Borel, 1896); *L'Ombre Ardente* (*The Fiery Shadow*; Fasquelle, 1897); *La Mandragore* (Pelletan, 1899); *Histoires de Masques* (*Stories of Masks*; Ollendorff, 1900); *Monsieur de Phocas* (Ollendorff, 1901; transl. 1994); *Princesses d'Ivoire et d'Ivresse* (*Princess of Ivory and Drunkenness*; Ollendorff, 1902); *Le Vice Errant* (*Wandering Vice*; AM, 1926); *La Ville Empoisonnée* (*The Poisoned City*; Crès, 1936); *Masques and Fantômes* (*Masks and Ghosts*; UGE, 1974); *Contes d'un Buveur d'Éther* (*Tales of an Ether Drinker*; Marabout, 1975); *Le Prince dans la Forêt* (*The Prince in the Forest*; ARCAM, 1977); *Histoires du Bord de l'Eau* (*Tales from the Water's Edge*; n.d.; *Note:* See Chapter IV. Also see **Grand-Guignol** and **Opéra**.

Lorraine, René (?-); *Le Roman du Capitaine Jean* (*The Novel of Captain John*; Mame, 1910); *Un Petit Monde d'Aviateurs en l'An 2000* (*A Small World of Aviators in the Year 2000*); Mame, 1912); *Note:* See Chapter V.

Lorris, Guillaume de (13th century); *Le Roman de la Rose* (*The Romance of the Rose*; c. 1230); *Note:* See Chapter I.

Lortac, Raoul *see* **Collard, Robert**

Lortie, Alain *see* **Sernine, Daniel**

Lorzac, Georges de (?-); *La Loque à Terre* (*The Wreck of a Tenant*; Brigandine, 1980); *Note:* See Chapter VIII.

Losfeld, Érik (?-1979); *Cerise, ou Le Moment Bien Employé* (*Cherry, or a Well-Used Moment*; as Dellfos; Los., 1969); *Note:* Light fantasy by the renowned publisher.

Lostin, Pierre (?-) *see* **Laumann, E.M.**

Loubet, Christophe (1969-); *La Saga des Bannis 1: Le Bâtard* (*The Saga of the Banished 1: The Bastard*; FNSF 17, 1997); *La Saga des Bannis 2: L'Exil* (*The Saga of the Banished 2: The Exile*; FNSF 18, 1997); *Note:* See Chapter VIII.

Louis-Combet, Claude (1932-); *Infernaux Paluds* (*Infernal Paluds*; Flamm., 1970); *Miroir de Léda* (*Leda's Mirror*; Flamm., 1971); *Tsé-Tsé* (Flamm., 1972); *Voyage au Centre de la Ville* (*Voyage to the Center of Town*; Flamm., 1974); *Le Roman de Mélusine* (*The Novel of Melusine*; AM, 1986); *Figures de Nuit* (*Night Figures*; Flamm., 1988); *Les Yeux Clos* (*Shut Eyes*; Deyrolle, 1991); *Le Boeuf Nabu ou les Métamorphoses du Roi des Rois* (*The Ox Nabu or Metamorphoses of the King of Kings*; Lettres Vives, 1992); *Dadomorphes and Dadopathes* (*Dadomorphs and Dadopaths*; Deyrolle, 1992); *Augias et Autres Infâmes* (*Augias and Other Infamous Actions*; Corti, 1993); *Note:* See Chapter VIII.

Lourbet, François (Lourdet, François; ?-); *Les Bagnes de l'Espace* (*The Space Penitentiaries*; Daniber 12, 1960); *Sortilège Temporel* (*Time Spell*; Daniber 14, 1960); *La Clef de l'Abîme* (*The Key of the Abyss*; L'Alouette 23, 1960); *Note:* See Chapter IX.

Louvigny, André *see* **Steiner, Kurt**

Louvres, Phyllis (?-); *Les Trigynes* (Los., 1969)

Louÿs, Pierre (1870-1925); *Aphrodite* (MdF, 1895; transl. 1900); *Les Aventures du Roi Pausole* (Fasquelle, 1901;

transl. as *The Adventures of King Pausole*, 1926); *Byblis* (A. Ferroud, 1901); *Sanguines* (*Bloody Tales*; Fasquelle, 1903; transl. 1932); *Ariane ou Le Chemin de la Paix Éternelle* (*Ariane, or the Path to Eternal Peace*; Meunier, 1904); *Le Crépuscule des Nymphes* (Montaigne, 1925; transl. as *The Twilight of the Nymphs*, 1928); *Note:* See Chapter IV. Also see **Opéra**.

Lowell, Richard (?-); *Sexe en Direct* (*Live Sex*; Edit & Public. Premières, Eroscope, 1980); *Note:* Erotic SF on the *Close Encounters* theme.

Lubert (Mademoiselle de; 1710-1779); Author of a number of fairy tales written from 1743 on: *Le Prince des Autruches (The Prince of Ostriches, Le Prince Glacé et la Princesse Étincelante (The Icy Prince and the Sparkling Princess, La Princesse Camion (Princess Camion, La Princesse Lionette et le Prince Coquerico (Princess Lionette and Prince Coquerico, La Princesse Couleur de Rose et le Prince Céladon (Princess Rose and Prince Celadon, Blancherose (Whiterose, La Princesse Sensible et le Prince Typhon (Princess Sensitive and Prince Typhoon*, etc. Also see **Cabinet des Fées** and Chapter III.

Luc, Anne-Marie-Suzanne *see* **Soulac, Anne-Marie**

Lucas, Gérald (?-); *L'Abcès* (*The Abcess*; Scorpion, 1961); *Le Bal des Machines* (*The Machines' Ball*; Le Pavé, 1972); *Note:* Swiss writer.

Lucas, Wilfrid (?-); *La Route de Lumière, Légende de l'Amour* (*The Road of Light, Legend of Love*; Figuière, 1927)

Luchet, Jean-Pierre Louis de la Roche du Maine, Marquis de (1740-1792); *La Reine de Benni* (*The Queen of Benni*; Grangé, 1766)

Lucien-Graux *see* **Graux, Lucien**

Luck, John *see* **Béra, Paul**

Luda (Schnitzer, Ludmilla; 1913-); *Le Cordonnier de Bagdad* (*The Cobbler of Baghdad*; LIRE, 1955); *Les Maîtres de la Forêt* (*The Masters of the Forest*; Messidor-La Farandole, 1958); *La Gardienne du Feu* (*The Guardian of the Fire*; Messidor-La Farandole, 1975); *La Chanteur des Tapis* (*The Carpet Singer*; Messidor-La Farandole, 1977); *Ce que disent les Contes* (*What the Tales Say*; Le Sorbier, 1981); *Yann ar lue* (Le Sorbier, 1981); *Les Morisques de Cambrai* (*The Morisques of Cambrai*; Le Sorbier, 1982); *La Dame du Lin* (*The Linen Lady*; Le Sorbier, 1982); *La Filleule de la Montagne de Feu* (*The Goddaughter of the Fire Mountain*; Le Sorbier, 1982); *Lise et le Lutin* (*Lise and the Goblin*; Hac., 1984); *Contes du Fleuve Amour* (*Tales from the River Love*; Messidor-La Farandole, 1984); *Le Palmier Menteur* (*The Lying Palm Tree*; Messidor-La Farandole,

1986); *Cet Endroit-là dans la Taïga* (*That Very Place in the Taiga*; Hatier, 1986); *Le Jardin de la Fille-Roi* (*The Garden of the King's Daughter*; Hatier, 1987); *L'Étrier d'Or* (*The Golden Spur*; Nathan, 1990); *Note:* Juveniles.

Luguet, Pierre (?-); *Une Descente au Monde Sous-Terrien* (*A Descent Into a Sub-Terranean World*; Libr. Éduc. Récré., 1906); *L'Invincible Kenyon* (*The Invincible Kenyon*; Hetzel, 1906); *La Flèche Rouge* (*The Red Arrow*; Lafitte, 1907); *Prisonnière de la Sierra* (*Prisoner of the Sierra*; Mame, 1913); *Note:* See Chapter V.

Lunel, Armand (?-?) *see* **Opéra**

Lutz, Émile *see* **Duthuit, Florent**

Luzel, François-Marie (?-) *see* ***Contes et Légendes***

Lys, Georges de (Bonnerive, Georges de; 1855-?); *La Vierge de Sedôm* (*The Virgin of Sedom*; Offenstadt, 1901); *Les Conquérants de l'Air* (*Conquerors of the Air*; Mame, 1910); *L'Île Envahie* (*The Invaded Island*; Mame, 1913); *L'Appel dans la Tourmente* (*The Call in the Storm*; Bonne Presse, 1922); *L'Âme Jalouse* (*The Jealous Soul*; Bonne Presse, 1927); *Note: Les Conquérants* was illustrated by **Robida**.

Maalouf, Amin (?-); *Le Premier Siècle Après Béatrice* (*The First Century After Beatrice*; Grasset-Fasquelle, 1992); *Note:* See Chapter IX.

MacDuff, Claude (1946-); *La Mort... De Toute Façons* (*Death... In Any Case*; La Presse, 1979); *1986: Mission Fantastique* (*1986: Fantastic Mission*; Québécor, 1980); *Note:* French-Canadian writer. In *Mission*, an asteroid buried in Arizona is responsible for evil on Earth.

Macé, Gérard (?-); *Bois Dormant* (*Sleeping Woods*; Gall., 1983); *Les Trois Coffrets* (*The Three Boxes*; Gall., 1985); *Pierrot, Valet de la Mort* (*Pierrot, Death's Butler*; Nitabah, 1986); *Le Dernier des Égyptiens* (*The Last of the Egyptians*; Gall., 1988); *Vies Antérieures* (*Previous Lives*; Gall., 1991); *L'Autre Hémisphère du Temps* (*The Other Half of Time*; Gall., 1995); *Note:* See Chapter VIII.

Machard, Alfred (1887-?); *Le Massacre des Innocents: Légende du Temps de Guerre* (*The Massacre of the Innocents: Legend of the War Time*; Ed. Fr. Ill., 1918); *L'Homme qui porte la Mort* (*The Man Who Carries Death*; Ren. du Livre, 1926); *L'Homme sans Coeur* (*The Man Without Heart*; Flamm., 1936); *Note:* Also see **Grand-Guignol**.

Macho, E. (?-); *L'Iceberg Mécanique* (*The Mechanical Iceberg*; RJ, 1934)

Macho, J.-E. (?-); *L'Île aux Étranges Mortes* (*The Island with Strange Dead*; CA, 1931)

MacKenzie, Nadine (1947-); *La Lumière dans la Nuit* (*The*

Light in the Night; Naaman, 1984); *Le Sosie de Nijinsky* (*Nijinsky's Twin*; Plaines, 1990); *Note:* French-Canadian writer. In the 1990 novel, a dancer is possessed by the spirit of the great master.

Mac Orlan, Pierre (Dumarchey, Pierre; 1882-1970); *La Maison du Retour Écoeurant* (*The House of the Disgusting Return*; Bibl. Humoristique, 1912); *Le Rire Jaune* (*The Yellow Laugh*; Méricant, 1914); *U-713, ou Les Gentilshommes d'Infortune* (*The Gentlemen of Ill Fortune*; SLF, 1917); *La Bête Conquérante* (*The Conquering Beast*; Crès, 1920); *Le Nègre Léonard et Maître Jean Mullin* (La Banderole, 1920); *La Cavalière Elsa* (*Elsa the Rider*; Gall., 1921); *Marguerite de la Nuit* (*Marguerite of the Night*; Émile-Paul, 1922); *Malice* (Crès, 1923); *L'Inhumaine* (*The Inhuman*; AM, 1924); *Sous la Lumière Froide* (*Under a Cold Light*; Émile-Paul, 1927); *Dina Miami* (CRT, 1928); *Masques sur Mesure* (*Masks to Fit*; Gall., 1937); *Note:* See Chapter VI. ***Marguerite de la Nuit*** was adapted into an eponymous 1955 film (see Book 1, Chapter I).

Mad, André *see* **Dazergues, Max-André**

Mada, Pierre *see* **Adam, Pierre**

Madelène, Jules de la (1820-1859); *Les Années en Peine* (*The Years of Pain*; 1857); *Note:* See Chapter IV.

Maël, Pierre (Causse, Charles (?-) & Vincent, Charles (?-)); *L'Alcyone* (Kolb, 1889); *L'Ondine de Ruiz* (*The Ondine of Ruiz*; Dentu, 1890); *La Roche qui Tue* (*The Killing Rock*; Mame, 1898); *Pilleurs d'Épaves* (*Looters of Shipwrecks*; Flamm., 1900); *Le Sous-Marin "Le Vengeur"* (*The Submarine "Avenger"*; JDV, 1902; rev. Ollendorff, 1912); *Au Pays du Mystère* (*In the Land of Mystery*; Ollendorff, 1904); *L'Énigme du Transtévère* (*The Transteverian Mystery*; Flamm., 1908); *La Main d'Ombre* (*The Hand of Shadow*; Roger & Chernoirz, 1909); *Le Forban Noir* (*The Dark Villain*; Hac., 1911); *Le Secret du Gouffre* (*The Secret of the Pit*; Hac., 1914); *La Légende de Moïna* (*The Legend of Moina*; Hac., 1915)

Maeterlinck, Maurice (1862-1949); *La Princesse Maleine* (*Princess Maleine*; Lacomblez, 1889; transl. 1894); *L'Intruse* (*The Intruder*; Lacomblez, 1890; transl. 1891); *Les Aveugles* (*The Blind*; Lacomblez, 1891; transl. 1891); *Les Sept Princesses* (*The Seven Princesses*; Lacomblez, 1891; transl. 1894); *Pelléas et Mélisande* (Lacomblez, 1892; transl. 1894); *La Mort de Tintagiles* (*The Death of Tintagiles*; Lacomblez, 1894; transl. 1899); *Alladine et Palomides* (Deman, 1894; transl. 1899); *Aglavaine et Sélysette* (MdF, 1896; transl. 1897); *Ariane et Barbe-Bleue* (*Ariadne and Blue-Beard*; Lacomblez, 1901; transl. 1901); *Le Temple Enseveli* (*The Buried Temple*; Charpentier & Fasquelle, 1902); *Le Double Jardin* (*The Twin Garden*; Fasquelle, 1904); *L'Oiseau Bleu* (*The*

Blue Bird; Charpentier & Fasquelle, 1908; transl. 1909); *La Mort* (*Death*; Fasquelle, 1913); *L'Hôte Inconnu* (*The Unknown Guest*; Fasquelle, 1917); *Intérieur* (*Interior*; Fasquelle, 1918); *Les Fiançailles* (*The Betrothal*; first publ. US 1918; first Fr. publ. Fasquelle, 1922); *Le Miracle de Saint Antoine* (*The Miracle of Saint Anthony*; Fasquelle, 1919; transl. 1919); *Le Grand Secret* (*The Great Secret*; Fasquelle, 1921); *La Vie de l'Espace* (*Life in Space*; Charpentier & Fasquelle, 1928); *La Grande Féerie* (*The Great Faery*; Fasquelle, 1929); *L'Araignée de Verre* (*The Glass Spider*; Fasquelle, 1932); *Note:* Belgian playwright. See chapters IV and VI. Also see **Opéra**.

Magini, Roger (1945-); *Un Homme Défait* (*A Defeated Man*; Herbes Rouges, 1995); *Les Miroirs Infinis* (*The Infinite Mirrors*; La Pleine Lune, 1997); *Note:* French-Canadian writer.

Magnard, Albéric (1865-1914) *see* **Opéra**

Magog, H.-J. (Jeanne, Henri-Georges; 1877-1947); *L'Oeil dans les Ténèbres* (*The Eye in the Darkness*; Tallandier, 1911); *L'Énigme de la Malle Rouge* (*The Mystery of the Red Trunk*; Tallandier, 1912); *L'Homme qui Devint Gorille* (*The Man Who Became a Gorilla;* Ollendorff, 1921; rev. as *La Fiancée du Monstre* (*The Monster's Fiancée*) and *Le Gorille Policier* (*The Policeman Gorilla*, 1930); *Extraordinaire Aventures de Deux Fiancés à travers le Monde* (*Extraordinary Adventures of Two Fiancés Across the World;* Ollendorff, 1922; rev. as *Les Buveurs d'Océan* (*The Ocean Drinkers,* BGA, 1926; rev. as *Le Secret du Pacifique* (*The Secret of the Pacific,* Simon, 1939); *Les Mystères de Demain* (*The Mysteries of Tomorrow*; with Paul **Féval** (Fils); serialized in 5 issues, Ferenczi, 1922-23): *1. Les Fiancés de l'An 2000* (*The Fiancés of the Year 2000*); *2. Le Monde des Damnés* (*The World of the Damned*); *3. Le Réveil d'Atlantide* (*Atlantis Awakens*); *4. L'Humanité Enchaînée* (*Mankind in Chains*); *5. Le Faiseur de Folles* (*The Maker of Madwomen*); *L'Île Tombée du Ciel* (*The Island Which Fell from the Sky;* Ollendorff, 1923, rev. as *La Conquête de l'Etoile* (*The Conquest of the Star,* BGA, 1934); *Trois Ombres sur Paris* (*Three Shadows Over Paris;* Gall., 1928; rev. as *Le Secret du Prof. Fringue* (*The Secret of Prof. Fringue,* Tallandier, 1941); *Le Village Ensorcelé* (*The Spellbound Village*; Plon, 1933); *L'Armée Invisible* (*The Invisible Army*; Hartoy, 1933); *La Vallée Ensevelie* (*The Buried Valley*; BGA, 1933); *Le Masque aux Yeux Rouges* (*The Mask with Red Eyes*; Baudinière, 1933); *L'Avion de Monsieur Personne* (*Mr. Nobody's Plane;* LPT, 1935; rev. as *L'Avion Sans Pilote* (*The Plane Without a Pilot,* BGA, 1935); *Le Bouddha Vivant* (*The Living Buddha*; PRA, 1936); *Le Crime du Fantôme* (*The Crime of the Ghost*; Simon, 1937); *La Vallée sous les Eaux* (*The Underwater Valley*; Tallandier, 1938); *La*

Tragique Épave (*The Tragic Shipwreck*; Simon, 1943); *L'Étreinte de la Pieuvre* (*The Hug of the Octopus*; Ed. Litt. Artistiques, 1942); *L'Invisible Assassin* (*The Invisible Assassin*; Sinmon, 1946); *L'Obus Surprise* (*The Surprise Shell;* LdA, 1953*); L'Île aux Calmars* (*Squid Island*; LdA, 1954); *Note:* See Chapter VII.

Magre, Maurice (?-); *Velleda* (Stock, 1908); *Le Sortilège* (*Drame Lyrique; The Spell*; Fasquelle, 1913); *La Mort Enchaînée* (*Death in Chains*; AM, 1920); *Sin* (Féerie; Librairie Théâtrale, 1921); *Priscillia d'Alexandrie* (*Priscilla of Alexandria*; AM, 1925); *La Luxure de Grenade* (*The Luxury of Granada*; AM, 1926); *Le Mystère du Tigre* (*The Mystery of the Tiger*; AM, 1927); *Le Poison de Goa* (*The Poison of Goa*; AM, 1928); Lucifer (AM, 1929); *La Mort et la Vie Future* (*Death and Future Life*; Fasquelle, 1932); *La Clef des Choses Cachées* (*The Key to Hidden Things*; Fasquelle, 1935); *Interventions Surnaturelles* (*Supernatural Interventions*; Fasquelle, 1939); *Note:* See Chapter VI.

Magué, Charles (?-); *Les Survivants de l'Atlantide* (*The Survivors of Atlantis*; BGA, 1929); *La Cuve aux Monstres* (*The Vat of Monsters*; BGA, 1930); *L'Archipel des Demi-Dieux* (*The Archipelago of Demigods*; BGA, 1931); *Au Souffle des Ailes* (*When the Wings Blow*; BGA, 1931); *Le Secret des Bouddhas* (*The Secret of the Buddhas*; BGA, 1932); *Note:* See Chapter VII.

Maguirre, P. P. (?-); *À Nous Deux, Dr. Mellor* (*To Me, Dr. Mellor*; Gautier-Languereau, 1952)

Maheux, Guy (1927-); *Une Sorcière dans mon Grain de Sable* (*A Witch in My Grain of Sand*; Maheux, 1976); *Note:* French-Canadian writer.

Maigrot, Henry *see* **Henriot, Émile**

Maillard, Lucien (?-); *Les Nuées d'Anaa* (*The Clouds of Anaa*; FNASF 1, 1995)

Maillart, Jean (?-); *Contes Chimériques* (*Chimerical Tales*; 1905); *Note:* Belgian writer. See Chapter VI.

Maillet, Andrée (1921-); *Le Lendemain n'est pas sans Amour* (*Tomorrow Is Not Without Love*; Beauchemin, 1963); *Le Chêne des Tempêtes* (*The Storm Oak*; Beauchemin, 1964); *Profil de l'Original* (*Profile of the Original*; Hexagone, 1974); *Lettres au Surhomme* (*Letters to the Superman*; La Presse, 1976); *Miroir de Salomé* (*Salome's Mirror*; La Presse, 1977); *Note:* French-Canadian writer.

Maillet, Antonine (1929-); *Pointe aux Conques* (Fidès, 1961); *Don L'Original* (Leméac, 1972; transl. as *The Tale of Don L'Original*, 1978); *On a Mangé la Dune* (*They Ate the Dune*; Leméac, 1977); *Les Drôlatiques, Horrifiques et Épouvantables Aventures de Panurge* (*The Funny, Horrific and Awful Adventures of Panurge*;

Leméac, 1983); *Garrochés en Paradis* (Leméac, 1986); *Note:* French-Canadian writer. *Don* is a Rabelaisian fantasy.

Maillet, Benoît de (1656-1728); *Telliamed* (Honoré, 1748); *Note:* See Chapter III.

Maillot (Abbé; ?-?); *Relation du Voyage Mystérieux de l'Île de la Vertu* (*Tale of the Mysterious Voyage to the Island of Virtue*; Besançon, 1683); *Note:* See Chapter III.

Mailly, Chevalier de (?-1724); *Voyage et les Aventures de Trois Princes de Serendib* (*Voyage and Adventures of Three Princes from Serendib*; 1719; rep. VI, 1788); *Illustres Fées* (*Illustrious Fairies*; 1786); *Note:* Also see Chapter III and **Cabinet des Fées**.

Mainard, Louis (1857-?); *Plus Haut! Plus Grand! Le Chicago* (*Bigger! Higher! the Chicago*; with Paul **Meyan**; Lecène-Oudin, 1892); *Fils de l'Océan* (*Son of the Ocean*; Dentu, 1894)

Maindron, (Georges-René) Maurice (1857-1911); *Saint-Cendre* (*Saint Ash*; Reine Blanche, 1898); *Blancador l'Avantageuse* (*Blancador the Advantageous*; Reine Blanche, 1900); *L'Arbre de Science* (*The Tree of Science*; Lemerre, 1906); *La Gardienne de l'Idole Noire* (*The Guardian of the Black Idol*; Lemerre, 1910); *Le Tournoi de Vauplassans* (*The Tourney of Vauplassans*; Plon, 1920); *Récits du Temps Passé* (*Tales of Past Times*; Mame, 1924); *Note:* See Chapter IV.

Maine, David *see* **Barbet, Pierre**

Maintigneux, Pierre Jean (?-); *Les Nouveaux Seigneurs* (*The New Lords*; Pensée Moderne, 1961); *Les Enfants de la Patrie* (*The Children of the Nation*; Pensée Moderne, 1964); *Les Douze Tombes de McTaylor* (*The Dozen Tombs of McTaylor*; Galliera 6, 1972); *Au Rendez-Vous de la Mort Joyeuse* (*Rendezvous with Joyous Death*; Galliera 8, 1973); *Note: Au Rendez-Vous* is a novelization of the eponymous 1972 film by Juan Luis **Buñuel**; Maintigneux was one of the film's writers.

Maizeroy, René (?-?); *L'Ange* (*The Angel;* Lemerre, 1895*); L'Amant de Proie* (*The Prey Lover*; AM, 1905); *Le Voleur d'Âmes* (*The Stealer of Souls*; JST, 1912); *L'Ensorceleur* (*The Caster of Spells*; AM, 1917); *La Croix Sanglante* (*The Bloody Cross*; as Léo Mora; RMY, 1930)

Major, Henriette (1933-); *Le Club des Curieux* (*The Club for Inquisitive Folks*; 1967); *À la Conquête du Temps* (*To Conquer Time*; Éd. Nouvelle, 1970); *Contes de Nulle Part et d'Ailleurs* (*Tales of Nowhere and Elsewhere*; École des Loisirs, 1975); *Histoires Autour du Poêle* (*Tales Around the Stove*; La Farandole, 1980); *Le Paradis des Animaux* (*The Animals' Paradise*; L'Amitié, 1984); *Ukalig au Pays des Affaires Perdues* (*Ukalig in the Land of Lost Cases*; Sorbier, 1985); *La Planète des*

Enfants (*The Planet of Children*; Héritage, 1991); *Note:* French-Canadian writer.

Major, René (?-); *Ivre Morte* (*Dead Drunk*; Aubier-Montaigne, 1981)

Makanine, Vladimir (?-); *Les Voix* (*The Voices*; Alinéa, 1988); *Le Précurseur* (*The Precursor*; Actes Sud, 1989); *La Perte* (*The Loss*; Alinéa, 1989); *Le Retardataire* (*The Late Comer*; Belfond, 1990); *La Brèche* (*The Break*; Belfond, 1991); *Le Citoyen en Fuite* (*The Fleeing Citizen*; Flamm., 1991); *La Rivière au Cours Rapide / La Vieille Cité* (*The Rapid River* / the *Old City*; Messidor, 1991); *La Route est Longue* (*The Road Is Long*; Gall., 1994); *Note:* See Chapter IX.

Malamud, Bernard (?-); *Les Locataires* (*The Tenants*; Seuil, 1976); *L'Homme dans le Tiroir* (*The Man in a Drawer*; Flamm., 1980); *La Vie Multiple de William D.* (*The Multiple Life of William D.*; Flamm., 1980); *La Grâce de Dieu* (*The Grace of God*; Flamm., 1983)

Malby, André (?-); *Massie… Etc.* (Egraz, 1972)

Malineau, Jean-Hugues (1945-); *Trois Histoires pour Aller Dormir* (*Three Stories to Go to Sleep*; Ecole des Loisirs, 1980); *Le Tue-Mouches* (*The Fly Killer*; Gall., 1981); *Le Coup d'État du Petit Prince* (*The Little Prince's Coup*; Messidor-La Farandole, 1985); *Note:* Juveniles.

Mallarmé, Stéphane (1842-1898); *Hérodiade* (1874); *L'Après-Midi d'un Faune* (*The Afternoon of a Faun*; 1876); *Note:* See Chapter IV.

Mallet-Joris, Françoise (?-); *Les Trois Âges de la Nuit* (*The Three Ages of Night*; Grasset, 1968)

Mallinus, Daniel (1939-); *Myrtis and Autres Histoires de Nuit and de Peur* (*Myrtis and Other Tales of Night and Fear*; MarF 433, 1973); *Note:* Belgian writer. See Chapter VIII.

Malouin, Bernard-Éric (?-); *Maléfices* (*Spells*; Odette, 1993); *Note:* French-Canadian writer.

Maltravers, Michaël (Bouvard, Roland; ?-); *La Maladie de Chooz* (*The Chooz Disease*; Gall. Série Noire 1013, 1966)

Maly, Michel (?-) *see* **Douay, Dominique**

Manceau, Marcelle (?-); *Le Talisman du Soleil* (*The Talisman of the Sun*; L'Amitié, 1966); *Le Mas Tortebesse* (*The House Tortebesse*; GP, 1969); *Note:* Juvenile fantasy. See Chapter IX.

Manchette, Jean-Patrick (1942-); *Les Chasses d'Aphrodite* (*Aphrodite's Hunt*; Or du Temps, 1970); *Nada* (Gall., 1972); *Morgue Pleine* (*Full Morgue*; Gall., 1973); *Folle à Tuer* (*Crazy Enough to Kill*; Gall., 1975); *Fatale* (Gall., 1977); *Mélanie White* (Hac., 1979); *La Princesse du Sang* (*Princess of Blood*; Rivages, 1996); *Note:* Popular thriller writer.

Manchez, Marcel (?-?) *see* **Grand-Guignol**

Mandelstamm, Valentin (1876-?); *Amoral* (La Plume, 1902); *Le Conte des Marennes* (Charpentier, 1909); *Le Conte du Cigare au Feu Vert* (*The Tale of the Cigar with a Green Flame*; JST, 1910); *L'Empire du Diamant* (*The Diamond Empire*; Lafitte, 1914); *V5* (Brentano's, New York, 1945)

Manier, Bernard (?-); *Histoires d'Ailleurs et de Nulle Part* (*Tales of Elsewhere and Nowhere*; Artistes, 1961); *Note:* Belgian writer. See Chapter VIII.

Mannoni, Octave (1901-1990); *La Machine* (Tchou, 1977)

Manoussi, Jean (?-?) *see* **Grand-Guignol**

Mantey, Christian (?-); *Transit pour l'Infini* (*Transit for Infinity*; FNA 728, 1976); *Black Planet* (FNA 755, 1976); *Palowstown* (as Jean-Christian Bergman/with Jean-Philippe **Berger**; FNA 914, 1979); *Homme, Sweet Homme…* (as Jean-Christian Bergman/with Jean-Philippe **Berger**; FNA 952, 1979); *Apocalypse Snow* (as Jean-Christian Bergman/with Jean-Philippe **Berger**; FNA 993, 1980); *Survivance* (*Survival*; as Budy Matieson/with Pierre **Dubois**; FNA 1019, 1980); *Titcht* (FNA 1093, 1981); *Shea* (as Budy Matieson/with Pierre **Dubois**; FNA 1135, 1982); *L'Effet Halstead* (*The Halstead Effect*; FNA 1193, 1983); *Wildlife Connection* (FNA 1219, 1983); *No Man's Land* (FNA 1280, 1984); as **Chillicothe, Zeb** (see above): Series *Jag*: Nos. 1 and others are by Christian Mantey. *Note:* See Chapter IX.

Marabini, Jean (?-); *Les Hommes du Futur* (*Future Men*; Cast., 1965); *Les Enfants Fous—An 2021* (*The Mad Children—Year 2021*); Plon, 1971); *Note:* See Chapter IX.

Maran, René (1887-1960); *Le Petit Roi de Chimérie* (*The Little King of Chimeria*; AM, 1924); Batouala (Guillot, 1947); *Bacouya le Cynocéphale* (AM, 1953)

Marbrouk, Alia (?-); *Le Futur est déjà là / Hurlement* (*The Future Is Already Here / Howling*; L'Entreligne, 1997); *Note:* Tunisian writer. Novellas written in 1992. See Chapter IX.

Marcel, Odile (?-); *L'Eau qui Dort* (*Sleeping Water*; Seuil, 1977); *L'Amazonie* (Seuil, 1981); *Note:* See Chapter VIII.

Marceron (Dr.) *see* **La Marche, Marc**

Marchand, Jacques-Laurent (?-); *Le Secret de Mesa Verde* (*The Secret of Mesa Verde*; Courteau, 1987); *Note:* French-Canadian writer. Esoteric novel.

Marchand, Léopold (?-?) *see* **Grand-Guignol**

Marchès, Léo (1870-1944) *see* **Grand-Guignol**

Marcotte, Gilles (1925-); *Le Poids de Dieu* (*The Weight of God*; Flamm., 1962); *Retour à Cooolbrook* (*Return to Coolbrook*; Flamm., 1965); *Un Voyage* (*A Journey*; Hurtubise, 1973); *La Vie Réelle* (*Real Life*; Boréal, 1989); *Note:* French-Canadian writer.

Marc-Py, Jean (?-) *see* **Deslinières, Lucien**

Marcy, Gérard (?-); *La Neige Bleue* (*The Blue Snow*; FNA 381, 1969); *La Force Secrète* (*The Secret Force*; FNA 409, 1970); *Vengeance en Symbiose* (*Symbiotic Revenge;* FNA 442, 1971); *Le Missile Hyperspatial* (*The Hyperspatial Missile*; FNA 491, 1972); *Note:* See Chapter IX.

Mardrus, Joseph-Charles-Victor (1868-1949); *La Reine de Saba* (*The Queen of Sheba*; Fasquelle, 1919); *Histoire d'Ali-Ben-Bekar et de la Belle Schamsennahar* (*Tale of Ali-Ben-Bekar and the Beautiful Schamsennahar*; Piazza, 1923); *Le Livre des Mille et Une Nuits* (*The Book of Thousand and One Nights*; Fasquelle, 1920-24); *Omrooulkays ou l'Homme à la Poigne d'Acier* (*The Man with the Hand of Steel*; Pensée Fr., 1924); *Histoire Charmante de l'Adolescente Sucre d'Amour* (*Charming Tale of the Young Love Sugar*; Fasquelle, 1927); *La Mariée Magique* (*The Magic Bride*; Sté. Bibl. Franco-Suisse, 1930); *Histoire de Kamaralzaman avec la Princesse Baudour* (*Tale of Kamaralzaman with the Princess Baudour*; Darantière, 1934); *Note:* See Chapter VI.

Marek, Lionel (?-); *L'An Prochain à Auschwitz* (*Next Year in Auschwitz*; Den., 1982); *Pourquoi Moi?* (*Why Me?*; Den., 1986)

Marès, Roland de (?-); *En Barbarie* (*Among the Barbarians*; 1895); *La Maison du Chanoine* (*The Priest's House*; MdF, 1936); *Note:* Belgian writer. See Chapter VI.

Marest Dampcourt, B. (?-); *La Découverte de l'Aérium* (*The Discovery of the Aerium*; "Bon Point Amusant," 1926); *Note:* Illustrated juvenile novel.

Marestan, Jean (?-); *Nora ou La Cité Interdite* (*The Forbidden City*; Provencia, 1950

Margerit, Robert (?-); *Nue et Nu* (*Naked Men and Women*; Le Grenier, 1936); *Une Âme Damnée* (*A Damned Soul*; Colbert, 1946); *Le Vin des Vendanges* (*Harvest Wine*; Cobert, 1946); *Phénix* (TR, 1946); *La Maison de la Mort* (*The House of Death*; Fayard, 1953); *La Salamandre Ernestine* (*Ernestine the Salamander*; Rougerie, 1953)**;** *Mont-Dragon* (*Mount Dragon*; Gall., 1973); *L'Île des Perroquets* (*Parrot Island*; LdP, 1974); *Par un Été Torride* (*In a Torrid Summer*; Rombaldi, 1978); *La Terre aux Loups* (*The Land of Wolves*; Phébus, 1986); *Le Château des Bois Noirs* (*The Castle of Dark Woods*;

Phébus, 1987); *Le Dieu Nu* (*The Naked God*; Phébus, 1988); *Les Hommes Perdus* (*The Lost Men*; Phébus, 1989); *L'Amour et le Temps* (*Love and Time*; Phébus, 1989); *Les Autels de la Peur* (*The Altars of Fear*; Phébus, 1989); *La Révolution* (*The Revolution*; Phébus, 1989); *Un Vent d'Acier* (*A Wind of Steel*; Phébus, 1989); *Les Amants* (*The Lovers*; Phébus, 1990); *Le Cortège des Ombres* (*The Procession of Shadows*; n.d.)

Maridat, Roger *see* **Verteuil, Éric**

Mariel, Pierre (Marie, Pierre-Maurice; 1897-?); *La Roue de la Mort* (*The Wheel of Death*; SET, 1926); *La Femme et la Nuit* (*The Woman and the Night*; SET, 1929); *Le Cargo de la Mort* (*The Cargo of Death*; with René **Jeanne**; RMY, 1929); *La Griffe du Lion* (*The Lion's Claw*; with René **Jeanne**; RMY, 1931); Robinson Junior (BGA, 1931); *Le Lévrier de la Mer* (*The Sea Greyhound*; BGA, 1930); *L'Éternelle Idole* (*The Eternal Idol*; Libr. Contemporaine, 1933); *La Couronne Brisée* (*The Broken Crown*; SEPIA, 1935); *Les Deux Visages* (*The Two Faces*; SEPIA, 1939)

Mariën, Marcel (1920-); *La Chaise de Sable* (*The Chair of Sand*; Invenion Collective, 1940); *L'Ance jetée dans le Doute* (*The Anchor Thrown in Doubt*; Lèvres Nues, 1972); *Figures de Poupe* (*Stern Figure*; Simoën, 1979); *Les Fantômes du Château de Cartes* (*The Phantoms of the House of Cards*; Julliard, 1981); *La Marche Palière* (*The Step March*; Le Temps qu'il fait, 1982); *La Licorne à Cinq Pattes* (*The Five-Legged Unicorn*; Lèvres Nues, 1986); *La Coupeuse de Souffle* (*The Breath Cutter*; Marée de la Nuit, 1987); *Troubles Têtes* (*Troubled Heads*; Lèvres Nues, 1988); *Dans la Peau du Miroir* (*In the Mirror's Skin*; Pierre d'Alun, 1988); *Note:* Belgian writer.

Marignac, Pascal (?-); *Mental* (as Kââ; FN, 1984); *Silhouettes de Mort sous la Lune Blanche* (*Dead Silhouettes Under a White Moon*; as Kââ; FN, 1984); *Il ne faut pas déclencher les Puissances Nocturnes et Bestiales* (*You Must Not Disturb the Nightly and Bestial Powers*; as Kââ; FN, 1985); *On Commencera à Tuer dans une Heure* (*They'll Start Killing in an Hour*; as Kââ; FN, 1986); *Respiration de la Haine* (*The Breathing of Hatred*; as Kââ; FN, 1986); *L'État des Plaies* (*The State of the Wounds*; as Corsélien; FNG 48, 1987); *Bruit Crissant du Rasoir sur les Os* (*The Grating Sound of Razor Over Bones*; as Corsélien; FNG 61, 1988); *Voyage au Bout du Jour* (*Voyage to the End of the Day*; as Béhémoth; Siry Maniac 3, 1988); *Retour du Bal à Dalstein* (*Back from the Ball in Dalstein*; as Corsélien; FNG 82, 1989); *Lésions Irréparables* (*Unrepairable Damages*; as Corsélien; FNG 106, 1990); *Trois Chiens Morts* (*Three Dead Dogs*; as Kââ; FN, 1992); *Dîner de Têtes* (*Dinner of Heads*; as Kââ; FN Angoisses 4, 1993); *Le Marteau* (*The Hammer*; as Kââ; FN, 1994); *Criant de*

Vérité (*Screaming with Truth*; as Kââ; FNFR 20, 1995); *24.000 Années* (*24,000 Years*; as Kââ; FNASF 10, 1996); *Note:* See Chapter VIII.

Marignac, Thierry (?-); *Milana* (FNASF 13, 1996)

Marillac, Alain (Legras, Alain; 1951-); Series *Dan Rixes*: *1. La Pyramide de l'Immatériel* (*The Pyramid of the Immaterial*; HMH, 1989); *2. La Nuit des Hougans* (*Night of the Hougans*; HMH, 1990); *3. OVNI à Matane* (*UFO in Matane*; HMH, 1990); *4.La Porte d'Émeraude* (*The Emerald Gate*; HMH, 1991); *5. La Loi du Miroir* (*The Law of the Mirror*; HMH, 1992); *6. Le Mur des Volontés* (*The Wall of Wills*; HMH, 1992); *Note:* French-Canadian writer. Series of young-adult novels featuring a stage magician who becomes the inheritor of the ancient Atlanteans' secrets.

Marivaux, Pierre Carlet de Chamblain de (1688-1763); *L'Île des Esclaves* (*The Islands of Slaves*; Noël Pissot, 1725); *L'Île de la Raison* (*The Island of Reason*; P. Prault, 1727); *Note:* Social utopias inspired by Swift.

Markalé, Jean (?-); *Les Celtes et la Civilisation Celtique* (*The Celts and Celtic Civilisation*; Payot, 1969); *L'Épopée Celtique d'Irlande* (*The Irish Celtic Sagas*; Payot, 1971); *La Tradition Celtique en Bretagne Armoricaine* (*Celtic Tradition in Armorican Britanny*; Payot, 1975); *Le Roi Arthur et la Société Celtique* (*King Arthur and the Celtic Society*; Payot, 1976); *Histoire Secrète de la Bretagne* (*Secret History of Britanny*; AM, 1977); *Contes Populaires de toutes les Bretagne* (*Popular Tales of the Entire Britanny*; Stock, 1980); *Merlin l'Enchanteur* (*Wizard Merlin*; Retz, 1981); *Le Graal* (*The Grail*; Retz, 1982); *Mélusine ou l'Androgyne* (*Melusine or the Androgyne*; Retz, 1983); *Siegfried ou l'Or du Rhin* (*Siegfried or the Rhine Gold*; Retz, 1984); *Le Christianisme Celtique et ses Survivances Populaires* (*Celtic Christianism and Its Popular Traditions*; Payot, 1984); *Lancelot et la Chevalerie Arthurienne* (*Lancelot and the Arthurian Chivalry*; Imago, 1985); *L'Épopée Celtique en Bretagne* (*Celtic Sagas in Britanny*; Payot , 1985); *Le Druidisme* (*The Druids*; Payot, 1985); *Gisors et l'Énigme des Templiers* (*Gisors and the Mystery of the Templars*; Pygmalion, 1986); *Montségur et l'Énigme Cathare* (*Montsegur and the Cathar Mystery*; Pygmalion, 1986); *Le Mont Saint-Michel et l'Énigme du Dragon* (*Mount Saint-Michael and the Mystery of the Dragon*; Pygmalion, 1987); *Carnac et l'Énigme de l'Atlantide* (*Carnac and the Atlantis Mystery*; Pygmalion, 1987); *Chartres et l'Énigme des Druides* (*Chartres and the Mystery of the Druids*; Pygmalion, 1988); *Brocéliande et l'Énigme du Graal* (*Broceliande and the Mystery of the Grail*; Pygmalion, 1989); *L'Énigme des Vampires* (*The Mystery of the Vampires*; Pygmalion, 1991); *Note:* See Chapters I and VIII.

Marlson, Pierre (Colson, Martial-Pierre; 1935-); *L'Empire du Peuple* (*The People's Empire*; with Michel **Jeury**/as Albert Higon; AMSF2 23, 1977); *Hyménophage* (Ponte Mirone, 1978); *Des Métiers d'Avenir* (*Future Jobs*; anthology; Ponte Mirone, 1979); *Désert* (Kes. I&M 6, 1979); *Les Compagnons de la Marciliague* (*The Companions of Marciliague*; Encre 3, 1979); *Note:* See Chapter IX.

Marmontel, Jean-François (1723-1799) *see* **Opéra**

Marois, Carmen (1951-); *L'Amateur d'Art* (*The Art Lover*; CdA 2, 1985); *Le Piano de Beethoven* (*Beethoven's Piano*; Q/A, 1991); *Un Dragon dans la Cuisine* (*A Dragon in the Kitchen*; Q/A, 1992); *Le Dossier Vert* (*The Green File*; HMH, 1992); *Le Fantôme de Mesmer* (*Mesmer's Ghost*; Q/A, 1993); *Le Bal des Ombres* (*Ball of Shadows*; anthology; Q/A, 1994); *Note:* French-Canadian writer. *L'Amateur* is a collection of fantastical tales. *Le Piano* is an amusing novel about young witches.

Marol (Marolle, Jean-Claude; 1946-); *Les Petits Chemins de la Veille-en-Bulle* (*The Little Roads of La Veille-en-Bulle*; Grasset, 1979); *Feudou Dragon Secret* (*Lowfire, Secret Dragon*; Ipomée, 1983); *La Tête Ailleurs* (*The Head Elsewhere*; Félin, 1984); *Pli Urgent* (*Urgent Letter*; L'Originel, 1985); *Le Saut de I'Ange Cascade* (*The Leap of the Angel Cascade*; Ipomée, 1985); *Secret* (Fourneau, 1986); *Le Blanc Vert* (*The Green White*; Terre Vivante, 1988); *Note:* Juveniles.

Marquet, Gabrielle (1923-); *Peau de Lapin* (*Rabbit Skin*; Den., 1952); *Les Oiseaux font bouger le Ciel* (*Birds Move the Sky*; Gall., 1961); *Le Sourd-Muet* (*The Deaf-Mute*; Gall., 1961); *La Cerise de Porcelaine* (*The Ceramic Cherry*; Flamm., 1966); *Les Martin-Pêcheurs* (*The King-Fishers*; Flamm., 1967); *Le Fauteuil à Bascule* (*The Rocking Chair*; Flamm., 1970); *L'Oeil de Déodat* (*Deodat's Eye*; Flamm., 1971); *La Boîte à Boutons* (*The Button Box*; Flamm., 1973); *Le Sine des Jumeaux* (*The Sign of the Twins*; Flamm., 1975); *Morte d'un Cadre* (*Executive Death*; Flamm., 1976); *La Poupée Phonographe* (*The Phonograph Doll*; Flamm., 1979); *Les Années Vermeil* (*The Vermilion Years*; Calmann-Lévy, 1984)

Marquis, Raoul *see* **Graffigny, Henry de**

Marrier, Guillemette (?-); *Nous n'irons plus au Bois* (*We Shall No Longer Go to the Woods*; Nlles. Presses Fr., 1946)

Marriott, Critenden (?-); *L'Île des Vaisseaux Perdus* (*The Island of Lost Ships*; Lafitte, 1923)

Marsais, Johanne (1946-1979); *Le Poids du Sang* (*The Weight of Blood*; Lueurs Mortes, 1995)

Marsan, Hugo (?-); *L'Arbre Mémoire* (*The Memory Tree*; Athanor, 1978)

Marsan, Stéphane (1970-); *L'Épreuve de l'Astramance* (*The Trial of the Astramance*; Mnemos 5, 1996); *La Cathédrale des Cimes* (*The Cathedral of the Summits*; Mnemos 8, 1996); *Les Miroirs de Cosme* (*The Mirrors of Cosme*; Mnemos 10, 1996); *Note:* See Chapter VIII.

Mars-Vallett, André-Édouard (?-); *Le Mystère du Foraisan* (*The Mystery of the Foraisan*; S&A 2, 1946)

Martel, Adrien (1914-); *Gil dans le Cosmos* (*Gil in the Cosmos*; Hatier JPA 9, 1971); *Gil Revient sur Terre* (*Gil Returns to Earth*; Hatier JPA 10, 1971); *Le Miracle du Fuji-Yama* (*The Miracle of the Fujiyama*; L'Amitié, 1974); *Fils du Mexique* (*Son of Mexico*; Messidor, 1982); *Note:* Juvenile SF. See Chapter IX.

Martel, Clément (1945-); *Magies du Temps et de l'Espace* (*Magics of Time and Space*; JCL, 1988); *Note:* French-Canadian writer. Collection of SF stories.

Martel, Dominique (?-) *see* **Klein, Gérard**

Martel, Julie (1973-); *Nadjal* (JP 96, 1995); *La Quête de la Crystale* (*The Quest of the Crystal*; JP 107, 1996); *Un Traître au Temple* (*A Traitor in the Temple*; JP, 1996); *Note:* French-Canadian writer.

Martel, Robert (1947-); *Louprecka* (Q/A, 1992); *Note:* French-Canadian writer. Juvenile fantasy.

Martel, Serge (?-); *L'Adieu aux Astres* (*Farewell to the Stars*; RF 57, 1958); *L'Aventure Alphéenne* (*The Alphean Adventure*; RF 67, 1960); *Les Fleurs Succombent en Arcadie* (*Flowers Die in Arcadia*; with Pierre **Dupriez**; Galliera 7, 1973); *Note:* See Chapter IX.

Martel, Suzanne (Chouinard, Suzanne; 1924-); *Surréal 3000* (*Quatre Montréalais en l'An 3000*); Jour, 1963; transl. as the *Underground City*, 1964); *Titralak, Cadet de l'Espace* (*Titralak, Space Cadet*; Héritage, 1974); *Nos Amis Robots* (*Our Friends the Robots*; Héritage, 1981); *L'Enfant de Lumière* (*The Child of Light*; Méridien, 1983); *Un Orchestre dans l'Espace* (*An Orchestra in Space*; Méridien, 1985); *Note:* French-Canadian writer. *Surréal* is about lifeunderground centuries after a nuclear war. *Un Orchestre* follows the adventures of young musicians on an alien world.

Martens, Thierri *see* **Varende, Yves**

Martial, Régine (?-?) *see* **Grand-Guignol**

Martigny, Comte de (?-); *Voyage d'Alcimédon, ou Naufrage qui Conduit au Port* (*Alcimedon's Journey, or Shipwreck That Led to the Harbor*; 1751; rep. VI, 1787); *Note:* Sub-titled "Story That Is More True Than Likely But That Could Provide Encouragement in the Search for Unknown Lands."

Martin, Christian (1962-); *Changement de Régime* (*Change of Regime*; L'A Venir, 1992); *L'Oeuf des Dieux* (*The Egg of the Gods*; Tisseyre, 1997); *Note:* French-Canadian writer. *Changement* is a collection of SF stories.

Martin, Sophie (1977-); *La Mission Einstein* (*The Einstein Mission*; with Annie **Millette**; Vents d'Ouest, 1996); *Note:* French-Canadian writer.

Martinès de Pasqually (?-?); *Traité de la Réintégration des Êtres dans leurs Premières Propriétés, Vertus et Puissances Spirituelles et Divines* (*Treatise of the Reintegration of Beings in Their First Properties, Virtues and Spiritual and Divine Powers*; Chacornac, 1899); *Note:* Satan succeeds in corrupting Adam and Eve.

Martini, Rodolphe (?-); *La Guerre Aérienne Berlin-Bagdad* (*The Aerial War Berlin-Baghdad*; Juven, 1907)

Martinigol, Danielle (?-); *L'Or Bleu* (*Blue Gold*; Hac., 1989); *Les Soleils de Bali* (*The Suns of Bali*; Hac., 1993); *Les Oubliés de Vulcain* (*Forgotten on Vulcan*; with Alain **Grousset**; LdP Jeunesse 541, 1995); *Kerri et Mégane et les Mange-Forêts* (*The Forest Eaters;* as Aldany, Kim/with Alain **Grousset**; Nathan, 1994) *Kerri et Mégane et les Transmiroirs* (*The Transmirrors*; as Aldany, Kim/with Alain **Grousset**; Nathan, 1996); *L'Enfant-Mémoire* (*The Memory Child*; as Aldany, Kim/with Alain **Grousset**; Hac., 1996); *Les Mondes Décalés* (*The Out-Of-Line Worlds*; with Alain **Grousset**; Flamm., 1997); *Kerri et Mégane—Brocantic Trafic* (as Aldany, Kim/with Alain **Grousset**; Nathan, 1997); *Note:* See Chapter IX.

Mas, André (?-); *Les Allemands sur Vénus* (*The Germans on Venus*; Pionnier?, 1914); Collection including: *Sous leur Double Soleil des Dryennes Chantent* (*Under Its Twin Suns, Dryans Sing*) / *Question* / *La Gardienne de la Double Lumière* (*The Guardian of the Double Light*) / *Sur le Vaisseau* (*Aboard the Ship*) / *La Reine Nyve aux Yeux Doux* (*Queen Nyve with Her Soft Eyes*) / *L'Obscur Devoir* (*The Obscure Duty*) / *La Mère* (*The Mother*) / *Le Cercle et la Croix* (*The Circle and the Cross*) / *Le Chant de l'Anniversaire* (*The Birthday Song*) / *La Bannière Étoilée qui Porte la Croix Blanche* (*The Star-Spangled Banner with a White Cross*; V. Attinger, 1922); *Dirméa, Le Monde des Vierges* (*Dimea, World of Virgins*; Chiberre, 1923); *Note:* See Chapter V.

Maskolo *see* **Natael**

Massacrier, Jacques (?-); *Le Goût du Temps qui Passe* (*The Taste of Time Passing*; AM, 1975); *Outre-Temps* (*Beyond Time*; Simoen, 1978); *Note:* See Chapter IX.

Massé, Johanne (1963-); *De l'Autre Côté de l'Avenir* (*From the Other Side of the Future*; JP 53, 1985; transl. as *Beyond the Future*, 1990); *Contre le Temps* (*Against Time*;

JP 58, 1987); *Le Passé en Péril* (*The Past in Danger*; JP 69, 1990); *Les Mots du Silence* (*The Words of Silence*; JP 84, 1993); *Note:* French-Canadian writer. All four books follow the adventures of space survivors and time-travelling Australians on a post-nuclear Earth and other eras.

Massepain, André (1917-); *La Fusée Mystérieuse* (*The Mysterious Rocket*; GP, 1959); *Le Derrick aux Abeilles* (*The Derrick of Bees*; GP, 1960); *Une Affaire Atomique* (*An Atomic Affair*; GP, 1961); *Le Secret de l'Étang* (*The Secret of the Pond*; GP, 1962); *La Grotte aux Ours* (*The Bear Cave*; GP, 1966); *L'Île aux Fossiles Vivants* (*The Island of the Living Fossils*; RL Plein Vent, 1967); *Les Flibustiers de l'Uranium* (*The Uranium Pirates*; RL Plein Vent, 1974); *Légends de la Grèce Antique and de Rome* (*Legends from Ancient Greece and Rome*; Hac., 1977); *Les Mille et Une Nuits* (*The 1001 Nights*; Bordas, 1979); *Un Lion chez le Coiffeur* (*A Lion at the Hairdresser*; Magnard, 1981); *Le Rayon des Étoiles* (*The Star Ray*; Magnard, 1982); *Note:* Juvenile SF. See Chapter IX.

Massiéra, Léopold (1920-); *L'Énigme des Soucoupes Volantes* (*The Mystery of the Flying Saucers*; MRA, 1953); *La Course aux Étoiles* (*Race for the Stars*; MRA, 1953); *Le Secret de l'Atome* (*The Secret of the Atom*; MRA, 1954); *Le Monde des Abîmes* (*The World of the Abyss*; MRA, 1954); *Les Troupeaux de la Lune* (*The Cattle of the Moon*; MRA, 1955); *Les Voleurs d'Océan* (*The Ocean Stealers*; MRA, 1955); *Les Chevaliers du Ciel* (*The Sky Knights*; MRA, 1955); *Le Guide de l'Avenir* (*The Guide from the Future*; MRA, 1956); *Note:* See Chapter IX.

Massieu, Léon (?-); *La Cité des Automates* (*City of Automatons*; 1923)

Massin, Paul *see* **Villette, André**

Masson, Émile (?-); *Utopie des Îles Bienheureuses dans le Pacifique en l'An 1980* (*Utopia of the Bienheureuses Islands in the Pacific in the Year 1980);* Rieder, 1921)

Masson, Gilles (?-); *La Machination* (*The Machination*; Ed. Fr. Réunis, 1973); *La Ballade d'Hiver* (*The Winter Ballad*; Ed. Fr. Réunis, 1976); *Aux Dernières Nouvelles* (*Latest News*; Sagittaire, 1978)

Mathieu, Claude (1930-1985); *La Mort Exquise* (*The Exquisite Death*; CLF, 1965); *Note:* French-Canadian writer. This is a collection of fantastical stories.

Mathon, Bernard (?-); *Locogringo Troisième* (*Third Locogringo*; CRNI, 1992); *Note:* Collection of SF stories.

Matieson, Budy *see* **Mantey, Christian**

Matignon, Bernard (1944-); *Les Soldats de Bois* (*The Wood Soldiers*; Fayard, 1972); *Une Mort qui fait du Bruit* (*A Noisy Death*; Fayard, 1974)

Matip, Benjamin (?-); *À la Belle Étoile* (*Under the Night Sky*; Présence Africaine, 1962); *Note:* Cameroon writer. See Chapter VIII.

Mativat, Daniel (1944-); *Ram, le Robot* (*Ram the Robot*; with Marie-Andrée **Boucher-Mativat**; Héritage, 1984); *Le Fantôme du Rocher* (*The Ghost of the Rock*; with Marie-Andrée **Boucher-Mativat**; Hurtubise, 1992); *L'Ankou ou l'Ouvrier de la Mort* (*The Ankou, or Death's Worker*; Tisseyre, 1996); *Note:* French-Canadian writer. *Ram* is a children's book about a robot who eventually becomes human.

Matthis, Charles-Émile (?-?); *Les Héros de l'Avenir* (*Heroes of the Future*; Jouvet, 1886); *Pique-Toto, La Paix et la Guerre* (*Peace and War*; Jouvet, 1888)

Mauclair, Camille (Faust, Camille Laurent Séverin; 1872-1945); *Couronne de Clarté, Roman Féerique* (*Crown of Light, a Novel of the Faery*; Ollendorff, 1895); *L'Orient Vierge, Roman Épique de l'An 2000* (*Virgin Orient, Epic Novel of the Year 2000);* Ollendorff, 1897); *Les Clefs d'Or* (*Le Triomphe dans les Ténèbres; The Gold Keys* (*Triumph in the Darkness)*; Ollendorff, 1897); *Le Soleil des Morts* (*The Sun of the Dead*; Ollendorff, 1898); *L'Ennemie des Rêves* (*The Dream Foe*; Ollendorff, 1900); *Note:* See Chapter IV.

Mauclère, Jean (?-); *La Voie qui Monte* (*The Uplifting Way*; Bonne Presse, 1917); *L'Infernale* (*The Infernal*; Plon, 1923); *La Sorcière d'Oya* (*The Witch of Oya*; Bonne Presse, 1924); *Tiotis aux Yeux de Mer* (*Tiotis of the Sea Eyes*; Plon, 1925); *La Maison du Solitaire* (*The House of the Lonely Man*; Mode Nationale, 1926); *Le Navire sans Nom* (*The Nameless Ship*; BGA, 1928); *La Mer Jasait* (*The Sea Whispered*; Gautier-Languereau, 1928); *La Fée aux Ruines* (*The Fairy of the Ruins*; Bonne Presse, 1931); *Le Talisman des Guernis* (*The Talisman of the Guernis*; Bonne Presse, 1941); *La Vision de Mona* (*Mona's Vision*; n.d.)

Maudru, P. (?-); *L'Homme aux Deux Têtes* (*The Man with Two Heads*; with H. **Lompech**; RMY, 1930

Mauffret, Yvon (1927-); *Le Mousse du Bateau Perdu* (*The Cabin Boy of the Lost Ship*; Amitié, 1973); *Benoit chez les Blubulles* (*Benoit Among the Blububbles*; Amitié, 1979); *Une Audacieuse Expédition* (*A Daring Expedition*; Amitié, 1982); *Contes de Noël* (*Christmas Tales*; Amitié, 1987); *Le Jardin des Enfants Perdus* (*The Garden of Lost Children*; Milan 1989); *Note:* Juveniles.

Mauhourat, Jean (?-); *Le Singe Jaune* (*The Yellow Monkey*; MOC 26, 1982)

Maupassant, Guy de (1850-1893); *Contes Fantastiques*

Complets (*Complete Fantastic Stories*; MarF 464, 1973); *Note:* See chapters IV and V. Also see **Grand-Guignol** for stage-play adaptations. Maupassant's genre tales include: "La Main Écorchée" ("The Flayed Hand"; 1875; rev. as "La Main" ("The Hand"; 1883), "Sur l'Eau" ("On the Water"; 1876), "Magnétisme" (1882), "La Peur" ("The Fear"; 1882), "Le Loup" ("The Wolf"; 1882), "Conte de Noël" ("Xmas Tale"; 1882), "Auprès d'un Mort" ("Near a Deadman"; 1882), "L'Apparition" ("The Ghost"; 1883), "Lui?" ("Him?"; 1883), "Un Fou?" ("A Madman?"; 1884), "L'Auberge" ("The Inn"; 1886), "Le Horla" (1886), "Le Diable" ("The Devil", "La Morte" ("The Dead Woman"; 1887), "La Nuit" ("The Night"; 1887), "L'Homme de Mars" ("The Man from Mars"; 1888), "L'Endormeuse" ("The Hypnotist"; 1889) and "Qui Sait?" ("Who Knows?"; 1890).

Maurel, Jean-Pierre (?-); *Le Diable sur la Neige* (*The Devil on the Snow*; Stock, 1981); *Note:* Collection of fantastical tales.

Maurette, Marcelle (?-?); *Le Roi Christine* (Billaudot, 1944); *Anastasia* (Buchet-Chastel, 1957); *La Possédée* (*The Woman Possessed*; Dauphin, 1972); *Note: Anastasia* is a fairy-tale play in 3 acts. Also see **Grand-Guignol**.

Maurevert, Georges (1869-?); *Légendes et Nouvelles Tragiques ou Folâtres* (*Legends and Tragic or Fantastical Stories*; H. Floury, 1910); *Note:* Also see **Grand-Guignol**.

Maurey, Max (1868-1947); *Les Aventures de M. Haps* (*The Adventures of Mr. Haps*; with George **Jubin**; Monde Ill., 1908); *Le Pharmacien* (*The Pharmacist*; Stock, 1933); *La Délaissée* (*The Abandoned Woman*; Libr. Théâtrale, 1991); *Note:* Also see **Grand-Guignol**.

Maurière, Gabriel *see* **Legrand, Henri**

Mauriès, Dominique (?-); *La Griffe* (*The Claw*; SdP 2 98, 1979); *Le Soleil Piétiné* (*The Trampled Sun*; SdP 2 143, 1989); *Note:* Juvenile.

Mauris, Jules (?-?) *see* **Grand-Guignol**

Maurois, André (Herzog, Émile Salomon; 1885-1967); *Le Chapitre Suivant* (*The Next Chapter*; Sagittaire, 1927); *Voyage au Pays des Articoles* (Schiffrin, 1927; rev. Gall., 1928; transl. as *A Voyage to the Island of the Articoles*, 1928); *Deux Fragments d'Une Histoire Universelle 1992* (*Two Fragments of an Universal History*; Portiques, 1928; transl. included in *The Weigher of Souls*; *Le Pays des 36.000 Volontés* (*The Country of 36,000 Wills*; Portiques, 1928); *Patapoufs et Filifers* (Hartmann, 1930); *Relativisme* (Kra, 1930; transl. as *A Private Universe*, 1932); *Le Peseur d'Âmes* (Gall., 1931; transl. as *The Weigher of Souls and the Earth Dwellers*, 1963); *Mes Songes Que Voici* (*Here Are My Dreams*; Grasset,

1932); *La Machine à Lire les Pensées* (Gall., 1937; transl. as *The Thought-Reading Machine*, 1938); *Toujours l'Inattendu Arrive* (*Always Expect the Unexpected*; Deux-Rives, 1946); *Les Mondes Impossibles* (*The Impossible Worlds*; Gall., 1947); *Nico, le Petit Garçon changé en Chien* (*Nico, the Little Boy Changed Into a Dog*; Calmann-Lévy, 1955); *Note:* See Chapter VII.

Mauvert, G. (?-?) *see* **Grand-Guignol**

Mauzan, L. A. (?-); *L'Hallucinant Pouvoir de Rupert Saint-Georges* (*The Mind-Boggling Power of Rupert Saint-Georges*; Arthaud, 1945)

Mauzens, Frédéric (1874-?); *Le Coffre-Fort Vivant* (*The Living Safe*; Flamm., 1907); *Les Reptiles de Paris* (*The Reptiles of Paris*; Flamm., 1910); *La Nouvelle Aventure du Coffre-Fort Vivant* (*The New Adventure of the Living Safe*; Flamm., 1925)

Max, Paul (?-); *Volcar le Terrible* (*Volcar the Terrible*; 1913); *Note:* See Chapter V.

Mayer, Chevalier Charles-Joseph de (?-?); Editor and publisher of the first specialized fantasy imprint in history: *Le Cabinet des Fées* (*Fairies' Cabinet*; 41 vols., 1785-89). See *Cabinet des Fées* and Chapter III.

Maynat, Nicole (?-); *Le Conte du Pays des Pas Perdus* (*The Tale of the Country of Lost Steps*; Nicole Maynat, 1974); *L'Histoire d'Héliacynthe* (*Heliacynth's Story*; Ipomée, 1979); *Le Gang des Chenilles Rouges* (*The Gang of the Red Caterpillars*; Ipomée, 1981); *L'Histoire de Lilas* (*Lilac's Story*; Ipomée, 1984); *Maco des Grands Bois* (*Maco of the Great Wood*; Ipomée, 1985); *Note:* Juveniles.

Maynial, Édouard *see* **Avril, Jean d'**

Mayviel, Guy (?-); *Au Beau Château Dormant* (*At the Beautiful Sleeping Castle*; A. Colin, 1924); *Le Grand Serpent de Mer* (*The Great Sea Serpent*; A. Colin, 1928)

Mazarin, Jean (Rey, René-Charles; 1934-); *Pas Même un Dieu* (*Not Even a God*; FNA 750, 1976); *Le Général des Galaxies* (*The Galactic General*; FNA 769, 1977); *Un Fils pour la Lignée* (*A Son for the Line*; FNA 790, 1977); *Un Monde de Chiens* (*A World of Dogs*; FNA 817, 1977); *L'Univers Fêlé* (*The Fractured*

Universe; FNA 865, 1978); *Libérez l'Homme!* (*Free Man!*; FNA 902, 1979); *Les Cités d'Apocalypse* (*The Cities of the Apocalypse*; FNA 940, 1979); *Greffe-moi l'Amour!* (*Graft Me Love!*; FNA 978, 1980); *Vive les Surhommes!* (*Long Live the Supermen!*; FNA 1007, 1980); *Avant-Poste* (*Outpost*; FNA 1090, 1981); *En Une Eternité...* (*In an Eternity...*; FNA 1103, 1981); *Haute-Ville* (*High-City*; FNA 1142, 1982); *Nausicaa* (FNA 1171, 1982); *Les Prophètes de l'Apocalypse* (*The Prophets of the Apocalypse*; FNA 1218, 1983); *Un Bonheur qui Dérape* (*A Stumbling Happiness*; FNA 1248, 1983); *L'Histoire Détournée* (*The Hijacked History*; FNA 1270, 1984); *Patrouilles* (*Patrols*; FNA 1310, 1984); *L'Âge à Rebours* (*The Backwards Age*; FNA 1358, 1985); *Poupée Tueuse* (*Killer Doll*; FNA 1386, 1985); *Blood Sex* (as Charles Nécrorian; FNG 5, 1985); *Poupée Cassée* (*Broken Doll*; FNA 1447, 1986); *Impacts* (as Charles Nécrorian; FNG 30, 1986); *Skin Killer* (as Charles Nécrorian; FNG 56, 1987); *L'Hiver en Juillet* (*Winter in July;* as Emmanuel Errer; Siry SF 7, 1988; rev. as *Le Baigneur* (*The Bather*; FN Angoisses 5, 1993); *Inquisition* (as Charles Nécrorian; FNG 63, 1988); *Blood Sex 2* (as Charles Nécrorian; FNG 91, 1989); *Note:* See chapters VIII and IX.

Meaulle, Fortuné-Louis (?-?); *Le Robinson des Airs* (*The Robinson of the Air*; Ducrocq, 1880); *Perdus dans la Grande Ville* (*Lost in the Big City*; Mame, 1891); *Petite Maga* (*Little Maga*; Ducrocq, 1891)

Meckert, Jean *see* **Amila, John**

Mège-Privet, Odile (?-) *see* ***Contes et Légendes***

Meheust, Bertrand (?-); *Science-Fiction et Soucoupes Volantes* (*Science-Fiction and Flying Saucers*; MdF, 1978)

Meilhac, Henri (1831-1897) *see* **Opéra**

Meirs, George (?-); *Le Cadavre Assassin* (*The Murderous Corpse*; RM, 1912); *Une Main dans la Nuit* (*A Hand in the Night*; RM, 1912); *Le Manoir Hanté* (*The Haunted Manor*; RM, 1912); *L'Antre d'Épouvante* (*The Lair of Terror*; RM, 1913); *L'Homme aux Deux Corps* (*The Man with Two Bodies*; RM, 1913); *L'Affolante Minute* (*The Alarming Minute*; RM, 1913); *La Main Fantôme* (*The Ghostly Hand*; RM, 1913); *L'Ombre qui Tue* (*The Killing Shadow*; RM, 1913); *Le Secret de la Momie* (*The Secret of the Mummy*; RM, 1913); *La Carte Sanglante* (*The Bloody Card*; RM, 1913); *Les Vampires* (with Louis **Feuillade**; serialized as 4 vols., Tallandier, 1916): *I. La Tête Coupée* (*The Cut-Off Head*); *2. Le Spectre; 3. Les Yeux Qui Fascinent* (*The Eyes That Fascinate*); *4. Satanas; Note:* Les Vampires is a novelization of **Feuillade**'s notorious serial (see Book 1, Chapter I).

Mélesville (Duveyrier, Anne-Honoré-Joseph; ?-?) *see* **Opéra**

Mendès, Catulle (?-?); *Zo'Har* (1886); *La Première Maîtresse* (*The First Mistress*; 1887); *Note:* See Chapter IV. Also see **Opéra**

Menez, Yann (?-); *Arphadax le Khour* (FNSL 4, 1974); *La Révolte des Logars* (*The Logars' Revolt*; FNA 660, 1975); *Un Monde de Héros* (*A World of Heroes*; FNSL 14, 1975); *Appelez-moi Dieu* (*Call Me God*; FNSL 18, 1976); *Demandez le Programme* (*Ask for the Program*; FNA 990, 1980); *Ballade pour un Glandu* (*Ballad for a Loser*; FNA 1010, 1980); *Note:* See Chapter IX.

Méon, D. M. (?-?); *Le Roman de Renart* (*The Novel of Reynart*; 4 vols.; Treuttel & Würtz, 1828); *Note:* See Chapter I.

Méra, Robert Georges *see* **Georges-Méra, Robert**

Merault, Maurice (?-); *Meurtres Transtemporels* (*Transtemporal Murders*; MOC 19, 1980); *L'Être de la Grande Spirale* (*The Being from the Great Spiral*; MOC 23, 1982); *Note:* See Chapter IX.

Mercier, Alain (?-); *Le Fantastique dans la Poésie Française* (*Fantasy in French Poetry*; anthology; La Pibole-J. Gouézec, 1980); *Note:* Collection of fantastical poems.

Mercier, André-Charles (?-?) *see* **Grand-Guignol**

Mercier, Louis-Sébastien (1740-1814); *L'An 2440, Rêve s'il en fut jamais* (*The Year 2440, a Dream If There Ever Was*; Van Harrevelt, 1771, rev. Lepetit & Gérard, 1786; transl. as *Memoirs of the Year 2500*, 1772); *Vathek* (Conte Arabe; Poinçot, 1787); *Voyages Imaginaires, Songes, Visions et Romans Cabalistiques* (*Imaginary Journeys, Dreams, Visions and Cabalistic Novels*; Paris & Amsterdam, 1788); *Note:* See Chapter III.

Mercier, Mario (?-); *La Cuvée de Singes* (*A Bucketful of Monkeys*; Civilisations Nouvelles, 1970); *Le Nécrophile* (Martineau, 1970); *L'Odyssée Fantastique d'Arthur Dément* (*Arthur Dement's Fantastic Odyssey*; Los., 1976); *Les Fêtes Cosmiques* (*Cosmic Feasts*; Dangles, 1985); *Le Souffle de l'Ange* (*The Angel's Breath*; Belles Lettres, 1996); *Note:* See Chapter VIII. Mario Mercier was one of the editors of the magazine *Horizons du Fantastique*; he also directed ***La Goulve*** (1971) and ***La Papesse*** (1974); see Book 1, Chapter I.

Méré, Charles (1883-1970) *see* **Grand-Guignol**

Méric, Victor (?-); *Les Bandits Tragiques* (*Tragic Bandits*; Kra, 1926); *Le Crime des Vieux* (*Old Folks' Crime*; Ed. De France, 1927); *La Der des Der* (*The Next Last War*; Ed. De France, 1929); *Les Compagnons de l'Escopette* (*The Brotherhood of the Rifle*; L'Épi, 1930); *Note:* See Chapter VII.

Merillac, Landry (1943-); *Les Sept Soleils de l'Archipel Humain* (*The Seven Suns of the Human Archipelago*; MarSF 449, 1973); *Note:* See Chapter IX.

Mérimée, Prosper (1803-1870); *Théâtre de Clara Gazul* (Sautelet, 1825); *La Guzla ou Choix de Poésies Illyriennes* (*La Guzla or Selection of Illyrian Poetry*; Levrault, 1827); *La Jaquerie (Scènes Féodales; The Jaquerie—Feudal Scenes*; Brissot-Thivars, 1828); *Chronique du Temps de Charles IX* (*Chronicles of the Times of Charles IX*; Alexandre Mesnier, 1829); *Vision de Charles X* (*Vision of Charles X*; in *Revue de Paris*, 1829); *Tamango* (in *Revue de Paris*, 1829); *Federigo* (in *Revue de Paris*, 1829); *Les Sorcières Espagnoles* (*The Spanish Witches*; in *Revue de Paris*, 1833); *Les Âmes du Purgatoire* (*The Souls of Purgatory*; in *Revue des Deux Mondes*, 1834); *La Vénus d'Ille* (*The Venus of Ille*; in *Revue des Deux Mondes*, 1837); *Lokis, le Manuscrit du Professeur Wittenbach* (*Lokis, or Prof. Wittenbach's Manuscript*; in *Revue des Deux Mondes*, 1869); *La Chambre Bleue* (*The Blue Room*; 1872); *Djoumâne* (wri. 1870); publ. in *Les Dernières Nouvelles de Prosper Mérimée* (*The Last Short Stories of Prosper Mérimee*, M. Lévy, 1873); *Il Viccolo di Madama Lucrezia* (in *Les Dernières Nouvelles de Prosper Mérimée* (*The Last Short Stories of Prosper Mérimee*, M. Lévy, 1873); *Note:* See Chapter IV.

Mérinos *see* **Mouton, Eugène**

Merle, Robert (1908-); *Un Animal Doué de Raison* (*An Animal Gifted with Reason*; Gall., 1968; transl. as *Day of the Dolphin*, 1969); *Derrière la Vitre* (*Behind the Glass*; Tallandier, 1971); *La Mort est mon Métier* (*Death Is My Business*; Gall., 1972); *Malevil* (Gall., 1972; transl. as *Malevil*, 1974); *L'Île* (*The Island*; Gall., 1974); *Les Hommes Protégés* (*The Protected Men*; Gall., 1974; transl. as *The Virility Factor*, 1977); *Madrapour* (Gall., 1976); *Le Prince que voilà* (*That Prince*; Plon, 1982); *Homme Invisible, Pour qui chantes-tu?* (*Invisible Man, for Whom Do You Sing?*; Grasset, 1984); *Flaminco: Sysyphe et la Mort* (*Sysyphus and Death*; Gall., 1986); *Le Jour ne se lève pas pour nous* (*Day Shall Not Rise for Us*; Plon, 1986); *L'Idole* (*The Idol*; Plon, 1987); *Le Propre de l'Homme* (*The Proper of Man*; Fallois, 1989); *Le Mort et le Vif / Nanterre la Folie* (*The Dead and the Quick / Crazy Nanterre*; Fallois, 1992); *L'Enfant-Roi* (*The Child-King*; Fallois, 1993); *Note:* See Chapter IX.

Day of the Dolphin was filmed by Mike Nichols in 1973. *Malevil* was adapted into an eponymous 1980 film (see Book 1, Chapter I).

Merrick, Hélène (1956-); *Les Larmes de Glace* (*The Tears of Ice*; Gall., 1988)

Merrien, Jean *see* **Paulin, Christophe**

Méry, G. (?-?) *see* **Opéra**

Meslin, Pascal (?-); *Accident de Référence* (*Referential Accident*; MdF, 1978)

Messac, Régis (1883-1943); *Quinzinzinzili* (Fenêtre Ouverte, 1935; rep. JCL, 1972); *Micromégas* (Imprim. La Laborieuse, 1936); *La Cité des Asphyxiés* (*The City of the Asphyxiated*; Fenêtre Ouverte, 1937; rep. JCL, 1972); *Pot-Pourri Fantôme* (*Ghostly Potpourri*; Bellenand, 1958); *Valcrétin* (JCL, 1973); *Note:* See Chapter VII.

Messager, Charles *see* **Vildrac, Charles**

Métayé, Jean (?-?) *see* **Grand-Guignol**

Métayer, Philippe (1946-); *L'Orpailleur de Blood Alley* (*The Gold Prospector of Blood Alley*; CLF, 1974); *Note:* French-Canadian writer.

Méténier, Oscar (1859-1913); *Barbe-Bleue* (*Blue-Beard*; Dentu, 1893); *Andrée: L'Amour qui Tue* (*The Killing Love*; Dentu, 1898); *Note:* Also see **Grand-Guignol**.

Mettais, Hippolyte (Dr.; ?-); *L'An 5865 ou Paris dans 4000 Ans* (*The Year 5865 or Paris in 4000 Years*; Libr. Centrale, 1865); *Paris avant le Déluge* (*Paris Before the Flood*; Libr. Centrale, 1866); *Le Secret des Catacombes* (*The Secret of the Catacombs*; Dentu, 1877); *Note:* See Chapter V.

Mettra (?-); *L'Ombre Inaccessible* (*The Unreachable Shadow*; with **Nubé**; L'Intrepide, 1931-32); *Note:* Sax Rohmer pastiche.

Meung, Jean (Clopinel) dit de (14th Century); *Le Roman de la Rose* (*The Romance of the Rose*; Le Roy, 1485); *Note:* See Chapter I.

Meurville, Louis de (?-); *La Cité Future* (*The Future City*; Plon, 1910); *Note:* See Chapter V.

Meyan, Paul (?-?) *see* **Mainard, Louis**

Meyer, J. (?-); *Le Bouchu et Ceux d'Ailleurs* (*The Bouchu and Those from Beyond*; Sat, 1960)

Meynard, Yves (1964-); *Sous des Soleils Étrangers* (*Under Alien Suns*; anthology/with Claude J. **Pelletier**; Ianus, 1989); *Orbite d'Approche 1* (*Near Orbit 1);* with Claude J. **Pelletier**; anthology; Ianus, 1992); *Orbite d'Approche 2* (*Near Orbit 2);* with Claude J. **Pelletier**; anthology; Ianus, 1993); *Orbite d'Approche 3* (*Near Orbit 3);* with

Claude J. **Pelletier**; anthology; Ianus, 1994); *La Rose du Désert* (*The Desert Rose*; Le Passeur, 1995); *Le Mage des Fourmis* (*The Magus of the Ants*; JP 105, 1995); *Chanson pour une Sirène* (*Song for a Siren*; with Élisabeth **Vonarburg**; Vents d'Ouest, 1995); *Escales sur Solaris* (*Shore Leave on Solaris*; anthology; with Joël **Champetier**; Vent d'Ouest, 1995); *Le Vaisseau des Tempêtes* (*The Ship of the Storms*; JP 113, 1996); *Le Prince des Glaces* (*The Prince of the Ice*; JP 114, 1996); *Un Oeuf d'Acier* (*An Egg of Steel*; Vents d'Ouest, 1997); *Le Fils du Margrave* (*The Son of the Margrave*; JP 118, 1997); *Orbite d'Approche 4* (*Near Orbit 4); with Claude J. **Pelletier**; anthology; Protoculture, 1997); *Note:* French-Canadian writer. Meynard's *The Book of Knights* was written in English and published in America by Tor in February 1998.

Meynier, Yvonne (?-); *L'Hélicoptère du Petit Duc* (*The Little Duke's Helicopter*; Magnard, 1962); *Erika des Collines* (*Erika of the Hills*; GP, 1964); *La Leçon de Silence* (*The Lesson of Silence*; Hatier, 1970); *Delphine, Reine de la Lumière* (*Delphine, Queen of Light*; Magnard, 1972); *Le Voyage Imaginaire* (*The Imaginary Journey*; Magnard, 1973); *L'Arbre aux Ancêtres* (*The Ancestors' Tree*; Magnard, 1976); *L'Aventure, Nathalie* (*The Adventure, Nathalie*; GP, 1976); *Le Petit Garçon qui avait perdu son Nom* (*The Little Boy Who Had Lost His Name*; Magnard, 1980); *Note:* Juvenile fantasy.

Meyrat, Nicolas (?-); *Le Faquir* (LPT/Hac., 1900)

Mézière, J. J. (?-); *Satellite Lune* (*Moon Satellite*; MarJ 63, 1955); *Note:* See Chapter IX.

Michaud, Nando (1943-); *Les Montres Sont Molles, Mais les Temps sont Durs* (*The Watches Are Soft, But Times Are Tough*; Tisseyre, 1988); *Le Mystère de la Chambre Froide* (*The Mystery of the Cold Room*; Balzac, 1995); *Note:* French-Canadian writer. *Les Montres* is a satirical time-travel story.

Michaux, Henri (1899-1984); *Fables des Origines* (*Fables from the Origins*; Disque Vert, 1924); *Ecuador* (Gall., 1929); *Un Certain Monsieur Plume* (*A Certain Mr. Feather*; Carrefour, 1930); *Un Barbare en Asie* (*A Barbarian in Asia*; Gall., 1932); *La Nuit Remue* (*Night Moves*; Gall., 1935); *Voyage en Grande Garabagne* (*Voyage in Great Garabagne*; Gall., 1936); *Entre Centre et Absence* (*Between Center and Absent*; Technique du Livre, 1936); *Sifflets dans le Temple* (*Whistles in the Temple*; GLM, 1936); *La Ralentie* (*Slowing Down*; GLM, 1937); *Au Pays de la Magie* (*In the Land of Magic*; Gall., 1941); *Je vous écris d'un Pays Lointain* (*I'm Writing to You from a Far-Away Land*; Bettencourt, 1942); *Épreuves, Exorcismes* (*Trials, Exorcisms*; Gall., 1943); *Labyrinthes* (Godet, 1944); *Le Lobe des Monstres* (*The Monsters' Lobe*; L'Arbalète, 1944); *Ici, Pod-*

dema (*Here, Poddema*; H.-L. Mermod, 1946); *Apparitions* (Point du Jour, 1946); *Ailleurs* (*Elsewhere*; Gall., 1948); *La Vie dans les Plis* (*Life in the Folds*; Gall., 1949); *Tranches de Savoir* (*Slices of Knowledge*; Les Pas Perdus, 1950); *Cas de Folie Circulaire* (*A Case of Circular Madness*; New York, 1952); *Nouvelles de l'Étranger* (*News from Abroad*; MdF, 1952); *Face aux Verrous* (*Facing the Deadbolts*; Gall., 1954); *Misérable Miracle* (*Miserable Miracle*; Rocher, 1956); *L'Infini Turbulent* (*The Turbulent Infinity*; MdF, 1957); *Vents et Poussières* (*Wind and Dust*; 1962); *Moments: Traversées du Temps* (*Moments: Crossing Through Time*; Gall., 1973); *Quand Tombent les Toits* (*When Roofs Fall*; GLM, 1973); *Les Ravagés* (*The Ravaged*; Fata Morgana, 1976); *Jours de Silence* (*Silent Days*; Fata Morgana, 1978); *Le Jardin Exalté* (*The Exalted Garden*; Fata Mogana, 1983); *Fille de la Montagne* (*Daughter of the Mountain;* M.D., 1984); *La Nuit Remue* (*Night Moves*; Gall., 1987); *En Songeant à l'Avenir* (*Thinking of the Future*; Échoppe, 1994); *Note:* Belgian writer and poet. See chapters VI and VIII.

Michel, André (?-); *L'Or Noir* (*The Black Gold*; Ferenczi, 1931); *Le Mystère de la Pyramide* (*The Mystery of the Pyramid*; PRA, 1936); *Le Royaume Imaginaire* (*The Imaginary Kingdom*; VA, 1936); *L'Oiseau du Pôle* (*The Bird of the Pole*; VA, 1937); *Le Secret de l'Hypogée* (*The Secret of the Hypogy*; VA, 1937); *Le Secret de Tokita* (*The Secret of Tokita*; Ferenczi, 1937); *La Danse du Sang* (*The Dance of Blood*; Ferenczi, 1937); *L'Homme du Hoggar* (*The Man from the Hoggar*; Ferenczi, 1938); *Le Maître des Sables* (*The Master of the Sands*; Ferenczi, 1938); *Au Coeur du Cyclone* (*In the Heart of the Hurricane*; Ferenczi, 1938); *Le Secret des Kerguelen* (*The Secret of the Kerguelen*; Ferenczi, 1938); *Le Pôle Tragique* (*The Tragic Pole*; PRA, 1939); *Le Trésor d'Angkor* (*The Treasure of Angkor*; Ferenczi, 1939); *Le Secret des Huit* (*The Secret of the Eight*; Ferenczi, 1939); *Le Dieu Vivant* (*The Living God*; VA, 1940); *Les Secrets du Yang-Tsé* (*The Secrets of the Yang-Tse*; Ferenczi, 1940); *Note:* See Chapter VII.

Michel, Francisque (?-?); *Tristan: Recueil de ce qui reste des poèmes relatifs à ses Aventures* (*Tristan: Collection of What Remains of the Poems Relating His Adventures*; Techener, 1835-39); *La Chanson de Roland* (*The Song of Roland*; Techener, 1837); *Note:* See Chapter I.

Michel, Jacques-Tristan (?-); *La Terre de chez Nous* (*Our Earth*; Debresse, 1939); *L'Odyssée Extraordinaire* (*The Extraordinary Odyssey*; Le Chardon, 1945); *La Vie Recommence* (*Life Begins Again*; Notre-Dame, 1945)

Michel, José (Carpouzis (Mme.); ?-); *La Dernière Fuite* (*The Last Flight*; FNAG 138, 1966); *Mon Fauteuil à Trois Roues* (*My Three-Wheeled Chair*; FNAG 149,

1968); *Le Démon qui m'habite* (*The Demon Inside Me*; FNAG 158, 1968); *Clinique pour Pauvres* (*Paupers' Clinic*; FNAG 168, 1969); *Mon Cimetière* (*My Cemetery*; FNAG 175, 1970); *L'Ostal du Mystère* (*The Hotel of Mystery*; FNAG 191, 1970); *Note:* See Chapter VIII.

Michel, Louise (1830-1905); *Légendes et Chants de Geste Canaques* (*Kanak Legends and Sagas*; Kéva, 1885); *Le Monde Nouveau* (*The New World*; Dentu, 1888); *Note:* See Chapter V.

Michel, Natacha (?-); *Le Repos de Penthésilée* (*Penthesileus' Rest*; Gall., 1980)

Michel, V. L. (?-); *L'Invention qui Tue* (*The Killing Invention*; Belles Éditions, 1937)

Michela, Ime (?-); *L'Aventure est au Coin du Ciel* (*Adventure Waits at the Sky's Corner*; STAEL, 1948); *Dyara, l'Homme-Panthère* (*Dyara, the Panther-Man*; STAEL, 1949)

Michelet, Victor Émile (?-); *La Possédée* (*The Possessed Woman*; Figuière, n.d.); *Contes Surhumains* (*Superhuman Tales*; Chamuel, 1900); *Contes aventureux, Contes et Récits de la Mer et de la Cité* (*Adventurous Tales, Tales and Stories of the Sea and the City*; Maisonneuve, 1900); *Le Coeur d'Alcyone* (*Alcyone's Heart*; Libr. Hermétique, 1910); *Les Portes d'Airain* (*The Brass Gates*; Figuière, 1919); *L'Amour et la Magie* (*Love and Magic*; Chacorna, 1926); *La Descente de Vénus aux Enfers* (*Venus' Descent Into Hell*; Messein, 1931); *Le Secret de la Chevalerie* (*The Secret of Chivalry*; Vega, 1985); *Note:* See Chapter IV.

Michel-Tyl, Edmond (?-?); *Marquita au Col d'Or* (*Marquita of the Golden Neck*; Tallandier, 1936); *La Vallée du Mystère* (*The Valley of Mystery*; Masque Émeraude 28, 1940); *Note:* Michel-Tyl translated Leslie Charteris' *Saint* novels in French for Fayard then went on to write new novels based on the *Saint* radio-plays and, later, Charteris' scripts for the New York *Herald-Tribune Saint* comic-strip. After his death, his wife Madeleine continued the series. In total, the Michel-Tyls produced 42 French *Saint* novels never published in English.

Micro, Jean (?-); *Drame au Studio D* (*Tragedy at Studio D*; Chantal, 1942); *L'Équipée Héroïque* (*The Heroic Adventure*; SEPE, 1944); *Le Maître de la Mort* (*The Master of Death*; SEPE, 1945); *Le Justicier Souriant* (*The Smiling Avenger*; SEPE, 1945); *La Dame au Turban Vert* (*The Woman with the Green Turban*; SEPE, 1946); *On a tué les Fiancés* (*They Killed the Fiances*; SEPE, 1949)

Migeat, François (?-); *Bourlingages* (*Wanderings*; FNASF 11, 1996)

Milan *see* **Bergal, Gilles**

Milési, Raymond (1947-); *Extra-Muros* (Aurore, Futurs

12, 1990); *Chien Bleu Couronné* (*Crowned Blue Dog*; FNA 1841, 1991); *Papa, J'ai Remonté le Temps* (*Dad, I've Travelled Back in Time*; Hac., 1996); *Salut Delcano!* (*Hello Delcano!*; SENO 4, 1996); *Futur sans Étoiles* (*Starless Future*; SENO 6, 1997); *Note:* See Chapter IX.

Millanvoy, Louis (?-); *Seconde Vie de Napoléon (1821-1830); Napoleon's Second Life*; 1913); *Note:* See Chapter V.

Mille, Pierre (1864-1941); *Quand Panurge Ressuscita* (*When Panurge Came Back to Life*; Cahiers de la Quinzaine, 1908); *L'Enfant et la Reine Morte* (*The Child and the Dead Queen*; Cahiers de la Quinzaine, 1908); *Histoires Exotiques et Merveilleuses* (*Exotic and Wondrous Tales*; Ferenczi, 1920); *L'Ange du Bizarre* (*The Angel of Bizarre*; Ferenczi, 1921); *Dans Trois Cents Ans* (*In 300 Years*; Fayard, 1922); *Le Diable au Sahara* (*The Devil in the Sahara*; AM, 1925); *Barnavaux, Soldat de France* (*Barnavaux, French Soldier*; Arts & Livre, 1927); *Comment la Baleine perdit ses Pieds* (*How the Whale Lost Its Feet*; Arts & Livre, 1928); *Barnavaux et Quelques Femmes* (*Barnavaux and Some Women*; Calmann-Lévy, 1931); *Les Aventuriers* (*The Adventurers*; Calmann-Lévy, 1937); *Note:* See Chapter VII. Also see **Grand-Guignol.**

Millemann, Jean (1960-); *Fumeterre* (*SmokeyEarth*; Ima Montis, 1994); *Note:* See Chapter IX.

Millette, Annie (?-) *see* **Martin, Sophie**

Milliet, Paul (?-?) *see* **Grand-Guignol** and **Opéra**

Minerath, Marc (?-); *L'Idole Perdue* (*The Lost Idol*; France-Édition, 1923); *L'Homme aux Huit Têtes* (*The Eight-Headed Man*; Baudinière, 1941); *Une Affaire de Termites* (*An Affair of Termites*; ABC, 1942); *Le Voleur des Mers* (*The Stealer of Seas*; Technique du Livre, 1945)

Minh, Yann (?-); *Thanatos 1: Les Récifs* (*The Reefs*; Florent Massot, 1997)

Miomandre, Francis de (Durand, François; 1880-1959); *Le Vent et la Poussière* (*The Wind and the Dust*; Calmann-Lévy, 1909); *Le Veau d'Or et la Vache Enragée* (*The Golden Calf and the Rabid Cow*; Émile-Paul, 1917); *Contes des Cloches de Cristal* (*Tales of the Crystal Bell*; Lesage, 1925); *Le Radjah de Mazulipatam* (*The Rajah of Mazulipatam*; Ferenczi, 1926); *Direction Étoile* (*Direction the Star*; Plon, 1937)

Miquel, André (?-); *Le Fils Interrompu* (*The Interrupted Son*; Flamm., 1971); *Vive la Suranie!* (*Long Live Surania!*; Flamm., 1978); *Les Dames de Bagdad* (*The Ladies of Baghdad*; Desjonquères, 1991)

Mir, M. (?-) *see* ***Contes et Légendes***

Miral-Viger (?-); *L'Anneau de Feu (The Ring of Fire;* Hac., 1922; rev. as *L'Anneau de Lumière (The Ring of Light,* Tallandier, 1922); *Note:* See Chapter VII.

Mirande, Jacqueline (Labrousse, Jacqueline; 1925-); *Le Bracelet aux Tourmalines (The Tourmaline Bracelet;* Hac., 1987); *Note:* Also see **Contes et Légendes**

Mirbeau, Octave (1848-1917); *Le Jardin des Supplices* (Fasquelle, 1899; transl. as *Torture Garden,* 1931); *Les Vingt et un Jours d'un Neurasthénique (The 21 Days of a Neurasthenic;* Fasquelle, 1901); *Contes de la Chaumière (Tales of the Cottage;* Flamm., 1923); *Contes Cruels (Cruel Tales;* Séguier, 1990); *Chroniques du Diable (The Devil's Chronicles;* Belles Lettres, 1995); *Note:* See Chapter IV. *Le Jardin* was adapted into a **Grand-Guignol** play by André de **Lorde** & Pierre **Chaine**; the play was published separately in 1929 (see André de **Lorde**).

Mirepoix, Levis (?-); *Montségur—Les Cathares* (AM, 1924)

Mirman, Louis (1916-); *Le Silex Noir (The Black Silex;* Gall., 1983); *Young* (Gall., 1985); *Grite parmi les Loups (Grite Among the Wolves;* Gall. 1987); *À la Recherche de Tiang (Looking for Tiang;* Gall., 1990); *Note:* Juveniles.

Mistler, Jean (1897-1988); *Ethelka* (Calmann-Lévy, 1929); *La Maison du Dr. Clifton (The House of Dr. Clifton;* Émile-Paul, 1932); *Aimés des Dieux (Loved By the Gods;* Hac., 1972); *Le Bout du Monde (The End of the World;* Hac., 1973); *Le Naufrage du Monte-Christo (The Shipwreck of the Monte-Christo;* Grasset, 1973); *L'Ami des Pauvres (The Friend of the Poor;* Grasset, 1974); *Anticipations and Utopies (Anticipations and Utopias;* Inst. De France, 1975); *Faubourg Antoine* (Grasset, 1982); *La Nuit de Gheel (Gheel's Night;* Nouveau Cercle Parisien du Livre, 1982); *Le Jeune Homme qui rôde (The Prowling Young Man;* Grasset, 1983); *Villes et Frontières (Cities and Frontiers;* Rocher, 1985)

Mistral, Frédéric (1830-1914); *Mireille* (Mireio; Roumanille, 1859); *Note:* See Chapter IV.

Mitchell, G. (?-?) *see* **Grand-Guignol**

Mochon, Jean-Philippe (?-); *Le Bel Effet Gore (A Nice Gory Effect;* anthology; FNG Special, 1988)

Mockel, Albert (1866-1945); *Clartés (Lights;* MdF, 1901); *Contes pour Enfants d'Hier (Tales for Yesterday's Children;* MdF, 1908); *Note:* Belgian writer.

Moessinger, Pierre (1943-); *Ping Pou I'Astronome (Ping Poo the Astronomer;* Ipomée, 1983); *Zéro Oxymoron* (Le Sorbier, 1984); *Les Gens du Cirque (The Circus Folks;* Berger-Levrault, 1985); *Ménagerie Nocturne (Night Menagerie;* Nathan, 1989); *Note:* Juveniles.

Moilin, Tony (Moilin, Jules-Antoine; 1832-1871); *Paris en l'An 2000 (Paris in the Year 2000);* Libr. Renaissance, 1869); *Note:* See Chapter V.

Moissard, Boris (1942-); *Contes à l'Envers (Upside Down Tales;* Ecole des Loisirs, 1979); *Le Coeur des Vastes Cités (The Heart of the Vast Cities;* Ecole des Loisirs, 1991); *Note:* Juveniles.

Moliner, Christian de (?-); *Quand Reviendront les Andes (When the Andes Returned;* Pensée U., 1984); *2052* (A. de Saint-Saulve, 1994); *Les Mondes du Serpent (The Worlds of the Serpent;* A. de Saint-Saulve, 1996)

Mollica, Anthony (1939-) & Elizabeth (?-); *Fleur de Lis* (with Donna **Stefoff**; Copp Clarck Pitman, 1973); *Note:* French-Canadian anthology.

Moncomble, Gérard (1951-); *L'Île à Malices (The Island of Tricks;* Milan, 1985); *Georges Bouton, Explomigrateur* (Milan, 1987); *L'Heure du Rat (The Hour of the Rat;* Milan, 1988); *Les Yeux d'Oo (The Eyes of Oo;* Milan, 1989); *L'Héritage de Georges Bouton (Georges Bouton's Inheritance;* Milan, 1989); *Note:* Juveniles.

Mondoloni, Jacques (?-); *Il faut partir Quilichini (We Must Leave Quilichini;* Matignon, 1973); *Je Suis Une Herbe (I Am an Herb;* JL 1341, 1982); *Papa 1er (Daddy 1st.;* PdF 367, 1983); *Les Goulags Mous (The Soft Gulags;* FNA 1289, 1984); *Carthage en Amérique (Carthago in America;* FNA 1343, 1984); *Les Idées Solubles (The Soluble Ideas;* FNA 1529, 1987); *Les Vitrines du Ciel (The Windows of the Sky;* FNA 1576, 1987); *Le Marchand de Torture (The Torture Merchant;* Den., 1989); *Tenue de Galère (Galley Suit;* Den., 1991); *Quand la Mer Reviendra (When the Sea Returned;* Messidor, 1991); *L'Ami Crados (My Friend Crados;* Syros, 1991); *Richard Coeur-de-Lièvre (Richard the Hare-Heart;* L'Atalante, 1993); *Jules et ses Cabanes (Jules and His Shacks;* Syros, 1993); *Le Jeu du Petit Poucet (Tom Thumb's Game;* Gall., 1994); *Corsica Blues* (L'Atalante, 1996); *Note:* See Chapter IX.

Mondoloni, Roger (1929-); *L'Aube du Temps qui Vient (The Dawn of the Times to Come;* Tisseyre, 1989); *Note:* French-Canadian writer.

Monjardin, Alin (?-?); *Un Drame au Fond de la Mer (A*

Tragedy at the Bottom of the Sea; RJ, 1933); *L'Extra-ordinaire Voyage* (*The Extraordinary Journey*; Petit Illustré, 1934); *Note:* See Chapter VII. Also see **Grand-Guignol**.

Monod, Jean-Louis (?-); *L'Appel* (*The Call*; Egraz, 1973); *Note:* Swiss writer.

Monsigny (Jacqueline; ?-); Series *Freddy Ravage*: *1. Freddy Ravage Passe à l'Attaque* (*Freddy Ravage Attacks*; Unide, 1975); *2. Freddy Ravage et les Diplodocus* (*Freddy Ravage and the Diplodocus*; Unide, 1975); *3. Freddy Ravage Prisonnier des Pharaons* (*Freddy Ravage Prisoner of the Pharaohs*; Unide, 1976); *4. Freddy Ravage et la Ville Dorée* (*Freddy Ravage and the Golden City*; Unide, 1976); *5. Freddy Ravage et les Agents Secrets* (*Freddy Ravage and the Secret Agents*; Unide, 1976); *6. Freddy Ravage et les Karatékas* (Unide, 1976); *7. La Jeunesse de Freddy Ravage* (*Young Freddy Ravage*; Unide, 1977); *Note:* Juvenile SF. See Chapter IX.

Montaigne, Michel de (Eyquem, Michel; 1533-1592); *Des Cannibales (Of Cannibals)* in *Essais* (*Essays*, Book 1 Impr. S. Millanges, 1580); *Note:* See Chapter II.

Montambault, André (1946-); *Étrangers!* (*Strangers*; AMAM 10, 1991); *Note:* French-Canadian writer.

Monteilhet, Hubert (1928-); *Les Pavés du Diable* (*The Devil's Cobblestones*; Hac., 1970); *Non-Sens* (*Nonsense*; Den, 1971); *Les Bourreaux de Cupidon* (*Cupid's Executioners*; Den., 1972); *Requiem pour une Noce* (*Requiem for a Wedding*; Den., 1973); *Esprit, es-tu la?* (*Spirit, Are You Here?*; Den., 1977); *Le Retour des Cendres* (*The Return of the Ashes*; JL, 1977); *Retour à Zéro* (*Return to Zero*; Ramsay, 1978); *Un Métier de Fantôme* (*A Ghostly Business*; Nathan, 1979); *Les Queues de Kallinaos* (*The Tails of the Kallinaos*; Ramsay, 1981); *Gus et les Hindous* (*Gus and the Hindus*; Nathan, 1982); *Néropolis* (Ramsay, 1984); *La Part des Anges* (*The Angels' Share*; Fallois, 1990); *Oedipe en Médoc* (*Oedipus in Medoc*; Fallois, 1993); *Note:* See Chapter VIII.

Monteils, Jean-Pierre (?-); *Le Dossier Secret de Rennes-le-Château* (*The Secret File of Rennes-le-Château*; Belfond, 1981); *Note:* A real-life priest spent over a billion francs betwen 1891 and 1917. Monteils offers a theory.

Montenis, André (?-?) *see* **Grand-Guignol**

Montesiste, Laurent (?-?); *Histoires Vertigineuses* (*Dazzling Tales*; MdF, 1896); *Note:* See Chapter IV.

Montesquieu, Charles-Louis de Secondat, Baron de la Brède et de (1689-1755); *Histoire des Troglodytes* (*History of the Troglodytes*) in *Lettres Persanes* (*Persan Letters*, Letters XI to XIV; P. Brunel, 1721); *Note:* See Chapter III.

Montfort, Élie *see* **Falcoz, André**

Montgon, Adhémar de (?-); *Les Deux Croquemitaines* (*The Two Bogeymen*; Hac., 1930); *Le Bâteau Fantôme* (*The Ghost Ship*; with Charles **Quinel**; Nathan, 1932); *Le Parfum Mystérieux* (*The Mysterious Perfume*; with Charles **Quinel**; Plon, 1932); *Un Cri dans l'Espace* (*A Scream in Space*; with Thérèse **Lenotre**; Mame, 1935); *La Cité des Femmes Nues* (*The City of Naked Women*; with Charles **Quinel**; Saillard, 1936); *La Magicienne Florentine* (*The Florentine Sorceress*; with Charles **Quinel**; Hac., 1936); *Note:* Also see ***Contes et Légendes***

Montignac, Georges (?-?); *Le Mystère plane* (*Mystery Lurks*; Tallandier, 1913); *La Disparition de Mona* (*Mona's Disappearance*; Mignot, 1914); *Note:* See Chapter VI and **Grand-Guignol**.

Montpetit, Charles (1958-); *Moi ou la Planète* (*Me or the Planet*; Actuelle, 1972); *Temps Perdu* (JP 50, 1984; transl. as *Lost Time*,1990); *Temps Mort* (*Dead Time*; JP 65, 1988); *Copie Carbone* (*Carbon Copy*; Q/A, 1993); *Note:* French-Canadian writer. *Temps Perdu* and *Temps Mort* tell the story of young Marianne who lives in accidental symbiosis with a time-travelling ghostly intelligence.

Montrel, Pierre (?-?) *see* **Grand-Guignol**

Mora, Léo *see* **Maizeroy, René**

Moralie, Pierre (?-); *L'Île Engloutie* (*The Sunken Island*; VA, 1936); *Le Rayon du Néant* (*The Void Ray*; VA, 1936); *La Caverne des Supplices* (*The Cave of Tortures*; VA, 1936); *Les Rescapés du "Météore"* (*The Survivors of the "Meteor"*; PRA, 1941); *Dans la Ville Séculaire* (*In the Secular City*; VA, 1941)

Morand, Eugène (?-?) *see* **Opéra**

Morax, René (?-?) *see* **Opéra**

More, Francis (?-); *Coma* (Plon, 1981)

Moré, Marcel (?-); *Les Noces Chymiques du Capitaine Némo et de Salomé* (*The Chymical Wedding of Captain Nemo and Salome*; written, 1930; publ. Gall., 1967); *Note:* Also the author of two essays on Jules **Verne**: *Le Très Curieux Jules Verne* (*The Very Strange Jules Verne*; 1960) and *Nouvelles Explorations de Jules Verne* (*New Explorations of Jules Verne*; 1963).

Moreau, Patrick (1945-); *...Et si l'Otage était Paris?* (*...And If the Hostage Was Paris?*; with Daniel **Saint-Hamont**; Tchou, 1978)

Moreaux, Michel (?-); *Nocturnales* (Cercle d'Or, 1974)

Morel, Eugène (1869-1934); *La Dernière Torture* (*The Last Torture*; Charpentier & Fasquelle, 1905); *Note:* Also see **Grand-Guignol**.

Morel, Maurice (?-); *Petite Jungle* (*Little Jungle*; Armand Colin, 1928); *Note:* Miniaturization.

Morel, Suzy (?-); *Célébration de la Neige* (*Celebrating Snow*; Morel, 1968); *L'Enfant Cavalier* (*The Child Rider*; Stock, 1977); *L'Éblouie* (*Stunned*; Stock, n.d.; *Les Pas d'Orphée* (*Orpheus' Steps*; Stock, 1982); *La Marie-Concorde* (Meylan, 1984); *Le Chemin des Loups* (*The Wolves' Path*; Calmann-Lévy, 1985); *L'Office des Ténèbres* (*The Office of Darkness*; Calmann-Lévy, 1989); *Note:* See Chapter VIII.

Morelly (?-?); *Naufrage des Isles Flottantes, ou Basiliade du Célèbre Pilpai* (*Wreck of the Floating Islands*; Paris-Messine, 1753); *Note:* See Chapter III.

Moreux, Abbé Théophile (1867-1954); *Les Reportages Extraordinaires de Julius Snow: Le Miroir Sombre—L'Énigme Martienne* (*The Extraordinary News Accounts of Julius Snow: The Dark Mirror—A Martian Enigma;* Lethielleux, 1911; rev. as *Mars Va Nous Parler* (*Mars Will Talk to Us*, JDV, 1924-25); *Note:* See Chapter V.

Morgan, Harry (?-); *La Reine du Ciel* (*The Queen of the Sky*; Rivages, 1997); *Note:* See Chapter VIII. French writer using a pseudonym.

Morgin de Kean (?-); *Le Continent Maudit* (*The Accursed Continent*; Den., 1939); *Les Chiens n'ont pas aboyé* (*The Dogs Didn't Bark*; Jean Renard, 1942); *La Maison près du Cimetière* (*The House Near the Cemetery*; Jean Renard, 1942); *Jouer avec le Feu* (*To Play with Fire*; Jean Renard, 1943)

Morgins, Jean-Louis (?-); *L'Île du Malheur* (*The Island of Woe*; RDA, 1926)

Morice, Émile (?-?); *La Griffe du Diable* (*The Devil's Claw*; in *Le Conteur*, Dumont, 1833)

Morin, Hugues (?-); *Les Veuves de Saint-Aubry* (*The Widows of Saint-Aubry*; Rocher, 1985)

Morin, Hugues (1966-); *Le Marchand de Rêves* (*The Dream Merchant*; Octa, 1994); *Sang Froid* (*Cold Blood*; anthology; Ashem Fictions, 1995); *Pot-Pourrire* (anthology; Ashem Fictions, 1996); *Note:* French-Canadian writer.

Morin, Jacqueline (1948-); *Molliger: Le Triomphe du Temps sur la Mort* (*The Triumph of Time Over Death*; Beauchemin, 1979); *La Filière du Temps: L'Histoire de Doucy Riverside* (*Time's Flow: The Tale of Doucy Riverside*; Inédi, 1980); *Note:* French-Canadian writer. *Molliger* is a novel about paranormal powers.

Morin, Lise (1964-); *L'Oiseau de Feu* (*The Bird of Fire*; Camédu, 1992); *Note:* French-Canadian writer.

Morineau, Alain (?-); *L'Île de Nulle Part* (*The Island from Nowhere*; JCL, 1980

Morora, Max (?-); *La Vengeance et l'Extase* (*Revenge and Ecstasy*; FN @lias 2, 1997)

Morris, Gilles (Dumoulin, Gilles-Maurice; 1924-); *Facteur Vie* (*Life Factor*; FNA 935, 1979); *...Ou Que La Vie Renaisse* (*...Or Let Life Be Reborn*; FNA 959, 1979); *Techniques de Survie* (*Survival Techniques*; FNA 979, 1980); *Untel, Sa Vie, Son Oeuvre* (*Someone, His Life, His Works*; FNA 988, 1980); *Les Malvivants* (*The Ill-Living*; FNA 1002, 1980); *La Vie en Doses* (*Life in Small Doses*; FNA 1012, 1980); *Les Vivants, les Morts et les Autres* (*The Living, the Dead and the Others*; FNA 1021, 1980); *Vecteur Dieu* (*God Vector*; FNA 1030, 1980); *Soucoupes Violentes* (*Violent Saucers*; FNA 1033, 1980); *La Guerre des Lovies* (*The War of the Lovies*; FNA 1045, 1981); *Les Plasmoïdes au Pouvoir* (*Power to the Plasmoids*; FN 1055, 1981); *Un Monde Impossible* (*An Impossible World*; FNA 1070, 1981); *Notre Chair Disparue* (*Our Disappeared Flesh*; FNA 1076, 1981); *...Ou Que La Mort Triomphe!* (*...Or Let Death Triumph!*; FNA 1087, 1981); *Planète-Suicide* (*Suicide Planet*; FNA 1095, 1981); *Une Secte Comme Beaucoup d'Autres* (*A Sect Like Many Other*; FNA 1109, 1981); *Fallait-il Tuer Dieu?* (*Should We Have Killed God?*; FNA 1121, 1982); *Examen de Passage* (*Transition Exam*; FNA 1129, 1982); *Cosmodrame* (*Cosmodrama*; FNA 1137, 1982); *La Vie, La Mort Confondues* (*Life and Death Combined*; FNA 1151, 1982); *Un Pour Tous... Tous Pourris!* (*One for All, All Corrupt!*; FNA 1165, 1982); *Une Odeur de Sainteté* (*A Scent of Holiness*; FNA 1174, 1982); *Et le Paradis en plus!* (*And Paradise on Top!*; FNA 1188, 1982); *Génération Clash* (FNA 1200, 1983); *La Frontière Indécise* (*The Uncertain Frontier*; FNA 1208, 1983); *Trop Pour un Seul Homme* (*Too Much for a Single Man*; FNA 1221, 1983); *Intervention Flash* (FNA 1230, 1983); *Evolution Crash* (FNA 1246, 1983); *Secteur Diable* (*Devil Sector*; FNA 1258, 1983); *Kamikazement Vôtres* (*Kamikazely Yours*; FNA 1269, 1983); *Les Métamorphes* (*The Metamorphs*; FNA 1282, 1984); *Survivre Ensemble* (*To Survive Together*; FNA 1287, 1984); *Un Avenir sur Commande* (*A Future to Order*; FNA 1301, 1984); *Vieillesse Délinquante* (*Delinquent Golden Agers*; FNA 1313, 1984); *L'Autre Côté du Vide* (*The Other Side of the Void*; FNA 1322, 1984); *Offensive Minérale* (*Mineral Attack*; FNA 1337, 1984); *À Moins d'un Miracle...* (*Unless a Miracle...*; FNA 1344, 1984); *Les Psychomutants* (FNA 1363, 1985); *La Pire Espèce* (*The Worst Kind*; FNA 1381, 1985); *Pour Une Dent, Toute La Gueule* (*For a Tooth, the Whole Face*; FNA 1409, 1985); *Feu sur Tout ce qui Bouge!* (*Fire on Anything That Moves!*; FNA 1416, 1985); *Retour en Avant* (*Return Forward*; FNA 1423, 1986); *Un Pied sur Terre* (*A Foot on the Ground*; FNA 1445, 1986); *Les Horreurs de la Paix* (*The Horrors of Peace*; FNA 1452, 1986); *La Barrière du Crâne* (*The Skull Barrier*;

FNA 1461, 1986); *Objectif: Surhomme* (*Target: Superman*; FNA 1478, 1986); *En Direct d'Ailleurs* (*Direct from Beyond*; FNA 1481, 1986); *La Piste des Écorchés* (*The Trail of the Flayed*; FNA 1488, 1986); *L'Agonie des Hommes* (*The Agony of Men*; FNA 1498, 1986); *Appelez-moi Einstein!* (*Call Me Einstein!*; FNA 1528, 1987); *Les Êtres Vagues* (*The Vague Beings*; FNA 1530, 1987); *La Longue Errance* (*The Long Wandering*; FNA 1546, 1987); *Le Commencement de la Fin* (*The Beginning of the End*; FNA 1564, 1987); *Le Fond de l'Abîme* (*The Bottom of the Abyss*; FNA 1577, 1987); *Le Bout du Tunnel* (*The End of the Tunnel*; FNA 1591, 1987); *Terre! Terre!* (*Earth! Earth!*; FNA 1595, 1987); *Psychosphère* (FNA 1864, 1992); Series *Vic Saint-Val* (as Vic Saint-Val): *1. VSV s'en occupe* (*VSV Will Take Care of It*; Espiomatic, 1971); *2. VSV sur un Volcan* (*VSV Over a Volcano*; Espiomatic, 1971); *3. VSV sans Visa* (*VSV Without a Visa*; Espiomatic, 1971); *4. VSV Dore la Pillule* (*VSV Paints a Rosy Picture*; Espiomatic, 1972); *5. VSV Vise à la Tête* (*VSV Aims for the Head*; Espiomatic, 1972); *6. VSV en Enfer* (*VSV in Hell*; Espiomatic, 1972); *7. VSV sur Orbite* (*VSV in Orbit*; Esiomatic, 1972); *8. VSV en Chute Libre* (*VSV in Free Fall*; Espiomatic, 1972); *9. VSV Annonce la Couleur* (*VSV Bids a Suit*; Espiomatic, 1972); *10. VSV contre VSV* (*VSV vs VSV*; Espiomatic, 1973); *11. VSV Rend la Monnaie* (*VSV Makes Change*; Espiomatic, 1973); *12. VSV Va à la Dame* (*VSV Plays Checkers*; Espiomatic, 1973); *13. VSV Entre Deux Eaux* (*VSV Between Waters*; Espiomatic, 1973); *14. VSV Donne le Feu Vert* (*VSV Greenlights*; Espiomatic, 1973); *15. VSV Brule les Étapes* (*VSV Misses All the Stops*; Espiomatic, 1973); *16. VSV Quitte ou Double* (*VSV Double or Nothing*; Espiomatic, 1973); 17. VSV Non Stop (Espiomatic, 1974); *18. VSV sous Pression* (*VSV Under Pressure*; Espiomatic, 1974); *19. VSV en Direct* (*VSV on Live TV*; Espiomatic, 1974); *20. VSV à Fond de Cale* (*VSV in the Brig*; Espiomatic, 1974); *21. VSV Période Fauve* (*VSV Fawn Period*; Espiomatic, 1974); *22. VSV Tous Azimuts* (*VSV in Every Direction*; Espiomatic, 1974); *23. VSV—Place aux Jeunes* (*VSV- Room for the Young*; Espiomatic, 1974); *24. VSV Vole dans les Plumes* (*VSV Beats the Crap*; Espiomatic, 1975); *25. VSV Force la Dose* (*VSV Increases the Dosage*; Espiomatic, 1975); *26. VSV Cousu Main* (*VSV Sown By Hand*; Espiomatic, 1975); *27. VSV au Finish* (*VSV to the Finish*; Espiomatic, 1975); *28. VSV Tranche dans le Vif* (*VSV Cuts to the Bone*; Espiomatic, 1975); *29. VSV Taille Adulte* (*VSV Adult Size*; Espiomatic, 1975); *30. VSV Priez Porno* (*VSV Prays for Porn*; Espiomatic, 1975); *31. Salut, la Mecque!* (*Hello, Mecca!*; Espiomatic, 1976); *32. Circuit Dracula* (*Dracula Circuit*; Espiomatic, 1976); *33. Aux Algues, Citoyens!* (*To Algae, Citizens!*; Espiomatic, 1976); *34. La Ruée vers Lore* (*Lore Rush*; Espiomatic, 1976); *35. Envoûtements sur Commande* (*Spells to Order*; Espiomatic, 1976); *36. Le Complexe de Frankenstein* (*The Frankenstein Complex*; Espiomatic, 1976); *37. Nostradamus au Pouvoir* (*Nostradamus in Power*; Espiomatic, 1976); *38. Monstres à Volonté* (*Monsters at Will*; Espiomatic, 1977); *39. Jusque là, ça va!* (*So Far, So Good*; Espiomatic, 1977); *40. Un Méchant Coup de Vieux!* (*A Nasty Old Man*; Espiomatic, 1977); *41. Société de Compromission* (*Compromised Society*; Espiomatic, 1977); *42. Pitié pour la Terre* (*Mercy for the Earth*; Espiomatic, 1977); *43. Course au Suicide* (*Suicide Race*; Espiomatic, 1977); *44. Nous Sommes tous des Cobayes* (*We're All Guinea Pigs*; Espiomatic, 1977); *45. Le Fer dans la Plaie* (*The Dagger in the Wound*; Espiomatic, 1977); *46. Violences sans Visages* (*Faceless Violence*; Espiomatic, 1977); *47. L'Équilibre de la Terreur* (*The Balance of Terror*; Espiomatic, 1978); *48. Partages en Frères* (*Brothers' Share*; Espiomatic, 1978); *49. Bienheureux les Doux* (*Blessed Be the Kind*; Espiomatic, 1978); *50. La Tête au Carré* (*The Head in a Square*; Espiomatic, 1978); *51. La Crainte du Gendarme* (*The Fear of the Policeman*; Espiomatic, 1978); *52. Massacre en Sourdine* (*Soft Massacre*; Espiomatic, 1978); *53. Debout, les Morts!* (*Stand Up, Deadmen*; Espiomatic, 1978); *54. La Boule à Zéro* (*Zero Ball*; Espiomatic, 1978); *55. Des Lendemains qui Hantent* (*Haunting Tomorrows*; Espiomatic, 1979); *56. Matraquage* (*Hammering*; Espiomatic, 1979); *57. Le Plus Dur Reste à Faire* (*The Hardest Remains to Be Done*; Espiomatic, 1979); *58. Casseurs, Chassez Casser!* (*Breakers, Hunters, Looters*; Espiomatic, 1979); *59. Exécution sur Mesure* (*Execution to Order*; Espiomatic, 1979); *60. Camouflage Express* (*Express Disguise*; Espiomatic, 1979); *Note:* See Chapter IX.

Morrisset, Franck (?-); *Alice qui dormait* (*Alice Who Slept*; FNA 1990, 1996); *L'Ange et la Mort* (*The Angel and Death*; FNA 1996, 1996); *La Résolution Andromède* (*The Andromeda Resolution*; FNSF 27, 1997); *Note:* See Chapter IX.

Morrisson, Roy *see* **Clauzel, Robert**

Mortemart (Baron de; ?-?); *Hallucination* (MdF, 1831)

Mortier, A. (?-?) *see* **Opéra**

Morvers, L. *see* **Falcoz, André**

Moselli, José (1882-1941); *Les Aventures Fantastiques d'un Jeune Policier* (*The Fantastic Adventures of a Young Policeman*; 1909-13; continued as Jean Flair, 1915); *W... Vert* (*W... Green*; 1910); *Le Chevalier de Marana* (*The Knight of Marana*; 1911); *Le Sultanat de Kazongo*

(*The Sultanate of Kazongo*; 1911); *John Strobbins* (*L'É-patant*, 1911-1933); *Le Pari du Milliardaire* (*The Billionnaire's Bet*; 1911); *Les Négriers des Mers du Sud* (*The Slavers of the Southern Seas*; 1912); Létio-Mousi (1912); *L'Anneau de Fer* (*The Iron Ring*; 1912); *Par le Fer et le Poison* (*By Iron and Poison*; 1912); *Le Roi des Boxeurs* (*The King of the Boxers*; 515 issues, *L'Épatant*, Series 1: 1912-28; Series 2: 1928-32; Series 3: 1932-35); *Le Baron Stromboli* (1912); *Des Galères à l'Échafaud* (*From the Galleys to the Gallows*; 1913); *Les Requins du Pacifique* (*The Sharks of the Pacific*; 1914; rev. as *Les Écumeurs des Mers Australes* (*The Reavers of the Southern Seas*, 1932); *Les Champs d'Or de l'Urubu* (*The Gold Fields of Urubu*; 1914); *Les Coeurs de Tigres* (*The Tiger Hearts*; 1915); *Les Compagnons de la Mort* (*The Brotherhood of Death*; 1915); *Le Maître de la Banquise* (*The Master of the Ice Shelf*; 1916; rev. as 2 vols., *La Cité du Pôle* (*The City at the Pole*) and *Les Robinsons de la Banquise* (*Robinsons of the Ice Shelf*, 1936-37); *Les Naufrageurs de l'Air* (*The Air Wreckers*; 1916; rev. as 5 vols., CdA, 1922): *1. Les Naufrageurs de l'Air* (*The Air Pirates*); *2. Les Espions de la Mer Jaune* (*The Spies of the Yellow Sea*); *3. La Prison Aérienne* (*The Aerial Prison*); *4. Les Étrangleurs de Batavia* (*The Stranglers of Batavia*); *5. Le Désert de Boue* (*The Desert of Mud*); *Face de Fer* (*Iron Face*; 1917); *Le Téléluz* (*L'Intrépide*, 1918); *L'Homme à la Carabine* (*The Carbine Man*; 1918); *Le Sire de Kergorec* (*The Lord of Kergorec*; 1918); *Les Mystères de la Mer de Corail* (*The Mysteries of the Coral Sea*; 1919); *Le Cadet de Crèvecoeur* (*The Cadet of Crevecoeur*; 1919); *Fifi l'Anguille* (*Fifi the Eel*; 1919); *Le Dragon d'Émeraude* (*The Emerald Dragon*; 1919); *Les Suppliciés du Hoang-Ho* (*The Tortured Men of the Hoang-Ho*; 1919); *Iko Térouka* (*Petit Illustré*, 1919-35); *La Prison de Glace* (*The Ice Prison*; S&V, 1919-20); *Le Clain 29* (1920); *La Fille aux Opales* (*The Opals Girl*; 1920); *Les Contrebandiers de l'île Holy* (*The Smugglers of Holy Island*; 1920); *Le Secret du Boucanier* (*The Secret of the Buccaneer*; 1920); *Le Récif des Tortues* (*The Turtles' Reef*; 1921); *La Dernière Affaire d'Alexandre Bullen* (*Alexander Bullen's Last Case*; S&V, 1921); *L'As du Cinéma* (*The Ace of Cinema*; 1921); *Le Rayon Phi* (*The Phi Ray*; S&V, 1921); *La Corde d'Acier* (*The Rope of Steel*; S&V, 1921); *Le Tchou King* (1921); *Le Maître de la Foudre* (*The Lightning Master*; *L'Intrépide*, 1921-22); *Les Conquérants de l'Abîme* (*The Conquerors of the Abyss*; S&V, 1922); *Le Lagon aux Requins* (*The Lagoon of Sharks*; 1922; rev. as *Le Mystère des Eaux Mortes* (*The Mystery of the Dead Waters*, 1936); *Les Barons de la Flibuste* (*The Barons of Piracy*; 1922; rev. as *Les Aventuriers de la Mer Caraïbe* (*The Adventurers of the Caribbean Sea*, 1936); *Browing & Cie.* (*Cri-Cri*, 1922-35); *Kermeur Vent Debout* (*Kermeur Upwind*; 1922); *L'Esclave Blanc* (*The White Slave*; 1922); *Les Démons de la Mer* (*The Demons of the Sea*; 1923); *Le Carcan de Cuivre* (*The Copper Prison*; 1923; rev. as *Le Collier Fatal* (*The Deadly Necklace*, 1937); *Le Bracelet de Jade* (*The Jade Bracelet*; 1923); *Le Voyage Éternel* (*The Eternal Voyage*; 1923; rev. as *Les Prospecteurs de l'Infini* (*Prospectors of Infinity*, 1923); *Triplix l'Insaisissable* (*Triplix the Uncatchable*; 1924); *Assiégés par les Convicts* (*Besieged By Convicts*; 1924); *Le Messager de la Planète* (*The Messenger of the Planet*; 1924); *Le Dernier Pirate* (*The Last Pirate*; 1924); *Alain Tête de Fer* (*Alan Iron Head*; 1924); *Cossard Belle Épée* (*Cossard Beautiful Sword*; 1924); *L'Idole Bleue* (*The Blue Idol*; 1924); *Le Roi des Convicts* (*The King of the Convicts*; 1924); *La Belle Créole* (*The Beautiful Creole*; 1924); *La Fin d'Illa* (*The End of Illa*; S&V, 1925; rep. MarSF 421, 1972); *La Momie Rouge* (*The Red Mummy*; 1925); *La Cité du Gouffre* (*The City of the Pit*; 1925); *Les Coureurs du Tour du Monde* (*The Racers Around the World*; 1925); *L'Archipel de l'Épouvante* (*The Archipelago of Terror*; *L'Intrépide*, 1925); *Les Mousquetaires de l'Océan* (*The Ocean Musketeers*; 1926); *La Flèche Sanglante* (*The Bloody Arrow*; 1926); *La Montagne des Dieux* (*The Mountain of the Gods*; S&V, 1926-27); *La Piste de l'Or* (*The Gold Trail*; 1927); *La Jarre de Cristal* (*The Crystal Jar*; *L'Intrépide*, 1928); *Radassar* (1928); *Batrracuda Inlet* (1928); *La Guerre des Océans* (*The War of the Oceans*; S&V, 1928-29; rep. MarSF 533, 1975); *Tavar la Hache* (*Tavar-The-Axe*; 1929); *Zaraga El Grande* (1930); *Les Tueurs de Chinatown* (*The Chinatown Killers*; 1931); *L'Empereur du Pacifique* (*The Emperor of the Pacific*; *L'Intrépide*, 1932-35); *Le Totem de l'Homme Mort* (*The Dean Man's Totem*; 1933); *Le Secret de Frederick Seymour* (*Frederick Seymour's Secret*; 1934); *M. Dupont Detective* (1935); *Scalp Rouge* (*Red Scalp*; 1935); *Les Compagons du Pelikan* (*The Companons of the Pelican*; 1935); *Le Club des Trois* (*The Club of Three*; 1935); *L'Avion Fantôme* (*The Phantom Airplane*; *L'Intrépide*, 1936); *Le Capataz de l'Île Perdue* (*The Capataz of the Lost Island*; 1936); *L'Héritier du Grand Lama* (*The Heir of the Great Lama*; 1936); *Les Rendez-Vous de Benguela* (*The Rendezvous of Benguela*; 1937); *La Disparition du Grand Tangarung* (*The Disappearance of the Great Tangarung*; 1937); *La Pyramide d'Or* (*The Gold Pyramid*; 1937); *Cicago Jim* (1937); *Lonely Reef* (1937); *La Racine de Kanjouk* (*The Kanjuk Root*; 1938); *L'Île des Hommes Bleus* (*The Island of the Blue Men*; *L'Épatant*, 1939); *Les Gangsters de l'Air* (*The Air Gangsters*; *L'As*, 1939); *Les Gangsters de l'Irrouady* (*The Gangsters of Irrouady*; 1939); *Les Compagnons de la Mort Subite* (*The Brotherhood of Sudden Death*; *Désiré*, 1967-68); *Note:* See Chapter VII. Most stories published in various publications of Editions Offenstadt.

Mottart, Raymond (?-); *Bételgeuse* (Ren. du Livre, 1956) *Note:* Belgian writer. See Chapter VIII.

Mottier, François (1952-); *Philip Jose Farmer Conquiert l'Univers* (*Philip Jose Farmer Conquers the Universe*; Glénat, 1980

Motus (Prof.; Rochard (Dr.); ?-); *L'Offensive des Microbes, Roman d'une Guerre Future* (*The Microbes' Attack, Novel of a Future War*; Tallandier, 1923); rep. as *La Guerre Microbienne, La Fin du Monde* (*The Microbian War, the End of the World*; as Prof. X, Tallandier, 1923); *Note:* See Chapter VII.

Mouëzy-Éon, André (1880-1967) *see* **Grand-Guignol**

Mouhy, Charles de Fieux, Chevalier de (1701-1784); *Lamékis, ou Les Voyages Extraordinaires d'un Égyptien dans la Terre Intérieure avec la Découverte de l'Île des Sylphides* (*Lamekis, or the Extraordinary Voyages of an Egyptian in the Inner Earth with the Discovery of Sylphides' Island*; Vol. 1: Poilly, 1735); Vol. 2: Neaulme, 1738; rep.VI, 1788); *Mille et Un Faveurs—Contes* (*A Thousand and One Favors—Tales*; Aux dépends de la Cie., Londres, 1740); *Le Masque de Fer, ou Les Aventures Admirables du Père et du Fils* (*The Iron Mask or the Admirable Adventures of the Father and the Son*; P. de Houdt, 1750); *Contes Nouveaux de Fées* (*New Fairy Tales*; Jarry, 1756); *Note:* See Chapter III.

Moulie, Christiane (?-); *La Machine à Remonter le Temps* (*The Time Machine*; Méridien, 1981)

Moulinasse, Julienne (?-); *Des Signes dans le Roc* (*Signs in the Rock*; Cap Burgonde, 1930)

Moulins, Maurice de *see* **Bonneau, Albert**

Mounié, Didier (?-); *Chausse-Trappes* (*Traps*; CRNI, n.d.; **Mounier, Jacques (?-?)** *see* **Grand-Guignol**

Mount, Norbert George (Moutier, Norbert; ?-); *Neige d'Enfer* (*Hellish Snow*; FNG 64, 1988); *L'Équarisseur de Soho* (*The Soho Equerry*; FNG 112, 1990); *Note:* See Chapter VIII. Under his real name, Moutier is a fanzine editor and also contributes to *L'Écran Fantastique*. In 1997, he became the publisher of *Fantastyka* magazine. He also wrote and directed the 1985 short feature **Hémophilia** (see Book 1, Chapter I).

Mourier, Maurice (1936-); *Le Miroir Mité* (*The Specked Mirror*; Gall., 1972); *Godilande ou le Journal d'un Mort* (*Diary of a Dead Man*; Gall., 1974); *Parcs de Mémoire* (*Memory Park*; PdF 394, 1985); *Note:* See Chapter IX.

Moussard, Jacqueline *see* **Cervon, Jacqueline**

Moussette, Marcel (1940-); *Les Patenteux* (Jour, 1974); *Note:* French-Canadian writer. Satirical science fiction.

Moutier, Norbert *see* **Mount, Norbert George**

Mouton, Eugène (1823-1902); *Fantaisies* (*Fantasies*; Charpentier, 1863); *Nouvelles et Fantaisies Humoristiques* (*Humorous Short Stories and Fantasies*; as Mérinos; Libr. Générale, 1872); *Chimère* (*Chimera*; Libr. Moderne, 1887); *Histoire de l'Invalide à la Tête de Bois* (*Tale of the Invalid with a Wooden Head*; L.Baschet, 1890); *Note:* See Chapters IV and V.

Moutonnet de Clairfons, Julien-Jacques (1740-1813); *Les Îles Fortunées, ou Les Aventures de Bathylle et de Cléobule* (Le Boucher, 1778; rev. VI, 1787); *Le Véritable Philanthrope, ou l'Île de la Philanthropie* (*The True Philanthroppist, or the Island of Philanthropia*; Philadelphia, 1790)

Mulinasse, Julienne (?-); *Des Signes dans le Roc* (*Signs in the Rock*; Cap Burgonde, 1930)

Muller, Charles (?-?) *see* **Grand-Guignol**

Muno, Jean (1924-); *L'Hipparion* (Julliard, 1962); *L'Homme qui s'efface* (*The Man Who Disappeared*; 1963); *L'Anti, Une Histoire de Fin du Monde* (*The Anti, a Tale of the End of the World*; P.J. Oswald, 1970); *Le Joker* (L. Musin, 1971); *La Brèche* (*The Breach*; St. Germain-des-Prés, 1973); *Ripple Marks* (J. Antoine, 1976); *Histoires Singulières* (*Singular Tales*; J. Antoine, 1979); *Histoire Exécrable d'un Héros Brabançon* (*Execrable Tale of a Brabant Hero*; J. Antoine, 1982); *Histoires Griffues* (*Clawed Tales*; AdH, 1985); *Jeu de Rôles* (*Role-Playing Games*; AdH, 1988); *Note:* Belgian writer. See Chapter VIII.

Murail, Lorris (?-); *Omnyle* (JCL, 1975); *La Secte* (*The Sect*; JCL, 1977); *L'Hippocampe* (*The Sea-Horse*; A&D 64, 1981); *Le Tombeau de Ridge* (*Ridge's Tomb*; F. Bourin, 1990); *Le Marchand de Cauchemars* (*The Nightmare Peddler*; Rouge & Or, 1990); *La Poubelle d'Ali-Baba* (*Ali-Baba's Dustbin*; Rouge & Or, 1991); *Le Professeur de Distractions* (*The Professor of Distractions*; École des Loisirs, 1993); *Note:* See Chapters VIII and IX.

Murail, Marie-Aude (1954-); *Graine de Monstre* (*Monster Seed*; Centurion, 1986); *Mystère* (*Mystery*; Gall., 1987); *Le Visiteur de Minuit* (*The Midnight Visitor*; Centurion, 1988); *Le Chien des Mers* (*The Sea Dog*; Ecole des Loisirs, 1988); *Jude et Jean* (Centurion, 1988); *Le Docteur Magicus* (Bayard, 1988); *La Nuit des Grottes* (*Cavern Night*; Nathan, 1990); *Les Secrets Véritables* (*The True Secrets*; Ecole des Loisirs, 1990); *Note:* Juveniles. See Chapter VIII.

Murat, Henriette Julie de Castelnau, Comtesse de (1670-1716); *Les Contes de Fées* (*The Fairy Tales*; Barbin, 1697); *Les Nouveaux Contes des Fées* (*The New Fairy Tales*; Barbin, 1698); *Les Lutins du Château de Kernosy* (*The Goblins of Castle Kernosy*; VI, 1788); *Note:* Also see Chapter III and *Cabinet des Fées*.

Murcie, Georges (1938-); *Garadania* (FNA 405, 1970); *Le Rendez-Vous aux 300.000 (Rendezvous at 300,000);* FNA 428, 1970); *La Puissance de l'Ordre (The Power of the Order;* FNA 450, 1971); *Les Rescapés du Futur (The Survivors of the Future;* FNA 467, 1971); *Motel 113* (FNA 483, 1971); *Objectif: La Terre! (Target: Earth!;* FNA 503, 1972); *Le Tunnelumière (The Lightunnel;* FNA 520, 1972); *Les Grottes de Phobos (The Caverns of Phobos;* FNA 536, 1972); *Les Possédés de Wolf 359 (The Possessed of Wolf 359);* FNA 552, 1973); *Mission au Futur Antérieur (Mission in a Previous Future;* FNA 569, 1973); *Arlyada* (FNA 580, 1973); *Vahanara* (FNA 594, 1974); *Oméga 5* (FNA 603, 1974); *De l'Autre Côté de l'Atome (On the Other Side of the Atom;* FNA 628, 1974); *Projet Apocalypse (Project Apocalypse;* FNA 639, 1974); *La Folie du Capitaine Sangor (The Madness of Captain Sangor;* FNA 655, 1975); *Opération Désespoir (Operation Despair;* FNA 663, 1975); *Les Naufragés du Temps (The Castaways in Time;* FNA 677, 1975); *Les Hybrides de Michina (The Hybrids of Michina;* FNA 686, 1975); *L'Homme de Lumière (The Man of Light;* FNA 704, 1975); *Mâa* (FNA 722, 1976); *Un Jour, l'Oubli (One Day, Oblivion;* FNA 733, 1976); *L'Etre Polyvalent (The Polyvalent Being;* FNA 752, 1976); *La Révolte de Zarmou (Revolt on Zarmou;* FNA 765, 1977); *Le Non-Etre (The Non-Being;* FNA 783, 1977); *Pari-Egar* (FNA 793, 1977); *La Courte Eternité d'Hervé Girard (The Short Eternity of Hervé Girard;* FNA 812, 1977); *Marga* (FNA 838, 1978); *La Mémoire du Futur (The Memory of the Future;* FNA 862, 1978); *Là-bas (Out There;* FNA 886, 1978); *Tetras* (FNA 969, 1980); *Note:* See Chapter IX.

Mure, André (?-); *Trahison Atomique (Atomic Betrayal;* Flamme d'Or, 1954); *Chronique d'une Mort Non-Programmée (Chronicles of an Unprogrammed Death;* Traitement de Textes, 1987); *Rue du Parfait-Silence (Street of Perfect Silence;* TR, 1991); *Montée de l'Observance (Observation Hill;* TR, 1992); *Le Chaudron du Diable (The Devil's Cauldron;* TR, 1994)

Murelli, Jean (Peheu, André; ?-); *L'Orgue de l'Epouvante (The Organ of Terror;* FNAG 49, 1959); *Ce Mur Qui Regardait (That Staring Wall;* FNAG 55, 1959); *De Mon Sarcophage (From My Sarcophagus;* FNAG 61, 1960); *Une Morte à Tuer (To Kill a Dead Woman;* FNAG 66, 1960); *Noir est ton Retour (Black Is Your Return;* FNAG 70, 1960); *Les Peaux Froides (The Cold Skins;* FNAG 79, 1961); *Requiem pour les Huit (Requiem for the Eight;* FNAG 89, 1962); *Ta Baraque à Malheurs (Your Unhappy House;* FNAG 98, 1963); *Les Noirs Paradis (The Black Paradises;* FNAG 110, 1964); *Des Faces Blêmes (Some Wan Faces;* FNAG 116, 1965); *La Nuit des Trépassés (The Night of the Dead;* FNAG 139, 1967); *Ma Peau de Fantôme (My Ghostly Skin;* FNAG 161, 1969); *Note:* See Chapter VIII.

Murey, Georges *see* **Arnaud, G.-J.**

Murphy, Francis (?-); *La Jeune Fille de Rattenberg (The Girl from Rattenberg;* FN, 1963); *Les Amants du Nil (The Nile's Lovers;* FN, 1965); *L'Invitée de Lorelei (Lorelei's Guest;* FNAG 162, 1969)

Mysor, Fernand (?-); *Les Semeurs d'Épouvante, Roman des Temps Jurassiques (The Sowers of Terror, Novel of Jurassic Times;* Grasset, 1923); *La Négresse dans la Piscine (The African Woman in the Swimming Pool;* Ed. du Siècle, 1924); *Va'Hour l'Illuminé (Va'Hour the Mad;* Baudinière, 1924); *La Ville Assassinée (The Murdered City;* Baudinière, 1925); *Par TSF (Via TSF;* Fasquelle, 1927); *Spasme (Spasms;* Baudnière, 1929); *Note:* See Chapter VII.

Nadal (Abbé) (?-?); *Les Voyages de Zulma dans le Pays des Fées (The Journefys of Zulma in the Land of the Fairies;* F. Changuion, 1734); *Note:* Children's fantasy.

Nadaud, Alain (1948-); *Archéologie du Zéro (Archeology of Zero;* Den., 1983); *L'Envers du Temps (The Other Side of Time;* Den., 1985); *Note:* See Chapter IX.

Nadaud, Marcel (1889-?); *Les Derniers Mousquetaires: Roman de la Guerre Aérienne (The Last Musketeers: a Novel of the War in the Air;* AM, 1917); *Frangipane et Cie.: Roman de la Guerre Aérienne (Frangipane and Co.: a Novel of the War in the Air;* AM, 1919); *Chignole au Paradis (Chignole in Paradise;* AM, 1923); *Les Morts Mystérieuses, les Sorciers Modernes (Mysterious Deaths, Modern Sorcerers;* Anquetil, 1926); *Note:* Also see **Grand-Guignol.**

Nagrien, X. (Audois, A.) (1825-); *Prodigieuse Découverte et ses Incalculables Conséquences sur les Destinées du Monde Entier (Prodigious Discovery and Its Incalculable Consequences on the Fate of the Entire World;* Hetzel, 1867); *Note:* See Chapter V.

Naïm, Robert *see* **Teldy-Naïm, Robert**

Narcejac, Thomas *see* **Boileau-Narcejac**

Nancey, Marcel (?-?) *see* **Grand-Guignol**

Natael & Maskolo (?-); *Les Enfants de l'Enfer (The Children from Hell;* Jean Goujon, 1978)

Nau, John-Antoine (Torquet, Eugène) (1860-1918); *Au Seuil de l'Espoir (On the Treshold of Hope;* Vannier, 1897); *La Force Ennemie (The Enemy Force;* La Plume, 1903); *Le Prêteur d'Amour (The Love Lender;* Fasquelle, 1905); *La Gennia* (Roman Spirite Hétérodoxe; Messein, 1906); *Vers la Fée Viviane (Towards Vivien the Fey;* La Phalange, 1908); *Les Galanteries d'Anthime Budin (The Gallant Gestures of Anthime Budin;* AM, 1923); *Note:* See Chapter V.

Ndiaye, Marie ?-); *La Sorcière (The Witch;* Minuit, 1996)

Nécrorian, Charles *see* **Mazarin, Jean**

Nedelec, François (1954-); *Mai 68 (Folie Douce, 1980); Empire Galactique (Galactic Empire*; RL, 1984); *Frontières de l'Empire (Frontiers of the Empire*; RL, 1985); *Encyclopédie Galactique (Galactic Encyclopedia*; RL, 1987); *Le Livre de la Licorne (The Book of the Unicorn*; Den., 1991); *Note:* Nedelec was one of the founders of the most popular French role-playing magazine, *Casus Belli.* The *Empire* titles were his attempt at creating a multi-game companion that could also be read and understood by non-RPG connoisseurs. the series is presented in an encyclopedia-like fashion.

Neilson, Francis (?-?) *see* **Grand-Guignol**

Neirynck, Jacques (1931-) *see* **Décotte, Alex**

Nemours, Henry (?-); *Mars en Avril (Mars in April*; Debresse, 1969); *Mars Revient (Mars Returns*; Pensée U., 1972)

Nennot, Dominique (?-); *Le Souffle du Mal (The Breath of Evil*; Karolus, 1961); *Déliriomas* (MOC 11, 1979)

Nepoty, Lucien (?-?) *see* **Opéra**

Nepveu, A. (Dr.) *see* **Durtain, Luc**

Ner, Henri *see* **Ryner, Han**

Nerval, Gérard de (Labrunie, Gérard) (1808-1855); *L'Alchimiste (The Alchemist*; with Alexandre **Dumas**; Dumont, 1839); *Voyage en Orient (Voyage in Orient*; Charpentier, 1851); *Les Illuminés (The Illuminated Ones*; V. Lecou, 1852); *Les Chimères (Chimeras*; Giraud, 1854); *Les Filles de Feu* (Giraud, 1854, transl. as *Daughters of Fire,* 1922); *Aurélia* (Michel Lévy, 1855); *Note:* See Chapter IV. De Nerval's genre tales include: "La Nuit du 31 Décembre" ("The Night of December 31st"; as Édouard de Puycousin; MdF, 1832), "La Main Enchantée" ("The Enchanted Hand"; in "Cabinet de Lecture," revised as "La Main de Gloire" ("The Glory Hand"), "Gautier," 1832), "Soirée d'Automne" ("Autum Evening"; 1836), "Le Portrait du Diable" ("The Devil's Portrait"; 1839), "Le Monstre Vert" ("The Green Monster"; 1849), "Histoire du Caliphe Hakem" ("Tale of Caliph Hakem") and "Histoire de la Reine du Matin et de Soliman," "Prince des Génies" ("Tale of the Queen of the Morning and of Soliman," "Prince of Djinns"; both incl. in "Voyage en Orient," 1851), and "La Pandora" (1854).

Néry, Gérard (?-); *In Extremis* (Martel, 1952); *Monsieur Cyber* (Los., 1969); *Thermotel **** (JCL, 1982); *Guide d'Ondes (Wave Guide*; JCL, 1982); *Thomas Loursin* (Grasset, 1983); *Iode 131* (FN, 1986); *La Chasse aux Cerveaux (Brain Hunt*; FN, 1987); *Panique à la Banque du Sperme (Panic at the Sperm Bank*; FNA 1663, 1989); *Pâques Sanglantes aux Caraïbes (Bloody Easter in the Caribbean*; FNA 1675, 1989); *Mort à l'Encre de Chine (Death with China Ink*; FNA 1688, 1989); *Terminus l'Enfer (Terminus: Hell*; FNA 1713, 1989); *Les Noyés du Fleuve Amour (Drowned in the River Love*; FNA 1724, 1989); *Scorpions* (FNA 1736, 1990); *Note:* See Chapter IX.

Nevers-Severin *see* **Bouquet, Jean-Louis**

Neveux, Georges (1900-1983) *see* **Grand-Guignol**

Nguyen, Jean-Jacques (?-); *Rêves d'Arkham (Arkham Dreams*; Oeil du Sphinx, n.d.); *Rêves d'Ailleurs (Elsewhere Dreams*; Oeil du Sphinx, n.d.); *Note:* See Chapter VIII.

Nicet, Max (1924-); *Quand Sonne Minuit (When Midnight Tolls*; Clocher, 1950); *Le Mystère de la Tour (The Mystery of the Tower*; Fleurus, 1952); *Les Brebis du Diable (The Devil's Ewes*; Hac., 1980); *Note:* Juveniles.

Nicot, Stéphane (?-); *Espaces Imaginaires 1 (Imaginary-Spaces 1*; anthology/with Jean-Marie **Gouanvic**; Imaginoïdes, 1983); *Espaces Imaginaires 2 (Imaginary-Spaces 2*; anthology/with Jean-Marie **Gouanvic**; Imaginoïdes, 1984); *Futurs Intérieurs (Internal Futures*; anthology; OF Special 34, 1984); *Espaces Imaginaires 3 (ImaginarySpaces 3*; anthology/with Jean-Marie **Gouanvic**; Imaginoïdes, 1985); *Espaces Imaginaires 4 (ImaginarySpaces 4*; anthology/with Jean-Marie **Gouanvic**; Imaginoïdes, 1986)

Nightingale, Charles (?-) *see* **Roche, Dominique**

Nimal, Henri de (1858-1925); *Légendes de la Meuse (Legends of the Meuse River*; 1898); *Note:* Belgian writer. See Chapter VI.

999; *L'Ordre Maçonnique de l'Himalaya (Manifeste K B L au Monde de la Surface) ; The Masonic Order of the Himalaya (Manifesto K B L to the Surface World;* 1966); *Note:* Collection of 1716 poems forming an esoteric pamphlet allegedly written in the year 701,966 of the Luciferian era and describing the secret order of the world.

Nino (Michel Veber) (?-?) *see* **Opéra**

Nizerolles, René-Marcel de (Priollet, Marcel) (1884-?); *Les Voyages Aériens d'un Petit Parisien à travers le Monde (The Aerial Voyages of a Little Parisian Across the World*; serialized in 111 isues (382 chapters, 1776 pages), Ferenczi, 1910-12; rev. as 100 issues (306 chapters, 1600 pages), Ferenczi, 1933-35; Titles of the Second Edition: *1. Un Match Sensationnel (An Extraordinary Match); 2. L'Avion Fantôme (The Ghost Plane); 3. Les Coupeurs de Têtes (The Head Cutters); 4. La Cité Mystérieuse (The Mysterious City); 5. Les Sauvages Blancs (The White Savages); 6. a la Merci du Traître (At the Traitor's Mercy); 7. Un Brave (A Brave); 8. Le*

Crime du Cafre (The Caphre's Crime); 9. Vers l'Inconnu (Towards the Unknown); 10. Prisonniers de la Banquise (Prisoners of the Ice Shelf); 11. Miracle sur Miracle (Double Miracle); 12. Aéroplanes et Sous-Marins (Airplanes and Submarines); 13. Les Pilleurs d'Épaves et le Mangeur d'Hommes (The Shipwreck Looters and the Man-Eater); 14. L'Inde Mystérieuse (Mysterious India); 15. La Folie de l'Inventeur (The Inventor's Madness); 16. Une Capture Mouvementée (An Event-Filled Capture); 17. L'Idole en Feu (The Idol on Fire); 18. Aviateurs et Policier (Airmen and Policemen); 19. Le Réveil du Volcan (The Volcano's Awakening); 20. En Mission! (On a Mission!); 21. Au Pays des Supplices (In the Land of Tortures); 22. Deux contre Mille (Two vs. a Thousand); 23. Rêve... ou Réalité? (Dream... or Reality?); 24. Une Poursuite Acharnée (A Fierce Pursuit); 25. Les Mangeurs d'Hommes (The Man-Eaters); 26. Un Duel Tragique (A Tragic Duel); 27. La Vengeance de la Bête (The Revenge of the Beast); 28. Le Secret du Cargo (The Secret of the Cargo); 29. Où Sont-Ils? (Where Are They?); 30. La Tombe de Glace (The Tomb of Ice); 31. L'Île au Trésor (Treasure Island); 32. L'Empereur des Andes (The Emperor of the Andes); 33. Tombé du Ciel! (Fallen from the Sky!); 34. La Vallée aux Condors (Condor Valley); 35. Résurrection (Rebirth); 36. Aux Mains de l'Ennemi (In Enemy Hands); 37. Moeurs de Sauvages (Savage Practices); 38. L'Attaque du Train (The Train Attack); 39. Le Combat dans les Airs (Battle in the Air); 40. Le Secret de l'Avion Fantôme (The Secret of the Ghost Plane); 41. Le Mystère du Nicaragua (The Mystery of Nicaragua); 42. La Terreur des Mers (The Terror of the Seas); 43. Les Apaches de Mexico (The Mexican Apaches); 44. Les Sorciers du Chiapas (The Chiapa Wizards); 45. Les Armes de l'Espion (The Weapons of the Spy); 46. L'Île qui Marche (The Walking Island); 47. Les Forcenés de Chicago (The Madmen of Chicago); 48. Pan! Dans le mille! (Bam! Bull's Eye!); 49. Prisonniers des Loups (Prisoner of the Wolves); 50. Une Intervention Inattendue (An Unexpected Intervention); 51. La Ville Morte (The Dead City); 52. La Chasse aux Gangsters (The Hunt for the Gangsters); 53. Un Coup de Théâtre (A Surprising Development); 54. Sous les Eaux du Niagara (Under the Niagara Waters); 55. Un Nouveau Robinson (A New Robinson); 56. La Torpille Infernale (The Torpedo from Hell); 57. La Lettre Z (Letter Z); 58. Le Mandarin Rouge (The Red Mandarin); 59. La Pagode Hantée (The Haunted Pagoda); 60. La Statue Vivante (The Living Statue); 61. Sous les Griffes du Monstre (Under the Claws of the Monster); 62. Un Combat de Géants (A Clash of Giants); 63. La Fièvre de l'Or (Gold Fever); 64. Les Yeux qu'on Brûle... (Burning Eyes...); 65. L'Énigme du Télégraphe (The Mystery of the Teleegraph); 66. Au Pays de la Soif (In the Land of Thirst); 67. Le Lac Empoisonné (The Poisoned Lake); 68. Le Vaisseau de la Terreur (The Ship of Terror); 69. Face à la Mort (Facing Death); 70. Une Prodigieuse Invention (A Prodigious Invention); 71. Un Combat sous la Terre (An Underground Battle); 72. Le Pont sur l'Abîme (The Bridge Over the Abyss); 73. Au Pays des Esclaves (In the Land of Slaves); 74. Une Chasse à l'Homme (A Man Hunt); 75. Les Étrangleurs du Caire (The Cairo Stranglers); 76. Honneur de Soldat (Soldier's Honor); 77. Les Francs-Tireurs de l'Air (Mercenaries of the Air); 78. Aux Mains des Dissidents (In the Hands of the Rebels); 79. Le Linceul de Boue (The Shroud of Mud); 80. Toutes les Audaces (All the Dares); 81. La Maison Volante (The Flying House); 82. Perdus en Mer! (Lost at Sea!); 83. Une Arrestation Mouvementée (An Event-Filled Arrest); 84. Un Drame dans un Phare (Tragedy in the Lighthouse); 85. L'Avion sans Pilote (The Pilotless Plane); 86. Bas le Masque! (Take Off Your Mask!); 87. La Chasse aux Brigands (The Hunt for the Villains); 88. Dramatique Évasion (Dramatic Escape); 89. on ne passe pas! (No Trespassing!); 90. La Fusée Humaine (The Human Rocket); 91. Une Succession de Coups de Théâtre (A Series of Surprising Developments); 92. Un Marché Infâme (An Infamous Offer); 93. Le Maître de l'Air (Master of the Air); 94. Fatale Méprise (Fatal Mistake); 95. Le Monstre du Lac (The Lake Monster); 96. Le Voilier en Perdition (The Lost Sailship); 97. L'Iceberg à Hélice (The Helix-Propelled Iceberg); 98. Le Club des Rois Américains (The American Kings' Club); 99. Le Suprême Combat (The Battle Supreme); 100. Victoire et Châtiment (Victory and Punishment); Les Aventuriers du Ciel: Voyages Extraordinaires d'un Petit Parisien dans la Stratosphère, la Lune et les Planètes (The Adventurers of the Sky: ExtraordinaryVoyages of a Little Parisian in the Stratosphere, the Moon and the Planets; serialized in 108 isues, Ferenczi, 1935-37; rev. as 26 issues, Ferenczi, 1950-51); Titles of the First Edition: 1. Le Mystère de l'Observatoire de Paris (The Mystery of the Paris Observatory); 2. Où Sont-Ils? (Where Are They?); 3. Les Surprises de la Stratosphère (The Surprises of the Stratosphere); 4. Allo?Ici, la Lune (Hello? the Moon Speaking); 5. Le Trésor des Pharaons (The Treasure of the Pharaohs); 6. Arrivée chez les Martiens (Arrival on Mars); 7. Les Hommes de l'An 20000 (The Men from the Year 20000); 8. Le Secret de la Pyramide (The Secret of the Pyramid); 9. A l'Assaut de la Terre (To Assault the Earth); 10. La Révolte des Automates (Revolt of the Automatons); 11. Au Pays des Sorciers (In the Land of the Wizards); 12. Nains contre Géants (Dwarves vs. Giants); 13. L'Île aux Surprises (Suprise Island); 14. Le Réveil des Momies (The Mummies Awaken); 15. Le Bateau Magique (The Magic Boat); 16. Au Service de l'Ennemi (In the Enemy's Service); 17. Gavroche et Dictateur (The Dictator Kid); 18. L'Énigme de la Planète Rouge (The Mystery of the Red Planet); 19. Tragique Erreur (Tragic Mistake); 20. Les Mon-

tagnes à Roulettes (The Mountains on Wheels); 21. Hercule, Minerve... et Compagnie (Hercules, Minerva and Co); 22. Le Cratère Volant (The Flying Crater); 23. Gangsters en Uniformes (Gangsters in Uniforms); 24. Aux Prises avec les Cyclopes (Grappling with the Cyclops); 25. Le Corsaire Aérien (The Air Corsair); 26. En Montgolfière (In a Hot-Air Balloon); 27. L'Homme sans Nom (The Nameless Man); 28. Les Planetes Bombardées (The Bombed Planets); 29. Le Puits Enchanté (The Enchanted Well); 30. La Forêt qui Parle (The Talking Forest); 31. Coups de Théâtre (Surprising Developments); 32. Prisonnier d'un Arbre (Prisoner of a Tree); 33. Chasse à l'Homme (Man Hunt); 34. Le Dénicheur d'Arcs-en-ciel (The Rainbow Finder); 35. Voyage aux Enfers (Journey to Hell); 36. Un Passager Escamoté (The Vanished Passenger); 37. Fatale Bourrasque (Fatal Windstorm); 38. Le Piège Est Tendu! (The Trap Is Set!); 39. Le Tour d'un Monde en 80 Minutes (Around a World in 80 Minutes); 40. Le Chercheur d'Images (The Image Seeker); 41. Le Roi Solitaire (The Lonely King); 42. La Véridique histoire de Barbe-Bleue (The True Story of Blue-Beard); 43. Les Kidnappers de Paris (The Paris Kidnappers); 44. La Galerie des Phenomènes (The Gallery of Freaks); 45. Les Surprises du Phonographe (The Surprises of the Phonograph); 46. Le Mort-Vivant (The Living Dead); 47. L'Océan Vagabond (Wandering Ocean); 48. Voyage en Aérobulle (Journey in an Air Bubble); 49. Transformé en Statues! (Turned Into Statues!); 50. Les Robinsons de l'Île Errante (The Robinsons of the Wandering Island); 51. La Fin du Monde (The End of the World); 52. La Cible Habitée (The Inhabited Target); 53. Sa Majesté le Soleil (His Majesty the Sun); 54. Une Invention Prodigieuse (A Prodigious Invention); 55. Le Passager Clandestin (The Stowaway); 56. Face aux Monstres (Facing the Monsters); 57. Les Mammouths à Surprise (The Surprise Mastodons); 58. Radio-Mars vous parle... (Radio-Mars Calling...); 59. La Maison à l'Envers (The Inside-Out House); 60. Un Million de Dollars en Fumée (A Million Dollars Into Smoke); 61. L'Horloge Humaine (The Human Clock); 62. Empreintes sur la Neige (Footprints on the Snow); 63. Le Royaume de la Transparence (The See-Through Kingdom); 64. Perdu en Plein Ciel! (Lost in the Open Sky!); 65. a la Conquête de l'Or (The Conquest of Gold); 66. La Guerre des Fauves (War of the Beasts); 67. Les Idoles Profanées (The Desecrated Idols); 68. Malheureux... N'allez pas plus loin! (Fool! Don't Go Any Further!); 69. Le Piège à Hommes (The Man Trap); 70. Defense de Survoler! (Forbidden Fly-Over!); 71. ...Et le Jour ne se leva pas! (...And the Sun Did Not Rise!); 72. Un Génial Malfaiteur (A Brilliant Villain); 73. Nous... Dans Cinq Cent Mille Ans (We... in 500,000 Years); 74. Le Singe Descend de l'Homme (Ape Is Descended from Man); 75. Le Triomphe de l'Artificiel (The Triumph of the Artificial); 76. Le Soleil en Bouteilles (The Sun in a Bottle); 77. Prisonnier sur Parole (Free on Their Own Word); 78. Trahi par un Cri d'Enfant (Betrayed By a Child's Scream); 79. Le Miracle des Hommes-Luisants (The Miracle of the Shining Men); 80. Le Temple sous les Eaux (The Underwater Temple); 81. Un Duel à Mort (Duel to the Death); 82. Une Nuit Mouvementée (An Event-Filled Night); 83. Les Ombres Vivantes (The Living Shadows); 84. Le Pays des Sept Couleurs (The Land of Seven Colors); 85. La Catapulte (The Catapult); 86. Les Cavaliers sans Montures (The Horseless Riders); 87. La Princesse de Verre (The Glass Princess); 88. Un Redoutable Voisinage (A Fearsome Neighbor); 89. Galériennes et Bagnardes (The Women's Penitentiary); 90. Une Tentative Désespérée (A Desperate Attempt); 91. Héros malgre lui! (Hero in Spite of Himself!); 92. Un Pays de Cocagne (The Land of Plenty); 93. L'Ermite du Désert (The Desert Hermit); 94. La Roche Infernale (The Rock from Hell); 95. Justice est faite! (Justice Is Done!); 96. Le Marché aux Esclaves (The Slave Market); 97. Retour aux Âges Préhistoriques (Return to Prehistory); 98. Cent Siècles en une Journée (A Hundred Centuries in One Day); 99. Une Fenêtre Ouverte sur l'Avenir (An Open Window on the Future); 100. Amis... ou Ennemis? (Friends... or Foes?); 101. La Fosse aux Étincelles (The Spark Pit); 102. Trahir... ou Mourir! (Betrayal... or Death!); 103. Un Mal qui répand la Terreur (The Terrifying Disease); 104. Le Coeur Électrique (The Electric Heart); 105. Un + Un... = Un! (One + One... = One!); 106. L'Orgie au Clair des Lunes (Orgy By Moons' Light); 107. Disparus! (Vanished!); 108. Les Triomphateurs (The Triumphant Ones); Les Robinsons de l'Île Volante: Aventures Extraordinaires d'un Petit Parisien sur Terre, sur Mer, dans l'Air et dans l'Invisible (The Robinsons of the Flying Island: the ExtraordinaryAdventures of a Little Parisian on Land, on Sea, in the Air and in the Invisible; serialized in 28 isues, Ferenczi, 1937-38); 1. L'Énigme du Pacifique (The Mystery of the Pacific); 2. Le Fléau en Marche (The Walking Bane); 3. À l'Assaut du Mystère (To Attack the Mystery); 4. L'Homme qui Vient de Nulle Part (The Man from Nowhere); 5. Les Dreadnoughts de l'Air (The Air Dreadnoughts); 6. Chez l'Ennemi (With the Enemy); 7. Le Cheval d'Attila (Attila's Horse); 8. L'Inventeur du Fantôme (The Inventor of the Phantom); 9. L'Île d'Alabat vous parle! (Alabat Island Calling!); 10. on ne passe pas! (No Trespassing!); 11. Un Drame autour d'une Allumette (Drama Around a Match); 12. Escale au Pays des Oiseaux (Stop-Over in the Land of Birds); 13. À la Façon de Promethée (In Prometheus' Manner); 14. Le Piège Est Tendu! (The Trap Is Set!); 15. L'Étincelle Magique (The Magic Spark); 16. Les Mutins d'Arguello (The Mutiny of Arguello); 17. Le Laboratoire de Satan (Satan's Laboratory); 18. Feu à Volonté (Fire at Will); 19. L'Adversaire aux Mille Dards (The Foe with a Thousand Stingers);

20. *Les Maîtres du Cyclone (Masters of Hurricanes)*;
21. *Une Mort à Venger! (A Death to Avenge!)*; 22.
Panique à Hollywood (Panic in Hollywood); 23. *Un
Match Imprévu (An Unforeseen Match)*; 24. *Comité Secret (Secret Committee)*; 25. *Des Morts qui se portent
bien (Some Dead Men Who Are Doing Well)*; 26. *Comme
au temps de Buffalo-Bill (Like in the Days of Buffalo
Bill)*; 27. *La Sentence du Météore (The Meteor's Verdict)*; 28. *Lac Michigan: Tout le Monde descend!
(Everyone Get Off at Lake Michigan!)*; *L'Homme qui
n'est plus lui (The Man Who Is No Longer Himself;* as
Marcel Priollet; VA, 1935; rev. as *L'Homme qui a Perdu
son Corps (The Man Who Lost His Body)*, Ferenczi,
1947); *Les Bâtisseurs de Montagnes (The Builders of
Mountains*; MRA, 1942); *Note:* See Chapters V and VII.

Nocher, Jean (Charon, Gaston) (1908-1967); *Frankenstein, L'Âge d'Or ou la Fin du Monde (Frankenstein, the
Golden Age or the End of the World*; Ed. Nouvelles,
1935); *Plateforme 70 ou l'Âge Atomique (Platform 70,
or the Atomic Age*; SPER, 1946); *En Direct avec l'Avenir
(Direct Communication with the Future*; Del Duca,
1962); *Note: Plateforme 70* is the novelization of the
eponymous radio drama (see Book 1, Chapter III).

Nodier, Charles (1780-1844); *Les Proscrits (The Pro-
scribed*; Lepetit & Gérard, 1802); *Le Peintre de
Salzbourg (The Painter of Salzbourg*; Maradan, 1803);
*Les Méditations du Cloître (The Meditations of the
Cloister*; 1803); *Les Tristes ou Mélanges tirés des
tablettes d'un Suicide (The Sad Ones or Mixture Made
from the Tablets of a Suicide*; Demonville, 1806); *Lord
Rutwen ou le Vampire (Lord Ruthwen or the Vampire*;
Barba, 1820; translated/adapted as *The Vampire or the
Bride of the Isles*, 1820); *Smarra ou les Démons de la
Nuit (Smarra or the Demons of the Night*; Ponthieu,
1821; transl. 1993); *Trilby ou le Lutin d'Argail (Trilby
or the Goblin of Argail*; Ladvocat, 1822; transl. as *Trilby
or the Fairy of Argyle*, 1895); *Infernaliana (anthology*;
Sanson, 1822); *Histoire d'Hélène Gillet (The Story of
Helen Gillet*; in Revue de Paris, 1822); *L'Histoire du
Roi de Bohême et de ses Sept Châteaux (The Story of
the King of Bohemia and of His Seven Castles*; Delan-
gle, 1830); *Cent et Une Nouelles des Cent et Un (101
Stories of the 101*; Ladvocat, 1832); *La Fée aux Miettes
(The Crumb Fairy*; Renduel, 1832); *Le Nouveau Faust
et la Nouvelle Marguerite (The New Faust and the New
Marguerite*; Renduel, 1832); *La Combe de l'Homme
Mort (The Valley of the Dead Man*; in *Le Salmigondis*,
Fournier, 1832); *Le Songe d'Or (The Golden Dream*; in
Revue de Paris, 1832); *Baptiste Montauban ou L'Idiot
(in Le Conteur*, Dumont, 1833); *Hurlubleu, Grand Man-
ifafa d'Hurlubière (in Revue de Paris, 1833); Léviathan-
le-Long, Archikan des Patagons de l'Île Savante (in
Revue de Paris, 1833); Paul ou La Ressemblance (Paul
or the Similarity*; in Revue de Paris, 1836); *Le Génie*

*Bonhomme (Allardin, 1837); Ines de la Sierra (in Revue
de Paris, 1837); Trésor des Fèves et Fleur des Pois (Allardin, 1837; transl. as Bean Flower and Pea Blossom,
1946); La Légende de Soeur Beatrix (The Legend of Sister Beatrix; in Revue de Paris, 1837); Les Quatre Talismans (The Four Talismans; in Revue de Paris, 1838); La
Neuvaine de la Chandeleur (The Rosary of the Chandeleur; in Revue de Paris 1838); Lydie ou La Résurrection (Lydia or the Resurrection; in Revue de Paris,
1839); Histoire du Chien de Brisquet (Tale of Brisquet's
Dog; Blanchard, 1844; transl. as The Woodcutter's Dog,
1922); L'Amour et le Grimoire (Love and the Grimoir;
Charpentier, 1853); Lidivine (Libr. Sté. Bibl., 1877);
Note:* See Chapters IV and V.

Noël, Bernard (1945-); *Les Yeux Chimères (Chimera Eyes*;
Caractères, 1955); *À Vif enfin la Nuit (Live at Last at
Night*; Fata Morgana, 1968); *Les Fleurs Noires (The
Black Flowers*; Tisseyre, 1978); *Contes pour un Autre
Oeil (Tales for Another Eye*; Préambule, 1985); *Note:*
French-Canadian writer. Collections of fantastical tales.

Noel-Noel (Noël, Lucien) (1897-?); *Le Voyageur des Siècles
(The Traveller of the Centuries*; BV, 1971); *Note:* Novelization of the eponymous 1971 television mini-series
(see Book 1, Chapter II).

Noguès, Jean-Côme (1934-); *Papa Fantôme (Ghost Dad*;
Hac., 1987); *Le Voeu du Paon (The Peacock's Wish*;
Gall., 1987); *La Vieille Maison Mal Coiffée (The Old
Rumpled House*; Rouge et Or, 1974); *Mon Pays sous les
Eaux (My Underwater Land*; Rouge et Or, 1971); *Note:*
Juveniles.

Noguez, Dominique (?-); *Derniers Jours du Monde (Last
Days of the World*; RL, 1991)

Nolane, Richard D. (?-); *400 Mètres d'Angoisse (400 Me-
ters of Terror*; anthology; Crépuscule, 1979); *L'Heure de
l'Éventreur (The Hour of the Ripper*; anthology; Cré-
puscule, 1980); *Les Démons d'Abidjan (The Demons of
Abidjan*; FNG 118, 1990); *Le Cimetière des Rêves (The
Graveyard of Dreams*; VG, 1991); *Autrefois les Extra-
Terrestres (Yesterday's E.Ts*; VG, 1993); *Monstres des
Lacs et des Océans (Monsters of Lakes and Oceans*;
VG, 1993); *Sur les Traces du Yeti and Autres Animaux
Clandestins (On the Trail of the Yeti and Other Hidden
Beasts*; VG, 1994); *La Chair et le Sang: Vampires and
Vampirisme (Flesh and Blood: Vampires and Vampirism*;
UGE, 1994); *Extra-Terrestres: La Vérité sur Roswell
(E.Ts: the Truth About Roswell*; Plein Sud, 1995);
*Chroniques Cryptozoologiques (Cryptozoologic Chron-
icles*; Plain Sud, 1996); *1947: Les Soucoupes Volantes
Arrivent (1947: the Coming of Flying Saucers*; CG,
1997); *Note:* See Chapter IX. Also see Terence **Cor-
man**. Richard D. **Nolane** also writes a ***Harry Dickson***
comic-book adaptation (see Book 1, Chapter V).

Nolant de Fatouville (?-?); *Grapinian ou Arlequin Empereur de la Lune (Grapinian, or Harlequin, Emperor of the Moon*; C. Blageart, 1684)

Nolhac, Pierre de (1859-1936); *Saison en Auvergne (Season in Auvergne*; 1932); *Contes Philosophiques (Philosophical Tales*; Grasset, 1932); *Note:* See Chapter VII.

Noort, Philippe (?-); *La Piste de Flamme (The Fire Trail*; Tallandier, 1932); *L'Oule du Diable (The Devil's Cave*; Alcan, 1933)

Nori, Claude (?-); *Une Fille Instantanée (An Instant Girl*; Seuil, 1981); *Il me semble vous avoir déjà rencontré quelque part (It Seems I've Already Met You Somewhere*; Contrejour, 1983); *Lotus Park* (Contrejour, 1987)

Normand, Jean (?-); *Le Mystère du Bagne (The Mystery of the Penitentiary*; Reportages Populaires, 1924); *Les Vengeurs du Soleil (The Avengers of the Sun*, 1928); *Le Tour du Monde du Petit Mécano (The Little Mechanic Around the World*; Ed. Modernes, 1930); *Les Longues Oreilles (The Long Ears*; VLAE, 1929); *Le Maître de l'Étoile (The Star Master*; BGA, 1930); *L'Épave du Nicobar (The Wreck of the Nicobar*; CA, 1933); *L'Homme à la Sarbacane (The Man with the Blow Pipe*; Tallandier, 1934); *Le Kébir Blanc (The White Kebir*; Ferenczi, 1936); *Le Poignard de Verre (The Glass Dagger*, 1936); *Les Galions de Parias (The Galleons of Pariahs*; Tallandier, 1936); *La Cité du Mystère (The City of Mystery*; Ferenczi, 1937); *La Passagère de la Malaisie (The Passenger of the Malaysia*; Ferenczi, 1937); *Le Trésor des Oyampis (The Treasure of the Oyampis*; BGA, 1937); *Les Évadés de la Mort (Escape from Death*; Tallandier, 1937); *L'Homme à la Cicatrice (The Man with a Scar*; Tallandier, 1937); *La Mâchoire du Requin (The Shark's Jaws*; Tallandier, 1937); *L'Agence Euréka (The Eureka Agency*; Tallandier, 1937); *Arika, Fleur des Tropiques (Arika, Flower of the Tropics*; SEPIA, 1938); *L'Icône d'Argent (The Silver Icon*; SEPIA, 1938); *La Pagode aux Serpents (The Pagoda of Snakes*; VA, 1938); *La Pagode Infernale (The Inernal Pagoda*; PRA, 1938); *La Chaîne d'Or (The Gold Chain*; Tallandier, 1938); *Gentlemen des Îles (Gentlemen from the Islands*; Tallandier, 1938); *Le Maître de l'Étoile (The Master of the Star*; Tallandier, 1938); *Le Masque de Poix (The Pitch Mask*; Tallandier, 1941); *Le Vengeur des Incas (The Inca Avenger*; ABC, 1941); *Le Tatouage Rouge (The Red Tattoo*; ABC, 1942); *Note:* See Chapter VII.

Norwood, Sam P. *see* **Brooker, Edward**

Nöstlinger, Christine (?-); *Le Môme en Conserve (The Kid in a Can*; Hac., 1982); *Le Roi des Concombres (The King of Cucumbers*; Bordas, 1982); *Le Nouveau Pinocchio (The New Pinocchio*; Souffles, 1989); *Le Nain dans la Tête (The Dwarf in the Head*; École de Loisirs, 1992)

Nothomb, Pierre (1887-1966); *La Rédemption de Mars (The Redemption of Mars*; Plon, 1922); *Le Lion Ailé (The Winged Lion*; Plon, 1926); *Le Prince d'Olzhein (The Prince of Olzhein*; Rond-Point, 1945); *Le Prince du Dernier Jour (The Prince of the Last Day*; AM, 1960); *Les Miracles (The Miracles*; Brepols, 1962); *Morménil* (Plon, 1964); *Note:* Belgian writer. See Chapters VII and VIII.

Nour, Michel (?-); *Et la Flamme s'éteignit (And the Flame Died*; France-Édition, 1924); *L'Espionne Sanglante (The Bloody Spy*; LN, 1931); *Nous avions fait un beau rêve (We Dreamed a Pleasant Dream*; Libr. Contemporane, 1932); *Le Rayon Infernal (The Hellish Ray*; BGA, 1933); *Petit Démon (Little Demon*; Rouff, 1934); *Le Mystère du Vase de Chine (The Mystery of the China Vase*; Rouff, 1935)

Noury, Maurice (?-); *Satan et Cie. (Satan and Co*; Tallandier, 1939); *Tout le Bonheur du Monde (All the Happiness in the World*; SEPIA, 1939); *Le Mystère de la Tour St. Jacques (The Mystery of St. Jack's Tower*; Tallandier, 1940); *L'île de la Damnation (The Island of Damnation*; Tallandier, 1941); *La Maison des Épouvantes (The House of Horrors*; LN, 1950)

Novy, Michel (?-); *Le Châtiment des Rois Frères (The Punishment of the Brother Kings*; Oeil-du-Sphinx, 1994); *Note:* See Chapter VIII.

Nozière, Jean-Paul (1943-); *L'Abominable Destin des Areu-Areu (The Awful Destiny of the Areu-Areu*; Magnard, 1981); *Le Facteur à l'Envers (The Inside-Out Mailman*; Amitié, 1981); *Cher Vieux Cochise (Dear Old Cochise*; Duculot, 1986); *La Vie Sauvage (Wild Life*; Flamm., 1987); *Ma Vie c'est l'Enfer (My Life Is Hell*; Amitié, 1987); *Dossier Top Secret* (Amitié, 1988); *Histoire du Magicien qui aimait les Petits Lapins et les Grands Destins (Tale of the Magician Who Liked Small Rabbits and Great Destinies*; CNDP, 1990); *Le Ventre du Bouddha (The Buddha's Belly*; Hac., 1991); *Retour à Ithaque (Return to Ithaca*; Gall., 1992); *La Malédiction du Corbeau (The Curse of the Crow*; Bayard, 1992); *Note:* Juveniles. *Areu-Areu* is a prehistoric satire à la *Quest for Fire*.

Nubé *see* **Mettra**

Nunes, Robert (?-?) *see* **Grand-Guignol**

Nyst, Ray (?-); *Un Prophète (A Prophet*; Chamuel, 1895); *La Caverne* (Baillière, 1909); *Note:* See Chapter V.

Odene, Laure (?-); *White Chapel* (Florent Massot, 1997)

Odier, Daniel (?-); *Le Voyage de John O'Flaherty (John O'Flaherty's Journey*; Seuil, 1972); *La Voie Sauvage (The Savage Way*; Seuil, 1974); *Splendor Solis* (Stock, 1976); *Ming* (RL, 1976); *Gioconda* (Fayard, 1984); *Le Baiser Cannibale (The Cannibal Kiss*; Mazarine, 1987); *L'Illusioniste (The Illusionist*; JCL, 1997)

Olaf (Babinski, Joseph) (1857-1932) *see* **Grand-Guignol**

Olaf, Dominique (?-); *Adam and Eve Pilotes d'OVNI (Adam and Eve UFO Pilots;* Pensée U., 1981)

Olasso, Pierre (?-); *Les Disparus de l'Avenue de Messine (The Disappearances on Messine Avenue;* Tallandier, 1932); *Le Mystère des Trois Baignoires (The Mystery of the Three Bathtubs;* Libr. Contemporaine, 1932); *Le Crime Mystérieux du Cheval Blanc (The Mysterious Crime of the White Horse;* Libr. Contemporaine, 1933); *Les Divinités de l'Or (The Gods of Gold;* Ferenczi, 1938); *La Marque de Kandaï (The Mark of Kandai;* Ferenczi, 1938); *L'Idole des Maoris (The Idol of the Maoris;* VA, 1938); *Le Secret du Désert (The Secret of the Desert;* VA, 1938); *Le Sorcier de la Jungle (The Wizard of the Jungle;* VA, 1938); *L'Agresseur de Peter-le-Balafré (Scarface Pete's Attacker;* Ferenczi, 1940); *La Voix qui Trompe (The Misleading Voice;* ABC, 1941); *L'Emblème du Tigre (The Sign of the Tiger;* Livre Moderne, 1941); *Le Hurlement Mystérieux (The Mysterious Howling;* Livre Moderne, 1942); *Le Monstre Préhistorique (The Prehistoric Monster;* MRA, 1952); *Note:* See Chapter VII.

Olivier, Georges (?-); *Le Fétiche Parlant (The Talking Idol;* Rieder, 1934)

Olivier, Paul (1871-?) *see* **Grand-Guignol**

Olivier-Martin, Yves (1935-); *Le Voisin (The Neighbor;* n.d.); *Isolina* (Promotion & Édition, 1968); *Note:* See Chapter VIII.

Ollier, Claude (1923-); *La Mise en Scène (The Direction;* Minuit, 1958); *Été Indien (Indian Summer;* Minuit, 1963); *Navattes* (Gall., 1967); *La Vie sur Epsilon (Life on Epsilon;* Gall., 1972); *Enigma* (Gall., 1973); *Our ou Vingt Ans Après (Our or Twenty Years Later;* Gall., 1974); *Fuzzy Sets* (10/18, 1975); *Souvenirs Écran (Screen Memories;* Gall., 1981); *Nébules (Nebulae;* Flamm., 1981); *Mon Double à Malacca (My Twin in Malacca;* Flamm., 1982); *L'Échec de Nolan (Nolan's Failure;* Flamm., 1985); *Une Histoire Illisible (An Unreadable Story;* Flamm., 1986); *L'Ailleurs le Soir (Elsewhere at Night;* Colorature, 1987); *Déconnection (Disconnected;* Flamm., 1988); *Le Maintien de l'Ordre (Maintaining Order;* Flamm., 1988); *Mesures de Nuit (Night Measures;* La Sétérée, 1988); *Journée de Travail (Work Day;* Flamm., 1989); *Feuilleton (Serial;* Julliard, 1990); *Du Fond des Âges (From the Darkest Ages;* Maeght, 1991); *Truquage en Amont (Tricks Upriver;* Flamm., 1992); *Le Sycomore* (Garanjoud, 1994); *Outback ou l'Arrière Monde (Outback or the World Behind;* POL, 1995); *Note:* See Chapter IX.

Ollivier, Jean (1925-); *Le Chaudron d'Or (The Golden Cauldron;* GP, 1974); *Le Marteau de Thor (Thor's Ham-*mer; GP, 1974); *Le Maître de l'Olympe (The Master of Olympus;* GP, 1975); *Ayak 1: Le Loup Blanc (The White Wolf;* GP, 1980); *Ayak 2: La Piste de l'Or (The Trail of Gold;* GP, 1981); *Ayak 3: La Ruée sur le Yukon (The Yukon Rush;* GP, 1981); *Récit des Mers du Sud (Tales from the Southern Seas;* Chardon Bleu, 1983); *Histoire du Gaillard d'Avant (Tales from the Bridge;* Gall., 1984); *Une Expédition Viking (A Viking Expedition;* Nathan, 1985); *Colonie Viking au Groënland (Viking Colony in Greenland;* AM, 1985); *La Chambre de Cristal (The Crystal Chamber;* Edimonde-Hac., 1986); *Le Secret des Grands Marais (The Secret of the Big Swamps;* Messidor-La Farandole, 1987); *L'Âge d'Or de la Flibuste (The Golden Age of Corsairs;* Messidor-La Farandole, 1987); *Histoires de l'Or (Tales of Gold;* Messidor-La Farandole, 1987); *Histoires de la Lande et de la Brume (Tales of the Moor and Mist;* Chardon Bleu, 1988)

Ollivier, Mikaël (1968-) *see* **Clarinard, Raymond**

Omessa, Charles (?-) & Henri (?-); *Anaïtis, Fille de Carthage (Daughter of Carthago;* Ed. De France, 1922); *Le Troisième Oeil de Civa (The Third Eye of Shiva;* Tallandier, 1932); *Histoire de l'Autre Monde (Tale from Another World;* Ed. De France, 1934); *Note:* See Chapter VI.

O'Neil, Jean (1936-); *Giriki et le Prince de Quécan (Giriki And the Prince of Quecan;* Libre Expression, 1982); *Note:* French-Canadian writer. Offbeat satire and love story.

Opéra; *Note:* We have listed below most of the major genre operas, according to their writers, i.e., the authors of their librettos. This list is not exhaustive; however, it is reasonably comprehensive as far as the major authors of genre librettos are concerned. The authors whose names are followed with (q.v.) have separate entries in this chapter. We provide a separate listing of the quoted composers below. Also see chapters II and IV. Authors: **Albaret, d'** *Scylla et Glaucus* (1746); *Note:* Libretto for composer Jean-Marie Leclair Aîné, based on Greek mythology. **Apollinaire, Guillaume (q.v.)** *Les Mamelles de Tiresias (The Tits of Tiresias;* 1917); *Note:* Libretto for a surrealist opera-bouffe for composer Francis Poulenc. **Arnoux, Alexandre (q.v.)** *Le Chevalier Errant (The Wandering Knight;* 1950); *Note:* Libretto for composer Jacques Ibert. **Augé de Lassus** *Phryné* (1893); *Note:* Libretto for composer Camille Saint-Saëns. **Autreau, J.** *see* **Le Valois d'Orville, Adrien-Joseph. Avril, René d'** *Le Miracle de Saint Nicolas (The Miracle of St. Nicolas;* 1905); *Note:* Libretto for composer Jean-Guy Ropartz. **Barbier, Jules** *Benvenuto Cellini* (with Léon de **Wailly**; 1838); *Dinorah ou le Pardon de Ploërmel (Dinorah or the Forgiveness of Ploermel;* with Michel **Carré**; 1859); *Faust* (with Michel **Carré**; 1859); *Philemon et Baucis* (with Michel **Carré**; 1860); *La Statue (The Statue*; with Michel **Carré**; 1861); *La Reine de Saba (The Queen of Shebah*; 1862); *Hamlet* (with Michel **Carré**; 1868); *Les Contes d'Hoffmann* (with Michel **Carré**; 1881); *Note: Benvenuto* for composer Hector **Berlioz**. *Dinorah* was for composer Giacomo Meyerbeer, and is based on ancient Britannic fairy tales; *Faust* and *Philémon* were for composer Charles Gounod and are based respectively on tales by Goethe and Ovid. *La Statue* was for composer Ernest Reyer and is based on an Oriental tale. *La Reine* was for composer Charles Gounod. *Hamlet* was for composer Ambroise Thomas and was loosely based on Shakespeare's play; *Les Contes* was for composer Jacques Offenbach and adapted material from the renowned German gothic tales. **Beauplan, A. de** *see* **Leuven, Adolphe de; Berlioz, Hector** *La Damnation de Faust (Faust's Damnation*; 1846); *Les Troyens (The Trojans*; 1860; repr. 1890); *Note:* Famous composer and author of two genre operas (including their librettos), the first based on Goethe's renowned tale. Also see **Barbier, Jules. Bernard, Pierre-Joseph** *Castor et Pollux* (1737); *Les Fêtes d'Hébé (The Festivities of Hebe*; with Simon-Joseph **Pellegrin** & Antoine Gautier de Montdorge & Alexandre Le Riche de la Pouplinière; 1739); *Les Surprises de l'Amour (Cupid's Surprises*; 1748); *Note:* Librettos for composer Jean-Philippe Rameau, based on Greek mythology. **Blau, Alfred** *Sigurd* (with Camille de **Locle**; 1884); *Note:* Libretto for composer Ernest Reyer. **Blau, Édouard** *Le Roi d'Ys* (1888); *Esclarmonde* (with Louis de Gramont; 1889); *Note:* The first libretto was for composer Édouard Lalo (it is about the legendary sunken city off the coast of Britanny); and the second for composer Jules Massenet. **Bonifacy, Pierre (q.v.);** *Dédale et Icare* (1975); *Note:* Libretto written for composer Renaud Gagneux. **Boukay, Maurice** *see* **Spitzmuller, George. Bourgeois, Anicet** *La Nonne Sanglante (The Bloody Nun*; 1835); *Note:* Libretto for composer Charles Gounod. **Boyer (Abbé);** *Méduse* (1697); *Note:* Libretto for composer Charles-Hubert Gervais. **Bretonneau (Père);** *David et Jonathan* (1688); *Note:* Libretto for composer Marc-Antoine Charpentier. **Butor, Michel (q.v.);** *Votre Faust (Your Faust*; 1960-67); *Note:* Libretto for composer Henri Pousseur. **Cahusac, Louis de** *Les Fêtes de Polymnie (The Festivities of Polymnie*; 1745); *Les Fêtes de l'Hymen et de l'Amour, ou Les Dieux d'Égypte (The Festivities of Hymen and Love, or the Gods of Egypt*; 1747); *Zais* (1748); *Nais* (1749); *Zoroastre* (1749); *La Naissance d'Osiris (The Birth of Osiris*; 1754); *Les Boréades* (1764); *Note:* Librettos for composer Jean-Philippe Rameau, based on Greek and Egyptian mythologies. **Caillet, Gérard** *see* **Landowski, Marcel. Cain, Henri** *Cendrillon (Cinderella*; 1899); *Don Quichotte* (1910); *Note:* Another variation of the classic fairy tale by **Per-**

rault and a libretto based on Cervantes' classic novel; both written for composer Jules Massenet. **Carré, Michel** *Dinorah ou le Pardon de Ploërmel (Dinorah or the Forgiveness of Ploermel*; with Jules **Barbier**; 1859); *Faust* (with Jules **Barbier**; 1859); *Philemon et Baucis* (with Jules **Barbier**; 1860); *La Statue (The Statue*; with Jules **Barbier**; 1860); *Mireille* (1864); *Hamlet* (with Jules **Barbier**; 1868); *Les Contes d'Hoffmann* (with Jules **Barbier**; 1881); *Note: Mireille* was a libretto for composer Charles Gounod based on a novel by Frédéric **Mistral**. for details regarding the collaborations with Jules **Barbier**, see under **Barbier. Charpentier, Gustave** *Orphée* (1913); *Note:* Composer and author of a genre opera (including its libretto) about Orphéus. **Chausson, Ernest** *Le Roi Arthus (King Arthur*; 1903); *Note:* Composer and author of a genre opera (including its libretto) about King Arthur and Merlin. **Clairville (Nicolaie, Louis-François);** *Daphnis et Chloé* (with Jules Cordier; 1860); *Les Cloches de Corneville (The Bells of Corneville*; 1877); *Note:* The first libretto was for composer Jacques Offenbach and is based on Greek mythology; the second for composer Robert Planquette and is about a haunted castle. **Claretie, Jules (q.v.);** *Amadis* (1890? repr. 1922); *Note:* Libretto for composer Jules Massenet. **Claudel, Paul (q.v.);** *Danse des Morts (Dance of the Dead*; 1938); *Note:* Libretto for composer Arthur Honegger. **Cocteau, Jean (q.v.);** *Oedipus Rex* (1927); *Note:* Libretto for composer Igor Stravinsky. **Colette** *L'Enfant et les Sortilèges (The Child and the Spells*; 1925); *Note:* Famous mainstream novelist. Libretto for composer Maurice Ravel. **Cordier, Jules** *see* **Clairville. Corneille, Thomas (q.v.);** *Cadmus et Hermione* (1673); *Alceste* (1674); *Thésée* (1675); *Isis* (1677); *Psyché* (with Philippe **Quinault**; 1678); *Bellérophon* (with Philippe **Quinault** and Bernard Le Bovier de **Fontenelle**; 1679); *Circé* (1694); *Médée* (1700); *Note:* Librettos for composers Jean-Baptise Lully; the last two were for composers Henry Desmarets and Marc-Antoine Charpentier. **Crémieux, Hector** *see* **Halévy, Ludovic. Danchet, Antoine** *Tancrède* (1702); *Les Muses* (1703); *Les Fêtes Vénitiennes (Venetian Festivities*; 1710); *Idoménée* (1712); *Les Amours de Vénus et Mars (The Loves of Venus and Mars*; 1712); *Note:* Librettos for composer André Campra, based on Greek mythology. **Debussy, Claude** *Le Diable dans le Beffroi (The Devil in the Belfry*; 1912); *La Chute de la Maison Usher (The Fall of the House of Usher*; 1917; repr. 1977); *Note:* Composer and author of two genre operas (including their librettos) based on Edgar Allan Poe's stories. **Delavigne, Casimir** *see* **Scribe, Eugène. Deschamps, Jacques-Marie** *Ossian ou Les Bardes* (1804); *Note:* Libretto for composer Jean-François Lesueur. **Dumesnil, Robert** *Lucifer* (1948); *Note:* Libretto for composer Claude Delvincourt. **Étienne, Charles-Guillaume** *Cendrillon*

(Cinderella; 1810); *Aladin ou La Lampe Merveilleuse (Aladdin and the Magic Lamp;* 1822); *Note:* Librettos for composer Nicolo Isouard, based on the famous tales. **Étienne, Just-Jean** *Si j'étais Roi (If I Were King;* 1852); *Note:* Libretto for composer Charles-Adolphe Adam. **Fauchois, René** *Pénélope* (1913); *Note:* Libretto for composer Gabriel Fauré. **Fleg, Edmond** *Oedipe* (1936); *Note:* Libretto for composer Georges Enesco. **Françaix, Jean** *Le Diable Boiteux (The Lame Devil;* 1938); *Note:* Composer and author of a genre opera (including its libretto) based on Alain René **Lesage's** story about the devil Asmodeus. **Fuzelier, Louis** *Les Indes Galantes (Amorous Indies;* 1735); *Note:* Libretto for composer Jean-Philippe Rameau, based on Greek mythology. **Galbert de Campistron, Jean** *Acis et Galatée* (1686); *Note:* Libretto for composer Jean-Baptiste Lully. **Gallet, Louis** *Le Roi de Lahore (The King of Lahore;* 1877); *Déjanire* (1911); *Note:* Librettos for composers Jules Massenet and Camille Saint-Saëns. **Gautier de Montdorge, Antoine** *see* **Pellegrin, Simon-Joseph Gautron, Micheline** *Médis et Alyssio* (1975); *Note:* Libretto for an opera by renowned film composer Georges Delerue. **Gentil-Bernard, Pierre-Joseph** *Castor et Pollux* (1737); *Note:* Libretto for composer Jean-Philippe Rameau. **Gide, André (q.v.);** *Perséphone* (1934); *Note:* Libretto for composer Igor Stravinsky. **Gille, Philippe** *Le Docteur Ox* (1877); *Rip Van Winkle* (with Henri **Meilhac;** 1882); *Note:* Librettos for composers Jacques Offenbach and Robert Planquette, based on tales by Jules **Verne** and Washington Irving. **Godard d'Aucourt de Saint-Just** *Le Calife de Bagdad (The Caliph of Baghdad;* 1800); *Note:* Libretto for composer François-Adrien Boieldieu. **Gramont, Louis de** *see* **Blau, Alfred. Gremont, Henri** *see* **Milliet, Paul. Guillard** *Iphigénie en Tauride (Iphigenia in Tauridia;* 1779); *Note:* Libretto for composer Christoph Gluck. **Halévy, Ludovic** *Orphée aux Enfers (Orpheus in Hell;* with Hector Crémieux; 1858); *La Belle Hélène (Beautiful Helen of Troy;* with Henri **Meilhac;** 1864); *Barbe-Bleue (Blue-Beard;* with Henri **Meilhac;** 1866); *Carmen* (with Henri **Meilhac;** 1875); *Note:* Three librettos for composer Jacques Offenbach, based on the famous tales; the fourth for composer Georges Bizet. **Hérold, Ferdinand** *see* **Lorrain, Jean. Hoffmann, François-Bernard** *Médée* (1797); *Note:* Libretto for composer Luigi Cherubini. **Hoppenot, Henri** *Opéras Minutes: L'Enlèvement d'Europe (The Taking of Europa], L'Abandon d'Ariane (The Abandonment of Ariadne], La Délivrance de Thésée (The Deliverance of Theseus;* 1927); *Note:* Librettos for composer Darius Milhaud. **Houdar de la Motte, Antoine** *Alcyone* (1706); *Sémélé* (1709); *Pygmalion* (1748); *Note:* The first two librettos were for composer Marin Marais, based on Greek mythology; the third for composer Jean-Philippe Rameau. **Hugo, Victor (q.v.);** *Les Djinns* (1912); *Note:*

Libretto for composer Louis Vierne. **Humières, Robert d'** *Tragédie de Salomé (Tragedy of Salome;* 1907); *Note:* Libretto for composer Florent Schmitt. **Laloy, Louis** *Padmâvati* (1923); *Note:* Libretto for composer Albert Roussel. **Landowski, Marcel** *Le Rire de Nils Halérius (The Laughter of Nils Halerius;* with Gérard Caillet; 1951); *Note:* Libretto for composer Landowski. **Leblanc du Rollet** *Alceste* (1776); *Note:* Libretto for composer Christoph Gluck. **Le Clerc de la Bruyère, Charles-Antoine** *see* **Pellegrin, Simon-Joseph. Lemaire, Ferdinand** *Samson et Dalila* (1890); *Note:* Libretto for composer Camille Saint-Saëns. **Léna, Maurice** *Le Jongleur de Notre-Dame (The Juggler of Notre-Dame;* 1902); *Note:* Libretto for composer Jules Massenet, based on a tale by Anatole **France** and a medieval mystery play. **Le Riche de la Pouplinière, Alexandre** *see* **Pellegrin, Simon-Joseph Leterrier, E.** *see* **Vanloo, Albert Leuven, Adolphe de** *Le Songe d'une Nuit d'Été (Midsummer Night's Dream;* with Joseph-Bernard Rosier; 1850); *La Poupée de Nuremberg (The Nuremberg Doll;* with A. de Beauplan; 1852); *Note:* The first libretto was for composer Ambroise Thomas, and is not specifically based on, though it uses the same characters as, the play by William Shakespeare. The second libretto was for composer Adolphe Adam and was based on a Hoffmann tale. **Le Valois d'Orville, Adrien-Joseph** *Platée ou Junon Jalouse (with J. Autreau) (Jealous Juno;* 1749); *Note:* Libretto for composer Jean-Philippe Rameau, based on Greek mythology. **Locle, Camille de** *see* **Blau, Alfred** and **Méry G. Loiseleur de Longchamps, Guillaume** *Céphale et Proscris* (1694); *Note:* Libretto for composer Élisabeth Jacquet de la Guerre. **Lorrain, Jean (q.v.);** *Prométhée (Prometheus;* with Ferdinand Hérold; 1900); *Note:* Libretto for composer Gabriel Fauré. **Louÿs, Pierre (q.v.);** *Le Roi Pausle (King Pausole;* 1931); *Note:* Libretto for composer Arthur Honegger. **Lunel, Armand** *Les Malheurs d'Orphée (Orpheus' Woes;* 1926); *Note:* Libretto for composer Darius Milhaud. **Maeterlinck, Maurice (q.v.);** *Pelléas et Mélisande* (1902); *Ariane et Barbe-Bleue (Ariadne and Blue-Beard;* 1907); *Note:* Librettos for composers Claude Debussy and Paul Dukas. **Magnard, Albéric** *Guercoeur* (1900; repr. 1931); *Note:* Composer and author of a genre opera (including its libretto) about a dead man who returns to life. **Marmontel, Jean-François** *La Guirlande ou les Fleurs Enchantées (The Garland, or the Enchanted Flowers;* 1751); *Acanthe et Céphise* (1751); *Zémire et Azor* (1771); *Céphale et Procris* (1773); *Roland* (1778); *Atys* (1780); *Didon* (1783); *Note:* the first two librettos were for composer Jean-Philippe Rameau and were based on Greek mythology; the third and fourth (including *Zémire,* based on *Beauty and the Beast* by Madame **Leprince de Beaumont**) were for composer André-Modeste Grétry; and the fourth, fifth, and sixth (including

Roland, based on *Ariosto*) for composer Niccolo Piccinni. **Meilhac, Henri** *La Belle Hélène (Beautiful Helen of Troy*; with Ludovic **Halévy**; 1864); *Barbe-Bleue (Blue-Beard*; with Ludovic **Halévy**; 1866); *Rip Van Winkle* (with Philippe **Gille**; 1882); *Carmen* (with Ludovic **Halévy**; 1875); *Note:* The first two librettos were for composer Jacques Offenbach; the third for composer Robert Planquette and was based on Washington Irving's famous tale; the fourth for composer Georges Bizet. **Mélesville** *see* **Scribe, Eugène. Mendès, Catulle (q.v.);** *Gwendoline* (1893); *Note:* Libretto for composer Emmanuel Chabrier. Fairy tale. **Méry, G.** *Erostrate* (with Pacini; 1862); *Don Carlos* (with Camille de **Locle**; 1867); *Note:* Librettos for composers Ernest Reyer and Giuseppe Verdi. **Milliet, Paul** *Hérodiade* (with Henri Gremont; 1881); *Note:* Libretto for composer Jules Massenet. **Morand, Eugène** *see* **Silvestre, Armand. Morax, René** *Le Roi David (King David*; 1921); *Note:* Libretto for composer Arthur Honegger. **Mortier, A.** *see* **Vanloo, Albert. Nepoty, Lucien** *Marouf* (1914); *Note:* Libretto for composer Henri Rabaud. Oriental tale. **Nino** *Persée et Andromède* (1921); *Angélique* (1927); *Note:* Librettos for composer Jacques Ibert, based on Greek mythology. **Pacini** *see* **Méry, G. Pellegrin, Simon-Joseph (Abbé);** *Jepthté* (1732); *Hyppolite et Aricie* (1733); *Les Fêtes d'Hébé (The Festivities of Hebe*; with Pierre-Joseph Bernard & Antoine Gautier de Montdorge & Alexandre Le Riche de la Pouplinière; 1739); *Dardanus* (with Charles-Antoine Le Clerc de la Bruyère; 1739); *Note:* The first libretto was for composer Michel Pignolet de Montéclair; the other three for composer Jean-Philippe Rameau. They were all based on Greek mythology. **Quinault, Philippe** *Les Fêtes de l'Amour et de Bacchus (The Festivities of Cupid and Bacchus*; 1672); *Cadmus et Hermione* (1673); *Alceste, ou Le Triomphe d'Alcide (Alceste, or Alcie's Triumph*; 1674); *Thésée (Theseus*; 1675); *Atrys* (1676); *Isis* (1677); *Psyché* (with Thomas **Corneille**; 1678); *Bellérophon* (with Thomas **Corneille** and Bernard Le Bovier de **Fontenelle**; 1679); *Proserpine (Persephone*; 1680); *Persée (Perseus*; 1682); *Phaéton ou La Volonté de Briller (The Will to Shine*; 1683); *Amadis de Gaule* (1684); *Roland* (1685); *Armide et Renaud* (1686); *Armide* (1777); *Note:* Librettos for composer Jean-Baptiste Lully, except for the 1777 *Armide* written for composer Christoph Gluck. They were inspired by classic legends from Ovid, Apuleius, Ariosto, etc. The 1675 *Thésée* was recreated in 1756 by composer Jean-Joseph de Mondeville. **Richepin, Jean (q.v.);** *Le Mage (The Magus*; 1891); *Note:* Libretto for composer Jules Massenet. **Rollet, du** *Iphigénie en Aulide (Iphigenia in Aulidia*; 1774); *Note:* Libretto written for composer Christoph Gluck. **Rosier, Joseph-Bernard** *see* **Leuven, Adolphe de. Rousseau, Jean-Jacques** *Les Muses Galantes (The Gallant Muses*;

1744); *Le Devin du Village (The Village's Seer*; 1752); *Note:* Operas written and composed by this renowned writer-philosopher. **Schaeffer, Pierre** *Orphée 51* (1951); *Note:* Composer (with Pierre Henry) and author of a genre opera (including its libretto), which is a modern retelling of the classic story. **Scribe, Eugène** *La Dame Blanche (The White Lady*; 1825); *Le Loup-Garou (The Werewolf*; 1827); *Fra Diavolo* (1830); *Le Philtre* (1831); *Robert le Diable (Robert the Devil*; with Casimir Delavigne; 1831); *Ali-Baba et les Quarante Voleurs (Ali-Baba and the Forty Thieves*; 1833); *Le Cheval de Bronze (The Brass Horse*; 1835); *La Juive (The Jewess*; 1835); *Le Lac des Fées (The Fairy Lake*; 1839); *La Part du Diable (The Devil's Share*; 1843); Cagliostro (1843); *Le Puit d'Amour (The Love Well*; 1843); *Haÿdée ou Le Secret* (1847); *Le Prophète (The Prophet*; 1849); *La Fée aux Roses (The Rose Fairy*; 1849); *La Tempête (The Tempest*; based on the play by Shakespeare; 1851); *Le Juif Errant (The Wandering Jew*; with Jules-Henri **Vernoy de Saint-Georges**; 1852); *La Nonne Sanglante (The Bloody Nun*; Based on a novel by Anicet **Bourgeois**; 1854); *La Chatte Métamorphosée en Femme (The Cat Who Turned Into a Woman*; with Mélesville; wri. 1827; 1858); *Note:* Prolific author of genre librettos. *La Dame* was for composer François-Adrien Boieldieu and was based on Walter Scott's stories; *Robert, La Juive*, and *Le Prophète* were for by composer Giacomo Meyerbeer; *Ali-Baba* was for composer Luigi Cherubini and was based on the famous Arabian tale; *Fra Diavolo, Le Philtre, Le Cheval, Le Lac*, and *La Part* were for composer Daniel Auber (*La Part* takes place on planet Venus); *Le Juif* was for composer Fromental Halévy; *La Nonne* for composer Charles Gounod; *La Chatte* for composer Jacques Offenbach. **Scudery, Georges de** *Didon (Dido*; 1693); *Note:* Libretto for composer Henry Desmarets. **Sedaine, Michel Jean** *Le Diable à Quatre (The Devil in Four*; 1757); *Note:* Libretto for composer Philidor. **Ségalen, Victor** *Orphée Roi (Orpheus King*; 1921); *Note:* Libretto for composer Claude Debussy. **Silvestre, Armand (q.v.);** *Le Sabbat (The Sabbath*; 1877); *Griselidis* (with Eugène Morand; 1901); *Note:* The first libretto was for composer Emmanuel Chabrier; the second for composer Jules Massenet. **Spitzmuller, George (q.v.);** *Panurge* (with Maurice Boukay; 1913); *Note:* Author of the libretto of a genre opera by French composer Jules Massenet, based on **Rabelais'** tale. **Terrasse, C.** *Le Mariage de Télémaque (Telemachus' Wedding*; 1910); *Note:* Opera written and composed by this composer. **Tiercelin, Louis** *Le Diable Couturier (The Devil Taylor*; 1889); *Note:* Libretto for composer Jean-Louis Ropartz. **Valéry, Paul** *Amphion* (1929); *Note:* Famous poet. Libretto for composer Arthur Honegger. **Vanloo, Albert** *Le Voyage dans la Lune (The Journey to the Moon*; with E. Leterrier & A. Mortier; 1875); *L'Étoile (The Star*; with E. Leterrier; 1877); *Note:*

Librettos for composers Jacques Offenbach and Emmanuel Chabrier, the last based on an oriental tale, with the collaboration of renowned poet Verlaine. **Vernoy de Saint-Georges, Jules-Henri** *La Reine de Chype (The Queen of Cyprus*; 1841); *Le Juif Errant (The Wandering Jew*; with Eugène **Scribe**; 1852); *La Magicienn (The Sorceress*; 1858); **Vian, Boris (q.v.);** *Le Chevalier de Neige (The Snow Knight*; 1957); *Note:* Libretto for an opera composed by renowned film composer Georges Delerue. **Voltaire (q.v.);** *Les Fêtes de Ramire (The Parties of Ramire*; 1740); *La Princesse de Navarre (The Princess of Navarre*; 1745); *Le Temple de la Gloire (The Temple of Glory*; 1745); *Note:* Three librettos written for composer Jean-Philippe Rameau. In the second, the Pyrennees collapse; the first and third are based on Greek mythology. **Wailly, Léon de (q.v.)** *see* **Barbier, Jules** *Composers:* Adolphe Adam (1803-1856), Charles-Adolphe Adam (1803-1856), Daniel Auber (1782-1871), Georges Bizet (1838-1875), Hector Berlioz (1803-1869), François-Adrien Boieldieu (1775-1834), André Campra (1660-1744), Emmanuel Chabrier (1841-1894), Gustave Charpentier (1860-1956), Marc-Antoine Charpentier (1634-1704), Ernest Chausson (1855-1899), Luigi Cherubini (1760-1842), Claude Debussy (1862-1918), Georges Delerue (1925-1992), Claude Delvincourt (?-), Henry Desmaretz (1661-1741), Paul Dukas (1865-1935), Georges Enesco (1881-1955), Gabriel Fauré (1845-1924), Jean Françaix (1912-1997), Renaud Gagneux (?-), Charles-Hubert Gervais (1671-1744), Christoph Gluck (1714-1787), Charles Gounod (1818-1893), André-Modeste Grétry (1741-1813), Fromental Halévy (1799-1862), Pierre Henry (1927-), Arthur Honegger (1892-1955), Jacques Ibert (1890-1962), Nicolo Isouard (1775-1818), Élisabeth Jacquet de la Guerre (1666-1729), Édouard Lalo (1823-1892), Jean-Marie Leclair Aîné (1697-1764), Jean-François Lesueur (1760-1837), Jean-Baptiste Lully (1632-1687), Albéric Magnard (1865-1914), Marin Marais (1656-1728), Jules Massenet (1842-1912), Giacomo Meyerbeer (1791-1864), Darius Milhaud (1892-1974), Jacques Offenbach (1819-1880), Philidor (François-André Danican; 1726-1795), Niccolo Piccinni (1728-1800), Michel Pignolet de Montéclair (1667-1737), Robert Planquette (1848-1903), Francis Poulenc (1899-1963), Henri Pousseur (1929-), Henri Rabaud (?-), Jean-Philippe Rameau (1683-1764), Maurice Ravel (1875-1937), Ernest Reyer (1823-1909), Jean-Louis Ropartz (?-?), Albert Roussel (1869-1937), Camille Saint-Saëns (1835-1921), Pierre Schaeffer (1910-1995), Florent Schmitt (?-?), Igor Stravinsky (1882-1971), Ambroise Thomas (1811-1896), Giuseppe Verdi (1813-1901), Louis Vierne (1870-1937).

Ormesson, Jean d' (?-); *Histoire du Juif Errant (Story of the Wandering Jew*; Gall., 1991); *La Douane de Mer (The Customs of the Sea*; Gall., 1993); *Note:* See Chapter VIII.

Orsenna, Éric (?-); *Histoire du Monde en Neuf Guitares (History of the World with Nine Guitars*; Fayard, 1996)

Orval, Claude (?-?); *Un Visage dans la Nuit (A Face in the Night*; Marpon, 1929); *Note:* Also see **Grand-Guignol**.

Ossau, Jean d' (Botto, Ernest) (?-); *Les Mémoires d'un Cheval de Course (Memoirs of a Race Horse*; Grasset, 1912); *Henri Bar sur la Lune (Henri Bar on the Moon*; Figuère, 1927)

Osten, Malko von (1960-); *Hallucinogènes* (Prince du Mal, 1984); *Note:* French-Canadian writer. Collection of fantasy stories.

Ostroga, Yvonne (1897-1981); *Quand les Fées vivaient en France (When Fairies Lived in France*; Hac., 1921); *Fées et Petite Filles de la Vieille France (Fairies and Little Daughters of Old France*; Hac., 1948)

Otis, Gaston (1943-); *Le Tabacinum* (JP 31, 1978); *Note:* French-Canadian writer.

Ottange, Jules d' (?-); *Petit Bonhomme Vit Encore (Little Guy Lives Again*; Taffin-Lefort, 1898); *Le Conteur Intarissable (The Untiring Storyteller*; Taffin-Lefort, 1899); *Le Chemin des Écoliers (The Schoolboys' Path*; Taffin-Lefort, 1902); *La Chasse aux Milliards (The Hunt for the Billions*; 4 vols, Lethielleux); *1. L'Héritier du Milliardaire (The Billionaires's Heir*; 1926); *2. All Right!* (1928); *3. Le Poisson d'Acier (The Fish of Steel*; 1928); *4. Électroville* (1931); *Note:* See Chapter VII.

Ouellet, Pierre (1950-); *L'Attrait (The Attraction*; L'Instant Même, 1994); *Note:* French-Canadian writer. Collection of fantastical tales.

Ousmane, Smbeme (?-); *Le Dernier de l'Empire—K'harmattour (The Last of the Empire*; 2 vols.; Encres Noires, 1981); *Note:* Senegalese writer. See Chapter IX.

Owen, Thomas (Bertot, Gérald) (1910-); *Gordon Oliver Mène l'Enquête (Gordon Oliver Leads the Investigation*; as Stéphane Rey; Heures Bleues, 1941); *Ce Soir, Huit Heures (Tonight at 8;* as Stéphane Rey; Le Jury, 1941; rev. as *Les Invités de 8 Heures [The Guests of 8 O'Clock]*, Meddens, 1945); *Destination Inconnue (Destination Unknown*; Le Jury, 1941); *Un Crime Swing (A Swing Crime*; Le Jury, 1942); *Le Nez de Cléopâtre (Cleopatra's Nose;* Le Jury, 1942; rev. as *Portrait d'une Dame de Qualité [Portrait of a Classy Lady]*, Argonautes, 1948); *Duplicité (Duplicity*; Sphinx, 1942); *Initiation à la Peur (Initiation to Fear*; Auteurs Associés, 1942); *L'Or Indigo (Indigo Gold*; Wri. 1942; publ. Lefrancq, 1995); *Les Espalard* (De Kogge, 1943); *Hôtel Meublé (Furnished Hotel*; Auteurs Associés, 1943); *Les Chemins Étranges (The Strange Paths*; De Kogge, 1943); *Le Livre Interdit (The Forbidden Book*; De Kogge, 1944); *La Cave aux Crapauds (The Toad Cave*;

La Boëtie, 1945); *Le Jeu Secret (The Secret Game*; Renaissance du Livre, 1950); *Les Grandes Personnes (The Adults*; Audace, 1954); *Pitié pour les Ombres (Mercy for the Shadows*; Renaissance du Livre, 1961); *Cérémonial Nocturne (Night Ceremonies*; MarF 242, 1966); *La Truie (The Sow*; MarF 394, 1972); *Le Rat Kavar (Kavar the Rat*; MarF 515, 1975); *Les Maisons Suspectes (The Suspicious Houses*; Jacques Antoine, 1976); *Le Livre Noir des Merveilles (The Black Book of Wonders*; Cast., 1980); *Les Chambres Secrètes (The Secret Rooms*; Delta, 1983); *Les Fruits de l'Orage (The Fruits of the Storm*; Jacques Anoine, 1984); *Les Sept Péchés Capitaux (The Seven Capital Sins*; Jacques Antoine, 1984); *Le Tétrastome* (Lefebvre & Gillet, 1988); *Carla Hurla (Carla Screamed*; La Rose de Chêne, 1990); *Élégie Urbaine (Urban Elegy*; Centre d'Art, 1991); *La Ténèbre (The Darkness*; Lefrancq, 1994); *Note:* Belgian writer. See Chapter VIII. Also see Book 1, Chapter II under **Owen** for television adaptations.

Pacheco de Céspedes, Daria-Luisa *see* **Darios, Louise**

Pacini (?-?) *see* **Opéra**

Page, Alain (Conil, Jean-Emmanuel) (1930-); *Un Cerveau pour Calone (A Brain for Calone*; CLE, 1971); *Il est si tard, M. Calone (It Is So Late, Mr. Calone*; CLE, 1971); *En Attendant Calone (Waiting for Calone*; CLE, 1971); *Les Compagnons d'Eleusis (The Brotherhood of Eleusis*; AM, 1975); *Le Mutant (The Mutant*; AM, 1978); *Cristaux de Nuit (Night Crystals*; C. Raulin, 1984); *A Pleines Dents (With All My Teeth*; FN, 1990); *Sang d'Enfer (Hellish Blood*; Flamm., 1991); *Note:* **Les Compagnons** and **Le Mutant** are novelizations of Page's two eponymous television series (see Book 1, Chapter II). the *Calone* novels are spy thrillers with genre elements. Page is also the author of a series of novels featuring the character of *L'Ombre* (*The Shadow*) published by Fleuve Noir in their *L'Aventurier* (*The Adventurer*) imprint in the 1960s. *L'Ombre Gagne la Belle (The Shadow Wins the Last One*; FN, 1969) contains genre elements.

Page, Marie (?-); *Vincent, Sylvie et les Autres (Vincent, Sylvie and the Others*; Héritage, 1985); *Note:* French-Canadian writer. Time-travel story.

Pagel, Michel (1961-); *Demain Matin au Chant du Tueur! (Tomorrow Morning When the Killer Sings*; FNA 1294, 1984); *La Taverne de l'Espoir (The Inn of Hope*; FNA 1305, 1984); *Le Viêt-Nam au Futur Simple (Future Tense Vietnam*; FNA 1320, 1984); *L'Ange du Désert (The Desert Angel*; FNA 1403, 1985); *Les Flammes de la Nuit—Rowena (The Flames of Night*; FNA 1433, 1986); *La Ville d'Acier (The Steel City*; FNA 1457, 1986); *Le Fou (The Madman*; FNA 1493, 1987); *Les Cavaliers Dorés (The Golden Horsemen*; FNA 1513, 1987); *Soleil Pourpre, Soleil Noir (Purple Sun, Black Sun*; FNA 1563,

1987); *Pour Une Poignée d'Helix Pomatias (For a Fistful of Helix Pomatias*; FNA 1628, 1988); *Le Diable à Quatre (The Devil in Four*; FNA 1657, 1988); *Sylvana* (FNA 1687, 1989); *Désirs Cruels (Cruel Desires*; FNA 1725, 1989); *Les Ailes Tranchées (The Sliced-Off Wings*; as Félix Chapel; FNA 1739, 1990); *Le Temple de la Mort Turquoise (The Temple of the Purple Death*; as Félix Chapel; FNA 1757, 1990); *Le Sang de Fulgavy (The Blood of Fulgavy*; as Félix Chapel; FNA 1768, 1990); *Les Ephémères des Sables (The Ephemerals of the Sands*; as Félix Chapel; FNA 1786, 1990); *L'Antre du Serpent (The Lair of the Serpent*; FNA 1794, 1990); *Le Refuge de l'Agneau (The Refuge of the Lamb*; FNA 1801, 1991); *Les Fêtes de Hrampa (The Celebrations of Hrampa*; as Félix Chapel; FNA 1819, 1991); *Le Cimetière des Astronefs (The Graveyard of the Spaceships*; FNA 1833, 1991); *Orages en Terre de France (Storms Over the Land of France*; FNA 1851, 1991); *Le Crâne du Houngan (The Skull of the Houngan*; FNAV 2, 1995); *L'Héritier de Soliman (The Heir of Soliman*; FNAV 13, 1995); *Nuées Ardentes (Fiery Clouds*; Étoiles Vives, 1997); *Note:* See Chapters VIII and IX. Also see Terence **Corman**.

Pagery, François *see* **Klein, Gérard**

Pagès, Robert (?-); *L'Exigence (The Imperative*; RL, 1964); *LOrdre du Silence (The Order of Silence*; Rocher, 1980); *L'Homme-Frontière (The Frontier-Man*; Rocher, 1981)

Pairault, Pierre *see* **Wul, Stefan**

Pajon, Henri (?-1776); *Histoire du Prince Joly, surnommé Prénany, et de la Princesse Feslée (Tale of Prince Joly Nicknamed Prenany and of Princess Feslee*; 2 vols.; 1740; rep. VI, 1788); *Histoire du Roi Splendide et de la Princesse Hétéroclite (Tale of King Splendid and of Princess Heteroclite*; 1747)

Palau, Pierre (1883-1966); *L'Énigmatique Disparition de James Butler (The Mysterious Disappearance of James Butler*; Hac., 1933); *Note:* Also see **Grand-Guignol**.

Pallascio-Morin, Ernest (1909-1998); *L'Heure Intemporelle (The Intemporal Hour*; Garneau, 1965); *La Route de Champigny (The Road to Champigny*; Courteau, 1988); *Note:* French-Canadian writer. Collection of fantastical tales.

Panas, Jean-Michel (?-); *Chronique des Singuliers (Chronicles of the Singulars*; Debresse, 1960)

Panier, Claire (?-); *Scythir de Dungroft: Gardien des Immortels Oubliés (Guardian of the Forgotten Immortals*; Octa, n.d.)

Papoz, Micky (?-); *Pitèle-Chique* (Casteou Rignaou, Terre Profonde, 1986); *Les Malfairies* (Cachan Foyer des PTT,

1993); *Comme une Fleur Sauvage (Like a Wild Flower*; Cachan, Foyer des PTT, 1997)

Paquin, Ubald (1894-1962); *La Cité dans les Fers (The City in Chains*; 1926); *Note:* French-Canadian writer. Grim anticipation of a bid for Quebec independence.

Paradis, Nicole (1941-); *Amitié Cosmique (Cosmic Friendship*; JCL, 1988); *Note:* French-Canadian writer.

Parant, Jean-Luc (?-); *Les Boules Intouchables (The Untouchable Balls*; Encres Vives, 1973); *Les Yeux CIIICXXV (The Eyes CIIICXXV*; Fata Morgana, 1976); *Les Yeux MMDVI (The Eyes MMDVI*; Bourgois, 1976); *La Joie des Yeux (The Joy of the Eyes*; Bourgois, 1977); *Les Xueyetêterret ou les Boules de Tnarapculnaej* (Atelier des Grames, 1977); *Comment toucher mes Boules ou Les Yeux MDDCXLVI (How to Touch My Balls or the Eyes MCCCXLVI*; Marmourel, 1978); *Les Yeux de la Violence (The Eyes of Violence*; Cééditions, 1978); *Les Yeux du Rêve (The Eyes of Dream*; Bourgois, 1978); *Le Mot Boules (The Word Balls*; Fata Morgana, 1980); *La Couleur des Mains (The Color of the Hands*; Aencrages, 1981); *Comme une Petite Terre Aveugle (As a Little Blind Land*; Lettres Vives, 1983); *Le Hasard des Yeux ou La Main de la Providence (The Hazard of the Eyes or the Hand of Fate*; L'Originel, 1983); *Le Voyage des Yeux (The Journey of the Eyes*; Carte Blanche, 1984); *Le Chant des Yeux (The Song of the Eyes*; Tribu, 1984); *Aux temps des Boules (In the Times of the Balls*; with Titi Parant; Voix, 1987); *De Couple en Boule (Of Couple in a Ball*; Fata Morgana, 1989); *Le Voyage Immobile (The Motionless Journey*; Creaphis, 1989); *Nuit-Oiseau (Night-Bird*; Evidant, 1990); *Les Yeux Goinfres (The Gluttonous Eyes*; Voix, 1991); *Les Frontières de l'Insaisissable (The Frontiers of the Unknowable*; Spectre Familiers, 1994)

Paraz, Albert (1899-); *Le Couteau de Jeannot (Jeannot's Knife*; 1946)

Paré, Ambroise (1517-1590); *Les Monstres, Tant Terrestres que Marins, avec leurs Portraits (Monsters, Terrestrials as Well as Sea-Faring, with Their Portraits*; Buon, 1579); *Note:* See Chapter II.

Paré, Jason (1981-); *Combat par l'Esprit (Mind Battle*; D'Ici et d'Ailleurs, 1995); *Note:* French-Canadian writer.

Paré, Marc-André (1951-); *Le Mystère des Borgs aux Oreilles Vertes (The Mystery of the Green-Eared Borgs*; Boréal, 1990); *Note:* French-Canadian writer. Children's SF novel.

Parent, Jean-Marie (?-) *see* **Facon, Roger**

Parent, Nathalie (?-); *J'ai des Petites Nouvelles Pour Toi (I Have Some News for You*; Triptyque, 1988); *Note:* French-Canadian writer. Collection of fantastical tales.

Paris, Alain (1947-); *Le Commando des Salopards (The Bastards' Commando*; Belfond, 1980); *Chasseur d'Ombres (Shadows Hunter*; Plasma 4, 1983); *Le Complot Schellenberg (The Schellenberg Conspiracy*; Belfond, 1984); *Les Bannières de Persh (The Banners of Persh*; with Jean-Pierre **Fontana**; FNA 1308, 1984); *Dernier Étage avant la Frontière (Last Floor Before the Border*; with Jean-Pierre **Fontana**; FNA 1323, 1984); *Sarkô des Grandes Zunes (Sarko of the Great Zunes*; with Jean-Pierre **Fontana**; FNA 1341, 1984); *Impact (AM, 1985); *Le Syndrome Karelmann (The Karelmann Syndrome*; with Jean-Pierre **Fontana**; FNA 1359, 1985); *Le Temple du Dieu Mazon (The Temple of the Mazon God*; with Jean-Pierre **Fontana**; FNA 1398, 1985); *La Marque des Antarcidès (The Mark of the Antarcides*; FNA 1408, 1985); *Opération Gomorrhe (Operation Gomorrah*; AM, 1986); *Le Clan du Brouillard (The Clan of the Mists*; with Jean-Pierre **Fontana**; FNA 1419, 1986); *Soldat-Chien (Dog Soldier*; FNA 1434, 1986); *Ashermayam (FNA 1456, 1986); *"Reich" (FNA 1480, 1986); *Les Hommes Lézards (The Lizard Men*; with Jean-Pierre **Fontana**; FNA 1484, 1986); *L'Ombre des Antarcidès (The Shadow of the Antarcides*; FNA 1502, 1986); *La Cité des Hommes de Fer (The City of the Iron Men*; with Jean-Pierre **Fontana**; FNA 1515, 1987); *Le Sceau des Antarcidès (The Seal of the Antar-*

cides; FNA 1549, 1987); *Soldat-Chien 2 (Dog Soldier 2*; FNA 1600, 1987); *Daïren* (JL 2484, 1988); *Svastika* (FNA 1629, 1988); *Seigneur des Runes (Lord of the Runes*; FNA 1635, 1988); *Sur l'Épaule du Grand Dragon (On the Shoulders of the Great Dragon*; FNA 1640, 1988); *Les Hérétiques du Vril (The Heretics of the Vril*; FNA 1645, 1988); *Achéron* (Aurore, Futurs 5, 1988; rev. FNA 1915, 1993); *Le Dieu de la Guerre (The God of War*; FNA 1671, 1989); *Dal Refa'l* (FNA 1705, 1989); *Joal ban Kluane* (FNA 1711, 1989); *Sassar* (FNA 1717, 1989); *Le Dirigeable Certitude (The Dirigible Certainty*; FNA 1749, 1990); *Les Fils du Miroir Fumant (The Sons of the Smoking Mirror*; FNA 1754, 1990); *Le Peuple Pâle (The Pale People*; FNA 1760, 1990); *L'Homme du Sid (The Man from Sid*; FNA 1824, 1991); *L'Écume du Passé (The Froth of the Past*; FNA 1830, 1991); *Celui-Qui-N'est-Pas-Nommé (He-Who-Is-Not-Named*; FNA 1834, 1991); *Le Désert des Cendres (The Desert of Ashes*; with Jean-Pierre **Fontana**; FNA 1868, 1992); *AWACS* (FNA 1901, 1993); *Note:* See Chapters VIII and IX.

Paroutaud, Jean Marie Amédée (1912-); *La Ville Incertaine (The Uncertain City*; Robert Marin, 1950); *Temps Fou / Autre Évènement (Crazy Time / Another Event*; Puyraimond, 1977); *La Descente Infinie (The Infinite Descent*; Puyraimond, 1977); *Le Pays des Eaux (The Land of Waters*; Le Tout sur Tout, 1983); *Note:* See Chapter VIII.

Pasquet, Jacques (?-); *Mystère et Boule de Gomme (Mystery and Bubblegum*; Q/A, 1985); *Note:* French-Canadian writer. Juvenile fantasy.

Pasquier, Alex (1888-1963); *Le Secret de ne Jamais Mourir / Une Histoire d'Automates (The Secret of Never Dying / a Tale of Automatons*; Polmoss, 1913); *La Conquête (The Conquest*; Figuière, 1926); *Note:* Belgian writer. See Chapter V.

Pasquiez, Jean-Claude (?-); *Grand-Mère Agent Secret (Granny Secret Agent*; with **Ann** & **Gwen**; Dauphin, 1972); *Fantastique Atome (Fantastic Atom*; Cast., 1973); *Prodigieux Cosmos (Prodigious Cosmos*; Cast., 1974); *Au Coeur du Vivant (In the Heart of Life*; Cast., 1977); *Néant Aller-Retour (Return from Nothingness*; with **Ann** & **Gwen**; Cast., 1983); *La Conquête des Pôles (The Conquest of the Poles*; Dupuis, n.d.); *Automates et Robots (Automaton and Robots*; Dupuis, n.d.); *Note:* Juvenile SF.

Passegué, Bertrand (?-); *Le Dieu du Delta (The God of the Delta*; FNA 1658, 1988); *Argyll* (FNA 1677, 1989); *Le Septième Cycle (The Seventh Cycle*; FNA 1691, 1989); *La Forteresse Éternelle (The Eternal Fortress*; FNA 1707, 1989); *Le Grand Hiver (The Great Winter*; FNA 1720, 1989); *Le Monde d'En-Bas (The Under-world*; FNA 1805, 1991); *Les Maîtres des Souterrains (The Masters of the Tunnels*; FNA 1815, 1991); *Le Monolithe Noir (The Black Monolith*; FNA 1869, 1992); *Métacentre (Metacenter*; FNA 1873, 1992); *Note:* See Chapter IX.

Passover, Geoffrey X. (?-); *Joar de l'Espace (Joar of Space*; SdPSF 24, 1972); *Les Survivants de l'An 2000 (The Survivors of the Year 2000*; SdP 2 58, 1977); *Note:* Juvenile SF. See Chapter IX.

Pastor, Philippe (?-); *Les Yeux de la Terre Folle (The Eyes of the Crazy Earth*; FNA 1929, 1993)

Pastre, Jules-Louis-Gaston (?-1939); *La Neuvième Croisade (The Ninth Crusade*; Plon, 1926); *L'Austère M. de Barrac (The Austere Mr. De Barrac*; Valat, 1928); *La Ville Aérienne (The City in the Air*; Hac., 1928); *Le Secret des Sables (The Secret of the Sands*; Hac., 1928); *Le Palace à la Dérive (A Palace Adrift*; Hac., 1929); *Flammes sur la Neige (Flames Over the Snow*; Hac., 1931); *L'Île d'Épouvante (The Island of Terror*; Tallandier, 1932); *Les Puits Tragiques (The Tragic Wells*; LPT, 1932); *Les Pirates de la Hanse (The Pirates of the Hanse*; LPT, 1936); *L'Île Z (Z Island*; LPT, 1936); *Le Capitan Alvez* (Loisirs, 1939); *Le Grand Complot de 1950 (The Great Plot of 1950*; LPT, 1938); *Les Avions de la Mort (The Planes of Death*; LPT, 1939); *Les Sous-Marins Fantômes (The Ghost Submarines*; LPT, 1939); *Note:* See Chapter VII.

Paterson, Carol *see* **Juillet, Jacques-Henri**

Patmos, Jean de (?-); *Anthropthéose (Anthropotheosis*; Scorpion, 1958); *Note:* See Chapter IX.

Patoux, Danièle (?-); *Les Oubliés du Temps (Forgotten in Time*; with Franck **Trapéras**; Zoe, 1997)

Patrick, Roland (-Yann) *see* **Juillet, Jacques-Henri**

Paulhac, Jean (?-); *Sous le Soleil de Minuit (Under the Midnight Sun*; TR, 1953); *Un Bruit de Guêpes (The Sound of Wasps*; PdF 19, 1957); *Les Sentiers Obliques (The Oblique Path*; Den., 1958); *Note:* See Chapter IX.

Paulin, Christophe (Merrien, Jean) (1905-1972); *La Mort Jeune (Young Death*; Gall., 1938); *S'il n'en reste qu'un (If Only One Is Left*; Self, 1946); *Viking, la Mer est Grande! (Viking, Sea Is Vast!*; Gérard, 1957); *Le Légendaire de la Mer (The Legends of the Sea*; RL, 1969); *L'Oiseau Mort du Cap Horn (The Dead Bird of Cape Horn*; Hatier, 1982); *Note:* See Chapter VII.

Paulin, Jean (?-); *Lorraine s'évade (Lorraine Escapes*; MarJ 302, 1965)

Pauwels, Louis (?-) *see* **Bergier, Jacques**

Pavel, Thomas G. (1941-); *Le Miroir Persan (The Persian Mirror*; Quinze, 1977); *Note:* French-Canadian writer born in Romania. This is a collection of fantastical stories.

Pawlowski, Gaston (William Adam) de (1874-1933); *Polochon, Paysages Animés, Paysages Chimériques (Polochon, Animated Landscapes, Chemerical Landscapes*; Charpentier, 1909); *Contes Singuliers (Singular Tales*; Renaissance du Livre, 1912); *Voyage au Pays de la 4ème Dimension (Voyage in the Fourth Dimension*; Charpentier-Fasquelle, 1912); *Jeph, le Roman d'un as (Jeph, the Novel of An Ace*; Ed. Fr. Ill., 1917); *Note:* See Chapter V.

Pays, Jean-François (?-); *La Montagne Interdite (The Forbidden Mountain*; SdPSF 36, 1972); *Le Dieu du Nil (The God of the Nile*; SdP 2 13, 1975); *Le Sorcier aux Yeux Bleus (The Wizard with Blue Eyes*; SdP 2 73, 1977); Series *Sous le Signe de Rome (Under the Mark of Rome)*: *Toukaram, Taureau Sauvage (Tukaram, the Savage Bull*; GP, 1961); *La Dernière Charge (The Last Charge*; GP, 1962); *Marcus Imperator* (GP, 1963); *Note:* Juveniles. See Chapter VIII.

Péan, Stanley (1966-); *La Plage des Songes (The Beach of Dreams*; CIDIHCA, 1988); *Le Tumulte de mon Sang (The Tumult of My Blood*; Q/A, 1991); *Sombres Allées (Dark Alleys*; CIDIHCA, 1992); *L'Emprise de la Nuit (The Hold of the Night*; Courte Échelle, 1993); *La Mémoire Ensanglantée (The Bloodied Memory*; Courte Échelle, 1994); *Treize pas vers l'Inconnu (Thirteen Steps Into the Unknown*; Tisseyre, 1996); *Zombi Blues* (Courte Échelle, 1996); *L'Appel des Loups (The Call of the Wolves*; Courte Échelle, 1997); *Note:* French-Canadian writer born in Haiti. *La Plage* and *Sombres* are collections of fantastical tales. *Le Tumulte* is a Haitian reworking of Poe.

Pearson, Claude (?-); *La Mort Atomique (Atomic Death*; Reflets, 1947); *Note:* Swiss writer.

Péchin, Véronique (?-); *À Fleur de Couteau (On the Edge of the Blade*; AdH, 1980)

Peck, Alex (?-); *La Cité Ensevelie (The Buried City*; MRA, 1952)

Pécout, Roland (?-); *Les Mangeurs de Momies (The Mummy Eaters*; Belfond, 1981); *Portulan I and II* (Vent Terral, 1978-80); *Note: Les Mangeurs* is a documentary work about mummy-trafficking in the Middle Ages.

Peheu, André *see* **Murelli, Jean**

Peko, Dominique (?-); *La Planète des Norchats (Planet of the Norcats*; BV, 1981); *Note:* See Chapter IX.

Péladan, Joséphin (1859-1918); *Le Vice Suprême (The Supreme Vice*; Dentu, 1884); *La Victoire du Mari (The Husband's Victory*; Dentu, 1889); *L'Androgyne* (Dentu, 1891); *La Quête du Graal (The Quest for the Grail*;

Salon Rose-Croix, 1892); *Amphithéâtre des Sciences Mortes (Amphitheater of Dead Sciences*; Chamuel, 1893); *Mélusine* (Ollendorff, 1895); *Oedipe et le Sphinx (Oedipus and the Sphinx*; Imprim. Prof., 1897); *Semiramis* (MdF, 1904); *De Parsifal à Don Quichotte* (Sansot, 1906); *La Torche Renversée (The Spilled Torch*; Monde Moderne, 1925); *Note:* Also known as the Sâr Merodak, Princess Dinska, Miss Sarah, Marquis de Valognes. See Chapter IV.

Pelchat, Jean (1954-); *Le Lever du Corps (Taking Off the Body*; L'Instant Même, 1991); *Note:* French-Canadian writer. Collection of fantastical tales.

Pellegrin, Simon-Joseph (Abbé) (?-?) *see* **Opéra**

Pellerin, Georges (?-); *Le Monde dans 2000 Ans (The World in 2000 Years*; Dentu, 1878); *La Comtesse Rouge (The Red Countess*; Dentu, 1883); *Note:* See Chapter V.

Pellerin, Gilles (1954-); *Les Sporadiques Aventures de Guillaume Untel (The Sporadic Adventures of Guillaume Anybody*; Asticou, 1982); *Ni le Lieu, Ni l'Heure (NeitherThe Time, Nor the Place*; Instant Même, 1987); *Note:* French-Canadian writer.

Pelletier, Aimé *see* **Vac, Bertrand**

Pelletier, Claude J. (?-) *see* **Meynard, Yves**

Pelletier, Francine (1959-); *Les Temps des Migrations (The Time of Migrations*; CdF 11, 1987); *Le Rendez-Vous du Désert (The Rendezvous in the Desert*; JP 59, 1987); *Mort sur le Redan (Death on the Redan*; JP 64, 1988); *Le Crime de l'Enchanteresse (The Crime of the Enchantress*; JP 66, 1989); *Monsieur Bizarre* (JP 70, 1990); *Des Vacances Bizarres (Some Bizarre Holidays*; JP 74, 1991); *La Forêt de Métal (The Metal Forest*; HMH, 1991); *Par Chemins Inventés (Through Made-Up Roads*; anthology; Q/A, 1992); *Le Septième Écran (The Seventh Screen*; JP 80, 1992); *La Saison de l'Exil (The Season of Exile*; JP 82, 1992); *La Planète du Mensonge (The Planet of Lies*; JP 89, 1993); *La Bizarre Aventure (The Bizarre Adventure*; JP, 1993); *Une Nuit Bizarre (A Bizarre Night*; JP, 1994); *Cher Ancêtre (Dear Ancestor*; JP, 1996); *Damien, Mort ou Vif (Damien, Dead or Alive*; JP 119, 1997); *Nelle de Vilvèq (Le Sable et l'Acier 1) (The Sand and the Steel 1*; AL, 1997); *Note:* French-Canadian writer. *Le Temps* is a collection of science fiction stories. *Le Rendez-Vous* follows the journey of a young hero on a desert planet. A number of stories and novels (*Mort sur le Redan, Le Crime*) features Arialde, a young ornithologist in a near-future world.

Pelletier, Jean-Jacques (1947-); *L'Homme à qui il Poussait des Bouches (The Man Who Was Growing Mouths*; L'Instant Même, 1994); *L'Assassiné de l'Intérieur (Murdered from Inside*; L'Instant Même, 1997); *Note:* French-Canadian writer.

BRICE PELMAN

LE TRÉSOR DE LA CASBAH SOUIRA

FLEUVE NOIR

Pierre SURAGNE

L'ENFANT QUI MARCHAIT SUR LE CIEL

FLEUVE NOIR

Pierre SURAGNE

ET PUIS LES LOUPS VIENDRONT

fleuve noir

Pelman, Brice (1924-); *Le Trésor de la Casbah Souira (The Treasure of the Casbah Souira*; FNAV 12, 1995); *La Pierre Makatea (The Makatea Stone*; FNSF 13, 1997)

Pelosato, A. (?-); *La Compagnie des Clones (The Company of Clones*; Naturellement, 1997)

Pelot, Pierre (Grosdemange, Pierre) (1945-); *La Drave* (GP, 1970); *L'Unique Rebelle (The Only Rebel*; L'Amitié, 1971); *Les Étoiles Ensevelies (The Buried Stars*; L'Amitié, 1972); *Une Autre Terre (Another Earth*; Hatier, 1972); *La Septième Saison (The Seventh Season*; as Pierre Suragne; FNA 505, 1972); *Mal Iergo le Dernier (Mal Iergo the Last*; as Pierre Suragne; FNA 519, 1972); *L'Enfant qui Marchait sur le Ciel (The Child Who Walked on the Sky*; as Pierre Suragne; FNA 530, 1972); *La Nef des Dieux (The Ship of the Gods*; as Pierre Suragne; FNA 549, 1973); *Mecanic Jungle* (as Pierre Suragne; FNA 566, 1973); *L'Île aux Enragés (The Rabid Island*; Hatier, 1973); *La Peau de l'Orage (The Skin of the Storm*; as Pierre Suragne; FNAG 235, 1973); *Duz* (as Pierre Suragne; FNAG 243, 1973); *Les Légendes de la Terre (The Legends of Earth*; GP, 1973); *Le Pays des Rivières sans Nom (The Land of Nameless Rivers*; GP, 1973); *Et puis les Loups Viendront (And Then the Wolves Will Come*; as Pierre Suragne; FNA 577, 1973); *Je suis la Brume (I Am the Mist*; as Pierre Suragne; FNAG 251, 1974); *Mais si les Papillons Trichent? (But What If the Butterflies Cheat?*; as Pierre Suragne; FNA 612, 1974); *Le Coeur sous la Cendre (The Heart Under the Ash*; L'Amitié, 1974); *Le Dieu Truqué (The Phony God*; as Pierre Suragne; FNA 625,

1974); *Le Pain Perdu (The Lost Bread*; GP, 1974); *Ballade pour Presqu'un Homme (Ballad for Almost a Man*; as Pierre Suragne; FNA 633, 1974); *Du Plomb dans la Neige (Lead in the Snow*; as Pierre Suragne; FN Special Police 1138, 1974); *Suicide* (as Pierre Suragne; FNSL 1, 1974); *Je suis la Mauvaise Herbe (I Am a Bad Seed*; GP, 1975); *Une Si Profonde Nuit (Such a Deep Night*; as Pierre Suragne; FNSL 8, 1975); *Le Ciel Fracassé (The Shattered Sky*; L'Amitié, 1975); *Vendredi, Par Exemple (Friday, for Example*; as Pierre Suragne; FNA 695, 1975); *Brouillards (Fog*; as Pierre Suragne; FNSL 13, 1975); *Les Neiges du Coucou (Cuckoo's Snows*; GP, 1975); *Le Pantin Immobile (The Motionless Puppet*; L'Amitié, 1976); *Elle Était Une Fois (She Was Upon a Time*; as Pierre Suragne; FNSL 25, 1976); *Le Septième Vivant (The Seventh Living*; as Pierre Suragne; FNSL 27, 1976); *Les Barreaux de l'Éden (The Bars of Eden*; JL 728, 1977); *Foetus-Party* (PdF 225, 1977); *Le Renard dans la Maison (The Fox in the House]* L'Amitié, 1977); *Le Sourire des Crabes (The Smile of the Crabs*; PP 5003, 1977); *La Cité au Bout de l'Espace (The City at the End of Space*; as Pierre Suragne; FNA 797, 1977); *Transit* (A&D 47, 1977); *Les Aventures de Victor Piquelune (The Adventures of Victor Piquelune*; Hatier, 1977); *Les Grands Méchants Loufs (The Big Bad Wolves*; as Pierre Suragne; FN Special-Police

présence du futur
pierre pelot
la guerre olympique

denoël

SCIENCE-FICTION
Pierre Pelot
LE SOURIRE DES CRABES

ANTICIPATION
PIERRE PELOT
LE FILS DU GRAND KONNAR
Konnar et Compagnie – 1

FLEUVE NOIR
ANTICIPATION

1351, 1977); *Delirium Circus* (JL 773, 1977); *Le Canard à Trois Pattes (The Three-Legged Duck*; with William **Camus** & J. **Coué**; Duculot, 1978); *Canyon Street* (PdF 265, 1978); *Le Mauvais Coton (The Bad Cloth*; L'Amitié, 1978); *Le Sommeil du Chien (The Sleep of the Dog*;

Kes. I&M 5, 1978); *Les Canards Boîteux (The Lame Ducks*; GP, 1978); *La Rage dans le Troupeau (The Rage in the Flock*; PP 5060, 1979); *Virgules Téléguidées (Remote-Controlled Commas*; as Pierre Suragne; FNA 970, 1980); *Blues pour Julie (Blues for Julia*; Ponte Mirone, 1980); *La Guerre Olympique (The Olympic War*; PdF 297, 1980); *Parabellum Tango* (JL 1048, 1980); *Le Ciel Bleu d'Irockee (The Blue Sky of Irockee*; PP 5072, 1980); *Dérapages (Out of Control*; as Pierre Suragne; FNA 999, 1980); *Fou comme l'Oiseau (Crazy as a Bird*; L'Amitié, 1980); *La Dame (The Lady*; Crépuscule, 1980); *Kid Jesus* (JL 1140, 1981); *L'Été en Pente Douce (Summer on a Soft Incline*; Kes., 1980); *Les Îles du Vacarme (The Islands of Clamor*; PP 5096, 1981); *Un Bus Capricieux (A Capricious Bus*; L'Amitié, 1981); *Konnar le Barbant (Konnar the Boring; OF 320-321, 1981; rev. as Le Fils du Grand Konnar (The Son of Great Konnar]*, FNA 1788, 1990); *Les Mangeurs d'Argile (The Clay Eaters*; PP 5126, 1981); *Les Pieds dans la Tête (The Feet in the Head*; Dim. 48, 1982); *Nos Armes Sont De Miel (Our Weapons Are Made of Honey*; JL 1305, 1982); *Mourir au Hasard (To Die Randomly*; PdF 339, 1982); *La Forêt Muette (The Silent Forest*; AM, 1982); *Pauvre Zhéros (Poor Zeros*; FN Engrenage 48, 1982); *Saison de Rouille (Rusty Season*; PP 5135, 1982); *Soleils Hurlants (Screaming Suns*; PP 5157, 1983); *La Nuit sur Terre (Night on Earth*; Den., 1983); *Le Cri du Prisonnier (The Prisoner's Scream*; FN Engrenage, 1983); *La Foudre au Ralenti (The Slow-Motion Lightning*; JL 1564, 1983); *Le Père de Feu (The Fire-Father*; PP 5173, 1984); *Le Chien Courrait sur l'Autoroute en Criant son Nom (A Dog Was Running on the Highway Shouting Its Name*; PP 5190, 1984); *Paradis Zéro (Paradise Zero*; FNA 1355, 1985); *Le Bruit des Autres (The Sound of Others*; FNA 1369, 1985); *Roman Toc (Phony Novel*; FN Special-Police 1952, 1985); *L'Heure d'Hiver (Winter Time*; FN Special-Police 1956, 1985); *Le Méchant qui Danse (The Dancing Villain*; FN Special-Police 1964, 1985); *Ce Chasseur-Là (That Hunter There*; PP 5209, 1985); *Noires Racines (Black Roots*; Den., 1985); *Natural Killers* (Vertiges, 1985); *Les Passagers du Mirage (The Passengers of the Mirage*; FNA 1426, 1985); *Fou dans la Tête de Nazi Jones (Mad in Nazi Jones' Head*; FNA 1463, 1986); *Les Conquérants Immobiles (The Motionless Conquerors*; FNA 1469, 1986); *Mémoires d'un Épouvantail Blessé au Combat (Memories of a Scarecrow Wounded in Action*; FNA 1482, 1986); *Observation du Virus en Temps de Paix (Observation of the Virus During Peace Time*; FNA 1495, 1986); *Purgatoire (Purgatory*; FNG 34, 1986); *Elle qui ne sait pas dire Je (She Who Couldn't Say I*; Plon, 1987); *Alabama Un.Neuf.Neuf.Six (Alabama 1.9.9.6*; FNA 1553, 1987); *Sécession Bis* (FNA 1565, 1987); *Offensive du Virus sous le Champ de Bataille (Offensive of the Virus on the Battlefield*; FNA 1580,

1987); *Aux Chiens Écrasés (The Run-Over Dogs*; FNG 59, 1987); *Si loin de Caïn (So Far from Cain*; Flamm., 1988); *Une Jeune Fille au Sourire Fragile (A Young Girl with a Fragile Smile*; Siry SF 6, 1988); *Le Présent du Fou (The Madman's Gift*; FNA 1732, 1990); *Les Forains du Bord du Gouffre (The Carnival on the Edge of the Abyss*; FNA 1737, 1990); *Le Ciel sous la Pierre (The Sky Under the Stone*; FNA 1743, 1990); *Les Faucheurs de Temps (The Time Reapers*; FNA 1750, 1990); *Le Seizième Round (The Sixteenth Round*; Messidor, 1990); *Le Rêve de Lucy (Lucy's Dream*; with Yves **Coppens**; Seuil, 1990); *La Nuit du Sagittaire (The Night of Sagittarius*; PP 5338, 1990); *Sur la Piste des Rollmops (On the Trail of the Rollmops*; FNA 1796, 1990); *Rollmops Dream* (FNA 1802, 1991); *Gilbert le Barbant—Le Retour (Gilbert the Boring—the Return*; FNA 1811, 1991); *Ultimes Aventures en Territoires Fourbes (Last Adventures in Deceitful Lands*; FNA 1831, 1991); *Les Larmes de la Jungle (The Tears of the Jungle*; Rageot, 1991); *Le Bonheur des Sardines (Sardines' Happiness*; Den., 1993); *Le Père Noël s'appelle Basile (Santa Claus Is Named Basil*; Syros, 1993); *Ce Soir, les Souris sont Bleues (Tonight, the Mice Are Blue*; Den., 1994); *L'Expédition Perdue (The Lost Expedition*; Nathan, 1994); *Le Dernier des Misfits (Last of the Misfits*; Lueurs Mortes, 1994); *Une Autre Saison comme le Printemps (Another Season Like Spring*; Den., 1995); *Le Chant de l'Homme Mort (The Song of the Dead Man*; FNAV 5, 1995); *Après le Bout du Monde (After the Edge of the World*; FNASF 5, 1996); *Vincent, le Chien Terriblement Jaune (Vincent, the Very Yellow Dog*; Pocket, 1995); *Les Caimans sont des Gens comme les Autres (Caymans Are Just Like Other People*; Den., 1996); *Messager des Tempêtes Lointaines (Messenger of the Far Storms*; PdF 566, 1996); *Sous le Vent du Monde (Under the Wind of the World*; Den., 1997); *Note:* See Chapters VIII and IX. Several of Pelot's juvenile or mystery novels have been filmed for television; genre telefilms include **La Mission** and **Le Matin des Jokers** (see Book 1, Chapter II).

Pénard, Eugène (?-); *Le Déluge de Feu (The Fire Flood*; Pages Illustrées, 1911-12); *Trois Années dans les Glaces (Three Years in the Ice*; Delachaux-Niestlé, 1947); *Les Étranges Découvertes du Dr. Todd (Dr. Todd's Strange Discoveries*; Delachaux-Niestlé, 1948) *Note:* Swiss writer. Juvenile SF. See Chapter V.

Pennac, Daniel (Pennachioni, Daniel) (1944-); *Cabot Caboche* (Nathan, 1982); *L'Oeil du Loup (The Eye of the Wolf*; Nathan, 1984); *Le Grand Rex* (Centurion, 1986); *La Petite Marchande de Prose (The Little Prose Merchant*; Gall., 1989); *Monsieur Malaussène* (Gall., 1995); *Messieurs les Enfants (Mister Children*; Gall., 1997); *Note:* See Chapter VIII.

Pennes, Sébastien (1974-); *La Brûlure du Phénix (The Burn of the Phoenix*; Mnemos 2, 1995); *Le Pacte de Pierre (The Pact of Stone*; Mnemos 4, 1995); *Dans l'Oeil de l'Aleph (In the Eye of the Aleph*; Mnemos 7, 1996); *Le Sabre et le Fou (The Sabre and the Madman*; Mnemos 17, 1996); *Note:* See Chapter VIII.

Péol, Huguette (1930-); *L'Auberge des Guerilleros (The Inn of the Guerilleros*; Amitié, 1967); *L'Herbe de Bouddha (The Herb of Buddha*; Amitié, 1977); *La Jungle de l'Or Maudit (The Jungle of the Accursed Gold*; Amitié, 1978); *Contes d'Amazonie (Tales of Amazonia*; Hatier, 1979); *Le Pays des Femmes-Oiseaux (The Land of the Bird-Women*; Amitié, 1980); *La Reine Sorcière (The Witch Queen*; Amitié, 1984); *Note:* Juveniles.

Pépin, Pierre-Yves (1930-); *L'Homme Essentiel et La Ville Introuvable de l'Homme Perdu (The Essential Man and the Unfindable City of the Lost Man*; Hexagone, 1975); *L'Homme Gratuit (Essai) (The Free Man: Essay*; Hexagone, 1977); *L'Homme Éclaté (Essai) (The Shattered Man: Essay*; Hexagone, 1984); *La Terre Émue (The Moved Earth*; Triptyque, 1986); *Le Diable au Marais (The Devil in the Swamp*; Triptyque, 1987); *Note:* French-Canadian writer. *Le Diable* is a collection of fantastical tales.

Perceval, Jean (?-); *L'Âme Errante du Professeur Morel (The Wandering Soul of Prof. Morel*; L'Intercontinentale, 1945)

Perdhubert, Eugène (Bouchacourt, J.-L.) (?-); *Les Pionniers de l'Univers (The Pioneers of the Universe]*: *1. L'Enigme de Céres (The Enigma of Ceres*; Debresse, 1975); *5. La Nuit Enchanteresse (The Spellbound Night*; Debresse, 1976); *2. L'Uomo e la Donna (The Man and the Lady*; Subervie, Rodez, 1978); *6. L'Aventure de M. Chou sur Callisto (Mr. Chou's Adventure on Callisto*; Peintres & Poètes, 1984); *Le Bibisme (Perdhubert,* 1986); *La Ballade des Mammouths (The Ballad of the Mastodons*; Perdhubert, 1986); *Note:* Incomplete series, published randomly by different publishers.

Péret, Benjamin (1899-1959); *Et les Seins Mouraient (And the Breasts Died*; Cahiers du Sud, 1918); *Dormir, Dormir dans les Pierres (To Sleep, to Sleep Among the Stones*; Ed. Surreal., 1927); *Le Grand Jeu (The Big Game*; Gall., 1928); *Main Forte (Strong Hand*; Fontaine, 1946); *Dernier Malheur, Dernière Chance (Last Woe, Last Chance*; Fontaine, 1946); *Feu Central (Central Fire*; K Ed., 1947); *La Brebis Galante (The Gallant Ewe*; Los., 1959); *Les Couilles Enragées (The Rabid Balls*; Los., 1970); *Note:* See Chapter VI.

Périsset, Maurice (?-); *Cruauté des Abîmes (Cruelty from the Abyss*; Feuillets de l'Ilôt, 1943); *Les Eaux Noires (The Black Waters*; Janicot, 1946); *La Rage Noire (The Black Rage; La Tarente, 1951); Corps Interdits (For-*bidden Bodies*; La Salamandre, 1954); *Le Jeu de Satan (The Game of Satan*; Galliera 3, 1972); *Le Visage Derrière la Nuit (The Face Behind the Night*; Galliera 11, 1973; rev. FNA 1911, 1993); *Les Proies Immobiles (The Motionless Prey*; Monnet Terrific 7, 1974); *L'Oiseau de Proie (The Bird of Prey*; as Hubert Torrey; Monnet Terrific, 1978); *Les Statues d'Algues (The Algae Statues*; Milan, 1996); *Note:* See Chapter VIII.

Perney, Marguerite *see* **Grand-Guignol**

Pérochon, Ernest (1885-1942); *Les Ombres (The Shadows*; Plon, 1923); *Les Hommes Frénétiques (The Frenetic Men*; Plon, 1925); *Huit Gouttes d'Opium (Eight Drops of Opium*; Plon, 1925); *Le Crime Étrange de Lise Balzan (Lise Balzan's Strange Crime*; Plon, 1929); *L'Eau Courante (The Running Water*; Plon, 1932); *Contes des Cent Un Matins (Tales of 101 Mornings*; Delagrave, 1930); *Note:* See Chapters VI and VII.

Péron, Guy (?-); *Les Tribulations de Jacques Cravant, Inventeur, ou le Canot Invisible (The Tribulations of Jacques Cravant, Inventor, or the Invisible Boat*; S&V, 1924); *La Demoiselle qui est partie (The Damsel Who Left*; Pensée Française, 1925); *Le Capitaine Zapataz (*Ferenczi, 1929); *La Croisière du Tank Sous-Marin (The Cruise of the Underwater Tank*; BGA, 1931)

Pérot, Maurice (?-); *L'Expérience du Dr. Hortner (The Experiment of Dr. Hortner*; VA, 1937); *Le Royaume de l'Épouvante (The Kingdom of Terror*; VA, 1937); *La Guerre aux Diamants (The Diamond War*; Ferenczi, 1937); *Les Explorateurs de l'Espace (The Explorers of Space*; VA, 1938); *Les Contrebandiers de la Mort (The Smugglers of Death*; Ferenczi, 1938); *Le Testament Tragique (The Tragic Testament*; Ferenczi, 1938); *Sous la Botte du Conquérant (Under the Heel of the Conqueror*; Ferenczi, 1939); *La Cité des Réprouvés (The City of the Shunned*; Ferenczi, 1939); *Note:* See Chapter VII.

Perrard, Odile (?-); *Les Démons Capricornes (The Capricorn Demons*; Seuil, 1984)

Perrault, Charles (1628-1703); *Histoires ou Contes du Temps Passé (*Barbin, 1697; transl. as *Histories or Tales of Past Times,* 1729; aka *Contes de ma Mère l'Oie (Tales of Mother Goose)*; *Note:* See Chapter III.

Perret, Jacques (1901-1992); *Roucou (*Gall., 1936); *Le Vent dans les Voiles (Wind in the Sails*; Gall., 1948); *La Bête Mahousse (The Beast Mahousse*; Toion d'Or, 1954)

Perrier, E.-G. (?-); *La Merveilleuse Aventure de Sir Pickwick (Sir Pickwick's Marvellous Adventure*; Gédalge, 1929); *Le Beau Voyage de Barbassou (Barbassou's Beautiful Journey*; Gédalge, 1930); *En l'An 2000 (In the Year 2000*; Gédalge, 1931); *Note:* See Chapter VII.

Perrin, Jules (Laurent) (?-); *La Reine Artémise (Queen Artemise*; Calmann-Lévy, 1887); *L'Inquiétude (The Worry*; Charpentier-Fasquelle, 1893); *Les Bonhommes en Papier (The Little Men of Paper*; Fasquelle, 1905); *Deux Fantômes (Two Ghosts*; Fasquelle, 1908); *L'Hallucination de M. Forbes (Mr. Forbes' Hallucination;* JST, 1907; rev. as *La Terreur des Images (The Terror of Images*, Lafitte, 1910); *Brocéliande* (Fasquelle, 1910); *Un Monde sur le Monde (A World on the World*; with Henri **Lanos**; *Nos Loisirs*, 1910); *Le Mariage d'Abélard (Abelard's Wedding*; Fasquelle, 1921); *Le Retour des Barbares (The Return of the Barbarians*; Fasquelle, 1926); *L'Ermite de Montoire (The Montoire Hermit*; Fasquelle, 1929)

Perrin, Louis *see* **Gastine, Louis**

Perriod, Marcelle *see* **Grimaud, Michel**

Perron-Louis (?-) *see* ***Contes et Légendes***

Perrot, Louise (?-); *La Manade du Centaure (The Manade of the Centaur*; Flamm., 1995); *Note:* Juvenile fantasy.

Perrot-Bishop, Annick (1945-); *Les Maisons de Cristal (The Houses of Crystal*; AMAM 8, 1990); *Note:* French-Canadian writer. Collection of SF stories.

Pérye, André (?-?); *L'Île qui Meurt (The Dying Island*; with Renée **Lacascade**; Calmann-Lévy, 1930); *Note:* Also see **Grand-Guignol**.

Pescow, Gaspard-Georges *see* **Dumas, Alexandre**

Peslouan, Hervé de (?-); *L'Étrange Menace du Prof. Iouchkoff (The Strange Threat of Prof. Iouchkoff*; LPT/Hachette, 1931); *Le Russe et son Pantin (The Russian and His Dummy*; Lemerre, 1931); *L'Énigme de l'Élysée (The Mystery of Elysée Palace*; Ren. du Lire, 1932); *L'Amiral des Sables (The Admiral of the Sands*; Tallandier, 1934); *Un Train Sifflait dans la Nuit (A Train Whistled in the Night*; with J. **Jacquin**; Hac., 1935); *La Sirène des Neiges (The Siren of the Snows*; Tallandier, 1937); *Le Maître du Bonheur (The Master of Happiness*; Ed. des Loisirs, 1939)

Petis de la Croix, François (Père) (Father; 1633-1667); *Histoire du Grand Genghizcan (Tale of the Great Genghizcan*; Vve. Jombert, 1710)

Petis de la Croix, François (Fils) (Son; 1653-1713); *Les Mille et Un Jours (The Thousand and One Days*; 1710-14); *Histoire de Timur-Bec (Story of Timur-Bec*; 1722); *Note:* See Chapter III.

Petitcastelli, Claude (?-); *Chroniques Fantastiques (Fantastical Chronicles*; with Michelle Fitoussi; anthology) Encre, 1980); *Note:* Collection of stories submitted to the radio series *Magical Nights.*

Petithuguenin, Jean (?-); *Le Roi de la Mer (The King of the Sea*; Livre Moderne, 1913); *Houdini, le Maître du Mystère (Houdini, Master of Mystery*; Ferenczi, 1921); *Le Roi de l'Abîme (The King of the Abyss*; 3 vols., Baudinière, 1928-29): *1. Le Signe Mystérieux (The Mysterious Sign); 2. Une Énigme Vivante (A Living Enigma); 3. Les Pirates Fantômes (The Ghost Pirates); Une Mission Internationale sur la Lune (An International Mission to the Moon*; JDV, 1926; rev. RMY, 1933); *Faust* (Tallandier, 1927); *L'Amante Réincarnée (The Reincarnated Lover*; RMY, 1931); *Une Âme en Perdition (A Lost Soul*; Rouff, 1931); *Le Secret des Incas (The Secret of the Incas*; CA, 1931); *Le Grand Courant (The Great Current*; S&V/CA, 1931); *Le Visiteur Invisible (The Invisible Visitor*; Ferenczi, 1932); *Note:* See Chapter VII.

Petitjean de la Rosière, Marie & Frédéric *see* **Delly**

Petitpierre, F.-G. *see* **Price, Georges**

Petoud, Wildy (?-); *La Route des Soleils (The Road of the Suns*; FNA 1953, 1994); *Tigre au Ralenti (Tiger in Slow Motion*; Destination Crépuscule, 1996); *Note:* Swiss writer. See Chapter IX.

Pettex, Contant *see* **Arly, Dominique**

Pettigrew, Jean (1955-); *Le Glaïeul Noir (The Black Gladiolus*; serialized in *Journal de Quebec*, 1992); *Note:* French-Canadian writer/editor.

Peudefer de Parville, François-Henri (1838-1909); *Un Habitant de la Planète Mars (An Inhabitant of Planet Mars*; Hetzel, 1865); *Note:* See Chapter V.

Peveril (?-); *Mission sur Palémon (Mission to Palemon*; Satellite 27, 1960)

Peyramaure, Michel (1922-); *Paradis entre Quatre Murs (Paradise Between Four Walls*; RL, 1954); *Les Dieux de Plume (The Feather Gods*; PC, 1965); *La Vallée des Mammouths (The Valley of the Mastodons*; RL Plein Vent, 1966); *Les Colosses de Carthage (The Colossus of Carthage*; RL, 1967); *Cordillère Interdite (Forbidden Mountain Range*; RL Plein Vent, 1970); *Le Chevalier de Paradis (The Knight of Paradise*; Cast., 1971); *La Citadelle Ardente (The Fiery Citadel*; RL, 1978); *La Tête du Dragon (The Dragon's Head*; RL, 1978); *L'Empire des Fous (The Empire of Madmen*; RL, 1980); *Quand Surgira l'Étoile Absinthe (When the Absinthe Star Rises*; RL, 1980); *La Porte Noire (The Black Gate*; RL, 1985); *La Chair et le Bronze (The Flesh and the Bronze*; RL, 1985); *La Caverne Magique (The Magic Cavern*; RL, 1986); *La Montagne Terrible (The Awful Mountain*; RL, 1989); *L'Aigle et la Foudre (The Eagle and the Lightning*; RL, 1991); *L'Aigle des Deux Royaumes (The Eagle of Two Kingdoms*; L. Souny, 1993); *Note:* See Chapter IX.

Peyre, Marc (1912-); *Le Captif de Zour (The Prisoner of Zour*; Calmann-Lévy, 1964)

Peyresblanques, Jean (?-) *see Contes et Légendes*

Peyrol, Manuele (?-); *L'Oeil du Chat (The Eye of the Cat*; Julliard, 1979); *Note:* Collection of fantastical tales.

Peyssonié, Paul *see* **Sonniès, Paul**

Pézard, André (?-) *see Contes et Légendes*

Pézard, Fanette (?-); *L'Aventure Futuriste (The Futuriste Adventure*; as Roche-Pézard; Boccard, 1983); *Note:* Also see *Contes et Légendes*

Phabrey, Gille (?-); *Arnold Bart, Chevalier (Arnold Bart, Knight*; ADPL, 1952); *Bernard au Pays des Loups (Bernard in the Land of the Wolves*; SdP, 1960); *La Pierre de Soleil (The Sun Stone*; S&A 10, 1961)

Philéas (1940-); *Le Sexe des Anges (The Sex of Angels*; GdV, 1990); *L'Ange et la Putain (The Angel and the Whore*; GdV, 1992); *Le Grand Frisson (The Great Shiver*; GdV, 1994); *Note:* Erotic fantasies.

Philippe, Jean-Loup (?-); *O* (Castel d'Eau, 1992); *Mémoire de Sang (Memory of Blood*; FNFR 19, 1995)

Phillippart, Michel (1946-); *Monde 39 (World 39*; Nathan SF 1, 1980)

Picalausa, Louis C. (?-); *Chur le Silencieux (Chur the Silent*; La Thyrse, 1922); *Zi et Za de la Jungle (Zi and Za of the Jungle*; Cast., 1938); *Les Chasseurs de Mammouths (The Mastodon Hunters*; Cast., 1943); *Le Sel de la Mer (The Salt of the Sea*; Cast., 1943); *Les Yeux de la Jungle (The Eyes of the Jungle*; Cast., 1944); *L'Enfant des Bêtes (The Child of the Beasts*; Cast., 1945)

Picard, Gilbert (1937-); *Demain n'est qu'une Chimère (Tomorrow Is Only a Fantasy*; Libr. Champs-Élysées, 1976); *La France Envoûtée (Spellbound France*; FN Carrousel, 1985); *La Guerre des Bacilles (War of the Viruses*; FN, 1985); *Le Miroir du Passé (The Mirror of the Past*; FNA 1380, 1985); *A Quoi Bon Ressusciter? (Why Bother with Resurrection?*; FNA 1390, 1985); *Le Volcan des Sirènes (The Mermaids' Volcano*; FNA 1410, 1985); *Les Combattants des Abysses (The Fighters of the Abyss*; FNA 1471, 1986); *Note:* See Chapter IX.

Picard, Sylvie (?-); *Souterrains (Underground*; FN Angoisses 3, 1993); *Libres comme l'Air (Free as Air*; Monde Libertaire, 1995); *Serial Victime* (Baleine, 1997)

Picher, Clermont (1944-); *Le Signe de l'Étoile (The Sign of the Star*; Fidès, 1991); *Note:* French-Canadian writer.

Pichette, Henri (1924-); *Le Dernier Homme (The Last Man*; Disque Vert, 1924); *Le Point Vélique (The Velic Point*; MdF, 1950); *Les Épiphanies (Mystère Profane) (The Epiphanies: a Mundane Mystery*; Gall., 1969); *Fragments du Sélénite (Fragments of the Selenite*; La Rubeline, 1973); *Note:* Belgian writer.

Pichon, Jean-Charles (1920-); *La Vie Impossible (The Impossible Life*; Grasset, 1946); *L'Épreuve de Mammon (The Test of Mammon*; Grasset, 1947); *La Loutre (The Otter*; Corrêa, 1951); *Le Juge (The Judge*; Corrêa, 1952); *Les Clefs et la Prison (The Keys and the Jail*; Delamain & Boutelleau, 1954); *La Soif et la Mesure (Thirst and Measure*; Delamain & Boutelleau, 1955); *Nostradamus et le Secret des Temps (Nostradamus and the Secret of Time*; Prod. de Paris, 1959); *Joseph Maldonna* (Calmann-Lévy, 1961); *Le Temps du Verseau (The Time of Aquarius*; RL, 1962); *Les Cycles de l'Éternel Retour (The Cycles of Eternal Return*; RL, 1963); *1. Le Royaume et les Prophètes (The Kingdom and the Prophets*); *2. Les Jours et les Nuits du Cosmos (Days and Nights of the Cosmos*); *Les Témoins de l'Apocalypse (The Witnesses of the Apocalypse;* RL, 1964); *Le Dieu du Futur (The God of the Future*; Planète, 1966); *Borille* (Grasset, 1966); *Nostradamus en Clair (Nostradamus Made Clear*; Laffont, 1970); *La Vie des Dieux (The Life of the Gods*; Payot, 1972); *Un Homme en Creux (A Hollow Man*; Stock, 1973); *La Terrasse du Dôme (The Terrace of the Dome*; Camby, 1982)

Pidoux, Edmond (?-); *Une Île nommée New Begin (An Island Called New Begin*; La Baconnière, 1977); *Note:* Swiss writer.

Pierre, Victor (?-); *Le Dictateur du Sahara (The Sahara Dictator*; BGA, 1950); *Au Fond de l'Abîme (At the Bottom of the Abyss*; Tallandier, 1952)

Pierrefeux, Jean de (?-); *Dix Ans Après—Horoscopes Futuristes (Ten Years Later—Futuristic Horoscopes*; Ferenczi, 1930)

Pierre-Pain, Ch. M. (?-); *L'Homme qui Assassina les Peuples (The Man Who Murdered People*; Plon, 1925)

Pierroux, Jacques (?-); *Pilotes pour Demain (Pilots for Tomorrow*; MarJ 69, 1956); *La Mer de Corail (The Coral Sea*; MarJ, 1960); *Police Spatiale (Space Police*; MarJ 203, 1961); *Note:* Belgian writer. Juvenile SF. See Chapter IX.

Pieyre de Mandiargues, André (1909-1991); *Dans les Année Sordides (During the Sordid Years*; APM, 1943); *Le Musée Noir (The Black Museum*; RL, 1946; rev. Gall., 1974); *Soleil des Loups (The Sun of the Wolves*; RL, 1951); *Marbre ou les Mystères d'Italie (Marble or the Italian Mystery*; RL, 1953); *Le Monstre de Bomarzo (The Monster of Bomarzo*; Grasset, 1957); *Feu de Braise (Ember Fire*; Grasset, 1959); *La Marée (The Tide*; CLP, 1962); *La Motocyclette (The Motorbike*; Gall., 1963); *Porte Dévergondée (Vulgar Door*; Gall., 1965); *La Marge (The Margin*; Gall., 1967); *La Nuit de 1914 ou le style Liberty (The Night of 1914 or the Liberty Style*; L'Herne, 1971); *Le Cadran Lunaire (The Moon Dial*; Gall., 1972); *Le Lis de Mer (The Sea Lys*; Gall., 1972);

Croiseur Noir (Black Cruiser; Paroles Peintes, 1972); *Le Désordre de la Mémoire (The Disorder of Memory*; Gall., 1975); *Sous la Lame (Under the Blade*; Gall., 1976); *Arcimboldo le Merveilleux (Arcimboldo the Marvellous*; RL, 1977); *Le Trésor Cruel de Hans Bellma (The Cruel Treasure of Hans Bellma*; Sphinx, 1979); *La Nuit Séculaire (The Secular Night*; Gall., 1979); *Le Deuil des Roses (Roses in Mourning*; Gall., 1983); *Cuevas Blues* (Fata Morgana, 1986); *Tout Disparaîtra (All Shall Vanish*; Gall., 1987); *Monsieur Mouton* (Fata Morgana, 1993); *Note:* See Chapter VIII.

Pigault-Lebrun, Charles (?-?); *L'Enfant du Carnaval (The Carnival Child*; Vatican, Imprimerie du Saint-Père, 1796); *Les Barons de Flesheim (The Barons of Flesheim*; Barba, 1798); *Note:* See Chapter IV.

Pigeon, Daniel (1963-); *Hémisphère* (XYZ, 1994); *Note:* French-Canadian writer.

Pigeon, Pierre (1950-); *L'Ordinateur Égaré (The Misplaced Computer*; Q/A, 1984); *Le Grand Ténébreux (The Great Darkness*; Q/A, 1986); *Cauchemar au Pays d'Onyx (Nightmare in Onyx Land*; Coincidence, 1989); *L'Homme du Lac (The Man from the Lake*; Coincidence, 1989); *Super Débile 5 (Super Stupid 5*; Coincidence, 1991); *La Soucoupe Affolante (The Disturbing Saucer*; Coïncidence, 1992); *Pouvoir Surnaturel (Supernatural Power*; Coïncidence, 1992); *Note:* French-Canadian writer. Juvenile fantasies starring the Blondeau family and their computer, Onyx.

Pignot, Émile (?-); *Humanité (Mankind*; Figuière, 1922); *Le Lendemain du Grand Soir (The Day After the Big Night*; Anquetil, 1926); *La Prison de la Chair (The Prison of Flesh*; Figuière, 1932)

Pilhes, René-Victor (1934-); *L'Imprécateur (The Imprecator*; Seuil, 1974); *La Bête (The Beast*; Seuil, 1976); *Le Loum* (Seuil, 1991); *La Faux (The Scythe*; AM, 1993); *Le Fakir* (Flamm., 1995); *Note:* **L'Imprécateur** was made into an eponymous film in 1977 (see Book 1, Chapter I).

Pineau, Christian (?-); *Contes de Je Ne Sais Quand (Tales of I-Don't-Know-When*; Hac., 1952); *Cornerousse le Mystérieux (Cornerousse the Mysterious*; Hac., 1957); *La Planète aux Enfants Perdus (The Planet of Lost Children*; Hac., 1960); *L'Escalier des Ombres (The Staircase of Shadows*; Julliard, 1963); *Note:* See Chapter IX.

Pingon, Jean de (?-); *Les Mémoires du Roi Bérold (The Memoirs of King Berold*; Buchet-Chastel, 1991)

Pinguilly, Yves (?-); *Le Ballon d'Or (The Golden Ball*; Rageot, 1994); *Le Lièvre et la Soupe au Pili-Pili (The Hare and the Pili-Pili Soup*; Rageot, 1994); *Le Gros Grand Gri Gri (The Big Big Talisman*; L'Harmattan, 1995); *Le Secret de la Falaise (The Secret of the Cliff*; Nathan, 1995); *Rock Parking* (Cast., 1995); *Une Semaine au Cimetière (A Week in the Cemetary*; Cast., 1995); *Meurtre Noir et Gri Gri Blanc (Black Murder and White Talisman*; Magnard, 1997); *Note:* Juvenile fantasies. Also see **Contes et Légendes**

Piret, Daniel (1933-); *Année 500.000 (Year 500,000*; FNA 490, 1972); *Les Deux Soleils de Canaé (The Two Suns of Canae*; FNA 525, 1972); *Les Égarés du Temps (Lost in Time*; FNA 554, 1973); *Les Disques de Biem-Kara (The Disks of Biem-Kara*; FNA 575, 1973); *Le Maître de Phallaté (The Master of Phallate*; FNA 595, 1974); *Le Fils de l'Atlantide (The Son of Atlantis*; FNA 604, 1974); *Naître ou Ne Pas Naître (To Be Born or Not to Be Born*; FNA 621, 1974); *Ahouvati le Kobek* (FNA 640, 1974); *Le Grand Passage (The Great Passage*; FNA 649, 1974); *Le Tell de la Puissance (The Tell of Power*; FNA 668, 1975); *Le Onzième Satellite (The Eleventh Satellite*; FNA 680, 1975); *Les Egrégores* (FNA 687, 1975); *Sakkara* (FNA 702, 1975); *Les Survivants de Miderabi (The Survivors of Miderabi*; FNA 711, 1975); *Vae Victis!* (FNA 721, 1976); *La Dernière Mort (The Final Death*; FNA 727, 1976); *Le Rescapé du Gaurisankar (The Survivor from the Gaurisankar*; FNA 739, 1976); *Le Manuscrit (The Manuscript*; FNA 754, 1976); *Sogol* (FNA 761, 1976); *Xurantar* (FNA 781, 1977); *La Mort des Dieux (The Death of the Gods*; FNA 804, 1977); *L'Île des Bahalim (The Island of the Bahalim*; FNA 813, 1977); *Les Dévoreurs d'Ames (The Soul Devourers*; FNA 825, 1977); *L'Ancêtre d'Irskaa (The Ancestor of Irskaa*; FNA 848, 1978); *Interférence* (FNA 861, 1978); *Le Navire-Planète (The Planet-Ship*; FNA 878, 1978); *N'ooma* (FNA 947, 1979); *Péril Végétal (Vegetable Threat*; as Red Ilan; MOC 2, 1979); *Cholom* (as Red Ilan; MOC 7, 1979); *La Sphère des Templiers (The Sphere of the Templars*; as Red Ilan; MOC 9, 1979); *Diaspora Cosmique (Cosmic Diaspora*; as Red Ilan; MOC 13, 1979); *Univers Alpha* (as Red Ilan; MOC 17, 1980); *Strontium 90* (FNA 983, 1980); *Sloma de l'Abianta* (FNA 1113, 1981); *Les Envoyés de Méga (The Envoys from Mega*; FNA 1119, 1982); *Prométhée (Prometheus*; FNA 1140, 1982); *La 666ème Planète (The 666th Planet*; FNA 1201, 1983); *Le Fils de Prométhée (The Son of Prometheus*; FNA 1233, 1983); *La Parole (The Spoken Word*; FNA 1278, 1984); *Note:* See Chapter IX.

Piscaglia, Christian (?-); *SOS Radiations* (BV, 1978); *300.000 Tonnes de Brut pour Rotterdam (300,000 Tons of Crude for Rotterdam*; Hac., 1981)

Pithon, Juste (?-); *35 degrés au-dessous de Zéro (Thirty-Five Degrees Below Zero*; Payot, 1945); *La Croix Magique (The Magic Cross*; Delachaux-Niestlé, 1947); *La Huitième Merveille (The Eighth Wonder*; Payot, 1949)

Pittard, Hélène, née Dufour *see* **Roger, Noëlle**

Pittier, Jacques-Michel (?-); *La Corde Raide (Straight Rope*; AdH, 1981)

Pitz, L. (?-) *see* **Contes et Légendes**

Pividal, Rafael (?-); *Le Capitaine Nemo et la Science (Captain Nemo and Science*; Grasset, 1972); *Emily et une Nuit (Emily and One Night*; Seuil, 1974); *Contes Sages (Wise Tales*; Rupture, 1977); *La Tête de Louis XVI (Louis XVI's Head*; Rupture, 1978); *Le Faux Prêtre (The False Priest*; Renaissance, 1980); *La Découverte de l'Amérique (The Discovery of America*; Grasset, 1981); *La Montagne Fêlée (The Cracked Mountain*; Grasset, 1985); *Grotius* (Grasset, 1986); *Hugo, l'Enterré Vivant (Hugo Buried Alive*; Renaissance, 1990); *Le Goût de la Catastrophe (The Taste of Catastrophe*; Renaissance, 1991); *Les Aventures Extraordinaires de Jacques Lamare (Jacques Lamare's Extraordinary Adventures*; Quai Voltaire, 1992)

Pixérécourt, René-Charles-Guilbert de (1773-1844); *Victor ou l'Enfant de la Forêt (Victor or the Child of the Forest*; Barba, 1803); *Le Château des Appenins ou Le Fantôme Vivant (The Castle in the Appenins or the Living Ghost*; Barba, 1799); *Coelina ou l'Enfant du Mystère (Coelina or the Child of Mystery*; Au Théâtre, 1803); *Pizarre ou la Conquête du Pérou (Pizarro or the Conquest of Peru*; Barba, 1802); *Le Solitaire de la Roche Noire (The Hermit of Black Rock*; Barba, 1806); *Les Ruines de Babylone (The Ruins of Babylon*; Barba, 1810); *Note:* See Chapter IV. *Coelina* is based on a novel by **Ducray-Duminil**.

Planchat, Henry-Luc (?-); *Derrière le Néant (Behind the Void*; anthology; MarSF 458, 1973); *Dédale 1* (anthology; MarSF 521, 1975); *Dédale 2* (anthology; MarSF 559, 1976); *Les Fenêtres Internes (The Inner Windows*; anthology; 10/18 1236, 1978); *Note:* See Chapter IX.

Plançon, Paul (?-) *see* **Falk, Henri**

Planque, Jean-Pierre (?-); *La Quête des Racines (Quest for the Roots*; L'Oeuf, n.d.); *Le Vrai Visage de Gregory (Gregory's True Face*; with Patrick **Raveau**; Pegase, n.d.)

Plante, Jacques (?-); *Le Cristal Magique (The Magic Crystal*; HRW, 1995); *Le Village Fantôme (The Ghost Village*; HRW, 1995); *Note:* French-Canadian writer.

Plante, Marie (1954-); *La Barrière du Temps (Time's Barrier*; JP 36, 1979); *Note:* French-Canadian writer. Juvenile SF.

Pliya, Jean (1931-); *L'Arbre Fétiche (The Fetish Tree*; CLE, Yaoundé, 1963); *Kondo le Requin (Kondo the Shark*; CLE, Yaoundé, 1965); *La Fille Têtue (The Stubborn Girl*; Nlles. Ed. Africaines, 1982); *Les Tresseurs de Corde (The Rope Weavers*; CEDA, 1987); *Note:* Beninese writer. See Chapter VIII.

Plour, Guy René de *see* **Grenier, Armand**

Plourde, Josée (?-); *Hubert et les Vampires (Hubert and the Vampires*; Michel Quintin, 1994); *Note:* French-Canadian writer.

Podalire, R. S. (?-); *Hippocrate chez les Pingouins (Hippocrates Among the Penguins*; Ed. Indep., 1919)

Poidloué, Charles (?-?) *see* **Grand-Guignol**

Poinsot, Maffeo Charles (1872-); *Sur le Gouffre (Over the Pit*; SFIL, 1900); *La Mortelle Impuissance (The Deadly Powerlessness*; Fasquelle, 1903); *La Faillite du Rêve (The Bankruptcy of Dream*; Fasquelle, 1905); *Mâles* (Libr. U., 1906); *Le Coeur Ailé (The Winged Heart*; Ren. du Livre, 1919); *Les Ivresses Désespérées (Desperate Drunkenness*; Pensée Fr., 1924); *Sémiramis, Reine de Babylone (Semiramis, Queen of Babylon*; with Marcel **Schneider**; Gall., 1926)

Poirier, Jean (1956-); *Aventures en Fusée (Adventure in a Rocket*; Énergie Pure, 1987); *Note:* French-Canadian writer. SF satire.

Poirier, Louis *see* **Gracq, Julien**

Poitras, Anique (1961-); *La Deuxième Vie (The Second Life*; Q/A, 1994); *La Lumière Blanche (The White Light*; Q/A, 1994); *Note:* French-Canadian writer. Juvenile SF.

Poittevin, Alfred de (?-?); *Une Promenade de Bélial (Belial's Walk*; 1848); *Note:* See Chapter IV.

Pol, Anne-Marie (?-); *La Reine de l'Île (The Queen of the Island*; Flamm., 1986); *Lola et les Loups (Lola and the Wolves*; Hac., 1988); *Le Sang des Étoiles (Blood of the Stars*; Hac., 1988); *Note:* Juveniles.

Polac, Michel (1930-); *La Vie Incertaine (Uncertain Life*; Gall., 1956); *Les Vies Parallèles (Parallel Lives*; Flamm., 1969); *Le Q.I. ou le Roman d'un Surdoué (The I.Q. or a Novel of the Gifted*; Belfond, 1978); *Note:* See Chapter IX.

Pomès, Paul (?-); *À la Poursuite du Temps (Pursuing Time*; MOC 14, 1979)

Poncetton, François *see* **Boca, Gaston**

Pons, Maurice (1925-); *La Mort d'Éros (Eros' Death*; Julliard, 1953); *Le Cordonnier Aristote (Aristote the Cobbler*; Julliard, 1958); *Rosa* (Den., 1967); *Mademoiselle B.* (Den., 1973); *La Maison des Brasseurs (The House of the Brewers*; Den., 1978); *Patinir ou l'Harmonie du Monde (Patinir or the Harmony of the World*; RL, 1980); *Pourquoi pas Métrobate? (Why Not Metrobate?*; Balland, 1982); *Virginales (Virginals*; Bougois, 1983); *Douce-Amère (Bitter-Sweet*; Den., 1985); *Le Passager de la Nuit (The Passenger of the Night*; Rocher, 1991); *Note:* See Chapter VIII.

Pons, René see **Pujol, René**

Ponson du Terrail, Victor-Alexis (1829-1871); *La Baronne Trépassée (The Dead Baroness*; Baudry, 1852); *Le Castel du Diable (The Devil's Castle*; Prignet, 1853); *Le Trou de Satan (Satan's Hole*; L. de Potter, 1863); *Le Chambrion* (Dentu, 1865); *La Maison du Diable (The Devil's House*; A. Faure, 1867); *Amaury le Vengeur (Amaury the Avenger*; Lachaud, 1869); *La Messe Noire (The Black Mass*; Dentu, 1869); *Les Aventures d'un Valet de Coeur (The Adventures of the Jack of Heart*; Dentu, 1883); *La Comtesse d'Asti (The Countess of Asti*; Dentu, 1891); *La Dame au Gant Noir (The Lady with a Black Glove*; Dentu, 1891); *Le Roman de Fulmen (The Novel of Fulmen*; Dentu, 1891); *Les Spadassins de l'-Opera (The Spadassins of the Opera*; Dentu, 1891); *Les Aventures d'un Enfant de Paris (The Adventures of a Parisian Child*; Roy & Geffroy, 1893); *Le Château Mystérieux (The Mysterious Castle*; Geffroy, 1893); *Le Bal des Victimes (The Ball of Victims*; Dentu, 1896); *Le Serment des Hommes Rouges (The Oath of the Red Men*; Geffroy, 1898); *Le Forgeron de la Cour-Dieu (The Blacksmith of God's Court*; Fayard, 1915); Series *Rocambole/Les Drames de Paris (The Dramas of Paris)*: *1. Les Deux Frères (The Two Brothers) / L'Héritage Mystérieux (The Mysterious Inheritance)*; 58 eps., *La Patrie*, 1857; rep. in *Rocambole* Vol. 1, Rouff, 1883-86); *2. Le Club des Valets de Coeur (The Club of the Jack of Hearts*; 105 eps., *La Patrie*, 1858; rep. in *Rocambole* Vol. 1, Rouff, 1883-86); *3. Les Exploits de Rocambole (The Exploits of Rocambole*; 109 eps., *La Patrie*, 1858-59; rep. in *Rocambole* Vol. 1, Rouff, 1883-86); *4. La Revanche de Baccarat (The Revenge of Baccarat;* 36 eps., *La Patrie,* 1859; rep. in *Rocambole* Vol. 2 as *La Dernière Incarnation de Rocambole (The Last Incarnation of Rocambole)*, Rouff, 1883-86); *5. Les Chevaliers du Clair de Lune (The Knights of the Moon Light*; 58 eps., *La Patrie*, 1860; rep. in *Rocambole* Vol. 2, Rouff, 1883-86); *6. Le Testament de Grain de Sel (The Testament of Grain-Of-Salt) / Le Château de Bellecombe (The Castle of Bellecombe)*; 74 eps., *La Patrie,* 1862; rep. in *Rocambole* Vol. 2, Rouff, 1883-86); *7. La Résurrection de Rocambole (The Resurrection of Rocambole);* 223 eps., *Le Petit Journal*, 1865-66; rep. in *Rocambole* Vol. 2 as *Le Bagne de Toulon (The Penitentiary of Toulon)*, Rouff, 1883-86); *8. Le Dernier Mot de Rocambole (The Last Word of Rocambole;* 350 eps., *La Petite Presse,* 1866-67; rep. in *Rocambole* Vol. 3 as *Les Ravageurs (The Ravagers) / Les Millions de la Bohémienne (The Millions of the Gypsy Woman)*, Rouff, 1883-86); *9. Les Misères de Londres (The Miseries of London;* 237 eps., *La Petite Presse*, 1867-68; rep. in *Rocambole* Vol. 3 as *Le Club des Crevés (The Club of the Deceased) / Le Retour de Rocambole (The Return of Rocambole) / Le Bûcher de la Veuve (The Widow's Stake) / La Vérité sur Rocambole (The Truth About Rocambole)*, Rouff, 1883-86); *10. Les Démolitions de Paris (The Demolitions of Paris;* 122 eps., *La Petite Presse,* 1869; rep. in *Rocambole* Vol. 4 as *La Nourrisseuse d'Enfants (The Child Feeder) / L'Enfant Perdu (The Lost Child) / Le Cimetière des Suppliciés (The Graveyard of the Tortured)*, Rouff, 1883-86); *11. La Corde du Pendu (The Hanged Man's Rope;* 112 eps., *La Petite Presse,* 1870; rep. in *Rocambole* Vol. 4 as *La Captivité du Maître (The Captivity of the Master) / L'Homme en Gris (The Man in Grey) / Les Amours du Limousin (The Loves of the Limousin)*, Rouff, 1883-86); By Constant Guéroult: *Le Retour et la Fin de Rocambole (The Return and the End of Rocambole; La Petite Presse,* 1875; rep. Benoist, 1877); *Les Nouveaux Exploits de Rocambole (The New Adventures of Rocambole*; Capiomont, Calvet, 1880); By ??: *Cadet Fripouille: Rocambole, Aventures Inédites (Cadet Crook: Rocambole's Unpublished Adventures;* 114 eps., *Le Matin*, 1911; rep. Fayard, 1912); By Frédéric **Valade**: *Le Petit-Fils de Rocambole (Rocambole's Grand-Son;* 112 eps., *Le Gaulois*, 1921); rep. as *Le Testament de Rocambole (Rocambole's Testament) / Olivia contre Rocambole (Olivia vs. Rocambole) / La Justice de Rocambole (Rocambole's Justice) / La Belle Olivia (The Beautiful Olivia) / Les Larmes de Rocambole (Rocambole's Tears) / Le Châtiment d'Olivia (Olivia's Punishment)*, LN, 1931-33); *Note:* See Chapter IV. Also see Book 1, chapters I, II, III, and IV for film, television, radio, and comic-book adaptations.

Porée-Kurrer, Philippe (1954-); *Le Retour de l'Orchidée (The Return of the Orchid*; JCL, 1990); *La Fiancée du Lac (The Fiancée of the Lake*; Pygmalion, 1993); *Shalôm* (Sivori, 1996); *Note:* French-Canadian writer. *Le Retour* is about the events leading to a Third World War.

Port(rage), Red see **Prévot, Gérard**

Portail, Jean (?-); *La Femme Enchaînée (The Woman in Chains*; Crès, 1928); *Fruit d'Orage (Storm Fruit*; Crès, 1929); *Lumière sur la Montagne (Light on the Mountain*; Excelsior, 1933); *Un Secret bien Gardé (A Well-Kept Secret*; SEPIA, 1940); *Note:* Also see **Contes et Légendes**

Poslaniec, Christian (1944-); *Les Oiseaux Étranglés (The Strangled Birds*; Chambelland, 1973); *Nouvelles de la Terre et d'Ailleurs (Stories from Earth and Elsewhere*; Renard Poche, 1980); *Frédérique au Pays du Papiratillon Rouge (Frederique in the Land of the Red Papiratillon*; Léon Faure, 1980); *Farfadets et Folies Douces (Goblins and Sweet Madness*; Léon Faure, 1981); *Éléphantasmes (Elephantasms*; Encres Vives, 1981); *Le Chapeau à Claques (Top Hat*; Renard Poche, 1982); *Les Métamorphoses de Miss Pop-Corn (Miss Popcorn's Metamorphoses*; École des Loisirs, 1984); *Histoires*

Horribles et Pas si Méchantes (Awful and Not So Nasty Tales; Flamm., 1986); *Pistache (Le Sorbier, 1986); Le Collectionneur d'Images (The Image Collector*; Magnard, 1986); *L'Escargot de Cristal (The Crystal Snail*; Centurion, 1986); *Le Marchand de Mémoire (The Memory Merchant*; Hac., 1988); *Le Train Perdu (The Lost Train*; École des Loisirs, 1989); *La Neige Bleue de Noël (The Blue Snow of Christmas*; Sorbier, 1989); *Mystère-Marmaille (Mystery-Club*; Réunion, 1990); *D'Étranges Visiteurs (Strange Visitors*; École des Loisirs, 1991); *Le Treizième Chat Noir (The Thirteenth Black Cat*; École des Loisirs, 1992); *Le Jour des Monstres (The Day of the Monsters*; Epigones, 1994); *Il Était Arrivé Quelque Chose (Something Happened*; École des Loisirs, 1996); *Note:* Juveniles. See Chapter VIII.

Posznanski, Alfred *see* **Savoir, Alfred**

Potocki, Jan (1761-1815); *Manuscrit Trouvé à Saragosse (Ms. Found in Zaragoza*; 1813; rev. 1847; trans. as *The Saragossa Manuscript*, 1960); *Note:* See Chapter III.

Potz, France (?-); *Fusée X-II (Rocket X-II*; VF 1, 1952); *SOS Planète en Péril (SOS Planet in Danger*; VF 4, 1953)

Poujol, Auguste (?-) *see* **Arthaud, E.**

Poulain, Albert (?-) *see Contes et Légendes*

Poulet, Robert (1893-?); *Handji (Den./Steele, 1930); Le Trottoir (The Pavement*; Den./Steele, 1931); *Ténèbres (Darkness*; Den./Steele, 1934); *Prélude à l'Apocalypse (Prelude to the Apocalypse*; Den., 1944); *L'Enfer-Ciel (The Heaven-Hell*; Plon, 1952); *La Hutte de Cochenille (The Caterpillar's Hut*; Plon, 1953); *La Lanterne Magique (The Magic Lantern*; Debresse, 1956); *Les Sources de la Vie (The Sources of Life*; Plon, 1967); *La Rose d'Acier (The Steel Rose*; Aelberts, 1969); *Histoire de l'Être (History of the Being*; Den., 1973); *Dis-moi qui te hante (Tell Me Who Haunts You*; Nlles. Ed. Latines, 1977); *Flèches du Parthe (Parthian Slings*; Aelberts, 1981); *L'Homme qui n'avait pas compris (The Man Who Did Not Understand*; Didier-Hatier, 1988); *Note:* Belgian writer. See Chapters VI and VIII.

Pouliot, Luc (1961-); *Le Voyage des Chats (The Journey of the Cats*; JP 79, 1992); *Note:* French-Canadian writer.

Pouliot, Pierre (1939-); *Le Croissant de Cristal (The Crystal Crescent*; Barré & Dayez, 1989); *Note:* French-Canadian writer published in France.

Pouvourville, Albert de (?-); *Greffe (Graft*; Figuière, 1922); *Le Maître des Sentences (The Sentence Master*; Baudinière, 1932); *Pacifique 39 (Baudinière, 1934); La Guerre Prochaine (The Next War*; serial. in 30 issues; retitled/renumbered *L'Héroïque Aventure (The Heroic Adventure)* after No. 5, Baudinière, 1934-35; collected in six vols.): *1. Le Navigyre; 2. Alerte sur Paris! (Alert in Paris!); 3. Le Mur de la Lumière (The Light Barrier); 4. La Route de Feu (The Road of Fire); 5. Paris l'Invincible (Invincible Paris); 1. La Frontière d'Acier (The Frontier of Steel); 2. Les Canons Longs (The Long Guns); 3. Au Secours de Prague (To Rescue Prague); 4. Alpinistes et Sous-Marins (Mountaineers and Sub-Mariners); 5. Les Aquatanks; 6. Les Crimes de la Science (The Crimes of Science); 7. Nos Savants Répliquent (Our Scientists' Response); 8. La Marche vers Stuttgart (The March Towards Stuttgart); 9. Prise de Karlsruhe (The Taking of Karlsruhe); 10. Croiseurs et Torpilles (Cruisers and Torpedos); 11. L'Europe en Armes (Europe in Arms); 12. Tirs Stratosphériques (Stratospheric Targetting); 13. Les Métèques au Poteau! (Let's Hang the Dagos!); 14. Les Tricolores sur Munich (Tricolored Over Munich); 15. Le Rayon Orange (The Orange Ray); 16. La Bataille de Franche-Comté (The Battle of Franche-Comté); 17. La Fin d'un Reitre (The End of a Ruffian); 18. Combats dans la Mer du Nord (Clashes in the North Sea); 19. Vers la Ruhr (Towards the Ruhr); 20. La Bataille de Belgique (The Battle of Belgium); 21. La Victoire des Ailes (The Victory of the Wings); 22. Vers le Grand Duel (Towards the Great Duel); 23. La Ruée sur le Rhin (The Rush Towards the Rhine); 24. L'Aube du Grand Choc (The Dawn of the Great Clash); 25. L'Épopée (The Epic); Note:* See Chapter VII.

Pouy, Jean-Bernard (?-); *La Pêche aux Anges (Fishing for Angels*; Gall., 1986); *L'Homme à l'Oreille Croquée (The Man with a Bitten Ear*; Gall., 1987); *La Clef des Mensonges (The Key of Lies*; Gall., 1988); *La Chasse au Tatou dans la Pampa Argentine (Hunting for the Tatoo in the Argentinian Pampa*; Canaille, 1992); *R.N. 86 (Interstate 86*; Clô, 1992); *Le Bienheureux (The Happy Man*; Atalante, 1994); *Palmiers et Crocodiles (Palmtrees and Crocodiles*; Clô, 1994); *Plein Tarif (Full Fare*; 1001 Nuits, 1994); *L'ABC du Métier (The ABC of the Trade*; La Loupiote, 1995); *La Petite Écuyère a cafté (The Little Squire Girl Who Snitched*; Baleine, 1995); *54x13 (L'Atalante, 1996)

Pozner, Vladimir (1905-); *Le Mors aux Dents (The Bridle in the Teeth*; Den., 1937); *Le Temps est Hors des Gonds (Time Out of Tracks*; Julliard, 1969); *Mal de Lune (Moon Sickness*; Julliard, 1974); *Deuil en 24 Heures (24 Hour Mourning*; Temps Actuels, 1982); *Le Fond des Ormes (The Bottom of the Elms*; Actes Sud, 1986)

Pradeau, Jean (?-); *Tête d'Horloge (Clock-Head*; Solar, 1964); *Un Petit Truc de Rien du Tout (A Little Insignificant Thing*; Orban, 1975); *Note:* For *Tête*, see Book 1, Chapter II for a 1970 television adaptation.

Prassinos, Gisèle (1920-); *Le Feu Maniaque (The Maniacal Fire*; Sagesse, 1935; rev. Godet, 1944); *Facilité Cré-

pusculaire (Twilight Facility; Debresse, 1937); *Le Temps n'est rien (Time Is Nothing*; Plon, 1958); *La Voyageuse (The Traveller*; Plon, 1959); *Le Visage Effleuré de Peine (The Face Fraught with Sorrow*; Grasset, 1960); *Brelin le Fou (Brelin the Mad*; Belfond, 1975); *Le Ciel et la Terre se Marient (Earth and Heaven Are Getting Married*; Ed. Ouvrières, 1979); *Le Verrou (The Bolt*; Flamm., 1987); *La Lucarne (The Dormer Window*; Flamm., 1990)

Prat, Marcelle (?-); *Vivre (To Live*; Flamm., 1922); *L'Homme Rêvé (The Dreamed Man*; with Bertrand de **Jouvenel**; Flamm., 1930); *La Femme Dévorée (The Devoured Woman*; Flamm., 1932); *La Prochaine (The Next One*; with Bertrand de **Jouvenel**; Flamm., 1934)

Prat, Pierre-Maurice (?-); *La Croisière de l'Épouvante (Cruise of Terror*; SEC, 1944)

Pratte, François (1958-); *Le Secret d'Awa (The Secret of Awa*; Courte Échelle, 1988); *Note:* French-Canadian writer.

Pré, Jean-François (?-); *Le Cheval du Président (The President's Horse*; FNASF 19, 1996)

Préchac, Jean de (?-?); *Contes moins Contes que les Autres, Sans Paragon et la Reine des Fées (Tales Less Tales Than Others, Without Paragon, and the Fairy Queen*; Cie. Des Libraires Ass., 1724); *Note:* Also see **Cabinet des Fées** and Chapter III.

Preel, Bernard (?-); *Les Deux Songes de la Ville (The Two Dreams of the City; incl. La Mosaïque des Paroisses (The Mosaic of Parishes) and L'Archipel des Métropoles (The Archipelago of Metropols)*; Descartes, 1995); *Note:* Futurology.

Prestre, Willy André (?-); *Bohême Lacustre (Lake Bohemians*; Attinger, 1925); *La Lente Agonie (The Slow Agony*; Attnger, 1934); *Tocsins dans la Nuit (Bells in the Night*; Attinger, 1934); *Le Solitaire à l'Oreille Coupée (The Lonely Man with a Cut-Off Ear*; Baconnière, 1934); *La Piste de l'Or (The Trail of Gold*; Zeluck, 1946); *La Piste Inconnue (The Unknown Trail*; Attinger, 1946); *Cordée sans Corde (Climbers Without Rope*; Jeheber, 1957); *La Rose de Fer (The Iron Rose*; Jeheber, 1958); *La Lumière qui Tue (The Light That Kills*; Prestre, 1960); *La Croisière de l'Étoile (The Star Cruise*; Prestre, 1962); *Note:* Swiss writer.

Prêtre, Marcel Georges (Chabrey, François) (?-); *Deux Visas pour l'Enfer (Two Visas for Hell*; La Baconnière, 1955); *L'Étrange Monsieur Steve (The Strange Mr. Steve*; Pensée Moderne, 1957); *4h30 chez Belzebuth (16:30 at Beelzebub's*; Degué, 1964); *La Cinquième Dimension (The Fifth Dimension*; FNAG 165, 1969); *Matt et la Guerre dans l'Espace (Matt and the War in Space*; as François Chabrey; FN Espionnage 1400, 1978)

Préville, Bruno (?-); *Fémina-City* (Leroy, 1979); *Maso-Story* (Leroy, n.d.)

Prévot, André (?-); *Cieux Nouveaux, ou Quatre Hommes dans la Lune (New Skies, or Four Men in the Moon*; Figuière, 1931)

Prévot, Gérard (1921-1975); *La Race des Grands Cadavres (The Race of Tall Cadavers*; Den., 1956); *La Note Jaune (The Yellow Note*; SGE, 1967); *Le Démon de Février (The February Demon*; MarF 369, 1970); *L'Impromptu de Coye (The Unexpected at Coye*; J. Antoine, 1972); *La Fouille (The Search*; 1972); *Celui Qui Venait De Partout (That Which Came from Everywhere*; MarF 441, 1973); *L'Empan* (1973); *La Nuit du Nord (The Night of the North*; MarF 484, 1974); *Destination Flora (Destination Flora*; as Red Port; Mar. P2000 4, 1974); *Le Pont Vertical (The Vertical Bridge*; as Red Port; Mar. P2000 10, 1974); *Vénus en Maison 7 (Venus in House 7*; as Red Port; Mar. P2000 15, 1974); *La Grande Panne (The Great Breakdown*; as Red Port; Mar. P2000 17, 1975); *La Fin de Flora (The End of Flora*; as Red Port; Mar. P2000 22, 1975); *Le Spectre Large (The Large Spectre*; MarFan 553, 1975); *La Cité sur l'Abîme (The City on the Abyss*; as Red Port; MarP 143, 1975); *Le Point de Chute (The Point of Fall*; J. Antoine, 1985); *Contes de la Mer du Nord (Tales of the North Sea*; J. Antoine, 1986); *Note:* Belgian writer. See Chapter VIII.

Price, Georges (Petitpierre, F.-G.) (?-?); *Les Trois Disparus du "Sirius" (The Three Men Who Vanished from the "Sirius";* Mame, 1896); *La Rançon du Sommeil (The Ransom of Sleep*; Flamm., 1910); *L'Étoile du Pacifique (The Star of the Pacific*; Mame, 1912); *Les Chasseurs d'Épave (The Shipwrecks Hunters*; Mame, 1913); *La Grotte Mystérieuse (The Mysterious Cavern*; Mame, 1920); *La Mine d'Or Infernale (The Gold Mine from Hell*; Mame, 1921); *La Maison Neuve (The New House*; Mame, 1921); *Note:* Juvenile fantastic adventures; *La Grotte* and *L'Étoile* are illustrated by **Robida**.

Prieur, Jean (?-); *Oeuvres Imberbes (Beardless Works*; La Caravelle, 1932); *Navires pour l'Atlantide (Ships for Atlantis*; Myrte, 1947); *Les Visiteurs de l'Autre Monde (The Visitors from Another World*; Fayard, 1977); *Les Morts m'ont donné signe de vie (The Dead Spoke to Me*; Hac., 1979); *Le Mystère des Retours Éternels (The Mystery of Eternal Returns*; RL, 1994); *Note:* Author of numerous pseudo-documentary works on reincarnation, ghosts, etc.

Priollet, Marcel *see* **Nizerolles, René Marcel de**

Prioly, Lucien (?-); *L'Homme de la Lande (The Man on the Moor*; 1946); *Nous Étions Sept Astronautes (We Were Seven Astronauts*; Bordas, 1946); *L'Île des Hommes de Fer (The Island of the Iron Men*; Bordas, 1948); *Le Colonel Avait Perdu (The Colonel Lost*; La Bruyère,

1949); *Trois Morts dans un Fauteuil (Three Dead in An Armchair*; La Bruyère, 1950); *Alerte aux Martiens (Martian Alert*; André Martel, 1954); *Note:* Juvenile SF. See Chapter IX.

Probst, Pierre (?-); *Caroline sur la Lune (Caroline on the Moon*; Hac., 1965); *Caroline et la Petite Sirène (Caroline and the Little Mermaid*; Hac., 1977); *Caroline chez les Lilliputiens (Caroline in Lilliput*; Hac., 1984); *Caroline à travers les Âges (Caroline Throughout the Ages*; Hac., 1985); *Caroline et le Robot (Caroline and the Robot*; Hac., 1986); *Le Fantôme Gourmand (The Gluttonous Ghost*; Hac., 1995); *Note:* Juveniles. See Chapter IX.

Prou, Suzanne (1920-); *La Petite Fille sous la Rivière (The Little Girl Under the River*; Cast., 1983); *Les Couleurs du Monde (The Colors of the World*; Clancier-Guénaud, 1983); *Les Voyageurs de la Paix (The Travellers of Peace*; Messidor-La Farandole, 1986); *Le Roi des Chats (The King of Cats*; Syros, 1988); *Note:* Juveniles.

Proulx, Monique (1952-); *Sans Coeur et Sans Reproche (Without Heart Nor Complaint*; Q/A, 1983); *Homme Invisible à la Fenêtre (Invisible Man at the Window*; Boréal, 1993); *Les Aurores Montréales (Montreal Dawns*; Boréal, 1996); *Note:* French-Canadian writer.

Proumen, Henri-Jacques (1879-1962); *Sur le Chemin des Dieux (On the Path of the Gods*; Ren. du Livre, 1928); *La Boîte aux Marionnettes (The Puppet Box*; J. Vernault, 1930); *Le Sceptre Volé aux Hommes (The Scepter Stolen from Men*; Ren. du Livre, 1930); *Il Pleut Bergère (Contes) (It Is Raining, Shepherdess (Tales)*; Vanderlinden, 1932); *Le Nez de mon Oncle (Contes) (My Uncle's Nose (Tales)*; Vanderlinden, 1932); *Kiss aux Yeux d'Or (Contes) (Kiss of the Golden Eyes (Tales)*; Vanderlinden, 1932); *Ève, Proie des Hommes (Eve, Prey of Men*; Maison du Livre Fr.,, 1934); *Fables sur Tout et sur Rien (Fables on Everything and Nothing*; Picart, 1936); *Aubes Cruelles (Cruel Dawns*; Ren. du Livre, 1942); *La Brèche d'Enfer (The Hellish Breach*; Dupuis, 1946); *L'Homme qui a été mangé et Autres Récits d'Anticipation (The Man Who Was Eaten and Other Tales of Anticipation*; Off. de Pub., 1950); *La Tabatière d'Or (The Gold Tobacco Box*; Dupuis, 1951); *Armes Nouvelles dans une Guerre Future (New Weapons for a Future War*; Payot, 1950); *Annick et Poutinet* (1952); *Note:* Belgian writer. See Chapter VII.

Prudhomme, Jean (?-) *see* **Level, Maurice**

Puig, Franc (?-); *L'Etrange Monsieur Borman (The Strange Mr. Borman*; FNAG 71, 1961)

Pujade-Renaud, Claude (1932-); *La Révolte de la Chaussure à Lacets (The Revolt of the Shoe with Laces*; Messidor-La Farandole, 1988); *Le Maître du Feu (The Fire Master*; Messidor-La Farandole, 1989); *Note:* Juveniles.

Pujol, René (?-?); *L'Homme qui Gagne (The Man Who Wins*; Ed. Fr. Ill., 1919); *Le Soleil Noir (The Black Sun*; LPT, 1929); *L'Héritière de Genghis Khan (The Heiress of Genghis Khan*; Fayard, 1929); *Le Détective Bizarre* (Fayard, 1929); *La Planète Invisible (The Invisible Planet*; S&V, 1930); *Au Temps des Brumes (In the Times of the Mist*; S&V, 1931); *La Chasse aux Chimères (The Chimera Hunt*; Portiques, 1932); *André Piffe, Reporter* (Portiques, 1932); *Le Mystère de la Flèche d'Argent (The Mystery of the Silver Arrow*; Libr. Contemporaine, 1933) as René Pons. See Henri **Bernay**. *Note:* See Chapter VII.

Pulicani(-Varnier), Suzanne (?-); *Monsieur Touminou et les Visiteurs de l'Air (Mr. Pussycat and the Visitors from the Air*; Magnard, 1963); *Monsieur Touminou Cosmonaute (Mr. Pussycat Cosmonaut*; Magnard, 1964); *Note:* Children's stories. See Chapter IX.

Pussey, Gérard (1947-); *Les Citrouilles du Diable (The Devil's Pumpkins*; École des Loisirs, 1984); *Nicolas et son Robot (Nicolas and His Robot*; Centurion, 1985); *La Nuit du Boufadou (The Night of the Boufadou*; École des Loisirs, 1987); *Note:* Juveniles.

Puycousin, Édouard de *see* **Nerval, Gérard de**

Quadruppani, Serge (?-); *Je Pense donc Je Nuis (I Think Therefore I Harm*; FN @lias 1, 1997); *Note:* Thriller featuring the character of @lias, a modern *Fantômas*-like super-villain.

Quatremarre, Jean (?-); *Alors la Terre s'arrêta... (Then the Earth Stood Still*; S&V, 1934); *Note:* See Chapter VII.

Quatrepoint, Robert (?-); Oméga (Den., 1966); *Moi, le Serpent (I, the Serpent*; Den., 1973); *Les Yeux d'Orphée (The Eyes of Orpheus*; Den., 1978); *Le Vaisseau Fantôme (The Ghost Ship*; Sud, 1984); *Amazonie* (Ramsay, 1990)

Quéneau, Raymond (1903-1976); *Gueule de Pierre (Stone Face*; Gall., 1934); *Les Temps Mêlés (Mixed Times*; Gall., 1941); *Saint-Glinglin (Saint-Never*; Gall., 1948); *Les Fleurs Bleues (The Blue Flowers*; Gall., 1965); *Contes et Propos (Tales and Words*; Gall, 1980); *Un Conte à votre façon (A Tale Your Way*; Kickshaws, 1982); *Le Chien à la Mandoline (The Dog with a Guitar*; Gall., 1987); *Le Vol d'Icare (Icarus' Flight*; Gall., 1989); *Note:* *Le Vol d'Icare* was adapted for television (see Book 1, Chapter II).

Quénot, Katherine (?-); *Rien que des Sorcières (Nothing But Witches*; AM, 1993); *Blanc comme la Nuit (White as Night*; AM, 1993); *Le Livre Secret des Sorcières (The Secret Book of Witches*; AM, 1994); *Si tu m'aimes (If You Love Me*; AM, 1995); *Note:* See Chapter VIII.

Quentin-Bauchard, Maurice *see* **Berleux, Jean**

Quesemand, Anne (1946-); *Colporteur d'Images (Image Peddler*; Syros, 1987); *La Mort-Marraine (Godmother Death*; Ipomée, 1988); *Note:* Juveniles.

Quillerbet (?-?) *see* **Grand-Guignol**

Quilliet, Bernard (?-); *La Véritable Histoire de France (The True French History*; Pr. de la Renaissance, 1983); *Note:* Uchronia.

Quinault, Philippe (1635-1688) *see* **Opéra**

Quinel, Charles (1868-1942); *Cagliostro l'Enchanteur (Cagliostro the Enchanter*; Nathan, 1932); *Note:* Also see **Contes et Légendes** and **Montgon, Adhémar de.**

Quinet, Edgar (1803-1875); *Ahasvérus* (Comptoir Imprimeurs Réunis, 1833); *Prométhée (Prometheus*; F. Bonnaire, 1838); *Merlin l'Enchanteur (Merlin the Enchanter*; Hac., 1895); *Note:* See Chapter IV.

Quint, Jimmy G. *see* **Guieu, Jimmy**

Quintin, Émile (?-); *Marie-Reine, Fille de la Terre (Marie-Reine, Daughter of Earth*; Ferenczi, 1926); *L'Effrayante Lumière Noire (The Frightful Black Light*; SJPC, 1947)

Quirielle, Jean de (1880-1964); *L'Homme qui fit Parler les Bêtes / L'Homme qui ne Pouvait pas Mourir (The Man Who Made Animals Talk / The Man Who Could Not Die*; RM, 1910); *L'Oeuf de Verre (The Glass Egg*; RM, 1912); *La Joconde Retrouvée (The Mona Lisa Recovered*; RM, 1913); *Les Voleurs de Cerveaux (The Brain Stealers*; LPT, 1920); *Celui qu'on attendait pas (The Unexpected Man*; LPT, 1925); *Dieu et la Diable (God and the She-Devil*; Cahiers Bourbonnais, 1966); *Note:* See chapters V and VII.

Rabbe, Alphonse (?-?); *Album d'un Pessimiste (Album of a Pessimist*; Dumont, 1835); *Note:* See Chapter IV.

Rabelais, François (1494-1553); *Pantagruel, Roy des Dipsodes (Pantagruel, King of the Dipsodes*; J & E de Marnef, 1532; rev. 1542); *La Vie très Horrifique du Grand Gargantua, Père de Pantagruel (The Very Horrific Life of Great Gargantua, Father of Pantagruel*; F. Juste, 1534; rev. 1542); *Le Tiers Livre des Faits et Dits Héroïques du Bon Pantagruel (The Third Book of the Actions and Sayings of the Good Pantagruel*; C. Wechel, 1546; rev. 1552); *Le Quart Livre des Faits et Dits Héroïques du Noble Pantagruel (The Fourth Book of the Actions and Sayings of the Noble Pantagruel*; F. Juste, 1548; rev. 1552); *L'Île Sonnante (The Ringing Island*; 1562); *Le Cinquième Livre des Faits et Dits Héroïques du Bon Pantagruel (The Fifth Book of the Actions and Sayings of the Good Pantagruel*; J. Martin, 1565); *Note:* See Chapter II.

Rabier, C. (?-) *see* **Darnaudet, Boris & François**

Rabiniaux, Roger (Bellion, Roger) (1914-1986); *Les Faubourgs du Ciel (Heaven's Suburbs*; Barbier, 1943); *Le Bonheur est sur la Terre (Happiness Lies on Earth*; as Roger Bellion; Lardanchet, 1946); *L'Honneur de Pédonzigue (The Honor of Pedonzigue*; Corréa, 1951); *Les Vertus de Craboneraque (The Virtues of Craboneraque*; Scorpion, 1952); *Un Roi Fantôme (A Phantom King*; Seghers, 1954); *Le Soleil des Dortoirs (The Sun of the Sleepers*; Buchet-Chastel, 1965); *Les Enragés de Cornebourg (The Enraged Folks of Cornebourg*; Hac., 1974); *La Fin de Pédonzigue ou l'An Mil'Atome (The End of Pedonzigue or the Year Thous'Atom*; Simoën, 1978); *La Grande Réception (The Great Reception*; Baudinière, 1981)

Rabou, Charles Félix Henri (1803-1871); *Contes Bruns (Brown Tales*; anthology/with **Balzac** & **Chasles**; Guyot, 1832); *L'Allée des Veuves (Widows' Alley*; Recoules, 1845); *La Fille Sanglante (The Bloody Girl*; L. de Potter, 1857); *Les Grands Danseurs du Roi (The Great Dancers of the King*; L. de Potter, 1860); *Note:* See Chapter IV.

Rachilde (Eymery, Marguerite) (1860-1953); *Madame Adonis* (Monnier, 1888); *Monsieur Vénus* (Brossier, 1889); *L'Animale (The She-Beast*; H. Simonis, 1893); *Le Démon de l'Absurde (The Demon of the Absurd*; MdF, 1894); *La Princesse des Ténèbres (The Princess of Darkness*; Calmann-Lévy, 1896); *Contes et Nouvelles (Tales and Stories*; MdF, 1900); *L'Imitation de la Mort (The Imitation of Death*; MdF, 1903); *Dessous (Under*; MdF, 1904); *Le Meneur de Louves (The She-Wolves' Leader*; MdF, 1905); *Dans le Puits ou La Vie Inférieure (In the Well or Inferior Life*; MdF, 1918); *Le Grand Saigneur (The Great Bloodletter*; Flamm., 1922); *Au Seuil de l'Enfer (On the Treshold of Hell*; Flamm., 1924); *La Femme aux Mains d'Ivoire (The Woman with Ivory Hands*; Portiques, 1929); *L'Homme aux Bras de Fer (The Man with Iron Arms*; Ferenczi, 1930); *Le Val sans Retour (The Valley of No Return*; Crès, 1930); *L'Amazone Rouge (The Red Amazon*; Lemerre, 1932); *L'Aérophage (with J.-J. **Lauzach**; Écrivains Ass., 1934); *La Fiancée du Fossoyeur (The Grave-Digger's Fiancée*; Fourneau, 1984); *L'Étoile Filante (The Shooting Star*; Fourneau, 1985); *La Mort d'une Fille de Marbre (The Death of a Marble Girl*; Fourneau, 1985); *Un Rêve Infernal (A Hellish Dream*; Fourneau, 1985); *Note:* See Chapter IV.

Racine, Jean(-Baptiste) (1639-1699); *Andromaque* (1667); *Iphigénie* (1674); *Phèdre* (1676); *Note:* See Chapter II.

Raemdonck, Jean-Paul (1937-); *Han* (MarF 400, 1972); *À l'Étoile de Mer (To the Sea Star*; Duculot, 1973); *Note:* Belgian writer. See Chapter VIII.

Rahier, François (?-); *Le Crépuscule du Compagnon (The*

Twilight of the Companion; FNA 1660, 1988); *L'Ouragan des Enfants Dieux (The Storm of the God Children*; FNA 1853, 1991); *Note:* See Chapter IX.

Raisson, Horace-Napoléon (1798-1854); *L'Élixir de Jeunesse (The Elixir of Youth*; in *L'Artiste*, 1833)

Rajic, Négovan (1923-); *Les Hommes-Taupes* (CLF, 1978; transl. as the *Mole Men*, 1980); *Propos d'un Vieux Radoteur (Words from An Old Dotard*; Tisseyre, 1982; transl. as the *Master of Strappado*, 1984); *Sept Roses pour une Boulangère (Seven Roses for a Baker*; CLF, 1987); *Service Pénitentiaire National (National Penitentiary Service*; Beffroi, 1988); *Note:* French-Canadian writer born in Belgrade. *Les Hommes-Taupes* is a fantastic allegory about political oppression.

Ralph, Raoul (?-?); *Son Importance Auguste Pluchon (His Importance Auguste Pluchon*; with L. **Tailhade**; Offenstadt, 1902); *Note:* Also see **Grand-Guignol**.

Ramdane, Mengouchi (?-); *L'Homme qui Enjamba la Mer (The Man Who Stepped Over the Sea*; Henri Veyrier, 1978)

Rameau, Jean (1859-1942); *Fantasmagories (Phatasmagorias*; Ollendorff, 1887); *L'Ensorceleuse (The Sorceress*; Ollendorff, 1897); *Les Féries (Fairies*; Ollendorff, 1897); *Le Satyre (The Satyr*; Ollendorff, 1897); *La Montagne d'Or (The Gold Mountain*; Ollendorff, 1899); *Le Champion de Cythère (The Champion of Cyther*; P.Lamm., 1901); *La Bonne Étoile (The Lucky Star*; SELEA, 1906); *Le Fuseau d'Or (The Gold Spindle*; Plon, 1914); *L'Arrivée aux Étoiles (Arrival to the Stars*; Plon, 1922); *Les Chevaliers de l'Au-Delà (The Knights from Beyond*; AM, 1932); *Note:* See Chapter V.

Ramonet, Yves (1962-); *La Massacreuse (The Massacror*; as Axelman; FNG 74, 1988); *Aux Morsures Millénaires (At the Millennial Bites*; as Axelman; FNG 89, 1989); *Guillotine!* (as Céline W. Barney/with Fred **Chéreau**; FNG 95, 1989); *Dunes Sanglantes (Bloody Dunes*; as Axelman; FNG 109, 1990); *Labyrinth-Jungle* (as Oscar Valetti/with Jacques **Barbéri**; FNA 1880, 1992); *L'Ombre et le Fléau (The Shadow and the Plague*; as Oscar Valetti/ with Jacques **Barbéri**; FNA 1896, 1992); *Chair Inconnue (Unknown Flesh*; as Oscar Valetti/ with Jacques **Barbéri**; FNA 1913, 1993); *Incarnations* (as Axelman; FN Angoisses 9, 1994); *Perspectives du Mensonge (Perspectives of a Lie*; PdF 544, 1994); *Dislocation* (Den., 1996); *Note:* See chapters VIII and IX.

Ramsay, Richard (?-); *Le Roman de Tristehomme et Esseulée (The Novel of Tristehomme and Esseulée*; Q/A, 1990); *Note:* French-Canadian writer. Modern retelling of Tristan and Isolde.

Ramsey, Kevin H. *see* **Valéry, Francis**

Ramuz, Charles-Ferdinand (1878-1947); *Terre du Ciel (Earth in the Sky*; Crès, 1921); *Présence de la Mort (Presence of Death*; Georg, 1922); *La Guérison des Maladies (The Cure for Diseases*; Grasset, 1924); *La Grande Peur dans la Montagne (The Great Fear in the Mountain*; Grasset, 1926); *Adam et Eve* (Mermod, 1932); *Si le Soleil ne revenait pas (If the Sun Did Not Return*; Mermod, 1937); *Note:* Swiss writer.

Randa, Peter (Duquesne, André) (1911-1979); *L'Escalier de l'Ombre (The Shadow Staircase*; FNAG 11, 1955); *Le Banquet des Ténèbres (The Feast of Darkness*; FNAG 22, 1956); *Veillée des Morts (Wake for the Dead*; FNAG 26, 1956); *Survie (Survival*; FNA 152, 1960; rev. by Philippe **Randa**, FNSL 167, 1985); *Baroud (Battle*; FNA 158, 1960); *Les Frelons d'Or (The Golden Hornets*; FNA 168, 1960); *Parodie à la Mort (Death Parody*; FNAG 62, 1960); *Les Rescapés de Demain (The Survivors of Tomorrow*; FNA 176, 1961); *Cycle Zéro (Zero Cycle*; FNA 182, 1961); *Commando de Transplantation (Transplanted Commando*; FNA

185, 1961); *L'Entité Négative (The Negative Entity*; FNAG 84, 1962); *Fugitif de l'Espace (Space Fugitive*; FNA 194, 1962); *Les Ephémères (The Ephemereals*; FNA 202, 1962); *Deucalion* (FNA 209, 1962); *Les Apprentis Sorciers (The Sorcerer's Apprentices*; FNA 213, 1962); *Les Ancêtres (The Ancestors*; FNA 220, 1963); *Plate-Forme de l'Eternité (Platform of Eternity*; FNA 227, 1963); *Humains de Nulle Part (Humans from Nowhere*; FNA 234, 1963); *Sédition (Revolt*; FNA 245, 1964); *La Loi de Mandralor (The Law of Mandralor*; FNA 249, 1964); *Zone de Rupture (Breaking Zone*; FNA 253, 1964); *Retour en Argara (Return to Argara*; FNA 258, 1964); *Reconquête (Reconquest*; FNA 265, 1965); *Qui Suis-Je? (Whom Am I?*; FNA 271, 1965); *Disparus dans l'Espace (Disappeared in Space*; FNA 272, 1965); *Le Secret des Antarix (The Secret of the Antarix*; FNA 276, 1965); *La Solitude des Dieux (The Loneliness of the Gods*; FNA 286, 1966); *Commando de Non-Retour (No-Return Commando*; FNA 297, 1966); *Vagues d'Invasion (Invading Waves*; FNA 299, 1966); *Objectif Tamax (Target Tamax*; FNA 305, 1966); *La Grande Dérive (The Great Drift*; FNA 316, 1967); *Les Survivants de Kor (The Survivors of Kor*; FNA 323, 1967); *Les Ides de Mars (The Ides of Mars*; FNA 331, 1967);

La Jungle d'Araman (The Jungle of Araman; FNA 336, 1967); *La Révolte des Inexistants (The Revolt of the Unbeings*; FNA 346, 1968); *L'Escale des Dieux (The Port of Call of the Gods*; FNA 355, 1968); *L'Héritier des Sars (The Heir of the Sars*; FNA 363, 1968); *Les Aventuriers de l'Espace (The Adventurers of Space*; FNA 369, 1968); *La Grande Chasse des Kadjars (The Great Hunt of the Kadjars*; FNA 378, 1969); *L'Homme Éparpillé (The Scattered Man*; FNA 390, 1969); *Les Damnés d'Altaban (The Damned of Altaban*; FNA 396, 1969); *Les Boucles du Temps (The Loops of Time*; FNA 401, 1969); *Enjeu Deterna (Deterna at Stake*; FNA 410, 1970); *Et le Dernier Humain Mourut (And the Last Human Died*; FNA 420, 1970); *La Trève du Sacre (The Coronation Truce*; FNA 432, 1970); *L'Univers des Torgaux (The Universe of the Torgaux*; FNA 440, 1970); *Le Cycle du Recommencement (The Cycle of a New Beginning*; FNA 449, 1971); *Le Dépositaire de Thana (The Depository of Thana*; FNA 460, 1971); *Les Astronefs du Pouvoir (The Spaceships of Power*; FNA 476, 1971); *Planète de Désolation (Desolated Planet*; FNA 478, 1971); *Les Immortels (The Immortals*; FNA 492, 1972); *Le Grand Cristal de Terk (The Great Crystal of Terk*; FNA 510, 1972); *La Loi des Ancêtres (The Law of the Ancestors*; FNA 522, 1972); *Les Témoins de l'Eternité (The Witnesses of Eternity*; FNA 534, 1972); *Le Rendez-Vous de Nankino (The Rendezvous of Nankino*; FNA 546, 1973); *Les Marées du Temps (The Tides of Time*; FNA 561, 1973); *Génération Spontanée (Spontaneous Generation*; FNA 576, 1973); *La Planète Perdue (The Lost Planet*; FNA 589, 1973); *Complot à Travers le Temps (Time Plot*; FNA 605, 1974); *Métamorphose (Metamorphosis*; FNA 619, 1974); *Les Sept Cryptes d'Hibernation (The Seven Hibernation Crypts*; FNA 632, 1974); *Les Massacres du Commencement (The Massacres of the Beginning*; FNA 645, 1974); *La Barrière du Grand Isolement (The Great Isolation Barrier*; FNA 659, 1975); *Les Résidus du Temps (The Remains of Time*; FNA 669, 1975); *La Brigade du Grand Sauvetage (The Great Rescue Brigade*; FNA 682, 1975); *L'Enjeu Galactique (The Galactic Stakes*; FNA 698, 1975); *Périls sur la Galaxie (Galaxy in Peril*; FNA 724, 1976); *L'Éternité Moins Une (Eternity Minus One*; FNA 734, 1976); *Les Assaillants (The Attackers*; FNA 746, 1976); *Elteor (FNA 757, 1976); *Les Arches de Noé (Noah's Arks*; FNA 787, 1977); *Les Couloirs de Translation (The Translation Corridors*; FNA 799, 1977); *Le Cycle des Algoans (The Algoan Cycle*; FNA 819, 1977); *L'Homme Venu Des Étoiles (The Man Who Came from the Stars*; FNA 843, 1978); *L'Homme Qui Partit Pour Les Étoiles (The Man Who Left for the Stars*; FNA 855, 1978); *Sanctuaire 1 (Sanctuary 1*; FNA 866, 1978); *Anastasis (FNA 880, 1978); *Les Pleïades d'Artani (The Pleiades of Artani*; FNA 890, 1978); *La Peste Sauvage (The Wild Plague*; FNA 916, 1979); *Les Bagnards d'Alboral (The Convicts of Alboral*; FNA 923, 1979); *Les Ilotes d'En-Bas (The Slaves from Below*; FNA 931, 1979); *Branle-Bas d'Invasion (Mobilisation for An Invasion*; FNA 937, 1979); *Venu de l'Infini (It Came from Infinity*; FNA 957, 1979); *Escale à Hango (Stop-Over in Hango*; FNA 973, 1980); *Note:* See Chapters VIII and IX. a number of Randa's novels were adapted into digest-sized graphic novels (see Book 1, Chapter V under **Fleuve Noir**). *Parodie à la Mort (FNAG 62)* was adapted into a **Grand-Guignol** play by M. **Renay**.

Randa, Philippe (Duquesne, Philippe) (?-); *Les Fusils d'Ekaistos (The Guns of Ekaistos*; FNA 1052, 1981); *L'Expérience du Grand Cataclysme (The Experience of the Great Cataclysm*; FNA 1066, 1981); *Le Réveil des Dieux (The Gods Awaken*; FNA 1075, 1981); *Le Palais du Roi Phédon (The Palace of King Phedon*; FNA 1080, 1981); *Mission sur Terre (Mission on Terra*; FNA 1101, 1981); *Baroud sur Bolkar (Battle on Bolkar*; FNA 1124, 1982); *La Planète Noire de Lothar (The Black Planet of Lothar*; FNA 1146, 1982); *Les Conjurés de Shargol (The Plotters of Shargol*; FNA 1155, 1982); *Folle Meffa (Crazy Meffa*; FNA 1173, 1982); *Les Écologistes de Combat (The Fighting Ecologists*; FNA 1187, 1982); *Aléas à travers le Temps (Incidents Through Time*; FNA 1232, 1983); *Mon Pote, le Martien... (My Pal the Martian*; FNA 1238, 1983); *La Démone de Karastan (The Demon-Lady of Karastan*; FNA 1264, 1983); *Camarade Yankee! (Comrade Yankee!*; FNA 1354, 1985); *Les Contrebandiers du Futur (The Smugglers of the Future*; FNA 1372, 1985); *Le Diable Soit avec Nous! (The Devil Be with Us*; FNA 1436, 1986); *Métamorphosa (FNA 1462, 1986); *U.S. Go Home... Go, Go! (FNA 1514, 1987); *Baroud pour le Genre Humain (Battle for Mankind*; FNA 1533, 1987); *Les Sirènes d'Almadia (The Sirens of Almadia*; FNA 1550, 1987); *Périls sur Mû (Perils on Mu*; FNA 1601, 1987); *Le Mal d'Ibrator (The Disease of Ibrator*; FNA 1626, 1988); *Alaïs (Pardès, 1989); *Contes d'Europe (Tales of Europe*; Le Flambeau, 1989); *Le Rêve Éclaté (The Shattered Dream*; PC, 1989); *Corps et Biens (Bodies and Goods*; La Thibaudière, 1994); *Les Légendes Païennes du Poitou (Pagan Legends of the Poitou*; L'Aencre, 1995); *Les Parques de l'Île d'Yeu (The Fates of Yeu Island*; Ambassy, 1996); *Note:* See Chapter IX. Philippe Randa is Peter **Randa**'s son. Philippe Randa also wrote a number of novels published under Jimmy **Guieu**'s name in the Jimmy **Guieu** imprint.

Randal, M. (?-) *see* **Grand-Guignol**

Ranne, G. Elton (Guéro, Gérard (?-) & Anne (?-)); *Frères de Sang (Blood Brothers*; Descartes, 1992); *La Mâchoire du Dragon (The Jaws of the Dragon*; FNA 1991, 1996); *Scales 1: Un Regard Vertical (A Vertical Glance*; Khom-Heidon, 1996); *Scales 2: Le Silence est

d'Or (Silence Is Golden; Khom-Heidon, 1996); *Scales
3: Bruits Blancs (White Noises*; Khom-Heidon, 1997);
Double Jeu (Double Game; FNSF 3, 1997); *Chute Libre
(Free Fall*; FNSF 20, 1997); *Note:* See Chapters VIII
and IX. G. Elton Ranne is also the author of the comic-
book series **Les Crocs d'Ébène (The Ebony Teeth)** and
Les Héritiers (The Inheritors). See Book 1, Chapter V.

Ransan, André (?-); *Le Royaume d'Alexandre (The Kingdom of Alexander*; Monde Moderne, 1925); *Durandal,
ou La Candeur Merveilleuse (Durandal, or Marvellous
Candor*; Balzac, 1943); *Note:* Also see **Grand-Guignol**.

Rapin, Christian (1931-); *Lo Libre* (Princi Negre, 1973);
Note: Collection of fantastical tales written in Occitan.

Raspail, Jean (1925-); *Le Tam-Tam de Jonathan
(Jonathan's Tom-Tom*; RL, 1971); *Le Camp des Saints*
(RL, 1973; transl. as the *Camp of the Saints*, 1975); *La
Hache des Steppes (The Axe of the Steppes*; RL, 1974);
Le Jeu du Roi (The King's Game; RL, 1976); *Septentrion*
(RL, 1979); *Les Yeux d'Irène (Irene's Eyes*; AM, 1984);
Pêcheur de Lune (Moon Fisher; RL, 1990); *Sire* (Fal-
lois, 1991); *L'Anneau du Pêcheur (The Ring of the Fish-
erman*; AM, 1994); *Note:* See Chapter IX.

Rastouin, Bernard (?-); *Shaan 1 (Le Cercle des Réaliés)
– Trois Lunes ((Circle of Realities) Three Moons*;
Khom-Heidon, 1996); *Shaan 2 – Éclipse* (Khom-Hei-
don, 1996); *Shaan 3 – Lumière du Matin (Morning
Light*; Khom-Heidon, 1997); *Note:* See Chapter VIII.

Ravalec, Vincent (?-); *Nostalgie de la Magie Noire (Nostalgia of Black Magic*; Flamm., 1997)

Raveau, Patrick (?-); *Ciel Ouvert (Open Sky*; Vague à
l'âme, 1991); *D'Avant la Fracture (Before the Fracture*;
La Bartavelle, 1994); *L'Ultime Songe de la Cité (The
City's Last Dream*; Destination Crépuscule, n.d.); *Le
Vrai Visage de Gregory (Gregory's True Face*; with
Jean-Pierre **Planque**; Pegase, n.d.)

Ravignant, Patrick (1943-); *La Peau de l'Ombre (The Skin
of the Shadow*; Calmann-Lévy, 1963); *Les Mutants de
la Voie (The Mutants of the Way*; AMSF 5, 1972); *Idiot
Cherche Village (Le Livre du Chaos) (Idiot Seeks Village (The Book of Chaos)*; TR, 1976); *La Comtesse des
Ténèbres (The Countess of Darkness*; Encre, 1979); *Les
Empires Secrets de Napoléon (Napoleon's Secret Empires*; Encre, 1979); *L'Église des Fous (The Church of
the Insane*; TR, 1982); *Les Oracles (The Oracles*; M.A.,
1983); *Les Fous de Dieu (The Madmen of God*; M.A.,
1984); *Histoire des Sorcières (History of Witches*; Bartillat, 1987); *Note:* See chapters VIII and IX.

Ray, Hélène (?-); *Pourquoi cet Étrange Pont sur la Rivière
de Cristal? (Why This Strange Bridge on the Crystal
River?*; Magnard, 1982)

**Ray, Jean (Kremer, Jean Raymond de) (1887-1964); 1.
Writing as Jean Ray:** *Les Contes du Whisky (The Tales
of Whiskey*; Ren. du Livre, 1925; rev. Atalante, 1946);
La Croisière des Ombres (The Cruise of Shadows; Ed.
De Belgique, 1932); *Le Grand Nocturne (The Great
Darkness*; Auteurs Ass., 1942); *Les Cercles de l'Epou-
vante (The Circles of Terror*; Auteurs Ass., 1943);
Malpertuis (Auteurs Ass., 1943; transl. Atlas Press,
1998); *La Cité de l'Indicible Peur (The City of the Un-
speakable Fear*; Auteurs Ass., 1943); *Les Derniers Con-
tes de Canterbury (The Last Tales of Canterbury*; Au-
teurs Ass., 1944); *La Gerbe Noire* (anthology; La
Sixaine, 1947); *Le Livre des Fantômes (The Book of
Ghosts*; La Sixaine, 1947; rev. MarF 247, 1966); *25 His-
toires Noires et Fantastiques (25 Dark and Fantastic
Tales*; MarF 114, 1961); *Le Carrousel des Maléfices (The
Spellbound Merry-Go-Round*; MarF 197, 1964); *Les
Contes Noirs du Golf (Dark Tales of Golf*; MarF 208,
1964); *Saint Judas-de-la-Nuit (St. Judas-Of-The-Night*;
1964; rep. in *Le Livre des Fantômes*, MarF 247, 1966);
Bestiaire Fantastique (Fantastic Bestiary; MarF 500,
1974); *Visages et Choses Crépusculaires (Faces and
Things of Dusk*; NéO 63, 1982); *Note:* Belgian writer.
See chapters VI and VIII. **Malpertuis** and **La Cité de
l'Indicible Peur** were both adapted into films (see Book
1, Chapter I). Jean Ray's story "Le Chemin du Songe"
("The Path of Dreams") was adapted into a **Grand-
Guignol** play in 1914. Another story, "L'Homme qui
Osa" was made into a 1966 short feature (see Book 1,
Chapter I). **2. Writing as John Flanders:** *Le Secret de
la Roche qui Gronde (The Secret of the Growling Rock*;
Altiora/Bonne Presse, 1936); Presto-Films Series (novel-
las published by Belgian publisher Bonne Presse be-
tween 1934 and 1939; titles listed are by Jean **Ray**): *15.
Les Prisonniers de Morstanhill (The Prisoners of
Morstanhill*; 1934); *19. Le Château du Péril (The Cas-
tle of Danger*; 1935); *20. Tempest le Terrible (Tempest the
Terrible*; 1935); *26. La Griffe dans la Neige (The Claw
in the Snow*; 1935); *60. La Nuit Tragique (The Tragic
Night*; 1935); *64. Le Roman de la Mer (The Novel of the
Sea*; 1935); *77. La Bête de Loch Boo (The Beast of Loch
Boo*; 1936); *81. L'Oiseau Mystérieux (The Mysterious
Bird*; 1936); *84. La Singulière Babet Brown (The Sin-
gular Babet Brown*; 1936); *87. Le Vallon qui Chante (The
Singing Valley*; 1936); *89. Le Feu Vert (The Green Fire*;
1936); *91. Hiro, L'Enfant de la Jungle (Hiro, Child of the
Jungle*; 1936); *95. Vacances Américines (American Hol-
idays*; 1936); *98. Dans la Grande Nuit du Pôle (In the
Great Polar Night*; 1936); *103. Aux Tréfonds du Mystère
(In the Deepest of Mysteries*; 1936); *108. L'Auberge
du Roi Gourmand (The Inn of the Glutton King*; 1936);
*112. Le Formidable Secret du Pole (The Formidable Se-
cret of the Pole*; 1938); *118. L'Ennemi dans l'Île (The
Enemy on the Island*; 1938); *123. Le Nègre de l'Ascenseur (The Negro in the Elevator*; 1937); *125. L'Aven-

ture Espagnole (The Spanish Adventure; 1937); *130. La Neuvaine d'Épouvante (The Prayer of Terror*; 1937); *135. La Jonque Noire (The Black Junk*; 1937); *136. L'Étrange Nuit du 1er Décembre (The Strange Night of December 1st*; 1937); *139. L'Enfer de Neige (The Snowy Hell*; 1937); *148. Le Pays des Sept Mille Merveilles (The Land of 7000 Wonders*; 1937); *153. Miss Volcan (Miss Volcano*; 1937); *154. Jim la Corneille (Jim Crow*; 1937); *172. Un Roi de la Mer (A King of the Sea*; 1938); *175. Quatre de l'Armée du Christ (Four from Christ's Army*; 1938); *178. L'Énigme Mexicaine (The Mexican Enigma*; 1938); *179. Le Dernier Loup (The Last Wolf*; 1938); *191. Le Salut de Torrington (Torrington's Salute*; 1938); *217. L'Aventure Énigmatique (The Enigmatic Adventure*; 1938); *221. Le Dernier Triton (The Last Triton*; 1938); *228. Un Homme Allait Mourir (A Man Was About to Die*; 1939); *232. Le Professeur Invisible (The Invisible Professor*; 1939); *237. La Statue Assassinée (The Murdered Statue*; 1939); *242. L'Oeil de la Nuit (The Night Eye*; 1939); *247. Le Carrefour de la Lune Rousse (The Intersection of the Rusty Moon*; 1939); *265. Le Mail Hanté (The Haunted Mall*; 1939); *272. Le Sous-Marin Assassiné (The Murdered Sub-Marine*; 1939); *Le Secret des Sargasses (The Secret of the Sargasso*; translated into French by Jacques **Van Herp** writing as Michel Jansen; *Bravo*, 1938-39); *De Zilveren Kaap (The Silver Cap*; in Flemish, Ed. De Piji, 1946); *Mystères et Aventures (Mysteries and Adventures;* incl. Presto-Films 123, 125, 140, 135, 237 and 247; Atalante, 1946; rev. as *La Neuvaine d'Épouvante (The Prayer of Terror)*, Beckers, 1966); *La Bataille d'Angleterre (The Battle for England*; Altiora, 1947); *Spoken Op De Ruwe Heide (Ghosts on the Wild Briar*; in Flemish, Goede Pers, 194?); *Het Zwarte Eiland (The Black Island;* in Flemish, Goede Pers, 194?; rev. as *L'Île Noire (The Black Island)*, NéO 182, 1987); *Geheimen Van Het Noorden (The Secrets of the North*; in Flemish, Goede Pers, 194?); *Les Sept Robinsons de la Mer (The Seven Robinsons of the Sea*; Lombard, 1955); *Bioj De Roodhuiden (Among the Red-Skins*; in Flemish, Altiora, 1956); *Un Roman de la Mer (A Novel of the Sea*; rev. of Presto Film 64; Altiora, 1957); *Les Prisonniers de Morstanhill (The Prisoners of Morstanhill*; rev. of Presto Films 15; Altiora, 1959); *Hiro, L'Enfant de la Jungle (Hiro, Child of the Jungle*; rev. of Presto Films 91; Altiora, 1959); *La Porte sous les Eaux (The Gate Under the Sea*; with Jacques **Van Herp** writing as Michel Jansen; adaptation by **Van Herp** of Presto-Films 103 & 112; Spès, 1960); *Vlucht Naar Bradford (Fugue in Bradford*; in Flemish, Van In, 1964); *De Koperen Duivelsklauw (The Diabolical Copper Claw*; in Flemish, Van In, 1964); *La Griffe du Diable (The Devil's Claw*; AELP, 1966); *Le Carrousel du Suspense (The Carrousel of Suspense*; Beckers, 1970); *Terres d'Aventures (Lands of Adventures*; The Skull, 1972); *Contes d'Horreur et d'Aventures (Tales of Horror and*

Adventure; 10/18 681, 1972); *Le Monstre de Borough / Le Mystérieux Homme de la Pluie (The Monster of Borough / the Mysterious Man from the Rain*; 10/18 908, 1974); *Visions Nocturnes (Nocturnal Visions*; NéO 100, 1984); *Visions Infernales (Infernal Visions*; NéO 103, 1984); *La Malédiction de Machrood (The Machrood Curse*; NéO 122, 1984); *La Brume Verte (The Green Mist*; NéO 151, 1985); *Les Feux Follets de Satan (Satan's Fireflies*; NéO 160, 1986); *Les Contes du Fulmar (Tales of the Fulmar*; NéO 171, 1986); *La Nef des Bourreaux (The Ship of Executioners*; Néo 193, 1987); *Note:* Jean Ray used the pseudonym of "John Flanders" to write juvenile adventure and fantastical novels (in both French and Flemish), as well as an estimated 300 stories in various French, Belgian and Flemish magazines, including the famous *Vlaamse Filmkens* (1930-45). Some of these stories have been translated into French and collected by 10/18 and NéO in a series of volumes listed above. 3. The *Harry Dickson* Series: (Titles attributed to Jean Ray are indicated with a (JR)); *1. Échappé à une Mort Terrible (Escape from a Dreadful Death*; 1929); *2. L'Hôtel Borgne du Caire (The Shady Hotel of Cairo*; 1929); *3. Idolatrie Chinoise (Chinese Idol-Worshipping*; 1929); *4. Le Testament du Détenu (The Prisoner's Testament*; 1929); *5. Le Secret du Gobelin (The Secret of the Gobelin*; 1929); *6. L'École pour Meutriers à Pittsburgh (The Pittsburgh Murder School*; 1929); *7. L'Europe en Péril (Europe in Danger*; 1929); *8. Un Cadeau de Noces Horrible (An Awful Wedding Gift*; 1929); *9. Le Roi des Malandrins (The King of Burglars*; 1930); *10. Le Mystère de la Tour (The Mystery of the Tower*; 1930); *11. Le Drame au Cirque Bianky (The Tragedy of Circus Bianky*; 1930); *12. Le Modèle du Faux Monnayeur (The Counterfeiter's Model*; 1930); *13. Le Dogue de Soho (The Mastiff of Soho*; 1930); *14. Les Douze Coeurs Morts (The Twelve Dead Hearts*; 1930); *15. Les Bandits de la Fête Populaire (The Robbers of the Popular Festivities*; 1930); *16. Un Chevauchée à la Mort par le St. Gothard (The St. Gothard Death Ride*; 1930); *17. Le Capitaine Disparu (The Disappeared Captain*; 1930); *18. Le Professeur Flax, Monstre Humain (Prof. Flax, Human Monster*; 1930); *19. Une Poursuite à travers le Désert (Desert Pursuit*; 1930); *20. La Femme à Quatre Faces (The Woman with Four Faces*; 1930); *21. Le Repaire aux Bandits de Corfou (The Lair of the Corfu Bandits*; 1930); *22. La Prisonnière du Clocher (The Prisoner of the Bell Tower*; 1930); *23. Sur la Piste d'Houdini (On the Trail of Houdini*; 1930); *24. La Sautoir Volé ou Les Mystérieux Voleurs de Bijoux*

(The Stolen Necklace or the Mysterious Jewel Thieves; 1930); *25. Dans la Vienne Souterraine (In Underground Vienna;* 1930); *26. Le Rajah Rouge (The Red Rajah;* 1930); *27. Le Bourreau de Londres (The Executioner of London;* 1930); *28. Le Roi des Contrebandiers d'Andorre (The King of the Andorra Smugglers;* 1930); *29. La Malédiction des Walpole (The Curse of the Walpoles;* 1930); *30. Une Fumerie d'Opium Parisienne (A Parisian Opium-Smoking Den;* 1930); *31. Le Toréador de Grenade (The Toreador of Granada;* 1930); *32. Le Musée des Horreurs (The Horror Museum;* 1930); *33. Miss Mercédes, la Reine de l'Air (Miss Mercedes, Queen of the Air;* 1931); *34. Le Docteur Criminel (The Criminal Doctor;* 1931); *35. Sous le Poids d'une Forfaiture (The Burder of Betrayal;* 1931); *36. Un Réveillon au Dragon Rouge (New Year's Eve at the Red Dragon;* 1931); *37 (JR?). L'Ermite du Marais du Diable (The Hermit of the Devil Swamp;* 1931; rep. HD8, MarF309; NéO 3); *38. L'Intrigante Démasquée (The Schemer Unmasked;* 1931); *39. Les Voleurs Volés ou Le Carnaval Tragique (The Stolen Thieves or Tragic Carnival;* 1931); *40. Les Détrousseurs de Cadavres (The Corpse Robbers;* 1931); *41. Autour d'un Trône (Around the Throne;* 1931); *42. Une Nuit d'Épouvante au Château Royal (A Night of Terror at the Royal Castle;* 1931); *43. Le Sosie d'Harry Dickson (Harry Dickson's Look-Alike;* 1931); *44. L'Agence des Fausses Nouvelles (The Phony News Agency;* 1931); *45. Le Double Crime ou La Montagne Sanglante (The Double Crime or the Bloody Mountain;* 1931); *46. Le Crucifié (The Crucified Man;* 1931); *47. Le Mauvais Génie du Cirque Angelo (The Evil Genius of Circus Angelo;* 1931); *48. La Mystérieuse Maison du Lutteur (The Wrestler's Mysterious House;* 1931); *49. Le Repaire de Palerme (The Lair of Palermo;* 1931); *50 (JR?). La Veuve Rouge (The Red Widow;* 1931); *51. Une Bête Humaine (A Human Beast;* 1931); *53 (JR). Le Signe de la Mort (The Sign of Death;* 1931; rep. NéO 3); *52. Le Tripot Clandestin de Franklin Street (The Secret Speakeasy of Franklin Street;* 1931); *54. La Fatale Ressemblance (Deadly Resemblance;* 1931); *55. Le Gaz Empoisonné (The Poisoned Gas;* 1931); *56. Le Pari Fatal (The Fatal Bet;* 1931); *57 (JR). Les Feux Follets du Marais Rouge (The Fireflies of the Red Swamp;* 1932; rep. NéO 21); *58. Tom Wills, Femme de Chambre (Tom Wills, Chambermaid;* 1932); *59. Les Treize Balles (The Thirteen Bullets;* 1932); *60. Harry Dickson s'amuse (Harry Dickson Has Fun;* 1932); *61. Joly, Chien Policier (Police Dog;* 1932); *62 (JR). Les Voleurs de Femmes de Chinatown (The Girl Snatchers of Chinatown;* 1932; rep. HD7, MarF 300); *63 (JR). L'Effroyable Fiancé (The Awful Fiancé;* 1932; rep. HD13, MarF 416); *64 (JR). Le Trésor du Manoir de Streetham (The Treasure of Streetham Manor;* 1932; rep. NéO 4); *65 (JR). on a Volé Un Homme (They Stole a Man;* 1932; rep. HD14, MarF 437); *66 (JR). Au Sec-*

ours de la France (To Rescue France; 1932); *67 (JR). Le Fantôme des Ruines Rouges (The Phantom of the Red Ruins;* 1932; rep. HD13, MarF 416; NéO 4); *68 (JR). Les Vengeurs du Diable (The Devil's Avengers;* 1932; rep. HD4, MarF 275; NéO 4); *69 (JR). L'Étrange Lueur Verte (The Strange Green Light;* 1932; rep. HD2, MarF 265; NéO 4); *70. Le Secret de la Jeune Veuve (The Secret of the Young Widow;* 1932); *71. L'Énigme du Tapis Vert (The Mystery of the Green Carpet;* 1932); *72. La Fille de l'Usurier (The Usurer's Daughter;* 1932; *73 (JR). Le Monstre Blanc (The White Monster;* 1932; rep. NéO 4); *74. Le Flair du Maître d'Hôtel (The Butler's Flair;* 1932); *75 (JR). Le Mystère de la Vallée d'Argent (The Mystery of the Silver Valley aka Les Chevaliers de la Lune (The Moon Knights;* 1932; rep. NéO 5); *76 (JR). Le Démon Pourpre (The Purple Devil;* 1932; rep. HDF14, MarF 437; NéO 5); *77 (JR). Les Gardiens du Gouffre (The Guardians of the Pit;* 1932; rep. NéO 5); *78. Le Fiancé Disparu (The Missing Fiancé;* 1932); *79. La Vie Criminelle de Lady Likeness (Lady Likeness' Criminal Life;* 1932); *80 (JR). La Dame au Diamant Bleu (The Lady with the Blue Diamond;* 1932; rep. NéO 21); *81 (JR). Le Vampire aux Yeux Rouges (The Red-Eyed Vampire;* 1933; rep. HD4, MarF 275; NéO 5); *82 (JR). La Flèche Fantôme (The Phantom Arrow;* 1933; rep. NéO 5); *83 (JR). Les Trois Cercles de l'Épouvante (The Three Circles of Terror;* 1933; rep. HD10, MarF 371; NéO 6); *84 (JR). La Maison du Scorpion (The House of the Scorpion;* 1933; rep. NéO 6); *85 (JR). La Bande de l'Araignée (The Gang of the Spider;* 1933; rep. HD 1, MarF 259; NéO 6); *86 (JR). Les Spectres-Bourreaux (The Ghost Executioners;* 1933; rep. HD1, MarF 259; NéO 6); *87 (JR). Le Mystère des Sept Fous (The Mystery of the Seven Madmen;* 1933; rep. HD3, MarF 269; NéO 6); *88 (JR). Les Étoiles de la Mort (The Stars of Death;* 1933; rep. HD13, MarF 416; NéO 7); *89 (JR). La Pierre de Lune (The Moonstone;* 1933; rep. HD5, MarF 283; NéO 7); *90 (JR). Le Mystère de la Forêt (The Mystery of the Forest;* 1933; rep. HD15, MarF 456; Néo 7); *91 (JR). L'Île de la Terreur (The Island of Terror;* 1933; rep. HD6, MarF 292; NéO 7); *92 (JR). La Maison Hantée de Fulham Road (The Haunted House of Fulham Road;* 1933; rep. HD11, MarF 379; NéO 7); *93 (JR). Le Temple de Fer (The Iron Temple;* 1933; rep. HD6, MarF 292; NéO 8); *94 (JR). La Chambre 113 (Room 113;* 1933; rep. HD13, MarF 416; NéO 8); *95 (JR). La Pieuvre Noire (The Black Octopus;* 1933; rep. HD2, MarF 265; NéO 8); *96 (JR). Le Singulier Mr. Hingle (The Strange Mr. Hingle;* 1933; rep. HD7, MarF 300; NéO 8); *97 (JR). Le Dieu Inconnu (The Unknown God;* 1933; rep. HD12, MarF 389; NéO 8); *98 (JR). Le Royaume Introuvable (The Hidden Kingdom;* 1933; rep. NéO 9); *99 (JR). Les Mystérieuses Études du Dr. Drumm (The Mysterious Studies of Dr. Drumm;* 1933; rep. HD3, MarF 269; NéO 9); *100 (JR). La Mort Bleue*

(The Blue Death; 1933; rep. NéO 9); *101 (JR). Le Jardin des Furies (The Garden of the Furies*; 1933; rep. HD5, MarF 283; NéO 9); *102 (JR). Les Maudits de Heywood (The Accursed of Heywood*; 1933; rep. HD12, MarF 389; NéO 9); *103 (JR). ??Mystéras??* (1933; rep. HD7, MarF 300; NéO 10); *104 (JR). La Cour d'Épouvante (The Court of Terror*; 1933; rep. HD7, MarF 300; NéO 10); *105 (JR). Le Roi de Minuit (The King of Midnight*; 1934; rep. HD14, MarF 437; NéO 10); *106 (JR). Le Chemin des Dieux (The Path of the Gods*; 1934; rep. HD2, MarF 265; NéO 10); *107. Blackwell, le Pirate de la Tamise (Blackwell, Pirate of the Thames*; 1934); *108. Les Dentelles de la Reine (The Queen's Lace*; 1934); *109. Le Sosie du Banquier (The Banker's Look-Alike*; 1934); *110. Le Trésor du Marchand d'Esclaves (The Treasure of the Slave Merchant*; 1934); *111 (JR). Les Blachclaver* (1934; rep. NéO 2); *112 (JR). Le Fantôme du Juif Errant (The Ghost of the Wandering Jew*; 1934; rep. HD4, MarF 275; Néo 10); *113 (JR). Messire l'Anguille (Sir Eel*; 1934; rep. HD15, MarF 456; NéO 11); *114 (JR). Le Châtiment des Foyle (The Punishment of the Foyles*; 1934; rep. HD6, MarF 292; NéO 11); *115 (JR). La Grande Ombre (The Great Shadow*; 1934; rep. HD11, MarF 379; NéO 11); *116 (JR). Les Eaux Infernales (The Infernal Waters*; 1934; rep. HD8, MarF 309; NéO 11); *117 (JR). Le Vampire qui Chante (The Singing Vampire*; 1934; rep. HD1, MarF 259; NéO 11); *118 (JR). Le Mystère de Bantam House (The Mystery of Bantam House*; 1934; rep. NéO 12); *119 (JR). La Cigogne Bleue (The Blue Stork*; 1934; rep. HD15, MarF 456; NéO 12); *120 (JR). Ce Paradis de Flower Dale (That Paradise of Flower Dale*; 1934; rep. NéO 2); *121 (JR). L'Esprit du Feu (The Fire Spirit; 1934; rep. NéO 2) 122 (JR). Turckle-le-Noir (Turckle-The-Black*; 1934; rep. HD14, MarF 437; NéO 12); *123 (JR). Les Yeux de la Lune (The Eyes of the Moon*; 1934; rep. HD10, MarF 371; NéO 12); *124 (JR). L'Île de Mr. Rocamir (The Island of Mr. Rocamir*; 1934; rep. HD8, MarF 309; NéO 12); *125 (JR). X-4* (1934; rep. HD6, MarF 292; NéO 13); *126 (JR). La Maison des Hallucinations (The House of Hallucinations*; 1934; rep. HD3, MarF 269; NéO 13); *127 (JR). Le Signe des Triangles (The Sign of the Triangles*; 1934; rep. HD12, MarF 389; NéO 13); *128 (JR). L'Hôtel des Trois Pèlerins (The Hotel of the Three Pilgrims*; 1934; rep. NéO 1); *129 (JR). La Menace de Khâli (The Threat of Khâli*); *130 (JR). Les Illustres Fils du Zodiaque (The Illustrious Sons of the Zodiac*; 1935; rep. HD12, MarF 389; NéO 21); *131 (JR). Le Spectre de Mr. Biedermeyer (The Ghost of Mr. Biedermeyer*; 1935; rep. NéO 3); *132 (JR). La Voiture Démoniaque (The Devil Car*; 1935; rep. NéO 1); *133 (JR). L'Aventure d'un Soir (An Evening's Adventure*; 1935; rep. NéO 13); *134 (JR). Le Dancing de l'Épouvante (The Night Club of Terror*; 1935; rep. HD9, MarF 358; NéO 13); *135 (JR). Les Plus Difficiles de mes Causes (My Most Difficult Cases*; 1935; rep. HD14,

MarF 437; NéO 14); *136 (JR). L'Homme au Mousquet (The Man with the Musket*; 1935; rep. HD9, MarF 358; NéO 14); *137 (JR). Le Savant Invisible (The Invisible Scientist*; 1935; rep. HD6, MarF 292; NéO 14); *138 (JR). Le Diable au Village (The Devil in the Village*; 1935; rep. NéO 3); *139 (JR). Le Cabinet du Dr. Selles (The Surgery of Dr. Selles*; 1935; rep. HD11, MarF 379; NéO 14); *140 (JR). Le Loup-Garou (The Werewolf*; 1935; rep. HD11, MarF 379; NéO 14); *141 (JR). L'Étoile à Sept Branches (The Seven-Pointed Star*; 1935; rep. HD8, MarF 309; NéO 15); *142 (JR). Le Monstre dans la Neige (The Snow Monster*; 1935; rep. NéO 3); *143 (JR). Le Cas de Sir Evans (The Case of Sir Evans*; 1935; rep. NéO 1); *144 (JR). La Maison du Grand Péril (The House of the Great Peril*; 1935; rep. HD9, MarF 358; NéO 15); *145 (JR). Les Tableaux Hantés (The Haunted Paintings*; 1935; rep. HD11; MarF 379; NéO 15); *146 (JR). Cric-Croc, le Mort en Habit (Cric-Croc, the Deadman Who Wore a Dinner Jacket*; 1935; rep. HD1, MarF 259; NéO 15); *147 (JR). Le Lit du Diable (The Devil's Bed*; 1935; rep. HD4, MarF 275; NéO 15); *148 (JR). L'Affaire Bardouillet (The Bardouillet Case*; 1935; rep. HD10, MarF 371; NéO 16); *149 (JR). La Statue Assassinée (The Murdered Statue*; 1935; rep. NéO 1); *150 (JR). Les Effroyables (The Frightful Ones*; 1935; rep. HD5, MarF 283; NéO 16); *151 (JR). L'Homme au Masque d'Argent (The Man in the Silver Mask*; 1936; rep. HD12, MarF 389; NéO 16); *152 (JR). Les Sept Petites Chaises (The Seven Little Chairs*; 1936; rep. HD3, MarF 269; NéO 16); *153 (JR). La Conspiration Fantastique (The Fantastic Conspiracy*; 1936; rep. HD9, MarF 358; NéO 16); *154 (JR). La Tente aux Mystères (The Tent of Mysteries*; 1936; rep. NéO 17); *155 (JR). Le Véritable Secret du Palmer Hotel (The True Secret of the Palmer Hotel*; 1936; rep. NéO 17); *156 (JR). Le Mystère Malais (A Malaysian Mystery*; 1936; rep. NéO 17); *157 (JR). Le Mystère du Moustique Bleu (The Mystery of the Blue Mosquito*; 1936; rep. NéO 2); *158 (JR). L'Énigmatique Tiger Brand (The Enigmatic Tiger Brand*; 1936; rep. HD15, MarF 456; NéO 17); *159 (JR). La Mitrailleuse Musgrave (The Musgrave Machine Gun*; 1936; rep. HD7, MarF 300; NéO 17); *160 (JR). Les Nuits Effrayantes de Felston (The Frightful Nights of Felston*; 1936; rep. NéO 18); *161 (JR). Les Vingt-Quatre Heures Prodigieuses (The Prodigious 24 Hours*; 1936; rep. HD8, MarF 309; NéO 18); *162 (JR). Dans les Griffes de l'Idole Noire (In the Clutches of the Black Idol*; 1936; rep. NéO 1); *163. La Résurrection de la Gorgone (The Resurrection of the Gorgon*; 1937; rep. HD2, MarF 265; NéO 18); *164 (JR). La Cité de l'Étrange Peur (The City of the Strange Fear*; 1937; rep. HD13, MarF 416; NéO 18); *165 (JR). Les Énigmes de la Maison Rules (The Enigmas of Rules House*; 1937; rep. HD2, MarF 265; NéO 18); *166 (JR). Le Studio Rouge (The Red Studio*; 1937; rep. HD9, MarF358; NéO 19); *167 (JR). La Terrible Nuit du Zoo*

(The Dreadful Night of the Zoo; 1937; rep. HD5, MarF283; NéO 19); *168 (JR)*. *La Disparition de Mr. Byslop (The Disappearance of Mr. Byslop*; 1937; rep. NéO 19); *169 (JR)*. *Les Momies Évanouies (The Vanished Mummies*; 1937; rep. NéO 19); *170 (JR)*. *L'Aventure Espagnole (The Spanish Adventure*; 1937; rep. NéO 19); *171 (JR)*. *La Tête à Deux Sous (The Two-Pennies Head*; 1937; rep. HD4, MarF 275; NéO 20); *172 (JR)*. *Le Fauteuil 27 (Seat 27*; 1937; rep. HD10, MarF 371; NéO 20); *173 (JR)*. *L'Affaire du Pingouin (The Penguin Affair*; 1937; rep. NéO 2); *174 (JR)*. *La Nuit du Marécage (The Night of the Swamp*; 1937; rep. NéO 20); *175 (JR)*. *on a Tué Mr. Parkinson (They Killed Mr. Parkinson*; 1938; rep. HD3, MarF 269; NéO 20); *176 (JR)*. *La Rue de la Tête Perdue (The Street of the Missing Head*; 1938; rep. HD1, MarF259; NéO 20); *177 (JR)*. *L'Énigme du Sphinx (The Sphinx Enigma*; 1938; rep. HD10, MarF 371; NéO 21); *178 (JR)*. *Usines de Mort (Death Factories*; 1938; rep. HD5, MarF 283; NéO 21); *Note:* See Chapter VI. The *Harry Dickson* series was reprinted twice (a) in 15 vols. by Marabout in the 1970s (HD 1-15); and (b) in 21 vols. by NéO in the 1980s (NéO 1-21). There are currently two competing series of graphic novels featuring **Harry Dickson** (see Book 1, Chapter V).

Rayjean, Max-André (Lombard, Jean) (?-); *Attaque Sub-Terrestre (Subterranean Attack*; FNA 71, 1956); *Base Spatiale 14 (Space Base 14*; FNA 86, 1957); *Les Parias de l'Atome (The Pariahs of the Atom*; FNA 104, 1957); *Chocs en Synthèse (Synthetic Shocks*; FNA 108, 1958); *La Folie Verte (The Green Madness*; FNA 114, 1958); *L'Anneau des Invincibles (The Ring of the Invincibles*; FNA 122, 1958); *Soleils: Échelle Zéro (Suns at Zero Scale*; FNA 127, 1959); *Le Monde de l'Éternité (The World of Eternity*; FNA 137, 1959); *Ere Cinquième (Fifth Era*; FNA 142, 1959); *Le Péril des Hommes (The Peril of Men*; FNA 151, 1960); *L'Ultra-Univers (The Ultra-Universe*; FNA 161, 1960); *Invasion "H"* (FNA 167, 1960); *Puissance: Facteur 3 (Power: Factor 3*; FNA 171, 1961); *Les Magiciens d'Andromède (The Wizards of Andromeda*; FNA 177, 1961); *L'Étoile de Goa (The Star of Goa*; FNA 189, 1961); *Planètes Captives (Captive Planets*; FNA 197, 1962); *L'Oasis du Rêve (The Dream Oasis*; FNA 217, 1962); *Terrom, Âge "Un" (Terrom Age One*; FNA 221, 1963); *La Fièvre Rouge (The Red*

FLEUVE NOIR

Fever; FNA 229, 1963); *Projet Kozna (Project Kozna*; FNA 240, 1964); *Round Végétal (Vegetable Battle*; FNA 247, 1964); *L'Escale des Zulhs (The Stop-Over of the Zuhls*; FNA 254, 1964); *L'Astre Vivant (The Living Star*; FNA 261, 1965); *Les Forçats de l'Energie (The Energy Convicts*; FNA 270, 1965); *Le Cerveau de Silstar (The BraIn of Silstar*; FNA 275, 1965); *Le Zoo des Astors (The Zoo of the Astors*; FNA 284, 1966); *Plan S-03* (FNA 291, 1966); *Les Clés de l'Univers (The Keys of the Universe*; FNA 303, 1966); *Les Anti-Hommes (The Anti-Men*; FNA 311, 1967); *Le Septième Continent (The Seventh Continent*; FNA 322, 1967); *Le Quatrième Futur (The Fourth Future*; FNA 333, 1967); *Contact "Z"* (FNA 344, 1968); *Civilisation "Omega"* (FNA 353, 1968); *Le Zor-Ko de Fer (The Iron Zor-Ko*; FNA 364, 1968); *L'An Un des Kreols (Year One of the Kreols*; FNA 375, 1969); *Relais Kéra (The Kera Relay*; FNA 387, 1969); *SOS Cerveaux (SOS Brains*; FNA 403, 1969); *Le Sang et la Chair (Flesh and Blood*; FNAG 178, 1969); *Prisonniers du Temps (Prisoners of Time*; FNA 414, 1970); *Retour au Néant (Return to Nothingness*; FNA 431, 1970); *Base Djeos (Djeos Base*; FNA 437, 1970); *La Bête du Néant (The Beast from the Void*; FNAG 184, 1970); *La Seconde Vie (The Second Life*; FNA 451, 1971); *Cellule 217 (Cell 217*; FNA 466, 1971); *Les Psycors de Paal Zuick (The Psycors of Paal Zuick*; FNA 477, 1971); *Dans les Griffes du Diable (In the Clutches of the Devil*; FNAG 202, 1971); *Les Statues Vivantes (The Living Statues*; FNA 506, 1972); *L'Arbre de Cristal (The Crystal Tree*; FNA 512, 1972); *L'Autre Passé (The Other Past*; FNA 528, 1972); *La Malédiction des Vautours (The Curse of the Vultures*; FNAG 222, 1972); *La Loi du Cube (The Cubic Law*; FNA 542, 1973); *La Révolte de Gerkanol (The Revolt of Gerkanol*; FNA 565, 1973); *Le Monde Figé (The Paralyzed World*; FNA 587, 1973); *La Dent du Loup (The Tooth of the Wolf*; FNAG 229, 1973); *Les Feux de Siris (The Fires of Siris*; FNA 610, 1974); *Le Secret des Cyborgs (The Secret of the Cyborgs*; FNA 629, 1974); *Le Grand Retour (The Great Return*; FNA 644, 1974); *Barrière Vivante (Living Barrier*; FNA 653, 1974); *Le Squelette de Volupté (The Voluptuous Skeleton*; FNAG 261, 1974); *L'Astronef Rouge (The Red Spaceship*; FNA 670, 1975); *Segregaria* (FNA 692, 1975); *Les Géants de Komor (The Giants of Komor*; FNA 712, 1975); *Les Germes de l'Infini (The Germs of Infinity*; FNA 753, 1976); *Les Irréels (The Unreals*; FNA 778, 1977); *Les Métamorphosés de Spalla (The Metamorphs of Spalla*; FNA 796, 1977); *Le Piège de Lumière (The Trap of Light*; FNA 815, 1977); *La Onzième Dimension (The Eleventh Dimension*; FNA 847, 1978); *La Chaîne des Symbios (The Chain of the Symbios*; FNA 867, 1978); *Génération Alpha* (FNA 887, 1978); *Les Maîtres de la Matière (The Masters of Matter*; FNA 896, 1979); *Les Singes d'Ulgor (The Monkeys of Ulgor*; FNA 925,*

1979); *Groupe "Géo" ("Geo" Group*; FNA 1004, 1980); *Déchéa* (FN 1054, 1981); *Jaïral* (FNA 1079, 1981); *Le Monde Noir (The Black World*; FNA 1098, 1981); *L'Ordre des Vigiles (The Order of Vigils*; FNA 1177, 1982); *Alpha-Park* (FNA 1253, 1983); *L'Âge de Lumière (The Age of Light*; FNA 1296, 1984); *Le Flambeau de l'Univers (The Universal Torch*; FNA 1329, 1984); *Les Acteurs Programmés (The Programmed Actors*; FNA 1400, 1985); *La Guerre des Loisirs (The Leisure Wars*; FNA 1435, 1986); *Citéléem* (FNA 1467, 1986); *Le Dernier Soleil (The Last Sun*; FNA 1587, 1987); *Note:* See chapters VIII and IX.

Raynaud, Claudine *see* **Cénac, Claude**

Razat, Claude (Bouyxou, Jean-Pierre) (?-); *Frankenstein de Fille en Aiguilles (Frankenstein, from Girls to Needles*; Bébé Noir, 1980); *Sorcellerie Rémoulade (Blended Witchcraft*; Brigandine, 1981)

Reberg, Évelyne (1939-); *L'Immeuble qui pêchait (The Building Which Went Fishing*; La Farandole, 1979); *Le Chipolate: Histoire d'un Défilé de Monstres qui se Termine bien (The Chipolate: Story of a Monsters' Parade That Ended Well*; La Farandole, 1980); *Le Dragon Chanteur (The Singing Dragon*; Bayard, 1980); *La Princesse Muette (The Silent Princess*; Duculot, 1980); *Le Képi Fantôme (The Phantom Helmet*; Nathan, 1980); *La Machine à Contes (The Storytelling Machine*; Magnard, 1981); *Un Diable au Garage (A Devil in the Garage*; Bayard, 1981); *La Vieille Dame et le Fantôme (The Old Lady and the Ghost*; Centurion, 1982); *Le Robot de Noël (The Christmas Robot*; Centurion, 1987); *Note:* Juveniles. See Chapter VIII.

Redon, Jean (?-); *Les Yeux Sans Visage (The Eyes Without a Face*; FNAG 56, 1959); *Note:* See Chapter VIII. This novel was adapted into the classic eponymous 1959 horror film (see Book 1, Chapter I). It was also adapted into a **Grand-Guignol** play by M. **Renay**.

Regina, Norbert (?-); *Les Rives du Potomac (The Shores of the Potomac*; Mazarine, 1980)

Régis, Herbert (?-); *L'Éclipse* (Den., 1939)

Régnier, Henri de (1864-1936); *Le Bosquet de Psyché (Psyche's Grove*; Lacomblez, 1894); *Contes à Soi-Même (Tales to Oneself*; Libr. Art Indep., 1894); *La Canne de Jaspe (The Stick of Jaspe*; MdF, 1897); *La Cité des Eaux (The City of Waters*; MdF, 1902); *Le Miroir des Heures (The Mirror of the Hours*; MdF, 1911); *L'Amphisbaine* (MdF, 1912); *Histoires Incertaines (Uncertain Tales*; MdF, 1919); *Marceline ou la Punition Fantastique (Marceline or the Fantastic Punishment*; AM, 1921); *Les Bonheurs Perdus (The Lost Happiness*; MdF, 1924); *Contes pour Chacun de Nous (Tales for Everyone of Us*;

Lapina, 1926); *Contes Vénitiens (Venetian Tales*; Le Livre, 1927); *Note:* See Chapter IV.

Régnier, Henri de (Madame) (Marie-Louise Antoinette de Hérédia) *see* **Houville, Gérard d'**

Régnier, Yves (?-); *L'Office de Six Heures (The Mass of 18:00*; GLM 1949); *Un Monde Aveugle (A Blind World*; GLM, 1952); *Le Sourire (The Smile*; Grasset, 1960); *Les Ombres (The Shadows*; Grasset, 1963); *Paysages de l'Immobilité (Motionless Landscapes*; Gall., 1975)

Régnier-Bohler, Danielle (?-); *La Légende Arthurienne (The Arthurian Legend*; anthology; RL, 1989); *Note:* See Chapter I.

Rehm, Pierre-Louis (?-?); *Les Bestiales (The Bestials*; Figuière, 1927); *Note:* Also see **Grand-Guignol**.

Reichen, Charles-Albert (?-); *La Fin du Monde est pour Demain (The End of the World Is for Tomorrow*; Erel-Lausanne, 1949); *Note:* Swiss writer.

Remize, Félix (?-) *see* ***Contes et Légendes***

Rémy, Jean-Charles (?-); *La Randonnée (The Journey*; Stock, 1970); *L'Arborescence* (Den., 1977); *La Nuée de Sarah (Sarah's Cloud*; Den., 1978); *Note:* See Chapter VIII.

Rémy, Pierre-Jean (Angremy, Jean-Pierre) (1937-); *Une Figure dans la Pierre (A Figure in the Stone*; Gall., 1976); *Cordélia, ou l'Angleterre (Cordelia, or England*; Gall., 1979); *Pandora* (AM, 1980); *Une Ville Immortelle (An Immortal City*; AM, 1986); *Et Gulliver mourut de Sommeil (And Gulliver Died from Sleep*; Julliard, 1989); *La Rose et le Blanc (The Rose and the White*; AM, 1997); *Note:* See Chapter VIII.

Rémy, Yves (1936-) & Ada (1939-); *Les Soldats de la Mer (The Soldiers from the Sea*; Julliard, 1968); *Le Grand Midi (The Great South*; Bourgois, 1971); *La Maison du Cygne (The House of the Swan*; A&D 51, 1978); *Note:* See chapters VIII and IX.

Renard, Christine (1929-1979); *À Contre-Temps (Against Time*; RF 113, 1963); *La Planète des Poupées (The Planet of Dolls*; Galliera 2, 1972); *Utopies 75 (Utopia '75*; anthology/with Jean-Pierre **Andrevon**, Philippe **Curval** & Michel **Jeury**; A&D 36, 1975); *La Treizième Royale (The Thirteenth Royal*; Hac., 1975); *En Cherchant Sybil (Looking for Sibyl*; Hac., 1975); *Les Maraudeurs du Petit Matin (The Dawn Rovers*; Hac., 1977); *La Mante au Fil des Jours (The Mantis on the Flow of the Days*; MarSF 621, 1977); *Des Métiers d'Avenir (Jobs for the Future*; Ponte Mirone, 1979); *La Nuit des Lumineux (The Night of the Light Beings*; Nathan SF 4, 1980); *Le Temps des Cerises (The Time of Cherries*; Kes., 1980); *À la Croisée des Parallèles (Crossing the Parallels*; with Claude **Cheinisse**; PdF 318, 1981); *Doc-*

teur Bizarre (PP, 1992); *L'Enfance des Dieux (The Childhood of the Gods)*; *Note:* See chapters VIII and IX. Christine Renard was married to Claude **Cheinisse**.

Renard, Maurice (1875-1939); *Fantômes et Fantôches (Ghosts and Puppets*; as Vincent Saint-Vincent; Plon, 1905); *Le Docteur Lerne, Sous-Dieu (Doctor Lerne, Undergod*; MdF, 1908; transl. as *New Bodies for Old*, 1923); *Le Voyage Immobile (The Motionless Journey*; MdF, 1909; transl. as *The Flight of the Aerofix*, 1932); *Le Péril Bleu (The Blue Peril*; Michaud, 1912); *M. D'Outremort (Mr. Beyonddeath*; Michaud, 1913; rev. as *Suite Fantastique*, Crès, 1920); *Les Mains d'Orlac* (Nilsson, 1920; transl. as *The Hands of Orlac*, 1929); *L'Homme Truqué / Le Château Hanté / La Rumeur dans la Montagne (The Phony Man / The Haunted Castle / The Rumor in the Mountain*; Crès, 1921); *L'Homme Qui Voulait Être Invisible (The Man Who Wanted to Be Invisible*; Oeuvres Libres, 1923); *Deux Contes à la Plume d'Oie (Two Tales with a Quill Pen*; Crès, 1923); *Le Singe (The Monkey*; with Albert **Jean**; Crès, 1925; transl. as *Blind Circle*, 1928); *L'Invitation à la Peur (The Invitation to Fear*; Crès, 1926; rev. as *Le Papillon de la Mort (Butterfly of Death)*, NéO, 1985); *Lui? Histoire d'un Mystère (Him? Tale of a Mystery*; Crès, 1927); *Un Homme chez les Microbes: Scherzo (A Man Amongst the Microbes: Scherzo*; Crès, 1928); *Le Carnaval du Mystère (The Merry-Go-Round of Mystery;* Crès, 1929; rep. in *Le Papillon de la Mort (The Butterfly of Death)*, NéO, 1985); *La Jeune Fille du Yacht (The Young Girl from the Yacht*; Crès, 1930); *Celui Qui n'a pas Tué (He Who Did Not Kill*; Crès, 1932); *Notre-Dame Royale* (Crès, 1933); *Le Maître de la Lumière (The Light Master*; *Journal de la Femme*, 1933; RMY, 1947); *Le Bracelet d'Émeraude (The Emerald Armband*; *Journal de la Femme*, 1934); *Le Mystère du Masque (The Mystery of the Mask*; *Le Petit Parisien*, 1934; Libr. Champs-Élysées Masque 175, 1935); *Le Mousquetaire des Halles (The Musketeer of the Halles*; *Le Petit Parisien*, 1935); *Fleur dans la Tourment (Flower in the Storm*; *Le Petit Parisien*, 1936); *Le Signe du Coeur (The Sign of the Heart*; *Le Petit Parisien*, 1937); *Les Trois Coups du Destin (The Three Blows of Fate*; *Le Petit Parisien*, 1938); *La Redingote Grise (The Grey Coat*; *Le Petit Parisien*, 1939); *Note:* Also see **Grand-Guignol** and chapters IV, V, and VII. **Le Docteur Lerne** and **Les Mains d'Orlac** have been adapted as films and television movies (see Book 1, Chapters I and II).

Renaud, Alexandre (?-); *La Fiancée du Holm (The Fiancee of Holm*; Pathé, 1946); *Le Dernier Jour (The Last Day*; Nef de Paris, 1960)

Renaud, Alix (1945-); *Carême* (St. Germain des Prés, 1972); *Extase Exacte (Accurate Ecstasy*; Pensée U., 1976); *Le Mari (The Husband*; Namaan, 1980); *Dix Sec-*

ondes de Sursis (Ten Seconds Delay; Temps Parallèle, 1983); *Merdiland* (Temps Parallèle, 1983); *Note:* French-Canadian writer born in Haiti. *Le Mari* and *Dix Secondes* are collections of fantastical stories. *Temps Parallèle* is a Marseilles-based publisher. *Dix Secondes* was also published simultaneously in Canada by Éditions Laliberté.

Renaud, Bernadette (1945-); *La Dépression de l'Ordinateur (The Computer's Depression*; Fidès, 1982); *Note:* French-Canadian writer.

Renaud, Christian (1944-); *Le Voyage en Coquillage (The Seashell Journey*; Cast., 1984); *Les Chaussures Magiques (The Magic Shoes*; Cast., 1986); *Note:* Juveniles.

Renaud, Jacques (1943-); *L'Espace du Diable (The Devil's Space*; Guérin, 1989); *Note:* French-Canadian writer.

Renaud, Janine (?-); *La Base Interdite (The Forbidden Base*; MOC 12, 1979); *Les Suppliciés d'Iryknos (The Tortured Men of Iryknos*; MOC 25, 1982)

Renaud, Jean-Joseph see **Joseph-Renaud, Jean**

Renaud, Maurice (?-); *Et Le Monde Faillit Changer (And the World Almost Changed*; VF 8, 1953)

Renay, M. (?-?) see **Grand-Guignol**

René (Commandant) (?-); *Les Carnets du Commandant: Le Manoir des Trépassés, Le Fantôme Sanglant (The Commanant's Notebooks: the Castle of the Dead, the Bloody Ghost*; Martel, 1953); *Le Froid qui Tue (The Cold That Kills*; Martel, 1954); *Le Marché du Diable (The Devil's Trade*; Sogedide, 1955); *L'Infernale Poursuite (The Infernal Pursuit*; Sogedide, 1956); *Eve, Fille de Satan (Eve, Satan's Daughter*; Martel, 1957)

Renez, Joachim (?-); *La Fin du Monde (The End of the World*; Tallandier, 1930); *Note:* Novelization of Abel **Gance**'s and Camille **Flammarion**'s eponymous 1930 film (see Book 1, Chapter I).

Renford, Philippe (1941-); *Plus Proche que vous ne Pensez (Closer Than You Think*; FNSF 9, 1997); *Note:* See Chapter IX.

Rengade, Jules (1841-?); *Aventures Extraordinaires de Trinitus: Voyage sous les Flots rédigé d'après le Journal de Bord de l'Éclair (Extraordinary Adventures of Trinitus: Underwater Journey Based on the Log of the Eclair*; as Aristide Roger; Brunet, 1868; rev. SI, 1889-90);

Renoult, Robert (?-); *L'Envers du Monde (The Other Side of the World*; MdF, 1965)

Renouvier, Charles (1815-1903); *Uchronie (L'Utopie dans l'Histoire): Esquisse Historique Apocryphe du Développement de la Civilisation Européenne tel qu'il n'a pas* *été, tel qu'il aurait pu être (Uchronia (Utopia in History): Apocryphal Sketch of the Development of European Civilization, as It Was Not, as It Could Have Been*; Bureau Critique Philosophique, 1876); *Note:* See Chapter V.

Reouven, René *see* **Sussan, René**

Restif de la Bretonne, Nicolas-Edmé (1734-1806); *Le Nouvel Abéliard (The New Abeliard*; Duchesne, 1778); *La Découverte Australe par un Homme Volant ou Le Dédale Français (The Southern Discovery By a Flying Man or the French Daedalus*; Leipsick, 1781); *Les Ving Épouses des Vingt Associés (The Twenty Brides of the Twenty Partners*; L. Boulanger, 1781); *Les Veillées du Marais: Histoire du Grand Prince Oribeau, Roi de Mommonie (The Evenings in the Marais: History of the Great Prince Oribeau, King of Mommonia*; Waterford, 1785); *Les Nuits de Paris (Parisian Nights*; London, 1788-89); *L'An 2000 (The Year 2000*; 1789); *Les Posthumes (Posthumous Writings*; 4 vols.; Duchêne, 1802); *Les Voyages de Multipliandre (The Journeys of Multipliandre*; Ulysse fin de Siècle, 1990); *Note:* See Chapter III.

Retamosa, Henri de (?-); *Les Yeux Bleus de la Mort (The Blue Eyes of Death*; Galliera 12, 1973)

Reuze, André (?-); *La Première Image (The First Image*; Fayard, 1923); *La Vénus d'Asnières, ou Dans les Ruines de Paris (The Venus of Asnieres, or in the Ruins of Paris*; Fayard, 1924); *La Tour de Souffrance (The Tower of Suffering*; Fayard, 1925); *Le Trésor de la "Fulgurante" (The Treasure of "Lightning Bolt";* Ferenczi, 1929); *Deux Femmes Pirates (Two Pirate Women*; Colbert, 1942); *L'Inconnue du Rempart (The Unknown Woman on the Ramparts*; Colbert, 1945); *L'Héroïne aux Cent Mousquets (The Heroine with a Hundred Muskets*; Plon, 1946); *Le Revenant du Tertre Feuillet (The Ghost of Feuillet Hill*; Le Maire, 1991)

Reveroni Saint-Cyr, Jacques-Antoine, baron (1767-1829); *Pauliska, ou La Perversité Moderne, Mémoires Récents d'une Polonaise (Pauliska, or Modern Perversity, Recent Memoirs of a Polish Lady*; Lemerre, 1798); *Note:* See Chapter IV.

Rex, Lionel *see* **Limat, Maurice**

Rey, Étienne (1879-?) *see* **Grand-Guignol**

Rey, René-Charles *see* **Mazarin, Jean**

Rey, Stéphane *see* **Owen, Thomas**

Reybaud, Louis (?-?); *Jérôme Paturot à la Recherche de la Meilleure des Républiques (Jerome Paturot in Search of the Best Republic*; M. Lévy, 1849); *Athanase Robichon, Candidat Perpétuel à la Présidence de la République (Athanase Robichon, Perpetual Candidate to the Presidency of the Republic*; M. Lévy, 1851)

Reynier, Marguerite (?-) *see* **Humble, Pierre**

Rey-Dussueil, Antoine-François-Marius (?-); *La Fin du Monde, Histoire du Temps Présent et des Choses à Venir (The End of the World: Story of the Present Times and Things to Come*; Renduel, 1830); *Le Monde Nouveau, Histoire Faisant Suite à la Fin du Monde (The New World: Story Following the End of the World*; Renduel, 1831); *Estrella* (Gosselin, 1843); *Note:* See Chapter V.

Rezvani, Géza (1928-); *Les Américanoiaques* (Bourgois, 1970); *La Voie de l'Amérique (The American Way*; Bourgois, 1970); *Coma* (Bourgois, 1970); *Note:* Iranian writer.

Rhomm, Patrice (?-); *Au Service du Diable (In the Devil's Service*; Galliera 1, 1972); *Note:* Novelization of the 1971 film ***La Plus Longue Nuit Du Diable*** *(The Devil's Longest Night* by Jean Brismée; Patrice Rhomm was one of the film's writers. Patrice Rhomm is a pseudonym of Rondard, Patrice (q.v.).

R'Hoone (Lord) *see* **Balzac, Honoré de**

Ribes, F.-H. *see* **Richard-Bessière**

Ribon, Robert de (?-); *Le Chemin du Mauvais Sort ou les 21 Jours de Julien Cazalis (The Path of Misfortune, or the 21 Days of Julien Cazalis*; Centième Étage, 1932); *L'Assassinat du Président (The Assassination of the President*; with André **Cayatte**; Maréchal, 1933)

Ricard, Charles (?-); *La Dernière des Révolutions (The Last of the Revolutions*; L'Amitié par le Livre, 1967)

Ricard, Christian (?-); *La Dextre des Titans (The Right Hand of the Titans*; Farran, 1971); *Au-Delà du Réel (Beyond Reality*; Farran, 1971); *Le Berceau des Maudits (The Cradle of the Accursed*; Farran, 1972); *Le Vénusien (The Venusian*; Farran, 1972)

Ricard, J. (?-) *see* **Fontis, Henri**

Ricardo (Capitaine) (?-); *La Reine Karati (Queen Karati*; D'Honat & De Grave, n.d.); *L'Atlantide (Atlantis*; D'Honat & De Grave, n.d.); *Monde contre Monde (World vs. World*; Van Loo, n.d.)

Ricardou, Jean (?-); *La Prise de Constantinople (The Taking of Constantinople*; Minuit, 1965)

Rich, Frank (?-); *L'Ange de la Vengeance—Jack Strait 1 (The Angel of Revenge*; FNSF 6, 1997); *Note:* in spite of the biography printed on the back cover, this is a French author "hiding" behind an American identity.

Richard, François (1913-) *see* **Richard-Bessière**

Richard, Gaston-Charles (1875-); *Le Tzar Rouge (The Red Czar*; Lemerre, 1920); *Rihana, Fille d'Islam (Rihana, Daughter of Islam*; Tallandier, 1930); *Sur le Toit du Monde (On the Roof of the World*; RMY, 1931); *Apocalypse* (Tallandier, 1934); *Le Jugement de Dieu (The*

Judgment of God; Tallandier, 1936); *Sous le Signe de Caïn* (*Under the Mark of Cain*; Tallandier, 1936); *La Chevalière de l'Air* (*The She-Knight of the Air*; Tallandier, 1937); *Josiane* (Tallandier, 1937); *La Revanche de Roland* (*Roland's Revenge*; Tallandier, 1937); *Le Roi Maudit* (*The Accursed King*; Tallandier, 1937); *Les Roses du Calvaire* (*The Roses of the Calvary*; Tallandier, 1938); *La Danse de Satan* (*Satan's Dance*; Tallandier, 1938); *Le Glaive et l'Archange* (*The Sword and the Archangel*; Tallandier, 1938); *La Nuit de Sang* (*The Night of Blood*; Tallandier, 1938); *L'Étoile Volée* (*The Stolen Star*; Tallandier, 1939); *L'Homme de Minuit* (*The Midnight Man*; Tallandier, 1939); *La Magie de l'Or* (*The Magic of Gold*; Tallandier, 1939); *Note:* Also see **Grand-Guignol**.

Richard, Jean-Marius *see* **Rim, Carlo**

Richard-Bessière (Bessière, Henri-Richard) (1923-); *Les Conquérants de l'Universe* (*The Conquerors of the Universe*; FNA 1, 1951); *À l'Assaut du Ciel* (*To Assault the Sky*; FNA 2, 1951); *Retour du Météore* (*Return of the Meteor*; FNA 3, 1951); *La Planète Vagabonde* (*The Wandering Planet*; FNA 4, 1952); *Croisière dans le Temps* (*Time Cruise*; FNA 6, 1952); *Sauvetage Sidéral* (*Interstellar Rescue*; FNA 37, 1954); *SOS Terre* (*SOS Earth*; FNA 55, 1955); *Vingt Pas dans l'Inconnu* (*Twenty Steps Into the Unknown*; FNA 60, 1955); *L'Aîle de l'Abîme* (*The Wing of the Abyss*; as Dominique H. Keller; FNAG 9, 1955); *Feu dans le Ciel* (*Fire in the Sky*; FNA 64, 1956); *Objectif Soleil* (*Target: the Sun*; FNA 69, 1956); *Altitude Moins X* (*Elevation Minus X*; FNA 75, 1956); *Route du Néant* (*Road Into the Void*; FNA 81, 1956); *Cité de l'Esprit* (*City of Mind*; FNA 85, 1957); *Création Cosmique* (*Cosmic Creation*; FNA 89, 1957); *Planète de Mort* (*Death Planet*; FNA 93, 1957); *La Deuxième Terre* (*The Second Earth*; FNA 97, 1957); *Via Dimension 5* (FNA 101, 1957); *Fléau de l'Univers* (*Universal Scourge*; FNA 105, 1958);

Carrefour du Temps (*Time's Crossroad*; FNA 111, 1958); *Relais Minos III* (*Relay Minos III*; FNA 117, 1958); *Bang!* (FNA 121, 1958); *Zone Spatiale Interdite* (*Forbidden Space Zone*; FNA 126, 1958); *Panique dans le Vide* (*Panic in the Void*; FNA 129, 1959); *Le Troisième Astronef* (*The Third Spaceship*; FNA 135, 1959); *Ceux de Demain* (*Those from Tomorrow*; FNA 139, 1959); *Réaction Déluge* (*Reaction Flood*; FNA 144, 1959); *On a Hurlé dans le Ciel* (*They Screamed in the Sky*; FNA 148, 1959); *Terre Degré "0"* (*Earth Degree 0*; FNA 153, 1960); *Générations Perdues* (*Lost Generations*; FNA 157, 1960); *Les Pantins d'Outre-Ciel* (*The Puppets from Beyond the Sky*; FNA 162, 1960); *Escale chez les Vivants* (*Stop-Over Among the Living*; FNA 166, 1960); *Les Lunes de Jupiter* (*The Moons of Jupiter*; FNA 169, 1960); *Destination Moins J.-C.* (*Destination Minus J.-C.*; FNA 175, 1961); *Plus Égale Moins* (*Plus Equals Minus*; FNA 179, 1961); *Légion Alpha* (FNA 183, 1961);

Les Mutants Sonnent le Glas (*The Mutants Bring Down the Curtain*; FNA 188, 1961); *La Guerre des Dieux* (*The War of the Gods*; FNA 192, 1961); *La Halte du Destin* (*The Halt of Fate*; as Dominique H. Keller; FNAG 72, 1961); *L'Ombre qui tue* (*The Killing Shadow*; as Dominique H. Keller; FNAG 74, 1961); *Suite Lugubre* (*Lugubrious Suite*; as Dominique H. Keller; FNAG 76, 1961); *L'Infernale Puissance* (*The Infernal Power*; as Dominique H. Keller; FNAG 78, 1961); *Les Poumons de Ganymède* (*The Lungs of Ganymede*; FNA 198, 1962); *Les Derniers Jours de Sol 3* (*The Last Days of Sol 3*; FNA 201, 1962); *Les Sept Anneaux de Rhéa* (*The Seven Rings of Rhea*; FNA 205, 1962); *Micro-Invasion* (FNA 210, 1962); *La Mort vient des Étoiles* (*Death Comes from the Stars*; FNA 214, 1962); *Visa pour Antarès* (*Visa for Antares*; FNA 222, 1963); *Les Jardins de l'Apocalypse* (*The Gardens of the Apocalypse*; FNA 228, 1963); *Planète à Vendre* (*Planet for Sale*; FNA 232, 1963); *Pas De Gonia Pour Les Gharkandes* (*No Gonia for the Gharkands*; FNA 238, 1964); *Alerte en Galaxie* (*Galactic Alert*; FNA 244, 1964); *Un Futur pour M. Smith* (*A Future for Mr. Smith*; FNA 250, 1964); *La Planète Géante* (*The Giant Planet*; FNA 255, 1964); *N'accusez pas le Ciel* (*Don't Accuse the Sky*; FNA 259, 1965); *Les Pionniers du Cosmos* (*The Pioneers of the Cosmos*; FNA 264, 1965); *Le Chemin des Étoiles* (*The Path to the Stars*; FNA 268, 1965); *Les Maîtres du Silence* (*The Masters of Silence*; FNA 279, 1965); *Je m'appelle... Tous* (*I'm Called... All*; FNA 280, 1965); *Les Mages de Dereb* (*The Wizards of Dereb*; FNA 289, 1966); *Agent Spatial No. 1* (*Space Agent No. 1*; FNA 293, 1966); *Cerveaux Sous Contrôle* (*Brains Under Control*; FNA 300, 1966); *Inversia* (FNA 306, 1966); *Cette Lueur Qui Venait Des Ténèbres* (*That Light Which Came from the Dark*; FNA 320, 1967); *L'Enfer dans le Ciel* (*Hell in the Sky*; FNA 329, 1967); *Chaos sur la Génèse* (*Chaos Over*

Genesis; FNA 335, 1967); *Ne Touchez Pas Aux Borloks (Don't Touch the Borloks*; FNA 342, 1968); *Tout Commencera... Hier (It All Began... Yesterday*; FNA 359, 1968); *Des Hommes, Des Hommes Et Encore Des Hommes (Men, Men and Always Men*; FNA 365, 1968); *La Machine Venue d'Ailleurs (The Machine from Beyond*; FNA 372, 1969); *Cauchemar dans l'Invisible (Invisible Nightmare*; FNA 380, 1969); *Les Marteaux de Vulcain (The Hammers of Vulcan*; FNA 400, 1969); *On Demande un Cobaye (Guinea-Pig Wanted*; FNA 406, 1970); *Les Prisonniers de Kazor (The Prisoners of Kazor*; FNA 422, 1970); *Quatre "Diables" Au Paradis (Four Devils in Paradise*; FNA 438, 1970); *Concerto pour l'Inconnu (Concerto for the Unknown*; FNA 461, 1971); *La Loi d'Algor (The Law of Algor*; FNA 473, 1971); *Variations sur une Machine (Variations on a Machine*; FNA 482, 1971); *Le Vaisseau de l'Ailleurs (The Ship from Beyond*; FNA 501, 1972); *Energie—500 (Energy—500*; FNA 516, 1972); *Quand les Soleils s'éteignent (When the Suns Die*; FNA 531, 1972); *1973... Et La Suite (1973... and the Rest*; FNA 555, 1973); *Les Seigneurs de la Nuit (The Lords of Night*; FNA 591, 1973); *Les Ruches de M.112 (The Hives of M.112*; FNA 615, 1974); *Les Sources de l'Infini (The Sources of Infinity*; FNA 636, 1974); *Quand la Machine s'emmêle (When the Machine Meddles*; FNA 646, 1974); *Les Portes du Futur (The Gates of the Future*; FNA 696, 1975); *Et La Nuit Fut... (And Night Fell...*; FNA 700, 1975); *Déjà Presque La Fin (Already Almost the End*; FNA 773, 1977); *Cette Machine est Folle (That Machine Is Mad*; FNA 809, 1977); *L'Homme Qui Vécut Deux Fois (The Man Who Lived Twice*; FNA 852, 1978); *Tout Va Très Bien, Madame La Machine (All's Well, Mrs. Machine*; FNA 903, 1979); *Les Quatre Vents de l'Eternité (The Four Winds of Eternity*; FNA 964, 1980); *Quand la Machine Fait "Boum"! (When the Machine Goes Boom!*; FNA 1032, 1980); *N'Aboyez Pas Trop Fort, Mr. Benton (Don't Bark Too Loudly, Mr. Benton*; FNA 1114, 1981); *Les Survivants de l'Au-Delà (The Survivors from Beyond*; FNA 1136, 1982); *Avant les Déluges (Before the Floods*; FNA 1214, 1983); *Après les Déluges (After the Floods*; FNA 1228, 1983); *A La Découverte du Graal (Searching for the Grail*; FNA 1261, 1983); *Les Maîtres de l'Horreur (The Masters of Horror*; FNA 1293, 1984); *Les Pierres de la Mort (The Stones of Death*; FNA 1346, 1984); *Silence... on Meurt! (Silence... People Are Dying!*; FNA 1370, 1985); *Cadavres à tout faire (Handy Corpses*; FNA 1411, 1985); *Note:* See chapters VIII and IX. a number of Richard-Bessière's novels were adapted into digest-sized graphic novels (see Book 1, Chapter V under **Fleuve Noir**).

Richaud, André de (1909-1968); *Comparses (Buddies*; Ed. des Heures, 1927); *La Création du Monde (The Cre-*

ation of the World; Grasset, 1930); *La Douleur (Pain*; Grasset, 1931); *La Fontaine des Lunatiques (The Fountain of the Lunatics*; Grasset, 1932); *La Barette Rouge (The Red Barrette*; Grasset, 1938); *La Nuit Aveuglante (The Blinding Night*; RL, 1945); *Je ne suis pas mort (I Am Not Dead*; Morel, 1965); *L'Étrange Visiteur (The Strange Visitor*; Grasset, 1984); *Le Mal de la Terre (The Sickness of Earth*; Le Temps qu'il fait, 1985); *La Part du Diable (The Devil's Share*; Le Temps qu'il fait, 1986); *Note:* See Chapter VIII.

Riche, Étienne de (?-); *Le Rocher Infernal (The Hellish Rock*; BGA, 1928); *Le Raid Fantastique (The Fantastic Raid*; CRT, 1931); *Vers les Sources Inconnues (Towards the Unknown Sources*; Tallandier, 1938); *Le Record Fabuleux (The Fabulous Record*; BGA, 1939); *Note:* See Chapter VII.

Richebourg, Charles (?-); *Le Vampire des Andes (The Vampire of the Andes*; MRA, 1957)

Richepin, Jean (1849-1926); *Les Morts Bizarres (The Bizarre Deaths*; Decaux, 1876); *Cauchemars (Nightmares*; Fasquelle, 1892); *Théâtre Chimérique (Chimerical Theater*; Fasquelle, 1896); *Le Monstre (The Monster*; Fasquelle, 1896); *Lagibasse (Roman Magique) (Lagibasse (Magical Novel)*; Fasquelle, 1900); *L'Aile, Roman des Temps Nouveaux (The Wing, Novel of Modern Times*; Lafitte, 1911); *Le Coin des Fous (Madmen's Corner*; Flamm., 1921); *Miarka, la Fille à l'Ourse (Miarka, the Bear-Girl*; Fasquelle, 1948); *L'Homme-Peste (The Plague-Man*; L'Hydre, 1986); *Note:* See Chapter IV. Also see **Opéra**.

Richet, Charles (1850-1935); *Possession* (as Charles Epheyre; 1887); *Dans 100 Ans (In 100 Years*; as Charles Epheyre; La Revue Scientifique, 1891-92); *Le Microbe du Professeur Bakermann, Récit des Temps Futurs (Prof. Bakermann's Microbe, Novel of Future Times*; SI, 1892); *Note:* See Chapter IV.

Richoufftz, E. (?-); *Les Russes Arrivent—Un Officier d'active raconte (The Russians Are Coming—An Officer Tells All*; AM, 1987)

Richter, Anne (1939-); *La Fourmi a fait le Coup (The Ant Did It*; 1955); *Les Locataires (The Tenants*; Belfond, 1967); *La Grande Pitié de la Famille Zintram (The Great Mercy of the Zintram Family*; J. Antoine, 1986); *Histoires de Doubles (Stories of Twins*; Complexe, 1995); *Note:* Belgian writer. See Chapter VIII.

Richter, Anne (1951-); *Cauchemar dans la Ville (Nightmare in the City*; HRW, 1995); *La Malédiction de l'Île des Brumes (The Curse of Misty Island*; HRW, 1995); *Note:* French-Canadian writer.

Richter, Charles de (1887-1970); *Le Signe de la Bête (The Mark of the Beast*; RMY, 1932); *La Menace Invisible*

(The Invisible Threat; Ed. de France, 1934; transl. as *The Fall of the Eiffel Tower*, 1934); *Les Vierges du Soleil (The Virgins of the Sun*, 1944); *L'Homme qui Voulut le Déluge (The Man Who Wanted the Flood*; Gutenberg, 1945); *La Robe de Lune (The Moon Dress*; Chantal, 1946); *Le Signe de la Lente Mort (The Mark of Slow Death*; Hac., 1978); *Note:* See Chapter VII.

Rienzi, Raymond de (?-); *Les Formiciens (The Ant-Men*; Tallendier, 1932); *Note:* See Chapter VII.

Rieu, Marcel (?-?) *see* **Grand-Guignol**

Rigaud, André (?-); *L'Étrange Voyage de Teddy Hubarth (Teddy Hubbarth's Strange Journey*; AM, 1926); *Le Logis de la Dame Blanche (The Home of the White Lady*; Janicot, 1944); *Adam, Ève et Cie. (Adam, Eve and Co.*; AM, 1947)

Rigaud, Gaston (?-); *L'Épopée Terrienne (The Terran Saga*; CPE, 1954)

Rigaut, Jacques (?-); *Un Brillant Sujet (A Brilliant Subject*; Littérature, 1921)

Rignac, Jean (?-); *Le Réveil des Titans (The Titans Awake*; AM, 1967); *Note:* See Chapter IX.

Rigoni, Francis (?-); *Goutte à Goutte (Drop By Drop*; Ima Montis, 1994)

Rihoit, Catherine (1950-); *Les Petites Annonces (The Classified*; Gall., 1981); *Tentation (Temptation*; Den., 1983); *Soleil (Sun*; Gall., 1985); *Retour à Cythère (Return to Cythera*; Gall., 1988); *La Petite Princesse de Dieu (God's Little Princess*; Plon, 1992)

Rillier, Louis (?-); *Le Voleur Invisible (The Invisible Thief*, as Williamson; JST, 1907)

Rim, Carlo (Richard, Jean-Marius) (1905-1989); *Mélisande et l'Automate (Melisande and the Automaton*; Gall., 1954); *Mémoire d'une Vieille Vague (Memoirs of An Old Wave*; Ramsay, 1990)

Riotor, Léon (1865-1942); *L'Univers en Feu (The Universe on Fire*; Lemerre, 1933)

Rioux, Michel (?-); *Le Cristal Fou (The Mad Crystal*; with Gilbert Tanugi; Hac., 1980)

Rittaud-Hutinet, Jacques (?-); *Légende pour le Temps Futur (Legend for a Future Time*; Comp'Act, 1997)

Rivane, Jean (?-); *Pour Félina (For Felina*; SdP Jr 7, 1960); *Note:* Juvenile.

Rivages, Philippe V. (?-); *La Planète de l'Eau Bleue (The Planet of Blue Water*; SdPSF 64, 1973); *Note:* Juvenile SF. See Chapter IX.

Rivail, Hippolyte *see* **Kardec, Alan**

Rivais, Yak (1939-); *Les Sorcières sont N.R.V. (The Witches Are Annoyed*; École des Loisirs, 1988); *Les Contes du Miroir (Tales of the Mirror*; École des Loisirs, 1988); *Rik et la Sorcière (Rik and the Witch*; Belfond, 1989); *Contes de la Rue de Bretagne (Tales from Britanny Street*; TR, 1990); *Quelle Affaire! Nouveaux Contes de la Rue Marcel-Aymé (What a Story! New Tales from Marcel-Aymé Street*; École des Loisirs, 1990); *Le Géant des Mers (The Sea Giant*; Picollec, 1991); *Mouche et la Sorcière (Mouche and the Witch*; École des Loisirs, 1991); *Contes du Cimetière après la Pluie (Tales from the Cemetery After the Rain*; Nathan, 1997); *Note:* Juveniles. See Chapter VIII.

Rivard, Gilles (1949-1991); *La Planète Guenille (The Rag Planet*; with Jean **Clouatre**; Inedi, 1980); *Note:* French-Canadian writers. Juvenile SF.

Rivelac, Jean de (?-); *Vitesse 93.600 KmH (Speed 93,600 KmH*; Ed. Art. Docum., 1945)

Rivet, Charles (1881-?); *Le Triomphe de Lénine (Anno Diaboli 310) 2227—Roman Soviétique (The Triumph of Lenin (Anno Diaboli 310) Yr. 2227—Soviet Novel*; with Michel **Goriellof**; Perrin, 1927); *Note:* See Chapter VII.

Rivière, François (1949-); *Le Manuscrit d'Orvileda (The Orvileda Manuscript*; Hac., 1980); *Profanations* (Seuil, 1982); *Tabou (Taboo*; Seuil, 1985); *Jonathan Cap Superstar* (Nathan, 1986); *Le Labyrinthe du Jaguar (The Jaguar's Labyrinth*; Nathan, 1986); *La Samba du Fantôme (The Ghost's Samba*; Nathan, 1986); *La Clinique du Docteur K. (Dr.K's Clinic*; Nathan, 1986); *Jonathan Cap contre les Chevaliers de Satan (Jonathan Cap vs. Satan's Knights*; Nathan, 1986); *Les Formules de Zoltan (Zoltan's Formulas*; Nathan, 1986); *La Guitare Survoltée (The High-Powered Guitar*; Nathan, 1987); *Le Spectre du Mandarin (The Mandarin's Ghost*; Nathan, 1988); *Le Gorille de Kivou (The Kivu Gorilla*; Nathan, 1988); *Le Fiancé de la Pirate (The Pirate's Fiance*; Nathan, 1988); *Bus pour l'Enfer (Bus to Hell*; Nathan, 1989); *Les Mystères de Ker-even, Enquête Extralucide (The Mysteries of Ker-Even, Supernatural Investigation*; Nathan, 1990); *Julius Exhumé (Julius Exhumed*; Seuil, 1990); *Kafka* (Calmann-Lévy, 1992); *Note:* See Chapter VIII.

Rivière, Henri (1827-1883); *Pierrot, Cain* (Hac., 1860); *La Main Coupée (The Severed Hand*; M. Lévy, 1862); *La Possédée, ou La Seconde Vie du Dr. Roger (The Possessed Woman, or the Second Life of Dr. Roger*; M. Lévy, 1863); *Le Colonel Pierre* (M. Lévy, 1863); *Les Méprises du Coeur (The Mistakes of the Heart*; M. Lévy, 1865); *L'Envoûtement (The Spell*; M. Lévy, 1870); *Note:* See Chapter IV.

Robban, Randolph (?-); *Si l'Allemagne Avait Vaincu (If Germany Had Won*; Tour du Guêt, 1949-50); *Le Robot Germanophile Télécommandé (The Remote-Controlled German-Loving Robot*; Tour du Guêt, 1956)

Robbe-Grillet, Alain (1922-); *Dans le Labyrinthe (In the Labyrinth*; Minuit, 1959); *Instantanés (Snap Shots*; Minuit, 1962); *La Maison de Rendez-Vous (The House of Rendezvous*; Minuit, 1965); *Topologie pour une Cité Fantôme (Topology for a Phantom City*; Minuit, 1976); *Djinn* (Minuit, 1981); *Note:* See Chapter VIII. Also see Book 1, chapters I and VI.

Roberge, Marc (1927-); *Les Affres des Ressuscités des Trois-Cimes (The Sufferings of the Resurrected of Trois-Cimes*; Maheux, 1975); *Note:* French-Canadian writer.

Robert-Dumas, Charles (?-); *Contes de l'Heure Présente (Tales of the Present Times*; with Maurice **Level**; Diesterweg, 1914); *L'Élixir de Suicide (The Suicide Elixir*; Fayard, 1934); *L'Embardée (The Sharp Turn*; Fayard, 1935); *L'Idole de Plomb (The Idol of Lead*; Fayard, 1935); *Le Masque de Vitriol (The Mask of Acid*; Fayard, 1935); *La Marque du Triangle (The Mark of the Triangle*; Fayard, 1937); *L'Usine Fatal (The Deadly Factory*; Fayard, 1937); *La Machine à Prédire la Mort (The Death-Predicting Machine*; with Roger-Francis **Didelot**; Fayard, 1938); *Face au Destin (Face-To-Face with Destiny*; Fayard, 1938); *L'Homme à la Manche Vide (The Man with the Empty Sleeve*; Fayard, 1941); *Le Témoin Invisible (The Invisible Witness*; Fayard, 1941)

Robida, Albert (1848-1926); *Voyages Très Extraordinaires de Saturnin Farandoul dans les 5 ou 6 Parties du Monde et dans tous les Pays Connus et même Inconnus de M. Jules Verne (The Very Extraordinary Voyages of Saturnin Farandoul in the 5 or 6 Continents of the World and in All the Lands Known or Even Unknown to Mr. Jules Verne*; Libr. Ill. Dreyfous, 1879; rev. Dentu, 1883); *Le Vingtième Siècle (The 20th Century*; G. Decaux, 1882-83; rev. Dentu, 1895); *La Guerre au Vingtième Siècle (War in the 20th Century*; La Caricature, 1883; rev. Libr. Ill., 1887); *La Vie Électrique (The Electric Life*; Libr.Ill., 1890); *Voyage au Pays des Saucisses (Journey to the Land of Sausages*; A. Colin, 1892); *Le Mystère de la Rue Carême-Prenant (The Mystery of Careme-Prenant Street*; A. Colin, 1897); *L'Horloge des Siècles (The Clock of the Centuries*; La Vie Ill./Juven, 1902); *Le Patron Nicklaus (Nicklaus the Boss*; A. Colin, 1909); *L'Île des Centaures (The Island of the Centaurs*; Laurens, 1912); *Un Potache en 1950 (A Student in 1950*; Mon Journal, 1917); *L'Ingénieur von Satanas (Engineer Von Satanas*; Ren. du Livre, 1919); *Voyage et Aventures de la Famille Noë dans l'Arche (Travels and Adventures of the Noah Family in the Ark*; Armand Colin, 1922); *Un Chalet dans les Airs (A Cabin in the Air*; Armand Colin, 1925); *Note:* See Chapter V.

Robitaille, Louis-Bernard (1946-); *La République de Monte-Carlo* (Denoël, 1990); *Note:* French-Canadian writer. Political fiction about the near-future.

Robitaillie, Henriette (1909-); *Le Château des Malices (The Castle of Tricks*; Montsouris, 1945); *Le Lac de l'Oubli (The Lake of Oblivion*; Publ. Techniques & Artistiques, 1946); *Contes des Bois et de la Lande (Tales of Woods and Moors*; Boivin, 1949); *Le Secret de l'Oeil Jaune (The Secret of the Yellow Eye*; Bonne Presse, 1949); *Le Monstre des Abîmes (The Monster from the Abyss*; Bonne Presse, 1951); *Voyage au Bout de la Mer (Voyage to the End of the Sea*; Nlles. Éditions Latines, 1952); *La Ferme du Loup Blanc (The Farm of the White Wolf*; Fleurus, 1953); *La Tribu des Bords du Feu (The Tribe at the Edge of Fire*; Apostolat de la Prière, 1955); *Luciole chez les Pirates (Firefly and the Pirates*; Gautier-Languereau, 1956); *La Maison des Sourires (The House of Smiles*; Gautier-Languereau, 1957); *Norr le Mystérieux (Norr the Mysterious*; SdP Jr 5, 1957); *Norr et le Confiseur (Norr and the Candy-Maker*; Mame-Fleurus, 1957); *La Route Secrète (The Secret Road*; Apostolat de la Presse, 1958); *Algue (Algae*; SdP Jr 15, 1959); *Les Sept Portes d'Ebène (The Seven Ebony Doors*; SdPJr 18, 1959); *La Piste Nouvelle (The New Trail*; Fleurus, 1960); *Le Village Abandonné (The Abandoned Village*; Deux Coqs d'Or, 1969); *Note:* Juveniles. See Chapters VIII and IX.

Roc, Gil (?-); *L'Univers des Gouffres (The Universe of the Pits*; MRA, 1955); *L'Étrange Peuple du Kintchindjinga (The Strange People of Kintchindjinga*; MRA, 1956); *L'Horrible Planète (The Awful Planet*; MRA, 1956); *Akérs* (Grassin, 1972); *La Sphère de Feu (The Sphere of Fire*; Nlle. Proue, 1987); *Le Styx Aller-Retour (The Styx and Back*; Les Dits du Pont, 1994); *Note:* See Chapter IX.

Roche, Aimé (?-); *Chantelouve* (SdP 2 102, 1980); *Le Chef à l'Oeil d'Ivoire (The Chief with An Ivory Eye*; SdP 2 126, 1982); *Note:* Juveniles.

Roche, Dominique (1948-); *Sous l'Araignée du Sud (Under the Southern Spider*; with Charles **Nightingale**; RL, 1978); *Note:* See Chapter VIII.

Roche, Thérèse (1930-); *L'Arbre, La Bache et le Grand Météo (The Tree, Its Cover and the Great Weather*; Magnard, 1978); *Garlone et les Snils (Garlone and the Snils*; Magnard, 1982); *Le Naviluk* (Magnard, 1983); *Les Extra-Chats (The Extra-Cats*; Magnard, 1984); *Elodie de la Vallodie* (Magnard, 1987); *Lily Moon et la Lucarne (Lily Moon and the Small Window*; Magnard, 1988); *Appoline et la Porte du Temps (Appoline and the Gate of Time*; Magnard, 1989); *Note:* Juvenile SF. See Chapter IX.

Roche-Pézard *see* **Pézard, Fanette**

Rochefort, Christiane (1917-); *Archaos, ou Le Jardin Étincelant (Archaos, or the Shining Garden*; Grasset, 1972); *La Porte du Fond (The Back Door*; Grasset,

1988); *Adieu Andromède (Good-Bye, Andromeda*; Grasset, 1997)

Rocher, Dominique (1929-); *Délire (Delirium*; FNAG 167, 1969); *Boomerang* (FNAG 174, 1969); *Les Voyances du Docteur Basile (The Visions of Dr. Basile*; FNAG 179, 1970); *Le Pacte du Sang (The Pact of Blood*; FNAG 186, 1970); *Le Docteur Soigne la Veuve (The Doctor Cares After the Widow*; FNAG 198, 1971); *L'Homme aux Lunettes Noires (The Man with the Dark Glasses*; FNAG 209, 1971); *Le Monstre Sans Visage (The Monster Without a Face*; FNAG 221, 1972); *Humeur Rouge (Red Mood*; FNAG 231, 1973); *La Clinique de la Mort (The Clinic of Death*; FNAG 257, 1974); *La Nuit des Morphos (The Night of the Morphos*; FNA 685, 1975); *De Sable et de Sang (Of Sand and Blood*; Debresse, 1990); *L'Être aux Yeux d'Améthyste (The Being with Amethyst Eyes*; Maison Rhodanienne, 1994); *La Voix du Seppuku (The Voice of Seppuku*; Rive Droite, 1996); *Note:* See Chapter VIII.

Rochon, Esther (1948-); *En Hommage aux Araignées (In Homage to Spiders;* Actuelle, 1974; rev. as *L'Étranger sous la Ville (The Stranger Under the City*, JP 56, 1986); *L'Épuisement du Soleil (The Exhaustion of the Sun*; CdF 8, 1985); *Coquillage* (Pleine Lune, 1985; transl. as *The Shell*, 1990); *Le Traversier (The Ferry*; Pleine Lune, 1987); *L'Espace du Diamant (The Diamond Space*; Pleine Lune, 1990); *Le Piège à Souvenirs (The Memories Trap*; Pleine Lune, 1991); *L'Ombre et le Cheval (The Shadow and the Horse*; JP 78, 1992); *Lame (Blade*; Q/A, 1995); *Aboli (Abolished*; AL, 1996); *Ouverture (Opening*; AL, 1997); *Note:* French-Canadian writer. Both *En Hommage* and *L'Épuisement* are remarkable fantasy sagas with Buddhist overtones, and take place in the same universe.

Rocque, Marie (1965-); *Etuk et Piqati* (Éd. des Plaines, 1993); *Note:* French-Canadian writer. Juvenile.

Rodiet, Antony (Dr.) (?-); *L'Avion Sous-Marin (The Underwater Plane*; same text, two editions: 1) as Dr. Rodiet/with Émile **Lutz**; 2) as Antoine Teidor/with Florent **Duthuit**; Tallandier, 1928); *L'Île Ressuscitée (The Resurrected Island*; BGA, 1937)

Roger, Aristide *see* **Rengade, Jules**

Roger, Noëlle (Pittard, Hélène, née Dufour) (1874-1953); *Les Disciples (The Disciples*; Payot, 1921); *Le Nouveau Déluge (The New Flood*; Calmann-Lévy, 1922); *Le Nouvel Adam (The New Adam*; AM, 1924); *L'Hôte Invisible (The Invisible Host*; LPT, 1926); *Celui Qui Voit (He Who Sees*; Calmann-Lévy, 1926); *Le Livre qui fait Mourir (The Book That Kills*; Calmann-Lévy, 1927); *Le Soleil Enseveli (The Buried Sun*; Calmann-Lévy, 1928; rev. 1951); *Princesse de Lune (Moon Princess*; Calmann-Lévy, 1929); *Le Chercheur d'Ondes (The Wave Seeker*;

Calmann-Lévy, 1931); *Le Nouveau Lazare (The New Lazarus*; Calmann-Lévy, 1935); *La Vallée Perdue (The Lost Valley*; Payot, 1940); *Au Seuil de l'Invisible (On the Treshold of the Unseen*; Attinger-Nauchâtel, 1949); *Note:* Swiss writer. See Chapter VII.

Roger, Marie-Sabine (1957-); *Les Sources du Mal (The Sources of Evil*; Hac., 1997); *Note:* Juvenile fantasy.

Roger (Prof.) (?-?) *see* **Grand-Guignol**

Rogers, Rose-Annie (?-); *L'Île Abandonnée (The Abandoned Island*; Kra, 1928)

Rogissard, Jean (?-); *Le Clos des Noires Présences (The Garden of the Black Presences*; Fayard, 1961)

Rogliano, Jean-Claude (?-); *Le Berger des Morts (Mal'-Concilio) (The Shepherd of the Dead*; in Corsican: Maison de la Culture de la Corse, 1975; in French: Belfond, 1980); *Cinq Contes pour une Île (Five Tales for An Island*; Delta-Amitié, 1979); *Contes et Légendes de Corse (Tales and Stories from Corsica*; with Agnès Rogliano; France-Empire, 1997); *Note:* Corsican writer. See Chapter VIII.

Roisel, Godefroy de (?-?); *Les Atlantes (The Atlanteans*; Germier-Baillere, 1874); *Note:* See Chapter V.

Roland, Claude (?-?) *see* **Grand-Guignol**

Roland, Claudine (1955-) *see* **Grosjean, Didier**

Roland, Marcel (1879-1941); *Le Presqu'Homme, Roman des Temps Futurs (The Almost-Man, Novel of Future Times*; Méricant, 1907); *Le Déluge Futur: Journal d'un Survivant (The Future Flood: Diary of a Survivor*; Fayard, 1910); *La Conquête d'Anthar: Roman des Temps Futurs (The Conquest of Anthar: Novel of Future Times*; Lafitte, 1913); *Faiseur d'Or (Gold Maker*; Flamm., 1915); *Osmant le Rajeunisseur (Osmant the Rejuvenator*; AM, 1925); *Note:* See Chapter V.

Rolin, Dominique (1913-); *Le Fauteuil Magique (The Magic Armchair*; Cast., 1971); *L'Enragé (The Enraged*; Ramsay, 1978); *L'Infini chez Soi (Infinity at Home*; Den., 1980); *Le Gâteau des Morts (The Cake of the Dead*; Den., 1982); *L'Enfant-Roi (The Child-King*; Den., 1986); *Les Marais (The Swamps*; Gall., 1991); *Train de Rêves (Dream Train*; Gall., 1994)

Rolin, Olivier (?-); *Phénomène Futur (Future Phenomenon*; Seuil, 1983); *Bar des Flots Noirs (Bar of the Black Waves*; Seuil, 1987); *L'Invention du Monde (The Invention of the World*; Seuil, 1993)

Roll, Jean (?-); *Échec à l'Agent 10-ter (Agent 10c in Check*; STAEL, 1948); *Note:* Juvenile.

Rolland, Romain (1866-1944); *La Révolte des Machines ou La Pensée Déchaînée (The Revolt of Machines, or

Thought Unbound; Worms, 1947); *Note:* See Chapter IX.

Rollet, du (?-?) *see* **Opéra**

Rollet, Serge (?-); *Sirène (Siren*; Sang du Dragon, 1993)

Rollet, Thierry (?-); *Kraken, ou Les Fils de l'Océan (Kraken, or the Sons of the Ocean*; SdP 2 116, 1980); *Note:* Juvenile.

Rollin, Jean (1938-); *Une Petite Fille Magique (A Magical Little Girl*; L'Hors-du-Temps, 1988); *Les Demoiselles de l'Étrange (The Damsels of the Weird*; Filipacchi, 1990; rev. with a sequel, *La Résurrection des Demoiselles (The Resurrection of the Damsels)*, Florent Massot, 1997); *Les Deux Orphelines Vampires (The Two Orphan Vampire Girls*; FN Angoisses 6, 1993); *Anissa (FNFR 10, 1994); Les Voyageuses (The Travellers*; FNFR 12, 1995); *Les Pillardes (The Female Looters*; FNFR 17, 1995); *Les Incendiaires (The Female Arsonists*; FNFR 24, 1995); *Bestialité (Bestiality*; FNFR 28, 1995); *La Petite Ogresse (The Little Ogress*; Florent Massot, 1996); *La Momie Sanglante (The Bloody Mummy*; Florent Massot, 1997); *Note:* See Chapter VIII. Jean Rollin is also a renowned horror-film director (see Book 1, Chapters I and VI).

Rolon, Jean (1938-); *L'Or du Scaphandier (The Deep-Sea Diver's Gold*; JCL, 1983); *Enfer Privé (Private Hell*; Lumière Noire, 1988); *Cyrille et Méthode* (Gall., 1994); *Zones* (Gall., 1996); *L'Organisation* (Grand Livre du Mois, 1996)

Romagny, A. (?-); *La Torpille Aérienne (The Aerial Torpedo*; CDAv, 1924); *Timor le Pirate (Timor the Pirate*; CDAv, 1924)

Romains, Jules (Farigoule, Louis) (1885-1972); *Psyché* (Gall., 1922-27); *Les Créateurs (The Creators*; Flamm., 1932); *Violation de Frontières (Border Violation*; Flamm., 1951); *Passagers de cette Planète, Où allons-nous? (Passengers of This Planet, Where Are We Going?*; Grasset, 1955); *Note:* See Chapter IX.

Romano, F. (?-); *Le Temple sous les Flots (The Underwater Temple*; VA, 1936); *Le Mirage de l'Île Dorée (The Mirage of the Golden Island*; VA, 1937)

Romazières, Edmond *see* **Keyser, Édouard de**

Rondard, Patrice *see* **Calixte, Hervé; Klein, Gérard**

Roneker, Jean-Paul (?-); *Apparence (Appearance*; Phénix, 1990)

Ronssin, Jean-Pierre (1953-); *La Vengeance du Chat Mouzoul (The Revenge of Muzul the Cat*; Gall., 1983); *Cervantès, le Manchot de Lépante (Cervantes, the One-Armed Man from Lepante*; Gall., 1986); *Note:* Juveniles.

Ronze, Charles (?-); *Le Maître des Neiges (The Snow Master*; SFEP Oeil-de-Faucon, 1941); *Les Démons de la Mine (The Demons of the Mine*; SFEP Oeil-de-Faucon, 1941); *La Horde des Monstres (The Horde of Monsters*; SFEP Oeil-de-Faucon, 1941); *Le Kraken de l'Océan Glacial (The Kraken of the Icy Ocean*; SFEP Oeil-de-Faucon, 1942); *Le Secret des Mers Australes (The Secret of the Southern Seas*; SFEP Oeil-de-Faucon, 1942); *Que se passe-t-il? (What Is Happening?*; SFEP Oeil-de-Faucon, 1942)

Roques, René (?-); *Ita* (Gérard, 1927)

Rosart, Jean-Paul (?-); *Le Roi Bissextile (The Leap Year King*; NéO, 1979); *Note:* Surreal fable.

Rose, Claude (1947-) *see* **Touati, Lucien-Guy**

Rosel, Michel (?-); *Montagnards de la Mer (Mountaineers of the Sea*; Arabesque 128, 1960); *Trafic de Cerveaux (Brain Traffic*; Arabesque 134, 1960); *Orbite de Mort (Deadly Orbit*; Arabesque 141, 1960); *Note:* See Chapter IX.

Rosensteel, F. C. (?-); *1+1 = 1* (RMY, 1913)

Rosier, Joseph-Bernard (?-?) *see* **Opéra**

Rosmer, Jean (1890-?); *Les Trois Désirs de Fleurette (Fleurette's Three Desires*; Firmin-Didot, 1903); *La Roche aux Fées (The Rock of Fairies*; Firmin-Didot, 1909); *Le Manoir de Glace (The Castle of Ice*; Gautier-Languereau, 1927); *L'Héritière du Soleil (The Heir of the Sun*; BGA, 1928); *720-C-13* (with V. d'**Entrevaux**; Hac., 1929); *Le Cadran Magique (The Magic Dial*; with V. d'**Entrevaux**; Hac., 1929); *L'Idole aux Bras Fermés (The Idol with Closed Arms*; Gautier-Languereau, 1929); *La Tour de Cristal (The Crystal Tower*; Tallandier, 1930); *Le Secret du Cosaque (The Secret of the Cossack*; Tallandier, 1930); *L'Avion Fulgurant (The Lightning Plane*; Paul Duval, 1931); *Le Manoir Perdu (The Lost Castle*; Mame, 1931); *Maléchamp* (SEPIA, 1933); *Le Dragon de Feu (The Dragon of Fire*; Tallandier, 1933); *L'Errante Mystérieuse (The Mysterious Wanderer*; SEPIA, 1935); *Le Palais aux Lépreux (The Palace of Lepers*; Clocher, 1936); *L'Écharpe d'Iris (The Scarf of Iris*; Bonne Presse, 1937); *La Tour Maudite (The Accursed Tower*; SEPIA, 1937); *Les Frères du Soleil (The Brothers of the Sun*; SEPIA, 1938); *L'Homme aux Chiens-Loups (The Man with the German Shepherds*; SEPIA, 1938); *L'Homme aux Cheveux*

Rouges (The Man with Red Hair; Clocher, 1940); *Les Chevalier des la Délivrance (The Knights of Deliverance*; Arc-en-Ciel, 1940); *Lady Sphinx* (Dup., 1940); *Le Secret des Ruines (The Secret of the Ruins*; Clocher, 1942)

Rosny Aîné, J. H. (Boëx, Joseph-Henri) (1856-1940); *Les Xipehuz* (Savine, 1887; transl. as *The Shapes*, 1968; retransl. in *The Xipehuz and the Death of the Earth*, 1978); *Vamireh, Roman des Temps Primitifs (Vamireh, Novel of Primitive Times*; *Revue Hebdomadaire*, 1892; Kolb, 1895); *Eyrimah* (*Le Bambou*, 1893; Plon, 1926); *Nymphée* (1893; SFIL, 1909); *Elem d'Asie (Elem of Asia*; Guillaume-Lotus Alba, 1896); *Nomai, Amours Lacustres (Nomai, Love on the Lake*; Guillaume-Lotus Alba, 1897); *Les Profondeurs de Kyamo (The Depths of Kyamo*; Plon, 1896); *Les Femmes de Setné (The Women of Setné*; as Enacryos; Ollendorff, 1903); *La Guerre du Feu (The War for Fire*; JST, 1909; Charpentier, 1911; transl. as *The Quest for Fire*, 1967); *Le Trésor dans la Neige (The Treasure in the Snow*; Flamm., 1910); *La Mort de la Terre (The Death of the Earth*; Plon, 1910; transl. as *The Xipehuz and the Death of the Earth*, 1978); *La Force Mystérieuse (The Mysterious Force*; JST, 1913; Plon, 1914); *Perdus? Aventures Héroïques (Lost? Heroic Adventures*; Flamm., 1916); *L'Aube du Futur (The Dawn of the Future*; Crès, 1917); *L'Énigme de Givreuse (The Enigma of Givreuse*; Flamm., 1917); *Le Félin Géant* (LPT, 1918; Plon, 1920; transl. as *The Giant Cat*, 1924; retransl. as *Quest of the Dawn Man*, 1964); *La Grande Énigme (The Great Enigma*; 1920); *L'Étonnant Voyage d'Hareton Ironcastle (The Amazing Journey of Hareton Ironcastle*; Flamm., 1922; transl./ adapted by Philip Jose Farmer as *Ironcastle*, 1976); *Les Autres Vies, les Autres Mondes (Other Lives, Other Worlds*; Crès, 1924); *L'Assassin Surnaturel (The Supernatural Assassin*; Flamm., 1924); *Les Navigateurs de l'Infini (The Navigators of Infinity*; Oeuvres Libres, 1925); *La Terre Noire (The Black Earth*; Nlle. Revue Critique, 1925); *Le Trésor Lointain (The Far-Away Treasure*; Arts & Livre, 1926); *La Femme Disparue (The Vanished Woman*; Nlle. Revue Critique, 1926); *Les Conquérants du Feu (The Conquerors of Fire*; Portiques, 1929); *Les Hommes-Sangliers (The Boar-Men*; Portiques, 1929); *Helgvor du Fleuve Bleu (Helgvor of the Blue River*; Flamm., 1929); *Au Château des Loups*

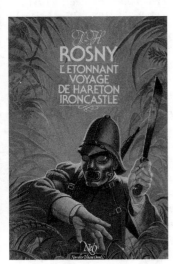

Rouges (At the Castle of the Red Wolves; Nlle. Revue Critique, 1929); *L'Initiation de Diane (Diana's Initiation*; Plon, 1930); *Le Fauve et sa Proie (The Beast and Its Prey*; Flamm., 1930); *Tabubu (Roman Egyptien) (Tabubu: An Egyptian Novel*; Meynal, 1932); *Ambor, le Loup Vainqueur de César (Ambor, the Wolf Who Defeated Caesar*; Stock, 1932); *Les Compagnons de l'Univers (The Companions of the Universe*; MdF, 1934); *La Sauvage Aventure (The Savage Adventure*; 1932; AM, 1935); *Le Vampire de Bethnal Green (The Vampire of Bethnal Green*; Albert, 1935); *La Vengeance (The Revenge*; Flamm., 1935); *Les Astronautes (The Astronauts; in Les Navigateurs de l'Infini (The Navigators of Infinity)*, RF 69, 1960); *Récits de Science-Fiction de J.-H. Rosny Aîné* (anthology by Jean-Baptise **Baronian**; MarSF 523, 1975) includes the following novels, novellas and short stories: *Les Xipehuz* (1887); *L'Immolation (The Immolation*; 1887); *La Sorcière (The Witch*; 1887); *Le Cataclysme* (1888); *La Légende Sceptique (The Skeptical Legend*; 1889); *Nymphée* (1893); *Un Autre Monde* (1895; transl. as *Another World*, 1962); *Le Jardin de Mary (Mary's Garden*; 1895); *Les Profondeurs de Kyamo (The Depths of Kyamo*; 1896); *La Contrée Prodigieuse des Cavernes (The Prodigious Land of the Caverns*; 1896); *Le Voyage (The Journey*; 1900); *L'Épave (The Wreck*; 1903); *La Mort de la Terre (The Death of the Earth*; 1910); *Le Trésor dans la Neige (The Treasure in the Snow*; 1910); *La Jeune Vampire (The Young Vampire*; 1920); *L'Assassin Surnaturel (The Supernatural Assassin*; 1924); *La Jeune Sorcière (The Young Witch*; 1924); *Les Navigateurs de l'Infini (The Navigators of Infinity*; 1925), *Les Hommes-Sangliers (The Boar-Men*; 1929); *Dans le Monde des Variants (In the Variants' World*; 1939); *Note:* Belgian writer. See Chapter V.

Rosny Jeune, J. H. (Boëx, Séraphin-Justin) (1859-1948); *La Contrée aux Embûches (The Ambush Country*; Crès, 1920); *Ls Furies (The Furies*; Ferenczi, 1928); *L'Énigme du Redoutable (The Enigma of the Redoutable*; Crès, 1930); *La Cité Infernale (The Hellish City*; Ed. de France, 1933); *Le Banquet de Platon (Plato's Banquet*; Plon, 1942); *Le Destin de Martin Lafaille (The Fate of Martin Lafaille*; AM, 1945); *Note:* Brother of J. H. **Rosny** Aîné. See Chapter VII.

Rotrou, Jean de (1609-1650); *La Bague d'Oubli (The Ring of Oblivion*; 1628); *Crisante* (A. de Sommanville, 1640); *Note:* See Chapter II.

Roudene, Alex (?-); *La Lanterne Bleue (The Blue Lantern*; Paul Mari, 1980); *Note: Documentary genre works include Les Extra-Terrestres (The Extra-Terrestrials; CELT, 1977), Envoûtement et Exorcisme (Spells and Exorcisms*; Magellan, 1994) and a few more titles about witchcraft, black magic, etc.

Roudy, Pierre (1927-); *Le Journal (The Diary*; Grames, 1971); *Et nous verrons la Mer encore (And We'll Still Sea the Sea*; Magnard, 1974); *Le Dernier Loup (The Last Wolf*; Magnard, 1977); *Et l'Homme tua la Femme (And Man Killed Woman*; Ed. Fr. Réunis, 1980); *La Florisane* (Papiers, 1985)

Roueche, Berton (?-); *La Révolte des Carnassiers (The Revolt of the Carnivores*; Hac., 1976); *Note:* Juvenile SF.

Rouff, Marcel (?-); *Ce qui Plane sur la Ville (What Hangs Over the City*; Rouff, 1921); *Voyage au Monde à l'Envers (Journey to the Upside Down World*; Crès, 1923); *Les Étranglés (The Strangled*; Émile Paul, 1927); *La Peau Peinte (The Painted Skin*; Nlle. Revue Critique, 1930)

Rouger, Gustave (?-); *Une Découverte Sensationelle (A Sensational Discovery*; Émile Paul, 1919); *L'Esclave aux Bêtes (The Slave with Beasts*; Émile Paul, 1919); *La Si Bonne... (The So Good...*; Ferenczi, 1925); *Les Intégrales de la Mort (The Integrals of Death*; J. Laffont, 1930)

Rougeron, Gérard (?-); *Opéra Machine* (Résonances, 1979); *Les Confettis Noirs (Black Confetti*; Ramsay, 1981)

Roumier-Robert, Marie-Anne de (?-?); *Voyage de Milord Céton dans les Sept Planètes ou Le Nouveau Mentor (Voyage of Lord Ceton in the Seven Planets or The New Mentor*; Despilly, 1765; VI 1787); *Les Ondins* (Delavain, 1768); *Note:* See Chapter III.

Rouquette, Louis-Frédéric (?-); *La Cité des Vieilles (The City of Old Women*; AM, 1918); *L'Homme qui Vint... (The Man Who Came...*; AM, 1921); *Le Grand Silence Blanc (The Great White Silence*; Ferenczi, 1921); *L'Épopée Blanche (The White Epic*; Ferenczi, 1926); *Le Secret du Pôle (The Secret of the Pole*; Ferenczi, 1926); *L'Île d'Enfer (The Hellish Isle*; Ed. de Paris, 1995); *La Bête Errante (The Wandering Beast*; Climats, 1996); *Note:* See Chapter VII.

Roure, Henry du *see* **Du Roure, Henry**

Rousseau, Jean-Jacques (1712-1778) *see* **Opéra**

Rousseau, Normand (1939-); *Les Pantins (The Puppets*; Pensée U., 1973); *Piège pour un Rat (ou Le Printemps est encore Possible) (Trap for a Rat (or Spring Is Still Possible);* University of Ottawa, 1979; rev. as *Le Déluge Blanc (The White Flood)*, Leméac, 1981); *La Tourbière (The Bog*; La Presse, 1982); *Dans la Démesure du Possible (In the Extravagance of the Possible*; Tisseyre, 1983); *Le Grand Dérangement (The Great Upset*; Stanké, 1984); *Note:* French-Canadian writer. *Le Déluge* is about the battle that pits a man against a rat. It was adapted as a 1983 motion picture entitled *Of Un-*

known Origin (Dir: George Pan Cosmatos), starring Peter Weller.

Rousseau, René (?-?) *see* **Grand-Guignol**

Roussel, Raymond (1877-1933); *Impressions d'Afrique (Impressions of Africa*; Lemerre, 1910); *Locus Solus* (Lemerre, 1914); *Nouvelles Impressions d'Afrique (New Impressions of Africa*; Lemerre, 1932); *Épaves (Wrecks*; Pauvert, 1973)

Rouzade, Léonie (?-?); *Le Monde Renversé (The World Upside Down*; Lachaud, 1872); *Voyage de Théodosie à l'Île d'Utopie (Voyage of Theodosie on the Island of Utopia*; Lachaud, 1872)

Rouzé, Michel (1910-); *La Forêt de Quokelunde ou le Mystère du Mont Saint-Michel (The Forest of Quokelunde, or the Mystery of Mount Saint-Michael*; Bourrelier, 1953)

Roy, Yvon *see* **Adam, E**

Royat, Maurice *see* **Toesca, Maurice**

Royer, Alain (?-) *see* **Baudry, Emmanuel**

Royer, Alphonse (?-?); *Braunsberg le Charbonnier (Braunsberg the Coal Peddler*; in *Revue des Deux Mondes*, 1832)

Royet (Colonel) (?-); *La Patrie en Danger (France Threatened*; with Paul d'**Ivoi**; Juven, 1905); *Un, La Mystérieuse (One, the Mysterious*; with Paul d'**Ivoi**; serialized in 88 issues, rev. as 2 vols. Juven, 1905); *1. Les Briseurs d'Épées (The Sword Breakers)*; *2. Le Capitaine Matraque (Captain Bludgeon)*; *La Tempête Universelle de l'An 2000 (The Universal Tempest of the Year 2000*; AA, 1921); *L'Idole de Pahli (The Idol of Pahli*; BGA, 1927); *À Deux Doigts de la Fin du Monde (Two Inches Away from the End of the World*; RDA, 1929); *Le Troupeau de Neptune (Neptune's Cattle*; VLAE, 1928); *L'Île d'Acier (The Island of Steel*; VLAE, 1929); *1932: La Guerre est Déclarée (1932: War Is Declared*; serialized in 20 issues, Tallandier, 1931): *1. Les Dernières Cartouches (The Last Cartridges)*; *2. La Science au Service de la France (Science in France's Service)*; *3. L'Armée de l'Ombre (The Army of Shadows)*; *4. L'Invasion Traîtresse (The Traitorous Invasion)*; *5. Paris Pollué (Polluted Paris)*; *6. Les Reptiles; 7. Les Forces Invisibles (The Invisible Forces)*; *8. Un contre Mille (One vs. a Thousand)*; *9. Nuit Tragique (Tragic Night)*; *10. La Veillée des Armes (The Wake Before the Weapons)*; *11. Sus à l'Agresseur (Attacking the Aggressor)*; *12. L'Heure H (The H Hour)*; *13. Le Sacrifice Héroïque (The Heroic Sacrifice)*; *14. Servir la France! (To Serve France!)*; *15. Premières Revanches (First Revenge)*; *16. Le Bombardement de Londres (The Bombing of London)*; *17. Terre d'Afrique (Land of Africa)*; *18.*

La Flotte Invisible (The Invisible Fleet); 19. Le Secret des Pharaons (The Secret of the Pharaohs); 20. Justice Immanente (Imminent Justice); Le Tunnel de Gibraltar (The Gibraltar Tunnel; BGA, 1933); *Le Défi d'un Boy-Scout (A Boy Scout's Challenge;* Tallandier, 1935); *Note:* See Chapter V.

Rudigoz, Roger (1922-); *La Souris Chauve Est née coiffée (The Bald Mouse Was Born Lucky;* École des Loisirs, 1983); *Les Contes de la Souris Chauve (Tales of the Bald Mouse;* École des Loisirs, 1983); *Zogidur* (École des Loisirs, 1985); *Note:* Juveniles.

Ruellan, André *see* **Steiner, Kurt**

Ruelle, Yves *see* **Dartois, Yves**

Ruf, Michel (?-); *Le Tableau Cinq (Table 5;* Parcours-Nomine, 1996)

Ruffin, Constant (?-); *L'Écu de Sobieski (Sobieski's Coin;* Ruffin, 1971); *Les Gouttes Noires (The Black Drops;* Ruffin, 1974); *Quand on téléphone à Dieu, il y a de la friture (When You Phone God, There's Static on the Line;* Cahiers Froissart, 1978)

Russell, Christian (?-); *Les Voyants (The Seers;* Métal 23, 1956)

Rustaing de Saint-Jory, Louis (1703-1752); *Les Femmes Militaires, Relation d'une Île Nouvellement Découverte par le C.D. *** (Military Women, Story of An Island Newly Discovered By C.D. ***;* Simon, 1735)

Ryner, Han (Ner, Henri) (1861-1938); *Un Roman Historique (An Historical Novel;* as Henri Ner; 1896); *L'Homme-Fourmi (The Ant-Man;* Figuière, 1901); *Les Voyages de Psychodore, Philosophe Cynique (The Travels of Psychodore, Cynical Philosopher;* Chacomac, 1903); *Le Sphinx Rouge, Roman Individualiste (The Red Sphinx, Individualistic Novel;* Figuière, 1905); *Les Pacifiques (The Pacifics; Figuière, 1914); La Tour des Peuples (The Tower of Peoples;* Figuière, 1919); *Les Apparitions d'Ahasvérus (Ahasverus' Appearances;* Figuière, 1920); *Le Père Diogène (Father Diogenes;* Figuière, 1920); *Les Paraboles Cyniques (The Cynical Parables;* Athena, 1922); *La Vie Éternelle, Roman du Mystère (Eternal Life, Novel of Mystery;* Radot, 1926); *Les Surhommes, Roman Prophétique (The Supermen, Prophetic Novel;* Crès, 1929); *Songes Perdus (Lost Dreams;* Messein, 1929); *Les Orgies sur la Montagne (Orgies on the Mountain;* Figuière, 1935); *Contes (Tales;* Pavillon, 1960); *Note:* See Chapter V.

Sabatier, Roland (?-?) *see* **Dubois, Pierre**

Sabran, Guy (?-); *La Croisière du Nébulor, Fusée Atomique (The Cruise of the Nebulor, Atomic Rocket;* GP, 1946); *Cornebus and Cie. (Cornebuse and Co.;* GP, 1946); *Note:* Also an illustrator.

Sabran, Jean *see* **Berna, Paul**

Sacchi, Henri (?-); *L'Empereur de Jade (The Jade Emperor;* Seuil, 1997)

Sade, Donatien Alphonse François, Marquis de (1740-1814); *Justine ou Les Malheurs de la Vertu* (Libr. Associés, 1791; transl. as *Justine or the Misfortunes of Virtue,* 1966); *Les 120 Journées de Sodome, ou l'École du Libertinage* (1784; transl. as *The 120 Days of Sodom,* 1966); *Juliette* (1797); *Note:* See Chapter IV.

Sadeur, Jacques *see* **Foigny, Gabriel de**

Sadinet, Jean *see* **Bettencourt, Pierre**

Sadoul, Jacques (1934-); *La Passion Selon Satan (The Passion According to Satan;* Pauvert, 1960; rev. 1978); *Hier, l'An 2000 (Yesterday, 2000 AD;* non-fiction; AM, 1973; transl. as *2000 AD,* 1975); *Histoire de la Science-Fiction Moderne (History of Modern Science Fiction;* non-fiction; AM, 1973; rev. RL, 1984); *Le Jardin de la Licorne (The Garden of the Unicorn;* Pauvert, 1977); *Les Hautes Terres du Rêve (The High Country of Dreams;* Pauvert, 1979); *L'Héritage Greenwood (The Greenwood Legacy;* Pr. de la Renaissance, 1981); *La Chute de la Maison Spencer (The Fall of the House of Spencer;* Pr. de la Renaissance, 1982); *L'Inconnue de Las Vegas (The Stranger of Las Vegas;* Pr. de la Renaissance, 1982); *La Mort du Héros (Death of a Hero;* Den., 1984); *Trois Morts au Soleil (Three Deaths in the Sun;* Rocher, 1986); *La Mort et l'Astrologue (Death and the Astrologer;* Rocher, 1987); *La Cité Fabuleuse (The Fabulous City;* Rocher, 1991); *Baron Samedi* (Belfond, 1994); *Le Sang du Dragonnier (The Blood of the Dragoneer;* Belfond, 1995); *Les Sept Masques (The Seven Masks;* AM, 1996); *Une Aventure de Carol Evans (A Carol Evans Adventure;* AM, 1997); *Note:* See chapters VIII and IX. Sadoul also wrote a number of documentary works about the occult: *Le Trésor des Alchimistes (The Treasure of the Alchemists;* Publ. Premières, 1970), *L'Énigme du Zodiaque (The Enigma of the Zodiac;* Den., 1971) and *Le Grand Art de l'Alchimie (The Great Art of Alchemy;* AM, 1972).

Sadyn, Jean (1924-); *La Nuit des Mutants (The Night of the Mutants;* MarF 347, 1970); *Haute Magie (High Magic;* MOC 20, 1980); *Cosmos* (MOC 27, 1982); *Dementiapolis* (MOC 28, 1982); *Haute Magie 2 (High Magic 2;* MOC 29, 1982); *Fables et Contes Flamands (Fables and Flemish Tales;* Houtland, 1993); *Flandres Fantastiques (Fantastic Flanders;* M. Loosen, 1994); *Shylock* (Houtland, 1995); *Les Nouveaux Dieux (The New Gods;* Houtland, 1996); *L'Oeil du Monde (The Eye of the World;* Houtland, 1996); *Humour et Fantasmes Flamands (Humor and Flemish Fantasies;* Houtland, 1997); *Note:* Belgian writer. See Chapter VIII.

Sageret, Jules (1861-1943); *La Race qui Vaincra (The Race Which Will Win*; MdF, 1908); *Paradis Laïque* (MdF, 1909); *Curiosités Aquatiques (Aquatic Curiosities*; Stock, 1938); *Le Nouvel Univers (The New Universe*; Gall., 1940); *Le Monde Agrandi (The Enlarged World*; Stock, 1941); *Note:* See Chapter V.

Saint-Aubin, Horace de *see* **Balzac, Honoré de**

Saint-Cloud, Pierre de (?-?); *Le Roman de Renart (The Novel of Reynart*; c. 1175); *Note:* See Chapter I.

Sainte-Marie, Jacques (1941-); *L'Astra-1 Appelle la Terre (Astra-1 is Calling Earth*; Centre Pédagogique, 1962); *Note:* French-Canadian writer. Juvenile SF.

Saint-Exupéry, Antoine de (1900-1944); *Le Petit Prince* (Reynal & Hitchcock, 1943; transl. as the *Little Prince*, 1945); *La Citadelle (The Citadel*; Gall., 1948); *Note:* See Chapter VI.

Saint-Géours, Jean (?-); *Les Traîtres (The Traitors*; as Jean Saint-Vernon; Julliard, 1959); *Ls Visages contre la Vitre (The Faces Against the Glass*; as Jean Saint-Vernon; Julliard, 1962); *Les Morphèvres* (as Jean Saint-Vernon; Julliard, 1964); *Les Masques de Famille (The Family Masks*; as Jean Saint-Vernon; Julliard, 1967); *L'Élction de Turdigal (Turdigal's Election*; Tchou, 1979); *L'Ultime Mort de Carlo Moore (The Ultimate Death of Carlo Moore*; RL, 1984); *La Ville au Coeur (The City in the Heart*; Bourgois, 1985); *Le Taureau Masqué (The Masked Bull*; Julliard, 1988); *La Vie dans tous les Sens (Life in Every Direction*; JCL, 1994); *Laisse tes Dieux Tranquilles! (Let Your Gods in Peace!*; JCL, 1995)

Saint-Gilles *see* **Arnaud, G.-J.**

Saint-Granier (Granier de Cassagnac, Jean) (1890-); *La République des Muets (The Republic of the Dumb*; Ed. de France, 1925); *Le Monde sans Amour (The Loveless World*; with Max **Aghion**; Delpeuch, 1930); *Le Chasseur d'Étoiles (The Star Hunter*; Marchot, 1950); *Adieu Vénus (Good-Bye Venus*; Fayard, 1957)

Saint-Hamont, Daniel (1945-) *see* **Moreau, Patrick**

Saintine, Xavier-Boniface de (1798-1865); *Le Mutilé (The Mutilated Man*; Dupont, 1832); *La Mythologie du Rhin (Rhine Mythology*; Hac., 1862); *La Seconde Vie: Rêves et Rêveries, Visions et Cauchemars (The Second Life: Dreams and Daydreams, Visions and Nightmares*; Hac., 1864); *Seul! (Alone!*; Hac., 1891); *Picciola* (Hac., 1899); *Note:* See Chapter IV. Also wrote under the pseudonym of "Xavier Boniface."

Saint-Martin, Louis-Claude de (1743-1803); *L'Homme de Désir (The Man of Desire*; Behmer, 1790); *Le Nouvel Homme (The New Man*; Cercle Social, 1797); *Le Crocodile, ou La Guerre du Bien et du Mal (The Crocodile, or the War Between Good and Evil*; Libr. Cercle Social,

1799); *Le Cimetière d'Amboise (The Amboise Cemetery*; Impr. De Laran, 1801); *Le Ministère de l'Homme-Esprit (The Ministery of the Spirit-Man*; Migneret, 1802); *Note:* See chapters III and IV.

Saint-Moore, Adam (Douyau, Jacques) (1926-); *La Marche au Soleil (Walking Under the Sun*; FN, 1964); *Le Parfum du Diable (The Devil's Perfume*; FN, 1979); *Les Lois de l'Orga (The Laws of the Orga; FNA 953, 1979); Les Jours de la Montagne Bleue (The Days of the Blue Mountain*; FNA 980, 1980); *3087* (FNA 987, 1980); *La Mémoire de l'Archipel (The Memory of the Archipelago*; FNA 1014, 1980); *La Vingt-Sixième Réincarnation (The 26th Reincarnation*; FNA 1049, 1981); *La Traque d'Eté (The Summer Hunt*; FNA 1078, 1981); *L'Hérésiarque (La Quête de l'Épée) (The Heresiarch (The Quest for the Sword)*; FNA 1159, 1982); *Une Petite Fée dans la Nuit (A Little Fairy in the Night*; FN, 1982); *Les Ombres de la Mégapole (The Shadows of the Megapolis*; FNA 1300, 1984); *Les Clans de l'Étang Vert (The Clans of the Green Pond*; FNA 1368, 1985); *Note:* See chapter IX.

Saint-Ogan, Alain (1895-1974) *see* **Ducray, Camille**; *also* see Book 1, Chapters V and VI.

Saint-Romain, Michel (?-); *Les Trois Griffes (The Three Claws*; FNAG 196, 1971); *Le Monstre de mes Nuits (The Monster of My Nights*; FNAG 204, 1971); *L'Enfant Muet (The Dumb Child*; FNAG 212, 1972); *La Vénus de Mort (The Venus of Death*; FNAG 218, 1972); *Note:* See Chapter VIII.

Saint-Val, Vic *see* **Morris, Gilles**

Saint-Vernon, Jean *see* **Saint-Géours, Jean**

Saint-Vincent, Vincent *see* **Renard, Maurice**

Saint-Yves, Claude (?-); *Les Mystérieuses Cités des Sables (The Mysterious Cities of the Sands*; BGA, 1930); *Le Marabout des Atlantes (The Priest of Atlantis*; BGA, 1932); *Rivales (Rivals*; Ferenczi, 1937); *Vengée! (Avenged!*; Ferenczi, 1938); *L'Amoureuse Masquée (The Masked Lover*; Ferenczi, 1939); *Le Signe de Lilith (The Mark of Lilith*; RL, 1947); *Les Aventures du Dernier Atlante (The Adventures of the Last Atlantean*; Bonne Presse, 1950); *La Fiancée du Dernier Atlante (The Fiancee of the Last Atlantean*; Bonne Presse, 1953); *Note:* See chapters VII and IX.

Salardenne, Roger (?-); *L'Île aux Femmes Nues (The Island of Naked Women*; Coll. Gauloise, 1927); *L'Aiguille d'Aphrodite (Aphrodite's Needle*; Coll. Gauloise, 1928); *Les Yeux qui Meurent (The Dying Eyes*; Ferenczi, 1928); *La Sphère Mystérieuse (The Mysterious Sphere*; BGA, 1929); *Le Disparu de la Huche à Pain (The Bread Basket Vanishings*; SPE, 1945)

Salaün-Ar-Fol (?-); *Le Festin des Dieux (The Feast of the Gods*; Camédu, 1993); *Note:* French-Canadian writer.

Salle, Antoine de la (?-?); *Le Paradis de la Reine Sybille (Queen Sybil's Paradise*; c. 1200); *Note:* See Chapter I.

Sallenave, Danièle (1940-); *Passage de Ruines avec Personnages (Passage Through the Ruins with Some Characters*; Flamm., 1975); *Les Portes de Gubbis (The Gates of Gubbis*; Hac., 1980); *Un Printemps Froid (A Cold Spring*; POL, 1983); *La Vie Fantôme (The Ghost Life*; POL, 1986); *Adieu (Good-Bye*; POL, 1987); *Le Principe de Ruine (The Ruin Principle*; Gall., 1994); *Les Trois Minutes du Diable (The Devil's Three Minutes*; Gall., 1994); *Note:* See Chapter VIII.

Salomon, Fernand (?-?) *see* **Grand-Guignol**

Salva, Pierre (1917-); *Les Mercenaires de l'Enfer (Mercenaries of Hell*; Scorpion, 1954); *Les Sauvages (The Savages*; Scorpion, 1960); *Quinze Heures pour Sauver Paris (15 Hours to Save Paris*; PC, 1969); *Le Diable dans la Tête (The Devil in the Head*; Den., 1970); *Quatre Jours en Enfer (Four Days in Hell*; Den., 1970); *L'Enfer les attend (Hell Awaits Them*; Den., 1971); *Je suis un pauvre Diable (I Am a Poor Devil*; Den., 1971); *La Fille du Lac au Diable (The Girl of Devil's Lake*; Den., 1972); *Les Griffes du Diable (The Devil's Clutches*; Den., 1973); *La Main à Couper (To Cut Off One's Hand*; Den., 1974); *Le Mammouth a la Peau Dure (The Mastodon Has a Tough Skin*; Eurédif, 1974); *Le Diable dans la Sacristie (The Devil in the Chapel*; Libr. Champs-Élysées, 1975); *Pas de Crédit avec le Diable (No Credit for the Devil*; Den., 1976); *Tous les Chiens de l'Enfer (All the Dogs of Hell*; Libr. Champs-Élysées, 1976); *Le Trou du Diable (The Devil's Hole*; Libr. Champs-Élysées, 1977); *Le Diable me guette (The Devil Is Watching Me*; Libr. Champs-Élysées, 1978); *Qui est le Diable? (Who Is the Devil?*; Libr. Champs-Élysées, 1978); *Des Clients pour l'Enfer (Clients for Hell*; Libr. Champs-Élysées, 1979); *Le Sourire du Diable (The Devil's Smile*; Libr. Champs-Élysées, 1979); *Le Diable est Mort (The Devil Is Dead*; Libr. Champs-Élysées, 1980); *Le Souper avec le Diable (The Supper with the Devil*; Den., 1980); *Mes Trois Nuits Infernales (My Three Hellish Nights*; Libr. Champs-Élysées, 1980); *Le Hideux Visage du Diable (The Devil's Hideous Face*; Libr. Champs-Élysées, 1981); *La Danse avec le Diable (The Dance with the Devil*; Libr. Champs-Élysées, 1981); *La Trinité du Diable (The Devil's Trinity*; Libr. Champs-Élysées, 1981); *Les Vieilles Dames vont en Enfer (Old Women Go to Hell*; Libr. Champs-Élysées, 1981); *L'Enfer derrière la Porte (Hell Behind the Door*; Libr. Champs-Élysées, 1982); *Sardines à la Sauce Diable (Sardines with Devil's Sauce*; Libr. Champs-Élysées, 1982); *Le Diable et son Train Électrique (The Devil and His Electric Train*; Libr. Champs-Élysées, 1983); *Quand le Diable ricane (When the Devil Laughs*; Libr. Champs-Élysées, 1984); *Le Diable au Paradis Perdu (The Devil in the Paradise Lost*; Libr. Champs-Élysées, 1986)

Salverte, Anne Joseph Eusèbe Baconnière (?-?); *Essai sur la Magie, les Prodiges et les Miracles (Essay on Magic, Prodigies and Miracles*; Sédillot, 1829)

Samat, Jean-Toussain (1871-1944); *Sangar, Taureau (Sangar, Bull*; Ren. du Livre, 1923); *Cartacalha la Grue (Ferenczi, 1926); *Razava, la Fille qui aimait jouer avec les Hommes Forts (Razava, the Girl Who Liked to Play with Strong Men*; Fasquelle, 1929); *Les Trois ou Mac Allan—Trois Acrobates à Transformations (The Three or Mac Allan—Three Transforming Acrobats*; Arlequin, 1932); *Les Vaisseaux en Flammes (The Ships on Fire*; LPT/Hac., 1933); *L'Amiral des Vaisseaux Morts (The Admiral of Dead Ships*; Baudinière, 1935); *Le Mystère du Mas des Rièges (The Mystery of Rieges House*; Baudinière, 1935); *L'Espionne au Corps de Bronze (The Spy with a Brass Body*; Baudinière, 1937); *La Mort trop tôt (Death Too Soon*; Baudinière, 1937); *Le Mage de l'Hippodrome (The Magus of the Racetrack*; Agence Paris. Distrib., 1938); *La Mort à la Fenêtre (Death at the Window*; Agence Paris. Distrib., 1938); *L'Éléphant de Poche (The Pocket Elephant*; Loisirs, 1939); *Mangamah, la Fille aux Yeux Bleus (Mangamah, the Girl with Blue Eyes*; Ren. du Livre, 1943)

Samivel (1907-1992); *Samovar et Baculot dans Parade de Diplodocus (Samovar and Baculot in Diplodocus Parade*; Hartmann, 1934); *Les Blagueurs de Bagdad (The Jokers of Baghdad*; Hartmann, 1935); *La Grande Nuit de Merlin (Merlin's Great Night*; Imprimerie Artistique, Lyon, 1943); *Ayorpok et Ayounghila, Conte Eskimo (Imprimerie Artistique, 1950)

Sanciaume, Joseph Louis (1903-1976); *L'Astre Pourpre (The Purple Star*; Baudinière, 1934); *Fortune Maudie (Accursed Fortune*; Baudinière, 1936); *Le Spectre Bleu (The Blue Spectre*; Baudinière, 1937); *L'Ombre dans les Flammes (The Shadow in the Flames*; Dupuis, 1938); *La Mort aux Mains Blanches (Death with White Hands*; Dupuis, 1939); *La Fugitive (The Fugitive*; Chantal, 1944); *Le Mystère des Serpentes (The Mystery of the Serpentes*; La Bruyère, 1946)

Sand, George (Dupin, Aurore) (1804-1876); *Mauprat (Bonnaire, 1837); *Consuelo (L. de Potter, 1842); *La Contesse de Rudolstadt (The Countess of Rudolstadt*; L. de Potter, 1844); *La Mare au Diable (The Devil's Pond*; Desessart, 1846); *Le Château des Déserts (The Caste of Deserts*; Lévy, 1851); *Les Maîtres Sonneurs (The Master Ringers*; Libr. Nouvelle, 1857); *Légendes Rustiques (Country Legends*; Calmann-Lévy, 1858); *La Nuit de Noël (Christmas Night*; 1863); *Laura ou le Voyage dans* *le Cristal (Laura or the Voyage Inside the Crystal*; Lévy, 1865); *Contes d'une Grand-Mère (Tales of a Grandmother*; Calmann-Lévy, 1872); *Le Géant Yeous (Yeous the Giant*; Lévy, 1873); *Le Château de Pictordu (The Castle of Pictordu*; Lévy, 1873); *La Reine Coax (Queen Coax*; Lévy, 1873); *Le Marteau Rouge (The Red Hammer*; Lévy, 1876); *La Ville Noire (The Black City*; Calmann-Lévy, 1882); *Le Chêne Parlant (The Talking Oak*; Nelson, 1933); *Note:* See Chapters IV and V.

Sandkühler, Conrad (?-) *see Contes et Légendes*

Sandoz, Maurice Yves (1892-); *Souvenirs Fantastiques et Trois Histoires Bizarres (Fantastic Remembances and Three Bizarre Tales*; Payot, 1941); *La Maison sans Fenêtres (The Windowless House*; Payot, 1943); *Le Labyrinthe* (Mermod, 1949); *La Limite (The Limit*; TR, 1951); *La Salière de Cristal (The Crystal Salt Shaker*; TR, 1952); *Contes Suisses (Swiss Tales*; Miroirs Partagés, 1956); *Note:* Swiss writer. Both *La Maison* and *Le Labyrinthe* were illustrated by Salvador Dali.

Sandre, Yves (1913-); *Le Dévorant (The Devurer*; Cast., 1980); *Terremoto (Motorearth*; Cast., 1984); *L'Enfant de Cristal (The Crystal Child*; Cast., 1990); *Note:* Juveniles.

Sandy, Isabelle (Xardel, Isabelle) (1866-1938); *La Descente de Croix (The Descent from the Cross*; Plon, 1920); *Dans la Ronde des Faunes (In the Dance of the Fauns*; Delalain, 1921); *L'Heure Folle (The Mad Hour*; Plon, 1922); *Andorra ou Les Hommes d'Airain (Andorra, or the Men of Brass*; Plon, 1923); *L'Homme et la Sauvageonne (The Man and the Wild Girl*; Plon, 1925); *Llivia ou Les Coeurs Tragiques (Llivia, or the Tragic Hearts*; Plon, 1926); *La Ronde Invisible (The Invisible Dance*; Vraie France, 1927); *Les Soutanes Vertes (The Green Cassocks*; Plon, 1927); *Le Dieu Noir (The Black God*; Plon, 1929); *Kaali, La Déesse de l'Amour et de la Mort (Kaali, Goddess of Love and Death*; Spès, 1930); *La Vierge au Collier (The Virgin with a Necklace*; Fasquelle, 1931); *Un Homme à la Mer (Man Overboard*; Fasquelle, 1932); *L'Homme qui Fabriquait de l'Or (The Man Who Made Gold*; Madeleine, 1932); *La Soutane Sanglante (The Bloody Cassock*; Plon, 1935); *La Petite Fille au Fantôme (The Little Girl and the Ghost*; Petit Écho de la Mode, 1936); *Quand les Loups ont Faim (When Wolves Hunger*; Tallandier, 1937); *Le Serpent autour du Monde (The Snake Around the World*; Bloud & Gay, 1938); *L'Enchantement (The Spell*; Cahiers d'Art & d'Amitié, 1938); *La Dactylo Masquée (The Masked Typist*; Tallandier, 1939)

Sanschagrin, Joceline (1950-); *Atterrissage Forcé (Forced Landing*; Courte Échelle, 1987); *La Fille aux Cheveux Rouges (The Girl with Red Hair*; Courte Échelle, 1989); *Le Karatéka* (Courte Échelle, 1990); *Mission Auda-*

cieuse (Daring Mission; Courte Échelle, 1991); *Note:* French-Canadian writer. a series of novels about the adventures of a super-powered girl named Wondeur in a strange, fantasy universe.

Santelli, César (1889-1971); *La Mystérieuse Aventure (The Mysterious Adventure*; Grasset, 1928); *Le Pain Mal Partagé (The Bread Ill Shared*; Portiques, 1932); *L'Escabeau Volant (The Flying Ladder*; Bourrelier, 1935); *Le Secret de l'Oiseau de Feu (The Secret of the Firebird*; Nathan, 1938); *Chacun son Mensonge (To Each His Lie*; Scorpion, 1959)

Santini, Gilles (?-); *Morte Chair (Dead Flesh*; FNG 101, 1989); *Éventrations (Disembowelings*; VG, 1990); *Miasmes de Mort (Death Miasma*; Florent Massot, 1996); *Note:* See Chapter VIII.

Sanvoisin, Éric (1962-); *Les Fées (The Fairies*; Hac., 1991); *Jalouve* (Nathan, 1995); *Bizarre le Bizarre* (Nathan, 1996); *Le Nain et la Petite Crevette (The Dwarf and the Little Shrimp*; Nathan, 1997); *Les Chasseurs d'Ombre (The Shadow Hunters*; Magnard, 1997); *Note:* Juvenile fantasy. See Chapter VIII.

Sarawak, Jean (?-); *Les Nouveaux Barbares (The New Barbarians*; Athanor, 1977)

Sarcus, Pierre de (?-); *La Ville Souterraine (The Underground City*; Fleurus, 1957)

Sardanti, Reg (?-); *Cadavres Laqués Sévices Gratuits* (FNG 94, 1989); *Kali-Yuga Le Relief de la Mort* (FNG 111, 1990)

Sardou, Victorien (1831-1908); *Les Diables Noirs (The Black Devils*; Lévy, 1864); *Les Ondines au Champagne (Champagne Ondines*; Dentu, 1865); *La Sorcière (The Witch*; 13 rue St. Georges, 1904); *Carlin* (Mouly, 1932)

Sarkel, François (Laselle, Jean-Pol) (1946-); *Dépression* (FNA 1745, 1990); *La Chair sous les Ongles (The Flesh Under the Nails*; FNG 116, 1990); *Silence Rouge (Red Silence*; FN Angoisses 7, 1993); *La Vallée Truquée (The Valley of Tricks*; FNAV 3, 1995); *Les Chasseurs de Chimères (The Hunters of Chimeras*; FNAV6, 1995); *Note:* See Chapter VIII. Under the pseudonym of "Brice Tarvel," François Sarkel is also the writer of the graphic novel series *Mortepierre* and *Sylve* (see Book 1, Chapter V).

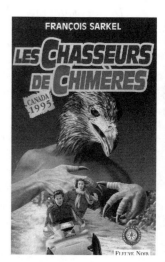

Sarrazin, Claude-Gérard (1936-); *Phosphores* (Guérin, 1978); *La Porte des Dieux (The Gateway of the Gods*; Presses Sélect, 1980); *Le Retour des Atlantes (The Return of the Atlanteans*; Courteau, 1984); *Note:* French-Canadian writer born in Algiers. Esoteric novels.

Sarrel, Urbain (?-); *Orgies Spatiales (Space Orgies*; GdV, 1990); *Note:* Erotic SF.

Sartène, Jean (?-?) *see* **Grand-Guignol**

Sarthoulet, Guy (?-); *Explosive! New York* (Simoën, 1977); *La Voie Tantrique (The Tantric Way*; Courrier du Livre, 1988)

Sauerwein, Christian (?-); *Incarnata, Histoire Étrange (Incarnata, a Strange Story*; AM, 1947)

Saunier, Marc (?-); *Au-Delà du Capricorne (Beyond Capricorn*; Sansot, 1914); *Fiancé à une Invisible (Engaged to an Invisible*; Sansot, 1925)

Saurat, Denis (1890-?); *La Mort et le Rêveur (Death and the Dreamer*; Vieux Colombier, 1947); *L'Expérience de l'Au-Delà (The Experience of Beyond*; Vieux Colombier, 1951); *L'Atlantide et le Règne des Géants (Atlantis and the Reign of Giants*; Den., 1954); *Note:* See Chapter VIII.

Saurel (de Cabrières), Pierre (Daignault, Pierre) (1925-); Series *Les Aventures Étranges de l'Agent Ixe-13, l'As des Espions Canadiens (The Strange Adventures of Agent X-13, the Ace of Canadian Spies)*: 1st Series: *1. Le Repaire de la Mort (The Lair of Death*; 1947); *2. La Tigresse (The Tigress*; 1947); *3. Aux Mains de la Gestapo (In the Hands of the Gestapo*; 1947); *4. L'Évasion du Dr. Woodbrock (The Escape of Dr. Woodbrock*; 1948); *5. Le Mystérieux Fauteuil No. 24 (The Mysterious Seat No. 24*; 1948); *6. Le Secret du Coffre-Fort (The Secret of the Safe*; 1948); *7. Un Piège (A Trap*; 1948); *8. Une Nuit en Italie (A Night in Italy*; 1948); *9. La Disparition de T-4 (The Disappearance of T-4*; 1948); *10. Au Secours de Madame Cornu (To Rescue Mrs. Cornu*; 1948); *11. En Mission au Maroc (Mission to Morocco*; 1948); 2nd Series: *1. L'Homme à la Cagoule (The Hooded Man*; 1948); *2. Le Silence de la Mort (The Silence of Death*; 1948); *3. Prisonnier des Jaunes (Prisoner of the Asians*; 1948); *4. Aventures au Pôle Nord (Adventures at the North Pole*; 1948); *5. La Chasse aux Espions (Spy Hunt*; 1948); *6. Dans l'Océan Atlantique (Under the Atlantic Ocean*; 1948); *7. L'Étrange Monsieur Villiers (The Strange Mr. Villiers*; 1948); *8. Fiancée en Péril (Fiancée in Danger*; 1948); *9. Le Sosie d'Herman Roterberg (Herman Roterberg's Lookalike*; 1948); *10. L'Invention du Père Flonko (Father Flonko's Invention*; 1948); *11. Cent contre Un (Hundred to One*; 1948); *12. L'Homme sans Nom (The Nameless Man*; 1948); *13. La Revanche d'Ixe-13 (The Revenge of X-13*; 1948); *14. L'Étrangleur*

(The Strangler; 1948); *15. Le Bourreau Japonais (The Japanese Executioner*; 1948); *16. Dans la Gueule du Loup (In the Wolf's Jaws*; 1948); *17. Le Mariage d'Ixe-13 (The Wedding of X-13*; 1948); *18. Horreurs Nazies (Nazi Horrors*; 1948); *19. Le Saboteur* (1948); *20. Le Mystère de la Femme Blonde (The Mystery of the Blonde Woman*; 1949); *21. Le Piège de Hans Loberg (Hans Loberg's Trap*; 1949); *22. Le Dictateur de Valparaiso (The Dictator of Valparaiso*; 1949); *23. Mystification (Mystified*; 1949); *24. À la Recherche de Sing Lee (Looking for Sing Lee*; 1949); *25. Le Fauteuil de Malheur (The Unlucky Seat*; 1949); *26. Sir George Assassiné (The Assassination of Sir George*; 1949); *27. Le Secret de la Bombe (The Secret of the Bomb*; 1949); *28. La Maison Numéro 13 (House No. 13*; 1949); *29. Le Rayon de la Mort (The Death Ray*; 1949); *30. La Lentille qui Tue (The Killing Lens*; 1949); *31. La Fille-Gas (The Gas-Girl*; 1949); *32. Jany, Voleuse d'Espion (Jany the Spy Thief*; 1949); *33. La Guerre des Enfants (The War of the Children*; 1949); *34. L'Espion-Quêteux (The Beggar Spy*; 1949); *35. Le Faux Coiffeur (The Phony Hairdresser*; 1949); *36. La Trappe Électrique (The Electric Trapdoor*; 1949); *37. La Bande Noire (The Black Band*; 1949); *38. L'Homme au Bras Coupé (The Man with the Severed Arm*; 1949); *39. L'Aéroport Invisible (The Invisible Airport*; 1949); *40. Le Yacht de la Mort (The Yacht of Death*; 1949); *41. Le Portrait d'un Fou (The Portrait of a Madman*; 1949); *42. Nazis à Ottawa (Nazis in Ottawa*; 1949); *43. Prisonniers sous l'Eau (Prisoners Under Water*; 1949); *44. Les Îles Traîtresses (The Traitor Islands*; 1949); *45. La Guerre des Yeux (The War of the Eyes*; 1949); *46. La Danse du Feu (The Dance of Fire*; 1949); *47. La Reine de l'Hypnotisme (The Queen of Hypnotism*; 1949); *48. Le Chien qui Vole (The Flying Dog*; 1949); *49. Le Gas de l'Épouvante (The Terror Gas*; 1949); *50. L'Espion du 1er Janvier (The Spy of January 1st.*; 1949); *51. La Beauté du Diable (The Devil's Beauty*; 1950); *52. Le Pauvre aux Deux Visages (The Pauper with Two Faces*; 1950); *53. L'Asile sans Fous (The Asylum Without Lunatics*; 1950); *54. L'Espion H-87 (Spy H-87*; 1950); *55. Les Morts Ambulants (The Walking Dead*; 1950); *56. Le Vol du Collier de Perles (The Stealing of the Pearl Necklace*; 1950); *57. La Bande des Capuchons (The Gang of the Hooded Men*; 1950); *58. L'Île Fantôme (The Phantom Island*; 1950); *59. Le Plafond qui Tue (The Murderous Ceiling*; 1950); *60. Caresses d'Espionne (Caresses of a Female Spy*; 1950); *61. Le Nègre Bali (Bali the Negro*; 1950); *62. Double Espionne (Double Spy*; 1950); *63. Susan, la Menteuse (Susan the Liar*; 1950); *64. La Croix de Sang (The Cross of Blood*; 1950); *65. Le Retour de l'Étrangleur (The Return of the Strangler*; 1950); *66. La Swastika Fatidique (The Fateful Swastika*; 1950); *67. Complot Jaune (Yellow Plot*; 1950); *68. Monsieur Unknown* (1950); *69. L'Écriture Secrète (The Secret*

Writing; 1950); *70. Pincés (Caught*; 1950); *71. Le Châtiment d'un Traître (The Punishment of a Traitor*; 1950); *72. Sir Arthur, Domestique (Sir Arthur, Domestic*; 1950); *73. Les Deux Ixe-13 (The Two X-13s*; 1950); *74. La Jalouse Espionne (The Jealous Female Spy*; 1950); *75. Les Bombes Volantes (The Flying Bombs*; 1950); *76. L'Enlèvement d'Ixe-13 (The Kidnapping of X-13*; 1950); *77. Chambre 28 (Room 28*; 1950); *78. Prisonnier au Japon (Prisoner in Japan*; 1950); *79. La Nouvelle Recrue (The New Recruit*; 1950); *80. Toute une Femme (A Whole Woman*; 1950); *81. Le Livre Rouge (The Red Book*; 1950); *82. La Fatale Distraction (The Fatal Distraction*; 1950); *83. La Cave de la Mort (The Cave of Death*; 1950); *84. La Bombe Atomique (The Atom Bomb*; 1950); *85. L'Espion A-1 (The A-1 Spy*; 1950); *96. Le Tibet Noir (Black Tibet*; 1950); *87. L'Impossible Évasion (The Impossible Escape*; 1950); *88. L'Inconcevable Piège (The Inconceivable Trap*; 1950); *89. L'Oeil de Vitre (The Glass Eye*; 1950); *90. Le Cas 18 (Case 18*; 1950); *91. La Guerre des Narcotiques (The War of the Narcotics*; 1950); *92. Rosita, l'Intrigante (Rosita the Schemer*; 1950); *93. Seul! (Alone!*; 1950); *94. La Main Jaune (The Yellow Hand*; 1950); *95. Un Pas, Un Mort (One Step, One Dead*; 1950); *96. L'Étranger du Mexique (A Stranger in Mexico*; 1950); *97. Mission Suicide (Suicide Mission*; 1950); *98. La Dôpe fait parler (Drugs Make You Talk*; 1950); *99. Monsieur Canada* (1950); *100. Le Traîneau Noir (The Black Sled*; 1950); *101. Prisonnier en Vacances (Prisoner on Holidays*; 1950); *102. Le Faux Départ (The False Departure*; 1950); *103. Le Voyage de la Mort (The Journey of Death*; 1951); *104. Manouk, le Mystérieux (Manook the Mysterious*; 1951); *105. La Mort de Francine (Francine's Death*; 1951); *106. Le Roi du Maquillage (The King of Make-Up*; 1951); *107. Sir Arthur Enlevé (Sir Arthur Kidnapped*; 1951); *108. Le Retour de Rosita (The Return of Rosita*; 1951); *109. Ixe-13 fait rire de lui (X-13 Makes People Laugh*; 1951); *110. Musée d'Espions (Spy Museum*; 1951); *111. Au Milieu des Jaunes (Among the Asians*; 1951); *112. Le Baiser de la Mort (The Kiss of Death*; 1951); *113. Les Dépouilleurs de Cadavres (The Grave Robbers*; 1951); *114. Le Mari de Gisèle (Gisele's Husband*; 1951); *115. Le Prêtre Espion (The Spy Priest*; 1951); *116. La Plus Belle Victoire (The Most Beautiful Victory*; 1951); *117. Le Jumeau d'Ixe-13 (X-13's Twin*; 1951); *118. La Vipère (The Viper*; 1951); *119. L'Atroce Supplice (The Awful Torture*; 1951); *120. À la Recherche de Von Tracht (Looking for Von Tracht*; 1951); *121. Document H-34* (1951); *122. Lili, la Dôpée (Lili the Drug Addict*; 1951); *123. Sus à Hitler (To Attack Hitler*; 1951); *124. Mariage d'un Mourant (A Dying Man's Wedding*; 1951); *125. La Caverne des Laurentides (The Cavern of Laurentides*; 1951); *126. L'Ombre de Gisèle (The Shadow of Gisele*; 1951); *127. L'Île des 22 Morts (The Island of the 22 Dead Men*; 1951); *128. Gisèle Revient (Gisele Returns*; 1951); *129.*

Josette, l'Espionne (Josette the Spy; 1951); *130. Les Cadavres Décapités (The Beheaded Corpses*; 1951); *131. Von Tracht et Bouritz s'évadent (Von Tract and Bouritz Escape*; 1951); *132. La Bombe Diabolique (The Diabolical Bomb*; 1951); *133. Le Rapt de Gisèle (The Kidnapping of Gisele*; 1951); *134. Ixe-13 Infirme (X-13 Disabled*; 1951); *135. La Négresse Arkia (Arkia the Black Woman*; 1951); *136. L'École Rouge (The Red School*; 1951); *137. L'Invention d'un Fou (A Madman's Invention*; 1951); *138. Espions Communistes (Communist Spies*; 1951); *139. Le Train de la Mort (The Death Train*; 1951); *140. Derrière le Rideau de Fer (Behind the Iron Curtain*; 1951); *141. Caresses Communistes (Communist Caresses*; 1951); *142. Ixe-13, Espion Russe (X-13, Russian Spy*; 1951); *143. La Trahison de Nadia (Nadia's Betrayal*; 1951); *144. L'Homme au Sou Percé (The Man with the Pierced Coin*; 1951); *145. La Machine à Tuer (The Killing Machine*; 1951); *146. Ixe-13 en Corée (X-13 in Korea*; 1951); *147. Taya, l'Espionne Communiste (Taya, Communist Spy*; 1951); *148. La Danseuse du Red Bird (The Dancing Girl of the Red Bird*; 1951); *149. Boiron Assassiné (Boiron Murdered*; 1951); *150. Jane, la Mystérieuse (Jane the Mysterious*; 1951); *151. Erre-19* (1951); *152. La Boule de Verre (The Glass Ball*; 1951); *153. Amour ou Devoir (Love or Duty*; 1951); *154. Fini pour Toujours (Forever Ended*; 1952); *155. Taya se venge (Taya's Revenge*; 1952); *156. Adoujah, l'Hypnotiseur (Adoujah the Hypnotist*; 1952); *157. Le Singe Vert (The Green Monkey*; 1952); *158. La Montre Mystérieuse (The Mysterious Watch*; 1952); *159. Le Mardi-Gras Tragique (Tragic Mardi-Gras*; 1952); *160. Le Secret de la Princesse (The Princess' Secret*; 1952); *161. L'Épouse du Traître (The Traitor's Wife*; 1952); *162. La Maison des Inventions (The House of Inventions*; 1952); *163. La Guerre aux Ours (The Bear Wars*; 1952); *164. La Pluie Magique (The Magic Rain*; 1952); *165. Le Document Introuvable (The Unfindable Document*; 1952); *166. Les Monstres Marins (The Sea Monsters*; 1952); *167. Herman, le Peureux (Herman the Fearful*; 1952); *168. Len Shu, le Traître (Len Shu the Traitor*; 1952); *169. Les Deux Capitaines Grant (The Two Captain Grants*; 1952); *170. Gisèle Tuboeuf Revient (Gisele Tuboeuf Returns*; 1952); *171. Le Cigare Mystérieux (The Mysterious Cigar*; 1952); *172. L'Invention Diabolique (The Diabolical Invention*; 1952); *173. Au Secours de Jane (To Rescue Jane*; 1952); *174. Le Cousin de Marius (Marius' Cousin*; 1952); *175. Mission-Suicide en Corée (Suicide Mission in Korea*; 1952); *176. Le Déserteur (The Deserter*; 1952); *177. La Déesse Égyptienne (The Egyptian Goddess*; 1952); *178. Le Supplice de la Goutte d'Eau (The Water Torture*; 1952); *179. Traître ou Prisonnier? (Traitor or Prisoner?*; 1952); *180. Marius, l'Assassin (Marius the Killer*; 1952); *181. Lana, l'Enjôleuse (Lana the Charmer*; 1952); *182. Taya s'évade (Taya Escapes*; 1952); *183. Au Milieu des Fous (Among Mad-*

men; 1952); *184. Le Mystérieux Niki (The Mysterious Niki;* 1952); *185. Marlov, Roi des Espions Russes (Marlov King of the Russian Spies;* 1952); *186. Le Composé Z (Compound Z;* 1952); *187. Marius devient Lutteur (Marius Becomes a Wrestler;* 1952); *188. La Soeur de Roxanne (Roxanna's Sister;* 1952); *189. Ixe-13 Amoureux de Taya (X-13 in Love with Taya;* 1952); *190. Les Saboteurs de Craigville (The Craigville Saboteurs;* 1952); *191. Meurtre chez les Esquimaux (Murders Among the Eskimoos;* 1952); *192. Roxanne, Espionne Communiste (Roxanna, Communist Spy;* 1952); *193. Michel ou Gilbert? (Michel or Gilbert?;* 1952); *194. L'École des Espions (The Spy School;* 1952); *195. La Fête-Surprise (The Surprise Party;* 1952); *196. Pensionnaires Dangereux (Dangerous Guests;* 1952); *197. Les Deux Majors de la Mort (The Two Deadly Majors;* 1952); *198. Hitler Vivant? (Hitler Alive?;* 1952); *199. L'Homme au Bras Tatoué (The Man with the Tattooed Arm;* 1952); *200. Nitchka, Beauté Ruse (Nitchka, Russian Beauty;* 1952); *201. L'Enlèvement de la Russe (The Kidnapping of the Russian Woman;* 1952); *202. Le Spécialiste Allemand (The German Specialist;* 1952); *203. Le Cigare qui ne fume pas (The Cigar That Didn't Burn;* 1952); *204. L'Étoile Noire (The Black Star;* 1952); *205. L'Assassinat de Minuit (The Midnight Assassination;* 1952); *206. Un Défi (A Challenge;* 1952); *207. Le Bossu Prisonnier (The Hunchback Prisoner;* 1953); *208. Évasion (Escape;* 1953); *209. L'Oeil de Vitre (The Glass Eye;* 1953); *210. L'Assassinat de l'Oncle Birdens (The Murder of Uncle Birdens;* 1953); *211. Le Mort qui Vit Toujours (The Deadman Who Is Still Alive;* 1953); *212. Sans Espoir (Without Hope;* 1953); *213. Amour et Trahison (Love and Betrayal;* 1953); *214. La Prochaine Victime (The Next Victim;* 1953); *215. Les Prisonniers de Corée (The Prisoners of Korea;* 1953); *216. Un Ixe-13 de trop (One X-13 Too Many;* 1953); *217. Face au Danger (Face-To-Face with Danger;* 1953); *218. Saboteurs à Vancouver (Saboteurs in Vancouver;* 1953); *219. Les Assassins de la Montagne (The Mountain Assassins;* 1953); *220. Le Château de la Mort (The Castle of Death;* 1953); *221. La Mystérieuse Madame Bohen (The Mysterious Mrs. Bohen;* 1953); *222. Il faut assassiner Marius (We Must Kill Marius;* 1953); *223. Le Dentiste Japonais (The Japanese Dentist;* 1953); *224. La Conversion de Taya (Taya's Conversion;* 1953); *225. Roxanne, la Danseuse (Roxanna the Dancer;* 1953); *226. Prisonniers sous la Terre (Prisoners Underground;* 1953); *227. L'Enlèvement du Général Barkley (The Kidnapping of General Barkley;* 1953)* (Nos. 228 to 274 were skipped by the publisher.) *275. Captifs en Sibérie (Prisoners in Siberia;* 1953); *276. Destination: Outre-Tombe (Destination: Beyond the Grave;* 1953); *277. La Guerre aux Honneurs (War with Honors;* 1953); *278. on a Rasé le Cadavre (They Shaved the Corpse;* 1953); *279. Le Savant à la Mémoire Courte (The Scientist with a Short Memory;* 1953); *280. La Reine des Rouges (The Queen of the Reds;* 1953); *281. Le Journaliste Espion (The Spy Journalist;* 1953); *282. Heures d'Angoisse sur l'Océan (Hours of Terror on the Ocean;* 1953); *283. Les Cadavres aux Mains Coupées (The Corpse with Severed Hands;* 1953); *284. Les Fabricants d'Argent (The Money Makers;* 1953); *285. L'Assassin Amnésique (The Amnesiac Assassin;* 1953); *286. Cadavre sans Tête (Headless Corpse;* 1953); *287. Roxanne Disparaît (Roxanna Vanishes;* 1953); *288. Ixe-13 chez les Russes (X-13 in Russia;* 1953); *289. L'Artiste-Espionne (The Female Artist Spy;* 1953); *290. Madame Watson se venge (Mrs. Watson's Revenge;* 1953); *291. L'École du Vice (The School of Vice;* 1953); *292. La Revanche des Communistes (The Communists' Revenge;* 1953); *293. Les Nègres Agresseurs (The Aggressor Negroes;* 1953); *294. La Femme-Fantôme (The Ghost-Woman;* 1953); *295. La Guerre de la Faim (The War of Hunger;* 1953); *296. Fuite vers Berlin (Flight to Berlin;* 1953); *297. Les Deux Frères Lokampf (The Two Lokampf Brothers;* 1953); *298. Les Pirates de la Mer (The Sea Pirates;* 1953); *299. Qui est le Numéro 1? (Who Is Number 1?;* 1953); *300. Le Manchot du 3ème Wagon (The One-Armed Man of the Third Railcar;* 1953); *301. La Voix Voilée (The Veiled Voice;* 1953); *302. Le Traître Chinois (The Chinese Traitor;* 1953); *303. Linwa, la Petite Chinoise (Linwa the Little Chinese;* 1953); *304. L'Affaire Cati Bayo (The Cati Bayo Case;* 1953); *305. La Secrétaire de l'Avocat Crémard (The Secretary of the Attorney Cremard;* 1953); *306. L'Amant de Marlène (Marlene's Lover;* 1954); *307. La Garce Espionne (The Spying Bitch;* 1954); *308. Trop Parler Nuit (Too Much Talk Is Bad;* 1954); *309. Le Gaz du Sommeil (The Sleeping Gas;* 1954); *310. À Mort, Ixe-13! (To Kill X-13!;* 1954); *311. Échec à Paris (Checkmate in Paris;* 1954); *312. L'Engin de Mort (The Engine of Death;* 1954); *313. Le Rapt Violent (The Violent Kidnapping;* 1954); *314. La Cave aux Rouges (The Reds' Cave;* 1954); *315. Le Supplice du Feu (The Torture By Fire;* 1954); *316. Marius Lamouche, Bigame (Marius Lamouche Bigamist;* 1954); *317. Le Bourreau du Camp 18 (The Executioner of Camp 18;* 1954); *318. La Serviette de Cuir (The Leather Briefcase;* 1954); *319. Les Saboteurs (*1954); *320. Agents Secrets en Chine (Secret Agents in China;* 1954); *321. La Photo du Scandale (The Scandalous Photo;* 1954); *322. Les Avions Fantômes (The Ghost Planes;* 1954); *323. L'Allemand Communiste (The German Communist;* 1954); *324. L'Araignée (The Spider;* 1954); *325. Le Secret de l'Horloge (The Secret of the Clock;* 1954); *326. Poignardé Deux Fois (Stabbed Twice;* 1954); *327. Mission au Mexique (Mission in Mexico;* 1954); *328. Complot à la Cabane (Plot in the Cabin;* 1954); *329. Une Morte chez la Voisine (A Dead Woman at My Neighbor's;* 1954); *330. Mission Sanglante (Bloody Mission;* 1954); *331. Le Cercueil Vide (The Empty Coffin;* 1954);*

*332. Mission à Hollywood (Mission in Hollywood;
1954); 333. Espion au Service Secret (Spy in the Secret
Service; 1954); 334. Chasse au Coffret (The Hunt for the
Box; 1954); 335. L'Épinglette d'Etta Hotzel (Etta
Hotzel's Pin; 1954); 336. La Folle de Berlin (The Mad-
woman of Berlin; 1954); 337. La Caisse de Bois (The
Wodden Crate; 1954); 338. Escapade à l'Hospice (Es-
cape at the Rest Home; 1954); 339. Le Papier Chiffré
(The Cyphered Paper; 1954); 340. Le Tube Noir (The
Black Tube; 1954); 341. La Garce et l'Hypnose (The
Bitch and Hypnosis; 1954); 342. La Moustache Noire
(The Black Mustache; 1954); 343. La Bombe D (The D
Bomb; 1954); 344. La Rage (1954); 345. Les Yeux Noirs
(The Black Eyes; 1954); 346. L'Espion Boxeur (The Box-
ing Spy; 1954); 347. Don Juan d'Hollywood (1954);
348. L'Opium sous les Tentures (Opium Under the
Drapes; 1954); 349. Le Sous-Marin Fantôme (The
Ghost Submarine; 1954); 350. L'Aveugle de Marrakech
(The Blind Man of Marrakech; 1954); 351. Trois Blancs
chez les Mau-Mau (Three White Men Among the Mau-
Mau; 1954); 352. Les Yeux Perçants du Kenya (The
Piercing Eyes of Kenya; 1954); 353. L'Araignée aux 100
Visages (The Spider with a Hundred Faces; 1954); 354.
Mystère dans les Airs (Mystery in the Air; 1954); 355.
Les Chevaliers de l'Alphabet (The Knights of the Al-
phabet; 1954); 356. Les Charmes de l'Espionne (The
Charms of the Female Spy; 1954); 357. Les Sournois du
Japon (The Japanese Deceivers; 1954); 358. Il faut
sauver le Patron (We Must Save the Boss; 1955); 359.
Les Marchands de Communisme (The Merchants of
Communism; 1955); 360. Péril chez les Barbares (Dan-
ger Among the Barbarians; 1955); 361. Trois Sacs à
l'Eau (Three Sacks in the Water; 1955); 362. L'Espion
de 11 ans (The 11-Year-Old Spy; 1955); 363. Le Savant
Aime les Rousses (The Scientist Loves Red Heads;
1955); 364. Rendez-Vous (1955); 365. Un Secret dans la
Plume (A Secret in the Pen; 1955); 366. Battue par les
Russes (Beaten By the Russians; 1955); 367. Il faut
sauver Roxanne! (We Must Save Roxanna!; 1955); 368.
La Lettre E (The Letter E; 1955); 369. Le Chinois d'As-
trakan (The Astrakan Chinese; 1955); 370. Les Uni-
formes Verts (The Green Uniforms; 1955); 371.
L'Héritage de Marius (Marius' Inheritance; 1955); 372.
Trois Missions dans Une (Three Missions in One; 1955);
373. Mission en Prison (Mission in Jail; 1955); 374.
Les Barbares de la Montagne (The Mountain Barnari-
ans; 1955); 375. L'Avion Z-Spécial (The Z-Special
Plane; 1955); 376. Lolita Perez de Panama (1955); 377.
À la Recherche du Disparu (Searching for the Man Who
Disappeared; 1955); 378. La Tache sur le Talon (The
Spot on the Heel; 1955); 379. Prisonniers de la Jungle
(Prisoners of the Jungle; 1955); 380. L'Italien a Soif
d'Amour (The Italian Is Thirsty for Love; 1955); 381.
Courrier Diplomatique (Diplomatic Mail; 1955); 382.
Le Bourreau Cicatrisé (The Scarred Executioner;*

*1955); 383. Amour et Espionnage (Love and Spying;
1955); 384. L'Agent A-27 (1955); 385. On veut un Ca-
davre (They Want a Corpse; 1955); 386. Marius contre
Ixe-13 (Marius vs. X-13; 1955); 387. Vendue aux Com-
munistes (Sold to the Communists; 1955); 388. Mission
en Espagne (Mission in Spain; 1955); 389. Emmurés!
(Walled Up!; 1955); 390. Mission-Suicide (Suicide Mis-
sion; 1955); 391. Attentat à la Mitraillette (Machine Gun
Assassintion Attempt; 1955); 392. Ruse de Vipère (A
Viper's Ruse; 1955); 393. Le Coffret d'Acier (The Steel
Box; 1955); 394. Le Don Juan de Las Vegas (1955); 395.
Le Bâton de Rouge (The Lipstick Stick; 1955); 396. Le
Chimiste Allemand (The German Chemist; 1955); 397.
Hitler au Canada! (Hitler in Canada!; 1955); 398. on
veut ses Secrets (They Want His Secrets; 1955); 399.
Trois Tueurs au Yukon (Three Killers in the Yukon;
1955); 400. SOS de France (SOS from France; 1955);
401. L'Amant de Paris (The Parisian Lover; 1955); 402.
Les Partisans de la Liberté (The Partisans of Freedom;
1955); 403. Ixe-13 Roulé par le Charme (X-13 Bam-
boozled By a Charmer; 1955); 404. La Main Pendait
(The Hanging Hand; 1955); 405. Espions en Skis (Spies
on Skis; 1955); 406. La Maîtresse a Peur (The Mistress
Is Afraid; 1955); 407. Les Fantômes Volants (The Fly-
ing Ghosts; 1955); 408. Les Bas-Fonds de Tokyo (The
Tokyo Underworld; 1955); 409. Les Démons de la Nuit
(The Demons of Night; 1955); 410. Le Serpent Vénéneux
(The Venomous Snake; 1955); 411. Disparition de Pris-
onniers (Prisoners' Disappearances; 1956); 412. Crim-
inels Incendiaires (Incendiary Criminals; 1956); 413.
Question de Vie ou de Mort (Question of Life and
Death; 1956); 414. Traîtrise ou Déshonneur (Betrayal
or Dishonor; 1956); 415. Les Gredins de Russie (The
Russian Crooks; 1956); 416. Ixe-13 à l'Asile (X-13 in
the Asylum; 1956); 417. La Sorcière Bolshéviste (The
Bolchevist Witch; 1956); 418. Agent Double (Double
Agent; 1956); 419. Espion au Kremlin (Spy in the Krem-
lin; 1956); 420. X-13, l'Insaisissable (X-13 the Un-
catchable; 1956); 421. Une Femme Dangereuse (A Dan-
gerous Woman; 1956); 422. L'Ermite de la Cabane (The
Cabin Hermit; 1956); 423. Criminel Allemand (German
Criminal; 1956); 424. Dans la Main du Mort (In the
Deadman's Hand; 1956); 425. L'Espion Borgne (The
One-Eyed Spy; 1956); 426. Au Pays du Mystère (In the
Land of Mystery; 1956); 427. Assaillie au Tibet (As-
saulted in Tibet; 1956); 428. Le Barbier Japonais (The
Japanse Barber; 1956); 429. La Fausse Lisette Tournel
(The Phony Lisette Tournel; 1956); 430. Drame au Lab-
oratoire (Tragedy in the Laboratory; 1956); 431. L'En-
fant du Naufrage (The Child from the Shipwreck; 1956);
432. Le Docteur au Crâne Chauve (The Doctor with a
Bald Head; 1956); 433. Revanche Communiste (Com-
munist Revenge; 1956); 434. Rendez-Vous au Point
Rouge (Rendezvous at the Red Dot; 1956); 435. Jane en
Prison (Jane in Jail; 1956); 436. Une Heure pour s'é-*

vader (An Hour to Escape; 1956); *437. Les Chandails Rouges* (The Red Sweaters; 1956); *438. Trois Portes, Trois Alarmes* (Three Doors, Three Alarms; 1956); *439. L'Explosion sur la Rive* (Explosion on the Shore; 1956); *440. Herman la Brute!* (Herman the Brute; 1956); *441. Deux Comprimés pour Ixe-13* (Two Pills for X-13; 1956); *442. Sous-Marin au Labrador* (Sub-Marine in Labrador; 1956); *443. Coup de Feu la Nuit* (Gunfire at Night; 1956); *444. Le Noyé à l'Oeil Crevé* (The One-Eyed Drowned Man; 1956); *445. La Cave Chinoise* (The Chinese Cave; 1956); *446. L'Expédition Taya* (The Taya Expedition; 1956); *447. L'Impossible Évasion* (The Impossible Escape; 1956); *448. Le Secret du Mort* (Deadman's Secret; 1956); *449. Thibault au Secours* (Thibault to the Rescue; 1956); *450. Le Secret dans l'Horloge* (The Secret of the Clock; 1956); *451. Un Marché avec les Russes* (A Trade with the Russians; 1956); *452. Danseuse à la Pomme d'Ève* (Dancing Girl at Eve's Apple; 1956); *453. L'Amant d'Hélène* (Helen's Lover; 1956); *454. L'Étrange Docteur Sucayo* (The Strange Dr. Sucayo; 1956); *455. Course à l'Enveloppe Jaune* (Race for the Yellow Envelope; 1956); *456. Le Journal d'un Prisonnier* (A Prisoner's Diary; 1956); *457. Le Vengeur* (The Avenger; 1956); *458. Les Russes à la Cabane* (The Russians at the Cabin; 1956); *459. La Liberté qui Tue* (The Freedom That Kills; 1956); *460. Nadia Démasquée* (Nadia Unmasked; 1956); *461. Ixe-13 en Hongrie* (X-13 in Hungary; 1956); *462. Tortures à Budapest* (Tortures in Budapest; 1957); *463. L'Ange Bleu* (The Blue Angel; 1957); *464. Zalec de Hongrie* (Zalec of Hungary; 1957); *465. Drogué sur une Mission* (Drugged on a Mission; 1957); *466. L'Allemande Effrontée* (The Brazen German Woman; 1957); *467. Le Secret dans le Canal* (The Secret in the Canal; 1957); *468. Horreurs Communistes* (Communist Horrors; 1957); *469. Sonia, Fille d'Amour* (Sonia, Love Girl; 1957); *470. Une Femme en Danger* (A Woman in Danger; 1957); *471. Baisers de Judas* (Judas' Kisses; 1957); *472. Zito, la Sirène* (Zito the Siren; 1957); *473. Les Brutes Attaquent* (The Brutes Attack; 1957); *474. Les Traîtres Communistes* (The Communist Traitors; 1957); *475. Société Secrète* (Secret Society; 1957); *476. L'Être Diabolique* (The Diabolical Entity; 1957); *477. Les Évadés* (The Escapees; 1957); *478. Le Gong de la Mort* (The Gong of Death; 1957); *479. Russe et Rusé* (Russian and Crafty; 1957); *480. L'Infâmie d'un Militaire* (The Infamous Act of a Soldier; 1957); *481. Le Témoin ne parlera plus* (The Witness Shall No Longer Talk; 1957); *482. Sadisme Effroyable* (Frightful Sadism; 1957); *483. Sérum contre la Mort* (Serum Against Death; 1957); *484. Judas chez les Espions* (Judas Among the Spies; 1957); *485. Témoin en Danger* (Witness in Danger; 1957); *486. La Main d'un Mort* (A Deadman's Hand; 1957); *487. La Rose Thé* (The Tea Rose; 1957); *488. Vedette Sexée à Hollywood* (Sexy Star in Hollywood; 1957); *489. Violée par un* Monstre (Raped By a Monster; 1957); *490. Le Sheik du Harem* (The Harem Sheik; 1957); *491. Les Voiles d'Arabie* (The Veils of Arabia; 1957); *492. La Médaille de Plomb* (The Lead Medal; 1957); *493. Gaby, Fille Perdue* (Gaby, Lost Girl; 1957); *494. Les Îles du Diable* (The Devil's Islands; 1957); *495. Morts à la Douzaine* (Dead By the Dozen; 1957); *496. La Morsure Venimeuse* (The Venomous Bite; 1957); *497. Les Visages à Deux Faces* (The Two-Sided Face; 1957); *498. Mission derrière les Barreaux* (Mission Behind Bars; 1957); *499. Les Femmes Séquestrées* (The Captive Women; 1957); *500. L'Imposteur* (The Impostor; 1957); *501. Fuite Impossible* (Impossible Ecape; 1957); *502. Mission aux Folies Bergères* (Mission at the Folies Bergeres; 1957); *503. L'Homme que l'on croyait mort* (The Man They Believed Dead; 1957); *504. Je me cherche un Amant* (I Seek a Lover; 1957); *505. Le Métal Mystère* (The Mystery Metal; 1957); *506. Le Secret de Mike* (Mike's Secret; 1957); *507. Le Survivant* (The Survivor; 1957); *508. L'Assassin aux Cheveux Roux* (The Red-Haired Assassin; 1957); *509. Les Loisirs Amoureux de Myriam* (Myriam's Love Leisures; 1957); *510. La Langue trop longue* (A Well-Hung Tongue; 1957); *511. Les Assassins du Grand Nord* (The Assassins of the Great North; 1957); *512. Roxanne, Danseuse Nue* (Roxanna, Nude Dancer; 1957); *513. Dupont, l'Invisible* (Dupont the Invisible; 1957); *514. Séductrice Orientale* (Oriental Seductress; 1958); *515. Les Masseuses Japonaises* (The Japanese Masseuses; 1958); *516. Les Deux Colosses* (The Two Colossi; 1958); *517. L'Affront* (The Insult; 1958); *518. Attaque Traîtresse* (Traitorous Attack; 1958); *519. L'Espionne à Deux Faces* (The Two-Faced Female Spy; 1958); *520. Empreintes Digitales* (Finger Prints; 1958); *521. L'Ombre de Nicolas* (Nicolas' Shadow; 1958); *522. Névrosée en Sibérie* (Neurotic in Siberia; 1958); *523. La Cité sans Femmes* (City Without Women; 1958); *524. Le Sosie de Staline* (Stalin's Double; 1958); *525. Ixe-13 se marie!* (X-13 Gets Married!; 1958); *526. La Piste de Sang* (The Trail of Blood; 1958); *527. Kati, la Sauvagesse* (Kati the Savage Girl; 1958); *528. Une Brute sur Roxanne* (A Brute on Top of Roxanna; 1958); *529. Ixe-13 contre Taya* (X-13 vs. Taya; 1958); *530. L'Amant Jaloux* (The Jealous Lover; 1958); *531. L'Ennemi Numéro Un* (Public Enemy Number One; 1958); *532. Le Retour de la Femme en Vert* (The Return of the Woman in Green; 1958); *533. Scandale!* (Scandal; 1958); *534. La Taya Canadienne* (The Canadian Taya; 1958); *535. L'Homme à l'Oeil de Vitre* (The Man with a Glass Eye; 1958); *536. Jambe de Bois* (Wooden Leg; 1958); *537. Déesse aux Cheveux Roux* (Red-Haired Goddess; 1958); *538. La Souris Blanche* (The White Mouse; 1958); *539. Le Vengeur* (The Avenger; 1958); *540. Le Futur Fuhrer* (The Future Fuhrer; 1958); *541. Le Piège d'Ixe-13* (X-13's Trap; 1958); *542. Meurtres au Couteau* (Murders By Knife; 1958); *543. Mission Place Pigalle* (Mission

Pigalle Square; 1958); *544. Un Cheveu de Trop (One Hair Too Many;* 1958); *545. Le Polonais au Coeur d'Or (The Golden-Hearted Polish Man;* 1958); *546. L'Île Maudite (The Accursed Island;* 1958); *547. Mission en Orient (Mission to the Orient;* 1958); *548. Odyssée en Mandchourie (Odyssey in Manchuria;* 1958); *549. Le Fils de Lang Mee (Lang Mee's Son;* 1958); *550. Les Jeunes Fous (The Young Madmen;* 1958); *551. La Dernière Nuit d'Amour (The Last Night of Love;* 1958); *552. La Fille de Vie Assassinée (The Murdered Prostitute;* 1958); *553. Prisonnier des Rebelles (Prisoner of the Rebels;* 1958); *554. L'Assassin à Deux Faces (The Two-Faced Assassin;* 1958); *555. L'Assassin d'un Communiste (A Communist's Murderer;* 1958); *556. Plaisirs à Vendre (Pleasures for Sale;* 1958); *557. Le Bain de la Mort (The Bath of Death;* 1958); *558. Une Fille Facile (An Easy Girl;* 1958); *559. La Vengeance de l'Amant (The Lover's Revenge;* 1958); *560. Charmes de Malheur (Unlucky Charms;* 1958); *561. Ixe-13, le tueur (X-13 the Killer;* 1958); *562. Troubles en Sibérie (Trouble in Siberia;* 1958); *563. Au Secours de Gisèle (To Rescue Gisele;* 1958); *564. Von Licken est pris! (Von Licken Is Caught!;* 1958); *565. L'Homme au Parapluie (The Man with the Umbrella;* 1958); *566. L'Enlèvement de Daniel (Daniel's Kidnapping;* 1958); *567. Roxanne assassine Marius (Roxanna Kills Marius;* 1959); *568. Voyage vers la Mort (Journey Towards Death;* 1959); *569. Espionnage en Fa Mineur (Spying in F Minor;* 1959); *570. Le Démon du Midi (The Noon Demon;* 1959); *571. L'Union des Assassins (The Murderers' Union;* 1959); *572. Le Silence de la Mort (The Silence of Death;* 1959); *573. Vengeance!* (1959); *574. Le Secret du Faux Malade (The Secret of the Phony Sick Man;* 1959); *575. Le Mort qui Bouge (The Dead Who Moves;* 1959); *576. Nadine de Moscou (Nadine of Moscow;* 1959); *577. La Femme de Malheur (The Unlucky Woman;* 1959); *578. Ixe-13 va-t-il se marier? (Will X-13 Marry?;* 1959); *579. L'Invitée Surprise (The Surprise Guest;* 1959); *580. L'Évasion d'Ixe-13 (X-13 Escapes;* 1959); *581. La Preuve (The Proof;* 1959); *582. L'Insaisissable Chinois (The Uncatchable Chinese;* 1959); *583. Le Sérum de Vérité (The Serum of Truth;* 1959); *584. Espionnage derrière les Barreaux (Spying Behind Bars;* 1959); *585. Perdus dans les Alpes (Lost in the Alps;* 1959); *586. Voyage de Noces Mouvementé (Event-Filled Honeymoon;* 1959); *587. L'Homme à la Poigne de Fer (The Man with An Iron Grip;* 1959); *588. Le Journaliste Indiscret (The Indiscreet Journalist;* 1959); *589. Le Joueur Assassin (The Gambling Assassin;* 1959); *590. La Geisha de Vancouver (The Geisha of Vancouver;* 1959); *591. La Ville du Mystère (The City of Mystery;* 1959); *592. La Déesse de la Montagne (The Mountain Goddess;* 1959); *593. Fleur de Lilas (Lilac Flower;* 1959); *594. Le Parchemin de la Mort (The Scroll of Death;* 1959); *595. Agents Libres (Free Agents;* 1959); *596. La Bonne Aventure (Good Fortune;* 1959); *597. Les Rebelles d'Algérie (The Algerian Rebels;* 1959); *598. Ixe-13 Prisonnier (X-13 Prisoner;* 1959); *599. La Serviette Disparue (The Vanished Briefcase;* 1959); *600. Les Croix Gammées d'Eva Braun (Eva Braun's Swastikas;* 1959); *601. L'Épouse de Quelques Heures (The Bride of a Few Hours;* 1959); *602. Victime de la Névrose (Victim of Neuroses;* 1959); *603. Mort Subite (Sudden Death;* 1959); *604. Le Prisonnier de la Jungle (Prisoner in the Jungle;* 1959); *605. Alerte à Hollywood (Alert in Hollywood;* 1959); *606. Le Piège de Taya (Taya's Trap;* 1959); *607. Dans la Gueule du Loup (In the Jaws of the Wolf;* 1959); *608. La Dernière Manche (The Last Battle;* 1959); *609. La Bombe à Retardement (The Time Bomb;* 1959); *610. Le Bagarreur (The Fighter;* 1959); *611. Révolte en Mer (Revolt at Sea;* 1959); *612. Escarmouche en Arabie (Skirmish in Arabia;* 1959); *613. Un Drame au Chèque (A Check Drama;* 1959); *614. L'Enjôleuse (The Spellbinding Girl;* 1959); *615. Derrière les Barreaux (Behind Bars;* 1959); *616. Espions Russes à Ottawa (Russian Spies in Ottawa;* 1959); *617. Le Noël d'un Espion (A Spy's Christmas;* 1959); *618. Les Meurtres de Saïgon (Murders in Saigon;* 1959); *619. L'Odieux Chantage (The Odious Blackmail;* 1960); *620. La Conduite Étrange de M. Brounoff (The Strange Behavior of Mr. Brounoff;* 1960); *621. Le Mari Infidèle (The Unfaithful Husband;* 1960); *622. Au Coeur de l'Afrique (In the Heart of Africa;* 1960); *623. La Déesse Blanche (The White Goddess;* 1960); *624. Zoteck, l'Insaisissable (Zoteck the Uncatchable;* 1960); *625. Meurtre aux Jeux Olympiques (Murder at the Olympic Games;* 1960); *626. Condamné à Mort (Condemned to Death;* 1960); *627. Taya en Danger (Taya in Danger;* 1960); *628. Un Réseau d'Espionnage (Spy Network;* 1960); *629. Celui que l'on attendait pas (The Unexpected Man;* 1960); *630. Brûlé Vif (Burned Alive;* 1960); *631. Le Bourreau Féminin (The Female Executioner;* 1960); *632. Nuit d'Orgie (Orgy Night;* 1960); *633. Les Cagoules Jaunes (The Yellow Hoods;* 1960); *634. Les Évadés des Rocheuses (Escape from the Rockies;* 1960); *635. Le Repaire de la Montagne (The Mountain Lair;* 1960); *636. La Ville Souterraine (The Underground City;* 1960); *637. Le Fou à l'Oeil Crevé (The Madman with a Gouged Eye;* 1960); *638. Prisonnier des Neiges (Prisoner of the Snows;* 1960); *639. La Femme à Barbe (The Bearded Lady;* 1960); *640. La Tête Coupée (The Severed Head;* 1960); *641. La Patiente Mystérieuse (The Mysterious Female Patient;* 1960); *642. Les Révoltés (The Revolutionaries;* 1960); *643. Espionnage Aérien en Russie (Air Spying Over Russia;* 1960); *644. Le Sang des Innocents (The Blood of the Innocents;* 1960); *645. Filles de Rue (Street Girls;* 1960); *646. Pionnier de la Mort (Pioneer of Death;* 1960); *647. La Vengeance de Dolorès (Dolores' Revenge;* 1960); *648. Au Secours de Denis (To Rescue Denis;* 1960); *649. Pleurs dans la*

Nuit (Tears in the Night; 1960); *650. Les Saboteurs du Pionnier 1 (The Saboteurs of Pioneer 1;* 1960); *651. Les Naufragés de l'Espace (Shipwrecked in Space;* 1960); *652. Les Déesses de Vesta (The Goddesses of Vesta;* 1960); *653. Les Pirates de l'Air (The Air Pirates;* 1960); *654. Les Petits Monstres Blancs (The Little White Monsters;* 1960); *655. Le Robot Vengeur (The Avenging Robot;* 1960); *656. Les Trois Plaies d'Utano (The Three Plagues of Ultano;* 1960); *657. Les Vampires de l'Espace (The Space Vampires;* 1960); *658. L'Ermite de l'Espace (The Space Hermit;* 1960); *659. La Dictatrice de l'Espace (The Female Dictator of Space;* 1960); *660. Le Serpent à Deux Têtes (The Two-Headed Serpent;* 1960); *661. Roi et Maître de l'Espace (King and Master of Space;* 1960); *662. La Révolte des Planètes (The Planets Revolt;* 1960); *663. La Déesse Vena (The Goddess Vena;* 1960); *664. La Planète Errante (The Wandering Planet;* 1960); *665. La Planète Mystère (aka Les Sons qui Hurlent) (The Mystery Planet (aka the Screaming Sounds);* 1960); *666. La Revanche des Zortiens (The Revenge of the Zortians;* 1960); *667. Retour sur la Terre (Return to Earth;* 1960); *668. Taya, l'Indomptable (Taya the Indomitable;* 1960); *669. Enquête au Congo (Investigation in Congo;* 1960); *670. Sabotage à Léopoldville (Sabotage in Leopoldville;* 1960); *671. Les Suspects Intouchables (The Untouchable Suspects;* 1961); *672. La Déesse Tempête (The Storm Goddess;* 1961); *673. La Vengeance de Miki (Miki's Revenge;* 1961); *674. Film Révolutionnaire (Revolutionary Film;* 1961); *675. Les Voyages Suicides (Suicide Journeys;* 1961); *676. La Mort ou l'Amour (Death or Love;* 1961); *677. Deux Femmes en Péril (Two Women in Danger;* 1961); *678. Piraterie en Haute Mer (Piracy on the High Seas;* 1961); *679. Le Bouddha qui Rit (The Laughing Buddha;* 1961); *680. L'Espion Sadique (The Sadistic Spy;* 1961); *681. Le Laboratoire de la Mort (The Laboratory of Death;* 1961); *682. Disparition en Plein Ciel (Vanished in Open Sky;* 1961); *683. Le Berceau Vide (The Empty Cradle;* 1961); *684. Terreur au Congo (Terror in the Congo;* 1961); *685. Le Journaliste Agent-Double (The Double-Agent Journalist;* 1961); *686. Ixe-13 Knockout (X-13 K.O.;* 1961); *687. Un Assassin à l'Hôpital (An Assassin at the Hospital;* 1961); *688. La Collection de Cadavres (The Corpses Collection;* 1961); *689. La Reine de la Jungle (The Queen of the Jungle;* 1961); *690. Boomerang* (1961); *691. Mission Gagarine* (1961); *692. La Fille aux Cheveux d'Ange (The Angel-Haired Girl;* 1961); *693. Le Couteau sur la Gorge (The Knife on the Throat;* 1961); *694. Trois Jours d'Angoisse (Three Days of Terror;* 1961); *695. Le Cadavre Démembré (The Dismembered Corpse;* 1961); *696. Le Quêteux aux Lunettes Noires (The Beggar with Dark Glasses;* 1961); *697. La Déesse sans Voile (The Goddess Without Veils;* 1961); *698. L'Ombre de la Mort Plane (The Shadow of Death Lurks;* 1961); *699. Espions à Vancouver (Spies in Vancouver;* 1961); *700. L'Île du Silence (The Island of Silence;* 1961); *701. Le Secret de Sing Lee (Sing Lee's Secret;* 1961); *702. Le Faux Pas de Marius (Marius' Misstep;* 1961); *703. Le Rideau Rouge (The Red Curtain;* 1961); *704. Neuf sur Dix (Nine Out of Ten;* 1961); *705. Une Fille dans la Nuit (A Girl in the Night;* 1961); *706. Aventure à Berlin (Adventure in Berlin;* 1961); *707. Bombe à Retardement (Time Bomb;* 1961); *708. La Guerre des Dôpés (The War of the Addicts;* 1961); *709. Le Train Fantôme (The Ghost Train;* 1961); *710. Justice est faite (Justice Is Served;* 1961); *711. Trafic d'Armes (Gun Running;* 1961); *712. Meurtre en Noir et Blanc (Murder in Black and White;* 1961); *713. Les Pillards de la Montagne (The Mountain Looters;* 1961); *714. Accusé sans Preuves (Accused Without Evidence;* 1961); *715. Taya en Amérique (Taya in America;* 1961); *716. Les Deux Taya (The Two Tayas;* 1961); *717. Mission Défendue (Forbidden Mission;* 1961); *718. Les Forçats Révoltés (The Revolt of the Convicts;* 1961); *719. La Fille aux Serpents (The Snake Girl;* 1961); *720. L'Ingrate (The Ungrateful Girl;* 1961); *721. 500 Pieds sous Terre (500 Feet Underground;* 1961); *722. Une Ombre dans la Nuit (A Shadow in the Night;* 1961); *723. La Clef du Mystère (The Key to the Mystery;* 1962); *724. Meurtre à Calcutta (Murder in Calcutta;* 1962); *725. Le Secret du Major (The Major's Secret;* 1962); *726. Un Homme Marqué (A Marked Man;* 1962); *727. Le Prix du Silence (The Price of Silence;* 1962); *728. La Mort n'a pas de Frontière (Death Has No Frontier;* 1962); *729. L'Innocente Victime (The Innocent Victim;* 1962); *730. Une Poupée qui danse bien (A Doll Who Danced Well;* 1962); *731. La Beauté dans l'Ombre (Beauty in the Shadow;* 1962); *732. Prisonniers de la Mer (Prisoners of the Sea;* 1962); *733. Spectacle Immoral (Immoral Spectacle;* 1962); *734. Du Sang dans le Noir (Blood in the Dark;* 1962); *735. L'Appareil de l'Autre Monde (The Device from Another World;* 1962); *736. Les Pendus sont Silencieux (Hanged Men Are Silent;* 1962); *737. Le Sosie d'Ixe-13 (X-13's Lookalike;* 1962); *738. Leçon de Meurtre (Murder Lesson;* 1962); *739. Enlèvement dans le Ciel (Kidnapping in the Sky;* 1962); *740. Les Voix Mystérieuses (The Mysterious Voices;* 1962); *741. Incroyables Révélations (Incredible Revelations;* 1962); *742. Meurtre au Japon (Murder in Japan;* 1962); *743. L'Américaine de Shanghaï (The American Girl from Shanghai;* 1962); *744. Ixe-13 est disparu (X-13 Has Vanished;* 1962); *745. La Femme en Vert (The Woman in Green;* 1962); *746. Vengeance sur le Tard (Late Revenge;* 1962); *747. La Valise aux Microbes (The Suitcase with Microbes;* 1962); *748. Sabotage en Haute Mer (Sabotage on the High Sea;* 1962); *749. Les Assassins Assassinés (The Murdered Assassins;* 1962); *750. Les Dessous de Chinatown (The Underworld of Chinatown;* 1962); *751. Le Mystère des Six (The Mystery of the Six;* 1962); *752. La Dent en or (The Gold Tooth;* 1962); *753.*

Explosions dans la Neige (Explosions in the Snow; 1962); *754. Les Cadavres Gelés (The Frozen Corpses;* 1962); *755. Le Singe Assassin (The Murderous Ape;* 1962); *756. Meurtre sous l'Eau (Murder Underwater;* 1962); *757. César, l'Assassin (Caesar the Killer;* 1962); *758. La Fugue de Marius (Marius' Escape;* 1962); *759. Le Mur de la Honte (The Wall of Shame;* 1962); *760. Ixe-13 Trahi par sa Femme (X-13 Betrayed By His Wife;* 1962); *761. Coupable d'Avance (Guilty Beforehand;* 1962); *762. L'Homme à la Perruque (The Man with the Wig;* 1962); *763. La Mort ou la Trahison (Death or Betrayal;* 1962); *764. Dans la Main du Mort (In the Deadman's Hand;* 1962); *765. Trois Heures d'Angoisse (Three Hours of Terror;* 1962); *766. Maniaque au Couteau (Knife-Wielding Maniac;* 1962); *767. Le Chien Naufragé (The Shipwrecked Dog;* 1962); *768. Le Harem des Disparitions (Disappearances in the Harem]*(1962); *769. Les Enfants-Espions (The Spy-Children;* 1962); *770. Sabotage* (1962); *771. Meurtres sous l'Eau (Murders Underwater;* 1962); *772. Emmurés Vivants (Walled-Up Alive;* 1962); *773. Le Secret du Décapité (The Secret of the Beheaded Man;* 1962); *774. Dans la Gueule du Loup (In the Jaws of the Wolf;* 1962); *775. Vengeance de Femme (A Woman's Revenge;* 1963); *776. Le Visiteur de Nankin (The Visitor from Nankin;* 1963); *777. Le Rendez-Vous de Minuit (The Midnight Rendezvous;* 1963); *778. L'Amnésique de Tokyo (The Tokyo Amnesiac;* 1963); *779. Les Fantômes-Espions (The Spy-Ghosts;* 1963); *780. Le Fou Éternel (The Eternal Madman;* 1963); *781. Le Salon des Espions (The Spy Saloon;* 1963); *782. Rencontre Fatidique (Fateful Encounter;* 1963); *783. La Maîtresse d'Ixe-13 (X-13's Mistress;* 1963); *784. La Danseuse de Pigalle (The Pigalle Dancing Girl;* 1963); *785. L'Espionne Aime trop les Hommes (The Female Spy Loved Men Too Much;* 1963); *786. Homme aux Femmes (A Woman's Man;* 1963); *787. La Sirène (The Siren;* 1963); *788. Le Cercle Vicieux (The Vicious Circle;* 1963); *789. Pas trop Petite pour l'Amour! (Not Too Small for Love!;* 1963); *790. Le Square du Péché (The Square of Sin;* 1963); *791. Seins et Saints (Breasts and Saints;* 1963); *792. Nuit d'Orgie chez Taya (Orgy Night at Taya's;* 1963); *793. La Vamp de Tokyo (The Tokyo Vamp;* 1963); *794. Les Passions Déchaînées (Unchained Passions;* 1963); *795. L'Esquimaude au Corps Chaud (The Eskimo Girl with a Hot Body;* 1963); *796. La Poupée d'Haïti (The Haitian Doll;* 1963); *797. Échange de Femmes (Women Exchange;* 1963); *798. Maniaque Sexuel ou Espion? (Sex Maniac or Spy?;* 1963); *799. Regardez mais ne touchez pas (Look But Don't Touch;* 1963); *800. Le Paquebot des Ivresses (The Steamboat of Drunks;* 1963); *801. Maison Close (Bordello;* 1963); *802. Folle des Hommes (Man Crazy;* 1963); *803. Elle n'aime que les Femmes (She Only Likes Women;* 1963); *804. Le Cirque des Amours Perverses (The Circus of Perverse*

Loves; 1963); *805. Les Caresses de Gina (Gina's Caresses;* 1963); *806. La Secrétaire aux Belles Jambes (The Secretary with Beautiful Legs;* 1963); *807. Le Robot en Amour (The Robot in Love;* 1963); *808. Corps contre Corps (Body Against Body;* 1963); *809. Voluptées Orientales (Oriental Passions;* 1963); *810. La Chair est Faible (The Flesh Is Weak;* 1963); *811. Passion Interdite (Forbidden Passion;* 1963); *812. La Masseuse Japonaise (The Japanese Masseuse;* 1963); *813. Treize Hommes, Une Femme (13 Men, 1 Woman;* 1963); *814. L'Espion et la Vicieuse (The Spy and the Vicious Lady;* 1963); *815. Un Piège de Femme (A Woman Trap;* 1963); *816. Étreintes à la Russe (Russian Hugs;* 1963); *817. La Timide Effeuilleuse (The Shy Strip-Teaser;* 1963); *818. La Journaliste Fait du Strip-Tease (The Woman Journalist Does Strip-Tease;* 1963); *819. La Garde-Malade a trop de Sex-Appeal (The Nurse Has Too Much Sex Appeal;* 1963); *820. La Patiente a Soif d'Amour (The Patient Is Thirsty for Love;* 1963); *821. La Faute de Gisèle (Gisele's Fault;* 1963); *822. La Capitale du Vice (The Capital of Vice;* 1963); *823. Parmi les Femmes (Among Women;* 1963); *824. Marius chez les Nudistes (Marius and the Nudists;* 1963); *825. Les Call-Girls de Londres (The London Call-Girls;* 1963); *826. Intrigues sur l'Océan (Schemes Over the Ocean;* 1963); *827. Les Caresses Infernales (The Infernal Caresses;* 1964); *828. Fuite Scandaleuse (Scandalous Escape;* 1964); *829. La Mexicaine a le Sang Chaud (The Hot-Blooded Mexican Girl;* 1964); *830. Il a assassiné sa Maîtresse (He Murdered His Mistress;* 1964); *831. Isabelle, la Lutteuse (Isabelle the Fighter;* 1964); *832. Trop belle pour être vraie (Too Beautiful to Be True;* 1964); *833. La Fille Sauvage des Rocheuses (The Wild Girl from the Rockies;* 1964); *834. Plaisirs d'Après Minuit (After Midnight Pleasures;* 1964); *835. La Pêche aux Femmes (Fishing for Women;* 1964); *836. Filles de Nuit (Night Girls;* 1964); *837. L'Amour qui rend fou (Mad Love;* 1964); *838. En Service, la Nuit (In Service at Night;* 1964); *839. L'Espionne sans Scrupules (The Female Spy Without Scruples;* 1964); *840. Vie de Débauche (Life of Debauchery;* 1964); *841. Le Viol de Gisèle (The Rape of Gisele;* 1964); *842. La Fille des Îles (The Island Girl;* 1964); *843. Amours de Jeunesse (Young Love;* 1964); *844. Elle Préfère l'Amour (She Prefers Love;* 1964); *845. La Sirène (The Siren;* 1964); *846. Les Petites Amies du Capitaine (The Captain's Girl-Friends;* 1964); *847. L'Amour en Double (Double Love;* 1964); *848. Trop de Femmes pour un Homme (Too Many Women for a Man;* 1964); *849. Cinq Hommes, Une Femme (5 Men, 1 Woman;* 1964); *850. Le Retour du Sadique (The Return of the Sadist;* 1964); *851. Le Sérum Miracle (The Miracle Serum;* 1964); *852. La Confession d'une Folle (A Madwoman's Confession;* 1964); *853. Ixe-13 chez les Nudistes (X-13 and the Nudists;* 1964); *854. Le Candidat de la Mort (The Candidate of Death;* 1964); *855. Ta*

Femme te trompe (Your Woman Is Cheating on You; 1964); *856. Dans les Bras d'un Autre (In Another's Arms;* 1964); *857. Intrigues en Plein Océan (Schemes on a Full Ocean;* 1964); *858. Les Ondes Meurtrières (The Killing Waves;* 1964); *859. L'Aveugle qui voit trop (The Blind Man Who Saw Too Much;* 1964); *860. L'Empreinte de la Mort (The Mark of Death;* 1964); *861. Le Bal des Maudits (The Ball of the Accursed;* 1964); *862. L'Enfant du Péché (The Child of Sin;* 1964); *863. La Poupée de Tokyo (The Tokyo Doll;* 1964); *864. Parmi les Cadavres (Among the Corpses;* 1964); *865. Mademoiselle Scandale (Miss Scandal;* 1964); *866. Le Roi de la Torture (The King of Torture;* 1964); *867. L'Île du Péché (The Island of Sin;* 1964); *868. Le Repaire des Amants (Lovers' Lair;* 1964); *869. L'Appel de la Passion (The Call of Passion;* 1964); *870. La Fermière en Amour (The Farming Girl in Love;* 1964); *871. Le Disparu de Chypre (Disappearance in Cyprus;* 1964); *872. La Loi des Amants (Lovers' Law;* 1964); *873. L'Espionne en Monokini (The Spy in Monokini;* 1964); *874. La Poupée de Pigalle (The Doll from Pigalle;* 1964); *875. Prostitution au Service Secret (Prostitution in the Secret Service;* 1964); *876. La Chinoise Invisible (The Invisible Chinese Woman;* 1964); *877. La Mort Tient le Volant (Death at the Wheel;* 1964); *878. Le Père Noël Espion (The Spying Santa Claus;* 1964); *879. La Déesse des Îles (The Island Goddess;* 1964); *880. L'Ermite de la Montagne (The Mountain Hermit;* 1965); *881. L'Éléphant Cramoisi (The Purple Elephant;* 1965); *882. Gisèle, Espionne Ennemie (Gisele, Enemy Spy;* 1965); *883. Vengeance! (Revenge!;* 1965); *884. L'Étrange Monsieur Pinard (The Strange Mr. Pinard;* 1965); *885. Le Numéro Un (Number On;* 1965); *886. À Bas les Masques! (Take Off the Masks!;* 1965); *887. Les Scandales Politiques (Political Scandals;* 1965); *888. Le Remède-Miracle (The Miracle-Pill;* 1965); *889. Trop Belle pour Être Esclave (Too Beautiful to Be a Slave;* 1965); *890. Mission au Vietnam (Mission in Vietnam;* 1965); *891. Gisèle, Fille de Vie (Gisele, Prostitute;* 1965); *892. La Madone aux Plaisirs (The Lady of Pleasures;* 1965); *893. Débauche à New York (Debauchery in New York;* 1965); *894. L'Impossible Évasion (The Impossible Escape;* 1965); *895. Elle est Prête à Tout (She Is Prepared to Do Anything;* 1965); *896. La Chinoise de Paris (The Chinese Girl of Paris;* 1965); *897. Le Secret dans la Tombe (The Secret in the Tomb;* 1965); *898. L'Espionne Fait du Nudisme (The Nudist Female Spy;* 1965); *899. Les Amours Illicites (Illicit Loves;* 1965); *900. La Disparition de Sing Lee (Sing Lee Disappears;* 1965); *901. Le Fils de Womee (The Son of Womee;* 1965); *902. Taya Trahit (Taya Betrays;* 1965); *903. Le Fils du Docteur Reynolds (Dr. Reynolds' Son;* 1965); *904. Pas de Bonheur pour Brenda (No Happiness for Brenda;* 1965); *905. La Cellule 192 (Cell 192;* 1965); *906. Les Plus Belles du Monde (The Most Beautiful in the World;*

1965); *907. Espionnage à la Manicouagan (Spying in Manikwagan;* 1965); *908. Le Code de l'Amour (The Code of Love;* 1965); *909. Espionnage en Gondole (Spying in a Gondola;* 1965); *910. Les Mystères de Calcutta (The Mysteries of Calcutta;* 1965); *911. L'Oeil du Lion (The Eye of the Lion;* 1965); *912. La Vengeance Rouge (The Red Revenge;* 1965); *913. Voyage vers la Mort (Journey Towards Death;* 1965); *914. Le Serpent de Las Vegas (The Snake of Las Vegas;* 1965); *915. Douze Heures d'Angoisse (Twelve Hours of Terror;* 1965); *916. Filles à l'Enchère (Girls on Auction;* 1965); *917. Chasse aux Espions (Spy Hunt;* 1965); *918. Le Poignard de Glace (The Ice Dagger;* 1965); *919. Espions sur Patins (Spies in Slippers;* 1965); *920. Judas en Jupon (Judas in a Skirt;* 1965); *921. Les Bas-Fonds de Pékin (The Underworld of Beijing;* 1965); *922. Traqué à Pékin (Hunted in Beijing;* 1965); *923. L'Amour à la Japonaise (Love Japan-Style;* 1965); *924. Pluie de Cadavres (Rain of Corpses;* 1965); *925. La Fin du Monde (The End of the World;* 1965); *926. 24 Heures d'Orgie (The 24-Hour Orgy;* 1965); *927. Le Pendu qui Parle (The Talking Hanged Man;* 1965); *928. Allo, Ici la Mort! (Hello! Death Here!;* 1965); *929. La Torche Vivante (The Living Torch;* 1965); *930. Les Secrets de l'Himalaya (The Secrets of the Himalayas;* 1965); *931. Le Camp des Atrocités (The Camp of Atrocities;* 1965); *932. La Coiffeuse Japonaise (The Japanese Hairdresser;* 1966); *933. L'Étrange Sabotage (The Strange Sabotage;* 1966); *934. Suicides en Série (A Series of Suicides;* 1966); *935. Elle avait trop d'Amants (She Had Too Many Lovers;* 1966); *936. Au Secours de Gisèle (To Rescue Gisele;* 1966); *937. La Vamp de St-Domingue (The Vamp of St. Domingo;* 1966); *938. Course contre la Montre (Race Against Death;* 1966); *939. Marius chez les Fous (Marius Among the Madmen;* 1966); *940. L'Homme au Monocle (The Man with the Monocle;* 1966); *941. L'Espionne de Berlin (The Female Spy from Berlin;* 1966); *942. Trop belle pour être Espionne (Too Beautiful to Be a Female Spy;* 1966); *943. L'Escouade des Beautés (The Beauty Squadron;* 1966); *944. L'Homme au Coeur Artificiel (The Man with An Artificial Heart;* 1966); *945. La Fugue de Marius (Marius' Escape;* 1966); *946. La Marchande d'Oiseaux (The Bird Merchant;* 1966); *947. Scandale à Ottawa (Scandal in Ottawa;* 1966); *948. La Chinoise en Amour (The Chinese Girl in Love;* 1966); *949. Le Sadique (The Sadist;* 1966); *950. Le Nouvel Allié de Taya (Talya's New Ally;* 1966); *951. Le Malade d'Amour (Love Sick;* 1966); *952. La Tombe du Docteur Blake (The Tomb of Dr. Blake;* 1966); *953. L'Astronaute se volatilise (The Astronaut Vanishes;* 1966); *954. Le Mort n'a plus froid (Death Is No Longer Cold;* 1966); *955. Maniaque Sexuel (Sex Maniac;* 1966); *956. Le Rayon Invisible (The Invisible Ray;* 1966); *957. La Potiche qui Griffe (The Clawing Vase;* 1966); *958. Le Signe de la Mort (The Mark of Death;* 1966); *959. Rox-*

anne Folle (Crazy Roxanna; 1966); *960. La Serviette de Cuir de Lydia (Lydia's Leather Briefcase*; 1966); *961. Du Sexe à Revendre (Sex for Sale*; 1966); *962. L'Invasion de la Terre (The Invasion of Earth*; 1966); *963. Mission dans la Jungle (Mission in the Jungle*; 1966); *964. Prisonnier des Pygmées (Prisoner of the Pygmies*; 1966); *965. Le Parchemin Chinois (The Chinese Scroll*; 1966); *966. Détournement de Mineure (Statutory Rape*; 1966); *967. Le Rat de Cale (The Hull Rat*; 1966); *968. Ixe-13 Assassiné? (X-13 Murdered?*; 1966); *969. Le Baiser de Katia (Katia's Kiss*; 1966); *970. La Cagoule Jaune (The Yellow Hood*; 1966); *Note:* Popular French-Canadian adventure series featuring a *James Bond*–like hero code named *Ixe-13.* in addition to the traditional superweapons, futuristic gadgets, mad scientists and villains trying to take over the world, the saga went "space opera" for 18 issues, from No. 650 to 667. A feature film was made in 1971.

Sauriol, Louise-Michelle (1938-); *Monde 008 sur la Pointe Claire (World 008 on the Clear Pointe*; HMH, 1989); *SOS Maya* (HMH, 1991); *Ookpik* (HMH, 1994); *Note:* French-Canadian writer. Children's fantasies.

Sautereau, François (1943-); *Un Trou dans le Grillage (A Hole in the Fence*; Nathan, 1977); *Le Roi sans Armes (The Weaponless King*; Nathan, 1979); *Train M* (Nathan, 1979); *La Cinquième Dimension (The Fifth Dimension*; GP, 1979); *Léonie et la Pierre de Lumière (Leonie and the Stone of Light*; Envol 1, 1980); *Nicolas et la Montre Magique (Nicolas and the Magic Watch*; Amitié, 1981); *Les Indiens de la Rue Jules Ferry (The Indians from Jules Ferry Street*; Amitié, 1982); *Prisonniers des Médias (Prisoner of the Media*; Amitié, 1983); *L'Étrange Noël de Jonas (Jonas' Strange Christmas*; Amitié, 1984); *L'Héritier de la Nuit (The Night Heir*; Nathan, 1985); *La Cité des Brumes (The City of Mists*; Amitié, 1986); *La Vallée des Esprits (The Valley of Minds*; Hatier, 1988); *La Forteresse de la Nuit (The Fortress of Night*; Rageot, 1989); *Classe de Lune (Moon Class*; Rageot, 1989); *Au Pays des Knops (In the Land of the Knops*; Nathan, 1989); *La Petite Planète (The Small Planet*; Milan, 1989); *La Fontaine Maléfique (The Evil Fountain*; Rageot, 1990); *Le Cahier Jaune (The Yellow Notebook*; Hac., 1990); *Les Allumeurs de Souvenirs (The Memories Lighters*; Lezay, 1995); *Racamiel and Rigobert* (Nathan, 1995); *Terminal Park* (Flamm., 1996); *La Montre Infernale (The Watch from Hell*; Nathan, 1996); *Note:* Juveniles. See Chapter VIII. Also see ***Contes et Légendes***

Sauty, Louis (?-); *Dans l'Antre des Dieux (In the Lair of the Gods*; Ed. Littéraires, 1925); *Le Ténéré* (Julliard, 1945)

Sauvage, Marcel (?-); *Le Premier Homme que j'ai tué (The First Man I Killed*; Ren. du Livre, 1929); *La Fin de Paris, ou La Révolte des Statues (The End of Paris, or the Statues' Revolt*; Den., 1932); *Sous le Feu de l'Équauteur: Les Secrets de l'Afrique Noire (Under the Equator's Fire: the Secrets of Dark Africa*; Den., 1937); *Sous le Masque des Sorciers (Under the Witch-Doctors' Masks*; Pigelet, 1946); *Les Gardiens de la Parole (The Guardians of the Word*; Élan, 1948)

Sauvestre, Jean (?-); *La Grotte Enchantée (The Enchanted Cavern*; Nlles. Presses Fr., 1946)

Savage, Michel (1947-); *Colomb d'Outre-Tombe (Columbus of Beyond the Grave*; Héritage, 1992); *Note:* French-Canadian writer.

Savoir, Alfred (Posznanski, Alfred) (1883-1934) *see* **Grand-Guignol**

Scapin, Jean (?-); *La Matraque du Fantôme (The Ghost's Club*; Ferenczi, 1938); *La Maison du Frisson (House of Shivers*; MOC 24, 1982)

Scarron, Paul (1610-1660); *Typhon ou la Gigantomachie* (Quinet, 1644); *Le Virgile Travesti (The Disguised Virgil*; Luyne, 1667)

Schaeffer, Pierre (1910-1995) *see* **Opéra**

Scheffer, R. (1864-?) *see* **Grand-Guignol**

Scheirs, Jef (?-); *Les Derniers Jours du Monde (The Last Days of the World*; Dupuis, n.d.); *Note:* Belgian writer.

Schinkel, David (?-) *see* **Beauchesne, Yves**

Schmitt, Bernard (?-); *Le Triomphe du Dr. Barbier (Dr. Barbier's Triumph*; Garance, 1959); *Phénix* (Garance, 1960); *Au Sud de Mostar (South of Mostar*; Kent-Segep, 1963); *Et à l'Aube, Walhall... (And at Dawn, Walhall...*; Pensée U., 1974)

Schneegans, Nicole (1941-); *L'Enfant et la Maison Bulle (The Child and the Bubble House*; Le Cerf, 1977); *Le Pêcheur d'Oiseaux (The Bird Fisher*; Bayard, 1980); *Les Jumeaux du Roi (The King's Twins*; Centurion, 1982); *Le Géant aux Étoiles (The Giant and the Stars*; Amitié, 1983); *Le Roi Amoureux (The King in Love*; Centurion, 1986); *Au Secours Balthazar (Help, Balthazar*; Amitié, 1988); *Mystérieuse Garance (Mysterious Garance*; Flamm., 1988); *Note:* Juveniles.

Schneider, Marcel (1913-); *Sémiramis, Reine de Babylone (Semiramis, Queen of Babylon*; with M. C. **Poinsot**; Gall., 1926); *La Première Île (The First Island*; AM, 1951); *Le Sang Léger (The Light Blood*; AM, 1952); *Aux Couleurs de la Nuit (In the Colors of Night*; AM, 1953); *Les Deux Miroirs (The Two Mirrors*; AM, 1956); *Le Sablier Magique (The Magic Hourglass*; Cast., 1960); *La Branche de Merlin (Merlin's Branch*; Plon, 1962); *Les Colonnes du Temple (The Columns of the Temple*; Grasset, 1962); *Histoire de la Littérature Fantastique en France (History of Fantastic Literature in France*; non-fiction; Fayard, 1964; rev. 1985); *Histoires Fantastiques d'Aujourd'Hui (Contemporary Fantastic Tales*; anthology; Cast., 1965); *Opéra Massacre (Opera Slaughter*; Grasset, 1965); *La Sybille de Cumes (The Sybil of Cumes*; Grasset, 1966); *La Nuit de Longtemps (The Night of Longtime*; Grasset, 1968); *Le Guerrier de Pierre (The Stone Warrior*; Grasset, 1969); *Le Lieutenant Perdu (The Lost Lieutenant*; Grasset, 1972); *La Belle Hollandaise (The Beautiful Dutch Girl*; PC, 1972); *Le Chasseur Vert (The Green Hunter*; PC, 1973); *Déjà la Neige (Already the Snow*; Grasset, 1974); *Le Vampire de Düsseldorf (The Vampire of Dusseldorf*; Pygmalion, 1975); *Sur une Étoile (Upon a Star*; Grasset, 1976); *Le Harem Impérial de Topkapi (The Imperial Harem of Topkapi*; AM, 1977); *Le Prince de la Terre (The Prince of the Earth*; Grasset, 1980); *L'Apparition de la Rose (The Appearance of the Rose*; Balland, 1980); *La Symphonie Imaginaire (The Imaginary Symphony*; Seuil, 1981); *La Lumière du Nord (The Light of the North*; Grasset, 1982); *Mère Merveille (Mother Wonder*; Grasset, 1983); *Histoires à Mourir Debout (Stories to Die Standing Up*; anthology; Grasset, 1985); *La Fin du Carnaval (The End of the Carnival*; Grasset, 1987); *Un Été sur le Lac (A Summer on the Lake*; Grasset, 1989); *L'Eternité Fragile (Fragile Eternity*; Grasset, 1989); *Le Palais des Mirages (The Palace of Mirages*; Lib. Gen. Fr., 1994); *La Jeune Fille au Sablier (The Young Girl and the Hourglass*; Rocher, 1996); *Paris, Lanterne Magique (Paris, Magic Lantern*; Grasset, 1997); *Note:* See Chapter VIII.

Schlockoff, Alain (?-) *see* **Andrevon, Jean-Pierre**

Schmidt, Joel (?-); *Le Fleuve des Morts (The River of the Dead*; Julliard, 1975); *La Ténébreuse (The Dark One*; AM, 1980); *La Reine de la Nuit (The Queen of Night*; Balland, 1983); *Le Flambeau des Ombres (The Torch of the Shadows*; AM, 1985); *Le Pavillon de l'Aurore (The Pavilion of Dawn*; Rocher, 1993); *La Métamorphose du Père (The Metamorphosis of the Father*; Rocher, 1996)

Schnitzer, Ludmilla *see* **Luda**

Schopfer, Jean *see* **Anet, Claude**

Schwabacher, Henri-Simon *see* **Duvernois, Henri**

Schwob, Marcel (1867-1905); *Coeur Double (Twin Hearts*; Ollendorff, 1891); *Le Roi au Masque d'Or (The King in the Golden Mask*; Ollendorf, 1892); *Vies Imaginaires (Imaginary Lives*; Charpentier-Fasquelle, 1896); *La Croisade des Enfants (The Children's Crusade*; MdF, 1896); *Mimes (Mimics*; MdF, 1964); *Vie de Morphiel, Démiurge (Life of Morphiel, Demiurge*; Cendres, 1994); *Note:* See Chapter IV.

Scovel, Guy *see* **Fontana, Jean-Pierre**

Scribe, Eugène (1791-1861) *see* **Opéra**

Scriven, Gérard (Père) (?-); *Wopsy, Mémoires d'un Ange Gardien (Wopsy, Memories of a Guardian Angel*; Grands Lacs, 1946); *Wopsy Continue (Wopsy Continues*; La Savane, 1957)

Scudery, Georges de (1601-1667) *see* **Opéra**

Seabury, Don A. (?-) *see* **Corman, Terence**

Sébillot, Paul Yves (?-); *Contes et Légendes du Pays de Gouarec (Tales and Legends from the Land of Gouarec*; Lafolye, 1897); *L'Île Volante (The Flying Island*; serialized as 4 vols., France Ed., 1923); *1. Le Bolide Mystérieux (The Mysterious Rocket*); *2. La Terreur de l'Humanité (The Terror of Mankind*); *3. Dans les Griffes du Bandit (In the Clutches of the Bandit*); *4. La Lutte Suprême (The Supreme Clash*; *Les Aventures de Gobela-Lune (The Adventures of Moon-Gulper*; France Ed., 1924); *Le Roi de l'Épouvante (The King of Terror*; BGA, 1930); *Le Mystère de Venise (The Mystery of Venice*; Tallandier, 1932); *L'Étreinte de l'Invisible (The Clutches of the Invisible*; Baudinière, 1935); *Mythologie and Folklore de Bretagne (Mythology and Folklore from Britanny*; Terre de Brume, 1995); *Note:* See Chapter VII.

Sedaine, Michel Jean (1712-1778) *see* **Opéra**

Sédillot, René (?-); *La France de Babel-Welche (The France of Babel-Welche*; Calmann-Lévy, 1983)

Ségalen, Victor (1878-1919) *see* **Opéra**

Segond, Aude (?-); *Le Sceau du Daghestan (The Seal of Daghestan*; SdP 2 69, 1977); *Note:* Juvenile.

Segrais, Jean Regnault de (?-?); *Nouvelles Françaises, ou les Divertissements de la Princesse Aurélie (French News, or the Entertainment of Princess Aurelia*; A. de Sommanville, 1656-1657); *Relation de l'Île Imaginaire et Histoire de la Princesse de Paphlagonie (Tale of the Imaginary Island and Story of the Princess of Paphlagonia*; A. de Sommanville, 1659; rep. VI, 1788)

Séguin, Pierre (1949-); *Les Métamorphoses du Choupardier (The Metamorphoses of the Choupardier*; HMH, 1976); *Caliban (HMH, 1977); *Note:* French-Canadian writer. Novel about a mythical beast.

Ségur, Nicolas (?-); *Le Paradis des Hommes (The Paradise of Men*; AM, 1930)

Séguret, Serge (1960-); *Le Cri de l'Asphalte (The Scream of the Tar*; FNSF 4, 1997); *La Cité des Motards (The City of Bikers*; FNSF 12, 1997); *Hors-Piste (Out of Runway*; FNSF 21, 1997); *Note:* See Chapter IX.

Seignolle, Claude (1917-); *Le Folklore du Hurepoix* (with Jacques Seignolle; Maisonneuve, 1937); *En Sologne* (Maisonneuve, 1945); *Les Fouilles de Robinson (The Digs of Robinson*; Maisonneuve, 1945); *Le Rond des Sorciers (The Circle of Sorcerers*; Quatre Vents, 1945);

Contes Populaires de Guyenne (Popular Tales of Guyenne; 2 vols.; Maisonneuve, 1946); *Marie La Louve* (Quatre-Vents, 1947; transl. as *Mary the Wolf* in *The Accursed*, 1967); *La Malvenue (The Illcome*; Maisonneuve, 1952; rev. MarF 215, 1965; transl. as *Malvenue* in *The Accursed*, 1967); *Le Bahut Noir (The Black Dresser*; Los., 1958); *Le Diable en Sabots (The Devil in Clogs*; Los., 1959); *La Brume ne se lèvera plus (The Mist Will No Longer Rise*; Los., 1959; rev. MarF 199, 1963); *La Gueule (The Jaws*; Los., 1959; partially rep. as *Les Loups Verts (The Geen Wolves)*, MarF 353, 1970); *Le Diable dans la Tradition Populaire (The Devil in Popular Traditions*; Maisonneuve, 1959); *Le Folklore du Languedoc* (Maisonneuve, 1960); *Le Galoup* (Ed. Pedagog. Mod., 1960); *Le Chupador* (EPM, 1960); *L'Événement (The Event*; Los., 1960); *Un Homme Nu (A Naked Man*; EPM, 1961); *Un Corbeau de Toutes les Couleurs (A Crow of All Colors*; Den., 1962); *Les Malédictions (The Curses*; Maisonneuve, 1963); *Le Folklore de la Provence* (Maisonneuve, 1963); *Miettes pour un Bestiaire (Crumbs for a Bestiary*; Dynamo, 1964); *Les Évangiles du Diable (The Devil's Gospel*; Maisonneuve, 1964); *La Nuit des Halles (The Night of the Halles*; Maisonneuve, 1965); *Histoires Maléfiques (Maleficent Tales*; MarF 230, 1965); *Contes Macabres (Macabre Stories*; MarF 244, 1966); *Les Chevaux de la Nuit (The Night Horses*; MarF 282, 1967; rev. Aventure Cartonnée, 1988); *Récits Fantastiques de Sologne* (Sologne, 1967); *Le Berry Traditionnel* (Maisonneuve & Larose, 1969); *Contes de Sologne* (Sologne, 1969); *Contes Fantastiques de Bretagne* (Maisonneuve & Larose, 1969); *Invitation au Château de l'Étrange (Invitation to the Castle of the Weird*; Maisonneuve & Larose, 1969); *Histoires Atroces (Atrocious Tales*; Publinex, 1970); *Histoires Vénéneuses (Poisonous Tales*; Belfond, 1970; rep. MarF 419, 1973); *Diables et Enchanteurs de Guyenne and Gascogne (Devils and Wizards of Guyenne and Gascony*; Tchou, 1973); *Contes Sorciers (Sorcerous Stories*; MarF 465, 1974); *Folklore du Hurepoix (Folklore from the Hurepoix*; Maisonneuve & Larose, 1978); *Le Meneur de Loups (The Wolf Leader*; J'aime Lire, 1979); *Histoires Étranges (Strange Stories*; Hac., 1980); *À l'Enseigne de l'Étrange (Under the Sign of the Strange*; Minerve, 1989); *L'Homme aux Sept Loups (The Man with Seven Wolves*; Bayard, 1990); *Une Enfance Sorcière (A Witch's Childhood*; Royer, 1994); *La Morsure de Satan (Satan's Bite*; Phébus, 1994); *Le Conteur de Loups (The Storyteller of Wolves*; Hesse, 1995); *Contes du Périgord (Perigord Stories*; Maisonneuve & Larose, 1996); *Note:* See Chapter VIII. a number of Claude Seignolle's stories have been adapted as short features or television movies (see Book 1, **Le Faucheur** under Short Features in Chapter I, **Marie la Louve** in Chapter II, and **Delphine** in Chapter III).

Sélènes, Pierre de (?-?); *Un Monde Inconnu, Deux Ans sur la Lune (An Unknown World, Two Years on the Moon*; Flamm., 1896); *Note:* See Chapter V.

Semant, Paul de (1855-1915); *Le Lac d'Or du Docteur Sarbacane (Dr. Sarbacane's Golden Lake*; Flamm., 1900); *Gaëtan Faradel, Explorateur malgré lui (Gaetan Faradel, Explorer in Spite of Himself*; Flamm., 1900); *Gaëtan Faradel, Champion du Tour du Monde (Gaetan Faradel, Champion of Going Around the World*; Flamm., Flamm., 1904); *Le Dernier Raid de Nelly Sanderson (Nelly Sanderson's Last Raid*; Flamm., 1908); *Le Fulgur* (Flamm., 1910)

Senard, Maurice (?-); *K.B.X. Métal* (Diderot, 1946)

Senécal, Patrick (1967-); *5150 Rue des Ormes (5150 Elm St.*; Guy Saint-Jean, 1994); *Note:* French-Canadian writer.

Sérane, Philippe (Abbé) (?-?); *L'Heureux Naufrage (The Fortunate Shipwreck*; Denonville, 1789); *Note:* Utopia.

Serge (Feaudière, Maurice) (?-); *L'Île aux Merveilles (The Island of Wonders*; Libr. Champs-Élysées, 1945); *Londres Secret et ses Fantômes (Secret London and Its Ghosts*; ERGÉ, 1946)

Sériel, Jerôme (Vallée, Jacques) (1939-); *Le Sub-Espace (The Sub-Space*; RF 82, 1961); *Le Satellite Sombre (The Dark Satellite*; PdF 59, 1963); *Alintel* (as Jacques Vallée; MdF, 1986); *Note:* See Chapter IX. Jacques Vallée is also the author of a number of celebrated non-fiction works analyzing the UFO phenomenon: *Challenge to Science: The UFO Enigma* (with Janine Vallee; 1966); *UFO in Space: Anatomy of a Phenomenon; Passport to Magonia* (1969); *The Invisible College; Messengers of Deception* (1979); *Dimensions: A Casebook of Alien Contact* (1988); *Confrontations: A Scientist's Search for Alien Contact* (1990); *Revelations: Alien Contact & Human Deception* (1991); *Forbidden Science (Journals 1957-69; 1992)*; etc.

Sernine, Daniel (Lortie, Alain) (1955-); *La Fresque aux Trois Démons (The Fresco with Three Demons*; Requiem, 1978; rev. HMH, 1991); *Les Contes de l'Ombre (Tales of Shadows*; Presses Sélect, 1979); *Légendes du Vieux Manoir (Legends of the Old Manor*; Presses Sélect, 1979); *Organisation Argus* (JP 38, 1979; transl. as *Those Who Watch Over the Earth*, 1990); *Le Trésor du Scorpion* (JP 40, 1980; transl. as *Scorpion's Treasure*, 1990); *L'Épée Arhapal* (JP 44, 1980; transl. as *The Sword of Arhapal*, 1990); *Le Vieil Homme et l'Espace (The Old Man and Space*; CdF 4, 1981); *La Cité Inconnue (The Unknown City*; JP, 1982); *Ludovic* (Tisseyre, 1983); *Quand Vient la Nuit (When Night Comes*; CdA 1, 1983); *Argus Intervient* (JP, 1983; transl. as *Argus Steps In*, 1990); *Les Méandres du Temps (The Meanders* *of Time*; CdF 6, 1983); *Le Cercle Violet (The Indigo Circle*; Tisseyre, 1984); *Les Envoûtements (The Bewitchments*; JP, 1985); *Aurores Boréales 2 (Northern Lights*; anthology; CdF 9, 1985); *Argus: Mission Mille (Argus: Mission One Thousand*; JP 63, 1988); *La Nef dans les Nuages (The Ship in the Clouds*; JP 67, 1989); *Nuits Blêmes (Wan Nights*; XYZ, 1990); *Quatre Destins (Four Destinies*; JP 72, 1990); *Les Rêves d'Argus (The Dreams of Argus*; JP 77, 1991); *Le Cercle de Khaleb (The Circle of Khaleb*; Héritage, 1991); *Boulevard des Étoiles (Boulevard of the Stars*; Ianus, 1991); *À la Recherche de M. Goodtheim (Looking for Mr. Goodtheim*; Ianus, 1991); *La Magicienne Bleue (The Blue Magician*; Tisseyre, 1991); *Chronoreg* (Q/A, 1992); *La Couleur Nouvelle (The New Color*; Q/A, 1993); *Les Portes Mystérieuses (The Mysterious Gates*; Héritage, 1993); *Manuscrit Trouvé dans un Secrétaire (Manuscript Found in a Secretary*; Tisseyre, 1994); *L'Arc-en-Cercle (The Rainbow Ring*; Héritage, 1995); *La Traversée de l'Apprenti Sorcier (The Crossing of the Sorcerer's Apprentice*; JP 100, 1995); *Sur la Scène des Siècles (On the Stage of the Centuries*; Ianus, 1995); *Note:* French-Canadian writer. The *Granverger* series is a juvenile gothic saga taking place in Neubourg, an imaginary Quebec. The series starts in *Légendes* and continues in *Le Trésor*, *L'Épée*, *Le Cercle*, *Les Envoûtements*, *Quatre Destins*, and *Le Cercle*. Sernine's other series, the *Argus* saga, is about the Erymeans, benevolent aliens watching Earth. (Both series cross over in *La Nef.*) *Ludovic* is a heroic fantasy novel. *Boulevard* and *À la Recherche* form a new cycle, collecting stories about a future Earth depopulated by the aliens of the *Argus* series.

Sernine, Paul (?-); *La Dame Mauve (The Mauve Lady*; Revue des Indépendants, 1922)

Servage, Patrice (?-); *Le Rescapé des Concluses (The Survivor from the Concluses*; Rocher, 1981); *Note:* Novel about UFO abductions.

Servant, Stéphane (?-); *Les Joyeuses et Émerveillantes Aventures des Six Frères du Petit Poucet (The Happy and Wondrous Adventures of Tom Thumb's Six Bothers*; Fontane, 1910)

Servat, Gilles (?-); *Les Chroniques d'Arcturus 1: Skinn Mac Dana (The Chronicles of Arcturus*; Atalante, 1995); *Les Chroniques d'Arcturus 2: La Navigation de Myrdhinn (Myrdhinn's Navigation*; Atalante, 1996); *Les Chroniques d'Arcturus 3: Arcturus* (Atalante, 1997); *Note:* See Chapter VIII.

Servier, Jean (?-); *Histoire de l'Utopie (History of Utopia*; non-fiction; Gal., 1968); **Servranckx, M. L. (?-);** *Une Révolution à Lilliput (A Revolution in Lilliput*; Portiques, 1930); *Note:* Belgian writer.

Seuhl, Antonin (?-); *Le Jaguar Rouge (The Red Jaguar*;

L'Intrépide, n.d.); *Les Gaités de la République de Patati et Patata (The Gaieties of the Republic of Patati et Patata*; Ollendorf, 1922); *Patati et Patata en Guerre: Aux Hommes de 2222 s'il en reste (Patati et Patata at War: to the Men of the Year 2222 If There Are Any Left*; Ollendorf, 1922); *La Victoire de Patati et Patata (The Victory of Patati et Patata,* Ollendorf, 1922); *La Grève des Machines (The Machines on Strike*; Baudinière, 1924; rev. as *Le Rayon d'Amour (The Love Ray)*, Baudinière, 1925); *La Femme sans Voile (The Woman Without Veil*; Baudinière, 1925); *L'Amour par TSF (Wireless Love*; Radot, 1927); *Gabone* (Baudinière, 1933); *Note:* See Chapter VII. Also see **Adam, Pierre**.

Sève, André de (1961-); *Les Conquérants de Shaddaï (The Conquerors of Shaddai*; Courteau, 1989); *Note:* French-Canadian writer.

Séverac, Guy (Chassin, F.) (?-); *Les Conquérants de l'Infini (The Conquerors of Infinity*; Lajeunesse, 1945); *Note:* See Chapter IX. Also used the pseudonym "Colonel Chassin."

Séverin, Jean (?-); *La Jalousie de Dieu (God's Jealousy*; RL, 1955); *L'Enfant et la Nuit (The Child and the Night*; RL, 1958); *L'Étoile des Baux (The Star of the Baux*; RL, 1966); *Les Enfants Éblouis (The Stunned Children*; RL, 1968); *SOS Tournebise* (SdP, 1972); *Qand Chassent les Vautours (When Hunt the Vultures*; RL, 1974); *Le Soleil d'Olympie (The Sun of Olympia*; RL, 1976)

Sévestre, Norbert (1879-); *Le Trèfle Rouge (The Red Clover*; Hac, 1908; rev., RMY, 1930); *Les Revenants de la Pierre aux Noyés (The Ghosts of the Drowned Men's Stone*; Hac., 1913); *La Main Rouge (The Red Hand*; Hac., 1915); *Le Masque qui Tombe (The Falling Mask*; Delagrave, 1919); *Le Tour du Monde en 14 Jours (Around the World in 14 Days*; Hac., 1921); *Trois Jeunes Aéronautes au Pôle Sud (Three Young Airmen at the South Pole*; Hac., 1927); *La Révolte des Monstres (The Revolt of the Monsters*; BGA, 1928); *La Sombre Affaire de la Croix Basse (The Dark Affair of the Low Cross*; RMY, 1931); *Terre Disparue (Vanished Land*; Tallandier, 1931); *Tsao le Pirate* (Montsouris, 1933); *Le Val Tragique (The Tragic Valley*; Montsouris, 1933); *L'Hydre de l'Amazonie (The Hydra of the Amazon*; Tallandier, 1936); *Pillards de l'Arctique (Reavers of the Arctic*; Tallandier, 1938); *Terres Mortelles (Deadly Lands*; Montsouris, 1938); *L'Île Sanguinaire (The Blood-Thirsty Island*; Tallandier, 1939); *L'Avion Rouge (The Red Plane*; Tallandier, 1942); *Note:* See Chapter VII.

Sévigny, Marc (1953-); *Vertige chez les Anges (Vertigo Among Angels*; VLB, 1988); *Note:* French-Canadian writer. Collection of fantastical tales.

Seyr, Jacques *see* **Vernes, Henri**

Shannon, Lew *see* **Vernes, Henri**

Sheldon, S. K. (Campos, Elisabeth) (?-); *Musée des Horreurs (Museum of Horrors*; FNG 60, 1987)

Shenandoo (?-); *Ceux de l'Ombre (Those in the Shadows*; André Martel, 1958); *Radiations de Mort (Deadly Radiations*; André Martel, 1958); *Avions sans Espoir (Planes Without Hope*; André Martel, 1958)

Sibres, Abel (?-); *L'Héritage de Sans-Patience, un Raid Transatlantique (The Sans-Patience Inheritance, a Transtalantic Raid*; Romans Populaires, 1913); *Dans les Ténèbres (In the Darkness*; Romans Populaires, 1913); *Le Prisonnier du Zeppelin-IV (The Prisoner of Zeppelin-IV*; Romans Populaires, 1917); *L'Insaisissable Fugitif (The Uncatchable Fugitive*; Romans Populaires, 1918); *Grippe Espagnole? (Spanish Flu?*; Romans Populaires, 1921); *Le Secret du Dactylo (The Secret of the Typist*; Bonne Presse, 1923); *Les Évadés de l'île sans Maître (Escape from the Island Without a Master*; Bonne Presse, 1926)

Sieffert, René (?-); *Contes de Pluie et de Lune (Tales of Rain and Moon*; Publ. Orient. De Fr., 1970); *Le Cycle Épique des Taïras et des Minamoto (The Epic Saga of the Tairas and the Minamoto*; Publ. Orient. De Fr., 1976); *Contes de Yamato (Tales from Yamato*; Publ. Orient. De Fr., 1979); *Le Conte du Coupeur de Bambou (The Tale of the Bamboo Cutter*; Publ. Orient. De Fr., 1992); *Histoire de Demoiselle Joruri (Story of Miss Joruri*; Publ. Orient. De Fr., 1994)

Sillig, Olivier (?-); *Bzjeurd* (Atalante, 1995)

Silva-Coronel, Paul (?-); See **Vercors**.

Silvain, Pierre (?-); *Les Éoliennes (The Wind Machines*; MdF, 1971); *Mélodrame (Melodrama*; Gall., 1971); *Le Grand Théâtre (The Great Theater*; MdF, 1973); *Les Espaces Brûlés (The Burned Spaces*; MdF, 1977); *Mémoire d'un Autre (Memory of Another*; MdF, 1977); *Le Regard du Serpent (The Serpent's Stare*; Mazarine, 1985); *Le Guetteur Invisible (The Invisible Watcher*; Noésis, 1991); *L'Empire Fortuné (The Wealthy Empire*; Manya, 1993); *La Gloire Éphémère de Joao Matos (The Ephemeral Glory of Joao Matos*; Julliard, 1994)

Silve de Ventavon, Jean (?-); *Le Coffret d'Ébène (The Ebony Box*; Los., 1968)

Silvestre, Armand (?-?); *Contes Pantagruéliques and Galants (Gallant and Gluttonous Tales*; Arnould, 1884); *Contes à la Brune (Tales of Mist*; Marpon & Flamm., 1889); *Contes Audacieux (Audacious Tales*; Kolb, 1892-1902); *Contes Divertissants (Entertaining Tales*; Libr. Illustrée, 1892); *Contes Hilarants (Hilarious Tales*; Libr. Illustrée, 1892); *Histoires Abracadabrantes (Alakazam Tales*; Libr. Illustrée, 1893); *Contes Désopilants (Funny Tales*; Libr. Illustrée, 1893); *Facéties Galantes: Contes Joyeux (Gallant Fantasies: Joyful Tales*; Fayard, 1893); *La Planète Enchantée (The Enchanted Planet*; Floury, 1896); *Contes Irrévérencieux (Irreverent Tales*; Flamm., 1896); *Contes Tragiques and Sentimentaux (Tragic and Sentimental Tales*; Flamm., 1897); *Grisélidis* (Stock, 1901); *Contes Incongrus (Incongruous Tales*; Libr. Contemporaine, 1902); *Note:* See Chapter IV. Also see **Opéra**.

Sim, Georges (Simenon, Georges) (1903-1989); *Le Roi des Glaces (The King of the Ice*; BGA, 1927); *Les Nains des Cataractes (The Dwarves of the Waterfalls*; BGA, 1928); *Le Secret des Lamas (The Secret of the Lamas*; BGA, 1928); *L'Île des Hommes Roux (The Island of the Red-Haired Men*; BGA, 1929); *Le Roi du Pacifique (The King of the Pacific*; LA, 1929); *Le Gorille Roi (The King of the Gorillas*; BGA, 1929); *Marie-Mystère (Mary Mystery*; PC, 1931); *La Fiancée du Diable (The Devil's Fiancée*; PC, 1932); *Note:* Belgian writer. See Chapter VII.

Simard, Danielle (1952-); *La Revanche du Dragon (The Dragon's Revenge*; Héritage, 1992); *Lia dans l'Autre Monde (Lian in the Other World*; Héritage, 1996); *Mes Parents sont Fous! (My Parents Are Mad!*; Héritage, 1996); *Note:* French-Canadian writer. Juvenile fantasies.

Simard, David (1977-); *Nouvelles Nouvelles (New Tales*; Françoise Marois, 1994); *Note:* French-Canadian writer.

Simard, Jean (1916-); *Mon Fils Pourtant Heureux (My Son Still Happy*; CLF, 1956); *Les Sentiers de la Nuit (The Paths of Night*; CLF, 1958); *L'Ange Interdit (The Forbidden Angel*; CLF, 1961); *13 Récits (13 Tales*; HMH, 1964); *Le Singe et le Perroquet (The Monkey and the Parrot*; Tisseyre, 1983); *Note:* French-Canadian writer.

Simart, Hélène *see* **Laurent, Agnès**

Simon, Valérie (1963-); *Arkem, La Pierre des Ténèbres 1: Yanis, Déesse de la Mort (Arkem, the Stone of Darkness 1: Yanis, Goddess of Death*; FNSF 22, 1997); *Arkem, La Pierre des Ténèbres 2: Sinen, Déesse de la Vie (Arkem, the Stone of Darkness 2: Sinen, Goddess of Life*; FNSF 23, 1997); *Note:* See Chapter VIII.

Simonay, Bernard (?-); *Phenix* (Rocher, 1986); *Graal* (Rocher, 1988); *La Malédiction de la Licorne (The*

Curse of the Unicorn; Rocher, 1990)La Porte de Bronze (The Gate of Brass; Rocher, 1994); *Les Enfants de l'Atlantide 1— Le Prince Déchu (The Children of Atlantis 1—the Fallen Prince*; Rocher, 1994); *Les Enfants de l'Atlantide 2—L'Archipel du Soleil (The Archipelago of the Sun; Rocher, 1995)Les Enfants de l'Atlantide 3—Le Crépuscule des Géants (The Twilight of the Giants; Rocher, 1996)La Lande Maudite (The Accursed Moor; Rocher, 1996) La Première Pyramide (The First Pyramid*; Rocher, 1996); *La Jeunesse de Djoser (Djoser's Youth*; Rocher, 1996)*Note:* See Chapter VIII.

Simoneau, Raymond *see* **Wilshcocqkst**

Simonet, Jean (?-); *Le Mystère du Lac en Flammes (The Mystery of the Lake on Fire*; STAEL, 1948); *Le Maître du Desert (The Master of the Desert*; STAEL, 1949); *La Vengeance de Ben-R'bi (Ben R'bi's Revenge*; STAEL, 1950); *Le Vampire des Sables (The Vampire of the Sands*; STAEL, 1951); *Note:* Also used the pseudonym "Frédy."

Simpson, Danièle (1946-); *Le Voleur d'Étoiles (The Star Thief*; Paulines, 1971); *L'Arbre aux Tremblements Roses (The Tree with Pink Shakings*; JP 49, 1984); *Note:* French-Canadian writer. *L'Arbre* is a juvenile novel about the adventures of two children, a bird, and an alien tree on a (literally) colorful planet.

Sinclair, Jacques (?-); *Le Destin s'amuse (Fate Has Fun*; Vigneau, 1946); *Le Voyageur (The Traveller*; TR, 1983)

Slang, Martin *see* **Béra, Paul.**

Smit Le Bénédicte, Jean-Claude (?-); With Jean **Lhassd**: *Hushan (Malpertuis,* 1978); *Le March and de Souvenirs* (c. d'Art Ix.; 1983); *Maasterstein* (1984); *Lion St. Pierre* (1985); *Delicatesses Montelles* (1989). With Frank **Andriat**: *Juridiction Zéro* (Alé; 1980); *Duckstone* (Memor; 1995); *Le Voleur d'Ans* (Memor; 1995); *Les Légions du Neant* (Memor; 1995). *Note:* Belgian writer.

Snorra, Robert (?-); *Les Nouveaux Troglodytes (The New Troglodytes*; Bonne Presse, 1947)

Sobra, Adrien *see* **Agapit, Marc**

Sodler, Éric (?-); *Raid sur Pluton (Raid Over Pluto*; Daniber 15, 1960)

Solar, Fabien (?-?) *see* **Grand-Guignol**

Solari, Émile (1873-1961); *Le Manoir des Roches Bleues (The Manor of Blue Rocks*; Bibl. Coop., 1906); *La Cité Rebâtie (The Rebuilt City*; Libr. Universelle, 1907);

Aventures au Maroc de Grain d'Or et de Sourcil de Loup (Adventures of Grain-Of-Gold and Wolf's Brow in Morocco; Firmin-Didot, 1907); *La Découverte du Dr. Maffle (The Discovery of Dr. Maffle*; Firmin Didot, 1911); *L'Envoyé des Forces Obscures (The Envoy of the Dark Forces*; Flamm., 1919); *La Compagne (The Companion*; Fasquelle, 1924); *Le Palais Bleu (The Blue Palace*; Fayard, 1925); *Le Crime de Sulpice (Sulpice's Crime*; Fasquelle, 1929); *A-t-elle Rêvé? (Did She Dream It?*; Tallandier, 1933); *Contes (Tales*; L. Jean à Carqueiranne, 1934); *Note:* See Chapter V.

Soler, Michel (?-); *L'Inconnu de la Montagne (The Unknown Man on the Mountain*; MRA, 1956)

Solet, Bertrand (1933-); *Les Révoltés de Saint-Domingue (The Revolutionaries of St. Domingue*; RL, 1967); *Le Seigneur des Sables (The Lord of the Sands*; Amitié, 1970); *Un Tambour dans la Nuit (A Drum in the Night*; Amitié, 1974); *Le Serment du Berger (The Shepherd's Oath*; Farandole, 1975); *Les Frères des Nuages (The Brothers of the Cloud*; TF 3, 1977); *15 Récits de SF* (anthology; Gautier-Languereau, 1978); *Le Talisman de Vanina (Vanina's Talisman*; J'Aime Lire, 1980); *Les Pionniers de l'Île Franche (The Pioneers of Free-Island*; BV, 1982); *Le Secret du Comte (The Count's Secret*; Hac., 1992); *Note:* Juveniles.

Solier, René de (?-); *La Corde à Puits (The Well's Rope*; Gall., 1948); *Les Gardes (The Guards*; Gall., 1952); *Chaises et Voyeurs de Ida Barbarigo (Chairs and Voyeurs of Ida Barbarigo*; Alfiéri, 1970); *Ljubo* (Musée de Poche, 1971); *Kijno* (Musée de Poche, 1972)

Sologne, Jean (?-); *L'Homme qui Change de Corps (The Man Who Switched Bodies*; Colbert, 1942)

Solomon, Michel (1909-); *La Troisième Greffe du Coeur (The Third Heart Transplant*; Humanitas, 1987); *Note:* French-Canadian writer. Apocalyptic near-future.

Somain, Jean-François *see* **Somcynsky, Jean-François**

Somcynsky, Jean-François (1943-); *Les Grimaces (Grimaces*; Tisseyre, 1975); *Le Diable du Mahani (The Devil of Mahani*; Tisseyre, 1978); *La Frontière du Milieu (The Frontier of the Middle*; 1980); *Peut-être à Tokyo (Maybe in Tokyo*; Naaman, 1981); *La Planète Amoureuse (The Planet in Love*; CdF 5, 1982); *J'ai Entendu Parler d'Amour (I Heard Love Mentioned*; Asticou, 1984); *Un Tango Fictif (Virtual Tango*; Naaman, 1986); *Les Visiteurs du PôleNord (The North Pole Visitors*; Tisseyre, 1987); *Dernier Départ (Last Departure*; as Jean-François Somain; Tisseyre, 1989); *Vivre en Beauté (To Live Beautifully*; as Jean-François Somain; AMAM 6, 1989); *La Nuit du Chien-Loup (The Night of the Wolf*; as Jean-François Somain; Tisseyre, 1990); *Tu Peux Compter Sur Moi (You Can Count on*

Me; as Jean-François Somain; Tisseyre, 1990); *Le Baiser des Étoiles (The Kiss of the Stars*; as Jean-François Somain; HMH, 1992); *Le Secret le Mieux Gardé (The Best Kept Secret*; as Jean-François Somain; Tisseyre, 1993); *Le Sourire des Mondes Lointains (The Smile of the Far Worlds*; as Jean-François Somain; Tisseyre, 1994); *Le Jour de la Lune (The Day of the Moon*; as Jean-François Somain; Vermillon, 1997); *Note:* French-Canadian writer. The theme of love and relationships is often central to his works. He is also the author of *Il n'y a pas de dernier amour (There Is No Last Love)*, a radio play about vampires, broadcast on Radio-Canada in 1985.

Sonet, Philippe (Father) (?-); *La Révolte chez le Petit Peuple (Revolt Among the Little People*; Durendal, 1939); *Guy Barclay, Général des Fourmis (General of the Ants*; Dupuis, 1951)

Sonkin, François (?-); *La Dame (The Lady*; Julliard, 1964); *Le Mief* (Den., 1967); *Les Gendres (The In-Laws*; Den., 1970); *Le Petit Violon (The Small Violin*; Gall., 1981); *Un Homme Singulier et Ordinaire (A Singular and Ordinary Man*; Gall., 1990); *Note:* See Chapter VIII.

Sonniès, Paul (Peyssonié, Paul) (?-?); *L'Histrianon* (Ollendorff, 1917); *Vortex le Cheval Fou (Vortex the Mad Horse*; Ren. du Livre, 1926); *Note:* Also see **Grand-Guignol.**

Sorel, Charles (1602-1674); *Le Berger Extravagant (The Extravagant Shepherd*; 3 vols.; T. du Bray, 1627); *La Maison des Jeux* (incl. *Récit du Voyage de Brisevent) (The House of Games;* incl. *Tale of Brisevent's Journey*; N. de Sercy, 1642; rev. 1657); *Recueils de Pièces en Prose (Collections of Prose Plays*; 2 vols.; N. de Sercy, 1644, 1658); *Description de l'Île de Portraiture et de la Ville des Portraits (Description of the Island of Portraiture and the City of Portraits*; N. de Sercy, 1659; rep. VI, 1788); *Note:* See Chapter III.

Sorez, Roger (?-); *La Tentation Cosmique (The Cosmic Temptation*; Métal 3, 1954)

Sorèze, Paul (?-); *Le Maître du Tonnerre (The Master of Thunder*; LA, 1928)

Soria, Georges (?-); *La Grande Quincaillerie (The Great Hardware*; PdF 209, 1976); *Note:* See Chapter IX.

Soriano, Marc (1918-); *Contes de la Fée Crapette (Tales of the Fairy Crapette*; Vigneau, 1945); *Le Colonel Introuvable (The Unfindable Colonel*; Hac., 1962); *L'Homme du Vendredi (The Friday Man*; Hac., 1963); *Le Mystère de la Cigogne Jaune (The Mystery of the Yellow Stork*; Hac., 1965); *Note:* Juveniles.

Sorokine, Dimitri (?-) *see* ***Contes et Légendes***

Soucy, Gaétan (1948-); *L'Immaculée Conception (The Im-*

maculate Conception; Lanterna Magica, 1994); *Note:* French-Canadian writer.

Soucy, Jean-Yves (1945-); *Un Dieu Chasseur (A Hunting God*; Presses de l'Université de Montréal, 1976); Chevaliers de la Nuit (La Presse, 1980; transl. as *Knights of Darkness*, 1994); *L'Étranger au Ballon Rouge (The Stranger with a Red Balloon*; La Presse, 1981); *Érica* (Libre Expression, 1984); *Un Été sans Aube (A Summer Without Dawn*; PC, 1992); *Note:* French-Canadian writer.

Soulac, Anne-Marie (Las Vergnas, Anne-Marie-Suzanne née Luc) (?-); *Une Nuit comme celle-ci (A Night Such as This One*; AM, 1952); *Le Passage des Vivants (The Passage of the Living*; AM, 1953); *L'Ange et la Bête (The Angel and the Beast*; AM, 1955); *Le Printemps des Monstres (The Spring of Monsters*; Den., 1960)

Soulat, Robert (?-); *Odette et le Mandarin (Odette and the Mandarin*; Den., 1984)

Soulès, Jean-Jacques *see* **Abellio, Raymond**

Soulié, Frédéric (1800-1847); *Les Deux Cadavres (The Two Corpses*; Boulé, 1832); *Le Vicomte de Béziers (The Viscount of Beziers*; Boulé, 1834); *Les Mémoires du Diable (The Devil's Memoirs*; Boulé, 1838); *Coelina* (Boulé, 1843-45); *Le Lion Amoureux (The Lion in Love*; Libr. Illustrée, 1876); *Contes Choisis (Selected Tales*; Gédalge, 1891); *Bébrix la Celte* (Ardant, 1891); *La Lanterne Magique (The Magic Lantern*; SFIL, 1904); *Note:* See Chapter IV. Also see François-Guillaume **Ducray-Duminil.**

Soulier, Jacky (?-) *see* **Camus, William**

Soulières, Robert (1960-); *Le Visiteur du Soir (The Visitor of the Evening*; 1980); *Planéria* (anthology; CLF, 1985); *L'Homme qui Venait de la Mer (The Man Who Came from the Sea*; Gamma-Jeunesse, 1991); *Note:* French-Canadian writer.

Soulodre, Henri (?-?); *L'Électro-Rêve (The Electro-Dream*; Desclée de Brouwer, 1895)

Sourbieu, Marcel (?-); *SOS Myriam* (MES, 1961)

Sourdoire, Claude (?-); *Aï Güo* (Or du Temps, 1971)

Souvelier, Charles L. (Bracops, Charles) (?-); *La Fantastique Expédition Star (The Fantastic Star Expedition*; Fleurus, 1957)

Souvestre, Émile (1805-1854); *La Maison Rouge (The Red House*; Charpentier, 1837); *Le Monde Tel Qu'il Sera (The World as It Will Be*; Coquebert, 1846); *Un Mystère (A Mystery*; Dondey-Dupré, 1851); *Le Foyer Breton (Contes et récits Populaires) (Britannic Hearth (Tales and Popular Stories)*; Lévy, 1853); *Contes et Nouvelles (Tales and Stories*; Lévy, 1855); *Les Anges du Foyer*

(The Angels of the Hearth; Lévy, 1858); *Les Contes du Foyer (Tales of the Hearth*; Haguenthal, 1859); *Les Anges du Logis (The Angels of the Home*; Haguenthal, 1862); *Les Merveilles de la Nuit de Noël (The Wonders of Christmas Night*; Lévy, 1868); *Contes et Légendes de Basse Bretagne (Tales and Legends from Lower Britanny*; Sté. Bibl. Bretons, 1891); *Les 1001 Nuits de la Bretagne (The 1001 Nights of Britanny*; Oeuvres Repr'sentatives, 1929); *Les Contes d'Outre-Mort (Tales from Beyond Death*; Montsouris, 1942); *Note:* See Chapter V. Also see ***Contes et Légendes***

Souvestre, Pierre (1874-1914); *Le Tour* (with Marcel **Al-lain**; Libr. de l'Auto, 1909); *Jojo 1er Roi de l'Air (Jojo the 1st King of the Air*; Libr. Aéronautique, 1910); *Les Hommes-Oiseaux (The Bird-Men*; Ed. & Librairie, 1910); The *Fantômas* series (with Marcel **Allain**); *Note:* See **Allain, Marcel.**

Spehner, Norbert (1943-); *Aurores Boréales 1 (Northern Lights*; anthology; CdF 7, 1983); *Écrits sur la Science-Fiction (Articles About SF*; non-fiction; Préambule, 1988); *Note:* French-Canadian writer born in France. Spehner is also one of the founders/editors of *Requiem.*

Spens, Willy de (?-); *La Nuit des Long Museaux (The Night of the Long Snouts*; TR, 1978); *La Palette Tragique (The Tragic Palette*; AdH, 1984); *La Loi des Vainqueurs (The Winners' Law*; TR, 1986); *Note:* See Chapter IX.

Spifame, Raoul (?-?); *Dicacarchia Henrici, Regis Christianissimi, Progymnasmata* (1556); *Note:* See Chapter II.

Spiraux, Alain (?-); *Le Délire de Gilles Frimousse (The Delirium of Gilles Frimousse*; Los., 1966); La Dénonciation (Sédimo, 1967); *Délirium à la Une (Front-Page Delirium*; Los., 1970)

Spitz, Jacques (1896-1963); *La Croisière Indécise (The Indecisive Cruise*; Gall., 1926); *La Mise en Plis (The Hairdo*; Ed. du Logis, 1928); *Le Vent du Monde (The Wind of the World*; Gall., 1928); *Le Voyage Muet (The Silent Voyage*; Gall, 1930); *Les Dames de Velours (The Velvet Ladies*; Gall., 1933); *L'Agonie du Globe (The Agony of the Globe*; Gall., 1935; transl. as *Sever the Earth*, 1936); *Les Évadés de l'An 4000 (The Escapees from Year 4000*; Gall., 1936); *La Guerre des Mouches (The War of the Flies*; Gall., 1938); *L'Homme Élastique (The Elastic Man*; Gall., 1938); *L'Expérience du Dr. Mops (The Experiment of Dr. Mops*; Gall., 1939); *La Parcelle "Z" (Particle Z*; Vigneau, 1942); *Les Signaux du Soleil (The Signals of the Sun*; Vigneau, 1943); *L'Oeil du Purgatoire (The Eye of Purgatory*; Nouvelle France, 1945); *La Forêt des Sept Pies (The Forest of the Seven Magpies*; Maréchal, 1946); *Ceci Est Un Drame (This Is a Tragedy*; Nouvelle France, 1947); *Note:* See Chapter VII.

Spitzmuller, Georges (1867-1925); *Satanas, Roi des Canons (Satanas, King of the Cannons*; Rouff, 1918); *Histoire d'un 75 (Story of a 75*; Rouff, 1918); *La Marche à l'Abîme (Marching Into the Abyss*; Ferenczi, 1921); Le Sacrifice (Copuette, 1922); *Le Grand Secret (The Great Secret*; Tallandier, 1922); *Le Cabinet du Docteur Caligari (The Cabinet of Dr. Caligari*; French novelization of film script; Cine-Collect., 1922); *Le Secret du Vieux Château (The Secret of the Old Castle*; Mode Nationale, 1923); *Le Capitaine La Garde de Jarzac* (Fayard, 1923); *Les Maîtres de l'Océan (The Masters of the Ocean*; Libr. Contemporaine, 1923); *Une Expédition aux Ruines de Paris (An Expedition to the Ruins of Paris*; France-Edition, 1923); *Héliodora en Atlantide (Heliodora in Atlantis*; with J.-A. **Barbier-Daumont**; France-Edition, 1923); *Les Secrets du Ciel (The Secrets of the Sky*; Rouff, 1925); *Le Crime du Docteur (The Doctor's Crime*; Fayard, 1926); *La Fatale Passion (The Fatal Passion*; S.E.T., 1926); *La Tempête (The Tempest*; Ferenczi, 1928); *Les Fiançailles Rouges (The Red Engagement*; Libr. Contemporaine, 1932); *Épisode de la Vie d'un 400 (Episode in the Life of One of the 400*; Rouff, n.d.); *Note:* See Chapter VII. Also see **Opéra.**

Splash, Brain (?-); *La Cervelle contre les Murs (Brains Against the Walls*; FNG 100, 1989)

Sprigel, Olivier *see* **Barbet, Pierre**

Spronck, Maurice (1861-1927); *L'An 330 de la République (The Year 330 of the Republic*; Chailley, 1894); *Note:* See Chapter V.

SR 27 (Ex-Agent) (?-); *Pagaille au Pentagone (A Mess at the Pentagon*; Arabesque 118, 1960); *Ici, Base Spatiale 15 (Here, Space Base 15*; Arabesque 121, 1960); *Le Temps des Poussins (The Time of the Chicks*; Arabesque 148, 1960); *Note:* See Chapter IX.

Srelsen, Axel (?-); *Le Retour des Guzreh (The Return of the Guzrch*; Daniber 16, 1960)

Stahl, P. J. (Hetzel, Pierre-Jules) (?-?); *Voyage où il vous plaira (Voyage Where You Please*; Hetzel, 1842-43); *Contes de la Tante Judith (Tales of Aunt Judith*; Hac., 1938); *Les Aventures de Tom Pouce (The Adventures of Tom Thumb*; CLF, 1957)

Stanislas-Meunier (Mme) (?-); *L'Attentat de la Rue de Courcelles (The Terrorist Action of Courcelles Street*; RMY, 1930)

Stanley, Éric *see* **Léonnec, Félix**

Star, André *see* **Dazergues, Max-André**

Starr, Mark *see* **Klein, Gérard**

Steeman, Stanislas-André (1908-1970); *L'Assassin Assas-*

siné *(The Murdered Murderer*; Libr. Champs-Élysées, 1933); *Les Fils de Balaoo (The Sons of Balaoo*; with Gaston **Leroux**; *Paris-Soir*, 1934; rev. Libr. Champs-Élysées, 1937); *Le Démon de Sainte-Croix (The Demon of St.Croix*; Dupuis, 1936); *Ennemi sans Visage (Faceless Enemy*; Dupuis, 1938; rev. as *Monsieur Wens et l'Automate (Mr. Wens and the Automaton*; Guy Le Prat, 1943); *Une Veuve Dort Seule (A Widow Sleeps Alone*; PC, 1949); *Madame la Mort (Mrs. Death*; PC, 1951); *Des Cierges au Diable (Candles for the Devil*; PC, 1959); *La Morte survit au 13 (The Dead Woman Lives at No.13*; PC, 1974); *Dix-Huit Fantômes (Eighteen Ghosts*; Libr. Champs-Élysées, 1989); *Note:* Belgian writer. See Chapter VII. Author of famous mysteries starring Monsieur Wens. His most famous thriller is probably *L'Assassin Habite Au 21 (The Murderer Lives at No.21)*, a novel about a serial killer, later made into an eponymous 1942 film by H.-G. Clouzot starring Pierre Fresnay as Wens.

Steimer (?-); *Le Petit Roi des Bruyères (The Little King of the Briar*; n.d.); *Les Aventures Fantastiques d'Oliver Gerfault (Oliver Gerfaut's Fantastic Adventures*; n.d.)

Steiner, Kurt (Ruellan, André) (1922-); *Alerte aux Monstres (Alert, Monsters*; as Kurt Wargar; VF 6, 1953); *Le Bruit du Silence (The Sound of Silence*; FNAG 13, 1955); *Pour Que Vive Le Diable (For the Devil to Live*; FNAG 17, 1956); *Fenêtres sur l'Obscur (Windows Into Darkness*; FNAG 20, 1956); *De Flamme et d'Ombre (Of Flame and Shadow*; FNAG 23, 1956); *Le Seuil du Vide (The Threshold of the Void*; FNAG 25, 1956); *Les Rivages de la Nuit (The Shores of Night*; FNAG 27, 1957); *Je Suis Un Autre (I Am Other*; FNAG 29, 1957); *Les Dents Froides (The Cold Teeth*; FNAG 31, 1957); *L'Envers du Masque (The Other Side of the Mask*; FNAG 33, 1957); *Les Pourvoyeurs (The Purveyors*; FNAG 35, 1957); *Sueurs (Sweat*; FNAG 37, 1957); *L'Herbe aux Pendus (The Herb of the Hanged Men*; FNAG 39, 1958); *La Marque du Démon (The Mark of the Demon*; FNAG 42, 1958); *Lumière de Sang (Blood Light*; FNAG 44, 1958); *Syncope Blanche (White Faint*; FNAG 45, 1958); *La Village de la Foudre (The Village of Lightning*; FNAG 47, 1958); *Le Prix du Suicide (The Price of Suicide*; FNAG 48, 1958); *Menace d'Outre-Terre (Menace from Beyond*; FNA 124, 1958); *La Chaîne de Feu (The Chain of Fire*; FNAG 52,

1959); *Dans un Manteau de Brume (In a Cloak of Mist*; FNAG 57, 1959); *Mortefontaine (Deadfountain*; FNAG 59, 1959); *Salamandra* (FNA 131, 1959); *Le 32 Juillet (July 32nd*; FNA 146, 1959); *Glace Sanglante (Bloody Ice*; FNAG 64, 1960); *Le Masque des Regrets (The Mask of Regrets*; FNAG 68, 1960); *Aux Armes d'Ortog (Under Ortog's Arms*; FNA 155, 1960); *S.O.S. Passé (SOS Past*; as André Louvigny; Satellite 28, 1960); *Manuel du Savoir-Mourir (Manual of How-To-Die*; as André Ruellan; Horay, 1963); *Les Improbables* (FNA 269, 1965); *Les Océans du Ciel (The Oceans of the Sky*; FNA 315, 1967); *Ortog et les Ténèbres (Ortog and the Darkness*; FNA 376, 1969); *Les Enfants de l'Histoire (The Children of History*; FNA 388, 1969); *Le Disque Rayé (The Scratched Record*; FNA 424, 1970); *Tunnel* (as André Ruellan; A&D 25, 1973); *Brebis Galeuses (Black Sheep*; FNA 596, 1974); *Un Passe Temps (A Pastime*; FNA 944, 1979); *Les Chiens (The Dogs*; as André Ruellan; Titres 1, 1979); *Le Livre d'Or de Philippe Curval (The Golden Book of Philippe Curval*; anthology; PP 5079, 1980); *Mémo* (as André Ruellan; PdF 390, 1984); *Grand-Guignol 36-88* (FNG 62, 1988); *Le Terme* (as André Ruellan; L'Astronaute Mort, 1995); *Albert et Georgette* (as André Ruellan; L'Astronaute Mort, 1995); *On a Tiré sur le Cercueil (They Shot at the Coffin*; as André Ruellan; Den., 1997); *Note:* See Chapters VIII and IX. André Ruellan has written a number of genre films for director Alain **Jessua** (see Book 1, Chapters I and VI). *Le Seuil du Vide* was adapted into an eponymous 1971 film (see Book 1, Chapter I). a number of Steiner's FNAG novels were adapted into digest-sized graphic novels (see Book 1, Chapter V under **Fleuve Noir**).

Steinmetz, Jean-Luc (?-); *La France Frénétique de 1830* (anthology; Phébus, 1978)

Sterlanges, Jean (?-); *Les Hommes Déchaînés (The Men Unbound*; Plon, 1947)

Sternberg, Jacques (1923-); *La Géométrie dans l'Impossible (The Impossible Geometry*; Los., 1953); *Le Délit (The Infraction*; Plon, 1954); *La Sortie est au Fond de l'Espace (The Exit Lies at the End of Space*; PdF 15, 1956); *Entre Deux Mondes Incertains (Between Two Uncertain Worlds*; PdF 21, 1957); *La Géométrie dans la Terreur (The Terror Geometry*; Los., 1958); *L'Employé (The Employee*; Minuit, 1958); *L'Architecte (The Architect*; Los., 1960); *Manuel du Parfait Secrétaire Commercial (Handbook of the Perfect Commercial Secretary*; Los., 1960); *La Banlieue (The Suburbs*; Los., 1961); *Un Jour Ouvrable (A Working Day*; Los., 1961); *Toi, Ma Nuit (You, My Night*; Los., 1965; transl. as *Sexualis '95*, 1967); *C'est la Guerre, Mr. Gruber (It's War, Mr. Gruber*; Los., 1968); *Attention, Planète Habitée (Beware, Inhabited Planet*; Los., 1969); *Je t'aime, Je t'aime (I Love You, I Love You*; Los., 1969); *Univers Zéro

(Universe Zero; MarSF 362, 1970); *Le Coeur Froid (The Cold Heart*; UGE, 1971); *Dictionnaire du Diable (Devil's Dictionary*; Calmann-Lévy, 1973); *Futurs sans Avenir* (A&D 12, 1971; transl. as *Future Without Future*, 1974); *Contes Glacés (Icy Tales*; Marabout, 1974); *Lettre Ouverte aux Terriens (Open Letter to the Earthmen*; AM, 1974); *Sophie, la Mer, la Nuit (Sophie, the Sea, the Night*; AM, 1976); *La Banlieue (The Suburb*; MarSF 569, 1976); *Vivre en Survivant (To Live as a Survivor*; Tchou, 1977); *Le Navigateur (The Navigator*; AM, 1977); *Mai 86* (AM, 1978); *Kriss l'Emballeur (Kriss the Packer*; Bourgois, 1979); *Suite pour Evelyne Sweet Evelyne (Suite for Evelyne Sweet Evelyne*; AM, 1980); *Le Supplice des Week-Ends (The Torture of Week-Ends*; UGE, 1981); *L'Anonyme (The Anonymous*; AM., 1982); *Dictionnaire des Idées Revues (Dictionary of Reviewed Ideas*; Den., 1985); *188 Contes à Régler (188 Tales on Account*; PdF 474, 1988); *Histoires à Dormir sans Vous (Stories to Sleep Without You*; Den., 1990); *Histoire à Mourir de Vous (Story to Die of You*; Den., 1991); *Contes Griffus (Clawed Tales*; Den., 1993); *Dieu, Moi et les Autres (God, I and Others*; Den., 1995); *Note:* Belgian writer. See chapters VIII and IX. Sternberg also wrote Alain **Resnais'** 1968 film *Je t'aime, Je t'aime* (see Book 1, Chapter I) and the animated short La Planète Verte (see Book 1, Chapter IV).

Stiernet, Hubert (1863-1939); *Contes au Perron (Tales of the Balcony*; 1893); *Histoires Hantées (Haunted Stories*; Libr. Moderne, 1907); *Note:* Belgian writer. See Chapter VI.

Stolze, Pierre (1952-); *Le Serpent d'Éternité (The Serpent of Eternity*; OGB 63, 1979); *Kamtchatka* (OGB 67, 1980); *Marilyn Monroe et les Samourais du Père Noël (Marilyn Monroe and Santa Claus' Samurais*; JL 1962, 1986); *Cent Mille Images ou Les Reines Mages de la Montagne Ardente (One Hundred Thousand Images or the Wizard Queen of the Fiery Mountain*; Philippe Olivier, 1990); *Intrusions* (Aurore, Futurs 11, 1990); *Le Déménagement (The Move*; La Geste, 1994); *Theophano 960* (FNA 1964, 1995); *Volontaire Désigné (Designated Volunteer*; UPNT, 1995); *La Maison Usher ne Chutera pas (The House of Usher Shall Not Fall*; Destination Crépuscule, 1996); *Gréta Garbo et les Crocodiles du Père Fouettard (Greta Garbo and the Nasty Santa's Crocodiles*; Hors Commerce, 1996); *Note:* See Chapter IX.

Stone, William *see* **Cambri, Gérard**

Storga, Ran (?-); *Vihila Planète de la Débauche (Vihila, Planet of Debauchery*; Python 3, 1971); *Note:* Erotic SF.

Stork, Christopher (Jouravieff, Ovide) (1925-1995); *La Peau de l'Auroch (The Auroch's Skin*; as Stéphane Jourat; Plon, 1954); *Le Dernier Soleil (The Last Sun*; as Stéphane Jourat; Plon, 1968); *L'Ordre Établi (The Established Order*; FNA 907, 1979); *Enjeu: Le Monde (The World at Stake*; FNA 926, 1979); *Dormir? Rêver Peut-être... (To Sleep, Perchance to Dream...*; FNA 938, 1979); *Achetez Dieu! (Buy God!*; FNA 960, 1980); Terra-Park (FNA 986, 1980); *L'Usage de l'Ascenseur est Interdit aux Enfants de Moins de Quatorze Ans Non Accompagnés (The Use of the Elevator Is Forbidden to Unaccompanied Children Under 14*; FNA 1001, 1980); *Il y a un Temps Fou... (It's Been a Crazy Time...*; FNA 1024, 1980); *Demain, les Rats (Tomorrow, the Rats*; FNA 1041, 1981); *Les Derniers Anges (The Last Angels*; FN 1053, 1981); *Vatican 2000* (FNA 1074, 1981); *Le Bon Larron (The Good Thief*; FNA 1092, 1981); *Les Petites Femmes Vertes (The Little Green Women*; FNA 1094, 1981); *La Femme Invisible (The Invisible Woman*; FNA 1108, 1981); *L'An II de la Mafia (Year II of the Mafia*; FNA 1130, 1982); *Tout le Pouvoir aux Étoiles (All the Power to the Stars*; FNA 1154, 1982); *La Machine Maîtresse (The Master Machine*; FNA 1172, 1982); *Dis, Qu'as-tu fait, Toi que Voilà... (Say, What Did You Do, You There...*; FNA 1186, 1982); *La Quatrième Personne du Pluriel (Fourth Person Plural*; FNA 1217, 1983); *L'Article de la Mort (The Article of Death*; FNA 1222, 1983); *La Dernière Syllabe du Temps (The Last Syllable of Time*; FNA 1229, 1983); *Un Peu, Beaucoup, à la Folie (A Little, a Lot, Madly*; FNA 1242, 1983); *Le XXIème Siècle n'aura pas lieu (The 21st Century Will Not Happen*; FNA 1256, 1983); *Mais n'anticipons pas... (Let's Not Anticipate...*; FNA 1263, 1983); *Pièces Détachées (Spare Parts*; FNA 1274, 1984); *Virus Amok* (FNA 1292, 1984); *Le Passé Dépassé (The Passed Over Past*; FNA 1299, 1984); *Pieuvres (Octopus*; FNA 1312, 1984); *L'Envers Vaut l'Endroit (The Two Sides Are the Same*; FNA 1319, 1984); *Terre des Femmes (Land of Women*; FNA 1340, 1984); *Le Rêve du Papillon Chinois (The Dream of a Chinese Butterfly*; FNA 1367, 1985); Made in Mars (FNA 1375, 1985); *Les Lunatiques (The Lunatics*; FNA 1383, 1985); *Billevesées et Calembredaines (Nonsense and Gobbledygook*; FNA 1389, 1985); Babel Bluff (FNA 1412, 1985); *L'Enfant de l'Espace (The Space Child*; FNA 1417, 1985); *Demi-Portion (Short Ration*; FNA 1432, 1986); *Ils Étaient Une Fois... (Once Upon Many Times...*; FNA 1448, 1986); *Psys Contre Psys (Psys vs. Psys*; FNA 1459, 1986); *De Purs Esprits... (Pure Minds...*; FNA 1476, 1986); *Don Quichotte II (Don Quixote II*; FNA 1485, 1986); *Contretemps (Countertime*; FNA 1501, 1986); *Le Lit à Baldaquin (A Bed with Canopy*; FNA 1522, 1987); *Je Souffre Pour Vous... (I Suffer for You...*; FNA 1543, 1987); *Une Si Jolie Petite Planète (Such a Pretty Little Planet*; FNA 1556, 1987); *Le Trillionnaire* (FNA 1569, 1987); *Les Enfants du Soleil (The Children of the Sun*; FNA 1588, 1987); *Alter Ego* (FNA 1604, 1988); Series *Marc Avril,* written as Marc Avril: *Avril sur Orbite*

(Avril in Orbit; FN Espionnage 1044, 1973); *Avrillico Presto* (FN Espionnage 1083, 1974); *Avril et le Diable (Avril and the Devil*; FN Espionnage 1203, 1975); *Faites l'Avril, pas la Guerre (Make Avril, Not War*; FN Espionnage 1247, 1976); *Avril à l'Asile (Avril in the Asylum*; FN Espionnage 1459, 1979); *Secte d'Avril (Avril's Sect*; FN Espionnage 1509, 1979); *Avril et les Ectoplasmes (Avril and the Ghosts*; FN Espionnage 1561, 1980); *Avril et le Nouvel Ordre des Assassins (Avril and the New Order of Assassins*; FN Espionnage 1588, 1981); *Avril chasse l'Aigle à Quatre Têtes (Avril Hunts the Four-Headed Eagle*; FN Espionnage 1606, 1981); *Avril et la Petite Fille Modèle (Avril and the Little Model Girl*; FN Espionnage 1611, 1981); *Avril en trompe l'oeil (Avril and the Trompe l'Oeil*; FN Espionnage 1630, 1982); *Le Phantasme d'Avril (Avril's Fantasy*; FN Espionnage 1642, 1982); *Note:* See Chapter IX.

Straitur, Pierre (?-); *La Cellule de la Mort (The Cell of Death*; Fleurus, 1945); *Chez les Touaregs au Litham Bleu (Among the Tuaregs and the Blue Litham*; Fleurus, 1947)

Straram, Patrick (1934-1988); *Irish Coffees au No Name Bar* (L'Hexagène-L'Obscène-Nyctalope, 1972); *La Faim de l'Énigme (The Hunger of the Enigma*; Aurore, 1975); *Blues Clair* (Noroît, 1984); *Note:* French-Canadian writer.

Stuntman, J. (?-); *Projet Apocalypse (Project Apocalypse*; FN, 1982); *La Bataille des Dieux (The Battle of the Gods*; FNA 1192, 1982); *Furie à Paris (Fury in Paris*; FN, 1983)

St-Yves, Glenn (1965-); *Trois Vieilles (Three Old Women*; Arion, 1992); *Note:* French-Canadian writer.

Suard, François (1937-); *Les Aventures du Chevalier Huon (The Adventures of Knight Huon*; Flamm., 1997); *Note:* See Chapter I.

Suberville, Jean (1887-1932); *Le Fifre de Bertrandou (Bertrandou's Pipes*; Édit. & Libr., 1919); *L'Homme Qui Fait Sauter le Monde (The Man Who Blew Up the World*; Chiron, 1927)

Sue, Eugène (1804-1857); *Kernock le Pirate* (Renduel, 1830); *Atar-Gull* (Renduel, 1831); *La Salamandre* (Renduel, 1832); *La Vigie de Koat-Ven (The Watchman of Koat-Ven*; Vimont, 1833); *Le Morne au Diable (The Devil's Morn*; Dondrey-Dupré, 1840); *Jean Cavalier ou Les Fanatiques des Cévennes (The Fanatics of the Cevennes*; Gosselin, 1840); *Paula Monti ou L'Hotel Lambert* (Gosselin, 1842); *Les Mystères de Paris (The Mysteries of Paris*; Schlesinger, 1842-43; transl. 1844); *Le Juif Errant (The Wandering Jew*; Beck, 1844-45; transl. 1845); *Le Diale à Paris (The Devil in Paris*; Hetzel, 1845-46); *Note:* See Chapter IV.

Sullivan, Vernon *see* **Vian, Boris**

Supervielle, Jules (1884-1960); *L'Homme de la Pampa (The Man from the Pampa*; Gall., 1923); *Le Survivant (The Survivor*; Gall., 1928); *Trois Mythes (Three Myths*; Amigo del Libro de Arte, 1929); *L'Enfant de la Haute Mer (The Child of the High Sea*; Gall., 1931); *La Belle au Bois (Beauty in the Wood*; Gall., 1932); *La Première Famille (The First Family*; 1934); *L'Arche de Noë (Noah's Ark*; Gall., 1938); *La Fable du Monde (The Fable of the World*; Gall., 1938); *Les Contes du Petit Bois (Tales of the Little Wood*; Quetzal, Mexico, 1942); Orphée (Ides & Calendes, 1946); *L'Enlèvement d'Europe (The Taking of Europa*; 13 rue St. Georges, 1947); *Les B.B.V.* (Minuit, 1949); *Schéhérazade* (Gall., 1949); *Premiers Pas dans l'Univers (First Steps Into the Universe*; Gall., 1950); *Note:* See Chapter VI.

Suquet, Henri (?-); *La Maison sous les Eaux (The Underwater House*; Loisirs, 1928); *On Va Faire Sauter Paris (We're Going to Blow Up Paris*; Boivin, 1935); *Le Mystère du Tour de France (The Mystery of the Tour of France*; Loisirs, 1939); *Les Quatre du Grand Crassier (The Four of the Big Junkyard*; Clocher, 1940); *L'Île à Pédales (The Pedal-Powered Island*; ABC, 1941); *Panique sur le Monde (Panic Over the World*, 1939; Clocher, 1942); *S.O.S.! Ici Paris (SOS! Paris Calling*; Clocher, 1942); *La Main qui Saisit (The Hand That Grips*; Montsouris, 1942); *L'Énigme de la Rame 34 (The Mystery of Subway Train 34*; Clocher, 1943); *Le Rayon du Sommeil (The Sleep Ray*; Montsouris, 1943); *Dans la Roue du Moulin (Inside the Miller's Wheel*; Montsouris, 1944); *Les Trois Triangles d'Émail (The Three Enamel Triangles*; Montsouris, 1945); *Onze et Une (Eleven and One*; Montsouris, 1945); *Le Canoë Mystère (The Mystery Canoe*; Clocher, 1945); *S.O.S. Pétrolier 27 (SOS Tanker 27*; Montsoris, 1946); *On a volé le 2 de la Rue (They Stole No.2 of the Street*; Marly, 1947); *La Perle Noire de Ceylan (The Black Pearl of Ceylon*; Clocher, 1949); *Ciel de Cuivre (Copper Sky*; SdP, 1949); *La Maison du Vent (The House of Wind*; Fleurus, 1954); *Le Secret du Diamant (The Diamond's Secret*; Mame, 1954); *Note:* Juveniles. See chapters VII.

Suragne, Pierre *see* **Pelot, Pierre**

Surget, Alain (1948-); *Prisonnier de la Rivière Noire (Prisoner of the Dark River*; Amitié, 1987); *Les Flèches du Silence (The Silent Arrows*; Gall., 1988); *Gare à la Bête! (Beware the Beast!*; Amitié, 1989); *Le Fils des Loups (The Son of the Wolves*; Rageot, 1989); *L'Abominable Gosse des Neiges (The Abominable Snow Kid*; Rageot, 1990); *Le Bal des Sorcières (Witches' Ball*; Rageot, 1994); *Le Gouffre aux Fantômes (The Ghost Pit*; Rageot, 1994); *Quand on Parle du Loup... (When We Cry Wolf...*; Rageot, 1994); *Qui a vu Turluru? (Who Saw Turluru?*;

Rageot, 1994); *Le Renard de Morlange (The Fox of Morlange*; Nathan, 1995); *L'Hôtel Maudit (The Accursed Hotel*; Rageot, 1996); *Note:* Juveniles. See Chapter VIII.

Sussan, René (1925-); *La Route des Voleurs (The Road of Thieves*; Den., 1959); *Les Confluents (The Confluence*; PdF 41, 1960); *Histoire de Farczi (Story of Farczi*; Den., 1964); *Dupont et le Bonheur des Hommes (Dupont and Man's Happiness*; Den., 1965); *L'Étoile des Autres (The Star of Others*; Den., 1967); *La Ville sans Fantômes (The Ghostless City*; Den., 1968); *L'Anneau de Fumée (The Smoke Ring*; PdF 188, 1974); *Le Bouton du Mandarin (The Mandarin's Button*; as René Réouven; Den., 1976); *Un Tueur en Sorbonne (A Killer at the Sorbonne;* as René Reouven; Den., 1980); *Élémentaire, mon cher Holmes (Elementary, My Dear Holmes*; as René Réouven; Den., 1982); *Les Insolites (Strange Tales*; PdF 386, 1984); *L'Assassin du Boulevard (The Boulevard Murderer*; as René Réouven; Den., 1985); *La Raison du Meilleur est Toujours la Plus Forte (The Best Reason Is Always the Strongest*; as René Réouven; Den., 1986); *Le Bestiaire de Sherlock Holmes (Sherlock Holmes' Bestiary*; as René Réouven; Den., 1987); *Le Détective Volé (The Stolen Detective*; as René Réouven; Den., 1988); *Les Passe-Temps de Sherlock Holmes (Sherlock Holmes' Passtimes*; as René Réouven; Den., 1989); *Les Grandes Profondeurs (The Lower Depths*; as René Réouven; Den., 1991); *Les Rénégats de l'An Mil (The Renegades of the Year 1000*; Den., 1992); *Histoires Secrètes de Sherlock Holmes (Secret Histories of Sherlock Holmes*; as René Réouven; Den., 1993); *Les Nourritures Extra-Terrestres (Extra-Terrestrial Food*; with Donna Sussan; PdF 550, 1994); *Voyage au Centre du Mystère (Journey to the Center of Mystery*; as René Réouven; Den., 1995); *Souvenez-Vous de Monte-Cristo (Remember Monte-Cristo*; as René Réouven; Den., 1996); *Les Survenants (The Overghosts*; Den., 1996); *Note:* See Chapters VIII and IX.

Sutal, Louis (Côté, Normand) (1939-); *La Mystérieuse Boule de Feu (The Mysterious Ball of Fire*; JP 3, 1971); *Menace sur Montréal (Threat Over Montreal*; JP 9, 1972); *Le Piège à Bateaux (The Boat Trap*; JP 14, 1973); *Révolte Secrète (Secret Revolt*; JP 18, 1974); *La Planète sous le Joug (The Planet Under the Yoke*; JP 24, 1976); *Panne dans l'Espace (Breakdown in Space*; JP 30, 1977); *Note:* French-Canadian writer. Juveniles.

Svenn, Patrick (?-); *L'Heure Funèbre (The Funeral Hour*; FNAG 2, 1954); *Le Fantôme Aveugle (The Blind Ghost*; FNAG 8, 1955); *Vengeance de l'Inconnu (Revenge of the Unknown*; FNAG 21, 1956)

Swann, Ingo (?-); *Le Maître de la Mort (The Death Master*; Belfond, 1981)

Swilawtor, John Edward (?-); *Homo Eroticus Rex* (Los., 1969)

Sylf, Christia (?-); *Kobor Tigan't* (PdE, 1969); *Le Règne de Ta (The Reign of Ta*; PdE, 1971); *Markosamo le Sage (Markosamo the Wise*; PdE, 1973); *La Patte de Chat (The Cat's Paw*; RL, 1974); *La Reine au Coeur Puissant (The Strong-Hearted Queen*; PdE, 1979); *Note:* See Chapter VIII.

Sylvestre, Pierre (?-); *Épouvante sur le Pacifique (Terror Over the Pacific*; Nlles. Presses Fr., 1946); *L'Île Maudite (The Accursed Island*; Nlles. Presses Fr., 1947); *Profil du Songe (Profile of the Dream*; Encres Vives, 1971); *Les Couleurs de la Vie (The Colors of Life*; Pensée U., 1976)

Szucsany, Désirée (1955-); *Les Filets (The Nets*; Pleine Lune, 1984); *Note:* French-Canadian writer. This is a collection of fantastical stories.

Tabachnik, Maud (?-); *A l'Horizon, les Ténèbres (Darkness on the Horizon*; Les Presses du Temps 3, 1996)

Taggart, Marie-Françoise (1968-); *Une Affaire de Vie ou de Mort (A Matter of Life and Death*; HMH, 1991); *Note:* French-Canadian writer. Novel about the afterlife.

Taieb, Héliane *see* **Verlanger, Julia**

Tailhade, L. (?-?) *see* **Ralph, Raoul**

Talabot, Jean T. (?-); *R'Adam et R'Eve ou Le Vestige (R'Adam and R'Eve or the Remains*; Mercure U., 1934); *Note:* See Chapter VII.

Talbert, Michel *see* **Bernanos, Michel**

Tallemand (Abbé) (?-?); *Voyage de l'Île d'Amour (Voyage to the Island of Love*; L. Billaine, 1663; rep. VI, 1788); *Le Second Voyage de l'Île d'Amour (The Second Voyage to the Island of Love*; L. Billaine, 1663; rep. VI, 1788)

Tallian, Pierre (?-); *Coralie Passée, Coralie Camée* (Flamm., 1968); *Le Grand Jour de Joseph Junior (Joseph Jr.'s Great Day*; Fayard, 1971); *Le Plaisir Rouge (The Red Pleasure*; Fayard, 1972)

Talmours, André (?-?) *see* **Grand-Guignol**

Tanaka, Béatrice (1932-); *La Fille du Grand Serpent (The Daughter of the Great Serpent*; Messidor-La Farandole, 1973); *Maya ou la 53ème Semaine de l'Année (Maya, or the Year's 53rd Week*; Messidor-La Farandole, 1975); *Contes d'Étoiles et de Lune (Tales of Stars and Moon*; Messidor-La Farandole, 1976); *La Montagne aux Trois Questions (The Mountain of Three Questions*; Messidor-La Farandole, 1976); *Le Crapaud et la Pluie (The Toad and the Rain*; Messidor-La Farandole, 1978); *Le Tonneau Enchanté (The Enchanted Barrel*; Messidor-La Farandole, 1982); *Ytch et les Choumoudoux (Ytch and the Choomoodoos*; Messidor-La Farandole, 1982); *Très Incroyable et Véridique Histoire de Bouffe-Boeuf et Bang (Very Incredible Yet True Story of Eat-Beef and*

Bang; Messidor-La Farandole, 1982); *Savitri la Vaillante (Savitri the Brave*; Messidor-La Farandole, 1984); *Contes en F. (Tales in F*; Messidor-La Farandole, 1985); *Chen du Grand Large (Chen of the Deep Sea*; Messidor-La Farandole, 1987); *La Princesse aux Deux Visages (The Princess with Two Faces*; Vif Argent, 1987); *Trois Sorcières (Three Witches*; Syros, 1988); *La Légende de Chico Rey (The Legend of Chico Rey*; Vif Argent, 1990); *La Quête du Prince de Koripan (The Quest of the Prince of Koripan*; Syros, 1992); *Les Manguiers d'Antigone (The Mango Trees of Antigone*; Flamm., 1993); *Note:* Juveniles. See Chapter VIII.

Tanase, Virgil (1945-); *Le Bal autour du Diamant Magique (The Ball About the Magic Diamond*; Gall., 1987); *Le Bal sur la Goélette du Pirate Aveugle (The Ball on the Blind Pirate's Ship*; Gall., 1987); *Note:* Juveniles.

Tansi, Sony Labou (?-); *Conscience de Tracteur (Tractor Consciousness*; Seuil, 1979); *La Vie et Demie (Life and a Half*; Seuil, 1979); *L'État Honteux (The Shameful State*; Seuil, 1981); *L'Anté-Peuple (The Pre-People*; Seuil, 1983); *Les Sept Solitudes de Lorsa Lopez (The Seven Solitudes of Lorsa Lopez*; Seuil, 1985); *Les Yeux du Volcan (The Eyes of the Volcano*; Seuil, 1988); *Le Coup de Vieux (An Old Man's Blow*; Présence Africaine, 1988); *Le Commencement des Douleurs (The Beginnings of Pain*; Seuil, 1995); *L'Autre Monde (The Other World*; Revue Noire, 1997); *Note:* Congolese writer. See Chapter VIII.

Tanugi, Gilbert (?-); See **Rioux, Michel**.

Tarassov, Lev *see* **Troyat, Henri**

Tarde, Jean Gabriel de (1843-1904); *Fragment d'Histoire Future (Fragment of Future History*; Giard & Brière, 1894; transl. as *Underground Man*, 1905); *Note:* See Chapter V.

Tardieu, Jean (1903-1995); *Le Témoin Invisible (The Invisible Witness*; Gall., 1943); *Histoires Obscures (Obscure Tales*; Gall., 1961); *La Part de l'Ombre (The Shadow's Share*; Gall., 1972); *Le Parquet se soulève (The Floor Is Pulling Up*; Apeïros, 1973); *Le Professeur Froeppel* (Gall., 1978); *Il était une fois, deux fois, trois fois (Once, Twice, Thrice Upon a Time*; Gall., 1978); *Les Tours de Trébizonde (The Towers of Trebizonde*; Gall., 1983); *La Cité sans Sommeil (The Sleepless City*; Gall., 1984); *Des Idées et des Ombres (Of Ideas and Shadows*; RLD, 1984); *Le Fleuve Caché (The Hidden River*; Gall., 1988); *L'Archipel sans Nom (The Nameless Archipelago*; Avant-Scène, 1990)

Tardivel, Jules-Paul (1851-1905); *Pour la Patrie* (Cadieux & Derome, 1895; transl. as *For My Country*, 1975); *Note:* French-Canadian writer. One of the first French-language Canadian science fiction novels. It advocates the founding of a reborn New France.

Tarvel, Brice *see* **Sarkel, François**

Tavera, Matteo (?-) & François (?-); *L'Ogive du Monde (The World Cone*; RF 64, 1959)

Tavernier, René (?-); *Avez-vous vu le Président? (Have You Seen the President?*; Den., 1975)

Taxil, Léo (Jogand-Pagès, Gabriel Antoine) (1854-1906); *Le Diable au XIXème Siècle ou Les Mystères du Spiritisme (The Devil in the 19th Century*; Delhomme & Briguet, 1892-95); *Note:* See Chapter IV.

Tefri (?-); *Le Docteur Olfa (Dr.Olfa*; Imprim. Réunies, 1953); *Le Succès du Docteur Olfa (Dr.Olfa's Success*; Imprim. Réunies, 1956); *Au Gravitor* (Scorpion, 1962); *Au Piladoc* (Scorpion, 1963); *Au Roulamort* (Promotion & Édition, 1968); *Note:* Swiss writer.

Teidor, Antoine *see* **Rodiet, Antoine**

Teissier, François (?-); *Une Nuit dans les Nuages (A Night in the Clouds*; Ardant, 1878); *Voyage Aérien de New York à Yokohama (Aerial Journey from New York to Yokohama*; Ardant, 1878); *Voyages Comiques de John Gilpin (Comical Journeys of John Gilpin*; Ardant, 1878); *Les Merveilles et Mystères de l'Océan, ou Voyage Sous-Marin de Southampton au Cap Horn (Wonders and Mysteries of the Ocean, or Underwater Journey from Southampton to the Cape Horn*; Ardant, 1900); *Note:* See Chapter V.

Teldy-Naïm, Robert (Naïm, Robert) (?-); *Paradis Atomiques (Atomic Paradises*; Horizons Fantastiques 1, 1949); *Cela Arrivera Hier (It Will Happen Yesterday*; Horizons Fantastiques 4, 1954); *Sept Soleils sur la Neige (Seven Suns on the Snow*; Bourrelier, 1954); *Bille-de-Clown, Cheval de Cirque (Clown-Face, Circus Horse*; Bourrelier, 1958); *La Croisière de la "Sirène" (The Cruise of the "Mermaid"*; Plon, 1960); *Chasse Gardée (Restricted Hunting*; Bellenand, 1960); *L'Ère des Truands (The Era of Crooks*; Den., 1972); *Note:* See Chapter IX. Also used the pseudonym of "Robert Tescher."

Tenand, Suzanne (1909-); *Contes de mon Pays (Tales from My Country*; À l'Enfant Poète, 1945)

Téramond, Guy de (Gautier de Téramond, François) (1869-1957); *L'Homme qui peut tout (The Man Who Could Do Anything*; Vermot, 1900; rev. as *Le Miracle du Professeur Wolmar (Prof. Wolmar's Miracle)*, Monde Illustré, 1910); *L'Adoration Perpétuelle (Perpetual Worship*; Simonis Empis, 1902); *Maison de Science (House of Science*; Lafitte, 1911); *Le Secret du Sous-Marin (The Secret of the Sub-Marine*; serialized as 2 vols: *La Fille du Savant (The Scientist's Daughter* and *Bertha l'Espionne (Bertha the Spy)*, Ferenczi, 1922); *Ravengar* (Ferenczi, 1922); *L'Homme qui Voit à travers les Murailles*

(The Man Who Could See Through Walls, 1913; Tallandier, 1923); *Vingt Mille Lieues à travers le Monde (20,000 Leagues Across the World*; serialized as 25 issues, Ferenczi, 1923-24); *1. Un Vieux Savant (An Old Scientist); 2. La Conquête du Pôle (The Conquest of the Pole); 3. Le Royaume des Pieuvres (The Kingdom of the Octopus); 4. Le Bouddha qui parle (The Talking Buddha); 5. Chez les Nains (Among the Dwarves); 6. Les Galions de Vigo (Vigo's Galleons); 7. Prisonnier chez les Fous (Prisoner Among the Madmen); 8. Au Pays des Fakirs (In the Land of the Fakirs); 9. Un Voyage au Centre de la Terre (A Journey to the Center of the Earth); 10. L'Île des Perroquets (Parrots Island); 11. L'Atlantide (Atlantis); 12. L'Île de Laputa (The Island of Laputa); 13. La Télépathie sans Fil (Wireless Telepathy); 14. L'Avion sans Pilote (The Pilotless Plane); 15. Le Grand Serpent de Mer (The Great Sea Serpent); 16. Au Milieu des Vampires (Amongst Vampires); 17. À la Recherche du Plésiosaure (In Search of the Plesiosaurus]; 18. L'Île aux Pavots (Poppy Island); 19. Aventures de Trois Boches (Adventure of Three Germans); 20. Un Voyage Accidenté sur l'Océan (An Event-Filled Journey on the Ocean); 21. Prisonniers des Boches (Prisoners of the Germans); 22. Perdus sur l'Amazone (Lost on the Amazon); 23. La Grotte aux Squelettes (The Cavern of Skeletons); 24. Au Pays des Géants (In the Land of Giants); 25. Le Mystère de l'Homme Tatoué (The Mystery of the Tattoed Man); À la Recherche du Plésiosaure (In Search of the Plesiosaurus*; JDV, 1925); *Le Faiseur de Monstres (The Monster Maker*; Tallandier, 1930); *Le Poste Mystérieux (The Mysterious Post*; Tallandier, 1932); *L'Énigme du Doigt Coupé (The Mystery of the Severed Finger*; Baudinière, 1935); *Note:* See chapters V and VII.

Ternoise, Paul (?-) *see* **Lavaur, Pierre**

Terrasse, C. (?-?) *see* **Opéra**

Terrasson, Jean (Abbé) (1670-1750); *Sethos, Histoire ou Vie tirée des Monuments, Anecdotes de l'Ancienne Égypte (Sethos, Tale or Life Drawn from the Monuments and Anecdotes of Ancient Egypt*; Desaint, 1731); *Note:* See Chapter III.

Tersac, Hélène (1946-); *Petit Jean va dans la Lune (Little John Goes to the Moon*; Grasset, 1976); *Les Loups du Bal (The Wolves of the Ball*; La Marelle, 1980); *Note:* Juveniles.

Tessier, François (?-); *La Cité des Âmes (The City of Souls*; Khom-Heidon, 1996); *Polaris 1 (Les Foudres de l'Abîme) – La Directive Exeter ((The Lightning from the Abyss) the Exeter Directive*; Khom-Heidon, 1997); *Note:* See Chapter IX.

Tessier, Maurice *see* **Dekobra, Maurice**

Tétreau, Jean (1923-); *Les Nomades (The Nomads*; Jour, 1967); *Volupté de l'Amour et de la Mort (Voluptuousness of Love and Death*; Jour, 1968); *Treize Histoires en Noir et Blanc (Thirteen Black and White Stories*; Jour, 1970); *Le Réformateur (The Reformer*; Ville St. Laurent, 1973); *Prémonitions* (Tisseyre, 1978); *Note:* French-Canadian writer. *Les Nomades* is a post-cataclysmic novel. *Volupté* is a collection of fantastical stories.

Texel, Jean (?-); *Parisgrad* (RL, 1982)

Thaillard, René (?-); *I.F. 2* (PRA, 1937); *Bébert Mécano* (Rouff, 1937); *L'Homme au Chien (The Man with a Dog*; Ferenczi, 1937)

Thalasso, Adolphe (?-?); *La Faim (The Hunger*; Tresse & Stock, 1893); *Note:* Also see **Grand-Guignol**.

Thébault, Eugène (?- 1942); *Les Maîtresses-Femmes (The Master Women*; Flamm., 1922); *Les Robinsons de la Somme (The Robinsons of the Somme*; Hac., 1925); *Radio-Terreur (Radio-Terror*; Fayard, 1928); *Nira, Australe Mystérieuse (Nira, Mysterious Australian*; Gédalge, 1930; rev. as *Les Deux Reines du Pôle Sud (The Two Queens of the South Pole]*, BGA, 1932); *Le Soleil Ensorcelé (The Spellbound Sun*; BGA, 1930); *Note:* See Chapter VII.

Thellier-Vallerand (Thellier (?-) & Vallerand, Jacques (1947-)); *Des Masques et des Miroirs (Of Masks and Mirrors*; Courteau, 1988); *Note:* Thellier is a French author; Vallerand is a French-Canadian writer. Collection of SF stories.

Thérenty (?-); *La Ronde des Lettres (The Dance of the Letters*; Nlles. Presses Fr., 1946)

Thériault, Adrien *see* **Thério, Adrien**

Thériault, Marie José (1945-); *Notre Royaume est de Promesses (Our Kingdom Is of Promises*; Fidès, 1974); *La Cérémonie* (La Presse, 1978; transl. as *The Ceremony*, 1980); *Invariance* (Noroît, 1982); *Les Demoiselles de Numidie (The Maidens of Numidia*; Boréal, 1984); *L'Envoleur de Chevaux (The Flyer of Horses*; Boréal, 1986); *Portraits d'Elsa (Portraits of Elsa*; Quinze, 1990); *Note:* French-Canadian writer, daughter of Yves **Thériault**.

Thériault, Yves (1915-1983); *Contes pour un Homme Seul (Tales for a Man Alone*; L'Arbre, 1944); *Les Commettants de Caridad (The Committers of Caridad*; Inst. Litt. Du Québec, 1961); *Le Vendeur d'Étoiles (The Seller of Stars*; Fidès, 1961); *Ashini* (Fidès, 1961); *Cul-de-Sac (Dead End*; Club des Livres à Succès, 1961); *Si la Bombe m'était Contée (If the Bomb Was Told to Me*; Jour, 1962); *Les Vendeurs du Temple (The Merchants of the Temple*; L'Homme, 1964); *Le Dompteur d'Ours (The Bear Tamer*; L'Homme, 1965); *L'Appelante (The Caller*; Jour, 1967); *L'Île Introuvable (The Unfindable Island*;

Jour, 1968); *Mahigan* (Leméac, 1968); *N'tsuk* (L'Homme, 1968); *Antoine et sa Montagne (Antoine and His Mountain*; Jour, 1969); *La Passe-au-Crachin (Misty Pass*; Ferron, 1972); *Le Haut Pays (The High Country*; René Ferron, 1973); *Agoak* (Quinze, 1975); *Le Partage de Minuit (The Sharing of Midnight*; Québecor, 1980); *Tayaout* (Quinze, 1981); *La Femme Anna (The Woman Anna*; VLB, 1981); *Valère et le Grand Canot (Valere and the Big Boat*; VLB, 1981); *L'Herbe de Tendresse (The Herb of Tenderness*; VLB, 1983); *Agakuk* (Grasset, 1992); The *Volpek* series: *1. La Montagne Creuse (The Hollow Mountain*; Lidec, 1965); *2. Le Secret de Mufjarti (The Secret of Mufjarti*; Lidec, 1965); *3. Les Dauphins de Monsieur Yu (Mister Yu's Dolphins*; Lidec, 1966); *4. Le Château des Petits Hommes Verts (The Castle of the Little Green Men*; Lidec, 1966); *5. Le Dernier Rayon (The Last Ray*; Lidec, 1966); *6. La Bête à 300 Têtes (The Beast with 300 Heads*; Lidec, 1967); *7. Les Pieuvres (The Octopus*; Lidec, 1967); *8. Les Vampires de la rue Monsieur le Prince (The Vampires of Monsieur-Le-Prince Street*; Lidec, 1968); *Note:* French-Canadian writer. Contes are fairy tales based on Native American legends. *Le Vendeur, Si la Bombe, L'Île, La Femme,* and *Valère* are collections of fantastical tales. *Le Haut-Pays* is about a mythical, parallel world. The *Volpek* series stars a secret agent in the James Bond mold who uses a lot of gadgets and tangles a few times with extraterrestrials.

Thério, Adrien (Thériault, Adrien) (1925-); *Brèves Années (Brief Years*; Fidès, 1953); *La Soif et le Mirage (The Thirst and the Mirage*; CLF, 1960); *Mors aux Flancs (Bolting*; Jumonville, 1965); *Un Païen chez les Pingouins (A Pagan Among the Penguins*; CLF, 1970); *Les Fous d'Amour (The Love Crazies*; Jumonville, 1973); *La Colère du Père (The Wrath of the Father*; Jour, 1974); *La Tête en Fête (Party in the Head*; Jumonville, 1975); *C'est ici que le Monde a commencé (It Is Here That the World Began*; Jumonville, 1978); *Note:* French-Canadian writer.

Thévenin, René (?-1967); *La Cité des Tortures (The City of Tortures*; JDV, 1906); *La Tête Ensorcelée (The Bewitched Head*; JDV, 1907); *L'Auto Fantôme (The Ghost Car*; Plein Air, 1909; rev. RMY, 1913); *Les Proies de la Sirène (The Siren's Preys*; JDV, 1910); *Le Mystère de la Bernina (The Mystery of Bernina*; JDV, 1911); *Le Collier de l'Idole de Fer (The Necklace of the Iron Idol*; Plein Air, 1912; rev. BGA, 1924); *Le Château Hanté d'Owlesfear (The Haunted Castle of Owlesfear*; JDV, 1912); *Barnabé Tignol et sa Baleine (Barnabe Tignol and His Whale*; AM, 1922); *Le Maître des Vampires (The Master of Vampires*; BGA, 1923); *La Jungle Insurgée (The Insurgent Jungle*; RDA, 1926); *Sous les Griffes du Monstre (Under the Claws of the Monster*; BGA, 1926); *La Forêt Sanglante (The Bloody Forest*; LA, 1927); *Les Chas-*

seurs d'Hommes (The Manhunters; S&V, 1929-30); *L'Ancêtre des Hommes (The Ancestor of Men*; S&V, 1932); *A L'Est de la Route 13 (East of Route 13*; S&V, 1933-34); *Le Pilote Fantôme (The Ghost Pilot*; Tallandier, 1937); *Note:* Also see Chapters V and VII, and André **Valérie**. Thévenin also wrote the comic book series **Durga Rani** *Futuropolis* (see Book 1, Chapter V).

Thiaudière, Edmond (1837-?); *Le Voyage en Bubaterbo, ou Pays des Jolis Boeufs (The Journey to Bubaterbo, Land of the Pretty Ox*; as Lord Humour; Ghio, 1874); *Les Voyages de Lord Humour—Le Pays des Rétrogrades, Île de Servat-Abus (Lord Humour's Journeys—the Land of the Retrogrades, Island of Servat-Abus*; Ghio, 1876); *Le Dindon Blanc (The White Turkey*; Ghio, 1877); *La Maison Fatale (The Deadly House*; Rouff, 1883); *La Proie du Néant (The Void's Prey*; Ollendorff, 1886); *De l'Une à l'Autre (From One to the Other*; Dentu, 1891); *Le Chien du Bon Dieu (God's Dog*; A. Robert, 1894); *Contes d'un Éleveur de Chimères (Tales of a Chimera Breeder*; Lemerre, 1902); *La Réponse du Sphinx (The Sphinx's Answer*; Fischbacher, 1905); *Note:* Also used the pseudonyms "Frédéric Stampf" and "Edmond Thy."

Thibault, François-Anatole *see* **France, Anatole**

Thibaux, Jean-Michel (?-); *L'Or du Diable (The Devil's Gold*; Orban, 1988)

Thiberge, Guillaume (?-); *L'Appel de l'Espace (The Call from Space*; Destination Crépuscule, 1996); *Note:* See Chapter IX.

Thibon, Gustave (?-); *Face à la Peur—La Fin du Monde est pour Demain (Facing the Fear—The End of the World Is for Tomorrow*; Bonnes Presses du Midi, 1947); *Vous serez comme des Dieux (You Will Be Like Gods*; Fayard, 1954); *L'Ignorance Étoilée (The Starry Ignorance*; Fayard, 1974); *Le Voile et le Masque (The Veil and the Mask*; Fayard, 1985); *L'Illusion Féconde (The Fertile Illusion*; Fayard, 1995); *Note:* See Chapter IX.

Thieblement, Françoise (?-) *see* *Contes et Légendes*

Thierry, Augustin (1870-?) *see* **Grand-Guignol**

Thierry, G. (?-) *see* **Duguet, Roger**

Thiéry, François (1952-); *L'Astrologie des Insectes (The Astrology of Insects*; Aubépine, 1987); *Trafics à l'Anglaise (English Traffic*; Aubépine, 1987); *L'Amour des Jaguars (The Love of Jaguars*; Magnard, 1987); *La Jungle aux Poisons (The Jungle of Poisons*; Magnard, 1988); *Attention! Pirates! (Beware! Pirates!*; Magnard, 1988); *L'Enfer du Désert (The Desert Hell*; Magnard, 1988); *Les Rhinocéros du Kilimandjaro (The Rhinoceros of Kilimandjaro*; Magnard, 1988); *Le Trésor sous la Mer (The Undersea Treasure*; Magnard, 1988); *Note:* Juveniles.

Thiès, Paul (1958-); *Les Forbans, des Caraïbes (The Caribbean Bandits;* Amitié, 1983); *Les Aventuriers de Saint-Corentin (The Adventurers from Saint-Corentin;* Amitié, 1985); *Histoire Farfelue d'un Fabuleux Éléphant (Funny Tale of a Fabulous Elephant;* Amitié, 1985); *Ali de Bassora* (Amitié, 1986); *Amad, les Dés du Hasard (Amad, the Dices of Chance;* Cast., 1988); *Le Sorcier aux Loups (The Wolf Wizard;* Amitié, 1988); *Le Magicien des Antilles (The Antilles Wizard;* Rageot, 1990); *L'Héritage d'Hercule—Achille Ravageur (Hercule's Inheritance—Achilles the Destroyer;* Milan, 1990); *Pas de Whisky pour Méphisto (No Whiskey for Mephisto;* Rageot, 1991); Series *Abdallah: Abdallah et les Sorcières du Bazar (Abdallah and the Bazaar Witches;* BR, 1995); *Abdallah et le Gâteau Diabolique (Abdallah and the Diabolical Cake;* BR, 1995); *Deux Princesses pour Abdallah (Two Princesses for Abdallah;* BR, 1995); *Abdallah et la Cité des Rêves (Abdallah and the City of Dreams;* BR, 1995); *Abdallah au Galop (Abdallah on the Run;* BR, 1995); *Abdallah et l'Oeuf d'Éléphant (Abdallah and the Elephant's Egg;* BR, 1995); *Abdallah et l'Enfant de Neige (Abdallah and the Snow Child;* BR, 1995); *Abdallah et la Flèche Blanche (Abdallah and the White Arrow;* BR, 1995); *Abdallah et le Quarante-et-Unième Voleur (Abdallah and the Forty-First Thief;* BR, 1995); *Abdallah et l'Île Atlantide (Abdallah and the Island Atlantis;* BR, 1995); *Abdallah et le Cavalier de la Steppe (Abdallah and the Rider from the Steppe;* BR, 1996); *Abdallah et la Forteresse des Sables (Abdallah and the Fortress of Sand;* BR, 1996); *Note:* Juveniles. See Chapter VIII.

Thilliez, Henry F. (?-); *La Grande Aventure des Fusées (The Great Adventure of Rockets;* UGE, 1963); *La Planète sans Rivage (Planet Without Shores;* Delagrave, 1964); *Les Pionniers du Cosmos (Pioneers of the Cosmos;* Hac., 1970); *Des Cieux et des Hommes (Of Skies and Men;* Hac., 1971); *Note:* Juvenile SF. See Chapter IX.

Thinès, Georges (?-); *Les Effigies (The Statues;* Gall., 1970); *Le Tramway des Officiers (The Officers' Tram;* Gall., 1974); *L'Oeil de Fer (The Eye of Iron;* Balland, 1977); *Les Objets vous Trouveront (Objects Will Find You;* Balland, 1979); *L'Homme Troué (The Holed Man;* CRI, 1981); *Les Vacances de Rocroi (Rocroi's Holidays;* Balland, 1982); *Théorèmes pour un Faust (Theorems for a Faust;* Le Cormier, 1983); *Le Désert d'Alun (The Alun Desert;* J. Antoine, 1986); *La Face Cachée (The Hidden Face;* AdH, 1994); *Note:* Belgian writer. See Chapter VIII.

Thirion, Jean-Benoît (1952-); *Les Échymoses Champêtres (The Farming Bruises;* Pensée U., 1973); *Liquidation Totale: Choses Mortes 78 (Total Liquidation: Dead Things 78;* EDEN, 1978); *Le Potentiel Recrucifié (The*

Recrucified Potential; Eden, 1979); *Ersatz d'Alsace* (anthology; Budderflade, 1979); *Le Vengeur (The Avenger;* Glénat, 1980); *Contes de l'Échiquier (Tales of the Chessboard;* Plein Chant, 1988)

Thirion, Louis (?-); *Waterloo, Morne Plaine (Waterloo, Sad Plain;* Scorpion, 1964); *Un Guepard pour Olga (A Leopard for Olga;* SEG, 1966); *Le Guepard se mouille (The Leopard Gets Wet;* SEG, 1966); *Les Stols (FNA 354, 1968); La Résidence de Psycartown (The Psycartown Residence;* Losfeld, 1968); *Les Naufragés de l'Alkinoos (The Survivors from the Alkinoos; FNA 377, 1969); Les Whums se Vengent (The Revenge of the Whums;* FNA 393, 1969); *Ysée-A (FNA 427, 1970); Sterga la Noire (Sterga-The-Black;* FNA 456, 1971); *Le Secret d'Ipavar (The Secret of Ipavar;* FNA 543, 1973); *Métrocéan 2031 (FNA 590, 1973); Chevaliers du Temps (Time Knights;* FNA 599, 1974); *Solaise* (Hermetoc 4-5, 1975; portions of this novel were incorporated in *Accident Temporel,* see below); *Chez Temporel (FNA 998, 1980); Le Répertoire des Époques de cette Galaxie et de Quelques Autres (The Repertory of the Epochs of This Galaxy and a Few Others;* FNA 1182, 1982); *Expérimentation Alpha (Experiment Alpha;* FNA 1204, 1983); *Ticket Aller-Retour pour l'Hyperespace (Return Ticket for Hyperspace;* FNA 1283, 1984); *Lorsque R'saanz Parut (When R'saanz Rise;* FNA 1339, 1984); *Galactic Paranoia (FNA 1348, 1985); Que l'Eternité Soit avec Vous! (May Eternity Be with You!;* FNA 1442, 1986); *Le Temps des Rats (The Time of the Rats;* FNA 1455, 1986); *Accident Temporel (Tempo-*

YSEE - A

FLEUVE NOIR

STERGA LA NOIRE

FLEUVE NOIR

LE SECRET D'IPAVAR

FLEUVE NOIR

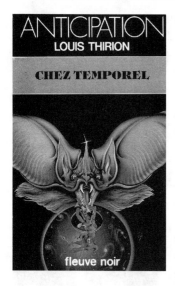

ral Accident; FNA 1509, 1986); *Réalité 2 (Reality 2*; FNA 1644, 1988); *Les Guerrières de Arastawar (The Warrior-Women of Arastawar*; FNA 1673, 1989); *Cette Chose qui vivait sur Véra (That Thing That Lived on Vera*; FNA 1701, 1989); *Requiem pour une Idole de Cristal (Requiem for a Crystal Idol*; FNA 1800, 1991); *Note:* See Chapter IX. Also see **Théâtre de l'Étrange** in Radio (Book 1, Chapter III).

Thiry, Marcel (1897-1977); *L'Enfant Prodigue (The Prodigal Child*; 1927); *La Mer de la Tanquillité (The Sea of Tranquility*; G. Thone, 1937); *Échec au Temps (Time in Check*; written in 1939; pub. Ed. Nlle. France, 1945; rev. Ren. du Livre, 1962); *Le Concerto pour Anne Queur (Concerto for Anne Queur*; 13 rue St. Georges, 1949); *Nouvelles du Grand Possible (Tales of the Great Possible*; L'Inter, 1949); *Trois Longs Regrets du Lis des Champs (Three Long Regrets of the Lily of the Fields*; Flûte Enchantée, 1955); *Commes Si (As If*; Monde du Livre, 1959); *Voie Lactée (Milky Way*; Rache, 1961); *Simul et Autre Cas (Simul and Other Cases*; Ed. du Large, 1963); *L'Égo des Neiges (The Ego of the Snows*; Rache, 1972); *Note:* Belgian writer. See chapters VII and VIII.

Thomas (sieur d'Embry), Artus (?-?); *Description de l'Île des Hermaphrodites (Description of the Island of Hermaphrodites*; written 1605; publ. Demen, 1724)

Thomas, Bernard (?-); See **Van Parys, Georges.**

Thomas, Gilles *see* **Verlanger, Julia**

Thomas, Henri (1912-1993); *La Chasse aux Trésors (The Treasures' Hunt*; Gall., 1961); *Les Tours de Notre-Dame (The Towers of Notre-Dame*; Gall., 1977); *Le Croc des Chiffoniers (The Junkman's Hook*; Gall., 1985); *Une Saison Volée (A Stolen Season*; Gll., 1986); *Le Promontoire (The Point*; Gall., 1987); *Un Détour par la Vie (Deviation Through Life*; Gall., 1988); *Le Goût de l'Éternel (The Taste of the Eternal*; Gall., 1990); *Le Crapaud dans la Tour (The Toad in the Tower*; Fata Morgana, 1992); *La Défeuillée (The Unleaving*; Le Temps qu'il faut, 1994)

Thomas, Jean (?-); *Le Robot Amoureux (The Robot in Love*; Phénix, 1980); *La Foulée Blanche (The White Step*; with Sabine **Fourquez**; Daniel, 1981)

Thomasset, René (?-); *Mephisto n'y fut pour rien (Mephisto Was for Nothing*; Baudinière, 1947); *Note:* Also see ***Contes et Légendes***

Thompson, Danièle (?-); See **Châteaureynaud, Georges-Olivier.**

Thylienne, Léon-Marie (?-); *Celui qui ressuscita (He Who Came Back to Life*; Schaert, 1924); *Note:* Belgian writer. Also used the pseudonym "Dr. Léon Wauthy."

Tiercelin, Louis (?-?) *see* **Grand-Guignol** and **Opéra**

Tilman, Pierre (?-); *L'île Flottante (The Floating Island*; Galilée, 1979); *Le Blouson (The Jacket*; L'Évidence, 1994)

Tilmans, Ege *see* **Tilms, Ege**

Tilms, Ege (Tilmans, Ege) (?-); *Hodomur, l'Homme de l'Infini (Hodomur, Man of Infinity*; Revue Mondiale, 1934); *Note:* Belgian writer. See Chapter VII.

Tinseau, (Comte Antoine-Joseph-) Léon de (?-); *Le Chemin de Damas (The Road to Damas*; Calmann-Lévy, 1894); *Vers l'Idéal (Towards the Ideal*; Calmann-Lévy, 1896); *La Princesse Errante (The Wandering Princess*; Calmann-Lévy, 1903); *La Clef de la Vie (The Key to Life*; Calmann-Lévy, 1907); *Les Deux Consciences (The Two Consciences*; Calmann-Lévy, 1910); *Le Duc Rollon (Duke Rollon*; Calmann-Lévy, 1913); *Jeanne la Mystérieuse (Jeanne the Mysterious*; Calmann-Lévy, 1921)

Tiphaigne de la Roche, Charles-François (1729-1774); *L'Amour Dévoilé ou le Mystère des Sympathistes (Love Unveiled, or the Mystery of the Sympathetists*; 1749); *Amilec, ou La Graine d'Hommes qui Sert à Peupler les Planètes (Amilec, or the Seed of Man Who Is Used to Seed the Planets*; Lambert, 1753); *Zamar, Député à la Lune par Amilec, Grand-Maître de la Manufacture (Zamar, Deputy to the Moon By Amilec, Grand-Master of the Factory*; Lambert, 1754); *Bigarrures Philosophiques (Philosophical Bizarreties*; Arkstée-Merkus, 1759); *Giphantie (Babylone-Durand, 1760; transl. 1761); *L'Empire des Zaziris sur les Humains ou la Zazirocratie (The Empire of the Zaziris Over Mankind, or the Zazirocracy*; Pékin, 1761); *Histoire des Galligènes (History of the Galligenes*; 1763); *Sanfrein, ou mon Dernier Séjour à la Campagne (Sanfrein, or My Last Stay in the Country*; Amsterdam, 1765); *Note:* See Chapter III.

Toepffer, Rodolphe (1799-1846); *Voyages et Aventures du Docteur Festus (Voyages and Adventures of Dr. Festus*; Cherbuliez, 1833); *Histoire de Monsieur Cryptogame (Story of Mr. Cryptogame*; Joubochet, 1846); *Le Presbytère (The Presbytery*; Hac., 1891); *Note:* See Chapter V. Toepffer is also the pioneer of modern comic books (see Book 1, Chapters V and VI).

Toesca, Maurice (Royat, Maurice) (1904-); *Perlimpimpin* (Stock, 1944); *Le Tournesol de Monsieur Picture (Mr.Picture's Sunflower*; Gall., 1944); *Le Singe Bleu*

(The Blue Monkey; Bader-Dufour, 1948); *Le Bruit Lointain du Temps (Time's Far-Away Sound*; CLF, 1961); *Les Loups-Garous (The Werewolves*; AM, 1966); *Voyage autour de l'Homme et Au-Delà (Journey Around Man and Beyond*; Planète, 1967); *Les Scorpionnes* (France-Empire, 1977); *Histoires Surnaturelles (Supernatural Tales*; AM, 1978); *Note:* See Chapter VIII. Toesca also wrote **Thanatos Palace Hotel** and **Les Voyageurs de l'Espace** (based on his play) for television (see Book 1, Chapter II) and **Tête à Tête** for radio (see Book 1, Chapter III).

Tollet, Pierre Jack (?-); *Meurtre en Soucoupe Volante (Murder on a Flying Saucer*; Pensée Moderne, 1953)

Topffer, Pierre (?-); *Les Messes Noires (Black Masses*; Belfond, 1980); *Note:* Documentary work about witchcraft.

Topor, Roland (1938-1997); *Le Locataire Chimérique (The Imaginary Tenant*; Buchet Chastel, 1964); *Quatre Roses pour Lucienne (Four Roses for Lucienne*; Bourgois, 1967); *Le Clown Tant Pis (The Clown Too Bad*; Daily-Bul, 1968); *Joko Fête son Anniversaire (Joko Celebrates His Birthday*; Buchet Chastel, 1969); *La Cuisine Cannibale (Cannibal Cooking*; Seuil, 1970); *Le Tâchier de l'Amateur (The Taskbook of the Amateur*; Daily-Bul, 1971); *L'Épikon* (Y. Rivière, 1974); *Café Panique (Panic Café*; Seuil, 1982); *Taxi Stories* (Safrat, 1987); *À Rebrousse-Poil (Against the Grain*; with Henri **Xhonneux**; Seuil, 1987); *Les Combles Parisiens (Parisian Attic*; Séguier, 1989); *Marquis* (Impr. Nationale, 1990); *Le Sacré Livre de Pronto (Pronto's Holy Book*; Syros, 1990); *Alice au Pays des Lettres (Alice in the Land of the Letters*; Seuil Jeunesse, 1991); *Le Courrier des Lettres (The Mail of the Letters*; Seuil, 1992); *Pense Bêtes (Reminders*; Cherche-Midi, 1992); *Pavé (Cobble Stone*; Baudouin, 1994); *Courts Termes (Short Terms*; Dumerchez, 1994); *Jachère Party* (Julliard, 1996); *Made in Taiwan Copyright in Mexico* (Rocher, 1997); *La Véritable Nature de la Vierge Marie (The True Nature of the VirgIn Mary*; Rocher, 1996); *Note:* See Chapter VIII. **Le Locataire Chimérique** was adapted into a 1976 film by Roman Polanski (see Book 1, Chapter I). **Topor** was also a renowned cartoonist who designed René **Laloux**'s animated feature, **La Planète Sauvage** (see Book 1, Chapter IV) and **Marquis** (See Book 1, Chapter I). He also acted in Werner Herzog's *Nosferatu*.

Torquet, Eugène *see* **Nau, John-Antoine**

Torrey, Hubert *see* **Périsset, Maurice**

Touati, Lucien-Guy (1947-); Motus (TF 11, 1979); *Guillou dans les Étoiles (Guillou Among the Stars*; with Claude **Rose**; GP, 1979); *La Marmite a Disparu (The Pot Is Gone*; Flamm., 1983); *La Voiture qui Parlait Trop (The Car Which Spoke Too Much*; GP, 1988); *Note:* Juvenile SF. See Chapter IX.

Toudouze, Georges G(ustave) (1877-1972); *La Conquête des Mers (The Conquest of the Seas*; Schleicher Frères, 1901); *Le Petit Roi d'Ys (The Little King of Ys*; Hac., 1913); *Filleule de Merlin (Merlin's God-Daughter*; Hac., 1916); *Tragique Réveil (Tragic Awakening*; Le Bon Livre, 1920); *Les Sous-Marins Fantômes (The Phantom Sub-Marines*; Hac. 1921); *Les Compagnons de l'Iceberg en Feu (The Companions of the Burning Iceberg*; Ollendorff, 1922); *Le Bateau des Sorcières (The Boat of Witches*; Ollendorff, 1923); *De Paris à New York en Autochenille (From Paris to New-York in a Tractor*; La Presse, 1926-27); *La Sorcière du Vésuve (The Witch of Mount Vesuvius*; Hac., 1927); *Le Corsaire du Pacifique (The Corsair of the Pacific*; Hac., 1929); *Une Femme parmi les Loups (A Woman Among Wolves*; Gall., 1929); *Carnaval en Mer (Carnival at Sea*; Ren. du Livre, 1932); *Le Secret de l'Île d'Acier (The Secret of the Island of Steel*; LPT, 1934; rev. BGA, 1938); *L'Inconnue de Ras Guardian (The Unknown Woman of Ras Guardia*; Tallandier, 1938); *La Reine des Pêcheurs de Perle (The Queen of the Pearl Divers*; Tallandier, 1938); *Le Seigneur du Temple Englouti (The Lord of the Sunken Temple*; Tallandier, 1938); *Gait la Mystérieuse (Gait the Mysterious*; BGA, 1940); *Anne et le Mystère Breton (Anne and the Briton Mystery*; Hac., 1942); *Faik de Kerloc'h, Pupille de l'Océan (Son of the Ocean*; Urz Goanaz Breiz-dolé, 1943); *Prisonniers du Serpent de Mer (Prisoners of the Sea Serpent*; Tallandier, 1946); *Le Diable Noir de l'Abîme (The Black Devil of the Abyss*; JDV, 1948); *Héritière de Neptune (Heir of Neptune*; BV, 1952); *Les Derniers Jours de la Villle d'Ys (The Last Days of the City of Ys*; Terre de Brume, 1994); Series *Les Aventuriers de la Science (The Adventurers of Science]: 1. L'Homme qui Volait le Gulf-Stream (The Man Who Stole the Gulf-Stream*; Gall., 1925; rev. as *Le Sorcier des Abîmes (Wizard of the Abyss)*, BGA, 1949); *2. L'Éveilleur de Volcans (The Awakwener of Volcanos*; Gall., 1926); *3. Une Femme parmi les Loups (A Woman Among Wolves*; Gall., 1930); *4. Pour Tout l'Or de la Mer (For All the Gold in the Sea*; Gall., 1932); *5. Le Maître de la Mort Froide (Master of the Cold Death*; Ren. du Livre, 1953); *Note:* See Chapter VII. Toudouze is also the author of a popular juvenile series featuring *Les Cinq Jeunes Filles (The Five Young Girls*; BV, 1960s-70s). Also see **Contes et Légendes**

Toufik, El Hadj-Moussa (1948-); *Le Passage (The Passage*; Naaman, 1980); *Les Collines de l'Épouvante (The Hills of Terror*; Desclez, 1981); *Note:* Algerian-born writer published in Quebec. Collections of fantastical tales.

Toulouse, Gilbert (?-); *La Montagne Retrouvée (The Found Mountain*; B. Arthaud, 1957); *Le Passage du Roi (The King's Passage*; Belfond, 1966); *Le Prisonnier dans l'Île (The Prisoner on the Island*; Belfond, 1968);

La Fin des Temps (The End of Time; Belfond, 1972); *Putsch* (Belfond, 1975); *Mont-Perdu (Lost Mountain*; Belfond, 1977); *Crystal-Palace* (Belfond, 1980); *Le Mercenaire (The Mercenary*; Belfond, 982); *L'Imposteur (The Imposter*; Belfond, 1985)

Touraine, Yves (?-); *L'Été sur la Grange Haute (Summer on the High Barn*; Charlot, 1947); *Le 5ème Coup de Trompette (The Fifth Blow of the Horn*; Arcanes, 1954); *L'Oiseleur des Songes (The Bird-Watcher of Dreams*; Debresse, 1956); *Le Ressuscité (The Man Who Came Back to Life*; Los., 1960); *Le Soliste des Sources (The Solo Singer of the Sources*; Caractères, 1989); *Orchestration Minérale (Mineral Orchestration*; Fragments, 1995)

Tournier, Michel (1924-); *Vendredi, ou Les Limbes du Pacifique (Friday, or Limbo of the Pacific*; Gall., 1967); *Le Roi des Aulnes (The King of the Elms*; Tallandier, 1970); *Amandine ou les Deux Jardins (Amandine, or the Two Gardens*; GP, 1977); *Le Cop de Bruyère (The Briar Patch*; Gall., 1978); *Pierrot ou les Secrets de la Nuit (Pierrot, or the Secrets of the Night*; Gall., 1979); *Barbedor (Goldenbeard*; Gall., 1980); *Gaspard, Melchior et Balthazar: Les Rois Mages (The Three Wise Kings*; Gall., 1980); *Le Vol du Vampire (The Vampire's Flight*; MdF, 1981); *Sept Contes (Seven Tales*; Gall., 1984); *Barbedor (Goldenbeard*; Gall., 1985); *La Goutte d'Or (The Golden Drop*; Gall., 1985); *La Fugue du Petit Poucet (Tom Thumb's Escape*; Hac., 1988); *Angus* (SdP, 1988); *Les Contes du Medianoche (Tales from the Medianoche*; Gall., 1989); *Le Medianoche Amoureux (The Medianoche in Love*; Gall., 1989); *Le Crépuscule des Masques (The Twilight of the Masks*; Hoëbecke, 1992); *La Couleuvrine (The Grass Snake*; Gall., 1994); *Le Miroir à Deux Faces (The Mirror with Two Faces*; Seuil, 1994); *Note:* See Chapter VIII.

Toussaint, Yvon (?-); *Un Incident Indépendent de notre Volonté (A Technical Incident*; AM, 1974); *La Mort est dans la Ville (Death Is in the City*; AM, 1978)

Toussaint-Juge *see* **Véry, Pierre**

Toussaint-Samat, Maguelonne (?-); *La Mort et sa Fille (Death and His Daughter*; with Jean Toussain-Samat; Les Deux Mondes, 1949); *Concerto pour Meurtre et Orchestre (Concerto for Murder and Orchestra*; Les Deux Mondes, 1950); *L'Extravagante Madame Doucet (The Extravagant Mrs. Doucet*; Calmann-Lévy, 1952); *Note:* Also see **Contes et Légendes**

Trans, H. F. (?-); *L'Île des Ténèbres (The Island of Darkness*; Presses d'Outremer, 1974)

Trapéras, Franck (?-); See **Patoux, Danièle**.

Trassard, Jean-Loup (?-); *L'Érosion Intérieure (The Inner Erosion*; Gall., 1965); *L'Ours Fariné (The Floured Bear*;

École des Loisirs, 1974); *L'Ancolie (The Ancoly*; Gall., 1975); *Des Cours d'Eau Peu Considérables (Some Small Waterways*; Gall., 1981); *Histoires Fraîches (Fresh Tales*; École des Loisirs, 1981); *Rana, la Menthe (Rana the Mint*; Ipomée, 1984); *Caloge* (Le Temps qu'il faut, 1991); *L'Espace Antérieur (Anterior Space*; Gall., 1993); *Traquet Motteux ou L'Agronome Sifflottant (Traquet Motteux, or the Whistling Agronomist*; Le Temps qu'il faut, 1994); *Note:* See Chapter VIII.

Traynel, (Marquis) Olivier de (1857-1921); *La Bête Loripai (The Beast Loripai*; Ollendorff, 1892); *La Découverte du Docteur Faldras (The Discovery of Dr. Faldras*; Ollendorff, 1908); *Élisabeth Faldras* (Ollendorff, 1909); *La Boussole Merveilleuse (The Wonderful Compass*; Boivin, 1923); *Note:* Also wrote under the pseudonym "Jean de Neltray."

Trébal (?-?) *see* **Grand-Guignol**

Treignier, Michel (?-); *Spectrales* (Cercle d'Or, 1974); *Le Chemin des Abîmes (The Path to the Abyss*; MarFan 578, 1976); *Note:* See Chapter VIII.

Tremblay, Clément (1974-); *La Maison des Sacrifices (The House of Sacrifices*; Guy Saint-Jean, 1995); *Note:* French-Canadian writer.

Tremblay, Gilles (1947-); *Les Nordiques Sont Disparus (The Nordiques Are Gone*; Proteau, 1983); *Note:* French-Canadian writer. After being exposed to an alien beam, children gain super-powers. The *Nordiques* are a hockey team.

Tremblay, Michel (1942-); *Contes pour Buveurs Attardés* (Jour, 1966; transl. as *Stories for Late Night Drinkers*, 1977); *La Cité dans l'Oeuf (The City in the Egg*; Jour, 1969); *La Nuit des Princes Charmants (The Night of Prince Charmings*; Leméac, 1995); *Note:* French-Canadian writer. *La Cité* features a mix of folklore, Greek myths, and original ideas.

Trendel, Guy (?-); *Dragons, Fantômes et Trésors Cachés (Dragons, Ghosts and Hidden Treasures*; Coprur, 1988); *Note:* Folk tales.

Trigon, Jean le Marchant de (1902-1968); *La Pierre de Lune (The Moonstone*; Rageot, 1944); *L'Homme qui Vivra dans Mille Ans (The Man Who Will Live in a Thousand Years*; Fleurus, 1957); *Un Ange Cornu avec des Ailes de Tôle (A Horned Angel with Metal Wings*; Actes-Sud, 1994)

Trintzius, René (1898-1953); *Le Soleil du Père (The Sun of the Father*; Gall., 1927); *Poudre d'Or (Golden Dust*; with Amédée **Valentin**; Gall., 1928); *Le Septième Jour (The Seventh Day*; Gall., 1931); *La Bête Écarlate (The Scarlet Beast*; Gall., 1934); *Les Clés du Désordre (The Keys to Disorder*; MdF, 1941); *Défense de Mourir (For-*

bidden to Die; with **Armory**; Jean Renard, 1943); *Babel des Ombres (Babel of Shadows*; Jean Renard, 1944); *Voyageur des Ténèbres (Voyager of Darkness*; Maréchal, 1946); *La Grande Peur (The Great Fear*; Arthaud, 1946)

Triolet, Elsa (1896-1970); *Le Cheval Roux (The Red Horse*; Ed. Fr. Réunis, 1953)

Tristan, Frédérick (1931-); *Le Dieu des Mouches (The God of the Flies*; Grasset, 1959); *Les Sept Femmes de Barbe-Bleue (The Seven Wives of Bluebeard*; Boîte Noire, 1966); *La Curieuse Histoire de la Geste Serpentine (The Curious Tale of the Serpent Saga*; Différence, 1978); *Les Tribulations Héroïques de Balthasar Kober (The Heroic Tribulations of Balthasar Kober*; Balland, 1980); *L'Histoire Sérieuse et Drolatique de l'Homme sans Nom (The Serious and Funny Tale of the Nameless Man*; Balland, 1980); *L'Oeil d'Hermès (The Eye of Hermes*; Arthaud, 1982); *La Cendre et la Foudre (Ash and Lightning*; Balland, 1982); *Les Égarés (The Lost Ones*; Balland, 1983); *Naissance d'un Spectre (Birth of a Spectre*; Balland, 1983); *Le Fils de Babel (The Son of Babel*; Balland, 1985); *Méduse (Medusa*; Distique, 1985); *Le Singe Égal du Ciel (The Ape Equal to Heaven*; Bourgois, 1986); *La Femme Écarlate (The Scarlet Woman*; Fallois, 1988); *L'Ange dans la Machine (The Angel in the Machine*; TR, 1989); *L'Atelier des Rêves Perdus (The Workshop of Lost Dreams*; Aube, 1991); *L'Obsédante (The Obsession*; Cherche-Midi, 1992); *Le Dernier des Hommes (The Last Man*; RL, 1993); *L'Énigme du Vatican (The Vatican Enigma*; Fayard, 1995); *Stéphanie Phanistée* (Fayard, 1997); *Note:* See Chapter VIII.

Trombert, Georges (?-); *L'Énigme Vivante (The Living Enigma*; Flamm., 1931); *L'Atome Complice (The Accomplice Atom*; STAEL, 1936); *Note:* Also used the pseudonyms "Rosita d'Arnay," "René Morny," "Michèle Rivière," and "George Sanzès."

Tron, Dominique (1950-); *De la Science-Fiction c'est nous à l'Interpénétration des Corps (From SF It's Us to the Interpenetration of Bodies*; Los., 1972)

Tronche, Philippe *see* **Curval, Philippe**

Trotet de Bargis, René (?-); *L'Éternelle Étreinte (The Eternal Hug*; France-Édit., 1923); *Kh'ia, la Fille des Gorilles (Kh'ia, Daughter of Gorillas*; RDA, 1923); *La Mission de Quatre Savants (The Mission of Four Scientists*; RDA, 1925); *Note:* See Chapter VII.

Troyat, Henri (Tarassov, Lev) (1911-); *L'Araigne* (Plon, 1938); *Le Mort Saisit le Vif (The Dead Catches the Living*; Plon, 1942); *La Geste d'Ève (The Saga of Eve*; Flamm., 1964); *Les Ailes du Diable (The Wings of the Devil*; Flamm., 1973); *À Quatre Pas du Soleil (Four Steps from the Sun*; Ramsay, 1982); *Le Marchand de Masques (The Merchant of Masks*; Flamm., 1994)

Trubert, Roger (?-); *L'Astre Rouge (The Red Star*; Montsouris, 1945); *Note:* Juvenile SF. See Chapter IX.

Truchaud, François (?-); *Retour à Bakaan (Return to Bakaan*; Chêne, 1976); *Note:* Illustrated by Philippe **Druillet**.

Trudel, Jean-Louis (1967-); *Le Ressuscité de l'Atlantide (Resurrection from Atlantis*; Imagine, 1985-86; rev. FNA 1955, 1994); *Pour des Soleils Froids (For Some Cold Suns*; Temps Tôt, 1991-92; rev. FNA 1942, 1994); *Aller Simple pour Saguenal (One-Way Ticket for Saguenal*; JP 91, 1994); *Un Trésor sur Serendib (A Treasure on Serendib*; JP 94, 1994); *Les Voleurs de Mémoire (The Memory Thieves*; JP 97, 1995); *Les Rescapés de Serendib (The Survivors from Serendib*; JP 102, 1995); *Le Prisonnier de Serendib (The Prisoner of Serendib*; JP 103, 1995); *Les Princes de Serendib (The Princes of Serendib*; JP 110, 1996); *Des Colons pour Serendib (Colonizers for Serendib*; JP 111, 1996); *Fièvres sur Serendib (Fevers on Serendib*; JP 116, 1996); *Un Printemps à Nigelle (A Spring in Nigelle*; JP 117, 1997); *Un Été à Nigelle (A Summer in Nigelle*; JP 120, 1997); *Un Hiver à Nigelle (A Winter in Nigelle*; JP 124, 1997); *Note:* French-Canadian writer.

Trumelet, Corneille (?-?); *Un Amour Sous-Marin (An Underwater Love*; Tiffy-Jullian, 1877); *Blida: Récits selon la Légende (Blida: Tales According to the Legends*; Jourdan, 1887)

Truong, Jean-Michel (?-); *Reproduction Interdite (Forbidden Reproduction*; Orban, 1989)

Trystram, Florence (?-); *Le Procès des Étoiles (The Stars on Trial*; Seghers, 1979); *La Nuit du Motard (The Night of the Biker*; Hac., 1986); *L'Épopée du Méridien Terrestre (The Saga of the Earth Meridian*; Flamm., 1986); *Lancelot* (Seguier, 1987); *Comme un Rêve de Pierre (As a Dream of Stone*; Seghers, 1987); *L'Enfant sans Nom (The Nameless Child*; Seghers, 1989); *Note:* See Chapter VIII.

T'Serstevens, Albert (1885-1974); *Le Dieu qui dance (The Dancing God*; AM, 1921); *Béni 1er, Roi de Paris (Blessed the 1st., King of Paris*; AM, 1926); *Note:* Belgian writer.

Tur, Jean (?-); *Mémoires de l'Arkonn Tecla (Memoirs of the Arkonn Tecla*; Idéale, 1969); *L'Archipel des Guerrières (The Archipelago of the Warrior-Women*; PdE, 1973); *La Harpe des Forces (The Harp of Power*; PdE, 1974); *Sterne Dorée (Golden Sterne*; PdE, 1976); *Aggin et Mavaé* (Jean Tur, 1986); *Le Nautile Solitaire (The Lonely Nautile*; Jean Tur, 1986); *Note:* See Chapter VIII.

Turgeon, Pierre(1947-); *Prochainement sur cet Écan (Soon on This Screen*; Jour, 1973); *Un, Deux, Trois (One, Two, Three*; Quinze, 1980); *La Première Personne (The First*

Person; Quinze, 1982); *Les Torrents de l'Espoir (The Rapids of Hope*; PC, 1996); *Note:* French-Canadian writer. *Un, Deux, Trois* is about a strange being who haunts a ghost town.

Turin, Philippe Henri (?-) *see* **Belfiore, Robert**

Tyssot de Patot, Simon (1655-1727); *Voyages et Aventures de Jacques Massé (Voyages and Adventures of Jacques Massé*; Jacques l'Aveugle, 1710); *La Vie, les Aventures et le Voyage de Groenland du Révérend Père Cordelier Pierre de Mésange (The Life, Adventures and Trip to the Greenland of the Rev. Father Pierre de Mesange*; Étienne Roger, 1720); *Note:* See Chapter III.

Ulbach, Louis *see* **Ferragus**

Urfé, Honoré d' (1561-1625); *L'Astrée* (Barbin, 1607-28); *Note:* See Chapter II.

Uzureau, Yves (?-) *see* **Ichbiah, Daniel**

Vac, Bertrand (Pelletier, Aimé) (1914-); *Le Carrefour des Géants (The Crossroads of Giants*; Livre de France, 1974); *Bizarres* (Guérin, 1988); *Note:* French-Canadian writer.

Vaes, Guy (1927-); *Octobre, Long Dimanche (October, Long Sunday*; Plon, 1957); *Les Cimetières de Londres (London's Cemeteries*; J. Antoine, 1978); *L'Envers (Upside Down*; J. Antoine, 1983); *Note:* Belgian writer. See Chapter VIII.

Vaillancourt, Lise (1954-); *L'Été des Eiders (The Summer of Eiders*; Leméac, 1996); *Note:* French-Canadian writer.

Vairasse d'Allais, Denis *see* **Veiras, Denis**

Valade, Frédéric (Jagot, Henry) (?-); *L'Affaire Jomini (The Jomini Case*; Gautier-Languereau, 1926); *L'Araignée Verte (The Green Spider*; BGA, 1926); *L'Étrange Aventure de M. de Permarc (The Strange Adventue of Mr. De Permarc*; Gautier-Languereau, 1929); *Le Tragique Secret de Jean Forbin (The Tragic Secret of Jean Forbin*; Gautier-Languereau, 1931); *La Folle de l'Étang Noir (The Madwoman of the Black Pond*; Gautier-Languereau, 1932); *La Reine des Invisibles (The Queen of the Invisibles*; CA, 1932); *Le Petit-Fils de Rocambole (Rocambole's Grand-Son*; 6 vols., LN, 1931-33); *Les Chauffeurs du Nord (The Drivers of the North*; Tallandier, 1937); *Les Mystères de la Croix-Salluste (The Mysteries of the Sallustic Cross*; Dupuis, 1937); *Note:* Also see **Ponson du Terrail**.

Valandré, Marianne (1937-); *Le Jour où le Soleil a oublié de se lever (The Day the Sun Forgot to Rise*; Grasset, 1979); *L'Arbre de Jérôme (Jerome's Tree*; Grasset, 1983); *Note:* Juveniles.

Valcros, William (?-?) *see* **Grand-Guignol**

Valcq, Philippe (?-); *Le Menestrel de Marie, Chroniques d'une Ville Magique (Mary's Minstrel: Chronicles of a Magical City*; Ramuel, 1997)

Valentin, Amédée (?-) *see* **Trintzius, René**

Valérie, André (?-); *Sur l'Autre Face du Monde (On the Other Side of the World*; S&V, 1935); *Note:* Some scholars believe that André **Valérie** was a pseudonym of René **Thévenin**.

Valéry, Francis (1955-); *La Nuit Tous Les Martiens Sont Verts (At Night All Martians Are Green*; as Kevin H. Ramsey; CNRI, n.d.); *Pas de Panique (Don't Panic*; as Kevin H. Ramsey; Editions de l'Hydre, n.d.); *L'Horreur des Collines (The Horror in the Hills*; DLM, 1988); *L'Arche des Rêveurs (The Ark of the Dreamers*; Aurore, 1991); *Altneuland* (Hydre, 1995); *Les Voyageurs sans Mémoires (The Travellers Without Memories*; Encrage, 1997); *Les Messagers de Saumwatu (The Messengers of Saumwatu*; DLM, Arkham 1, 1997); *La Mémoire du Monde (The Memory of the World*; DLM, Arkham 6, 1997); *Note:* See Chapters VIII and IX.

Valéry, Paul (1871-1945) *see* **Opéra**

Valetti, Oscar *see* **Barberi, Jacques & Ramonet, Yves**

Valiant, Daniel (?-); Series *La Légende du Goéland Blanc (The Legend of the White Seagull)*: *Ciel des Sables (Sky of the Sands*; SdP 2 18, 1976); *La Caverne du Temps (The Cavern of Time*; SdP 2 56, 1977); *Note:* Juvenile SF. See Chapter IX.

Valle, Jo (?-); *La Vengeance du Condamné (The Revenge of the Condemned Man*; Férenczi, 1914); *L'Aigle des Andes (The Eagle of the Andes*; Offenstadt, 1915); *Les Vautours contre l'Aigle (The Vultures vs. the Eagle*; Offenstadt, 1915); *Les Mille et Un Tours de l'Espiègle Lili (The 1001 Tricks of Facetious Lili*; Offenstadt, 1917); *Le Héros de Fachoda (The Hero of Fachoda*; Rouff, 1937); *Le Voeu de Couedic (Couedic's Wish*; n.d.)

Vallée, Danièle (1956-); *La Caisse (The Crate*; Vermillon, 1994); *Note:* French-Canadian writer.

Vallée, Jacques *see* **Seriel, Jérôme**

Vallène, Paul (?-); *Aller-Simple pour l'Anadyr (One-Way Ticket for Anadyr*; MarJ 267, 1964)

Vallerand, Jacques *see* **Thellier-Vallerand**

Vallerey, Tancrède (?-); *Le Mystère des Ruines (The Mystery of the Ruins*; Gedalge, 1929); *Celui qui Viendra (He Who Shall Come*; Oeuvres Libres, 1929); *L'Île au Sable Vert (The Island with Green Sand*; Hac., 1930); *L'Avion Fantastique (The Fantastic Plane*; Nathan, 1936); *Un Mois sous les Mers (A Month Undersea*; Nathan, 1937); *Le Manoir de Montsonore (The Manor of Montsonore*; BGA, 1951); *Note:* See Chapter VII.

Vallières, Alain (1951-); *Le Cité d'Atéra (The City of Atera*; Rocher Blanc, 1992); *La Quête de Trébor (Trebor's Quest*; Vallières, 1995); *Note:* French-Canadian writer.

Valojie, Marilyn (?-); *Les 3 C* (Baron chef d'oeuvre, 1972); *Capitaine Nickie contre l'Homme-Loup (Captain Nickie vs. the Wolf-Man*; Cadmium, 1973); *Mary Gold Initie à la Magie (Mary Gold Inititiates to Magic*; ODEPI, 1976); *Prophétie pour l'An 2000 (Prophecy for the Year 2000*; Valojie, 1976)

Valona , Louis (?-?) *see* **Grand-Guignol**

Valorbe, François (Hurault de Vibraye, Ludovic-François) (?-); *Soleil Intime (Intimate Sun*; GLM, 1949); *Carte Noire (*Black Card; Arcanes, 1953); *La Vierge aux Chimères (The Virgin with Chimeras*; Los., 1957); *Magirisée (Magicized*; Los., 1964*); L'Apparition Tangible (The Tangible Apparition*; Los., 1969); *Voulez-Vous Vivre en Eps? (Do You Want to Live in Eps?*; Bourgois, 1969); *Note:* See Chapter VIII.

Valpierre, Guy (?-); *Le Rendez-Vous du Cauchemar (Nightmare Rendezvous*; Hac., 1996); *Le Tarot du Diable (The Devil's Tarot*; Hac., 1997)

Vanasse, André (1942-); *La Saga des Lagacé* (Libre Expression, 1980); *Note:* French-Canadian writer. Satire about a super-powered family.

Van Brussel, Gust (1924-); *L'Anneau (The Ring*; MarFan 542, 1975); *Note:* Belgian writer.

Vandel, Jean-Gaston (Libert, Jean (1913-1995) & Vandenpanhuyse, Gaston (1913-)); *Les Chevaliers de l'Espace (The Space Knights*; FNA 7, 1952); *Le Satellite Artificiel (The Artificial Satellite*; FNA 10, 1952); *Les Astres Morts (The Dead Stars*; FNA 11, 1952); *Alerte aux Robots (Alert: Robots*; FNA 15, 1952); *Frontières du Vide (Frontiers of the Void*; FNA 17, 1953); *Le Soleil sous la Mer (The Undersea Sun*; FNA 19, 1953); *Attentat Cosmique (Cosmic Strike*; FNA 21, 1953); *Incroyable Futur (Incredible Future*; FNA 24, 1953); *Agonie des Civilisés (Agony of the Civilized*; FNA 26, 1953); *Pirate de la Science (Pirate of Science*; FNA 29, 1954); *Fuite dans l'Inconnu (Flight Into the Unknown*; FNA 34, 1954); *Naufrages des Galaxies (Wreckage of the Galaxies*; FNA 39, 1954); *Territoire Robot (Robot Territory*; FNA 43, 1955); *Les Titans de l'Energie (The Energy Titans*; FNA 48, 1955); *Raid sur Delta (Raid Over Delta*; FNA 52, 1955); *Départ pour l'Avenir (Departure for the Future*; FNA 56, 1955); *Bureau de l'Invisible (Office of the Invisible*; FNA 61, 1956); *Les Voix de l'Univers (The Voices of the Universe*; FNA 67, 1956); *La Foudre Anti-D (The Anti-D Lightning*; FNA 73, 1956); *Le Troisième Bocal (The Third Jar*; FNA 77, 1956); *Note:* See Chapter IX. Under the pseudonym of Paul **Kenny**, Libert and Vandenpanhuyse created the popular spy hero *Coplan FX-18*, also published by Fleuve Noir in its *Espionnage* imprint. Some of these (such as *Bataillon Fantôme (Ghostly Battalion*; FN Espionnage 194, 1959) featured genre elements. **Coplan** was the subject of several films and television adaptations (see Book 1, Chapters 1 and 2). A number of Vandel's novels were adapted into digest-sized graphic novels (see Book 1, Chapter V under **Fleuve Noir**).

Vandenpanhuyse, Gaston (1913-) *see* **Vandel, Jean-Gaston**

Vander, Guy (?-); *Les Compagnons du Claire de Lune (The Brotherhood of Moonlight*; France-Édition, 1923); *Au Son de l'Angelus (At the Sound of the Angelus*; France-Édition, 1924); *Le Roi du Bagne (The King of Convicts*; Férenczi, 1925); *Le Défilé des Serpents à Sonettes (The Canyon of Rattlesnakes*; Édit. Modernes, 1928); *L'Éclipse de Lune (The Lunar Eclipse*; Édit. Modernes, 1928); *Le Saut dans l'Abîme (The Jump Into the Abyss*; Édit. Modernes, 1928); *L'Envers du Bonheur (The Other Side of Happiness*; Bons Romans Populaires, 1929); *Le Capitaine Noir (The Black Captain*; Tallandier, 1930); *Le Maître de la Jungle (The Master of the Jungle*; Férenczi, 1930); *L'Araignée Rouge (The Red Spider*; BGA, 1931); *L'Âme en Peine (A Soul in Pain*; Tallandier, 1932); *Les Apaches de l'Ocean (The Apaches of the Ocean*; Baudinière, 1934); *La Mascotte de Bonaparte (Bonaparte's Mascot*; Baudinière, 1934); *La Fille de Satan (Satan's Daughter*; Police 81, 1935); *La Chasse à l'Homme (The Man Hunt*; Police 87, 1935)

Vandermeulen, Pierre (?-); *Contes Métaphysiques (Metaphysical Tales*; Arthaud, 1945); *L'Antéchrist et le Potier (The Antichrist and the Potter*; Arthaud, 1947)

Van Ermenghem, Frédéric *see* **Hellens, Franz**

Van Gaert, Hugo (?-); *Une Planète pour Copponi (A Planet for Copponi*; FNA 1959, 1995)

Van Herck, Paul (1938-); *Caroline, Oh! Caroline* (MSF 42, 1976); *Crésudi Dernier? (Sam of de Pluterdag*, 1968; MSF 56, 1977; transl. as *Where Were You Last Pluterday?*, 1973); *Note:* Belgian (Flemish) writer. These are French translations of Flemish novels.

Van Herp, Jacques (1923-); *Les Raiders de l'Espace (Space Raiders*; as Michel Jansen/with Jean **Erland**; SPES, 1955); *Le Prince Milou* (as André Jouly; SPES, 1957); *Le Port des Brumes (The Harbor of Mists*; as Michel Jansen; SdP 74, 1957); *La Porte sous les Eaux (The Gate Under the Sea*; as Michel Jansen/with Jean **Ray** writing as John Flanders; SPES, 1960); *Mer des Pluies (Sea of Rains*; as Michel Jansen; SPES, 1961); *Rona sur l'Amazone (Rona of the Amazon*; as Michel Goissert; SPES, 1963); *Panorama de la Science-Fiction* (non-fiction; Gérard, 1973); *La Nuit de St. Eutrope (The*

Night of St. Eutrope; Soleil des Lièvres, 1978); *Note:* Belgian writer. See Chapter IX.

Van Lerberghe, Charles (1861-1907); *Selection Surnaturelle (Supernatural Selection*; 1905); *Note:* Belgian writer. See Chapter VI.

Vanloo, Albert (?-?) *see* **Opéra**

Van Luggene, Bernard (?-); *Le Cartable Noir (The Black Briefcase*; St. Germain-des-Prés, 1986); *Le Veilleur de Licornes (The Unicorn Watcher*; GEMAP, 1995)

Van Offel, Horace (1876-1944); *Les Nuits de Gardes (The Watch Nights*; AM, 1917); *Le Tatouage Bleu (The Blue Tattoo*; AM, 1917); *La Terreur Fauve (The Fawn Terror*; AM, 1922); *Les Deux Ingénus ou Le Voyage aux Îles Fortunées (The Two Ingenues or the Journey to the Fortunate Islands*; Grasset, 1924); *Sylvia et le Cremnobate (Sylvia and the Cremnobate*; AM, 1929); *Le Chevalier de Batavia (The Knight of Batavia*; Libr. Champs-Élysées, 1929); *La Dépouille du Lion (The Lion's Skin*; Cosmopolites, 1930); *Le Jongleur d'Épées (The Juggler of Swords*; Portiques, 1930); *Le Casse-Tête Malais (The Malaysian Head-Clubber*; Libr. Champs-Élysées, 1931); *Le Chemin de Ronde (The Watch Path*; Portiques, 1932); *L'Oiseau de Paradis (The Bird of Paradise*; Portiques, 1932); *La Flûte Corsaire (The Corsair Flute*; Denoël & Steele, 1933); *L'Incendie de Chicago (The Chicago Fire*; Tallandier, 1938); *Le Capitaine du Vaisseau-Fantôme (The Captain of the Ghost-Ship*; Libr. Champs-Élysées, 1943); *Note:* Belgian writer. See Chapter VI.

Van Parys, Georges (1902-1971); *Les Atomistes (The Atom Smashers*; with Bernard **Thomas**; Den., 1968); *Note:* Famous film music composer. Novelization of an eponymous 1968 television series written by Bernard **Thomas** and Agnès **Van Parys** (see Book 1, Chapter II).

Van Remoortere, Julien (?-); *Le Livre Interdit de Krista O (The Forbidden Book of Krista O*; TF 12, 1979)

Varazze, Jacques de *see* **Voragine, Jacques de**

Varende, Yves (Martens, Thierri) (1942-); *Le Gadget de l'Apocalypse (The Apocalypse Gadget*; AMSF2 33, 1978); *Tamaru (*Glénat, 1980); *Les Tueurs de l'Ordre (The Killers of Order*; Glénat, 1980); *Tuez-les Tous! (Kill Them All!*; Glénat, 1980); *Lord Lister, Le Mystérieux Inconnu (Lord Lister, the Mysterious Unknown*; Hac., 1995); *Sherlock Holmes Revient (Sherlock Holmes Returns*; FN, 1996); *Le Requin de la Tamise (The Shark of the Thames*; Lefrancq, 1996); *Le Tueur dans le Fog (The Killer in the Fog*; Lefrancq, 1997); *Note:* Belgian writer. See chapters VIII and IX. Former editor of *Spirou.* Also see *Aryanne* in Book 1, Chapter V.

Varennes de Mondasse (?-?); *La Découverte de l'Empire*

de Cantahar (The Discovery of the Cantahar Empire; Prault, 1730)

Varlet, Théo (Varlet, Louis Théodore Étienne) (1878-1938); *La Bella Venere (*Malfère, 1920); *Les Titans du Ciel (The Titans of the Sky*; with Octave **Jonquel**; Malfère, 1921); *L'Agonie de la Terre (The Agony of Earth*; with Octave **Jonquel**; Malfère, 1922); *La Belle Valence (The Beautiful Valence;* with André **Blandin**; Malfère, 1923; rep. as *L'Épopée Martienne (The Martian Epic*, Encrage, 1996); *Le Démon dans l'Âme (The Demon in the Soul*; Malfère, 1923); *Le Dernier Satyre (The Last Satyr*; Malfère, 1923); *Aux Îles Bienhereuses (To the Blessed Islands*; Artisan, 1925); *Le Roc d'Or (The Golden Rock*; Plon, 1927); *Ad Astra (*Albert Messein, 1929); *La Grande Panne (The Great Breakdown*; Portiques, 1930); *Florilège de Poésie Cosmique (Flower Arrangement of Cosmic Poetry*; Mercure U., 1933); *Aurore Lescure, Pilote d'Astronef (*Amitié par le Livre, 1943); *Note:* See Chapter VII.

Vattel, Emmerich (1714-1767); *Les Fourmis (The Ants*; Arkstée & Merkus, 1757); *Note:* Swiss writer. See Chapter III.

Vaubourg, Marie (?-); *La Petite Fille aux Mains Coupées (The Little Girl with Cut-Off Hands*; Des Femmes, 1980)

Vaucaire, Maurice (?-?); *Le Masque de Sable: Histoire Véritable du Grand Sphinx (The Mask of Sand: True Story of the Great Sphinx*; Joanin, 1905); *Note:* Also see **Grand-Guignol**.

Vaulet, Clément *see* **Vautel, Clément**

Vaury, Louis *see* **Epuy, Michel**

Vautel, Clément (Vaulet, Clément) (1876-1954); *Monsieur Mézique (*with Georges de **La Fouchardière**; AM, 1914); *La Réouverture du Paradis Terrestre (The Reopening of Paradise on Earth*; AM, 1919); *La Machine à Fabriquer des Rêves (The Dream-Making Machine*; Lafitte, 1923); *La Grande Rafle (The Great Dragnet*; with Georges de **La Fouchardière**; AM, 1929); *Note:* See Chapter VII. Also see **Grand-Guignol**.

Vauthier, Maurice (1921-); *Écoute, Petit Loup (Listen, Little Wolf*; SdP Jr 23, 1960); *Wong (*Flamm., 1960); *La Terrible Bombe X (The Dreaded X Bomb*; SdP 165, 1964); *La Planète Kalgar (The Planet Kalgar*; Hac., 1966); *Quand Chantera l'Oiseau Quetzal (When the Quetzal Bird Sings*; SdPSF 73, 1974); *Croisade en Fraude (Fraudulent Crusade*; SdP 2, 1977); *Je t'appelle Zabur (I Dub You Zabur*; Cerf, 1996); *L'Homme de "Citadelle" (The Man from "Citadel"*; P. Téqui, 1997); Series *Amaël*: *Amaël (*SdP 2, 1981); *Le Sang des Amaël (The Blood of Amael*; SdP 2 124, 1984); *Amaël, Prince de la Jeunesse (Amael, Prince of Youth*; SdP, 1985); *Note:* Juvenile SF. See Chapter IX.

Vauzière, Claude *see* **Guieu, Jimmy**

Veber, Michel *see* **Nino**

Véber, Pierre-Eugène (1869-1942); *L'Homme qui Vendit son Âme au Diable (The Man Who Sold His Soul to the Devil*; Calmann-Lévy, 1918); *La Seconde Vie de Napoléon 1er (Napoleon's Second Life*; Férenczi, 1923); *Note:* See Chapter VII. *L'Homme* was twice adapted into films (see Book 1, Chapter I). Pierre *Veber* (see Book 2) also wrote ***Rouletabille Aviateur*** (see Book 1, Chapter I). He also used the pseudonym "Bill Sharp."

Veer, Olenka de (?-) *see* **Barjavel, René**

Végor, Maïk (?-); *Maïk et le Château Sanglant (Maik and the Bloody Castle*; Monnet Terrific 1, 1974); *Maïk et le Rajah Pourpre (Maik and the Purple Rajah*; Monnet Terrific 2, 1974); *Maïk et les Maîtres de Shambala (Maik and the Masters of Shamballah*; Monnet Terrific 3, 1974); *Le Dieu Vert (The Green God*; Monnet Terrific 4, 1974); *Maïk chez les SS (Maik with the SS*; Monnet Terrific 8, 1974); *Note:* See Chapter VIII.

Veilleux, Florent (1941-); *La Fiancée d'Archi (Archi's Fiancée*; Q/A, 1993); *Note:* French-Canadian writer.

Veillot, Claude (1925-); *Un Refuge en Galilée (A Refuge in Galilee*; Den., 1964); *L'Homme à la Carabine (The Man with a Rifle*; Hac., 1966); *Misandra (JL 558, 1974); La Machine de Balmer (Balmer's Machine*; JL 807, 1978); *L'Enfant qui Venait du Froid (The Child Who Came in from the Cold*; PC, 1993); *Note:* See Chapter IX.

Veiras, Denis (Vairasse d'Allais, Denis) (1635-1685); *Histoire des Sévarambes (The History of the Serarites or Sevarambi*; 4 vols; Barbin, 1677-79; rev. VI, 1787); *Note:* See Chapter III.

Velan, Yves (1925-); *La Statue de Condillac Retouchée (Condillac's Touched-Up Statue*; Seuil, 1973); *Soft Goulag* (Bertil-Galland, 1977); *Je: Roman (I: Novel*; AdH, 1990); *Note:* Swiss writer.

Velle, Louis (?-); *Ma Petite Femme (My Little Woman*; Calmann-Lévy, 1953); *Note:* See Chapter IX.

Venisse, Alain (1944-); *Le Clown de Minuit (The Midnight Clown*; FNFR 1, 1994); *Symphonie pour l'Enfer (Symphony for Hell*; FNFR 5, 1994); *Dans les Profondeurs du Miroir (In the Depths of the Mirror*; FNFR 8, 1994); *Cimetière des Chats (Cat Cemetery*; FNFR 11, 1995);

L'Étreinte de la Bête (The Hug of the Beast; FNFR 22, 1995); Déviation (Detour; FNFR 32, 1995); *Le Camescope Fantôme (The Phantom Camescope*; Magnard, 1996); *Monitor Man* (Florent Massot, 1997); *Note:* See Chapter VIII.

Ventteclaye, Marie-Louise (?-); *Le Merveilleux Voyage de Jacqueline (Jacqueline's Wonderful Journey*; "Fillette," n.d.); *Le Disque Enchanté (The Enchanted Disk*; "Fillette," n.d.)

Veraldi, Gabriel (1926-); *À la Mémoire dun Ange (In the Memory of An Angel*; Gall., 1953); *La Machine Humaine (The Human Machine*; Gall, 1954); *Le Chasseur Captif (The Captive Hunter*; Gall., 1956); *Note:* Also used the pseudonym "William Schmidt."

Véran, Régine (?-); *Le Rubis de Discorde (The Ruby of Discord*; Offenstadt, 1912)

Vercors (Bruller, Jean) (1902-1991); *Le Silence de la Mer (The Silence of the Sea*; Panthéon, Schiffrin, 1942; transl. as *Put Out the Light*, 1944); *La Marche à l'Étoile (The Walk to the Star*; Minuit, 1943); *Les Animaux Dénaturés (The Unnatural Animals*; AM, 1952; transl. as *You Shall Know Them*; aka *Borderline*; aka *The Murder of the Missing Link*, 1953); *Colères (Wrath*; AM, 1956; transl. as *The Insurgents*, 1957); *Sylva* (PP, 1961; transl. 1962); *Quota ou Les Pléthoriens* (with **Coronel**; Stock, 1966); *Les Chevaux du Temps (The Horses of Time*; Tchou, 1977); *Note:* See Chapter IX. As Jean Bruller, Vercors illustrated several genre novels by André **Maurois**.

Verdet, André (1913-); *La Nuit n'est pas la Nuit (Night Is Not Night*; Pré aux Clercs, 1948); *Le Loup et Moi (The Wolf and I*; Nlle. Ed., 1950); *L'Oiseau d'Or Chantera (The Golden Bird Will Sing*; GLM, 1951); *L'Oiseau et le Barrage (The Bird and the Dam*; Edit. Fr. Réunis, 1954); *Provence Noire (Dark Provence*; Cercle d'Art, 1955); *La Cité et son Fantôme (The City and Its Ghost*; Galilée, 1975)

Verdilhac, Yves de *see* **Dalens, Serge**

Verdot, Guy (?-); *Le Vieil Ulysse (Old Ulysses*; Gutenberg, 1945); *Je Ne Suis Pas d'Ici (I'm Not from Here*; R. Marin, 1951); *Le Chemin de Nulle Part (The Path to Nowhere*; R. Marin, 1951); *Demain à Pompei (Tomorrow in Pompei*; Gall., 1958); *Journal d'un Mort-Vivant (Diary of a Living Dead*; Plon, 1964)

Verdun (Commandant) (?-); *Face à l'Ennemi (Facing the Enemy*; Den., 1939); *1. La Guerre Souterraine (The Underground War*]; *2. L'Escadron Cyclone (The Tornado Squad*); *Note:* See Chapter VII.

Vergriete, Jean (?-); *Le Val du Grand Bison (The Valley of the Great Buffalo*; SdP, 1941); *Le Cavalier d'Ibn Saoud*

(Ibn Saoud's Rider; SdP, 1943); *Oulgwy des Sables Verts (Ulgwy of the Green Sands*; SdP, 1945); *La Maison qui Bouge (The House That Moves*; SdP, 1945); *Joël sous les Étoiles (Joel Under the Stars*; SdP, 1971); *Note:* Juveniles. Also used the pseudonym "Jean Vegh."

Verlanger, Julia (Taieb, Héliane, née Grimaître) (1929-

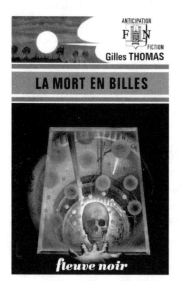

1985); *Les Portes Sans Retour (The Gates of No Return*; MF 3, 1976; rep. as Gilles Thomas, FNA 1941, 1994); *La Flûte de Verre Froid (The Flute of Cold Glass*; MF 9, 1976; rep. as Gilles Thomas, FNA 1934, 1994); *Les Hommes Marqués (The Marked Men*; as Gilles Thomas; FNA 737, 1976); *L'Autoroute Sauvage (The Savage Highway*; as Gilles Thomas; FNA 742, 1976); *La Croix des Décastés (The Cross of the Outcasts*; as Gilles Thomas; FNA 767, 1977); *La Mort en Billes (The Marbled Death*; as Gilles Thomas; FNA 772, 1977); *Magie Sombre (Dark Magic*; as Gilles Thomas; FNSL 35, 1977); *Les Ratés (The Losers*; as Gilles Thomas; FNA 818, 1977); *Les Voies d'Almagiel (The Ways of Almagiel*; as Gilles Thomas; FNA 832, 1978); *La Légende des Niveaux Fermés (The Legend of the Closed Levels*; as Gilles Thomas; FNA 841, 1978); *L'Ange aux Ailes de Lumière (The Angel with Wings of Light*; as Gilles Thomas; FNA 873, 1978); *L'Ile Brûlée (The Burned Island*; as Gilles Thomas; FNA 910, 1979); *D'un Lieu Lointain Nommé Soltrois (From a Far Place Called Solthree*; as Gilles Thomas; FNA 928, 1979); *La Jungle de Pierre (The Stone Jungle*; as Gilles Thomas; FNA 949, 1979); *Horlemonde (Worldbeyond*; as Gilles Thomas; FNA 991, 1980); *La Porte des Serpents (The Gate of the Serpents*; as Gilles Thomas; FNA 1013, 1980); *Les Cages de Beltem (The Cages of Beltem*; as Gilles Thomas; FNA 1191, 1982); *Acherra (Les Cages de Beltem, Vol.1*; as Gilles Thomas; FNA 1968, 1995); *Offren (Les Cages de Beltem, Vol.2*; as Gilles Thomas; FNA 1969, 1995); *Les Oiseaux de Cuir (The Birds of Leather*; as Gilles Thomas; FNA 1999, 1996); *La Révélation (The Revelation*; with **Gudule**; Hac., 1996); *Note:* See chapters VIII and IX.

Verlomme, Hugo (?-); *Mermère (*Ed. Maritimes, 1978); *Larima Baie (*JCL, 1985); *La Ville (The City*; Fleurus, 1992); *L'Homme des Vagues (The Man of the Waves*; Gall., 1992); *Les Indiens de la Ville Lumière (The Indians of the City of Lights*; Gall., 1995); *La Nuit des Dauphins (The Night of the Dolphins*; JCL, 1996); *Note:* See Chapter IX.

Vermeylen, August (1872-1945); *Le Juif Errant (The Wandering Jew*; MdF, 1906); *Note:* Belgian writer.

Vernay, Jean-Pierre (1958-); *L'Enfer en ce Monde (Hell in This World*; Ponte Mirone, 1980); *Thomas et le Rat (Thomas and the Rat*; Nathan SF 7, 1981); *Le Sang des Mondes (The Blood of the Worlds*; Plasma 6, 1983; rev. FNA 1927, 1993); *Dites-le avec des Mots (Say It with Words*; with Emmanuel **Jouanne**; PdF 410, 1985); *Les Chemins du Monde (The Paths of the World*; Dernier Cercle, 1985); *La Saga de l'Ennemi (The Enemy's Saga*; Dernier Cercle, 1985); *Fragments du Rêve (Dream Fragments*; PdF 504, 1989); *Note:* See Chapter IX.

Verne, Jules (1828-1905); *Cinq Semaines en Ballon (*VE, 1863; transl. as *Five Weeks in a Balloon*, 1869); *Voyage au Centre de la Terre (*VE, 1864; transl. as *Journey to the Center of the Earth*, 1872); *De la Terre à la Lune (*VE, 1865; transl. as *From the Earth to the Moon*, 1873); *Les Aventures du Capitaine Hatteras (Vol.1: Les Anglais au Pôle Nord; Vol.2: Le Désert de Glace) (The Adventures of Captain Hatteras*; VE, 1866; transl. as *The English at the North Pole* and *The Field of Ice*, 1874); *Les Enfants du Capitaine Grant (The Children of Captain Grant*; 3 vols.; VE, 1867-68; transl. as *In Search of the Castaways*, 1873); *Vingt Mille Lieues Sous les Mers (2* vols.; VE, 1870; transl. as *Twenty Thousand Leagues Under the Seas*, 1872); *Autour de la Lune (Around the Moon*; VE 1870; transl. included in *From the Earth to the Moon*, 1873); *Une Ville Flottante / Les Forceurs de Blocus (*VE, 1871; transl. as *A Floating City / The Blockade Runners*, 1874); *Aventures de Trois Russes et de Trois Anglais dans l'Afrique Australe (*VE, 1872; transl. as *Meridiana: the Adventures of Three Englishmen and Three Russians in South Africa*, 1873); *Le Pays des Fourrures (*VE, 1873; transl. as *The Fur Country*, 1873); *Le Tour du Monde en Quatre-Vingt Jours (*VE, 1873; transl. as *Around the World in Eighty Days*, 1874); *Une Fantaisie du Dr. Ox / Maître Zacharius (*VE, 1874; transl. as *Doctor Ox and Other Stories*, 1874); *Un Drame dans les Airs (*VE, 1874; transl. as *A Drama in the Air*, 1874); *L'Île Mystérieuse (3* vols.; VE, 1874-75; transl. as *The Mysterious Island*, 1875); *Le "Chancellor" (*VE, 1875; transl. as *Survivors of the "Chancellor,"* 1875); *Michel Strogoff (2* vols.; VE, 1876; transl. 1877); *Hector Servadac (2* vols.; VE, 1877; transl. 1877); *Les Indes Noires (The Black Indies*; VE, 1877; transl. as *The Child of the Cavern*, 1877); *Un Capitaine de Quinze Ans (*VE, 1878; transl. as *Dick Sand: A Captain at Fifteen*, 1878); *Les Tribulations d'un Chinois en Chine (*VE, 1879; transl. as *The Tribulations of a Chinaman in China*, 1879); *Les Cinq Cent Millions de la Begum (*with André **Laurie**; VE, 1879; transl. as *The 500 Millions of the Begum*, 1879); *La Maison à Vapeur (2* vols.; VE, 1880; transl. as *The Steam House*, 1881); *La Jangada (2* vols.; VE, 1881; transl. as *The Giant Raft*, 1881); *Le*

Rayon Vert (VE, 1882; transl. as *The Green Ray*, 1883); *L'École des Robinsons (The Robinsons School*; VE, 1882; transl. as *Godfrey Morgan: A Californian Mystery*, 1883); *Kéraban le Têtu* (2 vols.; VE, 1883; transl. as *The Headstrong Turk*, 1884); *L'Étoile du Sud (The Southern Star*; with André **Laurie**; VE, 1884; transl. as *The Vanished Diamond*, 1885); *L'Archipel en Feu* (VE, 1884; transl. as *The Archipelago on Fire*, 1885); *L'Épave du "Cynthia"* (with André **Laurie**; RA, 1885; transl. as *Salvage from the "Cynthia,"* 1958); *Mathias Sandorf* (3 vols.; VE, 1885; transl. 1885); *Robur le Conquerant* (VE, 1886; transl. as *The Clipper of the Clouds*, aka *Robur the Conqueror*, 1887); *Un Billet de Loterie: No. 9672* (VE, 1886; transl. as *Ticket No. 9672*, 1886); *Le Chemin de France* (VE, 1887; transl. as *The Flight to France*, 1888); *Nord contre Sud* (2 vols.; VE, 1887; transl. as *Texar's Vengeance, or North vs. South*, 1887); *Deux Ans de Vacances (A Two Years' Vacation*; 2 vols.; VE, 1888; transl. as *Adrift in the Pacific*, 1889); *Sans Dessus Dessous* (VE, 1889; transl. as *Topsy-Turvy*, 1890); *Famille Sans Nom* (2 vols.; VE, 1889; transl. as *A Family Without Name*, 1889); *César Cascabel* (2 vols.; VE, 1890; transl. 1890); *Mistress Branican* (2 vols.; VE, 1891; transl. 1891); *Le Château des Carpathes* (VE, 1892; transl. as *Castle of the Carpathians*, 1893); *Claudius Bombarnac* (VE, 1892; transl. 1894); *P'tit Bonhomme* (2 vols.; VE, 1893; transl. as *Founding Mick*, 1895); *Les Mirifiques Aventures de Maître Antifer* (2 vols.; VE, 1894; transl. as *Captain Antifer*, 1985); *L'Île à Hélice* (2 vols.; VE, 1895; transl. as *Floating Island*, 1896); *Face au Drapeau* (VE, 1896; transl. as *Facing the Flag*, 1897); *Clovis Dardentor* (VE, 1896; transl. 1897); *Le Sphinx des Glaces (2 vols.) (The Sphinx of the Ices*; VE, 1897; transl. as *An Antarctic Mystery*, 1898); *Le Superbe Orénoque (2 vols.) (The Superb Orinoco*; VE, 1898); *Le Testament d'un Excentrique* (2 vols.; VE, 1899; transl. as *The Will of an Eccentric*, 1900); *Seconde Patrie (Second Home*; 2 vols.; VE, 1900; transl. as *Their Island Home*, 1924); *Le Village Aérien* (2 vols.; VE, 1901; transl. as *The Village in the Tree Tops*, 1964); *Les Histoires de Jean-Marie Cabidoulin* (VE, 1901; transl. as *The Sea Serpent*, 1967); *Les Frères Kip (The Kip Brothers*; 2 vols.; VE, 1902); *Bourses de Voyage (Travelling Scholarships*; 2 vols.; VE, 1903); *Maître du Monde* (VE, 1904; transl. as *Master of the World*, 1914); *Un Drame en Livonie* (VE, 1904; transl. as *A Drama in Livonia*, 1967); *L'Invasion de la Mer (The Invasion of the Sea*; VE, 1905); *Le Phare du Bout du Monde* (VE, 1905; transl. as *The Lighthouse at the End of the World*, 1923); *Le Volcan d'Or* (2 vols.; VE, 1906; transl. as *The Golden Volcano*, 1962); *L'Agence Thompson and Co.* (2 vols.; VE, 1907; transl. as *The Thompson Travel Agency*, 1965); *La Chasse au Météore* (VE, 1908; transl. as *The Chase of the Golden Meteor*, 1909); *Le Pilote du Danube* (VE, 1908; transl. as *The Danube Pilot*, 1967);

Les Naufragés du "Jonathan" (2 vols.; VE, 1909; transl. as *Survivors of the "Jonathan,"* 1962); *Le Secret de Wilhelm Storitz* (VE, 1910; transl. as *The Secret of Wilhelm Storitz*, 1963); *Hier et Demain* (VE, 1910; transl. as *Yesterday and Tomorrow*, 1965); *L'Étonnante Aventure de la Mission Barsac* (2 vols.; Hac., 1914; transl. as *The Barsac Mission*, 1960); *Voyage à Travers l'Impossible (Journey Through the Impossible*; with A. d'Ennery; publ. Pauvert, 1981); *Paris au XXème Siècle* (written 1863; publ. Hac., 1994; transl. as *Paris in the 20th Century*, 1996); *Note:* See Chapter V. For film and television adaptations, see Book 1, chapters I and II.

Vernes, Henri (Dewisme, Charles-Henri) (1918-); *La Porte Ouverte (The Open Door*; as Charles-Henri Dewisme; Ren. du Livre, 1944); *Le Goût du Malheur (The Taste of Unhappiness*; as Charles-Henri Dewisme; wri. 1945; publ. Ed. Centre d'Art Ixelles, 1994); *La Belle Nuit pour un Homme Mort (Beautiful Night for a Dead Man*; as Charles-Henri Dewisme; Le Triolet, 1949); *Rendez-Vous au Pélican Vert (Rendezvous at the Green Pelican;* as Lew Shannon; Dernière Heure, 1950; rev. as *Drôle de Business (Funny Business*, Heroic-Albums, 1954); *L'Aventure est dans la Forêt (The Adventure Is in*

the Forest; as Jacques Seyr; Journal de Mickey, 1952); *Dix Mille Ans après l'Atome (Ten Thousand Years after the Atom*; as Jacques Seyr; Heroic-Albums, 1955); *Intrigues de Paris à Miami (Intrigues from Paris to Miami*; as Lew Shannon; Heroic-Albums, 1955); *Le Secret de l'Homme en Noir (The Secret of the Man in Black*; Journal de Tintin, 1955); *Le Démon Gris (The Grey Demon*; Journal de Tintin, 1956); *Les Rescapés de l'Eldorado (Rescued from Eldorado*; Hac., 1957); *Base Clandestine (Secret Base)*; Hac., 1957; rev. as *Des Dinosaures pour la Contesse (Dinosaurs for the Countess*, Hac., 1972); Series *Don: Le Fauve de Rangoon (The Wild Beast of Rangoon*; FN, 1983); *L'Épouvantable Épouvantail (The Awful Scarecrow*; FN, 1983); *Ixy-*

L'OMBRE
JAUNE 2

LEFRANCQ

greczed (Exwhyzee; FN, 1983); *Chromozome Y* (FN, 1983); *L'Ange de Managua (The Angel of Managua;* FN, 1983); *La Queue du Dragon (The Dragon's Tail;* FN, 1983); *Cafe no! Marimba si!* (FN, 1984); *K comme Tueur (K as in Killer;* FN, 1984); *Manneken-pis sur Jungle (Manneken-pis Over the Jungle;* FN, 1984); *Palomita Paloma* (FN, 1986); *Super Tueur (Super Killer;* FN, 1986); *Note:* Don is a James Bond-like hero involved in marginal SF adventures. Only the titles ghostwritten by **Vernes** are listed here. Series *Bob Morane: 1. La Vallée Infernale (The Infernal Valley;* MarJ 16, 1953); *2. La Galère Engloutie (The Sunken Galley;* MarJ 21, 1954); *3. Sur la Piste de Fawcett (On the Trail of Fawcett;* MarJ 26, 1954); *4. La Griffe de Feu (The Fire Claw;* MarJ 30, 1954); *5. Panique dans le Ciel (Panic in the Sky;* MarJ 34, 1954); *6. L'Héritage du Flibustier (The Pirate's Inheritance;* MarJ 38, 1954); *7. Les Faiseurs de Désert (The Desert Makers;* MarJ 42, 1955); *8. Le Sultan de Jarawak (The Sultan of Jarawak;* MarJ 46, 1955); *9. Oasis K Ne Répond Plus (Oasis K Does Not Answer;* MarJ 50, 1955); *10. La Vallée des Brontosaures (The Valley of the Brontosaurus;* MarJ 54, 1955); *11. Les Requins d'Acier (The Steel Sharks;* MarJ 58, 1955); *12. Le Secret des Mayas (The Secret of the Mayas;* MarJ 62, 1955); *13. La Croisière du Mégophias (The Cruise of the Megophias;* MarJ 66, 1956); *14. Opération Atlantide (Operation Atlantis;* MarJ 70, 1956); *15. La Marque de Kali (The Mark of Kali;* MarJ 74, 1956); *16. Mission pour Thulé (Mission for Thule;* MarJ 78, 1956); *17. La Cité des Sables (The City of the Sands;* MarJ 82, 1956); *18. Les Monstres de l'Espace (The Monsters from Space;* MarJ 86, 1956); *19. Le Masque de Jade (The*

L'OMBRE
JAUNE 3

LEFRANCQ

Jade Mask; MarJ 90, 1957); *20. Les Chasseurs de Dinosaures (The Dinosaur Hunters;* MarJ 94, 1957); *21. Échec à la Main Noire (The Black Hand in Check;* MarJ 98, 1957); *22. Les Démons des Cataractes (The Demons of the Waterfalls;* MarJ 102, 1957); *23. La Fleur du Sommeil (The Flower of Sleep;* MarJ 106, 1957); *24. L'Idole Verte (The Green Idol;* MarJ 110, 1957); *25. L'Empereur de Macao (The Emperor of Macau;* MarJ 114, 1958); *26. Tempête sur les Andes (Storms Over the Andes;* MarJ 118, 1958); *27.*

L'Orchidée Noire (The Black Orchid; MarJ 122, 1958); *28. Les Compagnons de Damballah (The Companions of Damballah;* MarJ 126, 1958); *29. Les Géants de la Taïga (The Giants of the Taiga;* MarJ 130, 1958); *30-31. Les Dents du Tigre (2 vols.) (The Teeth of the Tiger;* MarJ 134, 1958); *32. Le Gorille Blanc (The White Gorilla;* MarJ 138, 1959); *33. La Couronne de Golconde (The Crown of Golconde;* MarJ 142, 1959); *34. Le Maître du Silence (The Master of Silence;* MarJ 146, 1959); *35. L'Ombre Jaune (The Yellow Shadow;* MarJ 150, 1959); *36. L'Ennemi Invisible (The Invisible Enemy;* MarJ 154, 1959); *37. La Revanche de l'Ombre Jaune (The Revenge of the Yellow Shadow;* MarJ 158, 1959); *38. Le Châtiment de l'Ombre Jaune (The Punishment of the Yellow Shadow;* MarJ 162, 1960); *39. L'Espion aux Cent Visages (The Spy with a Hundred Faces;* MarJ 166, 1960); *40. Le Diable du Labrador (The Labrador Devil;* MarJ 170, 1960); *41. L'Homme aux Dents d'Or (The Man with the Teeth of Gold;* MarJ 174, 1960); *42. La Vallée des Mille Soleils (The Valley of a Thousand Suns;* MarJ 178, 1960); *43. Le Retour de l'Ombre Jaune (The Return of the Yellow Shadow;* MarJ 182, 1960); *44. Le Démon Solitaire (The Lonely Demon;* MarJ 186, 1960); *45. Les Mangeurs d'Atome (The Atom Eaters;* MarJ 190, 1961); *46. Le Temple des Crocodiles (The Temple of the Crocodiles;* MarJ 194, 1961); *47. Le Tigre des Lagunes (The Lagoon Tiger;* MarJ 198, 1961); *48. Le Dragon des Fenstone (The Fenstone Dragon;* MarJ 202, 1961); *49. Trafic aux Caraïbes (Traffic in the Caribbean;* MarJ 206, 1961); *50. Les Sosies de l'Ombre Jaune (The Duplicates of the Yellow Shadow;* MarJ 210, 1961); *51. Formule X 33 (Formula X 33;* MarJ 214, 1962); *52. Le Lagon aux Requins (The Shark Lagoon;* MarJ 218, 1962); *53. Le Masque Bleu (The Blue Mask;* MarJ 222, 1962); *54. Les Semeurs de Foudre (The Sowers of Lightning;* MarJ 226, 1962); *55. Le Club des Longs Couteaux (The Club of the Long Knives;* MarJ 230, 1962); *56. La Voix du Mainate (The Mynah's Voice;* MarJ 234, 1962); *57. Les Yeux de l'Ombre Jaune (The Eyes of the Yellow Shadow;* MarJ 238, 1962); *58. La Guerre des Baleines (The War of the Whales;* MarJ 242, 1963); *59. Les Sept Croix de Plomb (The Seven Lead Crosses;* MarJ 246, 1963); *60. Opération Wolf* (MarJ 250, 1963); *61. La Rivière de Perles (The River of Pearls;* MarJ 254, 1963); *62. La Vapeur du Passé (The Mists of the Past;* MarJ 258, 1963); *63. L'Héritage de l'Ombre Jaune (The Inheritance of the Yellow Shadow;* MarJ 262, 1963); *64. Mission à Orly (Mission at Orly;* MarJ 266, 1964); *65. L'Oeil d'Émeraude (The Emerald Eye;* MarJ 270, 1964); *66. Les Joyaux de Maharadjah (The Maharadjah's Jewels;* MarJ 274, 1964); *67. Escale à Felicidad (Stop-Over in Felicidad;* MarJ 278, 1964); *68. L'Ennemi Masqué (The Masked Enemy;* MarJ 282, 1964); *69. S.S.S. (Secret Service Saucers;* MarJ 286, 1964); *70. Le Camion Infernal (The Infernal Truck;* MarJ 290, 1964); *71. Ter-*

reur à la Manicouagan (Terror in Manikwagan; MarJ 294, 1965); *72. Les Guerriers de l'Ombre Jaune (The Warriors of the Yellow Shadow*; MarJ 298, 1965); *73. Le Président Ne Mourra Pas (The President Shall Not Die*; MarJ 306, 1965); *74. Le Secret de l'Antarctique (The Secret of the Antarctic*; MarJ 310, 1965); *75. La Cité de l'Ombre Jaune (The City of the Yellow Shadow*; MarJ 314, 1965); *76. Les Jardins de l'Ombre Jaune (The Gardens of the Yellow Shadow*; MarJ 315, 1965); *77. Le Collier de Civa (The Necklace of Shiva*; MarJ 318, 1966); *78. Organisation Smog* (MarJ 322, 1966); *79. Le Mystérieux Dr. Xhatan (The Mysterious Dr. Xhatan*; MarJ 328, 1966); *80. Xhatan, Maître de la Lumière (Xhatan, Master of Light*; MarJ 340, 1966); *81. Le Roi des Archipels (The King of the Archipelagos*; MarJ 346, 1966); *82. Le Samouraï aux Mille Soleils (The Samurai of a Thousand Suns*; MarJ 352, 1967); *83. Un Parfum d'Ylang-Ylang (A Scent of Ylang-Ylang*; MarP 6, 1967); *84. Le Talisman des Voïvodes (The Talisman of the Voivoids*; MarP 13, 1967); *85. Le Cratère des Immortels (The Crater of the Immortals*; MarP 24, 1967); *86. Les Crapauds de la Mort (The Toad Men of Death*; MarP 30, 1967); *87. Les Papillons de l'Ombre Jaune (The Butterflies of the Yellow Shadow*; MarP 39, 1968); *88. Alias M.D.O.* (MarP 45, 1968); *89. L'Empreinte du Crapaud (The Mark of the Toad Men*; MarP 49, 1968); *90. La Forteresse de l'Ombre Jaune (The Fortress of the Yellow Shadow*; MarP 54, 1968); *91. Le Satellite de l'Ombre Jaune (The Satellite of the Yellow Shadow*; MarP 57, 1968); *92. Les Captifs de l'Ombre Jaune (The Captives of the Yellow Shadow*; MarP 60, 1968); *93. Les Sortilèges de l'Ombre Jaune (The Spells of the Yellow Shadow*; MarP 66, 1969); *94. Les Mangeurs d'Âmes (The Soul Eaters*; MarP 70, 1969); *95. La Terreur Verte (Green Terror*; MarP 74, 1969); *96. Menace sous la Mer (The Undersea Menace*; MarP 78, 1969); *97. Les Masques de Soie (The Silk Masks*; MarP 80, 1969); *98. L'Oiseau de Feu (The Firebird*; MarP 81, 1969); *99. Les Bulles de l'Ombre Jaune (The Bubbles of the Yellow Shadow*; MarP 83, 1970); *100. Commando Epouvante (Terror Commando*; MarP 85, 1970); *101. La Piste de l'Ivoire (The Ivory Trail*; MarP 87, 1970); *102. Les Tours de Cristal (The Towers of Crystal*; MarP 88, 1970); *103. Les Cavernes de la Nuit (The Caverns of Night*; MarP 90, 1970); *104. L'Île du Passé (The Island of the Past*; MarP 91, 1970); *105. Une Rose pour l'Ombre Jaune (A Rose for the Yellow Shadow*; MarP 93, 1970); *106. Rendez-vous à Nulle Part (Rendezvous at Nowhere*; MarP 95, 1971); *107. Les Contrebandiers de l'Atome (The Atom Smugglers*; MarP 97, 1971); *108. L'Archipel de la Terreur (The Archipelago of Terror*; MarP 99, 1971); *109. La Vallée des Crotales (The Valley of the Rattlesnakes*; MarP 101, 1971); *110. Les Spectres d'Atlantis (The Spectres from Atlantis*; MarP 103, 1972); *111. Ceux-Des-Roches-Qui-Parlent (Those-From-The-Talking-Rocks*; MarP 105, 1972); *112. Poison Blanc (White Poison*; MarP 107, 1972); *113. Krouic* (MarP 109, 1972); *114. Piège au Zacaldago (Trap in Zacaldago*; MarP 111, 1972); *115. La Prison de l'Ombre Jaune (The Prison of the Yellow Shadow*; MarP 112, 1973); *116. Le Secret des Sept Temples (The Secret of the Seven Temples*; MarP 114, 1973); *117. Zone "Z"* (MarP 116, 1973); *118. Panne Sèche à Serado (Out of Gas in Serado*; MarP 117, 1973); *119. L'Epée du Paladin (The Sword of the Paladin*; MarP 119, 1973); *120. Le Sentier de la Guerre (The Warpath*; MarP 120, 1973); *121. Les Voleurs de Mémoire (The Memory Thieves*; MarP 121, 1973); *122. Les Poupées de l'Ombre Jaune (The Dolls of the Yellow Shadow*; MarP 122, 1974); *123. Opération Chevalier Noir (Operation Black Knight*; MarP 124, 1974); *124. La Mémoire du Tigre (The Tiger's Memory*; MarP 126, 1974); *125. La Colère du Tigre (The Tiger's Wrath*; MarP 128, 1974); *126. Les Fourmis de l'Ombre Jaune (The Ants of the Yellow Shadow*; MarP 129, 1974); *127. Les Murailles d'Ananké (The Walls of Ananke*; MarP 130, 1974); *128. Les Damnés de l'Or (The Gold Curse*; MarP 132, 1975); *129. Le Masque du Crapaud (The Mask of the Toad Men*; MarP 133, 1975); *130. Les Périls d'Ananké (The Perils of Ananke*; MarP 135, 1975); *131. Guerilla à Tumbaga (Guerilla in Tumbaga*; MarP 136, 1975); *132. La Tête du Serpent (The Serpent's Head*; MarP 138, 1975); *133. El Matador* (MarP 139, 1975); *134. Les Anges d'Ananké (The Angels of Ananke*; MarP 141, 1976); *135. Le Poison de l'Ombre Jaune (The Poison of the Yellow Shadow*; MarP 144, 1976); *136. Le Revenant des Terres Rouges (The Ghost of the Red Lands*; MarP 145, 1976); *137. Les Jeux de l'Ombre Jaune (The Games of the Yellow Shadow*; MarP 146, 1976); *138. La Malle à Malices (The Chest of Tricks*; MarP 147, 1976); *139. L'Ombre Jaune Fait Trembler la Terre (The Yellow Shadow Makes the Earth Quake*; MarP 148, 1976); *140. Mise en Boîte Maison (House Wrapping*; MarP 149, 1977); *141. Les Caves d'Ananké (The Caverns of Ananke*; MarP 150, 1977); *142. Dans le Triangle des Bermudes (In the Bermuda Triangle*; MarP 151, 1977); *143. La Prisonnière de l'Ombre Jaune (The Prisoner of the Yellow Shadow*; MBN 4, 1978); *144. La Griffe de l'Ombre Jaune (The Claw of the Yellow Shadow*; MBN 6, 1978); *145. La Tanière du Tigre (The Tiger's Lair*; MBN 9, 1978); *146. Les Plaines d'Ananké (The Plains of Ananke*; MBN 12, 1979); *147. Le Trésor de l'Ombre Jaune (The Treasure of the Yellow Shadow*; MBN 15, 1979); *148. L'Ombre Jaune et l'Héritage du Tigre (The Yellow Shadow and the Tiger's Inheritance*; MBN 20, 1979); *149. Le Soleil de l'Ombre Jaune (The Sun of the Yellow Shadow*; MBN 23, 1979); *150. Trafics à Paloma (Traffic in Paloma*; MBN 26, 1980); *151. Des Loups sur la Piste (Wolves on the Trail*; MBN 29, 1980); *152. Snake* (MBN 31, 1980); *153. Trois Petits Singes (Three Little Monkeys*; MBN 34, 1980); *154. L'Oeil du*

Samouraï (The Samurai's Eye; BV 4, 1982); *155. Les Yeux du Brouillard (The Eyes in the Fog*; BV 8, 1983); *156. L'Arbre de la Vie (The Tree of Life*; FNBM 1, 1988); *157. L'Ombre Jaune s'en va t'en Guerre (The Yellow Shadow Goes to War*; FNBM 9, 1988); *158. L'Exterminateur (The Exterminator*; FNBM 13, 1989); *159. Les Berges du Temps (The Shores of Time*; FNBM 18, 1989); *160. La Nuit des Négriers (The Night of the Slavers*; FNBM 21, 1989); *161. Le Jade de Séoul (The Jade from Seoul*; FNBM 26, 1990); *162. La Cité des Rêves (The Dream City*; FNBM 33, 1990); *163. Rendez-Vous à Maripasoula (Rendezvous at Maripasoula*; FNBM 41, 1991); *164. La Panthère des Hauts Plateaux (The Panther of the High Plains*; Lefrancq 4, 1992); *165. La Guerre du Cristal (The Crystal War*; Lefrancq 8, 1992); *166. Les Larmes du Soleil (The Tears of the Sun*; Lefrancq 12, 1993); *167. Les Démons de la Guerre (The Demons of War*; Lefrancq 16, 1993); *168. Les Déserts d'Amazonie (The Amazonian Desert*; Lefrancq 19, 1994); *169. Bételgeuse et Companie (Betelgeuse and Co.*; Lefrancq 20, 1994); *170. Le Réveil de Kukulcan (Kukulcan Awakens*; Lefrancq 22, 1994); *171. L'Anneau de Salomon (The Ring of Solomon*; Lefrancq 24, 1995); *172. Les Mille et Une Vies de l'Ombre Jaune (The Thousand and One Lives of the Yellow Shadow*; Lefrancq 26, 1995); *173. La Bête Hors des Âges (The Beast Out of the Ages*; Lefrancq 32, 1995); *174. L'Antre du Crapaud (The Lair of the Toad Men*; Lefrancq 36, 1996); 175. *Yang et Yin* (Lefrancq 42, 1997); *176. Les Pièges de Cristal (The Crystal Traps*; Lefrancq 46, 1997); *177. La Guerre du Pacifique n'aura pas lieu (The War in the Pacific Shall Not Take Place*; Lefrancq, 1997); *Note:* See Chapter IX. Henri Vernes is also the author of the graphic novel **Karga, le 7ème Univers** *(Karga, 7th Universe)* illustrated by André Beautemps (see Book 1, Chapter V).

Vernet, Madeleine (1878-1948); *La Fille du Diable (The Devil's Daughter*; L'Avenir Social, 1921)

Verneuil, Louis (1893-?) *see* **Grand-Guignol**

Verniculus (?-?); *Histoire de la Fin du Monde, ou La Comète de 1904 (Story of the End of the World, or the Comet of 1904*; 1882); *Note:* Swiss writer. See Chapter V.

Vernières, André (?-?) *see* **Grand-Guignol**

Vernon, Maurice (?-); *Les Savants dans l'Arène (The Scientists in the Arena*; Métal 17, 1955); *Balle de Sept (Bullet Seven*; Gerfaut, 1963); *Un Bon Coup de Malais (Malaysian Broom*; Gerfaut, 1963); *La Toile d'Araignée (The Spider's Web*; Galliera 5, 1973); *La Pierre aux Vierges (The Virgins' Stone*; Plaisir de Lire, 1976)

Vernou, Pierre (?-); *Les Pirates de l'Air (The Air Pirates*; Hac., 1913); *Aventures de Deux Scouts Alsaciens (Adventures of Two Alsatian Scouts*; Hac., 1926); *Les Yeux de Rubis (The Ruby Eyes*; Fayard, 1928)

Vernoy de Saint-Georges, Jules-Henri (1801-1875) *see* **Opéra**

Verseau, Dominique *see* **Guieu, Jimmy**

Versins, Pierre (Chamson, Jacques) (1923-); *Les Étoiles ne s'en foutent pas (The Stars Do Care*; Métal 9, 1954); *En Avant Mars! (Towards Mars*; Métal 14, 1955); *Feu d'Artifice (Fireworks*; Métal 19, 1956); *Le Professeur (The Professor*; Métal, 1956); *Outrepart (Beyond*; anthology; La Proue, 1971); *Encyclopédie de l'Utopie et de la Science-Fiction* (non-fiction; AdH, 1972); *Les Transhumains (The Transhumans*; Kes., 1980); *Note:* See Chapter IX. Pierre Versins edited the fanzine *Ailleurs (Elsewhere;* 1957-62) and produced the radio show **Passeport pour l'Inconnu** *(Passport for the Unknown]* in Geneva (see Book 1, Chapter III). He is also the curator of the science fiction museum, La Maison d'Ailleurs, located in Yverdon, Switzerland.

Vert, Marie-Louise (?-); *Le Bal des Étoiles (Ballroom of the Stars*; Magnard, 1962); *Les Histoires du Moulin à Huile (The Tales from the Oil Mill*; Magnard, 1970); *En Tapis Volant (On a Flying Carpet*; Magnard, 1972); *Un Grillon dans la Lune (A Cricket on the Moon*; Magnard, 1973); *Contes de Perrette (Perrette's Tales*; Studia, 1977); *Note:* See Chapter IX.

Verteuil, Éric (Bernier, Alain (?-) & Maridat, Roger (?-); *Au Bout, la Mort (At the End, Death*; FNAG 247, 1974); *La Mémoire Rongée (The Gnawed Memory*; FNAG 256, 1974); *Fascinée (Fascinated*; FNSL 9, 1975); *Horreur à Maldoror (Horror in Maldoror*; FNG 52, 1987); *Un Festin de Rats (A Feast of Rats*; as Berma; Siry Maniac 2, 1988); *Grillades au Feu de Bois (Grilled on Firewood*; FNG 68, 1988); *Monstres sur Commande (Monsters to Order*; FNG 75, 1988); *À la Recherche des Corps Perdus*  *(Looking for Lost Bodies*; FNG 80, 1988); *Les Horreurs de Sophie (The Horrors of Sophie*; FNG 87, 1989); *Les Charmes de l'Horreur (The Charms of Horror*; FNG 98, 1989); *Le Tour du Monde en Quatre-Ving Cadavres (Around the World with Eighty Corpses*; FNG 105, 1990); *Sang Frais pour le Troyen (Fresh Blood for the Trojan*; FNG 113, 1990); *Note:* See Chapter VIII.

Véry, Pierre (1900-1960); *Pont Égaré (Lost Bridge*; Gall.,

LES HÉRITIERS D'AVRIL
PAR
PIERRE VÉRY

1929); *Le Testament de Basil Crookes (The Testament of Basil Crookes*; as Toussaint-Juge; Libr. Champs-Élysées Masque 60, 1930); *Danse à l'Ombre (Dance in the Shadows*; Gall., 1930); *Les Métamorphoses de Jean Sucre (The Metamorphoses of Jean Sucre*; Gall., 1931); *Clavier Universel (Universal Keyboard*; Gall., 1933); *Le Meneur de Jeu (The Game Master*; Gall., 1934); *Meurtre Quai des Orfèvres (Murder Quai Des Orfevres*; Gall., 1934); *Monsieur Marcel des Pompes Funèbres (Mr. Marcel the Undertaker*; Gall., 1934); *L'Assassinat du Père Noël (The Murder of Santa Claus*; Gall., 1934); *Les Quatre Vipères (The Four Vipers*; Libr. Champs-Élysées, 1934); *La Moto Rouge (The Red Motorcycle; L'Aero*, 1934; rev. as *L'Inspecteur Max (Inspector Max)*, Gall., 1937); *L'Ennemi du Temps (Time's Enemy; L'Intransigeant*, 1935; rev. as *Le Reglo (The Straight Man)*, Gall., 1935); *Les Disparus de Saint-Agil (The Saint-Agil Disappearances*; Gall., 1935); *Le Gentleman des Antipodes (The Gentleman from the Other Side of the World*; Gall., 1936); *Les Trois Claude (The Three Claude*; Gall., 1936); *Le Thé des Vieilles Dames (The Tea of the Old Ladies*; Gall., 1937); *Goupi Mains-Rouges (Goupi Red-Hands*; Gall., 1937); *Les Veillées de la Tour Pointue (The Wakes of Pointed Tower*; Gall., 1937); *Mam'zelle Bécot (Miss Kiss*; Gall., 1937); *Monsieur Malborough est mort (Mr. Malborough Is Dead*; Gall., 1937); *Série de Sept (Series of Seven*; Gall., 1938); *Madame et le Mort (Madame and the Dead Man*; Gall., 1940); *Hallali chez les Fossiles (Hunt Among the Fossils; Tout and Tout*, 1940; rev. as *Mort Depuis 100.000 Ans (Dead for 100,000 Years)*, Gall., 1941); *L'Assassin a Peur la Nuit (The Murderer Is Scared at Night*; Fayard, 1942); *L'Inconnue du Terrain Vague (The Unknown Woman on the Commons*; Fayard, 1943); *Histoire de Brigands (Crooked Tales*; Maréchal, 1943); *Les Anciens de Saint-Loup (The Alumni of Saint-Loup*; Fayard, 1944); *Le Pays sans Étoiles (The Starless Country*; Maréchal, 1945); *Au Royaume des Feignants (In the Kingdom of Lazy Men*; Bateau Ivre, 1946); *Léonard ou Les Délices du Bouquiniste (Leonard, or the Joys of the Used Books Sales-*

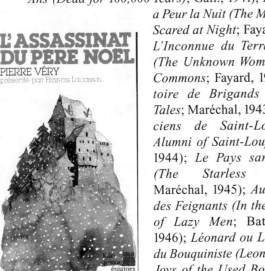

L'ASSASSINAT DU PÈRE NOËL
PIERRE VÉRY
présenté par Francis Lacassin

man; Maréchal, 1946); *Le Costume des Dimanches (Sunday Suit*; Fayard, 1948); *Goupi Mains-Rouges à Paris (Goupi Red-Hands in Paris*; Flore, 1949); *La Route de Zanzibar (The Road to Zanzibar*; TR, 1949); *Un Grand Patron (A Great Boss*; Julliard, 1951); *Le Guérisseur (The Witch Doctor*; Julliard, 1954); *Cinéma, Cyanure et Cie. (Cinema, Cyanide and Co.*; Libr. Champs-Élysées Masque 468, 1954); *La Révolte des Pères Noël (The Revolt of Santa Claus*; Julliard, 1959); *Signé Alouette (Signed: Alouette*; BV 152, 1960); *Les Héritiers d'Avril (The Heirs of April*; BV 168, 1960); *Tout Doit Disparaître le 5 Mai (Everything Must Go on May 5th*; PdF 48, 1961); *Note:* See chapters VI and VII.

Veuzit, Max du (?-); *L'Automate (The Automaton*; Tallandier, 1935); *Note:* See Chapter VII. With **Delly** and Guy des **Cars**, one of the most popular writers of romance novels.

Vial, José (?-); *Le Dernier Dictateur (The Last Dicator*; Lelubre, 1947)

Vialatte, Alexandre (?-); *Battlung le Ténébreux ou la Muse Périlleuse (Battlung the Dark or the Perilous Muse*; Gall., 1928); *Les Fruits du Congo (The Fruits of the Congo*; Gall., 1951); *L'Empereur a dépêché un de ses Messagers (The Emperor Sent One of His Messengers*; Dynamo, 1968); *Dernières Nouvelles de l'Homme (Latest News of Man*; Julliard, 1978); *Histoires et Légendes de l'Auvergne (Tales and Legends of the Auvergne*; Kogan, 1978); *L'Éléphant est Irréfutable (The Elephant Is Irrefutable*; Julliard, 1980); *Badonce et les Créatures (Badonce and the Creatures*; Julliard, 1982); *Le Fidèle Berger (The Faithful Shepherd*; Gall., 1984); *Bananes de Königsberg (Bananas from Konigsberg*; Julliard, 1985); *Les Champignons du Détroit de Behring (The Mushroom from the Behring Straits*; Julliard, 1985); *La Porte de Bath-Rabbin (The Gate of Bath-Rabbin*; Julliard, 1986); *La Maison du Joueur de Flûte (The House of the Flute Player*; Arléa, 1986); *La Dame du Job (The Job Lady*; Arléa, 1987); *Eloge du Homard et Autres Insectes (Praise of the Lobster and Other Insects*; Julliard, 1987); *Jean Dubuffet et le Grand Magma (Jean Dubuffet and the Great Magma*; Arléa, 1988); *Chronique des Grands Micmacs (Chronicle of the Great Stings*; Julliard, 1989); *Antiquité du Grand Chosier (Antiquity of the Great Catalog*; Presses Pockett, 1990); *Le Fluide Rouge (The Red Fluid*; Dilettante, 1990); *Profitons de l'Ornithorynque (Taking Advantage of the Ornithorynque*; Julliard, 1991); *Salomé* (Belles Lettres, 1992); *Chronique des Immenses Possibilités (Chronicle of the Immense Possibilities*; Julliard, 1993); *Dires Étonnants des Astrologues (Amazing Sayings of the Astrologers*; Dilettante, 1993); *Camille et les Grands Hommes (Camille and the Great Men*; Belles-Lettres, 1994); *Légendes Vertigineuses du Dauphiné (Vertigi-*

nous Legends of the Dauphiné; Bartillat, 1995); *L'Oiseau du Mois* (*The Bird of the Month*; Dilettante, 1995); *Pas de H pour Natalie* (*No H for Natalie*; Julliard, 1995)

Vian, Boris (1920-1959); *L'Écume des Jours* (Gall., 1947; transl. as *Froth on the Daydream*, aka *Mood Indigo*, 1967); *L'Automne à Pékin* (*Autumn in Peking*; Halluin, 1947); *Et on Tuera Tous Les Affreux* (*And We'll Kill All the Awful People*; as Vernon Sullivan; Scorpion, 1948); *Les Fourmis* (*The Ants*; D'Halluins, 1949; rev. Los., 1968; transl. as *Blues for a Black Cat*, 1992); *L'Herbe Rouge* (*The Red Grass*; Toutain, 1950); *L'Arrache-Coeur* (Pro Francia, 1953; transl. as *Heartsnatcher*, 1968); *Note:* See Chapter VIII. ***L'Écume des Jours*** was adapted into an eponymous 1968 feature film (see Book 1, Chapter I). ***L'Herbe Rouge*** was adapted for television in 1985 by Pierre **Kast** (see Book 1, Chapter II). Boris Vian also translated A. E. Van Vogt's classic *The World of Null-A* into French. Also see **Opéra**.

Viard, Henri *see* **Ward, Henry**

Vibert, Edmond Célestin Paul (1851-1918); *Pour Lire en Automobile, Nouvelles Fantastiques* (*To Read in a Car, Fantastical Short Stories*; Berger-Levrault, 1901); *Pour Lire en Bateau-Mouche, Nouvelles Surprenantes* (*To Read on a Bateau-Mouche, Surprising Short Stories*; Berger-Levrault, 1905); *Pour Lire en Sous-Marin, Nouvelles Énivrantes* (*To Read in a Sub-Marine, Inebriating Short Stories*; Berger-Levrault, 1914); *Note:* See Chapter IV.

Vicas, Victor (1918-1985); *L'Homme au Cerveau Greffé* (*The Man with a Brain Transplant*; RL, 1969); *L'Inconnu de la Mer Morte* (*The Unknown Man from the Dead Sea*; RL, 1969); *Note:* *L'Homme* was made into an eponymous 1974 film, also written by Vicas (see Book 1, Chapter I). Vicas was one of the co-writers on the series ***Aux Frontières du Possible*** (see Book 1, Chapter II).

Vickers, Nancy (1946-); *La Montagne de Verre* (*The Mountain of Glass*; Vermillon, 1993); *Le Trône des Maléfices* (*The Spellbound Throne*; Vermillon, 1994); *Les Sorcières de Chanterelles* (*The Witches of Chanterelle*; Vermillon, 1996); *Note:* French-Canadian writer. Fantasy trilogy.

Vicq, Alex (?-); *L'Enfant Gigogne* (*The Child Inside*; Encre, 1980); *Hard Top* (Encre, 1983)

Victor, René-Jacques (?-); *Les Doigts du Hasard* (*The Fingers of Chance*; MSF 46, 1976)

Vidal, Adolphe (?-) *see* ***Contes et Légendes***

Vidal, Florence (?-); *L'Aolès férox* (Rupture, 1978); *Note:* See Chapter IX.

Vidal, Jean-Pierre (1944-); *Histoires Cruelles et Lamentables* (*Cruel and Sorry Tales*; Logiques, 1991); *Note:* French-Canadian writer.

Vidal, Nicole (1928-); *Le Prince des Steppes* (*The Prince of the Steppes*; Amitié, 1967); *Les Jours Dorés de Kaï-Yuan* (*The Golden Days of Kai-Yuan*; Amitié, 1970); *La Conspiration des Parasols* (*The Conspiracy of Umbrellas*; Amitié, 1972); *Miguel de la Faim* (*Miguel of Hunger*; Amitié, 1973); *Nam de la Guerre* (*Nam of War*; Amitié, 1975); *Les Cartes Postales Magiques* (*The Magic Postcards*; Amitié, 1979); *Les Trois Souhaits d'Aisha* (*Aysha's Three Wishes*; Amitié, 1980); *La Nuit des Iroquois* (*The Night of the Iroquois*; Amitié, 1983); *Tsou l'Effrayeur de Dragons* (*Tsou the Frightener of Dragons*; Amitié, 1983); *Le Destin aux Mille Visages* (*The Destiny of a Thousand Faces*; Amitié, 1988); *Note:* Juveniles.

Vidal-Loria (?-); *La Terre va Mourir* (*Earth Is Going to Die*; Pensée U., 1980)

Vielle, Eugène-Émile (?-); *Le Tunnel sous la Manche* (*The Tunnel Under the Channel*; RL Plein Vent, 1970)

Viellerglé, M.A. de *see* **Balzac, Honoré de**

Vignaud, Jean (Mrs.) *see* **Bruno-Ruby, J.**

Vignon, Claude (1832-1888); *Minuit! Récits de la Veillée* (*Midnight! Tales of the Watch*; Amyot, 1856); *Note:* Claude Vignon was the wife of occultist Eliphas **Lévi**; also see Chapter IV.

Viguier, Laurent (Dr.) (?-); *L'Extraordinaire Prophétie du Moine Hermann* (*The Extraordinary Prophecy of Hermann the Monk*; Brossard, 1933)

Vilà, Christian (1950-); *Banlieues Rouges* (*Red Suburbs*; anthology/with Joël **Houssin**; ON 12, 1976); *Sang Futur* (*Future Blood*; as Kriss Vila; Los., 1977); *Noël Noir* (*Black Christmas*; as Jean Viluber/with Jean-Pierre **Hubert**; Sanguine, 1979); *Hamburgers et Coïncidences* (AM, 1982); *Clip de Sang* (*Bloody Video Clip*; FNG 16, 1985); *L'Océan Cannibale* (*The Cannibal Ocean*; FNG 32, 1987); *Coupes Sombres* (*Dark Cuts*; as Jean Viluber/with Jean-Pierre **Hubert**; FNG 42, 1987); *La Mort Noire* (*The Black Death*; FNG 66, 1988); *Décharges* (*Discharges*; as Jean Viluber/with Jean-Pierre **Hubert**; FNG 93, 1989); *Greffes Profondes* (*Deep Grafts*; as Jean Viluber/with

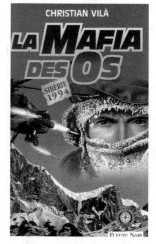

Jean-Pierre **Hubert**; FNG 110, 1990); *La Mafia des Os (The Bone Mafia*; FNAV 4, 1995); *La Montagne de Noé (Noah's Mountain*; FNAV 11, 1995); *L'Odeur de l'Or (The Smell of Gold*; FNSF 7, 1997); *Ice Flyer* (FNSF 19, 1997); *Note:* See Chapters VIII and IX.

Vildrac, Charles (Messager, Charles) (1882-1971); *Images et Mirages* (L'Abbaye, 1908); *L'Île Rose (The Pink Island*; AM, 1924); *Les Jouets du Père Noël (Santa Claus' Toys*; Bourrelier, 1946); *Le Jardinier de Samos (The Gardener of Samos*; Raison d'Être, 1947); *D'Après l'Écho (After the Echo*; AM, 1949); *Les Lunettes du Lion (The Lion's Spectacles*; GP, 1972)

Vilgensofer, A. (?-); *La Terre dans Cent Mille Ans (Earth in 100,000 Years*; Simonis-Empis, 1893); *Note:* See Chapter V.

Vilier, Jean-Louis (?-); *Siderelle* (Japyx, 1971); *La Planète de l'Amour (The Planet of Love*; GdV, 1986); *Apolline aux Enfers (Apolline in Hell*; Garancière, 1986); *Note:* Erotic SF.

Villaret, Bernard (1909-); *Seul, le Corail Reste (Only the Coral Remains*; AM, 1950); *Les Îles de la Nuit (The Islands of Night*; Bibliophiles du Faubourg & du Papier, 1964); *Mort au Champ d'Étoiles (Death on a Field of Stars*; MarSF 341, 1970); *Deux Soleils pour Artuby (Two Suns for Artuby*; PdF141, 1971); *Sept Histoires des Mers du Sud (Seven Tales of the Southern Seas*; Pacifique, 1972); *Le Chant de la Coquille Kalasai (The Song of the Kalasai Shell*; PdF170, 1976); *Visa pour l'Outre-Temps (Visa for Beyond Time*; PdF 213, 1976); *Pas d'Avenir pour les Sapiens (No Future for Homo Sapiens*; Nathan SF 3, 1980); *L'Infini Plus Un Mètre (Infinity Plus One Meter*; Nathan SF 5, 1981); *Quand Reviendra l'Oiseau-Nuage (When the Cloud Bird Returns*; AMSF 2 57, 1983); *Note:* See Chapter IX.

Villars, Nicolas-Pierre-Henri de Montfaucon de (Abbé) (?-1675); *Le Comte de Gabalis ou Entretiens sur les Sciences Secrètes (The Count of Gabalis, or Conversations on Secret Sciences*; Barbin, 1670; rep. VI, 1788); *Note:* See Chapter III.

Ville d'Avray, A. de (?-); *Voyage dans la Lune avant 1900 (Journey to the Moon Before 1900*; Fume, 1890); *Note:* See Chapter V.

Villedeuil (Comte de) (?-); *Paris à l'Envers (Paris Upside Down*; Libr. Nouvelle, 1853)

Villemaire, Yolande (1949-); *Ange Amazone (Angel Amazonia*; Herbe Rouge, 1982); *Les Coïncidences Terrestres (Terrestrial Coincidences*; Pleine Lune, 1983); *La Constellation du Cygne (The Swan Constellation*; Pleine Lune, 1985); *Meurtres à Blanc (Blank Murders*; Herbe Rouge, 1986); *Le Dieu Dansant (The Dancing God*; L'Hexagone, 1995); *Note:* French-Canadian writer.

Villemarqué, Hersart de la (?-); *Barzaz-Breiz, Légende Celtique (Barzaz-Breiz, Celtic Legend*; Charpentier, 1839); *Contes Populaires des Anciens Bretons (Popular Tales of Ancient Britons*; W. Coquelert, 1842)

Villemure, Pierre (1935-); *Quand le Diable s'en mêle (When the Devil Meddles*; Presses Laurentiennes, 1988); *Note:* French-Canadian writer. Collection of religious fantasy.

Villeneuve, Daniel de *see* **Listonai**

Villeneuve, Jocelyne (1941-); *Les Friperies (The Rags*; Prise de Parole, 1989); *Note:* French-Canadian writer.

Villette, André (Massin, Paul) (?-); *Les Perceurs de Planètes (The Planet Diggers*; Ed. Ouvrières, 1947)

Villiers de l'Isle-Adam, Jean-Marie-Matthias-Philippe Auguste, Comte de (1838-1889); *Isis* (Dentu, 1862); *Morgane* (Guyon Francisque, 1866); *Claire Lenoir* (in Revue des Lettres & des Arts, 1867); *L'ntersigne* (in Revue des Lettres & des Arts, 1868); *La Révolte (The Revolt*; Lemerre, 1870); *Contes Cruels (Cruel Tales*; Lévy, 1883; transl. as *Sardonic Tales*, 1927); *Véra* (in La Semaine Parisienne, 1884); *Axel* (Jeune France, 1885; transl. 1925); *L'Ève Future* (Brunhoff, 1886; transl. as *The Eve of the Future*, 1981); *L'Amour Suprême (The Supreme Love*; Brunhoff, 1886); *Tribulat Bonhomet* (Tresse & Stock, 1887; transl. 1925); *Histoires Insolites (Strange Tales*; Quantin, 1888); *Le Secret de l'Échafaud (The Secret of the Gallows*; Marpon & Flammarion, 1888); *Nouveaux Contes Cruels (New Cruel Tales*; Calmann-Lévy, 1893); *Akëdysseril* (Aujourd'hui, 1978); *Note:* See Chapters IV and V. *Le Secret de l'Échafaud* was adapted into a **Grand-Guignol** play by Charles **Hellem** & Pol d'**Estoc**.

Villois, Florent (?-); *Le Manuscrit Retrouvé (The Found Manuscript*; with Y. du **Jacquier**; L'Essor, 1942); *Le Pharaon des Andes (The Andes Pharaoh*; L'Essor, 1943); *Note:* Belgian writer.

Viluber, Jean *see* **Hubert, Jean-Pierre** & **Vilà, Christian**

Vimereu, Paul (?-); *César dans l'Île de Pan (Caesar on the Island of Pan*; 1923); *Note:* See Chapter VII.

Vincent, Charles (?-) *see* **Maël, Pierre**

Vincent, Guillaume (?-) *see* **Gaborit, Mathieu**

Vincent, Lucy *see* **Carrière, Huguette**

Vincent, Paul (?-); *Le Fantôme Vert (The Green Phantom*; Hac., 1927); *Le Dragon Rouge (The Red Dragon*; Hac., 1929)

Vindry, Noël (?-); *La Bête Hurlante (The Howling Beast*; RMY, 1949)

Vinet, David (?-); *Bombe Z ou La Prochaine Grande*

Derr... Nière (Z Bomb, or the Next Big Last One; Vinet, 1960)

Vion, Marc (?-); *La Peur du Stade (Fear of the Stadium*; G. Authier, 1977); *Panique au Pellerin (Panic in Pellerin*; Picollec, 1982); *Ballast au Clair de Lune (Ballast in Moonlight*; Picollec, 1985); *French Collection* (Picollec, 1988)

Viot, Henry-Gérard (?-); *L'Immortel Forban (The Immortal Villain*; Tallandier, 1933); *La Cité Fantastique (The Fantastic City*; NPF, 1947); *L'Écolier Invisible (The Invisible Schoolboy*; with Pierre **Devaux**; S&A 4, 1950); *La Minute Dérobée (The Purloined Minute*; with Pierre **Devaux**; S&A 5, 1952; transl. in *Science Fiction + magazine*, ed. Hugo Gernsback, 1953); *Chronastro* (S&A 6, 1953); *La Conquête d'Almériade (The Conquest of Almeriade*; with Pierre **Devaux**; S&A 7, 1954); *Explorations dans le Micro-monde (Explorations in the Microworld*; with Pierre **Devaux**; S&A 8, 1957); *Le Narcisse Tardif (The Late Narcissus*; Demn., 1974); *Note:* See Chapter IX.

Viscardini, Mario (?-); *La Maison du Genre Humain (The House of Mankind*; Delforge, 1944)

Viterbo, Max (?-?) *see* **Grand-Guignol**

Vivier, Robert (?-) *see* ***Contes et Légendes***

Vizerie, Bruno (?-); *La Porcelaine de l'Univers (Ceramics of the Universe*; Magnard, 1982)

Vladimir (?-); *Monsieur Afrique et le Rat de Brousse (Mister Africa and the Bush Rat*; FNASF 7, 1995)

Vogüe, Eugène-Melchior, Vicomte de (1848-1910); *Les Morts qui Parlent (The Talking Dead*; Plon, 1889); *Le Maître de la Mer (The Master of the Sea*; Plon, 1903)

Vois, Ernest (?-?) *see* **Grand-Guignol**

Voisin, Michel (?-) *see* ***Contes et Légendes***

Volkoff, Vladimir (1932-); *Métro pour l'Enfer (Metro for Hell*; RF 118, 1963); *Le Retournement (The Turning*; Julliard, 1979); *Le Tire-Bouchon du Bon Dieu (The Corkscrew of God*; PP 5142, 1982); *Le Montage (The Machination*; Julliard, 1982); *Le Trêtre (The Traitor*; AdH, 1983); *La Guerre des Pieuvres (The War of the Octopuses*; PP 5169, 1983); *Le Bouclage (The Wrap-Up*; AdH, 1990); *Chroniques Angéliques (Angelic Chronicles*; AdH, 1997); *Note:* See Chapter IX. *Le Retournement* and *Le Montage* are two famous John Le Carré-like spy thrillers. Volkoff

is also the author of the popular juvenile spy series, *Langelot*, written using the pseudonym "Lieutenant X" (see below). Series *Langelot* (as Lieutenant X): *1. Langelot Agent Secret (Langelot Secret Agent*; BV 284, 1965); *2. Langelot et les Espions (Langelot and the Spies*; BV 293, 1966); *3. Langelot et le Satellite (Langelot and the Satellite*; BV 297, 1966); *4. Langelot et les Saboteurs (Langelot and the Saboteurs*; BV 301, 1966); *5. Langelot et le Gratte-Ciel (Langelot and the Skyscraper*; BV 318, 1967); *6. Langelot contre Monsieur T (Langelot vs. Mr. T*; BV 334, 1967); *7. Langelot Pickpocket* (BV, 1967); *8. Une Offensive Signée Langelot (An Attack Signed Langelot*; BV 353, 1968); *9. Langelot et l'Inconnue (Langelot and the Unknown Girl*; BV 363, 1968); *10. Langelot contre Six (Langelot vs. Six*; BV

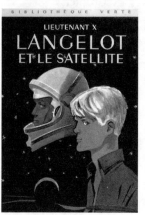

372, 1968); *11. Langelot et les Crocodiles (Langelot and the Crocodiles*; BV 386, 1969); *12. Langelot chez les Pa-Pous (Langelot Among the Pa-Pous*; BV 403, 1969); *13. Langelot Suspect* (BV 420, 1970); *14. Langelot et les Cosmonautes (Langelot and the Astronauts*; BV, 1970); *15. Langelot et le Sous-Marin Jaune (Langelot and the Yellow Submarine*; BV 456, 1971); *16. Langelot Mène la Vie de Château (Langelot Lives a Kingly Life*; BV, 1971); *17. Langelot et la Danseuse (Langelot and the Ballerina*; BV, 1972); *18. Langelot et l'Avion Détourné (Langelot and the Hijacked Plane*; BV, 1972); *19. Langelot fait le Malin (Langelot Plays Smart*; BV, 1972); *20. Langelot et les Exterminateurs (Langelot and the Exterminators*; BV, 1973); *21. Langelot et le Fils du Roi (Langelot and the King's Son*; BV, 1974); *22. Langelot fait le Singe (Langelot Plays with the Apes*; BV, 1974); *23. Langelot Kidnappé (Langelot Kidnapped*; BV, 1975); *24. Langelot et la Voyante (Langelot and the Medium*; BV, 1975); *25. Langelot sur la Côte d'Azur (Langelot on the French Riviera*; BV, 1976); *26. Langelot à la Maison Blanche (Langelot at the White House*; BV, 1976); *27. Langelot sur l'Île Déserte (Langelot on the Desert Island*; BV, 1977); *28. Langelot et le Plan Rubis (Langelot and the Ruby Plan*; BV, 1977); *29. Langelot passe à l'Ennemi (Langelot Defects*; BV,

1978); *30. Langelot chez le Présidentissime (Langelot and the Presidentissime*; BV, 1978); *31. Langelot en Permission (Langelot on Leave*; BV, 1979); *32. Langelot Garde du Corps (Langelot Bodyguard*; BV, 1979); *33. Langelot Gagne la Dernière Manche (Langelot Wins the Last Hand*; BV, 1980); *34. Langelot Mauvais Esprit (Langelot and the Evil Spirits*; BV, 1980); *35. Langelot et la Clef de la Guerre (Langelot and the War Key*; BV, 1982); *36. Langelot contre la Marée Noire (Langelot vs. the Black Tide*; BV, 1981); *37. Langelot et le Général Kidnappé (Langelot and the Kidnapped General*; BV, 1983); *38. Langelot aux Arrêts de Rigueur (Langelot Confined to Quarters*; BV, 1984); *39. Langelot Donne l'Assaut (Langelot Launches the Attack*; BV, 1985); *40. Langelot et le Commando Perdu (Langelot and the Lost Commando*; BV, 1986)

Volodine, Antoine (1950-); *Biographie Comparée de Jorian Murgrave (Comparative Biography of Jorian Murgrave*; PdF 397, 1985); *Un Navire de Nulle Part (A Ship from Nowhere*; PdF 413, 1986); *Rituel du Mépris, Variante Moldscher (Ritual of Contempt, the Moldscher Variation*; PdF 430, 1987); *Des Enfers Fabuleux (Some Fabulous Hells*; PdF 454, 1987); *Lisbonne, Dernière Marge (Lisbon, Last Margin*; Minuit, 1990); *Alto Solo* (Minuit, 1991); *Le Nom des Singes (The Name of the Apes*; Minuit, 1994); *Le Port Intérieur (The Inner Harbor*; Minuit, 1996); *Nuit Banche en Balkhyrie (White Night in Balkiria*; Gall., 1997); *Note:* See Chapter IX.

Volta, H. de (?-); *L'Île Merveilleuse (Miraculas) (The Marvelous Island*; serialized in 20 issues, Tallandier, 1921); *1. L'Art d'escamoter les Gens (The Art of Making People Disappear); 2. Le Tonnerre dans une Boîte (Thunder in a Box); 3. Milliardaire en une Minute (Billionaire in One Minute); 4. Au Pays de la Peur (In the Land of Fear); 5. La Taupe d'Acier (The Steel Mole); 6. Cinq Cent Lieues sous la Terre (500 Leagues Underground); 7. Ressuscités après 100.000 Ans (Brought Back to Life After 100,000 Years); 8. Les Miroirs qui trahissent (The Betraying Mirrors); 9. Le Mystère de Franklin Hill (The Mystery of Franklin Hill); 10. Les Hélices Paralysées (The Paralyzed Propellers); 11. La Fin des Guerres (The End of the Wars); 12. L'Obus Habité (The Inhabited Shell); 13. Au Secours d'une Vie Humaine (To Rescue a Human Life); 14. L'Attaque du Convoi d'Or (The Attack of the Gold Convoy); 15. Vers les Mondes Inconnus (Towards the Unknown Worlds); 16. La Découverte de l'Atlantide (The Discovery of Atlantis); 17. Le Taureau Pétrifié (The Petrified Bull); 18. Invulnérable ; 19. Une Révolution Géographique (A Geographic Revolution); 20. Scientific City ; Note:* See Chapter VII.

Voltaire (Arouet, François-Marie) (1694-1778); *Zadig* (1747; transl. 1778); *Micromégas* (1752; transl. 1753); *Candide* (Cramen, 1759; transl. 1760); *Note:* See Chapter III. Also see **Opéra**.

Vonarburg, Élisabeth (1947-); *L'Oeil de la Nuit (The Eye of Night*; CdF 1, 1980); *Le Silence de la Cité (The Silence of the City*; PdF 327, 1982; transl. as *The Silent City*, 1988); *Janus* (PdF 388, 1984); *Histoire de la Princesse et du Dragon (Story of the Princess and the Dragon*; Q/A, 1990); *Ailleurs et au Japon (Elsewhere and in Japan*; Q/A, 1991); *Chroniques du Pays des Mères (Chronicles of the Land of the Mothers*; Q/A, 1992; rep. LdP 7187, 1996; transl. as *In the Mothers' Land*, 1992); *Les Contes de la Chatte Rouge (The Tales of the*

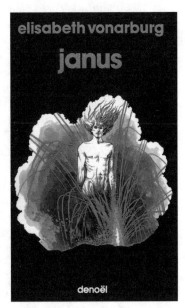

Red Mother-Cat; Q/A, 1993); *Les Voyageurs Malgré Eux (The Voyagers in Spite of Themselves*; Q/A, 1994; transl. as *Reluctant Voyagers*, 1995); *Contes de Tyranaël (Tales of Tyranael*; Q/A, 1994); *Chanson pour une Sirène (Song for a Siren*; with Yves **Meynard**; Vents d'Ouest, 1995); *Tyranaël 1: Les Rêves de la Mer (The Dreams of the Sea*; AL, 1996); *Tyranaël 2: Le Jeu de la Perfection (The Game of Perfection*; AL, 1996); *Tyranaël 3: Mon Frère, l'Ombre (My Brother, the Shadow*; AL, 1997); *Tyranaël 4: L'Autre Rivage (The Other Shore*; AL, 1997); *Tyranaël 5: La Mer Allée avec le Soleil (The Sea Gone with the Sun*; AL, 1997); *Note:* French-Canadian writer born in France.

Von Osten, Malko *see* **Osten, Malko von**

Voragine, Jacques de (1228-1298); *La Légende Dorée (The Golden Legend*; 1250); *Note:* See Chapter I.

Voussac, Jean *see* **Bonneau, Albert**

Vox, Vincent (?-); *Prométhée de l'Ombre (Prometheus of Shadow*; FNFR 27, 1995)

Voyages Imaginaires; A table of contents (compiled by

Pierre **Versins**) of this remarkable imprint, edited and published by Charles-Georges-Thomas **Garnier**, follows, with the original dates of publication when applicable: 1-3. De Foë, Daniel. *Robinson Crusoe.* 4. Quarll, Philippe. *Le Solitaire Anglais (The Lonely Englishman).* 5. **Veiras, Denis.** *Histoire des Sévarambes* (1677-79); 6. Berington, Simon. *Mémoires de Gaudence de Luques (Memoirs of Gaudence of Lucques*; 1737). 7-9. **Grivel, Guillaume.** *L'Île Inconnue, ou Mémoires du Chevalier des Gastines (The Unknown Island, or Memoirs of the Chevalier des Gastines*; 1783); 10. **Martigny (Comte de).** *Voyage d'Alcimédon, ou Naufrage qui Conduit au Port (Alcimedon's Journey, or Shipwreck That Led to the Harbor*; 1756); **Moutonnet de Clairfons, Julien-Jacques.** *Les Îles Fortunées, ou Les Aventures de Bathylle et de Cléobule* (1778); **Montesquieu.** *Histoire des Troglodytes* (1721); Pinto, Menez. *Aventures d'un Corsaire Portugais (Adventures of a Portuguese Corsair*; 1614); 11-12. *Voyages et Aventures du Capitaine Robert Boyle (Voyages and Adventures of Captain Robert Boyle*); *Naufrage et Aventures de Pierre Viaud (Shipwreck and Adventures of Pierre Viaud*); *Relation du Naufrage de Madame Godin sur la Rivière des Amazones (Tale of the Shipwreck of Mrs. Godin on the River of the Amazons*); 13. Lucien. *Histoire Véritable (True Story*; c. 180 A.D.), continued by Perrot d'Ablancourt. **Cyrano de Bergerac.** *Etats et Empires de la Lune / Etats et Empires du Soleil (The States and Empires of the Moon the Sun*; 1657, 1662); 14. Jonathan Swift. *Gulliver* (1726); 15. **Desfontaines (Abbé).** *Le Nouveau Gulliver (The New Gulliver*; 1730); 16. *Voyages Récréatifs du Chevalier de Quevedo (Recreative Journeys of the Knight of Quevedo*); **Béthune (Chevalier de).** *Relation du Monde de Mercure (Tale of the World Mercury*; 1750); 17-18. **Roumier-Robert, Marie-Anne de.** *Voyage de Milord Céton dans les Sept Planètes ou Le Nouveau Mentor (Voyage of Lord Ceton in the Seven Planets or the New Mentor*; 1765); 19. Holberg, Ludvig. *Voyage de Nikolas Klimius (Voyage of Nikolas Klimius*; 1741); *Relation d'un Voyage du Pôle Arctique au Pôle Antarctique par le Centre du Monde avec la Description de ce Périlleux Passage et les Choses Merveilleuses et Étonnantes qu'on a découvertes sous le Pôle Antarctique (Tale of a Journey from the North Pole to the South Pole Through the Center of the Earth, with the Description of This Dangerous Passage and the Wondrous and Amazing Things We Discovered Under the South Pole*; 1721); 20-21. **Mouhy (Chevalier de).** *Lamékis, ou Les Voyages Extraordinaires d'un Égyptien dans la Terre Intérieure avec la Découverte de l'Île des Sylphides (The Extraordinary Voyages of An Egyptian in the Inner Earth with the Discovery of Sylphides' Island*; 1737-38); **Aunillon, Pierre-Charles-Fabiot.** *Azor, ou Le Prince Enchanté, Histoire Nouvelle pour Servir de Chronique à celle de la Terre des Perroquets (Azor, or*

the Enchanted Prince, New Story Serving as a Chronicle to the Land of Parrots; 1750); 22-23. Robert Paltock. *Les Hommes Volants (The Flying Men*; 1750); **Legrand, Marc-Antoine.** *Les Aventures du Voyageur Aérien (The Adventures of An Aerial Traveler*; 1724); **Voltaire.** *Micromégas* (1752); 24. **Foigny, Gabriel de.** *La Terre Australe Connue, ou Les Aventures de Jacques Sadeur dans la Découverte et le Voyage de la Terre Australe (A New Discovery of Terra Incognita Australis*; 1676); 25. **Pajon, Henri.** *Histoire du Prince Soly, surnommé Prénany, et de la Princesse Feslée (Tale of Prince Soly Nicknamed Prenany and of Princess Feslee*; 1740); **Mailly (Chevalier de).** *Voyage et les Aventures de Trois Princes de Serendib (Voyage and Adventures of Three Princes from Serendib*; 1719); 26. **Bougeant, Guillaume-Hyacinthe.** *Voyage Merveilleux du Prince Fan-Féredin dans la Romancie contenant plusieurs Observations Historiques, Géographiques, Physiques, Critiques et Morales (Marvellous Voyage of Prince Fan-Feredin in Romancia Containing Several Historical, Geographical, Physical, Critical and Moral Observations*; 1735); **Segrais.** *Relation de l'Île Imaginaire et Histoire de la Princesse de Paphlagonie (Tale of the Imaginary Island and Story of the Pincess of Paphlagonia*; 1659); **Tallemand (Abbé).** *Voyages de l'Île d'Amour (Voyages to the Island of Love*; 1663); **Aubignac (Abbé d').** *Relation du Royaume de Coquetterie (Tale of the Kingdom of Coquettishness*; 1654); **Sorel, Charles.** *Description de l'Île de Portraiture et de la Ville des Portraits (Description of the Island of Portraiture and the City of Portraits*; 1659); 27. Camoëns. *La Lusiade: L'Île Enchantée (The Enchanted Island*); **Aulnoy (Baronne d').** *L'Île de la Félicité (The Island of Happiness);* **La Dixmerie, M. de.** *L'Île Taciturne et l'Île Enjouée, ou Voyage du Génie Alaciel dans ces Deux Îles (Taciturn Island and Happy Island, or the Journey of the Djinn Alaciel in These Two Islands*; 1759); Caraccioli (Marquis de). *Voyage de la Raison en Europe (Voyage of Reason in Europe*); 28-30. *Voyage Sentimental en France (Sentimental Journeys Throughout France)* 31. **Lévesque, Pierre-Charles.** *Les Rêves d'Aristobule, Philosophe Grec (The Dreams of Aristobule, Greek Philosopher*; 1761); **Mercier, Louis-Sébastien.** *Songes d'un Hermite (Dreams of a Hermit*; 1770); 32. **Mercier, Louis-Sébastien.** *Songes et Visions Philosophiques (Philosophical Dreams and Visions*; 1768); 33. Apulée. *Les Métamorphoses (Metamorphoses*); 34. **Villars, Nicolas-Pierre-Henri de Montfaucon de (Abbé).** *Comte de Gabalis* (1670); Robert (Madame). *Les Ondins (The Water Sprites*); 35. Hamilton. *L'Enchanteur Faustus (Faustus the Enchanter*). **Cazotte, Jacques.** *Le Diable Amoureux (The Devil in Love*); **Murat (Comtesse de).** *Les Lutins du Château de Kernosy (The Goblins of Castle Kernosy*; VI, 1788); 36. Bordelon (Abbé). *Histoire de M. Oufle (Tale of Mr. Oufle)*

Vrigny, Roger (1920-); *Une Vie Brève (A Brief Life*; Gall., 1972); *La Nuit de Mougins (The Night at Mougins*; Gall., 1974); *Un Ange Passe (An Angel Passes*; Gall., 1979); *Accident de Parcours (Accident in Transit*; Gall., 1985); *Le Bonhomme d'Ampère (The Ampere Guy*; Gall., 1988); *Les Coeurs Sensibles: Arban, Laurence, Barbegal (The Sensitive Hearts*; Gall., 1990); *Le Garçon d'Orage (The Storm Boy*; Gall., 1994); *Instants Dérobés (Purloined Moments*; Gall., 1996); *Note:* See Chapter VIII.

Vulbeau, Alain (?-); *Mox* (Cahiers d'Utopie, 1980)

Vylars, Cilia de (?-?); *Vers la Force (Towards the Force*; 1905); *Note:* Also see **Grand-Guignol**.

Wagner, Paul (?-); *Graine d'Ortie (Nettles Seed*; TR, 1971); *L'Enfant et les Magiciens (The Child and the Wizards*; TR, 1977); *Le Temps des Marguerites (The Time of the Daisies*; Cercle d'Or, 1980); *Note:* See Chapter VIII.

Wagner, Roland C. (1960-); *Le Serpent d'Angoisse (The Terror Snake*; FNA 1585, 1987); *Un Ange s'est Pendu (An Angel Hanged Himself*; FNA 1614, 1988); *La Mémoire des Pierres (The Memory of the Stones*; FNA 1649, 1988); *Prisons Intérieures (Inner Prisons*; FNA 1654, 1988); *Les Futurs Mystères de Paris (The Future Mysteries of Paris*; FNA 1659, 1988); *Le Paysage Déchiré (The Torn Landscape*; FNA 1678, 1989); *Un Navire Ancré dans le Ciel (A Ship Anchored in the Sky*; FNA 1695, 1989); *La Mort Marchait dans les Rues (The Death That Walked the Streets*; FNA 1702, 1989); *Les Psychopompes de Klash (The Psychopumps of Klash*; as Red Deff; FNA 1733, 1990); *Le Rêveur des Terres Agglutinées (The Dreamer of the Clotted Lands*; FNA 1770, 1990); *L'Autoroute de l'Aube (The Highway of Dawn*; FNA 1787, 1990); *Viper* (as Red Deff; FNA 1806, 1991); *Chroniques du Désespoir (Chronicles of Despair*; FNA 1820, 1991); *Ganja* (as Red Deff; FNA 1825, 1991); *Cette Crédille Qui Nous Ronge (That Gnawing Credille*; FNA 1847, 1991); *Quelqu'un Hurle Mon Nom (Someone Howls*

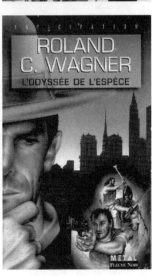

My Name; Editions de l'Hydre, 1993); *H. P. L. (1890-1991);* L'Astronaute Mort, 1996); *La Balle du Néant (The Bullet from the Void*; FNA 1988, 1996); *Les Ravisseurs Quantiques (The Quantum Kidnappers*; FNA 1998, 1996); *Le Nombril du Monde (The Navel of the World*; DLM, Arkham 2, 1997); *L'Odyssée de l'Espèce (A Species Odyssey*; FNA 2001, 1997); *L'Aube Incertaine (Uncertain Dawn*; FNSF 15, 1997); *Note:* See chapters VIII and IX. Roland C. Wagner (using the pseudonym of Richard Wolfram) also wrote a number of novels published under Jimmy **Guieu**'s name for the Jimmy **Guieu** imprint.

Wailly, Gaston de (Commandant) (1857-); *Le Brick Sanglant (The Bloody Ship*; Kolb, 1890); *Le Serment de Lucette (Lucette's Oath*; Calmann-Lévy, 1899); *Le Monde de l'Abîme (The World of the Abyss*; À Travers le Monde, 1904; rev., BGA, 1924); *Le Roi de l'Inconnu (The King of the Unknown*; À Travers le Monde, 1905; rev. BGA, 1925); *Le Meurtrier du Globe (The Murderer of the Globe*; JDV, 1910; rev. BGA, 1925); *L'Île Mystère (Mystery Island*; BGA, 1926); *L'Allié Mystérieux (The Mysterious Ally*; BGA, 1926); *Note:* See Chapter V.

Wailly, Léon de (?-?); *L'Autre Chambre (The Other Room*; Revue des Deux Mondes, 1831); *Note:* Also see **Opéra**.

Waldor, Mélanie (?-?); *L'Écuyer Dauberon (The Squire Dauberon*; Moutardier, 1832); *La Coupe de Corail (The Coral Cup*; L. de Potter, 1842); *Le Château de Ramsberg (The Castle of Ramsberg*; L. de Potter, 1844); *L'Eglise Tendue de Noir (The Church Dressed in Black*; Nancy, 1846); *Note:* See Chapter IV.

Walker, J. Bernard *see* **Bernard-Walker, J.**

Walter, Jean-Jacques (?-); *L'Étoile des Sables (The Star of the Sands*; Belfond, 1975); *Planètes Pensantes (Thinking Planets*; Den., 1980)

Walther, Daniel (1940-); *Mais l'Espace, Mais le Temps... (But Space, But Time...*; Bodson, 1972; rev. FNA 1089, 1982); *Les Soleils Noirs d'Arcadie (The Black Suns of Arcadia*; anthology; ON 2, 1975); *Requiem pour Demain (Requiem for Tomorrow*; MarSF 571, 1976); *Krysnak, ou le Complot (Krysnak, or the Conspiracy*; PdF 258, 1978); *L'Épouvante (The Terror*; JL 976, 1979); *Hallo Jack, Où est donc passé Artie? on dit*

qu'il fourgue des flingues chez le Négus? (Hullo Jack, Where Is Artie? They Say He's Smuggling Guns to the Negus?; Ponte Mirone, 1979); *Étrangers à Utopolis (Strangers in Utopolis*; L'Ancrier, 1980); *Les Quatre Saisons de la Nuit (The Four Seasons of the Night*; NéO 20, 1980); *L'Hôpital et Autres Fables Cliniques (The Hospital and Other Clinical Fables*; NéO 37, 1982); *Happy End* (PdF 343, 1982); *Le Livre de Swa* (FNA 1132, 1982; transl. as *The Book of Shai*, 1984); *Le Destin de Swa* (FNA 1158, 1982; transl. as *Shai's Destiny*, 1985); *La Légende de Swa (Shai's Legend*; FNA 1202, 1983); *Embuscade sur Ornella (Ambush on Ornella*; FNA 1227, 1983); *Apollo XXV* (FNA 1262, 1983); *Nocturne sur Fond d'Epées (Nocturne on a Field of Swords*; NéO 110, 1984); *Coeur Moite et Autres Maladies Modernes (Moist Heart and Other Modern Diseases*; NéO 125, 1984); *La Pugnace Revolution de Phagor (The Pugnacious Revolution of Phagor*; FNA 1317, 1984); *Le Veilleur à la Lisière du Monde (The Watcher on the Edge of the World*; FNA 1385, 1985); *Sept Femmes de mes Autres Vies (Seven Women of My Other Lives*; PdF 398, 1985); *La Marée Purulente (The Foul Tide*; FNG 18, 1986); *Le Rêve du Scorpion (The Scorpion's Dream*; NéO 200, 1987); *Tigre (Tiger*; FNA 1605, 1988); *La Planète Jaja (The Jaja Planet*; FNA 1721, 1989); *Le Village (The Village*; L'Ancrier, 1989); *L'Iris de Perse (The Persian Iris*; L'Ancrier, 1993); *La Terre sans Souffrance (Earth Without Suffering*; FNAV 10, 1995); *Les Rapiéceurs de Néant (The Void Patchers*; Alfil, 1997); *Note:* See Chapters VIII and IX.

Ward, Henry (Viard, Henri) (1921-); *Les Soleils Verts (The Green Suns*; Jeheber, 1956); *L'Enfer est dans le Ciel (Hell is in the Sky*; Del Duca, 1958); *Le Secret du Président (The President's Secret*; as Henri Viard; Den., 1967); *Rira Bien qui Mourra le Dernier (The Last to Laught Is the Last to Die*; RL, 1970); *Le Mytheux (The Mythous*; Gall., 1972); *Le Roi des Mirmidons (The King of the Myrmidons*; Gall., 1982); *Note:* See Chapter IX. Henri Viard also wrote the television series ***Aux Frontières Du Possible** (To the Frontiers of the Possible)* and the teleplay ***Mars: Mission Accomplie*** (see Book 1, Chapter II).

Ward, Philippe (Laguerre, Philippe) (1958-); *Artahe* (CyLibris, 1997); *Note:* See Chapter VIII.

Wargar, Kurt *see* **Steiner, Kurt**

Warnant-Côté, Marie-Andrée (1946-); *La Cavernale (The Cavernal*; CLF, 1983); *Note:* French-Canadian writer.

Warney, Lucien (Weill, Lucien-Élie) (?-); *L'Homme qui vécut sa Mort (The Man Who Lived His Death*; Redier, 1928)

Warren, Raoul de (1905-1994); *L'Énigme du Mort Vivant (The Mystery of the Living Dead*; Bordas, 1950); *La Bête de l'Apocalypse (The Beast of the Apocalypse*; RL, 1956); *Le Village Assassin (The Murderous Village*; AELP, 1967); *L'Insolite Aventure de Marina Sloty (Marina Sloty's Strange Adventure*; L'Herne, 1981); *Rue du Mort-qui-Trompe (Street of the Dead Who Cheats*; L'Herne, 1984); *Et le Glas Tinta Trois Fois (And the Bell Tolled Three Times*; L'Herne, 1989); *Les Portes de l'Enfer (The Gates of Hell*; L'Herne, 1991); *La Clairière des Eaux Mortes (The Clearing of the Dead Waters*; L'Herne, n.d.); *Note:* See Chapter VIII.

Watteau, Monique(-Alika) (1929-); *La Colère Végétale (The Vegetable Wrath*; Plon, 1954); *La Nuit aux Yeux de Bête (The Night with Eyes of Beasts*; Plon, 1956); *L'Ange à Fourrure (The Angel with Fur*; Plon, 1958); *Je Suis le Ténébreux (I Am the Dark One*; Julliard, 1962); *Le Cimetière des Cachalots (The Graveyard of the Cachalots*; RL, 1966); *Note:* Belgian writer. See Chapter VIII.

Wattyne, P. de (?-?) *see* **Grand-Guignol**

Weill, Lucien-Élie *see* **Warney, Lucien**

Werber, Bernard (1961-); *Les Fourmis (The Ants*; AM, 1991; transl. as *Empire of the Ants*, 1996); *Le Jour des Fourmis (The Day of the Ants*; AM, 1992); *Les Thanatonautes (The Thanatonauts*; AM, 1994); *La Révolution des Fourmis (The Revolution of the Ants*; AM, 1996); *Note:* See Chapter IX. *Les Fourmis* was adapted into a graphic novel (see Book I, Chapter V).

Wermelinger, Raymond (1938-); *Soyez donc Maçon ou K 522 (Be a Mason, or K 522*; Baudinière, 1978); *Note:* Collection of fantastical tales prefaced by Claude **Klotz**.

Wersinger, Marc (1909-); *La Chute dans le Néant (The Fall Into Nothingness*; Pré-aux-Clercs, 1947); *Note:* See Chapter VII.

Westphal, Éric (1929-); *La Manifestation (The Demonstration*; Gall., 1967); *On n'est plus chez soi (Dialogues Lunaires) (We're Not at Home (Lunatic Dialogues)*; Buchet-Chastel, 1972); *Bactéries Blues* (Maison de la Culture de Rennes, 1974); *Toi et tes Nuages / Pollufission 2000 (You and Your Clouds*; Gall., 1976); *Le Naufrage (The Shipwreck*; Papiers, 1985); *De Tout pour Faire un Monde (A Bit of Everything to Make a World*; Papiers, 1986); *Le Caillou Blanc (The White Pebble*; Libr. Théâtrale, 1990); *Armistice au Pont de Grenelle (Armistice at Grenelle Bridge*; Libr. Théâtrale, 1990); *Note: Pollufission* is a stage play.

Weulersse, Odile (1938-); *Les Pilleurs de Sarcophages (The Looters of Sarcophagus;* Hac., 1984); *Le Messager d'Athènes (The Messenger from Athens;* Hac., 1985); *Le Secret des Catacombes (The Secret of the Catacombs;* Hac., 1986); *Le Cavalier de Bagdad (The Rider of Baghdad;* Hac., 1988); *Le Chevalier au Bouclier Vert (The Knight with a Green Shield;* Hac., 1990); *L'Aigle de Mexico (The Eagle from Mexico;* Hac., 1992); *Note:* Juveniles. See Chapter VIII.

Wietzel, Élie (?-); *La Porte des Limbes (The Gate of Limbo;* Mnemos 25, 1997); *Note:* See Chapter VIII.

Wild, René Herbert (?-); *L'Ambassade Oubliée (The Forgotten Embassy;* AM, 1931); *Le Triangle de Feu (The Triangle of Fire;* Tallandier, 1935)

Williamson *see* **Rillier, Louis**

Wilshcocqkst (Simoneau, Raymond) (1962-); *Hautes Brumes (High Mists;* Guy Saint-Jean, 1994); *Note:* French-Canadian writer.

Wintrebert, Joelle (1949-); *Les Olympiades Truquées (The Trick Olympics;* Kes I&M 9, 1980; rev. FNA 1573, 1987); *Les Maîtres-Feu (The Fire Masters;* JL 1408, 1982); *Nunatak (AdP 57, 1983); Chromoville (JL 1576, 1983); La Fille de Terre Deux (The Girl from Earth-Two;* Bordas, 1987); *Bébé-Miroir (Mirror Baby;* FNA 1624, 1988); *Le Créateur Chimérique (The Chimerical Creator;* JL 2420, 1988); *Kidnapping en Télétrans (Kidnaping By Teletrans;* Hac., 1988); *Comme un Feu de Sarments (As a Vine Fire;* Hac., 1990); *L'Océanide (Hac. Jeunesse, 1992); Hurlegriffe (Screamclaw;* Encrage, 1996); *Les Diables Blancs (The White Devils;* Gall. Jeunesse, 1993); *Les Ouraniens de Brume (The Ouranians of Mist;* Nathan, 1996); *Les Gladiateurs de Thule (The Gladiators of Thule;* Castor Poche, 1997); *Note:* See Chapter IX.

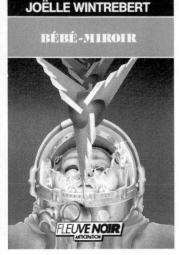

Wisner, René (?-?) *see* **Grand-Guignol**

Wissant, Georges de (?-?) *see* **Grand-Guignol**

Wittkop(-Menardeau), Gabrielle (?-); *Le Nécrophile (Régine Desforges, 1972); La Mort de C. Christian (The Death of C. Christian;* Bourgois, 1975); *Les Rajahs Blancs (The White Rajahs;* Presses de la Ren., 1986); *Hemlock, ou Les Poisons (Presses de la Ren., 1988); Al-*manach Perpétuel des Harpies (Perpetual Almanach of the Harpies;* P. Thierry, 1995); *Les Départs Exemplaires (Exemplary Departures;* Ed. De Paris, 1996); *Note:* See Chapter VIII.

Wolff, Roby (?-); *Le Robinson de la Tour (The Robinson of the Tower;* France-Empire, 1980)

Wolfram, Richard *see* **Wagner, Roland C**.

Wolinski, Maryse (?-); *Les Sorcières du Boisjoli (The Witches of Boisjoli;* Messidor-La Farandole, 1981)

Wolmark, Nina (?-) *see* **Chalopin, Jean**

Wul, Stefan (Pairault, Pierre) (1922-); *Retour à "O" (Return to "0";* FNA 78, 1956); *Niourk (FNA 83, 1957); Rayons pour Sidar (Rays for Sidar;* FNA 90, 1957); *La Peur Géante (The Giant Fear;* FNA 96, 1957); *OMS en Serie (OMS in Series;* FNA 102, 1957); *Le Temple du Passé (FNA 106, 1958; transl. as the Temple of the Past, 1973); L'Orphelin de Perdide (The Orphan of Perdide;* FNA 109, 1958); *La Mort Vivante (The Living Death;* FNA 113, 1958); *Piège sur Zarkass (Trap on Zarkass;* FNA 119, 1958); *Terminus 1 (FNA 130, 1959); Odyssée Sous Contrôle (Odyssey Under Control;* FNA 138, 1959); *Noô*

(2 vols.; PdF 236-237, 1977); *Note:* See Chapter IX. *OMS en Série* was adapted into the animated feature ***La Planète Sauvage*** *(Fantastic Planet;* 1973). *L'Orphelin de Perdide* was adapted into the animated feature ***Les Maîtres du Temps*** *(The Time Masters;* 1981); see Book 1, Chapter IV. Stéfan Wul also worked on the television series ***Mycènes*** (see Book 1, Chapter II).

Wybert, Armand (?-); *Demain le Soleil se lèvera (Tomorrow the Sun Shall Rise;* Scorpion, 1960)

Wyl, Jean-Michel (1942-1980); *Québec Banana State (Beauchemin, 1978); À l'Été des Indiens (To the Indian Summer;* Libre Expression, 1980); *Note:* French-Canadian writer. In *Banana State,* communists take power in Quebec.

X (Groupe des); *Chaos Puissance 5 (Chaos Power 5;* Mnemos18, 1997)

X (Lieutenant) *see* **Volkoff, Vladimir**

X (Prof.) *see* **Motus (Prof.)**

Xardel, Isabelle *see* **Sandy, Isabelle**

Xhonneux, Henri (?-); See **Topor, Roland.**

Yance, Claude-Emmanuelle (Lachance, Lise) (1941-); *Mourir comme un Chat (To Die Like a Cat*; L'Instant Même, 1987); *Note:* French-Canadian writer. Collection of fantastical tales.

Yanne, Jean (1933-); *L'Apocalypse Est Pour Demain (The Apocalypse Is for Tomorrow*; Simoen, 1977); *Note:* Novelisation of the eponymous radio serial (see Book 1, Chapter III). Yanne also directed **Les Chinois à Paris** (see Book 1, Chapter I) and wrote the graphic novel series *Les Dossiers du B.I.D.E.* (see Book 1, Chapter V).

Yawache, Alain (1932-) *see* **Kijé (Lieutenant)**

Yelnick, Claude (?-); *L'Homme Cette Maladie (Man, This Disease*; Métal 7, 1954; transl. as the *Trembling Tower*, 1956); *Croisière sans Retour (Cruise of No Return*; Plon, 1962); *Note:* See Chapter IX.

Yergeau, Pierre (1957-); *1999* (L'Instant Même, 1995); *Note:* French-Canadian writer.

Younes, Georges (?-); *Poids Atomique 238.2 (Atomic Weight 238.2*; Corne d'Or, 1953)

Yourcenar, Marguerite (Crayencour, Marguerite de) (1903-1987); *Le Jardin des Chimères (The Garden of Chimeras*; Perrin, 1921); *Feux* (1936; rev. 1968; transl. as *Fires*, 1981); *Nouvelles Orientales* (Gall., 1938; rev. 1963, 1978; transl. as *Oriental Tales*, 1985); *Mémoires d'Hadrien* (Plon, 1951; transl. as *Memoirs of Hardian*, 1954); *L'Oeuvre au Noir (The Dark Work*; Gall., 1968; transl. as the *Abyss*, 1976); *Note:* See Chapter VIII.

Yvelise, Jean d' (?-); *L'Océan de Lumière (The Ocean of Light*; VA, 1940); *La Séquestrée de Ker-Armor (The Captive Woman of Ker-Armor*; SEPIA, 1940); *Le Soleil sur le Rêve Mort (The Sun Over the Dead Dream*; SEPIA, 1940)

Zarka, Albert (?-); *Un jour tout changea (One Day Everything Changed*; SIPEP, 1961)

Zelde, Jacques (?-); *La Chanson de l'Amibe (The Amoeba's Song*; Plasma, 1976); *Les Hordes (The Hordes*; Balland, 1988); *Gribiche* (Balland, 1989)

Zola, Émile (1840-1902); *Fécondité (Fecundity*; Flamm., 1899; transl. 1900); *Travail (Labor*; Flamm., 1901; transl. 1902); *Vérité (Truth*; Flamm., 1903; transl. 1903); *Note:* See Chapter V.

Zorn, Jacqueline (?-) *see* **Groc, Léon**

Zuylen de Nyevelt, Hélène, Baronne de (née de Rotschild) (1863-1947) *see* **Grand-Guignol**

CHAPTER XII

Major Awards

1. France

"Prix Jules Verne" (1927–33; 1958–63) (Jury)
(Books published by Hachette only)
1927—Octave Béliard—*La Petite Fille de Michel Strogoff* (*The Grand-Daughter of Michel Strogoff*)
Max Begouën—*Quand Le Mammouth Ressuscita* (*When the Mastodon Revived*) (runner-up)
1928—Jules-Louis-Gaston Pastre—*Le Secret des Sables* (*The Secret of the Sands*)
1929—Albert Bailly—*L'Éther-Alpha*
1930—Tancrède Vallerey—*L'Île au Sable Vert* (*The Island with Green Sand*)
1931—Hervé De Peslouan—*L'Étrange Menace du Prof. Iouchkoff* (*The Strange Threat of Prof. Iouchkoff*)
1932—Pierre Palau—*L'Énigmatique Disparition de James Butler* (*The Mysterious Disappearance of James Butler*)
1933—Jean-Toussain Samat—*Les Vaisseaux en Flammes* (*The Ships on Fire*)
1958—Serge Martel—*L'Adieu Aux Astres* (*Farewell to the Stars*)
1959—Daniel Drode—*Surface De La Planète* (*Surface of the Planet*)
1960—Michel Jeury (As "Albert Higon")—*La Machine du Pouvoir* (*The Machine of Power*)
1961—Jérôme Sériel—*Le Sub-Espace* (*The Sub-Space*)
1962—Philippe Curval—*Le Ressac de l'Espace* (*The Breakers of Space*)
1963—Vladimir Volkoff—*Métro pour l'Enfer* (*Metro for Hell*)

"Grand Prix du Roman d'Anticipation Scientifique"
(a.k.a. *"Prix Rosny Aîné"*) (1954) (Jury) (Books published by Métal only)
1954—Charles Henneberg—*La Naissance des Dieux* (*The Birth of the Gods*)

"Grand Prix du Roman de la Science Fiction"
(1954–57) (Jury) (Books published by Fleuve Noir only)
1954—Jimmy Guieu—*L'Homme de l'Espace* (*The Man from Space*)
1955—Jean-Gaston Vandel—*Bureau de l'Invisible* (*Office of the Invisible*)
1956—Stéfan Wul—*Retour à "O"* (*Return to "0"*)
1957—Max-André Rayjean—*Les Parias de l'Atome* (*The Pariahs of the Atom*)

"Prix Apollo" (1972–90) (Jury) (French/Foreign Novels/Short Stories—Only French authors & novels are listed)
1977—Philippe Curval—*Cette Chère Humanité* (*That Dear Mankind*)
1983—Michel Jeury—*L'Orbe et la Roue* (*The Orb and the Wheel*)
1984—Serge Brussolo—*Les Semeurs d'Abîmes* (*The Abyss Sowers*)
1988—G.-J. Arnaud—*La Compagnie des Glaces* (*The Ice Company*) (series)
1990—Joël Houssin—*Argentine*

"Grand Prix de l'Imaginaire" (1974–) (Jury) (formerly known as *"Grand Prix de la Science Fiction Française"*; name changed in 1991) (Novels/Short Stories—Only novels are listed)
1974—Michel Jeury—*Le Temps Incertain* (*The Uncertain Time*)
1975—Philippe Curval—*L'Homme à Rebours* (*The Backwards Man*)
1976—Philip Goy—*Le Livre-Machine* (*The Machine-Book*) (special award)
Daniel Walther—*Les Soleils Noirs d'Arcadie* (*The Black Suns of Arcadia*) (anthology)

1977—Michel Demuth—*Les Galaxiales* (*The Galaxials*)

Yves Dermèze (lifetime)

1978—Pierre Pelot—*Delirium Circus*

1979—Yves & Ada Rémy—*La Maison du Cygne* (*The House of the Swan*)

1980—Daniel Walther—*L'Épouvante* (*The Terror*)

1981—Serge Brussolo—*Vue en Coupe d'une Ville Malade* (*Cut-Out View of a Sick City*)

1982—Élisabeth Vonarburg—*Le Silence de la Cité* (*The Silence of the City*)

Jean-Pierre Andrevon—*La Fée et le Géomètre* (*The Fairy and the Surveyor*) (juvenile)

G.-J. Arnaud—*La Compagnie des Glaces* (*The Ice Company*) (special award/series)

1983—Pierre Billon—*L'Enfant du Cinquième Nord* (*The Child of the Fifth North*)

Michel Grimaud—*Le Tyran d'Axilane* (*The Tyrant of Axilane*) (juvenile)

1984—Jean-Pierre Hubert—*Le Champ du Rêveur* (*The Dreamer's Field*)

Thérèse Roche—*Le Naviluk* (juvenile)

1985—André Ruellan—*Mémo*

Robert Escarpit—*L'Enfant qui Venait de l'Espace* (*The Child Who Came from Outer Space*) (juvenile)

1986—Joël Houssin—*Les Vautours* (*The Vultures*)

Charles Dobzynski—*Le Commerce des Mondes* (*The Trade of Worlds*) (juvenile)

1987—Antoine Volodine—*Rituel du Mépris, Variante Moldscher* (*Ritual of Contempt, the Moldscher Variation*)

Emmanuel Carrère—*Le Détroit de Behring* (*The Straits of Behring*) (special award)

1988—Serge Brussolo—*Operation "Serrures Carnivores"* (*Operation "Carnivorous Locks"*)

Georges-Olivier Châteaureynaud—*Le Combat d'Odiri* (*Odiri's Fight*) (juvenile)

1989—Joelle Wintrebert—*Le Créateur Chimérique* (*The Chimerical Creator*)

Christian Grenier—*Le Coeur en Abîme* (*The Heart in the Abyss*) (juvenile)

Dominique Douay & Michel Maly—*Les Voyages Ordinaires d'un Amateur de Tableaux* (*The Ordinary Voyages of a Painting Lover*) (special award)

1990—Jean-Pierre Andrevon—*Sukran*

Colette Fayard—*Les Chasseurs au Bord de la Nuit* (*The Hunters at the Edge of Night*) (story collection)

Roger Leloup—*Le Pic des Ténèbres* (*The Peak of Darkness*) (juvenile)

Philippe Curval (lifetime)

1991—Francis Berthelot—*Rivage des Intouchables* (*Beach of the Untouchables*)

Liliane Korb—*Temps sans Frontières* (*Time Without Borders*) (juvenile)

1992—Joël Houssin—*Le Temps du Twist* (*The Time of Twist*)

Pierre Pelot & Yves Coppens—*Le Rêve de Lucy* (*Lucy's Dream*) (juvenile)

1993—Ayerdhal—*Demain, une Oasis* (*Tomorrow, an Oasis*)

François Coupry—*Le Fils du Concierge de l'Opera* (*The Son of the Concierge of the Opera*) (juvenile)

1994—Pierre Bordage—*Les Guerriers du Silence* (*The Warriors of Silence*)

Alain Grousset—*Les Chasse-Marée* (*The Tide Hunters*) (juvenile)

1995—Laurent Genefort—*Arago*

René & Dona Sussan—*Les Nourritures Extra-Terrestres* (*Extra-Terrestrial Food*) (special award)

1996—Maurice G. Dantec—*Les Racines du Mal* (*The Roots of Evil*)

1997—Jean-Marc Ligny—*Inner City*

Raymond Milési—*Papa, J'ai Remonté le Temps* (*Dad, I've Travelled Back in Time*) (juvenile)

1998—Serge Lehman—*F.A.U.S.T.*

Christian Grenier—Saga of the "*Multimonde*" (juvenile/series)

"Graoully d'Or" (1978-82) (Jury) (Metz SF Convention) (French/Foreign Novels—Only French authors are listed)

1978—Pierre Pelot—*Transit*

1979—no award

1980—Francis Berthelot—*La Lune Noire d'Orion* (*The Black Moon of Orion*)

1981—Jean Hougron—*Le Naguen*

1982—Serge Brussolo—*Sommeil de Sang* (*Sleep of Blood*)

"Prix Rosny Aîné" (1980-) (Popular Vote) (French SF Convention) (Novels/Short Stories—Only novels are listed)

1980—Michel Jeury—*Le Territoire Humain* (*The Human Territory*)

1981—Michel Jeury—*Les Yeux Géants* (*The Giant Eyes*)

1982—Élisabeth Vonarburg—*Le Silence de la Cité* (*The Silence of the City*)

1983—Emmanuel Jouanne—*Damiers Imaginaires* (*Imaginary Squares*)

1984—Jean-Pierre Hubert—*Le Champ du Rêveur* (*The Dreamer's Field*)

1985—Emmanuel Jouanne—*Ici-Bas* (*Here Below*)

1986—Jean-Pierre Hubert—*Ombromanies* (*Shadowmania*)

1987—Francis Berthelot—*La Ville au Fond de l'Oeil* (*The City at the Bottom of the Eye*)

1988—Roland C. Wagner—*Le Serpent d'Angoisse* (*The Terror Snake*)

Joëlle Wintrebert—*Les Olympiades Truquées* (*The Trick Olympics*)

1989—Roland C. Wagner—*Poupée aux Yeux Morts* (*Dead-Eyed Doll*) (trilogy comprised of *La Mémoire des Pierres* (*The Memory of the Stones*), *Prisons Intérieures* (*Inner Prisons*) and *Les Futurs Mystères de Paris* (*The Future Mysteries of Paris*))

1990—Yves Frémion—*L'Hétéradelphe de Gane* (*The Heteradelph of Gane*)

1991—Pierre Stolze—*Cent Mille Images ou Les Reines Mages de la Montagne Ardente* (*One Hundred Thousand Images or The Wizard Queen of the Fiery Mountain*)

1992—Jean-Claude Dunyach—*Étoiles Mortes* (*Dead Stars*) (trilogy comprised of *Nivôse*, *Aigue-Marine*, and *Voleurs de Silence* (*Thieves of Silence*))

1993—Alain le Bussy—*Deltas*

1994—Richard Canal—*Ombres Blanches* (*White Shadows*)

1995—Richard Canal—*Aube Noire* (*Black Dawn*)

1996—Maurice G. Dantec—*Les Racines du Mal* (*The Roots of Evil*)

1997—Serge Lehman—*F.A.U.S.T.*

1998—Roland C. Wagner—*L'Odyssée de l'Espèce* (*A Species Odyssey*)

"Prix Cosmos 2000" (1982–86) (Voted by customers of eponymous specialized bookstore) (French/Foreign Novels—Only French authors are listed)

1983—Michel Jeury—*L'Orbe et la Roue* (*The Orb and the Wheel*)

1987—Bernard Simonay—*Phénix*

1996—Pierre Bordage—*Les Guerriers du Silence 3: La Citadelle Hypénéros* (*The Warriors of Silence 3*)

"Prix Julia Verlanger" (1986–) (Jury) (French/Foreign Novels—Only French authors are listed)

1986—Michel Jeury—*Le Jeu du Monde* (*The World Game*)
Stefan Wul—*Noô*

1987—Bernard Simonay—*Phénix*

1989—Hugues Douriaux—*La Biche de la Forêt d'Arcande* (*The Doe from the Forest of Arcande*) (trilogy comprised of *Le Monde au-delà des Brumes* [*The World Beyond the Mists*], *Thorn le Guerrier* [*Thorn the Warrior*], and *Les Mortels et les Dieux* [*The Mortals and the Gods*])

1994—Pierre Bordage—*Les Guerriers du Silence* (*The Warriors of Silence*)

1995—Bernard Simonay—*La Porte de Bronze* (*The Gate of Brass*)

1996—Julia Verlanger (posthumously)—*Les Cages de Beltem* (*The Cages of Beltem*) (*Acherra* and *Offren*)
Pierre Grimbert—*Six Héritiers* (*Six Heirs*)

"Gérardmer-Fantastica" (1995–) (Jury) (*Fantastique* only)

1995—Anne Duguël—*Le Chien Qui Rit* (*The Dog That Laughs*)

1996—Benjamin Legrand—*La Mécanique des Ombres* (*The Mechanic of Shadows*)

1997- Max Dorra—*La Qualité du Silence* (*The Quality of Silence*)

"Prix Ozone" (1997-) (Voted by readers of eponymous magazine) (French/Foreign Novels, Short Stories, Films, Comics, etc.—Only French authors and novels are listed)

1997—Serge Lehman—*F.A.U.S.T.* (science fiction)
Anne Duguël—*Petite Chanson dans la Pénombre* (*Little Song in The Dark*) (*fantastique*)
Pierre Grimbert—*Six Héritiers* (*Six Heirs*) (fantasy)

1998—Roland C. Wagner—*L'Odyssée de l'Espèce* (*A Species Odyssey*) (science fiction)
Jeanne Faivre d'Arcier—*La Déesse Écarlate* (*The Scarlet Goddess*) (*fantastique*)
Ayerdhal—*Parleur, ou La Chronique d'un Rêve Enclavé* (*Speaker, or The Chronicle of an Embedded Dream*) (fantasy)

"Grand Prix de la Tour Eiffel" (1997–) (Jury)

1997—Pierre Bordage—*Wang*

2. French Canada

"Grand Prix de la Science-Fiction et du Fantastique Québécois" (1984–) (Jury)

1984—Denis Côté—*Les Hockeyeurs Cybernétiques* (*The Cybernetic Hockey-Players*), *Les Parallèles Célestes* (*The Celestial Parallels*)

1985—André Berthiaume—*Incidents de Frontière* (*Border-Incidents*)

1986—Esther Rochon—*L'Épuisement du Soleil* (*The Exhaustion of the Sun*)

1987—Esther Rochon—*Coquillage* (*Shell*)

1988—Gilles Pellerin—*Ni le Lieu, Ni l'Heure* (*Neither the Time, Nor the Place*)

1989—Evelyne Bernard—*La Vaironne*

1990—Jacques Brossard—*L'Oiseau de Feu 1: Les Années d'Apprentissage* (*The Firebird 1: The Years of Apprenticeship*)

1991—Esther Rochon—*L'Espace du Diamant* (*The Diamond Space*)

1992—Daniel Sernine—*Boulevard des Étoiles* (*Boulevard of the Stars*), *À la Recherche de M. Goodtheim* (*Looking for Mr. Goodtheim*), *Les Rêves d'Argus* (*The Dreams of Argus*)

1993—Élisabeth Vonarburg—*Chroniques du Pays des Mères* (*Chronicles of the Land of the Mothers*)

1994—Yves Meynard—various short stories

1995—Joël Champetier—*La Mémoire du Lac* (*The Memory of the Lake*), *Le Secret des Sylvaneaux* (*The Secret of the Sylvanans*)

1996—Daniel Sernine—*L'Arc-en-Cercle* (*The Rainbow Ring*), *La Traversée de l'Apprenti Sorcier* (*The Crossing of the Sorcerer's Apprentice*), *Sur la Scène des Siècles* (*On the Stage of the Centuries*)

1997—Élisabeth Vonarburg—*Tyranaël 1: Les Rêves de la Mer* (*The Dreams of the Sea*), *Tyranaël 2: Le Jeu de la Perfection* (*The Game of Perfection*)

"Prix Aurora" (formerly known as ***"Prix Casper"***; name changed in 1990) (Popular vote) (Canadian SF convention) (French-language works included since 1986) (Only French-language authors are listed)

1986—Daniel Sernine—*"Yadjine et la Mort"* (*Yardjine and Death*) (short story)

1987—Élisabeth Vonarburg—*"La Carte du Tendre"* (*The Lover's Map*) (short story)

1988—Alain Bergeron—*"Les Crabes de Vénus Regardent le Ciel"* (*The Venusian Crabs Look at the Sky*) (short story)

1989—Charles Montpetit—*Temps Mort* (*Dead Time*)

1990—Jacques Brossard—*L'Oiseau de Feu 1: Les Années d'Apprentissage* (*The Firebird 1: The Years of Apprenticeship*)

1991—Élisabeth Vonarburg—*Histoire de la Princesse et du Dragon* (*Story of the PrIncess and the Dragon*)

1992—Élisabeth Vonarburg—*Ailleurs et au Japon* (*Elsewhere and in Japan*)

1993—Élisabeth Vonarburg—*Chroniques du Pays des Mères* (*Chronicles of the Land of the Mothers*)

1994—Daniel Sernine—*Chronoreg*

1995—Joël Champetier—*La Mémoire du Lac* (*The Memory of the Lake*)

1996—Élisabeth Vonarburg—*Les Voyageurs Malgré Eux* (*The Voyagers in Spite of Themselves*)

1997—Yves Meynard—*La Rose du Désert* (*The Desert Rose*)

"Prix Boreal" (1980–) (Popular vote)

1980—Alain Bergeron—*Un Été de Jessica* (*A Summer of Jessica*)

1981—Jean-Pierre April—*La Machine à Explorer la Fiction* (*The Machine for Exploring Fiction*)

1982—Élisabeth Vonarburg—*Le Silence de la Cité* (*The Silence of the City*) (science fiction novel)

René Beaulieu—*Légendes de Virnie* (*Legends from Virnia*) (science fiction collection)

Michel Bélil—*Greenwich* (*fantastique* novel)

Michel Bélil—*Déménagement* (*Moving Day*) (*fantastique* collection)

1983—Pierre Billon—*L'Enfant du Cinquième Nord* (*The Child of the Fifth North*) (science fiction)

André Carpentier—*Du Pain, Des Oiseaux* (*Bread, Birds*) (*fantastique*)

1984—Denis Côté (lifetime)

1985—no award

1986—Esther Rochon—*L'Épuisement du Soleil* (*The Exhaustion of the Sun*)

1987—Esther Rochon—*Coquillage* (*Shell*)

1988—Francine Pelletier—*Les Temps des Migrations* (*The Time of Migrations*)

1989- Guy Bouchard—*Les Gélules Utopiques* (*The Utopian Capsules*)

1990—Jacques Brossard—*L'Oiseau de Feu 1: Les Années d'Apprentissage* (*The Firebird 1: The Years of Apprenticeship*)

1991—Joël Champetier—*La Mer au Fond du Monde* (*The Sea at the Bottom of the World*)

1992—Joël Champetier—*La Taupe et le Dragon* (*The Mole and the Dragon*)

Daniel Sernine—*Boulevard des Étoiles* (*Boulevard of the Stars*)

1993—Élisabeth Vonarburg—*Chroniques du Pays des Mères* (*Chronicles of the Land of the Mothers*)

1994—Jacques Brossard—*L'Oiseau de Feu 2B: Le Grand Projet* (*The Firebird 2B: The Great Project*)

1995—Daniel Sernine—*Manuscrit Trouvé dans un Secrétaire* (*Manuscript Found in a Secretary*)

1996—Yves Meynard—*La Rose du Désert* (*The Desert Rose*)

1997—Élisabeth Vonarburg—*Tyranaël 1: Les Rêves de la Mer* (*The Dreams of the Sea*)

Bibliography & Sources

In English:

BOOKS

Chronicle of the Cinema. Robyn Karney, ed. (Dorling Kindersley, 1995).

The Encyclopedia of Fantasy. John Clute & John Grant, eds. (Little Brown, 1997).

The Encyclopedia of Science Fiction. John Clute & Peter Nicholls, eds. (St. Martin's, 1993).

The Film Encyclopedia. Ephraim Katz (Harper Perennial, 1994).

The Great French Films. James Reid Paris (Citadel, 1983).

Horror and Science Fiction Films (3 vols.) Donald C. Willis (Scarecrow, 1980-84).

Immoral Tales: European Sex & Horror Movies (1956-1984). Cathal Tohill & Pete Thomas (St. Martin's, 1995).

Reference Guide to Fantastic Films (3 Vols.) Walt Lee & Bill Warren (Chelsea-Lee, 1974).

Science Fiction: The Illustrated Encyclopedia. John Clute, ed. (Dorling Kindersley, 1995).

TV Movies & Video Guide (1995). Leonard Maltin, ed. (Plume, 1995).

The World Encyclopedia of Cartoons. Maurice Horn, ed. (Chelsea, 1980).

The World Encyclopedia of Comics. Maurice Horn, ed. (Chelsea, 1976).

MAGAZINES

Cinefantastique. Fred Clarke, ed. (Cinefantastique).

Starlog. David Mcdonnell, ed. (Starlog Press).

In French:

BOOKS

À la Recherche de l'Empire Caché. Francis Lacassin (Julliard, 1991).

L'Affaire Jacobs. Gérard Lenne (Megawave, 1990).

L'Année de la Science-Fiction et du Fantastique Québécois (8 vols.). René Beaulieu, Denis Côté, Gaétan Godbout, Claude Janelle & Jean Pettigrew, eds. (Le Passeur, 1985-)

Les Années Cinquante. Henri Filippini (Glénat, 1977).

Les Années "Pilote" (1959-1989). Patrick Gaumer (Dargaud, 1996).

Les Années Radio. Jean-François Remonté & Simone Depoux (L'Arpenteur, 1989).

La Bande Dessinée. Gérard Blanchard (Marabout, 1969).

Bibliographie Analytique de la Science-Fiction et du Fantastique Québécois. Aurélien Boivin, Maurice Émond & Michel Lord (Nuit Blanche, 1992).

Catalogue des Âmes et des Cycles de la Science-Fiction. Stan Barets (Denoël, 1981).

Catalogue Analytique des Romans "Anticipation" du Fleuve Noir. Sylviane Collas (L'Annonce-Bouquins, 1988).

Catalogue Analytique des Romans de Terreurs / Frissons 2. Sylviane Collas (L'Annonce-Bouquins, 1985, 1995).

Cinéguide. Éric Leguèbe, ed. (Presses de la Cité, 1992).

Dictionnaire de la Bande Dessinée. Henri Filippini, ed. (Bordas, 1989).

Dictionnaire du Fantastique. Alain Pozzuoli & Jean-Pierre Krémer (Jacques Grancher, 1992).

Encyclopédie de l'Utopie, des Voyages Extraordinaires et de la Science-Fiction. Pierre Versins (L'Âge d'Homme, 1972).

Encyclopédie des Bandes Dessinées. Marjorie Alessandrini, ed. (Albin Michel, 1979).

Encyclopédie des Bandes Dessinées de Petit Format (2 Vols). Gérard Thomassian (Librairie Fantamask, 1994-95).

Escales sur l'Horizon. Serge Lehman, ed. (Fleuve Noir, 1998).

Et Franquin Créa La Gaffe. Numa Sadoul (Dargaud/Schlirff, 1986).

Les Feuilletons Historiques de la Télévision Française. Jacques Baudou & Jean-Jacques Schleret (Huitième Art, 1992).

Le Grand Guignol: Théâtre des Peurs de la Belle Époque. Agnès Pierron (Laffont, 1995).

Le Guide de la Bédé Francophone. Yves Frémion (Syros, 1990).

Guide des Films (1885-1995) (2 vols.) Jean Tulard, ed. (Robert Laffont, 1990).

Hergé et Tintin Reporters. Philippe Godin (Lombard, 1986).

Hier, L'an 2000. Jacques Sadoul (Denoël, 1973).

Histoire de la Litérature Fantastique en France. Marcel Schneider (Fayard, 1985).

Histoire de la Science-Fiction Moderne. Jacques Sadoul (Robert Laffont, 1984).

Histoire de "Spirou" et des Publications Dupuis. Philippe Brun (Glénat, 1980).

Histoire du Journal "Pilote" et des Publications des Éditions Dargaud. Henri Filippini (Glénat, 1977).

Histoire du Journal "Tintin." Alain Lerman (Glénat, 1979).

Histoire du Journal "Vaillant." Henri Filippini (Glénat, 1978).

Index des Collections Spécialisées. Francis Valery (F. Valery, 1977).

Le Livre d'Or du Journal "Pilote." Guy Vidal, ed. (Dargaud, 1980).

Le Lombard (1946-1996): Un Demi-Siècle d'Aventures (2 Vols). Jean-Louis Lechat (Lombard, 1996).

Les Maîtres de la Science-Fiction. Lorris Murail (Bordas, 1993).

Les Mémoires de "Spirou." Thierri Martens & Jean-Paul Tibéri (Dupuis, 1989).

Merveilleux et Fantastique à la Télévision Française. Jacques Baudou & Jean-Jacques Schleret (Huitième Art, 1995).

Meurtres en Série—Les Séries Policières de la Télévision Française. Jacques Baudou & Jean-Jacques Schleret (Huitième Art, 1990).

Mister Moebius et Docteur Gir. Numa Sadoul (Albin Michel, 1976).

Moebius: Entretiens avec Numa Sadoul. Numa Sadoul (Casterman, 1991).

Le Monde d'Hergé. Benoit Peeters (Casterman, 1984).

Panorama de la Bande Dessinée. Jacques Sadoul (J'ai Lu, 1976).

Panorama de la Litérature Fantastique de Langue Française. Jean-Baptiste Baronian (Stock, 1978).

Panorama de la Science-Fiction. Jacques Van Herp (Marabout, 1973).

Le Petit Bédéraste du 20ème Siècle—Catalogue des Récits Complets et des Petits Formats (2 Vols). M. Moutier (Moutier, 1980-81).

93 Ans de BD. Jacques Sadoul (J'ai Lu, 1989).

Le Rayon SF. Henri Delmas & Alain Julian (Milan, 1985).

La Science-Fiction. Denis Guiot, Jean-Pierre Andrevon & George Barlow (MA, 1987).

Télé Feuilletons. Jean-Jacques Jelot-Leblanc (MA, 1990)

Trésors de la Bande Dessinée (1995-1996). Michel Béra, Michel Denni & Philippe Mellot, ed. (L'Amateur, 1994).

MAGAZINES

Le Collectionneur de Bandes Dessinées. Numa Sadoul, ed. (Glénat).

L'Écran Fantastique. Alain Schlockoff, ed. (Imédia).

Europe. Charles Dobzynski, ed. (Europe).

Fantascienza. Alain Grousset, Dominique Martel & Serge Ecckerman, eds. (Fantascienza).

Fiction. Alain Dorémieux, ed. (Opta).

Horizons du Fantastique. Dominique Besse & Louis Guillon, eds. (Ekla).

Iblis. François Bazzoli & Alain Chareyre-Mejan, eds. (Iblis).

Otrante. Lambert Barthélémy, ed. (G.E.E.E.F.F.)

Revue de l'Imaginaire. Rémy Brument & Jérémi Sauvage , eds. (ACIER).

La Revue du Cinéma.

Index